WHAT
HISTORICAL
NOVEL DO I
READ
NEXT?

VOLUME 1
A-Z

WHAT HISTORICAL NOVEL

DO I READ NEXT?

VOLUME 1
A-Z

DANIEL S. BURT, PH.D

GALE

Detroit

New York

Toronto

London

Daniel S. Burt, Ph.D.

Gale Research Staff

Senior Editor: Debra M. Kirby
Associate Editors: Victoria A. Coughlin and Lydia Fink
Contributing Editors: Kathleen Dallas, Nancy Franklin, Arlene Johnson, Prindle
LaBarge, Sharon McGilvray, Charles B. Montney and Dana Shonta
Managing Editor: Ann V. Evory

Production Director: MaryBeth Trimper
External Production Assistant: Shanna Heilveil
Product Design Manager: Cynthia Baldwin
Graphic Designer: Mary Krzewinski

Manager Data Entry Services: Eleanor Allison
Data Entry Coordinator: Gwendolyn S. Tucker
Data Entry Associates: Maleka Imrana, Beverly Jendrowski

Manager, Technical Support Services: Theresa Rocklin
Programmer/Analyst: Joshua E. Cohen

Library of Congress Cataloging-in-Publication Data
Burt, Daniel S.
    What historical novel do I read next? / Daniel S. Burt.
        p.   cm.
    Includes indexes.
    ISBN 0-7876-0388-0 (set : alk. paper). -- ISBN
0-7876-1541-2 (vol. 1 : alk. paper)
    1. Historical fiction--Bibliography.   I. Title.
Z5917.H6B87   1997
[PN3441]
016.80863'81--dc21   97-10702
                                                              CIP

ISBN 0-7876-0388-0 (Complete set)
ISBN 0-7876-1541-2 (Volume 1)
ISBN 0-7876-1542-0 (Volume 2)
ISSN 1052-2212

Printed in the United States of America

Contents

Volume 1

Volume 2

Preface

Selection Criteria

Readers with a dual interest in history and fiction have a wealth of novels to choose from but few resources to help find them. This book is intended as a useful tool to explore a library's holdings of historical novels. For the first time, readers can track down historical fiction by author, subject, fictional and historical characters, time period, and place. Almost 7,000 novels by more than 3,000 authors are included.

Most of us use the phrase "historical novel" casually, never really needing an exact definition to make ourselves understood. We just know it when we see it. A reference book, however, requires a set of criteria to determine what's in and what's out. Otherwise the book has no boundaries. If the working definition of historical fiction is too loose, every novel set in a period before the present qualifies, and, except for science fiction, every novel becomes an historical novel immediately upon publication. If the definition is so strict that only books set in a time before the author's birth make the cut, then we would end up excluding countless works that critics, readers, librarians, and the authors themselves think of as historical novels.

The task in planning this book was to fashion a definition or set of criteria flexible enough to include novels that passed what can be regarded as the litmus test for historical fiction: Did the author use his or her imagination—and often quite a bit of research—to evoke another and earlier time than the author's own?

The selection could have been limited to those novels that concern a specific historical event or involve actual historical figures. This would, however, have excluded a number of fine re-creations of the past in which the characters do not intersect with important events or personages, but evoke everyday life in a past era. Some temporal measure was needed to distinguish between the recent past and what can be described as the historical past—the province of the historical novelist. Walter Scott, who is credited with inventing, or at least popularizing, the historical novel, offered a useful distinction. The subtitle of his first historical novel, *Waverley*, is "'Tis Sixty Years Since" and this provides a possible formula for separating the created past from the remembered past. What is unique about the historical novel is its attempt to imagine a distant period of time before the novelist's lifetime, a past not recalled but created. Scott's 60-year span (the same, incidentally, used by Leo Tolstoy in *War and Peace*) between a novel's composition and its imagined era offers an arbitrary but useful way to distinguish between the personal and the historical past. The distance of two generations or nearly a lifetime provides a necessary span for the past to emerge as history and forces the writer to rely on more than recollection or invention to uncover the patterns and textures of the past.

This book adopts Scott's formula but adjusts it to 50 years, including those books in which the bulk of the plot is set in a period 50 years or more before the novel was written. The date of authorship rather than the date of publication has been used to rule out a contemporaneous manuscript from qualifying merely because it sat in a desk drawer for 50 years before being published. The word "bulk" is used because otherwise family sagas and the like which may end in the present but are largely about the past would otherwise have been excluded.

Because a rigid application of this 50-year guide might rule out quite a few books intended by their authors and regarded by their readers to be historical novels, two other tests have been applied to books written about more recent periods:

● Is the book commonly thought of as an historical novel, typically because actual historical events and personalities are central to its plot? (A book such as Don DeLillo's *Libra* qualifies under this criterion.)

● Did the author set out to write an historical novel evoking a bygone era? (Herman Wouk's *The Winds of War* and *War and Remembrance* thereby qualify, though within the 50-year limit. I admit this is a gray area and requires a good deal of subjective judgment to divine the author's intent.)

Even books that were undeniably historical novels by even the strictest definition had to meet one other of the overriding criteria. They had to be generally available to readers. This means that they must be found in the circulating collections of large public libraries and, therefore, be accessible to patrons, if not in every local library, then through the interlibrary loan system. This book has been written primarily to serve the needs of people who read historical fiction for pleasure, not those who study it for scholarly purposes. To list and describe books that can only be located in the restricted stacks of large research libraries would merely tantalize readers who have no access to such works.

I have tried to apply these criteria for the historical novel as a guide, not an inflexible rule, and have allowed some exceptions when warranted by special circumstances. Additionally, not every title in the Western or historical romance genres has been included. In some cases only a sampling of an author's books are represented—those that seemed most interesting for their historical elements. Finally, the scope of this work is limited to books for an adult audience, although many of these are certainly appropriate for younger readers.

With these restrictions in mind, the reader will be able to use this volume to venture through the entire range of human history to identify the best the genre has to offer on every era, locale, and subject, and to appreciate the many ways in which the past has been imaginatively repossessed.

After defining what an historical novel is, the next challenge was finding the many novels that fit the criteria. In this age of electronic databases, one might have expected that a few keystrokes would produce a comprehensive list. However, novels' subjects have never been consistently coded, and an electronic search reveals only an incomplete and spotty listing. Other bibliographical guides to historical novels, if far less extensive, have been published, but none more recently than twenty years ago, and they are of little help in determining what might still be held in the fiction collections of average public libraries. The solution was the low-tech expedient of going through the fiction holdings of seven public libraries of various sizes in Connecticut and Massachusetts over a three-year period to identify all the titles that fit the criteria for historical novels. Once authors were identified, additional titles were located based on a check of availability through Connecticut's statewide automated network of library catalogs. The experience was akin to trawling with progressively finer nets hoping that no important historical novel could escape capture. If a title has managed to elude me, it probably was because it was not widely held. While I believe my systematic trawling has pulled in all but the minnows, a few bigger fish may have escaped. Since I have no doubt that a few personal favorites have been omitted, I urge readers to send me additional titles that should be included in subsequent editions of this book or any comments and suggestions for enhancing and improving *What Historical Novel Do I Read Next?* Please address correspondence to: Daniel Burt, *What Historical Novel Do I Read Next?*, c/o Gale Research Inc., 835 Penobscot Bldg., Detroit, Michigan 48226-4094.

Using This Book

Several indexes have been included to provide readers with a variety of paths to approach historical fiction. Most bibliographic guides to historical fiction are organized by period alone. This book encourages the reader to follow interests by time (here by century but also by decade, beginning with the 18th century) and also by place and subject. If you do not recall a book's title or author but can remember an important character's name, you should be able to locate the book. Historical figures who have at least a speaking role in a novel are also indexed. Should you wish to locate only novels in which Napoleon or George Washington appear as characters, that is possible using the book's index of historical characters. The professions and types of characters are also categorized so it is possible to identify those historical novels in which a doctor or a lawyer, for example, appears as a principal character.

The listings include available biographical information on the authors as well as a short descriptive summary for each title. These summaries include an evaluative comment on the historical accuracy of each book. While I do not pretend to be an expert on all of the eras depicted, I have tried to offer a commonsense reaction to the vexing question of authenticity and truthfulness in a novel's use of the past. Because historical novels are fictions, certain liberties with the facts are not only allowable but inevitable. Yet, the quality of a historical novel is fairly measured by whether or not it presents a convincing version of the past.

Acknowledgments

I owe a great deal to others who assisted in the preparation and the production of this book. I am grateful for all the courtesies and kindness of the many individuals at the following libraries who rarely flinched on my regular visits when they saw me coming with my box of 35 books or more to check out: In Connecticut, Russell Library (Middletown), Meriden Public Library, Wallingford Public Library, and Westport Public Library; in Massachusetts, The Eldridge Public Library (Chatham), Snow Public Library (Orleans) and Brooks Free Library (Harwich). I was ably assisted by a number of undergraduate students at Wesleyan University who served as research assistants, including Jennifer Kaminsky, Matthew Larsen, Jill Kraus, Aaron Loewenstein, Alex Poolus, Carl Robichaud, Glen Shapiro, Daniella Thome, Georgiana Yeboah, and, in particular, Amanda Shurgin and Taylor Loeb whose skill and efforts in tracking down elusive authors were exceptional. I was also greatly assisted by my colleagues at Wesleyan, particularly Stella Beaudoin, Andrea Dine, and especially Lois Poissant. Thanks also to Edmund A. Rubacha, reference librarian at Wesleyan's Olin Memorial Library, for his always sensible advice, and to Jay Zocco for his many library runs and for his paying probably the first double-digit overdue fines of his life. I am also grateful for the editorial support I received from those at Gale Research: Lydia Fink, Victoria Coughlin, and Debra Kirby, my editor. I would like to acknowledge the great assistance of Patricia Noyes who helped with a number of the entries and in countless other ways that allowed this project to be completed, and Edward Knappman who provided not only the initial insight that the time was right for a comprehensive and up-to-date reference guide to the historical novel but great counsel in getting me started and keeping me on track. Finally, I owe a great debt to my wife, Deborah G. Felder, whose daily forbearance was matched only by her exceptional memory and mastery of the kings and queens of England.

About the Author

Daniel S. Burt has been an Associate Dean of the College at Wesleyan University where he also serves as an adjunct lecturer in the Department of English, teaching courses on the English novel and Dickens in London.   Before coming to Wesleyan in 1989, he was an assistant professor of English at New York University where he taught such courses as Major English Novelists, Post-World War II American Fiction, American Short Stories, the English Novel in the 19th Century, Dickens, Forms of Fictions, Literary Interpretation, and Realism and Non-realism in the English Novel.

He has written "A Victorian Gothic: G.W.M. Reynolds' Mysteries of London" for *The New York Literary Forum* (1980) and *The Miller Analogy Test* (Arco, 1981). He has also worked as a freelance editor for Times Books, Prentice Hall Press, Arco, and the World Almanac. He is currently at work on *The Literary 100: The Hundred Most Influential Literary Artists of All Time*.

Introduction

Background

Perhaps no other fictional genre has combined to such an extent reader interest, literary achievement, and critical controversy as the historical novel. Since its first appearance with Sir Walter Scott's Waverley novels in the early 19th century, the historical novel has been the best-selling fictional genre in America, England, and throughout much of the world. Arguably the greatest novel ever written—Tolstoy's *War and Peace*—is an historical novel, as is the world's most popular novel, Margaret Mitchell's *Gone With the Wind*. Readers of this book will note in the list of authors represented no fewer than fifteen Nobel Prize winners in literature. The best-known historical novelists are represented—Georgette Heyer, Rafael Sabatini, Gore Vidal, Jean Plaidy, Mary Renault, and James Michener—but so too are such unexpected writers of historical novels as Susan Sontag, Norman Mailer, and John Updike. The range and diversity of novelists included, as well as the number of titles, speak to the persistence and appeal of the historical novel form.

Yet the form has never fully shed its reputation as a hybrid whose market appeal is often at odds with critical valuation. What stands out after reading the reviews for hundreds of the novels listed in this volume is that the historical novelist cannot win for trying. Either historical novels are criticized for their errors and falsification of history or faulted for indulging in historical detail work at the expense of a novel's main job of plot and character development. Clearly, the historical novel is judged from a critical standard that makes it extremely difficult to satisfy the often contradictory goals of historical and imaginative truth. The historical novelist invites this criticism by invading the province of the historian with an intention to elucidate the past as well as to entertain. Not bound by the same restrictions as the historian to report what is known and verifiable, the historical novelist is free to look beneath the facts of history for insights, interpretations, and surmises. However, the novelist must always face judgment on his or her ability to reproduce the surface details of a past age and for the quality of the novel's manipulation and understanding of the past. In short, the writer of historical fiction must satisfy the contrary impulses of the historian *and* the novelist. It is not surprising that achieving the ideal balance between truth and invention makes success in the historical novel so difficult and elusive. Despite the finger-wagging of critics, venturing into history for fictional plots and settings continues to attract novelists, and the results have retained an avid audience for nearly two centuries.

Walter Scott and the Origins of the Historical Novel

It is a commonplace of literary history to locate the origin of the historical novel with Walter Scott. When Scott turned from poetry to the novel with the publication of *Waverley* in 1814, he captivated his audience with his colorful romance of Scottish life at the time of the Jacobite Rebellion of 1745 and opened up a new field for the novel. What was new or novel about prose fiction in the 18th century, the novel tradition thatScott inherited, was the replacement of the prose romance's conventions—exotic and vague settings, generic character types, and idealized action—with the realistic details of normal, everyday life in which the reader could recognize himself and his world reflected imaginatively. The novel substituted the romance's interest in the general and the ideal with an interest in the particular. As one early novelist observed, "The Novel is a picture of real life and manners, and of the times in which it was written. The Romance, in lofty and elevated language, describes what has never happened nor is likely to." The novel turned away from the romance's extravagant characters, its remote and exotic settings, and its heroic, implausible actions to represent the actual experiences of individuals in particular and contemporary settings. The long ago and far away was replaced by the here and the now as novelists attempted to chronicle the actual world accurately governed by the laws of probability.

What Scott did was to redirect the novel from the contemporary to the historical past and to explore it not as the romantic nether-world of the Gothic and romance writers but as believable and recognizable a place as his reader's contemporary world. Scott labored to provide an accurate historical setting for his novels and to equip his characters with plausible motives and behavior. Scottish customs, speech, and geography are carefully rendered. The past is used not for its eerie or romantic atmosphere but as a context for Scott's drama of actual men and "those passions common to men in all stages of society, and which have alike agitated the human heart, whether it throbbed under the steel corselet of the fifteenth century, the brocaded coat of the eighteenth, or the blue frock and white dimity waistcoat of the present day." Nothing like it had ever been done in the novel before—the past exposed with the immediacy and verisimilitude of the present.

Certainly, the past had been the province of the literary artist before Scott. In *The Iliad* Homer reflects his own times by locating his story in the

action of the Greeks centuries before on the plains of Troy. Other classical writers exploited the distancing effect of placing the action for their plays and stories in a remote and mythological time. The most immediate precedent for Scott, however, was unquestionably Shakespeare's History Plays. The essential ingredients of the historical novel are all contained in Shakespeare's English and Roman historical plays: the use of actual historical figures and events, the intersection of the public and the private, and the exploration of contemporary issues from the perspective of the past. Shakespeare also demonstrates the liberties Scott and future historical novelists could claim in their versions of the past. For Shakespeare history is not entombed by the details of the past but liberated from them to become a living presence. The distant is brought near, and the present is shown as an outgrowth of the past. But did it happen exactly as Shakespeare described? Such a question seems beside the point when locating the plays' truthfulness to character and theme. The Henry plays in particular (*Henry IV, parts 1 and 2* and *Henry V*) offered Scott a useful model that shaped all of the Waverley novels. Actual and invented characters are joined to suggest the ways in which public events are shaped by the personal, and vice versa. The world of the court and the tavern intersect, and Shakespeare makes both believable by the force of his imagination. The actual details of history—personages and events—are employed but are shaped by Shakespeare's artistic vision and themes, even to the extent of telescoping events and falsifying facts. Shakespeare's legacy to the historical novel is the repossession of the past with the artistic license to revivify history shaped by the imagination. What Shakespeare attempted in the drama, Scott adapted to the novel and created a new fictional form.

Because Scott's popularity has waned considerably in the 20th century, it is difficult for a modern reader to appreciate the influence of Scott's novels in England, America, and Europe during the 19th century. Only if we recognize the extent of Scott's popularity can we make sense of

Mark Twain's claim that Scott's portrait of the chivalric past was responsible for the American Civil War. James Fenimore Cooper, who would be labeled the "American Scott," began his writing career convinced that he could outdo the author of the Waverley novels at historical romances and in the process started America's novel tradition. In England during the Victorian period almost all of the important novelists—Charles Dickens, William Makepeace Thackerary, George Eliot, Wilkie Collins, Elizabeth Gaskell, Anthony Trollope, and Thomas Hardy—and a host of others who are rarely read today, such as Harrison Ainsworth, G.P.R. James, Charles Reade, and Edward Bulwer-Lytton, tried their hand or made their living writing historical novels. Beyond America and England, the historical novel in the 19th century was adapted and imitated throughout the world: by Victor Hugo, Honoré Balzac, and Gustave Flaubert in France, by Aleksandr Pushkin and Leo Tolstoy in Russia, by Alessandro Mazoni in Italy, and by Benito Pérez Galdós in Spain. Scott's success attracted a host of imitators, of varying degrees of artistic seriousness and talent. So popular would the historical novel become during the Victorian period that a young Anthony Trollope was advised by an editor to avoid it because "Your historical novel is not worth a damn."

Historical Romance

For the historical novel overproduction rapidly bred critical suspicion and contempt for the form as writers of considerable weaker aesthetic skills and less serious intentions began to dominate the field. The historical novel, like any other narrative genre, can easily sink into a formula fiction with stock characters and implausible action, stilted dialogue, and period details that are as real as a costume party. Instead of an instrument of truthtelling, the historical novel can easily become a means for escape into the past as an exotic locale for fantasy and wish fulfillment. The novel's psychological and social realism can regress to the older tendencies of the prose romance: remote and exotic settings and idealized character types, in which action and adventure are primary. The principal apologist in the 19th century for the historical romance, as opposed to the historical novel, was another Scotsman, Robert Lewis Stevenson. For Stevenson, the novel must entertain and has no responsibility to teach or persuade the reader of anything more than to turn the pages and enjoy the pleasure of suspense, adventure, mystery, and romance. In Stevenson's view incident, not character development or landscape and period painting, was the engine of the novel, and the novel required incidents, in his words, "animated with passion, passion clothed upon with situation. Neither exists for itself, but each inheres indissolubly with the other." By emphasizing adventure over truth in historical fiction Stevenson helped establish a second stream for the historical novel as it entered the 20th century.

Somewhere along the continuum between Scott and Stevenson, between the literary historian and the story-teller, between the realist and the romancer, historical novelists can be located. This is not to say that the tendencies of the story-teller are lacking in Scott or that Stevenson was willing to sacrifice all standards of verisimilitude in search of adventure in the past. Rather, the distinction between the predominant elements of both novelists provides a useful way of evaluating the intentions of historical novelists and establishing an appropriate standard for judging their work. As the historical fiction genre entered the 20th century, along with all prose fiction, it divided between high art and low, between truthtelling and entertainment, between the serious and the popular. I am not arguing here that popular historical genre fiction cannot have elements of truth or that serious historical novels cannot entertain, but I do contend each should be judged based on the author's intention and goal.

The Historical Novel in the 20th Century

What is most striking in surveying historical fiction in the 20th century is its multiplicity of forms. Historical fiction can be found in almost every section of the modern bookstore: shelved alongside the classics or serious contemporary fiction or in the romance, mystery, fantasy, and biographical sections. Each has its own set of conventions and standards as writers choose the historical past as the locale for their imagining, and each genre adds a new set of criteria to the evaluation of the novelist's performance, which may or may not be appropriate for another. A fictional biographer, for example, must be extremely careful about the degree of invention employed, whereas other historical novelists can claim a great deal of liberty to modify the past. E.L. Doctorow, for example, in discussing his novel *Ragtime*, observed "So my answer to the question—Is this really true? Did Morgan really meet Ford? Did Evelyn Nesbit really meet Emma Goldman?—My answer is, they have now."

What is remarkable in the collection of the authors and titles in this book are the range and diversity of the historical form, evidence of the continuing appeal both to readers and novelists of the past as a source of entertainment and illumination. There are examples of historical novels functioning as genre fiction, in which the past is used only as an exotic backdrop to enhance the novel's romance and in which stock elements and predictable outcomes reassure rather than stimulate the reader. There are other examples in which the past is exposed in original and challenging ways that provide new insights about what it must have been like to live in a past time, as well as how the past offers a reflection of present concerns. Attention to historical accuracy offered by historical novelists ranges from one extreme to the other. Mary Renault provides one side of the debate in arguing that "As a historical novelist I have a powerful horror of exploiting the dead. . . . I have tried to fill in the gaps, but never knowingly falsified. I would rather approach the graves of our forebears upon earth as a guardian and servant, than as a tomb-robber." The other

side points to the impossibility of ever reaching a satisfactory standard of historical accuracy and even contests that that should be a goal. Lion Feuchtwanger has argued that the historical novelist "has no other intention than to give expression to his own (contemporary) attitudes and a subjective (but in no sense historical) view of the world, and to do so in a way that these could be perceived directly by the reader. Whenever he chose to use historical wrappings, it was for the purpose of elevating the subject out of the personal and private realm in order to set it on a platform and achieve a degree of distance." Concerning historical accuracy, Feuchtwanger argues that "I cannot imagine that a serious novelist, when working with historical subject matter, could ever regard historical facts as anything other than a means of achieving distance, as a metaphor, in order to render his own feelings, his own era, his own philosophy, and himself as accurately as possible. . . . Asking the author of historical novels to teach you about history is like expecting the composer of a melody to provide answers about radio transmission. . . . Contrary to the scientist, the author of historical novels has the right to choose a lie that enhances illusion over a reality that distracts from it." Readers of historical novels should be mindful of both positions in assessing the utility of the form and the standards and goals of the novelist.

And what about the critical reputation of the historical novel in the 20th century? It is clear that the historical novel as a form has suffered for its popularity until fairly recently. Many critics have dismissed historical novels as being simply less truthful than history (begging the question of the nature and degree of illusion certainly present in any historical study). Critics have been slow to grant that instead of falling short of a standard of truth the historical novel offers something beyond factual data, which in the hands of a literary genius can become a masterpiece. Rather, the form itself has been condemned based on the lack of achievement by its weakest practitioners. There is no question that there are degrees of successes in the historical novel, as there are in poetry, drama, and other forms of novels. Few critics, however, reject the potential of tragedy, for example, when a play only reaches the level of the melodramatic.

The historical novel persists as both a serious literary form and as a form of popular entertainment. There are signs that critics have increasingly recognized this fact as the number of recent book-length critical studies cited in the "Suggestions for Further Reading" indicate. In recent years the various influences of popular culture have attracted critical scrutiny, and the historical novel has earned its share of attention. The historical novel has also been given a place in the literary canon both as a subject for serious critical inquiry and as a form for important literary achievement.

Controversy still surrounds the form, however, as the furor over William Styron's treatment of slavery in *The Confessions of Nat Turner* and over Gore Vidal's portrait of Abraham Lincoln reveals. Interpreting the past is risky business, as Oliver Stone discovered in his historical films *J.F.K.* and *Nixon*. In October 1992 *American Heritage* magazine published an issue devoted to the historical novel, entitled "Truth *and* Fiction: The Power of the Historical Novel" that summarizes

much of the controversy over the form. The issue includes a survey of novelists, journalists, and historians who were asked what their favorite American historical novel was and why. The results are a fascinating testimony both to the ambiguity of the historical novel and its continuing appeal. Almost every conceivable novel is mentioned for praise and sometimes is awkwardly made to fit into the historical fiction category. Several historians confess that historical novels first got them hooked on history; novelists argue over definitions but most maintain that the past remains a challenging and fertile terrain for fictional imagining. What is obvious in sampling the various opinions expressed is that the historical novel is far from being an outdated literary form and instead can still spark a lively debate on how the past should be recalled and imagined and the various pleasures that can be derived from a fictional encounter with history.

It is my hope that this book will add to the debate over the historical novel if only because it attempts to gather together so many novels that deal with the past for the reader's pleasure and edification. Far from being an old-fashioned fictional form whose best years are behind it, the historical novel seems far healthier than expected with the prognosis of a long, rich life ahead of it.

The Most Popular Historical Novels

This listing is based on data of best sellers compiled by *Publisher's Weekly* since 1895. Novels included appeared on at least one end-of-year top-ten hardcover fiction best seller list. Novels published before 1895 have certainly sold in excess of a million copies and in several instances are perennial best sellers.

Author	Title	Year of Publication
Allen, Hervey	*Anthony Adverse*	1933
	Action at Aquila	1938
	The Forest and the Fort	1943
Archer, Jeffrey	*As the Crow Flies*	1991
Asch, Sholem	*The Nazarene*	1939
	The Apostle	1943
	Mary	1949
	Moses	1951
Auchincloss, Louis	*The Rector of Justin*	1964
Auel, Jean	*The Valley of Horses*	1982
	The Mammoth Hunters	1985
Bacheller, Irving	*D'ri and I*	1901
	Light in the Clearing	1901
	A Man for the Ages	1919
Bellamann, Henry	*Kings Row*	1940
Bristow, Gwen	*Calico Palace*	1970
	Jubilee Trail	1950
Buck, Pearl S.	*The Good Earth*	1931
Bulwer-Lytton, Edward	*The Last Days of Pompeii*	1834
Caldwell, Taylor	*Never Victorious, Never Defeated*	1954
	Dear and Glorious Physician	1959
	Grandmother and the Priests	1963
	Captains and the Kings	1972
	Ceremony of the Innocent	1976
	Great Lion of God	1970
	A Pillar of Iron	1965
	Testimony of Two Men	1968
Carr, Caleb	*The Alienist*	1994
Churchill, Winston	*Richard Carvel*	1899
	The Crossing	1904
	Coniston	1906
Clavell, James	*Shogun*	1975
	Tai-Pan	1966

Cooper, James Fenimore	*The Spy*	1821
	The Last of the Mohicans	1826
	The Deerslayer	1841
Costain, Thomas B.	*The Black Rose*	1946
	The Moneyman	1947
	High Towers	1949
	The Silver Chalice	1952
	The Tontine	1955
	Below the Salt	1957
Crane, Stephen	*The Red Badge of Courage*	1895
Crichton, Michael	*The Great Train Robbery*	1975
Delderfield, R.F.	*God Is an Englishman*	1970
	Theirs Was the Kingdom	1971
Dickens, Charles	*A Tale of Two Cities*	1859
Doctorow, E.L.	*Ragtime*	1975
Douglas, Lloyd C.	*The Robe*	1942
	The Big Fisherman	1948
Du Maurier, Daphne	*Hungry Hill*	1943
	The King's General	1946
	Mary Anne	1954
	The Glass-Blowers	1963
Dumas, Alexandre	*The Three Musketeers*	1844
Eco, Umberto	*The Name of the Rose*	1983
Eden, Dorothy	*The Vines of Yarrabee*	1969
Edmonds, Walter D.	*Drums Along the Mohawk*	1936
Erskine, John	*The Private Life of Helen of Troy*	1925
Fast, Howard	*The Immigrants*	1977
	Second Generation	1978
	The Establishment	1979
	The Legacy	1981
Ferber, Edna	*Show Boat*	1926
	Cimarron	1930
	Saratoga Trunk	1941
Follett, Ken	*The Man From St. Petersburg*	1982
Ford, Paul L.	*Janice Meredith*	1899
Fowles, John	*The French Lieutenant's Woman*	1969
Gann, Ernest K.	*The Antagonists*	1970
Hawthorne, Nathaniel	*The Scarlet Letter*	1850
Hayden, Sterling	*Voyage: A Novel of 1896*	1976
Hill, Ruth Beebe	*Hanta Yo*	1979
Holt, Victoria	*The Queen's Confession*	1968
Hough, Emerson	*54-40 or Fight*	1909
Howatch, Susan	*Cashelmara*	1974
Jakes, John	*North and South*	1982
	Love and War	1984

Johnston, Mary	*To Have and to Hold*	1899
	Audrey	1902
	The Long Roll	1911
Jong, Erica	*Fanny*	1980
Kantor, MacKinlay	*Andersonville*	1955
Kaye, M.M.	*The Far Pavilions*	1978
	Shadow of the Moon	1979
Keyes, Frances P.	*I, the King*	1966
	Steamboat Gothic	1952
	Blue Camellia	1957
Koen, Karleen	*Through a Glass Darkly*	1986
L'Amour, Louis	*The Walking Drum*	1984
	Jubal Sackett	1985
Lampedusa, Giuseppe di	*The Leopard*	1960
Llewellyn, Richard	*How Green Was My Valley*	1940
Lockridge, Ross	*Raintree County*	1948
Lofts, Norah	*The Lost Queen*	1969
Lord, Betty Bao	*Spring Moon*	1981
Mailer, Norman	*The Executioner's Song*	1979
Malamud, Bernard	*The Fixer*	1966
Mason, F. Van Wyck	*Cutlass Empire*	1949
McMurtry, Larry	*Lonesome Dove*	1985
Meyer, Nicholas	*The Seven-Per-Cent Solution*	1974
	The West End Horror	1976
Michener, James	*Hawaii*	1959
	The Source	1965
	Centennial	1974
	Chesapeake	1978
	The Covenant	1980
	Poland	1983
	Texas	1985
	Alaska	1988
Mitchell, Margaret	*Gone with the Wind*	1936
Mitchell, S. Weir	*Hugh Wynne, Free Quaker*	1898
Mydans, Shelley	*Thomas*	1965
Page, Elizabeth	*The Tree of Liberty*	1939
Pasternak, Boris	*Doctor Zhivago*	1958
Portis, Charles	*True Grit*	1968
Price, Eugenia	*New Moon Rising*	1969
Renault, Mary	*The Mask of Apollo*	1966
	Fire From Heaven	1969
	The Persian Boy	1972
Ripley, Alexandra	*Scarlett*	1992

Roberts, Kenneth	*Northwest Passage*	1937
	Oliver Wiswell	1940
	Lydia Bailey	1947
	Boon Island	1956
Rolvaag, O.E.	*Peder Victorious*	1929
Rutherfurd, Edward	*Sarum*	1987
Sabatini, Rafael	*The Carolinian*	1925
Scott, Walter	*Ivanhoe*	1819
	Kenilworth	1821
Selinko, Annemarie	*Désirée*	1953
Seton, Anya	*Green Darkness*	1972
	The Winthrop Woman	1958
Shaara, Jeff	*Gods and Generals*	1996
Shellabarger, Samuel	*Captain From Castile*	1945
	Prince of Foxes	1947
	Lord Vanity	1953
Sienkiewicz, Henryk	*Quo Vadis*	1897
Solomon, Ruth F.	*The Candlesticks and the Cross*	1967
Solzhenitsyn, Alexander	*August 1914*	1972
Steel, Danielle	*Zoya*	1988
Steen, Marguerite	*The Sun Is My Undoing*	1941
Stevenson, Robert L.	*Treasure Island*	1883
Stewart, Mary	*The Crystal Cave*	1970
	The Hollow Hills	1973
	The Last Enchantment	1979
	The Wicked Day	1983
Stone, Irving	*Immortal Wife*	1944
	Love Is Eternal	1954
	The Agony and the Ecstasy	1961
	Those Who Love	1965
	The Passions of the Mind	1971
	The Greek Treasure	1975
	The Origin	1980
Styron, William	*The Confessions of Nat Turner*	1967
Thackeray, William M.	*Vanity Fair*	1848
Thompson, Maurice	*Alice of Old Vincennes*	1900
Tolstoy, Leo	*War and Peace*	1872
Uris, Leon	*Trinity*	1976
Vidal, Gore	*Julian*	1964
	Washington, D.C.	1967
	Burr	1973
	1876	1976
	Creation	1981
	Lincoln	1984
Wallace, Lew	*Ben-Hur*	1880

Walpole, Hugh	*Rogue Herries*	1930
Waltari, Mika	*The Egyptian*	1949
	The Adventurer	1950
	The Wanderer	1951
Werfel, Franz	*The Song of Bernadette*	1942
West, Jessamyn	*Except for Me and Thee*	1969
	The Massacre at Fall Creek	1975
Wilder, Thornton	*The Bridge of San Luis Rey*	1927
	Woman of Andros	1930
Williams, Ben Ames	*House Divided*	1947
	The Unconquered	1953
Winsor, Kathleen	*Forever Amber*	1944
Wouk, Herman	*The Winds of War*	1971
	War and Remembrance	1978
Yerby, Frank	*The Vixens*	1947
	The Golden Hawk	1948
	Pride's Castle	1949
	Floodtide	1950
	A Woman Called Fancy	1951
	The Saracen Blade	1952
	Benton's Row	1954
Young, Stark	*So Red the Rose*	1934

Pulitzer Prize Winning Historical Novels

Author	Title	Award Year
Wilder, Thornton	*The Bridge of San Luis Rey*	1928
Buck, Pearl S.	*The Good Earth*	1932
Davis, H.L.	*Honey in the Horn*	1936
Mitchell, Margaret	*Gone with the Wind*	1937
Guthrie, A.B.	*The Way West*	1950
Kantor, MacKinlay	*Andersonville*	1956
Taylor, Robert L.	*The Travels of Jaimie McPheeters*	1959
Malamud, Bernard	*The Fixer*	1966
Styron, William	*The Confessions of Nat Turner*	1968
Stegner, Wallace	*The Angle of Repose*	1972
Shaara, Michael	*The Killer Angels*	1975
Mailer, Norman	*The Executioner's Song*	1980
McMurtry, Larry	*Lonesome Dove*	1986

Recommended Historical Novels

Below is a selection from a great number of excellent historical novels contained in this book. Listed are those novels that in the author's opinion bring together a vivid and authentic re-creation of the past with a rousing fictional story and compelling characters and are particularly recommended.

Author	Title	Year of Publication

PREHISTORY

Author	Title	Year of Publication
Auel, Jean	*The Clan of the Cave Bear*	1980
	The Valley of Horses	1982
	The Plains of Passage	1991
	The Mammoth Hunters	1985
Gear, W. Michael and Gear, Kathleen O'Neal	*The First North Americans Series*	
Golding, William	*The Inheritors*	1962
Kurten, Bjorn	*Dance of the Tiger*	1980
	Singletusk	1986
Wolf, Joan	*Daughter of the Red Deer*	1991
	The Horsemasters	1993
	The Reindeer Hunters	1994

THE ANCIENT WORLD

Egypt

Author	Title	Year of Publication
Drury, Allen	*A God Against the Gods*	1976
	Return to Thebes	1977
Gedge, Pauline	*The Twelfth Transforming*	1984
	Lady of the Reeds	1995
Hawkes, Jacquetta	*King of the Two Lands*	1966
Mailer, Norman	*Ancient Evenings*	1983
McGraw, Eloise J.	*Pharaoh*	1958
Smith, Wilbur	*River God*	1993
Tarr, Judith	*Pillar of Fire*	1995
	King and Goddess	1996
Waltari, Mika	*The Egyptian*	1949

Greece

Duggan, Alfred	*Besieger of Cities*	1963
Mitchison, Naomi	*The Corn King and the Spring Queen*	1931
Parotti, Phillip	*The Greek Generals Talk*	1986
	The Trojan Generals Talk	1988
Paton Walsh, Jill	*Farewell Great King*	1972
Renault, Mary	*The Last of the Wine*	1956
	The King Must Die	1958
	The Mask of Apollo	1966
	Fire From Heaven	1969
	Funeral Games	1981
	The Persian Boy	1972
	The Praise Singer	1978
Rofheart, Martha	*My Name Is Sappho*	1974
Sutcliff, Rosemary	*The Flowers of Adonis*	1970
Warner, Rex	*Pericles the Athenian*	1963

Rome

Bryher	*Roman Wall*	1954
	The Coin of Carthage	1963
Duggan, Alfred	*Winter Quarters*	1956
	Three's Company	1957
	Children of the Wolf	1959
	Family Favorites	1960
Feuchtwanger, Lion	*Josephus*	1932
	The Jew of Rome	1936
	Josephus and the Emperor	1942
Gann, Ernest K.	*The Antagonists*	1970
Graves, Robert	*I, Claudius*	1934
	Claudius the God	1935
Green, Peter	*Sword of Pleasure*	1957
Hardy, William G.	*City of Libertines*	1957
Leckie, Ross	*Hannibal*	1996
Massie, Allan	*Augustus*	1986
	Tiberius	1993
	Caesar	1994
Sienkiewicz, Henryk	*Quo Vadis*	1897
Vidal, Gore	*Julian*	1964
Warner, Rex	*The Young Caesar*	1958
	Imperial Caesar	1960
	The Converts	1967

Wilder, Thornton	*Ides of March*	1948
Williams, John	*Augustus*	1972
Yourcenar, Marguerite	*Hadrian's Memoirs*	1954

Biblical and Christian Eras

Asch, Shalom	*The Nazarene*	1939
	Mary	1949
	Moses	1951
	The Prophet	1955
Bercovici, Konrad	*The Exodus*	1947
Berstl, Julius	*The Tentmaker*	1952
Buckmaster, Henrietta	*And Walk in Love*	1956
Buechner, Frederick	*The Son of Laughter*	1993
Burgess, Anthony	*Man of Nazareth*	1979
Mann, Thomas	*The Joseph Tetralogy*	
Martin, Malachi	*King of Kings*	1980
Mitchison, Naomi	*Blood of the Martyrs*	1948
Schmitt, Gladys	*David the King*	1946

THE DARK AGES

Bryher	*Ruan*	1960
Cornwell, Bernard	*The Winter King*	1995
Duggan, Alfred	*Conscience of the King*	1952
	The Right Line of Cerdic	1961
Gay, Laverne	*The Unspeakables*	1945
Stewart, Mary	*The Crystal Cave*	1970
	The Hollow Hills	1973
	The Last Enchantment	1979
	The Wicked Day	1983
	The Prince and the Pilgrim	1995
Sutcliff, Rosemary	*The Sword at Sunset*	1963
Tapsell, R.F.	*The Year of the Horsetails*	1967
Treece, Henry	*Great Captains*	1955
	Red Queen, White Queen	1958
White, T.H.	*The Once and Future King*	1958
Whyte, Jack	*The Singing Sword*	1996
	The Skystone	1996
Wolf, Joan	*The Road to Avalon*	1988
	The Edge of Light	1990

THE MIDDLE AGES

Andrew, Prudence	*The Hooded Falcon*	1961
	Ordeal by Silence	1961
	The Constant Star	1964
Bryher	*Fourteenth of October*	1952
	This January Tale	1966
Butler, Margaret	*The Lion of England*	1973
	The Lion of Justice	1975
	The Lion of Christ	1977
Closs, Hannah	*High Are the Mountains*	1959
	Deep Are the Valleys	1961
	The Silent Tarn	1963
Druon, Maurice	*The Poisoned Crown*	1957
	The Strangled Queen	1957
	Royal Succession	1958
	The She-Wolf of France	1960
Duggan, Alfred	*Cunning of the Dove*	1960
Eco, Umberto	*The Name of the Rose*	1983
Edmondston, C.M. and Hyde, M.L.F.	*King's Man*	1948
Graham, Alice Walworth	*Vows of the Peacock*	1955
	Shield of Honor	1957
Holland, Cecelia	*The Firedrake*	1966
	Kings in Winter	1968
	Antichrist	1970
Maughan, A.	*Harry of Monmouth*	1956
Muntz, Hope	*Golden Warrior*	1949
Mydans, Shelley	*Thomas*	1965
Oldenbourg, Zoe	*The World Is Not Enough*	1948
	The Cornerstone	1955
	Destiny of Fire	1961
	Cities of the Flesh	1961
	The Heirs of the Kingdom	1971
Palmer, Marian	*White Boar*	1968
Penman, Sharon Kay	*The Sunne in Splendour*	1982
	Here Be Dragons	1987
	Falls the Shadow	1988
	The Reckoning	1991
	When Christ and His Saints Slept	1995
Prescott, Hilda	*The Unhurrying Chase*	1955
	Son of Dust	1956
Schoonover, Lawrence	*Spider King*	1954

Seton, Anya	*Katherine*	1953
Simon, Edith	*Golden Hand*	1952
Tey, Josephine	*The Daughter of Time*	1952
Warner, Sylvia	*The Corner That Held Them*	1948
Weenolson, Hebe	*The Last Englishman*	1951
White, Helen C.	*Not Built with Hands*	1935

THE RENAISSANCE

Europe

Alexander, Sidney	*Michelangelo the Florentine*	1957
	The Hand of Michelangelo	1965
	Nicodemus	1987
Bellonci, Maria	*Private Renaissance*	1989
Dunnett, Dorothy	*The House of Niccolo Series*	
Eliot, George	*Romola*	1863
Ennis, Michael	*Duchess of Milan*	1992
Haase, Hella S.	*The Scarlet City*	1990
Holland, Cecelia	*City of God*	1979
Mann, Heinrich	*Young Henry of Navarre*	1937
Merle, Robert	*Vittoria*	1990
Seymour, Miranda	*The Bride of Sforza*	1975
Spinatelli, Carl	*The Florentine*	1953
Stone, Irving	*The Agony and the Ecstasy*	1961

Tudor and Elizabethan England

Brady, Charles	*Stage of Fools*	1952
Byrd, Elizabeth	*Immortal Queen*	1956
Davidson, Diane	*Feversham*	1969
Delves-Broughton, Josephine	*Heart of a Queen*	1950
Eckerson, Olive	*My Lord Essex*	1955
Finney, Patricia	*The Firedrake's Eye*	1992
Ford, Ford Maddox	*The Fifth Queen*	1963
Garrett, George	*Death of the Fox*	1971
	The Succession	1983
	Entered From the Sun	1990
George, Margaret	*The Autobiography of Henry VIII*	1986
	Mary, Queen of Scotland and the Isles	1992
Gidley, Charles	*Armada*	1987
Miles, Rosalind	*I, Elizabeth*	1994

| John Fowles | *The French Lieutenant's Woman* | 1969 |

20th CENTURY

Barker, Pat	*Regeneration*	1992
	The Eye in the Door	1994
	The Ghost Road	1996
Doctorow, E.L.	*Ragtime*	1976
Faulks, Sebastian	*Birdsong*	1996
Flannagan, Thomas	*The End of the Hunt*	1994
Pasternak, Boris	*Doctor Zhivago*	1958

UNITED STATES

Colonial Period

Allen, Hervey	*The Forest and the Fort*	1943
	Bedford Village	1944
	Toward the Morning	1948
Barth, John	*The Sot-Weed Factor*	1960
Bernhard, Virginia	*A Durable Fire*	1990
Edmonds, Walter D.	*In the Hands of the Senecas*	1947
Fletcher, Inglis	*Roanoke Hundred*	1948
Gebler, Ernest	*Plymouth Adventure*	1950
Mac, Gerard	*Pilgrims*	1994
Roberts, Kenneth	*Northwest Passage*	1937
Seton, Anya	*The Winthrop Woman*	1958
Settle, Mary Lee	*O Beulah Land*	1956
Stone, Grace	*The Cold Journey*	1934
Swanson, Neil	*The First Rebel*	1937
Thom, James Alexander	*Follow the River*	1981

The American Revolution

Giles, Janice	*Hannah Fowler*	1956
Barry, Jane	*Long March*	1955
	The Carolinians	1959
Boyd, James	*Drums*	1925
Churchill, Winston	*Richard Carvel*	1899
	The Crossing	1904
Edmonds, Walter D.	*Drums Along the Mohawk*	1936
Ellis, William	*Bounty Lands*	1952

Fast, Howard	*Conceived in Liberty*	1939
	Citizen Tom Paine	1943
	April Morning	1961
Fleming, Thomas	*Liberty Tavern*	1976
Flood, Charles	*Monmouth*	1961
Ford, Paul Leicester	*Janice Meredith*	1899
Graves, Robert	*Sergeant Lamb's America*	1940
	Proceed, Sergeant Lamb	1941
Lancaster, Bruce	*Guns of Burgoyne*	1939
	Trumpet to Arms	1944
	Blind Journey	1953
Mitchell, S. Weir	*Hugh Wynne, Free Quaker*	1897
Page, Elizabeth	*Tree of Liberty*	1939
Roberts, Kenneth	*Arundel*	1930
	Rabble in Arms	1933
	Oliver Wiswell	1940

19th Century

Davis, Harold	*Beulah Land*	1949
Ehrlich, Leonard	*God's Angry Man*	1932
Nelson, Turman	*Surveyor*	1960
Roberts, Kenneth	*Lively Lady*	1931
	Captain Caution	1934
	Lydia Bailey	1946
Settle, Mary Lee	*Know Nothing*	1960
Styron, William	*The Confessions of Nat Turner*	1967
Walker, Margaret	*Jubilee*	1966
Wallace, Willard M.	*Jonathan Dearborn*	1967
Williams, Ben Ames	*The Unconquered*	1952

The Civil War

Becker, Stephen	*When the War Is Over*	1969
Boyd, James	*Marching On*	1927
Churchill, Winston	*The Crisis*	1901
Crane, Stephen	*The Red Badge of Courage*	1895
Dowdey, Clifford	*The Bugles Blow No More*	1937
Foote, Shelby	*Shiloh*	1952
Jones, Douglas C.	*Elkhorn Tavern*	1980
	The Barefoot Brigade	1985
Kantor, MacKinlay	*Long Remember*	1934
	Andersonville	1955

Keneally, Thomas	*Confederates*	1981
Lancaster, Bruce	*Roll, Shenandoah*	1956
Lentz, Perry	*The Falling Hills*	1967
Mitchell, Margaret	*Gone with the Wind*	1936
Robertson, Don	*The Three Days*	1959
	By Antietam Creek	1960
Shaara, Michael	*The Killer Angels*	1975
Slotkin, Richard	*The Crater*	1980
Warren, Robert Penn	*Wilderness*	1961
Wicker, Tom	*Unto This Hour*	1984
Williams, Ben Ames	*House Divided*	1947
Young, Stark	*So Red the Rose*	1934

The West

Arnold, Elliott	*Time of the Gringo*	1952
Barton, Del	*A Good Day to Die*	1980
Bean, Amelia	*Fancher Train*	1958
	The Feud	1960
	Time for Outrage	1967
Berger, Thomas	*Little Big Man*	1964
Blacker, Irwin	*Taos*	1959
Cather, Willa	*Death Comes for the Archbishop*	1927
Chiaventone, Frederick J.	*A Road We Do Not Know*	1996
Clark, Walter	*The Ox-bow Incident*	1940
Davis, H. L.	*Honey in the Horn*	1935
Dexter, Pete	*Deadwood*	1986
Ferber, Edna	*Cimarron*	1930
Fisher, Vardis	*Children of God*	1939
	Tale of Valor	1958
Guthrie, A.B., Jr.	*The Big Sky*	1947
	The Way West	1949
Hall, Oakley	*Warlock*	1958
Hansen, Ron	*Desperadoes*	1980
Horgan, Paul	*A Distant Trumpet*	1960
LeMay, Alan	*The Searchers*	1954
Manfred, Frederick	*Lord Grizzly*	1954
McMurtry, Larry	*Lonesome Dove*	1985
Portis, Charles	*True Grit*	1968
Rolvaag, O.E.	*Giants in the Earth*	1927
Straight, Michael	*Carrington*	1959
	A Very Small Remnant	1963

AFRICA

Achebe, Chinua	*Things Fall Apart*	1959
Cloete, Stuart	*The Turning Wheel*	1937
Forbath, Peter	*Lord of the Kongo*	1996
Hagerfors, Lennart	*The Whales of Lake Tanganyika*	1989
Halkin, John	*Kenya*	1986
Harrison, William	*Burton and Speke*	1982

ASIA

China

Buck, Pearl S.	*The Good Earth*	1931
	Imperial Woman	1955
Clavell, James	*Tai-pan*	1966
Cooney, Eleanor and Altieri, Daniel	*The Court of the Lion*	1989
	Deception	1992
Elegant, Robert S.	*Dynasty*	1977
	Manchu	1980
	Mandarin	1983
	From a Far Land	1987
Grey, Anthony	*Peking*	1988
Levi, Jean	*The Chinese Emperor*	1987
	The Dream of Confucius	1992
Lord, Bette Bao	*Spring Moon*	1981
Oxnam, Robert B.	*Ming*	1995

India

Alter, Stephen	*Silk and Steel*	1980
Fast, Jonathan	*Golden Fire*	1986
Hoover, Thomas	*The Moghul*	1983
Kaye, M. M.	*Shadow of the Moon*	1957
	The Far Pavilions	1978
Masters, John	*Nightrunners of Bengal*	1950
	The Deceivers	1952
Mehta, Gita	*Raj*	1989
Scott, Paul	*The Raj Quartet*	

Japan

Clavell, James	*Shogun*	1975
	Gai-Jin	1993
Guest, Lynn	*Yedo*	1985
Robson, Lucia St. Clair	*Tokaido Road*	1991
Stacton, David	*Segaki*	1959
Tolosko, Edward	*Sakuran*	1978
Tsuji, Kunio	*The Signore*	
1990 Yoshikawa, Eija	*The Heike Story*	1956
	Musashi	1981
	Taiko	1992

AUSTRALIA AND THE PACIFIC

Bushnell, O.A.	*Molokai*	1965
Nordhoff, Charles & Hall, James	*The Bounty Trilogy*	
Wood, Barbara	*The Dreaming*	1991

SOUTH AMERICA, LATIN AMERICA, AND THE CARIBBEAN

Bell, Madison Smartt	*All Souls' Rising*	1995
Green, Gerald	*The Sword and the Sun*	1953
Jeffries, Bruce	*Drums of Destiny*	1947
Peters, Daniel	*The Luck of Huemac*	1981
	Tikal	1983
	The Incas	1991
Stacton, David	*A Signal Victory*	1960

The Most Popular Time Periods, Settings, Subjects, and Historical Figures

Based on the books included in *What Historical Novel Do I Read Next?*, here are the most popular historical novel categories by time, place, subject, and historical figures who appear as characters.

TIME PERIODS

Top 10 Centuries

	Number of titles
1. 19th century	1070
2. 17th century	449
3. 16th century	420
4 18th century	386
5. 20th century	354
6. 15th century	215
7. 1st century	168
8. 12th century	139
9. 13th century	112
10. 14th century	99

Top 10 Decades

	Number of titles
1. 1860s	500
2. 1810s	279
3. 1850s	264
4. 1910s	252
5. 1870s	229
6. 1770s	225
7. 1880s	208
8. 1780s	197
9. 1800s	195
10. 1840s	195

SETTINGS

Top 10 Countries

	Number of references
1. United States	3338
2. England	2343
3. France	722
4. American Colonies	421
5. Italy	297
6. Scotland	243
7. Russia	179
8. Roman Empire	168
9. Israel	164
10. Ireland	141

Top 10 Cities

	Number of references
1. London	787
2. Paris	249
3. New York	247
4. Rome	186
5. Washington, D.C.	111
6. Boston	100
7. New Orleans	90
8. Jerusalem	71
9. San Francisco	60
10. Vienna	52

SUBJECTS

Top 20 Subjects

	Number of references		Number of references
1. American West	598	11. Romance	355
2. Biography, Fictionalized	536	12. American Colonies	287
3. Indians	541	13. American Revolution	269
4. Mystery	504	14. Settlement of the American Frontier	268
5. Civil War--U.S.	416	15. Roman Empire	229
6. Middle Ages	415	16. Crime and Criminals	221
7. Family Saga	397	17. Napoleonic Wars	181
8. Victorian Period	391	18. World War I	178
9. Royalty--England	360	19. Regency Romance	172
10. Sea Story	357	20. Biblical Story	170

HISTORICAL FIGURES

Top 35 Historical Characters

	Number of titles		Number of titles
1. Elizabeth I	88	20. Arthur Wellesley, Duke of Wellington	27
2. George Washington	87	Edward VII	
3. Napoleon Bonaparte	80	22. Saint Peter	26
4. Henry VIII	60	23. David	25
Jesus Christ		Eleanor of Aquitaine	
6. Abraham Lincoln	57	Julius Caesar	
7. Benjamin Franklin	41	Winston Churchill	
8. Queen Victoria	40	27. James I	24
9. Ulysses S. Grant	39	Louis XIV	
10. Charles II	37	29. The Virgin Mary	23
11. Robert E. Lee	36	Sam Houston	
12. Pontius Pilate	33	William Shakespeare	
13. George Armstrong Custer	31	32. George Rogers Clark	22
14. Franklin Delano Roosevelt	30	33. Anne Boleyn	21
15. Horatio Nelson	29	Catherine of Aragon	
Mary, Queen of Scots		Charles I	
17. Benedict Arnold	28		
George IV			
Marquis de Lafayette			

SUGGESTIONS FOR FURTHER READING

Guides

Baker, Ernest A., *A Guide to Historical Fiction* (London: G. Routledge, 1914).

Bridgers, Emily, *English History Through Historical Novels* (Chapel Hill, North Carolina: North Carolina Library, 1957).

Gerhardstein, Virginia Brokaw, *Dickinson's American Historical Fiction*, 5th edition (Metuchen, New Jersey: Scarecrow Press, 1986).

Hartman, Donald K. and Gregg Sapp, *Historical Figures in Fiction* (Phoenix, Arizona: Oryx Press, 1994).

Herald, Diana Tixier, *Genreflecting: A Guide to Reading Interests in Genre Fiction* (Englewood, Colorado: Libraries Unlimited, 1995).

Irwin, Leonard B., *A Guide to Historical Fiction* (Brooklawn, New Jersey: McKinley, 1971).

Logasa, Hannah, *Historical Fiction: Guide for Junior and Senior High Schools and Colleges, also for General Readers*, 8th ed. (Philadelphia: McKinley, 1964).

McGarry, Daniel D. and Sarah Harriman White, *Historical Fiction Guide* (Metuchen, New Jersey: Scarecrow Press, 1963).

Neild, Jonathan, *A Guide to the Best Historical Novels and Tales* (New York: Macmillan, 1929).

Spearman, Walter Smith, *American History Through Historical Novels* (Chapel Hill, North Carolina: North Carolina Library, 1952).

VanMeter, Vandelia, *America in Historical Fiction: A Bibliographic Guide* (Englewood, Colorado: Libraries Unlimited, 1997).

Criticism

Allemano, Marina, *Historical Portraits and Visions* (New York: Garland, 1991).

Altick, Richard, *The English Common Reader* (Chicago: University of Chicago Press, 1957).

Broerman, Bruce M., *The German Historical Novel in Exile After 1933* (University Park: Pennsylvania State University Press, 1986).

Brown, David D., *Walter Scott and the Historical Imagination* (Boston: Routledge & Kegan Paul, 1979).

Butterfield, Herbert, *The Historical Novel: An Essay* (Cambridge: Cambridge University Press, 1924).

Cahalan, James M., *The Great Hatred, Little Room: The Irish Historical Novel* (New York: Syracuse University Press, 1983).

Cam, Helen, *Historical Novels* (London: Routledge, 1961).

Chapman, Raymond, *The Sense of the Past in Victorian Literature* (London: Croom Helm, 1986).

Cockburn, Claud, *Bestseller* (London: Sidgwick & Jackson, 1972).

Connor, Steven, *English Novel in History, 1950 to the Present* (New York: Routledge, 1945).

Cullen, Jim, *The Civil War in Popular Culture: A Reusable Past* (Washington, D.C.: Smithsonian Institution Press, 1995).

Dekker, George, *The American Historical Romance* (New York: Cambridge University Press, 1987).

Feuchtwanger, Lion, *The House of Desdemona, or, The Laurels and Limitations of Historical Fiction* (Detroit: Wayne State University Press, 1963).

Fisher, Philip, *Hard Facts: Setting and Form in the American Novel* (New York: Oxford University Press, 1987).

Fleishman, Avrom, *The English Historical Novel: Walter Scott to Virginia Woolf* (Baltimore: Johns Hopkins Press, 1971).

Foley, Barbara, *Telling the Truth: The Theory and Practice of Documentary Fiction* (Ithaca, New York: Cornell University Press, 1986).

Friedman, Barton R., *Fabricating History: English Writers on the French Revolution* (Princeton: Princeton University Press, 1988).

Gorgorza Fletcher, Madeleine de, *The Spanish Historical Novel, 1870-1970* (London: Tamesis Books, 1974).

Henderson, Harry B. III, *Versions of the Past* (New York: Oxford University Press, 1974).

Higdon, David Leon, *Shadows of the Past in Contemporary British Fiction* (Athens, Georgia: University of Georgia Press, 1984).

Hughes, Helen, *The Historical Romance* (New York: Routledge, 1993).

Hughson, Lois, *From Biography to History: The Historical Imagination in American Fiction, 1880-1940* (Charlottesville, Virginia: University Press of Virginia, 1988).

Jacobs, Naomi, *The Character of Truth: Historical Figures in Contemporary Fiction* (Cabondale, Illinois: Southern Illinois University Press, 1990).

Kantor, MacKinlay, *The Historical Novelist's Obligation to History* (Macon, Georgia: Wesleyan College, 1966).

Lascelles, Mary, *The Story-Teller Retrieves the Past: Historical Fiction and Fictitious History in the Art of Scott, Stevenson, Kipling, and Some Others* (New York: Oxford University Press, 1980).

Leasy, Ernest Erwin, *The American Historical Novel* (Norman, Oklahoma: Oklahoma University Press, 1950).

Leavis, Q.D., *Fiction and the Reading Public* (London: Chatto & Windus, 1932).

Levin, David, *In Defense of Historical Literature* (New York: Hill and Wang, 1967).

Lovell, Terry, *Consuming Fiction* (New York: Verso, 1988).

Lukacs, Georg, *The Historical Novel* (Lincoln, Nebraska: University of Nebraska Press, 1962).

Lukacs, John, *Historical Consciousness; or, The Remembered Past* (New York: Harper & Row, 1968).

Manzoni, Alessandro, *On the Historical Novel* (Lincoln, Nebraska: University of Nebraska Press, 1984).

Marriott, J.R.R., *English History in English Fiction* (New York: Dutton, 1941).

Martin, Michael, *The Big Domino in the Sky* (Amherst, New York: Prometheus Press, 1996).

Martin, Rhona, *Writing Historical Fiction* (New York: St. Martin's Press, 1988).

Matthews, Brander, *The Historical Novel, and Other Essays* (New York: Scribner's, 1914).

McEwan, Neil, *Perspective in British Historical Fiction Today* (Wolfeboro, New Hampshire: Longwood Academic, 1987).

Menton, Seymour, *Latin America's New Historical Novel* (Austin, Texas: University of Texas Press, 1993).

Onega, Susana, ed., *Telling Histories: Narrativizing History, Historicizing Literature* (Atlanta: Rodopi, 1995).

Orel, Harold, *The Historical Novel from Scott to Sabatini: Changing Attitudes Toward a Literary Genre* (New York: St. Martin's Press, 1995).

Radway, Janice, *Reading the Romance: Women, Patriachy and Popular Literature* (Chapel Hill, North Carolina: University of North Carolina Press, 1991).

Roberts, David, ed., *The Modern German Historical Novel: Paradigms, Problems, Perspectives* (New York: Berg, 1991).

Robertson, Fiona, *Legitimate Histories: Scott, Gothic, and the Authorities of Fiction* (New York: Oxford University Press, 1994).

Sanders, Andrew, *The Victorian Historical Novel, 1840-1880* (New York: Macmillan, 1979).

Sauerberg, Lars de, *Fact into Fiction: Documentary Realism in the Contemporary Novel* (New York: St. Martin's Press, 1991).

Scanlan, Margaret, *Traces of Another Time: History and Politics in Postwar British Fiction* (Princeton: Princeton University Press, 1990).

Shaw, Harry E., *The Forms of Historical Fiction: Sir Walter Scott and His Successors* (Ithaca, New York: Cornell University Press, 1983).

Sheppard, Alfred T., *The Art and Practice of Historical Fiction* (London: H. Toulmin, 1930).

Simmons, Clare A., *Reversing the Conquest: History and Myth in Nineteenth-century British Literature* (New Brunswick, New Jersey: Rutgers University Press, 1990).

Terry, R.C., *Victorian Popular Fiction, 1860-80* (Atlantic Highland, New Jersey: Humanities Press, 1983).

Wesseling, Elisabeth, *Writing History as a Prophet: Postmodernist Innovations of the Historical Novel* (Philadelphia: J. Benjamins, 1991).

Williams, John, *E.L. Doctorow in the Postmodern Age* (Columbia, South Carolina: Camden House, 1996).

Zimmerman, Everett, *The Boundaries of Fiction: History and the Eighteenth-century British Novel* (Ithaca, New York: Cornell University Press, 1996).

WHAT HISTORICAL NOVEL DO I READ NEXT?

VOLUME 1
A-Z

Volume 1

ANNE MERTON ABBEY
(PSEUD. OF JEAN BROOKS)

1 *Kathryn: In the Court of Six Queens*

Date of Publication: 1989
Subject(s): Tudor Period; Royalty—England
Fictional character(s): Kathryn Chase, Gentlewoman; John de Gael, Gentleman
Historical character(s): Henry VIII, Ruler (King of England); Catherine of Aragon, Royalty (queen consort of Henry VIII); Anne Boleyn, Royalty (queen consort of Henry VIII); Jane Seymour, Royalty (queen consort of Henry VIII); Anne of Cleves, Royalty (queen consort of Henry VIII); Catherine Howard, Royalty (queen consort of Henry VIII); Catherine Parr, Royalty (queen consort of Henry VIII)
Time Period(s): 16th century
Locale(s): England

Summary: The intrigue and marital complications of Henry VIII's reign are dramatized from the perspective of the fictional Kathryn Chase. As a lady-in-waiting to the king's six wives, Kathryn is in a position to witness a good deal of the behind-the-scenes details of both historical fact and imaginative speculation.

Historical Accuracy: The novel both animates historical fact and embellishes it with some intriguing possibilities.

MARGARET ABBEY
(PSEUD. OF MARGARET ELIZABETH YORK, 1927-)

Born in Leicester, England, educator and author Margaret Abbey taught history, drama, and English for 25 years and was the head of the English department at a comprehensive school in Leicester. Her novels include *Flight of the Kestrel*, *Brothers in Arms*, and *Amber Promise*. She has also written under the names Joanna Makepeace and Elizabeth York.

2 *Blood of the Boar*

Date of Publication: 1979
Subject(s): War of the Roses; Royalty—England
Fictional character(s): Catherine Newberry, Spouse (of Kingsford); Sir Hugh Kingsford, Gentleman
Historical character(s): Richard III, Ruler (King of England)
Time Period(s): 15th century (1484-1486)
Locale(s): England

Summary: This romantic novel continues the story of Catherine Newberry during the reign of Richard III. Her husband's resentment of Catherine's love for the king leads to his banishment, while Catherine is forced to reveal the true parentage of her son and protect him from his enemies.

Historical Accuracy: The story is a fictional one with only a slight connection to actual events.

3 *The Flight of the Kestrel*

Date of Publication: 1973
Subject(s): Elizabethan Period; Pirates; Sea Story
Fictional character(s): Donna Carlotta de Rodriguez, Gentlewoman; Sir Robin Maldry, Gentleman
Historical character(s): Elizabeth I, Ruler (Queen of England)
Time Period(s): 16th Century
Locale(s): *Kestrel*, At Sea; England

Summary: This romantic adventure tale set during the conflict between England and Spain concerns the beautiful Donna Carlotta de Rodriguez who loses her heart to a mysterious pirate captain.

Historical Accuracy: The story has some convincing period elements, but the emphasis is on romantic adventure rather than documenting particular historical events.

4 *The Heart Is a Traitor*

Date of Publication: 1978
Subject(s): War of The Roses; Royalty—England
Fictional character(s): Catherine Newberry, Ward; Sir Hugh Kingsford, Gentleman

Historical character(s): Richard, Duke of Gloucester, Royalty (Duke of Gloucester)
Time Period(s): 15th century (1480s)
Locale(s): England; Lille, France

Summary: This romantic triangle set during the War of the Roses involves Catherine Newberry, a ward of the crown, who is married to Sir Hugh Kingsford at the request of Richard of Gloucester. Catherine, however, is in love with Richard.

Historical Accuracy: The story is fanciful and the period elements are only lightly sketched.

5   *The Son of York*

Date of Publication: 1971
Subject(s): War of the Roses
Fictional character(s): Sir Charles Beaumont, Gentleman; Margaret Woollatt, Servant
Historical character(s): Richard, Duke of Gloucester, Royalty (Duke of Gloucester)
Time Period(s): 15th century (1479)
Locale(s): England

Summary: This tale of political intrigue takes as its background the succession controversy that brings Richard, Duke of Gloucester, to the throne as Richard III. Sir Charles Beaumont returns to England on a secret mission and is plunged into a tangle of intrigue.

Historical Accuracy: The novel accepts the debated contention that Perkin Warbeck was indeed Richard, Duke of York.

6   *The Warwick Heiress*

Date of Publication: 1970
Subject(s): War of the Roses; Royalty—England
Fictional character(s): Piers Langham, Knight
Historical character(s): Anne Neville, Noblewoman; Richard, Duke of Gloucester, Nobleman; Edward IV, Ruler (King of England)
Time Period(s): 15th century
Locale(s): England

Summary: The dynastic conflict of the War of the Roses is dramatized through the relationship between Anne Neville, the daughter of Warwick, the Kingmaker, and Richard, Duke of Gloucester, the ambitious younger brother of Edward IV. Their love, which flourishes despite the enmity between their families, is seen through the eyes of Piers Langham, a knight in Richard's household.

Historical Accuracy: The dialogue and details are invented, though the story does capture the period conflict between the Houses of York and Lancaster.

JANE LUDLOW ABBOT (1881-)

An American writer born in Buffalo, New York, Abbott attended Cornell University. Abbott's other books include *Angels May Weep*.

7   *River's Run*

Date of Publication: 1950

Subject(s): War of 1812
Fictional character(s): Quint Darby, Young Man
Time Period(s): 1810s
Locale(s): New York

Summary: During the War of 1812 Quint Darby falls under suspicion because of the British sympathies of his father and brother.

Historical Accuracy: The actual events of the war are remote and sketchily drawn. The characters are melodramatic.

MARGOT ABBOTT

8   *The Last Innocent Hour*

Date of Publication: 1991
Subject(s): World War II; Nazis
Fictional character(s): Sally Jackson, Military Personnel (intelligence officer); Christian Mayr, Military Personnel
Historical character(s): Reinhard Heydrich, Military Personnel; Adolf Hitler, Political Figure
Time Period(s): 1930s; 1940s (1933-1946)
Locale(s): Berlin, Germany

Summary: Sally Jackson returns to Berlin in 1946 as an army intelligence officer helping to prosecute war criminals. Memories take her back to 1933 when as the naive daughter of the American ambassador she falls in love and marries Nazi Christian Mayr. Both come under the special attention of General Reinhard Heydrich, Himmler's protege.

Historical Accuracy: The story is based loosely on U.S. Ambassador William Dodd's daughter Martha.

ROBERT H. ABEL (1941-)

An American novelist and professor of English, Abel is the author of several collections of short stories, including *Skin and Bones*, *Full-Tilt Boogie*, and *Ghost Traps*. His novel *The Progress of Fire* appeared in 1985.

9   *Freedom's Dues*

Date of Publication: 1980
Subject(s): American Revolution; Slavery; American Colonies
Fictional character(s): Jonathan Dunhill, Journalist, Businessman; Lydia Dunhill, Heroine; Gwanga, Slave
Historical character(s): John Hancock, Patriot, Businessman; Benjamin Franklin, Political Figure, Businessman; John Adams, Political Figure; Samuel Adams, Patriot
Time Period(s): 18th century (1751-1770s)
Locale(s): Boston, Massachusetts, American Colonies; Northampton, Massachusetts, American Colonies

Summary: Chronicling two decades of colonial life, the novel is written in the form of the memoirs of Jonathan Dunhill, publisher of the *Boston Oracle* and *Dockside Advertiser*. With the help of his fiery wife, Lydia, and his slave, Gwanga (whose attempt to earn his freedom provides the novel's title), Dunhill operates his newspapers and observes the opening political intrigues of the American Revolution.

Historical Accuracy: The narrator is far from worshipful of the historical figures, which makes the novel a lively and controversial take on the period.

CECIL ABERNETHY (1908-)

Born in Charleston, South Carolina, Abernethy received his Ph.D. from Vanderbilt University and has taught at several colleges. He is the author of several scholarly works.

10　*Mr. Pepys of Seething Lane*

Date of Publication: 1957
Subject(s): Restoration Period; Biography, Fictionalized
Historical character(s): Samuel Pepys, Writer, Government Official
Time Period(s): 17th century
Locale(s): London, England

Summary: Based on the 3,000-page diary of Samuel Pepys, the novel reconstructs the story of this tailor's son who becomes Secretary of the Affairs of the Admiralty during the Restoration of Charles II. The novel offers a vivid look at 17th-century London and the politics of the period.

Historical Accuracy: This is neither a biography nor a history but a narrative with only occasional invented dialogue.

PETER ABRAHAMS (1919-)

Abrahams, the son of an Ethiopian father and a mother of mixed French and African ancestry, was born near Johannesburg, South Africa. He began working at the age of nine as a tinsmith's helper and was educated while working at such jobs as kitchen helper, dishwasher, porter, and clerk. After failing in his attempt to start a school for poor Africans, Abrahams worked as an editor, a journalist, and for two years as a stoker at sea. Eventually, he imigrated to Jamaica, where he became a radio news commentator, magazine editor, and the chair of Radio Jamaica. His works include *A Blackman Speaks of Freedom*, *Return to Goli*, and *This Island Now*.

11　*The View From Coyaba*

Date of Publication: 1985
Subject(s): Racial Conflict
Fictional character(s): Samson, Slave; Jacob Brown, Religious (bishop); David Batara, Revolutionary
Time Period(s): 19th century; 20th century (1833-1980)
Locale(s): Jamaica; United States; Africa

Summary: This wide-ranging panoramic novel spans 150 years of racial history centered in Jamaica but extending to the U.S. in 1912, Liberia in 1932, Uganda and Kenya in 1953, Uganda in 1972, and finally Jamaica in 1980. The novel chronicles the effect on black lives of emancipation and the emerging struggles for identity in the Third World.

Historical Accuracy: The novel captures its various eras and regions with skill and conviction.

12　*Wild Conquest*

Date of Publication: 1950
Subject(s): Frontier—Africa; Great Trek; Boers
Fictional character(s): Kaspar Jansen, Landowner; Anna Jansen, Spouse; Moshesh, Chieftain (Basutos)
Time Period(s): 1830s
Locale(s): South Africa

Summary: The novel depicts the conflict in South Africa during the 1830s, capturing the perspective of both the Boers and the British. The story concentrates on the Jansens who join the Great Trek when the freeing of their slaves erupts into violence. The novel dramatizes the adventure of their journey and the clash with the Africans who attempt to stop their encroachment.

Historical Accuracy: Unlike other accounts of the Great Trek, this version is well-rounded and authentic, fair to both sides in the conflict.

WILLIAM M. ABRAHAMS (1919-)

13　*Imperial Waltz*

Date of Publication: 1954
Subject(s): Royalty—Austria
Historical character(s): Franz Josef I, Ruler (Emperor of Austria); Elizabeth of Bavaria, Royalty (consort of Franz Joseph); Julius Andrassy, Nobleman (count), Political Figure
Time Period(s): 19th century
Locale(s): Austria

Summary: This romantic novel is based on the early life of the Empress Elizabeth of Austria. It begins with her career as a young Bavarian princess and follows the early years of her marriage to Franz Joseph and her relationship with Count Andrassy. Elizabeth's dedication to an independent Hungary is also depicted.

Historical Accuracy: The novel effectively captures its period and documents the various evidence about the Empress Elizabeth.

ALAIN ABSIRE (1950-)

Born in Rouen, France, Absire's novel, *God's Equal*, received the prestigious Prix Femina award. He lives in Paris.

14　*God's Equal*

Date of Publication: 1987
Subject(s): Middle Ages
Fictional character(s): Odilon de Bernay, Religious (monk); Liebaut de Malbray, Knight; Mathilde, Healer
Time Period(s): 11th century
Locale(s): Normandy, France

Summary: Odilon de Bernay, a French monk, narrates the story of his youth as the squire of knight Liebaut de Malbray. The pair battle Frisian pirates on the coast of Normandy and come into conflict when Liebaut falls in love with a peasant girl who is a healer.

Historical Accuracy: The novel is set against a believable medieval background.

15 *Lazarus*

Date of Publication: 1988
Subject(s): Biblical Story
Historical character(s): Lazarus, Biblical Figure; Jesus Christ, Biblical Figure
Time Period(s): 1st century
Locale(s): Israel

Summary: This tale, based on John's Gospel story, focuses on Lazarus after he is brought back from the dead by Jesus. He goes in search of Jesus to demand to know the reason for his condition, a kind of suspended animation between life and death.

Historical Accuracy: The novel, based on the New Testament story, is more a meditation on the nature of miracles and life without meaning.

CHINUA ACHEBE (1930-)

Achebe is a Nigerian novelist, poet, short story writer, and essayist. His first novel, *Things Fall Apart*, is considered by many to be the beginning of contemporary African literature.

16 *Things Fall Apart*

Date of Publication: 1958
Subject(s): Tribal Life—African; English Colonies
Fictional character(s): Okonkwo, Chieftain
Time Period(s): 19th century
Locale(s): Umuofia, Nigeria

Summary: The novel describes the cost of change to a traditional African village with the coming of British colonization. Okonkwo's inability to change causes a tragedy. When he accidentally kills a tribe member, he is exiled for seven years. When he returns, he resists the changes brought about by European missionaries.

Historical Accuracy: Nigerian Ibo tribal rituals and customs are detailed with care. Achebe shows both the good and the bad of traditional African village life.

PETER ACKROYD (1949-)

An English novelist, poet, and literary critic, Ackroyd is also a biographer of T.S. Eliot and Charles Dickens. His works all show an amazing virtuosity and inventiveness, often using the past in interesting ways. Ackroyd has stated that he is less interested in writing historical fiction than in writing about the nature of history itself.

17 *Chatterton*

Date of Publication: 1987
Subject(s): Mystery; Forgery; Literary Life
Fictional character(s): Charles Wychwood, Writer (poet); Harriet Scrope, Writer (novelist)

Historical character(s): Thomas Chatterton, Writer (poet); George Meredith, Writer (novelist); Henry Wallis, Artist
Time Period(s): Multiple Time Periods
Locale(s): London, England; Bristol, England

Summary: The discovery of a lost manuscript, presumably by the poet and plagiarist Thomas Chatterton, suggests that he did not commit suicide and may have forged most of the English poetry of the 18th century. This literary mystery animates a group of contemporary literary figures and affords an interesting meditation on literary originality and appropriation.

Historical Accuracy: Ackroyd is able to shuttle convincingly among contemporary London and the the 18th and 19th centuries, detailing each period with conviction.

18 *English Music*

Date of Publication: 1992
Subject(s): Childhood; Theatrical Life
Fictional character(s): Timothy Harcombe, Psychic; Clement Harcombe, Entertainer
Historical character(s): Charles Dickens, Writer (novelist); William Hogarth, Artist; Edward Campion, Writer (poet)
Time Period(s): 1930s
Locale(s): London, England

Summary: Clement Harcombe and his son Timothy perform acts of spiritual healing at a theater. Timothy has remarkable psychic gifts, and when he is abruptly separated from his father he begins to exist in a realm of visions sweeping across time and history. He plunges into the creations of Dickens, Blake, Malory, Defoe, Bunyan, and Doyle accompanied by fictional and historical figures. Timothy learns to hear the "English music"—the workings of the English imagination throughout history.

Historical Accuracy: The novel is a tour de force of imaginative re-possession of the past, both historical and artistic.

19 *The Last Testament of Oscar Wilde*

Date of Publication: 1983
Subject(s): Literary Life; Victorian Period
Historical character(s): Oscar Wilde, Writer
Time Period(s): 1900s (1900)
Locale(s): Paris, France; London, England

Summary: Ackroyd's novel offers the reflections of Oscar Wilde in the final year of his life. After serving a prison sentence for a sodomy conviction in England, Wilde retreats to Paris in despair, his career is shambles. The novel captures the seemingly authentic voice of Wilde in his moving and insightful recollections.

Historical Accuracy: The novel is utterly convincing as a first-person narrative of a remarkable literary figure and the times he helped to shape.

20 *Milton in America*

Date of Publication: 1997
Subject(s): American Colonies; Religious Conflict; Puritans
Historical character(s): John Milton, Writer (poet)
Time Period(s): 17th century (1660s)

Locale(s): New England, American Colonies

Summary: The premise of this fascinating exercise in imaginative reconstruction is what might have happened had John Milton come to Puritan America in 1660. Milton becomes the leader of a community of Puritan settlers and wages a holy war on a neighboring town inhabited by Roman Catholics.

Historical Accuracy: Although the story is imagined, the period elements are convincing.

21 *The Trial of Elizabeth Cree: A Novel of the Limehouse Murders*

Date of Publication: 1994
Subject(s): Victorian Period; Crime and Criminals; Theatrical Life
Fictional character(s): Elizabeth Cree, Actress
Historical character(s): George Gissing, Writer; Dan Leno, Entertainer; Karl Marx, Philosopher
Time Period(s): 1880s (1880-1881)
Locale(s): London, England

Summary: In 1880 a series of grisly murders in London's Limehouse is thought to be the work of a golem, a savage creature of Jewish folklore. The murders are mysteriously connected to the actress Elizabeth Cree who stands accused of murdering her husband. Karl Marx, George Gissing, and the famous music hall comedian Dan Leno all have an interest in the investigation and Elizabeth's fate.

Historical Accuracy: The novel excells at re-creating with utter believability the Victorian period atmosphere.

ALICE ACLAND
(PSEUD. OF ANNE WIGNALL, 1912-)

English writer Wignall was born in London and began writing in 1949. She has called herself a compulsive writer who has turned to re-creating the past and to storytelling rather than to the study of character.

22 *The Secret Wife*

Date of Publication: 1976
Subject(s): Royalty—France
Historical character(s): Francoise d'Aubigne, Noblewoman (consort of Louis XIV); Louis XIV, Ruler (King of France)
Time Period(s): 17th century; 18th century
Locale(s): France

Summary: Francoise d'Aubigne, Madame de Maintenon, the second wife of French King Louis XIV, tells her story. The granddaughter of Agrippa d'Aubigne, the Huguenot hero, she is a devout Catholic. Married to the French poet Paul Scarron, she becomes a prominent figure in the intellectual and artistic world of Paris, and gradually gains influence over Louis XIV, whom she secretly marries after Scarron's death.

Historical Accuracy: The novel captures the atmosphere of the French court of the period with convincing details.

DORIS SUTCLIFFE ADAMS

23 *No Man's Son*

Date of Publication: 1961
Subject(s): Middle Ages; Crusades
Fictional character(s): Landry de Parolles, Knight; Rodriga de Parolles, Young Woman
Historical character(s): Richard I, Ruler (King of England)
Time Period(s): 12th century
Locale(s): Palestine

Summary: During the siege of Acre by Richard the Lionheart's army, a poor knight, Landry de Parolles, scrambles to find a suitable husband for his daughter, Rodriga, before he dies. The pair face both perils and betrayal.

Historical Accuracy: The story is a fanciful one, though the details of the Crusades are authentic.

24 *The Price of Blood*

Date of Publication: 1962
Subject(s): Vikings; Christianity; Dark Ages
Fictional character(s): Niall Southfarer, Sailor, Prisoner; Odda, Landowner
Historical character(s): Alfred the Great, Ruler (King of Wessex)
Time Period(s): 9th century
Locale(s): Devon, England; Wessex, England

Summary: In this tale of the Viking invasion of England, Niall is a Christian Dane from Ireland who is shipwrecked on the Devon coast. There he is taken prisoner and sees firsthand the results of his kinsmen's assaults. He is pressed into battle, forced to choose between loyalty toward his kinsmen and the people of his Christian faith.

Historical Accuracy: The period detail is convincing and expertly delivered.

HAROLD ADAMS (1923-)

An American mystery writer from South Dakota, Adams graduated from the University of Minnesota and has worked as the assistant director of the Better Business Bureau of Minneapolis. He is the executive director of the Charities Review Council of Minnesota. Adams is known for his sharp dialogue, complex characterizations, and wry humor.

25 *The Man Who Missed the Party*

Date of Publication: 1989
Subject(s): Mystery
Fictional character(s): Carl Wilcox, Hotel Worker
Time Period(s): 1930s (1934)
Locale(s): Corden, South Dakota

Summary: On the tenth anniversary of the Corden High School football team, a murder occurs, and Carl Wilcox must investigate.

Historical Accuracy: The novel offers some convincing period elements to create its setting.

JANE ADAMS (1940-)

Jane Adams was born in New London, Connecticut, and received her degree from Smith College in 1960. She is the author of *Sex and the Single Parent* and *Women on Top*, as well as the novel *Good Intentions* and the play *The Promised Land*.

26　*Seattle Green*

Date of Publication: 1987
Subject(s): Family Saga; Settlement of the American Frontier
Fictional character(s): Maddy Douglas, Settler; Catherine Blanchard, Socialite; Natalie Blanchard, Journalist
Time Period(s): 19th century; 20th century (1866-1962)
Locale(s): Seattle, Washington

Summary: Nearly 100 years of Seattle history is detailed in this story of three generations of women. Maddy Douglas comes west as a mail-order bride in 1866 and begins the Blanchard dynasty. Its history, described in the lives of Maddy, her daughter Catherine, and granddaughter Natalie, illustrates the colorful history of Seattle from settlement to city.

Historical Accuracy: Many of the characters and incidents described have historical antecedents, and Adams captures the development of a community in this chronicle.

RICHARD ADAMS (1920-)

Adams is an English writer who served from 1947 to 1974 in the British Civil Service. He began writing his first novel, *Watership Down*, to amuse his children. It was rejected by numerous publishers but eventually became a surprise bestseller. His other works include *Plague Dogs*, *Shardik*, *Maia*, and *The Girl on the Swing*.

27　*Traveller*

Date of Publication: 1988
Subject(s): Civil War—U.S.; Animals
Fictional character(s): Traveller, Animal (Robert E. Lee's horse); Tom, Animal (cat)
Historical character(s): Jefferson Davis, Political Figure; Robert E. Lee, Military Personnel (general); Thomas Jonathan Jackson, Military Personnel; James Ewell Brown Stuart, Military Personnel; James Longstreet, Military Personnel
Time Period(s): 1860s (1861-1868)
Locale(s): Virginia; Pennsylvania

Summary: Adams offers a unique perspective on the events and personalities of the Civil War through the eyes of Robert E. Lee's closest companion, his horse, Traveller. Traveller's recollections of "Marse Robert" and their adventures cover the Seven Days campaign, Gettysburg, the siege of Petersburg, the fall of Richmond, and the surrender at Appomattox. The horse keenly observes men and details from an angle (he thinks the General has won the war) that is odd, refreshing, and moving.

Historical Accuracy: The ingenuity of the novel is its unique angle of vision. Knowledge of the events and characters helps interpret Traveller's perspectives.

SAMUEL HOPKINS ADAMS (1871-1958)

Adams was an American novelist and muckraking journalist for *McClure's*, *Collier's*, and the *New York Tribune*. His works include *The Great American Fraud*, about patent nostrums; *The Godlike Daniel*, a biography of Daniel Webster; *Revelry*; and *Incredible Era*, about the Harding administration.

28　*Banner by the Wayside*

Date of Publication: 1947
Subject(s): Theatrical Life; Canal Building
Fictional character(s): Drurie Andrew, Orphan, Actress; Jans Quintard, Actor
Time Period(s): 1830s
Locale(s): Erie Canal, New York

Summary: Drurie, a foundling, and Jans, an expelled Harvard student, find romance and adventure as their theatrical troupe tours the Erie Canal country in the 1830s. The novel captures the pungent and brawling atmosphere of the canal days.

Historical Accuracy: Adams' dialogue and scenes convincingly create the atmosphere of the period.

29　*Canal Town*

Date of Publication: 1944
Subject(s): Canal Building; Medical Profession
Fictional character(s): Horace Amlie, Doctor; Araminta Jerrold, Gentlewoman
Time Period(s): 1820s
Locale(s): Palmyra, New York

Summary: Life in a fictional New York town in the 1820s is chronicled through the experience of a country doctor. He must contend with the community's superstitions and traditions in the face of changes brought by the Erie Canal.

Historical Accuracy: Adams succeeds well in his reconstruction of a phase in American life that has received little historical attention.

30　*The Gorgeous Hussy*

Date of Publication: 1934
Subject(s): Politics; War of 1812
Historical character(s): Peggy Eaton, Gentlewoman (aka Peggy O'Neale), Political Figure (protege of Andrew Jackson); Andrew Jackson, Political Figure; Rachel Jackson, Spouse (of Andrew); Daniel Webster, Political Figure; Henry Clay, Political Figure; Anne Royall, Journalist
Time Period(s): 19th century (1812-1861)
Locale(s): Washington, District of Columbia

Summary: Washington politics from the 1810s to the Civil War are chronicled from the perspective of Peggy Eaton, protege of Andrew Jackson, who Adams claims altered the course of our nation's destiny. Washington's rough-and-tumble political world of the period is vividly dramatized.

Historical Accuracy: Adams warns the reader not to try to reconcile his story with historical facts and admits to taking many liberties with the chronology.

31   *The Harvey Girls*

Date of Publication: 1942
Subject(s): American West; Railroads
Fictional character(s): Deborah Rapalje, Waiter/Waitress; Alma ''Cricket'' Seelye, Waiter/Waitress; Hazel Biggs, Waiter/Waitress
Time Period(s): 1890s
Locale(s): Sandrock, Southwest

Summary: Fred Harvey's restaurants followed the Sante Fe Railroad from Kansas to California. To staff them, Harvey recruited girls from the East and the Midwest. The novel tells the story of three of those recruits who come to the fictional town of Sandrock to ''feed the trains.'' Their adventures and conflict with the Alhambra Dance Hall form the novel's story.

Historical Accuracy: The novel is a faithful rendering both of the Harvey restaurant operation and the change of customs brought west by the arrival of the railroad.

32   *Sunrise to Sunset*

Date of Publication: 1950
Subject(s): Crime and Criminals; Labor Movement
Fictional character(s): Becky Webb, Worker; Guy Roy, Businessman; Gordon Stockwell, Businessman
Time Period(s): 1830s
Locale(s): Troy, New York

Summary: The novel offers the romantic story of the love between an ambitious factory girl, Becky Webb, and a wealthy manufacturer, Guy Roy. The story's background depicts the exploitation of female labor and the establishment of the first humane laws regulating working conditions in the cotton mills.

Historical Accuracy: Adams has invented some non-historical elements, but the essential atmosphere of the period is clearly depicted.

33   *Tenderloin*

Date of Publication: 1959
Subject(s): Crime and Criminals; Gay Nineties
Fictional character(s): Dr. Brockholst Farr, Religious; Tommy Howatt, Journalist; Dan Adriance, Journalist
Time Period(s): 1890s
Locale(s): New York, New York

Summary: New York City during the Gay Nineties is the subject of this novel concerning a clergyman, Dr. Farr, who sets out to rid the city of corruption. He disguises himself to gain entrance to the city's dens of iniquity and scandal follows.

Historical Accuracy: History redefined as nostalgia is the key ingredient here with the city's raw edges softened for the smooth running of the novel's romantic elements.

YVONNE ADAMSON
(PSEUD. OF YVONNE MONTGOMERY; MARY JO ADAMSON, 1935-)

Yvonne Adamson is the pseudonym for two Colorado writers, Yvonne Montgomery and Mary Jo Adamson.

Adamson was born in Illinois and graduated from Marycrest College and Humboldt State College. She received her Ph.D. in English literature from the University of Denver. She is the author of a number of mysteries, including *A February Face* and *JApril When I Woo*.

34   *Bridey's Mountain*

Date of Publication: 1993
Subject(s): Family Saga; Inheritance—Disputed
Fictional character(s): Morna Gregory, Heroine; Bridget Isobel, Heroine; Ariana McAllister, Heroine
Time Period(s): 20th century (1900-1990s)
Locale(s): Telluride, Colorado

Summary: Three generations of women's lives are detailed beginning with Morna, a beautifu Irish woman who comes to Telluride, Colorado, in 1900. Her legacy is a mountain named for her daughter, who in turn will pass it down to the present generation. A threat by developers causes it to be defended and in the process much is learned about the mountain's symbolic significance.

Historical Accuracy: The scenes of Telluride are convincingly detailed.

ROBERT H. ADELMAN (1919-)

An American author and television scriptwriter, Adelman was born in Philadelphia. After 15 years as a Philadelphia newspaperman, Adelman wrote his first book, *The Devil's Brigade*, a bestseller, which became a film starring William Holden. Adelman's other books include *The Bloody Benders*, *The Black Box*, and *Alias Big Cherry*.

35   *The Bloody Benders*

Date of Publication: 1970
Subject(s): American West; Crime and Criminals
Historical character(s): Kate Bender, Outlaw
Time Period(s): 19th century
Locale(s): Kansas

Summary: This western tale is based on the actual exploits of Kate Bender, who preyed upon visitors to her family's inn on the Kansas frontier.

Historical Accuracy: The novel's background is realistic and authentic and based on fact.

36   *Sweetwater Fever*

Date of Publication: 1984
Subject(s): American West; Mining; Racial Conflict
Fictional character(s): Sam Hume, Teenager; Chung Lin, Immigrant; Celina Sewell, Prostitute
Time Period(s): 1850s (1853)
Locale(s): Jacksonville, Oregon

Summary: This western adventure story is set against a backdrop of the goldstrike in Jacksonville, Oregon, during the 1850s. The novel captures all the color of a mining boom town, including the Tong wars among the Chinese laborers.

Historical Accuracy: Although the primary characters are fictional, the majority of the scenes are based on actual events.

RICHARD ADICKS (1932-)

Adicks grew up in Cole City, Florida, and attended the University of Florida. He earned a Ph.D. in English from Tulane University and has taught at Georgia Tech and the University of Central Florida. Adicks has written on Alfred Tennyson, Walt Whitman, James Joyce, and others.

37 *A Court of Owls*

Date of Publication: 1989
Subject(s): Civil War—U.S.; Battle of Gettysburg
Historical character(s): Lewis Powell, Military Personnel (Confederate soldier); John Wilkes Booth, Actor, Murderer
Time Period(s): 1860s (1861-1865)
Locale(s): Washington, District of Columbia; Florida; Virginia

Summary: The novel traces the Civil War career of Confederate soldier Lewis Powell, whose path crosses that of John Wilkes Booth and eventually leads to Powell's trial as a conspirator in the assassination of Abraham Lincoln. The novel follows Powell's adventures at Gettysburg and as one of Mosby's Rangers and the role he plays in the conspiracy to kill the president.

Historical Accuracy: The author insists that the novel is historical fiction and not history. Some events have been invented; others have been rearranged. The novel offers a plausible version of what might have happened.

MARK ADLARD (1932-)

British author Mark Adlard wrote three science fiction novels set in the 22nd century before turning to historical fiction. He has cited one of the main preoccupations of his work as the way economic activity seems to give meaning to individual lives, but usually does not succeed.

38 *The Greenlander*

Date of Publication: 1978
Subject(s): Sea Story; Whaling; Coming of Age
Fictional character(s): Arthur Storm, Sailor; Peter Gill, Sailor; Jim Richardson, Sailor
Time Period(s): 19th century
Locale(s): *William Scoresby Sr.*, At Sea (en route from England to Greenland); Greenland

Summary: This is a coming of age novel set in the whaling days. Young Arthur Storm ships out on a voyage to the Greenland Sea. The crew is a colorful cast of characters, and the novel is filled with exciting action, including an encounter with a shark, a whaleboat lost at sea, and the ship becoming frozen in arctic ice.

Historical Accuracy: The naval and whaling details are convincingly and colorfully presented.

ELIZABETH ADLER (1914-)

Born in Yorkshire, England, Adler is a romance novelist who has been praised for avoiding the formulas of the genre. Her novels include *Leonie*, *Private Desires*, and *Peach*, which is set during the Nazi invasion of France.

39 *Fortune Is a Woman*

Date of Publication: 1992
Subject(s): Business Building; Disasters—Natural; Earthquakes
Fictional character(s): Francie Harrison, Heiress—Dispossessed; Annie Aysgarth, Businesswoman; Lai Tsin, Businessman
Time Period(s): 19th century; 20th century (1890-1960s)
Locale(s): San Francisco, California; Hong Kong

Summary: The novel tells the story of three friends—a disowned daughter of a San Francisco millionaire, a dutiful daughter of a widowed father, and a mysterious Chinese mandarin. They meet in the aftermath of the 1906 San Francisco earthquake and form an alliance that brings them vast wealth.

Historical Accuracy: The scenes of San Francisco in the 1900s are realistically drawn.

GEOFF AGGELER (1939-)

An American writer and professor of English, Aggeler was trained as a specialist in Renaissance literature. He has written a biography of writer Anthony Burgess.

40 *Confessions of Johnny Ringo*

Date of Publication: 1987
Subject(s): Crime and Criminals; Civil War—U.S.; American West
Historical character(s): Johnny Ringo, Outlaw; Wyatt Earp, Lawman; Cole Younger, Outlaw; William Clarke Quantrill, Military Personnel (Confederate guerrilla leader); John Henry Holliday, Gambler, Dentist
Time Period(s): 19th century (1860-1882)
Locale(s): Arizona; Texas; Missouri

Summary: The novel takes the form of the memoirs of the western outlaw Johnny Ringo, renowned for both his savagery and his education. Ringo narrates his life story, from his violent childhood, to becoming one of Quantrill's Raiders during the Civil War, to the Arizona territory and a final confrontation with Wyatt Earp.

Historical Accuracy: Aggeler fills in the unknown details of Ringo's life with plausible surmises. His knowledge of the period gives the story the ring of authenticity.

DEMETRIO AGUILERA MALTA (1909-)

An Ecuadorian journalist, diplomat, educator, and writer, Aguilera Malta was born in Guayaquil, Ecuador, and attended the University of Guayaquil. His works include the novels *Don Goya*, *La Isla Virgen*, and *Seven Moons and Seven Serpents*.

41   *Manuela, La Caballeresa Del Sol*

Date of Publication: 1967
Subject(s): Independence—South America
Historical character(s): Simon Bolivar, Military Personnel (general); Manuela Saenz, Political Figure, Lover
Time Period(s): 1820s; 1830s (1822-1831)
Locale(s): Lima, Peru; Caracas, Venezuela

Summary: The novel describes the relationship between Simon Bolivar and his mistress Manuela Saenz, who comes to play an important role as Bolivar's political adviser. The novel recreates events on and off the battlefield and the unusual partnership of the great liberator and his unconventional mistress.

Historical Accuracy: The novel is faithful to the events of the period, and the characterization of Bolivar is convincing.

GAMAL AHITANI

42   *Zayni Barakat*

Date of Publication: 1990
Subject(s): Ottoman Empire
Fictional character(s): Zayni Barakat, Government Official
Time Period(s): 16th century (1516)
Locale(s): Cairo, Egypt

Summary: In 1516 the Mamluk dynasty in Egypt is under increasing pressure from the Ottoman Turks. Zayni Barakat attempts to maintain his power in the face of Turkish military advance and an ever-shifting political climate.

Historical Accuracy: The era is evoked with convincing details and an authentic atmosphere.

JOAN AIKEN (1924-)

Prolific American novelist Joan Aiken is the daughter of writer Conrad Aiken. She has written critically acclaimed and popular children's fiction, historical novels, and mysteries.

43   *Castle Barebane*

Date of Publication: 1976
Subject(s): Mystery; Crime and Criminals; Victorian Period
Fictional character(s): Val Montgomery, Heroine; Lord Clanreydon, Nobleman; Marcus Cusak, Editor
Time Period(s): 1880s
Locale(s): New York, New York; London, England; Edinburgh, Scotland

Summary: Val Montgomery leaves New York in the 1880s to journey to London to help her spendthrift half-brother and his ailing wife. She arrives to find only her nephew and niece, apparently abandoned. She takes the children to Scotland to stay with their mother's nurse and is embroiled in threats and revelations.

Historical Accuracy: The story's background is colorfully depicted with figures from the Victorian underworld, music halls, and streets.

44   *Eliza's Daughter*

Date of Publication: 1994
Subject(s): Regency Romance
Fictional character(s): Eliza Williams, Governess; Elinor Dashwood, Gentlewoman; Marianne Dashwood, Gentlewoman
Historical character(s): William Wordsworth, Writer; Samuel Taylor Coleridge, Writer
Time Period(s): 18th century; 19th century (1797-1814)
Locale(s): England; Portugal

Summary: Aiken's third novel modeled on Jane Austen reintroduces Austen's characters from *Sense and Sensibility*. The impetuous and spirited heroine Eliza finds herself living in Austen's milieu with the Dashwood sisters. She soon sets out on her own, creating her own way with determination.

Historical Accuracy: The era is authentically drawn if Eliza is somewhat of an anomaly. She comes across as a modernist alternative to Austen's conformity.

45   *Emma Watson*

Date of Publication: 1996
Subject(s): Regency Period
Fictional character(s): Emma Watson, Young Woman
Time Period(s): 1810s
Locale(s): England

Summary: This novel completes Jane Austen's novel fragment, *The Watsons*. Elaborating Austen's original characters, the novel follows the experiences of 19-year-old Emma Watson who is adopted by her aunt after the death of her mother.

Historical Accuracy: The novel features a convincing re-creation of the Austen style and era.

46   *The Five-Minute Marriage*

Date of Publication: 1978
Subject(s): Regency Romance; Inheritance—Disputed
Fictional character(s): Delphie Carteret, Heiress—Dispossessed; Gareth Penistone, Heir
Time Period(s): 19th century (1800-1820)
Locale(s): London, England

Summary: Delphie Carteret, the disinherited daughter of a viscount, finds that an imposter has claimed her fortune. To win back what is rightfully hers, she agrees to a counterfeit marriage to the principal heir, her cousin Gareth. The scheme backfires, and Delphie becomes enmeshed in a web of family rivalries and deceit.

Historical Accuracy: The plot contrivances overwhelm the period details.

47   *The Girl From Paris*

Date of Publication: 1982
Subject(s): Victorian Period; Literary Life; Inheritance—Disputed
Fictional character(s): Ellen Paget, Governess; Comte De La Ferte, Nobleman; Germaine De Rhetoree, Writer
Historical character(s): Gustave Flaubert, Writer
Time Period(s): 1850s (1859)

Locale(s): Paris, France; Brussels, Belgium; England

Summary: Ellen Paget is thrust into literary Paris as governess in the home of the Comte de la Ferte. She is introduced to the leading intellectuals and writers of the age and slowly loses her conventional upbringing. She is then called home to England to attend to her father's affairs and settle a dispute over an inheritance.

Historical Accuracy: Ellen, who has never heard of Edgar Allen Poe, does know that George Eliot is a female, though this was not well known until long after the time of the story. This slip aside, the milieu is colorfully created.

48   *The Haunting of Lamb House*

Date of Publication: 1991
Subject(s): Literary Life; Supernatural
Fictional character(s): Toby Lamb, Child
Historical character(s): E.F. Benson, Writer; Henry James, Writer; William James, Scholar, Writer; Hugh Walpole, Writer; Edith Wharton, Writer
Time Period(s): Multiple Time Periods
Locale(s): Rye, England

Summary: The novel tells the story of Lamb House, home of writers Henry James and E.F. Benson. The house is haunted, and its history is re-created when Toby Lamb's childhood journal falls into the hands of James and Benson, releasing his ghostly spirit.

Historical Accuracy: The novel ingeniously re-creates local history and the atmosphere of both 18th century Rye and the literary inhabitants of Lamb House.

49   *If I Were You*

Date of Publication: 1987
Subject(s): Regency Romance; Identity—Concealed
Fictional character(s): Alvey Clement, Student; Louisa Winship, Student
Time Period(s): 1810s (1815)
Locale(s): Northumberland, England

Summary: Louisa Winship dreams of becoming a missionary in India. Since her parents disapprove, she devises a scheme whereby her school friend Alvey will impersonate her, and she will fulfill her dream. Alvey struggles to keep the secret while penetrating the deeper secrets of the Winship family.

Historical Accuracy: The premise of the story is far-fetched and contrived, more fairy tale romance than historical.

50   *Jane Fairfax*

Date of Publication: 1990
Subject(s): Regency Romance
Fictional character(s): Jane Fairfax, Gentlewoman; Emma Woodhouse, Gentlewoman; Frank Churchill, Gentleman
Time Period(s): 1800s
Locale(s): Hampshire, England

Summary: Aiken offers Jane Austen's *Emma* from the perspective of Jane Fairfax, the outsider who threatens Emma's social predominance. Here she is seen not as a foil to Emma but as a complex and compelling individual in her own right.

Historical Accuracy: The novel is a worthy echoing of the Austen original, widening the context and offering an interesting slant on the customs and period details.

51   *Mansfield Revisited*

Date of Publication: 1984
Subject(s): Regency Romance
Fictional character(s): Susan Price, Gentlewoman; Edmund Bertram, Gentleman; Fanny Bertram, Gentlewoman
Time Period(s): 1800s
Locale(s): Hampshire, England

Summary: In this sequel to Jane Austen's *Mansfield Park*, Joan Aiken speculates on what happened after Fanny Price married Edmund Bertram. Susan Price comes to live at Mansfield and the emphasis is on her struggle to overcome class obstacles.

Historical Accuracy: Aiken provides a convincing re-possession of Austen's atmosphere and the Regency period.

52   *Midnight Is a Place*

Date of Publication: 1974
Subject(s): Mystery; Childhood; Victorian Period
Fictional character(s): Lucas, Teenager; Anna-Marie Murgatroyd, Teenager
Time Period(s): 1840s (1842)
Locale(s): Blastburn, England

Summary: Fourteen-year-old Lucas is bored and lonely in Midnight Court, a brooding manor house in Victorian England. He is joined by a French girl, Anna-Marie, and both are suddenly thrown out on their own to survive the winter. To do so, they enter the Victorian world of work and suffering.

Historical Accuracy: Aiken's version of Victorian factory life is convincingly drawn, even if the story is more fanciful than realistic.

53   *The Smile of the Stranger*

Date of Publication: 1978
Subject(s): French Revolution
Fictional character(s): Juliana Paget, Gentlewoman; Charles Elphinstone, Historian; Count Van Welcker, Nobleman
Historical character(s): George, Prince of Wales, Royalty
Time Period(s): 1780s
Locale(s): Florence, Italy; England

Summary: Juliana Paget is the young, only daughter of an English historian living in Florence. When the turbulence of the French Revolution breaks out, they flee across France to England, crossing the channel in a balloon. In England Juliana is far from safe. She finds herself at the mercy of her inheritance, which attracts a succession of menacing strangers.

Historical Accuracy: The plot is fast-paced and entertaining, and there is scant time for a full rendering of period details. Aiken admits to manipulating the time scheme to allow an appearance by the Prince Regent.

54   *The Weeping Ash*

Date of Publication: 1980

Subject(s): Suspense; Georgian Period
Fictional character(s): Fanny Paget, Heroine; Scylla Paget, Heroine; Carloman Paget, Hero
Time Period(s): 1770s (1775)
Locale(s): India; Middle East (Persia, Turkey); England

Summary: Two tales are connected in this novel of adventure and suspense. Fanny Paget endures a loveless marriage in England. Meanwhile, twin cousins of her husband flee soldiers of a vengeful maharajah across India, Afghanistan, Persia, and Turkey before reaching England and a violent confrontation.

Historical Accuracy: The novel offers fast-paced action and suspense, which predominate over historical details.

EDWARD MADDIN AINSWORTH
(1902-1968)

An American journalist, editor, columnist, documentary film producer, and author, Ainsworth was born in Waco, Texas, and attended the Texas Agricultural and Mechanical College and the University of California, Los Angeles. His books include *Potluck*, *Death Cues the Pageant*, and *The Cowboy in Art*.

55   *Eagles Fly West*
Date of Publication: 1946
Subject(s): American West; Gold Rush—California
Fictional character(s): Shane Malone, Journalist
Time Period(s): 1840s; 1850s
Locale(s): California; New York, New York

Summary: A young newspaperman, Shane Malone, joins the fight for American control of California and witnesses the discovery of gold and the push for statehood.

Historical Accuracy: The historical elements presented here are faithful to the facts.

WILLIAM HARRISON AINSWORTH
(1805-1882)

Ainsworth is an English author of the Victorian period who published 39 novels during his productive career. He was a popular writer of the period, now considered a minor figure. He has the distinction of being the first writer to introduce actual historical figures in his novels. Ainsworth's antiquarian interests helped insure that his novels were filled with interesting historical details, even if his plots are implausible and his characters idealized.

56   *Jack Sheppard*
Date of Publication: 1839
Subject(s): Crime and Criminals
Fictional character(s): Owen Wood, Carpenter; Thames Darrell, Gentleman, Heir—Dispossessed
Historical character(s): Jack Sheppard, Criminal (notorious jailbreaker); Jonathan Wild, Criminal, Bounty Hunter
Time Period(s): 18th century (1702-1724)
Locale(s): London, England

Summary: Ainsworth's novel is a romance of criminality. Sheppard is an actual burglar and jailbreaker, greatly idealized. The implausible story and romance of Sheppard's exploits prompted William Makepeace Thackeray's scathing satire, *Catherine*, which was meant to deflate the so-called "Newgate Novel"—novels that romanticized criminals and crime.

Historical Accuracy: There are scattered references to historical incidents. However, the novel is more romance than realistic.

57   *Old St. Paul's*
Date of Publication: 1841
Subject(s): Plague; Fires; Royalty—England
Fictional character(s): Stephen Bloundel, Store Owner (grocer); Amabel Bloundel, Young Woman; Leonard Holt, Apprentice
Historical character(s): Charles II, Ruler (King of England); John Wilmot, Nobleman (Earl of Rochester); Sir George Etherege, Nobleman
Time Period(s): 17th century (1665-1666)
Locale(s): London, England

Summary: This is a melodramatic story that uses the Plague of London in 1665 and the Great Fire as part of the novel's climax. Ainsworth, master of atmosphere and setting, tells the improbable story of a grocer's apprentice who becomes a baron after he saves the life of his king.

Historical Accuracy: There are strong details of London life, at odds with the overheated and contrived melodrama of the story.

58   *The Tower of London*
Date of Publication: 1840
Subject(s): Elizabethan Period; Royalty—England
Fictional character(s): Cuthbert Cholmondeley, Knight; Cicely, Young Woman
Historical character(s): Mary I, Ruler (Queen of England); Elizabeth Tudor, Royalty (later Elizabeth I); Lord Guilford Dudley, Nobleman; Sir Thomas Wyatt, Nobleman, Writer (poet); Lady Jane Grey, Royalty
Time Period(s): 16th century (1550-1560)
Locale(s): London, England

Summary: The novel offers a fictionalized account of the various claimants to the English throne on the death of Edward VI—Mary, Lady Jane Grey, and Elizabeth. Plot and counterplot take place inside and outside the Tower of London. History shares the stage with the romance between Cuthbert, Lord Dudley's squire, and Cicely.

Historical Accuracy: Ainsworth offers historical facts embroidered for the service of romance and drama. Events depicted are only partially true.

59   *Windsor Castle*
Date of Publication: 1843
Subject(s): Tudor Period; Royalty—England
Fictional character(s): Herne the Hunter, Demon, Spirit; Morgan Fenwolf, Servant (gamekeeper)

Historical character(s): Henry VIII, Ruler (King of England); Anne Boleyn, Royalty; Thomas Wolsey, Religious (cardinal), Political Figure (Lord Chancellor); Sir Thomas Wyatt, Nobleman, Writer (poet); Jane Seymour, Noblewoman, Royalty
Time Period(s): 16th century (reign of Henry VIII, 1509-1547)
Locale(s): Windsor, England

Summary: This novel concerns the reign of Henry VIII combined with elements of the Gothic romance in the form of a spectral demon called Herne the Hunter who serves as a kind of vague symbol of conscience in Henry's court as Anne Boleyn is executed to make way for Jane Seymour.

Historical Accuracy: There is little historical accuracy here although it is interesting to see historical characters take the roles of Gothic romance heroes and heroines.

ORIANA AKINSON

60   *The Golden Season*
Date of Publication: 1953
Subject(s): Settlement of the American Frontier; War of 1812; Coming of Age
Fictional character(s): Freedom Ware, Young Woman
Time Period(s): 18th century; 19th century (1790s-1810s)
Locale(s): Catskill Mountains, New York

Summary: This is the story of young Freedom Ware, the daughter of an innkeeper in the Catskill Mountains, from the 1790s through the War of 1812. As the migration to Ohio accelerates, Freedom struggles to reach maturity.

Historical Accuracy: This is a effective evocation of the period and the region, filled with authentic details of life and customs of the times.

VASSILY AKSYONOV (1932-)

Russian-born writer Aksyonov came to the U.S. in 1980. His parents spent 18 years in exile in Siberia as political prisoners during the Stalinist era. He spent his first 18 years in an ophanage for "Children of Enemies of the State." After initially training as a doctor, he turned to writing and has been a popular, though harassed and censored, literary figure in the Soviet Union for 20 years. He has been called the Slavic J.D. Salinger.

61   *Generations of Winter*
Date of Publication: 1994
Subject(s): World War II; Family Saga; Stalinism
Fictional character(s): Boris Gradov, Doctor (surgeon); Mary Gradov, Musician (pianist); Nikita Gradov, Military Personnel
Historical character(s): Joseph Stalin, Political Figure; Lavrenty Beria, Government Official (head of secret police)
Time Period(s): 20th century (1925-1945)
Locale(s): Moscow, Union of Soviet Socialist Republics

Summary: This vast panoramic novel covers the years of Stalin's growing power and unprecedented intrigue and oppression. At the center of the story is the Gradov family who reflect the period in their struggles, victories, and losses.

Historical Accuracy: The novel is utterly convincing in its depiction of the era. Newspaper headlines are interspersed as a reflection of current events.

PEDRO ANTONIO DE ALARCON
(1833-1891)

A Spanish writer, politician, and diplomat. Alarcon's *The Three-Cornered Hat* was the basis of the popular ballet by Manuel de Folla. Alarcon wrote novels characterized by keen powers of observation and humor.

62   *The Three-Cornered Hat*
Date of Publication: 1874
Subject(s): Rural Life—Spain
Fictional character(s): Lucas, Worker (miller); Don Eugenio, Nobleman; Frasquita, Spouse (of Lucas)
Time Period(s): 19th century (early)
Locale(s): Spain

Summary: This is a folk tale of Spanish life in the early years of the 19th century. Don Eugenio falls in love with the miller's wife and plots a seduction. In retaliation, the miller, dressed in the Don's clothes, visits the Don's wife, with expected comic complications.

Historical Accuracy: Despite the farcical situations, the characters are remarkably real, if one-dimensional, and the depiction of Spanish village life is convincing.

BILL ALBERT

Born in New York, Albert grew up in southern California and moved to England in 1964 where he taught history at the University of Norwich. Albert is active in the disability movement. His first novel was *Desert Blues*.

63   *Castle Garden*
Date of Publication: 1996
Subject(s): Picaresque Adventure; American West; Labor Movement
Fictional character(s): Meyer Liebermann, Adventurer
Historical character(s): William F. Cody, Frontiersman, Entertainer; William "Big Bill" Haywood, Labor Organizer
Time Period(s): 19th century; 20th century (1887-1907)
Locale(s): New York, New York; West

Summary: Young Meyer Liebermann narrates this picaresque adventure tale about his journey West from New York. During the trip he encounters Buffalo Bill Cody's Wild West Show and is later involved in the famous trial of Big Bill Haywood, leader of the IWW and the Western Federations of Miners.

Historical Accuracy: The novel constructs its fanciful story around actual events that capture the passing of the Western frontier and the betrayal of its dream.

NOBUKO ALBERY

Born in Ashiya, Japan, Albery attended Waseda University and received her M.A. from New York University. She has worked as a representative for a Tokyo theater company, an interpreter for the U.S. State Department's Protocol Agency, and as a theater producer in London.

64 *The House of Kanze*

Date of Publication: 1985
Subject(s): Theatrical Life; Royalty—Japan
Historical character(s): Fujiwaka Motokiyo Zeami, Actor, Writer (playwright); Kiyotsugu Kanami, Actor; Ashikaga Yoshimitsu, Ruler (shogun)
Time Period(s): 14th century
Locale(s): Japan

Summary: Set in 14th century Japan, the novel traces the life of Zeami, the great Japanese actor/playwright who established and perfected the tradition of the Noh play. Zeami is shown as a young player acclaimed by the Shogun Yoshimitsu. Court and theatrical life are interwoven as Zeami struggles to express his genius in Japanese theater.

Historical Accuracy: Like Shakespeare, little is known about Zeami, the Japanese theatrical equivalent of the Bard. The author admits to imagining and inventing a great many of the characters and events and much of the background of the story, which must be considered historical fiction with the emphasis on fiction.

HARRY ALBRIGHT

65 *Gettysburg: Crisis of Command*

Date of Publication: 1989
Subject(s): Civil War—U.S.; Battle of Gettysburg
Historical character(s): Robert E. Lee, Military Personnel (general); Thomas Jonathan Jackson, Military Personnel (general); A.P. Hill, Military Personnel; George Meade, Military Personnel (Union army commander); John Buford, Military Personnel (cavalry officer); James Ewell Brown Stuart, Military Personnel (cavalry officer); James Longstreet, Military Personnel (general)
Time Period(s): 1860s (1862-1863)
Locale(s): Virginia; Gettysburg, Pennsylvania

Summary: The pivotal battle of the Civil War is chronicled more from the perspective of the commanders and their strategies than of the ordinary combatants. Albright's version of the events casts Longstreet as the brooding, reluctant agent of Lee's faulty battle plan. Sorely missed is the heroic Stonewall Jackson.

Historical Accuracy: Besides created dialogue, this is less a novel than a critique. The chronology is carefully rendered, although the interpretations are questionable.

CLIFFORD LINDSEY ALDERMAN
(1902-)

American novelist Alderman was born in Massachusetts and graduated from the U.S. Naval Academy. He is a chemical engineer as well as the author of books for both adults and juveniles.

66 *The Arch of Stars*

Date of Publication: 1950
Subject(s): American Revolution
Fictional character(s): Jared French, Young Man
Historical character(s): Ethan Allen, Military Personnel (Revolutionary soldier), Leader (Green Mountain Boys); Ira Allen, Military Personnel (Revolutionary soldier)
Time Period(s): 1770s
Locale(s): Vermont; New York

Summary: This novel set during the Revolutionary War in the Hampshire Grants, later the state of Vermont, concerns Jared French, a minister's son with a proclivity for adventure. Various exploits in romance and at war occur, with the French assisting Ethan Allen and the Green Mountain Boys.

Historical Accuracy: The novel's rapid-fire adventure competes with a period background that convincingly captures the lives of the wilderness settlers in Vermont.

67 *To Fame Unknown*

Date of Publication: 1954
Subject(s): French and Indian War; American Colonies
Fictional character(s): Esek Warren, Settler
Historical character(s): James Wolfe, Military Personnel (general)
Time Period(s): 18th century
Locale(s): Northampton, Massachusetts, American Colonies

Summary: The loves of Esek Warren of Northampton, Massachusetts, are described against a backdrop of the final days of the French and Indian War. British General James Wolfe makes a memorable appearance in the story.

Historical Accuracy: The background of the military, social, and economic conflicts are authentically presented.

BRIAN ALDISS (1925-)

An English author of criticism, essays, and travelogues, Aldiss' primary reputation is that of science fiction writer. His novels have won virtually every major award in the science fiction field. His most ambitious effort is the *Helliconia* trilogy.

68 *Frankenstein Unbound*

Date of Publication: 1973
Subject(s): Time Travel; Gothic Romance; Fantasy
Fictional character(s): Joe Bondenland, Time Traveller; Victor Frankenstein, Scientist
Historical character(s): George Gordon Byron, Writer, Nobleman (Lord Byron); Percy Bysshe Shelley, Writer; Mary Wollstonecraft Godwin, Writer
Time Period(s): 2020s (2020); 1810s (1816)
Locale(s): Switzerland

Summary: Joe Bondenland is able to go back in time from the 21st century to 1816 to discover that Frankenstein was not a creation of Mary Shelley's imagination but an actual person, as real as his monster.

Historical Accuracy: This is an ingenious mixture of forms: science fiction, Gothic romance, and historical fiction. The Regency period is convincingly rendered.

BESS STREETER ALDRICH (1881-1954)

Iowa novelist Aldrich was the author of a number of novels dealing with pioneer life. She also wrote *The Man Who Caught the Weather*, a collection of short stories.

69 *A Lantern in Her Hand*

Date of Publication: 1928
Subject(s): Settlement of the American Frontier
Fictional character(s): Abbie Deal, Frontierswoman
Time Period(s): 1850s; 1860s (1854-1865)
Locale(s): Nebraska; Iowa

Summary: The novel concerns pioneer life in Nebraska. At the center of the story is Abbie Deal, who in 1854 travels by covered wagon to the Nebraska territory. There she marries and settles in a sod house. The novel chronicles her struggle against adversity.

Historical Accuracy: Abbie Deal is modelled on Aldrich's mother. The details of frontier life are convincing.

70 *The Lieutenant's Lady*

Date of Publication: 1942
Subject(s): American West; Indians; Settlement of the American Frontier
Fictional character(s): Norman Stafford, Military Personnel; Linnie Stafford, Settler
Time Period(s): 1860s (1867)
Locale(s): Omaha, Nebraska; Dakota Territory, United States

Summary: Norman Stafford, a young army officer, eagerly awaits the arrival of his beloved to his Nebraska fort during the 1860s. Linnie arrives instead, and Stafford learns that his beloved has married another. A loveless marriage between Linnie and Stafford follows, but hardship and danger on the frontier eventually bring them together.

Historical Accuracy: The novel offers a full and authentic look at the frontier life of the period.

71 *Miss Bishop*

Date of Publication: 1933
Subject(s): College Life; Education
Fictional character(s): Ella Bishop, Teacher; Delbert Thompson, Businessman
Time Period(s): 19th century; 20th century (1880-1930)
Locale(s): Midwest

Summary: Ella Bishop is a young teacher at a midwestern college. Knowing that her impending marriage will force her to forfeit her teaching career, she breaks her engagement. Her devotion to career over marriage is considered startlingly unusual, which speaks volumes about the time in which the novel was written. The foregone marriage sets the bittersweet tone of the story.

Historical Accuracy: The novel is more nostalgic than historical.

72 *Song of Years*

Date of Publication: 1939
Subject(s): Settlement of the American Frontier; Civil War—U.S.
Fictional character(s): Suzanne Martin, Settler; Jeremiah Martin, Settler; Wayne Lockwood, Military Personnel, Settler
Time Period(s): 1850s; 1860s (1854-1865)
Locale(s): Iowa

Summary: Pioneer life in Iowa before and during the Civil War is depicted in this story of the seven daughters of the Martin family. A love story between Wayne Lockwood and Suzanne Martin is played out against the daily challenges of pioneer life and the events of the time that impact the prairie community.

Historical Accuracy: The author details pioneer life with authenticity.

73 *Spring Came on Forever*

Date of Publication: 1935
Subject(s): Settlement of the American Frontier; Family Saga
Fictional character(s): Matthias Meier, Settler; Amelia Stoltz, Settler
Time Period(s): 19th century; 20th century (1866-1933)
Locale(s): Nebraska

Summary: The novel chronicles four generations of lives on the Nebraska prairie from the 1860s to the late 1930s. The interconnected lives of two families, beginning with Matthias Meier and Amelia Stoltz, German pioneers who come to Nebraska by wagon in 1866, are depicted.

Historical Accuracy: The novel provides an authentic portrait of the times and the region.

JAMES ALDRIDGE (1918-)

74 *One Last Glimpse*

Date of Publication: 1977
Subject(s): Literary Life
Fictional character(s): Kit Quayle, Journalist
Historical character(s): Ernest Hemingway, Writer; F. Scott Fitzgerald, Writer; Zelda Fitzgerald, Socialite
Time Period(s): 1920s (1929)
Locale(s): Paris, France; Brittany, France

Summary: Kit Quayle, an aspiring Australian writer, is employed as a driver by Ernest Hemingway and F. Scott Fitzgerald on a motor tour through Brittany. The trip is a wild ride as two huge and damaged egos clash, testing the limits of their friendship.

Historical Accuracy: Aldridge's story is pure fiction, but his story of Hemingway and Fitzgerald's friendship is as valid as any of the other myriad explanations of what happened between the two men.

MIGUEL ALEMAN VELASCO

Mexican author Aleman Velasco is an expert on the ancient history of Mexico.

75   *Copilli, Aztec Prince*

Date of Publication: 1981
Subject(s): Aztec Empire
Fictional character(s): Copilli, Royalty (prince)
Historical character(s): Axayacatl, Ruler (Aztec); Montezuma II, Ruler (Aztec)
Time Period(s): 16th century
Locale(s): Mexico

Summary: The novels offers the autobiography of Copilli, an Aztec prince during the time of Montezuma. His training as well as the beliefs and customs of the Aztecs are depicted. He struggles to build a great pyramid as a record of the history of his people, who are about to be destroyed by the arrival of the conquistadors.

Historical Accuracy: Aztec life and beliefs are genuinely reconstructed.

BRUCE ALEXANDER

76   *Blind Justice*

Date of Publication: 1994
Subject(s): Mystery; Crime and Criminals; Georgian Period
Fictional character(s): Jeremy Proctor, Servant, Teenager
Historical character(s): Sir John Fielding, Judge, Handicapped (blind); Samuel Johnson, Writer, Scholar; James Boswell, Writer; David Garrick, Actor
Time Period(s): 1760s (1768)
Locale(s): London, England

Summary: This mystery's detective is Sir John Fielding, judge and half brother of novelist Henry Fielding, who founded London's first police force, the Bow Street Runners. Fielding possesses a keen intellect and skill as a detective, even more remarkable because he is blind. Assisted by 13-year-old Proctor, Fielding investigates the death of a lord and reveals foul play and conspiracy.

Historical Accuracy: The period setting and characters, historical and otherwise, are vividly and wittily rendered.

77   *Murder in Grub Street*

Date of Publication: 1995
Subject(s): Mystery; Georgian Period
Fictional character(s): Jeremy Proctor, Servant, Teenager; John Clayton, Writer (poet)
Historical character(s): Sir John Fielding, Judge, Handicapped (blind)
Time Period(s): 18th century
Locale(s): London, England

Summary: In this second installment of a mystery series based on the historical figure of Sir John Fielding, the hero investigates what seems to be a clear case of murder. Poet John Clayton is caught wielding an axe when a bookseller, his wife, and two sons are murdered in their Grub Street shop. Fielding, however, is not so sure, and his investigation leads to a complex conspiracy of politics, religion, and greed.

Historical Accuracy: The period elements are exact and convincingly detailed. Fielding was a blind magistrate who co-founded London's first police force, the Bow Street Runners.

78   *Watery Grave*

Date of Publication: 1996
Subject(s): Mystery; Georgian Period
Fictional character(s): Jeremy Proctor, Servant, Teenager
Historical character(s): Sir John Fielding, Judge, Handicapped (blind)
Time Period(s): 1760s (1769)
Locale(s): London, England

Summary: In the third of the historical mystery novels involving Sir John Fielding, the co-founder of London's Bow Street Runners and a blind magistrate, he is asked to investigate a relative's tale of murder at sea. Fielding uncovers a number of secrets that some would prefer remain buried.

Historical Accuracy: The novel's period ambience is persuasive and authentic.

KARL ALEXANDER (1944-)

A native of Los Angeles, California, Alexander attended Brown University and San Francisco State College. He received his M.F.A. from the University of Iowa. He served in the Marine Corps from 1968 to 1971 and has worked as a college professor, screenwriter, and television writer.

79   *Papa and Fidel*

Date of Publication: 1989
Subject(s): Literary Life; Independence—Cuba
Historical character(s): Ernest Hemingway, Writer (novelist), Adventurer; Fidel Castro, Revolutionary
Time Period(s): 1950s; 1960s (1957-1960)
Locale(s): Havana, Cuba; New York, New York

Summary: The novel imagines what might have happened if, instead of the single meeting between Hemingway and Castro that occurred in 1961, the two had met and become friends in 1957 in the Cuban hills. As Castro plots his revolution, Hemingway is allowed a final reliving of his own heroic past.

Historical Accuracy: The premise of the novel is imagining what might have happened between two dynamic personalities. Both main characters are turned into glamorous and idealized versions of their historical selves.

80   *Time After Time*

Date of Publication:
Subject(s): Time Travel; Crime and Criminals
Fictional character(s): Amy Robbins, Clerk (in a bank); Leslie John Stephenson, Murderer (aka Jack the Ripper), Doctor
Historical character(s): H.G. Wells, Writer (novelist)
Time Period(s): 1890s (1893); 1970s (1979)
Locale(s): London, England; San Francisco, California

Summary: H. G. Wells allows his friend, Dr. Stephenson, to use his time machine. When Stephenson turns out to be Jack the Ripper, Wells must follow him to San Francisco in 1979 to halt his killing spree. Wells meets a young bank clerk, Amy

Robbins, and must adjust to a future that even he could not have imagined. Amy becomes one of Stephenson's intended victims and must be saved with some sleight of hand in the space/time continuum.

Historical Accuracy: The novel is a dizzying juxtaposition of 1893 and 1979 as Wells brings his perspective to bear on the modern world. The novel is a smart and knowing evocation of both eras.

KATE ALEXANDER
(PSEUD. OF TILLY ARMSTRONG, 1927-)

Born in Sutton, England, Alexander attended commercial school in Wimbledon and worked as a secretary for the World Health Organization and for the British Steel Corp. before becoming a full-time writer.

⬛ 81 *Palaces of Desire*

Date of Publication: 1978
Subject(s): French Revolution; Royalty—France; Napoleonic Era
Fictional character(s): Nicole de Clervaux, Noblewoman, Ward; William Falkland, Nobleman (Duke of Falkland)
Historical character(s): Louis XVI, Ruler (King of France); Marie Antoinette, Royalty (Queen of France); Napoleon Bonaparte, Military Personnel (general), Ruler (Emperor of France)
Time Period(s): 18th century; 19th century (1789-1800s)
Locale(s): Bordeaux, France; Paris, France; Alexandria, Egypt

Summary: French noblewoman Nicole de Clervaux is the ward of the English Duke of Falkland, with whom she falls in love. Caught up in the French Revolution, she is imprisoned but is sustained by her passion for the duke which continues despite his marriage to another. Infatuated with Nicole, Napoleon takes her to Egypt where she is reunited with Falkland.

Historical Accuracy: The scenes of court and prison are convincing, but the presence in the story of so many important figures strains credibility.

LAWRENCE ALEXANDER (1939-)

⬛ 82 *The Big Stick*

Date of Publication: 1986
Subject(s): Gay Nineties; Mystery
Historical character(s): Theodore Roosevelt, Government Official (police commissioner); William F. Cody, Entertainer, Frontiersman; Antonin Dvorak, Composer; Thomas Alva Edison, Inventor; Lillian Russell, Actress
Time Period(s): 1890s
Locale(s): New York, New York; Long Island, New York

Summary: New York Police Commissioner Teddy Roosevelt investigates a series of robberies that affect some of New York's leading citizens, including Buffalo Bill, Dvorak, Edison, and Lillian Russell. T.R.'s investigation provides an impressive tour of Gay Nineties' New York.

Historical Accuracy: That Roosevelt was in fact Police Commissioner is the only historical fact, other than the impressive background reconstruction of the period.

⬛ 83 *Speak Softly*

Date of Publication: 1987
Subject(s): Gay Nineties; Mystery
Historical character(s): Theodore Roosevelt, Government Official (police commissioner); Franklin Delano Roosevelt, Gentleman; Edith Roosevelt, Gentlewoman, Spouse
Time Period(s): 1890s (1895)
Locale(s): New York, New York; Long Island, New York

Summary: New York's Police Commissioner, Teddy Roosevelt, is called in to investigate a series of murders linked to organized crime and narcotics. The "Black Hand" killers threaten his young cousin, F.D.R., and the game is afoot, climaxing in a submarine chase in New York harbor.

Historical Accuracy: Every fact, date, and event is based on historical record, except for a few instances where discretion or dramatic effect dictate a departure from what actually happened.

⬛ 84 *The Strenuous Life*

Date of Publication: 1991
Subject(s): Mystery; Gay Nineties
Historical character(s): Theodore Roosevelt, Government Official (police commissioner); John D. Rockefeller, Financier, Businessman; Geronimo, Indian (Apache), Chieftain
Time Period(s): 1890s (1895)
Locale(s): New York, New York; Fort Sill, Oklahoma

Summary: A theft at New York's armory leads to New York Police Commissioner Theodore Roosevelt's investigation of an ever-widening conspiracy that involves him with such disparate personalities as John D. Rockefeller and Geronimo.

Historical Accuracy: The inventive situation is fanciful, but the atmosphere is precisely and vividly rendered.

SIDNEY ALEXANDER (1912-)

American author and translator Alexander was a journalist and foreign correspondent from 1948-1968. He has written poetry, a number of radio plays and a biography of Marc Chagall.

⬛ 85 *The Hand of Michelangelo*

Date of Publication: 1977
Subject(s): Biography, Fictionalized; Artistic Life; Renaissance
Historical character(s): Michelangelo Buonarotti, Artist
Time Period(s): 16th century (1505-1525)
Locale(s): Florence, Italy; Rome, Italy

Summary: This is the second of three novels based on the life and career of Italian Renaissance artist and sculptor Michelangelo. The years of Michelangelo's greatest artistic achievements are depicted, as well as a portrait of Renaissance Jewish history.

Historical Accuracy: The novel is meticulous in its research and authenticity.

86   *Michelangelo the Florentine*

Date of Publication: 1957
Subject(s): Renaissance; Artistic Life; Biography, Fictionalized
Fictional character(s): Andrea del Medigo, Artist
Historical character(s): Michelangelo Buonarotti, Artist; Leonardo da Vinci, Artist; Sandro Botticelli, Artist; Alexander VI, Religious (pope); Cesare Borgia, Nobleman; Lucrezia Borgia, Noblewoman; Niccolo Machiavelli, Political Figure, Writer
Time Period(s): 15th century; 16th century (1493-1505)
Locale(s): Florence, Italy; Rome, Italy

Summary: This is the first volume of Alexander's trilogy on the life of Michelangelo. It covers the first 30 years of his life, culminating in his sculpting of David. The novel, though, is far more than a biography of a great Renaissance artist; it is also the history of the period, connecting Michelangelo with the turbulent politics of the Medicis and the Borgias. In Alexander's picture of the Jew Andrea, a graphic picture of the treatment of the Jews during the period is also offered.

Historical Accuracy: The novel is a hallmark of historical reconstruction. The language, customs, and politics are joined into a comprehensive panorama.

87·   *Nicodemus: The Roman Years of Michelangelo Buonarroti, 1534-1564*

Date of Publication: 1984
Subject(s): Artistic Life; Renaissance; Biography, Fictionalized
Historical character(s): Michelangelo Buonarotti, Artist
Time Period(s): 16th century (1534-1564)
Locale(s): Rome, Italy

Summary: In this moving final volume of Alexander's Michelangelo trilogy, the artist's final years in Rome at work for a succession of popes are chronicled from the perspective of Michelangelo himself and several eyewitnesses. The novel is a convincing depiction both of the artist's genius and of his time.

Historical Accuracy: The novel, like its predecessors, is a masterwork of historical reconstruction.

MARY BETHELL ALFRIEND

88   *Juan Ortiz: Gentleman of Seville*

Date of Publication: 1941
Subject(s): Exploration
Historical character(s): Juan Ortiz, Explorer; Hernando de Soto, Explorer
Time Period(s): 16th century
Locale(s): Florida

Summary: The novel offers a fictional account of the actual Spanish explorer Juan Ortiz. As a member of an earlier expedition, Ortiz survives for ten years among the Florida Indians before being rescued by De Soto. Ortiz then joins De Soto's expedition as an interpreter and guide.

Historical Accuracy: The known facts about Juan Ortiz' life and career are blended with imaginary details and an essentially romantic plot.

MARGARET ALLAN (1922-)

Allan's books include *A Portrait of Joy*, *Doctor David*, and *Son of Hamish*.

89   *The Last Mammoth*

Date of Publication: 1995
Subject(s): Prehistory; Tribal Life—Prehistoric
Fictional character(s): Gotha, Shaman, Prehistoric Human; Rising Sun, Prehistoric Human; Running Deer, Prehistoric Human
Time Period(s): 180th century B.C. (17,953 B.C.)
Locale(s): Green Valley, Earth

Summary: The prehistoric People of the Mammoth face extinction for the Great Maya has died and the sacred mammoth stone is shattered. Hope rests with the youth Rising Sun and the rebellious girl Running Deer who together must make a perilous journey to save their people.

Historical Accuracy: The background of the story is solidly rooted in convincing details of what prehistoric life might have been like.

90   *The Mammoth Stone*

Date of Publication: 1993
Subject(s): Prehistory; Tribal Life—Prehistoric
Fictional character(s): Wolf, Prehistoric Human, Warrior; Maya, Prehistoric Human, Shaman
Time Period(s): 180th century B.C.
Locale(s): North America (modern Pennsylvania)

Summary: In this tale of prehistoric life in America, the People of the Mammoth are nomadic hunters who follow the mammoth herds. Great changes and challenges transpire with the birth of twin children. Wolf grows up to become a warrior, while Maya has the sign (one blue eye and one green) that marks her as the wielder of the Mammoth Stone, a talisman of great power.

Historical Accuracy: The story has fantasy elements, but does depend on a credible version of prehistoric life.

PAULA ALLARDYCE
(PSEUD. OF URSULA TORDAY, 1888-)

An English author who was born in London and attended the London School of Economics, Torday wrote under a series of pseudonyms including Charity Blackstock, Lee Blackstock, and Charlotte Keppel.

91   *Miss Philadelphia Smith*

Date of Publication: 1977
Subject(s): Romance; Georgian Period

Fictional character(s): Philadelphia Smith, Heroine; Atherton, Rake, Gentleman
Time Period(s): 1750s
Locale(s): London, England

Summary: Class differences form the subject of this romantic novel in which a street in London is divided between the odd-numbered houses of the wealthy and the modest even numbers. Philadelphia Smith lives in an even-numbered cottage and attracts the attention of a rake, the grandest of the odds. The two come together before retreating to their appropriate social worlds.

Historical Accuracy: The novel accurately portrays the social disparities of the period, but romance takes precedence over the historical details.

KEITH ALLDRITT (1935-)

Born in Wolverhampton, England, Alldritt received his degree from St. Catherine's College of Cambridge University. He has worked as a professor of English at the University of Illinois and the University of British Columbia.

92 *Elgar on the Journey to Hanley*
Date of Publication: 1979
Subject(s): Musical Life; Victorian Period
Fictional character(s): Dora Penny, Gentlewoman
Historical character(s): Edward William Elgar, Composer
Time Period(s): 20th century (turn of the century)
Locale(s): Wolverhampton, England

Summary: British composer Edward Elgar stops off at Wolverhampton on a journey to Hanley and meets the young daughter of a rector, Dora Penny. The novel tells the story of their relationship while examining provincial English life at the turn of the century. The novel also offers insights into Elgar's development as a composer.

Historical Accuracy: Alldritt has been justly praised for his ability to capture life in the English Midlands with familiarity and intimacy.

MARJORIE ALLEE

93 *Judith Lankester*
Date of Publication: 1930
Subject(s): Quakers
Fictional character(s): Judith Lankester, Settler
Time Period(s): 1840s
Locale(s): Indiana

Summary: Life in a Quaker community in Indiana is depicted in this story of Judith Lankester. After her father's death, Judith goes by covered wagon to Indiana to her grandfather's frontier home. There she must learn to cope with frontier life.

Historical Accuracy: The story is a forceful one with a solid background of period frontier life.

DEXTER ALLEN

94 *The Coil of the Serpent*
Date of Publication: 1955
Subject(s): Aztec Empire
Historical character(s): Nezahual, Ruler (Aztec)
Time Period(s): 15th century
Locale(s): Mexico

Summary: This is the sequel to *The Jaguar and the Golden Stag*, the author's chronicle of Aztec life before the Spanish conquest. It continues the story of Nezahual, who has overthrown the regent to claim the throne of Texcuco. The novel recounts Nezahual's military campaigns to repel invasions and maintain his power.

Historical Accuracy: The novel interweaves poetic elements with a graphic depiction of Aztec life and customs.

95 *The Jaguar and the Golden Stag*
Date of Publication: 1954
Subject(s): Aztec Empire
Historical character(s): Nezahual, Royalty (Aztec prince)
Time Period(s): 15th century
Locale(s): Mexico

Summary: This poetic and forceful story of the Aztecs shortly before the arrival of the Spanish concerns the young prince Nezahual, who climbs to power as emperor of Anahuac.

Historical Accuracy: This lyrical portrait of Nezahual is at variance with the Aztec chieftain of history.

96 *Valley of Eagles*
Date of Publication: 1957
Subject(s): Aztec Empire
Historical character(s): Nezahual, Ruler (lord of Tezcuco)
Time Period(s): 16th century
Locale(s): Mexico

Summary: The third novel of a trilogy about the reign of Nezahual, enigmatic lord of Tezcuco. The novel features a vivid depiction of Aztec customs and concludes with the arrival of Cortez and the Spanish.

Historical Accuracy: The events and most of the characters are drawn from William H. Prescott's *The Conquest of Mexico*.

HERVEY ALLEN (1889-1949)

An American novelist and poet, Allen achieved remarkable popular success with his novel of the Napoleonic era, *AnthonyAdverse*. He also produced a carefully-researched biography of Edgar Allen Poe, *Israfel* (1926). His trilogy of novels about 18th-century American frontier life (listed below) is still highly regarded.

97 *Action at Aquila*
Date of Publication: 1937
Subject(s): Civil War—U.S.; Shenandoah Valley Campaign

Fictional character(s): Nathaniel Franklin, Military Personnel (Union colonel); Elizabeth Crittenden, Spouse (Confederate officer's wife)
Historical character(s): James Buchanan, Political Figure (former president); Philip H. Sheridan, Military Personnel (Union general)
Time Period(s): 1860s (1864-1865)
Locale(s): Pennsylvania; Maryland; Shenandoah Valley, Virginia

Summary: In this novel about the Civil War's Shenandoah Valley campaign of 1864-1865, Colonial Franklin returns to the Sixth Pennsylvania Cavalry after a furlough. He then participates in a minor, though significant, military action.

Historical Accuracy: There are good, if at times overly romantic, details of combat and the period.

98   *Anthony Adverse*

Date of Publication: 1933
Subject(s): Napoleonic Era; Slavery; Picaresque Adventure
Fictional character(s): Anthony Adverse, Adventurer, Bastard Son; Bonnyfeather, Businessman; Don Luis, Nobleman (Spanish)
Historical character(s): Napoleon Bonaparte, Military Personnel; Jean Laffite, Pirate; Aaron Burr, Political Figure
Time Period(s): 18th century; 19th century (1775-1804)
Locale(s): Europe (Switzerland, Spain, Italy, France); Africa; North America (Cuba, Louisiana, New Mexico)

Summary: This massive picaresque adventure begins in 1775. It involves the illegitimate son of an Irish-French noble and the Scottish wife of a Spanish noble. The hero travels and launches financial schemes throughout Europe, Africa, and America. His adventures are cast in a brooding, lyrical light.

Historical Accuracy: The novel seems more poetic and symbolic than realistic, despite the presence of historical characters.

99   *Bedford Village*

Date of Publication: 1944
Subject(s): Settlement of the American Frontier; American Colonies
Fictional character(s): Salathiel Albine, Frontiersman; Captain Ecuyer, Military Personnel; Garrett Pendergass, Businessman
Time Period(s): 1760s (1763-1764)
Locale(s): Bedford, Pennsylvania, American Colonies

Summary: This second volume of Allen's trilogy concerns the settling of Bedford, the colonies' western-most outpost. Albine continues to learn the ways of civilization in the frontier of Pennsylvania.

Historical Accuracy: There are strong details of frontier life and a poetic rendering of the gradual disappearance of the American wilderness.

100   *The Forest and the Fort*

Date of Publication: 1943
Subject(s): American Colonies; Settlement of the American Frontier; French and Indian War

Fictional character(s): Salathiel Albine, Frontiersman; Big Turtle, Indian; James McArdle, Religious
Time Period(s): 18th century
Locale(s): Pennsylvania, American Colonies (western territory)

Summary: A frontiersman, Albine is captured and raised by the Shawnees in the American colonies' western frontier of Pennsylvania. This first volume of a trilogy evokes frontier life and the formation of an American identity.

Historical Accuracy: The novel offers dramatic scenes from the French and Indian War, especially the siege of Fort Pitt.

101   *Toward the Morning*

Date of Publication: 1948
Subject(s): Settlement of the American Frontier; American Colonies
Fictional character(s): Salathiel Albine, Frontiersman; Frances Melissa O'Toole, Settler, Spouse
Time Period(s): 1760s (1764-1765)
Locale(s): Pennsylvania, American Colonies

Summary: This final volume of a trilogy describes frontier life in western Pennsylvania during the 1760s. As the wilderness is settled and civilization causes a clash of interests, Albine journeys east to Philadelphia and an uncertain future.

Historical Accuracy: The depiction of the wilderness diminishes over the series into an elegy for a lost era.

MERRIT PARMALEE ALLEN

102   *Battle Lanterns*

Date of Publication: 1949
Subject(s): American Revolution
Historical character(s): Francis Marion, Military Personnel (American officer)
Time Period(s): 1780s
Locale(s): South Carolina

Summary: Set during the American Revolution, the novel chronicles the exploits of Francis Marion, the Swamp Fox, and his guerrilla campaign against the British in the southern campaign of the war.

Historical Accuracy: The novel is effective and believable in capturing the atmosphere of the times and is faithful to historical events.

T.D. ALLEN

(PSEUD. OF TERRY D. ALLEN, 1908- ; DON B. ALLEN)

Terry Allen was born in Oklahoma and graduated from Phillips University. A professor of creative writing at the Institute of American Indian Arts in Santa Fe, Allen has also lectured on American Indians at the University of California at Santa Cruz.

103   *Doctor in Buckskin*

Date of Publication: 1951

Subject(s): Settlement of the American Frontier; Indians; Religious Life

Historical character(s): Marcus Whitman, Doctor, Religious (missionary); Narcissa Whitman, Spouse, Religious (missionary)

Time Period(s): 19th century

Locale(s): Oregon; Pacific Northwest

Summary: This is the story of Marcus and Narcissa Whitman who are among the first whites to venture into the Oregon wilderness. They open a missionary outpost among the Cayuse Indians whom they assist during an epidemic spread by the arrival of settlers. The novel recounts their tragic history.

Historical Accuracy: The novel stays close to the actual events that occurred to the Whitmans.

104 *Troubled Border*

Date of Publication: 1954

Subject(s): American West; Biography, Fictionalized

Historical character(s): John McLoughlin, Businessman

Time Period(s): 19th century

Locale(s): Pacific Northwest

Summary: The early days of the settlement of the Pacific Northwest are described in the fictionalized biography of John McLoughlin, the chief superintendent for the Hudson's Bay Company at Fort Vancouver on the Columbia River.

Historical Accuracy: The story stays close to the facts, though the characters tend toward the melodramatic.

WALTER ALLEN (1911-)

A literary and radio critic, college professor, journalist, and biographer as well as a novelist, Allen was born and raised in Birmingham, England. Allen is a fellow of the Royal Society of Literature. He has been called one of the last of a school of critics who focus on the whole rather than a narrow aspect of life.

105 *Threescore and Ten*

Date of Publication: 1959

Subject(s): Family Saga

Fictional character(s): Billy Ashted, Artisan (silversmith); George Thompson, Political Figure; Rose Thompson Ashted, Spouse

Time Period(s): 19th century; 20th century (1875-1951)

Locale(s): Manchester, England

Summary: Billy Ashted reviews his life at age 76, forming a social chronicle from the Victorian period to World War II and a personal philosophy that attempts to cope with a long history of disappointments. Ashted rises from poverty in the Manchester slums to become a silversmith. Friendship with George Thompson, who becomes a socialist Member of Parliament, connects Billy to the larger world.

Historical Accuracy: The novel offers a convincing portrait of a life and time.

MARGUERITE ALLIS (1887-1958)

106 *All in Good Time*

Date of Publication: 1944

Subject(s): Business Building

Fictional character(s): Job Hubbard, Artisan (clockmaker); Elvira Hubbard, Gentlewoman

Time Period(s): 18th century; 19th century (1795-1820s)

Locale(s): Connecticut

Summary: Set in the early years of the young American nation, the novel describes Job Hubbard who stays home in Connecticut instead of heading west to Ohio like so many of his peers. Job is a clockmaker who establishes his business at the beginning of mass production. The novel recounts this and other factors of business at the time, such as the effects of the Embargo Act of 1807.

Historical Accuracy: Allis knows the locale intimately and is able to capture the period with authentic details.

107 *Brave Pursuit*

Date of Publication: 1954

Subject(s): Women's Rights; Family Saga; Education

Fictional character(s): Ashbel Field, Settler; Connie Field, Settler, Feminist

Time Period(s): 1810s

Locale(s): Cincinnati, Ohio

Summary: The third of Allis' novels concerning the Field family takes place in Ohio in the years following the War of 1812. Connie Field is denied the education she desires as well as the chance to marry whom she likes. She is determined to be independent, and to do so she must run away.

Historical Accuracy: Allis' sense of place and customs are convincing in this drama about women's rights and education.

108 *The Bridge*

Date of Publication: 1949

Subject(s): Business Building; Civil War—U.S.; Railroads

Fictional character(s): Lucius Lord, Businessman; Sarah Lord, Gentlewoman

Historical character(s): Clara Barton, Nurse; Dorothea Dix, Nurse

Time Period(s): 19th century (1840-1870)

Locale(s): Middletown, Connecticut; New Haven, Connecticut; Washington, District of Columbia

Summary: Prominent in the shipping industry, the Lords find themselves in the midst of conflict when the townspeople of Middletown decide to build a railroad bridge. It helps to revive the town's economy, but it also brings problems with neighboring towns and the shipping industry. Civil War scenes add to the drama.

Historical Accuracy: The novel is an interesting picture of city rivalries in a time when the railroad transformed the landscape and customs of America.

109 *Charity Strong*

Date of Publication: 1945

Subject(s): Musical Life
Fictional character(s): Charity Strong, Gentlewoman; Perry Green, Worker
Time Period(s): 1820s; 1830s (1825-1832)
Locale(s): Connecticut; New York, New York

Summary: The prejudice of New Englanders, particularly to those with artistic gifts, is Allis' theme in this novel of Connecticut and New York life in the 1820s and 1830s. Charity Strong is a young woman who rebels against the "older school" of music. Charity is torn between the wider cultural opportunities of New York and the familiarity of her hometown.

Historical Accuracy: There are solid and convincing scenes of period Connecticut and period New York.

110   *Free Soil*

Date of Publication: 1958
Subject(s): Settlement of the American Frontier; Slavery
Fictional character(s): Lafayette Field, Settler; Eve Field, Southern Belle, Settler
Historical character(s): John Brown, Abolitionist
Time Period(s): 1840s
Locale(s): Cincinnati, Ohio; Lawrence, Kansas

Summary: Lafe and Eve Field move west to the Kansas frontier, where the border battle between free state and slave state occurs. The events in the novel lead directly to the Civil War.

Historical Accuracy: The details of the period and its issues are described in convincing human terms as the Fields are once again swept up in the country's history.

111   *Law of the Land*

Date of Publication: 1948
Subject(s): Women's Rights
Fictional character(s): Arabella Barlow, Gentlewoman; Ben Barlow, Worker; Mark Dudley, Gentleman
Historical character(s): Lucretia Mott, Feminist; Elizabeth Cady Stanton, Feminist
Time Period(s): 1850s
Locale(s): Connecticut; New York

Summary: The novel features an ill-fated love affair set against the backdrop of the emerging struggle for women's rights. Arabella Barlow is in love with a man who is not her husband. She fights her way into the Connecticut General Assembly to make her case to reform divorce laws.

Historical Accuracy: The novel's romantic story is reinforced by solid period details.

112   *Now We Are Free*

Date of Publication: 1952
Subject(s): Settlement of the American Frontier; Immigrants
Fictional character(s): Ashbel Field, Military Personnel, Explorer; Ezra Pomeroy, Military Personnel, Explorer; Silas Marvin, Military Personnel, Explorer
Historical character(s): Moses Cleaveland, Explorer; Rufus Putnam, Military Personnel
Time Period(s): 1780s; 1790s

Locale(s): Connecticut; Pennsylvania; Ohio (Northwest territory)

Summary: The novel describes the opening of America's original Northwest territory: western Pennsylvania and Ohio. A group of young Revolutionary War veterans embarks on an epic journey to survey the territory, beginning and ending in their native Connecticut.

Historical Accuracy: Allis' history and period detail are authentic.

113   *The Rising Storm*

Date of Publication: 1955
Subject(s): Slavery; Underground Railroad
Fictional character(s): Lafayette Field, Gentleman, Twin; Lancelot Field, Gentleman, Twin
Time Period(s): 1830s
Locale(s): Cincinnati, Ohio

Summary: Antislavery agitation splits the Field family, specifically dividing twin brothers Lafayette and Lancelot Field, the former raised in Cincinnati and committed to the concept of equality, the latter raised on a Louisiana plantation. An escaped slave who takes refuge in the Field's home, a station on the underground railroad, brings on a family crisis.

Historical Accuracy: Allis vividly recreates the customs and daily habits of the era, on the borderline between free and slave states.

114   *The Splendor Stays: An Historic Novel Based on the Lives of the Seven Hart Sisters of Saybrook*

Date of Publication: 1942
Subject(s): War of 1812; Family Saga
Historical character(s): Elisha Hart, Sea Captain; Ann Hart, Gentlewoman; Mary Hart, Gentlewoman; Jeanette Hart, Gentlewoman; Isaac Hull, Military Personnel (naval officer); Simon Bolivar, Military Personnel, Revolutionary; James Fenimore Cooper, Writer; Fritz-Greene Halleck, Writer (poet)
Time Period(s): 19th century (1806-1840s)
Locale(s): Saybrook, Connecticut; New York, New York; South America

Summary: American history in the first several decades of the 19th century is chronicled through the perspective of the Hart family, who become associated with the great events and personalities of the age. The Hart sisters' experiences represent the change in social customs and politics of the period.

Historical Accuracy: The novel offers a convincing panorama of the first half of the 19th century grounded in the facts of the Hart family history.

115   *To Keep Us Free*

Date of Publication: 1953
Subject(s): Settlement of the American Frontier; War of 1812; Indians
Fictional character(s): Ashbel Field, Settler; Faith Field, Settler

Historical character(s): William Henry Harrison, Military Personnel, Political Figure
Time Period(s): 18th century; 19th century (1797-1815)
Locale(s): Cleveland, Ohio; Marietta, Ohio (Northwest territory)

Summary: The pioneering Field family has migrated from Connecticut to the Ohio wilderness to settle the territory. They must contend with threats from the Indians, the British, and fellow settlers. There are scenes involving the settlements of Marietta and Cleveland specifically. The action climaxes with the battles of the War of 1812.

Historical Accuracy: Allis' depiction of Ohio during this period is both compelling and authentic.

116 *Water over the Dam*

Date of Publication: 1947
Subject(s): Canal Building
Fictional character(s): Titus Todd, Clerk (store clerk), Landowner; Benoni Dickinson, Landowner, Businessman; Deborah Dickinson, Gentlewoman
Historical character(s): James Hillhouse, Political Figure
Time Period(s): 19th century (1825-1848)
Locale(s): Connecticut

Summary: The novel centers on the building of the ill-fated Farmington Canal from 1825 to 1848, a grand project meant to open up trade within Connecticut. Titus Todd is a young store clerk whose life and love are tied to the building of the canal.

Historical Accuracy: The political intrigue and town rivalry are captured convincingly.

E.M. ALMEDINGEN (1898-1971)

Novelist and biographer Almedingen was born in St. Petersburg, Russia, and graduated from Xenia Nobility College in 1913. She was a lecturer on English medieval history and literature at the University of Petrograd and on Russian history and literature at Oxford. Almedingen wrote over 60 books, the most popular being her biographical and autobiographical novels. Books include *The Emperor Alexander I*, *Lion of the North*, and *Catherine: Empress of Russia*.

117 *The Ladies of St. Hedwig's*

Date of Publication: 1967
Subject(s): Russian Empire; Religious Life
Fictional character(s): Dame Louise Thurston, Religious (prioress)
Time Period(s): 1860s
Locale(s): St. Petersburg, Russia

Summary: Set during the Polish Mutiny in the 1860s, the novel concerns the conflict between a group of Polish nuns in a convent in St. Petersburg and the Russian authorities. The story centers on the prioress, Dame Louise, who faces the challenge of resisting the reprisals against the order.

Historical Accuracy: The story is based in part on an actual community of nuns in St. Petersburg. The novel succeeds in re-creating the atmosphere of the era and the customs of the convent during the period.

118 *Young Catherine*

Date of Publication: 1938
Subject(s): Russian Empire; Royalty—Russia; Biography, Fictionalized
Historical character(s): Catherine II, Ruler (Empress of Russia)
Time Period(s): 18th century
Locale(s): Russia; Germany

Summary: This biographical novel recounts the rise to power of Catherine the Great of Russia, beginning with her childhood and the arranged marriage that brings her to Russia, and ending with the coup in 1762 that brings her to the throne.

Historical Accuracy: The basic outline of the story follows the actual facts.

JUDY ALTER (1938-)

American western writer Alter was born in Chicago and received her Ph.D. from Texas Christian University. She is the author of *Luke and the Van Zandt County War* and *Women of the Old West*.

119 *Cherokee Rose: A Novel of America's First Cowgirl*

Date of Publication: 1996
Subject(s): American West
Fictional character(s): Tommy Jo Burns, Frontierswoman, Entertainer
Historical character(s): Theodore Roosevelt, Political Figure
Time Period(s): 19th century; 20th century
Locale(s): Oklahoma

Summary: The novel is inspired by the life of western trick roper and entertainer Lucille Mulholt, for whom President Theodore Roosevelt coined the term "cowgirl." Her story takes her around the world with Buffalo Bill's Wild West Show and the 101 Ranch Show.

Historical Accuracy: The story is not intended as a biography but bases many of its events and situations on several western women, creating a composite portrait.

120 *Jessie: A Novel Based on the Life of Jessie Benton Fremont*

Date of Publication: 1995
Subject(s): American West; Biography, Fictionalized
Historical character(s): Jessie Benton Fremont, Spouse; John C. Fremont, Frontiersman, Political Figure; Thomas Hart Benton, Political Figure
Time Period(s): 19th century
Locale(s): California; Panama; Arizona

Summary: Jessie Benton defies her father, Senator Thomas Hart Benton, and elopes with the handsome frontier explorer John Charles Fremont. She stands with him through his incredible career in Panama, during the California Gold Rush, and at his near capture of the White House. The novel allows Jessie to tell her own story and emerge from her husband's long shadow.

Historical Accuracy: The author admits to taking small liberties with history for the sake of dramatic storytelling and also to simplify what was an unbelievably complex life.

121 *Libbie*

Date of Publication: 1994
Subject(s): Settlement of the American Frontier; Military Life—U.S. Cavalry; Indians
Historical character(s): George Armstrong Custer, Military Personnel; Elizabeth Bacon Custer, Gentlewoman, Spouse
Time Period(s): 1860s; 1870s
Locale(s): Monroe, Michigan; Dakota Territory, United States; Kansas

Summary: This first-person narrative of Elizabeth Custer tells the story of her courtship and married life with the flamboyant boy-general up to his disaster at the Little Bighorn. Elizabeth follows her beloved ''Autie'' from post to post. He is an enigma whose tragic end seems foretold.

Historical Accuracy: Alter tries to deepen the portrait of Mrs. Custer, the devoted keeper of her husband's grand reputation. Her suggestion of Custer's flaws and domestic conflict is speculative. There are some slight deviations from history.

STEPHEN ALTER (1956-)

Alter was born in India of American missionaries. His first book, *Neglected Lives*, was published in 1978.

122 *Silk and Steel*

Date of Publication: 1980
Subject(s): Religious Conflict; Indian Empire
Fictional character(s): Augustine, Military Personnel (mercenary); Webley, Military Personnel (mercenary); Khasturba, Prostitute
Time Period(s): 1810s
Locale(s): Lucknow, India

Summary: India before the dominance of the British Raj is the setting for this novel. Muslims and Sikhs are at war with each other, aided by mercenary bands; all are fighting the British for control. Augustine is half-English, half-Indian, caught between conflicting loyalties. His friend is the the brilliant soldier Webley. They both love the prostitute Khasturba.

Historical Accuracy: The novel creates an authentic sense of time and place, of divided loyalties, and an India in transition.

JULIA COOLEY ALTROCCHI (1893-1972)

An American poet, novelist, and lecturer, Altrocchi was born in Connecticut and attended Vassar College. She is the author of *Snow Covered Wagons: A Pioneer Epic.*

123 *Wolves Against the Moon*

Date of Publication: 1940
Subject(s): War of 1812

Historical character(s): Joseph Bailly, Trader (fur)
Time Period(s): 18th century; 19th century (1794-1835)
Locale(s): Canada; Great Lakes

Summary: The novel depicts the adventurous career of the actual Joseph Bailly who, though an heir to a great fortune, chooses to venture into the Great Lakes region as a fur-trader. His exploits take him throughout the Northwest Territory and involve him in such events as the Detroit fire of 1805 and the Chicago and Raisin River massacres.

Historical Accuracy: The portraits and the events described are based on fact, although the author has occasionally departed from the historical record in the interest of her story.

FRANCIS AMES (1900-)

Born in Omaha, Nebraska, Ames is the son of a rancher and was raised on a Montana cattle ranch. There he worked as a cowpuncher and fur trapper. Ames is the author of more than 600 stories and articles in magazines such as *The Saturday Evening Post* and *Field and Stream*. He is an authority on outdoor life and Montana. His books include *Fishing the Oregon Country* and *The Callahans' Gamble*, as well as several television scripts.

124 *That Callahan Spunk!*

Date of Publication: 1965
Subject(s): American West; Homesteading
Fictional character(s): John Conway, Settler; Clara Conway, Spouse; Tom Conway, Young Man
Time Period(s): 1900s (1908)
Locale(s): Montana

Summary: The novel describes the lot of homesteaders in Montana during the 1900s. John Conway brings his family west from New England, and the novel records their efforts to survive and thrive as pioneers.

Historical Accuracy: This is an authentic portrait of pioneer life of the period and the region.

JOHN EDWARD AMES

125 *The Golden Circle*

Date of Publication: 1996
Subject(s): Civil War—U.S.; Slavery
Fictional character(s): Noah Flemming, Adventurer; Ursula D'Antoni, Southern Belle
Time Period(s): 1860s
Locale(s): New Orleans, Louisiana; San Francisco, California

Summary: At the beginning of the Civil War, a group of Southern cotton magnates and Northern financiers plot to seize control of California and make it the center of a vast slave empire stretching from the Pacific Northwest to South America. Noah Fleming recruits a ragtag army to oppose the threat from the powerful cabal.

Historical Accuracy: The story is fanciful, but filled with believable period elements.

VALERIE ANAND (1937-)

British novelist Anand confesses that she developed an interest in history at the age of 15 after seeing the movie *Ivanhoe*.

`126` *The Cherished Wives*

Date of Publication: 1994
Subject(s): Family Saga; Georgian Period
Fictional character(s): Lucy-Anne Whitmead, Spouse; George Whitmead, Businessman
Time Period(s): 18th century; 19th century (1740-1801)
Locale(s): Surrey, England

Summary: This is the fifth volume of the Bridges Over Time series tracing the Whitmead family from the time of Magna Carta. The story concerns the married life of Lucy-Anne Whitmead. Her parents arrange for her to marry a distant cousin whom she hardly knows. Her experiences as a wife, mother, and grandmother are detailed as she struggles for independence and fulfillment.

Historical Accuracy: The novel interweaves a convincing period background with its impact on the novel's domestic and family drama.

`127` *Crown of Roses*

Date of Publication: 1989
Subject(s): War of the Roses; Royalty—England
Fictional character(s): Petronel Faldene, Gentlewoman; Lionel Eynesby, Gentleman
Historical character(s): Edward IV, Ruler (King of England); Richard, Duke of Gloucester, Nobleman (later Richard III); Richard Neville, Nobleman (Earl of Warwick); John Alcock, Religious; Anne Neville, Noblewoman; George, Duke of Clarence, Nobleman; Edward V, Ruler (King of England); Henry Stafford, Nobleman (Duke of Buckingham)
Time Period(s): 15th century (1466-1486)
Locale(s): England; France

Summary: Public and private lives are woven together in the dynastic struggle between Edward IV and his brother Richard of Gloucester. Petronel, who is married off to the unloving Lionel Eynesby, is recruited by the king as an emissary to his brother, the Duke of Clarence, to check the kingmaking plans of Warwick. The turbulent events leading up to the reign of Richard III are dramatized in all their intrigue and violence.

Historical Accuracy: Anand convincingly clarifies the confusing allegiances and personalities. Her Richard III stands in marked contrast to the villainous figure offered by the Tudor apologists.

`128` *The Disputed Crown*

Date of Publication: 1982
Subject(s): Middle Ages; Norman Conquest; Royalty—England
Fictional character(s): Brand, Knight; Wulfhild, Young Woman; Simon Inconnu, Knight
Historical character(s): William I, Ruler (King of England); Hereward the Wake, Outlaw, Revolutionary; Matilda of Flanders, Royalty, Spouse (of William)
Time Period(s): 11th century (1066-1086)
Locale(s): Sussex, England; York, England; Ely, England

Summary: After William is crowned king in 1066, the English people must decide whether to serve the Norman invaders or rebel; the novel explores both sides. Brand of Followdene joins with Hereward the Wake in open rebellion. His daughter, Wulfhild, chooses the different course of marrying a Norman knight and securing her estate.

Historical Accuracy: The novel's feel for the period is strong and realistic. Some invention has been done with the historical figure of Hereward.

`129` *The Faithful Lovers*

Date of Publication: 1993
Subject(s): Family Saga; Civil War—England; Restoration Period
Fictional character(s): Ninian Whitmead, Landowner; Parvati, Outcast
Time Period(s): 17th century; 18th century (1639-1710)
Locale(s): Cornwall, England

Summary: In Book IV of the Bridges Over Time series tracing the history of England and the Whitmead family from medieval times, Ninian Whitmead is resigned to living alone on his Cornish estate. When a shipwrecked pirate ship leaves Parvati, a young Indian girl, stranded, Ninian takes her in and eventually marries her. Parvati adapts to English life and customs as the events of the 17th century create considerable upheaval.

Historical Accuracy: The novel captures with skill the customs and the culture of the period.

`130` *Gildenford*

Date of Publication: 1977
Subject(s): Middle Ages; Royalty—England; Anglo-Saxon Period
Fictional character(s): Brand, Servant
Historical character(s): Alfred Atheling, Royalty; Edward the Confessor, Ruler (King of England); Godwin, Nobleman (Earl of Wessex); Harold Harefoot, Ruler (Danish king of England)
Time Period(s): 11th century (1036-1052)
Locale(s): Gildenford, England; Winchester, England

Summary: In 1036, 600 sympathizers of Alfred Atheling, the younger brother of Edward the Confessor, were cruelly slaughtered at Guildenford by Harold Harefoot, the Danish ruler of England. Implicated in the massacre is Godwin, Earl of Essex. The novel shows the effects of the massacre from the perspective of a member of Godwin's household, who must balance feudal loyalty and moral duty.

Historical Accuracy: Anand's research is evident in bringing to life this distant period in English history.

`131` *King of the Wood*

Date of Publication: 1988
Subject(s): Middle Ages; Royalty—England; Norman Conquest

Fictional character(s): Ralph De Aix, Knight; Sybil, Gentlewoman
Historical character(s): William II, Ruler (King of England)
Time Period(s): 11th century (1068-1100)
Locale(s): England

Summary: After the death of William the Conqueror, one of his three sons—William Rufus—ascends to the throne. It is he that the young Norman Ralph de Aix serves, and Ralph is rewarded with an isolated and rundown estate. To maintain it, Ralph is drawn into the clash between Norman and Saxon.

Historical Accuracy: The era has become Anand's specialty, and she shows her research in this exciting and moving tale of cultural clashes and assimilation.

132 *The Norman Pretender*
Date of Publication: 1979
Subject(s): Norman Conquest; Middle Ages; Anglo-Saxon Period
Historical character(s): Harold II, Ruler (Saxon King of England); Edward the Confessor, Ruler (King of England); William the Conqueror, Nobleman; Aldith, Royalty (wife of Harold II)
Time Period(s): 11th century (1053-1066)
Locale(s): England; Normandy, France

Summary: The novel chronicles the final tumultuous years of Saxon England, climaxing in the Battle of Hastings and the victory of the Norman Pretender, William, Duke of Normandy. Edward the Confessor has named Harold, Saxon Earl of Wessex, as his successor, producing a threat from William and rivalry and jealousy among his own followers.

Historical Accuracy: Anand constructs her story with masterful precision, detailing the period and animating her research into a dramatic story.

133 *The Proud Villeins*
Date of Publication: 1990
Subject(s): Middle Ages; Slavery; Anglo-Saxon Period
Fictional character(s): Ivon De Clairpont, Knight, Slave; Eric Olafson, Knight; Gunnor, Slave
Historical character(s): Alfred Atheling, Royalty
Time Period(s): 11th century; 12th century (1040-1144)
Locale(s): Gildenford, England; Norfolk, England; Northumbria, England

Summary: Ivon de Clairpont survives the bloody massacre at Gildenford in the 11th century only to be sold into servitude on a Dane's farm. He ceaselessly plots his escape and refuses to give up his past and his desire for freedom. His descendents must then deal with his cruel legacy.

Historical Accuracy: The era is detailed with accomplished care.

134 *The Ruthless Yeomen*
Date of Publication:
Subject(s): Middle Ages; Peasants' Revolt; Royalty—England
Fictional character(s): Isabel of Northfield, Young Woman; Nicola, Young Woman; Thomas Woodcarver, Landowner

Historical character(s): Wat Tyler, Revolutionary; Richard II, Ruler (King of England); Edward I, Ruler (King of England)
Time Period(s): 13th century; 14th century (1271-1399)
Locale(s): Northfield, England; London, England

Summary: The second of Anand's Bridges over Time series, the novel covers the period of the 13th and 14th centuries from the perspective of a serf, Isabel of Northfield, who battles for status and independence against a backdrop of dynastic turmoil. The novel culminates with the Peasants Revolt of 1381.

Historical Accuracy: Historical change is played out both on the domestic and political level with the life of the ordinary peasant compellingly drawn.

135 *Women of Ashdon*
Date of Publication: 1992
Subject(s): Elizabethan Period; Royalty—England; Tudor Period
Fictional character(s): Susannah Whitmead, Young Woman; James Weston, Gentleman; Christina Trefusis, Young Woman
Historical character(s): Henry VIII, Ruler (King of England); Margaret Beaufort, Royalty; Perkin Warbeck, Imposter (pretender to the throne); Elizabeth I, Ruler; Sir Francis Walsingham, Government Official, Spy (spymaster)
Time Period(s): 15th century; 16th century (1472-1586)
Locale(s): Ashdon, England; London, England

Summary: In this third volume of Anand's Bridges over Time series, the Tudor period is chronicled focussing on two women, Susannah and Christina. The are the guardians of Ashdon manor against the political upheaval that surrounds them as Henry VIII and Elizabeth I make their mighty presences felt.

Historical Accuracy: The novel is a model of historical scholarship set to the service of a highly energized dramatic story.

ALSTON ANDERSON (1924-)

Anderson's books include *Lover Man*.

136 *All God's Children*
Date of Publication: 1965
Subject(s): Civil War—U.S.; Reconstruction Period; Slavery
Fictional character(s): October Pruitt, Slave
Time Period(s): 19th century
Locale(s): Georgia; New Orleans, Louisiana; Virginia

Summary: This story set before, during, and after the Civil War, chronicles the experiences of slave October Pruitt. He escapes to Philadelphia via the Underground Railroad and joins the Union Army during the war. He finally settles in New Orleans during Reconstruction where tragedy continues to follow him.

Historical Accuracy: This is an authentic depiction of the period and its attitudes.

CATHERINE ANDERSON

137 *Comanche Moon*

Date of Publication: 1991
Subject(s): American West; Romance; Indians
Fictional character(s): Loretta Simpson, Handicapped (mute); Hunter of the Wolf, Indian (Comanche), Warrior
Time Period(s): 1860s
Locale(s): Texas

Summary: In the first novel of a trilogy set in the American West, the destiny of the Comanche Hunter of the Wolf, is joined to that of mute Loretta Simpson, silent since her parents were massacred when she was a child. Their love for each other must overcome many cultural and social obstacles.

Historical Accuracy: Though the emphasis is on the emotional not the historical, there are some convincing period details and an authentic atmosphere.

PAUL LEWIS ANDERSON (1880-1956)

Born in Trenton, New Jersey, and educated at Lehigh University, Anderson became an important photographer. His writings on the subject include *Pictorial Landscape Photography* and *The Fine Art of Photography*. He also authored short stories and the novels *Swords in the North* and *A Slave of Cataline*.

138 *Swords in the North*

Date of Publication: 1936
Subject(s): Roman Empire
Fictional character(s): Gaius, Nobleman, Military Personnel (Roman soldier); Brighde, Royalty (princess)
Historical character(s): Julius Caesar, Military Personnel (general)
Time Period(s): 1st century B.C.
Locale(s): England; Rome, Roman Empire

Summary: Set during Julius Caesar's invasion of Britain, the story centers on the experience of a Roman aristocrat, Gaius, who is captured and marked for sacrifice by the Druids. He is saved by the British princess Brighde, whom he marries. They return together to Rome.

Historical Accuracy: Solid scholarship provides a factual basis for the period and its customs.

PRUDENCE ANDREW (1924-)

An English novelist of historical fiction set in the medieval period, Andrew taught history for a time before turning to writing.

139 *The Constant Star*

Date of Publication: 1964
Subject(s): Middle Ages; Peasants' Revolt
Fictional character(s): Thomas Adam, Farmer
Time Period(s): 14th century (1381)
Locale(s): Gloucestershire, England

Summary: Set during the Peasants Revolt of 1381, the novel shows how the revolt affected a village in Gloucestershire. One peasant, Thomas Adams, is unwilling to join in the rebellion and stands for the old ways against the self-seeking opportunism of his neighbors.

Historical Accuracy: The novel graphically captures village life and customs of a time in transition as the medieval world struggles to modernize.

140 *The Hooded Falcon*

Date of Publication: 1961
Subject(s): Middle Ages; Wales-England Conflict; Coming of Age
Fictional character(s): Simon Beaumont, Nobleman; Huw, Servant; Philip Win, Tailor
Historical character(s): Harry Monmouth, Royalty (later Henry V)
Time Period(s): 15th century
Locale(s): Wales; London, England

Summary: This coming of age novel is set during the border wars between England and Wales. Young Simon Beaumont is the son of an English baron fascinated by the Welsh—their speech, songs, and customs. He experiences love, heresy, and the plague before being forced to choose where his true loyalty lies.

Historical Accuracy: The novel offers good details of medieval life, particularly Welsh customs.

141 *A New Creature*

Date of Publication: 1968
Subject(s): Religious Conflict; Georgian Period
Fictional character(s): Will Beckford, Businessman (merchant)
Historical character(s): John Wesley, Religious (evangelical preacher)
Time Period(s): 1730s (1739)
Locale(s): Bristol, England

Summary: The social and personal effects of the new religion of Methodism are explored in this novel. Will Beckford is a prominent merchant and slave trader who is inspired when he hears John Wesley preach. The novel traces the effects of Beckford's conversion to Methodism on his friends, business associates, and the Bristol community.

Historical Accuracy: The novel offers a convincing psychological portrait as well as an authentic picture of the age.

142 *Ordeal by Silence*

Date of Publication: 1961
Subject(s): Middle Ages; Religious Life
Fictional character(s): Philip of Evesham, Servant, Religious; Pierre Fulbert, Religious
Historical character(s): Henry II, Ruler (King of England)
Time Period(s): 12th century
Locale(s): Gloucestershire, England

Summary: In consideration of the canonizing of Philip of Evesham, the Devil's Advocate reviews the testimony of many witnesses to Philip's life and work: his upbringing, his association with Henry II, and the miracles that he presumably accomplished. Is he a saint or an ordinary man?.

Historical Accuracy: The novel's many witnesses present a convincing panorama of the medieval world.

143 *A Question of Choice*

Date of Publication: 1962
Subject(s): War of the Roses; Religious Life
Fictional character(s): Brother Mark, Religious (monk); Brother Joseph, Religious (monk)
Historical character(s): Edward IV, Ruler (King of England); Richard Neville, Nobleman (Earl of Warwick)
Time Period(s): 15th century (1468)
Locale(s): Gloucestershire, England; London, England

Summary: The turmoil of the War of the Roses is played out in ecclesiastical circles as both Edward IV and Warwick put forward candidates for abbot of Woodchester Abbey. The decision falls to six monks, each with his own private reason for preferring one or the other candidate. The welfare of the abbey hangs in the balance.

Historical Accuracy: This is a dramatic and insightful depiction of the politics of the period reflected in the faithfully re-created monastic setting.

144 *A Sparkle From the Coal*

Date of Publication: 1964
Subject(s): Middle Ages; Religious Conflict
Fictional character(s): Benjamin Carpenter, Student—College, Recluse
Time Period(s): 14th century (1318-1380)
Locale(s): England

Summary: Benjamin Carpenter is a student at Oxford who, in a desperate search for faith, abandons the university for the life of a hermit on a desolate island. There he endures the suspicions of the villagers and the extremes of nature, recording a spiritual autobiography while waiting for a sign from God.

Historical Accuracy: The story offers an intimate and convincing portrait of the medieval mind.

ANNULET ANDREWS (1866-1943)

Born in Washington, Georgia, Andrews first made her reputation as a poet, publishing in leading magazines and newspapers. She was also a correspondent for the New York *Herald*. Her books include *The Wife of Narcissus*, *Immortal Marriage*, and *Dido, Queen of Hearts*.

145 *Melissa Starke*

Date of Publication: 1935
Subject(s): Reconstruction Period
Fictional character(s): Melissa Starke, Young Woman
Time Period(s): 1860s
Locale(s): Georgia

Summary: Set during the Reconstruction Period, this novel follows the experiences of Melissa Starke on a Georgia plantation. Despite hardships and the cruelty of her aunts, Melissa remains true to her ideals and gains a career and true love.

Historical Accuracy: The story's romance dominates the historical scene, which establishes primarily a nostalgic sense of the past.

GINA ANDREWS

146 *Esther: The Star and the Sceptre*

Date of Publication: 1980
Subject(s): Biblical Story; Jews; Ancient Israel
Historical character(s): Xerxes I, Ruler (King of Persia); Esther, Royalty (wife of Xerxes I), Biblical Figure; Mordecai, Lawyer, Biblical Figure
Time Period(s): 5th century B.C.
Locale(s): Persia

Summary: The novel dramatizes the story behind the Jewish tradition of Purim. Esther is taken in bondage to serve the desires of the Persian emperor Xerxes. She becomes his queen and must balance her passion for him and her love for her people. She alone stands between the Jews of Persia and a bloody massacre.

Historical Accuracy: The novel is based on the Old Testament Book of Esther, backed by research on the the period that is convincingly presented.

JOHN ANDREWS (1941-)

A physicist at Brookhaven laboratories on Long Island, New York, Andrews holds degrees from MIT and Notre Dame.

147 *A Viking's Daughter*

Date of Publication: 1989
Subject(s): Vikings; Exploration; Middle Ages
Fictional character(s): Gudrid, Young Woman (Viking)
Historical character(s): Erik Thorvaldsson, Explorer; Leif Eriksson, Explorer
Time Period(s): 11th century
Locale(s): Iceland; Greenland; Vinland, North America

Summary: Gudrid is a Viking maiden whose experiences reflect the heroic age of the Viking explorers. She travels from her native Iceland to Erik the Red's colony in Greenland before finally setting sail for Leif Eriksson's Vinland, where she bears the first European child born in the New World.

Historical Accuracy: Based on Icelandic sagas and actual persons and events, the novel is a convincing re-creation of the period.

ROBERT HARDY ANDREWS (1908-)

Born in Kansas, Andrews has worked as a reporter and city editor for the *Minneapolis Journal* and as a writer and producer for motion pictures and television. In his estimation he has traveled some 250,000 miles since 1953. His books include *The Unbeliever* and *A Lamp for India*. *Great Day in the Morning* was made into a film in 1956.

148 *Burning Gold*

Date of Publication: 1945

Subject(s): Sea Story; Pirates
Historical character(s): William Dampier, Explorer, Sea Captain; Thomas Dover, Doctor; Daniel Defoe, Writer
Time Period(s): 18th century
Locale(s): England; Tortuga, West Indies; Panama

Summary: Dr. Thomas Dover goes to sea with Captain Dampier and falls in with buccaneers in the West Indies. After crossing the isthmus of Panama, Dover rejoins Dampier and returns to England a wealthy man.

Historical Accuracy: The novel intermingles facts and fiction with an authentic depiction of the buccaneers' commonwealth on Tortuga.

149 *Great Day in the Morning*

Date of Publication: 1950
Subject(s): American West; Civil War—U.S.
Fictional character(s): Owen Pentecost, Young Man
Time Period(s): 1850s; 1860s (1850-1860)
Locale(s): Colorado

Summary: The conflict between Northerners and Southerners in the American West is dramatized in the experiences of Owen Pentecost, who arrives in Denver in 1858. He is a major figure in the ''Georgia Conspiracy'' to bring Colorado into the conflict on the Southern side.

Historical Accuracy: The fictional elements are balanced by factual contemporary records and official documents of the day.

IVO ANDRIC (1892-1975)

Yugoslavian writer Andric was born in Bosnia and attended the University of Zagreb, Vienna University, and the University of Krakow. He received a doctorate in philosophy from Graz University, Austria. Andric was a member of the group that shot and killed Archduke Ferdinand of Austria, igniting World War I. He was imprisoned during the war for his role in the plot. Andric was a member of the diplomatic service in Rome, Geneva, Madrid, Budapest, Trieste, Graz, Belgrade, and Berlin. He received the Nobel Prize for Literature in 1951 for his distinguished writing career recording the troubled history of his native Bosnia.

150 *Bosnian Chronicle*

Date of Publication: 1945
Subject(s): Napoleonic Era
Fictional character(s): M. Jean DaVille, Diplomat (French consul-general); Joseph Von Mitterer, Diplomat (Austrian consul-general)
Historical character(s): Husref Mehmed Pasha, Ruler (Turkish Vezir); Selim III, Ruler (Ottoman sultan)
Time Period(s): 1800s; 1810s (1807-1814)
Locale(s): Travik, Bosnia-Hercegovina

Summary: Set in Bosnia during the era of Napoleon, the novel chronicles the community of Travik, made up of Muslim Turks, Christians, and Jews. The opening of French and Austrian consulates is the catalyst for an exploration of the differences among the groups. The consuls of France and Austria try to secure the area for their respective emperors.

Historical Accuracy: The background of the period and regional details are authentically delivered.

151 *The Bridge on the Drina*

Date of Publication: 1945
Subject(s): Bridge Building; World War I
Fictional character(s): Mehmed Pasha Sokolovici, Ruler (Turkish Grand Vezir); Abidaga, Businessman; Fata Osmanagic, Young Woman
Time Period(s): Multiple Time Periods
Locale(s): Visegrad, Bosnia-Hercegovina

Summary: Four hundred years of Bosnian history are chronicled in this story of a bridge constructed in 1516 across the Drina. The brutal history of its construction and the sweep of history that crosses the bridge are dramatized until its destruction at the outbreak of World War I.

Historical Accuracy: The novel offers an authentic look at a stretch of history little known beyond Bosnia.

152 *Devil's Yard*

Date of Publication: 1962
Subject(s): Religious Conflict
Fictional character(s): Brother Petar, Religious (monk); Djamic, Nobleman
Time Period(s): 19th century; 20th century (turn of the century)
Locale(s): Constantinople, Ottoman Empire

Summary: When a Bosnian monk travels to Constantinople on church business, he is imprisoned for no apparent reason in the infamous ''Devil's Yard.'' There Brother Petar hears the stories of several inmates, including Djamic, who reflects on an ancestor's similar imprisonment 500 years before.

Historical Accuracy: More a parable than an accurate and historically-based story, the novel is nonetheless a compelling and believable fable of innocence and aggression.

JERZY ANDRZEJEWSKI (1909-1983)

A Polish writer born in Warsaw, Andrzejewski was a former member of the Polish Communist Party but left in 1957 after the party banned a new literary magazine. Andrzejewski helped fund the Worker's Defense Committee to assist families of jailed workers. A major figure in Polish literary circles, Andrzejewski is best known for his novel *Ashes and Diamonds*.

153 *The Inquisitors*

Date of Publication: 1960
Subject(s): Inquisition; Jews
Fictional character(s): Diego Manentes, Religious
Historical character(s): Tomas de Torquemada, Religious
Time Period(s): 15th century
Locale(s): Spain

Summary: The novel presents the story of the Spanish Inquisition and its Grand Inquisitor, Tomas de Torquemada, as seen through the eyes of his secretary, Diego Manentes. The novel veers toward the allegorical with obvious parallels drawn between 15th-century Spain and modern Communism. In the end the dying Torquemada, in conversation with the devil, is revealed as an agent of Satan.

Historical Accuracy: The novel imagines Torquemada's thoughts and the inner workings of the Inquisition.

BARBARA ANNANDALE
(PSEUD. OF JEAN BOWDEN, 1925-)

Scottish author Jean Bowden, who has also worked as a book and magazine editor, uses many pseudonyms, including Barbara Annandale.

154 *The Bonnet Laird's Daughter*

Date of Publication: 1977
Subject(s): American Revolution; Georgian Period
Fictional character(s): Margaret Menteith, Heroine; Gavin Napier, Military Personnel
Historical character(s): Samuel Johnson, Writer, Scholar; James Boswell, Writer; Fanny Burney, Writer; John Paul Jones, Military Personnel (naval officer); Benjamin Franklin, Diplomat, Political Figure; David Garrick, Actor; George III, Ruler (King of England); Charlotte of Mecklenburg-Strelitz, Royalty (Queen of England)
Time Period(s): 1770s; 1780s (1775-1780)
Locale(s): Dumfrieshire, Scotland; London, England; Paris, France

Summary: Margaret Menteith, daughter of the laird of Dumfrieshire, falls in love with Gavin Napier, an American rebel, and protege of John Paul Jones. She secretly marries him and he leaves her pregnant to contend alone with her family and her condition. She escapes her father's wrath, rather implausibly aided by Dr. Johnson. Various complications threaten the lovers' reunion.

Historical Accuracy: The cameo appearances here are not convincing. The novel connects too many important historical figures to the romantic tale to be believable.

MILFORD E. ANNESS (1918-)

Born in Indiana, Anness is a graduate of Indiana University and was an Indiana state senator from 1946 to 1952. He became a circuit court judge in 1955 and has been a practicing attorney since leaving the bench in 1962.

155 *Song of Metamoris: A Story That Remains of a People Who Passed This Way*

Date of Publication: 1964
Subject(s): Indians; Settlement of the American Frontier
Fictional character(s): Metamoris, Indian (Delaware), Chieftain

Historical character(s): Tecumseh, Indian (Shawnee), Chieftain
Time Period(s): 1810s
Locale(s): Indiana

Summary: The novel tells the story of a young Delaware chief, Metamoris, who works with the great Indian leader Tecumseh to unite the tribes against further encroachment by white settlement. Their efforts are thwarted by the attack on Tippecanoe in 1811, which ultimately leads to the Indians' defeat.

Historical Accuracy: The novel's period and historical elements are accurately presented.

RODERICK ANSCOMBE

156 *The Secret Life of Laszlo, Count Dracula*

Date of Publication: 1994
Subject(s): Medical Profession; Gothic Romance
Fictional character(s): Lazlo, Nobleman (Count Dracula), Doctor
Historical character(s): Jean-Martin Charcot, Doctor, Scientist
Time Period(s): 19th century (1866-1888)
Locale(s): Paris, France; Hungary

Summary: The testimony of Count Dracula, aristocrat, doctor, and helpless killer of young women, is portrayed in this non-supernatural version of the famous vampire story. Lazlo, Count Dracula, is shown studying with the renowned pioneer of hypnotism, Charcot. He then returns to Hungary where an epidemic and the politics of the Austro-Hungarian Empire make him a hero by day, a killer by night.

Historical Accuracy: This is an ingenious and realistic clinical version of the Count with authentic period touches.

EVELYN ANTHONY
(PSEUD. OF EVELYN WARD-THOMAS, 1928-)

English novelist Anthony calls her first seven novels "animated history," based on real people and their contemporary relations and motives. Feeling that the historical vein was running thin, she turned to modern thrillers, the most famous being *The Tamarind Seed*.

157 *All the Queen's Men*

Date of Publication: 1960
Subject(s): Elizabethan Period; Royalty—England
Historical character(s): Elizabeth I, Ruler; Mary Stuart, Royalty (Queen of Scotland); Robert Dudley, Nobleman (Earl of Leicester), Courtier; Sir Francis Walsingham, Government Official, Spy (spymaster); Edmund Campion, Religious; Robert Cecil, Government Official
Time Period(s): 16th century (1558-1588)
Locale(s): England; Scotland

Summary: The novel chronicles the first 30 years of the reign of Elizabeth I. She is depicted as an astute, clever, and at times ruthless sovereign who must carefully negotiate through treacherous domestic and international politics. The crisis produced by the challenge of Mary, Queen of Scots provides the novel's climax.

Historical Accuracy: The historical details are faithfully detailed.

158 *Anne Boleyn*
Date of Publication: 1957
Subject(s): Tudor Period; Royalty—England
Historical character(s): Anne Boleyn, Royalty; Henry VIII, Ruler; Thomas Wolsey, Religious (cardinal), Political Figure; Catherine of Aragon, Royalty; Mary Tudor, Royalty; Clement VII, Religious (pope); Thomas Cranmer, Religious (archbishop); Sir Thomas More, Political Figure; Thomas Cromwell, Political Figure
Time Period(s): 16th century
Locale(s): Greenwich, England; London, England; Windsor, England

Summary: The novel details the courtship and marriage of Henry VIII and Anne Boleyn, as well as her eventual execution. The political and religious crisis the affair caused is also highlighted. The novel is a succinct and restrained view of the political manueverings that surround the king's divorce and remarriage.

Historical Accuracy: All the major players are convincingly presented, and the complicated political landscape is helpfully sorted out.

159 *The Cardinal and the Queen*
Date of Publication: 1968
Subject(s): Royalty—France
Historical character(s): Louis XIII, Ruler (King of France); Anne of Austria, Royalty (Queen of France); Armand-Jean Du Plessis, Religious (Cardinal Richelieu), Political Figure (minister); Marie de' Medici, Noblewoman; George Villiers, Nobleman (Duke of Buckingham); Henri Coeffier-Ruze d'Effiat, Nobleman (Marquis de Cinq-Mars); Jules Mazarin, Religious, Political Figure
Time Period(s): 17th century (1617-1642)
Locale(s): Paris, France

Summary: Intrigue and romance in the court of Louis XIII is the subject of this novel, which describes Richelieu's passion for the queen, Anne of Austria. She is caught between the cardinal's passion and her husband's hatred. She responds with a desperate love affair with the English Duke of Buckingham and a series of narrow escapes.

Historical Accuracy: Anthony bases some of her conclusions on rumors, namely that Richelieu was the father of Louis XIV and that Buckingham's death was orchestrated by the cardinal.

160 *Charles the King*
Date of Publication: 1961
Subject(s): Civil War—England; Royalty—England
Historical character(s): Charles I, Ruler (King of England); Oliver Cromwell, Military Personnel, Revolutionary; Henrietta-Maria, Royalty (wife of Charles); George Villiers, Nobleman (Duke of Buckingham)

Time Period(s): 17th century (1640s)
Locale(s): England

Summary: The novel chronicles the reign of Charles I, the last absolute monarch of England, and his romance with Henrietta Maria, daughter of the King of France. Charles' absolutism plunges the country into civil war and conflict with Oliver Cromwell, parliament, and the Puritans.

Historical Accuracy: The confusing events of the English Civil War are carefully delineated. Charles is sympathetically treated, which is unconventional.

161 *Clandara*
Date of Publication: 1962
Subject(s): Jacobite Rebellion; Feuds
Fictional character(s): Katherine Fraser, Gentlewoman; James Macdonald, Gentleman
Historical character(s): Charles Edward Stuart, Royalty
Time Period(s): 1740s
Locale(s): Scotland

Summary: A Scottish family feud between the Frasers of Clandara and the Macdonalds complicates the romance of Katherine Fraser and James Macdonald. Their love affair coincides with the call of Prince Charles for the clans to join him to win back the Scottish and English thrones for the Stuart cause. The conflicting demands of self, family, and country are examined in scenes on the battlefield of Scotland.

Historical Accuracy: The novel ably interweaves the personal and the historical in strong scenes of the Stuart Rebellion.

162 *Far Flies the Eagle*
Date of Publication: 1955
Subject(s): Napoleonic Wars; Royalty—Russia; Russian Empire
Historical character(s): Alexander I, Ruler (Czar of Russia); Napoleon Bonaparte, Ruler (French emperor), Military Personnel; Catherine, Grand Duchess of Russia, Royalty (Czar Alexander's sister); Josephine, Royalty (Empress of France), Spouse; Marie Louise of Austria, Royalty (Napoleon's second wife); Charles Maurice de Talleyrand-Perigord, Diplomat, Government Official; Clemens von Metternich, Political Figure; Joachim Murat, Military Personnel (general), Royalty (King of Naples); Mikhail Illarionovich Kutuzov, Military Personnel (commander of the Russian army)
Time Period(s): 19th century (1807-1820)
Locale(s): Russia; Austria

Summary: Czar Alexander versus Napoleon is the subject of this novel, which details Alexander's life from his treaty with Napoleon at Tilsit in 1807 until his death. Anthony offers an unconventional portrait of the czar: not the weak-willed autocrat history has labeled him, but a worthy adversary in the diplomatic and military struggle with Napoleon.

Historical Accuracy: The rush of great events allows only some quick character sketches, not full portraits. The novel reduces the complex to clear lines and issues, if somewhat simplified for dramatic effect.

163   *The French Bride*

Date of Publication: 1964
Subject(s): Romance; Royalty—France
Fictional character(s): Charles Macdonald, Gentleman; Anne De Bernard, Gentlewoman; Louise De Vitale, Gentlewoman
Historical character(s): Louis XV, Ruler (King of France); Jeanne du Barry, Lover (the king's mistress), Noblewoman
Time Period(s): 1750s
Locale(s): Versailles, France; Paris, France

Summary: Charles Macdonald, a Scottish member of Louis XV's court, contracts a marriage of convenience with Anne de Bernard for her fortune. Anne falls in love with her husband and is soon caught up in the intrigue of Louis' court and a conspiracy that leads her to the Bastille.

Historical Accuracy: Court customs are featured in this romance that plausibly employs historical figures.

164   *Rebel Princess*

Date of Publication: 1953
Subject(s): Royalty—Russia; Biography, Fictionalized; Russian Empire
Historical character(s): Catherine II, Ruler (empress of Russia); Elizabeth, Ruler (Empress of Russia); Peter III, Ruler (Czar of Russia); Frederick the Great, Ruler (King of Prussia)
Time Period(s): 18th century (1743-1762)
Locale(s): Germany; Russia

Summary: This is the story of the remarkable rise to power of Catherine the Great of Russia from her youth as an obscure German princess who becomes the wife of the ineffectual and boyish Grand Duke Peter. She must contend with the autocratic and unpredictable Empress Elizabeth until Catherine finally seizes control of all Russia.

Historical Accuracy: The essential facts of Catherine's life are delivered faithfully.

165   *Valentina*

Date of Publication: 1966
Subject(s): Napoleonic Wars; Espionage; Russian Empire
Fictional character(s): Valentina Grunowski, Noblewoman, Spy; Colonel De Chavel, Military Personnel; Alexandra, Royalty (princess)
Historical character(s): Napoleon Bonaparte, Ruler, Military Personnel; Joachim Murat, Military Personnel (general), Royalty (King of Naples); Michel Ney, Military Personnel (general), Royalty (prince)
Time Period(s): 1810s (1812)
Locale(s): Poland; Russia

Summary: The Countess Valentina's Polish husband forces her to spy on the French as Napoleon prepares to invade Russia. She is found out and rescued by Colonel de Chavel, the head of French Intelligence. His protection angers the Count. Amidst Napoleon's disastrous retreat from Russia, Valentina falls in love with Chavel and sets out with her sister to find him again.

Historical Accuracy: The novel uses the historical details of the invasion and retreat from Russia as a backdrop for this

romantic story, and the historical characters seem more idealized than realistic.

166   *Victoria and Albert*

Date of Publication: 1958
Subject(s): Victorian Period; Royalty—England
Historical character(s): Victoria, Ruler (Queen of England); Albert of Saxe-Coburg-Gotha, Royalty (prince consort); William Lamb, Political Figure (prime minister), Nobleman; Henry John Temple, Political Figure (foreign minister), Nobleman; Robert Peel, Political Figure; Lord John Russell, Political Figure (prime minister)
Time Period(s): 19th century (1830s-1850s)
Locale(s): London, England; Windsor, England

Summary: Queen Victoria's reign is described as the story of a marriage. Victoria is impetuous and extreme, blindly in love with Albert, who does not share her devotion. The novel combines the political maneuvering of the period with a clearly developed portrait of the private lives of the royals.

Historical Accuracy: The novel's historical background is well-developed, though Anthony's interpretation of Albert is controversial.

PIERS ANTHONY

(PSEUD. OF PIERS ANTHONY DILLINGHAM JACOB, 1934-)

A native of Oxford, England, Anthony emigrated to the U.S. in 1940 and attended Goddard College and the University of South Carolina. He has been nominated for numerous awards and honors, including the Nebula Award of the Science Fiction Writers of America, the Hugo Award, and the British Fantasy Award.

167   *Isle of Woman*

Date of Publication: 1993
Subject(s): Fantasy; Reincarnation; Prehistory
Fictional character(s): Blaze, Blacksmith; Ember, Parent (mother), Leader; Stone, Artisan
Time Period(s): Multiple Time Periods
Locale(s): Africa; North America

Summary: In a series of vignettes, the novel moves from the origins of humanity on the plains of Africa to futuristic America through the experiences of a group of people reincarnated over time. Blaze's true love is Ember whom he encounters repeatedly in a variety of guises.

Historical Accuracy: This is a remarkable panorama of human history depicting the continuity of human traits over time.

168   *Shame of Man*

Date of Publication: 1994
Subject(s): Fantasy; Reincarnation; Prehistory
Fictional character(s): Hugh, Musician; Ann, Dancer
Time Period(s): Multiple Time Periods
Locale(s): Earth

Summary: In the second volume of Anthony's Geodyssey series which began with *Isle of Woman*, another man and woman, both artists, are followed through a series of reincarnations from the dawn of mankind. They live in the caves of prehistoric Europe, the Holy Land of King David, and third century Japan. They also experience Central Asia under Genghis Khan, Easter Island, and finally a future world devastated by ecological ruin.

Historical Accuracy: This panorama is so broad that it is like looking at history from space. From that vantage point the author is able to explore broad trends and repeated themes over vast stretches of human time.

169 *Tatham Mound*

Date of Publication: 1991
Subject(s): Indians; Spanish Conquest; Tribal Life—Native American
Fictional character(s): Hotfoot, Indian (aka Throat Shot/Tale Teller); Trader, Indian
Historical character(s): Hernando de Soto, Explorer
Time Period(s): 16th century
Locale(s): North America; Central America

Summary: The novel offers the life-story of an Indian called first Hotfoot, then Throat Shot, and finally Tale Teller. Apprenticed to an Indian trader, he journeys throughout the Americas, meeting other tribes and collecting their stories. When the Spanish arrive, he serves as the interpreter for De Soto on his march through the Southeast, which will bring an end to the lives of the native peoples celebrated in the memory of Tale Teller.

Historical Accuracy: The novel attempts to show the pre-contact world of America as filled with real people. It succeeds in painting a genuine portrait of the times and native customs.

ALLEN APPEL (1945-)

Appel is an American photographer, illustrator, and writer who has received considerable critical acclaim for his science fiction novels involving the character Alex Balfour, a historian who becomes an unwilling time traveller.

170 *Till the End of Time*

Date of Publication: 1990
Subject(s): Time Travel; World War II
Fictional character(s): Alex Balfour, Historian, Time Traveller; Molly Glenn, Journalist
Historical character(s): Albert Einstein, Scientist; John F. Kennedy, Military Personnel (naval officer); Betty Grable, Actress; William J. "Wild Bill" Donovan, Political Figure; Franklin Delano Roosevelt, Political Figure
Time Period(s): 1940s; 1980s
Locale(s): New York, New York

Summary: Time travelling historian Alex Balfour slips into the years of the Second World War and is given the opportunity of preventing the atomic bombing of Japan. Meanwhile, in the present, Molly Glenn is researching a story on Japanese biochemical warfare unaware that Alex's experiences in the past are partially responsible for her findings. Confusion in the time-space continuum heads toward an explosive climax.

Historical Accuracy: The novel is an ingenious blending of fantasy and actual events and personalities, with a knowledgeable sense of the period.

171 *Time After Time*

Date of Publication: 1985
Subject(s): Russian Revolution; Time Travel; Royalty—Russia
Fictional character(s): Alex Balfour, Historian (history professor), Time Traveller
Historical character(s): Grigori Efimovich Rasputin, Religious (monk and mystic); Vladimir Ilich Lenin, Revolutionary, Political Figure; Nicholas II, Ruler (Czar of Russia); Alexandra Feodorovna, Royalty
Time Period(s): 1910s
Locale(s): New York, New York; Russia

Summary: Alex Balfour, a young history professor, has the ability to imaginatively go back in time. He winds up in Russia during the revolution. Trapped and on the run, he confronts the period's leading figures and finds himself involved in the fate of the Romanovs.

Historical Accuracy: The novel's interest stems from its modern perspective on the past, but the contrivance overburdens the re-creation of the past.

172 *Twice upon a Time*

Date of Publication: 1988
Subject(s): Time Travel; Indians; Literary Life
Fictional character(s): Alex Balfour, Historian (historian), Time Traveller; Molly Glen, Journalist (reporter)
Historical character(s): Mark Twain, Writer (novelist); George Armstrong Custer, Military Personnel (cavalry officer)
Time Period(s): 1970s (1976); 1870s (1876)
Locale(s): New York, New York; Philadelphia, Pennsylvania; Rapid City, South Dakota

Summary: Alex Balfour, an historian with the ability to travel in time, goes back to 1876 where he discusses Mark Twain's writings with the author himself and tries to affect the course of history by persuading the Indians to avoid the encounter with Custer and the violent retribution that will follow. While he visits 1876, Molly Glenn, a reporter in the present, covers an Indian uprising to commemorate the 100th anniversary of Custer's Last Stand.

Historical Accuracy: The novel is an ingenious blend of history, suspense, and fantasy with an authentic sense of the past.

AHARON APPELFELD (1932-)

Born in Russia, Appelfeld was deported to a concentration camp at age eight. He escaped and spent the next three years hiding from the Nazis in the Ukraine. He eventually joined the Russian army, and in 1946 he emigrated to Israel. He is considered one of the finest novelists writing about the Jewish experience during the Second World War.

173 *The Age of Wonders*

Date of Publication: 1981
Subject(s): Jews; Anti-Semitism
Fictional character(s): Bruno, Hero; Louise, Prostitute
Time Period(s): 1930s
Locale(s): Austria

Summary: In pre-war Austria, a Jewish family watches the effects of anti-Semitism taking control of their lives. The father is an intellectual who refuses to accept the implication of what is happening and retreats into Jewish self-hatred and eventual derangement. Years later, the narrator of the first part of the novel returns to Austria and observes the devastating effects of the war before making peace with the ghosts from his childhood.

Historical Accuracy: As in most of Appelfeld's work, the details of time and place are suggested rather than revealed in depth. Atmosphere and psychological insight dominate over historical elements.

174 *Badenheim 1939*

Date of Publication: 1980
Subject(s): Holocaust; Jews; World War II
Fictional character(s): Dr. Pappenheim, Entertainer; Dr. Fussholdt, Historian; Sally, Prostitute
Time Period(s): 1930s (1939)
Locale(s): Austria

Summary: In the spring and summer of 1939 before the outbreak of World War II, life in a resort town near Vienna goes on as normal. A collection of Jewish middle class vacationers, entertainers, hotel staff, and townspeople are absorbed in the trivial daily routine until the forced arrival of other Jews turns the resort town into a nightmare.

Historical Accuracy: The author excells in re-creating a world in collapse, chronicling social customs under pressure of mostrous evil.

175 *For Every Sin*

Date of Publication: 1989
Subject(s): Holocaust; World War II; Jews
Fictional character(s): Theo, Wanderer; Mina, Wanderer
Time Period(s): 1940s (1945)
Locale(s): Europe

Summary: Theo is a young survivor of a concentration camp who sets out across Europe intent on journeying home. He enters a nightmare world of fellow uprooted survivors. Theo is forced to come to grips with his past and the human condition from which he cannot escape.

Historical Accuracy: The novel is written with a simple directness that reaches levels of universal significance.

176 *The Healer*

Date of Publication: 1990
Subject(s): Anti-Semitism; Jews
Fictional character(s): Felix Katz, Businessman; Henrietta Katz, Heroine; Helga Katz, Child
Time Period(s): 1930s

Locale(s): Vienna, Austria; Carinthian Mountains, Austria

Summary: On the eve of World War II, a Viennese businessman and his family travel to the Carpathian Mountains in search of a famous healer to aid their ailing daughter. The thoroughly assimilated and self-hating Jewish businessman is shocked to learn that the healer is an old rabbi who preaches a return to the old values of faith. The businessman endures six snow bound months in the mountain village before leaving his wife and daughter to return to Vienna. He finds it plagued with the same anti-Semitism that has already infected him.

Historical Accuracy: Told simply with the elements of a fable, the novel creates a symbolic and psychological atmosphere rather than a full depiction of the period.

177 *Katerina*

Date of Publication: 1992
Subject(s): Jews; Holocaust
Fictional character(s): Katerina, Servant, Housekeeper
Time Period(s): 1930s; 1940s
Locale(s): Europe

Summary: The Holocaust is depicted from the perspective of a simple Gentile housekeeper who works in a succession of Jewish households before World War II. In them she discovers culture, love, and values. Her employers disappear, leave, or are killed, and Katerina is left on her own attempting to make sense of her loss.

Historical Accuracy: This is a moving evocation of the vacuum left by the Holocaust told simply from the perspective of a woman trying to understand.

178 *The Retreat*

Date of Publication: 1984
Subject(s): Anti-Semitism; Jews
Fictional character(s): Lotte Schloss, Heroine; Herbert Kuntz, Journalist
Time Period(s): 1930s
Locale(s): Austria

Summary: The retreat is a hill-top hotel, and its patrons are all Jews who receive lessons in assimilation: how to look, act, and talk like a Gentile. The patrons' attempt to shed their identity in a pre-war world that will allow no escape from one's heritage is the novel's moving theme.

Historical Accuracy: Fable-like, the story provides a psychological inquiry into the nature and effects of assimilation. The historical period is suggested rather than elaborately revealed.

179 *To the Land of the Cattails*

Date of Publication: 1986
Subject(s): Holocaust; Jews
Fictional character(s): Toni Strauss, Outcast, Wanderer; Rudi Strauss, Outcast, Wanderer
Time Period(s): 1930s (1938)
Locale(s): Austria; Russia

Summary: In 1938 a Jewish woman living in Austria journeys eastward to her native land accompanied by her son. Just short of their goal, the boy discovers that his mother, along with the other Jews in the village, has been shipped off in a train to an unspecified destination. He sets out to find her.

Historical Accuracy: Written as a dream-like evocation of Europe on the brink of the cataclysm of World War II, the novel creates an atmosphere of impending crisis and moral uncertainty that rings true to the period.

180   *Tzili: The Story of a Life*

Date of Publication: 1983
Subject(s): World War II; Jews; Holocaust
Fictional character(s): Tzili Kraus, Heroine
Time Period(s): 1940s
Locale(s): Europe

Summary: The novel is a story of survival. Tzili is considered slow and simple-minded, more like the neighboring peasants than the Jewish community to which she belongs. When war breaks out, Tzili's simplicity and endurance are her means of self-preservation as she survives in the forest.

Historical Accuracy: The tale is simply told, almost like a folk tale with a minimum of details of time and place.

181   *Unto the Soul*

Date of Publication: 1994
Subject(s): Jews; Adolescence
Fictional character(s): Amalia, Young Woman, Orphan; Gad, Young Man, Orphan
Time Period(s): 20th century

Summary: Gad and Amalia are an orphaned brother and sister who have inherited positions as caretakers of a Jewish cemetery on a remote mountain top in turn-of-the-century Eastern Europe. Their lives, isolated and without meaning, are filled with loneliness and guilt from the lust they feel for each other.

Historical Accuracy: The novel is told with the simplicity of a fable and reaches a timeless quality of universal meanings rather than a particularization of time and place.

LOUIS ARAGON (1897-1982)

Louis Aragon was a French novelist, poet, Resistance fighter, and political activist. He was a leader of the Surrealist Movement and much of his early work reflects a surrealist tone. In 1927, Aragon became attracted to Communism and visited the Soviet Union in 1930. Although he spoke out against the injustices in the communist world, Aragon remained faithful to communist ideals. His series of four novels collectively titled *Le Monde reel* (1934-1944) describes class struggle in French society.

182   *Holy Week*

Date of Publication: 1961
Subject(s): Napoleonic Era; Royalty—France
Historical character(s): Louis XVIII, Ruler (King of France); Napoleon Bonaparte, Ruler (exiled emperor of France); Charles Philippe, Nobleman (Comte d'Artois); Theodore Gericault, Military Personnel (officer in the musketeers), Art-

ist; Louis-Alexander Berthier, Military Personnel (captain of the Life Guards)
Time Period(s): 1810s (1815)
Locale(s): France

Summary: The title refers to the week between Palm Sunday and Easter, 1815, during which Napoleon returned from exile on Elba and began his march toward Paris while Louis XVIII fled north, abandoning his throne. This vast panoramic epic, which has been compared to the novels of Leo Tolstoy and Victor Hugo, examines the effects this moment in time had on a huge cast of historical personalities, posing complex dramatic answers to questions such as whom to follow and what is loyalty.

Historical Accuracy: Aragon insists that this is not a historical novel but a work of the imagination. As such it is a major achievement of historical re-creation.

JEFFREY ARCHER (1940-)

English author Archer was a Conservative Member of Parliament from 1969-1974 and the deputy chairman of the British Conservative Party in 1985-1986. On the verge of bankrupcy, he wrote his first novel, aptly titled, *Not a Penny More, Not a Penny less*. His novel *Kane & Abel* was the first of a string of bestsellers. Archer doesn't consider himself a writer but a storyteller in the old English tradition. His bestsellers are unusual in that they have no bad language, explicit sex, or gratuitous violence.

183   *As the Crow Flies*

Date of Publication: 1991
Subject(s): World War I; Business Building
Fictional character(s): Charlie Trumper, Businessman; Guy Trentham, Military Personnel (army officer)
Time Period(s): 20th century
Locale(s): London, England

Summary: Young Charlie Trumper greatly admires his grandfather, who sells produce from a barrow. World War I interrupts Charlie's ambition to own a great shop, and the enmity between himself and Guy Trentham complicates his plans after the war.

Historical Accuracy: The period details are convincing.

ELLEN ARGO
(PSEUD. OF ELLEN ARGO JOHNSON, 1933-1983)

American author Argo was the daughter of an Army officer who claims that Argo was always a storyteller. Her fictional trilogy takes as its subject sailing and the sea, which was her first love.

184   *The Crystal Star*

Date of Publication: 1979
Subject(s): Sea Story; Clipper Ships; Business Building
Fictional character(s): Julia Howard Logan, Businesswoman, Sailor; Stephen Logan, Sea Captain; David Baxter, Sea Captain

Time Period(s): 1840s; 1850s (1842-1850)
Locale(s): Hong Kong; *Crystal Star*, At Sea

Summary: Following *Jewel of the Sea*, this second volume of Argo's trilogy sees Julia Howard Logan set sail with her husband on a ship that she helped design and build during the age of the great clipper ships and the China trade. She endures storms, pirate attack, and childbirth at sea while trying to maintain a dual love: the sea and her husband. Her story concludes in *The Yankee Girl*.

Historical Accuracy: The naval details are closely and convincingly rendered.

185   *Jewel of the Sea*

Date of Publication: 1977
Subject(s): Sea Story; Clipper Ships; Business Building
Fictional character(s): Julia Howard, Sailor; Jason Thatcher, Sailor; David Baxter, Sea Captain
Time Period(s): 19th century (1827-1842)
Locale(s): Cape Cod, Massachusetts; At Sea

Summary: In this first novel of a trilogy of ship building and clipper ships, Julia Howard, a shipmaster's daughter, refuses to wait on land to hear of others' tales of foreign ports and sea adventures. A number of men help her reach her goal of owning her own ship and living a life at sea. Her story continues in *The Crystal Star*.

Historical Accuracy: The details of the early days of Cape Cod ship building and the merchant marine are fully presented.

186   *The Yankee Girl*

Date of Publication: 1980
Subject(s): Sea Story; Clipper Ships; Business Building
Fictional character(s): Julia Howard Logan, Sea Captain, Businesswoman; Stephen Logan, Sea Captain; David Baxter, Sea Captain
Time Period(s): 1850s; 1860s (1850-1863)
Locale(s): Cape Cod, Massachusetts; San Francisco, California; *Crystal Star*, At Sea

Summary: In this concluding volume of Argo's trilogy of clipper ship days, Julia Logan and her husband, Stephen, embark on a voyage to China. They lose most of their crew to the lure of gold fever when they put in at San Francisco. On the voyage across the Pacific they face mutiny and other trials and domestic tragedy that tests Julia's resolve.

Historical Accuracy: The details of sailing life are faithfully described.

HOMERO ARIDJIS (1940-)

Aridjis is one of Mexico's foremost poets and novelists. Two of his poetry collections have appeared in English, *Blue Spaces* and *Exaltation of Light*. He has taught at Columbia, NYU, and Indiana University, and has been the Mexican ambassador to the Netherlands and Switzerland. Aridjis is the founder and president of the Group of 100, an international environmental group of writers, authors, and students.

187   *1492: The Life and Times of Juan Cabezon of Castile*

Date of Publication: 1991
Subject(s): Inquisition; Religious Conflict; Jews
Fictional character(s): Juan Cabezon, Orphan; Isabel de la Vega, Fugitive
Time Period(s): 15th century (1492)
Locale(s): Spain

Summary: The expulsion of the the Jews from Spain in the 15th century is dramatized through the experiences of Juan Cabezon, a descendant of converted Jews, who is orphaned at an early age by a series of accidents. He agrees to hide the beautiful Isabel de la Vega with whom he falls in love. When Isabel is driven to madness by her forced seclusion and fear of discovery by the agents of the Inquisition, she vanishes, and Juan sets off in search of her across Spain and into the heart of the Jewish communities where he becomes the target of the Inquisition.

Historical Accuracy: The novel expertly captures the atmosphere of the period.

188   *The Lord of the Last Days: Visions of the Year 1000*

Date of Publication: 1994
Subject(s): Middle Ages; Religious Conflict
Fictional character(s): Alfonso, Artisan (scribe and illuminator); Abh Allah, Warrior (Muslim)
Time Period(s): 10th century (999)
Locale(s): Spain

Summary: On the birth of the new millennium, Christian and Moorish armies battle for control of medieval Spain. The cultural conflict is mirrored in the experiences of two brothers who find themselves on opposite sides: Alfonso, a Christian like his mother, and Abh Allah, a Muslim warrior like his father. Their story is told in a series of scenes that captures life in the year 999.

Historical Accuracy: The novel is an artful blend of realistic details, historical events, and imagination. The author's bibliography shows the extensive research that created the novel's compelling and disturbing reality.

LESLIE ARLEN
(PSEUD. OF CHRISTOPHER NICOLE, 1930-)

Born in Georgetown, British Guiana, Nicole was educated there and in Barbados. He has worked for the Royal Bank of Canada in their West Indies branches. His many adventure novels offer a full history of the West Indies. He has also written under the names Leslie Arlen, Robin Cade, Peter Grange, Carline Gray, Simon McKay, C.R. Nicholson, Christina Nicholson, Robin Nicholson, Alison York, and Andrew York.

189   *Love and Honor*

Date of Publication: 1980
Subject(s): Family Saga; Russian Revolution; Russian Empire

Fictional character(s): George Hayman, Journalist; Ilona Borodin, Gentlewoman

Historical character(s): Alexandra Feodorovna, Royalty (Tsarina of Russia); Grigori Efimovich Rasputin, Religious (monk)

Time Period(s): 1900s; 1910s

Locale(s): Russia

Summary: This first novel in a series on the Russian aristocratic Borodin family is set in the years leading up to the Russian Revolution. The story concerns Ilona Borodin who falls in love with American journalist George Hayman.

Historical Accuracy: The novel presents a believable period backdrop for this family story.

ELLIOTT ARNOLD (1912-1980)

Born in New York City, Arnold attended New York University and worked as a journalist and editor for the *New York World-Telegram* and the *American Indian*. Arnold was the recipient of numerous prizes and awards, including the Screen Writers Guild Prize and the National Conference of Christians and Jews Brotherhood Award. Arnold is best known for his western novels.

190 *Blood Brother*

Date of Publication: 1947

Subject(s): American West; Indians; Civil War—U.S.

Fictional character(s): Sonseeahray, Indian (Apache)

Historical character(s): Cochise, Indian (Apache), Chieftain; Oliver Otis Howard, Military Personnel (general); Thomas Jeffords, Frontiersman, Scout

Time Period(s): 19th century (1849-1874)

Locale(s): New Mexico; Arizona

Summary: The novel tells the story of the Apache Wars in the Southwest and how Cochise broke with other Apaches and made peace for the Chiricahua tribe. It is also the story of Cochise's friend, and later blood brother, Thomas Jeffords, and his love affair with the Apache maiden Sonseeahray.

Historical Accuracy: The events and personalities are authentic. Jeffords' love affair is, however, an invention.

191 *The Camp Grant Massacre*

Date of Publication: 1976

Subject(s): American West; Indians

Historical character(s): Emerson Whitman, Military Personnel (cavalry officer); Eskiminzin, Indian (Apache), Chieftain

Time Period(s): 1870s (1871)

Locale(s): Tucson, Arizona; Camp Grant, Arizona

Summary: The fragile peace between the settlers and the Apaches arranged by cavalry officer Emerson Whitman and Apache Chief Eskiminzin is broken when the townspeople of Tucson mount an attack on the unarmed Indians, and Whitman is unable to prevent the slaughter. The novel avoids simplifying the situation into heroes and villains, even granting the townspeople some sympathy.

Historical Accuracy: The story is convincing, and other than some invented dialogue, its details are based on actuality.

192 *Deep in My Heart: A Story Based on the Life of Sigmund Romberg*

Date of Publication: 1949

Subject(s): Biography, Fictionalized; Musical Life

Historical character(s): Sigmund Romberg, Composer

Time Period(s): 19th century; 20th century

Locale(s): Vienna, Austria; United States

Summary: This fictional biography of composer Sigmund Romberg traces his career from his student days in Vienna, to his coming to America, and his successes as a composer, conductor, radio star, and concert performer.

Historical Accuracy: The novel mixes fact and invention here, particularly in the details of Romberg's early life. With its comprehensive index and lists of Romberg's performances, scores, and songs, it comes close to being a definitive biography, at least in regards to the events of Romberg's career. The interpretation of character is more subjective, however.

MICHAEL ARNOLD

193 *Against the Fall of Night*

Date of Publication: 1975

Subject(s): Byzantine Empire; Crusades

Fictional character(s): Nicetas Acominatus, Government Official

Historical character(s): Andronicus I Comnenus, Ruler (Byzantine emperor); Theodora, Royalty

Time Period(s): 12th century

Locale(s): Byzantine Empire

Summary: This massive historical novel chronicles the little-known reign of Andronikus Comnenus, ruler of the Byzantine Empire at the time of its conquest by the Crusaders. Comnenus attempts to halt the slow decline of his empire through military might and bloody court intrigue.

Historical Accuracy: The novel is an impressive and elaborate reconstruction of Byzantine politics and the era.

194 *The Archduke*

Date of Publication: 1967

Subject(s): Royalty—Austria; Austro-Hungarian Empire

Historical character(s): Francis Joseph I, Ruler (Emperor of Austria); Rudolf Rudolf, Crown Prince of Austria, Royalty; Maria Vetsera, Noblewoman (baroness), Lover

Time Period(s): 1880s (1888-1889)

Locale(s): Vienna, Austria

Summary: The novel tells the tragically romantic story of Crown Prince Rudolf and his mistress, the 17-year-old Baroness Vetsera, which culminates in her death and his suicide. Written in diary form, the novel chronicles the last five months of Rudolf's life and the court intrigue that contributed to the tragedy.

Historical Accuracy: The novel provides a convincing portrait of the House of Hapsburg although the author admits to taking certain liberties with historical fact.

HARRIETTE SIMPSON ARNOW
(1908-1986)

Born in Kentucky, Arnow attended Berea College and received her B.S. from the University of Louisville. She was a member of the Women's International League for Peace and Freedom and was the 1955 recipient of the *Women's Home Companion* Silver Distaff Award for "unique contribution by a woman to American life." She also wrote under the name Harriette Simpson.

195 *The Kentucky Trace: A Novel of the American Revolution*

Date of Publication: 1974
Subject(s): American Revolution; Settlement of the American Frontier
Fictional character(s): Leslie Collins, Frontiersman, Surveyor; William David, Child; Little Brother, Indian
Time Period(s): 1770s
Locale(s): Kentucky

Summary: The impact of the American Revolution on the Kentucky mountain country is chronicled. Leslie Collins is a Daniel Boone-like central character who fights on the rebel side. He is captured by bandits and rescued, and returns home to find his farm deserted and his family gone. While searching for them he encounters a woman and her unwanted son, William David, whom Leslie is determined to save.

Historical Accuracy: The author shows that she knows both the locale and the historical period in this dramatic story.

BEN ARONIN (1904-1980)

An American author, Hebrew scholar, and lawyer, Aronin taught Hebrew and Bible classes at the College of Jewish Studies in Chicago for many years. He was also known as "Uncle Ben" in the children's television program the "Magic Door," which he created. Aronin is the author of a Hebrew epic, *The Abramiad* and numerous children's books.

196 *Walt Whitman's Secret*

Date of Publication: 1955
Subject(s): Literary Life; Biography, Fictionalized; Civil War—U.S.
Historical character(s): Walt Whitman, Writer (poet); Stephen Foster, Composer; Henry David Thoreau, Writer, Philosopher; Ralph Waldo Emerson, Writer, Philosopher; Herman Melville, Writer
Time Period(s): 19th century (1840s-1860s)
Locale(s): New Orleans, Louisiana; New York, New York; Washington, District of Columbia

Summary: This biographical portrait of American poet Walt Whitman chronicles his career and personal life from his early years to his literary success following the publication of *Leaves of Grass*. Throughout, Whitman's unorthodoxy creates opposition and controversy.

Historical Accuracy: The novel is faithful to the facts of Whitman's life.

SHOLEM ASCH (1880-1957)

Sholem Asch, a Polish-born writer who emigrated to the United States in 1909, is one of the most widely known Yiddish writers. His plays, stories, and novels depict Jewish life in Europe and America, and his series of historical novels traces the common spiritual heritage of Jews and Christians.

197 *The Apostle*

Date of Publication: 1943
Subject(s): Christianity; Biblical Story
Historical character(s): Simon Bar Jonah, Religious, Biblical Figure; Saul of Tarsus, Biblical Figure; Reb Istephan, Religious; Nero, Ruler
Time Period(s): 1st century
Locale(s): Jerusalem, Israel; Roman Empire (Antioch, Corinth, Ephesus, Cyprus, Damascus, and Rome)

Summary: The novel attempts a faithful chronicle of the early years of Christianity, centered on the lives of Peter and Paul. Paul's conversion, his preaching mission throughout the Roman Empire to Rome itself, and his martyrdom are depicted.

Historical Accuracy: Asch's story is supported by a carefully presented history of the period and contemporary events.

198 *Mary*

Date of Publication: 1949
Subject(s): Biblical Story
Historical character(s): Mary, Biblical Figure; Joseph, Biblical Figure, Carpenter; Yeshua, Biblical Figure
Time Period(s): 1st century (1-33)
Locale(s): Nazareth, Israel; Bethlehem, Israel; Jerusalem, Israel

Summary: The New Testament story of Jesus' birth, youth, mission, and final crucifixion is retold as a domestic family story with a focus on Jesus' mother. Jesus is depicted as a kind of precocious genius in this retelling. The novel roused criticism from Jewish readers as a reverent apology to Christianity—a charge that Asch denied.

Historical Accuracy: The details from the New Testament are combined with believable details of everyday life.

199 *Moses*

Date of Publication: 1951
Subject(s): Biblical Story; Ancient Egypt; Pharaohs
Historical character(s): Moses, Biblical Figure, Royalty; Ramses II, Ruler (pharaoh); Aaron, Biblical Figure
Time Period(s): 13th century B.C.
Locale(s): Egypt; Palestine

Summary: Moses is depicted as a young prince of the pharaoh's court who discovers his past among Hebrew slaves. In exile, Moses marries and tends his flocks before being called by a vision to deliver Israel from Egypt. The great battle with the pharaoh to free the Hebrews and the exodus from Egypt are depicted.

Historical Accuracy: Asch offers the well-known story of Exodus with clear details of life during the period.

200 *The Nazarene*

Date of Publication: 1939
Subject(s): Fantasy; Biblical Story
Fictional character(s): Pan Vladomsky, Scholar; Jochanan, Student
Historical character(s): Jesus Christ, Biblical Figure; Pontius Pilate, Government Official, Biblical Figure; Cornelius the Ciliarch, Political Figure, Government Official (military governor of Jerusalem)
Time Period(s): 1st century; 20th century
Locale(s): Jerusalem, Israel; Warsaw, Poland

Summary: The novel attempts to tell the story of Christ from an eyewitness account, made possible by the uncanny reincarnation of Cornelius the Ciliarch, as an anti-semitic Polish antiquarian. Cornelius is the military governor of Jerusalem, and possesses a manuscript written by Judas Iscariot.

Historical Accuracy: Asch's knowledge of the historical era and its customs anchors the fantastical framework of the tale.

201 *The Prophet*

Date of Publication: 1955
Subject(s): Biblical Story; Jews; Religious Life
Historical character(s): Daniel, Biblical Figure; Isaiah, Biblical Figure (prophet); Cyrus the Great, Ruler (King of Persia); Cambyses II, Ruler (King of Persia); Narbonidus, Ruler (King of Babylon)
Time Period(s): 6th century B.C.
Locale(s): Babylon

Summary: Isaiah is the voice of the Jews in captivity in Babylon. As the Persian king Cyrus invades the kingdom, Isaiah proclaims his people's deliverance and Cyrus as their liberator. But Cyrus' god is not the God of the Jews, and Isaiah despairs until he has another vision of a deliverer, not a powerful king but an ordinary man who will redeem mankind through his own suffering.

Historical Accuracy: The novel offers a remarkably detailed look at court life in Babylon and its customs.

202 *Salvation*

Date of Publication: 1934
Subject(s): Napoleonic Wars; Jews; Religious Life
Fictional character(s): Reb Yechiel, Religious (rabbi); Rivke Yechiel, Worker (peasant); Wydawski, Nobleman
Time Period(s): 1810s
Locale(s): Poland

Summary: This is the story of a Jewish community in a small Polish village in the years following the retreat of Napoleon's army. Reb Yechiel searches for the God and salvation in scenes that re-create a culture persecuted out of existence in Poland.

Historical Accuracy: The novel has the simplicity of a fable and the timeless quality of folklore, but describes with some care and certain authenticity a past age and culture.

MARY ELLEN ASHCROFT (1952-)

Ashcroft is an Associate Professor of English at Bethel College in Minnesota. Her previous books include *Bearing Our Sorrows* and *Temptations Women Face*.

203 *The Magdalene Gospel*

Date of Publication: 1995
Subject(s): Biblical Story
Historical character(s): Mary Magdalene, Biblical Figure; Jesus Christ, Biblical Figure
Time Period(s): 1st century
Locale(s): Jerusalem, Israel

Summary: The novel offers an imaginative retelling of the gospel stories from the perspective of Jesus' women followers. Banding together after Jesus' crucifixion and led by Mary Magdalene, they share their feelings of love for Jesus and their reasons for following him.

Historical Accuracy: This version of the gospels provides an original slant on the familiar story. The author provides a list of biblical passages on which the novel's stories are based and the historical details that serve to elucidate them.

HELEN ASHFIELD
(PSEUD. OF PAMELA BENNETTS, 1922-)

Helen Ashfield is a pseudonym used by English novelist Pamela Bennetts. She is a full-time member of the staff of the London Diocesan fund of the Church of England. She writes historical novels in her spare time since she finds the modern world unsatisfactory and unromantic.

204 *Beau Barron's Lady*

Date of Publication: 1980
Subject(s): Regency Romance
Fictional character(s): Charles Baron, Gentleman, Rake; Bess Hathaway, Streetperson, Madam (brothel owner); Thomas Crayford, Nobleman (Earl of Crayford)
Historical character(s): George Bryan Brummell, Gentleman (dandy and fashion arbiter)
Time Period(s): 19th century (Regency period)
Locale(s): London, England

Summary: In this Pygmalion story, Bess is a girl of the London slums who is taken up by rake and dandy Charles Barron. Bess gets on in the world as an owner of a brothel but uses her beauty to wed the Earl of Crayford. Her heart remains with Charles, and, when widowed a second time, Bess must save him from poverty as he saved her.

Historical Accuracy: The story is a far-fetched fantasy of wish fulfillment. There are some solid period details however.

205 *Crystal*

Date of Publication: 1987

Subject(s): Regency Romance
Fictional character(s): Crystal Yorke, Streetperson; Basil Corry, Store Owner; Stuart Haversham, Nobleman
Time Period(s): 18th century; 19th century (1795-1810)
Locale(s): London, England

Summary: Crystal Yorke is rescued from the London slums by a kindhearted shopkeeper. She becomes the mistress of a nobleman. To ensure the success of her benefactor's shop, she agrees to participate in a cruel joke which has unfortunate consequences.

Historical Accuracy: This book, and the entire series, contain convincing background details, even as the foreground action veers toward the implausible.

206 *Emerald*

Date of Publication: 1983
Subject(s): Romance; Business Building
Fictional character(s): Emily Tregellan, Seamstress (dressmaker), Servant; Nicholas Ronan, Nobleman (Viscount Asterly)
Time Period(s): 1830s
Locale(s): Cornwall, England; London, England

Summary: Emily Tregellan is determined to escape her humble origins and become a fashionable dressmaker. She rises from scullery maid to seamstress in her employer's household and eventually becomes Madame Emerald, dressmaker to the aristocracy. Nicholas Ronan, an aristocrat, falls in love with her, but the secrets of the past threaten their happiness.

Historical Accuracy: There is some authentic period painting, but the essence of the work is an unlikely jump from servant to peeress.

207 *Garnet*

Date of Publication: 1985
Subject(s): Romance
Fictional character(s): Garnet Bradley, Store Owner; Jonathan Heathcote, Nobleman (Earl of Derebrook); Frances Heathcote, Noblewoman
Time Period(s): 1830s (1834)
Locale(s): Oxfordshire, England

Summary: Garnet Bradley, a shopkeeper, is loved by the dashing Earl of Derebrook. Their affair continues even when the earl marries another. His wife convinces the earl that Garnet is having an affair with his brother. An illegitimate child adds to the complications.

Historical Accuracy: The period detail is clear though the situation is neither probable nor original.

208 *The Marquis and Miss Jones*

Date of Publication: 1982
Subject(s): French Revolution; Romance; Identity—Concealed
Fictional character(s): Martina Howe, Gentlewoman, Imposter ("Miss Jones"); Natalie Trowbridge, Gentlewoman; Adrian Rothwell, Nobleman (Marquis of Rothwell)
Time Period(s): 1770s; 1780s (1779-1780)
Locale(s): London, England; Paris, France

Summary: The Marquis of Rothwell and Lady Martina Howe are secretly engaged, yet do not know each other. When they do meet, Martina is tricked into pretending to be a harlot, Miss Jones. Later, as Lady Howe, she is exposed by the Marquis as an imposter; a harlot pretending to be a lady. She has sworn not to reveal the truth. The action climaxes in the outbreak of the French Revolution and a daring rescue.

Historical Accuracy: The plot is far too tortuously contrived to be believed, and the historical scenes function as little more than additional plot stimulants.

209 *The Michaelmas Tree*

Date of Publication: 1982
Subject(s): Romance; Servants; Georgian Period
Fictional character(s): Patrick Kinnersley, Gentleman; Caroline Castleman, Seamstress, Governess
Time Period(s): 1770s (1773-1774)
Locale(s): England

Summary: In this riches to rags story, Patrick Kinnersley is in love with Caroline Castleman. He is forced to marry another, and Caroline leaves her father's home in shame. She takes a position in service in Patrick and his wife's household with predictably explosive results.

Historical Accuracy: The contrivances here defy probability or logic regardless of historical era.

210 *Opal*

Date of Publication: 1986
Subject(s): Romance; Victorian Period; Theatrical Life
Fictional character(s): Opal Shannon, Thief (pickpocket), Actress; Edward Adare, Nobleman; Gillian Wintour, Gentlewoman
Time Period(s): 1850s (1853)
Locale(s): London, England

Summary: In this rags to riches story, Opal Shannon, a pickpocket, falls in love with a nobleman, Edward Adare. She emerges from the workhouse to stardom. In the musical hall, Opal has a second encounter with Adare whose fiancee does not approve.

Historical Accuracy: The novel's premise is unrealistic. The period detail is employed largely to heighten the melodrama.

211 *Pearl*

Date of Publication: 1984
Subject(s): Romance; Victorian Period
Fictional character(s): Pearl Cartwright, Young Woman; Bruce Sackville, Gentleman; James Sackville, Gentleman
Time Period(s): 1830s; 1840s (1833-1843)
Locale(s): London, England

Summary: Pearl Cartwright is savagely raped by Bruce Sackville, the brother of the man with whom she falls in love, James Sackville. When she discovers his complicity in a plan to take the child she bears from the rape, Pearl seeks revenge in a manipulation of her own. But their love will out even when James is obligated to marry another.

Historical Accuracy: The novel presents some authentic period details.

`212` *Regency Rogue*
Date of Publication: 1982
Subject(s): Regency Romance; Royalty—England; Mystery
Fictional character(s): Anthony St. Romer, Nobleman (Earl of Dunmorrow); Davina Temple, Gentlewoman; Christmas Dee, Nobleman
Historical character(s): George, Prince Regent, Royalty (later George IV)
Time Period(s): 1810s
Locale(s): London, England; Brighton, England

Summary: The Earl of Dunmorrow is asked by the Prince Regent to investigate the mysterious disappearance of Sir Christmas Dee. The Earl is joined in his search by Lady Temple with whom he falls in love. The solution to the mystery is discovered with the help of two escaped convicts.

Historical Accuracy: Ashfield has mastered the period details and reproduces the era well.

`213` *Ruby*
Date of Publication: 1984
Subject(s): Romance; Georgian Period
Fictional character(s): Ruby Travers, Heiress; Lionel Whitcombe, Businessman; Sebastian Stratton, Nobleman (Earl of Stratton)
Time Period(s): 1790s
Locale(s): Lancashire, England

Summary: The daughter of the housekeeper of a manor house, Ruby Travers, inherits the estate. She, like the former owner, is unwilling to sell the estate to Lionel Whitcombe, a nouveau riche industrialist. Their conflict increases as Ruby falls in love with the Earl of Stratton; secrets from the past play a role in their romance.

Historical Accuracy: The antagonism between Whitcombe, the representative of the new industrial age, and Ruby, a landowner, seems more fairy tale than history.

`214` *Sapphire*
Date of Publication: 1985
Subject(s): Regency Romance
Fictional character(s): Sapphire Grant, Teacher; Ashton Howard, Gentleman; Arminta Howard, Gentlewoman
Time Period(s): 1820s (1820)
Locale(s): Lancashire, England; London, England

Summary: Sapphire Grant is a poor parson's daughter who is in love with Ashton Howard, son of the Earl of Stonehurst. Her sister falls in love with a handsome stranger, and jealousy mars the romance.

Historical Accuracy: The action is standard romantic fare with a clear period background.

`215` *Topaz*
Date of Publication: 1987
Subject(s): Regency Romance; Gypsies

Fictional character(s): Topaz Chilcott, Gypsy; Rossmayne, Nobleman (Marquis of Rossmayne); Oswin Lovat, Nobleman
Time Period(s): 1800s (1807)
Locale(s): Dartmoor, England; London, England

Summary: This Regency romance involves a beautiful gypsy girl in love with a marquis who rejects her. She marries a lord and becomes the toast of the London season, but the marquis is still in her thoughts.

Historical Accuracy: The novel is more a fairy tale of social wish fulfillment than any kind of accurate historical story.

HELEN ASHTON (1891-1958)
Ashton studied medicine at London University and served as a nurse during World War I.

`216` *Footman in Powder*
Date of Publication: 1954
Subject(s): Royalty—England; Servants; Georgian Period
Fictional character(s): Jem Wyatt, Servant
Historical character(s): George, Prince of Wales, Royalty; Caroline of Brunswick, Royalty (princess); George III, Ruler (King of England)
Time Period(s): 18th century; 19th century (1779-1830)
Locale(s): London, England; Brighton, England

Summary: Life in the household of George, Prince of Wales (later George IV) is detailed from the perspective of Jem Wyatt, who begins his career as a kitchen helper in the prince's summer household in Brighton. He is on hand for the tumultuous history of the two Georges, providing a behind the scenes look at the royals.

Historical Accuracy: Convincing in its sources and details, the novel provides some authentic looks at the royal family.

`217` *The Hedge of Thorns*
Date of Publication: 1958
Subject(s): Disasters—Natural; Rural Life—Ireland; Irish Potato Famine
Fictional character(s): Alicia Brendan, Young Woman; Captain Roderick Kirwan, Landowner
Historical character(s): Alfred, Lord Tennyson, Writer (poet)
Time Period(s): 19th century (1825-1850)
Locale(s): Cheltenham, England; Mayo, Ireland

Summary: In 1844, 19-year-old Alicia Brendan runs away to Ireland with her lover, Captain Kirwan. There she runs a grand manor house in County Mayo without an income to support it. The potato famine further complicates the domestic situation and produces the novel's climax.

Historical Accuracy: The scenes of Irish life are well-presented and authentic, if secondary to the novel's romantic complications.

`218` *Letty*
Date of Publication: 1951
Subject(s): Biography, Fictionalized; Literary Life
Historical character(s): Letitia Elizabeth Landon, Writer (poet)

Time Period(s): 19th century
Locale(s): England

Summary: This fictional biography is based on the life of minor English poet Letty Landon, whose literary success was compromised by a series of scandals. The novel is filled with details of the literary and social customs of the day.

Historical Accuracy: The facts of Landon's life and the period background are faithfully depicted.

219 *Parson Austen's Daughter*

Date of Publication: 1949
Subject(s): Biography, Fictionalized; Literary Life
Historical character(s): Jane Austen, Writer
Time Period(s): 18th century; 19th century (1775-1817)
Locale(s): Steventon, England; Bath, England; Winchester, England

Summary: Based on family papers, letters, and biographies, the novel offers a fictional account of the life of Jane Austen. In a life in which so little that was dramatic or sensational happened, the appeal here is a look at the novelist as she must have appeared from the perspective of her family, friends, and relatives. The customs, clothing, and pastimes of the period are vividly depicted.

Historical Accuracy: The author invents nothing here but stays strictly within the confines of what is known about Austen.

220 *The Swan of Usk*

Date of Publication: 1940
Subject(s): Biography, Fictionalized; Literary Life; Medical Profession
Historical character(s): Henry Vaughan, Writer (poet), Doctor
Time Period(s): 17th century
Locale(s): Wales; England

Summary: Seventeenth-century English poet Henry Vaughan is the subject of this biographical novel. An important metaphysical poet, Vaughan attended Oxford but did not complete his degree. He studied law before turning to medicine and becoming a respected physician. The novel captures the details of Vaughan's life and career as well as the impact of historical events.

Historical Accuracy: The novel is based on unpublished biographical material used to create a faithful portrait of Vaughan's life and times.

MARY LOUISE ASWELL (1902-1984)

Descended from a Philadelphia Quaker family, Aswell attended Bryn Mawr and later did graduate work at Yale and Radcliffe. She worked for twelve years as the literary editor of *Harper's Bazaar* and wrote a number of Quaker sketches for the *New Yorker*. She also wrote a suspense novel, *Far to Go*.

221 *Abigail*

Date of Publication: 1959
Subject(s): American Colonies; Quakers

Fictional character(s): Abigail Harrison, Young Woman
Time Period(s): 18th century (1700-1775)
Locale(s): Philadelphia, Pennsylvania, American Colonies

Summary: Rebellious Abigail Harrison struggles against the rigid tenets of the Philadelphia Friends Society.

Historical Accuracy: The novel provides an authentic portrait of Quaker life in Philadelphia before the American Revolution.

GERTRUDE ATHERTON (1857-1948)

A native of San Francisco, Atherton moved to England and received critical acclaim for her historical novels, particularly *The Conqueror* (1902), a fictional biography of Alexander Hamilton. Also the author of short stories, Atherton set many of her novels in California during Spanish rule. She returned to San Francisco and wrote a two-volume history of California. She also wrote the autobiographies *My San Francisco* and *Adventures of a Novelist*.

222 *The Conqueror: Being the True and Romantic Story of Alexander Hamilton*

Date of Publication: 1902
Subject(s): Biography, Fictionalized; American Revolution; Politics
Historical character(s): Alexander Hamilton, Political Figure; Thomas Jefferson, Political Figure; James Madison, Political Figure; Aaron Burr, Political Figure; Eliza Jumel, Spouse (of Aaron Burr)
Time Period(s): 18th century; 19th century
Locale(s): United States

Summary: The novel offers a dramatized biography of Alexander Hamilton that traces his career: his early life in the West Indies; his education at King's College, where he became a leader among the young patriots in favor of American independence; his military activities during the Revolution; and his political life following independence. The novel concludes with an account of Hamilton's famous duel with Aaron Burr.

Historical Accuracy: Although the author contends she has kept within the probabilities, her portraits of many historical characters are largely imagined.

223 *Dido, Queen of Hearts*

Date of Publication: 1929
Subject(s): Myths and Legends
Fictional character(s): Dido, Ruler (Queen of Carthage); Aeneas, Wanderer
Time Period(s): Indeterminate Past
Locale(s): Carthage, Ancient Civilization

Summary: The mythological story of Dido, Queen of Carthage, and her tragic love for Trojan wanderer Aeneas is told in novel form. The author borrows details from Virgil and others to produce a romantic tale in which Dido emerges as a tragic figure, and Aeneas is shown as somewhat less deserving of her devotion.

Historical Accuracy: The novel is more colorful than accurate in its depictions, with its primary emphasis on exotic romance.

224   *Golden Peacock*

Date of Publication: 1936
Subject(s): Roman Empire
Fictional character(s): Pomponia, Teenager
Historical character(s): Augustus, Ruler (Emperor of Rome); Horace, Writer
Time Period(s): 1st century B.C. (20 B.C.)
Locale(s): Rome, Roman Empire

Summary: In this adventure story, 16-year-old Pomponia plays a major role in saving Augustus from a conspiracy. When Pomponia's parents are murdered, she is taken in by her father's friend, Horace, and the search for the person behind the killings leads to the royal palace.

Historical Accuracy: The details provide a colorful background, but the novel fails to capture credibly the spirit of the times.

225   *The Immortal Marriage*

Date of Publication: 1927
Subject(s): Ancient Greece
Historical character(s): Pericles, Political Figure; Aspasia, Gentlewoman; Socrates, Teacher, Philosopher; Sophocles, Writer (playwright); Phidias, Artist (sculptor); Alcibiades, Political Figure, Military Personnel (general)
Time Period(s): 5th century B.C.
Locale(s): Athens, Greece

Summary: The novel provides a factual re-creation of the love affair between Athenian statesman Pericles and beautiful courtesan Aspasia, who it is said became Pericles' mistress and advisor after the death of his wife. The novel offers scenes from the main events of Pericles' life.

Historical Accuracy: The novel features an authentic depiction of the period with many accurate details about life and customs.

A.A. ATTANASIO (1951-)

An American writer educated at the University of Pennsylvania, Columbia, and New York University, Attanasio has received awards for both his poetry and his science fiction novels, which include *Rodix*, *In Other Worlds*, and *Arc of the Dream*.

226   *Kingdom of the Grail*

Date of Publication: 1992
Subject(s): Middle Ages; Identity—Concealed
Fictional character(s): Ailena Valaise, Noblewoman; Guy Valaise, Nobleman; Erec, Revolutionary
Time Period(s): 12th century (1187-1188)
Locale(s): Wales

Summary: Ten years after the aged Baroness Valaise was banished from her castle by her son and sent off on a pilgrimage to the Holy Land, a woman arrives at the castle claiming that she is the baroness. She is not the aged dowager, but a young maiden. She claims that she has drunk from the Holy Grail, has been restored to her youth, and has been compelled to return to Wales and end her son's tyrannical reign. Is she an imposter or living miracle?.

Historical Accuracy: With the Normans trying to subdue Wales in the background, the novel is an intriguing blend of history and legend.

227   *Wyvern*

Date of Publication: 1988
Subject(s): Sea Story; Pirates
Fictional character(s): Jaki Gefjon, Outcast, Adventurer; Jabalwan, Teacher
Time Period(s): 17th centure (1609-1630)
Locale(s): *Silenos*, At Sea

Summary: Jaki Gefjon is the son of a native woman of Borneo and a Dutch trader. Caught in the clash between two cultures, he is befriended by a mystic named Jabalwan, who teaches him the ways of his ancestors. Jaki travels to the distant corners of the earth in search of a home.

Historical Accuracy: The novel presents a magical world, less historical than legendary and mythical.

LOUIS AUCHINCLOSS (1917-)

An American author of novels, short stories, and criticism, Auchincloss was for many years a practicing attorney. His work has largely concentrated on the lives of New York's wealthy and business families. Critics have seen Auchincloss as continuing to mine territory formerly explored by Henry James and Edith Wharton. Few modern writers have been so successful in continuing the novel of manners.

228   *The Book Class*

Date of Publication: 1984
Subject(s): Friendship
Fictional character(s): Polly Travers, Political Figure; Georgia Bristed, Socialite; Leila Lee, Socialite
Time Period(s): 20th century (1908-1968)
Locale(s): New York, New York

Summary: The novel describes the lives of a dozen women who form a book club in 1908 and meet regularly for the next 60 years. Well-to-do and secure, each woman shows the limits of her talent and ambition as their lives, filled with passion, betrayal, and loyalty, are revealed.

Historical Accuracy: Auchincloss is at home in these scenes of fashionable New York life, probing them for psychological and human meaning.

229   *The Cat and the King*

Date of Publication: 1981
Subject(s): Royalty—France

Historical character(s): Louis XIV, Ruler (King of France); Louis de Rouvroy, Nobleman; Francoise d'Aubigne, Royalty (second wife of Louis XIV), Noblewoman (marquise)
Time Period(s): 17th century; 18th century (1690s-1749)
Locale(s): Versailles, France

Summary: Daily life at Versailles at the court of Louis XIV, is the subject of the novel. Auchincloss offers an extension of the chronicler Saint-Simon's memoirs, revealing the private lives, factions, liaisons, and dalliances of Louis' court.

Historical Accuracy: The novel is convincing in its depiction of the period and its personalities, particularly Saint-Simon himself.

230 *Exit Lady Masham*
Date of Publication: 1983
Subject(s): Royalty—England; Politics
Historical character(s): Abigail Masham, Noblewoman, Courtier; Anne, Ruler (Queen of England); Sarah Churchill, Noblewoman (Duchess of Marlborough); John Churchill, Nobleman (Duke of Marlborough); Robert Harley, Political Figure, Nobleman (Earl of Oxford); Jonathan Swift, Writer
Time Period(s): 17th century; 18th century (1680-1733)
Locale(s): London, England

Summary: The drama of court life and power politics during the reign of Queen Anne is recreated here. To increase their power and influence over the queen, John and Sarah Churchill arrange for Abigail, Sarah's young cousin, to serve as a lady-in-waiting to Anne. Abigail finds herself at the center of the era's pivotal events.

Historical Accuracy: Auchincloss' portrait of Queen Anne is masterful, and the period details are solidly presented.

231 *The House of Five Talents*
Date of Publication: 1960
Subject(s): Family Saga
Fictional character(s): Julius Millinder, Gentleman; Augusta Millinder, Gentlewoman; Oswald Millinder, Gentleman
Time Period(s): 19th century; 20th century (1873-1948)
Locale(s): New York, New York; Newport, Rhode Island; Bar Harbor, Maine

Summary: The effects of a vast fortune on five generations of the Millinder family are chronicled in this novel. The family's founder, Julius Millinder, is a German immigrant who makes his fortune by financial maneuverings of a questionable nature. The story is told by Augusta Millinder, the granddaughter of Julius and one of the last survivors of the older generation. She describes the past and comments on the present, thus detailing wealthy American society from the post-Civil War era to the modern day.

Historical Accuracy: Auchincloss is at home in this milieu of New York society and American wealth. Both are shown with a close psychological awareness.

232 *Portrait in Brownstone*
Date of Publication: 1962
Subject(s): Family Saga; Business Building

Fictional character(s): Geraldine Brevoort, Gentlewoman; Derrick Hartley, Businessman; Ida Trask Hartley, Gentlewoman
Time Period(s): 20th century (1901-1951)
Locale(s): New York, New York; Paris, France

Summary: The novel explores the family history of the Denisons during the first half of the 20th century. A prosperous middle-class family, the Denisons make the move from Brooklyn to Manhattan and climb toward respectability and social prominence.

Historical Accuracy: The author portrays this milieu with care and psychological penetration. The book excels in creating the atmosphere of a New York now disappeared.

233 *The Rector of Justin*
Date of Publication: 1964
Subject(s): Education
Fictional character(s): Francis Prescott, Religious (clergyman), Teacher; Harriet Prescott, Spouse
Time Period(s): 19th century; 20th century (1876-1946)
Locale(s): New England

Summary: The novel offers a picture of life in a New England preparatory school for boys and a character study of its founder and headmaster, Francis Prescott, a complex man of both good qualities and petty weaknesses. The story is told through a collection of diaries, interviews, and notes written by those who knew Prescott.

Historical Accuracy: The novel is a masterful collection of different perspectives on a complex character that animates the character and his era.

234 *Watchfires*
Date of Publication: 1982
Subject(s): Underground Railroad; Civil War—U.S.; Women's Rights
Fictional character(s): Dexter Fairchild, Lawyer; Rosalie Fairchild, Spouse
Time Period(s): 19th century (1850s-1895)
Locale(s): New York, New York; Washington, District of Columbia

Summary: New York before, during, and after the Civil War is the novel's setting. Dexter Fairchild and his wife Rosalie become involved in the underground railroad and the struggle for women's legal rights.

Historical Accuracy: The novel is absolutely convincing in its period details and the political forces of the time are well integrated into the domestic drama.

235 *The Winthrop Covenant*
Date of Publication: 1976
Subject(s): Puritans; Family Saga
Fictional character(s): Samuel Shaw Russell, Diplomat; Winthrop Ward, Businessman
Historical character(s): Anne Hutchinson, Religious; John Winthrop, Political Figure (colonial administrator); Charles Maurice de Talleyrand-Perigord, Diplomat, Government Official

Time Period(s): Multiple Time Periods
Locale(s): Boston, Massachusetts; New York, New York; Paris, France

Summary: This series of vignettes spans three centuries of the Winthrop family in America and traces the rise and fall of the Puritan ethic. The story begins with the trial of Anne Hutchinson in the Massachusetts Bay Colony and follows over time characters who collectively define the Puritan sense of mission.

Historical Accuracy: Auchincloss is sure of his theme, and each era is carefully and believably displayed.

JEAN M. AUEL (1936-)

Auel was born in Chicago and received her B.A. degree from the University of Portland. She was a technical writer before she published her first novel in 1980. The first of her Earth's Children series about prehistoric life, *Clan of the Cave Bear*, the novel proved to be a major popular success. Her speculations about early human life are supported by anthropological and archeological research, as well as survival training. Despite some criticism about the occasional lapses into anachronism, the series has been widely praised.

236 *The Clan of the Cave Bear*
Date of Publication: 1980
Subject(s): Prehistory; Tribal Life—Prehistoric
Fictional character(s): Ayla, Prehistoric Human; Brun, Chieftain, Prehistoric Human; Iza, Healer, Prehistoric Human
Time Period(s): Indeterminate Past
Locale(s): Europe

Summary: This is the first of Auel's saga of prehistoric people. The author tells a fascinating story of tribal life of individuals with fears, hopes, triumphs, and tragedies comparable to those in so-called civilized times. Ayla is the central figure, and her story comes alive with many details describing the lives and customs of an ancient people.

Historical Accuracy: With information gathered from archeological and anthropological sources, the author has produced a novel rich in prehistoric details.

237 *The Mammoth Hunters*
Date of Publication: 1985
Subject(s): Prehistory; Tribal Life—Prehistoric
Fictional character(s): Ayla, Prehistoric Human; Jondalar, Lover (to Ayla), Prehistoric Human; Ranec, Hunter, Prehistoric Human
Time Period(s): Indeterminate Past
Locale(s): Europe

Summary: In this third novel of the Earth's Children series, the independent heroine Ayla and Jondalar meet the Mamutoi (Mammoth Hunters). Ayla finds herself torn between her strong feelings for Ranec and Jondalar.

Historical Accuracy: The novel is convincing in its detailed descriptions of the time and place. It is difficult to believe that the author did not experience the era she describes.

238 *The Plains of Passage*
Date of Publication: 1990
Subject(s): Prehistory; Tribal Life—Prehistoric
Fictional character(s): Ayla, Prehistoric Human; Jondalar, Lover, Prehistoric Human; Attaroa, Chieftain (S'Armunai clan), Prehistoric Human
Time Period(s): Indeterminate Past
Locale(s): Europe

Summary: In the fourth of the Earth's Children series, Ayla and her male companion, Jondalar, have mastered the domestication of animals; and their horsemanship has other hunter-gatherers awe-struck and frightened. They experience savagery and support as they search for a home.

Historical Accuracy: The novel, based on solid research from archeological and anthropological sources, provides a fascinating and convincing reconstruction of the distant past of humanity.

239 *The Valley of Horses*
Date of Publication: 1982
Subject(s): Prehistory; Tribal Life—Prehistoric
Fictional character(s): Ayla, Prehistoric Human; Jondalar, Prehistoric Human; Thonolan, Prehistoric Human
Time Period(s): Indeterminate Past
Locale(s): Europe

Summary: In this second novel of the Earth's Children series, Ayla explores new territory. She finds a unique friendship with animals as vulnerable as she is. Surviving the elements, however, is not as difficult as the emotional turmoil she experiences as she becomes close to another human.

Historical Accuracy: The novel is strongly grounded by an extensive knowledge of prehistory from anthropological and archeological sources.

HELEN AUGUR

240 *Tall Ships to Cathay*
Date of Publication: 1951
Subject(s): Sea Story; Chinese Empire; Clipper Ships
Historical character(s): Seth Low, Businessman; Charles Porter Low, Sea Captain; William Henry Low, Businessman
Time Period(s): 19th century
Locale(s): China; Salem, Massachusetts

Summary: The story of America's clipper ship days and the China trade is told through the actual experiences of the Low family who establish a shipping and commercial empire. The novel captures the details of the trade and the fortunes of the Low family.

Historical Accuracy: The novel is based on the actual letters of the Low family and is faithful to their lives and the history of the clipper ship era.

DIANE AUSTELL

241   *Lights Along the Shore*

Date of Publication: 1992
Subject(s): American West; Ranching; Civil War—U.S.
Fictional character(s): Marin Gentry, Young Woman; Stuart Severance, Rancher; Vail Severance, Rancher
Time Period(s): 1840s; 1860s
Locale(s): San Francisco, California; Washington, District of Columbia

Summary: In this western tale, Marin Gentry marries Stuart Severance although she is pregnant by Vail Severance. The couple succeeds in the booming California, but when the Civil War breaks out the pressure on the family increases. Vail's return produces the novel's climax.

Historical Accuracy: The historical background is genuine, though the emphasis is more on the emotional than the historical.

242   *While the Music Plays*

Date of Publication: 1996
Subject(s): Civil War—U.S.; Espionage
Fictional character(s): Laura Chandler, Spy, Widow(er); Chase Girard, Spy
Historical character(s): Judah P. Benjamin, Political Figure, Government Official (Confederate); Varina Howell Davis, Spouse (of Jefferson Davis)
Time Period(s): 1860s
Locale(s): Washington, District of Columbia; Richmond, Virginia

Summary: This tale of romance and espionage is set during the American Civil War. Southern belle Laura Chandler is recruited by Chase Girard as a Union spy despite her family's loyalties to the Southern cause.

Historical Accuracy: Some of the fictional characters in the story are based on historical figures and the actual events are described accurately.

JOAN AUSTEN-LEIGH

The great-grandaughter of Jane Austen's nephew, Austen-Leigh is a playwright, novelist, and co-founder of the Jane Austen Society of North America.

243   *A Visit to Highbury*

Date of Publication: 1993
Subject(s): Regency Period
Fictional character(s): Mary Goddard, Teacher (boarding school); Charlotte Pinkney, Spouse
Time Period(s): 1810s (1813-1814)
Locale(s): Highbury, England; London, England

Summary: This epistolary novel acts as a companion to Jane Austen's *Emma*, offering the events of Austen's novel as seen through the perspective of boarding school mistress Mary Goddard. She writes to her sister in London whose hasty second marriage is marred by misunderstanding. The novel offers an interesting slant on the original Austen story.

Historical Accuracy: The author captures the Regency era and the Jane Austen flavor with skill.

PAUL AUSTER (1947-)

A graduate of Columbia University, Auster has had a varied career as a merchant seaman, a census taker, a tutor, a telephone operator for the Paris Bureau of the *New York Times*, a translator, critic, poet, and teacher of creative writing. He has been nominated for an Edgar Award and a *Boston Globe* Literary Press Award.

244   *Mr. Vertigo*

Date of Publication: 1994
Subject(s): Depression Era; Magic; Baseball
Fictional character(s): Walter Claireborne Rawley, Orphan, Magician; Yehudi, Magician, Teacher
Historical character(s): Jay Hanna Dean, Sports Figure (baseball pitcher)
Time Period(s): 20th century (1927-1970s)
Locale(s): Midwest; Chicago, Illinois; St. Louis, Missouri

Summary: This is a picaresque story of Walter Rawley, an orphan from St. Louis who becomes ''Walter the Wonder Boy,'' once Master Yehudi trains him in the world of magic and showmanship. Their adventures across America are chronicled in a series of near misses and sleights of hand.

Historical Accuracy: The novel is both a rousing and compelling adventure, convincing in its period details and sense of time and place.

FREDERICK BRITTEN AUSTIN
(1885-1941)

Novelist Frederick Austin is the author of *Forty Centuries Look Down*, a biographical novel of Napoleon; *The Red Flag*, set during the American Revolution; and a novel about prehistoric man *When Mankind Was Young*.

245   *Forty Centuries Look Down*

Date of Publication: 1937
Subject(s): Napoleonic Wars
Historical character(s): Napoleon Bonaparte, Military Personnel (general); Josephine, Spouse
Time Period(s): 1790s (1798)
Locale(s): Paris, France; Egypt

Summary: Napoleon's Egyptian campaign and marital affairs are depicted. After his triumph in Italy, Napoleon sets off to conquer Egypt, leaving behind his wife, Josephine, whom he suspects of being unfaithful to him. On his return he learns that his suspicions are true, but the two are eventually reconciled.

Historical Accuracy: The novel's historical framework is accurate, with dialogue crafted from Napoleon's correspondence.

246   *The Road to Glory*

Date of Publication: 1935

Subject(s): Napoleonic Wars
Historical character(s): Napoleon Bonaparte, Military Personnel (general)
Time Period(s): 1790s
Locale(s): France; Italy

Summary: The novel recounts the achievements of Napoleon's first Italian campaign and the beginnings of his legendary military successes. The story is told exclusively from Napoleon's point of view.

Historical Accuracy: Despite the rendering of Napoleon's thoughts and imaginings, the novel's factual basis is clear.

DORA AYDELOTTE (1878-1968)

Born in Altamont, Illinois, Aydelotte was educated at the Chicago Art Institute and the Women's College of Richmond, Virginia. Her books deal with the codes and characters of the old Southwest, as well as natural disasters (floods, drought, and dust storms), and ranching life. Her novels include *Trumpets Calling*, *Texas Triggers*, and *Full Harvest*.

247 *Run of the Stars*

Date of Publication: 1940
Subject(s): American West; Settlement of the American Frontier
Fictional character(s): Sela Burchard, Teacher; Clint Aragon, Farmer
Time Period(s): 1890s
Locale(s): Oklahoma

Summary: The scene for this western novel is the Oklahoma territory in the 1890s. The novel describes pioneer life through the experiences of young Sela Burchard, and details her relationship with Clint Aragon.

Historical Accuracy: The novel provides an authentic portrait of the period and the region.

248 *Trumpets Calling*

Date of Publication: 1938
Subject(s): Settlement of the American Frontier; Farming
Fictional character(s): Martha Prawl, Settler; David Prawl, Settler
Time Period(s): 1890s
Locale(s): Oklahoma

Summary: Homesteading in the Cherokee Strip of Oklahoma during the 1890s is the novel's subject. Settlers David and Martha Prawl struggle against poverty and drought.

Historical Accuracy: The novel provides a convincing and essentially non-romanticized depiction of frontier life.

ROSE AYERS

(PSEUD. OF LILLIAN BETHEL GREENWOOD, 1932-)

A native of Saskatchewan, Canada, Ayers received her B.A. and M.A. degrees from the University of British Columbia. She has worked as a high school English teacher and a college instructor in creative writing. She sold her first stories to the Canadian Broadcasting Corporation.

249 *The Street Sparrows*

Date of Publication: 1978
Subject(s): Victorian Period; Crime and Criminals
Fictional character(s): Meg Smith, Foundling, Streetperson; Jamie, Foundling, Streetperson; Geordie McCannon, Criminal; Charles Stuart, Gentleman
Time Period(s): 19th century (Victorian period)
Locale(s): London, England

Summary: London street life during the Victorian period is captured in this novel that revisits the domain of Charles Dickens' *Oliver Twist* with a harder, more realistic edge. Meg Smith is a foundling who earns her living on the London streets along with a friend, Jamie. They fall into the hands of Geordie McCannon who keeps a team of boys and girls for various licit and illicit activities. When Jamie is hanged for theft, Meg turns to Lord Charlie Stuart, and a romance follows.

Historical Accuracy: The novel is a far more realistic portrait of Victorian street life than Dickens managed in *Oliver Twist*. The period details and customs are faithfully delivered.

MICHAEL AYRTON (1921-1975)

Born in London, Ayrton left school at fourteen to study art in Vienna and Paris. He worked as a novelist, essayist, art historian, illustrator, sculptor, painter, theater designer, documentary filmmaker, and professor of fine art and English literature. He was the recipient of the 1958 Gran Premio di Bergamo for his film, *Greek Sculpture*, and the 1968 Heinmann Award from the Royal Society for Literature.

250 *The Maze Maker*

Date of Publication: 1967
Subject(s): Myths and Legends
Fictional character(s): Daedalus, Artisan; Icarus, Young Man (son of Daedalus); Minos, Ruler (King of Crete)
Time Period(s): Indeterminate Past
Locale(s): Athens, Greece; Crete, Greece

Summary: This is an autobiography of the famous artificer, Daedalus, who builds the labyrinth at Knossos and fashions the wings that kill his son Icarus when he flies too close to the sun. Daedalus becomes the archetype of the artist-craftsman and reveals himself to be a blend of cunning, vanity, and insecurity.

Historical Accuracy: The novel offers a magical evocation of the world of Greek myths and legends described in human and psychologically believable terms.

BERNIE BABCOCK (1868-1962)

Babcock was born in Unionville, Ohio, but moved with his family to Arkansas when he was ten years old. He was a journalist as well as a novelist and wrote the books *Soul of*

Abe Lincoln, Lincoln's Mary and the Babies, and *The Heart of George Washington*.

251   *Soul of Abe Lincoln*

Date of Publication: 1923
Subject(s): Civil War—U.S.
Fictional character(s): Del Norcrosse, Military Personnel (Union soldier); Ann Laury, Young Woman
Historical character(s): Abraham Lincoln, Political Figure
Time Period(s): 1860s
Locale(s): Washington, District of Columbia

Summary: Set during the Civil War, the novel traces the influence of Abraham Lincoln on a young southern couple, Del Norcrosse and Ann Laury. Norcrosse is committed to the Union and joins the Northern Army. The lovers are on the verge of reconciliation when Lincoln is assassinated.

Historical Accuracy: Though the story is essentially an invented romance, the details of its historical events, particularly of Lincoln's assassination, are realistically presented.

252   *The Soul of Ann Rutledge*

Date of Publication: 1919
Subject(s): Settlement of the American Frontier; Biography, Fictionalized
Historical character(s): Abraham Lincoln, Political Figure; Ann Rutledge, Young Woman
Time Period(s): 1830s (1831-1835)
Locale(s): Illinois

Summary: This romantic re-creation of the early years in the life of Abraham Lincoln is set during the 1830s and concerns Lincoln's first love, Ann Rutledge, and his determination to succeed as a lawyer and politician.

Historical Accuracy: This is an idealized version of Lincoln's biography with scenes invented and the majority of the story based in imagination rather than on facts.

NAOMI LANE BABSON (1895-)

Born in Rockport, Massachusetts, Babson attended Radcliffe College and went to China shortly after graduation. She is the author of *The Yankee Bodleys*, *All the Tomorrows*, and *Look Down From Heaven*.

253   *I Am Lidian*

Date of Publication: 1951
Subject(s): American West; Theatrical Life; Wagon Trains
Fictional character(s): Lidian Dorie, Actress, Pioneer
Time Period(s): 1850s; 1860s (1856-1868)
Locale(s): Montana

Summary: Massachusetts-born Lidian Dorie joins a theatrical troupe and heads west with a wagon train heading for San Francisco. She makes it as far as Montana where she settles down to the life of a pioneer.

Historical Accuracy: The novel captures the era and its atmosphere of frontier life during the period.

RICCARDO BACCHELLI (1891-1985)

An Italian poet and novelist, Bacchelli's literary reputation rests primarily on his historical novels, of which *The Mill on the Po* is the most famous. Bacchelli has not been widely translated.

254   *The Mill on the Po*

Date of Publication: 1940
Subject(s): Independence—Italy; Napoleonic Wars
Fictional character(s): Lazzaro Scacerini, Worker (miller); Dosolina Scacerini, Spouse (of Scacerini); Cecilia, Orphan
Time Period(s): 19th century (1807-1872)
Locale(s): Ferrara, Italy

Summary: The great events of 19th century Italy are portrayed from the perspective of a single family who operate a mill on the river Po. Lazzaro, who receives a legacy from a dying soldier on Napoleon's retreat from Russia, opens the mill and then must contend with smugglers, trouble with Austria, and Italian partisans. The family drama serves as a metaphor for political struggle during a difficult time in Italian history.

Historical Accuracy: The details of ordinary life make this an impressive chronicle of the time.

255   *Nothing New under the Sun*

Date of Publication: 1955
Subject(s): Rural Life—Italy; World War I
Fictional character(s): Giuseppe Scacerni, Mentally Ill Person; Cecilia Scacerni, Businesswoman (manager of mill); Giovanni Scacerni, Worker (mill)
Time Period(s): 19th century; 20th century (1872-1918)
Locale(s): Po River Valley, Italy (near Ferrara)

Summary: This is the third volume of the author's trilogy, *The Mill on the Po*. The story of the Scacerni family and their mill continues into the next generation and Italy's emergence as a modern nation. The action culminates with the impact of the Great War.

Historical Accuracy: The novel, along with the previous two volumes in the trilogy, is a convincing panorama of a people caught in the tide of political events.

IRVING A. BACHELLER (1859-1950)

American novelist Bacheller was born in Pierpont, New York, and graduated from St. Lawrence University. In 1884 he founded the first newspaper syndicate in the U.S. His novels are largely historical romances concerned with early American life.

256   *A Candle in the Wilderness*

Date of Publication: 1930
Subject(s): American Colonies; Puritans
Fictional character(s): William Heydon, Fugitive; Robert Heathers, Fugitive
Historical character(s): John Cotton, Religious (minister); Sir Henry Vane, Political Figure; John Winthrop, Political Figure
Time Period(s): 17th century (1634)

Locale(s): Boston, Massachusetts, American Colonies; New York, New York, American Colonies

Summary: This novel describes early life in the American Colonies while following the adventures of two young fugitives from England. Misconduct with a servant girl causes Robert Heathers to flee to Quebec. He escapes capture by the Indians, and finally reaches New York. Meanwhile, in Boston, William Heydon achieves prominence.

Historical Accuracy: The novel features an elaborate and authentic period background, with the original sources duly noted by the author.

257　*D'ri and I*

Date of Publication: 1901
Subject(s): War of 1812; Battle of Lake Erie
Fictional character(s): Darius Olin, Backwoodsman, Military Personnel; Ramon Bell, Military Personnel; Louise de Lambert, Gentlewoman
Historical character(s): Oliver Hazard Perry, Military Personnel (admiral)
Time Period(s): 18th century; 19th century (1790s-1810s)
Locale(s): Vermont; Lake Erie, Great Lakes

Summary: Friendship and adventure during the War of 1812 is the novel's subject as Darius Olin, nicknamed "D'ri," a brawny, raw-boned backwoodsman, accompanies Ramon Bell, the son of his employer, into battle with Admiral Perry on Lake Erie. A romance between Ramon and two daughters of a French nobleman complicates matters, but D'ri is stalwart on behalf of his friend.

Historical Accuracy: The scenes of battle are lively and believable, if D'ri is somewhat too simple and unassuming to be true.

258　*Father Abraham*

Date of Publication: 1925
Subject(s): Civil War—U.S.; Antebellum South
Fictional character(s): Randall Hope, Young Man
Time Period(s): 1860s
Locale(s): South

Summary: The influence of Abraham Lincoln on the thoughts and actions of several characters is explored. The story centers on a young Northerner, Randall Hope, who moves to the South to live with his uncle. There he experiences the clash of ideas between the North and South, intensified as war breaks out.

Historical Accuracy: The period background is reliably, if conventionally, presented.

259　*In the Days of Poor Richard*

Date of Publication: 1922
Subject(s): American Colonies; American Revolution; Indians
Fictional character(s): Jack Irons, Frontiersman; Margaret Hare, Young Woman
Historical character(s): Benjamin Franklin, Political Figure
Time Period(s): 18th century
Locale(s): American Colonies; England; France

Summary: This is a panoramic view of the events of the American Revolution. Benjamin Franklin is at the center of the novel's historical action, and a fictional story of Jack Irons and Margaret Hare provides the novel's romantic element. The account of Indian fighting and the depiction of Franklin are the strongest aspects of the novel.

Historical Accuracy: The novel's romantic events and details are based on letters and family records, and the historical events are accurately presented.

260　*Light in the Clearing*

Date of Publication: 1917
Subject(s): Politics
Fictional character(s): Barton Baynes, Young Man
Historical character(s): Silas Wright, Political Figure
Time Period(s): 1840s; 1850s
Locale(s): New York

Summary: This tale of life in northern New York state concerns the career of Silas Wright, governor of the state. The story is told by Barton Baynes, who has come under Wright's influence.

Historical Accuracy: The details of the past have a nostalgic and sentimental quality that casts the tale in a particularly unrealistic light.

261　*A Man for the Ages*

Date of Publication: 1919
Subject(s): Biography, Fictionalized; Underground Railroad
Historical character(s): Abraham Lincoln, Political Figure
Time Period(s): 1830s; 1840s (1837-1847)
Locale(s): Illinois

Summary: This blend of fact and fancy chronicles the youth and pioneer experiences of Abraham Lincoln. The future president's skills and abilities are developed and demonstrated in a series of adventures. The story concludes with Lincoln's courtship of Mary Todd.

Historical Accuracy: The novel blends accurate historical details with invention.

262　*The Master of Chaos*

Date of Publication: 1932
Subject(s): American Revolution
Fictional character(s): Colin Cabot, Military Personnel (soldier); Patience Fayerweather, Loyalist
Historical character(s): George Washington, Military Personnel (army commander)
Time Period(s): 1770s
Locale(s): American Colonies

Summary: This tale of the American Revolution concerns a young Harvard graduate, Colin Cabot, who falls in love with Patience Fayerweather, the daughter of a Loyalist. Colin joins the rebel army and serves as George Washington's secretary.

Historical Accuracy: The novel's period elements are well defined and based on evident research.

SAMUEL G. BAGGETT (1894-1964)

Born in Coryell County, Texas, Baggett was admitted to the Texas bar in 1919 and later worked for the United Fruit Company. He wrote extensively on the law.

263 *Gods on Horseback*

Date of Publication: 1952
Subject(s): Aztec Empire; Exploration
Fictional character(s): Teotl, Outlaw, Revolutionary; Mitla, Young Woman
Historical character(s): Hernando Cortez, Military Personnel (conquistador), Explorer
Time Period(s): 16th century
Locale(s): Mexico

Summary: The background of this romantic adventure story is the conquest of the Aztec Empire by Cortez. Teotl, an Aztec outlaw plotting the downfall of Montezuma, falls in love with one of the ruler's vestal virgins, Mitla. The climax of the story is the capture of Tenochtitlan by Cortez.

Historical Accuracy: The novel features an insightful view of Aztec life and customs woven into an adventure story that features both actual and fanciful circumstances.

JOAN BAGNEL

264 *Gone the Rainbow, Gone the Dove*

Date of Publication: 1973
Subject(s): Independence—Ireland
Fictional character(s): Jamie Daley, Revolutionary; Margaret Culhaney, Young Woman; Ian Riordan, Revolutionary (captain of the IRA)
Time Period(s): 1910s; 1920s (1910s-1920s)
Locale(s): Ireland

Summary: This tragic love story is set during the Irish Rebellion and concerns Jamie Daley and his love for Margaret Culhane. Love for country will eventually come between the two as each is plunged into the violence of the period.

Historical Accuracy: The novel offers some clear and compelling pictures of the ''Troubles'' with the inevitable bittersweet blend of beauty and violence.

ANTHONY BAILEY (1933-)

An English-born author, Bailey was educated at Oxford University and served as an officer in the British army. Since 1956, he has been a staff writer at *The New Yorker*.

265 *Major Andre*

Date of Publication: 1987
Subject(s): American Revolution; Espionage
Historical character(s): John Andre, Military Personnel (British officer); Benjamin Tallmadge, Military Personnel; Benedict Arnold, Military Personnel, Traitor; Nathanael Greene, Military Personnel (American general)
Time Period(s): 1780s (1780)
Locale(s): Tappan, New York

Summary: Benedict Arnold's plan to surrender West Point to the British is described by a British officer being held by American forces prior to his execution for espionage. John Andre, a charming soldier, amateur actor, and poet provides his perspectives on the war's most notorious treason, which, had it been successful, might have altered the course of history.

Historical Accuracy: The novel captures Andre's personality and his times with sophistication and perceptiveness.

CHARLES W. BAILEY (1929-)

American writer Bailey is a career journalist, serving as the Washington correspondent for the *Minneapolis Tribune*. He also was the Washington editor for National Public Radio and the chairman of its Washington Journalism Center. Bailey is the co-author, with Fletcher Knebel, of the best-sellers, *Seven Days in May* and *Convention*.

266 *The Land Was Ours: A Novel of the Great Plains*

Date of Publication: 1991
Subject(s): Politics; Social Chronicle
Fictional character(s): Dan Woods, Journalist; Grace Woods, Spouse; George Norton, Banker
Historical character(s): William Jennings Bryan, Political Figure, Lawyer; Mark Hanna, Businessman, Political Figure; William McKinley, Political Figure; Theodore Roosevelt, Political Figure; Franklin Delano Roosevelt, Political Figure; Calvin Coolidge, Political Figure; Sam Rayburn, Political Figure
Time Period(s): 19th century; 20th century (1873-1938)
Locale(s): Nebraska; South Dakota; Minneapolis, Minnesota

Summary: The novel offers a history of American life focused on the great political struggles of the the 20th century. Dan Woods is born in a sod house and becomes a newspaper editor. He marries Grace, his counselor and critic. George Norton is a publisher and powerbroker. Together they reflect the times as America changes from an agrarian society to a modern industrial power. The change and its cost to the heartland of America form the novel's theme.

Historical Accuracy: This broad sweep of history is illustrated with many historical figures portrayed with insight and authenticity.

HENRY CHRISTOPHER BAILEY
(1878-1961)

Bailey was born in London and educated at Oxford. While attending Oxford, he published his first book, which would become the first in a series of historical novels. He later went to work for the London *Daily Telegraph*. During World War I, he began to write detective stories, creating the well known character of Mr. Fortune.

267 *The Merchant Prince*

Date of Publication: 1929

Subject(s): War of the Roses; Business Building
Fictional character(s): Hugh Camboys, Businessman (merchant)
Time Period(s): 15th century
Locale(s): England

Summary: Set in England during the period of the War of the Roses, the novel describes the career of Hugh Camboys, who rises from poverty by marketing his mother's embroideries.

Historical Accuracy: The novel provides a convincing and accurate portrait of daily life of the period.

PAUL BAILEY (1937-)

An English author, Bailey was born in London, attended the Central School of Speech and Drama, and was an actor on television and with the Stratford and Royal Court theaters in England. He left a job as a salesman at a large Knightsbridge store to write full-time.

`268` *For Time and All Eternity*

Date of Publication: 1964
Subject(s): Mormons; American West
Fictional character(s): Nancy Corey, Gentlewoman; Joel Scott, Military Personnel
Historical character(s): Brigham Young, Religious (Mormon leader), Political Figure
Time Period(s): 1870s; 1880s
Locale(s): Utah

Summary: The campaign against the Mormon practice of multiple marriages is illustrated in the story of Nancy Corey, a devout Mormon who neither accepts polygamy nor accepts being selected by one of the Elders to be his fourth or fifth wife. She escapes that fate when she marries a ''heathen,'' Joel Scott, only to find him falling under the influence of the Mormon way of life.

Historical Accuracy: The novel offers a convincing view of a little known episode of Western history when federal law compelled Mormon men to disenfranchise all their wives except the first, and marshals were offered rewards for every ''cohab'' they could root out.

BERYL BAINBRIDGE (1933-)

Born in Liverpool, Bainbridge was an actress on radio and in repertory theater and the host of the BBC series, ''English Journey'' and ''Forever England.'' She is considered one of the half-dozen most inventive and interesting novelists in Britain today. Her other novels include *Another Part of the Wood*, *Harriet Said*, *Sweet William*, and *The Dressmaker*.

`269` *The Birthday Boys*

Date of Publication: 1991
Subject(s): Polar Exploration
Historical character(s): Robert Falcon Scott, Explorer; Lawrence Edward Oates, Explorer; Edgar Evans, Explorer; Edward Wilson, Explorer, Doctor; Henry Robertson Bowers, Explorer
Time Period(s): 1910s (1910-1912)

Locale(s): Antarctica

Summary: This is the story of the doomed Antarctic expedition led by Robert Scott in 1912. Told by Scott and four members of his team, the explorers' optimism and genteel amateurism become a metaphor for the foolish carnage to come in the Great War.

Historical Accuracy: Bainbridge imaginatively recreates both the events of the expedition and the ethos of the explorers that doom them to their deaths.

`270` *Every Man for Himself*

Date of Publication: 1996
Subject(s): Ocean Liners; Shipwrecks
Fictional character(s): Morgan, Gentleman
Time Period(s): 1910s (1912)
Locale(s): *Titanic*, At Sea; England

Summary: The novel provides a fictional reconstruction of the maiden voyage of the *Titanic* in 1912. Told from the perspective of J. Pierpont Morgan's nephew, the novel captures the glittery voyage, and the events that join crew and passengers as the unsinkable *Titanic* meets its destiny.

Historical Accuracy: The novel offers a convincing and human portrait of the voyage.

`271` *Watson's Apology*

Date of Publication: 1984
Subject(s): Victorian Period; Crime and Criminals; Trials
Historical character(s): John Selby Watson, Religious (clergyman), Murderer; Anne Watson, Spouse
Time Period(s): 19th century (1844-1884)
Locale(s): Surrey, England; London, England

Summary: This novel is based on the true story of a notorious Victorian murder case in which clergyman J.S. Watson bludgeoned his wife to death after their return from church. The event allows the author to present a devastating portrait of a Victorian marriage and a meditation on male/female relations.

Historical Accuracy: The actual persons, events, and documents of the case are employed. The motives of the characters, their conversations, and their feelings are the invention of the author.

`272` *Young Adolf*

Date of Publication: 1979
Subject(s): Biography, Fictionalized
Historical character(s): Adolf Hitler, Political Figure
Time Period(s): 1910s (1912)
Locale(s): Liverpool, England

Summary: The author has taken a diary entry that recorded the fact that Adolf Hitler visited his brother in Liverpool for five months in 1912 and imagines how this period of his life had an impact on Hitler's later development. Young Adolf emerges as an outsider and a dead weight, a fairly pathetic figure whose later career seems to compensate for a host of inadequacies.

Historical Accuracy: The novel is an imaginative exercise rather than a historical account. The period details are, however, quite convincing.

GEORGE BAKER

273 *Paris of Troy*

Date of Publication: 1947
Subject(s): Trojan War; Myths and Legends; Ancient Greece
Fictional character(s): Achates, Warrior; Paris, Royalty (prince of Troy); Helen of Troy, Royalty (Queen of Sparta); Oenone, Young Woman
Time Period(s): 13th century B.C.
Locale(s): Troy, Ancient Civilization; Egypt

Summary: Achates, a Trojan warrior and friend of Paris, tells the story of the siege of Troy. The war is precipitated by the tragic love affair of Paris, son of King Priam of Troy, and Helen, wife of the King of Sparta. The story invents a prior love between Paris and Oenone, who is also loved by Achates.

Historical Accuracy: The novel blends together legend, history, and myth in a convincing and believable interpretation of the Homeric tale.

KARLE WILSON BAKER (1878-1961)

Born in Little Rock, Arkansas, and educated at the University of Chicago and Columbia University, Baker wrote for popular magazines, contributing both poetry and fiction. His novels *Star of the Wilderness* and *Old Coins* are set in the Southwest and integrate military life with romance.

274 *Star of the Wilderness*

Date of Publication: 1942
Subject(s): Texas Revolution
Fictional character(s): Paul McAlpine, Settler; Jesse McAlpine, Spouse
Historical character(s): James Grant, Political Figure
Time Period(s): 1830s
Locale(s): Nacogdoches, Texas

Summary: The story of the Texas Revolt and the formation of the Texas Republic is told from the perspective of Jesse McAlpine. Jesse and her husband, Paul, are persuaded by James Grant to leave Cincinnati for a new life in the southwest. They find themselves caught up in the politics and violence of the uprising against Mexico.

Historical Accuracy: The historical background is accurately rendered, as are the manners and customs of the era.

LUCINDA BAKER (1916-)

Born in Illinois and the daughter of an Indian trader, Baker attended Arizona State College and began her career as a freelance writer in 1936. She is the author of numerous mysteries and gothic novels.

275 *The Place of Devils*

Date of Publication: 1976

Subject(s): American West; Romance
Fictional character(s): Raphael de Casta, Rancher; Lalia Cortland, Governess; Carmen de Casta, Child
Time Period(s): 1870s (1879)
Locale(s): Tucson, Arizona

Summary: Lalia Cortland is a young missionary's daughter who agrees to to care for a rancher's young daughter, Carmen. Marriage to Raphael de Costa follows but much complicates their happiness. Lalia is brutally attacked, a neighbor is suddenly murdered, and Carmen disappears. Lalia must act to reverse this chain of disasters.

Historical Accuracy: The story is a fairly conventional romance but enhanced with some vivid background details.

MADELINE BAKER

276 *A Whisper on the Wind*

Date of Publication: 1991
Subject(s): American West; Time Travel; Indians
Fictional character(s): Elayna O'Brien, Young Woman; Michael Wolf, Time Traveller, Indian (Cheyenne)
Time Period(s): 1950s (1955); 1870s (1875)
Locale(s): South Dakota

Summary: By chance, Michael Wolf leaves the 1950s and travels back in time to the 1870s to experience life as a Cheyenne Indian during the fateful Indian Wars. The experience has a profound influence on his future life.

Historical Accuracy: The novel offers good historical details.

NIGEL BALCHIN

277 *Borgia Testament*

Date of Publication: 1949
Subject(s): Renaissance
Historical character(s): Cesare Borgia, Military Personnel, Diplomat
Time Period(s): 15th century; 16th century
Locale(s): Italy

Summary: Cast in the form of a journal written by Cesare Borgia while he is imprisoned in the Castle San Angelo waiting to be executed, the novel chronicles his career in flashbacks. The man who was the model for Machiavelli's *The Prince*, Borgia attempted to reach the highest level of power in Renaissance Italy. He reveals himself as a complex blend of guile and need.

Historical Accuracy: The novel is effective in capturing the struggle for dominance in 15th-century Italy. The central character, however, lacks depth, which undermines believability.

JOHN LLOYD BALDERSTON
(1889-1954)

SYBIL BOLITHO

Born in Philadelphia, journalist, editor, playwright, and screenwriter Balderston was a correspondent for the New York *World* and a lecturer in drama at the University of Southern California. He also wrote *A Goddess to a God: An Historical Reconstruction* and *Julius Caesar*.

`278` *A Goddess to a God*

Date of Publication: 1948
Subject(s): Roman Empire
Historical character(s): Cleopatra, Ruler (Queen of Egypt); Julius Caesar, Military Personnel (Roman general), Political Figure
Time Period(s): 1st century B.C.
Locale(s): Egypt; Rome, Roman Empire

Summary: The novel takes the form of a series of letters exchanged between Cleopatra and Julius Caesar, from his invasion of Egypt to his assassination. The novel captures the emotional side of each figure as well as some vivid details of the period and its customs.

Historical Accuracy: The novel is successful in its ability to create a believable historical atmosphere.

BATES BALDWIN
(PSEUD. OF JOHN EDWARD JENNINGS, 1906-1973)

Born in Brooklyn, Jennings was a lieutenant commander in the Navy. He worked as a freelancer, penned short stories for magazines, and wrote historical novels. Jennings writes under the pseudonyms Bates Baldwin and Joel Williams.

`279` *Tide of Empire*

Date of Publication: 1952
Subject(s): Politics
Fictional character(s): Nick Valmy, Sea Captain
Historical character(s): Jerome Bonaparte, Nobleman; Elizabeth Patterson, Spouse (of Jerome Bonaparte); Napoleon Bonaparte, Ruler (Emperor of France); Thomas Jefferson, Political Figure; James Madison, Political Figure
Time Period(s): 1800s
Locale(s): Washington, District of Columbia; Paris, France; Haiti

Summary: The relationship between America and France in the early years of the 19th century forms the background for this historical adventure tale concerning American sea captain Nick Valmy. When he contests his ship's seizure by the French, he is plunged into a series of romantic adventures that take him from Washington to Paris and Haiti, encountering several historical figures.

Historical Accuracy: The novelist's romantic-adventure bent takes a number of liberties with the historical events depicted.

LELAND DEWITT BALDWIN (1897-1981)

An American educator, librarian, editor, historian, and author, Baldwin worked as a professor and librarian at the University of Pittsburgh and as an editor for the University of Pittsburgh Press. Baldwin wrote several history books, including *Whiskey Rebellion: The Story of a Frontier Uprising*, *The Stream of American History*, and *Reframing the Constitution*.

`280` *The Delectable Country*

Date of Publication: 1939
Subject(s): Settlement of the American Frontier; Whiskey Rebellion
Fictional character(s): David Braddee, Sailor, Religious (preacher)
Time Period(s): 1790s
Locale(s): Ohio River, United States; Pittsburgh, Pennsylvania

Summary: The frontier of the Ohio and Mississippi Valleys during the 1790s is depicted in the adventures of David Braddee, who begins as a riverman and later becomes a Methodist preacher.

Historical Accuracy: The novel's romanctic plot and stock characters mar an otherwise respectable version of the historical era and the frontier life of the time.

WILLIAM BALDWIN

`281` *The Hard to Catch Mercy*

Date of Publication: 1993
Subject(s): Rural Life—U.S.
Fictional character(s): Colonel Allson, Veteran; Captain Allson, Sea Captain; Anna Maum, Slave (former), Servant
Time Period(s): 1910s (1916)
Locale(s): South Carolina

Summary: This wild and comic tale is set in the Carolina Low Country in 1916, the fateful year that two milk cows, Ruth and Naomi, wander off and get stuck in the mud. An entire community is revealed in the blending of old Confederate nobility with southern white-trash, all expecting high times to come with the electrification of the region.

Historical Accuracy: Weirdly comic, the novel successfully creates a believable regional world, familiar yet strange.

BEVERLY BALIN

`282` *King in Hell: A Novel of Bothwell and Mary, Queen of Scots*

Date of Publication: 1971
Subject(s): Royalty—Scotland
Historical character(s): James Hepburn, Nobleman (Earl of Bothwell); Mary, Queen of Scots, Ruler (Queen of Scotland)
Time Period(s): 16th century
Locale(s): Scotland

Summary: The novel dramatizes the story of James Hepburn, Earl of Bothwell, the third husband of Mary, Queen of Scots.

The novel offers a number of controversial interpretations of their relationship and the events which clouded it, making the assertion that Bothwell was innocent of the murder of Mary's second husband, Lord Darnley. The author also accepts the dubious Casket letters that suggested Bothwell and Mary were having an affair before Darnley's murder.

Historical Accuracy: The novel's interpretations are contrary to historical consensus on Bothwell's role in Darnley's murder.

ZACHARY BALL
(PSEUD. OF FRANKIE-LEE JANAS, 1908-)

Born in Appleton City, Missouri, Janas attended the University of Texas and pursued work in publishing, amateur dramatics, and radio. She has published under several pseudonyms, including Lisa Bremer, Francesca Gree, and Saliee O'Brien.

`283` *Pull Down to New Orleans*

Date of Publication: 1946
Subject(s): Riverboats; Antebellum South
Fictional character(s): Zadok Grainger, Sea Captain (riverboat)
Time Period(s): 1800s (1802)
Locale(s): Mississippi River; Ohio River, United States

Summary: The passengers of a riverboat captained by Zadok Grainger undertake the perilous journey to New Orleans. The Spanish have closed the river to American commerce, and one of the passengers holds the key to breaking the Spanish blockade.

Historical Accuracy: Romance predominates in this adventure tale, with some authentic period elements.

TODHUNTER BALLARD (1903-1980)

The author of more than fifty novels, mostly Westerns, Ballard was born in Cleveland and attended Wilmington College. Balllard's novel *Gold in California!* won the Spur Award as the best historical novel of 1966. Ballard also wrote a number of television scripts.

`284` *The Californian*

Date of Publication: 1971
Subject(s): Gold Rush—California; Stagecoaches
Fictional character(s): Mitchell Randolph, Businessman
Time Period(s): 19th century
Locale(s): California

Summary: Mitchell Randolph attempts to make his fortune by creating an express stagecoach service. The novel follows his success and his competition with the mighty Wells Fargo company.

Historical Accuracy: The story is fictional, but does create an authentic period atmosphere.

L. CHRISTIAN BALLING

`285` *Champion*

Date of Publication: 1988
Subject(s): Middle Ages; Crusades; Royalty—England
Historical character(s): William Marshal, Knight, Nobleman (Earl of Pembroke); Isabelle de Claire, Noblewoman, Heiress; Richard I, Ruler (King of England); John, Royalty (prince); Eleanor of Aquitaine, Royalty; Henry II, Ruler (King of England)
Time Period(s): 12th century (1153-1189)
Locale(s): England; Palestine; France

Summary: William Marshal, knighthood's greatest champion, is shown in the story of his career as a Knight Templar during the Crusades and his love for Isabelle de Claire. William, though great in battle and in the lists, is without land or wealth. He finds himself caught up in the dynastic struggle between Richard Lionhearted and Prince John. Marshal's code of chivalry is strained by the selfish manipulations of his liege lords.

Historical Accuracy: The novel is a full and authentic rendering of the politics and customs of the times, with Marshal emerging as a kind of chivalric anachronism in a new brutal age.

W.A. BALLINGER
(PSEUD. OF WILFRED MCNEILLY, 1921-)

Born in Scotland, Ballinger has been a journalist in Northern Ireland, a writer, and a cameraman for the BBC.

`286` *The Men That God Made Mad: A Novel about Ireland's Easter Rising*

Date of Publication: 1966
Subject(s): Independence—Ireland; World War I; Easter Rising
Fictional character(s): Declan O'Donovan, Revolutionary; Margaret Kengston, Gentlewoman; Peadar Casey, Revolutionary
Historical character(s): James Connolly, Revolutionary
Time Period(s): 1910s (1916)
Locale(s): Dublin, Ireland

Summary: This is an account of the Irish Easter Rising of 1916 in which a small band of Irish rebels took on the might of the British army and proclaimed an Irish Republic. Their act was doomed to fail, but their martyrdom inspired the nation, turning the bumbled rebellion into the stuff of myth and legend. The same process is at work here as Declan O'Donovan proves himself in the struggle.

Historical Accuracy: The events are fictional but do capture the atmosphere of the period.

V.J. BANIS (1937-)

American novelist Banis also writes suspense fiction under the name of Jon Alexander.

287   *The Earth and All It Holds*

Date of Publication: 1980
Subject(s): Family Saga; Business Building; World War I
Fictional character(s): Philip De Brussac, Heir—Dispossessed, Businessman; Jolene Perreira, Heroine; Sloan Morrow, Gambler
Time Period(s): 19th century; 20th century (1892-1916)
Locale(s): San Francisco, California; Los Angeles, California; France

Summary: This sequel to *This Splendid Earth* chronicles two new generations of the De Brussac family at the turn of the century. Philip, the dispossessed heir of the wine-making dynasty, falls in love with Jolene Perreira. Betrayal separates them in a California beset by labor unrest and the onset of World War I.

Historical Accuracy: The California of the period is convincingly depicted.

288   *San Antone*

Date of Publication: 1985
Subject(s): Family Saga; American West; Business Building
Fictional character(s): Joanna Harte, Rancher; Lewis Harte, Rancher; Webb Price, Military Personnel
Time Period(s): 19th century; 20th century (1850s-1900s)
Locale(s): San Antonio, Texas

Summary: Joanna Harte and her husband leave genteel plantation life in South Carolina for the adventure and challenge of Texas. Joanna is attracted to the state's independence and opportunity, and their ranch becomes one of the most successful in the state. Meanwhile they watch San Antonio change from a frontier town to a dynamic city.

Historical Accuracy: The story dominates the historical details, but the atmosphere of early Texas statehood is dramatically reproduced.

289   *This Splendid Earth*

Date of Publication: 1978
Subject(s): Family Saga; Business Building
Fictional character(s): Anne De Brussac, Gentlewoman; Claude De Brussac, Businessman; Philip De Brussac, Heir—Dispossessed
Time Period(s): 19th century (1830s-1860s)
Locale(s): France; California

Summary: The novel chronicles the success of the wine-making De Brussac family. The second generation must flee from France to America with the vines to start over in the new world.

Historical Accuracy: This family saga offers some clear details about the wine industry.

LYNNE REID BANKS (1929-)

An English author born in London, Banks attended the Royal Academy of Dramatic Art and was an actress in repertory companies from 1949-1959. She then became a freelance journalist and television writer. Her children's book, *The Indian in the Cupboard*, is regarded as a classic.

Besides her children's books, Banks is the author of plays and novels, Including *The L-Shaped Room*.

290   *Dark Quartet: The Story of the Brontes*

Date of Publication: 1976
Subject(s): Literary Life; Biography, Fictionalized; Victorian Period
Historical character(s): Charlotte Bronte, Writer (novelist); Emily Bronte, Writer (novelist and poet); Anne Bronte, Writer (novelist); Branwell Bronte, Artist (painter); Patrick Bronte, Religious (clergyman)
Time Period(s): 19th century (1821-1849)
Locale(s): Haworth, England (in Yorkshire); Brussels, Belgium

Summary: This biographical novel chronicles the short and tragic lives of the Brontes—Charlotte, Emily, Anne, and Branwell—who live with their eccentric clergyman father in Yorkshire. The children endure their father's harsh discipline by constructing endless tales of adventure and wish fulfillment, the basis for Charlotte and Emily's later novels. Three-fourths of the quartet die within a year of the staggering success of Charlotte's *Jane Eyre*.

Historical Accuracy: The novel stays close to the sources for the most part but does engage in some speculations when the sources fail.

291   *Path to the Silent Country*

Date of Publication: 1977
Subject(s): Literary Life; Biography, Fictionalized; Victorian Period
Historical character(s): Charlotte Bronte, Writer (novelist); Harriet Martineau, Writer, Abolitionist; William Makepeace Thackeray, Writer (novelist); Patrick Bronte, Religious (clergyman); Elizabeth Gaskell, Writer (novelist)
Time Period(s): 1840s; 1850s (1849-1855)
Locale(s): Haworth, England (in Yorkshire); London, England

Summary: The novel continues the author's biographical portrait of the Bronte family, recording Charlotte Bronte's years alone after the deaths of her sisters and brother. Enjoying the success that *Jane Eyre* brings her, Charlotte visits London and meets many of the literary lions of the age before an unexpected marriage with her father's curate. The novel ends with her untimely death at age 39.

Historical Accuracy: The fictional account is based for the most part on letters and biographical sources, though some speculation is also evident.

POLAN BANKS (1906-)

Banks' novel, *The Great Lie*, was made into a 1941 film starring Bette Davis. A 1951 film, *My Forbidden Past*, was based on Banks' novel, *Carriage Entrance*.

292   *Black Ivory*

Date of Publication: 1926
Subject(s): War of 1812; Pirates; Battle of New Orleans

Historical character(s): Jean Laffite, Pirate
Time Period(s): 1810s
Locale(s): New Orleans, Louisiana

Summary: The novel offers a story of Jean Lafitte and his career as pirate and slaverunner. The story climaxes with the defense of New Orleans against the British, as Lafitte must decide whose side to support in the conflict.

Historical Accuracy: The emphasis here is on romance, not realism, in presenting characters and events.

293   *The Gentleman From America*

Date of Publication: 1930
Subject(s): Biography, Fictionalized
Historical character(s): Benjamin Franklin, Diplomat; Temple Franklin, Bastard Son (Franklin's grandson); Cunegonde Brillon, Gentlewoman; Blanchette Caillot, Gentlewoman
Time Period(s): 18th century
Locale(s): Paris, France

Summary: This dramatization of episodes and situations from Benjamin Franklin's life while serving as ambassador to the court of France, concentrates on the romantic adventures of Franklin's illegitimate grandson, Temple. He is welcomed in fashionable society until he begins to contemplate marriage.

Historical Accuracy: The story invents very little. Franklin's speeches and statements are drawn from his letters and writings.

DON BANNISTER (1928-)

An English author, Bannister was born in Birmingham and received his Ph.D. in psychology from the University of London. He has served as the head of the psychology department of Bexley Hospital in Kent.

294   *Long Day at Shiloh*

Date of Publication: 1981
Subject(s): Civil War—U.S.; Battle of Shiloh; Military Life
Historical character(s): Ulysses S. Grant, Military Personnel (Union commander); William Tecumseh Sherman, Military Personnel (general)
Time Period(s): 1860s (1862)
Locale(s): Pittsburg Landing, Tennessee (Shiloh battlefield)

Summary: On April 6, 1862, just before dawn, Confederate forces attack Grant's Union army encamped at Pittsburgh Landing on the Tennessee River. This novel tells the story of the furious and bloody first day of the Battle of Shiloh from the perspective of dozens of the combatants.

Historical Accuracy: The authenticity of the eyewitness accounts is masterful. Bannister convinces the reader that the events must have transpired as narrated.

ANNA BANTI
(PSEUD. OF LUCIA LOPRESTI, 1895-1978)

295   *Artemesia*

Date of Publication: 1947

Subject(s): Artistic Life; World War II; Women's Rights
Historical character(s): Artemisia Gentileschi, Artist (painter)
Time Period(s): 17th century; 1940s (1944)
Locale(s): Rome, Italy; Naples, Italy; Florence, Italy

Summary: The novel tells the experiences of Artemisia Gentileschi, an esteemed painter whose devotion to her craft, despite rejection and persecution, becomes emblematic of women's pursuit of creative careers. The novel shuttles between Artemisia's life in the 17th century and the experiences of the author during World War II.

Historical Accuracy: The novel effectively captures life in the 17th century combined with modern psychological inquiry.

JOHN BANVILLE (1945-)

An Irish writer, Banville was an editor for the *Irish Press* and the *Irish Times*. With the publication of his first novel, *Long Lankin*, he was dubbed a ray of hope for the future of fiction. His poetic and experimental style is often joined with meticulous historical documentation. His books have drawn comparisons with the works of Samuel Beckett and James Joyce.

296   *Doctor Copernicus*

Date of Publication: 1976
Subject(s): Science; Biography, Fictionalized
Historical character(s): Nicolaus Copernicus, Scientist (astronomer)
Time Period(s): 15th century; 16th century (1473-1543)
Locale(s): Germany (Prussia); Italy

Summary: By demonstrating that the Earth is not the center of the universe, Copernicus changed forever the medieval conception of the cosmos with man at its center and introduced the modern world view of relativity and uncertainty. This fictional version of his life explores the terrible cost of his terrifying discovery in personal terms.

Historical Accuracy: The medieval world view that Copernicus' discovery threatened is sharply and meticulously detailed.

297   *Kepler: A Novel*

Date of Publication: 1981
Subject(s): Science; Biography, Fictionalized
Historical character(s): Johannes Kepler, Scientist (mathematician/astronomer); Tycho Brahe, Scientist (astronomer)
Time Period(s): 17th century
Locale(s): Germany; Prague, Czechoslovakia

Summary: In these scenes from the life of Kepler, who laid the scientific foundation for the modern view of the universe, an intellectual hero emerges. Kepler struggles to reduce the muddle and chaos of the late medieval world to modern order. He stands as an outsider whose passion for the truth is heroic.

Historical Accuracy: Banville makes the scientific issues and the thought of the era come into dramatic and authentic focus.

ELSIE BARBER (1914-)

Born in Massachusetts, Barber is the author of *The Wall Between*, *The Trembling Years*, *Hunt for Heaven*, and *Jenny Angel*.

298 *Hunt for Heaven*

Date of Publication: 1950
Subject(s): Labor Movement; Religious Life
Fictional character(s): John Bliss, Religious (minister)
Time Period(s): 1880s; 1890s
Locale(s): Chicago, Illinois; Pennsylvania

Summary: The novel describes the efforts of a Chicago minister, John Bliss, to lead a group of believers out of labor-torn Chicago to establish an ideal community on a Pennsylvania farm. The novel depicts the community's initial success but eventual failure to live up to its ideals.

Historical Accuracy: The historical background of the labor unrest in Chicago is factual and believable.

PHYLLIS BARBER (1943-)

Born in Nevada, Barber attended Brigham Young University and earned a M.F.A. from Vermont College. She is a professional pianist and journalist. The two major influences on her writing have been the Nevada desert in which she grew up and the Mormon religion.

299 *And the Desert Shall Bloom*

Date of Publication: 1991
Subject(s): Depression Era; Religious Life
Fictional character(s): Esther Jenson, Spouse; Alfred Jenson, Worker (construction)
Time Period(s): 1930s (1930-1935)
Locale(s): Hoover Dam, Nevada

Summary: The Jenson family is driven by the Depression to find work on the monumental Hoover Dam Project in Nevada. Their personal struggles are juxtaposed with the day-to-day details of the construction project and the unforgiving western landscape. The dam and the effort to build it become a metaphor for human achievement and possibility.

Historical Accuracy: The details of the Hoover Dam Project are faithfully presented.

JOHN BARCHILON

300 *The Crown Prince*

Date of Publication: 1984
Subject(s): Musical Life; Biography, Fictionalized; World War I
Historical character(s): Paul Wittgenstein, Musician (concert pianist); Maurice Ravel, Composer
Time Period(s): 19th century; 20th century (1890s-1920s)
Locale(s): Vienna, Austria; Paris, France; Berlin, Germany

Summary: This is the story of concert pianist Paul Wittgenstein whose spectacular musical career is tragically halted in the Great War by a devastating injury. He battles despair and attemps to regain his artistry in a postwar Germany of plagues, runaway inflation, and rising Nazism. The novel also depicts Wittgenstein's friendship with Maurice Ravel, despite their having been on opposite sides in the war.

Historical Accuracy: The author's intent here is to write a novel, not an authoritative biography.

TESSA BARCLAY
(PSEUD. OF JEAN BOWDEN, 1928-)

Bowden is an English writer who has worked as a book and magazine editor. She is the author of several multi-volume family sagas, each centering around a particular industry.

301 *The Wine Widow*

Date of Publication: 1984
Subject(s): Family Saga; Business Building; Franco-Prussian War
Fictional character(s): Nicole Berthois, Farmer (peasant), Spouse (of Philippe); Philippe de Tramont, Nobleman, Writer
Time Period(s): 19th century (1850s-1870s)
Locale(s): France

Summary: A peasant girl, Nicole Berthois, weds Philippe de Tramont. His early and tragic death leaves her in charge of the family winery, and she struggles to secure the reputation of the family business by producing the greatest champagne ever made. Her business and family fortune are affected by the Franco-Prussian War.

Historical Accuracy: The scant historical details here are only a generalized background to the domestic story.

JAMES BARKE (1905-1958)

Barke was a Scottish writer, best known for his multi-volume fictional biography of Robert Burns.

302 *Crest of the Broken Wave*

Date of Publication: 1953
Subject(s): Biography, Fictionalized; Literary Life
Historical character(s): Robert Burns, Writer (poet)
Time Period(s): 1780s; 1790s
Locale(s): Scotland

Summary: This volume of the author's fictional life of Scottish poet Robert Burns the years of Burns' retirement to a farm at Ellisland. Burns struggles to turn a profit from the land with his wife and an ever-growing family.

Historical Accuracy: Despite the clear partisanship of the author for his subject, the evidence of the novel's solid research is apparent. The author claims to have verified all facts and taken no liberties with them.

303 *Song in the Green Thorn Tree*

Date of Publication: 1947
Subject(s): Biography, Fictionalized; Literary Life
Historical character(s): Robert Burns, Writer (poet)
Time Period(s): 1780s
Locale(s): Scotland

Summary: The second in a series of five novels on the life of Scottish poet Robert Burns describes his years as a farmer before his first great literary success. Burns struggles to make a living on the Mossgiel farm, and his conflict with the church is described. The volume ends with the death of his fiancee, Mary Campbell, and Burns' abandoning his plans to emigrate to Jamaica.

Historical Accuracy: The novel provides a faithful rendering of the facts and events of Burns' life, though Burns is too often a target of the author's unobjective affection.

304 *Well of the Silent Harp*
Date of Publication: 1954
Subject(s): Biography, Fictionalized; Literary Life
Historical character(s): Robert Burns, Writer (poet)
Time Period(s): 1790s
Locale(s): Scotland

Summary: The fifth and final volume of the author's series chronicling the life of Scottish poet Robert Burns concludes the story of Burns, his family, and friends. The novel provides a good deal of source material for Burns' poetry as well as a thorough depiction of his genius.

Historical Accuracy: The novel's facts are faithful to history. The interpretation occasionally betrays a clear partisanship.

305 *The Wind That Shakes the Barley*
Date of Publication: 1947
Subject(s): Literary Life; Biography, Fictionalized
Historical character(s): Robert Burns, Writer; William Burns, Farmer
Time Period(s): 18th century (1750s-1784)
Locale(s): Scotland

Summary: The first in a series of novels based on the life of poet Robert Burns describes his early years. The novel covers the period of Burns' childhood and youth up to the death of his farmer father, William. The novel captures the hardships of Burns' life and the origin of his poetic genius.

Historical Accuracy: The novel shows evidence of the author's familiarity with Burns' poetry and letters, as well as sources about Burns' life and conditions in 18th-century Scotland.

306 *Wonder of All the Gay World*
Date of Publication: 1949
Subject(s): Literary Life; Georgian Period; Biography, Fictionalized
Historical character(s): Robert Burns, Writer (poet); Jean Armour, Spouse (of Burns)
Time Period(s): 1780s (1786-1788)
Locale(s): Edinburgh, Scotland

Summary: The third volume in a five-part fictional biography of Scottish poet Robert Burns covers Burns' Edinburgh years and the difficulties of his courtship of Jean Armour that finally ends in their marriage. Burns' romantic life predominates over his poetry.

Historical Accuracy: The novel offers a convincing re-creation of Edinburgh life in the 1780s and the poet's background. The essential facts are observed.

PAT BARKER (1943-)
Baker is a British novelist who has been a teacher of history and politics. Her novels include *Union Street*, which was filmed as *Stanley and Iris*, *Blow Your House Down*, *The Century's Daughter*, and *The Man Who Wasn't There*.

307 *The Eye in the Door*
Date of Publication: 1993
Subject(s): World War I; Psychiatry; Medical Profession
Fictional character(s): Billy Prior, Military Personnel; Charles Manning, Military Personnel, Homosexual
Historical character(s): Siegfried Sassoon, Military Personnel, Writer; W.H.R. Rivers, Psychologist; Robert Ross, Writer, Homosexual
Time Period(s): 1910s (1918)
Locale(s): London, England; Salsford, England

Summary: In this sequel to Barker's *Regeneration*, many of the same characters return including poet Sassoon and a veteran, Prior, who suffers from fugue states of memory loss. Barker sees this as symptomatic of a wider social illness that requires individuals to disassociate themselves from identities considered disturbing (like violence) or deviant (like homosexualty).

Historical Accuracy: All the events of the novel are rooted in actuality, as Baker's appendix shows. The novel is a brilliant psychological study in the guise of historical fiction.

308 *The Ghost Road*
Date of Publication: 1995
Subject(s): World War I; Psychiatry; Medical Profession
Fictional character(s): Billy Prior, Military Personnel (lieutenant)
Historical character(s): W.H.R. Rivers, Doctor (psychologist); Wilfred Owen, Military Personnel (British officer), Writer (poet)
Time Period(s): 1910s (1918)
Locale(s): London, England; France

Summary: This title concludes Barker's trilogy of novels on the psychological costs of World War I. It is 1918, and Billy Prior considers himself cured of shellshock. He is anxious to join his friend and fellow former patient Wilfred Owen back at the front as the war climaxes. Meanwhile, Dr. Rivers continues to face the moral dilemma of certifying his patients as sufficiently cured to resume the madness of the war.

Historical Accuracy: The novel blends the fictional with the actual figures of Rivers and Owen. Barker captures the feeling and the background of the period with skill.

309 *Regeneration*
Date of Publication: 1991
Subject(s): World War I; Psychiatry; Medical Profession
Fictional character(s): Billy Prior, Military Personnel

Historical character(s): W.H.R. Rivers, Psychologist; Siegfried Sassoon, Writer, Military Personnel; Robert Graves, Writer, Military Personnel
Time Period(s): 1910s (1917)
Locale(s): Edinburgh, Scotland

Summary: Barker explores the psychological cost of combat using an actual event from the First World War. The English poet and officer Siegfried Sassoon has decided that the war is unjust. Instead of being court-martialed, he is sent to an army hospital for treatment for shellshock by the psychologist W.H.R. Rivers who restores his willingness to return to the front. The historical situation becomes an occasion for Barker to explore the meaning of the war and how its casualties can be treated.

Historical Accuracy: The novel is a brilliant joining of a modern sensibility to an historical period with illumination of both.

SHIRLEY BARKER (1911-1965)

Barker is an American writer who was born in New Hampshire. She attended the University of New Hampshire and Radcliffe College. She worked for a number of years as a librarian at the New York Public Library in the American history department.

310 *Corner the Moon*

Date of Publication: 1961
Subject(s): Napoleonic Wars; Witchcraft and Sorcery
Fictional character(s): Blaise Everden, Military Personnel; Mary Everden, Spouse; Anne Campion, Gentlewoman
Time Period(s): 1800s (1804)
Locale(s): Kent, England

Summary: Set in the Kentish countryside in 1804 when invasion by Napoleon seems imminent, the novel concerns Blaise Everden and his new wife, Mary. Blaise's first love is the strange Anne Campion who is suspected of being a witch. Mary, a Londoner, must learn the strange ways of the country folk while all await the arrival of the French invaders.

Historical Accuracy: The novel is perceptive in rendering the customs of the times and the historical moment of the threatened French invasion.

311 *Fire and the Hammer*

Date of Publication: 1953
Subject(s): American Revolution; Quakers; American Colonies
Fictional character(s): Lass Marvayne, Young Woman; Mahlon Dorn, Outlaw, Religious (Quaker)
Time Period(s): 1770s
Locale(s): Bucks County, Pennsylvania; Trenton, New Jersey; Philadelphia, Pennsylvania

Summary: This story of the American Revolution describes an interesting aspect of the conflict: the adventures of a band of Quaker outlaws who wage a private war against both the British and the authority of the Continental Congress. The story centers on Mahlon Dorn, the band's leader, and the woman who loves him, Lass Marvayne, the daughter of a blockade runner.

Historical Accuracy: The historical background for the novel's fictional story is accurate and faithful to both the time and its events.

312 *The Last Gentleman*

Date of Publication: 1960
Subject(s): American Revolution; American Colonies; Politics
Historical character(s): Thomas Gage, Military Personnel (British general), Political Figure (colonial governor); John Wentworth, Political Figure (colonial governor), Loyalist
Time Period(s): 1770s (1774-1775)
Locale(s): Portsmouth, New Hampshire, American Colonies

Summary: This novel offers a rare sympathetic portrait of a Loyalist during the American Revolution. John Wentworth is the Portsmouth-born colonial governor of New Hampshire. His loyalties are divided between his duty to the king and to his native country. He stands firmly with the former, sending aid to General Gage in Boston, despite overwhelming opposition from his countrymen.

Historical Accuracy: The novel's depiction of the period and the locale is authentic, and Wentworth withstands the heroic elevation he is given.

313 *Liza Bowe*

Date of Publication: 1956
Subject(s): Elizabethan Period; Theatrical Life
Fictional character(s): Liza Bowe, Saloon Hostess (barmaid); Dick Buckerel, Worker (boatman); Philip Fineaux, Scholar
Historical character(s): Christopher Marlowe, Writer (poet and playwright); Thomas Nash, Writer (playwright); William Shakespeare, Writer (poet and playwright); Thomas Kyd, Writer (playwright)
Time Period(s): 16th century (1580s)
Locale(s): Cambridge, England; London, England

Summary: Literary London during the Elizabethan period is the subject of this novel that centers on a young barmaid at the famous Mermaid Tavern who becomes the friend of virtually all the important literary figures of the time. Liza is in love with Philip Frineau, a devotee of the Faust legend who gives Christopher Marlowe some good ideas for his play, and a young Thames boatman.

Historical Accuracy: More colorful than accurate, the novel offers a genuine atmosphere but hardly a reliable version of events.

314 *Peace, My Daughters*

Date of Publication: 1949
Subject(s): American Colonies; Witchcraft and Sorcery
Fictional character(s): Remember Winster, Spouse (of Jonathan); Jonathan Winster, Farmer; John Horne, Artisan (shoemaker)
Historical character(s): Tituba, Witch, Slave; Cotton Mather, Religious (clergyman)
Time Period(s): 17th century (1691-1697)
Locale(s): Salem, Massachusetts, American Colonies

Summary: Evil and deviltry seem to be infecting the community of Salem in the 1690s. Remember Winster thinks that she knows the source of the trouble—the devil incarnate impersonating a shoemaker, John Horne. Horne desires Remember, who tries to stand firm but wavers. She is finally saved when on the brink of capitulation.

Historical Accuracy: Barker's romantic and supernatural tale is developed in the interstices of history with actual personages forming an authentic historical background.

315   *Rivers Parting*

Date of Publication: 1950
Subject(s): Settlement of the American Frontier; American Colonies; Fires
Fictional character(s): John Scarlock, Settler; Joan Scarlock, Settler; Will Scarlock, Settler; Doll Trasper, Entertainer (ballad singer); Nan Knight, Spinster
Time Period(s): 17th century (1628-1660s)
Locale(s): Nottingham, England; Portsmouth, New Hampshire, American Colonies; London, England

Summary: The novel concerns the settlement of New Hampshire and the colonists' struggle with Massachusetts for control of the colony. John and Joan Scarlock journey from Nottingham to the American wilderness. Their son, Will, returns to London where he witnesses the plague and the Great Fire of London. Returning to America, he is torn between his affections for the spinster, Nan, and a London ballad singer, Doll.

Historical Accuracy: The novel is packed with period details, at odds at times with the novel's rather romanticized and hyper-inflated style.

316   *The Road to Bunker Hill*

Date of Publication: 1962
Subject(s): American Revolution; Battle of Bunker Hill; American Colonies
Fictional character(s): Sally Rose Townsend, Teenager; Kitty Greenleaf, Teenager
Time Period(s): 1770s
Locale(s): Boston, Massachusetts, American Colonies; Newburyport, Massachusetts, American Colonies

Summary: The novel dramatizes the events leading up to the Battle of Bunker Hill as seen from the perspective of two young girls, Sally Rose Townsend and Kitty Greenleaf. It features a vivid portrait of everyday life in the first few weeks of the American Revolution.

Historical Accuracy: The historical background is convincingly displayed.

317   *Strange Wives*

Date of Publication: 1963
Subject(s): American Revolution; Jews
Fictional character(s): Ruben Bravo, Trader; Jenny Tupper, Farmer; Riva Gold, Gentlewoman; Stephen Pryde, Gentleman

Historical character(s): Ezra Stiles, Scholar, Professor; George Washington, Military Personnel (American commander)
Time Period(s): 1760s; 1770s
Locale(s): Newport, Rhode Island, American Colonies

Summary: This novel focusing on the rarely depicted Jewish community in colonial America portrays Ruben Bravo and Riva Gold's marriages to Gentiles Jenny Tupper and Stephen Pryde respectively. Persecution and cultural differences are dramatized, and the action culminates with George Washington's promise of freedom of religion to the Jews and his invitation to them to join the Revolution.

Historical Accuracy: The colonial scenes of the Jewish community are realistically depicted.

318   *Swear by Apollo*

Date of Publication: 1958
Subject(s): Medical Profession; Witchcraft and Sorcery; Georgian Period
Fictional character(s): Randall Woodbury, Doctor, Widow(er); Comyn Rhinn, Laird; Andra Deveron, Sorceress; Margery Rhinn, Gentlewoman; Ellen Deveron, Young Woman
Time Period(s): 1770s (1773)
Locale(s): Hebrides, Scotland; Edinburgh, Scotland

Summary: Randall Woodbury, a young recently widowed physician, journeys to Scotland to further his medical studies. There, he agrees to an offer made by the Laird of the Isle of Rona in the Hebrides and serves as the island's doctor. He is attracted to the laird's daughter, Margery, but finds himself the object of the schemes of Ellen Deverton, daughter of the island's seer, Andra. The novel's climax represents a clash between science and magic.

Historical Accuracy: The atmosphere of a brooding, uncanny Scottish landscape of the period is well-developed and convincing.

319   *Tomorrow the New Moon*

Date of Publication: 1955
Subject(s): American Colonies; Puritans; Religious Conflict
Fictional character(s): Kevin Quill, Settler; Samuel Osborn, Teacher
Time Period(s): 1710s
Locale(s): Cape Cod, Massachusetts, American Colonies; Martha's Vineyard, Massachusetts, American Colonies

Summary: Life in the Massachusetts Bay Colony in the early years of the 18th century is depicted as newcomers from England attempt to adjust to the customs and values of the ''Old Comers.'' The novel offers a varied picture of colonial values as well as the tension of religious conflict in the forging of American identity.

Historical Accuracy: The novel is a colorful and believable recreation of the period and the region.

ROBERT BARNARD (1936-)

An English writer born in Essex and a graduate of Oxford, Barnard has been a lecturer of English in Australia and

Norway, a mystery writer, and a literary critic. He has been called one of the deftest stylists in the mystery field, and his books have drawn praise for his wit, social satire, and well-drawn characters.

`320` *The Skeleton in the Grass*

Date of Publication: 1988
Subject(s): Mystery; Civil War—Spain
Fictional character(s): Sarah Lausley, Governess; Dennis Hallam, Journalist, Pacifist
Time Period(s): 1930s (1936)
Locale(s): Oxfordshire, England

Summary: While the Spanish Civil War rages and Hitler marches his troops into the Rhineland, Sarah Lausley serves as the governess for the Hallams, a wealthy family who are pacificists. A Fascist in the neighborhood stirs up animosity toward Dennis Hallam and his family until events lead to murder.

Historical Accuracy: This is an ingenious story set in a fully-realized period setting.

JOANNA BARNES (1934-)

Born in Boston, Barnes attended Smith College. Since 1956 she has been a popular actress in movies and television series.

`321` *Pastora*

Date of Publication: 1980
Subject(s): American West; Civil War—U.S.
Fictional character(s): Lucy Cade, Orphan, Businesswoman
Time Period(s): 19th century (1840s-1890s)
Locale(s): San Francisco, California

Summary: This is the story of Lucy Cade, an orphan at fifteen and a survivor of the trek west from Missouri to California. She settles in San Francisco during the Gold Rush. She succeeds as a rancher, businesswoman, and socialite. California is shown transforming from a wilderness to a center of business and culture.

Historical Accuracy: The historical details of the period form a convincing backdrop for this saga.

MARGARET CAMPBELL BARNES
(1891-1962)

An English author, Barnes began her career writing short stories and articles for women's magazines and newspapers. She lived for most of her life on the Isle of Wight.

`322` *Brief Gaudy Hour*

Date of Publication: 1949
Subject(s): Tudor Period; Royalty—England
Historical character(s): Anne Boleyn, Royalty (second wife of Henry VIII); Henry VIII, Ruler (King of England); Mary Tudor, Royalty (later Mary I); Sir Thomas Wyatt, Writer (poet), Gentleman; Thomas Cranmer, Religious (Archbishop of Canterbury)

Time Period(s): 16th century
Locale(s): England; France

Summary: The story of Anne Boleyn from her girlhood to her execution is the novel's subject. Throughout Anne's courtship and short married life with Henry VIII until the moment of her death, Anne is shown as a compelling human figure, a victim in a deadly political world.

Historical Accuracy: The historical figures and court scenes are convincingly described.

`323` *Isabel the Fair*

Date of Publication: 1957
Subject(s): Middle Ages; Royalty—England
Historical character(s): Edward II, Ruler (King of England); Isabel of France, Royalty; Roger de Mortimer, Nobleman; Piers Gaveston, Gentleman
Time Period(s): 14th century
Locale(s): London, England

Summary: French princess Isabel the Fair marries Edward II of England, who is a weak, ineffectual leader and an indifferent husband. Isabel first turns for assistance to Piers Gaveston, who is murdered, and then to the dashing Roger de Mortimer, a Welsh border lord.

Historical Accuracy: The sense of the period is expertly rendered.

`324` *The King's Bed*

Date of Publication: 1961
Subject(s): War of the Roses; Royalty—England
Fictional character(s): Tansy Marsh, Young Woman; Robert Marsh, Innkeeper
Historical character(s): Richard III, Ruler (King of England)
Time Period(s): 15th century (1485)
Locale(s): Leicester, England

Summary: Tansy Marsh is thrust onto the center stage of history when Richard III spends the night on the eve of the Battle of Bosworth Field at her father's inn. The novel's title refers to Richard's massive travelling bed. Tansy is given the dangerous task of delivering the king's final message.

Historical Accuracy: The novel is framed by authentic events, with legend and fiction filling in the details.

`325` *King's Fool*

Date of Publication: 1959
Subject(s): Tudor Period; Royalty—England
Historical character(s): Will Somers, Entertainer (court jester); Henry VIII, Ruler (King of England); Katherine of Aragon, Royalty (first wife of Henry VIII); Anne Boleyn, Royalty (second wife of Henry VIII); Jane Seymour, Royalty (third wife of Henry VIII); Anne of Cleves, Royalty (fourth wife of Henry VIII); Katherine Howard, Royalty (fifth wife of Henry VIII); Katherine Parr, Royalty (sixth wife of Henry VIII)
Time Period(s): 16th century
Locale(s): England

Summary: The novel offers a perspective on Henry VIII, his court, and his wives, seen through the eyes of his jester, Will Somers. Somer's history is chronicled from his Shropshire country background to his arrival in the court. Will brings wit and impudence into his description of the royal world of the Tudor dynasty.

Historical Accuracy: The perspective is original and unique, convincing in its historical details.

MARGARET CAMPBELL BARNES
(1891-1962)

HEBE ELSNA
(PSEUD. OF DOROTHY P. ANSLE)

An English author, Barnes began her career writing short stories and articles for women's magazines and newspapers. She lived for most of her life on the Isle of Wight.

326 *Lady on the Coin*

Date of Publication: 1963
Subject(s): Restoration Period; Royalty—England
Fictional character(s): Francis Stuart, Gentlewoman
Historical character(s): Charles II, Ruler (King of England); Henrietta-Maria, Royalty; Barbara Villiers, Gentlewoman, Lover (Charles II's mistress)
Time Period(s): 17th century (1660s)
Locale(s): Paris, France; London, England

Summary: Francis Stuart is a distant cousin of Charles II, the banished King of England. After Charles' restoration, Francis becomes a maid-of-honor and is swept up in the intrigue of Charles' court. She remains the king's favorite and his choice for the model of Britannia on the coins of the realm.

Historical Accuracy: The novel is filled with believable court politics and gossip.

MARGARET CAMPBELL BARNES
(1891-1962)

An English author, Barnes began her career writing short stories and articles for women's magazines and newspapers. She lived for most of her life on the Isle of Wight.

327 *Mary of Carisbrooke*

Date of Publication: 1956
Subject(s): Civil War—England; Royalty—England
Fictional character(s): Richard Osborne, Military Personnel; Libby, Servant
Historical character(s): Charles I, Ruler (King of England); Charles II, Ruler (King of England); Mary Floyd, Servant (laundress)
Time Period(s): 1640s
Locale(s): Wight, England; Netherlands

Summary: The story concerns the captivity of Charles I in Carisbrooke Castle on the Isle of Wight during the months preceding his trial and execution. He is loyally served by the laundress Mary Floyd. By smuggling his secret correspon-

dence in and out of the castle, she becomes caught up in the murderous intrigue between the loyalists and Parliament.

Historical Accuracy: The services rendered by Mary Floyd to Charles are authentic; her subsequent activities and love affair are imaginary.

328 *My Lady of Cleves*

Date of Publication: 1946
Subject(s): Tudor Period; Royalty—England; Artistic Life
Historical character(s): Henry VIII, Ruler (King of England); Anne of Cleves, Royalty (fourth wife of Henry VIII); Hans Holbein the Younger, Artist
Time Period(s): 16th century
Locale(s): London, England; Germany; Calais, France

Summary: The brief and disastrous fourth marriage of Henry VIII to Anne of Cleves is described in this novel. The brief courtship of Henry and Anne is facilitated by a flattering portrait by Holbein that does not match reality as Henry quickly discovers when he actually meets Anne. Anne nobly accepts the king's displeasure.

Historical Accuracy: Barnes suggests an infatuation between Anne and Holbein as one of the reasons for the tragic misperception of the king, which seems fanciful.

329 *The Tudor Rose*

Date of Publication: 1953
Subject(s): War of the Roses; Royalty—England; Tudor Period
Historical character(s): Elizabeth of York, Royalty; Henry VII, Ruler (King of England); Henry Tudor, Royalty (later Henry VIII); Perkin Warbeck, Imposter (claimant to the throne)
Time Period(s): 15th century
Locale(s): England

Summary: The novel offers the story of Elizabeth of York, daughter of a king, wife of a king, and mother of Henry VIII. At the climax of the War of the Roses, Elizabeth agrees to a political marriage with Henry VII, and the Tudor dynasty begins. She battles pretenders to the throne while watching her son grow to manhood and the destiny that awaits him.

Historical Accuracy: The novel provides a rare look at this important figure. Events are described with convincing details of the period.

330 *With All My Heart*

Date of Publication: 1951
Subject(s): Restoration Period; Royalty—England; Biography, Fictionalized
Historical character(s): Charles II, Ruler (King of England); Catherine of Braganza, Royalty (consort of Charles II); Nell Gwynne, Actress
Time Period(s): 17th century
Locale(s): London, England

Summary: Catherine Braganza, Charles II's cloistered queen, provides a capsule history of the Restoration, seen through a royal lens. The great events of Charles II's colorful reign—

the plague and Great Fire of London—are reported at second-hand.

Historical Accuracy: In this biographical account, the romantic and the historical are intermixed, with the former dominating.

331 *Within the Hollow Crown*

Date of Publication: 1947
Subject(s): Middle Ages; Royalty—England
Historical character(s): Richard II, Ruler; Henry Bolingbroke, Royalty (later Henry IV); Anne of Bohemia, Royalty; Geoffrey Chaucer, Writer; John of Gaunt, Royalty; Wat Tyler, Revolutionary, Worker (peasant)
Time Period(s): 14th century
Locale(s): London, England; Ireland

Summary: The tragic reign of Richard II is chronicled in this novel that paints a positive picture of Richard in contrast to the ineffectual and self-absorbed monarch of tradition. Richard is presented as sensitive, an advocate of the peasant, and an adoring husband. He is unfortunately beset by intrigue and jealousy from all sides.

Historical Accuracy: Barnes' portrait of a gallant Richard is debatable. The historical truth probably lies somewhere between this flattering depiction and Shakespeare's highly critical portrayal of the king.

PERCY RAYMOND BARNES

332 *Crum Elbow Folks*

Date of Publication: 1938
Subject(s): Quakers; Rural Life—U.S.
Fictional character(s): Huldah Sheldon, Religious (Quaker)
Time Period(s): 1830s (1838)
Locale(s): Hudson River, New York

Summary: Life in a Quaker community along the Hudson River during the 1830s is depicted in this story of Huldah Sheldon's love for a non-Quaker and the conflict this brings.

Historical Accuracy: The novel depends on an accurate depiction of Quaker life and the customs of the period.

HELEN C. BARNEY (1890-)

Born in Towson, Maryland, Barney was educated at Johns Hopkins University. She served on the Board of Directors of the Clearwater Conservatory of Music and was active in the League of Women Voters. Her novels include *Fruit in His Season*, *Green Rose of Furley*, and *The White Dove*.

333 *Fruit in His Season*

Date of Publication: 1951
Subject(s): Quakers; Settlement of the American Frontier
Fictional character(s): Obadiah Roberts, Settler; Patience Roberts, Spouse
Time Period(s): 1780s
Locale(s): Ohio; Virginia

Summary: In the years following the American Revolution, the Roberts family, Virginia Quakers who oppose slavery, set out for the free territory of Ohio. There they must contend with Indians and a smallpox epidemic.

Historical Accuracy: The author has drawn on the memories and records of her Quaker ancestors, which provide a realistic and authentic basis for the story.

334 *Green Rose of Furley*

Date of Publication: 1953
Subject(s): Slavery; Quakers; Civil War—U.S.
Fictional character(s): Susan Coale, Young Woman; Calvin Pancoast, Military Personnel (Union officer)
Historical character(s): Abraham Lincoln, Political Figure
Time Period(s): 1860s
Locale(s): Baltimore, Maryland

Summary: The novel explores the relationship between Quaker Susan Coale and a Union officer, Calvin Pancoast, with whom she falls in love. Their relationship tests her faith and produces a family crisis.

Historical Accuracy: The novel is based on authentic details of Quaker life and customs.

ALEXANDER BARON (1917-)

Born Alec Berstein, novelist, journalist and screenwriter Baron is the author of *Queen of the East*, *Franco Is Dying*, and *From the City, From the Plough*, which is set during World War II.

335 *The Golden Princess*

Date of Publication: 1954
Subject(s): Exploration; Aztec Empire
Historical character(s): Hernando Cortez, Explorer, Military Personnel (conquistador); Marina, Royalty (Aztec princess), Guide (interpreter); Montezuma II, Ruler (Aztec emperor)
Time Period(s): 16th century (1519-1521)
Locale(s): Mexico

Summary: The conquest of Mexico by the Spanish under Cortez is dramatized in the story of the Aztec woman named Dona Marina who assists Cortez as a guide and translator. The action covers a two year span from the establishment of Vera Cruz to the assault on Mexico City and the humiliation and death of Montezuma.

Historical Accuracy: The author has manipulated the historical chronology to include some important events within the book's scope. Otherwise, the author cites sources for most of the details of the story.

336 *Queen of the East*

Date of Publication: 1956
Subject(s): Roman Empire
Historical character(s): Zenobia, Ruler (Queen of Palmyra); Aurelian, Ruler (Roman emperor)
Time Period(s): 3rd century
Locale(s): Palmyra, Syria; Rome, Roman Empire

Summary: The novel chronicles the conflict between Queen Zenobia of Palmyra and the Roman Emperor Aurelian. When Zenobia dares to call her son emperor, the Romans under Aurelian march against her, defeating Palmyra and bringing her back to Rome as a captive.

Historical Accuracy: The historical incidents portrayed are accurate. The novel's colorful details create a believable atmosphere of the time.

ELISABETH BARR

337   *Castle Heritage*

Date of Publication: 1978
Subject(s): Romance; Inheritance—Disputed; Victorian Period
Fictional character(s): Caroline Spencer, Gentlewoman; Malvina Blaise, Noblewoman; Drew Pendellow, Gentleman, Heir
Time Period(s): 1890s (1896)
Locale(s): Cornwall, England; London, England

Summary: Carolyn Spencer, on a visit to Castle Heritage in Cornwall, marries the son of Lady Malvina despite her strong attraction to the castle's heir, Drew Pendellow. She is caught up in a loveless marriage and family intrigue.

Historical Accuracy: Though set in the Golden Jubilee year of 1896, there are few period details in this breathless romantic tale.

338   *The Sea Treasure*

Date of Publication: 1979
Subject(s): Romance; Pirates
Fictional character(s): Leonora, Survivor, Amnesiac; Dominic Pengallion, Gentleman, Landowner
Time Period(s): 1790s (1790)
Locale(s): Cornwall, England

Summary: A band of brigands arranges a shipwreck off the coast of Cornwall and murders the passengers. One woman survives the wreck, but she loses her memory. Squire Pengallion names her Leonora or the "sea treasure." As the only witness to the crime, her life is in danger as she struggles to remember the identity of the criminals.

Historical Accuracy: This is a gripping suspense tale with solid and believable period details of Cornish life.

339   *The Storm Witch*

Date of Publication: 1976
Subject(s): Romance; Inheritance—Disputed; Napoleonic Wars
Fictional character(s): Isabella St. Clair, Young Woman; Dorien Mallary, Highwayman, Gentleman; Amy Hart, Spy
Time Period(s): 1810s
Locale(s): London, England

Summary: In this novel of romantic suspense, a young woman, Isabella St. Clair, gets involved with a dashing highwayman who is intent on exposing the person who robbed him of his inheritance. Together they find themselves in the middle of intrigue during the war with Napoleon.

Historical Accuracy: The novel is too romantically overheated to provide much thorough period grounding. This is romanticized villainy with idealized heroes.

GLADYS H. BARR

340   *Cross, Sword, and Arrow*

Date of Publication: 1955
Subject(s): Middle Ages; Crusades; Children's Crusade
Fictional character(s): Bertran de Born, Young Man; Pieteria, Young Woman
Time Period(s): 13th century (1212)
Locale(s): Europe; Palestine

Summary: This tale of the Children's Crusade recounts the experiences of Bertran de Born, who, while serving Pope Innocent III, participates in the pilgrimage to the Holy Land. Captured by the Saracens, he is sustained by his faith and is finally freed to marry his beloved Pieteria.

Historical Accuracy: The period elements are accurately presented, though the story is more romantic than historic.

341   *The Master of Geneva: A Novel Based on the Life of John Calvin*

Date of Publication: 1961
Subject(s): Biography, Fictionalized; Religious Life
Historical character(s): John Calvin, Philosopher (theologian)
Time Period(s): 16th century (1521-1559)
Locale(s): France; Geneva, Switzerland

Summary: This biographical novel traces the career of the French-born Protestant theologian John Calvin. The novel follows his life from his boyhood, through his conversion experience and his devotion to the cause of the Reformation, to his days of acceptance in Geneva.

Historical Accuracy: The novel is faithful to the facts of Calvin's life and the period.

342   *Monk in Armour*

Date of Publication: 1950
Subject(s): Religious Life; Biography, Fictionalized
Historical character(s): Martin Luther, Religious (priest), Leader (Protestant Reformation)
Time Period(s): 15th century; 16th century (1490s-1525)
Locale(s): Germany

Summary: This fictional biography of the life of Martin Luther traces his career from boyhood to his marriage. The novel details the religious developments that lead Luther to break with the Roman Catholic Church and the beginnings of the Protestant Reformation.

Historical Accuracy: The novel is marred by oversimplification.

343   *The Pilgrim Prince*

Date of Publication: 1964

Subject(s): Biography, Fictionalized; Civil War—England; Literary Life
Historical character(s): John Bunyan, Religious (preacher), Writer
Time Period(s): 17th century
Locale(s): England

Summary: This biographical novel based on the life of English writer John Bunyan traces his career from his difficult childhood, to his joining the Parliamentary Army during the English Civil War, to his days as an itinerant preacher. While imprisoned for a number of years, Bunyan writes his famous work *Pilgrim's Progress.*

Historical Accuracy: The novel is filled with historical details that create a solid period background.

PAT BARR (1934-)

Barr is an English author who attended the University of Birmingham and University College, London, and then taught English for a number of years in Japan. She has produced two important nonfiction books on Japan, *The Coming of the Barbarians* and *The Deer Cry Pavilion.* She is also the author of other works on India and China.

344 *Jade*
Date of Publication:
Subject(s): East/West Relations; Chinese Empire
Fictional character(s): Alice Greenwood, Captive, Gentlewoman; Frank Greenwood, Gentleman; James Galbraith, Journalist (war correspondent)
Time Period(s): 19th century (1870s)
Locale(s): Peking, China; Kweichow, China; Shanghai, China

Summary: This is the tale of a young English woman trapped in China after the massacre of Christians in 1870. First a servant, then a concubine, Alice Greenwood's mingling of two cultures make her notorious among both the Chinese and the English. Finding love and losing it more than once, her story is one of romantic adventure.

Historical Accuracy: Set in China during the most turbulent years in the 19th century, the novel captures the rich variety of Chinese and colonial life.

JUNE BARRACLOUGH (1930-)

A graduate of Oxford and the University of London, June Barraclough was born in Yorkshire, England. She has worked as a teacher of languages in grammar schools as well as a lecturer in French and French literature at the University of London and other institutions. Barraclough uses her family history and Yorkshire background in her historical novels, which are usually concerned with young women on the threshold of adult life.

345 *Familiar Acts*
Date of Publication: 1993
Subject(s): Mystery; Victorian Period; Childhood

Fictional character(s): Hetty Coppen, Gentlewoman; Orso Orsini, Singer (opera); Simon Voyle, Gentleman, Ward
Time Period(s): 19th century (1850-1870)
Locale(s): Kent, England; Florence, Italy; London, England

Summary: What secrets lurk behind the respectable facade of a Victorian family? Young Hetty Coppen discovers many questions and eventually the answers to her family's odd behavior toward her and her brother. Love with an operatic tenor in Florence must be interrupted to face crises at home.

Historical Accuracy: The domestic details of a Victorian childhood are convincingly described.

346 *The Heart of the Rose*
Date of Publication: 1985
Subject(s): Romance; Servants; Victorian Period
Fictional character(s): Anne Tesseyman, Servant (maid); George Harlow, Nobleman, Heir
Time Period(s): 19th century (1818-1848)
Locale(s): Yorkshire, England

Summary: Set in Yorkshire, England, this romance tells the story of Anne Tesseyman, a simple country girl employed as a servant in the great house of the noble Harlow family. Her promotion to work in the nursery brings her into contact with George, the heir to the earldom, and the two fall in love.

Historical Accuracy: Despite the fairytale upstairs-downstairs romance, the details of life in a great house during the period are convincing and authentic.

347 *Kindred Spirits*
Date of Publication: 1988
Subject(s): Romance; Literary Life
Fictional character(s): Jane Bantham, Writer; Philip March, Editor; Charles Fitzpercy, Writer (poet); Fred Digby, Gentleman
Time Period(s): 1820s (1823-1824)
Locale(s): London, England

Summary: Jane Bantham is a young woman who comes to London to live with her uncle. There, she is introduced to the literary circles of the 1820s and encouraged in her own writing. She falls in love with a dashing poet and is admired by a man trapped in an unhappy marriage.

Historical Accuracy: The novel is filled with period references and is particularly rich in literary allusions of the period.

MAUDE BARRAGAN

348 *John Howard Payne, Skywalker*
Date of Publication: 1953
Subject(s): Biography, Fictionalized; Literary Life
Historical character(s): John Howard Payne, Actor, Writer (playwright); Washington Irving, Writer; Charles Lamb, Writer
Time Period(s): 18th century; 19th century
Locale(s): United States; England

Summary: American actor and playwright John Howard Payne is remembered principally as the composer of the song

"Home, Sweet, Home." The novel chronicles his career in America and abroad.

Historical Accuracy: The facts of Payne's life are faithfully depicted, but the novel fails to convince the reader of the naturalness and lifelikeness of the characters presented.

JOSE BARREIRO

349   *The Indian Chronicles*

Date of Publication: 1993
Subject(s): Exploration
Historical character(s): Christopher Columbus, Explorer, Sea Captain; Diego Colon, Indian (Taino), Linguist; Bartolome de Las Casas, Religious (missionary), Historian
Time Period(s): 16th century (1532-1533)
Locale(s): Cuba

Summary: The novel dramatizes the arrival of Columbus in Cuba and its effect on the native people. The novel is cast in the form of the fictional diary of Diego Colon, a Taino Indian who becomes Columbus' principal interpreter. Diego's initial admiration for the Spaniards gradually erodes when he witnesses their obsessive quest for gold.

Historical Accuracy: The novel is based on the actual 16th-century diaries of Colon with some obvious fictional embellishments.

JULIA BARRETT

(PSEUD. OF GABRIELLE DONNELLY; JULIA BRAUN KESSLER)

350   *Presumption: An Entertainment*

Date of Publication: 1993
Subject(s): Regency Romance
Fictional character(s): Georgiana Darcy, Gentlewoman; Elizabeth Darcy, Gentlewoman; Thomas Heywood, Military Personnel (army officer)
Time Period(s): 19th century (Regency period)
Locale(s): England

Summary: In this sequel to Jane Austen's *Pride and Prejudice*, scandal besets the Bennet family and Georgiana Darcy is tested in her vow to give her heart to no man. The novel delightfully re-engages all the favorite characters of Austen's novel for both a reprise and variations on Austen's themes.

Historical Accuracy: The novel succeeds in capturing the Regency atmosphere of the Austen era in a flattering imitation of the original.

351   *The Third Sister*

Date of Publication: 1996
Subject(s): Regency Period
Fictional character(s): Margaret Dashwood, Gentlewoman
Time Period(s): 19th century
Locale(s): Devonshire, England

Summary: This sequel to Jane Austen's *Sense and Sensibility* takes up the story of the overlooked third Dashwood sister,

Margaret. In the course of romantic entanglements, Margaret emerges as an equal to her more famous sisters.

Historical Accuracy: The novel offers an authentic echo of the Austen original and a convincing portrait of the period.

MONTE BARRETT (1897-1949)

352   *Tempered Blade*

Date of Publication: 1946
Subject(s): Biography, Fictionalized; Texas Revolution; Battle of the Alamo
Historical character(s): Jim Bowie, Frontiersman
Time Period(s): 19th century (1815-1836)
Locale(s): Texas; Louisiana

Summary: The life and frontier career of Jim Bowie are depicted from his years as a noted frontiersman in the backwoods of Louisiana through his years in Texas. A leader of the American settlers who oppose the Mexican government, Bowie joins in the Nacogdoches disturbance of 1832 and, when the revolution begins, is made a colonel. Bowie dies at the Battle of the Alamo.

Historical Accuracy: The novel mixes some fictional elements with its facts and occasionally distorts history in the interest of the narrative.

WILLIAM E. BARRETT (1900-1986)

Born in New York City, advertising executive and author William Barrett attended Manhattan College. He was a prolific author of inspirational works. Two of Barrett's most popular novels, *The Left Hand of God* and *Lilies of the Field* were adapted into successful motion pictures. His other books include *The Glory Tent*, a sequel to *Lilies of the Field*, and *The Fools of Time*, a science fiction novel.

353   *Lady of the Lotus*

Date of Publication: 1975
Subject(s): Biography, Fictionalized; Religious Life; Ancient India
Historical character(s): Siddhartha Gautama, Philosopher; Yasodhara, Spouse (of Gautama)
Time Period(s): 6th century B.C.; 5th century B.C.
Locale(s): India

Summary: The novel describes the married life of Siddharta Gautama who becomes the Buddha, and his wife, Yasodhara. Pieced together from fact and legend, the story recounts their youthful romance, married life, the birth of their son, and the departure of Gautama in pursuit of spiritual enlightenment. Yasodhara remains with Siddharta's family and awaits her husband's return.

Historical Accuracy: The novel is based on evident extensive research into the period and supplements what is known with plausible surmises of what might have been.

CLARE BARROLL

354 *The Iron Crown*

Date of Publication: 1975
Subject(s): Vikings; Byzantine Empire; Inheritance—Disputed
Fictional character(s): Eric, Bastard Son, Warrior (Viking); Ulf, Warrior (Viking); Signy, Royalty (princess)
Historical character(s): Harald, Royalty (Prince of Norway)
Time Period(s): 11th century
Locale(s): Hebrides, Scotland; Norway; Byzantium, Byzantine Empire

Summary: Eric, a young Viking robbed of his inheritance by his half-brother, is in love with Princess Signy of the Hebrides. In search of honor and a fortune with which to woo her, Eric sets out on a journey to the imperial court of Byzantium. There he attempts to free Harald of Norway from prison while also attempting to learn the precious formula for Greek fire—gunpowder.

Historical Accuracy: The novel is convincingly detailed, and includes notes that indicate sources for the events and personalities.

STEPHANIE BARRON

Barron is a mystery writer who lives in Evergreen, Colorado. She is a lifelong admirer of Jane Austen's works.

355 *Jane and the Man of the Cloth*

Date of Publication: 1997
Subject(s): Mystery; Regency Period
Fictional character(s): Geoffrey Sidmouth, Religious (clergyman)
Historical character(s): Jane Austen, Writer
Time Period(s): 1800s (1804)
Locale(s): Lyme Regis, England

Summary: In this second mystery novel with Jane Austen as sleuth, the Austen family is on holiday at Lyme Regis. There they meet the mysterious Mr. Geoffrey Sidmouth who seems to be connected with a pair of murders and a smuggling ring. Jane is determined to solve the mystery of his secret life, while risking her heart on him.

Historical Accuracy: The novel's background is faithful to Austen's life and characters are drawn from references in her letters. The story is based in part on the rumor that Jane Austen had an unfortunate love affair with a clergyman she met during a seaside holiday.

356 *Jane and the Unpleasantness at Scargrave Manor*

Date of Publication: 1996
Subject(s): Mystery; Georgian Period
Fictional character(s): Isobel Payne, Noblewoman (Countess of Scargrave), Widow(er); Fitzroy Payne, Nobleman (viscount)
Historical character(s): Jane Austen, Writer, Detective—Amateur
Time Period(s): 1800s (1802-1803)
Locale(s): Bath, England; Hertfordshire, England

Summary: This English country house murder mystery features Jane Austen as the sleuth. When the Earl of Scargrave dies mysteriously, accusations of adultery and murder are directed at his widow, Isobel Payne. She turns to her friend Jane Austen for help in investigating the motives of Scargrave Manor's guests.

Historical Accuracy: The fictional story is set within a realistic framework from Austen's biography and shows clear expertise in the details of the period, with one exception: when Jane hears Big Ben strike 40 years too soon.

JANE BARRY (1915-1979)

357 *The Carolinians*

Date of Publication: 1959
Subject(s): American Revolution; Battle of Cowpens; Battle of Kings Mountain
Fictional character(s): Orne Savage, Military Personnel; Sabrina Quantrell, Gentlewoman
Time Period(s): 1780s
Locale(s): North Carolina

Summary: The American Revolution is depicted here as a civil war that divided families. The Quantrells are a loyalist family in the Carolinas who shelter a wounded rebel, Orne Savage. His presence splits the family and forces the Quantrells to choose political sides. The action culminates in the battles of Cowpens and Kings Mountain.

Historical Accuracy: The novel is carefully detailed in its period pictures and politics.

358 *The Long March*

Date of Publication: 1955
Subject(s): American Revolution; Battle of Cowpens
Fictional character(s): Mary Craig, Spy
Historical character(s): Daniel Morgan, Military Personnel (American officer); Horatio Gates, Military Personnel (general); Francis Marion, Military Personnel (American officer); Nathanael Greene, Military Personnel (general)
Time Period(s): 1770s; 1780s (1779-1781)
Locale(s): Virginia; North Carolina; South Carolina

Summary: American Revolutionary commander Dan Morgan is in retirement in 1779 after the rigors of the battles of Quebec and Saratoga. A beautiful Patriot spy, Mary Craig, convinces him to return to the army and join the Carolina campaign. Morgan leads the rebel army to victory at the Battle of Cowpens.

Historical Accuracy: The novel is filled with action and portraits of military leaders, both realistically depicted.

359 *Maximilian's Gold*

Date of Publication: 1966
Subject(s): Civil War—U.S.; Treasure Hunt; Indians
Fictional character(s): Jake Starke, Mountain Man; Boyd Walker, Military Personnel; Shelby, Frontiersman

Time Period(s): 1860s (1867)
Locale(s): Missouri; Texas; Mexico

Summary: In 1867, former Confederate soldiers and a mountain man set out to find gold supposedly hidden by the Emperor Maximilian. Each has his own motive for possessing the treasure. Ahead lie Comanches, hijackers, Texas Rangers, and a Mexican wagon train that will alter their plans.

Historical Accuracy: The novel is a fast-paced adventure story with convincing atmosphere and period background.

360 *A Shadow of Eagles*

Date of Publication: 1964
Subject(s): American West; Ranching; Cattle Drives
Fictional character(s): Ramon Dominguez, Rancher; Cayetana Dominguez, Young Woman; Uremay, Rancher
Time Period(s): 1870s
Locale(s): Texas; Montana

Summary: Ranching life on the Texas-Mexican border is the subject of this novel centered around the hacienda Tres Reyes, its Spanish owner, and his daughter, Cayetana, who is torn between her Spanish heritage and her Texas home. The novel features a cattle drive into Montana.

Historical Accuracy: The novel's details are convincing and vividly drawn.

361 *A Time in the Sun*

Date of Publication: 1962
Subject(s): American West; Indians
Fictional character(s): Anna Stillman, Captive; Linus Degnan, Military Personnel
Historical character(s): Cochise, Indian (Apache), Chieftain; Victorio, Indian, Chieftain; Nane, Indian, Chieftain
Time Period(s): 1870s
Locale(s): Arizona

Summary: Anna Stillman is on her way to Tucson to marry Linus Degnan when she is captured by an Apache raiding party. A complicated negotiation follows to release her, but she no longer wants to be rescued. A clash of cultures and personalities marks this Western tale, which details the encroachment upon Indian life by Americans and Mexicans.

Historical Accuracy: Apache culture is presented in vivid and convincing detail.

JOHN BARRY

362 *The Michaelmas Girls*

Date of Publication: 1975
Subject(s): Victorian Period; Crime and Criminals; Mystery
Fictional character(s): Christopher Keele, Social Worker
Time Period(s): 1880s
Locale(s): London, England

Summary: This fictional reconstruction of the Jack the Ripper case offers a solution to the mystery suggesting that the killer had an accomplice, a woman who helped procure the Ripper's victims. The details are recounted through the discoveries of Christopher Keele, a social worker.

Historical Accuracy: The novel achieves a high level of authenticity of atmosphere.

LINDA LANG BARTELL (1948-)

An American romance writer born in Cleveland and a graduate of Cleveland State University, Bartell taught French and history in several high schools in Ohio. She won the Romance Writers of America Golden Heart Award for *Brianna* in 1985. Her life-long interest in European history prompted her to write historical romances.

363 *Caressa*

Date of Publication: 1990
Subject(s): Romance; Renaissance
Fictional character(s): Caressa Rugger, Widow(er), Noblewoman; Dante de Allesandro, Nobleman
Time Period(s): 15th century (1475)
Locale(s): Tuscany, Italy

Summary: Set in Renaissance Italy during the 15th century, this romance dramatizes Caressa Rugger's attempt to avenge the death of her brother. She kidnaps his supposed murderer, Dante de Allesandro, and finds herself forced to marry Dante to end the family feud.

Historical Accuracy: More colorful than historical, the novel captures some of the atmosphere of the period.

JOHN BARTH (1930-)

An American writer, Barth grew up in Cambridge, Maryland, on the Chesapeake Bay, the setting for much of his work. Barth attended Johns Hopkins and returned there in 1971 to teach creative writing. Considered one of the major modernist writers, his novels include *The Floating Opera*, *The End of the Road*, *Giles Goat-Boy*, and *Letters*.

364 *The Sot-Weed Factor*

Date of Publication: 1966
Subject(s): American Colonies; Literary Life; Picaresque Adventure
Fictional character(s): Henry Burlingame, Teacher; Anna Cooke, Gentlewoman, Twin
Historical character(s): Ebenezer Cooke, Writer, Twin; Pocahontas, Indian; John Smith, Settler
Time Period(s): 18th century
Locale(s): Chesapeake Bay, Maryland, American Colonies

Summary: In the author's wildly inventive and comic parody of the 18th-century picaresque novel, Ebenezer Cooke, an actual historical figure who was the poet laureate of Maryland, tells his life story that includes his twin sister Anna and their tutor Henry Burlingame.

Historical Accuracy: Barth turns a dizzying blend of fiction and authentic historical documentary evidence into a tour de force of literary devices and historical perception.

DONALD BARTHELME (1931-1989)

Barthelme was an American writer who was born in Philadelphia and worked as a newspaper reporter and the director of the Contemporary Arts Museum of Houston. He is widely considered to be one of the most original and influential American writers of short fiction since Ernest Hemingway. His work is marked by technical experimentation and a darkly absurdist viewpoint. His novels include *Snow White*, *The Dead Father*, and *Paradise*.

`365` *The King*

Date of Publication: 1990
Subject(s): Arthurian Legends; World War II; Fantasy
Fictional character(s): Arthur, Ruler (King of England); Guinevere, Royalty (Queen of England); Lancelot, Knight
Historical character(s): Ezra Pound, Writer (poet)
Time Period(s): 1940s (during World War II)
Locale(s): England

Summary: In this weird and dazzling juxtaposition of eras, World War II rages in Europe and King Arthur and his knights struggle to keep the kingdom going. Modern and Arthurian cultures are blended together with the expected comic results as each perspective illuminates the other.

Historical Accuracy: Inventive and amusing, the novel is built out of details from both Arthurian legends and wartime Britain. The author is convincing in both worlds.

LANIER BARTLETT (1830-1918)

A novelist and autobiographer, Bartlett is the author of *Adios*, *On the Old West Coast: Being Further Reminiscences of a Ranger*, and *Major Horace Bell*.

`366` *Adios!*

Date of Publication: 1929
Subject(s): American West; Crime and Criminals
Fictional character(s): Pancito Delfino, Outlaw; Harry Howard, Lawman
Time Period(s): 1840s (1846)
Locale(s): California

Summary: Set in California in the days following its acquisition by the United States, the novel tells the story of a young Californian of Spanish descent, Pancho Delfino, who refuses to accept the American conquest. He forms a band of outlaws to harass the hated gringos and is opposed by the American ranger Captain Harry Howard.

Historical Accuracy: The period elements create a plausible historical background for the novel's action.

PAUL BARTLETT (1909-)

Born in Missouri, Bartlett has worked as a freelance writer and artist. He has been an instructor of creative writing at Georgia State College.

`367` *When the Owl Cries*

Date of Publication: 1960
Subject(s): Mexican Revolution
Fictional character(s): Don Raul Medina, Landowner
Time Period(s): 1900s
Locale(s): Mexico

Summary: This novel explores the injustices of the hacienda-system that became a major cause of the Mexican Revolution. Don Raul Medina takes over the management of his estate from his father, who has treated his peasants cruelly. Raul, filled with democratic zeal, attempts reforms but finds out that it is too late to undo past ways.

Historical Accuracy: The novel's analysis and characterization are at times superficial. The story succeeds better in capturing the atmosphere of the time.

DEL BARTON (1925-1971)

Born on an Indian reservation, Barton is the great-grandaughter of the Sioux warrior Grey Wolf. She based her novel, *A Good Day to Die*, on stories told by Grey Wolf.

`368` *A Good Day to Die*

Date of Publication: 1980
Subject(s): American West; Indians; Tribal Life—Native American
Historical character(s): Grey Wolf, Indian (Sioux), Warrior; Crazy Horse, Indian (Sioux), Warrior; George Armstrong Custer, Military Personnel (cavalry officer)
Time Period(s): 19th century
Locale(s): West

Summary: During his 107 years, Sioux warrior Grey Wolf struggles against white encroachment and the decline of Indian life and customs. This story depicts the tragic history of the Plains Indians, whose culture is displaced by white settlement.

Historical Accuracy: The novel is based on extensive research and first-hand accounts, which provide an authentic and convincing background.

FLORENCE WHITFIELD BARTON

`369` *The Sage and the Olive*

Date of Publication: 1953
Subject(s): Religious Conflict; Protestant Reformation; Biography, Fictionalized
Historical character(s): Robert Estienne, Printer
Time Period(s): 16th century
Locale(s): Paris, France

Summary: The beginning of the Protestant Reformation in France is depicted through the story of printer Robert Estienne, member of a prominent family of Paris and Geneva printers. Robert is a capable scholar who is fired with enthusiasm for the Lutheran ideas of religious reform.

Historical Accuracy: The novel shows evidence of solid research in capturing Estienne's life and times.

JAMES BARWICK
(PSEUD. OF JAMES DONALD, 1931- ; ANTHONY BARWICK, 1934-)

James Barwick is a pseudonym for two prominent film and television writers. Anthony Barwick has worked on several feature films including two James Bond movies. Donald James has also written for British and American television, including the ''Mission: Impossible'' series.

370 *The Hangman's Crusade*

Date of Publication: 1981
Subject(s): World War II; Holocaust
Fictional character(s): Jim Franklyn, Journalist
Historical character(s): Reinhard Heydrich, Government Official (Nazi); Adolf Hitler, Leader (Nazi); Pius XII, Religious (pope); Winston Churchill, Political Figure
Time Period(s): 1940s
Locale(s): Germany; Czechoslovakia

Summary: This speculative fiction attempt to answer the historical mysteries behind the assassination of Nazi architect of the Holocaust Reinhard Heydrich and the reason behind the silence of Pius XII in the face of the Nazis' persecution of the Jews. Journalist Jim Franklyn investigates and is led into a tangled conspiracy.

Historical Accuracy: Although the novel is a work of fiction, it is based on some actual events and provides a plausible, if highly speculative, account.

371 *Shadow of the Wolf*

Date of Publication: 1979
Subject(s): World War II; Espionage
Fictional character(s): Alfred Horn, Pilot
Historical character(s): Rudolf Hess, Leader (Nazi)
Time Period(s): 1940s
Locale(s): England

Summary: In this historical thriller, Nazi leader Rudolph Hess undertakes his notorious peace mission to England. Although Hess is captured, flier Alfred Horn attempts to deliver Hess' plan to the Americans. The Americans, however, are not receptive and the full force of the FBI comes down on Horn. The peace plan is never invoked and America enters the war against Germany.

Historical Accuracy: The novel's story is imaginary but does utilize convincing and authentic period elements.

CYNTHIA BASS

372 *Maiden Voyage*

Date of Publication: 1996
Subject(s): Ocean Liners; Shipwrecks
Fictional character(s): Sumner Jordan, Child
Time Period(s): 1910s (1912)
Locale(s): Titanic, At Sea

Summary: This coming of age story is set aboard the ill-fated *Titanic*. 12-year-old Sumner Jordan, son of a suffragette, is rewarded for his precocity with a trip to England in 1912. The novel describes his experiences on the return trip aboard the unsinkable *Titanic*.

Historical Accuracy: The novel is meticulously researched and features an authentic period background as well as a faithful version of the sinking of the *Titanic*.

373 *Sherman's March*

Date of Publication: 1994
Subject(s): Civil War—U.S.; Sherman's March to the Sea; Military Life
Fictional character(s): Nicholas J. Whiteman, Military Personnel (Union army captain); Annie Saunders Baker, Widow(er), Refugee
Historical character(s): William Tecumseh Sherman, Military Personnel (Union general)
Time Period(s): 1860s (1864)
Locale(s): Georgia

Summary: Sherman's devastating march to the sea, which redefined warfare into total war by bringing the civilian population onto the front lines of the conflict for the first time, is explored from the perspective of three participants: Sherman himself, a captain in the Union army, and a widowed southern farmwife and refugee.

Historical Accuracy: The details of the engagement and the period are genuine and grippingly realistic.

JEAN BASSAN

374 *The Wrong Horse*

Date of Publication: 1961
Subject(s): Middle Ages
Fictional character(s): Crespi, Leader (Guelph); Gagini, Military Personnel
Time Period(s): 12th century
Locale(s): Italy

Summary: This tale of an Italian town's disintegration is set during the 12th century during the conflict between the Guelph and the Ghibelline. Crespi assumes leadership in the campaign against a neighboring town that has fallen into the hands of the Ghibelline. His authority is challenged with the arrival of the militarist Gagini.

Historical Accuracy: The novel's theme aims at modern and universal significance, which tends to undermine the specificity of its historical background.

HAMILTON BASSO (1904-1964)

Born in New Orleans, Basso attended Tulane University and worked as a journalist and advertising copywriter before becoming an editor for the *New Republic*, *Time*, and the *New Yorker*. Impressions of his native South are his principal subjects in novels such as *The View From Pompey's Head*, *Days Before Lent*, and *Sun in Capricorn*. He is also the author of a biography of Confederate general Pierre Beauregard.

375 *The Light Infantry Ball*

Date of Publication: 1959

Subject(s): Civil War—U.S.; Antebellum South; Confederate States of America

Fictional character(s): John Bottomley, Gentleman, Plantation Owner; Cameron Bottomley, Gentleman; Ules Monckton, Journalist, Military Personnel (Confederate officer)

Time Period(s): 1850s; 1860s (1851-1865)

Locale(s): South Carolina; Richmond, Virginia

Summary: Life in the South before and during the Civil War is seen through the experiences of a South Carolina planter family, particularly John Bottomley who serves in the Confederate war cabinet. John and his family become casualties of the Southern tradition.

Historical Accuracy: This is a highly detailed psychological study of multiple characters who convincingly make up the South of the period.

JOHN CALVIN BATCHELOR (1948-)

Born in Pennsylvania, Batchelor earned his B.A. from Princeton. He also attended the University of Edinburgh and Union Theological Seminary. He has served as the editor of the *SoHo Weekly News* and as a book reviewer for the *Village Voice*. His novels include *The Further Adventures of Halley's Comet* and *The Birth of the People's Republic of Antarctica*.

376 *American Falls*

Date of Publication: 1985

Subject(s): Civil War—U.S.; Espionage

Fictional character(s): John Oliphant, Spy; Amaziah Butter, Spy, Military Personnel (Union soldier)

Time Period(s): 1860s (1864-1865)

Locale(s): Niagara Falls, New York; Washington, District of Columbia; New York, New York

Summary: On the eve of the election of 1864, the Confederate secret service, based in Canada, launches teams of saboteurs to disrupt it. Two agents, Confederate John Oliphant and Yankee Amaziah Butter, are locked in the shadow game of pursuit and capture. The enemies are shown to have a great deal in common in a world of shifting allegiances and constant infidelities.

Historical Accuracy: The novel is a masterwork of believable historical recreation, utterly convincing and rooted in the events of the period.

LOIS BATTLE (1942-)

Australian writer Battle graduated from UCLA and has worked as an actress, a nursery school teacher, a probation officer, and a dance instructor. Battle's novels primarily concern women's lives and have a realistic edge.

377 *Storyville*

Date of Publication: 1993

Subject(s): Prostitution; Romance

Fictional character(s): Kate Cavanaugh, Prostitute; Julia Randsome, Gentlewoman; Charles Randsome, Businessman

Time Period(s): 1890s (1898-1899)

Locale(s): New Orleans, Louisiana

Summary: The novel describes the parallel lives of two women, one a prostitute in New Orleans' notorious red-light district, Storyville, and the other a transplanted Yankee, Julia Randsome, who has married into one of New Orleans' most prominent families. Julia's husband owns property in Storyville where the two women's stories converge.

Historical Accuracy: New Orleans at the end of the 19th century is drawn with precision and gusto.

FLORENCE M. BAUER

378 *Abram, Son of Terah*

Date of Publication: 1948

Subject(s): Biblical Story

Fictional character(s): Eber, Slave

Historical character(s): Abram, Biblical Figure

Time Period(s): 20th century B.C.

Locale(s): Ur, Mesopotamia

Summary: The novel depicts the life of Abraham and his search for one God over the many offered by the priests of Mesopotamia 4,000 years ago. The novel offers a detailed picture of life in the ancient city of Ur and Abraham's search for meaning.

Historical Accuracy: The story is imagined, but the modes and the manners of the people are convincing.

379 *Behold Your King*

Date of Publication: 1945

Subject(s): Biblical Story

Fictional character(s): Jonathan of Cyrene, Young Man

Historical character(s): Jesus Christ, Biblical Figure; Joseph of Arimathea, Biblical Figure; Barabbas, Biblical Figure, Outlaw

Time Period(s): 1st century (27-33 A.D.)

Locale(s): Jerusalem, Israel

Summary: Jonathan of Cyrene comes to Judea in 27 A.D. and is persuaded to believe that Jesus of Nazareth is the true messiah. He relates the story of Jesus's ministry and the events leading up to the crucifixion.

Historical Accuracy: The novel's principle source is the New Testament, which is skillfully interwoven with the story's fictional elements. Elaborations and inventions are reserved for minor events and characters.

HANS BAUMANN (1914-)

Born in Bavaria, Baumann was a teacher there and also worked as a manual laborer in postwar Germany before becoming a full-time writer. He has won many awards for his children's books. His works include *The Dragon Next Door*, *I Marched*, and *The Stolen Fire*.

380   *Sons of the Steppe: The Story of How the Conqueror Genghis Khan Was Overcome*

Date of Publication: 1957
Subject(s): Mongol Empire; Middle Ages; Chinese Empire
Fictional character(s): Arik-Buka, Warrior
Historical character(s): Genghis Khan, Warrior, Leader (Mongol); Kublai Khan, Ruler (Mongol emperor)
Time Period(s): 13th century
Locale(s): Mongolia; China; Asia

Summary: The world of Genghis Khan, on the march and at war, is dramatized in the story of two of the Khan's grandsons. Arik-Buka embraces the life of the Mongol warrior, while Kublai Khan, sickened by constant battle, yearns for peace. The clash of ideology is played out in the conflict of the two brothers, against a vivid backdrop of life in camp and in the campaigns of Genghis Khan's hordes.

Historical Accuracy: The novel blends actual incidents with legend and invention creating the theme of cultural and ideological conflict against a convincing historical backdrop.

FREDERIC BAUME

381   *Yankee Woman*

Date of Publication: 1945
Subject(s): American West; Sea Story
Fictional character(s): Harriet Spilsbury, Sea Captain
Time Period(s): 19th century
Locale(s): San Francisco, California

Summary: This tale of California during the gold rush years tells the story of Harriet Spilsbury, the wife of a sadistic Maine sea captain. When he conveniently dies, Harriet takes over as ship's captain and later as the owner of one of the most notorious dives on the Barbary Coast.

Historical Accuracy: The novel aims only at capturing the colorful spirit of the era rather than fully documenting the past.

GEORGE BAXT (1923-)

New York-born Baxt attended City and Brooklyn College. He has earned a reputation as a knowledgeable motion picture and theater historian, and uses his expertise to his advantage in series of mysteries involving theatrical personalities.

382   *The Alfred Hitchcock Murder Case*

Date of Publication: 1986
Subject(s): Mystery; Motion Picture Industry
Historical character(s): Alfred Hitchcock, Director; Alma Hitchcock, Writer
Time Period(s): 1920s; 1930s (1925-1936)
Locale(s): Munich, Germany; London, England

Summary: In 1925 the set for the movie Alfred Hitchcock is making in Munich, Germany, becomes a stage for a real murder. With few clues the crime remains unsolved. Eleven years later in London, while Hitchcock is at work on *The Lady Vanishes*, a phone call brings back the past, and the director is charged with a crime he did not commit.

Historical Accuracy: The novel's story is fictitious. However, the novel's era and references to Hitchcock and his works are authentically drawn.

383   *The Bette Davis Murder Case*

Date of Publication: 1994
Subject(s): Mystery; Motion Picture Industry
Historical character(s): Bette Davis, Actress; Agatha Christie, Writer
Time Period(s): 1930s (1936)
Locale(s): London, England

Summary: While on sabbatical from Hollywood negotiating a new contract, Bette Davis rents the London mansion of the famous Egyptologist Virgil Wynn. When he is found murdered in the house, Bette finds herself embroiled in a bitter and deadly family feud and an ancient curse. Aid is provided in sorting out the crime by her neighbor, Agatha Christie.

Historical Accuracy: The story is fanciful but a delightfully rendered combination of period details and the frisson provided by the volatile Ms. Davis.

384   *The Dorothy Parker Murder Case*

Date of Publication: 1984
Subject(s): Mystery; Literary Life
Fictional character(s): Jacob Singer, Detective—Police
Historical character(s): Dorothy Parker, Writer; George S. Kaufman, Writer; Alexander Woolcott, Writer; Robert Benchley, Writer
Time Period(s): 1920s (1926)
Locale(s): New York, New York

Summary: In 1926, Dorothy Parker takes up a murder investigation when a show girl is found killed in George S. Kaufman's apartment. Parker enlists the aid of other Round Table denizens in an increasingly complicated and dangerous series of events.

Historical Accuracy: The novel features convincing period details.

385   *The Greta Garbo Murder Case*

Date of Publication: 1992
Subject(s): Mystery; Motion Picture Industry; World War II
Historical character(s): Greta Garbo, Actress; Peter Lorre, Actor; Bela Lugosi, Actor; Erich Von Stroheim, Director, Actor; Marion Davies, Actress
Time Period(s): 1940s
Locale(s): Hollywood, California

Summary: During World War II, Greta Garbo's movie career diminishes with the decline of her films' biggest markets in Europe and Asia. She agrees to star in an independent production of a film on Joan of Arc that employs a number of German expatriates. She soon finds herself in the middle of a cast that includes spies and a drama that includes murder.

Historical Accuracy: The novel is knowing and convincing in the details of the film business and the era.

386 *The Mae West Murder Case*

Date of Publication: 1993
Subject(s): Mystery; Motion Picture Industry
Historical character(s): Mae West, Actress
Time Period(s): 1930s (1936)
Locale(s): Hollywood, California

Summary: In 1936 someone is leaving a trail of murdered Mae West impersonators and getting ever closer to the original. Mae herself takes up the investigation, and winds up in the middle of a web of blackmail and corruption in scenes from the golden days of Hollywood.

Historical Accuracy: The period details are authentically delivered.

387 *The Noel Coward Murder Case*

Date of Publication: 1992
Subject(s): Mystery; Literary Life
Fictional character(s): Abraham Wang, Detective—Police
Historical character(s): Noel Coward, Writer, Entertainer; Dorothy Parker, Writer
Time Period(s): 1930s (1935)
Locale(s): Shanghai, China; New York, New York

Summary: Noel Coward agrees to perform at the opening night of a new nightclub in New York City. When a showgirl meets her death on stage, Coward turns to sleuthing and uncovers a white slavery ring and gangster activities.

Historical Accuracy: The novel offers convincing details of the period.

388 *The Talking Pictures Murder Case*

Date of Publication: 1990
Subject(s): Mystery; Motion Picture Industry
Fictional character(s): Herbert Villon, Detective—Police; Hazel Dickson, Journalist (gossip reporter)
Historical character(s): Louis B. Mayer, Businessman (studio executive); Samuel Goldwyn, Businessman (studio executive); Adolph Zukor, Businessman (studio executive); Jack Warner, Businessman (studio executive)
Time Period(s): 1920s (1929)
Locale(s): Hollywood, California

Summary: In 1929, Hollywood is in turmoil at the arrival of "talkies." Studio executives are busy dropping silent stars whose voices don't deliver, and a murderer is on the loose. Police detective Herbert Villon investigates, as does gossip columnist Hazel Dickson.

Historical Accuracy: The novel offers well-researched and convincing period details about the film business.

389 *The Tallulah Bankhead Murder Case*

Date of Publication: 1987
Subject(s): Mystery; Theatrical Life

Fictional character(s): Jacob Singer, Detective—Police
Historical character(s): Tallulah Bankhead, Actress
Time Period(s): 1950s (1952)
Locale(s): New York, New York

Summary: At the beginning of the McCarthy Era, Tallulah Bankhead is enjoying a comeback as the star of a popular radio program. But the witchhunt for communists intervenes when a scheduled guest kills himself after his name is given to the Un-American Actitivities Committee. Tallulah herself is threatened with the blacklist, and the first of a series of murders occurs. Tallulah joins detective Jacob Singer in the investigation.

Historical Accuracy: Although the murderer and his victims are fictitious, the atmosphere of the McCarthy Era and its complications are factual.

390 *The William Powell and Myrna Loy Murder Case*

Date of Publication: 1996
Subject(s): Mystery; Motion Picture Industry
Fictional character(s): Herbert Villon, Detective—Police; Jim Mallory, Detective—Police
Historical character(s): William Powell, Actor; Myrna Loy, Actress; Jean Harlow, Actress; Lillian Hellman, Writer; Dashiell Hammett, Writer; Louis B. Mayer, Businessman (studio head)
Time Period(s): 1930s (1936)
Locale(s): Hollywood, California

Summary: When a Hollywood madam threatens to blackmail many of the film capital's leading men, William Powell and Myrna Loy, fresh from their success in *The Thin Man*, reprise their roles as Nick and Nora Charles for real in a case of gossip and murder.

Historical Accuracy: The novel features a genuine insider's feel for the period and the movie community.

SARAH BAYLIS (1956-1987)

Baylis was an English writer who also wrote two novels for teenagers, *Vila* and *The Tomb of Reeds*.

391 *Utrillo's Mother*

Date of Publication: 1987
Subject(s): Artistic Life; Biography, Fictionalized
Historical character(s): Suzanne Valadon, Artist (painter); Maurice Utrillo, Artist (painter); Edgar Degas, Artist (painter)
Time Period(s): 19th century; 20th century (1810s-1930s)
Locale(s): France

Summary: In this first-person narrative, Suzanne Valadon, known primarily as the mother of Maurice Utrillo, tells of her peasant upbringing and her working-class life in Paris. She works for a time as a circus performer and artist's model, eventually becoming an artist herself. Overshadowed by her more famous son, her lovers, and her artistic colleagues, this novel gives Valadon her say, and resurrects an interesting and provocative life.

Historical Accuracy: The novel is a convincing portrait of an overlooked artist, filled with period detail that vividly captures the era.

REX BEACH

392   *The World in His Arms*

Date of Publication: 1946
Subject(s): American West
Fictional character(s): Jonathan Clark, Outlaw, Sea Captain; Marina Selanova, Noblewoman (countess); Semyon Petrovsky, Royalty (prince)
Time Period(s): 1850s
Locale(s): San Francisco, California; Sitka, Alaska

Summary: This romantic adventure tale is set in Russian Alaska. Jonathan Clark, who is engaged in illicit poaching of the seal herds in the Pribilofs and Aleutians, and the Countess Marina, kinswoman of the Czar's governor of Alaska, fall in love. When Jonathan is captured, only his Russian rival for Marina's affections has the power to save his life.

Historical Accuracy: This is a colorful romantic tale with an authentic period backdrop.

SUSAN HICKS BEACH (1866-)

Beach is the author of *An Inland Ferry, Shuttered Doors,* and *A Cardinal of the Medici.*

393   *A Cardinal of the Medici*

Date of Publication: 1937
Subject(s): Renaissance
Historical character(s): Ippolito de' Medici, Religious (cardinal), Bastard Son; Clement VII, Religious (pope); Leo X, Religious (pope); Catherine de' Medici, Noblewoman
Time Period(s): 16th century
Locale(s): Italy

Summary: Renaissance politics and culture are depicted in the career of Ippolito de' Medici, the illegitimate son of Giuliano de' Medici, duke of Nemours, and an unknown mother. His story is related through the reminiscences of his mother, who describes his rise to cardinal at age 19 and his death at age 22 by poison.

Historical Accuracy: The novel is well documented and, except for minor details, thoroughly accurate in its depiction of the period.

CARLETON BEALS (1893-1979)

Born in Kansas, Beals graduated from the University of California and Columbia, with additional study at universities in Madrid, Rome, and Mexico. A foreign correspondent who has visited 42 countries and covered numerous revolutions and uprisings, Beals has been called ''the dean of correspondents in Latin America.'' Beals' books include *The Stones Awake, Drums over the Amazon,* and *The Incredible Incas.*

394   *Taste of Glory*

Date of Publication: 1956
Subject(s): Biography, Fictionalized; Independence—South America
Historical character(s): Bernardo O'Higgins, Revolutionary, Ruler (dictator of Chile)
Time Period(s): 18th century
Locale(s): Chile; England; Peru

Summary: This biographical novel dramatizes the career of South American revolutionary Bernardo O'Higgins. The illegitimate son of an Irish adventurer, O'Higgins is raised in England where he joins a group dedicated to the establishment of a new Incan Empire in Peru. O'Higgins leaves for South America determined to establish American-style independence there and, for a time, is the Supreme Dictator of Chile.

Historical Accuracy: Use of invented dialogue causes the novel to fall short of a careful and reliable account of O'Higgins. However, the essential outline of his story is observed, and the atmosphere of the time is vividly captured.

AMELIA BEAN

395   *The Fancher Train*

Date of Publication: 1958
Subject(s): American West; Wagon Trains; Mormons
Fictional character(s): Jed Smith, Scout; Melissa Boller, Young Woman
Time Period(s): 1850s (1857)
Locale(s): Utah

Summary: This is a factual account of the infamous Mountain Meadows Massacre of 1857 in which an entire wagon train of over 120 adults was murdered by Mormons and Indians. The novel includes a conventional love story between the wagon train's scout, Jed Smith, and young Melissa Boller, who are allowed to survive the massacre.

Historical Accuracy: Accounts differ on who was responsible for the massacre, but this version is based on the most accepted interpretation, carefully researched and marred only by an overly conventional love story.

396   *The Feud*

Date of Publication: 1960
Subject(s): American West; Ranching
Fictional character(s): Jonathan Tewkbury, Rancher; Andy Cooper, Outlaw (rustler)
Time Period(s): 1880s
Locale(s): Arizona

Summary: This western tale is based on the actual Graham-Tewkbury feud during the 1880s in Arizona. When a Graham runs off with a Tewkbury girl and deserts her, violence explodes. Raids, counter-raids, and killings escalate.

Historical Accuracy: The basis for the novel is factual, and the story is delivered with authenticity.

397 *Time for Outrage*

Date of Publication: 1967
Subject(s): American West; Lincoln County War
Fictional character(s): Luke Pender, Cowboy
Historical character(s): William Bonney, Outlaw
Time Period(s): 1870s (1878)
Locale(s): Lincoln County, New Mexico

Summary: The novel captures the events of the Lincoln County War that exploded in New Mexico in 1878 when the murder of John Henry Tunstall led to a full-scale battle against corrupt law and government officials. The story centers on a young friend of William Bonney, better known as Billy the Kid.

Historical Accuracy: The main parts of the novel are true and faithful to history.

FRED BEAN (1941-)

Western novelist Bean's books include *Bloody Trail*, *Hard Luck*, *Gunfight at Eagle Springs*, and *Tom Spoon*.

398 *Pancho And Black Jack*

Date of Publication: 1995
Subject(s): Revolution—Mexico; World War I
Fictional character(s): Will Johnson, Cowboy; Eliza Griewson, Spy
Historical character(s): Francisco Villa, Outlaw, Revolutionary; John J. Pershing, Military Personnel (general); George S. Patton, Military Personnel (army officer); Tasker Bliss, Military Personnel (army officer), Government Official
Time Period(s): 1900s (1916)
Locale(s): Mexico; Texas; New Mexico

Summary: When Pancho Villa is suspected of leading a raid across the U.S. border and attacking a New Mexico town, General John J. Pershing is sent south of the border. His campaign is both the last full-scale cavalry campaign and the first motorized fighting in U.S. History.

Historical Accuracy: The novel attempts to stay close to the historical facts and offers some speculative conclusions regarding the activities of Pancho Villa.

399 *The Pecos River*

Date of Publication: 1995
Subject(s): American West; Indians; Settlement of the American Frontier
Fictional character(s): Buck Wallace, Adventurer; Goyah, Indian (Comanche), Warrior; Asa, Indian (Kiowa), Young Woman
Time Period(s): 19th century
Locale(s): Pecos River, New Mexico

Summary: In this installment of the Rivers West series, Buck Wallace, a sailor, journeys west into New Mexico to settle beside the Pecos River in the land of the Comanche. To create his home he must contend with the legendary warrior Goyah, who is sustained by the support of a Kiowa woman, Asa.

Historical Accuracy: The novel offers excellent details of western life.

400 *Trail's End*

Date of Publication: 1994
Subject(s): American West; Cattle Drives; Indians
Fictional character(s): Buck Smith, Leader (trail boss)
Time Period(s): 19th century
Locale(s): Texas; Chisholm Trail, United States; Abilene, Kansas

Summary: Adventure along the legendary Chisholm Trail is described as Buck Smith assembles a crew of cowboys to drive 1,200 longhorns from Matamoros to Abilene. They must contend with river crossings, storms, stampedes, outlaws, and Indians, as well as internal dissent.

Historical Accuracy: The details and the mechanics of the cattle drive are captured with authenticity.

JOHN BEATTY (1922-1975)

PATRICIA BEATTY (1922-1991)

An American historian, biographer, and novelist, John Beatty was born in Portland, Oregon, and graduated from Reed College, Stanford, and the University of Washington, Seattle. He was a professor of history and humanities at the University of California, Riverside, an authority on 17th- and 18th-century English history. Patricia Beatty grew up in the Pacific Northwest after living on an Indian reservation. A librarian and teacher, she authored more than 50 books for children.

401 *Campion Towers*

Date of Publication: 1965
Subject(s): Civil War—England; Religious Conflict; Puritans
Fictional character(s): Penitence Hervey, Teenager
Historical character(s): Charles, Royalty (prince)
Time Period(s): 17th century
Locale(s): England

Summary: Set during Cromwellian times, the story follows the adventures of a young Puritan girl from the Massachusetts Bay Colony. On a visit to England she comes to believe that her relatives are Papists. She agrees to inform on them, a decision which plunges her into the intrigues of the period.

Historical Accuracy: The first-person narrative restricts the novel's view and prevents a full presentation of the period. However, much of the period's atmosphere is rendered convincingly.

DAVID BEATY (1919-)

BETTY BEATY

David Beaty was born in Sri Lanka and attended Oxford University and University College, London. He was a senior captain of BOAC. His wife, Betty, was born in Yorkshire and was a stewardess for British European Airways.

402   *Wings of the Morning*

Date of Publication: 1982
Subject(s): Aviation; World War I; World War II
Fictional character(s): Amelia Jerningham, Gentlewoman, Pilot; James March, Engineer, Pilot; Frederick Haybury, Gentleman
Time Period(s): 20th century (1903-1970s)
Locale(s): England; Europe; United States

Summary: The history of aviation is detailed in the lives of two people fascinated by the adventure of flight. Amelia Jerningham helps the local blacksmith's son, James March, build one of the first airplanes in Britain. They share a passion for flying and for each other, but class differences separate them until years later. Amelia becomes one of the female pioneers of aviation and James a war hero.

Historical Accuracy: The novel is filled with convincing details of airplanes and the aviation industry's progression throughout the century.

K.K. BECK

(PSEUD. OF KATHRINE MORRIS, 1950-)

An American mystery writer whose full name is Kathrine Kristine Beck Morris, she was born in Seattle, Washington and received her B.A. degree from San Francisco State University. Beck has worked as a radio time salesperson, an advertising copywriter, and a trade magazine editor.

403   *Death in a Deck Chair*

Date of Publication: 1984
Subject(s): Mystery
Fictional character(s): Iris Cooper, Detective—Amateur; Jack Clancy, Journalist
Time Period(s): 1920s
Locale(s): *Irenia*, At Sea (Southampton to Montreal)

Summary: Iris Cooper, on a round-the-world cruise with her aunt, finds herself assisting in the investigation of a shipboard murder. Many of the passengers have a motive for the killing, and her search for the truth may prove deadly.

Historical Accuracy: The period details of a transatlantic liner are authentically presented.

404   *Peril under the Palms*

Date of Publication: 1989
Subject(s): Mystery
Fictional character(s): Iris Cooper, Detective—Amateur; Antoinette Caulfield, Heiress; Jack Clancy, Journalist
Time Period(s): 1920s (1928)
Locale(s): Honolulu, Hawaii

Summary: Iris Cooper, on a holiday to Honolulu with her aunt and schoolmate Antoinette Caulfield, an heiress to one of Hawaii's great fortunes, is soon swept up in a series of baffling events. First, Antoinette is approached by a mysterious woman in white who claims to be her long-dead mother. Then a ship's passenger is found dead on the beach, followed by the discovery of another body, and all seems connected to the Caulfield fortune.

Historical Accuracy: The details of the period are delightfully and convincingly portrayed.

405   *Young Mrs. Cavendish and the Kaiser's Men*

Date of Publication: 1987
Subject(s): Espionage; World War I
Fictional character(s): Maude Teasdale Cavendish, Journalist; Louise Arbor, Socialite
Time Period(s): 1910s (1916)
Locale(s): San Francisco, California; Arizona

Summary: Maude Cavendish, a society reporter, is swept up in an elaborate German plot before America's entry into World War I. She is kidnapped by mistake, taken for a debutante whose father is a famous scientist. This is only the beginning of Maude's adventures which will ultimately lead her to the desert of Arizona and a plot of global significance.

Historical Accuracy: The novel is a fast-paced intrigue with solid period background of pre-war America.

BERIL BECKER (1901-)

Born in Russia, Becker emigrated to the U.S. where he attended Columbia University. He served as a radio operator in the U.S. Merchant Marines during World War II, and his career has included work as an industrial reporter and researcher. Becker's books reflect his belief in the future importance of technology.

406   *Whirlwind in Petticoats*

Date of Publication: 1947
Subject(s): Biography, Fictionalized; Women's Rights
Historical character(s): Victoria Claflin Woodhull, Feminist
Time Period(s): 19th century; 20th century
Locale(s): New York, New York

Summary: This fictional biography records the controversial career of early feminist Victoria Woodhull. Her advocacy of women's rights and free love made her one of the most notorious women of her day. The novel depicts her private and public encounters with some famous contemporaries.

Historical Accuracy: The novel's emphasis on the sensational and sentimental counteracts its usefulness as a reliable biographical account.

STEPHEN BECKER (1927-)

Becker is an American writer from Mount Vernon, New York, who graduated from Harvard. He has worked as a free-lance writer, translator, and editor. His novels have been consistently praised for their inventive style. Works include *A Covenant with Death*, *Shanghai Incident*, the nonfiction *Comic Art in America*, and a biography of Marshall Field.

407   *A Rendezvous in Haiti*

Date of Publication: 1987

Subject(s): World War I; Independence—Haiti
Fictional character(s): Caroline Barbour, Captive (kidnapping victim); McAllister, Military Personnel (U.S. army soldier); Father Scarron, Religious (priest)
Time Period(s): 1910s (1919)
Locale(s): Haiti

Summary: McAllister, a veteran of World War I, is on duty in Haiti trying to put down a peasants' revolt. Caroline Barbour is kidnapped, and McAllister, assisted by a local priest, pursues her and her kidnapper for a climactic rendezvous in the jungle with revelations about all the characters.

Historical Accuracy: Becker masterfully captures the era and the locale.

408 When the War Is Over

Date of Publication: 1969
Subject(s): Civil War—U.S.; Trials
Fictional character(s): Marius Catto, Military Personnel (Union soldier); Thomas Martin, Military Personnel (Confederate soldier), Spy (accused)
Historical character(s): Joseph Hooker, Military Personnel (Union general)
Time Period(s): 1860s (1865)
Locale(s): Kentucky; Cincinnati, Ohio

Summary: In 1865, after Lee's surrender, a rebel soldier, Thomas Martin, is executed on a charge of being a Confederate guerilla. The impact of his death on Catto, a Union soldier, is the subject of the novel. It explores in moral and human terms the nature of warfare and punishment, of walking the line between war and murder, military justice and vengeance.

Historical Accuracy: The voices of the characters are real and authentic.

REXANNE BECNEL

409 My Gallant Enemy

Date of Publication: 1990
Subject(s): Middle Ages; Romance
Fictional character(s): Lady Lilliane of Orrick, Noblewoman; Corbett of Colchester, Nobleman
Time Period(s): 13th century (1273)
Locale(s): England

Summary: This romantic adventure novel concerns Lady Lilliane of Orrick who is abducted by crusader Corbett of Colchester when she refuses to marry him. They eventually reconcile and then must endure the obstacles of the political intrigue of the times.

Historical Accuracy: The medieval atmosphere is genuine if somewhat underdeveloped in favor of the romance.

410 Thief of My Heart

Date of Publication: 1991
Subject(s): Reconstruction Period; Romance; Identity—Concealed
Fictional character(s): Lacie Montgomery, Teacher, Imposter; Dillon Lockwood, Heir

Time Period(s): 1870s (1872)
Locale(s): Louisiana; Denver, Colorado

Summary: In an attempt to keep her school open, Lacie Montgomery pretends to be the widow of the former school master. When his brother, Dillon Lockwood, arrives, complications occur. He is determined to gain his inheritance and reveal Lacie's deception. The scene shifts from Reconstruction era Lousiana to frontier Denver as love and deception produce exciting climaxes.

Historical Accuracy: The novel's premise is a stretch, but the period background helps the solidity of the story.

411 Where Magic Dwells

Date of Publication: 1994
Subject(s): Middle Ages; Romance; Witchcraft and Sorcery
Fictional character(s): Wynne ab Gruffydd, Sorceress; Sir Cleve FitzWarin, Knight
Time Period(s): 12th century (1172)
Locale(s): Radnor Forest, Wales

Summary: Wynne ab Gruffyd, the Seeress of Radnor, is raising five war orphans. When the English knight Sir Cleve FitzWarin arrives to claim one of the children, he must contend with Wynne's magic, her fierce protection of the orphans, and his growing attraction to the mysterious beauty.

Historical Accuracy: The novel is more picturesque than detailed in its historical elements, but does supply a believable period atmosphere.

DONALD F. BEDFORD
(PSEUD. OF DONALD FRIEDE; H. BEDFORD JONES; KENNETH FEARING, 1902-1961)

American poet and novelist Fearing was born in Oak Park, Illinois and attended the University of Wisconsin. He is best known for his 1946 suspense novel *The Big Clock*, which was produced as a motion picture in 1948.

412 John Barry

Date of Publication: 1947
Subject(s): American West; Gold Rush—California
Fictional character(s): John Barry, Businessman
Time Period(s): 1840s; 1850s (1846-1850)
Locale(s): San Francisco, California

Summary: John Barry travels to California from Maine and becomes a prominent businessman who plays a role in the development of San Francisco. The novel captures the gold rush experience and the aftermath of the Donner party disaster.

Historical Accuracy: Bedford provides an accurate sketch of the period and its events.

DAVID BEE

413 Curse of Magira

Date of Publication: 1964
Subject(s): World War I; Mystery

Fictional character(s): Pete Disley, Police Officer (superintendant); Manfred Von Thieleman, Police Officer
Time Period(s): 1910s (1914-1918); 1960s
Locale(s): Tanzania (then Tanganyika)

Summary: In Tanganyika in the 1960s, the newly appointed superintendent of police, Pete Dilsey, examines a skull of a Boer prospector missing for more than 40 years. His predecessor, Manfred von Thieleman, offers clues to the mystery, and the story shifts to the East African campaign during World War I and the four year struggle between Britain and Germany for control of the area.

Historical Accuracy: The novel offers an ingenious reconstruction of the past.

THOMAS BEER (1889-1940)

American novelist Beer attended Yale, then studied law at Columbia University, becoming a sixth-generation lawyer. He fought in World War I and began to write on his return to America. He gave up the practice of law soon after.

414 *Sandoval: A Romance of Bad Manners*

Date of Publication: 1924
Subject(s): Social Chronicle
Fictional character(s): Thorold Gaar, Teenager; Christian Cody de Sandoval, Adventurer
Time Period(s): 1870s
Locale(s): New York, New York

Summary: Social life in New York forms the background for this story of two brothers. When a shady business deal is brought to light, both brothers become disillusioned.

Historical Accuracy: The novel's period background is authentic and believable.

ROBERT J. BEGIEBING

415 *The Strange Death of Mistress Coffin*

Date of Publication: 1991
Subject(s): American Colonies; Mystery; Witchcraft and Sorcery
Fictional character(s): Richard Browne, Detective—Amateur; Kathrin Coffin, Settler; Elizabeth Higgins, Settler
Time Period(s): 17th century (1640s)
Locale(s): New Hampshire, American Colonies

Summary: Based on an actual unsolved murder case in colonial America, the novel dramatizes the investigation by Richard Browne into the murder of Kathrin Coffin. Her death is a baffling mystery entangled with the motives and beliefs of the colonists. Kathrin's own journal reveals a complex and human voice untimely silenced.

Historical Accuracy: The novel offers a fascinating and authentic evocation of life in early America that goes well beyond the cliches of Puritan life.

LOUIS BEGLEY (1933-)

Born in Poland, Begley immigrated to the U.S. in 1948, becoming an American citizen in 1953. He attended Harvard and became an attorney specializing in international corporate law.

416 *Wartime Lies*

Date of Publication: 1991
Subject(s): World War II; Holocaust; Childhood
Fictional character(s): Maciek, Orphan; Tania, Gentlewoman
Time Period(s): 1930s; 1940s (1939-1945)
Locale(s): Warsaw, Poland

Summary: Maciek and his Aunt Tania survive the German invasion of Poland in 1939, outwitting both the Gestapo and Polish Jew hunters before being taken. They escape from a train bound for Auschwitz and take refuge on a peasant farm. At the war's end, Maciek faces adulthood with his childhood permanently lost and a past that must be expiated.

Historical Accuracy: The novel is intimate, shrewdly observant, and authentic in its power to capture the experience of the Holocaust.

EMERY BEKESSY

417 *Barabbas: A Novel of the Time of Jesus*

Date of Publication: 1946
Subject(s): Biblical Story
Historical character(s): Barabbas, Biblical Figure, Thief; Jesus Christ, Biblical Figure; Pontius Pilate, Government Official, Biblical Figure; Mary Magdalene, Biblical Figure; Joseph of Arimathea, Biblical Figure
Time Period(s): 1st century
Locale(s): Jerusalem, Israel

Summary: In this speculation about why Barabbas was chosen to be released rather than Jesus, Barabbas is portrayed not as a common thief but as a revolutionary leader. Barabbas' call for the violent overthrow of Roman rule contrasts with Jesus' message of peace.

Historical Accuracy: There is no historical basis for the novel's portrait of Barabbas. As an example of the clash of factions during the period, the novel does have some historical validity.

CEDRIC BELFRAGE (1904-1990)

An English author born in London, Belfrage attended Cambridge University. During World War II, he served in British Intelligence. A radical journalist for a variety of newspapers and magazines, Belfrage was a target of congressional investigators during the McCarthy era in the 1950s. His works include *A Faith to Free the People*, *Seeds of Destruction*, and *The Man at the Door with the Gun*.

418 *My Master Columbus*

Date of Publication: 1961
Subject(s): Exploration; Indians
Fictional character(s): Yayael, Servant, Indian
Historical character(s): Cristobal Colon, Explorer, Sea Captain
Time Period(s): 15th century; 16th century (1492-1506)
Locale(s): West Indies (Haiti, Cuba, Bahamas); Spain

Summary: Columbus is seen from the perspective of a Native American whom he "discovers" in 1492. Yayael accompanies Columbus back to Spain and on his return voyages to the New World. On either side of the Atlantic, the cultural conflict is explored as the new world meets the old with tragic consequences for some.

Historical Accuracy: The novel is more a satire than an actual depiction of the historical Columbus, but the details of the voyages are realistically shown.

ANTHEA BELL

419 *The Floral Companion*

Date of Publication: 1988
Subject(s): Romance
Fictional character(s): Caroline Elliott, Widow(er), Artist; William Gerard, Gentleman; Clarissa Gerard, Gentlewoman
Time Period(s): 1830s (1830)
Locale(s): East Anglia, England; London, England

Summary: The recently widowed Caroline Elliott avoids the London season by accepting an invitation from her cousin, Clarissa, to join her in East Anglia. There Caroline hopes to get on with her book of paintings of wild flowers. Instead of the pastoral retreat she craves she finds a conspiracy to match her with Clarissa's son, William, as well as strange country happenings including a peasant uprising and gossip surrounding the vicarage.

Historical Accuracy: The novel is a delightful comedy of manners with a well-grounded period background.

420 *A London Season*

Date of Publication: 1983
Subject(s): Romance; Servants
Fictional character(s): Elinor Radley, Governess; Sir Edmund Grafton, Nobleman; Persephone Grafton, Ward, Heiress
Time Period(s): 1820s (1826)
Locale(s): England

Summary: Elinor Radley, a governess with a secret, is hired to serve as the chaperone of Sir Edmund's 18-year-old ward, Persephone. A series of secrets complicates the situation. Why is Persephone so reluctant to make her debut in society? How can Elinor keep her past hidden as her affection for Sir Edmund grows?.

Historical Accuracy: The novel shows an impressive sense of the period and faithfully depicts that background.

CLARE BELL (1952-)

A science fiction and fantasy writer, Bell's novels include *Clan Ground*, *People of the Sky*, *Ratha and Thistle-Chaser*, *Ratha's Creature*, and *Tomorrow's Sphinx*.

421 *The Jaguar Princess*

Date of Publication: 1993
Subject(s): Aztec Empire; Fantasy
Fictional character(s): Mixcatl, Royalty (princess); Wise Coyote, Royalty (prince), Architect; Nine-Lizard, Writer (scribe)
Time Period(s): Indeterminate Past
Locale(s): Tenochtitlan, Mexico

Summary: Set in the pre-Columbian Aztec Empire, the novel tells the story of Mixcatl, the Jaguar Princess. She is a former slave who rises up to challenge the rigid and violent codes of the Aztecs. In a blend of magic and power, she withstands the treachery of the Aztec court.

Historical Accuracy: The novel's fantasy elements are solidly based on the culture and the atmosphere of the pre-Columbian world view and its customs.

MADISON SMARTT BELL (1957-)

Born in Nashville, Tennessee, Bell attended Princeton University and Hollins College. He has been a teacher of writing and the director of a media arts organization. Bell is the author of two collections of short stories and several novels, including *Save Me, Joe Louis*, *Dr. Sleep*, and *Soldier's Joy*.

422 *All Souls' Rising*

Date of Publication: 1995
Subject(s): Independence—Haiti; Slavery; French Colonies
Fictional character(s): Antoine Hebert, Doctor; Claudine Arnaud, Gentlewoman
Historical character(s): Pierre Dominique Toussaint l'Ouverture, Revolutionary, Political Figure
Time Period(s): 1790s (1791-1793); 1800s (1802)
Locale(s): Haiti

Summary: The story of the slave revolt that freed Haiti from French colonial rule is dramatized in scenes of harrowing violence and suffering. The story follows a large group of characters from different social strata during the events of the period. At the center of this story is Toussaint L'Ouverture, a self-educated and determined African slave who leads the insurrection.

Historical Accuracy: The novel offers a convincing internal and external view of the revolt and its central player.

NEIL BELL
(PSEUD. OF STEPHEN SOUTHWOLD, 1887-1964)

English novelist and children's writer Southwold fought in World War I and also worked as an artist, art teacher, freelance journalist, shipwright, and English teacher. Besides Neil Bell, Southwold also published under the names Miles and Paul Martens.

423   *So Perish the Roses*

Date of Publication: 1940
Subject(s): Biography, Fictionalized; Literary Life
Historical character(s): Charles Lamb, Writer; Mary Ann Lamb, Writer
Time Period(s): 18th century; 19th century
Locale(s): England

Summary: This fictional biography traces the careers of Charles and Mary Ann Lamb. The novel attempts to portray Charles Lamb as a complete human being rather than as the idealized figure created by Coleridge and Wordsworth. It also deals with the fit of insanity that leads Mary Lamb to wound her father and kill her mother, as well as the literary associations of both brother and sister.

Historical Accuracy: The novel is balanced in its portrait of the Lambs and convincing in rendering fully-rounded characters.

SALLIE BELL

An American writer born in New Orleans, Bell attended Newcomb College.

424   *Marcel Armand*

Date of Publication: 1935
Subject(s): War of 1812; Pirates
Fictional character(s): Marcel Armand, Pirate; Elbee Rochelle, Gentlewoman; Andre Fournier, Military Personnel (captain)
Historical character(s): Jean Laffite, Pirate
Time Period(s): 1810s
Locale(s): New Orleans, Louisiana

Summary: This historical romance set in New Orleans during the War of 1812 concerns the aristocratic Elbee Rochelle, who is torn between the love of two men, Captain Andre Fournier and Marcel Armand, a lieutenant of pirate leader Jean Lafitte. Treachery and misunderstanding must be cleared away before true love can flourish.

Historical Accuracy: Despite the premium on romantic situations, the novel stays close to actual facts and accurately reports historical events.

THOMAS BELL (1902-1961)

425   *Out of This Furnace*

Date of Publication: 1941
Subject(s): Immigrants; Labor Movement
Fictional character(s): Djuro Kracha, Immigrant; Mike Dobrejcak, Worker (steel); Mary Dobrejcak, Spouse; Dobie Dobrejcak, Labor Organizer
Time Period(s): 19th century; 20th century (1880s-1930s)
Locale(s): Braddock, Pennsylvania

Summary: The story of America's steel industry is reflected in the experiences of three generations of an immigrant family. The novel begins in the 1880s with the arrival of Djaro Kracha who finds work in the steel mills of Braddock, Pennsylvania. The family drama shares the stage with the develop-

ment of the labor movement and the creation of the Congress of Industrial Organizations.

Historical Accuracy: The novel is an authentic picture of the period and region.

JAMES WARNER BELLAH (1899-1976)

An American writer, Bellah was born in New York City and attended Columbia and the University of Pennsylvania. He worked as an advertising copywriter, a college instructor, and a foreign correspondent. He was the author of various screenplays about the American West, including the classics *Fort Apache*, *She Wore a Yellow Ribbon*, and *The Man Who Shot Liberty Valance*.

426   *The Journal of Colonel De Lancey*

Date of Publication: 1967
Subject(s): Revolution—Central America
Fictional character(s): Christopher De Lancey, Military Personnel, Mercenary
Historical character(s): William Walker, Adventurer, Revolutionary
Time Period(s): 19th century (1832-1850)
Locale(s): London, England; Nicaragua

Summary: De Lancey is a subaltern in the Duke of Cornwall's Regiment when an indiscretion with a royal princess forces him out of the army. He offers his services to American soldier of fortune William Walker, joining Walker in his grand campaign to conquer all of Central America.

Historical Accuracy: The novel offers an interesting portrait of the enigmatic but fascinating Walker, but the emphasis is on romantic adventure rather than historical events.

427   *The Valiant Virginians*

Date of Publication: 1953
Subject(s): Civil War—U.S.; Military Life
Fictional character(s): Roan Catlett, Military Personnel (Confederate cavalry trooper); Davin Ancrum, Military Personnel (Confederate cavalry trooper); Forney Manigault, Military Personnel (Confederate cavalry trooper)
Time Period(s): 1860s
Locale(s): Virginia

Summary: This Civil War story tells the adventures of three young Confederate cavalry troopers in the Army of the Shenandoah under the command of Jubal Early. They participate in a number of engagements in the early years of the war.

Historical Accuracy: The novel portrays the military life and engagements of the period with a meticulous authority.

HENRY BELLAMANN

428   *Kings Row*

Date of Publication: 1940
Subject(s): Rural Life—U.S.; Medical Profession
Fictional character(s): Parris Mitchell, Young Man, Student (medical)

Time Period(s): 1890s; 1900s
Locale(s): Midwest

Summary: Life in a small midwestern town at the turn of the century is this novel's subject. Seen through the eyes of Parris Mitchell, the story covers his life up to the point when he goes off to study medicine. The novel's theme is the degeneration of the town's former pioneer spirit into cynicism and greed.

Historical Accuracy: The novel captures small town life during the period convincingly.

PAMELA BELLE (1952-)

English novelist Belle was an elementary school teacher before turning to writing full-time in 1985. Because her characters are so real to her, she places great importance on proper historical research, desiring to make every detail of their lives accurate.

429 *Alethea*

Date of Publication: 1985
Subject(s): Artistic Life; Family Saga; Restoration Period
Fictional character(s): Alathea Heron, Artist; Jasper Sewell, Doctor; Kit Drakelon, Gentleman
Historical character(s): John Wilmot, Nobleman (Earl of Rochester)
Time Period(s): 17th century (1660-1674)
Locale(s): London, England

Summary: In the concluding volume of Belle's Heron family chronicle, the scene shifts to Restoration London and Alathea Heron's career as a famous painter, loved both by a young doctor, her step-brother, and John Wilmot, Earl of Rochester.

Historical Accuracy: The Restoration scenes are colorfully depicted.

430 *The Chains of Fate*

Date of Publication: 1984
Subject(s): Civil War—England; Family Saga; Romance
Fictional character(s): Thomazine Heron, Gentlewoman; Francis Heron, Military Personnel
Time Period(s): 17th century (1642-1660)
Locale(s): Scotland; Suffolk, England

Summary: In this second volume of Belle's Heron family chronicle, Thomazine travels north into Scotland in search of her lover, Francis Heron. The next generation of characters begins to increase in importance as the action of the English Civil War reaches its climax.

Historical Accuracy: The social and political scene is fully detailed and forms a solid background for the novel's romance.

431 *A Falling Star*

Date of Publication: 1990
Subject(s): Monmouth's Rebellion; Family Saga; Restoration Period
Fictional character(s): Silence St. Barbe, Gentlewoman; Alexander St. Barbe, Gentleman; Charles St. Barbe, Gentleman
Historical character(s): James Scott, Nobleman

Time Period(s): 17th century (1680s)
Locale(s): Bath, England

Summary: Silence St. Barbe, now a grandmother who has held her estate and family together through the English Civil War, must face the domestic challenge of who will inherit Wintercombe as rebellion breaks out again when the Protestant Duke of Monmouth challenges the Catholic James II for the throne.

Historical Accuracy: Belle successfully blends the domestic and the political into a full and accurate depiction of the times.

432 *The Lodestar*

Date of Publication: 1987
Subject(s): War of the Roses; Royalty—England; Middle Ages
Fictional character(s): Christopher Heron, Gentleman, Courtier; Julian Bray, Gentlewoman
Historical character(s): Richard, Duke of Gloucester, Royalty (later Richard III); Edward IV, Ruler (King of England); Henry Tudor, Nobleman (later Henry VII)
Time Period(s): 15th century
Locale(s): Northumbria, England; London, England

Summary: Christopher Heron is determined to rise in the world and joins the household of Richard, Duke of Gloucester, becoming a trusted member of the Duke's retinue. Christopher ascends to the pinnacle of power as Richard wins the scramble for the throne following the death of Edward IV. The treason, rebellion, and betrayal Christopher witnesses cause him to reassess his ambition.

Historical Accuracy: Belle ably dramatizes the torturous politics of the War of the Roses. The known facts are the bones of the story, but conjecture fleshes out certain gaps.

433 *The Moon in the Water*

Date of Publication: 1983
Subject(s): Civil War—England; Family Saga; Romance
Fictional character(s): Thomazine Heron, Heiress, Orphan; Francis Heron, Gentleman; Dominic Drakelon, Gentleman
Time Period(s): 17th century (1635-1642)
Locale(s): Suffolk, England; Banbury, England; Oxfordshire, England

Summary: This romantic tale of thwarted love is set during the turmoil of the English Civil War. Thomazine Heron becomes the ward of the Heron family. She is betrothed to Dominic Drakelon but is in love with the Heron's scapegrace son, Francis. The battles of the Civil War separate the lovers, and Francis is feared dead.

Historical Accuracy: The novel is solidly based on historical fact, and the period details are authentic.

434 *Treason's Gift*

Date of Publication: 1992
Subject(s): Glorious Revolution; Family Saga
Fictional character(s): Alexander St. Barbe, Gentleman, Rake; Louise Chevalier, Gentlewoman; Charles St. Barbe, Gentleman

Historical character(s): William of Orange, Royalty (Dutch ruler); James II, Ruler (King of England)
Time Period(s): 17th century (1680s)
Locale(s): Bath, England; Amsterdam, Netherlands; London, England

Summary: The St. Barbe family is swept up in the events leading to the Glorious Revolution of 1688. After the death of his son, Alexander St. Barbe returns to his rakish ways, while his exiled cousin Charles returns to claim the family estate and its mistress. Alex is employed by William of Orange as a spy, and England slides once again into civil war while trying to rid itself of its Catholic king, James II.

Historical Accuracy: Belle has made this period her own, and her research is both solid and convincing.

435 *Wintercombe*

Date of Publication: 1988
Subject(s): Civil War—England; Family Saga
Fictional character(s): Silence St. Barbe, Gentlewoman; Ridgeley, Military Personnel; Colonel Hellier, Military Personnel
Time Period(s): 17th century (1640s)
Locale(s): Bath, England

Summary: Lady St. Barbe is left on her own at the estate of Wintercombe while her husband and eldest son are fighting for the Parliamentary forces in the English Civil War. Her home is suddenly invaded by the King's forces, and she must maintain her household while tempted by the offer of love to abandon everything.

Historical Accuracy: The novel offers a marvelous reconstruction of daily life in a great house during the 17th century. The details are elaborate and totally convincing.

MARIA BELLONCI (1902-1986)

Italian journalist and reviewer Bellonci is best known for her psychologically insightful historical novels.

436 *Private Renaissance*

Date of Publication: 1985
Subject(s): Renaissance; Politics
Historical character(s): Isabella d'Este, Noblewoman; Francesco Gonzaga, Nobleman; Lucrezia Borgia, Noblewoman
Time Period(s): 16th century (1500-1533)
Locale(s): Ferrara, Italy; Rome, Italy; Mantua, Italy

Summary: The Italian Renaissance is viewed through the perspective of Isabella d'Este, Marchesa of Mantua and roving ambassador, who maintains the independence of Mantua despite shifting political allegiances. At the center of the storm that rages throughout Italy, Isabella creates a cultural locus for the artistic and intellectual achievement of the Renaissance.

Historical Accuracy: The historical detail is exact and compelling. Great events and personalities are believably captured.

CLARENCE BENADUM (1889-)

Born in Delaware County, Indiana, Benadum was educated at Valparaiso University. He hunted gold, worked as a cowboy, practiced law, and served in the field artillery in World War I.

437 *Bates House*

Date of Publication: 1951
Subject(s): Civil War—U.S.
Fictional character(s): David Stone, Lawyer; Margaret Manning, Southern Belle
Time Period(s): 1860s
Locale(s): United States

Summary: This romance set during the American Civil War reflects the war years from the point of view of a northern lawyer, David Stone, and a young southern girl, Margaret Manning. The romantic complications compete with battle and prison scenes.

Historical Accuracy: The atmosphere is authentic, documented from period speeches, editorials, and other sources.

NATHANIEL BENCHLEY (1915-1981)

American journalist, novelist, and humorist Nathaniel Benchley is the son of well-known humorist Robert Benchley and the father of Peter Benchley, the author of the best-selling *Jaws*. Benchley began his career as a reporter for the *New York Herald Tribune*. He is the author of plays, biographies, novels, screenplays, short stories, and works for juveniles, such as *Red Fox and His Canoe* and *Sam, the Minuteman*. He is probably best-known for his novel *The Off-Islanders*, which was made into the 1966 film *The Russians Are Coming, the Russians Are Coming*.

438 *Portrait of a Scoundrel*

Date of Publication: 1979
Subject(s): Business Building; American Revolution
Historical character(s): Robert Morris, Financier; James Greenleaf, Financier; George Washington, Political Figure; John Adams, Political Figure; John Hancock, Political Figure; Noah Webster, Scholar (lexicographer)
Time Period(s): 1780s; 1790s
Locale(s): Boston, Massachusetts; Philadelphia, Pennsylvania

Summary: The novel is a satirical and comic depiction of America's founding fathers and the early years of the young American Republic. It is based on the scandal created by a land speculation syndicate led by Robert Morris, the Superintendent of Finance during the Revolution, and Boston businessman James Greenleaf. Their greed leads to bankruptcy and financial ruin for many who trusted them.

Historical Accuracy: The novel is based on fact with an uncanny sense of the customs and details of period life. The novel's portraits of familiar figures are original and lacking the usual trappings of heroism.

DON BENDELL

439 Chief of Scouts

Date of Publication: 1993

Subject(s): Indians; Military Life—U.S. Cavalry; Battle of the Little Bighorn

Fictional character(s): Chris Colt, Frontiersman, Scout

Historical character(s): George Armstrong Custer, Military Personnel (cavalry officer); Crazy Horse, Indian (Sioux), Chieftain

Time Period(s): 1870s (1876)

Locale(s): Little Bighorn River, Montana

Summary: Chris Colt, a scout for the Seventh Cavalry, is also a blood brother of Crazy Horse. His loyalties clearly divided, Colt leads Custer into what he knows will be a tragic and deadly encounter. Courage and skill will be needed to survive the battle.

Historical Accuracy: The novel offers an unbiased version of the famous Last Stand.

LAURA BENET (1884-1979)

An American social worker, newspaper editor, poet, and author, Benet is the sister of Stephen Vincent and William Rose Benet. After retiring from social work, Benet worked for several New York newspapers, including the *New York Post*. Benet is the author of children's books, novels, and literary biographies.

440 Come Slowly Eden: A Novel about Emily Dickinson

Date of Publication: 1942

Subject(s): Biography, Fictionalized; Literary Life

Historical character(s): Emily Dickinson, Writer (poet), Recluse

Time Period(s): 19th century (1830s-1850s)

Locale(s): Amherst, Massachusetts

Summary: The novel presents a factual account of the life of poet Emily Dickinson. It traces her childhood in Amherst, Massachusetts, and ends in her disappointment with love, the suggested cause for her withdrawal from society and life as a recluse.

Historical Accuracy: The novel is faithful to the known facts of Dickinson's life and does not stray too far afield in suggesting the basis for her artistic genius or motivations.

STEPHEN VINCENT BENET (1898-1943)

American poet and novelist Benet was born in Pennsylvania and graduated from Yale University. Benet is best remembered for his poetry, especially for his long narrative poem on the Civil War, *John Brown's Body*, which won the Pulitzer Prize in 1929, and for his short story "The Devil and Daniel Webster" Benet also wrote the librettos for two one-act folk operas.

441 Spanish Bayonet

Date of Publication: 1926

Subject(s): American Revolution

Fictional character(s): Sebastian Zafortezas, Sea Captain; Andrew Beard, Young Man

Time Period(s): 1770s

Locale(s): New York, American Colonies; Florida

Summary: This adventure novel is set during the outbreak of the American Revolution and concerns young Andrew Beard, who finds himself in Spanish Florida when the hostilities begin. Divided loyalties produce a series of dramatic adventures.

Historical Accuracy: The emphasis is on colorful adventure and an exotic setting that predominates over a carefully detailed historical background.

FRANS GUNNAR BENGTSSON
(1894-1954)

Bengtsson is one of the most distinguished figures in 20th-century Swedish literature. He grew up in a farming and seafaring region in the southern province of Skane, which is featured in his best work, *The Long Ships*, a novel of medieval Sweden. His other works include *The Sword Does Not Jest: The Heroic Life of Charles XII of Sweden, A Walk on the Ant Hill, and Other Essays*, and *Red Orm*.

442 The Long Ships

Date of Publication: 1954

Subject(s): Vikings; Dark Ages; Byzantine Empire

Fictional character(s): Red Orm, Warrior, Adventurer; Toke, Warrior, Adventurer

Time Period(s): 10th century

Locale(s): Spain; Asia Minor; Byzantine Empire

Summary: The novel offers a saga of Viking adventure, chronicling the various exploits of Red Orm in Spain, as a galley slave of the Muslims, and at the court of the Byzantine emperor. In all, Orm proves himself to be a brave and clever warrior fired by the thrill of adventure.

Historical Accuracy: The novel's events are invented, but the story offers an authentic version of Viking life.

ANTONIO BENITEZ-ROJO (1931-)

Born in Havana, Cuba, Antonio Benitez-Rojo emigrated to the U.S. in 1980. He attended the Colegio de Belen, the University of Havana, and American University. Benitez-Rojo worked for the Ministry of Labor, the Latin American Center for Literary Research, and as a publisher in Cuba prior to his defection. In the U.S. he has taught at several colleges and universities. He is currently a professor of Romance languages at Amherst College. Benitez-Rojo is the author of the award-winning book of short stories *Tute de Reyes* and the novel *The Enigma of the Esterlines*.

443   *Sea of Lentils*

Date of Publication: 1990
Subject(s): Exploration; Spanish Colonies; Slavery
Fictional character(s): Anton Babtista, Military Personnel (Spanish soldier)
Historical character(s): Philip II, Ruler (King of Spain); Don Pedro de Valdes, Gentleman, Military Personnel (Spanish soldier); Don Pedro de Ponte, Businessman
Time Period(s): 16th century
Locale(s): Spain; West Indies; St. Augustine, Florida

Summary: The novel weaves together a variety of perspectives on Spain's ventures in America. The fragmented narration includes the story of the fictional Anton Babtista who accompanies Columbus on his second voyage to America, the founding of St. Augustine and the American slave trade, and the death-bed reflections of Spanish King Philip II.

Historical Accuracy: Called a deconstructionist novel, the text combines the factual and the imaginary and serves to demythologize the Spanish colonial experience. The novel does not aspire to a balanced portrait but is thesis-documented in its treatment of colonialism.

JOHN BENNETT (1865-1956)

Bennett was born in Ohio and settled in Charleston, South Carolina. In addition to *So Shall They Reap*, he is best known for *Skylark*, a boy's book set in Shakespeare's time. His work on South Carolina folklore and African-American life is collected in *The Doctor to the Dead: Grotesque Legends & Folk Tales of Old Charleston.*

444   *So Shall They Reap*

Date of Publication: 1944
Subject(s): Civil War—U.S.
Fictional character(s): Sam Mitchell, Military Personnel (Confederate soldier)
Time Period(s): 1860s
Locale(s): Alabama

Summary: This Civil War-era tale portrays the non-slave holding Southerners who defined the attitude, ''rich man's war, poor man's fight.'' The novel concerns a feud between the Mitchells and the Crombies that plays itself out against the events of the Civil War.

Historical Accuracy: The perspective on the fighting and military life of the time is original and believable, though different from other fictional treatments. The author is clearly at home in the region, among the southern poor whites whose interests are very different from the plantation owners who fight for the preservation of their way of life.

PAMELA BENNETTS (1922-)

English novelist Bennetts writes her books in her spare time. She works full-time on the staff of the London Diocesan fund of the Church of England. Bennetts prefers historical novels as she finds the modern world unsatisfactory and vastly unromantic.

445   *The Barons of Runnymede*

Date of Publication: 1974
Subject(s): Middle Ages; Royalty—England
Historical character(s): John, Ruler (King of England); Isabella of Angouleme, Royalty (Queen of England), Spouse (of John); Stephen Langton, Religious (archbishop); Philip II, Ruler (King of France)
Time Period(s): 13th century (1200s)
Locale(s): England; France

Summary: The troubled reign of King John is chronicled in this novel that climaxes with his grudging signing of Magna Carta and a redefinition of royal power in England. John is shown as a complex blend of shrewdness and incompetence, headstrong but often wrong in gauging both his support and his opposition. He is also plagued by an unfaithful wife.

Historical Accuracy: This is a balanced portrait of John, a combination of differing historical views of his reign.

446   *The Borgia Prince*

Date of Publication: 1968
Subject(s): Renaissance; Politics
Fictional character(s): Bianca Di Marco, Prisoner, Gentlewoman; Beltrame Di Marco, Prisoner, Gentleman
Historical character(s): Cesare Borgia, Military Personnel, Nobleman; Niccolo Machiavelli, Diplomat, Political Figure
Time Period(s): 15th century
Locale(s): San Severo, Italy; Imola, Italy

Summary: Cesare Borgia faces rebellion among his condottieri who fear his growing power. He crushes the rebellion at San Severo and captures a beautiful young woman, Bianca, who desperately tries to save her brother's life. She falls in love with the scheming but charismatic Borgia. Machiavelli, a diplomat from Florence, is on hand to keep watch on the prince.

Historical Accuracy: The details of Renaissance power politics are vividly presented, as is the human side of Borgia, too often shown as a monster.

447   *The De Montfort Legacy*

Date of Publication: 1973
Subject(s): Middle Ages; Royalty—England; Baron's War
Historical character(s): Henry III, Ruler (King of England); Simon de Montfort, Nobleman (Earl of Leicester); Edward I, Ruler (King of England)
Time Period(s): 13th century (1264-1272)
Locale(s): England; Wales

Summary: Simon de Montfort leads England's barons in a revolt against Henry III to counter his claim of absolute power. Henry is defeated at the Battle of Lewes and for a short time Simon holds power until he is overthrown by Edward I, Henry's son, at Evesham. This is the story of these tumultuous times that saw the first ever Parliament that included representatives of the common people of England.

Historical Accuracy: The facts are well-grounded in historical research.

448 *Death of the Red King*

Date of Publication: 1976

Subject(s): Middle Ages; Mystery; Royalty—England

Historical character(s): William Rufus, Ruler (King of England); Walter Tirel, Nobleman; Henry Beauclerc, Nobleman (later Henry I)

Time Period(s): 12th century (1100)

Locale(s): New Forest, England; Winchester, England

Summary: In 1100 while hunting in England's New Forest, William Rufus, King of England, is accidentally killed with an arrow through the heart. But was it an accident? The novel offers a fascinating speculation on William's death and the conspiracy that may have been behind it.

Historical Accuracy: The interpretation of the event is speculative, yet the historical background is knowledgeably established, and Bennetts makes a dramatic case.

449 *Don Pedro's Captain*

Date of Publication: 1978

Subject(s): Middle Ages; Royalty—England

Historical character(s): Edward, the Black Prince, Royalty; Pedro the Cruel, Ruler (King of Castile)

Time Period(s): 14th century (1360s)

Locale(s): Aquitaine, France; Najera, Spain; Bordeaux, France

Summary: The last great adventure of Edward, the Black Prince is to aid the deposed King of Castile in reclaiming his throne. Edward achieves a great military success at Najera, but, after restoring Don Pedro to his throne, Edward and his army are betrayed when Pedro fails to pay Edward's debts. Edward returns to his weakened province of Aquitaine disappointed and stricken by the illness that will kill him.

Historical Accuracy: The story is an accurate account of the final gallant adventure of Edward.

450 *A Dragon for Edward*

Date of Publication: 1975

Subject(s): Middle Ages; Royalty—England

Historical character(s): Edward I, Ruler (King of England); Llywelyn ap Gruffydd, Royalty (Prince of Wales)

Time Period(s): 13th century (1270s)

Locale(s): England; Wales

Summary: The novel dramatizes the struggle between England and Wales as Edward I attempts to subdue the Welsh led by Llywelyn ap Gruffydd. Against this historical background is a fictional story involving one of Edward's marcher lords and a Welsh girl whose brother has a deep-seated hatred for the English.

Historical Accuracy: Richly evocative of the period, the story is set against a historical backdrop that is faithful to the facts.

451 *Envoy From Elizabeth*

Date of Publication: 1973

Subject(s): Elizabethan Period; Royalty—England; Espionage

Fictional character(s): Nicholas Rokesby, Military Personnel, Spy; Catalina, Ward, Gentlewoman

Historical character(s): Elizabeth I, Ruler (Queen of England); Sir Francis Drake, Sea Captain, Military Personnel

Time Period(s): 16th century (1580s)

Locale(s): London, England; Spain

Summary: As the Spanish fleet prepares to invade England, King Philip sends an assassin to kill Elizabeth I. The queen responds by sending Nicholas Rokesby to Philip's court as a spy to learn the identity of the assassin. Nicholas loses his heart to Catalina, Philip's beautiful ward, who has her own secret.

Historical Accuracy: The action is fast-paced and exciting with convincing depictions of the English and Spanish courts.

452 *The Lords of Lancaster*

Date of Publication: 1973

Subject(s): Middle Ages; War of the Roses; Royalty—England

Historical character(s): Richard II, Ruler (King of England); John of Gaunt, Royalty; Henry Bolingbroke, Nobleman, Ruler (King of England); Isabella of France, Royalty (queen consort of Richard); Anne of Bohemia, Royalty (Richard's first wife)

Time Period(s): 14th century

Locale(s): England

Summary: The causes and origin of the War of the Roses are chronicled in this story of the reign of Richard II. Richard becomes increasingly despotic and indifferent to laws and customs. When he banishes his cousin Henry Bolingbroke, the seeds for his destruction are planted as Henry returns and full-scale rebellion breaks out.

Historical Accuracy: The story is plausibly researched with convincing historical details of the period.

453 *My Dear Lover England*

Date of Publication: 1975

Subject(s): Elizabethan Period; Royalty—England

Fictional character(s): Lady Damaris Wyngarde, Noblewoman; Lord Randal Cavendish, Nobleman

Historical character(s): Elizabeth I, Ruler (Queen of England); Robert Dudley, Nobleman (Earl of Leicester)

Time Period(s): 16th century

Locale(s): England

Summary: The intrigue of Elizabeth I's court is seen from the perspective of Damaris Wyngarde who becomes a maid of honor to the queen. The court is scandalized by the intimate relationship between Elizabeth and Lord Dudley. When Dudley's wife dies suspiciously, the central question is whether Elizabeth intends to make Dudley her husband.

Historical Accuracy: The fictional story of Damaris is set within a convincing version of the events surrounding Amy Robsart's death and the question of Elizabeth's marital intentions.

454 *Richard and the Knights of God*

Date of Publication: 1973

Subject(s): Middle Ages; Crusades; Royalty—England

Fictional character(s): Simon Fitzalan, Knight; Latisse de Vaudemont, Captive
Historical character(s): Richard I, Ruler (King of England); Saladin, Ruler (Muslim)
Time Period(s): 12th century
Locale(s): Palestine

Summary: In this tale of the Crusades, Simon Fitzalan sails to join Richard in his struggle against Muslim leader Saladin. Simon is in search of a priceless relic taken from the first crusaders years before. He saves the life of Saladin's nephew, and as a reward Saladin gives Simon one of his French captives, the fiery and beautiful Latisse de Vaudemont.

Historical Accuracy: The romance and adventure is supported by evident research and accurate details of the events and the period.

455   *Royal Sword at Agincourt*

Date of Publication: 1971
Subject(s): Middle Ages; Royalty—England; Battle of Agincourt
Fictional character(s): Tracy de Redvers, Knight, Courtier; Felice Ashville, Traitor
Historical character(s): Harry Monmouth, Royalty (prince), Ruler (King of England); Henry IV, Ruler (King of England); Charles VI, Ruler (King of France)
Time Period(s): 15th century
Locale(s): London, England; Normandy, France

Summary: Pleasure-loving Prince Harry is transformed into dutiful Henry V on his father's death. Determined to exalt the crown his father seized, he earns a great victory over the French at Agincourt. There are, however, still conspirators, and his faithful vassal Tracy de Redvers is torn between his loyalty to the king and his passion for Felice Ashville, a conspirator.

Historical Accuracy: This is essentially Shakespeare's Henry with a somewhat implausible romantic story of intrigue added.

456   *The She-Wolf*

Date of Publication: 1975
Subject(s): Middle Ages; Royalty—England
Historical character(s): Edward II, Ruler (King of England); Isabella of France, Royalty (queen consort of Edward II); Roger de Mortimer, Nobleman; Edward III, Ruler (King of England); Piers Gaveston, Companion (of Edward II); Hugh Dispenser, Companion (of Edward II); Charles IV, Ruler (King of France)
Time Period(s): 14th century
Locale(s): England; France

Summary: The novel dramatizes the troubled reign of Edward II and his conflict with his wife, Isabella of France. With the help of her lover, Roger Mortimer, Isabella forces Edward's abdication and arranges his murder. Isabella's son eventually seizes control as Edward III and brings Isabella and Mortimer to justice. Isabella is one of the most vilified figures in English history, and the novel shows why this is so.

Historical Accuracy: The novel's reconstruction of history is accurate.

457   *Stephen and the Sleeping Saints*

Date of Publication: 1977
Subject(s): Middle Ages; Royalty—England
Fictional character(s): Leonia FitzAdeline, Gentlewoman
Historical character(s): Matilda, Royalty (empress); Geoffrey de Mandeville, Nobleman (Earl of Essex)
Time Period(s): 12th century (1144)
Locale(s): East Anglia, England

Summary: England is in the midst of civil war as Matilda challenges Stephen's right to the English throne. Geoffrey de Mandeville, Earl of Essex, in defiance of Stephen, has embarked on a campaign of plunder and destruction in East Anglia. Love proves to be a casualty of the war as a tragic romance occurs between Geoffrey and one of his prisoners.

Historical Accuracy: The novel is a convincing drama of conflicting egos in the period setting.

ROBERT HUGH BENSON (1871-1914)

English author Benson was the son of Edward White Benson, an Archbishop of Canterbury, and the brother of writers A.C. and E.F. Benson. In 1903 he joined the Roman Catholic Church and was ordained as a priest a year later. In 1911 he was made a monsignor and became privy chamberlain to Pope Pius X.

458   *Come Rack! Come Rope!*

Date of Publication: 1912
Subject(s): Elizabethan Period; Religious Conflict
Fictional character(s): Robin Audrey, Religious (priest); Marjorie Manners, Gentlewoman
Historical character(s): Mary, Queen of Scots, Ruler (Queen of Scotland); Edmund Campion, Religious (priest)
Time Period(s): 16th century
Locale(s): England; Rheims, France

Summary: The novel's title refers to Edmund Campion's defiant rallying cry of hunted priests in Elizabethan England. The era is dramatized in the story of Robin Audrey and Marjorie Manners, lovers whose break-up causes Robin to become a priest. On his return to England, the odds are against his survival, as well as the Catholic Church and the Stuart cause.

Historical Accuracy: The novel is a convincing dramatic portrait of Elizabethan England and the fate of priests during the Reformation.

459   *The King's Achievement*

Date of Publication: 1905
Subject(s): Tudor Period; Religious Life; Religious Conflict
Fictional character(s): Christopher Torridon, Religious (monk); Ralph Torridon, Gentleman
Historical character(s): Beatrice Atherton, Gentlewoman; Sir Thomas More, Government Official; Henry VIII, Ruler (King of England); Thomas Cromwell, Government Official

Time Period(s): 16th century
Locale(s): England

Summary: The destruction caused by the Protestant Reformation is dramatized in the conflict of the Torridon brothers—Christopher, a monk, and Ralph, the opportunistic agent of Thomas Cromwell. The dissolution of the monasteries and religious persecution are depicted in this sweeping novel that animates many historical figures of the era.

Historical Accuracy: The novel is as faithful to the religious atmosphere as it is to the political era.

BARBARA BENTLEY

460 *Mistress Nancy*

Date of Publication: 1980
Subject(s): Trials
Historical character(s): Nancy Randolph, Gentlewoman (aka Anne Cary Morris); Gouverneur Morris, Political Figure, Diplomat; Patrick Henry, Lawyer; John Marshall, Lawyer; John Randolph, Political Figure
Time Period(s): 18th century; 19th century
Locale(s): New York; Virginia

Summary: Based on the life of Nancy Randolph, the novel explores the sensational 18th-century scandal in which Randolph faces trial for murder. She is defended by Patrick Henry and John Marshall (later to become Chief Justice of the Supreme Court). Although acquitted, she is plagued by rumors that threaten to ruin her marriage with prominent politician Gouverneur Morris.

Historical Accuracy: The novel is based on actual journals and court documents and no major character or situation has been invented.

PHYLLIS BENTLEY (1894-1977)

An English writer born in Halifax, Bentley graduated from the University of London. A former teacher and government secretary during World War I and II, Bentley was a prominent regional novelist who devoted her career to writing almost exclusively about the West Riding of Yorkshire, her lifelong home. She regarded her trilogy—*Inheritance, The Rise of Henry Morcar,* and *A Man of His Time*—as her most significant accomplishment.

461 *Freedom, Farewell*

Date of Publication: 1936
Subject(s): Roman Empire; Biography, Fictionalized
Historical character(s): Julius Caesar, Military Personnel (general), Political Figure; Pompey, Military Personnel (general), Political Figure; Marcus Tullius Cicero, Lawyer; Marcus Licinius Crassus, Political Figure, Military Personnel (general); Marcus Junius Brutus, Political Figure; Marcus Porcius Cato, Political Figure
Time Period(s): 1st century B.C.
Locale(s): Rome, Roman Empire; Gaul; Africa

Summary: This fictional biography of Julius Caesar traces his career from his youth to his assassination and the accession of Augustus. The novel offers a vivid portrait of Julius Caesar's rise to power as well as a close look at Roman customs and politics of the period. .ACCACC The novel's panoramic approach provides coverage in breadth rather than depth. Yet the basic framework is accurately depicted in a series of believable portraits.

462 *The Power and the Glory*

Date of Publication: 1940
Subject(s): Civil War—England; Restoration Period
Fictional character(s): Penninah Clarkson, Young Woman; John Thorpe, Businessman (clothier); Francis Ferrand, Gentleman
Time Period(s): 17th century (1620s-1660s)
Locale(s): Yorkshire, England

Summary: The story of the English Civil War is described from the perspective of two Puritan families in Yorkshire. Penninah Clarkson in old age narrates her autobiography, including her marriage to fellow Puritan John Thorpe and her love for the Royalist Francis Ferrand. The novel captures with some skill the period and its clash of religious and political ideas.

Historical Accuracy: The novel succeeds in capturing ordinary daily life and customs as well as showing the effects of the major historical events of the day.

KENNETH BENTON (1909-)

British author Benton was born in South Coldfield, England, and was educated at the University of London, the University of Florence, and the University of Vienna. From 1937 to 1968, Benton served with the British Foreign Service as a diplomat in Austria, Latvia, Italy, Peru, and Brazil. He is the author of *Twenty-Fourth Level, Spy in Chancery,* and *Craig and the Living Dead.*

463 *Death on the Appian Way*

Date of Publication: 1974
Subject(s): Roman Empire
Historical character(s): Marcus Tullius Cicero, Political Figure, Lawyer; Clodia, Gentlewoman; Marcus Caelius, Gentleman; Publius Clodius Pulcher, Political Figure
Time Period(s): 1st century B.C.
Locale(s): Rome, Roman Empire

Summary: Life in the Roman Republic in the years before the political coalition of Pompey, Caesar, and Crassus is dramatized through the feud between Cicero and Clodius. The novel is narrated by Marcus Caelius, Cicero's pupil and the lover of Clodius' sister, Clodia.

Historical Accuracy: The novel's characterizations are not entirely convincing though the atmosphere is authentic.

PAUL BENTON

464 *The Gentleman From America*

Date of Publication: 1957

Subject(s): Regency Period
Fictional character(s): Captain Jack Newbury, Adventurer; Alastair MacPhiggan, Nobleman
Historical character(s): Arthur Wellesley, Nobleman (Duke of Wellington); Alexander I, Ruler (Czar of Russia)
Time Period(s): 1810s
Locale(s): London, England; Paris, France; St. Petersburg, Russia

Summary: This adventure tale in the Alexandre Dumas tradition dramatizes the exploits of American Jack Newbury who, after ten years trapping in the Rockies, joins forces with his cousin Alastair MacPhiggan for a series of European adventures. They include a duel in Regency England, intrigue in Paris, and a secret mission for the Duke of Wellington to Russia.

Historical Accuracy: The novel traces its historical background lightly with an emphasis on fast-paced adventure.

JULIETTE BENZONI (1920-)

Benzoni is a Paris-born French writer. Her series of historical novels featuring strong female central characters have been praised both for their liveliness and historical backgrounds.

465 *The Lure of the Falcon*

Date of Publication: 1978
Subject(s): American Revolution; Indians
Fictional character(s): Gilles Goelo, Bastard Son, Military Personnel; Judith de Saint Melaine, Noblewoman
Historical character(s): George Washington, Military Personnel (commander of American forces); Marie Joseph Paul de Lafayette, Military Personnel, Nobleman (Marquis de Lafayette); Alexander Hamilton, Military Personnel; Benedict Arnold, Military Personnel, Traitor
Time Period(s): 1770s; 1780s (1779-1781)
Locale(s): France; New York; Pennsylvania

Summary: Gilles Goelo's mother pressures him to join the priesthood, hoping to atone for the affair which left her with a bastard son. The identity of Gilles' father remains a secret, and he rebels against his mother. He joins Lafayette and goes to America where his daring attracts the attention of General Washington who sends him on a mission in which his true identity as a hero is revealed.

Historical Accuracy: The novel offers non-stop adventure with historical touches. The period is vividly depicted.

466 *Marianne*

Date of Publication: 1969
Subject(s): Napoleonic Era; Espionage; Romance
Fictional character(s): Marianne d'Asselnat, Orphan, Noblewoman; Francis Cranmere, Nobleman; Jason Beaufort, Sea Captain
Historical character(s): Joseph Fouche, Government Official (minister of Police); Napoleon Bonaparte, Military Personnel, Ruler (Emperor of France); Charles Maurice de Talleyrand-Perigord, Government Official, Diplomat
Time Period(s): 1790s; 1800s (1793-1809)

Locale(s): Paris, France; England

Summary: The novel begins the adventures of Marianne d'Asselnat during the Napoleonic Era. Marianne is orphaned during the Reign of Terror. Her marriage to an English lord ends in disaster when her fortune and virginity are lost to Beaufort, an adventuring sea captain. She flees to France where she is employed as a spy in the home of Tallyrand before becoming one of Napoleon's mistresses.

Historical Accuracy: What separates this novel from other romantic adventure stories is the evident research into the period that creates an authentic atmospere.

467 *Marianne and the Crown of Fire*

Date of Publication: 1976
Subject(s): Napoleonic Wars
Fictional character(s): Marianne d'Asselnat, Royalty (princess); Jason Beaufort, Gentleman
Historical character(s): Napoleon Bonaparte, Ruler (Emperor of France)
Time Period(s): 1810s (1812-1813)
Locale(s): Moscow, Russia

Summary: In the sixth volume of the romantic adventure series featuring Marianne D'Asselnat, Napoleon has invaded Russia. Marianne follows with a message to save the emperor, her former lover. She is swept up in the chaos of the invasion and the destruction of Moscow.

Historical Accuracy: The story is fanciful but does employ accurate details of Napoleon's campaign in Russia.

468 *Marianne and the Lords of the East*

Date of Publication: 1975
Subject(s): Napoleonic Era; Romance
Fictional character(s): Marianne d'Asselnat, Noblewoman (Princess Sant'Anna); Jason Beaufort, Sea Captain; Corrado Sant'Anna, Nobleman (prince)
Time Period(s): 1810s
Locale(s): Constantinople, Ottoman Empire; Russia

Summary: Marianne's mission in Constantinople is to enlist the aid of the Sultana of the Ottoman Empire in Napoleon's secret invasion of Russia. At the Ottoman court Marianne is plunged into intrigue and conspiracy. Danger dogs her personal affairs as well as Prince Corrado threatens, and Jason Beaufort is in peril.

Historical Accuracy: The novel is irrepressible in its adventure but solidly supported by background details of the period.

469 *Marianne and the Masked Prince*

Date of Publication: 1970
Subject(s): Napoleonic Era; Romance
Fictional character(s): Marianne d'Asselnat, Noblewoman, Singer (opera); Francis Cranmere, Nobleman; Corrado Sant'Anna, Nobleman
Historical character(s): Joseph Fouche, Government Official (minister of police); Charles Maurice de Talleyrand-Perigord,

Government Official, Diplomat; Napoleon Bonaparte, Ruler (Emperor of France)
Time Period(s): 1800s
Locale(s): Paris, France; Lucca, Italy

Summary: In the second novel of Marianne's adventures, Napoleon has helped her to a high place in Paris society and a career as an opera singer. When her husband, Lord Cranmere, believed dead, appears at her debut, Marianne flees to Italy where she becomes involved with a mysterious prince.

Historical Accuracy: The novel is exceptionally well researched with period details that bolster the story's romance.

470　*Marianne and the Privateer*

Date of Publication: 1972
Subject(s): Napoleonic Era; Romance
Fictional character(s): Marianne d'Asselnat, Noblewoman (Princess Sant'Anna); Jason Beaufort, Sea Captain
Historical character(s): Charles Maurice de Talleyrand-Perigord, Government Official, Diplomat; Napoleon Bonaparte, Ruler (Emperor of France), Military Personnel
Time Period(s): 1800s
Locale(s): Paris, France; Brittany, France

Summary: Back in Paris after her Italian adventure, Marianne is now a princess, and she is reunited with Jason Beaufort. She quickly finds herself enmeshed in a conspiracy that threatens their love and the fate of Napoleon himself.

Historical Accuracy: Well-researched and presented, the novel exceeds the romance-adventure genre with its documentation.

471　*Marianne and the Rebels*

Date of Publication: 1972
Subject(s): Napoleonic Era; Romance
Fictional character(s): Marianne d'Asselnat, Noblewoman (Princess Sant'Anna); Jason Beaufort, Sea Captain; Corrado Sant'Anna, Nobleman (prince)
Historical character(s): Napoleon Bonaparte, Ruler (Emperor of France), Military Personnel
Time Period(s): 1810s
Locale(s): Venice, Italy; Constantinople, Ottoman Empire; Greece

Summary: Marianne is in Italy anticipating a reunion with Beaufort and a journey with him to America. Her past reappears in the form of her husband, Prince Corrado, and her former lover, Napoleon. Napoleon sends Marianne on a secret mission that takes her through Greece and on to the capital of the Ottoman Empire.

Historical Accuracy: The action is fast-paced and non-stop, but all is supported by accurate details of the period.

EVELYN BERCKMAN (1900-1978)

Evelyn Berckman was a writer whose work often combined elements from many genres including mystery, psychological suspense, romance, gothic, and historical fiction. In addition to being a writer, she was also a concert pianist and composer whose works were performed by the Philadelphia Orchestra and the Rochester Symphony. She was born in Philadelphia and educated at Columbia University.

472　*A Finger to Her Lips*

Date of Publication: 1971
Subject(s): Suspense; Romance; Servants
Fictional character(s): Sybilla-Marie, Royalty (princess); Karl-Eberhard, Nobleman (Duke of Volingen-Ilm)
Time Period(s): 1790s (1798)
Locale(s): Germany

Summary: Princess Sybilla-Marie is divorced and cast out by her husband after having an affair with an English diplomat. Her son, fathered by her lover, is threatened by her ex-husband so Sybilla-Marie returns to the Duke's castle disguised as a servant to kidnap her son. She discovers in the closely regimented hierarchical world of the castle's servants that she has a difficult time even gaining a glimpse of her son.

Historical Accuracy: The emphasis is on suspense rather than history. The German royalty is portrayed with considerable simplification to suit the novel's melodramatic situation.

KONRAD BERCOVICI (1882-1961)

Bercovici was born in Romania and raised among gypsies. He came to the U.S. in 1916 and worked on the staff of the New York *World*, then the New York *Evening Post*. He authored novels, plays, and short stories, many with a gypsy theme. *It's the Gypsy in Me* is his autobiography.

473　*The Exodus*

Date of Publication: 1947
Subject(s): Biblical Story; Ancient Egypt; Pharaohs
Historical character(s): Moses, Biblical Figure, Leader (of Hebrews)
Time Period(s): 13th century B.C.
Locale(s): Egypt

Summary: The novel dramatizes the Biblical story of the exodus of the Hebrews from Egypt and the leadership of Moses. The main account stays close to the Old Testament sources, but considerable invention is employed to fill out the early history of Moses, about which little is known. The novel does offer a convincing portrait of what life must have been like for the Hebrews in Egypt.

Historical Accuracy: The Old Testament account has been embellished with a romanticized fictional background.

474　*Savage Prodigal*

Date of Publication: 1948
Subject(s): Biography, Fictionalized; Literary Life
Historical character(s): Arthur Rimbaud, Writer (poet); Paul Verlaine, Writer (poet)
Time Period(s): 19th century (1854-1891)
Locale(s): France; Africa

Summary: The novel is based on the life of French poet Arthur Rimbaud, whose hallucinatory verses had a great influence on the symbolist movement. It records Rimbaud's strange relationship with the poet Verlaine and Rimbaud's years of wandering in North Africa.

Historical Accuracy: Some of the dialogue is taken from Rimbaud's own works.

RACHEL BERDACH

475 *The Emperor, the Sages and Death*

Date of Publication: 1968
Subject(s): Middle Ages; Jews
Historical character(s): Frederick II, Ruler (German emperor); Jacob Chalif Benaron, Religious (rabbi)
Time Period(s): 13th century
Locale(s): Sicily, Italy

Summary: This philosophical and ethical inquiry begins as Frederick II returns from the Crusades to his palace in Sicily. The emperor's desire for truth causes him to bring to his court Jewish and Moslem philosophers and theologians. The book is a series of short tales and discursive conversations prompted by the Emperor's questions. Rabbi Benaron tells most of the stories, defending his views and faith against the papal legate.

Historical Accuracy: This is a poetic and philosophical exploration with an atmosphere of the time used primarily to uncover timeless universal truths.

CONSTANCE BERESFORD-HOWE
(1922-)

Canadian writer Beresford-Howe was born in Montreal, attended McGill University, and received her Ph.D. in English from Brown University. She has taught English at Ryerson Polytechnic Institute in Toronto.

476 *My Lady Greensleeves*

Date of Publication: 1955
Subject(s): Elizabethan Period
Fictional character(s): Avys Winter, Gentlewoman; Henry Brandon, Gentleman; Piers Winter, Gentleman
Time Period(s): 16th century
Locale(s): Hungerford, England; London, England

Summary: Life in Elizabethan England is displayed in the unhappy marriage between Avys and Piers Winter and Avys' love affair with her cousin Henry. The results of their affair are followed in scenes that attempt to paint a portrait of ordinary life of the period. The novel's major focus is the daily life of middle-class people who are not involved in the intrigues of Elizabeth's court or the threat of Spanish invasion, but in their own human problems.

Historical Accuracy: The incidents are based on the actual record of the divorce suit between Sir Walter Hungerford and his wife Anne, though freely adapted for the novel's purpose.

THOMAS BERGER (1924-)

This American novelist is noted for his comedic touch and mastery of fictional forms and genres: the Western (*Little*

Big Man), the detective novel (*Who is Teddy Villanova?*), and surburban life (*Neighbors*). His Reinhart novels (*Reinhart in Love, Reinhart's Women*) have been justly praised.

477 *Arthur Rex: A Legendary Novel*

Date of Publication: 1978
Subject(s): Dark Ages; Arthurian Legends
Fictional character(s): Arthur, Ruler; Guinevere, Royalty; Launcelot, Knight
Time Period(s): 5th century
Locale(s): England

Summary: Berger retells the Arthurian legends from a modern viewpoint. His female characters—Guinevere, the two Isoldes, and others—get their due as the true powers behind the throne and in the bedroom. Arthur, Merlin, Launcelot, and other male characters suffer from very 20th century maladies. The novel features a previously unrecorded battle to the death between the two greatest Knights of the Round Table, Gawayne and Launcelot.

Historical Accuracy: Berger's language and atmosphere are authentic, if occasionally modern. The psychology of the characters is contemporary.

478 *Little Big Man*

Date of Publication: 1964
Subject(s): American West; Indians
Fictional character(s): Jack Crabb, Frontiersman, Gunfighter; Old Lodge Skins, Indian (Cheyenne chief); Mrs. Pendrake, Gentlewoman
Historical character(s): George Armstrong Custer, Military Personnel; Wyatt Earp, Lawman; James Butler Hickok, Frontiersman, Gunfighter; Martha Jane Cannary Burk, Frontierswoman
Time Period(s): 19th century (1852-1876)
Locale(s): West (Nebraska, Dakota Territory, Wyoming, Montana); Leavenworth, Kansas

Summary: 111-year-old Jack Crabb narrates this picaresque tall tale of the West. Captured and raised by the Cheyenne, he is later rescued. He becomes a shopkeeper, a con-man, a gunfighter, a wrangler and jester for Custer, and the only white survivor of the Last Stand.

Historical Accuracy: Berger's rollicking story punctures most Western myths. His ironic and modern perspective creates a believable and authentic Wild West.

TED BERKMAN (1914-)

An American writer born in Brooklyn, Berkman attended Cornell, Columbia, the Contemporary School of Music, and UCLA. He has worked as an assistant city editor and foreign editor for the *New York Daily Mirror*. Berkman was the author of the filmscripts for *Fear Strikes Out* and *Bedtime for Bonzo*. A talented musician and composer, his works have been performed at the White House.

479   *To Seize the Passing Dream*

Date of Publication: 1972

Subject(s): Artistic Life; Victorian Period; Biography, Fictionalized

Historical character(s): James Abbott McNeill Whistler, Artist; George Du Maurier, Artist, Writer; Oscar Wilde, Writer; Algernon Swinburne, Writer; Dante Gabriel Rossetti, Artist; Aubrey Beardsley, Artist; John Singer Sargent, Artist; Henri de Toulouse-Lautrec, Artist; Marcel Proust, Writer; Edgar Degas, Artist

Time Period(s): 19th century; 20th century (1875-1903)

Locale(s): London, England; Paris, France

Summary: In this biographical novel of James McNeill Whistler, the notorious American painter and wit is portrayed along with a virtual ''who's who'' of the 19th century. Whistler emerges as a more complex and troubled figure than the cynical wit he presented as his public persona, appearing as an iconoclast wracked by self-doubt.

Historical Accuracy: The novel is a convincing display of Whistler's life and times.

VIRGINIA BERNHARD (1937-)

An American writer, Bernhard was born in Austin, Texas, and educated at Rice and the University of Pennsylvania. She has been a history professor at the University of St. Thomas, Houston, Texas, with a specialty in colonial America.

480   *A Durable Fire*

Date of Publication: 1990

Subject(s): American Colonies; Settlement of the American Frontier; Indians

Fictional character(s): Temperance Yardley, Settler; George Yardley, Military Personnel; Will Sterling, Settler

Historical character(s): John Smith, Leader; Pocahontas, Indian; John Rolfe, Settler

Time Period(s): 17th century (1607-1622)

Locale(s): Jamestown, Virginia, American Colonies; London, England

Summary: This is a brilliant re-creation of life in the Jamestown settlement including the wreck of the *Sea Venture*, the difficult times during the winter of 1609-1610, and the massacre of the James River settlers. The drama revolves around Temperance Yardley, her husband George, and George's friend Will who form a triangular relationship.

Historical Accuracy: The novel carefully sticks to the known facts, offering them in a history of Virginia appendix. The story is an artful blend of the historical and probable surmises.

DON BERRY (1932-)

Minnesota novelist Berry has also lived in Oregon, the setting of *Trask*, a story of Indian and white relations in the mid-19th century. He also wrote a history of the Rocky Mountain Fur Company, *A Majority of Scoundrels.*

481   *Moontrap*

Date of Publication: 1962

Subject(s): Settlement of the American Frontier

Fictional character(s): Johnson Monday, Mountain Man; Webb, Mountain Man

Time Period(s): 1850s

Locale(s): Oregon

Summary: The conflict between the trappers and the settlers in the Oregon Territory is dramatized in the story of two mountain men, Monday and Webb. They are feared and rejected by the settlers who hope to establish civilization in the wilderness that the two men have helped tame. The trappers' customs fade as the land they opened up is settled.

Historical Accuracy: The novel provides strong scenes of life in the wilderness and the clash of ideologies between trappers and settlers.

482   *To Build a Ship*

Date of Publication: 1963

Subject(s): Settlement of the American Frontier; Indians

Fictional character(s): Ben Thaler, Frontiersman; Warren Vaughn, Frontiersman; Sam Howard, Frontiersman

Time Period(s): 1850s

Locale(s): Oregon

Summary: In the Oregon Territory during the 1850s, a settlement is dependent on a ship for contact with the outside and trade. When the only captain to enter their harbor once a year dies, they decide to build their own schooner. The novel details the obstacles and complications met in this endeavor, including a death, a murder trial, and Indian trouble.

Historical Accuracy: The novel is an accurate rendering of frontier life and times.

483   *Trask*

Date of Publication: 1960

Subject(s): Settlement of the American Frontier; Indians

Fictional character(s): Eldridge Trask, Mountain Man, Settler; Charley Kehwa, Indian, Guide

Time Period(s): 1840s

Locale(s): Oregon

Summary: Eldridge Trask is one of the first settlers of the Oregon Territory in the 1840s. He abandons his life as a mountain man to settle south of the Columbia River. After five years, his restlessness stirs and, with Charley Kehwa, an Indian guide, he ventures southward to Murderer's Harbor in the land of the Killamooks. The novel offers a day-to-day account of their ordeal that culminates in a final test of endurance.

Historical Accuracy: The novel is convincing in its depiction of the early settlement of Oregon and the wilderness.

JIM BERRY

484   *The Moon Stallion*

Date of Publication: 1982

Subject(s): Indians; Tribal Life—South American
Fictional character(s): Harkana, Indian (Tehuelche); Pandra, Indian (Tehuelche)
Time Period(s): 1870s (1879)
Locale(s): Patagonia, Argentina

Summary: The novel is based on the historical details of the Tehuelche tribe that fought South American settlers in Patagonia in the 19th century. Harkena is exiled for killing his father. When he returns, he possesses the knowledge of the white settlers and an awareness of the coming great battle which will decide his people's fate.

Historical Accuracy: The novel offers an authentic version of tribal life and customs.

JULIUS BERSTL (1883-)

Born in Bernburg, Germany, Berstl was educated at the universities of Goettingen and Leipzig. He worked for the BBC and authored several plays.

485 *Kean: The Imaginary Memoirs of an Actor*
Date of Publication: 1962
Subject(s): Theatrical Life; Biography, Fictionalized
Historical character(s): Edmund Kean, Actor
Time Period(s): 19th century
Locale(s): England; United States

Summary: The novel offers an autobiographical account of the life and career of the legendary Shakespearean actor Edmund Kean. Kean revolutionizes acting with his energy and violent emotional approach. His offstage life is no less dramatic, and the novel provides both a synopsis of his career and insights into Kean's nature and the sources of his genius.

Historical Accuracy: The framework of the novel's story is fictional. The various interpretations the author ascribes to his central character are questionable, and the author's clear sympathy occasionally results in partisanship and special pleading.

486 *The Tentmaker*
Date of Publication: 1951
Subject(s): Biblical Story
Historical character(s): Saul of Tarsus, Biblical Figure; Pontius Pilate, Government Official, Biblical Figure
Time Period(s): 1st century
Locale(s): Tarsus, Middle East; Jerusalem, Israel; Damascus, Syria

Summary: The novel tells the story of St. Paul, originally Saul, from his early years in Tarsus through his fanatically anti-Jesus period in Jerusalem to his final revelation on the road to Damascus. Paul is depicted as a complex individual, a product of the three worlds in which he lives: Jewish, Greek, and Roman.

Historical Accuracy: The novel offers a remarkably detailed and authentic depiction of the period and the personality of Paul.

ARTHUR BEVERLY-GIDDINGS
(1899-1970)

Beverly-Giddings is an English author of *Larrish Hundred*, *Broad Margin*, and *River of Rogues*.

487 *The Rival Shores*
Date of Publication: 1956
Subject(s): American Revolution; American Colonies
Fictional character(s): Sir John Whytting, Loyalist; Phyllida Wyman, Young Woman
Time Period(s): 1770s (1774)
Locale(s): Maryland, American Colonies; Delaware, American Colonies; Virginia, American Colonies

Summary: This adventure story describes the workings of the underground railroad that transported loyalists on the Eastern Shore of Maryland and Delaware to safety in the days before the outbreak of the American Revolution. Sir John Whytting is the leader of the loyalist underground.

Historical Accuracy: The novel draws on surviving family records to provide an authentic period background for the story.

BASIL BEYEA (1910-)

An American writer born in New York and educated at Princeton and the New York School of Social Work, Beyea served as a family case worker in New York, Boston, and Honolulu. He has also been a freelance TV writer and author of documentary and educational films.

488 *The Golden Mistress*
Date of Publication: 1975
Subject(s): Biography, Fictionalized
Historical character(s): Eliza Jumel, Socialite
Time Period(s): 1790s
Locale(s): Providence, Rhode Island

Summary: The novel covers the early years of the notorious Eliza Jumel, the illegitimate child of a prostitute, who rises from the wharfs of Providence, Rhode Island, to become the most famous courtesan of her day. Eventually she becomes the mistress, then the wife, of Aaron Burr. The novel depicts her life up to her departure for New York.

Historical Accuracy: The novel is based on scrupulous research. The characters and details are as accurate as possible; however, the author admits that since many parts of Jumel's life remain a mystery, the interpretation of Eliza herself is fiction.

489 *Notorious Eliza*
Date of Publication: 1978
Subject(s): Biography, Fictionalized; Politics
Historical character(s): Eliza Jumel, Socialite; Stephen Jumel, Plantation Owner, Businessman; Aaron Burr, Political Figure; Alexander Hamilton, Political Figure; Napoleon Bonaparte, Ruler (Emperor of France), Military Personnel
Time Period(s): 18th century; 19th century (1794-1834)

Locale(s): New York, New York; Saratoga Springs, New York; Paris, France

Summary: In the continuation of Beyea's adventures of Eliza Jumel begun in *The Golden Mistress*, Eliza's story is taken up at age 19 when she enters New York society. She becomes Aaron Burr's mistress, tricks merchant Stephen Jumel into marriage, is accepted into the great salons of Paris, and finally weds and divorces Burr. The novel features the famous Burr-Hamilton duel and a rich evocation of the era.

Historical Accuracy: The story is solidly rooted in fact, except for the years in which the history is unknown, when it offers carefully constructed surmises.

TOM BEZZI

490 *Hubble Time*

Date of Publication: 1987
Subject(s): Science; Biography, Fictionalized
Fictional character(s): Jane Hubble, Writer
Historical character(s): Edwin Powell Hubble, Scientist (astronomer)
Time Period(s): 20th century
Locale(s): Los Angeles, California

Summary: A fictional granddaughter of American astronomer Edwin Hubble interweaves excerpts from her grandmother's diary with her own reflections. The novel offers a portrait of Hubble and his wife, as well as the famous circle of friends they socialized with, including Aldous Huxley and Charlie Chaplin.

Historical Accuracy: The novel lacks the focus to provide a fully believable portrait of either Hubble or his times.

JOHN BIGGINS (1949-)

Biggins was born in South London but grew up in the Welsh border country. Educated at University College in Swansea, Biggins spent four years in Poland as a research student and lecturer.

491 *The Emperor's Coloured Coat*

Date of Publication: 1992
Subject(s): World War I; Austro-Hungarian Empire
Fictional character(s): Otto Prohaska, Military Personnel (officer)
Time Period(s): 1910s (1912-1914)
Locale(s): Austria

Summary: The novel continues the story of Austrian naval officer Otto Prohaska introduced in *A Sailor in Austria*. Shortly before the start of World War I, Prohaska, after going AWOL after a liaison with a Polish actress, finds himself at the center of the conspiracy to assassinate the Archduke Franz Ferdinand. Prohaska's adventures serve to reflect the collapse of the Austro-Hungarian Empire.

Historical Accuracy: The atmosphere is captured with authentic details.

492 *A Sailor of Austria*

Date of Publication: 1991
Subject(s): Sea Story; World War I; Submarines
Fictional character(s): Otto Prohaska, Military Personnel (naval officer)
Time Period(s): 1910s
Locale(s): At Sea

Summary: In 1986 a 101-year-old survivor of the Austro-Hungarian Navy recounts his exploits as a submarine captain. His adventures take him from the Adriatic to the coast of Albania, and include transporting the pretender to the throne, convoy patrol, and a final escape from the coast of Palestine at the end of the war.

Historical Accuracy: The details of submarine life in the Austrian Navy are believable and authentic.

493 *The Two-Headed Eagle*

Date of Publication: 1993
Subject(s): World War I; Aviation
Fictional character(s): Otto Prohaska, Military Personnel, Pilot
Time Period(s): 1910s (1916)
Locale(s): Italy

Summary: In this installment of the adventures of Otto Prohaska, it is the summer of 1916. Prohaska joins the Royal Austro-Hungarian Flying Service for the Italian campaign of World War I in the skies above the Alps.

Historical Accuracy: The novel provides an authentic depiction of the era and a convincing historical background.

LLOYD BIGGLE JR. (1923-)

Biggle is an American science fiction and mystery writer who was born in Waterloo, Iowa. He attended Wayne State University and received a Ph.D. in musicology from the University of Michigan. Biggle sees himself primarily as a storyteller in whatever genre he attempts.

494 *The Glendower Conspiracy*

Date of Publication: 1990
Subject(s): Mystery; Edwardian Period
Fictional character(s): Edward Porter Jones, Detective—Private; Sherlock Holmes, Detective—Private
Time Period(s): 1900s (1904)
Locale(s): Wales

Summary: Edward Porter Jones, the former Baker Street Irregular and now apprentice detective under Sherlock Holmes, is sent by the master to Wales. There he investigates the murder of a Welsh landowner that seems linked to the secretive Robert Owen Study League. Jones needs his famous mentor's help in solving the case.

Historical Accuracy: The novel offers an authentic re-creation of both the era and the Sherlock Holmes genre.

495 *The Quallsford Inheritance*

Date of Publication: 1986

Subject(s): Mystery; Victorian Period
Fictional character(s): Edward Porter Jones, Detective—Private; Sherlock Holmes, Detective—Private; John H. Watson, Doctor
Time Period(s): 1900s (1900)
Locale(s): London, England

Summary: Edward Porter Jones is a former Baker Street Irregular turned apprentice detective under Sherlock Holmes. Their case begins with an odd request for an exotic fruit at London's Spitalfields Market. An investigation into the puzzle leads to a woman in distress, and Porter goes to the rescue.

Historical Accuracy: The novel accurately captures the flavor of Victorian London, as well as the Holmesian background.

CHRISTOPHER BIGSBY (1941-)

Scottish-born Bigsby attended the University of Sheffield and received his Ph.D. from the University of Nottingham. He has taught American literature at British universities and has worked as a presenter for the BBC. He is the author of critical works on American playwrights Edward Albee and David Mamet, as well as a critical study of black writers of the 1960s and 1970s, *The Second Black Renaissance.*

496   *Hester*

Date of Publication: 1994
Subject(s): Puritans; American Colonies
Fictional character(s): Hester Prynne, Spouse; Roger Chillingworth, Doctor; Arthur Dimmesdale, Religious (clergyman)
Time Period(s): 17th century
Locale(s): Norwich, England; Boston, Massachusetts, American Colonies

Summary: The novel is a retelling and imaginative extension of Nathaniel Hawthorne's *The Scarlet Letter*, in which Bigsby extends the story into the year preceding the events of Hawthorne's novel. We learn of Hester Prynne's ill-fated married life to Chillingworth and her journey to America where her affair with Reverend Dimmesdale culminates in Hester's growing selfhood and tragedy.

Historical Accuracy: The novel offers a modernist perspective on the characters and events, less a re-creation of the past than a meditation on its meaning.

497   *Pearl*

Date of Publication: 1995
Subject(s): American Colonies
Fictional character(s): Pearl Prynne, Bastard Daughter; Hester Prynne, Spouse, Outcast
Time Period(s): 17th century
Locale(s): London, England; Norfolk, England; Boston, Massachusetts, American Colonies

Summary: The author continues his fictional elaboration of Nathaniel Hawthorne's *The Scarlet Letter*, here imagining the fate of Hester Prynne's daughter Pearl. She returns to England to claim an estate and sets in motion a conspiracy against her.

Historical Accuracy: The novel provides a believable atmosphere of the period and the region of Norfolk, England, during the 17th century.

RACHEL BILLINGTON (1942-)

An English author born in Oxford, Billington is the daughter of the seventh Earl of Longford (a former leader of the House of Lords) and a member of a literary family that includes her mother, historian Elizabeth Longford, and her sister, historian and mystery writer Lady Antonia Fraser.

498   *Theo and Matilda*

Date of Publication: 1990
Subject(s): Dark Ages; Tudor Period; Victorian Period
Fictional character(s): Theo, Religious; Matilda, Royalty (princess); Matilda Whitfield, Gentlewoman; Theodore, Religious
Time Period(s): Multiple Time Periods
Locale(s): England

Summary: The novel is a love story sequence played out by five different couples, all named Theo and Matilda, from 770 to the present. Each couple's relationship is affected by the history of the period in which they live in this fascinating blend of universal truth and particularized history.

Historical Accuracy: This is an ingenious study of love over time and under the pressure of history. The eras of each section are convincingly drawn.

499   *A Woman's Age*

Date of Publication: 1979
Subject(s): Family Saga
Fictional character(s): Violet Hesketh, Gentlewoman; Eleanor Hesketh, Gentlewoman
Time Period(s): 20th century (1910-1980)
Locale(s): Northumberland, England; Ireland

Summary: The novel depicts the lives of four generations of women in an upperclass English family, covering 70 years and the major events of the 20th century. Violet Hesketh's father is killed in the Great War, and it is not until the Second World War that she emerges from her isolation. Her daughter, also named Violet, settles into the security of the 1950s, while her daughter survives the social upheavals of the 1970s.

Historical Accuracy: The novel offers a panorama of the 20th century seen through the social lens of the upperclass.

ARCHIE BINNS (1899-1971)

A novelist and historian, Binns was born in Washington and served on a light ship crew near Cape Flattery before attending Stanford University. He has worked as a journalist, editor, and creative writing instructor at the University of Seattle. During his writing career, he produced more than 15 fiction and nonfiction works, many based on historical events in the Pacific Northwest.

500 *The Head Waters*

Date of Publication: 1957
Subject(s): American West
Fictional character(s): Tom Wells, Pioneer; Constance Wells, Spouse
Time Period(s): 1890s
Locale(s): Pacific Northwest

Summary: This novel describes the struggles of a young pioneer couple, Tom and Constance Wells, in the Pacific Northwest during the 1890s. The story features the activities of smugglers during the period.

Historical Accuracy: This is an authentic tale, faithful to the period and the region.

501 *The Land Is Bright*

Date of Publication: 1939
Subject(s): American West; Wagon Trains
Fictional character(s): Gideon Black, Teacher, Pioneer; Case Ford, Pioneer; Nancy Ann Greenfield, Pioneer
Time Period(s): 1850s (1854)
Locale(s): Oregon Trail, United States

Summary: Schoolmaster Gideon Black leads the westward crossing of a group of Illinois farmers. The group faces all the hardships and difficulties of the epic journey along the Oregon Trail, which is captured in vivid detail.

Historical Accuracy: The novel provides an authentic chronicle of life along the Oregon Trail, showing evident research into the period and geography.

502 *Mighty Mountain*

Date of Publication: 1940
Subject(s): Settlement of the American Frontier; Indians; American West
Fictional character(s): Elmer Hale, Sailor, Settler; Lisette Hale, Settler, Spouse; Leschi, Indian
Time Period(s): 1850s
Locale(s): Washington

Summary: Life on the frontier of Washington in the 1850s is the setting for this novel that follows the ordeals of Elmer Hale and his wife, Lisette. It describes encounters with the Indians as well as the inevitable arrival of civilization and the changes it brings for the pioneers.

Historical Accuracy: The novel is sharply and convincingly descriptive of the period and the time.

503 *You Rolling River*

Date of Publication: 1947
Subject(s): Settlement of the American Frontier; American West
Fictional character(s): John Fortune, Government Official (customs agent); Willard Pearson, Sailor; Rita Collins, Gentlewoman
Time Period(s): 1860s (1865)
Locale(s): Astoria, Oregon

Summary: The novel portrays the lives and stories of many inhabitants of Astoria, Oregon, a port town on the Columbia River. It describes the obstacles for those trying to forge a respectable life amidst the rough and tumble of the waterfront, with its sailors' attractions, ladies of easy virtue, and the threat of being shanghaied for a trip around the Horn.

Historical Accuracy: The novel is atmospheric and honest in its portrayal of frontier town life of the period.

ROBERT MONTGOMERY BIRD
(1806-1854)

This American novelist and dramatist was also a doctor. He began his career writing romantic tragedies and comedies set in Philadelphia. His finest novel is *Nick of the Woods*. Because of ill health, he stopped writing in 1839.

504 *The Hawks of Hawk-Hollow*

Date of Publication: 1835
Subject(s): American Revolution
Fictional character(s): Herman Hunter, Artist; Catherine Loring, Heroine; Henry Falconer, Hero
Time Period(s): 1780s
Locale(s): Delaware Water Gap, Pennsylvania

Summary: The Gilbert and Falconer families feud in the Delaware Water Gap region during the American Revolution. A love triangle ends in tragedy and reveals hidden identities.

Historical Accuracy: There is little period detail but much romantic maneuvering.

505 *Nick of the Woods; or, The Jibbenainosay*

Date of Publication: 1837
Subject(s): Settlement of the American Frontier; Indians
Fictional character(s): Roland Forrester, Military Personnel, Settler; Edit Forrester, Orphan; Nathan Slaughter, Trapper
Time Period(s): 1780s
Locale(s): Kentucky

Summary: In this famous tale of the American frontier, the setting is the wilds of Kentucky. The Forresters, two cousins in an emigrant band, meet a variety of frontier types, including a Quaker trapper who warns them about an Indian uprising. They also learn of the spectral Nick of the Woods, a mysterious Indian avenger. An Indian attack, capture, and the revelation of Nick's secret follow.

Historical Accuracy: The novel was written in part to correct James Fenimore Cooper's heroic and sentimentalized characterization of Indians.

MARGARET BIRKHEAD

506 *Trust and Treason*

Date of Publication: 1989
Subject(s): Elizabethan Period; Family Saga
Fictional character(s): Thomas Woodfall, Gentleman; Robert Cooper, Government Official; Cecily Woodfall, Gentlewoman

Historical character(s): Elizabeth I, Ruler (Queen of England); Sir Philip Sidney, Gentleman; Robert Cecil, Nobleman; Christopher Hatton, Gentleman, Political Figure; Sir Francis Walsingham, Government Official
Time Period(s): 16th century (1558-1585)
Locale(s): Sussex, England; London, England

Summary: In this tale of two generations of the Woodfall family during the Elizabethan period, the political intrigue surrounding Elizabeth's reign eventually surrounds the family. Robert Cooper must investigate a suspected plot by his father, Thomas Woodfall, to assassinate the queen. Divided loyalties and treacherous rivalries complicate his task.

Historical Accuracy: The historical detail is meticulous, and the court politics are fascinatingly connected with the family drama.

HOFFMAN BIRNEY (1891-1958)

An American writer born in New Jersey, Birney's books include *Ann Carmeny, Brothers of Doom: The Story of the Pizarros of Peru, Dead Man's Trail*, and *Vigilantes*, a chronicle of the rise and fall of the Plummer gang of outlaws in and about Virginia City, Montana in the early 1860s. He also wrote a history of the Mormons, *Zealots of Zion*.

507   *The Dice of God*

Date of Publication: 1956
Subject(s): American West; Indians; Military Life—U.S. Cavalry
Fictional character(s): Frederick C. Tuthill, Military Personnel (lieutenant colonel)
Time Period(s): 1860s; 1870s (1866-1876)
Locale(s): North Dakota; Montana

Summary: This *roman a clef* tells in fictional form the story of George Armstrong Custer's Indian fighting days, culminating in the Battle of the Little Bighorn. Set in the Dakota and Montana territory during the Indian Wars, the novel chronicles the military career of Lieutenant Colonel Frederick Tuthill and the events leading up to the Indian massacre.

Historical Accuracy: The novel is fiction placed in a historical frame with clear parallels to the story of Custer and the Seventh Cavalry.

508   *Eagle in the Sun*

Date of Publication: 1935
Subject(s): Mexican War
Fictional character(s): John Chain, Trader; Sandra Tarranti, Spy (suspected)
Time Period(s): 1840s
Locale(s): Santa Fe, New Mexico

Summary: Set during the war with Mexico, the novel concerns a young trader, John Chain. Chain becomes involved with the mysterious Sandra Tarranti, who is suspected of being a spy for the Mexicans. The novel features a vivid depiction of Sante Fe during the period.

Historical Accuracy: The story is invented, but the atmosphere is authentic.

509   *Grim Journey*

Date of Publication: 1935
Subject(s): American West; Wagon Trains; Donner Party
Historical character(s): William H. Eddy, Pioneer
Time Period(s): 1840s (1846)
Locale(s): Oregon Trail, United States

Summary: The story of the ill-fated Donner Party is told by one of its survivors, William H. Eddy. He offers a factual account of the group's trip west in 1846 from Missouri. Poorly led and disorganized, they are trapped in the mountains, where to survive they are forced to resort to cannibalism.

Historical Accuracy: The novel emphasizes the factual over the sensational.

ILSE BISHCOFF (1903-1990)

Illustrator and author Bischoff's works include *Carl and Anna, The Street of the Islands*, and *Proud Heritage*.

510   *Proud Heritage*

Date of Publication: 1949
Subject(s): Artistic Life; American Revolution
Historical character(s): Gilbert Stuart, Artist
Time Period(s): 18th century
Locale(s): Rhode Island, American Colonies; England

Summary: The novel is based on the life of portrait painter Gilbert Stuart, the son of a royalist snuff maker in Rhode Island. The novel traces his career as the most celebrated portrait painter of his day.

Historical Accuracy: The novel is distinguished by its faithful presentation of the facts of Stuart's career and his motivations as an artist.

ROSANNE BITTNER (1945-)

An American historical romance novelist whose settings are mainly in the West, Bittner was born in Indiana and worked as a secretary before becoming a full-time writer in 1984. She has earned high praise for her western settings.

511   *Arizona Ecstasy*

Date of Publication: 1989
Subject(s): American West; Romance; Indians
Fictional character(s): Lisa Powers, Captive; Chaco, Indian (half-Apache)
Time Period(s): 19th century
Locale(s): Southwest

Summary: Set during the final days of the free Apache nation, this Western romance tells the story of Chaco, who returns to the Apache way of life and his doomed love for the white captive Lisa Powers.

Historical Accuracy: The novel offers a blend of authentic period description and passion.

512 Embers of the Heart

Date of Publication: 1990
Subject(s): American West; Civil War—U.S.
Fictional character(s): Anna Kelly, Businesswoman; Nate Foster, Lawman (U.S. marshall)
Time Period(s): 1860s
Locale(s): Abilene, Kansas

Summary: Anna Kelly's husband, a member of the Quantrell Raiders, is killed in the Civil War. After the war, Anna moves to Abilene to order a restaurant. She falls in love with Marshall Nate Foster but faces a challenge when her husband reappears, damaged by the war.

Historical Accuracy: The story offers a convincing period setting and an original woman's perspective on the period.

513 Montana Woman

Date of Publication: 1990
Subject(s): American West; Romance
Fictional character(s): Joline Masters, Widow(er), Settler; Clint Reeves, Settler
Time Period(s): 1860s
Locale(s): Montana

Summary: Following the death of her father and husband in the Civil War, Joline Masters heads west to Montana Territory for a new start with Clint Reeves.

Historical Accuracy: The period details are present but the emphasis is less on documentation than it is on romance.

514 Oregon Bride

Date of Publication: 1990
Subject(s): American West; Romance; Wagon Trains
Fictional character(s): Mary Beth MacKinder, Widow(er); Josh Rivers, Guide
Time Period(s): 1850s (1851)
Locale(s): Oregon Trail, United States

Summary: In this Western romance, Mary Beth MacKinder joins a westbound wagon train after the death of her husband. She finds love with trail guide Josh Rivers. Along the Oregon Trail she must endure Indians, tornadoes, and her in-laws.

Historical Accuracy: Western life of the period is captured with verve and color.

515 Sioux Splendor

Date of Publication: 1990
Subject(s): American West; Indians; Romance
Fictional character(s): Cynthia Ann Wells, Captive, Gentlewoman; Red Wolf, Indian (Sioux), Warrior
Time Period(s): 1860s (1865)
Locale(s): South Dakota; Washington, District of Columbia

Summary: Cynthia Wells is captured by the Sioux and falls in love with Red Wolf. When she is rescued and returns east, she is hopeful that she and Red Wolf will be reunited. Circumstances keep them apart, but they eventually overcome opposition to their union.

Historical Accuracy: The story offers authentic depiction of Sioux culture though it seems more wish fulfillment than reality.

516 Sweet Mountain Magic

Date of Publication: 1990
Subject(s): American West; Romance
Fictional character(s): Venado, Amnesiac; Sage MacKenzie, Mountain Man
Time Period(s): 1840s (1846)
Locale(s): Rocky Mountains

Summary: Mountain man Sage MacKenzie finds "Venado" near a burnt wagon. She has no memory and will not speak, and MacKenzie cares for her. When her memory returns, they must deal with her husband.

Historical Accuracy: More romance than history, the novel does provide some convincing background painting.

517 Thunder on the Plains

Date of Publication: 1992
Subject(s): American West; Romance; Railroads
Fictional character(s): Sunny Landers, Gentlewoman, Businesswoman; Colt Travis, Frontiersman
Historical character(s): Dr. Thomas Durant, Businessman; John Casewent, Military Personnel, Businessman
Time Period(s): 1850s; 1860s (1857-1869)
Locale(s): Great Plains

Summary: This Western romance between Sunny Landers and Colt Travis is set against the background of the building of the transcontinental railroad from Nebraska to Utah. Sunny is devoted to her father's dream of opening the Great Plains by rail. Travis is a frontiersman devoted to Sunny. The action follows the struggle to build the railroad and to forge their relationship.

Historical Accuracy: The details of the negotiations and the complications of building the Union Pacific are well-grounded in fact.

BJORNSTJERNE BJORNSON (1832-1910)

A Norwegian writer and one of the major figures of Norwegian literature, Bjornson succeeded Henrik Ibsen as the director of the Ole Bull Theater in Bergen and became the national poet of Norway. In 1903 he won the Nobel Prize for Literature.

518 Arne

Date of Publication: 1858
Subject(s): Rural Life—Norway; Feuds
Fictional character(s): Nils, Tailor, Musician; Margit, Heroine; Arne, Worker (peasant)
Time Period(s): 19th century
Locale(s): Norway

Summary: Arne is the story of a young peasant boy in a Norwegian village. His father is a wicked fiddler who provides a troubling legacy for the young boy. Eventually a feud with his father's enemy is overcome when Arne marries the enemy's daughter.

Historical Accuracy: This is something of an allegory of the life of Norse peasants. Good details of ordinary life are given a tragic and symbolic significance.

LAURA BLACK

Born in Edinburgh, Black sets her novels in West Perthshire, Scotland in the 1860s amid upper-class society. The books do not form a series, although a few minor characters and imaginary places reappear throughout her work.

519 *Albany*

Date of Publication: 1984
Subject(s): Romance; Inheritance—Disputed
Fictional character(s): Leondra Albany, Gentlewoman, Heiress; Simon Donaldson, Gentleman; Jack Avington, Nobleman; Duncan Glenalban, Nobleman (Earl of Glenalbin)
Time Period(s): 19th century
Locale(s): Scotland

Summary: Who exactly is Leonora Albany? Is she the rightful heir of the Glenalbin estate, the descendant of Bonnie Prince Charlie, and therefore the lost queen of Scotland? Is she the dupe of a cunning schemer? Or is she simply an adventuress? Leonora arrives at Glenalbin to claim her birthright and is surrounded by deceit and self-interest that must be untangled before the final romantic conclusion.

Historical Accuracy: The novel is an amusing version of the familiar story of a disputed inheritance, full of period details.

520 *Falls of Gard*

Date of Publication: 1986
Subject(s): Romance
Fictional character(s): Arabella Gordon, Gentlewoman; Geoffrey Nicholls, Gentleman; Rupert Fraser, Gentleman; Peter McCallum, Gentleman; Charles, Nobleman (Marquess of Gard)
Time Period(s): 19th century
Locale(s): Scotland

Summary: When Arabella Gordon returns from Australia to her native Scotland, she is considered uncultured and hoydenish. As she struggles to gain the polish needed to come out in polite society, she attracts a number of admirers. Not numbered among her suitors is the aloof Marquess of Gard who remembers an earlier encounter years before at the Falls of Gard. History repeats itself with some romantic implications.

Historical Accuracy: The courtship rituals and customs are convincingly depicted.

521 *Glendraco*

Date of Publication: 1977
Subject(s): Romance; Victorian Period
Fictional character(s): Cristina Drummond, Gentlewoman; Lord Draco, Nobleman
Time Period(s): 1860s (1860)

Locale(s): Edinburgh, Scotland; Glasgow, Scotland; Highlands, Scotland

Summary: Cristina Drummond searches out the secrets of her grandfather's terrible past. The trail leads to the estate of Glendraco and an ever-widening series of secrets and revelations concerning the aristocratic Draco family. Her adventures expose her to rape, murder, and white slavery amidst the slums of Glasgow.

Historical Accuracy: The story offers strong and vivid portraits of Scotland, but the adventures veer toward the melodramatic not the realistic.

522 *Ravenburn*

Date of Publication: 1978
Subject(s): Romance; Victorian Period
Fictional character(s): Katherine Irvine, Heiress, Gentlewoman; Isabella Irvine, Widow(er); Tom Ravenburn, Outcast
Time Period(s): 1860s
Locale(s): Scotland

Summary: Katherine Irvine, heiress to a large Scottish estate, finds herself in the center of a web of conspiracy and suspense involving a mysterious stranger who comes to live on an island in the nearby lake and a past that refuses to stay buried.

Historical Accuracy: This suspenseful romance is grounded in a solid and believable sense of locale.

523 *Strathgallant*

Date of Publication: 1981
Subject(s): Romance; Victorian Period
Fictional character(s): Perdita Sinclair, Heiress, Orphan; Colin Ramsay, Military Personnel; Harry Ramsay, Gentleman; Jamie Ramsay, Lawyer; Alex Ramsay, Student—College
Time Period(s): 1850s
Locale(s): Highlands, Scotland

Summary: Perdita Sinclair is an orphan and heiress to a vast Scottish estate. She must marry, and the likeliest candidates for a husband are her cousins. Each is invited for a visit, and a competition for Perdita's affections and her hand ensues. Before the issue is resolved, intrigue, treachery, and violence occur.

Historical Accuracy: The novel is solidly placed in its Scottish locale with the appropriate customs of the period.

524 *Wild Cat*

Date of Publication: 1979
Subject(s): Romance; Victorian Period; Gypsies
Fictional character(s): Catriona Douglas, Gentlewoman; Alexander Carnmore, Nobleman; Richard Grant, Gentleman
Time Period(s): 1860s (1862)
Locale(s): Highlands, Scotland

Summary: On her wedding night, Catriona Douglas learns that her husband is a drunkard and a brute. Fleeing, she hides among a band of gypsies where she witnesses a murder. She is then hunted by two adversaries: her husband and the murderer.

Historical Accuracy: The novel's appeal is romantic suspense with some convincing regional painting.

THOMAS WAKEFIELD BLACKBURN

525 A Good Day to Die

Date of Publication: 1967
Subject(s): American West; Indians; Battle of Wounded Knee
Fictional character(s): Chance Easterbrook, Journalist; Beau Lane, Linguist, Indian (half-breed)
Historical character(s): William F. Cody, Frontiersman; John J. Pershing, Military Personnel (army officer); Frederic Remington, Artist; Sitting Bull, Indian (Sioux), Chieftain
Time Period(s): 1890s (1890-1891)
Locale(s): Wounded Knee, South Dakota

Summary: The novel dramatizes the Battle of Wounded Knee, the last major action against the Sioux in 1890. Chance Easterbrook is a reporter sent to the Dakota reservation to interview Sitting Bull, and he is on hand for the Seventh Cavalry's revenge for the Custer massacre.

Historical Accuracy: The novel portrays Indian customs with more authenticity than actual historical figures, who are thinly sketched.

IRWIN R. BLACKER (1919-1985)

Born in Ohio, Blacker was educated at Ohio University and Western Reserve University and joined the faculty of Purdue University. He is the author of over 40 network television programs, including episodes of ''Bonanza.'' His novels include *The Kilroy Gambit* and *The Golden Conquistadors*.

526 Days of the Gold

Date of Publication: 1961
Subject(s): Gold Rush—Klondike
Fictional character(s): Simon Coit, Prospector; Tom Tlingit, Prospector
Time Period(s): 1890s
Locale(s): Yukon Territory, Canada; Alaska

Summary: Life in the Alaskan gold fields during the Klondike Gold Rush in the 1890s forms the background for this adventure tale. The story centers on the experience of an ex-schoolteacher, Simon Coit, who joins the gold prospectors.

Historical Accuracy: The atmosphere of the period is faithful to the historical facts, and the claim trial depicted is derived from an actual case.

527 Taos

Date of Publication: 1959
Subject(s): Pueblo Revolt; Spanish Colonies; Indians
Historical character(s): Pope, Indian, Shaman; Don Antonio Ostermin, Government Official (colonial governor)
Time Period(s): 17th century (1680)
Locale(s): Taos, New Mexico; Santa Fe, New Mexico

Summary: This is a fictional reconstruction of the rebellion of the Pueblo Indians in the Spanish province of Nueva Mexico in 1680. The conflict is seen from the perspective of both the Indian insurgents and the Spanish overlords, particularly the two leading figures: Indian shaman and rebel leader Pope and the Spanish governor, Antonio Ostermin.

Historical Accuracy: The author has taken certain liberties with history in reconstructing his story though the essential historical background is accurate and shows evidence of considerable research.

R.D. BLACKMORE (1825-1900)

Educated at Blundell's School, Tiverton, and Exeter College, Oxford, Blackmore trained as a lawyer but abandoned his legal career because of ill health. His most popular novel is *Lorna Doone*, but he also wrote 13 other novels and several volumes of poetry.

528 Lorna Doone

Date of Publication: 1869
Subject(s): Crime and Criminals; Monmouth's Rebellion
Fictional character(s): John Ridd, Adventurer; Lorna Doone, Captive (kidnapped girl), Ward; Carver Doone, Outlaw
Historical character(s): James II, Ruler (King of England)
Time Period(s): 17th century
Locale(s): Exmoor, England

Summary: John Ridd returns from school to learn that his father has been killed by the Doones, a band of outlaws. They have also kidnapped a young girl who becomes the Doones' ward. Ridd attempts to save Lorna from the clutches of the evil Carver Doone. Lorna turns out to be an heiress, and she lives for a time at the court of James II. John eventually becomes involved in Monmouth's Rebellion, and the climax is a battle to the death with Carver.

Historical Accuracy: The novel is one of the hallmarks of the historical adventure story, a compendium of high action and period detail.

529 The Maid of Sker

Date of Publication: 1872
Subject(s): Napoleonic Wars; Sea Story
Fictional character(s): Davy Llewellyn, Sailor, Fisherman; Maid of Sker, Outcast; Rodney Bluett, Gentleman, Military Personnel
Time Period(s): 18th century; 19th century (1780-1800)
Locale(s): Wales; Bristol Channel, England

Summary: ''Fisherman Davy'' Llewellyn, a sailor and one of Lord Nelson's bravest, while fishing along the shore of the Bristol Channel discovers a two-year-old child adrift in a boat—the Maid of Sker. She turns out to be Bertha, the long-lost daughter of an aristocratic family, which allows her marriage to the noble Rodney Bluett.

Historical Accuracy: The appeal of the novel is the first-person recollection of past naval engagements, which are remembered with an authenticity and charm.

CHARITY BLACKSTOCK
(PSEUD. OF URSULA TORDAY, 1888-)

English novelist Torday graduated from the London School of Economics and worked for seven years as an assistant in the placement of Jewish refugee children. In 1954 she published her first novel, *After the Lady*, under the pseudonym of Pamela Allardyce. *Miss Fanny*, published in 1957, was the first of many historical romances she wrote under the name of Charity Blackstock.

530 *The English Wife*

Date of Publication: 1964
Subject(s): Regency Romance; Highland Clearances
Fictional character(s): Meg Rowland, Gentlewoman; Ringan Kerr, Businessman (estate manager)
Time Period(s): 1800s; 1810s (1805-1816)
Locale(s): Inverness, Scotland; London, England; Sutherland, Scotland

Summary: Englishwoman Meg Rowland falls in love with Ringan Kerr, the chief factor for the Duke of Scotland. She is delighted with her Scottish husband and their life in the Highlands until she sees the effect of her husband's duty to his master as the Highland Clearances wreaks its havoc on traditional Scottish life. Meg is divided between her love for her husband and her abhorrence of his actions.

Historical Accuracy: The Scottish scenes are vivid and authentic as is the depiction of the tragic era of the Highland Clearance.

531 *The Lonely Strangers*

Date of Publication: 1972
Subject(s): Romance; Jacobite Rebellion
Fictional character(s): Call MacDonnell, Fugitive; Grizel Ryder, Widow(er)
Time Period(s): 1780s
Locale(s): Paris, France

Summary: The novel concerns Call MacDonnell and Grizel Ryder, Scottish exiles in Paris, victims of the failed Stuart Rebellion and Bonnie Prince Charlie's cause. Call is separated from his wife and is marked by a death sentence; Grizel is widowed by the cause. They come together for support in tumultuous Paris, engulfed in revolutionary fervor and the fantastic dreams of the Scottish exiles who plot their return to their homeland.

Historical Accuracy: The novel's strength is the atmosphere of doom and menace that hangs over the relationships and a convincing rendering of the historical background.

FORRESTER BLAKE (1912-)

American author Blake has written novels about mountain men, the Mexican-American War, the desert, and other classic Western locations and subjects. His books include *Riding the Mustang Trail* and *Wilderness Passage*.

532 *The Franciscan*

Date of Publication: 1963
Subject(s): Religious Life; Indians; American West
Fictional character(s): Lorenzo de Escalona, Religious (Franciscan priest); Manuel de Vargas, Military Personnel (Spanish sergeant); Estrella Guerrero, Young Woman (half-breed)
Time Period(s): 17th century (1675)
Locale(s): New Mexico

Summary: A Franciscan priest finds himself an unwilling member of a group whose job is to search out renegade Indians in Spanish New Mexico in the 1670s. Padre Lorenzo is a staunch supporter of the Indians and opposed to Sergeant Vargas. The story features an ambush, a long march, and finally a revealing climax.

Historical Accuracy: The period is effectively presented in this re-creation of the Spanish West and Indian life.

533 *Johnny Christmas*

Date of Publication: 1948
Subject(s): American West
Fictional character(s): Johnny Christmas, Mountain Man
Time Period(s): 1830s; 1840s (1836-1846)
Locale(s): Southwest

Summary: Set in the Southwestern frontier in the years of Mexican control and growing American settlement, the novel dramatizes the coming of age experiences of Johnny Christmas. The story includes abundant material about trapping, the customs of the Ute Indians, and the declining control of the Spanish in New Mexico and California.

Historical Accuracy: The novel features an expert and authentic reconstruction of frontier customs and the region's landscape.

534 *Wilderness Passage*

Date of Publication: 1953
Subject(s): American West; Mormons; Indians
Fictional character(s): Johnny Christmas, Mountain Man
Time Period(s): 1840s
Locale(s): Utah; Oregon Trail, United States

Summary: In this story of conflict with Indians and Mormons in the Utah Territory and along the Oregon trail, mountain man Johnny Christmas finds himself unwillingly forced into the dispute.

Historical Accuracy: The novel is authoritative in its knowledge of emigrant trains and trappers of the period.

JAMES CARLOS BLAKE (1950-)

Born in Texas, James Carlos Blake was an army paratrooper who now teaches writing and literature at Dade County Community College in Miami.

535 *The Friends of Pancho Villa*

Date of Publication: 1996
Subject(s): Mexican Revolution
Fictional character(s): Rodolfo Fierro, Revolutionary

Historical character(s): Francisco Villa, Revolutionary
Time Period(s): 1910s; 1920s
Locale(s): Mexico

Summary: The novel provides a first-hand account of the Mexican Revolution from the perspective of one of its participants, Rodolfo Fierro, who is on hand for Pancho Villa's meteoric rise and fall.

Historical Accuracy: The details of the Mexican Revolution are close to the facts, and the atmosphere of the period is genuine.

536 *The Pistoleer*

Date of Publication: 1995
Subject(s): American West; Crime and Criminals; Biography, Fictionalized
Historical character(s): John Wesley Hardin, Outlaw, Gunfighter; James Butler Hickok, Lawman
Time Period(s): 19th century (1855-1896)
Locale(s): Texas

Summary: The novel reconstructs the life and times of one of the West's most famous gunmen, John Wesley Hardin. Various voices of friends and enemies provide eye-witness accounts of Hardin's wild days and life as a Texas gunman.

Historical Accuracy: The novel is impressive as a convincing reconstruction of genuine western voices and the western era.

MICHAEL BLAKE (1945-)

An American novelist and screenwriter, Blake, attended the University of New Mexico. He was living in his car and at a friend's house while working on *Dances with Wolves*. The film was hailed as offering the most accurate cinematic presentation of Plains Indian culture and the best western since the days of John Ford. It earned Blake an Academy Award for best adapted screen play.

537 *Dances with Wolves*

Date of Publication: 1988
Subject(s): American West; Indians
Fictional character(s): John Dunbar, Military Personnel (lieutenant); Stands with a Fist, Indian, Young Woman; Kicking Bird, Indian (Comanche), Warrior
Time Period(s): 1860s
Locale(s): West

Summary: In the years following the Civil War, Lieutanant John Dunbar is ordered to an abandoned army post in the West where he learns the ways of the Comanche.

Historical Accuracy: The novel offers an authentic and sympathetic depiction of Indian culture.

538 *Marching to Valhalla: A Novel of Custer's Last Days*

Date of Publication: 1996
Subject(s): American West; Indians; Military Life—U.S. Cavalry

Historical character(s): George Armstrong Custer, Military Personnel (cavalry officer); Elizabeth Bacon Custer, Spouse
Time Period(s): 1870s (1876)
Locale(s): Dakota Territory, United States

Summary: Cast in the form of a journal kept by George Armstrong Custer during the weeks leading up to the Battle of the Little Bighorn, the novel portrays Custer as a dashing, driven soldier who rides headlong to meet his destiny.

Historical Accuracy: The novel offers a believable impersonation of Custer's voice and character, supported by evident factual and geographical details.

MIKE BLAKELY

539 *Too Long at the Dance*

Date of Publication: 1996
Subject(s): American West; Johnson County War; Cattle Drives
Fictional character(s): Caleb Holcomb, Cowboy, Musician; Amelia Holcomb, Widow(er)
Time Period(s): 1880s; 1890s (1884-1891)
Locale(s): Colorado; New Mexico

Summary: In this sequel to *Shortgrass Story*, cowboy and musician Caleb Holcomb becomes involved in the Johnson County War and the Arapaho uprising, while courting his brother's widow. The novel offers a vivid portrait of the last great cattle drives and the settlement of the Indian Territory.

Historical Accuracy: Actual historical events provide an authentic background.

RICHARD BLAKER (1893-1940)

English novelist Blaker was born in India and educated at Oxford. At the outbreak of World War I, he enlisted in the Royal Field Artillery and fought in France, Egypt, and Palestine. He began his writing career after the war with *The Voice in the Wilderness*.

540 *The Needle-Watcher*

Date of Publication: 1932
Subject(s): Japanese Empire; Elizabethan Period; East/West Relations
Historical character(s): William Adams, Sailor; Tokugama Ieyasu, Ruler (shogun)
Time Period(s): 16th century; 17th century
Locale(s): Japan

Summary: The novel tells the story of William Adams, the first Englishman to visit Japan. In 1598 Adams sails aboard a Dutch ship as pilot-major (navigator or "needle-watcher") for a two-year trading voyage to the East. Shipwrecked, Adams becomes the vassal of the Shogun Ieyasu and proves his skill with a sword and in the intrigues of feudal Japan.

Historical Accuracy: The novel interweaves actual details of Adams' life and invented adventures.

MICHAEL BLANKFORT (1907-1982)

An American psychologist, screenwriter, playwright, and novelist, Blankfort trained as a psychologist at Princeton and worked as a college instructor and prison psychologist. He devoted himself to writing in 1937. His screenwriting credits include *The Caine Mutiny*, *The Plainsman*, and *Broken Arrow*. *The Juggler* won the Daroff Award in 1952 and was made into a film by Stanley Kramer, the first American movie to be shot in Israel.

541 *Behold the Fire*

Date of Publication: 1965
Subject(s): World War I; Espionage; Jews
Fictional character(s): Naftali Brandt, Writer (poet), Farmer; Saul Wilner, Peddler; Rachel Singer, Young Woman
Historical character(s): Edmund Henry Hynman Allenby, Military Personnel (British general); T.E. Lawrence, Military Personnel (British colonel); Jemel Pasha, Military Personnel (commander of the Turkish Army); Chaim Weitzman, Leader (Zionist), Scientist
Time Period(s): 1910s; 1920s (1914-1928)
Locale(s): Palestine; London, England; Cairo, Egypt

Summary: Set during World War I, the novel dramatizes the efforts of NILI, a small, secret group of Palestinian Jews who act as spies for the British in the war against the Turks. The novel features authentic descriptions of battles in the desert and in the mountains of Palestine where General Allenby completes his historic capture of Jerusalem.

Historical Accuracy: The novel is faithful to the morality of the past time and the spirit of the people who lived through it, even though some scenes and incidents have been invented, and names and places changed, added, or omitted for the sake of the story.

WYATT BLASSINGAME (1909-1985)

Born in Alabama and a graduate of the University of Alabama, Blassingame wrote in several genres, including juvenile nonfiction and adult novels. He contributed to such periodicals as *Dime Mystery* and *Terror Tales* in the 1930s. His books include *Halo of Spears* and *For Better, for Worse*.

542 *Live From the Devil*

Date of Publication: 1959
Subject(s): Ranching
Fictional character(s): Matt Prescott, Rancher
Time Period(s): 20th century (1900s-1950s)
Locale(s): Florida

Summary: Matt Prescott becomes a powerful cattle baron in the fictional Tonekku County, in this novel of ranching in early 20th-century Florida.

Historical Accuracy: The regional background is convincingly evoked, but the story rarely rises above the conventional.

WILLIAM JAMES BLECH
(PSEUD. OF WILLIAM J. BLAKE)

543 *The Angel: A Novel Based on the Life of Alexander I of Russia*

Date of Publication: 1950
Subject(s): Russian Empire; Royalty—Russia; Napoleonic Wars
Historical character(s): Alexander I, Ruler (Czar of Russia)
Time Period(s): 18th century; 19th century (1777-1825)
Locale(s): Russia; Europe

Summary: The novel chronicles the life and times of Russia's enigmatic Czar Alexander I, who along with Napoleon dominated the European scene from 1802 to 1818. A mystic and an autocrat, Alexander was the grandson of Catherine the Great and was convinced that he was destined to be the savior of all Europe. The novel vividly captures the enigma of this curious Russian despot.

Historical Accuracy: The author relies on historical facts and surmise.

544 *The Copperheads*

Date of Publication: 1941
Subject(s): Civil War—U.S.; Draft Riots
Fictional character(s): Maria Meinhardt, Young Woman; Frank Doughty, Military Personnel (Union soldier); Jurgen Van Rensselaer, Financier
Time Period(s): 1860s
Locale(s): New York, New York

Summary: Maria Meinhardt, the daughter of a German immigrant, is loved by several men, including Frank Doughty, a Union soldier, and Jurgen Van Rensselaer, a wealthy businessman and Copperhead.

Historical Accuracy: The atmosphere of Civil War-era New York City is authoritatively drawn, and the novel features a vivid depiction of the New York Draft Riot.

WINFRED BLEVINS (1938-)

An American writer born in Little Rock, Arkansas, Blevins graduated from the University of Missouri and Columbia University. He has been an instructor of American literature at Purdue University as well as a music and stage reviewer for various Los Angeles newspapers.

545 *The High Missouri*

Date of Publication: 1994
Subject(s): American West; Indians
Fictional character(s): Dylan Campbell, Wanderer, Trapper; Morgan Bleddyn, Wanderer; Cree Medicine, Indian (Piegan), Captive
Time Period(s): 1820s
Locale(s): Three Forks, Montana; Rocky Mountains
Summary: In this installment of the Rivers West series, Dylan Campbell heads west as a member of the Northwest Trading Company. He is instructed in wilderness life by the enigmatic

wanderer Morgan Bleddyn, known as the Druid. Campbell's journey takes on many elements of the mythic quest for meaning and identity in the wilds.

Historical Accuracy: The novel is less historical than archetypal. However, the period background is authentic.

546 *The Powder River*

Date of Publication: 1990
Subject(s): American West; Indians
Fictional character(s): Adam Smith Maclean, Doctor; Elaine Maclean, Spouse, Teacher
Historical character(s): Little Wolf, Indian (Cheyenne)
Time Period(s): 1870s (1878-1879)
Locale(s): Cheyenne Reservation, Oklahoma; Powder River, Montana

Summary: The Cheyenne are dying on the Oklahoma reservation where they have been confined since their surrender. They make a desperate attempt to return to their Powder River homeland 1,500 miles away. They are accompanied by Doctor Adam Maclean and his wife who are determined to save as many lives as possible.

Historical Accuracy: The story is fictional but authentic in its depiction of the era and the region.

547 *The Snake River*

Date of Publication: 1992
Subject(s): American West; Indians; Settlement of the American Frontier
Fictional character(s): Flare O'Flaherty, Mountain Man; Margaret Jewel, Teacher; Sima, Indian (Shoshone), Teenager
Time Period(s): 1830s
Locale(s): Snake River, Oregon

Summary: Mountain man Flare O'Flaherty guides a party of missionaries to the Willamette Valley. He is attracted to teacher Margaret Jewel. The story details their journey and how the wilderness changes people in ways they cannot foresee.

Historical Accuracy: The novel offers a convincing depiction of the frontier and the period.

548 *Stone Song: A Novel of the Life of Crazy Horse*

Date of Publication: 1995
Subject(s): American West; Indians; Biography, Fictionalized
Historical character(s): Crazy Horse, Indian (Sioux), Warrior; Red Cloud, Indian, Chieftain
Time Period(s): 19th century (1854-1877)
Locale(s): Great Plains

Summary: The novel tells the story of the great Lakota Sioux warrior Crazy Horse. Spurned from childhood for his light hair, Crazy Horse grows up to lead his people to their greatest victory, the one over General Custer at the Battle of Little Big Horn. The novel dramatizes Crazy Horse's life, his defense of Sioux values, and his faithfulness to his vision.

Historical Accuracy: Though the author claims fidelity to the facts, he admits to employing some speculation and imagination as appropriate in his role as a novelist.

549 *The Yellowstone*

Date of Publication: 1988
Subject(s): American West; Indians
Fictional character(s): Robert Burns Maclean, Mountain Man, Trader
Time Period(s): 19th century (1843-1865)
Locale(s): Wyoming; Montana

Summary: Trader and mountain man Maclean comes to the Yellowstone River and begins to trade with the Cheyenne. Over 20 years the changes he sees mirror the development of the West.

Historical Accuracy: The novel is exact and convincing in its details of Western life of the period.

JAMES BLISH (1921-1975)

An American writer of mainly science fiction, Blish was born in New Jersey and was educated at Rutgers and Columbia. He was a newspaper editor and public relations counsel. He is best known for adapting the ''Star Trek'' television scripts to book form. His 1958 novel *A Case of Conscience* won a Hugo award. Blish has been rated as one of the finest science fiction writers of his generation.

550 *Doctor Mirabilis*

Date of Publication: 1964
Subject(s): Middle Ages; Science; Biography, Fictionalized
Historical character(s): Roger Bacon, Religious (friar), Scholar; Albertus Magnus, Scholar; Henry III, Ruler (King of England)
Time Period(s): 13th century (1231-1294)
Locale(s): England; France; Italy

Summary: Friar Roger Bacon was one of the greatest scholars of the Middle Ages, and this novel offers a plausible account of his life. Since little is known of Bacon's life, the author surmises much, relying on his extraordinary sense of the 13th century for plausible scenes and subjects.

Historical Accuracy: What makes this novel so reliable is not the biography of Bacon, which is mostly speculation, but the authentic sense of the period that anchors the story.

ROBERT BLOCH (1917-)

A native of Chicago, Bloch worked as an advertising copywriter. He began his career in horror and science fiction writing at the suggestion of writer H.P. Lovecraft, and he published his first story in *Weird Tales* magazine at the age of 17. Most famous as the author of *Psycho*, Bloch has written two dozen novels of mystery and horror and over 60 scripts for television series, including ''I Spy,'' ''Star Trek,'' and ''Night Gallery.''

551 *The Night of the Ripper*

Date of Publication: 1984
Subject(s): Mystery; Victorian Period
Fictional character(s): Mark Robinson, Doctor; Frederick Abberline, Detective—Police
Historical character(s): Arthur Conan Doyle, Writer; George Bernard Shaw, Writer; Oscar Wilde, Writer
Locale(s): London, England

Summary: The novel offers an ingenious new solution to the famous Jack the Ripper case. Doctor Robinson and Detective Abberline work against the clock to stop the series of grisly Whitechapel murders. Some historical figures have supporting roles.

Historical Accuracy: The novel is a clever puzzle with sufficient period details to convince the reader of its authenticity.

ROBERT S. BLOOM

Robert Bloom is Deputy Administrative Assistant to the Supreme Judicial Court of Massachusetts.

552 *A Generation of Leaves*

Date of Publication: 1991
Subject(s): War of 1812; Napoleonic Wars
Fictional character(s): Daniel Carey, Printer, Historian
Historical character(s): Gouverneur Morris, Diplomat, Political Figure; Nancy Randolph, Spouse (of Gouverneur Morris), Gentlewoman; Charles Maurice de Talleyrand-Perigord, Diplomat; Marie Joseph Paul de Lafayette, Nobleman (Marquis de Lafayette), Military Personnel (general); John Randolph, Political Figure
Time Period(s): 18th century; 19th century (1792-1833)
Locale(s): New York; Virginia; Europe (Leipzig, Paris)

Summary: This massive panoramic novel attempts to depict the history of the young American nation from the 1790s to the 1830s. A young historian, Daniel Carey, forms a relationship with statesman Gouverneur Morris. He participates in the disastrous Niagara Campaign of 1812, and undertakes a diplomatic mission for Morris to Europe where he witnesses the Battle of Leipzig and the fall of Paris. Finally, he investigates the facts surrounding the murder trial of Nancy Randolph, Morris' wife.

Historical Accuracy: The novel is an impressive reconstruction of the past with supporting documents that convince the reader of the novel's veracity.

URSULA BLOOM (1893-1984)

English journalist and author Bloom produced more than 500 books, making her one of England's most prolific writers. She completed her first book at age seven. After her first husband died in 1918, she began working as a crime reporter. She began in earnest as a novelist in 1924 and continued writing into the 1970s, working on her books 16 hours a day. Her titles include *Secret Lover*, *The Rose of Norfolk*, and *Judas Iscariot, Traitor?*

553 *The Romance of Charles Dickens*

Date of Publication: 1960
Subject(s): Literary Life; Biography, Fictionalized; Victorian Period
Historical character(s): Charles Dickens, Writer
Time Period(s): 1830s; 1850s
Locale(s): London, England

Summary: This biographical novel, based on an episode in the life of Charles Dickens, records Dickens' first love affair with Maria Beadnell before his success as a writer. Maria's banker father objects, and Dickens is left brokenhearted. Years later Maria is transformed into Dora in *David Copperfield*, and during the 1850s Dickens meets the matronly Maria Beadnell again, to his great disappointment.

Historical Accuracy: The novel's facts are based on Dickens' life; the dialogue is invented.

GODFREY BLUNDEN (1906-)

Blunden's novels include *The Looking-Glass Conference* and *The Time of the Assassins*. He is also the author of *The Land and People of Australia* and the co-author with Maria Blunden of *Impressionists and Impressionism*.

554 *Charco Harbour*

Date of Publication: 1968
Subject(s): Exploration; Sea Story
Historical character(s): James Cook, Explorer, Sea Captain
Time Period(s): 1760s (1768)
Locale(s): At Sea; Australia

Summary: The novel describes Captain Cook's voyage to the South Seas and the first landfall in Australia. Cook's ship is wrecked, and the crew are marooned in Charco Harbour where contact is made with the indigenous people. Cook emerges as a complex individual, far more interesting than his legendary status.

Historical Accuracy: The novel is scrupulously researched and the results are evident in the believability of the scene and the personalities.

JULIET BLYTH

555 *The Parfit Knight*

Date of Publication: 1986
Subject(s): Regency Romance
Fictional character(s): Lord Amberley, Nobleman, Rake; Rosalind Vernon, Gentlewoman, Handicapped (blind)
Time Period(s): 19th century (Regency period)
Locale(s): Hertfordshire, England; London, England

Summary: When his coach is attacked by a highwayman, the Marquis of Amberley takes shelter with the Vernon family. Amberley falls in love with the handsome Rosalind Vernon, who is blind. He arranges for Rosalind to have a social season in London, and she proves to be a brilliant success. Complications from Amberley's past slow the course of love.

Historical Accuracy: The Regency period details are present with an unusual heroine for the genre.

LEGETTE BLYTHE (1900-)

An American writer born in North Carolina, Blythe attended the University of North Carolina and was a public school teacher, a newspaper reporter, and writer in residence at the University of North Carolina at Charlotte. His biblical novels and series of children's books on biblical characters have been translated into many languages.

556 *Brothers of Vengeance*

Date of Publication: 1969
Subject(s): Biblical Story; Roman Empire
Fictional character(s): Onesimus, Government Official
Historical character(s): Barabbas, Thief, Biblical Figure; Jesus Christ, Biblical Figure, Religious; Pontius Pilate, Government Official (procurator of Judea), Biblical Figure; Herod Antipas, Ruler (Tetrarch of Galilee); Tiberius, Ruler (Roman emperor); Caligula, Ruler (Roman emperor); Claudius I, Ruler (Roman emperor); Nero, Ruler (Roman emperor); Paul, Biblical Figure, Religious
Time Period(s): 1st century
Locale(s): Rome, Roman Empire; Jerusalem, Israel

Summary: The events surrounding Jesus' arrest and execution are played out from the perspective of Barabas, the thief released instead of Jesus, and Onesimus, whose parents are murdered by a band that includes Barabas. Onesimus' campaign of vengeance against Barabas is matched by the thief's hatred of the Romans. Both will be affected by the death of the Galilean in Jerusalem.

Historical Accuracy: The familiar story is well told and solidly detailed in this novel which blends the actual with the fabricated.

557 *Hear Me, Pilate!*

Date of Publication: 1961
Subject(s): Biblical Story; Roman Empire
Fictional character(s): Longinus, Military Personnel (Roman tribune); Claudia, Gentlewoman, Spouse (of Pilate)
Historical character(s): Pontius Pilate, Government Official (procurator of Jerusalem), Biblical Figure; Lucius Aelius Sejanus, Political Figure; Herod Antipas, Ruler (King of Judea), Biblical Figure
Time Period(s): 1st century
Locale(s): Jerusalem, Israel; Rome, Roman Empire

Summary: The crucifixion story of Jesus is told from the perspective of Pontius Pilate; the Roman tribune Longinus, Christ's executioner; and Pilate's wife, Claudia. Pilate is shown as weak and corrupt, a pawn of the ambitious Sejanus who secures for him the post of procurator of Judea. Conspiracy and intrigue lead to the arrest and execution of Jesus.

Historical Accuracy: The author combines a solid sense of place and time with inventions to fashion his story.

558 *Man on Fire: A Novel on the Life of St. Paul*

Date of Publication: 1964
Subject(s): Biography, Fictionalized; Roman Empire; Christianity
Fictional character(s): Longinus, Military Personnel (Roman tribune); Claudia, Gentlewoman, Spouse (of Pilate)
Historical character(s): Paul, Religious, Biblical Figure; Pontius Pilate, Government Official (procurator of Judea), Biblical Figure; Peter, Religious, Biblical Figure; Tiberius, Ruler (Roman emperor); Caligula, Ruler (Roman emperor); Herod Agrippa II, Ruler (King of Judea); Nero, Ruler (Roman emperor); Timothy, Religious, Biblical Figure
Time Period(s): 1st century (30s-60s)
Locale(s): Jerusalem, Israel; Middle East; Rome, Roman Empire

Summary: The novel offers both a fictional biography of St. Paul as well as a history of the early Christian church and its impact on the Roman Empire. The novel follows Paul as he develops the formal structure of the Church and Christian dogma until his martyrdom.

Historical Accuracy: The author blends together the historical, the legendary, and the fictional.

559 *A Tear for Judas*

Date of Publication:
Subject(s): Biblical Story; Roman Empire
Fictional character(s): Longinus, Military Personnel (Roman centurion)
Historical character(s): Judas Iscariot, Biblical Figure; Nicodemus, Biblical Figure; John the Baptist, Biblical Figure; Jesus Christ, Biblical Figure; Pontius Pilate, Biblical Figure, Government Official
Time Period(s): 1st century
Locale(s): Jerusalem, Israel

Summary: This version of Jesus' ministry and crucifixion is told from the perspective of Judas who is portrayed as a zealot who follows Jesus in the hopes that he will lead the Hebrews in revolt against the Romans.

Historical Accuracy: The novel offers a convincing depiction of the familiar Biblical story with a plausible background of the political turmoil of the period.

PHILIP BOAST (1952-)

Born in London and a graduate of Northeastern University, Boast has worked in sales, as a sanitary inspector, a chicken farmer, and a chauffeur to pay for his writing. At age 16 he left school to sail to the Galapagos Islands to study wildlife. He has suggested that all his novels are interconnected and are intended to be read as a single book.

560 *London's Child*

Date of Publication: 1987
Subject(s): Childhood; World War I; Aviation

Fictional character(s): Ben London, Foundling, Military Personnel; Ria Price, Streetperson, Actress; Vane Leibig, Gentleman
Time Period(s): 20th century (1900s-1930s)
Locale(s): London, England

Summary: Ben London is a foundling, born in a graveyard. His mother is a servant girl seduced by the lord of the manor. After Ben endures the workhouse and life on the street, he's saved by an East End girl, Ria. Her betrayal causes him to embark on a career marked as much by revenge as ambition, first as a flyer in World War I and then as the owner of a clothing store.

Historical Accuracy: The rags to riches story is marked by a vivid background of period details.

JOHAN BOJER (1872-1959)

This Norwegian novelist visited the U.S. in 1923 to gather material for his novel, *The Emigrants*. His other works feature Norwegian settings.

561 *The Emigrants*

Date of Publication: 1925
Subject(s): Settlement of the American Frontier; Immigrants
Fictional character(s): Erik Foss, Immigrant; Morten Kvidal, Immigrant, Carpenter; Kal Skaret, Immigrant, Farmer
Time Period(s): 1890s
Locale(s): Dakota Territory, United States; Norway

Summary: Erik Foss leads a group of Norwegian families to the Dakota wilderness, where they cultivate the land and become Americans.

Historical Accuracy: Bojer, a Norwegian writing an American story, is nevertheless convincing in his details of pioneer life.

562 *The Great Hunger*

Date of Publication: 1919
Subject(s): Immigrants; Farming
Fictional character(s): Peer Holm, Immigrant, Farmer
Time Period(s): 1850s
Locale(s): Norway; Midwest

Summary: This tale of immigrant life in America concerns Norwegian Peer Holm, who journeys to the Midwest in the 1850s to farm and continue his search for spiritual meaning and fulfillment.

Historical Accuracy: The novel provides an authentic portrait of immigrant life and Norwegian culture and customs.

563 *The Last of the Vikings*

Date of Publication: 1921
Subject(s): Sea Story; Fishing
Fictional character(s): Kristaver Myran, Sea Captain, Fisherman; Lars Myran, Fisherman, Sailor
Time Period(s): 1800s
Locale(s): Norway; *Seal*, At Sea

Summary: Norwegian cod fishermen Kristaver Myran and his son endure a year of great hardship and danger.

Historical Accuracy: Bojer realistically describes the passing era of the heroic independent fisherman.

PAUL DARCY BOLES (1916-1984)

An Indiana-born author of novels, short stories, and criticism, Boles was a high school dropout who began writing at age nine.

564 *The Limner*

Date of Publication: 1975
Subject(s): Picaresque Adventure; Mystery
Fictional character(s): Luke Applegate, Artist, Wanderer; Letty Eisner, Young Woman
Time Period(s): 1870s
Locale(s): East Coast

Summary: The novel offers the picaresque adventures of Luke Applegate, a wandering painter, or limner, who meets and falls in love with Letty Eisner. When her father is murdered, Luke searches for his killer. The mystery is eventually resolved after a dramatic balloon flight.

Historical Accuracy: The novel is a convincing evocation of the period.

565 *The Mississippi Run*

Date of Publication: 1977
Subject(s): Horse Racing; Horses; Reconstruction Period
Fictional character(s): Tom Broome, Jockey; Francia Broome, Young Woman
Historical character(s): Bret Harte, Writer
Time Period(s): 19th century (late)
Locale(s): Mississippi

Summary: The world of harness racing is the backdrop for this picaresque novel set in the South following the Civil War. Tom Broome wants to enter his stallion, Greyboy, at the Yadkin Fair. His adventures in getting there and the climactic races involve a large cast of Southern Rabelaisian types.

Historical Accuracy: The novel is full to bursting with character types that invoke an authentic time and place.

GUY BOLTON (1884-1979)

English playwright, screenwriter, and novelist, Bolton often collaborated with P.G. Wodehouse and Oscar Hammerstein and is the author of more than 50 plays and musicals. His best remembered works are *Anastasia*, *Lady Be Good*, and *Anything Goes*.

566 *The Olympians*

Date of Publication: 1961
Subject(s): Literary Life; Regency Period
Historical character(s): Percy Bysshe Shelley, Writer; Mary Wollstonecraft Shelley, Writer
Time Period(s): 1810s; 1820s (1814-1822)
Locale(s): England; Europe

Summary: The novel dramatizes the relationship between poet Percy Shelley and Mary Wollstonecraft Godwin, the daughter of Shelley's idol William Godwin and feminist writer Mary Wollstonecraft. In 1814 the two fall in love and, although Shelley is already married, they elope together to the continent facing social ostracism. They are later married after Shelley's first wife committs suicide.

Historical Accuracy: The novel features a wealth of historical details and anecdotes that provide a solid framework, despite an often lush and romanticized style.

MURIEL RAY BOLTON (1909-1983)

An American author and writer for film and television, Bolton is best known as the head writer and story consultant for the popular TV series ''The Millionaire.''.

567 *The Golden Porcupine*

Date of Publication: 1947
Subject(s): Royalty—France
Historical character(s): Louis XII, Ruler (King of France)
Time Period(s): 15th century
Locale(s): France

Summary: This royal tale of France in the 15th century describes the tangled route of Louis, Duke of Orleans, to the throne as Louis XII. He is pursued by Louis XI, the ''Spider King,'' who attempts to break feudalism and create a unified French nation. The duke resists, becomes a royal prisoner and falls in love with both the king's daughter and his queen. Eventually, he gains the crown.

Historical Accuracy: The novel handles its complicated politics and succession issues with care and authenticity.

BASIL BONALLACK

Educated at Clare College, Cambridge, Bonallack has worked as a freelance journalist. In 1974 he won the Malta Short Story Competition.

568 *The Flame in the Dark*

Date of Publication: 1976
Subject(s): Dark Ages; Anglo Saxon Period; Royalty—England
Fictional character(s): Edward of Kent, Knight
Historical character(s): Alfred the Great, Ruler (King of Wessex)
Time Period(s): 9th century
Locale(s): England

Summary: This chronicle of the career of Alfred the Great is told by his companion-in-arms, Edward of Kent, who describes Alfred's rise to power and his struggles against the Danes. The novel captures Alfred's military successes in the famous victory of Ashdown and the climatic Battle of Ethandun.

Historical Accuracy: The novel mixes actual events and figures with some deliberate anachronisms for purposes of clarity, but it is meant to be a tale, not a history.

PARRIS AFTON BONDS

569 *Blue Moon*

Date of Publication: 1985
Subject(s): Mexican Revolution
Fictional character(s): Roxana Van Buren, Journalist, Detective—Private; Sam Brady, Cowboy
Historical character(s): Francisco Villa, Revolutionary
Time Period(s): 1910s (1916)
Locale(s): Texas; Mexico

Summary: Roxana Van Buren takes a job as a private investigator in Texas to support herself; and her first case draws her into the turmoil of the Mexican Revolution. During the Revolution she sets out to interview revolutionary leader Pancho Villa.

Historical Accuracy: The story is more ingenious and entertaining than historical.

570 *Dream Time*

Date of Publication: 1993
Subject(s): Business Building; Frontier—Australia
Fictional character(s): Nan Briscoll, Convict, Businesswoman (shipping company); Tom Livingston, Sea Captain; Miles Randolph, Villain
Time Period(s): 19th century
Locale(s): Australia

Summary: Nan Briscoll is betrayed by her lover, Miles Randolph, and sent to Australia as a convict. There she prospers as a trader, marrying sea captain Tom Livingston. When Miles appears on the scene, Nan turns to revenge.

Historical Accuracy: The novel, although melodramatic, is filled with accurate period details of frontier Australia.

CINDY BONNER (1953-)

Born in Corpus Christi, Texas, Cindy Bonner is the daughter of an oil company accounting executive and a U.S. Navy comptroller. She attended the University of Southern Mississippi and San Antonio College. Bonner has worked variously as a yoga teacher, a computer operator, a real estate manager, a blues/rock band manager, a co-owner of a wholesale nursery, and a volunteer worker in a school library.

571 *Lily*

Date of Publication: 1992
Subject(s): American West; Crime and Criminals; Romance
Fictional character(s): Lily DeLong, Young Woman; Marion Beatty, Young Man
Time Period(s): 1880s
Locale(s): Texas

Summary: This western tale describes the love affair between Lily DeLong and Marion Beatty, the youngest son of one of the oulaw Beatty brothers.

Historical Accuracy: This romantic tale provides some convincing period elements.

572 *Looking After Lily*

Date of Publication: 1994
Subject(s): American West; Crime and Criminals; Romance
Fictional character(s): Lily DeLong, Young Woman; Haywood Beatty, Young Man
Time Period(s): 1880s
Locale(s): Texas

Summary: In the sequel to *Lily*, when her lover, Marion Beatty, is sent to jail, a pregnant Lily DeLong is placed under the care of Marion's brother Haywood. Love blossoms with important consequences.

Historical Accuracy: The novel's romance is paramount, but there are some authentic period elements.

THEODORE BONNET

573 *The Mudlark*

Date of Publication: 1949
Subject(s): Victorian Period; Royalty—England
Fictional character(s): Wheeler, Outcast
Historical character(s): Benjamin Disraeli, Political Figure; Victoria, Ruler (Queen of England)
Time Period(s): 1870s (1875)
Locale(s): London, England

Summary: This Victorian era tale describes the role played by a London urchin who accidentally finds himself in the company of Queen Victoria and her prime minister, Benjamin Disraeli, and comes to play a role in convincing the queen to end her seclusion after 14 years of mourning for Prince Albert.

Historical Accuracy: The novel blends historically accurate details with fancy.

ARNA BONTEMPS (1902-1973)

Bontemps was an American educator, anthropologist, poet, and author of plays, novels, biographies, and juvenile fiction on African-American life and culture. He was one of the last surviving members of the Harlem Renaissance that included such writers as Langston Hughes, Countee Cullen, and James Weldon Johnson.

574 *Black Thunder*

Date of Publication: 1936
Subject(s): Slavery; Gabriel's Insurrection; Antebellum South
Historical character(s): Gabriel, Slave
Time Period(s): 1800s; 1810s
Locale(s): Richmond, Virginia

Summary: The novel dramatizes the events of Gabriel's Insurrection. In 1810, a large group of slaves plot to seize power and take control of Richmond, Virginia. The novel captures the motives of the insurgents and the conditions that set off their attempt to win their freedom.

Historical Accuracy: The novel is reliable in its depiction of the historical events and the atmosphere of the period.

575 *Drums at Dusk*

Date of Publication: 1939
Subject(s): Independence—Haiti; French Revolution
Fictional character(s): Diron Desautels, Nobleman
Historical character(s): Pierre Dominique Toussaint l'Ouverture, Revolutionary, Political Figure
Time Period(s): 1790s (1791)
Locale(s): Haiti

Summary: This story is set in Haiti at the beginning of the rebellion led by Toussaint L'Ouverture. The story is seen from the perspective of a young French aristocrat, Diron Desautels, who befriends Toussaint L'Ouverture and finds himself drawn into the conflict.

Historical Accuracy: The novel's manner of presentation and its emphasis on the exotic and romantic mar any careful consideration of the historical background.

MARTIN BOOTH (1944-)

Both a poet and a writer, Booth was born in Lancashire, England, and later moved to Hong Kong. He was educated at the University of London and St. Peter's College, Oxford. He is a teacher of English and a much published poet whose works are represented in more than 25 anthologies.

576 *Dreaming of Samarkand*

Date of Publication: 1989
Subject(s): Homosexuality; Literary Life
Historical character(s): T.E. Lawrence, Archaeologist, Military Personnel (British officer); James Elroy Flecker, Writer (poet); Helle Flecker, Spouse (of James)
Time Period(s): 1910s (1911-1914)
Locale(s): Beirut, Lebanon; England; Switzerland

Summary: The novel describes a love triangle involving T.E. Lawrence, English poet James Elroy Flecker, and his wife, Helle. Flecker is a consular official in Beirut, desperate to make his mark as a poet. He meets and falls in love with Lawrence. Theirs is a spiritual bond that cannot prevent Flecker's disappointment. In the end he is sustained only by his love for Lawrence, his wife, and his poetry.

Historical Accuracy: The novel is a convincing version of an early event in Lawrence's life and the ultimate event in Flecker's.

ALICE BORCHARDT

577 *Beguiled*

Date of Publication: 1997
Subject(s): Middle Ages; Vikings; Witchcraft and Sorcery
Fictional character(s): Elin, Young Woman; Owen, Religious (bishop); Hakon, Warrior (Viking)
Time Period(s): 10th century
Locale(s): Chantalon, France

Summary: This sequel to *Devoted* continues the story of Elin, a woman of the pagan Forest People who marries Owen, the young Christian bishop of Chantalon. Now they must resist a Viking invasion in a clash of heroism and magic.

Historical Accuracy: The novel is filled with period elements though it is more fantasy than history.

578 *Devoted*

Date of Publication: 1995
Subject(s): Dark Ages; Supernatural; Vikings
Fictional character(s): Elin, Young Woman; Owen, Religious (bishop)
Time Period(s): 10th century
Locale(s): France

Summary: Set in 10th century France where pagan customs contend with Christianity and the myths of the Vikings, the novel tells the story of Elin. A woman of the Forest People of northern France, Elin is rescued from Viking captivity by Owen, Bishop of Chantalon. They marry, and when Owen is captured, Elin must defend her home and rescue her husband.

Historical Accuracy: The novel is atmospheric rather than strictly historic.

LUCILLE BORDEN (1873-)

An American novelist and essayist, Borden's books include *From Out of Magdala*, *White Hawthorn*, *Starforth*, and *King's Highway*.

579 *Sing to the Sun*

Date of Publication: 1933
Subject(s): Middle Ages; Religious Life
Fictional character(s): Adriano Guriandio, Young Man; Vittoria Ziani, Young Woman
Historical character(s): Francis of Assisi, Religious (monk)
Time Period(s): 13th century
Locale(s): Assisi, Italy

Summary: The life of Saint Francis of Assisi is depicted through the perspective of two young lovers, Adriano Guriandio and Vittoria Ziani, who narrates their story in which Francis plays a prominent role. The novel captures the effect Francis of Assisi had on his countrymen.

Historical Accuracy: The novel provides an authentic background for this depiction of Francis.

RAYMOND C. BOREL (1927-)

Born of American parents in France, Borel was educated at the Sorbonne and has worked as an assistant to various motion picture directors in Africa, Brazil, and Mexico. He is a television screenwriter and correspondent for several European newspapers.

580 *Death at the French Creek*

Date of Publication: 1975
Subject(s): Napoleonic Wars; Indians; American West
Fictional character(s): Edmund Grail, Veteran (Napoleonic Guard); Sophie de Dupuy-Preaux, Noblewoman

Historical character(s): Napoleon Bonaparte, Ruler (French emperor), Military Personnel (army commander)
Time Period(s): 1810s
Locale(s): France; Texas

Summary: The novel offers the story of a regiment of Napoleon's army after the defeat at Waterloo. Edmund Grail is a loyal officer of the Napoleonic Guard who journeys to America with a group of fellow veterans and Sophie, the wife of a French noble. Their plan is to liberate Mexico and prepare it for Bonapartist rule. The scheme meets its end in an encounter with the Creek Indians.

Historical Accuracy: Rather than a realistic depiction of history, this is an adventure story with the appeal of the romantic lost cause.

BARBARA DODGE BORLAND
(1904-1991)

An American writer and editor, Borland was born in Connecticut and attended Oberlin College and Columbia University School of Journalism. She worked for a variety of publishers and was the author of numerous articles, short stories, and poems in various magazines, alone and in collaboration with her husband, Hal Borland. She also produced a newspaper gardening column.

581 *The Greater Hunger*

Date of Publication: 1962
Subject(s): American Colonies; Religious Conflict
Fictional character(s): Samuel Downing, Scientist (horticulturist); Hetty Downing, Young Woman; Nathaniel Trumbull, Religious (minister)
Historical character(s): John Winthrop, Political Figure (colonial governor); Roger Williams, Religious (clergyman)
Time Period(s): 17th century (1629-1630s)
Locale(s): England; Salem, Massachusetts, American Colonies; Boston, Massachusetts, American Colonies

Summary: Early American life in the Massachusetts Bay Colony is depicted. The story centers on Hetty Downing, the daughter of a horticulturist who has come to America to develop experimental gardens in the settlement. She is attracted to the minister, Nathaniel Trumbull, who attempts to unify the diverse colonists—Puritans, Anglicans, and Catholics—with mixed results.

Historical Accuracy: The novel offers a vivid and convincing portrait of early American colonial life.

HAL BORLAND (1900-1978)

An American novelist who was born in Nebraska and grew up in eastern Colorado, Borland served as the outdoor writer for the *New York Times* for many years. He was also the author of documentary film scripts.

582 *The Amulet*

Date of Publication: 1957
Subject(s): Civil War—U.S.; American West

Fictional character(s): Quincy Scott, Military Personnel (Confederate volunteer); Buffalo Jake, Mountain Man; Porter Hayes, Military Personnel (Confederate volunteer)
Time Period(s): 1860s (1861)
Locale(s): Denver, Colorado; Great Plains; Missouri

Summary: At the start of the Civil War, Quincy Scott joins a column of irregular Confederate volunteers in Denver for the long trek east to the fighting in Missouri. The action culminates in the Battle of Wilson's Creek, on the western front of the Civil War.

Historical Accuracy: The novel is evocative and realistic in its depiction of the Western frontier and the period.

583 *The Seventh Winter*

Date of Publication: 1959
Subject(s): American West; Ranching
Fictional character(s): Jeff Ross, Rancher; Loretta Ross, Spouse
Time Period(s): 1870s (1871)
Locale(s): Colorado

Summary: Jeff Ross' seventh winter in Colorado is a bitter one. His dreams of a happy marriage and family and a successful ranch come apart as he struggles to hold on in this bitter winter of his discontent.

Historical Accuracy: The details of ranching life in a Colorado winter are graphically and authentically portrayed.

584 *When the Legends Die*

Date of Publication: 1963
Subject(s): American West; Indians; Rodeos
Fictional character(s): Thomas Black Bull, Indian (Ute); Blue Elk, Indian (Ute)
Time Period(s): 1910s
Locale(s): Colorado (southwest); Odessa, Texas

Summary: This is the story of a Ute Indian boy, Thomas Black Bull. When his parents die, he endures prejudice and conflict at a reservation school and later on the rodeo circuit. Throughout, Black Bull tries to make peace with his identity and his place in a world that refuses to see or value his heritage.

Historical Accuracy: The scene and characters are genuinely and realistically drawn.

MARVIN BOROWSKY

585 *The Queen's Knight*

Date of Publication: 1955
Subject(s): Dark Ages; Myths and Legends; Arthurian Legends
Fictional character(s): Arthur, Ruler (King of the Britons); Guinevere, Royalty (queen consort of Arthur); Lancelot, Knight; Lucan, Knight; Jocelyn, Maiden
Time Period(s): 5th century
Locale(s): England

Summary: This version of King Arthur and Camelot is stripped of the chivalrous and poetic trappings of Malory and Tennyson to offer a more realistic interpretation. The fall of Camelot is portrayed from the perspective of two lovers, Lucan and Jocelyn, who find themselves close observers of the royal tragedy involving Arthur, Guinevere, and Lancelot. Arthur is portrayed not as a great hero or tragic figure but as a plain man protecting a kingdom torn by strife and petty jealousies.

Historical Accuracy: The novel is a literary amalgam of actual life of the fifth century, the chivalric traditions of the 12th century, and some very clear 20th-century ideas. The overall effect is to break the conventional pattern of Arthur's story in interesting, if not always believable, ways.

ELIZABETH BORTON
(PSEUD. OF ELIZABETH BORTON DE TREVINO, 1904-)

Born in California, Trevino graduated from Stanford University and studied violin at the Boston Conservatory of Music. She later worked as a journalist, a publicist for the Mexico City Tourist Department, and First Violinist in the Vivaldi Orchestra. An author of books for adults and children, her best-known juvenile book is *I, Juan de Pareja*, which won the Newbery Medal in 1966. Her adult novels include *The Greek of Toledo: A Romantic Narrative about El Greco* and *Among the Innocent*.

586 *The Greek of Toledo: A Romantic Narrative of El Greco*

Date of Publication: 1959
Subject(s): Biography, Fictionalized; Artistic Life; Inquisition
Historical character(s): Domenikos Theotokopoulos, Artist (El Greco); Titian, Artist; Tintoretto, Artist
Time Period(s): 16th century; 17th century
Locale(s): Venice, Italy; Toledo, Spain; Rome, Italy

Summary: This biographical account of the life of painter El Greco follows his career from his departure from Crete to his apprenticeship in Italy under Titian and Tintoretto, his days in Rome, and his final move to Toledo where he creates his masterpieces during the time of the Inquisition.

Historical Accuracy: The novel imaginatively embellishes the few documented facts about El Greco's life, adding romance and an invented inner life for the artist that is plausible but by no means certain.

MALCOLM BOSSE (1933-)

Bosse is an American author born in Detroit and educated at Yale, the University of Michigan, and NYU where he received a Ph.D. in English in 1969. He is a professor of English at City College of the City University of New York. His mysteries and young adult books have received critical praise.

587 *The Examination*

Date of Publication: 1994
Subject(s): Chinese Empire
Fictional character(s): Lao Hong, Young Man; Lao Chen, Student

Time Period(s): 16th century
Locale(s): China

Summary: Set in 16th-century China during the Ming dynasty, the novel records the adventures of two brothers who journey across China to Beijing where the scholarly Lao Chen intends to sit for the examination that will lead to a position as a government official. His worldly-wise brother Lao Hong protects him from the dangers of the journey.

Historical Accuracy: The novel provides an authentic period backdrop.

588 *The Vast Memory of Love*

Date of Publication: 1992
Subject(s): Crime and Criminals; Picaresque Adventure; Georgian Period
Fictional character(s): Ned Carleton, Criminal; Robert Scarrat, Criminal (kidnapper); Jenny Rivers, Criminal
Historical character(s): Henry Fielding, Writer, Judge (magistrate); John Montagu, Nobleman (Earl of Sandwich); John Wilkes, Political Figure
Time Period(s): 1750s
Locale(s): London, England

Summary: This is the picaresque tale of a young shepherd, Ned Carleton, who is forced to earn his living off the London streets in the 1750s. There he is introduced to all elements of the criminal underworld and becomes a notorious outlaw bent on revenge. His target is the Earl of Sandwich, who forced Ned into crime by dismissing Ned from his household.

Historical Accuracy: The details of 18th-century London life—both the fashionable world and the criminal underworld—are described with relish and conviction.

589 *The Warlord*

Date of Publication: 1983
Subject(s): Chinese Revolution
Fictional character(s): Shan-Teh Tang, Military Personnel, Warlord; Vera Rogacheva, Gentlewoman; Erich Luckner, Businessman; Philip Embree, Adventurer
Historical character(s): Chiang Kai-Shek, Military Personnel (Chinese commander), Political Figure; Mao Tse-tung, Revolutionary, Political Figure
Time Period(s): 1920s (1927)
Locale(s): Shanghai, China; Hunan, China

Summary: As China emerges into the modern world, it becomes a war zone of competing factions. General Tang is a warlord trying to keep European greed, Japanese expansion, and Bolshevik revolutionary zeal in check. He is connected to a group of foreigners whose personal stories become bound up in the larger political events.

Historical Accuracy: The novel is an extensive panorama of the period. Covering so much ground, the novel inevitably gives short shrift to some events.

ALLAN R. BOSWORTH (1901-1986)

Born in San Angelo, Texas, Bosworth was a former U.S. Navy captain, a newspaperman, and the author of more than 500 short stories and books, including *New Country* and *The Crows of Edwina Hill*.

590 *Storm Tide*

Date of Publication: 1965
Subject(s): Sea Story; Whaling
Fictional character(s): Scon Bailey, Sea Captain; Susan Marcy, Heiress
Time Period(s): 1880s
Locale(s): New Bedford, Massachusetts; *Bedford Lass*, At Sea

Summary: Captain Scon Bailey is set on taking the first sail-and-steam whaling ship on a four-year voyage around the world. To do so, he must bring along Susan Marcy, who has inherited her father's fleet. The novel chronicles their adventures.

Historical Accuracy: Though the author admits to taking certain liberties in recording the voyage of the first steam whaling ship, he has faithfully described whaling details and techniques.

CAROLINE BOURNE

591 *Allegheny Captive*

Date of Publication: 1990
Subject(s): Romance; Riverboats
Fictional character(s): Charissa Sherwood, Heiress; Andrew Donovan, Sea Captain (riverboat)
Time Period(s): 1820s
Locale(s): Mississippi River; New Orleans, Louisiana; Allegheny Mountains, Pennsylvania

Summary: In this romantic adventure story, gentlewoman Charissa Sherwood is kidnapped and sold into slavery to work in a New Orleans brothel. She escapes on board Andrew Donovan's riverboat, where love triumphs amidst conflict as the two head up the Mississippi and east to Donovan's Pennsylvania home.

Historical Accuracy: Love is all in this period story with some lightly-sketched period details.

PETER BOURNE
(PSEUD. OF GRAHAM JEFFERS, 1900-1982)

An English author born in London, Bourne began his career as a writer in 1920. He was also a freelance journalist, literary agent, and film writer and producer. Under the pseudonym Bruce Graeme, he wrote crime novels featuring Blackshirt, a cracksman and adventurer.

592 *The Courts of Love: A Romance of Medieval France*

Date of Publication: 1958
Subject(s): Middle Ages; Royalty—England
Fictional character(s): Raymond de Prissac, Nobleman (Comte de Prissac); Joscelin de Sabres, Knight; Ghislaine, Young Woman

Historical character(s): Eleanor of Aquitaine, Royalty (queen consort of Henry II); Henry II, Ruler (King of England); Richard the Lionhearted, Royalty (prince)
Time Period(s): 12th century (1172-1173)
Locale(s): France

Summary: Joscelin, the cousin and squire of Raymond de Prissac, reluctantly agrees to abduct a young maiden with a fortune so that the comte can marry her. During their adventures together Joscelin falls in love with Ghislaine and goes to Queen Eleanor's Court of Love to plead his case.

Historical Accuracy: The story is a fanciful one, constructed loosely within the confines of historical events.

593   *Drums of Destiny*

Date of Publication: 1947
Subject(s): Slavery; Independence—Haiti
Fictional character(s): Duncan Stewart, Doctor
Historical character(s): Henri Christophe, Ruler, Revolutionary; Pierre Dominique Toussaint l'Ouverture, Revolutionary, Political Figure; Alexandre Petion, Revolutionary, Political Figure; Jean-Jacques Dessalines, Military Personnel, Revolutionary
Time Period(s): 18th century; 19th century (1768-1820s)
Locale(s): Scotland; Haiti

Summary: This novel depicts the slave revolt that led to the independence of Haiti. Doctor Duncan Stewart journeys to Haiti where he encounters Toussaint L'Ouverture, Christophe, and others and is on hand during the struggle that ends French control of the island and during the civil war between blacks and mulattoes that follows.

Historical Accuracy: The novel is a vivid and reliable interpretation of the events and a believable dramatization of the historical personalities.

594   *Flames of Empire*

Date of Publication: 1949
Subject(s): Civil War—U.S.; Royalty—France
Fictional character(s): Martin Ravenel, Spy, Adventurer
Historical character(s): Maximilian, Ruler (Emperor of Mexico); Carlota, Royalty (consort of Maximilian); Napoleon III, Ruler (Emperor of France)
Time Period(s): 19th century (1847-1864)
Locale(s): New Orleans, Louisiana; Paris, France; Mexico

Summary: Martin Ravenel, secret agent, Confederate patriot, and adventurer, journeys to the court of Napoleon III seeking support for the Confederate cause. He is recruited to assist in the installation of Maximilian as Emperor of Mexico and to serve him during his short and tragic reign.

Historical Accuracy: Colorful and romantic, the emphasis here is on adventure rather than a careful rendering of the facts. The atmosphere is, however, genuine.

595   *Soldiers of Fortune*

Date of Publication: 1962
Subject(s): Sea Story; American Colonies
Fictional character(s): George Flower, Nobleman; Mounslic, Military Personnel; Jeremy Alicock, Farmer

Historical character(s): John Smith, Leader, Military Personnel
Time Period(s): 17th century (1606)
Locale(s): *Susan Constant*, At Sea (between England and Virginia)

Summary: The novel provides a profile of the first colonists of Virginia as they sail across the Atlantic. The crew includes Captain John Smith, a young aristocrat who is fleeing England after killing one of the King's musketeers; a mercenary soldier; and a gentleman farmer accidently involved in Guy Fawkes' plot to blow up Parliament. Their stories and others offer a panorama of English history and of the character of America's first colonists.

Historical Accuracy: The novel ingeniously offers a range of character types and personalities, revealing along the way the period's history and customs.

596   *Twilight of the Dragon*

Date of Publication: 1954
Subject(s): East/West Relations; Boxer Rebellion; Royalty—China
Fictional character(s): Wen Chin, Government Official; Randall Lockhart, Gentleman; Evelyn Stangeway, Gentlewoman
Historical character(s): Kuang-Hsu, Ruler (Emperor of China); Tz'u-hsi, Royalty (Dowager Empress of China)
Time Period(s): 1900s (1900)
Locale(s): Peking, China

Summary: The novel concerns the Boxer Rebellion in China and the palace intrigue that led to the siege of the foreign legations in Beijing. It is also a dual love story. Wen Chin, an interpreter for the American legation, struggles to free his beloved, who has been abducted into concubinage, while Randall Lockhart strives to win the hand of Evelyn Stangeway.

Historical Accuracy: The novel is primarily a romance with a historical backdrop. The atmosphere of Chinese court politics is convincing.

597   *When God Slept*

Date of Publication: 1956
Subject(s): Middle Ages; East/West Relations
Fictional character(s): Michael de Bernay, Servant (squire), Slave; William Long-Arm, Knight; Jayarajadevi, Royalty (princess); Tilaki, Slave
Time Period(s): 12th century
Locale(s): Cambodia; England

Summary: En route to the Crusades, a young squire named Michael de Bernay is captured by Arabs and turned into a galley slave. He journeys east to Kambuja (now Cambodia) where he becomes the house slave of Princess Jayarajadevi. He dreams of escape while absorbing the strange and exotic customs of a truly foreign people.

Historical Accuracy: The emphasis here is more on exoticism than historical accuracy. However, the clash of culture between Medieval Europe and the East is interesting and well-developed.

MARJORIE BOWEN

(PSEUD. OF MARGARET CAMPBELL, 1886-1952)

English historical novelist, playwright, and short story writer Campbell published under several pseudonyms, including Marjorie Bowen, George Preedy, and Robert Paye. Subjects of her biographical novels include Mary, Queen of Scots; Emma, Lady Hamilton; Mary Wollstonecraft Godwin; John Wesley; and John Paul Jones.

598 *The Lady and the Arsenic*

Date of Publication: 1937
Subject(s): Crime and Criminals; Biography, Fictionalized
Historical character(s): Marie LaFarge, Murderer
Time Period(s): 19th century (1816-1852)
Locale(s): France

Summary: The novel offers a fictional biography of Frenchwoman Marie LaFarge, who in 1840 was convicted of poisoning her husband. The novel describes her life, her 12 years in prison, and death at the age of 37. LaFarge insists on her innocence but is unable to re-open her case or to prove that she is not guilty.

Historical Accuracy: The novel is faithful to the source material of contemporary accounts and LaFarge's own memoirs.

599 *Queen's Caprice*

Date of Publication: 1934
Subject(s): Royalty—Scotland
Historical character(s): Mary, Queen of Scots, Ruler; Henry Stewart, Nobleman (Lord Darnley), Spouse (consort of Mary)
Time Period(s): 16th century (1565-1567)
Locale(s): Scotland

Summary: The novel dramatizes the story of the crucial years in the career of Mary, Queen of Scots, from her first meeting with Lord Darnley to her imprisonment in Lochleven Castle.

Historical Accuracy: The interpretation offered fits the facts of history, though some liberties have been taken with the motivations of the characters.

PETER BOWEN

600 *Imperial Kelly*

Date of Publication: 1992
Subject(s): Spanish-American War; Boer War
Fictional character(s): Luther "Yellowstone" Kelly, Adventurer
Historical character(s): Theodore Roosevelt, Political Figure; Winston Churchill, Political Figure; Jennie Jerome, Gentlewoman
Time Period(s): 1890s
Locale(s): Cuba; South Africa; Philippines

Summary: The novel recounts the adventures of Luther "Yellowstone" Kelly, who ventures beyond the western frontier to help Theodore Roosevelt recruit Rough Riders for the Cuban campaign, goes to South Africa during the Boer War, and finally travels to the Philippines for adventures among the Igorote tribesmen.

Historical Accuracy: The novel is more burlesque than accurate in its historical details with a fine sense of revisionist comedy in its repossession of history.

601 *Kelly Blue*

Date of Publication: 1991
Subject(s): American West; Civil War—U.S.; Indians
Fictional character(s): Luther "Yellowstone" Kelly, Adventurer
Historical character(s): William F. Cody, Frontiersman; Jim Bridger, Frontiersman; Crazy Horse, Indian (Sioux), Warrior; Brigham Young, Leader (Mormon); Kit Carson, Frontiersman; Red Cloud, Indian (Sioux), Chieftain; Ulysses S. Grant, Political Figure
Time Period(s): 19th century; 20th century (1865-1917)
Locale(s): West

Summary: Luther "Yellowstone" Kelly, army scout, Indian fighter, and adventurer, continues the story of his exploits during the Civil War and out west. He becomes an apprentice to Jim Bridger, is pursued by Brigham Young, and is in the thick of the fighting during the Indian Wars of the 1870s.

Historical Accuracy: The emphasis here is on the comic and the anti-heroic, producing a rollicking revisionist version of historical events and figures emphasizing the absurd and the all too human.

602 *Yellowstone Kelly*

Date of Publication: 1987
Subject(s): American West; Zulu War; Indians
Fictional character(s): Luther "Yellowstone" Kelly, Adventurer
Historical character(s): Nelson Appleton Miles, Military Personnel (general); Sitting Bull, Indian (Sioux), Chieftain; Theodore Roosevelt, Political Figure; William F. Cody, Frontiersman, Entertainer; Cetewayo, Ruler (Zulu king); Jack Johnson, Sports Figure (boxer)
Time Period(s): 19th century; 20th century (1870s-1900s)
Locale(s): United States; Africa

Summary: The novel begins the memoirs of Luther Sage "Yellowstone" Kelly, Indian fighter and adventurer. He narrates an offbeat and irreverent account of his involvement in the Nez Perce War in the American Northwest and the Zulu War in Africa.

Historical Accuracy: This is history repossessed with an emphasis on the comic and outrageous. The background is solidly historical but the treatment is unique and idiosyncratic.

TRUE BOWEN

603 *And the Stars Shall Fall*

Date of Publication: 1951
Subject(s): Russian Empire; Royalty—Russia; Russian Revolution

Historical character(s): Alexandra Feodorovna, Royalty (consort of Czar Nicholas II); Nicholas II, Ruler (Czar of Russia)
Time Period(s): 19th century; 20th century
Locale(s): Russia

Summary: The life and times of Russia's last czarina, Alexandra, consort of Nicholas II, are described. The sympathy of the author is clearly pro-Romanov in this documentation of the breakup of both a family and a regime.

Historical Accuracy: The novel offers an accurate picture of the events. Some interpretation is evident in ascribing motives.

GEORGE BOWERING (1935-)

A Canadian novelist and poet, Bowering was born in British Columbia. He was educated at the University of British Columbia. He is the author of numerous poetry collections, including *Rocky Mountain Foot* and *The Gangs of Kosmos*. Bowering's novels include *Concentric Circles* and *Burning Water*. He has won the Canadian Governor General's Award twice.

604   *Shoot!*

Date of Publication: 1994
Subject(s): Crime and Criminals
Historical character(s): Allan McLean, Outlaw; Charlie McLean, Outlaw; Archie McLean, Outlaw
Time Period(s): 1870s (1879)
Locale(s): Victoria, British Columbia, Canada

Summary: Based on fact, the novel recounts the experiences of the McLean Gang, three brothers of mixed white and Indian blood who operated around Victoria, British Columbia during the 1870s. The novel offers a wry alternative to the American western story in its portrait of young outcasts.

Historical Accuracy: The novel uses history as the starting point for a largely imaginary reconstruction of the period and the events surrounding the McLean Gang.

JOHN CLARKE BOWMAN

605   *Powhatan's Daughter*

Date of Publication: 1973
Subject(s): American Colonies; Indians
Historical character(s): Pocahontas, Indian; John Smith, Settler; Powhatan, Indian, Chieftain; John Rolfe, Settler, Landowner; Ben Johnson, Writer; Anne of Denmark, Royalty (Queen of England); James I, Ruler (King of England); Charles Stuart, Royalty (prince)
Time Period(s): 17th century (1607-1617)
Locale(s): Jamestown, Virginia, American Colonies; England

Summary: This is the tale of Pocahontas, who intercedes on behalf of the Jamestown colonists with her father, Powhatan, the strongest chief on the Chesapeake. The legend of the tragic love affair between Pocahontas and John Smith is described both in Virginia and in England as Pocahontas is celebrated at the court of James I.

Historical Accuracy: The love affair is based on legend rather than historical fact. Despite this, the story is solidly grounded in the historical records of the Jamestown colony.

BURKE BOYCE (1901-)

An American writer born in St. Louis, boyce attended and was a professor at Harvard. His is an Olympic-class fencer and has travelled around the world in competitions. Boyce's novels include *Cloak of Folly*, *The Emperor's Arrow*, and *The Perilous Night*.

606   *Cloak of Folly*

Date of Publication: 1949
Subject(s): Elizabethan Period; Literary .Life
Historical character(s): Edward de Vere, Nobleman (Earl of Oxford)
Time Period(s): 16th century; 17th century
Locale(s): England

Summary: This novel is based on the life of Elizabethan poet, courtier, and soldier Edward de Vere, 17th earl of Oxford. The author describes de Vere's literary side, his adventures with Sir Francis Drake, and the intrigue for which he was imprisoned.

Historical Accuracy: The portrait of the times is authentic and believable.

607   *Man From Mt. Vernon*

Date of Publication: 1961
Subject(s): American Revolution; Biography, Fictionalized
Historical character(s): George Washington, Military Personnel (commander of American army), Political Figure; Martha Washington, Spouse; John Adams, Political Figure; Charles Lee, Military Personnel (army officer); Benedict Arnold, Military Personnel (army officer); Nathanael Greene, Military Personnel (army officer); Horatio Gates, Military Personnel (army officer); Marie Joseph Paul de Lafayette, Military Personnel (army officer), Nobleman (Marquis de Lafayette)
Time Period(s): 1770s; 1780s (1775-1781)
Locale(s): Mount Vernon, Virginia; New Jersey; New York

Summary: This fictional biography of George Washington follows the general through the crucial events of the American Revolution. Its aim is to create a rounded portrait of Washington the man, not the legend. Family obligations, self-doubt, and remarkable determination mark the portrayal.

Historical Accuracy: The novel offers a convincing and reliable portrait of the man and his times.

608   *Morning of a Hero*

Date of Publication: 1963
Subject(s): American Colonies; French and Indian War; Biography, Fictionalized
Historical character(s): George Washington, Military Personnel (army officer), Landowner; Edward Braddock, Military Personnel (army officer); Sally Fairfax, Gentlewoman; Martha Custis, Gentlewoman
Time Period(s): 1750s

Locale(s): Virginia, American Colonies; Ohio

Summary: The novel describes George Washington's early years as a surveyor, as a member of a diplomatic mission to the French, and as a colonial officer during the French and Indian Wars. He emerges from General Braddock's defeat as a hero. Washington is also shown failing in love with Sally Fairfax but marrying instead her friend Martha Custis.

Historical Accuracy: The novel is distinctive in that it attempts to render Washington as very much a creature of his times. The details of colonial life are authentic.

609 *The Perilous Night*

Date of Publication: 1942
Subject(s): American Revolution; Farming; American Colonies
Fictional character(s): Asa Howell, Farmer; Tempy Ann Howell, Young Woman
Time Period(s): 1770s; 1780s
Locale(s): Hudson River Valley, New York, American Colonies

Summary: Through the experiences of the Howell family, the author presents the effects of the American Revolution on a prosperous farming community in the Hudson River Valley.

Historical Accuracy: The novel provides details of everyday life during the period and describes the conflict of loyalty between patriots and Tories.

BRENDAN BOYD

610 *Blue Ruin: A Novel of the 1919 World Series*

Date of Publication: 1991
Subject(s): Baseball; Crime and Criminals
Historical character(s): Arnold Rothstein, Criminal, Gambler; Charles Comiskey, Businessman; Ring Lardner, Writer, Gambler; Joseph Sullivan, Criminal, Gambler
Time Period(s): 1910s (1919)
Locale(s): Chicago, Illinois

Summary: In 1919 the unimaginable happens: the invincible Chicago White Sox throw the World Series. The story of the conspiracy is dramatized with an emphasis on the prominent players behind the scenes, including gamblers Sullivan and Rothstein, White Sox owner Charles Comiskey, and writer Ring Lardner.

Historical Accuracy: The novel provides a faithful recreation of the events of 1919.

JAMES BOYD (1888-1944)

This American novelist used his experience in World War I as the basis for two major novels, *Drums* and *Marching On*. They are set, respectively, in the Revolutionary War and the Civil War, since Boyd was convinced that a writer needs the perspective of years. His other novels are *Roll River*, *Long Hunt*, and *Bitter Creek*.

611 *Drums*

Date of Publication: 1925
Subject(s): American Revolution; Sea Story
Fictional character(s): John Fraser, Gentleman
Historical character(s): John Paul Jones, Military Personnel
Time Period(s): 1770s; 1780s
Locale(s): North Carolina; London, England; *Bonhomme Richard*, At Sea (Baltic)

Summary: Boyd depicts the American Revolution through the experience of a young North Carolina country gentleman who goes to London on family business and winds up joining John Paul Jones in naval actions.

Historical Accuracy: The author attempts a panoramic view of all classes of American society during the Revolution.

612 *Marching On*

Date of Publication: 1927
Subject(s): Civil War—U.S.
Fictional character(s): James Fraser, Farmer; Steward Prevost, Southern Belle; Charles Prevost, Gentleman
Time Period(s): 1860s (1860-1865)
Locale(s): North Carolina

Summary: James Fraser, a poor Carolina farmer, falls in love with a rich planter's daughter. He is imprisoned during the Civil War, then returns home for the novel's climax.

Historical Accuracy: This is an interesting take on the usual social portrait of the South, which ignores class differences.

MARTIN BOYD (1893-1972)

An Australian painter and novelist, Boyd grew up in Melbourne and lived in Australia before emigrating to England and Italy in 1920. Boyd served in the Royal Flying Corps during World War I as an observer. His works include *Nuns in Jeopardy*, *A Difficult Young Man*, *Outbreak of Love*, and *When the Blackbirds Sing*.

613 *Lucinda Brayford*

Date of Publication: 1946
Subject(s): Family Saga
Fictional character(s): Lucinda Brayford, Gentlewoman; Hugo Brayford, Gentleman; Arthur Brayford, Nobleman
Time Period(s): 19th century; 20th century (1858-1940s)
Locale(s): England

Summary: Four generations of a wealthy English family are portrayed in a story that offers a vivid picture of upper-class English life from the 1850s to the 1940s. At the center of the family drama is Lucinda, who marries into the Brayford family and struggles to maintain herself in the midst of rivalry and the challenging ideal of English genteel life.

Historical Accuracy: As a panorama of English manners the novel is convincing, reminiscent of John Galsworthy's Forsythe saga.

THOMAS ALEXANDER BOYD
(1898-1935)

Boyd was born in Ohio and left school at 18 to join the marines. He fought in World War I and was wounded in France. After his discharge, he went to work for a Minnesota newspaper and wrote his first novel. In his short career he authored mainly historical and biographical works.

614   *Samuel Drummond*

Date of Publication: 1925
Subject(s): Civil War—U.S.; Farming
Fictional character(s): Samuel Drummond, Farmer
Time Period(s): 1860s
Locale(s): Ohio

Summary: The novel offers a portrait of family life in Ohio during the Civil War. It chronicles the fate of Samuel Drummond and his family, whose fortunes are affected through the war years.

Historical Accuracy: The novel provides accurate details of period and rural life.

615   *Shadow of the Long Knives*

Date of Publication: 1928
Subject(s): American Revolution
Fictional character(s): Angus McDermott, Frontiersman, Scout
Time Period(s): 1770s
Locale(s): Ohio

Summary: Pioneer life in the Ohio wilderness before and during the American Revolution is depicted in the adventures of Angus McDermott. McDermott's Indian upbringing makes him of great use to the British as an interpreter and peacemaker. When the Revolution begins, a crisis of loyalties occurs.

Historical Accuracy: The novel's depiction of the period and frontier life is restrained and genuine.

WILLIAM BOYD (1952-)

Boyd is an English novelist who was born in Ghana and educated at universities in Nice, Glasgow, and Oxford. He has been a literary critic and lecturer in English at St. Hilda's College, Oxford University. With the publication of his first novel, *A Good Man in Africa*, Boyd was acclaimed as one of England's brightest literary talents.

616   *An Ice-Cream War*

Date of Publication: 1983
Subject(s): World War I
Fictional character(s): Felix Cobb, Military Personnel (British soldier); Gabriel Cobb, Military Personnel (British soldier); Charis Cobb, Spouse (of Gabriel)
Time Period(s): 1910s
Locale(s): Dar-Es-Salaam, Tanzania (then German East Africa); Kent, England; Nairobi, Kenya (then British East Africa)

Summary: The fighting in the East African colonies during the First World War is the subject of this novel that focuses on two brothers, Gabriel and Felix Cobb, who both love Charis, Gabriel's wife. Their domestic conflict mirrors the military one as the old ways of life disappear in the face of new realities.

Historical Accuracy: The African scenes are fully detailed and convincing.

617   *The New Confessions*

Date of Publication: 1988
Subject(s): World War I; Motion Picture Industry
Fictional character(s): John James Todd, Military Personnel (infantry soldier), Director (film)
Time Period(s): 19th century; 20th century (1899-1972)
Locale(s): Scotland; Europe; United States

Summary: John James Todd is a Scotsman born in 1899 whose experiences reflect the history of the 20th century. After service in World War I, he begins a career as a filmmaker that takes him to the Weimar Republic of Germany and, ultimately, to Hollywood.

Historical Accuracy: The novel is an amusing chronicle of one man's life and times, convincing in the details of its history.

T. CORAGHESSAN BOYLE (1948-)

Born in Peekskill, New York, Boyle earned an M.F.A. and a Ph.D. from the University of Texas. Boyle is widely considered to be one of the best American comic writers.

618   *The Road to Wellville*

Date of Publication: 1993
Subject(s): Business Building; Medical Profession
Fictional character(s): Will Lightbody, Gentleman; Eleanor Lightbody, Spouse
Historical character(s): John Harvey Kellogg, Doctor
Time Period(s): 1900s (1907)
Locale(s): Battle Creek, Michigan

Summary: In 1907 the rich and famous journey to Battle Creek, Michigan, drawn by the nutritional guru, Dr. John Harvey Kellogg. Will and Eleanor Lightbody join their ranks, resulting in a wicked send-up of health fads and the profits to be derived from the dream of a longer and healthier life.

Historical Accuracy: The comedy is rooted in the actual details of turn-of-the-century fashion and the exploitation of people's vanity and dreams.

619   *Water Music*

Date of Publication: 1980
Subject(s): Exploration; Frontier—Africa
Fictional character(s): Ned Rise, Thief
Historical character(s): Mungo Park, Explorer
Time Period(s): 1790s; 1800s (1795-1806)
Locale(s): Niger River, Africa; London, England

Summary: This novel tells the exploits of Scottish explorer Mungo Park and his expedition to chart the course of the Niger River in Western Africa. Park is joined by a London thief and scoundrel, Ned Rise, whose resources prove invaluable when dealing with the hostile natives and Muslims.

Historical Accuracy: The novel is a comic send-up that manipulates the factual to fit the comedy. The author admits to reshaping historical fact to serve his purpose.

WALTER J. BOYNE (1929-)

An American born in St. Louis, Boyne is a graduate of the University of California, Berkeley, and received his M.B.A. from the University of Pittsburgh. Boyne is a curator and director of the National Air and Space Museum in Washington, D.C. and has devoted his writing career to aviation.

620 *Eagles at War*

Date of Publication: 1991
Subject(s): Aviation; World War II
Fictional character(s): Frank Bandfield, Military Personnel (major), Pilot; Hadley Roget, Engineer (aviation); Bruno Hafner, Pilot, Engineer (aviation)
Time Period(s): 1930s; 1940s
Locale(s): Germany; United States; England

Summary: The rise of the modern aviation industry is dramatized in this novel. The story focuses on the work of Americans Frank Bandfield and Hadley Roget and their German counterpart Bruno Hafner. Hafner has a personal reason to want to best Bandfield, and their animosity is played out in the battles of World War II.

Historical Accuracy: The technical details of aviation design and the flying scenes are authentic and convincing.

LEIGH BRACKETT (1915-1978)

An American author and screenwriter, Brackett was born in Los Angeles, California. She is best known for her science fiction books, including *Alpha Centauri or Die!* and *The Sword of Rhiannon*. Brackett worked with William Faulkner on the screenplay for *The Big Sleep*. She also wrote the screenplays for *Hatari*, *The Long Goodbye*, and *The Empire Strikes Back*.

621 *Follow the Free Wind*

Date of Publication: 1963
Subject(s): American West; Indians; Biography, Fictionalized
Historical character(s): Jim Beckwourth, Indian (Crow), Chieftain
Time Period(s): 19th century
Locale(s): West

Summary: This Western story is based on the actual events in the life of James Beckwourth, the son of a Virginia landowner father and a mulatto mother who journeys west where he is adopted by the Crow Indians. He eventually rises to the position of chief and participates in the Crow's war against white encroachment.

Historical Accuracy: The novel is faithful to the facts surrounding Beckwourth and provides an authentic period background.

ROARK BRADFORD (1896-1948)

Tennessee-born Bradford served in World War I and then worked as a journalist in Atlanta and New Orleans. He wrote several stories about African Americans.

622 *Kingdom Coming*

Date of Publication: 1933
Subject(s): Civil War—U.S.; Slavery
Fictional character(s): Grammy, Slave
Time Period(s): 1860s
Locale(s): Louisiana

Summary: The novel depicts life on a Louisiana plantation during the Civil War. When his master leaves for the war, young Grammy is left in charge of the plantation. As most of the slaves begin to drift away, Grammy also starts down river to New Orleans where he is captured and interned.

Historical Accuracy: There are some anachronisms in this otherwise authentic tale of the period and slave life in the South.

623 *Three-Headed Angel*

Date of Publication: 1937
Subject(s): Civil War—U.S.; Antebellum South
Fictional character(s): Richard Whiting, Gentleman, Landowner; Bas Younger, Landowner
Time Period(s): 19th century
Locale(s): Phinizy County, Tennessee

Summary: The Younger and Whiting families are at the center of this story of the settlement of Phinizy County, Tennessee. The novel depicts early pioneer days in the area, the effects of the Civil War, and the development that characterizes the second and third generations of settlers.

Historical Accuracy: The novel features an authentic look at the region and the period.

MARION ZIMMER BRADLEY (1930-)

An American-born science fiction and fantasy writer, Bradley attended the New York State College for Teachers and Hardin-Simmons College. She is the author of one of the best-loved science fiction series, the Darkover novels, comprised of more than 20 books. She won a Locus award for the best fantasy novel in 1984 for *The Mists of Avalon*, which has been called the most ambitious retelling of the Arthurian legend in the 20th century. Bradley is also very active in feminist and gay rights causes.

624 *The Firebrand*

Date of Publication: 1987
Subject(s): Myths and Legends; Trojan War
Fictional character(s): Kassandra, Royalty (Princess of Troy); Helen of Troy, Noblewoman; Paris, Royalty (Prince of Troy)

Time Period(s): 13th century B.C.
Locale(s): Troy, Ancient Civilization

Summary: The fall of Troy is told from the perspective of Kassandra, twin of Paris. Kassandra lives in a time when the old matriarchal traditions and the worship of the Earth Mother is giving way to a new world view where male rules and gods are dominant. These new forces plunge Troy into the quarrel that will destroy it.

Historical Accuracy: The novel is an ingenious blend of archeological fact with myth and legend. The author skillfully fashions an ancient world view that is coherent and compelling.

625 *The Forest House*

Date of Publication: 1994
Subject(s): Roman Empire; Fantasy; Druids
Fictional character(s): Eilan, Young Woman, Religious (priestess); Gaius Marcellius, Military Personnel (Roman officer)
Time Period(s): 1st century
Locale(s): England

Summary: Eilan is a young Druidic priestess caught between her duty to guard the ancient rites of learning, healing, and prophecy and her love for the Roman soldier Gaius Marcellius, whose duty is to subdue the Britons.

Historical Accuracy: The novel captures the mystery and the romance of Druidic Britian and the period of Roman occupation.

626 *The Mists of Avalon*

Date of Publication: 1983
Subject(s): Dark Ages; Arthurian Legends; Witchcraft and Sorcery
Fictional character(s): Arthur, Ruler (King of the Britons); Gwenhwyfar, Royalty (queen consort of Arthur); Morgan, Witch
Time Period(s): 5th century
Locale(s): England

Summary: This retelling of the Arthurian legend highlights the perspective of the women in the story. Arthur is caught between the Christian world, represented by Gwenhwyfar, and the old pagan religion of Avalon, represented by his sister, Morgan. The battle between new and old, Briton and Saxon, is played out as well in this story of Camelot's fall.

Historical Accuracy: History is shown indirectly in this novel. The cultural clash between the Saxons and the Britons is convincingly depicted.

GILLIAN BRADSHAW (1956-)

American author Bradshaw received her B.A. degree from the University of Michigan and her M.A. from Cambridge University.

627 *The Beacon of Alexandria*

Date of Publication: 1986
Subject(s): Roman Empire; Medical Profession; Christianity

Fictional character(s): Charis, Doctor; Philon, Doctor; Athanasios, Religious
Time Period(s): 4th century (371-378)
Locale(s): Alexandria, Egypt; Ephesus, Middle East; Thrace, Greece

Summary: Charis, a woman determined to become a physician, flees her home in Ephesus to enter the medical world in Alexandria. Immediately, she is plunged into the collapsing world of the Roman Empire, wracked by factional disputes between Arian and Nicene Christians. She finds her way to Thrace on the crumbling borders of the Empire, which is besieged by the Visigoths.

Historical Accuracy: The period is ably depicted from the vantage point of Bradshaw's unusual heroine. The author admits to some distortion of the chronology.

628 *The Bearkeeper's Daughter*

Date of Publication: 1987
Subject(s): Byzantine Empire; Roman Empire
Fictional character(s): John, Courtier; Narses, Servant (eunuch)
Historical character(s): Theodora, Ruler (Byzantine empress), Spouse (of Justinian); Justinian I, Ruler (Byzantine emperor)
Time Period(s): 6th century
Locale(s): Constantinople, Byzantine Empire

Summary: During the late Roman period in Constantinople, the capital of the empire in the east, a young man arrives from Arabia. He quickly earns the empress' favor and at the same time becomes embroiled in court politics, factional conflicts, and finally, warfare on the eastern frontier.

Historical Accuracy: Bradshaw has made this period her own. The details of court and customs of the time are convincingly depicted.

629 *Hawk of May*

Date of Publication: 1980
Subject(s): Myths and Legends; Dark Ages; Arthurian Legends
Fictional character(s): Gwalchmai, Knight; Arthur, Ruler; Morgawse, Sorceress; Aldulf, Sorcerer
Time Period(s): 6th century
Locale(s): England (southwest); Orkney Islands, Scotland

Summary: Gwalchmai is King Arthur's nephew, the son of the sorceress Morgawse. After rejecting his mother's world, he attempts to win the confidence and trust of his uncle. First, he must battle with the Saxons, the pursuing demons of Morgawse, a white stallion that cannot be tamed, and an evil sorcerer.

Historical Accuracy: The historical background is not entirely accurate. There are anachronisms and some complete departures from what is known about Britain between the Roman withdrawal and the Saxon conquest.

630 *Horses of Heaven*

Date of Publication: 1991
Subject(s): Royalty—Bactria; Ancient Greece; Fantasy

Fictional character(s): Mauakes, Ruler; Heliokleia, Royalty; Itaz, Royalty
Time Period(s): 2nd century B.C. (140 B.C.)
Locale(s): Bactria, Asia (Central Asian kingdom); Afghanistan

Summary: Mauakes rules over the Hellenistic Greek kingdom of Bactria. His wife, Heliokleia, is attracted to Mauakes' son, Itaz, and a tale of forbidden passion and high politics unfolds.

Historical Accuracy: The book, although a fantasy set in a real time and place, is thoroughly grounded in historical research. Bradshaw's epilogue, a defense against claims of anachronisms, makes this clear.

631 *Imperial Purple*

Date of Publication: 1988
Subject(s): Byzantine Empire
Fictional character(s): Demetrias, Artisan (silk-weaver); Chrysaphos, Servant
Historical character(s): Theodosius II, Ruler (Eastern Roman emperor); Pulcheria, Royalty
Time Period(s): 5th century
Locale(s): Constantinople, Byzantine Empire; Tyre, Lebanon

Summary: Demetrias is a talented silk-weaver in Tyre in the 5th century who is ordered to weave a cloak of imperial purple. Because of the importance of her task, Demetrias is kidnapped and taken to Constantinople. There, she finds herself involved in a conspiracy to overthrow the emperor. At the center of the conspiracy is the possession of the valuable and symbolic purple cloak.

Historical Accuracy: Bradshaw's knowledge of the period is convincing, and the setting is ably displayed.

632 *In Winter's Shadow*

Date of Publication: 1982
Subject(s): Myths and Legends; Dark Ages; Arthurian Legends
Fictional character(s): Arthur, Ruler (King of the Britons); Gwynhwyfar, Royalty (queen consort of Arthur); Bedwyr, Knight
Time Period(s): 6th century
Locale(s): England (southwest); Brittany, France

Summary: In the final volume of Bradshaw's Arthurian trilogy, the fall of Camelot is dramatized. Queen Gwynhwyfar (Guinevere) narrates the tragic story of her fatal love affair with Bedwyr, the perfect knight. It is the queen's human perspective that supplies the originality to this familiar tragedy.

Historical Accuracy: The Arthurian legend is put into a historical context that convinces the reader that it might have been as described.

633 *Kingdom of Summer*

Date of Publication: 1981
Subject(s): Myths and Legends; Dark Ages; Arthurian Legends
Fictional character(s): Gwalchmai, Knight; Elidan, Royalty (princess); Arthur, Ruler

Time Period(s): 6th century
Locale(s): England (southwest)

Summary: In the second volume of Bradshaw's Arthurian trilogy, Gwalchmai is sent by Arthur to conquer his strongest opposition. Gwalchmai falls in love with Princess Elidan. When Gwalchmai kills her brother, Elidan flees to a convent, and Gwalchmai pursues his lost love.

Historical Accuracy: Bradshaw's world of Britain before the Saxon conquest is solidly grounded in historical detail.

CHARLES ANDREW BRADY (1912-)

An American educator and author, Brady was born in Buffalo, New York, and graduated from Canisius College and Harvard. A professor of English, Brady has produced television programs on Joseph Conrad, Walt Whitman, and other literary subjects. His books include *Cat Royal*, *Stage of Fools*, and *Crown of Grass*.

634 *Crown of Grass*

Date of Publication: 1964
Subject(s): Literary Life
Historical character(s): Francois Rene de Chateaubriand, Writer, Diplomat; Leo XII, Religious (pope); Francois Eugene Vidocq, Detective—Police
Time Period(s): 1820s
Locale(s): Rome, Italy

Summary: In post-Napoleonic Rome at the end of the 1820s, French writer Chateaubriand is serving as the French ambassador to the Papal States. He is caught in a triangle of love and politics that turns murderous.

Historical Accuracy: The novel intermingles the factual with the imagined and the fanciful in a suspenseful tale that does offer a convincing period background.

635 *Stage of Fools*

Date of Publication: 1953
Subject(s): Tudor Period; Royalty—England; Religious Conflict
Historical character(s): Sir Thomas More, Writer, Political Figure; Henry VIII, Ruler (King of England)
Time Period(s): 15th century; 16th century (1480s-1530s)
Locale(s): England

Summary: Based on the life of Sir Thomas More, the novel dramatizes his rise to power as chancellor of Henry VIII and his opposition to the king's divorce and break with the Catholic Church. In a world in which the court and clergy are corrupt and self-serving, More emerges as a man of principle, too principled for his own good.

Historical Accuracy: The novel blends facts, imaginative speculations, and evident advocacy on behalf of More into an authentic portrait of the man and his age.

636 *This Land Fulfilled*

Date of Publication: 1958
Subject(s): Exploration; Vikings

Fictional character(s): Thrand, Religious (priest); Grainne, Ruler (Irish queen)
Historical character(s): Leif Eriksson, Explorer
Time Period(s): 11th century
Locale(s): Norway; Ireland; North America

Summary: In 1066 Thrand, a priest and chief counselor to the Irish queen Grainne, is asked to relate his experiences 50 years earlier with Leif Ericson on his voyage to North America. Thrand's story begins in Norway and chronicles his voyage across the Atlantic and the explorer's three-year stay in Vinland.

Historical Accuracy: Considerable liberties have been taken with sources in which details from various Vinland sagas are transposed.

JOAN BRADY (1939-)

Born in San Francisco, Brady graduated from Columbia University and pursued a career in dance before turning to writing. She performed with the San Francisco Ballet and the New York City Ballet.

637   *Theory of War*

Date of Publication: 1993
Subject(s): Slavery; Reconstruction Period; Railroads
Fictional character(s): Johnathan Carrick, Slave; College, Outcast
Historical character(s): George Stoke, Political Figure
Time Period(s): 19th century; 20th century (1860s-1920s)
Locale(s): Sweetbriar, Kansas; Denver, Colorado; Cheyenne, Wyoming

Summary: Jonathan Carrick, a white boy, is sold into slavery to a Kansas tobacco farmer after the Civil War. He endures the grinding work and bullying from the son of the farm family, George Stoke. Jonathan escapes to the West for a career on the railroad. His rage and hatred for George Stoke keeps him going and reveals the enormous cost of slavery to the human spirit.

Historical Accuracy: The psychological profiles are convincingly dramatized as is the post-Civil War period in the West.

BILL BRAGG (1922-)

R.C. HOUSE

Bragg is an American writer born in Casper, Wyoming, and educated at the University of Wyoming. He held various positions in publishing and sales, was a member of the Wyoming House of Representatives, and served as an historian at the Fort Laramie National Monument. In his view, all his work has been aimed at telling the true story of his native state. House was born in Ohio and attended Bowling Green University and Kent State. He was a communication specialist for Ford Motor Company and a former president of the Western Writers of America.

638   *Drumm's War*

Date of Publication: 1992
Subject(s): Military Life—U.S. Cavalry; American West; Mexican War
Fictional character(s): Andrew Drumm, Military Personnel (cavalry officer)
Time Period(s): 1840s (1846)
Locale(s): New Mexico; St. Louis, Missouri; Mexico

Summary: Cavalry captain Andrew Drumm is sent on a reconnaissance mission into the Southwest on the eve of the Mexican War. He encounters Mexican opposition that seems to know the mission's plans in advance. When Drumm manages to bring his men back to St. Louis, he faces a court martial.

Historical Accuracy: The details of western and military life are graphically depicted.

MELVYN BRAGG (1939-)

Born in Carlisle, Cumberland, England, broadcaster, screenwriter, and novelist Melvyn Bragg is a graduate of Oxford University where he received a B.A. with honors in history. Since 1961 he has worked for the BBC as a television producer. He is the author of *For Want of a Nail*, *The Second Inheritance*, and *A Place in England* (the sequel to *The Hired Man*). He also wrote the film scripts for such movies as *Isadora*, and *The Music Lovers*.

639   *The Hired Man*

Date of Publication: 1970
Subject(s): Rural Life—England; Mining
Fictional character(s): John Tallentire, Worker (farm laborer)
Time Period(s): 1890s; 1900s
Locale(s): Cumberland, England

Summary: This tale of rural life in England at the turn of the century concerns farm laborer John Tallentire, who is forced by circumstances to leave the farm and seek employment in a coal town. The novel provides a vivid look at a traditional rural society in transition.

Historical Accuracy: The novel features a convincing portrayal of the period and the region.

CARYL BRAHMS
(PSEUD. OF DORIS CAROLINE ABRAHAMS, 1901-1982)

S.J. SIMON

Caryl Brahms is a pseudonym used by British author Doris Abrahams who was born in Surrey, England, and educated at the Royal Academy of Music. She has worked as a journalist, playwright, and novelist. She is best known for her successful collaborations with S.J. Simon including *A Bullet in the Ballet*. She also co-wrote *Sing a Rude Song* and *The Mitford Girls* with satirist Ned Sherrin.

640   *No Bed for Bacon*

Date of Publication: 1941

Subject(s): Elizabethan Period; Literary Life
Historical character(s): William Shakespeare, Writer; Sir Francis Bacon, Lawyer
Time Period(s): 17th century
Locale(s): England

Summary: History is reinterpreted as farce in this send-up of the Elizabethan period. Shakespeare is shown as a commercial hack and Sir Francis Bacon, rather than the genius behind Shakespeare's plays, is an ineffectual dandy.

Historical Accuracy: History is considerably warped and altered to accommodate this wry view of the past.

DONALD BRAIDER (1923-1976)

Braider, an American businessman, educator, editor, and writer, served with U.S. Army Intelligence and produced several books on art, as well as a biography of Sam Houston.

`641` *Color From a Light Within: A Novel Based on the Life of El Greco*

Date of Publication: 1967
Subject(s): Artistic Life; Inquisition; Renaissance
Historical character(s): Domenikos Theotokopoulos, Artist (painter); Tiziano Vecelli, Artist; Alessandro Farnese, Religious (cardinal); Philip II, Ruler (King of Spain)
Time Period(s): 16th century; 17th century (1541-1614)
Locale(s): Crete, Greece; Italy (Venice, Rome); Toledo, Spain

Summary: This fictional biography of El Greco follows his life from his birth on Crete to his study under the master Titian in Renaissance Italy to his life in the Spain of Philip II. Braider's life of the artist offers not only insights into El Greco's great genius and its personal cost but also thoughtful portraits of Italy during the Renaissance and Spain during the Inquisition.

Historical Accuracy: Braider's sense of time, place, and personalities is utterly convincing and on target. This is one of the best portraits of an artist and his age.

`642` *An Epic Joy: A Novel Based on the Life of Rubens*

Date of Publication: 1971
Subject(s): Artistic Life; Thirty Years War; Biography, Fictionalized
Historical character(s): Peter Paul Rubens, Artist, Diplomat; Armand-Jean Du Plessis, Religious (Cardinal Richelieu), Political Figure (chief minister to Louis XIII); Charles I, Ruler (King of Spain); Michelangelo da Caravaggio, Artist
Time Period(s): 16th century; 17th century (1587-1637)
Locale(s): Antwerp, Belgium; Italy; Spain

Summary: The novel tells the story of artist Pieter Paul Rubens who, in addition to being one of the world's greatest artists, was also an important diplomat who represented the court of the Spanish Netherlands during the Thirty Years' War. The novel chronicles Rubens career and blends his artistic achievement with the political turmoil of the period.

Historical Accuracy: The novel is completely convincing as a life of a great creative genius and as a description of the period.

`643` *Rage in Silence: A Novel Based on the Life of Goya*

Date of Publication: 1969
Subject(s): Napoleonic Wars; Artistic Life; Biography, Fictionalized
Historical character(s): Francisco Jose de Goya y Lucientes, Artist (painter); Maria Cayetana, Noblewoman (Duchess of Alba); Charles IV, Ruler (King of Spain); Arthur Wellesley, Military Personnel, Nobleman (Duke of Wellington)
Time Period(s): 18th century; 19th century (1795-1824)
Locale(s): Madrid, Spain

Summary: Goya's life is depicted from his rebirth as an artist at the age of 50 and his love affair with the Duchess of Alba. Goya endures the vicissitudes of the Spanish court and goes beyond his status as a respected portrait painter to become a great visionary artist, whose work reflects the horrors of the Napoleonic Wars in Spain.

Historical Accuracy: This biographical novel is a believable account of a fascinating figure and period in history.

FORBES BRAMBLE (1939-)

A graduate of the University of London, Bramble is a successful playwright as well as a novelist and a professional architect. He enjoys the variety of his careers and is unwilling to give up one for the others.

`644` *The Iron Roads*

Date of Publication: 1981
Subject(s): Victorian Period; Railroads
Fictional character(s): Henry Kelleway, Lawyer
Historical character(s): George Hudson, Financier; George Stephenson, Engineer; Victoria, Ruler (Queen of England); Albert of Saxe-Coburg-Gotha, Royalty (prince consort of Victoria)
Time Period(s): 1840s
Locale(s): England

Summary: The novel captures the railroad mania of the Victorian period and its "Railway King," George Hudson. As Hudson's advisor, Henry Kelleway finds himself enmeshed in Hudson's shady dealings until he decides to help bring Hudson down.

Historical Accuracy: The novel effectively and convincingly captures the period and atmosphere of the time.

`645` *Regent Square*

Date of Publication: 1977
Subject(s): Family Saga; Legal Profession; Victorian Period
Fictional character(s): Thomas Kelleway, Lawyer; John Kelleway, Adventurer; William Kelleway, Artist (painter); Henry Kelleway, Lawyer
Time Period(s): 19th century (1820s-1850s)
Locale(s): London, England

Summary: This novel chronicles the Kelleway family whose patriarch, Thomas, is a distinguished lawyer and a firm advocate of the old school. His family continually threatens his desire for order and tradition. John, the eldest, is an adventurer; William, a painter and freethinker; and Henry, a lawyer like his father. Henry will risk the honor of the family's name.

Historical Accuracy: The novel is filled with convincing details of legal London.

646 The Strange Case of Deacon Brodie

Date of Publication: 1975
Subject(s): Crime and Criminals
Historical character(s): William Brodie, Thief, Artisan (cabinet maker)
Time Period(s): 1780s
Locale(s): Edinburgh, Scotland; London, England

Summary: William Brodie, the inspiration for Robert Lewis Stevenson's *Dr. Jekyll and Mr. Hyde*, is ostensibly an upstanding citizen of Edinburgh. He is a cabinet maker and a member of the town council. He is also, however, a master thief who cases his clients' homes and businesses during the day and robs them at night.

Historical Accuracy: The novel is scrupulous in its historical research and authentic in rendering the period.

HOUSTON BRANCH

FRANK WATERS (1902-)

American author Waters was born in Colorado Springs, Colorado, and attended Colorado College. During World War II, he served in the U.S. Army where he prepared training films on weapons. He is the author of *The Man Who Killed the Deer, Pike's Peak: A Family Saga,* and *River Lady,* which was made into a film in 1949.

647 Diamond Head

Date of Publication: 1948
Subject(s): Civil War—U.S.; Sea Story; Whaling
Fictional character(s): Cameron Richards, Military Personnel (Confederate naval officer); Abigail Macy, Young Woman
Time Period(s): 1860s (1864)
Locale(s): New Bedford, Massachusetts; Hawaii; Pacific Ocean

Summary: This Civil War-era adventure story is based on the actual exploits of the Confederate cruiser *Shenandoah*, which is sent into the Northern Pacific to destroy the New England whaling fleet. To the adventures of the *Shenandoah* at sea is added a romance between Confederate naval officer Cameron Richards and the daughter of a whaling tycoon, Abigail Macy.

Historical Accuracy: The authors claim that almost every event in the book is true and based on the historical record. There is, however, no record of the *Shenandoah* refitting in Hawaii.

ANNA BRAND

648 Thunder Before Seven

Date of Publication: 1941
Subject(s): Texas Revolution; Battle of San Jacinto
Fictional character(s): Blazely Tyler, Revolutionary
Time Period(s): 1820s; 1830s
Locale(s): Brazos River, Texas

Summary: The story of the original American settlers around the Brazos River during the time of the Texas Revolt is recounted in a tale of pioneer life and rebellion. The catalyst for the growing conflict with Mexico is the firebrand Blazely Tyler. The novel's climax is the tragic Sabine Trek and the victory at San Jacinto.

Historical Accuracy: The novel's strength lies in its period background and setting, which seem genuine.

STEPHEN E. BRANSFORD (1949-)

Born in Medford, Oregon, Stephen Bransford attended Bethany Bible College and Arizona State University. He has worked for the PTL Television Network and is a writer and television producer at Bransford Associates, Inc. He is the author of the novel *High Places*.

649 Riders of the Long Road

Date of Publication: 1984
Subject(s): Religious Life; Settlement of the American Frontier
Fictional character(s): Jonathan Barratt, Young Man; Silas Will, Religious (itinerant preacher)
Historical character(s): Francis Ashbery, Religious (preacher); Tecumseh, Indian (Shawnee), Chieftain
Time Period(s): 1780s
Locale(s): Kentucky

Summary: The novel dramatizes the exploits of American circuit riders, itinerant preachers who travelled through the American wilderness spreading Methodist teachings. The story involves the search by Jonathan Barratt for circuit rider Silas Will whom he is convinced is a fraud and a scoundrel.

Historical Accuracy: Based in part on the actual experiences of the most famous of the circuit riders, Francis Ashbery, the story is in keeping with what is known from history.

HENRY C. BRANSON

650 Salisbury Plain

Date of Publication: 1965
Subject(s): Civil War—U.S.; Military Life; Arthurian Legends
Fictional character(s): John Lake, Military Personnel (Union captain)
Time Period(s): 1860s
Locale(s): Virginia

Summary: This Civil War story is narrated by a young Union captain, John Lake, who serves as an aide to an army major-general on an imaginary 10-week campaign. The campaign's events are raised to the level of the symbolic by establishing a correspondence with the myth of the *Morte d'Arthur* in which Salisbury Plain was the site of King Arthur's final battle.

Historical Accuracy: The novel's symbolic parallels are strained, yet the description of army life and military action are convincing.

IRVING BRANT (1885-1976)

A native of Iowa, Brant graduated from the University of Iowa and worked as a newspaper reporter on a variety of big city papers, including the *St. Louis Star*, the *Des Moines Register*, and the *Chicago Sun*. He became a full-time writer in the 1940s. He is best known for his six-volume biographical study of James Madison on which he worked for 23 years.

`651` *Friendly Cove*

Date of Publication: 1963
Subject(s): Sea Story
Fictional character(s): Rodrigo Alvarez, Sailor, Carpenter; John Meares, Sea Captain
Time Period(s): 1780s; 1790s (1786-1790)
Locale(s): Pacific Northwest, North America (northwest coast); Vancouver, British Columbia, Canada

Summary: The novel details the adventures of a Spanish sailor, Rodrigo Alvarez, who is drawn to the northwest coast of North America at the end of the 18th century. As a carpenter's apprentice he suffers hardship at sea, endures a shipwreck, and makes a 1,000-mile trip in a dugout canoe to Friendly Cove, now Vancouver. He is on hand when the English and Spanish maneuver for the possession of the Pacific coast.

Historical Accuracy: The novel blends adventure with an authentic reconstruction of the period.

MATT BRAUN

`652` *The Stuart Women*

Date of Publication: 1980
Subject(s): Antebellum South; Business Building; Riverboats
Fictional character(s): Tom Stuart, Shipowner (riverboat captain); Jouette St. Vrain, Gentlewoman; Maria, Heroine
Historical character(s): Zachary Taylor, Military Personnel (army officer)
Time Period(s): 1840s (1847)
Locale(s): New Orleans, Louisiana; Rio Grande, Texas

Summary: In the Antebellum South, Tom Stuart is a riverboat captain drawn to opportunity on the Texas frontier. He is also attracted to a Mexican girl, Maria, and then to the Creole Jouette as he sets his sights on New Orleans. There he is involved in a duel and a clash with the French aristocracy of the city.

Historical Accuracy: The novel is an exuberant adventure on the booming frontier recently opened up by the Mexican War, featuring plenty of convincing atmosphere.

`653` *Wyatt Earp*

Date of Publication: 1994
Subject(s): American West; Crime and Criminals; Biography, Fictionalized
Historical character(s): Wyatt Earp, Lawman; Doc Holliday, Dentist, Gunfighter; Ike Clanton, Rancher, Outlaw
Time Period(s): 1880s
Locale(s): Tombstone, Arizona

Summary: The life and times of western legend Wyatt Earp are portrayed in this novel that concentrates on Earp's career in Tombstone and the fateful showdown with the Claytons that made Earp s reputation. The famous gun-fight at the OK Corral takes on mythical overtones in a combat between two ways of life.

Historical Accuracy: The facts of Earp's career are authentic, though the novel is a blend of the factual and the legendary.

WALLACE BREEM

An English author who served in the Indian Army, Breem held a variety of jobs including unskilled laborer in a tannery, rent collector in London's East End, and veterinarian's assistant. He was a law librarian in London's Inns of Court before turning to writing.

`654` *Eagle in the Snow*

Date of Publication: 1970
Subject(s): Roman Empire; Military Life; Barbarians
Fictional character(s): Maximus, Military Personnel (legion commander)
Time Period(s): 5th century (406)
Locale(s): Germany

Summary: As the Roman Empire collapses, a single Roman legion led by Maximus guards the Empire's Rhine frontier. His devotion to duty and Roman training keep him steadfast against incredible odds. He holds the frontier at great human and emotional cost.

Historical Accuracy: The novel is convincing in its re-creation of the time. The details of military life are assured and authentic.

`655` *The Leopard and the Cliff*

Date of Publication: 1978
Subject(s): British Colonies; Military Life—British Army; Afghan War
Fictional character(s): Charles Sandeman, Military Personnel (army officer)
Time Period(s): 1910s (1919)
Locale(s): North-West Frontier, India

Summary: The novel describes the withdrawal of a small British column from its outpost on the Northwest Frontier of India. They are surrounded by tribes in revolt, and Sandeman takes charge when his commanding officer is killed. He must contend with desertion, the wounded, short supplies, and treachery.

Historical Accuracy: The novel's depiction of both the locale and the military is genuine and revealing.

GLORIA HOWE BREMKAMP (1924-)

Born in Hugo, Oklahoma, Bremkamp is a graduate of the University of Oklahoma. She had a successful career as a public relations executive.

656 *Merari*

Date of Publication: 1986
Subject(s): Biblical Story
Fictional character(s): Merari, Young Woman
Historical character(s): Elisha, Biblical Figure, Religious (prophet); Jezebel, Royalty (queen consort of King Ahab), Biblical Figure; Jorum, Biblical Figure
Time Period(s): Indeterminate Past
Locale(s): Jerusalem, Israel

Summary: This tale from the Old Testament is the story of Merari, who, with the prophet Elisha, opposes the idol worship of the day and incurs the wrath of Jezebel and her son, Jorum. Merari's story is one of great bravery and faith under adversity.

Historical Accuracy: The novel is an effective evocation of the Biblical period.

J.H. BRENNAN (1940-)

A prolific science fiction and fantasy writer, Brennan's novels include *Ancient Evil*, *The Castle of Darkness*, and *The Crypts of Terror*.

657 *Shiva: An Adventure of the Ice Age*

Date of Publication: 1990
Subject(s): Prehistory; Tribal Life—Prehistoric
Fictional character(s): Shiva, Prehistoric Human (Cro-Magnon), Orphan; Hiram, Prehistoric Human (Cro-Magnon); Doban, Prehistoric Human (Neanderthal), Child
Time Period(s): Indeterminate Past
Locale(s): Europe

Summary: In this tale of prehistoric tribal conflict, Shiva, to the disapproval of her tribe, adopts a lost Neanderthal child, Doban. Shiva and the child have a series of adventures as she attempts to restore Doban to his tribe.

Historical Accuracy: The novel offers an interesting and convincing look at prehistoric life.

JACQUES BRENNER

658 *Nephew to the Emperor: A Novel Based on the Life of Beethoven*

Date of Publication: 1959
Subject(s): Musical Life; Biography, Fictionalized
Historical character(s): Ludwig van Beethoven, Composer; Karl Beethoven, Ward
Time Period(s): 1810s; 1820
Locale(s): Vienna, Austria

Summary: The novel portrays the great composer Beethoven from the perspective of his nephew Karl. When Beethoven's brother dies, his nine-year-old son is left in the care of the 40-year-old bachelor Beethoven. Their relationship is dramatized as Beethoven fights his sister-in-law for custody, and Karl presents a number of trials for the great composer.

Historical Accuracy: The author has drawn extensively on Beethoven's letters and the notebooks of his conversations to build a strong authenticity in the story.

MADELEINE BRENT

Madeleine Brent is a pseudonym for a romance and suspense novelist who was a recipient of the Romantic Novelists Association Major Award in 1978.

659 *The Capricorn Stone*

Date of Publication: 1979
Subject(s): Romance; Theatrical Life; Victorian Period
Fictional character(s): Bridie Chance, Orphan, Actress
Time Period(s): 1890s
Locale(s): London, England; Paris, France

Summary: Upon discovering that her father is a criminal, Bridie Chance is suddenly penniless. She makes a new life for herself as a comic in London, and must continually contend with the past.

Historical Accuracy: The details of Victorian theatrical life are well imagined and displayed.

660 *A Heritage of Shadows*

Date of Publication: 1984
Subject(s): Romance; Identity—Concealed
Fictional character(s): Hannah McLeod, Waiter/Waitress, Teacher (French tutor); Toby Kent, Artist; Sebastian Ryder, Gentleman
Time Period(s): 1890s
Locale(s): Paris, France; England; Mexico

Summary: Hannah McLeod is an Englishwoman with a secret living in Paris. Financial circumstances force her back to England to work as a French tutor in the household of Sebastian Ryder. He seems to know far more about Hannah than she does about herself.

Historical Accuracy: The novel is a taut suspense story with some authentic touches to illustrate the 1890s atmosphere.

661 *Moonraker's Bride*

Date of Publication: 1973
Subject(s): Romance; Boxer Rebellion; Treasure Hunt
Fictional character(s): Lucy Waring, Orphan; Nicholas Sabine, Adventurer; Robert Falcon, Gentleman
Time Period(s): 1900s
Locale(s): China; England

Summary: Lucy Waring, an orphan raised in China, marries adventurer Nicholas Sabine the night before he is to be executed by a local warlord. Returning to England, Lucy finds out more about her late husband. She becomes involved with his arch-rival, Robert Falcon, who was seeking the same treasure as Nick. The outbreak of the Boxer Rebellion sends Lucy back to China to rescue old friends and solve the riddle of the treasure's whereabouts.

Historical Accuracy: The period is primarily an exotic background with suspense and romance the foreground concern.

662 *Stormswift*

Date of Publication: 1985
Subject(s): Romance; Victorian Period; Afghan War
Fictional character(s): Jemimah Lawley, Heiress
Time Period(s): 1870s (1879)
Locale(s): Afghanistan; England

Summary: Jemimah Lawley, sole heiress to an English estate, is taken captive by Afghan soldiers. She survives her life of captivity in the remote Afghan kingdom of Shul and eventually escapes. Returning to England, she learns more about her past and the meaning of Stormswift.

Historical Accuracy: The novel's adventures, despite their exoticism, are remarkably controlled by the details of the period.

663 *Stranger at Wildings*

Date of Publication: 1976
Subject(s): Romance; Circus Life
Fictional character(s): Chantal, Entertainer (circus performer); Martin Verne, Vagrant, Amnesiac
Time Period(s): 19th century
Locale(s): Hungary; England

Summary: Disowned by her family, Chantal join the circus and becomes a trapeze artist. She meets a mysterious young man with amnesia, and their paths lead them both to startling revelations.

Historical Accuracy: The contrivance here strains credibility. The details of circus life are interesting and authentic.

HOWARD BRESLIN

664 *The Bright Battalions*

Date of Publication: 1953
Subject(s): French and Indian War; American Colonies
Fictional character(s): Kevin O'Connor, Military Personnel (soldier), Adventurer
Historical character(s): Louis Joseph de Montcalm, Military Personnel (French general)
Time Period(s): 1750s (1756-1759)
Locale(s): New York, American Colonies; Montreal, Quebec, Canada

Summary: This romantic adventure tale depicts the exploits of Irishman Kevin O'Connor who fights for the French in the French and Indian Wars. Action includes the conflict in colonial New York and New France.

Historical Accuracy: The story is fanciful but set against a plausible period background.

665 *Concert Grand*

Date of Publication: 1963
Subject(s): Musical Life; Civil War—U.S.; Biography, Fictionalized
Historical character(s): Louis Moreau Gottschalk, Musician (pianist), Composer; Phineas T. Barnum, Entertainer, Businessman
Time Period(s): 19th century (1848-1865)
Locale(s): Paris, France; New Orleans, Louisiana

Summary: The novel is based on the life of Louis Moreau Gottschalk, America's first native classical musician and composer. His career is traced from his first success in Paris during the Second Republic to his triumphant return to America on the eve of the Civil War.

Historical Accuracy: While the events are based on fact, Gottschalk's motivations and character are, for the most part, the author's creations.

666 *The Gallowglass*

Date of Publication: 1958
Subject(s): Vikings; Middle Ages; Celtic Ireland
Fictional character(s): Ronan MacHugh, Mercenary; Nuala, Young Woman
Historical character(s): Malachy Mor, Ruler (High King of Ireland); Brian Boru, Chieftain (clan leader)
Time Period(s): 10th century; 11th century (990-1014)
Locale(s): Ireland

Summary: Ronan MacHugh is a gallowglass, or mercenary, in Ireland with a grudge against the Irish chieftain, Brian Boru. Ronan offers his services to the Irish high king Malachy Mor. The Irish are divided into rival clans that are united only by their hatred of the Danes, who rule from their stronghold of Dublin. The novel is a colorful story of battles, duels, escapes, and love.

Historical Accuracy: The novel blends the historical with the legendary. The atmosphere of early Ireland is convincing.

667 *A Hundred Hills*

Date of Publication: 1960
Subject(s): Civil War—U.S.; Siege of Vicksburg
Fictional character(s): Alexandra Kittering, Southern Belle; Bryce Furlong, Military Personnel (Confederate officer); Tempe Dixon, Military Personnel (Confederate soldier)
Time Period(s): 1860s (1861-1863)
Locale(s): Vicksburg, Mississippi

Summary: Detailing the Siege of Vicksburg, this novel focuses on the inhabitants of the city. Alexandra Kittering is a young southern belle who must deal with the punishing siege and accept the destruction of the southern way of life.

Historical Accuracy: The novel is convincing in its depictions of the events and the atmosphere of the time.

668 *Shad Run*

Date of Publication: 1955
Subject(s): Politics; Fishing

Fictional character(s): Lancey Quist, Young Woman; Dirk Van Zandt, Young Man
Time Period(s): 1780s (1788)
Locale(s): Hudson River Valley, New York; Poughkeepsie, New York

Summary: Life among the shad fishermen of the Hudson valley is profiled in this story. Lancey Quist, the daughter of a fisherman, falls in love with Dirk Van Zandt as notable figures of New York state arrive for a convention to ratify the Constitution.

Historical Accuracy: The novel offers a convincing regional portrait and captures the politics which revolved around ratifying the Constitution.

669 *The Silver Oar*

Date of Publication: 1954
Subject(s): American Colonies; Pirates; Trials
Fictional character(s): Cormac Doyle, Pirate, Convict; Jill Murdoch, Young Woman
Historical character(s): Cotton Mather, Religious (clergyman); Edward Andros, Political Figure (governor)
Time Period(s): 17th century (1689)
Locale(s): Boston, Massachusetts, American Colonies

Summary: The title refers to the oar that was carried before a condemned pirate on the way to his execution. Cormac Doyle is a condemned pirate who tells his story in the American colonies of 1689, the year of the Boston Revolution against Governor Andros.

Historical Accuracy: Events are described just as they occured. The narrator who tells us of these events, however, is not objective in his telling.

670 *Tamarack Tree*

Date of Publication: 1947
Subject(s): Politics; Rural Life—U.S.
Historical character(s): Daniel Webster, Political Figure; William Henry Harrison, Political Figure
Time Period(s): 1840s (1840)
Locale(s): Stratton, Vermont

Summary: A political convention is organized on top of Stratton Mountain to solidify the candidacy of William Henry Harrison. Daniel Webster is the featured speaker. The novel details the effects of the convention on a small New England community.

Historical Accuracy: The novel is an authentic dramatization of the period and its leading political personalities.

JOHN BRICK (1922-1973)

American novelist Brick was born in Newburgh, New York, and attended NYU and Columbia University. Brick was a magazine editor and was a member of the U.S. Senate Permanent Investigating Subcommittee from 1963-1973.

671 *Eagle of Niagara: The Story of David Harper and His Indian Captivity*

Date of Publication: 1955
Subject(s): American Revolution; Indians
Fictional character(s): David Harper, Military Personnel (soldier), Captive
Historical character(s): Joseph Brant, Indian (Mohawk), Chieftain
Time Period(s): 1770s
Locale(s): New York

Summary: The novel describes the adventures of a young American Revolutionary War soldier, David Harper, who is captured by Indian leader Joseph Brant. Harper comes to admire and understand Brant's loyalty to the English, producing a conflict in his own loyalty to the American cause.

Historical Accuracy: The novel offers a convincing presentation of period details.

672 *Jubilee*

Date of Publication: 1956
Subject(s): Civil War—U.S.; Battle of Gettysburg; Battle of Atlanta
Fictional character(s): Jefferson Barnes, Military Personnel (Union officer); Kate Barnes, Spouse
Historical character(s): William Tecumseh Sherman, Military Personnel (Union general)
Time Period(s): 1860s (1862-1865)
Locale(s): New York; South (Georgia, Tennessee, and South Carolina); Gettysburg, Pennsylvania

Summary: Jefferson Barnes commands the 195th New York. They first see action at Gettysburg and then join Sherman's army for the Battle of Lookout Mountain and the Battle of Atlanta. Barnes and his men also join Sherman's march to the sea. Scenes on the homefront in New York are also described.

Historical Accuracy: Brick Renders the battle scenes vividly and convincingly.

673 *The Raid*

Date of Publication: 1951
Subject(s): American Revolution; Indians; Settlement of the American Frontier
Historical character(s): Tom Currie, Frontiersman; Jessica Currie, Spouse; William Desmond, Military Personnel (British loyalist); Joseph Brant, Indian (Mohawk chief), Loyalist
Time Period(s): 1770s (1779)
Locale(s): New York

Summary: Tom Currie, recently wed and on leave from the American army, finds his wife taken hostage by a party of Indians and Loyalists. The militia sets out to rescue her and the other settlers who were taken. Exciting scenes of combat and pursuit in the wilderness follow.

Historical Accuracy: The chronology and events are loosely based on the actual Battle of Minisink in July, 1779 in Orange County, New York.

674 *The Richmond Raid*

Date of Publication: 1963
Subject(s): Civil War—U.S.
Historical character(s): Hugh Judson Kilpatrick, Military Personnel (Union cavalry officer); Ulrich Dahlgren, Military Personnel (Union cavalry officer)
Time Period(s): 1860s (1864)
Locale(s): Richmond, Virginia

Summary: The novel tells the story of a daring plan to get behind the Confederate lines, enter Richmond, burn the city, free the prisoners on Belle Isle and in Libby prison, and capture and kill Jefferson Davis. The ambitious plan is executed by three very different officers who each contribute to the fate of the mission.

Historical Accuracy: The story is tautly described and realistically presented, based on actual events and characters.

675 *The Rifleman*

Date of Publication: 1953
Subject(s): American Revolution; Battle of Saratoga; Indians
Historical character(s): Timothy Murphy, Military Personnel (rifleman); Daniel Morgan, Military Personnel (American officer); Benedict Arnold, Military Personnel (American officer)
Time Period(s): 1770s; 1780s
Locale(s): Saratoga, New York; Schoharie, New York; Seneca County, New York

Summary: Timothy Murphy is a rifleman from the backwoods of Pennsylvania under Daniel Morgan. Major battles of the American Revolution, most notably the Battle of Saratoga, are reccounted here. murphy's ong-running feud with the Indians is also featured.

Historical Accuracy: The action is based on the actual details of Murphy's life during the Revolution. His early history is unknown and accordingly what is shown is the author's invention.

676 *Rogue's Kingdom*

Date of Publication: 1965
Subject(s): Civil War—U.S.; Crime and Criminals
Fictional character(s): Ben Lawton, Outlaw; Ruth Sherman, Teacher
Time Period(s): 1860s
Locale(s): Pennsylvania; Madison County, New York; Washington, District of Columbia

Summary: The novel concerns the Lawtons, an outlaw family who specialize in horse theft throughout Pennsylvania and New York. Their sanctuary is a tract of wilderness called the Kingdom. Ben Lawton marries a schoolteacher who is intent on reforming him. Conflicting family loyalty and his duty as a husband are further complicated by the outbreak of the Civil War.

Historical Accuracy: This is an interesting and unusual tale of eastern outlaws. The atmosphere of the period is authentic.

677 *The Strong Men*

Date of Publication: 1959
Subject(s): American Revolution; Military Life—U.S. Army
Fictional character(s): Matt Hill, Military Personnel (American soldier); Marion Hill, Military Personnel (American soldier)
Historical character(s): Anthony Wayne, Military Personnel (American general); Friedrich von Steuben, Military Personnel (advisor to Washington); Marie Joseph Paul de Lafayette, Military Personnel, Nobleman (Marquis de Lafayette)
Time Period(s): 1770s (1777-1778)
Locale(s): Valley Forge, Pennsylvania; Monmouth, New Jersey

Summary: A company of Rangers survive the bleak winter at Valley Forge and emerge as an army to fight the decisive Battle of Monmouth. A young recruit narrates their story.

Historical Accuracy: Brick's bibliography attests to the research that makes this a faithful account of the events.

678 *Troubled Spring*

Date of Publication: 1950
Subject(s): Civil War—U.S.
Fictional character(s): Samuel Bellnap, Veteran; Robert Bellnap, Businessman; Martha Bellnap, Spouse (of Robert)
Time Period(s): 1860s (1865)
Locale(s): Hudson River Valley, New York

Summary: Union soldier Samuel Bellnap is released from the Confederate prison camp in Andersonville. He returns to his home in the Hudson Valley where his family believes him to be dead. He finds that his sweetheart has married his brother. Samuel must reconcile the changes made by the war both to himself and those around him.

Historical Accuracy: This is a convincing portrait of a Civil War veteran. The author admits to deliberately including anachronisms.

ALAN BRIEN

679 *Lenin: The Novel*

Date of Publication: 1987
Subject(s): Russian Revolution; Biography, Fictionalized
Historical character(s): Vladimir Ilich Ulyanov, Political Figure (Nikolai Lenin), Revolutionary; Leon Trotsky, Revolutionary; Alexandr Feodorovich Kerensky, Revolutionary, Political Figure; Joseph Stalin, Revolutionary, Political Figure
Time Period(s): 19th century; 20th century (1886-1924)
Locale(s): Moscow, Russia; Switzerland (Berne, Zurich); St. Petersburg, Russia

Summary: Told in the form of a diary, the novel describes Lenin's life his boyhood, his exile in Siberia, the Russian Revolution, and the birth of the Soviet Union. The great figures and events of the period are reflected, but at the center is the enigma of Lenin himself. The novel attempts to create a plausible human side to his character.

Historical Accuracy: Brien's absorption in Lenin's life and the history of Russia are obvious. There is a remarkable sense of the inside view in the novel.

JEAN BRIGGS (1925-)

English novelist Briggs is a graduate of Kings College, London, and she has worked as a teacher of English and as an educational adviser in London. Her first novel, *The Flame of the Borgias*, was stimulated by an addiction to Venice and was based on 15th- and 16th-century letters. Her interest in the Renaissance reflects her focus on the conflict between personal relationships and professional commitments.

680   *The Flame of the Borgias*

Date of Publication: 1974
Subject(s): Renaissance
Historical character(s): Pietro Bembo, Nobleman, Religious (cardinal); Lucrezia Borgia, Noblewoman; Raphael Sanzio, Artist
Time Period(s): 16th century (1502-1505)
Locale(s): Venice, Italy; Ferrara, Italy

Summary: The novel tells the story of the relationship between Pietro Bembo, Venetian nobleman, poet, scholar, and later cardinal, and the notorious Lucrezia Borgia. Their doomed love affair is set against the intrigues of Renaissance Italy.

Historical Accuracy: The account is based on letters written by Bembo and Borgia, and the period detail is enthusiastically and authentically delivered.

EMILY BRIGHTWELL

681   *The Ghost and Mrs. Jeffries*

Date of Publication: 1993
Subject(s): Mystery; Victorian Period
Fictional character(s): Mrs. Jeffries, Housekeeper; Gerald Witherspoon, Detective—Police
Time Period(s): 1880s (1887)
Locale(s): London, England

Summary: The death of Mrs. Hoges is predicted at a seance, and that night she is murdered. Inspector Witherspoon investigates, but it is Mrs. Jeffries, his housekeeper, who is able to penetrate the spirit world.

Historical Accuracy: This period mystery creates a believable period background.

682   *The Inspector and Mrs. Jeffries*

Date of Publication: 1993
Subject(s): Mystery; Victorian Period
Fictional character(s): Mrs. Jeffries, Housekeeper; Gerald Witherspoon, Detective—Police
Time Period(s): 1880s
Locale(s): London, England

Summary: In the first novel in the series, the reader is introduced to Scotland Yard Inspector Gerald Witherspoon, whose

reputation depends in no small measure upon the sleuthing ability of his housekeeper, Mrs. Jeffries.

Historical Accuracy: The series features an authentic period background for the historical mystery.

683   *Mrs. Jeffries and the Missing Alibi*

Date of Publication: 1996
Subject(s): Mystery; Victorian Period
Fictional character(s): Mrs. Jeffries, Housekeeper; Gerald Witherspoon, Detective—Police
Time Period(s): 1880s
Locale(s): London, England

Summary: The killer who attacks Peter Hornsby hits him with a policeman's truncheon and tells the night watchman that he is Inspector Witherspoon. The real Witherspoon has a shaky alibi, and as the chief suspect, he is prevented from investigating the case. It is up to Mrs. Jeffries to clear the inspector.

Historical Accuracy: The period elements are convincingly drawn.

684   *Mrs. Jeffries Dusts for Clues*

Date of Publication: 1993
Subject(s): Mystery; Victorian Period
Fictional character(s): Mrs. Jeffries, Housekeeper; Gerald Witherspoon, Detective—Police
Time Period(s): 1880s
Locale(s): London, England

Summary: The disappearance of a servant girl begins a mysterious puzzle for Inspector Witherspoon and his trusty housekeeper, Mrs. Jeffries. A valuable brooch disappears at the same time as the servant, and when it is found pinned to the dress of a murdered woman, the case becomes complicated.

Historical Accuracy: The period elements are believably presented.

685   *Mrs. Jeffries on the Ball*

Date of Publication: 1994
Subject(s): Mystery; Victorian Period
Fictional character(s): Mrs. Witherspoon, Housekeeper; Gerald Witherspoon, Detective—Police
Time Period(s): 1880s (1887)
Locale(s): London, England

Summary: At the Jubilee Ball in honor of Queen Victoria, Hannah Greenwood is found murdered. As she was a member of the Hyde Park Literary Circle, her fellow members become the likely suspects. As Inspector Witherspoon plods through the case, it is Mrs. Jeffries who manages to save the day.

Historical Accuracy: The novel features authentic period details.

686   *Mrs. Jeffries on the Trail*

Date of Publication: 1955
Subject(s): Mystery; Victorian Period
Fictional character(s): Mrs. Jeffries, Housekeeper; Gerald Witherspoon, Detective—Police
Time Period(s): 1880s

Locale(s): London, England

Summary: The murder of a London girl on one of the foggiest nights of the year presents a puzzle for Inspector Witherspoon that requires his housekeeper Mrs. Jeffries' assistance.

Historical Accuracy: The mystery is ingenious and features a convincing period background.

687 *Mrs. Jeffries Plays the Cook*

Date of Publication: 1995
Subject(s): Mystery; Victorian Period
Fictional character(s): Mrs. Jeffries, Housekeeper; Gerald Witherspoon, Detective—Police
Time Period(s): 1880s
Locale(s): London, England

Summary: The murder of Minerva Kelly, a kleptomaniac, presents a problem for Mrs. Jeffries, who must double as a cook and a sleuth to get to the truth.

Historical Accuracy: The period elements are authentic in this mystery.

688 *Mrs. Jeffries Stands Corrected*

Date of Publication: 1996
Subject(s): Mystery; Victorian Period
Fictional character(s): Mrs. Jeffries, Housekeeper; Gerald Witherspoon, Detective—Police
Time Period(s): 19th century
Locale(s): London, England

Summary: In this installment of the Victorian-era mystery series featuring Scotland Yard Inspector Witherspoon and his detective housekeeper Mrs. Jeffries, the murder of a local publican provides a puzzle to test Mrs. Jeffries' mettle and Inspector Witherspoon's patience.

Historical Accuracy: The mystery is set against a convincing period background.

689 *Mrs. Jeffries Takes Stock*

Date of Publication: 1994
Subject(s): Mystery; Victorian Period
Fictional character(s): Mrs. Jeffries, Housekeeper; Gerald Witherspoon, Detective—Police
Time Period(s): 1880s
Locale(s): London, England

Summary: The murder of a businessman who may have deceived stockholders gives several a motive for murder in Inspector Witherspoon's next case. Again, it is Mrs. Jeffries who solves the puzzle.

Historical Accuracy: The late-Victorian setting is credibly re-created.

LOUISE BRINDLEY

690 *In the Shadow of the Brontes*

Date of Publication: 1983
Subject(s): Literary Life; Victorian Period

Fictional character(s): Lizzie Godolphin, Servant (scullery maid)
Historical character(s): Charlotte Bronte, Writer; Emily Bronte, Writer; Anne Bronte, Writer
Time Period(s): 1840s
Locale(s): Haworth, England (in Yorkshire)

Summary: This evocation of the life of the Bronte sisters is provided by a scullery maid from a local workhouse, Lizzie Godolphin, whose physical resemblance to Anne Bronte is only one of several links to the Brontes that gives her the ability to see into the sisters' future and to discover the inspiration for their writing.

Historical Accuracy: The novel is faithful to what is known about the Brontes and offers a number of plausible suggestions about the factual basis for their fiction.

CAROL BRINK (1895-1981)

Born in Moscow, Idaho, Brink attended the University of Idaho and the University of California at Berkeley. A writer of books for children and adults, Brink is best known for her bestselling children's historical novel *Caddie Woodlawn*, which earned a Newbery Medal in 1936 and is considered a children's classic. Brink's novels for adults include *Snow in the River* and *The Bellini Look*.

691 *Buffalo Coat*

Date of Publication: 1944
Subject(s): American West
Fictional character(s): Jenny Walden, Teenager; Willard J. Hawkins, Doctor
Time Period(s): 1880s; 1890s (1888-1896)
Locale(s): Idaho

Summary: The frontier community of Opportunity, Idaho, during the 1880s and 1890s is the scene for this western novel that traces the intersecting lives of a number of characters.

Historical Accuracy: The novel offers a believable treatment of the period.

692 *Caddie Woodlawn*

Date of Publication: 1935
Subject(s): Farming; Rural Life—U.S.
Fictional character(s): Caddie Woodlawn, Teenager
Time Period(s): 1860s
Locale(s): Wisconsin

Summary: Pioneer life on a Wisconsin farm in the 1860s is the subject of this novel that centers on tomboyish Caddie Woodlawn. The story dramatizes one year on a pioneer farm and features a variety of adventures for the reckless Caddie.

Historical Accuracy: The novel is based on the reminiscences of the author's grandmother, which provide the novel's vivid and believable background.

JACQUELINE BRISKIN (1927-)

Born in London, England, Briskin grew up in Beverly Hills, California, and studied at UCLA. Her other books include *California Generation* and *Rich Friends*.

693   *Paloverde*

Date of Publication: 1978
Subject(s): Family Saga; Motion Picture Industry; Aviation
Fictional character(s): Amelie Deane, Young Woman; Bud Van Vliet, Heir; 3vee Van Vliet, Heir
Time Period(s): 19th century; 20th century (1884-1917)
Locale(s): Los Angeles, California

Summary: This family saga is set against the background of the development of California from the 1880s through the power of the railroads, the discovery of oil in Los Angeles, the emergence of the motion-picture industry, and the coming of aviation. These changes are played out while two brothers—Bud and 3vee Van Vliet—compete for the love of Amelie Deane.

Historical Accuracy: The novel's period and regional background is true to the history of California.

GWEN BRISTOW (1903-1980)

An American born in South Carolina, Bristow was a reporter for many years for the New Orleans *Times-Picayune*. She started her fiction career working with her husband on mystery stories. She is best known for her Plantation Trilogy, a collection of tales about antebellum plantation life.

694   *Calico Palace*

Date of Publication: 1970
Subject(s): American West; Gold Rush—California
Fictional character(s): Kendra Logan, Young Woman; Marny Randolph, Saloon Keeper/Owner; Hiram Boyd, Miner (gold), Banker
Historical character(s): John A. Sutter, Businessman
Time Period(s): 1840s; 1850s (1847-1851)
Locale(s): San Francisco, California

Summary: This novel tells the story of the California Gold Rush and the boom town that became the city of San Francisco.

Historical Accuracy: The search for gold among the young, eager prospectors, and the excitement of the gold rush is well described, as is the growth of San Francisco from boom town to city.

695   *Celia Garth*

Date of Publication: 1959
Subject(s): American Revolution; Espionage
Fictional character(s): Celia Garth, Seamstress, Spy; Luke Ansell, Military Personnel (captain); Vivian Lacy, Plantation Owner
Historical character(s): Francis Marion, Military Personnel (colonel)
Time Period(s): 1770s; 1780s (1779-1782)
Locale(s): Charleston, South Carolina

Summary: While working as a dressmaker for plantation owner Vivian Lacy, Celia Garth becomes caught up in the events which occur during the British capture of Charleston. After the death of her finacee, militiaman Jimmy Rand, Celia is recruited as a spy for the patriot cause, sending information to Francis Marion's guerrilla troops by way of one of Marion's men, handsome daredevil Luke Ansell.

Historical Accuracy: This novel is well-researched concerning the facts of Charleston and South Carolina's involvement during the Revolution. The writing style veers between phrasing pertinent to the Revolutionary era and mid-twentieth century speech.

696   *Deep Summer*

Date of Publication: 1937
Subject(s): Antebellum South
Fictional character(s): Judith Sheramy, Settler; Philip Larne, Gentleman
Time Period(s): 18th century
Locale(s): Louisiana

Summary: Judith Sheramy, the daughter of a New England farmer, meets Philip Larne, a South Carolina gentleman. They marry and create a great Louisiana plantation out of the wilderness.

Historical Accuracy: The novel captures late 18th-century Louisiana convincingly.

697   *The Handsome Road*

Date of Publication: 1938
Subject(s): Antebellum South; Civil War—U.S.; Reconstruction Period
Fictional character(s): Corrie May Upjohn, Young Woman; Ann Sheramy, Young Woman
Time Period(s): 19th century (1859-1885)
Locale(s): Louisiana

Summary: This sequel to *Deep Summer* depicts life in a small river town in Louisiana before, during, and after the Civil War. The story chronicles the changes brought on by the war as reflected in the stories of two different woman, Corrie May Upjohn and Ann Sheramy.

Historical Accuracy: The author knows the region well and presents an authentic portrait of the period.

698   *Jubilee Trail*

Date of Publication: 1950
Subject(s): American West; Mexican War
Fictional character(s): Garnet Cameron, Young Woman; Oliver Hale, Trader; John Ives, Trader, Rancher
Time Period(s): 1840s
Locale(s): New York, New York; Santa Fe, New Mexico; Los Angeles, California

Summary: Garnet Cameron travels across America along the Jubilee Trail with her new husband, Oliver Hale. She finds adventure, betrayal, and romance in California and New Mexico, as the U.S. struggles to wrest the west from Mexican control.

Historical Accuracy: The language tends to be somewhat contemporary, but the Mexican War and the emergence of the Bear Flag Republic of California as a state are historical events that are well told here.

HERMANN BROCH (1886-1951)

German novelist Broch grew up in Austria, where he studied mathematics and philosophy. He worked as the director of a textile company and became well known for his first novel, *The Sleepwalkers*, published in 1931. During World War II Broch moved to the U.S.

`699` *The Death of Virgil*

Date of Publication: 1945
Subject(s): Roman Empire; Literary Life
Historical character(s): Publius Vergilius Maro, Writer (poet)
Time Period(s): 1st century B.C.
Locale(s): Roman Empire

Summary: This is a poetic exploration of the final days of the Roman poet Virgil, author of the epic *Aeneid*. Virgil's dying thoughts provide an opportunity for an inquiry into the values of the Augustan Age and a symbolic examination of more modern themes.

Historical Accuracy: This dense and symbolic work operates on many levels, including a believable evocation of the period and the poet.

DARRYL BROCK

`700` *If I Never Get Back*

Date of Publication: 1990
Subject(s): Time Travel; Baseball; Sports
Fictional character(s): Sam Fowler, Time Traveller, Journalist
Historical character(s): Mark Twain, Writer; George Wright, Sports Figure (baseball pitcher)
Time Period(s): 1860s (1869)
Locale(s): New York

Summary: Crime reporter Sam Fowler travels back in time to 1869 and finds himself surrounded by players of the Cincinnati Red Stocking baseball team who are beginning their legendary 64-0 season. Fowler joins the team and "invents" the bunt, the intentional walk, hot dogs, and Cracker Jacks. He tours Manhattan with Mark Twain and finds himself in the center of intrigue with gamblers and Fenian revolutionaries.

Historical Accuracy: Widely inventive, the novel owes it success to its ability to plausibly animate these early days of baseball and the post-Civil War era.

ROSE BROCK
(PSEUD. OF JOSEPH HANSEN, 1923-)

Mystery writer and poet Joseph Hansen has also published under the pseudonyms James Colton and James Coulton, as well as Rose Brock. He was born in Aberdeen, South Dakota, and was educated in South Dakota and California. Hansen has taught fiction writing at the Beyond Baroque Foundation in Venice, California, and at UCLA. His first novel as Rose Brock was *Tara House* published in 1971.

`701` *Longleaf*

Date of Publication: 1974
Subject(s): Romance; Identity—Concealed
Fictional character(s): Bird Thatcher, Heiress—Lost; Lorna Thatcher, Widow(er)
Time Period(s): 1880s
Locale(s): Tennessee; New Orleans, Louisiana

Summary: Bird Thatcher's mother, the widow of a Confederate cavalry officer, confesses on her deathbed that Bird is not her child but was found during the war. The only clue to her identity was some old letters signed "Andre Dutrane." Bird sets out to discover her identity and her heritage, a journey that will take her to New Orleans and a tangled past and threatened future.

Historical Accuracy: The romantic suspense here is supported by vivid and convincing historical details.

MAX BROD (1884-1968)

A Czech author, dramatist, biographer, composer, and lawyer, Brod was born in Prague and attended the University of Prague. After fleeing to Palestine in 1939 at the outbreak of World War II, Brod worked as the dramaturge of the Hebrew National Theatre, a post that he held until his death. Brod was responsible for the publication of Franz Kafka's novels *The Trial* and *The Castle* after Kafka's death. Brod's works include *Kafka: A Biography*, *The Redemption of Tycho Brahe*, and *Reubeni: Prince of the Jews*.

`702` *The Master*

Date of Publication: 1951
Subject(s): Biblical Story
Fictional character(s): Meleager, Writer (poet); Shoshana, Young Woman
Historical character(s): Jesus Christ, Biblical Figure; Peter, Biblical Figure, Religious
Time Period(s): 1st century
Locale(s): Israel

Summary: Set during the ministry of Jesus, the novel attempts to place the birth of Christianity in the context of the philosophical and religious ideas of the times. The story involves the exposure to Jesus and his disciples of a young Greek poet, Meleager, who is working as a scribe for Pilate.

Historical Accuracy: The novel alters or departs from traditional interpretations of Jesus based on the Biblical record.

GLORIA KURIAN BRODER

BILL BRODER (1931-)

703 *Remember This Time*

Date of Publication: 1983
Subject(s): World War I; Russian Revolution
Fictional character(s): Kala Chodorov, Young Woman
Time Period(s): 1910 (1914-1919)
Locale(s): Russia

Summary: Set during the First World War and the Russian Revolution, the novel describes the impact of these great events on the Chodorov family who finds their home in the Pale of Jewish settlement in Western Russia destroyed. Young Kala Chodorov experiences life as a refugee and in Moscow during the revolution and civil war.

Historical Accuracy: The novel provides an authentic period background based on evident research that is faithful to reliable sources.

LOUIS BROMFIELD (1896-1956)

Born in Ohio, Bromfield served in World War I and was employed as a New York journalist and foreign correspondent, living for many years in France. *Early Autumn*, his fourth novel, won the Pulitzer Prize for Fiction in 1927.

704 *Wild Is the River*

Date of Publication: 1941
Subject(s): Civil War—U.S.
Fictional character(s): James Wicks, Military Personnel (Union general); Tom Bedloe, Military Personnel (Union major); Elaine de Leche, Southern Belle
Time Period(s): 1860s (1862)
Locale(s): New Orleans, Louisiana

Summary: Cultures clash in occupied New Orleans when Union Major Tom Bedloe falls in love with Creole beauty Elaine de Leche.

Historical Accuracy: Except for occasional references there is little effort to re-create the past.

TERESA BROOKE

705 *Under the Winter Moon*

Date of Publication: 1958
Subject(s): Middle Ages; Crusades
Fictional character(s): Lady Anne of Meziere, Noblewoman; Denys de Seconnet, Knight
Time Period(s): 11th century
Locale(s): France; Jerusalem, Palestine

Summary: Denys de Seconnet goes on a pilgrimage to the Holy Land with Peter the Hermit during the First Crusade. His lover, Lady Anne of Meziere, awaits his return, but when he fails to come back, she goes to Jerusalem herself to search for him.

Historical Accuracy: The novel offers a strong background of medieval details and a convincing period atmosphere, though at times it displays an overly modern sensibility.

BERTRAM BROOKER (1888-1955)

Born in Croydon, England, Brooker's family immigrated to Manitoba, Canada in 1905. At 17 he worked on the Grand Trunk Pacific Railway. He also worked as a journalist, book editor, and painter and in advertising. He was elected to the Ontario Society of Artists in 1936. His work includes *The Tangled Mirage: A Mortimer Hood Mystery* and *Sounds Assembling*, a collection of poetry.

706 *The Robber: A Tale of the Time of the Herods*

Date of Publication: 1946
Subject(s): Biblical Story
Historical character(s): Barabbas, Biblical Figure, Outlaw; Joseph of Arimathea, Biblical Figure; Judas Iscariot, Biblical Figure
Time Period(s): 1st century
Locale(s): Jerusalem, Israel

Summary: This biblical story is based on the lives of Barabbas, Joseph of Arimathea, and Judas Iscariot. In this version Barabbas is a Robin Hood-like outlaw who robs to help the less fortunate. He is befriended by Joseph of Arimathea, who also befriends a sympathetically portrayed Judas. The novel ends with Jesus' crucifixion.

Historical Accuracy: Despite the obvious invention of characterization, the novel's period background is convincing.

SUSANNAH BROOME

707 *The Pearl Pagoda*

Date of Publication: 1980
Subject(s): Romance; Opium War; Chinese Empire
Fictional character(s): Megan Jones, Young Woman; Robert Hawkes, Sea Captain
Time Period(s): 19th century
Locale(s): Macao; England

Summary: Megan Jones goes to China to become a missionary's wife only to find upon her arrival that her fiance has died. She is swept up in China's Opium Wars, imprisoned, and held for ransom. Eventually she marries a ship captain whose history shakes their marriage.

Historical Accuracy: The Chinese setting and period are more an exotic backdrop for this romantic adventure than historical documentation.

JOHN BROPHY (1899-1965)

English author Brophy was born in Liverpool and graduated from the universities of Liverpool and Durham. He taught in Egypt for two years during the 1920s, worked in a general store, and was an advertising agency copywriter prior to becoming a full-time writer. Brophy is best known for his war novels drawn from his own experiences during World War II. Four of his novels were made into films: *Immortal Sergeant*, *Waterfront*, *Turn the Key Softly*, and *The Day They Robbed the Bank of England*.

708 *Gentleman of Stratford*

Date of Publication: 1940
Subject(s): Elizabethan Period; Biography, Fictionalized; Theatrical Life
Historical character(s): William Shakespeare, Writer
Time Period(s): 16th century; 17th century
Locale(s): Stratford-on-Avon, England; London, England

Summary: This biographical novel chronicles the life of William Shakespeare, staying close to the known facts and interpreting Shakespeare's character through his writing. The novel excels in rendering the Elizabethan period and its customs. But adhering to the known is a decided limitation in creating a full-scale and imaginative portrait of Shakespeare.

Historical Accuracy: The novel is careful in its faithful presentation of what is known. Unfortunately, what we do not know about Shakespeare is what is needed to create a compelling portrait.

DOROTHY KATHLEEN BROSTER

709 *The Dark Mile*

Date of Publication: 1934
Subject(s): Jacobite Rebellion
Fictional character(s): Ian Stewart, Young Man; Olivia Campbell, Young Woman
Historical character(s): Charles Edward Stuart, Royalty
Time Period(s): 1740s (1745)
Locale(s): Highlands, Scotland

Summary: The novel continues the story of a group of Jacobites begun in *The Flight of the Heron*. Ian Stewart, the cousin of Ewen Cameron of the earlier novel, falls in love with Englishwoman Olivia Campbell, whose father commanded the English troops at the Battle of Culloden.

Historical Accuracy: The novel is most authentic in its Scottish Highlands setting.

710 *The Flight of the Heron*

Date of Publication: 1930
Subject(s): Jacobite Rebellion; Georgian Period; Battle of Culloden
Fictional character(s): Ewen Cameron, Laird; Keith Windham, Military Personnel (English captain)
Historical character(s): Charles Edward Stuart, Royalty
Time Period(s): 1740s (1745)
Locale(s): Scotland

Summary: The backdrop for this novel is the unsuccessful attempt by Bonnie Prince Charlie to seize the Hanoverian throne in 1745. The action centers on the divided loyalty and test of friendship between Scottish chief Ewen Cameron and English army captain Keith Windham.

Historical Accuracy: The historical background for the story is authentic and faithful to the facts.

DEE BROWN (1908-)

Brown was raised in Arkansas where he developed his interest in the Western experience and Indian culture. A librarian, Brown achieved major popular success with the nonfiction title *Bury My Heart at Wounded Knee*, and went on to write more works of fiction and nonfiction about the American West.

711 *Conspiracy of Knaves*

Date of Publication: 1986
Subject(s): Civil War—U.S.; Espionage
Fictional character(s): Belle Rutledge, Actress, Spy; Charley Heywood, Spy; John Truscott, Military Personnel (Confederate officer)
Time Period(s): 1860s (1864)
Locale(s): Kentucky; Chicago, Illinois; Cincinnati, Ohio

Summary: In this tale of Civil War espionage and conspiracy, an actress, Belle Rutledge, is recruited as a Union spy. However, she is actually a double agent who is involved in a plot to free Rebel soldiers being held in Chicago and to use them to force the Northwest Territories to join the Confederate cause.

Historical Accuracy: Brown constructs a rousing story, anchored by period details, including newspaper headlines that document the era.

712 *Creek Mary's Blood*

Date of Publication: 1980
Subject(s): Indians; Family Saga
Fictional character(s): Creek Mary, Indian; Opothle, Indian; Talasi, Indian
Historical character(s): James Edward Oglethorpe, Military Personnel, Political Figure (founder of Georgia); Andrew Jackson, Military Personnel, Political Figure; Theodore Roosevelt, Political Figure; Red Cloud, Indian, Chieftain; Crazy Horse, Indian, Warrior; Sitting Bull, Indian, Chieftain; Tecumseh, Indian, Chieftain
Time Period(s): 18th century; 19th century (1770-1890)
Locale(s): Georgia; Midwest (Nebraska, Kansas, Missouri, Illinois); West (Oklahoma, New Mexico, Colorado, Wyoming, Montana)

Summary: This epic tale of Indian life follows a single familys participation in several major events: the American Revolution, the Cherokee relocation of the 1830s, and the Battles of Little Big Horn and Wounded Knee. As the indomitable Creek Mary's family moves from Georgia to the Great Plains, their history mirrors that of a people and a nation.

Historical Accuracy: The novel truly earns the adjective epic. The historical detail is exact and convincing.

713 *Killdeer Mountain*

Date of Publication: 1983
Subject(s): American West; Indians; Mystery

Fictional character(s): Sam Morrison, Journalist; Charles Rawley, Military Personnel, Frontiersman
Time Period(s): 1860s (1866)
Locale(s): Missouri; Dakota Territory, United States

Summary: A reporter for the *St. Louis Herald* aboard a steamboat on the Missouri in 1866 investigates the story of Charles Rawley, Civil War hero and Indian fighter. Many witnesses debate whether he was in fact a hero or a coward in a battle with the Indians at Killdeer Mountain. Rawley's story and the stories of those who knew him reveal much about life on the frontier.

Historical Accuracy: Brown's mystery concerning Rawley's past illuminates a carefully presented picture of Western life, filled with authentic portraits and period details.

714 *Wave High the Banner*

Date of Publication: 1942
Subject(s): Biography, Fictionalized; Texas Revolution; Battle of the Alamo
Historical character(s): Davy Crockett, Frontiersman
Time Period(s): 18th century; 19th century (1786-1836)
Locale(s): Tennessee; Texas

Summary: The novel dramatizes the life of frontiersman Davy Crockett from his boyhood in the Tennessee wilderness to his death at the Battle of the Alamo. The author has refashioned the various legends of the Crockett myth into a believable biographical account.

Historical Accuracy: The novel stays close to the known facts about Crockett's career with some fictional elements added in the interest of the story.

715 *Yellowhorse*

Date of Publication: 1956
Subject(s): American West; Military Life—U.S. Cavalry; Indians
Fictional character(s): Tom Easterwood, Military Personnel (cavalry officer); Spotted Wolf, Indian (Sioux); Major Quill, Military Personnel (cavalry officer)
Time Period(s): 1870s
Locale(s): West

Summary: Captain Tom Easterwood served as a balloonist in the Civil War. Now, as a cavalry officer in the middle of the Indian Wars, his special qualifications are put to service to save his unit during a Sioux uprising.

Historical Accuracy: Brown knows his characters and the period. The dialogue and the details are convincing even if the situation—a surveillance balloon in the middle of the western frontier—is a bit far-fetched.

DIANA BROWN (1928-)

Brown was born in England and emigrated to the U.S. in 1949, becoming a naturalized citizen in 1957. She received her college degrees from San Jose State University. Brown has served in a variety of consulate posts in public relations and library work in the U.S., the Far East, and Europe. She writes of women in the past in order to gain an understanding of the position of women throughout history. She is the author of *The Hand of a Woman*, *The Sandalwood Fan*, and *St. Martin's Summer*.

716 *The Blue Dragon*

Date of Publication: 1988
Subject(s): Romance; East/West Relations
Fictional character(s): Marigold Wilder, Religious (missionary); Mark Banning, Adventurer
Historical character(s): Lafcadio Hearn, Writer
Time Period(s): 1890s
Locale(s): England; Seoul, Korea

Summary: Marigold Wilder embarks on a career as a missionary in Korea, newly opened to outsiders. Her story is intertwined with that of an American adventurer, Mark Banning, who comes to Korea in search of gold. Both must contend with an alien culture and are swept up in the political intrigue that besets Korea during the scramble for power.

Historical Accuracy: The background of Korean history is well established with a solid sense of both the culture and the era.

717 *Come Be My Love*

Date of Publication: 1981
Subject(s): Regency Romance; Literary Life
Fictional character(s): Alexandra Cox-Neville, Gentlewoman, Writer; Darius Wentworth, Heir
Historical character(s): Sydney Smith, Religious (clergyman), Writer; Samuel Rogers, Writer (poet); Thomas Moore, Writer (poet)
Time Period(s): 1810s; 1820s
Locale(s): Wiltshire, England; London, England

Summary: Alexandra Cox-Neville is in love from childhood with Darius Wentworth, heir to the Wentworth estate. He regards her as a sister and weds another. Alexandra flees an unwanted marriage to London where she fashions a literary career. Scandal follows the publication of a volume of her poetry.

Historical Accuracy: The novel is filled with insights into literary London of the period including the presence of major and minor figures.

718 *The Emerald Necklace*

Date of Publication: 1980
Subject(s): Regency Romance
Fictional character(s): Leonora Fordyce, Noblewoman; Etienne Lambert, Bastard Son
Time Period(s): 1810s (Regency period)
Locale(s): London, England; Yorkshire, England; Dordogne, France

Summary: Leonora Fordyce marries the illegitimate and self-made Etienne Lambert to pay her father's gambling debts. She begins to fall in love with her husband, but a tangle of secrets must be solved before their marriage can succeed.

Historical Accuracy: The novel offers some conventional romantic complications with some period painting of Regency

London and Yorkshire. The emphasis here, however, is on romance and not history.

719 *The Hand of a Woman*

Date of Publication: 1984
Subject(s): Romance; Civil War—U.S.; Medical Profession
Fictional character(s): Damaris Fanshawe, Child-Care Giver (nursemaid), Doctor; Templeton Caylew, Businessman; Guy Parrish, Landowner
Time Period(s): 1860s; 1870s
Locale(s): New York, New York; Memphis, Tennessee

Summary: Damaris Fanshawe is the nursemaid in the home of New York businessman Templeton Caylew. Seduced and then discharged, she enters the Episcopal sisterhood of St. Catherine. She trains as one of the first female physicians in America, and during the yellow fever epidemic in Memphis meets Guy Parrish, a cotton planter. Damaris must make an agonizing choice between duty and her love.

Historical Accuracy: The amazing career of the heroine strains credibility, yet the details of period life are strongly and convincingly painted.

720 *The Sandalwood Fan*

Date of Publication: 1983
Subject(s): Regency Romance
Fictional character(s): Charles Mortimer, Military Personnel (army officer), Nobleman; Georgina Staverton, Gentlewoman; Penelope Bransom, Widow(er)
Time Period(s): 1810s
Locale(s): London, England

Summary: Lord Mortimer, a hero of the battle of Waterloo, is one of London's most eligible bachelors. He resists all matches, preferring to nurse his unrequited love for Lady Staverton. When a young widow, Penelope Bransom, comes to London for her sister's debut, she unexpectedly attracts Mortimer. Their unusual romance forms the novel's story.

Historical Accuracy: The period detail is solid, particularly on the courtship machinations and the London social scene.

ESTHER FISHER BROWN

721 *Gaul Is Divided*

Date of Publication: 1952
Subject(s): Roman Empire; Gallic War
Historical character(s): Julius Caesar, Military Personnel (Roman general); Vercingetorix, Chieftain, Leader (of the Gauls)
Time Period(s): 1st century B.C. (52 B.C.)
Locale(s): Gaul (modern France)

Summary: This account of the Gallic War between Rome and the Gauls is told from the perspective of Vercingetorix, the great Arvernian chieftain and Julius Caesar's greatest opponent. He is shown from his 14th birthday to his assumption of the leadership of the Gauls in the fight against Roman occupation.

Historical Accuracy: The novel authentically describes the era and the events of the Gallic War.

HARRY BROWN (1917-1986)

An American poet, novelist, playwright, and screenwriter, Brown was born in Portland, Maine, and attended Harvard. His works include *A Walk in the Sun*, *The Wild Hunt*, and *Stars in Their Courses*. Brown won an Academy Award for his script for *A Place in the Sun*.

722 *The Stars in Their Courses*

Date of Publication: 1960
Subject(s): American West
Fictional character(s): Percy Randal, Rancher; Arch Eastmere, Gunfighter
Time Period(s): 1870s (1879)
Locale(s): West

Summary: This novel attempts nothing less than to translate Homer's *Iliad* into a western. Percy Randal is a powerful rancher who is opposed by a band of his neighbors with the help of a hired gun, Arch Eastmere. The Homeric parallels are unmistakable in this story that is inflated to the level of an epic.

Historical Accuracy: The novel's reliance on types in the interest of reaching universal levels aides the poetical quality of the work but undermines its realism and particularity.

KARL BROWN (1897-1990)

An American cinematographer, director, screenwriter, and author, Brown chronicled his experiences as a pioneering filmmaker in his 1973 autobiography, *Adventures with D.W. Griffith*. Brown was Griffith's assistant cameraman on such classic films as *Birth of a Nation* and *Intolerance*.

723 *The Cup Trembling*

Date of Publication: 1953
Subject(s): Civil War—U.S.
Historical character(s): Frederick William Stowe, Military Personnel (Union captain); Harriet Beecher Stowe, Writer
Time Period(s): 1860s
Locale(s): Washington, District of Columbia

Summary: This psychological-historical study examines the Civil War career of Frederick William Stowe, son of Harriet Beecher Stowe. Frederick goes to war compelled by his mother's crusading vision, but the experience of war seems to free him from his mother's grasp and recasts her as a more malevolent spirit.

Historical Accuracy: The basic facts are accurately observed, but the interpretation of Stowe's relationship with her son is decidedly modern.

KATHARINE HOLLAND BROWN
(1876-1931)

Born in Alton, Illinois, Brown graduated from the University of Michigan and taught school before turning to full-time writing. Several of her novels feature historical figures. She published *White Roses*, *Uncertain Irene*, and *The Messenger*.

724 *The Father*

Date of Publication: 1928
Subject(s): Slavery
Fictional character(s): John Stafford, Abolitionist
Historical character(s): Abraham Lincoln, Political Figure
Time Period(s): 1850s (1850)
Locale(s): Springfield, Illinois

Summary: This tale of the abolition movement during the 1850s describes the anti-slavery activity of John Stafford. He outrages the community but attracts the support of young Springfield lawyer Abraham Lincoln.

Historical Accuracy: The novel provides a vivid portrait of the years preceding the Civil War.

LINDA BEATRICE BROWN

Brown is a professor of Humanities at Bennett College in Greensboro, North Carolina. She is also a poet and author of the collection *A Love Story to Black Man.*

725 *Crossing over Jordan*

Date of Publication: 1995
Subject(s): Slavery; Family Saga
Fictional character(s): Georgia McCloud, Slave; Sadie Temple, Young Woman; Story Temple, Young Woman
Time Period(s): Multiple Time Periods
Locale(s): United States

Summary: This family chronicle set in the years following the Civil War to the 21st century details the crippling influence of slavery on several generations of black women. Though Georgia McCloud lives through slavery to emancipation, her daughter Sadie finds herself in an abusive relationship, and her other daughter Story limits her options in a search for safety. The cycle of oppression and restraint is repeated from one generation to the next.

Historical Accuracy: The novel offers convincing psychological portraits and a sweeping saga of African-American history.

MARY BROWN (1929-)

726 *Playing the Jack*

Date of Publication: 1984
Subject(s): Theatrical Life; Georgian Period; Picaresque Adventure
Fictional character(s): Jack, Entertainer; Sprat, Orphan
Time Period(s): 1780s (1785)
Locale(s): England

Summary: In this picaresque novel, a runaway orphan is adopted by travelling entertainers led by the enigmatic Jack. Christened ''Sprat,'' the boy is abducted from the London streets into a children's brothel and gaming house. The novel ingeniously develops an elaborate connection of characters whose double identities complicate the novel's plot.

Historical Accuracy: The novel is a convincing evocation of life on the city streets and country lanes of 18th-century England.

RITA MAE BROWN (1944-)

American novelist Brown was born in Pennsylvania and attended New York University, receiving her Ph.D. from the Institute for Policy Studies in Washington, D.C. Her first and most popular novel, *Rubyfruit Jungle*, was published in 1973 to great critical acclaim. Brown is a member of the board of directors of Sagaris, a feminist school.

727 *Dolley*

Date of Publication: 1994
Subject(s): Biography, Fictionalized; War of 1812; Politics
Historical character(s): Dolley Madison, Spouse, Political Figure; James Madison, Political Figure; Henry Clay, Political Figure; John C. Calhoun, Political Figure; Daniel Webster, Political Figure; George Cockburn, Military Personnel (British admiral); William Winder, Military Personnel (American general); John Armstrong, Political Figure
Time Period(s): 18th century; 19th century (1781-1814)
Locale(s): Washington, District of Columbia

Summary: Dolley Madison, wife of the fourth president of the United States, tells her own story in the pages of her diary. She emerges as a thoroughly modern and complex woman, a savvy politician with the ability to see through many of the male politicos. She faces her sternest test in 1814 as British forces invade Washington and the fate of the young nation hangs in the balance.

Historical Accuracy: This is a remarkable effort in historical re-creation. The extensive bibliography shows the thoughtful research that helps establish the novel's authenticity.

728 *High Hearts*

Date of Publication: 1986
Subject(s): Civil War—U.S.; Identity—Concealed; Slavery
Fictional character(s): Geneva Chatfield, Spouse (of Nash), Military Personnel (Confederate Soldier); Nash Hart, Military Personnel (Confederate officer); Mars Vickers, Military Personnel (Confederate major); Di-Peachy, Slave
Time Period(s): 1860s (1861-1862)
Locale(s): Virginia

Summary: During the Civil War, Geneva Chatfield disguises herself as a boy and follows her husband, Nash Hart, into battle on the Confederate side. Although Nash shrinks from the horrors of war, Geneva is invigorated by it. The novel presents an ingenious portrait of the effect of the war on women and blacks, a factor too often left out of consideration.

Historical Accuracy: The author's notes and bibliography show evidence of meticulous research, creating an authentic period background for her unusual story.

729 *Riding Shotgun*

Date of Publication: 1996
Subject(s): Time Travel; American Colonies

Fictional character(s): Pryor Deyhle Blackwood, Widow(er), Time Traveller
Time Period(s): 1990s; 17th century (1699)
Locale(s): Virginia

Summary: While on a fox hunt, Pryor Deyhle Blackwood, or ''Cig,'' finds herself transported back in time to Virginia in 1699. She is accepted into the family of another young woman named Pryor Deyhle. The contrast between eras plays an important role in answering many of Cig's lingering questions both about the past and the present.

Historical Accuracy: The novel is inventive in its contrast between the past and the present and presents a number of believable historical details.

730 *Southern Discomfort*

Date of Publication: 1982
Subject(s): Antebellum South
Fictional character(s): Banana Mae Parker, Prostitute; Blue Rhonda Latrec, Prostitute; Hortensia Banastre, Gentlewoman
Time Period(s): 19th century
Locale(s): Montgomery, Alabama; Chicago, Illinois

Summary: This is a tender, bawdy tale of the lives and loves of two first-class southern whores who live their lives with gusto and humor. In contrast to them is Hortensia Banastre, a beautiful woman trapped in a loveless marriage, who is infatuated with a young prize fighter.

Historical Accuracy: The novel captures the flavor of the era with an emphasis on the outrageous and absurd.

RUSSELL A. BROWN (1934-)

Sherlock Holms and the Mysterious Friend of Oscar Wilde is Brown's first novel.

731 *Sherlock Holmes and the Mysterious Friend of Oscar Wilde*

Date of Publication: 1988
Subject(s): Mystery; Victorian Period; Literary Life
Fictional character(s): Sherlock Holmes, Detective—Private; John H. Watson, Doctor, Sidekick
Historical character(s): Oscar Wilde, Writer
Time Period(s): 1890s (1895)
Locale(s): London, England

Summary: In this Victorian-era mystery, Sherlock Holmes aids Oscar Wilde in helping a Swedish inventor avoid blackmailers. The case throws Holmes and Watson into Wilde's world where Holmes must contend with the vengeful Marquess of Queensberry and Watson must be rescued from a pederast hangout in London.

Historical Accuracy: The novel is more ingenious than believable with a forced conjunction of the Holmes and Wilde milieux.

WESLEY BROWN (1945-)

Brown was born in New York City and is a graduate of Oswego State University. His first novel was *Tragic Magic*.

732 *Darktown Strutters*

Date of Publication: 1994
Subject(s): Minstrel Shows; Slavery; Civil War—U.S.
Fictional character(s): Jim Crow, Dancer; Jack Diamond, Dancer; Tom Rice, Entertainer
Historical character(s): William Lane, Entertainer; Frederick Douglass, Abolitionist
Time Period(s): 19th century (1830-1876)
Locale(s): Kentucky (Louisville, Lexington, Paducah); Midwest (St. Louis, Cincinnati); New York, New York

Summary: This novel chronicles the life and times of a black dancer, Jim Crow, who performs in minstrel shows. Crow is a slave taught to dance by his father. He is the only black in an all-white minstrel show and endures humiliation and violence from audiences that are alternately fascinated and disgusted with his performances.

Historical Accuracy: This is a fascinating and moving depiction of minstrel life. The authenticity derives from Brown's appropriate sounding dialogue.

HOWARD BROWNE (1908-)

733 *Scotch on the Rocks*

Date of Publication: 1991
Subject(s): Mystery; Crime and Criminals; Depression Era
Fictional character(s): Lee Vance, Con Artist
Time Period(s): 1930s (1932)
Locale(s): Texas; Oklahoma; Kansas

Summary: A family recently dispossessed in a farm foreclosure finds a bootlegger's cache of liquor. Con man Lee Vance convinces them to go on the road to Kansas City to sell the cache. The novel details their road adventures that include a crooked cop and a bank robbery.

Historical Accuracy: The Depression-era atmosphere is convincingly displayed.

JOSEPH BRUCHAC III (1942-)

Bruchac is an American poet, storyteller, and novelist who taught for a time in Africa. Much of his work is influenced by Native American experience and folktales.

734 *Dawn Land*

Date of Publication: 1993
Subject(s): Indians; Prehistory; Tribal Life—Prehistoric
Fictional character(s): Young Hunter, Indian, Warrior; Bear Talker, Indian; Medicine Plant, Indian
Time Period(s): Indeterminate Past
Locale(s): North America

Summary: Set about 10,000 years ago among the Abenaki, the novel concerns a young brave's perilous journey to prevent a threat to his homeland.

Historical Accuracy: This is a richly lyrical and believeable evocation of the culture of native peoples.

VINCENZ BRUN

735   *Alcibiades, Beloved of Gods*

Date of Publication: 1935
Subject(s): Ancient Greece
Historical character(s): Alcibiades, Political Figure, Military Personnel (general); Pericles, Ruler (Greek); Socrates, Philosopher; Aspasia, Gentlewoman; Aristophanes, Writer; Phidias, Artist (sculptor)
Time Period(s): 5th century B.C.
Locale(s): Athens, Greece

Summary: This tale of 5th-century Athens centers on the remarkable career of Alcibiades, the ward of Pericles and student of Socrates. The novel traces his development up to the time of his departure for the attack on Syracuse.

Historical Accuracy: The novel's historical elements are uneven. Some of the presentations are accurate and genuine, while others appear incredible.

JOHN BRUNNER (1934-)

English novelist Brunner was educated at Cheltenham College and published his first novel in 1951. His most famous book is *Stand on Zanzibar*, which won the Hugo Award from the World Science Fiction Society for best novel in 1969.

736   *The Great Steamboat Race*

Date of Publication: 1983
Subject(s): Riverboats; Reconstruction Period
Fictional character(s): Miles Parbury, Sea Captain (riverboat), Handicapped (blind); Hosea Drew, Sea Captain (riverboat); Cato Woodley, Sea Captain (riverboat)
Time Period(s): 1870s
Locale(s): Mississippi River; New Orleans, Louisiana

Summary: Based on the famous steamboat race between the *Natchez* and the *Robert E. Lee*, this novel chronicles life on the river in the 1870s. The riverboat captains, owners, pilots, and passengers form a full representation of people of the period.

Historical Accuracy: This is not a historical novel, but rather a depiction of what science fiction writers call a retrospective parallel world. The historical facts have been altered to fit the novel's drama.

WILL BRYANT (1923-)

An American novelist, Bryant was born in Arizona and spent his childhood travelling throughout the West. He served as a naval aviator during World War II. In addition to his writing, he has been a book illustrator, art director, and graphic designer.

737   *The Big Lonesome*

Date of Publication: 1971
Subject(s): American West; Indians
Fictional character(s): Tobin Shattuck, Prospector; Joe Horn, Mountain Man
Time Period(s): 1860s
Locale(s): Idaho; Montana

Summary: Tobin Shattuck accompanies his father, a Civil War deserter, west into the Rockies guided by an old trapper's memory of a gold-rich stream. Tobin is attacked by a grizzly and is rescued by the Blackfoot Indians. He is introduced to Indian ways and customs.

Historical Accuracy: The novel offers an authentic look at frontier life of the period.

738   *Blue Russell*

Date of Publication: 1976
Subject(s): American West; Crime and Criminals; Railroads
Fictional character(s): Blue Russell, Orphan; Packy Disbrow, Thief, Handicapped; Clay Russell, Outlaw
Time Period(s): 1890s (1899)
Locale(s): St. Louis, Missouri; Wyoming; Utah

Summary: Blue Russell is the only one who believes he killed his uncle in self-defense. While on the run, he teams up with Packy Disbrow, a one-eyed crippled safecracker. They head west, joining Blue's brother Clay to tackle the ''Invincible,'' a triple-locked safe, on a daring train robbery. The novel's climax is a chase along the Owlhoot trail.

Historical Accuracy: The novel is full of period detail and a vivid depiction of the West.

739   *Escape From Sonora*

Date of Publication: 1973
Subject(s): American West; Mexican Revolution; Crime and Criminals
Fictional character(s): John Perrell, Vagrant; Clint, Convict (former); Costello, Detective—Private (Pinkerton)
Time Period(s): 1910s (1916)
Locale(s): California; Arizona; Sierra Madre, Mexico

Summary: In 1916 a group of drifters riding the rails are accosted by a sadistic railroad bull. When he is killed, they are pursued into Mexico by Costello, a Pinkerton detective. A band of renegades from Pancho Villa's army captures them. Their only hope for escape is to get an old 1907 Thomas Flyer automobile running.

Historical Accuracy: The atmosphere and the locale are authentic and realistic.

BRYHER

(PSEUD. OF ANNIE WINIFRED ELLERMAN, 1894-1983)

English novelist Bryher, born Annie Winifred Ellerman, took her pseudonym from one of the Scilly Islands where she spent holidays as a student. At the outbreak of World War I, she gave up the study of archaeology and turned to writing. From 1921 on, she lived on Lake Geneva.

740   *The Coin of Carthage*

Date of Publication: 1963

Subject(s): Roman Empire; Punic Wars
Fictional character(s): Zonas, Trader; Dasius, Trader
Time Period(s): 3rd century B.C. (218-202 B.C.)
Locale(s): Roman Empire; Carthage, Ancient Civilization

Summary: The novel offers the experiences of two Greek traders who travel with Hannibal's invading army during the second Punic War and are then lured to Carthage on the eve of its destruction.

Historical Accuracy: Bryher's poetic and evocative method is to capture the feel of the period rather than its facts and events. She successfully creates a human context for history.

741 *The Colors of Vaud*

Date of Publication: 1969
Subject(s): Independence—Switzerland; French Revolution
Fictional character(s): Philippe Masson, Revolutionary; Laurent Perrin, Farmer; Sophie Perrin, Young Woman
Time Period(s): 18th century; 19th century (1792-1802)
Locale(s): Vaud, Switzerland; Lausanne, Switzerland

Summary: The novel describes the Canton of Vaud's struggle for independence from the rule of Bern. Revolutionary fervor arrives with emigres from France who suggest that independence is possible. The local elders fear, however, that this might mean the end of tradition. Sophie and Philippe are two young people who insist that equality and independence are the future.

Historical Accuracy: The novel captures the atmosphere and the setting of this traditional society in the throes of the new and potentially dangerous idea of freedom.

742 *The Fourteenth of October*

Date of Publication: 1952
Subject(s): Norman Conquest; Battle of Hastings; Vikings
Fictional character(s): Wulf, Captive, Warrior; Rafe, Warrior
Time Period(s): 11th century
Locale(s): Yorkshire, England; Normandy, France; Hastings, England

Summary: The title refers to the date of the Battle of Hastings in 1066 and the Norman victory over the Saxons. The novel tells of a Saxon warrior, Wulf who becomes a hostage of the Danes. Following a period of servitude, Wulf escapes with his friend Rafe and they join in the Battle of Hastings. Bryher attempts to show that much was lost when the Saxons were defeated, and the novel attempts to reconstruct the sense of culture altered by the Norman Conquest.

Historical Accuracy: The novel's first-person narration helps produce an authentic voice and a vivid evocation of the period.

743 *Gate to the Sea*

Date of Publication: 1958
Subject(s): Ancient Greece; Religious Life; Barbarians
Fictional character(s): Harmonia, Religious (priestess); Archias, Outcast; Lykos, Slave
Time Period(s): 5th century B.C.
Locale(s): Paestum, Italy

Summary: This is a vivid description of the events which led to the fall of Paestum to invading barbarians. After eight years of struggling to coexist with barbarian invaders, Harmonia reflects on her life and city before and after the invasion. She details the conflict of preserving the sacred relics and rituals against the forces of ignorance and savagery.

Historical Accuracy: Using allegory and fable, the story's moral is solidly imagined against a clear backdrop of classical life.

744 *The Player's Boy*

Date of Publication: 1953
Subject(s): Jacobean Period; Theatrical Life
Fictional character(s): John Sands, Actor
Historical character(s): Francis Beaumont, Writer (playwright); John Fletcher, Writer (playwright)
Time Period(s): 17th century (1605-1620s)
Locale(s): London, England

Summary: This is an imaginative reconstruction of theatrical life during the Jacobean period. The story follows the carrer of actor-apprentice John Sands and his relationship with dramatist Francis Beaumont.

Historical Accuracy: The novel faithfully catches the spirit of the 17th-century English stage.

745 *Roman Wall*

Date of Publication: 1954
Subject(s): Roman Empire; Barbarians
Fictional character(s): Valerius, Military Personnel (Roman soldier); Demetrius, Trader; Vinodius, Government Official; Veria, Gentlewoman
Time Period(s): 3rd century (265)
Locale(s): Switzerland

Summary: In the 3rd century, Switzerland is an outpost in an ever-shrinking Roman Empire. The people in the settlements anticipate the arrival of the barbarians from the north. They understand this means the destruction of their way of life. A large cast includes Valerius, a soldier; Demetrius, a trader; and Vinodius, the governor, who organizes games to distract the worried populace.

Historical Accuracy: The novel successfully captures a sense of the imminent change of the Roman Empire during its long decline.

746 *Ruan*

Date of Publication: 1960
Subject(s): Dark Ages; Sea Story; Druids
Fictional character(s): Ruan, -Adventurer; Erbin, Sailor; Moram, Ruler (Saxon king)
Time Period(s): 6th century
Locale(s): Cornwall, England; Scilly, England; Ireland

Summary: Ruan, although raised to be a Druid priest, desires the adventures of the sea. He is able to achieve this dream, and through him we glimpse the sights and sounds of England in the 6th century. There are scenes of a Cornish fair, Druid rituals, and the burial of a king on the mysterious Island of the Dead.

Historical Accuracy: The novel intimately and poetically captures the atmosphere and ethos of the period.

747   *This January Tale*

Date of Publication: 1966
Subject(s): Norman Conquest; Middle Ages; Anglo Saxon Period
Fictional character(s): Eldred, Knight; Godric, Knight; Elfreda, Young Woman
Time Period(s): 11th century (1066)
Locale(s): Exeter, England

Summary: The Saxon perspective is depicted in this novel as events move toward the climactic Battle of Hastings. Exeter is beseiged and taken as the Saxons scatter, exiles in their own country. The novel describes the events as they affect a number of Saxons under the pressure of great events and change.

Historical Accuracy: The novel faithfully captures the atmosphere and the ethos of the period. It makes a compelling claim that much was lost as well as gained with the coming of the Normans.

JOHN GORDON BRYSON (1900-)

Bryson writes robust stories of the criminal element in colonial North America.

748   *Valiant Libertine*

Date of Publication: 1942
Subject(s): American Revolution
Fictional character(s): Ian MacFarlane, Adventurer, Loyalist; Felicity Madden, Spy
Historical character(s): John Burgoyne, Military Personnel (British general); William Howe, Military Personnel (British general); Henry Clinton, Military Personnel (British general)
Time Period(s): 1770s (1775)
Locale(s): Boston, Massachusetts, American Colonies; Quebec, Canada

Summary: This swashbuckling tale set during the early days of the American Revolution concerns the adventures of Loyalist Ian MacFarlane. MacFarlane returns from Europe to Boston, where he is plunged into a series of intrigues and duels.

Historical Accuracy: The author's statement that the book was written not as historical but as romantic fiction should be noted. Despite the presence of historical figures, the story's costume adventures predominate over a careful presentation of the era and its events.

JOHN BUCHAN (1875-1940)

Scottish author and statesman Buchan was elected to Parliament in 1927 and was appointed as governor general of Canada. In 1935 he was raised to the peerage as Baron Tweedsmuir. His works include a four-volume history of World War I and biographies of Julius Caesar, Walter Scott, and Oliver Cromwell, as well as the adventure novels *The Thirty-nine Steps* and *Greenmantle*.

749   *The Blanket of the Dark*

Date of Publication: 1931
Subject(s): Royalty—England; Tudor Period
Fictional character(s): Peter Pentecost, Adventurer, Scholar
Historical character(s): Henry VIII, Ruler (King of England)
Time Period(s): 16th century
Locale(s): England

Summary: This adventure tale, set during the Tudor period, describes a plot to overthrow Henry VIII. Peter Pentecost, a young scholar, finds himself in the center of the political intrigue that threatens Henry's hold on power.

Historical Accuracy: The novel's story is fanciful, but filled with believable period elements.

750   *The Free Fishers*

Date of Publication: 1934
Subject(s): Napoleonic Wars; Fishing; Espionage
Fictional character(s): Anthony Lammas, Religious (minister)
Time Period(s): 1800s
Locale(s): Scotland; England

Summary: The Free Fishers of Forth are a secret organization of Scottish fishermen who serve on the side of England against the French during the Napoleonic Wars. Anthony Lammas, the honorary chaplain of the order, is given the task of rescuing a young lord from a dangerous involvement with a French spy.

Historical Accuracy: This romance in the manner of Robert Louis Stevenson has an authentic atmosphere of the time and the region.

751   *Midwinter*

Date of Publication: 1923
Subject(s): Jacobite Rebellion; Georgian Period
Fictional character(s): Alasdair MacLean, Gentleman; Sir John Norrey, Gentleman; Claudia Grevel, Gentlewoman
Historical character(s): Samuel Johnson, Writer, Scholar
Time Period(s): 1740s (1746)
Locale(s): England

Summary: This romantic adventure tale is set during Bonnie Prince Charlie's rebellion. It employs the eminent Doctor Johnson in an important role in a plot that forces Captain Alasdair MacLean to choose between Sir John Norrey and the Stuart cause.

Historical Accuracy: The novel is a spirited blend of history and romance, with the former providing a believable backdrop.

752   *Salute to Adventurers*

Date of Publication: 1917
Subject(s): American Colonies
Fictional character(s): Andrew Garuald, Adventurer, Businessman
Time Period(s): 17th century (1690s)
Locale(s): American Colonies; Scotland

Summary: Set in the Virginia colony during the 1690s, the novel describes the adventures of a young Scotsman, who seeks his fortune in the colonies. For the hand of a lady, he embarks on an adventurous journey deep into the heart of the American wilderness and encounters Indians.

Historical Accuracy: The emphasis on derring-do and romance predominates over any careful documentation of the period.

PERDITA BUCHAN (1940-)

English-born writer Buchan recieved her B.A. degree from Radcliffe College. She pursued a career in book publishing and has worked as an English teacher at the Lenox School in New York City and at Concord Academy. Her short stories have appeared in such publications as *The New Yorker* and *Ladies Home Journal.*

753 *Called Away*

Date of Publication: 1980
Subject(s): Time Travel; Rural Life—U.S.
Fictional character(s): Jared, Young Man; Clover, Young Woman; Curt Mudspell, Peddler, Deity (Pan)
Time Period(s): 1980s; 1810s (1815-1816)
Locale(s): Vermont

Summary: Jared and Clover are two back-to-nature youths who retreat to Circe, Vermont, for the natural life. There Clover is attracted to an itinerant peddler, Curt Mudspell, who turns out to be an modern equivalent of Pan, the god of the woods. He transports Clover back in time to 1815 where she experiences Vermont's worst year, when summer never came. She also discovers the harsh and powerful forces of nature that she and Jared naively seek to control.

Historical Accuracy: The novel offers some authentic looks at the region and its heritage during the memorable winter of 1815-1816.

PEARL S. BUCK (1892-1973)

Born in West Virginia, Buck grew up in China where her parents were missionaries. She was educated at Randolph Macon and Cornell but returned to China to be a missionary teacher at Chinese universities. Her best-known novel about China, *The Good Earth*, won the Pulitzer Prize in 1931. Buck won the Nobel Prize for Literature in 1938. In 1949 she founded Welcome House, which provides care for children of Asian women and American soldiers. The Pearl Buck Foundation, the recipient of all of her royalties, aids in the adoption of Amerasian children.

754 *The Good Earth*

Date of Publication: 1931
Subject(s): Rural Life—China; Chinese Empire
Fictional character(s): Wang Lung, Farmer; O-Lan, Slave; Lotus Blossom, Prostitute (concubine)
Time Period(s): 19th century
Locale(s): China

Summary: The trials of a farm family in rural China are dramatized as Wang Lung and a slave girl, O-Lan, struggle to survive on his farm and in the city. With stolen money Wang

Lung buys a mistress, Lotus Blossom. He repents his treatment of O-Lan on his deathbed.

Historical Accuracy: Buck's depiction of traditional Chinese life is authentic and free of moral judgment. The story accurately renders the personal and spiritual life of ordinary people.

755 *Imperial Woman*

Date of Publication: 1956
Subject(s): Boxer Rebellion; Royalty—China; Chinese Empire
Historical character(s): Tz'u-hsi, Ruler (Empress of China); Hsien Feng, Ruler (Emperor of China); Tung Chih, Ruler (Emperor of China); Kiwang Hsi, Ruler (Emperor of China); Li Lien Ying, Servant (court eunuch)
Time Period(s): 19th century; 20th century (1840-1908)
Locale(s): China

Summary: This biographical novel concerns the last Empress of China, T'zu-Hsi, and her attempt to preserve the Manchu dynasty. T'zu-Hsi is best known for her support of the Boxer Rebellion of 1900, but the novel traces the whole career of this remarkable woman, from her start as the favorite concubine of the Emperor Hsien Feng, through her reign as the empress of three emperors.

Historical Accuracy: The period and scene are richly detailed. The author's obvious preference for her central character, however, sacrifices some objectivity.

756 *The Living Reed*

Date of Publication: 1963
Subject(s): Family Saga; Independence—Korea; World War II
Fictional character(s): Kim Il-Han, Gentleman; Kim Yul-Chun, Revolutionary
Time Period(s): 19th century; 20th century (1881-1952)
Locale(s): Korea

Summary: Modern Korea from the closing days of the 19th century to the Korean War, is the subject of the author's story about four generations of the upperclass Kim family. The family's patriarch, Kim Il-Han, reflects the changes that beset his country, from the scramble for control by Russia, China, and Japan to the Japanese persecution and the Communist triumph in the north.

Historical Accuracy: The novel shows evidence of extensive research that included a trip by jeep through much of South Korea.

FERGUS REID BUCKLEY (1930-)

Born in Paris, Buckley graduated from Yale University. A successful businessman, he operated businesses in exports and travel in Madrid.

757 *Eye of the Hurricane*

Date of Publication: 1967
Subject(s): Sea Story; Fishing; Disasters—Natural

Fictional character(s): Jonathan Wright, Sailor, Fisherman; August Baxter, Sailor, Fisherman
Time Period(s): 19th century; 20th century (1898-1938)
Locale(s): Fair Haven, New York (on Long Island); Great South Bay, New York (on Long Island)

Summary: This massive saga of the sea and the fishing industry on Long Island concerns two rivals, Jonathan Wright and August Baxter, who both try to halt the changes that threaten their seagoing heritage as they battle their own demons. The adventure closes with the great hurricane of 1938.

Historical Accuracy: The novel's sense of both the time and the place is exact and convincing.

HENRIETTA BUCKMASTER
(PSEUD. OF HENRIETTA HENKLE STEPHENS, 1909-1983)

An American editor and writer born in Cleveland Ohio, Buckmaster is remembered for the highly acclaimed nonfiction work *Let My People Go: The Story of the Underground Railroad and the Growth of the Abolition Movement* She served on the staff of the Christian Science Monitor as the editor for the fine arts and literary page.

758   *All the Living: A Novel of One Year in the Life of William Shakespeare*

Date of Publication: 1962
Subject(s): Elizabethan Period; Theatrical Life; Biography, Fictionalized
Historical character(s): William Shakespeare, Writer
Time Period(s): 17th century (1600)
Locale(s): London, England

Summary: The novel reconstructs events in Elizabethan London of 1600 that involved William Shakespeare. In this fateful year, Shakespeare is most involved with the Dark Lady of his sonnets and, along with his company, participates in the political intrigue that ends with the execution of the Earl of Essex for treason in 1601. The experience sends Shakespeare back to his wife in Stratford.

Historical Accuracy: The novel's portrait of Elizabethan England is genuine, and the narrative observes the known facts, or at least plausible possibilities.

759   *And Walk on Love: A Novel Based on the Life of the Apostle Paul*

Date of Publication: 1956
Subject(s): Christianity; Religious Life; Biography, Fictionalized
Historical character(s): Paul, Biblical Figure
Time Period(s): 1st century (33-64 A.D.)
Locale(s): Middle East; Roman Empire

Summary: This fictional biography of St. Paul traces his career from the crucifixion of Christ to Paul's death. His missionary travels take him throughout the ancient world as the fundamentals of Christian theology emerge.

Historical Accuracy: The interpretation is not rigorously doctrinaire in its re-creation. The known facts are used to reach an original and believable interpretation of Paul's character and personality.

760   *Deep River*

Date of Publication: 1944
Subject(s): Antebellum South; Slavery
Fictional character(s): Simon Bliss, Landowner, Political Figure; Savanna Bliss, Spouse
Time Period(s): 1850s (1859)
Locale(s): Georgia

Summary: The conflict within Southern society over the issue of slavery is dramatized in this story set in Georgia during the 1850s. The novel explores the differences between the plantation Georgians, who see slavery as essential for their economy and culture, and the Georgia mountaineers, like the novel's hero, Simon Bliss, who are opposed to slavery. The focus is on Simon's plantation-born wife, Savanna, who is faced with conflicted loyalties.

Historical Accuracy: The novel features a convincing depiction of the region and the era.

761   *Fire in the Heart*

Date of Publication: 1948
Subject(s): Antebellum South; Theatrical Life; Victorian Period
Historical character(s): Fanny Kemble, Actress; Sarah Siddons, Actress; Pierce Butler, Plantation Owner
Time Period(s): 1830s; 1840s
Locale(s): London, England; Sea Islands, Georgia

Summary: English actress Fanny Kemble achieves theatrical success in Victorian London and makes an unsuccessful marriage to a Southern plantation owner. Kemble's opposition to slavery alienates her from her husband and her southern neighbors.

Historical Accuracy: The novel is faithful to Kemble's life and the events of her marriage.

FREDERICK BUECHNER (1926-)

Buechner was born in New York City and attended Princeton and Union Theological Seminary. He is an ordained Presbyterian minister. His works include *A Long Day's Dying*, *The Season's Difference*, and *The Book of Bebb*. He is also the author of collections of meditations and autobiographical studies.

762   *Brendan*

Date of Publication: 1987
Subject(s): Exploration; Religious Life; Dark Ages
Historical character(s): Brendan the Navigator, Religious, Explorer
Time Period(s): 5th century; 6th century
Locale(s): Ireland; At Sea

Summary: This novel chronicles the life of Brendan the Navigator, a priest and founder of many monasteries. He also made many voyages in search of Tir-Na-N-Og, the terrestrial paradise. Legend and speculation trace his voyages as far as Florida. Brendan is revealed as a complex individual; heroic yet filled with self-doubt.

Historical Accuracy: While most of the sources are legendary, the author shapes them into a convincing and brilliant re-creation of ancient Ireland.

763 *Godric*

Date of Publication: 1980
Subject(s): Middle Ages; Religious Life
Historical character(s): Godric, Religious, Recluse (hermit); Ranulf Flambard, Religious (bishop)
Time Period(s): 12th century
Locale(s): Finchale, England

Summary: Godric narrates the story of his life of varied occupations. He works as a peddler and a trader, then makes two pilgrimages, one to Rome and the other to Jerusalem. He ends his life as a hermit. Godric's story becomes an occasion for a religious exploration.

Historical Accuracy: Few historical novels succeed as well in capturing the thoughts of an individual in the past. Godric emerges as a totally believable character.

764 *The Son of Laughter*

Date of Publication: 1993
Subject(s): Biblical Story
Historical character(s): Jacob, Biblical Figure; Abraham, Biblical Figure; Joseph, Biblical Figure
Time Period(s): Indeterminate Past
Locale(s): Middle East

Summary: The novel offers a contemporary retelling of the Biblical story from Genesis of Abraham, Sarah, Isaac, and Joseph and his brothers. The story is narrated by Jacob who helps humanize the Biblical figures.

Historical Accuracy: This retelling is faithful to the Biblical original and elaborated with authentic details.

BARTLE BULL

Born in London, Bull has been a student of Africa for over 30 years. He is the author of the authoritative history of the African safari *Safari: A Chronicle of Adventure*. He is a lawyer, living in New York.

765 *The White Rhino Hotel*

Date of Publication: 1992
Subject(s): British Colonies
Fictional character(s): Olivio Fonseca Alavedo, Saloon Keeper/Owner; Alan Rider, Adventurer; Gwen Llewelyn, Young Woman
Time Period(s): 1910s; 1920s (1918-1920)
Locale(s): Kenya

Summary: In the aftermath of World War I, veterans and their families sail for Kenya to stake claims to estates of virgin land. The crossroads for many of them is the White Rhino Hotel that features a scheming bartender, Olivio Alavedo, and

a clientele seeking adventure and passion, including Alan Rider and Gwen Llewelyn.

Historical Accuracy: The novel is evocative of the period with a clear knowledge of the terrain.

EDWARD BULWER-LYTTON (1803-1873)

Bulwer-Lytton was an English author who was also a member of Parliament and secretary for the colonies, created Baron Lytton of Knebworth in 1866. A versatile author, he wrote, besides historical novels, novels of manners, a Utopian novel, ghost stories, and plays. In addition to the novels listed, notable works include *Pelham*, *Ernest Maltravers*, *The Caxtons*, *The Lady of Lyons*, and *Richelieu*.

766 *Eugene Aram*

Date of Publication: 1832
Subject(s): Crime and Criminals; Georgian Period
Fictional character(s): Houseman, Murderer; Madeline Lester, Gentlewoman
Historical character(s): Eugene Aram, Murderer, Teacher
Time Period(s): 1750s
Locale(s): Knaresborough, England (English town near York); York, England

Summary: The novel is based on the actual case of schoolmaster Eugene Aram who was tried and executed for murder. Bulwer-Lytton turns the historical Aram into a romantic figure wracked with guilt. He settles in a remote village and is on the verge of marrying when his accomplice reappears and betrays Aram.

Historical Accuracy: The novel can be grouped as one of the "Newgate Novels" celebrating crime and criminals, far more an idealization than an actual portrait of criminality.

767 *Harold, the Last of the Saxon Kings*

Date of Publication: 1848
Subject(s): Norman Conquest; Anglo-Saxon Period; Middle Ages
Historical character(s): Harold II, Ruler (King of England); William the Conqueror, Ruler (later William I); Edith the Fair, Noblewoman
Time Period(s): 11th century (1050-1066)
Locale(s): Hastings, England; Normandy, France

Summary: The novel concerns the final days of the reign of Edward the Confessor and the scramble for power after his death. Harold is the last of the Saxon Kings, and his career is dramatized up to his death at Hastings and William the Conqueror's triumph. Connected to these great historical events is the romantic story of Harold's love for Edith the Fair who for political reasons he does not marry.

Historical Accuracy: Edith did in fact visit the fallen Harold on the battlefield of Hastings but not to die beside him, only to identify the body.

768   *The Last Days of Pompeii*

Date of Publication: 1834
Subject(s): Roman Empire; Disasters—Natural
Fictional character(s): Glaucus, Young Man (Greek); Ione, Ward; Arbaces, Guardian; Nydia, Peddler (flowerseller), Handicapped (blind)
Time Period(s): 1st century (79)
Locale(s): Pompeii, Roman Empire

Summary: The novel takes place shortly before Pompeii's destruction in the eruption of Mount Vesuvius and centers on the love of two young Greeks, Glaucus and Ione, and the villainy of Arbaces, Ione's guardian.

Historical Accuracy: This is a highly-detailed and convincing picture of Roman life and times. There are exciting scenes of palace life, gladiatorial games, and ordinary life of the time before the catastrophe.

769   *The Last of the Barons*

Date of Publication: 1843
Subject(s): Royalty—England; War of the Roses; Witchcraft and Sorcery
Fictional character(s): Adam Warner, Philosopher, Inventor; Sibyll Warner, Young Woman; Friar Bungey, Religious, Astrologer
Historical character(s): Richard Neville, Nobleman (Earl of Warwick), Political Figure ("The Kingmaker"); Edward IV, Ruler (King of England); Henry VI, Ruler (King of England); Lord William Hastings, Nobleman
Time Period(s): 15th century (1467-1471)
Locale(s): London, England; Tewkesbury, England; France

Summary: The novel depicts the last years of the feudal period, following the War of the Roses and Edward IV's feud with Warwick, one of the last of the great feudal barons. Court and political intrigue and the Battle of Tewkesbury are interwoven with the tragic story of a poor philosopher-inventor and his daughter who are persecuted because of popular prejudice and superstition.

Historical Accuracy: The novel is a complex and fascinating drama of a turning point in England, richly packed with period details.

770   *Rienzi, or The Last of the Tribunes*

Date of Publication: 1835
Subject(s): Middle Ages
Fictional character(s): Walter de Montreal, Mercenary; Cecco del Vecchio, Blacksmith
Historical character(s): Cola di Rienzo, Political Figure (aka Rienzi)
Time Period(s): 14th century (1347-1354)
Locale(s): Rome, Italy

Summary: This novel chronicles the rise and fall of Italian Cola di Rienzi, Roman tribune who, in 1347, established a republic but was forced to abdicate. He later returned from exile only to be assassinated. Rienzi is presented in a fascinating portrait of an able politician crippled by arrogance and grandiosity.

Historical Accuracy: The novel follows the historical facts closely and gives a good depiction of the life and times of the period.

ANITA RICHMOND BUNKLEY

771   *Black Gold*

Date of Publication: 1994
Subject(s): Oil Industry; Racial Conflict
Fictional character(s): Leela Wilder, Orphan, Spouse; T.J. Wilder, Farmer; Carey Logan, Gambler; Victor Beaufort, Prospector (oil)
Time Period(s): 1920s
Locale(s): Texas

Summary: The novel's background is the Texas oil boom of the 1920s and the rarely depicted African-Americans whose lives were affected by the discovery of oil on their land. Leela Wilder is one of these. An orphan, she marries T.J. Wilder but loves Carey Logan, T.J.'s half-brother. When oil is discovered, the bank and drillers force Leela into a fight for her land. She turns to Victor Beaufort, the only black wildcatter in Texas.

Historical Accuracy: The period and the locale are authentically depicted.

LOLAH BURFORD (1931-)

Born in Dallas, Texas, Burford received her undergraduate degree from Bryn Mawr and an M.A. from S.M.U., where she was an instructor in the English department from 1954-1956.

772   *Edward, Edward*

Date of Publication: 1973
Subject(s): Picaresque Adventure; Homosexuality; Napoleonic Wars
Fictional character(s): James Noel Holland, Nobleman (Earl of Tyne); Edward Clare, Ward
Historical character(s): George, Royalty (prince); John Wesley, Religious (Methodist leader); George Bryan Brummell, Gentleman
Time Period(s): 18th century; 19th century (1795-1816)
Locale(s): Northumberland, England; London, England; Vienna, Austria

Summary: This picaresque tale is the story of the strange romance between James Holland, the Earl of Tyne, and his young ward Edward. Educated at Oxford and fitted out to make his mark on London society by Beau Brummell himself, Edward must contend with a relationship with his guardian that is both illicit and, as it turns out, incestuous. The result is a breakdown and recovery in Vienna.

Historical Accuracy: The period details are remarkably well-developed.

773   *MacLyon*

Date of Publication: 1974
Subject(s): American Colonies; Jacobite Rebellion

Fictional character(s): Diarmid MacLyon, Gentleman; Mary Elisabeth Grant, Gentlewoman
Time Period(s): 1740s (1746-1748)
Locale(s): Highlands, Scotland; Georgia, American Colonies

Summary: Diarmid MacLyon abducts and marries Mary Elisabeth Grant. His father disapproves and disowns him. Diarmid is arrested by the king's soldiers and transported to the Georgia colony as an indentured servant. Incredibly, Mary Elisabeth follows him, using her beauty to gain information on her husband's whereabouts.

Historical Accuracy: The picture of Scotland and the Georgia colony are based on documented sources. The heroine's devotion to her caddish husband is implausible.

`774` *Vice Avenged: A Moral Tale*

Date of Publication: 1971
Subject(s): Gambling; Georgian Period
Fictional character(s): Bysshe Gore, Nobleman (marquis), Rake; Cressida Salisbury, Gentlewoman; Duke of Salisbury, Nobleman
Time Period(s): 18th century
Locale(s): England

Summary: Bysshe Gore makes a wager that he can ravish any virgin from a good family. Chosen by lot, his victim is Cressida, daughter of the Duke of Salisbury. Gore wins the wager but does not anticipate the cunning actions of the duke, and retribution and expiation take their course.

Historical Accuracy: Although the author calls the novel unrealistic, the sorts of wagers depicted are unfortunately based on fact.

`775` *The Vision of Stephen: An Elegy*

Date of Publication: 1972
Subject(s): Dark Ages; Victorian Period; Time Travel
Fictional character(s): Stephen, Royalty (prince); Margery, Child
Time Period(s): 7th century (674); 1820s (1822)
Locale(s): Northumbria, England

Summary: In this historical fantasy, Stephen is a young prince from the 7th century who is transported in time to 1822 and becomes involved in the life of an English family. The juxtaposition allows for an examination of the two eras and a contrast of life styles, customs, and beliefs.

Historical Accuracy: The author convinces with the details of both eras.

ANTHONY BURGESS
(PSEUD. OF JOHN BURGESS WILSON, 1917-1993)

English writer, critic, and intellectual, Burgess was born in Manchester and attended Manchester University. He began his writing career while teaching English in the British colony of Malaya. His most popular novel is *A Clockwork Orange*. Burgess claimed that he tried to bring a variety of subject matter into fiction as well as exploit words and language.

`776` *A Dead Man in Deptford*

Date of Publication: 1993
Subject(s): Elizabethan Period; Espionage; Theatrical Life
Historical character(s): Christopher Marlowe, Writer, Spy; Thomas Kyd, Writer; William Shakespeare, Writer, Actor; Sir Walter Raleigh, Gentleman, Courtier; Robert Devereux, Nobleman (Earl of Essex)
Time Period(s): 16th century (1593)
Locale(s): London, England

Summary: The short and ultimately tragic life of Elizabethan poet and playwright Christopher Marlowe is dramatized. Burgess offers both a panoramic portrait of the age as well as an informed speculation about Marlowe who is shown seduced into the devious world of Elizabethan espionage that leads to his murder in a Deptford tavern.

Historical Accuracy: The author asserts that all the historical facts are verifiable, yet the truth about Marlowe's end and his espionage work is shrouded in controversy and is ultimately speculative.

`777` *The End of the World News*

Date of Publication: 1983
Subject(s): Fantasy
Historical character(s): Sigmund Freud, Doctor (psychiatrist); Leon Trotsky, Revolutionary; Carl Jung, Doctor (psychiatrist)
Time Period(s): 1910s (1917)
Locale(s): Vienna, Austria; New York, New York

Summary: Burgess weaves three stories in this novel: the life of Sigmund Freud, Trotsky's visit to New York, and the future destruction of the earth from the distant galaxy of Lynx. Burgess believes that Freud's discovery of the unconscious, Trotsky's vision of a socialist state, and humanity's first steps into outer space are the greatest events of the 20th century. The novel offers a dramatic meditation on all three.

Historical Accuracy: Inventive and erudite, the novel is a fantasy with a core of historical background.

`778` *The Kingdom of the Wicked*

Date of Publication: 1985
Subject(s): Roman Empire; Christianity; Jews
Fictional character(s): Sadoc, Writer
Historical character(s): Jesus Christ, Biblical Figure, Religious (teacher); Tiberius, Ruler (Roman emperor); Caligula, Ruler (Roman emperor); Nero, Ruler (Roman emperor); Herod Agrippa I, Ruler (King of Judea); Peter, Biblical Figure; Paul, Biblical Figure; Pontius Pilate, Government Official (procurator of Jerusalem), Biblical Figure; Lucius Annaeus Seneca, Writer (playwright), Philosopher; Vespasian, Ruler (Roman emperor)
Time Period(s): 1st century (33-80)
Locale(s): Israel; Roman Empire

Summary: The conflict between Christianity and the Roman Empire is chronicled by an aging and pessimistic shipping clerk. He records with unflinching honesty the birth and growth of Christianity beginning with the resurrection of Jesus. The novel's range is dizzying, as it catalogues all the major players from the disciples to the Caesars.

Historical Accuracy: The author's evident research and erudition do not detract from the narrative. The era and the issues of church and state are brought to dramatic life.

779 *Man of Nazareth*

Date of Publication: 1979
Subject(s): Biblical Story; Roman Empire; Biography, Fictionalized
Historical character(s): Jesus Christ, Biblical Figure, Religious (teacher); Mary, Biblical Figure; Joseph, Biblical Figure; Herod the Great, Ruler (King of Judea); Pontius Pilate, Government Official (procurator of Jerusalem); Peter, Biblical Figure; Judas Iscariot, Biblical Figure
Time Period(s): 1st century
Locale(s): Jerusalem, Israel; Nazareth, Israel

Summary: This is the novelization of Burgess' screenplay for the Franco Zeffirelli television production, ''Jesus of Nazareth,'' which attracted one of the largest audiences in television history when it was first broadcast. Burgess' version of the well-known story of Jesus' birth, childhood, ministry, and death is narrated with verve in a succession of memorable scenes.

Historical Accuracy: Burgess' grasp of period detail and events is impressive and convincing.

780 *Napoleon Symphony*

Date of Publication: 1974
Subject(s): Napoleonic Era; Royalty—France
Historical character(s): Napoleon I, Ruler (Emperor of France), Military Personnel (French commander); Josephine, Royalty (consort of Napoleon); Antoine Gros, Artist; Alexander I, Ruler (Czar of Russia); Charles Maurice de Talleyrand-Perigord, Diplomat, Government Official
Time Period(s): 18th century; 19th century (1796-1821)
Locale(s): Paris, France; Europe (Italy, Austria, Russia, Prussia); Egypt

Summary: The career of Napoleon is dramatized not as an epic but as a comic symphony in four movements. The tale moves from Napoleon's first campaigns, through marriage, power, and exile, to final defeat and death. A chorus of voices captures the era and the emperor whose exuberance and audacity make for a virtuoso performance.

Historical Accuracy: Endlessly inventive, Burgess' picture is comically exaggerated, more like an opera performance than history. Its essence is nonetheless revealing and convincing.

781 *Nothing Like the Sun*

Date of Publication: 1967
Subject(s): Elizabethan Period; Theatrical Life; Biography, Fictionalized
Historical character(s): William Shakespeare, Writer, Actor; Anne Hathaway, Spouse; Richard Burbage, Actor; Will Kempe, Actor; Richard Alleyne, Actor
Time Period(s): 16th century (1570s-1599)
Locale(s): Stratford-on-Avon, England; London, England

Summary: In Burgess' fictionalized life of William Shakespeare, the emphasis is on Shakespeare's love life, considered the inspiration for his poetry and the basis for his tragedies. We follow the poet from his days in Stratford and his first love to the forced and loveless marriage to Ann Hathaway. His move to London and the stage and the unleashing of his literary passion are also described.

Historical Accuracy: Few writers other than Burgess could imitate so well the language and poetic vision of Shakespeare. The speculation here is backed by the author's authoritative ability to render the period and the personalities.

JACKSON BURGESS (1927-)

Born in Atlanta, Georgia, Burgess graduated from the University of Chicago and the University of North Carolina. He is a professor of English at the University of California, Berkeley.

782 *Pillar of Cloud*

Date of Publication: 1957
Subject(s): American West
Fictional character(s): Garvin Cooper, Settler; Bob McVey, Settler; Ned Drum, Guide
Time Period(s): 1850s (1858)
Locale(s): Kansas

Summary: Persuaded by their guide Ned Drum, two young men, Garvin Cooper and Bob McVey, set out on a new trail West between the Sante Fe trail to the south and the Oregon trail to the north. The frontier take its terrible toll and tests the character of each of the travellers.

Historical Accuracy: The novel's portrait of the western plains is vivid and convincing.

MALLORY BURGESS

783 *Ballenrose*

Date of Publication: 1991
Subject(s): Romance
Fictional character(s): Molly Flowers, Young Woman; Ballenrose, Gentleman
Historical character(s): George Villiers, Nobleman (Duke of Buckingham), Courtier
Time Period(s): 17th century
Locale(s): London, England

Summary: In this rag to riches romantic story, flowergirl Molly Flowers is taken in by the Duke of Buckingham as his long lost niece, Lady Mary Catherine Villiers. Molly is thrust into 17th-century society. But all is not what it seems, and Molly and Ballenrose, the man she loves, must contend with Buckingham's intrigues.

Historical Accuracy: The story is fanciful and rather far-fetched, more costume drama than a carefully detailed historical novel.

COLIN BURKE (1936-)

An American professor of history, Burke was born in San Francisco and attended San Francisco State University and Washington University.

784 *Kimberley*

Date of Publication: 1985
Subject(s): Boer War
Fictional character(s): Emma Stevenson, Spouse; Geoffrey Stevenson, Military Personnel; Bart Bannock, Horse Trainer
Time Period(s): 1890s; 1900s (1899-1900)
Locale(s): Kimberley, South Africa

Summary: This romantic adventure is set during the siege of Kimberley during the Boer War. Emma Stevenson is trapped in a stifling marriage to war hero Geoffrey, while attracted to the horse trainer Bart Bannock. The novel's romance climaxes as the siege tightens.

Historical Accuracy: The details of the siege and the period are solidly presented.

BRIAN BURLAND (1931-)

Born in Bermuda, Burland attended the University of Western Ontario. After serving as the company director of his family's business in Bermuda, Burland became a full-time writer. He is the author of The Bermudians novel series that includes *A Fall From Aloft*, which was nominated for an American Academy of Arts and Letters Award.

785 *Surprise*

Date of Publication: 1974
Subject(s): Slavery; Racial Conflict; Sea Story
Fictional character(s): Surprise Billinghurst, Sailor
Time Period(s): 1840s (1842-1844)
Locale(s): Bermuda; West Indies

Summary: Surprise Billinghurst, a black seaman from Bermuda, builds a small ship and, with his wife, child, and a small crew, sails to an uninhabited island and creates a settlement. Two years later, the British send a warship to put down this rebellion and the blacks' proclaimed republic.

Historical Accuracy: The story of the British repression of the black population on Bermuda is authentic as are the details of nautical life of the period.

FRANK BURLESON

786 *Desert Hawks*

Date of Publication:
Subject(s): Indians; American West; Revolution—Mexico
Fictional character(s): Nathanial Barrington, Military Personnel (lieutenant)
Historical character(s): Mangas Coloradas, Indian (Apache), Chieftain
Time Period(s): 1840s (1846)
Locale(s): Southwest

Summary: In the first novel of the author's Apache Wars Saga, Nathanial Barrington is a young lieutenant thrust into the conflict both with Mexico and with the Apaches.

Historical Accuracy: The fictional story captures the era and details of frontier life with conviction.

787 *Savage Frontier*

Date of Publication: 1995
Subject(s): American West; Indians
Fictional character(s): Nathanial Barrington, Military Personnel (lieutenant)
Time Period(s): 1850s (1854)
Locale(s): Southwest

Summary: In the third volume of the author's Apache Wars trilogy, Nathanial Barrington faces his severest test as a new generation of Apache leaders mount a growing resistance.

Historical Accuracy: Although the emphasis is on fast-paced action, the background of frontier life of the period is genuine.

788 *War Eagles*

Date of Publication: 1995
Subject(s): American West; Indians
Fictional character(s): Nathanial Barrington, Military Personnel (lieutenant); Jocita, Indian (Apache), Warrior
Historical character(s): Mangas Coloradas, Indian (Apache), Chieftain
Time Period(s): 1850s (1851)
Locale(s): Southwest; Santa Fe, New Mexico

Summary: In the second volume of the author's Apache Wars trilogy, First Lieutenant Nathanial Barrington faces his first test as a professional soldier in an undeclared war against the Apaches. He meets his match in a Apache woman warrior, Jocita.

Historical Accuracy: The novel is atmospheric and convincing in its details of military and frontier life.

ROGER BURLINGAME (1889-1967)

An American writer born in New York City, Burlingame graduated from Harvard and studied at the Sorbonne. He worked as a book editor at Scribner's and was the author of novels and histories, including *Benjamin Franklin, the First American*.

789 *Whittling Boy: The Story of Eli Whitney*

Date of Publication: 1941
Subject(s): Biography, Fictionalized; Inventions
Historical character(s): Eli Whitney, Inventor
Time Period(s): 18th century; 19th century
Locale(s): Massachusetts; Connecticut

Summary: This biographical novel based on the life of Eli Whitney shows his development from his youth as a Massachusetts farmboy to his achievements as an inventor. His invention of the cotton gin revolutionizes agricultural production. Later Whitney's firearms company is the first manufacturer to utilize interchangeable parts which paves the way for modern industrial mass production.

Historical Accuracy: This is a serviceable and faithful biographical treatment of Whitney's career and achievements.

EDWARD BURMAN (1947-)

Burman was born in England and educated at the University of Leeds. He worked as a lecturer at the University of Rome before turning to writing full time. A strong interest in music and poetry led to his desire to write. He is interested in all things medieval, especially architecture.

790   *The Image of Our Lord*

Date of Publication: 1990
Subject(s): Middle Ages; Religious Life; Religious Conflict
Fictional character(s): Jacques Fournier, Religious (inquisitor, monk); Nicholas Lirey, Nobleman, Heir—Dispossessed; Pietro di Ocre, Religious (Knight Templar)
Historical character(s): Philip the Fair, Ruler (King of France); Clement VII, Religious (pope)
Time Period(s): 14th century
Locale(s): Avignon, France; Paris, France; Italy

Summary: Jacques Fournier, a young monk, is sent by his patron to interrogate Pietro di Ocre, once a leading figure in the secretive Knights Templars. Fournier is joined by dispossessed aristocrat Nicholas de Lirey. They learn of a hidden relic, the Shroud of Turin, which could upset the balance of power in Europe.

Historical Accuracy: The novel is exact in its history and convincing in its depiction of the era.

WILLIAM R. BURNETT (1899-1982)

Novelist and screenwriter Burnett was born in Springfield, Ohio, and attended the Miami Military Institute and Ohio University. After early attempts at vaudeville and professional boxing, Burnett became a factory shop steward, an insurance salesman, and a statistician for the Ohio Department of Labor Relations. He received Academy Award nominations for his screenplays *Wake Island* and *The Great Escape*. *The Great Escape* also won the Edgar Allen Poe award and the Screen Writers award for best drama. His novels *High Sierra* and *The Asphalt Jungle* were adapted by him for the screen. Both films were named among the ten best films of the year they were released.

791   *Adobe Walls: A Novel of the Last Apache Rising*

Date of Publication: 1953
Subject(s): American West; Indians
Fictional character(s): Walter Grein, Scout
Time Period(s): 1880s (1886)
Locale(s): Arizona

Summary: The story of the Apache uprising in 1886 is dramatized through the experiences of Walter Grein, chief of scouts.

The novel shows a great familiarity with the southwestern territory and the customs of the Apaches.

Historical Accuracy: The basis for the novel's situation is historical and accurately presented.

792   *Captain Lightfoot*

Date of Publication: 1954
Subject(s): Crime and Criminals
Fictional character(s): John "Thunderbolt" Doherty, Highwayman; Michael Martin, Young Man
Time Period(s): 18th century
Locale(s): Ireland; Scotland

Summary: The life and adventures of an Irish highwayman in the 18th century are detailed. Young Michael Martin is renamed Captain Lightfoot by the notorious criminal John "Thunderbolt" Doherty, who introduces the young man into criminal life in a series of exploits.

Historical Accuracy: The author admits to a number of historical inaccuracies which are of little consequence in this entertaining adventure yarn.

793   *The Dark Command*

Date of Publication: 1938
Subject(s): Slavery; Civil War—U.S.
Fictional character(s): John Seton, Young Man; Mary McCloud, Young Woman
Time Period(s): 1860s
Locale(s): Ohio; Kansas

Summary: This adventure novel is set against the backdrop of the Free Soilers' fight against the pro-slavery forces in Kansas before and during the Civil War. The novel features the activities of Quantrill's guerrillas and the burning of Lawrence, Kansas.

Historical Accuracy: The story's period and regional background is authentic and believable.

794   *The Goldseekers*

Date of Publication: 1962
Subject(s): Gold Rush—Klondike
Fictional character(s): Jim Hardy, Prospector; Hoxie Thicke, Prospector
Time Period(s): 1890s (1896-1897)
Locale(s): Alaska; Seattle, Washington

Summary: In 1896, two young men, Jim Hardy and Hoxie Thicke, journey from Ohio to the Alaskan gold fields with a group of men stricken with gold fever. They are thrust into a series of adventures.

Historical Accuracy: The novel effectively creates a picture of the era and the Alaskan scene.

795   *Mi Amigo*

Date of Publication: 1959
Subject(s): American West; Indians; Military Life—U.S. Cavalry
Fictional character(s): John Desportes, Military Personnel (sergeant), Scout; Bud Smith, Teenager

Time Period(s): 19th century
Locale(s): Southwest

Summary: This tale of the Southwest describes the relationship between veteran cavalry sergeant John Desportes and teenager Bud Smith. Their respective mettle is tested against the threat posed by the Apaches.

Historical Accuracy: The novel provides an authentic portrait of period and regional life.

796 *Saint Johnson*

Date of Publication: 1930
Subject(s): American West; Crime and Criminals
Fictional character(s): Wayt Johnson, Lawman; Brant White, Gunfighter, Gambler
Time Period(s): 1880s
Locale(s): Tombstone, Arizona

Summary: This western tale offers a fictional version of the famous Earp-Clanton feud that culminates in the gunfight at the OK Corral. In this version Wayt Johnson is based on Wyatt Earp and Brant White on Doc Holliday.

Historical Accuracy: The story is faithful to the events in Tombstone during the period.

OLIVE ANN BURNS (1930-1990)

An American author born in Georgia, Burns received her B.A. degree from the University of North Carolina at Chapel Hill. She has worked as a writer and journalist. It was after being diagnosed with cancer that she decided to begin the novel which became *Cold Sassy Tree*. It took her eight and a half years to complete while she battled the effects of chemotherapy.

797 *Cold Sassy Tree*

Date of Publication: 1984
Subject(s): Family Saga; Rural Life—U.S.
Fictional character(s): Will Tweedy Blakeslee, Teenager; E. Rucker Blakeslee, Veteran (Confederate), Store Owner; Love Simpson Blakeslee, Spouse (of E. Rucker)
Time Period(s): 1900s (1906-1907)
Locale(s): Cold Sassy, Georgia

Summary: The novel offers a comic and passionate portrait of small-town southern life through the voice of adolescent Will Tweedy. A family crisis occurs when Will's grandfather marries a young woman three weeks after the death of his first wife. This May-December romance affects the entire Blakeslee family and the whole town of Cold Sassy.

Historical Accuracy: The novel offers an accurate sense of small-town southern life at the turn of the century.

798 *Leaving Cold Sassy*

Date of Publication: 1992
Subject(s): Family Saga; Rural Life—U.S.
Fictional character(s): Will Tweedy Blakeslee, Young Man; Sanna Klein, Teacher
Time Period(s): 1910s (1917)

Locale(s): Cold Sassy, Georgia

Summary: In this unfinished sequel to *Cold Sassy Tree*, it is 1917 and Will Tweedy is 25. He is about to fall in love with school teacher Sanna Klein, and grapples with the changes that have taken place in his hometown. The novel follows Will and Sanna's relationship up to the beginning of their married life.

Historical Accuracy: The author has been justly praised for her ability to animate the past and present a compelling and convincing portrait of small-town southern life.

PATRICIA BURNS

799 *Kezzy*

Date of Publication: 1988
Subject(s): Railroads; Romance; Stagecoaches
Fictional character(s): Daniel Pyner, Heir; Keziah Heath, Servant; Laura Harris, Gentlewoman
Time Period(s): 1820s (1821)
Locale(s): England

Summary: Daniel Pyner, heir to his father's coaching company, understands that he must accommodate the burgeoning railroad in order to salvage the company. His soulmate, Kezzy, is a young servant who also wants to better herself. Pyner has even grander plans regarding Laura Harris, daughter of the owner of Upthorpe Hall.

Historical Accuracy: The novel is filled with vivid historical details of England adjusting to the modern world of steam.

800 *Stacey's Flyer*

Date of Publication: 1986
Subject(s): Stagecoaches; Romance; Business Building
Fictional character(s): Stacey Brown, Young Woman; Simon Keating, Young Man
Time Period(s): 19th century
Locale(s): England

Summary: Stacey Brown is the daughter of a man who runs a stagecoach out of Norwich, England. She is anxious to join him in running the company, but finds her place taken by Simon Keating, who becomes a bitter rival. Romance and adventure culminate in a thrilling race, the outcome of which will decide the fate of the company.

Historical Accuracy: The novel offers some interesting looks at the customs of England's coaching days.

RON BURNS

801 *Enslaved*

Date of Publication: 1994
Subject(s): Mystery; Slavery; Earthquakes
Fictional character(s): Harrison Hull, Military Personnel (army officer), Explorer
Historical character(s): Thomas Jefferson, Political Figure
Time Period(s): 1810s
Locale(s): Virginia; Kentucky; Missouri

Summary: Army officer and explorer Harrison Hull is asked by former president Thomas Jefferson to investigate the disappearance of two slaves from his nephew's Kentucky plantation. Hull uncovers a complex tangle of corruption and betrayal, marauding outlaws, and a set of discoveries that will become a rallying cry for the early abolitionists.

Historical Accuracy: Although the central character is invented, and the story has been embellished and expanded, the basic facts of the case are true.

802 The Mysterious Death of Meriwether Lewis

Date of Publication: 1993
Subject(s): Mystery; War of 1812
Fictional character(s): Harrison Hull, Military Personnel (army captain), Explorer
Historical character(s): Meriwether Lewis, Explorer; John James Audubon, Naturalist (ornithologist), Artist (illustrator); Alexander Wilson, Naturalist (ornithologist)
Time Period(s): 1810s (1810-1812)
Locale(s): Tennessee; St. Louis, Missouri

Summary: The death of Meriwether Lewis in a rustic inn while on his way to meet President James Madison is the occasion for this mystery. Lewis' friend Alexander Wilson and the explorer and army captain Harrison Hull attempt to solve the mystery. Ruling out suicide, they uncover a wide-ranging conspiracy with murder at its starting point.

Historical Accuracy: The novel is firmly grounded in historical fact, and the surmises are plausible, if inventive.

803 Roman Nights

Date of Publication: 1991
Subject(s): Roman Empire; Politics; Mystery
Fictional character(s): Livinius Severus, Lawyer, Detective—Private
Historical character(s): Lucius Aelius Aurelius Commodus, Royalty (emperor designate); Marcus Aurelius, Ruler (emperor); Galen, Doctor
Time Period(s): 2nd century (180)
Locale(s): Rome, Roman Empire

Summary: Livinius Severus, a stoic and respected lawyer, serves the philosopher-emperor Marcus Aurelius. He finds himself thrust into the intrigue that surrounds Rome and threatens to plunge it into violence and debauchery. Severus embarks on a hopeless quest to stop a rush to anarchy and the dissolution of the empire.

Historical Accuracy: The novel is a convincing evocation of the period. The author's careful research into Roman customs, Roman places, and events of the time are apparent.

804 Roman Shadows

Date of Publication: 1992
Subject(s): Roman Empire; Mystery
Fictional character(s): Livinius Severus, Political Figure (senator)

Historical character(s): Marcus Tullius Cicero, Political Figure, Philosopher; Augustus, Ruler (Roman emperor); Gaius Scribonius Curio, Political Figure
Time Period(s): 1st century B.C. (50-43 B.C.)
Locale(s): Roman Empire

Summary: Emperor Augustus has asked Gaius Severus, a close friend of Cicero, what he knows of certain events which occured nine years earlier. Severus' account details a complex mystery, the solution of which determines the future of Rome.

Historical Accuracy: The novel offers a remarkably detailed and authentic re-creation of ancient Rome.

JOHN BURRESS

805 Bugle in the Wilderness

Date of Publication: 1958
Subject(s): Civil War—U.S.
Fictional character(s): Billy Goforth, Teenager
Time Period(s): 1860s
Locale(s): Missouri

Summary: This story dramatizes life on the Missouri frontier during the Civil War. Billy Goforth has a mother who has lost her mind from an accident and a father whose drinking and carousing hide a deep secret. Billy struggles to keep the family together in the face of overwhelming odds.

Historical Accuracy: The novel features an authentic regional background.

EDGAR RICE BURROUGHS (1875-1950)

American publisher and author Edgar Rice Burroughs was born in Chicago, Illinois, and attended the Michigan Military Academy. He served in the U.S. Cavalry from 1896 to 1897. Best known as the creator of Tarzan, one of the most enduring characters of popular adventure fiction, Burroughs achieved such success that he was able to found his own publishing company and motion picture studio.

806 Apache Devil

Date of Publication: 1933
Subject(s): American West; Indians
Fictional character(s): Shoz-Dijiji, Indian (Apache), Warrior; Wichita Billings, Young Woman
Historical character(s): Geronimo, Indian (Apache), Chieftain
Time Period(s): 1880s
Locale(s): Southwest

Summary: This sequel to *The War Chief* describes the last days of Apache freedom during Geronimo's final campaigns before his surrender to General Nelson Miles at Skeleton Canyon in 1886. The novel continues the story of the white infant adopted by Geronimo and named Shoz-Dijiji, and his relationship with Wichita Billings.

Historical Accuracy: The final pursuit of Geronimo is faithful to historical facts.

807 *I Am a Barbarian*

Date of Publication: 1967
Subject(s): Roman Empire
Fictional character(s): Brittanicus, Slave
Historical character(s): Caligula, Ruler (Roman emperor)
Time Period(s): 1st century (16-41)
Locale(s): Rome, Roman Empire

Summary: This adventure tale set during the reign of Caligula is told from the point of view of a young English slave, Brittanicus, who grows up with the notorious emperor.

Historical Accuracy: The novel's dates and historical events are accurate, though the modernized colloquialisms of the language have a jarring quality.

WILLIAM S. BURROUGHS (1914-)

Born in St. Louis, Missouri, and descended on his mother's side from Civil War general Robert E. Lee, Burroughs was educated at Harvard University, the University of Vienna, and Mexico City College. His career has included stints as an advertising copywriter, a bartender, an exterminator, and a private detective. Burroughs embodies for many the archetypal artist as outsider and rebel. He has had a major influence as one of the Beat generation of writers. His most famous novel is *Naked Lunch*.

808 *The Place of Dead Roads*

Date of Publication: 1983
Subject(s): American West; Fantasy
Fictional character(s): Kim Carsons, Adventurer, Writer
Time Period(s): 19th century (1849-1899)
Locale(s): Colorado

Summary: The novel opens with a gunfight in 1899 in Boulder, Colorado. One of the participants writes novels under the pen name Kim Carsons, and the novel follows him from his boyhood days to the fateful gunfight half a century later. Carsons' picaresque story is twisted in characteristic Burroughs fashion into a strange meditation on good versus evil.

Historical Accuracy: The West in this novel is largely a symbol for some time-bending fantasy.

PHILIP BURTON (1904-)

The foster father of actor Richard Burton, Philip Burton was born in Wales and graduated with high honors in pure mathematics and history from the University of Wales. He was a senior master at a secondary school in Port Talbot, Wales, served in the RAF during World War II, and went on to direct, act in, and lecture on theatrical works. Burton was a founding member of the British Drama Board and a member of the Order of the British Empire. He is the author of four books and has written more than 100 scripts for the BBC.

809 *You, My Brother*

Date of Publication: 1973

Subject(s): Elizabethan Period; Theatrical Life
Fictional character(s): Edward Shakespeare, Actor
Historical character(s): William Shakespeare, Writer, Actor; Ben Jonson, Writer; Elizabeth I, Ruler (Queen of England); Robert Devereux, Nobleman (Earl of Essex)
Time Period(s): 16th century; 17th century (1596-1606)
Locale(s): London, England; Stratford-on-Avon, England

Summary: This richly textured and solidly researched novel details the relationship between William Shakespeare and his younger brother Edward. Shakespeare is at the peak of his fame when Edward convinces him to allow Edward to become an apprentice at the Globe Theatre. Edward joins the company and is plunged into the complex world of the theater, court, and rivalry with his famous sibling.

Historical Accuracy: The novel is authentic in its depiction of the period and masterful in its knowledge of both the theater and Shakespeare.

IAN BURUMA (1951-)

Dutch writer Buruma was born in The Hague and graduated from Leiden University. He has worked as the cultural editor for *Far Eastern Economic Review*. His book *Behind the Masks* looks at the fantasy life of the Japanese and how it reflects Japanese society.

810 *Playing the Game*

Date of Publication: 1991
Subject(s): Victorian Period; Sports; British Raj
Historical character(s): Benjamin Disraeli, Political Figure; Oscar Wilde, Writer; K.S. Ranjitsinhji, Sports Figure (cricketer)
Time Period(s): 19th century
Locale(s): England; India

Summary: This hybrid novel offers in part a fictional autobiography of K.S. Ranjitsinhji, the great Indian cricketer who dominated English cricket at the end of the 19th century. The other half of the novel is the author's search for traces of Ranjitsinhji, who ruled the princely state of Nawanagar. The novel provides the opportunity to explore Anglo-Indian relations in the context of England's most famous sport.

Historical Accuracy: The novel's imagined conversations between Ranjitsinhji, Disraeli, and Wilde are fanciful. Historical chronology does not allow even the possibility of such a meeting.

FREDERICK BUSCH (1941-)

Busch was born in Brooklyn, New York, and graduated from Muhlenberg College and Columbia University. He is a professor of English at Colgate University and the author of a number of highly-regarded novels and short story collections, including *Manual Labor*, *Harry and Catherine*, *Closing Arguments*, and *Too Late American Boyhood Blues*.

811 *The Mutual Friend*

Date of Publication: 1975

Subject(s): Literary Life; Victorian Period; Biography, Fictionalized
Historical character(s): Charles Dickens, Writer; George Dolby, Manager; Ellen Ternan, Actress
Time Period(s): 19th century
Locale(s): United States; England

Summary: This imaginative biographical reconstruction of the life of Charles Dickens is directed by George Dolby, the manager for Dickens' final tour of America. Scenes from Dickens' past provide a psychological profile of the inimitable author, as well as the time period. Dickens' genius is joined with his obsessions to create a fully-realized portrait.

Historical Accuracy: The novel's background is convincing in its documentation of elements from Dickens' life combined with a good deal of imaginative elaboration.

NIVEN BUSCH (1903-1991)

An American film producer, educator, rancher, journalist, screenwriter, and novelist, Busch was born in New York City and attended Princeton University. He is best known for his screenplays, some of which became classic Hollywood films, and for his novels, such as *Duel in the Sun*, which were successfully adapted for films. Among his novels are *The Furies*, *The Hate Merchant*, and *Continent's Edge*.

812   *Duel in the Sun*

Date of Publication: 1944
Subject(s): American West; Ranching
Fictional character(s): Jesse McConles, Rancher; Pearl Chavez, Young Woman
Time Period(s): 1880s
Locale(s): Texas

Summary: This western tale is set in the Texas frontier during the 1880s and concerns the conflict of the cattlemen against incursion by the railroad and the homesteaders.

Historical Accuracy: The novel offers a genuine evocation of place and the period.

ADELYN BUSHNELL (1834-)

Born in Maine, Bushnell has been an actress, writer, and director for vaudeville headliners and radio stars. She is the author of a play, *I, Myself*.

813   *Tide-Rode*

Date of Publication: 1947
Subject(s): Sea Story
Fictional character(s): Caleb Dow, Sea Captain; Delight Dow, Spouse; John Dow, Young Man
Time Period(s): 1870s
Locale(s): Tranquility, Maine; *Sophronia*, At Sea

Summary: In the 1870s the Dow family is dominated by Captain Caleb Dow. He forces his son John to go to sea and forces his daughter into an unwanted marriage. Conflict both at sea and at home forms the novel's domestic drama.

Historical Accuracy: The novel offers some convincing period details of the region.

OSWALD ANDREW BUSHNELL
(1913-)

Bushnell is a novelist and historian of Hawaii. *The Return of Lono* concerns Captain Cook's last voyage. *Ka'a'awa* is the story of Hawaii from the 1850s to the 1890s. *The Gifts of Civilization: Germs and Genocide in Hawaii* is set in 18th and 19th century Hawaii.

814   *Ka'a'awa: A Novel about Hawaii in the 1850s*

Date of Publication: 1972
Subject(s): Royalty—Hawaii; Tribal Life—Hawaiian
Fictional character(s): Hiram Nihoa, Spy; Saul Bristol, Settler
Historical character(s): Kamehameha III, Ruler (King of Hawaii)
Time Period(s): 1850s (1853)
Locale(s): Oahu, Hawaii

Summary: The novel presents two related stories of Hawaii during the 1850s. In the first, Hawaiian Hiram Nihoa is asked by King Kamehameha III to investigate rumors that Californian filibusters are planning to invade the island. The second is the story of New Englander Saul Bristol, who attempts to save the people in the valley of Ka'a'awe from the first epidemic of smallpox to reach Hawaii.

Historical Accuracy: The novel presents a faithful version of Hawaii during the period.

815   *Molokai*

Date of Publication: 1963
Subject(s): Medical Profession; Religious Life
Fictional character(s): Dr. Newman, Doctor; Keanu, Convict; Caleb, Invalid (leper)
Historical character(s): Joseph de Veuster, Religious (priest)
Time Period(s): 1870s
Locale(s): Molokai, Hawaii

Summary: The novel depicts life in the Hawaiian leper colony of Molokai and the work of Belgian missionary Father Damien. The events are told from multiple points of view, including those of Dr. Newman, a medical expert seeking the cure for leprosy, Keanu, a condemned criminal who agrees to Dr. Newman's medical experiments; and the leper Caleb.

Historical Accuracy: The Hawaii scene is depicted convincingly. The novel provides a realistic picture of island life and of Father Damien, who often receives legendary treatment.

816   *The Return of Lono: A Novel of Captain Cook's Last Voyage*

Date of Publication: 1956
Subject(s): Exploration; Sea Story
Fictional character(s): John Forrest, Sailor (midshipman)

Historical character(s): James Cook, Explorer, Military Personnel (naval officer); William Bligh, Military Personnel (naval officer)
Time Period(s): 1770s (1779)
Locale(s): Hawaii; *Resolution*, At Sea

Summary: The novel describes the final voyage of English explorer and navigator Captain James Cook when he meets his bloody end on the shores of Hawaii's Kealakekua Bay. Hailed first as ''Lono'' or god to the islanders, Cook's arrival sets off a chain of events culminating in his murder.

Historical Accuracy: The novel is steeped in the atmosphere of the period, and the events are based on many journal accounts of the voyage.

BEVERLY BUTLER (1932-)

A native of Milwaukee who lost her eyesight at an early age, Butler attended Mount Mary College and Marquette University, and has worked as a teacher and librarian. She was the 1955 winner of the Dodd Mead prize for *Song of the Voyageur*, and her *Feather in the Wind* brought her an award for distinguished service to history from the State Historical Society of Ohio.

`817` *My Sister's Keeper*

Date of Publication: 1980
Subject(s): Fires
Fictional character(s): Mary James, Young Woman; Clara Cody, Young Woman; Ellery Cody, Worker (factory)
Time Period(s): 1870s (1871)
Locale(s): Peshtigo, Wisconsin

Summary: Mary James travels to Peshtigo, Wisconsin, in the drought year of 1871. There she is attracted to her sister's husband, Ellery, and comes into conflict with her sister over his affection. The domestic drama is affected by the forest fire that consumes the town and shatters their lives.

Historical Accuracy: The novel is based on the historical details of the disaster of Peshtigo in 1871.

DAVID BUTLER

`818` *Lillie*

Date of Publication: 1978
Subject(s): Victorian Period; Royalty—England; Biography, Fictionalized
Historical character(s): Lillie Langtry, Actress; Edward, Prince of Wales, Royalty; Oscar Wilde, Writer (playwright); John Everett Millais, Artist (painter); Randolph Churchill, Gentleman; James Abbott McNeill Whistler, Artist (painter); Leopold II, Ruler (King of the Belgians)
Time Period(s): 19th century; 20th century (1870s-1902)
Locale(s): London, England; Jersey, England

Summary: This biographical novel describes the career of English actress Lillie Langtry who was called the world's most beautiful woman. The novel tells Lillie's story from her youth on the Channel Island of Jersey to her triumph in London where she becomes Edward VII's mistress and pre-

sides over a fashionable artistic circle that includes Wilde, Millais, and Whistler.

Historical Accuracy: The novel invents conversations and situations but is generally faithful to Langtry's history.

`819` *Lusitania*

Date of Publication: 1982
Subject(s): World War I; Shipwrecks; Sea Story
Historical character(s): Will Turner, Sea Captain; Woodrow Wilson, Political Figure; William Jennings Bryan, Political Figure; Winston Churchill, Political Figure; Wilhelm II, Ruler (German kaiser); Walther Schwieger, Military Personnel (U-boat commander); Alfred von Tirpitz, Military Personnel (German Grand Admiral); Sir Edward Grey, Political Figure
Time Period(s): 1910s (1915)
Locale(s): *Lusitania*, At Sea; New York, New York; Germany

Summary: The sinking of the *Lusitania* in 1915 is described from a variety of perspectives: the ship's captain, Will Turner; the U-boat commander Schwieger; and from the political perspective of Germany, England, and America. America's entry into the war hangs in the balance, and the tragedy of the unsinkable *Lusitania* could alter the course of the war.

Historical Accuracy: The novel is exhaustive in its research and convincing in its portraits of the key players in the ship's drama, at center stage in global affairs.

GWENDOLINE BUTLER (1922-)

English author Butler received her M.A. from Oxford. Her police procedural novels and historical mysteries, set in Victorian and Edwardian England, are widely acclaimed. She has been called the Jane Austen of the crime story by many.

`820` *Meadowsweet*

Date of Publication: 1977
Subject(s): Romance; Victorian Period; Mystery
Fictional character(s): Daisy Adair, Gentlewoman; Trelawney Adair, Gentlewoman; Frederick Von Friedberg, Royalty (prince)
Time Period(s): 1900s
Locale(s): England; Berlin, Germany; Friedberg, Germany

Summary: When her sister Daisy marries the German Prince Frederick von Friedberg, Trelawney Adair follows her to Germany as secretary to the German Empress. There she finds herself in the middle of a series of suspicious events that suggest a deadly conspiracy.

Historical Accuracy: The emphasis is on romantic intrigue and suspense with a backdrop of period history that is rather confusingly presented.

`821` *Sarsen Place*

Date of Publication: 1974
Subject(s): Mystery; Victorian Period; Servants
Fictional character(s): Mary Lamont, Governess; Adelaide Demarest, Gentlewoman

Time Period(s): 1890s
Locale(s): Oxford, England

Summary: Mary Lamont, the daughter of a freethinking portrait painter, takes a position as governess for the Demarest family at Sarsen Place in Oxford. The Demarest family hides many secrets, the exposure of which leads to kidnapping and murder.

Historical Accuracy: The novel offers an authentic evocation of Victorian Oxford.

822   *The Vesey Inheritance*

Date of Publication: 1975
Subject(s): Mystery; Victorian Period
Fictional character(s): Errol Vesey, Gentlewoman; Geraldine Maurice, Gentlewoman
Historical character(s): Victoria, Ruler (Queen of England)
Time Period(s): 1870s
Locale(s): London, England; Windsor, England

Summary: Young Errol Vesey is placed by her aunt in attendance on Queen Victoria. She is caught up in a tangle of intrigue that involves kidnapping. At the center of the story are several mysteries surrounding Errol's background.

Historical Accuracy: The novel offers an authentic look at Victoria's court at Windsor.

MARGARET BUTLER

823   *The Lion of Christ*

Date of Publication: 1977
Subject(s): Middle Ages; Royalty—England; Religious Conflict
Historical character(s): Henry II, Ruler (King of England); Thomas Becket, Religious (Archbishop of Canterbury); Eleanor of Aquitaine, Royalty (queen consort of Henry II)
Time Period(s): 12th century (1164-1171)
Locale(s): London, England; Canterbury, England

Summary: The final tumultuous years of conflict between the king and his former best friend, Thomas a Becket, now Archbishop of Canterbury, are chronicled here. Henry asserts his authority over all courts, including the ecclesiastical courts previously under Becket's jurisdiction. Becket's adamant refusal to defer to the king seals his fate.

Historical Accuracy: The novel is solidly based on historical record, except for some surmises. Eleanor is given a far greater role in the quarrel than has been traditionally recognized.

824   *The Lion of England*

Date of Publication: 1973
Subject(s): Middle Ages; Royalty—England
Historical character(s): Henry II, Ruler (King of England); Eleanor of Aquitaine, Royalty (queen consort of Henry II); Hikenai, Prostitute (mistress of Henry II); Thomas Becket, Lawyer, Religious (Archbishop of Canterbury)
Time Period(s): 12th century (1152-1160)
Locale(s): France; England

Summary: The opening years of the reign of Henry II are chronicled here. To the anguish of Henry's wife, Eleanor of Aquitaine, Henry is having an affair with the Saxon Hikenai. Henry's friendship with Thomas a Becket is an additional wedge between the king and the queen.

Historical Accuracy: The novel's history is convincingly delivered and accurate except for some minor tampering with the chronology. There is also much speculation about Hikenai, of whom little is known.

825   *The Lion of Justice*

Date of Publication: 1975
Subject(s): Middle Ages; Royalty—England; Religious Conflict
Historical character(s): Henry II, Ruler (King of England); Eleanor of Aquitaine, Royalty (queen consort of Henry II); Thomas Becket, Religious (Archbishop of Canterbury)
Time Period(s): 12th century (1161-1164)
Locale(s): London, England; Canterbury, England

Summary: In the second volume of Butler's trilogy on the reign of Henry II, the rift that will cost the king his best friend, Thomas a Becket, begins to open. Appointed Archbishop of Canterbury to serve the king's interest, Thomas chooses to serve the church instead. When Henry claims secular jurisdiction over clerics, Thomas considers this a violation of ecclesiastical privilege and stands against the king.

Historical Accuracy: The facts of the quarrel between Henry and Becket are documented. The gaps in the historical record are filled in by the author's imagination.

MILDRED ALLEN BUTLER (1897-)

Born in Massachusetts, Butler graduated from Wellesley College and the University of Oregon. She was a high school teacher of English in Massachusetts and New Hampshire.

826   *Ward of the Sun King*

Date of Publication: 1970
Subject(s): Royalty—France
Fictional character(s): Adrienne Lavelle, Young Woman
Historical character(s): Louis XIV, Ruler (King of France); Francoise d'Aubigne, Royalty (consort of Louis XIV)
Time Period(s): 1700s
Locale(s): Versailles, France; England; Quebec, Quebec, Canada

Summary: This novel set in the court of French King Louis XIV tells the story of Adrienne Lavelle, a student in a school for impoverished girls of the nobility created by Madame de Maintenon, the puritanical wife of the king. Adrienne resists the school's severe treatment and flees to England and then to New France.

Historical Accuracy: The novel's depiction of court life is historically accurate.

RAGAN BUTLER

827 *Captain Nash and the Honour of England*

Date of Publication: 1976
Subject(s): Mystery; Georgian Period
Fictional character(s): Captain George Nash, Detective—Private
Time Period(s): 1770s
Locale(s): London, England

Summary: The second case for England's first private detective, Captain George Nash, involves him in a royal scandal that reaches to the king himself. At the center of the puzzle is the identity of a mysterious woman and the results of a duel to the death. Nash contends with attempts on his own life as he penetrates the secrets that could jeopardize the honor of the nation.

Historical Accuracy: The story is a fanciful one but filled with authentic period elements.

828 *Captain Nash and the Wroth Inheritance*

Date of Publication: 1976
Subject(s): Mystery; Inheritance—Disputed
Fictional character(s): Captain George Nash, Detective—Private; Sir Harry Pelham, Gentleman; Oliver Wroth, Gentleman
Time Period(s): 1770s (1771)
Locale(s): London, England

Summary: In 1771, Captain George Nash, late of His Majesty's 5th Regiment of Dragoons, decides to offer his services "for the gathering of information and the detection of crimes," thus becoming England's first private detective. His first case is an elaborate triangle of blackmail and murder and a scandalous plot involving the vast Wroth inheritance.

Historical Accuracy: The period details are sharply presented.

RICHARD BUTLER (1925-)

Born in England, Butler spent five years in the Royal Air Force before emigrating to Australia, where he embarked on a career as an actor before turning to writing.

829 *The Men That God Forgot*

Date of Publication: 1976
Subject(s): Crime and Criminals
Fictional character(s): James Porter, Convict; John Barker, Convict; William Shiers, Gentleman
Time Period(s): 1830s (1833-1839)
Locale(s): Sarah's Island, Australia; At Sea; Chile

Summary: Based on a true story, the novel tells of a daring escape from a desolate penal colony in Australia in the 1830s. The men seize a vessel and flee across the Pacific to Chile where they begin a new life.

Historical Accuracy: The novel offers its sources as evidence of the factual basis of the story, but the characters are imaginary.

SUZANNE BUTLER
(PSEUD. OF SUZANNE BUTLER PERREARD, 1919-)

Canadian-born Butler has operated a nursery school in Geneva. She writes for both children and adults. Her novels include *Starlight in Tourrone* and *My Pride, My Folly*.

830 *My Pride, My Folly*

Date of Publication: 1953
Subject(s): Romance
Fictional character(s): Michael Shea, Sailor; Kirstina Brandt, Spouse (of Shea); James Collingwood, Gentleman
Time Period(s): 19th century (1850s-1870s)
Locale(s): Boston, Massachusetts; Montreal, Quebec, Canada

Summary: Kirstina Brandt falls in love with sailor Michael Shea on the voyage from Denmark to Boston. She marries him, but disappointment follows. After Michael is reportedly lost at sea, she goes to Montreal to work as a nursemaid and then becomes the wife of James Collingwood, who takes her to his estate in the wilderness of Upper Canada. Finally, a man arrives from California who will alter the course of her life yet again.

Historical Accuracy: The emphasis is on the romantic complications rather than the historical details.

831 *Vale of Tyranny*

Date of Publication: 1954
Subject(s): Romance; Franco-Prussian War
Fictional character(s): Thorn Drayton, Heiress; Rhys Vaughan, Gentleman; Edmond Laurignac, Nobleman (Comte de Laurignac)
Time Period(s): 19th century (1850s-1870s)
Locale(s): Wales; Paris, France

Summary: This love story shuttles between Wales and Paris of the Second Empire. Thorn Drayton inherits a Welsh ironworks that she wishes to run along with her lover, Rhys Vaughan. His behavior, however, causes her to flee to Paris, where she is swept up in the glittering world of the haute monde. The Franco-Prussian War and the siege of Paris force her back home to a confrontation with Rhys.

Historical Accuracy: The details of fashionable society during the Second Empire are accurately detailed.

CORDIA BYERS

832 *Desire and Deceive*

Date of Publication: 1990
Subject(s): Middle Ages; Romance
Fictional character(s): Megan Wakesfield, Noblewoman, Highwayman; Richard St. Clare, Nobleman, Highwayman
Time Period(s): 14th century (1337)
Locale(s): England

Summary: This medieval romantic adventure depicts Megan Wakefield who, to save her estate, robs travellers along the King's wool route in 14th-century England. When her would-be suitor, Richard St. Clare, in disguise, joins her in her adventures, love ensues.

Historical Accuracy: Despite the novel's plot that strains credibility, the story convinces with its period elements and authentic background.

ELIZABETH BYRD (1912-)

An American writer born in St. Louis, Byrd attended NYU and has worked as a newswriter for CBS, a literary agent, and a freelance writer.

833 *The Famished Land*

Date of Publication: 1972
Subject(s): Rural Life—Ireland; Irish Potato Famine; Disasters—Natural
Fictional character(s): Moira McFlaherty, Farmer; Liam Lenihan, Farmer
Time Period(s): 1840s (1845)
Locale(s): Ireland

Summary: Set in Ireland during the years of the potato famine, the novel describes its impact on Moira McFlaherty and her family who struggle to survive as the potatoes begin to rot in their fields. Her love for Liam Lenihan must await their survival.

Historical Accuracy: The novel is convincing both in its depiction of the era and in portraying Irish customs and character.

834 *Immortal Queen*

Date of Publication: 1956
Subject(s): Elizabethan Period; Royalty—England; Biography, fictionalized
Historical character(s): Mary, Queen of Scots, Ruler (Queen of France and Scotland); Catherine de' Medici, Royalty (queen consort of Henri II); Henri II, Ruler (King of France); Elizabeth I, Ruler (Queen of England); Henry Stewart, Nobleman (Lord Darnley), Spouse (second husband of Mary); James Hepburn, Nobleman (Earl of Bothwell), Spouse (third husband of Mary); Sir Francis Walsingham, Government Official (spymaster)
Time Period(s): 16th century (1557-1587)
Locale(s): France; Edinburgh, Scotland; England

Summary: This biographical novel of Mary, Queen of Scots begins and ends on the day of her execution in 1587. As she awaits death, her life unfolds, including her three marriages and her role as queen of both France and Scotland. Mary emerges as a complex creation of her age, imperious but dependent on support and approval and no match for Elizabeth.

Historical Accuracy: The novel is an impressive and authentic historical reconstruction.

835 *Lady of Monkton*

Date of Publication: 1975
Subject(s): Middle Ages; Witchcraft and Sorcery
Fictional character(s): Cathryn Grandison, Gentlewoman; Micheal Scot, Servant; Roger Douglas, Gentleman
Time Period(s): 15th century
Locale(s): Scotland

Summary: Cathryn Grandison is engaged to a man she has never seen and marries him by proxy. Now, as the Lady of Monkton, she is entangled in a complex web of intrigue and betrayal. A trusted servant is revealed to be a witch, and Cathryn must find an antidote to her potions.

Historical Accuracy: The period setting makes the sorcery of the tale believable.

836 *Maid of Honour: A Novel Set in the Court of Mary, Queen of Scots*

Date of Publication: 1978
Subject(s): Royalty—Scotland; Elizabethan Period
Historical character(s): Mary, Queen of Scots, Ruler (Queen of Scotland); Mary Seton, Gentlewoman; James Hepburn, Nobleman (Earl of Bothwell), Spouse (third husband of Mary)
Time Period(s): 16th century (1560s-1587)
Locale(s): Paris, France; Edinburgh, Scotland

Summary: Intrigue in the court of Mary, Queen of Scots is described from the first-hand source of Mary Seton, is the queen's maid of honor. Mary Seton is not an impartial witness, but she has a unique perspective on the long and drawn-out wrangle with Elizabeth, and Mary's attempt to stay on her throne.

Historical Accuracy: The novel offers an authentic first-hand viewpoint.

MAX BYRD (1942-)

An American writer born in Georgia, Byrd has worked as a professor of English at Yale University and the University of California at Davis. His academic specialty is the 18th century. Byrd won the Shamus Award in 1982 for his mystery *California Thriller*.

837 *Jackson: A Novel*

Date of Publication: 1997
Subject(s): Biography, Fictionalized; War of 1812; Politics
Fictional character(s): David Chase, Writer; Emma Colden, Feminist
Historical character(s): Andrew Jackson, Military Personnel (general), Political Figure; Aaron Burr, Political Figure; Thomas Jefferson, Political Figure; Sam Houston, Political Figure; Rachel Jackson, Spouse
Time Period(s): 18th century; 19th century
Locale(s): United States

Summary: The novel offers a portrait of the life and times of the complex and contradictory American leader Andrew Jackson. On the eve of his bid for the presidency, Jackson's chances are threatened by an uncomplimentary biography written by David Chase. Chase is joined by activist Emma Colden, and the pair discover a secret that could alter the future of America.

Historical Accuracy: The novel ingeniously blends the fictional with the historical, relying for its facts on the standard sources with some compression of events and speculation.

838 *Jefferson: A Novel*

Date of Publication: 1993
Subject(s): American Revolution; Politics
Historical character(s): Thomas Jefferson, Political Figure; William Short, Secretary; John Adams, Political Figure; Abigail Adams, Spouse; Benjamin Franklin, Political Figure, Inventor; Marie Joseph Paul de Lafayette, Nobleman (marquis)
Time Period(s): 1780s
Locale(s): Paris, France; Charlottesville, Virginia

Summary: In 1784 Thomas Jefferson arrives in Paris as the newly appointed ambassador to the court of Louis XVI. We see the events and players through the eyes of Jefferson's secretary, William Short. He offers some rare glimpses of Jefferson's struggles to build his dream for America while suffering from a crisis of the heart.

Historical Accuracy: Byrd is convincing in his scholarship, offering a deep and compelling portrait of Jefferson.

SIGMAN BYRD

JOHN SUTHERLAND

839 *The Valiant*

Date of Publication: 1955
Subject(s): American West; Indians
Fictional character(s): Joel, Indian (Nez Perce), Chieftain; Stella Kendrick, Young Woman
Time Period(s): 1870s
Locale(s): Oregon

Summary: This is a fictional story based on the actual events surrounding the betrayal of the Nez Perce Indians in the Pacific Northwest. In this version, Chief Joel is a young replacement for the historical Chief Joseph. A romance involving Stella Kendrick, the daughter of an army general, is added to the story of the Indians' conflict with the army.

Historical Accuracy: The novel's basic story of the Nez Perce is historical, but the fictional plot predominates.

DONN BYRNE

(PSEUD. OF BRIAN OSWALD DONN BYRNE, 1889-1928)
Born in New York City but educated in Dublin, Byrne excelled in romantic stories tinged with Celtic mysticism. His series of historical romances maintains a decidedly Irish perspective.

840 *Messer Marco Polo*

Date of Publication: 1921

Subject(s): Picaresque Adventure
Fictional character(s): Golden Bells, Royalty (Kubla Khan's daughter)
Historical character(s): Marco Polo, Explorer; Kublai Khan, Ruler
Time Period(s): 13th century
Locale(s): Venice, Italy; China

Summary: Marco Polo visits the court of Kublai Khan and falls in love with the Emperor's daughter.

Historical Accuracy: Loosely based on history, this is actually an exotic romance (in the style of a folk-tale) about the East's mystery and attractions.

JAMES BRANCH CABELL (1879-1958)

American novelist Cabell was born in Richmond, Virginia, and graduated from the College of William and Mary. He worked as a journalist and a coal miner before turning to writing novels. Many of his most popular novels are set in the imaginary medieval kingdom of Poictesme and are considered satirical moral allegories. Titles include *The Cream of the Jest*, *Jurgen*, and *The Silver Stallion*.

841 *The First Gentleman of America: A Comedy of Conquest*

Date of Publication: 1942
Subject(s): Spanish Colonies
Fictional character(s): Nemattanon, Indian, Chieftain
Time Period(s): 16th century
Locale(s): North America; Spain; France

Summary: This highly satirical work on the clash of cultures between the Western Europeans and the Native Americans is based on the partly legendary and partly historical story of a young Indian chieftain who visited Spain in the 16th century. Nemattanon learns the ways of civilized life and returns to defend his people from its destructive effects.

Historical Accuracy: The novel's purpose is satire rather than history, but it does depend heavily on historical elements to create its targets.

GEORGE W. CABLE (1844-1925)

Born in New Orleans, Cable served in the Confederate army during the Civil War before he turned to a writing career. His books celebrate the local color of New Orleans. Works include *Madame Delphine*, *Dr. Sevier*, *John March, Southerner*, and *The Cavalier*.

842 *The Grandissimes*

Date of Publication: 1880
Subject(s): Antebellum South
Fictional character(s): Honore Grandissime, Nobleman, Businessman; Aurora Nanconou, Widow(er); Joseph Frowenfeld, Pharmacist
Time Period(s): 1800s
Locale(s): New Orleans, Louisiana

Summary: The novel is a complex and complicated tale of family fortune in early 19th century Creole New Orleans. Honore Grandissime is the patriarch determined to hold his family together and do right by a young widow. An outsider, the American Frowenfeld, becomes the catalyst for the novel's dramatic climax.

Historical Accuracy: Cable offers an authentic recreation of Creole society that includes accurately rendered dialect.

MARY CABLE (1920-)

Born in Cleveland, Ohio, Mary Cable attended the Cas'Alta School in Florence, Italy, and Barnard College. She has worked on the editorial staff of the *New Yorker*, *Harper's Bazaar*, and for the American Heritage Publishing Company. Cable is the author of *Lost New Orleans*, *Top Drawer: American High Society From the Gilded Age to the Roaring Twenties*, and *Blizzard of '88*.

843   *Avery's Knot*

Date of Publication: 1981
Subject(s): Crime and Criminals; Trials
Historical character(s): Ephraim Avery, Religious (clergyman); Sarah Maria Cornell, Worker (in a cotton mill)
Time Period(s): 1830s (1830)
Locale(s): Fall River, Massachusetts

Summary: Based on an actual event, the novel records the circumstances that lead to a Methodist minister, Ephraim Avery, being charged with the murder of a young cotton-mill worker, Sarah Cornell. This was the first time a clergyman in America was tried for murder.

Historical Accuracy: The principal events are faithful to the facts. However, when the facts are not known, the author has made educated guesses.

JEAN CABRIES (1929-)

Cabries is a French author.

844   *Jacob*

Date of Publication: 1958
Subject(s): Biblical Story
Historical character(s): Esau, Biblical Figure; Jacob, Biblical Figure; Joseph, Biblical Figure (son of Jacob); Isaac, Biblical Figure; Leah, Biblical Figure; Rachel, Biblical Figure
Time Period(s): Indeterminate Past
Locale(s): Middle East

Summary: This novel offers a factual re-telling of the Old Testament story of Jacob beginning with Isaac, passing his blessing on to Jacob and not to his brother Esau. Fleeing his brother's vengeance, Jacob struggles to marry Rachel, only to find her sister, Leah, substituted at the wedding. Jacob finally is reunited with Rachel, who bears his son, Joseph, and after wrestling all night with God, Jacob receives the name Israel.

Historical Accuracy: The novel is purposely anachronistic in order to cast Jacob in the role of a searcher for universal meaning in the world.

JAMES M. CAIN (1892-1977)

American novelist Cain is best known for his mystery crime books, including *The Postman Always Rings Twice*, *Double Indemnity*, and *Mildred Pierce*. Cain also worked as a screenwriter, newspaper reporter, and professor of journalism. He began his writing career at the age of 42 after being fired by Paramount. His writing style is said to have influenced Albert Camus.

845   *Mignon*

Date of Publication: 1962
Subject(s): Civil War—U.S.
Fictional character(s): Bill Cresap, Veteran (Union Army); Mignon Landry, Young Woman
Time Period(s): 1860s (1864)
Locale(s): New Orleans, Louisiana

Summary: This tale of Civil War-era New Orleans follows the exploits of Bill Cresap, invalided out of the Union Army and in search of the main chance in New Orleans as the war draws to a close. He is approached by Creole Mignon Landry to assist in getting her father out of a military prison where he has been sent for trading with the enemy. Cresap is thereby launched into a series of adventures dealing with shady trading in confiscated cotton.

Historical Accuracy: The novel's setting and situations are equally short on authenticity and plausibility.

MOYRA CALDECOTT (1927-)

Born in South Africa, Caldecott emigrated to England in 1951. She was educated at the University of Natal and has worked as a teacher and in an art gallery.

846   *The Lily and the Bull*

Date of Publication: 1979
Subject(s): Myths and Legends; Minoan Civilization
Fictional character(s): Ierii, Young Woman; Thyloss, Young Man
Time Period(s): 10th century B.C.
Locale(s): Crete, Greece

Summary: Ierii is the daughter of the chief gardener of the royal palace on Minoan Crete, and Thyloss the son of the keeper of the queen's bull. Their love is threatened as the entire island is shaken by the willfulness of the queen following the death of her son. Ierii and Thyloss are drawn into an escalating cycle of grief and destruction.

Historical Accuracy: Less a summary of the historical than the mythical and symbolic, the novel reaches the abstract appeal of universals.

847   *Shadows on the Stones*

Date of Publication: 1978
Subject(s): Prehistory; Bronze Age; Myths and Legends
Fictional character(s): Kyra, Religious (priestess); Khu-Ren, Religious (priest), Prehistoric Human; Isar, Captive, Prehistoric Human; Lark, Child, Prehistoric Human

Time Period(s): Indeterminate Past
Locale(s): England

Summary: In the final volume of the author's Sacred Stones trilogy, the powers of darkness spread in the form of a new god, Groth. Peril and evil influences infect all before the final, climactic confrontation.

Historical Accuracy: This imaginative fantasy is supported by the author's research into ancient British mythology and society.

`848` *The Tall Stones*

Date of Publication: 1977
Subject(s): Prehistory; Bronze Age; Myths and Legends
Fictional character(s): Wardyke, Sorcerer, Prehistoric Human; Kyra, Psychic, Prehistoric Human
Time Period(s): Indeterminate Past
Locale(s): England

Summary: The first of the author's Sacred Stones trilogy is set in a small isolated community in Bronze Age Britain. The village is threatened by Wardyke, a corrupt priest. He is challenged by Kyra, a young girl possessed of great psychic powers.

Historical Accuracy: The novel offers an interesting and imaginative re-creation of the spiritual past of prehistoric tribes.

`849` *The Temple of the Sun*

Date of Publication: 1977
Subject(s): Prehistory; Bronze Age; Myths and Legends
Fictional character(s): Kyra, Psychic; Wardyke, Sorcerer, Prehistoric Human; Lord Guidron, Religious (high priest), Prehistoric Human
Time Period(s): Indeterminate Past
Locale(s): England

Summary: In the second volume of the author's Sacred Stones trilogy, Kyra journeys to the distant Temple of the Sun to train for the priesthood. But the Temple and its lord, Guidron, are challenged by the evil Wardyke, and Kyra must test her fledgling powers against his.

Historical Accuracy: The fantasy offers an imaginative speculation of what might have taken place in prehistoric Britian.

TAYLOR CALDWELL (1900-1985)

British-born author Caldwell settled in America in 1906 and published her first novel in 1938. She produced a string of bestsellers, many concerned with business families around the turn of the century. She proved herself equally adept at writing about ancient times.

`850` *The Arm and the Darkness*

Date of Publication: 1943
Subject(s): Religious Conflict
Fictional character(s): Arsene de Richepane, Nobleman; Louis Richepane, Religious (priest)
Historical character(s): Armand-Jean Du Plessis, Religious (Cardinal Richelieu), Political Figure; Louis XIII, Ruler (King of France)

Time Period(s): 17th century
Locale(s): Paris, France

Summary: Conflict between Catholics and Huguenots during the reign of French King Louis XIII is dramatized in this story of the two Richepane brothers. Arsene is a young nobleman struggling to do the right thing; his brother Louis is a villainous priest. Richelieu emerges as the mastermind of this period that the author presents as a precursor to the French Revolution.

Historical Accuracy: The thesis that dominates the story is questionable and undermines the author's reliability in interpreting historical facts.

`851` *Captains and the Kings*

Date of Publication: 1972
Subject(s): Family Saga; Politics
Fictional character(s): Joseph Armagh, Immigrant, Financier; Bernadette Armagh, Spouse; Rory Armagh, Gentleman
Historical character(s): Abraham Lincoln, Political Figure; Theodore Roosevelt, Political Figure
Time Period(s): 19th century; 20th century
Locale(s): Philadelphia, Pennsylvania; Virginia

Summary: An Irish immigrant, Joseph Armagh, is taken under the wing of a powerful entrepreneur. Upon the entrepreneur's death, Joseph inherits his great wealth and business. The novel details the effect of wealth on Joseph and his family and describes his involvement in politics from the Civil War to the Woodrow Wilson era.

Historical Accuracy: The historical background is solidly presented and backed by extensive research.

`852` *Ceremony of the Innocent*

Date of Publication: 1976
Subject(s): Politics; World War I
Fictional character(s): Jeremy Porter, Political Figure; Ellen Watson Porter, Spouse
Time Period(s): 19th century; 20th century (1890s-1930s)
Locale(s): Pennsylvania; New York, New York; Washington, District of Columbia

Summary: This is a tale of political corruption and betrayal. Ellen Watson marries Jeremy Porter and enters his world of politics, wealth, and power. Their story illustrates America's loss of innocence during the turbulent opening decades of the 20th century.

Historical Accuracy: The personal tone and autobiographical nature of the story affects the objectivity.

`853` *Dear and Glorious Physician*

Date of Publication: 1959
Subject(s): Biblical Story; Christianity; Roman Empire
Historical character(s): Luke, Biblical Figure, Doctor; Mary, Biblical Figure; Pontius Pilate, Government Official (procurator of Jerusalem), Biblical Figure; Tiberius, Ruler (Roman emperor)
Time Period(s): 1st century
Locale(s): Jerusalem, Israel; Athens, Greece; Rome, Roman Empire

Summary: This is the story of St. Luke from his childhood and youth as an apprentice to his career as a physician. His later career as a disciple of Jesus and gospel writer is also described.

Historical Accuracy: Most of the events described are authenticated by secondary sources.

854   *Dynasty of Death*

Date of Publication: 1938
Subject(s): Family Saga; Business Building
Fictional character(s): Joseph Barbour, Businessman; Martin Barbour, Businessman; Gregory Sessions, Businessman
Time Period(s): 19th century (1837-1898)
Locale(s): England; Pennsylvania

Summary: Two American families build a small firearms business into a huge munitions empire during the 19th century. Their success has a cost, however, as rivalry, jealousy, and conflict become by-products of the company.

Historical Accuracy: The story details accurately the history of the 19th century.

855   *The Earth Is the Lord's: A Tale of the Rise of Genghis Khan*

Date of Publication: 1941
Subject(s): Mongol Empire; Tribal Life—Mongol; Biography, Fictionalized
Historical character(s): Genghis Khan, Warrior
Time Period(s): 12th century
Locale(s): Gobi Desert, Mongolia

Summary: The story of the great Mongol conqueror Genghis Khan is dramatized from his birth and childhood as the son of a petty tribal chieftain in the Gobi desert to his first great victory over the Turks and his success in consolidating the nomadic Mongol tribes into a fearsome army. The novel captures the setting and the customs of the Mongols and shows Genghis Khan's determined rise to power.

Historical Accuracy: More operatic than historically accurate, the novel is colorful and filled with action that emphasizes the spectacular and is sometimes at odds with the facts.

856   *Glory and the Lightning*

Date of Publication: 1974
Subject(s): Ancient Greece; Women's Rights
Historical character(s): Aspasia, Lover (of Pericles); Pericles, Political Figure; Anaxagoras, Philosopher; Zeno, Philosopher; Socrates, Philosopher; Sophocles, Writer (dramatist)
Time Period(s): 5th century B.C. (480-410 B.C.)
Locale(s): Athens, Greece; Damascus, Syria; Persia

Summary: In this novel of ancient Greece, the author attempts to show the low status of women of the time. The story follows the experiences of Aspasia, travelling as the companion of a Persian satrap. She experiences a life of great riches and pleasure but no power, and decides to pursue an independent life. Eventually she becomes the companion by choice of Pericles, the great Greek leader.

Historical Accuracy: The novel is richly textured with period characters and details, bringing the era to life.

857   *Grandmother and the Priests*

Date of Publication: 1963
Subject(s): Religious Life
Fictional character(s): Rose Mary O'Driscoll Cullen, Widow(er); Edward Albert Harrington, Religious (monsignor); Rose McConnell, Young Woman
Time Period(s): 1900s
Locale(s): England; Scotland

Summary: A young woman recalls the stories told to her grandmother about a succession of Catholic priests. The various adventures of the priests form a vivid portrait of faith and devotion in the face of opposition that would overwhelm lesser people.

Historical Accuracy: The period details in this story cycle are solidly grounded.

858   *Great Lion of God*

Date of Publication: 1970
Subject(s): Biblical Story; Biography, Fictionalized
Historical character(s): Saul of Tarsus, Biblical Figure, Religious; Jesus Christ, Biblical Figure, Teacher; Pontius Pilate, Government Official (procurator of Jerusalem), Biblical Figure; Joseph of Arimathea, Biblical Figure; Peter, Biblical Figure, Religious (apostle)
Time Period(s): 1st century (15-65)
Locale(s): Tarsus, Middle East; Jerusalem, Israel; Roman Empire

Summary: The author recreates the life of St. Paul. He is the intellectual son of a wealthy Roman-Jewish family, and his life is chronicled from his early teenage years to his death as a martyr. Paul emerges as a complex blend of religious faith and human frailities.

Historical Accuracy: The novel is rich in historical background and solidly based on the documented record, as indicated by an extensive bibliography.

TAYLOR CALDWELL (1900-1985)

JESS STEARN

British born, Caldwell settled in America in 1906 and published her first novel in 1938. She produced a string of best sellers, many concerned with business families around the turn of the century. She is equally adept at writing about ancient times. Stearn is an American writer, biographer, and expert in the occult. She has produced a best-selling book on Edgar Cayce.

859   *I, Judas*

Date of Publication: 1977
Subject(s): Biblical Story
Historical character(s): Jesus Christ, Biblical Figure; Judas Iscariot, Biblical Figure, Traitor; John the Baptist, Biblical

Figure; Mary, Biblical Figure; Mary Magdalene, Biblical Figure; Pontius Pilate, Government Official (procurator of Jerusalem), Biblical Figure
Time Period(s): 1st century
Locale(s): Jerusalem, Israel

Summary: Judas Iscariot tells his own story and emerges not as the wicked villain of legend. The son of a rich and powerful Pharisee Jewish family, Judas becomes a zealot opposing Roman rule. He becomes a disciple of Jesus, and his ultimate betrayal of Jesus is far more complex than the desire for a few pieces of silver.

Historical Accuracy: This is an ingenious and modernized version of the Biblical story, rooted more in the period's politics than in dogma. The interpretation of Judas' motives is, of course, speculative.

TAYLOR CALDWELL (1900-1985)

British-born author Caldwell settled in America in 1906 and published her first novel in 1938. She produced a string of bestsellers, many concerned with business families around the turn of the century. She proved herself equally adept at writing about ancient times.

860 *Never Victorious, Never Defeated*

Date of Publication: 1954
Subject(s): Family Saga; Railroads
Fictional character(s): Aaron deWitt, Businessman; Stephen deWitt, Businessman; Rufus deWitt, Businessman
Time Period(s): 19th century; 20th century (1866-1935)
Locale(s): Pennsylvania

Summary: A family battles for control of the Interstate railroad line. The sides form around brothers Stephen and Rufus deWitt, and the battle continues with their offspring. The story covers nearly 100 years of American capitalism.

Historical Accuracy: The novel effectively evokes several historical eras, from the Johnson administration to the New Deal.

861 *A Pillar of Iron*

Date of Publication: 1965
Subject(s): Roman Empire; Politics
Historical character(s): Marcus Tullius Cicero, Political Figure, Philosopher; Julius Caesar, Political Figure, Military Personnel (army commander); Lucius Sergius Catilina, Political Figure; Lucius Cornelius Sulla, Military Personnel (army officer)
Time Period(s): 1st century B.C.
Locale(s): Rome, Roman Empire

Summary: The novel offers a detailed and compelling portrait of Cicero: poet, orator, lawyer, politician, and philosopher. His life in Rome during the first century B.C. and his unflagging defense of the Republic are played out against a backdrop of deadly conspiracy that pushes Rome to the brink of political chaos.

Historical Accuracy: This is an impressive effort of historical re-creation based on years of research.

862 *A Prologue to Love*

Date of Publication: 1961
Subject(s): Business Building
Fictional character(s): Caroline Ames, Businesswoman; John Ames, Businessman
Time Period(s): 19th century; 20th century (1880-1914)
Locale(s): Boston, Massachusetts

Summary: Caroline Ames is the daughter of an unscrupulous businessman, John Ames, who instills in her a horror of poverty and a faith in the power of money. His fortune makes her one of the richest women in the world, but also one of the loneliest. The withering effects of great wealth are dramatized.

Historical Accuracy: This lesson novel offers some convincing period details of Boston at the turn of the century.

863 *Testimony of Two Men*

Date of Publication: 1968
Subject(s): Medical Profession; Crime and Criminals
Fictional character(s): Robert Morgan, Doctor; Jonathon Ferrier, Doctor
Time Period(s): 19th century; 20th century (turn of the century)
Locale(s): Pennsylvania

Summary: Sheltered and naive, Robert Morgan is a young physician just out of medical school. He begins work with a small-town doctor, Jonathan Ferrier. Ferrier has been acquitted in the mysterious death of his wife, adding suspense to the story.

Historical Accuracy: The locale and era are painted with some authenticity.

864 *The Wide House*

Date of Publication: 1945
Subject(s): Politics; Racial Conflict; Religious Conflict
Fictional character(s): Janie Cauder, Widow(er); Stuart Coleman, Gentleman
Time Period(s): 1850s
Locale(s): New York

Summary: This domestic drama is set in a small upstate New York town in the 1850s. The author depicts religious and racial conflict against a backdrop of the ''Know-Nothing'' party and social and political issues of the day. At the center of the action are unconventional widow Janie Cauder and her Irish cousin, Stuart Coleman.

Historical Accuracy: The period atmosphere is believable, though at times somewhat superficially presented.

CHARLES J. CALITRI (1916-)

Born in New York City, Calitri graduated from New York University. A high school teacher of English and a professor of education, Calitri's works include *Rickey*, *Strike Heaven on the Face*, and *Father*.

865   *The Goliath Head*

Date of Publication: 1972
Subject(s): Artistic Life; Biography, Fictionalized
Historical character(s): Michelangelo da Caravaggio, Artist (painter)
Time Period(s): 16th century; 17th century (1590-1610)
Locale(s): Rome, Italy

Summary: This fictionalized life of the Italian painter Caravaggio depicts his loves and artistic career starting with his arrival in Rome in 1590. Caravaggio's insistence on realism in art leads to criticism and struggle. The novel captures the artistic issues of the day and the turbulent love life of Caravaggio.

Historical Accuracy: The novel is faithful to the details of Caravaggio's life and to the era, particularly in rendering period Rome.

MORLEY CALLAGHAN (1903-1990)

Canadian journalist and author Callaghan is best known for beating Ernest Hemingway in a controversial fight in 1929 in Paris when the timekeeper, F. Scott Fitzgerald, failed to end the first round at the agreed-upon time. Among his novels are *Strange Fugitive*, *More Joy in Heaven*, and *The Loved and the Lost*.

866   *A Time for Judas*

Date of Publication: 1984
Subject(s): Biblical Story
Fictional character(s): Philo of Crete, Servant (scribe)
Historical character(s): Jesus Christ, Biblical Figure; Judas Iscariot, Biblical Figure; Pontius Pilate, Government Official, Biblical Figure; Mary Magdalene, Biblical Figure
Time Period(s): 1st century
Locale(s): Jerusalem, Israel

Summary: The story of Jesus' ministry and crucifixion is given a nontraditional treatment by Philo of Crete, Pontius Pilate's Greek scribe. His version treats Judas not as a villain but as a devoted friend of Jesus who assists him in initiating events to fulfill his spiritual mission.

Historical Accuracy: The novel parts company with Biblical sources and its philosophical bearings are at times confused.

ITALO CALVINO (1923-1985)

An Italian author who graduated from the University of Turin, Calvino served in the Italian Resistance during World War II. He is best known for his monumental collection of Italian fables that he both edited and wrote. His writing embraces a wide variety of literary styles, and he has been called one of modern literature's greatest fabulists. Titles include *The Path to the Nest of Spiders*, *Cosmic Comics*, *The Nonexistent Knight*, and *The Seasons in the City*.

867   *Invisible Cities*

Date of Publication: 1972
Subject(s): Fantasy; Chinese Empire; Exploration

Historical character(s): Marco Polo, Explorer; Kublai Khan, Ruler (Chinese emperor)
Time Period(s): 13th century
Locale(s): China

Summary: The novel takes the form of a coversation between Marco Polo and an aged Kublai Khan as Polo describes to the emperor 55 imaginary, symbolic cities. Each city is named for a woman and provides a subject for moral and philosophical speculation.

Historical Accuracy: The novel is a tour de force of inventiveness as Calvino blends the fantastic with a solid sense of the world into an endlessly provocative speculation.

KENNETH M. CAMERON (1931-)

An American writer, Cameron was born in Indiana and graduated from the University of Rochester and Carnegie Institute of Technology. He has worked as a professor of English and theater and has written a number of suspense novels under the pen name George Bartram.

868   *Our Jo, or The Chronicle of a Coming Man*

Date of Publication: 1974
Subject(s): Picaresque Adventure; Restoration Period; Fires
Fictional character(s): Jo Haynes, Bastard Son, Adventurer
Historical character(s): Charles II, Ruler (King of England); Titus Oates, Leader (Popish Plot); George Villiers, Nobleman (Duke of Buckingham), Courtier; Barbara Villiers, Noblewoman
Time Period(s): 17th century
Locale(s): London, England

Summary: In the best *Tom Jones* tradition, Jo Haynes is a bastard who makes his way in Restoration London. He is cast into prison for mimicking the Duke of York and is enlisted by the king to uncover a Puritan conspiracy. His fortune is won and lost while he mixes with the greats of the day and endures the Great Plague and the Fire of London. Through it all, he is irrepressible as well as philosophical.

Historical Accuracy: This comic send-up of the picaresque novel is filled with authentic period details, personalties, and events that create a realistic texture.

WILLIAM CAMERON

869   *Day Is Coming*

Date of Publication: 1944
Subject(s): Victorian Period; Socialism; Politics
Fictional character(s): Arthur Cullen, Worker
Historical character(s): Oscar Wilde, Writer; William Morris, Writer, Artisan
Time Period(s): 19th century; 20th century (1887-1939)
Locale(s): England

Summary: The novel traces the development of the socialist and craft movements in England from the celebration of Queen Victoria's jubilee in 1887 to the beginning of World War II. The novel's hero, Arthur Cullen, is a member of the

Guild of English Craftsmen and joins William Morris in the English countryside. The novel features a detailed discussion of Morris' ideals and efforts to achieve them.

Historical Accuracy: The novel captures its era with skill. However, the author's thesis on the dignity and ideals of the common workman tends toward idealization and abstraction.

DEBORAH CAMP

870 *Belle Starr*

Date of Publication: 1987
Subject(s): Crime and Criminals; American West; Civil War—U.S.
Historical character(s): Belle Starr, Outlaw; Cole Younger, Outlaw; Jesse James, Outlaw; William Clarke Quantrill, Outlaw, Military Personnel (Confederate guerilla leader)
Time Period(s): 19th century (1864-1885)
Locale(s): Missouri; Oklahoma; Texas

Summary: The novel offers Western outlaws as romantic adventurers. Belle Starr, Cole Younger, and Jesse James are shown as Confederate compatriots fighting for a lost cause. Their life of crime is depicted as a Robin Hood-like revenge of the little people over the government. All is larger than life and considerably idealized.

Historical Accuracy: The elevation of criminals into romantic legends requires a good deal of obfuscation of the facts.

871 *Black-Eyed Susan*

Date of Publication: 1990
Subject(s): American West; Romance
Fictional character(s): Susan Armitage, Governess; Logan Vance, Journalist, Publisher (newspaper owner)
Time Period(s): 1890s
Locale(s): St. Louis, Missouri; Tulsa, Oklahoma

Summary: In the 1890s, Susan Armitage accompanies her widowed brother-in-law to the Oklahoma territory to care for his two children. Propriety forces them to marry; however, love enriches and complicates matters as the two are forced to deal with their growing relationship and a variety of frontier problems.

Historical Accuracy: The emphasis is squarely on relationships over the historical.

872 *Fallen Angel*

Date of Publication: 1989
Subject(s): American West; Romance
Fictional character(s): Justine Drussard, Actress, Prostitute; York Master, Detective—Private (Pinkerton agent)
Time Period(s): 19th century
Locale(s): Tombstone, Arizona

Summary: Abandoned by her fellow actors and stranded out west, Justine Drussard resorts to prostitution to support herself. Pinkerton agent York Master seeks her assistance in locating his missing sister.

Historical Accuracy: This is a colorful romantic story rather than a thorough historical one, but it has some genuine period touches.

GRACE CAMPBELL (1895-1963)

Born near Williamstown in Glengarry County, Ontario, on a farm, Campbell went to Queen's University and earned a gold medal in English literature. She taught school, married, and moved to Montreal. She published short stories and novels, including *Highland Heritage* and *Torbeg*.

873 *Torbeg*

Date of Publication: 1953
Subject(s): Jacobite Rebellion
Fictional character(s): Finlay Ban Grant, Laird
Time Period(s): 1740s (1745)
Locale(s): Scotland

Summary: This tale about Bonnie Prince Charlie's ill-fated rising to capture the British throne concentrates on the old ways of clan life destroyed by the Stuart cause. Finlay Ban Grant answers the call to arms but with tragic consequences.

Historical Accuracy: The story is a fanciful one, but does present the historical background with accuracy.

PATRICIA CAMPBELL (1901-)

Campbell was born and raised in Washington where she attended the University of Washington, Seattle. A writer and teacher, Campbell was the author of a weekly newspaper column, "The History of North Olympic Peninsula.".

874 *Cedarhaven*

Date of Publication: 1965
Subject(s): American West; Settlement of the American Frontier
Fictional character(s): Darrie Starkweather, Gentlewoman; Belle Starkweather, Gentlewoman; Genia Starkweather, Gentlewoman
Time Period(s): 1850s (1859)
Locale(s): Port Townsend, Washington

Summary: Three sisters—Darrie, Belle, and Genia Starkweather—journey to the Washington Territory in 1859. The novel tells the stories of the men they find and their lives in a boom town of sailors and adventurers in the pioneer Northwest.

Historical Accuracy: The author is intimate with her locale, and the era is truthfully depicted.

875 *The Royal Ann Tree*

Date of Publication: 1956
Subject(s): Settlement of the American Frontier
Fictional character(s): Louise Vane, Orphan
Time Period(s): 1850s
Locale(s): Puget Sound, Washington

Summary: At the age of 15, Louise Vane finds herself alone, when she is orphaned by the death of her parents. The novel captures her life on an isolated homestead.

Historical Accuracy: This is an authentic look at the period and the region.

876   *Silver Fruit*

Date of Publication: 1959
Subject(s): Family Saga; American West
Fictional character(s): Louise Stacy, Gentlewoman; Dee Cummings, Businesswoman; Amory Cummings, Businessman
Time Period(s): 1900s; 1910s (1900s-1918)
Locale(s): Port Garry, Washington

Summary: Two contrasting families, the patriarchal Cummingses and the Wolfkills, are gradually connected by the friendship between Louise and Dee. Lou's envy of the wealth and elegance of the Cummings family gradually changes as they are revealed to be self-absorbed and unfulfilled.

Historical Accuracy: Campbell's knowledge of the locale anchors the story in a particular setting and time that is well-described.

THOMAS CAMPBELL

877   *Old Miss*

Date of Publication: 1929
Subject(s): Antebellum South; Civil War—U.S.
Fictional character(s): Charlotte Steppleton, Southern Belle; Robert Tirwell, Spouse (of Charlotte)
Time Period(s): 19th century
Locale(s): Virginia

Summary: Plantation life in Virginia before and during the Civil War is presented in this family story of Charlotte Steppleton. The novel portrays Charlotte from childhood to her marriage to Robert Tirwell and describes their family. By the end of the war, all has been altered.

Historical Accuracy: As a presentation of Southern life during the period, the novel achieves a high standard of believability.

JANE CAMPION

KATE PULLINGER

Campion, daughter of a performance director and actress, was born in Wellington, New Zealand, and has become a world-renowned filmmaker and writer. She is a former art school student who developed her filmmaking skills at the Australian Film, Television, and Radio School. Her film *The Piano* was a surprise box office hit. She was the second woman to be nominated for an Academy Award for Best Director, and won an Oscar for the Best Screenplay.

878   *The Piano*

Date of Publication: 1994
Subject(s): Victorian Period

Fictional character(s): Ada McGrath, Young Woman, Handicapped (mute); Stewart McGrath, Landowner; Baines, Landowner
Time Period(s): 19th century
Locale(s): New Zealand

Summary: In the novelization of the award-winning film, the story of Ada McGrath and her arranged marriage in remote New Zealand is described as a sexual journey. Ada's husband refuses to transport her prized piano and their illiterate neighbor, Baines, agrees to let Ada earn her piano back.

Historical Accuracy: The novel reveals details that the movie left unstated. The novel excels in capturing the era's repressions and strangled emotions.

MARSHA CANHAM

879   *The Blood of Roses*

Date of Publication: 1989
Subject(s): Jacobite Rebellion; Espionage; Romance
Fictional character(s): Catherine Ashbrooke, Gentlewoman; Alexander Cameron, Spy (Jacobite)
Time Period(s): 1740s (1745)
Locale(s): England

Summary: In the sequel to *The Pride of Lions*, the love between Catherine Ashbrooke and Alexander Cameron is severely tested when she learns that he is a Scottish spy during the Jacobite uprising.

Historical Accuracy: Romance predominates over a careful and convincing period or historical presentation.

880   *In the Shadow of Midnight*

Date of Publication: 1994
Subject(s): Middle Ages; Romance
Fictional character(s): Lady Ariel de Clare, Noblewoman; Eduard FitzRandwulf d'Amboise, Knight, Bastard Son
Historical character(s): John, Ruler (King of England); William Marshal, Nobleman (Earl of Pembroke)
Time Period(s): 13th century (1200s)
Locale(s): Wales; England; France

Summary: The headstrong niece of William Marshal, Ariel de Clare, comes under the protection of knight Eduard FitzRandwulf d'Amboise who is pledged to see her safely to Wales. Connected to their growing attraction to one another is a dangerous plan to rescue Princess Eleanor from the king.

Historical Accuracy: The story is a fanciful one, employing some actual historical figures in fictional circumstances. The novel does offer some authentic period touches.

881   *The Pride of Lions*

Date of Publication: 1988
Subject(s): Jacobite Rebellion; Espionage; Romance
Fictional character(s): Catherine Ashbrooke, Gentlewoman; Alexander Cameron, Spy
Time Period(s): 1740s (1745)
Locale(s): England

Summary: This romance set against the backdrop of the Jacobite Rebellion of 1745 concerns Catherine Ashbrooke, who is forced by her father to marry the winner of a duel, Alexander Cameron. Despite this inauspicious beginning, Catherine is determined to win his love.

Historical Accuracy: The novel's story strains credibility but does employ some authentic period elements.

VICTOR CANNING (1911-1986)

English author Canning was born in Plymouth and served as a major in the Royal Artillery during World War II. He is the author of over 50 mysteries and thrillers. Most feature moral conflict as a central theme.

882 *The Crimson Chalice*

Date of Publication: 1978
Subject(s): Myths and Legends; Dark Ages; Arthurian Legends
Fictional character(s): Arthur, Warrior, Ruler (King of the Britons); Merlin, Sorcerer
Time Period(s): 5th century
Locale(s): England

Summary: The book's version of the Arthurian saga chronicles the career of Arthur from his childhood to his unification of the Britons in an effort to resist the Saxon invaders. The emphasis is on an historical Arthur, and the novel attempts to find the realistic basis for the legends.

Historical Accuracy: The author did not follow the accepted Arthurian legend because he felt there was little truth in it.

883 *Raven's Wind*

Date of Publication: 1983
Subject(s): Dark Ages; Vikings; Anglo-Saxon Period
Fictional character(s): Justus, Slave; Riada, Young Woman
Historical character(s): Alfred the Great, Ruler (King of Wessex)
Time Period(s): 9th century (870s)
Locale(s): Wessex, England; Denmark

Summary: Justus, a young man living in Wessex in the 9th century, is captured by the Vikings and taken back to Denmark as a slave. There he learns Viking ways, including the craft of shipbuilding, which he uses to escape. He eventually convinces King Alfred that England must build warships to repulse the Viking raiders.

Historical Accuracy: The novel effectively evokes the reality of Anglo-Saxon England and the heroic age of the Vikings.

LE GRAND CANNON (1899-1979)

An American novelist best known for *Look to the Mountain*, Cannon received an MBA from Harvard and pursued a business career until 1932 when he became a full-time writer. Among his works are *The Kents*, *A Mighty Fortress*, *Come Home at Even*.

884 *Come Home at Even*

Date of Publication: 1951
Subject(s): American Colonies; Puritans
Fictional character(s): Robert Cargill, Carpenter
Historical character(s): Roger Williams, Religious (clergyman)
Time Period(s): 17th century (1630s)
Locale(s): Lancashire, England; Salem, Massachusetts, American Colonies

Summary: Colonial life in Salem, Massachusetts, during the days of the Puritans is described through the experiences of an English carpenter, Robert Cargill, who seeks a better life in America. Roger Williams plays a central role in Cargill's decision whether to stay in America or return to England.

Historical Accuracy: This quiet domestic story is both compelling and convincing in its picture of colonial life and customs.

885 *Look to the Mountain*

Date of Publication: 1942
Subject(s): American Colonies; American Revolution
Fictional character(s): Whit Livingston, Trapper; Jonas Moore, Frontiersman; Melissa Butler, Spouse (of Whit)
Time Period(s): 18th century (1709-1777)
Locale(s): New Hampshire, American Colonies

Summary: Pioneer life in New Hampshire before and during the American Revolution is depicted in the experiences of trapper Whit Livingston and his wife Melissa. Events of the war reach them only as distant echoes; the majority of their concerns are focused on the daily tasks of survival in the woods.

Historical Accuracy: The period elements are convincingly presented.

JAY CANTOR (1950-)

Cantor is the author of fantasy and historical novels, including *The Death of Che Guevara* and *Krazy Kat*, and the nonfiction titles, *On Giving Birth to One's Own Mother: Essays on Art and Society* and *The Space Between: Literature and Politics*.

886 *The Death of Che Guevara*

Date of Publication: 1983
Subject(s): Biography, Fictionalized
Historical character(s): Che Guevara, Revolutionary
Time Period(s): 20th century
Locale(s): Cuba; Bolivia

Summary: The novel takes the form of a fragmentary autobiography of the revolutionary leader Che Guevara. The second part of the novel is made up of diary entries based on the actual records kept by Guevara in the Bolivia campaign, in which he was captured and executed.

Historical Accuracy: The novel is skillful and authentic in presenting the background and biographical details of Guevara's life and times.

BENJAMIN CAPPS (1922-)

An American writer born in Texas and educated at the University of Texas, Capps has been an instructor of English and journalism, a tool and die maker, and a surveyor. His western novels have won many awards.

887 The Brothers of Uterica

Date of Publication: 1967
Subject(s): American West; Utopian Communities
Fictional character(s): Jean Bossereau, Leader (community); Harriet Edwards, Feminist; Dr. Valentin, Doctor
Time Period(s): 1850s
Locale(s): Texas

Summary: In the 1850s a band of settlers journey into the Texas frontier to establish a utopian community. Uterica is to run on the principles of reason, brotherly love, and communal property. The novel details the discrepancy between the ideal and the real as the community finds itself ill-prepared to deal with foul weather, drought, Indians, stampedes, their lack of skills, and conflict within the community.

Historical Accuracy: Uterica is based on ideal communities established in the 19th century. The western wilderness is realitically described.

888 Sam Chance

Date of Publication: 1965
Subject(s): American West; Ranching; Reconstruction Period
Fictional character(s): Sam Chance, Veteran (Civil War), Rancher
Time Period(s): 19th century; 20th century (1865-1922)
Locale(s): Texas

Summary: This western story traces the career of a Confederate sergeant who becomes a Texas cattle rancher immediately following the end of the Civil War. The novel dramatizes his rise to power until his death in the 1920s.

Historical Accuracy: The novel captures the era and the atmosphere of the region convincingly.

889 The Trail to Ogallala

Date of Publication: 1964
Subject(s): American West; Cattle Drives
Fictional character(s): Billy Scott, Cowboy
Time Period(s): 19th century
Locale(s): Texas; Kansas; Nebraska

Summary: This is a day-to-day account of a three-month-long cattle drive from South Texas to Ogallala, Nebraska. Billy Scott is the young skilled cattleman who drives a herd of cattle north. On the way they encounter dangerous river crossings, sudden storms, drought, and a seemingly never ending expanse of frontier before reaching their final destination.

Historical Accuracy: The details of the cattle drive are realistic and reliable.

890 The True Memoirs of Charley Blankenship

Date of Publication: 1972
Subject(s): American West; Ranching
Historical character(s): Charley Blankenship, Cowboy
Time Period(s): 1880s; 1890s
Locale(s): West

Summary: The novel is based on the actual Charles E. Blankenship's account of ten years of his life as a cowboy. His experiences are representative of actual western life at the time, and his memoirs are filled with a colorful gallery of realistic western types.

Historical Accuracy: There are few better actual representations of what ordinary life must have been like in the West.

891 The White Man's Road

Date of Publication: 1969
Subject(s): Indians
Fictional character(s): Joe Cowbone, Indian (Comanche)
Time Period(s): 1890s
Locale(s): Southwest

Summary: This tale of the maturation of a young Comanche, Joe Cowbone, shows his struggle to find his identity in the face of the declining vitality of Indian life. Joe's assertion of self becomes fixed on a horse-stealing raid.

Historical Accuracy: The novel features an authentic presentation of the period and setting.

892 Woman Chief

Date of Publication: 1979
Subject(s): American West; Indians; Tribal Life—Native American
Historical character(s): Woman Chief, Indian (Crow)
Time Period(s): 19th century
Locale(s): Great Plains

Summary: In the male-dominated world of Indian life on the Great Plains, this novel details the extraodinary tale of an Atsina Indian child. Beginning her life among the Crow Indians as a ''slave girl,'' the child wins such respect that she is later revered as ''Woman Chief.'' The novel, derived from stories handed down by white traders, traces Woman Chief's career and her rise to a great leader of her people.

Historical Accuracy: The novel is convincing in its depiction of Native American Indian life and customs.

893 A Woman of the People

Date of Publication: 1966
Subject(s): American West; Indians; Tribal Life—Native American
Fictional character(s): Helen Morrison, Captive; Old Woman, Indian (Comanche); Ute Killer, Indian (Comanche), Warrior
Time Period(s): 19th century (1850s-1870s)
Locale(s): Texas

Summary: A white girl, age nine, is captured in 1854 by the Comanches. She adapts to Indian ways while secretly planning her escape, but cannot help being caught up in Comanche life. In the end, she has a divided loyalty as the settlers' encroachment means an end to the way of life that has become her own.

Historical Accuracy: The novel attempts to depict the Comanches as neither noble savages nor as the brutes of other western novels. The novel creates a realistic sense of a complex culture existing in a harsh and demanding environment.

PETER CAREY (1943-)

Australian author Carey was educated at Monash University. He has worked in advertising and as a free-lance writer. His works, which include *The Fat Man in History*, *War Crimes*, *Bliss*, and *Illywhacker* have been widely praised. He was honored with England's Booker Prize in 1988 for *Oscar and Lucinda*.

`894` *Oscar and Lucinda*

Date of Publication: 1988
Subject(s): Victorian Period; Religious Life
Fictional character(s): Oscar Hopkins, Religious (defrocked Anglican priest); Lucinda Leplastrier, Businesswoman (glass factory owner)
Time Period(s): 1860s (1866)
Locale(s): England; Australia

Summary: Oscar Hopkins is a defrocked Anglican priest and a compulsive gambler. He and Lucinda Leplastrier, owner of a glass factory in Sydney, construct a small church made of iron and glass that they ship to a remote location. The novel offers an odd group of misfits and fanatics that collectively provide an off-beat look at the Victorian age and its blend of love, commerce, religion, and colonialism.

Historical Accuracy: Perhaps too eccentric to be regarded as historical, the novel is insightful in its symbolic creation of Victorian angst and atmosphere.

HENRY CARLISLE (1926-)

An American writer, Carlisle was born in San Francisco and attended the University of Paris and Stanford University. He worked for a number of years as a trade book editor. His novel *Voyage to the First of December* won the Putnam Award in 1972.

`895` *The Jonah Man*

Date of Publication: 1984
Subject(s): Sea Story; Whaling
Historical character(s): George Pollard, Sea Captain; Mary Pollard, Spouse; Ralph Waldo Emerson, Writer, Philosopher
Time Period(s): 19th century (1808-1847)
Locale(s): *Essex*, At Sea; Nantucket, Massachusetts

Summary: The novel tells the story of the actual whaling ship *Essex* that was struck and sunk by a sperm whale in the Pacific. The survivors endure three months in an open boat before being rescued 4,000 miles from the site of the disaster. The captain of the *Essex* narrates the story of his life as an outcast after the adventure. The actual sinking of the ship was

the inspiration for the climax of Herman Melville's *Moby Dick*.

Historical Accuracy: The novel is a convincing version of the actual events with speculations about Pollard's life after his famous adventure.

`896` *The Land Where the Sun Dies*

Date of Publication: 1975
Subject(s): Indians; Seminole Wars; Slavery
Fictional character(s): Laird Caffrey, Military Personnel; Eliza Hutchins, Spouse (of Caffrey); John Hutchins, Government Official
Historical character(s): Andrew Jackson, Military Personnel, Political Figure; James Monroe, Political Figure; Martin Van Buren, Political Figure; Osceola, Indian (Seminole), Chieftain
Time Period(s): 19th century (1818-1838)
Locale(s): Florida; Tennessee

Summary: The novel chronicles the cruel Indian removal policy masterminded by Andrew Jackson that resulted in the Seminole War led by Chief Osceola. Events are seen through the perspectives of a government agent, John Hutchins; his daughter, Eliza; and her husband, Laird Coffrey, who must carry out the assignment to put down the Indian rising.

Historical Accuracy: The novel convincingly details a shameful period in American history that is rarely presented.

`897` *Voyage to the First of December*

Date of Publication: 1976
Subject(s): Sea Story; Mutiny; Trials
Historical character(s): Philip Spencer, Military Personnel (midshipman); Alexander Slidell Mackenzie, Military Personnel (naval captain); Robert Leacock, Doctor
Time Period(s): 1840s (1842)
Locale(s): *Somers*, At Sea; New York, New York

Summary: This is a fictional reconstruction of the notorious Somers Mutiny Affair. Midshipman Philip Spencer, son of President Tyler's Secretary of War, and two other sailors are hanged for mutiny aboard the U.S. brig *Somers* on a training cruise to the African coast. The ship's surgeon offers a view of the events and the ensuing court of inquiry while raising some provocative questions of whether there was a mutiny at all.

Historical Accuracy: This novel about a fascinating naval incident is solidly based on the evidence of the case with credible speculations about motive and intention.

CARL LAMSON CARMER (1893-1976)

An American professor of English, journalist, and author, Carmer was a historian specializing in upstate New York. His published books includes volumes of poetry and novels for juveniles and adults, many with a New York setting.

`898` *Genesee Fever*

Date of Publication: 1941
Subject(s): Whiskey Rebellion

Fictional character(s): Nathan Hart, Teacher
Time Period(s): 1790s
Locale(s): Genesee Valley, New York

Summary: The novel tells of the settlement of upstate New York and the conflict between farmers and those who wished to establish landed status in the Genesee Valley. The hero is Nathan Hart, a school teacher who escapes from the Whiskey Rebellion only to find himself in the struggle between wealthy and small landowners.

Historical Accuracy: The book's strength is in detailing the settlement of upstate New York with authentic regional period details.

EMILY CARMICHAEL
(PSEUD. OF EMILY KROKOSZ)

899 *Visions of a Heart*

Date of Publication: 1990
Subject(s): War of 1812; Romance
Fictional character(s): Miriam Sutcliffe, Gentlewoman, Fugitive; Jordan Scott, Indian (part Chippewa), Frontiersman
Time Period(s): 1810s
Locale(s): Michilimackinac, Michigan; Ontario, Canada

Summary: Miriam Sutcliffe is a fugitive from an English treason charge during the War of 1812. She meets another fugitive, Jordan Scott, who has abandoned life in Boston to live among the Chippewas. The two, with little in common, come together eventually.

Historical Accuracy: The novel is more fantasy than realistic. There are some period elements that are believable.

NICHOLAS CARNAC
(PSEUD. OF F.H.M. EDWARDS)

900 *Indigo*

Date of Publication: 1982
Subject(s): Inheritance—Disputed; British Raj; Indian Mutiny
Fictional character(s): Alasdair Lindsay, Landowner; Craig Lindsay, Heir; John Douglas, Landowner
Time Period(s): 1850s (1856-1859)
Locale(s): Bengal, India; Calcutta, India; London, England

Summary: Craig Lindsay is named heir to his uncle's vast indigo plantation in India. From the moment Craig arrives to claim his inheritance he is caught in a web of conspiracy and intrigue and an apparent plot by the Douglas family to take control of the estate. Meanwhile, India explodes in violence, mutiny, and rebellion.

Historical Accuracy: The glimpse of British colonial life and the India of the mutiny are compellingly described.

901 *Tournament of the Shadows*

Date of Publication: 1978
Subject(s): Espionage; Victorian Period
Fictional character(s): Mark Aspern, Military Personnel (captain); Vassily Danin, Spy; Mei Ling, Royalty (princess)

Time Period(s): 1880s (1884-1887)
Locale(s): St. Petersburg, Russia; Calcutta, India; Peking, China

Summary: Captain Mark Aspern finds himself playing in the "Great Game" of global politics with Asia hanging in the balance. His opponent is the daring Russian intelligence agent Vassily Danin. Aspern's secret mission takes him from Russia to India and China. At each step danger lurks in a web of conspiracy and betrayal with the fates of nations in peril.

Historical Accuracy: The novel is filled with details of the period that buttress the high stakes adventure.

WALTER CARNAHAN (1891-)

Born in Indiana, Carnahan graduated from Oakland City College and Indiana University. A high school teacher, Carnahan is the author of several mathematics textbooks, as well as novels.

902 *Hoffman's Row*

Date of Publication: 1963
Subject(s): Biography, Fictionalized
Historical character(s): Abraham Lincoln, Lawyer; Mary Todd Lincoln, Spouse
Time Period(s): 1840s
Locale(s): Springfield, Illinois

Summary: This novel is based on an actual incident during the courtship of Abraham Lincoln and Mary Todd. Lincoln is challenged to a duel by a rival. The incident is filled-out with an elaborate set of contrivances involving a runaway slave and scoundrels.

Historical Accuracy: Although the incident has some basis in fact, the emphasis on romance strains plausibility at several points.

OTIS CARNEY (1922-)

Born in Chicago, Carney worked as a newspaper reporter and a free-lance novelist and television screenwriter. He served in the U.S. Marine Corps for four years, where he earned the rank of captain. Other works include *Love at First Flight*, *When the Bough Breaks*, *Yesterday's Hero*, *Good Friday 1963*, and *The Paper Bullet*, which won the Friends of the American Writers Best Book Award in 1960.

903 *Chihuahua 1916*

Date of Publication: 1980
Subject(s): American West; Mexican Revolution
Fictional character(s): Sam Eagle, Cowboy; Ora Scalley, Cowboy; Lottie Pruitt, Young Woman
Historical character(s): John J. Pershing, Military Personnel (army officer)
Time Period(s): 1910s (1915-1916)
Locale(s): Columbus, New Mexico; Chihuahua, Mexico

Summary: A small group is caught in the crossfire as General Pershing pursues Pancho Villa into Mexico. The campaign is a mistake from the start as Mexican-American relations are played out on the border of the vanishing American frontier on the eve of World War I.

Historical Accuracy: The account is based on interviews with participants, giving the story solidity and credibility.

ANNABEL CAROTHERS

904 *Kilcaraig*

Date of Publication: 1982
Subject(s): Family Saga
Fictional character(s): Catriona Lamont, Gentlewoman; Grania Lamont, Gentlewoman; Rorie Lamont, Gentleman
Time Period(s): 20th century (1913-1978)
Locale(s): Mull, Scotland; London, England

Summary: This family saga, set mainly on the tiny Scottish island of Mull, tells the story of the Lamonts of Castle Kilcaraig, who struggle to maintain their world despite 20th century changes. Catriona's secret love begins a chain of events, and her descendents each must be measured by the hold Kilcaraig has on them.

Historical Accuracy: The locale painting is effective and genuine.

ALEJO CARPENTIER (1904-1980)

A Cuban journalist, editor, musicologist, and author, Carpentier is an important figure in Latin American literature who coined the term ''magical realism.'' After spending many years in self-imposed exile, Carpentier returned to Cuba after the revolution in 1959. During the last years of his life, he was the cultural attache for the Cuban Embassy in France. His books include *The Lost Steps*, *The War of Time*, and *Reasons of State*.

905 *The Harp and the Shadow*

Date of Publication: 1990
Subject(s): Exploration
Historical character(s): Christopher Columbus, Explorer; Pius IX, Religious (pope); Jules Verne, Writer; Leon Bloy, Writer; Bartolome de Las Casas, Religious (missionary); Friedrich Schiller, Writer
Time Period(s): Multiple Time Periods
Locale(s): Europe; At Sea; West Indies

Summary: This experimental inquiry into the character of Christopher Columbus is divided into three parts. The first is set in the 19th century as Pope Pius IX is preparing to canonize Columbus; the second is the confessional account of Columbus himself; and the third is an imaginary debate on Columbus by such figures as Jules Verne and Friedrich Schiller.

Historical Accuracy: Columbus emerges as a credible figure and the novel displays a convincing encyclopedic grasp of the periods and issues.

906 *Kingdom of This World*

Date of Publication: 1957

Subject(s): Independence—Haiti; Slavery
Fictional character(s): Ti Noel, Slave
Time Period(s): 18th century
Locale(s): Haiti

Summary: The story of the Haitian revolution is told through the experiences of Ti Noel, a slave of a wealthy planter. The events capture the overthrow of the French government, the kingship of Henri Christophe, and his downfall.

Historical Accuracy: The novel provides an accurate depiction of the events of the Haitian revolt.

CALEB CARR (1955-)

An American writer born in New York City and educated at New York University, Carr is the author of short stories and articles on military history, as well as an historical work, *America Invulnerable: The Quest for Absolute Security From 1812 to Star Wars*. He also wrote *The Devil Soldier: The Story of Frederick Townsend Ward*, a biography of a participant in the Taiping Rebellion.

907 *The Alienist*

Date of Publication: 1994
Subject(s): Mystery; Psychology
Fictional character(s): John Schuler Moore, Journalist; Dr. Lazlo Kreizler, Psychologist, Detective—Amateur; Sara Howard, Secretary
Historical character(s): Theodore Roosevelt, Political Figure (New York police commissioner); John Pierpont Morgan, Financier; Franz Boas, Anthropologist; Anthony Comstock, Political Figure (anti-vice crusader); Paul Kelly, Organized Crime Figure; Lincoln Steffens, Journalist
Time Period(s): 1890s (1896)
Locale(s): New York, New York; Washington, District of Columbia

Summary: A serial killer is murdering boy prostitutes in Manhattan in 1896. Police commissioner Theodore Roosevelt brings in an ''alienist,'' an expert in mental pathology, to catch the killer by attempting to understand the context of his life. Dr. Kreizler assembles a team that includes a *New York Times* reporter, a young police secretary, and two eccentric detectives to solve the mystery of who did it and why.

Historical Accuracy: The novel is a close reconstruction of turn-of-the-century New York even if the narrator, John Schuler Moore, offers too contemporary a voice.

JOHN DICKSON CARR (1906-1977)

An An American mystery writer born in Pennsylvania and a graduate of Haverford College, Carr is credited with being the creator of the historical mystery story. He is the official biographer of Arthur Conan Doyle and is recognized as one of the foremost practitioners of the ''locked room'' or ''impossible crime'' mystery form. Carr's formula for a successful mystery is to merely state the evidence to the reader and the reader will mislead him or herself.

908 *Captain Cut-Throat*

Date of Publication: 1955

Subject(s): Mystery; Napoleonic Era

Fictional character(s): Allan Hepburn, Spy

Historical character(s): Joseph Fouche, Political Figure (police chief), Revolutionary; Napoleon Bonaparte, Military Personnel (army commander), Ruler (Emperor of France); Charles Maurice de Talleyrand-Perigord, Government Official, Diplomat

Time Period(s): 1800s (1805)

Locale(s): Paris, France; Boulogne, France

Summary: This historical mystery is set during Napoleon's preparations for the invasion of England. A murderer, who leaves a calling card next to his victims signed ''Captain Cut-Throat,'' is on the loose. When one of Napoleon's sentries falls victim to the murderer, wily Paris police chief Joseph Fouche recruits British spy Allan Hepburn to ferret out the killer.

Historical Accuracy: Many authentic period touches create a believable background.

909 *The Devil in Velvet*

Date of Publication: 1951

Subject(s): Mystery; Restoration Period; Time Travel

Fictional character(s): Nicholas Fenton, Professor (history), Time Traveller; Mary Genville, Young Woman; Meg York, Young Woman

Historical character(s): Charles II, Ruler (King of England)

Time Period(s): 17th century (1670s); 1920s

Locale(s): London, England

Summary: Nicholas Fenton, a 1920s historian, finds himself inhabiting the body of a nobleman in Restoration. With his knowledge of future events, Nicholas is at the center of the Popish plot against Charles II, while two different women compete for his favors.

Historical Accuracy: The novel's background is firmly grounded as the novel's extensive documentation makes clear.

910 *Fire, Burn!*

Date of Publication: 1957

Subject(s): Mystery; Regency Period; Time Travel

Fictional character(s): John Cheviot, Detective—Police, Time Traveller; Lady Flora Drayton, Gentlewoman

Historical character(s): Robert Peel, Political Figure, Government Official

Time Period(s): 1820s (1829)

Locale(s): London, England

Summary: Police Detective John Cheviot of Scotland Yard finds himself transported back in time to 1829 where he assists Robert Peel in establishing the London Metropolitan Police Force. He also finds himself accused of murder. The future of the force hangs in the balance in this ingenious time tangle.

Historical Accuracy: The author's evident knowledge of the period creates a convincing picture of the times.

911 *The Hungry Goblin: A Victorian Detective Novel*

Date of Publication: 1972

Subject(s): Victorian Period; Mystery

Fictional character(s): Christopher Farrell, Journalist; Nigel Seagrave, Explorer

Historical character(s): Wilkie Collins, Writer (novelist); Edmund Henderson, Detective—Police

Time Period(s): 1860s (1869)

Locale(s): London, England

Summary: In this Victorian-era mystery, Wilkie Collins acts as detective in a complicated tale involving journalist Christopher Farrell, recently returned to London from America; his friend, the explorer Nigel Seagrave; and two mysterious women. The complicated mystery plot is a collection of ingenious enigmas, including Carr's speciality, the locked-room puzzle.

Historical Accuracy: The details of period life are authentically drawn, as Carr's notes make clear.

912 *Most Secret*

Date of Publication: 1964

Subject(s): Restoration Period; Picaresque Adventure

Fictional character(s): Roderick Kinsmere, Adventurer; Dolly Landis, Actress

Historical character(s): Charles II, Ruler (King of England)

Time Period(s): 17th century (1670)

Locale(s): London, England; France

Summary: This is a rollicking and picaresque tale set in the London of Charles II. Adventurer Roderick Kinsmere finds himself in an escalating tangle of conspiracies and challenges that take him from the Palace Yard to Drury Lane and the appealing actress Dolly Landis.

Historical Accuracy: The period background of this fictional story is credible.

913 *The Murder of Sir Edmund Godfrey*

Date of Publication: 1936

Subject(s): Mystery; Restoration Period; Popish Plot

Historical character(s): Charles II, Ruler (King of England); Sir Edmund Godfrey, Judge; Titus Oates, Rebel

Time Period(s): 17th century (1678)

Locale(s): London, England

Summary: The novel considers one of history's great unsolved mysteries: the disappearance and death of Sir Edmund Godfrey in 1678. Godfrey is a well-known London magistrate who vanishes after taking a deposition from Titus Oates on the Catholic plot to take over England. When his body is later found, Catholics are blamed, and Godfrey's presumed murder is used as the excuse to force Charles II to change the line of succession and prevent his brother James, a Catholic, from succeeding him. The novel recreates the mystery surrounding Godfrey's death with an ingenious solution.

Historical Accuracy: Although the novel is based on fact and bolstered by evident scholarship, it does not presume to be history, except insofar as it tries to be true to the atmosphere and spirit of the time.

914 *Papa La-Bas*

Date of Publication: 1968
Subject(s): Mystery; Witchcraft and Sorcery; Antebellum South
Fictional character(s): Dick Macrae, Diplomat (English consul); Margot de Sancerre, Young Woman; Isabelle de Sancerre, Gentlewoman
Historical character(s): Judah P. Benjamin, Political Figure
Time Period(s): 1850s (1858)
Locale(s): New Orleans, Louisiana

Summary: This ingenious and unusual mystery is set in New Orleans during the 1850s. It's a complex tale involving the British Consul, Dick Macrae, and creole voodoo. On the scene to investigate is Louisiana Senator Judah P. Benjamin who will later serve during the Civil War in Jefferson Davis' cabinet.

Historical Accuracy: The mystery is solidly based on factual details of the period as the author's notes indicate.

915 *Scandal at High Chimneys: A Victorian Melodrama*

Date of Publication: 1959
Subject(s): Mystery; Victorian Period
Fictional character(s): Clive Strickland, Lawyer, Writer; Victor Damon, Gentleman; Kate Damon, Gentlewoman
Historical character(s): Jonathan Whicher, Detective—Police
Time Period(s): 1860s (1865)
Locale(s): London, England

Summary: Clive Strickland is invited by his friend Victor Damon to visit his family's estate to advise on the prospective marriage of one of Victor's sisters. While there, strange happenings begin to occur, including the apparition of a ghost-like figure and the murder of the family patriarch. As one of the suspects, Clive must solve the crimes.

Historical Accuracy: The period details are authentic and convincing.

PHILIPPA CARR
(PSEUD. OF ELEANOR HIBBERT, 1906-1993)

Philippa Carr is one of many pseudonyms for prolific British author Eleanor Burford Hibbert. One of the most popular romance writers of this century, she is perhaps better known for her novels written as Jean Plaidy and Victoria Holt. The novels written as Philippa Carr combine the gothic and historical styles of fiction.

916 *The Adulteress*

Date of Publication: 1982
Subject(s): Romance; Family Saga; Georgian Period
Fictional character(s): Zipporah Ransome, Gentlewoman
Time Period(s): 1750s
Locale(s): England

Summary: When the family estate is at risk, Zipporah Ransome is called back to her ancestral home, Eversleigh Court. There, she is caught up in a vicious web of family scandal and menace.

Historical Accuracy: The historical period is secondary to the Gothic tangle of threat and menace.

917 *The Black Swan*

Date of Publication: 1990
Subject(s): Independence—Ireland; Victorian Period; Family Saga
Fictional character(s): Lucie Lansdon, Orphan, Gentlewoman; Joel Greenham, Fiance(e), Gentleman; Roland Fitzgerald, Gentleman
Time Period(s): 1880s
Locale(s): Cornwall, England; London, England

Summary: In this sequel to *The Changeling*, Lucie Lansdon witnesses her father's murder by an Irish terrorist. Disaster and death seem to follow Lucie when her fiance, Joel Greenham, dies suddenly. All appears calm when she marries Roland Fitzgerald, but their life together is also marred by disaster, real and imagined.

Historical Accuracy: The historical setting of the agitation surrounding Irish Home Rule is accurately described.

918 *The Changeling*

Date of Publication: 1989
Subject(s): Romance; Victorian Period; Family Saga
Fictional character(s): Rebecca Mandeville, Orphan, Gentlewoman; Benedict Lansdon, Gentleman, Step-Parent; Belinda Mandeville, Orphan, Gentlewoman
Time Period(s): 1870s
Locale(s): London, England; Cornwall, England

Summary: In a sequel to Carr's *The Pool of St. Branok*, Rebecca and Belinda Mandeville lose their mother and are forced to live with their stepfather, Benedict Lansdon, whom Rebecca despises. The family scene erupts in conflict and tension that escalates into violence.

Historical Accuracy: The Victorian scene forms a believable backdrop to the novel's melodramatic story.

919 *Daughters of England*

Date of Publication: 1995
Subject(s): Restoration Period; Religious Conflict
Fictional character(s): Sarah Standish, Actress; Lord Rosslyn, Nobleman; Kate Rosslyn, Young Woman
Time Period(s): 17th century (1660-1689)
Locale(s): England

Summary: Set during the 17th century against the backdrop of Catholic-Protestant conflict, the novel tells the story of Sarah Standish who runs off to become an actress. She weds Lord Rosslyn and is pregnant by the time she learns that he is already married. After she dies, the story continues with the adventures of her daughter Kate who becomes a pawn in Lord Rosslyn's plot to secure Rosslyn Manor.

Historical Accuracy: Although the romantic adventure elements predominate, there is a strong and authentic picture of the era and its conflicts.

920   *Knave of Hearts*

Date of Publication: 1983
Subject(s): Romance; Family Saga
Fictional character(s): Lottie, Gentlewoman; Charles de Tourville, Gentleman; Dickson Frenshaw, Gentleman
Time Period(s): 18th century
Locale(s): Paris, France; England

Summary: Lottie is a young English girl who travels with her mother and new stepfather to Paris where she is quickly swept up in the glitter and intrigue of the French court. Passion comes in the form of a new lover and an old one who is on a secret mission, as France moves steadily toward revolution.

Historical Accuracy: The historical detail here is presented in passing, more as costumes and setting for the novel's tangled suspense and romance.

921   *Lament for a Lost Lover*

Date of Publication: 1977
Subject(s): Civil War—England; Restoration Period; Fires
Fictional character(s): Arabella Tolworthy, Gentlewoman, Widow(er); Harriet Main, Actress; Edwin Eversleigh, Heir
Time Period(s): 17th century (1658-1660s)
Locale(s): France; London, England

Summary: Arabella Tolworthy and her family flee England when Charles I is dethroned and serve the exiled Charles II. She accompanies the king back to England as a widow in control of the Eversleigh estate. The past returns in the form of actress Harriet Main, and the suspense culminates in the St. Giles Plague and the Great Fire of London.

Historical Accuracy: Carr cuts a wide historical swath through the 17th century as an authentic background to the novel's romantic complications.

922   *The Lion Triumphant*

Date of Publication: 1974
Subject(s): Elizabethan Period; Romance; Spanish Armada
Fictional character(s): Catherine Farland, Young Woman; Jake Pennlyon, Sea Captain
Time Period(s): 16th century (1580s)
Locale(s): Plymouth, England; Spain

Summary: This romantic adventure novel is set during the Elizabethan period and culminates with the defeat of the Spanish Armada. Catherine Farland is loved by dashing sea-captain Jake Pennlyon. Their happiness is interrupted by the arrival of a strange spectral ship and abduction before eventual rescue.

Historical Accuracy: This is a solid depiction of the Elizabethan era that is rarely as well documented in other historical romances.

923   *The Love Child*

Date of Publication: 1978

Subject(s): Popish Plot; Romance; Monmouth's Rebellion
Fictional character(s): Priscilla Eversleigh, Gentlewoman; Jocelyn Frinton, Gentleman; Beaumont Granville, Gentleman
Time Period(s): 1760s
Locale(s): England

Summary: Blackmail, intrigue, murder, romance, and lust during the period of the English "Popish plot" form the novel's story. Priscilla Eversleigh falls in love with the fugitive Jocelyn Frinton. Her illegitimate daughter by him complicates her family's life as does the lecherous Granville who tests Priscilla's fortitude.

Historical Accuracy: The historical background is solidly established and leads to many of the romantic complications.

924   *Midsummer's Eve*

Date of Publication: 1986
Subject(s): Romance; Victorian Period
Fictional character(s): Annora Cadorson, Gentlewoman; Rolf Hanson, Gentleman; Joe Cresswell, Gentleman
Time Period(s): 1830s (1837)
Locale(s): Cornwall, England; London, England; Australia

Summary: Annora Cadorson, the daughter of a lord, is initiated into the world of tragedy and disillusion. Her love for the dashing Rolf Hanson is destroyed on a fateful midsummer's eve. She flees her home in Cornwall for London and a romance with Joe Cresswell until scandal erupts. Along with her family, Annora sails to Australia where she is forced to confront her disturbing past.

Historical Accuracy: In reality, few could endure such a melodramatically punishing history. Adversity is all in this period romance that owes very little to the historical period.

925   *The Miracle at St. Bruno's*

Date of Publication: 1972
Subject(s): Tudor Period; Romance; Religious Life
Fictional character(s): Damask Farland, Gentlewoman; Bruno, Orphan, Religious
Time Period(s): 16th century (1523-1553)
Locale(s): England

Summary: This romantic story of suspense is set during the tumultuous reign of Henry VIII and concerns Damask Farland, daughter of a lawyer whose land stands next to St. Bruno's Abbey. Shortly before her birth, a child is found at the door of the abbey. Taken in and named Bruno, he will play the central role in a romantic tangle of concealed identities, treasure, and blighted love.

Historical Accuracy: The details of the period are strongly presented.

926   *The Pool of St. Branok*

Date of Publication: 1987
Subject(s): Romance; Victorian Period; Frontier—Australia
Fictional character(s): Angelet Mandeville, Gentlewoman; Gervaise Mandeville, Gentleman; Benedict Lansdon, Gentleman
Time Period(s): 1850s
Locale(s): Cornwall, England; London, England; Australia

Summary: Angelet, haunted by painful childhood memories, marries the charming Gervaise Mandeville and follows him to the Australian gold fields. There she meets Benedict Lansdon, a figure from her troubled past who forces her to confront and overcome the tragedy she witnessed at the pool of St. Branok.

Historical Accuracy: The scenes of Australian frontier life are compelling and convincing, but the emphasis here is on the heroine's haunted past, not history.

927   *The Return of the Gypsy*

Date of Publication: 1985
Subject(s): Regency Romance; Napoleonic Wars; Gypsies
Fictional character(s): Romany Jake, Gypsy; Jessica Frenshaw, Gentlewoman
Time Period(s): 1800s; 1810s (1805-1815)
Locale(s): England

Summary: Romany Jake is an irresistible gypsy who attracts the passion of Jessica Frenshaw. He is exiled after his murder trial. Following Napoleons fall, he returns and is revealed to be neither a criminal nor a gypsy.

Historical Accuracy: The period details here form a plausible background to the romantic tale.

928   *Saraband for Two Sisters*

Date of Publication: 1976
Subject(s): Civil War—England; Romance
Fictional character(s): Angelet Landor, Gentlewoman, Twin; Bersaba Landor, Gentlewoman, Twin; Richard Tolworthy, Gentleman
Time Period(s): 17th century (1640s)
Locale(s): England

Summary: Twin sisters experience love and life during the English Civil War. Angelet and Bersaba are as opposite in temperament as they are alike in appearance. Angelet is bound for social success in London and a fashionable marriage to the king's general, Richard Tolworthy. Beneath the surface, however, secrets are hidden, and history intervenes, determining the fates of both sisters.

Historical Accuracy: The period history is detailed and authentic, serving as a trigger for the novel's suspense.

929   *The Song of the Siren*

Date of Publication: 1979
Subject(s): Romance; Jacobite Rebellion; Family Saga
Fictional character(s): Carlotta Eversleigh, Gentlewoman; Damaris Eversleigh, Gentlewoman; Lord Hessenfield, Nobleman
Time Period(s): 17th century
Locale(s): Paris, France; England

Summary: Lord Hessenfield, a dashing Jacobite leader, runs off with Carlotta Eversleigh. When he leaves her pregnant, Carlotta has an affair with her sister's suitor. Carlotta eventually reunites with Lord Hessenfield in France, and moral retribution ensues.

Historical Accuracy: The historical details are mainly costumes and melodrama rather than an accurate representation of the past.

930   *A Time for Silence*

Date of Publication: 1991
Subject(s): Romance; World War I
Fictional character(s): Lucinda Greenham, Student; Annabelinda Denver, Student
Time Period(s): 1910s (1913-1918)
Locale(s): France; London, England; Belgium

Summary: Two school friends—Lucinda and Annabelinda—leave London for finishing school on the continent. There a secret affair and childbirth are further complicated by the German invasion of Belgium and the beginning of World War I. The girls flee to England, burying their secret, but blackmail and eventual murder result.

Historical Accuracy: The historical scenes of the German invasion and the evacuation of Belgium are compelling and authentic, but they are used primarily as accelerators of the novel's melodramatic plot.

931   *Voices in a Haunted Room*

Date of Publication: 1984
Subject(s): Romance; Napoleonic Wars
Fictional character(s): Claudine de Tourville, Gentlewoman; David Frenshaw, Gentleman; Jonathan Frenshaw, Gentleman
Time Period(s): 1790s; 1800s (1790s-1805)
Locale(s): England

Summary: Claudine de Tourville flees Revolutionary France to her mother's ancestral English home. There she is torn between her two step-brothers, the steady, scholarly David and the passionate Jonathan. Their triangular relationship is played out against the backdrop of the Napoleonic Wars.

Historical Accuracy: The history is accurate, but is referred to in an indirect context rather than as a major element of the story.

932   *Will You Love Me in September?*

Date of Publication: 1981
Subject(s): Romance; Jacobite Rebellion; Family Saga
Fictional character(s): Lance Clavering, Military Personnel; Clarissa Field, Gentlewoman; Dickson Frenshaw, Gentleman
Time Period(s): 1710s (1715)
Locale(s): England

Summary: Clarissa Field is drawn into a dark tangle of family secrets and rivalry as the Jacobite Rebellion divides the country. She is attracted to Lance Clavering, a dashing soldier. But is he a charming lover or someone plotting to seize her fortune at the cost of her life? Dickson Frenshaw's motives are equally ambiguous. Is he Clarissa's protector or her jailer?.

Historical Accuracy: The romantic suspense is blended with plausibly rendered period details.

933   *The Witch From the Sea*

Date of Publication: 1975

Subject(s): Elizabethan Period; Gothic Romance
Fictional character(s): Linnet Pennlyon, Gentlewoman; Colum Casvellyn, Adventurer
Time Period(s): 16th century; 17th century (1588-1610s)
Locale(s): Plymouth, England

Summary: This gothic romance is set during the Elizabethan period. Linnet Pennlyon is seduced by and marries the Byronic adventurer, Colum Casvellyn, who alternately attracts and repels her. They live in his sinister castle-like fortress. The arrival of a shipwrecked Spanish woman who develops an uncanny influence on the household brings on the novel's dramatic climax.

Historical Accuracy: Despite the high gothic melodrama, there are accurate period elements in the novel.

ROBYN CARR (1951-)

Carr was born in Minnesota and currently lives in Arizona. She trained as a nurse. At the center of her books are female characters who adhere to the customs of their time yet possess some contemporary values.

934   *The Bellerose Bargain*

Date of Publication: 1982
Subject(s): Romance; Restoration Period; Identity—Concealed
Fictional character(s): Alicia Tilden, Saloon Hostess (barmaid); Geoffrey Perry, Sea Captain; Culver Perry, Gentleman
Historical character(s): Charles II, Ruler (King of England)
Time Period(s): 17th century (1660s)
Locale(s): London, England; American Colonies

Summary: A pygmalion-like transformation occurs when a young tavern maid, Alicia, agrees to impersonate Lady Charlotte Bellamy so Lord Seavers can claim the Bellamy fortune. Alicia appears as Lady Bellamy at the court of Charles II but falls in love with her mock husband. The complications are sorted out in America where Alicia's past and her secret catch up with her.

Historical Accuracy: The novel's premise owes more to the fairytale and to romantic wish fulfillment than to any actual historical past.

935   *The Blue Falcon*

Date of Publication: 1981
Subject(s): Middle Ages; Crusades; Romance
Fictional character(s): Conan de Corbney, Knight; Udele de Corbney, Gentlewoman; Chandra Ellard, Gentlewoman; Tedric, Knight
Historical character(s): Richard I, Ruler (King of England)
Time Period(s): 12th century (1187)
Locale(s): England; Palestine

Summary: Lovers Conan de Corbney, knight of King Richard, and Chandra Ellard are separated by the machinations of Conan's mother, Lady Udele. Each marries another with disastrous consequences. Treachery and intrigue complicate the novel's romance as the action culminates during the Third Crusade. The fate of the lovers becomes entwined with that of King Richard himself.

Historical Accuracy: Chivalry and medieval customs are vividly and authentically displayed.

936   *The Braeswood Tapestry*

Date of Publication: 1984
Subject(s): Restoration Period; Romance; Feuds
Fictional character(s): Jocelyn Cutler, Young Woman (peasant); Trent Westcott, Gentleman; Stephen Kerr, Gentleman
Historical character(s): Charles II, Ruler (King of England)
Time Period(s): 17th century (1660s)
Locale(s): England

Summary: Jocelyn Cutler, an innocent peasant girl, is rescued from the advances of Stephen Kerr by Kerr's fiercest enemy, Sir Trent Westcott. Jocelyn is indebted to Westcott, and she joins forces with him to avenge the cruelties of the Kerr family.

Historical Accuracy: The Restoration period is only lightly suggested here in this tale of romantic family feuding.

937   *By Right of Arms*

Date of Publication: 1986
Subject(s): Middle Ages; Romance
Fictional character(s): Aurelie de Pourure, Gentlewoman, Widow(er); Hyatt Laidley, Knight
Historical character(s): Edward, the Black Prince, Royalty (Prince of Wales); Edward III, Ruler (King of England)
Time Period(s): 14th century (1355-1356)
Locale(s): Windsor, England; France

Summary: Sir Hyatt, a knight serving Edward III and the Black Prince, is sent to claim the stronghold of De La Noye in France. Lady Aurelie, recently a widow, weds Sir Hyatt, and the two, initially distrustful of each other, eventually build a relationship despite threats from within and without.

Historical Accuracy: The medieval atmosphere is fully drawn, and the novel's romance builds its friction from the clash of cultures between the French and the English.

938   *Chelynne*

Date of Publication: 1980
Subject(s): Romance; Restoration Period
Fictional character(s): Chelynne Mondeloy, Gentlewoman; Chadwick Hawthorne, Heir, Nobleman
Historical character(s): Charles II, Ruler (King of England)
Time Period(s): 17th century (1660s)
Locale(s): London, England

Summary: Chelynne Mondeloy cannot understand her husband Chadwick's indifference. While trying to discover the reason, she is caught up in the intrigue and scandal of Charles II's court, including an encounter with the king himself.

Historical Accuracy: The novel is overfilled with romantic adventure that strains credibility. The portrait of Charles' scandal-ridden court is, however, colorfully and authentically presented.

939 *The Everlasting Covenant*

Date of Publication: 1987
Subject(s): War of the Roses; Romance
Fictional character(s): Anne Gifford, Gentlewoman; Dylan de Frayne, Gentleman
Time Period(s): 15th century (1460-1484)
Locale(s): England

Summary: Love during the War of the Roses is the subject of this novel. Anne Gifford is in love with Dylan de Frayne though their families are locked in a fierce rivalry exacerbated by the War of the Roses. They are separated, and the political and dynastic struggle must conclude before a reunion is possible.

Historical Accuracy: The history is delivered as context for the novel's complications. Although plausible, the historical scenes are of less interest than the romance.

940 *The Troubadour's Romance*

Date of Publication: 1985
Subject(s): Middle Ages; Romance
Fictional character(s): Felise Scelfton, Heiress; Royce Leighton, Knight
Historical character(s): Henry II, Ruler (King of England); Eleanor of Aquitaine, Royalty
Time Period(s): 12th century (1184)
Locale(s): London, England; Poitiers, France

Summary: Felise Scelfton, a lady of property, is forced by command of Henry II to marry Sir Royce Leighton. She is determined to win her husband's love, but his dark past and her own mysterious parentage complicate their relationship.

Historical Accuracy: The atmosphere of Eleanor of Aquitaine's court and the medieval setting serve as a plausible backdrop for the novel's romantic complications.

941 *Woman's Own*

Date of Publication: 1990
Subject(s): Romance; Family Saga
Fictional character(s): Emily Armstrong, Heroine; Amanda Armstrong, Heroine; Lilly Armstrong, Heroine
Time Period(s): 19th century (1859-1876)
Locale(s): Philadelphia, Pennsylvania

Summary: Three generations of Armstrong women are chronicled in this historical romance set in 19th century Philadelphia. Emily Armstrong quarrels with her mother Amanda over her choice of a husband. She forsakes the family's wealth and endures grinding poverty while raising her daughters. When calamity arrives, help is offered by the mother Emily thought she had lost.

Historical Accuracy: The emphasis here is on relationships with some accurate period painting.

EMMANUEL CARRERE

942 *Gothic Romance*

Date of Publication: 1990

Subject(s): Literary Life; Supernatural
Historical character(s): Mary Wollstonecraft Shelley, Writer; Percy Bysshe Shelley, Writer
Time Period(s): 1810s (1816)
Locale(s): Lake Geneva, Switzerland

Summary: This novel is based on the events surrounding the composition of Mary Shelley's *Frankenstein*. The atmosphere of Gothic chills predominates in this story that blends the real and the imaginary.

Historical Accuracy: Real-life events are only the starting point in this grotesque and eerie story.

SALLY CARRIGHAR

Born in Cleveland, Ohio, Carrigher attended Wellesley and has pursued a dual career as a writer and a naturalist. She won a Guggenheim fellowship for field work in the Arctic to study Eskimos and wild animals. She stayed nine years in a primitive and isolated village, which formed the basis for several books. She has written an autobiography, *Home to the Wilderness*.

943 *The Glass Dove*

Date of Publication: 1962
Subject(s): Slavery; Underground Railroad; Civil War—U.S.
Fictional character(s): Andrew MacIntosh, Farmer, Abolitionist; Sarah MacIntosh, Young Woman; Daniel Colling, Military Personnel (soldier)
Time Period(s): 1860s
Locale(s): Jericho, Ohio (fictional town)

Summary: Andrew MacIntosh turns his Ohio farm into a station on the underground railroad to assist slaves escaping to Canada. When the war breaks out, he leaves the farm and the slave-running in the hands of his daughter Sarah. She becomes involved in a romance with a wounded soldier who is suspected of being a Confederate spy.

Historical Accuracy: The author's attention to details contributes to the sense of authenticity in this story.

ROBERT CARSE (1902-1971)

Born in New York City, Carse was a writer of fiction and nonfiction for adults and children. He was also a journalist and a professional merchant mariner. He is the author of *A Cold Corner of Hell: The Story of the Murmansk Convoys* and the novels *The Wicked Blade* and *Drums of Empire*.

944 *The Beckoning Waters*

Date of Publication: 1953
Subject(s): Immigrants; Business Building
Fictional character(s): Alan Kennard, Sailor, Businessman
Time Period(s): 19th century; 20th century (1876-1932)
Locale(s): Great Lakes

Summary: This panoramic novel of life on the Great Lakes follows the experiences of a young Irish sailor, Alan Kennard, who jumps ship in New York and makes his way to Buffalo where he signs aboard a Great Lakes schooner. The novel depicts his career as he makes his way to become a shipping tycoon.

Historical Accuracy: This is an authentic depiction of the region and the period.

FORREST CARTER (1927-1979)

An American author of Western fiction, Carter was born in Tennessee and was half Cherokee Indian. He spent most of his life moving from one job to another, including stints as a ranch hand and wood chopper. At the age of 40, he paid for the printing of his first book, *The Rebel Outlaw: Josey Wales*. Clint Eastwood produced and starred in the movie version.

945   *Gone to Texas*

Date of Publication: 1975
Subject(s): American West; Crime and Criminals; Reconstruction Period
Fictional character(s): Josey Wales, Outlaw
Time Period(s): 1860s
Locale(s): Missouri

Summary: First published in 1973 as *The Rebel Outlaw*, the novel describes the Border War in Missouri that spawned so many outlaws, such as Jesse James. Like James, Josey Wales joins the guerrilla soldiers of Missouri and becomes a fugitive and wanted man. The novel dramatizes his attempt to escape west to Texas through dangerous Comanche territory.

Historical Accuracy: This is an authentic evocation of the period and the region.

946   *The Vengeance Trail of Josey Wales*

Date of Publication: 1976
Subject(s): American West; Crime and Criminals
Fictional character(s): Josey Wales, Outlaw
Time Period(s): 19th century
Locale(s): Texas; Mexico

Summary: The novel is the sequel to the author's *Gone to Texas* and continues the story of outlaw Josey Wales. His tranquil life on the Texas-Mexico border is broken when a band of Mexican bandits kidnaps a friend. He sets out into Mexico to even the score and is beset by Mexican bandits and the Commanches.

Historical Accuracy: The novel is graphically realistic in its details of period western life.

947   *Watch for Me on the Mountain*

Date of Publication: 1978
Subject(s): American West; Indians; Biography, Fictionalized
Historical character(s): Geronimo, Indian (Apache), Chieftain
Time Period(s): 19th century; 20th century (1829-1909)
Locale(s): Southwest

Summary: This fictionalized biography of Apache chief Geronimo chronicles his career and the war waged by the Chiricahua Apaches against the settlers in the Southwest.

Geronimo is presented as a religious mystic compelled to follow higher, spiritual laws.

Historical Accuracy: The novel's portrait of the Indian leader is somewhat romanticized, but the overall treatment of both the Indians and their opposition is balanced and convincing.

WINIFRED CARTER (1917-)

Born in Seattle, Washington, Carter worked for several newspapers.

948   *Dr. Johnson's Dear Mistress*

Date of Publication: 1949
Subject(s): Biography, Fictionalized; Literary Life; Georgian Period
Historical character(s): Hester Lynch Thrale Piozzi, Writer; Samuel Johnson, Writer; Oliver Goldsmith, Writer; David Garrick, Actor
Time Period(s): 18th century; 19th century
Locale(s): England

Summary: The novel is based on the life of Hester Thrale, later Mrs. Piozzi, who was a close friend and associate of Dr. Samuel Johnson. The novel captures Johnson and his circle as well as their times.

Historical Accuracy: The treatment of the personalities and the period rarely rises above the level of the superficial.

JACQUES CARTON (1903-)

Carton is a French author.

949   *La Belle Sorel*

Date of Publication: 1956
Subject(s): Royalty—France; Biography, Fictionalized; Middle Ages
Historical character(s): Agnes Sorel, Lover (mistress of Charles VII); Charles VII, Ruler (King of France)
Time Period(s): 15th century
Locale(s): France

Summary: This biographical account of Agnes Sorel, the mistress of French King Charles VII, chronicles the powerful influence she had over the king and the politics of the period.

Historical Accuracy: The novel captures with skill the atmosphere of medieval France.

JOSEPHINE CASE

950   *Written in Sand*

Date of Publication: 1945
Subject(s): Tripolitan War; Pirates
Historical character(s): William Eaton, Military Personnel (general)
Time Period(s): 1800s (1801-1805)
Locale(s): Tripoli, Africa

Summary: The story of America's war against the Barbary pirates of Tripoli is dramatized through the military experiences of American general William Eaton. He is successful in suppressing the Barbary pirates, but most of his gains are offset by government appeasement.

Historical Accuracy: The careful documentation of the historical background is enlivened by imagined conversations.

VICTORIA CASE (1897-)

Born in Texas, Case worked for newspapers in Oregon, including the *Portland Journal*. She contributed short stories and articles to numerous magazines. Her books include *Last Mountains*, *Applesauce Needs Sugar*, and *A Finger in Every Pie*.

951 *The Quiet Life of Mrs. General Lane*

Date of Publication: 1952
Subject(s): Biography, Fictionalized; Mexican War; American West
Historical character(s): Joseph Lane, Military Personnel (general), Political Figure; Polly Lane, Spouse
Time Period(s): 19th century
Locale(s): Oregon

Summary: This fictionalized biography traces the lives of Joseph Lane and his wife, Polly. The story of his illustrious career as a hero in the Mexican War and governor of the Oregon Territory is contrasted with Polly Lane's raising of ten children. Her strength of character balances her husband's greater notoriety.

Historical Accuracy: The author has taken her materials from family notes on General Lane's career, but has employed her imagination in depicting Polly Lane.

JACK CASEY (1950-)

Born in Troy, New York, Casey is a graduate of Yale University and attended the University of Edinburgh and Albany Law School. He is the deputy director of planning of Rensselaer County, New York.

952 *Lily of the Mohawks*

Date of Publication: 1984
Subject(s): Indians; Religious Life; American Colonies
Historical character(s): Kateri Tekakwitha, Indian (Mohawk), Religious (saint)
Time Period(s): 17th century
Locale(s): New York, American Colonies

Summary: The novel provides an account of the life of Mohawk Indian Kateri Tekakwitha, the first native American to be canonized as a saint. Orphaned as a small child and scarred by smallpox, Kateri is severely tested in her Catholic faith, and the novel offers many instances of her devotion and goodness.

Historical Accuracy: This is hagiography with a sharply realized period background and graphic descriptions of Indian customs.

JOHN CASHMAN
(PSEUD. OF TIMOTHY DARWIN, 1941-)

An Indian writer born in Simla and educated at Beaumont College, Cashman is a barrister in London with a strong interest in Victorian crime, history, and military studies.

953 *The Gentleman From Chicago*

Date of Publication: 1973
Subject(s): Medical Profession; Mystery; Crime and Criminals
Historical character(s): Thomas Neill Cream, Doctor
Time Period(s): 19th century (1850-1892)
Locale(s): Montreal, Quebec, Canada; Chicago, Illinois; London, England

Summary: This is the confession of the historical doctor and murderer Thomas Neill Cream. Cream was born in Scotland, educated in Canada, and practiced medicine in Chicago. He killed for pleasure, mostly in London, with poison his preferred method. When he was hanged, the assembled crowd cheered. The novel offers a psychological study of Cream.

Historical Accuracy: Though based on the factual Victorian killer, the majority of this story is fictitious.

VIRGINIA C. CASSEL

Born in Pittsburgh, Cassel attended Beaver College, Western Reserve University, and the University of New Mexico. She has worked as an educational administrator in the U.S. Office of Education, where she concentrated on Native American programs.

954 *Juniata Valley*

Date of Publication: 1981
Subject(s): French and Indian War; American Colonies; Battle of Fort Duquesne
Fictional character(s): John Graves, Settler; Francis Wilson, Settler; Mary Ann Eldridge, Captive
Historical character(s): George Washington, Military Personnel (army officer)
Time Period(s): 1750s (1756)
Locale(s): Juniata Valley, Pennsylvania, American Colonies

Summary: The novel portrays frontier life in western Pennsylvania during the French and Indian Wars. Five families of settlers are determined to keep their homes despite Indian raids and the Quaker farmers' reluctance to fight back. The novel's climax is the Battle of Fort Duquesne.

Historical Accuracy: Cassel offers an accurate and authentic account of the struggle between the natives and the settlers in mid-18th century Pennsylvania.

R.V. CASSILL (1919-)

Born in Cedar Falls, Iowa, Cassill received his M.A. from the University of Iowa and taught writing there. He was a lecturer at Columbia University and an editor at Collier's Encyclopedia.

955 *After Goliath*

Date of Publication: 1985
Subject(s): Biblical Story; Ancient Israel
Historical character(s): David, Biblical Figure; Bathsheba, Biblical Figure; Absalom, Biblical Figure; Joab, Biblical Figure; Solomon, Biblical Figure
Time Period(s): 10th century B.C.
Locale(s): Israel

Summary: The reign of King David of ancient Israel is given a modernized interpretation. Stripped of any supernatural elements, David's regime is recast into a scramble for power by deeply flawed individuals. Only Joab emerges with dignity as the more famous figures are diminished to the level of the petty and the neurotic.

Historical Accuracy: This is a revision of the past with a particularly modern sensibility dominating.

HENRY CASTOR (1909-)

Born in Philadelphia, Pennsylvania, Castor graduated from the University of Pennsylvania and worked in publishing. He is the author of such nonfiction works as *Teddy Roosevelt and the Rough Riders*, *Fifty-four Forty or Fight!*, and *The Tripolitan War*.

956 *The Year of the Spaniard*

Date of Publication: 1950
Subject(s): Spanish-American War
Fictional character(s): Caleb Hawkins, Military Personnel (soldier); Warren Spangler, Journalist
Historical character(s): Stephen Crane, Writer
Time Period(s): 1890s (1898)
Locale(s): Cuba; Puerto Rico; Philippines

Summary: Events of the Spanish-American War are seen through the experiences of two Philadelphia college friends. Caleb Hawkins serves with the Rough Riders in Cuba, while newspaper reporter Warren Spangler covers the war and meets writer Stephen Crane.

Historical Accuracy: The novel manages to capture the atmosphere of the war with conviction.

WILLA CATHER (1876-1947)

Born in Virginia, Cather moved as a child to Nebraska, the scene of many of her novels. She worked for a time as a magazine editor before turning to fiction. Her principal works include *O Pioneers!*, *My Antonia*, *One of Ours*, and *A Lost Lady*.

957 *Death Comes for the Archbishop*

Date of Publication: 1927
Subject(s): American West; Christianity; Settlement of the American Frontier
Fictional character(s): Jean Marie Latour, Religious (archbishop); Joseph Vaillant, Religious (priest)
Historical character(s): Kit Carson, Frontiersman
Time Period(s): 19th century (1851-1870s)

Locale(s): Santa Fe, New Mexico; Southwest

Summary: This novel chronicles the development of the Catholic Church in the Southwest. Cather describes church activities in New Mexico, capturing much of the spirit of the American West—its bleak desert landscape and Indian, Mexican, and Spanish customs.

Historical Accuracy: Reflecting over 300 years of Spanish colonial history and primitive tribal life, this is a moving regional and cultural portrait. Archbishop Latour and Father Vaillant are based on historical figures.

958 *Sapphira and the Slave Girl*

Date of Publication: 1940
Subject(s): Antebellum South; Slavery
Fictional character(s): Henry Colbert, Businessman (miller); Nancy Till, Slave; Sapphira Colbert, Gentlewoman
Time Period(s): 1850s (1856); 1880s (1881)
Locale(s): Virginia; Canada

Summary: Nancy Till, a mulatto slave girl, is persecuted by Sapphira, the invalid wife of a pious miller who befriends the slave girl. After resisting a seduction attempt by Sapphira's philandering nephew, Nancy escapes to Canada by way of the underground railroad. She returns a respectable and successful woman.

Historical Accuracy: The novel is based on an incident Cather recollected from her Virginia childhood.

959 *Shadows on the Rock*

Date of Publication: 1931
Subject(s): French Colonies; Frontier—Canada
Fictional character(s): Euclide Auclair, Pharmacist; Cecile Auclair, Heroine; Pierre Charron, Trader (of furs)
Historical character(s): Louis de Buade, Nobleman (Comte de Frontenac), Political Figure (governor of New France)
Time Period(s): 17th century (1697-1698)
Locale(s): Quebec, Quebec, Canada

Summary: Cather follows one family—a father and daughter—through a single year, describing their daily routines, food, and housing in Canada's New France colony.

Historical Accuracy: This depiction of a little-known segment of 17th-century North American history is rendered with sympathy and precision.

NANCY CATO (1917-)

Born in Adelaide, South Australia, Cato has worked as a journalist, art critic, and free-lance writer. Her other works include *Jindyworobak Anthology*, *Time Flow Softly*, *Green Grows the Vine*, *But Still the Stream: A Novel of the River Murray*, *The Sea Ants, and Other Stories*, and *North-West by South*. She won the Northern Territory Poetry Prize and the Poetry Society Award in 1963, and the Commonwealth Literature Fund fellowship in 1968.

960 *Forefathers*

Date of Publication: 1982

Subject(s): Family Saga; Frontier—Australia
Fictional character(s): Josh Forbes, Farmer, Rancher (sheep); Jamie Brown, Convict; Sam King, Prospector
Time Period(s): 19th century; 20th century (1824-1970s)
Locale(s): Tasmania, Australia

Summary: In this immense family saga that traces three families through seven generations and over 150 years, the history of Australia is dramatized from the perspective of the Forbes, Brown, and King families who intermarry, succeed, and fail with a rugged determination.

Historical Accuracy: The novel offers a fascinating look at 150 years of Australian history from the perspective of an ever-growing family.

961 *The Heart of the Continent*

Date of Publication: 1989
Subject(s): Frontier—Australia; Medical Profession; Aviation
Fictional character(s): Alix MacFarlane, Nurse; Jim Manning, Rancher; Caro Manning, Nurse, Pilot
Time Period(s): 20th century (1900s-1940s)
Locale(s): Queensland, Australia

Summary: Alix MacFarlane rejects her expected life as a society wife to work as a nurse in an isolated outland settlement of Queensland, Australia. There she marries rancher Jim Manning. After he is killed in World War I, she returns to Queensland. Her daughter Caro fulfills Alix's dream of providing medical care by becoming a pilot and nurse in the newly formed flying doctor service on the eve of World War II.

Historical Accuracy: The sense of place is well established and convincing.

962 *North-West by South*

Date of Publication: 1965
Subject(s): Exploration; Biography, Fictionalized
Historical character(s): Sir John Franklin, Explorer
Time Period(s): 1840s
Locale(s): Arctic; Tasmania, Australia

Summary: This biographical account of English arctic explorer Sir John Franklin reconstructs the last years of his life as the Lieutenant-Governor of Van Dieman's Land (now Tasmania) and his doomed search for the North-West Passage.

Historical Accuracy: The novel is faithful to the facts of Franklin's life.

BRUCE CATTON (1899-1978)

Born in Michigan, Catton attended Oberlin College and served with the U.S. Navy during World War I. During World War II, Catton worked with the U.S. War Information Board; and he held other government posts until 1952. Catton's nonfiction book, *A Stillness at Appomattox*, won the Pulitzer Prize and the National Book Award in 1954. An authority on the Civil War, his other books include *Mr. Lincoln's Army* and *Terrible Swift Sword*.

963 *Banner at Shenandoah*

Date of Publication: 1955
Subject(s): Civil War—U.S.; Shenandoah Valley Campaign; Battle of Missionary Ridge
Fictional character(s): Bob Hayden, Military Personnel (Union soldier)
Historical character(s): Philip H. Sheridan, Military Personnel (Union general)
Time Period(s): 1860s
Locale(s): Shenandoah Valley, Virginia

Summary: The novel describes the Shenandoah Campaign at the end of the Civil War from the perspective of young Bob Hayden, who serves as the color-bearer for General Philip Sheridan's fighting cavalry. Action includes the battles at Boonville, Missionary Ridge, and Cedar Creek.

Historical Accuracy: The military action is faithful to the facts, but the characters are largely invented.

HARRY M. CAUDILL (1922-1990)

An American legislator, educator, and author, Caudill was born in Kentucky. He is best known for his 1963 book *Night Comes to the Cumberlands: A Biography of a Depressed Area* that prompted Federal relief to the area. A lawyer and a member of the Kentucky state legislature from 1954 to 1970, Caudill became a professor of Appalachian studies at the University of Kentucky in 1977. His other books include *Darkness at Dawn* and *Theirs Be the Power: The Moguls of Eastern Kentucky*.

964 *Dark Hills to Westward*

Date of Publication: 1969
Subject(s): Indians; Settlement of the American Frontier
Historical character(s): Jennie Sellards Wiley, Captive
Time Period(s): 1780s (1789)
Locale(s): Virginia; Kentucky

Summary: The novel is based on the true stoy of Jennie Wiley. Captured by Indians in the wilderness of western Virginia, Wiley must assert considerable resources to win her freedom. The novel provides an honest and vivid portrait of frontier life and Indian customs that is more realistic than idealized.

Historical Accuracy: The novel is convincing in its re-creation of life in the wilderness.

DARIO CECCHI (1918-)

Cecchi is an Italian writer whose books include biographies of Antonio Mancini and Giovanni Boldini.

965 *Titian*

Date of Publication: 1958
Subject(s): Renaissance; Artistic Life; Biography, Fictionalized
Historical character(s): Titian, Artist
Time Period(s): 15th century; 16th century (1477-1567)
Locale(s): Italy

Summary: This fictionalized biography traces the career of the great Italian painter Titian against the background of Renaissance Italy. The novel dramatizes Titian's long and distinguished career and gives ample evidence of his greatness as an artist and his influence on later artists.

Historical Accuracy: The novel occasionally embellishes the biographical facts with invented scenes and dialogue.

ELIZABETH CHADWICK

966   *First Knight*

Date of Publication: 1995
Subject(s): Myths and Legends; Dark Ages; Arthurian Legends
Fictional character(s): Arthur, Ruler (King of the Britons); Guinevere, Royalty (queen consort of Arthur); Lancelot du Lac, Knight
Time Period(s): Indeterminate Past
Locale(s): England

Summary: This novelization of the 1995 film tells the story of Camelot with a few differences: Lancelot is a drifting mercenary, and Guinevere is depicted as a warrior queen.

Historical Accuracy: A New Age Arthurian saga, the novel does, however, attempt to capture a believable historical background.

967   *The Leopard Unleashed*

Date of Publication: 1992
Subject(s): Middle Ages; Crusades
Fictional character(s): Renard, Knight, Heir; Olwen, Entertainer, Dancer; Eleanor, Gentlewoman, Fiance(e) (of Renard)
Time Period(s): 12th century (1139-1141)
Locale(s): Antioch, Syria; Welsh Marches, Wales

Summary: Renard is a crusader enthralled by Olwen, a dancing girl with a boundless ambition. Renard is betrothed to Eleanor, and when he returns home from Palestine to his duty, Olwen refuses to be left behind. Renard is caught in a triangle complicated by civil war in which his life will depend on his former mistress and his wife.

Historical Accuracy: Well imagined, the novel is grounded in accurate historical details.

968   *The Running Vixen*

Date of Publication: 1991
Subject(s): Middle Ages; Romance
Fictional character(s): Adam de Lacey, Knight; Heulwen, Widow(er); Warrin de Mortimer, Knight
Time Period(s): 12th century (1126-1128)
Locale(s): Welsh Marches, Wales

Summary: Adam de Lacey returns home in 1126 to the Welsh Marches still in love with his widowed foster sister, Heulwen. She plans to marry Adam's rival, Warrin de Mortimer, but Adam discovers that Mortimer is involved in a deadly conspiracy aimed at thwarting King Henry. Before Adam and Heulwen can be united, they must deal with Warrin's vengeance and the treachery of the rebel barons.

Historical Accuracy: The romance is authentic in its historical details.

969   *The Wild Hunt*

Date of Publication: 1990
Subject(s): Middle Ages
Fictional character(s): Judith of Ravenstow, Gentlewoman; Guyon, Nobleman (lord of Ledworth); Robert de Belleme, Nobleman
Time Period(s): 11th century; 12th century (1098-1102)
Locale(s): Welsh Marches, Wales

Summary: A marriage of convenience between Judith of Ravenstow and Guyon, Lord of Ledworth, grows into a deeper, more passionate relationship as the two must join together to defeat King William Rufus' baron, Robert de Belleme. The scene is the Welsh March wars of the 12th century.

Historical Accuracy: The novel is a well-observed and authentic rendering of the time and place.

GEORGE CHALLIS
(PSEUD. OF FREDERICK FAUST, 1892-1944)

Born in Seattle, Washington, and killed in action during World War II, Faust was best known as Max Brand, the popular Western novelist. His best-known novel is *Destry Rides Again*. He also wrote historical novels, including *The Golden Knight*, and invented the character of Dr. Kildare.

970   *The Bait and the Trap*

Date of Publication: 1951
Subject(s): Renaissance
Fictional character(s): Tizzo, Young Man
Historical character(s): Cesare Borgia, Military Personnel, Political Figure
Time Period(s): 16th century
Locale(s): Italy

Summary: Tizzo, the hero of *The Firebrand*, returns in this novel of intrigue and betrayal set in Renaissance Italy. Tizzo enters the service of Cesare Borgia believing in the duke's virtues. Events soon teach him a lesson about Borgia's true colors.

Historical Accuracy: This is a romanticized version of history with an emphasis on costumed adventure.

971   *The Golden Knight*

Date of Publication: 1937
Subject(s): Middle Ages; Royalty—England
Historical character(s): Richard I, Ruler (King of England); Blondel de Nesle, Minstrel (troubadour); Leopold IV, Nobleman; Henry VII, Ruler (Holy Roman Emperor)
Time Period(s): 12th century (1190s)
Locale(s): Austria

Summary: The novel dramatizes the story of Richard the Lionhearted's imprisonment in Austria. The tale sticks close to the facts of Richard's capture by his bitter enemy, Leopold of Austria, and his eventual rescue, aided by his faithful troubadour, Blondel, who sets out across Europe to find his master.

Historical Accuracy: The novel intermingles the factual, the legendary, and the invented into a rousing adventure story with a good deal of believability in its portraits and period details.

HARVEY CHALMERS (1890-1971)

Chalmers was an American industrialist and novelist.

972 *Drums Against Frontenac*

Date of Publication: 1949
Subject(s): French and Indian War
Fictional character(s): Robin Blagden, Diplomat
Historical character(s): John Bradstreet, Military Personnel (colonel)
Time Period(s): 1750s
Locale(s): New York, American Colonies; Quebec, Quebec, Canada

Summary: A young Londoner, Robin Blagden, is sent by William Pitt the Elder to report on James Abercrombie's march to Montreal in 1758. His experiences during the campaign culminate in the capture of Fort Frontenac by the British Colonel Bradstreet and his band of regulars and colonial troops.

Historical Accuracy: The facts are accurately presented in the story of the campaign.

973 *West to the Setting Sun*

Date of Publication: 1943
Subject(s): Indians; American Revolution; Biography, Fictionalized
Historical character(s): Joseph Brant, Indian (Mohawk), Chieftain; Sir William Johnson, Government Official
Time Period(s): 18th century
Locale(s): New York, American Colonies

Summary: This fictional biography of the great Mohawk chieftain Joseph Brant traces his leadership throughout the French and Indian Wars and the American Revolution. Brant leads the Indians of the Six Nations, the Iroquois, against the French. When the Revolution breaks out he remains loyal to the British, leading many famous raids on the colonial settlements of New York.

Historical Accuracy: Where data does not exist, the author has invented motives, dialogue, and actions to offer a version of what Brant might have done and said under the circumstances. The result is something between an authentic biography and an adventure story.

ANN CHAMBERLIN (1917-)

Born in Marietta, Ohio, Chamberlin attended Marietta College and the University of Cincinnati and worked for several newspapers as a book reviewer. She has also taught creative writing and published several novels, including *The Tall Dark Man* and *The Soldier's Room*.

974 *Sofia*

Date of Publication: 1996
Subject(s): Ottoman Empire
Fictional character(s): Giorgio Veniero, Sailor; Sofia Baffo, Gentlewoman, Captive; Esmikan, Royalty (princess)
Time Period(s): 16th century (1560s)
Locale(s): Venice, Italy; Constantinople, Ottoman Empire

Summary: This exotic story describes the adventures of Sofia Baffo, daughter of a Venetian nobleman, who is captured by corsairs and sold into slavery in the great harem of the sultan. With her is a young Italian sailor who falls in love with the sultan's daughter.

Historical Accuracy: The novel's atmosphere both of period and place is convincing.

975 *Tamar*

Date of Publication: 1994
Subject(s): Biblical Story
Fictional character(s): Tamar, Noblewoman, Heiress
Historical character(s): David, Ruler (King of Israel), Biblical Figure; Absalom, Royalty (prince), Biblical Figure; Amnon, Royalty (prince), Biblical Figure
Time Period(s): 10th century B.C.
Locale(s): Israel

Summary: Set in the court world of King David of Israel, the novel describes the life of Tamar, the daughter of one of David's wives and a princess in her homeland. She is loved by Amnon, David's heir, and hated by Absalom, who regards her as a threat.

Historical Accuracy: The era is imaginatively constructed so that the politics and customs are believable.

ROBERT W. CHAMBERS (1865-1933)

New York novelist Chambers began his career as a painter and illustrator but soon turned to writing primarily historical romances.

976 *Cardigan*

Date of Publication: 1901
Subject(s): American Revolution; American Colonies; Indians
Fictional character(s): Michael Cardigan, Bodyguard
Historical character(s): Sir William Johnson, Government Official; John Hancock, Patriot
Time Period(s): 1770s (1774-1775)
Locale(s): New York, American Colonies; Massachusetts, American Colonies

Summary: This is the first in a series of historical romances of frontier life in upstate New York before and during the American Revolution. The story follows the adventures of Michael Cardigan, the bodyguard of Sir William Johnson, Commissioner of Indian Affairs, in the negotiations with the Indians as the outbreak of the Revolution tests the loyalty of all on the frontier.

Historical Accuracy: The author advises readers of this romance who are interested in history to go directly to the sources on which the imagined story is based.

977   *The Happy Parrot*

Date of Publication: 1929
Subject(s): War of 1812; Sea Story
Fictional character(s): Eric Strake, Sea Captain
Time Period(s): 1810s
Locale(s): *Happy Parrot*, At Sea

Summary: This nautical adventure story is set during the War of 1812 and involves Eric Strake, commander of the schooner *The Happy Parrot*, which is involved in the slave trade. Conflict with slaves, pirates, and the navy makes for a thrilling romantic story.

Historical Accuracy: The novel's romantic adventure largely overwhelms other considerations; and the depiction of the slave trade is cavalier at best.

978   *Hidden Children*

Date of Publication: 1914
Subject(s): American Revolution; Indians
Fictional character(s): Evan Loskiel, Military Personnel (soldier)
Time Period(s): 1770s
Locale(s): New York

Summary: This tale, set in western New York during the American Revolution, describes the border warfare between American troops and the English with their Indian allies. Evan Loskiel of Morgan's Rifles is introduced to Indian intrigue by a young gypsy girl who follows his regiment.

Historical Accuracy: The novel's depiction of Native American Indian life and customs is convincing.

979   *Little Red Foot*

Date of Publication: 1921
Subject(s): American Revolution; Indians
Fictional character(s): John Drogue, Military Personnel (soldier); Penelope Grant, Gentlewoman
Time Period(s): 1770s; 1780s (1774-1782)
Locale(s): New York

Summary: During the American Revolution, the Tories and their Iroquois allies fight the colonials and their Oneida allies. The plot includes Indian and Tory raids, along with a romance between former loyalist John Drogue and Penelope Grant.

Historical Accuracy: Indian warfare and the Tory raids are accurately described.

980   *Painted Minx*

Date of Publication: 1930
Subject(s): American Revolution
Fictional character(s): Marie Guest, Actress, Loyalist
Time Period(s): 1770s; 1780s (1777-1782)
Locale(s): New York, New York

Summary: Marie Guest is a Tory actress in the John Street Theater. Her experiences provide a vivid and authentic account of New York City during the American Revolution.

Historical Accuracy: The novel's romance and adventure take place against a convincing period backdrop.

981   *The Rake and the Hussy*

Date of Publication: 1930
Subject(s): War of 1812; Battle of New Orleans
Fictional character(s): Joshua Brooke, Rake
Historical character(s): Andrew Jackson, Military Personnel (general)
Time Period(s): 1810s
Locale(s): New Orleans, Louisiana

Summary: This romantic adventure novel concerns the exploits of Joshua Brooke, who assists Andrew Jackson in defending New Orleans against the British.

Historical Accuracy: Despite weak fictional elements, the novel presents vivid and believable historical portraits and captures the events accurately.

982   *Secret Service Operator 13*

Date of Publication: 1934
Subject(s): Civil War—U.S.; Espionage; Draft Riots
Fictional character(s): Gail Loveless, Spy (Union), Actress; Jack Galliard, Spy (Confederate)
Historical character(s): Allan Pinkerton, Military Personnel (intelligence officer); James Ewell Brown Stuart, Military Personnel (Confederate general)
Time Period(s): 1860s
Locale(s): New York, New York; Virginia

Summary: Gail Loveless is a talented Union spy who uses her skills as an actress to work undercover as a young mulatto girl, a stable boy, and a nun. Her espionage work is complicated when she falls in love with Confederate secret agent Jack Galliard. The novel also provides a vivid picture of New York's Draft Riots.

Historical Accuracy: The story is more colorful and entertaining than plausible, and more a romance than a carefully documented examination of Civil War espionage work.

983   *War Paint and Rouge*

Date of Publication: 1931
Subject(s): French and Indian War; American Colonies
Fictional character(s): John Cardess, Military Personnel (army officer)
Time Period(s): 1750s (1757-1758)
Locale(s): New York, American Colonies; Canada

Summary: This romantic adventure story depicts the events surrounding the French capture of Fort William Henry and the French loss of Louisburg during the French and Indian War. The action is described by a young New Yorker and officer in Major Roger's Rangers.

Historical Accuracy: The events are accurately captured, but the background is vague and lightly sketched.

984   *Whistling Cat*

Date of Publication: 1932
Subject(s): Civil War—U.S.
Fictional character(s): Juan Maddox, Military Personnel (Union soldier)

Historical character(s): Ulysses S. Grant, Military Personnel (Union commander)
Time Period(s): 1860s
Locale(s): United States

Summary: This Civil War novel looks at the war from the perspective of young Juan Maddox. Detailed to the telegraph division of the Union army. as a telegrapher, Maddox is privy to the strategy and the secret operations of the war.

Historical Accuracy: The novel follows actual events faithfully, though the romance elements are improbable.

CLARA LONGWORTH DE CHAMBRUN (1873-1954)

Born in Cincinnati, Ohio, Clara Longworth de Chambrun is the author of *The Sonnets of William Shakespeare*, *The Making of Nicholas Longworth*, and *Shadows Like Myself* (an autobiography).

985 *Two Loves Have I*

Date of Publication: 1934
Subject(s): Elizabethan Period; Literary Life; Biography, Fictionalized
Historical character(s): William Shakespeare, Writer; Anne Hathaway, Spouse; Ben Jonson, Writer; Michael Drayton, Writer
Time Period(s): 16th century; 17th century
Locale(s): England

Summary: The novel gives a biographical portrait of William Shakespeare, filling in the considerable gaps in our knowledge of his life with plausible conjecture. Shakespeare's literary genius is given a sense of place and time, and the identity of the Dark Lady of the sonnets is revealed.

Historical Accuracy: The considerable speculation needed to fill in the gaps, though based on evident research, is not convincing in every instance.

FRANCOISE CHANDERNAGOR

Chandernagor lives in Paris and has worked as the legal adviser for the French Counsel of State. *The King's Way* is her first novel.

986 *The King's Way*

Date of Publication: 1981
Subject(s): Biography, Fictionalized; Royalty—France
Historical character(s): Louis XIV, Ruler (King of France); Francoise d'Aubigne, Royalty (queen consort of Louis XIV)
Time Period(s): 17th century; 18th century (1635-1719)
Locale(s): France

Summary: Madame de Maintenon, the mistress and later the wife of Louis XIV, provides her recollections of France's golden age under the Sun King. From her birth in a prison and her destitute childhood in the French West Indies, she rises to become the most powerful woman in France. She emerges as a complex mixture of ambition and self-doubt.

Historical Accuracy: This fictional autobiography makes frequent use of Maintenon's own words from her voluminous letters and diaries. The novel includes a list of sources and notes in which the author explains how closely her version is patterned on history.

HSIN-HAI CHANG (1898-)

Chinese author Chang was born in Shanghai and educated at Tsinghua College, Johns Hopkins, and Harvard. A professor of comparative literature at various colleges and universities, Chang served as a diplomat for the Republic of China to Portugal, Czechoslovakia, and Poland during the 1930s. His works include *The Life and Times of Chiang Kai-shek* and *Letters from a Chinese Diplomat*.

987 *The Fabulous Concubine*

Date of Publication: 1956
Subject(s): Chinese Empire; Boxer Rebellion
Fictional character(s): Golden Orchard, Young Woman; Shen Wen-Ching, Scholar, Diplomat
Time Period(s): 1900s
Locale(s): Peking, China; Soochow, China; Berlin, Germany

Summary: This tale of Chinese life is set at the turn of the century during the violence of the Boxer Rebellion. It concerns the career of Golden Orchard, who becomes the concubine of scholar Shen Wen-ching. When he is appointed ambassador to Germany, Golden Orchard accompanies him there, and the novel dramatizes her ascension into the high circles of power and politics.

Historical Accuracy: The novel provides an accurate depiction of upper-class life in China at the turn of the century.

ARTHUR CHAPMAN (1873-1935)

An American journalist, poet, and novelist, Chapman was born in Rockford, Illinois. His books include *Out Where the West Begins*, *The Story of Colorado*, and *The Pony Express*.

988 *John Crews*

Date of Publication: 1926
Subject(s): American West; Mormons; Indians
Fictional character(s): John Crews, Trapper; Annabel Drayton, Captive
Time Period(s): 19th century
Locale(s): Fort Laramie, Wyoming

Summary: Annabel Drayton is rescued from a Danite Mormon sect by trapper John Crews. Together they have a series of adventures with friendly and hostile Indians before reaching safety at Fort Laramie.

Historical Accuracy: The details of Indian and Mormon customs are plausible.

HESTER W. CHAPMAN (1899-1976)

An English historical novelist and biographer, Chapman worked for the Fighting French and the American Red Cross during World War II. Her biographies of such figures as

Edward Tudor, Lady Jane Grey, and Charles I have been praised for their accuracy, in-depth research, and vivid characterization, the same qualities that mark her historical novels.

`989` *Eugenie*

Date of Publication: 1961
Subject(s): Biography, Fictionalized; Royalty—France
Fictional character(s): Miss Flowers, Governess, Companion (of Eugenie)
Historical character(s): Eugenie, Royalty (Empress of France); Napoleon III, Ruler (Emperor of France)
Time Period(s): 19th century
Locale(s): France; Spain

Summary: This biographical novel dramatizes the life of Eugenie who, as the wife of Napoleon III, became the celebrated Empress of France and helped to define the age. Her life, from her childhood in Spain to her years on the throne, is described by her English governess, Miss Flowers, who becomes her companion and an eyewitness to the events of her reign.

Historical Accuracy: The age is re-created with skill and accuracy, though some manipulation of events has been done to accommodate the narrative device.

`990` *Fear No More*

Date of Publication: 1968
Subject(s): French Revolution; Royalty—France
Historical character(s): Louis XVI, Ruler (King of France); Marie Antoinette, Royalty (queen consort of Louis XVI); Louis Charles, Royalty (French dauphin), Heir
Time Period(s): 1780s; 1790s
Locale(s): Versailles, France; Paris, France

Summary: The fall of Louis XVI and Marie Antoinette is seen from the perspective of their son, Louis, the dauphin. He is only dimly aware of the upheaval that is going on around him, but he increasingly finds himself at center stage. It will be his testimony about his mother that will result in her death on the guillotine.

Historical Accuracy: Louis XVII, who is only five when the story begins, shows a level of maturity in his perceptions and comments that go far beyond precociousness and undermines believability.

`991` *Limmerston Hall*

Date of Publication: 1973
Subject(s): Suspense; Gothic Romance; Victorian Period
Fictional character(s): Neville Quarrendon, Artist, Widow(er); Anne Nilson, Gentlewoman
Time Period(s): 19th century (Victorian period)
Locale(s): England

Summary: This gothic romance set during the Victorian period has the required sensitive heroine, Anne Nilson, and a brooding and enigmatic hero, artist Neville Quarrendon. To what lengths will he go to possess Limmerston Hall? Is he a conspirator, or only the victim of vicious rumors? Anne's suspicions are tested in this mystery of character and gothic atmosphere.

Historical Accuracy: The period background is convincingly drawn.

`992` *Lucy*

Date of Publication: 1965
Subject(s): Restoration Period; Theatrical Life
Fictional character(s): Lucy Browne, Actress, Foundling; Richard Nash, Actor
Historical character(s): Charles II, Ruler (King of England)
Time Period(s): 1760s
Locale(s): London, England

Summary: Life in the Restoration theater is portrayed through the career of Lucy Browne, a foundling turned successful actress. The life of actors and their companions, dependent on the patronage of the court, is depicted. Actor-manager Richard Nash must navigate a tangled field of shifting allegiances, and Lucy must deal with an equally vexing romantic career.

Historical Accuracy: The author knows the era intimately and provides a great deal of authentic material on both the period and the stage.

MARISTAN CHAPMAN
(PSEUD. OF MARY CHAPMAN, 1895- ; JOHN HIGHAM STANTON CHAPMAN, 1891-1972)

Maristan Chapman is a pseudonym for husband and wife John Stanton Chapman and Mary Chapman. John Chapman was born in England and came to the U.S. in 1917, giving up a career in aeronautical engineering to become a full-time writer. Mary Chapman was born in Chattanooga, Tennessee and worked as a missionary, lecturer, and engineering technologist. Under the joint pseudonyms Maristan Chapman, Kirk Connell, Dent Ilsley, and Jane Selkirk, they published numerous books for adults and young people, including biographies, historical novels, and chronicles of the medieval world. Their novels include *Flood in Glen Hazzard*, *The Happy Mountain*, and.

`993` *Rogue's March*

Date of Publication: 1949
Subject(s): American Revolution; Battle of King's Mountain
Fictional character(s): Margaret Brooke, Young Woman; Lantry Ward, Military Personnel (soldier)
Historical character(s): John Sevier, Political Figure
Time Period(s): 1770s; 1780s
Locale(s): Carolinas, United States; Tennessee

Summary: Set during the final years of the American Revolution, the novel follows the adventures of Lantry Ward of Tennessee, an express rider for the colonists, in skirmishes in the Carolinas and Tennessee that culminate in the Battle of King's Mountain. The love interest is provided by Margaret Brooke, the daughter of a Tory landowner.

Historical Accuracy: The novel captures with skill and credibility the atmosphere of Lantry Ward's life and the events of the pivotal Battle of King's Mountain.

994 *Tennessee Hazard*

Date of Publication: 1953

Subject(s): Settlement of the American Frontier; Spanish Colonies

Fictional character(s): Tom Hazard, Frontiersman

Historical character(s): James Wilkinson, Military Personnel (general); John Sevier, Political Figure, Frontiersman

Time Period(s): 1780s (1788)

Locale(s): Tennessee; New Orleans, Louisiana

Summary: In the years immediately following the American Revolution, a conspiracy threatens to make the Tennessee frontier fall into the hands of the Spanish in Louisiana. Tom Hazard sets out for New Orleans to intercept a message that will further the Spanish cause.

Historical Accuracy: The political background is true, as is the evocation of frontier life during the period.

W.J. CHAPUT

995 *The Man on the Train*

Date of Publication: 1986

Subject(s): World War II; Espionage

Fictional character(s): Frank Kemper, Military Personnel (naval intelligence officer); Paul Striecher, Spy; Hannah Doll, Young Woman

Historical character(s): Winston Churchill, Political Figure (British prime minister)

Time Period(s): 1940s (1941)

Locale(s): Vermont

Summary: Winston Churchill, after meeting with President Roosevelt and Congress in December 1941, is heading by train to Ottawa, Canada. A German spy is determined to kill the British prime minister. Frank Kemper of naval intelligence must foil the plot in this spy thriller.

Historical Accuracy: Winston Churchill did travel through Vermont by train in 1941. The rest of the events are the author's creation.

EILEEN CHARBONNEAU

Charbonneau is an award-winning young adult novelist. She has written for the *New York Times*, and her novels include *The Ghost of Stony Clove*, *In the Time of the Wolves*, and *Honor to the Hills*.

996 *Waltzing in Ragtime*

Date of Publication: 1996

Subject(s): American West; Earthquakes

Fictional character(s): Olana Whittaker, Journalist; Matthew Hart, Ranger (forest ranger)

Time Period(s): 1900s (1900-1906)

Locale(s): San Francisco, California

Summary: The novel describes the relationship between Olana Whittaker, the daughter of a lumber baron, and forest ranger Matthew Hart. They are trapped together in a blizzard, and

Olana learns to appreciate Matthew's environmental sentiments. The novel's climax is the San Francisco earthquake.

Historical Accuracy: Despite the modern sensibility regarding the protection of the environment, the novel does offer a convincing depiction of the period and the region.

LOUIS CHARBONNEAU (1924-)

American western and science fiction writer Charbonneau was born in Detroit. He has been a staff writer for the *Los Angeles Times* and a book editor for Security World Publishing Company in Los Angeles. In addition to his novels, Charbonneau is the author of numerous radio and television plays, including several scripts for the TV series ''Outer Limits.'' Charbonneau prefers writing about the West because of its mythic qualities and its limitless possibilites for strong drama in which right and wrong are so clearly perceived.

997 *Down From the Mountain*

Date of Publication: 1969

Subject(s): American West; Wagon Trains; Indians

Fictional character(s): Gage Pardee, Frontiersman; Anne Locke, Immigrant; Eban Pardee, Frontiersman

Time Period(s): 1860s (1866)

Locale(s): Pacific Northwest

Summary: Nineteen-year-old Gage Pardee is elected leader of a wagon train heading west and racing against time to cross the mountains before the first snows. A bitter confrontation ensues when another train is met. One must give way, the other will be caught in the snow and certainly perish.

Historical Accuracy: The novel is historical not in its facts but in its fidelity to its time and place. Conflicts and challenges like those in the story did occur in similar mountain passes.

998 *Trail: The Story of the Lewis and Clark Expedition*

Date of Publication: 1989

Subject(s): Lewis and Clark Expedition; Exploration; Dogs

Fictional character(s): Seaman, Animal (dog)

Historical character(s): William Clark, Explorer, Military Personnel; Meriwether Lewis, Explorer, Military Personnel; Thomas Jefferson, Political Figure; James Monroe, Political Figure; George Rogers Clark, Military Personnel (army officer); Sacajawea, Indian (Shoshone), Guide

Time Period(s): 1800s (1803-1806)

Locale(s): Pacific Northwest; West

Summary: The Lewis and Clark Expedition is dramatized through the experiences of a valued member of the team, Meriwether Lewis' dog, Seaman. The dog is part of Lewis and Clark's great journey to chart the Louisiana Territory. They endure hostile Indians, stampeding buffalo, and the wilderness. Seaman is kidnapped and comes to the rescue of his master.

Historical Accuracy: The author based the events on the historical record and probability but fills in the gaps with speculation.

DOROTHY CHARQUES (1899-1976)

An English biographer and novelist, Charques was born in Warwickshire and graduated from the University of Sheffield with honors in history and economics. Her historical novels have been acclaimed by critics.

999   *The Dark Stranger*

Date of Publication: 1957
Subject(s): Civil War—England; Witchcraft and Sorcery
Fictional character(s): Elizabeth Devize, Orphan; Sir Rafe Gilles, Gentleman
Time Period(s): 17th century
Locale(s): England

Summary: This novel of intrigue is set during the English Civil War, the conflict between the Royalists and the Roundheads. The action centers on Elizabeth Devize, an orphan whose father died at Marston Moor, and the mysterious Sir Rafe Gilles.

Historical Accuracy: The novel effectively builds its suspense and action around an authentic core of period religious and political elements.

1000   *Men Like Shadows*

Date of Publication: 1953
Subject(s): Middle Ages; Crusades
Fictional character(s): John of Oversley, Knight; Melisande Preaux, Gentlewoman; Gui de Pasay, Knight
Historical character(s): Richard the Lionhearted, Ruler (King of England)
Time Period(s): 12th century
Locale(s): England; Palestine

Summary: In this adventure tale, John of Oversley and his comrades accompany Richard the Lionhearted to Palestine to win back Jerusalem for Christendom.

Historical Accuracy: The novel offers an impressive and believable reconstruction of the Third Crusade.

1001   *The Nunnery*

Date of Publication: 1959
Subject(s): Tudor Period; Religious Life
Fictional character(s): Jane Ingham, Orphan, Ward; Cecilia Wayte, Religious (prioress); Sir John Acock, Gentleman
Historical character(s): Thomas Cromwell, Government Official
Time Period(s): 16th century (1630s)
Locale(s): Warwickshire, England

Summary: The novel's historical background is the Tudor period and the seizure by Henry VIII of England's monasteries and convents. The story concerns a Warwickshire nunnery and its struggle to survive. Jane Ingham is an orphan and ward of Cecilia Wayte, the Lady Prioress of Cokehill Priory. Jane resists a life in the convent due to her love for the courtier Sir John Acock, who finds himself embroiled in court politics and intrigue.

Historical Accuracy: The novel captures with skill the Tudor period, both its political climate and the daily life of the people.

SAMUEL CHARTERS (1929-)

An American ethnomusicologist, poet, and writer, Charters was born in Pittsburgh, Pennsylvania, and was educated at Sacramento City College, Tulane University, and the University of California at Berkeley. He has worked in the music recording industry and received a Grammy Award for producing Clifton Chenier's recording of "I'm Here." He is the author of *The Roots of the Blues*; the biographies *I Love: The Story of Vladimir Mayakovsky* and *Lili Bruk*; and the novels *Mr. Jabi and Mr. Smythe* and *Louisiana Black*.

1002   *Jelly Roll Morton's Last Night at the Jungle Inn: An Imaginary Memoir*

Date of Publication: 1984
Subject(s): Musical Life; Biography, Fictionalized
Historical character(s): Joseph Ferdinand Morton, Musician
Time Period(s): 20th century
Locale(s): United States

Summary: The novel provides an autobiographical account of the life and career of jazz great Jelly Roll Morton. Although little is known for sure about Morton's early career, this version, which depends on interviews with Morton, attempts to sort out the factual from the legendary.

Historical Accuracy: The novel is able to provide a convincing voice and makes strong use of the known facts.

NICHOLAS CHASE
(PSEUD. OF ANTHONY HYDE, 1946-)

Nicholas Chase is a pseudonym for Canadian novelist and short-story writer, Anthony Hyde, who is best known for his international thrillers, *The Red Fox* and *China Lake*. Hyde was born in Ottawa, Ontario, and attended Carleton University. He has also co-written with his brother, Christopher Hyde.

1003   *Locksley*

Date of Publication: 1983
Subject(s): Middle Ages; Crime and Criminals; Myths and Legends
Fictional character(s): Robert of Locksley, Outlaw (aka Robin Hood)
Time Period(s): 12th century
Locale(s): Nottinghamshire, England

Summary: Robert of Locksley recounts his career as the outlaw Robin Hood in this realistic interpretation of the legendary story. In this version, Robin Hood is less heroic and more human, a man who finds himself the reluctant leader of a band of outcasts.

Historical Accuracy: Although psychologically and atmospherically convincing, some modifications of historical fact have been necessary to place Locksley at the center of important events.

BARBARA CHASE-RIBOUD

`1004` *Echo of Lions*

Date of Publication: 1989
Subject(s): Slavery; Trials; Politics
Fictional character(s): Vivian Braithwaite, Abolitionist; Henry Braithwaite, Abolitionist
Historical character(s): Joseph Cinque, Slave, Revolutionary; John Quincy Adams, Lawyer, Political Figure; Martin Van Buren, Political Figure; Louisa Adams, Spouse (of John Quincy Adams)
Time Period(s): 1830s; 1840s (1839-1842)
Locale(s): *Amistad*, At Sea; Connecticut (New Haven, Hartford); Washington, District of Columbia

Summary: In 1839 slaves aboard the *Amistad* mutiny, killing the captain and crew, and try unsuccessfully to sail home to Africa. They are captured and imprisoned. Their leader, Joseph Cinque, is both vilified as a murdering pirate and hailed as an abolitionist hero who has mounted the only successful slave revolt in American history. John Quincy Adams comes to his defense in a trial that eventually becomes the first civil rights case decided by the Supreme Court, which holds that escaped slaves should be treated as free men.

Historical Accuracy: The novel is based on solid and impressive research into the events and period. This is a riveting and important aspect of American history, here animated into troubling and insightful life.

`1005` *The President's Daughter*

Date of Publication: 1994
Subject(s): Civil War—U.S.; Slavery; Battle of Gettysburg
Fictional character(s): Harriet Hemings, Abolitionist, Nurse; Thance Wellington, Businessman
Historical character(s): Sally Hemings, Slave; Thomas Jefferson, Political Figure; Abraham Lincoln, Political Figure
Time Period(s): 19th century (1822-1876)
Locale(s): Monticello, Virginia; Philadelphia, Pennsylvania; Gettysburg, Pennsylvania

Summary: In this sequel to *Sally Hemings*, the author tells the story of the daughter of Thomas Jefferson's supposed slave mistress. At age 21 Harriet Hemings leaves Monticello for Philadelphia where she finds love but also learns what freedom in the North for blacks really means. Her activities lead her from abolition and women's rights to a role in the Battle of Gettysburg.

Historical Accuracy: The novel's historical basis is debatable. More speculation than history, it is still convincing as a plausible version of the facts.

`1006` *Sally Hemings*

Date of Publication: 1979
Subject(s): Slavery; American Revolution

Historical character(s): Sally Hemings, Slave; Thomas Jefferson, Political Figure, Diplomat; John Adams, Political Figure, Diplomat; Abigail Adams, Gentlewoman, Spouse; Martha Jefferson, Gentlewoman, Spouse; John Quincy Adams, Political Figure; James Madison, Political Figure
Time Period(s): 18th century; 19th century (1787-1835)
Locale(s): Monticello, Virginia; Paris, France

Summary: The novel is based on the long-held suspicion that Thomas Jefferson had an affair with his slave Sally Hemings and that she bore him children. The novel details the affair over a 38-year period, an ingenious speculation on race and national identity revealed in the domestic arrangements of one of the creators of the American consciousness.

Historical Accuracy: The novel raised a firestorm of protest from Jefferson scholars who denied the novel's central premise. In her defense, the author supports her claims with solid research.

`1007` *Valide: A Novel of the Harem*

Date of Publication: 1986
Subject(s): Slavery; Ottoman Empire; Napoleonic Wars
Fictional character(s): Black Eunuch, Slave
Historical character(s): Mahmud II, Ruler (sultan, Ottoman Empire); Naksh-i-dil, Slave, Royalty; Catherine II, Ruler (Empress of Russia); Napoleon Bonaparte, Ruler, Military Personnel; Abdulhamid I, Ruler (sultan, Ottoman Empire)
Time Period(s): 18th century; 19th century (1781-1839)
Locale(s): Constantinople, Ottoman Empire; St. Petersburg, Russia; Crimea, Russia

Summary: This is the extraordinary story of an American Creole girl who is captured by pirates and sold into slavery, entering the harem of Topkapi during the reign of Sultan Abdulhamid. She becomes the mother of Sultan Mahmud II, which makes her the Empress Mother, or Valide, of the Ottoman Empire. The novel offers a realistic reconstruction of harem life of the period and a portrait of a remarkable woman, a match for Catherine the Great and Napoleon.

Historical Accuracy: The novel is utterly convincing in presenting the history of the period and the customs of royal life in the Ottoman Empire.

FRANCOIS RENE DE CHATEAUBRIAND (1768-1848)

A French writer who was one of the pioneers of the French romantic movement, Chateaubriand's most famous work is *Le Genie du Christianisme*, an apology for Christianity.

`1008` *Atala*

Date of Publication: 1801
Subject(s): Indians; Settlement of the American Frontier
Fictional character(s): Atala, Indian, Young Woman; Chactas, Indian
Historical character(s): Aubrey, Religious (missionary priest)
Time Period(s): 1720s
Locale(s): Louisiana

Summary: Chateaubriand uses the American wilderness as a setting for this tale of the noble savage. Chactas is captured by

Atala's tribe. She loves him, but they cannot wed because he is not a Christian. Chactas' conversion and Atala's tragic end illustrate the author's philosophical point about Christian faith and God's goodness.

Historical Accuracy: This is more a philosophical romance than a historical novel, but the wilderness scenes are at least based on the author's travels in the American frontier.

BRUCE C. CHATWIN (1940-1989)

British art consultant, journalist, and author Bruce Chatwin is known for his distinctive travel books and novels. He was hailed as an elegant and accomplished writer from his first publication, *In Patagonia*, a record of his impressions of the desolate southern regions of South America. Chatwin worked for the art auction firm of Sotheby's, but left after eight years to study anthropology. His works include the travel book *Songlines*, the novels *On the Black Hill* and *Utz*, and a collection of essays, *What Am I Doing Here?*.

1009 *The Viceroy of Ouidah*

Date of Publication: 1980
Subject(s): Slavery
Fictional character(s): Francisco Da Silva, Trader (slave)
Time Period(s): 19th century
Locale(s): Brazil; Africa

Summary: The West African slave trade in the 19th century forms the background for this novel that began as a nonfictional account of the actual white Brazilian slave trader Francisco da Souza. His rise from a poor orphan in Brazil to Viceroy of Ouidah and the richest man in West Africa is translated into a fictional version that vividly captures the slave trade and period African life.

Historical Accuracy: The novel's grasp of its exotic setting and the details of the period provide a believable context for the story.

LILLIAN CHEATHAM

1010 *Portrait of Emma*

Date of Publication: 1975
Subject(s): Suspense; Romance; Witchcraft and Sorcery
Fictional character(s): Emma Ashton, Orphan; Silence Southwick, Businesswoman, Widow(er)
Time Period(s): 18th century (post-American Revolution)
Locale(s): Boston, Massachusetts

Summary: Young Emma Ashton takes a position in the household of Silence Southwick, a moneylender and owner of a thriving pottery business. She finds herself caught in a web of family secrets and suspected witchcraft and learns that she is the intended next victim.

Historical Accuracy: The emphasis is on romantic suspence with some period details that make a plausible background.

1011 *The Secret of Saramount*

Date of Publication: 1978

Subject(s): Suspense; Romance
Fictional character(s): Colin Mountain, Young Man; Sarah Mountain, Young Woman
Time Period(s): 1910s
Locale(s): Charleston, South Carolina

Summary: When Sarah Mountain's beloved cousin Colin returns after having disappeared 12 years ago, doubt remains. Although he looks and acts like the Colin Sarah remembers, there are lapses in his recollections that cause suspicion that this man may be an imposter, a fraud attempting to take the plantation of Saramount from its rightful heirs.

Historical Accuracy: The southern background is plausible, but the emphasis here is contrived romantic suspense rather than fully developed historical events.

JUDITH CHERNAIK (1934-)

Chernaik was born in New York City and received her B.A. from Cornell and her Ph.D from Yale. She has taught English at such institutions as Columbia, Tufts, and the University of London.

1012 *The Daughter: A Novel Based on the Life of Eleanor Marx*

Date of Publication: 1979
Subject(s): Victorian Period; Literary Life
Historical character(s): Eleanor Marx, Activist (socialist); Edward Aveling, Actor, Writer (playwright); Olive Schreiner, Feminist; Havelock Ellis, Scientist; George Bernard Shaw, Writer; May Morris, Writer
Time Period(s): 1890s
Locale(s): London, England

Summary: The novel describes the life of Eleanor Marx, the youngest daughter of Karl Marx, who became a great socialist heroine in the 1880s and a member of London's bohemian intellectual set that included George Bernard Shaw and Havelock Ellis. In 1898, Eleanor took her own life after her common-law husband, actor Edward Aveling, deserted her for a young actress. The novel explores in interesting ways the difficulty of both revolution and liberation.

Historical Accuracy: Though based on historical details and a fully realized period, the author admits her novel is not meant to be a literal reconstruction of real events.

1013 *Love's Children*

Date of Publication: 1992
Subject(s): Literary Life; Regency Period
Historical character(s): Percy Bysshe Shelley, Writer; Mary Wollstonecraft Shelley, Writer; Claire Clairmont, Gentlewoman; Harriet Westbrook, Gentlewoman, Spouse (first wife of Shelley); George Gordon Byron, Writer, Nobleman; Fanny Godwin, Bastard Daughter; Thomas Love Peacock, Writer; Leigh Hunt, Writer
Time Period(s): 1810s (1816-1817)
Locale(s): Geneva, Switzerland; Marlow, England; London, England

Summary: Four women are connected with the poet Percy Shelley: Harriet Westbrook, Mary Shelley, Fanny Godwin, and Claire Clairmont. Told in jounal entries from all four, the novel is the story of Shelley's stay in Geneva with Lord Byron and Mary Shelley, and Claire's return to England. They launch a revolutionary way of living before suicide, family conflict, and a custody suit drive Shelley from England permanently.

Historical Accuracy: The novel is an impressive blending of history and the imagination. Though the perspectives are invented, they ring true as a reflection of the personalities and the era.

MARION CHESNEY (1936-)

Scottish novelist Chesney was born in Glasgow and worked as a women's fashion editor, theater critic, and reporter before turning to writing novels full-time. She has written more than 30 Regency romances. Her research skills as a reporter help her accurately render the customs and details of the period.

1014 *The Adventuress*

Date of Publication: 1987
Subject(s): Regency Romance; Servants
Fictional character(s): John Rainbird, Servant (butler); Emily Goodenough, Gentlewoman; Sir George Goodenough, Gentleman
Time Period(s): 1810s (1811)
Locale(s): London, England

Summary: Sir George and Emily Goodenough, father and daughter, are not the genteel society folks they seem, but rather a former butler and a runaway chambermaid. The staff at Number 67 joins forces to protect the Goodenoughs' social fraud and win Emily the man of her choice.

Historical Accuracy: Despite the implausible premise, there are good realistic details of Regency England and its social customs.

1015 *Animating Maria*

Date of Publication: 1990
Subject(s): Regency Romance
Fictional character(s): Amy Tribble, Spinster; Effy Tribble, Spinster; Maria Kendall, Gentlewoman
Time Period(s): 19th century (Regency period)
Locale(s): London, England

Summary: The Tribble sisters' fifth London season offers them a seemingly easy challenge in Maria Kendall— beautiful, refined, and possessing a fortune—a perfect candidate for marriage. The challenge for the sisters is not Maria as much as her impossibly gauche parents.

Historical Accuracy: The novel is supported by a sure sense of the social background of the London marriage market of the time.

1016 *At the Sign of the Golden Pineapple*

Date of Publication: 1987
Subject(s): Regency Romance; Business Building
Fictional character(s): Henrietta Bascombe, Heiress, Businesswoman (confectioner); Guy Clifford, Gentleman; Rupert Carrisdowne, Nobleman (Earl of Carrisdowne)
Time Period(s): 19th century (Regency period)
Locale(s): London, England

Summary: With an inheritance, Henrietta Bascombe decides to open a London sweetshop to rival the famous Gunter's. One of the appeals of the shop is Henrietta's beauty which attracts Guy Clifford, the best friend of the Earl of Carrisdowne. The earl sets out to put a stop to Guy's dalliance and loses his heart to the fair Henrietta.

Historical Accuracy: The novel is a romantic fantasy yet possesses strong details of period London.

1017 *Back in Society*

Date of Publication: 1994
Subject(s): Regency Romance; Hotels; Business Building
Fictional character(s): Lady Jane Fremney, Noblewoman; Miss Tonks, Gentlewoman, Spinster; Philip Sommerville, Nobleman
Time Period(s): 1810s
Locale(s): London, England

Summary: All seems to be going well for the Poor Relation Hotel. The rooms are all filled; the Prince of Wales' patronage assures the hotel's status as one of the most fashionable in London. However, one guest, Lady Jane Fremney, has decided to commit suicide in despair over her father's insistence that she marry a man not of her choosing. When Miss Tonks uncovers her plans, she enlists the poor relations to assist Lady Jane in overcoming her troubles.

Historical Accuracy: The novel is filled with accurate period details.

1018 *The Banishment*

Date of Publication: 1995
Subject(s): Regency Romance
Fictional character(s): Isabella Beverley, Gentlewoman; Ajax Judd, Gentleman; Viscount Fitzpatrick, Nobleman
Time Period(s): 19th century (Regency period)
Locale(s): England

Summary: In the first volume of The Daughters of Mannerling series, the proud Beverley family loses their fortune and the estate of Mannerling due to Sir Beverley's gambling. The eldest daughter, Isabella, has no choice but to try to court Mr. Judd who now holds the property. However, her heart is set on the Irish peer, Lord Fitzgerald.

Historical Accuracy: The novel provides a serviceable period background for the romantic complications.

1019 *Beatrice Goes to Brighton*

Date of Publication: 1992
Subject(s): Regency Romance; Stagecoaches

Fictional character(s): Hannah Pym, Housekeeper (retired), Matchmaker; Beatrice Marsham, Gentlewoman, Widow(er); Alistair Munro, Nobleman
Time Period(s): 19th century (Regency romance)
Locale(s): Brighton, England

Summary: After enduring a brutal, abusive marriage, recent widow Beatrice Marsham is in no hurry to remarry. She flees by stagecoach to Brighton to avoid an unwanted engagement. Hannah Pym is determined to find her a proper match and settles on Lord Munro as the perfect candidate. She sets out to show him that Beatrice is not the heartless flirt Munro knew in the past.

Historical Accuracy: The period details are strongly and vividly presented.

1020 *Belinda Goes to Bath*

Date of Publication: 1991
Subject(s): Regency Romance; Stagecoaches
Fictional character(s): Hannah Pym, Housekeeper (retired), Matchmaker; Belinda Earle, Gentlewoman; Marquess of Fenton, Nobleman
Time Period(s): 19th century (Regency period)
Locale(s): England (en route to Bath)

Summary: Hannah Pym's second attempt at matchmaking takes place on the Quicksilver coach to Bath. Passenger Belinda Earle is being banished for attempting to run off with a footman. There is no eligible suitor for her aboard until the coach lands in the river near Baddell Castle. Its owner, Fenton, might just answer the need with a little manipulation by Hannah.

Historical Accuracy: The novel is a delightful romantic comedy with good period detail of coaching in England.

1021 *Colonel Sandhurst to the Rescue*

Date of Publication: 1994
Subject(s): Regency Romance; Business Building; Hotels
Fictional character(s): Colonel Sandhurst, Military Personnel (retired), Businessman; Lord Bewley, Nobleman; Frederica Gray, Gentlewoman
Time Period(s): 1810s
Locale(s): London, England

Summary: Colonel Sandhurst's scheme to rescue the financially strapped Poor Relation Hotel is to concoct a fraudulent kidnapping of a peer's daughter to force him to settle his bill with the hotel and to prevent Frederica's unwanted marriage to Lord Bewley. The plan goes awry when Bewley shows up at the wrong moment.

Historical Accuracy: The novel offers solid period details to bolster its comedy and misadventures.

1022 *Daphne*

Date of Publication: 1984
Subject(s): Regency Romance; Family Saga
Fictional character(s): Daphne Armitage, Gentlewoman; Cyril Archer, Gentleman; Simon Garfield, Nobleman
Time Period(s): 1810s

Locale(s): Hopeworth, England (rural village); London, England

Summary: The fourth daughter of the Reverend Charles Armitage is the vain and empty-headed Daphne who has fixed her heart on a match with the equally superficial Cyril Archer. Her father, however, has other ideas, namely the noble Simon Garfield.

Historical Accuracy: Romantic complications dominate, yet the novel's dialogue sounds realistic, and the period touches create a plausible atmosphere.

1023 *Deborah Goes to Dover*

Date of Publication: 1992
Subject(s): Regency Romance; Stagecoaches; Boxing
Fictional character(s): Hannah Pym, Housekeeper (retired), Matchmaker; Deborah Western, Noblewoman; Lord Ashton, Nobleman
Time Period(s): 19th century (Regency romance)
Locale(s): England (en route to Dover)

Summary: On her way to Dover Hannah Pym steps into a prize-fight ring to save her footman from harm. There she discovers a woman in disguise watching the fight and decides that this tomboy, Lady Deborah Western, might make a suitable match for Lord Ashton.

Historical Accuracy: The novel offers an interesting glimpse at the Regency sporting world.

1024 *Deirdre and Desire*

Date of Publication: 1983
Subject(s): Regency Romance; Family Saga
Fictional character(s): Deirdre Armitage, Gentlewoman; Harry Desire, Nobleman; Guy Wentwater, Gentleman
Time Period(s): 1810s (1815)
Locale(s): Hopeworth, England (rural village); London, England

Summary: The third daughter of Reverend Armitage to enter the marriage market is the headstrong, red-haired Deirdre, who resists her father's choice of a husband for her, Lord Desire, when she finds herself falling in love with the dashing Guy Wentwater. Her father's scheme to restore the family fortune through the marriage seems doomed to failure.

Historical Accuracy: There are detailed observations about dress and customs that provide realistic touches to the romantic comedy.

1025 *The Desirable Duchess*

Date of Publication: 1993
Subject(s): Regency Romance
Fictional character(s): Alice Lacey, Gentlewoman; Gerald Warby, Gentleman; Duke of Ferrant, Nobleman (Duke of Ferrant)
Time Period(s): 1810s
Locale(s): England

Summary: Alice Lacey is separated from her love, Gerald Warby, and she eventually succumbs to the attractions of the

Duke of Ferrant. They marry, but the duke is unfaithful, and Gerald returns, putting Alice to the test.

Historical Accuracy: The author's period details ground the story convincingly to the era.

1026 *Diana the Huntress*

Date of Publication: 1985
Subject(s): Regency Romance; Family Saga; Hunting
Fictional character(s): Diana Armitage, Gentlewoman; Charles Armitage, Religious (country vicar); Charles Dantry, Nobleman
Time Period(s): 1810s
Locale(s): Hopeworth, England (rural village); London, England

Summary: The fifth Armitage daughter shares her father's passion for fox hunting and craves a man's independence of action, particularly to indulge in the sport. A romatic adventure ensues, and Diana the huntress becomes the hunted in a marriage chase.

Historical Accuracy: There are accurate details of hunting and town life in this romance.

1027 *Emily Goes to Exeter*

Date of Publication: 1990
Subject(s): Regency Romance; Stagecoaches
Fictional character(s): Hannah Pym, Housekeeper (retired), Matchmaker; Emily Freemantle, Gentlewoman, Heiress; Ranger Harley, Nobleman
Time Period(s): 19th century (Regency period)
Locale(s): England (en route to Exeter)

Summary: Middle-aged spinster and housekeeper Hannah Pym receives a legacy that allows her to fulfill a secret dream of travelling throughout England by stagecoach. She sets out on her first trip to Exeter, and the coach is set upon by a highwayman and overturns. The passengers are stranded by a snow storm, giving Miss Pym the opportunity to untangle the romantic situation of a young heiress in disguise who is fleeing from an unwanted betrothal.

Historical Accuracy: The series' conceit of a travelling matchmaker is charming, and the novel offers some interesting views of England during the age of coaching.

1028 *Enlightening Delilah*

Date of Publication: 1989
Subject(s): Regency Romance
Fictional character(s): Amy Tribble, Spinster; Effy Tribble, Spinster; Delilah Wraxall, Gentlewoman
Time Period(s): 19th century (Regency period)
Locale(s): London, England

Summary: The Tribble sisters take up the marriage cause of Delilah Wraxall, a beautiful but cynical heart-breaker who is not anxious to marry anyone except the one man who spurned her love. She enters the London social season and flirts shamelessly, until her true love appears and the game turns serious.

Historical Accuracy: The author creates a believable social scene as the background for her romantic story.

1029 *Finessing Clarissa*

Date of Publication: 1989
Subject(s): Regency Romance
Fictional character(s): Amy Tribble, Spinster; Effy Tribble, Spinster; Clarissa Vevian, Gentlewoman
Time Period(s): 19th century (Regency period)
Locale(s): London, England

Summary: Clarissa Vevian is wealthy, beautiful, and well-bred but embarrassingly clumsy and accident prone. The Tribbles take her on to restore her confidence and guide her safely to marriage. Their efforts are unwittingly aided by a highwayman.

Historical Accuracy: There is good period detail of the London social scene.

1030 *The First Rebellion*

Date of Publication: 1989
Subject(s): Regency Romance
Fictional character(s): Fanny Waverly, Gentlewoman
Time Period(s): 19th century (Regency period)
Locale(s): England

Summary: The Waverly sisters are raised to be staunch feminists who know little about men or life. When the Earl of Tredair comes into their lives and courts Fanny, their philosophy undergoes a challenging reassessment.

Historical Accuracy: The feminism of the Waverly sisters is difficult to accept as historical.

1031 *The Folly*

Date of Publication: 1996
Subject(s): Regency Romance
Fictional character(s): Rachel Beverley, Gentlewoman; Charles Blackwood, Widow(er)
Time Period(s): 1800s
Locale(s): England

Summary: The novel continues the Daughters of Mannerling series as Rachel Beverley is drawn to Mannerling's new tenant, widower Charles Blackwood. Complications occur but all is resolved, as expected, by multiple marriage proposals.

Historical Accuracy: Chesney's accomplished period painting serves a fairly formulaic plot.

1032 *Frederica in Fashion*

Date of Publication: 1985
Subject(s): Regency Romance; Family Saga
Fictional character(s): Charles Armitage, Religious (country vicar); Frederica Armitage, Gentlewoman; Duke of Pembury, Nobleman
Time Period(s): 1810s
Locale(s): Hopeworth, England (rural village); London, England

Summary: Frederica is the last of the Armitage daughters, the ugly duckling whom her five elder sister despair of ever marrying off. She resists their scheming and surprisingly arranges her own match that eclipses those of her sisters.

Historical Accuracy: The period is re-created with authentic vocabulary and local details.

1033 *Her Grace's Passion*

Date of Publication: 1991
Subject(s): Regency Romance
Fictional character(s): Matilda Hadshire, Noblewoman (Duchess of Hadshire); Charles Torridon, Nobleman (Earl of Torridon)
Time Period(s): 19th century (Regency period)
Locale(s): London, England

Summary: Matilda is trapped in a marriage to a cruel and unfaithful husband. She dreams instead of the dashing Earl of Torridon. He too is locked in a loveless marriage, and both must free themselves from their unwanted partners before getting together.

Historical Accuracy: The romantic complication and contrivance here strains credibility.

1034 *The Intrigue*

Date of Publication: 1995
Subject(s): Regency Romance; Inheritance—Disputed
Fictional character(s): Jessica Beverley, Gentlewoman; Robert Sommerville, Professor; Harry Devers, Heir
Time Period(s): 19th century (Regency period)
Locale(s): England

Summary: In the second volume of The Daughters of Mannerling series, the Beverley family tries to regain Mannerling, the 17th century mansion gambled away by Sir Beverley. Hope rests on Jessica Beverley to attract the attention of Henry Devers, the present heir of Mannerling. But her real love is Oxford don Robert Sommerville. How will Jessica resolve the conflict between family loyalty and her heart's desire?.

Historical Accuracy: The story is an engaging one with convincing period trappings.

1035 *Lady Fortescue Steps Out*

Date of Publication: 1992
Subject(s): Regency Romance; Business Building; Hotels
Fictional character(s): Lady Fortescue, Noblewoman; Colonel Sandhurst, Military Personnel (retired); Harriet James, Cook
Time Period(s): 1810s
Locale(s): London, England

Summary: Lady Fortescue and Colonel Sandhurst, both impoverished members of the upper class, hatch a plan for financial solvency. They turn Lady Fortescue's Bond Street home into a posh hotel staffed by poor relations of the nobility, and the Poor Relation Hotel is born. Lady Fortescue's nephew is appalled at his aunt's entry into trade until he meets the hotel's chef, Harriet James.

Historical Accuracy: This is a delightful Regency fantasy. If the premise is far-fetched, the authentic period background creates the realism.

1036 *Marrying Harriet*

Date of Publication: 1990
Subject(s): Regency Romance
Fictional character(s): Amy Tribble, Spinster; Effy Tribble, Spinster; Harriet Brown, Gentlewoman
Time Period(s): 19th century (Regency period)
Locale(s): London, England

Summary: The Tribble sisters' final challenge as chaperones-for-hire is the overly virtuous Harriet Brown, who is beset by a rake. The sisters, however, are surprised to learn that Harriet is plotting to arrange suitors for them in this finale to the series.

Historical Accuracy: The novel offers some delightful comic romance with an accurate background of period details.

1037 *Minerva*

Date of Publication: 1982
Subject(s): Regency Romance; Family Saga
Fictional character(s): Charles Armitage, Religious (country vicar); Minerva Armitage, Gentlewoman; Sylvester Comfrey, Nobleman
Time Period(s): 1810s (1811)
Locale(s): Hopeworth, England (rural village); London, England

Summary: *Minerva* is the first of six volumes recounting the romantic courtship of the six daughters of a country vicar during the Regency Period. Minerva, the eldest daughter, is a prude who is sent to London to marry a man of fortune. Her first London season shocks the moralizing Minerva when she finds herself surrounded by the rakes and dandies of the ton.

Historical Accuracy: Chesney's familiarity with period details and emphasis on the comedy of manners over the romance make this story more believable than other Regency romances.

1038 *The Miser of Mayfair*

Date of Publication: 1986
Subject(s): Regency Romance; Servants
Fictional character(s): John Rainbird, Servant (butler); Roderick Sinclair, Gentleman; Fiona Sinclair, Gentlewoman, Ward
Time Period(s): 1800s (1807)
Locale(s): London, England

Summary: The Mayfair house at Number 67 Clarges Street is deemed an unlucky address and remains vacant season after season to the disappointment of the staff. No tenant means no parties and no tips. When Mr. Sinclair lets the house for the season, all are delighted until they discover that he is a notorious miser. Rainbird, the clever butler of Number 67, comes to the rescue of Sinclair's ward and arranges a fashionable match for her.

Historical Accuracy: Chesney has mastered the atmosphere of the Regency Period which she delivers in full details.

1039 *Miss Davenport's Christmas*

Date of Publication: 1993
Subject(s): Regency Romance
Fictional character(s): Gillian Davenport, Gentlewoman, Orphan; Amanda Davenport, Gentlewoman, Orphan; Ranger Marden, Nobleman
Time Period(s): 19th century (Regency period)
Locale(s): London, England

Summary: Two sisters, Gillian and Amanda Davenport, are raised by their strict Puritan parents in a sober regimen which eschews luxury and festivities. When the sisters are on their own, they rebel, celebrating Christmas in fine style. Fashionable gentlemen join the celebration.

Historical Accuracy: The Puritan opposition to Christmas is a bit overplayed for the novel's romantic point.

1040 *Miss Fiona's Fancy*

Date of Publication: 1987
Subject(s): Regency Romance
Fictional character(s): Fiona Grant, Gentlewoman; Charles Cleveden, Nobleman (Marquess of Clevedon)
Time Period(s): 19th century (Regency period)
Locale(s): London, England; Scotland

Summary: Fiona Grant arrives in London from her native Scotland and is goaded into a wager. She risks losing a fortune she does not possess unless she is able to win the hand of the Marquess of Clevedon, the most eligible but elusive catch in London. It is a high-stakes romance with an uncertain outcome.

Historical Accuracy: The novel offers a good deal of period detail that is convincingly displayed.

1041 *Miss Tonks Turns to Crime*

Date of Publication: 1993
Subject(s): Regency Romance; Business Building; Hotels
Fictional character(s): Miss Tonks, Gentlewoman, Spinster; Colonel Sandhurst, Military Personnel (retired); Lady Fortescue, Noblewoman
Time Period(s): 1810s
Locale(s): London, England

Summary: To keep the Poor Relation Hotel afloat, funds are needed, and shy spinster Miss Tonks is persuaded to steal something of value from her rich sister. A more unlikely thief cannot be imagined, but Miss Tonks surprises everyone.

Historical Accuracy: The novel offers period fun with a believable background of Regency customs.

1042 *Mrs. Budley Falls From Grace*

Date of Publication: 1993
Subject(s): Regency Romance; Business Building; Hotels
Fictional character(s): Eliza Budley, Widow(er); Marquess of Porterhouse, Nobleman; Philip Sommerville, Nobleman
Time Period(s): 1810s
Locale(s): London, England

Summary: The Poor Relation Hotel is again in need of funds to survive, and it is Eliza Budley who comes to the aid of the enterprise. She has no relatives to borrow from, but the Marquess of Porterhouse is rumored to be so rich and senile that he might not remember whether Mrs. Budley is one of his relatives or not.

Historical Accuracy: This is an amusing caper, one of the most engaging of the series, with a clear period background.

1043 *Penelope Goes to Portsmouth*

Date of Publication: 1991
Subject(s): Regency Romance; Stagecoaches
Fictional character(s): Hannah Pym, Housekeeper (retired), Matchmaker; Penelope Wilkins, Gentlewoman; Augustus Railton, Nobleman
Time Period(s): 19th century (Regency period)
Locale(s): England (en route to Portsmouth)

Summary: While on her way to Portsmouth, the irrepressible travelling matchmaker Hannah Pym sets out to match up the sheltered and naive Penelope and the worldly Lord Railton. A footman charged with a crime he did not commit provides the opportunity for a rescue and, perhaps, the sparks to ignite a romance between the unwilling couple.

Historical Accuracy: The romantic comedy is bolstered by period details that enliven the story.

1044 *Perfecting Fiona*

Date of Publication: 1989
Subject(s): Regency Romance
Fictional character(s): Amy Tribble, Spinster; Effy Tribble, Spinster; Fiona MacLeod, Gentlewoman, Heiress
Time Period(s): 19th century (Regency period)
Locale(s): London, England

Summary: The Tribble sisters' second challenge in their school for manners is Fiona MacLeod, an heiress whose various marriage proposals have all fallen through at the last moment. It turns out that Fiona is an incorrigible flirt, and the Tribbles have their work cut out for them in salvaging Fiona's and their own reputation for marrying the unmarriageable.

Historical Accuracy: The novel, like the series, is filled with authentic details of the London social scene during the Regency.

1045 *Plain Jane*

Date of Publication: 1986
Subject(s): Regency Romance; Mystery; Servants
Fictional character(s): Jane Hart, Gentlewoman; Euphemia Hart, Gentlewoman; Lord Tregarthan, Nobleman
Time Period(s): 1800s (1808)
Locale(s): London, England

Summary: The Hart sisters—beautiful, ambitious Euphemia and her plainer, quieter younger sister, Jane—move into Number 67 Clarges Street for the London season. Jane turns away from the social whirl to investigate the mysterious death of a past tenant of the house, aided by the dashing Lord Tregarthan.

Historical Accuracy: The novel features some fascinating details of life in Regency London.

1046 *Rainbird's Revenge*

Date of Publication: 1988
Subject(s): Regency Romance; Servants
Fictional character(s): John Rainbird, Servant (butler); Duke of Pelham, Nobleman; Jenny Sutherland, Gentlewoman
Time Period(s): 1810s (1812)
Locale(s): London, England

Summary: In this finale to Chesney's series about Number 67 Clarges Street, Mayfair, the house's owner, the Duke of Pelham, returns determined to find a suitable wife. One possibility is the vain Jenny Sutherland, whom Rainbird befriends. He schemes to produce a marriage which will determine the fate of all at Number 67.

Historical Accuracy: Chesney's picture of Regency London is masterfully displayed.

1047 *Rake's Progress*

Date of Publication: 1987
Subject(s): Regency Romance; Servants
Fictional character(s): John Rainbird, Servant (butler); Lord Guy Carlton, Nobleman, Rake; Esther Jones, Gentlewoman
Time Period(s): 1810s (1810)
Locale(s): London, England

Summary: This season's tenant at Number 67 Clarges Street is the notorious rake Lord Carlton who seems destined to die of dissipation unless the staff can reform him. They identify the prim Esther Jones as a likely candidate to assist, but inevitable complications present themselves.

Historical Accuracy: The novel and the series show Chesney's ability to animate the social world of Regency England.

1048 *Refining Felicity*

Date of Publication: 1988
Subject(s): Regency Romance
Fictional character(s): Amy Tribble, Spinster; Effy Tribble, Spinster; Felicity Baronsheath, Gentlewoman
Time Period(s): 19th century (Regency period)
Locale(s): London, England

Summary: Amy and Effy Tribble are impoverished spinster sisters who advertise as professional chaperones and guarantee to prepare even the most difficult young ladies for the marriage market. Their first customer and challenge is Felicity, a spoiled brat indifferent to the idea of marriage.

Historical Accuracy: Chesney's conceit of a school for marriage manners offers a good opportunity to observe the London Regency social scene.

1049 *The Scandalous Lady Wright*

Date of Publication: 1990
Subject(s): Regency Romance; Mystery
Fictional character(s): Sir Benjamin Wright, Nobleman; Emma Wright, Noblewoman; Jules Saint-Juste, Nobleman (Comte Saint-Juste)
Time Period(s): 19th century (Regency period)
Locale(s): London, England

Summary: Sir Benjamin Wright is an honored member of the aristocracy, but his wife, Emma, knows him to be a drunken brute. His murder is a welcome release from a bad marriage, but suspicion about his death falls on Emma. The Comte Saint-Juste comes to her rescue. He helps Emma discover Sir Benjamin's secrets and wins her heart at the same time.

Historical Accuracy: The period painting is well done in this story with far more substance than the expected romantic fare.

1050 *The Scandalous Marriage*

Date of Publication: 1991
Subject(s): Regency Romance
Fictional character(s): Lucy Blish, Gentlewoman; Belinda Blish, Gentlewoman; Lucifer Wardshire, Nobleman (Duke of Wardshire)
Time Period(s): 19th century (Regency period)
Locale(s): London, England

Summary: Lucy Blish's sister Belinda is intent on marrying the Duke of Wardshire, a nobleman with a scandalous reputation. Lucy attempts to protect her sister from his dubious charms only to succumb to them herself.

Historical Accuracy: The novel is filled with details of the costumes and customs of the period.

1051 *Sir Philip's Folly*

Date of Publication: 1993
Subject(s): Regency Romance; Business Building; Hotels
Fictional character(s): Philip Sommerville, Nobleman; Lady Carruthers, Noblewoman; Mary Budge, Widow(er)
Time Period(s): 1810s
Locale(s): London, England

Summary: The Poor Relation Hotel is disrupted by the vulgar Mrs. Budge, who refuses to do any work around the hotel. Amidst the commotion she causes, Lady Carruthers comes to stay at the hotel and tries to pass herself off as much younger than she is. It is up to the poor relations to deal with the lazy Mrs. Budge, vanquish Lady Carruthers, and arrange a match for her daughter.

Historical Accuracy: The novel and the series are precise in their period details and social niceties.

1052 *The Taming of Annabelle*

Date of Publication: 1983
Subject(s): Regency Romance; Family Saga
Fictional character(s): Charles Armitage, Religious (country vicar); Annabelle Armitage, Gentlewoman; Marquis of Brabington, Nobleman
Time Period(s): 1810s (1812)
Locale(s): London, England; Hopeworth, England (rural village)

Summary: Annabelle is the second oldest marriageable daughter of the Armitage family. Like her older sister Minerva, Annabelle has her London debut. As willful and reckless as Minerva is modest, Annabelle scandalizes society and her sister before agreeing to marry the Marquis of Brabington, but complications develop.

Historical Accuracy: Chesney accurately details the London social scene in this romantic comedy of manners.

1053 *The Wicked Godmother*

Date of Publication: 1987
Subject(s): Regency Romance; Servants
Fictional character(s): John Rainbird, Servant (butler); Harriet Metcalf, Gentlewoman, Heiress
Time Period(s): 1800s (1809)
Locale(s): London, England

Summary: The new tenant at Number 67 Clarges Street, Mayfair, is young Harriet Metcalf, an heiress with a dubious reputation. Rainbird and the staff must intercede to combat the vicious gossip that threatens to spoil the chances of their new mistress to find romantic happiness.

Historical Accuracy: The novel is built on the details of domestic life during the Regency, which are rendered with precision.

1054 *Yvonne Goes to York*

Date of Publication: 1992
Subject(s): Regency Romance; Stagecoaches
Fictional character(s): Hannah Pym, Housekeeper (retired), Matchmaker; Yvonne Grenier, Gentlewoman; Mrs. Clarence, Gentlewoman
Time Period(s): 19th century (Regency period)
Locale(s): England (en route to York)

Summary: Hannah Pym goes to see her former employer, Mrs. Clarence, who has left a loveless marriage and gone to York with her footman. On the way, Hannah assists a young Frenchwoman as well as her former mistress while surprisingly finding herself in a match that will end her career on the road.

Historical Accuracy: The series delightfully concludes with period details of Regency England.

DEBORAH CHESTER (1957-)

Born in Chicago, Chester graduated from the University of Oklahoma. Her novel *The Sign of the Owl* was named the best book for young adults in 1981. She was the Oklahoma Writer of the Year in 1985. Her goal as a writer is to produce books that her readers cannot put down.

1055 *French Slippers*

Date of Publication: 1981
Subject(s): Regency Romance
Fictional character(s): Julia Swanton, Orphan; Lucien Arouet, Nobleman (Marquis du Vallon)
Time Period(s): 1810s
Locale(s): London, England

Summary: When her father is killed in a duel, Julia Swanton is left penniless. She returns to London pretending her father is still alive, thus maintaining her hope for a financially rewarding marriage. She must contend, however, with Lord du Vallon, a Frenchman suspected of being a spy for Napolean. He knows her secret.

Historical Accuracy: Though contrivance predominates, the period details are well presented and authentic.

1056 *A Love So Wild*

Date of Publication: 1980
Subject(s): Regency Romance
Fictional character(s): Mary Clampton, Convict; Aubrey Menton, Nobleman (Earl of Menton)
Historical character(s): George, Prince Regent, Royalty (Prince of Wales)
Time Period(s): 19th century (Regency period)
Locale(s): Brighton, England; London, England

Summary: Mary Clampton finds herself going from prison to high Regency society, contracted to marry the son of the villainous noble who conspired to imprison her. Despite this, she is attracted to the Earl of Menton, and Mary is swept up in a rivalry and a conspiracy with major repercussions.

Historical Accuracy: The contrivance strains credibility, but the period details are convincing.

FREDERICK J. CHIAVENTONE

A retired cavalry officer, army strategist, and expert on guerilla warfare, Chiaventone was a professor of international security affairs at the U.S. Army Command and General Staff College.

1057 *A Road We Do Not Know: A Novel of Custer at the Little Bighorn*

Date of Publication: 1996
Subject(s): Battle of the Little Bighorn; Indians; Military Life—U.S. Cavalry
Historical character(s): George Armstrong Custer, Military Personnel (cavalry officer); Frederick Benteen, Military Personnel (cavalry officer); Crazy Horse, Indian (Sioux), Warrior; Sitting Bull, Indian (Sioux), Chieftain; Gall, Indian (Sioux), Warrior; Charles Varnum, Military Personnel (lieutenent)
Time Period(s): 1870s (1876)
Locale(s): Dakota Territory, United States; Little Bighorn River, Montana

Summary: This novel provides an hour-by-hour account of the events leading up to and including the Battle at the Little Bighorn in which Custer's command is massacred in the greatest Indian victory of the Sioux War. It offers a detailed and objective perspective on both sides of the conflict with emphasis on the ordinary participants and the human dimension of the battle.

Historical Accuracy: Based on extensive research, this account is faithful to the firsthand reports of the actual participants. Slight liberties have been taken with some details.

DONALD BARR CHIDSEY (1902-1981)

An American writer born in New Jersey, Chidsey was a newspaperman for ten years on many different papers. He served with the American Field Service in the Middle East. Besides his novels, he was also the author of nonfiction studies including *Elizabeth I, Aaron Burr and His Strange Doings in the West, Bonnie Prince Charlie,* and *The World of Samuel Adams.*

1058 *Captain Adam*

Date of Publication: 1953
Subject(s): Sea Story; Pirates; American Colonies
Fictional character(s): Adam Long, Sea Captain; Lady Maisie Treadway, Noblewoman; Deborah Selden, Young Woman
Time Period(s): 18th century
Locale(s): Rhode Island, American Colonies; West Indies; London, England

Summary: This romantic adventure story of the high seas records the exploits of Adam Long, who becomes the captain of a schooner built in Rhode Island in the early 1700s. His adventures with pirates, smugglers, and a beautiful passenger from London form the novel's swashbuckling action.

Historical Accuracy: The novel is more colorful and atmospheric than careful in its period documentation.

1059 *Captain Bashful*

Date of Publication: 1955
Subject(s): Elizabethan Period
Fictional character(s): Kit Peverel, Adventurer; Jane Mautravers, Gentlewoman
Historical character(s): Elizabeth I, Ruler (Queen of England)
Time Period(s): 16th century
Locale(s): England; France

Summary: Kit Peverel returns from service abroad as a mercenary to find that his family estate in Dorset has been seized. The novel follows his exploits in regaining his estate and winning the hand of his love, Jane Mautravers.

Historical Accuracy: The novel's thrilling action predominates over a careful and credible historical background.

1060 *The Edge of Piracy*

Date of Publication: 1964
Subject(s): American Revolution; Sea Story
Fictional character(s): Ezra Bond, Sailor
Time Period(s): 1770s
Locale(s): West Indies; At Sea

Summary: This nautical adventure tale, set during the American Revolution, tells the story of seaman Ezra Bond who is pressed into service on a British man-of-war, escapes, and embarks on a smuggling career in the West Indies.

Historical Accuracy: The novel's nautical scenes are authentic and believable.

1061 *His Majesty's Highwayman*

Date of Publication: 1958
Subject(s): Crime and Criminals; Georgian Period
Fictional character(s): Tom Savage, Adventurer; Harry Tewkes, Highwayman; Molly Evans, Young Woman
Historical character(s): William Pitt the Elder, Political Figure
Time Period(s): 1770s (1775)
Locale(s): England

Summary: Tom Savage, unfortunately, resembles the infamous highwayman Harry Tewkes, a coincidence which nearly costs him his life. Arrested and nearly executed by mistake, he is rescued by Harry's gang. To clear his name, Tom impersonates the highwayman until a final confrontation with his look-alike nemesis.

Historical Accuracy: Pure swashbuckling fun, the novel does offer some realistic period details.

1062 *The Legion of the Lost*

Date of Publication: 1967
Subject(s): Sea Story; Pirates
Fictional character(s): Toby Franklin, Servant; Eve Shackleton, Young Woman
Historical character(s): Captain William Kidd, Pirate
Time Period(s): 17th century
Locale(s): New York, New York, American Colonies; At Sea; Madagascar

Summary: Toby Franklin, an indentured servant, is ordered by his master to accompany pirate Captain William Kidd on a voyage to Madagascar. When he discovers a beautiful young woman in a treasure chest, he jumps ship with Eve Shackleton, beginning a series of swashbuckling adventures.

Historical Accuracy: The emphasis is on adventure and exotic locales rather than an accurate depiction of historical events.

1063 *Lord of the Isles*

Date of Publication: 1954
Subject(s): Adventure
Fictional character(s): Johnny Lamb, Adventurer, Sailor; Ann Mathewson, Widow(er)
Historical character(s): Kaahumanu, Ruler (Queen of Hawaii)
Time Period(s): 1820s
Locale(s): Hawaii (formerly the Sandwich Islands)

Summary: Johnny Lamb, a fugitive from a murder charge in Connecticut, ships out aboard a whaling ship and winds up in the Sandwich Islands. There he achieves success as a trader and becomes the common-law consort of Queen Kuaahumanu. His true interest, however, is Ann Mathewson, the young widow of one of America's first Christian missionaries in Hawaii, and a woman more than a match for the irrepressible Lamb.

Historical Accuracy: This is a charming romantic adventure tale with a vivid period Hawaiian setting.

1064 *Reluctant Cavalier*

Date of Publication: 1960
Subject(s): Elizabethan Period; Sea Story; Spanish Armada
Fictional character(s): George Fitzwilliam, Diplomat
Historical character(s): Mary, Queen of Scots, Ruler (Queen of Scotland); Elizabeth I, Ruler (Queen of England); Sir Francis Drake, Sea Captain
Time Period(s): 16th century (1571-1588)
Locale(s): England; Spain; Scotland

Summary: During the years preceding the defeat of the Spanish Armada, George Fitzwilliam becomes the courier in secret negotiations between England and Spain and between Queen

Elizabeth and Mary, Queen of Scots. Fitzwilliam dislikes the duplicity of his missions and the danger. He joins Drake for adventures at sea in action that culminates in the defeat of the Armada.

Historical Accuracy: This is a lively and colorful evocation of the period.

1065 *Stronghold*

Date of Publication: 1948
Subject(s): Sea Story; War of 1812
Fictional character(s): Habakkuk Jones, Sailor; John Rellison, Sailor; Deliverance Watts, Young Woman
Time Period(s): 1810s
Locale(s): Connecticut; Martinique

Summary: This is the story of the friendship and rivalry between Habakkuk Jones and John Rellison from Connecticut who both take to the sea. Hab is impressed into the British Navy on his way home from Martinique. He escapes and makes it home to Deliverance Watts, but when John returns as well, conflict breaks out between the two former comrades.

Historical Accuracy: The novel offers some convincing period details of naval life during the War of 1812.

1066 *This Bright Sword*

Date of Publication: 1957
Subject(s): Middle Ages; Royalty—England
Fictional character(s): Guy fitz Warren, Knight; Maud, Young Woman; Guernes de Pont Ste. Maxence, Nobleman
Historical character(s): John, Ruler (King of England)
Time Period(s): 13th century
Locale(s): England

Summary: Guy fitz Warren, a knight of considerable skill, is chosen by Lord Ste. Maxence to be the constable and defender of Pingry Castle and the husband of the lord's niece, Maud. It is a marriage of convenience, but Guy labors to arouse the interest of his aloof bride. His daring exploits culminate in an important role in coercing King John to sign Magna Carta.

Historical Accuracy: The author attempts to present the age of chivalry in a realistic light. Accordingly, there are some authentic details of ordinary life amongst the romantic adventures.

1067 *The Wickedest Pilgrim*

Date of Publication: 1961
Subject(s): American Colonies; Pilgrims
Fictional character(s): Salathiel Boyd, Sailor, Pirate
Historical character(s): Miles Standish, Leader (pilgrim); Priscilla Mullins, Settler; John Alden, Leader (pilgrim)
Time Period(s): 17th century (1620s)
Locale(s): *Mayflower*, At Sea; Plymouth, Massachusetts, American Colonies

Summary: In 1620, a drunken pirate named Sal Boyd climbs aboard his ship after a night of carousing. The ship he boards is not his, but the *Mayflower* as it heads across the Atlantic on her voyage to the New World. The novel describes how this odd pilgrim fares and how he contributes to life and survival in the Plymouth colony.

Historical Accuracy: The story is a comic invention with some realistic and credible touches of Pilgrim life.

LAURENE CHINN (1902-1978)

Chinn was born in Iowa. Her father was a clergyman, which may explain the Biblical subjects of her fiction. She attended Hastings College and West Texas State College, and taught in the Kansas school system. She began her writing career in 1938 and had forty stories published within a year and a half.

1068 *Marcus*

Date of Publication: 1965
Subject(s): Biblical Story; Christianity; Roman Empire
Historical character(s): Mark, Biblical Figure, Religious; Jesus Christ, Biblical Figure; Paul, Biblical Figure, Religious; Peter, Biblical Figure, Religious
Time Period(s): 1st century (30-65)
Locale(s): Jerusalem, Israel; Cyprus; Rome, Roman Empire

Summary: The novel tells the story of Mark, youngest of the 12 disciples and one of the first people to write about the life of Jesus. We see Mark's devotion to Jesus and his ministry first with Paul on Cyprus and then with Peter in Rome. Mark emerges as very much a representative of his age.

Historical Accuracy: The author has been careful to keep to the historical record when it is known and to speculate when necessary.

1069 *The Soothsayer*

Date of Publication: 1972
Subject(s): Biblical Story; Christianity
Fictional character(s): Merza, Sorceress (soothsayer)
Historical character(s): Paul, Biblical Figure, Religious; Timothy, Religious, Biblical Figure
Time Period(s): 1st century
Locale(s): Asia Minor; Macedonia; Greece

Summary: Two people enter the life of 13-year-old Timothy: Saint Paul, and Merza, a soothsayer. Timothy is determined to follow Paul in his missionary work, but he also searches for Merza. His quest takes him from Asia Minor through Thessalonica, to Corinth and Ephesus where Timothy becomes a bishop of the early church.

Historical Accuracy: The evocation of the ancient world is convincing if the actual details of the story are fictional.

1070 *The Unanointed*

Date of Publication: 1958
Subject(s): Biblical Story; Jews; Ancient Israel
Historical character(s): David, Biblical Figure, Ruler (King of Israel); Joab, Biblical Figure, Military Personnel (general); Solomon, Biblical Figure, Ruler (King of Israel); Bathsheba, Biblical Figure, Spouse; Absalom, Biblical Figure
Time Period(s): 10th century B.C.
Locale(s): Jerusalem, Israel; Bethlehem, Israel

Summary: This is the story of King David's kinsman and military commander, Joab. He carries out David's commands and fights Israel's enemies so that Israel grows from a scattering of warring tribes to a unified nation.

Historical Accuracy: This is a blend of the actual and the imagined, anchored by a convincing reconstruction of the period.

P.F. CHISHOLM

1071 *A Famine of Horses*

Date of Publication: 1994
Subject(s): Mystery; Elizabethan Period
Fictional character(s): Sir Robert Carey, Nobleman, Government Official (deputy warden); Lady Elizabeth Widdrington, Noblewoman
Historical character(s): James Hepburn, Nobleman (Earl of Bothwell)
Time Period(s): 16th century
Locale(s): Carlisle, England

Summary: Sir Robert Carey is the newly appointed Deputy Warden of the West March in the border country between England and Scotland. The murder of Sweetmilk Geordie Graham could start a civil war, and Carey must find the killer and at the same time solve the theft of hundreds of horses that have been stolen.

Historical Accuracy: The novel offers a convincing look at the 16th century English borders and the conflicts surrounding them.

1072 *A Season of Knives*

Date of Publication: 1996
Subject(s): Elizabethan Period; Mystery
Fictional character(s): Sir Robert Carey, Nobleman, Government Official (deputy warden); Lady Elizabeth Widdrington, Noblewoman
Time Period(s): 16th century (1592)
Locale(s): Carlisle, England

Summary: In this second Elizabethan-era mystery Sir Robert Carey is the new deputy warden of Carlisle, in the West Marches, along the troubled border between Scotland and England. His amorous adventures in foiling the kidnapping of Lady Elizabeth Widdrington are interrupted when he returns to Carlisle to discover that he is being accused of murder. The crime plunges Carey into a tangle of intrigue.

Historical Accuracy: Although there was an actual Sir Robert Carey, all the characters and events portrayed are fictitious. The novel does feature an authentic regional and period background.

SYNNOVE CHRISTENSEN

1073 *Lindeman's Daughters*

Date of Publication: 1958
Subject(s): Family Saga

Fictional character(s): Hans Jacob Lindeman, Artist; Anne Pernille Oleson, Spouse; Anders Oleson, Sea Captain
Time Period(s): 18th century
Locale(s): Norway

Summary: This domestic melodrama about the fate of the Lindeman family is set in Norway during the 18th century when the first demands for independence are being heard. After his wife dies, the care of Hans Jacob Lindeman falls on long-suffering Anne Pernille who must endure her father's eccentricities and an unwanted marriage to a sea captain in his sixties.

Historical Accuracy: The novel's vivid portrait of the period is authentic, even as the story strains credibility by its melodramatic excesses.

JOHN CHRISTGAU (1934-)

Born in Minnesota, author and English teacher John Christgau attended San Francisco State University. His first novel, *Spoon*, has been compared by one critic to *Candide* and was named best novel of the year in 1978 by the Society of Midland Authors.

1074 *Spoon*

Date of Publication: 1978
Subject(s): Indians; Picaresque Adventure
Fictional character(s): Alexander Featherstone, Artist; Spoon, Indian, Guide
Historical character(s): Abraham Lincoln, Political Figure
Time Period(s): 1860s (1862)
Locale(s): Minnesota

Summary: This tragicomic tale concerns the Sioux-Santee uprising in Minnesota in 1862. Artist Alexander Featherstone has come to sketch the Santees. His interpreter is the idiosyncratic Indian, Spoon. They find themselves at the center of events that lead to the trial and execution of 38 Indians at Mankato.

Historical Accuracy: Factual elements in the novel are based on a close examination of testimony about the events.

CATHERINE CHRISTIAN (1901-)

Christian is the author of fantasy novels and historical fiction, including *The Pharaoh's Secret* and *The Pendragon*.

1075 *The Pendragon*

Date of Publication: 1976
Subject(s): Myths and Legends; Dark Ages; Arthurian Legends
Fictional character(s): Guinevere, Royalty (queen consort of Arthur); Bedivere, Knight; Launcelot, Knight; Arthur, Ruler (king of the Britons)
Time Period(s): 6th century
Locale(s): England

Summary: Told by Bedivere, Arthur's boyhood companion and comrade, the novel chronicles the familiar story of Camelot, told not as legend but as historical fact, as it might have happened. The tragic failure of Arthur's attempt to bring order to the anarchy of Britain after the Romans' departure is told as a great personal and political drama.

Historical Accuracy: The research into the factual basis of the Arthurian legend lends credibility to this version.

AGATHA CHRISTIE (1890-1976)

Arguably the bestselling novelist of all time, British mystery writer Dame Agatha Christie was born in Torquay, England, and was tutored by her mother until the age of 16. She later studied singing and piano in Paris. From the publication of her first popular success, *The Murder of Roger Ackroyd*, Christie produced a long string of mystery stories that made her name synonymous with the genre, and made her fictional detectives Miss Marple and Hercule Poirot household names. Among her many works are *The A.B.C. Murders*, *Murder on the Orient Express*, and the longest running play in history, *The Mousetrap*.

`1076` *Death Comes as the End*

Date of Publication: 1944
Subject(s): Ancient Egypt; Mystery
Fictional character(s): Renisenb, Widow(er); Hori, Secretary (scribe); Imhotep, Religious (priest)
Time Period(s): 20th century B.C.
Locale(s): Thebes, Egypt

Summary: Christie's detective story set in ancient Egypt focuses on a series of murders that strike members of a wealthy family. Renisenb, the family's young, widowed daughter, and Hori, the family scribe and business adviser, become the detectives who try to deduce the identity of the murderer.

Historical Accuracy: There tends to be an English country-house feel to the story, but the era and its customs have been well researched and are successfully rendered here.

J.D. CHRISTILIAN

`1077` *Scarlet Women*

Date of Publication: 1996
Subject(s): Mystery; Women's Rights
Fictional character(s): Harp, Detective—Private
Historical character(s): Victoria Claflin Woodhull, Feminist
Time Period(s): 1870s (1871)
Locale(s): New York, New York

Summary: A prostitute's murder in New York City in 1871 sends private detective Harp into the shadowy labyrinth of corrupt politicians, mobsters, and the demimonde. The novel features a remarkable re-creation of period Manhattan.

Historical Accuracy: The period background is authentic and believable.

WINSTON CHURCHILL (1871-1947)

Churchill was born in St. Louis but lived mainly in New Hampshire. His most famous works are historical novels. Other works include *Mr. Crewes' Career*, *A Far Country*, *A*

Modern Chronicle, *The Inside of the Cup*, and *The Dwelling-Place of Light*.

`1078` *Coniston*

Date of Publication: 1906
Subject(s): Politics
Fictional character(s): Jethro Bass, Political Figure; Cynthia Ware, Heroine
Time Period(s): 1830s
Locale(s): Coniston, Vermont

Summary: Jethro Bass, an eccentric but popular politician, quarrels with his love and they part. Eventually, he befriends her orphan daughter, and his sharp dealings are revealed.

Historical Accuracy: This is an interesting look at early 19th-century New England town life.

`1079` *The Crisis*

Date of Publication: 1901
Subject(s): Civil War—U.S.
Fictional character(s): Stephen Brice, Lawyer, Military Personnel; Virginia Carvel, Southern Belle; Clarence Colfax, Gentleman, Military Personnel
Historical character(s): Abraham Lincoln, Political Figure; Stephen A. Douglas, Political Figure; William Tecumseh Sherman, Military Personnel; Ulysses S. Grant, Military Personnel
Time Period(s): 1850s; 1860s
Locale(s): St. Louis, Missouri; Springfield, Illinois; Virginia

Summary: The events of the Civil War and the regional differences that caused it are studied through a group of characters from St. Louis, a crossroads in the dispute. Stephen Brice meets Lincoln, Grant, and Sherman and witnesses some of the pivotal events of the war, while attempting to woo his southern sweetheart.

Historical Accuracy: This is one of the best Civil War novels to integrate the fictional and the historical. It also examines Northern and Southern culture in detail.

`1080` *The Crossing*

Date of Publication: 1904
Subject(s): American Revolution; Settlement of the American Frontier
Fictional character(s): David Ritchie, Orphan, Lawyer
Historical character(s): George Rogers Clark, Military Personnel; Daniel Boone, Frontiersman
Time Period(s): 1770s; 1780s
Locale(s): North Carolina; Kentucky; Charleston, South Carolina

Summary: This historical adventure tells the story of David Ritchie, orphaned when his father is killed in the American Revolution. Only 11, David serves as George Rogers Clark's drummer boy and aide and participates in the Wilderness campaign in Kentucky. He later becomes a lawyer.

Historical Accuracy: This is Churchill's finest novel, full of historical characters and details that support an exciting story of development in the American wilderness.

1081 *Richard Carvel*

Date of Publication: 1900

Subject(s): American Revolution; Sea Story

Fictional character(s): Richard Carvel, Gentleman, Military Personnel (sailor); Dorothy Manners, Gentlewoman

Historical character(s): John Paul Jones, Military Personnel; Horace Walpole, Writer; George Fox, Religious

Time Period(s): 1760s; 1770s

Locale(s): Maryland, American Colonies; London, England

Summary: In this novel of the American Revolutionary period, Richard Carvel is kidnapped by pirates and later captured by John Paul Jones, who befriends him. Carvel's subsequent career in London introduces him to many prominent figures but doesn't help him arrange a marriage to his sweetheart. The Revolution forces him into action with Jones, and Carvel is wounded during the victory of the *Bonhomme Richard* over the *Serapis*.

Historical Accuracy: The book's implausible coincidences contrast with its historical throughness.

JOHN CLAGETT (1916-)

Born in Kentucky, Clagett graduated from the U.S. Naval Academy and Yale University. A professor of English at Middlebury College, Clagett's books include *The Rebel*, *Island of Dragons*, and *Typhoon*.

1082 *Buckskin Cavalier*

Date of Publication: 1954

Subject(s): Indians

Fictional character(s): Lynn Cameron, Gentleman; Dawn Woodbridge, Captive

Historical character(s): Simon Girty, Frontiersman, Scout; Daniel Boone, Frontiersman

Time Period(s): 18th century

Locale(s): Northwest Territory, United States; Fort Pitt, Pennsylvania; Kentucky

Summary: Set during the Indian Wars in the Northwest Territory, this frontier tale describes the efforts of a young gentleman, Lynn Cameron, who sets out along the Wilderness Road to free Dawn Woodbridge, who has been captured by the Indians.

Historical Accuracy: The story provides a number of authentic period details and a believable atmosphere of frontier life.

1083 *Cradle of the Sun*

Date of Publication: 1952

Subject(s): Mayan Empire; Spanish Colonies; Inquisition

Fictional character(s): Juan de Moncada, Military Personnel (Spanish soldier)

Time Period(s): 16th century

Locale(s): Dominican Republic (Santo Domingo); Yucatan, Mexico; Spain

Summary: This story of Spain's colonies in the New World describes the adventures of an officer in the Spanish army, Juan de Moncada. Fleeing from the Inquisition, he goes to Santo Domingo and then to the Yucatan. There he is taken in by the Mayans and aids them in their resistance against the Spanish invaders.

Historical Accuracy: The novel largely succeeds in creating a believable historical background for the story.

CARLILE CLANCY (1930-)

Son of a half-Cherokee father, Clancy was born on the Choctaw Indian Reservation in Oklahoma and raised in California. Clancy worked as a newspaper reporter, college instructor, musician, and forest ranger. His novel *Honkeytonk Man* was made into a film starring Clint Eastwood.

1084 *Children of the Dust*

Date of Publication: 1995

Subject(s): American West; Oklahoma Land Rush; Ku Klux Klan

Fictional character(s): Gypsy Smith, Gunfighter, Lawman; John Maxwell, Teacher; Rachel Maxwell, Young Woman; Colby, Indian (Cheyenne)

Time Period(s): 1880s

Locale(s): Oklahoma

Summary: Set against the background of the Oklahoma land rush of the 1880s, the novel tells the story of Gypsy Smith, a mixed-blood black Cherokee, who on the eve of his wedding is attacked by the Ku Klux Klan. This prompts a killing frenzy on the part of Smith. His story is joined to that of John Maxwell, a school teacher whose enlightened attitudes toward the Indians are tested when his daughter Rachel falls in love with a young Cheyenne boy.

Historical Accuracy: Missing.

GAIL CLARK (1944-)

Clark was born in Waynesburg, Pennsylvania, and attended California State College in Pennsylvania and California State University. She has worked as a dialogue replacement editor for TV and feature films. She began her creative writing inventing fantasy stories as a child. Clark admits to a fascination with historical trivia.

1085 *The Baroness of Bow Street*

Date of Publication: 1979

Subject(s): Regency Period; Mystery

Fictional character(s): Dulcie Bligh, Noblewoman; Leda Langtry, Editor, Feminist; Ivor Jessop, Nobleman (Viscount Jeffries); Mignon Montague, Gentlewoman

Time Period(s): 19th century (Regency period)

Locale(s): London, England

Summary: When a 19th century feminist and editor of the *London Apocalypse*, Leda Langtry, is jailed for slandering a fashionable lord, Dulcie Bligh secures her release. But when the lord is found murdered, Leda becomes the prime suspect. Dulcie begins her investigation while at the same time trying to identify a suitor for her flirtatious niece.

Historical Accuracy: In this ingenious blend of genres, the tale is filled with convincing period details.

1086 Dulcie Bligh

Date of Publication: 1978
Subject(s): Regency Period; Mystery
Fictional character(s): Dulcie Bligh, Noblewoman (baroness); Benedict Trench, Nobleman (Earl of Dorset); Lavender Lytton, Companion
Time Period(s): 19th century (Regency period)
Locale(s): London, England

Summary: In this mystery set during the Regency period in London, a society beauty of great wealth has been found strangled. The chief suspect is Benedict Trench, Earl of Dorset, Dulcie Bligh's nephew. She decides to prove his innocence and to find the jewels that disappeared the night of the murder.

Historical Accuracy: The era is colorfully and vividly evoked in this Regency tale.

HOWARD CLARK

(PSEUD. OF)

Clark wrote about the Industrial Revolution in Connecticut during the early 19th century.

1087 The Mill on Mad River

Date of Publication: 1948
Subject(s): Business Building
Fictional character(s): Ashton Holt, Businessman
Time Period(s): 1810s
Locale(s): Waterbury, Connecticut

Summary: Waterbury, Connecticut, is the scene for this novel that traces the business successes of Ashton Holt. His childhood dreams of owning his own brass factory are later realized. The novel features a history of Connecticut's brass and clock-making industries.

Historical Accuracy: The novel captures the historical atmosphere with authenticity.

JEAN CLARK (1920-)

A high school English teacher, Clark was born in Connecticut and educated at Western Connecticut State College and Wesleyan University. She won an award from the League of Connecticut Historical Societies for her first novel, Untie the Winds.

1088 The Marriage Bed

Date of Publication: 1983
Subject(s): American Colonies; French and Indian War; Farming
Fictional character(s): Margaretta Van Dyck, Young Woman; Stephen Warner, Farmer; Nicolaus Van Baden, Gentleman
Time Period(s): 18th century (1740s-1760s)
Locale(s): Hudson River Valley, New York, American Colonies

Summary: The background of this dramatic story is the Dutch tenant farmers' uprising in protest of the restrictive manorial system that kept them in poverty during the 18th century. Margaretta is the young wife of tenant farmer Stephen Warner. To better her family and to win their independence, she risks scandal in a desperate bargain with the lord of the Van Baden estate.

Historical Accuracy: The novel is convincing in its details of Dutch family life in the Hudson River Valley of the period.

1089 Until the Winds

Date of Publication: 1976
Subject(s): American Colonies; Puritans
Historical character(s): Anne Eaton, Gentlewoman, Spouse; Theophilus Eaton, Government Official; John Davenport, Religious (minister)
Time Period(s): 17th century (1688-1664)
Locale(s): New Haven, Connecticut, American Colonies

Summary: The novel recounts the history of the New Haven colony from its founding to its merger with the Connecticut colony in 1664. The story centers on the experiences of Anne Eaton, the wife of the governor, who comes into conflict with the predominant Puritan values.

Historical Accuracy: This historical account is based on events derived from church and town records, but the human emotions and relationships are largely invented.

JUSTUS KENT CLARK (1917-)

A Blue Creek, Utah, native, Clark earned a Ph.D. from Stanford University, where he taught English. He has also taught at the California Institute of Technology. In addition to fiction, he has written a three-act musical, Take Your Medicine, and a biography, Goodwin Wharton.

1090 King's Agent

Date of Publication: 1958
Subject(s): Royalty—England; Glorious Revolution
Fictional character(s): Sir Ralph Barnard, Gentleman
Historical character(s): James II, Ruler (King of England); William III, Ruler (King of England); James FitzJames Berwick, Nobleman (duke)
Time Period(s): 17th century (1680s)
Locale(s): France; England

Summary: The exile of James II following the Glorious Revolution is dramatized from the perspective of a follower of the exiled king, Sir Ralph Barnard. He is torn by shifting allegiances and a recognition of the hopelessness of James' cause. The novel features a vivid portrait of the period as well as an adventure story filled with spies, betrayal, and intrigue.

Historical Accuracy: The novel's framework is historical and accurately constructed.

L.D. CLARK (1922-)

Clark was born in Gainesville, Texas, and received his degrees from Columbia University. He is a professor of

English at the University of Arizona, Tucson, and an expert on the work of D.H. Lawrence.

1091 *A Bright Tragic Thing*

Date of Publication: 1992
Subject(s): Civil War—U.S.; American West
Fictional character(s): Todd Blair, Teenager
Time Period(s): 1860s
Locale(s): Gainesville, Texas

Summary: Based on the actual events surrounding the hanging of Union sympathizers in Gainesville, Texas, the novel focuses on Todd Blair, whose family are Unionists. At first his father and 40 others are detained. When it is apparent that they are to be executed, Todd tries unsuccessfully to free his father and then turns to vengeance on his executioners.

Historical Accuracy: This taut drama of the Civil War is accurate in its background and details.

NORMA LEE CLARK

1092 *Lady Jane*

Date of Publication: 1982
Subject(s): Regency Romance; Servants
Fictional character(s): Jane Coombes, Servant (maid); Jasper Montmorency, Nobleman; Sebastian Payton, Invalid; Leach, Servant (butler)
Time Period(s): 19th century (Regency period)
Locale(s): England

Summary: Jane Coombes loses her place as an underhouse maid when she tries on her employer's luxurious negligee and rips it while repelling the advances of Lord Jasper. She finds another position and marriage to a reclusive cripple, Sebastian Payton. As a widow she enters London society only to re-encounter Lord Jasper and the butler that betrayed her in the past.

Historical Accuracy: The novel's details of the period are well-drawn and convincing.

1093 *The Tynedale Daughters*

Date of Publication: 1981
Subject(s): Regency Romance
Fictional character(s): Norrie Tynedale, Gentlewoman; Millie Tynedale, Gentlewoman; Kitty Tynedale, Gentlewoman; Anthony Beaumont, Gentleman
Time Period(s): 19th century (Regency period)
Locale(s): England

Summary: Marital complications are in store for the three Tynedale sisters—Norrie, Millie, and Kitty—in an elaborate and complicated courtship dance of exchanged partners. There is also a threat of the loss of the Tynedale estate as Anthony Beaumont could become the next owner of Tynedale.

Historical Accuracy: The period is effectively evoked.

RONALD CLARK (1916-1987)

British journalist and writer Clark served as a war correspondent with the British United Press and a foreign correspondent. He is the author of numerous books on mountaineering, as well as respected biographies of such figures as Sigmund Freud and Albert Einstein.

1094 *Queen Victoria's Bomb*

Date of Publication: 1967
Subject(s): Victorian Period; Science
Fictional character(s): Franklin Huxtable, Scientist
Historical character(s): Alfred, Lord Tennyson, Writer (poet); Victoria, Ruler (Queen of England); Albert of Saxe-Coburg-Gotha, Royalty (prince consort of Queen Victor); Edward, Prince of Wales, Royalty
Time Period(s): 1850s
Locale(s): England; Africa

Summary: The question that this novel poses is, what would have happened if the atom bomb had been built a century earlier? This was at least conceivable, as the novel suggests in the disclosures of Professor Franklin Huxtable, whose invention of an ultimate weapon creates for the Victorians the moral question of our times.

Historical Accuracy: What makes the novel so ingenious is the careful support for what might have been and what was.

TOM CLARK (1941-)

An American poet, biographer, sportswriter, and novelist, Clark was born in Chicago, and attended John Carroll University, the University of Michigan, Cambridge University, and the University of Essex. He was the poetry editor for the *Paris Review* from 1963-1973 and has been an instructor in poetics at the New College of California. His works include many anthologies of poetry, biographies of Robert Creeley and Jack Kerouac, and the novels *The Master* and *Who Is Sylvia?*.

1095 *The Exile of Celine*

Date of Publication: 1987
Subject(s): Literary Life; World War II
Historical character(s): Louis-Ferdinand Celine, Writer
Time Period(s): 1940s; 1950s
Locale(s): France; Germany; Denmark

Summary: Accused of collaborating with the Nazis, French writer Celine flees Paris as World War II draws to a close, first for Germany and then to Denmark where he lives in exile until he is granted amnesty in 1951. The novel offers a fictional account of Celine's life in exile, the story of a determined survivor.

Historical Accuracy: The novel presents a believable portrait of the controversial French writer that convincingly captures his complexity.

WALTER VAN TILBURG CLARK
(1909-1971)

Clark was an American writer who grew up in Nevada and was a professor of English. Besides the bestselling *The Ox-Bow Incident*, his works include *The City of Trembling Leaves*, *The Track of the Cat*, and *The Watchful Gods*.

1096 *The Ox-Bow Incident*

Date of Publication: 1940
Subject(s): American West; Crime and Criminals; Vigilantes
Fictional character(s): Carter Gil, Cowboy; Art Croft, Rancher; Tetley, Rancher
Time Period(s): 1880s
Locale(s): Nevada

Summary: Clark turns the Western into a taut and moving drama of mob violence and retribution as he describes a posse that searches for rustlers and administers rough justice with tragic consequences.

Historical Accuracy: The novel raises the standard conventions of the Western into the stuff of tragedy. The details of western life are presented with unflinching honesty.

WILLIAM KENDALL CLARKE (1911-1981)

An American author of television dramas and novels, Clarke wrote numerous scripts for serials. His best known novels are *Tomfool's Pike* and *The Robber Baroness*.

1097 *The Robber Baroness*

Date of Publication: 1979
Subject(s): Business Building; Civil War—U.S.
Historical character(s): Hetty Green, Financier; Andrew Carnegie, Financier; Mark Twain, Writer; Herman Melville, Writer; Victoria, Ruler (Queen of England); Edward, Prince of Wales, Royalty
Time Period(s): 1850s; 1860s
Locale(s): New York, New York; London, England; New Bedford, Massachusetts

Summary: The early years of the notorious miser and financier Hetty Green are depicted. Known as ''The Witch of Wall Street,'' Hetty is shown in youth as passionate and determined, able to dominate events. The novel features scenes from the Civil War and the visit of the Prince of Wales to New York City.

Historical Accuracy: Although biographical data and history have been scrupulously respected, the author admits that the novel is fiction, not history.

TOM CLARKSON (1913-)

Born in Birmingham, England, Clarkson worked as a professional actor, painter, and writer, publishing in periodicals. His books include *The Wounded* and *The Angel of My Bed*, a book of poems.

1098 *Love Is My Vocation: An Imaginative Study of St. Therese of Lisieux*

Date of Publication: 1952
Subject(s): Biography, Fictionalized; Religious Life
Historical character(s): Therese of Lisieux, Religious (nun)
Time Period(s): 19th century (1873-1897)
Locale(s): Lisieux, France

Summary: The novel is a fictional account of the life of Therese of Lisieux who was canonized in 1925. It attempts to capture the human story of the Carmelite nun who entered the convent at Lisieux at the age of 15 where she spent the remaining nine years of her life until her death from tuberculosis.

Historical Accuracy: The novel is derived, at least, in part, from Therese's autobiography, which creates a strong sense of authenticity.

BERNARD CLAVEL (1923-)

French writer Clavel apprenticed as a pastry cook at the age of 14. He worked as a painter and at other odd jobs before becoming a full-time writer.

1099 *Lord of the River*

Date of Publication: 1972
Subject(s): Riverboats
Fictional character(s): Christian Merlin, Sea Captain (riverboat)
Time Period(s): 1840s
Locale(s): Rhine River, Europe

Summary: In the 1840s generations of barge sailors were being replaced by steam-powered ships. Christian Merlin, captain and owner of a train of barges, is determined that his way of life on the river will not disappear, and he mounts one final, grand journey to prove his worth and his heritage.

Historical Accuracy: The period is convincingly detailed in this exciting adventure story.

JAMES CLAVELL (1924-1994)

Clavell was born in Australia and later became a U.S. citizen. During World War II he served in the armed forces and was a prisoner of war of the Japanese. Clavell was an author, screenwriter, producer, director, and playwright. His novels collectively represent what he called ''The Asian Saga,'' and include, besides those listed below, *King Rat* (set in World War II), *Noble House* (concerning modern Hong Kong), and *Whirlwind* (dealing with the Middle East).

1100 *Gai-Jin: A Novel of Japan*

Date of Publication: 1993
Subject(s): East/West Relations; Business Building; Japanese Empire

Fictional character(s): Angelique Richaud, Gentlewoman; Malcolm Struan, Businessman, Trader; Tess Straun, Businesswoman, Trader; Yoshi, Nobleman, Warlord
Time Period(s): 1860s (1862)
Locale(s): Yedo, Japan (present day Tokyo); Yokohama, Japan; Hong Kong

Summary: Set in Japan in 1862, *Gai-Jin*, which means foreigner, is really the sequel to both *Tai-Pan* and *Shogun*. Lord Toranaga's military victory at the end of *Shogun* has secured 250 years of peace and domination by his heirs as Shoguns, but the Toranaga Shogunate is in decline, and new opposition, violently hating gai-jin influence in Japan, is pushing Japan back toward civil war. Dirk Straun's short-lived marriage to Angelique Richaud has a profound impact on the Noble House trading empire.

Historical Accuracy: Clavell ingeniously connects the court and feudal world of Japan with the family business of the Noble House, all meticulously grounded in the Japan of the 19th century.

1101 *Shogun*

Date of Publication: 1977
Subject(s): Japanese Empire; Samurai; East/West Relations
Fictional character(s): John Blackthorne, Sailor; Lord Yoshi Toranaga, Nobleman, Warlord; Lady Mariko Toda, Noblewoman
Time Period(s): 17th century
Locale(s): Japan

Summary: English pilot, or navigator, John Blackthorne wrecks his ship in Japan in 1600. He becomes a key player in the dynastic struggle between Lords Toranaga and Ishido to become Shogun, or military ruler, of Japan. Blackthorne is tutored in the ways of the Japanese and the samurai by Lady Mariko, with whom he falls in love. He must also guard against the intrigues of the Portuguese and the Jesuits who regard him as a heretic and a serious threat to their influence.

Historical Accuracy: The novel's chief characters have a basis in fact, and the novel offers a convincing description of the period.

1102 *Tai-Pan*

Date of Publication: 1966
Subject(s): Business Building; East/West Relations
Fictional character(s): Dirk Struan, Businessman, Trader; Gordon Chen, Businessman, Trader; Tyler Brock, Businessman, Trader
Time Period(s): 1840s
Locale(s): Hong Kong

Summary: Set in China in the aftermath of the Opium Wars and against the backdrop of the colonial scramble for economic control of China, the story concerns Dirk Straun and his ruthless intrigues to secure Hong Kong, the center of the lucrative China trade, as a Crown colony of Britain. In the process, he becomes *tai-pan*, or supreme leader, of the mercantile Noble House.

Historical Accuracy: Clavell's great strength is storytelling supported by rich details of Chinese life and colonial customs.

PAUL CLAYTON

1103 *Flight of the Crow*

Date of Publication: 1996
Subject(s): Spanish Colonies; Indians
Fictional character(s): Calling Crow, Indian
Time Period(s): 17th century (1650s)
Locale(s): Georgia, American Colonies

Summary: In the second novel of a trilogy describing Indian life in Georgia during the 17th century, Calling Crow has escaped from enslavement by the Spanish and has settled along the coast. When Spanish ships arrive, Calling Crow leads in the battles that will decide the fate of the native people.

Historical Accuracy: The novel's atmosphere is believable in capturing the times and the customs of Indian life.

JON CLEARY (1917-)

An Australian writer of adventure novels, Cleary was born in Sydney and left school at the end of his second year of high school. He worked at a variety of jobs prior to World War II. During the war he served in the Middle East and in the New Guinea and New Britain campaigns. Cleary is the author of over 35 novels and has probably earned the greatest sales of any novelist in Australia. He attributes his success to his ability to tell a captivating story.

1104 *The Faraway Drums*

Date of Publication: 1981
Subject(s): British Raj; Assassination
Fictional character(s): Clive Farnol, Government Official (intelligence officer); Bridie O'Brady, Journalist
Historical character(s): George V, Ruler (King of England)
Time Period(s): 1910s (1911)
Locale(s): Delhi, India; Simla, India

Summary: In 1911 on the eve of George V's coronation as Emperor of India, Clive Farnol, a British intelligence officer, and Bridie O'Brady, a young American newspaperwoman, uncover a plot to assassinate the king. They must make their way from the northern hill country of Simla to Delhi, fending off ambush attempts and betrayal, to prevent the assasination.

Historical Accuracy: Though fanciful, the adventure is fully realized in a convincing atmosphere of India and the times.

1105 *The Golden Sabre*

Date of Publication: 1981
Subject(s): Adventure; Russian Revolution
Fictional character(s): Matt Cabell, Engineer (oil); Eden Penfold, Governess
Time Period(s): 1920s
Locale(s): Siberia, Russia; Tiflis, Russia

Summary: In revolutionary Russia, Matt Cabell, an American oil engineer, rescues an English governess, Eden Penfold, in a stolen Rolls-Royce Silver Ghost. They are trailed by a murderous dwarf during a 1000-mile journey from Siberia to Tiflis and freedom.

Historical Accuracy: The emphasis is on high adventure rather than history, but the scenery is believable.

1106 *High Road to China*

Date of Publication: 1977
Subject(s): Aviation; Adventure; Crime and Criminals
Fictional character(s): Eve Tozer, Heiress; William Bede O'Malley, Pilot; Bradley Tozer, Businessman
Historical character(s): Mustafa Kemal, Political Figure; Mao Tse-tung, Political Figure, Revolutionary
Time Period(s): 1920s
Locale(s): London, England; China; Europe (France, Germany)

Summary: Eve Tozer's father, an American tycoon, is kidnapped in China by a warlord who demands as ransom a priceless statuette that Eve must transport from London in 18 days. The only hope is to fly to China, and she recruits an ex-RFC pilot to make the journey. What follows is a non-stop adventure halfway around the world and encounters with events and personalities of the period.

Historical Accuracy: This is a matchless adventure tale with some interesting glimpses of the period.

BRIAN CLEEVE (1921-)

Born in Essex, England, Cleeve received his B.A. from the University of South Africa, and his Ph.D. from the National University of Ireland, where he resides. Cleeve has been a broadcaster for Radio Telefís Eireann. His novels up to 1980 were largely romances. With *The House on the Rock* and *The Secret Mansions*, his work has taken on a deeper tone of mysticism and metaphysics.

1107 *Hester*

Date of Publication: 1980
Subject(s): French Revolution; Royalty—France
Fictional character(s): Hester Broadhurst, Gentlewoman; Michel Vernet, Gentleman; Prince De Talmond, Royalty
Historical character(s): Louis XVI, Ruler (King of France); Napoleon Bonaparte, Military Personnel (general)
Time Period(s): 1780s; 1790s
Locale(s): Paris, France; Vendee, France

Summary: Hester Broadhurst, in Paris on the eve of the Revolution, is a fervent republican, until she shelters the royalist Michel Vernet. Hester begins to experience the darker side of the Revolution, including the prison massacre of 1792 and the battles in the Vendee.

Historical Accuracy: Few could expect to live through all the adventures Hester endures, which strains credibility.

1108 *Judith*

Date of Publication: 1978
Subject(s): Romance; Georgian Period
Fictional character(s): Judith Mortimer, Orphan, Gentlewoman; Robert Barnabas, Smuggler

Time Period(s): 1790s (1796)
Locale(s): London, England; Essex, England

Summary: In order to support herself, Judith Mortimer gets involved with a band of smugglers, allowing them to use her barn to conceal their goods. She also is attracted to the son of the smugglers' chief, Robert Barnabas. Discovery and an arranged marriage cause her to flee to London. She finds her way first to a fancy house of prostitution, then she is held in a private madhouse.

Historical Accuracy: This is a far more realistic period romance than the usual fare and creates somewhat more believability in the scenes described.

1109 *Kate*

Date of Publication: 1977
Subject(s): French Revolution; Theatrical Life; Crime and Criminals
Fictional character(s): Kate Herriot, Actress; The Squire, Smuggler
Time Period(s): 1790s
Locale(s): London, England

Summary: Kate Herriot is a young actress orphaned in France during the Revolution who escapes from a French prison and makes her way illegally to London. There, determined to continue her career as an actress, she falls prey to "The Squire," lord of the London underworld, and is caught up in a dangerous smuggling venture. The ultimate survivor, Kate endures imprisonment in Newgate and finally triumphs on the London stage.

Historical Accuracy: The scenes of London theatrical and underworld life are convincing.

1110 *Sara*

Date of Publication: 1976
Subject(s): Regency Romance
Fictional character(s): Sara Pownall, Orphan; Harry Summers, Gentleman
Time Period(s): 1810s (1814)
Locale(s): Essex, England; London, England; Wales

Summary: In 1814 Sara Pownall makes her way from the Essex countyside to Regency London. She finds a position in a gaming house where the upper class gather. There she meets Harry Summers and has a romance that will transform her life.

Historical Accuracy: The novel features a genuine background of rural Essex and upper and lower-class Regency London.

HUGH CLEVELY

1111 *Stranger in Two Worlds*

Date of Publication: 1959
Subject(s): Fires; Independence—Ireland; Fenians
Fictional character(s): Justin Kelly, Adventurer; Molly Fay, Revolutionary (Fenian)
Time Period(s): 19th century
Locale(s): Ireland; London, England; Chicago, Illinois

Summary: Young Justin Kelly survives the 1857 siege of Lucknow which takes the lives of his parents. His further adventures take him to Ireland where he becomes involved with the Fenians; London; and Chicago at the time of the Great Fire.

Historical Accuracy: The period elements are convincing and rousingly displayed.

HOWARD CLEWES (1912-1988)

An English dramatist, screenwriter, and novelist, Clewes is best known for his screenwriting work in the 1962 remake of the film *Mutiny on the Bounty*. His other works include *The Unforgiven*, plays *Quay South* and *Image in the Sun*, and the film scripts *The Long Memory* and *The Day They Robbed the Bank of England*.

1112 *I, the King*

Date of Publication: 1979
Subject(s): Inca Empire; Spanish Colonies
Historical character(s): Charles V, Ruler (King of Spain); Gonzalo Pizarro, Military Personnel (conquistador), Explorer; Pedro de la Gasca, Religious (missionary)
Time Period(s): 16th century (1542)
Locale(s): Peru; Spain

Summary: In 1542 Gonzalo Pizarro, a conquistador and the last of the adventurer Pizarro brothers, leads a revolt against Charles V of Spain in protest of the genocide committed by his fellow Spaniards against the Incas. His opposition is the priest Pedro de la Gasca, who has the absolute power of the emperor. A clash of wills and vision between the two is dramatized.

Historical Accuracy: The scenes of colonial life in Peru are based on fact; some minor liberties have been taken, primarily in dramatizing meetings whose conversations actually happened in letters.

WINSTON CLEWES
(PSEUD. OF DAVID ARMSTRONG, 1906-1957)

British author Clewes was born in Leeds and educated at Foyle College in Northern Ireland. His novel *Troy and the Maypole* is base don his childhood recollections of Derry where his family moved in 1914. Clewes is the author of the fantasy novel, *Sweet River in the Morning* and *Epitaph for Love*.

1113 *Violent Friends*

Date of Publication: 1945
Subject(s): Biography, Fictionalized; Literary Life
Historical character(s): Jonathan Swift, Writer, Religious (clergyman); Esther Johnson, Gentlewoman; Esther Vanhomrigh, Gentlewoman
Time Period(s): 1720s
Locale(s): Dublin, Ireland

Summary: The story covers the relationships between satirist Jonathan Swift and the two significant women in his life

celebrated in his journals and poems as ''Vanessa'' and ''Stella.'' The novel dramatizes the period from Swift's return to Ireland as Dean of St. Patrick's in Dublin to the death of Stella.

Historical Accuracy: Some liberties of time and place have been taken, but the central facts are consistent with Swift's biography.

ROY CLEWS (1937-)

Born in London, Clews has been a professional soldier serving with the Royal Marine Commandos in Cyprus and with the Spanish Foreign Legion in the Sahara. He spent 12 years travelling around the world working as a seaman, copper miner, laborer, and actor.

1114 *Drums of War*

Date of Publication: 1979
Subject(s): Napoleonic Wars; Peninsular War; Military Life—British Army
Fictional character(s): Jethro Stanton, Military Personnel (corporal); Sarah Stanton, Spouse (common-law wife of Jethro); Sophia Dennetry, Young Woman
Time Period(s): 1810s (1813)
Locale(s): Portugal; Spain

Summary: This novel about the Napoleonic Penninsular Campaign describes a small band of British soldiers travelling with their wives and mistresses to the battleground on the plains of Vitoria for the decisive battle of the campaign. Jethro Stanton is accompanied by his common-law wife, Sarah, but his attention strays to Sophia, sister of one of his commanding officers.

Historical Accuracy: The novel convincingly portrays the lot of the common foot soldier and the details of the struggle in Portugal and Spain.

1115 *The Valiant and the Daunted*

Date of Publication: 1976
Subject(s): Regency Period; Luddites; Labor Movement
Fictional character(s): Jethro Stanton, Worker; Abigail Bartleet, Young Woman; Peter Stanton, Labor Organizer (Luddite), Worker; Bronwen Elliot, Young Woman, Abuse Victim
Time Period(s): 1810s
Locale(s): Worchestershire, England

Summary: In England during the Regency period, the Luddites battle the mill owners for improved working conditions. Jethro Stanton is the son of Luddite leader Peter Stanton who is framed for murder by the mill owners. Jethro pursues his father and must make important choices regarding his father's cause. He is also attracted to two very different women: Abigail Bartleet, the daughter of a mill owner, and Bronwen Elliot, who is auctioned off by her brutal husband.

Historical Accuracy: The novel is faithful to the period and filled with convincing details that capture the atmosphere and spirit of the times.

MICHELLE CLIFF (1946-)

Jamaican-born journalist and author Cliff has worked as a reporter and researcher for *Life* magazine and as an editor in publishing specializing in history, politics, and women's studies. Her books include *Abeng*, *No Telephone to Heaven*, and *Bodies of Water*.

1116 *Free Enterprise*

Date of Publication: 1993
Subject(s): Slavery; Racial Conflict
Fictional character(s): Anne Christmas, Abolitionist
Historical character(s): Mary Ellen Pleasant, Abolitionist
Time Period(s): 19th century
Locale(s): United States

Summary: The novel tells the story of the black abolitionist and entrepreneur Mary Ellen Pleasant. Pleasant and the fictional Jamaican woman Anne Christmas become collaborators with John Brown in the struggle to create an African-American state. After the failure at Harper's Ferry, both women are forced to flee: Pleasant to open a hotel staffed by runaway slaves and Christmas to a Mississippi leper colony.

Historical Accuracy: The novel assumes a good deal of history to make sense of its story of racial conflict.

NICHOLAS R. CLIFFORD (1930-)

An American writer and historian, Clifford was born in Pennsylvania and educated at Princeton and Harvard universities. He is a history professor at Middlebury College in Vermont.

1117 *The House of Memory: A Novel of Shanghai*

Date of Publication: 1994
Subject(s): Chinese Revolution
Fictional character(s): Matthew Walker, Historian; Simon Larsen, Gentleman
Time Period(s): 1920s; 1980s (1989)
Locale(s): Shanghai, China

Summary: In 1989 a young American scholar travels to Shanghai to complete his research on a book about the city's turbulent past. He also investigates the disappearance of Simon Larsen, who vanished from Shanghai three weeks before the Nationalists crushed the Communist uprising in 1927. With Larsen's journal, we travel back in time to the Shanghai of the 1920s and witness curious parallels with China today.

Historical Accuracy: The author contends that the novel is primarily about history. The events described are accurately depicted.

CHARMIAN CLIFT (1923-1969)

GEORGE JOHNSTON

Clift was an Australian writer.

1118 *The Big Chariot*

Date of Publication: 1953
Subject(s): Chinese Empire
Fictional character(s): Cheng Yuan, Nobleman; Cheng Wei, Nobleman
Time Period(s): 17th century (1640s-1660s)
Locale(s): China

Summary: Set in China as the Ming Dynasty falls to the Manchus, the novel centers on the rivalry of two brothers, Cheng Yuan and Cheng Wei.

Historical Accuracy: The historical background to the story is authentic and reliable.

WILLIAM CLIVE
(PSEUD. OF RONALD BASSETT, 1924-)

Born in London, Clive was a career army officer until 1954 when he entered the public relations field before turning to writing full time. His book *Witchfinder General* was the basis for the feature film *The Conqueror Worm*, starring Vincent Price.

1119 *Dando on Delhi Ridge*

Date of Publication: 1971
Subject(s): Indian Mutiny; British Raj; Military Life—British Army
Fictional character(s): Joseph Dando, Military Personnel (rifleman)
Time Period(s): 1850s (1857)
Locale(s): India

Summary: The novel offers a view of the life and times of an ordinary English soldier, Joseph Dando, during the Sepoy revolt in India in 1857. Dando is a cockney charity waif and petty thief who endures disease and the desert as well as fierce fighting with a characteristic determination and aplomb.

Historical Accuracy: Far less heroic than Kipling's romanticized version of the British soldier, Dando is a more realistic and truthful portrait, and the incidents are based on fact.

1120 *The Tune That They Play*

Date of Publication: 1973
Subject(s): Zulu War; Military Life—British Army
Fictional character(s): Sibindi, Warrior (Zulu); Charles "Noggs" Norris-Newman, Journalist; Edwin Dyson, Military Personnel (British soldier)
Time Period(s): 1870 (1879)
Locale(s): Isandhlwana, Africa (Zululand); England; Ireland

Summary: In 1879 six companies of British infantry face an attack by 20,000 Zulu warriors. The British stand and fight to the last man. Their deaths are a testimony to an arrogant general staff and a failure to respect the proud and accomplished Zulu warriors. The novel dramatizes the lives and perspectives of some of the combatants.

Historical Accuracy: The action is factual. The personal histories of the combatants are invented.

STUART CLOETE (1897-1976)

Born in France, Cloete was a member of the Coldstream Guards of the British Army during World War I. He has described his life as being divisible into three parts: soldier, cattle rancher, and writer. His novels, with their themes of interracial love and religious disillusionment, were not well received in his home country of South Africa. The ban on his books in South Africa was only lifted two years before his death in 1974.

1121 The Abductors

Date of Publication: 1966
Subject(s): Victorian Period; Prostitution; Slavery
Fictional character(s): Edward Lenton, Nobleman; Lavinia Lenton, Noblewoman; Ellen Pickford, Governess, Prostitute
Time Period(s): 1870s; 1880s
Locale(s): London, England; Paris, France

Summary: The novel offers an expose of white slavery during the Victorian period. Lord Lenton seduces the family's governess. When he tires of her, he consigns her to a London brothel he frequents. Lavinia Lenton is appalled by her husband's behavior and hypocrisy and begins a crusade to stop the trafficking in young girls for the pleasure of the ostensibly respectable Victorians.

Historical Accuracy: The novel is sensational in its approach, with an appendix of press clippings attesting to the persistence of white slavery and a bibliography of sources. Despite the documentation, the effect is more melodramatic than factual.

1122 The Fiercest Heart

Date of Publication: 1960
Subject(s): Frontier—Africa; British Colonies; Afrikaaners
Fictional character(s): Oom Prinsloo Willem, Settler, Farmer; Maria Tante, Settler, Farmer; John Cedric Robinson, Military Personnel (British officer)
Time Period(s): 1830s
Locale(s): South Africa

Summary: The novel chronicles the great Boer trek during the 1830s in which 10,000 Boers left the Cape Colony for the African interior and freedom from British rule. The story of the trek and its hardships along with conflicts with the Zulus and the British, who regard the Boers as outlaws, are depicted in strong portraits of Boer determination and heroism.

Historical Accuracy: The details of African life and Boer belief are solidly and authentically presented; the basis of the Boers' intolerance is, however, soft-pedaled.

1123 The Hill of Doves

Date of Publication: 1942
Subject(s): Frontier—Africa; Family Saga
Fictional character(s): Lena du Toit, Young Woman; Dirk Van der Berg, Young Man
Time Period(s): 1880s
Locale(s): Transvaal, South Africa

Summary: The novel continues the family saga begun in *Watch for the Dawn* and concerns the relationship between Lena du Toit and Dirk Van der Berg during the War of 1880.

Historical Accuracy: The novel is exact and convincing in rendering the period and region.

1124 How Young They Die

Date of Publication: 1969
Subject(s): World War I; Military Life—British Army
Fictional character(s): Jim Hilton, Military Personnel (British soldier)
Time Period(s): 1910s (1916-1918)
Locale(s): London, England; France; Flanders, Belgium

Summary: The First World War on the Western front and on the homefront is the subject of this novel that focuses on the combat career of Jim Hilton. The carnage of trench warfare and the break-up of conventional English life are given equal treatment here.

Historical Accuracy: The combat scenes are authentically delivered as are the cultural and daily details of life during the war.

1125 The Mask

Date of Publication: 1957
Subject(s): Frontier—Africa; Family Saga; Afrikaaners
Fictional character(s): Simon Van der Berg, Trader
Historical character(s): Paul Kruger, Leader (Boer), Political Figure
Time Period(s): 1850s (1852-1854)
Locale(s): South Africa

Summary: In the fourth novel dealing with the Van der Berg family of South Africa, young Simon Van der Berg comes of age against the historical background of the Voortrekkers' conflict with the Kaffir Warriors led by the chieftains Mapela and Makapan.

Historical Accuracy: The events described are historically accurate, and the period atmosphere is convincingly captured.

1126 Rags of Glory

Date of Publication: 1963
Subject(s): Boer War; Victorian Period; Military Life
Fictional character(s): Boetie Van der Berg, Military Personnel (Boer soldier); John Turnbull, Military Personnel (British officer); Moolman, Hunter (ivory)
Historical character(s): Paul Kruger, Political Figure (leader of Transvaal Republic), Military Personnel (Boer commander); Louis Botha, Political Figure, Military Personnel (Boer commander); Horatio Herbert Kitchener, Military Personnel (British general); Christiaan de Wet, Military Personnel (Boer leader); Joseph Chamberlain, Political Figure (British M.P.); David Lloyd George, Political Figure (British M.P.)
Time Period(s): 1890s; 1900s (1899-1902)
Locale(s): South Africa; England

Summary: Cloete's panorama of the Boer War ranges from England to South Africa, detailing the personal dramas of participants on both sides of the conflict—young Boetie Van der Berg; Turnbull, an English cavalry officer; Moolman, an ivory hunter; and dozens more in this sweeping history. Cloete argues that the Boer War represents the death of the 19th century.

Historical Accuracy: The history is bolstered by an impressive bibliography. The issues and the personalities are convincingly shown.

1127 *The Turning Wheels*

Date of Publication: 1937
Subject(s): Frontier—Africa; Afrikaaners; British Colonies
Fictional character(s): Hendrik Van der Berg, Settler; Sannie Van Reenen, Settler; Zwart Piete du Plessis, Hunter
Time Period(s): 1830s
Locale(s): South Africa

Summary: The novel offers the story of one band of Boers who, incensed by the actions of the British in the Cape Colony which they founded, set out into the interior of Africa. They endure ambush, bush fire, and animal attacks before scaling the final mountain range to reach the promised land of their dreams.

Historical Accuracy: Cloete knows this locale and the customs of the Boers and fashions his story into a gripping and authentic period adventure.

1128 *Watch for the Dawn*

Date of Publication: 1939
Subject(s): Frontier—Africa; English Colonies; Afrikaaners
Fictional character(s): Kaspar Van der Berg, Settler; Frederik Bezvidenhout, Settler; Aletta, Settler
Time Period(s): 1810s
Locale(s): South Africa

Summary: Resentment over British rule in South Africa explodes when an old farmer is shot. Kaspar Van der Berg, a young Boer in love with Aletta, finds himself in the center of the conflict. There are strong scenes of Afrikaner life set against the background of clashing cultures: Boer, English, and African.

Historical Accuracy: Cloete's sense of both time and place is convincingly depicted.

HANNAH CLOSS

1129 *Deep Are the Valleys*

Date of Publication: 1961
Subject(s): Middle Ages; Religious Conflict; Albigensian Crusade
Fictional character(s): Wolf of Foix, Bastard Son
Historical character(s): Simon de Montfort, Nobleman; Raymond VI of Toulouse, Nobleman
Time Period(s): 13th century
Locale(s): France

Summary: The novel continues the story of Wolf of Foix and his part in the Albigensian Crusade. On the side of Raymond of Toulouse against Simon de Montfort, leader of the Crusade, Wolf is determined to avenge the death of his friend.

Historical Accuracy: The author takes some minor liberties with historical fact but is, in the main, faithful to the events of the Albigensian Crusade.

1130 *High Are the Mountains*

Date of Publication: 1959
Subject(s): Middle Ages; Religious Conflict; Albigensian Crusade
Fictional character(s): Wolf of Foix, Bastard Son
Historical character(s): Raymond VI of Toulouse, Nobleman; Simon de Montfort, Nobleman
Time Period(s): 13th century
Locale(s): France

Summary: In 1208 Pope Innocent III proclaims a crusade against the Albigensian heretics of the Languedoc region of France. The novel dramatizes the events of the period, including the siege of Carcassonne. The story is told from the vantage point of young Wolf of Foix.

Historical Accuracy: The novel does not aim at exactitude of archaeological and historical detail. However the story does capture convincingly the spirit and atmosphere of the time and its philosophical and religious conflicts.

1131 *The Silent Tarn*

Date of Publication: 1963
Subject(s): Middle Ages; Albigensian Crusade
Fictional character(s): Wolf of Foix, Bastard Son
Time Period(s): 13th century
Locale(s): France

Summary: The novel, left unfinished upon the author's death, completes a trilogy on the period of the Albigensian Crusade. The central character in all three books is Wolf of Foix, the bastard son of a great family, who seeks his identity on the battlefield. Here he reaches his maturity faced with the conflict between his Cathar vow of non-violence and his desire to protect the rebels.

Historical Accuracy: The novel is marred by an incomplete knowledge of Catharism, which results in several thematic errors.

PATRICIA CLOUD
(PSEUD. OF PAT WALLACE STROTHER, 1929-)

Born in Alabama, Cloud attended the University of Tennessee and Columbia University and has worked in radio as a program director, copy chief, and announcer. She is primarily a romance novelist and invented the astrological novel genre out of her interest in the occult. She uses a variety of pseudonyms.

1132 *This Willing Passion*

Date of Publication: 1978
Subject(s): Romance; Theatrical Life; Trials
Fictional character(s): Maeve Heron, Actress, Widow(er); Fingal Pearse, Military Personnel (captain); William Morgan, Gentleman
Time Period(s): 1870s

Locale(s): New York, New York; Ireland; New Orleans, Louisiana

Summary: Maeve Heron, an orphan and widow from Ireland, rises to success as an actress in New York during the 1870s. She is pursued by two different men, Captain Pearse and William Morgan. Eventually the situation explodes in violence, and Maeve faces trial for murder.

Historical Accuracy: The period settings are genuine.

MICHAEL CLYNES
(PSEUD. OF P.C. DOHERTY)

An English mystery writer, Clynes was born in Middlesbrough and studied history at Liverpool and Oxford universities. He obtained his doctorate at Oxford for his thesis on Edward II and Queen Isabella. He is currently a headmaster of a school in northeast London. He has written a number of historical mysteries under several pseudonyms.

1133   *A Brood of Vipers*

Date of Publication: 1994
Subject(s): Tudor Period; Mystery; Royalty—England
Fictional character(s): Roger Shallot, Servant; Benjamin Daunbey, Gentleman
Historical character(s): Henry VIII, Ruler (King of England); Thomas Wolsey, Religious (cardinal), Government Official; Giulio de' Medici, Religious (cardinal)
Time Period(s): 16th century (1523)
Locale(s): London, England; Florence, Italy

Summary: When a Florentine envoy to London is murdered, Roger Shallot and Benjamin Daunbey are sent to Florence to discover the identity of the assassin and to deliver a secret message from Henry VIII to Giulio de' Medici. They encounter murder, pursuit by Turkish corsairs, black magic, and a conspiracy that will have enormous consequences.

Historical Accuracy: Although Shallot, who narrates the story, is a confessed liar, the author's notes point out the firm basis in fact of the novel's circumstances.

1134   *The Gallows Murder*

Date of Publication: 1996
Subject(s): Mystery; Tudor Period; Plague
Fictional character(s): Roger Shallot, Servant; Benjamin Daunbey, Gentleman
Historical character(s): Thomas Wolsey, Religious (cardinal), Government Official
Time Period(s): 16th century
Locale(s): London, England

Summary: Roger Shallot is trapped in London during an outbreak of the Plague. The murder of the royal executioner and another member of the guild of hangmen point to a conspiracy that Shallot and his master, Benjamin Daunbey, investigate. The case is connected with a blackmail scheme aimed at Henry VIII, and the pair must solve a 40-year-old mystery to expose the murderer and the conspiracy.

Historical Accuracy: The novel makes convincing use of period elements.

1135   *The Grail Murders*

Date of Publication: 1993
Subject(s): Tudor Period; Mystery
Fictional character(s): Roger Shallot, Servant; Benjamin Daunbey, Gentleman
Historical character(s): Edward Stafford, Nobleman (Duke of Buckingham); Henry VIII, Ruler (King of England); Thomas Wolsey, Religious (cardinal), Government Official
Time Period(s): 16th century (1522)
Locale(s): London, England; Glastonbury, England

Summary: The Duke of Buckingham is killed because he was searching for two precious relics: the Holy Grail and Excalibur. Benjamin Daunbey and Roger Shallot are ordered to find the relics for the king.

Historical Accuracy: The corruption and scandal of the Tudor court of Henry VIII are effectively described.

1136   *The Poisoned Chalice*

Date of Publication: 1992
Subject(s): Mystery; Tudor Period; Espionage
Fictional character(s): Roger Shallot, Servant; Benjamin Daunbey, Gentleman
Historical character(s): Thomas Wolsey, Religious (cardinal), Government Official; Henry VIII, Ruler (King of England)
Time Period(s): 16th century (1520-1521)
Locale(s): London, England; Paris, France

Summary: In the second installment of the historical mystery series involving Roger Shallot, the murder of a diplomat at the English embassy in Paris sends Shallot and his master, Benjamin Daunbey, on a secret mission to France. A spy is suspected of passing information to the French king and must be found, and a ring must be retrieved from Francis I on behalf of Henry VIII himself.

Historical Accuracy: The author's notes help untangle Shallot's exaggerations from historical truth and establish the factual basis for the novel's circumstances.

1137   *The White Rose Murders*

Date of Publication: 1991
Subject(s): Mystery; Tudor Period; Royalty—England
Fictional character(s): Roger Shallot, Gentleman; Benjamin Daunbey, Gentleman; Selkirk, Doctor
Historical character(s): Thomas Wolsey, Religious (cardinal), Government Official (chancellor); Henry VIII, Ruler (King of England); Margaret Tudor, Royalty (queen of James IV of Scotland); Catherine of Aragon, Royalty (queen consort of Henry VIII); Mary Tudor, Royalty (princess)
Time Period(s): 16th century (1502-1517)
Locale(s): London, England; Canterbury, England; Paris, France

Summary: Roger Shallot, with his Master Benjamin Daunbey, investigates a murder in the court of Henry VIII. Selkirk, a half-mad physician imprisoned in the Tower, is found murdered and the only clue is a poem of riddles. Other victims follow, each found with a white rose, the mark of a secret society that plots the overthrow of the Tudors.

Historical Accuracy: The novel's sense of period is impressive. Many of the narrator's claims, no matter how outlandish, can be verified by historical fact.

ELIZABETH COATSWORTH (1893-1986)

Born in Buffalo, New York, Coatsworth is a graduate of Vassar College and Columbia University. Coatsworth began her career as a poet, but achieved acclaim for her children's books. *The Cat Who Went to Heaven* won the Newbery Medal in 1931. Most of her books are set in rural New England where she resided.

`1138` *Here I Stay*

Date of Publication: 1938
Subject(s): Settlement of the American Frontier; Farming
Fictional character(s): Margaret Winslow, Settler, Orphan; Captain Bob Bandylegs, Indian; John Grant, Naturalist
Time Period(s): 1810s (1817)
Locale(s): Maine

Summary: Margaret Winslow declines to move west to the Ohio country in the Western Reserve like her neighbors and instead stays alone on her isolated farm. The novel describes her year in the Maine wilderness and the considerable challenges that she faces.

Historical Accuracy: The novel is filled with details of frontier life that give an authentic feel to the story.

`1139` *A Toast to the King*

Date of Publication: 1940
Subject(s): American Colonies; American Revolution
Fictional character(s): Judith Willard, Loyalist, Orphan; Abigail Willard, Loyalist, Orphan; Georgianna Willard, Loyalist, Orphan
Time Period(s): 1770s
Locale(s): Boston, Massachusetts, American Colonies

Summary: Set in Boston following the Boston Tea Party, the novel concerns the three Willard Sisters—Judith, Abigail, and Georgianna—who remain staunch Tories despite the sympathies of their community in favor of independence. Their loyalty to the crown costs them their lovers, and their lives are endangered when they rescue a British Officer.

Historical Accuracy: The period elements are convincingly drawn.

HAMILTON COCHRAN (1898-1977)

An American historian and author of 13 books, Cochran was born in Philadelphia and graduated from the University of Michigan. In addition to his writing career, Cochran worked in sales and in advertising.

`1140` *The Dram Tree*

Date of Publication: 1961
Subject(s): Civil War—U.S.; Sea Story
Fictional character(s): Jeff Ryall, Sea Captain, Blockade Runner; Dulcie Dubois, Southern Belle; Tina Tyler, Shipowner

Time Period(s): 1860s
Locale(s): *Banshee*, At Sea; Bermuda; Wilmington, North Carolina

Summary: This story of Confederate blockade running during the Civil War follows the exploits of dashing sea captain Jeff Ryall as he challenges the Union blockade to import weapons and export cotton out of Wilmington, North Carolina. On shore his affections are divided between the aristocratic beauty Dulcie Dubois and Tina Tyler, the owner of his ship, *The Banshee*. The action culminates in the battle for Fort Fisher.

Historical Accuracy: The methods used by Southern blockade runners are authentic, and the description of the second battle of Fort Fisher is based on official reports.

`1141` *Rogue's Holiday*

Date of Publication: 1947
Subject(s): Sea Story; Pirates
Fictional character(s): Robert Maynard, Military Personnel (naval lieutenant); Molly Molloy, Young Woman
Historical character(s): Edward Teach, Pirate
Time Period(s): 1710s (1718)
Locale(s): England; Carolinas, American Colonies; At Sea

Summary: This rousing pirate adventure tells the story of a young British naval lieutenant, Robert Maynard, who, in a series of adventures, finds himself captured by pirate Edward Teach, better known as Blackbeard. Maynard avoids being flogged to death, endears himself to Blackbeard's latest wife (his 13th), and is on hand for the pirate captain's demise.

Historical Accuracy: The emphasis here is on fast-paced adventure rather than careful historical accuracy. The period is suggested, but there is more fiction than fact connected to Blackbeard.

`1142` *Silver Shoals*

Date of Publication: 1945
Subject(s): American Colonies; Sea Story; Treasure Hunt
Historical character(s): William Phipps, Sea Captain; James II, Ruler (King of England)
Time Period(s): 17th century
Locale(s): London, England; Boston, Massachusetts, American Colonies; Bahamas

Summary: This historical adventure novel is based on an actual treasure hunt that took place in the Bahamas during the late 17th century. It is financed by the Duke of Abermarle and James II and led by Captain William Phips. A conventional romance between Phips' secretary and a Massachusetts girl is added to the action scenes of the expedition that nets a fortune in siver and jewels from a sunken Spanish galleon.

Historical Accuracy: The novel is a blend of fiction and history with the greatest credibility in the nautical and colonial scenes.

`1143` *Windward Passage*

Date of Publication: 1942
Subject(s): Pirates; Sea Story
Historical character(s): Henry Morgan, Sea Captain, Pirate

Time Period(s): 17th century (1671)
Locale(s): Caribbean; Panama

Summary: The exploits of English buccaneer Sir Henry Morgan are celebrated in this account of Morgan's daring raid on Panama in 1671. Morgan is shown objectively as a complex figure of great skill as well as brutality.

Historical Accuracy: The essential details of the story's action are truthful with some imagined scenes and situations.

LOUIS COCHRAN (1899-)

Born in Mississippi, Cochran received his law degree from Cumberland University and served as a Special Agent for the FBI and as an intelligence agent during World War II.

1144 *Fool of God: A Novel Based on the Life of Alexander Campbell*

Date of Publication: 1958
Subject(s): Religious Life; Biography, Fictionalized
Historical character(s): Alexander Campbell, Leader (religious); Henry Clay, Political Figure; Thomas Jefferson, Political Figure; Thomas Campbell, Leader (religious)
Time Period(s): 18th century; 19th century (1788-1866)
Locale(s): Scotland; United States

Summary: This fictionalized biography traces the life and causes of Alexander Campbell, founder of the Disciples of Christ. Campbell and his father Thomas emigrate from Scotland to America where their advocacy for the return to scriptural simplicity attracts a group of followers known as the Reformers.

Historical Accuracy: The novel stays close to the biographical sources.

1145 *Raccoon John Smith*

Date of Publication: 1963
Subject(s): Settlement of the American Frontier; Religious Life
Fictional character(s): Raccoon John Smith, Religious (preacher)
Time Period(s): 19th century
Locale(s): Kentucky

Summary: The novel presents the fictional biography of a pioneer Kentucky preacher, Raccoon John Smith. A follower of Alexander Campbell, Smith faces dangers in the wilderness as well as the challenges of Calvinism to instill a message of brotherhood and tolerance on the frontier.

Historical Accuracy: Although Smith is invented, his story and the period are accurately and faithfully rendered.

AMANDA COCKRELL
(PSEUD. OF AMANDA COCKRELL CROWE, 1948-)

An American born in Louisiana, Cockrell graduated from Hollins College. She has worked as a newspaper reporter and radio copywriter. For Cockrell, fiction is entertainment with a subliminal message. She is fascinated by history and

intends her books to be a window on another world as well as a journey through a different landscape.

1146 *The Deer Dancers*

Date of Publication: 1995
Subject(s): Prehistory; Tribal Life—Prehistoric
Fictional character(s): Deer Shadow, Prehistoric Human, Shaman; Wind Caller, Prehistoric Human
Time Period(s): 50th century B.C.
Locale(s): Rio Grande Valley, North America

Summary: In Book One of the Daughter of the Sky series, Deer Shadow is a young shaman of the Yellow Grass People. She seems to have lost some power when her people are threatened by a hostile tribe. When a handsome outcast arrives bearing new ideas and sacred seeds, the stage is set for Deer Shadow's defense of tradition.

Historical Accuracy: The prehistoric customs and cultures are credible.

MARIAN COCKRELL (1909-)

Born in Alabama, Cockrell has been writing fiction since the 1930s.

1147 *The Misadventures of Bethany Price*

Date of Publication: 1979
Subject(s): American West; Picaresque Adventure; Women's Rights
Fictional character(s): Bethany Price, Orphan; Styler Brown, Journalist
Time Period(s): 1860s (1868-1869)
Locale(s): Bright Prairie, Colorado

Summary: Bethany Price leaves the Blanche P. Tinoca Home of Mercy at age 16 for a disastrous marriage to a man 20 years her senior. She flees west disguised as a boy and meets up with Styler Brown, who is headed for Bright Prairie, Colorado. There they publish a radical newspaper that advocates women's suffrage, and Bethany causes quite a stir in the conservative town.

Historical Accuracy: The comedy is based on Bethany's rather modern challenge to conventional society.

1148 *The Revolt of Sarah Perkins*

Date of Publication: 1965
Subject(s): American West; Education; Women's Rights
Fictional character(s): Sarah Perkins, Teacher
Time Period(s): 1860s (1869)
Locale(s): Colorado

Summary: This unusual story of the western frontier chronicles one woman's rebellion against contemporary mores. Sarah Perkins, a schoolteacher from the East, is recruited by a town in the Colorado Territory because she is considered unmarriageable and will stay and teach. She appears to fit their need, until she begins to challenge conventional wisdom and behavior.

Historical Accuracy: This story is honest and telling in its suggestions that the West was far more conservative than usually described.

ANDREI CODRESCU (1946-)

Born in Transylvania, Romania, Codrescu was expelled from the University of Bucharest for his criticism of the communist government. He came to the United States and is now considered to be one of America's most imaginative poets. He is a writer, journalist, translator, and regular commentator on National Public Radio's ''All Things Considered.'' He is also the editor of *Exquisite Corpse: A Journal of Books and Ideas*.

1149 *The Blood Countess*

Date of Publication: 1995
Subject(s): Crime and Criminals
Fictional character(s): Drake Bathory-Kereshtur, Young Man
Historical character(s): Elizabeth Bathory, Noblewoman (countess)
Time Period(s): 16th century; 20th century
Locale(s): Hungary; New York, New York

Summary: This darkly psychological novel of eroticism and murder tells the story of Countess Elizabeth Bathory of Hungary who, to preserve her youth, bathes in the blood of virgins she has murdered. Her descendant, Drake Bathory-Kereshtur, a Hungarian emigre in New York, is haunted by the horrifying legacy of his ancestor.

Historical Accuracy: Wildly inventive and suggestive, the picture of the 16th century strains credibility with its emphasis on the bizarre.

AL CODY

1150 *Bitter Creek*

Date of Publication: 1939
Subject(s): American West; Ranching; Indians
Fictional character(s): Ray Talcott, Young Man; Antelope, Doctor; Many Clouds, Indian
Time Period(s): 1870s
Locale(s): Illinois; West

Summary: Ranching life in the West of the 1870s is the novel's subject. The story follows young Ray Talcott from his home in Illinois west to a series of adventures including the Indian Wars.

Historical Accuracy: The novel offers an authentic depiction of western life of the times.

VIRGINIA COFFMAN (1914-)

An American born in San Francisco, Coffman attended the University of California at Berkeley. She worked as a secretary and writer for movie and television studios and has also been an actress and a drama teacher. Coffman is the author of many romance and mystery novels, including *Moura* and the Lucifer Cove series.

1151 *The Dark Palazzo*

Date of Publication: 1973
Subject(s): Gothic Romance; French Revolution
Fictional character(s): Rachel Carewe, Gentlewoman; Maitland Carewe, Diplomat; Mira Teotochi, Servant (housekeeper)
Time Period(s): 1790s (1797)
Locale(s): Venice, Italy

Summary: Rachel Carewe, daughter of the British ambassador to Venice, escapes from revolutionary France only to find her father strangely changed and controlled by the sinister housekeeper, Mira Teotochi. Rachel finds herself enmeshed in the intrigues of French and Austrian spies and is accused in her father's murder. The answer to her predicament is hidden in a crypt in the cemetery of San Michelle.

Historical Accuracy: The atmosphere of Gothic threat is perfectly connected to the Venice of the period and its political scene.

1152 *Dark Winds*

Date of Publication: 1985
Subject(s): Gothic Romance; Victorian Period
Fictional character(s): Cecilly Wentworth, Gentlewoman; Jason Bourne, Businessman (mill owner)
Time Period(s): 19th century (1837-1850)
Locale(s): Leeds, England; Yorkshire, England

Summary: Cecilly Wentworth's romantic attachment to Jason Bourne, mill owner and master of Bourne Hall, is strained as Jason is discovered to be other than the man she thought he was, and the Bourne family is beset by ominous secrets.

Historical Accuracy: The Yorkshire locale is atmospheric and believable.

1153 *The Gaynor Women*

Date of Publication: 1978
Subject(s): Romance; Family Saga
Fictional character(s): Ellen Gaynor, Gentlewoman; Maggilee Gaynor, Gentlewoman; Varina Dunmore Gaynor, Gentlewoman
Time Period(s): 1880s
Locale(s): Virginia

Summary: Set in Virginia in the 1880s, this novel traces the lives of three strong characters in the Gaynor family. Varina is the grandmother and matriarch, the protector of the southern tradition. Maggilee is a celebrated beauty, and Ellen, her daughter, must struggle to emerge from her mother's shadow.

Historical Accuracy: The social world of the period is ably and believably detailed.

1154 *Hyde Place*

Date of Publication: 1974
Subject(s): Romance; Earthquakes; Disasters—Natural
Fictional character(s): Merideth Hyde, Young Woman
Time Period(s): 1910s (1919)
Locale(s): San Francisco, California

Summary: This novel of romantic suspense is set in San Francisco 13 years after the devestating earthquake. Merideth Hyde returns to the city to dispose of inherited property and search for her mother, thought to have perished in the disaster. She is beset by imposters and fortune hunters from all sides as the past must be reassembled and sorted out from the wreckage.

Historical Accuracy: The novel's atmosphere and details of period San Francisco are convincing.

1155 *Marsanne*

Date of Publication: 1976
Subject(s): Romance; Regency Period; Napoleonic Era
Fictional character(s): Marsanne de Vaudraye, Heiress, Gentlewoman; Philip Justin, Gentleman
Time Period(s): 1810s
Locale(s): France; England

Summary: Marsanne de Vaudraye finds herself in jeopardy, threatened by those bent on seizing her inheritance. She flees to the safety of England but falls into a tangle of intrigue and deceit. She must rely on the assistance of Philip Justin, who introduces her to the world of smugglers and pirates.

Historical Accuracy: The romance uses a clearly described picture of Regency England and France on the eve of Napoleon's return from Elba as a background.

1156 *Mistress Devon*

Date of Publication: 1972
Subject(s): American Colonies; Theatrical Life
Fictional character(s): Devon Howard, Seamstress, Actress
Time Period(s): 1770s (1774)
Locale(s): American Colonies

Summary: Tory and Patriot conflict in the years preceding the American Revolution is seen from the perspective of actress Devon Howard, who tours the American Colonies in a repertory company. Conflict in love and politics forms the novel's romantic drama.

Historical Accuracy: The novel creates a credible though strictly functional atmosphere of the period.

1157 *Pacific Cavalcade*

Date of Publication: 1981
Subject(s): Family Saga; World War II; Depression Era
Fictional character(s): Randi Lombard, Gentlewoman; Leo Prysing, Director
Time Period(s): 20th century (1918-1941)
Locale(s): California; Hawaii; Europe

Summary: This family saga concerns Randi Lombard, who rises from a humble background to marry into one of San Francisco's best families. Her history reflects the events of the years between the end of World War I and the beginning of World War II and includes scenes of the 1933 California earthquake, Nazi-occupied Vienna, and a seaborne departure hours before the attack on Pearl Harbor.

Historical Accuracy: The novel is packed with historical details, though the characters' proximity to so many important events strains credibility.

1158 *Veronique*

Date of Publication: 1975
Subject(s): Romance; French Revolution; Reign of Terror
Fictional character(s): Veronique de Vaudraye, Gentlewoman; Gilles Marsan, Revolutionary
Historical character(s): Maximilien Francois de Robespierre, Revolutionary, Political Figure; Georges-Jacques Danton, Revolutionary, Political Figure
Time Period(s): 1780s; 1790s
Locale(s): Paris, France

Summary: Veronique de Vaudraye is a young French woman of a noble family swept up in the events of the French Revolution and the ensuing Reign of Terror. She is in love with a hero of the revolution in this romance of the clash between the old and the new.

Historical Accuracy: The emphasis is on romance and adventure, but the details of the important events and figures are described with some skill.

MATT COHEN (1942-)

A Canadian writer and teacher, Cohen was born in Ontario and attended the University of Toronto. He has been the writer-in-residence and a professor of creative writing at the University of Western Ontario and the University of Victoria. A prolific writer of experimental prose, Cohen has shown his versatility in various literary forms—short stories, poetry, songs, novellas, and novels.

1159 *The Spanish Doctor*

Date of Publication: 1984
Subject(s): Inquisition; Religious Conflict; Medical Profession
Fictional character(s): Avram Halevi, Doctor; Rodrigo Velasquez, Religious (cardinal); Gabriela Hasdai, Young Woman
Time Period(s): 14th century; 15th century (1391-1445)
Locale(s): Toledo, Spain; Montpellier, France; Kiev, Russia

Summary: Avram Halevi is a Spanish doctor, a Jew forced to convert to Catholicism during the Spanish Inquisition. He turns to science to counter superstition and prejudice. His medical skill is put to use in plague-ridden Europe, while religious persecution causes him to flee to France, Italy, and finally Russia.

Historical Accuracy: The details of 14th-century life for a physician and a Jew are ably and authentically described.

OCTAVUS ROY COHEN (1891-1959)

An American journalist, lawyer, and writer, Cohen was born in Charleston, South Carolina. Cohen is the creator of private detective Jim Hanley, featured in a number of mysteries. He is the author of *Danger in Paradise*, *My Love Wears Black*, and *Love Can Be Dangerous*.

1160 *Borrasca*

Date of Publication: 1953
Subject(s): American West; Mining
Fictional character(s): Malcolm Douglas, Young Man
Time Period(s): 1860s; 1870s
Locale(s): Virginia City, Nevada

Summary: Set during the boom time of the Comstock Lode, the novel describes development in Virginia City as fortunes are made, lost, and re-made in the mining frenzy.

Historical Accuracy: The details surrounding the mining boom during the period are authentically described.

ELIZABETH BOATWRIGHT COKER
(1909-1993)

An American born in South Carolina, Coker attended Converse and Middlebury colleges. She was a professor of English and began her career as a novelist at the age of 40.

1161 *La Belle*

Date of Publication: 1959
Subject(s): Civil War—U.S.
Historical character(s): Marie Boozer, Southern Belle
Time Period(s): 19th century
Locale(s): Columbia, South Carolina; New York, New York; Europe

Summary: The novel dramatizes the life of southern belle Marie Boozer from the Civil War, when she and her mother become camp followers of Sherman's troops, to her years of notoriety and scandal in New York and Europe.

Historical Accuracy: The life of Marie Boozer is reconstructed from letters, diaries, newspaper accounts, and contemporary records which help supply an authentic background.

1162 *The Big Drum*

Date of Publication: 1957
Subject(s): American Colonies; Slavery; Indians
Fictional character(s): Simon Blake, Artist (draftsman); Raven, Slave
Time Period(s): 17th century (1678-1683)
Locale(s): London, England; Barbados; Charleston, South Carolina, American Colonies

Summary: Simon Blake is a young draftsman and apprentice to Christopher Wren who journeys to Barbados in the 17th century. He enjoys a series of adventures, including becoming one of the early settlers of Charleston where he endures the perils of Carolina Indians.

Historical Accuracy: This spirited adventure is strong on regional flavor in the depictions of Barbados and of Carolina, but less convincing in its English period scenes.

1163 *Blood Red Roses*

Date of Publication: 1977
Subject(s): Civil War—U.S.
Fictional character(s): Angelica Berrien, Southern Belle; Beau Berrien, Plantation Owner, Military Personnel (Confederate officer); Frederick Pierce, Spy, Military Personnel (Union soldier)
Time Period(s): 1860s (1860-1865)
Locale(s): Albermarle County, Virginia; Hilton Head Island, South Carolina

Summary: Angelica marries Beau Berrien, a rich planter from Hilton Head, South Carolina. When the war begins, he enlists, and she is left on the island after the entire white population flees during the Union occupation. She is protected by Frederick Pierce, a Union soldier and former admirer, as she struggles to survive and awaits Beau's return.

Historical Accuracy: The locale and the events described are authentic.

1164 *Daughter of Strangers*

Date of Publication: 1950
Subject(s): Antebellum South; Slavery; Civil War—U.S.
Fictional character(s): Charlotte La Jeune, Young Woman, Slave; Inigo Galliard, Gentleman
Time Period(s): 19th century (1830-1865)
Locale(s): South Carolina; Mississippi

Summary: This romantic tale of slavery and the South in the years before and during the Civil War concerns Charlotte Le Jeune, the daughter of a quadroon who, because she is one-eighth black, is sold into slavery. Intended to be the mistress of a Mississippi gentleman, Charlotte struggles against the rigid caste system of the south.

Historical Accuracy: The novel is convincing in its depiction of Southern society and its stratified social hierarchy and customs.

1165 *The Grasshopper King*

Date of Publication: 1981
Subject(s): Reconstruction Period; Independence—Mexico
Fictional character(s): Angelica Berrien, Spouse; Beau Berrien, Gentleman
Historical character(s): Maximilian, Ruler (Emperor of Mexico); Carlota, Royalty (empress consort of Maximilian)
Time Period(s): 1860s
Locale(s): Mexico

Summary: In the sequel to *Blood Red Roses*, Angelica and Beau Berrien flee the post-Civil War turmoil of South Carolina for Mexico where they enter the court world of Maximilian and Carlota. Both are drawn into the ill-fated imperial regime, which is under attack by anti-Maximilian forces.

Historical Accuracy: The novel's history is not successfully integrated with the fictional story.

1166 *Lady Rich*

Date of Publication: 1963
Subject(s): Elizabethan Period; Royalty—England
Historical character(s): Penelope Devereux, Noblewoman; Robert Dudley, Nobleman (Earl of Leicester); Elizabeth I, Ruler (Queen of England); Sir Philip Sidney, Gentleman, Writer (poet); Robert Rich, Nobleman; Robert Cecil, Government Official
Time Period(s): 16th century; 17th century (1575-1607)

Locale(s): England

Summary: This is the remarkable first-person recollections of Penelope Devereaux, daughter of the Earl of Essex, descended from the Plantagenets and related to both Anne Boleyn and Queen Elizabeth. Her great enemy is Robert Dudley, the Queen's favorite, who forces her to marry Robert Rich thereby keeping her from Philip Sidney. Her story offers an intimate look at Elizabeth's court.

Historical Accuracy: The details of Elizabethan customs and the court politics of Elizabeth's reign are genuinely described.

MERLE ESTES COLBY (1902-1969)

Colby was born in Lodi, Wisconsin. His novels portray the migration of settlers from the Northeast to the Midwest, life in covered wagons, the adventures of bargemen, stories of frontier outposts, the development of new communities, and the depredations of outlaws. Colby's novels include *All Ye People* and *The Big Secret.*

1167 *All Ye People*

Date of Publication: 1931
Subject(s): Settlement of the American Frontier
Fictional character(s): John Bray, Settler
Time Period(s): 1810s (1810)
Locale(s): Vermont; Ohio

Summary: The western migration during the early 19th century is depicted in the experiences of a young Vermonter, John Bray, who leaves his home for Ohio. His adventures along the way capture the color and spirit of the age.

Historical Accuracy: The novel's portrait of the life and customs of the period is believable.

1168 *New Road*

Date of Publication: 1933
Subject(s): Settlement of the American Frontier
Fictional character(s): Martin Ward, Settler; Hagar Ward, Pioneer, Widow(er)
Time Period(s): 19th century (1820-1840)
Locale(s): Ohio

Summary: Pioneer life in Ohio is depicted in the story of Martin Ward from Maryland who marries Hagar, a pioneer. She introduces Martin to pioneer life and together they help build the town of Toward.

Historical Accuracy: This is a convincing chronicle of pioneer life and customs.

DON COLDSMITH (1926-)

Coldsmith is an American novelist who served as a combat medic in World War II and received his M.D. from the University of Kansas. He has been a rancher and horse breeder, as well as a teacher at Emporia State University in Kansas.

1169 *Bearer of the Pipe*

Date of Publication: 1995
Subject(s): Indians; Tribal Life—Native American
Fictional character(s): Wolf Pup, Indian (Elk-Dog People), Healer (medicine man)
Time Period(s): 18th century
Locale(s): Great Plains, North America

Summary: In this installment of the Spanish Bit Saga, the young brave Wolf Pup begins the training necessary to become a medicine man and future bearer of the Story Skins, pipe, and the sacred Spanish bit. He must endure a vision quest and deal with the devastating impact of a massive tornado that leaves his village in ruins and drives away the buffalo upon which the Elk-Dog People depend.

Historical Accuracy: The depiction of Indian life and culture is authentic and believable.

1170 *Bride of the Morning Star*

Date of Publication: 1991
Subject(s): Indians; Tribal Life—Native American
Fictional character(s): Calling Bird, Indian, Captive; Tall Bull, Indian, Warrior; Bear Paws, Indian, Warrior
Time Period(s): 1720s (1725)
Locale(s): Great Plains, North America

Summary: In the nineteenth volume of the Spanish Bit saga, Calling Bird, a young woman of the Elk-dog People is kidnapped by the Pawnees to become a human sacrifice to their most powerful god, the Morning Star. Tall Bull leads a party of warriors to rescue her.

Historical Accuracy: The Pawnee ceremony of the Morning Star is historical, and the incident is based on a similar factual event.

1171 *Buffalo Medicine*

Date of Publication: 1981
Subject(s): Indians; Tribal Life—Native American
Fictional character(s): Owl, Indian; Old White Buffalo, Indian, Shaman
Time Period(s): 16th century (1559-1561)
Locale(s): Great Plains, North America

Summary: The second volume of the Spanish Bit saga shows Owl, the younger son of the chief of the Elk-dog People, serving as an apprentice to the tribe's medicine man, Old White Buffalo. While on his vision quest, he is captured by the Head Splitters, the People's sworn enemies. This is the beginning of a long and harrowing odyssey that tests his courage.

Historical Accuracy: The novel provides a convincing background of tribal life and customs.

1172 *Child of the Dead*

Date of Publication: 1995
Subject(s): Indians; Tribal Life—Native American
Fictional character(s): Running Deer, Indian, Widow(er); Gray Mouse, Indian, Child
Time Period(s): 18th century

Locale(s): Great Plains, North America

Summary: The novel dramatizes the devastating impact contact with Europeans had on the Indians. Disease spreads rapidly through the tribes, the most dreaded of which is smallpox. The novel describes how Running Deer, a grieving widow, cares for a young girl of another tribe afflicted with the disease. She is nursed back to health but wishes to rejoin her own people rather than adopt the ways of Running Deer's people.

Historical Accuracy: The novel's ability to capture tribal life and the impact of change on traditional ways is remarkably detailed and convincing.

1173 *Daughter of the Eagle*

Date of Publication: 1984
Subject(s): Indians; Tribal Life—Native American
Fictional character(s): Eagle Woman, Indian, Warrior (female); Long Walker, Indian, Warrior
Time Period(s): 16th century (1583-1584)
Locale(s): Great Plains, North America

Summary: In the sixth volume of the Spanish Bit saga, Eagle Woman, at 19, is the oldest unmarried woman in the tribe. As a warrior sister she has taken a vow of chastity, and now instead of marrying Long Walker, she wants to become a full-fledged warrior, equal to the men. She achieves her goal and leads a war party on a dangerous mission.

Historical Accuracy: The details of customs and locale are authentically drawn.

1174 *The Elk-Dog Heritage*

Date of Publication: 1982
Subject(s): Indians; Tribal Life—Native American
Fictional character(s): Heads Off, Indian, Chieftain (formerly Juan Garcia); Coyote, Indian, Warrior
Time Period(s): 16th century (1544-1545)
Locale(s): Great Plains, North America

Summary: In the third volume of the Spanish Bit saga, the former Spanish outsider, Juan Garcia, is now the chief Heads Off. He has brought horses, or elk-dogs, to the People, transforming them into fierce warriors. The horses help Heads Off's people become the victors over their traditional enemy, the Head Splitters. But the gift is an ambiguous and troubling one as Heads Off must keep some of the tribe's warriors on the path of peace.

Historical Accuracy: The background of tribal life is authentic.

1175 *The Flower in the Mountains*

Date of Publication: 1988
Subject(s): Indians; Tribal Life—Native American
Fictional character(s): Jean "Woodchuck" Cartier, Frontiersman; Red Feather, Indian; Sky-Eyes, Frontiersman (aka Andre Du Pres)
Time Period(s): 17th Century (1660s)
Locale(s): Great Plains, North America

Summary: The thirteenth volume of the Spanish Bit saga concerns Woodchuck, a former French explorer and now a tribal member of the Elk-dog People. Here, he introduces his son, Red Feather, to the world of the whites. Woodchuck and his companion, Sky-Eyes, find themselves in danger of capture by the same French men they have deserted for tribal life.

Historical Accuracy: The novel is both atmospheric and authentic in its details of the locale and the customs.

1176 *Follow the Wind*

Date of Publication: 1983
Subject(s): Indians; Tribal Life—Native American; Spanish Colonies
Fictional character(s): Pedro Garcia, Gentleman; Heads Off, Indian (aka Juan Garcia), Chieftain; Ramon Cabeza, Military Personnel (Spanish officer)
Time Period(s): 16th century (1547-1548)
Locale(s): Southwest, North America; Great Plains, North America

Summary: In the fourth volume of the Spanish Bit saga, a reconnaissance group of Spaniards attempts to learn the fate of Don Pedro Garcia's son, Juan, who is rumored to be living with the Indians. They confront the seemingly endless track of wilderness, watched by cautious Indians. Finally, they reach the end of their quest and find the answers they are seeking.

Historical Accuracy: The author's ability to render a believable scene is first-rate.

1177 *Fort De Chastaigne*

Date of Publication: 1990
Subject(s): Indians; Tribal Life—Native American; Exploration
Fictional character(s): White Fox, Indian, Shaman; Captain LeFever, Military Personnel (French officer); Baptiste DuBois, Frontiersman (voyageur)
Time Period(s): 1700s
Locale(s): Missouri River, North America; Great Plains, North America

Summary: In the sixteenth volume of the Spanish Bit saga, the French Captain LeFever sets out from the new Fort de Chastaigne on the Missouri River to establish trade with the Spanish of Sante Fe. He is accompanied by White Fox, his guide, and they attempt to earn the trust and friendship of the tribes downriver. But the voyageur Baptiste DuBois incites trouble among the Indians.

Historical Accuracy: The details of frontier life are authentic, as is the conflict between the French and the Spanish.

1178 *Man of the Shadows*

Date of Publication: 1983
Subject(s): Indians; Tribal Life—Native American
Fictional character(s): Eagle, Indian, Warrior; Old Man, Indian, Recluse
Time Period(s): 16th century (1565-1566)
Locale(s): Great Plains, North America

Summary: In the fifth volume of the Spanish Bit saga, Eagle, a young warrior of the Elk-dog People, is separated from the tribe during a hunt, his leg broken. He is helped by a mysterious, tribe-less old recluse. Eagle begins to think that he has found the legendary trickster whom the People call the Old Man of the Shadows.

Historical Accuracy: The story is based on solid anthropological details of primitive customs.

1179 *Medicine Knife*

Date of Publication: 1988

Subject(s): Indians; Tribal Life—Native American; Spanish Colonies

Fictional character(s): Sky-Eyes, Frontiersman (aka Andre Du Pres); Pale Star, Indian

Time Period(s): 17th Century (1660s)

Locale(s): Great Plains, North America; Santa Fe, New Mexico (New Spain)

Summary: In the twelfth volume of the Spanish Bit saga, Sky-Eyes journeys with his wife, Pale Star, to the Spanish settlement of Sante Fe to trade pelts for Spanish metal. The journey is perilous, and Sky-Eyes must rely on both his white man's knowledge and his Indian skills to save himself and his wife from the Spanish.

Historical Accuracy: The period details are convincing and reliable.

1180 *Moon of Thunder*

Date of Publication: 1985

Subject(s): Indians; Tribal Life—Native American

Fictional character(s): Rabbit, Indian, Teenager; Heads Off, Indian (formerly Juan Garcia), Chieftain; Blue Paints, Indian

Time Period(s): 17th century (1600-1601)

Locale(s): Great Plains, North America

Summary: In this, the seventh novel of the Spanish Bit saga, Rabbit is a 17-year-old Indian who must complete his vision quest before being accepted as an adult member of the tribe. His grandfather, the great tribal chief Heads Off, entrusts him with the Spanish bit, the tribe's powerful talisman. What happens to Rabbit and the Spanish bit forms the novel's exciting narrative.

Historical Accuracy: The details of tribal life are remarkably detailed and convincing.

1181 *Pale Star*

Date of Publication: 1986

Subject(s): Indians; Tribal Life—Native American

Fictional character(s): Pale Star, Indian, Teenager; Three Owls, Indian, Warrior

Time Period(s): 17th century (1630-1631)

Locale(s): Great Plains, North America

Summary: This ninth volume of the Spanish Bit saga concerns the adventures of Pale Star, the granddaughter of Running Eagle. At 13 she is kidnapped by an enemy tribe and sold into captivity where she encounters a cruel warrior, Three Owls, who wants to make her his slave wife.

Historical Accuracy: The novel's story is informed by a credible background of Indian life and customs.

1182 *Quest for the White Bull*

Date of Publication: 1990

Subject(s): Indians; Tribal Life—Native American

Fictional character(s): Red Horse, Indian, Shaman; Digging Owl, Indian, Shaman

Time Period(s): 1700s

Locale(s): Great Plains, North America

Summary: In the seventeenth volume of the Spanish Bit saga, the buffalo, upon which the Elk-dog People depend, do not return in the spring. Their disappearance is connected with that of a sacred white buffalo. Red Horse, the tribe's medicine man, embarks on a quest to find the white buffalo and return with its miraculous skin. He meets Digging Owl, a medicine man from a southern tribe on a similar mission, and together they endure great hardships on their quest.

Historical Accuracy: The novel features convincing details of tribal life and customs.

1183 *Return of the Spanish*

Date of Publication: 1991

Subject(s): Indians; Tribal Life—Native American; Spanish Colonies

Fictional character(s): Don Pedro de Villasur, Military Personnel (Spanish officer); Strong Bow, Indian, Guide

Time Period(s): 1720s

Locale(s): Great Plains, North America

Summary: In 1720, Don Pedro de Villasur leads an expedition of Spanish soldiers onto the Great Plains to root out French settlements along the Platte River. They acquire the services of Strong Bow, who is ignorant of the real purpose of the Spanish, as a guide. Villasur distrusts Strong Bow and disregards his advice, leading his men into a trap set by the Pawnees.

Historical Accuracy: The details of western life and tribal customs are authentic.

1184 *Return to the River*

Date of Publication: 1987

Subject(s): Indians; Tribal Life—Native American

Fictional character(s): Jean Cartier, Frontiersman; Pale Star, Indian; Sky-Eyes, Military Personnel (French officer), Frontiersman (aka Andre Du Pres)

Time Period(s): 17th century (1642-1644)

Locale(s): Great Plains, North America

Summary: In the eleventh volume of the Spanish Bit saga, Jean Cartier, acting as guide for a party of French explorers searching for the mouth of the Mississippi, embarks on a journey back to the Elk-dog People whom he left years before. The journey is perilous and climaxes with his reunion with the son he left behind.

Historical Accuracy: The novel's details about wilderness life and Indian customs are convincing and authentic.

1185 *River of Swans*

Date of Publication: 1986

Subject(s): Indians; Tribal Life—Native American; Exploration
Fictional character(s): Andre Du Pres, Military Personnel (French officer), Explorer; Pale Star, Indian
Time Period(s): 17th century (1636-1638)
Locale(s): Mississippi River, North America; Great Plains, North America

Summary: The tenth volume of the Spanish Bit saga describes an expedition into the North American wilderness by French officer Andre Du Pres. He is accompanied by Pale Star, an Indian woman kidnapped as a child and brought east. She knows that this might be her only chance to rejoin her people. The expedition endures storms and attack, and survival depends on reaching Pale Star's home among and the Elk-dog People. Du Pres must then decide whether to continue his mission or remain with the woman he now loves.

Historical Accuracy: The novel effectively and convincingly captures wilderness life of the period.

1186 *Runestone*

Date of Publication: 1995
Subject(s): Exploration; Vikings; Indians
Fictional character(s): Nils Thorsson, Sea Captain; Svenson, Sailor; Odin, Indian, Guide
Time Period(s): 11th century
Locale(s): North America

Summary: Norseman Nils Thorsson pilots two longships along the route to North America navigated by Leif Ericson. There they encounter the native people who resist the invaders. Only Thorsson, the sailor Svenson, and a one-eyed native guide whom they call Odin survive, and they begin an epic trek across the continent.

Historical Accuracy: The novel is a blend of extensive archaeological and anthropological research and speculation. The story is plausible and convincing.

1187 *The Sacred Hills*

Date of Publication: 1985
Subject(s): Indians; Tribal Life—Native American
Fictional character(s): Looks Far, Indian, Shaman; Wolf's Head, Indian, Shaman
Time Period(s): 17th century (1625-1627)
Locale(s): Great Plains, North America

Summary: In the eighth volume of the Spanish Bit saga, the Elk-dog People are threatened by a new enemy, the previously unknown Blue Paint People, who kill for pleasure. When the wife of Looks Far is killed, he proposes joining forces with the tribe's traditional enemy, the hated Head Splitters.

Historical Accuracy: Although fictional, the background of tribal life and customs is convincing.

1188 *The Smoky Hill*

Date of Publication: 1989
Subject(s): American West; Settlement of the American Frontier; Indians

Fictional character(s): Gabe Booth, Mountain Man; Lemuel Booth, Prospector; Jesse Booth, Military Personnel (corporal)
Historical character(s): John C. Fremont, Explorer, Frontiersman
Time Period(s): 19th century (1844-1876)
Locale(s): Smoky Hill River, Kansas

Summary: The locus is the Smoky Hill River country of Kansas which is depicted through the experiences of three members of the Booth family. Gabe is a mountain man who maps the unexplored area with Captain John Fremont in the 1840s; Lem is an Illinois farm boy who comes to the area in search of gold; and Jesse is a young army corporal involved in the Indian wars of the 1870s.

Historical Accuracy: The novel offers an evocative and authentic picture of the locale and the various eras.

1189 *Song of the Rock*

Date of Publication: 1989
Subject(s): Indians; Tribal Life—Native American
Fictional character(s): White Fox, Indian; Southwind, Indian
Time Period(s): 17th century (1690)
Locale(s): Great Plains, North America

Summary: While on a vision quest, White Fox stumbles upon the body of a dead warrior laid out for burial. He is suddenly and viciously attacked by a woman. He rejoins his tribe but is haunted by the woman and has a premonition that she is in danger. He is compelled to find her and uncover the mystery that surrounds her.

Historical Accuracy: The novel provides reliable details about Indian life and customs.

1190 *Thunderstick*

Date of Publication: 1993
Subject(s): Indians; Tribal Life—Native American
Fictional character(s): Singing Wolf, Indian; Rain, Indian; White Feathers, Indian
Time Period(s): 18th century
Locale(s): Great Plains, North America

Summary: As important as the horse has been to the fate of the Elk-dog People, the musket proves to be an equally ambiguous legacy. It arrives with a stranger from the eastern band of the People, White Feathers, who becomes Singing Wolf's rival for the love of Rain. Singing Wolf must put his rivalry aside to learn the secrets of the thunder stick and help save the tribe from the Shaved-head People who have mastered the new technology.

Historical Accuracy: The novel's depiction of tribal life and customs is convincing.

1191 *Track of the Bear*

Date of Publication: 1994
Subject(s): Indians; Tribal Life—Native American
Fictional character(s): Singing Wolf, Indian (Elk-Dog People), Shaman; Rain, Indian (Elk-Dog People)
Time Period(s): 18th century
Locale(s): Great Plains, North America

Summary: The author continues his Spanish Bit Saga chronicling the history of the Elk-Dog People. When a bear kills one of the People, the event seems to presage misfortune. Singing Wolf, the son of Walks in the Sun, sets out to discover whether the attack is in fact an evil omen.

Historical Accuracy: The presentation of Indian customs is convincing.

1192 *Trail From Taos*

Date of Publication: 1989
Subject(s): Indians; Spanish Colonies; Pueblo Revolt
Fictional character(s): Red Feather, Indian
Time Period(s): 17th century (1680)
Locale(s): Santa Fe, New Mexico (New Spain)

Summary: The historical background to the fourteenth volume of the Spanish Bit saga is the Pueblo Revolt in New Mexico in 1680. The southern tribes rise up against the Spanish occupiers of their lands and beat them back to Mexico for over a decade. Red Feather, on a trading trip to Sante Fe, is swept up in the conflict which further embroils the Elk-dog People when they try to rescue him.

Historical Accuracy: The basis of the story is historical. The details are authentic and reliable.

1193 *Trail of the Spanish Bit*

Date of Publication: 1980
Subject(s): Spanish Colonies; Indians; Tribal Life—Native American
Fictional character(s): Juan Garcia, Military Personnel (Spanish officer); Coyote, Indian, Warrior; Tall One, Indian
Time Period(s): 16th century (1540-1544)
Locale(s): Great Plains, North America

Summary: This is the first volume of the author's Spanish Bit saga, which chronicles the history of an Indian tribe of the Great Plains from the 16th to the 18th century. Juan Garcia, a Spanish soldier and explorer, is stranded alone among Indians as curious about him as he is about them. The novel shows his assimilation of tribal ways and his adoption by the tribe.

Historical Accuracy: Although fictional, the story is solidly based on anthropological and archaeological evidence.

1194 *Walks in the Sun*

Date of Publication: 1992
Subject(s): Indians; Tribal Life—Native American
Fictional character(s): Walks in the Sun, Indian, Explorer; Blue Jay, Indian, Explorer
Time Period(s): 1720s
Locale(s): Great Plains, North America; Mexico

Summary: In the twentieth volume of the Spanish Bit saga, Walks in the Sun accompanies his friend Blue Jay and nine followers on a journey further south than any of the Elk-dog People have previously gone. They are eventually captured by fierce warriors who practice cannibalism. This tale of their epic journey and return home forms an exciting adventure.

Historical Accuracy: The basis of the story is a factual expedition mounted by the Kiowas.

1195 *World of Silence*

Date of Publication: 1992
Subject(s): Indians; Tribal Life—Native American
Fictional character(s): Speaks-Not, Indian, Handicapped (deaf); South Wind, Indian, Young Woman
Time Period(s): 18th century
Locale(s): Great Plains, North America; Rocky Mountains, North America

Summary: In the 18th century, Speaks-Not is deaf yet able to learn the skills he needs to survive, earning the respect of his tribe. When a raid by the Forest People destroys all he has built, he must begin again, aided only by his granddaughter, South Wind, who also provides his link with the past.

Historical Accuracy: The novel's details of tribal life are authentic and convincing.

ALLAN COLE (1943-)

CHRIS BUNCH (1943-)

Born in Philadelphia, Pennsylvania, Cole is the son of a CIA agent and grew up in Europe and the Far East. He has worked as a chef, a journalist, and an editor. Chris Bunch is a science fiction novelist who collaborates with Cole. Together Cole and Bunch have written a number of science fiction and fantasy novels, including *The Court of a Thousand Sons*, *Fleet of the Damned*, and *Revenge of the Damned*. They also co-wrote *A Reckoning for Kings: A Novel of the Tet Offensive*.

1196 *A Daughter of Liberty*

Date of Publication: 1993
Subject(s): American Revolution; War of 1812
Fictional character(s): Diana Shannon, Servant (indentured); Emmett Shannon, Military Personnel (soldier)
Historical character(s): Dolley Madison, Spouse (of James Madison), Political Figure
Time Period(s): 18th century; 19th century (1778-1814)
Locale(s): Valley Forge, Pennsylvania; Philadelphia, Pennsylvania; Washington, District of Columbia

Summary: In the first volume of the Shannon Family Saga, Diana, a fifteen-year-old indentured servant, escapes her abusive master. She meets and eventually marries Emmett Shannon, a deserter from Washington's beleagured army at Valley Forge. The novel traces Diana Shannon's rise to respectibility as a businesswoman, a confidante of the powerful, and a champion of freedom.

Historical Accuracy: The historical period is captured with some authenticity, though too often as a thin background for the novel's drama.

ISABEL COLEGATE (1931-)

An English author, Colegate was born in Lincolnshire and attended boarding schools in Shropshire and Norfolk. She has a strong reputation as an elegant stylist with a talent for capturing the British upperclasses prior to World War I and during the social transformation that followed.

1197 *The Shooting Party*

Date of Publication: 1980
Subject(s): Hunting; World War I
Fictional character(s): Randolph Nettleby, Nobleman; Tom Harker, Worker; Cornelius Cardew, Gentleman
Time Period(s): 1910s (1913)
Locale(s): Oxfordshire, England

Summary: In the autumn of 1913 a shooting party on Sir Randolph's Oxfordshire estate becomes a metaphor for the tragic breakup of the aristocratic world that will come in August, 1914. Beneath the surface glitter, gentlemanly code, and sporting rivalry there is moral and social breakdown.

Historical Accuracy: The novel brilliantly captures English social life and plumbs its recesses for deeper meaning.

1198 *Statues in a Garden*

Date of Publication: 1964
Subject(s): World War I; Politics
Fictional character(s): Aylmer Weston, Political Figure; Alice Benedict, Gentlewoman; Edmund Weston, Gentleman
Time Period(s): 1910s (1914)
Locale(s): London, England

Summary: This novel describes the family of Sir Alymer Weston, a prominent politician and a member of Prime Minister Herbert Asquith's cabinet. Beneath the calm surface of a beautiful summer, all is falling apart, and family tragedy becomes a microcosm for the global tragedy that is to come.

Historical Accuracy: The era is evoked with telling details and grace notes that set the scene convincingly in its historical context.

1199 *The Summer of the Royal Visit*

Date of Publication: 1991
Subject(s): Victorian Period
Fictional character(s): Stephen Collingwood, Religious (clergyman); Edwin Hanbury, Engineer
Time Period(s): 1890s
Locale(s): Bath, England

Summary: The novel offers a portrait of Bath, England, on the eve of a royal visit by Queen Victoria. Beyond the peaceful surface and glittery preparations are secrets and conflict. At the center of the story is the architectural contest for the design of a new hotel intended to restore the city's fading reputation.

Historical Accuracy: Colegate's sense of the social drama of a city is set within the clear context of the Victorian past.

BOB COLEMAN (1951-)

An American writer and businessman from San Diego, California, Coleman graduated from the University of California at San Diego and received his Ph.D. from the University of Washington. He is the vice president of a small

brokerage and consulting firm in San Diego. His novel, *The Latter Adventures of Tom Jones* was written after five years of graduate work in 18th-century literature.

1200 *The Latter Adventures of Tom Jones*

Date of Publication: 1985
Subject(s): Picaresque Adventure; American Revolution; American Colonies
Fictional character(s): Tom Jones, Landowner; Amelia Jones, Young Woman; Hacksem Jones, Gentleman
Historical character(s): Benjamin Franklin, Political Figure
Time Period(s): 1770s (1774-1775)
Locale(s): Somerset, England; London, England; Boston, Massachusetts, American Colonies

Summary: Tom Jones, about 30 years after the events in Henry Fielding's novel, finds himself a widower beset by three troublesome children, and sets out for new adventures in America on the eve of the Revolution. His daughter sets off on her own adventure to avoid the machinations of her villainous brother.

Historical Accuracy: Coleman's knowledge of 18th-century customs and life are evident in this literary re-possesion of Fielding's masterpiece.

JANE CANDIA COLEMAN (1939-)

Born in St. Paul, Minnesota, Coleman graduated from the University of Pennsylvania. A short story and poetry writer, Coleman is the co-founder and director of the Women's Writing Center at Carlow College in Pittsburgh. She lives on a ranch in Arizona, trains and rides her own horses, and was inducted into the Cowboy Hall of Fame in 1990 for *No Roof but Sky*.

1201 *Doc Holliday's Woman*

Date of Publication: 1995
Subject(s): American West; Biography, Fictionalized
Historical character(s): Kate Elder, Frontierswoman, Orphan; John Henry Holliday, Gunfighter, Gambler; Wyatt Earp, Lawman
Time Period(s): 19th century (1866-1887)
Locale(s): Dodge City, Kansas; Tombstone, Arizona

Summary: The novel offers a fictionalized biography of the actual Kate Elder, who came West when her parents followed the Emperor Maximilian to Mexico. Left an orphan as a teenager, she becomes a saloon entertainer and the mistress of gambler Doc Holliday. She travels with Doc on his doomed odyssey and witnesses his showdown with the Clantons at the OK Corral.

Historical Accuracy: The novel is a blend of the actual and the invented. The period details are authentic.

LONNIE COLEMAN (1920-1982)

Born in Georgia and a graduate of the University of Alabama, Coleman was an editor for *Ladies' Home Journal*,

Collier's, Good Housekeeping, and *McCall's.* His Beulah Land trilogy sold over one million copies.

1202 *Beulah Land*

Date of Publication: 1973
Subject(s): Antebellum South; Slavery; Family Saga
Fictional character(s): Arnold Kendrick, Plantation Owner; Deborah Kendrick, Spouse; Lovey, Slave
Time Period(s): 19th century (1820-1861)
Locale(s): Savannah, Georgia

Summary: In this first volume of the author's trilogy, the Kendrick family is introduced. They are Georgia plantation owners with 150 slaves. Their intertwined lives characterize Southern plantation life in the Antebellum period.

Historical Accuracy: The drama is somewhat overheated and veers in the direction of the soap opera rather than an accurate portrait of the antebellum south.

1203 *The Legacy of Beulah Land*

Date of Publication: 1980
Subject(s): Family Saga; Reconstruction Period
Fictional character(s): Leon Marsh, Bastard Son, Heir; Eugene Betchley, Gentleman; Frankie-Julia Saxon, Southern Belle
Time Period(s): 19th century (1879-1895)
Locale(s): Savannah, Georgia

Summary: In the concluding volume of the author's plantation trilogy, the Kendrick-Davis clan emerges from the Reconstruction period. They have endured and prospered; now, their greatest challenge will be to hold onto their plantation and heritage against threats from within and without.

Historical Accuracy: The novel is sensationalistic rather than convincingly historical.

1204 *Look Away, Beulah Land*

Date of Publication: 1977
Subject(s): Civil War—U.S.; Family Saga; Reconstruction Period
Fictional character(s): Sarah Kendrick, Plantation Owner; Benjamin Davis, Gentleman; Daniel Todd, Military Personnel
Time Period(s): 1860s; 1870s (1864-1874)
Locale(s): Savannah, Georgia

Summary: In the second volume of the author's plantation trilogy, the aftermath of the Civil War is explored in the experiences of the Kendrick family. Their plantation has been devastated by Sherman's rampaging soldiers. An era has died, and a turbulent new age is being born.

Historical Accuracy: The author's grasp of period details creates a panorama of the people and the times; occasionally, however, the sensational predominates over the historical.

1205 *Mark*

Date of Publication: 1981
Subject(s): Depression Era; Coming of Age; Homosexuality
Fictional character(s): Mark Bowman, Orphan, Homosexual
Time Period(s): 1920s; 1930s

Locale(s): Montgomery, Alabama

Summary: This is a coming of age story set in Depression era Montgomery, Alabama. Mark is an orphan who goes from adolescence to adulthood in the course of the story. The novel deals frankly with the central character's homosexuality.

Historical Accuracy: The sights and sounds of the era are clearly created with all the appropriate movie titles, brand names, and events of the period creating a convincing background.

TERRY COLEMAN (1931-)

An English author, Coleman was born in Bournemouth and attended the University of Exeter and the University of London. He has been a lecturer in medieval law, a journalist for five English newspapers, and a historian. His nonfictional *The Railway Navvies* offer a picture of the construction of England's railroads in the 19th century.

1206 *Southern Cross*

Date of Publication: 1979
Subject(s): Frontier—Australia
Fictional character(s): Susannah King, Gentlewoman
Historical character(s): Nicholas Baudin, Explorer; William Bligh, Military Personnel (naval officer), Government Official; Philip Gidley King, Political Figure (colonial governor)
Time Period(s): 19th century (1802-1854)
Locale(s): Sydney, Australia

Summary: The novel portrays the first tumultuous decades of the 19th century in Australia, detailed through the experience of Susannah King, the Governor's daughter. She becomes the lover of French explorer Nicholas Baudin. The novel offers an accurate look at the settlement of Australia and includes descriptions of the Botany Bay convicts and the Ballarat goldfield riots.

Historical Accuracy: The events and the personalities are firmly rooted in historical fact that is plausibly described.

1207 *Thanksgiving*

Date of Publication: 1981
Subject(s): American Colonies; Pilgrims; Settlement of the American Frontier
Fictional character(s): Wolsey Lowell, Settler; Francis Wheaton, Settler; Wild O'Brien, Adventurer
Historical character(s): William Bradford, Leader (colonial); Miles Standish, Military Personnel; Charles I, Ruler (King of England); Peter Stuyvesant, Political Figure (Governor of New Amsterdam); Samuel Pepys, Writer
Time Period(s): 17th century
Locale(s): England; Plymouth, Massachusetts, American Colonies; New York, New York, American Colonies

Summary: The novel tells the story of some of the first European settlers of America. Wolsey Lowell crosses the Atlantic to America with the pilgrims on the *Mayflower*, and establishes the custom of Thanksgiving after the first harvest at Plymouth. He then moves on to the Dutch island of Manhattan before heading further west to the Mississippi.

Historical Accuracy: The novel is a picture only framed by fact. Although much is invented, the picture of colonial life is convincing.

BILL COLLETT

Bill Collett is a chemist and an amateur yachtsman.

1208 *The Last Mutiny: The Further Adventures of Captain Bligh*

Date of Publication: 1993
Subject(s): Mutiny; Sea Story; Napoleonic Wars
Historical character(s): William Bligh, Military Personnel (vice admiral); Fletcher Christian, Military Personnel (naval officer)
Time Period(s): 18th century; 19th century
Locale(s): Kent, England; New South Wales, Australia; At Sea

Summary: In 1817, the year of his death, William Bligh, in retirement in Kent, reflects on his extraordinary life. He offers his own unique perspective on Captain Cook's last voyage, the famous naval battles of Camperdown and Copenhagen, his tenure as governor of New South Wales, and, of course, the *Bounty* mutiny.

Historical Accuracy: As the author's notes make clear, the story stays close to the historical record, but the interpretation of Bligh's character is the author's.

RICHARD OLIVER COLLIN (1940-)

An American from Buffalo, New York, Collin earned his B.A. degree from Canisius College. He has been an intelligence analyst with the Defense Intelligence Agency and an adviser to the Saudi Arabian Defense Forces. He is a lecturer in history at Oxford University.

1209 *Contessa*

Date of Publication: 1994
Subject(s): Family Saga; World War I
Fictional character(s): Achille Leone, Gentleman; Rosaria Combardi, Farmer (peasant)
Time Period(s): 1910s; 1920s (1911-1922)
Locale(s): Italy

Summary: This love story of Achille, the son of an Italian count, and Rosaria, a peasant girl, is played out during the tumultuous years of World War I and the post-war rise of Italian fascism. Historical events tear the lovers apart, and the story details their struggle and eventual triumph.

Historical Accuracy: The novel employs convincing period details.

MAX ALLAN COLLINS (1948-)

An American born in Iowa, Collins earned his B.A. and M.F.A. from the University of Iowa. A professional rock musician and instructor of English, journalism, and creative writing, Collins also writes comic strips, particularly Dick Tracy. In his novels, his speciality is the period private eye novel.

1210 *Carnal Hours*

Date of Publication: 1994
Subject(s): Mystery; World War II
Fictional character(s): Nate Heller, Detective—Private; Sir Harry Oakes, Financier; Alfred de Marigny, Gentleman
Historical character(s): Meyer Lansky, Organized Crime Figure; Erle Stanley Gardner, Writer; Edward, Duke of Windsor, Royalty; Wallis Warfield Simpson, Noblewoman (Duchess of Windsor)
Time Period(s): 1940s (1943)
Locale(s): Bahamas

Summary: Chicago detective Nate Heller takes a case in the Bahamas on behalf of a millionaire, Harry Oakes, who winds up murdered. His philandering son-in-law, Alfred de Marigny, is the obvious suspect, but Heller attempts to prove him innocent, aided by writer Erle Stanley Gardner and some famous island denizens.

Historical Accuracy: The novel's period details and background are authentic and convincing.

1211 *The Dark City*

Date of Publication: 1987
Subject(s): Crime and Criminals; Depression Era
Historical character(s): Eliot Ness, FBI Agent
Time Period(s): 1930s
Locale(s): Cleveland, Ohio

Summary: After his success in Chicago bringing Al Capone to justice, FBI agent Elliott Ness is working alone in Cleveland attempting to clean up a corrupt police force and a city government with strong ties to the underworld.

Historical Accuracy: The novel mixes factual details of Ness' actual career with an imagined set of events against an authentic period background.

1212 *Murder by the Numbers*

Date of Publication: 1993
Subject(s): Mystery; Depression Era; Crime and Criminals
Fictional character(s): Toussaint Johnson, Police Officer
Historical character(s): Eliot Ness, FBI Agent
Time Period(s): 1930s (1938)
Locale(s): Cleveland, Ohio

Summary: After breaking Al Capone in Chicago, Eliot Ness tries to bring to justice the Mayfield Road Mob, Cleveland's black gangsters who control the numbers racket. The mob is moving in and threatens to produce a full-scale racial gang war. With the help of Toussaint Johnson, a black police officer, Ness tries to keep the lid on an extremely volatile situation.

Historical Accuracy: The novel is based on events in the life of Eliot Ness, mixed well with speculation and fiction.

1213 *Stolen Away*

Date of Publication: 1991
Subject(s): Mystery; Depression Era; Crime and Criminals
Fictional character(s): Nate Heller, Detective—Private
Historical character(s): Charles Lindbergh, Pilot

Time Period(s): 1930s (1932-1936)
Locale(s): New Jersey

Summary: When private detective Nate Heller comes to New Jersey to assist the police in the Lindbergh kidnapping case, his presence is resented. When a child's body turns up, it is assumed that it is the Lindbergh baby. Answers to the many questions raised take years to resolve.

Historical Accuracy: Although based in fact, the novel offers its own highly-speculative account of the famous kidnapping.

1214 *True Crime*

Date of Publication: 1984
Subject(s): Mystery; Crime and Criminals; Depression Era
Fictional character(s): Nate Heller, Detective—Private
Historical character(s): John Dillinger, Criminal, Murderer; Sally Rand, Dancer; Melvin Purvis, FBI Agent; Frank Nitti, Organized Crime Figure, Criminal; Kate ''Ma'' Barker, Criminal; Alvin Karpis, Criminal; Charles Arthur Floyd, Criminal; J. Edgar Hoover, Government Official
Time Period(s): 1930s (1934)
Locale(s): Chicago, Illinois

Summary: Nate Heller, a private eye in Chicago in 1934, finds himself in the middle of the FBI's attempt to establish its reputation. The FBI hopes to bring those on its list of Public Enemies, including Dillinger, Karpis, Pretty Boy Floyd, and the Barker gang, to justice.

Historical Accuracy: The period and the personalities are based on factual record.

1215 *True Detective*

Date of Publication: 1983
Subject(s): Mystery; Crime and Criminals; Depression Era
Fictional character(s): Nate Heller, Police Officer, Detective—Private
Historical character(s): Eliot Ness, Police Officer; Frank Nitti, Organized Crime Figure, Criminal; Al Capone, Organized Crime Figure, Criminal; Anton Cermak, Political Figure (Mayor of Chicago); George Raft, Actor; Franklin Delano Roosevelt, Political Figure (President of the U.S.); Barney Ross, Sports Figure (boxer)
Time Period(s): 1930s (1932-1933)
Locale(s): Chicago, Illinois; Miami, Florida

Summary: Nate Heller is the youngest cop on the Chicago police force of the 1930s. He quits because of the corruption to become a private investigator. Hired by Al Capone to help him maintain control of his operation, Heller becomes involved in the assassination attempt on Franklin Roosevelt. The novel ends with a deadly climax at the Chicago World's Fair.

Historical Accuracy: The period is vividly depicted although the facts are not exact.

NORMAN COLLINS (1907-1982)

An English broadcasting executive, publisher, editor, and novelist, Collins served for ten years as deputy chairman of Victor Gollancz Ltd., a London publishing house. For the BBC, Collins was the director general of overseas service and controller of the television division. Collins was the author of numerous popular books, including *Flames Coming Out of the Top*, *I Shall Not Want*, and *Children of the Archbishop*.

1216 *Quiet Lady*

Date of Publication: 1942
Subject(s): Franco-Prussian War; Siege of Paris; Paris Commune
Fictional character(s): Anna Karlin, Young Woman, Widow(er)
Historical character(s): Otto von Bismarck, Political Figure (German chancellor); Napoleon III, Ruler (Emperor of France)
Time Period(s): 19th century
Locale(s): Paris, France; England

Summary: This long historical novel follows the adventures of Anna Karlin through the Siege of Paris and the Commune, several love affairs, and two marriages. She ends her life as a respectable widow living quietly in England. Her story is interspersed with monologues from Bismarck and Napoleon III, two historical giants of the period.

Historical Accuracy: The novel provides an authentic portrait of the siege of Paris, but other events are not successfully supported by the weak frame of the fictional story.

WARWICK COLLINS

Collins is a British writer and yacht designer who lives in Lymington, Hampshire. His first three novels were thrillers set in the world of sailboat racing.

1217 *The Rationalist*

Date of Publication: 1993
Subject(s): Medical Profession; Suspense
Fictional character(s): Silas Grange, Doctor; Celia Quill, Widow(er)
Time Period(s): 18th century
Locale(s): England

Summary: A respected small-town doctor, Silas Grange, is drawn into the mysterious world of a beautiful widow, Mrs. Quill, and her daughter. He finds himself trapped in an erotic game in which he is the unwilling victim.

Historical Accuracy: The plot depends on the formality of the 18th century; the background of small-town English life is carefully detailed.

ALICE MARY COLVER (1892-)

Born in New Jersey, Colver graduated from Wellesley College. She is the author of juvenile and adult fiction. Her titles include *The Measure of the Years*, *The Parson*, and *The Dear Pretender*. She also writes under the pseudonym Mary Randall.

1218 *The Measure of the Years*

Date of Publication: 1954
Subject(s): American Colonies; French and Indian War; American Revolution
Fictional character(s): Mark Martin, Settler, Sea Captain; Esther Richardson, Spouse (of Mark)
Time Period(s): 18th century (1739-1785)
Locale(s): Stockbridge, Massachusetts, American Colonies

Summary: The novel describes the history of Stockbridge, Massachusetts, from its beginnings as Indian Town to 1785. The town's development is seen through the experiences of sea captain Mark Martin who, along with his wife Esther, settles in Stockbridge during the French and Indian Wars. The novel chronicles their life and daily events during the period.

Historical Accuracy: The historical events are based on town, church, and family records, although there are some deviations from established facts.

1219 *There Is a Season*

Date of Publication: 1957
Subject(s): American Colonies
Fictional character(s): Mary Martin, Young Woman
Time Period(s): 18th century (1756-1770)
Locale(s): Stockbridge, Massachusetts, American Colonies; Charleston, South Carolina, American Colonies

Summary: The sequel to *The Measure of the Years* depicts life and conditions in colonial Stockbridge, Massachusetts, and Charleston, South Carolina. The story centers on Mary Martin, whose elopement with an irresponsible peddler eventually leads to happiness with another man.

Historical Accuracy: The period background is minimal.

ANNE COLVER (1908-)

Born in Cleveland, Ohio, Colver is a graduate of Whitman College. She is the author of a number of juvenile and adult novels, including *Theodosia, Daughter of Aaron Burr* and *Mr. Lincoln's Wife*.

1220 *Listen for the Voices*

Date of Publication: 1939
Subject(s): Literary Life
Fictional character(s): Albert Shipman, Gentleman; Laura Shipman, Spouse
Historical character(s): Ralph Waldo Emerson, Writer; Henry David Thoreau, Writer
Time Period(s): 1840s; 1850s (1848-1851)
Locale(s): Concord, Massachusetts

Summary: Life in Concord, Massachusetts, is depicted as a group of fictitious characters interact with the literary luminaries, like Emerson and Thoreau, who gave Concord its reputation as a center for literary and intellectual achievement.

Historical Accuracy: The novel captures its setting and its famous residents effectively.

1221 *Mr. Lincoln's Wife*

Date of Publication: 1943
Subject(s): Biography, Fictionalized; Civil War—U.S.
Historical character(s): Mary Todd Lincoln, Spouse; Abraham Lincoln, Political Figure
Time Period(s): 19th century (1840-1865)
Locale(s): Springfield, Illinois; Washington, District of Columbia

Summary: This fictional biography of Mary Todd Lincoln tells her story from the days of her courtship and marriage to Lincoln in Springfield, Illinois, through the years of the Civil War to Lincoln's assassination.

Historical Accuracy: The historical background is genuine, and the author's treatment of Mary Todd Lincoln is fair and balanced. The novel is, however, marred by several factual errors.

HENRY JOHN COLYTON
(PSEUD. OF SAMUEL ZIMMERMANN)

1222 *Sir Pagan*

Date of Publication: 1947
Subject(s): Middle Ages; Crusades
Fictional character(s): Pagan de Fitz-Stephen, Bastard Son, Knight
Historical character(s): Baldwin I, Ruler (King of Jerusalem)
Time Period(s): 12th century
Locale(s): Palestine

Summary: Set during the First Crusades, this novel of romance and adventure concerns the natural son of Count Stephen du Blois, Pagan de Fitz-Stephen, who must make his way with his wits and resources rather than his noble connection.

Historical Accuracy: The novel's period background is credible and authentic.

HARRY COMBS (1913-)

Combs is an American novelist who spent most of his career in the aviation industry. He wrote the nonfiction book, *Kill Devil Hill: Discovering the Secret of the Wright Brothers.*

1223 *Brules*

Date of Publication: 1992
Subject(s): American West; Indians; Crime and Criminals
Fictional character(s): Cat Brules, Cowboy, Outlaw; Wild Rose, Indian; Pedro Gonzalez, Outlaw
Time Period(s): 19th century; 20th century (1867-1909)
Locale(s): Hays, Kansas; Southwest

Summary: This tough and moving novel tells the story of cowboy Cat Brules. He loses his love to the Comanches, which sets him on his life-long search for justice in a western landscape with precious little to spare.

Historical Accuracy: This is a meticulously documented western story, far more convincing in its details than other "epic" westerns.

1224 *The Scout*

Date of Publication: 1995
Subject(s): American West; Indians; Battle of the Little Bighorn
Fictional character(s): Cat Brules, Frontiersman; White Antelope, Indian (Crow); Melisande Brules, Spouse
Historical character(s): George C. Crook, Military Personnel (general); George Armstrong Custer, Military Personnel (cavalry officer)
Time Period(s): 1870s; 1880s
Locale(s): Wyoming; Santa Fe, New Mexico; Colorado

Summary: The story of Cat Brules, gunman turned army scout, is continued. Brules is on hand for the Indian Wars of the 1870s and 1880s with General Crook and Custer, the pursuit of Chief Joseph and the the Nez Perce, and the hunting down of Geronimo. In the process, a way of life is seen passing as remembered by the older Brules telling his story to an eleven-year-old in 1909.

Historical Accuracy: The novel offers a remarkably detailed and unvarnished portrait of the American West and its history.

SIGRID COMBUCHEN (1942-)

Born in Germany of Russian-Lithuanian and German parents, Combuchen has lived in Sweden since age six. She is one of Sweden's leading literary critics and has won several important fiction prizes in Sweden. Her books include *A Housebroke Society*, *In Northern Europe*, and *Warmth*.

1225 *Byron: A Novel*

Date of Publication: 1988
Subject(s): Literary Life; Biography, Fictionalized
Historical character(s): George Gordon Byron, Writer, Nobleman
Time Period(s): 19th century; 1930s (1938)
Locale(s): England; Italy; Greece

Summary: In 1938 members of the Byron Society present sketches that capture Byron's career to commemorate the 150th anniversary of the poet's birth. This intriguing fictional biography creates a richly textured portrait of Byron as well as a convincing frame of England and Europe in the 1930s.

Historical Accuracy: The novel's biographical mosaic is fashioned out of factual details and invention. The novel's preface indicates some deliberate inaccuracies.

WILL COMFORT (1878-1932)

Journalist and fiction writer Comfort wrote about his experiences in the Russo-Japanese War in *Routledge Rides Again*. He wrote a candid autobiography, *Midstream*, and the historical novel *Apache*.

1226 *Apache*

Date of Publication: 1931
Subject(s): American West; Indians; Biography, Fictionalized

Historical character(s): Mangas Coloradas, Indian (Apache), Chieftain
Time Period(s): 19th century
Locale(s): Southwest

Summary: This biography of the Apache chief Mangas Colorados tracks his rise to tribal leadership and his efforts to reunite the Indians and drive out the white settlers.

Historical Accuracy: The facts that are known about Colorados are accurately preserved, and the treatment is an honest one which avoids idealization.

RALPH COMPTON

1227 *The Goodnight Trail*

Date of Publication: 1992
Subject(s): Cattle Drives; American West; Ranching
Fictional character(s): Benton McCaleb, Cowboy, Gunfighter; Will Elliot, Cowboy
Historical character(s): Charles Goodnight, Rancher
Time Period(s): 1860s (1866)
Locale(s): Staked Plains, New Mexico; Colorado (eastern slope); Texas

Summary: In the aftermath of the Civil War, the Texas economy is in shambles. Rancher Charles Goodnight hatches a plan to restore prosperity by rounding up the thousands of half-wild cattle from the plains and driving them to Denver. To do so, Goodnight and his team must contend with hostile Indians, strengthened by the lack of a military presence during the war years.

Historical Accuracy: The novel is both an exciting and an accurate depiction of life on the range and an historic cattle drive.

IVY COMPTON-BURNETT (1884-1969)

English author Compton-Burnett is widely held to be one of the premier modern English writers. Her characteristic subject was the genteel world of England before the Great War with a focus on the Victorian and Edwardian family as a model for civilization as a whole. Compton-Burnett was a master of suggestion, pointing to extremes and violence that reside beneath the quiet surface of good breeding and civility.

1228 *A Father and His Fate*

Date of Publication: 1958
Subject(s): Victorian Period; Inheritance—Disputed
Fictional character(s): Miles Mowbray, Landowner; Ellen Mowbray, Spouse (of Miles); Malcolm Mowbray, Gentleman, Heir
Time Period(s): 19th century; 20th century (turn of the century)
Locale(s): England

Summary: English country life at the turn of the century is the author's setting in this domestic drama of Miles Mowbray, an English squire whose entailed estate is to be inherited by his nephew Malcolm. Beneath the surface of respectable upper-class life lurks hypocrisy, betrayal, and deceit.

Historical Accuracy: The novel is understated and expert in detailing English life of the period.

1229 *A Heritage and Its History*

Date of Publication: 1960
Subject(s): Victorian Period; Inheritance—Disputed
Fictional character(s): Edwin Challoner, Heir; Simon Challoner, Heir; Hamish Challoner, Gentleman
Time Period(s): 19th century (late)
Locale(s): England

Summary: Compton-Burnett uses a characteristic setting of an English country house and village at the turn of the century to explore family affairs. The affairs of the Challoner family illustrate greed, deceit, and betrayal. The disposition of the Challoner estate produces almost grotesque warping of normal human relations.

Historical Accuracy: The author is remarkably able to capture the period.

1230 *The Mighty and Their Fall*

Date of Publication: 1962
Subject(s): Family Saga
Fictional character(s): Nina Middleton, Widow(er); Egbert Middleton, Young Man; Lavinia Middleton, Young Woman
Time Period(s): 1900s
Locale(s): England

Summary: Nina Middleton's desire to remarry sets in motion a chain of deceit and betrayal.

Historical Accuracy: The author traces her locale and setting with precision, bringing to it the universality of a Sophocles or Thomas Hardy.

1231 *Mother and Son*

Date of Publication: 1955
Subject(s): Victorian Period
Fictional character(s): Miranda Hume, Gentlewoman; Julius Hume, Gentleman; Rosebery Hume, Gentleman; Hester Wolsey, Companion, Housekeeper
Time Period(s): 19th century (late)
Locale(s): England

Summary: Set in late Victorian times, the novel is a character study of a domestic tyrant, Miranda Hume; her meek husband, Julius; and their son, Rosebery. A family secret traps them in a sinister realm of guilt and betrayal.

Historical Accuracy: Few writers have achieved such levels of imagination; her setting is authentically detailed.

MARYSE CONDE
(PSEUD. OF MARYSE BOUCOLON, 1937-)

West Indian writer Conde was born in Guadeloupe and educated at the Sorbonne. Her imaginative fictions show a blending of West Indian and continental influences.

1232 *The Children of Segu*

Date of Publication: 1989
Subject(s): Religious Conflict; French Colonies
Fictional character(s): Tiekoro Traore, Young Man
Historical character(s): El-Hadj Omar, Warrior (Islamic)
Time Period(s): 19th century
Locale(s): Segu, Africa (near present-day Mali)

Summary: This sequel to *Segu* continues the history of the African city of Segu in the second half of the 19th century, now conquered by the great Islamic warrior El-Hadj Omar who has unleashed a bloody holy war. The war's effects on the Traore family are depicted.

Historical Accuracy: The author's notes indicate the historical basis for the novel's domestic story.

1233 *I, Tituba, Black Witch of Salem*

Date of Publication: 1992
Subject(s): American Colonies; Witchcraft and Sorcery; Puritans
Fictional character(s): Mama Yaya, Spirit, Healer; Indian John, Slave, Spouse (Tituba's)
Historical character(s): Tituba, Witch, Slave
Time Period(s): 17th century (1690s)
Locale(s): Salem, Massachusetts, American Colonies; Barbados

Summary: In this novel of early colonial life, Tituba, the property of the minister of Salem, Massachusetts, is accused of and confesses to practicing witchcraft. She is imprisoned before being sold to pay for her chains and keep. The novel is a gripping look at both slavery and witchcraft in the American colonies.

Historical Accuracy: Based on the historical Tituba, the novel is a convincing portrait of the age.

1234 *Segu*

Date of Publication: 1987
Subject(s): Slavery; Religious Conflict; Family Saga
Fictional character(s): Dousika Traore, Nobleman
Time Period(s): 18th century; 19th century (1797-1860)
Locale(s): Segu, Mali

Summary: This depiction of African history focuses on the period in which native customs and beliefs yield to the influence of Islam. The story concerns Segu's Bambara tribe and the family of nobleman Dousika Traore which is torn apart by the actions of his four sons. One fights for the old pagan ways, one coverts to Islam, one is sold into slavery in Brazil, and one becomes a mercenary.

Historical Accuracy: Native customs and the workings of the slave trade are treated authentically.

RICHARD CONDON (1915-)

American novelist Condon was born in New York City and has worked as a publicist in New York and Hollywood for a number of movie studios. Condon began his writing career at age 42, specializing in political thrillers. Bestselling titles include *The Manchurian Candidate*, *The Oldest Confession*, and *Winter Kills*. His novel *Prizzi's Honor* was made into a highly successful film starring Jack Nicholson and Kathleen Turner.

1235   *The Abandoned Woman*

Date of Publication: 1977
Subject(s): Royalty—England
Historical character(s): George IV, Ruler (King of England); Caroline of Brunswick, Royalty (queen consort of George IV)
Time Period(s): 18th century; 19th century (1795-1821)
Locale(s): England

Summary: The novel dramatizes the relationship between George IV and Caroline of Brunswick. They married in 1795 and almost never saw each other over the next 26 years. George charged her with bearing an illegitimate child, but Caroline was cleared of the charge. After George was crowned king, Caroline returned to England to claim her rights as queen and was charged with adultery.

Historical Accuracy: The facts are considerably distorted by a modernist perspective and a satirical impulse.

ROBERT J. CONLEY (1940-)

A Native American writer born in Oklahoma, Conley attended Midwestern University and has been an instructor of English at a variety of colleges and universities. An expert in Cherokee Indian culture and history, his novels depict the Cherokee experience with considerable authority.

1236   *The Actor*

Date of Publication: 1987
Subject(s): American West; Theatrical Life
Fictional character(s): Bluford ''Blue'' Steele, Actor (aka John Berringer Temple); Brice Seagraves, Actor; Bluff Luton, Lawman (town marshal)
Time Period(s): 1880s
Locale(s): Iowa

Summary: Bluford Steele is part Cherokee, educated in the East, and finds his true calling as an actor. Traveling with a small acting troupe in the West, he is forced to play his most demanding role, impersonating a cold-blooded gunfighter to recover the stolen proceeds of the troupe's performances.

Historical Accuracy: The situation is fictional, but Steele is based on a number of actual Cherokees who were sent East for an education, one of whom became a professional actor in New York in the 1850s.

1237   *Back to Malachi*

Date of Publication: 1986
Subject(s): American West; Indians
Fictional character(s): Charlie Black, Indian (half-breed Cherokee); Mose Pathkiller, Indian (Cherokee); Malachi, Indian (Cherokee)
Time Period(s): 19th century
Locale(s): Oklahoma

Summary: Charlie Black is a young half-breed Cherokee pulled between assimilation to white culture and his loyalty to his Cherokee heritage. When his friend Mose Pathkiller gets into trouble with the law, Charlie must choose between his future and his friend.

Historical Accuracy: The fictional story owes some of its details to the actual Cherokee outlaw Ned Christie.

1238   *Border Line*

Date of Publication: 1993
Subject(s): American West; Indians
Fictional character(s): Dhu Walker, Indian (Cherokee), Rancher; Ben Franklin Lacey, Rancher; Newt Trainor, Outlaw
Time Period(s): 1860s (post Civil War)
Locale(s): Preston, Texas; Iowa

Summary: Dhu Walker and Ben Lacey, the reluctant companions in the author's *Strange Company*, have survived the Civil War, and taken up ranching in Texas. When there is trouble in Lacey's family back in Iowa, the two go to help. The gold they carry makes them an attractive prey for a Confederate guerilla, Newt Trainor.

Historical Accuracy: The regional and period details are realistic and believable.

1239   *Colfax*

Date of Publication: 1990
Subject(s): American West; Mystery
Fictional character(s): Bluff Luton, Lawman (Marshall); Oliver Colfax, Outlaw, Gunfighter
Time Period(s): 1880s
Locale(s): Riddle, Iowa; St. Louis, Missouri; Texas

Summary: Oliver Colfax is a hired gun who finds himself in the middle of a murder investigation when his friend Marshall Bluff Luton is killed. His pursuit of the killer takes him first into Indian territory in Texas and eventually back home to Iowa.

Historical Accuracy: The period details are authentic and convincing.

1240   *Crazy Snake*

Date of Publication: 1994
Subject(s): American West; Indians; Civil War—U.S.
Fictional character(s): Fahnee, Indian (Creek), Healer (medicine woman)
Historical character(s): Chitto Harjo, Indian (Creek), Chieftain
Time Period(s): 19th century; 20th century (1861-1900)
Locale(s): Oklahoma

Summary: The story of the Creek people is dramatized through the experiences of the Creek warrior chief called Crazy Snake who comes of age during the Civil War and struggles to preserve his people's sovereignity in the face of strong opposition.

Historical Accuracy: Based on actual events, the story is more fictional than factual, and the author alerts the reader that it should not be confused with truth.

1241 *The Dark Way*

Date of Publication: 1993
Subject(s): Indians; Tribal Life—Native American
Fictional character(s): Standing-in-the-Doorway, Indian (Cherokee), Shaman (priest); Two Heads, Indian (Cherokee); Edohi, Indian (Cherokee), Warrior
Time Period(s): Indeterminate Past
Locale(s): Southeast, North America

Summary: In the second book of the author's Real People saga, one of the most dramatic events in Cherokee lore is depicted: the overthrow of the Ani-kutani, the powerful ruling priesthood. A drought threatens the tribe, and the priests design a four-day ceremony to divert an increasingly disenchanted populace. The ceremony instead becomes the catalyst for rebellion.

Historical Accuracy: The account of tribal customs are authentic and realistic.

1242 *Geronimo: An American Legend*

Date of Publication: 1994
Subject(s): American West; Indians; Biography, Fictionalized
Historical character(s): Geronimo, Indian (Apache), Chieftain; George C. Crook, Military Personnel (general); Al Sieber, Scout
Time Period(s): 1880s (1885-1886)
Locale(s): Arizona; Mexico

Summary: The career of Geronimo, one of the last and greatest war leaders of the Chiricahua Apaches, is dramatized from his escape from the reservation to his final surrender two years later. The novel offers a speculative account of the events of Geronimo's early years as well as a full depiction of Geronimo's revolt and his inevitable failure.

Historical Accuracy: The novel is solidly based on documented evidence. The surmises about Geronimo's sketchy past are plausible.

1243 *Go-Ahead Rider*

Date of Publication: 1990
Subject(s): American West; Indians
Fictional character(s): George Tanner, Indian (Cherokee), Lawman (deputy); Go-Ahead Rider, Indian (Cherokee), Lawman (sheriff)
Time Period(s): 1860s
Locale(s): Tahlequah, Oklahoma (Cherokee Nation, Indian Territory)

Summary: Harvard graduate and half-Cherokee George Tanner returns home to the Cherokee Nation and is hired by Go-Ahead Rider to be his deputy. The Indian Council is debating whether the railroad should be permitted to come into town or not. When one of the key voters disappears, Tanner finds himself in the middle of political intrigue, blackmail, and bootlegging.

Historical Accuracy: The politics of the Cherokees are authentically presented.

1244 *Killing Time*

Date of Publication: 1988
Subject(s): American West; Crime and Criminals
Fictional character(s): Bluff Luton, Lawman (town marshal); Oliver Colfax, Outlaw, Gunfighter; Bluford "Blue" Steele, Lawman (town marshal)
Time Period(s): 1880s
Locale(s): Riddle, Iowa; Texas

Summary: When Marshall Bluff Luton of Riddle, Iowa, receives word that his brother's murderers are in Wichita County, he sets off on a hazardous trek into Texas. Oliver Colfax, a hired gun out to kill Luton, winds up saving his life, waiting until he can find the right "killing time" for the deed.

Historical Accuracy: The details of western life and the region are convincing.

1245 *The Long Trail North*

Date of Publication: 1993
Subject(s): American West; Indians
Fictional character(s): Dhu Walker, Indian (Cherokee), Rancher; Thane Savage, Outlaw; Herd McLellan, Rancher
Time Period(s): 19th century (post-Civil War)
Locale(s): Texas; Kansas City, Missouri; South Dakota

Summary: When Herd McLellan is ambushed by his old nemesis, Thane Savage, Dhu Walker, his partner, trails the outlaw. Walker's route takes him back to Cherokee country for a visit with a shaman and then on a trek through Arkansas, Missouri, and finally South Dakota for the final showdown.

Historical Accuracy: The novel offers convincing western and period scenes.

1246 *Mountain Windsong*

Date of Publication: 1992
Subject(s): Indians; Tribal Life—Native American; Trail of Tears
Fictional character(s): Oconechee, Indian (Cherokee), Young Woman (chief's daughter); Waguli, Indian (Cherokee), Warrior
Time Period(s): 1830s
Locale(s): North Carolina; Cherokee Nation, Oklahoma

Summary: This is a love story set during Andrew Jackson's Indian removal policy, which uprooted the Cherokees from their North Carolina homeland. Oconechee manages to escape the forced removal, but Waguli joins the exodus of the Trail of Tears. The two spend years searching for one another before they are finally reunited.

Historical Accuracy: This moving story is gripping and convincing in its details of Indian life of the period.

1247 *Ned Christie's War*

Date of Publication: 1990
Subject(s): Indians; American West
Fictional character(s): Sam Maples, Lawman
Historical character(s): Ned Christie, Indian (Cherokee), Outlaw; Isaac C. Parker, Judge
Time Period(s): 1880s

Locale(s): Cherokee Nation, Oklahoma; Fort Smith, Arkansas

Summary: The novel describes the tragic career of Ned Christie, a Cherokee patriot who struggles to prevent the government from taking the last of the Cherokee's land. For some, he was a troublemaker who needed to be kept in check. He is framed for the murder of a deputy, and in the pursuit that follows Ned takes on both Federal lawmen and the dead man's son.

Historical Accuracy: Although based on historical events, the story is not intended to be accurate in all details.

1248 *Nickajack*

Date of Publication: 1992
Subject(s): American West; Indians; Trials
Fictional character(s): Nickajack, Indian (Cherokee); Coffee Soldier, Indian (Cherokee)
Time Period(s): 1840s (1841)
Locale(s): Cherokee Nation, Oklahoma

Summary: In the 1840s the Cherokee Nation is split into two factions: those who sign the treaty with the U.S. government and those who refuse. Nickajack, an apolitical Cherokee, is drawn into the web of political intrigue when he is ambushed by a resister and kills him. His trial demonstrates the consequences of a divided Cherokee Nation.

Historical Accuracy: Based on a true incident, the story convincingly details the little-known politics of the period.

1249 *Quitting Time*

Date of Publication: 1989
Subject(s): American West; Theatrical Life; Mystery
Fictional character(s): Oliver Colfax, Outlaw, Gunfighter
Time Period(s): 1870s
Locale(s): St. Louis, Missouri; Pullman, Colorado

Summary: Upon seeing a performance of Shakespeare's *Titus Adronicus*, Oliver Colfax is persuaded to leave retirement and work as a hired gun for a rancher. While fighting off rustlers, Colfax is soon involved in shady business with the acting troupe whose performance influenced him so.

Historical Accuracy: The novel's situation is fanciful and somewhat far-fetched, but the western details are authentic.

1250 *The Saga of Henry Starr*

Date of Publication: 1989
Subject(s): American West; Crime and Criminals; Biography, Fictionalized
Historical character(s): Henry Starr, Outlaw (bank robber), Indian (Cherokee)
Time Period(s): 19th century; 20th century (1880s-1920s)
Locale(s): Arkansas; Oklahoma

Summary: This is the story of the notorious bank robber Henry Starr who begins his career as a Cherokee cowboy and is arrested for a crime he did not commit. Branded a criminal, he decides to become one in earnest. It is said that he robbed more banks than any other man in history, and his exploits are described here.

Historical Accuracy: Although based on the actual life of Henry Starr, some liberties have been taken with the facts.

1251 *Strange Company*

Date of Publication: 1991
Subject(s): American West; Civil War—U.S.
Fictional character(s): Dhu Walker, Indian, Military Personnel (Confederate soldier); Ben Franklin Lacey, Military Personnel (Union soldier); Gordon Early, Military Personnel (Confederate officer)
Time Period(s): 1860s
Locale(s): Pea Ridge, Alaska; Texas; Indian Territory

Summary: Half-Cherokee Dhu Walker is an unwilling Confederate soldier who, along with captured Union soldier Ben Lacey, breaks away from the army. They strive for freedom as well as for a chance for revenge against the Confederate officer whom both blame for their predicament.

Historical Accuracy: The novel offers convincing western and period details.

1252 *To Make a Killing*

Date of Publication: 1994
Subject(s): American West; Indians
Fictional character(s): Go-Ahead Rider, Lawman (town marshall), Indian (Cherokee); Beehunter, Lawman (deputy), Indian (Cherokee); George Tanner, Lawman (deputy), Indian (Cherokee)
Time Period(s): 19th century (post Civil War)
Locale(s): Cherokee Nation, Oklahoma

Summary: The murder of a prisoner in Sheriff Go-Ahead Rider's jail presents a troubling puzzle. At first, deputy Beehunter is the prime suspect, but soon the hunt for the killer leads north and into a tangled plot of smuggling, murder, and evil spirits.

Historical Accuracy: The details of life in the Cherokee Nation of the period is authentic and well-drawn.

1253 *The Way of the Priests*

Date of Publication: 1992
Subject(s): Indians; Tribal Life—Native American
Fictional character(s): Corn Flower, Indian (Cherokee), Captive; Edohi, Indian (Cherokee), Warrior; Standing-in-the-Doorway, Indian (Cherokee), Shaman (priest)
Time Period(s): Indeterminate Past
Locale(s): Southeast, North America

Summary: A Cherokee village celebrates the safe return of Corn Flower, who had been kidnapped by the Choctaws. Her return, however, adds to the turmoil surrounding the Ani-Kutani, the ruling priesthood. The Ani-Kutani struggle to maintain power, fighting the doubt among their people brought on by an extended drought.

Historical Accuracy: The depiction of tribal life is believable and convincing.

1254 *The White Path*

Date of Publication: 1993

Subject(s): Indians; Tribal Life—Native American
Fictional character(s): Edohi, Indian (Cherokee), Warrior; Dancing Rabbit, Indian (Cherokee)
Time Period(s): Indeterminate Past
Locale(s): Southeast, North America

Summary: In book three of the author's Real People saga, which concerns the Cherokees in pre-Columbian America, the Ani-Kutani, the despotic class of priests, has been overthrown. Internal conflict threatens to tear the tribe apart in the current vacuum of leadership and tradition. The last of the Ani-Kutani, Edohi, possesses the secrets that can possibly save the Real People. Meanwhile the Suwali people prepare to wage a war of conquest against the Cherokee.

Historical Accuracy: The use of Cherokee lore and tribal customs is authentic.

PHOEBE CONN

`1255` *By Love Enslaved*

Date of Publication: 1989
Subject(s): Dark Ages; Romance; Vikings
Fictional character(s): Dana, Landowner; Brendan, Slave (Celt)
Time Period(s): 9th century (886)
Locale(s): Isle of Fyn, Denmark

Summary: Dana is left in charge of her father's household in his absence, and she must deal with the Celtic slave Brendan. Romance develops, but not without problems.

Historical Accuracy: This period romance is more particular and convincing in its setting and details than others.

EVAN S. CONNELL (1924-)

Born in Kansas City, Missouri, Connell graduated from the University of Kansas and did graduate work at Stanford, Columbia, and San Francisco State College. Connell was a U.S. Navy pilot and flight instructor. His fictions have been enthusiastically heralded by critics as some of the best modern texts. His non-fiction study, *Son of the Morning Star: Custer and the Little Big Horn*, was a surprise bestseller, the fruit of four years of research. It has been called an American classic.

`1256` *The Alchymist's Journal*

Date of Publication: 1991
Subject(s): Alchemy; Middle Ages; Occult
Historical character(s): Philippus Aureolus Paracelsus, Philosopher
Time Period(s): 16th century
Locale(s): Europe

Summary: The author imagines the journals of seven alchemists, beginning with the famous 16th-century alchemist Paracelsus. Each reflect on alchemy and the world in a kind of chorus of voices and perspectives that collectively render both a philosophy and an understanding of the medieval world.

Historical Accuracy: The novel is a tour de force of impersonation of period voices and of the medieval world view.

MABEL CONQUIST

`1257` *Bianca*

Date of Publication: 1956
Subject(s): Renaissance
Fictional character(s): Bianca Tedelli, Gentlewoman, Spouse; Vittorino Tedelli, Gentleman
Time Period(s): 15th century
Locale(s): Italy

Summary: This tale of intrigue set in Renaissance Italy during the age of the city-states concerns Bianca Tedelli and her husband Vittorino. Famous historical figures are mentioned but are very much in the background. The period is suggested by intrigue and brutality that could only have happened during the Renaissance. The murder of Galeazzo Maria Sforza in the Milan Cathedral, an actual event, provides the novel's turning point.

Historical Accuracy: This is a convincing tale of the Renaissance with a credible period background.

ROBERT CONROY
(PSEUD. OF ROBERT GOLDSTON, 1927-)

An American writer born in New York City, Conroy attended Columbia University and has been a professional writer living abroad mainly in Spain, France, and England since 1953. He is the author of numerous fictional and historical studies.

`1258` *1901*

Date of Publication: 1995
Subject(s): Diplomacy; Alternate History
Fictional character(s): Patrick Mahan, Military Personnel (army major)
Historical character(s): Theodore Roosevelt, Political Figure; James Longstreet, Veteran (Confederate general); Joe Wheeler, Veteran (Civil War); Douglas MacArthur, Military Personnel (army officer); Wilhelm II, Ruler (German kaiser); William McKinley, Political Figure; Elihu Root, Diplomat, Government Official (cabinet member); Alfred von Tirpitz, Military Personnel (German admiral); Alfred von Schlieffen, Military Personnel (German field marshal)
Time Period(s): 1900s (1901)
Locale(s): Long Island, New York; New York, New York; Danbury, Connecticut

Summary: The novel imagines a German invasion of the U.S. in 1901 when President McKinley refuses to give up the newly-aquired territories of Guam, Puerto Rico, Cuba, and the Philippines from the Spanish-American War. Kaiser Wilhelm launches an invasion, landing on Long Island, and burning Manhattan. The war concludes in the climactic Battle of Danbury, Connecticut. Many historical figures are featured, responding to imaginary events in a manner consistent with their personalities.

Historical Accuracy: The story is based on an actual German war scare, but the dialogue and incidents described are from the author's imagination.

SARAH BOOTH CONROY (1927-)

Conroy was formerly a foreign correspondent for the *Washington Post* stationed in Switzerland, Belize, and Austria. She continues to write occasionally for the *Post* and other newspapers and magazines in addition to heading a multi-million-dollar communications firm.

1259 *Refinements of Love: A Novel about Clover and Henry Adams*

Date of Publication: 1993
Subject(s): Mystery; Literary Life; Politics
Historical character(s): Marian "Clover" Adams, Socialite, Writer; Henry Adams, Writer; John Hay, Political Figure (secretary of state); Grover Cleveland, Political Figure; Henry James, Writer
Time Period(s): 1880s (1885)
Locale(s): Washington, District of Columbia

Summary: The novel is a speculative account of the strange death in 1885 of Henry Adam's wife, Clover. Was she murdered? If so, why? The novel offers an astonishing theory to suggest that Clover's genius may have led to her undoing.

Historical Accuracy: Conroy's theory is bolstered by an elaborate defense in her afterword. The novel is convincing in its depiction of the era, but her sensational interpretation of the events must be seen as more fictional than historical.

ALBERTA CONSTANT (1908-1981)

Born in Texas, Constant served as the educational director of Phi Eta Sorority from 1938 to 1950 and the poetry editor for *Veteran Voices*, a writing project for hospitalized veterans. Constant is the author of a number of children's books as well as adult fiction. Her books include *Those Miller Girls*, and *Paintbox on the Frontier: The Life and Times of George Caleb Bingham*. She also wrote the narrative material for Jack Kilpatrick's symphony *OK*.

1260 *Oklahoma Run*

Date of Publication: 1955
Subject(s): Settlement of the American Frontier
Fictional character(s): Bushrod Sheridan, Settler; Lainey Sheridan, Young Woman; Allegra Sheridan, Settler, Spouse (of Bushrod)
Time Period(s): 1890s
Locale(s): Oklahoma

Summary: During the homesteading days in the Oklahoma Territory, the Sheridan family stakes a claim to some land. Pioneer life is a trial to Allegra, Bushrod Sheridan's wife, but their daughter, Lainey, thrives.

Historical Accuracy: The depiction of frontier life is authentic and convincing.

MAURICE CONSTANTIN-WEYER
(1881-1964)

Born Maurice Constantin (he later appended his second wife's maiden name, Weyer) in Boubonne-les-Bains, France, this writer of 60 volumes of fiction, biography, criticism, history, and memoirs immigrated to Canada in 1904. He settled in Manitoba and drew heavily upon his experiences there to create the historical novels for which he is most remembered. One of these, *Un Homme Se Penche Sur Son Passe* (translated as *A Man and His Past*) won him the French Prix Goncourt. He is also the author of *La Bourrasque* (translated as *A Martyr's Folly*) and *Les Compagnons de la Boule*.

1261 *The Half Breed*

Date of Publication: 1930
Subject(s): Red River Rebellion; Indians; Frontier—Canada
Historical character(s): Louis Riel, Revolutionary
Time Period(s): 19th century
Locale(s): Canada

Summary: The novel tells the story of Louis Riel, Canadian insurgent and leader of two rebellions against the Canadian government. Born of French and metis parents, he leads the rebellion of the Red River settlements against the transfer of power from the Hudson's Bay Company to Canada in 1870. In the 1880s he leads an uprising of Indians and metis in Saskatchewan, for which he is captured, tried for treason, and hanged.

Historical Accuracy: The novel is faithful to the actual events of Riel's life and the issues that drove him to rebellion.

BEATRICE COOGAN

1262 *The Big Wind*

Date of Publication: 1969
Subject(s): Irish Potato Famine; Independence—Ireland; Labor Movement
Fictional character(s): Roderick O'Carroll, Landowner
Historical character(s): Daniel O'Connell, Political Figure
Time Period(s): 1830s; 1840s
Locale(s): Ireland

Summary: This story of 19th century Ireland begins on the night of the famous Big Wind of 1839, the greatest storm ever recorded in Ireland. The story continues in strong scenes of the Irish Famine and the Fenian Land War between the starving Irish peasants and the Anglo-Irish landlords.

Historical Accuracy: The events are solidly based on actuality.

JUDITH COOK (1933-)

An English author born in Manchester, Cook has worked as a writer for the *Guardian*, a freelance investigator, and a political journalist. She won the 1980 Margaret Rhondda Award of the Society of Authors for investigative reporting on the effects of Agent Orange.

1263 *The Slicing Edge of Death*

Date of Publication: 1993
Subject(s): Elizabethan Period; Mystery; Espionage
Historical character(s): Christopher Marlowe, Writer (playwright)
Time Period(s): 16th century (1593)
Locale(s): London, England

Summary: The novel offers a fictional solution to the actual historical mystery of the death of Elizabethan playwright Christopher Marlowe's death. Marlowe's ignominious end in a Deptford tavern after a night of gambling and carousing may have resulted from his involvement in a clandestine espionage mission for the queen and with Sir Walter Raleigh's secret society, the School of Night.

Historical Accuracy: Cook offers a credible solution to the enigma of Marlowe's end, mixing fiction and fact in an entertaining fashion.

ROBERTA ST. CLAIR COOK

1264 *The Thing about Clarissa*

Date of Publication: 1958
Subject(s): Settlement of the American Frontier
Fictional character(s): Clarissa Cameron, Young Woman
Time Period(s): 1830s (1837)
Locale(s): Ohio

Summary: This tale of life along the Ohio frontier in the 1830s concerns Clarissa Cameron who returns home from Mme. Gaillard's Female Academy in Philadelphia fully educated in the ways of correct female behavior. The novel's plot contrasts this education with the practical one she receives.

Historical Accuracy: The author has derived many of her facts from the papers and records of her grandmother to capture authentically the atmosphere of the era.

WILL COOK

1265 *Elizabeth, By Name*

Date of Publication: 1958
Subject(s): American West; Reconstruction Period
Fictional character(s): Elizabeth Rettig, Young Woman
Time Period(s): 1870s
Locale(s): Texas

Summary: On the north Texas prairie during the 1870s, Elizabeth Rettig survives a buffalo stampede that kills her brother. Despite the threat of Indian attack, she starts a trading company on the cattle trail to Dodge City.

Historical Accuracy: This is an authentic and believable portrait of the period and the region.

DAVID COXE COOKE (1917-)

Born in Delaware, Cooke served as a war correspondent in Europe during World War II. A magazine editor as well as a freelance writer, Cooke won an Edgar Award for his outstanding contribution to the detective story.

1266 *The Post of Honor*

Date of Publication: 1958
Subject(s): American West; Indians
Fictional character(s): Calhoun Smith, Young Man; Louise Hunt, Young Woman
Time Period(s): 1860s (1868)
Locale(s): Arizona

Summary: Calhoun Smith, a man bent on vengeance, and Louise Hunt, a young woman from Philadelphia, come together at an outpost in the Arizona Territory. Their growing love for each other is threatened by marauding Apaches.

Historical Accuracy: The novel's melodramatic romance shares the stage with an authentic depiction of Indian fighting during the period.

JOHN BYRNE COOKE

1267 *The Snowblind Moon*

Date of Publication: 1985
Subject(s): American West; Indians
Fictional character(s): Chris Hardeman, Scout; Lisa Putnam, Rancher; Sun Horse, Indian (Sioux), Chieftain
Time Period(s): 1870s
Locale(s): Powder River, Wyoming

Summary: This western novel concerns the conflict between white settlers and the Indians. A huge cast of characters is employed, including Chris Hardeman, a former army scout; Lisa Putnam, a rancher sympathetic to the Indians; and the Sioux Chief Sun Horse, who is being forced onto a reservation.

Historical Accuracy: The novel excels in capturing the atmosphere of the period with convincing historical details.

1268 *South of the Border*

Date of Publication: 1989
Subject(s): American West; Crime and Criminals; Mexican Revolution
Historical character(s): Charlie Siringo, Lawman; Butch Cassidy, Outlaw
Time Period(s): 1910s (1919)
Locale(s): Delgado, Mexico

Summary: This autobiographical account of Charlie Siringo, an actual ex-Pinkerton agent, tells how he and outlaw Butch Cassidy found themselves guarding a film company's payroll in Mexico. Siringo alone knows the true identity of Cassidy. The story features a battle between the Mexican troops and Pancho Villa's rebels.

Historical Accuracy: The novel's research is evident in this authentic portrait of the period.

JOHN ESTEN COOKE (1830-1886)

An author of romances set in his native Virginia, Cooke joined the Confederate army in the Civil War and published *The Life of Stonewall Jackson*. His Civil War romances include *Surry of Eagle's Nest*, *Hilt to Hilt*, and *Mohun*. In all his work, the past is highly idealized and entertaining.

1269 *The Virginia Comedians*

Date of Publication: 1854
Subject(s): American Colonies
Fictional character(s): Champ Effingham, Gentleman (dandy); Beatrice Hallam, Actress; Charles Waters, Gentleman
Time Period(s): 1760s (1763)
Locale(s): Williamsburg, Virginia, American Colonies

Summary: Cooke's story is a romance of hidden identities and melodramatic action set in colonial Virginia. Champ, the young son of a Virginia planter, falls in love with an actress, prompting predictable disapproval from the gentry. He has a rival for the woman's affection, and when they fight Champ leaves Virginia thinking he has killed his opponent. Happy marriages are finally arranged as news of the passing of the Stamp Act shifts attention to the political struggle ahead.

Historical Accuracy: Cooke's tale is well-grounded in the history of Virginia, and the picture of time and place compensates for the contrivance and sentimentality.

JOHN PEYTON COOKE

1270 *Torsos*

Date of Publication: 1994
Subject(s): Mystery; Homosexuality; Depression Era
Historical character(s): Eliot Ness, Government Official (FBI agent)
Time Period(s): 1930s (1933-1938)
Locale(s): Cleveland, Ohio

Summary: This mystery is based on the actual torso murders by a serial killer who terrorized Cleveland during the 1930s, pursued by FBI agent Eliot Ness. The novel's thesis is that the killer was a homosexual sadist who chose his victims from among the city's underworld of pimps and prostitutes.

Historical Accuracy: The novel stays close to the known facts and the historical chronology but elaborates with speculation and a sensationalism that overpowers an otherwise genuine look at Depression-era Cleveland.

WILLIAM VICTOR COOKE (1942-)

A British poet, novelist, literary critic, biographer, and historian, Cooke has taught at several British private schools. His books include *Edward Thomas: A Critical Biography*; *Builder*, a book of poetry; and *The Keys of England*, a historical novel.

1271 *The Keys of England*

Date of Publication: 1929
Subject(s): Middle Ages; Barons' War
Fictional character(s): Garth Alysin, Sailor
Time Period(s): 13th century
Locale(s): England

Summary: This romantic adventure story is set in England during the Barons' War. The novel concerns the exploits of Garth Alysin in scores of narrow escapes, sea battles, and a very complicated romantic dilemma.

Historical Accuracy: The novel mixes fact and history into an exciting adventure tale that is unfortunately betrayed by a number of modern turns of thought and speech.

CATHERINE COOKSON (1906-)

Cookson was born in Tyne Dock, England. She received the Winifred Holtby Award for the best regional novel from the Royal Society of Literature in 1968 for *The Round Tower*. Her books are read avidly in 30 countries. In the early 1980s sales in paperbacks alone reached 27 million. No fewer than 50 titles of her books have been in print at any one time over the last decade.

1272 *The Bannaman Legacy*

Date of Publication: 1985
Subject(s): Romance; Family Saga
Fictional character(s): Roddy Greenback, Orphan; Mary Ellen Lee, Young Woman
Time Period(s): 19th century
Locale(s): Northumberland, England

Summary: The story spans three generations in the 19th century. The violent death of Roddy Greenback's father in 1807 is the catalyst for a tale of vengeance that plays itself out in succeeding generations. Roddy is raised an orphan but is haunted by the truth of what happened to his father, alienating him from those who care for him.

Historical Accuracy: The novel features good locale and period details.

1273 *The Black Candle*

Date of Publication: 1989
Subject(s): Class Conflict; Victorian Period
Fictional character(s): Bridget Mordaunt, Businesswoman (candle and blacking factory); Joseph Skinner, Worker (factory worker); Douglas Filmore, Gentleman
Time Period(s): 19th century; 20th century (1883-1925)
Locale(s): England

Summary: Bridget Mordaunt oversees a candle factory she inherited as a young girl. She becomes involved in the fate of Joseph Skinner, a factory employee who is unjustly accused of murder. She also finds herself connected to the fate of a fading aristocratic family in this novel of class conflict and village life.

Historical Accuracy: The novel offers well-rounded and believable characters and a convincing setting.

1274 *The Black Velvet Gown*

Date of Publication: 1984
Subject(s): Romance; Class Conflict
Fictional character(s): Maria Millican, Widow(er), Servant; Biddy Millican, Servant; Laurence Gullington, Gentleman
Time Period(s): 1820s

Locale(s): Northumberland, England

Summary: Class difference and the limited opportunity for the poor in the 19th century set the tension in this story of a mother and her daughter. Maria Millican is a widow who works at the manor house where her daughter, Biddy, is encouraged to learn. Knowledge, however, can be a curse in this world where servants need only limited skills.

Historical Accuracy: The class differences and regional details are strongly and authentically presented.

1275 *The Cinderpath*

Date of Publication: 1978
Subject(s): World War I; Edwardian Period; Childhood
Fictional character(s): Edward MacFell, Gentleman; Charlie MacFell, Military Personnel (British soldier)
Time Period(s): 1900s; 1910s (1900s-1918)
Locale(s): England; Western Front, France (during World War I)

Summary: The pain of an Edwardian childhood dominated by a strict disciplinarian, Edward MacFell, is played out in the development of his son, Charlie, who shows himself to be a man of substance after all by enduring the tortures of the western front in World War I.

Historical Accuracy: The novel's period details are convincingly presented in this story of childhood pain with adult consequences.

1276 *The Gambling Man*

Date of Publication: 1975
Subject(s): Victorian Period
Fictional character(s): Rory Connor, Businessman (rent collector), Gambler; Charlotte Kean, Gentlewoman; Janie Waggett, Servant (nursemaid)
Time Period(s): 1870s
Locale(s): Tyneside, England

Summary: The rise and fall of Rory Connor, the son of a steelworker in the north of England, is depicted. Connor is ambitious and daring, which causes others to either love or hate him. Two women are connected with his story, Janie, a childhood friend, and Charlotte, the daughter of the property owner for whom Rory works.

Historical Accuracy: The novel is a remarkably honest depiction of mixed characters and full of realistic regional and period painting.

1277 *The Girl*

Date of Publication: 1977
Subject(s): Victorian Period; Romance
Fictional character(s): Hannah Boyle, Bastard Daughter; Anne Thornton, Gentlewoman; Fred Loam, Gentleman
Time Period(s): 1850s
Locale(s): England

Summary: Hannah Boyle's mother reveals to her that her father is one of the well-born Thornton family. Hannah is taken in by the family and must endure the cruelty of Anne Thornton and a marriage to Fred Loam, a man she does not

love. Hannah's story is one of adversity that must be surmounted before any ultimate happiness is possible.

Historical Accuracy: Cookson is best in the locale painting that renders the period customs with precision and authenticity.

1278 *The Harrogate Secret*

Date of Publication: 1988
Subject(s): Childhood; Suspense
Fictional character(s): Freddie Musgrave, Worker (errand boy); Maggie Hewitt, Businesswoman
Time Period(s): 19th century (1815-1850s)
Locale(s): Tyneside, England

Summary: A young boy, Freddie Musgrave, who supports himself by running messages, ventures one night to the great house of the The Towers. There he witnesses something that will alter his life. He is bribed into silence, but years later the past returns with important consequences.

Historical Accuracy: There are good details of a coal-mining and ship-building town of the period.

1279 *The Love Child*

Date of Publication: 1990
Subject(s): Romance; Victorian Period
Fictional character(s): Nathaniel Martell, Gentleman; Maria Dagshaw, Gentlewoman; Anna Dagshaw, Young Woman; Timothy Barrington, Gentleman
Time Period(s): 1880s
Locale(s): Northumberland, England

Summary: The Dagshaw family is stigmatized by the fact that Nathaniel Martell and Maria Dagshaw never married. Their eldest daughter, Anna, meets and falls in love with Timothy Barrington and must contend with prejudice and persecution in trying to fulfil a relationship with him.

Historical Accuracy: The novel's premise is somewhat strained, but there are strong regional and period details.

1280 *The Mallen Girl*

Date of Publication: 1973
Subject(s): Family Saga; Victorian Period; Romance
Fictional character(s): Anna Brigmore, Governess; Barbara Mallen, Ward, Gentlewoman; Daniel Bensham, Gentleman
Time Period(s): 1870s
Locale(s): England

Summary: In this second volume of the Mallen family saga, the emphasis is on the second generation, especially the imperious Barbara Mallen. She is only slightly controlled by her governess, Anna Brigmore. Anna also serves the new owners of High Bank Hall, the Benshams, who provide some well-needed normalcy to the dark strains of the Mallens' story.

Historical Accuracy: The novel offers some convincing details of period and regional life.

1281 *The Mallen Lot*

Date of Publication: 1974
Subject(s): Family Saga; Romance; World War I

Fictional character(s): Barbara Mallen, Gentlewoman; Katie Bensham, Gentlewoman; Benjamin Bensham, Military Personnel (British soldier)
Time Period(s): 19th century; 20th century (1880-1917)
Locale(s): England; France

Summary: The Mallen curse, which holds that the Mallens bring trouble and grief to all, is carried on in the next generation in this final novel of Cookson's Mallen trilogy. Barbara Mallen has embarked on a disastrous affair, and her son, Ben, suffers the strains of the First World War.

Historical Accuracy: The novel is a complicated family saga with a strong background of historical events from the Great War.

1282 *The Mallen Streak*

Date of Publication: 1973
Subject(s): Family Saga; Victorian Period; Romance
Fictional character(s): Thomas Mallen, Gentleman; Anna Brigmore, Governess; Donald Radlet, Gentleman
Time Period(s): 1850s; 1860s (1851-1862)
Locale(s): England

Summary: In this first novel of a trilogy about the Mallen family and the tangled branches of their family tree, patriarch Thomas Mallen, who possesses the distinctive family streak of white hair, tries to avoid financial ruin. When scandal arises, he is forced to live in a small cottage with his nieces and their governess, Anna Brigmore. A catalyst for conflict arrives in the form of Donald Radlet who also has the distinctive Mallen streak.

Historical Accuracy: The emphasis is on the family dynamics rather than the historical period. However, the regional description is convincing.

1283 *The Maltese Angel*

Date of Publication: 1992
Subject(s): Rural Life—England; Victorian Period
Fictional character(s): Ward Gibson, Farmer; Fanny McQueen, Dancer; Daisy Mason, Young Woman
Time Period(s): 19th century; 20th century (1880s-1920s)
Locale(s): Durham, England

Summary: Ward Gibson takes up his inheritance of a Durham farm in the 1880s. Expected to marry Daisy Mason, he instead loses his heart to a dancer, Fanny McQueen, whom he marries. This sets off a series of retaliations by the local community who feel Ward has betrayed their expectations and deserted Daisy. The consequences of these circumstances are followed through subsequent decades and generations.

Historical Accuracy: The author's ability to capture rural and period customs is exceptional.

1284 *The Moth*

Date of Publication: 1986
Subject(s): Romance; World War I
Fictional character(s): Robert Bradley, Carpenter; Millie Thorman, Child; Agnes Thorman, Young Woman
Time Period(s): 1910s
Locale(s): Northumberland, England

Summary: This is a love story set in the north of England at the beginning of World War I. Robert Bradley works in his uncle's carpentry shop. He is introduced to the Thorman family by the child Millie. An involvement with Agnes Thorman follows in which class difference, a troubled family, and the war all play important roles.

Historical Accuracy: The novel excels in both period and regional depictions.

1285 *My Beloved Son*

Date of Publication: 1991
Subject(s): Childhood; Inheritance—Disputed
Fictional character(s): Ellen Jebeau, Gentlewoman, Widow(er); Joseph Jebeau, Military Personnel; Arthur Jebeau, Lawyer, Widow(er)
Time Period(s): 1920s; 1930s (1926-1937)
Locale(s): England

Summary: A mother's passionate determination that her young son should succeed is the basis of the novel's tragedies. Ellen Jabeau and her son Joseph, installed in her brother-in-law's estate, set off a series of family conflicts. Years later, Joseph tries to emerge from his mother's control and achieve his own independence.

Historical Accuracy: The novel is set in a locale that Cookson knows intimately, and the period is carefully represented.

1286 *The Parson's Daughter*

Date of Publication: 1987
Subject(s): Romance; Victorian Period
Fictional character(s): Nancy Ann Howard, Young Woman; Dennison Harpcore, Landowner, Rake
Time Period(s): 19th century (late)
Locale(s): Northumberland, England

Summary: Nancy Ann Howard is a parson's daughter who marries Dennison Harpcore, a gambler and a rake. Their marriage is far from happy. When Nancy insists on changes, she sets in motion a chain of events that destroys the great House of Harpcore and alters the course of her life.

Historical Accuracy: The novel features strong regional details.

1287 *The Rag Nymph*

Date of Publication: 1991
Subject(s): Childhood; Victorian Period
Fictional character(s): Agnes Winkowski, Businesswoman (rag merchant); Millie Forester, Abandoned Child; Ben, Orphan, Worker
Time Period(s): 1850s (1854)
Locale(s): England

Summary: Millie Forester is abandoned by her mother and taken in by Agnes Winkowski, a rag woman. A growing relationship and mutual dependency develops between Agnes, who has adapted to the harsh Victorian world of grinding poverty and indifference, and Millie, whose development is traced across the backdrop of the Victorian period.

Historical Accuracy: The novel is solidly based on period details that vividly display the fate of unprotected children in a rough and tumble age.

1288 *Tilly*

Date of Publication: 1980
Subject(s): Romance; Family Saga; Class Conflict
Fictional character(s): Tilly Trotter, Young Woman; Mark Sopwith, Gentleman
Time Period(s): 1830s
Locale(s): Tyneside, England

Summary: Tilly Trotter lives with her grandparents in a cottage near the Sopwith estate in the north of England. She endures ostracism, crushing poverty, and the accusation of witchcraft. Through it all Tilly is determined and steadfast. She agrees to become Mark Sopwith's mistress, but not to marry him and bring disgrace to his family.

Historical Accuracy: The novel is firmly rooted in Cookson's native region and offers a compelling and convincing look at the class differences of the period.

1289 *Tilly Alone*

Date of Publication: 1982
Subject(s): Family Saga; Class Conflict
Fictional character(s): Tilly Sopwith, Heroine; Simon Bentwood, Gentleman; Steve McGrath, Gentleman
Time Period(s): 1850s
Locale(s): Tyneside, England (in Northumberland)

Summary: In the concluding novel of the trilogy, Tilly returns home from Texas, now the lady of Sopwith Manor. She is hated by the gentry and the villagers as an upstart and worse. She endures all, including her old nemesis, Simon Brentwood, before finding happiness with another old friend, Steve McGrath.

Historical Accuracy: The novel, like the two preceding volumes, is a long exercise in adversity for Tilly. Here the class differences of Cookson's familiar regional locale are demonstrated with credibility.

1290 *Tilly Wed*

Date of Publication: 1981
Subject(s): American West; Indians; Family Saga
Fictional character(s): Tilly Trotter, Young Woman; Matthew Sopwith, Gentleman
Time Period(s): 1840s
Locale(s): Tyneside, England (in Northumberland); Texas

Summary: Adversity continues for Tilly Trotter in the second volume of Cookson's Tilly trilogy. Her lover, Mark Sopwith, dies, and Tilly agrees to marry his son, Matthew, and accompany him to Texas. There, frontier life must be surmounted, as well as the constant threat of Indian attacks. As at home, Tilly shows herself to be ever determined and resourceful.

Historical Accuracy: Cookson admits that her foray into the Texas frontier represents foreign territory and that the details owe a great debt to published sources rather than first-hand experience.

1291 *The Whip*

Date of Publication: 1983
Subject(s): Romance
Fictional character(s): Emma Molinero, Orphan; Ralph Bowman, Artist; Barney Yorkless, Farmer; Henry Granger, Religious (parson)
Time Period(s): 19th century
Locale(s): Tyneside, England (in Northumberland)

Summary: The orphan daughter of a local farm girl and an itinerant Spanish carnival performer, Emma Molinero is sent to live with her maternal grandmother in Northumberland. She becomes a figure of fascination, particularly for her skill with a whip, a legacy from her performing father. Emma has relationships with a variety of suitors: an artist, a farmer, and ultimately, the village parson.

Historical Accuracy: The regional details are authentic and convincing.

1292 *The Wingless Bird*

Date of Publication: 1991
Subject(s): Romance; World War I
Fictional character(s): Agnes Conway, Worker; Jessie Conway, Student; Charles Farrier, Gentleman
Time Period(s): 1910s; 1920s (1913-1923)
Locale(s): England

Summary: Agnes Conway's struggle to keep her family together and make a better life form the novel's drama. She works selflessly in her parents' small store while her sister Jessie is pampered and sent to secretarial school to better her lot in life. Those plans are halted when Jessie becomes pregnant. Success seems secure when Agnes marries Charles Farrier, but World War I intervenes. The novel is a character study in determination and coping with adversity.

Historical Accuracy: There are strong regional details and a convincing war background.

DANE COOLIDGE (1873-1940)

Born in Massachusetts, novelist and naturalist Coolidge graduated from Stanford University in 1898 and became a field collector of animals, birds, and reptiles in the western United States and elsewhere. His novels of the old West include *Hidden Water*, *The Fighting Fool*, *The Fighting Danites*, *Hell's Hip Pocket*, and *Gringo Gold*.

1293 *Gringo Gold*

Date of Publication: 1939
Subject(s): Gold Rush—California; Crime and Criminals
Historical character(s): Joaquin Murieta, Outlaw
Time Period(s): 1840s (1849)
Locale(s): California

Summary: This tale of California during the Gold Rush is based on the actual experiences of Mexican bandit Joaquin Murrieta. The source for the novel is an account of Murrieta given to the author by the daughter of a Texas Ranger who was captured during the war with Mexico.

Historical Accuracy: The novel's authenticity is evident in the period elements and events.

ELEANOR COONEY

DANIEL ALTIERI

1294 *The Court of the Lion*

Date of Publication: 1989
Subject(s): Chinese Empire; Royalty—China
Historical character(s): Hsuan-tsung, Ruler (Chinese emperor); An Lu-Shan, Military Personnel; Kao Li-shih, Political Figure
Time Period(s): 8th century (738)
Locale(s): China

Summary: This novel of the T'ang dynasty in the 8th century tells a story of intrigue in the court of Emperor Hsuan-tsung, whose weakness provides an opening for others intent on seizing power. It falls to the eunuch Kao Li-shih to protect the dynasty from threats within and without.

Historical Accuracy: This is a massive re-creation of a fascinating period of Chinese history told with conviction and insight.

1295 *Deception*

Date of Publication: 1993
Subject(s): Chinese Empire; Royalty—China; Mystery
Historical character(s): Dee Jen-dieh, Judge; Wu Chao, Ruler (Chinese empress)
Time Period(s): 7th century; 8th century (651-706)
Locale(s): China

Summary: In the imperial court, Lady Wu Chao, the favorite concubine of the emperor, is climbing to power. Meanwhile, Judge Dee Jen-chen begins an investigation of a series of grotesque and inexplicable murders of wealthy families.

Historical Accuracy: The novel vividly chronicles a colorful period of Chinese history.

COURTNEY RYLEY COOPER (1886-1940)

A press agent, journalist, and novelist, Cooper is known for his graphic accounts of the old West and homesteading, set in unruly Oklahoma, Colorado, and Oregon in the 1840s. His novels include *Circus Day*; *Designs in Scarlet*, a crime novel; *Here's to Crime*; and *The Pioneers*.

1296 *The Pioneers*

Date of Publication: 1938
Subject(s): American West; Wagon Trains
Fictional character(s): Judith Barton, Young Woman
Historical character(s): Kit Carson, Frontiersman
Time Period(s): 1840s (1842)
Locale(s): Oregon Trail, United States

Summary: This western romance concerns a wagon train expedition across the Oregon Trail led by Kit Carson. The details of the crossing are joined with the conspiracy of a U.S. senator to betray the settlers to the fur trading interests.

Historical Accuracy: The details are too often implausible and the plot too far-fetched to be taken as an authentic picture of actual events along the Oregon Trail.

J. CALIFORNIA COOPER

An American writer born in Berkeley, California, Cooper is the author of plays, short stories, and novels for children and adults.

1297 *Family*

Date of Publication: 1991
Subject(s): Antebellum South; Slavery; Fantasy
Fictional character(s): Clora, Slave, Spirit
Time Period(s): 19th century; 20th century
Locale(s): South

Summary: When Clora, a slave in the pre-Civil War South, commits suicide to stop the continual debasement she endures from her master, she becomes a ghost who watches over her family for the next hundred years as they become free and prosperous.

Historical Accuracy: Though fantastical, the novel does feature an authentic depiction of the various eras represented.

JAMES FENIMORE COOPER (1789-1851)

Cooper was an American author who grew up at his family's estate at Cooperstown in upstate New York. He entered the Navy in 1805 after being expelled from Yale for misconduct. He served for six years and based many of his stories on his naval experiences. Cooper took up a literary career at age 30 when his wife challenged his claim that he could write a better book than the English novel he was reading. His novels are mostly set in the past, and his Leather-stocking Tales, five novels depicting early frontier America, are his most enduring works. Cooper is considered the first major American novelist.

1298 *The Bravo*

Date of Publication: 1831
Subject(s): Renaissance; Espionage
Fictional character(s): Jacopo Frontoni, Spy, Criminal (hired assassin); Don Camillo Monforte, Nobleman; Violetta Tiepolo, Heiress
Time Period(s): 15th century
Locale(s): Venice, Italy

Summary: A departure for Cooper from his American wilderness and sea adventures, the novel is set in Venice during the Renaissance and centers on the intrigues of Jacopo Frontoni who, to win the release of his imprisoned father, agrees to serve as a secret agent for the Venetian Senate. Pretending also to be a bravo, or hired assassin, he is suspected of committing a number of political murders. His assistance of a Neapolitan to win the hand of a rich heiress brings on his tragic downfall.

Historical Accuracy: This is an extremely colorful though thin and implausible romance of the Renaissance.

1299 *The Deerslayer*

Date of Publication: 1841
Subject(s): Settlement of the American Frontier; Indians; French and Indian War
Fictional character(s): Natty Bumppo, Frontiersman, Guide; Chingachgook, Indian; Thomas Hutter, Backwoodsman
Time Period(s): 1740s (1740)
Locale(s): Lake Otsego, New York, American Colonies (northern Adirondacks)

Summary: In this first of the Leather-stocking Tales in chronological order, Natty Bumppo, a young woodsman known as Deerslayer, journeys to Lake Otsego to warn another woodsman and his daughters that the Iroquois are on the warpath and to meet his Indian friend Chingachgook. An exciting series of confrontations with the hostiles follows, including dramatic captures and rescues.

Historical Accuracy: Cooper's strength was generating exciting action and the atmosphere of the frontier. Realism of character and incident is far less developed than tone.

1300 *The Headsman; or, The Abbaye des Vignerons*

Date of Publication: 1833
Subject(s): Identity—Concealed; Crime and Criminals
Fictional character(s): Balthazar, Parent; Sigismund, Young Man; Adelheid de Willading, Noblewoman
Time Period(s): 1700s
Locale(s): Berne, Switzerland

Summary: This is a fairytale romance of 18th-century Switzerland concerning the attempt of the executioner of Berne to conceal the identity of his supposed son so that he will not be forced to continue in the family business. A love story between the son and a noble's daughter completes the romance.

Historical Accuracy: There is little of the historical over the make-believe.

1301 *The Heidenmauer*

Date of Publication: 1832
Subject(s): Religious Conflict; Religious Life
Fictional character(s): Count Emich of Leiningen-Hartenburg, Nobleman; Berchtold Hintermayer, Servant (forester); Meta Frey, Young Woman
Time Period(s): 16th century
Locale(s): Durkheim, Bavaria

Summary: The novel dramatizes the battle for control of a Bavarian town in the 16th century between the Benedictines of the abbey of Limburg and a feudal lord. Cooper's theme is the transition from superstition and Catholicism to secular rule and skeptical Protestantism. A love story subplot between the Count's forester and the daughter of a leading citizen is connected to the larger theme.

Historical Accuracy: The novel is more a thesis than a convincing narrative, with thin and idealized characters and situations.

1302 *The Last of the Mohicans*

Date of Publication: 1826
Subject(s): French and Indian War; Indians; Settlement of the American Frontier
Fictional character(s): Natty Bumppo, Frontiersman (aka Hawkeye), Guide; Chingachgook, Indian; Cora Munro, Young Woman; Alice Munro, Young Woman; Magua, Indian (Huron renegade); Uncas, Indian (last of the Mohicans)
Historical character(s): Louis Joseph de Montcalm, Military Personnel (commander French forces/Canada)
Time Period(s): 1750s (1757)
Locale(s): Lake George, New York, American Colonies

Summary: In the second of the Leather-stocking Tales, Cora and Alice Munro journey to join their father, the English commander of Fort William Henry on Lake George in New York during the French and Indian War. Pursuit and capture dominates their story, complicated by the renegade Huron, Magua, and assisted by Hawkeye, Chingachgook, and his son Uncas, whose love for Cora produces the novel's tragic climax.

Historical Accuracy: Cooper's characterization is thin and awkward, yet the details of Indian and wilderness life are appealing and absorbing.

1303 *Lionel Lincoln; or, The Leaguer of Boston*

Date of Publication: 1825
Subject(s): American Revolution; Battle of Bunker Hill; Battle of Lexington
Fictional character(s): Lionel Lincoln, Military Personnel (British officer), Loyalist; Job Pray, Military Personnel (American soldier); Cecil Dynever, Heroine
Time Period(s): 1770s (1775)
Locale(s): Boston, Massachusetts, American Colonies; Lexington, Massachusetts, American Colonies

Summary: This tangled family drama is set in and around Boston during the opening of the American Revolution. Lionel Lincoln's family is split apart as his father and stepbrother take up the rebel cause, and Lincoln serves as a British soldier. There are scenes of the battles at Lexington and Bunker Hill.

Historical Accuracy: Implausible and far-fetched romance elements mar the period detail.

1304 *Mercedes of Castile*

Date of Publication: 1840
Subject(s): Exploration; Sea Story
Fictional character(s): Mercedes, Noblewoman; Don Luis, Gentleman
Historical character(s): Christopher Columbus, Sea Captain, Explorer; Isabella I, Ruler (Queen of Castile); Ferdinand V, Ruler (King of Aragon)
Time Period(s): 15th century (1492)

Locale(s): Spain (Granada, Barcelona, Castile, Aragon); *Santa Maria*, At Sea (across the Atlantic); Haiti

Summary: The novel concerns Columbus' first voyage and the securing of support by Isabella and Ferdinand. Connected to the mission is the romance of Don Luis and Mercedes of Castile, who refuses his love unless he agrees to accompany Columbus on his voyage.

Historical Accuracy: Cooper's sea experience and his reliance on Columbus' journals help the story's authenticity.

1305 *The Pathfinder; or, The Inland Sea*

Date of Publication: 1840
Subject(s): French and Indian War; Settlement of the American Frontier; Indians
Fictional character(s): Natty Bumppo, Frontiersman, Guide; Chingachgook, Indian; Mabel Dunham, Young Woman
Time Period(s): 1750s (1759)
Locale(s): Oswego, New York, American Colonies (on Lake Ontario); Thousand Islands, New York, American Colonies

Summary: This is the third of the Leather-stocking Tales, and it shows Natty Bumppo at the height of his powers and in love for the first and last time. The action takes place around the British fort at Oswego, one of the western-most frontier posts, during an attack by the Iroquois and the French.

Historical Accuracy: Exciting action and authentic atmosphere of the American colonial frontier bolster Cooper's romance.

1306 *The Pilot*

Date of Publication: 1823
Subject(s): American Revolution; Sea Story
Fictional character(s): Richard Barnstable, Sea Captain, Military Personnel; Colonel Howard, Loyalist, Gentleman; Edward Griffith, Military Personnel (naval lieutenant)
Historical character(s): John Paul Jones, Military Personnel (unnamed pilot or navigator)
Time Period(s): 1770s; 1780s (1775-1783)
Locale(s): England (northeast coast)

Summary: An unnamed American naval pilot, known to be John Paul Jones, is involved in an exciting series of land and sea adventures in England during the American Revolution. The action is centered at the home of a former South Carolina loyalist whose two nieces are loved by two of the American naval officers. Cooper set out to prove that a former navy man could write a more convincing sea story than Sir Walter Scott had achieved in *The Pirate*.

Historical Accuracy: This is the first genuine sea story. The novel's accuracy in nautical details owes much to Cooper's six year service in the U.S. Navy.

1307 *The Pioneers; or, The Sources of the Susquehanna*

Date of Publication: 1823
Subject(s): Identity—Concealed; Settlement of the American Frontier
Fictional character(s): Natty Bumppo, Frontiersman, Hunter; John Mohegan, Indian (aka Chingachgook); Marmaduke

Temple, Judge, Landowner; Oliver Edwards, Imposter (aka Edward Oliver Effingham), Heir—Lost; Elizabeth Temple, Gentlewoman
Time Period(s): 1790s
Locale(s): Templeton, New York (fictional Cooperstown, New York); Otsego County, New York (upstate New York)

Summary: This is the first of Cooper's Leather-stocking Tales but the fourth in the chronology of the tales and the life of their central character, Natty Bumppo. An aging Bumppo and Chingachgook find their freedom threatened by encroaching civilization during the decade following the American Revolution. To this elegy for a passing way of life is added a rather implausible romance of concealed identities and lovers' complications.

Historical Accuracy: The novel is the first true romance of the frontier in American literature. Despite a tendency toward the ideal, the novel's details of hunting and trapping life show considerable realism.

1308 *The Prairie*

Date of Publication: 1827
Subject(s): Settlement of the American Frontier; Indians
Fictional character(s): Natty Bumppo, Frontiersman, Guide; Ishmael Bush, Kidnapper; Hard-Heart, Indian
Time Period(s): 1800s (1804)
Locale(s): Western Plains, North America

Summary: The fifth and final of the Leather-stocking Tales chronicles the end of Natty Bumppo's frontier career on the Western Plains. Bumppo, nearly 90, is still resourceful enough to save travellers on a wagon train from Indian attack, prairie fire, and a buffalo stampede. The plot contrivances involve a kidnapping.

Historical Accuracy: There is excessive reliance on coincidence, which diminishes the authenticity of the western atmosphere and the pathos of Bumppo's passing.

1309 *The Red Rover*

Date of Publication: 1827
Subject(s): American Revolution; Sea Story; Pirates
Fictional character(s): Red Rover, Sea Captain (aka Captain Heidegger), Pirate; Henry Ark, Military Personnel (naval lieutenant); Mrs. Wyllys, Governess
Time Period(s): 1770s; 1790s
Locale(s): Newport, Rhode Island; At Sea

Summary: During the American Revolution, Lieutenant Henry Ark, disguised as a common sailor, tracks down the notorious pirate, the Red Rover. Disguises, secret identities, and exciting naval action accelerate this nautical romance.

Historical Accuracy: The romantic coincidences and revelations of secrets jar with the details of naval life, which Cooper based on first-hand experience.

1310 *The Spy: A Tale of the Neutral Ground*

Date of Publication: 1821
Subject(s): American Revolution; Espionage

Fictional character(s): Harvey Birch, Peddler, Spy; Major Peyton Dunwoodie, Patriot, Military Personnel (American army); Captain Henry Wharton, Loyalist, Military Personnel (British army)
Historical character(s): George Washington, Military Personnel (as Mr. Harper)
Time Period(s): 18th century; 19th century (1780s-1810s)
Locale(s): Westchester County, New York; New Jersey

Summary: The story concerns the activities of a peddler, Harvey Birch, who is suspected of being a Loyalist spy during the American Revolution. He is actually in the service of George Washington who appears in the novel in disguise as Mr. Harper. Both Harper and Birch visit a Loyalist family and become involved in complicated family affairs and military action.

Historical Accuracy: The novel is more idealized than realistic. Cooper's purpose is unapologetically patriotic, and his characters are designed to represent ideal types.

1311 *The Water Witch*
Date of Publication: 1830
Subject(s): Pirates; American Colonies; Sea Story
Fictional character(s): Skimmer of the Seas, Sea Captain, Pirate; Alinda de Barberie, Heiress, Fiance(e); Captain Ludlow, Sea Captain, Military Personnel (English naval officer)
Time Period(s): 17th century
Locale(s): New York, New York, American Colonies; Long Island Sound, New York, American Colonies

Summary: The novel describes how a pirate captain, called "The Skimmer of the Seas," abducts an heiress, eludes capture by her suitor—an English captain—and finally becomes a patriotic pirate when the French threaten New York.

Historical Accuracy: This is a fanciful romance relieved only by nautical details that ring true.

1312 *The Wept of Wish-Ton-Wish*
Date of Publication: 1829
Subject(s): American Colonies; Indians; King Philip's War
Fictional character(s): Mark Heathcote, Settler; Narra-mattah, Indian (kidnapped child)
Historical character(s): Metacomet, Indian, Chieftain (of the Wampanoags); Canonchet, Indian, Chieftain (of the Narragansetts)
Time Period(s): 17th century (1666-1676)
Locale(s): Wish-ton-Wish, Connecticut, American Colonies

Summary: The novel is set during King Philip's War, the most successful Indian rising in southern New England. The story concerns a young girl who is abducted by an Indian who turns out to be Canonchet, Chief of the Narragansetts. His intercession on behalf of the Heathcotes results in tragic consequences.

Historical Accuracy: This treatment is a blend of accurate American colonial details and a romantic plot.

JAMIE LEE COOPER
Author and illustrator Cooper was born in Richmond, Indiana, and attended Fairfax Hall and the Cincinnati Art Academy. Cooper's ancestors were among the first settlers in the old Northwest Territory. She wrote *The Castaways* and *The Great Dandelion*.

1313 *The Horn and the Forest*
Date of Publication: 1963
Subject(s): Indians; War of 1812; Battle of Tippecanoe
Fictional character(s): Jonathan Raoul, Widow(er), Doctor; Nathan Raoul, Young Man
Time Period(s): 18th century; 19th century
Locale(s): Indiana

Summary: This story of frontier life in the old Northwest Territory chronicles two generations of pioneers. Jonathan Raoul, a doctor from the East, marries a half-breed woman who bears him twins. His son Nathan's dual heritage prevents him from fighting the Indians when Tecumseh battles the forces of General Benjamin Harrison.

Historical Accuracy: The novel offers an authentic look at the region and its history during the period leading up to the Battle of Tippecanoe.

1314 *Rapaho*
Date of Publication: 1967
Subject(s): American West; Indians
Fictional character(s): Rapaho, Trapper, Frontiersman
Time Period(s): 19th century
Locale(s): West

Summary: Frontiersman Rapaho reminisces about his life as a preacher's son, buffalo hunter, Indian fighter, and trapper. The novel evokes the vanishing American frontier and portrays an individual caught between two conflicting cultures.

Historical Accuracy: This is a genuine picture of frontier life, filled with authentic details and customs.

1315 *Shadow of a Star*
Date of Publication: 1965
Subject(s): Spanish Colonies; Indians
Fictional character(s): Matyeh, Trader; Patche, Trapper, Outlaw; Shonti, Religious (priest)
Time Period(s): 17th century (1680s)

Summary: Set in Spanish New Mexico during the 1680s, the story follows the experiences of three brothers who are forced to flee the Basque region of Spain when their sister is burned as a witch. One becomes a trader, another an outlaw fur trapper, and the third a priest.

Historical Accuracy: The novel is rich in atmosphere and convincing in its details of period life.

KENT COOPER (1880-1965)
An American journalist and publisher, Cooper was born in Columbus, Indiana. From 1943 until his death, Cooper worked as the executive director of the Associated Press and during his tenure there introduced the use of the telephone and the wirephoto. An outspoken advocate of freedom of the press, Cooper wrote *Barriers Down* and *The Right to Know*.

1316 *Anna Zenger: Mother of Freedom*

Date of Publication: 1946

Subject(s): American Colonies; Biography, Fictionalized; Trials

Historical character(s): Anna Zenger, Spouse; Peter Zenger, Journalist; Andrew Hamilton, Lawyer

Time Period(s): 18th century

Locale(s): New York, New York, American Colonies

Summary: This fictionalized biography about Anna Zenger, the wife of colonial New York printer and journalist John Zenger, contends that she wrote the articles in *The New York Weekly Journal* that resulted in her husband's imprisonment and trial.

Historical Accuracy: Though the novel fails to make a case about Anna Zenger, it offers a convincing depiction of colonial New York.

CLAIRE COOPERSTEIN

Cooperstein is also a prize-winning painter, sculptor, and poet.

1317 *Johanna: A Novel of the Van Gogh Family*

Date of Publication: 1995

Subject(s): Biography, Fictionalized; Artistic Life

Historical character(s): Johanna Van Gogh-Bonger, Gentlewoman, Widow(er)

Time Period(s): 19th century; 20th century (1888-1913)

Locale(s): Paris, France; Netherlands

Summary: The role of Vincent Van Gogh's sister-in-law in saving his paintings and reputation from obscurity is recorded in the imagined diary of Johanna Van Gogh, the young widow of Vincent's brother Theo. When Vincent commits suicide, the tragedy leads to Theo's eventual collapse and death six months later. Johanna is left with an infant son and an art collection that few value. She sets out to maintain her independence and in the process helps reclaim Van Gogh's legacy.

Historical Accuracy: The novel's letters and diary entries are invented but based on the known facts.

BONNIE COPELAND (1919-)

Born in Indiana, Copeland graduated from Weber State College and pursued a career in public relations. She regards the research for her historical work as her delight, spending a year or more on background research for each book.

1318 *Lady of Moray*

Date of Publication: 1979

Subject(s): Middle Ages; Royalty—Scotland

Fictional character(s): Gruoch, Royalty, Spouse (of Macbeth); Boite, Nobleman (Earl of Moray)

Historical character(s): Macbeth, Ruler (King of Scotland); Duncan I, Ruler (King of Scotland)

Time Period(s): 11th century (1050s)

Locale(s): Scotland

Summary: The novel attempts to paint a fuller historical account of Shakespeare's cold-blooded murderer, Lady Macbeth. Little is known in fact about the actual Lady Macbeth, but the novel offers a plausible account of Gruoch, daughter of Boite, Earl of Moray. When King Malcolm illegally names his grandson Duncan his heir, Gruoch begins her own climb to the throne that involves an ambitious pact with Duncan's lieutenant, Lord Macbeth.

Historical Accuracy: The novel's account is fictional but rooted in the atmosphere of the period.

ALFRED COPPEL (1921-)

Born in California, Coppel attended Stanford University. He served as a fighter pilot during World War II. Although his novels cover a range of genres, his forte is espionage fiction.

1319 *The Marburg Chronicles*

Date of Publication: 1985

Subject(s): Family Saga; Civil War—U.S.

Fictional character(s): Adriana Santana, Gentlewoman; Micah Marburg, Banker; Aaron Marburg, Military Personnel

Time Period(s): 19th century (1860-1899)

Locale(s): Santanilla, Spain; San Francisco, California; Mexico

Summary: Three generations and over 50 years of family history are chronicled, beginning with Adriana Santana, who falls in love with a Jewish banker, Micah Marburg. Their destiny together takes them to America, where their son Aaron fights in the Battle of the Wilderness in the Civil War. The dynasty is continued in San Francisco.

Historical Accuracy: The scope of the novel is vast and panoramic, covering many years and a myriad of characters. The atmosphere and period details are solidly depicted.

HENRY W. CORAY (1904-)

1320 *Son of Tears*

Date of Publication: 1957

Subject(s): Roman Empire; Religious Life; Biography, Fictionalized

Historical character(s): Augustine, Religious (bishop), Philosopher; Monica, Gentlewoman

Time Period(s): 4th century; 5th century

Locale(s): Hippo, Africa (in present-day Algeria); Carthage, Ancient Civilization; Rome, Roman Empire

Summary: This biographical novel captures the career of St. Augustine, who is considered second only to St. Paul as the founder of Western theology. Augustine's youth in North Africa, his defiance of his mother, and his flirtation with Manichaeism are dramatized, as well as Augustine's conversion experience and his years as the bishop of Hippo.

Historical Accuracy: The novel is scrupulous in its research and documentation of Augustine's life and times.

ELIZABETH CORBETT (1887-1981)

A prolific American novelist, poet, and author, Elizabeth Corbett was born in Aurora, Illinois, and attended the University of Wisconsin. She wrote a number of historical novels that were often set during the Civil War. Among her books are *Puritan and Pagan*, *Out at the Soldiers Home* (an autobiography), and *Sunday at Six*.

1321 *The Far Down*

Date of Publication: 1939
Subject(s): Family Saga
Fictional character(s): Tim Malone, Veteran (Civil War); Madge Malone, Young Woman; Tessie Malone, Young Woman
Time Period(s): 1870s
Locale(s): Midwest

Summary: Life in the Midwest during the 1870s is dramatized in the experiences of the Malone family. Tim Malone is a veteran of the Civil War, and after his death, his large family must struggle to make their way in the world.

Historical Accuracy: The novel features a great deal of accurate period painting.

1322 *Faye's Folly*

Date of Publication: 1941
Subject(s): Civil War—U.S.; Rural Life—U.S.
Fictional character(s): Sheba Faye, Farmer
Time Period(s): 1860s
Locale(s): Illinois

Summary: The Civil War era is reflected as it affects the Faye family on their Illinois farm. The novel provides a vivid portrait of the politics of the period as the great events of the war make their impact on the homefront.

Historical Accuracy: The novel provides a genuine look at the region and the period.

CHARLES CORCORAN

1323 *Blackrobe*

Date of Publication: 1938
Subject(s): Exploration; Indians
Historical character(s): Jacques Marquette, Explorer, Religious (missionary); Louis Jolliet, Explorer
Time Period(s): 17th century
Locale(s): Mississippi River, Mississippi River, North America; Canada

Summary: Based on Jacques Marquette's discovery of the Mississippi River, the novel recounts the adventures of the Jesuit missionary and explorer. He and Louis Jolliet were the first to confirm the existence of the great river running south to the Gulf of Mexico. The novel captures the hardships of the journeys.

Historical Accuracy: The novel blends the invented with the factual, but stays close to known history.

WILLIAM CORCORAN

1324 *Golden Horizons*

Date of Publication: 1937
Subject(s): Settlement of the American Frontier; Farming
Fictional character(s): Allan Harper, Farmer
Time Period(s): 1870s
Locale(s): Kansas

Summary: This western tale concerns the clash between settlement and frontier life. Allan Harper, a Yankee farmer, struggles to introduce winter wheat, which will remake the prairie, while attempting to clean up the area's lawlessness.

Historical Accuracy: The novel's setting and situations are authentic.

ALEXANDER CORDELL
(PSEUD. OF GEORGE ALEXANDER GRABER, 1914-)

Sri Lankan author Cordell was born in Colombia, Ceylon, into a family of English soldiers. He grew up in North China, Egypt, Hong Kong, and Ceylon, and has worked as a civil surveyor in Wales. Cordell began writing in 1950.

1325 *The Rape of the Fair Country*

Date of Publication: 1959
Subject(s): Chartist Revolt; Labor Movement
Fictional character(s): Iestyn Mortymer, Worker (iron worker); Hywel Mortymer, Worker (iron worker)
Time Period(s): 1820s; 1830s (1826-1837)
Locale(s): Wales

Summary: The Chartist uprising of the 1830s is seen through its effects on a family of Welsh iron workers. The Mortymer family struggles with the impact of the industrial revolution and the workers' lack of power. Labor disputes and dissatisfaction explode into the political action of the Chartists, advocates of a "People's Charter" for universal suffrage, secret ballots, and other voting reforms.

Historical Accuracy: The novel is an authentic re-creation of the period and its effect on a family.

1326 *This Sweet and Bitter Earth*

Date of Publication: 1977
Subject(s): Labor Movement; Mining
Fictional character(s): Toby Davies, Miner
Time Period(s): 1900s; 1910s
Locale(s): Wales

Summary: Toby Davies flees the harsh slate quarries in the north of Wales only to become involved in the bitter miners' struggle that explodes into the notorious riots of 1910. The novel details the events and the lives of the Welsh miners in a story of courage and endurance.

Historical Accuracy: The novel is convincing in its ability to render both the historical events and the customs of the miners.

MARIE CORELLI
(PSEUD. OF MARY MACKAY, 1855-1924)

British pianist and writer Corelli was the illegitimate daughter of the songwriter Charles Mackay. In 1884, she made her successful musical debut. Corelli was shunned by the literary establishment of her day but was an enormously popular writer. She has been called the first modern bestselling author. Her most famous book, *The Sorrows of Satan*, was praised by Queen Victoria and at the time of Corelli's death had gone through 60 editions.

1327 *Barabbas: A Dream of the World's Tragedy*

Date of Publication: 1893
Subject(s): Biblical Story
Fictional character(s): Judith Iscariot, Young Woman
Historical character(s): Barabbas, Biblical Figure, Outlaw; Judas Iscariot, Biblical Figure
Time Period(s): 1st century
Locale(s): Jerusalem, Israel

Summary: This biblical romance dramatizes the last days of Christ—his betrayal, crucifixion, and resurrection. The true villain of the story is not the thief Barabbas but Judas Iscariot's sister, Judith, who is responsible both for Barabbas' crimes and for her brother's betrayal of Christ. Barabbas dies in prison after being converted to Christianity.

Historical Accuracy: The story is more of a fanciful invention than a faithful depiction of the biblical story. It does, however, show a certain amount of study of period Jewish manners and customs.

LUCY CORES

1328 *Katya*

Date of Publication: 1980
Subject(s): Romance; Russian Empire
Fictional character(s): Lisa Vorontzou, Gentlewoman; Katya Vorontzou, Bastard Daughter
Time Period(s): 1800s
Locale(s): St. Petersburg, Russia; Moscow, Russia

Summary: This is a tale of glamour and intrigue in Russian high society at the beginning of the 19th century. It is the story of two daughters of Count Vorontzou: Lisa and the illegitimate Katya. When the count dies, Katya is ousted from her home and must make her own way.

Historical Accuracy: The period touches are well done and convincing.

1329 *The Year of December*

Date of Publication: 1974
Subject(s): Royalty—Russia; Decembrist Uprising
Fictional character(s): Grisha Volynski, Royalty (prince)
Historical character(s): Claire Clairmont, Gentlewoman, Governess; Ivan Pushchin, Revolutionary
Time Period(s): 1820s (1825)

Locale(s): Moscow, Russia

Summary: The novel tells the fascinating story of Claire Clairmont, stepsister of Mary Shelley and mistress of Lord Byron. In 1825 Claire is employed as a governess in a wealthy Moscow household. There she becomes involved in the ferment of protest against the repression of Czar Alexander I, which culminates in the tragic and doomed Decembrist Uprising.

Historical Accuracy: The timetable of Claire Clairmont's presence in Moscow is accurate, though the suggestion of her affairs and involvement in the uprising is speculative.

EDWIN CORLE (1906-1956)

Born in New Jersey, Corle was the author of a number of books on the Southwest. His novels include *Fig Tree John*, about a 19th- century Apache's troubled relationships with whites, and *People on Earth*, a less tragic handling of the same theme. His desert stories are collected in *Mohave*; his nonfiction includes *Desert Country* and *The Gila, River of the Southwest*.

1330 *Billy the Kid*

Date of Publication: 1953
Subject(s): American West; Biography, Fictionalized; Lincoln County War
Historical character(s): William Bonney, Outlaw (Billy the Kid); Pat Garrett, Lawman; Lew Wallace, Political Figure, Writer
Time Period(s): 19th century (1859-1881)
Locale(s): Lincoln County, New Mexico

Summary: The short and murderous outlaw career of Billy the Kid is dramatized. Dead at the age of 21 and credited with 21 murders, William H. Bonney is shown as a product and a victim of his times, at the center of the Lincoln County cattle war.

Historical Accuracy: The novel is for the most part faithful to the known facts. Occasionally, incidents are invented, such as Billy's meeting with New Mexico governor Lew Wallace.

MARIBELLE CORMACK (1902-1984)

WILLIAM P. ALEXANDER

Born in Buffalo, New York, Cormack graduated from Cornell University and received a master's degree from Brown University. She is known for her strong interest in astronomy and is the author of *First Book of Stones*, *Road to Down Under*, and *Land for My Sons*.

1331 *Land for My Sons*

Date of Publication: 1939
Subject(s): American Revolution; Indians
Fictional character(s): Michael Marshall, Scout
Time Period(s): 1770s
Locale(s): Pennsylvania, American Colonies

Summary: This tale of the western frontier during the American Revolution centers on the young surveyor and scout, Michael Marshall, who joins Washington's army when the fighting begins. Marshall is charged with making contact with Cornplanter, the chief of the Senecas.

Historical Accuracy: The novel is an authentic portrait of the period.

DOROTHY HELEN CORNISH

1332 *These Were the Brontes*

Date of Publication: 1940
Subject(s): Victorian Period; Literary Life
Historical character(s): Charlotte Bronte, Writer; Emily Bronte, Writer; Anne Bronte, Writer
Time Period(s): 19th century
Locale(s): Haworth, England (Yorkshire)

Summary: The novel sets out to capture the strange and tragic story of the Bronte family in this semi-biographical account. At the center of the tale is Charlotte Bronte's growth to maturity and literary genius.

Historical Accuracy: The novel observes the basic outlines of the Brontes' lives, with plausible surmises offered when facts fail.

BERNARD CORNWELL (1944-)

Born in London, Cornwell worked for the B.B.C. before turning to writing full-time. He moved to the United States in 1980. His series of novels involving Richard Sharp is modeled after C.S. Forester's Horatio Hornblower books and spring from Cornwell's life-long fascination with the Duke of Wellington and his armies. Cornwell is currently in the middle of a new series of novels concerning the American Civil War.

1333 *Battle Flag*

Date of Publication: 1995
Subject(s): Civil War—U.S.; Battle of Bull Run; Military Life
Fictional character(s): Nate Starbuck, Military Personnel (Confederate officer); William Faulconer, Military Personnel (Confederate general); Elial Starbuck, Religious (clergyman)
Historical character(s): Robert E. Lee, Military Personnel (Confederate commander); Thomas Jonathan Jackson, Military Personnel (Confederate officer)
Time Period(s): 1860s (1862)
Locale(s): Virginia

Summary: The third volume of the author's Starbuck Chronicles is set against the background of the decisive Civil War military action of 1862 that culminates in the second Battle of Bull Run. Starbuck, now a Confederate officer, distinguishes himself at the Battle of Cedar Mountain but conflict with General Faulconer, his former patron who is now his brigade commander, reaches a climax at Dead Mary's Ford.

Historical Accuracy: The battle action is based on actual events and some of the activities attributed to the fictional characters are based on actuality as well.

1334 *The Bloody Ground*

Date of Publication: 1996
Subject(s): Civil War—U.S.; Battle of Antietam; Military Life
Fictional character(s): Nate Starbuck, Military Personnel (Confederate officer); Adam Faulconer, Military Personnel (Union officer)
Historical character(s): George McClellan, Military Personnel (Union commander); Thomas Jonathan Jackson, Military Personnel (Confederate general); Robert E. Lee, Military Personnel (Confederate commander); Allan Pinkerton, Detective—Private
Time Period(s): 1860s (1862)
Locale(s): Maryland; Virginia; Washington, District of Columbia

Summary: The fourth volume in "The Starbuck Chronicles" moves from the Confederate victory at Second Bull Run/Manassas to the Battle of Antietam, the bloodiest single day in the Civil War. Lee decides to cross the Potomac in the South's first invasion of the North. Starbuck is sent to Richmond in charge of a punishment battalion before taking part in Stonewall Jackson's capture of Harper's Ferry and Antietam.

Historical Accuracy: The fictional elements are interwoven with accurately described historical events.

1335 *Copperhead*

Date of Publication: 1994
Subject(s): Civil War—U.S.; Military Life; Peninsular Campaign
Fictional character(s): Nate Starbuck, Military Personnel (Confederate soldier); Thomas Truslow, Military Personnel (Confederate soldier); Adam Faulconer, Military Personnel (Confederate soldier)
Historical character(s): Oliver Wendell Holmes, Military Personnel (Union soldier), Judge; Jefferson Davis, Political Figure (President of the Confederacy); George McClellan, Military Personnel (Union commander); Joseph E. Johnston, Military Personnel (Confederate general)
Time Period(s): 1860s (1862)
Locale(s): Virginia

Summary: In the second year of the Civil War, Nate Starbuck, a young Bostonian fighting for the Confederacy, is accused of being a Yankee spy. To clear himself and discover the identity of the real secret agent, he undertakes a hazardous ride through the Union lines as the Peninsular Campaign rages.

Historical Accuracy: The author's description of the military scenes are first rate and accurate.

1336 *Rebel*

Date of Publication: 1993
Subject(s): Civil War—U.S.; Military Life; Battle of Bull Run
Fictional character(s): Nate Starbuck, Military Personnel; Washington Faulconer, Landowner, Military Personnel
Time Period(s): 1860s (1861)
Locale(s): Richmond, Virginia; Manassas, Virginia

Summary: Nate Starbuck runs away from his stern father's control and arrives in Richmond, Virginia, on the eve of the Civil War. Rescued from a Yankee-hating mob by Washington Faulconer, he joins Faulconer's regiment out of gratitude and finds himself in the first great battle of the war, Bull Run.

Historical Accuracy: The scenes of military action are accurately and convincingly rendered.

1337 *Redcoat*

Date of Publication: 1988
Subject(s): American Revolution; Military Life—British Army; American Colonies
Fictional character(s): Sam Gilpin, Military Personnel; Jonathon Becket, Orphan, Patriot; Caroline Fisher, Gentlewoman
Historical character(s): William Howe, Military Personnel (British general)
Time Period(s): 1770s (1777-1778)
Locale(s): Philadelphia, Pennsylvania

Summary: Two opponents—a British soldier, Sam Gilpin, and an American patriot, Jonathon Becket—are linked as the British under General Howe occupy Philadelphia during the winter of 1777. Love and war are connected as the stakes in the birth of the new nation are dramatically high.

Historical Accuracy: The historical elements are carefully detailed although Cornwell admits to taking some liberties with the chronology of the Revolution.

1338 *Sharpe's Battle*

Date of Publication: 1995
Subject(s): Napoleonic Wars; Peninsular War; Military Life—British Army
Fictional character(s): Richard Sharpe, Military Personnel (army officer); Thomas Harper, Military Personnel (army sergeant); Guy Loup, Military Personnel (French general)
Historical character(s): Arthur Wellesley, Military Personnel (British general), Nobleman (Duke of Wellington)
Time Period(s): 1810s (1811)
Locale(s): Spain; Portugal

Summary: The author returns to the story of Richard Sharpe. It is 1811 and the eve of one of the bitterest battles of the Peninsular War. Sharpe is in command of an Irish battalion of the King of Spain's household guard. They are poorly equipped and trained, and up against crack French troops commanded by Sharpe's nemesis, General Guy Loup. After Loup's attack, Sharpe finds his reputation in ruins, to be redeemed only on the battlefield.

Historical Accuracy: The military and period details are convincingly rendered.

1339 *Sharpe's Company*

Date of Publication: 1982
Subject(s): Napoleonic Wars; Peninsular War; Military Life—British Army
Fictional character(s): Richard Sharpe, Military Personnel; Patrick Harper, Military Personnel; Obadiah Hakeswill, Military Personnel
Historical character(s): Arthur Wellesley, Military Personnel, Nobleman (Duke of Wellington)
Time Period(s): 1810s (1812)
Locale(s): Badajoz, Spain

Summary: The route into Spain is blocked by two fortress cities—Ciudad Rodrigo and Badajoz. Sharpe must push through to Badajoz for personal as well as military reasons in competition with the loathsome Sergeant Hakeswill, who is determined to humiliate Sharpe.

Historical Accuracy: The siege and sack of Badajoz is described with careful attention to historical facts.

1340 *Sharpe's Devil*

Date of Publication: 1992
Subject(s): Spanish Colonies; Revolution—South America
Fictional character(s): Richard Sharpe, Military Personnel (retired); Blas Vivar, Nobleman, Government Official; Patrick Harper, Military Personnel (retired)
Historical character(s): Napoleon Bonaparte, Ruler, Military Personnel; Thomas Cochrane, Military Personnel, Political Figure
Time Period(s): 1820s (1820-1821)
Locale(s): St. Helena; Valdivia, Chile

Summary: Sharpe and Harper come out of retirement to find an old friend, Vivar, who has disappeared in Chile. On the way, they stop at St. Helena to see the exiled Emperor Napoleon who asks them to carry a gift to an admirer in Chile. There they find themselves in the midst of a war for the independence of Chile and possibly a new empire for Napoleon, led by the charismatic Englishman Lord Cochrane.

Historical Accuracy: Cochrane and his rebellion in Chile that featured a planned rescue of Napoleon from exile to form the United States of South America are historically based.

1341 *Sharpe's Eagle*

Date of Publication: 1981
Subject(s): Napoleonic Wars; Peninsular War; Military Life—British Army
Fictional character(s): Richard Sharpe, Military Personnel; Patrick Harper, Military Personnel; Josefina Lacosta, Gentlewoman
Historical character(s): Arthur Wellesley, Military Personnel, Nobleman (Duke of Wellington)
Time Period(s): 1800s (1809)
Locale(s): Talavera, Spain

Summary: This first novel in the series introduces Richard Sharpe, temporary captain in the 95th Light Infantry of Wellington's army in Spain. He is one of the few officers promoted from the ranks for bravery. He must now redeem the honor of the regiment that has lost its colors in combat by capturing one of the gold eagles given by Napoleon to each of his battalions. The action culminates in the Battle of Talavera.

Historical Accuracy: The military details are solidly researched and displayed.

1342 *Sharpe's Enemy*

Date of Publication: 1984
Subject(s): Napoleonic Wars; Peninsular War; Military Life—British Army

Fictional character(s): Richard Sharpe, Military Personnel; Obadiah Hakeswill, Military Personnel; Patrick Harper, Military Personnel
Time Period(s): 1810s (1812)
Locale(s): Adrados, Spain

Summary: It is Christmas 1812, and Sharpe, now a major, is in the thick of a fight in a mountain pass in western Spain. He must contend with the French, an army of deserters who have seized a convent, and an old nemesis, Hakeswill. The military encounter concludes with the unveiling of a new secret weapon never before tested in battle.

Historical Accuracy: The military action here is fictional, but the facts of a deserter army and the rocket troop are true.

`1343` *Sharpe's Gold*

Date of Publication: 1981
Subject(s): Napoleonic Wars; Peninsular War; Military Life—British Army
Fictional character(s): Richard Sharpe, Military Personnel; Patrick Harper, Military Personnel; El Catolico, Revolutionary, Military Personnel
Historical character(s): Arthur Wellesley, Military Personnel, Nobleman (Duke of Wellington)
Time Period(s): 1810s (1810)
Locale(s): Almeida, Portugal

Summary: Sharpe undertakes a secret mission to gain a fortune in gold, enough to reverse the tide in the Peninsular campaign. He must battle both the French and a Spanish guerilla leader to reach the fortress town of Almeida which is fated to be destroyed in one of the biggest explosions in history.

Historical Accuracy: The Almeida explosion is factual though its cause is adapted to the fictional story.

`1344` *Sharpe's Honour*

Date of Publication: 1985
Subject(s): Napoleonic Wars; Peninsular War; Military Life—British Army
Fictional character(s): Richard Sharpe, Military Personnel; Pierre Ducos, Spy; La Marquesa, Prostitute, Widow(er)
Historical character(s): Arthur Wellesley, Military Personnel, Nobleman (Duke of Wellington); Joseph Bonaparte, Ruler (King of Spain)
Time Period(s): 1810s (1813)
Locale(s): Vitoria, Spain

Summary: As the war in Spain draws to a close, a French plot aimed at breaking the alliance between England and Spain is hatched. The pawn in this high-stakes gambit is Richard Sharpe, who is arrested as an assassin and sentenced to death by public hanging. The novel concludes with the Battle of Vitoria, in which Wellington defeated the French, driving them from Spain.

Historical Accuracy: The novel, like the series, is meticulously researched and correct in its details of military life and the period.

`1345` *Sharpe's Regiment*

Date of Publication: 1986

Subject(s): Napoleonic Wars; Military Life—British Army
Fictional character(s): Richard Sharpe, Military Personnel; Patrick Harper, Military Personnel; Jane Gibbons, Gentlewoman
Historical character(s): George, Prince Regent, Royalty
Time Period(s): 1810s (1813)
Locale(s): Spain; England; France

Summary: Major Richard Sharpe returns home to England on the eve of the invasion of France. There he is embroiled in intrigue that threatens his command and the life of Jane Gibbons. Disguised as a new recruit, he sets out to untangle the conspiracy.

Historical Accuracy: The history is brilliantly realized, accurately presenting the British military during the Napoleonic Wars.

`1346` *Sharpe's Revenge*

Date of Publication: 1989
Subject(s): Napoleonic Wars; Peninsular War; Military Life—British Army
Fictional character(s): Richard Sharpe, Military Personnel; William Frederickson, Military Personnel; Patrick Harper, Military Personnel
Time Period(s): 1810s (1814)
Locale(s): Toulouse, France; Bordeaux, France; London, England

Summary: As the British and Spanish armies push into southwestern France, the war is almost over. One great battle remains: the taking of Toulouse. After the battle, Richard Sharpe is prepared to enjoy the peace. Instead, he is the victim of an elaborate plot, charged with the theft of a portion of Napoleon's baggage en route to Elba. Sharpe and his comrade, Frederickson, must escape their captors and clear Sharpe's name.

Historical Accuracy: Cornwell's history is accurately delivered as are the period details that add to the novel's texture.

`1347` *Sharpe's Rifles*

Date of Publication: 1988
Subject(s): Napoleonic Wars; Peninsular War; Military Life—British Army
Fictional character(s): Richard Sharpe, Military Personnel; Patrick Harper, Military Personnel; Blas Vivar, Nobleman
Time Period(s): 1800s (1809)
Locale(s): Galicia, Spain

Summary: In 1809 the British army is in retreat, and the French threaten to capture all of Spain and Portugal. Another prize they are after is in the strongbox of a Spanish nobleman. Sharpe joins with Vivar in an uneasy alliance against their common enemy.

Historical Accuracy: The retreat to Corunna is historically accurate as is the brutal French invasion of Galicia.

`1348` *Sharpe's Siege*

Date of Publication: 1987
Subject(s): Napoleonic Wars; Military Life—British Army

Fictional character(s): Richard Sharpe, Military Personnel; Pierre Ducos, Military Personnel; Cornelius Killick, Military Personnel, Mercenary
Time Period(s): 1810s (1814)
Locale(s): Bay of Biscay, France; Bordeaux, France

Summary: Sharpe's mission in the winter of 1814 is to capture a small unguarded French fort, cut off Napoleon's supply lines, and retreat across the sea. Waiting for him is Sharpe's old enemy, Ducos, and an unexpected battalion of French soldiers. Sharpe finds himself abandoned by the navy, and he must find his own way home aided by an unscrupulous American mercenary, Cornelius Killick.

Historical Accuracy: The era is skillfully depicted, and, though the events are fictional, they are described as if they might have happened.

1349 *Sharpe's Sword*

Date of Publication: 1983
Subject(s): Napoleonic Wars; Peninsular War; Military Life—British Army
Fictional character(s): Richard Sharpe, Military Personnel; Patrick Harper, Military Personnel; Captain Leroux, Military Personnel
Historical character(s): Arthur Wellesley, Military Personnel, Nobleman (Duke of Wellington)
Time Period(s): 1810s (1812)
Locale(s): Salamanca, Spain

Summary: Sharpe must protect an important spymaster from a French assassin, Captain Leroux, in the occupied city of Salamanca on the eve of the great, pivotal battle of the Peninsular campaign. Secrecy and deception put Sharpe in mortal danger.

Historical Accuracy: Cornwell's ability to capture military history and period detail are impressive.

1350 *Waterloo*

Date of Publication: 1990
Subject(s): Napoleonic Wars; Battle of Waterloo; Military Life—British Army
Fictional character(s): Richard Sharpe, Military Personnel; Patrick Harper, Military Personnel; John Rossendale, Nobleman
Historical character(s): Frederick, Royalty (Prince of Orange), Military Personnel; Arthur Wellesley, Military Personnel, Nobleman (Duke of Wellington)
Time Period(s): 1810s (1815)
Locale(s): Brussels, Belgium; Waterloo, Belgium

Summary: At the culmination of Sharpe's military career he finds himself on the personal staff of Frederick, Prince of Orange, who has no military experience but has been given command of a large portion of the allied forces. Personal conflict is prelude to the greatest battle of the 19th century and the climax of Sharpe's adventures.

Historical Accuracy: Cornwell's version of the battle is convincingly drawn with a solid sense of eyewitness accounts.

1351 *The Winter King*

Date of Publication: 1996
Subject(s): Dark Ages; Myths and Legends; Arthurian Legends
Fictional character(s): Arthur, Ruler (King of the Britons); Guinevere, Royalty (queen consort of Arthur); Launcelot, Knight; Galahad, Knight; Merlin, Sorcerer
Time Period(s): 5th century
Locale(s): England

Summary: In Cornwell's interpretation of the Arthurian legend, Arthur is a complex individual, less the hapless victim of his own strengths than someone largely responsible for his own difficulties. His impetuousness causes him to seize Guinevere for his queen, an act with bloody consequences.

Historical Accuracy: The novel is particularly strong and convincing in its period battle scenes.

JOHN WILLIAM CORRINGTON
(1932-1988)

Born in Tennessee, Corrington earned both a Ph.D. and a J.D. degree, working as a professor of English at Louisiana State University and in private law practice in New Orleans. A novelist, short story writer, and poet, Corrington's works include *Where We Are*, which won the Charioteer Poetry Prize in 1962; *To Carthage Then I Came*, which won an NEA Award in 1968 for the short story; and the novels *The Upper Hand* and *The Bombardier*.

1352 *And Wait for the Night*

Date of Publication: 1964
Subject(s): Civil War—U.S.; Reconstruction Period
Fictional character(s): Edward Malcolm Sentell, Military Personnel (Confederate soldier); Morrison Stevens, Military Personnel (Confederate soldier); Philippe Crowninshield, Military Personnel (Union soldier)
Historical character(s): Nathan Bedford Forrest, Military Personnel (Confederate general)
Time Period(s): 1860s (1863-65)
Locale(s): Shreveport, Louisiana; Vicksburg, Mississippi

Summary: The South in defeat is the novel's subject. It chronicles the tragic fall of Vicksburg, the occupation of Shreveport, and the beginning of Reconstruction. The historical events are played out with a large cast that includes Sentell, an honorable Confederate major; Stevens, a bitter rebel veteran; and Crowninshield, the son of a freedman who returns home at the head of a column of black Union troops. The novel makes it clear that the war was not over with the surrender.

Historical Accuracy: The novel is vividly evocative of the period, although the author denies that it is a historical novel. He claims he made no attempt to accurately re-create the military events.

DIANE CORY

1353 *A Token of Jewels*

Date of Publication: 1989
Subject(s): World War I; Romance
Fictional character(s): Annastatia Brassova, Socialite; Joseph Sutherland, Military Personnel (British officer)
Time Period(s): 1910s (1914)
Locale(s): St. Petersburg, Russia; England; Milwaukee, Wisconsin

Summary: Set in Russia on the brink of World War I, Annastatia Brassova flees a deteriorating political situation assisted by British officer Sutherland. As war breaks out, she is pursued by an enemy of England and America.

Historical Accuracy: The novel is historically atmospheric and convincing in its period details.

HUBERT CORYELL (1889-)

Born in Cornwell, New York, Coryell was educated at Harvard and taught in public and private schools. He wrote several books for boys and historical novels, including *Indian Brother*, a captivity narrative, and *The Scalp Hunters*.

1354 *Indian Brother*

Date of Publication: 1935
Subject(s): American Colonies; Indians
Fictional character(s): Sam Hilton, Captive; Martha Hilton, Captive; Sosepsis, Indian, Warrior
Time Period(s): 1710s (1713)
Locale(s): Maine

Summary: This tale of capture by Indians is set in the Maine wilderness and concerns Sam Hilton's attempt to rescue his twin-sister, Martha. Sam is in turn captured by the Indians but is assisted by Sosepsis, who becomes his Indian brother.

Historical Accuracy: Although accurate in its depiction of Indian customs and the times, the novel makes little attempt to reproduce 18th-century speech.

MARJORIE CORYN (1894-)

Coryn's books include *The Chevalier d'Eon* and *The House of Orleans*.

1355 *Alone Among Men*

Date of Publication: 1947
Subject(s): Napoleonic Era; Politics
Historical character(s): Napoleon Bonaparte, Military Personnel (army officer); Josephine, Spouse
Time Period(s): 1790s (1799)
Locale(s): France

Summary: The time period is the 32 days in 1799 following Napoleon's return from Egypt and the coup d'etat that made him First Consul of France. The novel concentrates on the relationship between Napoleon and Josephine and the political manuevering that results in Napoleon's ascension to power.

Historical Accuracy: The novel handles the personal and political interplay with some skill, creating believable portraits and an authentic period background.

1356 *Good-Bye My Son*

Date of Publication: 1943
Subject(s): Biography, Fictionalized; Napoleonic Era
Historical character(s): Maria Letizia Bonaparte, Parent (Napoleon's mother), Spouse (of Carlo); Napoleon Bonaparte, Military Personnel (general), Ruler (Emperor of France); Carlo Bonaparte, Revolutionary, Political Figure
Time Period(s): 18th century; 19th century
Locale(s): France

Summary: This biographical novel traces the history of the Bonaparte family from the vantage point of Napoleon's mother, Maria Letizia. The story begins before Napoleon's birth as Maria and Carlo Bonaparte flee to the mountains of Corsica from the invading French. The novel continues the family's story through Napoleon's final defeat and exile.

Historical Accuracy: The novel depends on a faithful depiction of the facts although the story is romanticized at times.

1357 *The Incorruptible*

Date of Publication: 1943
Subject(s): French Revolution; Reign of Terror
Historical character(s): Maximilien Francois de Robespierre, Revolutionary; Camille Desmoulins, Revolutionary; Paul Barras, Revolutionary; Jean Lambert Tallien, Revolutionary; Georges Couthon, Revolutionary; Georges-Jacques Danton, Revolutionary
Time Period(s): 1790s (1794)
Locale(s): Paris, France

Summary: This novel of the French Revolution focuses on the last five months in the life of Robespierre. The architect of the Reign of Terror is seen from a variety of vantage points, including friends and enemies such as Danton, Barras, and Desmoulin.

Historical Accuracy: The historical portrait is faithful to the facts, but readers may question the author's interpretations of Robespierre's character.

1358 *The Marriage of Josephine*

Date of Publication: 1945
Subject(s): French Revolution; Napoleonic Era
Historical character(s): Josephine, Spouse (of Napoleon); Napoleon Bonaparte, Military Personnel (army commander), Ruler (Emperor of France)
Time Period(s): 1790s
Locale(s): France

Summary: The relationship between Napoleon and his first wife, Josephine, is dramatized. The story follows Josephine's career from her imprisonment during the French Revolution to her marriage with Napoleon and the first few years of their life together, with hints of the trouble to come.

Historical Accuracy: History is somewhat idealized in this novel, and the novel's interpretation of Josephine's character is questionable.

1359 *Sorrow by Day*

Date of Publication: 1950
Subject(s): Royalty—France
Historical character(s): Louis XIV, Ruler (King of France); Louise de Bourbon, Noblewoman; Antonin-Nompar de Caumont La Force, Nobleman (Duc de Lauzun), Courtier
Time Period(s): 17th century
Locale(s): France

Summary: Intrigue and romance in the court of Louis XIV are featured in this story of the king's cousin, Louise de Bourbon's romantic pursuit of the Gascon Duc de Lauzun. Lauzun makes his way in court circles by blackmailing the king's mistress and finally agrees to marry ''La Grande Mademoiselle.''.

Historical Accuracy: The author's use of historical background elements is adroit.

MARCH COST

(PSEUD. OF MARGARET MACKIE MORRISON, ?-1973)

Scottish born Cost was a novelist, biographer, and short story writer.

1360 *The Countess*

Date of Publication: 1963
Subject(s): Biography, Fictionalized
Historical character(s): Sarah Thompson, Noblewoman (Countess Rumford); Benjamin Thompson, Nobleman (Count Rumford)
Time Period(s): 18th century
Locale(s): London, England; Paris, France; Munich, Germany

Summary: This biographical novel offers the story of Sarah Thompson, the daughter of Benjamin Thompson, Count Rumford, who was born in Massachusetts in 1753. He married a beautiful rich widow and became a soldier, a spy, and commander-in-chief of the Bavarian Army, as well as a scientist. His daughter's story is no less impressive. She moves through the capitals of Europe in a life filled with intrigue and adventure.

Historical Accuracy: The novel is scrupulously researched with many first-hand documents consulted.

1361 *I, Rachel*

Date of Publication: 1957
Subject(s): Biography, Fictionalized; Theatrical Life
Historical character(s): Elisa Felix, Actress; Napoleon III, Ruler (Emperor of France)
Time Period(s): 19th century (1821-1857)
Locale(s): Paris, France

Summary: The novel offers an autobiographical account of one of the greatest actresses of the 19th century, Elisa Felix, whose stage name was Rachel. A peddler's daughter, she begins performing as a street singer. She goes on to become one of the most adored performers of her time.

Historical Accuracy: The author calls the book an interpretation, but claims to have followed the facts as closely as posssible.

THOMAS B. COSTAIN (1885-1965)

Born in Ontario, Canada, Costain worked as a journalist in Canada before coming to the U.S. in 1920 and becoming the associate editor of *The Saturday Evening Post*. Costain published the first of his many popular historical romances when he was 57 years old. His novels *The Black Rose* and *The Silver Chalice* were made into films. Costain is the father of the historical novelist Molly Costain Haycraft.

1362 *Below the Salt*

Date of Publication: 1957
Subject(s): Middle Ages; Barons' War
Fictional character(s): Richard of Rawen, Knight; Tostig, Knight
Historical character(s): Innocent III, Religious (pope); William Marshal, Nobleman (Earl of Pembroke)
Time Period(s): 12th century; 13th century (1175-1215)
Locale(s): England; France; Rome, Italy

Summary: This exciting tale of adventure and intrigue recreates the events that led King John to sign the Magna Carta in 1215. Within the rather awkward modern frame of the story of a U.S. senator who believes he was one of the period characters in a previous life, the novel focuses on Sir Richard of Rawen and Sir Tostig, who embark on a number of perilous missions, including the rescue of John's niece from a fortress. The knights also participate in the Barons' War, which culminates in King John's capitulation at Runnymede.

Historical Accuracy: Costain rejects the notion of medieval glamour and offers instead a believable and realistic portrait of the times.

1363 *The Black Rose*

Date of Publication: 1945
Subject(s): Middle Ages; Norman Conquest; Chinese Empire
Fictional character(s): Walter of Gurnie, Student, Bastard Son; Tristram Griffen, Student; Lady Maryam, Noblewoman
Historical character(s): Edward I, Ruler (King of England); Roger Bacon, Religious (friar), Philosopher
Time Period(s): 13th century (1270s)
Locale(s): Oxford, England; Kinsai, China (modern Hangchow); London, England

Summary: Walter of Gurnie, the illegitimate son of an earl, with his friend and fellow student Tristram Griffen, travels to Cathay (China) to make his fortune and secure his honor in England. In Cathay Walter marries the Lady Maryam, whom he has saved from Kublai Khan's harem, and becomes a spy for the Khan's general. After Walter and Maryam are separated during a battle, Walter returns to England, where he works to restore the Gurnie lands appropriated by the Normans.

Historical Accuracy: The novel emphasizes colorful adventure with much rich detail concerning medieval English and Chinese customs.

1364 *Darkness and the Dawn*

Date of Publication: 1959

Subject(s): Dark Ages; Roman Empire
Fictional character(s): Nicolas, Young Man; Ildico, Young Woman
Historical character(s): Attila the Hun, Ruler (king of the Huns); Aetius, Military Personnel (Roman general)
Time Period(s): 5th century
Locale(s): Gaul; Italy

Summary: The novel's setting is Europe under attack by Attila and his Hun army. Nicholas and Ildico, the fictional hero and heroine, are swept up in the tide of war and conquest. Nicholas is carried off as a slave in the household of Aetius, the Roman general who defeats Attila at the battle of Chalons. Ildico, whom Attila covets as a member of his harem, escapes to Constantinople on her magnificent black stallion. How the lovers are reunited forms the novel's climax.

Historical Accuracy: The novel offers a blend of fiction and fact with fiction predominant.

`1365` For My Great Folly

Date of Publication: 1942
Subject(s): Jacobean Period; Sea Story; Pirates
Fictional character(s): Roger Blease, Pirate, Sailor; Katie Ladland, Young Woman; Sir Sigismund Hill, Businessman (merchant)
Historical character(s): John Ward, Sea Captain, Pirate; Ann Turner, Store Owner (shopkeeper), Murderer (poisoner); Archie Armstrong, Courtier (court jester of James I); John Smith, Sea Captain, Explorer; Sir Francis Bacon, Philosopher, Political Figure; James I, Ruler (King of England); Anne of Denmark, Royalty (queen consort of James I)
Time Period(s): 17th century
Locale(s): London, England; Africa; At Sea

Summary: The novel depicts the exploits of English seaman and pirate John Ward and his Free Rovers at sea, in the London underworld, and in the court of James I. The story is told from the perspective of a young sailor and freebooter, Roger Blease.

Historical Accuracy: The customs, culture, and atmosphere of the times are well-rendered.

`1366` High Towers

Date of Publication: 1949
Subject(s): Family Saga; Exploration; Indians
Fictional character(s): Felicite-Anne Halay, Ward; Philippe Girard, Carpenter
Historical character(s): Jean-Baptiste Le Moyne, Explorer, Settler; Pierre Le Moyne, Explorer, Settler; Charles Le Moyne, Settler, Landowner
Time Period(s): 18th century
Locale(s): France; North America; Louisiana

Summary: The novel tells the business, naval, administrative, and personal exploits of the Le Moyne family. It is founded by Charles Le Moyne, whose 11 sons greatly influence the settlement of New France and the development of Louisiana and New Orleans. The novel depicts the achievements of the Le Moynes and dramatizes the issues of co-existence with the native peoples during the period.

Historical Accuracy: The historical frame for the story is accurate. The elements of the personal stories of the various characters are largely fictional.

`1367` The Last Love

Date of Publication: 1963
Subject(s): Napoleonic Era
Historical character(s): Napoleon Bonaparte, Ruler (Emperor of France); Betsy Balcombe, Young Woman; Hudson Lowe, Government Official
Time Period(s): 1810s; 1820s
Locale(s): St. Helena

Summary: The story of Napoleon's exile on St. Helena is dramatized through his relationship with a young Englishwoman, Betsy Balcombe. The story depicts Napoleon's life on the island under the tyrannical governor Sir Hudson Lowe, flashbacks to his youth and campaigns, and his continual hope for escape from the dismal island.

Historical Accuracy: The novel is based on some established facts, but liberties have been taken with the sequence of events and some imagined characters have been introduced.

`1368` The Moneyman

Date of Publication: 1947
Subject(s): Royalty—France
Historical character(s): Jacques Coeur, Courtier (financial adviser), Financier; Charles VII, Ruler (King of France); Agnes Sorel, Gentlewoman, Lover
Time Period(s): 15th century (1436)
Locale(s): France

Summary: Set in the French court of Charles VII, the novel describes the role played by Jacques Coeur. Born a commoner, Coeur becomes one of the first great merchant princes and amasses a personal fortune greater than had ever been earned by a private citizen. A financial adviser to the king, Coeur directs the war against the English that drives them from Normandy. The novel describes Coeur's eventual downfall, as well as the story of the king's mistress, Agnes Sorel.

Historical Accuracy: The novel blends a romantic story with a faithful picture of Charles' court and the events of the period.

`1369` Ride with Me

Date of Publication: 1944
Subject(s): Napoleonic Wars; Peninsular War
Fictional character(s): Francis Ellery, Publisher; Gabrielle de Salle, Gentlewoman
Historical character(s): Sir Robert Wilson, Military Personnel (English officer)
Time Period(s): 1800s; 1810s
Locale(s): Spain; Russia; London, England

Summary: Sir Robert Wilson's military exploits in the Peninsular Campaign and during Napoleon's retreat from Moscow are the subject of this book. They are combined with a fictional story about Francis Ellery, publisher of a London newspaper, and Gabrielle de Salle, a French refugee.

Historical Accuracy: The actual exploits of war hero Wilson co-exist somewhat uncomfortably with the romance plot.

1370 *The Silver Chalice*

Date of Publication: 1952
Subject(s): Biblical Story; Christianity
Fictional character(s): Basil of Antioch, Artisan (silversmith), Slave; Deborah, Gentlewoman
Historical character(s): Simon Magus, Magician; Joseph of Arimathea, Biblical Figure; Paul, Biblical Figure, Religious (apostle); Luke, Biblical Figure, Religious (evangelist); Nero, Ruler (Roman emperor); Peter, Biblical Figure, Religious (apostle)
Time Period(s): 1st century
Locale(s): Antioch, Syria; Jerusalem, Israel; Rome, Roman Empire

Summary: Basil, a silversmith cheated out of his inheritance, is enslaved. He is purchased and freed by Luke, who hires him to make a likeness of the dying Joseph of Arimathea. Basil is then commissioned to design a silver chalice to house the cup used by Jesus during the Last Supper. While carrying out his commission, Basil works to regain his inheritance, is torn between two beautiful women, and experiences the promise of Christianity versus the charlatanism of the false messiah, Simon Magus.

Historical Accuracy: The era is faithfully recreated here, particularly the growing danger which faced the early Christians.

1371 *The Tontine*

Date of Publication: 1955
Subject(s): Regency Period; Victorian Period; Family Saga
Fictional character(s): Samuel Carboy, Businessman (merchant); Helen Groody, Activist (social reformer); Jonathan Bade, Lawyer
Historical character(s): Joseph Bonaparte, Political Figure; Louis Napoleon Bonaparte, Ruler (Emperor of France)
Time Period(s): 19th century (1815-1850s)
Locale(s): London, England; Kingston, Jamaica; New Jersey

Summary: Wealthy merchant Samuel Carboy establishes a tontine—part lottery, part bank, part insurance scheme—in which the proceeds go to the surviving shareholders over a period of years until there is just one beneficiary left. The novel follows the fates of several characters over the course of the 19th century.

Historical Accuracy: The Battle of Waterloo figures in the plot as it pertains to the financial speculation and the creation of the tontine. The fictional story interweaves the fate of the Bonaparte family and its attempts to reassert its influence. The novel also captures credibly the social reform movements of the period.

RALPH W. COTTON

1372 *While Angels Dance*

Date of Publication: 1994
Subject(s): Civil War—U.S.; Crime and Criminals
Fictional character(s): Jeston Nash, Outlaw
Historical character(s): Jesse James, Outlaw; Frank James, Outlaw; Cole Younger, Outlaw
Time Period(s): 1860s; 1870s
Locale(s): Missouri; Kansas

Summary: Jeston Nash, the central character of this novel, resembles Jesse James' actual cousin Jesse Woodrow James. After killing a Yankee soldier in self-defense, Jeston meets his cousins Frank and Jesse James and joins Quantrill's Raiders. After the war, Jeston rides with the James-Younger gang while seeking vengeance against the man responsible for the death of his child.

Historical Accuracy: The novel creates a plausible fictional story within a framework of facts involving the James family.

NORBERT COULEHAN

1373 *Fourth King*

Date of Publication: 1960
Subject(s): Roman Empire; Sea Story
Fictional character(s): Titus Terentius, Sea Captain
Time Period(s): 1st century
Locale(s): At Sea; Rome, Roman Empire

Summary: Set during the reign of Roman Emperor Augustus, the novel describes the efforts of Titus Terentius to deliver distant kings to a summit meeting called by Augustus. Titus' journey takes him to Norway, Africa, and the Middle East. He must contend with storms, pirates, and court intrigues to accomplish his mission.

Historical Accuracy: The story is fanciful and the presentation of characters and the period is marred by simplification and stereotyping.

CATHERINE COULTER

Romance novelist Coulter was born in Texas and received her B.A. from the University of Texas and an M.A. from Boston College. She worked in human resources for firms in New York City and San Francisco and began writing in the 1970s when her husband was in medical school. At the time, she was reading 20 to 30 romances a week and decided that she could write better ones herself. Coulter is a history buff whose favorite period is the Napoleonic Era, but her historical romances have been set from the first century to the present.

1374 *Earth Song*

Date of Publication: 1990
Subject(s): Middle Ages; Romance
Fictional character(s): Philippa de Beauchamp, Noblewoman; Dienwald de Fortenberry, Nobleman
Time Period(s): 13th century (1275)
Locale(s): England

Summary: To evade her father's arranged marriage for her, Philippa de Beauchamp leaves home in a wool wagon disguised as a peasant. She is kidnapped and held for ransom by nobleman Dienwald de Fortenberry. Philippa, however, takes charge of Dienwald's castle, and romance ensues.

Historical Accuracy: The attitudes expressed seem more modern than medieval.

`1375` *The Heiress Bride*

Date of Publication: 1993
Subject(s): Regency Romance; Mystery
Fictional character(s): Joan ''Sinjin'' Sherbrooke, Heiress; Colin Kincross, Widow(er), Nobleman (Earl of Ashburnham)
Time Period(s): 1810s
Locale(s): England; Scotland

Summary: In the third of the Bride Trilogy, set during the Regency period, a conventional romance is joined to a murder plot with supernatural elements. Young Sinjin Sherbrooke sets her cap at Colin Kinross, despite her brother's determination that she may not even see him. Her marital goal is reached but not before she is almost killed.

Historical Accuracy: The novel is packed with more plot elements than the standard Regency romance. The period details create a plausible backdrop.

`1376` *Lord of Hawkfell Island*

Date of Publication: 1993
Subject(s): Dark Ages; Romance; Vikings
Fictional character(s): Mirana, Royalty (princess), Captive; Rorik Heraldsson, Warrior (Viking)
Time Period(s): 10th century (910)
Locale(s): Ireland

Summary: This romantic tale set in 10th century Ireland involves the kidnapped Mirana who winds up marrying her captor, Viking warrior Rorik, when she learns that her brother intended her to marry another against her will. She is kidnapped again, this time by her brother, and Rorik must come to the rescue.

Historical Accuracy: Romance predominates over historical details, and the background is only lightly sketched.

`1377` *Night Shadow*

Date of Publication: 1989
Subject(s): Regency Romance
Fictional character(s): Lily Tremaine, Governess; Knight Winthrop, Nobleman (Viscount Castlerosse), Rake
Time Period(s): 1810s (1814)
Locale(s): London, England

Summary: When her fiance is murdered, Lily Tremaine seeks help from his cousin, Knight Winthrop, a notorious rake and a confirmed bachelor. He has no intention of changing his lifestyle, but does not count on falling in love with Lily.

Historical Accuracy: This is a charming romantic contrivance with some period touches, although the intent is clearly not documentary.

`1378` *Night Storm*

Date of Publication: 1990
Subject(s): Regency Romance
Fictional character(s): Eugenia Paxton, Businesswoman (shipyard owner), Imposter (disguised as a man); Alec Carrick, Sea Captain, Nobleman (Baron Shepard)
Time Period(s): 1810s (1819)
Locale(s): England; Chesapeake Bay, Maryland

Summary: In this Regency romance that combines murder, amnesia, revenge, and passion, the complications begin when Eugenia Paxton enters into a partnership with sea captain Alec Carrick to save her shipyard.

Historical Accuracy: The emphasis is on romantic contrivance over history.

`1379` *The Nightingale Legacy*

Date of Publication: 1994
Subject(s): Regency Romance
Fictional character(s): Caroline Derwent-Jones, Young Woman; Frederic North Nightingale, Nobleman
Time Period(s): 1810s (1814)
Locale(s): Cornwall, England

Summary: Mystery and romance are feature in this second novel of the Legacy Trilogy that begins with *The Wyndham Legacy*. Caroline Derwent-Jones manages to escape from her guardian and is drawn into the mystery surrounding Frederic North Nightingale.

Historical Accuracy: The novel offers an atmospheric period background that is credible.

`1380` *Rosehaven*

Date of Publication: 1996
Subject(s): Middle Ages; Romance
Fictional character(s): Severin of Langthorne, Nobleman (baron); Hastings of Trent, Heiress
Time Period(s): 13th century (1270s)
Locale(s): England

Summary: During the reign of Edward I in the 13th century, Severin of Langthorne contracts a marriage to the heiress Hastings of Trent. It is a marriage between opposites, and they must work out their relationship while solving the riddle of the mysterious property of Rosehaven.

Historical Accuracy: The novel features a plausible sense of the period.

`1381` *Secret Song*

Date of Publication: 1991
Subject(s): Middle Ages; Romance
Fictional character(s): Daria de Fortesque, Noblewoman, Heiress; Roland de Tourney, Knight
Time Period(s): 13th century (1275)
Locale(s): England

Summary: The final volume of the Song Trilogy, set in 13th-century England, describes the romantic adventures that ensue when Roland de Tourney is hired to rescue Daria de Fortesque. He accomplishes his mission and captures the lady's heart, but after their affair, loses his memory of it. When Daria becomes pregnant, Roland does not believe the baby is his. Love will out, however, due to Daria's persistence.

Historical Accuracy: The romantic situation strains credibility, and the atmosphere is more approximate than historically precise.

1382 *The Sherbrooke Bride*

Date of Publication: 1992
Subject(s): Regency Romance
Fictional character(s): Alexandra Chambers, Noblewoman; Douglas Sherbrooke, Nobleman (Earl of Northcliffe)
Time Period(s): 1800s (1807)
Locale(s): England

Summary: In the first book of the Bride Trilogy the setting is Regency England. Romantic complications develop when Douglas Sherbrooke decides to marry a society beauty but winds up married to her sister, Alexandra Chambers, instead.

Historical Accuracy: The novel's premise is incredible, and the period elements are little more than serviceable.

STEPHEN COULTER (1914-)

Coulter is a British author who has also had a long career as a journalist. In the 1930s he served as Reuter's parliamentary correspondent. From 1945-1965, he was Kemsley Newspapers' correspondent in Paris. During World War II, Coulter served as one of Dwight D. Eisenhower's staff officers at Allied headquarters. Under the pseudonym James Mayo, he was the creator of secret agent Charles Hood, the protagonist of a series of crime novels. His works include *The Loved Enemy*, *Embassy*, and *The Man Above Suspicion*.

1383 *The Chateau*

Date of Publication: 1974
Subject(s): Romance; Business Building
Fictional character(s): Francis Gautier, Landowner; Susannah Gautier, Spouse
Time Period(s): 1850s
Locale(s): Bordeaux, France

Summary: Susannah, the young American bride of Francis Gautier, becomes mistress of a chateau in the Gautier family's vineyard. She is resented and causes scandal in the bourgeoisie society of Bordeaux. However, when disease threatens the grapes and the family's future, it is her determination that saves the day.

Historical Accuracy: The novel is filled with authentic details about viticulture.

1384 *Damned Shall Be Desire: The Passionate Life of Guy de Maupassant*

Date of Publication: 1858
Subject(s): Biography, Fictionalized; Literary Life
Historical character(s): Guy de Maupassant, Writer
Time Period(s): 19th century
Locale(s): France

Summary: This biographical novel traces the career of Guy de Maupassant, who bursts on the French literary scene in 1880 and achieves great fame for his short stories and novels. His love life is no less renowned, but with the consequences of early death in an insane asylum as the victim of syphilis.

Historical Accuracy: The details of Maupassant's life and times are accurately recounted.

1385 *The Devil Inside: A Novel of Dostoevsky's Life*

Date of Publication: 1960
Subject(s): Biography, Fictionalized; Literary Life; Russian Empire
Historical character(s): Feodor Mikhailovich Dostoevsky, Writer; Polina Suslova, Gentlewoman
Time Period(s): 19th century (1839-1881)
Locale(s): Russia

Summary: This account of the life of Russian writer Dostoevsky begins prior to his father's brutal slaying by his serfs and ends with his own death in 1881. Dostoevsky's continual run-in with his debtors, his spiritual torments, and his obsession with gambling are vividly portrayed.

Historical Accuracy: The novel combines elements from biographical sources and from Dostoevsky's works.

HAROLD COURLANDER (1908-)

American novelist Courlander is a specialist in the oral traditions of African and Caribbean cultures. He was born in Indiana and graduated from the University of Michigan. He is the author of more than 35 books, including the bestselling *The Cow-Tail Switch and Other West African Stories* and *The Drum and the Hoe: Life and Lore of the Haitian People*. Courlander is a former editor for the United Nations and a political analyst for the Voice of America. His novel *The African* was the subject of a successful copyright infringement suit brought against Alex Haley, who acknowledged that portions of his novel *Roots* had been taken from Courlander's.

1386 *The African*

Date of Publication: 1967
Subject(s): Slavery; Antebellum South
Fictional character(s): Hwesuhunu, Slave; Ookumi, Slave
Time Period(s): 1800s (1802)
Locale(s): Africa (West); St. Lucia; Georgia

Summary: The novel describes the experiences of a young West African boy, Hwesuhunu, who is taken by American slave traders. He endures the voyage across the Atlantic, shipwreck on the island of St. Lucia, and enslavement on a Georgia plantation.

Historical Accuracy: The novel convinces the reader that this is indeed what it must have been like to be seized into slavery.

GAY COURTER (1944-)

Born in Pittsburgh, Courter is a graduate of Antioch College, and worked for many years as a free-lance film writer and producer before turning to novels.

1387 *Flowers in the Blood*

Date of Publication: 1991
Subject(s): Jews; British RAJ
Fictional character(s): Dinah Sassoon, Young Woman; Edwin Salen, Gentleman
Time Period(s): 19th century (1878-1898)
Locale(s): Calcutta, India; Darjeeling, India; Hong Kong

Summary: When her mother is mysteriously murdered, Dinah Sassoon, daughter of an affluent opium trader in 19th-century Calcutta, is left dishonored and unmarriageable. Her adventures take her to the rajah's court where she eventually falls in love. The novel offers a vivid portrait Jewish community.

Historical Accuracy: Although the story is fictional, it is based on real events in Calcutta's Baghdadi Jewish community in the 19th century.

1388 *The Midwife*

Date of Publication: 1981
Subject(s): Medical Profession; Jews
Fictional character(s): Hannah Blau, Nurse, Midwife
Time Period(s): 1900s (1904-1908)
Locale(s): Russia; New York, New York

Summary: Hannah Blau is a young Jewish woman in Russia who practices midwifery. Her career takes her from the Imperial Palace to New York's Lower East Side and fashionable Fifth Avenue mansions. Through romances and hostility, she maintains her career, although she is seen as an economic threat to the emerging male specialty of obstetrics.

Historical Accuracy: The period details are convincing, and the medical details are meticulously presented.

1389 *The Midwife's Advice*

Date of Publication: 1992
Subject(s): Medical Profession; Women's Rights
Fictional character(s): Hannah Blau Sokolow, Nurse, Midwife
Time Period(s): 1910s; 1920s (1913-1922)
Locale(s): New York, New York

Summary: In the sequel to *The Midwife*, Hannah Blau Sokolow continues her career as a midwife in New York's Bellevue Hospital. Compelled by her patients' needs, she increasingly becomes involved in the new and radical ideas of birth control, sex education, and health care.

Historical Accuracy: The novel gives an authentic factual account of the opposition to the innovations launched by women such as Margaret Sanger.

1390 *River of Dreams*

Date of Publication: 1984
Subject(s): Romance
Fictional character(s): Margaret Claiborne, Gentlewoman, Musician (pianist); Erik Larson, Gentleman; Joaquin Freire, Composer
Time Period(s): 19th century; 20th century (1895-1927)
Locale(s): Rio de Janeiro, Brazil

Summary: Margaret Claiborne is a southern-born American who settles in Rio de Janeiro and marries Erik Larson. Her husband's affairs send her to Joaquin Freire, Brazil's most celebrated composer. The novel's drama deals with Margaret's struggle for identity in a Brazil with a unique mix of race, class, and morality.

Historical Accuracy: The author admits she adapted the Brazilian setting to her own needs.

JAMES COWAN (1942-)

Born in Melbourne, Cowan lives in Western Australia where he directs a major arts program aimed at increasing the appreciation of Aboriginal art. He spent many years living among the indigenous peoples of Morocco, Libya, Tahiti, and Japan. His books include *Letters From a Wild State*, *Mysteries of Dreamtime: The Spiritual Life of the Australian Aborigine*, and two collections of poetry.

1391 *A Mapmaker's Dream*

Date of Publication: 1996
Subject(s): Renaissance; Religious Life; Exploration
Historical character(s): Fra Mauro, Religious (monk), Cartographer
Time Period(s): 16th century
Locale(s): Venice, Italy

Summary: This unusual novel—part historical fiction, part philosophical meditation—records the efforts of the Venetian monk, Fra Mauro, confined to his cell on an island monastery, to create a perfect map of the world. His project attracts a series of explorers, pilgrims, and travellers who share with him their accounts of the world. Mauro's map grows to incorporate both the real and the imagined.

Historical Accuracy: The story is invented, but depends on a believable picture of the period.

A.E. COWDREY (1933-)

Born in New Orleans, Cowdrey received his B.S. degree from Tulane in 1956 and his M.A. in history from Johns Hopkins. Cowdrey taught at Tulane and at Newcomb College before becoming a full-time writer. He is the author of *The Delta Engineers: A History of the Army Corps of Engineers in the New Orleans District*.

1392 *Elixir of Life*

Date of Publication: 1965
Subject(s): Antebellum South
Fictional character(s): John Samson Donnelly, Businessman (patent medicine salesman)
Time Period(s): 1850s (1853)
Locale(s): New Orleans, Louisiana

Summary: New Orleans in 1853 in the grip of a yellow fever epidemic is the scene for this comic novel that describes the misadventures of patent-medicine salesman John Samson Donnelly who produces a cure for the disease.

Historical Accuracy: The novel presents the rakish and colorful atmosphere of period New Orleans as a backdrop to the story.

STEPHANIE COWELL

An American novelist and Elizabethan scholar, Cooke is a classical singer and balladeer who co-founded a chamber opera company and produced several Renaissance festivals. *Nicholas Cooke* is her first novel and is intended to be the first in a fictional series.

1393 *Nicholas Cooke: Actor, Soldier, Physician, Priest*

Date of Publication: 1993
Subject(s): Elizabethan Period; Theatrical Life; Literary Life
Fictional character(s): Nicholas Cooke, Actor, Military Personnel
Historical character(s): John Heminges, Actor, Businessman (manages theater company); Thomas Pope, Actor; William Shakespeare, Actor; Robert Devereux, Military Personnel, Nobleman (Earl of Essex); Christopher Marlowe, Writer (playwright); Henry Wriothesley, Nobleman (Earl of Southampton); Thomas Hariot, Scientist (astronomer)
Time Period(s): 16th century; 17th century (1593-1617)
Locale(s): London, England; Ireland

Summary: This is the first-person narrative of Nicholas Cooke, who as a young boy in 1593 runs off to London. There he meets and is seduced by poet Christopher Marlowe. He joins a theater company whose members include Shakespeare. After seducing the manager's wife, Cooke enlists to fight with Essex in Ireland. On his return he embarks on careers as both a priest and a scientist.

Historical Accuracy: Cowell shows a remarkable historical imagination in this first novel of a proposed trilogy. The historical accuracy never detracts from an exciting human drama.

1394 *The Physician of London*

Date of Publication: 1995
Subject(s): Jacobean Period; Medical Profession; Civil War—England
Fictional character(s): Nicholas Cooke, Doctor, Religious (priest); Thomas Wentworth, Landowner
Historical character(s): William Laud, Religious (archbishop); William Harvey, Doctor
Time Period(s): 17th century (1617-1645)
Locale(s): London, England; Yorkshire, England; Oxford, England

Summary: In the second volume of the story of Nicholas Cooke, physician, priest, actor, and soldier, it is 1617 and Cooke, now in his mid-thirties, is determined to continue his scientific research by building a successful magnifying instrument. His friendship with Thomas Wentworth brings him into the center of a growing animosity between the power of the king and that of the gentry and landowners that will explode into the English Civil War.

Historical Accuracy: The era is captured with skill and authority as the fictional story is interwoven with actual figures and real events faithfully presented.

HAROLD COYLE (1952-)

American career army officer Coyle has become well-known as the author of military thrillers. His novels include *Sword Point*, *Bright Star*, *The Ten Thousand*, *Trial by Fire*, and *Code of Honor*.

1395 *Look Away*

Date of Publication: 1995
Subject(s): Civil War—U.S.; Battle of Gettysburg; Military Life
Fictional character(s): James Bannon, Student—College, Military Personnel (Confederate soldier); Kevin Bannon, Student—College, Military Personnel (Union soldier); Harriet Shields, Young Woman; Mary Beth McPherson, Gentlewoman
Historical character(s): Thomas Jonathan Jackson, Professor, Military Personnel (Confederate officer)
Time Period(s): 1850s; 1860s (1856-1863)
Locale(s): Virginia; New Jersey; Pennsylvania

Summary: The campaigns of the early years of the Civil War, up to and including the Battle of Gettysburg, are dramatized in the parallel experiences of two brothers, James and Kevin Bannon, who find themselves on opposite sides in the conflict. Battlefields and the homefront are vividly depicted in the Bannons' involvement with the war and the two women in their lives.

Historical Accuracy: The novel mixes fiction and fact. The author has carefully placed his fictional characters in events that actually occurred, using actual first-person accounts to capture the action and the reactions of the characters.

1396 *Until the End*

Date of Publication: 1996
Subject(s): Civil War—U.S.
Fictional character(s): James Bannon, Military Personnel (Confederate soldier); Kevin Bannon, Military Personnel (Union soldier); Mary Beth McPherson, Gentlewoman; Harriet Shields, Nurse
Time Period(s): 1860s (1863-1865)
Locale(s): Virginia; New Brunswick, New Jersey

Summary: The novel concludes the story of James and Kevin Bannon who find themselves serving on opposite sides in the Civil War. This sequel to *Look Away* picks up their story after their fateful meeting on the Gettysburg battlefield. The final bloody years of the conflict are described.

Historical Accuracy: The novel's notes show the closeness of the narrative to actual events.

ALFRED LELAND CRABB (1884-)

Born in Kentucky, Crabb graduated from George Peabody College for Teachers and Columbia University. He was a public school teacher and principal in Kentucky and Louisiana before becoming a professor of education. Most of his books deal with the history of Nashville and his interest in cookery.

1397 *Breakfast at the Hermitage*

Date of Publication: 1945
Subject(s): Reconstruction Period
Fictional character(s): Hunt Justice, Architect
Historical character(s): Sarah Polk, Widow(er) (of James K. Polk)
Time Period(s): 1870s
Locale(s): Nashville, Tennessee

Summary: Nashville, Tennessee, is shown rebuilding after the Civil War. The novel's symbol for the city is the renovation of the Hermitage, the house Andrew Jackson planned for his beloved wife, Rachel. Neglected during the war, its revitalization reflects the fate of the city. The novel follows architect Hunt Justice as he contributes to the city's rebuilding.

Historical Accuracy: The novel features authentic period details.

1398 *Dinner at Belmont*

Date of Publication: 1942
Subject(s): Antebellum South; Civil War—U.S.
Fictional character(s): Adelicia Acklen, Southern Belle; Joseph Acklen, Gentleman
Historical character(s): William Walker, Adventurer; Sarah Polk, Widow(er) (of James K. Polk)
Time Period(s): 1850s; 1860s (1858-1865)
Locale(s): Nashville, Tennessee

Summary: This is the story of Nashville, Tennessee, before and during the Civil War. The novel artfully interweaves fictional and historical characters, such as William Walker and the widow of President John K. Polk. Adelicia Acklen is the hostess of Belmont. Her soirees during the eventful years of the Civil War chronicle the history of a city and its inhabitants.

Historical Accuracy: The historical elements are authentic and convincingly developed.

1399 *Home to Kentucky: A Novel of Henry Clay*

Date of Publication: 1953
Subject(s): Politics; Biography, Fictionalized
Historical character(s): Henry Clay, Lawyer, Political Figure
Time Period(s): 18th century; 19th century (1790s-1852)
Locale(s): Virginia; Kentucky; Washington, District of Columbia

Summary: The life of American statesman Henry Clay is shown from his days as a young lawyer in western Virginia and Kentucky to his distinguished and contentious career in politics. Clay comes close to winning the presidency and plays an important role in preserving the Union.

Historical Accuracy: The author is convincing in rendering the period and the biographical details of Clay's remarkable career.

1400 *Home to Tennessee*

Date of Publication: 1952
Subject(s): Civil War—U.S.; Espionage

Fictional character(s): Beasley Nichol, Military Personnel (Confederate officer), Spy; Hume Crockett, Military Personnel (Confederate officer), Spy
Historical character(s): Nathan Bedford Forrest, Military Personnel (Confederate general); Sarah Polk, Widow(er) (of James K. Polk)
Time Period(s): 1860s (1864)
Locale(s): Nashville, Tennessee; Florence, Alabama

Summary: The background of the story is the ill-fated Confederate campaign to retake Nashville in 1864. General Nathan Bedford Forrest's favorite secret agent and intelligence officer, Beasley Nichol, spends most of the story behind enemy lines as the action mounts to its climax at Spring Hill, the Battle of Franklin, and the final two-day Battle of Nashville.

Historical Accuracy: The novel is an artful blend of the actual events and fictional accounts.

1401 *Home to the Hermitage*

Date of Publication: 1948
Subject(s): Biography, Fictionalized; Politics
Historical character(s): Andrew Jackson, Military Personnel (general), Political Figure; Rachel Jackson, Spouse
Time Period(s): 19th century (1815-1829)
Locale(s): Nashville, Tennessee

Summary: The novel tells the story of Andrew Jackson and his wife, Rachel, from Jackson's return from the War of 1812 to his election as president in 1828. The author attempts to paint a gentler, more domestic Jackson in his devotion to his wife and their Tennessee home, the Hermitage.

Historical Accuracy: The author's admiration for Jackson sacrifies objectivity.

1402 *Journey to Nashville*

Date of Publication: 1957
Subject(s): Settlement of the American Frontier; Indians
Historical character(s): James Robertson, Settler; John Donelson, Settler
Time Period(s): 1770s; 1780s
Locale(s): Nashville, Tennessee

Summary: The founding of Nashville, Tennessee, is chronicled. A group of settlers from the Wautanga Settlement of East Tennessee journey through the wilderness to a site on the Cumberland chosen by James Robertson, the party's leader. Another group, led by John Donelson, travel by river. They meet in April 1780. The novel details vividly their hardships and dangers.

Historical Accuracy: The novel effectively creates a sense of the wilderness and the efforts of the party to reach their destination.

1403 *Lodging at the Saint Cloud*

Date of Publication: 1946
Subject(s): Civil War—U.S.; Espionage
Fictional character(s): Adelicia Acklen, Southern Belle; Beasley Nichol, Military Personnel (Confederate officer), Spy; Hume Crockett, Military Personnel (Confederate officer), Spy

Historical character(s): Sarah Polk, Widow(er) (of James K. Polk); Nathan Bedford Forrest, Military Personnel (Confederate general)
Time Period(s): 1860s (1862)
Locale(s): Nashville, Tennessee

Summary: The novel is set in the occupied city of Nashville, Tennessee, during the Civil War. To gather intelligence on the Union forces, Nathan Bedford Forrest sends spies into the city. Their adventures are interwoven with characters from *Dinner at Belmont*, Alicia Acklen and the widow of James K. Polk.

Historical Accuracy: The novel's local details are exact and authentic, as are the historical events surrounding Nashville's occupation.

1404 *Mockingbird Sang at Chickamauga*
Date of Publication: 1949
Subject(s): Civil War—U.S.; Battle of Chickamauga; Espionage
Fictional character(s): Beasley Nichol, Military Personnel (Confederate officer), Spy; Hume Crockett, Military Personnel (Confederate officer), Spy
Historical character(s): Nathan Bedford Forrest, Military Personnel (Confederate general); William S. Rosecrans, Military Personnel (Union general); James Longstreet, Military Personnel (Confederate general)
Time Period(s): 1860s (1863)
Locale(s): Chattanooga, Tennessee

Summary: Military action around Chattanooga, including the battles of Chickamauga, Missionary Ridge, and Lookout Mountain, are featured in this story that involves Nathan Bedford Forrest's intelligence agents Lieutenant Beasley Nichol and Captain Hume Crockett. The action moves between the battlefield and the homefront.

Historical Accuracy: The military action is carefully and authentically detailed.

1405 *Peace at Bowling Green*
Date of Publication: 1955
Subject(s): Civil War—U.S.; Antebellum South; Settlement of the American Frontier
Fictional character(s): Jacob Skiles, Settler; Rumsey Skiles, Landowner; Ella Skiles, Spouse (of Rumsey)
Time Period(s): 19th century (1803-1860s)
Locale(s): Bowling Green, Kentucky

Summary: In 1803 Jacob Skiles and his family settle in their frontier home in the isolated village of Bowling Green, Kentucky. The novel depicts the growth and development of their community into a thriving city. The Civil War splits the border community, turning neighbors into enemies.

Historical Accuracy: The locale is painted with assurance, and the historical events are convincingly reflected in their effects on the community.

1406 *Reunion at Chattanooga*
Date of Publication: 1950
Subject(s): Reconstruction Period

Fictional character(s): Grandma Blevins, Businesswoman; Clay Blevins, Businessman; Ruth Blevins, Young Woman
Time Period(s): 19th century (1876-1890)
Locale(s): Chattanooga, Tennessee

Summary: The post-Civil War development of Chattanooga, Tennessee, is depicted as Yankees come to settle in the community and an eventual harmonious truce takes place. Grandma Blevins is the spirit of the old South shown adapting to the future.

Historical Accuracy: The locale is colorfully and authentically depicted.

1407 *Supper at the Maxwell House*
Date of Publication: 1943
Subject(s): Reconstruction Period; Ku Klux Klan
Fictional character(s): Weaver Cole, Businessman
Historical character(s): Nathan Bedford Forrest, Veteran (Confederate general); Sarah Polk, Widow(er) (of James K. Polk)
Time Period(s): 1860s (post-Civil War)
Locale(s): Nashville, Tennessee

Summary: Nashville during Reconstruction forms the novel's background, as the city attempts to rebuild while being victimized by Yankee carpetbaggers out for quick profits. General Nathan Bedford Forrest is shown organizing the nightriders, or Ku Klux Klan, to exact revenge for Northern injustices.

Historical Accuracy: The novel mingles the fictional and the factual into an authentic depiction of the life of the city. The Klan is cast in an heroic role that leaves unsaid its racial supremicist component.

JIM CRACE (1946-)

English writer Crace is an honors graduate of London's Birmingham College of Commerce. Crace spent the late 1960s as a producer and writer for Sudanese Educational Television, and as an English teacher in Botswana. Author of *Continent*, *The Gift of Stones*, and *Arcadia*, Crace won the Whitbread First Novel Prize, the David Higham Prize, and the Guardian Fiction Award. Crace is known for his original fiction probing the social and political nature of human beings.

1408 *Signals of Distress*
Date of Publication: 1995
Subject(s): Sea Story; Slavery
Fictional character(s): Aymer Smith, Businessman; Otto, Slave, Cook
Time Period(s): 1830s
Locale(s): England

Summary: The novel details the effects on a small town in England when an American vessel, *The Belle of Wilmington*, runs aground offshore. Aboard is Otto, the ship's slave-cook, whose presence is a catalyst for the town's troubled reaction, particularly that of soap manufacturer and reformer Aymer Smith.

Historical Accuracy: The novel offers a convincing evocation of 19th-century town life.

FANNY CRADOCK

1409 *The Lormes of Castle Rising*

Date of Publication: 1975
Subject(s): Edwardian Period; Family Saga; Servants
Fictional character(s): Justin Henry de Lorme, Nobleman (Lord Aynthorp); Alicia de Lorme, Noblewoman (Lady Aynthorp); Sawby, Servant (butler)
Time Period(s): 1900s; 1910s (1907-1910)
Locale(s): England

Summary: Life on a great estate during the Edwardian period is depicted in this first volume of the history of the Lorme family, headed by Lord Aynthorp. Upstairs and downstairs are described in this novel of domestic life involving family members and servants and an era that is headed for great changes.

Historical Accuracy: The period social details are accurately pictured.

1410 *Shadows over Castle Rising*

Date of Publication: 1976
Subject(s): Edwardian Period; Family Saga; World War I
Fictional character(s): Henry Lorme, Gentleman; Petula Danement, Gentlewoman; Alicia de Lorme, Noblewoman (Lady Aynthorp)
Time Period(s): 1900s; 1910s (1910-1914)
Locale(s): England

Summary: The second volume of the author's saga of the aristocratic Lorme family is set between 1910 and 1914, from the death of Edward VII to the onset of the First World War. Henry Lorme's marriage to Petula Danement is at the center of the domestic story, but all is interrupted with the outbreak of war and the end of an era.

Historical Accuracy: The novel provides a good social history of the period.

1411 *War Comes to Castle Rising*

Date of Publication: 1978
Subject(s): World War I; Family Saga
Fictional character(s): Gyles Lorme, Nobleman (Lord Aynthorp); Christine Lorme, Spouse
Time Period(s): 1910s (1914-1918)
Locale(s): England

Summary: War arrives in the third volume of the author's saga of the noble Lorme family. One wing of the castle is turned into a convalescent home for wounded soldiers, and the family struggles to maintain its traditions as the war takes its terrible toll.

Historical Accuracy: The novel captures its era with skill and believability.

1412 *Wind of Change at Castle Rising*

Date of Publication: 1979
Subject(s): Family Saga
Fictional character(s): Sue Ellen Blenkinsop, Heiress, Widow(er); Sawby, Servant (butler); Henry Lorme, Gentleman
Time Period(s): 1910s; 1920s
Locale(s): England

Summary: Post-World War I England is depicted in the fourth volume of the saga concerning the Lorme family. Change is the novel's theme as the Lormes must cope with a new and formerly unknown family member: an American heiress and widow of the family's black sheep.

Historical Accuracy: The social history reflected by the family history is solidly detailed and accurate.

JOHN KENNY CRANE (1942-)

Crane is the Dean of the College of Humanities and the Arts at San Jose State University in California. *The Legacy of Ladysmith* (1986), about a Scottish family and its role in the Boer War, is his first novel.

1413 *The Legacy of Ladysmith*

Date of Publication: 1986
Subject(s): Boer War; Siege of Ladysmith
Fictional character(s): Roberts Menzies, Doctor; Jason Glass, Writer
Historical character(s): Louis Botha, Military Personnel (Boer general), Political Figure; Piet Cronje, Military Personnel (Boer military commander)
Time Period(s): 1890s; 1900s (1899-1900)
Locale(s): Scotland; Ladysmith, South Africa

Summary: Jason Glass, an American writer, journeys to Scotland in 1975 to research a biography of Roberts Menzies, a key figure in the siege of Ladysmith, South Africa, during the Boer War. In delving into the past, Glass discovers a tangled tale of intrigue and deception.

Historical Accuracy: The working together of the historical details of the siege and the fictional story is well done. The period material is convincing.

STEPHEN CRANE (1871-1900)

This American writer championed literary realism. Paradoxically, though he later served as a war correspondent, he had no personal military experience when he created his masterpiece of combat, *The Red Badge of Courage*. His other works include *Maggie: A Girl of the Streets* and the short story "The Open Boat." He died of tuberculosis in Germany.

1414 *The Red Badge of Courage*

Date of Publication: 1895
Subject(s): Civil War—U.S.

Fictional character(s): Henry Fleming, Military Personnel (soldier); Jim Conklin, Military Personnel (soldier); Wilson, Military Personnel (soldier)

Time Period(s): 1860s

Locale(s): United States (unidentified Civil War battlefield)

Summary: Crane views war from the perspective of a young soldier who experiences cowardice, guilt, fear, and finally triumph on an unnamed Civil War battlefield.

Historical Accuracy: His psychological realism set the tone for one of the greatest treatments of war in modern fiction.

TERESA CRANE

1415 *Freedom's Banner*

Date of Publication: 1994

Subject(s): Civil War—U.S.; Antebellum South; Slavery

Fictional character(s): Johnny Sherwood, Gentleman, Military Personnel (Confederate soldier); Mattie Henderson, Spouse (of Johnny); Harry Sherwood, Adventurer

Time Period(s): 19th century (1860s-1899)

Locale(s): Bath, England; Georgia; Egypt

Summary: Englishwoman Mattie Henderson marries the handsome Southerner Johnny Sherwood and settles with him on the Sherwood Plantation in Georgia on the eve of the Civil War. The novel depicts the devastation and conflict the war produces for Mattie, a fervent abolitionist. Her actions provide an important legacy for her son Harry.

Historical Accuracy: The novel's themes are strongly expressed, with some well-aimed period depictions.

1416 *The Hawthorne Legacy*

Date of Publication: 1988

Subject(s): Regency Romance; Inheritance—Disputed; Slavery

Fictional character(s): Jessica Hawthorne, Gentlewoman; Robert Fitzbolton, Gentleman; Daniel O'Donnel, Artist

Time Period(s): 1810s; 1820s (1810-1826)

Locale(s): Suffolk, England; Florence, Italy

Summary: Jessica Hawthorne's parents made their fortune in the slave trade. Love and romance are complicated by jealousy and betrayal, and Jessica must endure a disastrous marriage to Robert Fitzbolton before she can reclaim her legacy and rediscover a lost love.

Historical Accuracy: The period details are convincingly presented.

1417 *Molly*

Date of Publication: 1982

Subject(s): Boer War; Business Building; World War I

Fictional character(s): Molly O'Dowd, Secretary, Businesswoman; Harry Benton, Military Personnel; Adam Jefferson, Military Personnel

Time Period(s): 19th century; 20th century (1898-1918)

Locale(s): London, England

Summary: Molly O'Dowd is a determined Irish girl who arrives in London penniless and manages to escape the poverty and vice of London's East End to found her own employment agency. Love and romance are interrupted first by the Boer War and then by the Great War.

Historical Accuracy: The novel offers a convincing depiction of the London of the period and the personal effects of the wars.

1418 *Sweet Songbird*

Date of Publication: 1987

Subject(s): Victorian Period; Theatrical Life; Franco-Prussian War

Fictional character(s): Kitty Daniels, Orphan, Singer; Moses Smith, Criminal; Matt Daniels, Thief; Luke Peveral, Gypsy, Thief

Time Period(s): 1860s; 1870s (1863-1870s)

Locale(s): Suffolk, England; London, England; Paris, France

Summary: Kitty and Matt Daniels, both orphans, flee from the English countryside to London. There Matt takes up a career as a thief, while Kitty resists a descent into vice. With the help of gypsy Luke Peveral, she becomes a successful music hall performer, finding her way to Paris under siege in the Franco-Prussian War.

Historical Accuracy: There are authentic period details in this story of Victorian adversity and resolution.

PAUL F. CRANSTON

1419 *To Heaven on Horseback*

Date of Publication: 1952

Subject(s): American West; Biography, Fictionalized

Historical character(s): Marcus Whitman, Doctor; Narcissa Whitman, Spouse

Time Period(s): 1830s; 1840s

Locale(s): Oregon

Summary: In the 1830s, Narcissus Whitman, the wife of medical missionary Marcus Whitman, became one of the first white women ever to reach Oregon. This novel, based on the actual letters and journals of Narcissus, reenacts their journey west, ending before the massacre in which both the Whitmans were killed.

Historical Accuracy: The novel's factual basis is evident in its use of primary source material.

MAX CRAWFORD (1938-)

Born in Lubbock, Texas, Crawford earned his B.A. degree from the University of Texas.

1420 *Lords of the Plains*

Date of Publication: 1985

Subject(s): American West; Military Life—U.S. Cavalry; Indians

Fictional character(s): Philip Chapman, Military Personnel (cavalry soldier); James John Macswain, Military Personnel (cavalry soldier)

Historical character(s): Tehana Storm, Indian (Comanche), Chieftain

Time Period(s): 1870s (1875)
Locale(s): Texas; New Mexico

Summary: After the bitter failure of the Second U.S. Cavalry to subdue the Comanches in 1874, a second campaign is launched the following year. The events of this campaign are narrated by Captain Chapman, whose company endures forced marches, a tragic ambush, and a decisive battle that defeats Tehana Storm, the legendary half-white Comanche chieftain.

Historical Accuracy: The details of Western and military life are expertly depicted.

AILEEN CRAWLEY

1421 *The Bride of Suleiman*

Date of Publication: 1981
Subject(s): Ottoman Empire
Fictional character(s): Khurrem, Slave, Seamstress
Historical character(s): Suleiman I, Ruler (Sultan of the Turks); Hafise, Spouse (of Suleiman)
Time Period(s): 16th century
Locale(s): Constantinople, Ottoman Empire

Summary: Khurrem is a Russian slave girl brought to the harem of Suleiman by the Sultana Hafise due to her skill at needlework. Impetuous and honest, Khurrem succeeds in pleasing Hafise as well as Suleiman the Magnificent, who finally, after a series of adventures, pays her the ultimate compliment by asking her to be his bride.

Historical Accuracy: The details of court life in the Ottoman Empire are well-researched and presented.

1422 *The Shadow of God*

Date of Publication: 1983
Subject(s): Ottoman Empire
Historical character(s): Suleiman I, Ruler (Sultan of the Turks); Hafise, Spouse (of Suleiman)
Time Period(s): 16th century (1520s)
Locale(s): Constantinople, Ottoman Empire; Rhodes, Greece

Summary: In the sequel to *The Bride of Suleiman*, Khurrem, the former slave girl and now Suleiman's bride, must learn the intricacies of court politics and prepare to one day rule the harem. The novel colorfully recreates the palace of the Ottoman sultan.

Historical Accuracy: Well-researched and convincing in its period details, the novel provides a reliable version of the past.

JOHN CREASY (1908-1973)

English mystery novelist Creasy began writing at a young age; by the age of 17 he had collected a total of 743 rejection slips. He went on to write nearly 600 books, making him the world's most prolific writer of crime fiction in English. He was given the Grand Master Award in 1969 from the Mystery Writers of America for outstanding contribution to the mystery novel genre. At his death, 60 million copies of his books had been sold worldwide.

1423 *The Masters of Bow Street*

Date of Publication: 1974
Subject(s): Crime and Criminals; Family Saga
Fictional character(s): James Furnival, Judge (chief magistrate); James Marshall, Detective—Police; Jacob Rackham, Thief
Historical character(s): Henry Fielding, Writer, Judge (magistrate); Arthur Wellesley, Military Personnel, Nobleman (Duke of Wellington); Robert Peel, Political Figure
Time Period(s): 18th century; 19th century (1739-1829)
Locale(s): London, England

Summary: The history of the creation of a professional police force in London is chronicled through the story of a single family. John Furnival, Chief Magistrate of Bow Street, and his adopted son, John Marshall, share a dream of police work. Over time, their dream is made a reality, as 18th-century London gives way to the Victorian period.

Historical Accuracy: This is a remarkable and convincing evocation of the period, filled with Dickensian touches that bring the past to life.

WILL CREED

1424 *The Sword of Il Grande*

Date of Publication: 1948
Subject(s): Renaissance
Fictional character(s): Gano Grande, Mercenary; Cosimo di Modena, Banker
Time Period(s): 15th century
Locale(s): Italy

Summary: The novel is set in Renaissance Italy in a city similar to Florence after the nobles have been expelled and before the Modenas have established themselves. It describes the adventures of a young mercenary swordsman, Gano Grande, who is hired to head the police.

Historical Accuracy: The novel interweaves a great many period details and establishes a believable background for the novel's adventures.

MICHAEL CRICHTON (1942-)

Born in Chicago, Crichton received his A.B. and M.D. degrees from Harvard. A sickly child who liked to play with electric trains, Crichton published his first article at age 14, a travel piece in the *New York Times*. Crichton began to write thrillers while he was in medical school, and he has produced some of the biggest selling books in U.S. history, such as *The Andromeda Strain*, *Congo*, and *Jurassic Park*.

1425 *Eaters of the Dead*

Date of Publication: 1976
Subject(s): Vikings; Dark Ages
Fictional character(s): Herger, Warrior
Historical character(s): Ahmad Ibn Fadlan, Diplomat (Arab), Captive
Time Period(s): 10th century (922)

Locale(s): Bagdad, Persia; Russia; Europe

Summary: In 922 Arab diplomat Ibn Fadlan, on a mission to the king of the Bulgars, is captured by a band of Vikings. His adventures include real and mythical encounters of the most startling kinds. The novel's originality is the sophisticated Arab perspective on the barbarian Vikings.

Historical Accuracy: The author offers an elaborate framework of scholarship to bolster his invention and connect it to the real.

1426 *The Great Train Robbery*

Date of Publication: 1975
Subject(s): Victorian Period; Crime and Criminals; Railroads
Fictional character(s): Edward Pierce, Thief; Robert Agar, Thief (safe cracker)
Time Period(s): 1850s (1854-1855)
Locale(s): London, England

Summary: In 1855 a group of resourceful thieves plot to steal a fortune in gold bullion being shipped to the British troops fighting in Russia. The gold is secured in a guarded railroad carriage in two safes with four separate keys needed to unlock them. The scheme to gain the keys and the gold is masterful.

Historical Accuracy: The novel is accomplished in its authentic depiction of the period.

IAIN CRICHTON SMITH

1427 *The Alien Light*

Date of Publication: 1969
Subject(s): Rural Life—Scotland; Highland Clearances
Fictional character(s): Mrs. Scott, Widow(er)
Time Period(s): 19th century
Locale(s): Highlands, Scotland

Summary: This tale of the Highland Clearances tells the story of an aging widow, Mrs. Scott, whose husband was killed during the Peninsular Campaign in the service of the Duke of Sutherland. Expecting a pension from the duke, Mrs. Scott instead is evicted.

Historical Accuracy: The novel is expert in capturing regional atmosphere and details.

GEORGE WILLIAM CRONYN
(1888-1969)

A native of Anderson, Indiana, Cronyn was educated at Harvard, Cornell, and Columbia. He taught English and held various jobs in theaters as well as writing several plays. His books have been praised for their use of local color and evocation of the California Gold Rush. They include *American Indian Poetry: An Anthology of Songs and Chants*, *The Fool of Venus*, and *Mermaid Tavern: Kit Marlowe's Story*.

1428 *The Fool of Venus*

Date of Publication: 1934
Subject(s): Middle Ages; Crusades

Historical character(s): Peire Vidal, Entertainer (troubadour)
Time Period(s): 12th century
Locale(s): Provence, France; Palestine; Constantinople, Byzantine Empire

Summary: This novel of the Middle Ages is based on the life of Peire Vidal, the greatest of the troubadours of Provence. Vidal is shown both in his native Provence and involved in the Third Crusade, that includes the siege and sacking of Constantinople and the siege of Jerusalem.

Historical Accuracy: Story features events in which there is no historical evidence that Vidal actually participated. However, the novel is loaded with period elements that capture the events and the atmosphere of the Third Crusade.

1429 *Mermaid Tavern*

Date of Publication: 1937
Subject(s): Literary Life; Elizabethan Period
Historical character(s): Christopher Marlowe, Writer
Time Period(s): 16th century
Locale(s): London, England; Cambridge, England; France

Summary: The novel offers a factual and swashbuckling account of the life of English poet and playwright Christopher Marlowe. The novel invents a romantic explanation for Marlowe's shady adventures and his controversial demise.

Historical Accuracy: The period elements are authentic, but the novel should not be taken as a biographical account of Marlowe's life.

ELIZABETH CROOK (1959-)

1430 *Promised Lands*

Date of Publication: 1994
Subject(s): Texas Revolution; American West
Fictional character(s): Domingo de la Rosa, Rancher (Mexican); Hugh Kenner, Doctor, Farmer; Katie Kenner, Young Woman; Callum Mackay, Immigrant
Historical character(s): Sam Houston, Military Personnel, Political Figure
Time Period(s): 1830s (1835-1836)
Locale(s): Texas

Summary: The novel tells the story of the Texas Revolution of 1835-1836 from both sides of the struggle. Domingo de la Rosa, a rancher; Hugh Kenner and his daughter, Katie; Callum Mackay, a Scottish immigrant; and others are caught up in the events that culminate in the Goliad massacre.

Historical Accuracy: The author's reconstruction of the events and the scene is masterfully done and authentic in its details.

1431 *The Raven's Bride*

Date of Publication: 1991
Subject(s): Politics
Historical character(s): Sam Houston, Political Figure (Governor of Tennessee); Eliza Allen, Gentlewoman, Spouse (of Houston)
Time Period(s): 1820s (1824-1829)
Locale(s): Tennessee

Summary: In 1829 Sam Houston, the governor of Tennessee, marries Eliza Allen, the daughter of a prominent landholder. Eleven weeks after the wedding, Eliza inexplicably leaves her husband, creating a scandal that causes the governor to resign and move on to his destiny in Texas. Neither ever reveal the reason for their separation. The author supplies speculation that paints a portrait of a failed marriage.

Historical Accuracy: The author admits to inventing many of her characters' motives and actions.

CHARLENE CROSS

1432 *Masque of Enchantment*

Date of Publication: 1990
Subject(s): Romance; Victorian Period
Fictional character(s): Alissa Ashford, Imposter (alias Miss Pembroke), Governess; Jared Braxton, Gentleman
Time Period(s): 1840s
Locale(s): England; Hawkstone, Scotland

Summary: To avoid being charged with murder, actress Alissa Ashford leaves London passing as the new governess for Jared Braxton. In Scotland, instead of the security she expects, she finds danger and intrigue.

Historical Accuracy: The story emphasizes romantic suspense with a slight period backdrop.

DONNA WOOLFOLK CROSS (1947-)

Born in New York City, Cross is a graduate of the University of Pennsylvania. She is a professor of English and a director of the writing center at Onondaga Community College in upstate New York. Cross has written two books on language, *Word Abuse* and *Mediaspeak*.

1433 *Pope Joan*

Date of Publication: 1996
Subject(s): Dark Ages; Religious Life; Battle of Fontenoy
Historical character(s): John VIII, Religious (pope)
Time Period(s): 9th century
Locale(s): Rome, Italy

Summary: This novel is based on the life of a 9th-century woman who, assuming the identity of her dead brother, gained the throne of St. Peter. A distinguished religious scholar, Joan proves to be a shrewd politician as well. The novel provides dramatic scenes of 9th-century events such as the sacking of St. Peter's, the fire that destroyed a third of the Vatican, and the Battle of Fontenoy.

Historical Accuracy: Joan's identity and career are controversial and disputed by the Church. The author claims to have accurately portrayed the main events of Joan's adult life, using imagination only to fill in some of the missing pieces of her story . Notes indicate where the author has deviated from the factual record.

ANN CROWLEIGH
(PSEUD. OF BARBARA CUMMINGS)

1434 *Clively Close: Dead as Dead Can Be*

Date of Publication: 1993
Subject(s): Mystery; Victorian Period
Fictional character(s): Miranda Clively, Spinster; Clare Clively-Murdoch, Widow(er)
Time Period(s): 1870s (1875)
Locale(s): London, England

Summary: The Clively twins are forced by financiers to rent out part of their family home. Renovations uncover the skeleton of a baby, a family secret, and a dilemma. When the family is assembled a fresh corpse is the result. What is the truth that someone desperately wants to hide?.

Historical Accuracy: The drawing room manners and customs are authentic.

DUANE CROWLEY

1435 *Riddle Me a Murder*

Date of Publication: 1987
Subject(s): Middle Ages; Mystery
Historical character(s): Geoffrey Chaucer, Writer; John of Gaunt, Royalty (Duke of Lancaster)
Time Period(s): 14th century
Locale(s): London, England

Summary: This mystery set in 14th-century England employs poet Geoffrey Chaucer as its sleuth. Chaucer must warn John of Gaunt that a conspiracy is underway, while the duke is contending with the poisioning of his latest mistress.

Historical Accuracy: The mystery features a convincing look at court life and the political intrigue of the period.

ELAINE CROWLEY

1436 *The Ways of Women*

Date of Publication: 1993
Subject(s): World War I; Independence—Ireland; Civil War—Ireland
Fictional character(s): Jack Harte, Veteran (World War I); Julia Harte, Spouse; Sarah Quinlaw, Young Woman; Barney Daly, Veteran (World War I)
Time Period(s): 20th century (1918-1930s)
Locale(s): Dublin, Ireland

Summary: Ireland's tragic history after the First World War is reflected in its effect on four residents of a neighborhood in Dublin. Jack Harte and his boyhood friend Barney Daly return from the war to Jack's wife, Julia, and her best friend, Sarah. Together they must endure tragic events in the aftermath of the war.

Historical Accuracy: The sense of place and period are effectively and authentically drawn.

GERTRUDE CROWNFIELD (1867-1945)

Born in Baltimore, Maryland, Crownfield taught school in Ohio and earned a nursing degree in New York City. She wrote novels set in colonial America that feature stories of immigrants in New York, Indians in Ohio, and historical figures such as Mad Anthony Wayne. Her work includes *Where Glory Waits* and *Proud Lady*.

1437 *Where Glory Waits*

Date of Publication: 1934
Subject(s): Biography, Fictionalized
Historical character(s): Anthony Wayne, Military Personnel (general); Mary Vining, Gentlewoman
Time Period(s): 1790s
Locale(s): United States

Summary: This episode in the life of American Revolutionary War general Anthony Wayne describes his love affair with Mary Vining. When they meet and fall in love, Wayne is already married. Upon the death of his wife, the two are to be married when Wayne is killed attempting to quell an Indian uprising.

Historical Accuracy: The novel adheres mainly to historical facts, though the characterization of Wayne tends toward idealization.

HOMER CROY (1883-1965)

An American humorist, reporter, and author, Croy worked as a reporter for Missouri's *St. Joseph Gazette* before moving to New York to work as a writer. One of his books, *They Had to See Paris*, became Will Roger's first talking picture, and Rogers used Croy's stories for his movies more than those of any other writer. His novels include *West of the Water Tower* and *Mr. Meek Marches On*. Croy was the first person to tour the world shooting motion pictures.

1438 *Wheels West*

Date of Publication: 1955
Subject(s): American West; Wagon Trains; Donner Party
Historical character(s): James Frazier Reed, Pioneer; George Donner, Pioneer; Tamsen Donner, Pioneer
Time Period(s): 1840s (1846-1847)
Locale(s): Oregon Trail, United States; Sierra Nevada Mountains, California

Summary: Along the Oregon Trail, the ill-fated Donner Party is trapped by the snows and resorts to cannibalism to survive. James Frazier Reed, one of the pioneers, is banished from the wagon train without food or weapons but survives and returns to help save his family.

Historical Accuracy: The novel's extensive notes indicate the factual source for the details.

WILLIAM CROZIER

1439 *The Fates Are Laughing*

Date of Publication: 1945
Subject(s): Roman Empire; Christianity
Fictional character(s): Metella, Noblewoman
Time Period(s): 1st century (40)
Locale(s): Rome, Roman Empire

Summary: Ancient Rome during the reigns of Tiberius and Caligula is dramatized through the experiences of a Roman senatorial family, particularly Metella, whose advanced notions about freedom for the slaves produce difficulties. Later she becomes afraid that her son may be overly influenced by Christianity.

Historical Accuracy: The novel provides a fascinating and thoroughly believable portrait of the period.

JOHN H. CULP (1907-)

Born in Meridian, Mississippi, Culp attended the University of Oklahoma. After graduating, he worked as a public school teacher and a music store manager in Oklahoma. During World War II, he served in the U.S. Army Air Forces as a sergeant. He is the author of a number of historical novels on the American West.

1440 *Born of the Sun*

Date of Publication: 1959
Subject(s): American West; Cattle Drives
Fictional character(s): Kid Martin, Orphan, Rancher
Time Period(s): 1870s
Locale(s): Texas; Abilene, Kansas

Summary: This western story narrated by Kid Martin describes the first cattle drive during the 1870s from Northwest Texas to Abilene, Kansas. The novel describes the adventures of the journey.

Historical Accuracy: The novel features an authentic depiction of ranching and the cattle drives of the period.

1441 *The Bright Feathers*

Date of Publication: 1965
Subject(s): American West; Picaresque Adventure
Fictional character(s): Scrape Dawkins, Teenager; Scot Benton, Teenager; Ham Esposita McGook, Teenager
Historical character(s): Belle Starr, Outlaw
Time Period(s): 1870s (1871)
Locale(s): Kansas; Oklahoma; Texas

Summary: This picaresque tale records the adventures of three young cowhands from Texas who are trying to get home after a cattle drive to Kansas. They are taken for horse thieves, impressed into the army, meet Belle Starr and her band of outlaws, and travel by railroad, steamboat, and stagecoach in a colorful evocation of the West.

Historical Accuracy: This is a convincing look at the period and its customs.

1442 *The Men of Gonzales*

Date of Publication: 1960
Subject(s): Texas Revolution; Battle of the Alamo
Fictional character(s): Juan White, Teenager
Time Period(s): 1830s (1836)
Locale(s): Gonzales, Texas

Summary: Set during the Texas war of independence, the story describes the efforts of a small group from Gonzales, Texas, where the first shots were fired against Mexico, who set out to join the men in the besieged garrison at the Alamo.

Historical Accuracy: The story is based on the relief effort for the Alamo, led by John W. Smith. The story, however, is not meant as a literal reflection of the actual events. The characters are fictional, and incidents have been invented or modified.

1443 *Oh, Valley Green*

Date of Publication: 1972
Subject(s): American West; Espionage
Fictional character(s): Jacob Key, Spy
Time Period(s): 1840s (1842)
Locale(s): Santa Fe, New Mexico; Sante Fe Trail, West

Summary: In this tale of pioneer days, Jacob Key moves his family west from Virginia along the Santa Fe Trail. His secret mission is to set up an undercover network in New Mexico Territory to aid the American government's move to annex Texas and California.

Historical Accuracy: The novel offers an authentic look at the various groups who contended for power in the Southwest during the period.

1444 *The Restless Land*

Date of Publication: 1962
Subject(s): American West; Indians; Cattle Drives
Fictional character(s): Martin Cameron, Orphan, Teenager
Time Period(s): 1870s
Locale(s): Texas

Summary: In the sequel to *Born of the Sun*, the scene is the northwest Texas frontier of the 1870s. Martin Cameron, known as Kid, has returned home from a cattle drive to find the area under attack by the Comanches. He must journey alone across the southern plains in search of a young girl captured by the Indians.

Historical Accuracy: The history is faithfully recorded, and the details are authentic.

1445 *Timothy Baines*

Date of Publication: 1969
Subject(s): American West; Indians; Medical Profession
Fictional character(s): Dorch McIntyre, Doctor; Timothy Baines, Servant; Denna Cart, Young Woman
Time Period(s): 1870s
Locale(s): Texas; Indian Territory

Summary: This western story, set in the Indian Territory of Oklahoma and Texas during the 1870s, describes the experience of part Indian Dorch McIntyre, who comes to practice

medicine among the Chickasaws and Choctaws to atone for a crime he committed during the Civil War.

Historical Accuracy: The period is recorded authentically.

1446 *The Treasure of the Chisos*

Date of Publication: 1971
Subject(s): Treasure Hunt; American West
Fictional character(s): Colin O'Reiley, Adventurer
Time Period(s): 19th century
Locale(s): Mississippi River; Texas

Summary: This adventure tale is the story of a treasure hunt undertaken by young Colin O'Reiley who travels down the Mississippi and along the old Chisholm Trail to southwestern Texas into the mysterious Chisos Mountains.

Historical Accuracy: The novel is convincing in its period elements.

1447 *A Whistle in the Wind*

Date of Publication: 1968
Subject(s): American West; Indians
Fictional character(s): Chafin, Trader, Captive
Time Period(s): 19th century (1850s-1870s)
Locale(s): Texas

Summary: This tale of frontier life in Texas among the Comanches centers on the trader Chafin, who is captured by the Indians and forced to become a liaison between the Comanches and the Comancheros. The novel captures Indian life as the Comanches are driven off the plains and into the reservations.

Historical Accuracy: Action predominates over a full presentation of historical elements. The novel does feature a convincing realism of detail.

BETTY SUE CUMMINGS (1918-)

Born in Virginia, Cummings graduated from Longwood College and the University of Washington, Seattle. She has worked as a teacher of English in public schools in Virginia, Wyoming, and Florida.

1448 *Say These Names (Remember Them)*

Date of Publication: 1984
Subject(s): Indians; Seminole Wars
Fictional character(s): See-Ho-Kee, Indian
Time Period(s): 1830s
Locale(s): Florida

Summary: Set during the Second Seminole War in Florida that destoyed the native people, the novel describes the experiences of See-Ho-Kee, a young Indian woman, who flees south into the Everglades. She is sustained by her memory of the life that the war wipes away.

Historical Accuracy: The novel is based on a carefully reconstructed historical background. It blends the factual with the fictional to capture a period and a people.

JACK CUMMINGS (1940-)

1449 *Sergeant Gringo*

Date of Publication: 1984
Subject(s): Military Life; Mexican Revolution
Fictional character(s): Matt Dunn, Military Personnel (sergeant)
Historical character(s): Francisco Villa, Revolutionary
Time Period(s): 1910
Locale(s): New Mexico; Mexico

Summary: During Pancho Villa's raid on the U.S. border, Sergeant Matt Dunn's wife is raped and brutally murdered. He deserts his post in New Mexico to search for her killer while he is in turn pursued by the army for desertion.

Historical Accuracy: The main character and events are fictional but based on the actual expedition by General Pershing into Mexico in pursuit of Pancho Villa.

JOHN CUNNINGHAM

1450 *The Rainbow Runner*

Date of Publication: 1992
Subject(s): American West; Revolution—Mexico
Fictional character(s): Jack O'Donohue, Detective—Private
Time Period(s): 1910s (1913)
Locale(s): Los Angeles, California; Mexico

Summary: Jack O'Donohue is hired to transport a priceless jewelled monstrance to a church in revolution-torn Mexico. The church is seen as an enemy of the revolution, and O'Donohue is set upon by Pancho Villa's army. He struggles to complete his mission in the chaos of factional intrigue and betrayal.

Historical Accuracy: The novel is full of genuine atmospheric elements of Mexico during the revolution.

1451 *Warhorse*

Date of Publication: 1956
Subject(s): American West; Ranching
Fictional character(s): Buford Allen, Rancher
Time Period(s): 1880s (1882)
Locale(s): Montana; Ogalalla, Nebraska

Summary: This tale of ranching life in Montana during the 1880s tells the story of Buford Allen and his conflict with the law and rivals during the period of the great Western cattle boom.

Historical Accuracy: This is an authentic and believable story of western life.

JAMES OLIVER CURWOOD (1878-1927)

A Michigan journalist and novelist, Curwood was extremely popular for his stories of the North Woods, which have been compared to Jack London's works. Curwood's novels include *The Country Beyond*, *The Gold Hunters*, and *Nomads of the North*.

1452 *The Plains of Abraham*

Date of Publication: 1928
Subject(s): French and Indian War
Fictional character(s): Toinette Tonteur, Orphan; Jeems Bulain, Orphan
Time Period(s): 1750s
Locale(s): Canada

Summary: This historical romance is set during the French and Indian War and concerns Toinette Tonteur and Jeems Bulain, both orphaned by an Indian massacre. Their story is set against the military campaign that climaxes with the fall of Quebec to the English.

Historical Accuracy: The factual events are accurately described.

DAN CUSHMAN (1909-)

American author Dan Cushman was born in Michigan and attended the University of Montana. Cushman has worked as an assayer, geologist's assistant, miner, and camp cook. He is best known for his novel *Stay Away, Joe*, which was produced as a movie called *Four for Texas*.

1453 *The Silver Mountain*

Date of Publication: 1957
Subject(s): American West; Mining; Business Building
Fictional character(s): John Ballard, Mine Owner; Grattan O'More, Mine Owner; Neva Rush, Young Woman
Time Period(s): 1880s; 1890s
Locale(s): Montana

Summary: John Bullard rises to power and vies with his partner, Grattan O'More, for the love of the ambitious and dangerous Neva Rush.

Historical Accuracy: The story is fictitious, but the novel believably portrays Montana's silver mining region in the late 19th century.

JANET DAILEY (1944-)

Born in Iowa, Dailey worked as a secretary in Nebraska and Iowa. She began her writing career when she and her husband decided to sell their successful construction business and set out on a journey across America in a trailer. Her first novel, *No Quarter Asked*, sold more than a million copies. She has followed up this success with a string of bestsellers that have made her the top female novelist in the U.S.

1454 *The Great Alone*

Date of Publication: 1986
Subject(s): Settlement of the American Frontier; Gold Rush—Klondike; Family Saga
Fictional character(s): Luka Karakou, Hunter; Winter Swan, Indian (Aleut); Larissa Tarakandu, Spouse; Caleb Stone, Sea Captain; Glory St. Clair, Prostitute
Time Period(s): Multiple Time Periods
Locale(s): Alaska

Summary: This ambitious fictional chronicle offers 200 years of Alaskan history, from the Russian settlement to statehood, seen through a seven generation family saga. Through their perspective the panorama of Alaskan history emerges with its blending of different cultures: Russian, Indian, English, and American.

Historical Accuracy: The history of Alaska is convincingly portrayed in this massive historical chronicle.

`1455` *The Pride of Hannah Wade*

Date of Publication: 1985
Subject(s): American West; Indians
Fictional character(s): Hannah Wade, Spouse, Captive; Stephen Wade, Military Personnel (major); Lutero, Indian (Apache), Warrior; Jake Cutter, Military Personnel (captain)
Time Period(s): 1870s (1876)
Locale(s): New Mexico

Summary: Hannah Wade, the wife of Major Stephen Wade, is kidnapped by renegade Apaches under the leadership of Lutero. She endures hardship and humiliation until she is finally rescued by Captain Jake Cutter. On her return, her suffering continues as she is punished for her will to survive at the cost of her honor.

Historical Accuracy: The novel offers some convincing details both of the western frontier and Indian life, though the Apaches are portrayed with scant sympathy or objectivity.

`1456` *The Proud and the Free*

Date of Publication: 1994
Subject(s): Indians; Antebellum South
Fictional character(s): Temple Gordon, Southern Belle, Indian (half Cherokee); Eliza Hall, Teacher; Stuart, the Blade, Indian (Cherokee)
Time Period(s): 1830s
Locale(s): Georgia; Cherokee Nation, Oklahoma

Summary: The novel is set in the Cherokee Nation on the eve of the Trail of Tears. Temple Gordon, raised a southern belle on a Georgia plantation, is half Cherokee. She is caught up in the government's Indian removal policy that sweeps the old world away in a crossfire of vigilantes, tribal bickering, and government betrayal.

Historical Accuracy: The main characters and their stories are invented, but the background is factual and authentic.

JOSEPH A. DALEY (1927-)

Born in Rome, New York, Daley has worked as an editor on a U.S. Navy newspaper, a labor arbitrator on the Boston docks, and a public relations executive in New York. In 1962, Daley ran for Congress in New York. He is the author of the novel *Spicy Lady*.

`1457` *Exit with Drums*

Date of Publication: 1970
Subject(s): Civil War—U.S.

Fictional character(s): James Merrick, Military Personnel (Confederate major); Adam Tucker, Military Personnel (Union colonel)
Time Period(s): 1860s (1865)
Locale(s): Luxor, Georgia; Virginia

Summary: This Civil War tale is set in a peaceful backwater of coastal Georgia where an unofficial truce between the Union and Confederate armies explodes into violence when two Union soldiers are found dead.

Historical Accuracy: The novel is fanciful but convincing in its atmosphere and period elements.

KARA DALKEY

`1458` *Goa*

Date of Publication: 1996
Subject(s): Elizabethan Period; Inquisition
Fictional character(s): Thomas Chinnery, Adventurer
Time Period(s): 16th century
Locale(s): Goa, India

Summary: This adventure tale set during the Elizabethan period concerns the journey of Thomas Chinnery into the Portuguese-controlled waters of East Africa and India to establish trade in medicinal herbs. Events bring him to the Portuguese colony city of Goa at the height of its Inquisition.

Historical Accuracy: The novel's notes make clear the basis of fact from which this largely fictional tale derives its background.

ROBERT WELTER DALY (1916-1975)

An American educator, historian, editor, and author, Daly taught at the U.S. Coast Guard Academy and the U.S. Naval Academy. An expert on naval history, Daly's works include *Raphael Semmes, Confederate Admiral* and the novels *To the Vigilant* and *Guns of Roman Nose*.

`1459` *Broadsides*

Date of Publication: 1940
Subject(s): Napoleonic Wars; Sea Story; Military Life—British Navy
Fictional character(s): Edward O'Corboy, Military Personnel (naval officer)
Time Period(s): 1790s; 1800s
Locale(s): At Sea

Summary: This naval adventure story set during the Napoleonic Wars concerns Irishman Edward O'Corboy, who rises through the ranks to become a captain in the British navy. His adventures at sea dramatize several actual engagements, including the Battle of Trafalgar.

Historical Accuracy: The novel is a fairly comprehensive depiction of the naval history of the era.

`1460` *Soldier of the Sea*

Date of Publication: 1942
Subject(s): Sea Story; Military Life—British Navy

Fictional character(s): Peter Dickoe, Military Personnel (naval lieutenant)
Time Period(s): 1790s (1795-1797)
Locale(s): *Pegasus*, At Sea; France

Summary: This story of military action set during the war with France in the 1790s involves the scholarly Peter Dickoe, who, due to the deaths of his brothers, must live up to family tradition by joining the military. He becomes a lieutenant of marines and is assigned to lead a landing in France, where he must meet and escort back to the ship a mysterious passenger. The novel is filled with military action as young Dickoe proves his mettle.

Historical Accuracy: The novel is best in its depiction of period naval life, which is delivered with authenticity.

DON DANDREA (1936-)

Dandrea is from Colorado Springs, Colorado, and is a graduate of Colorado State College. He has worked as a physicist at the White Sands Missile Range in New Mexico and as an electronic engineer at various defense establishments.

1461 *Orlok*

Date of Publication: 1986
Subject(s): Mongol Empire
Historical character(s): Subotai, Military Personnel (Mongol general); Genghis Khan, Ruler (Mongol emperor)
Time Period(s): 13th century
Locale(s): Asia (China, Korea, India); Persia; Russia

Summary: The military master-mind behind Genghis Khan's conquering of half the known world in the 13th century was Subotai, called Orlok, or eagle. The novel imagines Subotai's early life on the Asian steppes, his study with an Indian warrior, and his brilliant military exploits.

Historical Accuracy: The author acknowledges that his novel makes certain departures from the generally accepted data on the historical characters and events.

CLEMENCE DANE
(PSEUD. OF WINIFRED ASHTON, 1888-1965)

British portraitist, actress, and author Ashton was born in Blackheath, England. She took the pseudonym Clemence Dane from St. Clements Dane church in London, which was bombed during World War II. *Legend*, her 1949 novel, was adapted into the successful play *A Bill of Divorcement*. Ashton also wrote *Broome Stages* and *The Moon is Feminine*.

1462 *He Brings Great News*

Date of Publication: 1945
Subject(s): Napoleonic Wars; Sea Story; Battle of Trafalgar
Fictional character(s): John Richards Lapenotiere, Military Personnel (naval officer)
Time Period(s): 1800s (1805)
Locale(s): At Sea; England

Summary: The turning point in England's naval war with France, the Battle of Trafalgar, is the background for this novel in which Lieutenant John Lapenotiere brings the news of Admiral Nelson's great victory and his death back to England.

Historical Accuracy: The novel effectively uses its naval elements.

KATHLEEN DANIELS
(PSEUD. OF GEORGE SCHWARTZ; KATHLEEN SCHWARTZ)

1463 *Minna's Story: The Secret Love of Doctor Sigmund Freud*

Date of Publication: 1992
Subject(s): Biography, Fictionalized; Medical Profession
Historical character(s): Sigmund Freud, Doctor, Writer; Minna Bernay, Gentlewoman
Time Period(s): 1890s (1895-1898)
Locale(s): Vienna, Austria

Summary: Cast in the form of a diary kept by Minna Bernay, Sigmund Freud's sister-in-law, the novel recounts her relationship with Freud and her influence on the development of Freud's theories on hysteria, sexuality, and dreams.

Historical Accuracy: The novel has employed carefully researched historical and biographical facts to reconstruct this story of Freud's domestic life. The interpretation of Freud's relationship with Bernay is controversial and subject to considerable debate.

PETER DANIELSON (1928-)

Born in the Deep South, Danielson worked as a newspaper reproter before becoming a musician. In the 1970s he achieved his first success as a novelist.

1464 *Children of the Lion*

Date of Publication: 1989
Subject(s): Biblical Story
Fictional character(s): Sneferu, Military Personnel (soldier); Zakir, Artisan; Ahuna, Young Woman, Artisan
Historical character(s): Abraham, Biblical Figure; Hagar, Biblical Figure, Slave
Time Period(s): Indeterminate Past
Locale(s): Canaan, Palestine

Summary: In the first book of the author's Biblical series, the founding of the line of Abraham is traced from the fiery destruction of Sodom. As Abraham leads his people, his love for the slave girl Hagar is a source of complication. Meanwhile, a family of artisans plays an important role in the history of Abraham's tribe as it is fashioned into a nation.

Historical Accuracy: The story is mainly fictional with some convincing background details.

1465 *The Death of Kings*

Date of Publication: 1994

Subject(s): Biblical Story
Fictional character(s): Eri, Artisan (armorer); Tania, Royalty (princess)
Historical character(s): Saul, Biblical Figure, Ruler (King of Israel); Jonathan, Biblical Figure; David, Biblical Figure
Time Period(s): Indeterminate Past
Locale(s): Israel

Summary: As Saul's victories over the Philistines make him the first King of Israel, he must deal with a rival in the form of warrior-hero David. Civil war breaks out as Saul's reign degenerates into tyranny and cruelty.

Historical Accuracy: Derived in part from the Biblical account, there is also considerable invention in the story.

`1466` *Departed Glory*

Date of Publication: 1993
Subject(s): Biblical Story; Ancient Egypt
Fictional character(s): Eri, Slave, Warrior
Historical character(s): Saul, Biblical Figure; Samuel, Biblical Figure, Judge
Time Period(s): Indeterminate Past
Locale(s): Egypt

Summary: The Israelites versus the Philistines is the theme in this installment of the Children of the Lion saga. A former slave, Eri, joins with King Saul to unite the divided tribes of Israel in defense. The action includes political intrigue in the court of the Egyptian pharaoh.

Historical Accuracy: The novel is more a colorful costume drama than an accurate historical account of the era, but the atmosphere is often credible.

`1467` *The Exodus*

Date of Publication: 1989
Subject(s): Family Saga; Biblical Story; Ancient Egypt
Fictional character(s): Seth, Artisan (armorer)
Historical character(s): Moses, Biblical Figure; Aaron, Biblical Figure; Miriam, Biblical Figure
Time Period(s): 13th century B.C.
Locale(s): Egypt

Summary: Book Ten of the Children of the Lion series describes the exodus of the Hebrews from Egypt. The clan of the Children of the Lion use their talents as sword makers to help the Egyptian prince, Moses, lead his people out of slavery.

Historical Accuracy: The Biblical story is repossessed in a fictional narrative that does offer some plausible period elements.

`1468` *The Golden Pharaoh*

Date of Publication: 1985
Subject(s): Ancient Egypt; Family Saga; Pharaohs
Fictional character(s): Shobai, Artisan (armorer); Mereet, Spouse (of Shobai)
Historical character(s): Joseph, Biblical Figure
Time Period(s): 14th century B.C.
Locale(s): Egypt

Summary: In volume five of the Children of the Lion saga, the clan assists the true ruler of Egypt, who has been exiled to the Upper Nile. To the north, the Golden Pharaoh, usurper of the throne, has enslaved many, and rebellion and war are spreading.

Historical Accuracy: The novel weaves together a colorful mix of history, legend, Biblical elements, and the imagination into an atmospheric evocation of the period.

`1469` *The Invaders*

Date of Publication: 1991
Subject(s): Family Saga; Ancient Israel; Ancient Greece
Fictional character(s): Helen of Troy, Noblewoman; Pepi, Artisan (armorer); Achilles, Warrior
Historical character(s): Deborah, Biblical Figure
Time Period(s): 12th century B.C.
Locale(s): Israel; Troy, Ancient Civilization

Summary: In the 13th volume of the Children of the Lion series, war continues to rage in Troy and the Israelites fall under the control of a sadistic, power-hungry general. He is opposed by Deborah, a seeress and prophet, who inspires the nation.

Historical Accuracy: The novel blends Biblical details and Greek legends into a plausible reconstruction of the ancient past.

`1470` *The Lion in Egypt*

Date of Publication: 1984
Subject(s): Ancient Egypt; Family Saga; Biblical Story
Fictional character(s): Ben-Hadad, Artisan (armorer); Shobai, Artisan (armorer)
Historical character(s): Joseph, Biblical Figure
Time Period(s): 14th century B.C.
Locale(s): Egypt

Summary: Book four of the Children of the Lion series concerns the conquest of Egypt by the armies of the Shepherd Kings and the enslavement of Joseph by a foreign tribe. The key to Egypt's liberation is held by the Children of the Lion.

Historical Accuracy: The story is fanciful but filled with the colorful atmosphere of the era.

`1471` *The Promised Land*

Date of Publication: 1990
Subject(s): Family Saga; Ancient Greece; Ancient Israel
Fictional character(s): Iri, Artisan (armorer), Wanderer; Helen of Troy, Noblewoman
Historical character(s): Joshua, Biblical Figure
Time Period(s): 12th century B.C.
Locale(s): Israel; Troy, Ancient Civilization

Summary: As the saga of the Children of the Lion continues, the Israelites are at war in Canaan and the Greeks are in conflict with the Trojans. Warfare drives away the Children of the Lion, while Iri travels the Aegean in search of his beloved.

Historical Accuracy: The novel blends together Biblical elements and Greek legends in a story that is a plausible reconstruction of the era.

1472 *The Prophecy*

Date of Publication: 1986
Subject(s): Ancient Egypt; Family Saga; Pharaohs
Fictional character(s): Kamose, Bastard Son; Teti, Artisan (armorer)
Historical character(s): Joseph, Biblical Figure
Time Period(s): 14th century B.C.
Locale(s): Egypt

Summary: In the seventh installment of the Children of the Lion saga, rebellion against the Hai oppressors of Egypt spreads. Teti, a female member of the Children of the Lion clan, forges a special sword that will affect the course of the conflict.

Historical Accuracy: The story is invented, but convincing in its atmosphere.

1473 *Prophets and Warriors*

Date of Publication: 1992
Subject(s): Biblical Story
Fictional character(s): Abimelech, Warrior; Talus, Warrior; Luti, Sorceress
Time Period(s): Indeterminate Past
Locale(s): Palestine; Greece; Babylon

Summary: Gideon's illegitimate son, Abimelech, tries to gain power and causes violence across Canaan. In Thrace, Talus gathers a following to regain the Children of the Lion's stone fortune. In Babylon, Luti is ordered to spy while her daughter is taken as a hostage to ensure Luti's cooperation.

Historical Accuracy: There is little here that is directly historical.

1474 *The Sea Peoples*

Date of Publication: 1989
Subject(s): Biblical Story; Family Saga
Fictional character(s): Iri, Artisan (armorer); Keturah, Captive, Spouse (of Iri); Minotaur, Pirate
Historical character(s): Joshua, Biblical Figure, Warrior
Time Period(s): 11th century B.C.
Locale(s): Israel

Summary: The Hebrews are now led by the fierce warrior Joshua and face a number of challenges as they move against the enemies that block their path into Canaan. One comes from a mysterious pirate called the Minotaur and his seagoing people who are equally determined to seize Canaan. The clan of the Children of the Lion is in the middle of the conflict.

Historical Accuracy: The novel interweaves the historical, the legendary, and the invented into a rousing adventure that captures the color and atmosphere of the age.

1475 *The Shepherd Kings*

Date of Publication: 1985
Subject(s): Biblical Story
Fictional character(s): Hadad, Artisan; Kirta, Artisan
Historical character(s): Jacob, Biblical Figure; Esau, Biblical Figure
Time Period(s): Indeterminate Past

Locale(s): Canaan, Palestine; Crete, Greece

Summary: In the second volume of the author's Biblical series, Jacob, though heir of the kingdom of Canaan, is forced to flee north of Damascus to a city under assault by rampaging nomads. Meanwhile, the artisan Kirta discovers the secret of iron at the court of Minos in Crete.

Historical Accuracy: The main outlines of the novel are imagined, though the atmosphere is derived from Biblical stories.

1476 *The Shining King*

Date of Publication: 1995
Subject(s): Biblical Story; Ancient Egypt
Fictional character(s): Sunu, Warrior
Historical character(s): David, Biblical Figure, Ruler (King of Israel); Joab, Biblical Figure
Time Period(s): Indeterminate Past
Locale(s): Israel; Egypt

Summary: When King Saul dies, chaos reigns throughout a divided Israel, and the Philistines take advantage of it to ravage the countryside. Sunu forms an alliance with David to rescue the Israelites.

Historical Accuracy: The atmosphere is authentic, even if the actual story is more imagined than actual.

1477 *Sword of Glory*

Date of Publication: 1987
Subject(s): Family Saga; Ancient Egypt
Fictional character(s): Seth, Artisan (armorer); Kamose, Bastard Son, Ruler (Egyptian king); Mara, Spouse (of Kamose)
Time Period(s): 13th century B.C.
Locale(s): Mesopotamia; Egypt

Summary: In Volume Eight of the Children of the Lion series, conflict arises in Egypt when Kamose embraces the cult of an evil goddess and becomes a murderous tyrant. Seth, a Child of the Lion, searches Mesopotamia for a weapon upon which the destiny of Egypt depends.

Historical Accuracy: The fictional story relies on a believably constructed period background.

1478 *Triumph of the Lion*

Date of Publication: 1995
Subject(s): Biblical Story
Fictional character(s): Sunu, Warrior
Historical character(s): David, Biblical Figure; Bathsheba, Biblical Figure
Time Period(s): 10th century B.C.
Locale(s): Israel

Summary: In this installment of the author's biblical-era series, ultimate victory is within reach as David amasses an army to march on Jerusalem. Sunu, a fearless young warrior bearing the Mark of the Lion, leads a raid into the city that could determine the final outcome of the battle.

Historical Accuracy: The background details are believable, but the story is fanciful.

`1479` *The Trumpet and the Sword*

Date of Publication: 1991
Subject(s): Biblical Story
Fictional character(s): Zalmunnah, Chieftain (King of the Bedouins); Luti, Sorceress
Historical character(s): Gideon, Biblical Figure
Time Period(s): Indeterminate Past
Locale(s): Palestine

Summary: War with the Phoenicians and the Bedouins is the challenge for the celebrated warrior and prophet Gideon. He attempts to lead his people into the promised land while pursued by Zalmunnah, who is bent on destroying the Israelites.

Historical Accuracy: There is a sense of authentic atmosphere even if the story itself is imagined.

`1480` *Vengeance of the Lion*

Date of Publication: 1983
Subject(s): Family Saga; Biblical Story; Ancient Egypt
Fictional character(s): Shobai, Artisan (armorer)
Historical character(s): Joseph, Biblical Figure
Time Period(s): 14th Century B.C.
Locale(s): Israel; Egypt

Summary: The third volume of the Children of the Lion series dramatizes the struggle for power in Canaan and Egypt as the armies of the Shepherd Kings move south, and overcome Egypt's army. The fictional saga of Children of the Lion, renowned weapon-makers, is connected to events in Egypt and the Biblical story of Joseph, son of Jacob.

Historical Accuracy: The story blends Biblical, historical, and imaginary material together in a colorful presentation of the period.

JACK DANN (1945-)

A Johnson City, New York, native, Dann was educated at the State University of New York at Binghamton. He has taught writing and appeared on television and radio. He has won several awards for his science fiction. His novels include *Starhiker* and *The Memory Cathedral*.

`1481` *The Memory Cathedral: A Secret History of Leonardo Da Vinci*

Date of Publication: 1995
Subject(s): Renaissance; Artistic Life; Fantasy
Historical character(s): Leonardo da Vinci, Artist, Inventor
Time Period(s): 15th century (1480s)
Locale(s): Italy; Syria

Summary: This imaginative historical fantasy speculates on what might have happened had Leonardo da Vinci journeyed to Syria and built for a local potentate the marvelous military inventions recorded in his notebooks. The effect on warfare is deadly and the result produces a moral quandary for da Vinci.

Historical Accuracy: The situation is imaginary, but the details from da Vinci's biography and the elements of Renaissance life are authentic.

CATHERINE DARBY
(PSEUD. OF MAUREEN PETERS, 1935-)

Born in Caernarvon, Wales, Darby graduated from University College of North Wales. She is a teacher of English to retarded children. In her writing she is interested in the influence of the past over the present and her specific interests include hagiography, the Tudor period, and the theater.

`1482` *The Love Knot*

Date of Publication: 1989
Subject(s): Middle Ages; Literary Life
Historical character(s): Geoffrey Chaucer, Writer; John of Gaunt, Royalty; Philippa de Roet, Gentlewoman; Katherine de Roet, Gentlewoman
Time Period(s): 14th century (1349-1360)
Locale(s): London, England

Summary: Two sisters, Phillippa and Katherine de Roet, lose their mother to the plague and journey to England, where their father introduces them to English society. Phillipa contracts a loveless marriage with the poet Geoffrey Chaucer, while Katherine's affairs take her to the center stage of England's most important houses.

Historical Accuracy: The story is based in large measure on fact with the details of English life in the 14th century presented with authenticity.

CLARE DARCY

American romance novelist Darcy is a prolific author of mainly Regency-era romances. Reviewers have designated her the heir apparent to Georgette Heyer.

`1483` *Allegra*

Date of Publication: 1974
Subject(s): Regency Romance; Napoleonic Wars; Battle of Waterloo
Fictional character(s): Allegra Herington, Gentlewoman; Derek Herington, Military Personnel; Hilary Herington, Gentlewoman
Time Period(s): 1810s (1815)
Locale(s): Brussels, Belgium; Bath, England

Summary: In the spring of 1815, Allegra Herington and her sister Hilary find themselves in Brussels in the days leading up to the Battle of Waterloo. The greatest battle in the 19th century becomes the ultimate complication in this romantic tangle involving the proud Allegra and the stalwart Sir Derek.

Historical Accuracy: The costumes and dialogue are right, if somewhat trivial compared to the battlefield drama that remains in the background.

`1484` *Caroline and Julia*

Date of Publication: 1982
Subject(s): Regency Romance; Inheritance—Disputed; Theatrical Life

Fictional character(s): Caroline Devereaux, Gentlewoman, Orphan; Julia Daventry, Widow(er), Actress; Neville Devereaux, Gentleman; Lord Redvers Wrexham, Nobleman
Time Period(s): 19th century (Regency period)
Locale(s): London, England

Summary: A complicated plot featuring a hidden will and a disputed fortune tangles the romance as Caroline Devereaux turns to her mother's actress friend, Julia Daventry, for support. A forced marriage and threats of violence must be overcome before the final satisfactory conclusion.

Historical Accuracy: The Regency atmosphere is aided by some behind-the-scenes looks at the theater world of the time.

1485 *Cressida*

Date of Publication: 1977
Subject(s): Regency Romance
Fictional character(s): Cressida Calverton, Gentlewoman; Deverell Rossiter, Military Personnel; Kitty Chenevix, Gentlewoman
Time Period(s): 19th century (Regency period)
Locale(s): London, England; Gloucestershire, England

Summary: When Cressida Calverton again meets Captain Deverell Rossiter, who jilted her years before, he has made a fortune and become a social lion. The sparks fly as he becomes interested in Kitty Chenevix.

Historical Accuracy: The novel is loaded with Regency elements that create the proper background.

1486 *Elyza*

Date of Publication: 1976
Subject(s): Regency Romance
Fictional character(s): Elyza Leigh, Gentlewoman; Cleve Redmayne, Gentleman; Corinna Mayfield, Gentlewoman
Historical character(s): George, Prince Regent, Royalty (prince regent)
Time Period(s): 19th century (Regency period)
Locale(s): London, England; Brighton, England

Summary: Elyza Leigh escapes from London to Bath. She is befriended by Cleve Redmayne, who has returned from India to marry Corinna Mayfield. In Bath a duel, a kidnapping, a chase, and numerous proposals all complicate the romance.

Historical Accuracy: The novel is somewhat over-stuffed with Regency elements, though the dialogue and costumes are convincing.

1487 *Eugenia*

Date of Publication: 1977
Subject(s): Regency Romance
Fictional character(s): Eugenia Liddiard, Young Woman; Richard Liddiard, Young Man; Gerald Liddiard, Young Man
Time Period(s): 1810s
Locale(s): London, England; Kent, England

Summary: This Regency period romance features the romantic maneuverings of Eugenia Liddiard. She encounters a long-lost cousin who resembles another cousin, a scapegrace wanted on a charge of highway murder. Eugenia helps keep

both men out of the hands of the Bow Street Runners while generating a great deal of confusion that is only untangled in the novel's happy conclusion.

Historical Accuracy: The novel features genuine period elements that create a convincing sense of the era.

1488 *Georgina*

Date of Publication: 1971
Subject(s): Regency Romance
Fictional character(s): Georgina Power, Heiress; Mark Shannon, Bastard Son, Widow(er)
Time Period(s): 19th century (Regency period)
Locale(s): Bath, England; Kerry, Ireland

Summary: Georgina is exiled to Ireland from Bath when she rejects an eligible but dull suitor. There she meets Shannon, the bastard son of a lord, and the romantic complications must be worked through until the expected harmonious conclusion.

Historical Accuracy: The Irish scenes are interesting and convincing, if the romance is conventional Regency fare.

1489 *Gwendolen*

Date of Publication: 1978
Subject(s): Regency Romance
Fictional character(s): Henry Belville, Military Personnel (captain); Gwendolen Quarters, Gentlewoman; Lyndale, Nobleman (Marquis of Lyndale)
Time Period(s): 1810s (1814)
Locale(s): England

Summary: Gwendolen Quarters falls madly in love with the gallant Captain Henry Belville, but later discovers him to be pompous and overbearing. She must help untangle the love affairs of her sisters while attracted to Lyndale, her sister's choice.

Historical Accuracy: The Regency atmosphere is convincing, if unoriginal.

1490 *Lady Pamela*

Date of Publication: 1975
Subject(s): Regency Romance
Fictional character(s): Pamela Frayne, Gentlewoman; Carlin Dalven, Nobleman (baron); Lord Babcock, Nobleman
Time Period(s): 19th century (Regency period)
Locale(s): Wiltshire, England; London, England

Summary: In this romantic tangle Lady Pamela Frayne, engaged to Lord Babcock, is involved in an intrigue dealing with a missing memorandum from the Foreign Office. Lord Dalven both assists and complicates the plot.

Historical Accuracy: The atmosphere of Regency society is clearly depicted.

1491 *Letty*

Date of Publication: 1980
Subject(s): Regency Romance
Fictional character(s): Harry Tyne, Gambler, Gentleman; Max von Bergheim, Nobleman; Letty Montressor, Singer
Time Period(s): 1810s

Locale(s): London, England; Vienna, Austria

Summary: Harry Tyne is a disgraced gentleman, wrongfully accused of being a card cheat, who embarks for Vienna with Letty, a young singer, to open a gaminghouse. Letty falls in love with Harry and tries to clear his name.

Historical Accuracy: The romantic world clashes somewhat with that of the Congress of Vienna, where the fate of Europe is being decided as well as the story's romantic complications.

1492 *Lydia, or Love in Town*

Date of Publication: 1973
Subject(s): Regency Romance
Fictional character(s): Lydia Leyland, Gentlewoman; Christopher Brome, Nobleman (Viscount Northover)
Time Period(s): 1810s
Locale(s): London, England

Summary: Lydia Leyland is the daughter of a family from Louisiana. She comes to England with a small inheritance to find a rich husband. She is befriended by Lord Northover, who rescues Lydia from her social blunders.

Historical Accuracy: Scenes at the Vauxhall Gardens and the theater create a strong sense of period atmosphere.

1493 *Victoire*

Date of Publication: 1974
Subject(s): Regency Romance
Fictional character(s): Victoire Duvernay, Gentlewoman; Lewis Fearon, Nobleman (Marquis of Tarn)
Time Period(s): 19th century (Regency period)
Locale(s): London, England

Summary: The novel is a romantic combat of wits between the Marquis of Tarn and Victoire Duverny, daughter of an Irish colonel killed in battle. A London season becomes the stage for the action that includes a disputed inheritance and an attempted murder.

Historical Accuracy: The Regency feel and atmosphere are genuine if the drama is somewhat conventional.

ELEANOR DARK

1494 *Storm of Time*

Date of Publication: 1950
Subject(s): Frontier—Australia; Rum Rebellion
Fictional character(s): Stephen Mannion, Landowner
Historical character(s): William Bligh, Government Official (governor of New South Wales); John MacArthur, Military Personnel (captain)
Time Period(s): 18th century; 19th century (1759-1808)
Locale(s): Australia

Summary: The novel chronicles the early days of the Australian colony and the conflicts of Captain John MacArthur with a succession of colonial governors. The last is William Bligh, of *Bounty* fame, who proves to be MacArthur's toughest adversary. It takes the Rum Rebellion of 1808 to unseat him.

Historical Accuracy: The historical elements of the story are accurate and convincing.

1495 *The Timeless Land*

Date of Publication: 1941
Subject(s): Frontier—Australia
Fictional character(s): Andrew Prentice, Convict
Historical character(s): Arthur Phillip, Government Official (colonial governor); Benilong, Chieftain (aborigine)
Time Period(s): 1790s
Locale(s): Sydney, Australia

Summary: The early years of the settlement of Australia are shown from the points of view of its native aborigines and settlers, convicts, and government officials of the colony at Sydney. The three main characters—Arthur Phillip, the first governor of New South Wales, the aborigine Benilong (both taken from history), and the convict Andrew Prentice—represent the three clashing interests that form the earliest Australian colonial experience.

Historical Accuracy: The novel's details are carefully based on the record.

ELIZABETH DARRELL
(PSEUD. OF EDNA DAWES)

English writer Dawes spent her early childhood in Hong Kong. Darrell is one of several pseudonyms. Her other novels include *And in the Morning*, *At the Going Down of the Sun*, and *Burn All Your Bridges*.

1496 *The Gathering Wolves*

Date of Publication: 1980
Subject(s): Russian Revolution; Civil War—Russia; Bridge Building
Fictional character(s): Paul Anderson, Engineer; Alexander Swardovsky, Military Personnel (colonel); Lyudmilla Zapalova, Dancer (ballet)
Time Period(s): 1910s (1918-1919)
Locale(s): Russia

Summary: The background of this story is the Russian Revolution and its subsequent civil war. In the arctic forests of North Russia, along the important railway from Mirmansk to Petrograd, a British engineer, Paul Anderson, struggles to repair an important railway bridge while getting involved with the White Russian cause.

Historical Accuracy: The novel imagines what might have happened in this setting during this time. The speculation is convincing and effective.

1497 *The Jade Alliance*

Date of Publication: 1979
Subject(s): East/West Relations; English Colonies
Fictional character(s): Nadja Brusilov, Young Woman; Andrew Stanton, Government Official (British)
Time Period(s): 1900s
Locale(s): Hong Kong

Summary: The Brusilovs are refugees from the turmoil of Czarist Russia who settle in Hong Kong and enter the thriving jade business. Nadja Brusilov falls in love with British agent Andrew Stanton, who is investigating the connection between the jade business and the Russian-Chinese alliance. What he uncovers could have global consequences.

Historical Accuracy: This novel of intrigue features a vividly imagined and convincing period Hong Kong.

COLETTE DAVENAT

French author Davenat has a particular interest in the Renaissance and the Elizabethan period.

1498 *Deborah*

Date of Publication: 1973
Subject(s): Elizabethan Period; Espionage
Fictional character(s): Deborah Mason, Spy; Kit Belstone, Nobleman
Historical character(s): Elizabeth I, Ruler (Queen of England)
Time Period(s): 16th century (1580s)
Locale(s): England

Summary: This adventure tale set during the Elizabethan period, concerns Deborah Mason, the young ward of one of Queen Elizabeth's maids, who becomes a secret agent for the Queen. Her first mission is to take a secret message to the imprisoned Mary, Queen of Scots, an adventure that introduces her to a wider world of intrigue and danger.

Historical Accuracy: The novel's story is fanciful, but it is authentic in some of its period elements.

1499 *Deborah and the Many Faces of Love*

Date of Publication: 1974
Subject(s): Elizabethan Period; Espionage; Spanish Armada
Fictional character(s): Deborah Mason, Spy, Noblewoman (countess)
Historical character(s): Sir Francis Drake, Military Personnel (naval officer); Robert Cecil, Nobleman, Courtier; Elizabeth I, Ruler (Queen of England)
Time Period(s): 16th century (1588)
Locale(s): London, England; Flanders

Summary: This sequel to *Deborah* continues the exploits of the trusted agent of Queen Elizabeth, Deborah Mason (now Countess of Norland) who is sent on a mission to Spanish-occupied Flanders as the Spanish Armada is preparing to invade England. She is unmasked but escapes in the hold of a Spanish ship from which she views the great sea battle. On her return to England she faces a charge of high treason.

Historical Accuracy: The story is fanciful and full of romantic adventures that depend on a clear background of period events and figures.

1500 *Deborah and the Siege of Paris*

Date of Publication: 1976
Subject(s): Elizabethan Period; Espionage
Fictional character(s): Deborah Norland, Noblewoman (countess), Spy; Sir William Tremor, Gentleman; Perceval de War, Gentleman

Historical character(s): Elizabeth I, Ruler (Queen of England); Robert Cecil, Courtier, Government Official; Henri IV, Ruler (King of France)
Time Period(s): 16th century (1590s)
Locale(s): London, England; Paris, France; Cornwall, England

Summary: In the third of the Elizabethan adventure novels involving Queen Elizabeth's agent, Deborah, Countess of Norland, she is given the task of infiltrating and thwarting a conspiracy to overthrow the throne. Escaping from the ruthless leader of the conspiracy, Sir William Tremor, Deborah flees to France where she finds herself in the thick of Henri IV's struggle to secure his throne.

Historical Accuracy: The story is fictional but is set against an authentic period background.

GWEN DAVENPORT (1910-)

Born in Colon, Panama, Davenport is the daughter of a vice admiral in the U.S. Navy. She was educated at Vassar College and is the author of *The Wax Foundation* and *Great Loves in Legend and Life. Belvedere*, her novel and play, was adapted into the film *Sitting Pretty* and the television series ''Mr. Belvedere.''.

1501 *Time and Chance*

Date of Publication: 1993
Subject(s): Victorian Period; Family Saga
Fictional character(s): Maria Wrox Hampden, Gentlewoman
Time Period(s): 1840s
Locale(s): England

Summary: The Wrox family are members of the landed gentry during the early years of Queen Victoria's reign. The family and their matriarch, Maria Wrox-Hampden, attempt to cope with changes brought about by the arrival of the railroad and other social disruptions.

Historical Accuracy: The novel offers a believable portrait of Victorian customs.

EVAN JOHN DAVID (1881-)

David is the author of *As Runs the Glass* and editor of *Leonard Wood on Nation Issues: The Many-Sided Mind of a Great Executive Shown by His Public Utterances.*

1502 *As Runs the Glass*

Date of Publication: 1944
Subject(s): French Revolution; Sea Story
Fictional character(s): Dodpher Tudor, Bastard Son; Jared Tudor, Young Man
Time Period(s): 1790s
Locale(s): Maine; Brest, France

Summary: Set during the French Revolution, this adventure tale involves a seafaring family, the Tudors, and the rivalry between Dodpher and Jared Tudor. Jared finds himself in a series of adventures at sea and in revolutionary France.

Historical Accuracy: The period background is historically accurate.

DIANE DAVIDSON (1924-)
An American teacher, actress, and author, Davidson was born in Los Angeles, California, and attended the University of California, Berkeley, and Sacramento College.

`1503` *Feversham*
Date of Publication: 1969
Subject(s): Tudor Period; Mystery
Historical character(s): Alice Arden, Gentlewoman; Sir Thomas Cheyney, Government Official
Time Period(s): 16th century (1550s)
Locale(s): England

Summary: Based on an actual murder case recorded in Raphael Holinshed's *Chronicle* and dramatized in a Tudor play, *Arden of Feversham*, the novel reconstructs the attempt of Alice Arden to have her lover murder her husband. The case is investigated by Sir Thomas Cheyney whose inquiries take him through the Tudor underworld and into a complicated tangle of seduction and betrayal.

Historical Accuracy: The author's notes indicate the minor alterations from the actual events and chronology. The period accuracy is of a high standard.

LOUIS B. DAVIDSON

EDDIE DOHERTY (1890-1975)
Davidson has worked as a lawyer in New York. He is a collector of law cases and ship's logs involving pirates. Doherty was an American journalist, war correspondent, and an ordained priest of the Byzantine Catholic Church of the Melchite rite. His books include *Strange Crimes at Sea* (with Louis B. Davidson), *I Cover God*, and *King of Sinners*.

`1504` *Captain Marooner*
Date of Publication: 1952
Subject(s): Sea Story; Whaling; Mutiny
Fictional character(s): George Comstock, Sailor; Sam Comstock, Sailor
Time Period(s): 1820s
Locale(s): *Globe*, At Sea

Summary: Based on the voyage of the New England whaling ship *Globe* in the 1820s, the novel recounts the events that lead up to a mutiny. Told by a young Quaker seaman, George Comstock, the story evokes life aboard a whaler and the factors that lead to mutiny and violence.

Historical Accuracy: The incidents leading up to the mutiny, the actual mutiny itself, and its aftermath are based on the records of the testimony of the surviving crew members.

L.S. DAVIDSON JR.

`1505` *The Disturber*
Date of Publication: 1964
Subject(s): American Colonies; Pilgrims; Puritans

Fictional character(s): David Ratcliffe, Doctor
Historical character(s): Thomas Morton, Adventurer, Trader; Ben Jonson, Writer; William Blackstone, Settler; Miles Standish, Leader (pilgrim)
Time Period(s): 17th century
Locale(s): Merry Mount, Massachusetts, American Colonies; Plymouth, Massachusetts, American Colonies; London, England

Summary: The founding of Merry Mount, not far from the Plymouth Colony, is the novel's subject. The libertine Thomas Morton establishes Merry Mount to defy the austere Puritans, and their reaction is swift and severe. Morton is sent back to England in chains. David Ratcliffe, a young indentured apprentice, comes under Morton's influence and meets him again in London while completing his medical training.

Historical Accuracy: The novel's history is reliable, based on documented sources.

JUNE WYNDHAM DAVIES
Born in Liverpool, England, Davies has written fiction for women's magazines.

`1506` *Golden Destiny*
Date of Publication: 1992
Subject(s): American West; Gold Rush—California
Fictional character(s): Alicia Langdon, Young Woman; Chen Kai Tsu, Immigrant; Colonel Jack Cornish, Landowner
Time Period(s): 1850s
Locale(s): San Francisco, California; Sierra Nevada Mountains, California

Summary: Alicia Langdon flees from a violent past, seeking refuge in the High Sierras, where she becomes attracted to landowner Colonel Jack Cornish. The discovery of valuable mineral deposits on Cornish's land threatens to endanger his property and expose Alicia's past.

Historical Accuracy: The story has a basis in historical fact, and the period background is rendered convincingly.

`1507` *Storm Before Sunrise*
Date of Publication: 1993
Subject(s): Immigrants; Medical Profession
Fictional character(s): Adam Kingsley, Doctor; Melisande Stevens, Orphan, Immigrant
Time Period(s): 19th century
Locale(s): New York

Summary: Orphan Melisande Stevens comes to America from England to work as a maid. She attracts the attention of Doctor Adam Kingsley, who sets out to discover the truth about her past.

Historical Accuracy: The novel provides a believable reconstruction of its period and region.

SHIRLEY DAVIES-OWENS (1937-)
Born in Cheshire, England, Davies-Owens moved to the United States in 1963 and became a naturalized citizen in 1977. She received a diploma from the Liverpool College of

Commerce in 1955 and worked as an office manager and writer before becoming a full-time novelist in 1982.

1508 *Silver Linings*
Date of Publication: 1986
Subject(s): Victorian Period; Romance
Fictional character(s): Emma Cadman, Young Woman; Ewan McKenzie, Gentleman
Time Period(s): 1870s; 1880s (1877-1888)
Locale(s): London, England

Summary: Emma Cadman is a young woman whose home hides a dark secret that puts Emma in physical and emotional jeopardy. Circumstances force her into poverty and diminishing expectations until a further change of fortune and the restorative power of love help heal old wounds.

Historical Accuracy: The novel's period details are accurately and convincingly depicted.

MARIA THOMPSON DAVIESS
(1872-1924)

Born in Harrodsburg, Kentucky, Daviess attended Wellesley College. She was a painter and jewelry maker. Daviess wrote *Treasure Babies*, *The Tinder Box*, *Bluegrass and Broadway*, and *The Matrix*, a pious and sincere treatment of the romance of Thomas Lincoln and Nancy Hanks.

1509 *The Matrix*
Date of Publication: 1920
Subject(s): Settlement of the American Frontier
Historical character(s): Thomas Lincoln, Settler; Nancy Hanks, Spouse
Time Period(s): 19th century
Locale(s): Kentucky

Summary: The novel memorializes the relationship between Thomas Lincoln and Nancy Hanks, parents of Abraham Lincoln. Through their experiences, the novel presents a vivid portrait of pioneer life in Kentucky.

Historical Accuracy: Put together from both documentary evidence and legend, the story is told with more piety than realism.

GORDON DAVIOT
(PSEUD. OF ELIZABETH MACKINTOSH, 1896-1952)

A Scottish writer, Mackintosh was a teacher until her mother's death. She returned home and turned to writing. She is best known by her pseudonym Josephine Tey and for her detective/historical novel, *The Daughter of Time*, which provides an arresting portrait of Richard III.

1510 *The Privateer*
Date of Publication: 1952
Subject(s): Pirates; Sea Story
Historical character(s): Henry Morgan, Pirate
Time Period(s): 17th century
Locale(s): West Indies

Summary: The novel tells the story of British pirate Henry Morgan from his early days as a young bondsman in Barbados to his becoming a privateer attacking Spanish shipping on behalf of English interests. Morgan's exploits are fully detailed against a realistic backdrop of contemporary events.

Historical Accuracy: The period is captured faithfully.

BURKE DAVIS (1913-)

Born in North Carolina, Davis is a graduate of the University of North Carolina. He has worked as a newspaper reporter in Maryland and North Carolina. He is the author of biographies on Stonewall Jackson, Robert E. Lee, and Jeb Stuart, and his novels include *Whisper My Name*, *The Rugged Ones*, and *The Summer Land*.

1511 *The Ragged Ones*
Date of Publication: 1951
Subject(s): American Revolution; Battle of Cowpens
Historical character(s): Nathanael Greene, Military Personnel (general); Daniel Morgan, Military Personnel (general)
Time Period(s): 1780s
Locale(s): Carolinas, United States

Summary: The story of the Southern campaign of 1781 is described beginning with the American victory at the battle of Cowpens to the costly British victory at Guilford Courthouse. The novel describes the strategy of General Nathanael Greene, which paves the way for the American victory at Yorktown.

Historical Accuracy: The novel features an unheroic, though convincing, portrait of the American army which is very different from other more idealized depictions.

1512 *To Appomattox: Nine April Days, 1865*
Date of Publication: 1959
Subject(s): Civil War—U.S.
Historical character(s): Robert E. Lee, Military Personnel (Confederate commander); Ulysses S. Grant, Military Personnel (Union commander)
Time Period(s): 1860s (1865)
Locale(s): Virginia

Summary: The final nine days of the Civil War are described in this documentary novel that leads up to the climactic meeting between Lee and Grant at Appomattox Court House. Based on newspaper accounts, letters, and diaries, the novel achieves a vivid picture of the collapse of the Confederacy.

Historical Accuracy: The novel is faithful in its realistic depiction of the events and the era.

1513 *Yorktown*
Date of Publication: 1952
Subject(s): American Revolution; Battle of Yorktown; American Colonies

Fictional character(s): Peter Spargo, Military Personnel (sergeant); Eve Cooper, Young Woman
Historical character(s): George Washington, Military Personnel (army commander); Marie Joseph Paul de Lafayette, Military Personnel (general), Nobleman (Marquis de Lafayette); Henry Clinton, Military Personnel (general); Charles Cornwallis, Military Personnel (general); Anthony Wayne, Military Personnel (general)
Time Period(s): 1770s; 1780s (1778-1781)
Locale(s): Yorktown, Virginia

Summary: The story of the events leading up to the decisive Battle of Yorktown in the American Revolution are described through the experiences of Peter Spargo. He escapes from a prison ship, rejoins his former commander, ''Mad'' Anthony Wayne, and participates in the action against Cornwallis that leads to the Colonists' victory.

Historical Accuracy: The historical elements are accurately presented, and the character sketches of the many historical figures are convincing.

CHRISTOPHER DAVIS (1928-)

Born in Philadelphia, Davis has worked as a professor of creative writing at the University of Pennsylvania. His novel *First Family* was chosen by *Time* magazine as one of the best novels of 1961. The stage adaptation of his novel *Last Summer* became Jane Fonda's first Broadway starring role under the title ''There Was a Little Girl.''.

1514 *Belmarch: A Legend of the First Crusade*

Date of Publication: 1964
Subject(s): Middle Ages; Crusades; Jews
Fictional character(s): Belmarch, Military Personnel (soldier); Annas, Leader (Jewish)
Time Period(s): 11th century (1096)
Locale(s): Europe

Summary: The novel depicts the efforts by soldier Belmarch to recall and expiate his role in the massacre of Jews by the Crusaders on their way to the Holy Land. Unable to recall the crime, Belmarch is hounded by the Jew Annas to relive the events.

Historical Accuracy: Despite the novel's dream-like and fable-like quality, the story does capture the period atmosphere and customs authentically.

1515 *A Peep into the 20th Century*

Date of Publication: 1971
Subject(s): Crime and Criminals; Inventions
Historical character(s): Rupert Weber, Murderer; Thomas Alva Edison, Inventor, Scientist; George Westinghouse, Inventor, Businessman
Time Period(s): 1890s
Locale(s): New York

Summary: Based on fact, the novel concerns the fate of ax murderer Rupert Weber who was the first man to die in the electric chair. This invention becomes a metaphor for the new century's ingenuity and perfection of violence.

Historical Accuracy: The novel's scenes are invented, but the basic facts are historically accurate.

CLYDE BRION DAVIS (1894-1962)

An American journalist and author, Davis was born in Nebraska. He was a reporter for newspapers in Colorado and Washington. His books include *Jeremy Bell*, *Shadow of a Tiger*, and *Unholy Uproar*.

1516 *Nebraska Coast*

Date of Publication: 1939
Subject(s): Settlement of the American Frontier
Fictional character(s): Jack MacDougall, Settler, Farmer
Time Period(s): 1860s (1861)
Locale(s): Nebraska; New York

Summary: With the outbreak of the Civil War, New York farmer Jack MacDougall's anti-war sentiment causes him to head west to a Nebraska frontier town. The novel, based on the experiences of the author's grandfather, dramatizes his life on the frontier.

Historical Accuracy: The details of pioneer life are well drawn and believable.

DOROTHY DAVIS (1916-)

Born in Chicago, Illinois, and a graduate of Barat College, Davis received the 1985 Grandmaster Award for lifetime achievement from the Mystery Writers of America. Her books include *The Habit of Fear*, *Scarlet Night*, and *A Day in the Life*.

1517 *Men of No Property*

Date of Publication: 1956
Subject(s): Immigrants; Racial Conflict
Fictional character(s): Margaret Hickey, Immigrant; Vincent Dunne, Immigrant; Dennis Lavery, Sailor; Norah Hickey, Immigrant
Time Period(s): 1840s; 1850s
Locale(s): New York, New York

Summary: Life in New York City for a group of recent immigrants from Ireland is dramatized. The years are the 1840s and 1850s when the Irish face prejudice and persecution from the Know-Nothing party. The politics and the violence of the era are vividly portrayed.

Historical Accuracy: The depiction of period New York is convincing and authentic.

ELMER HOLMES DAVIS (1890-1958)

An Indiana journalist and novelist, Davis was the director of the Office of War Information from 1942-1945. In 1921, while on the staff of *The New York Times*, he wrote the newspaper's history. His novels include *Gilman of Redford* and *Show Window*. His essays are collected in *Not to Mention the War*.

1518   *Giant Killer*

Date of Publication: 1928
Subject(s): Biblical Story; Ancient Israel
Historical character(s): David, Ruler (King of Israel), Biblical Figure; Joab, Biblical Figure, Military Personnel (general)
Time Period(s): 10th century B.C.
Locale(s): Israel

Summary: The novel portrays David, King of ancient Israel, as an opportunist, always ready to take credit for someone else's achievement. The real hero in the story is David's kinsman Joab, the commander-in-chief of the army, who builds up the nation for David to rule.

Historical Accuracy: The novel is built upon a framework of solid biblical scholarship with a strikingly modern interpretation.

GENEVIEVE DAVIS (1928-)

An American writer born in Philadelphia, Davis attended the International School in Geneva and the Sorbonne.

1519   *A Passion in the Blood*

Date of Publication: 1977
Subject(s): Renaissance
Historical character(s): Lucrezia Borgia, Noblewoman; Cesare Borgia, Military Personnel, Political Figure; Alexander VI, Religious (pope)
Time Period(s): 15th century
Locale(s): Italy

Summary: This romanticized account of Lucrezia Borgia as a young woman portrays her as an innocent victim of her political father, of Pope Alexander VI, and of the incestuous jealousies of her brother Cesare. The result is a somewhat modernized portrait of the dysfunctional Borgia family.

Historical Accuracy: Idealized and romanticized, the novel should not be relied on for historical accuracy.

HAROLD LENOIR DAVIS (1896-1960)

An American author from Oregon, Harold Lenior Davis' work reflects the frontier experience of the Pacific Northwest. His novel *Honey in the Horn* won the Pulitzer Prize. He also wrote poetry and essays about the Pacific Northwest.

1520   *Beulah Land*

Date of Publication: 1949
Subject(s): American West; Settlement of the American Frontier
Fictional character(s): Ewen Warne, Settler, Frontiersman; Ruhama, Indian; Askwani, Indian
Time Period(s): 1850s
Locale(s): North Carolina; Natchez, Mississippi; Midwest (Kansas, Missouri)

Summary: The novel tells the story of western migration as Ewen Warne together with his half-Indian daughter, a white boy raised by the Indians, and an outcast Cherokee woman begin the long trek west. Their epic journey is filled with danger.

Historical Accuracy: Davis provides both the feel of the period and credible personalities.

1521   *Distant Music*

Date of Publication: 1957
Subject(s): American West; Family Saga; Settlement of the American Frontier
Fictional character(s): Ranse Mulock, Frontiersman
Time Period(s): 19th century (1850s-1890s)
Locale(s): Clarke's Landing, Oregon   .

Summary: Three generations of pioneers illustrate the opening of the Pacific Northwest in the second half of the 19th century. Ranse Mulock is the patriarch who first arrives at Clarke's Landing on the Columbia River. His story and his family's struggles show that they all hear "the distant music" of the beauty of the land, which sustains them.

Historical Accuracy: Davis writes with conviction and certainty about a setting with which he is intimately acquainted.

1522   *Harp of a Thousand Strings*

Date of Publication:
Subject(s): Settlement of the American Frontier; French Revolution; Pirates
Fictional character(s): Melancthon Crawford, Settler; Apeyahola, Indian; Jean-Lambert Tallien, Revolutionary
Time Period(s): 1780s; 1790s (1780s-1790s)
Locale(s): Great Plains; Tripoli, Africa; Paris, France

Summary: The novel provides an ingenious interweaving of history—the harp of the novel's title—connecting the founding of a western prairie town, the war with the Barbary pirates, and the French Revolution. Three escaped American prisoners in Tripoli hear the story of a Frenchman and his tragic love affair in the midst of the revolution. Each of the Americans illustrates an aspect of the Frenchman's story.

Historical Accuracy: There are good details of the French Revolution in this thesis novel about the interconnections of history.

1523   *Honey in the Horn*

Date of Publication: 1935
Subject(s): American West; Settlement of the American Frontier; Homesteading
Fictional character(s): Clay Calvert, Outlaw; Lucie, Settler
Time Period(s): 1900s (1906-1908)
Locale(s): Oregon

Summary: Set in Oregon during the homesteading period, the novel follows the adventures of Clay Calvert, who unwillingly assists in a jailbreak and then evades the law, traveling throughout the Oregon countryside. Through his travelling a convincing portrait of the era is created.

Historical Accuracy: Davis effectively captures the people and the Oregon scene.

JAMES F. DAVIS

1524 *The Road to San Jacinto*

Date of Publication: 1936
Subject(s): Texas Revolution
Fictional character(s): Mark Lyle, Young Man
Historical character(s): Jim Bowie, Frontiersman; Davy Crockett, Frontiersman; Sam Houston, Political Figure
Time Period(s): 1830s (1835-1836)
Locale(s): Texas

Summary: The story of Texas' struggle for independence from Mexico is told from the perspective of Mark Lyle, who travel to Texas from Georgia in search of his father's murderer. He is soon involved in the struggle against Santa Anna.

Historical Accuracy: The novel is faithful to the historical events and characters.

JULIA DAVIS (1900-1993)

An American social worker, journalist, and writer, Davis was born in West Virginia and graduated from Barnard College. She worked as a reporter for the Associated Press and as the chairman of the child adoption service for the Children's Aid Society. Her books focus on the history of Virginia and her family's role in its history. They include *Sword of the Vikings*, *The Shenandoah*, and *A Valley and a Song*.

1525 *Bridle the Wind*

Date of Publication: 1953
Subject(s): Antebellum South; Slavery
Fictional character(s): Lucy MacLeod, Spouse; Angus MacLeod, Plantation Owner
Time Period(s): 1830s; 1840s (1835-1840s)
Locale(s): New York, New York; Virginia

Summary: The novel, set in the years before the Civil War, describes the efforts of Lucy MacLeod, the wife of a Virginia plantation owner, to atone for her role in helping a slave escape to freedom. She is banished from her home and children and then must struggle to be accepted.

Historical Accuracy: The novel effectively presents attitudes of the time and the atmosphere of the period.

1526 *Cloud on the Land*

Date of Publication: 1951
Subject(s): Antebellum South; Slavery; Indians
Fictional character(s): Angus MacLeod, Plantation Owner; Lucy MacLeod, Spouse
Time Period(s): 19th century
Locale(s): Virginia; West

Summary: This novel, set in the years following the War of 1812, traces the experiences of Virginia plantation owner Angus MacLeod, who heads west, marries, and seeks his fortune in fur trading. The second half of the story, *Bridle the Wind*, returns to Virginia and takes up the issue of slavery.

Historical Accuracy: The novel features a believable historical background.

1527 *Eagle on the Sun*

Date of Publication: 1956
Subject(s): Antebellum South; Mexican War; Slavery
Fictional character(s): Angus MacLeod, Plantation Owner; Junius MacLeod, Military Personnel (army officer)
Time Period(s): 1840s
Locale(s): Virginia; Mexico

Summary: This sequel to the author's *Bridle the Wind* continues the story of the MacLeod family of Virginia into the events of the Mexican War. Agitation over slavery gives way to the jingoism of a foreign war as Angus and Junius MacLeod join the invading American army in action in Mexico.

Historical Accuracy: The novel captures the era and its conflicts with credibility.

LINDSEY DAVIS

1528 *The Iron Hand of Mars*

Date of Publication: 1992
Subject(s): Mystery; Roman Empire; Barbarians
Fictional character(s): Marcus Didius Falco, Detective—Private; Julius Civilis, Leader (rebel); Helena Justina, Noblewoman
Historical character(s): Vespasian, Ruler (Roman emperor); Titus, Royalty (son of the emperor), Heir
Time Period(s): 1st century (70s)
Locale(s): Rome, Roman Empire; Germany

Summary: Ancient Rome's private eye, Marcus Didius Falco, is sent on an undercover mission to Roman Germany. He is sent by Titus, largely to get him out of the way so Titus can pursue Helena, Falco's patrician girlfriend. In Germany, he faces a rebel chieftain, Civilis, and the members of the XIV Legion, who hold a grudge against him. Falco crosses into barbarian territory with more challenges to face.

Historical Accuracy: The novel is a combination of modern sensibility and convincing period details.

1529 *Last Act in Palmyra*

Date of Publication: 1994
Subject(s): Mystery; Roman Empire; Theatrical Life
Fictional character(s): Marcus Didius Falco, Detective—Private; Anacrites, Spy; Helena Justina, Noblewoman
Historical character(s): Vespasian, Ruler (Roman emperor)
Time Period(s): 1st century (72)
Locale(s): Rome, Roman Empire; Syria

Summary: In this historical mystery set in the 1st century, private detective Marcus Didius Falco and Helena Justina leave Rome for the eastern Mediterranean and Syria. There they stumble upon a dead Roman playwright and join the dead man's acting troupe in which Falco accepts a writing assignment. A killer, however, is on the loose, and the next victim seems to be a member of the cast.

Historical Accuracy: The novel curiously mixes a modern sensibility with authentic period elements.

1530 *Poseidon's Gold*

Date of Publication: 1992
Subject(s): Mystery; Roman Empire
Fictional character(s): Marcus Didius Falco, Detective—Private; Marcus Didius Festus, Adventurer; Censorinus, Veteran (Roman soldier)
Time Period(s): 1st century
Locale(s): Rome, Roman Empire

Summary: Marcus Didius Falco, Imperial spy and informer, returns home to Rome after a six-month mission among the German legions. He finds his home in turmoil and an ex-legionnaire demanding money Falco's brother owes him. When the man is found stabbed to death, Falco is the prime suspect. He must clear his name by finding his long-lost father, the only one who may know what his brother Festus was really up to.

Historical Accuracy: Witty and sophisticated, the novel's period details are also convincing.

1531 *Shadows in Bronze*

Date of Publication: 1990
Subject(s): Mystery; Roman Empire
Fictional character(s): Marcus Didius Falco, Detective—Private; Barnabas, Revolutionary; Helena Justina, Noblewoman
Historical character(s): Vespasian, Ruler (Roman emperor)
Time Period(s): 1st century (70s)
Locale(s): Rome, Roman Empire; Bay of Naples, Roman Empire

Summary: Marcus Didius Falco, chief informer and detective for the Emperor Vespasian, is on the trail of the conspirator Barnabas, intent on toppling both the emperor and Falco. The pursuit takes him to the Bay of Naples and a painful encounter with his ex-love Helena Justina.

Historical Accuracy: The sensibility here is hard-boiled and modern, but the period details are authentic.

1532 *The Silver Pigs*

Date of Publication: 1989
Subject(s): Mystery; Roman Empire
Fictional character(s): Marcus Didius Falco, Detective—Private; Sosia Camillina, Young Woman; Versus Camillus Decimus, Political Figure (senator)
Historical character(s): Vespasian, Ruler (Roman emperor); Titus, Royalty (emperor's son), Heir
Time Period(s): 1st century (70s)
Locale(s): Rome, Roman Empire

Summary: In the first of the author's mystery novels set in ancient Rome, Marcus Didius Falco, informer and detective, literally runs into Sosia Camillina as she is chased by kidnappers. She is pursued because she knows where ignots, or silver pigs, intended to fund a plot against the emperor are

hidden. Falco looks into the case, a labyrinth of greed, deceit, and danger.

Historical Accuracy: The novel features delightfully re-created period backdrops, turning ancient Rome into a very modern city.

1533 *Time to Depart*

Date of Publication: 1995
Subject(s): Mystery; Roman Empire
Fictional character(s): Marcus Didius Falco, Detective—Private; Helena Justina, Noblewoman; Pius Balbinius, Organized Crime Figure
Historical character(s): Vespasian, Ruler (Roman emperor)
Time Period(s): 1st century (72)
Locale(s): Rome, Roman Empire

Summary: In this installment of the detective cases of private investigator Marcus Didius Falco in Emperor Vespasian's Rome, the prosecution of underworld organizer Pius Balbinius results in a scramble for power to claim his operation. He is allowed ''time to depart,'' avoiding his death sentence by going into exile. However, should Pius reappear, it will mean certain death for Falco.

Historical Accuracy: The novel mixes tongue-in-cheek anachronisms with an authentic look at Rome during the period.

1534 *Venus in Copper*

Date of Publication: 1991
Subject(s): Mystery; Roman Empire
Fictional character(s): Marcus Didius Falco, Detective—Private; Hortensius Novus, Businessman (real estate developer), Fiance(e); Severina Zotica, Fiance(e)
Historical character(s): Titus, Royalty (son of the emperor), Heir
Time Period(s): 1st century (70s)
Locale(s): Rome, Roman Empire

Summary: Falco, under-appreciated and underpaid informer for the emperor, sets out on his own as a private investigator. He is hired by the family of a prominent real estate developer, Hortensius, to investigate the background of his fiancee, Serverina. When Hortensius is poisoned, Severina hires Falco to solve the mystery.

Historical Accuracy: This is a delightful blend of authentic period details and modern sensibility which turns ancient Rome into a thoroughly contemporary city.

LOU ELLEN DAVIS (1936-)

Born in Pennsylvania and a graduate of NYU, Davis was a reporter for the *Village Voice* and an actress in TV and radio commercials. Her novels include *Along Came a Spider* and *There Was an Old Woman*, which was made into the TV movie *Revenge* in 1972.

1535 *Clouds of Destiny*

Date of Publication: 1978
Subject(s): American Revolution

Fictional character(s): Isabel Browne, Prostitute; James Devant, Smuggler; Sarah Carrington, Loyalist
Time Period(s): 1770s
Locale(s): Connecticut

Summary: Three characters—an English prostitute, a staunch American loyalist, and a smuggler—find themselves caught up in the events of the American Revolution. Isabel Browne has acquired an important letter from the lord she has murdered, and both rebels and loyalists try to gain the document. James Devant at first tries to profit from the conflict but eventually joins the fight on the side of the rebels.

Historical Accuracy: The details of the period are convincingly presented.

MAGGIE DAVIS

Born in Norfolk, Virginia, Davis is a former radio and TV script writer and producer, public relations agent, and newspaper feature writer. She was named Georgia Writer of the Year in 1964.

1536 *The Far Side of Home*

Date of Publication: 1963
Subject(s): Civil War—U.S.; Battle of Kennesaw Mountain; Battle of Atlanta
Fictional character(s): Johnny McLeod, Military Personnel (Confederate soldier); Annabella Hammond, Spouse (of McLeod)
Time Period(s): 1860s (1863-1864)
Locale(s): Jonesboro, Georgia; Augusta, Georgia; Atlanta, Georgia

Summary: The novel details the experiences of a private in a Georgia regiment during the Civil War. In 1863, Johnny McLeod sets out on leave for home in Jonesboro. On the way he meets and marries Annabella Hammond before returning to the fighting in the Battle of Kennesaw Mountain. He eventually reunites with Annabella during the Battle of Atlanta.

Historical Accuracy: Realistic in detail, the novel delivers an unsentimental and reliable picture of the war.

M.H. DAVIS

Born in Norfolk, Virginia, Davis worked as a radio and television script writer and producer, a public relations agent, and newspaper feature writer. He was named Georgia Writer of the Year for 1964. His works include *The Far Side of Home*, *Rommel's Gold*, *The Shiek*, and *Eagles*.

1537 *The Winter Servant*

Date of Publication: 1958
Subject(s): Dark Ages; Vikings
Fictional character(s): Doireann, Young Woman; Thorsten, Warrior
Time Period(s): 9th century
Locale(s): Scotland

Summary: Doireann, the daughter of a Scottish chieftain, is sold to the Vikings by her jealous foster brother. She must adapt to the strange customs of the Norsemen.

Historical Accuracy: The novel is convincing in its details of Viking lore and customs.

MILDRED B. DAVIS

KATHERINE A. DAVIS ROOME

Davis started writing at the age of ten because of her love of reading; mysteries were her favorite books. She received the Edgar Award from the Mystery Writers of America for Best First Novel by an American author in 1949 for *The Room Upstairs*. Roome graduated from Williams College in 1974 and Cornell Law School in 1977. She is Mildred Davis' daughter.

1538 *Lucifer Land*

Date of Publication: 1977
Subject(s): American Revolution
Fictional character(s): Cassie Bedham, Young Woman
Time Period(s): 1770s; 1780s
Locale(s): Bedford, New York

Summary: The novel portrays the effects of the American Revolution on a family in Bedford, New York. The Revolution is more accurately described as a Civil War between rebels and Tories. Its effects on young Cassie Bedham are dramatized showing how her world is transformed in the process of the war.

Historical Accuracy: The period details and atmosphere are realistically presented.

PAXTON DAVIS

1539 *The Seasons of Heroes*

Date of Publication: 1967
Subject(s): Family Saga; Civil War—U.S.
Fictional character(s): Bobby Gibboney, Military Personnel (Confederate soldier); Matthew Gibboney, Military Personnel (Confederate soldier); William Gibboney, Government Official
Time Period(s): 19th century; 20th century (1822-1912)
Locale(s): Virginia

Summary: The novel is made up of stories from three generations of the Gibboney family. Each story relates the turning point of the characters' lives and connects them to the moral implications of the Civil War. Each of the three Gibboneys defines his values set against the pressure of time and history.

Historical Accuracy: The novel interweaves its historical elements faithfully into the story by demonstrating their impact on the characters.

W.E. DAVIS (1951-)

1540 *The Gathering Storm*

Date of Publication: 1996
Subject(s): American West

Fictional character(s): Matt Page, Lawman
Time Period(s): 1870s
Locale(s): Bodie, California

Summary: This tale of California during the 1870s concerns the experiences of young Matt Page who is named deputy of a mining boom town. When a large vein of gold is discovered, Page must contend with desperadoes, gamblers, conflict between rival miners, and escaped convicts.

Historical Accuracy: Some of the characters and incidents described are based on fact, as the author's notes make clear.

WILLIAM STEARNS DAVIS (1877-1930)

Massachusetts novelist and scholar Davis taught for many years at the University of Minnesota. His scholarly works include *A Short History of the Near East* and *Life in Elizabethan Days*. His romantic novels based on historical study include *A Friend of Caesar*, *God Wills It*, *Falaise of the Blessed Voice*, and *The Whirlwind*.

1541 *Gilman of the Redford*

Date of Publication: 1927
Subject(s): American Revolution; American Colonies
Fictional character(s): Roger Gilman, Student—College
Historical character(s): Paul Revere, Artisan (silversmith), Patriot; Samuel Adams, Patriot
Time Period(s): 1770s (1770-1775)
Locale(s): Boston, Massachusetts, American Colonies

Summary: The scene is Boston and Harvard College in the days leading up to the outbreak of the American Revolution. Roger Gilman is a young Harvard undergraduate who finds himself involved with the patriots' cause. Many of the famous figures of the period are featured, including Paul Revere and Sam Adams.

Historical Accuracy: The novel is more romance than careful history. The book does provide some authentic period elements of undergraduate life of the times.

CECIL DAWKINS (1927-)

1542 *The Live Goat*

Date of Publication: 1971
Subject(s): Antebellum South; Crime and Criminals
Fictional character(s): Duncan McElroy, Farmer; Toliver Pullen, Farmer
Time Period(s): 1840s
Locale(s): South; Texas

Summary: When a woman is found murdered and a half-wit boy flees with a neighbor's prize mule, community members form a posse to bring the murderer to justice.

Historical Accuracy: The novel offers an authentic portrait of the frontier landscape from Carolina to Texas.

DIANNE DAY (1938-)

A native of Mississippi and a graduate of Stanford and the University of North Carolina, Day first worked as a

psychologist and a hospital administrator before beginning to write in 1985. Her goal in her writing is to entertain, and also, occasionally, to educate.

1543 *Fire and Fog*

Date of Publication: 1996
Subject(s): Mystery; Earthquakes
Fictional character(s): Fremont Jones, Businesswoman
Time Period(s): 1900s (1906)
Locale(s): San Francisco, California

Summary: Unconventional heroine and sleuth Fremont Jones must deal with the aftermath of the San Francisco earthquake in this historical mystery novel. Joining the Red Cross to assist quake victims, Jones encounters a woman who winds up murdered. The corpse disappears, along with all the evidence.

Historical Accuracy: The novel provides a colorful and believable depiction of period San Francisco.

1544 *The Strange Files of Fremont Jones*

Date of Publication: 1995
Subject(s): Mystery
Fictional character(s): Caroline Fremont Jones, Secretary; Justin Cameron, Lawyer; Edgar Allen Patridge, Writer
Time Period(s): 1900s (1905)
Locale(s): San Francisco, California

Summary: Bostonian and Wellesley graduate Caroline Jones escapes her family's control for a new life and a career as a typist in turn-of-the-century San Francisco. There she becomes involved with the personal lives of her clients, providing a series of adventures.

Historical Accuracy: The novel features convincing period details and an authentic setting.

DOUGLAS DAY (1932-)

American author Day was born in Colon, Panama, the son of an officer in the U.S. Navy. He is a graduate of the University of Virginia, where he now serves as a professor of English. Day is best known for his National Book Award-winning *Malcolm Lowry: A Biography*. He has also written the novel *Journey of the Wolf* and *Swifter than Reason: The Poetry and Criticism of Robert Graves*.

1545 *The Prison Notebooks of Ricardo Flores Magon*

Date of Publication: 1991
Subject(s): Biography, Fictionalized; Mexican Revolution; Politics
Historical character(s): Ricardo Flores Magon, Activist (anarchist), Revolutionary; Francisco Villa, Revolutionary; Emma Goldman, Activist (anarchist); Emiliano Zapata, Revolutionary
Time Period(s): 19th century; 20th century
Locale(s): Mexico

Summary: This is a fictional autobiography of Mexican anarchist Ricardo Flores Magon, who narrates the story of his career and involvement in the Mexican Revolution. Flores Magon's writings and theories had a major impact in the clash of ideas that shaped the Mexican Revolution. The novel captures Flores Magon's commitment to the cause and illustrates some fundamental qualities of the Mexican identity.

Historical Accuracy: In this fictional memoir, Day captures with skill the clash of ideas and the atmosphere of the time.

ELDOROUS L. DAYTON (1906-1987)

American speechwriter, journalist, scriptwriter, and biographer, Dayton is a former newspaperman who covered such major news stories as the Lindbergh kidnapping. He wrote speeches for President Herbert Hoover and presidential candidate Thomas E. Dewey. Dayton also wrote scripts and documentaries for television, including ''The Secret Life of Adolf Hitler,'' and ''Castro, Communism, and Cuba,'' both of which received Emmy nominations. His several biographies include one on Harry S Truman entitled *Give Em Hell, Harry.*

1546 *Chantefable*

Date of Publication: 1982
Subject(s): Roman Empire; Literary Life; Biography, Fictionalized
Historical character(s): Gaius Valerius Catullus, Writer (poet); Clodia, Noblewoman
Time Period(s): 1st century B.C.
Locale(s): Rome, Roman Empire

Summary: This biographical account of the Roman poet Catullus attempts to offer an interpretation of Catullus' poetry, particularly the origin of his love poems to the fictional Lesbia, inspired by the actual Roman noblewoman Clodia.

Historical Accuracy: The novel offers a believable reconstruction of period Rome and a plausible analysis of Catullus and his poetic influences.

CELESTE DE BLASIS (1946-)

California-born novelist De Blasis was raised on a ranch in the high desert of southern California. She attended Wellesley College, Oregon State University, and Pomona College.

1547 *The Proud Breed*

Date of Publication: 1978
Subject(s): American West; Family Saga; Horses
Fictional character(s): Tessa Ramsay, Gentlewoman; Gavin Ramsay, Trader
Time Period(s): 19th century (1830s-1890s)
Locale(s): California

Summary: This generational saga is set in California and centers on the love between Tessa and Gavin Ramsay. She is the daughter of a California aristocrat, and he is a Yankee trader. Together they build a great ranch breeding golden palominos. Their story reflects the history of California in the 19th century.

Historical Accuracy: The historical background is solidly researched and developed.

1548 *A Season of Swans*

Date of Publication: 1989
Subject(s): Family Saga; Reconstruction Period; Horses
Fictional character(s): Gincie Carrington, Landowner; Travis Culhane, Landowner; Lexy Culhane, Journalist
Time Period(s): 19th century (1870-1892)
Locale(s): Maryland; Sonoma Valley, California; Saratoga Springs, New York

Summary: This novel is the last in the author's trilogy on the Wild Swan horse farm in Maryland. This volume follows the family fortune from the 1870s to 1890s as Gincie and Travis Culhane, heirs to the dynasty, struggle to rebuild their fortune during the aftermath of the Civil War. Their children venture far afield, and become involved in the period's important events.

Historical Accuracy: The historical events are faithfully, if briefly, presented in the onrush of family complications.

1549 *Swan's Chance*

Date of Publication: 1985
Subject(s): Civil War—U.S.; Family Saga; Slavery
Fictional character(s): Alexandra Thaine Falconer, Landowner; Rane Falconer, Landowner; Gincie Carrington, Abolitionist
Time Period(s): 19th century (1836-1865)
Locale(s): Maryland

Summary: In the second volume of the family saga of the Falconer family, Alex and Rane Falconer struggle to maintain their horse farm, Wild Swan, in the midst of the north and south conflict. At the same time, their children pursue different careers.

Historical Accuracy: The political events of the period are detailed only in passing.

1550 *Wild Swan*

Date of Publication: 1984
Subject(s): Family Saga; Napoleonic Era; Horses
Fictional character(s): Alexandra Thaine, Young Woman; Rane Falconer, Young Man; St. John Carrington, Military Personnel
Time Period(s): 19th century (1813-1831)
Locale(s): Devon, England; Maryland

Summary: In this first volume of a trilogy, Alexandra Thaine is torn between her love for Rane Falconer and her duty to St. John Carrington. The novel dramatizes the founding of Wild Swan, a Maryland horse farm that breeds throughbred race horses.

Historical Accuracy: This family saga is remarkably detailed in its historical background, far more so than other generational sagas.

HELMA DE BOIS

Born in Amsterdam, De Bois worked for the United Nations in Geneva, Switzerland.

1551 *The Incorruptible*

Date of Publication: 1965
Subject(s): French Revolution; Reign of Terror; Russian Empire
Fictional character(s): Marc de Guemont, Young Man
Historical character(s): Maximilien Francois de Robespierre, Revolutionary, Political Figure; Catherine the Great, Ruler (Czarina of Russia); Georges-Jacques Danton, Revolutionary, Political Figure
Time Period(s): 1780s; 1790s (1788-1794)
Locale(s): France; Germany; St. Petersburg, Russia

Summary: The events of the French Revolution and the Reign of Terror that followed are depicted in the journal of Marc de Guemont. The grandson of a French duke, his friendships with many important figures, particularly Robespierre, provide behind-the-scenes access to some of the great events of the day.

Historical Accuracy: The novel provides a faithful chronology and a believable historical background for the story.

EDITH DE BORN

Born in Vienna, De Born is a graduate of the University of Vienna. During the German occupation of France, she and her French banker husband lived in Paris. At that time she began writing and was active in the French Resistance. Her books include *The Imperfect Marriage*, *The Engagement*, and *The House in Vienna*.

1552 *Felding Castle*

Date of Publication: 1957
Subject(s): Family Saga; Austro-Hungarian Empire
Fictional character(s): Maria Amalia Elizabeth Theresa, Noblewoman (countess)
Time Period(s): 19th century; 20th century
Locale(s): Austria

Summary: During the waning years of the Hapsburg Empire, the aristocratic Maria Amalia Elizabeth Theresa, called Milli, visits Felding Castle. There she is introduced to a very different life than that of her quiet childhood.

Historical Accuracy: The novel is convincing in its portrait of the declining Austrian nobility.

L. SPRAGUE DE CAMP (1907-)

An American writer born in New York City, De Camp graduated from the California Institute of Technology and worked as an editor and freelance writer. Besides his historical fiction, De Camp is the author of many science fiction books and several volumes in the Conan the Barbarian series. De Camp has been called the master of the humorous tale, and is one of the few historical novelists that mine history for its comedy.

1553 *The Arrows of Hercules*

Date of Publication: 1965
Subject(s): Military Life
Fictional character(s): Zopyros, Engineer
Historical character(s): Dionysios the Great, Ruler (dictator of Syracuse)
Time Period(s): 4th century B.C.
Locale(s): Syracuse, Ancient Civilization; Carthage, Ancient Civilization

Summary: The novel records the foundation of the world's first military ordnance department by Dionysios the Great of Syracuse in the 4th century B.C. Zopyrus, a young engineer, is recruited to design new and deadlier weapons, and his creation, the catapult, is put to use against the Carthaginians.

Historical Accuracy: The novel's notes indicate the factual basis and sources for the story.

1554 *The Bronze God of Rhodes*

Date of Publication: 1960
Subject(s): Wonders of the World; Macedonian Empire
Historical character(s): Antigonus I, Ruler (Asian), Military Personnel (general); Chares, Artist (Sculptor); Demetrius I, Ruler (King of Macedon); Ptolemy I, Ruler (King of Egypt)
Time Period(s): 4th century B.C.
Locale(s): Rhodes, Greece; Egypt

Summary: The history of the construction of the Colossus of Rhodes, one of the Seven Wonders of the World, is described by Chares, the Greek sculptor who built it. In the background are the wars between the successors of Alexander the Great, notably Antigonus and his son Demetrius in their struggle for power with Ptolemy I of Egypt.

Historical Accuracy: The novel's scholarship is impressive, a convincing re-creation of the period.

1555 *The Dragon of the Ishtar Gate*

Date of Publication: 1961
Subject(s): Witchcraft and Sorcery
Fictional character(s): Myron, Adventurer; Bessas, Adventurer
Historical character(s): Xerxes I, Ruler (King of Persia)
Time Period(s): 5th century B.C. (456 B.C.)
Locale(s): Persia; Africa

Summary: This adventure tale describes the exploits of Myron, a Greek, and Bessas, a Persian, who are sent into the Congo to capture a dragon whose blood will provide a life elixir for King Xerxes. The pair face innumerable challenges, including ambushes, cannibals, pygmies, and assassins.

Historical Accuracy: The novel mixes the fantastic with accurate historical details that create a believable, if exotic, background for the story's many adventures.

1556 *An Elephant for Aristotle*

Date of Publication: 1958
Subject(s): Macedonian Empire; Ancient Greece
Fictional character(s): Leon of Atrax, Military Personnel (cavalry officer)

Historical character(s): Alexander the Great, Ruler (Macedonian king); Aristotle, Philosopher, Teacher
Time Period(s): 4th century B.C. (326 B.C.)
Locale(s): Athens, Greece; Middle East; India

Summary: This comic adventure imagines the complications if Alexander the Great had presented his former teacher Aristotle with the first elephant brought from India to Greece. Alexander's cavalry officer, Leon of Atrax, is given the commission to transport the beast across several thousand miles of desert, mountains, and sea, braving sandstorms, quicksand, and numerous attacks.

Historical Accuracy: The emphasis here is on comedy rather than authenticity. To differentiate the multitude of nationalities in Alexander's empire, the author gives each a particularly modern accent or dialect. Leon of Atrax, from northern Greece, speaks with a Scottish brogue.

1557 *Lest Darkness Fall*

Date of Publication: 1941
Subject(s): Time Travel; Dark Ages
Fictional character(s): Martin Padway, Time Traveller, Archaeologist
Time Period(s): 6th century
Locale(s): Italy

Summary: While archaeologist Martin Padway is studying in the Piazza del Pantheon, lightning strikes and transports him back in time to 6th century Italy. Padway uses his knowledge of history and his 20th century skills to deal with his new existance.

Historical Accuracy: The novel offers an ingenious and convincing reconstruction of the past.

CHARLES THEODORE HENRI DE COSTER (1827-1879)

De Coster was a Belgian writer who specialized in collecting legends from Flemish folklore. His literary use of the archaic style earned him a reputation as a medievalist.

1558 *The Legend of Tyl Ulenspiegel*

Date of Publication: 1867
Subject(s): Picaresque Adventure; Independence—Netherlands
Fictional character(s): Tyl Ulenspiegel, Wanderer, Military Personnel; Lamme Goedzak, Military Personnel
Historical character(s): Philip II, Ruler (King of Spain)
Time Period(s): 16th century
Locale(s): Netherlands; Flanders

Summary: In this story, based on folk legend and history, the author tells of the adventures of Ulenspiegel, a Flemish hero. He joins the army of William of Orange to fight King Philip of Spain. Ever resourceful, trusting in faith and home, Ulenspiegel comes to symbolize his native land.

Historical Accuracy: This is an interesting blend of legend and history with a suggested parallel between Ulenspiegel, the patriot savior, and King Philip, the destroyer.

TOM DE HAVEN (1949-)

Born in New Jersey and a graduate of Rutgers and Bowling Green University, De Haven is an associate professor of American studies and creative writing at Virginia Commonwealth University. He is the author of highly imaginative, often bizarre fictions. He originally intended to be a cartoonist, but since his drawing talent was minimal, he turned to writing.

1559 *Funny Papers*

Date of Publication: 1985
Subject(s): Journalism; Artistic Life; Comic Strips
Fictional character(s): Pinfold, Streetperson; Fuzzy, Animal (dog); Georgie Wreckage, Artist
Time Period(s): 1890s (1895)
Locale(s): New York, New York

Summary: This comic novel is set in 1895 and concerns the origins of the funny papers. A street vagrant, Pinfold, and a dog, Fuzzy, become the inspiration of young sketch artist Georgie Wreckage. Success as a cartoonist sends Wreckage on an exhilerating ride through Gay Nineties New York, where life is as colorful as anything one finds in the comics.

Historical Accuracy: The novel is filled to the brim with period details. The result is a fantasy anchored by its era that the author admits is not a factual account of the birth of the funnies.

MAZO DE LA ROCHE (1879-1961)

A Canadian novelist, short-story writer, and playwright, de la Roche was born in Newmarket, Ontario, and attended the University of Toronto and Toronto's School of Art. Her masterwork is the Jalna Chronicles series, which follows several generations of the Whiteoak family in Ontario. The series sold more than 11 million copies during the author's lifetime.

1560 *Morning at Jalna*

Date of Publication: 1960
Subject(s): Family Saga; Civil War—U.S.
Fictional character(s): Curtis Sinclair, Gentleman; Adeline Whiteoak, Spouse; Philip Whiteoak, Landowner
Time Period(s): 1860s
Locale(s): Canada

Summary: Chronologically the second novel in the Jalna Chronicles, this installment is set during the American Civil War and concerns the visit to Jalna of a group of Southern refuges from the Union invasion of Carolina.

Historical Accuracy: The novel captures the period authentically.

TERESA DE LUCA

1561 *A Distant Thunder*

Date of Publication: 1990

Subject(s): Civil War—Spain; Romance
Fictional character(s): Dolores Carrasquez, Gentlewoman; Jack Austin, Journalist; Lorenzo Montanis, Gentleman; Tomas Garcia, Revolutionary
Time Period(s): 1930s; 1940s (1930-1940)
Locale(s): Spain; England

Summary: This is a story of love and coming of age against the backdrop of the Spanish Civil War. Dolores Carrasquez is the only daughter of a wealthy Spanish landowner. She finds herself pulled in conflicting directions by three men—Lorenzo, a Spanish gentleman; Tomas, a revolutionary writer; and Jack Austin, an English journalist.

Historical Accuracy: Despite the novel's background of the Spanish Civil War, the author admits to altering history in the interest of readability. The result is purely fictional.

COLIN DE SILVA

De Silva was born in Ceylon. In 1962 he emigrated to Honolulu.

1562 *The Winds of Sinhala*

Date of Publication: 1982
Subject(s): Sinhala Empire
Fictional character(s): Rodana, Royalty (prince), Teacher; Gaminini, Heir, Royalty (prince)
Time Period(s): 2nd century B.C.
Locale(s): Ceylon

Summary: The novel captures the culture and customs of the Sinhala nation of Ceylon in the 2nd century B.C. Gaminini is the king's son and heir, and his story is narrated by Rodana, who serves as Gaminini's tutor. The story is one of political intrigue and family treacheries, forming an epic history of an ancient culture.

Historical Accuracy: Though based on what little is known of the period, the author explains that the novel includes fictional characters, incidents, customs, and ceremonies to complete the story.

LOUIS DE WOHL (1903-1963)

Born in Berlin, De Wohl's father was a Hungarian nobleman and diplomat, his mother an Austrian baroness. A writer of renown in Germany, De Wohl left for England when Hitler came to power. He served during World War II as the British Army Head of the Department of Psychological Warfare.

1563 *Citadel of God: A Novel of Saint Benedict*

Date of Publication: 1959
Subject(s): Roman Empire; Religious Life; Biography, Fictionalized
Historical character(s): Benedict, Religious; Anicius Severinus, Philosopher
Time Period(s): 6th century
Locale(s): Rome, Italy; Ravenna, Italy

Summary: The Roman Empire after its fall is the setting for this novel that concerns the life of St. Benedict. The novel details Benedict's disillusionment in a conquered Rome, his years as a hermit, and his work establishing the monastic order that would help preserve learning and scholarship.

Historical Accuracy: The novel is faithful to the facts of Benedict's life and captures the atmosphere of Rome at the end of its grand history.

1564 *David of Jerusalem*

Date of Publication: 1963
Subject(s): Biblical Story; Ancient Israel; Biography, Fictionalized
Historical character(s): David, Ruler (King of Israel), Biblical Figure; Samuel, Religious (prophet), Biblical Figure; Saul, Ruler (King of Israel), Biblical Figure; Bathsheba, Royalty (queen consort of David), Biblical Figure; Solomon, Ruler (King of Israel), Biblical Figure; Jonathan, Biblical Figure
Time Period(s): 10th century B.C.
Locale(s): Israel

Summary: The novel tells the story of David, a shepherd boy who rises to rule Israel. David's career is depicted from his childhood to his years of service to King Saul and on to his own long reign. Many important Biblical figures—Jonathan, Bathsheba, and Solomon—are portrayed.

Historical Accuracy: The novel is faithful to the Biblical account, and the period details are supported by evident research.

1565 *The Glorious Folly: A Novel of the Time of St. Paul*

Date of Publication: 1957
Subject(s): Biography, Fictionalized; Christianity; Religious Life
Historical character(s): Paul, Biblical Figure, Religious; Pontius Pilate, Government Official, Biblical Figure; Herod Agrippa II, Ruler (King of Judea); Claudius I, Ruler (Roman emperor); Nero, Ruler (Roman emperor)
Time Period(s): 1st century (36-67)
Locale(s): Antioch, Syria; Jerusalem, Israel; Rome, Roman Empire

Summary: The life of St. Paul is depicted from his days as a virulent anti-Christian to his conversion and ministry. The scene shifts from the Middle East to Rome for Paul's final test and martyrdom.

Historical Accuracy: The period details are convincing in this life of Paul.

1566 *The Golden Thread*

Date of Publication: 1952
Subject(s): Religious Life; Biography, Fictionalized
Historical character(s): Ignatius Loyola, Military Personnel, Religious; Francis Xavier, Religious
Time Period(s): 16th century (1521-1556)
Locale(s): Spain; Rome, Italy; Middle East

Summary: The transformation of Ignatius Loyola from worldly nobleman and soldier to the founder of the Jesuit order is chronicled here. He is seriously wounded at the siege of Pamplona in 1521, and the experience changes the course of his life. The novel traces his later career and his pilgrimage to the Holy Land.

Historical Accuracy: The period is depicted with skill and authenticity.

1567 *Imperial Renegade*

Date of Publication: 1950
Subject(s): Roman Empire; Christianity
Historical character(s): Julian the Apostate, Ruler (Roman emperor)
Time Period(s): 4th century (348-363)
Locale(s): Byzantium, Roman Empire

Summary: The novel tells the story of Julian the Apostate, a young monk who converts to paganism and becomes Roman emperor. The story details Julian's efforts to restore the worship of the gods and suppress Christianity.

Historical Accuracy: The novel is authentic in its presentation of period details and the facts surrounding Julian's reign.

1568 *The Joyful Beggar: A Novel of St. Francis of Assisi*

Date of Publication: 1958
Subject(s): Middle Ages; Religious Life; Biography, fictionalized
Historical character(s): Francis of Assisi, Religious (monk); Frederick II, Ruler (Holy Roman emperor); Innocent III, Religious (pope)
Time Period(s): 13th century (1202-1226)
Locale(s): Assisi, Italy

Summary: This biographical novel traces the life of St. Francis of Assisi from his realization of his religious calling and the founding of the Franciscan order of monks. Interwoven with Francis' story is the political background involving Frederick II, the Holy Roman Emperor and the fate of Italy.

Historical Accuracy: The period details are convincing.

1569 *The Last Crusader*

Date of Publication: 1956
Subject(s): Royalty—Spain; Religious Conflict; Battle of Lepanto
Historical character(s): Juan of Austria, Royalty (son of Charles V); Philip II, Ruler (King of Spain); Charles V, Ruler (Holy Roman Emperor)
Time Period(s): 16th century (1554-1571)
Locale(s): Spain

Summary: The Spanish military hero, Don Juan of Austria, is presented here during the crusade against the Moslems. Juan is the son of Emperor Charles V and spent his childhood in a Spanish peasant's hut before being recognized by Philip II as his half-brother. Juan plays a pivotal role in the climactic victory at Lepanto.

Historical Accuracy: The era is effectively and convincingly rendered.

1570 *Lay Siege to Heaven: A Novel of Saint Catherine of Siena*

Date of Publication: 1961
Subject(s): Middle Ages; Religious Life; Biography, Fictionalized
Historical character(s): Catherine of Siena, Religious; Gregory XI, Religious (pope)
Time Period(s): 14th century (1347-1380)
Locale(s): Siena, Italy; Avignon, France

Summary: This biographical novel traces the remarkable career of Catherine of Siena. She is the daughter of a prosperous dyer in 14th century Italy, and a mystical experience in her youth leads her to a religious calling. She plays an important role as a religious leader, persuading Pope Gregory to return from Avignon to Rome, and in politics, helping to subdue warfare in the Italian City-States.

Historical Accuracy: The novel is a thorough and convincing chronicle of both the life and the times of Catherine.

1571 *The Living Wood*

Date of Publication: 1947
Subject(s): Roman Empire; Christianity
Historical character(s): Constantine I, Ruler (Roman Emperor); Helena, Religious; Constantius I, Military Personnel (tribune)
Time Period(s): 3rd century; 4th century (272-326)
Locale(s): England; Rome, Roman Empire; Middle East

Summary: The novel describes the family history of Emperor Constantine and the search for the true cross. Tribune Constantius is a Roman officer in Britain who marries Helena, the daughter of the King of Britain. Helena is determined that their son, Constantine, should be a great warrior, but her conversion to Christianity alters her plans and she sets out in search of the true cross.

Historical Accuracy: Although a novel first, this book includes many events and personalities based on historical fact.

1572 *The Quiet Light*

Date of Publication: 1950
Subject(s): Middle Ages; Religious Life; Biography, Fictionalized
Historical character(s): Thomas Aquinas, Religious, Philosopher; Frederick II, Ruler (Holy Roman Emperor); Louis IX, Ruler (King of France)
Time Period(s): 13th century
Locale(s): Italy

Summary: This biographical novel chronicles the remarkable life of Thomas Aquinas. Rather than follow his family's ambition and become a major power in the church, he takes a vow of poverty and joins the Dominicans. Very much connected to the world of the 13th century, and a favorite of kings and emperors, Aquinas remains true to his mission and becomes the most important theologian of the Middle Ages.

Historical Accuracy: Unfortunately, the novel's objectivity is sacrificed in creating a foil to Thomas, producing a biased portrait of Frederick II.

1573 *The Restless Flame*

Date of Publication: 1951
Subject(s): Roman Empire; Religious Life; Biography, Fictionalized
Historical character(s): Augustine, Religious (bishop), Philosopher; Ambrose, Religious (bishop); Monica, Noblewoman
Time Period(s): 4th century; 5th century (370-430)
Locale(s): Africa; Rome, Roman Empire; Milan, Roman Empire

Summary: Based on St. Augustine's *Confessions*, the novel tells the story of this great doctor of the Church. He is transformed from a vain and sensual young man in Africa by his conversion by Ambrose in 387. Augustine then becomes one of the great theologians of history, dying as the Bishop of Hippo while the Vandals attack his city.

Historical Accuracy: The novel stays close to the sources, and the author skillfully depicts the period.

1574 *Set All Afire: A Novel of St. Francis Xavier*

Date of Publication: 1953
Subject(s): Religious Life; Biography, Fictionalized
Historical character(s): Francis Xavier, Religious (missionary); Ignatius Loyola, Religious (founder of the Jesuit order)
Time Period(s): 16th century (1520s-1557)
Locale(s): Paris, France; India; Japan

Summary: St. Francis Xavier is renowned as the greatest of all missionaries. Urged by Ignatius Loyola to "set all afire" in the Orient, Francis departs on year-long voyage to India. After great success, he moves on to Japan, dying suddenly on the eve of setting out to bring Christianity to China. The novel offers a vivid dramatization of Francis' extraordinary life.

Historical Accuracy: The account of both Francis Xavier and the period is genuine.

1575 *Throne of the World*

Date of Publication: 1949
Subject(s): Roman Empire; Barbarians
Historical character(s): Attila the Hun, Ruler (King of the Huns); Honoria, Royalty (princess); Leo I, Religious (pope)
Time Period(s): 5th century (425-452)
Locale(s): Roman Empire; Asia

Summary: As the Roman Empire declines in the 5th century, the love affair between Attila and the Roman princess Honoria, the daughter of the Roman Empress Placidia, provides the motivation for the Huns' invasion of the Western Empire. The role played by Pope Leo I in halting the Huns' advance is prominently displayed.

Historical Accuracy: The version of history presented is highly romanticized and idealized. The historical facts do not support the novel's case about the love between Honoria and Attila or Leo's eloquence in halting the Huns.

MALCOLM DECKER (1893-)

Decker is an author of several histories of the American Revolution and biographies, including *Benedict Arnold* and *Brink of Revolution: America in Crisis, 1765-1776*.

1576 *The Rebel and the Turncoat*

Date of Publication: 1949
Subject(s): American Revolution; American Colonies; Espionage
Fictional character(s): Henry Prince, Young Man
Historical character(s): Nathan Hale, Patriot, Military Personnel (colonial spy)
Time Period(s): 1770s
Locale(s): New York, New York; Philadelphia, Pennsylvania

Summary: This tale of divided loyalties during the American Revolution tells the story of Henry Prince, the nephew of a New York Tory bookseller, who is gradually persuaded to embrace the American cause. Nathan Hale plays a key role in his decision.

Historical Accuracy: The atmosphere of the period is captured in a well-told story.

WARWICK DEEPING (1877-1950)

Born in Essex, England, Deeping was trained as a physician, but he practiced medicine for just one year. A successful series of historical novels allowed him to devote himself entirely to writing, and he produced approximately 70 novels during his lifetime. Best known for the post-World War I tale *Sorell and Son*, he also wrote *Love Among the Ruins*, *Old Pybus*, *The Man Who Went Back*, and *Martin Valiant*.

1577 *The Man on the White Horse*

Date of Publication: 1934
Subject(s): Roman Empire; Christianity
Fictional character(s): Geraint, Landowner, Warlord; Guinevra, Orphan
Time Period(s): 4th century (363)
Locale(s): England

Summary: This romantic tale is set in Britain as Roman power is waning and conflict among the Welsh, Picts, and Saxons turns the country into a deadly battlefield. The story concerns the struggle of a warlord, Geraint, whose rescue of a beautiful orphan, Guinevra, threatens to start a rebellion.

Historical Accuracy: The sense of the 4th-century life is unconvincing. The characters are given a modern sensibility and language.

1578 *Martin Valliant*

Date of Publication: 1939
Subject(s): War of the Roses
Fictional character(s): Martin Valliant, Religious (monk), Knight
Time Period(s): 15th century
Locale(s): England

Summary: This romantic novel describes the adventures of Martin Valliant, a monk. Out of love he leaves the cloister and embarks on a career as a knight.

Historical Accuracy: With some authority the novel captures the corrupt conditions in the church and politics of the period.

JIM DEFELICE (1956-)

An American novelist, journalist, and college professor, DeFelice's novels include *Coyote Bird*, *War Breaker*, and *The Iron Chain*.

1579 *The Iron Chain*

Date of Publication: 1995
Subject(s): American Revolution; Espionage
Fictional character(s): John Gibbs, Spy, Patriot
Time Period(s): 1770s (1777)
Locale(s): New York

Summary: Lieutenant Colonel John Gibbs, General Washington's secret agent, is given the mission of finding out how the British plan to defeat the iron chain placed across the Hudson River to prevent the movement of their fleet. Gibbs attempts to halt the British invasion while trying to survive when he is exposed as a spy.

Historical Accuracy: The action surrounding the iron chain across the Hudson during the Revolution is invented, though the chain itself did exist.

WILLIAM DEGENHARD

1580 *The Regulators*

Date of Publication: 1943
Subject(s): Shays' Rebellion
Fictional character(s): Warren Hascott, Veteran (Revolutionary War); Judith Burdock, Gentlewoman; Beulah Crane, Farmer
Historical character(s): Daniel Shays, Veteran (Revolutionary War), Leader (insurrectionist)
Time Period(s): 1780s (1786-1787)
Locale(s): Boston, Massachusetts; Worcester, Massachusetts

Summary: When Warren Hascott returns home to Boston after the Revolution, he finds everything changed. The country is in a depression, and the new regime seems far more repressive than the British. Discontent explodes in Shays' Rebellion, a populist revolt of farmers in western Massachusetts that helps force Massachusetts to ratify the federal constitution.

Historical Accuracy: The novel is well-researched and persuasive in its details of an important and little-understood period of American history.

THEODORA DEHON

1581 *Heroic Dust*

Date of Publication: 1940
Subject(s): French Revolution; Chouan Revolt

Fictional character(s): Louis-Auguste de Boisdesert, Gentleman; Alexandrine de Royville, Gentlewoman
Time Period(s): 1790s (1792)
Locale(s): Normandy, France

Summary: The novel provides a dramatic account of the Chouan Revolt, the Royalist uprising against the French Revolution. The story focuses on the aristocratic Boisdesert family of Normandy and chronicles the events of the rising.

Historical Accuracy: The novel captures the flavor of the region and the period expertly.

JOSEPH JAY DEISS (1915-)

Deiss grew up in Texas and received his B.A. and M.A. degrees from the University of Texas. He worked as a writer for the U.S. government and as a public relations executive before leaving business in 1954 to write full time. During his five years of research for *The Great Infidel* Deiss learned to read 13th-century Italian and acquired a falcon to learn the art of hawking. His other books include *Washington Story*, *The Blue Chips*, and the nonfiction work *Herculaneum: Italy's Buried Treasure*.

1582 *The Great Infidel*

Date of Publication: 1963
Subject(s): Middle Ages; Biography, Fictionalized
Historical character(s): Frederick II, Ruler (Holy Roman Emperor)
Time Period(s): 13th century
Locale(s): Italy; Germany

Summary: This autobiographical account describes the life and career of Frederick II, Holy Roman Emperor and King of Sicily. Frederick narrates the story of his coming to power and the attitudes which set him apart from his contemporaries. Frederick's tragedy is that he was a Renaissance man who lived 200 years too early.

Historical Accuracy: The novel stays close to historical facts, as is made clear by extensive notes.

MARGARET DELAND

1583 *The Kays*

Date of Publication: 1926
Subject(s): Civil War—U.S.
Fictional character(s): Agnes Kay, Gentlewoman; Arthur Kay, Young Man
Time Period(s): 1860s
Locale(s): Pennsylvania

Summary: This Civil War era tale describes the experiences of the Kay family and its iron-willed matriarch, Agnes Kay, who is a pacifist and stubbornly opposes the war sentiment that sweeps the country.

Historical Accuracy: The novel provides a believable portrait of the northern homefront during the Civil War.

SVEN DELBLANC

1584 *Speranza*

Date of Publication: 1983
Subject(s): Sea Story; Slavery
Fictional character(s): Malte Moritz Von Putbus, Nobleman
Time Period(s): 18th century
Locale(s): *Speranza*, At Sea

Summary: This moral fable takes the form of a diary kept by a young Swedish nobleman sailing aboard the *Speranza* toward the Dutch West Indies with a cargo of slaves. The experience provides an opportunity to explore the diarist's idealism under the strain of the corrupting voyage.

Historical Accuracy: The novel presents a believable portrait of the age and its attitudes.

R.F. DELDERFIELD (1912-1972)

English author Ronald Frederick Delderfield worked in various capacities on the country newspaper his father owned. He served in the R.A.F. as a public relations officer during the Second World War. Delderfield began his career as a writer and playwright following the war. From that point, he estimated that he wrote 4,000 words a day, every day of the year. Besides his novels and plays, Delderfield is the author of numerous historical works on Napoleon and the Napoleonic Era.

1585 *Farewell the Tranquil*

Date of Publication: 1950
Subject(s): French Revolution; Espionage
Fictional character(s): Davy Trelcar, Smuggler
Time Period(s): 1780s
Locale(s): England; France

Summary: English smuggler Davy Trelcar is accused of killing an exciseman and being a French spy. He flees to France where he takes part in the Revolution. In exchange for clemency, Trelcar's wife hands over French military information to the British.

Historical Accuracy: There are a number of mistakes evident in the rendering of the historical facts, but the novel does capture its period atmosphere with conviction.

1586 *Give Us This Day*

Date of Publication: 1973
Subject(s): Family Saga; World War I
Fictional character(s): Adam Swann, Veteran, Businessman; Alexander Swann, Military Personnel (major); Giles Swann, Businessman
Historical character(s): David Lloyd George, Political Figure (prime minister)
Time Period(s): 1910s
Locale(s): London, England; Dublin, Ireland

Summary: This is the continuation of the Swann family history begun in *God Is an Englishman* and *Theirs Was the Kingdom*. The chronicle brings the Swann family to World War I and

the destruction of the Victorian values which have sustained them.

Historical Accuracy: Through the Swann family, the author reflects the making of the modern world and the destructive impact of change. The period's major events are convincingly detailed.

1587 *God Is an Englishman*

Date of Publication: 1970
Subject(s): Family Saga; Victorian Period
Fictional character(s): Henrietta Rawlinson, Gentlewoman; Adam Swann, Businessman
Time Period(s): 1850s; 1860s (1857-1866)
Locale(s): London, England

Summary: This is the first of three volumes that chronicle the history of the Swann family and 19th and 20th century English history. Adam Swan parlays a necklace captured on the battlefield in India into a vast commercial enterprise and family dynasty. The novel shows his rise to success and respectability.

Historical Accuracy: The world of Victorian England in the throes of commercial expansion and imperialism is authentically depicted.

1588 *A Horseman Riding By*

Date of Publication: 1966
Subject(s): Family Saga; World War I; World War II
Fictional character(s): Paul Craddock, Veteran (of the Boer War); Grace Lovell, Spouse (of Craddock); Claire Dernent, Spouse (of Craddock)
Time Period(s): 20th century (1902-1940)
Locale(s): Devonshire, England

Summary: The novel offers a personal counterattack on behalf of the British way of life between 1902 and 1940. Seen from the perspective of Paul Craddock, a young soldier in the Boer War who becomes the squire of Shallowford, the novel dramatizes his and his family's history as they are affected by the great events of the 20th century.

Historical Accuracy: The novel is expert in capturing the regional and period details. The author's evident partisanship, however, results in some muting of the picture by nostalgia for a departed way of life.

1589 *Seven Men of Gascony*

Date of Publication: 1949
Subject(s): Napoleonic Wars; Military Life
Fictional character(s): Gabriel Guilame, Military Personnel (infantryman), Artist; Jean Ticquet, Military Personnel (sergeant)
Historical character(s): Michel Ney, Military Personnel (French marshal); Napoleon Bonaparte, Military Personnel (French commander), Ruler (Emperor of France); Jean Lannes, Military Personnel (French marshal)
Time Period(s): 1800s; 1810s (1808-1815)
Locale(s): Europe (France, Austria, Germany, Portugal); Russia; England

Summary: The novel offers the experience of typical infantrymen in Napoleon's Grande Armee during his campaigns, including the invasion of Russia and the final defeat at Waterloo. The company represents a cross-section of character types, and their experiences give an instructive ground-eye view of Napoleon's army and its impressive morale.

Historical Accuracy: The details are convincing and authentic.

`1590` *Theirs Was the Kingdom*

Date of Publication: 1971
Subject(s): Family Saga; Business Building
Fictional character(s): Adam Swann, Businessman; Henrietta Swann, Spouse; George Swann, Businessman
Time Period(s): 19th century; 20th century
Locale(s): London, England; Vienna, Austria

Summary: This family saga focusses on several members of the large Swann family, showing a diversified blend of English life during the late 1800s and early 1900s. The fortune of the family business is connected to the political and social situations of the period.

Historical Accuracy: The novel is convincing in its depiction of the period.

`1591` *To Serve Them All My Days*

Date of Publication: 1972
Subject(s): Family Saga; Education
Fictional character(s): David Powlett-Jones, Teacher; Elizabeth Marwood, Nurse, Spouse (to Powlett-Jones); J.D. Alcock, Teacher (headmaster)
Time Period(s): 20th century (1916-1939)
Locale(s): England

Summary: The novel follows the career of David Powlett-Jones as a history teacher at an English public school. The story shows his slow rise from a shell-shocked World War I veteran to instructor, housemaster, and finally headmaster as England faces another war.

Historical Accuracy: The novel is convincing in rendering the details of the period between the wars.

MIGUEL DELIBES (1920-)

Spanish writer Delibes was born in Valladolid and attended its university. He is considered one of Spain's most important novelists, a writer of stark realism with rural subject matter and well-developed characters.

`1592` *The Stuff of Heroes*

Date of Publication: 1990
Subject(s): Civil War—Spain
Fictional character(s): Gervasio Garcia de la Lastra, Military Personnel (naval officer)
Time Period(s): 1930s
Locale(s): Spain

Summary: In this coming of age novel Gervasio Garcia de la Lastra is tested by the events of the Spanish Civil War, as the country is split apart into opposing camps.

Historical Accuracy: The events depicted are drawn from fact and dramatized with authenticity.

DON DELILLO (1936-)

Born in New York City, DeLillo ranks with the best of contemporary American novelists, highly acclaimed for his inventive and provocative books that display a wide range of interests, including football, science, political conspiracies, and terrorism. All share a common theme of the disintegration of order and the rise of paranoia. DeLillo won an American Book Award in 1985 for *White Noise*. Other books include *Ratner's Star*, *End Zone*, and *Players*.

`1593` *Libra*

Date of Publication: 1988
Subject(s): Assassination; Crime and Criminals
Historical character(s): John F. Kennedy, Political Figure; Lee Harvey Oswald, Criminal (alleged assassin); Jack Ruby, Murderer
Time Period(s): 1960s (1963)
Locale(s): Dallas, Texas

Summary: This re-creation of the assassination of President Kennedy is based on the thesis that it was a CIA conspiracy. Alarmed by the growing rapprochement with Cuba, CIA operatives seized upon Lee Harvey Oswald to commit the deed. This familiar theory is deepened fictionally by an imaginative exploration of the central players in the events at Dallas in 1963. At the center is the strange figure of Oswald and his odd drift toward his destiny.

Historical Accuracy: The plausibility of the novel's conspiracy theory is less convincing than the treatment of Oswald, who emerges in all his troubling paradoxes as a true individual.

FLOYD DELL (1887-1969)

Dell was among the influential Chicago School of midwestern writers that included Carl Sandburg, Ben Hecht, and Charles MacArthur. A socialist, Dell was the editor of the radical *Masses*. His novels include *Moon-Calf*, *The Briary Bush*, and *The Golden Spike*.

`1594` *Diana Stair*

Date of Publication: 1932
Subject(s): Women's Rights; Abolition Movement
Fictional character(s): Diana Stair, Widow(er), Abolitionist
Time Period(s): 1840s
Locale(s): Boston, Massachusetts

Summary: The novel dramatizes a heroine ahead of her time, Diana Stair, who is drawn into the Abolitionist Movement, and later becomes a labor leader, and member of a socialist colony. Her modern notions cause both controversy and conflict.

Historical Accuracy: The novel makes a case that 20th-century radicalism has its roots in the 19th century. Despite some anachronisms, the novel does capture the social scene believably.

GEORGE DELL (1901-)

1595 *The Earth Abideth*

Date of Publication: 1986
Subject(s): Reconstruction Period; Farming
Fictional character(s): Thomas Linthorne, Farmer; Sara Linthorne, Spouse
Time Period(s): 19th century; 20th century (1866-1903)
Locale(s): Fairfield County, Ohio

Summary: This realistic tale of farm life begins in 1866 with Thomas and Sara Linthorne starting their life together following the Civil War. The novel follows their family history as they claim their land, build a house, and start their family.

Historical Accuracy: The author is uncompromising in his portrayal of ordinary life in a particular time and place.

GENELL DELLIN

1596 *Cherokee Dawn*

Date of Publication: 1990
Subject(s): American West; Civil War—U.S.; Indians
Fictional character(s): Lacey Longbaugh, Orphan; Ridge Chekote, Indian (part Cherokee)
Time Period(s): 1860s
Locale(s): Oklahoma

Summary: With a background of the West during the Civil War, this romantic story concerns the adventures of Lacey Longbaugh, who journeys into the Oklahoma Territory after her parents are killed. There she encounters the part-Cherokee Ridge Chekote.

Historical Accuracy: The period background is convincing.

DAVID DELMAN (1924-)

Delman worked in advertising and wrote several mystery novels, including *He Who Digs a Grave* and *The Nice Murderers*.

1597 *Ain't Goin' to Glory*

Date of Publication: 1991
Subject(s): Civil War—U.S.; Draft Riots; Racial Conflict
Fictional character(s): Stephen Jardine, Journalist; Margaret Jardine, Spouse; John Brautigan, Police Officer (chief of police)
Historical character(s): Horace Greeley, Journalist, Editor; James Gordon Bennett, Journalist, Editor
Time Period(s): 1860s (1863)
Locale(s): New York, New York

Summary: The events of New York's Draft Riots of 1863 are dramatized in this fictional account which centers on Stephen Jardine, a reporter for the *New York Tribune*, and his wife, Margaret. They are caught up in the violence in which a black orphanage is sacked and burned, and black men are hanged from lamp posts.

Historical Accuracy: The author admits to taking some slight liberties with the chronology but every incident is based on something that actually happened.

1598 *The Bluestocking*

Date of Publication: 1994
Subject(s): Trials; Theatrical Life
Fictional character(s): Henry Stewart, Journalist; Serena Blaylock, Artist
Historical character(s): Edwin Forrest, Actor; Catherine Forrest, Gentlewoman, Spouse
Time Period(s): 1850s (1852)
Locale(s): New York, New York

Summary: The divorce case in 1852 of actor Edwin Forrest and his wife, Catherine, was the longest divorce suit ever to be tried in New York. Scandal abounded in charges and counter-charges to the fascination of New York society. The novel follows this trial of the century closely with the actual testimony plus a sidebar of a *New York Tribune* reporter in love with artist and freethinker Serena Blaylock.

Historical Accuracy: The novel is a marvelous reconstruction of this trial and scandal with evident use of primary materials.

VINA DELMAR (1905-1990)

Born in New York City, Delmar worked as a typist, switchboard operator, usher, actress, and movie theater manager. Her novels such as *Bad Girl* and *Kept Woman*, and short story collection *Loose Ladies* were notorious for their frank treatment of Jazz Age morality. Her later work shows her interest in the 19th-century South.

1599 *Beloved*

Date of Publication: 1956
Subject(s): Civil War—U.S.; Biography, Fictionalized; Politics
Historical character(s): Judah P. Benjamin, Political Figure (Confederate cabinet member); Jefferson Davis, Political Figure (President of the Confederacy)
Time Period(s): 19th century (1816-1884)
Locale(s): New Orleans, Louisiana; Charleston, South Carolina; Richmond, Virginia

Summary: This biographical novel describes the career of Judah P. Benjamin who, as Secretary of War and State under Jefferson Davis, was widely regarded as the brains of the Confederacy. Benjamin's rise to power and prominence is chronicled from his childhood in Charleston, including his studies at Yale and his first law practice. The novel also covers his political career, from his service as Senator for Louisiana to his terms as the Secretary of War and of State in the Confederacy. He is forced into exile, ending his life in England.

Historical Accuracy: The novel's sources are impressive, and the life is both reliable and believable.

1600 *The Big Family*

Date of Publication: 1961

Subject(s): American Revolution; Civil War—U.S.; Family Saga
Historical character(s): John Slidell, Political Figure (Confederacy); Alexander Slidell Mackenzie, Military Personnel (naval officer); Matthew Perry, Military Personnel (naval officer); Andrew Jackson, Political Figure; James Buchanan, Political Figure; Judah P. Benjamin, Political Figure (Confederate Cabinet Member); Louis Napoleon Bonaparte, Ruler (Emperor of France); Eugenie, Royalty (consort of Louis Napoleon)
Time Period(s): 18th century; 19th century (1770s-1870s)
Locale(s): New Orleans, Louisiana; France; Japan

Summary: This family saga chronicles the remarkable Slidell family. It opens during the American Revolution and continues through the Civil War. At the center of the story is John Slidell, who flees to New Orleans after a scandalous duel to become the city's most influential citizen, U.S. senator, and Confederate Commissioner to France. Others in the family include Captain Alexander Mackenzie who becomes involved in the Somers mutiny, and Commodore Perry, who opened up Japan.

Historical Accuracy: Although the early years of the Slidells are invented, little else in the novel is.

`1601` *The Laughing Stranger*
Date of Publication: 1953
Subject(s): Civil War—U.S.; Reconstruction Period
Fictional character(s): Brett Carpenter, Military Personnel, Veteran; Elizabeth Carpenter, Spouse; Brandon Coberley, Southern Belle
Time Period(s): 1860s
Locale(s): New Jersey

Summary: This domestic drama is set immediately following the Civil War and involves the Carpenter family. When Brett Carpenter returns from the war, his family moves to the New Jersey coast for him to recover from the trauma of battle. There their lives are entangled with the beautiful and mysterious Brandon Coberley from Carolina.

Historical Accuracy: The atmosphere of impending doom vividly captures the period in this suspense novel.

`1602` *A Time for Titans*
Date of Publication: 1974
Subject(s): Louisiana Purchase; Independence—Haiti; Diplomacy
Historical character(s): Napoleon Bonaparte, Ruler (Emperor of France); Thomas Jefferson, Political Figure; Pierre Dominique Toussaint l'Ouverture, Revolutionary, Political Figure; James Madison, Political Figure, Diplomat; James Monroe, Political Figure, Diplomat; Henri Christophe, Revolutionary, Political Figure
Time Period(s): 1800s
Locale(s): Paris, France; Washington, District of Columbia; Haiti

Summary: The complicated diplomatic maneuverings that led to the Louisiana Purchase are seen as the clash among three titans of history: Napoleon, Jefferson, and Toussaint L'Ouverture. The novel dramatizes the connections between Napoleon's aspirations in Europe, Haiti's freedom, and the greatest land acquistion ever achieved by means other than conquest.

Historical Accuracy: Historical reality has not been altered here, but rather trimmed down to avoid confusion.

JOSEPHINE DELVES-BROUGHTON
(1916-)

Born in Hampstead, England, Delves-Broughton was educated at the Sherbourn School for Girls and has written *The World is a Bridge*, *The Siege*, and an historical novel, *Heart of a Queen*.

`1603` *Heart of a Queen*
Date of Publication: 1950
Subject(s): Elizabethan Period; Royalty—England; Biography, Fictionalized
Historical character(s): Elizabeth I, Ruler (Queen of England); Robert Dudley, Courtier, Nobleman (Earl of Leicester); Robert Devereux, Courtier, Nobleman (Earl of Essex)
Time Period(s): 16th century; 17th century
Locale(s): England

Summary: The reign of Elizabeth I is dramatized through her relationship with the two principal men in her life—the earls of Leicester and Essex. Elizabeth's inner life shares the stage with the intrigue of her court and the sweep of history that marked the Elizabethan period. In the end it is Elizabeth's dedication to England and her duty as its queen that predominates.

Historical Accuracy: The novel makes use of the letters and actual conversations and incidents to create an authentic portrait of the queen and her era.

`1604` *Officer and Gentleman*
Date of Publication: 1951
Subject(s): Victorian Period; Crimean War; Military Life
Fictional character(s): Quinton Arrowe, Military Personnel (army officer); Thomas Arrowe, Military Personnel (army officer)
Time Period(s): 19th century
Locale(s): England; Crimea, Russia

Summary: This family and military tale concerns the attempt of Quinton Arrowe to live up to the reputation of his father, ''Flogging Tom'' Arrowe, a renowned general and one of the greatest rakes of his day. Quinton's military experiences include riding with the Light Brigade at Balaclava during the Crimean War.

Historical Accuracy: The novel makes use of authentic period elements in its detailing of military life and customs.

PHYLLIS GORDON DEMAREST
(1911-1969)

An English novelist and short story writer, Demarest was born in London. Her books include *The Naked Risk* and *Angelic City*.

1605 *The Wilderness Brigade*

Date of Publication: 1957
Subject(s): Civil War—U.S.
Fictional character(s): Roark Bradford, Military Personnel (Union soldier); Beau Herrick, Military Personnel (Confederate major); Emmeline Herrick, Southern Belle
Time Period(s): 1860s
Locale(s): Wilkes County, North Carolina

Summary: This Civil War tale tells the story of Union prisoner of war Roark Bradford, who escapes and assists Confederate major Beau Herrick, who was blinded at Malvern Hill. Herrick hides Bradford and Bradford falls in love with Herrick's sister Emmeline. Encounters with bushwackers and the Home Guards mark the action.

Historical Accuracy: Romance predominates over careful and believable documentation of the era.

ROBERT DEMARIA (1928-)

De Maria is an American writer and college professor who taught at the University of Oregon, Columbia University, and Hofstra University. He served as an editor at Macmillan and as a dean for the New School for Social Research. His other works include *Carnival of Angels*.

1606 *Clodia*

Date of Publication: 1965
Subject(s): Roman Empire; Literary Life
Historical character(s): Gaius Valerius Catullus, Writer (poet); Clodia, Noblewoman; Publius Clodius Pulcher, Political Figure; Marcus Tullius Cicero, Political Figure, Philosopher
Time Period(s): 1st century B.C.
Locale(s): Rome, Roman Empire

Summary: Catullus, one of the greatest Latin poets, tells the story of his life and affair with the notorious Clodia, the beautiful sister of the despot Clodius. In the final days of the Roman Republic, as Rome drifts toward civil war, Catullus is caught up in the intrigues and politics of the period.

Historical Accuracy: The relationship between Catullus and Clodia is based on tradition rather than fact. However, the voice of the poet and the sense of the period are convincing.

1607 *To Be a King*

Date of Publication: 1976
Subject(s): Elizabethan Period; Theatrical Life; Espionage
Historical character(s): Christopher Marlowe, Writer; Sir Francis Walsingham, Government Official; Sir Walter Raleigh, Gentleman, Courtier; Thomas Kyd, Writer; William Shakespeare, Writer
Time Period(s): 16th century (1570s-1590s)
Locale(s): Canterbury, England; Cambridge, England; London, England

Summary: The novel offers the story of one of the most enigmatic figures of English literature and the Elizabethan period, Christopher Marlowe, poet, playwright, and, it is said, espionage agent. The novel chronicles Marlowe's life from childhood to Cambridge, to literary London and the court politics of Elizbeth's reign, and finally his death at an inn at Deptford under very suspicious circumstances.

Historical Accuracy: Historians are by no means certain of Marlowe's espionage activities. This version of the events has a plausible historical background, but its premises and conclusions are speculative.

AL DEMPSEY

1608 *Path of the Sun*

Date of Publication: 1992
Subject(s): American West; Railroads
Fictional character(s): James Hill, Financier; Zack Horton, Heir; Leah Page, Businesswoman
Time Period(s): 1880s
Locale(s): Rapid City, South Dakota; Great Plains

Summary: The transformation of the American West by the railroad and by statehood are the parallel themes in this novel. Railroad tycoon James Hill is driven to build a railroad empire, recruiting support from a variety of sources. He encounters danger from those who wish things to be left as they are.

Historical Accuracy: The novel is a colorful evocation of the closing of the American West and the forces of both change and the status quo.

1609 *What Law There Was*

Date of Publication: 1991
Subject(s): American West; Mining
Fictional character(s): Henry Plummer, Lawman (sheriff)
Time Period(s): 1860s (1862-1864)
Locale(s): Bannack, Montana

Summary: The discovery of gold in Montana brings a wave of miners, prostitutes, preachers, and settlers to the tiny town of Bannack. Townspeople elect Henry Plummer as the sheriff. However, Plummer is worse than the outlaws he is hired to police, and his gang kills over 100 before the townspeople form a vigilante committee to hang Plummer.

Historical Accuracy: The story is based on well-researched period details.

HENRY DENKER (1912-)

An American novelist born in New York City, Denker graduated from NYU and was a practicing lawyer in addition to being a playwright and TV, film, and radio scriptwriter. Denker is the recipient of a Peabody and a Christopher award.

1610 *The Healers*

Date of Publication: 1983
Subject(s): Medical Profession; Civil War—U.S.
Fictional character(s): David Lilliendahl, Doctor; Mary Sinclair, Doctor
Time Period(s): 19th century (1848-1885)
Locale(s): Vienna, Austria; New York, New York

Summary: This is the love story of two early medical pioneers of the 19th century. David Lilliendahl is a Jewish medical student who emigrates to New York and works at the Jews Hospital. He works with Mary Sinclair, the daughter of a prominent family and the first female doctor accepted to L'Ecole de Medicine in Paris. Together they tend the sick through the Civil War and after.

Historical Accuracy: The novel is an effective and convincing look at the medical profession of the period.

1611 *Salome, Princess of Galilee*

Date of Publication: 1952
Subject(s): Biblical Story
Historical character(s): Salome, Biblical Figure
Time Period(s): 1st century
Locale(s): Israel

Summary: This fanciful tale of Biblical times shows Salome after the death of John the Baptist. Consumed by guilt after her responsibility in his beheading, Salome repents and joins the early Christians after the death of Christ.

Historical Accuracy: The story has no basis in the New Testament story.

ALBERTO DENTI DI PIRAJNO
(1886-1968)

Denti di Pirajno wrote his first novel at the age of 75.

1612 *Ippolita*

Date of Publication: 1961
Subject(s): Independence—Italy
Fictional character(s): Ippolita von Grueber, Gentlewoman
Time Period(s): 19th century
Locale(s): Italy (north)

Summary: This is the story of Ippolita, a stubborn, self-centered woman. She is the richest woman in a small town and a miser. Her story is set against the turmoil brought on by the revolution of Garibaldi.

Historical Accuracy: The novel features a well-described historical background.

MAURICE DENUZIERE (1926-)

Denuziere has worked as the chief correspondent for the French newspaper *Le Monde*. He has covered a significant number of conflicts throughout the world beginning with World War II.

1613 *Bagatelle*

Date of Publication: 1978
Subject(s): Civil War—U.S.; Antebellum South
Fictional character(s): Caroline Tregan, Orphan; Clarence Dandridge, Plantation Owner
Time Period(s): 19th century (1830s-1860s)
Locale(s): New Orleans, Louisiana

Summary: The novel concerns life in New Orleans before and during the Civil War. The story centers on the experiences of a young French orphan girl, Caroline Tregan, and her relationship with the mysterious Clarence Dandridge.

Historical Accuracy: Derived from archival records, the novel's story is based on fact and provides an authentic depiction of the era and the region.

AUGUST DERLETH (1909-1971)

An American novelist, poet, and mystery writer, Derleth was the author of many books set in his native Wisconsin, including two long series of novels, The Sac Prairie Saga and The Wisconsin Saga.

1614 *Bright Journey*

Date of Publication: 1940
Subject(s): Settlement of the American Frontier; War of 1812
Historical character(s): John Jacob Astor, Trader, Financier; Hercules Dousman, Trader, Frontiersman
Time Period(s): 19th century (1812-1843)
Locale(s): Pacific Northwest; Mackinac Island, Michigan

Summary: The fur trade in the Pacific Northwest is depicted in the adventures of Hercules Dousman, an agent for John Jacob Astor. The first section of the story deals with Dousman's boyhood on Mackinac Island during the War of 1812 and the second, his employment with the American Fur Company.

Historical Accuracy: The novel offers a poetic yet believable rendering of the locale and the period.

1615 *The Hills Stand Watch*

Date of Publication: 1960
Subject(s): Settlement of the American Frontier; Mining
Fictional character(s): David Pengellen, Businessman (merchant); Tamsen Bishop, Young Woman
Time Period(s): 1840s
Locale(s): Wisconsin

Summary: This tale of frontier life in a small town in the Wisconsin territory during the 1840s captures the problems of the day, details of lead mining, and trouble with the Indians. At the center of the story is the young merchant David Pengellen.

Historical Accuracy: The activities centering around Wisconsin's pursuit of statehood follow the events of history, as do the details of lead mining.

1616 *The House on the Mound*

Date of Publication: 1958
Subject(s): Settlement of the American Frontier
Historical character(s): Hercules Dousman, Trader, Businessman; Jane Dousman, Spouse
Time Period(s): 19th century (1848-1868)
Locale(s): Wisconsin

Summary: This sequel to *Bright Journey* continues the story of fur trader and railroad builder Hercules Dousman. The novel is set in Wisconsin from the time of its admission to the Union to Hercules' death. The story concerns Dousman's attempt to reclaim his illegitimate son.

Historical Accuracy: The novel captures the regional background with skill and authority.

1617 *Restless Is the River*

Date of Publication: 1940
Subject(s): Settlement of the American Frontier
Fictional character(s): Augustin Brogmar, Nobleman (count)
Time Period(s): 19th century (1839-1850)
Locale(s): Sac Prairie, Wisconsin

Summary: This third installment of the author's Sac Prairie Saga continues the story of pioneer life in the mid-19th century. The story centers on a Hungarian nobleman, Count Brogmar, who seeks his fortune in the wilderness.

Historical Accuracy: The novel provides an authentic background of the region and period.

1618 *The Shadow in the Glass*

Date of Publication: 1963
Subject(s): Biography, Fictionalized; Politics
Historical character(s): Nelson Dewey, Political Figure
Time Period(s): 19th century
Locale(s): Wisconsin; New York

Summary: This biographical novel chronicles the career of Nelson Dewey, the first governor of Wisconsin. The novel captures life in the Wisconsin territory and the events leading to statehood in which Dewey plays an important role.

Historical Accuracy: The novel is faithful to the actual events of the period and Dewey's life.

1619 *Still Is the Summer Night*

Date of Publication: 1937
Subject(s): Settlement of the American Frontier
Fictional character(s): Ratio Halder, Farmer; Julie Halder, Spouse (of Ratio); Alton Halder, Farmer
Time Period(s): 1880s
Locale(s): Sac Prairie, Wisconsin

Summary: The novel features an intimate look at small town life on the Wisconsin prairie during the 1880s. The action concerns a romantic triangle between the two Halder brothers—Ratio and Alton—and Ratio's wife Julia.

Historical Accuracy: The novel captures the region and the period convincingly.

1620 *Wind over Wisconsin*

Date of Publication: 1938
Subject(s): Black Hawk War; Indians
Fictional character(s): Pierre Chalfonte Pierneau, Frontiersman
Historical character(s): Black Hawk, Indian (Sauk), Chieftain
Time Period(s): 1830s
Locale(s): Wisconsin

Summary: Set during the last decade of the Indian wars in Wisconsin the novel centers on Pierre Pierneau, a friend of the great Sauk chief Black Hawk. Pierneau's experiences dramatize the transition of the Wisconsin wilderness from fur trading to farming and settlement.

Historical Accuracy: The author is a master of his region, and a vast amount of research has gone into the book to create a believable historical background.

ROBERT S. DEROPP (1913-)

Born in London, England, and educated at the University of London, De Ropp immigrated to the united States, where he worked as a scientist at the Rockefeller Institute and the New York Botanical Garden before settling in California. From 1961 until he retired, he was a research biochemist at the University of San Francisco. In addition to publishing numerous scientific works, he is the author of *If I Forget Thee*, a novel about the siege of Jerusalem in 70 A.D.

1621 *If I Forget Thee*

Date of Publication: 1956
Subject(s): Roman Empire; Jews
Fictional character(s): Lucius Cimber, Young Man; Rebecca, Young Woman
Time Period(s): 1st century (66 A.D.)
Locale(s): Israel

Summary: The unrest between the Jews and the Romans that culminates in the destruction of Jerusalem and the Temple is the historical backdrop for this romantic novel. Lucius Cimber, son of a Roman patrician, and Rebecca, the daughter of the High Priest of the Jews fall in love despite the differences between their peoples.

Historical Accuracy: The novel attempts, with some success, to capture authentically the events and customs of the period.

PETER DEROSA (1932-)

Born in London and a former Jesuit priest, DeRosa taught philosophy at Corpus Christi College, London. He has worked as a radio producer for the BBC. DeRosa is also the author of scripts for the British Television series ''Bless Me, Father,'' based on his experiences.

1622 *Rebels: The Irish Rising of 1916*

Date of Publication: 1990
Subject(s): Easter Rising; World War I; Independence—Ireland
Historical character(s): Roger Casement, Government Official, Revolutionary; Tom Clarke, Revolutionary; James Connolly, Labor Leader, Revolutionary; Sean McDermott, Revolutionary; Patrick Henry Pearse, Teacher, Revolutionary; Joseph Plunkett, Revolutionary; Constance Markievicz, Noblewoman, Revolutionary; Eamon De Valera, Revolutionary; Arthur Griffith, Journalist, Revolutionary
Time Period(s): 1910s (1914-1916)
Locale(s): Dublin, Ireland

Summary: This is a fascinating and detailed account of the Easter 1916 Irish Rising, in which a group of amateurs, ill-organized and poorly equipped, challenge the might of the British and declare an Irish Republic. They are soundly criticized by the Irish populace as traitors and tools of the German enemy during wartime. The execution of 16 of the rebel leaders turns them into martyred heroes and accelerates Irish independence.

Historical Accuracy: The novel is a brilliant and detailed reconstruction of the events and the personalities, well-researched and utterly convincing.

ALICE CURTIS DESMOND (1897-)

Born in Connecticut, Desmond was a writer primarily for young people. She found material for her books on three world tours and trips to Alaska, South America, and Australia.

`1623` *Alexander Hamilton's Wife*

Date of Publication: 1952
Subject(s): Biography, Fictionalized; American Colonies
Historical character(s): Elizabeth Schuyler, Gentlewoman, Spouse (of Hamilton); Alexander Hamilton, Political Figure
Time Period(s): 18th century; 19th century
Locale(s): New York

Summary: This fictional biography narrates the story of Alexander Hamilton and his wife, Elizabeth Schuyler. She is the daughter of the famous Revolutionary War general, Philip Schuyler. The story of Hamilton's political career and Elizabeth's support is dramatized, along with a vivid portrait of the times.

Historical Accuracy: Based on evident research, the novel captures with skill life in colonial New York.

JOANNA DESSAU (1921-)

An English writer born in London, Dessau studied at the Royal Academy for Music. She has worked as a nursery school teacher. A descendant of a courtier to Elizabeth I, Dessau has authored a number of historical novels set in the Elizabethan period. Her books include *Amazing Grace*, *The Constant Lover*, *Crown of Sorrows*.

`1624` *Absolute Elizabeth*

Date of Publication: 1979
Subject(s): Elizabethan Period; Royalty—England
Historical character(s): Elizabeth I, Ruler (Queen of England)
Time Period(s): 16th century
Locale(s): England

Summary: In the sequel to *The Red Haired Brat*, the author continues a biographical account of Elizabeth I. The novel shifts between Elizabeth in old age, a brilliant and formidable monarch and in her youth, temperamental and giddy, with little to suggest her future strength of character.

Historical Accuracy: The intended contrast between young Elizabeth and her elder self is so stark that it undermines credibility.

`1625` *The Blacksmith's Daughter*

Date of Publication: 1983
Subject(s): Biography, Fictionalized; Napoleonic Wars

Historical character(s): Lady Emma Hamilton, Spouse; Sir William Hamilton, Diplomat; Horatio Nelson, Military Personnel (naval officer)
Time Period(s): 18th century; 19th century (1781-1814)
Locale(s): England; Italy

Summary: The novel traces the remarkable story of Lady Emma Hamilton, wife of British diplomat and archaeologist Sir William Hamilton and the mistress of England's greatest naval hero, Horatio Nelson. The novel recounts her rise from humble beginnings as she parlays her great beauty into respectability, fame, and finally notoriety as Lord Nelson's paramour.

Historical Accuracy: The novel is faithful to the basic outline of Emma Hamilton's story, with a number of invented scenes and conversations.

`1626` *Lord of the Ladies*

Date of Publication: 1981
Subject(s): Literary Life; Regency Period
Historical character(s): George Gordon Byron, Writer (poet), Nobleman; Lady Caroline Lamb, Noblewoman; Annabella Millbanke, Spouse (of Byron); Percy Bysshe Shelley, Writer (poet); Claire Clairmont, Gentlewoman; Teresa Guiccioli, Gentlewoman
Time Period(s): 19th century
Locale(s): England; Italy; Greece

Summary: The novel concentrates on the many notorious love affairs of Bryon as described by a number of his intimates. The perspectives include Lady Caroline Lamb; Byron's wife, Annabella Millbanke; and his mistresses, Claire Clairmont and Teresa Guiccioli.

Historical Accuracy: The various narrative voices are unconvincingly differentiated, and little of Byron's genius survives the concentration on romance.

`1627` *The Red-Haired Brat*

Date of Publication: 1978
Subject(s): Tudor Period; Royalty—England; Biography, Fictionalized
Historical character(s): Elizabeth Tudor, Royalty (princess); Henry VIII, Ruler (King of England); Catherine Howard, Royalty (queen consort of Henry VIII); Mary Tudor, Royalty (princess); Robert Dudley, Nobleman (Earl of Leicester); Catherine Parr, Royalty (queen consort of Henry VIII); Edward Tudor, Royalty (prince)
Time Period(s): 16th century (1536-1558)
Locale(s): England

Summary: The novel offers an autobiography of Elizabeth I from age three until being crowned queen in 1558. She grows up in the uncertain and dangerous reign of her father, Henry VIII. As the daughter of Anne Boleyn, she is also distrusted by her older half-sister, Princess Mary. A virtual prisoner when Mary becomes queen, Elizabeth survives, learning patience and guile, which will equip her well when she comes to rule.

Historical Accuracy: Elizabeth's voice is convincing and the sense of the period is authentic and reliable.

JEAN DETRE (1935-)

Born in Oakland, California, Detre was educated at San Francisco State University and has worked as a journalist and a critic. His publications include a book of poems, *Extensions*, and two novels, *The Honey Dwarf* and *A Most Extraordinary Pair: Mary Wollstonecraft and William Godwin*.

1628 *A Most Extraordinary Pair*

Date of Publication: 1975
Subject(s): Literary Life; Georgian Period
Historical character(s): Mary Wollstonecraft Godwin, Writer; William Godwin, Writer
Time Period(s): 1790s (1796-1797)
Locale(s): London, England

Summary: Told in the form of letters and a journal kept by writer Mary Wollstonecraft, the novel records her romance with fellow writer William Godwin, which spans a one-year period ending with Mary Wollstonecraft's death in childbirth. The novel mixes actual letters written by the pair with an invented journal to explore their relationship and to introduce the feminist thinking of Wollstonecraft.

Historical Accuracy: The novel combines actual details of Wollstonecraft and Godwin's biography with some imaginative interpretations and speculative leaps.

BABETTE DEUTSCH (1895-1982)

American novelist, critic, editor, and author, Deutsch is best remembered for her work with her husband Avram Yarmolinsky, with whom she translated Pushkin and anthologies of Russian and German poetry. Her own imagist poetry is printed in several collections.

1629 *Rogue's Legacy: A Novel about Francois Villon*

Date of Publication: 1942
Subject(s): Biography, Fictionalized; Hundred Years War
Historical character(s): Francois Villon, Writer (poet)
Time Period(s): 15th century (1431-1463)
Locale(s): Paris, France

Summary: This novel is based on the life of 15th-century vagabond, thief, and poet Francois Villon. What little is known of the facts of Villon's life are pieced together from his poems and from police records, which include a murder he committed and his involvement with a band of thiefs after his banishment from Paris.

Historical Accuracy: The novel faithfully presents the known details and creates a believable backdrop of 15th-century life.

JUDE DEVERAUX
(PSEUD. OF JUDE GILLIAM WHITE, 1947-)

American romance writer Deveraux was born in Louisville and attended Murray State University, the College of Sante Fe, and the University of New Mexico. She began writing romances when she grew tired of reading what she calls

"rape sagas." She tries to make her books feature women who have some power and can make things happen. She considers herself both a feminist and a romantic, which she contends is not a contradiction.

1630 *The Conquest*

Date of Publication: 1991
Subject(s): Middle Ages; Romance
Fictional character(s): Zared Peregrine, Noblewoman; Tearle Howard, Nobleman
Time Period(s): 15th century
Locale(s): England

Summary: In the sequel to *The Taming*, the action is set during the 15th century as nobleman Tearle Howard pursues Zared Peregrine, despite the corrosive effects of a family feud. The romance is joined with supernatural elements.

Historical Accuracy: The novel is a combination of genres: fantasy, history, but fundamentally romance. The period elements are lightly drawn.

1631 *A Knight in Shining Armor*

Date of Publication: 1989
Subject(s): Romance; Time Travel; Tudor Period
Fictional character(s): Dougless Montgomery, Teacher (elementary); Nicholas Stafford, Nobleman (Earl of Thornwyck)
Time Period(s): 1980s; 16th century (1560s)
Locale(s): England

Summary: Elementary school teacher Dougless Montgomery finds herself stranded in England at the tomb of a Tudor nobleman, who materializes and takes her back in time for romance and adventure.

Historical Accuracy: Romance is at the core of this fantasy, with some authentic period touches.

1632 *Mountain Laurel*

Date of Publication: 1990
Subject(s): American West; Romance
Fictional character(s): Maddie Worth, Singer (opera); Ring Montgomery, Military Personnel (army captain)
Time Period(s): 1850s (1859)
Locale(s): Rocky Mountains

Summary: When her younger sister is kidnapped, opera singer Maddie Worth tries to win her freedom while performing in mining towns in the Rockies during the 1850s. She falls in love with Captain Ring Montgomery, who has been assigned to safeguard her town.

Historical Accuracy: The period is suggested rather than fully defined in this historical romance.

1633 *The Taming*

Date of Publication: 1989
Subject(s): Romance; Middle Ages
Fictional character(s): Liana Neville, Heiress; Rogan Peregrine, Landowner
Time Period(s): 15th century (1440s)

Locale(s): England

Summary: In this romance set during the 1440s, Rogan Peregrine marries wealthy heiress Liana Neville to support his feud with the Howard family. Liana is far more than Rogan has bargained for. She organizes his chaotic household and wins his affection.

Historical Accuracy: There's a good deal of charm to this romantic story that offers some authentic details of the period.

JOHN ANTHONY DEVON
(PSEUD. OF ROBERT PAYNE, 1911-1983)

Devon is a pseudonym for English writer Robert Payne, who was born in Cornwall and educated at St. Paul's School, the University of Capetown, the University of London, the University of Liverpool, and the Sorbonne. He worked as a tax inspector, a shipwright, a London *Times* correspondent during the Spanish Civil War, and an English professor. Payne conspired to assassinate Hitler during the occupation of Vienna. He began his writing career as a poet but established his reputation as the author of popular biographies of Karl Marx, Charlie Chaplin, Greta Garbo, Adolph Hitler, and others. His novels focus on East/West relations.

1634 *O Western Wind*

Date of Publication: 1957
Subject(s): American Colonies; Puritans; Religious Conflict
Fictional character(s): Damon, Young Man; Sapphira Trelawney, Young Woman
Historical character(s): Miles Standish, Leader (Pilgrim); William Bradford, Government Official (colonial governor)
Time Period(s): 17th century
Locale(s): Cornwall, England; Plymouth, Massachusetts, American Colonies

Summary: This novel examines some of the least attractive features of the Puritan founders of the Pilgrim colony of Plymouth. The fictional story begins in Cornwall as Damon, a Cornish farmhand, flees his home after a dispute over his love for Sapphira. He joins the Pilgrims on the *Mayflower*. The novel describes the destruction of Merry Mount by Miles Standish and the Puritan leaders who expose this bigotry and intolerance.

Historical Accuracy: The novel provides a realistic background of colonial times which is credible, though unusual and very different from other more traditional treatments.

LOUIS DEVON

1635 *Aide to Glory*

Date of Publication: 1952
Subject(s): Civil War—U.S.; Biography, Fictionalized
Historical character(s): Ulysses S. Grant, Military Personnel (Union general); John Aaron Rawlins, Military Personnel (Union officer)
Time Period(s): 1860s; 1870s
Locale(s): United States

Summary: This is a fictional biography of Union officer John Rawlins who served as Grant's aide-de-camp. The novel follows Rawlins' career with Grant through the war and into politics as Rawlins becomes Grant's Secretary of War.

Historical Accuracy: The novel is meticulous in its research and adheres scrupulously to the evidence, derived from Rawlins' own letters and other period sources.

KEITH DEWHURST (1931-)

English writer Dewhurst was born in Oldham and graduated from Cambridge. He has worked as a sportswriter, TV presenter, and a columnist. He has achieved acclaim for both his plays and his novels.

1636 *Captain of the Sands*

Date of Publication: 1981
Subject(s): Sea Story; Slavery
Fictional character(s): Tom Derker, Sailor; Henry Dingwall, Sailor; William Derker, Sea Captain
Time Period(s): 18th century (1749-1760s)
Locale(s): England; At Sea

Summary: When he loses both his parents, 12-year-old Tom Derker decides to go to sea on his uncle's ship. It turns out to be a slave ship, and Tom comes of age on the voyage from the Ivory Coast to Antigua and America. His adventures eventually uncover his secret heritage.

Historical Accuracy: The nautical and period details are authentic and convincing.

CHARLES DEXTER

1637 *The Street of Kings*

Date of Publication: 1957
Subject(s): Jacobean Period; Crime and Criminals
Historical character(s): James I, Ruler (King of England); Thomas Overbury, Writer; Frances Howard, Noblewoman; Robert Carr, Nobleman
Time Period(s): 17th century
Locale(s): London, England

Summary: The novel records the scandal surrounding the death of writer Sir Thomas Overbury. Overbury disapproves of Robert Carr's marriage to Frances Howard, the divorced wife of the Earl of Essex. Imprisoned in the Tower by James I, Overbury is slowly poisoned to death, and Carr and Howard are convicted of the murder.

Historical Accuracy: The novel mixes fact and fancy in its reconstruction of the famous scandal. The atmosphere of the time is captured convincingly.

PETE DEXTER (1943-)

Born in Michigan and raised in Georgia, Illinois, and South Dakota, Dexter has worked as a truck driver, gas station attendant, mail sorter, construction worker, and salesman. Dexter achieved notoriety for his opinionated newspaper columns. He turned to fiction after nearly being beaten to death by readers who were infuriated by one of his *Daily News* columns. His novels have been praised for his mixture of violence and humor, his sharp ear for dialogue, and eye for local color. His novel *Paris Trout* won the National Book Award in 1988.

1638 *Deadwood*

Date of Publication: 1986
Subject(s): American West
Historical character(s): James Butler Hickok, Frontiersman; Martha Jane Cannary Burk, Frontierswoman (Calamity Jane)
Time Period(s): 1870s (1876-1878)
Locale(s): Deadwood, South Dakota

Summary: Life in Deadwood, South Dakota, is depicted in this Western novel that features Wild Bill Hickok. He is pursued by Calamity Jane and a series of other colorful western characters, who present a rogue's gallery of Western life before the fire that destroys Deadwood and the assassination of Hickok.

Historical Accuracy: Inventive and vivid in capturing an authentic aura, the novel is based on actual events and characters.

GEORGIA DI DONATO (1932-)

Born in Seattle, Di Donato graduated from the University of Washington, Seattle. She has worked as a production assistant on the "Today Show," and has been a producer and writer for film and TV. She was a late starter as a novelist, publishing her first novel at age 47.

1639 *Woman of Justice*

Date of Publication: 1980
Subject(s): American West; Legal Profession; Crime and Criminals
Historical character(s): Temperance Smith, Judge; Isaac C. Parker, Judge; Ulysses S. Grant, Political Figure; Susan B. Anthony, Suffragette
Time Period(s): 1870s
Locale(s): Fort Smith, Arkansas

Summary: This is the story of the first female judge in the American West, Temperance Smith. In 1875 she was assigned by President Grant to be the assistant to the notorious Isaac Parker, the hanging judge. In the rugged Fort Smith of the Arkansas Territory, Justice Smith attempts to establish the rule of law in the frontier.

Historical Accuracy: The basis of the story is factual. However, the author admits that license was taken in the portrayal of certain incidents and events.

ISABEL DICK

1640 *Wild Orchid*

Date of Publication: 1945
Subject(s): Frontier—Australia

Fictional character(s): Jan Halifax, Settler; Harriat Bracken, Spouse
Time Period(s): 1840s
Locale(s): Tasmania, Australia (then Van Diemen's Land)

Summary: In 1840 Harriat Bracken marries Jan Halifax and goes with him to Van Diemen's Land (now Tasmania) where they struggle to establish their home and future. They must contend with a fire that destroys their home and the lawlessness of the wilderness.

Historical Accuracy: The evocation of the period is authentically realized.

CHARLES DICKENS (1812-1870)

Dickens was an English author who is considered the "greatest dramatic writer since Shakespeare." As a child he endured the humiliation of his father's imprisonment for debt. He was forced to work in a factory for meager wages, an experience that had a profound effect on his work. His strength as a writer lies in his ability to animate character and scene; weaknesses include a sometimes damaging tendency toward sentimentality and idealization, particularly of his female characters. Notable works include *Pickwick Papers*, *Oliver Twist*, *A Christmas Carol*, *David Copperfield*, *Bleak House*, and *Great Expectations*.

1641 *Barnaby Rudge: A Tale of the Riots of Eighty*

Date of Publication: 1841
Subject(s): Georgian Period; Religious Conflict; Gordon Riots
Fictional character(s): Gabriel Varden, Repairman (locksmith); Sir John Chester, Nobleman; John Haredale, Gentleman (Catholic)
Historical character(s): Lord George Gordon, Nobleman, Fanatic (anti-Catholic)
Time Period(s): 1770s; 1780s (1775-1780)
Locale(s): London, England

Summary: The first of Dickens' two attempts at historical novels. Subtitled "A Tale of the Riots of Eighty," the story is set during the Gordon anti-Popery riots in London in 1780. Its plot centers on a murder; the conflict between Geoffrey Haredale, a Catholic, and the villainous Sir John Chester; and a romance between the former's niece and the latter's son.

Historical Accuracy: Dickens' achievement is his thrilling and vivid depiction of the riots, climaxing in the burning of Newgate Prison. Customs and attitudes are more Victorian than 18th century.

1642 *A Tale of Two Cities*

Date of Publication: 1859
Subject(s): French Revolution; Reign of Terror
Fictional character(s): Sydney Carton, Lawyer; Lucie Manette, Gentlewoman, Spouse (of Darnay); Charles Darnay, Nobleman; Alexander Manette, Doctor, Political Prisoner
Time Period(s): 18th century (1775-1793)
Locale(s): London, England; Paris, France

Summary: Set during the French Revolution and the Reign of Terror, the plot concerns Dr. Manette, who has been wrongfully confined to the Bastille for eighteen years by the villainous Marquis de St. Everemonde, and the love triangle between Manette's daughter Lucie, Darnay, who is the nephew of the marquis, and the wastrel English lawyer Sydney Carton whose heroic sacrifice provides the novel's climax.

Historical Accuracy: The novel owes much to Carlyle's *The French Revolution* in attitude but features Dickens' incomparably vivid descriptions of characters, action, and setting.

WILLIAM DIETER (1929-)

Born in Richland County, Wisconsin, Dieter attended the University of Wisconsin. He worked in sales for the National Cash Register Company until 1968 and as a purchasing manager for Coors Container Company in Golden, Colorado, until 1980. He is the author of *Hunter's Orange* and *Beyond the Mountain*.

1643 The White Land

Date of Publication: 1970
Subject(s): American West; Ranching
Fictional character(s): Marc Robbarde, Rancher; Griffith, Businessman (cattle driver)
Time Period(s): 1880s
Locale(s): Montana

Summary: Marc Robbarde, a rancher, and Griffith, a wealthy cattle driver, are rivals on Montana's winter range. Their struggle intensifies when a blizzard threatens to destroy their herds and the men themselves.

Historical Accuracy: The novel provides an authentic depiction of the period and the region.

ANNIE DILLARD (1945-)

Born in Pittsburgh and a graduate of Hollins College, Dillard is a writer in residence at Wesleyan University. She is best known as a writer of non-fiction books of essays, memoirs, and literary criticism. She won a Pulitzer Prize for *Pilgrim at Tinker Creek*. Dillard has earned a reputation for excellence in every genre she has attempted.

1644 The Living

Date of Publication: 1992
Subject(s): Settlement of the American Frontier; American West; Crime and Criminals
Fictional character(s): Claire Fishburn, Businessman; John Sharp, Orphan, Teacher; Beal Obenchain, Murderer; Minta Honer, Settler
Historical character(s): James J. Hill, Financier (railroad); Frederick Weyerhaeuser, Financier (timber industry)
Time Period(s): 19th century (1855-1897)
Locale(s): Bellingham Bay, Washington; Seattle, Washington

Summary: The novel offers the communal history of a settlement on the northwest coast of Washington that becomes the town of Whatcan. The community is chronicled centering on the connected lives of three men: Claire Fishburn, John Sharp, and Beal Obenchain. Violence keeps pace with development as settlers arrive along with the railroad. The wilderness gives way to a particularly American version of civilization.

Historical Accuracy: Sharply detailed and imagined, the novel is a vivid picture of a region over time.

ANNA DILLON

1645 Seasons

Date of Publication: 1988
Subject(s): Independence—Ireland; Easter Rising
Fictional character(s): Katherine Lundy, Servant (maid); Dermot Corcoran, Journalist; John Lewis, Military Personnel (captain)
Historical character(s): Constance Markievicz, Noblewoman, Revolutionary
Time Period(s): 19th century; 20th century (1898-1916)
Locale(s): Ireland

Summary: The novel traces the steps leading up to the Irish Easter Rebellion of 1916, in which a small band proclaim an Irish Republic and take on the might of the English army. Katherine Lundy comes to work for the dashing English Captain Lewis. She is at first captivated but learns that he is not quite what he pretends to be. Slowly she is swept up in the events that lead to the glorious tragedy of Easter 1916.

Historical Accuracy: The events and atmosphere of the period are convincingly detailed.

EILIS DILLON (1920-)

An Irish writer born in Galway, Dillon has been a lecturer in creative writing at Trinity College and University College, Dublin. Dillon first began writing in Irish Gaelic and has been a prolific author of children's fiction and mysteries. Dillon became the first author to receive the Irish Book of the Year Award for *The Island of Ghosts*.

1646 Across the Bitter Sea

Date of Publication: 1973
Subject(s): Independence—Ireland; Easter Rising; Irish Potato Famine
Fictional character(s): Morgan Connolly, Revolutionary; Samuel Flaherty, Landowner; Alice Flaherty, Spouse
Time Period(s): 19th century; 20th century (1851-1916)
Locale(s): Ireland

Summary: The novel spans three generations and covers Irish history from the famine in the 1850s to the Easter Rising in 1916. It is the love story of Alice Flaherty for both her husband, Samuel, and the revolutionary Morgan Connolly. Her love for two very different men is played out during a tragic period of Ireland's struggle for identity and freedom.

Historical Accuracy: Richly detailed, the novel is an authentic reflection of the times and the customs.

1647 *Wild Geese*

Date of Publication: 1980
Subject(s): Independence—Ireland; American Revolution; Georgian Period
Fictional character(s): Robert Brien, Fugitive, Military Personnel (French soldier); Louise Brien, Fugitive
Time Period(s): 18th century (1736-1782)
Locale(s): Ireland; Paris, France; United States

Summary: The Wild Geese were members of the Irish nobility who fled their country in the 18th century to escape the repression of the English. The novel tells the story of two Wild Geese, Robert and Louise Brien, brother and sister, who join their French cousins in the decadent society of pre-revolutionary Paris. Robert joins the French army in the American Revolution, and Louise is trapped in a loveless marriage. Through many vicissitudes they struggle to sustain the severed ties with their homeland and identity.

Historical Accuracy: The 18th-century atmosphere and events are convincingly displayed.

THOMAS M. DISCH (1940-)

CHARLES NAYLOR (1940-)

Disch is an American writer born in Des Moines, Iowa. He won the O. Henry Prize in 1975 for "Getting into Death" and in 1979 for "Xmas." He is the author of science fiction, poetry, historical novels, opera librettos, and computer-interactive fiction. Born in Des Moines, Iowa, Naylor is an award-winning freelance writer, poet, and lecturer who lives in New York City. His writing includes a children's book, *The Brave Little Toaster.*

1648 *Neighboring Lives*

Date of Publication: 1981
Subject(s): Victorian Period; Literary Life
Historical character(s): Thomas Carlyle, Writer; Jane Carlyle, Writer, Spouse; Leigh Hunt, Writer; John Stuart Mill, Writer, Philosopher; Robert Browning, Writer; Lewis Carroll, Writer; William Norris, Writer, Artist
Time Period(s): 19th century (1830s-1870s)
Locale(s): London, England; Oxford, England

Summary: The novel captures the literary life of Thomas Carlyle and his wife and the circle of writers and artists with whom they have contact. The novel offers a multiplicity of details that serve to evoke the time and place.

Historical Accuracy: The novel captures effectively the literary atmosphere of the period.

DAVID DIVINE
(PSEUD. OF ARTHUR DURHAM DIVINE, 1904-1987)

Born in Cape Town, South Africa, Divine was a war correspondent for the *Sunday Times* of London and later its defense correspondent. He received a distinguished service medal for his wartime activities. He is the author of more than 40 books—thrillers, adventure stories, historical accounts, and studies of military politics. His novel *Boy on a Dolphin* was adapted for film and became an American box office hit.

1649 *The Golden Fool*

Date of Publication: 1954
Subject(s): Mining
Fictional character(s): Jacques Lemaire, Farmer; Anthony Stopford, Prospector
Time Period(s): 1860s
Locale(s): South Africa

Summary: This adventure tale set in the African Transvaal involves the discovery of gold by Englishman Anthony Stopford on Boer Jacques Lemaire's farm. Lemaire tries to conceal the gold strike. Stopford falls in love with Lemaire's daughter but alienates Lemaire's greedy son.

Historical Accuracy: The novel believably conveys the locale and atmosphere of the period.

1650 *Thunder on the Chesapeake*

Date of Publication: 1961
Subject(s): Civil War—U.S.; Sea Story; Battle of the *Monitor* vs. the *Merrimac*
Fictional character(s): Linden Cleave, Southern Belle; Revell Jordan, Military Personnel (Confederate soldier); Stephen Knott, Military Personnel (naval officer)
Historical character(s): John Ericsson, Inventor, Engineer
Time Period(s): 1860s
Locale(s): Portsmouth, Virginia; Chesapeake Bay, Virginia; New York, New York

Summary: This Civil War novel involves three individuals: Linden Cleave, a vehemently pro-South belle, and her two suitors. Revell Jordan enlists in the Confederate Army and Stephen Knott retains his commission in the U.S. Navy. Knott is on hand for the construction of the U.S.S. *Monitor*, and the story climaxes in the *Monitor*'s epic battle with the *Merrimack*.

Historical Accuracy: The details of the period and the naval history are authentic.

PIERSON DIXON (1904-1965)

Born in Surrey, Dixon graduated from Cambridge University and studied at the British School of Archaeology in Athens. Dixon worked in the British Foreign Service serving in embassies in Madrid, Ankara, and Rome and becoming an ambassador to Czechoslovakia and the permanent representative of the U.K. to the United Nations.

1651 *Farewell, Catullus*

Date of Publication: 1953
Subject(s): Roman Empire; Literary Life
Historical character(s): Gaius Valerius Catullus, Writer (poet); Publius Clodius Pulcher, Political Figure; Clodia, Gentlewoman
Time Period(s): 1st century B.C. (63-54 B.C.)
Locale(s): Rome, Roman Empire

Summary: The novel provides a fictional account of the career of Roman lyric poet Catullus. Although very little is known of Catullus beyond what is revealed in his writings, the novel offers an imaginative reconstruction of his life and of the waning days of the Roman Republic.

Historical Accuracy: The novel helpfully includes commentary indicating where and why the author's interpretation of events differs from other accounts.

MICHAEL DOBBS (1950-)

Dobbs was a key adviser to British Prime Minister Margaret Thatcher. His books include *Wall Games* and *House of Cards*.

1652 Last Man to Die

Date of Publication: 1992
Subject(s): World War II; Espionage
Fictional character(s): Peter Hencke, Military Personnel (German soldier)
Historical character(s): Adolf Hitler, Political Figure; Eva Braun, Spouse (of Hitler); Paul Joseph Goebbels, Political Figure
Time Period(s): 1940s (1945)
Locale(s): England; Germany

Summary: In this World War II-era thriller, Peter Hencke escapes from an English prison camp and makes his way back to Germany where he is hailed as a hero of the Third Reich. He joins the SS and is introduced to the subterranean world of Hitler's bunker.

Historical Accuracy: The background for the novel is faithful to actual events and sources concerning the end of the war, but the author is clear that the novel is intended as entertainment rather than history.

ALFRED DOBLIN (1878-1957)

German author Doblin practiced medicine from 1911 to 1933. He escaped from Germany to the U.S. in 1940. Perhaps best known for the classic *Berlin Alexanderplatz*, Doblin is considered one of the most influential novelists of the 20th century.

1653 Karl and Rosa

Date of Publication: 1983
Subject(s): World War I; Socialism; Revolution—Germany
Fictional character(s): Friedrich Becker, Veteran, Teacher
Historical character(s): Karl Liebknecht, Revolutionary; Rosa Luxemburg, Revolutionary; Vladimir Ilich Lenin, Revolutionary; Leon Trotsky, Revolutionary; Friedrich Ebert, Political Figure; Philipp Scheidemann, Political Figure
Time Period(s): 1910s (1918-1919)
Locale(s): Berlin, Germany; Russia

Summary: In the second volume of Doblin's massive *November 1918: A German Revolution* that began with *A People Betrayed*, the focus is on two of the key players in the immediate post-war period in Germany. Karl Liebknecht and Rosa Luxemburg are the leaders of the radical Spartan League that spearheads the proletarian revolution that erupts in Germany following World War I. Their fate becomes a tragic and moving personal, rather than political, story.

Historical Accuracy: The cumulative effect of Doblin's massive orchestration is a symphony of voices and characters that effectively captures the time and the place.

1654 A People Betrayed

Date of Publication: 1983
Subject(s): World War I; Revolution—Germany; Socialism
Fictional character(s): Friedrich Becker, Veteran, Teacher
Historical character(s): Karl Liebknecht, Revolutionary; Woodrow Wilson, Political Figure; Rosa Luxemburg, Revolutionary; Friedrich Ebert, Political Figure (Reich president)
Time Period(s): 1910s (1918)
Locale(s): Berlin, Germany; United States

Summary: It is 1918, and Germany is tottering on the brink of chaos. The fighting is over, but the revolution has begun. Leaders of the military have entered an uneasy alliance with the socialist leaders who have assumed control over the government and proclaim a new German Republic. Throughout Berlin, rival political groups jockey for power. Doblin captures the moment in a kind of cinematic panorama, weaving fictional and historical characters and events into an amazing portrayal of the period.

Historical Accuracy: This is a masterful reconstruction of the historical and human moment.

JAN DOBRACZYNSKI (1910-)

A Polish author and former member of the Polish parliament, Dobraczynski was born in Warsaw and attended the High School of Commerce there. During World War II, he served as captain of cavalry in the Polish Underground Army and was awarded a Silver Cross for merit. He is the recipient of several awards in Poland for his work, and his books have been translated into many languages, including English. His novels include *Overtaken*, *Martin Come Back from Afar*, and *The Burnt Bridges Left Behind*.

1655 The Letters of Nicodemus

Date of Publication: 1958
Subject(s): Biblical Story; Roman Empire; Jews
Historical character(s): Nicodemus, Biblical Figure
Time Period(s): 1st century
Locale(s): Israel

Summary: Told in the form of letters from the New Testament figure Nicodemus to his former tutor, the novel traces the impact of Jesus Christ on the skeptical Nicodemus as he tries to come to terms with his belief in Christ as the true Messiah.

Historical Accuracy: The novel offers a vivid and authentic treatment of the political atmosphere of the period and a faithful presentation of the known Biblical events.

E.L. DOCTOROW (1931-)

Doctorow is an American novelist and playwright known for his inventive use of historical figures in his fictional works. His other works include a science-fiction novel, *Big as Life*, and the play, *Drinks Before Dinner*.

1656 *Billy Bathgate*

Date of Publication: 1989
Subject(s): Depression Era; Crime and Criminals
Fictional character(s): Billy Behan, Hero; Lulu Rosencrantz, Organized Crime Figure
Historical character(s): Arthur Flegenheimer, Organized Crime Figure
Time Period(s): 1930s
Locale(s): New York, New York

Summary: The title character is a young boy from the Bronx who is adopted into the inner circle of the notorious Dutch Schultz gang as an apprentice and finally a protege of the legendary gangster. The occasion offers Doctorow an opportunity at historical re-creation of New York in the 1930s.

Historical Accuracy: Doctorow has a rare ability to transform fact into fiction, raising history to the level of sustaining myth.

1657 *Loon Lake*

Date of Publication: 1979
Subject(s): Depression Era
Fictional character(s): Penfield, Writer; Joe Korzeniowski, Hero; F.W. Bennet, Businessman
Time Period(s): 1930s
Locale(s): Adirondacks, New York; New York, New York

Summary: In this marvelous conjunction of personalities, a young hobo and carnival roustabout finds his way to Loon Lake, the hidden wilderness estate of one of the country's richest men. There he meets a poet, a gangster, and a woman aviator. Their encounter serves to illustrate American life between the wars.

Historical Accuracy: The novel is in turns lyrical and magical as history is re-processed into a human drama.

1658 *Ragtime*

Date of Publication: 1975
Subject(s): Crime and Criminals
Fictional character(s): Tateh, Artist; Coalhouse Walker, Revolutionary
Historical character(s): Harry Houdini, Magician; Evelyn Nesbit, Socialite; Sigmund Freud, Doctor; Emma Goldman, Revolutionary; John Pierpont Morgan, Businessman; Henry Ford, Businessman; Booker T. Washington, Political Figure, Teacher
Time Period(s): 1900s; 1910s (1906-1914)
Locale(s): New Rochelle, New York; New York, New York

Summary: The novel is a tour de force recreation of New York at the beginning of the 20th century. A respectable family is swept up in the drama of the times with appearances by a host of historical characters. The novel's drama turns on a black

man's rage directed at the emblem of American wealth and power, J.P. Morgan.

Historical Accuracy: Doctorow delights with his ability to reanimate history. Some critics have resisted his manipulation of historical characters arguing that they are historical in name only. The author has claimed only that his book is a mingling of fact and fiction.

1659 *The Waterworks*

Date of Publication: 1994
Fictional character(s): McIlvane, Journalist; Martin Pemberton, Writer
Time Period(s): 1870s
Locale(s): New York, New York

Summary: Doctorow's novel is set in Boss Tweed's New York of corrupt officials and rapacious capitalism. A newspaper writer has seen his father, thought to be dead, riding in an omnibus. He investigates the truth and uncovers a New York landscape that is less the backdrop for the story than its main character, a city filled with the living dead and the walking wounded.

Historical Accuracy: Doctorow resuscitates the past into a magical transformation of fact and fiction that is brooding and at times terrifying.

1660 *Welcome to Hard Times*

Date of Publication: 1960
Subject(s): American West; Crime and Criminals
Fictional character(s): Blue, Political Figure (mayor); Molly Riordan, Prostitute; Bad Man From Bodie, Outlaw
Time Period(s): 1890s
Locale(s): Dakota Territory, United States

Summary: A tale of violence and destruction in the Dakota Territory at the close of the 19th century, the novel concerns the town of Hard Times where an outlaw destroys the town. It is rebuilt by the mayor, but the spectre of impending doom and moral weakness haunt the inhabitants.

Historical Accuracy: Doctorow transforms the Western into a vehicle of serious writing and moral exploration. The details of Western life are fresh and convincing.

1661 *World's Fair*

Date of Publication: 1985
Subject(s): Depression Era
Fictional character(s): Dave, Businessman; Rose, Housewife
Time Period(s): 1930s
Locale(s): New York, New York (mainly the Bronx)

Summary: The novel is a full and evocative recreation of childhood in New York City during the 1930s. A first-person narrative by the young son of a poor family in the Bronx, the boy's recollections rebuild the past into a sustaining shape. The novel culminates in a visit to the future promise of the New York World's Fair of 1939.

Historical Accuracy: Doctorow's eye for period detail breathes life into this boyhood memoir.

CHRISTINA DODD

1662 *Candle in the Window*

Date of Publication: 1991
Subject(s): Middle Ages; Romance
Fictional character(s): William of Miraval, Nobleman, Handicapped (blind); Saura of Roget, Noblewoman, Handicapped (blind)
Time Period(s): 12th centry (1153)
Locale(s): England

Summary: This romantic story set during the 12th century involves the love that transpires between Sir William, who loses his sight in battle and Lady Saura, blind since birth, who tries to help him adjust to his new handicap.

Historical Accuracy: This unusual love story is convincing in most of its period elements.

SUSAN DODD (1946-)

Born in Chicago, Dodd received a B.S. degree from Georgetown, an M.A. from the University of Louisville, and an M.F.A. from Vermont College. She has worked as a speech writer for Senator Thomas J. Dodd and as an instructor in creative writing.

1663 *Mamaw*

Date of Publication: 1988
Subject(s): Crime and Criminals; Civil War—U.S.; Biography, Fictionalized
Historical character(s): Zerelda Cole James, Frontierswoman; Jesse James, Outlaw; Frank James, Outlaw
Time Period(s): 19th century; 20th century (1825-1911)
Locale(s): Missouri

Summary: The novel tells the story of the mother of Jesse and Frank James. Zerelda Cole James leaves a convent at age 15 to marry. She is jailed as a Confederate spy during the Civil War and fiercely defends her land and her family after the death of her husband.

Historical Accuracy: Based on solid research, the novel captures the particulars of the James family as well as their era.

CONSTANCE DODGE (1896-)

Born in Boston, Massachusetts, Dodge was educated at Smith College. a traveller and mountain climber, she published several novels including *The Dark Stranger*, *The Weather Cock*, and *Graham of Claverhouse*.

1664 *The Dark Stranger*

Date of Publication: 1940
Subject(s): Jacobite Rebellion; American Colonies; American Revolution
Fictional character(s): Lachlan MacLean, Laird; Dugald MacLean, Military Personnel (soldier)
Time Period(s): 18th century (1740s-1770s)
Locale(s): Scotland; North Carolina, American Colonies

Summary: This panoramic adventure tale spans more than 30 years and two generations of the Scottish family the MacLeans. The story begins with the Jacobite Rising and the Stuarts' defeat at the Battle of Culloden. Lachlan MacLean escapes with his family to Carolina and a new life. His son, Dugald, however, resists the easy prosperity of plantation life for Indian fighting and service in the Revolution. The climax of the story is the naval battle between the *Bonhomme Richard* and the *Serapis*.

Historical Accuracy: The historical events described are accurate, though considerable plot manipulation was needed to work out the chronology.

1665 *Graham of Claverhouse*

Date of Publication: 1936
Subject(s): Restoration Period; Religious Conflict
Historical character(s): John Graham of Claverhouse, Nobleman
Time Period(s): 17th century
Locale(s): Scotland

Summary: Set during the reign of Charles II, the novel concerns the efforts of John Graham of Claverhouse to establish the Episcopal Church in Scotland on behalf of the Stuart cause. Graham is given the task of hunting down the Covenanters.

Historical Accuracy: The story is largely invented with a foundation of truth and believable period details.

1666 *In Adam's Fall*

Date of Publication: 1946
Subject(s): American Colonies; Puritans; Witchcraft and Sorcery
Fictional character(s): Damaris Horn, Young Woman
Time Period(s): 17th century (1690s)
Locale(s): Salem, Massachusetts, American Colonies

Summary: The Salem witch hunt in the closing years of the 17th century is depicted. Damaris Horn, the novel's heroine, finds herself caught up in the Puritan fury to uncover witchcraft.

Historical Accuracy: This version of events is simplified and somewhat idealized, convincing in minor details only.

1667 *The Pointless Knife*

Date of Publication: 1937
Subject(s): Feuds
Fictional character(s): Neil Roy MacGregor, Fugitive; Mary Logan, Gentlewoman
Time Period(s): 17th century
Locale(s): Scotland

Summary: After a fight with the Cocquhouns at Glen Fruin, the MacGregor clan is outlawed and prohibited from carrying any arms except a pointless knife. Neil Roy MacGregor finds refuge in the household of Lady Mary Logan. His interest in her granddaughter leads her to conspire against him.

Historical Accuracy: The plot is contrived and formulaic, but does feature some authentic period elements.

1668 *Weathercock*

Date of Publication: 1942
Subject(s): American Colonies; American Revolution; Battle of Alamance
Fictional character(s): Carrington Pryde, Military Personnel (soldier); Clotilda Pryde, Widow(er)
Time Period(s): 1760s; 1770s
Locale(s): Cape Fear, North Carolina, American Colonies

Summary: Class conflict in North Carolina during the American Revolution forms the background for this story of the Pryde family. The story centers on young Carrington Pryde, who eventually goes against his family to enlist in General Greene's colonial army. The other major character is Carrington's grandmother, the imperious Clotilda Pryde. The novel dramatizes the complex sympathies of the plantation owners and the backwoodsmen in choosing sides during the conflict.

Historical Accuracy: This is a well-drawn and convincing portrait of the period and its events.

LOUIS DODGE (1870-)

Born in Burlington, Iowa, and educated in Arkansas, Dodge began his career as a journalist. He also served in the Spanish American War and wrote several novels, including *The American*, *Children of the Desert*, and *Wagon Ruts*.

1669 *The American*

Date of Publication: 1934
Subject(s): American West
Fictional character(s): Leander Calvert, Prospector
Time Period(s): 1850s
Locale(s): Illinois; West

Summary: This story of the American West is told through the experiences of Illinois farmer Leander Calvert, who decides to seek his fortune in the western gold fields.

Historical Accuracy: The novel provides a catalogue of authentic period elements.

P.C. DOHERTY

An English mystery writer, Doherty was born in Middlesbrough and studied history at Liverpool and Oxford universities. He obtained is doctorate at Oxford for his thesis on Edward II and Queen Isabella. He is currently a headmaster of a school in northeast London. He has written a number of historical mysteries under several pseudonyms.

1670 *Angel of Death*

Date of Publication: 1990
Subject(s): Mystery; Middle Ages; Royalty—England
Fictional character(s): Hugh Corbett, Government Official (clerk), Detective—Amateur; Ranulf, Servant, Thief (former)
Historical character(s): Edward I, Ruler (King of England)
Time Period(s): 13th century (1299)
Locale(s): London, England

Summary: Hugh Corbett, is asked to solve the mystery of the death of the dean of St. Paul's Cathedral. Corbett's investigation leads him to uncover ecclesiastical and political conspiracies.

Historical Accuracy: The novel offers details that render the smells, sights, and sounds of medieval London.

1671 *The Crown in Darkness*

Date of Publication: 1988
Subject(s): Middle Ages; Mystery; Royalty—Scotland
Fictional character(s): Hugh Corbett, Government Official (clerk), Detective—Amateur; Ranulf, Servant, Thief (former); James Selkirk, Knight
Historical character(s): Robert the Bruce, Nobleman (Earl of Carrick), Patriot (Scottish); John Comyn, Patriot (Scottish)
Time Period(s): 13th century (1286)
Locale(s): Edinburgh, Scotland

Summary: Hugh Corbett, investigates the mysterious death of Scotland's king, Alexander III, whose empty throne attracts a number of ambitious claimants. He is drawn into a series of devious political maneuvers upon which the fate of an independent Scotland depends.

Historical Accuracy: The novel is an artful blend of the actual and the fictional with an authentic look at medieval life.

1672 *The Death of a King*

Date of Publication: 1985
Subject(s): Middle Ages; Mystery; Royalty—England
Fictional character(s): Edmund Beche, Government Official (royal clerk); Thomas Tweng, Knight, Government Official (sheriff); Jean Raspale, Government Official (French clerk)
Historical character(s): Edward III, Ruler (King of England); Isabella of France, Royalty (wife of Edward II)
Time Period(s): 14th century
Locale(s): England

Summary: Edmund Beche is commissioned by the king to investigate the circumstances surrounding the death of his father, Edward II, who died 18 years earlier. He uncovers intrigue, violence, and murder.

Historical Accuracy: The novel is an accomplished blend of fact and fiction. The premise of the mystery is speculative, but the period details and the medieval atmosphere are authentic.

1673 *The Fate of Princes*

Date of Publication: 1990
Subject(s): War of the Roses; Mystery; Royalty—England
Fictional character(s): Thomas Belknap, Spy, Religious (former priest); Giles Argentine, Doctor, Gentleman; Richard Scarisbrooke, Government Official (sergeant, constable of prison)
Historical character(s): Francis Lovell, Nobleman, Political Figure (chamberlain of England); Richard III, Ruler (King of England); John Howard, Nobleman (Duke of Norfolk); Henry Stafford, Nobleman (Duke of Buckingham)
Time Period(s): 15th century
Locale(s): London, England

Summary: The fate of Richard III's two young nephews is the novel's subject and the source of an investigation by Francis, Viscount Lovell, the close associate of Richard III. The novel exposes the bloody politics of the War of the Roses and offers a dramatic and intriguing solution to one of the most baffling of historical mysteries, the fate of the two princes in the Tower.

Historical Accuracy: The speculations here are supported by documentary and archeological evidence.

1674 *The Masked Man*

Date of Publication: 1991
Subject(s): Mystery; Crime and Criminals
Fictional character(s): Ralph Croft, Outlaw, Detective—Amateur; Captain D'Estivet, Military Personnel; Maurepas, Scholar, Librarian
Time Period(s): 18th century (early)
Locale(s): Paris, France

Summary: An unlikely protagonist, Ralph Croft is a murderer, forger, smuggler, and outlaw from England. He is chosen by the French to discover the true identity of the Man in the Iron Mask, a prisoner in France during the reign of Louis XIV. Croft sets out to solve one of the most famous mysteries in French history; however, not everyone wishes the truth to be learned.

Historical Accuracy: The novel is based on the unsolved historical mystery celebrated in Alexandre Dumas' novel, *The Man in the Iron Mask*. An excellent costume mystery.

1675 *The Prince of Darkness*

Date of Publication: 1992
Subject(s): Mystery; Middle Ages; Royalty—England
Fictional character(s): Hugh Corbett, Government Official (clerk), Detective—Amateur; Ranulf, Servant, Thief (former); Eleanor Belmont, Gentlewoman
Historical character(s): Edward, Prince of Wales, Royalty; Piers Gaveston, Gentleman; Edward I, Ruler (King of England); Philip IV, Ruler (King of France)
Time Period(s): 14th century (1300-1301)
Locale(s): Oxfordshire, England; London, England

Summary: Eleanor Belmont, the former mistress of the Prince of Wales, is found murdered in a convent, and Hugh Corbett is sent to investigate. The leading suspects are the prince himself and his current lover.

Historical Accuracy: The blending of fiction and fact creates an authentic atmosphere and a mystery that is historically plausible.

1676 *Satan in St. Mary's*

Date of Publication: 1986
Subject(s): Middle Ages; Mystery; Royalty—England
Fictional character(s): Hugh Corbett, Government Official (clerk), Detective—Amateur; Ranulf, Servant, Thief (former); Nigel Couville, Gentleman
Historical character(s): Edward I, Ruler (King of England)
Time Period(s): 13th century
Locale(s): London, England

Summary: A man is found hanged in the London church of St. Mary's. Was it suicide or murder? Hugh Corbett is assigned the task of determining the truth. The intrigue ensnares him, and the king's life is treatened.

Historical Accuracy: The novel features accurate descriptions of medieval life and customs, particularly the contrasts between society's upper and lower classes.

1677 *Satan's Fire*

Date of Publication: 1996
Subject(s): Mystery; Middle Ages; Royalty—England
Fictional character(s): Hugh Corbett, Government Official (master of clerks), Detective—Amateur
Historical character(s): Edward I, Ruler (King of England)
Time Period(s): 13th century
Locale(s): England

Summary: In this installment of the medieval mystery series featuring royal clerk and master spy Sir Hugh Corbett, a counterfeiting and assassination ring threatens King Edward I's rule and life. Sir Hugh must unmask the counterfeiter and expose the conspiracy. His investigation leads him to the sacred Order of Templars.

Historical Accuracy: The novel is convincingly grounded in historical facts, creating an authentic and believable period background.

1678 *The Serpent Amongst the Lilies*

Date of Publication: 1990
Subject(s): Middle Ages; Hundred Years War; Mystery
Fictional character(s): Matthew Jankyn, Thief, Spy
Historical character(s): Joan of Arc, Warrior; Henry Beaufort, Religious, Government Official (guardian of Henry VI)
Time Period(s): 15th century (1429)
Locale(s): Paris, France; Orleans, France; Shropshire, England

Summary: Matthew Jankyn, English war hero, rogue, and thief, is chosen by the ruthless Beaufort to determine the true identity and designs of Joan of Arc. He becomes part of her campaign on and off the battlefield, revealing the horrors, misery, and splendor of medieval France.

Historical Accuracy: The novel ingeniously mixes fact with fiction. The details of medieval battle are particularly well done.

1679 *The Song of a Dark Angel*

Date of Publication: 1994
Subject(s): Mystery; Middle Ages
Fictional character(s): Hugh Corbett, Government Official (master of clerks), Detective—Amateur
Time Period(s): 14th century (1302)
Locale(s): Norfolk, England

Summary: In 1302 Sir Hugh Corbett, King Edward I's keeper of the Secret Seal, a clerk and spy, is sent to the icy region of Norfolk where the bitter winter wind called the Dark Angel is blowing. A man's corpse is found on the beach with his head impaled on a pole, while the young wife of a local baker is found hanging. Corbett is drawn into these mysteries and an ever deadlier conspiracy.

Historical Accuracy: Rich in period details, the novel offers a convincing picture of the era and the locale.

1680 *Spy in Chancery*

Date of Publication: 1988
Subject(s): Middle Ages; Espionage; Mystery
Fictional character(s): Hugh Corbett, Government Official (clerk of the royal chancery), Detective—Amateur; Maeve, Young Woman; Lord Morgan, Nobleman
Historical character(s): Edward I, Ruler (King of England); Philip IV, Ruler (King of France)
Time Period(s): 13th century
Locale(s): London, England; Neath, Wales; Paris, France

Summary: Hugh Corbett, clerk of the royal chancery in 13th century England, is commissioned by Edward I to travel to France and Wales to discover the identity of a spy who is thought to be someone in high office and close to the king. There follows danger on sea and land as Hugh enters the underworld of medieval Paris and the hostile wilderness of Wales, where he falls in love.

Historical Accuracy: The novel is rich and precise in details of medieval times: language, dress, and customs.

1681 *The Whyte Harte*

Date of Publication: 1988
Subject(s): Mystery; Middle Ages; Royalty—England
Fictional character(s): Matthew Jankyn, Spy, Military Personnel; Edmund Luttrell, Religious (defrocked priest), Thief
Historical character(s): Henry IV, Ruler (King of England); Richard II, Ruler (King of England); John Oldcastle, Religious
Time Period(s): 15th century (1400s-1410s)
Locale(s): England; Agincourt, France; Scotland

Summary: Doherty examines one of history's most tantalizing mysteries—the death of Richard II. Did he die when history says he did? Matthew Jankyn is hired to spy on the Whyte Harte, a secret society whose aim is to overthrow Henry IV and restore Richard to the throne. This involves Jankyn in the extremes of medieval society—church, court, and slums—and a tangled web of conspiracy in the past and the present.

Historical Accuracy: While the novel's conspiracy premises are speculative, the period atmosphere is authentic and reliable.

IVAN DOIG (1939-)

Doig is an American writer born in Montana. He has written largely on American themes, Montana, and the Pacific Northwest. His work includes a memoir, *This House of Sky*, and the nonfiction work, *Winter Brothers*.

1682 *Dancing at the Rascal Fair*

Date of Publication: 1987
Subject(s): Settlement of the American Frontier; Family Saga; Immigrants
Fictional character(s): Angus McCaskill, Immigrant; Rob Barclay, Immigrant; Adair Barclay, Immigrant

Time Period(s): 19th century; 20th century (1889-1919)
Locale(s): English Creek, Montana (actually based on Dupuyer, Montana); Scotland

Summary: The second in Doig's family saga trilogy tells the story of the first generation immigrants who sail from Scotland to settle in Montana. The novel covers their 30 years of enduring brutal winters and their losses and triumphs.

Historical Accuracy: The novel is enriched with much research including first-hand accounts of the early settlement of the state.

1683 *English Creek*

Date of Publication: 1984
Subject(s): Family Saga
Fictional character(s): Jick McCaskill, Rancher; Varick McCaskill, Ranger (forest); Beth McCaskill, Housewife
Time Period(s): 1930s
Locale(s): English Creek, Montana (actually based on Dupuyer, Montana)

Summary: In this first novel of a trilogy, we follow the McCaskill family in the 1930s on the Montana range. The young narrator describes rodeos, family rifts, range riding, and forest fires.

Historical Accuracy: The author used historical societies' sources to create as authentic a setting and atmosphere as possible.

1684 *Ride with Me, Mariah Montana*

Date of Publication: 1990
Subject(s): Family Saga; Settlement of the American Frontier
Fictional character(s): Jick McCaskill, Rancher; Mariah McCaskill, Photographer; Riley Wright, Journalist
Time Period(s): 1980s (1989)
Locale(s): Montana

Summary: The McCaskill family saga is brought to the present as Mariah, the daughter of Jick McCaskill, is assigned to document the state's history to celebrate the centennial of statehood. Mariah, Jick, and journalist Wright crisscross the state and uncover the past.

Historical Accuracy: The historical accounts taken from newspapers of the time are interspersed with the narrative which provides an interesting double focus of the past and the present.

1685 *The Sea Runners*

Date of Publication: 1982
Subject(s): Settlement of the American Frontier
Fictional character(s): Nils Karlsson, Backwoodsman; Melander, Settler; Braaf, Thief
Time Period(s): 1850s (1852-1853)
Locale(s): New Archangel, Alaska; Astoria, Oregon

Summary: This adventure novel involves four Swedes indentured in Russian Alaska in the 1850s who escape down the Pacific Northwest coast to Oregon by canoe. On both land and sea the men encounter danger from the elements, from others, and from themselves.

Historical Accuracy: The events are based on an actual journey. The details are admirably rendered.

MARY DOLAN

`1686` *Hannibal of Carthage*

Date of Publication: 1955
Subject(s): Punic Wars; Roman Empire; Carthaginian Empire
Fictional character(s): Sosylos, Slave
Historical character(s): Hannibal, Military Personnel (Carthaginian general); Mago, Spouse (of Hannibal)
Time Period(s): 3rd century B.C.; 2nd century B.C.
Locale(s): Carthage, Ancient Civilization; Roman Empire

Summary: The novel offers a portrait of the great Carthaginian general Hannibal from the perspective of a slave and eyewitness, Sosylos. He records Hannibal's exploits as he crosses the Alps with his elephant corps and then marches through Italy to the gates of Rome itself. Hannibal emerges as a great tactical military genius and patriot of limitless resources and determination.

Historical Accuracy: The main events are from recorded history but are amplified with the author's speculation. There are so few facts known about Hannibal's life, experts hold a wide range of opinions as to actual events.

MAURICE DOLBIER (1912-1993)

Dolbier was from Skowhegan, Maine, and attended Whitehouse Academy of Dramatic Arts. He toured as an actor with Shakespearean companies. He was also a news editor and announcer in radio and a book critic for a variety of newspapers.

`1687` *Benjy Boone*

Date of Publication: 1967
Subject(s): Picaresque Adventure; Theatrical Life
Fictional character(s): Benjy Boone, Actor; Crassus Cornelius Boone, Actor
Time Period(s): 1830s (1839)
Locale(s): Erie Canal, New York; Mississippi River; Philadelphia, Pennsylvania

Summary: This picaresque novel concerns Benjy Boone's search for his father, the infamous thespian Crassus Cornelius Boone, who has disappeared after being accused of murder. Benjy joins an acting troupe whose tour takes them down the Erie Canal, acroos the Great Lakes to Chicago, and then down the Mississippi, where he has a series of adventures. Eventually the mysteries surrounding his father are revealed. father are revealed.

Historical Accuracy: The novel features meticulous attention to historical detail of the period and theatrical life of the time.

`1688` *The Mortal Gods*

Date of Publication: 1971
Subject(s): Theatrical Life; Victorian Period
Fictional character(s): Robert Jovian, Actor, Businessman (theater company manager); June Jovian, Actress

Time Period(s): 1890s (1895)
Locale(s): London, England

Summary: Robert Jovian is the actor-manager of a theatrical company at Victorian London's Olympia Theatre. For the 1895 season he proposes, at age 60, to mount a production of *Romeo and Juliet* with himself as the young lover. The reaction and complications provide an amusing plot that vividly captures the world of the London theater.

Historical Accuracy: The theatrical details of the period are authentically drawn.

FRIEDRICH DONAUER (1884-)

Donauer is a German writer.

`1689` *Swords Against Carthage*

Date of Publication: 1933
Subject(s): Roman Empire; Punic Wars
Historical character(s): Publius Cornelius Scipio Africanus, Military Personnel (Roman general)
Time Period(s): 3rd century B.C. (218-201 B.C.)
Locale(s): Spain

Summary: This historical romance is set during the Second Punic War and concerns the military career of Scipio Africanus, the commander-in-chief of the Roman legion in Spain. A romantic sub-plot of a young tribune and his cousin who are captured by the Carthaginians is appended to his story.

Historical Accuracy: The military campaigns and political situation of the period are vividly and accurately detailed.

ANTON DONCHEV (1930-)

Bulgarian writer Donchev originally trained to be a lawyer. *Time of Parting* won the Dimitrov Prize, the highest literary distinction in Bulgaria.

`1690` *Time of Parting*

Date of Publication: 1967
Subject(s): Ottoman Empire
Fictional character(s): The Venetian, Nobleman (French); Karaibrahim, Military Personnel (janissary); Aligorko, Religious (monk)
Time Period(s): 17th century (1668)
Locale(s): Rhodope Mountains, Bulgaria

Summary: The novel details the tragic invasion of Bulgaria by the Turks in the 17th century. Karaibrahim is the commander of a Turkish detachment that has been sent to convert the Bulgarians to Islam. A French nobleman known as the Venetian is taken prisoner by the Turks and converts to Islam. He serves as a translator for Karaibrahim. The novel is made up of separate chronicles by the Venetian and a Bulgarian monk named Aligorko. They become eyewitnesses to the torture, rape, and massacre of the Turkish invasion.

Historical Accuracy: The novel is artful in evoking and documenting the period and the struggle.

SUSAN DONNELL

Born in Manila, the Philippines, Donnell attended the University of Rome, Lausanne University, and the New York School of Drama. She has worked as a model, publicist, and film actress. Her main interest has been history, which she has explored while living in China, Hawaii, Mexico, England, France, Switzerland, Germany, Italy, and Portugal.

1691 *Pocahontas*

Date of Publication: 1991
Subject(s): Settlement of the American Frontier; American Colonies; Indians
Historical character(s): Powhatan, Indian, Chieftain; Pocahontas, Indian; John Smith, Settler; James I, Ruler (King of England)
Time Period(s): 17th century (1607-1617)
Locale(s): Jamestown, Virginia, American Colonies; London, England

Summary: History records that when Pocahontas saw John Smith again after several years in England, she was overpowered by emotion. The author uses this observation to speculate on a love affair. The novel details Pocahontas' relationship with Smith and her assistance of the Jamestown colonists.

Historical Accuracy: The love affair between Pocahontas and John Smith is speculative. The emphasis here is romance over historical accuracy.

ELISABETH DORED

A Norwegian author educated in Oslo, Paris, and Vienna, Dored has been a painter, newspaperwoman, and lecturer.

1692 *I Loved Tiberius*

Date of Publication: 1959
Subject(s): Roman Empire
Historical character(s): Augustus, Ruler (Roman emperor); Claudius I, Ruler (Roman emperor); Livia, Royalty (consort of Augustus); Julia, Royalty (daughter of Augustus); Tiberius, Ruler (Roman emperor)
Time Period(s): 1st century B.C.
Locale(s): Rome, Roman Empire; Spain; Gaul

Summary: This is an account of the first family of the Roman Empire by Julia, the daughter of Augustus. She becomes attached to her stepbrother Tiberius, but before she is allowed to marry him, she is forced into two other marriages. Through Julia the life of the Empire is reflected, culminating in tragedy.

Historical Accuracy: The author's interpretation of Julia is at variance from other accounts. However, this version is convincingly supported by evident research.

PRINCE THIBAUT D'ORLEANS

PRINCESS MARION D'ORLEANS

1693 *A Castle in Bavaria*

Date of Publication: 1973
Subject(s): World War I; Nazis; Royalty—Germany
Historical character(s): Aurora Hartburg, Widow(er), Royalty; Gottfried von Hartburg, Royalty (prince); Ruprecht Hartburg, Royalty (prince); Frederick Leopold, Ruler (archduke)
Time Period(s): 1910s; 1920s (1918-1924)
Locale(s): Bavaria, Germany; Vienna, Austria; Berlin, Germany

Summary: The fate of a great European family, the Hartburgs of Bavaria, is depicted from the end of World War I to the rise of Hitler and Nazism. The ancient and noble Hartburg family is caught up in the turmoil of history, and their intrigues, sexual scandals, and transitions are played out against a backdrop of post-war Germany and the forces that allow Hitler's triumph.

Historical Accuracy: The period is evoked with conviction.

ROBERTA KELLS DORR

1694 *Abraham and Sarah: The Long Journey*

Date of Publication: 1995
Subject(s): Biblical Story; Ancient Egypt
Historical character(s): Abraham, Biblical Figure; Sarah, Biblical Figure; Hagar, Biblical Figure
Time Period(s): Indeterminate Past
Locale(s): Middle East; Egypt

Summary: The novel dramatizes the Biblical story of Abraham and Sarah and their years of wandering in search of the land promised by God. Their journey takes them to the Nile delta where Sarah's beauty attracts the attention of the pharaoh. Eventually Sarah and Abraham, along with Hagar, are ordered from Egypt, and Sarah conceives a child.

Historical Accuracy: The novel is faithful to its Biblical sources, with obvious fictional elaboration and an authentic period background.

1695 *Bathsheba*

Date of Publication: 1980
Subject(s): Biblical Story; Ancient Israel
Historical character(s): David, Ruler (King of Israel), Biblical Figure; Bathsheba, Royalty (consort of David), Biblical Figure; Uriah, Biblical Figure; Absalom, Biblical Figure
Time Period(s): 10th century B.C.
Locale(s): Israel

Summary: This retelling of the Biblical story of David and Bathsheba dramatizes King David's passion for the already married Bathsheba and the steps he takes to make her his queen. The novel reveals as well the resulting struggle over David's throne within his household and among his advisers.

Historical Accuracy: The novel is faithful to the Biblical sources with fictional elements added to develop the period background.

1696 *The Queen of Sheba*

Date of Publication: 1990
Subject(s): Biblical Story; Ancient Israel
Historical character(s): Queen of Sheba, Ruler, Biblical Figure; Solomon, Ruler (King of Israel), Biblical Figure
Time Period(s): 10th century B.C.
Locale(s): Jerusalem, Israel

Summary: The novel reconstructs the Biblical story of the Queen of Sheba's visit to the magnificent court of Solomon in Jerusalem. Based on a few lines from the Bible and other sources and legends, the novel expands the story into a fully-realized portrait of the era and its figures.

Historical Accuracy: The novel's reconstruction is supported by meticulous research and knowledge of the region and the era.

1697 *Solomon's Song*

Date of Publication: 1989
Subject(s): Biblical Story; Ancient Israel
Historical character(s): Solomon, Royalty (prince), Biblical Figure; David, Ruler (King of Israel), Biblical Figure; Shulamit, Biblical Figure, Shepherd
Time Period(s): 10th century B.C.
Locale(s): Israel

Summary: This Biblical story dramatizes the relationship that inspired the Old Testament's Song of Solomon. Solomon, the young Prince of Israel, falls in love with a young shepherdess, Shulamit, only to find that she has been chosen as the newest wife of his father, King David.

Historical Accuracy: The novel is faithful to the biblical narrative and provides a good deal of authentic period elements.

CAROLE NELSON DOUGLAS (1944-)

Born in Washington state, Douglas attended the College of St. Catherine. She has worked as a reporter and a feature writer for newspapers in St. Paul, Minnesota. The author of mysteries, romances, and science fiction, her work rests on the fine line between serious and popular fiction.

1698 *Good Morning, Irene*

Date of Publication: 1991
Subject(s): Mystery; Victorian Period
Fictional character(s): Irene Adler, Singer (opera); Penelope Huxleigh, Companion; Geoffrey Norton, Lawyer
Historical character(s): Bram Stoker, Writer; Sarah Bernhardt, Actress
Time Period(s): 1880s (1888)
Locale(s): Paris, France

Summary: Irene Adler, opera singer and amateur sleuth, reads her own obituary, in which she is described as the victim of a train accident. She is soon very much alive, cracking a baffling case that includes Bram Stoker and Sarah Bernhardt.

Historical Accuracy: The scenes of Paris of the era are well developed and convincing.

1699 *Good Night, Mr. Holmes*

Date of Publication: 1990
Subject(s): Mystery; Victorian Period
Fictional character(s): Irene Adler, Singer (opera); Penelope Huxleigh, Companion; Godfrey Norton, Lawyer
Historical character(s): Lillie Langtry, Actress; Bram Stoker, Writer; Oscar Wilde, Writer; Antonin Dvorak, Composer
Time Period(s): 1890s (1894)
Locale(s): London, England

Summary: Irene Adler, the beautiful American opera singer who captures Sherlock Holmes heart in ''Scandal in Bohemia,'' is here an amateur detective who gets involved with many leading figures of the period. Her adventures are narrated by Penelope Huxleigh, a parson's daughter, who is often shocked by the forthright and flamboyant Irene.

Historical Accuracy: The novel excels in replicating authentically the late-Victorian milieu.

1700 *Irene at Large*

Date of Publication: 1992
Subject(s): Mystery; Victorian Period; Espionage
Fictional character(s): Irene Adler, Singer (opera); Penelope Huxleigh, Companion; Quentin Stanhope, Military Personnel (British officer)
Historical character(s): Oscar Wilde, Writer; Sarah Bernhardt, Actress
Time Period(s): 1880s
Locale(s): Paris, France; Afghanistan; London, England

Summary: Irene Adler and Penelope Huxleigh meet Quentin Stanhope, who tells them a story of treachery and murder during the Afghan campaign and the battle of Maiwand. A secret agent, code name Tiger, is still a threat both to Quentin and to a physician named Watson. The game is most definitely afoot.

Historical Accuracy: Period details are captured with authenticity.

1701 *Irene's Last Waltz*

Date of Publication: 1994
Subject(s): Mystery; Victorian Period
Fictional character(s): Irene Adler, Singer (opera); Godfrey Norton, Lawyer; Penelope Huxleigh, Companion; Sherlock Holmes, Detective—Private; John H. Watson, Doctor
Time Period(s): 1880s (1889)
Locale(s): Paris, France; Prague, Bohemia

Summary: At home in Paris, Irene Adler is approached by a princess beset by a loveless husband and a scandal which could have international implications. The husband turns out to be none other than the King of Bohemia, the man whose advances Irene once spurned.

Historical Accuracy: The novel is solidly grounded in period details and Holmesian atmosphere.

LLOYD C. DOUGLAS (1877-1951)

An American Lutheran minister and writer, Douglas is best remembered for his two inspirational historical novels, *The Big Fisherman* and *The Robe*, which were considerable popular successes. *The Robe* became a popular film that spawned a film sequel, *Demetrius and the Gladiators*.

1702 *The Big Fisherman*

Date of Publication: 1948
Subject(s): Christianity; Biblical Story
Fictional character(s): Fara, Royalty (Arabian princess); Voldi, Nobleman (Arabian); Nicator Mencius, Government Official (Roman proconsul)
Historical character(s): Peter, Biblical Figure; Jesus Christ, Biblical Figure; Herod Antipas, Ruler (Tetrarch of Judea); John the Baptist, Biblical Figure
Time Period(s): 1st century
Locale(s): Arabia; Jerusalem, Israel

Summary: This story of early Christianity and Jesus's later life, teachings, miracles, death, resurrection, and the gathering of the disciples is told from the point of view of Peter; Fara, the half-Arabian, half-Jewish daughter of Antipas; Voldi, Fara's betrothed; and Mencius, a sympathetic Roman proconsul. John the Baptist's last days and death are also described.

Historical Accuracy: The book is true to the biblical accounts of Jesus; the author has made his own determinations of character regarding these biblical figures.

1703 *The Robe*

Date of Publication: 1942
Subject(s): Biblical Story; Christianity; Roman Empire
Fictional character(s): Marcellus Gallio, Military Personnel (Roman tribune); Demetrius, Slave; Diana Gallus, Young Woman
Historical character(s): Tiberius, Ruler (Roman emperor); Caligula, Ruler (Roman emperor); Pontius Pilate, Government Official (procurator of Jerusalem); Peter, Biblical Figure; Salome, Biblical Figure
Time Period(s): 1st century
Locale(s): Rome, Roman Empire; Jerusalem, Israel; Athens, Greece

Summary: The novel provides a fictional account of Marcellus Gallio, an upperclass Roman tribune assigned to crucify Jesus. When Marcellus wins Jesus' robe in a dice game and dons the garment in a fit of drunkenness, he becomes emotionally distraught over the crucifixion. The robe's healing powers later restore Marcellus' equanimity, and with his loyal, resourceful slave, Demetrius, he embarks upon a quest to learn all he can about Jesus and his teachings, eventually becoming a Christian in defiance of Roman law.

Historical Accuracy: This story is essentially a celebration of early Christianity but Roman and Jewish culture and politics are detailed fairly well. The history of the crucifixion, its aftermath, and its effect on the populace of the region is in accord with what is known from the Bible and traditional historical speculation concerning the era.

CLIFFORD DOWDEY (1904-)

An American born in Virginia, Dowdey attended Columbia University and began his career as a reporter and book reviewer for the *Richmond News Leader*. Dowdey is a recognized authority on the Civil War and the Army of Northern Virginia.

1704 *Bugles Blow No More*

Date of Publication: 1937
Subject(s): Civil War—U.S.
Fictional character(s): Paul Kirby, Military Personnel (Confederate soldier); Elizabeth Kirby, Southern Belle; Ambrose Kirby, Military Personnel (Confederate soldier)
Time Period(s): 1860s (1861-1865)
Locale(s): Richmond, Virginia

Summary: Life in Richmond, Virginia, the capitol of the Confederacy, is depicted in this novel, centering on the life of the Kirby family. Events range from the opening days of Virginia's secession through the battles of the war and the devestating siege and evacuation of the city in 1865.

Historical Accuracy: The novel offers an authentic and convincing look at the homefront during the Civil War.

1705 *Gamble's Hundred*

Date of Publication: 1939
Subject(s): American Colonies
Fictional character(s): Sydney Frane, Plantation Owner; Christopher Ballard, Surveyor; Evelyn Frane, Spouse
Time Period(s): 1730s
Locale(s): Williamsburg, Virginia, American Colonies

Summary: The novel concerns a love triangle between plantation owner Sydney Frane, his wife, and surveyor Christopher Ballard. The social background of the story is the conflict between the big landowners and the small planters who are being driven by economic distress to open rebellion.

Historical Accuracy: The novel's story is invented, but for the events and attitudes the author went largely to the existing records or to a few secondary sources based wholly upon records.

1706 *The Proud Retreat*

Date of Publication: 1953
Subject(s): Civil War—U.S.
Historical character(s): Jefferson Davis, Political Figure; Judah P. Benjamin, Political Figure; Frances Malvern, Military Personnel (colonel); John Reagan, Military Personnel (Confederate officer); Delcie Rawls, Southern Belle
Time Period(s): 1860s (1865)
Locale(s): Richmond, Virginia; South

Summary: When Richmond falls during the Civil War, Jefferson Davis boxes up the Confederate treasury in a wagon train and heads south. He tries to reach Texas, avoiding Sherman's army and bands of marauders. In the first few days immediately following the war, the treasure vanishes, and its whereabouts enters the realm of legend. The novel depicts the events leading up to its disappearance and offers one version of its fate.

Historical Accuracy: The novel blends the factual with the imagined. The atmosphere of the era is convincing.

`1707` A Question of Honour

Date of Publication: 1962
Subject(s): Reconstruction Period
Fictional character(s): Ballard Edwards, Artist, Veteran; Madeleine Edwards, Spouse (of Ballard); Louis Roche, Veteran; Joan Harbin, Young Woman
Time Period(s): 1860s (post Civil War)
Locale(s): James River, Virginia

Summary: Life after the Civil War is depicted as a Virginia family attempts to remake their lives on their plantation. The marriage of Ballard and his wife Madeleine dissolves under the pressure of the struggle and with the acquaintance of Louis Roche and Joan Harbin.

Historical Accuracy: The atmosphere of the South in ruins is convincingly presented.

`1708` Sing for a Penny

Date of Publication: 1941
Subject(s): Business Building
Fictional character(s): Kirby Harron, Businessman; Nancy Pendleton, Young Woman
Time Period(s): 1880s; 1890s
Locale(s): Richmond, Virginia

Summary: The novel follows Kirby Harran and his determination to gain success. He begins as a clerk in a paper factory and eventually takes over the management of the mill and gets involved in unscrupulous dealings to achieve his goal, tangling with Richmond's financiers in the process.

Historical Accuracy: The social scene of period Richmond is authentically drawn.

`1709` Tidewater

Date of Publication: 1943
Subject(s): Settlement of the American Frontier
Fictional character(s): Caffey Wade, Gentleman; Libby Gamble, Young Woman; Philip Cherrill, Landowner
Time Period(s): 1830s
Locale(s): Virginia; Tennessee

Summary: A former Virginia planter, Caffey Wade, attempts to carve a plantation out of the frontier of Tennessee in the 1830s. He is quick to learn the difference between the civilization he left and the wide-open frontier, where a new set of ethics emerge in his rivalry with a prominent landowner.

Historical Accuracy: The details of frontier life, particularly the land speculation of the period, are authentically presented.

`1710` Where My Love Sleeps

Date of Publication: 1945
Subject(s): Civil War—U.S.; Battle of Petersburg
Fictional character(s): Blount Mathis, Military Personnel (Confederate captain)

Time Period(s): 1860s (1864-1865)
Locale(s): Richmond, Virginia; Petersburg, Virginia

Summary: The fighting around Petersburg and the fall of Richmond provide the setting for the novel. The background story presents the experiences of a Confederate captain, Blount Mathis, who is an officer on the staff of A.P. Hill. During the last years of the Civil War Mathis becomes more aware of the true nature of the conflict and its costs.

Historical Accuracy: The events of the battle around Petersburg and the fall of Richmond are handled accurately.

ANNE MILLER DOWNES (?-1964)

Born in Utica, New York, Downes earned a degree at the Columbia School of Journalism and wrote feature articles for newspapers and magazines. Her novels include *The Quality of Mercy*, *Mary Donovan*, and *The Eagle's Song*.

`1711` The Pilgrim Soul

Date of Publication: 1952
Subject(s): Settlement of the American Frontier; Indians
Fictional character(s): Dolly Copp, Settler; Hayes Copp, Settler
Time Period(s): 1820s
Locale(s): New Hampshire

Summary: The novel depicts pioneer life in the New Hampshire wilderness of the 1820s. Dolly Copp travels with her husband, Hayes, into the virgin forest at the foot of Mount Madison, and the novel recounts their struggle to clear the land and their encounters with Indians, bears, mountain lions, and winter.

Historical Accuracy: The novel is convincing in its detailing of the frontier life of the period.

`1712` The Quality of Mercy

Date of Publication: 1959
Subject(s): Settlement of the American Frontier; Indians; Immigrants
Fictional character(s): James Eaton, Immigrant; Susan Blair, Spouse
Time Period(s): 1810s
Locale(s): Philadelphia, Pennsylvania; Tennessee

Summary: James Eaton and his wife, Susan, leave their Philadelphia home and join the migration of settlers opening up the Tennessee wilderness beyond the Cumberland Mountains. They find themselves contending with the land, as well as war with the English and the Indians, as Andrew Jackson mounts his campaign against the Creek Indians.

Historical Accuracy: The depiction of frontier life is convincing and based on actual events.

JOHN HYATT DOWNING (1888-)

`1713` Anthony Trant

Date of Publication: 1941

Subject(s): Settlement of the American Frontier; Business Building
Fictional character(s): Anthony Trant, Businessman
Time Period(s): 19th century; 20th century
Locale(s): Sioux City, Iowa

Summary: This sequel to *Sioux City* continues the story of Anthony Trant whose rising fortunes mirror the development of the city.

Historical Accuracy: The novel convincingly depicts the life of Sioux City as it was during the period.

1714 *Sioux City*

Date of Publication: 1940
Subject(s): Settlement of the American Frontier
Fictional character(s): Anthony Trant, Young Man
Time Period(s): 1880s
Locale(s): Sioux City, Iowa

Summary: The novel depicts the growth of Sioux City, Iowa, in the 1880s through the experiences of young Anthony Trant, who comes there from college determined to make his fortune outside his overbearing father's shadow.

Historical Accuracy: The novel provides a faithful portrait of frontier times in Sioux City during the period.

SIR ARTHUR CONAN DOYLE
(1859-1930)

Though remembered chiefly for his creation of the amateur detective Sherlock Holmes, this English author and physician also wrote a number of historical romances. His later years were marked by an interest in spiritualism.

1715 *Micah Clarke*

Date of Publication: 1888
Subject(s): Monmouth's Rebellion
Fictional character(s): Micah Clarke, Fisherman; Decimus Saxon, Military Personnel
Historical character(s): Henry Beaufort, Nobleman; James Scott, Nobleman, Military Personnel
Time Period(s): 17th century (1685)
Locale(s): Portsmouth, England; Taunton, England

Summary: When the Duke of Monmouth—a Protestant—attempts to seize the English throne from Catholic James II, Micah Clarke becomes enmeshed in the conspiracy.

Historical Accuracy: This stirring adventure carefully reconstructs the events of 1685, offering a good collection of period details and portraits.

1716 *The White Company*

Date of Publication: 1891
Subject(s): Middle Ages
Fictional character(s): Alleyne Edricson, Military Personnel; John Hordle, Military Personnel; Nigel Loring, Nobleman, Knight
Historical character(s): Edward, the Black Prince, Royalty
Time Period(s): 15th century

Locale(s): England; Bordeaux, France; Pyrenees, Spain

Summary: In this tale of chivalry, young Edricson leaves an abbey to enter the feudal world. He encounters bowman John and becomes squire to the valiant Sir Nigel. They journey to France to join the White Company of English bowmen making war on the Spanish. Scenes of battles and sieges accelerate to a dramatic and ultimately happy conclusion.

Historical Accuracy: This is more a romance than a history, but the story includes good background details of the age of chivalry.

HARRY SINCLAIR DRAGO (1888-1979)

American author Drago attended the University of Toledo and worked as a cub reporter and Sunday columnist for the *Toledo Bee* before moving to New York, where he worked in publishing. He has written more than 100 western novels, some under pseudonyms. He spent five years in Hollywood during the 1920s writing for cowboy screen stars Tom Mix, Buck Jones, and Ken Maynard. His fiction includes *Whispering Saga* and *Oh, Susannah*, a 60,000-word novel he wrote in 11 days, and the western histories *Road Agents and Train Robbers* and *The Great Range Wars*, for which he received the Western Heritage Award in 1970.

1717 *Montana Road*

Date of Publication: 1935
Subject(s): American West; Battle of the Little Bighorn; Indians
Fictional character(s): Melissa Stafford, Young Woman; Stephen Glen, Government Official (Indian agent); Wick Flood, Trader
Historical character(s): George Armstrong Custer, Military Personnel (cavalry officer)
Time Period(s): 1870s
Locale(s): Dakota Territory, United States

Summary: The novel depicts the opening up of the Dakota Territory, the gold rush in the Black Hills, and the Indian Wars, which climax with Custer's Last Stand. The actual events form the background for a fictional story involving three individuals who meet on board a riverboat and whose lives become entwined.

Historical Accuracy: The novel attempts to do justice to the Sioux and reliably depicts the events described.

SHANNON DRAKE
(PSEUD. OF HEATHER GRAHAM POZZESSERE)

American romance novelist Pozzessere has authored more than 50 romances under the names Shannon Drake and Heather Graham. She won an award for the best sensual romance set during the American Civil War in 1988 for *Darker Stranger*. She has said that she strives to write books that are fun to read.

1718 *Princess of Fire*

Date of Publication: 1989

Subject(s): Romance; Middle Ages; Norman Conquest
Fictional character(s): Fallon Godwinson, Royalty (princess); Alaric of Anion, Nobleman (count)
Time Period(s): 11th century (1066)
Locale(s): England

Summary: The conflict betwen Saxons versus Normans forms the background for this which Norman Alaric of Anion is attracted to Saxon Princess Fallon Godwinson. Friction between the two eventually turns to attraction, but not before political and cultural differences are resolved.

Historical Accuracy: The novel offers more period background than is usual in a historical romance. The period details are put to good effect in the drama.

JOHN W. DRAKEFORD (1914-)

A Baptist pastor, psychologist, educator, and author, Drakeford was born in Sydney, Australia, and came to the U.S. in 1954. He has worked as a professor of psychology and counseling and as a director of the counseling center at Southwestern Baptist Theological Seminary. Drakeford is widely known as an authority on John Wesley with an important collection of Wesleyana. His many writings include *Wisdom for Today's Family*, *People to People Therapy*, and *Marriage: How to Keep a Good Thing Growing*.

`1719` *Take Her, Mr. Wesley*

Date of Publication: 1973
Subject(s): American Colonies; Religious Life; Biography, Fictionalized
Historical character(s): John Wesley, Religious (missionary)
Time Period(s): 1730s (1736-1737)
Locale(s): Georgia, American Colonies

Summary: This journal account of a year in the life of John Wesley describes his experiences in the Georgia colony with Governor Oglethorpe who plays the role of matchmaker by arranging for Wesley to tutor Miss Sophia Hopkey. Although she falls in love with him, Wesley is unable to see marriage as compatible with his spiritual commitment.

Historical Accuracy: The novel is based on Wesley's private diaries and other first hand reports.

THEODORE DREISER (1871-1945)

Dreiser was an American novelist and leading figure among American naturalists. His chief works are *Sister Carrie*, *Jenny Gerhardt*, and *An American Tragedy*.

`1720` *The Financier*

Date of Publication: 1912
Subject(s): Business Building
Fictional character(s): Frank A. Cowperwood, Businessman; Aileen Butler, Gentlewoman; Edward Butler, Political Figure, Businessman
Time Period(s): 19th century (1850-1874)
Locale(s): Philadelphia, Pennsylvania; Chicago, Illinois

Summary: The novel tells of businessman Frank Cowperwood's stellar career, his failed marriage, his mistress, and his downfall after the Panic of 1871. Through it all, Cowperwood adapts to his circumstances, the ultimate capitalist.

Historical Accuracy: Cowperwood is modeled after businessman Charles T. Yerkes.

JOAN DRUETT (1939-)

Born and raised in New Zealand, Druett is a writer of science fiction and nonfictional studies of the 19th century, as well as fiction. She received a B.A. from Victoria University in Wellington and was a teacher of biology and English until 1983, when she began writing full time. She has an interest in the unusual subject of women and whaling.

`1721` *Abigail*

Date of Publication: 1988
Subject(s): Sea Story; Treasure Hunt; Pirates
Fictional character(s): Abigail Sherman, Adventurer; Seth Morgan, Sea Captain
Time Period(s): 1850s
Locale(s): New Zealand; New Bedford, Massachusetts; At Sea

Summary: Abigail Sherman, the daughter of a whaling captain, is raised in New Zealand but is sent to New England when her mother dies. There she receives from her father the title to his ship and the clues to lead her to a vast fortune. She embarks on the treacherous voyage home to claim her legacy, a voyage in which she must contend with gamblers, pirates, fortune hunters, and false friends.

Historical Accuracy: The adventure is solidly anchored by period detail that is convincing.

EMMA DRUMMOND
(PSEUD. OF ELIZABETH DARRELL, 1931-)

Drummond comes from an English military family. She spent her early years in Hong Kong, where she graduated from a military academy and served as a training officer.

`1722` *Beyond All Frontiers*

Date of Publication: 1983
Subject(s): British Raj; Victorian Period; Afghan War
Fictional character(s): Charlotte Scott, Gentlewoman; Richard Lingarde, Military Personnel (British officer), Engineer
Time Period(s): 1830s; 1840s (1837-1843)
Locale(s): Meerpore, India; Kabul, Afghanistan

Summary: Having completed her schooling in England, Charlotte Scott returns to India at the outbreak the first Afghan War. She marries Richard Lingarde who seems to understand that British rule in India will be defeated. He is sent to war-torn Kabul, and Charlotte journeys through the Khyber Pass to join him.

Historical Accuracy: The author knows the locale and the military matters and renders them with conviction.

1723 *The Bridge of a Hundred Dragons*

Date of Publication: 1986
Subject(s): Chinese Revolution; Bridge Building
Fictional character(s): Alexandra Mostyn, Artist; Mark Rawlings, Military Personnel (major), Engineer
Time Period(s): 1920s
Locale(s): Shanghai, China; Nanking, China; Hong Kong

Summary: Set during the Shanghai emergency of 1927 and the advance of the Kuomintang army led by Chiang Kai-Shek, the novel tells the story of Alexandra Mostyn, a would-be artist, and her relationship with British Army engineer Major Rawlings who, in the midst of the turmoil, attempts to rebuild a strategic bridge. The pair gets swept up in the revolution that spreads all around them.

Historical Accuracy: The author bases her version of the events in Nanking and Shanghai on the personal reminiscences of her relatives. This helps create a sense of authenticity and believability.

1724 *A Captive Freedom*

Date of Publication: 1987
Subject(s): Boer War; Victorian Period; Theatrical Life
Fictional character(s): Vivian Veasey-Hunter, Military Personnel (captain of lancers); Leila Duncan, Actress
Time Period(s): 1890s; 1900s (1896-1901)
Locale(s): London, England; Kimberley, South Africa

Summary: Vivian Veasey-Hunter, an army captain recently returned to London from the Ashanti War, falls in love with an actress Leila Duncan. Their pasts kept them apart, but they meet again in South Africa during the siege of Kimberley.

Historical Accuracy: The details of both theatrical and military life are convincingly delivered.

1725 *Forget the Glory*

Date of Publication: 1985
Subject(s): Crimean War; Victorian Period; Military Life—British Army
Fictional character(s): Mary Clarke, Widow(er); Rowan DeMayne, Military Personnel (captain); Lydia Moorfield, Gentlewoman
Time Period(s): 1850s (1853-1855)
Locale(s): India; Crimea, Russia

Summary: Two British cavalry regiments stationed in India make the 6,000 mile trip across two continents to reinforce the troops in the Crimean War. Mary Clarke is a trooper's wife, twice widowed, who accompanies the regiment. Captain DeMayne, who is in love with the flirtatious society beauty Lydia Moorfield befriends Mary. Their fate will be determined in the days leading up to the fall of Sebastopol.

Historical Accuracy: The events are based on personal accounts and regimental records.

1726 *A Question of Honour*

Date of Publication: 1991
Subject(s): Victorian Period; Family Saga; Military Life—British Army

Fictional character(s): Gilliard Ashleigh, Gentleman, Veteran (former general); Vere Ashleigh, Gentleman; Valentine Ashleigh, Gentleman
Time Period(s): 1890s
Locale(s): England

Summary: An iron-willed former general, Sir Gilliard Ashleigh, is determined to continue his family's heroic military heritage in succeeding generations. His heirs, Vere and Valentine Ashleigh, both resist the military future laid out for them, and the novel explores the effects on the family of divided loyalties and the conflict between duty and selfhood.

Historical Accuracy: This family drama is informed by the author's clear familiarity with the military ethos and background of the period.

1727 *Some Far Elusive Dawn*

Date of Publication: 1988
Subject(s): World War I; British Colonies
Fictional character(s): Alex Beresford, Businessman; Martin Linwood, Veteran (ex-Army officer); Lydia Beresford, Young Woman
Time Period(s): 1920s
Locale(s): Singapore

Summary: Alex Beresford is the unwilling heir to a shipping line in Singapore in the 1920s. Alex resents his dominating father for having denied him participation in the Great War. The relationship drama is complicated when the Berefords get involved with a shell-shocked army veteran to whom Alex's sister Lydia is attracted.

Historical Accuracy: The novel features an authentic look at British colonial life in Singapore during the period.

1728 *That Sweet and Savage Land*

Date of Publication: 1990
Subject(s): Romance; British Colonies; Military Life—British Army
Fictional character(s): Elizabeth de Rioches, Gentlewoman; William Delacourt, Military Personnel (army officer); John Stavenham, Military Personnel (army officer)
Time Period(s): 19th century
Locale(s): England; India

Summary: Marriage, for Elizabeth de Rioches, is confining and a disappointment. Her husband, William Delacourt leaves her with his family when he departs with the army for India, and she meets another soldier, John Stavenham, with whom she has an affair. He also is posted to India and serves under Delacourt. Elizabeth joins them in India as the country erupts in war.

Historical Accuracy: The details of colonial and military life of the period are convincingly presented.

JUNE DRUMMOND (1923-)

Drummond is a South African writer of thrillers whose first book, *The Black Unicorn*, was published in 1959. She has written a book a year since then. Drummond was a

provincial candidate for the Progressive Party in Durban in 1974.

1729 *The Bluestocking*

Date of Publication: 1985
Subject(s): Regency Romance
Fictional character(s): Davina Wakeford, Gentlewoman; Lucas Rowan, Nobleman (Earl of Rigg); Jocellin Clare, Gentlewoman
Time Period(s): 1810s (1816)
Locale(s): London, England

Summary: When her father dies, Davina Wakeford is left with no fortune and a heavily mortgaged Palladian mansion. Her aunt sees the solution to Davina's problem as a rich husband and invites Davina to come to town for the London season. There she is a great success, but her relative's schemes could spoil her chances for romance and security.

Historical Accuracy: The romance is solidly imagined with period details.

1730 *The Unsuitable Miss Pelham*

Date of Publication: 1990
Subject(s): Regency Romance
Fictional character(s): Alexander Frome, Nobleman (Earl of Linslade), Diplomat; Lucilla Pelham, Gentlewoman
Time Period(s): 1820s (1821)
Locale(s): Cotswolds, England; London, England

Summary: Alexander Frome, on a visit to the Cotswolds, meets Lucilla Pelham, whose father had been an explorer. He is attracted to her, but romantic misunderstandings and complications present obstacles until the dramatic climax.

Historical Accuracy: The plot is intricately woven and the period details are unusually accurate and exact.

MAURICE DRUON (1918-)

A French writer and critic, Druon was born in Paris. During the Second World War, he served as a cavalry officer and escaped France through Spain during the German occupation. He fought with the Free French forces in England. He has served as a war correspondent and in 1973 was the French Minister of Cultural Affairs.

1731 *Alexander the God*

Date of Publication: 1960
Subject(s): Macedonian Empire; Biography, Fictionalized
Fictional character(s): Aristander, Religious (soothsayer)
Historical character(s): Alexander the Great, Ruler (Macedonian king)
Time Period(s): 4th century B.C.
Locale(s): Greece; Persia

Summary: The novel offers a biographical account of the astounding career of Alexander the Great, who in the 13 years after he succeeds his father, Philip of Macedonia, becomes master of most of the known world. The novel is cast in the form of a memoir of Aristander, soothsayer to Alexander.

Historical Accuracy: The novel mixes fact and fiction and pursues the theme of Alexander's conviction that he is a god, a theme that is urged beyond the historical evidence.

1732 *The Iron King*

Date of Publication: 1956
Subject(s): Middle Ages; Royalty—France
Historical character(s): Philip IV, Ruler (King of France); Jacques de Molay, Knight (Grand Master, Knights Templar); Isabella of France, Royalty (queen of Edward II of England); Robert of Artois, Nobleman
Time Period(s): 14th century (1313)
Locale(s): France; England

Summary: This is the first of the author's Accursed Kings series. At the beginning of the 14th century, Philip IV rules France with absolute and crushing power. His only adversary is the powerful and independent Order of the Knights Templar, which Philip persecutes. The novel details the result of Philip's actions and the curse delivered by the Grand Master, Jacques de Molay, which blights Philip and his descendants.

Historical Accuracy: This is a remarkable period reconstruction, authentic as well as dramatic.

1733 *The Lily and the Lion*

Date of Publication: 1961
Subject(s): Middle Ages; Royalty—England; Royalty—France
Historical character(s): Edward III, Ruler (King of England); Isabella of France, Royalty (queen consort of Edward II), Widow(er); Roger de Mortimer, Nobleman; Philip VI, Ruler (King of France); Robert of Artois, Nobleman; Mahaut, Noblewoman (Countess of Artois); Cola di Rienzo, Nobleman, Political Figure (tribune of Rome)
Time Period(s): 14th century
Locale(s): England; France; Italy

Summary: In this concluding volume of the Accursed Kings series, Edward III establishes his power by executing his mother's lover, Roger de Mortimer. In France, Philippe VI has gained the throne and becomes involved in the bitter feud between Robert of Artois and the Countess Mahaut.

Historical Accuracy: The history is scrupulously documented.

1734 *The Poisoned Crown*

Date of Publication: 1957
Subject(s): Middle Ages; Royalty—France
Historical character(s): Louis X, Ruler (King of France); Clemence of Hungary, Royalty (queen consort of Louis X); Charles of Valois, Nobleman; Robert of Artois, Nobleman
Time Period(s): 14th century (1310s)
Locale(s): France

Summary: The third of the author's Accursed Kings series deals with the last months of Louis X's reign. After having his first wife imprisoned and strangled, Louis marries Clemence of Hungry to ensure a successor to the crown. He brings her into the violent atmosphere of his intrigue-riddled court. In his short 18 month reign, Louis destroys his father's achievements while producing no heir and a legacy of rebellion.

Historical Accuracy: The author has the ability of Alexandre Dumas to animate his historical facts while keeping within the limits of the actual or probable.

1735 *The Royal Succession*

Date of Publication: 1958
Subject(s): Middle Ages; Royalty—France
Historical character(s): Clemence of Hungary, Royalty (queen consort of Louis X), Widow(er); Philippe, Nobleman (Count of Poitiers); Charles, Nobleman (Count de la Marche); Robert of Artois, Nobleman
Time Period(s): 14th century (1316)
Locale(s): France

Summary: In the fourth volume of the Accursed Kings series, France is left without a king and many claimants to the throne. At Lyons, the eldest brother of Louis X attempts to force the conclave of cardinals to elect a new pope. Philippe maneuvers to have himself named regent and then king. At the same time, a civil war rages, fulfilling the curse pronounced two years before by the Grand Master of the Templars.

Historical Accuracy: Druon's grasp of the historical details are remarkable in this authentic version of the period and its personalities.

1736 *The She-Wolf of France*

Date of Publication: 1960
Subject(s): Middle Ages; Royalty—France; Royalty—England
Historical character(s): Charles IV, Ruler (King of France); Edward II, Ruler (King of England); Isabella of France, Royalty (queen consort of Edward II); Roger de Mortimer, Nobleman; Edward, Royalty (prince)
Time Period(s): 14th century (1320s)
Locale(s): France; England

Summary: The title refers to Isabella, daughter of Philip the Fair and the wife of the English king Edward II. The novel deals with her love affair with Roger de Mortimer and their toppling of Edward II—one of the most heinous events in English history. This is power politics at its most treacherous and brutal.

Historical Accuracy: The author's notes attest to the care with which he has kept to the facts.

1737 *The Strangled Queen*

Date of Publication: 1956
Subject(s): Middle Ages; Royalty—France
Historical character(s): Louis X, Ruler (King of France); Marguerite de Bourgogne, Royalty (queen consort of Louis X); Robert of Artois, Nobleman; Charles of Valois, Nobleman
Time Period(s): 14th century (1310s)
Locale(s): Normandy, France; Paris, France

Summary: In the second volume of the Accursed Kings series Louis X's rule and his domestic problems are chronicled. Louis desires to be free of his wife in order to wed Clemence of Hungary. There is no pope, however, to annul the marriage, and another, more temporal, solution is found.

Historical Accuracy: The author is painstaking in the authenticity of the facts provided.

ALLEN DRURY (1918-)

An American journalist and novelist, Drury worked as the Washington correspondent for the New York Times. *Advise and Consent*, his popular and sensational novel about Washington politics, won the Pulitzer Prize in 1959.

1738 *A God Against the Gods*

Date of Publication: 1976
Subject(s): Pharaohs; Religious Conflict; Ancient Egypt
Historical character(s): Akhenaton, Ruler (pharaoh); Nefertiti, Royalty (Egyptian queen)
Time Period(s): 14th century B.C.
Locale(s): Egypt

Summary: Drury offers a fascinating depiction of ancient Egypt in this story of the reign of the Pharaoh Akhenaton, who challenges Egyptian belief by advocating a single diety as ruler of the universe.

Historical Accuracy: The political and philosophical climate are ingeniously re-created.

1739 *Return to Thebes*

Date of Publication: 1977
Subject(s): Pharaohs; Religious Conflict; Ancient Egypt
Historical character(s): Akhenaton, Ruler (Egyptian pharaoh); Nefertiti, Royalty (Egyptian queen); Tutankhamen, Royalty; Seti I, Ruler (pharaoh)
Time Period(s): 14th century B.C.
Locale(s): Egypt

Summary: Drury concludes the story of Akhenaton's reign and the end of the 18th dynasty. Akhenaton's desire to change the Egyptian order of belief is detailed as family and court politics distance him from his family and his people.

Historical Accuracy: The results of Drury's extensive research are evident in this re-animation of ancient times and culture.

THEODORA MCCORMICK DU BOIS
(1890-)

American educatior and novelist Du Bois was born in Brooklyn, New York. Her books include *The Cavalier's Corpse*, *The Listener*, and *Rich Boy, Poor Boy*.

1740 *Captive of Rome*

Date of Publication: 1962
Subject(s): Roman Empire
Fictional character(s): Marcus Fabatus, Military Personnel (Roman officer); Ethnea, Royalty (Irish princess), Captive
Historical character(s): Alaric I, Ruler (King of the Visigoths); Ataulf, Ruler (King of the Visigoths); Patrick, Religious (missionary); Honorius, Ruler (Roman emperor)
Time Period(s): 5th century
Locale(s): Ireland; Rome, Roman Empire

Summary: The fall of the Roman Empire is chronicled in this story of Roman soldier Marcus who wishes to marry Ethnea, the daughter of an Irish king. She is captured by the Goths and then becomes a Roman slave. Marcus and Ethnea are separated as the barbarians arrive at the gates of Rome.

Historical Accuracy: Many of the author's characters and events are historically accurate. The scenes involving St. Patrick are based on legend, not history.

1741 *The Emerald Crown*

Date of Publication: 1955
Subject(s): Dark Ages; Royalty—Ireland; Celtic Ireland
Fictional character(s): Niall Black-Knee, Royalty (prince); Fiann Sionna, Royalty (princess)
Time Period(s): 9th century
Locale(s): Ireland

Summary: In this adventure tale, Niall Black-Knee returns to Ireland after fighting the Danes with Alfred the Great in England. A son of an Irish king, Niall finds himself in the thick of the fighting against a marauding band of Danes. When the Danes sack a convent, Niall comes to the rescue, saving Sionna, the daughter of the High King. The novel chronicles years of struggle until Niall succeeds to the throne as the High King with Sionna as his queen.

Historical Accuracy: The story is an imagined one, but convincing in its atmosphere of the period.

1742 *Freedom's Way*

Date of Publication: 1953
Subject(s): American Colonies; American Revolution; Georgian Period
Fictional character(s): Caroline Matilda, Convict, Servant
Time Period(s): 1770s
Locale(s): Annapolis, Maryland

Summary: Caroline Matilda, a maid of honor at the court of George III, is unjustly accused of stealing the queen's jewels. She is transported as a convicted indentured servant to Maryland at the time of the outbreak of the American Revolution. Her experiences fending for herself in the American colonies and wilderness make for a high-spirited adventure.

Historical Accuracy: The novel is a mingling of fact and fiction. Most of the details are historically based and authentic to the period.

1743 *The Love of Fingin O'Lea*

Date of Publication: 1957
Subject(s): Medical Profession; Middle Ages
Fictional character(s): Fingin O'Lea, Doctor; Dermot, Ruler (King of Ireland)
Time Period(s): 12th century
Locale(s): Ireland; France; Italy

Summary: This novel of medieval Ireland and the medical profession portrays the adventures of a young medical student, Fingin O'Lea. O'Lea accompanies the Irish King Dermot on a raid which causes Henry II's invasion of Ireland. Through his experiences and travels, Fingin emerges as one of the most famous physicians in 12th-century Europe.

Historical Accuracy: The novel excels in portraying the state of medicine at the time.

DAPHNE DU MAURIER (1907-1989)

Du Maurier is the granddaughter of English artist and novelist George Du Maurier, the author of *Trilby*. Her father was the famous actor-manager Sir Gerald du Maurier who created the role of Bulldog Drummond on the stage. Her most famous novel is the classic suspense romance *Rebecca*.

1744 *Frenchman's Creek*

Date of Publication: 1941
Subject(s): Pirates; Restoration Period; Sea Story
Fictional character(s): Dona St. Columb, Noblewoman; Jean-Benoit Aubery, Pirate
Time Period(s): 17th century (1640s)
Locale(s): Cornwall, England; *La Mouette*, At Sea

Summary: This is the romantic adventure of the rebellious Lady Dona St. Columb. Bored by her life at the court of Charles II, she takes up with a French pirate who is in hiding near her Cornish estate. She tries to maintain her double life, feeling pressure from both sides to reveal her secret.

Historical Accuracy: The novel is more fantasy than history. The Cornish details provide the main realistic elements.

1745 *The Glass-Blowers*

Date of Publication: 1963
Subject(s): Family Saga; French Revolution
Fictional character(s): Robert Busson, Revolutionary; Michel Busson, Revolutionary; Sophie Duval, Young Woman
Time Period(s): 18th century; 19th century (1747-1811)
Locale(s): Cherigny, France; Paris, France

Summary: The novel tells the story of a family of glass blowers whose members become involved in the events of the French Revolution and the civil war that sweeps France in its aftermath. Their fortunes become intertwined with the course of the Revolution, from the Reign of Terror to the ascendancy of Napoleon.

Historical Accuracy: The novel is authentic in capturing the atmosphere of the period.

1746 *Hungry Hill*

Date of Publication: 1944
Subject(s): Family Saga
Fictional character(s): Copper John Brodrick, Landowner; Fanny Rosa Flowers, Young Woman; Henry Brodrick, Gentleman
Time Period(s): 19th century; 20th century (1820-1920)
Locale(s): Ireland

Summary: One hundred years of family and regional history are depicted in this novel. Copper John Brodrick, the owner of Clonmere, is determined to sink a copper mine into Hungry Hill, the domain of the Donovan family and other tenants who consider Brodrick an interloper. The feud that results and the intermingling of families over the generations form the novel's drama.

Historical Accuracy: The novel features a convincing look at the Irish countryside during the period.

1747 *Jamaica Inn*
Date of Publication: 1937
Subject(s): Suspense; Georgian Period
Fictional character(s): Mary Yellan, Young Woman; Joss Merlyn, Innkeeper; Francis Davey, Religious (preacher)
Time Period(s): 1790s
Locale(s): Cornwall, England; Bodmin, England

Summary: This classic novel of romantic suspense is set at the isolated Jamaica Inn, located on the Cornish moors. Mary Yellan comes to visit her aunt and finds herself involved in smuggling, murder, treachery, and love.

Historical Accuracy: The novel features a believable period atmosphere.

1748 *The King's General*
Date of Publication: 1946
Subject(s): Civil War—England; Family Saga
Historical character(s): Honor Harris, Young Woman; Sir Richard Grenville, Military Personnel (general); George Villiers, Nobleman (Duke of Buckingham); Charles Stuart, Royalty (Prince of Wales)
Time Period(s): 17th century (1622-1653)
Locale(s): Cornwall, England

Summary: This is a fictionalized account of the Harris and Grenville families of Cornwall and their involvement in the English Civil War. The romance between Honor Harris and Sir Richard Grenville, the title character, is highlighted.

Historical Accuracy: The events of the English Civil War, particularly Cornwall's part in it, have been well researched by the author; but she seems primarily concerned with character studies.

1749 *Mary Anne*
Date of Publication: 1954
Subject(s): Regency Period; Royalty—England
Historical character(s): Mary Anne Clarke, Lover (mistress of the Duke of York); Frederick Augustus, Royalty (Duke of York and Albany)
Time Period(s): 18th century; 19th century (1770s-1820s)
Locale(s): London, England

Summary: The novel tells the story of the author's ancestor, Mary Anne Clarke, who rises up from London's Fleet Street to become the mistress of George III's second son, the Duke of York. Her trading in military promotions creates one of England's greatest political scandals. The duke is charged and eventually cleared.

Historical Accuracy: The novel mixes the fictional and the factual. The basic story is faithful to history.

GEORGE DU MAURIER (1834-1896)
Du Maurier was a French-born English novelist and illustrator. He joined the staff of *Punch* in 1864 and produced drawings satirizing the upper- and middle-classes. His most famous novel is *Trilby*.

1750 *Peter Ibbetson*
Date of Publication: 1891
Subject(s): Crime and Criminals; Fantasy
Fictional character(s): Peter Ibbetson, Gentleman, Murderer; Colonel Ibbetson, Gentleman
Time Period(s): 1840s
Locale(s): Paris, France; London, England

Summary: This is the strange tale of an English boy who returns from living in Paris on the death of his parents. A cousin raises him to be a gentleman, but he has more affinity for art. He develops the ability to 'dream true,' to experience in dreams the fulfillments not possible in real life. Despite being condemned for murder, he is happy journeying back in time.

Historical Accuracy: The novel is an odd fantasy meant to question the nature of reality and the realm of dreams.

ELIZABETH NELL DUBUS (1933-)
Born in Louisiana, Dubus is a graduate of the University of Southwestern Louisiana and Louisiana State University. She has been a teacher of speech and drama. She won the Ione Burden Prize from the Deep South Writers Conference for her 1974 novel *Turnings*. Her other works include *To Love and Dream* and *Where Love Rules*.

1751 *Cajun*
Date of Publication: 1983
Subject(s): Family Saga
Fictional character(s): Claude Langlinais, Gentleman; Mathilde Langlinais, Spouse
Time Period(s): Multiple Time Periods
Locale(s): Canada; New Orleans, Louisiana

Summary: This multi-generational saga describes the history of the Langlinais clan beginning with the arrival from France of Claude Langlinais. Thrown out of the English colony with other Acadians, he immigrates with his wife Mathilde to New Orleans where subsequent generations are connected with the city's turbulent history.

Historical Accuracy: The novel offers many authentic period details to form a convincing background for the family saga.

1752 *Twilight of the Dawn*
Date of Publication: 1989
Subject(s): Civil War—U.S.; Slavery; Antebellum South
Fictional character(s): Gabrielle Cannon, Southern Belle; Alex St. Cyr, Gentleman; Tom Cannon, Gentleman
Time Period(s): 1860s (1860-1865)
Locale(s): Louisiana

Summary: Antebellum life in Louisiana is depicted in this family drama involving Gabrielle Cannon, her brother Tom, and Alex St. Cyr, a young man from a prominent New Orleans family. The issues that erupt to produce the Civil War eventually split brother and sister.

Historical Accuracy: The locale is authentically rendered.

JACQUES DUCHARME (1910-)

Born in holyoke, Massachusetts, Ducharme, a descendant of French Canadians who migrated to New England, was educated at Assumption College and at the sorbonne. he has authored *The Shadows of Trees: The Story of French Canadians in New England* and *The Delusson Family*.

1753 *The Delusson Family*

Date of Publication: 1939
Subject(s): Social Chronicle
Fictional character(s): Jean Baptiste Delusson, Settler; Cecile Delusson, Spouse
Time Period(s): 19th century
Locale(s): Holyoke, Massachusetts

Summary: This tale chronicles the history of the French-Canadian Delusson family, who in 1874, journey to Holyoke, Massachusetts, for a better life working in the mills. Their story and the French-Canadian customs they preserve are narrated in a quiet, authentic manner.

Historical Accuracy: The period elements are authentically reproduced.

ROBERT L. DUFFUS (1888-1972)

An American author and journalist, Duffus was born in Waterbury, Vermont and educated at Stanford University. His works include *Roads Going South*, a fictionalized account of his boyhood in Vermont, the novel *The Coast of Eden*, and an autobiographical work, *Innocents at Cedro*, which tells of his experiences during a year at Stanford University when he lived with social scientist Thorsten Veblen.

1754 *Jornada*

Date of Publication: 1935
Subject(s): American West; Mexican War; Wagon Trains
Fictional character(s): Mercedes Peyton, Gentlewoman; Martin Collins, Settler
Time Period(s): 1840s
Locale(s): Southwest; Santa Fe, New Mexico

Summary: This romantic adventure tale is set during the weeks leading up to the Mexican War. A wagon train loaded with arms intended to crush the rebellion travels from Missouri to Sante Fe. The difficulties of the journey are joined to a love triangle involving the expedition's leader, his wife Mercedes Peyton, and young Martin Collins. The latter two are separated from the group and must make their own way across La Jornada, the great desert on the way to Sante Fe.

Historical Accuracy: The historical background is authentic but secondary to the romance.

BRUCE DUFFY

1755 *The World as I Found It*

Date of Publication: 1967
Subject(s): Philosophy; Biography, Fictionalized; World War I
Historical character(s): Ludwig Wittgenstein, Philosopher; Bertrand Russell, Philosopher; G.E. Moore, Philosopher
Time Period(s): 20th century (1900s-1951)
Locale(s): Vienna, Austria; Cambridge, England

Summary: This biographical novel traces the career of philosopher Ludwig Wittgenstein and his relationships to the English philosophers Bertrand Russell and G.E. Moore. The novel is centered on three primary points of Wittgenstein's life: his first years at Cambridge, his service in World War I, and his return to England.

Historical Accuracy: The novel is faithful to the outlines of Wittgenstein's life, and despite the occasional lapses and invention, the story provides a believable portrait.

BILL DUGAN

1756 *Chief Joseph*

Date of Publication: 1992
Subject(s): American West; Indians; Biography, Fictionalized
Historical character(s): Chief Joseph, Indian (Nez Perce), Chieftain; Oliver Otis Howard, Military Personnel (general)
Time Period(s): 19th century (1805-1877)
Locale(s): Washington

Summary: The novel offers a biographical examination of Nez Perce leader Chief Joseph. Called "the Indian Napoleon," Joseph attempts to gain freedom for his people by leading them into Canada, pursued relentlessly by the U.S. Army.

Historical Accuracy: The author admits to altering or ignoring some facts in favor of more significant or dramatic truth.

1757 *Crazy Horse*

Date of Publication: 1992
Subject(s): Battle of the Rosebud; Indians; Biography, Fictionalized
Historical character(s): Crazy Horse, Indian (Sioux), Warrior; George Armstrong Custer, Military Personnel (cavalry officer); Red Cloud, Indian (Sioux), Chieftain
Time Period(s): 19th century (1841-1877)
Locale(s): Black Hills, South Dakota

Summary: This fictionalized biography of Crazy Horse follows his career as a warrior beginning in his early teens. The novel climaxes with his greatest triumph, leading the Sioux in the Battle of the Rosebud, which precedes the destruction of Custer at the Little Bighorn.

Historical Accuracy: The facts of Crazy Horse's life are well-supported and documented with care.

1758 *Geronimo*

Date of Publication: 1994

Subject(s): American West; Indians; Biography, Fictionalized
Historical character(s): Geronimo, Indian (Apache), Chieftain; George C. Crook, Military Personnel (general); Cochise, Indian (Apache), Warrior
Time Period(s): 19th century
Locale(s): Arizona; Fort Sill, Oklahoma; Skeleton Canyon, Mexico

Summary: The novel, part of the author's War Chiefs series, offers a fictional biography of Apache leader Geronimo. The story of his early years is based on multiple stories and legends about his origins and development. Later he wars with the Army and settlers who threaten the Apaches' heritage and homeland.

Historical Accuracy: The novel stays close to the sources, particularly in the later years of Geronimo about which much is known.

1759 *Quanah Parker*

Date of Publication: 1993
Subject(s): American West; Indians; Biography, Fictionalized
Historical character(s): Cynthia Ann Parker, Captive; Peta Nocona, Indian (Comanche), Chieftain; Quanah Parker, Indian (half Comanche), Chieftain
Time Period(s): 19th century (1840s-1890s)
Locale(s): Texas

Summary: This fictional biography of Quanah Parker, the half-Comanche war chief who led the last great Comanche war against the settlers, begins with the story of his mother, Cynthia Ann Parker, who is abducted as a child by the Comanches and becomes the wife of Chieftain Peta Nocona. Quanah is one of two children she bears before being forcibly returned to the white world. Parker rebels against his mother's race and mounts a desperate war against encroachment.

Historical Accuracy: The novel intermixes the factual with the legendary.

1760 *Sitting Bull*

Date of Publication: 1994
Subject(s): American West; Indians; Biography, Fictionalized
Historical character(s): Sitting Bull, Indian (Sioux), Chieftain; Crazy Horse, Indian (Sioux), Warrior; George C. Crook, Military Personnel (general)
Time Period(s): 19th century (1830s-1890s)
Locale(s): Montana; Wyoming

Summary: The life and career of famed Sioux shaman and chieftain Sitting Bull is chronicled. His enormous influence over the Sioux and role in the Indian Wars that produce both the great victory over Custer at the Little Big Horn and the disaster that follows are depicted.

Historical Accuracy: The novel provides a convincing look at Sitting Bull's career that is faithful to the facts.

ALFRED DUGGAN (1903-1964)

Duggan was born in Buenos Aires, Argentina, but grew up in England. He began his writing career in 1950 and produced a series of historical novels and histories for children. Duggan specialized in animating obscure and neglected historical periods and personalities.

1761 *Besieger of Cities*

Date of Publication: 1963
Subject(s): Ancient Greece
Historical character(s): Demetrius I, Ruler (King of Macedonia)
Time Period(s): 3rd century B.C. (294-285 B.C.)
Locale(s): Athens, Greece; Cyprus; Middle East

Summary: The reign of Demetrius I, the so-called Besieger of Cities, is described. His reputation is based on a lifetime of fighting to restore the extensive empire of Alexander the Great. Demetrius is revealed as a fascinating figure caught up in almost continual strife.

Historical Accuracy: Duggan's success lies in making the remote past seem immediate and convincing.

1762 *Children of the Wolf*

Date of Publication: 1959
Subject(s): Myths and Legends; Roman Empire
Fictional character(s): Romulus, Twin; Remus, Twin; Marcus, Military Personnel
Time Period(s): 8th century B.C.
Locale(s): Rome, Roman Empire

Summary: The founding of Rome is Duggan's subject; and he treats the legendary figures of twin brothers Romulus and Remus as actual historical figures. The site of the city is marked out by a ploughshare. Later, the city grows, with the inevitable problems familiar to all urban planners. Romulus proves to be more innovative than Remus when it comes to formulating solutions to Rome's growing pains.

Historical Accuracy: The speculation here is believable. Sabine and Etruscan life is convincingly displayed.

1763 *Conscience of the King*

Date of Publication: 1951
Subject(s): Dark Ages; Biography, Fictionalized; Anglo Saxon Period
Historical character(s): Cedric Elesing, Ruler (Saxon)
Time Period(s): 5th century; 6th century (451-531)
Locale(s): England; Germany

Summary: The story of the Saxon invasion of Britain is told in this fictional autobiography of Cedric Elesing, the founder of Wessex. Elesing, ''Woden-born like all German kings,'' is also part Roman Briton. He joins the invading Saxons and carves out his kingdom following the collapse of the Roman government in Britain.

Historical Accuracy: Duggan bolsters his story with archaeological and scholarly research although not all historians may agree with his interpretations.

1764 *Count Bohemond*

Date of Publication: 1965
Subject(s): Middle Ages; Crusades

Historical character(s): Bohemond, Nobleman; Robert Guiscard, Nobleman; Tancred, Nobleman
Time Period(s): 11th century (1058-1100)
Locale(s): Normandy, France; Greece; Middle East (Antioch, Jerusalem)

Summary: This is the story of the First Crusade and one of its great leaders, Bohemond, son of Robert Guiscard. He is a stalwart and indomitable leader, a master of the military arts and the diplomatic skills necessary to keep together the feuding coalition of allies. The action follows the campaign that conquered Antioch and finally Jerusalem.

Historical Accuracy: Duggan's strength is to make his characters and their era believable.

1765 *The Cunning of the Dove*

Date of Publication: 1960
Subject(s): Royalty—England; Anglo Saxon Period
Fictional character(s): Edgar, Servant (chamberlain to King Edward)
Historical character(s): Edward the Confessor, Ruler (King of England); Godwin, Nobleman (Earl of Wessex); Emma of Normandy, Royalty (mother of Edward the Confessor); William the Conqueror, Nobleman (later William I); Harold, Nobleman (later King of England)
Time Period(s): 11th century (1027-1075)
Locale(s): England

Summary: Duggan offers the story of the reign of Edward the Confessor, one of the last Anglo-Saxon kings of England, whose vow of chastity left the throne without an heir, making the Norman Conquest inevitable. Edward's reign is told from the perspective of Edgar, his chamberlain, who is on hand during the struggle with Earl Godwin for effective control of the country.

Historical Accuracy: Duggan is able to convince the reader what it must have been like to live during these times.

1766 *Family Favorites*

Date of Publication: 1961
Subject(s): Roman Empire; Royalty—Rome
Fictional character(s): Duratius, Military Personnel (praetorian guard)
Historical character(s): Elagabalus, Ruler (Roman emperor)
Time Period(s): 3rd century
Locale(s): Rome, Roman Empire

Summary: The short and decadent reign of the Roman emperor Elagabalus is described from the perspective of Duratius, a member of the Praetorian guard. Elagabalus is named emperor at the age of 14, and his extravagant behavior and the intrigue leading up to his assassination are depicted.

Historical Accuracy: The novel excels in capturing authentically the atmosphere of Rome in decline.

1767 *Knight with Armour*

Date of Publication: 1951
Subject(s): Middle Ages; Crusades
Fictional character(s): Sir Roger, Knight
Time Period(s): 11th century (1096-1099)

Locale(s): Palestine; Sussex, England

Summary: Sir Roger, a Norman knight, participates in the First Crusade. The military campaign trail takes him to Nicaea, Dorylaeum, Anatolia, and Antioch before the final assault on Jerusalem.

Historical Accuracy: The novel features a genuine look at period life.

1768 *The Lady for Ransom*

Date of Publication: 1954
Subject(s): Middle Ages; Byzantine Empire; Battle of Manzikent
Fictional character(s): Roussel de Balliol, Knight; Matilda, Spouse (of Balliol), Gentlewoman; Roger fitzOdo, Knight
Historical character(s): Romanus Diogenes, Ruler (Byzantine emperor); Alexius I Comnenus, Ruler (Byzantine emperor)
Time Period(s): 11th century (1070s)
Locale(s): Asia Minor; Constantinople, Byzantine Empire

Summary: This is a tale of Norman mercenaries who fight against the Turks for the tottering Byzantine Empire in the 11th century. Roussel de Balliol is convinced by his ambitious and practical wife to join an expedition against the Turks which becomes the decisive Battle of Manzikert in 1071, which broke the power of the Eastern Roman Empire. Roussel finds himself the victim of shifting power in Constantinople and lacking his wife's cunning and resolution.

Historical Accuracy: The author stays close to the actual facts, letting fancy take over only when his evident close research supplies no answers.

1769 *Leopards and Lilies*

Date of Publication: 1954
Subject(s): Middle Ages; Royalty—England
Fictional character(s): Margaret Fitz-Gerold, Gentlewoman; Count de Redvers, Nobleman; Falkes de Brealte, Knight
Historical character(s): Simon de Montfort, Military Personnel, Nobleman; John, Ruler (King of England)
Time Period(s): 13th century (1215-1252)
Locale(s): England; France

Summary: Margaret, the ambitious daughter of King John's chamberlain, weds Count de Redvers. On his death she comes to John's court and marries Falkes de Brealte, the captain of the king's crossbowmen. She joins him in the Angevin cause in the war of succession and is enmeshed in the intrigue it created.

Historical Accuracy: Duggan's portrait of medieval life at court is authentic and revealing.

1770 *The Little Emperors*

Date of Publication: 1953
Subject(s): Roman Empire
Fictional character(s): Caius Sempronius Felix, Government Official
Time Period(s): 5th century (407)
Locale(s): England

Summary: Roman civil servant Caius Sempronius Felix attempts to hold the empire together despite Britain's being cut off by the German conquest of Gaul and the political intrigue that produces three British emperors.

Historical Accuracy: The novel provides a remarkable and convincing portrait of the decline of Roman power in Britain.

1771 *Lord Geoffrey's Fancy*

Date of Publication: 1962
Subject(s): Middle Ages; Crusades
Fictional character(s): William de Briwerr, Knight; Geoffrey de Bruyere, Nobleman, Knight
Time Period(s): 13th century (1254-1272)
Locale(s): Greece; Constantinople, Byzantine Empire

Summary: Set during the Fourth Crusade, the novel offers a portrait of feudal life among the Frankish knights as they defend their captured land from the Byzantines. Lord Geoffrey, described here by his vassal, William, as "the best knight in all Romanie," is imprisoned in Constantinople and tried for treason and adultery.

Historical Accuracy: Duggan's picture of medieval customs and personalities is consistently believable as well as entertaining.

1772 *My Life for My Sheep*

Date of Publication: 1955
Subject(s): Middle Ages; Biography, Fictionalized; Religious Life
Historical character(s): Thomas Becket, Religious (archbishop of Canterbury); Henry II, Ruler (King of England); Philip II, Ruler (King of France); Alexander III, Religious (pope)
Time Period(s): 12th century (1118-1170)
Locale(s): England; France

Summary: This fictional biography of Thomas Becket applies Duggan's skill as a novelist to imagine scenes and thoughts for which there are no historical or documented evidence. He tells the story of Thomas' rise as knight and lawyer, his friendship with Henry II, and their epic falling out over the perogatives of church and state.

Historical Accuracy: Duggan is thorough in his presentation of the period and the issues as well as fair and balanced in his interpretation.

1773 *The Right Line of Cedric*

Date of Publication: 1961
Subject(s): Anglo Saxon Period; Royalty—England
Historical character(s): Alfred the Great, Ruler (King of Wessex); Ethelwulf, Ruler (King of Wessex); Leo IV, Religious (pope); Ethelred I, Ruler (King of Wessex)
Time Period(s): 9th century (858-899)
Locale(s): Rome, Italy; Canterbury, England; Winchester, England

Summary: Duggan here chronicles the life of Alfred the Great, King of Wessex. Originally only the fourth son of Ethelwulf, Alfred becomes a leading and unifying force among the feuding Saxon kingdoms.

Historical Accuracy: Duggan recreates this remote period of English history so that the era is clearly shown and the personalities are brought compellingly to life.

1774 *Three's Company*

Date of Publication: 1958
Subject(s): Roman Empire; Politics; Assassination
Historical character(s): Marc Antony, Military Personnel, Political Figure; Caius Julius Caesar Octavianus, Military Personnel, Political Figure; Marcus Aemilius Lepidus, Military Personnel, Political Figure; Gaius Julius Caesar, Ruler, Military Personnel
Time Period(s): 1st century B.C. (78-13 B.C.)
Locale(s): Rome, Roman Empire; Gaul; Africa

Summary: In the vacuum that follows the assassination of Julius Caesar, a triumvirate of Antony, Octavius, and Lepidus emerges to punish the conspirators and rule the Empire. Duggan focuses on Lepidus, the least known of the trio, whose career is chronicled as Roman noble, the most important civil magistrate of Rome, and the man whom both Antony and Octavius trust. Lepidus' failures of leadership illustrate a capable man pushed beyond the limits of his abilities.

Historical Accuracy: Duggan's reconstruction of the politics, customs, and personalities is remarkable.

1775 *Winter Quarters*

Date of Publication: 1956
Subject(s): Roman Empire; Military Life
Fictional character(s): Camillus, Military Personnel; Acco, Military Personnel; Publius Crassus, Military Personnel
Time Period(s): 2nd century B.C.
Locale(s): Rome, Roman Empire; Greece; Middle East

Summary: The novel offers a foot-soldier's view of the Roman Empire in the days when Caesar, Crassus, and Pompey competed for conquest and control. Camillus and Acco are two Gauls who follow the Roman army from Germany to Rome to Syria where an ill-considered war against the Parthians results in disaster.

Historical Accuracy: The details of military life are convincingly drawn, as are the beliefs and attitudes of two of the Empire's citizens.

ANN DUKTHAS
(PSEUD. OF P.C. DOHERTY)

1776 *The Prince Lost to Time*

Date of Publication: 1995
Subject(s): French Revolution; Mystery
Fictional character(s): Nicholas Segalla, Immortal, Scholar
Historical character(s): Louis Charles, Royalty (dauphin); Marie Antoinette, Royalty (queen consort of Louis XVI); Napoleon Bonaparte, Military Personnel (officer)
Time Period(s): 1790s (1793); 1810s (1815)
Locale(s): Paris, France

Summary: In the second mystery featuring the immortal Nicholas Segalla, Nicholas attempts to solve one of history's

greatest mysteries: what became of the lost Dauphin, Louis Charles. Segalla discovers the fate of Louis XVII in a mystery shrouded by violence and secrets at the heart of revolutionary France.

Historical Accuracy: The novel's solution to the historical puzzle is speculative but plausible, backed by evident research and a solid grounding in the period and its events.

1777 *A Time for the Death of a King*

Date of Publication: 1994
Subject(s): Mystery; Royalty—Scotland
Fictional character(s): Nicholas Segalla, Immortal, Scholar (Jesuit priest)
Historical character(s): Mary Stuart, Ruler (Queen of Scotland); Henry Stewart, Nobleman (Lord Darnley); James Hepburn, Nobleman (Earl of Bothwell)
Time Period(s): 16th century (1567)
Locale(s): Scotland; Dublin, Ireland; Paris, France

Summary: This novel takes up the historical mystery of who killed Lord Darnley, the dissolute husband of Mary, Queen of Scots. The investigator is Nicholas Segalla, a mysterious, possibly immortal, scholar who is a Jesuit priest in Mary's time. Segalla uncovers answers to questions that have baffled historians since the 16th century: How was Darnley killed? Was Mary Stuart a murderess? And who wrote the damning Casket Letters?.

Historical Accuracy: This is an ingenious mystery with some provocative speculations. Grounded in fact, the novel's solutions are imaginary.

1778 *The Time of Murder at Mayerling*

Date of Publication: 1996
Subject(s): Mystery; Hapsburg Empire
Fictional character(s): Nicholas Segalla, Immortal, Scholar
Historical character(s): Franz Josef I, Ruler (Austrian emperor)
Time Period(s): 1890s
Locale(s): Austria

Summary: Based on an actual historical mystery, the novel sends the immortal Nicholas Segalla to the decadent court of the Hapsburgs in the late 19th century. There he investigates the apparent murder-suicide of the Archduke Rudolph and his mistress, while the emperor and his agents destroy crucial evidence that could reveal a deeper plot.

Historical Accuracy: The novel makes ingenious use of the details of the death of Archduke Rudolph, but the conclusions reached are speculative.

ALEXANDRE DUMAS (1802-1870)

Dumas was the son of Napoleon's famous mulatto general. He was largely self-educated and traded on his gifts for storytelling to pursue a writing career. His first successes were historical dramas; he achieved his greatest success with *The Three Musketeers* and its sequels. Scorned by critics as lacking in style and depth of characterization, his novels have been enormously popular for generations and translated into nearly every language. Dumas set the pattern for the historical adventure novel.

1779 *Les Quarant Cinq*

Date of Publication: 1894
Subject(s): Royalty—France
Fictional character(s): Crillon, Military Personnel (French soldier)
Historical character(s): Henri III, Ruler (King of France); Catherine de' Medici, Royalty (queen consort of Henri II)
Time Period(s): 16th century (1585-1586)
Locale(s): Paris, France

Summary: The title refers the guardsmen of French King Henri III, and the novel dramatizes his turbulent reign and the ambitions of his mother, Catherine de Medici. The story begins with the execution of a convicted murderer who provided Henri with evidence of the innocence of the Guises, which the king ignored. The novel follows the tangled plot of conspiracy and betrayal.

Historical Accuracy: The story is invented but relies on a believable portrait of the era and its central figures.

1780 *Queen Margot*

Date of Publication: 1845
Subject(s): Royalty—France; Saint Bartholomew's Day Massacre
Historical character(s): Marguerite de Valois, Royalty (queen consort of Henri IV); Henri IV, Ruler (King of France); Catherine de' Medici, Royalty (queen consort of Henri II); Charles IX, Ruler (King of France); Henri of Anjou, Royalty (King of France)
Time Period(s): 16th century (1570s)
Locale(s): France

Summary: The background of this story is the political intrigue and religious conflict initiated by the marriage in 1572 between Marguerite de Valois and Henri IV of France. Marguerite, Charles IX's sister and the daughter of Henri II and Catherine de Medici, is a Catholic. Henri is a Protestant, and the wedding produces the infamous Saint Bartholomew's Day Massacre in which thousands of Protestants are killed. The novel is a nonstop adventure story of intrigue and power politics featuring poisonings, assassination, romance, pomp, and ceremony.

Historical Accuracy: Dumas is a master of mixing romantic adventure with historical events. Readers should be cautioned not to accept his version of history as reliable.

1781 *The Queen's Necklace*

Date of Publication: 1848
Subject(s): Royalty—France
Fictional character(s): Philippe de Taverney, Courtier; Andree de Taverney, Courtier; Count de Charny, Military Personnel (naval officer)
Historical character(s): Marie Antoinette, Royalty (Queen of France); Louis de Rohan, Religious (cardinal), Political Figure; Jeanne de la Motte, Noblewoman, Adventurer; Count

Alessandro Cagliostro, Adventurer, Nobleman; Franz Anton Mesmer, Doctor
Time Period(s): 1780s
Locale(s): France

Summary: The novel provides a fictional retelling of the affair of the diamond necklace, in which Marie Antoinette was the target of court intrigue perpetrated by her enemies. A young woman resembling the queen is persuaded to impersonate her to purchase, but not pay for, an expensive diamond necklace, and to dupe Cardinal de Rohan into an amorous adventure with the false queen. The result is a royal scandal surrounding Marie Antoinette.

Historical Accuracy: The affair of the diamond necklace and the ensuing scandal is said to have been a contributing factor to the negative attitude of the public toward the monarchy during the last few years before the French Revolution. The actual details are blended with Dumas' inventions.

1782 *The Three Musketeers*

Date of Publication: 1844
Subject(s): Royalty—France
Fictional character(s): D'Artagnan, Military Personnel (musketeer in training); Athos, Military Personnel (musketeer); Porthos, Military Personnel (musketeer); Aramis, Military Personnel (musketeer); Milady de Winter, Spy; Rochefort, Nobleman (count)
Historical character(s): Armand-Jean Du Plessis, Religious (Cardinal Richelieu), Political Figure (Duc de Richelieu); Louis XIII, Ruler (King of France); Anne of Austria, Royalty (queen consort of Louis XIII); George Villiers, Nobleman (Duke of Buckingham), Courtier
Time Period(s): 17th century (1620s)
Locale(s): Paris, France; La Rochelle, France; England

Summary: While training to become a musketeer, the young, clever Gascon D'Artagnan joins forces with Athos, Porthos, and Aramis to save the queen's honor from a trap set by the scheming Cardinal Richelieu. Their adversaries include the arrogant Count Rochefort and the malevolent Milady de Winter.

Historical Accuracy: Fiction and romance are interwoven with such historical events as the siege of La Rochelle and the murder of Buckingham, all reworked into a fast-paced adventure and a classic historical romance.

1783 *Twenty Years After*

Date of Publication: 1845
Subject(s): Civil War—England; Royalty—France; The Fronde
Fictional character(s): D'Artagnan, Military Personnel (King's Musketeers); Athos, Veteran (King's Musketeers); Porthos, Veteran (King's Musketeers); Aramis, Veteran (King's Musketeers), Nobleman; Raoul de Bragelonne, Nobleman (viscount)
Historical character(s): Jules Mazarin, Religious (cardinal), Political Figure; Anne of Austria, Royalty (queen regent of France); Charles I, Ruler (King of England); Francois de Vendome de Bourbon, Courtier (Duc de Beaufort), Leader

(Frondist); Oliver Cromwell, Political Figure; Henrietta-Maria, Royalty (queen consort of Charles I)
Time Period(s): 17th century (1648)
Locale(s): Paris, France

Summary: Twenty years after the events of *The Three Musketeers* D'Artagnan, Athos, Porthos, and Aramis are swept up in new adventures concerning the Fronde, a revolt of the masses and the nobles against Cardinal Mazarin and the royal family. They also attempt to foil Oliver Cromwell's plot to capture and execute King Charles I. Aiding Cromwell in his political machinations is the son of the vicious Milady De Winter, who has sworn vengeance on the four men who murdered his mother.

Historical Accuracy: The Fronde and Cromwell's overthrow of the monarchy are historical fact, but the book is riddled with inaccuracies as to the dates when some events actually occurred, such as the attaining of Louis XIV's majority and a battle fought by Charles I that took place three years earlier than reported. Mazarin is also characterized as having no virtues, only vices, when he actually achieved much greatness during his tenure as France's first minister.

DAVID DUNCAN (1913-)

Born in Montana, Duncan worked for the U.S. Department of Agriculture, as a field director of the American Red Cross, and as a labor economist. He is the author of 15 screenplays, including an adaptation of H.G. Wells' *The Time Machine*.

1784 *The Trumpet of God*

Date of Publication: 1956
Subject(s): Middle Ages; Crusades; Children's Crusade
Fictional character(s): Ulric, Teenager
Time Period(s): 13th century (1212)
Locale(s): Europe

Summary: The novel dramatizes the story of the Children's Crusade to liberate the Holy Land. It relates the events of the ill-fated pilgrimage as well as the background of peasant life in the feudal villages. According to this analysis, the desire to escape the bleak prospects for the average person may have provided as much of the incentive for the Crusade as did religious zeal.

Historical Accuracy: The novel achieves a high degree of authenticity and realism in its presentation of the events and the social background of the period.

HARLEY DUNCAN

1785 *West of Appomattox*

Date of Publication: 1961
Subject(s): Civil War—U.S.; American West
Fictional character(s): Dan Kilbourne, Military Personnel (Confederate soldier), Veteran; Jane Morgan, Young Woman; Mavis Todd, Southern Belle
Historical character(s): Joseph Orville Shelby, Military Personnel (Confederate general)
Time Period(s): 1860s (1865)

Locale(s): San Antonio, Texas; Mexico

Summary: This is the story of the Confederate Iron Brigade under General Joseph Shelby. Shelby leads his group of volunteers on a march to Mexico to avoid surrendering at the end of the Civil War. The novel dramatizes the story of some members of the Brigade and their adventures in Mexico as they attempt to keep their cause and the past alive.

Historical Accuracy: The situation is based on historical facts.

THOMAS WILLIAM DUNCAN
(1905-1985)

Born in Iowa, Duncan graduated from Harvard University. A reporter, feature writer, and book reviewer for the *Des Moines Register* and the *Des Moines Tribune*, Duncan was a professor of English at Grinnell College and became a full-time writer in 1944.

1786 *Big River, Big Man*

Date of Publication: 1959
Subject(s): Business Building; Civil War—U.S.
Fictional character(s): Jim Buckmaster, Frontiersman; Caleb McSwasey, Businessman; Rolfe Torkelsen, Immigrant, Lawyer
Time Period(s): 19th century
Locale(s): Wisconsin; New Mexico; New England

Summary: This massive novel sprawls across America describing western and business expansion in the 19th century. The novel begins with a depiction of the lumber industry on the Upper Mississippi and the careers of three "big men"—Jim Buckmaster, Caleb McSwasey, and Rolfe Torkelsen—who are launched on a pursuit of power. The novel concludes with events of the Civil War.

Historical Accuracy: The novel covers so much ground in telling its story that there are a number of hits and misses in capturing the era and its preoccupations.

1787 *The Labyrinth*

Date of Publication: 1967
Subject(s): Rural Life—U.S.
Fictional character(s): Hugo Wickett, Editor; Spicy Dawson, Young Woman
Time Period(s): 1890s (1897)
Locale(s): Litchfield, Iowa

Summary: This is a tale of small town life in Iowa at the end of the 19th century and the ramifications that arise when newspaper editor Hugo Wickett marries Spicy Dawson.

Historical Accuracy: The historical background of actual events and a genuine period atmosphere provide a convincing look at Midwestern life in the 19th century.

1788 *The Sky and Tomorrow*

Date of Publication: 1974
Subject(s): World War I; Aviation
Fictional character(s): Mark Cockfoster, Pilot
Time Period(s): 1910s (1910-1919)

Locale(s): Iowa; California

Summary: Mark Cockfoster dreams of flying from a young age. He builds a plane and learns to fly, participating in the early years of aviation as a barnstormer and a stunt pilot. When World War I begins, he learns other uses for his airplane and becomes haunted by friends and family lost and killed.

Historical Accuracy: This is a richly detailed evocation of early aviation and small town midwestern life of the period.

KATHARINE DUNLAP

Born in Washington, D.C., dunlap attended private school and earned a diploma from the Sorbonne. She is a recipient of the French Legion of Honor and is the author of several novels, including *Lady Be Good*, *The Glory and the Dream*, and *Twice the New Moon*.

1789 *The Glory and the Dream*

Date of Publication: 1951
Subject(s): Theatrical Life
Historical character(s): Adrienne Lecouvreur, Actress; Maurice, Comte de Saxe, Military Personnel, Nobleman
Time Period(s): 1730s
Locale(s): France

Summary: This is a fictional account of the love affair between French actress Adrienne Lecouvreur and nobleman and military leader Comte de Saxe, one of the greatest French generals of his age. The liaison ends tragically with Lecouvreur's death by poisoning.

Historical Accuracy: The novel is authentic in its presentation of the factual details.

CAROLA DUNN (1946-)

An English writer born in London, Dunn attended Victoria University in Manchester and has worked as a secretary, sales clerk, bookkeeper, market research interviewer, construction worker, and building designer. Dunn began writing with the determination to produce better romance novels than those she had read. Her romances are marked by extensive research in which she is very particular about every detail.

1790 *Angel*

Date of Publication: 1984
Subject(s): Regency Romance; Identity—Concealed
Fictional character(s): Evangelina Brenthaven, Gentlewoman (aka Evelyn Brand); Elizabeth Markham, Gentlewoman; Dominic Markham, Nobleman, Military Personnel (army officer)
Time Period(s): 1800s
Locale(s): Lake District, England

Summary: Lady Evangelina Brenthaven, convinced that all her suitors are only interested in her fortune, goes in disguise as plain Evelyn Brand for a summer in the Lake District. There she spends her time assisting in the courtship of her new friend, Elizabeth Markham, but soon finds herself in the middle of arrangements that she has difficulty controlling.

Historical Accuracy: This romantic story does provide some convincing regional and period details.

1791   *The Black Sheep's Daughter*

Date of Publication: 1989
Subject(s): Regency Romance
Fictional character(s): Teresa Danville, Gentlewoman; Andrew Graylin, Gentleman; Muriel Parr, Gentlewoman
Time Period(s): 19th century (Regency period)
Locale(s): Costa Rica; England

Summary: This unusually situated Regency romance begins in Costa Rica where Teresa Danville has grown up on her father's coffee plantation. She now accompanies Sir Andrew Graylin back to England for her debut. They experience adventures on the way, and Teresa is a major social sensation, due to her individuality and independence. Graylin is affianced to proper Muriel Parr, but Teresa's attractions are formidable.

Historical Accuracy: The novel's setting is a refreshing change and seemingly authentic.

1792   *The Frog Earl*

Date of Publication: 1992
Subject(s): Regency Romance; Identity—Concealed
Fictional character(s): Simon Hurst, Servant (gamekeeper), Nobleman (earl); Lakshmi Lassiter, Royalty (princess)
Time Period(s): 19th century (Regency period)
Locale(s): England

Summary: Simon Hurst is an earl in disguise. Weary of the London marriage market, he has become his aunt's gamekeeper. The Princess Lakshmi is unlikely to exchange kisses with a servant but such is the case in a bargain for the return of her bracelet.

Historical Accuracy: The story is a fairytale rather than a realistic depiction of the period.

1793   *Lady in the Briars*

Date of Publication: 1990
Subject(s): Regency Romance; Russian Empire
Fictional character(s): Rebecca Parr, Young Woman; Teresa Graylin, Gentlewoman; John Danville, Nobleman
Time Period(s): 1810s; 1820s (1819-1820)
Locale(s): St. Petersburg, Russia

Summary: Rebecca Parr accompanies her friend Teresa Graylin and her diplomat husband to St. Petersburg. Lord John Danville has arranged the trip to be near her. She, however, is more interested in Russian affairs and gets herself embroiled in intrigue which lands her in the Peter Paul fortress, an occasion for Lord John's heroics.

Historical Accuracy: The story is a rare departure for the genre, as it is set outside society London. The Russian scenes are well-described.

1794   *Lavender Lady*

Date of Publication: 1983
Subject(s): Regency Romance
Fictional character(s): Hester Godric, Gentlewoman; David Fairfax, Nobleman (earl)
Time Period(s): 19th century (Regency period)
Locale(s): Henley, England; London, England

Summary: After a coaching accident, David Fairfax recuperates in the comfort of the Godric family. The family of orphans is run by the sensible Hester. David neglects to inform the family that he is an earl. After involving himself in the Godric's domestic affairs and falling in love with middle-class Hester, Fairfax leaves, certain he will forget her. However, they are destined to meet again.

Historical Accuracy: This lively romantic story is informed by solid details of the domestic habits of the period.

1795   *Lord Iverbrook's Heir*

Date of Publication: 1986
Subject(s): Regency Romance; Inheritance—Disputed
Fictional character(s): Hugh Carrick, Nobleman (Viscount Iverbrook); Selena Whitton, Gentlewoman; Peter Carrick, Orphan, Child
Time Period(s): 19th century (Regency period)
Locale(s): England

Summary: Viscount Iverbrook returns from Jamaica determined to claim his brother's son and install him in the family estate. The boy, Peter, is under the guardianship of Selena Whitton who is just as determined to keep the child. Iverbrook is slowly swept up in the Whitton family, and Selena finds herself falling in love with him. A series of crises involving young Peter bring them together.

Historical Accuracy: There are many period touches that help establish the novel's era.

1796   *Miss Hartwell's Dilemma*

Date of Publication: 1988
Subject(s): Regency Romance
Fictional character(s): Amaryllis Hartwell, Gentlewoman, Student; Bertram Pomeroy, Nobleman, Heir; Daniel Winterbourne, Nobleman
Time Period(s): 19th century (Regency period)
Locale(s): England

Summary: Amaryllis Hartwell's dilemma is between two suitors, dashing Lord Pomeroy and dark, brooding Lord Winterbourne. In addition, her father, who is under a pall of scandal, is threatening to reappear in her life, and a sinister-looking Spaniard has been seen lurking about her school. All must be dealt with.

Historical Accuracy: This is fairly standard romantic fair with some authentic period touches.

1797   *Two Corinthians*

Date of Publication: 1989
Subject(s): Regency Romance

Fictional character(s): Bertram Pomeroy, Nobleman, Heir; Claire Sutton, Gentlewoman; George Winterbourne, Gentleman

Time Period(s): 19th century (Regency period)

Locale(s): England

Summary: In this complicated courtship tangle, Lord Bertram Pomeroy, recently rejected by Amaryllis (in *Miss Hartwell's Dilemma*), has decided on Claire Sutton. Claire's sister is interested in George Winterbourne, brother to Amaryllis' fiance. George, however, becomes attracted to Claire, while Bertram grows fond of another. The elaborate mating dance gets sorted out eventually.

Historical Accuracy: The emphasis is on the romantic tangle, but there are some convincing period touches.

OLAV DUNN (1876-1939)

Norwegian author Dunn's books include *The Big Wedding*.

1798 *The People of Juvik*

Date of Publication: 1923

Subject(s): Family Saga; Rural Life—Norway

Fictional character(s): Per Anders Juvika, Landowner, Farmer; Anders Haaberg, Farmer; Odin Setran, Carpenter

Time Period(s): 19th century; 20th century (1800-1918)

Locale(s): Norway

Summary: *The People of Juvik* is a family chronicle of more than six generations of Norwegian life made up of six novels: *The Trough of the Wave*, *The Blind Man*, *The Big Wedding*, *Odin in Fairyland*, *Odin Grows Up*, and *The Storm*. The novels are filled with local color, superstition, customs, crafts, and daily routine of rural life.

Historical Accuracy: The language Dunn uses is that of the common people of Norway which helps establish the novels' realistic background.

DOROTHY DUNNETT (1923-)

A Scottish author of historical novels and thrillers, Dunnett worked in the British Civil Service and was a successful professional portrait painter. Her historical novels have been consistently cited as models of the genre for their painstaking research and re-creation of the past.

1799 *Checkmate*

Date of Publication: 1975

Subject(s): Tudor Period; Royalty—Scotland

Fictional character(s): Francis Crawford, Adventurer (aka Lymond); Philippa Somerville, Gentlewoman

Historical character(s): Mary, Queen of Scots, Ruler (Queen of Scotland)

Time Period(s): 16th century (1550s)

Locale(s): Lyon, France

Summary: Francis Crawford's concluding adventure takes place in the middle of a whirlwind of conspiracy in the French court. Mary, Queen of Scots becomes a pawn in a much larger power play between France and England. Crawford must settle things with his brother and his estranged wife, Philippa.

Historical Accuracy: This is an adult adventure tale with convincing historical background and psychologically realistic characters.

1800 *The Disorderly Knights*

Date of Publication: 1966

Subject(s): Tudor Period; Royalty—Scotland

Fictional character(s): Francis Crawford, Adventurer (aka Lymond)

Historical character(s): Cormac O'Connor, Chieftain

Time Period(s): 16th century (1551-1552)

Locale(s): Scotland; Malta; Tripoli, Libya

Summary: In the third novel of the Lymond saga, Francis Crawford journeys to Malta where the Turkish fleet has orders to destroy the Christian bastion, home of the Knights of the Order of St. John. The Order is wracked by internal division and corruption, and Lymond's life and reputation are endangered.

Historical Accuracy: The attacks on Malta and Tripoli are factual.

1801 *The Game of Kings*

Date of Publication: 1961

Subject(s): Tudor Period; Royalty—Scotland

Fictional character(s): Francis Crawford, Adventurer (aka Lymond); Christian Stewart, Gentleman; Richard Crawford, Nobleman (Baron Cutler)

Historical character(s): Mary, Queen of Scots, Ruler (Queen of Scotland); Mary of Guise, Royalty (queen of James V of Scotland), Widow(er); Edward Seymour, Nobleman (Duke of Somerset)

Time Period(s): 16th century (1547)

Locale(s): Scotland

Summary: This is the first of the author's Lymond series, which chronicles the life of Francis Crawford of Lymond in the 16th century. Crawford is a soldier, a former galley slave, and a mercenary who returns home a proclaimed traitor with a price on his head. He finds himself in the middle of a feud with his brother, border skirmishes, and conspiracies aimed against the child-queen, Mary.

Historical Accuracy: The novel is a remarkable combination of stirring adventure, reliable history, and period details.

1802 *King Hereafter*

Date of Publication: 1982

Subject(s): Middle Ages; Royalty—Scotland; Vikings

Historical character(s): Macbeth, Ruler (King of Scotland); Harold Harefoot, Ruler (King of England); Canute, Ruler (of England, Denmark, Norway); Groa, Royalty (queen consort of Macbeth); Duncan I, Ruler (King of Scotland); Edward the Confessor, Ruler (King of England); Lady Godiva, Noblewoman

Time Period(s): 11th century

Locale(s): Scotland

Summary: The author removes the tale of the Scottish king Macbeth from the influence of Shakespeare's play, to offer a different, far more accurate historical figure. Macbeth rules the Orkney Islands and begins to forge a Scottish kingdom with his wife Groa, to whom he is devoted. The novel is a vast panorama of life and politics in the 11th century with many historical characters appearing.

Historical Accuracy: The novel blends fact and legend into a vivid and convincing historical portrait of the age.

1803 *Niccolo Rising*

Date of Publication: 1986
Subject(s): Renaissance; Business Building
Fictional character(s): Marian de Charetty, Widow(er), Businesswoman; Claes vander Poele, Ward (aka Nicholas or Niccolo), Apprentice
Historical character(s): Louis, Royalty (French dauphin), Heir (of Charles VII); Cosimo de' Medici, Financier
Time Period(s): 15th century (1450s–1460s)
Locale(s): Bruges, Belgium; Italy; Switzerland

Summary: This first volume of the House of Niccolo series begins in 1459 in Bruges and concerns a trading company headed by a widow, Marian de Charetty. Her apprentice is the wily Claes, who is forever getting into trouble in this center of trade, gossip, and spying. He becomes the confidential messenger for the Medicis and the Dauphin of France in an increasingly complex series of schemes and counter-schemes.

Historical Accuracy: The era is richly and authentically detailed in this sweeping blend of suspense and action with a vivid historical background.

1804 *Pawn in Frankincense*

Date of Publication: 1969
Subject(s): Tudor Period; Ottoman Empire
Fictional character(s): Francis Crawford, Adventurer (aka Lymond); Oonagh O'Dwyer, Captive; Graham Reid Mallett, Gentleman
Historical character(s): Suleiman I, Ruler (Ottoman sultan)
Time Period(s): 16th century (1550s)
Locale(s): *Dauphine*, At Sea (Mediterranean); Constantinople, Ottoman Empire

Summary: In the fourth of Dunnett's novels chronicling the adventures of Francis Crawford of Lymond, Lymond is the special envoy of the King of France to the Sultan of the Ottoman Empire. The official mission, however, is only a pretext for a more personal one. Graham Mallett is holding Crawford's illegitimate son and his mother captive, and Crawford tracks them down across the Mediterranean in the middle of the conflict between Muslims and Christians.

Historical Accuracy: The story is an ingenious adventure with solid details of the period.

1805 *Queen's Play*

Date of Publication: 1964
Subject(s): Tudor Period; Royalty—Scotland; Royalty—France
Fictional character(s): Francis Crawford, Adventurer (aka Lymond); Richard Crawford, Nobleman (Baron Cutler)
Historical character(s): Mary of Guise, Royalty (queen of James V of Scotland), Widow(er); Mary, Queen of Scots,

Ruler (Queen of Scotland); Henri II, Ruler (King of France); Catherine de' Medici, Royalty (Queen of France); Francois, Royalty (dauphin of France)
Time Period(s): 16th century (1550)
Locale(s): Scotland; France; England

Summary: In the second volume of Dunnett's Lymond saga, Francis Crawford is sent by Mary of Guise to France to protect the child-queen Mary from harm from various conspirators. He makes his way to the most treacherous court in Europe where he is the target of several adversaries while Mary's life hangs in the balance.

Historical Accuracy: Dunnett provides breathless adventure rooted in exhaustive research and a solid grasp of the period.

1806 *Race of Scorpions*

Date of Publication: 1990
Subject(s): Renaissance; Business Building
Fictional character(s): Nicholas vander Poele, Adventurer, Businessman; Tobias Beventini, Doctor
Historical character(s): Carlotta de Lusignon, Royalty (daughter of John II of Cyprus); James de Lusignan, Royalty, Bastard Son (of John II of Cyprus)
Time Period(s): 15th century (1460s)
Locale(s): Venice, Italy; Genoa, Italy; Cyprus

Summary: Nicholas, now a widower living in Venice, becomes involved in a bitter and ruthless power struggle in Cyprus among the royals, who are known to their people as the race of scorpions. As in the past, Nicholas is ever-resourceful in love, danger, and intrigue.

Historical Accuracy: The historical background is solidly grounded and is not sacrificed in the interest of the novel's adventure.

1807 *The Ringed Castle*

Date of Publication: 1971
Subject(s): Tudor Period; Royalty—Russia; Royalty—England
Fictional character(s): Francis Crawford, Adventurer (aka Lymond); Philippa Somerville, Gentlewoman
Historical character(s): Ivan the Terrible, Ruler (Czar of Russia); Osep Grigorievich Nepeda, Diplomat; Mary I, Ruler (Queen of England)
Time Period(s): 16th century (1556-1557)
Locale(s): Moscow, Russia; Scotland; London, England

Summary: In the fifth of the author's Lymond saga, Francis Crawford is in Moscow as the right hand man of Czar Ivan. He is training the Czar's army and administering rough justice to Ivan's enemies. In England, his wife, Philippa, awaits the annullment of their marriage in the court of Bloody Mary. The two meet again when Crawford joins the first diplomatic envoys from Russia to the English court.

Historical Accuracy: Dunnett delivers the period details of Czarist Russia as convincingly as she does those of the Tudor court.

1808 *Scales of Gold*

Date of Publication: 1992

Subject(s): Renaissance; Business Building
Fictional character(s): Nicholas vander Poele, Adventurer, Businessman; Gelis van Borselen, Gentlewoman; Godscale of Cologne, Religious (chaplain)
Time Period(s): 15th century (1464-1468)
Locale(s): Venice, Italy; Timbuktu, Mali

Summary: In Venice, unknown enemies threaten Nicholas vander Poele's banking and trading company. To secure his fortune, Nicholas sets sail for Africa. With him is Gelis van Borselen, who holds Nicholas responsible for the death of her sister. Together they experience a series of hair-raising adventures as they reach exotic Timbuktu.

Historical Accuracy: The novel is a rousing adventure anchored by solid period details so richly textured that they convince the reader of the story's authenticity.

`1809` The Spring of the Ram

Date of Publication: 1988
Subject(s): Renaissance; Business Building; Byzantine Empire
Fictional character(s): Nicholas vander Poele, Adventurer, Businessman; Marian de Charetty, Widow(er), Businesswoman; Catherine de Charetty, Young Woman
Historical character(s): Cosimo de' Medici, Financier
Time Period(s): 15th century (1460s)
Locale(s): Bruges, Belgium; Florence, Italy; Byzantine Empire

Summary: Nicholas vander Poele, bastard, apprentice, rogue, code-breaker, and confidential messenger to the Medicis and the Dauphin of France, is now married to his former employer, Marian de Charetty. Having placed her company in jeopardy, he flees Bruges for Florence, eventually venturing to the terminus of the silk route. Trouble mars his voyage, but this is only a prelude to the intrigue he must face when he reaches his destination.

Historical Accuracy: The novel features a historically accurate sense of period and personalities, which is not sacrificed in the interest of the novel's considerable adventure.

`1810` To Lie with Lions

Date of Publication: 1996
Subject(s): Renaissance
Fictional character(s): Nicholas vander Poele, Banker; Gelis van Borselen, Gentlewoman (wife of Nicholas)
Historical character(s): James de Lusignan, Ruler (King of Jerusalem); James III, Ruler (King of Scotland); Louis XI, Ruler (King of France); Charles, Duke of Burgundy, Nobleman
Time Period(s): 15th century (1470s)
Locale(s): Venice, Italy; Edinburgh, Scotland; Cyprus

Summary: The ninth installment of the House of Niccolo saga continues the story of banker, soldier of fortune, and secret agent, Nicholas Vander Poele (aka Nicholas de Fleury). He engages in a battle of wits with his wife, Gelis van Borselen, and in diplomatic missions for Louis XI, Scotland's James III, and Charles of Burgundy. One diplomatic mission takes him to Cyprus.

Historical Accuracy: The novel's adventures are placed against a solidly documented period background.

`1811` The Unicorn Hunt

Date of Publication: 1994
Subject(s): Renaissance; Business Building
Fictional character(s): Nicholas vander Poele, Adventurer, Businessman
Historical character(s): James III, Ruler (King of Scotland); Edward IV, Ruler (King of England); Louis XI, Ruler (King of France)
Time Period(s): 15th century (1468-1471)
Locale(s): Europe (Flanders, Tyrol, Venice); Edinburgh, Scotland; Middle East (Egypt, Sinai, Cyprus)

Summary: Nicholas vander Poele returns from his adventures in Africa and begins to build a new trading empire in Edinburgh. When his new wife disappears, Nicholas pursues her and also seeks vengeance for past betrayals. His search takes him across a Europe threatened from without by the Turks and from within by shifting allegiances.

Historical Accuracy: The period details are convincing in their authenticity.

CHARLES DUNSCOMB (1914-)

Dunscomb is the author of such books as *The Bond and the Free*.

`1812` Behold, We Live

Date of Publication: 1956
Subject(s): Christianity; Roman Empire
Fictional character(s): Cedonius, Slave
Time Period(s): 2nd century
Locale(s): Roman Empire (Rome, Sardinia, Antium)

Summary: This novel re-creates the Roman Empire during the second century and the early days of Christianity. The story focuses on the slave Cedonius, a nominal Christian, who, after years of testing and trials, converts in earnest. The novel climaxes in the anti-Christian riots in Antium.

Historical Accuracy: The realistic portrait of the period and early Christianity is at times marred by the polemics.

`1813` The Bond and the Free

Date of Publication: 1955
Subject(s): Biblical Story; Roman Empire; Christianity
Fictional character(s): Lavinia, Young Woman
Historical character(s): Pontius Pilate, Government Official, Biblical Figure
Time Period(s): 1st century
Locale(s): Jerusalem, Israel

Summary: The story of Jesus and the early years of Christianity is presented from the vantage point of a young Roman woman, the niece of Pontius Pilate's wife. She visits Jerusalem during the years of Jewish unrest and is on hand for Jesus' sentencing before Pilate. The story of her reaction and eventual conversion is described in a series of letters to a friend back in Rome.

Historical Accuracy: The novel is skilled in capturing the atmosphere of the Roman colonial empire and the impact of the new religion.

CHARLES DURBIN

1814 *The Mercenary*

Date of Publication: 1963
Subject(s): Renaissance
Historical character(s): Giampaolo Baglioni, Mercenary
Time Period(s): 16th century
Locale(s): Italy

Summary: Giampaolo Baglioni is a condottiere, or mercenary, in Renaissance Italy who offers his services to both sides in the factional dispute between the Borgias and the Medicis. The novel is told in the form of a diary written by him in 1520 while he is awaiting execution.

Historical Accuracy: The novel excels at evoking the atmosphere of Renaissance Italy and its many military campaigns and betrayals.

MARILYN DURHAM (1930-)

An American writer born in Iowa, Durham attended the University of Evansville. She was a housewife when she turned novelist at the age of 42.

1815 *Dutch Uncle*

Date of Publication: 1973
Subject(s): American West
Fictional character(s): Jake Hollander, Lawman (sheriff); Carrie Hand, Publisher; Frank Becker, Outlaw
Time Period(s): 1880s (1880)
Locale(s): Arredondo, New Mexico; Arizona

Summary: Jake Hollander, former gunslinger and cardsharp, is on his way from Arizona to El Paso to begin a new life as a saloon keeper. He reaches New Mexico with two Mexican orphans in his care. Rather than leave them to the care of the ladies of the Golden Moon Saloon, he stays in Arredondo as sheriff, contending with both publisher Carrie Hand and the escaped outlaw Frank Becker.

Historical Accuracy: The period details are well developed and authentic in this wryly funny western tale.

1816 *Flambard's Confession*

Date of Publication: 1982
Subject(s): Middle Ages; Royalty—England
Historical character(s): William Rufus, Ruler (King of England); Ranulf Flambard, Religious (priest), Government Official (tax collector)
Time Period(s): 11th century
Locale(s): England

Summary: William the Conqueror is succeeded by his third son, William Rufus, a man who has been called the worst king in all of English history. A man of temper, pride, and ambition, Rufus's reign is chronicled here from the perspective of

his chaplain, Ranulph Flambard, the son of a poor priest in Normandy, who becomes one of the most successful administrators in English history as the king's "prince of tax collectors.".

Historical Accuracy: This is a rousing tale of medieval life and intrigue, convincingly detailed to create a vivid sense of the period.

1817 *The Man Who Loved Cat Dancing*

Date of Publication: 1972
Subject(s): American West; Indians
Fictional character(s): Jay Grobart, Veteran (army officer), Outlaw; Catherine Crocker, Captive; Washakie, Indian (Shoshone), Chieftain
Time Period(s): 1880s
Locale(s): Wyoming

Summary: A train robbery orchestrated by Jay Grobart, a former army officer and convict, is disrupted by Catherine Crocker, who is fleeing from her husband. Taking Catherine captive, Grobarts flees into Indian territory and a possible meeting with his daughter by the Shoshone girl Cat Dancing.

Historical Accuracy: The novel features strong details of western life.

JAROSLAV DURYCH

1818 *The Descent of the Idol*

Date of Publication: 1936
Subject(s): Thirty Years War; Religious Conflict
Historical character(s): Albrecht von Wallenstein, Military Personnel (general)
Time Period(s): 17th century
Locale(s): Europe

Summary: This enormous chronicle of the Thirty Years War captures in exhausting detail the intrigue and conflict of the period. Centering on the career of Albrecht of Wallenstein, the novel describes the warfare fueled by religious fanaticism and the scramble for power that defined the period.

Historical Accuracy: The period is rendered with a multiplicity of authentic details.

WILMA DYKEMAN

An American writer and lecturer born in North Carolina, Dykeman graduated from Northwestern University. She is the author of fiction and nonfiction titles with a strong regional interest. Her books include *The Far Family*, *Return the Innocent Earth*, and *Tennessee: A History*.

1819 *The Tall Woman*

Date of Publication: 1962
Subject(s): Civil War—U.S.; Reconstruction Period
Fictional character(s): Lydia McQueen, Mountain Woman
Time Period(s): 19th century (1864-1890s)
Locale(s): Smokey Mountains, North Carolina

Summary: The hard life of a North Carolina mountain woman, Lydia McQueen, is described from her marriage at the time of the Civil War, to her death 30 years later. Rich in regional details, the novel presents a series of setbacks that Lydia surmounts with determination.

Historical Accuracy: The novel provides an authentic tone and solid regional background.

CAROL MAXWELL EADY

1820 *Her Royal Destiny*

Date of Publication: 1985
Subject(s): Tudor Period; Royalty—England; Biography, Fictionalized
Historical character(s): Henry VIII, Ruler (King of England); Katherine Parr, Royalty (queen consort of Henry VIII); Thomas Seymour, Gentleman
Time Period(s): 16th century
Locale(s): England

Summary: This novelization of the life of Katherine Parr, Henry VIII's sixth wife, begins in 1525 during Katherine's childhood. Told mainly in her voice, the novel describes her marriages, the birth of her daughter, Mary, and her sudden death. Katherine emerges as an outspoken and strong individual, very different from Henry's other wives.

Historical Accuracy: The novel convinces in its characterization and the account of the period and its events.

TERRENCE EAGLETON (1943-)

Widely regarded the foremost young Marxist literary thinker in England, British writer Eagleton was born in Salford and received his M.A. and Ph.D. from Trinity College, Cambridge. He is the author of the critical works *Literary Theory: An Introduction*, *The Function of Criticism*, and a biography of William Shakespeare.

1821 *Saints and Scholars*

Date of Publication: 1987
Subject(s): Easter Rising; Independence—Ireland; Philosophy
Fictional character(s): Leopold Bloom, Businessman
Historical character(s): Ludwig Wittgenstein, Philosopher; James Connolly, Revolutionary; Nikolai Bakhtin, Philosopher
Time Period(s): 1910s (1916)
Locale(s): Ireland

Summary: The novel imagines a fanciful meeting in Ireland in 1916 of philosopher Ludwig Wittgenstein; Irish revolutionary James Connolly, who is on the run after the Easter Uprising; Nikolai Bakhtin, the Marxist aesthetician; and the fictional hero of John Joyce's *Ulysses*, Leopold Bloom. The conjunction produces a philosophical debate on various matters.

Historical Accuracy: The novel features an accurate sketch of the political and social issues of the times.

TOM EARLY
(PSEUD. OF ELMER KELTON, 1926-)

Tom Early is a pseudonym for Elmer Kelton, who also writes as Alex Hawk and Lee McElroy. Kelton worked for the *Standard-Times* of San Angelo, Texas from 1948-1963. He began writing novels under his real name in 1955. As Tom Early, Kelton has published *Sons of Texas*, *Honor at Daybreak*, *Slaughter*, and *The Far Canyon*.

1822 *Sons of Texas*

Date of Publication: 1989
Subject(s): Independence—Mexico; American West; Spanish Colonies
Fictional character(s): Mordecai Lewis, Frontiersman; Elizandra Saragosa, Military Personnel (Spanish soldier); Michael Lewis, Frontiersman
Time Period(s): 1810s; 1820s (1816-1821)
Locale(s): San Antonio, Texas

Summary: Texas under the domination of Spain is the scene for the story of Mordecai Lewis, a veteran of the Battle of New Orleans, who settles with his brother Michael in Texas and must decide whether to join in the struggle for Mexican independence from Spain.

Historical Accuracy: The novel captures the locale and the political atmosphere of the period.

WILLIAM EASTLAKE (1917-)

An American born in New York City, Eastlake was educated in New Jersey and at the Alliance Francaise in Paris. He has been a lecturer at USC, the University of Arizona, and the U.S. Military Academy. During the war in Vietnam he was a correspondent for *The Nation*. In the 1950s he settled on a ranch in New Mexico which became the setting for several of his novels.

1823 *The Long Naked Descent into Boston*

Date of Publication: 1977
Subject(s): American Revolution
Fictional character(s): Hieronymous Poxe, Editor, Journalist; Isaac Braxton, Journalist
Historical character(s): George Washington, Military Personnel (army commander); Benjamin Franklin, Political Figure; John Hancock, Political Figure, Revolutionary; John Adams, Political Figure; Nathan Hale, Patriot; Samuel Adams, Patriot, Revolutionary; Paul Revere, Patriot; John Burgoyne, Military Personnel (British general), Writer (playwright); Benedict Arnold, Military Personnel (American officer); Thomas Paine, Patriot, Revolutionary
Time Period(s): 1770s (1775-1776)
Locale(s): Boston, Massachusetts, American Colonies

Summary: This decidedly unhistorical and comic send-up of the events in Boston in 1775 on the eve of the Revolution features the reporting of the *New Boston Times* on the gathering conflict and its major players. Several historical figures are portrayed, all shown as a good deal more human than history and heroism have cast them.

Historical Accuracy: This is a comic fantasy not intended as history and it skewers many figures that American history portrays as the paragons they certainly were not.

ROBERT EASTON (1915-)

American writer Easton graduated from Harvard and the University of California, Santa Barbara. He was formerly employed as a ranch hand, day laborer, and a civil engineer. An editor, writer, and biographer, Easton has concentrated on the American West.

1824   *This Promised Land*

Date of Publication: 1982
Subject(s): American West; Spanish Colonies; Indians
Fictional character(s): Lospe, Indian (Chumash), Young Woman; Antonio Boneu, Military Personnel (Spanish soldier)
Historical character(s): Junipero Serra, Religious (Franciscan missionary); Gaspar de Portola, Military Personnel (general)
Time Period(s): 18th century
Locale(s): California

Summary: This is the story of the settlement of New Spain, California, in the 18th century. Against the background of General Gaspar Portola's expedition, the novel traces the love affair between Antonio, a Spanish soldier, and Lospe, a Chumash Indian girl. Through stong details, the conflict of cultures and beliefs that defined Old California is portrayed.

Historical Accuracy: Remarkable in its depiction of Indian life, the novel offers a convincingly balanced portrait of both the invaders and the natives.

EVELYN EATON (1902-)

Born in Switzerland, Eaton became a U.S. citizen in 1944. She attended the Sorbonne. A poet and a novelist, Eaton also served as a war correspondent in the China-Burma-India theater during World War II. She is the author of a number of highly popular historical romances.

1825   *Give Me Your Golden Hand*

Date of Publication: 1951
Subject(s): American Revolution; American Colonies; Quakers
Fictional character(s): Axford Daigle, Bastard Son
Time Period(s): 18th century
Locale(s): England; American Colonies

Summary: The purported illegitimate son of George III, Axford Daigle, is kept in disguise by a group of English peers for their own purposes. Daigle makes his way to the colonies, where he joins the Quakers and the colonial cause.

Historical Accuracy: The novel excels in its authentic depiction of 18th century life and customs.

1826   *Go Ask the River*

Date of Publication: 1969
Subject(s): Chinese Empire; Literary Life
Historical character(s): Hung Tu, Writer (poet); Meng Chaio, Writer (poet)
Time Period(s): 8th century; 9th century (760-824)
Locale(s): Shu Province, China

Summary: This biographical account traces the career of Hung Tu, a woman who became the poet laureate of the Province of Shu in the 9th century. Hung Tu trains as a courtesan and, when she meets the poet Meng Chaio, develops her gift for poetry. She later becomes the official hostess of the provincial governor.

Historical Accuracy: The author's depiction of 9th-century China may not stand up to a scholarly standard.

1827   *Heart in Pilgrimage*

Date of Publication: 1948
Subject(s): Biography, Fictionalized; Religious Life
Historical character(s): Elizabeth Ann Seton, Teacher, Religious (nun); William Seton, Gentleman
Time Period(s): 18th century; 19th century (1774-1821)
Locale(s): Maryland; New York, New York

Summary: The novel is based on the life of Elizabeth Ann Seton, the first native-born American to be canonized as a saint. She is a New York belle who converts to Catholicism after her husband dies, even though her family ostracizes her. She later founds the order of the Sisters of Charity. The novel depicts her married life, her conversion, and her religious career.

Historical Accuracy: The novel is based on Seton's journals. The liberties taken with the facts are minor.

1828   *In What Torn Ship*

Date of Publication: 1944
Subject(s): Independence—Corsica
Historical character(s): Pasquale Paoli, Patriot; Carlo Bonaparte, Patriot; Maria Letizia Bonaparte, Spouse
Time Period(s): 1760s
Locale(s): Corsica, France

Summary: The novel chronicles the career of Corsican patriot Pasquale Paoli, who fought for the independence of Corsica from the Genoese and the French. The story begins with Paoli's return to Corsica from exile and culminates in his desperate and unsuccessful stand against the French. Carlo Bonaparte, the father of Napoleon, at first is loyal to Paoli but later sides with the French.

Historical Accuracy: The novel is a blend of fact and imagination with an authentic historical background.

1829   *Quietly My Captain Waits*

Date of Publication: 1940
Subject(s): Frontier—Canada; Biography, Fictionalized
Historical character(s): Louise de Freneuse, Gentlewoman
Time Period(s): 17th century; 18th century
Locale(s): Canada

Summary: Madame Louise de Freneuse, a widow of property, ingratiates herself with three successive provincial governors and assists in the management of the colony. The novel reconstructs her colorful life with a solid period background.

Historical Accuracy: The novel benefits from evident research into the period.

1830 *Restless Are the Sails*

Date of Publication: 1941
Subject(s): French and Indian War; Siege of Louisburg
Fictional character(s): Paul de Morpain, Young Man; Anne du Chambon, Young Woman
Historical character(s): Pierre de Morpain, Pirate
Time Period(s): 1740s (1744-1746)
Locale(s): Louisbourg, Nova Scotia, Canada

Summary: The story of the crucial siege of Louisburg, the French fortress on Cape Breton Island, during the French and Indian Wars is told by a cast of historical and fictional characters. Pirate-privateer Pierre de Morpain learns of the New Englanders' planned invasion. His nephew, Paul, carries the news to Louisburg but he is ignored. Paul also gets involved with the daughter of the governor.

Historical Accuracy: The novel's romance and fictional elements overpower the history here, though the essential background is accurate.

DIKKON EBERHART (1946-)

An American born in Boston and a graduate of Dartmouth, the Pacific School of Religion, and the Theological Union, Berkeley, Eberhart has worked as a teacher and headmaster at private schools. He is the son of poet Richard G. Eberhart.

1831 *Paradise*

Date of Publication: 1983
Subject(s): Sea Story; Exploration; Dark Ages
Fictional character(s): Finbar, Outcast, Artisan (ironsmith); Barinthus, Sailor; Ide, Religious (abbess)
Historical character(s): Brendan the Navigator, Religious (monk), Explorer
Time Period(s): 6th century
Locale(s): At Sea; North America

Summary: The novel describes a voyage in the 6th century by Irishman Brendan and a small crew in a tiny curragh. They rescue a black man, Finbar, who accompanies them to Thule (present-day Iceland) and beyond to the shores of North America.

Historical Accuracy: Though based on Brendan's exploits, chronicled in early Latin manuscripts, the novel takes artistic license with this saga.

MIGNON G. EBERHART (1899-)

An American writer born in Lincoln, Nebraska, Eberhart attended Nebraska Wesleyan University. She has been a writer since the 1930s and is the author of over 50 mystery novels. Many of her stories are set in exotic locales with carefully detailed settings. Eberhart is a past president of the

Mystery Writers of America and received their Grand Master Award in 1970.

1832 *The Bayou Road*

Date of Publication: 1979
Subject(s): Civil War—U.S.
Fictional character(s): Marcy Chastain, Southern Belle; John Farrell, Military Personnel (Union major)
Time Period(s): 1860s (1863)
Locale(s): New Orleans, Louisiana

Summary: This suspense novel is set during the Civil War in Union occupied New Orleans. Part Creole Marcy Chastain falls in love with a Union major, John Farrell, and contends with divided loyalties when she is recruited to gain secrets from Farrell.

Historical Accuracy: The novel provides an authentic period background.

1833 *The Cup, the Blade or the Gun*

Date of Publication: 1961
Subject(s): Civil War—U.S.; Mystery
Fictional character(s): Sarah Salter, Spouse
Time Period(s): 1860s (1863)
Locale(s): Mississippi

Summary: The experiences of Sarah Salter of Connecticut who marries a Confederate officer and lives on his family's plantation while he is away at the front forms the background for this suspense-romance. Sarah experiences hostility and threats, including a murder plot, against the backdrop of the siege of Vicksburg.

Historical Accuracy: The novel is well-ground and convincing in its depiction of Civil War history.

1834 *Family Fortune*

Date of Publication: 1976
Subject(s): Romance; Civil War—U.S.; Inheritance—Disputed
Fictional character(s): Lucinda Chance, Heiress; Jeff Chance, Guardian
Time Period(s): 1860s (Civil War period)
Locale(s): Virginia (western)

Summary: When the patriarch of the Chance family dies in western Virginia during the Civil War, he leaves half his estate to his daughter by his second marriage, Lucinda, but her half brother is made her guardian until she turns 18 or marries. Jeff Chance is determined that she will not inherit her fortune, and Lucinda must withstand his schemes.

Historical Accuracy: Puzzle and suspense predominate over the period detail here.

GERTRUDE EBERLE

1835 *Charioteer: A Story of Old Egypt in the Days of Joseph*

Date of Publication: 1946

Subject(s): Ancient Egypt; Biblical Story
Fictional character(s): Raanah, Slave
Historical character(s): Joseph, Biblical Figure
Time Period(s): Indeterminate Past
Locale(s): Egypt

Summary: The novel tells the story of the Old Testament figure Joseph in captivity in Egypt. It combines the Biblical story with an imagined one of a slave, Raanah, who dreams of becoming a charioteer.

Historical Accuracy: The novel achieves believability in its period background.

FRANK ECCLES (1923-)

An Englishman born in Manchester, Eccles has been a teacher and headmaster at various schools in England and Germany. His love of the sea turned him to fiction. Although he could not afford a boat, he read everything he could to capture the technical details of sailing for his first novel, *The Barbary Run*. He was able to buy a sailing cruiser out of the royalties and has been sailing ever since.

1836   *Mutiny Run*

Date of Publication: 1994
Subject(s): Sea Story; Mutiny; Military Life—British Navy
Fictional character(s): John Lawson, Military Personnel (midshipman); Brewster, Military Personnel (naval captain)
Time Period(s): 1790s (1797)
Locale(s): *Adamant*, At Sea; Brest, France

Summary: The novel is set against the historical backdrop of the Nore Mutiny that infected England's Channel Fleet in 1797. Captain Brewster is in command of the *Adamant* on a daring raid near Brest where he is able to successfully convince the French that the Royal Navy is still intact and not in shambles from the mutiny. Admiralty politics call him away from the ship, and the mutiny spreads.

Historical Accuracy: The author is exact and convincing in the nautical details of the period.

OLIVE ECKERSON (1901-)

Eckerson was born in England and came to the U.S. in her teens. She taught high school English and wrote a number of historical novels.

1837   *The Golden Yoke: A Novel of the War of the Roses*

Date of Publication: 1961
Subject(s): War of the Roses; Royalty—England; Royalty—France
Historical character(s): Richard, Duke of Gloucester, Royalty (Duke of Gloucester); Anne Neville, Noblewoman (wife of Richard); Edward IV, Ruler (King of England); Richard Neville, Nobleman (Earl of Warwick); Louis XI, Ruler (King of France); George, Duke of Clarence, Nobleman
Time Period(s): 15th century
Locale(s): England; France

Summary: The complicated dynastic struggle between the Houses of York and Lancaster is depicted in the love story between Richard, Duke of Gloucester, and Anne Neville. They find themselves on opposite sides of the War of the Roses as Richard remains loyal to his brother Edward IV. Anne is the daughter of Edward's principal rival, the Earl of Warwick, and is torn between Richard and her father.

Historical Accuracy: The novel offers a sympathetic treatment of Richard III that is supported by convincing details.

1838   *My Lord Essex*

Date of Publication: 1955
Subject(s): Elizabethan Period; Royalty—England
Historical character(s): Robert Devereux, Nobleman (Earl of Essex); Elizabeth I, Ruler (Queen of England); William Cecil, Nobleman, Courtier; Robert Cecil, Government Official (Queen's secretary); Sir Francis Bacon, Lawyer; Sir Francis Walsingham, Government Official; Sir Walter Raleigh, Courtier, Gentleman; Robert Dudley, Nobleman (Earl of Leicester), Courtier
Time Period(s): 16th century; 17th century (1575-1601)
Locale(s): England

Summary: The novel dramatizes the tragic course of Elizabeth's romance with Essex, and his transformation from queen's favorite to traitor. Essex's career is marked with privilege and power, which become the basis for his ambition that causes him to look even beyond the role of consort to the queen. The novel characterizes the court politics that lead to Essex's rise and fall.

Historical Accuracy: The novel is an impressive re-creation of the times and personalities that dominated the Elizabethan period.

ALLEN W. ECKERT (1931-)

An American writer born in Buffalo, Eckert attended the University of Dayton and Ohio State University. He has worked as a painter, private detective, fireman, salesman, trapper, and commercial artist, among many other occupations. A winner of a Newbery-Caldecott award, his 'Winning of the West' series has been nominated for the Pulitzer Prize on several occasions. A committed environmentalist and author of nature books, Eckert is the author of over 200 TV scripts for the series "Wild Kingdom." His historical novels have been called "documentary fiction," close to history but with invented dialogue to tell his story.

1839   *The Conquerors*

Date of Publication: 1970
Subject(s): Settlement of the American Frontier; Indians
Historical character(s): Pontiac, Indian (Ottawa), Chieftain; Henry Boquet, Military Personnel (general); Henry Gladwin, Military Personnel (army officer); Sir William Johnson, Government Official (colonial administrator)
Time Period(s): 18th century (1758-1789)
Locale(s): Northwest Territory, United States

Summary: In the third volume of the author's Narratives of America, the English victory over the French in the French and Indian Wars opens up a vast new empire. The settlers who rush in to occupy the newly acquired territory encounter hostile Indians who regard them as intruders on their ancestral lands. The action climaxes with the fierce Pontiac uprising.

Historical Accuracy: The factual basis of this documentary narrative is sure and authentic. The author prides himself on inventing no detail and scrupulously documents all facts.

1840 *The Court Martial of Daniel Boone*

Date of Publication: 1973
Subject(s): American Revolution; Indians; Trials
Historical character(s): Daniel Boone, Frontiersman
Time Period(s): 1770s (1778)
Locale(s): Boonesborough, Kentucky

Summary: In 1778, as a captain during the Revolutionary War, Daniel Boone is court-martialed on charges of having betrayed his command to the Indians and having conspired with the British to surrender Boonesborough. Boone pleads guilty to all charges except treason, and the novel records the famous trial and Boone defense.

Historical Accuracy: The novel is based on a scrupulous review of the known sources with little invented material.

1841 *The Frontiersmen*

Date of Publication: 1967
Subject(s): Settlement of the American Frontier; Indians
Historical character(s): Simon Kenton, Frontiersman; Tecumseh, Indian (Shawnee), Chieftain; Daniel Boone, Frontiersman
Time Period(s): 18th century; 19th century (1755-1836)
Locale(s): Northwest Territory, United States

Summary: The first of the author's Narratives of America series describes frontier life in the old Northwest Territory and centers on a woodsman, Indian fighter, and scout named Simon Kenton. His experiences are matched with those of Tecumseh, the great Shawnee chief whose Indian confederacy came close to halting western expansion.

Historical Accuracy: Written with the authority of history this book is actually more fact than fiction.

1842 *Gateway to Empire*

Date of Publication: 1983
Subject(s): Settlement of the American Frontier; War of 1812; Indians
Historical character(s): John Kinzie, Trader; Tecumseh, Indian (Shawnee), Chieftain; George Rogers Clark, Military Personnel (general); William Henry Harrison, Military Personnel, Political Figure; William Wells, Military Personnel (army captain)
Time Period(s): 18th century; 19th century (1763-1816)
Locale(s): Great Lakes; Chicago, Illinois

Summary: In the fifth volume of the Narratives of America, the scene is the struggle to control the Chicago Portage, which is a vital link between the east and western expansion. The protagonists are John Kinzie, a successful trader, and Tecum-

seh, the Shawnee chief who is determined to halt further settlement.

Historical Accuracy: Dozens of historical figures are featured with nothing invented, according to the author. The elaborate documentation attests to the reliability of that assertion.

1843 *Johnny Logan: Shawnee Spy*

Date of Publication: 1983
Subject(s): Indians; Biography, Fictionalized; Espionage
Historical character(s): Spemica Lawba, Indian (Shawnee), Spy; Benjamin Logan, Military Personnel (general); Tecumseh, Indian (Shawnee), Chieftain
Time Period(s): 18th century
Locale(s): Ohio

Summary: Based on fact, the novel tells the story of Spemica Lawba, a Shawnee Indian who is captured by white soldiers and adopted by General Benjamin Logan. A spy for the Americans, Lawba becomes the only Indian in Ohio history to be buried with military honors.

Historical Accuracy: The novel's familiarity with the era and its events guarantee an authentic and believable depiction of the time.

1844 *A Sorrow in Our Heart*

Date of Publication: 1992
Subject(s): War of 1812; Indians; Biography, Fictionalized
Historical character(s): Tecumseh, Indian (Shawnee), Chieftain; William Henry Harrison, Military Personnel, Political Figure
Time Period(s): 18th century; 19th century
Locale(s): Southeast

Summary: In this biography of the great Indian leader Tecumseh, the author employs fictional techniques such as imagined conversations and shifting viewpoints to qualify it as a novel. Tecumseh emerges as a great visionary who dreams of uniting tribes in a great battle against the settlers, a battle that will decide the fate of the Indians in America.

Historical Accuracy: The book has all the features of a history text with facts carefully documented and notes to support conjecture.

1845 *That Dark and Bloody River*

Date of Publication: 1995
Subject(s): American Colonies; Settlement of the American Frontier; Indians
Historical character(s): George Washington, Military Personnel; Daniel Boone, Frontiersman; Lewis Wetzel, Frontiersman; George Rogers Clark, Military Personnel; Simon Girty, Frontiersman
Time Period(s): 18th century (1768-1799)
Locale(s): Ohio Valley, United States

Summary: Eckert's narrative history chronicles the settlement of the Ohio River Valley. Ranging from the 1760s to the 1790s, the novel features dozens of the key players in the settlement of America's first western wilderness. For settlers and explorers like Boone and Wetzel, the Ohio offers limitless possibilities. For the Indians whom they displace, it is the end of an era and their way of life.

Historical Accuracy: The author supplements the facts of history with reconstituted dialogue.

`1846` *Twilight of Empire*

Date of Publication: 1988
Subject(s): Settlement of the American Frontier; Indians; Black Hawk War
Historical character(s): Black Hawk, Indian, Chieftain; Lewis Cass, Political Figure; Andrew Jackson, Military Personnel, Political Figure; Abraham Lincoln, Political Figure; John Reynolds, Political Figure; Zachary Taylor, Military Personnel, Political Figure
Time Period(s): 19th century (1801-1838)
Locale(s): Mississippi River; Illinois

Summary: In the sixth volume of the Narratives of America series, westward expansion moves into the Illinois territory, provoking a bloody confrontation with the legendary war chief Black Hawk. John Reynolds, the governor of the territory, leads a group of settlers and soldiers to sieze the land from the Indians.

Historical Accuracy: More history text than fiction, the facts are scrupulously documented.

`1847` *Wilderness Empire*

Date of Publication: 1969
Subject(s): Settlement of the American Frontier; Indians; French and Indian War
Historical character(s): Sir William Johnson, Settler; George Washington, Military Personnel (army officer); Edward Braddock, Military Personnel (army officer); Daniel Boone, Frontiersman; George Clinton, Political Figure; Simon Girty, Frontiersman; Robert Rogers, Frontiersman
Time Period(s): 18th century (1715-1774)
Locale(s): New York, American Colonies; Northwest Territory, United States

Summary: The second volume of the author's Narratives of America series covers the Indian wars, in which the Iroquois were incited by the French to halt the expansion of the American colonies. Dozens of important figures appear in this documentary narrative history.

Historical Accuracy: Every date and event is historically accurate and every character actually lived the role in which he or she is portrayed.

`1848` *The Wilderness War*

Date of Publication: 1978
Subject(s): Settlement of the American Frontier; Indians; American Revolution
Historical character(s): Thayendanegea, Indian (Iroquois), Chieftain; Joseph Brant, Indian, Loyalist; Sir William Johnson, Government Official (colonial administrator); John Sullivan, Military Personnel (general)
Time Period(s): 18th century (1763-1780)
Locale(s): New York, American Colonies

Summary: During the Revolutionary War, Thayendanegea, the Iroquois war chief, allies his tribes with the one white man they trust, Sir William Johnson. The Iroquois play an important role as British allies in the war against the colonists.

Historical Accuracy: The author provides all the documentation of a history text.

UMBERTO ECO (1932-)

An Italian academic and literary critic, Eco is a renowned specialist in semiotics. A master of a number of foreign languages, he has written on popular culture (comic strips, Superman, James Bond movies). All his work shows considerable ingenuity and great erudition.

`1849` *The Island of the Day Before*

Date of Publication: 1994
Subject(s): Sea Story; Thirty Years War
Fictional character(s): Roberto della Griva, Sailor
Time Period(s): 17th century (1643)
Locale(s): Pacific Ocean (South Pacific)

Summary: This dense and rich meditation on time and history is set in 1643. After a violent storm in the South Pacific, Roberto della Griva finds himself aboard a fully provisioned ship anchored in the bay of a beautiful island. As he explores the ship, he reviews his life, which becomes an encyclopedic journey through his times.

Historical Accuracy: The novel excells in reconstructing the past believably.

`1850` *The Name of the Rose*

Date of Publication: 1980
Subject(s): Middle Ages; Religious Life; Mystery
Fictional character(s): William of Baskerville, Religious (English Franciscan monk), Scholar; Adso da Melck, Religious (scribe); Jorges da Burgos, Religious
Time Period(s): 14th century (1327)
Locale(s): Italy (northern)

Summary: This surprise international bestseller tells of the visit of Brother William of Baskerville and his young scribe to an Italian monastery in the early years of the 14th century. There they investigate a series of grisly murders that reveal the deadly factional intrigues during the time and, finally, a shattering literary secret.

Historical Accuracy: Eco's massive erudition is part of the fun here, as he masterfully recreates time and place and the cultural and intellectual issues that defined the medieval world on the verge of the Renaissance.

MAURICE EDELMAN (1911-1975)

Born in Wales, Edelman attended Trinity College, Cambridge, and worked for a time as a research and development supervisor in the plastic and timber industry. He served as a member of Parliament from 1950 to 1974, enjoying the distinction of being the first novelist member of the British parliament since Disraeli himself.

1851 *Disraeli in Love*

Date of Publication: 1972
Subject(s): Politics; Literary Life; Biography, Fictionalized
Historical character(s): Benjamin Disraeli, Writer, Political Figure; Henrietta Sykes, Gentlewoman; Daniel O'Connell, Political Figure; Daniel Maclise, Artist; Robert Peel, Political Figure
Time Period(s): 1830s (1832-1837)
Locale(s): London, England

Summary: The early life of writer and politician Benjamin Disraeli is dramatized. He bursts on the London scene as a novelist with a daring ambition to be the first English Jew to succeed in politics. Disraeli falls in love with Lady Henrietta Sykes, whose husband is indifferent to her. Disraeli must balance his heart and his ambition as the scandal of their affair threatens to derail his career.

Historical Accuracy: The sense of period and the politics of the era are believable and convincing.

1852 *Disraeli Rising*

Date of Publication: 1975
Subject(s): Victorian Period; Politics; Biography, Fictionalized
Historical character(s): Benjamin Disraeli, Political Figure; Robert Peel, Political Figure; Louis Philippe, Ruler (King of France); William Gladstone, Political Figure
Time Period(s): 19th century (1838-1850s)
Locale(s): London, England; Paris, France

Summary: The novel continues the story of British dandy, novelist, and politician Benjamin Disraeli, begun in *Disraeli in Love*. Disraeli begins his political ascent to prime minister though beset by domestic conflict. Forever the outsider, Disraeli masters the political game to become the most powerful man in England.

Historical Accuracy: The details of the Victorian period are thorough and convincingly presented.

MARJORIE EDELSON

1853 *Malkeh and Her Children*

Date of Publication: 1992
Subject(s): Jews; Russian Revolution; Immigrants
Fictional character(s): Malkeh Mandelkern, Spouse; Yoysef Mandelkern, Tailor
Time Period(s): 19th century; 20th century (1878-1923)
Locale(s): St. Petersburg, Russia; Moscow, Russia; California (San Francisco, Sacramento)

Summary: This is the story of the survival of the Jewish Mandelkern family as they endure tsarist persecution in Russia and then the Russian Revolution. At the center of the story is the indomitable Malkeh whose dedication to tradition and family sustains them in Russia and America.

Historical Accuracy: The novel is richly pictured, capturing the period customs and details with skill and conviction.

DOROTHY EDEN (1912-1982)

A New Zealand-born novelist, Eden is one of the best-known contemporary historical romance writers. She has been praised for her solidly researched backgrounds and intriguing plots.

1854 *The American Heiress*

Date of Publication: 1980
Subject(s): World War I; Shipwrecks; Identity—Concealed
Fictional character(s): Clemency Jervis, Heiress; Harriet Brown, Servant; Hugo Hazzard, Nobleman
Time Period(s): 1910s
Locale(s): New York, New York; London, England

Summary: In this improbable romantic tale, a lady's maid assumes her mistress' identity when she is lost in the sinking of the *Lusitania*. As the American heiress, she marries an English nobleman, and she must then deal with the guilt and attempt to earn love in her own right.

Historical Accuracy: The romantic situation here defies credibility.

1855 *An Important Family*

Date of Publication: 1982
Subject(s): Frontier—New Zealand
Fictional character(s): Kate O'Connor, Gentlewoman; John Devenish, Nobleman
Time Period(s): 1860s
Locale(s): England; New Zealand

Summary: Kate O'Connor marries into a prominent English family. Her husband surprises all with the announcement that the entire clan is to re-locate to the wilderness of New Zealand. Kate manages the long sea voyage and begins to create a home in the wilderness, but family secrets break to the surface.

Historical Accuracy: Eden is best here in the details of New Zealand life.

1856 *Lady of Mallow*

Date of Publication: 1962
Subject(s): Inheritance—Disputed; Romance
Fictional character(s): Sarah Mildway, Governess, Fiance(e); Blane Mallow, Heir, Gentleman; Ambrose Mallow, Heir—Dispossessed
Time Period(s): 1890s
Locale(s): London, England; Mallow, England (country estate)

Summary: In this romantic tangle a long-lost heir appears to claim his inheritance, dispossessing the nephew of the late master of Mallow and his fiancee. She gains a position in the household as a governess to help expose the imposter as a fraud and promptly gets caught up in a series of mysteries that climax in madness and murder.

Historical Accuracy: Although set in the Victorian era, there is little period specific detail. The romantic mystery is all in this exciting story.

1857 *Melbury Square*

Date of Publication: 1970
Subject(s): Romance; Artistic Life
Fictional character(s): Maude Lucie, Model; James Lucie, Artist; Guy Beauchamp, Nobleman
Time Period(s): 1910s
Locale(s): London, England

Summary: Maude Lucie is a great beauty and her father's favorite model. He is one of London's fashionable portrait painters. The romantic drama is joined when Maude is forced to choose between her doting and demanding father and a penniless young aristocrat with whom she has fallen in love.

Historical Accuracy: There are good details of artistic London though the romantic complications here are standard.

1858 *The Millionaire's Daughter*

Date of Publication: 1974
Subject(s): Romance
Fictional character(s): Christabel Spencer, Socialite, Noblewoman; Earl of Monkshood, Nobleman; Matthew Smith, Artist, Writer
Time Period(s): 1900s
Locale(s): New York, New York; London, England; Wiltshire, England

Summary: Christabel is the daughter of a New York millionaire. She triumphs in the New York social scene but a larger stage is needed and a title. She is sent off to London for the social season and captures an Earl. As the Countess of Monkshood she discovers that all that glitters is not gold, and love enters in the form of a young artist and writer.

Historical Accuracy: History extends here little further than the fashionable locales for the romance.

1859 *Never Call It Loving*

Date of Publication: 1966
Subject(s): Victorian Period; Politics; Independence—Ireland
Historical character(s): Charles Stewart Parnell, Political Figure; Katherine O'Shea, Gentlewoman, Lover (Parnell's mistress); William Gladstone, Political Figure
Time Period(s): 1880s
Locale(s): London, England; Ireland

Summary: The novel dramatizes the tragic love affair between Parnell and Kitty O'Shea, which ends Parnell's political career. Parnell is holding together the Irish Home Rule party and is a major irritant to the English government. The scandal that broke when the affair became public split Ireland apart.

Historical Accuracy: The focus here is on the two lovers instead of a full depiction of the politics of the time.

1860 *Ravenscroft*

Date of Publication: 1964
Subject(s): Victorian Period; Mystery; Crime and Criminals
Fictional character(s): Guy Raven, Gentleman, Political Figure; Bella Raven, Orphan; Lally, Orphan
Time Period(s): 1870s
Locale(s): London, England

Summary: Guy Raven, a young reform politician, rescues and shelters two sisters who were forced to seek their fortune on the streets of London. To save his reputation he marries the eldest, Bella, and she attempts to win his love. Her past and criminal associates return for revenge and besiege Ravenscroft.

Historical Accuracy: The mystery romance owes little to the actual sights and sounds of London life, though the urban scenes of low life are a departure in the expected fashionable world of the romance.

1861 *The Salamanca Drum*

Date of Publication: 1977
Subject(s): Family Saga; Military Life—British Army; World War I
Fictional character(s): Matilda Dunncastle, Gentlewoman; Joshua Webb, Banker
Time Period(s): 19th century; 20th century (1890-1939)
Locale(s): Somerset, England

Summary: Matilda Duncastle is a child of a distinguished British military family. She makes a marriage of convenience with a rich man to pay her father's debts and to save her family estate. Her plan is to raise children to share her family's military heritage. The horror of war in the 20th century sobers her image of heroic sacrifice and glory.

Historical Accuracy: There is little direct history here, just enough to illustrate the lesson of the novel that the glory of war needs to be reassessed by its cost.

1862 *Speak to Me of Love*

Date of Publication: 1972
Subject(s): Business Building
Fictional character(s): Beatrice Bonnington, Businesswoman; William Overton, Gentleman
Time Period(s): 19th century; 20th century (1881-1939)
Locale(s): London, England

Summary: Beatrice Bonnington is the daughter of a London tradesman who marries a distinguished gentleman. She is patronized by society and unloved by her husband. She turns her energy into building up a mercantile empire. The suggestion here is that women enter business largely because love has failed.

Historical Accuracy: The period detail is here, sufficient to provide a setting for the romantic complications.

1863 *The Time of the Dragon*

Date of Publication: 1975
Subject(s): Boxer Rebellion; Chinese Empire
Fictional character(s): Amelia Carrington, Gentlewoman, Collector (antique); Nathaniel Carrington, Gentleman, Collector
Historical character(s): Tz'u-hsi, Ruler (Dowager Empress of China)
Time Period(s): 1890s; 1900s
Locale(s): Peking, China

Summary: The Carrington family, collectors of antiques, journey to Peking during the Boxer Rebellion. There they endure the siege of the legation district and the hatred of the "foreign devils'' in an explosion of Chinese nationalism. The Carringtons are seen as chief desecrators of the Chinese heritage.

Historical Accuracy: There are good details here of Chinese life and the period of the Boxer Rebellion.

1864 *The Vines of Yarrabee*

Date of Publication: 1969
Subject(s): Frontier—Australia
Fictional character(s): Gilbert Massingham, Plantation Owner; Eugenia Massingham, Gentlewoman; Molly Jarvis, Servant
Time Period(s): 19th century (1827-1864)
Locale(s): New South Wales, Australia

Summary: Australian plantation life in the 19th century is the subject of this novel that finds refined Englishwoman Eugenia brought to New South Wales to become the mistress of Yarrabee. She is appalled by the life she finds there, dependant on convict slave labor.

Historical Accuracy: This is a domestic drama set in an interesting locale, although given a predictable romantic treatment.

MATTHEW EDEN

1865 *The Murder of Lawrence of Arabia*

Date of Publication: 1979
Subject(s): Mystery
Historical character(s): T.E. Lawrence, Writer, Adventurer; Ramsay MacDonald, Political Figure
Time Period(s): 1930s (1935)
Locale(s): England

Summary: This mystery novel looks at the facts surrounding the fatal motorcycle crash that took the life of T.E. Lawrence. The novel speculates that Lawrence's death is no accident and is connected with Middle Eastern and English politics. The novel reconstructs the last 11 weeks of Lawrence's life, when he is at the center of plots involving Palestinian Jews and Arabs.

Historical Accuracy: Fiction supplements facts here, and the novel's plot is primarily fanciful, though it shows evidence of scholarship and research.

ROSEMARY EDGHILL

1866 *Fleeting Fancy*

Date of Publication: 1992
Subject(s): Regency Romance
Fictional character(s): Primula Greetwell, Gentlewoman; Lord Severn, Nobleman, Rake
Time Period(s): 1800s; 1810s (1807-1817)
Locale(s): London, England

Summary: In this Regency romance, Lord Severn, who tricks Primula Greetwell into a false marriage, forces his father to put his foot down. Severn is given a choice: marry sight unseen the bride of his father's choice or be cut off from his

family and fortune forever. Severn chooses the former, and his father's choice is an older and wiser Primula, who has motives of her own.

Historical Accuracy: The situation defies credibility, but it is anchored in believable period detail.

1867 *Two of a Kind: An English Trifle*

Date of Publication: 1988
Subject(s): Regency Romance
Fictional character(s): Juliette Devereaux, Gentlewoman; Jack Barham, Nobleman (Marquess of Barham)
Time Period(s): 1810s (1819)
Locale(s): London, England; Sussex, England

Summary: Juliette Devereaux endures a disappointing London season with no marriage proposals. She is self-reliant and independent and too pragmatic for romance. At a party in Sussex she meets the hapless Marquess of Barham, banished from his ancestral home and her opposite in every way. But complications bring them together.

Historical Accuracy: The plot depends on a full sense of time and place.

JANET EDMONDS

1868 *Rivers of Gold*

Date of Publication: 1990
Subject(s): Gold Rush—Klondike
Fictional character(s): Amity Jones, Young Woman
Time Period(s): 19th century
Locale(s): England; Alaska

Summary: Amity Jones answers an advertisement for marriageable women in Alaska. She finds herself in the middle of the Klondike Gold Rush and must quickly adapt to a new and challenging environment of bears, dog sleds, and the rough and tumble of frontier life.

Historical Accuracy: The novel offers some convincing details of Alaskan frontier experience.

1869 *Sarah Camberwell Tring*

Date of Publication: 1993
Subject(s): American Colonies; Inheritance—Disputed
Fictional character(s): Sarah Camberwell Tring, Businesswoman, Widow(er); Kieron Roade, Rake, Heir
Time Period(s): 1750s (1750)
Locale(s): Yorktown, Virginia, American Colonies; London, England

Summary: Virginia widow and businesswoman Sarah Tring learns that she has been named an heir of her father's former employer, under the condition she gets to London in time to claim her legacy. She decides to undertake the journey. When she arrives, she meets Kieron Roade, the second heir of the disputed fortune, and complications ensue.

Historical Accuracy: The story is an entertaining romance rather than a genuine look at the period.

1870 *Turn of the Dice*

Date of Publication: 1989
Subject(s): American Colonies; Slavery
Fictional character(s): Abigail Broughton, Gentlewoman, Servant (indentured); Jasper Cuddesdon, Nobleman; Lance Howarth, Servant (indentured), Landowner
Time Period(s): 18th century (second half)
Locale(s): Williamsburg, Virginia, American Colonies

Summary: Abigail Broughton is the genteel daughter of a father with insurmountable gambling debts. She is sold as a bond-slave to Lord Jasper Cuddesdon in Virginia, a man whose offer of marriage Abigail once spurned. In Virginia, Abigail must gamble to gain her freedom and control her fate in America.

Historical Accuracy: Although it was possible for a debtor or his relation to become a bond-slave in the 18th century, the author has no historical precedent for the heroine's situation.

WALTER D. EDMONDS (1903-)

American novelist Edmonds is best known for his historical novels set in his native New York State. *Drums Along the Mohawk* is widely regarded as a classic.

1871 *The Boyds of Black River*

Date of Publication: 1953
Subject(s): Family Saga; Horses
Fictional character(s): Doone Boyd, Young Man; John Callant, Servant (groom); Ledyard Boyd, Gentleman
Time Period(s): 20th century (turn of the century)
Locale(s): New York

Summary: The horse-centered life of a gentry family in upstate New York at the turn of the century is the novel's subject. The Boyds have a comfortable and prosperous life that is centered around the great pacer Blue Dandy. The novel depicts their domestic routine on the brink of change from horse-dominated to horse-less.

Historical Accuracy: More nostalgic than historical, the past here is bathed in a tender sentimental wistfulness.

1872 *Cadmus Henry*

Date of Publication: 1949
Subject(s): Civil War—U.S.; Balloons; Peninsular Campaign
Fictional character(s): Cadmus Henry, Military Personnel (confederate soldier)
Historical character(s): Joseph E. Johnston, Military Personnel (Confederate general)
Time Period(s): 1860s (1862)
Locale(s): Virginia

Summary: Cadmus Henry is a young Confederate soldier who dreams of glory but is assigned as a clerk, copying endless reports on the progress of the Peninsular Campaign in 1862. He volunteers for special duty that turns out to be aerial reconaissance in a balloon. Drifting over enemy lines in which both sides look remarkably the same and his encounter with an abolitionist girl help to change his attitude about the war.

Historical Accuracy: The period details are accurate and reliable.

1873 *Chad Hanna*

Date of Publication: 1940
Subject(s): Circus Life; Erie Canal
Fictional character(s): Chad Hanna, Orphan, Worker (hostler); Elias Proops, Veteran (American Revolution); Ike Wayfish, Entertainer (clown)
Time Period(s): 1830s (1836)
Locale(s): Erie Canal, New York

Summary: The title character is an orphan who runs away to become a horse boy on the Erie Canal. He is now the hostler at the Yellow Bud Tavern in upstate New York, dreaming of the larger world beyond his tiny village. Then a circus comes to town, and Chad is hooked as the circus tries to survive in uncertain times.

Historical Accuracy: The locale and period details are ably depicted.

1874 *Drums Along the Mohawk*

Date of Publication: 1936
Subject(s): American Revolution; Indians
Fictional character(s): Gilbert Martin, Farmer, Military Personnel (militiaman); Lana Martin, Spouse
Time Period(s): 1770s; 1780s (1776-1784)
Locale(s): Mohawk Valley, New York, American Colonies

Summary: This is one of the classics of its genre, a remarkably detailed evocation of the effects of the American Revolution in the wilderness of New York's Mohawk Valley. Gilbert and Lana Martin are newlyweds who get swept up in the struggles between Tories, Rebels, British soldiers, and the Iroquois.

Historical Accuracy: Edmonds has scrupulously attempted to render life as it was, down to using contemporary records of the weather during the period depicted. This is a model of historical accuracy.

1875 *Erie Water*

Date of Publication: 1933
Subject(s): Canal Building; Erie Canal
Fictional character(s): Jerry Fowler, Worker (canal); Mary Goodhill, Immigrant
Time Period(s): 1810s; 1820s (1817-1825)
Locale(s): New York

Summary: Mary Goodhill is one of a group of redemptioners who have put themselves into bondage to pay their passage to America in the 1810s. Jerry Fowler, on his way to buy a farm, redeems Mary and acquires a wife. Their lives become connected with the building of the Erie Canal and the changes it produces.

Historical Accuracy: Edmonds' sense of place and the customs of the time are convincing and authentic.

1876 *In the Hands of the Senecas*

Date of Publication: 1947
Subject(s): Settlement of the American Frontier; Indians

Fictional character(s): Martha Dysart, Captive; Caty Breen, Captive; Delia Borst, Captive
Time Period(s): 1770s (1778)
Locale(s): New York, American Colonies (upstate)

Summary: Set in the wilderness of upstate New York in 1778, the novel describes an Indian raid by the Senecas on a Mohawk Valley community. A group of women and children are captured and taken west, deep inside Indian territory along the Great Central Trail of the Iroquois. The novel offers a vivid depiction of endurance and danger.

Historical Accuracy: The author has gone to painstaking details to provide a realistic and plausible historical background.

1877 *Rome Haul*

Date of Publication: 1929
Subject(s): Canal Building; Erie Canal
Fictional character(s): Dan Harrow, Farmer; Molly Larkins, Cook; Gentleman Joe Calash, Outlaw
Time Period(s): 1850s (1850)
Locale(s): Albany, New York; Rome, New York; Erie Canal, New York

Summary: The novel depicts the people and the customs along the Erie Canal. Dan Harrow is a farmer drawn to the canal for work. There he encounters a variety of characters including a cook, a canal bully with whom he has an epic fist-fight, and a canal highwayman.

Historical Accuracy: This is a classic historical novel with vivid details of a bygone era.

1878 *The Wedding Journey*

Date of Publication: 1947
Subject(s): Erie Canal
Fictional character(s): Roger Wilcox, Young Man; Bella Wilcox, Spouse
Time Period(s): 1830s (1835)
Locale(s): Erie Canal, New York

Summary: The novel describes the honeymoon trip of Roger and Bella Wilcox from Schenectady to Buffalo, a three-day journey on the Erie Canal. In Richard's impatience to reach their destination, the stages of the their journey and their fellow travellers are vividly detailed.

Historical Accuracy: The author has mastered this period and locale and recreates it with color and verve.

1879 *Young Ames*

Date of Publication: 1942
Subject(s): Business Building
Fictional character(s): John Ames, Businessman; Christine Chevalier, Gentlewoman
Historical character(s): Andrew Jackson, Political Figure
Time Period(s): 1830s (1833-1835)
Locale(s): New York, New York

Summary: Life in New York City in the 1830s is depicted in the story of young John Ames' rise to success in business and his marriage to the senior partner's daughter. Young Ames'

adventures in business paint a colorful portrait of period New York.

Historical Accuracy: Although the author lays no claims to historical value of any sort for the novel it is clear that sources were consulted, and that the period details have been shaped by the facts.

C.M. EDMONDSTON

M.L.F. HYDE

1880 *King's Man*

Date of Publication: 1948
Subject(s): Middle Ages; Crusades; Royalty—England
Historical character(s): Henry II, Ruler (King of England); Eleanor of Aquitaine, Royalty (queen consort of Henry II); William Marshal, Knight, Nobleman; Richard the Lionhearted, Royalty (prince)
Time Period(s): 12th century (1169-1189)
Locale(s): England; France; Palestine

Summary: The novel depicts events in the reign of Henry II from the perspective of Henry's loyal retainer William Marshal. The political maneuvering of the Plantagenets forms the background as Henry attempts to consolidate and hold his kingdom in both England and France.

Historical Accuracy: The story is largely based on fact with some events and conversations imagined.

ANNE EDWARDS (1927-)

1881 *Haunted Summer*

Date of Publication: 1972
Subject(s): Literary Life; Regency Period
Historical character(s): Percy Bysshe Shelley, Writer (poet); Mary Wollstonecraft Shelley, Writer; George Gordon Byron, Writer (poet); John Polidori, Doctor
Time Period(s): 1810s (1816)
Locale(s): Lake Geneva, Switzerland

Summary: Shelley and his second wife, Mary, spent the summer of 1816 in Switzerland with Bryon. This historical situation becomes the occasion for a gothic tale narrated by Marry Shelley of haunted castles and strange and tragic goings-on.

Historical Accuracy: The situation is historical but everything else is fanciful.

1882 *The Hesitant Heart*

Date of Publication: 1974
Subject(s): Biography, Fictionalized; Literary life
Historical character(s): Emily Dickinson, Writer (poet), Recluse
Time Period(s): 19th century
Locale(s): Amherst, Massachusetts

Summary: The author sets out to solve the various mysteries of poet Emily Dickinson's emotional attachments by imaginatively revealing her interior life in private correspondence.

Historical Accuracy: The novel makes frequent use of Dickinson's verse and letters and convincingly establishes the atmosphere of the poet's house, family, and possibilities.

1883 *Wallis: The Novel*

Date of Publication: 1991
Subject(s): Royalty—England; Biography, Fictionalized
Historical character(s): Edward VIII, Ruler (King of England); Wallis Warfield Simpson, Socialite
Time Period(s): 19th century; 20th century (1899-1937)
Locale(s): United States; England; China

Summary: The novel details the life of Wallis Simpson, who becomes the Duchess of Windsor and for whom Edward VIII relinquishes his crown. Her life is described from her youth in Baltimore, to her two marriages before becoming the Prince of Wales' mistress. This is very much an insider's view, and Mrs. Simpson emerges as a strong and determined woman while Edward VIII is shown as weak and lacking.

Historical Accuracy: The events and details are credible; the imagined and private conversations are very much speculations on the part of the author.

JAROLDEEN EDWARDS

1884 *Harvest of Dreams*

Date of Publication: 1994
Subject(s): American Colonies; Settlement of the American Frontier; American Revolution
Fictional character(s): Nathan Fairchild, Settler; Ainsley Windsor, Young Woman; Talmadge Fairchild, Captive
Time Period(s): 1770s
Locale(s): Marshfield, Massachusetts, American Colonies

Summary: Set during the early years of the American Revolution, the novel tells the story of Nathan Fairchild, a settler in colonial Massachussetts. His home is burned, his wife murdered, and his children stolen by a French and Indian raiding party. He rebuilds and is surprised to find a rival for the love of Ainsley Windsor—his son Talmadge, returned from captivity.

Historical Accuracy: The evocation of period life is convincing.

RHODA S. EDWARDS

1885 *The Broken Sword*

Date of Publication: 1976
Subject(s): War of the Roses; Royalty—England
Historical character(s): Richard III, Ruler (King of England); Anne Neville, Royalty (queen consort of Richard III); Elizabeth of York, Royalty (princess)
Time Period(s): 15th century (1483-1485)
Locale(s): England

Summary: The complex and enigmatic Richard III is the subject of this novel that depicts the two years of his troubled reign from the perspective of a variety of eye witnesses, including the king himself. What emerges is a more balanced

portrait than that given by Shakespeare and subsequent historical interpretations.

Historical Accuracy: The period details show evident research and support the novel's view of Richard III and his times. The author is clearly a partisan of Richard, which affects interpretation.

1886 *Fortune's Wheel*

Date of Publication: 1979
Subject(s): War of the Roses; Royalty—England
Historical character(s): Edward IV, Ruler (King of England); Richard, Duke of Gloucester, Nobleman (Duke of Gloucester); Richard Neville, Nobleman (Earl of Warwick); Anne Neville, Noblewoman (consort of Richard III); Louis XI, Ruler (King of France)
Time Period(s): 15th century (1468-1472)
Locale(s): England; France

Summary: The novel offers a view of the young Richard, Duke of Gloucester, who will become Richard III. Instead of Shakespeare's villainous monster, Richard is shown here as a man torn between his brother Edward IV and the Earl of Warwick whose daughter, Anne, he loves.

Historical Accuracy: The author's evident intimacy with the period supports her interpretation of the events and the personalities.

SAMUEL EDWARDS
(PSEUD. OF NOEL B. GERSON, 1914-1988)

Samuel Edwards is a pseudonym for prolific author Noel B. Gerson. An American writer, Gerson was born in Chicago and educated at the University of Chicago. During World War II, Edwards served in military intelligence. He was a newspaper reporter, radio and TV scriptwriter, and the author of over 100 books. His historical novels feature a lively and entertaining blend of fact and fiction.

1887 *The King's Messenger*

Date of Publication: 1956
Subject(s): American Colonies
Fictional character(s): Terence Haliwell, Government Official (king's messenger)
Historical character(s): Louis de Buade, Government Official (governor-general of Canada), Nobleman (Comte de Frontenac)
Time Period(s): 17th century (1695)
Locale(s): England; American Colonies; Quebec, Canada

Summary: Set in Quebec and the American Colonies during the 17th century, this adventure novel follows the experiences of Terence Halliwell, an agent of King William III, in the intrigue between the English and the French.

Historical Accuracy: The story is fanciful but filled with believable period touches.

1888 *Master of Castile*

Date of Publication: 1962

Subject(s): Royalty—Spain
Historical character(s): Alvaro de Luna, Government Official (constable of Castile); Juan II, Ruler (King of Castile); Juan Hurtado de Mendoza, Government Official (minister-in-chief); Francisco Ruminez, Religious (cardinal); Isabel of Portugal, Royalty (queen consort of Juan II)
Time Period(s): 15th century (1410s-1430s)
Locale(s): Toledo, Spain; Granada, Spain

Summary: The novel chronicles the life and times of Alvaro de Luna, a favorite of Juan II of Castile, who, as constable and grand master of the Order of Santiago, virtually rules the kingdom. He achieves victories over the Moors and the rebellious nobles. Enmity with Juan's second wife leads to his trial and execution.

Historical Accuracy: The novel accurately captures the court intrigue and the period Spanish setting.

1889 *The Queen's Husband*
Date of Publication: 1960
Subject(s): Royalty—England; Independence—Netherlands; Glorious Revolution
Historical character(s): William of Orange, Nobleman (Duke of Orange); Mary Stuart, Royalty (princess), Ruler (Queen of England); John de Witt, Political Figure; John Churchill, Nobleman (Duke of Marlborough); Anne, Royalty (princess)
Time Period(s): 17th century (1669-1688)
Locale(s): Netherlands; England

Summary: The novel offers a sympathetic portrait of William of Orange, who challenges the invincibility of Louis XIV for the freedom of his native Netherlands. He makes a political marriage with the fifteen-year-old niece of England's Charles II. William gradually learns to love Mary, and in 1688 topples James II and takes her home to be crowned queen.

Historical Accuracy: The novel's historical background is accurately portrayed. The interpretation of William, however, is unusual. He is shown as far more human and heroic than history usually records him.

1890 *The Scimitar*
Date of Publication: 1955
Subject(s): Ottoman Empire
Fictional character(s): Julian Hamilton, Military Personnel (captain); Celia Vinton, Gentlewoman; Laya Fayema, Noblewoman
Time Period(s): 18th century
Locale(s): Constantinople, Ottoman Empire; Belgrade, Ottoman Empire

Summary: Captain Julian Hamilton, a veteran of the Duke of Marlborough's campaigns, agrees to become a military adviser to the Turks and travels to Constantinople. There he gets involved with two women: Celia Vinton, a young Englishwoman; and Laya Fayema, a powerful Turkish noblewoman. The resolution of Hamilton's romantic dilemma is played out during the Battle of Belgrade.

Historical Accuracy: The period history is well-researched and presented, though the emphasis is more on romantic adventure than historical precision.

1891 *Theodora*
Date of Publication: 1969
Subject(s): Byzantine Empire
Historical character(s): Theodora, Ruler (Byzantine empress); Justinian I, Ruler (Byzantine emperor)
Time Period(s): 6th century
Locale(s): Constantinople, Byzantine Empire

Summary: The novel dramatizes the remarkable story of Theodora and Justinian who together rejuvenated the faltering Eastern Roman Empire. Theodora was a courtesan who schemed to win the scholarly Justinian. Together they reformed the legal codes, drove the barbarians out of Italy, and sparked major theological controversies. Through it all they created an important political partnership with far-reaching consequences.

Historical Accuracy: The scholarship is evident in this authentic look at Byzantine politics and the personalities of Theodora and Justinian.

FEROL EGAN (1923-)

Born in Sonora, California, Egan grew up on a cattle ranch and has been a teacher, science writer, lumberjack, longshoreman, and historian. His books, *The El Dorado Trail* and *Sand in a Whirlwind*, won the Commonwealth Medal.

1892 *The Taste of Time*
Date of Publication: 1977
Subject(s): American West; Wagon Trains
Fictional character(s): Jedediah Wright, Farmer, Widow(er)
Time Period(s): 1850s (1859)
Locale(s): California; Oregon Trail, United States

Summary: Jedediah Wright, a New York state farmer and widower, decides to head West. Traveling in a mule-drawn wagon, he falls in with a pair of young men; and together they deal with Indians and Mormons before Jed's final remarkable adventures in California.

Historical Accuracy: The novel captures its era and the region with authenticity.

JUDITH EGAN (1942-)

1893 *Elena*
Date of Publication: 1981
Subject(s): Russian Revolution; World War I
Historical character(s): Elena Islavina, Gentlewoman; Ivan Shatagin, Military Personnel (captain)
Time Period(s): 20th century (1900-1920s)
Locale(s): Russia; Turkey

Summary: This is a tale of love and survival during the Russian Revolution based on the true story of Elena Islavina, the daughter of Russian aristocrats, and Ivan Shatagin, a young captain in the Czar's army. They overcome parental opposition to their marriage but then must contend with the overwhelming forces of the Revolution.

Historical Accuracy: Based on a true story, the novel interweaves fact and fiction and offers a personal and human interpretation of the great events of Russian history.

JOHN EHLE (1925-)

Born in Asheville, North Carolina, Ehle attended the University of North Carolina. He served in the U.S. Army during World War II. A former associate professor at his alma mater and special assistant to North Carolina's governor Terry Sandford, Ehle has served on the boards of several organizations and foundations. His novels include *Move Over, Mountain*, *Kingstree Island*, and *Lion on the Hearth*.

1894 *The Journey of August King*
Date of Publication: 1971
Subject(s): Antebellum South; Slavery
Fictional character(s): August King, Mountain Man; Williamsburg, Slave
Time Period(s): 19th century
Locale(s): North Carolina

Summary: The novel describes the unusual relationship between North Carolina mountain man August King and a 15-year-old runaway slave girl named Williamsburg. What to do with her becomes a dilemma for King, as he must deal with the culture of rural North Carolina before the Civil War.

Historical Accuracy: The novel presents a convincing portrait of the time and the region.

1895 *The Land Breakers*
Date of Publication: 1964
Subject(s): American Colonies; Settlement of the American Frontier
Fictional character(s): Mooney Wright, Settler; Tinkler Harrison, Settler
Time Period(s): 1770s; 1780s (1779-1784)
Locale(s): North Carolina

Summary: Mooney Wright, the first settler to arrive in a remote North Carlonia mountain region, begins to clear the land. Tinkler Harrison follows, bringing his slaves and some vestiges of civilization. The novel describes their personal crises, hunt for a massive bear, and attempt to drive livestock to market over the mountains.

Historical Accuracy: This is an authentic depiction of pioneer life and customs in rural North Carolina.

1896 *The Road*
Date of Publication: 1967
Subject(s): Railroads
Fictional character(s): Weatherby Wright, Engineer, Railroad Worker
Time Period(s): 1870s
Locale(s): North Carolina

Summary: This novel continues the history of the North Carolina mountain region begun in *The Land Breakers*. While overseeing construction of the region's first railroad in the 1870s, Weatherby Wright must contend with engineering problems and the use of convict labor.

Historical Accuracy: The story is faithful to the spirit and atmosphere of the region and its development.

1897 *Time of Drums*
Date of Publication: 1970
Subject(s): Civil War—U.S.; Battle of Chancellorsville; Battle of Gettysburg
Fictional character(s): Owen Wright, Military Personnel (Confederate colonel)
Time Period(s): 1860s (1862-1863)
Locale(s): Virginia; North Carolina

Summary: The novel chronicles the Civil War experiences of a North Carolina mountain regiment during the critical campaigns of 1863. Confederate Colonel Owen Wright, after spending time in winter camp with his family, leads his regiment in the battles at Chancellorsville and Gettysburg.

Historical Accuracy: This is a believable and authentic novel, with a strong sense of the Civil War period and its customs.

LEONARD EHRLICH (1905-)

Born in New York City, Ehrlich is a powerful novelist of social processes and their impact on individuals. He has been lauded as well for his poetic sensibility and his portraits of figures in the abolition movement such as William Lloyd Garrison.

1898 *God's Angry Man*
Date of Publication: 1932
Subject(s): Slavery; Biography, Fictionalized
Historical character(s): John Brown, Abolitionist; James Ewell Brown Stuart, Military Personnel (officer); Henry David Thoreau, Writer
Time Period(s): 1850s
Locale(s): Kansas; Virginia

Summary: This biographical novel dramatizes the violent career of abolitionist John Brown during his participation in the Free Soil movement in Kansas. The novel's climax is Brown's attack on Harper's Ferry and his ensuing trial and execution.

Historical Accuracy: Though some elements have been invented or altered, the basic narrative remains close to the known facts, and the dialogue is based on evident research.The author's forward makes clear that its intention is not strictly historical, but a free and vigorous adaptation of historical facts.

TOM EIDSON (1944-)

An executive at the public relations firm of Hill & Knowlton in New York, Eidson was formerly CEO of that firm but stepped down in order to devote more time to his writing. He published his first novel, the Spur award-winning *St. Agnes' Stand*, in 1994. Eidson was born in southern California and graduated from Texas A & M University.

1899 *The Last Ride*

Date of Publication: 1995
Subject(s): American West; Indians
Fictional character(s): Samuel Jones, Frontiersman; Maggie Baldwin, Young Woman
Time Period(s): 1880s (1886)
Locale(s): Southwest

Summary: In this western tale, Samuel Jones abandons his daughter, Maggie, to live with the Indians. When he returns, years later, his plans to make peace with her are interrupted by a band of renegade Apaches who kidnap Maggie's daughter to sell to slave traders in Mexico. Father and daughter set out in pursuit.

Historical Accuracy: The novel is exact in its regional and period details.

1900 *St. Agnes' Stand*

Date of Publication: 1994
Subject(s): American West; Indians
Fictional character(s): Nat Swanson, Fugitive; Sister St. Agnes, Religious (nun)
Time Period(s): 1880s
Locale(s): New Mexico

Summary: Nat Swanson is on the run from having killed a man in self-defense. Deep in the New Mexico desert, he encounters the survivors of an Apache ambush—three nuns and seven orphans. Sister St. Agnes regards Nat as the answer to their prayers, and Nat must deal with the burden that her trust in him produces.

Historical Accuracy: The novel captures the setting with skill and authenticity.

KARL V. EIKER

1901 *Star of Macedon*

Date of Publication: 1957
Subject(s): Macedonian Empire
Fictional character(s): Gyges, Slave
Historical character(s): Alexander the Great, Ruler (King of Macedonia); Philip II, Ruler (King of Macedonia)
Time Period(s): 4th century B.C.
Locale(s): Macedonia; Persia

Summary: It is said that no man is a hero to his valet, and Alexander the Great is no hero to his slave, Gyges. This portrait of Alexander's entire career reduces the legend to very human dimensions.

Historical Accuracy: The basic framework of the events is factual, but there are far more surmises and interpretations than documented facts.

ROBERT S. ELEGANT (1928-)

Born in New York City and educated at the University of Pennsylvania, Yale, and Columbia, Elegant was a foreign correspondent in Japan, Korea, and China for *Newsweek* and the chief of the Hong Kong bureau for the *Los Angeles*

Times. His novels were written with the hope of giving Western readers a view of China's recent history and the character of the Chinese that they would not have received otherwise.

1902 *Dynasty*

Date of Publication: 1977
Subject(s): East/West Relations; Business Building; Chinese Revolution
Fictional character(s): Jonathan Sekloong, Bastard Son, Trader; Charles Sekloong, Businessman; Mary Osgood, Young Woman
Historical character(s): Sun Yat-Sen, Political Figure; Chiang Kai-Shek, Political Figure; Mao Tse-tung, Political Figure
Time Period(s): 20th century (1900-1970)
Locale(s): Hong Kong; China

Summary: The novel traces Chinese history during the first 70 years of the 20th century from the perspective of the Sekloong family, founded by Jonathan Sekloong, illegitimate son of a Chinese woman and an Irish soldier of fortune. His trading empire is created during the turbulence of the Chinese Revolution while two of his grandsons pursue opposite paths in the political struggle.

Historical Accuracy: The novel is authentic in its delivery of both the personalities and events of the period.

1903 *From a Far Land*

Date of Publication: 1987
Subject(s): Chinese Revolution
Fictional character(s): Julia Pavernen, Young Woman; Emily Howe, Young Woman; Tommy Howe, Revolutionary
Historical character(s): Chiang Kai-Shek, Political Figure; Chou En-lai, Political Figure; Mao Tse-tung, Political Figure
Time Period(s): 20th century (1921-1952)
Locale(s): Shanghai, China

Summary: This dramatic saga combines a love story with the violent birth of modern China. Two recent Bryn Mawr graduates sail to Shanghai where they find class differences and unrest which will eventually explode into the Chinese Revolution. The struggle between the Nationalists and the Communists, the epic Long March, and the Sino-Japanese War are all depicted.

Historical Accuracy: The historical events are in the forefront, authentically described.

1904 *Manchu*

Date of Publication: 1980
Subject(s): East/West Relations; Chinese Empire; Espionage
Fictional character(s): Francis Arrowsmith, Mercenary, Adventurer; Marta Soo, Gentlewoman
Historical character(s): Paul Hsu, Political Figure
Time Period(s): 17th century (1624-1652)
Locale(s): China; Korea

Summary: Francis Arrowsmith is a British mercenary drawn to China in the 17th century to recoup his fortune. He stays in China for over 30 years as the Ming dynasty falls to the

Manchus. He is connected with court intrigue and romance with several strong and powerful women.

Historical Accuracy: The author has carefully based his characters and events on historical precedents.

⬛1905⬛ *Mandarin*

Date of Publication: 1983
Subject(s): East/West Relations; Chinese Empire; Business Building
Fictional character(s): Aisek Lee, Businessman (merchant); Sal Haleevie, Businessman (merchant); Fronah Haleevie, Young Woman; Gabriel Hyde, Military Personnel (American naval officer)
Historical character(s): Yenehala, Ruler (Dowager Empress)
Time Period(s): 19th century (1852-1875)
Locale(s): Shanghai, China; Peking, China

Summary: Set during the tumultuous years of mid-19th century China that saw the Taiping rebellion and the rise of the formidable Dowager Empress, the novel tells the story of two merchantile families. The families are headed by Aisek Lee, one of the few Chinese-born Jews, and Saul Haleevie, a Jewish merchant who has fled from in persecution in Persia and India. Saul's daughter, Fronah, provides the story's romantic interest in her love affair with Gabriel Hyde, an American naval officer. All are swept up in the violent events that wrack all of China.

Historical Accuracy: The novel is an impressive historical account of the times; credible and fully developed.

⬛1906⬛ *The Seeking*

Date of Publication: 1969
Subject(s): Mongol Empire
Fictional character(s): Harrap, Royalty (Prince of Kamardol); Ambiala, Lover (courtesan)
Time Period(s): 2nd century B.C.
Locale(s): Asia (central Asia)

Summary: To escape the murderous intrigue of his kingdom, Harrap, Prince of Kamardol sets off on a year-long pilgrimage called The Seeking. He and a small band of warriors follow The Horse, avatar of the gods, into the great plains of Central Asia where they encounter a variety of cultures: Indian, Chinese, Greek, Jewish, and Nomad.

Historical Accuracy: The novel is a remarkable depiction of the past with a convincing animation of ancient customs.

ETHEL COOK ELIOT (1893-)

Born in North Gage, New York, Eliot is the author of *The Little House in Fairy Wood*, *The Wind Boy*, and *Roses for Mexico*.

⬛1907⬛ *Roses for Mexico*

Date of Publication: 1946
Subject(s): Religious Life
Historical character(s): Juan Diego, Indian; Juan de Zumarraga, Religious (bishop)
Time Period(s): 16th century (1531)

Locale(s): Mexico City, Mexico

Summary: The novel tells the story of the revelation of the Virgin Mary to an Indian convert, Juan Diego, on his way to mass in Mexico City. She instructs him to build a church on the site of her appearance. The Guadalupe shrine is one of the holiest sites in North America, and the novel helps explain its significance to Mexican life.

Historical Accuracy: The dialogue ascribed to Juan Diego is unconvincing.

GEORGE ELIOT
(PSEUD. OF MARY ANN EVANS, 1819-1880)

Born Mary Ann Evans, George Eliot was raised on a farm in the English Midlands. In 1851, she became assistant editor of the *Westminster Review* and met some of London's leading literary figures, including writer and intellectual George Henry Lewes. Although unable to marry since Lewes was legally prohibited from divorcing his estranged wife, Eliot and Lewes fell in love and lived together until his death. Her other major novels include *The Mill on the Floss*, *Felix Holt*, and *Daniel Deronda*.

⬛1908⬛ *Adam Bede*

Date of Publication: 1859
Subject(s): Crime and Criminals; Georgian Period
Fictional character(s): Adam Bede, Carpenter; Dinah Morris, Religious (Methodist lay-preacher); Arthur Donnithorne, Gentleman, Military Personnel; Hetty Sorrel, Criminal (child-murderer)
Time Period(s): 1790s (1799)
Locale(s): Hayslope, England (English village in the Midlands); Midlands, England

Summary: The seduction of Hetty Sorel by the young squire Arthur Donnithorne is the core of the drama. Hetty is loved by the stalwart Adam Bede and befriended by itinerant Methodist lay-preacher Dinah Morris. Hetty is convicted of child murder and is saved from the gallows by Arthur's intervention. Eliot's lesson here is the inevitable working of moral consequence.

Historical Accuracy: Eliot's picture of rural English life is convincing, based on her childhood memories.

⬛1909⬛ *Middlemarch*

Date of Publication: 1872
Subject(s): Politics; Medical Profession
Fictional character(s): Dorothea Brooke, Gentlewoman; Tertius Lydgate, Doctor; Edward Casaubon, Religious, Scholar
Time Period(s): 1830s
Locale(s): Middlemarch, England (based on Coventry, England); Rome, Italy

Summary: *Middlemarch* is George Eliot's masterpiece, a complex panoramic portrait of English provincial life around the time of the passage of the Reform Bill of the 1830s that began the shift of political power from the upperclass to the middleclass. The disappointment of two idealists—Dorothea

Brooke and Doctor Lydgate—are contrasted in an intricate web of interdependent social customs.

Historical Accuracy: Eliot's skill is capturing all aspects of English life. Few novels have ever attempted such an ambitious social documentation.

1910 *Romola*

Date of Publication: 1863
Subject(s): Renaissance; Crime and Criminals
Fictional character(s): Romola, Scholar; Tito Melema, Adventurer, Criminal
Historical character(s): Charles VIII, Ruler (King of France); Niccolo Machiavelli, Philosopher; Girolamo Savonarola, Religious
Time Period(s): 15th century (1492-1498)
Locale(s): Florence, Italy

Summary: Set in 15th-century Florence following the expulsion of the Medici, *Romola* utilizes the arrival of Charles VIII and the fanatical preaching of Savonarola as the historical background for a plot involving a thoroughly wicked adventurer, Tito Melema, and the thoroughly good Romola, whom he marries. Eliot shows the working of nemesis in the form of the return of Tito's former benefactor whom he has cheated and ignored.

Historical Accuracy: Eliot renders the historical figures and period with great care.

1911 *Silas Marner*

Date of Publication: 1861
Subject(s): Rural Life—England; Crime and Criminals
Fictional character(s): Silas Marner, Artisan (linen weaver); Eppie Cass, Orphan, Heir—Lost; Dunstan Cass, Gentleman, Criminal
Time Period(s): 18th century
Locale(s): Raveloe, England (rural village)

Summary: The redemption of the miserly Marner by the love of a child whom he adopts is the theme of the novel. The mysteries of her identity and Marner's cache of gold are eventually unravelled. The story's unrelenting somberness of tone is relieved by humorous vignettes of rural village life.

Historical Accuracy: The melodramatic complications are at odds with the more precisely imagined scenes of English village life at the turn of the 18th century.

GEORGE FIELDING ELIOT

1912 *Caleb Pettengill U.S.N.*

Date of Publication: 1956
Subject(s): Civil War—U.S.; Sea Story
Fictional character(s): Caleb Pettengill, Military Personnel (naval captain); Emma Harrifield, Abolitionist; Terry Seabright, Southern Belle
Time Period(s): 1860s
Locale(s): Chesapeake Bay, Virginia; At Sea (Carolina Coast)
Summary: This is the story of the development of the modern steam navy seen through Caleb Pettengill's experiences in the

Civil War. With the outbreak of hostilities, he delivers reinforcements to Fort Monroe in Virginia, attempts the removal of the steam frigate *Merrimac* from the Navy Yard at Norfolk, and takes up blockade duty along the Carolina coast.

Historical Accuracy: The details of naval history and the military action are convincing.

GERHART ELLERT
(PSEUD. OF GERTRUD SCHMIRGER, 1900-)

Ellert is a German writer.

1913 *Gregory the Great*

Date of Publication: 1963
Subject(s): Biography, Fictionalized; Roman Empire; Religious Life
Fictional character(s): Damianus, Secretary
Historical character(s): Gregory I, Religious (pope)
Time Period(s): 6th century; 7th century (540-640)
Locale(s): Rome, Italy

Summary: This fictional life of Pope Gregory I is narrated by his secretary, Damianus. Gregory is one of the architects of papal power in the church, insisting on the temporal authority of the pope, which has significant historical consequences.

Historical Accuracy: For a purported biography, Gregory's life is only dimly sketched. There is also evident omission of details to create a more harmonious portrait of Gregory.

EDWARD E. ELLIOTT (1911-)

1914 *The Devil and the Mathers*

Date of Publication: 1989
Subject(s): American Colonies; Puritans; Witchcraft and Sorcery
Historical character(s): Cotton Mather, Religious (clergyman); Increase Mather, Religious (clergyman)
Time Period(s): 17th century (1692)
Locale(s): Salem, Massachusetts, American Colonies

Summary: The novel captures the events of the 1692 Salem witchcraft trials. When a number of young girls accuse a West Indian servant of sorcery, the hysteria, fueled by the zealous Puritan religious leaders Cotton and Increase Mather, produces a number of executions of the "minions of Satan."

Historical Accuracy: The novel provides an accurate version of the events of 1692.

JANICE ELLIOTT (1931-)

An English author born in Derby, Elliott graduated from Oxford University. She has worked as a journalist, novelist, and critic. *Secret Places* won the Southern Arts Award for Literature.

1915 *Angels Falling*

Date of Publication: 1969
Subject(s): Family Saga

Fictional character(s): Lilian Candish, Young Woman; Andrew Garland, Journalist
Time Period(s): 20th century (1900s-1960s)
Locale(s): England

Summary: This English family saga follows the life of Lilian Candish, who is born on the day of Queen Victoria's funeral and dies in the 1960s. The novel records her marriage to journalist Andrew Garland and their children's search for success and meaning in their lives.

Historical Accuracy: English history forms the background for the novel's story, including World War I, the women's suffrage movement, the Spanish Civil War, and World War II.

JOHN ELLIOTT (1918-)

1916　*Blood on the Snow*

Date of Publication: 1977
Subject(s): Russo-Japanese War; Russian Revolution
Fictional character(s): Sophia Petrovna, Noblewoman, Widow(er); George Gapon, Religious (priest); Boris Volkov, Military Personnel
Historical character(s): Maxim Gorky, Writer; Leon Trotsky, Revolutionary; Vladimir Ilich Lenin, Revolutionary
Time Period(s): 19th century; 20th century (1899-1906)
Locale(s): Russia; Manchuria, China

Summary: The novel chronicles the early stages of the Russian Revolution—the 1905 Bloody Sunday Procession to the Winter Palace, the mutiny of the *Potemkin*, and the murderous struggle between the Bolsheviks and the Czar's secret police. Sophia Petrovna is an aristocrat, widowed by an assassin, who is converted to the cause of the revolution. Boris Volkov is an officer in the Czar's army whose reaction against the suppression of the Jews and rebels condemns him to death.

Historical Accuracy: The canvas is very broad but realistic in its depiction of the era's great events and issues.

AMANDA MAE ELLIS (1898-1969)

Born in Missouri, Ellis graduated from Colorado College and the University of Iowa and was a professor of English at the University of Illinois and Colorado College. She is the author of textbooks and historical studies, as well as novels, including *The Strange, Uncertain Years* and *Rebels and Conservatives*.

1917　*Elizabeth, the Woman*

Date of Publication: 1951
Subject(s): Elizabethan Period; Royalty—England; Biography, Fictionalized
Historical character(s): Elizabeth I, Ruler (Queen of England)
Time Period(s): 16th century; 17th century (1543-1603)
Locale(s): England

Summary: The reign of Elizabeth I is depicted in this fictional biography that follows her career from age ten to her death 60 years later. The novel offers both a psychological portrait of the queen and a vivid look at her age.

Historical Accuracy: The biographical details are faithful to the facts of Elizabeth's life and the events of her reign.

JULIE ELLIS (1933-)

An American writer born in Columbus, Georgia, Ellis moved to New York for a theatrical career before turning to writing. She has written nearly 150 books under different names. Her romances are respected for their strong historical backgrounds.

1918　*Eden*

Date of Publication: 1975
Subject(s): Antebellum South; Slavery
Fictional character(s): Michael Eden, Heir, Plantation Owner; Victoria Wickersham, Spouse (of Michael)
Time Period(s): 19th century
Locale(s): New Orleans, Louisiana

Summary: Michael Eden brings his new bride, Victoria, to the plantation world of the South prior to the Civil War. She causes bitter animosity among Michael's family as she tries to win his love. They join an antislavery campaign that brings them closer together but causes conflict and resentment with others.

Historical Accuracy: The novel offers a convincing portrait of a particular time and place.

1919　*Glorious Morning*

Date of Publication: 1982
Subject(s): Theatrical Life; Motion Picture Industry; World War I
Fictional character(s): Rissa Lindowska, Immigrant, Actress; Max Miller, Businessman; Phillip Cambridge, Nobleman
Time Period(s): 20th century (1906-1922)
Locale(s): Poland; London, England; New York, New York

Summary: When Rissa Lindowska flees the pograms in Poland, she first goes to London where she becomes romantically involved with an English lord. Later she moves to New York and establishes herself on the Yiddish stage. Her career is set against the backdrop of both World War I and the birth of the movie industry.

Historical Accuracy: The period details, particularly those of theatrical life, are convincingly displayed.

1920　*The Hampton Heritage*

Date of Publication: 1978
Subject(s): Family Saga; Business Building; Spanish-American War
Fictional character(s): Caroline Hampton, Heiress, Orphan; Josiah Hampton, Businessman; Eric Hampton, Political Figure; Tina Hampton, Spouse (of Eric)
Time Period(s): 1890s
Locale(s): Atlanta, Georgia

Summary: Caroline Hampton journeys to Atlanta to claim her inheritance, but her grandfather, Josiah, refuses to acknowledge their kinship. She works to be accepted and succeeds, but her happiness in her love for Eric Hampton is complicated by his scheming wife, Tina.

Historical Accuracy: This family saga has a surprisingly full depiction of the period events of the Spanish-American War.

1921 *The Hampton Women*

Date of Publication: 1980
Subject(s): World War I; Family Saga; Shipwrecks
Fictional character(s): Caroline Hampton, Businesswoman; Elizabeth Hampton, Teenager; Maureen Hampton, Bastard Daughter
Time Period(s): 1910s (1913-1918)
Locale(s): Atlanta, Georgia; Washington, District of Columbia

Summary: The novel offers portraits of three strong women, Caroline, Elizabeth, and Maureen Hampton, set against the backdrop of the events from 1913 to 1918 as America drifts toward involvement in World War I. Domestic and personal history mix with larger political themes.

Historical Accuracy: The novel offers a fairly detailed look at some of the social and political issues of the period.

1922 *The Magnolias*

Date of Publication: 1976
Subject(s): Antebellum South; Slavery; Romance
Fictional character(s): Jeannie Fleming, Orphan; Kevin Ransome, Plantation Owner; Dennis Mitchell, Heir
Time Period(s): 1840s
Locale(s): Charleston, South Carolina; Georgia (coastal)

Summary: Orphaned when her mother dies suddenly, Jeannie Fleming becomes the ward of her cousin, Kevin Ransome. She flees his unwanted advances to marry Dennis Mitchell, an heir to The Magnolias, a Charleston plantation. There, Jeannie experiences the decay that seems to infect all.

Historical Accuracy: Romance is predominant in this antebellum tale with some authentic period details.

1923 *The Only Sin*

Date of Publication: 1986
Subject(s): Romance; Business Building
Fictional character(s): Lilli Landau, Bastard Daughter, Businesswoman; Jacques Laval, Adventurer; Mischa Lamsaloff, Royalty (prince)
Time Period(s): 20th century (1903-1979)
Locale(s): Marienbad, Germany; Australia; London, England

Summary: The novel spans three-quarters of the 20th century and three continents. It is the story of Lilli Landau's rise to power and fame as the founder of a great cosmetics empire. She is the illegitimate daughter of an unknown father whose search for her identity takes her from Germany to Australia and finally America in scenes that capture great events of the period.

Historical Accuracy: The novel is filled with historical details of the 1920s, the Depression, World War II, and the Red Scare. All are interwoven with the novel's story of love and business.

1924 *Savage Oaks*

Date of Publication: 1977
Subject(s): Antebellum South; Romance
Fictional character(s): Suzanne Dupree, Orphan, Heiress; Keith Savage, Heir, Plantation Owner; Phillip Savage, Gentleman
Time Period(s): 1850s
Locale(s): New Orleans, Louisiana; Savannah, Georgia

Summary: Orphan Suzanne Dupree finds herself heiress to a Louisiana estate. There, she meets and marries Keith Savage, heir to a neighboring plantation, Savage Oaks. He has married her only to secure his property, and Suzanne, in despair, begins a search for the identity of her parents.

Historical Accuracy: The emphasis is on romantic suspense with a slight period background.

KENNETH M. ELLIS

1925 *Guns Forever Echo*

Date of Publication: 1941
Subject(s): Middle Ages; Hundred Years War; Plague
Fictional character(s): Geoffrey Ellis, Gentleman
Time Period(s): 14th century
Locale(s): Yarmouth, England

Summary: This historical novel centers on the English town of Yarmouth and the Ellis family. The story follows the adventures in love and war of Geoffrey Ellis and features a vivid description of the Black Death which hit Yarmouth in 1349.

Historical Accuracy: The novel captures period life authentically and convincingly.

PETER BERRESFORD ELLIS (1943-)

Born in Coventry, England, Ellis studied at Brighton College and has worked as a journalist and editor. A full-time writer since 1975, Ellis is the author of numerous novels of adventure, horror, and fantasy under a variety of pseudonyms. His books include *A Voice from the Infinite: The Life of Sir Henry Rider Haggard* and *The Hound of Frankenstein*. Ellis has also contributed articles on the problems of national minorities to journals in many countries.

1926 *The Rising of the Moon*

Date of Publication: 1987
Subject(s): Independence—Ireland; Fenians
Fictional character(s): Gavin Devlin, Veteran (Union army); John-Joe Devlin, Veteran (Union army)
Historical character(s): Andrew Johnson, Political Figure
Time Period(s): 1860s (1866-1868)
Locale(s): Ireland; Canada; New York

Summary: The novel tells the actual story of the little-known invasion of Canada by an army of Irish-Americans, many of them former Union officers from the Civil War. The novel moves from New England to Ireland, and finally Canada, as the operation in support of freedom for Ireland is planned and executed.

Historical Accuracy: The events are based on extensive research into the facts.

WILLIAM DONOHUE ELLIS (1918-)

Born in Massachusetts, Ellis is a graduate of Wesleyan University. His novel *The Bounty Lands* won an Ohioana Literary Award. He received a Pulitzer Prize nomination for *Jonathan Blair*.

1927　*The Bounty Lands*

Date of Publication: 1952
Subject(s): Settlement of the American Frontier; Homesteading
Fictional character(s): Jonathan Woodbridge, Veteran (American Revolution), Settler
Time Period(s): 18th century; 19th century (1790s-1810s)
Locale(s): Ohio

Summary: Set during the period following the American Revolution, the novel dramatizes the land disputes between speculators and settlers in Ohio over the homesteads granted to veterans for their war service. The story centers on the adventures of Jonathan Woodbridge, a former private in the American army, whose 100 acres in the Northwest Territory become a battle zone.

Historical Accuracy: The novel effectively and convincingly captures the era and the locale.

1928　*The Brooks Legend*

Date of Publication: 1958
Subject(s): Medical Profession; War of 1812; Settlement of the American Frontier
Fictional character(s): Saul Brooks, Doctor; Felicia Jordan, Widow(er)
Time Period(s): 1810s
Locale(s): Mesopotamia, Ohio

Summary: During the War of 1812, Saul Brooks refuses to operate on Colonel Jordan who is certain to die. Brooks is branded with a reputation for neglect that follows him to the Ohio settlement of Mesopotamia where he meets Colonel Jordan's widow, Felicia.

Historical Accuracy: The novel is a colorful story of frontier life and an authentic look at the medical profession of the time.

1929　*Jonathan Blair, Bounty Lands Lawyer*

Date of Publication: 1954
Subject(s): Settlement of the American Frontier; Legal Profession
Fictional character(s): Jonathan Blair, Lawyer
Time Period(s): 1800s
Locale(s): Ohio

Summary: The author continues his history of the Ohio frontier begun in *The Bounty Lands* with the story of frontier lawyer Jonathan Blair who is instrumental in the formation of the Mesopotamia Territory in Ohio.

Historical Accuracy: The novel provides an authentic depiction of frontier life in the Ohio territory during the period.

EDWARD ELLSBERG

1930　*Captain Paul*

Date of Publication: 1941
Subject(s): Sea Story; American Revolution
Fictional character(s): Tom Folger, Sailor
Historical character(s): John Paul Jones, Military Personnel (captain); Benjamin Franklin, Political Figure, Diplomat
Time Period(s): 18th century; 19th century (1773-1808)
Locale(s): Nantucket, Massachusetts; At Sea

Summary: The novel depicts the life and adventures of John Paul Jones from the point of view of a Nantucket sailor. The novel chronicles Jones' remarkable career that includes stints as a pirate and slaver, and his rise to the position of captain by the age of 21. He becomes the first commander of a vessel to fly the American flag. The story climaxes in the epic battle between the *Bonhomme Richard*, captained by Jones, and the British ship *Serapis*.

Historical Accuracy: The author notes the few instances in which he has deviated from the known facts.

HEBE ELSNA
(PSEUD. OF DOROTHY P. ANSLE)

1931　*The Elusive Crown*

Date of Publication: 1973
Subject(s): Royalty—England
Fictional character(s): Christy Merryn, Companion
Historical character(s): Mary, Royalty (princess); Anne, Royalty (princess); James II, Ruler (King of England); Sarah Churchill, Noblewoman (Duchess of Marlborough); William of Orange, Royalty
Time Period(s): 17th century
Locale(s): England

Summary: This is the story of the two daughters of James II, Mary and Anne. The political intrigue surrounding the succession to the English throne is dramatized from the perspective of Christy Merryn, a companion to both royal sisters.

Historical Accuracy: The novel blends factual details of the period with the fictional story of Christy Merryn.

1932　*The King's Bastard*

Date of Publication: 1971
Subject(s): Restoration Period; Royalty—England
Historical character(s): Charles II, Ruler (King of England); James Scott, Nobleman (Duke of Monmouth), Bastard Son; Catherine of Braganza, Royalty (queen consort of Charles II)
Time Period(s): 17th century
Locale(s): England

Summary: This story of Restoration England and the court of King Charles II focuses on the early life of James Scott, later the Duke of Monmouth, the King's illegitimate son. James' curious place in his father's court and his friendship with Charles' queen, Catherine of Braganza, is explored.

Historical Accuracy: The novel is based on fact, but events and details are simplified and idealized into a more romantic tale.

1933 *The Queen's Ward*

Date of Publication: 1967
Subject(s): Elizabethan Period; Royalty—England
Fictional character(s): Morag Trevenna, Ward
Historical character(s): Elizabeth I, Ruler (Queen of England); Robert Dudley, Nobleman (Earl of Leicester)
Time Period(s): 16th century
Locale(s): England

Summary: This tale of intrigue in the court of Elizabeth I revolves around the mysterious death of Amy Robsart, the wife of the queen's favorite, Lord Robert Dudley. Morag Trevenna, Amy's 15-year-old cousin, is taken into the royal household though she holds Dudley and the Queen responsible for Amy's death.

Historical Accuracy: The story is fanciful with imagined dialogue and an invented story line. The details of the Robsart affair are speculation and contradictory.

1934 *The Wise Virgin*

Date of Publication: 1967
Subject(s): Tudor Period; Royalty—England
Fictional character(s): Jocelyn Randhurst, Gentlewoman
Historical character(s): Henry VIII, Ruler (King of England); Jane Seymour, Royalty (queen consort of Henry VIII); Thomas Cranmer, Religious (archbishop); Katherine Howard, Royalty (queen consort of Henry VIII); Anne of Cleves, Royalty (queen consort of Henry VIII)
Time Period(s): 16th century
Locale(s): England

Summary: This fanciful story records how Lady Jocelyn Randhurst fails to win the affection of Henry VIII and to become his queen but also avoids the fate of several of her rivals for the king's attention.

Historical Accuracy: The novel is only occasionally faithful to the period, with a modern sensibility predominating.

MURIEL ELWOOD (1902-)

An English writer born in London, Elwood worked as a secretary prior to 1934 when she became a full-time writer. Her books include *Toward the Sunset*, *Against the Tide*, *Dorothea*, and *The Deluge*.

1935 *Against the Tide*

Date of Publication: 1950
Subject(s): American West
Fictional character(s): Philip Mackay, Young Man; Francisca de Gomez, Young Woman
Time Period(s): 19th century (1879-1896)

Locale(s): Los Angeles, California

Summary: The novel describes the cultural conflict between California's Spanish ranch owners and the American settlers in the closing decades of the 19th century. Philip Mackay is a young American who seeks his fortune and the love of Francisca de Gomez, against her family's wishes.

Historical Accuracy: The novel provides an authentic portrait of the era and the cultural clashes of the period.

1936 *Deeper the Heritage*

Date of Publication: 1947
Subject(s): Frontier—Canada; Indians; Queen Anne's War
Fictional character(s): Elise de Courville-Boissart, Young Woman; Antoine de Brevaux, Military Personnel (naval officer)
Time Period(s): 1710s (1710-1713)
Locale(s): Montreal, Quebec, Canada

Summary: Elise de Courville-Boissart, the daughter of one of Montreal's prominent families, falls in love with Antoine, a French naval officer. Complicating this marriage is the mystery surrounding Antoine's parentage. Trouble from the Indians and the English also interferes.

Historical Accuracy: The novel offers a convincing depiction of life in the French colony.

1937 *Heritage of the River*

Date of Publication: 1945
Subject(s): Frontier—Canada; Indians
Fictional character(s): Paul Boissart, Twin, Trapper; Marguerite Boissart, Twin, Captive
Historical character(s): Louis de Buade, Government Official (colonial governor)
Time Period(s): 17th century (1680s)
Locale(s): Montreal, Quebec, Canada; Quebec, Quebec, Canada

Summary: This tale of life in the New France frontier town of Montreal centers on the Boissart family, specifically twins Paul and Marguerite. Their adventures with the Indians and in romance are related.

Historical Accuracy: The period elements, which are convincing, are undermined by artificial dialogue, thin characterization, and an implausible plot.

1938 *So Much as Beauty Does*

Date of Publication: 1941
Subject(s): Napoleonic Era; Royalty—France
Historical character(s): Charles Ferdinand de Bourbon, Nobleman (Duc de Berry); Amy Brown, Gentlewoman
Time Period(s): 18th century; 19th century
Locale(s): London, England; Paris, France

Summary: Set during the Napoleonic era and the Bourbon restoration, the novel is based on the actual love affair between Amy Brown, the daughter of an English clergyman, and the Duke de Berry, a French exile in London. When Napoleon falls and the duke becomes heir to the French throne, their relationship is doomed.

Historical Accuracy: The historical background is only lightly sketched when real events have a direct impact on the central characters.

1939 *Web of Destiny*

Date of Publication: 1951
Subject(s): French and Indian War; Battle of Quebec
Fictional character(s): Philippe Courville-Boissart, Military Pèrsonnel (French soldier); Nancy Walker, Young Woman
Historical character(s): Louis Joseph de Montcalm, Military Personnel (French general); James Wolfe, Military Personnel (English general)
Time Period(s): 1750s
Locale(s): Canada

Summary: This installment of the Canadian series continues the story of the fortunes of the Courville-Boissart family during the final years of the French control of Canada. Philippe participates in the French defense of Fort Ticonderoga and rescues his cousin, Nancy Walker, from the Indian massacre at Fort William Henry.

Historical Accuracy: The historical events are accurately described and the portraits of the historical figures are believable.

DELLA F. EMMONS (1890-1983)

Born in Minnesota, Emmons is best known for her stories about pioneer days. Her first book, *Sacajawea of the Shoshones*, was written while travelling in the west with her husband. It was made into a film, *The Far Horizon*. Her other books include *Nothing in Life Is Free* and *Northwest History in Action*.

1940 *Sacajawea of the Shoshones*

Date of Publication: 1943
Subject(s): Lewis and Clark Expedition; Indians; Biography, Fictionalized
Historical character(s): Sacajawea, Indian (Shoshone), Guide; Meriwether Lewis, Explorer; William Clark, Explorer
Time Period(s): 18th century; 19th century
Locale(s): Missouri River, United States; Rocky Mountains; Pacific Northwest

Summary: This historical novel is based on the life of the Shoshone Indian guide Sacajawea who helped guide the Lewis and Clark Expedition. It offers a rather romanticized portrait whose basis is the journals of Lewis and Clark and other contemporaries. The novel traces her childhood, the expedition, her later years in St. Louis, and her return to the reservation.

Historical Accuracy: The novel is a blend of the factual and the imagined. The considerable gaps in the biographical record are filled with plausible surmises.

SHUSAKU ENDO (1923-)

A Japanese novelist born in Tokyo, Endo received a degree in French Literature from Keio University and studied for several years at the University of Lyons. Endo is regarded as one of Japan's foremost writers. His Catholic background has helped shape his perspective to encompass the Western traditions, and his work explores how East and West really meet. The result is some of Japan's finest writing.

1941 *The Samurai*

Date of Publication: 1982
Subject(s): East/West Relations; Christianity; Japanese Empire
Fictional character(s): Velasco, Religious (Franciscan missionary)
Historical character(s): Rokuemon Hasekura, Warrior (samurai), Diplomat; Paul V, Religious (pope)
Time Period(s): 17th century (1613-1617)
Locale(s): Japan; Mexico; Europe

Summary: In the 17th century the Japanese respond to the West's scramble for control and influence with a diplomatic mission. Rokuemon Hasekura, a samurai, joined by an ambitious Franciscan missionary, Father Velasco, embark on a journey around the world to Mexico, Spain, and Italy. When Hasekura returns, he finds that the political tide has shifted to an isolationist policy and a violent repression of Western influence.

Historical Accuracy: Though based on actual historical fact, Endo's motive extends far deeper than merely recording the past. The historical background becomes an occasion for a deeper meditation on human motive and frailty.

GUY ENDORE

1942 *King of Paris*

Date of Publication: 1956
Subject(s): Literary Life; Biography, Fictionalized
Historical character(s): Alexandre Dumas, pere, Writer; Alexandre Dumas, fils, Writer; Jules Verne, Writer
Time Period(s): 19th century
Locale(s): Paris, France

Summary: The novel offers the life of Alexandre Dumas with all the verve and panache of a Dumas story. Dumas' assault on literary Paris is described in a way that captures not only his talent and multi-dimensional character but also the period in which Dumas and his son played such major roles.

Historical Accuracy: The novel captures the essence, as opposed to the substance, of Dumas' life.

1943 *Voltaire! Voltaire!*

Date of Publication: 1961
Subject(s): Literary Life; Biography, Fictionalized
Historical character(s): Francois Marie Arouet, Philosopher, Writer (aka Voltaire); Jean Jacques Rousseau, Philosopher, Writer
Time Period(s): 18th century
Locale(s): Paris, France; Geneva, Switzerland

Summary: The novel offers the parallel lives of two 18th-century intellectual giants : Voltaire and Rousseau. The story jumps from one to the other but is connected by the intense rivalry and jealousy Rousseau feels for Voltaire.

Historical Accuracy: All of the characters in the book are real and the background is well documented.

ELIZABETH ENGSTROM
(PSEUD. OF LYNN GUTZMER ENGSTROM, 1951-)

Engstrom is the author of fantasy novels and historical fiction, including *Black Ambrosia*, and *When Darkness Loves Us*.

1944 *Lizzie Borden*

Date of Publication: 1991
Subject(s): Crime and Criminals
Historical character(s): Lizzie Borden, Murderer (accused)
Time Period(s): 1890s (1892)
Locale(s): New Bedford, Massachusetts

Summary: This novel provides a fictional treatment of the notorious Lizzie Borden, who was charged and acquitted in the brutal murder of her father and stepmother. The novel offers a psychological story of the Borden family and their passions and repressions that moves inexorably toward the novel's bloody climax.

Historical Accuracy: While staying close to the basic facts of the case, the novel does employ some speculation as well as a supernatural solution to the crime.

MICHAEL ENNIS

1945 *Byzantium*

Date of Publication: 1989
Subject(s): Byzantine Empire; Vikings
Fictional character(s): Maria, Noblewoman
Historical character(s): Haraldr Sigurdarson, Royalty (Viking prince); Zoe, Ruler (Eastern Roman Empress)
Time Period(s): 11th century (1030-1066)
Locale(s): Constantinople, Byzantine Empire; Norway; Danube River, Europe

Summary: Set in Constantinople in the 11th century, this is a tale of palace intrigue and adventure involving Haraldr Sigurdarson, a dispossessed Viking prince who enters the world of the Viking protectors of the Byzantine Empire.

Historical Accuracy: Extensively researched, the novel is an artful blend of the imagined and the historically reliable.

1946 *Duchess of Milan*

Date of Publication: 1992
Subject(s): Renaissance; Politics
Historical character(s): Isabella d'Aragona, Noblewoman (Duchess of Milan); Ludovico Sforza, Political Figure (regent), Nobleman (Duke of Bari); Beatrice d'Este, Gentlewoman; Gian Galeazzo Sforza, Nobleman (Duke of Milan); Charles VIII, Ruler (King of France); Ferrante of Aragon, Ruler (King of Naples); Leonardo da Vinci, Artist
Time Period(s): 15th century; 16th century (1490-1524)

Locale(s): Milan, Italy; Naples, Italy; Venice, Italy

Summary: Set in Renaissance Italy, the novel details the political intrigue in the Duchy of Milan. Isabella and Beatrice are cousins who are married, respectively, to the Duke of Milan and his uncle, the regent. Both are ambitious and cunning and this story re-creates the scandals and maneuvering of the period.

Historical Accuracy: The novel is meticulously researched and based on fact. The story represents a novelist's answers to questions that have kept historians guessing for five hundred years.

LESLIE EPSTEIN (1938-)

An American born in Los Angeles, Epstein graduated from Yale, Oxford, and UCLA. He is a lecturer in English and directs the creative writing program of Boston University. He has been praised for tackling difficult and weighty moral subjects in his novels. For example, in *King of the Jews* he explores the role some European Jews played in betraying their own people to the Nazis.

1947 *Pinto and Sons*

Date of Publication: 1990
Subject(s): Medical Profession; Gold Rush—California; Indians
Fictional character(s): Adolph Pinto, Doctor, Teacher
Time Period(s): 1840s
Locale(s): Boston, Massachusetts; California

Summary: Adolph Pinto, a young medical student in Boston in 1846, is inspired by a demonstration of anesthesia to search for ways of alleviating pain in the world. His journey takes him to the gold fields of California and a role as a teacher to the boys of the Modac tribe whose fathers toil in the mines. The Indians finally revolt, and Pinto returns to his calling as a surgeon, ministering to the suffering people he sees only too frequently all around him. The novel follows his quest for meaning and value in a world with little interest in his mission.

Historical Accuracy: Although some of the names and events are based on historical fact, characters and incidents are largely the product of the author's imagination.

LOULA GRACE ERDMAN (?-1976)

Born in Missouri, Erdman graduated from the University of Wisconsin and taught in public schools in Texas and at Texas State University as a writer-in-residence. She began to write as a hobby, and her first novel, *The Years of the Locust*, won the Dodd, Mead-Redbook Prize in 1947.

1948 *Another Spring*

Date of Publication: 1966
Subject(s): Civil War—U.S.
Fictional character(s): Susan Nicols, Refugee; Pete Carroway, Refugee
Time Period(s): 1860s (1863)
Locale(s): Missouri

Summary: In the contested border country of western Missouri during the Civil War, the conflict forces families from their homes. This novel tells the stories of three such families and their experiences as refugees.

Historical Accuracy: The eviction order covering Cass, Bates, and Jackson counties in Missouri is actual; and the author accurately represents his time and region.

1949 *The Edge of Time*

Date of Publication: 1950
Subject(s): American West; Farming
Fictional character(s): Wade Cameron, Settler; Bethany Cameron, Settler
Time Period(s): 1880s
Locale(s): Panhandle, Texas

Summary: Homesteaders Bethany and Wade Cameron carve a small farm out of the prairie of the Texas Panhandle in the 1880s. The novel dramatizes their daily struggle with blizzards, droughts, and incredible loneliness.

Historical Accuracy: This is an authentic account of frontier life during the period.

1950 *The Far Journey*

Date of Publication: 1955
Subject(s): American West
Fictional character(s): Catherine Montgomery, Gentlewoman; Edward Delaney, Gentleman
Time Period(s): 1890s
Locale(s): Missouri; Texas

Summary: Genteel Catherine Montgomery falls in love with Edward Delaney and joins him for the dangerous and challenging trip west from Missouri to Texas.

Historical Accuracy: The novel is filled with authentic details of pioneer life.

1951 *Many a Voyage*

Date of Publication: 1960
Subject(s): Slavery; Civil War—U.S.; Biography, Fictionalized
Historical character(s): Edward Ross, Political Figure
Time Period(s): 19th century (1848-1889)
Locale(s): Kansas; Washington, District of Columbia; New Mexico

Summary: This biographical novel describes the career of Edward G. Ross, an anti-slavery newspaper editor in Kansas during the free-soil movement. Ross serves in the Civil War and later enters politics. As a senator from Kansas he casts the deciding vote in Andrew Jackson's impeachment trial. Later he becomes the territorial governor of New Mexico.

Historical Accuracy: The novel is faithful to the facts of Ross' life.

CAROLLY ERICKSON (1943-)

An American born in Los Angeles, Erickson is a graduate of the University of Washington, Seattle, and Columbia University. She is a professor of medieval history at Brooklyn College. She is best known for her biographical lives of the Tudor family, Henry VIII, Mary, and Elizabeth. The author has been praised for her historical expertise and her eye for relevant and revealing details.

1952 *Mistress Anne*

Date of Publication: 1984
Subject(s): Tudor Period; Royalty—England; Biography, Fictionalized
Historical character(s): Anne Boleyn, Royalty (queen consort of Henry VIII); Henry VIII, Ruler (King of England); Katherine of Aragon, Royalty (queen consort of Henry VIII); Sir Thomas Wyatt, Writer, Courtier
Time Period(s): 16th century
Locale(s): England

Summary: Though perhaps as much a biography as a novel, this life of Anne Boleyn offers enough imagined dialogue and interpretation of the title character's thoughts to be considered fictional. Anne emerges as a complex individual at the center of a richly pictured and treacherous Tudor court.

Historical Accuracy: All the elements of documentation lend this life a compelling and convincing reliability.

STEVE ERICKSON (1950-)

An American born in California and a graduate of UCLA, Erickson has been a freelance editor and writer in London, Paris, Rome, Venice, Amsterdam, and Los Angeles. His experimental and science fiction stories have been widely praised for their inventiveness and originality.

1953 *Arc d'X*

Date of Publication: 1993
Subject(s): Fantasy; Slavery; Reincarnation
Fictional character(s): Etcher, Thief
Historical character(s): Sally Hemings, Slave; Thomas Jefferson, Diplomat, Political Figure
Time Period(s): 18th century; 21st century
Locale(s): Paris, France; Los Angeles, California; Berlin, Germany

Summary: This fantasy novel of reincarnation has a strong historical component. Sally Hemings, after killing her master, is burned at the stake but returns to life as Thomas Jefferson's slave and mistress. She accompanies Jefferson to Paris. The novel jumps ahead to 21st century Los Angeles where the theme of master and slave is repeated.

Historical Accuracy: Though historical accuracy is hardly the point here, the customs of the 18th century are accurately depicted.

BARBARA ERSKINE (1944-)

An Englishwoman born in Nottingham and a graduate of the University of Edinburgh, Erskine is a freelance writer, editor, and historical research editor. She was nominated for an award from the Romantic Novelists Association in 1987 for *Lady of May*. She has written many historical romances under the pseudonym Kate Buchan. Erskine considers the settings for her novels of great importance and she sees herself as filling in the gaps of history with her fiction.

1954 *Kingdom of Shadows*

Date of Publication: 1988
Subject(s): Romance; Time Travel; Middle Ages
Fictional character(s): Clare Royland, Landowner, Psychic; Paul Royland, Spouse
Time Period(s): 20th century; 14th century
Locale(s): Scotland

Summary: Time shifts between the 20th and the 14th centuries in this romantic novel. Clare Royland has visions of her long-dead ancestor, as her husband plots to convince everyone that Clare is mad.

Historical Accuracy: The novel features a great deal of Scottish history that creates a plausible historical background.

1955 *Lady of Hay*

Date of Publication: 1986
Subject(s): Middle Ages; Time Travel
Fictional character(s): Jo Clifford, Time Traveller, Journalist
Historical character(s): John, Ruler (King of England); Matilda Bradse, Noblewoman
Time Period(s): 12th century; 20th century
Locale(s): Wales; England

Summary: This novel shuttles between the present and the 12th century as journalist Jo Clifford finds herself reliving the experiences of Matilda, Lady of Hay, the wife of a baron at the time of King John.

Historical Accuracy: The novel's notes indicate the historical sources for the actual story of Matilda and King John.

JOHN ERSKINE (1879-1951)

A critic, musician, and professor of English at Columbia University, Erskine was the author of popular novels such as *Give Me Liberty*, the story of Patrick Henry, and *The private Life of Helen of Troy*. He also published several books on music and literature. He wrote an autobiography, *My Life as a Writer*.

1956 *Give Me Liberty: The Story of an Innocent Man*

Date of Publication: 1940
Subject(s): American Colonies; American Revolution
Fictional character(s): David Farrill, Young Man
Historical character(s): Patrick Henry, Patriot, Political Figure; George Washington, Military Personnel; Thomas Jefferson, Political Figure
Time Period(s): 18th century (1750s-1770s)
Locale(s): Virginia, American Colonies

Summary: This novel set in colonial Virginia in the years leading up to the American Revolution features young David Farrill, an admirer of Patrick Henry. As Henry preaches

sedition and revolution more openly, Farrill finds himself in a conflict of loyalty and friendship.

Historical Accuracy: The novel provides a light and entertaining look at the period with touches of period accuracy.

1957 *The Private Life of Helen of Troy*

Date of Publication: 1925
Subject(s): Ancient Greece; Myths and Legends; Trojan War
Fictional character(s): Helen of Troy, Royalty (queen consort of Menelaus); Menelaus, Ruler (King of Sparta); Hermione, Young Woman
Time Period(s): Indeterminate Past
Locale(s): Sparta, Greece

Summary: The novel imagines what happens to Helen and Menelaus after the fall of Troy when they return to Sparta. There they must deal with the conflict caused by their daughter Hermione and the problems of her marriage. Written entirely in dialogue, the story offers an entertaining domestic drama in which Helen's particular philosophy of life and love predominates.

Historical Accuracy: The novel offers little background or atmosphere of the period, and the conversations take on a curiously modern resonance.

SUSAN ERTZ (1894-1985)

English-born short story and novel writer, Ertz was raised in the U.S. and England. Her novels include *Madam Claire*, *Nina*, *After Noon*, and *The Philosopher's Daughter*.

1958 *The Proselyte*

Date of Publication: 1933
Subject(s): American West; Mormons
Fictional character(s): Zillah Purdy, Settler
Time Period(s): 19th century
Locale(s): Utah

Summary: The hardships faced by the Mormons are presented in the story of Zillah Purdy, who marries a Mormon missionary and accompanies him to Utah. There they must deal with the difficulties of the land and the Mormon tenet of polygamy.

Historical Accuracy: The pro-Mormon sympathies are obvious and dictate the presentation. The period details and dialogue, however, are accurate and convincing.

ANTHONY ESLER (1934-)

Born in New London, Connecticut, Esler was educated at the University of Arizona and Duke. Esler is a professor of history at the College of William and Mary.

1959 *Babylon*

Date of Publication: 1980
Subject(s): Jews; Babylonian Empire
Fictional character(s): Leah, Young Woman; Nabu, Military Personnel (Babylonian soldier)
Historical character(s): Belshazzar, Royalty (Babylonian prince); Daniel, Biblical Figure

Time Period(s): 6th century B.C.
Locale(s): Babylon

Summary: After the Babylonians destroy Jerusalem in 586 B.C., the captured Hebrews are forced to live in exile in Babylon for 40 years. The novel tells a story of their captivity. Leah is a young Jewish woman who is, at first, attracted to the opulence and luxury of the Babylonians. In the end, however, she becomes a warrior for her people and leads them back to Israel.

Historical Accuracy: The details of the story are convincing.

1960   *The Blade of Castlemayne*

Date of Publication: 1974
Subject(s): Elizabethan Period
Fictional character(s): Walter Castlemayne, Gentleman; Arabella Traherne, Gentlewoman; Malcolm Devereux, Gentleman
Time Period(s): 16th century (1590)
Locale(s): England

Summary: This swashbuckling adventure during the Elizabethan period puts Walter Castlemayne in deadly combat against Sir Malcolm Devereux, called the Great Captain, a man with the reputation of being a ruthless cutthroat. Hanging in the balance is a commission as captain of *The Golden Fortune*, a ship which is to join Sir Francis Drake's armada to collect Spanish treasure.

Historical Accuracy: The novel's adventures are solidly anchored by an accurate sense of the period.

1961   *For Love of a Pirate*

Date of Publication: 1978
Subject(s): Pirates; Sea Story; Elizabethan Period
Fictional character(s): Tamar De la Barca, Gentlewoman; John Burrows, Pirate
Historical character(s): Sir Walter Raleigh, Courtier; Robert Cecil, Government Official (advisor to Elizabeth I), Courtier; William Cecil, Government Official (advisor to Elizabeth I), Courtier
Time Period(s): 16th century
Locale(s): Havana, Cuba; At Sea; London, England

Summary: Tamar, the daughter of Cuba's Spanish governor, is captured by the English privateer, Sir John Burrows, when he mounts an assault on Havana's Custom House. His goal is King Philip's treasure from the New World, but it is on its way to Spain aboard a galleon. Burrows gives chase with Tamar in tow. How the treasure is gained and how Tamar goes from enemy to lover is the source of the novel's romantic adventure.

Historical Accuracy: The emphasis here is on swashbuckling adventure with a modicum of authentic period touches.

1962   *Forbidden City*

Date of Publication: 1977
Subject(s): Chinese Empire; Boxer Rebellion
Fictional character(s): Elizabeth Rowntree, Student (medical); Chen Li, Doctor; Michael Connor, Military Personnel (marine sergeant)

Time Period(s): 1890s (1899)
Locale(s): Peking, China

Summary: Elizabeth Rowntree leaves her medical studies to visit her missionary father in China. When she arrives, she finds herself in the midst of the Boxer Rebellion. Her father has been brutally murdered, and she finds herself drawn to two different men: the Chinese doctor Chen Li and a battle-worn marine sergeant, Michael Connor.

Historical Accuracy: The historical details of the Boxer Rebellion authentically form the novel's backdrop.

1963   *Hellbane*

Date of Publication: 1975
Subject(s): Witchcraft and Sorcery; Trials; Jacobean Period
Fictional character(s): Nicholas Hellbane, Fanatic (witch-finder); Alys, Witch
Time Period(s): 17th century (1613)
Locale(s): Devonshire, England

Summary: Nicholas Hellbane, a witch-finder, comes to a small Devonshire fishing village to rout out the satanic elements in their midst. He drives the community to enmity and madness before encountering his nemesis in the darkly passionate and bewitching Alys.

Historical Accuracy: The regional and period details and dialogue are realistic as is the psychological exploration of the divided Hellbane.

1964   *Lord Libertine*

Date of Publication: 1976
Subject(s): French Revolution; Romance; Georgian Period
Fictional character(s): Christopher Arundel, Nobleman, Rake; Barbara MacFarlane, Gentlewoman
Time Period(s): 1790s (1792)
Locale(s): London, England; Paris, France

Summary: Lord Arundel is a notorious rake, duelist, and gambler. In 1792, he rescues a damsel in distress, the unseducible Lady MacFarlane. Arundel's reputation is at stake and a wager ''to bed her inside of a month'' produces the novel's romantic adventure, taking the characters from Georgian London to revolutionary Paris.

Historical Accuracy: The emphasis here is on high romantic adventure, yet the period background is authentic and convincing.

NORBERT ESTEY

1965   *All My Sins: A Novel of the Life and Loves of Ninon de Lenclos*

Date of Publication: 1954
Subject(s): Biography, Fictionalized
Historical character(s): Ninon de Lenclos, Gentlewoman
Time Period(s): 17th century
Locale(s): France

Summary: This biographical account is based on the life of famous courtesan and beauty Ninon de Lenclos, whose career spanned much of the 17th century and the reigns of Louis XIII and XIV. The novel captures the spirit of the age, her many romances, and her assistance to such men of letters as Moliere, Racine, and Corneille.

Historical Accuracy: The novel captures both the life of Lenclos and the period with authenticity.

HAMMON ESTHER

1966 *Road to Lendor*

Date of Publication:
Subject(s): American Colonies; Witchcraft and Sorcery; Biography, Fictionalized
Historical character(s): Samuel Parris, Religious (minister)
Time Period(s): 17th century
Locale(s): London, England; Barbados; Salem, Massachusetts, American Colonies

Summary: Concentrating on Salem's village pastor, Reverend Samuel Parris, the novel captures the spirit and events of the Salem witchcraft trials. The novel provides a biographical study of Parris, tracing his career from England, to Barbados, to his clerical life in the American Colonies.

Historical Accuracy: Despite a full and authentic background to accompany the drama, at times too much material is displayed to be developed fully.

LOREN D. ESTLEMAN (1952-)

An American novelist, Estleman was born in Ann Arbor, Michigan and attended Eastern Michigan University. He has worked as a cartoonist and reporter for a variety of newspapers. He won a Golden Spur Award for best western historical novel in 1982 for *Aces & Eights* and a Pulitzer Prize nomination for *This Old Bill*. He is best known for his series of hard-boiled mysteries that authentically evoke Detroit. He alternates between writing mysteries and westerns, calling both genres America's contributions to world literature.

1967 *Aces and Eights: A Novel of the Legend of Wild Bill Hickok*

Date of Publication: 1981
Subject(s): American West; Crime and Criminals; Trials
Historical character(s): James Butler Hickok, Frontiersman, Gunfighter; Jack McCall, Murderer; William F. Cody, Frontiersman; John Quincy Adams Crandall, Lawyer
Time Period(s): 1870s (1876)
Locale(s): Deadwood, South Dakota

Summary: In 1876 the legendary gunslinging marshal Wild Bill Hickok is shot in the back as he plays poker in Deadwood's Saloon Number 10. He is clutching two pairs of aces and eights, which will become famous as "The Dead Man's Hand." Hickok's murderer is Jack McCall, and the novel details the events of his trial and the circumstances surrounding Hickok's murder.

Historical Accuracy: The novel is not intended to be a factual account of the trial of Jack McCall, although parts of it are based on existing transcripts. The particulars of Hickok's life have been recorded faithfully.

1968 *Bloody Season*

Date of Publication: 1988
Subject(s): American West; Crime and Criminals
Historical character(s): Johnny Ringo, Outlaw; Wyatt Earp, Lawman; John Henry Holliday, Gunfighter, Gambler; William Barclay "Bat" Masterson, Lawman
Time Period(s): 1880s (1881)
Locale(s): Tombstone, Arizona

Summary: Probably no other single event in western history has been celebrated as much as the gunfight at the OK Corral, which has become the apotheosis of the Western legend. This version provides an in-depth and factual telling of the events with an emphasis on what really happened.

Historical Accuracy: Riveting and realistic, this version of the familiar story rings true at every stage. However, this is fiction based on fact and not pure history.

1969 *City of Widows*

Date of Publication: 1994
Subject(s): American West; Crime and Criminals
Fictional character(s): Page Murdock, Lawman
Historical character(s): Lew Wallace, Military Personnel (general), Writer; Pat Garrett, Lawman; Geronimo, Indian (Apache), Warrior
Time Period(s): 1880s (1881)
Locale(s): New Mexico

Summary: Lawman Page Murdock is sent to New Mexico to track down a man and bring him to justice. This becomes the beginning of a long and dangerous odyssey of treachery and betrayal.

Historical Accuracy: The locale is convincingly presented.

1970 *Dr. Jekyll and Mr. Holmes*

Date of Publication: 1979
Subject(s): Mystery; Victorian Period; Supernatural
Fictional character(s): Sherlock Holmes, Detective—Private; John H. Watson, Doctor; Henry Jekyll, Doctor, Murderer (aka Edward Hyde)
Time Period(s): 1880s (1884)
Locale(s): London, England

Summary: The murder of a member of Parliament leads Holmes and Watson into an investigation that involves the prominent doctor Henry Jekyll who, of course, is also the vicious murderer Edward Hyde. The novel ingeniously combines both Arthur Conan Doyle's characters and Robert Louis Stevenson's story into an exciting and entertaining pastiche of both authors' work.

Historical Accuracy: The author has mastered the period details as well as the styles of both Doyle and Stevenson.

1971 *Gunman*

Date of Publication: 1985
Subject(s): American West; Crime and Criminals
Historical character(s): John Miller, Outlaw
Time Period(s): 19th century (1841-1880)
Locale(s): West

Summary: The novel tells the life story of gunman John Miller who as an orphaned youth begins to use his gun to earn his living. He falls in with a band of night riders and bank robbers and makes his name with his skill on the draw, earning the nickname ''Killer Miller.''

Historical Accuracy: The novel is rich in western flavor and period details.

1972 *The Hider*

Date of Publication: 1978
Subject(s): American West
Fictional character(s): Jack Butterworth, Frontiersman; Jeff Curry, Young Man
Time Period(s): 1890s (1898)
Locale(s): Oregon

Summary: Young Jeff Curry encounters an apparition from the past in Jack Butterworth, former scout in the Indian Wars who fought in Texas, worked for the Union Pacific Railroad, and hunted buffalo. Curry joins Butterworth for a final hunt, but after getting involved with a runaway Indian, finds himself hunted by the law.

Historical Accuracy: The period Western locale is convincing.

1973 *The High Rocks*

Date of Publication: 1979
Subject(s): American West
Fictional character(s): Bear Anderson, Mountain Man; Page Murdock, Lawman
Time Period(s): 1880s
Locale(s): Montana

Summary: Bear Anderson is a legend in the Montana of the 1890s. When his family is killed by Flathead Indians, he mounts a campaign of vengeance against them. Most assume that he perishes in the worst winter Montana has ever seen, but deputy sheriff Page Murdock finds himself on Bear's trail.

Historical Accuracy: The locale and the period are authentically drawn.

1974 *Mister St. John*

Date of Publication: 1983
Subject(s): American West; Crime and Criminals
Fictional character(s): Irons St. John, Lawman
Time Period(s): 1900s (1906)
Locale(s): Cheyenne, Wyoming

Summary: Irons St. John is not the same man he was 20 years before when he was a young deputy for Hanging Judge Parker. But the Union Pacific Railroad offers him $15,000 to bring an outlaw gang to justice, and St. John sets out with a ragtag posse to prove that his best days are not behind him.

Historical Accuracy: This is an amusing variation on the standard Western pursuit theme with some authentic period details.

1975 *Murdock's Law*

Date of Publication: 1982
Subject(s): American West; Crime and Criminals; Ranching
Fictional character(s): Page Murdock, Lawman; Chris Shedwell, Outlaw
Time Period(s): 1880s
Locale(s): Breen, Montana

Summary: Special U.S. Deputy Page Murdock, while in pursuit of outlaw Chris Shadwell, unexpectedly finds himself the marshall of Breen, Montana. The town is a lawless place ready to explode into a range war between the big and small ranchers. Murdock must keep the peace as best he can.

Historical Accuracy: The novel is more formulaic than distinctively historical.

1976 *Sherlock Holmes vs. Dracula*

Date of Publication: 1978
Subject(s): Mystery; Victorian Period; Supernatural
Fictional character(s): Sherlock Holmes, Detective—Private; John H. Watson, Doctor; Dracula, Vampire
Time Period(s): 1890s (1890)
Locale(s): London, England; Whitby, England

Summary: In 1890 when a deserted ship is beached on the English coast, its cargo is discovered to be fifty boxes of earth, and its only passenger an enormous black dog that vanishes into the night. Dracula has arrived in England. Luckily, Sherlock Holmes is on hand to challenge him in this ingenious blending of Bram Stoker and Arthur Conan Doyle.

Historical Accuracy: The author has clearly mastered the atmosphere of both novelists and the period effectively.

1977 *Stamping Ground*

Date of Publication: 1980
Subject(s): American West; Indians
Fictional character(s): Page Murdock, Lawman; Ghost Shirt, Indian (Cheyenne); A.C. Hudspeth, Lawman
Time Period(s): 1880s
Locale(s): Dakota Territory, United States

Summary: Deputy Page Murdock signs on for a seemingly impossible assignment: infiltrate Indian territory and capture the Cheyenne leader Ghost Shirt who has escaped from prison and is gathering the tribes for war. His assistance comes in the form of aging federal marshal Hudspeth.

Historical Accuracy: The story is somewhat far-fetched, but the locale is precisely rendered.

1978 *The Stranglers*

Date of Publication: 1984
Subject(s): American West; Crime and Criminals
Fictional character(s): Page Murdock, Lawman; Harlan A. Blackthorne, Judge; Sugar Jim Creel, Outlaw
Time Period(s): 1890s

Locale(s): Helena, Montana

Summary: While in pursuit of outlaw Sugar Jim Creel, Deputy Page Murdock gets ambushed by an Indian tracker. Page must bring Creel in, but Creel is hooked up with a gang of stranglers, outlaws who lynch lawmen.

Historical Accuracy: Although action-packed, the story is more formula than history.

1979 *Sudden Country*

Date of Publication: 1991

Subject(s): American West; Treasure Hunt; Indians

Fictional character(s): David Grayle, Teenager; Jonathan Flynn, Veteran (Confederate soldier); Ben Wedlock, Outlaw

Time Period(s): 1890s

Locale(s): Panhandle, Texas; Black Hills, South Dakota

Summary: When young David Grayle comes into possession of a treasure map from former Quantrill Raider Jonathan Flynn, he sets off into the Black Hills in the heart of Sioux country on a treasure-hunting expedition that includes the mystery of one-eyed Ben Wedlock.

Historical Accuracy: This is an ingenious western *Treasure Island* with an emphasis on adventure, not history.

1980 *This Old Bill*

Date of Publication: 1984

Subject(s): American West; Theatrical Life

Historical character(s): William F. Cody, Frontiersman, Entertainer; Ned Buntline, Writer; George Armstrong Custer, Military Personnel (cavalry officer); Victoria, Ruler (Queen of England)

Time Period(s): 19th century; 20th century (1854-1917)

Locale(s): West; Europe

Summary: The novel offers a biographical history of Buffalo Bill Cody, who by the age of 23 was one of the best hunters and Indian scouts in the West. His fame was cultivated by journalist Ned Buntline and by Cody himself, first as an actor and then as the impresario of the travelling Wild West Show.

Historical Accuracy: Some distortion in this account is deliberate and it should not be read for biographical exactness.

1981 *Whiskey River*

Date of Publication: 1990

Subject(s): Mystery; Crime and Criminals; Prohibition Era

Fictional character(s): Constantine Minor, Journalist; John Dance, Organized Crime Figure

Time Period(s): 1920s; 1930s (1928-1932)

Locale(s): Detroit, Michigan

Summary: Prohibition-era Detroit is the scene for this novel that tells the story of bootlegging, police corruption, and gang warfare through the perspective of newspaper reporter Minor. The novel centers on the rise and fall of gangster Jack Dance.

Historical Accuracy: The novel offers an authentic portrait of the era.

WILLIE SNOW ETHRIDGE (1900-1983)

An American journalist, writer, and lecturer, Ethridge was born in Savannah, Georgia, and graduated from Wesleyan College in Macon. She is best known as a travel writer and historian. Her travel books include *It's Greek to Me* and *Going to Jerusalem*. She is also the author of the biography *Strange Fires: the True Story of John Wesley's Love Affair in Georgia*. In 1983 she received the North Carolina Award for literature.

1982 *Summer Thunder*

Date of Publication: 1959

Subject(s): American Colonies; Spanish Colonies

Fictional character(s): Heather Forsyth, Settler; Bart Calloway, Sea Captain

Historical character(s): James Edward Oglethorpe, Military Personnel (general), Leader (colonial)

Time Period(s): 1730s (1733)

Locale(s): Savannah, Georgia, American Colonies

Summary: Life in the settlement of Georgia in the 1730s is depicted. General James Oglethorpe is the determined, and at times stubborn, leader of the colony. The novel centers on the experiences of a young couple, Heather Forsyth and Bart Calloway. The action includes the Battle of Bloody Marsh in which the Spanish on the colony's southern frontier are defeated.

Historical Accuracy: The period details are credible and realistic.

ELENA YATES EULO

1983 *A Southern Woman*

Date of Publication: 1993

Subject(s): Civil War—U.S.

Fictional character(s): Elizabeth Allen Crocker, Young Woman; Ama Hadley, Landowner

Time Period(s): 1860s

Locale(s): Tennessee

Summary: Elizabeth Allen Crocker is ostracized when her husband leaves Tennessee to fight for the Yankees during the Civil War. She is left to fend for herself in the backwoods until Ama Hadley takes her in and begins to show her a new life. Elizabeth battles bigotry and injustice.

Historical Accuracy: The regional details establish an authentic period background.

JEAN EVANS (1939-)

English author Evans began to write in her thirties after her children had grown. She has produced three books a year ever since. Titles include *The King's Own*, *Uncrowned King*, and *Nine Days a Queen*.

1984 *The Phoenix Rising*

Date of Publication: 1977

Subject(s): Royalty—England

Historical character(s): Charles I, Ruler (King of England); Charles Stuart, Royalty (prince)
Time Period(s): 17th century (1649)
Locale(s): England

Summary: This historical novel is set in the final months before the execution of Charles I and involves the efforts of Charles Stuart, the future Charles II, to regain the throne. Stuart forges a futile alliance with the Scots before he is forced to flee into exile.

Historical Accuracy: The framework of the story is historical, but it lacks in depth and specificity.

HAL GEORGE EVARTS (1915-)

Evarts was born in Kansas and after graduating from Stanford in the 1930s, set out on a knapsack trip around the world. He worked as a screenwriter in Hollywood and as a reporter for trade journals and newspapers. In 1939, Evarts returned to Europe, where he wrote for the *Herald Tribune* in Paris until the Nazi occupation. He became a full-time writer in 1940, principally of western novels.

1985　*Fur Brigade*

Date of Publication: 1928
Subject(s): American West; Indians
Fictional character(s): Hunter Breckenridge, Trapper
Time Period(s): 19th century (1815-1835)
Locale(s): Pacific Northwest

Summary: The fur trade in the Pacific Northwest is portrayed in the experiences of frontiersman Hunter Breckenridge. His adventures include some ghastly encounters with the Indians.

Historical Accuracy: The action is based on incidents that actually happened, and the novel captures its period convincingly.

1986　*Shaggy Legion*

Date of Publication: 1930
Subject(s): American West
Fictional character(s): Breck Coleman, Frontiersman; Sue Carrolton, Young Woman
Historical character(s): George Armstrong Custer, Military Personnel (cavalry officer); Philip H. Sheridan, Military Personnel (general); James Butler Hickok, Frontiersman; William F. Cody, Frontiersman
Time Period(s): 1870s
Locale(s): West

Summary: The novel depicts the wave of settlers on the Western Plains that pushed out the great buffalo herds. It features several actual figures and a love affair between a young plainsman, Breck Coleman, and the daughter of a settler, Sue Carrolton.

Historical Accuracy: The novel presents a faithful picture of the region and its history, though the story itself is a fanciful one.

DAVID EVERITT (1952-)

An American novelist and screenwriter, Everitt was born in New York City and graduated from the State University of New York, Buffalo. He has worked as a bookstore clerk and an editor for *Fangoria* magazine. He is also the author of *The Manly Handbook.*

1987　*The Story of Pat Garrett and Billy the Kid*

Date of Publication: 1990
Subject(s): Crime and Criminals; American West
Historical character(s): Pat Garrett, Lawman; William Bonney, Outlaw
Time Period(s): 1880s
Locale(s): Lincoln County, New Mexico

Summary: Billy the Kid's short and violent life is brought to an abrupt end by lawman Pat Garrett. Everitt's re-telling attempts to offer a realistic version of the story, shorn of romantic trappings.

Historical Accuracy: The novel succeeds in delivering an authentic version of the well-known Western story.

1988　*The Story of the Sundance Kid*

Date of Publication: 1990
Subject(s): American West; Crime and Criminals
Historical character(s): Harry Longabaugh, Outlaw; Butch Cassidy, Outlaw; Etta Place, Outlaw
Time Period(s): 1890s; 1900s
Locale(s): Wyoming; Utah; Bolivia

Summary: Harry Longabaugh, the Sundance Kid, is shown from the time he joins Butch Cassidy's Wild Bunch until his death in Bolivia.

Historical Accuracy: Everitt attempts to show the western outlaws stripped of the romance and legend that have accrued to their stories. As a result, this version seems far more authentic than others.

ELIZABETH EYRE
(PSEUD. OF JILL STAYNES, 1927- ; MARGARET STOREY, 1926-)

Elizabeth Eyre is the joint pseudonym used by English authors Jill Staynes and Margaret Storey. Storey is an English teacher who has also written children's books.

1989　*Axe for an Abbot*

Date of Publication: 1995
Subject(s): Mystery; Renaissance
Fictional character(s): Sigismondo, Mercenary, Detective—Amateur; Benno, Servant
Time Period(s): 15th century
Locale(s): Italy

Summary: A missing relic is at the center of this installment of the historical mystery series featuring the mercenary Sigismondo. An abbot is found murdered with Sigismondo's axe sticking out of his back. There follows a rush to recover a fabled jewel-encrusted cross said to bring fertility to its owner.

Historical Accuracy: Despite the novel's occasional outrageousness, the period elements are convincing.

1990 *Bravo for the Bride*

Date of Publication: 1994
Subject(s): Mystery; Renaissance
Fictional character(s): Sigismondo, Mercenary, Detective—Amateur; Benno, Servant
Time Period(s): 15th century
Locale(s): Italy

Summary: In this installment of the historical mystery series involving the mercenary Sigismondo, the wedding of Prince Galeotto and Princess Ariana becomes the occasion for murder. First a statue falls from the matrimonial arch almost killing the couple; then the bride is found strangled. Sigismondo is asked to investigate.

Historical Accuracy: The period elements are authentic and believable.

1991 *Curtains for the Cardinal*

Date of Publication: 1992
Subject(s): Mystery; Renaissance
Fictional character(s): Sigismondo, Mercenary, Detective—Amateur; Benno, Servant; Minerva, Royalty (princess)
Time Period(s): 16th century
Locale(s): Italy

Summary: In this Renaissance mystery, Sigismondo prevents Princess Minerva from being killed by her own father. He arranges for her protection in the villa of a blind lord who may in fact be Minerva's true father. When the cardinal arrives to officiate at the wedding between Lord Astorre and the now missing Minerva, the cardinal is murdered, and Sigismondo attempts to solve the case.

Historical Accuracy: The details of Italian Renaissance life are richly and accurately developed.

1992 *Death of the Duchess*

Date of Publication: 1992
Subject(s): Mystery; Renaissance
Fictional character(s): Sigismondo, Mercenary, Detective—Amateur; Benno, Servant
Time Period(s): 16th century
Locale(s): Italy

Summary: Sigismondo is assigned by the Duke of Rocca to investigate the kidnapping of Jacob Di Torre's daughter. When the Duchess is found dead in her bedroom, his assignment becomes more difficult.

Historical Accuracy: The details of Renaissance life are ably and accurately presented.

JOHAN FABRICIUS (1899-)

Prolific Java-born Dutch author Johan Fabricius attended art academies in The Hague and in Amsterdam and worked as a painter on the Austro-Italian front in 1918. During World War II, Fabricius was a freelance broadcaster in Dutch, English, German, and Malay for the BBC in Europe. His first novel, *The Girl in the Blue Hat*, was produced as a motion picture and a television series. His other works include *Comedians Passed By*, several plays, including *Stock Treatment*, and a number of juvenile works.

1993 *Mortal Pageant*

Date of Publication: 1956
Subject(s): Middle Ages; Plague
Fictional character(s): Giacopo Orlandini, Gentleman
Time Period(s): 14th century (1347)
Locale(s): Florence, Italy

Summary: This tale of the Plague Years in Italy attempts to record what life must have been like under the threat of such a deadly contagion. Giacopo Orlandini, with his family and friends, flees Florence for a villa in the country but the disease follows them. In the crisis that ensues, the characters all reveal their true natures.

Historical Accuracy: The period elements are accurate and authentically reproduced.

ELIZABETH FACKLER (1947-)

Born in Michigan, Fackler is a graduate of the University of California, San Diego. She has worked as a librarian and writer.

1994 *Billy the Kid: The Legend of El Chivato*

Date of Publication: 1995
Subject(s): American West; Crime and Criminals; Lincoln County War
Historical character(s): William Bonney, Outlaw; Pat Garrett, Lawman
Time Period(s): 1870s; 1880s (1874-1881)
Locale(s): Silver City, New Mexico; Arizona; Lincoln County, New Mexico

Summary: The short and violent life of William Bonney, known as Billy the Kid, is described, tracing his involvement in the violent Lincoln County War in New Mexico. Billy is shown as a scapegoat for the sins of his Anglo contemporaries, and as a freedom fighter on the western frontier against corruption and big business.

Historical Accuracy: The author is faithful to historical reality, but bases her story on the belief that folk heroes do not achieve public adulation without a reason.

EDWIN FADIMAN (1925-)

Fadiman is an American novelist whose books include *The One-Eyed Kings*, *The Professional*, and *The Feast Day*. He has been a reviewer for the *Saturday Review*.

1995 *The Voice and the Light*

Date of Publication: 1949
Subject(s): Hundred Years War; Biography, Fictionalized; Religious Life
Historical character(s): Joan of Arc, Warrior
Time Period(s): 15th century
Locale(s): France

Summary: The novel presents the early years of Joan of Arc before she comes to the aid of the dauphin, later Charles VII, during the Hundred Years War. The novel dramatizes her growing awareness of a divine calling in the voices she hears that urge her to take up the career of a warrior.

Historical Accuracy: The novel presents a believable portrait of the locale.

MARIA FAGYAS

Hungarian-born Fagyas is a U.S. novelist, playwright, and screenwriter for a variety of motion picture studios. She won an Edgar Allen Poe Award for *The Fifth Woman.*

1996 *Court of Honor*

Date of Publication: 1978
Subject(s): Military Life; Homosexuality
Fictional character(s): Alexa de Rethy, Gentlewoman; Hans Gunther von Godenhausen, Military Personnel (captain)
Historical character(s): Wilhelm II, Ruler (German kaiser); Kuno von Molke, Military Personnel (general)
Time Period(s): 1900s (1900)
Locale(s): Germany

Summary: Scandal in the court of Kaiser Wilhelm of Germany is touched off by young Alexa de Rethy. Her marriage to Captain von Godenhausen sets in motion a crisis that implicates some of the leading figures in Germany and threatens the Kaiser himself. The scandal brings disgrace to the elite Gardes du Corps regiment, whose traditions and foibles are vividly described.

Historical Accuracy: The atmosphere of the Prussian military is accurately depicted, as are the period details.

1997 *Dance of the Assassins*

Date of Publication: 1973
Subject(s): Politics
Fictional character(s): Michael Vassilovich, Military Personnel (captain)
Historical character(s): Draga Lunyevitza-Mashin, Royalty (queen consort of Alexander); Alexander of Serbia, Ruler (King of Serbia)
Time Period(s): 1900s (1903)
Locale(s): Belgrade, Serbia

Summary: In 1903 Captain Vassilovich must decide whether to join a conspiracy to assassinate the king and queen of Serbia. The king is a tyrannical despot and his queen is just as bad. However, Draga Mashin is also the woman Vassilovich almost married. Should he help or hinder the conspiracy?.

Historical Accuracy: The period details are authentic and realistically drawn, even though the story is a fictional one.

1998 *The Devil's Lieutenant*

Date of Publication: 1970
Subject(s): Austro-Hungarian Empire; Military Life; Trials
Fictional character(s): Emile Kunze, Judge; Peter Dorfrichter, Military Personnel (lieutenant)
Historical character(s): Franz Ferdinand, Royalty (archduke)
Time Period(s): 1900s (1909)
Locale(s): Vienna, Austria

Summary: In 1909 a scandal erupts in the officer corps of the Austro-Hungarian army. A young officer, Lieutenant Dorfrichter, having been passed over for promotion, is accused of sending poisioned ''aphrodisiac'' capsules to ten members of the Senior Staff. One senior officer dies as a result. On trial for the crime, Dorfrichter must combat Judge Advocate Kunze in a tautly described battle of wits.

Historical Accuracy: The novel captures with precision and color the atmosphere of the Austro-Hungarian army and Vienna in the 1900s.

ZOE FAIRBAIRNS (1928-)

Irish writer Fairburns worked as a freelance fashion designer for numerous magazines before beginning her writing career in 1961. She is the author of historicals, romances, and crime novels under a variety of pseudonyms.

1999 *Stand We at Last*

Date of Publication: 1983
Subject(s): Family Saga; Victorian Period; Women's Rights
Fictional character(s): Helena Croft, Gentlewoman; Sarah Croft, Gentlewoman; Ruby Barrington, Worker
Time Period(s): 19th century; 20th century (1855-1978)
Locale(s): England; Australia

Summary: This ''feminist saga'' spans 120 years and four generations of women from Victorian times to the 1970s. Helena Craft and her sister Sarah are trapped by a limited vision of women's places and possibilities. Sarah heads out for life in Australia and, when she returns to England, joins the campaign for women's rights. Her descendants carry on the fight.

Historical Accuracy: Though ideologically biased, the authentic and vivid scenes dramatize a bro ad reach of modern history.

JANET FAIRBANK (1879-1951)

Chicago novelist Fairbank's novels include *The Lion's Den* and *The Bright Land*, the story of a mid-19th century woman who grows up in New Hampshire and travels to the Illinois frontier. *Rich Man, Poor Man* is about the suffragette movement and the Progressive Party. Her stories are collected in *Idle Hands.*

2000 *The Bright Land*

Date of Publication: 1932
Subject(s): Settlement of the American Frontier; Civil War—U.S.

Fictional character(s): Abby-Delight Flagg, Settler
Time Period(s): 19th century
Locale(s): Galena, Illinois

Summary: The novel tells the life story of Abby-Delight Flagg from her girlhood during Jackson's presidency to the Civil War. It provides a chronicle of life in the 19th century around Galena, Illinois, where the impact of history is dramatized.

Historical Accuracy: The novel provides a solid background of historical details.

2001 *The Cortlandts of Washington Square*

Date of Publication: 1922
Subject(s): Civil War—U.S.
Fictional character(s): Anne Byrne, Nurse
Time Period(s): 1860s
Locale(s): New York, New York

Summary: The New York social scene during the Civil War is the setting for this novel, in which Anne Byrne's widowed mother marries into the fashionable Cortlandt family. When war breaks out, Anne is determined to become a nurse, much to the horror of the proper Cortlandts, who disapprove of such work for a young lady of fashion.

Historical Accuracy: The novel presents a vivid and authentic picture of life in New York before and during the Civil War.

2002 *The Smiths*

Date of Publication: 1925
Subject(s): Family Saga
Fictional character(s): Peter Smith, Businessman; Ann Smith, Spouse
Time Period(s): 19th century; 20th century (1860s-1920s)
Locale(s): Chicago, Illinois

Summary: The novel attempts to describe the growth and development of Chicago from the Civil War period to the 1920s. The history of the city is reflected in the experiences of businessman Peter Smith, whose ambition is to become an iron master, and his wife Ann.

Historical Accuracy: The novel captures a good deal of Chicago's history in passing, but the past is superficially rendered.

ELEANOR FAIRBURN (1928-)

British author Fairburn has worked as a tutor in practical writing at the University of Leeds Education Centre. Her novels include *The Green Popinjays*, *The White Seahorse*, and *Winter's Rose*.

2003 *The Rose at Harvest End*

Date of Publication: 1975
Subject(s): War of the Roses; Royalty—England; Witchcraft and Sorcery
Historical character(s): Edward IV, Ruler (King of England); Richard Neville, Nobleman (Earl of Warwick); Elizabeth Woodville, Royalty (queen consort of Edward IV); Richard,

Duke of Gloucester, Nobleman; George, Duke of Clarence, Nobleman; Cecily Neville, Noblewoman
Time Period(s): 15th century (1461-1483)
Locale(s): England

Summary: The troubled reign of Edward IV and the Lancastrian victory in the War of the Roses is chronicled, focusing on Edward's queen, Elizabeth Woodville. She had spurned him before he was king, and now she is determined to use his infatuation to advance her interests. But as queen, Elizabeth alienates powerful Warwick the Kingmaker, and the dynastic struggle continues.

Historical Accuracy: The story is delivered with authenticity and evident research into the period.

WILLIAM FAIRCHILD

A British writer born in Cornwall, Fairchild attended the Royal Naval College and was a British naval officer in World War II. He is a playwright, screenwriter, and film director, as well as the author of more than 50 short stories.

2004 *No Man's Land*

Date of Publication: 1987
Subject(s): World War I; Fantasy
Fictional character(s): Adrian Garrard, Military Personnel (British officer)
Time Period(s): 1910s; 1920s (1917-1920s)
Locale(s): Ypres, Belgium; England

Summary: Adrian Garrard, a young British officer, is wounded at Passchendaele in 1917. As he lays near death in No Man's Land he sees a group of spectral figures—deserters from both sides—scavenging among the corpses from the day's fighting. After the war, he is asked to investigate the underground community of men living in the abandoned tunnels below the surface of the Western Front. His investigation leads him to a shattering truth that will translate into a second war to come.

Historical Accuracy: The basis of the story is, of course, fantasy, but the World War I details are genuine.

RICHARD FALKIRK
(PSEUD. OF DEREK LAMBERT, 1929-)

An Englishman born in London, Falkirk attended Epsom College in Surrey and has worked as a newspaper reporter and foreign correspondent in Africa and Moscow for the *Daily Express*. A disciplined writer, Falkirk sets himself a quota of at least ten pages a day.

2005 *Beau Blackstone*

Date of Publication: 1973
Subject(s): Mystery; Railroads
Fictional character(s): Edmund Blackstone, Detective—Police
Historical character(s): George Stephenson, Engineer (railroad)
Time Period(s): 1820s (1825)
Locale(s): England

Summary: Bow Street Runner Edmund Blackstone goes undercover to investigate who has been stealing the wages of railway workers and to foil a plot to pull off history's first train robbery. Danger and complications abound in this suspenseful adventure set during the construction of the first rail lines.

Historical Accuracy: The author admits to some anachronisms here, but the essence of the story's railroad atmosphere is authentic.

2006 *Blackstone*

Date of Publication: 1972
Subject(s): Mystery; Regency Period; Royalty—England
Fictional character(s): Edmund Blackstone, Detective—Police
Historical character(s): Alexandrina Victoria, Royalty (princess)
Time Period(s): 1820s
Locale(s): London, England

Summary: This first in a series of historical mysteries featuring Bow Street Runner Beau Blackstone has the detective assigned to protect the child Princess Alexandrina Victoria (later to become Queen Victoria). When she disappears, Blackstone is faced with a royal crisis and mystery.

Historical Accuracy: The story is, of course, fanciful, but it is set in an identifiable era with convincing period touches.

2007 *Blackstone and the Scourge of Europe*

Date of Publication: 1974
Subject(s): Mystery; Royalty—England
Fictional character(s): Edmund Blackstone, Detective—Police
Historical character(s): George IV, Ruler (King of England); Napoleon Bonaparte, Ruler (exiled emperor of France)
Time Period(s): 1820s (1820-1821)
Locale(s): Brighton, England; St. Helena

Summary: Blackstone is sent by George IV to investigate the security arrangements on St. Helena to make sure that the island's most famous inhabitant, Napoleon, stays put. On the island, Blackstone uncovers conflicting evidence of an escape plot and possibly other nefarious schemes as well. Is Napoleon being poisoned, and is he even the patient being treated at Longwood House?.

Historical Accuracy: The period details are convincing if the plot is more fanciful than historical.

2008 *Blackstone's Fancy*

Date of Publication: 1973
Subject(s): Mystery; Boxing
Fictional character(s): Edmund Blackstone, Detective—Police
Time Period(s): 1820s
Locale(s): England

Summary: Bow Street Runner Edmund Blackstone is assigned to help stamp out illegal prizefighting. The fight promoters will stop at nothing to keep their lucrative business going, and kidnapping, blackmail, and murder become obstacles in Blackstone's way.

Historical Accuracy: The period details are authentic and convincing.

LEONARD FALKNER (1900-)

Born in Cleveland, Ohio, Falkner has worked as a newspaper writer and editor in New York. His books include *Forge of Liberty*, *John Adams: Reluctant Patriot of the Revolution*, and *For Jefferson and Liberty*.

2009 *Painted Lady: Eliza Jumel, Her Life and Times*

Date of Publication: 1962
Subject(s): Biography, Fictionalized
Historical character(s): Eliza Jumel, Spouse (of Jumel and Burr); Aaron Burr, Political Figure; Stephen Jumel, Businessman (wine merchant)
Time Period(s): 19th century
Locale(s): New York, New York; Paris, France

Summary: This biographical novel traces the rise of Elizabeth Jumel from poor, illegitimate child to one of New York's wealthiest women, first married to wine merchant Stephen Jumel and then to Aaron Burr. The novel captures the social life of New York during the early 1800s.

Historical Accuracy: The novel excels in establishing a genuine historical background.

THOMAS FALL
(PSEUD. OF DONALD CLIFFORD SNOW, 1917-)

An American writer, Fall was born in New York City and is primarily an author of books for young adults. Many reflect his Cherokee heritage.

2010 *The Justicer*

Date of Publication: 1959
Subject(s): American West; Trials; Indians
Fictional character(s): Angus DeWolfe, Lawyer; Willard Ring, Judge; Marcus Maywood, Indian (Shawnee)
Time Period(s): 1880s (1889)
Locale(s): Kansas (Indian Territory)

Summary: In the Kansas Indian Territory of 1889, justice is swift and is doled out by one man, Judge Rising, who has a reputation for sentencing to death any Indian unlucky enough to come before him. Angus DeWolfe takes on the judge in the trial of an Indian charged with murder. More than a man's life is at stake here; the law itself is on trial.

Historical Accuracy: Though the story is fictional, the background details are based on fact.

FREDERIC FALLON (1944-1970)

An American born in Boston, Fallon received his B.A. degree from California State College. He was a doctoral candidate at the University of California, Davis, where he taught English. Fallon sold paintings to help finance his education.

2011 *The White Queen*

Date of Publication: 1972
Subject(s): Elizabethan Period; Royalty—Scotland
Historical character(s): John Knox, Religious; James Stewart, Nobleman, Bastard Son (of James V); William Maitland, Political Figure, Diplomat; Mary, Queen of Scots, Ruler (Queen of Scotland); James Hepburn, Nobleman (Earl of Bothwell); Henry Stewart, Nobleman (Lord Darnley); Elizabeth I, Ruler (Queen of England)
Time Period(s): 16th century
Locale(s): Edinburgh, Scotland; England

Summary: This is the story of Mary, Queen of Scots' troubled reign after her return from France. While matters of state prove difficult because her court is full of conflicting allegiances, matters of the heart prove impossible when she is linked to the weak Lord Darnley but loved by the Earl of Bothwell.

Historical Accuracy: This is a novel, not a biography; and the author has taken liberties with certain historical facts.

DANA FARALLA (1909-)

Faralla was born in Minnesota and attended the University of Minnesota and the Williams School of Drama. She has worked as an actress, private secretary, screen story analyst, and associate editor of *Poet* magazine. Her novels include *The Madstone*, *Children of Lucifer*, and *The Straw Umbrella*. She has also written children's books.

2012 *A Circle of Trees*

Date of Publication: 1955
Subject(s): Settlement of the American Frontier; Immigrants
Fictional character(s): Gunnar Neilson, Immigrant, Settler; Kersti Neilson, Immigrant, Settler
Time Period(s): 1880s
Locale(s): Minnesota

Summary: A Danish immigrant family, the Neilsons, experiences pioneer life on the Minnesota prairie in the 1880s. The family must contend with wilderness conditions very different from life in their native land.

Historical Accuracy: The novel captures believably the atmosphere of the period and the region.

JEFFREY FARNOL (1878-1952)

Born in Warwickshire, England, Farnol grew up aspiring to be a novelist. He was unable to attend university but began writing stories, and after considerable struggle, attained success with his first novel, *The Broad Highway*.

2013 *The King Liveth*

Date of Publication: 1944
Subject(s): Anglo-Saxon Period; Royalty—England

Fictional character(s): Ranulf, Nobleman (earl); Lady Morwenna, Noblewoman
Historical character(s): Alfred the Great, Ruler (King of Wessex)
Time Period(s): 9th century
Locale(s): England

Summary: In Anglo-Saxon England, Alfred the Great defeats the Danes under the leadership of Guthram and drives them out of Wessex. The novel blends these factual events with an invented romance between Ranulf and the Lady Morwenna.

Historical Accuracy: The novel skillfully presents an authentic look at the period.

JUDITH FARR (1937-)

An author and English professor, Farr was born in New York City and was educated at Marymount Manhattan College and Yale University. A professor of English at American University, Farr is the author of *The Life and Art of Elinor Wylie* and *The Passion of Emily Dickinson*, which was listed as a *New York Times* Notable Book of 1992.

2014 *I Never Came to You in White*

Date of Publication: 1996
Subject(s): Biography, Fictionalized; Literary Life
Historical character(s): Emily Dickinson, Writer (poet); Thomas Wentworth Higginson, Religious (minister), Abolitionist
Time Period(s): 19th century (1847-1886)
Locale(s): Amherst, Massachusetts

Summary: The novel reconstructs the inner and private life of Emily Dickinson in a series of 66 imagined letters from 1847 when Dickinson was 17 to the end of her life. The letters capture both Dickinson's unique sensibility and the perplexing aspects of her character as reflected by those who knew her.

Historical Accuracy: The novel contains some modifications and compression of actual events.

ROWENA RUTHERFORD FARRAR (1903-)

An American writer and teacher of fiction writing, Farrar was born in Nashville, Tennessee, and attended Vanderbilt University and New York University. She is the author of *A Wondrous Moment Then* and *Grace Moore and Her Many Worlds*.

2015 *Bend Your Heads All*

Date of Publication: 1965
Subject(s): American Colonies; Settlement of the American Frontier; American Revolution
Fictional character(s): Adele Overman, Pioneer; Seth Overman, Pioneer
Time Period(s): 1770s
Locale(s): Nashville, Tennessee

Summary: The novel describes emigration to Tennessee and the settlement of Nashville before and during the American Revolution. The pioneer Overman family withstands Indian attacks and wilderness conditions.

Historical Accuracy: Although the characters are fictional, the incidents and background are drawn from history and are authentic.

J.G. FARRELL (1935-1979)

Born in Liverpool, England, Farrell lived for long periods in France and Ireland where he spent much of his childhood. Best known for his novels about the British Empire, Farrell is the author of *A Girl in the Hand*. *Troubles* won the Faber Memorial Prize for 1970. It is the first of a trilogy that includes *The Siege of Krishnapur* and *The Singapore Grip*.

2016 *The Siege of Krishnapur*

Date of Publication: 1973
Subject(s): British Raj; Indian Mutiny
Fictional character(s): Mr. Hopkins, Government Official (head of administration); Tom Willoughby, Judge; George Flevry, Military Personnel (English Officer)
Time Period(s): 1850s
Locale(s): Krishnapur, India

Summary: This darkly cosmic indictment of the British in India depicts an imaginary mutiny in Krishnapur in the 1850s. When the sepoys attack, the British defense is organized by Mr. Hopkins the Collector, the head of administration for the district. A varied group of Britons expose their strengths and weaknesses under the pressure of the siege. By the time relief arrives, they have few illusions left to support the high calling of England's imperial mission.

Historical Accuracy: The period elements are convincingly presented.

2017 *Troubles*

Date of Publication: 1970
Subject(s): Independence—Ireland
Fictional character(s): Brendan Archer, Military Personnel (major)
Time Period(s): 1910s (1919)
Locale(s): Ireland

Summary: Set during the period of Ireland's struggle for independence, the story takes place at a resort hotel on the Irish coast. The hotel becomes the locus for action that comes to symbolize the passing of an age.

Historical Accuracy: The novel is convincing in its period details and its reflection of the times.

MICHAEL FARRELL (1944-)

An Irish writer born in County Derry and a graduate of Queen's University, Belfast, Farrell was the founding member of the People's Democracy (a Marxist group dedicated to achieving a united socialist Ireland). Farrell was jailed in 1971 and 1973 for his political activities but won

his release after a 35-day hunger strike. Farrell teaches history and general studies at Belfast College of Technology.

2018 *Thy Tears Might Cease*

Date of Publication: 1962
Subject(s): Independence—Ireland; Easter Rising; Civil War—Ireland
Fictional character(s): Martin Reilly, Patriot, Orphan; Millie Bannon, Worker (factory)
Time Period(s): 1910s; 1920s (1910-1920)
Locale(s): Ireland

Summary: Martin Reilly comes of age during the Irish "troubles." Martin finds himself swept up in the events of the Easter Uprising of 1916 and its bloody aftermath, which progressively strip away his beliefs about himself and the Irish character.

Historical Accuracy: The novel is an honest and balanced view of a complex subject that can ably serve as either a social history of the time or a psychological portrait of a participant in the events.

GENE FARRINGTON (1931-)

An American novelist and playwright, Farrington worked as an advertising manager for a number of firms. He won the Prose Award in 1977 for "The Mass According to Saint Lester" and the Sherrill C. Corwin-Metropolitan Theatres Corporation Award in 1980 for "Halek.".

2019 *The Breath of Kings*

Date of Publication: 1982
Subject(s): Middle Ages; Royalty—England; Anglo Saxon Period
Historical character(s): Edward the Confessor, Ruler (King of England); Emma of Normandy, Royalty (mother of Edward); Ethelred II the Unready, Ruler (King of England)
Time Period(s): 11th century (1012-1066)
Locale(s): England; Normandy, France; Rouen, France

Summary: The novel details the turbulent era of English history prior to the Norman Conquest and focuses on the relationship of powerful and ambitious Emma of Normandy and her son Edward. He is the "albino monster" who will eventually rule as Edward the Confessor, but Emma rejects his claim and allies herself with the Danish invader, Canute, to breed a more desirable heir.

Historical Accuracy: The confusing dynastic maneuvering is dramatized with a convincing display of the politics and the period background.

ROBERT FARRINGTON (1925-)

2020 *The Killing of Richard the Third*

Date of Publication: 1971
Subject(s): War of the Roses; Royalty—England; Espionage

Fictional character(s): Henry Morane, Government Official (privy clerk)
Historical character(s): Richard III, Ruler (King of England); Edward IV, Ruler (King of England); Christopher Urswick, Government Official; William Stanley, Nobleman
Time Period(s): 15th century
Locale(s): England

Summary: Henry Morane is the privy clerk to Richard III's secretary as the War of the Roses rushes to its bloody climax on Bosworth Field. The king is surrounded by rivals and enemies, and Morane undertakes several secret missions as Richard's special agent, including one to kidnap Henry Tudor. The climax of the novel is Richard's downfall at Bosworth.

Historical Accuracy: Although the story is fanciful, the period is ingeniously and realistically depicted.

`2021` *The Traitors of Bosworth*

Date of Publication: 1978
Subject(s): Tudor Period; Espionage; Royalty—England
Fictional character(s): Henry Morane, Government Official (privy clerk); Matilda Morane, Spouse
Historical character(s): William Stanley, Nobleman; Henry Percy, Nobleman (Earl of Northumberland); Henry VII, Ruler (King of England); Elizabeth of York, Royalty (queen consort of Henry VII)
Time Period(s): 15th century (1480s-1490s)
Locale(s): England; Flanders

Summary: Henry Morane, clerk and secret agent to the court of Henry VII, though loyal to the king, is determined to bring justice to those who betrayed Richard III and contributed to his death at Bosworth Field. New conspiracies as well are growing in Flanders, where a pretender to the throne is being trained by Richard's sister. Can Morane's duties be combined with his obsession to bring Northumberland and Stanley to justice?.

Historical Accuracy: The historical details are credible and the atmosphere convincing.

`2022` *Tudor Agent*

Date of Publication: 1974
Subject(s): Tudor Period; Espionage; War of the Roses
Fictional character(s): Henry Morane, Government Official (privy clerk); Matilda Morane, Spouse
Historical character(s): Christopher Urswick, Government Official; Henry VII, Ruler (King of England); Elizabeth of York, Royalty (queen consort of Henry VII)
Time Period(s): 15th century (1485-1487)
Locale(s): England

Summary: Henry Morane, the resourceful clerk in the court of Richard III whose exploits the author describes in *The Killing of Richard the Third*, returns. Having survived the Battle of Bosworth Field, Henry now attempts to prove his worthiness to serve the new king, Henry VII. He is employed by Christopher Urswick, the creator of the Tudor espionage system, on a series of hazardous missions.

Historical Accuracy: The period details are authentically created.

JACK FARRIS (1921-)

Born in Texas, Farris attended Ouachita Baptist University and the University of Michigan. During World War II, he served in the U.S. Navy as a chief fire control man in the South Pacific. Farris has worked as a professor of English. His books include *Ramey, A Man to Ride With*, and *The Abiding Gospel of Claude Dee Moran, Jr.*

`2023` *Me and Gallagher*

Date of Publication: 1982
Subject(s): American West; Crime and Criminals; Vigilantes
Fictional character(s): Thomas "Grubber" Graves, Teenager, Orphan; Gallagher, Lawman
Time Period(s): 1860s (1863)
Locale(s): Virginia City, Montana

Summary: This western novel describes how the Montana vigilante movement developed to counteract corruption and lawlessness in the territory. Teenager Grubber Graves describes his relationship with wagonmaster and itinerant lawman Gallagher, who agrees to help fight crime in Virginia City.

Historical Accuracy: The story and characters are fictional, but the atmosphere is authentic.

DANIEL FARSON (1927-)

An English writer and television personality, Farson is the great-nephew of Bram Stoker, the author of *Dracula*, and was at age 17 the youngest ever lobby correspondent in the House of Commons. He has been a journalist, photographer, merchant seaman, and pub owner. Voted in 1960 as the best TV interviewer by British critics, Farson has hosted such TV shows as "Farson's Guide to Britain" and "Farson in Australia.".

`2024` *Swandowne*

Date of Publication: 1986
Subject(s): Crime and Criminals; Frontier—Australia
Fictional character(s): Augustus Stowe, Gentleman, Landowner; Poland Stowe, Gentleman; Sarah Stowe, Gentlewoman; Dick Stanton, Sailor, Convict
Historical character(s): Victoria, Ruler (Queen of England); Albert of Saxe-Coburg-Gotha, Royalty (prince consort of Victoria)
Time Period(s): 1840s
Locale(s): Tasmania, Australia; England

Summary: The Stowe family, as a result of gambling debts, are forced to flee to Van Dieman's Land (Tasmania) in the 1840s. There they meet Dick Stanton, a former sailor condemned to the infamous Port Arthur prison and assigned to the Stowes as a bond servant. The novel details their struggle to build a new life in their new home.

Historical Accuracy: The novel is backed by evident research and some eye witness accounts of Tasmania's troubled history.

HOWARD FAST (1914-)

A prodigious American historical novelist, Fast has written on American and ancient themes, all with a strong commitment to issues of human justice, the nature of moral and political leadership, and personal courage. Fast was a war correspondent during World War II, a member of the U.S. Peace Council from 1950-1955, and was an American Labor Party candidate for the U.S. Congress in 1952. He has also published detective novels under the pseudonym E.V. Cunningham.

2025 *Agrippa's Daughter*

Date of Publication: 1964
Subject(s): Roman Empire; Jews; Jewish Revolt
Historical character(s): Berenice Basagrippa, Royalty (princess); Herod Agrippa I, Ruler (King of Judea); Titus Flavius Vespasianus, Ruler (Roman emperor)
Time Period(s): 1st century
Locale(s): Jerusalem, Israel; Rome, Roman Empire

Summary: This tale, set during the first century in Jerusalem and Rome, tells the story of Berenice Basagrippa, the daughter of Herod Agrippa. Irrepressible and adaptable as she negotiates factional disputes during the Jewish War of 66 A.D., Berenice deals with Roman intervention, surviving three husbands and multiple lovers, including the Roman Emperor Titus.

Historical Accuracy: Some liberties are taken with historical events to enhance the drama, but it contains good local color.

2026 *The American*

Date of Publication: 1946
Subject(s): Politics; Biography, Fictionalized
Historical character(s): John Peter Altgeld, Judge, Political Figure (Governor of Illinois); Clarence Darrow, Lawyer; Samuel Gompers, Labor Leader; Grover Cleveland, Political Figure; Eugene V. Debs, Political Figure (socialist leader); William Jennings Bryan, Political Figure, Lawyer
Time Period(s): 19th century; 20th century (1850-1902)
Locale(s): Chicago, Illinois; Springfield, Illinois

Summary: This is a biographical novel on the life of John Peter Altgeld, liberal judge and governor of Illinois. Altgeld pardons the Haymarket anarchists and opposes President Cleveland in the Pullman Strike. Branded a Communist, he fails to halt the Democratic party's flight to William Jennings Bryan after the famous ''Cross of Gold'' speech.

Historical Accuracy: Fast's thesis depicting a progressive hero sometimes distorts historical facts.

2027 *April Morning*

Date of Publication: 1961
Subject(s): American Revolution; Battle of Lexington; Battle of Concord

Fictional character(s): Adam Cooper, Patriot, Military Personnel (minute-man); Moses Cooper, Patriot, Military Personnel (minute-man)
Time Period(s): 1770s (1775)
Locale(s): Lexington, Massachusetts, American Colonies; Concord, Massachusetts, American Colonies

Summary: The opening shots of the American Revolution at Lexington and Concord are dramatized from the perspective of 15-year-old Adam Cooper, his family, and the community as they debate what is to be done now that the British army is on the march.

Historical Accuracy: There are good details of domestic life.

2028 *Citizen Tom Paine*

Date of Publication: 1943
Subject(s): American Revolution; French Revolution; Biography, Fictionalized
Historical character(s): Thomas Paine, Patriot, Revolutionary; Benjamin Franklin, Inventor, Diplomat; John Hancock, Patriot; Thomas Jefferson, Patriot, Diplomat; George Washington, Military Personnel; Napoleon Bonaparte, Military Personnel; Georges-Jacques Danton, Revolutionary, Political Figure; James Monroe, Political Figure
Time Period(s): 18th century; 19th century (1775-1809)
Locale(s): Philadelphia, Pennsylvania; Paris, France

Summary: In this fictionalized biography of Revolutionary patriot Tom Paine, we follow him from poverty in England and his arrival in America with the assistance of Ben Franklin, to his role as a writer who inspired the new nation to struggle for independence. Paine next goes to France where he becomes involved in the French Revolution.

Historical Accuracy: This is an accurate though reverent account of an American patriot.

2029 *Conceived in Liberty*

Date of Publication: 1939
Subject(s): American Revolution
Fictional character(s): Allen Hale, Military Personnel
Historical character(s): George Washington, Military Personnel; Anthony Wayne, Military Personnel; Friedrich von Steuben, Military Personnel, Nobleman; Marie Joseph Paul de Lafayette, Military Personnel, Nobleman; Charles Lee, Military Personnel
Time Period(s): 1770s (1777-1778)
Locale(s): Valley Forge, Pennsylvania; Monmouth, New Jersey

Summary: Set during the American Revolution, the novel realistically depicts life at Valley Forge during the terrible winter of 1777-1778. Fast's characteristic social concerns are evident in the contrast shown between the daily life of the officers and the common soldiers.

Historical Accuracy: This is an authentic portrait of everyday life during Revolutionary times.

2030 *The Establishment*

Date of Publication: 1979
Subject(s): Family Saga; McCarthy Era; Communism

Fictional character(s): Barbara Lavette, Writer; Bernie Cohen, Adventurer (soldier of fortune)
Time Period(s): 1940s; 1950s
Locale(s): Palestine; San Francisco, California; Washington, District of Columbia

Summary: In this, the third volume of the Lavette family saga, the story centers on Barbara Lavette, author and correspondent, who finds herself on hand for the birth of Israel and in a confrontation with Congress during the McCarthy communist witch hunt.

Historical Accuracy: Fast covers so much ground that the history reads like highlights rather than a fully developed portrait.

2031 *Freedom Road*

Date of Publication: 1944
Subject(s): Reconstruction Period; Slavery
Fictional character(s): Gideon Jackson, Slave (former), Political Figure
Historical character(s): Ulysses S. Grant, Political Figure, Military Personnel
Time Period(s): 1860s; 1870s (1865-1877)
Locale(s): South Carolina; Washington, District of Columbia

Summary: This novel, set in South Carolina, is a scorching polemic about the failure of the promise of freedom for freed slaves and poor whites following the Civil War. Gideon Jackson is a freed slave who is elected to participate in the state constitutional convention. He educates himself, becomes a congressman, and serves his rural community in securing land and self-respect until federal troops are withdrawn, and klansmen seek revenge.

Historical Accuracy: Fast's moral drives his facts here. Villainy and virtue are unmistakable.

2032 *Haym Solomon, Son of Liberty*

Date of Publication: 1941
Subject(s): American Revolution; Biography, Fictionalized
Historical character(s): Haym Solomon, Financier, Patriot
Time Period(s): 18th century (1740-1785)
Locale(s): United States

Summary: This is a fictionalized life story of the Jewish financier, Haym Solomon, who plays an important role in raising money to pay for the American Revolution and the launching of the American republic. The novel dramatizes both the intricate financial dealings that transpire and the role of the Jewish community in the cause.

Historical Accuracy: Solomon's story is set in a semi-fictional frame that establishes an accurate account of trade and currency issues of the time.

2033 *The Hessian*

Date of Publication: 1972
Subject(s): American Revolution; Trials
Fictional character(s): Feversham, Doctor; Packenham, Military Personnel (general)
Time Period(s): 1780s
Locale(s): Ridgefield, Connecticut

Summary: Set during the Revolutionary War, the novel concerns a community seeking revenge on a troop of Hessian soldiers, particularly one young drummer boy who is accused of murder. Fast explores the ethical dilemma of moral accountability during wartime in this taut drama.

Historical Accuracy: Attitudes of the characters seem more modern than historical.

2034 *The Immigrants*

Date of Publication: 1977
Subject(s): Immigrants; Family Saga; Earthquakes
Fictional character(s): Dan Lavette, Fisherman, Businessman; Jean Lavette, Socialite; May Ling, Heroine
Historical character(s): Alfred E. Smith, Political Figure (Governor of New York)
Time Period(s): 19th century; 20th century (1880-1930)
Locale(s): San Francisco, California; Los Angeles, California

Summary: This novel, first in a series of five, tells the story of the Lavette family, who come to America in the 1880s, and their son's struggle in San Francisco until the 1930s. He gains and loses a fortune and a Nob Hill wife.

Historical Accuracy: The novel features good details of California life, including the earthquake of 1906.

2035 *The Immigrant's Daughter*

Date of Publication: 1985
Subject(s): Family Saga
Fictional character(s): Barbara Lavette, Writer, Political Figure
Time Period(s): 1970s; 1980s
Locale(s): San Francisco, California; San Salvador, El Salvador

Summary: The final installment of the Lavette family saga includes the fourth generation during the 1970s and 1980s. Barbara Lavette runs for Congress and gets swept up in the events of the period, including the violence in Central America.

Historical Accuracy: The novel reads more like highlights of the era than a fully-created portrait.

2036 *The Last Frontier*

Date of Publication: 1941
Subject(s): Settlement of the American Frontier; Indians; American West
Fictional character(s): Dull Knife, Indian (Cheyenne); Little Wolf, Indian (Cheyenne)
Time Period(s): 1870s (1878)
Locale(s): Kansas; Nebraska

Summary: In 1878 a tribe of Cheyenne led by Dull Knife and Little Wolf escape starvation, disease, and oppression on a government reservation and flee to their northern homeland. They are ruthlessly pursued through Kansas and Nebraska by whites intent on either enslaving the Indians or exterminating them.

Historical Accuracy: Fast presents a heartbreaking account of the closing of the West to the Indian way of life in this early and carefully documented "revisionist" view.

2037 *The Legacy*

Date of Publication: 1981
Subject(s): Family Saga
Fictional character(s): Barbara Lavette, Writer
Time Period(s): 1960s
Locale(s): San Francisco, California; Israel

Summary: The Lavette family saga continues into the 1960s. Barbara Lavette finds herself involved in the women's movement and protests over the war in Vietnam. The Lavette's third generation find themselves at the center of some of the decade's great events—a civil rights lynching in the South, the Arab-Israeli Six Day War, urban riots, and the Nixon presidency.

Historical Accuracy: Comprehensiveness forces a sacrifice in both credibility and thoroughness.

2038 *Max*

Date of Publication: 1982
Subject(s): Business Building; Motion Picture Industry
Fictional character(s): Max Britsky, Businessman (movie mogul)
Historical character(s): Mary Pickford, Actress; Douglas Fairbanks, Actor; Charlie Chaplin, Actor
Time Period(s): 19th century; 20th century (1891-1937)
Locale(s): New York, New York (lower East Side); Hollywood, California

Summary: This is the story of Max Britsky who struggles up from poverty on the Lower East Side of New York to create and build the motion picture industry.

Historical Accuracy: This is a colorful evocation of turn of the century New York and early Hollywood.

2039 *Moses, Prince of Egypt*

Date of Publication: 1958
Subject(s): Biblical Story; Pharaohs; Jews
Historical character(s): Moses, Leader, Biblical Figure; Ramses II, Ruler (pharaoh)
Time Period(s): 13th century B.C.
Locale(s): Egypt; Kush, Ancient Civilization (present day Ethiopia)

Summary: This entertaining and informative novel tells the story of the young Moses from age 10 to 23, as he progresses from young Egyptian prince in the palace world of Ramses II to learning his heritage as a child of the tribe of Levi.

Historical Accuracy: There are many interesting details of ancient Egyptian life including its medicine, engineering, and warfare.

2040 *The Passion of Sacco and Vanzetti: A New England Legend*

Date of Publication: 1953

Subject(s): Crime and Criminals; Trials
Historical character(s): Nicola Sacco, Murderer; Bartolomeo Vanzetti, Murderer; Benito Mussolini, Political Figure; Felix Frankfurter, Lawyer, Professor; Calvin Coolidge, Political Figure (U.S. president)
Time Period(s): 1920s (1927)
Locale(s): Boston, Massachusetts; New York, New York

Summary: The story takes place on the day of the execution of Sacco and Vanzetti for payroll robbery and murder in Boston in 1927. A number of historical personalities reflect on the case.

Historical Accuracy: Fast offers a recreation of events that provides a meditation on justice in an America under threat from internal and external sources.

2041 *Power*

Date of Publication: 1962
Subject(s): Labor Movement; Mining
Fictional character(s): Benjamin Holt, Miner (Labor Leader); Dorothy Aimesley, Young Woman
Historical character(s): Franklin Delano Roosevelt, Political Figure (U.S. president)
Time Period(s): 20th century (1914-1937)
Locale(s): West Virginia; Pomax, Illinois; Pennsylvania

Summary: This is the story of Ben Holt, coal miner and labor leader. Holt builds a labor movement of mine workers and endures violence and strikes to protect his power.

Historical Accuracy: Holt is a thinly disguised portrait of John L. Lewis, President of the United Mine Workers. The story contains good details of labor struggles of the 1920s and 1930s.

2042 *The Proud and the Free*

Date of Publication: 1950
Subject(s): American Revolution; Battle of Yorktown
Fictional character(s): Jamie Stuart, Patriot, Military Personnel (sergeant)
Historical character(s): Anthony Wayne, Military Personnel (American general)
Time Period(s): 1780s
Locale(s): Pennsylvania; New Jersey; Yorktown, Virginia

Summary: Jamie Stuart, sergeant of the 11th Regiment of the Pennsylvania Line during the Revolution, tells his story. The Eleventh, made up of Scottish, Irish, English, Germans, Blacks, Poles, and Jews, revolt because of poor treatment by their officers. The story of their revolt paints a graphic picture of the lot of the common citizen-soldier during the Revolution and the contradictions in the ideals of the new republic.

Historical Accuracy: Stuart's first-person narration lends credibility to his story.

2043 *Second Generation*

Date of Publication: 1978
Subject(s): Family Saga; Depression Era; World War II
Fictional character(s): Dan Lavette, Businessman; Barbara Lavette, Writer
Time Period(s): 1930s; 1940s

Locale(s): San Francisco, California; Paris, France; Berlin, Germany

Summary: This second volume of what one critic has called Fast's "soap history" concerns the fortunes of Dan Lavette and his family from the Depression to the close of World War II. The central figure is Barbara Lavette, who journeys to Europe on the verge of war as a correspondent.

Historical Accuracy: The complexity of the period is simplified for the drama.

2044 *Spartacus*

Date of Publication: 1952
Subject(s): Roman Empire; Servile War; Gladiators
Fictional character(s): Varinia, Slave; Gracchus, Political Figure
Historical character(s): Spartacus, Slave, Revolutionary (leader of slave revolt); Marcus Licinius Crassus, Military Personnel (Roman general); Marcus Tullius Cicero, Political Figure, Philosopher
Time Period(s): 1st century B.C. (71 B.C.)
Locale(s): Rome, Roman Empire; Capua, Roman Empire

Summary: Set in Capua and Rome in 71 B.C., the novel chronicles the Servile War—the slave revolt led by gladiator and third generation slave, Spartacus. Prominent Romans—Crassus, Cicero, and Gracchus—explore the enigma of the slave who took on the might of Rome.

Historical Accuracy: The novel is strong on details of gladiator and Roman life, but should not be trusted as a faithful depiction of history.

2045 *Torquemada*

Date of Publication: 1966
Subject(s): Inquisition; Jews
Fictional character(s): Alvero de Rafel, Nobleman; Mendoza, Religious (rabbi)
Historical character(s): Tomas de Torquemada, Religious (Grand Inquisitor); Christopher Columbus, Explorer, Sea Captain; Isabella I, Ruler (Queen of Castile); Ferdinand V, Ruler (King of Aragon)
Time Period(s): 15th century (1483)
Locale(s): Segovia, Spain; Seville, Spain

Summary: In this exploration of the human actors in the Spanish Inquisition, Thomas de Torquemada is appointed Grand Inquisitor by Isabella and Ferdinand. His lifelong friend, the nobleman Alvero, is suspected of being a Jewish sympathizer. Columbus makes a brief appearance on the eve of his famous voyage.

Historical Accuracy: This is more a historical sketch than a full portrait.

2046 *The Unvanquished*

Date of Publication: 1942
Subject(s): American Colonies; American Revolution
Historical character(s): George Washington, Military Personnel; Alexander Hamilton, Patriot; Aaron Burr, Patriot; Charles Lee, Military Personnel; John Adams, Patriot; John Hancock, Patriot

Time Period(s): 1770s (1776)
Locale(s): New York, New York, American Colonies; Trenton, New Jersey, American Colonies

Summary: "These are the times that try men's souls": the novel is set in 1776 and concerns the disastrous Battle of Brooklyn and the subsequent retreat by the rebel American army. Washington, an unsure Virginia foxhunter, grows in leadership, enduring a succession of setbacks to his new army, until the tide turns after he defeats the Hessians at Trenton on Christmas, 1776. All the key figures of the American Revolution are represented.

Historical Accuracy: Fast renders the events with unadorned authenticity that rings true.

JONATHAN FAST (1948-)

An American novelist, Fast is the son of prolific writer Howard Fast. He was born in New York and received his B.A. from Sarah Lawrence College. He has produced fiction on a wide range of subjects from modern Hollywood to India in the 7th century.

2047 *Golden Fire*

Date of Publication: 1986
Subject(s): Royalty—India; Indian Empire
Fictional character(s): Candra Gupta, Royalty (prince); Rama Gupta, Royalty (prince); Dhruvadeva, Royalty (princess)
Time Period(s): 4th century
Locale(s): India

Summary: This tale of ancient India in the 4th century dramatizes the story of Prince Rama who is born with a harelip and jealous of his brother Candra. For his protection Candra is raised in secret by a silk merchant's family. He meets the child princess Dhruvadeva who is bound to be married to Prince Rama. Tragedy and conflict prevent their getting together.

Historical Accuracy: Based largely on Indian legend, the story nonetheless is believable in its creation of court and ordinary life of the period.

2048 *The Jade Stalk*

Date of Publication: 1988
Subject(s): Royalty—China; Chinese Empire
Fictional character(s): Huai-i, Sports Figure (boxer), Farmer (peasant)
Historical character(s): Wu Chao, Ruler (empress)
Time Period(s): 7th century
Locale(s): China

Summary: The powerful Empress Wu of China's T'ang dynasty shocks Mandarin society by taking as her lover a common peasant, Huai-i, a boxer and a gift from the Empress' daughter. His talents for pleasing a woman insure his place in the Empress' affections and certain displeasure from court factions.

Historical Accuracy: The novel offers a compelling evocation of Chinese court life and the factional disputes of the period.

WILLIAM FAULKNER (1897-1962)

Faulkner, considered the greatest American novelist of the 20th century, was born in Mississippi, educated at the University of Mississippi, and a resident for most of his life of Oxford, Mississippi. His many memorable characters populate the fictional Yoknapatawpha County, which Faulkner used to explore themes of Southern life and values in transition. His challenging and stylistically experimental works include *Sound and the Fury*, *As I Lay Dying*, and *Light in August*.

2049 *Absalom, Absalom!*

Date of Publication: 1936
Subject(s): Antebellum South; Family Saga; Civil War—U.S.
Fictional character(s): Thomas Sutpen, Plantation Owner
Time Period(s): 19th century; 20th century
Locale(s): Jefferson, Mississippi

Summary: Tracing the rise and fall of Thomas Sutpen and his family, the novel covers nearly a hundred years of Southern and American history. Sutpen's attempts to create a dynasty through force of will are doomed as history and his past block his efforts. The novel deals with themes of incest, miscegenation, and guilt. A number of narrators explore Sutpen's enigmatic personality and monomania as well as the forces of time and place that he cannot control.

Historical Accuracy: Faulkner uses the past as an expressionistic and mythical medium to reveal the personal and social tragedy of Southern life.

2050 *The Unvanquished*

Date of Publication: 1938
Subject(s): Civil War—U.S.; Coming of Age
Fictional character(s): Bayard Sartoris, Young Man; Colonel John Sartoris, Military Personnel (Confederate officer); Ringo, Companion (of Bayard)
Time Period(s): 1860s
Locale(s): Mississippi

Summary: This coming-of-age tale traces the experiences of Bayard Sartoris and his black companion Ringo. Both young men learn about violence and the code of the Southern cause through the ambiguous inspiration of Bayard's father, colonel John Sartoris, and other Sartoris family members during the Civil War. Bayard must contend with the murder of both his grandmother and his father as the war produces a collapse of the old Southern order and inadequate values to replace it.

Historical Accuracy: Richly evocative of the time and place, the novel provides one of the best reconstructions of Southern life and attitudes during the Civil War and its aftermath.

SEBASTIAN FAULKS (1953-)

English writer Faulks is a graduate of Emmanuel College, Oxford University. He was a teacher of English and French at the International School of London. Faulks worked as a journalist and editor for 14 years before becoming a full-time writer in 1991. He was voted the Author of the Year by the British Book Awards for *Birdsong*.

2051 *Birdsong*

Date of Publication: 1993
Subject(s): World War I
Fictional character(s): Stephen Wraysford, Businessman, Military Personnel (soldier); Isabelle Azaire, Gentlewoman; Jack Firebrace, Military Personnel (soldier), Miner
Time Period(s): 20th century (1978-1979)
Locale(s): Amiens, France

Summary: The novel tells the story of a young Englishman, Stephen Wraysford, who journeys to France on business in 1910 and becomes entangled in a clandestine love affair. When World War I breaks out, he joins the army and is given the command of a brigade of miners assigned to tunnel deep beneath the enemy lines. The novel captures an entire subterranean world of death but also one of love and loyalty. The novel shuttles between Wraysford's diary account and his granddaughter's attempt in the 1970s to penetrate the past.

Historical Accuracy: The novel details with conviction the world of trench warfare and its curious reversal of norms and behavior. The novel is far less believable in its modern scenes.

RAOUL COHEN FAURE (1909-)

Born in Havana, Cuba, Feuille was a University of Texas graduate and a lawyer, holding several important government positions, including acting governor of the Pananma Canal Zone. He wrote for publications in three languages.

2052 *Lady Godiva and Master Tom*

Date of Publication: 1948
Subject(s): Middle Ages; Myths and Legends
Historical character(s): Lady Godiva, Noblewoman; Leofric, Nobleman (Earl of Mercia)
Time Period(s): 11th century
Locale(s): Coventry, England

Summary: The novel offers alternative circumstances for Lady Godiva's famous naked ride through the streets of Coventry. In this version, Lady Godiva's motivation is far from an altruistic attempt to reduce the taxation of the citizens. Instead she intends to drive her husband, whom she despises, to destruction.

Historical Accuracy: The novel's characterizations are far more modern than medieval.

IRVIN FAUST (1924-)

Born in New York City, Faust graduated from City College and Columbia University and has combined a career as a high school guidance counselor with that of a writer. His literary success began with the publication of the short story collection *Roar Lion Roar and Other Stories*. His novels include *The Struggle* and *Willy Remembers*.

2053 *Foreign Devils*

Date of Publication: 1973
Subject(s): Boxer Rebellion; Time Travel

Fictional character(s): Norris Blake, Journalist
Time Period(s): 1900s; 1970s
Locale(s): China; New York, New York

Summary: In this book-within-a-book, a New York writer exorcises his writer's block with a novel about New York *World* correspondent Norris Blake, who reports on the Boxer Rebellion in China for Joseph Pulitzer. As the novel reaches its conclusion, the scenes of China in the 1900s and New York City in the 1970s merge.

Historical Accuracy: The writer calls his Boxer Rebellion story "fictionally oriented history." Despite a number of accurate period elements, the retreat to the past seems more for the sake of nostalgia and comparison than a genuine attempt at recovery.

QUINN FAWCETT
(PSEUD. OF CHELSEA QUINN YARBRO, 1942-)

Quinn Fawcett is a pseudonym for American supernatural and horror writer Chelsea Quinn Yarbro. An American novelist born in Berkeley, California, Yarbro has written books in a number of genres: fantasy, gothic, science fiction, Western, and suspense. She is best known for her historical vampire novels. A believer in the occult, Yarbro often incorporates magic and mysticism into her stories, but rarely is the historical sacrificed.

`2054` *Napoleon Must Die*
Date of Publication: 1993
Subject(s): Napoleonic Wars; Mystery
Fictional character(s): Victoire Vernet, Spouse; Lucien Vernet, Military Personnel (aide to Napoleon)
Historical character(s): Napoleon Bonaparte, Military Personnel (French commander), Ruler (Emperor of France)
Time Period(s): 1800s
Locale(s): Egypt

Summary: Napoleon's military expedition to Egypt has captured a vast cache of treasure. When a guard is killed and the treasure disappears, suspicion falls on Major Vernet. His wife is determined to prove him innocent. She uncovers more than just greed and deception.

Historical Accuracy: The period details of both Egypt and the French forces are authentically delivered.

JANE FEATHER

`2055` *Brazen Whispers*
Date of Publication: 1990
Subject(s): Middle Ages; Romance
Fictional character(s): Magdalen de Brese, Noblewoman; Guy de Servais, Nobleman
Time Period(s): 14th century (1370s)
Locale(s): England; France

Summary: Set during the 14th century and the conflict between France and England, the novel concerns the love between Magdalen de Brese and Guy de Gervais. Despite com-

plications, including marriage to other partners and political intrigue, Magdalen eventually wins the man she loves.

Historical Accuracy: The period background is detailed with some conviction.

`2056` *Reckless Angel*
Date of Publication: 1989
Subject(s): Civil War—England
Fictional character(s): Henrietta Ashby, Young Woman; Sir Daniel Drummond, Gentleman, Widow(er)
Time Period(s): 17th century (1648)
Locale(s): England; Netherlands

Summary: The background to this romantic adventure story is the Royalist versus Roundhead conflict during the English Civil War in the 17th century. Sir Daniel Drummond rescues Henrietta Ashby from the battlefield, and he marries her. Together they are swept up in passion and political intrigue on behalf of the Royalist cause.

Historical Accuracy: The period background is effectively and convincingly drawn.

JURG FEDERSPIEL (1931-)

`2057` *The Ballad of Typhoid Mary*
Date of Publication: 1983
Subject(s): Immigrants
Historical character(s): Mary Mallon, Immigrant, Cook
Time Period(s): 19th century; 20th century (1867-1907)
Locale(s): United States

Summary: The novel presents an imaginative chronicle of the life and career of Mary Mallon, a German immigrant and a typhoid carrier who spread the disease throughout the U.S. as a cook. The novel imagines what Typhoid Mary felt and did from her arrival in America to her incarceration.

Historical Accuracy: The story is based partly on fact with the author's suggested ratio: 85 percent fiction, 15 percent fact.

ANDREW J. FENADY (1928-)

An American author, screenwriter, film and television producer, Fenady was born in Toledo, Ohio, and attended the University of Toledo. His novels include *Claws of the Eagle*, *The Man with Bogart's Face*, and *The Secret of Sam Marlowe*.

`2058` *The Summer of Jack London*
Date of Publication: 1985
Subject(s): Biography, Fictionalized; Sea Story; Gold Rush—Klondike
Historical character(s): Jack London, Writer, Sailor
Time Period(s): 1890s (1895)
Locale(s): San Francisco, California

Summary: This novel recreates the events of one summer in the life of novelist Jack London. Not yet 20, London has returned to San Francisco after a disastrous sea voyage and sets out to work on his first novel. A relationship with a society beauty and a failed kidnapping attempt form the action before London heads off to the Alaskan gold fields.

Historical Accuracy: Although based on actual details of London's life, the story is more fictional than factual but does provide a credible character portrait of the young Jack London.

EDWARD FENTON (1917-)

An American writer of books for adults and children, Fenton was born in New York City and attended Amherst College. His adult novels include *The Double Darkness*, and his many juvenile works include *The Nine Questions*, *The Phantom of Walkaway Hill*, and *Petros's War*.

2059   *Anne of the Thousand Days*

Date of Publication: 1970
Subject(s): Tudor Period; Royalty—England
Historical character(s): Henry VIII, Ruler (King of England); Anne Boleyn, Royalty (queen consort of Henry VIII); Thomas Wolsey, Religious (cardinal), Political Figure; Catherine of Aragon, Royalty (queen consort of Henry VIII); Thomas Cromwell, Political Figure
Time Period(s): 16th century (1530s)
Locale(s): England

Summary: Based on the screenplay of the film version of Maxwell Anderson's play, the novel recounts the tempestuous and eventually tragic courtship and marriage of Henry VIII and Anne Boleyn. The novel dramatizes as well the political manuevering needed to bring about Henry's divorce from Catherine of Aragon and the split that leads to Anne's execution.

Historical Accuracy: This is a simplified, though historically accurate, version of the events and the period.

EDNA FERBER (1887-1968)

An American novelist and playwright, Ferber was born in Kalamazoo, Michigan. At the age of 17 she started working full-time as a newspaper reporter. In the 1920s and 1930s Ferber was considered the greatest American woman novelist. In 1924 her novel *So Big* won the Pulitzer Prize. Ferber's literary influence was so great that it is said that her novel *Ice Palace* played an important role in Alaska gaining statehood.

2060   *American Beauty*

Date of Publication: 1931
Subject(s): American Colonies; Family Saga
Fictional character(s): Orrange Oakes, Settler; Jude Oakes, Farmer; Orrange Olszak, Worker
Time Period(s): Multiple Time Periods
Locale(s): Connecticut

Summary: American history is reflected in the chronicle of a Connecticut estate from its earliest settlement in the 1700s to its decline and regeneration as the earliest colonial settlers give way to later immigrants from Poland, who share with their predecessors a great love for the land.

Historical Accuracy: The locale painting is effective and convincing in this massive social chronicle.

2061   *Cimarron*

Date of Publication: 1954
Subject(s): American West; Indians
Fictional character(s): Sabra Venable, Frontierswoman, Political Figure; Yancey Cravat, Frontiersman, Journalist
Time Period(s): 19th century; 20th century (1889-1900s)
Locale(s): Oklahoma; Kansas

Summary: The story of the settling of Oklahoma is depicted from the land rush of 1889 to the striking of oil. Sabra Venable marries adventurer Yancey Cravat, and they set out for the Oklahoma territory where their experiences reflect the progress of the state. Yancey establishes a newspaper and becomes a crusader for reform.

Historical Accuracy: The author has made no attempt to set down an actual history of Oklahoma.

2062   *Saratoga Trunk*

Date of Publication: 1941
Subject(s): Business Building
Fictional character(s): Clio Dulaine, Young Woman; Clint Mardon, Businessman; Bartholomew Van Fleet, Financier
Time Period(s): 1880s
Locale(s): New Orleans, Louisiana; Saratoga Springs, New York

Summary: This is a love story between Clio Dulaine and Clint Mardon, who set out to make a fortune among the robber barons of the 1880s in fashionable Saratoga Springs. Their story describes the social and business life of the period.

Historical Accuracy: The novel offers convincing period details of fashionable life.

2063   *Show Boat*

Date of Publication: 1926
Subject(s): Riverboats; Theatrical Life
Fictional character(s): Magnolia Ravenal, Actress; Kim Ravenal, Actress; Gaylord Ravenal, Gambler
Time Period(s): 19th century; 20th century (1870s-1920s)
Locale(s): Mississippi River; Chicago, Illinois; New Orleans, Louisiana

Summary: The novel was the basis of one of the most successful stage and screen productions, capturing life on board a Mississippi River showboat. Magnolia Ravenal is the stalwart performer on Captain Hawkin's *Cotton Blossom* showboat as it cruises the river and dramatizes river life of the period.

Historical Accuracy: The author admits to manipulating details and the chronology, claiming that her goal was nothing but fiction.

CHARLES FERGUS

2064   *Shadow Catcher*

Date of Publication: 1991

Subject(s): American West; Indians; Photography
Fictional character(s): Ansel Fry, Photographer
Historical character(s): Joseph Dixon, Photographer; James McLaughlin, Frontiersman
Time Period(s): 1910s (1913)
Locale(s): West

Summary: The novel depicts the historical Wanamaker Expedition that chronicled life on the Indian reservations of the West. While the expedition's official photographer, Joseph Dixon, takes carefully posed pictures of the Indians as the Noble Savage, Ansel Fry secretly photographs reservation life as it truly is.

Historical Accuracy: Based on an actual event, the novel accurately documents Indian life of the period.

ADAM FERGUSSON (1932-)

A Scottish writer, educated in history at Cambridge, Fergusson has worked as a journalist since 1956. He was a regular broadcaster with the BBC foreign service.

2065 *Roman Go Home!*

Date of Publication: 1969
Subject(s): Roman Empire
Fictional character(s): Marcus Probus, Nobleman; Imogen, Royalty (Celtic princess)
Historical character(s): Honorius, Ruler (Roman Emperor)
Time Period(s): 5th century
Locale(s): England

Summary: This comic satire is set in 5th century Britain as the collapsing Roman Empire prepares to abandon its British colony and hand over power to the savage Britons. A love affair between the Roman patrician Marcus and a Celtic princess, Imogen, is complicated by the political intrigue of disengagement, with obvious parallels to the dismantling of the British Empire fifteen centuries later.

Historical Accuracy: The historical errors here are deliberate distortions that are necessary to advance the novel's plot.

HARVEY FERGUSSON (1890-1971)

An American novelist born in New Mexico, Fergusson graduated from Washington and Lee University. Fergusson worked as a reporter in Washington, D.C., Chicago, and in Savannah, Georgia. His grandfather was a Sante Fe merchant who became a Congressman. Fergusson moved east when he was young and returned infrequently except in his books. His books include *Followers of the Sun, The Conquest of Don Pedro,* and *The Life of Riley.*

2066 *The Conquest of Don Pedro*

Date of Publication: 1954
Subject(s): American West; Social Chronicle
Fictional character(s): Leo Mendes, Store Owner; Magdalena Mendes, Spouse
Time Period(s): 1860s
Locale(s): New Mexico

Summary: The novel provides a chronicle of life in a small town in New Mexico on the lower Rio Grande Valley shortly after the end of the Civil War. The scene is shown from the perspective of Leo Mendes, the town's storekeeper, who reflects both the continuity and changes in the community.

Historical Accuracy: This is an authentic look at the region during the period with a careful avoidance of the extraordinary and the exceptional.

2067 *Grant of Kingdom*

Date of Publication: 1950
Subject(s): American West
Fictional character(s): Jean Ballard, Mountain Man; Dona Consuelo Coronel, Gentlewoman; Clay Tighe, Lawman
Time Period(s): 1850s
Locale(s): New Mexico

Summary: This tale of Old New Mexico involves mountain man Jean Ballard who marries the beautiful and aristocratic Dona Consuelo Coronel. Her dowry is 2000 square miles of the New Mexican wilderness, and the novel traces the effect of the Ballard Grant, as several characters are tested by crisis and the demands of power.

Historical Accuracy: The novel offers good and genuine period details in this atmospheric Western tale.

2068 *In Those Days*

Date of Publication: 1929
Subject(s): American West
Fictional character(s): Robert Jayson, Settler
Time Period(s): 19th century; 20th century
Locale(s): Southwest

Summary: Robert Jayson who journeys from New England to settle in an adobe town beside the Rio Grande. The novel follows his life story and the eventual growth and development of the region as the time of the frontier passes.

Historical Accuracy: The novel captures its setting and period with authenticity.

2069 *Wolf Song*

Date of Publication: 1927
Subject(s): American West
Fictional character(s): Sam Lash, Mountain Man; Lola Salazar, Young Woman; Lone Wolf, Indian
Historical character(s): Kit Carson, Frontiersman
Time Period(s): 1830s
Locale(s): Southwest

Summary: This western tale of mountain man Sam Lash describes his life in the Southwest in pursuit of beaver and the conflict of cultures between the Anglos, Spanish, and Indians. His relationship with the Spanish maiden Lola Salazar civilizes Sam.

Historical Accuracy: The novel is precise in its reproduction of the period and its customs.

ELIZABETH FERRELL

MARGARET FERRELL

2070 *Full of Thy Riches*

Date of Publication: 1944
Subject(s): Civil War—U.S.; Business Building; Oil Industry
Fictional character(s): India Culpepper, Young Woman; Brian Kilpatrick, Adventurer
Historical character(s): John D. Rockefeller, Financier
Time Period(s): 1860s
Locale(s): West Virginia

Summary: India Culpepper's elderly husband takes her into West Virginia's new oil country, where she falls in love with Brian Kilpatrick. The story's climax is a Confederate raid on the oil wells.

Historical Accuracy: The novel is full of cliches and lacking in authentic detail.

LION FEUCHTWANGER (1884-1958)

Feuchtwanger was a German novelist whose historical novels were extremely popular in the 1940s and 50s. He escaped from Nazi Germany and lived in the United States after 1940.

2071 *The Jew of Rome*

Date of Publication: 1936
Subject(s): Roman Empire; Jews
Historical character(s): Flavius Josephus, Historian; Vespasian, Ruler (Roman emperor)
Time Period(s): 1st century
Locale(s): Rome, Roman Empire

Summary: This second volume of a trilogy on the life of Josephus describes his career as a historian as well as his emerging struggle between loyalty to Rome and Jewish nationalism.

Historical Accuracy: The novel's details of Roman court life and culture are strongly presented.

2072 *Josephus*

Date of Publication: 1932
Subject(s): Roman Empire; Jews
Historical character(s): Flavius Josephus, Military Personnel, Courtier; Vespasian, Ruler (Roman emperor); Nero, Ruler (Roman emperor)
Time Period(s): 1st century
Locale(s): Rome, Roman Empire; Alexandria, Egypt; Jerusalem, Israel

Summary: In this first novel of a trilogy on the life of Josephus, a Jew who earned the favor of Roman emperors, we follow the first stage of Josephus' interesting career as a soldier and politician. The scene shifts from Rome to Alexandria and then to Jerusalem for the siege and fall of the city.

Historical Accuracy: The novel is convincing in its details of Imperial Rome.

2073 *Josephus and the Emperor*

Date of Publication: 1942
Subject(s): Roman Empire; Jews
Historical character(s): Flavius Josephus, Historian, Political Figure; Domitian, Ruler (Roman emperor); Lucia, Royalty (Roman empress)
Time Period(s): 1st century
Locale(s): Rome, Roman Empire; Israel

Summary: In this final volume of a trilogy on the life of Josephus, he has finished his universal history of the Jews and has fallen out of favor with the new emperor. Josephus tries unsuccessfully to be both a Jewish teacher and a Roman knight. He is forced to decide with which side to align himself.

Historical Accuracy: The novel expertly details Roman life and the political issues of the day.

2074 *Power*

Date of Publication: 1925
Subject(s): Politics; Religious Conflict; Jews
Fictional character(s): Josef Suss Oppenheimer, Courtier; Rabbi Gabriel, Religious; Karl Alexander, Nobleman
Time Period(s): 1750s
Locale(s): Germany

Summary: This story of court intrigue in Germany involves Suss, a half-Christian Jew, and the Prussian nobles he assists. The author uses the story to ask what is a Jew and why does one remain Jewish despite persecution. Suss is shown transformed from crass materialist to true believer.

Historical Accuracy: There are good details of German court life.

2075 *The Ugly Duchess*

Date of Publication: 1923
Subject(s): Middle Ages
Historical character(s): Meinhard, Royalty (prince); Margaret of Tyrol, Noblewoman (countess); Johann, Royalty (son of King John of Bohemia)
Time Period(s): 14th century
Locale(s): Tyrol, Austria; Bohemia; Munich, Germany

Summary: This is a complex tale of the reign of Margaret, Countess of Tyrol, in the 14th century. She is a powerful leader trying to withstand innumerable pressures inside and outside the country. Margaret, John Tenniel's model for the duchess in his illustration for *Alice in Wonderland*, is a remarkable character study in greed and evil.

Historical Accuracy: This is a confusing tale because of the complexity of 14th-century politics; however, the novel's characters are well-developed and plausible.

LEWIS S. FEUER

2076 *The Case of the Revolutionist's Daughter: Sherlock Holmes Meets Karl Marx*

Date of Publication: 1983
Subject(s): Mystery; Victorian Period
Fictional character(s): Sherlock Holmes, Detective—Private; John H. Watson, Doctor; Eleanor Tussy, Relative (daughter of Karl Marx); James Moriarty, Criminal, Professor
Historical character(s): Friedrich Engels, Philosopher
Time Period(s): 1890s
Locale(s): England

Summary: The celebrated sleuth Sherlock Holmes agrees to search for Eleanor Tussy, the missing daughter of Karl Marx. She is living happily with an evil colleague of Holmes' nemesis, Professor Moriarty. The novel's climax pits Holmes against Moriarty against a backdrop of late-19th-century socialists and social reformers.

Historical Accuracy: The novel's melodrama and suspense are at odds with an attempt to capture the atmosphere of the period.

FRANK FEUILLE

2077 *The Cotton Road*

Date of Publication: 1954
Subject(s): Civil War—U.S.
Fictional character(s): Timmie O'Shea, Teenager; Lance Godfrey, Businessman
Time Period(s): 1860s
Locale(s): Brownsville, Texas

Summary: In an attempt to break the Union blockade that prevents cotton from reaching English markets, Southerners are shipping it overland through Texas to Mexico. Young, crippled Timmie O'Shea joins forces with Englishman Lance Godfrey to haul a shipment of cotton along the dangerous Cotton Road contending with outlaws and Indians.

Historical Accuracy: The novel sheds a convincing light on a little-known aspect of the Civil War.

BRADDA FIELD (1904-)

Field is the author of *The Earthen Lot* and *Small Town*. She won the Femina Vie Heureuse Prize, 1932-1933.

2078 *Bride of Glory*

Date of Publication: 1942
Subject(s): Napoleonic Wars; Biography, Fictionalized
Historical character(s): Lady Emma Hamilton, Gentlewoman; Sir William Hamilton, Diplomat; Horatio Nelson, Military Personnel (British admiral)
Time Period(s): 18th century; 19th century
Locale(s): England; Naples, Italy

Summary: The novel tells the story of Emma Lyon, a blacksmith's daughter. She becomes the notorious Emma Hamil-ton, wife of the British envoy to Napoleon's court and mistress of England's greatest naval hero, Admiral Horatio Nelson.

Historical Accuracy: The novel is packed with historical and political details, but the characters fail to emerge as truly living portraits.

DAWN STEWART FIELD (1940-)

An American writer born in West Virginia, Field is a graduate of the University of Kentucky and Harvard. She has worked for the Library of Congress as a supervisor of Russian translation in the fields of biology and medicine.

2079 *Luise*

Date of Publication: 1974
Subject(s): Gothic Romance; War of 1812
Fictional character(s): Luise Von Doring, Noblewoman; Peter Tarlton, Businessman (merchant); Jeremy Morris, Gentleman, Lawyer
Time Period(s): 1810s
Locale(s): Alexandria, Virginia; Washington, District of Columbia

Summary: In this Gothic historical romance set in Alexandria and Washington during the War of 1812, the Baroness Luise Von Doring, who has fled the Napoleonic Wars for a new life in America, has two rivals for her affections. She is also haunted by a vivid imagination and the suspicion that someone is trying to drive her insane. The novel climaxes with the British attack on Washington.

Historical Accuracy: The hybrid of history and Gothic romance is unusual, giving a sense that the novel is split in its interests. The historical details are colorfully evoked.

RACHEL FIELD (1894-1942)

An American novelist, poet, playwright, editor, and illustrator, Field was born in New York City and attended Radcliffe College. She was the first woman to win the prestigious Newbery Award in 1930 for *Hitty: Her First Hundred Years*. *All This, and Heaven Too* was adapted into a film starring Bette Davis.

2080 *All This, and Heaven Too*

Date of Publication: 1938
Subject(s): Literary Life; Crime and Criminals
Historical character(s): Rachel, Actress; Samuel Morse, Scientist; Harriet Beecher Stowe, Writer; William Cullen Bryant, Writer; Henry M. Field, Religious (clergyman), Writer; Henriette Deluzy-Desportes, Governess; Fanny Kemble, Actress; Peter Cooper, Inventor, Financier
Time Period(s): 19th century (1841-1875)
Locale(s): France; New York, New York

Summary: This remarkable story of Henriette Deluzy-Desportes, the author's great-aunt, begins with her involvement in the notorious Praslin murder case. After she takes refuge in America, the novel's focus shifts to the American literary scene of the 1850s and 1860s with very important historical figures appearing.

Historical Accuracy: The story is carefully based on actuality.

2081 *Time out of Mind*

Date of Publication: 1935
Subject(s): Family Saga
Fictional character(s): Nathaniel Fortune, Heir; Kate Fernald, Young Woman
Time Period(s): 19th century
Locale(s): Maine

Summary: The dissolution of a Maine shipbuilding family is detailed in the story of the Fortunes. Major Fortune is determined that his fourth, frail son, Nathaniel, should carry on the family business, but Nathaniel is more interested in music than shipping. This family tragedy is played out against the end of the era of sailing ships.

Historical Accuracy: The novel masters an authentic regional atmosphere.

WILLIAM FIFIELD (1916-1987)

An American writer, actor, producer-director, and former bullfighter, Fifield was born in Chicago, Illinois, and was educated at Whitman College. The winner of the O'Henry Memorial Award for his short story, "Fishermen of Patzcuaro," Fifield's other works include biographies of Jean Cocteau and Amedeo Modigliani, as well as *The Encyclopedia of Wines and Spirits*, written with Alexis Lichine.

2082 *The Devil's Marchioness*

Date of Publication: 1957
Subject(s): Crime and Criminals
Historical character(s): Marie Madeleine Brinvilliers, Noblewoman (marquise), Murderer
Time Period(s): 17th century
Locale(s): France

Summary: The novel records everything that is known of the notorious Marquise De Brinvilliers who poisoned her father and her two brothers.

Historical Accuracy: The novel provides an exact chronology of the facts, but some invented conversations and the thoughts of the characters make this case study a novel.

EVA FIGES (1932-)

English author Figes was born in Berlin, Germany, and graduated from Queen Mary College, London. She has worked as an editor in publishing. In 1967 she won the Guardian Prize for *Winter Journey*. Other novels include *Equinox*, *B*, and *Waking*. She is also a children's book author and a translator.

2083 *Light*

Date of Publication: 1983

Subject(s): Artistic Life
Historical character(s): Claude Monet, Artist
Time Period(s): 1900s (1900)
Locale(s): Giverny, France

Summary: The novel offers a day in the life of French painter Claude Monet in 1900 as he completes his "Waterlilies." The novel functions as a kind of prose poem and literary impressionist study of various themes and layers of meaning, including the nature of light.

Historical Accuracy: The novel uses details of Monet's life and career as the starting point for a wider speculation.

2084 *The Seven Ages*

Date of Publication: 1986
Subject(s): Middle Ages; Victorian Period; Georgian Period
Fictional character(s): Lady Blanche, Noblewoman; Henry Dinsdale, Doctor
Time Period(s): Multiple Time Periods
Locale(s): England

Summary: Nearly 1,000 years of English and women's history are reflected in this poetic novel that captures the voices of seven women whose lives span the centuries from the Middle Ages to the present. The novel skillfully interweaves historical background, folk tradition, and the history of childbirth and midwifery into a series of fascinating glimpses of an alternative view of history.

Historical Accuracy: The novel's period elements are authentic, but the novel's objectivity is often sacrificed for its theme. The males here are particularly maligned.

2085 *The Tree of Knowledge*

Date of Publication: 1990
Subject(s): Literary Life; Women's Rights
Historical character(s): John Milton, Writer (poet); Deborah Milton, Gentlewoman
Time Period(s): 17th century
Locale(s): England

Summary: This novel offers a vivid portrait of women's lot in 17th-century England in an extended monologue by one of John Milton's daughters, whom he ignores and exploits. Milton is presented as a cruel misogynist, insensitive and intolerant of his daughters. The novel depicts the lack of options for women at the time and their hopeless attempts to find fulfillment.

Historical Accuracy: The novel offers a feminist reading of both Milton and his times. Though supported by biographical record, the novel provides little to mitigate the stark and negative portrait.

MERTON FINCH
(PSEUD. OF MERTON FINK, 1921-)

Born in Liverpool, England, Merton Fink attended the University of Liverpool. A dental surgeon in private practice, Fink has written several books on dentistry as well as other titles such as *The Empire Builder* and *Josephus Flavius*.

2086 *Simon Bar Cochba: Rebellion in Judea*

Date of Publication: 1969
Subject(s): Roman Empire; Jewish Revolt
Historical character(s): Simon Bar Kokhba, Leader (of the Jewish Revolt)
Time Period(s): 2nd century (118-135)
Locale(s): Israel

Summary: The novel recounts the events of the Jewish Revolt against Roman domination in A.D. 132-135 led by Simon Bar Cochba. Although the rebellion failed, it came close to ending Roman control. The novel focuses on the charismatic leadership of Bar Cochba, thought by some to be the Messiah.

Historical Accuracy: The story is based on ancient sources and modern archaeological evidence and is close to historical fact with a fictional element to join the facts together.

PHILLIP FINCH

2087 *Birthright*

Date of Publication: 1979
Subject(s): Gold Rush—California; American West; Mining
Fictional character(s): Joshua Belden, Heir, Gambler; Elizabeth Burgess, Orphan, Madam; Crooked Fingers, Indian (Washo)
Time Period(s): 1840s (1848)
Locale(s): Virginia City, Nevada

Summary: This caper novel is set during the boom town scramble of the California Gold Rush. It features an unlikely trio of characters: a disinherited gambler, Joshua Belden; a madam, Elizabeth Burgess; and an Indian, Crooked Fingers. They become the main conspirators in a sting that captures the spirit of the Virginia City boom.

Historical Accuracy: The story is fanciful but authentic in its depiction of the region and the era.

IRVING FINEMAN (1893-)

Born in New York City, Fineman graduated from MIT and Harvard as an engineer. He worked as a professor of literature at Bennington College and as a writer for several motion picture studios.

2088 *Jacob: An Autobiography*

Date of Publication: 1941
Subject(s): Biblical Story; Ancient Israel
Historical character(s): Isaac, Biblical Figure; Jacob, Biblical Figure; Esau, Biblical Figure; Rachel, Biblical Figure; Joseph, Biblical Figure
Time Period(s): Indeterminate Past
Locale(s): Israel

Summary: The Old Testament story of Isaac, Jacob, Essau, and Rachel is depicted. Jacob tells the story to his young son, Joseph. The novel is a lyrical evocation of the Biblical story with a concentration on characterization over a fully realized background.

Historical Accuracy: The novel does not attempt to re-create a primitive society. This is a modernized Biblical story.

2089 *Ruth*

Date of Publication: 1949
Subject(s): Biblical Story; Ancient Israel
Historical character(s): Ruth, Biblical Figure; Naomi, Biblical Figure; Boaz, Biblical Figure
Time Period(s): Indeterminate Past
Locale(s): Bethlehem, Israel; Moab, Ancient Civilization

Summary: This novel, based on the Biblical book of Ruth, tells the story of the Moabite widow Ruth and her fidelity to her widowed mother-in-law, Naomi. Ruth returns with Naomi to Bethlehem, where she marries Naomi's kinsman, Boaz.

Historical Accuracy: This novelized version remains close to the Biblical original and employs direct scriptural quotations as well as a convincing depiction of life in Israel more than 3,000 years ago.

LUCILE FINLAY (1897-)

An American writer born in Greenville, Mississippi, Finlay decided as a young woman to become a lawyer. She studied on her own before passing the bar exam.

2090 *The Coat I Wore*

Date of Publication: 1947
Subject(s): American Revolution
Fictional character(s): Anthony Hastings, Military Personnel (British colonel)
Time Period(s): 1770s
Locale(s): Louisiana; Natchez, Mississippi; England

Summary: This story, set during the American Revolution, takes the perspective of British sympathizers. Colonel Anthony Hastings leads a small group of settlers from the Carolinas to Natchez. Then the scene shifts to England where Hastings rescues his son from a cruel mother.

Historical Accuracy: The novel's central character is based on an actual figure, Anthony Hutchins, who experienced all the things described in the story.

GERTRUDE E. FINNEY (1892-)

Born in Morocco, Indiana, Finney attended the State College of Washington. Her books include *Yes, a Homestead*, *One Woman's Land*, and *To Survive We Must Be Clever*.

2091 *The Plums Hang High*

Date of Publication: 1955
Subject(s): Farming; Immigrants
Fictional character(s): Hannah Maria Howard, Immigrant, Spouse; Jethro Howard, Farmer, Immigrant
Time Period(s): 19th century (1868-1890)
Locale(s): Midwest

Summary: The novel describes the experiences of a family of English immigrants who journey to the Midwest during the

19th century. Hannah Maria and Jethro Howard struggle as farmers.

Historical Accuracy: This is a believable description of period life.

JACK FINNEY
(PSEUD. OF WALTER BRADEN FINNEY, 1921-1996)

American writer Finney was born in Milwaukee, Wisconsin, and attended Knox College. He achieved distinction as a writer of science fiction and thrillers. His *The Body Snatchers* inspired the classic science fiction film *Invasion of the Body Snatchers*. His time travel novel *Time and Again* has reached cult status in popularity. His other books include *The Night People*, *The Woodrow Wilson Dime*, and *Good Neighbor Sam*.

2092 *From Time to Time*

Date of Publication: 1995
Subject(s): Time Travel; Shipwrecks
Fictional character(s): Simon Morley, Time Traveller; Major Ruben Prien, Military Personnel, Historian; Helen Metzner, Time Traveller
Historical character(s): Theodore Roosevelt, Political Figure; Al Jolson, Entertainer
Time Period(s): 1880s (1886-1887); 1910s (1911-1912)
Locale(s): New York, New York; Belfast, Ireland; *Titanic*, At Sea

Summary: Simon Morley, the hero of *Time and Again*, is now happily married and living in the New York of the 1880s. He ventures back into the 20th century, first to reluctantly rejoin the U.S. government's time travel project, and then to try to prevent the sinking of the *Titanic*. The architects of the project hope that the successful voyage of the ship will secure the life of a diplomat who could be instrumental in preventing World War I.

Historical Accuracy: Life in the 1880s and early 1900s is carefully detailed, as are the events relating to the sinking of the *Titanic*.

2093 *Time and Again*

Date of Publication: 1970
Subject(s): Time Travel; Gilded Age
Fictional character(s): Simon Morley, Artist (illustrator), Time Traveller; Julia Charbonneau, Young Woman; Major Ruben Prien, Military Personnel (army officer); Thomas Byrnes, Detective—Police
Time Period(s): 1880s (1882)
Locale(s): New York, New York

Summary: Simon Morley joins a U.S. government-sponsored time-travel project and travels back to the New York of 1882. There he uncovers a blackmail plot that leads to danger for him and the woman with whom he has fallen in love. When Morley ultimately learns that the project wants him to manipulate the course of history, by preventing the blackmailer from becoming a trusted foreign affairs adviser to President Grover Cleveland, he is faced with an ethical dilemma.

Historical Accuracy: Except for a few deliberate inaccuracies for the sake of story telling, the author's depiction of 19th-century New York is factually correct.

PATRICIA FINNEY (1958-)

An Englishwoman born in London, Finney graduated from Waldham College, Oxford. She was only seventeen when she completed her first novel, *A Shadow of Gulls*.

2094 *The Crow Goddess*

Date of Publication: 1978
Subject(s): Dark Ages; Roman Empire
Fictional character(s): Lugh MacRomain, Bastard Son, Warrior; Cuchulain MacSualtim, Warrior; Julius Karus, Military Personnel (cavalry officer)
Historical character(s): Hadrian, Ruler (Roman emperor)
Time Period(s): 2nd century (117-121)
Locale(s): England; Ireland

Summary: In the sequel to the author's *A Shadow of Gulls*, Lugh MacRomain has settled in Britain, but the Emperor Hadrian is determined that he go back to Ireland. There Lugh has both a powerful enemy and a loyal friend, Cuchulain. He is swept up in a cycle of battle and betrayal.

Historical Accuracy: The author has blended the legendary, the historical, and the imagined into a convincing version of the second century.

2095 *The Firedrake's Eye*

Date of Publication: 1992
Subject(s): Elizabethan Period; Espionage
Fictional character(s): Tom O'Bedlam, Mentally Ill Person; David Becket, Military Personnel
Historical character(s): Elizabeth I, Ruler (Queen of England); Sir Walter Raleigh, Courtier; Sir Philip Sidney, Courtier, Writer; Sir Francis Walsingham, Government Official
Time Period(s): 16th century (1583)
Locale(s): London, England

Summary: In Elizabethan London, Tom O'Bedlam, the mad son of a prominent Catholic family, discovers evidence of a conspiracy to assassinate Queen Elizabeth during festivities to commemorate her ascension to the throne. The conspiracy reaches to the highest levels of Elizabeth's court.

Historical Accuracy: The novel is a remarkable evocation of Elizabethan politics and the look and smell of Elizabethan London. The fruits of the author's considerable research are well displayed.

2096 *A Shadow of Gulls*

Date of Publication: 1977
Subject(s): Dark Ages; Myths and Legends
Fictional character(s): Lugh MacRomain, Bastard Son, Warrior; Otter, Young Woman; Cuchulain MacSualtim, Warrior
Historical character(s): Conchubar, Ruler (King of Ulster)
Time Period(s): 2nd century (113)
Locale(s): Ireland

Summary: This is a rich and evocative adventure set in Celtic Ireland during the 2nd century. Lugh MacRomain is the bastard son of a Roman centurion and an Irish princess. He accidentally kills the king of Ulster and flees, involving himself in the famous Cattle Raid of Cooley and the clash between Ulster and the south.

Historical Accuracy: The events are based on the Ulster cycle of hero-tales and the story stays close to the original.

RACHEL ANN FISH

`2097` *The Running Iron*
Date of Publication: 1957
Subject(s): American West; Settlement of the American Frontier; Ranching
Fictional character(s): Robert Forge, Veteran (Confederate colonel); Fonella Forge, Spouse
Time Period(s): 19th century; 20th century (1860s-1910s)
Locale(s): Wyoming; Alabama; Texas

Summary: Western American history from the 1860s to World War I is reflected in the experiences of former Confederate Colonel Robert Forge, who leaves his Alabama plantation for life in Wyoming as a rancher. This family chronicle shows the Forges adjusting to pioneer life, Indian fighting, and cattle ranching.

Historical Accuracy: The novel's history is strongest in the cattle war scenes.

ROBERT L. FISH (1912-1981)

American engineer and author Fish worked in the plastics industry as a consulting engineer. He wrote his first novel, *The Fugitive*, at the age of 48, and won three Edgar Awards for his mysteries. Titles include *The Diamond Bubble*, *Whirligig*, and *The Wager*. The movie *Bullitt* was based on Fish's *Mute Witness*. He also collaborated with the soccer star Pele on his autobiography.

`2098` *Rough Diamond*
Date of Publication: 1981
Subject(s): Frontier—Africa
Fictional character(s): Barney Barnet, Adventurer
Historical character(s): Cecil John Rhodes, Political Figure
Time Period(s): 1870s; 1880s
Locale(s): South Africa

Summary: In 1872 Barney Barnet leaves London's East End to seek his fortune in South Africa's diamond field. In his adventures, an encounter with Cecil Rhodes, the discovery of gold in the Transvaal, and a vivid re-creation of colonial Africa are featured.

Historical Accuracy: The region and its history are well-drawn and convincing.

ANNE FISHER (1898-1967)

Born in Denver, Colorado, Fisher was educated at the University of Denver and the Colorado Medical School. She travelled extensively and published several works of nonfiction and fiction, including *The Salinas* (Rivers of America Series), *Stories California Indians Told*, and an historical novel, *Oh Glittery Promise*.

`2099` *Oh Glittering Promise*
Date of Publication: 1949
Subject(s): American West; Gold Rush—California
Fictional character(s): Charles Morgan, Prospector
Time Period(s): 19th century (1849-1869)
Locale(s): California

Summary: This tale of the California Gold Rush describes the adventures of a young Welsh miner, Charles Morgan, who, compelled by his wife's greed, leaves his job and family to search for gold.

Historical Accuracy: The background details give evidence of careful research, but the story rarely reaches beyond the level of the melodramatic.

EDWARD FISHER (1902-)

An American scientist and writer, Fisher was educated at Harvard, the University of Paris, and the Corcoran School of Art. He has worked as an instructor of English and as an administrative officer and speech writer for various federal agencies.

`2100` *The Best House in Stratford*
Date of Publication: 1965
Subject(s): Elizabethan Period; Biography, Fictionalized; Literary Life
Historical character(s): William Shakespeare, Writer; Ben Jonson, Writer; Anne Hathaway, Spouse; Richard Burbage, Actor
Time Period(s): 16th century (1590s-1600s)
Locale(s): London, England; Stratford-on-Avon, England

Summary: In the concluding volume of the author's trilogy on the life of William Shakespeare, his life as a playwright and actor in London is depicted. The novel dramatizes his rivalry and friendship with Ben Jonson, his feelings of inadequacy as a husband and father, and his return to Stratford to purchase the town's greatest house.

Historical Accuracy: Like its predecessors, this novel, though based on factual details, is largely speculative. It is convincing nonetheless in its atmosphere and in the credibility of the personalities depicted.

`2101` *Love's Labour's Won*
Date of Publication: 1963
Subject(s): Biography, Fictionalized; Elizabethan Period; Literary Life
Historical character(s): William Shakespeare, Writer
Time Period(s): 16th century (1580s)
Locale(s): England

Summary: The second volume of a trilogy on the life of Shakespeare covers his lost years from his departure from

Stratford to his emergence in London as an actor/playwright. The novel attempts to answer the vexing question of how a boy from a small town with no university education and no prospects could have emerged in less than ten years as the greatest writer of his age.

Historical Accuracy: Since nothing is known for sure of Shakespeare's life during this period, the novel must be regarded as speculative. The evident research into the period, however, at least lends a weight of plausibility to Fisher's interpretation.

2102 *Shakespeare & Son*

Date of Publication: 1962
Subject(s): Biography, Fictionalized; Elizabethan Period; Literary Life
Historical character(s): William Shakespeare, Writer; Anne Hathaway, Spouse
Time Period(s): 16th century (1579-1582)
Locale(s): Stratford-on-Avon, England

Summary: The novel offers an intriguing speculation about William Shakespeare's youth. The story covers the years in Stratford between Shakespeare's fifteenth and eighteenth birthdays and shows young William's conflict with his father and his courtship of and marriage to Anne Hathaway.

Historical Accuracy: The author warns that this is a novel and that the reader interested in fact should consult scholarly sources. His account of Shakespeare's life is an invention.

FRANCES HOPE FISHER

2103 *Written in the Stars: A Novel about Albrecht Durer*

Date of Publication: 1951
Subject(s): Artistic Life; Renaissance
Historical character(s): Albrecht Durer, Artist; Agnes Durer, Spouse; Giovanni Bellini, Artist (sculptor)
Time Period(s): 15th century; 16th century
Locale(s): Nuremberg, Germany; Venice, Italy

Summary: The novel portrays the great artist Albrecht Durer and his marriage. Characterized by history as a shrew and a tyrant, Agnes Durer is shown here from a more balanced and sympathetic perspective. In the process of dramatizing Durer's married life, the novel offers a fully realized depiction of medieval Nuremberg, a city haunted by secret tribunals and plagues, and of Venice in the earliest days of the Renaissance.

Historical Accuracy: The novel is accomplished in its attention to detail and evokes a realistic portrait of the artist and his era.

GRAHAM FISHER (1920-)

Born in King's Lynn, England, Fisher also writes as George Heather. An Historian and biographer, he is the author of *The Crown and the Ring: The Story of the Queen's Years of Marriage and Monarchy, Monarch: A Biography of Elizabeth II*, and *The Plot to Kill Wallis Simpson*.

2104 *The Plot to Kill Wallis Simpson: A Work of Faction*

Date of Publication: 1989
Subject(s): Royalty—England; Assassination
Historical character(s): Edward VIII, Ruler (King of England); Wallis Warfield Simpson, Noblewoman (Duchess of Windsor); Winston Churchill, Political Figure
Time Period(s): 1930s (1936)
Locale(s): England; France

Summary: A discovered manuscript reveals why Wallis Simpson fled England shortly before the abdication of Edward VIII in 1936. The manuscript's author, an English aristocrat determined to prevent their marriage, describes an assassination attempt that is prevented by the efforts of the king, Winston Churchill, and others.

Historical Accuracy: This work of "faction" is more ingenious than believable. The historical figures employed remain shadowy and sketchy.

RICHARD FISHER (1936-)

An American writer born in New York City, Richard Fisher has worked in public relations, journalism, television, and as a writer of documentaries for the U.S. Information Agency. He is the author of *The Very First Time*.

2105 *Judgment in July*

Date of Publication: 1962
Subject(s): American West; Mining; Indians
Fictional character(s): Jason Kyle, Prospector
Time Period(s): 1870s
Locale(s): Deadwood, South Dakota

Summary: Set in the Dakotas in the period following Custer's defeat at the Little Bighorn, the novel describes the conflict between the gold miners and the Indians, as well as life in the frontier boom town of Deadwood, as the settlers await an attack by the Sioux.

Historical Accuracy: This is an authentic description of western life during the period.

VARDIS FISHER (1895-1968)

Vardis Fisher was born in Idaho and taught as a college professor in Utah and New York. His novels are generally set either in the American West or in ancient times concerned with Old and New Testament themes.

2106 *Children of God*

Date of Publication: 1939
Subject(s): Settlement of the American Frontier; Religious Conflict; Mormons
Historical character(s): Joseph Smith, Religious (founder of Mormonism); Brigham Young, Religious, Political Figure; John Taylor, Religious
Time Period(s): 19th century (1820-1890)
Locale(s): Palmyra, New York; Midwest (Ohio, Illinois, Missouri); Utah

Summary: Called by its author an American epic, the novel describes the founding of the Mormon Church and its turbulent early history. Beginning with John Smith's vision, the novel details the early church's persecution in the Midwest and the epic trek west led by Brigham Young to the settlement of Utah and continued conflict with the federal government.

Historical Accuracy: Based on fact, Fisher rounds out the personalities and events so that they take on a compelling and believable life.

2107　*City of Illusion*

Date of Publication: 1941
Subject(s): American West; Mining
Fictional character(s): Eilley Bowers, Young Woman; Luff McCoy, Prospector
Time Period(s): 1850s (1850)
Locale(s): Virginia City, Nevada

Summary: The novel describes the events surrounding the discovery of the Comstock Lode and the sudden development of the boom town of Virginia City, Nevada. The novel follows the effect of the immense silver strike on a number of characters whose fortunes rise and fall with that of the mine.

Historical Accuracy: This is an authentic depiction of life during the period, though many of the events and characters are more the stuff of legend than verifiable fact.

2108　*The Island of the Innocent: A Novel of Greek and Jew in the Time of the Maccabees*

Date of Publication: 1952
Subject(s): Ancient Israel; Jews
Fictional character(s): Philemon, Wanderer; Judith, Dancer
Time Period(s): 2nd century B.C.
Locale(s): Jerusalem, Israel

Summary: Set in Jerusalem during the 2nd century B.C., the novel describes the conflict between various factions within the Jewish community. Philemon, a Greek, is drawn to Judith, a beautiful ceremonial dancing girl. The novel pits the Hellenist Jews against the Jews who strictly obey the laws of the Torah.

Historical Accuracy: The novel is filled with authentic period elements creating a believable portrait of the age and its beliefs.

2109　*The Mothers*

Date of Publication: 1943
Subject(s): American West; Donner Party; Wagon Trains
Historical character(s): George Donner, Settler; Tamsen Donner, Settler; James Frazier Reed, Settler; Margaret Reed, Settler
Time Period(s): 1840s (1846)
Locale(s): Sierra Nevada Mountains, California

Summary: In the High Sierras in 1846, the Donner Party is trapped by winter and finally destroyed by hunger and cold. The novel details their tragic story of heart-breaking suffering

and determination to survive despite mounting challenges as conditions lead to madness and cannibalism.

Historical Accuracy: The novel blends the facts of the written accounts and the survivor's stories with a fictional interpretation of motives and behavior.

2110　*Mountain Man*

Date of Publication: 1965
Subject(s): American West; Indians
Fictional character(s): Sam Minard, Mountain Man; Lotus, Indian; Kate Bowden, Widow(er)
Time Period(s): 1850s
Locale(s): Rocky Mountains

Summary: The novel details the life of mountain man Sam Minard in the Rockies of the the 1850s. Minard struggles to survive in the wilderness with Lotus, an Indian girl, battling the ferocious Crow Indians. A parallel story follows the experiences of Kate Burden whose entire family is massacred by the Indians.

Historical Accuracy: Sam and Kate are based on John Johnson and Jane Morgan, actual figures who today are almost completely lost in legends.

2111　*Pemmican*

Date of Publication: 1956
Subject(s): Frontier—Canada; Indians; Pemmican War
Fictional character(s): David MacDonald, Frontiersman; Sunday, Indian (Blackfoot)
Time Period(s): 1810s
Locale(s): Rocky Mountains, Canada

Summary: The background of the novel is the early 19th century conflict between the Hudson's Bay Company and the North Westers called the Pemmican War. David MacDonald is a frontiersman with the Hudson's Bay Company who discovers a white woman captive among the Blackfoot Indians. With her he endures life in the wilderness that includes Indian attack, starvation, and a buffalo stampede.

Historical Accuracy: The events and characters are fictional but they do capture the atmosphere of the period.

2112　*Tale of Valor*

Date of Publication: 1958
Subject(s): American West; Lewis & Clark Expedition; Exploration
Historical character(s): Meriwether Lewis, Explorer; William Clark, Explorer; Sacajawea, Indian, Guide
Time Period(s): 1800s (1804-1806)
Locale(s): West

Summary: Lewis and Clark's epic trek across half a continent, the fruits of Jefferson's Louisiana Purchase, is dramatized. The novel offers a convincing day-to-day account and details the enormous challenges of the trip.

Historical Accuracy: Although the trip is shrouded in controversy and conflicting testimony, this version seems both plausible and reliable.

2113 *The Valley of Vision: A Novel of King Solomon and His Time*

Date of Publication: 1951
Subject(s): Biblical Story
Historical character(s): Solomon, Biblical Figure, Ruler (King of Israel); David, Biblical Figure, Ruler (King of Israel); Bathsheba, Biblical Figure
Time Period(s): 10th century B.C.
Locale(s): Israel

Summary: The novel dramatizes the reign of King Solomon beginning with the death of David. In the early years of Solomon's reign, conflict develops between the cosmopolitan Solomon and his provincial subjects.

Historical Accuracy: The author offers an impressive list of sources as background for his interpretation of Solomon and his reign.

NANCY FITZGERALD (1951-)

Born in California and a graduate of the University of California, Santa Barbara, Fitzgerald worked for a time as a high school English teacher and as a member of the creative writing faculty at UCLA, as well as a teacher of pre- and post-natal care.

2114 *Chelsea*

Date of Publication: 1979
Subject(s): Victorian Period; Artistic Life
Fictional character(s): Cecily Hawthorne, Orphan, Servant; Devin Sheridan, Artist
Historical character(s): Oscar Wilde, Writer; James Abbott McNeill Whistler, Artist
Time Period(s): 19th century (Victorian period)
Locale(s): London, England

Summary: Cecily Hawthorne is rescued from a life of drudgery as a servant by artist Devin Sheridan. When she models for his paintings, they create a sensation in Victorian London. Suddenly, Cecily is the talk of the town, but what will the effect of all the notoriety be on the artist who made her famous?.

Historical Accuracy: The novel's depiction of the Victorian art world is authentic and believable.

2115 *Mayfair*

Date of Publication: 1978
Subject(s): Romance; Victorian Period
Fictional character(s): Sibilla Corrough, Gentlewoman; Sophia Corrough, Gentlewoman
Time Period(s): 1850s
Locale(s): London, England

Summary: The travails of the London social season during the Great Exhibition of 1850 are depicted in the experiences of Sibilla and Sophia, the last of the daughters of the Earl and Countess of Corrough. Their older sisters have achieved mixed successes in their marriages so the stakes and challenges are high as the two negotiate the perilous marriage market.

Historical Accuracy: The period is convincingly reflected in this witty romance.

2116 *St. John's Wood*

Date of Publication: 1977
Subject(s): Victorian Period; Prostitution
Fictional character(s): Thalia Hurrocks, Writer; Guenvere Shallot, Prostitute; Stacey Parrington, Nobleman (marquis)
Time Period(s): 19th century (Victorian period)
Locale(s): London, England

Summary: Thalia Horrock rebels against the stifling gentility of her conventional Victorian parents and dreams of adventure and independence. She sets out to write a novel on the "pretty horsebreakers," London's fashionable prostitutes. While researching her book, she creates.a scandal that may jeopardize any chance she will have to make a fashionable match.

Historical Accuracy: The premise is far-fetched with overly modern attitudes displayed.

VALERIE FITZGERALD (1927-)

Canadian novelist Fitzgerald was born in India. She left India in 1947 and has lived in England, Switzerland, Ireland, Kenya, and Italy. Her novel *Zemindar* won the Georgette Heyer Award, the Romantic Association Major Award, and the Elizabeth Godge Historical Trophy.

2117 *Zemindar*

Date of Publication: 1981
Subject(s): Indian Mutiny; British Raj; Victorian Period
Fictional character(s): Oliver Erskine, Gentleman; Laura Hewitt, Gentlewoman
Time Period(s): 1850s (1857)
Locale(s): Oudh, India; Lucknow, India

Summary: Laura Hewitt is a young Englishwoman who journeys in the 1850s to northern India, where she meets Oliver Erskine, the zemindar of a fiefdom. Laura is both attracted and repelled by Oliver's world, his private kingdom that is suddenly engulfed by the rebellion of the Indian Mutiny.

Historical Accuracy: The author lists the few deviations taken from the historical facts. In the main, the historical record is observed.

CONSTANTINE FITZGIBBON (1919-)

Born in Lenox, Massachusetts, to British parents, FitzGibbon attended Wellington College, the University of Munich, the Sorbonne, and Exeter College, Oxford. He worked as a schoolmaster in Bermuda from 1946-1947 and thereafter was a professional writer. His novels include *The Arabian Bird*, *The Fair Game*, and *Going to the River*.

2118 *High Heroic*

Date of Publication: 1969
Subject(s): Independence—Ireland; Biography, Fictionalized; Civil War—Ireland

Historical character(s): Michael Collins, Political Figure, Revolutionary; Patrick Henry Pearse, Revolutionary, Patriot; Arthur Griffith, Revolutionary, Patriot; William Butler Yeats, Writer; David Lloyd George, Political Figure; Winston Churchill, Political Figure; Frederick Edwin Smith, Political Figure, Nobleman (Earl of Birkenhead)
Time Period(s): 19th century; 20th century (1890-1922)
Locale(s): Ireland; England

Summary: The novel presents the story of Ireland's struggle for independence based on the experiences of Sinn Fein leader Michael Collins. He is one of the central figures in Ireland's battle with Britain for self-government, and the novel examines Collins' contribution and philosophy. Many historical figures are on hand to act out their parts in the drama.

Historical Accuracy: The novel is effective in capturing the spirit of the times, and the main events of the narrative are faithful to the facts.

THOMAS FLANAGAN (1923-)

American novelist and academic Thomas Flanagan returned to fiction writing after a 30 year hiatus to produce *The Year of the French,* which is thought by many to be one of the finest historical novels written by an American in more than a decade. He followed this success with two more novels. Collectively the three re-create over 100 years of turbulent Irish history.

2119 *The End of the Hunt*

Date of Publication: 1994
Subject(s): Independence—Ireland; Civil War—Ireland; Politics
Fictional character(s): Patrick Prentiss, Lawyer; Christopher Black, Political Figure, Revolutionary; Frank Lacy, Revolutionary; Janice Nugent, Gentlewoman
Historical character(s): Michael Collins, Political Figure, Revolutionary; Eamon De Valera, Political Figure; Winston Churchill, Political Figure; David Lloyd George, Political Figure
Time Period(s): 1910s; 1920s (1919-1924)
Locale(s): Ireland; London, England

Summary: This third novel of Flanagan's Irish trilogy covers the period of the Irish Uprising, the Black and Tan War, and the Irish Civil War. Flanagan tells this tragic and heroic story from the perspective of several participants: an Irish barrister, a Republican gunman, and an important rebel leader and his mistress. At the center of the drama is the enigmatic and powerful figure of Michael Collins.

Historical Accuracy: Flanagan is convincing and masterful in the historical details and the human stories behind the headlines. His theme is the dream of an independent republic under assault by history and reality.

2120 *The Tenants of Time*

Date of Publication: 1988
Subject(s): Independence—Ireland; Politics; Fenians

Fictional character(s): Patrick Prentiss, Historian, Writer; Ned Nolan, Revolutionary (Fenian); Robert Delaney, Revolutionary, Political Figure; Hugh MacMahon, Teacher, Revolutionary
Historical character(s): Joseph Chamberlain, Political Figure; Charles Stewart Parnell, Political Figure; Michael Davitt, Revolutionary; James Abbott McNeill Whistler, Artist
Time Period(s): 19th century; 20th century (1867-1908)
Locale(s): Kilpeder, Ireland; Dublin, Ireland; London, England

Summary: A Fenian leader heads a failed uprising in the small town of Kilpeder in 1867. Patrick Prentiss is writing a history of the rebellion and uncovers patterns and connections that reveal the human drama of the Irish struggle for independence.

Historical Accuracy: Flanagan expertly weaves fiction and history, reaching a new level of achievement for the historical novel.

2121 *The Year of the French*

Date of Publication: 1979
Subject(s): Independence—Ireland; Politics; Georgian Period
Fictional character(s): Owen McCarthy, Writer, Teacher; Arthur Broome, Religious (Protestant minister); George Moore, Historian, Writer
Historical character(s): Charles Cornwallis, Military Personnel (general), Nobleman; Maria Edgeworth, Writer; Theobald Wolfe Tone, Revolutionary; Jean-Joseph Humbert, Military Personnel
Time Period(s): 1780s (1789)
Locale(s): Mayo, Ireland; Dublin, Ireland; Paris, France

Summary: The French attempt an invasion of Ireland and fail. They are assisted in their efforts by an insurrection of the United Irishmen, who proclaim an Irish Republic. The troops land on the primitive western coast of Mayo, and the tragic and bloody events are then described by a number of participants: a schoolmaster, a clergyman, a United Irishman, and a British soldier.

Historical Accuracy: Flanagan accurately captures Irish life at a pivotal moment in history. The events he describes cause the abolition of the Irish Parliament and spark the next 100 years of struggle for home rule and independence.

ROY CATESBY FLANNAGAN
(1897-1952)

Flannagan's books include *The Story of Lucky Strike*, a book on the U.S. cigarette industry.

2122 *Forest Cavalier: A Romance of America's First Frontier and of Bacon's Rebellion*

Date of Publication: 1952
Subject(s): American Colonies; Bacon's Rebellion
Fictional character(s): Lance Clayborn, Settler, Hunter
Historical character(s): Nathaniel Bacon, Leader (Bacon's Rebellion)

Time Period(s): 17th century (1670s)
Locale(s): Jamestown, Virginia, American Colonies

Summary: The adventure tale of young Lance Clayborn, who comes to the Virginia colony to avenge his uncle's death, is told against the background of Bacon's Rebellion. Lance learns the ways of the wilderness and becomes a hunter and participant in Bacon's uprising against the colonial government of Sir William Berkeley. In the end Lance avenges his uncle, finds love, and clears his own honor.

Historical Accuracy: For the most part the novel's history is authentic, vividly capturing Bacon's Rebellion.

GUSTAVE FLAUBERT (1821-1880)

Flaubert was a French novelist whose *Madame Bovary* is considered one of the greatest 19th-century French novels, a landmark in realistic depiction of provincial life. His work set a high standard for objectivity and scrupulously realistic documentation.

2123 *Salammbo*

Date of Publication: 1862
Subject(s): Roman Empire; Punic Wars
Fictional character(s): Salammbo, Noblewoman, Religious (priestess); Matho, Chieftain (Libyan)
Historical character(s): Hamilcar Barca, Military Personnel
Time Period(s): 3rd century B.C.
Locale(s): Carthage, Ancient Civilization

Summary: The novel tells a tragic story about the defense of Carthage before a vast army of mercenaries. One, a Libyan chief, falls in love with Salammbo, priestess of the moon goddess and daughter of the Carthaginian leader. Salammbo risks all to recover a stolen sacred veil.

Historical Accuracy: Flaubert put five years of research into every detail about Carthage during the Punic Wars. The result is a vast reconstruction of the past.

FRANCES FLEETWOOD (1902-)

Born in London and educated at the Sorbonne, Fleetwood has worked as a political journalist's secretary and participated in Carol of Romania's abortive attempt to return to his throne in 1928. Her books include *Conquest* and a book of verse, *The Threshold*.

2124 *Concordia*

Date of Publication: 1972
Subject(s): Middle Ages
Fictional character(s): Concordia Malatesta, Young Woman
Historical character(s): Francesca da Rimini, Noblewoman; Paolo Malatesta, Nobleman (Francesca's brother-in-law); Giovanni Malatesta, Nobleman (Francesca's husband)
Time Period(s): 13th century
Locale(s): Rimini, Italy

Summary: Celebrated by Dante, the tragic love affair between Francesca da Rimini and her brother-in-law, Paolo Malatesta, is recounted in the journal of Francesca's daughter, Con-

cordia. Concordia is torn by the love she still feels for her father, even after he kills her mother and his brother.

Historical Accuracy: The novel excels at capturing the atmosphere of 13th-century Italian life and customs.

GLEN H. FLEISCHMANN (1909-)

Born in Nebraska, Fleischmann attended Vogue School of Art in Chicago and became an illustrator. His work appeared in *The Saturday Evening Post*, *Good Housekeeping*, and *Collier's* and in ads for General Foods, General Mills, and the Ford Motor Co. He is the author of the nonfictional *The Cherokee Removal*, the research for which began when he examined the archives at Fort Belvoir, where he was stationed during World War II. Some of Fleischmann's relatives were among the evictors and the evicted under the Indian removal policy.

2125 *While Rivers Flow*

Date of Publication: 1963
Subject(s): Indians
Fictional character(s): James Burke, Military Personnel (army officer); Otis Whitaker, Political Figure (Georgia senator); Rene Jo Whitaker, Spouse (of Burke)
Time Period(s): 1830s
Locale(s): Georgia; Tennessee; Washington, District of Columbia

Summary: The Cherokee Indians were forced to move from their ancestral lands in Georgia and Tennessee during the 1830s. This historical event is seen through the experience of army officer James Burke, who is given the unpleasant task of carrying out the government's repressive policy. He marries the daughter of a Georgia senator who is a leader in the movement to evict the Indians and faces a severe test of his loyalty and duty.

Historical Accuracy: The details of the period and the facts of the Indian removal policies are accurately presented.

GEORGINA FLEMING

2126 *Beyond the Shadowlands*

Date of Publication: 1993
Subject(s): Gypsies; Victorian Period
Fictional character(s): Alice Brennan, Captive; Milly Toole, Servant (nursemaid); Luke Durant, Outlaw
Time Period(s): 1860s (1867)
Locale(s): England

Summary: In this Victorian suspense story, Alice Brennan is consigned to a lunatic asylum by her scheming husband. She escapes and joins a gypsy troupe of performers under the protection of the dashing Luke Durant. Eventually, Alice begins to unravel the mysteries of her past.

Historical Accuracy: The Victorian atmosphere is authentically drawn as is the Romany community.

H.K. FLEMING (1901-)

English author Fleming was an editorial assistant on various English newspapers before coming to the U.S. He worked for the *Baltimore Sun* and in Washington for various government agencies.

`2127` *The Day They Kidnapped Queen Victoria*

Date of Publication: 1978
Subject(s): Victorian Period; Crime and Criminals
Historical character(s): Victoria, Ruler (Queen of England); Benjamin Disraeli, Political Figure; Alfred, Lord Tennyson, Writer (poet)
Time Period(s): 1860s
Locale(s): England

Summary: On its way from Balmoral, Queen Victoria's train is highjacked, and she is kidnapped. To rescue her, a daring plan is launched by Prime Minister Benjamin Disraeli, who recruits the help of Alfred, Lord Tennyson. A highly amusing historical thriller results.

Historical Accuracy: The story is, of course, fanciful, but it does show an authentic sense of the period and its figures.

JOAN FLEMING (1908-1980)

An English author born in Lancashire, Fleming attended the University of Lausanne. Though she wrote some historical novels, she preferred mysteries because they did not require time-consuming historical research. She authored numerous witty crime and gothic novels as well as the travel guide *Shakespeare's Country in Colour.*

`2128` *Too Late! Too Late! The Maiden Cried*

Date of Publication: 1975
Subject(s): Picaresque Adventure; Victorian Period
Fictional character(s): Thomas Nateby-Dyce, Gentleman; Nokomis Pennyform, Young Woman, Indian (half)
Time Period(s): 1840s
Locale(s): London, England

Summary: When Thomas Nateby-Dyce's mother dies, he discovers that he has inherited a valuable moonstone. He also takes responsibility for Nokomis Pennyform, the half-American Indian daughter of his mother's lover. She arrives to claim the moonstone and thoroughly disrupts the conventional Victorian family.

Historical Accuracy: This is an amusing story of Victorian society disrupted by an American outsider. The period details are authentic.

THOMAS FLEMING (1927-)

A biographer, historian, and novelist, Fleming is a Jersey City, New Jersey native who received his B.A. degree from Fordham University. He has written biographies of Thomas Jefferson (American Book Award winner), George

Washington, and Benjamin Franklin as well as respected historical works on the colonial and revolutionary periods.

`2129` *Liberty Tavern*

Date of Publication: 1976
Subject(s): American Revolution; American Colonies
Fictional character(s): Jonathan Gifford, Saloon Keeper/Owner; Sarah Gifford, Spouse; Caroline Skinner, Gentlewoman
Time Period(s): 1770s
Locale(s): New Jersey, American Colonies

Summary: The American Revolution is seen from the perspective of New Jersey tavern keeper Jonathan Gifford. A former British soldier, Gifford must decide between his loyalty to England and his family's growing support for the Revolution. The focus of the novel's action is the tavern, a crossroads in the events of the times.

Historical Accuracy: Detailed and convincing, the novel offers a picture of the issues and conflicts among ordinary people of the time that is authentic.

`2130` *Over There*

Date of Publication: 1992
Subject(s): World War I
Fictional character(s): Polly Warden, Nurse; Paul Lebrun, Doctor (surgeon); Malvern Hill Bliss, Military Personnel (general)
Historical character(s): John J. Pershing, Military Personnel (general); Georges Clemenceau, Political Figure; Douglas Haig, Military Personnel (general)
Time Period(s): 1910s (1915-1918)
Locale(s): United States; France

Summary: The American experience in World War I is the novel's subject, which blends fictional and historical characters. Polly Warden is a young woman determined to make a contribution to the war effort, while General Pershing struggles to maintain the independence of the American army in the face of Allied manipulation.

Historical Accuracy: The novel's events and interpretations are supported by solid research. The novel is filled with period details.

`2131` *The Spoils of War*

Date of Publication: 1985
Subject(s): Reconstruction Period; Family Saga; Spanish-American War
Fictional character(s): Jonathan Stapleton, Veteran (general), Businessman; Cynthia Legrand Stapleton, Spouse; Rawdon Stapleton, Businessman, Military Personnel
Historical character(s): Ulysses S. Grant, Political Figure; Rutherford B. Hayes, Political Figure; James A. Garfield, Political Figure; Jay Gould, Financier; William Randolph Hearst, Financier
Time Period(s): 19th century (1866-1900)
Locale(s): New York, New York; Washington, District of Columbia

Summary: The events in the lives of the Stapleton family form a complex social history of the period from 1866 to 1900. Jonathan Stapleton is a former Union general who marries his brother's southern-born widow. Through them and their son Rawdon, the post-war world is detailed.

Historical Accuracy: The author, an historian, is careful and accurate in his documentation.

INGLIS FLETCHER (1888-1969)

American novelist Inglis Fletcher produced an impressive chronicle of her native North Carolina in a series of historical novels. Her novels depict the earliest settlement of the American wilderness and the following turbulent years of the development and creation of the American nation.

2132 *Bennett's Welcome*

Date of Publication: 1950
Subject(s): American Colonies; Civil War—England; Royalty—England
Fictional character(s): Richard Monington, Nobleman; Kathryn Audley, Gentlewoman; Nicholas Holder, Gentleman
Historical character(s): Charles II, Ruler (later King of England); Oliver Cromwell, Political Figure
Time Period(s): 17th century (1651)
Locale(s): Worcester, England; James River, Virginia, American Colonies; Albemarle County, North Carolina, American Colonies

Summary: Fletcher depicts the Cromwellian period in America and dramatizes the adventures of Richard Monington, a Cavalier whose side is defeated by Cromwell. He escapes to Virginia as an indentured servant. There the effects of the Civil War are played out among the planters as a new national identity is being formed.

Historical Accuracy: The novel is well-researched and documented. Although Fletcher claims that the story is not history, historical details of this neglected period in American history are presented.

2133 *Cormorant's Brood*

Date of Publication: 1959
Subject(s): American Colonies; Espionage; Identity—Concealed
Fictional character(s): Dick Chapman, Settler; Anthony Dawson, Settler, Spy; Deirdra Treffrey, Governess
Time Period(s): 1720s (1725)
Locale(s): Edenton, North Carolina, American Colonies

Summary: In the Albemarle settlement of Edenton, the wilderness is giving way to a prosperous community. Resentment of the "cormorant brood" of greedy and irresponsible colonial governors is growing. A young settler is recognized as one of the proprietors of the colony investigating dissent. Political turmoil breaks out as control of the colony hangs in the balance.

Historical Accuracy: Fletcher gives a vivid portrait of the period and the personalities who made up the Edenton community.

2134 *Lusty Wind for Carolina*

Date of Publication: 1944
Subject(s): American Colonies; Settlement of the American Frontier; Pirates
Fictional character(s): Robert Fountaine, Landowner (planter)
Historical character(s): Anne Bonny, Pirate; Woodes Rogers, Sea Captain, Political Figure (governor of the Bahamas); Charles Vane, Pirate; Edward Teach, Pirate
Time Period(s): 1710s; 1720s (1718-1725)
Locale(s): Cape Fear, North Carolina, American Colonies; Nassau, Bahamas

Summary: Pirate adventures dominate this installment of Fletcher's Carolina chronicle. It is the 1710s, and a settlement has been created on the Cape Fear River. If the settlement is to survive, the pirates who haunt the area ·must be controlled. Woodes Rogers leads a convoy to destroy their power. The struggle of the fledgling Carolina colony and a stormy love story are interwoven with the nautical action.

Historical Accuracy: Fletcher is convincing with her accurate research, and her romantic and fast-moving story ignites the period details.

2135 *Men of Albemarle*

Date of Publication: 1942
Subject(s): American Colonies; Settlement of the American Frontier
Fictional character(s): Roger Mainwairing, Landowner (planter); Mary Tower, Gentlewoman
Time Period(s): 1710s (1710-1712)
Locale(s): Queen Anne's Town, North Carolina, American Colonies

Summary: The settlement of Carolina from 1710 to 1712 is the setting for Fletcher's chronicle. The establishment of the rich planter families and their growing insistence on self-government culminate with the establishment of the Common Laws, the basis for what would develop into a revolution and a new nation. Several families' histories are connected here to create the sense of community.

Historical Accuracy: Fletcher ingeniously blends romance with politics and period detail.

2136 *Queen's Gift*

Date of Publication: 1952
Subject(s): Politics
Fictional character(s): Adam Rutledge, Landowner (planter); Ann Rutledge, Spouse
Historical character(s): Anne Stuart, Noblewoman; James Iredell, Political Figure; Sam Johnston, Political Figure
Time Period(s): 1780s (1788-1789)
Locale(s): Edenton, North Carolina; Hillsborough, North Carolina

Summary: The town of Edenton, North Carolina, is divided over which type of government will replace British rule. The Rutledge family is equally divided between the need for a new constitution with a strong central government and the fear that the plan could ignore the rights of the common man. Fletcher captures the debate played out by a wide cross-section of personalities.

Historical Accuracy: The details and issues are sharply drawn in this portrait of the earliest days of the American nation.

2137 *Raleigh's Eden*

Date of Publication: 1940
Subject(s): American Revolution; American Colonies
Fictional character(s): Adam Rutledge, Landowner (planter)
Historical character(s): Charles Cornwallis, Military Personnel (general); Nathanael Greene, Military Personnel (general); John Paul Jones, Military Personnel (naval officer); Flora MacDonald, Settler; Banastre Tarleton, Military Personnel (British officer)
Time Period(s): 18th century (1765-1782)
Locale(s): Albemarle County, North Carolina

Summary: The story covers the period before the American Revolution to after Cornwallis' surrender in 1782. The scene is coastal North Carolina. Fletcher's cast is over 100 strong, including several major historical figures of the period. All the various characters and scenes paint a full and colorful scene of American life in conflict.

Historical Accuracy: Fletcher spent years researching the book and then blending her assembled facts into a dramatic fiction. The result is an impressive re-creation of the past.

2138 *Roanoke Hundred*

Date of Publication: 1948
Subject(s): Elizabethan Period; Sea Story; Settlement of the American Frontier
Historical character(s): Elizabeth I, Ruler (Queen of England); Sir Richard Grenville, Nobleman, Explorer; Sir Philip Sidney, Nobleman, Writer (poet); Thomas Hariot, Scientist (astronomer); John White, Political Figure (governor of Roanoke Island); Richard Hooker, Religious (Anglican theologian); Sir Francis Drake, Military Personnel, Explorer
Time Period(s): 16th century (1580s)
Locale(s): England; Roanoke Island, North Carolina, American Colonies

Summary: This panoramic story tells the tale of the founding of the first English settlement in North America, on Roanoke Island off the coast of North Carolina. Richard Grenville successfully petitions Elizabeth to approve the venture, then leads his small pirate fleet against the Spanish and to the settlement in the New World.

Historical Accuracy: The novel offers an impressive re-creation of the New World as it must have looked to the Elizabethans and an animation of a huge cast of historical figures.

2139 *Rogue's Harbor*

Date of Publication: 1964
Subject(s): American Colonies; Pirates
Fictional character(s): Nathan Willoughby, Businessman; Buchanan, Laird, Teacher; Robin Willoughby, Sailor
Time Period(s): 1800s; 1810s
Locale(s): Perquimans District, North Carolina

Summary: The novel tells the story of the gentry Willoughby family in early 19th century North Carolina. Nathan Willoughby joins with other settlers in opposing government rule over trade. His youngest son is captured by pirates, and his only daughter elopes with a man who appears to be a poor Scottish schoolteacher.

Historical Accuracy: There is too much exciting action to develop the scenes as carefully as needed, but the novel does capture many period details.

2140 *The Scotswoman*

Date of Publication: 1954
Subject(s): American Revolution; Royalty—England; American Colonies
Historical character(s): Flora MacDonald, Revolutionary; Charles Edward Stuart, Royalty
Time Period(s): 1770s
Locale(s): Hebrides, Scotland; North Carolina, American Colonies

Summary: Fletcher tells the story of the amazing life of Scotswoman Flora MacDonald, who helped save the life of Prince Charles and would later help lead the Highlanders of North Carolina against the British in the American Revolution. Fletcher fills in the gaps in the documentation with plausible surmises and creates a fast-paced story with swordplay, a storm at sea, pirates, and a grand climax: the Battle of Widow Moore's Creek Bridge.

Historical Accuracy: The novel is thoroughly grounded in research and authenticity, including the dialect of the American Highlanders.

2141 *Toil of the Brave*

Date of Publication: 1946
Subject(s): American Revolution; American Colonies; Battle of Kings Mountain
Fictional character(s): Peter Huntley, Military Personnel; Anthony Allison, Military Personnel, Spy; Angela Ferrier, Heroine
Time Period(s): 1770s (1779)
Locale(s): Albemarle County, North Carolina

Summary: The scene is the American Revolution in North Carolina. The tale is a romantic triangle involving a beautiful woman loved by an American patriot and by a dashing British officer. The backdrop is the divided loyalties brought on by the Revolution that splits the community apart. The novel climaxes in a strong depiction of the Battle of Kings Mountain.

Historical Accuracy: Fletcher grounds her romance in solid facts and assembles a large cast to give a full treatment of the times.

2142 *Wicked Lady*

Date of Publication: 1962
Subject(s): American Revolution; American Colonies; Espionage
Fictional character(s): Baron Von Poellnitz, Nobleman

Historical character(s): Charles Cornwallis, Military Personnel (general); Anne Stuart, Noblewoman; Henry Clinton, Military Personnel; Marie Joseph Paul de Lafayette, Military Personnel, Nobleman (Marquis de Lafayette)

Time Period(s): 1780s

Locale(s): Edenton, North Carolina

Summary: Into the Edenton, North Carolina, community toward the close of the American Revolution come Lady Anne Stuart and her German husband. He wishes to settle as a planter; his wife has larger ambitions, involving espionage and a series of conquests.

Historical Accuracy: Fletcher ingeniously reflects the larger issues of the Revolution in her story of the new order in conflict with the old.

2143 The Wind in the Forest

Date of Publication: 1957

Subject(s): American Colonies

Historical character(s): William Troy, Political Figure (governor of Carolina); Harmon Husband, Frontiersman

Time Period(s): 1770s

Locale(s): North Carolina, American Colonies

Summary: The subject of this volume of Fletcher's chronicle of 18th-century North Carolina is the conflict between the conservative planters of the North Carolina Tidewater and the frontier farmers of the west, who are driven to revolt by what they perceive as oppression and injustice. Their uprising culminates in the battle of Alamance.

Historical Accuracy: The novel is solidly grounded in fact, which Fletcher uses to her advantage to capture the period.

CHARLES BRACELEN FLOOD (1929-)

Born in New York City, Flood graduated from Harvard and has worked as a writer and an instructor in creative writing. He was praised for his war reporting from Vietnam.

2144 Monmouth

Date of Publication: 1961

Subject(s): American Revolution; Battle of Monmouth

Fictional character(s): Nicholas Burk, Military Personnel (officer); Charity Avery, Widow(er), Spy

Historical character(s): George Washington, Military Personnel (army commander); Alexander Hamilton, Military Personnel (officer); Marie Joseph Paul de Lafayette, Nobleman, Military Personnel (general); William Howe, Military Personnel (English general); Casimir Pulaski, Military Personnel (commander), Patriot; Friedrich von Steuben, Military Personnel (Prussian officer), Nobleman; Henry Clinton, Military Personnel (British General)

Time Period(s): 1770s (1777-1778)

Locale(s): Philadelphia, Pennsylvania; Valley Forge, Pennsylvania; Monmouth, New Jersey

Summary: The fateful winter of 1777-1778 at Valley Forge is the low-point of the American Revolution. The American army endures its toughest challenge and emerges to fight the Battle of Monmouth, the turning point of the revolution. The events leading up to the battle are dramatized through the experiences of Nicholas Burk, an American officer, and Charity Avery, who risks her life spying on Sir William Howe's army.

Historical Accuracy: The historical events and personalities are authentically presented.

ROBERT FLYNN (1932-)

Born on a farm in Texas, Flynn has taught in the Trinity University Drama Department. He is the author of *Journey to Jefferson*, a dramatic adaptation of William Faulkner's *As I Lay Dying*. His novels include *In the House of the Lord* and *The Signs of Hope*.

2145 North to Yesterday

Date of Publication: 1967

Subject(s): American West; Cattle Drives

Fictional character(s): Lampassas, Store Owner

Time Period(s): 1870s

Locale(s): Texas

Summary: Storekeeper Lampassas assembles an odd company of hands to conduct a cattle drive from Texas to the railroad in Kansas.

Historical Accuracy: This is an authentic version of the cattle drive, with all its attendant dangers realistically and believably portrayed.

ANTONIO FOGAZZARO (1842-1911)

Fogazzaro was a Italian poet, essayist, and outstanding novelist. His masterpiece is *A Little World of Former Time*, set in the Valsolda region during the last ten years of Austrian rule (1850-1860). His humor has been called Dickensian, and his power of characterization has been justly praised.

2146 The Patriot

Date of Publication: 1896

Subject(s): Independence—Italy

Fictional character(s): Don Franco Maironi, Patriot; Marchesa Orsola, Noblewoman; Luisa Rigey, Heroine

Time Period(s): 1850s

Locale(s): Italy

Summary: Set during the turmoil surrounding Italy's attempt to gain its independence from Austria and unify, the novel is a family drama of a matriarch, the Marchesa Orsola, opposed to her grandson's love of a neighborhood girl. They marry secretly, and he is disowned. The family struggles parallel the nation's as Franco joins the rebellion against Austria.

Historical Accuracy: This is more a personal story than a larger nationalistic one. Historical events form only a general background for the family story.

KEN FOLLETT (1949-)

An English master of thrillers, Follett was born in Wales and graduated from the University of London. He worked as a reporter and a music columnist. His novel *The Eye of the*

Needle won the Edgar Award in 1978, causing him to be called the most popular and interesting writer of spy thrillers since Le Carre, Forsyth, Deighton, and Fleming. He began writing while working as a reporter for London's *Evening News*, joining a publishing company to learn the inside of the business. His forte is novels that offer variations on history.

`2147` *A Dangerous Fortune*

Date of Publication: 1993
Subject(s): Victorian Period; Business Building
Fictional character(s): Augusta Pilaster, Gentlewoman; Edward Pilaster, Gentleman; Solly Greenbourne, Heir; Micky Miranda, Financier
Time Period(s): 19th century (1866-1892)
Locale(s): England

Summary: This story of business intrigue and family secrets is set in motion when a young student drowns in a mysterious accident. The implications are traced through a number of characters over a period of three decades. At the center of the story is the Pilaster family, whose banking empire is threatened.

Historical Accuracy: The story offers a convincing evocation of the Victorian period.

`2148` *The Man From St. Petersburg*

Date of Publication: 1982
Subject(s): World War I; Espionage
Fictional character(s): Walden, Nobleman (Earl of Walden); Feliks Kischessinsky, Spy; Aleksey Orlov, Royalty (Prince)
Historical character(s): Winston Churchill, Political Figure
Time Period(s): 1910s (1914)
Locale(s): London, England

Summary: Follett's thriller is set at the outbreak of World War I as a secret Russian emissary is due in England to seal an alliance between Russia and England. Also in England from Russia is an assassin whose success could mean ruin for England.

Historical Accuracy: The author's ability to create an authentic atmosphere is impressive.

`2149` *The Pillars of the Earth*

Date of Publication: 1989
Subject(s): Middle Ages; Religious Life; Architecture
Fictional character(s): Tom, Artisan; Aliena, Noblewoman; Philip, Religious (prior); William of Sens, Artisan
Historical character(s): Thomas Becket, Religious (Archbishop of Canterbury)
Time Period(s): 12th century (1135-1174)
Locale(s): England

Summary: The political, spiritual, and human aspects of building a Gothic cathedral in 12th century England are examined in this tale of betrayal, love, and revenge. Several characters, noble as well as humble, are drawn into the events.

Historical Accuracy: The novel is a masterful adventure that reveals the period in depth.

`2150` *A Place Called Freedom*

Date of Publication: 1995
Subject(s): American Colonies; Crime and Criminals
Fictional character(s): Mack McAsh, Miner; Lizzie Hallim, Gentlewoman
Time Period(s): 1760s
Locale(s): Highlands, Scotland; London, England; Virginia, American Colonies

Summary: As the American Colonies move toward revolution, Mack McAsh is a bound servant working in the coal mines of Scotland. His longing to escape to freedom causes him to be transported as a criminal to colonial Virginia, where he meets an unlikely ally, aristocratic Lizzie Hallim.

Historical Accuracy: The novel effectively captures the customs of the period and events that helped produce the American Revolution.

DOROTHY NORRIS FOOTE (1908-)

Born in Iowa, Foote graduated from the University of Iowa. She worked as a professor of English at the University of Redlands, California State College at Los Angeles, and San Jose College.

`2151` *The Constant Star*

Date of Publication: 1959
Subject(s): Elizabethan Period
Historical character(s): Sir Philip Sidney, Writer, Courtier; Robert Devereux, Nobleman (Earl of Essex); Frances Walsingham, Gentlewoman
Time Period(s): 16th century
Locale(s): England

Summary: This novel set during the Elizabethan period focuses on Frances Walsingham, the daughter of Queen Elizabeth's secretary of state and chief of her secret service, Sir Francis Walsingham. Frances marries two of Elizabethan England's most famous men, the poet and courtier Sir Philip Sidney and the Earl of Essex. The novel attempts to explain her love for each and her connection with the major events of the period.

Historical Accuracy: The novel is not reliable as history and the characters lack the naturalness to be taken as believable portraits.

SHELBY FOOTE (1916-)

An American novelist and historian, Foote was born in Mississippi and lives in Memphis, Tennessee. Foote wrote the monumental study *The Civil War: A Narrative* as well as a number of novels that celebrate his Delta home.

`2152` *Jordan County: A Landscape in Narrative*

Date of Publication: 1954
Subject(s): Settlement of the American Frontier; Indians; Civil War—U.S.

Fictional character(s): Colonel Frisbie, Military Personnel; Chisahahoma, Indian; Isaac Jameson, Frontiersman
Time Period(s): Multiple Time Periods
Locale(s): Jordan County, Mississippi

Summary: Foote develops a fictional chronicle in seven chapters going back in time from 1950 to 1797. Using the experiences of several individuals, he assembles a narrative about a community and its inhabitants, including frontiersmen, Indians, aristocrats, blacks, and whites. His theme is the personal cost of history on human life.

Historical Accuracy: Foote knows his ground and traces its dimensions with assurance.

2153 *Shiloh*

Date of Publication: 1952
Subject(s): Civil War—U.S.; Battle of Shiloh; Military Life
Fictional character(s): Palmer Metcalfe, Military Personnel; Walter Fountain, Military Personnel; Otto Flickner, Military Personnel
Historical character(s): Nathan Bedford Forrest, Military Personnel (cavalry officer); Albert Sidney Johnston, Military Personnel (general); Ulysses S. Grant, Military Personnel (commanding general); William Tecumseh Sherman, Military Personnel (officer)
Time Period(s): 1860s (1862)
Locale(s): Pittsburg Landing, Tennessee

Summary: The murderous Civil War battle of Shiloh is described by several participants on both sides. In the spare and specific language of first-hand reporting, Foote creates a sense of battle from the foot soldier's vantage point, filled with horror and chaos, and occasional acts of great personal courage.

Historical Accuracy: The historical figures' words and actions are documented. Foote's monumental narrative history of the Civil War shares with this novel the power of the particular.

PETER FORBATH (1931-1996)

In addition to writing five books, Forbath was a foreign correspondent who covered, among other areas, Africa, the Middle East, and Europe. Among his books are *The River Congo*, about the discovery and exploration of the Congo.

2154 *The Last Hero*

Date of Publication: 1988
Subject(s): Victorian Period; Exploration
Historical character(s): Henry Morton Stanley, Journalist, Explorer; Emin Pasha, Explorer
Time Period(s): 1880s (1885-1887)
Locale(s): Sudan; Congo River, Africa

Summary: After the fall of Khartoum in 1885, the northernmost province of Equatoria is still holding out. A relief expedition is arranged, led by the great explorer Henry Morton Stanley, the man who discovered the source of the Nile, traced the course of the Congo, and found Dr. Livingstone. The novel tells the true story of the epic journey up the Congo River to Emin Pasha's beleaguered garrison.

Historical Accuracy: The novel is scrupulous in its truthfulness and utterly convincing in its details.

2155 *Lord of the Kongo*

Date of Publication: 1996
Subject(s): Exploration; Frontier—Africa; Slavery
Historical character(s): Affonso I, Ruler (Lord of the Congo); Gil Eanes, Servant
Time Period(s): 15th century; 16th century
Locale(s): Congo, Africa

Summary: This novel of the Portuguese exploration of the Congo tells the story of a young Portuguese page and cabin boy, Gil Eanes, who is sent by his captain on a dangerous journey to the capital of the Congo. There he must survive court politics by his wits and his friendship with one of the king's sons, who becomes King Affonso I, the black Catholic ruler. The novel describes the clash of cultures as European values corrupt the Africans.

Historical Accuracy: The central events and characters are real, taken from 16th-century Portuguese chronicles.

ESTHER FORBES (1891-1967)

Born in Massachusetts, Forbes was a member of the editorial staff of Houghton Mifflin Co. She won a 1942 Pulitzer Prize for *Paul Revere and the World He Lived In* and a Newbery Award for the acclaimed children's book *Johnny Tremaine*. Her books have been translated into at least ten foreign languages.

2156 *The General's Lady*

Date of Publication: 1938
Subject(s): American Revolution; Mystery
Fictional character(s): Morganna Bale, Loyalist, Spouse (of Milroy); Arnold Milroy, Military Personnel (British officer)
Time Period(s): 1780s
Locale(s): Massachusetts

Summary: During the final days of the American Revolution, Morganna Bale, a proud Tory, agrees to marry the American General Arnold Milroy to save her family fortune. When Morganna falls in love with a young British officer and General Milroy is found dead, tragedy follows.

Historical Accuracy: The novel provides an understated though totally convincing period background.

2157 *A Mirror for Witches*

Date of Publication: 1928
Subject(s): American Colonies; Witchcraft and Sorcery
Fictional character(s): Jared Bilby, Sea Captain; Doll, Orphan, Witch; Bloody Shad, Pirate, Demon
Time Period(s): 17th century
Locale(s): Salem, Massachusetts, American Colonies

Summary: In this tale of witchcraft in the Massachusetts colony, a sea captain rescues and adopts a young girl from Brittany whose parents have been burned as witches. In Massachusetts the girl shows supernatural powers and a capacity for evil that convince her she is a witch. She joins forces with a strange demon pirate and is finally tried for her crimes.

Historical Accuracy: The background of the Massachusetts colony is fully described, and the tale of witchcraft is put to the service of psychological realism.

2158 *Paradise*

Date of Publication: 1937
Subject(s): American Colonies; King Philip's War; Indians
Fictional character(s): Jude Parre, Settler; Johnny Pigge, Young Man
Time Period(s): 17th century (1670s)
Locale(s): Canaan, Massachusetts, American Colonies

Summary: Life in the small community of Canaan near Boston during the period of King Philip's war is dramatized. The customs and culture of colonial America are depicted in the various lives of the members of the small community who are drawn together by the threat of warfare with the Indians.

Historical Accuracy: The regional and period elements are authentically drawn.

2159 *Rainbow on the Road*

Date of Publication: 1954
Subject(s): Picaresque Adventure
Fictional character(s): Jude Rebough, Artist; Eddie Creamer, Companion; Rudy Lambkin, Outlaw
Time Period(s): 1850s
Locale(s): New England

Summary: The life of the itinerant peddlers of New England is depicted in the wanderings of Jude Rebough, a limner, or portrait painter, and his young helper, Eddie Creamer. Jude is mistaken for the outlaw Rudy Lambkin. The emphasis here, however, is not on the story but on the re-creation of a past age.

Historical Accuracy: Forbes is masterful in detailing old New England customs and details bringing a past age and a region to vivid life.

2160 *The Running of the Tide*

Date of Publication: 1948
Subject(s): Shipbuilding; Sea Story; Japanese Empire
Fictional character(s): Dash Inman, Sea Captain; Polly Mompesson, Young Woman
Time Period(s): 1800s; 1810s
Locale(s): Salem, Massachusetts; *Victrix*, At Sea; Japan

Summary: The colorful story of the brief period when Salem, Massachussetts, was the center of trade with the Orient is detailed. Dash Inman, the captain of the *Victrix*, initiates American trade with Japan. But Salem's day is not long, and the embargo of the War of 1812 destroys the vigorous trading center.

Historical Accuracy: Although the *Victrix* was not the first American ship to trade with Japan, other period details are based on reliable sources.

FORD MADOX FORD (1873-1939)

An English author born in Merton, Ford was originally named Ford Hermann Madox Hueffer. His father was an eminent author and music critic for the London *Times*. Ford was the founder and editor of the *English Review* and *Transatlantic Review*. He wrote more than 60 books. His most celebrated work was his four-volume saga of World War I England: *Some Do Not*, *No More Parades*, *A Man Could Stand Up*, and *The Last Post*. Ford co-wrote novels with Joseph Conrad and supported the careers of D.H. Lawrence, James Joyce, and Ezra Pound.

2161 *The Fifth Queen*

Date of Publication: 1906
Subject(s): Royalty—England; Tudor Period
Historical character(s): Henry VIII, Ruler (King of England); Katherine Howard, Royalty (queen consort of Henry VIII); Anne of Cleves, Royalty (queen consort of Henry VIII); Thomas Cromwell, Government Official (Lord Priory Seal); Thomas Cranmer, Religious (Archbishop of Canterbury); Mary Tudor, Royalty (princess)
Time Period(s): 16th century (1539-1542)
Locale(s): England; France

Summary: The novel chronicles the brief, tragic marriage of Katherine Howard, Henry VIII's fifth queen. Katherine is the daughter of a poverty-stricken lord who is appointed one of the ladies-in-waiting to Princess Mary. With the appointment comes further contact with Henry and her fateful marriage. Katherine is depicted as too honest, too deeply religious for the world in which she had to live.

Historical Accuracy: This is one of the finest historical reconstructions of this period. The characters are full-bodied and believable.

2162 *Ladies Whose Bright Eyes*

Date of Publication: 1935
Subject(s): Time Travel; Middle Ages
Fictional character(s): William Sorrell, Publisher
Time Period(s): 14th century (1326); 20th century
Locale(s): England

Summary: English publisher William Sorrell is injured in a train crash and finds himself transported back in time to the 14th century. He is transformed into a slave from Palestine seeking to restore a holy cross fashioned by Joseph of Arimathea to the Egerton family. Conflict over the cross and Sorrell's inability to exploit his knowledge of history and technology form the novel's ingenious story.

Historical Accuracy: The novel skillfully re-creates the atmosphere of 14th-century England.

HILARY FORD
(PSEUD. OF SAMUEL YOUD, 1922-)

An English writer born in Lancashire, Ford headed the Industrial Diamond Information Bureau of the Diamond Corporation. He is the author of novels for both children and adults under several pseudonyms. He is most highly acclaimed for his science fiction work as John Christopher that includes the *Tripod*, *Sword*, and *Fireball* trilogies. His future worlds are modeled on medieval times and allow him to express his interest in the past.

2163 *Castle Malindine*

Date of Publication: 1975
Subject(s): Victorian Period; Inheritance—Disputed
Fictional character(s): Arabella Harley, Young Woman; Sir John Dungillis, Landowner
Time Period(s): 1860s
Locale(s): Ireland

Summary: When the prospect of an unexpected inheritance brings Arabella Harley to Ireland, she finds herself in the middle of a family dispute and an impending peasant revolt against harsh conditions. Before the rightful heir is recognized, Castle Malindine is attacked, and blood is spilled.

Historical Accuracy: Good authentic period details, particularly of the Irish scenes.

JESSE HILL FORD (1928-)

An American writer born in Alabama, Ford graduated from Vanderbilt and the University of Florida. He worked as the director of public service for the Tennessee Medical Association. He won an O. Henry Award in 1961 for "How the Mountains Are" and an Edgar Award in 1975 for "The Jail.".

2164 *The Raider*

Date of Publication: 1975
Subject(s): Civil War—U.S.; Antebellum South; Settlement of the American Frontier
Fictional character(s): Elias McCutcheon, Settler, Military Personnel (cavalry raider); Shokotee, Indian (Chickasaw), Chieftain; Sim Hornby, Outlaw
Time Period(s): 19th century (1830s-1860s)
Locale(s): Tennessee

Summary: With help from the Chickasaws, Elias McCutcheon builds a life in the Tennessee wilderness, only to see his plantation and his family destroyed by the Civil War. Through it all McCutcheon endures, and his experiences detail the history of western Tennessee.

Historical Accuracy: The events and characters are described with a realism and authority that create a believable historical background.

JOHN M. FORD (1957-)

John M. Ford is a versatile and prolific writer of fiction, science fiction, horror, poetry, and non-fiction. He has written several Star Trek novels and is also a game designer. *The Dragon in Waiting* won the World Fantasy Award for Best Novel in 1984.

2165 *The Dragon Waiting: A Masque of History*

Date of Publication: 1983
Subject(s): War of the Roses; Fantasy; Renaissance
Historical character(s): Edward IV, Ruler (King of England); Cecily of York, Noblewoman (Duchess of York); George, Duke of Clarence, Royalty; Richard, Duke of Gloucester, Royalty; Anne Neville, Noblewoman (consort of Richard III); Elizabeth Woodville, Royalty (consort of Edward IV); Louis VI, Ruler (King of Frnace); Francois Villon, Writer (poet); Margaret of Anjou, Royalty (consort of Henry VI of England)
Time Period(s): 15th century (1478)
Locale(s): England; France; Italy

Summary: This novel weaves various personalities into a tapestry of fanciful invention. The common thread is rebellion and strife, in which history is blended with magic to produce an imaginative conjunction of the real and the far-fetched.

Historical Accuracy: The novel makes use of historical characters and settings in a manner more usual to drama. Some events and all dialogue are invented, as of course are the overtly fantastic elements.

PAUL LEICESTER FORD (1865-1902)

Novelist, scholar, and bibliographer Ford began work in his father's library of Americana at the age of 11 and helped produce many scholarly editions of historical materials, including *The Writings of Thomas Jefferson* and *The True George Washington*. He died tragically at the hand of a disinherited brother.

2166 *Janice Meredith*

Date of Publication: 1899
Subject(s): American Revolution
Fictional character(s): Janice Meredith, Young Woman; John Brereton, Military Personnel (colonel), Patriot
Historical character(s): George Washington, Military Personnel (army commander); Martha Washington, Spouse; Charles Lee, Military Personnel (general); Alexander Hamilton, Military Personnel (officer)
Time Period(s): 1770s; 1780s
Locale(s): New Jersey; Virginia

Summary: The years of the American Revolution are captured in the romantic adventures of Janice Meredith, who finds herself in the thick of the action. Coquettish Janice captivates soldiers on both sides of the conflict before finally being won by patriot Colonel Brereton. George Washington appears as a major character in this classic romantic novel of the American Revolution.

Historical Accuracy: More idealized than accurate, the novel does offer some credible period customs and a convincing period atmosphere.

LEONARD L. FOREMAN (1901-)

Born in England, Foreman served in the British army before settling in Lakeport, California. Several of his books have been made in to movies and television plays. His novels include *The Road to San Jacinto*, *Return of the Texan*, *Spanish Grant*, and *Rawhiders of the Brasada*.

2167 *The Road to San Jacinto*

Date of Publication: 1943
Subject(s): Texas Revolution; Battle of the Alamo
Fictional character(s): Dain, Young Man; Cleo, Young Woman
Historical character(s): Davy Crockett, Frontiersman; Antonio Lopez de Santa Anna, Military Personnel (general)
Time Period(s): 1830s
Locale(s): Texas

Summary: This historical romance dramatizes the story of Davy Crockett and his end at the Battle of the Alamo. The fictional story involves a young couple, Dain and Cleo, who encounter Crockett and are persuaded to join him in Texas as the war for independence begins. The novel offers a series of adventures before the climax at the Alamo.

Historical Accuracy: Despite the fanciful fictional story, the historical elements are authentic and genuine.

RUSSELL FOREMAN (1921-)

Australian writer Foreman was born in Melbourne and worked as an aircraft project engineer. His historical novels attempt to explain the effect of European migration into the southwest Pacific. In *Ringway Virus*, Foreman explores the environmental impact of human interference on viruses such as influenza.

2168 *Long Pig*

Date of Publication: 1958
Subject(s): Sea Story
Fictional character(s): Oliver Slater, Sailor; Seyawa, Young Woman
Time Period(s): 19th century
Locale(s): Fiji

Summary: Based on the wreck of the American ship *Argo* at the beginning of the 19th century, the novel dramatizes the fate of the ship's crew who are stranded on a Fijian atoll and their clash with the natives. Oliver Slater escapes in a canoe with the Fijian Seyawa following violence on the island.

Historical Accuracy: Romance and horror dominate the story, which does offer some graphic depictions of native customs.

C.S. FORESTER (1899-1966)

Forester was an English novelist who was born in Cairo and studied medicine before giving it up to write poetry and fiction. He is best known for his Horatio Hornblower series which he began on a cruise in Central America at the opening of World War II. Forester decided to write about a comparable time in which England fought against a tyrant who dominated Europe. The Hornblower series has set the standard for naval adventure during the age of sail.

2169 *Admiral Hornblower in the West Indies*

Date of Publication: 1958
Subject(s): Disasters—Natural; Pirates; Military Life—British Navy
Fictional character(s): Horatio Hornblower, Military Personnel (admiral); Thomas Fell, Military Personnel (naval captain); Barbara Hornblower, Spouse
Time Period(s): 1820s (1821-1823)
Locale(s): At Sea (in the West Indies); England

Summary: Hornblower is in charge of His Majesty's ships in the West Indies station. He must contend with the aftermath of the Napoleonic Wars as revolutionaries, pirates, and competing nations scheme to possess the remnants of the French Empire. Hornblower is at the center of a series of adventures and close calls, culminating with a devastating hurricane.

Historical Accuracy: The period and nautical details are meticulously presented.

2170 *Beat to Quarters*

Date of Publication: 1937
Subject(s): Sea Story; Napoleonic Wars; Military Life—British Navy
Fictional character(s): Horatio Hornblower, Military Personnel (naval captain); William Bush, Military Personnel (naval lieutenant); Don Julian Alvarado, Landowner (aka El Supremo)
Time Period(s): 1800s (1808)
Locale(s): *Lydia*, At Sea; Panama

Summary: Captain Hornblower is on a delicate secret mission to form an alliance with a Spanish landowner who intends to raise a rebellion against the Spanish, Napoleon's allies. Hornblower's ship will equip the rebel army. In mid-rebellion, however, Hornblower receives the news that Spain is now England's ally, and the rebels are now the enemy.

Historical Accuracy: The novel is convincing in its nautical and political details.

2171 *The Captain From Connecticut*

Date of Publication: 1941
Subject(s): Sea Story; War of 1812; Military Life—U.S. Navy
Fictional character(s): Joshua Peabody, Military Personnel (naval captain); Anne de Villebois, Gentlewoman
Time Period(s): 1810s (1814)
Locale(s): *Delaware*, At Sea; West Indies

Summary: The novel's hero, Captain Joshua Peabody, commands the American frigate *Delaware*. During the War of 1812, he breaks through the British naval blockade and reaches the Caribbean. There, he attacks a British convoy, raids the British islands of the Antilles, has a romance with the daughter of the governor of Martinque, and is finally cornered by a British squadron.

Historical Accuracy: The nautical details are convincing in this exciting adventure tale.

2172 *Commodore Hornblower*

Date of Publication: 1945

Subject(s): Sea Story; Napoleonic Wars; Military Life—British Navy

Fictional character(s): Horatio Hornblower, Military Personnel (naval commodore); Barbara Hornblower, Spouse; William Bush, Military Personnel (naval captain)

Time Period(s): 1810s (1812)

Locale(s): England; At Sea (in the Baltic Sea)

Summary: Hornblower is in command of a squadron ordered to maintain the shaky alliance of Sweden and Russia with Britain against Napoleon. The appearance of his squadron in the Baltic has international repercussions.

Historical Accuracy: The nautical details and political intrigues are realistically and convincingly presented.

2173 *Flying Colours*

Date of Publication: 1938

Subject(s): Sea Story; Napoleonic Wars; Military Life—British Navy

Fictional character(s): Horatio Hornblower, Military Personnel (naval captain); William Bush, Military Personnel (naval lieutenant); Lady Barbara Wellesley, Noblewoman

Historical character(s): George, Prince Regent, Royalty

Time Period(s): 1810s (1810-1811)

Locale(s): France; England

Summary: Captain Hornblower makes a daring escape from the French. His wife, Maria, dies in childbirth, and Hornblower is now free to entertain hopes of marriage to Lady Barbara.

Historical Accuracy: The novel's adventure is bolstered by believable period details.

2174 *The Gun*

Date of Publication: 1933

Subject(s): Napoleonic Wars; Peninsular War; Military Life

Fictional character(s): El Bilbanto, Rebel; Luke Brett, Military Personnel (captain); Carlos O'Neill, Military Personnel (captain)

Time Period(s): 1810s (1813)

Locale(s): Spain

Summary: The gun is a 6,000 pound bronze cannon, and its history forms the novel's story. The gun is abandoned, rescued by Spanish villagers, and is used by a rebel army in various efforts against the French and ultimately, to help defeat Napoleon.

Historical Accuracy: The novel is strong on authentic, local details.

2175 *Hornblower and the Atropos*

Date of Publication: 1953

Subject(s): Sea Story; Napoleonic Wars; Military Life—British Navy

Fictional character(s): Horatio Hornblower, Military Personnel (naval captain); Maria Hornblower, Spouse

Time Period(s): 1800s (1805-1808)

Locale(s): England; *Atropos*, At Sea

Summary: Hornblower commands the *Atropos* in the naval procession for the funeral of Lord Nelson. He then conducts a search for Spanish treasure in Turkish waters and takes on a great Spanish frigate in the early days of the French Empire under Napoleon.

Historical Accuracy: The nautical details are admirably delivered.

2176 *Hornblower and the Hotspur*

Date of Publication: 1962

Subject(s): Sea Story; Napoleonic Wars; Military Life—British Navy

Fictional character(s): Horatio Hornblower, Military Personnel (naval commander); Maria Hornblower, Spouse; William Bush, Military Personnel (naval lieutenant)

Time Period(s): 1800s (1803-1805)

Locale(s): *Hotspur*, At Sea; France

Summary: Hornblower commands the frigate *Hotspur* and is on blockade duty along the French coast near Brest. His job is to keep Napoleon from invading England. To that end, he is involved in a series of naval encounters and a daring land raid to destroy a French signal station. The final encounter is with a Spanish fleet laden with treasure for Napoleon.

Historical Accuracy: The details of life aboard ship and naval strategy are convincing and authentic.

2177 *Hornblower During the Crisis*

Date of Publication: 1966

Subject(s): Sea Story; Napoleonic Wars; Military Life—British Navy

Fictional character(s): Horatio Hornblower, Military Personnel (naval captain); James Percival Meadows, Military Personnel (naval captain)

Time Period(s): 1800s (1805)

Locale(s): At Sea

Summary: In the final, and unfinished, Hornblower novel, the year is 1805, and Hornblower has been promoted and relieved of his command of the *Hotspur*. The new captain is James Meadows and within days the *Hotspur* is run aground and sunk. Meadows is found guilty in a court martial and joins Hornblower for the voyage to Plymouth. They intercept a French ship and discover secret French orders, leading to a complex espionage plot led by Hornblower.

Historical Accuracy: The naval action is meticulously described and the period is authentically rendered.

2178 *Lieutenant Hornblower*

Date of Publication: 1952

Subject(s): Sea Story; Napoleonic Wars; Military Life—British Navy

Fictional character(s): Horatio Hornblower, Military Personnel (naval lieutenant); William Bush, Military Personnel (naval lieutenant)

Time Period(s): 1800s (1802-1803)

Locale(s): *Renown*, At Sea (in the West Indies)

Summary: Action against the Spanish in the West Indies sets the background for this installment of Hornblower's adventures which follows his career as a young lieutenant to his promotion to captain. Aboard the *Renown*, Hornblower meets William Bush for the first time and shows his mettle both under fire and in a high-stakes game of whist.

Historical Accuracy: The novel features carefully detailed nautical scenes and ship-board life.

2179 *Lord Hornblower*

Date of Publication: 1946
Subject(s): Sea Story; Napoleonic Wars; Military Life—British Navy
Fictional character(s): Horatio Hornblower, Military Personnel (naval commodore); William Bush, Military Personnel (naval captain); Barbara Hornblower, Spouse
Time Period(s): 1810s (1813-1815)
Locale(s): London, England; France

Summary: Hornblower is assigned to put down a mutiny on a British ship where the crew is holding its officers hostage. After resolving the situation, he travels to Paris, following Napoleon's first abdication. While there, he witnesses the Hundred Days of Napoleon's return to power. When he attempts to escape from France, he is captured and sentenced to death.

Historical Accuracy: More a land than a sea story, the details of the tumultuous final days of the Napoleonic Wars are convincingly presented.

2180 *Mr. Midshipman Hornblower*

Date of Publication: 1950
Subject(s): Sea Story; Military Life—British Navy
Fictional character(s): Horatio Hornblower, Military Personnel (midshipman)
Time Period(s): 1790s (1794-1798)
Locale(s): *Indefatigable*, At Sea; France

Summary: Chronologically, this is the first of the Hornblower series, depicting him as a skinny and gawky youth of 17 when he is introduced to life aboard a British naval ship. A doctor's son, Hornblower must rely on his own merit, not influential connections, to rise in the ranks. He shows his mettle in action against the French and the Spanish and becomes a commissioned officer by the story's conclusion.

Historical Accuracy: Intimate and authentic, the novel is a marvel of historical nautical re-creation.

2181 *Rifleman Dodd*

Date of Publication: 1932
Subject(s): Napoleonic Wars; Peninsular War; Military Life—British Army
Fictional character(s): Matthew Dodd, Military Personnel (British rifleman)
Historical character(s): Arthur Wellesley, Military Personnel (general), Nobleman (Duke of Wellington)
Time Period(s): 1810s (1813)
Locale(s): Portugal

Summary: During the Peninsular Campaign, Rifleman Matthew Dodd is cut off from his company and attempts to rejoin them from behind enemy lines in Portugal. Falling in with a band of rebel guerillas, Dodd mounts a private war on the French and achieves an amazing success.

Historical Accuracy: The novel is convincing in its detailing of the period and the locale.

2182 *Ship of the Line*

Date of Publication: 1938
Subject(s): Sea Story; Napoleonic Wars; Military Life—British Navy
Fictional character(s): Horatio Hornblower, Military Personnel (naval captain); William Bush, Military Personnel (naval lieutenant); Maria Hornblower, Spouse
Time Period(s): 1810s (1810)
Locale(s): *Sutherland*, At Sea; Portsmouth, England; France

Summary: Captain Hornblower is on squadron duty against the French. He makes a daring attack on a French fortress and takes several prizes. The novel climaxes with the destruction of his ship and his capture by the French.

Historical Accuracy: The details of nautical and military life are expertly rendered.

2183 *To the Indies*

Date of Publication: 1940
Subject(s): Exploration; Spanish Colonies
Fictional character(s): Don Narciso Rich, Government Official
Historical character(s): Christopher Columbus, Explorer, Sea Captain
Time Period(s): 15th century; 16th century (1498-1500)
Locale(s): Hispaniola, West Indies

Summary: Don Narciso Rich, an agent of Ferdinand and Isabella, investigates conditions in the colony of Hispaniola under Columbus' rule. The Spaniards are portrayed as intent only on the search for gold and the visionary Columbus as incapable of keeping order. He is sent back to Spain in chains.

Historical Accuracy: The novel provides a faithful account of Columbus' third voyage and the events that led to his disgrace.

ANTHONY FORREST
(PSEUD. OF NORMAN MACKENSIE, 1921- ; ANTHONY BROWN, 1930-)

Anthony Forrest is the pseudonym for writers Norman MacKenzie and Anthony Brown. MacKenzie, with his wife Jeanne, is the author of several biographies of English figures including Charles Dickens, H.G. Wells, and the Fabians. Brown, a correspondent for *The Daily Mail*, *The London Times*, and *The Manchester Guardian*, has written several distinguished historical volumes on military intelligence. The inspiration for their historical espionage series and main character came when MacKenzie heard a ''Captain Justice'' paged at a Vancouver airport.

2184 *A Balance of Dangers*

Date of Publication: 1984

Subject(s): Napoleonic Wars; Battle of Copenhagen; Espionage

Fictional character(s): John Valcourt Justice, Military Personnel (naval officer), Spy

Historical character(s): Arthur Wellesley, Military Personnel (army commander), Nobleman (Duke of Wellington)

Time Period(s): 1800s (1807)

Locale(s): Copenhagen, Denmark

Summary: In 1807 with Europe dominated by Napoleon, Captain Justice is given the important mission of preventing the powerful Dutch fleet from falling into French hands. The fate of England hangs in the balance, and Justice's espionage work becomes the prelude for the important Battle of Copenhagen.

Historical Accuracy: The period details makes this historical thriller believable.

2185 *Captain Justice*

Date of Publication: 1981

Subject(s): Napoleonic Wars; Espionage

Fictional character(s): John Valcourt Justice, Military Personnel (naval officer), Spy; Lucienne Lamotte, Gentlewoman

Time Period(s): 1800s (1804)

Locale(s): London, England; Boulogne, France; Verdun, France

Summary: Captain John Justice is sent on a secret mission to find a missing British agent and learn his plan to destroy Napoleon's invasion fleet. Justice is seized as a suspected spy and taken to Verdun where hundreds of English citizens are interned. He picks up the trail of the agent and makes his way back to Boulogne for a spectacular attack on the French ships in the harbor.

Historical Accuracy: Bizarre as the story sometimes seems, the setting is based on the truth.

2186 *The Pandora Secret*

Date of Publication: 1982

Subject(s): Napoleonic Wars; Espionage

Fictional character(s): John Valcourt Justice, Military Personnel (naval officer), Spy

Historical character(s): Robert Fulton, Engineer, Inventor

Time Period(s): 1800s (1804)

Locale(s): Portsmouth, England; London, England

Summary: Captain Justice's second assignment is to protect American inventor Robert Fulton who is designing a secret weapon that could change the course of modern warfare. The French are busy trying to capture and destroy Fulton's *Pandora*.

Historical Accuracy: As far-fetched as the story may appear, it is based on fact, though Fulton's plan for a submarine was rejected by the British Admiralty as foolish.

WILLIAMS FORREST (1868-)

Born in Baltimore, Maryland, Forrest was educated at Transylvania University and the College of the Bible in Lexington, Kentucky. He wrote extensively on religious subjects. His novels include *Fires of Desire* and *Trail of Tears*.

2187 *Trail of Tears*

Date of Publication: 1959

Subject(s): Indians; Tribal Life—Native American; Trail of Tears

Historical character(s): John Ross, Indian (Cherokee), Chieftain; Major Ridge, Indian (Cherokee), Chieftain

Time Period(s): 1830s

Locale(s): Georgia

Summary: The novel dramatizes the story of the Indian removal policy of the 1830s which resulted in the forced migration of the Cherokee Indians from Georgia to the Oklahoma Territory. When gold is discovered on Indian land, whites demand the Indians' removal, which is supported by Andrew Jackson. The novel focuses on Cherokee leader John Ross, who first opposes removal and then leads his people west to help relieve their suffering.

Historical Accuracy: Clearly polemical in its attack on the injustice done to the Cherokees, the novel's objectivity is at times compromised. The portrait of Ross is believable.

MARGARET FORSTER (1938-)

Born in Cumberland, England, and a graduate of Oxford, Forster taught at a girls' school in London and was the literary critic for the London *Evening Standard*. She is the author of four biographies, including a life of Elizabeth Barrett Browning and *Significant Sisters*, the stories of eight women important to the history of feminism. Forster is married to writer and journalist Hunter Davies.

2188 *Lady's Maid*

Date of Publication: 1990

Subject(s): Victorian Period; Literary Life; Servants

Historical character(s): Elizabeth Barrett, Writer (poet); Elizabeth "Lily" Wilson, Servant, Companion; Robert Browning, Writer

Time Period(s): 19th century (1844-1861)

Locale(s): London, England; Italy

Summary: While researching her biography of Elizabeth Barrett Browning, the author discovered the existence of Elizabeth Wilson, Elizabeth Barrett's lady's maid. With few historical details to go on, this novel imagines the role Wilson played in facilitating one of the 19th century's most famous love affairs.

Historical Accuracy: The biographer's knowledge of her subject is evident, even in a work based on imagination.

2189 *Memoirs of a Victorian Gentleman: William Makepeace Thackeray*

Date of Publication: 1979

Subject(s): Victorian Period; Literary Life; Biography, Fictionalized

Historical character(s): William Makepeace Thackeray, Writer
Time Period(s): 19th century
Locale(s): England

Summary: The novel offers English novelist William Thackeray's own account of his life and career, based on his letters and diaries. Thackeray provides insights into his assault on literary fame, as well as his domestic heartbreak.

Historical Accuracy: The novel is faithful to the facts and invents little. Thackeray's thoughts are based on his own recorded reflections.

ROBERT H. FOWLER (1926-)

An American newspaper and magazine reporter and editor, Fowler was born in North Carolina and graduated from the University of North Carolina and Columbia University. He regards his writing largely as a hobby but one in which he takes particular pains to achieve accuracy.

2190 *Jason McGee*

Date of Publication: 1979
Subject(s): French and Indian War; American Colonies; Indians
Fictional character(s): Jason McGee, Teenager; Christopher Cadwell, Trapper; Ephraim Haworth, Religious (Quaker preacher)
Time Period(s): 1750s (1753-1754)
Locale(s): Pennsylvania, American Colonies

Summary: When his mother is killed by Indians and his brother captured, young Jason McGee heads west to find him and gain revenge. He is plunged into the events of the French and Indian War with colorful companions, namely an irrascible fur trapper and a Quaker preacher.

Historical Accuracy: The novel is based on solid research into the period and its customs, creating an authentic atmosphere.

2191 *Jeremiah Martin: A Revolutionary War Novel*

Date of Publication: 1989
Subject(s): American Revolution; American Colonies
Fictional character(s): Jeremiah Martin, Gentleman; Gerta McGee, Gentlewoman; Francis Bolton, Gentleman
Historical character(s): Benjamin Franklin, Diplomat; John Burgoyne, Military Personnel (general); Thomas Gage, Military Personnel (general)
Time Period(s): 1770s; 1780s (1770s-1780s)
Locale(s): Boston, Massachusetts; Barbados; Philadelphia, Pennsylvania

Summary: Jeremiah Martin finds himself in the middle of the American Revolution. He is on hand at Lexington and the seige of Boston. He agrees to serve as an American spy and is almost hanged for his troubles. He later commands a privateer and endures the winter at Valley Forge. He slowly sheds his self-interest on behalf of the cause of independence.

Historical Accuracy: This is a rousing story marked by accurate period details.

2192 *Jim Mundy: A Novel of the American Civil War*

Date of Publication: 1977
Subject(s): Civil War—U.S.; Military Life—Confederate
Fictional character(s): Jim Mundy, Military Personnel (Confederate soldier); Jane Ferro, Southern Belle
Time Period(s): 1860s (1861-1865)
Locale(s): North Carolina; Virginia; Canada

Summary: Jim Mundy is a young North Carolina volunteer in the Confederate army. His adventures include an escape from a federal prisoner of war camp to Canada, an ill-fated invasion of Vermont by Southern forces, and participation in some of the war's most critical battles. Mundy rises to the rank of captain and is able to woo Jane Ferro, the beautiful daughter of a plantation owner.

Historical Accuracy: This is a fairly rollicking, picaresque treatment of the Civil War with a wry and offbeat perspective of its events and personalities.

2193 *The Spoils of Eden*

Date of Publication: 1985
Subject(s): English Colonies; Slavery; Religious Conflict
Fictional character(s): Charlotte Foxley, Gentlewoman; Richard Bolton, Plantation Owner (sugar planter); David Higganbotham, Doctor
Historical character(s): Charles II, Ruler (King of England)
Time Period(s): 17th century (1660s-1670s)
Locale(s): Barbados; London, England

Summary: Charlotte Foxley, the bride of Sir Richard Bolton, journeys to her new home on a sugar plantation in Barbados. There she must adjust to the primitive conditions and the devastating effects of the slavery that supports the colonial system. The conditions explode into an uprising when a hurricane strikes the island.

Historical Accuracy: The exotic atmosphere is authentically rendered reflecting the period and the island's history.

JOHN FOWLES (1926-)

An English novelist, short story writer, poet, and essayist, Fowles was born in Essex and graduated (with honors in French) from Oxford University. His writing career has been marked by an impressive range and diversity. Fowles has written examples of the thriller, the development novel, and the historical novel—all on the theme of individuals acting independently in the face of social and psychological pressures. His books include *The Collector*, *The Magus*, *The Ebony Tower*, and *Daniel Martin*.

2194 *The French Lieutenant's Woman*

Date of Publication: 1969
Subject(s): Victorian Period
Fictional character(s): Charles Smithson, Gentleman; Sarah Woodruff, Young Woman; Ernestina Freeman, Gentlewoman
Time Period(s): 19th century
Locale(s): Lyme Regis, England

Summary: Charles Smithson is attracted to the mysterious Sarah Woodruff, whom the locals refer to as the French lieutenant's woman. Smithson breaks off his engagement to Ernestina Freeman and risks his inheritance to pursue Sarah. The novel concludes with three possible resolutions of the lovers' dilemma.

Historical Accuracy: The novel is ruled by a modernist sensibility but authentically reflects Victorian customs.

JOHN FOX (1862-1919)

Kentucky-born nvelist who grew up among Cumberland mountaineers, Fox's fiction draws on his own experience. He was a correspondent for *Harper's Weekly* during the Spanish-American War. His best known work is *The Trail of the Lonesome Pine*, a sentimental novel, but *Erskine Dale, Pioneer*, a romance set in Kentucky and Virginia during the American Revolution, is considered his finest work.

2195 *Erskine Dale, Pioneer*

Date of Publication: 1920
Subject(s): American Revolution; Indians; American Colonies
Fictional character(s): Erskine Dale, Frontiersman
Time Period(s): 18th century
Locale(s): Virginia, American Colonies; Kentucky

Summary: This historical adventure novel concerns the exploits of young Erskine Dale, who is captured by the Indians and brought up among them. He is also the heir to a great Virginia estate, and the action shuttles between wilderness life and the sophisticated life of the colonial towns before and during the Revolution.

Historical Accuracy: The novel vividly and believably recreates the atmosphere and social scene of its period.

PAUL HERVEY FOX

2196 *Daughter of Jairus*

Date of Publication: 1951
Subject(s): Biblical Story
Fictional character(s): Naomi, Young Woman
Historical character(s): Jesus Christ, Biblical Figure; Judas Iscariot, Biblical Figure
Time Period(s): 1st century
Locale(s): Israel

Summary: This Biblical story based on one of Jesus' miracles, the raising of Naomi, daughter of Jairus. It contrasts the faith of Naomi and that of Judas, who misunderstands and then refuses to accept Jesus' ministry. The story feature the events leading up to the crucifixion and their effects on Judas, Naomi, and the other disciples.

Historical Accuracy: Familiarity with the geography, customs, and life of the period is evident in this novel, which interweaves a fanciful story with New Testament events.

NIGEL FOXELL (1931-)

A British author, translator, and teacher, Foxell was born in London and educated at Exeter College, Oxford. A lecturer on the Metaphysical and Romantic poets, Foxell is the author of *Ten Poems Analysed*, *Sermon in Stone: Essays on the Statue of John Donne in St. Paul's Cathedral*, and the novel *The Marriage Seat*.

2197 *Loving Emma*

Date of Publication: 1986
Subject(s): Napoleonic Wars; Sea Story
Historical character(s): Lady Emma Hamilton, Gentlewoman; Sir William Hamilton, Diplomat; Horatio Nelson, Military Personnel (admiral)
Time Period(s): 18th century; 19th century
Locale(s): England; Naples, Italy

Summary: This fictional version of the relationship between Lady Emma Hamilton and Lord Nelson curiously ends at the beginning of their six year affair, as Nelson returns to Naples in triumph after the Battle of the Nile. The majority of the novel's story concerns Nelson's life leading up to his affair.

Historical Accuracy: The basic framework is factual, but some liberties have been taken in the interest of the fiction.

ANATOLE FRANCE
(PSEUD. OF JACQUES-ANATOLE-FRANCOIS THIBAULT, 1844-1924)

French man of letters best known for his satirical tales.

2198 *At the Sign of the Reine Pedauque*

Date of Publication: 1893
Subject(s): Picaresque Adventure
Fictional character(s): Jacques Menetrier, Scholar; D'Astrarac, Philosopher; Catherine, Femme Fatale
Time Period(s): 18th century
Locale(s): Paris, France

Summary: The novel is a rollicking story, similar in outline to Henry Fielding's *Tom Jones*, in which young scholar Jacques Menetrier experiences life as a succession of adventures both mental and physical. The humor is satirical and bawdy.

Historical Accuracy: The novel is more a satiric than a realistic depiction of the period. Nevertheless the characters are memorably described.

STEPHEN D. FRANCES

Francis was born in London and now lives in Spain.

2199 *La Guerra: A Spanish Saga*

Date of Publication: 1970
Subject(s): Civil War—Spain; Rural Life—Spain
Fictional character(s): Rafael Ledesma, Military Personnel (Loyalist); Emil Serra, Activist (communist); Benito Vigon, Military Personnel (Loyalist)
Time Period(s): 1930s
Locale(s): Spain

Summary: The novel is a panoramic account of the Spanish Civil War and its impact on the tiny fishing village of Escoleras. The village is taken over first by terrorists, then by government forces, and finally by Franco's army. The novel attempts to tell how the civil war affected every level of society, sweeping all up in its violence.

Historical Accuracy: The novel offers a believable account of all sides in the conflict, attempting to supply plausible and genuine motives to all.

BRUNO FRANK (1887-1945)

Born in Stuttgart, Germany of well-to-do Jewish family, Frank studied law, philosophy, and hsitory at several European universities, earning a doctoral degree in 1912. An exile in England during World War II, he later went to Hollywood and worked for several film studios. He first gainedhis reputation as a lyric poet and a playwright, but he is also a novelist (*The Days of the King*) and short story writer.

2200 *The Days of the King*

Date of Publication: 1927
Subject(s): Biography, Fictionalized; Royalty—Germany
Historical character(s): Frederick the Great, Ruler (King of Prussia)
Time Period(s): 1780s
Locale(s): Germany

Summary: Towards the end of his life Frederick the Great recalls his past and his attempts to introduce reforms in his country. The three episodes from his life illustrate the human side of the Prussian ruler.

Historical Accuracy: The episodes have a factual basis, intermingled with the imaginative.

2201 *A Man Called Cervantes*

Date of Publication: 1935
Subject(s): Biography, Fictionalized; Battle of Lepanto; Literary Life
Historical character(s): Miguel de Cervantes, Writer
Time Period(s): 16th century; 17th century
Locale(s): Seville, Spain; Rome, Italy

Summary: This biographical treatment of the life of Cervantes, the creator of *Don Quixote*, concentrates on the years leading up to the conception of his masterpiece. Cervantes is shown in Rome, teaching an Italian cardinal Spanish, and at the Battle of Lepanto, where Cervantes loses his hand. His attempts to escape from captivity in Algiers are presented, as well as his years as a tax-gatherer in southern Spain and his imprisonment in Seville where he is inspired to write *Don Quixote*.

Historical Accuracy: The novel builds Cervantes' life out of what is known, with the necessary fictional elaboration to fill in the gaps and to flesh out the scenes and situations.

EDWARD FRANKLAND (1884-)

Franklin worked as an archaeologist, painter, farmer, and scientist.

2202 *The Foster Brothers*

Date of Publication: 1954
Subject(s): Middle Ages; Vikings
Fictional character(s): Gunnar, Young Man; Arnvid, Young Man; Astrid, Young Woman
Time Period(s): 11th century (1002)
Locale(s): England; Wales; Scotland

Summary: This adventure tale set in the England of Ethelred the Unready concerns two foster brothers, Gunnar and Arnvid, who compete for the favors of Astrid, whom they rescue when all of the Danes in England are to be murdered. Their adventures take them through much of England.

Historical Accuracy: The novel provides a believable and evocative picture of the period and its customs.

GEORGE MACDONALD FRASER
(1928-)

Fraser is an English writer who served in a Highland regiment in India, Africa, and the Middle East and was also a journalist. His Flashman books have been critical and popular successes. He is also a screenwriter and wrote the screenplays for Richard Lester's films *The Three Musketeers* and *The Four Musketeers*.

2203 *Flash for Freedom*

Date of Publication: 1971
Subject(s): Victorian Period; Slavery
Fictional character(s): Harry Flashman, Gentleman, Adventurer; Susan Willinck, Prostitute
Historical character(s): William Gladstone, Political Figure; Abraham Lincoln, Lawyer, Political Figure
Time Period(s): 1840s
Locale(s): London, England; Dahomey (West Africa); New Orleans, Louisiana

Summary: Forced to flee England to avoid a scandal over cards, Flashman finds his way to Africa and involvement with the Anglo-American slave trade. He is captured by the U.S. Navy but escapes in New Orleans. He smuggles a girl up the Mississippi and obtains employment as a slave driver. He also meets Congressman Abraham Lincoln. Flashman discovers the country of his dreams, filled with brother charletans, braggarts, and cowards.

Historical Accuracy: Fraser's attempt to show the humorous side of slavery causes some major equivocation here.

2204 *Flashman*

Date of Publication: 1969
Subject(s): Victorian Period; Military Life—British Army; Afghan War
Fictional character(s): Harry Flashman, Military Personnel
Historical character(s): Arthur Wellesley, Political Figure; Victoria, Ruler (Queen of England); James Thomas Brudenell, Political Figure; Akbar Khan, Ruler
Time Period(s): 1830s; 1840s (1839-1842)
Locale(s): London, England; India; Kabul, Afghanistan

Summary: The conceit here is whatever became of the notorious school bully from Thomas Hughes' *Tom Brown's Schooldays?* The answer is contained in his memoirs, edited and annotated by Fraser. In this first volume, Flashman is off to India and adventure as a reluctant secret agent in Afghanistan and a participant in the historical disaster of the retreat from Kabul.

Historical Accuracy: Fraser calls Flashman the soft and seamy underbelly of the great Victorian epic. History is all here but always with Flashman's skewed and comic slant.

2205 *Flashman and the Angel of the Lord*

Date of Publication: 1995
Subject(s): Victorian Period; Slavery
Fictional character(s): Harry Flashman, Gentleman, Adventurer
Historical character(s): John Brown, Abolitionist, Revolutionary
Time Period(s): 1850s (1858-1859)
Locale(s): Calcutta, India; Harpers Ferry, Virginia

Summary: Flashman emerges from his experiences in the Indian Mutiny to find his way to America where he plays a pivotal role in where he John Brown's raid on Harper's Ferry. It all begins with a dropped handkerchief from a shady lady in a Calcutta hotel. In the balance is the impending American Civil War. Flashman must deal, in his inimitable fashion, with undercover agents, beauties, hooded villains, and finally Brown and his gang of fanatics.

Historical Accuracy: Flashy's tendency to exaggerate and frankly lie is corrected by clever notes that sort out the historically real from the imagined.

2206 *Flashman and the Dragon*

Date of Publication: 1986
Subject(s): Chinese Empire; Taiping Rebellion
Fictional character(s): Harry Flashman, Gentleman, Adventurer
Historical character(s): James Bruce, Political Figure; Charles George Gordon, Military Personnel; John Arbuthnot Fisher, Military Personnel
Time Period(s): 1860s
Locale(s): Peking, China; Shanghai, China; Nanking, China

Summary: Flashman finds his way to China at the time of the Taiping Rebellion of 1860. He blithely blunders through one of the bloodiest civil wars in history to the center of Imperial Chinese power. Along the way he encounters a number of historical figures at the beginning of their careers.

Historical Accuracy: Fraser's notes and appendices help explain the action and bolster the history.

2207 *Flashman and the Mountain of Light*

Date of Publication: 1990
Subject(s): British Raj; Indian Mutiny; Espionage
Fictional character(s): Harry Flashman, Military Personnel

Time Period(s): 1840s
Locale(s): India (northwest frontier)

Summary: Flashman is in India on the northwest frontier where the Sikhs are preparing to invade British India. A spy is needed to infiltrate the court of the Punjab, and Flashman is the luckless choice. There he meets a beautiful and lascivious widowed maharani. He is on hand for some of the bloodiest campaigns in India and the Indian Mutiny.

Historical Accuracy: Despite the humor, the history is accurately shown, at least with the emendations of Fraser's notes that help to correct some of Flashman's impressions.

2208 *Flashman and the Redskins*

Date of Publication: 1982
Subject(s): American West; Indians; Battle of the Little Bighorn
Fictional character(s): Harry Flashman, Gentleman, Adventurer
Historical character(s): Geronimo, Indian (Apache), Chieftain; Ulysses S. Grant, Political Figure; James Butler Hickok, Frontiersman; Crazy Horse, Indian (Sioux warrior); George Armstrong Custer, Military Personnel (cavalry officer)
Time Period(s): 1840s (1849); 1870s (1876)
Locale(s): West

Summary: Flashman's career in the American West is chronicled in two different periods. The first takes him to California with the 49ers, where he ships a brothel on wheels to the miners. He is captured by the Apaches and marries a princess of the tribe with Geronimo serving as best man. The second half of his western odyssey takes place in 1876 and includes his eye-witness account of the Battle of the Little Big Horn.

Historical Accuracy: Fraser's notes anchor the book, an ingenious mixture of history and outrageousness.

2209 *Flashman at the Charge*

Date of Publication: 1973
Subject(s): Victorian Period; Military Life—British Army; Crimean War
Fictional character(s): Harry Flashman, Military Personnel; Elsbeth Flashman, Gentlewoman
Historical character(s): James Thomas Brudenell, Political Figure; Fitzroy Somerset, Military Personnel; Albert of Saxe-Coburg-Gotha, Royalty (prince); Yakub Beg, Political Figure; Izzat Kutebar, Revolutionary
Time Period(s): 1850s
Locale(s): Crimea, Russia; London, England; Asia (central)

Summary: Flashman blunders into the Crimea where he is on hand for the charge of the Light Brigade. Taken prisoner, he ventures deeper into Russian Asia and finds himself at the center of the conflict on the top of the world with India hanging in the balance.

Historical Accuracy: Fraser's blend of history and the outrageous behavior of his main character is a delight.

2210 *Flashman's Lady*

Date of Publication: 1977
Subject(s): Victorian Period; Pirates

Fictional character(s): Harry Flashman, Gentleman, Adventurer; Elsbeth Flashman, Gentlewoman
Historical character(s): James Brooke, Adventurer; Ranavalona I, Ruler (Queen of Madagascar)
Time Period(s): 1840s
Locale(s): London, England; Madagascar; Sarawak, Malaysia

Summary: Isn't there any honor among bounders? Flashman, on a voyage to the Orient, finds his wife abducted by a handsome pirate. Her rescue takes him to Borneo and a meeting with the White Rajah, James Brooke, and to the court of the black queen of Madagascar.

Historical Accuracy: The scenes are exotic but given the expected Flashman treatment in this amusing historical send-up of British colonialism.

2211 *Mr. American*

Date of Publication: 1980
Subject(s): Edwardian Period; Crime and Criminals
Fictional character(s): Mark Franklin, Outlaw; Kid Curry, Outlaw
Historical character(s): Edward VII, Ruler (King of England); Alice Keppel, Gentlewoman, Lover (Edward's mistress); Winston Churchill, Political Figure
Time Period(s): 1900s; 1910s (1909-1914)
Locale(s): London, England; Norfolk, England

Summary: Who is the mysterious American who arrives in England with nothing to declare but an old saddle, two pistols, and a letter of credit for £50,000? Mark Franklin, a member of Butch Cassidy's gang, makes his way to the top of Edwardian society. He acts the complete gentleman until the past reasserts itself.

Historical Accuracy: Fraser offers a full, if comic, treatment of the Edwardian era from the slightly skewed perspective of an American desperado's assault on fashionable society.

2212 *The Pyrates*

Date of Publication: 1983
Subject(s): Pirates; Sea Story
Fictional character(s): Benjamin Avery, Sea Captain; Colonel Blood, Pirate
Historical character(s): Anne Bonny, Pirate
Time Period(s): 17th century
Locale(s): Barbary Coast, Africa; West Indies

Summary: In this send-up of pirate adventures, young Captain Avery is charged with delivering the fabulous Madagascar Crown to its owner. There follows, at breakneck speed, the loss, chase, recovery, loss, and chase of the treasure across the globe involving an assortment of colorful buccaneers.

Historical Accuracy: This is history repossessed by Hollywood played at comic speed—a treasure-trove of romantic adventure elements.

2213 *Royal Flash*

Date of Publication: 1970
Subject(s): Victorian Period; Revolution of 1848
Fictional character(s): Harry Flashman, Military Personnel

Historical character(s): Otto von Bismarck, Political Figure; Lola Montez, Spy, Dancer
Time Period(s): 1840s
Locale(s): London, England; Germany

Summary: After emerging from the First Afghan War quite accidentally a hero, Flashman finds himself in Germany at the center of political intrigue involving both Bismarck and the notorious Lola Montez.

Historical Accuracy: Fraser's annotations keep a check on Flashman's tendency to exaggerate and falsify history. The effect is history with a decidedly comic spin.

STEVE FRAZEE (1909-)

Born in Salida, Colorado, novelist and short-story writer Steve Frazee attended Western State College of Colorado. He is the author of several "Lassie" books. His other works include *Killer Lion*, *Outcasts*, and *Fire in the Valley*. Seven movies and fifteen television programs have been based on Frazee's stories.

2214 *Shining Mountains*

Date of Publication: 1951
Subject(s): American West; Mining
Fictional character(s): Jonathan Romig, Religious (lay preacher)
Time Period(s): 1860s
Locale(s): Colorado

Summary: Following the Civil War, a group of Confederate and Union veterans seek their fortune in the gold fields of Colorado. The novel describes their adventures and conflicts, centering on the experiences of lay preacher Jonathan Romig.

Historical Accuracy: The novel captures the period and the region authentically.

MARGARET FRAZER

2215 *The Bishop's Tale*

Date of Publication: 1994
Subject(s): Mystery; Middle Ages; Religious Life
Fictional character(s): Sister Frevisse, Religious (nun), Detective—Amateur; Clement Sharpe, Knight; Beaufort, Religious (bishop)
Time Period(s): 15th century (1430s)
Locale(s): England

Summary: Sister Frevisse goes to the funeral of her uncle. At the funeral feast, Sir Clement Sharpe dares God to strike him down and then collapses. Since all have eaten the same foods as Sir Clement, The Lord's vengeance is suspected, but Bishop Beaufort secretly orders Sister Frevisse to investigate a more wordly solution to the mysterious death.

Historical Accuracy: The medieval atmosphere is convincingly created.

2216 *The Boy's Tale*

Date of Publication: 1995

Subject(s): Mystery; Middle Ages; Religious Life
Fictional character(s): Sister Frevisse, Religious (nun), Detective—Amateur
Time Period(s): 15th century (1430s)
Locale(s): England

Summary: When sanctuary is given to a lady with two young boys, Sister Frevisse learns that the boys are half brothers of Henry VI. She takes them in and conceals them but attempts are made on the boys' lives from inside the walls of St. Frideswide's.

Historical Accuracy: The medieval atmosphere is authentically delivered.

2217 *The Novice's Tale*

Date of Publication: 1992
Subject(s): Mystery; Middle Ages; Religious Life
Fictional character(s): Sister Frevisse, Religious (nun), Detective—Amateur; Sister Thomasine, Religious (novice); Lady Ermentrude Fenner, Noblewoman
Time Period(s): 15th century (1431)
Locale(s): England

Summary: The peace of St. Frideswide priory is shattered by the arrival of Lady Ermentrude and her retinue. When she is found dead, Sister Frevisse, hosteler of the priory, investigates. The most likely suspect is the pious young novice Sister Thomasine, who is also Lady Ermentrude's niece.

Historical Accuracy: The period details are authentic and convincing.

2218 *The Outlaw's Tale*

Date of Publication: 1994
Subject(s): Mystery; Middle Ages; Religious Life
Fictional character(s): Sister Frevisse, Religious (nun), Detective—Amateur; Nicholas, Outlaw
Time Period(s): 15th century (1434)
Locale(s): England

Summary: While Sister Frevisse is on her way to a baptism, she is waylaid by a band of outlaws whose leader is her long-lost cousin Nicholas. He asks Frevisse to help him gain a pardon, but while she is lodging with Nicholas' business companion, a murder occurs, and Frevisse must uncover who robbed and killed a rich land owner, even as suspicion points clearly to Nicholas.

Historical Accuracy: The period is convincingly portrayed.

2219 *The Servant's Tale*

Date of Publication: 1993
Subject(s): Mystery; Middle Ages; Religious Life
Fictional character(s): Sister Frevisse, Religious (nun), Detective—Amateur; Sister Thomasine, Religious (nun)
Time Period(s): 15th century (1434)
Locale(s): England

Summary: During Christmas of 1434, a band of travelling actors seeks shelter at St. Frideswide's. With them is the wounded husband of the cloister's maid. The actors claim they found him drunk in a ditch, but the story does not hold

up. particularly when two more dead bodies are discovered. Sister Frevisse takes up the investigation.

Historical Accuracy: The period background is effectively and convicingly portrayed.

JOHN FREDMAN (1927-)

An English writer educated at Cambridge, Fredman was a practicing attorney before turning to writing full time.

2220 *The Wolf of Masada*

Date of Publication: 1979
Subject(s): Roman Empire; Siege of Masada; Jewish Revolt
Fictional character(s): Simon ben Eleazar, Gladiator, Military Personnel; Andrasta, Slave
Historical character(s): Vespasian, Ruler (Roman emperor); Flavius Josephus, Military Personnel, Historian; Nero, Ruler (emperor)
Time Period(s): 1st century (37-73)
Locale(s): Israel; Rome, Roman Empire; England

Summary: The novel describes the epic adventures of a Jewish shepherd boy, Simon ben Eleazar, who is captured by the Romans and becomes a gladiator and member of the Roman legion fighting in Britannia. His friendship with Vespasian is tested when he returns to Israel to participate in a Jewish revolt.

Historical Accuracy: The story is a mixture of the fictional and the factual.

ANNE FREMANTLE (1910-)

Born in France, Freemantle was educated at Oxford. She has worked as an editor and educatior at the BBC and Fordham University, and reviewed books for *The New York Times*. Her books include *The Little Band of Prophets: The Fabians*, *By Grace of Love*, and *James and Joan*.

2221 *James and Joan*

Date of Publication: 1948
Subject(s): Royalty—Scotland; Literary Life
Historical character(s): James I, Ruler (King of Scotland); Joan Beaufort, Royalty (consort of James I)
Time Period(s): 15th century
Locale(s): Scotland; England

Summary: The novel dramatizes the story of James I of Scotland, the son and successor of Robert III. Fearing for his safety, Robert sends James to France, but James is captured by the English and becomes their prisoner for 18 years. Shortly before his release to reclaim his throne, James falls in love with and marries Joan Beaufort, daughter of the Earl of Somerset, for whom he writes the famous poem "The King's Quair."

Historical Accuracy: The novel is solidly researched and accurate in its events and chronology.

JUDITH E. FRENCH

2222 *Lovestorm*

Date of Publication: 1990
Subject(s): American Colonies; Romance
Fictional character(s): Elizabeth Sommersett, Noblewoman; Cain Dare, Indian (Lenni Lappe)
Time Period(s): 17th century
Locale(s): Jamestown, Virginia, American Colonies

Summary: Lady Elizabeth Sommersett is shipwrecked and rescued by English-speaking Indian Cain Dare. Attraction ensues, but Lady Elizabeth returns to civilization. Then she is determined to go back to the frontier.

Historical Accuracy: The historical probability here is doubtful, but the essence is romance, not careful realism.

2223 *Moonfeather*

Date of Publication: 1990
Subject(s): American Colonies; Romance; Indians
Fictional character(s): Moonfeather Leah Stewart, Indian (half Shawnee), Noblewoman; Brandon, Nobleman
Time Period(s): 1700s (1706)
Locale(s): England; American Colonies

Summary: Moonfeather's mother is a Shawnee and her father is a Scottish earl. She is forced to marry an arrogant Englishman in order to save his life. Eventually, Moonfeather finds herself in England dealing with prejudice and suspicion.

Historical Accuracy: The story is not convincing as history.

2224 *Scarlet Ribbons*

Date of Publication: 1989
Subject(s): American Colonies; American Revolution; Romance
Fictional character(s): Sarah Turner, Innkeeper; Forest Irons, Spy
Time Period(s): 1770s (1777)
Locale(s): Maryland

Summary: This romance novel is set during the American Revolution and depicts Tory innkeeper Sarah Turner, who is persuaded to support the American cause through her attraction to American spy Forest Irons.

Historical Accuracy: The emphasis is on romance over historical details, but the period is colorfully captured.

PETER FRENCH (1918-)

An American novelist born in Wisconsin, French graduated from Boston University and was the managing news editor of *Business Week*. His major interest, outside of his writing, is sailing.

2225 *The Ocean Mistress*

Date of Publication: 1961
Subject(s): Sea Story
Fictional character(s): Simon Salter, Sea Captain; Carolina Salter, Spouse

Time Period(s): 1840s (1849)
Locale(s): New York, New York; *Ocean Mistress*, At Sea; Hong Kong

Summary: This novel of clipper ship days concerns Captain Simon Salter, who builds a new ship that can outrun all rivals in the China trade. At home in New York he finds his wife distant and increasingly unhappy. At sea, Salter's *Ocean Mistress* embarks on a perilous journey.

Historical Accuracy: The naval and period depiction is believable.

2226 *The Southern Cross*

Date of Publication: 1958
Subject(s): Sea Story
Fictional character(s): Samuel Wilson, Sea Captain; Stephen Hyatt, Sailor
Time Period(s): 1830s
Locale(s): New York, New York; *Southern Cross*, At Sea; Canton, China

Summary: Adventure aboard a clipper ship in the China trade of the 1830s is the novel's subject. Captain Samuel Wilson pilots the *Southern Cross* around the world and back. Life aboard ship and in Canton, China, is vividly described.

Historical Accuracy: The nautical and period details are believable.

PETER FREUCHEN (1886-1957)

Born in Denmark, explorer, journalist, and author, Freuchen lived with native peoples in the Artic and married and Eskimo woman, who died on one of his expeditions in 1921. An active anti-Nazi, Freuchen escaped from a concentration camp. His novels include *Artic Adventure* and *The Law of Larion*. He also wrote an autobiography, *Vagrant Viking*.

2227 *The Law of Larion*

Date of Publication: 1952
Subject(s): Indians; Tribal Life—Native American
Historical character(s): Larion, Indian, Chieftain
Time Period(s): 1850s
Locale(s): Alaska

Summary: Indian life in Alaska at the time of the Russian encroachment is described through the experiences of Indian Chieftain Larion. Larion initially welcomes the Russians but later attempts to halt the spread of settlement.

Historical Accuracy: The novel offers an authentic and believable account of Indian life and customs.

2228 *White Man*

Date of Publication: 1946
Subject(s): Tribal Life—Eskimo
Fictional character(s): Peter Haseman, Convict, Settler; Karen Haseman, Settler, Spouse
Time Period(s): 1720s
Locale(s): Denmark; Greenland

Summary: The novel dramatizes life in the Danish colony of Greenland during the 18th century during the reign of Frederick IV. Eskimo life and the travails of the settlements are shown through the experiences of Peter Haseman and his wife Karen.

Historical Accuracy: The novel expertly depicts the details of Eskimo life.

EDITH FREUND (1931-)

American author Freund was born in Illinois and has worked as a newspaper reporter.

2229 *Chicago Girls*

Date of Publication: 1985
Subject(s): Chicago World's Fair; Women's Rights
Fictional character(s): Margaret Marsh, Suffragette; Trudy Jahn, Young Woman
Time Period(s): 1890s
Locale(s): Chicago, Illinois; New York, New York

Summary: Set against the backdrop of America's first world's fair—Chicago's Columbian Exposition of 1893—the novel follows two women whose paths cross in many ways. Margaret Marsh is a confirmed suffragette who is afraid marriage will compromise her declared independence; Trudy Jahn has risen up from the slums of Chicago to become a precious commodity in the fashionable world of New York society. Their adventures explore the Gay Nineties era in scenes that portray the very rich and the very poor.

Historical Accuracy: The period backdrop is convincingly drawn.

RUBY FRAZIER FREY

2230 *Red Morning*

Date of Publication: 1946
Subject(s): French and Indian War; American Colonies; Indians
Fictional character(s): Jane Bell, Spouse (of Frazier), Captive; John Frazier, Trader
Historical character(s): Edward Braddock, Military Personnel (general); Robert Dinwiddie, Government Official (colonial administrator); Benjamin Franklin, Political Figure; George Washington, Military Personnel (army officer)
Time Period(s): 1750s
Locale(s): Ohio Valley, United States

Summary: This historical romance is set in the Ohio Valley during the French and Indian War. The heroine, Jane Bell, journeys into the Northwest Territory after her first husband dies and is captured by Indians. Her fictional story is connected to actual events and several real figures.

Historical Accuracy: The historical elements are more convincing than the romantic story, particularly the details of frontier life at the time.

KURT FRIEBERGER

2231 *Fisher of Men: A Novel of Simon Peter*

Date of Publication: 1954
Subject(s): Biography, Fictionalized; Christianity; Biblical Story
Historical character(s): Simon Peter, Biblical Figure, Religious (apostle); Jesus Christ, Biblical Figure
Time Period(s): 1st century
Locale(s): Jerusalem, Israel; Rome, Roman Empire

Summary: The novel follows the career of St. Peter beginning with his youth in Galilee. He is intent on revenge on the Romans for the death of his father, but instead he comes under the influence of Jesus and his alternatives to violence. The novel traces Peter's role in Jesus' passion and his part in the early church to his martyrdom in Rome.

Historical Accuracy: The novel relies on a variety of invented elements to fill in the gaps in Peter's biography. The novel is successful in creating a believable human portrait.

ALBERT FRIED

2232 *The Prescott Chronicles*

Date of Publication: 1976
Subject(s): Family Saga; American Revolution; Civil War—U.S.
Fictional character(s): Samuel Prescott, Settler; Bartholomew Prescott, Political Figure; Julian Prescott, Political Figure
Historical character(s): John Winthrop, Leader (colonial); Cotton Mather, Religious (clergyman); Benjamin Franklin, Political Figure; Ralph Waldo Emerson, Writer; Henry David Thoreau, Writer; Theodore Roosevelt, Political Figure; Franklin Delano Roosevelt, Political Figure; Eleanor Roosevelt, Political Figure; Felix Frankfurter, Lawyer, Judge
Time Period(s): Multiple Time Periods
Locale(s): United States

Summary: A panorama of American history is chronicled through the experiences of the Prescott family, who reflect the public and private events that shaped American history from the American Revolution, to the Civil War, to the McCarthy era. Dozens of historical characters are shown, and a sense of an insider's perspective on great events is captured.

Historical Accuracy: History passes at such speed that it cannot be detailed with great care. However, the historical elements are authentically drawn.

PAUL FRISCHAUER (1898-1977)

Born in Vienna, Frischauer studied law and later became a journalist, novelist, and playwright. During World War II, he became Chief Adviser to the Joint Broadcast Committee of the BBC for enemy and neutral countries. In 1941 Frischauer went to Brazil to work against the Nazi party there. His books include *Garibaldi: The Man and the Nation*, *A Great Lord*, and *Prince Eugene: A Man and a Hundred Years of History*.

2233 *A Great Lord*

Date of Publication: 1937
Subject(s): Napoleonic Wars
Fictional character(s): Andreas Raskonski, Nobleman
Historical character(s): Napoleon Bonaparte, Ruler (Emperor of France)
Time Period(s): 1800s; 1810s
Locale(s): Poland; Paris, France

Summary: Minor Polish noble Andreas Raskonski allies himself with Napoleon as part of his plan for uniting Poland and then works actively with the Russians to subvert Napoleon's power.

Historical Accuracy: The author claims that the story is based on actual family papers, though fictional characters and events have been created.

2234 *The Shepherd's Crook*

Date of Publication: 1951
Subject(s): Religious Conflict; Royalty—France; Huguenots
Fictional character(s): Isabeau Vezenobres, Young Woman; Guy D'Alais, Nobleman (marquis)
Historical character(s): Louis XIV, Ruler (King of France)
Time Period(s): 17th century (1680s)
Locale(s): France

Summary: This romantic tale is set during the persecution of the Huguenots in France following the Edict of Nantes in 1685. Isabeau Vezenobres, the daughter of a martyred Huguenot leader, learns about her father's faith after his death, a discovery that causes her to flee from the court of Louis XIV. A target of the King's Inquisitor, Isabeau must be rescued by her lover, the Marquis d'Alais, from the notorious Tower of Constance.

Historical Accuracy: The period elements are authentic, and the novel makes plausible use of actual figures and events.

2235 *So Great a Queen: The Story of Esther, Queen of Persia*

Date of Publication: 1950
Subject(s): Biblical Story; Persian Empire
Historical character(s): Haman, Biblical Figure, Courtier; Esther, Biblical Figure; Ahasuerus, Ruler (King of Persia); Mordecai, Biblical Figure
Time Period(s): 5th century B.C.
Locale(s): Persia

Summary: The novel retells the Biblical tale of Esther, the Hebrew woman who is chosen as queen by the Persian king Ahasuerus. Esther, aided by her cousin Mordecai, foils a plot by the courtier Haman to massacre the Jews.

Historical Accuracy: The novel embellishes on the Old Testament story, and unfortunately the result is rarely convincing.

NEWTON FROLICH

Frolich's books include *Making the Best of It: A Commonsense Guide to Negotiating a Divorce.*

2236 *1492*

Date of Publication: 1990
Subject(s): Inquisition; Exploration; Jews
Historical character(s): Christopher Columbus, Explorer, Sea Captain; Isabella I, Ruler (Queen of Spain)
Time Period(s): 15th century (1477-1492)
Locale(s): Spain

Summary: This tale of Christopher Columbus ends with his ships sailing west from Spain and is mainly concerned with the years leading up to his epic voyage. Spain during the time of the Inquisition is dramatized with Columbus, in this version a Jewish convert to Christianity, trying to avoid persecution.

Historical Accuracy: While the author's attention to detail is impressive, he also engages in some implausible speculation that undermines believability.

MARK FROST (1953-)

Frost was the co-creator of the television series *Twin Peaks*. He also wrote the acclaimed 1992 movie *Storyville*.

2237 *The List of Seven*

Date of Publication: 1993
Subject(s): Occult; Victorian Period; Mystery
Fictional character(s): Jim Sparks, Government Official (Queen's special agent)
Historical character(s): Arthur Conan Doyle, Writer, Doctor; Victoria, Ruler (Queen of England)
Time Period(s): 1880s (1884)
Locale(s): London, England

Summary: In 1884 Arthur Conan Doyle is a struggling physician, aspiring writer, and a debunker of the supernatural. He is involved in investigating a deadly conspiracy of Satanists—the Devil Brotherhood. His partner is secretive Jim Sparks, who claims to be an agent of the queen. Their only clue is a list of seven names, the leaders of the Brotherhood.

Historical Accuracy: The novel is a dizzying blend of adventure, supernatural horror, and period details, which are expertly delivered.

2238 *The Six Messiahs*

Date of Publication: 1995
Subject(s): Mystery; American West
Fictional character(s): Jack Sparks, Detective—Private
Historical character(s): Arthur Conan Doyle, Writer
Time Period(s): 1880s (1889)
Locale(s): New York, New York; Chicago, Illinois; Arizona

Summary: It is ten years after Arthur Conan Doyle first met Jack Sparks and solved the deadly case of *The List of 7*. Now Doyle is the wealthy and celebrated creator of Sherlock Holmes. On his first book tour of America, he finds himself stalked by assassins attempting to steal a book of ancient mysticism. Doyle tracks six mysterious strangers across America to the Arizona desert for a final confrontation with overwhelming evil.

Historical Accuracy: The story is an ingenious fantasy with some convincing period elements.

MARK FRUTKIN (1948-)

A Canadian writer, editor, journalist, and performance artist, Frutkin lives in Ottawa, Ontario. He was educated in the U.S. and Italy. He has published books of poetry as well as fiction and has been a speech-writer for a British member of parliament. His historical novels include *The Growing Dawn*, based on the life of Marconi, and *Atmospheres Apollinaire*, a fictionalized biography of the French poet Guillaume Apollinaire.

2239 *Invading Tibet*

Date of Publication: 1991
Subject(s): Military Life; East/West Relations
Fictional character(s): Edmund Candler, Journalist; J.R.L. Macdonald, Military Personnel (British officer); Sarge, Servant
Time Period(s): 1900s (1904)
Locale(s): Lhasa, Tibet

Summary: In 1904, a force of British troops invades Tibet and marches on Lhasa to seize the Dalai Lama and compel him to expel foreign provocateurs. The story of the invasion is told from the perspective of Edmund Candler, a journalist, who observes a military venture gone mad.

Historical Accuracy: The novel, which is based on actual events, is more metaphysical exploration than historical presentation. There is little concern for surface verisimilitude, and turn-of-the-century characters speak a modern patois that is disconcerting.

ELLEN FRYE

2240 *The Other Sappho*

Date of Publication: 1989
Subject(s): Ancient Greece; Literary Life; Homosexuality
Fictional character(s): Lykaina, Slave, Writer (poet); Maia, Religious (priestess)
Historical character(s): Sappho, Writer (poet)
Time Period(s): 7th century B.C.
Locale(s): Sparta, Greece; Lesbos, Greece

Summary: This novel tells the story of a young lesbian slave, Lykaina, who seeks out Sappho and her famous school of poetry. Instructed in the worship of the Earth Mother by Priestess Maia, Lykaina eventually leaves Lesbos, offended by the other poets' disdain for the poor. She rejoins Maia and creates her own school of poetry.

Historical Accuracy: This largely imaginative tale is bolstered by evident research into the period and its customs.

JOHN FRYE

HARRIET FRYE

2241 *North to Thule: An Imagined Narrative of the Famous "Lost" Voyage of Pytheas of Massalla in the Fourth Century B.C.*

Date of Publication: 1985
Subject(s): Sea Story; Ancient Greece
Historical character(s): Pytheas, Sailor (navigator)
Time Period(s): 4th century B.C.
Locale(s): At Sea

Summary: The novel offers a "fictionalized history" of Pytheas' voyage from the Mediterranean through the Straits of Gibraltar to Britain and up the coast of Northern Europe. Pytheas' account was lost when the library in Alexandria burned, and the novel provides a plausible version of what might have happened.

Historical Accuracy: The book's publisher insists that the meticulous research makes this work nonfiction. Despite evident scholarship, the basis for the events described is speculative.

PEARL FRYE (1917-)

Frye is the author of several novels, including *Narrow Bridge*, *Game for Empires*, and *Gallant Captain: A Biographical Novel Based on the Life of John Paul Jones*.

2242 *Gallant Captain*

Date of Publication: 1956
Subject(s): Sea Story; Biography, Fictionalized; American Revolution
Historical character(s): John Paul Jones, Sea Captain
Time Period(s): 18th century
Locale(s): At Sea; American Colonies

Summary: This biographical treatment of the naval career of John Paul Jones covers the years from Jones' service as a young commander of a British ship to his central role in the creation of the American Navy. The novel's climax is the famous battle of the *Bon Homme Richard* and the *Serapis*.

Historical Accuracy: The novel offers a convincing depiction of the era.

2243 *A Game for Empires*

Date of Publication: 1950
Subject(s): Sea Story; Battle of the Nile; Napoleonic Wars
Historical character(s): Horatio Nelson, Military Personnel (admiral)
Time Period(s): 1790s (1793-1798)
Locale(s): England; At Sea

Summary: This biographical account of the naval career of Horatio Nelson begins in 1793 when he is given command of the *Agamemnon* and ends in 1798 with the defeat of the

French fleet in the Battle of the Nile. The novel is insightful both in its battle scenes and in its portrait of Nelson.

Historical Accuracy: The author has drawn on Nelson's letters in aid of the novel's authenticity, creating a superior historical novel.

2244 *The Sleeping Sword: A Biographical Novel*

Date of Publication: 1952
Subject(s): Napoleonic Wars; Sea Story; Biography, Fictionalized
Historical character(s): Horatio Nelson, Military Personnel (admiral); Lady Emma Hamilton, Gentlewoman; Sir William Hamilton, Diplomat
Time Period(s): 1790s; 1800s (1799-1805)
Locale(s): Naples, Italy; At Sea (Mediterranean)

Summary: The naval career and romantic life of Horatio Nelson are described, including his assistance to the Two Sicilies kingdom, his first meeting with his later mistress, Lady Emma Hamilton, and his death at the Battle of Trafalgar. The novel excels in its depiction of the naval battles and its illustration of Nelson's formidable genius as a strategist.

Historical Accuracy: This is an accurate and authentic presentation of the period and its events.

CARLOS FUENTES (1929-)

Mexican author Fuentes was born in Panama City and graduated from the National University of Mexico. He was Mexico's ambassador to France from 1955 to 1957. Considered one of Mexico's greatest novelists, Fuentes was one of the principal forces in the internationalization of the Spanish-American novel. His novel *The Old Gringo* was the first novel by a Mexican author to appear on the *New York Times* bestseller list.

2245 *The Campaign*

Date of Publication: 1991
Subject(s): Independence—South America
Fictional character(s): Baltasar Bustos, Student, Revolutionary; Ofelia Salamanca, Noblewoman (Marquise de Cobra)
Time Period(s): 1810s
Locale(s): South America; Mexico

Summary: During South America's revolutionary decade of the 1810s—the so-called "romantic time"—Baltasar Bustos, the son of a wealthy Argentine ranch owner, commits a subversive act. He steals a child born of the Marquise de Cobra and replaces it with a black baby, the child of a prostitute who had just been publicly flogged. This revolutionary act becomes entangled with Bustos' passion for the Marquise and his long public and personal campaign of repentance and redemption.

Historical Accuracy: The details of the period are reliable and convincing.

2246 *The Death of Artemio Cruz*

Date of Publication: 1967
Subject(s): Revolution—Mexico
Fictional character(s): Artemio Cruz, Financier, Revolutionary; Catalina Cruz, Spouse
Time Period(s): 19th century; 20th century (1889-1959)
Locale(s): Mexico

Summary: On his deathbed, aged millionaire Artemio Cruz reflects on his life as a former revolutionary turned ruthless exploiter. Cruz achieved his success through blackmail, bribery, and exploitation of the workers, making Fuentes' point that the revolution has been betrayed by the common people who made it.

Historical Accuracy: Fuentes' obvious thesis dictates his account, which on the whole is compelling and authentic in its evocation of the period.

2247 *The Old Gringo*

Date of Publication: 1985
Subject(s): Revolution—Mexico
Fictional character(s): Harriet Winslow, Young Woman; Tomas Arroya, Military Personnel (general)
Historical character(s): Ambrose Bierce, Writer, Journalist; Pancho Villa, Revolutionary, Military Personnel (general)
Time Period(s): 1910s (1914)
Locale(s): Mexico

Summary: The novel, set in Mexico in the time of Pancho Villa, features three individuals whose paths intersect: Arroya, one of Villa's generals; Harriet Winslow, a young woman in search of her father, missing since the war in Cuba; and Ambrose Bierce, a writer and journalist who has come to Mexico to die.

Historical Accuracy: The atmosphere of the story is genuine, capturing the clash of two cultures.

SHEILA FUGARD (1932-)

Born in Birmingham, England, Fugard moved to South Africa when she was a young girl. There she attended the University of Cape Town. In 1956, she married South African playwright and director Athol Fugard. Her writings reflect a concern with clashing cultures, racial tensions, decaying civilization, and revolutionary nonviolence and retaliation. She is the author of the critically acclaimed novel *The Castaways* and two volumes of poetry, *Threshold* and *Mythic Things*.

2248 *A Revolutionary Woman*

Date of Publication: 1985
Subject(s): Racial Conflict; Boers; Vigilantes
Fictional character(s): Christina Ransome, Teacher
Time Period(s): 1920s
Locale(s): Karroo District, South Africa

Summary: Set in South Africa during the 1920s, the novel is told from the perspective of Christina Ransome, an English-speaking white radical teacher who angers the Boer community by her attitudes. The novel's conflict comes when one of her pupils seduces a young African girl, and a vigilante group seeks vengeance.

Historical Accuracy: The novel is convincing in capturing the atmosphere of the place and the time.

EDMUND FULLER (1914-)

American writer and teacher born in Delaware, Fuller taught at the New School for Social Research and Columbia University. He is the author of many books of literary criticism, among them *Man in Modern Fiction.*

2249 *John Milton*

Date of Publication: 1944
Subject(s): Biography, Fictionalized; Civil War—England
Historical character(s): John Milton, Writer (poet)
Time Period(s): 17th century
Locale(s): England

Summary: Fuller provides a fictionalized account of the life and times of English poet John Milton. Despite a fiercely Protestant viewpoint, the author invents little in this rendering of Milton's genius.

Historical Accuracy: The novel stays close to the facts of Milton's life, and its invented dialogue is plausible.

2250 *A Star Pointed North*

Date of Publication: 1946
Subject(s): Biography, Fictionalized; Slavery; Civil War—U.S.
Historical character(s): Frederick Douglass, Abolitionist, Journalist
Time Period(s): 19th century (1817-1895)
Locale(s): United States

Summary: This biographical novel traces the career of abolitionist leader Frederick Douglass. Born a slave, Douglass escapes to the North and becomes one of the central figures in the movement to abolish slavery. The novel captures with some skill Douglass' career and the era.

Historical Accuracy: The story is faithful to the facts of Douglass' life.

IOLA FULLER

(PSEUD. OF IOLA FULLER MCCOY, 1906-)

An American writer born in Michigan and a graduate of the University of Michigan, Fuller worked as a college teacher. Her guiding principles in her novels are accuracy in historical material used, a theme of universal importance, a carefully constructed plot, and careful character development.

2251 *All the Golden Gifts*

Date of Publication: 1966
Subject(s): Royalty—France
Fictional character(s): Anne-Marie Courtine, Gentlewoman; Guy de Mornay, Military Personnel (musketeer); Jean Pierre de Blecourt, Gentleman

Historical character(s): Louis XIV, Ruler (King of France)
Time Period(s): 17th century (1670s)
Locale(s): France

Summary: Anne-Marie Courtine is brought from the country by a scheming relative to the court of Louis XIV to become the king's favorite. She resists the Sun King's efforts to win her, drawn instead by the competing attractions of a young musketeer, Guy de Mornay, and a gentleman, Jean Pierre de Blecourt. Who will win the battle for Anne-Marie's heart and how will she survive the court intrigue?.

Historical Accuracy: The novel captures with conviction the period details and atmosphere of Louis' court.

2252 *The Gilded Torch*

Date of Publication: 1957
Subject(s): Exploration; Espionage
Fictional character(s): Victor de Correnes, Courtier, Spy; Marc de Lorrenes, Frontiersman
Historical character(s): Rene-Robert Cavelier de La Salle, Explorer; Louis XIV, Ruler (King of France); Louis de Buade, Government Official (governor of New France), Nobleman (Comte de Frontenac); Francoise Athenais Rochechouart de Mortemart, Noblewoman (Marquise de Montespan); Francoise d'Aubigne, Noblewoman (Marquise de Maintenon), Royalty (queen consort of Louis XIV)
Time Period(s): 17th century (1670s)
Locale(s): Versailles, France; New France, North America; Mississippi River, North America

Summary: Identical twins Marc and Vicor de Lorrenes become involved in the politics surrounding the explorations of LaSalle. Victor is sent by Louis XIV to spy on LaSalle, and while Marc becomes an immediate proponent of the French explorer's cause, Victor must endure four years of frontier hardships before he begins to support the French colonisation of America.

Historical Accuracy: The story adheres closely to the fragmentary chronicles of LaSalle's exploration while filling in gaps with colorful details of French court life and wilderness experiences.

2253 *The Loon Feather*

Date of Publication: 1940
Subject(s): Indians; Tribal Life—Native American
Fictional character(s): Baptiste Lamont, Trader (fur)
Historical character(s): Tecumseh, Indian, Chieftain; Oneta, Indian
Time Period(s): 19th century (1806-1830s)
Locale(s): Mackinac, Michigan; Detroit, Michigan

Summary: The fur trade in Michigan in the early decades of the 19th century is depicted from the perspective of the daughter of the great chief Tecumseh. Oneta's experiences describe the passing of the traditional ways and the fading of the world of the fur trappers to the onrush of settlement.

Historical Accuracy: This is largely a fictional story with some solid realistic background elements.

2254 *The Shining Trail*

Date of Publication: 1943
Subject(s): Indians; Black Hawk War
Fictional character(s): Chaske, Indian (Sauk), Warrior
Historical character(s): Black Hawk, Indian, Chieftain
Time Period(s): 1820s; 1830s
Locale(s): Mississippi River

Summary: The novel concerns the Sauk Indians and the events that lead up to the Black Hawk Wars as the great chief wages an unsuccessful war against settlement by the whites moving west. Increasing disruption of the traditional ways and the betrayal and treachery of the white traders lead to the outbreak of open warfare.

Historical Accuracy: The novel's incidents are based on historical facts, and the fictional characters are largely based on actual figures.

JAMIE FULLER

Fuller holds degrees in English and in Russian. She is a translator of Russian poetry and lives in Austin, Texas.

2255 *The Diary of Emily Dickinson: A Novel*

Date of Publication: 1993
Subject(s): Biography, Fictionalized; Literary Life
Historical character(s): Emily Dickinson, Writer (poet)
Time Period(s): 1860s (1867-1868)
Locale(s): Amherst, Massachusetts

Summary: This fictionalized diary of American poet Emily Dickinson chronicles the events in a single year from 1867 to 1868. It records both the everyday events of Dickinson's life and her reflections on God, death, and love that form the basis for her poetry.

Historical Accuracy: The novel obviously owes a great deal to the actual details of Dickinson's life and a thorough knowledge of her poetry.

LEN FULTON (1934-)

American publisher and author Fulton left his native New England for the University of Wyoming. He has worked as an editor and publisher with his own imprint, Dust Books, which publishes annually *The Directory of Little Magazines and Small Presses.* His books include *Two Short Stories, Dark Other Adam Dreaming*, and a travelogue, *American Odyssey.*

2256 *The Grassman*

Date of Publication: 1974
Subject(s): American West; Ranching
Fictional character(s): Ben Finn, Rancher
Time Period(s): 19th century
Locale(s): Ten Smoke River, Wyoming

Summary: In the closing days of Wyoming's open range, a conflict over water rights to the Ten Smoke River explodes into a full-scale range war. The disturbance jeopardizes Ben Finn's ranching empire.

Historical Accuracy: The novel's story is fanciful but is filled with authentic western lore and regional details.

J.C. FURNAS (1905-)

A native of Indianapolis, Indiana, Furnas graduated from Havard and has worked in publishing and as a publicist for movies and television. His books include *Voyage to Windward, The Road to Harper's Ferry*, and *Anatomy of Paradise*, which won the Annisfield Wolff award in 1948. Furnas also wrote a trilogy on the social history of the United States entitled *The Americans*, *Great Times*, and *Stormy Weather.*

2257 *The Devil's Rainbow*

Date of Publication: 1962
Subject(s): Mormons; Religious Conflict
Fictional character(s): Joe Pomeroy, Orphan
Historical character(s): Joseph Smith, Leader (Mormon), Religious; Brigham Young, Leader (Mormon), Religious
Time Period(s): 19th century (1830s-1840s)
Locale(s): Kirtland, Indiana; Nauvoo, Illinois

Summary: The novel offers a portrait of Mormon founder Joseph Smith as recalled by Joe Pomeroy, a protege of Smith's. Pomeroy tells his story from the period just after Smith's first revelation to his murder by a mob. The novel presents an interpretation of Smith as a paranoiac who helps bring his destruction upon himself.

Historical Accuracy: The historical and regional atmosphere is convincing, but the novel's story and characterizations are at times guilty of oversimplification and stereotyping.

MARTHEDITH FURNAS (1904-)

An American writer born in Indianapolis, Indiana, Furnas worked as a dress model in New York and as a fashion reporter. She lived for a time in Ceylon and India.

2258 *The Far Country*

Date of Publication: 1947
Subject(s): American West; Wagon Trains
Fictional character(s): Unwin Shaw, Pioneer
Time Period(s): 1840s
Locale(s): Oregon Trail, United States

Summary: The novel chronicles a trek by wagon train along the Oregon Trail from Kentucky to California in the 1840s. The struggle of the crossing is described by young Unwin Shaw.

Historical Accuracy: The novel features an authentic version of the actual details of a western crossing by wagon during the period.

MARGARET GAAN (1914-)

Chinese born, Gaan came to the U.S. in 1977 having attended convent schools in Shanghai. She served as the

Program Officer for UNICEF in Asia, helping to build the program throughout the continent. After retirement, Gaan began her writing career, citing writing as one of the few occupations in which age is an advantage as it allows the mature writer to create with compassion as well as passion.

2259 *Little Sister*

Date of Publication: 1983
Subject(s): Chinese Revolution; East/West Relations
Fictional character(s): Little Sister, Child; Grandmother, Heroine, Grandparent
Time Period(s): 1920s
Locale(s): Shanghai, China

Summary: Set in Shanghai during the great protest march of 1925, the opening of China's nationalist revolution, the novel focusses on the visit by Little Sister, a Chinese-American child, to her grandparents. The family is swept up in the coming change as Grandmother provides stability and continuity with the past and traditions.

Historical Accuracy: References to places in the novel are factual; the family events are fictional.

2260 *Red Barbarian*

Date of Publication: 1984
Subject(s): Chinese Empire; Opium War; East/West Relations
Fictional character(s): Charlie Tyson, Businessman; Ling-ling, Spouse
Time Period(s): 19th century (1816-1842)
Locale(s): Canton, China

Summary: The novel's background is the lucrative and destructive opium trade introduced into China by the British in order to finance the tea trade. Charlie Tyson arrives in Canton to serve the chairman of the East India Company. His marriage to Ling-ling splits her family as tension between the British and the Chinese grows into open warfare.

Historical Accuracy: Historically accurate elements form the basis of the story.

2261 *White Poppy*

Date of Publication: 1985
Subject(s): Opium War; Chinese Empire; Boxer Rebellion
Fictional character(s): Yin-Kwa, Businessman; Jin-See, Businessman; Donald Mathes, Businessman
Historical character(s): Tz'u-hsi, Ruler (Dowager Empress of China)
Time Period(s): 19th century; 20th century (1860-1906)
Locale(s): China

Summary: At the end of the Opium War, the drug is legalized, securing a vast market for the English. Yin-kwa, an opium smuggler in *Red Barbarian*, now embarks on a plan to halt the trade and produce a nationalistic uprising. He is aided by Donald Mathes, heir to the largest opium trading house, and Charlie Tyson's son, Jin-see.

Historical Accuracy: The period and atmosphere are accurate and convincing.

DIANA GABALDON (1952-)

Gabaldon has a Ph.D. in quantitative behavioral ecology and was a professor at Arizona State University until she left in 1992 to write full-time.

2262 *Dragonfly in Amber*

Date of Publication: 1992
Subject(s): Romance; Time Travel; Jacobite Rebellion
Fictional character(s): Claire Randall, Doctor, Widow(er); James Fraser, Military Personnel
Time Period(s): 1740s (1744); 1960s (1968)
Locale(s): Scotland; Paris, France

Summary: In the sequel to *Outlander*, Claire Randall returns to the Scottish Highlands twenty years after her last adventure. She is transported again into the 1740s and the Jacobite Rebellion. She and James Fraser get caught up in the intrigues of the French court of Charles Stuart and the violent uprising that culminates in the disaster at Culloden.

Historical Accuracy: The evocation of the 18th century Scottish past is authentic and compelling.

2263 *Drums of Autumn*

Date of Publication: 1997
Subject(s): Time Travel; American Colonies
Fictional character(s): Jamie Fraser, Adventurer, Spouse (of Claire); Claire Fraser, Time Traveller, Spouse (of Jamie)
Time Period(s): 1760s; 1770s
Locale(s): Cape Fear, North Carolina, American Colonies

Summary: The novel continues the time travel saga of Jamie and Claire Fraser, he a Highlander of the 18th century and she a visitor from the 20th century. They have made their way to the American colonies and a new beginning among the exiled Scots in the North Carolina colony, despite Claire's knowledge of the Revolution to come. They are pursued by the British Crown, Jamie's aunt, and their daughter from the 20th century who tries to save them from a future that she alone can foresee.

Historical Accuracy: The novel interweaves its fictional story against a believable period background of actual events and circumstances.

2264 *Outlander*

Date of Publication: 1991
Subject(s): Romance; Time Travel; Jacobite Rebellion
Fictional character(s): Claire Randall, Nurse; James Fraser, Military Personnel
Time Period(s): 1740s (1743); 1940s (1945)
Locale(s): Scotland

Summary: In 1945 Claire Randall, a former British combat nurse, is on holiday in Scotland with her husband. Through contact with an ancient stone circle she is hurtled back in time to the 1740s during the Jacobite Rebellion. She is accused of witchcraft and forced to marry James Fraser for her own protection. Their passion causes her a dilemma in choosing between the past and the future.

Historical Accuracy: The friction in the story stems from modern sensibility interjected into the past. The 1740s are evoked with considerable authenticity.

`2265` *Voyager*

Date of Publication: 1994
Subject(s): Romance; Time Travel; Pirates
Fictional character(s): Claire Randall, Doctor; James Fraser, Military Personnel
Time Period(s): 1740s (1746); 1960s (1968)
Locale(s): Scotland; West Indies

Summary: In the third volume of the author's series concerning time traveller Claire Randall, Claire decides to risk a return to the past to find her lover, James Fraser, who may have survived the Battle of Culloden. The scene changes to the West Indies, where Claire meets Highland smugglers and Caribbean pirates.

Historical Accuracy: This is a gripping adventure yarn filled with period details that effectively bring the past to life.

GILBERT WOLF GABRIEL (1890-1952)

Gabriel is noted for his naturalistic treatment of history, especially in stories about trading and Indian battles. His artful narratives are based on extensive research.

`2266` *I, James Lewis*

Date of Publication: 1932
Subject(s): Settlement of the American Frontier
Historical character(s): James Lewis, Frontiersman
Time Period(s): 1810s (1810-1811)
Locale(s): Pacific Northwest, North America; New York, New York

Summary: This account of James Lewis, a fur-trading expediter John Jacob Astor sent to the Pacific Northwest in the 1810s, is described from Lewis' perspective. Little is actually known about Lewis, except that he was a member of the crew of the *Tonquin*, participated in the founding of Astoria, and was massacred by the Indians.

Historical Accuracy: The novel's romantic adventure predominates over a careful documentation of the past, though period details give evidence of extensive research.

`2267` *I Thee Wed*

Date of Publication: 1948
Subject(s): French Revolution; Royalty—France
Fictional character(s): Alan Ruff, Engineer, Surveyor; Gay Leguay, Young Woman, Seamstress
Historical character(s): Marie Antoinette, Royalty (consort of Louis XVI); Hans Axel von Fersen, Nobleman (count), Diplomat
Time Period(s): 1790s
Locale(s): Pennsylvania; France

Summary: This historical romantic adventure novel is based on the building of a refuge for Marie Antoinette in the wilderness of Pennsylvania. The novel's hero is a young Scottish-American surveyor and engineer, Alan Ruff. The heroine is a young French sewing-girl who comes to America to act as the queen's double.

Historical Accuracy: The emphasis is on romantic adventure rather than on a careful depiction of the facts.

NICHOLAS GAGE
(PSEUD. OF NICHOLAS NGAGOYEANES, 1939-)

Born in Greece, Gage was educated at Boston University and Columbia. He is a leading investigative reporter for the *New York Times*. His works include the non-fictional *Portrait of Greece*, and the novel, *Bones of Contention*. His 1983 best-selling book *Eleni* describes his search for the truth about his mother's execution during the Greek Civil War.

`2268` *The Bourlotas Fortune*

Date of Publication: 1975
Subject(s): Business Building; Independence—Greece
Fictional character(s): Kosmas Bourlotas, Shipowner; Demo Malitas, Shipowner; Jason Venetis, Shipowner
Time Period(s): 19th century; 20th century (1821-1960s)
Locale(s): Greece; London, England; New York, New York

Summary: The novel decribes the world of Greek shipowners who, with skill, daring, and occasional larceny, parlay the shipping business into great wealth and power. The novel covers the period from the 1820s to the 1960s but centers on Kosmas Bourlotas, born into poverty in 1896. He goes to sea as a deckhand and slowly builds his shipping empire in London and New York.

Historical Accuracy: Most of the incidents in the novel took place, as it describes the experiences of a generation of Greek shipowners building large fleets and large fortunes in the postwar world.

DIANA GAINES (1912-)

An American from Chicago, Gaines attended Smith College and the University of Chicago. She began her writing career as a copywriter for an advertising agency and for Marshall Field & Co.

`2269` *Nantucket Woman*

Date of Publication: 1976
Subject(s): American Colonies; Whaling
Historical character(s): Kezia Coffin, Businesswoman
Time Period(s): 18th century (1723-1798)
Locale(s): Nantucket, Massachusetts, American Colonies; London, England; Philadelphia, Pennsylvania, American Colonies

Summary: The novel is based on the historical Kezia Coffin, a daring eccentric in the provincial community of Nantucket in the 1740s. She shocks the Quaker elders and becomes a free-thinking and independent merchant whose adventurous career takes her to London and Philadelphia.

Historical Accuracy: Solidly researched, the novel is based on actual persons and events; the unusual Kezia Coffin seems truly ahead of her time.

ERNEST J. GAINES (1933-)

An American writer born in Louisiana, Gaines received his B.A. degree from San Francisco State College and did graduate work at Stanford. He has been a professor of English at the University of Southwestern Louisiana, Lafayette, and Whittier College. Gaines grew up on a Louisiana plantation, which is the backdrop for many of his stories and has been favorably compared to William Faulkner's fictional Yoknapatawpha County. *The Autobiography of Miss Jane Pittman* is widely regarded as his masterpiece. The TV version of the novel that aired in 1974 won nine Emmy Awards. His novels are deeply rooted in black culture and storytelling tradions.

2270 *The Autobiography of Miss Jane Pittman*

Date of Publication: 1971
Subject(s): Civil War—U.S.; Racial Conflict; Reconstruction Period
Fictional character(s): Jane Pittman, Heroine
Time Period(s): 19th century; 20th century (1864-1964)
Locale(s): Louisiana

Summary: This is a fictionalized autobiography of a black woman, Jane Pittman, born in slavery. It begins in 1864 as she serves water to Confederate and Union troops and continues for 100 years. Through her life and times the struggles of African-Americans are reflected. Pittman emerges as a woman of undauntable strength committed to the cause of personal dignity and freedom.

Historical Accuracy: The novel offers a genuine and personal history of the period from the Civil War to the modern era.

FRANCES GAITHER

2271 *Double Moscadine*

Date of Publication: 1949
Subject(s): Antebellum South; Trials
Fictional character(s): Syke Berry, Lawyer
Time Period(s): 1850s
Locale(s): Mississippi

Summary: This novel exposes the reality of plantation life in Mississippi during the 1850s through a trial in which a young kitchen slave is accused of poisoning the plantation owner's family.

Historical Accuracy: The case is fictitious, but it is modeled on an actual case recorded in Mississippi during the period.

2272 *The Red Cock Crows*

Date of Publication: 1944
Subject(s): Antebellum South; Slavery
Fictional character(s): Adam Fiske, Gentleman

Time Period(s): 1830s
Locale(s): Mississippi

Summary: This novel, set in Mississippi during the 1830s, concerns a young New Englander, Adam Fiske, who, though sympathetic to the plight of the slaves, finds himself involved in suppressing a slave rebellion.

Historical Accuracy: The main events of the story are based in part on actual events that occurred in 1835 in Livingston, Mississippi.

DAVID GALLOWAY (1937-)

An American writer, educator, museum curator, and literary and art critic, Galloway was born in Memphis, Tennessee, and was educated at Harvard and the State University of New York. His novels include *Melody Jones*, *A Family Album*, and *Lamaar Ransom: Private Eye*.

2273 *Tamsen*

Date of Publication: 1983
Subject(s): American West; Wagon Trains; Donner Party
Historical character(s): George Donner, Pioneer; Tamsen Donner, Spouse
Time Period(s): 1840s
Locale(s): Oregon Trail, United States; Sierra Nevada Mountains, California

Summary: The novel describes the fate of the Donner Party who are trapped by winter storms as they try to cross the Sierra Nevadas and are reduced to cannibalism in order to survive.

Historical Accuracy: The novel provides a faithful account of the ill-fated Donner Party.

MANUEL DE JESUS GALVAN (1834-1911)

Born in Santo Domingo, Dominican Republic, Galvan wrote about the Spanish colonization of his native city, basing his writing on the work of Bartolome de las Casas.

2274 *The Cross and the Sword*

Date of Publication: 1954
Subject(s): Spanish Colonies; Indians
Fictional character(s): Enriquillo, Indian (Santo Domingo)
Time Period(s): 16th century
Locale(s): West Indies

Summary: Set in the Caribbean in the post-Columbian period, the novel dramatizes the attempt by a Santo Domingo Indian, Enriquillo, to save the Indians from slavery. The novel depicts the clash of cultures between the primitive innocence of the natives and the rapacious greed of the conquistadors.

Historical Accuracy: The novel's portrait of the period and the region is solid and believable.

JEAN GAMO

2275 *The Golden Chain*

Date of Publication: 1948
Subject(s): Middle Ages
Fictional character(s): Pe de Biraygue, Servant (squire); Bernat Lomassou, Nobleman (Conte de Heresmedan); Lady Juana-Maria, Noblewoman
Time Period(s): 15th century
Locale(s): Pyrenees, France

Summary: Set in medieval France, the novel is narrated by the squire to the Conte de Heresmedan, Pe de Biraygue. It captures life during war and peacetime on a great feudal estate in the 14th century.

Historical Accuracy: The attempt to render everyday life during the Middle Ages is only partially successful. The characters resort to romantic types.

ERNEST K. GANN (1910-1991)

An American writer born in Nebraska, Gann attended Yale University. He served in the U.S. Army Air Force and was decorated with the Distinguished Flying award. He worked as a pilot for American Airlines. The author of screenplays as well as novels, his work has been consistently praised for his painstaking attention to aeronautical details.

2276 *The Antagonists*

Date of Publication: 1970
Subject(s): Roman Empire; Jews; Siege of Masada
Historical character(s): Flavius Silva, Military Personnel (Roman general); Eleazar ben Yair, Leader
Time Period(s): 1st century (78)
Locale(s): Masada, Israel

Summary: In this novel about the siege of Masada, the Roman General Flavius Silva and his Jewish counterpart, Eleazar ben Yair, are enemies. Eleazar is the leader of the 900 Jews who resist the Roman army from the heights of their fortress at Masada. Silva works to complete the assault ramps that will end the resistance, while Eleazar struggles to keep the resistance alive in the face of crushing odds.

Historical Accuracy: The author's reconstruction of the events is rooted in contemporary accounts and archaeological research.

2277 *The Aviator*

Date of Publication: 1981
Subject(s): Aviation
Fictional character(s): Unnamed Character, Pilot; Heather, Child
Time Period(s): 1920s (1928)
Locale(s): Rocky Mountains, Colorado

Summary: Set in the pioneering days of the U.S. airmail service, an unnamed pilot and his young passenger crash in the Rockies. The novel depicts their struggle to survive and the bond that is created by their ordeal.

Historical Accuracy: The details of the period and the wilderness are convincing.

2278 *Gentlemen of Adventure*

Date of Publication: 1984
Subject(s): Aviation; World War I; World War II
Fictional character(s): Kiffen Draper, Pilot; Toby Bryant, Pilot
Time Period(s): 20th century (1915-1945)
Locale(s): United States; Europe

Summary: Two flyers, Kiffen Draper and Toby Bryant, achieve distinction as fighter pilots during World War I, fly in air shows, participate in the Spanish Civil War, and continue their aerial adventures during World War II.

Historical Accuracy: This is a convincing look at the history of aviation in the first half of the 20th century.

2279 *In the Company of Eagles*

Date of Publication: 1966
Subject(s): World War I; Aviation
Fictional character(s): Paul Chamay, Military Personnel, Pilot; Sebastian Kupper, Military Personnel, Pilot
Time Period(s): 1910s (1916-1917)
Locale(s): France

Summary: The air war of World War I is depicted in action involving both French and German pilots. As opposed to the anonymous slaughter in the trenches, the airmen of the First World War are the last heirs of the heroic and chivalric tradition of honorable combat. Chamay and Kupper duel in the air as heroic combatants in a struggle that has precious little meaning.

Historical Accuracy: The details of air combat and flight of the period are authentically presented.

2280 *The Triumph*

Date of Publication: 1986
Subject(s): Roman Empire; Jews
Fictional character(s): Domitillia, Royalty (daughter of the Roman emperor)
Historical character(s): Flavius Silva, Military Personnel (general), Government Official (governor of Judea); Vespasian, Ruler (Roman emperor); Titus, Ruler (Roman emperor); Domitian, Ruler (Roman emperor); Flavius Josephus, Military Personnel (general), Historian
Time Period(s): 1st century (73-79)
Locale(s): Rome, Roman Empire

Summary: In the sequel to *The Antagonists*, General Flavius Silva has triumphed at Masada but at an immense human cost. He returns to Rome to find himself in the center of the struggle to succeed the ailing Emperor Vespasian's impending death.

Historical Accuracy: The details of a corrupt and tottering Roman Empire are fully and convincingly detailed.

NORMAN GARBO (1919-)

An American born in New York City, Garbo attended City College and the New York Academy of Fine Arts. Garbo is an artist whose works have been exhibited at the

Metroplolitan Museum of Art, the Chicago Art Institute, and the Philadelphia Museum. He is also a syndicated columnist.

2281 *The Artist*

Date of Publication: 1978
Subject(s): Artistic Life
Fictional character(s): David Karlinsky, Artist
Time Period(s): 19th century; 20th century (1896-1945)
Locale(s): Russia; New York, New York

Summary: The novel chronicles the life of a Jewish artist, David Karlinsky, who is born in Russia and emigrates to New York's teeming lower East Side in the 1900s. He struggles to represent the life of the ghetto and becomes the first great Jewish-American painter. In his full life he also participates in both World Wars.

Historical Accuracy: The period background is genuine and authentically evoked.

GABRIEL GARCIA MARQUEZ (1928-)

Colombian author Garcia Marquez attended the Universidad Nacional de Colombia and the Universidad de Cartagena. He has worked as a journalist and received the Nobel Prize in Literature in 1982. His novel *One Hundred Years of Solitude* is generally considered his masterpiece, ensuring his place in the top rank of 20th-century literary masters.

2282 *The General in His Labyrinth*

Date of Publication: 1990
Subject(s): Independence—South America
Historical character(s): Simon Bolivar, Military Personnel (general), Revolutionary
Time Period(s): 1830s (1830)

Summary: In the last year of his life, Simon Bolivar makes a final seven-month voyage down the Magdalena River from Bogota, Colombia, to the sea. It becomes an occasion for the great general, who dreamed of a South America free from Spanish domination, to reexamine his life. The portrait that emerges is of a great and complex individual and a life of both triumph and disillusion.

Historical Accuracy: The novel is a remarkable blend of history and psychology.

DOROTHY GARDINER (1894-)

An American author of several historical and mystery novels, Gardiner was born in Buffalo, New York. Her favorite subjects are Colorado and the West.

2283 *The Golden Lady*

Date of Publication: 1936
Subject(s): Mining; American West
Fictional character(s): Vannie Swenk, Young Woman
Time Period(s): 19th century; 20th century (1880s-1930s)
Locale(s): Colorado; England

Summary: Gold mining in Colorado is the background for this novel that traces the adventures of Vannie Swenk. The daughter of a gambler, Swenk is given the title to the Golden Lady mine when she is a child. The influence of gold on a variety of characters is traced over the years from the 1880s to the Depression.

Historical Accuracy: The novel provides an authentic picture of mining life during the period.

2284 *The Great Betrayal*

Date of Publication: 1948
Subject(s): American West; Sand Creek Massacre; Indians
Fictional character(s): Kendall Lobach, Banker
Time Period(s): 1860s
Locale(s): Fort Lyon, Colorado

Summary: A regiment of volunteer cavalry massacres an encampment of friendly indians at Sand Creek in the Colorado territory. The novel chronicles the event and its aftermath, and connects it to a fictional story involving the banker Kendall Lobach.

Historical Accuracy: The novel is faithful to the actual events and is painstaking in its accuracy.

2285 *Snow-Water*

Date of Publication: 1939
Subject(s): Family Saga; American West
Historical character(s): Daniel Bartor, Pioneer
Time Period(s): 19th century; 20th century (1868-1934)
Locale(s): Bartorville, Colorado

Summary: The creation and development of a Western town is chronicled from its founding by pioneer Daniel Bartor, whose irrigation scheme to bring water from the snow cap of the mountains makes development possible.

Historical Accuracy: The novel is best in its portrait of the earliest days of the town's settlement and the details of frontier life.

JOHN ROLFE GARDINER (1937-)

American novelist and short-story writer Gardiner grew up in suburban Fairfax County, Virginia, and worked as a reporter for *Broadcasting Magazine* in Washington, D.C.

2286 *Great Dream From Heaven*

Date of Publication: 1974
Subject(s): Labor Movement; Mining
Fictional character(s): Eugene Daniels, Labor Leader
Time Period(s): 1880s
Locale(s): Coal Creek, Tennessee

Summary: Eugene Daniels, a young labor organizer, is sent by the Knights of Labor to Tennessee coal country to stir up interest in labor unions. The miners see him as a dreamer, while the coal companies see him as a dangerous rabblerouser. He sets off an explosion of violence and labor conflict in this novel set during the early years of the union movement.

Historical Accuracy: The story is fictional but backed by genuine regional and period details.

JOHN E. GARDNER (1926-)

An English writer born in Northumberland, Gardner graduated from St. John's College, Cambridge. He served as a commando in the Royal Marines during World War II in the Far and Middle East. Gardner now lives in the U.S. and is the author of mysteries and thrillers, including several James Bond adventures. His novels include *The Liquidator*, *Ice Breaker*, and *Nobody Loves Forever*.

2287 *The Return of Moriarty*

Date of Publication: 1974
Subject(s): Mystery; Victorian Period
Fictional character(s): James Moriarty, Criminal, Professor; Sherlock Holmes, Detective—Private; Angus McCready Crow, Police Officer (inspector)
Historical character(s): Edward, Prince of Wales, Royalty (Prince of Wales)
Time Period(s): 1890s (1894)
Locale(s): London, England

Summary: The archrival of Sherlock Holmes, Professor Moriarty, is back in London after his fatal Swiss rendezvous with Holmes in 1891. His criminal empire is in disarray, and the novel follows Moriarty's devious schemes aimed at destabilizing the world. Inspector Angus Crow's mission is to thwart and capture the criminal mastermind.

Historical Accuracy: The novel captures the era with skill.

MONA GARDNER (1900-)

Gardner was born in Seattle and received an A.B. from Stanford University in 1920. She has contributed articles to such periodicals as the *New Yorker*, *McCall's*, *Saturday Evening Post*, and the *Atlantic Monthly*.

2288 *Hong Kong*

Date of Publication: 1958
Subject(s): Opium War; East/West Relations; Chinese Empire
Fictional character(s): Gill Bennett, Trader; Zena d'Almada, Gentlewoman
Time Period(s): 1830s; 1840s
Locale(s): Hong Kong; China

Summary: The novel chronicles the founding of Hong Kong and the turmoil of the Opium Wars as the Chinese struggle to rid their country of outsiders. Gill Bennett is newly-arrived in Macao and plans to make his fortune from opium. He is quickly caught up in dangerous intrigue.

Historical Accuracy: Filled with period touches, the background to this fictional story is authentic.

RICHARD GARDNER (1931-)

An American born in Washington, Gardner graduated from Washington State College. He has worked for radio and TV stations as a performer, puppeteer, producer, and director. He became a full-time writer in 1961, and has lived in Spain, Turkey, and England. His novel *Scandalous John* was made into a film in 1974.

2289 *The Adventures of Don Juan*

Date of Publication: 1974
Subject(s): Royalty—Spain; Inquisition; Picaresque Adventure
Fictional character(s): Ripio de Rebombar, Businessman (theatrical producer); Don Juan Lucero, Gentleman
Historical character(s): Philip III, Ruler (King of Spain); Tirso de Molina, Writer (playwright), Religious (monk)
Time Period(s): 17th century (1620s)
Locale(s): Madrid, Spain

Summary: In the 1620s in Spain a play depicting the exploits of the infamous seducer Don Juan suggests that he is a member of Philip III's court. The basis of the play is a diary that details the exploits of one of the most fascinating figures of legend and presents his life from his childhood to his trial by the Spanish Inquisition.

Historical Accuracy: The novel features a convincing look at the political intrigues of Philip's court as well as the theatrical world of the period.

BRIAN GARFIELD (1939-)

Garfield grew up in Arizona, worked on a cattle ranch and rode in rodeos as well as working for a time as a professional jazz musician. Since 1970 he has written one or two books a year, what he calls ''suspense fiction''—not quite mysteries, not quite adventure tales, and not quite romances. He won an Edgar Award in 1976 for *Hopscotch* and an American Book Award nomination in 1980 for *Wild Times*, which was presented as a TV mini series in 1980. His books have sold over 12 million copies and have been translated into 17 languages.

2290 *Manifest Destiny*

Date of Publication: 1989
Subject(s): American West; Biography, Fictionalized
Historical character(s): Theodore Roosevelt, Rancher; Marquis de Mores, Rancher; Medora de Mores, Spouse
Time Period(s): 1880s (1884-1885)
Locale(s): Dakota Territory, United States

Summary: In 1884 Theodore Roosevelt's life is in shambles: his mother and bride die on the same day, and for consolation and recovery, T.R. heads west to the Badlands to take up ranching. He must contend with the Marquis De Mores and a band of night-riding vigilantes determined to rid the area of small ranchers like Roosevelt.

Historical Accuracy: The events are based on fact, but, in an attempt to put history in tidier order, events have been simplified.

2291 *Wild Times*

Date of Publication: 1978
Subject(s): American West
Fictional character(s): Hugh Cardiff, Frontiersman, Entertainer

Historical character(s): William F. Cody, Frontiersman, Entertainer; James Butler Hickok, Frontiersman; Wyatt Earp, Lawman
Time Period(s): 19th century; 20th century (1868-1922)
Locale(s): West; New York, New York

Summary: This is the fictional autobiography of western legend Hugh Cardiff, the champion rifle shot of the world, hero of dime novels and the Wild West Show. Cardiff sets the record straight and details western life that shows him as a sharpshooter, fugitive, Indian fighter, buffalo hunter, actor, moviemaker, and finally, genuine western myth.

Historical Accuracy: The author makes it clear that this is a work of fiction and even the historical figures who appear are not meant to be taken as actual. However, the incidents are based upon facts.

LEON GARFIELD (1921-)

An English novelist born in Brighton, Garfield's art teaching was interrupted by service in World War II in the medical corps. He has also worked as a biochemist. Garfield is generally considered one of the most innovative writers of historical fiction in the field of juvenile literature, though he sees his novels as written for all ages. Inspired by Greek myths, Bible stories, and Victorian novels, Garfield resists the notion that he writes historical fiction, calling the past more a locality than a time.

2292 *The House of Cards*

Date of Publication: 1982
Subject(s): Victorian Period
Fictional character(s): Mr. Dolly, Businessman; David Kozlowski, Young Man; Katerina Kropotka, Streetperson
Time Period(s): 1850s (1859)
Locale(s): London, England

Summary: In 1859 in Victorian London, Mr. Dolly gives a dinner party above his pickled herring shop. His guests include David Kozlowski, a young man newly arrived from Poland, and the unexpected, mysterious Katerina Kropotka who will be the agent for exposing some buried secrets and initiate the novel's intrigue and adventure.

Historical Accuracy: The novel offers an authentic version of Victorian London and a convincing echoing of both Charles Dickens and Joseph Conrad.

2293 *The Pleasure Garden*

Date of Publication: 1976
Subject(s): Crime and Criminals; Georgian Period
Fictional character(s): Orpheus Jones, Writer (poet); Martin Young, Religious (priest); Brisker, Child
Time Period(s): 18th century
Locale(s): London, England

Summary: This novel of blackmail and murder is set in the Mulberry Pleasure Gardens of London. A variety of characters find themselves the victims of a blackmail ring in this atmospheric evocation of Hogarthian London.

Historical Accuracy: Garfield is masterful and convincing in re-creating the atmosphere and setting of the period.

2294 *The Prisoners of September*

Date of Publication: 1975
Subject(s): French Revolution
Fictional character(s): Lewis Boston, Gentleman; Richard Mortimer, Nobleman, Revolutionary; Countess de la Motte-Valois, Noblewoman
Time Period(s): 1780s; 1790s (1789-1793)
Locale(s): Paris, France

Summary: Two young Englishmen, Lewis Boston and Richard Mortimer, by chance encounter a renegade French countess during the French Revolution, and all three are swept up in the horror of the September Massacre. Both Lewis and Richard lose their illusions under the pressure of the great events of the Revolution.

Historical Accuracy: The details of the September Massacre are authentically presented.

2295 *The Sound of Coaches*

Date of Publication: 1974
Subject(s): Stagecoaches
Fictional character(s): Sam, Foundling; Jenny, Servant (chambermaid); Daniel Coventry, Actor
Time Period(s): 18th century
Locale(s): England

Summary: A foundling is adopted by an old coachman and his wife in this tale of 18th century England. Sam dreams of his legacy and parentage. Was his father a daring highwayman? His progress toward his sense of identity is worked out in a series of complications and comedy that teach him more about his nature than his heritage.

Historical Accuracy: The novel is a tour de force in a convincing evocation of the period.

HAMLIN GARLAND (1860-1940)

Born in Wisconsin, Garland grew up in a middle western farming community that he celebrated in his poetry, stories, and autobiographies. His stories are collected in *Main-Travelled Roads*. Garland is best remembered for his two autobiographical works, *A Son of the Middle Border* and *A Daughter of the Middle Border*, which won the Pulitzer Prize in 1921. His realistic novels of prairie life include *A Little Norsk* and *Rose of Dutcher's Coolly*. Garland also wrote a biography of Ulysses S. Grant and several books on spiritualism.

2296 *Trail-Makers of the Middle Border*

Date of Publication: 1926
Subject(s): Biography, Fictionalized; Civil War—U.S.
Historical character(s): Richard Garland, Military Personnel (Union soldier)
Time Period(s): 19th century
Locale(s): Maine; Wisconsin; Illinois

Summary: This fictionalized biography of the author's father portrays his youth on a Maine farm, his pioneer days in Wisconsin, and his participation in the Civil War.

Historical Accuracy: The depiction of the period is authentic, particularly in its treatment of the Civil War.

DAVID GARNETT (1892-1981)

English author Garnett was the last surviving member of the Bloomsbury Group that included Virginia and Leonard Woolf. Garnett became a bookseller after service as a conscientious objector in World War I. His first novel, *Lady into Fox*, was an instant literary success. Garnett was a pilot during World War II and wrote graphic accounts of the Battle of Britain. He is best known as a writer of short fantasies. Among his books are *A Man in the Zoo*, *The Sailor's Return*, and *A Shot in the Dark*.

`2297` *Pocahontas; or, The Nonparell of Virginia*

Date of Publication: 1933
Subject(s): American Colonies; Indians
Historical character(s): Pocahontas, Indian; John Smith, Settler; John Rolfe, Settler
Time Period(s): 17th century
Locale(s): Jamestown, Virginia, American Colonies; England

Summary: The novel recounts the familiar tale of Indian princess Pocahontas, who is shown as a child growing up in the forests of Virginia. She rescues settler John Smith and aids the starving colonists. Later, married to John Rolfe, she voyages to England, where she dies of smallpox.

Historical Accuracy: The novel attempts a realistic portrait of Virginia during the period of its earliest settlement. In the main it succeeds, though its realism is augmented with a number of romantic inventions.

`2298` *Up She Rises*

Date of Publication: 1977
Subject(s): Napoleonic Wars
Fictional character(s): Clementina Carey, Spouse; Peter Lamond, Military Personnel (naval officer)
Time Period(s): 18th century; 19th century
Locale(s): Scotland; England; Russia

Summary: The novel tells the story of Clementina Carey, the daughter of a poor Scottish crofter, and her amazing rise to fortune. She marries Peter Lamont who in turn has risen from being press-ganged into the British Navy to become master of his own fleet. Clementina endures an epic trek on foot from Scotland to Portsmouth to join her husband. She then accompanies him to France, Germany, and the court of Nicholas I of Russia.

Historical Accuracy: The heroine of the novel is the author's great-grandmother and the events are based on fact.

MARY A. GARRATT

`2299` *The Asherwood Protegee*

Date of Publication: 1982
Subject(s): Regency Romance
Fictional character(s): Donna Thomas, Gentlewoman
Historical character(s): Arthur Wellesley, Nobleman (Duke of Wellington)
Time Period(s): 1810s (1816)
Locale(s): London, England

Summary: This adventure in fashionable Regency London centers on the first London season of young Donna Thomas. Her adventures take place at balls and in drawing rooms and include an appearance by the Duke of Wellington, fresh from his victory at Waterloo.

Historical Accuracy: The plot is conventional but offers more than the usual quota of period details.

GEORGE GARRETT (1929-)

A distinguished American writer of fiction, poetry, plays, and criticism, Garrett is a professor of creative writing at the University of Virginia. His trilogy (*Death of the Fox*, *The Succession*, and *Entered From the Sun*) meticulously and poetically recreates the life and times of Elizabethan England.

`2300` *Death of the Fox*

Date of Publication: 1971
Subject(s): Elizabethan Period; Royalty—England
Historical character(s): Sir Walter Raleigh, Nobleman, Courtier; Elizabeth I, Ruler (Queen of England); James I, Ruler (King of England and Scotland); Robert Cecil, Nobleman, Courtier; Sir Francis Bacon, Courtier, Nobleman; Robert Devereux, Nobleman, Courtier
Time Period(s): 16th century; 17th century (1577-1618)
Locale(s): London, England

Summary: The Fox is Sir Walter Raleigh, the consummate Renaissance man: courtier, explorer, poet, and intellectual. He is a great favorite of Elizabeth but a great enemy of the next king, James I. Garrett chronicles Raleigh's rise and fall in a "work of fiction, of the imagination, planted and rooted in fact.".

Historical Accuracy: Garrett's ability to evoke the Elizabethan era, while writing a highly imaginative modern work of fiction redefines the standard of the modern historical novel.

`2301` *Entered From the Sun*

Date of Publication: 1990
Subject(s): Elizabethan Period; Literary Life; Crime and Criminals
Fictional character(s): Joseph Hunnyman, Actor, Detective—Amateur; Captain Barfoot, Military Personnel (retired soldier), Detective—Amateur
Historical character(s): Ben Jonson, Writer (poet and playwright); William Shakespeare, Writer (poet and playwright)
Time Period(s): 16th century (1597)

Locale(s): London, England

Summary: In this completion of Garrett's trilogy of the Elizabethan period, the subject is a famous murder mystery: why was poet, playwright, and possible spy Christopher Marlowe killed in a dispute among friends at a tavern? This actual event and the little that is known about it fuels an investigation by two very different amateur detectives: an actor and an aging army veteran. They uncover much about Elizabethan life and culture in addition to some provocative speculation about Marlowe's demise.

Historical Accuracy: This is an impressive revival of the past that is in turn brutal, tender, sordid, and magical.

2302 *The Succession: A Novel of Elizabeth and James*

Date of Publication: 1983
Subject(s): Elizabethan Period; Royalty—England
Historical character(s): Elizabeth I, Ruler (Queen of England); James I, Ruler (King of England and Scotland); Robert Cecil, Nobleman, Courtier; Robert Carey, Nobleman, Courtier; Robert Devereux, Nobleman, Courtier
Time Period(s): 16th century; 17th century (1566-1626)
Locale(s): London, England; Scotland

Summary: The second of Garrett's Elizabethan trilogy, it takes as its theme the central political question of the time: Who will succeed the aging and heir-less Elizabeth, a Catholic or Protestant? A Scotsman or one of the many European pretenders to the throne? Told in a series of voices of real and imagined witnesses (a messenger, a priest, an actor), the effect is a kind of grand choral orchestration of an age.

Historical Accuracy: Garret redefines the way an historical period can be recreated as a modern novel of the past.

OMAR V. GARRISON (1913-)

Born in Colorado, Garrison worked as a newspaper reporter and editor for Reuters in London during World War II and as the science editor for the Los Angeles *Mirror-News*. His books include *Spy Government*, *Howard Hughes in Las Vegas*, and *The Hidden Story of Scientology*.

2303 *Balboa: Conquistador*

Date of Publication: 1971
Subject(s): Exploration
Historical character(s): Vasco Nunez de Balboa, Explorer
Time Period(s): 16th century (1501-1517)
Locale(s): Panama

Summary: This novel depicts Balboa's exploration of Panama and covers the years from 1501 to Balboa's death. In contrast to the other Spanish conquistadors, Balboa is shown as enlightened in his treatment of the Indians.

Historical Accuracy: The novel's account is believable, capturing the atmosphere of the Spanish conquest.

DAVID GARTH

2304 *Fire on the Wind*

Date of Publication: 1951
Subject(s): Reconstruction Period; Railroads; Lumber Industry
Fictional character(s): Wayne Preston, Veteran (Civil War)
Time Period(s): 1860s (post-Civil War)
Locale(s): Upper Peninsula, Michigan

Summary: In the Upper Peninsula of Michigan in the years following the Civil War, young Wayne Preston turns down a job with the Union Pacific to help his father develop Michigan's vast timber lands.

Historical Accuracy: The novel is filled with authentic details of logging and the timber industry that create a believable background for the story.

2305 *Gray Canaan*

Date of Publication: 1947
Subject(s): Civil War—U.S.; Battle of Bull Run; Espionage
Fictional character(s): Racewell Emery, Military Personnel (Confederate captain); Holly Charles, Young Woman
Time Period(s): 1860s (1862)
Locale(s): Richmond, Virginia; Washington, District of Columbia

Summary: This Civil War tale of espionage considers what might have been for Confederate fortunes in 1862 if Plan Canaan—the detachment of Jackson from Lee's company to strike the Union west of the Alleghenies—had been put into operation. The plan falls into Union hands, and Confederate cavalry officer Racewell Emery sets out to retrieve it against a contingent of Northern operatives.

Historical Accuracy: The novel's history is mainly fanciful, but the depictions of Richmond and Washington during the period contain many believable details.

CHLOE GARTNER (1916-)

Born in Kansas, Gartner attended the University of California, Berkeley, Mesa College, and Marin College. She worked for the *San Francisco Chronicle* as a research assistant. Her books include *The Drums of Khartoum*, *Woman of the Glen*, and *Greenleaf*.

2306 *Anne Bonny*

Date of Publication: 1977
Subject(s): Sea Story; Pirates; Biography, Fictionalized
Historical character(s): Anne Bonny, Pirate
Time Period(s): 18th century
Locale(s): Charleston, South Carolina; American Colonies; West Indies

Summary: The life story of pirate Anne Bonny is described beginning with her early years in Charlestown as the daughter of a well-to-do gentleman. She forsakes that world for the life of a pirate. What little is known about Bonny's notorious career supports a colorful tale of shipboard and outlaw life.

Historical Accuracy: The basic framework of the novel's story is historical. Considerable imaginative embellishments fill out the portrait of Bonny.

2307 *Drums of Khartoum*

Date of Publication: 1967
Subject(s): English Colonies; Siege of Khartoum
Fictional character(s): Victoria Hubbard, Gentlewoman; Gavin Graham, Military Personnel (British officer); Charles Blair, Doctor
Historical character(s): Charles George Gordon, Military Personnel (general); Muhammad Ahmad, Leader (Muslim), Fanatic; Horatio Herbert Kitchener, Military Personnel (British officer)
Time Period(s): 1880s (1884)
Locale(s): Khartoum, Sudan

Summary: In 1884, as the rest of Anglo-Egyptian Sudan falls to the forces of the Mahdi's Dervish army, Victoria Hubbard returns to her birth place at Khartoum. She finds herself at the center of the seige and the heroic resistance by General Gordon.

Historical Accuracy: The story is invented but the historical background is accurate and convincing.

2308 *The Infidels*

Date of Publication: 1960
Subject(s): Middle Ages; Crusades
Fictional character(s): Justin Le Noir, Knight
Time Period(s): 11th century (1099)
Locale(s): France; Palestine

Summary: This tale of the First Crusade follows the exploits of a young French knight, Justin Le Noir, on the long journey across Europe to the walls of Jerusalem. The novel provides a realistic portrait of the lot of the crusaders and the curious contradictions between their spiritual goal and its reality.

Historical Accuracy: Despite the realistic tone, the novel's historical basis is weak, and a number of inaccuracies are present.

2309 *Mistress of The Highlands*

Date of Publication: 1976
Subject(s): Civil War—England; Covenanters
Fictional character(s): Katrine Fraser, Young Woman; Nicholas Dunn, Laird; Sandy Dunn, Laird
Time Period(s): 17th century (1628-1650)
Locale(s): Scotland

Summary: This is the tale of the troubles of the Scottish Covenanters in the days of Charles I. Katrine Fraser must endure the turmoil and struggles of the times as she is caught up in the political events that climax in war.

Historical Accuracy: Katrine's story is invented but the events and customs of the time are authentic.

2310 *The Woman from The Glen*

Date of Publication: 1973

Subject(s): Jacobite Rebellion; Battle of Culloden; Georgian Period
Fictional character(s): Jennie MacAllan, Young Woman, Twin; Pollux MacAllan, Young Man, Twin
Historical character(s): Charles Edward Stuart, Royalty (prince)
Time Period(s): 1740s
Locale(s): Scotland

Summary: The novel describes the efforts to restore the Stuarts to the British throne. Jennie MacAllan and her twin brother Pollux join Bonnie Prince Charlie's cause and endure hunger, betrayal, and warfare culminating in the crushing defeat at Culloden.

Historical Accuracy: The story is fictional but the events described are based on fact.

JULIE GARWOOD (1946-)

An American from Kansas City, Missouri, Garwood attended Avila College. She is the author of historical novels, romances, and novels for young adults. Her works include *The Lion's Lady*, *Guardian Angel*, and *The Prize*.

2311 *The Bride*

Date of Publication: 1989
Subject(s): Romance; Middle Ages
Fictional character(s): Jamie Jamison, Noblewoman; Alec Kincaid, Laird
Time Period(s): 12th century (1102)
Locale(s): Scotland; England

Summary: Set in the cultural conflict between the Scots and the English in the 12th century, this romantic novel depicts the forced marriage between Scottish laird Kincaid and Englishwoman Jamie Jamison.

Historical Accuracy: The period background is authentically presented.

ELIZABETH GASKELL (1810-1865)

English novelist Gaskell was raised in Knutsford, Cheshire, the setting of several of her novels of provincial English life. She married a Unitarian minister and lived near Manchester where she raised a large family and produced several novels. Her major works are *Mary Barton*, *Cranford*, *North and South*, and *Wives and Daughters*. They are distinguished by their humor, perceptive characterization, and accurate descriptions of English life and customs. She also wrote the first biographical study of the Bronte family in *Life of Charlotte Bronte*.

2312 *Sylvia's Lovers*

Date of Publication: 1863
Subject(s): Napoleonic Wars
Fictional character(s): Sylvia Robson, Young Woman; Philip Hepburn, Clerk; Charley Kinraid, Sailor
Time Period(s): 1790s; 1800s
Locale(s): Yorkshire, England; Acre, Ottoman Empire

Summary: Mrs. Gaskell's only historical novel is set during the Napoleonic Wars and involves the conflict between Sylvia Robson's two suitors, Philip Hepburn, a draper's shop assistant, and seaman Charley Kinraid. When Kinraid is taken by a naval press gang, Philip reports to Sylvia that Kinraid has drowned so that he may win her hand. When Kinraid returns, Hepburn runs away to join the army. He meets his rival again at the siege of Acre where Hepburn saves Kinraid's life.

Historical Accuracy: The novel uses accurate historical background material and authentic period details, particularly concerning the workings of the naval press gangs.

CATHERINE GASKIN (1929-)

Irish writer Gaskin was born in Dundalk and educated at Holy Cross College, Sydney, Australia. She lives on the Isle of Man, and her novels have been translated into eleven languages, including Hebrew, Turkish, and Japanese.

2313 *Blake's Reach*

Date of Publication: 1958
Subject(s): French Revolution; Crime and Criminals
Fictional character(s): Jane Howard, Young Woman
Time Period(s): 1790s
Locale(s): Kent, England

Summary: This novel of suspense and romance is set during the French Revolution and involves the efforts of Jane Howard to restore a family manor in Kent. She finds herself involved with a smuggling ring.

Historical Accuracy: The historical background is only dimly suggested.

2314 *A Falcon for a Queen*

Date of Publication: 1972
Subject(s): Gothic Romance; Victorian Period
Fictional character(s): Kirsty Howard, Young Woman; Angus MacDonald, Gentleman; Gavin Campbell, Gentleman
Time Period(s): 1900s (1901-1902)
Locale(s): Highlands, Scotland

Summary: Kirsty Howard journeys from China to the Scottish Highlands when her brother mysteriously dies on a visit to the home of Kirsty's grandfather. Long hidden secrets bring Kirsty both revelations about her family and danger in this gothic tale of clan conflict.

Historical Accuracy: The standard gothic elements are featured, but the regional details provide a solid and convincing background.

2315 *I Know My Love*

Date of Publication: 1961
Subject(s): Frontier—Australia
Fictional character(s): Adam Langley, Sea Captain; Rose Maguire, Young Woman; Emma Brown, Spouse (of Langley)
Time Period(s): 1850s
Locale(s): Australia

Summary: This romantic tale set in mid-19th-century Australia during its gold rush days describes a romantic triangle involving sea captain Adam Langley. Langley marries the English Emma Brown but also loves Rose Maguire, an Irish girl. Their mutual attraction is played out over a number of years and disappointments.

Historical Accuracy: The novel blends its romantic plot with a realistically described period background.

2316 *Sara Dane*

Date of Publication: 1954
Subject(s): English Colonies; Crime and Criminals
Fictional character(s): Sara Dane, Convict; Andrew Maclay, Military Personnel (naval officer)
Historical character(s): William Bligh, Government Official (colonial governor)
Time Period(s): 18th century; 19th century
Locale(s): New South Wales, Australia

Summary: This story, based in part on an actual account, traces the experiences of a young woman, Sara Dane, who is transported as a convict from England in the 1790s and rises to prominence in the Australian Colony of New South Wales.

Historical Accuracy: The novel is not intended as an accurate account but as a general outline of the times.

WILLIAM H. GASS (1924-)

American writer Gass was born in North Dakota and graduated from Kenyon College and Cornell University. A professor of philosophy at Washington University, St. Louis, Gass is a distinguished and acclaimed essayist and fiction writer who has earned a reputation as a most accomplished stylist. His works include *The Tunnel, In the Heart of the Heart of the Country*, and *Fiction and the Figures of Life*.

2317 *Omensetter's Luck*

Date of Publication: 1966
Subject(s): Rural Life—U.S.; Religious Life
Fictional character(s): Brackett Omensetter, Farmer; Jethro Furber, Religious (clergyman); Henry Pimber, Landowner
Time Period(s): 1890s
Locale(s): Gilean, Ohio (fictional town)

Summary: This dense exploration of the nature of good and evil is set in Ohio during the 1890s. Brackett Omensetter comes to the small Ohio community of Gilean possessing a rare innocence and luck that disturbs many, including the Reverend Jethro Furber and Omensetter's landlord, Henry Pimber.

Historical Accuracy: Deeply felt and provocative, the novel reaches levels of the universal and the mythical, though based on a convincing period setting.

CATHERINE GAVIN (1907-)

A Scottish-born writer from Aberdeen, Gavin graduated from the University of Aberdeen and taught as a history professor at Aberdeen and the University of Glasgow. She also worked as a reporter and foreign correspondent for

London's *Daily Express* in the Middle East and Ethiopia. Active in Scottish politics in the 1930s, Gavin was twice elected as a Conservative candidate for Parliament.

`2318` *The Cactus and the Crown*

Date of Publication: 1962
Subject(s): Mexican Revolution
Fictional character(s): Andrew Lorimer, Doctor; Sally Lorimer, Young Woman; Pierre Franchet, Military Personnel (French soldier)
Historical character(s): Maximilian, Ruler (Emperor of Mexico); Carlota, Royalty (empress consort of Maximilian)
Time Period(s): 1860s (post Civil War)
Locale(s): Mexico

Summary: The tragic reign of Maximilian and Carlota in Mexico is the background for this novel involving the interlocked fates of three individuals—Americans Andrew and Sally Lorimer and French soldier Pierre Franchet. Andrew, a former field surgeon with the Confederate army has come to Mexico with his sister to start afresh. He becomes one of the doctors who tries to stop Carlota's drift into madness as Mexico teeters on the brink of revolution.

Historical Accuracy: The history of Maximilian and Carlota is authentically presented.

`2319` *The Devil in Harbour*

Date of Publication: 1968
Subject(s): World War I; Battle of Jutland; Espionage
Fictional character(s): Elena Petrovna, Dancer (ballet); David Flett, Military Personnel (sailor); Ingrid Sabiston, Gentlewoman
Historical character(s): John Rushworth Jellicoe, Military Personnel (British admiral)
Time Period(s): 1910s (1914-1916)
Locale(s): Petrograd, Russia; London, England; Scapa Flow, Scotland

Summary: This story of espionage and naval action in the First World War ranges from Petrograd to Scapa Flow and culminates in the war's only major naval battle at Jutland. The web of conspiracy involves a Russian ballerina, a young Scottish sailor, and his lover.

Historical Accuracy: The novel blends the factual and the fictional. The description of the Battle of Jutland is authentic and reliable.

`2320` *The Fortress*

Date of Publication: 1964
Subject(s): Crimean War; Sea Story
Fictional character(s): Brand Endicott, Sea Captain; Alexandra Gyllenlove, Patriot
Time Period(s): 1850s (1854-1855)
Locale(s): St. Petersburg, Russia; At Sea (in the Baltic); Finland

Summary: The Crimean War's other theater, the Baltic, is the scene for the novel's adventure and romance. An American merchant sea captain, out of love for a Finnish patriot, joins the British navy to fight the Russians. The action climaxes

with the victory over the Russians at the fortress of Sveaborg, the key to the Gulf of Finland.

Historical Accuracy: Well researched and detailed, the novel's operations are based on fact.

`2321` *Give Me the Daggers*

Date of Publication: 1972
Subject(s): World War I; Russian Revolution
Fictional character(s): Tom Fleming, Veteran; Boris Heiden, Revolutionary; Nancy Macpherson, Young Woman
Historical character(s): Gustaf Mannerheim, Military Personnel (general)
Time Period(s): 1910s (1917-1918)
Locale(s): Finland; London, England; Zurich, Switzerland

Summary: Set during the turmoil of the Russian Revolution, the novel details the adventures of a Canadian soldier, Tom Fleming, who is sent on a mission to bring two English agents out of Russia. Fleming is quickly involved in a clash of wills with a Russian revolutionary, Boris Heiden, and the strong-willed Nancy Macpherson.

Historical Accuracy: The author points out that the novel is a composite of fact and fiction.

`2322` *The House of War*

Date of Publication: 1970
Subject(s): Independence—Turkey
Fictional character(s): Evelyn Barrett, Young Woman
Historical character(s): Kemal Ataturk, Military Personnel (soldier), Political Figure
Time Period(s): 1920s (1922)
Locale(s): Turkey

Summary: The novel details the war for Turkish independence in which Kemal Ataturk's outnumbered forces win a great victory over the Greek generals. Ataturk is shown as a brilliant military commander. A fictional romance with an American journalist's wife shows a different side of this great military leader.

Historical Accuracy: Despite the fictional invention of the romance, the action and atmosphere are convincing.

`2323` *Madeleine*

Date of Publication: 1957
Subject(s): Canal Building; Franco-Prussian War; Royalty—France
Fictional character(s): Madeleine d'Arbonne, Gentlewoman; James Bruce, Engineer
Historical character(s): Eugenie, Royalty (Empress of France); Ferdinand Marie de Lesseps, Engineer
Time Period(s): 1860s; 1870s (1869-1871)
Locale(s): Suez Canal, Egypt; Paris, France

Summary: This love story set in France's Second Empire begins with the opening of the Suez Canal in 1869 by the Empress Eugenie. In her entourage is Madeleine d'Arbonne who meets and falls in love with James Bruce, a Scottish marine engineer. Their affair continues in Paris at the outbreak of the Franco-Prussian War and during the siege of Paris.

Historical Accuracy: The historical details are reliable and accurate with strong period touches.

2324 *The Snow Mountain*

Date of Publication: 1973
Subject(s): Russian Revolution; Royalty—Russia; World War I
Historical character(s): Nicholas II, Ruler (Czar of Russia); Olga, Grand Duchess of Russia, Royalty
Time Period(s): 1910s (1914-1918)
Locale(s): St. Petersburg, Russia; Siberia, Russia; Finland

Summary: The final years of Nicholas II and his family are chronicled from the perspective of his eldest daughter, Olga. The court world that is soon to be shattered by the revolution is detailed in this drama that graphically depicts the Bolshevik uprising and the beginning of the Soviet regime.

Historical Accuracy: The historical details are authentic and convincing.

THOMAS GAVIN

American writer Gaskin has taught in both elementary schools and high schools. He is currently a professor of English at Middlebury College.

2325 *Kingkill*

Date of Publication: 1977
Subject(s): Chess
Fictional character(s): William Schlumberger, Handicapped (hunchback); Henri Rouault, Gentleman; Louise Rouault, Spouse
Time Period(s): 1820s
Locale(s): Paris, France

Summary: This novel is based on the historical facts of a hoax by a Viennese confidence man who claimed to have created an automatic chess player which could beat chess champions. Hunchbacked William Schlumberger's obsession with Louise Rouault is the one thing to divert him from his passion for chess.

Historical Accuracy: Inventive and imaginative, the novel paints a convincing period picture of 19th century Paris.

LAVERNE GAY (1914-)

Born in Lodi, California, Gay learned her enthusiasm for historical subjects from her Irish grandfather. She was educated at the University of California and has tught high school. Her novels include *Wine of Satan*, *A Tale of Bohemond, Prince of Antioch* and *The Unspeakables*.

2326 *The Unspeakables: A Tale of Lombardy*

Date of Publication: 1945
Subject(s): Dark Ages
Fictional character(s): Theudelinda, Royalty (princess)
Historical character(s): Authari, Ruler (Lombard king); Gregory the Great, Religious (pope)

Time Period(s): 6th century
Locale(s): Lombardy, Italy; Rome, Italy

Summary: The story of the Lombards' rule in Northern Italy during the 6th century is described. The story focuses on the reign of Authari, the Lombard king and his wife, Theudelinda. The achievements of Gregory the Great are also chronicled.

Historical Accuracy: The author's knowledge of the history and the archaeology of the period is evident.

2327 *Wine of Satan*

Date of Publication: 1949
Subject(s): Crusades; Middle Ages; Byzantine Empire
Historical character(s): Bohemond I, Nobleman (Prince of Antioch), Leader (of the First Crusade); Robert Guiscard, Nobleman; Alexius I Comnenus, Ruler (Byzantine emperor)
Time Period(s): 11th century; 12th century
Locale(s): Italy; Antioch, Syria; Byzantine Empire

Summary: The novel tells the story of Bohemond I, the great military leader of the First Crusade. Bohemond is born Marc de Hauteville, son of Count Guiscard, who barely recognizes his offspring. Bohemond draws strength from this rejection and becomes the central figure in the Crusades and the battles against Alexius I.

Historical Accuracy: The novel is filled with exciting adventure yet careful in offering an attentive look at the period.

MARGARET COOPER GAY

2328 *Hatchet in the Sky*

Date of Publication: 1954
Subject(s): French and Indian War; Indians
Fictional character(s): David Caithris, Laird
Historical character(s): Henry Gladwin, Military Personnel (major); Pontiac, Indian (Ottawa), Chieftain
Time Period(s): 1760s
Locale(s): Northwest Territory, United States; Detroit, Michigan

Summary: Set during the French and Indian War and Pontiac's Rebellion, the novel is narrated by David Caithris, an exiled Scottish laird. His experiences reflect the scene on the western frontier following the British victory over the French and the Indian retaliation.

Historical Accuracy: The novel is filled with authentic period details, but the romantic plot undermines credibility with its over-reliance on coincidence and idealized characters.

KATHLEEN O'NEAL GEAR

Kathleen O'Neal Gear is a former state historian and archaeologist of Wyoming, Kansas, and Nebraska for the U.S. Department of the Interior. She is best known for her series of novels written with her husband W. Michael Gear chronicling North American prehistory.

2329 *Sand in the Wind*

Date of Publication: 1990

Subject(s): American West; Indians
Fictional character(s): Wounded Bear, Indian (Cheyenne), Shaman; Colleen Merrill, Young Woman; Matthew Douglas, Military Personnel (cavalry lieutenant)
Time Period(s): 1870s
Locale(s): Nebraska; Montana

Summary: Colleen Merrill, who has come west by wagon train with her abusive husband, is attracted to both Wounded Bear, a Cheyenne shaman, and Matthew Douglas, a cavalry officer.

Historical Accuracy: The novel offers an interesting situation, illustrated with convincing period details.

2330 *Thin Moon and Cold Mist*

Date of Publication: 1995
Subject(s): Civil War—U.S.; Battle of the Wilderness; American West
Fictional character(s): Robin Heatherton, Spy (Confederate); Thomas Corley, Military Personnel (Union officer)
Time Period(s): 1860s (1864-1865)
Locale(s): Virginia; Colorado

Summary: Set during the Civil War, the novel tells the story of Robin Heatherton, a spy for the Confederacy, who infiltrates the Union forces during the Battle of the Wilderness. When she is discovered, she must reach Confederate lines with vital information. Robin flees west after the war to work a mining claim, while Union major Thomas Corley is determined to find her and have her tried for treason.

Historical Accuracy: The background of the story is based on the actual career of a Confederate spy.

2331 *This Widowed Land*

Date of Publication: 1993
Subject(s): Indians; French Colonies; Religious Life
Fictional character(s): Andiora, Indian (Huron), Shaman; Marc Dupre, Religious (Jesuit missionary)
Historical character(s): Jean de Brebeuf, Religious (Jesuit missionary)
Time Period(s): 17th century
Locale(s): Canada

Summary: Set in New France in the 17th century, the novel tells the story of Father Marc Dupre, a French Jesuit missionary, and his mission to the Hurons. Andiora is a Huron shaman with whom he falls in love during a mysterious epidemic that ravages the Hurons.

Historical Accuracy: The novel is solidly researched and based on actual historical events.

W. MICHAEL GEAR

Gear has been a professor of archaeology since 1978. He also co-authors historical novels with his wife, Kathleen O'Neal Gear.

2332 *Bighorn Legacy*

Date of Publication: 1988
Subject(s): American West

Fictional character(s): Jeremiel Catton, Religious (minister); Bram Catton, Outlaw (horsetheif); Branton Brag, Murderer
Time Period(s): 1850s (1850)
Locale(s): St. Louis, Missouri; Sangre de Cristo Mountains, New Mexico

Summary: In this Western novel of vengeance, when Branton Brag settles an old score by killing Web Catton, the Catton family joins together to avenge the father's death and the lure of a fortune in gold.

Historical Accuracy: The period elements are authentic.

W. MICHAEL GEAR

KATHLEEN O'NEAL GEAR

W. Michael Gear holds an M.A. in anthropology and has worked as a professor of archaeology since 1978. His wife Kathleen O'Neal Gear is a former state historian and archaeologist for Wyoming, Kansas, and Nebraska for the U.S. Department of the Interior.

2333 *The Morning River*

Date of Publication: 1995
Subject(s): American West; Indians
Fictional character(s): Richard Hamilton, Student—College
Time Period(s): 1820s (1825)
Locale(s): St. Louis, Missouri; Great Plains

Summary: This is a revisionist frontier tale intended to debunk portraits of the Plains Indians as noble savages. Harvard philosophy student Richard Hamilton goes to St. Louis in 1825, where he is sold as an indentured servant for an adventure on the frontier. A series of brutal frontier encounters makes the author's realistic points clear.

Historical Accuracy: The novel provides a graphic and convincing portrait of life during the period.

2334 *People of the Earth*

Date of Publication: 1992
Subject(s): Prehistory; Tribal Life—Prehistoric
Fictional character(s): Brave Man, Prehistoric Human, Chieftain; Bad Belly/Still Water, Prehistoric Human; White Ash, Psychic (dreamer), Prehistoric Human
Time Period(s): 30th century B.C. (3000 B.C.)
Locale(s): North America

Summary: Tribal rivalries and territorial battles are prominent in this examination of prehistoric life in North America. As clans migrate southward along the Rocky Mountains, kidnapping and the powerful fetish, the Wolf Bundle, play important roles in the fate of the tribes.

Historical Accuracy: The narrative is backed up by solid research that makes this novel a vivid and believable reconstruction of the distant past.

2335 *People of the Fire*

Date of Publication: 1991
Subject(s): Prehistory; Tribal Life—Prehistoric

Fictional character(s): Little Dancer, Prehistoric Human; Hungry Bear, Prehistoric Human, Shaman
Time Period(s): 80th century B.C. (8000 B.C.)
Locale(s): Rocky Mountains, North America

Summary: In the second of the authors' series on North American prehistoric people, a small band of pioneers struggle to keep their ancestors' dreams alive in a drought stricken land.

Historical Accuracy: The background is solidly researched and convincing.

2336   *People of the Lakes*
Date of Publication: 1994
Subject(s): Indians; Tribal Life—Native American
Fictional character(s): Star Shell, Indian (Hopewell); Otter, Indian (Hopewell), Trader; Black Skull, Indian (Hopewell), Warrior
Time Period(s): 1st century
Locale(s): East, North America; Great Lakes, North America

Summary: In first century North America, the fate of the Hopewell Mound Builders is jeopardized by the corrupting influence of an evil totemic mask. Star Shell, the daughter of a Hopewell chief, is determined to save her people by carrying the mask northward across the Great Lakes to throw it into Niagra Falls. The novel describes her journey with a small band of companions.

Historical Accuracy: The novel's adventures are solidly backed by convincing evidence.

2337   *People of the Lightning*
Date of Publication: 1995
Subject(s): Prehistory; Tribal Life—Prehistoric
Fictional character(s): Pondwader, Prehistoric Human, Teenager; Musselwhite, Prehistoric Human, Warrior
Time Period(s): 50th century B.C.
Locale(s): North America (Florida)

Summary: The novel looks at prehistoric life in Florida. Pondwader, a teenager with white hair, pink eyes, and pale skin, is marked as the Lightning Boy, whose presence foretells disaster to come. His village trades him to the woman warrior Musselwhite, who is engaged in a battle to recapture her husband from the enemy. She underestimates the power of the Lightning Boy.

Historical Accuracy: The basis of the novel's fictional story is solidly detailed research that creates a credible sense of prehistoric tribal life.

2338   *People of the River*
Date of Publication: 1992
Subject(s): Indians; Tribal Life—Native American
Fictional character(s): Tharon, Indian, Chieftain; Nightshade, Indian, Shaman; Lichen, Indian, Young Woman; Fly Catcher, Indian, Warrior
Time Period(s): 6th century
Locale(s): Mississippi Valley, North America

Summary: The Mound Builders, a tribe of Indians living along the Mississippi, suffer from want and hunger. Their chief, Tharon, continues to demand his tribute. Lichen and Flycatcher come of age facing a future that is as unpredictable as the present is harsh and punishing.

Historical Accuracy: The novel offers a convincing portrait of tribal life.

2339   *People of the Sea*
Date of Publication: 1993
Subject(s): Prehistory; Tribal Life—Prehistoric
Fictional character(s): Sunchaser, Prehistoric Human, Shaman; Catchstraw, Prehistoric Human; Kestrel, Prehistoric Human, Runaway
Time Period(s): 130th century B.C. (13,000 B.C.)
Locale(s): Sierra Nevada Mountains, North America

Summary: In this portrait of life in North America 15,000 years ago, the glaciers are receding, and Sunchaser's people are deprived of large game with the disappearance of the mastodons. While Catchstraw uses witchcraft to undermine Sunchaser's authority, Kestrel, fleeing an abusive husband, joins the tribe. Many fear that she will bring retribution from the spirit world onto the tribe.

Historical Accuracy: The novel is based on anthropological and archaeological evidence that lends the story credibility.

2340   *People of the Silence*
Date of Publication: 1996
Subject(s): Indians; Tribal Life—Native American; Identity—Concealed
Fictional character(s): Cornsilk, Indian (Anasazi); Poor Singer, Indian (Anasazi)
Time Period(s): 12th century (1150)
Locale(s): Southwest, North America

Summary: As the Anasazi civilization in the Southwest collapses, the Great Sun Chief searches for a child his wife bore by another man. Unaware of the larger implications, Cornsilk and Poor Singer try to keep ahead of a killer who is stalking them.

Historical Accuracy: The era is evoked with characteristic thoroughness and confidence by the authors.

2341   *People of the Wolf*
Date of Publication: 1990
Subject(s): Prehistory; Tribal Life—Prehistoric
Fictional character(s): Heron, Prehistoric Human, Shaman; Runs in Light, Prehistoric Human, Hunter; Raven Hunter, Prehistoric Human, Warrior
Time Period(s): 130th century B.C. (Pleistocene Era (13,000 B.C.))
Locale(s): Asia; Bering Strait, Alaska, North America

Summary: In the first of the Gears' chronicle of prehistoric life in North America, Heron has a vision that Runs in Light will become Wolf Dreamer, a powerful shaman who will lead his people to a distant land. Raven Hunter is the rival for tribal power.

Historical Accuracy: The novel is an authentic depiction of prehistoric life supported by evident research and detailed anthropological and archaeological insights.

ERNEST GEBLER (1915-)

An Irishman born in Dublin, Gebler is a novelist, playwright, and screenwriter.

2342 *The Plymouth Adventure*

Date of Publication: 1950
Subject(s): Pilgrims; American Colonies
Historical character(s): John Alden, Settler (Pilgrim); William Bradford, Settler (Pilgrim); Miles Standish, Settler (Pilgrim); Massasoit, Indian (Wampanoag), Chieftain; Squanto, Indian (Pawtuxet), Guide
Time Period(s): 17th century (1620s)
Locale(s): Southampton, England; *Mayflower*, At Sea; Plymouth, Massachusetts, American Colonies

Summary: This is a story of the voyage of the *Mayflower* and the first few months of the Pilgrims' settlement in Massachusetts. The novel chronicles the personal conflicts and hardships suffered during the voyage as well as the struggles to carve a settlement out of the wilderness.

Historical Accuracy: This is a faithful representation of the *Mayflower* voyage.

PAULINE GEDGE (1945-)

Born in Aukland, New Zealand, Gedge lives in a rural community on the prairies of western Canada. She spent part of her childhood in England. She has received high praise for her series of novels recreating life in ancient Egypt.

2343 *Child of the Morning*

Date of Publication: 1977
Subject(s): Ancient Egypt; Pharaohs
Historical character(s): Hatshepsut, Ruler (Queen of Egypt); Senmut, Architect; Amun, Ruler (pharaoh)
Time Period(s): 15th century B.C.
Locale(s): Egypt

Summary: This is the fascinating story of Hatsheput, the youngest daughter of the Pharaoh who in an unprecedented move becomes his heir. She assumes the throne at the age of 15 and reigns for more than 20 years, defying opposition to rule by a woman. The novel offers a speculative history of her reign.

Historical Accuracy: More fictional than factual, the novel is nevertheless convincing in its re-creation of the ancient Egyptian customs.

2344 *The Eagle and the Raven*

Date of Publication: 1978
Subject(s): Roman Empire; Druids; Celtic Britain
Fictional character(s): Caradoc, Royalty (Celtic prince); Eurgain, Spouse (of Caradoc); Aricia, Royalty (queen of a northern tribe)

Historical character(s): Boadicea, Ruler (Celtic queen); Claudius I, Ruler (Roman emperor)
Time Period(s): 1st century (32-59)
Locale(s): England; Rome, Roman Empire

Summary: In Roman Britain the native Celts struggle to maintain their independence. Caradoc is the son of a Celtic king who attempts to unite the various Celtic tribes and lead them against the occupying Romans. He is joined in his campaign by the warrior queen Boadicea.

Historical Accuracy: This is an impressive evocation of Roman Britain and the customs of the Celts. The age is brought to vivid life in this account.

2345 *Lady of the Reeds*

Date of Publication: 1994
Subject(s): Ancient Egypt; Pharaohs
Fictional character(s): Thu, Young Woman; Hui, Nobleman
Historical character(s): Ramses III, Ruler (pharaoh of Egypt)
Time Period(s): 12th century B.C.
Locale(s): Egypt

Summary: A peasant girl, Thu, is determined to rise above her lot. She uses the assistance of the aristocrat Hui to break into the rarified world of the Pharaoh, becoming the beloved concubine of Ramses III. She plays an important role in the history of Dynastic Egypt.

Historical Accuracy: The novel blends a fictional story with a credible treatment of events during the reign of Ramses III.

2346 *Mirage*

Date of Publication: 1990
Subject(s): Ancient Egypt; Pharaohs
Historical character(s): Khaemwaset, Royalty (prince), Scholar; Ramses II, Ruler (pharaoh)
Time Period(s): 13th century (B)
Locale(s): Egypt

Summary: Khaemwaset is a son of Ramses II, a scholar in search of the mysteries contained in the Scroll of Thoth, a parchment believed to be the key to immortality. His search becomes connected with the arrival of a noblewoman whose powers rival anything Khaemwaset can imagine.

Historical Accuracy: This is an exciting and atmospheric story with an authentic background of the period.

2347 *The Twelfth Transforming*

Date of Publication: 1984
Subject(s): Ancient Egypt; Pharaohs
Historical character(s): Akhenaton, Ruler (pharaoh); Tiye, Royalty (mother of Akhenaton); Nefertiti, Royalty (queen consort of Akhenaton); Amenhotep III, Ruler (pharaoh); Horemheb, Military Personnel (general)
Time Period(s): 14th century B.C.
Locale(s): Egypt

Summary: The novel tells the story of the reign of Akhenaton who brings the Egyptian Empire to the edge of collapse and causes a struggle for power and control with his mother, Tiye, and Horemheb, the leader of the army.

Historical Accuracy: As sensational as the novel' material may appear, the author is faithful to Egyptian history and the customs of the period.

ALAN GELB (1950-)

American author Alan Gelb was born in New York City and attended Johns Hopkins University. He is the author of *The Janissary*, *Playgrounds*, and *Fever on the Wind* (under the pseudonym Adrien Lloyd).

2348 *Mussolini*

Date of Publication: 1985
Subject(s): Biography, Fictionalized; World War II
Historical character(s): Benito Mussolini, Leader (Italian Fascist); Adolf Hitler, Leader (Nazi)
Time Period(s): 19th century; 20th century (1880s-1945)
Locale(s): Italy

Summary: This novel, based on a screenplay by Stirling Silliphant, offers a fictionalized biography of the Italian fascist leader and dictator Benito Mussolini. The novel traces his rise to power and the events of World War II with an emphasis on both the public and private side of the Italian leader.

Historical Accuracy: The novel is faithful to the facts of history but does invent scenes and conversations in presenting this portrait of Mussolini.

ROBERTA GELLIS (1927-)

Gellis was born in New York City and graduated from Hunter College and Brooklyn Polytechnic Institute. She has worked as a chemist, biologist, and freelance editor. She has turned a lifelong interest in medieval history and literature into a successful writing career.

2349 *Bond of Blood*

Date of Publication: 1965
Subject(s): Middle Ages
Fictional character(s): Cain Radnor, Knight; Leah Pembroke, Gentlewoman; Lord Pembroke, Nobleman (Earl of Pembroke)
Historical character(s): Maud, Ruler (Empress)
Time Period(s): 12th century (1140s)
Locale(s): England; Wales

Summary: The novel is set during the dynastic struggle between Stephen and Maude in the 12th century. Cain is a Welsh knight who marries Leah, daughter of the Earl of Pembroke, as a gesture toward peace in the British-Welsh border conflict. However, he finds himself drawn into intrigue that reaches to the throne itself.

Historical Accuracy: The major political events of the novel are factual and drawn from the chronicle of the Gesta Stephani.

2350 *The Dragon and the Rose*

Date of Publication: 1977

Subject(s): War of the Roses; Tudor Period; Royalty—England
Historical character(s): Edward IV, Ruler (King of England); Richard III, Ruler (King of England); Henry VII, Ruler (King of England)
Time Period(s): 15th century
Locale(s): England

Summary: The novel depicts the War of the Roses, the dynastic struggle between the houses of York and Lancaster which raged in England during the 15th century. The Yorkist kings, Edward IV and Richard III, are eventually bested by Henry Tudor.

Historical Accuracy: The basic outlines of history are observed. However, the novel's flattering picture of Henry VII is at odds with the standard accounts.

2351 *Knight's Honor*

Date of Publication: 1964
Subject(s): Middle Ages; Royalty—England
Fictional character(s): Elizabeth Chester, Gentlewoman, Spouse (of Roger)
Historical character(s): Roger of Hereford, Nobleman (Earl of Hereford); Henry of Anjou, Nobleman; Ranulf de Gernons, Nobleman
Time Period(s): 12th century (1140s)
Locale(s): England

Summary: The civil war between King Stephen and Empress Maude is the background for this novel. Roger, Earl of Hereford, is a supporter of Henry of Anjou, later Henry II. The political intrigue of the period is blended with Roger's domestic relations with his wife, Elizabeth.

Historical Accuracy: The author has been careful to ground the story on the known historical facts whenever available.

2352 *Masques of Gold*

Date of Publication: 1988
Subject(s): Middle Ages; Romance
Fictional character(s): Lissa de Flael, Widow(er); Sir Justin FitzAilwin, Knight
Time Period(s): 13th century (1210s)
Locale(s): London, England

Summary: This romantic tale describes the relationship between Lissa de Flael, a noble's daughter and a widow, and Sir Justin FitzAilwin, warden of London. Their love affair is set against the danger of the clash between King John and his powerful barons.

Historical Accuracy: The novel offers a far more detailed and documented period background than other historical romances. The author's notes underscore the story's reliance on history.

2353 *A Silver Mirror*

Date of Publication: 1989
Subject(s): Romance; Middle Ages
Fictional character(s): Lady Barbara Bigod, Noblewoman, Bastard Daughter; Sir Alphonse D'Aix, Nobleman, Bastard Son

Time Period(s): 13th century (1260s)
Locale(s): England; France

Summary: The background of this medieval romance is the divisive wars of Henry II that pitted the French against the English. Political differences create conflict as Lady Barbara, an Englishwoman, falls in love with Sir Alphonse, a Frenchman. They must contend with war, intrigue, and divided loyalties, as well as their love for each other.

Historical Accuracy: The period details are richly and convincingly established.

GENEVIEVE GENNARI

2354 The Riven Heart

Date of Publication: 1956
Subject(s): French Revolution; Napoleonic Era; Reign of Terror
Fictional character(s): Constance Deschaumes, Young Woman; Maximilien Bergeron, Revolutionary
Time Period(s): 18th century; 19th century (1789-1815)
Locale(s): France

Summary: Constance Deschaumes' first husband, an aristocrat, is executed during the Reign of Terror. She then marries Maximilien Bergeron, a republican, who becomes an ardent follower of Napoleon. Their life together is affected by the major events of the period.

Historical Accuracy: The novel makes use of an authentic period background and is faithful to actual events.

MARGARET GEORGE (1943-)

An American writer born in Nashville, George graduated from Tufts University and Stanford. She worked for many years as a science writer for the National Institute for Health. She spent 15 years researching her first book length fiction, *The Autobiography of Henry VIII*, for which she won an Oppie Award for the best biographical novel. Her inspiration has been the big-screen epics of the 1950s, directed by such figures as David Lean. George has attempted the same sense of scope and elegance in her fiction.

2355 The Autobiography of Henry VIII

Date of Publication: 1986
Subject(s): Tudor Period; Biography, Fictionalized; Royalty—England
Historical character(s): Henry VIII, Ruler (King of England); Catherine of Aragon, Royalty (queen consort of Henry VIII); Anne Boleyn, Royalty (queen consort of Henry VIII); Jane Seymour, Royalty (queen consort of Henry VIII); Anne of Cleves, Royalty (queen consort of Henry VIII); Catherine Parr, Royalty (queen consort of Henry VIII); Mary Tudor, Royalty (princess); Elizabeth Tudor, Royalty (princess); Thomas Wolsey, Religious (cardinal); Will Somers, Entertainer (king's fool)
Time Period(s): 15th century; 16th century
Locale(s): England

Summary: In an imagined journal of King Henry VIII with notes from Will Somers, the King's fool, the author attempts to present an inside look at this controversial king and his times. Henry's reign and domestic life are shown with speculations about Henry's reactions to his various wives, his treatment of his officials and retainers, and his inner fears and contradictions.

Historical Accuracy: The novel is a model of integrated research and drama that catches the flavor of the era, with an evident sympathetic bias toward Henry.

2356 Mary, Queen of Scotland and the Isles

Date of Publication: 1992
Subject(s): Elizabethan Period; Royalty—Scotland; Biography, Fictionalized
Historical character(s): Mary, Queen of Scots, Ruler (Queen of Scotland); John Knox, Religious; James Hepburn, Nobleman (Earl of Bothwell); Henry Stewart, Nobleman (Lord Darnley); Marie de Guise, Royalty (mother of Mary, Queen of Scots); Elizabeth I, Ruler (Queen of England); Francois II, Royalty (French dauphin); Catherine de' Medici, Royalty (Queen of France)
Time Period(s): 16th century (1542-1587)
Locale(s): France; Scotland; England

Summary: Blending history and invention, the author re-creates the amazing life and times of Mary, Queen of Scots from the French court where her first husband is the royal heir, to her turbulent reign as Queen of Scotland, and her tragic confrontation with Elizabeth. Mary is shown from a variety of vantage points to create a credible picture of this complex monarch.

Historical Accuracy: The novel is a model of careful and precise rendering of both the historical period and its figures. The sheer comprehensiveness of the approach convinces the reader of its accuracy.

FRANCIS GERARD (1905-)

A science fiction and fantasy author, Gerard's books include *Secret Sceptre*.

2357 The Scarlet Beast

Date of Publication: 1935
Subject(s): Roman Empire; Punic Wars
Fictional character(s): Marcus Flaminius, Warrior
Historical character(s): Hannibal, Military Personnel (general); Publius Cornelius Scipio Africanus, Military Personnel (general)
Time Period(s): 2nd century B.C.
Locale(s): Spain; Gaul

Summary: The novel dramatizes events of the Second Punic War that pits Carthage against Rome. Marcus Flaminius is captured by the Carthaginians and taken as a slave to Carthage. The action climaxes in the final decisive battle won by Scipio Africanus, which sealed Carthage's fate.

Historical Accuracy: There is no mistaking which side the author prefers. To make his point, the Carthaginians are vilified, which undermines the novel's historical objectivity.

JO GERMANY

An English writer born in Cambridge, Germany worked as an office clerk and concert party artist. She is the author of gothic, romance, and historical novels with an insatiable curiosity for the way people lived and behaved during the 18th and 19th centuries.

2358 *City of Golden Cages*

Date of Publication: 1978
Subject(s): Romance; Royalty—Russia; Russian Empire
Fictional character(s): Charlotte Hammond, Orphan
Time Period(s): 1760s
Locale(s): St. Petersburg, Russia

Summary: The adventures of an English girl in Tsarist Russia in the 1760s are depicted. Charlotte Hammond hopes to start a new life in Russia but finds herself caught up in intrigue that affects her own happiness and the fate of the Romanov dynasty.

Historical Accuracy: The novel captures the period background of the Russian court and culture with skill.

2359 *Devil Child*

Date of Publication: 1977
Subject(s): Suspense; Russian Empire
Fictional character(s): Sergei Bibikov, Nobleman (count); Caroline Bibikov, Spouse
Time Period(s): 18th century
Locale(s): England; Russia

Summary: A marriage of convienence between an English woman and Count Bibikov of Russia plunges her into a dangerous mystery. Who killed the Count's first wife? Was it the Count's youngest son, known as the Devil Child, or the Count himself? Caroline attempts to answer these questions while trying to take charge of her husband's estate and contending with bands of rebel Cossacks.

Historical Accuracy: The Russian period background is genuine.

JACK GERSON

2360 *Death Squad London*

Date of Publication: 1990
Subject(s): Mystery
Fictional character(s): Ernst Lohmann, Refugee (former Berlin police inspector)
Time Period(s): 1930s (1936)
Locale(s): London, England

Summary: Former Berlin police inspector Ernst Lohmann, a Jewish refugee in London during the 1930s, is asked by a friend to investigate the suicide of a reporter. The reporter was working on a story involving the transfer of money from England to Hitler when she was found dead.

Historical Accuracy: The novel captures the pre-war scene with care and conviction.

NOEL B. GERSON (1914-1988)

An American writer, Gerson was born in Chicago and educated at the University of Chicago. During World War II, Gerson served in military intelligence. He was a newspaper reporter, radio and TV scriptwriter, and the author of over 100 books. His historical novels feature a lively and entertaining blend of fact and fiction.

2361 *The Anthem*

Date of Publication: 1967
Subject(s): Religious Conflict
Fictional character(s): Philippe de Montauban, Nobleman; Michel de Montauban, Nobleman; Maurice de Montauban, Nobleman
Historical character(s): Henri IV, Ruler (King of France); Louis XIV, Ruler (King of France); Francoise d'Aubigne, Noblewoman, Spouse (second wife of Louis XIV); Frederick the Great, Ruler (German emperor); Clement VIII, Religious (pope); Innocent XI, Religious (pope); Napoleon Bonaparte, Military Personnel, Ruler (Emperor of France); Francois Marie Arouet, Philosopher, Writer (aka Voltaire); Johann Wolfgang von Goethe, Writer; Armand-Jean Du Plessis, Religious (Cardinal Richelieu), Government Official (French minister)
Time Period(s): Multiple Time Periods
Locale(s): Europe; United States

Summary: This ambitious novel attempts no less than a history of the struggle for religious freedom over a 300-year period. The effects of the struggle on a single family, the Montaubans, are depicted in scenes involving dozens of historical figures that illustrate phases of the struggle.

Historical Accuracy: The perspective is so broad that the effect is, by design, a capsulized version of history.

2362 *Clear for Action!*

Date of Publication: 1970
Subject(s): Sea Story; War of 1812; Civil War—U.S.
Historical character(s): David Farragut, Military Personnel (naval officer)
Time Period(s): 19th century (1810-1865)
Locale(s): At Sea; New Orleans, Louisiana; Washington, District of Columbia

Summary: The story of David Farragut, America's greatest naval hero since John Paul Jones, is depicted. Farragut joins the navy at age 10 and receives his first command at 13. During the Civil War he achieves lasting fame in the Battle of Mobile Bay with his famous declaration, ''Damn the torpedoes! Full steam ahead!''.

Historical Accuracy: The details of Farragut's life and the period's history are delivered in workmanlike fashion.

2363 *The Conqueror's Wife*

Date of Publication: 1957
Subject(s): Middle Ages; Norman Conquest; Battle of Hastings
Historical character(s): William the Conqueror, Nobleman (Duke of Normandy); Matilda of Flanders, Noblewoman, Spouse (wife of William); Harold II, Ruler (King of England)
Time Period(s): 11th century
Locale(s): Normandy, France; England

Summary: This novel tells the story of the woman behind the man. In this case, the man is William the Conqueror and the woman is Matilda, his queen. Initially reluctant to marry the natural son of the Duke of Normandy, Matilda does so, and together the couple make a formidable alliance that moves from convenience and opportunity to affection and love.

Historical Accuracy: The atmosphere is reliably delivered though the story is unabashedly fictional rather than historically accurate, so much so that at the outset the author admits that his characters and incidents have no relation to any person or event in real life.

2364 *The Crusader*

Date of Publication: 1970
Subject(s): Women's Rights; Biography, Fictionalized
Historical character(s): Margaret Sanger, Nurse, Activist; Havelock Ellis, Doctor, Scientist; Mahatma Gandhi, Leader (for Indian independence)
Time Period(s): 20th century (1900-1930)
Locale(s): New York, New York

Summary: This biographical novel details the career of women's rights reformer Margaret Sanger. As a nurse in the tenements of New York she comes to the realization that a woman's control of reproduction is essential. The struggle to launch the birth control movement is described, and Sanger emerges as a complex amalgam of reformer and stubborn egoist. Her affair with scientist Havelock Ellis is also depicted.

Historical Accuracy: The author has carefully kept to the documented sources in his recontruction of Sanger's life and times.

2365 *The Cumberland Rifles*

Date of Publication: 1952
Subject(s): Settlement of the American Frontier
Fictional character(s): Elholm, Military Personnel
Historical character(s): Andrew Jackson, Military Personnel (general); John Sevier, Frontiersman, Political Figure
Time Period(s): 1790s (1796)
Locale(s): Tennessee

Summary: Elholm, a mercenary soldier, comes to America to fight for the Spanish but instead joins the American side in this romantic adventure story.

Historical Accuracy: The novel sticks to the basic historical facts about wilderness life in the future state of Tennessee.

2366 *Daughter of Eve*

Date of Publication: 1958

Subject(s): American Colonies; Indians; Settlement of the American Frontier
Historical character(s): John Smith, Settler, Leader (colonial); Pocahontas, Indian; John Rolfe, Settler; Sir Walter Raleigh, Courtier, Gentleman; Powhatan, Indian, Chieftain; James I, Ruler (King of England); Anne of Denmark, Royalty (Queen of England)
Time Period(s): 17th century (1606-1613)
Locale(s): Jamestown, Virginia, American Colonies; London, England

Summary: The novel tells the familiar story of Captain John Smith and his relationship with the Indian princess Pocahontas. Early life in the Jamestown settlement is detailed as well as the sad story of Smith's love for Pocahontas that ends in England with Pocahontas a celebrity and royal curiosity.

Historical Accuracy: The author took liberties with the creation of his characters just as John Smith took liberties in his depictions of events.

2367 *Emperor's Ladies*

Date of Publication: 1959
Subject(s): Napoleonic Era; Royalty—France
Historical character(s): Marie Louise of Austria, Royalty (princess); Napoleon Bonaparte, Ruler (Emperor of France), Military Personnel
Time Period(s): 18th century; 19th century
Locale(s): Europe; France

Summary: The novel looks at the domestic side of the life of Napoleon, centering on Marie Louise, the young Austrian princess who becomes his second wife. While Napoleon rises from obscurity as an artillery officer to conquer most of Western Europe, his role as husband and father is dramatized.

Historical Accuracy: The portrait of Napoleon is considerably sanitized, and the version of events is shaped more to an idealized rather than a realistic pattern.

2368 *The Forest Lord*

Date of Publication: 1955
Subject(s): American Colonies; Indians; Sea Story
Fictional character(s): Josiah Burney, Heir—Dispossessed; Obadiah Gaskell, Religious (clergyman), Sailor; Joanna Cochrane, Frontierswoman
Time Period(s): 1700s
Locale(s): Charleston, South Carolina, American Colonies; *Apollo*, At Sea

Summary: This is an adventure story whose background is the colonial settlement of Charleston and the Indian war that almost destroyed it. Josiah Burney is shanghaied into the English navy to prevent him from claiming the earldom that is rightfully his. He jumps ship in Charleston with others and attempts to rescue a white girl from the Westoe Indians who may hold a clue to the whereabouts of Josiah's missing father and the restoration of his birthright.

Historical Accuracy: The colonial background is authentic.

2369 *Give Me Liberty*

Date of Publication: 1966

Subject(s): American Revolution; American Colonies; Biography, Fictionalized
Historical character(s): Patrick Henry, Lawyer, Patriot; John Paul Jones, Sea Captain; Dorothea Dandridge, Spouse (of Patrick Henry); George Rogers Clark, Military Personnel
Time Period(s): 18th century (1747-1799)
Locale(s): Virginia

Summary: This biographical novel of the life of Patrick Henry follows his career as a lawyer and famous orator, earning his reputation as the ''great Virginia rebel'' in the struggle with the Crown. After his first wife dies, he wooes the beautiful Dorothea Dandridge, who is also pursued by John Paul Jones.

Historical Accuracy: The facts of Henry's life are well-researched and presented.

2370   *The Golden Eagle*

Date of Publication: 1953
Subject(s): Mexican War; Espionage
Fictional character(s): Jonathan Wyatt, Spy
Historical character(s): Robert E. Lee, Military Personnel (army officer)
Time Period(s): 1840s (1845-1848)
Locale(s): Mexico

Summary: This tale of espionage and adventure during the Mexican War involves Texan Jonathan Wyatt. He undertakes a spying mission into Mexico to map Vera Cruz (in anticipation of General Winfield Scott's invasion) and to pick up important intelligence in Mexico City.

Historical Accuracy: This fast-paced adventure tale interweaves a fanciful plot with authentic period elements and events.

2371   *The Golden Lyre*

Date of Publication: 1963
Subject(s): Macedonian Empire
Historical character(s): Alexander the Great, Ruler (King of Macedonia); Ptolemy, Military Personnel; Thais, Spouse (of Ptolemy)
Time Period(s): 4th century B.C. (338-328 B.C.)
Locale(s): Macedonia; Persia; Egypt

Summary: The novel follows the rise and stunning career of Alexander the Great. Events are told from the perspective of his trusted friend, Ptolemy, and the courtesan, Thais, who marries Ptolemy while scheming to become Alexander's mistress. The story follows Alexander's epic military campaign through Persia to his decline into despotism and madness.

Historical Accuracy: The story is grounded in historical sources, but, as the author points out, the sources are a blend of fact and legend.

2372   *The Highwayman*

Date of Publication: 1955
Subject(s): American Colonies; French and Indian War
Fictional character(s): Mercy Pepperell, Young Woman; Peter Staples, Young Man; Jack Duppan, Highwayman
Historical character(s): William Pepperell, Military Personnel (general); Peter Warren, Military Personnel (admiral)

Time Period(s): 1740s
Locale(s): Maine; Boston, Massachusetts, American Colonies; Louisbourg, Nova Scotia, Canada (then part of New France)

Summary: Mercy, the daughter of William Pepperell of Maine, is kidnapped by Jack Duppan. He has also stolen important military documents to aid the French in their war with the English colonists. The action culminates in the capture of Louisburg.

Historical Accuracy: The novel blends fact and fancy. The details about the campaign against Louisburg are authentic.

2373   *The Hittite*

Date of Publication: 1961
Subject(s): Hittites
Fictional character(s): Marduk, Military Personnel; Arinna, Spouse (of Marduk); Zia, Gentlewoman
Historical character(s): Muwatallis I, Ruler (Hittite king)
Time Period(s): 14th century B.C.
Locale(s): Asia Minor

Summary: Lord Marduk is a young army commander in the Hittite Empire and a confidant of the emperor, Muwatallis I. His wife, Arinna, in retaliation for having been caught in adultery, tricks Marduk into an indiscretion with Zia, the wife of a powerful merchant. As punishment, Marduk is banished, until a plot to overthrow the emperor returns him to favor.

Historical Accuracy: The romantic intrigue is backed up with some convincing details of this ancient culture.

2374   *I'll Storm Hell*

Date of Publication: 1967
Subject(s): American Revolution; Biography, Fictionalized
Historical character(s): Anthony Wayne, Military Personnel (American general); Benjamin Franklin, Political Figure; George Washington, Military Personnel (American commander); Benedict Arnold, Military Personnel; Marie Joseph Paul de Lafayette, Nobleman, Military Personnel; Nathanael Greene, Military Personnel (American general); Charles Lee, Military Personnel (American general)
Time Period(s): 18th century (1760-1796)
Locale(s): Pennsylvania; New York

Summary: The novel offers a biographical account of American Revolutionary hero ''Mad'' Anthony Wayne. Before the war, he is the chief surveyor for Benjamin Franklin. During the Revolution, Wayne is one of Washington's most indomitable generals. He reaches the height of his reputation in his headlong assault of Stony Point on the Hudson.

Historical Accuracy: Many of Wayne's papers and letters were destroyed by his son so certain aspects of the author's assertions are conjectural.

2375   *The Imposter*

Date of Publication: 1954
Subject(s): British Colonies
Fictional character(s): Jeremy Stone, Artisan (gunsmith), Imposter

Historical character(s): Caroline Stuart, Noblewoman (Duchess of Glasgow); Ian MacGregor, Gentleman; Thomas Murrah, Nobleman
Time Period(s): 17th century (1691-1692)
Locale(s): New York, New York, American Colonies; Port Royal, Jamaica

Summary: Jeremy Stone, a young gunsmith from New York, aspires to become a gentleman. Thus, when an opportunity comes to impersonate a member of the gentry, he does not hesitate and accompanies the Duchess of Glasgow's party to Port Royal, Jamaica, as the nephew of the governor. There he is caught up in intrigue, romance, and a daring rebellion, one of the greatest plots ever perpetrated in the colonies.

Historical Accuracy: The story is rooted in fact and captures with authority the atmosphere of colonial Port Royal.

2376 The Land Is Bright

Date of Publication: 1961
Subject(s): Settlement of the American Frontier; American Colonies; Pilgrims
Historical character(s): William Bradford, Leader (of Plymouth colony); Miles Standish, Military Personnel; John Alden, Leader (of Plymouth colony)
Time Period(s): 17th century (1620-1623)
Locale(s): *Mayflower*, At Sea; Cape Cod, Massachusetts, American Colonies; Plymouth, Massachusetts, American Colonies

Summary: The novel chronicles the events in the Plymouth colony of Massachusetts during its first fateful three years. At the center of the Pilgrims' struggle for survival is William Bradford who, more than any other single person, organized and molded the group of settlers into a community.

Historical Accuracy: The details of the period and events are based on substantial research. The interpretation of the characters is the author's.

2377 The Mohawk Ladder

Date of Publication: 1951
Subject(s): War of the Spanish Succession; Espionage
Fictional character(s): Joshua Peattie, Military Personnel (lieutenant); Diane D'Ancours, Spy; Old Bear Trap, Military Personnel
Historical character(s): John Churchill, Nobleman (Duke of Marlborough)
Time Period(s): 1700s (1707)
Locale(s): Lille, France; Netherlands (Oudenarde, Ghent); Flanders, Belgium

Summary: This fanciful and romantic story is set during the War of the Spanish Succession in the 18th century and involves a group of American volunteers led by Joshua Peattie. He leads his men in action against the French, torn between his loyalty to the Duke of Marlborough and his attraction to a beautiful French spy. The action climaxes in the storming of Ghent and the use of the American device, the Mohawk ladder.

Historical Accuracy: More swashbuckling than historical, the period is colorfully presented.

2378 The Naked Maja

Date of Publication: 1959
Subject(s): Artistic Life; Biography, Fictionalized
Historical character(s): Francisco Jose de Goya y Lucientes, Artist; Maria Cayetana, Noblewoman (Duchess of Alba); Charles IV, Ruler (King of Spain)
Time Period(s): 18th century; 19th century
Locale(s): Spain

Summary: This biographical account of the life of Spanish painter Goya follows his career, his relationship with the Duchess of Alba, and the intrigue in the court of Spanish King Charles IV.

Historical Accuracy: The novel is faithful to the facts of Goya's life and the events of the period.

2379 Old Hickory

Date of Publication: 1964
Subject(s): War of 1812; Biography, Fictionalized; American Revolution
Historical character(s): Andrew Jackson, Military Personnel, Political Figure; Rachel Jackson, Spouse (of Jackson)
Time Period(s): 18th century; 19th century (1781-1845)
Locale(s): Tennessee; Washington, District of Columbia

Summary: This biographical novel on the life of Andrew Jackson details his service as a 14-year-old combatant in the American Revolution, his devotion to his home state of Tennessee, and his passion for his wife, Rachel. He becomes a national hero after the Battle of New Orleans, which propels him into the White House.

Historical Accuracy: Somewhat of a hagiography, the rough edges of Jackson are smoothed into a flattering portrait.

2380 Sam Houston

Date of Publication: 1968
Subject(s): Texas Revolution; Civil War—U.S.; Biography, Fictionalized
Historical character(s): Sam Houston, Political Figure, Military Personnel; Andrew Jackson, Military Personnel, Political Figure; James K. Polk, Political Figure; Antonio Lopez de Santa Anna, Military Personnel (general); Stephen F. Austin, Political Figure; Thomas Hart Benton, Political Figure
Time Period(s): 19th century (1805-1863)
Locale(s): Tennessee; Texas; Washington, District of Columbia

Summary: The epic life of Sam Houston is chronicled from his early years in Tennessee under Andrew Jackson in the War of 1812, through his career as a congressman and governor of Tennessee, to his leadership in the Texas Revolution. After emerging as a great American hero, he is branded a traitor to the South because of his adamant opposition to Texas' secession during the Civil War.

Historical Accuracy: A short history cannot do justice to Houston's amazing career. Some evident speculation was needed for the Tennessee years.

2381 *Savage Gentleman*

Date of Publication: 1950
Subject(s): American Colonies; Indians; Queen Anne's War
Fictional character(s): Jeffrey Wyatt, Servant (bondsman), Military Personnel (militiaman); Leah Hill, Gentlewoman; Simon Willard, Military Personnel (lieutenant); Adiawano, Indian (Seneca), Royalty (princess)
Historical character(s): Benjamin Church, Military Personnel (colonel); Joseph Dudley, Government Official (colonial governor)
Time Period(s): 1700s
Locale(s): Schenectady, New York, American Colonies; Onondagas, New York, American Colonies; Port Royal, Nova Scotia, Canada (now Annapolis Royal)

Summary: The novel is an adventure set against the backdrop of Queen Anne's War. Two rivals for the love of Leah Hill— Jeffrey Wyatt and Simon Willard—participate in a dangerous mission to aid frontier settlers in the fight against the French and the Indians. The action culminates in the pivotal Battle of Port Royal, the first major battle of American colonial history.

Historical Accuracy: The research and documentation of the period are solidly established.

2382 *The Slender Reed*

Date of Publication: 1965
Subject(s): Texas Revolution; Mexican War; Biography, Fictionalized
Historical character(s): James K. Polk, Political Figure; Andrew Jackson, Political Figure; Martin Van Buren, Political Figure
Time Period(s): 19th century (1806-1849)
Locale(s): Tennessee; Washington, District of Columbia

Summary: This biographical novel about James K. Polk, eleventh president of the U.S., chronicles his life from his youth on the Tennessee frontier as a sharpshooter and Indian fighter to his political career as Speaker of the House, governor of Tennessee, and finally, president. His vision of an American Texas results in the declaration of war with Mexico.

Historical Accuracy: The details of Polk's life and times are well presented and researched.

2383 *The Swamp Fox, Francis Marion*

Date of Publication: 1967
Subject(s): American Revolution; Biography, Fictionalized
Historical character(s): Francis Marion, Military Personnel (colonel); William Moultrie, Military Personnel (general); Henry Lee, Military Personnel (colonel); Nathanael Greene, Military Personnel (general)
Time Period(s): 18th century (1752-1786)
Locale(s): South Carolina, American Colonies

Summary: The life of Francis Marion, the legendary Swamp Fox, is chronicled in this biographical novel. Marion is born to a Huguenot family in the Carolinas. When the Revolution breaks out he is promoted to the rank of colonel in the South Carolina militia. Marion perfects a new kind of fighting, guerilla warfare, in which he harasses British troops using his knowledge of tidal Carolina for hiding and safety.

Historical Accuracy: Gerson's story is supported by solid research.

2384 *That Egyptian Woman*

Date of Publication: 1956
Subject(s): Roman Empire
Historical character(s): Cleopatra, Ruler (Queen of Egypt); Julius Caesar, Military Personnel (general), Political Figure; Marc Antony, Military Personnel (general), Political Figure
Time Period(s): 1st century B.C.
Locale(s): Egypt; Rome, Roman Empire

Summary: This novel based on the lives of Cleopatra and Julius Caesar traces the meteoric rise of the ambitious queen of Egypt who led a revolt against her brother and gained a kingdom by enlisting the aid of Julius Caesar. Cleopatra follows Caesar to Rome, becomes his mistress, and after his murder, takes up with Marc Antony.

Historical Accuracy: The author has taken historical liberties in the interest of telling a captivating story. The dialogue and situations at times defy credibility.

2385 *TR*

Date of Publication: 1970
Subject(s): Spanish-American War; World War I; Biography, Fictionalized
Historical character(s): Theodore Roosevelt, Political Figure; Edith Roosevelt, Spouse; William Howard Taft, Political Figure
Time Period(s): 19th century; 20th century (1858-1918)
Locale(s): New York, New York; Dakota Territory, United States; Washington, District of Columbia

Summary: This biographical novel chronicles the life of Theodore Roosevelt. At age 42 he became America's youngest president, but he had already been a sportsman, hunter, rancher, soldier, and explorer in addition to his political career. A complex figure, Roosevelt was at the center of events as America emerged as a world power.

Historical Accuracy: This massive fictionalized version of Roosevelt's life is supported by solid research and an authentic re-creation of the period and personalities.

2386 *The Trojan*

Date of Publication: 1962
Subject(s): Hittites; Ancient Greece
Fictional character(s): Hiram, Warrior (army commander); Tros, Warrior; Anichis, Slave
Historical character(s): David, Ruler (King of Israel)
Time Period(s): 10th century B.C.
Locale(s): Troy, Ancient Civilization; Israel

Summary: This is the story of the first Greek invasion of Troy, 100 years before the events chronicled by Homer. Troy is captured by the barbaric Hellenes. Tros and the slave Anichis escape to recruit the assistance of Israel and Sheba. Meanwhile Hiram creates a guerilla army in the mountains surrounding Troy.

Historical Accuracy: The scene is colorfully evoked.

2387 *Yankee Doodle Dandy*

Date of Publication: 1965

Subject(s): American Colonies; American Revolution; Biography, Fictionalized

Historical character(s): John Hancock, Businessman, Patriot; Samuel Adams, Revolutionary; George Washington, Military Personnel (American commander); John Adams, Political Figure; Abigail Adams, Spouse (of John Adams)

Time Period(s): 18th century (1754-1793)

Locale(s): Boston, Massachusetts, American Colonies

Summary: This biographical novel tells the story of John Hancock, who amasses his fortune in the mercantile and shipping business. The taxation policies of the Crown move him toward the radical politics of Sam Adams, and Hancock becomes the leader in Massachusetts in the fight for independence.

Historical Accuracy: The facts of this biographical novel are supported by evident research.

2388 *The Yankee From Tennessee*

Date of Publication: 1960

Subject(s): Civil War—U.S.; Biography, Fictionalized; Reconstruction Period

Historical character(s): Andrew Johnson, Political Figure; James K. Polk, Political Figure; Andrew Jackson, Political Figure; Jefferson Davis, Political Figure; Martin Van Buren, Political Figure; Ulysses S. Grant, Military Personnel (Union general); Abraham Lincoln, Political Figure

Time Period(s): 19th century (1826-1875)

Locale(s): Tennessee; Washington, District of Columbia

Summary: This biographical novel traces Andrew Johnson's career including his stints as Tennessee governor, congressman, and Abraham Lincoln's vice president. Johnson's troubled presidency is detailed during the Reconstruction period as the radical Republican Congress attempts to impeach him.

Historical Accuracy: Although based on fact and historical record, the novel does invent some scenes and incidents based on the author's interpretations.

ROBERT GESSNER (1907-1968)

Born in Escanaba, Michigan, Gessner was a professor at New York University as well as an author. His novels include *Here Is My Home*, *Treason*, and *Youth Is the Time*.

2389 *Treason*

Date of Publication: 1944

Subject(s): Biography, Fictionalized; American Revolution

Fictional character(s): Matthew Clarkson, Military Personnel (soldier)

Historical character(s): Benedict Arnold, Military Personnel (general), Traitor

Time Period(s): 18th century

Locale(s): American Colonies

Summary: This biographical study attempts to explore the motives behind Benedict Arnold's famous act of treason during the American Revolution. The story is narrated partly from the perspective of a young aide to General Arnold whose initial hero worship must be painfully reassessed.

Historical Accuracy: The novel is faithful to the facts. It humanizes Arnold and treats him with sympathy without apologizing for his betrayal of the American cause.

WILLIAM GETZ

2390 *Sam Patch: Ballad of a Jumping Man*

Date of Publication: 1986

Subject(s): Theatrical Life; Picaresque Adventure; Animals

Fictional character(s): Bruin, Animal (bear)

Historical character(s): Sam Patch, Entertainer

Time Period(s): 1820s (1827)

Locale(s): Patterson, New Jersey; Niagara Falls, New York

Summary: This unusual novel is narrated by Bruin, a performing bear who meets the historical celebrity Sam Patch. Patch achieves notoriety in his death defying jumps off bridges, ships, and, in particular, waterfalls. They team up for a series of oddball adventures, including the ultimate challenge of Niagra Falls.

Historical Accuracy: This comic fantasy is filled with period information that creates a believable historical background.

MAURICE GHNASSIA (1920-)

A French writer born in Paris, Ghnassia immigrated to the U.S. in 1955. A graduate of the Sorbonne, Ghnassia has been an editor and a film producer and director. During World War II, Ghnassia fought in the French Resistance in the Groupe des Six.

2391 *Arena: A Novel of Spartacus and Crassus*

Date of Publication: 1969

Subject(s): Roman Empire; Servile War; Slavery

Historical character(s): Marcus Licinius Crassus, Military Personnel (general), Political Figure; Spartacus, Slave, Leader (revolt)

Time Period(s): 1st century B.C. (70 B.C.)

Locale(s): Roman Empire

Summary: The novel portrays the Servile War of the 1st century B.C., the slave revolt led by Spartacus, as a showdown between the oppressed and the powerful, represented by Spartacus and the sybaritic Crassus respectively. The novel is convincing in setting the human drama of the war into the context of Roman power politics.

Historical Accuracy: Carefully researched, the novel joins modern novelistic techniques to the service of history.

ZULFIKAR GHOSE (1935-)

Pakistani poet and novelist Ghose came to the U.S. in 1969, after having lived in England and Brazil. His books include the poetry collection *The Loss of India*, the novel *The*

Murder of Aziz Khan, and an autobiography, *Confessions of a Native-Alien*.

2392 *The Incredible Brazilian: The Native*

Date of Publication: 1972
Subject(s): Picaresque Adventure
Fictional character(s): Gregorio Peixoto da Silva Xavier, Adventurer
Time Period(s): 17th century
Locale(s): Brazil

Summary: Set in 17th-century Brazil, this picaresque tale sends Gregorio Peixoto da Silva Xavier, the son of a rich landowner, on a seemingly endless series of adventures across the geographical and social landscape of Brazil. He joins an expedition to capture Indian slaves, is imprisoned, sells arms to both sides during the civil war, and has a string of largely indistinguishable sexual encounters.

Historical Accuracy: The novel is at home in its period and region, and the adventures of the hero collectively paint a rich and varied period landscape.

DENISE GIARDINA (1951-)

An American from West Virginia, Giardina earned degrees from West Virginia Wesleyan College and the Virginia Theological Seminary. She has worked as a clerk, typist, and computer operator. She calls herself an Appalachian writer, interested in exploring the affinities between Appalachia and other exploited areas such as Poland and Central America.

2393 *Good King Harry*

Date of Publication: 1984
Subject(s): Royalty—England; Battle of Agincourt; Middle Ages
Historical character(s): Henry V, Ruler (King of England); John of Gaunt, Royalty; Henry IV, Ruler (King of England); Richard II, Ruler (King of England); Catherine of Valois, Royalty (queen consort of Henry V)
Time Period(s): 14th century; 15th century (1398-1422)
Locale(s): England; France; Wales

Summary: Henry V tells his own story in this autobiographical novel that traces his career as the rakish young Prince Hal to the national hero Henry V, victor at Agincourt. The novel captures medieval life and customs from the back alleys of London to the court and to the battlefields of Wales and France.

Historical Accuracy: The story is firmly rooted in history, captured with care.

2394 *Storming Heaven*

Date of Publication: 1987
Subject(s): Labor Movement; Mining; Battle of Blair Mountain

Fictional character(s): C.J. Marcum, Political Figure; Rondall Cloud, Labor Organizer; Carrie Bishop, Nurse; Rosa Angelelli, Immigrant
Time Period(s): 19th century; 20th century (1890-1921)
Locale(s): Justice County, West Virginia

Summary: The novel provides a gripping account of the years leading up to the Battle of Blair Mountain in which an army of 10,000 coal miners faced a division from the U.S. army. The rebellion is chronicled from the perspective of four participants—a mayor, a union organizer, a nurse, and an immigrant.

Historical Accuracy: The novel provides an authentic portrait of the region and the period.

MARY ANN GIBBS
(PSEUD. OF MARJORY ELIZABETH BIDWELL, 1900-)

An Englishwoman born in Sussex, Gibbs began her writing career in 1933. She has written more than 300 stories and articles for magazines as well as her novels.

2395 *The Admiral's Lady*

Date of Publication: 1974
Subject(s): Victorian Period; Romance
Fictional character(s): Sir John Farebrother, Military Personnel (admiral); Susanna Farebrother, Gentlewoman; Will Farebrother, Gentleman
Time Period(s): 1880s (1887)
Locale(s): England

Summary: This fanciful romance is set during the time of Queen Victoria's Golden Jubilee. Susanna Farebrother awaits the return of her father, the admiral. Instead, his twin brother Will appears, masquerading as the admiral while he carries out a secret mission for the queen. Will overcomes his reputation as the black sheep of the family.

Historical Accuracy: The novel's premise is difficult to accept, but the period flavor is genuine.

2396 *A Most Romantic City*

Date of Publication: 1976
Subject(s): Victorian Period; Romance
Fictional character(s): Cecily Forbes, Gentlewoman; Charles Pitborough, Banker, Widow(er); Barnaby Tilverton, Gentleman
Time Period(s): 1890s (1890)
Locale(s): Venice, Italy

Summary: Romantic complications in Venice during the 1890s form the novel's drama. Cecily Forbes turns down the proposal of banker Charles Pitborough who pursues her to Venice with his friend, the scoundrel Barnaby Tilverton. Venice works its magic in creating the novel's romantic complications and climaxes.

Historical Accuracy: The emphasis is on romantic adventure, not period painting, but the atmosphere is credible.

2397 *The Tempestuous Petticoat*

Date of Publication: 1977

Subject(s): Romance; Suspense; Georgian Period
Fictional character(s): Martha Lingford, Orphan; Henry Lingford, Gentleman; Drummond Connington, Gentleman
Time Period(s): 18th century (late)
Locale(s): England

Summary: When her father dies, Martha Lingford is responsible for her two younger siblings, and she seeks the support of her grandfather, Henry Lingford. He is a mysterious recluse involved in smuggling and possibly worse. Martha, and dandy Drummond Connington, set about solving a murder and falling in love.

Historical Accuracy: The novel is filled with period atmosphere rather than a carefully detailed historical background.

WILLA GIBBS (1917-)

Gibbs' novels include *Tell Your Sons*, *The Tender Men*, *The Twelfth Physician*, *Dedicated*, and *The Shadow of His Wings*. He was born in Alberta, Canada.

`2398` *According to Mary: A Novel of the Magdalene*

Date of Publication: 1962
Subject(s): Biblical Story; Roman Empire
Fictional character(s): Gaius, Military Personnel (centurion)
Historical character(s): Mary Magdalene, Biblical Figure; Mary, Biblical Figure; Jesus Christ, Biblical Figure; Lazarus, Biblical Figure
Time Period(s): 1st century
Locale(s): Israel

Summary: The life of Jesus is depicted through the eyes of one of his most devoted followers, the notorious courtesan Mary Magadalene. Her current lover, a Roman centurian, Gaius, sends her to the home of Mary to investigate the truth of the legends surrounding Jesus. Mary Magdalene is taken by his sanctity and teachings. The events of Jesus's miracles and his crucifixion are described.

Historical Accuracy: The novel blends the Biblical references to Mary Magdalene with her fictional presence at other events, real and imagined.

`2399` *The Dedicated*

Date of Publication: 1960
Subject(s): Medical Profession; Napoleonic Wars
Fictional character(s): Anne Warburton, Gentlewoman; Jeremy Sternes, Publisher (newspaper)
Historical character(s): Edward Jenner, Doctor; William Woodville, Doctor; Napoleon Bonaparte, Military Personnel (army commander), Ruler (emperor)
Time Period(s): 1800s
Locale(s): London, England; France

Summary: The novel depicts the battle against smallpox, seen in the struggle between two doctors, Edward Jenner and William Woodville, to unlock the solution to the disease. Jenner's cowpox vaccine is at first ridiculed, but it finds a powerful sponsor in Emperor Napoleon.

Historical Accuracy: The story blends fact and fiction, but the medical details are convincing.

`2400` *A Fig in Winter*

Date of Publication: 1963
Subject(s): Roman Empire; Christianity
Fictional character(s): Julian Quintus, Slave
Historical character(s): Marcus Aurelius, Ruler (Roman emperor), Writer
Time Period(s): 2nd century
Locale(s): Rome, Roman Empire

Summary: This tale of the reign of Roman Emperor Marcus Aurelius and the early Christian church involves Julian Quintus, who sets off to Rome to restore the social status of his family. Instead, he finds himself the personal slave of Marcus Aurelius. He witnesses the major events in Marcus Aurelius' reign and his dealings with the Christian church.

Historical Accuracy: The novel shows great attention to period details and an evident familiarity with Marcus Aurelius' *Meditations*, upon which much of the story is based.

`2401` *Seed of Mischief*

Date of Publication: 1953
Subject(s): French Revolution; Royalty—France
Fictional character(s): Jeanne de Villefont, Noblewoman
Historical character(s): Louis XVII, Royalty (Dauphin of France); Napoleon Bonaparte, Military Personnel (officer); Paul Barras, Revolutionary; Andoche Junot, Military Personnel (French general)
Time Period(s): 1790s
Locale(s): Paris, France

Summary: The novel speculates about the endlessly provocative mystery of the fate of the ''Lost Dauphin,'' Louis XVII. In this version, noblewoman Jeanne de Villefont, spared the guillotine, sets out to become the mother of the new king of France.

Historical Accuracy: Although the novel's story is fanciful, it does feature believable historical detail and a convincing atmosphere of the times.

`2402` *Tell Your Sons: A Novel of the Napoleonic Era*

Date of Publication: 1946
Subject(s): Napoleonic Era
Fictional character(s): Paul d'Avnay, Military Personnel (lieutenant)
Historical character(s): Napoleon Bonaparte, Ruler (Emperor of France)
Time Period(s): 18th century; 19th century
Locale(s): Europe

Summary: The novel offers a biographical account of Napoleon and his era told from the perspective of a young admirer, Paul d'Avnay, whose fortunes follow those of Napoleon. The scenes occur throughout Europe and dramatize the charismatic power and influence of the French leader.

Historical Accuracy: This is a highly romantic version of the emperor and his era, seen through the subjective lens of hero-worship. A strong portrait emerges of Napoleon, but everything else fades into the background.

2403 *The Twelfth Physician*

Date of Publication: 1954

Subject(s): French Revolution; Medical Profession; Reign of Terror

Fictional character(s): Charlot Florian, Doctor

Historical character(s): Napoleon Bonaparte, Military Personnel (general)

Time Period(s): 1780s; 1790s

Locale(s): France; Cayenne, Guyana; Egypt

Summary: During the French Revolution under Robespierre, to teach medicine was to risk the guillotine. When five young men seek a physician to instruct them, it is only the 12th they approach, Dr. Charlot Florian, who agrees to accept them as pupils. The decision is a costly one for Florian, and the novel traces the consequences to the Cayenne penal colony and Napoleon's Egyptian campaign.

Historical Accuracy: The novel vividly and believably recreates historical events and the atmosphere of the early Napoleonic era.

CHARLES GIDLEY

(PSEUD. OF GIDLEY WHEELER, 1938-)

An Englishman born in Bristol, Gidley joined the Royal Navy at age 16 and rose to captain and senior pilot. He left the navy in 1980 to write novels and produce dramatic scripts for British television.

2404 *Armada*

Date of Publication: 1987

Subject(s): Spanish Armada; Elizabethan Period; Sea Story

Fictional character(s): Harry Pascoe, Fisherman; Tristram Pascoe, Spy; Sara Hussey, Young Woman

Time Period(s): 16th century (1558-1588)

Locale(s): Cornwall, England; Lisbon, Portugal; At Sea (English coast)

Summary: The great events of the threatened Spanish invasion of England form the background of this romantic adventure. Tristram Pascoe becomes an English spy as the Spanish prepare their invasion fleet. He falls in love with Sara Hussey, an Irishwoman trapped in a failed marriage with her Portuguese cousin. The action culminates in the destruction of the Spanish fleet.

Historical Accuracy: The emphasis is not on the great figures or diplomatic manuevering but on a personal story of romance and adventure with a historical background.

ANNA GILBERT

(PSEUD. OF MARGUERITE LAZARUS, 1916-)

The child of a schoolmaster in a village in North England, Gilbert was a grammar school teacher until 1973. She began to write in the 1950s, setting most of her work in Victorian England, a society near enough in time to be well documented, but far enough away to offer an escape from the complications of modern life.

2405 *Flowers for Lilian*

Date of Publication: 1980

Subject(s): Victorian Period; Suspense

Fictional character(s): Maggie Ossian, Gentlewoman; Lilian Bellefleur, Gentlewoman; Daniel Hebworthy, Gentleman

Time Period(s): 1860s

Locale(s): England (north country)

Summary: In this novel of love and jealousy, Lilian Bellefleur is overprotected by her family. As the story progresses, her secrets are exposed, and retribution comes from an unexpected source.

Historical Accuracy: The novel offers a convincing evocation of Victorian England.

2406 *The Long Shadow*

Date of Publication: 1984

Subject(s): Victorian Period; Suspense

Fictional character(s): Hannah Medlar, Gentlewoman; Adrian Rudyard, Gentleman; Zilla Medlar, Gentlewoman

Time Period(s): 19th century (Victorian period)

Locale(s): England (north country)

Summary: In this novel of suspense, Hannah Medlar's hopes center on Adrian Rudyard, but a mysterious series of events shatters her plans. The frightening visit of a rag woman, the arrival of a strange girl, and the tragic fate of Hannah's sister-in-law accelerate the suspense.

Historical Accuracy: The novel features an authentic texture of Victorian life.

2407 *The Wedding Guest*

Date of Publication: 1993

Subject(s): Family Saga; World War I

Fictional character(s): Elinor Findon, Orphan; May Findon, Artist; Kelda Findon, Gentlewoman

Time Period(s): 1920s

Locale(s): Bidminster, England

Summary: During the 1920s, a young woman goes to live with her two aunts and uncovers family secrets related to the facade of quiet country life and the losses of the Great War.

Historical Accuracy: The novel focusses on relationships more than the period, but it does present an interesting portrait of post-war England in which loss and regret were constant.

ELLEN GILCHRIST (1935-)

Born in Vicksburg, Mississippi, Gilchrist is a graduate of Millsaps College. She is an author and journalist, as well as a frequent commentator on National Public Radio's ''Morning Edition.'' She lives in Fayetteville, Arkansas, and her works have been praised for their depiction of Southern life and culture.

2408 *Anabasis: A Journey to the Interior*

Date of Publication: 1994
Subject(s): Ancient Greece; Peloponnesian War
Fictional character(s): Auria, Slave; Philokrates, Teacher; Meion, Young Man
Time Period(s): 5th century B.C. (431 B.C.)
Locale(s): Greece

Summary: The novel tells the story of the slave girl Auria, who, in defiance of tradition, is raised by a philosopher and teacher. She develops her own sense of self-worth and identity. Her experiences are set in the decline of the Golden Age of Greece and the endless war with Sparta.

Historical Accuracy: Although the author does not feel this is a book of history, the period background seems genuine.

JANICE HOLT GILES (1909-1979)

An American writer born in Arkansas, Giles attended the University of Arkansas and Transylvania College. She worked for a time as a director of religious education in Arkansas before becoming a full-time and prolific writer in 1950.

2409 *The Believers*

Date of Publication: 1957
Subject(s): Settlement of the American Frontier; Shakers; Religious Conflict
Fictional character(s): Rebecca Fowler, Spouse (of Cooper); Richard Cooper, Settler
Time Period(s): 1800s
Locale(s): Kentucky

Summary: After the death of a child, Richard Cooper converts and moves to a Shaker community in Kentucky. His wife, Rebecca, dutifully tries to follow the strange customs of the community until she is forced to rebel.

Historical Accuracy: The novel offers a convincing portrait of everyday life in a Shaker village of the period.

2410 *The Great Adventure*

Date of Publication: 1966
Subject(s): American West
Fictional character(s): Joe Fowler, Mountain Man, Guide; Pierre Driant, Trapper; Johnny Fowler, Trader
Historical character(s): Jim Bridger, Mountain Man; Tom Fitzpatrick, Mountain Man; William Sublette, Mountain Man; Benjamin Bonneville, Military Personnel (captain); William Drummond, Military Personnel (captain)
Time Period(s): 1830s
Locale(s): Santa Fe, New Mexico; Pacific Northwest; Rocky Mountains

Summary: Joe Fowler leads a trapping party from Sante Fe to Oregon where he assists Captain Bonneville in his assignment to spy on the British during the Northwest border dispute.

Historical Accuracy: The novel is detailed in its history and authentic in its details of frontier life and the fur trade.

2411 *Hannah Fowler*

Date of Publication: 1956
Subject(s): Settlement of the American Frontier; American Colonies; Indians
Fictional character(s): Hannah Moore Fowler, Settler; Samuel Moore, Settler; Tice Fowler, Frontiersman
Time Period(s): 1770s (1778)
Locale(s): Kentucky

Summary: This is a story of pioneer life in Kentucky during the 1770s. Hannah Moore marries Tice Fowler, and they carve out a homestead in the wilderness. They must contend with Indian attacks and other frontier hardships.

Historical Accuracy: The details of frontier life and the sensibilities of the settlers are realistically drawn.

2412 *Johnny Osage*

Date of Publication: 1960
Subject(s): Settlement of the American Frontier; Indians
Fictional character(s): Johnny Fowler Osage, Trader; Judith Lowell, Teacher
Time Period(s): 1820s (1821)
Locale(s): Arkansas; Oklahoma

Summary: Johnny Fowler, the son of Hannah Fowler, travels west to the old Osage homeland in present day Oklahoma as a partner in a trading post. He is joined by a group of missionaries intent on "improving" the Indians as the bitter feud between the Osage and the Cherokee explodes into raids and massacres.

Historical Accuracy: The novel is convincing in its rendering of the period and customs.

2413 *The Kentuckians*

Date of Publication: 1953
Subject(s): Settlement of the American Frontier; American Colonies; American Revolution
Fictional character(s): David Cooper, Frontiersman; Bethia Jordan, Settler
Historical character(s): Daniel Boone, Frontiersman
Time Period(s): 1760s; 1770s (1769-1777)
Locale(s): Kentucky

Summary: The novel chronicles the struggles of the first pioneers in the Kentucky wilderness and the agitation of the Transylvania Company's push for separate statehood and freedom from the authority of Virginia. David Cooper loses Bethia to his enemy as the settlers battle the British and their Indian allies.

Historical Accuracy: This is a fascinating period of American history rendered with authenticity and conviction.

2414 *The Land Beyond the Mountains*

Date of Publication: 1958
Subject(s): Settlement of the American Frontier
Fictional character(s): Cassius Cartwright, Military Personnel (major)
Historical character(s): James Wilkinson, Military Personnel (general)

Time Period(s): 1780s; 1790s (1783-1792)
Locale(s): Kentucky

Summary: The background of the novel is the Spanish Conspiracy of General James Wilkinson who attempts to wrestle away Kentucky from the United States to create an independent empire in the wilderness. Cass Cartwright is initially attracted to Wilkinson's offer of aid to the embattled Kentucky settlers against Indian raids, but Wilkinson's shady dealings with the Spanish governor in New Orleans reveal his true intentions.

Historical Accuracy: This is a fascinating portrait of a little known period of frontier development and the elusive figure of Wilkinson.

2415 *Run Me a River*

Date of Publication: 1964
Subject(s): Civil War—U.S.; Riverboats
Fictional character(s): Bohannon Cartwright, Sailor (riverman)
Time Period(s): 1860s (1861)
Locale(s): Green River, Kentucky

Summary: As the Civil War begins, Bo Cartwright's desire to be left in peace to run his riverboat is challenged when Confederate troops occupy Bowling Green. There follows an exciting five day race upstream ahead of the Confederates and away from the federal gunboats to the safety of Evansville.

Historical Accuracy: The author admits to some slight manipulation of the chronology here.

2416 *Savanna*

Date of Publication: 1961
Subject(s): American West; Indians
Fictional character(s): Savanna Fowler, Widow(er)
Historical character(s): Sam Houston, Political Figure; Auguste Chouteau, Trader, Frontiersman
Time Period(s): 1830s
Locale(s): Fort Gibson, Arkansas

Summary: Savanna Fowler, a 19-year-old widow in the turbulent Arkansas Territory, runs her own trading store in fierce competition with Auguste Chouteau and Sam Houston. What precisely is Houston up to? Savanna is a remarkable portrait of a strong frontier woman on her own.

Historical Accuracy: The novel is authentic both in its history and its details of frontier life in the Arkansas Territory.

2417 *Six-Horse Hitch*

Date of Publication: 1969
Subject(s): American West; Stagecoaches; Indians
Fictional character(s): Starr Fowler, Driver (stage coach); Ed Westmoreland, Trader
Historical character(s): Ben Holladay, Businessman; Jack Slade, Outlaw
Time Period(s): 1850s (1859)
Locale(s): Utah; Colorado; Pacific Northwest

Summary: The story of the great Overland Mail and Stage line whose coaches ran from Missouri to the Pacific is told through the adventures of Starr Fowler, a stage coach driver. The hazards of nature, Indian attacks, and outlaw hold-ups are revealed dramatically and realistically.

Historical Accuracy: The atmosphere and details of the stage coaching days are accurately presented.

2418 *Voyage to Santa Fe*

Date of Publication: 1962
Subject(s): American West
Fictional character(s): Johnny Fowler, Trader; Janice Fowler, Spouse
Time Period(s): 1820s (1823)
Locale(s): Arkansas; Santa Fe, New Mexico

Summary: In this sequel to *Johnny Osage*, Johnny Fowler and his young wife, Janice, journey west from the Arkansas territory for Santa Fe with a 20-man mule train carrying trading goods. Johnny must contend with a rough collection of muleskinners, floods, droughts, wild animals, attacks, and treachery.

Historical Accuracy: The details of frontier life are exact and scrupulously presented.

DONNA GILLESPIE

2419 *The Light Bearer*

Date of Publication: 1994
Subject(s): Roman Empire; Tribal Life—Germanic
Fictional character(s): Auriane, Warrior, Religious (priestess); Marcus Julianus, Political Figure
Time Period(s): 1st century
Locale(s): Germany; Rome, Roman Empire

Summary: The cultural conflict between the Germanic tribes and the Roman Empire is dramatized in the adventures of Auriane, the daughter of a tribal chieftain, who takes the oath of a warrior to revenge herself on the Roman invaders. Her fate leads her to Rome itself and a surprisng connection with Roman statesmen Marcus Julianus.

Historical Accuracy: The tale emphasizes adventure, but the period elements are convincing.

JANE GILLESPIE (1923-)

2420 *Ladysmead: A Novel in the Jane Austen Tradition*

Date of Publication: 1982
Subject(s): Regency Romance
Fictional character(s): Thomas Cockley, Religious (clergyman); Sophia Lockley, Gentlewoman
Time Period(s): 19th century (Regency period)
Locale(s): Lancashire, England

Summary: The Reverend Thomas Lockley has several marriageable daughters, and when his wife dies the task to find suitable husbands for her sisters falls to Sophia. Her fate seems to be spinsterhood.

Historical Accuracy: The novel is a convincing echoing of the Jane Austen milieu with authentic period touches.

2421 *Teverton Hall*

Date of Publication: 1983
Subject(s): Regency Romance
Fictional character(s): William Collins, Religious (rector); George Dallow, Gentleman; Corinna Dallow, Gentlewoman
Time Period(s): 19th century (Regency period)
Locale(s): Essex, England; Bath, England

Summary: This Regency romance describes the courtship complications of the Dallows of Teverton Hall. It borrows characters from Jane Austen's *Pride and Prejudice*, including the awful Reverend William Collins.

Historical Accuracy: The author evokes the Austen-like scenes with skill and authentic period touches.

ELIAS GILNER (1888-1976)

Gilner was a Russian-born American playwright, novelist, and author of nonfiction works.

2422 *Prince of Israel*

Date of Publication: 1952
Subject(s): Jewish Revolt; Roman Empire; Jews
Historical character(s): Simon Bar Kokhba, Leader (Jewish revolt); Akiba ben Joseph, Religious (rabbi); Hadrian, Ruler (Roman Emperor)
Time Period(s): 2nd century
Locale(s): Israel; Rome, Roman Empire

Summary: This account of the Jewish Revolt against the Romans during the reign of Hadrian concentrates on two central figures in the conflict, military leader Simon Bar Kokhba and spiritual leader Rabbi Akiba Ben-Joseph. The novel chronicles the Jews' valiant stand against the might of the Roman Empire.

Historical Accuracy: The novel is faithful to the facts of history in its account of the revolt.

CHARLES JAMES LOUIS GILSON
(1878-1973)

Gilson is an author of science fiction and fantasy novels, including *The City of the Sorcerer* and *The Lost City*.

2423 *The White Cockade*

Date of Publication: 1924
Subject(s): French Revolution; Identity—Concealed
Fictional character(s): Henri de Savenay, Nobleman, Revolutionary
Time Period(s): 1780s
Locale(s): France

Summary: This historical romance set during the French Revolution concerns Henri de Savenay, son of a nobleman, who is brought up as a street gamin in the slums of Paris ignorant of his identity. Committed to the Revolution, he learns of his

identity and is faced with the conflict of remaining true to the cause or to his blood.

Historical Accuracy: The historical elements are well drawn and convincing.

JEAN GIONO (1895-1970)

A French author born in Monosque in the Basses-Alpes, Giono was a novelist, poet, and playwright. He made his small town life in provincial Southern France the locale for much of his work.

2424 *The Horseman on the Roof*

Date of Publication: 1954
Subject(s): Plague; Picaresque Adventure
Fictional character(s): Angelo Pardi, Military Personnel (colonel of hussars); Pauline Theus, Noblewoman (Marquise de Theus)
Time Period(s): 1830s (1838)
Locale(s): Provence, France

Summary: The novel describes the travels of Angelo Pardi, a fugitive Italian colonel of hussars, through Provence during an epidemic of cholera. Picaresque in tone, the description of the dying and the dead is realistically rendered as Angelo travels across the blighted landscape digging graves and helping the sick, accompanied by a noblewoman, Pauline Theus.

Historical Accuracy: The novel seems realistic and accurate in its descriptions of the plague and the period.

2425 *The Straw Man*

Date of Publication: 1959
Subject(s): Picaresque Adventure
Fictional character(s): Angelo Pardi, Military Personnel (hussar colonel)
Time Period(s): 1840s (1848)
Locale(s): Italy

Summary: This sequel to *Horsemen on the Roof* continues the picaresque adventures of Colonel Angelo Pardi. He finds himself involved in the Italian revolution against Austria in 1848 as a revolutionary group seeks to use him as a scapegoat.

Historical Accuracy: The novel's greatest success is in its convincingly painted background of Italian cities and countryside.

DIANE GLANCY (1941-)

An American poet, dramatist, short story writer, essayist, and novelist, Glancy was born in Kansas City, Missouri, and graduated from the University of Missouri and the University of Iowa. She is a professor of English at Macalester College and is the winner of an American Book Award for a book of essays, *Claiming Breath*. She has also published a volume of poetry, *One Age in a Dream*, and a collection of short stories, *Trigger Dance*.

2426 *Pushing the Bear: A Novel of the Trail of Tears*

Date of Publication: 1996
Subject(s): Indians; Tribal Life—Native American; Trail of Tears
Fictional character(s): Maritole, Indian (Cherokee)
Time Period(s): 1830s (1838-1839)
Locale(s): North Carolina; Oklahoma

Summary: The forced resettlement of the Cherokees from North Carolina to present-day Oklahoma along what came to be known as the Trail of Tears is recounted by a variety of the participants, Indians and whites, as well as from fragments of the actual historical record. The central narrator, Maritole, struggles with "pushing the bear," the heavy burden of anger, madness, and physical strain, along the brutal forced march of her people.

Historical Accuracy: The novel's picture of the Cherokees' exodus is honestly and convincingly drawn.

ALICE GLASGOW

2427 *The Twisted Tendril*

Date of Publication: 1928
Subject(s): Civil War—U.S.; Biography, Fictionalized; Assassination
Historical character(s): John Wilkes Booth, Actor, Murderer
Time Period(s): 1860s
Locale(s): United States

Summary: The novel is a fictional account of the Lincoln assassination and the conspiracy led by John Wilkes Booth. The story dramatizes the stages of Booth's involvement in the plot and the events leading to his death.

Historical Accuracy: The novel provides a believable version of the events, weaving together factual details with some invented scenes and dialogue.

PHILIP GLAZEBROOK (1937-)

An Englishman born in London, Glazebrook was educated at Eton and Trinity College, Cambridge. He was the honorary attache to the British Embassy in Rome and has worked as an advertising copywriter and film scriptwriter. He is the author of a travel book, *Journey to Kars.*

2428 *Captain Vinegar's Commission*

Date of Publication: 1987
Subject(s): Picaresque Adventure; Victorian Period
Fictional character(s): Tresham Pitcher, Young Man; Roland Farr, Gentleman
Time Period(s): 1840s; 1850s
Locale(s): England; Middle East; Asia Minor

Summary: This picaresque travel story is set during the Victorian period and involves young Tresham Pitcher. His friend Roland Farr invents for Pitcher the persona of "Captain Vinegar," and persuades a publisher to fund a book on the Captain's Middle East travels. The two embark on an over-

land journey from Vienna through Asia Minor to Palmyra with a series of adventures along the way.

Historical Accuracy: The novel is comically inventive and imaginative in capturing the world of 19th century travel and the Middle East.

MARY GLAZENER (1921-)

Glazener was born in Atlanta, Georgia, and graduated from Clemson University in 1975. She has worked as a legal secretary and as a producer and performer on a children's television program. She is the author of the plays *The Stumbling Block* and *The Slave Girl.*

2429 *The Cup of Wrath*

Date of Publication: 1991
Subject(s): Nazis; World War II
Historical character(s): Dietrich Bonhoeffer, Writer, Religious (theologian)
Time Period(s): 1930s; 1940s (1933-1945)
Locale(s): Berlin, Germany

Summary: Dietrich Bonhoeffer is the leader of a resistance movement during Hitler's rule. His opposition to the Nazis is dramatized into a realistic and truthful thriller.

Historical Accuracy: The situations described are based on actual events.

JUDITH GLEASON (1929-)

Gleason was born in California and graduated from Radcliffe College and Columbia University. She is a writer of adult and juvenile fiction. Her books include *This Africa* and *Leaf and Bone.*

2430 *Agotime, Her Legend*

Date of Publication: 1970
Subject(s): Slavery
Historical character(s): Agotime, Royalty (Dahomean queen)
Time Period(s): 19th century
Locale(s): Africa (west); Brazil; At Sea

Summary: The novel recounts the story of Dahomean queen Agotime, who, after the death of her husband, is sold into slavery. The novel graphically describes the infamous Middle Passage, or slave route, to America. Agotime is taken to Brazil, where she participates in a slave revolt.

Historical Accuracy: The novel blends the known facts with legend, and depends on the writer's imagination when facts and details are unknown.

VICTORIA GLENDINNING (1937-)

British biographer and novelist Glendinning was born in Yorkshire and attended Somerville College, Oxford. She received a diploma in social administration from Southampton University. A writer since 1969, Glendinning has also worked part-time in psychiatric social work. She is the author of biographies of Rebecca West, Vita Sackville-

West, Edith Sitwell, Elizabeth Bowen, and Anthony Trollope. Her biography of Trllope won the Whitehead Award.

`2431` *Electricity: A Novel*

Date of Publication: 1995
Subject(s): Victorian Period
Fictional character(s): Charlotte Mortimer, Young Woman; Peter Fisher, Engineer
Time Period(s): 1880s; 1890s
Locale(s): England

Summary: Electricity becomes a metaphor in this turn-of-the-century tale. Charlotte Mortimer marries a young electrical engineer and accompanies her husband while he wires the estate of a country gentleman. There she experiences a different kind of electricity. As new technology calls old values into question, Charlotte must adapt to changes in herself and in her world.

Historical Accuracy: The novel is adept at capturing the end of the 19th century and the atmosphere of social change.

JOHN GLOAG (1896-)

`2432` *Artorius Rex*

Date of Publication: 1977
Subject(s): Roman Empire; Arthurian Legends
Fictional character(s): Caius Geladius, Government Official; Merlin, Courtier; Gwinfreda, Royalty (Saxon princess); Artorius, Military Personnel (general)
Time Period(s): 6th century
Locale(s): England

Summary: The final volume of a trilogy on Roman Britain tells the story of Artorius, the historical original of the legendary King Arthur. Artorius struggles to unite Britain against the Irish, the Picts, and the Saxons. Artorius' success is undermined by his disastrous relationship with Gwinfrida, the daughter of a Saxon king. The story of Artorius' rise and fall is described by Caius Geladius in his report to the Roman Emperor Justinian.

Historical Accuracy: While the figure of Artorius has a basis in historical fact, his story is largely fanciful. Yet the novel makes reliable use of historical sources in reflecting the era.

`2433` *Caesar of the Narrow Seas*

Date of Publication: 1969
Subject(s): Roman Empire; Barbarians
Fictional character(s): Lucius Priscus, Military Personnel (centurion)
Historical character(s): Marcus Aurelius Carausius, Military Personnel (commander)
Time Period(s): 3rd century (286-291)
Locale(s): England

Summary: The novel describes the period in the 3rd century in which the Roman General Carausius ruled Britain as an independent empire. Told from the perspective of Lucius Priscus, a clenturion, the novel captures Carausius' struggles against invading barbarians who see Britain as an attractive prize weakly held by a declining Roman Empire.

Historical Accuracy: The novel is convincing in its historical background, a blend of fact and invention.

`2434` *The Eagles Depart*

Date of Publication: 1973
Subject(s): Roman Empire
Fictional character(s): Marcus Geladius, Military Personnel (centurian)
Historical character(s): Magnus Maximus, Ruler (Roman emperor)
Time Period(s): 5th century
Locale(s): England

Summary: In this installment of the author's series of novels on Roman Britain, Marcus Geladius, the son of a Roman father and native British mother, narrates his life story. He becomes a distinguished soldier, rising to the command of the XXth Legion, and struggles to maintain Roman control of Britain as the Empire's power wanes, and Britain is torn apart by civil war.

Historical Accuracy: The novel shows evident research into the period and its customs which are reproduced convincingly.

MOLLY GLOSS (1944-)

An American from Portland, Oregon, Gloss graduated from Portland State College. She was an elementary school teacher and a freelance writer. She has written both Western novels and science fiction.

`2435` *The Jump-Off Creek*

Date of Publication: 1989
Subject(s): American West; Homesteading
Fictional character(s): Lydia Sanderson, Frontierswoman
Time Period(s): 1890s
Locale(s): Oregon

Summary: Lydia Sanderson leaves an unhappy marriage to try homesteading on her own in Oregon during the 1890s. Told through her journal, the novel follows her development as she copes with harsh conditions and the few reclusive people she encounters.

Historical Accuracy: The story offers an authentic look at frontier life of the period.

DOUGLAS GLOVER (1948-)

Born in Canada, Glover is a graduate of the University of Edinburgh and the University of Iowa. He teaches creative writing at Skidmore College and is considered one of Canada's most talented writers. His short story collection, *The Mad River and Other Stories* began his literary career.

`2436` *The Life and Times of Captain N.*

Date of Publication: 1993
Subject(s): American Revolution; Indians

Fictional character(s): Hendrick Nellis, Loyalist, Military Personnel (captain); Mary Hunsacker, Immigrant, Captive; Oskar Nellis, Young Man
Time Period(s): 1770s; 1780s (1779-1781)
Locale(s): New York; Canada

Summary: Adventures during the American Revolution are described by Oskar Nellis, the young son of Captain Hendrick Nellis who is a Tory guerilla fighter and rescuer of captured whites from Indians. Captain Nellis captures his son Oskar and forces him to become a reluctant Loyalist in an adventure that involves Mary Hunsacker, a German immigrant captured by the Indians.

Historical Accuracy: Some of the events are based loosely on real incidents. This is a weirdly inventive modernist spin on the period, more phantasmagorical than actual.

JUDITH GLOVER (1943-)

Glover is an English writer who has worked as a reporter for the *Wolverhampton Express and Star*. She is fascinated by history, especially English rural history, and has written regional guidebooks as well as fiction.

2437 *The Imagination of the Heart*
Date of Publication: 1989
Subject(s): Romance; Victorian Period
Fictional character(s): Catherine March, Spouse; Oliver Van Der Kleve, Banker; Jonathan Rivers, Artist
Time Period(s): 1850s
Locale(s): England

Summary: The novel offers a portrait of a Victorian marriage. Catherine March, an orphan and former workhouse girl, marries a successful banker, Oliver Van Der Kleve, the governor of her charity school. She endures a loveless marriage and finds romance with the artist Jonathan Rivers, an affair that leads to tragedy.

Historical Accuracy: The novel is accomplished in capturing the Victorian atmosphere and many of its customs.

2438 *The Stallion Man*
Date of Publication: 1982
Subject(s): Romance; Victorian Period; Rural Life—England
Fictional character(s): Frank Morgan, Adventurer, Gypsy (part); Dinah Flynn, Saloon Hostess (barmaid); Rachel Bates, Gentlewoman
Time Period(s): 1850s (1852)
Locale(s): Sussex, England

Summary: Set in the 1850s in the Sussex countryside, the novel tells the story of Frank Morgan. Part gypsy, Morgan is a stallion man who visits farmers with mares for breeding but also wins the affection of numerous women. When he sets out to seduce Rachel Bates, the unhappy wife of Weatherfield's new rector, tragedy ensues.

Historical Accuracy: The novel offers an unusual and authentic look at rural customs and traditions of the period.

2439 *Tigerlilies*
Date of Publication: 1991
Subject(s): World War I
Fictional character(s): Flora Dennison, Gentlewoman; Roseen O'Connor, Gentlewoman, Widow(er)
Time Period(s): 1900s; 1910s
Locale(s): England

Summary: This is the story of a rivalry between two women. Flora Dennison is a gentle, privileged young woman and Roseen O'Connor is the daughter of her father's mistress. The two are opposites tempermentally, and when their paths cross during the outbreak of World War I, each has a major impact on the life of the other.

Historical Accuracy: This is a well plotted story with a solid period background.

CONSTANCE GLUYAS (1920-)

English-born Gluyas immigrated to the U.S. in 1944. She served in the British Royal Air Force during World War II.

2440 *Born to Be King*
Date of Publication: 1974
Subject(s): Jacobite Rebellion; Battle of Culloden
Fictional character(s): Christopher Moncrieff, Adventurer; Elizabeth Drummond, Young Woman
Historical character(s): Charles Edward Stuart, Royalty (prince)
Time Period(s): 1740s (1745)
Locale(s): Scotland; England

Summary: It is 1745 and the charismatic Bonnie Prince Charlie returns from exile in France. He gathers a Scottish army to wrest the English throne from George I and reinstate the Stuart line. The novel tells the story of the rebellion, climaxing in the defeat of the Stuart cause at Culloden. The narrative centers on adventurer Christopher Moncrieff and Elizabeth Drummond who disguises herself as a man to march with the prince.

Historical Accuracy: The novel is a blend of the fictional and the fanciful. The basic historical details are accurate though the plot is invented.

2441 *The King's Brat*
Date of Publication: 1972
Subject(s): Restoration Period; Royalty—England
Fictional character(s): Angel Dawson, Streetperson; Nicholas Tavington, Nobleman (Earl of Benbrook)
Historical character(s): Charles II, Ruler (King of England); Barbara Villiers, Lover (the king's mistress), Gentlewoman; Catherine of Braganza, Royalty (queen consort of Charles II)
Time Period(s): 17th century (1660s)
Locale(s): London, England

Summary: At the age of 15, Angel Dawson, a street waif, is released from Newgate Prison to carry a dying friend's message to his brother. The man turns out to be the Earl of Benbrook, and a pygmalion romance ensues that elevates Angel from the street and prison to the court of Charles II.

Historical Accuracy: More fairy tale romance than plausible story, the novel is, however, convincing in its period touches.

2442 *My Lady Benbrook*

Date of Publication: 1974
Subject(s): Restoration Period; Royalty—England; Fires
Fictional character(s): Angel Dawson, Gentlewoman, Spouse (of Tavington); Nicholas Tavington, Nobleman (Earl of Benbrook)
Historical character(s): Charles II, Ruler (King of England); Barbara Villiers, Lover (the king's mistress), Gentlewoman
Time Period(s): 17th century (1666)
Locale(s): London, England

Summary: The novel continues the story of Angel Dawson begun in *The King's Brat*. Angel is a former street urchin who goes from Newgate Prison to become the wife of Nicholas Tavington, the Earl of Benbrook. At the court of Charles II, she becomes a rival of the King's mistress, Barbara Castlemaine, who launches a plot to destroy her.

Historical Accuracy: The story is fanciful with some authentic period painting.

2443 *My Lord Foxe*

Date of Publication: 1976
Subject(s): Civil War—England; Royalty—England
Fictional character(s): Brett Foxefield, Nobleman (Earl of Foxefield); Meredith Hartford, Gentlewoman
Historical character(s): Charles I, Ruler (King of England); Henrietta-Maria, Royalty (queen consort of Charles I); George Villiers, Nobleman (Duke of Buckingham); Oliver Cromwell, Political Figure
Time Period(s): 17th century (1640s)
Locale(s): England

Summary: Set during the reign of Charles I and the growing power of opposition from Cromwell and the Puritans, the story centers on Cavalier Brett Foxefield, a favorite of the king who dutifully stands by Charles, and the intrigues of the Duke of Buckingham and Queen Henrietta Maria.

Historical Accuracy: The period flavor and historical background are reliable, though the story is fanciful.

ROBERT GODDARD (1954-)

An English writer born in Hampshire, Goddard graduated from Cambridge and the University of Exeter. He worked as an educational administrator in Devon, England before becoming a full-time writer. He received a Booker Prize nomination in 1986 for *Past Caring*. His work has been admired for his intriguing and suspenseful narratives, which have been compared to the novels of Daphne du Maurier. Most of Goddard's works show his preoccupation with the impact of the past on the present.

2444 *In Pale Battalions*

Date of Publication: 1988
Subject(s): World War I; Suspense

Fictional character(s): John Hallows, Military Personnel (captain), Heir; Leonora Hallows, Gentlewoman; Ralph Mompesson, Criminal (blackmailer)
Time Period(s): 1910s; 1920s
Locale(s): England; France

Summary: In 1916, Captain John Hallows is reported killed in action during the Battle of the Somme. His wife Leonora is blackmailed into marrying the American fortune hunter, Ralph Mompesson. After Leonora dies in childbirth and Mompesson is murdered, a man appears with an amazing story.

Historical Accuracy: The novel is an ingenious suspense story with a solid and realistic period background.

2445 *Painting the Darkness*

Date of Publication: 1985
Subject(s): Victorian Period; Identity—Concealed
Fictional character(s): James Norton, Heir; William Trenchard, Businessman; Constance Trenchard, Spouse
Time Period(s): 19th century
Locale(s): England

Summary: In this Victorian tale of disputed identity and buried secrets, James Norton appears in London claiming to be the long-presumed dead James Davenall. The revelation throws the Davenall family into an uproar of court cases and recriminations. James' former lover, Constance Trenchard, and her husband become embroiled in the dispute with tragic consequences.

Historical Accuracy: The novel displays authentic period elements.

PARKE GODWIN (1929-)

A former actor and New Yorker, Parke Godwin moved west to Auburn, California, and became a full-time writer. He has written more than a dozen books in the genres of science fiction, fantasy and historical fiction. Godwin won the World Fantasy Award for *Beloved Exile* (1984).

2446 *Beloved Exile*

Date of Publication: 1984
Subject(s): Dark Ages; Myths and Legends; Arthurian Legends
Fictional character(s): Guenevere, Royalty (queen consort of King Arthur); Launcelot, Knight; Bedivere, Knight
Time Period(s): 6th century
Locale(s): England

Summary: In this second volume of a trilogy based on Arthurian legend, Arthur has died, and Guenevere attempts to maintain the power that her love for Launcelot helped to undermine. The Celtic world that she inhabits slowly gives way to the new Saxon future.

Historical Accuracy: The novel is a fantasy, not history, but it is filled with period atmosphere that creates a plausible historical context for the events.

2447 *Firelord*

Date of Publication: 1980
Subject(s): Dark Ages; Myths and Legends; Arthurian Legends
Fictional character(s): Arthur, Ruler (king of the Britons); Guenevere, Royalty (queen consort of Arthur); Launcelot, Knight
Time Period(s): 6th century
Locale(s): England

Summary: King Arthur tells his own story in this autobiography that blends authentic history with myth and legend. The famous triangle of love and honor involving the king, Guenevere, and Launcelot is chronicled but with sufficient connection to the period to suggest what might have happened if their story was historical.

Historical Accuracy: Although the novel is a fantasy, it is placed in an historically accurate setting.

2448 *Robin and the King*

Date of Publication: 1993
Subject(s): Norman Conquest; Middle Ages; Crime and Criminals
Fictional character(s): Edward Aelredson, Outlaw (Robin Hood), Nobleman; Marian, Spouse
Historical character(s): William the Conqueror, Ruler (King of England); William II, Ruler (King of England)
Time Period(s): 11th century (1083-1100)
Locale(s): England

Summary: Robin and Marian, now middle-aged, are still battling the absolute rule of England's Norman conquerors. However, a new foreign threat causes Robin to join with William in a series of daring adventures.

Historical Accuracy: The period is rendered with a credible degree of authority.

2449 *Sherwood*

Date of Publication: 1991
Subject(s): Middle Ages; Norman Conquest; Crime and Criminals
Fictional character(s): Edward Aelredson, Nobleman (aka Robin Hood); Ralf FitzGerald, Knight (Sheriff of Nottingham); Marian, Young Woman
Historical character(s): William the Conqueror, Ruler (King of England); Matilda of Flanders, Royalty (queen consort of William I)
Time Period(s): 11th century (1060s)
Locale(s): Nottingham, England

Summary: This version of the Robin Hood story imagines a realistic basis for the legend and is set in the 11th century rather than the 12th of tradition. Robin is a Saxon landowner who must contend with the effects of the Norman Conquest. In this version, the Sheriff of Nottingham is a sympathetic Norman knight forced to impose King William's rigid laws on the Saxons who resist their fate.

Historical Accuracy: The author makes a strong case for her historical Robin Hood, and creates a plausible and fully detailed period and set of circumstances.

2450 *The Tower of Beowulf*

Date of Publication: 1995
Subject(s): Dark Ages; Myths and Legends
Fictional character(s): Beowulf, Warrior, Chieftain; Arothgar, Ruler (King of the Danes); Grendel, Monster
Time Period(s): 6th century
Locale(s): Denmark

Summary: The novel offers an adaptation of the Beowulf legend, tracing the career of the hero as he proves himself a remarkable leader in a series of adventures. His most fateful challenge is a battle to the death with the monster Grendel and his horrific mother. The author provides an interesting interpretation of the Beowulf story by turning Grendel and his mother into near-humans and Beowulf into a kind of reverse Hamlet. The effect is a modernized version of the epic story.

Historical Accuracy: The novel offers a blend of the realistic and the legendary, as well as an authentic version of the 6th century.

NIKOLAI V. GOGOL (1809-1852)

Gogol was a Russian writer born in the Ukraine whose customs and folklore he used as a basis for his tales. His masterpiece is *Dead Souls*. He also wrote several plays of which the best known is *The Inspector General*.

2451 *Taras Bulba*

Date of Publication: 1835
Subject(s): Russian Empire; Cossacks
Fictional character(s): Taras Bulba, Warrior (Cossack); Otap, Warrior (Cossack); Andru, Warrior (Cossack)
Time Period(s): 15th century
Locale(s): Russia; Poland (southeastern)

Summary: This novel of the Cossacks in Russia is centered on patriarch Bulba and his two sons. The younger falls in love with a Polish girl and betrays his people. The elder son is captured by the Poles.

Historical Accuracy: There are strong and convincing scenes of the Cossacks on the march and in battle.

MICHAEL GOLDING

2452 *Simple Prayers*

Date of Publication: 1994
Subject(s): Rural Life—Italy; Middle Ages
Fictional character(s): Albertino, Businessman (merchant); Ermenegilda, Gentlewoman; Miriam, Gentlewoman
Time Period(s): 14th century
Locale(s): Venice, Italy

Summary: On an island in the Venice lagoon, a corpse with bloody welts washes up on shore and brings about changes in the quiet life of the villagers.

Historical Accuracy: The texture of medieval life is ably and genuinely presented.

WILLIAM GOLDING (1911-1993)

An English writer born in Cornwall, Golding graduated from Oxford. He commanded a ship during World War II. His war experience was, in his view, a turning point when he began to see what people were capable of doing to one another. His novels attempt to portray man's constant struggle between a civilized self and a hidden, darker nature. His most famous novel is *Lord of the Flies*, which descibes the descent into violence and bestiality of a group of shipwrecked public school boys. Golding won the Nobel Prize for Literature in 1983.

`2453` *Close Quarters*

Date of Publication: 1987
Subject(s): Napoleonic Era; Sea Story
Fictional character(s): Edmund Talbot, Gentleman
Time Period(s): 1810s (1815)
Locale(s): At Sea (England to Australia)

Summary: In the second volume of a trilogy describing a voyage during the Napoleonic Era of an aged ship of the line carrying passengers to Australia, news reaches the ship of Napoleon's defeat and exile to Elba. Edmund Talbot, whose journal provides much of the narrative, falls in love.

Historical Accuracy: The period is evoked with authentic details.

`2454` *Fire Down Below*

Date of Publication: 1989
Subject(s): Sea Story; Napoleonic Era
Fictional character(s): Edmund Talbot, Gentleman
Time Period(s): 1810s (1815)
Locale(s): At Sea (England to Australia)

Summary: In the third and final volume describing a sea voyage during the Napoleonic era, the aged ship of the line struggles to reach port, while dissension among the passengers and crew reaches a climax.

Historical Accuracy: The period atmosphere is convincingly described.

`2455` *The Inheritors*

Date of Publication: 1955
Subject(s): Prehistory; Tribal Life—Prehistoric
Fictional character(s): Mal, Prehistoric Human, Chieftain; Lok, Prehistoric Human
Time Period(s): Indeterminate Past
Locale(s): Earth

Summary: A paleolithic tribe encounters more advanced humans in its trek from winter quarters to the sea. It is ill-prepared for either change in routine or the customs of the other tribe.

Historical Accuracy: The evocation of a primitive people is particularly compelling and believable.

`2456` *Rites of Passage*

Date of Publication: 1980

Subject(s): Napoleonic Era; Sea Story
Fictional character(s): Edmund Talbot, Gentleman; Robert Colley, Religious (clergyman)
Time Period(s): 1810s (1814-1815)
Locale(s): At Sea (England to Australia)

Summary: In the first volume of a trilogy describing a sea voyage during the Napoleonic Era, Edward Talbot, a young gentlemen narrates the events that take place during the passage of a ship from England to Australia.

Historical Accuracy: The novel features authentic period elements as the background for Golding's dark meditation.

`2457` *The Spire*

Date of Publication: 1964
Subject(s): Middle Ages; Religious Life
Fictional character(s): Jocelin, Religious (dean of Salisbury Cathedral); Roger Mason, Artisan; Anselm, Religious
Time Period(s): 13th century; 14th century
Locale(s): Salisbury, England

Summary: Under the direction of Jocelin, a visionary dean who is driven to glorify God no matter the cost to himself or others, Salisbury Cathedral's spire is built. Jocelin's megalomania results in insanity and tragedy.

Historical Accuracy: Along with penetrating psychological insights, the novel offers convincing medieval details, both in architecture and social customs.

JAMES GOLDMAN (1927-)

Born in Chicago, Goldman is a playwright, screenwriter, novelist, and lyricist. He won the Writers Guild Award in 1967 for his screenplay *The Lion in Winter* and a Tony Award for *Follies*.

`2458` *Myself as Witness*

Date of Publication: 1979
Subject(s): Middle Ages; Royalty—England
Fictional character(s): Giraldus, Religious (monk)
Historical character(s): John, Ruler (King of England)
Time Period(s): 13th century (1210s)
Locale(s): England

Summary: The novel offers a revisionist portrait of England's King John. The monk Giraldus chronicles the tumultuous final years of John's reign that culminates in the signing of the Magna Carta. John emerges not as the evil king of tradition but instead as a clever though inept monarch. His inferiority to his famous parents, Henry II and Eleanor of Aquitaine, and his illustrious brother, Richard the Lionhearted, produces an erratic and unstable king.

Historical Accuracy: Giraldus possesses an anachronistically modern sensibility that undermines the novel's period feel. Experts may question the novel's interpretations of King John's character.

LAWRENCE GOLDMAN

2459 *The Castrato*

Date of Publication: 1973
Subject(s): Biography, Fictionalized; Musical Life
Historical character(s): Carlo Broschi, Singer (opera)
Time Period(s): 18th century
Locale(s): Europe

Summary: This is a fictionalized account of the great 18th-century Italian soprano Farinelli. Castrated in his boyhood to preserve his high-pitched voice, Farinelli becomes an operatic sensation throughout Europe. His success comes at a high personal cost, however, and the novel traces the impact of his mutilation on his life.

Historical Accuracy: The novels shows evidence of solid research and stays close to the known facts.

GLORIA GOLDREICH

2460 *Leah's Journey*

Date of Publication: 1978
Subject(s): Immigrants; Jews; Depression Era
Fictional character(s): Leah Goldfeder, Immigrant; David Goldfeder, Immigrant; Aaron Goldfeder, Military Personnel (soldier)
Time Period(s): 20th century (1919-1956)
Locale(s): Russia; New York, New York; Israel

Summary: The novel chronicles three generations of the Jewish experience during the 20th century. The story begins as Leah and David Goldfeder leave the oppression of Russia in 1919 for Manhattan's Lower East Side. Their struggle and rise to success is played out against the major events of the century.

Historical Accuracy: The novel's scenes and characters are authentically drawn and convincing.

2461 *West to Eden*

Date of Publication: 1987
Subject(s): American West; Jews; Disasters—Natural
Fictional character(s): Emma Coen, Companion; Isaac Lewin, Immigrant
Time Period(s): 19th century; 20th century (1897-1940)
Locale(s): Amsterdam, Netherlands; Galveston, Texas; Phoenix, Arizona

Summary: The novel describes the Jewish immigrant experience in the American West at the turn of the century. Emma Coen ventures to Galveston, Texas, with a plan to promote Jewish resettlement. There she meets Isaac Lewin. They endure the tidal wave of 1900 before heading to Arizona and later to California.

Historical Accuracy: The novel is solidly based in historical details and convincingly authentic in its atmosphere and retelling of events that are not widely known.

2462 *The Year of Our War*

Date of Publication: 1994
Subject(s): World War II
Fictional character(s): Sharon Grossberg, Teenager, Student—High School
Time Period(s): 1940s (1944)
Locale(s): Brooklyn, New York; Woodstock, New York

Summary: This coming of age novel takes place in 1944, the last full year of the war and the year Sharon Grossberg's mother dies. Sharon is left in the care of an extended family in New York, and she learns a great deal about life in the days leading up to peace.

Historical Accuracy: The novel offers a remarkably detailed portrait of the period.

LISA GOLDSTEIN (1953-)

American fantasy writer Goldstein was born in Los Angeles and graduated from UCLA. She is a co-owner of the Dark Carnival Bookstore in Berkeley, California. Her novel *The Red Magician*, the story of a young Jewish woman's coming of age during the Holocaust, has been widely praised.

2463 *Strange Devices of the Sun and Moon*

Date of Publication: 1993
Subject(s): Elizabethan Period; Witchcraft and Sorcery
Fictional character(s): Ann Wood, Businesswoman (bookseller); Margery, Witch
Historical character(s): Christopher Marlowe, Writer, Spy
Time Period(s): 16th century
Locale(s): London, England

Summary: With her husband dead and her son missing, Ann Wood struggles as a London bookseller. She becomes involved with playwright Christopher Marlowe, who is a spy for a mysterious benefactor. Intrigue and conspiracy involve the fate of Alice's son and the Queen of the Fairies.

Historical Accuracy: The period detail is delivered with rare skill.

JOHN GOLDTHORPE

2464 *The Same Scourge*

Date of Publication: 1956
Subject(s): Biblical Story; Roman Empire
Fictional character(s): Dorio, Military Personnel (Roman soldier)
Historical character(s): Jesus Christ, Biblical Figure; Pontius Pilate, Government Official, Biblical Figure
Time Period(s): 1st century
Locale(s): Jerusalem, Israel

Summary: The story of Jesus is seen against a backdrop of the Roman occupation of Judea. The central figure is the Roman soldier Dorio, who is charged with investigating the anti-Roman activities among the Jews in Galilee. He comes into contact with Jesus of Nazareth, and what he learns from Jesus produces a moral crisis of divided loyalties and spiritual reassessment.

Historical Accuracy: The period detail is recorded with scrupulous attention to fact. Unfortunately, the characters and the dialogue are less convincing.

SERGEANNE GOLON
(PSEUD. OF SERGE GOLON, 1903-1972; ANNE GOLON)

Sergeanne Golon is the pseudonym for French husband and wife Serge and Anne Golon. Serge Golon was an engineer, prospector, chemist, and geologist before turning to writing. Anne Golon, the daughter of a French naval officer, became a journalist. The pair met while pursuing their separate careers in Africa. After returning to France in 1952 they devoted themselves to chronicling the adventures of Angelique, one of the world's most famous and bestselling fictional heroines. After Serge Golon died, Anne continued Angelique's adventures on her own.

2465 *Angelique*

Date of Publication: 1958
Subject(s): Royalty—France
Fictional character(s): Angelique de Sance, Noblewoman; Joffrey de Peyrac, Nobleman; Philippe du Plessis-Belliere, Government Official (marshal of France)
Historical character(s): Louis XIV, Ruler (King of France); Anne de Montpensier, Noblewoman (the king's cousin); Philippe I, Duc d'Orleans, Royalty (the king's brother); Louis de Conde, Military Personnel, Courtier
Time Period(s): 17th century (1648-1667)
Locale(s): Paris, France; Toulouse, France; Poitou, France

Summary: The first book in the series begins with Angelique's childhood and continues through her convent school days and arranged marriage to the brilliant, wealthy Comte de Peyrac, by whom she has two sons. When Peyrac is arrested on a trumped-up charge of sorcery and is executed, Angelique, reduced to poverty, joins the Parisien underworld. She rises from poverty to become a successful businesswoman and regains a place in court.

Historical Accuracy: The novel and the series is marked by historical accuracy and a clear depiction of French history and culture.

2466 *Angelique and the Demon*

Date of Publication: 1972
Subject(s): American Colonies; Indians
Fictional character(s): Angelique de Peyrac, Noblewoman; Joffrey de Peyrac, Nobleman; Ambroisine de Maudribourg, Noblewoman; Piksarett, Indian (Patsuikett), Chieftain
Historical character(s): William Phipps, Government Official (royal governor)
Time Period(s): 17th century (1690s)
Locale(s): Goldsboro, American Colonies

Summary: The Duchess de Maudribourg, a beautiful French noblewoman of dubious and devilish reputation, is sent to America to kill Angelique and destroy Peyrac. Angelique

battles the duchess with the help of her son and the chief of the Patsuiketts.

Historical Accuracy: The novel features accurate background details of the tenuous coexistence of the French and the English in Acadia and New England that explode in the French and Indian Wars.

2467 *Angelique and the Ghosts*

Date of Publication: 1976
Subject(s): Frontier—Canada
Fictional character(s): Angelique de Peyrac, Noblewoman; Joffrey de Peyrac, Nobleman; Nicholas de Bardagne, Diplomat
Time Period(s): 17th century (1690s)
Locale(s): St. Lawrence River, Canada

Summary: The Peyracs and their entourage sail up the St. Lawrence River toward Quebec to face what could be a hostile reception from the French. Along the way, Angelique must outwit her old admirer, Count de Bardagne, an agent of the king.

Historical Accuracy: There are details of cultural history here but few actual historical events. More attention is paid to romance.

2468 *Angelique and the King*

Date of Publication: 1960
Subject(s): Royalty—France
Fictional character(s): Angelique du Plessis-Belliere, Noblewoman; Philippe du Plessis-Belliere, Nobleman
Historical character(s): Louis XIV, Ruler (King of France); Francoise Athenais Rochechouart de Mortemart, Lover (mistress of the king), Gentlewoman
Time Period(s): 17th century (1667-1675)
Locale(s): Paris, France; Versailles, France

Summary: Angelique and her sons become deeply involved in the intrigues of Louis XIV's court. At the same time, Angelique tries to win the love of her handsome but emotionally distant husband, Philippe du Plessis-Belliere.

Historical Accuracy: The culture and customs of the Sun King's court are believably rendered here.

2469 *Angelique in Barbary*

Date of Publication:
Subject(s): Pirates; Slavery
Fictional character(s): Angelique du Plessis-Belliere, Noblewoman; Rescator, Pirate; Osman Faraji, Servant (vizier of the sultan)
Historical character(s): Mulai Ismail, Ruler (Sultan of Morocco); Victor de Vivonne, Military Personnel (admiral of the French fleet); Mezze-Morte, Pirate
Time Period(s): 17th century
Locale(s): Marseilles, France; Meknes, Morocco; Crete, Greece

Summary: To escape the king's attention and having learned that her first husband may still be alive, Angelique journeys through the Mediterranean to find him. Captured by pirates, she is sold as a slave and purchased by the sultan of Morocco.

She resists the vigilance of the sultan's vizier and embarks on a daring escape with a band of French captives.

Historical Accuracy: The book is less concerned with historical fact than others in the series, but it still provides a believable account of Muslim culture and life in the Mediterranean during the 1600s.

2470 *Angelique in Love*

Date of Publication: 1961
Subject(s): American Colonies; Pirates; Indians
Fictional character(s): Angelique du Plessis-Belliere, Noblewoman; Rescator, Pirate; Gabriel Berne, Businessman (Huguenot merchant)
Historical character(s): Massaswa, Indian, Chieftain
Time Period(s): 17th century (1670s)
Locale(s): Goldsboro, Maine; At Sea (enroute to America)

Summary: During the voyage to America, Angelique discovers the true identity of the pirate Rescator, and resists the courtship of Gabriel Berne. She also must diffuse tensions between the ethnically diverse pirate crew and the Huguenot passengers who plan a mutiny.

Historical Accuracy: Less concerned with historical events than with driving the series' plot forward, the novel does offer some convincing details of early American life.

2471 *Angelique in Revolt*

Date of Publication: 1961
Subject(s): Royalty—France; Huguenots; Religious Conflict
Fictional character(s): Angelique du Plessis-Belliere, Noblewoman; Honorine du Plessis-Belliere, Gentlewoman (Angelique's daughter); Gabriel Berne, Businessman (Huguenot merchant); Rochefort, Explorer
Historical character(s): Louis XIV, Ruler (King of France)
Time Period(s): 17th century (1670s)
Locale(s): Poitou, France; La Rochelle, France

Summary: Upon her return to France from Barbary, Angelique becomes one of the leaders of the Huguenot revolt in Poitou against the king. Condemned to death, she and her daughter seek refuge with the Bernes, a Huguenot family in La Rochelle. A daring escape to freedom in America forms the novel's climax.

Historical Accuracy: The fictional story is blended believably with the historical facts about the Huguenots' persecution and immigration to America.

2472 *The Countess Angelique*

Date of Publication: 1967
Subject(s): American Colonies; Indians
Fictional character(s): Angelique de Peyrac, Noblewoman; Joffrey de Peyrac, Nobleman; Outakke, Indian (Iroquois), Chieftain
Time Period(s): 17th century (1680s)
Locale(s): Maine

Summary: The reunited Peyrac family settle in Maine where they establish friendly relations with the British and the Indians, including the distrustful chief Outakke. They also endure a bitter winter. Viewed by the French-Canadian Cath-

olics as heretics, they are harassed, seen as a threat to French interests in the area.

Historical Accuracy: The conditions that led to the French and Indian Wars are obliquely suggested here. Indian and French-Canadian culture are well rendered.

2473 *The Temptation of Angelique*

Date of Publication: 1970
Subject(s): American Colonies; Indians
Fictional character(s): Angelique de Peyrac, Noblewoman; Joffrey de Peyrac, Nobleman; Gold Beard, Pirate
Time Period(s): 17th century (1680s)
Locale(s): Maine

Summary: While journeying to the British settlement at Brunswick, Angelique and Joffrey are separated by a string of false messages. Angelique is captured by Gold Beard, who has been sent from France to take the Peyracs' lands. Escape and subsequent capture by the Indians follow.

Historical Accuracy: This installment of the series is less concerned with historical events than the atmosphere of the tenuous relationship between the French and the English in America. The atmosphere is well documented.

LAURENCE GONZALES (1947-)

Raised in Houston, Texas, Gonzales studied trumpet at the Berkeley School of Music and travelled throughout the U.S. as a rock musician. He has been the editor of *Triquarterly* and the articles editor of *Playboy*. His books include *The Last Deal Jambeaux*, and *4.4.4.*

2474 *El Vago*

Date of Publication: 1983
Subject(s): Mexican Revolution
Fictional character(s): El Vago, Revolutionary
Historical character(s): Francisco Villa, Revolutionary; Emiliano Zapata, Revolutionary
Time Period(s): 19th century; 20th century (1894-1944)
Locale(s): Mexico; New Mexico

Summary: The story of the Mexican Revolution is told from the perspective of the fictional El Vago, bandit, cattle rustler, revolutionary, and the foster brother of Pancho Villa. The novel follows El Vago's career during the Revolution and his growing disillusion with war and its atrocities.

Historical Accuracy: The novel's perspective is clearly modern, which interferes with the authenticity of its history.

SUZANNE GOODWIN
(PSEUD. OF SUZANNE EBEL, 1916-)

Born in London, Goodwin has worked as a journalist and in advertising. She won a Romantic Novelists Association Major Award in 1964. She points out that many of the glamorous and exotic backgrounds for her stories are part of her own life. She lives in a flat close to the Thames, in an 18th-century house in the hills above Cannes, and in a flat in Stratford-on-Avon. Her husband, John Goodwin, is the former publicity director of the Royal Shakespeare Company.

2475 *Floodtide*

Date of Publication: 1983
Subject(s): Romance; Boer War; World War I
Fictional character(s): Stella Vredenburg, Young Woman; Rupert Flood Corydon, Military Personnel (British soldier)
Time Period(s): 1900s; 1910s (1902-1918)
Locale(s): South Africa; England; France

Summary: Stella Vredenburg saves the life of an enemy British soldier during the Boer War. When she becomes pregnant with Rupert Corydon's child, he marries her and brings her back to his family's estate in England. There she must adjust to a new life and Corydon's hostile family.

Historical Accuracy: The emphasis is on romance with some convincing period touches.

2476 *Lovers*

Date of Publication: 1988
Subject(s): Romance; Edwardian Period
Fictional character(s): Nelly Briggs, Worker (maid), Actress; Matthew Ayrton, Artist
Time Period(s): 1890s; 1900s
Locale(s): London, England; Paris, France

Summary: Nelly Briggs is a maid in a fashionable London brothel. When she witnesses the murder of a prostitute by a peer, she is hurried off to France, where she discovers a larger world of art and artists and a lover. Happiness, however, is threatened by surprising revelations.

Historical Accuracy: These are colorful and authentic scenes of the Edwardian era.

2477 *While the Music Lasts*

Date of Publication: 1992
Subject(s): Romance; Depression Era
Fictional character(s): Vivien Bryant, Gentlewoman; Claire Bryant, Gentlewoman; Julie Bryant, Socialite; Isobel Bryant, Artist
Time Period(s): 1920s; 1930s
Locale(s): England

Summary: This is the story of the four Bryant sisters, who each acquire an unexpected inheritance. They must cope with the stock market crash that costs them their fortune.

Historical Accuracy: The details of the period are well drawn.

CAROLINE GORDON (1895-1981)

Born in Trenton, Kentucky, American author Caroline Gordon attended Bethany College. An educator, literary critic, journalist, and novelist, Gordon's fiction examined life in the American Souoth and has been compared to the work of other Southern women writers such as Eudora Welty and Katherine Anne Porter. Gordon's novels, short story collections, and books of literary criticism include *Aleck Maury: Sportsman, The Garden of Adonis, The*

Malefactors, and *A Good Soldier: A Key to the Novels of Ford Madox Ford*.

2478 *None Shall Look Back*

Date of Publication: 1937
Subject(s): Civil War—U.S.; Battle of Chickamauga
Fictional character(s): Fontaine Allard, Landowner; Ned Allard, Military Personnel (Confederate soldier)
Historical character(s): Nathan Bedford Forrest, Military Personnel (Confederate general)
Time Period(s): 1860s (1862-1863)
Locale(s): Kentucky; Tennessee

Summary: Confederate cavalry legend Nathan Bedford Forrest dominates this novel concerned with the western campaign in Kentucky and Tennessee during the Civil War. The novel depicts the experience of the Allard family of Kentucky, whose lives are transformed by the war. The novel features scenes at the battle for Fort Danielson and at Chicamauga.

Historical Accuracy: The novel's accuracy about manners and customs of the period is exceptional. Unfortunately, the invented story does not achieve the same interest as the actual events.

2479 *Penhally*

Date of Publication: 1932
Subject(s): Antebellum South; Civil War—U.S.; Family Saga
Fictional character(s): Nicholas Llewellyn, Plantation Owner; Ralph Llewellyn, Plantation Owner
Time Period(s): 19th century; 20th century (1826-1930s)
Locale(s): Tennessee

Summary: This family saga depicts life on a Tennessee plantation, Penhally, over a 100 year period. The story begins and ends with a brothers' quarrel over the dispositon of the plantation. In between there are scenes of the effects of the Civil War, Reconstruction, and the rise of the New South in the 20th century.

Historical Accuracy: The novel's background is convincing, though the novel is weakened by attempting to cover so much ground and so many different historical eras.

CHARLES WILLIAM GORDON
(1860-1937)

Born in Indian Lands, Ontario, Canada, Gordon was an educator, Presbyterian minister and missionary, and author. He wrote under the pseudonym of Ralph Connor in books that conveyed his great fondness for Canada's untamed wilderness. His novels include *The Rebel Loyalist*, *The Doctor: A Tale of the Rockies*, and *The Sky Pilot in No Man's Land*, based on his own adventures in France during World War I.

2480 *The Rebel Loyalist*

Date of Publication: 1935
Subject(s): American Revolution

Fictional character(s): Roger Brandt, Military Personnel (soldier), Loyalist
Time Period(s): 1770s; 1780s
Locale(s): United States; Canada

Summary: This story of the American Revolution is told from the perspective of Roger Brandt, who remains loyal to the English cause during the conflict. Despite its clear British sympathies, the novel does do justice to both sides.

Historical Accuracy: Although romantic elements undercut the evident historical research, the novel is adept at capturing the atmosphere and the political and social aspects of the Revolution.

DAN GORDON (1947-)

Gordon's books include *Murder in the First*.

2481 *Wyatt Earp*

Date of Publication: 1994
Subject(s): American West; Biography, Fictionalized
Historical character(s): Wyatt Earp, Lawman; Virgil Earp, Lawman; Johnny Ringo, Outlaw
Time Period(s): 19th century (1860s-1880s)
Locale(s): Dodge City, Kansas; Tombstone, Arizona

Summary: Based on the screenplay of the Kevin Costner film, the novel offers a biographical examination of the career of western lawman Wyatt Earp from his adolescence and the Civil War through his marshalling days in Dodge City and Tombstone and the climactic gunfight at the OK Corral upon which Earp's legend is largely based.

Historical Accuracy: The novel tries to offer a more realistic and human side to the legendary figure and to that extent this version is likely closer to the truth than other versions of Earp's story.

NOAH GORDON (1926-)

Born in Massachusetts, Gordon is a journalism graduate of Boston University. He has worked as a science reporter and a book editor.

2482 *The Physician*

Date of Publication: 1986
Subject(s): Medical Profession; Middle Ages
Fictional character(s): Rob J. Cole, Doctor
Historical character(s): Avicenna, Doctor, Philosopher
Time Period(s): 11th century
Locale(s): England; Persia

Summary: Rob Cole, apprentice to a barber-surgeon in England, has an all-consuming passion to study medicine and become a great healer. He journeys to Persia, impersonating a Jew, to study with the legendary physician Avicenna. His adventures are vividly described.

Historical Accuracy: Though based on fact, many of the details of the 11th-century atmosphere are imagined.

2483 *Shaman*

Date of Publication: 1992
Subject(s): American West; Medical Profession; Indians
Fictional character(s): Rob J. Cole, Doctor; Makwa-Ikwa, Indian (Sauk), Shaman; Sarah Cole, Spouse (of Rob)
Historical character(s): Oliver Wendell Holmes, Doctor; Black Hawk, Indian (Sauk), Chieftain
Time Period(s): 19th century (1835-1864)
Locale(s): Great Plains; Boston, Massachusetts

Summary: This western saga follows the career of a young doctor, Rob J. Cole, from his days of training in Boston to the western frontier of Illinois and the battlefields of the Civil War. His encounter with the Sauk Indians and the medicine man Makwa-Ikwa proves crucial in his development as a doctor and as a white man coming to grips with the Indian tragedy.

Historical Accuracy: The novel is fictional, but supported by a solid period background.

RICHARD GORDON
(PSEUD. OF GORDON OSTLERE, 1921-)

An English writer born in London, Gordon received his degrees from Cambridge University. He is an anesthetist who worked as a ship's surgeon. On a trip to Australia, Gordon wrote his first comic novel, which he followed up with a series of well-received farces.

2484 *Jack the Ripper*

Date of Publication: 1980
Subject(s): Mystery; Victorian Period; Medical Profession
Fictional character(s): Sir Morrell Mackensie, Doctor; Oliver Wilberforce, Doctor; Bertram Randolph, Doctor
Historical character(s): Sigmund Freud, Doctor
Time Period(s): 1880s (1888)
Locale(s): London, England

Summary: The novel examines the Ripper murders from a medical perspective. Three doctors—Mackensie, Queen Victoria's surgeon; Wilberforce, a young surgeon; and Randolph, a pleasure-loving aesthete—become involved as bodies begin to turn up in London's Whitechapel district.

Historical Accuracy: The angle on the murders is original, and the period background is well-grounded and convincing.

2485 *The Private Life of Florence Nightingale*

Date of Publication: 1979
Subject(s): Victorian Period; Medical Profession; Crimean War
Fictional character(s): Tristram Darling, Journalist
Historical character(s): Florence Nightingale, Nurse, Gentlewoman
Time Period(s): 19th century
Locale(s): England; Crimea, Russia

Summary: Muckraking journalist Tristram Darling attempts to penetrate Florence Nightingale's public persona and reveal her private side.

Historical Accuracy: This novel is too sensational in its approach and does a disservice to Florence Nightingale's real accomplishments.

`2486` *The Sleep of Life*

Date of Publication: 1975
Subject(s): Victorian Period; Medical Profession
Fictional character(s): Guy Romilly, Journalist
Historical character(s): Robert Liston, Doctor
Time Period(s): 1840s (1846)
Locale(s): London, England; Hartford, Connecticut; Boston, Massachusetts

Summary: Journalist Guy Romilly leaves England for America to investigate the use of a new substance called ether. The discovery of anesthesia begins a long battle that revolutionizes surgery and transforms the medical profession.

Historical Accuracy: The basis of the story is factual.

JOSEPH N. GORES (1931-)

Born in Minnesota, Gores is a graduate of the University of Notre Dame. He is a novelist, short-story writer, and television scriptwriter. He worked as a private investigator in San Francisco for ten years, an experience he reflected in his novel *Hammett*, which won an Edgar Award and was made into a film in 1982.

`2487` *Hammett: A Novel*

Date of Publication: 1975
Subject(s): Mystery
Historical character(s): Dashiell Hammett, Writer, Detective—Private
Time Period(s): 1920s (1928)
Locale(s): San Francisco, California

Summary: This thriller is based on actual events in Dashiell Hammett's career as a private investigator. He is employed by a reform committee to investigate administrative corruption. The novel combines details of Hammett's career as a private eye with a suspense story.

Historical Accuracy: The novel features a careful evocation of the period and details from Hammett's life.

CHARLES ORSON GORHAM
(1911-1975)

An American publishing executive and novelist, Gorham was born in Philadelphia and attended Columbia University. He served as the publicity director of Doubleday. His titles include *Trial by Darkness* and *The Lion of Judah*.

`2488` *Gold of Their Bodies: A Novel about Gauguin*

Date of Publication: 1955

Subject(s): Biography, Fictionalized; Artistic Life
Historical character(s): Paul Gauguin, Artist; Camille Pissarro, Artist; Vincent Van Gogh, Artist
Time Period(s): 19th century; 20th century (1850s-1903)
Locale(s): France; Tahiti, French Polynesia; Marquesas Islands, French Polynesia

Summary: This fictional account of French artist Paul Gauguin traces his life from his youth in France to his death in the Marquesas Islands. In between, Gauguin's determination to succeed as a artist leads to his abandonment of his wife and family, his friendship with Van Gogh, and his decision to live primitively in the South Seas.

Historical Accuracy: The novel adheres closely to the known facts of Gauguin's life. However, the author's clear partisanship sometimes causes him to justify the unjustifiable in Gauguin's behavior.

`2489` *Wine of Life*

Date of Publication: 1958
Subject(s): Literary Life; Biography, Fictionalized
Historical character(s): Honore de Balzac, Writer
Time Period(s): 18th century; 19th century (1799-1850)
Locale(s): France

Summary: The life of French novelist Balzac is chronicled from his birth into a bourgeois family in Tours to his days as a struggling artist when he nearly starves in a Paris garret while writing from midnight to noon. Balzac is depicted as a complex mixture of amazing creative power, rage, and passion.

Historical Accuracy: The novel is faithful to the facts of Balzac's life and to his world. However, the author's partiality toward his subject veers toward hagiography and sacrifices objectivity.

HERBERT GORMAN

`2490` *Brave General*

Date of Publication: 1942
Subject(s): Biography, Fictionalized
Historical character(s): Georges Ernest Jean Marie Boulanger, Military Personnel (general), Political Figure
Time Period(s): 1880s
Locale(s): France

Summary: The novel deals with the rise and fall of Georges Boulanger, a French military leader and political adventurer who almost succeeds in becoming the dictator of France in the 1880s.

Historical Accuracy: Despite the author's admission to some liberties taken with the historical chronology, the events described are faithful to the facts. The novel succeeds primarily in capturing the atmosphere of the period convincingly.

`2491` *The Breast of the Dove*

Date of Publication: 1950
Subject(s): Independence—Mexico
Fictional character(s): Captain Balzane, Military Personnel

Historical character(s): Maximilian, Ruler (Emperor of Mexico), Royalty (Archduke of Austria); Carlota, Royalty (empress consort of Maximilian)
Time Period(s): 1860s
Locale(s): Mexico

Summary: This novel describes the reign of Maximilian and Carlota in Mexico through the perspective of French Captain Balzane, an intimate of the court. Napoleon III thrusts the unprepared royal couple into Mexico's turmoil, where their reign is doomed.

Historical Accuracy: The novel shows evidence of considerable research.

2492 *The Cry of Dolores*
Date of Publication: 1948
Subject(s): Independence—Mexico
Fictional character(s): Luz, Indian; Ciriaco, Indian
Historical character(s): Miguel Hidalgo y Costilla, Religious (priest), Revolutionary
Time Period(s): 1810s
Locale(s): Dolores, Mexico

Summary: The Mexican uprising of 1810 was led by Miguel Hidalgo y Costilla, whose advocacy of the Indians created a large peasant army that challenged the royalist forces. The fictional story of an Indian woman, Luz, and her mestizo son, Ciriaco, intersects with the historical events of Hidalgo y Costilla's ultimately failed rebellion.

Historical Accuracy: The novel provides an authentic portrait of the period and the issues.

2493 *The Wine of San Lorenzo*
Date of Publication: 1945
Subject(s): Texas Revolution; Mexican War
Fictional character(s): Charley Livingston, Captive
Historical character(s): Winfield Scott, Military Personnel (general); Antonio Lopez de Santa Anna, Military Personnel (general), Political Figure
Time Period(s): 1830s; 1840s
Locale(s): Mexico

Summary: The central character is an American boy, Charley Livingston, who is captured at the Alamo, adopted by General Santa Anna, and rechristened Juan Diego. Raised in the Mexican fashion, he joins the battle with the U.S. in the 1840s on the Mexican side.

Historical Accuracy: The novel offers a view of the Mexican War from the Mexican perspective and a thoughtful and convincing re-creation of period society.

ELIZABETH GOUDGE (1900-1984)

An English educator, artist, and author, Goudge was a prolific writer of books for children and adults, known for her depiction of small-town English life. Goudge taught handicrafts such as weaving, leatherwork, and embroidery. Her most famous novel was *Green Dolphin Street*, which was made into a film. Her other works include *Child from*

the Sea, *The City of Bells*, *Towers in the Mist*, and *The Bird in the Tree*.

2494 *Dean's Watch*
Date of Publication: 1960
Subject(s): Victorian Period; Religious Life
Fictional character(s): Isaac Peabody, Artisan (clockmaker); Adam Ayscough, Religious (dean)
Time Period(s): 1850s
Locale(s): England

Summary: Set in an English cathedral town during the Victorian period, the novel describes the relationship between Isaac Peabody, clockmaker, and Adam Ayscough, the dean of the cathedral. Through their friendship, Isaac discovers religious faith and Ayscough overcomes his reserve and wins the affection of the community.

Historical Accuracy: The novel sharply realizes its period background.

2495 *Towers in the Mist*
Date of Publication: 1938
Subject(s): Elizabethan Period
Fictional character(s): Gervas Leigh, Religious (canon)
Historical character(s): Elizabeth I, Ruler (Queen of England); Sir Walter Raleigh, Gentleman, Courtier; Sir Philip Sidney, Gentleman, Courtier
Time Period(s): 16th century
Locale(s): Oxford, England

Summary: Elizabethan Oxford is the scene for this novel that describes daily life of the period. The story centers on Canon Gervas Leigh of Christ Church College. Walter Raleigh and Philip Sidney appear as young scholars, and Queen Elizabeth arrives on a six-day royal visit to the university.

Historical Accuracy: The novel captures the flavor of the period and its personalities.

2496 *The White Witch*
Date of Publication: 1958
Subject(s): Civil War—England; Espionage
Fictional character(s): Francis Leyland, Spy, Nobleman; Jenny Haslewood, Young Woman; Froniga, Gypsy
Historical character(s): Charles I, Ruler (King of England); Oliver Cromwell, Political Figure
Time Period(s): 17th century
Locale(s): England

Summary: This tale set during the time of the English Civil War concerns Royalist spy Francis Leyland and the gypsy girl, Froniga. Together they have a series of adventures during some of the great events that pit Charles I against Cromwell.

Historical Accuracy: The author admits to some deliberate modification of what is known by having Oliver Cromwell capture the Royal Standard at Edgehill.

JOHN GOULD (1908-)

Born in London, Gould was educated as an engineer and worked as a journalist and military historian.

2497 *No Other Place*

Date of Publication: 1984
Subject(s): American Colonies
Fictional character(s): Jabez Knight, Settler; Elzada Knight, Young Woman
Time Period(s): 17th century
Locale(s): Maine

Summary: Set in colonial Maine during the 17th century, the novel centers on the experiences of the Knight family. They struggle to survive rivalries between Catholics and Protestants, French and British, and shipbuilders and landowners. The novel shows America's early settlers as the victims of political forces every bit as sinister as the wilderness itself.

Historical Accuracy: The novel provides a great deal of local history and customs that create a believable historical background.

BARBARA GOWDY

2498 *Through the Green Valley*

Date of Publication: 1988
Subject(s): Rural Life—Ireland; Fenians; Independence—Ireland
Fictional character(s): Michael Malone, Young Man
Time Period(s): 18th century; 19th century
Locale(s): Ireland; Wales; France

Summary: Irish life in the late 18th and early 19th century is captured in the coming-of-age story of Michael Malone. His family's poverty and persecution by the Anglo-Irish landowners lead him to become involved with the Fenian brotherhood and to eventual exile in Wales and France.

Historical Accuracy: The novel provides an authentic depiction of the Irish peasantry of the period.

IRIS GOWER

2499 *Fiddler's Ferry*

Date of Publication: 1987
Subject(s): Rural Life—England
Fictional character(s): Nerys Beynon, Young Woman
Time Period(s): 1920s
Locale(s): Swansea, Wales

Summary: In the fifth of a series on young women living in South Wales in the aftermath of World War I, the story concerns Nerys Beynon who is taken in by a ferry boatman's family. She finds herself at the center of conflicting domestic dynamics.

Historical Accuracy: The novel's regional and period elements are convincing.

2500 *Morgan's Woman*

Date of Publication: 1986
Subject(s): Rural Life—England

Fictional character(s): Catherine Preele, Spouse, Farmer; David Preele, Veteran (World War I), Handicapped; Martin Lloyd, Worker (farm laborer)
Time Period(s): 1920s
Locale(s): Swansea, Wales

Summary: The fourth of a series of novels on the lives of women in the early years of the 20th century in South Wales, is set in the years following the end of the Great War. Catherine Preele is left to manage the farm when her husband David comes home from the war crippled and confined to a wheelchair. When a young worker arrives, a passionate attraction threatens tragic consequences.

Historical Accuracy: The novel features an authentic period and regional background.

2501 *Proud Mary*

Date of Publication: 1985
Subject(s): Victorian Period; Edwardian Period; Crime and Criminals
Fictional character(s): Mary Jenkins, Young Woman; Billy Gray, Convict; Brandon Sutton, Businessman
Time Period(s): 1890s; 1900s
Locale(s): Wales

Summary: This atmospheric tale set in turn-of-the-century Wales centers on the struggles of young Mary Jenkins, who fights to clear Billy Gray from a charge of theft and murder brought by steel works owner Brandon Sutton.

Historical Accuracy: The novel is rich in convincing period atmosphere.

2502 *Spinners' Wharf*

Date of Publication: 1985
Subject(s): Rural Life—England; World War I
Fictional character(s): Rhian Gray, Worker (mill); Mansel Jack, Businessman (factory owner)
Time Period(s): 1910s
Locale(s): Swansea, Wales

Summary: In the third book of a series of life in South Wales, the period is the war years of World War I. Rhian Gray returns home to Wales to find the community disrupted by the war. She must decide between her affection for her former sweetheart and her attraction to Mansel Jack, a mill owner who opens a munitions factory.

Historical Accuracy: The region and period elements are drawn with a convincing authenticity.

DEBORAH GRABIEN

2503 *Fire Queen*

Date of Publication: 1990
Subject(s): Dark Ages; Romance
Fictional character(s): Maeve, Ruler (Irish Queen); Connal, Chieftain, Warrior
Time Period(s): Indeterminate Past
Locale(s): Ireland

Summary: Set in prehistoric Ireland, the romance pits Irish warriors Maeve and Connal against each other, although they are in love with each other. They join forces to hunt down a man who threatens them both.

Historical Accuracy: The legendary Irish setting is vividly created in this fictional tale.

C.L. GRACE
(PSEUD. OF P.C. DOHERTY)

C.L. Grace is a pseudonym for the English mystery writer P.C. Doherty, who was born in Middlesbrough and studied history at Liverpool and Oxford universities. He obtained his doctorate at Oxford for his thesis on Edward II and Queen Isabella. He is currently a headmaster of a school in northeast London. He has written a number of historical mysteries under several pseudonyms.

2504   *An Ancient Evil*
Date of Publication: 1994
Subject(s): Middle Ages; Mystery
Fictional character(s): Sir Godfrey Evesden, Gentleman; Alexander McBain, Clerk; Edith Mohun, Handicapped (blind)
Time Period(s): 14th century
Locale(s): London, England; Oxford, England

Summary: In a variation on the framework of Chaucer's *Canterbury Tales*, the Canterbury pilgrims pass the time during their journey telling stories of mystery and terror. The Knight's tale begins the sequence and tells a story of medieval Oxford where students are being murdered in bizarre ways. It is suspected that the murders are connected with a vampire cult that was active during the reign of William the Conqueror. Sir Godfrey Evesden, Alexander McBain, and a blind exorcist, Edith Mohun, investigate and uncover a plot with serious repercussions for Oxford, both the city and the university.

Historical Accuracy: The novel is convincing in its details of medieval life and customs.

2505   *The Book of Shadows*
Date of Publication: 1996
Subject(s): Mystery; War of the Roses; Medical Profession
Fictional character(s): Kathryn Swinbrooke, Detective—Amateur, Scientist (physician/chemist); Colum Murtagh, Government Official (king's commissioner)
Historical character(s): Edward IV, Ruler (King of England); Elizabeth Woodville, Royalty (queen consort of Edward IV)
Time Period(s): 15th century (1471)
Locale(s): Canterbury, England; London, England

Summary: The murder of the powerful Tenebrae, the keeper of the *Book of Shadows*, whose secrets include those of Edward IV and his queen, Elizabeth Woodville, provides a mystery for Kathryn Swinbrooke to solve. A succession of suspects become murder victims themselves.

Historical Accuracy: The novel is exact in its depiction of the period and its politics, offering plausible speculations based on historical fact.

2506   *The Eye of God*
Date of Publication: 1994
Subject(s): Middle Ages; Medical Profession; Mystery
Fictional character(s): Kathryn Swinbrooke, Detective—Amateur, Scientist (physician/chemist); Brandon, Military Personnel; Colum Murtagh, Military Personnel (Irish soldier)
Historical character(s): Richard Neville, Nobleman
Time Period(s): 15th century (1471)
Locale(s): Canterbury, England

Summary: Richard Neville, Earl of Warwick, asks a trusted soldier named Brandon to deliver a royal relic to the monks at Canterbury. When Brandon is captured and dies mysteriously, the relic disappears. Soldier Colum Murtagh and physician Kathryn Swinbrooke attempt to solve the crime and find themselves in a dangerous conspiracy.

Historical Accuracy: The mystery is solidly grounded in fact and period detail, particularly medieval medicine.

2507   *The Golden Wind*
Date of Publication: 1969
Subject(s): Exploration; Sea Story; Ancient Greece
Historical character(s): Eudoxus of Kyzikos, Explorer
Time Period(s): 2nd century B.C.
Locale(s): Africa

Summary: The novel records the voyages of discovery of Eudoxos of Kyzikos who ventures beyond the Mediterranean world across the Indian Ocean and along both coasts of Africa. Based on historical research, the novel has expanded and embellished an account of this early explorer.

Historical Accuracy: The novel's notes indicate the historical basis for this story that has been considerably expanded by a solid knowledge of life in the ancient world.

2508   *The Merchant of Death*
Date of Publication: 1995
Subject(s): Mystery; Medical Profession
Fictional character(s): Kathryn Swinbrooke, Detective—Amateur, Scientist (physician/chemist); Richard Blunt, Artist; Colum Murtagh, Military Personnel (soldier)
Time Period(s): 15th century
Locale(s): Canterbury, England

Summary: In the third historical mystery involving Kathryn Swinbrooke, a 15th-century physician and chemist, two crimes become linked. Painter Ricard Blunt too serenely confesses to the murder of his wife, while a tax collector is killed and his tax monies stolen. Kathryn investigates, joined by Colum Murtagh, a soldier of the Crown charged with recovery the lost revenue.

Historical Accuracy: The novel is rich in period details and convincing in its depiction of the era.

2509 *A Shrine of Murders*

Date of Publication: 1993

Subject(s): Mystery; Middle Ages; Medical Profession

Fictional character(s): Kathryn Swinbrooke, Detective—Amateur, Scientist (physician/chemist); Colum Murtagh, Military Personnel (Irish soldier)

Historical character(s): Edward IV, Ruler (King of England)

Time Period(s): 15th century (1471)

Locale(s): Canterbury, England

Summary: The novel introduces Kathryn Swinbrooke, a physician and chemist in 15th-century Canterbury. She is asked to investigate a series of poisonings announced by doggerel poems posted on Canterbury Cathedral's door. Irish soldier Colum Murtagh joins her in the investigation.

Historical Accuracy: The novel's convincing period details make a strong case for the existence of female doctors in the Middle Ages.

2510 *A Tapestry of Murders*

Date of Publication: 1994

Subject(s): Mystery; Middle Ages; Royalty—England

Fictional character(s): Nicholas Chirke, Lawyer

Historical character(s): Geoffrey Chaucer, Writer; Isabella of France, Royalty (queen consort of Edward II)

Time Period(s): 14th century

Locale(s): Kent, England

Summary: In this installment of medieval mysteries narrated by Chaucer's Canterbury Pilgrims, it is the Man of Law's turn. He describes the intrigue surrounding the reign of Edward II and his queen, Isabella, called the "She-Wolf of France." On her death, her trusted squire attempts to flee to France, possibly carrying a document discrediting the English king. A young lawyer, Nicholas Chirke, is hired to investigate, and he finds himself pursued by assassins and French agents while uncovering some deadly secrets.

Historical Accuracy: Many elements of the story reflect historical truths as the author's notes point out.

ALICE WALWORTH GRAHAM (1905-)

Born in Mississippi, Walworth attended Mississippi College for Women. She began writing at the age of seven. Her novels include *The Voices of the Peacock*, *The Natchez Woman*, and *Indigo Bond*.

2511 *Shield of Honor*

Date of Publication: 1957

Subject(s): Middle Ages; Royalty—England; Barons' War

Fictional character(s): Andrew de Astley, Knight

Historical character(s): Simon de Montfort, Nobleman; Henry III, Ruler (King of England)

Time Period(s): 13th century (1260)

Locale(s): England

Summary: The period of England's Barons' War against the tyranny of Henry III is dramatized. The hero is Andrew de Astley, one of Simon de Montfort's followers. The novel captures the various political maneuvers and battles that pro-

duced the famous Parliament of 1265, admitting for the first time representatives from England's boroughs.

Historical Accuracy: The novel is masterful in its ability to bring its period vividly to life.

2512 *The Summer Queen*

Date of Publication: 1973

Subject(s): War of the Roses; Royalty—England

Fictional character(s): Cicely Bonville, Gentlewoman

Historical character(s): Edward IV, Ruler (King of England); Elizabeth Woodville, Royalty (consort of Edward IV)

Time Period(s): 15th century

Locale(s): England

Summary: When Edward IV marries the woman he loves, commoner Elizabeth Woodville, he sets in motion a chain of events that will affect England through three subsequent reigns and plunge the nation into renewed civil war. The story of this royal romance is seen through the eyes of Cicely Bonville, one of the queen's ladies-in-waiting.

Historical Accuracy: The novel is exact and perceptive in its rendering of court life during the 15th century and the issues surrounding the dynastic struggles of the War of the Roses.

2513 *Vows of the Peacock*

Date of Publication: 1955

Subject(s): Middle Ages; Royalty—England

Historical character(s): Edward II, Ruler (King of England); Isabella of France, Royalty (queen consort of Edward II); Piers Gaveston, Companion (of Edward II); Roger de Mortimer, Nobleman (Earl of March); Elizabeth de Beauchamp, Gentlewoman; Thomas Astley, Gentleman; Guy de Beauchamp, Nobleman (Earl of Warwick)

Time Period(s): 13th century; 14th century

Locale(s): England

Summary: This vivid recreation of court intrigue and dynastic struggles during the reign of Edward II centers on two women. They are Isabella of France, who marries Edward, and Elizabeth de Beauchamp, the daughter of one of the powerful barons who plots against the king. The novel features insightful portraits of many of the leading figures in this fascinating period of English history.

Historical Accuracy: The novel's period background and details are painstakingly and faithfully depicted.

HEATHER GRAHAM
(PSEUD. OF HEATHER GRAHAM POZZESSERE)

American romance novelist Pozzessere has authored more than 50 romances under the names Shannon Drake and Heather Graham. She won an award for the best sensual romance set during the American Civil War in 1988 for *Darker Stranger*. She has said that she strives to write books that are fun to read.

2514 *And One Rode West*

Date of Publication: 1992

Subject(s): Reconstruction Period; American West

Fictional character(s): Christa Cameron, Young Woman; Jeremy McCauley, Military Personnel (colonel)
Time Period(s): 1860s
Locale(s): Virginia; Great Plains

Summary: In the conclusion of the Civil War trilogy chronicling the Cameron family of Virginia, in the aftermath of the war Christa Cameron, to save her plantation, agrees to marry Union officer Jeremy McCauley. She accompanies him west for a new life.

Historical Accuracy: The novel features a believable period background.

2515 *And One Wore Gray*

Date of Publication: 1992
Subject(s): Civil War—U.S.; Romance
Fictional character(s): Daniel Cameron, Military Personnel (Confederate colonel); Callie Michaelson, Young Woman
Time Period(s): 1860s (1862-1865)
Locale(s): Virginia; Sharpsburg, Maryland

Summary: The author continues her Civil War-era saga begun in *One Wore Blue*. Callie Michaelson, who despises the Southern cause, is nonetheless the object of desire of Confederate colonel Daniel Cameron. Their stormy relationship is played out against the backdrop of a number of Civil War engagements.

Historical Accuracy: The novel is faithful to the war's chronology and period details.

2516 *Love Not a Rebel*

Date of Publication: 1989
Subject(s): American Revolution; Romance
Fictional character(s): Amanda Sterling, Noblewoman, Spy; Eric Cameron, Patriot
Time Period(s): 1770s
Locale(s): New England, American Colonies

Summary: In this complex romantic adventure set during the American Revolution, Amanda Sterling is a reluctant English spy. She marries Eric Cameron, the American traitor she is in charge of investigating.

Historical Accuracy: The story is fanciful, and the romance dominates the history.

2517 *One Wore Blue*

Date of Publication: 1991
Subject(s): Civil War—U.S.; Romance
Fictional character(s): Kieran MacKay, Southern Belle, Widow(er); Jesse Cameron, Doctor, Military Personnel (Union officer)
Time Period(s): 1850s; 1860s (1859-1861)
Locale(s): Harpers Ferry, Virginia

Summary: When physician Jesse Cameron chooses to fight for the Union instead of his native South, Kieran MacKay can hardly believe that the man she has known and loved since childhood is deserting the Southern Cause. Lots of sparks fly before these two stubborn, highly principled people can reconcile their feelings, both political and personal, and begin to

see things from the other's point of view. Companion novel to *And One Wore Gray*.

Historical Accuracy: The novel contains interesting historical detail, particularly of the Harper's Ferry incident.

2518 *A Pirate's Pleasure*

Date of Publication: 1989
Subject(s): American Colonies; Romance; Pirates
Fictional character(s): Skye Kinsdale, Runaway; Roc ''Silver Hawk'' Cameron, Pirate
Time Period(s): 1710s
Locale(s): American Colonies

Summary: Swashbuckling romantic adventure ensues as reluctant bride Skye Kinsdale sails to America to escape her fate. She finds herself a pirate captain.

Historical Accuracy: The period details are thin, but the emphasis is clearly exotic romance over a carefully detailed historical setting and situation.

2519 *Runaway*

Date of Publication: 1994
Subject(s): Indians
Fictional character(s): Tara Brent, Fugitive; Jarrett McKenzie, Widow(er)
Historical character(s): Osceola, Indian (Seminole), Chieftain
Time Period(s): 1830s (1835-1836)
Locale(s): New Orleans, Louisiana; Florida

Summary: The background for this story of Florida in the 1830s is the brutal persecution of Florida's native people during the period. Tara Brent is on the run, framed for a crime she did not commit. She follows Jarret McKenzie to his home in the wilds of Florida and joins in his resistance to President Jackson's repressive Indian policy.

Historical Accuracy: The fictional story of Tara Brent and Jarrett McKenzie is set against an authentic period background and actual events.

2520 *The Viking's Woman*

Date of Publication: 1990
Subject(s): Dark Ages; Romance; Vikings
Fictional character(s): Rhiannon, Noblewoman; Eric of Dubhlain, Royalty (prince), Warrior
Time Period(s): 9th century (878)
Locale(s): Ireland

Summary: Rhiannon leads an attack on what is believed to be a Viking raiding party, wounding the Viking leader, Eric. The invaders, however, turn out not to be enemies but rather honored guests of the Irish king. To make amends, Rhiannon must marry Eric.

Historical Accuracy: The Irish elements of the story are believable, though the basic plot strains credibility.

WINSTON GRAHAM (1910-)

An English author born in Manchester, Graham became a full-time writer in 1934 and received the Order of the British

Empire in 1983 for his distinguished career. He is best known for his series of Poldark novels, which were made into a popular PBS television series. The central protagonist, Ross Poldark, has been called a kind of Heathcliffian Mr. Rochester and Cornwall's answer to Rhett Butler. Graham is also the author of several thrillers, including *Marnie*, which became a film directed by Alfred Hitchcock.

2521 *The Angry Tide*

Date of Publication: 1978
Subject(s): Georgian Period; Family Saga
Fictional character(s): Ross Poldark, Businessman (mine owner), Political Figure; Demelza Poldark, Spouse; George Warleggan, Businessman, Political Figure; Elizabeth Warleggan, Spouse; Osborne Whitworth, Religious (vicar); Morwenna Whitworth, Spouse; Drake Carne, Blacksmith; Mark Adderly, Political Figure, Rake
Time Period(s): 1790s (1798-1799)
Locale(s): Cornwall, England; London, England

Summary: The Warleggan-Poldark feud reaches new heights as George Warleggan sets in motion political and financial intrigues designed to destroy Ross Poldark. Adding to the melodramatic mix are Mark Adderly's less-than-gentlemanly interest in Demelza, Morwenna Whitworth's unhappy marriage, and Elizabeth's desperate attempt to convince her husband of her fidelity.

Historical Accuracy: The growing influence of Napoleon and its effect on England are discussed. However, the customs and culture of the era remain the focus.

2522 *The Black Moon*

Date of Publication: 1973
Subject(s): Georgian Period; Family Saga; French Revolution
Fictional character(s): Ross Poldark, Businessman (mine owner); Demelza Poldark, Spouse; George Warleggan, Businessman; Elizabeth Warleggan, Spouse; Drake Carne, Blacksmith; Morwenna Chynoweth, Gentlewoman; Agatha Poldark, Gentlewoman
Time Period(s): 1790s
Locale(s): Cornwall, England

Summary: The enmity between the Warleggans and the Poldarks continues. This time it is fueled by Ross' insistence on visiting his irascible Aunt Agatha, who lives with the Warleggans, and by Drake Carne's wooing of Elizabeth's cousin, Morwenna. Ross mounts an expedition to rescue Dr. Dwight Enys, who has been captured and imprisoned by the French while working as a military surgeon.

Historical Accuracy: The French Reign of Terror, England's war with France, and the English Wesleyan (Methodist) revival movement are lightly woven into the plot. Tom Paine's *Rights of Man* is briefly discussed. All help create a believable period background.

2523 *Cordelia*

Date of Publication: 1959
Subject(s): Victorian Period

Fictional character(s): Brook Ferguson, Businessman; Cordelia Ferguson, Spouse; Stephen Crossley, Writer (poet)
Time Period(s): 1860s
Locale(s): Manchester, England

Summary: When lovely young Cordelia Blake becomes the second wife of Brook Ferguson, she endures the onerous duties of a Victorian wife, the iron will of her scheming father-in-law, and the gloom of the Ferguson estate, Grove Hall, until the dashing poet Stephen Crossley enters her life.

Historical Accuracy: The customs and culture of the Victorian period are well rendered.

2524 *Demelza*

Date of Publication: 1953
Subject(s): Georgian Period; Family Saga
Fictional character(s): Ross Poldark, Businessman (mine owner); Demelza Poldark, Spouse; Francis Poldark, Businessman, Gentleman; Elizabeth Poldark, Spouse; Verity Poldark, Gentlewoman; Dwight Enys, Doctor; Captain Andrew Blamey, Sea Captain; George Warleggan, Businessman
Time Period(s): 1780s
Locale(s): Cornwall, England

Summary: In the second Poldark novel, Ross Poldark's business troubles mount and his feud with the unscrupulous George Warleggan begins. Demelza gives birth to a daughter, tries to reunite star-crossed lovers Verity Poldark and Captain Blamey, and attempts to reconcile the two branches of the Poldark family. Dr. Dwight Enys battles epidemics and embarks upon an ill-fated affair with the wife of a miner.

Historical Accuracy: Cornish customs and culture of the era are well rendered.

2525 *The Four Swans*

Date of Publication: 1976
Subject(s): Georgian Period; Family Saga
Fictional character(s): Ross Poldark, Businessman (mine owner), Political Figure; Demelza Poldark, Spouse; George Warleggan, Businessman; Elizabeth Warleggan, Spouse; Hugh Armitage, Military Personnel (naval officer); Morwenna Whitworth, Spouse; Drake Carne, Blacksmith; Osborne Whitworth, Religious (vicar)
Time Period(s): 1790s (1796-1797)
Locale(s): Cornwall, England

Summary: In this installment of the Poldark saga, the Poldark-Warleggan feud continues as Ross Poldark stands for Parliament. Demelza must fight her growing attraction to Hugh Armitage, while her brothers suffer love troubles of their own. Morwenna, still in love with Drake Carne, suffers an unbearable marriage to the brutal Reverend Osborne Whitworth.

Historical Accuracy: The author admits taking some liberty with the dates of the Truro elections, but states that the events recorded are otherwise very much as they actually occurred.

2526 *The Grove of Eagles*

Date of Publication: 1964
Subject(s): Elizabethan Period
Fictional character(s): Maugan Killigrew, Young Man

Historical character(s): Sir Walter Raleigh, Courtier; John Killigrew, Government Official
Time Period(s): 16th century (1590s)
Locale(s): Cornwall, England

Summary: The scene is Elizabethan England in the 1590s when a second Spanish Armada threatens invasion. The story centers on the Killigrew family of Cornwall. It is told from the perspective of Maugan Killigrew, son of the governor of Pendennis Castle, the most vital position on the Cornish coast. Treachery and treason are played out as the Spanish mount an attempt to conquer England in 1597.

Historical Accuracy: The author explains that whenever possible he has used original sources and has not distorted the known facts.

2527   *The Last Gamble*

Date of Publication: 1955
Subject(s): Georgian Period; Family Saga
Fictional character(s): Ross Poldark, Businessman (mine owner); Demelza Poldark, Spouse; Francis Poldark, Gentleman; Elizabeth Poldark, Spouse; George Warleggan, Businessman; Dwight Enys, Doctor; Caroline Penvennan, Heiress
Time Period(s): 1790s (1792-1793)
Locale(s): Cornwall, England

Summary: In this installment of the Poldark saga (also published as *Warleggan*), Ross and Francis Poldark struggle to make a new mine pay, and Ross is torn between his love for Elizabeth and Demelza. The unscrupulous George Warleggan insinuates himself further into the personal lives and business affairs of the Poldarks, and Doctor Dwight Enys becomes romantically involved with the wealthy Caroline Penvennan.

Historical Accuracy: The novel captures many period elements, including smuggling, the war with France, and the Revolution's Reign of Terror.

2528   *The Miller's Dance*

Date of Publication: 1982
Subject(s): Regency Period; Family Saga; Napoleonic Wars
Fictional character(s): Ross Poldark, Businessman (mine owner), Political Figure; Demelza Poldark, Spouse; Stephen Carrington, Businessman (miller); George Warleggan, Businessman, Political Figure; Jeremy Poldark, Relative; Clowance Poldark, Fiance(e)
Historical character(s): Richard Trevitnick, Engineer, Inventor
Time Period(s): 1810s (1812-1814)
Locale(s): Cornwall, England

Summary: The Industrial Revolution comes to Cornwall as Jeremy Poldark explores ways to work the Poldark mines using Richard Trevitnick's steam engine. Ross must decide whether to keep his seat in Parliament, while Demelza struggles with a late-term pregnancy, and daughter Clowance becomes engaged to the roguish miller Stephen Carrington. The Poldarks' old adversary, widower George Warleggan, embarks upon a second marriage with the independent Lady Harriet Carter and once again insinuates himself into the Poldarks' business affairs.

Historical Accuracy: The Industrial Revolution, the Napoleonic Wars, and the problem of press gangs figure in the plot. The senility of George III, the antics of the Prince Regent, the War of 1812, and the assassination of Prime Minister Spencer Perceval are also mentioned, creating a believable period background.

2529   *The Renegade: A Novel of Cornwall, 1783-1787*

Date of Publication: 1951
Subject(s): Georgian Period; Family Saga
Fictional character(s): Captain Ross Poldark, Veteran (Revolutionary War), Landowner; Demelza Carne, Servant; Francis Poldark, Gentleman; Elizabeth Poldark, Spouse; Verity Poldark, Gentlewoman
Time Period(s): 1780s (1783-1787)
Locale(s): Cornwall, England

Summary: In this first book in the Poldark saga, Ross Poldark returns to Cornwall after serving in the war in America to find his father dead, his home and finances in a shambles, and his sweetheart, Elizabeth, now engaged to his cousin. He works to rebuild his fortune and family relationships, and finds a new love in the lower classes when he meets upright Demelza Carne, a miner's daughter.

Historical Accuracy: The culture and customs of 18th-century England in general and Cornwall in particular are authentically realized.

2530   *The Stranger From the Sea*

Date of Publication: 1982
Subject(s): Regency Period; Family Saga
Fictional character(s): Ross Poldark, Businessman (mine owner), Political Figure; Demelza Poldark, Spouse; Stephen Carrington, Adventurer; George Warleggan, Businessman, Political Figure; Lady Harriet Carter, Widow(er), Gentlewoman
Historical character(s): George, Prince of Wales, Royalty; George Canning, Political Figure
Time Period(s): 1810s (1810-1811)
Locale(s): Cornwall, England; Portugal; London, England

Summary: In this continuation of the Poldark saga, Ross advises the Prince of Wales and George Canning on English strategy in Portugal and involves himself in politics. Demelza uneasily oversees the growing friendships of her son and daughter with adventurer Stephen Carrington, and George Warleggan woos Lady Harriet Carter.

Historical Accuracy: England's involvement in the Napoleonic Wars figures in the plot, as does King George III's second bout of madness and the political struggle connected to his demise. The period elements create a plausible backdrop.

2531   *The Twisted Sword*

Date of Publication: 1991
Subject(s): Family Saga; Napoleonic Wars; Battle of Waterloo

Fictional character(s): Ross Poldark, Businessman; Demelza Poldark, Spouse; Jeremy Poldark, Military Personnel (lieutenant)
Time Period(s): 1810s (1815)
Locale(s): France; Belgium

Summary: In the conclusion of the Poldark saga, the time is 1815, and Ross Poldark is sent to France to assess the strength of the Bonapartists. He and Demelza are swept up in the Parisian social whirl. Meanwhile, Jeremy Poldark, a lieutenant in the British army, honeymoons in Brussels. They are all fated to be reunited on the battlefield of Waterloo.

Historical Accuracy: As in all of the Poldark novels the characters connect believably with the historical events, which are convincingly depicted.

2532 *Venture Once More*

Date of Publication: 1950
Subject(s): Family Saga; Georgian Period
Fictional character(s): Ross Poldark, Businessman (mine owner); Demelza Poldark, Spouse; Francis Poldark, Gentleman; Elizabeth Poldark, Spouse; Dwight Enys, Doctor; Caroline Penvennan, Heiress; George Warleggan, Businessman
Time Period(s): 1790s
Locale(s): Cornwall, England

Summary: In this installment of the Poldark saga, Ross Poldark stands trial, falsely accused of inciting a shipwreckers' riot. Demelza attempts to clear Ross' name, hesitating to tell her nearly bankrupt husband she is expecting a child and worrying that he still loves Elizabeth. The estranged Ross and Francis are reconciled, begin a business venture together, and work to ruin the scheming George Warleggan. A subplot concerns the budding romance between selfless doctor Dwight Enys and the arrogant, aristocratic Caroline Penvennan.

Historical Accuracy: The customs and culture of the era, and particularly those of the Cornish working class, are carefully rendered. The novel also alludes to the coming war with France.

DOROTHY GRANT (1900-)

An American author born in New York City, Grant was a copywriter for radio and television in addition to a novelist.

2533 *Margaret Brent, Adventurer*

Date of Publication: 1944
Subject(s): American Colonies; Religious Conflict
Historical character(s): Margaret Brent, Settler
Time Period(s): 17th century (1638-1649)
Locale(s): Maryland, American Colonies

Summary: Based in part on the actual experiences of settler Margaret Brent, the novel provides a detailed portrait of life in the Catholic colony of Maryland during the 17th century. Brent is shown as a staunch Catholic and a champion of religious and individual liberty.

Historical Accuracy: The author indicates the instances of variance from the historical record.

2534 *Night of Decision: A Novel of Colonial New York*

Date of Publication: 1946
Subject(s): American Colonies; Religious Conflict
Fictional character(s): Becky Kartright, Young Woman
Historical character(s): Thomas Dongan, Political Figure
Time Period(s): 17th century (1683-1690)
Locale(s): New York, American Colonies

Summary: Catholic governor Thomas Dongan does his best to keep order over the Calvinist settlers in colonial New York. Religious intolerance, however, is rampant and forms the background for the fictional story involving young Becky Kartwright, who falls in love with an Irish Catholic.

Historical Accuracy: The novel does justice to its period, which it captures with some authenticity.

JOAN GRANT
(PSEUD. OF JOAN MARSHALL KELSEY, 1907-)

Born in London, Kelsey based her historical novels on the conviction that she formerly lived in the various eras depicted. Her books include *Scarlet Feather*, *Laird and the Lady*, and *Lord of the Horizon*.

2535 *Life as Carola*

Date of Publication: 1939
Subject(s): Renaissance; Picaresque Adventure
Fictional character(s): Carola, Bastard Daughter, Entertainer
Time Period(s): 16th century
Locale(s): Italy

Summary: Carola is the illegitimate daughter of an Italian nobleman who sets out to make her fortune. She travels with a troupe of strolling players for a while, enters a convent, and finally marries an elderly scholar.

Historical Accuracy: Despite the fact that the author claims to be offering the actual memories of a former incarnation of herself, the period details have an artificial quality, and there are several errors of fact.

2536 *Winged Pharaoh*

Date of Publication: 1938
Subject(s): Ancient Egypt; Pharaohs
Fictional character(s): Sekeeta, Royalty (princess), Heiress
Time Period(s): 40th century B.C.
Locale(s): Egypt

Summary: Ancient Egypt during the First Dynasty is the setting for this tale of Sekeeta, daughter of the pharaoh and co-heir with her brother to the throne of Egypt. She narrates her own story, from childhood to death, revealing a great deal of the customs and beliefs of the ancient Egyptians.

Historical Accuracy: The portrait of the daily life of the First Dynasty is faithful to what is known. Scholars may, however, disagree with many of the interpretations offered.

LAURIE GRANT

2537 *Emerald Fire*

Date of Publication: 1990
Subject(s): Middle Ages; Romance; Crusades
Fictional character(s): Joan of Hawkingham, Noblewoman; Richard of Kingsclere, Knight
Time Period(s): 12th century
Locale(s): England

Summary: While on a pilgrimage, Joan of Hawkingham finds herself in the company of Richard of Kingsclere, the man she believes is responsible for her sister's mysterious death. Joan seeks to learn the truth even as the two become attracted to one another, while enduring murder, kidnapping, and villainy before a true understanding can be gained.

Historical Accuracy: The emphasis is on romantic adventure, but the period elements are believable.

MAXWELL GRANT

Australian-born novelist Grant was formerly a newspaper and TV journalist.

2538 *Blood Red Rose*

Date of Publication: 1986
Subject(s): Revolution—China; Civil War—China
Fictional character(s): Kate Richmond, Doctor (surgeon); Sun Lung Shen, Revolutionary; Thomas Blake, Adventurer
Time Period(s): 20th century (1926-1949)
Locale(s): China (northern)

Summary: The novel's setting is China's bloody civil war. Kate Richmond, an American surgeon, slowly finds herself drawn to the Chinese Communist cause. The action includes a vivid re-creation of the famous Long March into northern China and scenes that capture the complexity of the Chinese social and political structure.

Historical Accuracy: The story is fictional, but the era and the details of Chinese life of the period are convincing.

2539 *Inherit the Sun*

Date of Publication: 1981
Subject(s): Frontier—Australia; Family Saga; Ranching
Fictional character(s): John Carlyon, Rancher; Beth Brennan Carlyon, Teacher; Anne Carlyon, Spouse (of John)
Time Period(s): 19th century; 20th century (1896-1974)
Locale(s): Outback, Australia

Summary: Three generations of the Carlyon family experience life in the Australian Outback. Their story is about creation of a great ranching empire carved out of the wilderness. It is also about progress and encroaching civilization that unalterably change the land.

Historical Accuracy: The author admits that his background is real, though the characters and events are imaginary.

GUNTHER GRASS (1927-)

A German novelist, poet, playwright, and graphic artist, Grass was born in the Free City of Danzig and attended the Berlin Academy of Fine Arts. During World War II, he was drafted into the German army and was a prisoner of war in Czechoslovakia. He has worked as a farm laborer, a miner, an apprentice stonecutter, and a drummer for a jazz band. Grass is one of the leading figures in post-World War II German literature. His first novel, *The Tin Drum*, created an international sensation.

2540 *The Tin Drum*

Date of Publication: 1963
Subject(s): Family Saga; World War II; Picaresque Adventure
Fictional character(s): Oskar Matzerath, Murderer (accused)
Time Period(s): 19th century; 20th century (1899-1954)
Locale(s): Poland; Germany

Summary: This enormous and important novel offers no less than a history of modern Germany as seen through the eyes of a dwarf being held for murder in an insane asylum. Oskar's story turns on his pivotal third birthday, when he wills himself to stop growing, defining his career as an outsider and a misfit.

Historical Accuracy: The novel is a surreal, mock-epic chronicle of 20th-century madness and upheaval delivered with an imaginative vitality.

PATRICIA GRASSO

An English teacher at Everett High School in Massachusetts for 23 years, Grasso lives in Winchester, Massachusetts. In her historical novels, the heroine gets to do things Grasso would like to do.

2541 *Highland Belle*

Date of Publication: 1991
Subject(s): Tudor Period; Romance
Fictional character(s): Brigitte Devereux, Bride (reluctant), Noblewoman; Ian MacArthur, Laird
Time Period(s): 16th century
Locale(s): Scotland; England

Summary: Cultural conflict between the English and Scots during the 16th century forms the basis of this romance in which English noblewoman Brigitte Devereux is startled to discover that her new Scottish husband does not even attend their wedding ceremony. She heads back to England where she encounters Ian MacArthur, the man she has just married by proxy.

Historical Accuracy: The improbability of the novel's plot is in fact based on actual Scottish marriage customs of the period.

RALPH GRAVES (1924-)

An American writer born in Washington, D.C., Graves is a graduate of Harvard and has worked as a reporter and writer for *Life* magazine. His books include *Shore of Honor*, a fictionalized account of his experiences during World War II, and *August*, a novel about family relationships.

2542 *The Lost Eagles*

Date of Publication: 1955
Subject(s): Roman Empire; Barbarians
Fictional character(s): Severus, Young Man
Time Period(s): 1st century (9-17)
Locale(s): Rome, Roman Empire; Germany

Summary: This adventure tale of Rome during the reigns of Augustus and Tiberius describes the exploits of young Severus, who sets off for Germany to retrieve three legion standards lost to the barbarians. To regain the final eagle, he poses as a deserter and infiltrates a German tribe.

Historical Accuracy: The story is fanciful but filled with plausible period elements.

ROBERT GRAVES (1895-1985)

An Irish-born poet and novelist, Graves was an officer in the First World War, during which he wrote his first poetry. *Goodbye to All That*, his autobiography written at age 36, is a wry reflection on his war experience and the war's effect on his generation. He is best known for his historical novels, his poetry, and his collected essays on poetry, *The White Goddess*.

2543 *Claudius the God*

Date of Publication: 1935
Subject(s): Roman Empire
Historical character(s): Claudius I, Ruler (Roman emperor); Valeria Messalina, Noblewoman (Claudius' wife); Herod Agrippa II, Royalty (prince), Courtier; Nero, Heir, Royalty
Time Period(s): 1st century (41-54)
Locale(s): Roman Empire; England

Summary: This continues Claudius' memoirs and covers his 14-year reign as Roman emperor that ends when he is killed by Nero's mother Agrippina. Roman life in the decline brought about by human greed, lust, and the corrupting influence of power is chronicled by Claudius, who truthfully writes a history like no other, from the inside and complete with family secrets.

Historical Accuracy: This is superb recreation of Roman life in its decline.

2544 *Count Belisarius*

Date of Publication: 1938
Subject(s): Roman Empire; Christianity; Barbarians
Historical character(s): Belisarius, Military Personnel (Roman general); Justinian I, Ruler (Eastern Roman emperor); Silverius, Religious (pope)
Time Period(s): 6th century (500-565)
Locale(s): Constantinople, Byzantine Empire; Carthage, Ancient Civilization; Rome, Italy

Summary: Set in the Roman Empire of the 6th century, the novel concerns the great general Belisarius and his campaigns in Persia and Africa, and against the Goths before the gates of Rome. His nemesis is the Emperor Justinian. Belisarius endures political intrigue and church schisms. He is portrayed as both the last noble Roman and the first chivalrous knight.

Historical Accuracy: Graves' erudition and eye for the authentic fill this long novel with vivid pictures of the final days of the Roman Empire.

2545 *Hercules, My Shipmate*

Date of Publication: 1945
Subject(s): Myths and Legends; Fantasy
Fictional character(s): Ancaeus, Sailor; Jason, Sea Captain; Hercules, Adventurer
Time Period(s): 13th century B.C.
Locale(s): *Argo*, At Sea (Mediterranean and Black Sea)

Summary: This is the epic tale of Jason and the Argonauts told as if the events were historical rather than mythological. Graves offers his characteristic brand of erudition, earthy humor, and vignettes of daily life to produce a lively and informative adventure story.

Historical Accuracy: A long "historical appendix" documents the sources of Graves' ingenious rendering of myth in historical terms.

2546 *Homer's Daughter*

Date of Publication: 1955
Subject(s): Myths and Legends; Fantasy
Fictional character(s): Nausicaa, Royalty (princess); Aethon, Adventurer
Time Period(s): 8th century B.C.
Locale(s): Sicily, Italy

Summary: Graves selects an incident from *The Odyssey* for treatment as an historical novel. Princess Nausicaa is beset by 120 suitors. It will take all her wily, and sometimes brutal, cunning and the assistance of a young man who washes ashore in a storm to rid herself of her unwanted suitors.

Historical Accuracy: Graves' tale is full of bawdy humor and glimpses of everyday life in legendary times.

2547 *I, Claudius*

Date of Publication: 1934
Subject(s): Roman Empire
Historical character(s): Claudius I, Writer, Nobleman; Augustus, Ruler (Roman emperor); Livia, Noblewoman (Augustus' wife); Tiberius, Ruler (Roman emperor); Caligula, Ruler (Roman emperor); Lucius Aelius Sejanus, Military Personnel; Herod Agrippa I, Royalty (prince), Courtier
Time Period(s): 1st century B.C.; 1st century
Locale(s): Roman Empire

Summary: Written in the form of a memoir of the Roman Emperor Claudius, this is an insider's view of the reigns of Augustus, Tiberius, and Caligula, detailing imaginatively the private side of the first family of the Roman Empire. The novel is filled with memorable portraits, particularly the dreadful Livia, the depraved Caligula, and power-mad Sejanus.

Historical Accuracy: Graves's scholarship and passion for the authentic never interferes with what is essentially a very modern story of corruption and evil.

2548 *Islands of Unwisdom*

Date of Publication: 1949

Subject(s): Spanish Colonies; Sea Story; Exploration

Historical character(s): Don Alvaro de Mendana de Neira, Military Personnel (general), Explorer; Ysabel Barreto, Gentlewoman

Time Period(s): 16th century (1595)

Locale(s): Solomon Islands

Summary: King Philip II sends a Spanish expedition to establish a colony in the Solomon Islands. The expedition encounters hardships, and leadership falls to Don Alvaro's wife, Ysabel Barreto.

Historical Accuracy: The novel recaptures the time and atmosphere authentically.

2549 *King Jesus*

Date of Publication: 1946

Subject(s): Jews; Biblical Story; Christianity

Historical character(s): Jesus Christ, Political Figure, Biblical Figure; Mary, Biblical Figure; Joseph, Carpenter, Biblical Figure; Herod I, Ruler

Time Period(s): 1st century

Locale(s): Israel

Summary: Graves retelling of the New Testament casts Jesus in the role of political, rather than spiritual, leader. His story deemphasizes the divine and the miraculous while depicting a Jesus caught up in the political and religious struggles of his time.

Historical Accuracy: Graves' version of Jesus is sure to offend the faithful but should be read as a tour de force of erudition and historical imagination.

2550 *Proceed, Sergeant Lamb*

Date of Publication: 1941

Subject(s): American Revolution; American Colonies; Military Life—British Army

Historical character(s): Robert Lamb, Military Personnel (British soldier); Charles Cornwallis, Military Personnel (British general); Charles Lee, Military Personnel (American general); Horatio Gates, Military Personnel (American general); George Washington, Military Personnel (army commander); Benedict Arnold, Military Personnel (general), Traitor

Time Period(s): 1770s; 1780s (1777-1782)

Locale(s): Boston, Massachusetts; New York, New York; Yorktown, Virginia

Summary: Graves' continuation of the memoirs of Sergeant Lamb begins in a prison camp near Boston. Lamb escapes and rejoins the British army in New York where he takes part in engagements in Connecticut and the Carolinas. As the confidential clerk to General Cornwallis, he is on hand for the British defeat at Yorktown. Lamb escapes once more and endures a thousand-mile march through hostile territory before reaching safety and home. Lamb's royalist views provide an original and sardonic perspective on the new American republic.

Historical Accuracy: Graves is particularly strong in military and regimental details.

2551 *The Real David Copperfield*

Date of Publication: 1933

Fictional character(s): David Copperfield, Writer; Wilkins Micawber, Gentleman (shabby); Little Emily, Orphan, Fiance(e)

Time Period(s): 1820s; 1830s

Locale(s): London, England; Dover, England; Norwich, England

Summary: Graves offers an edited and slightly altered version of Charles Dickens' masterpiece *David Copperfield* with a "tightening-up and a sorting of what is true from what is false." It is essentially Dickens' novel but with a decidedly unsentimental slant. The reader can judge whether this is an improvement.

Historical Accuracy: This Dickens' novel retold by Graves presents a pastiche of imitation and subtle changes of motivation and characterization. Some will view it as a literary theft, others as ingenious re-imagining.

2552 *Sergeant Lamb's America*

Date of Publication: 1940

Subject(s): American Revolution; Military Life—British Army; Indians

Fictional character(s): Kate Welldone, Heroine

Historical character(s): Robert Lamb, Military Personnel (British soldier); John Burgoyne, Military Personnel (British general); Benedict Arnold, Military Personnel; Horatio Gates, Military Personnel (American general)

Time Period(s): 18th century (1753-1777)

Locale(s): Dublin, Ireland; Ticonderoga, New York, American Colonies; Boston, Massachusetts, American Colonies

Summary: Graves depicts the military career of the actual Robert Lamb, born in Dublin, who enlists in the British army at age 17 and campaigns in Canada and New York. Lamb lives for a time among the Indians before rejoining the army and taking part in the attack on Fort Ticonderoga.

Historical Accuracy: The novel features a number of colorful scenes of the American frontier and of the United States' early history as a nation from a decidedly royalist perspective.

2553 *Wife to Mr. Milton*

Date of Publication: 1944

Subject(s): Literary Life; Civil War—England

Historical character(s): Marie Powell, Gentlewoman; John Milton, Writer (poet); Charles I, Ruler (King of England); Oliver Cromwell, Political Figure

Time Period(s): 17th century (1641-1652)

Locale(s): Oxford, England; London, England

Summary: This first-person narrative is the story of Marie Powell, an English gentleman's daughter and the first wife of poet John Milton. Her story of her relationship with one of England's greatest writers and intellects is told against the backdrop of the English Civil War that includes an eyewitness account of the execution of Charles I.

Historical Accuracy: Only Robert Graves would have the audacity of taking the reader into the bedroom of one of England's greatest poets. The novel is filled with convincing details of 17th-century daily life.

AUSTIN K. GRAY (1887-1945)

Gray's other books include *Benjamin Franklin's Library*.

2554 *Teresa, or Her Demon Lover*

Date of Publication: 1945
Subject(s): Literary Life; Biography, Fictionalized
Historical character(s): Teresa Guiccioli, Noblewoman, Lover; George Gordon Byron, Nobleman, Writer
Time Period(s): 19th century
Locale(s): Italy

Summary: The novel chronicles the full and interesting life of Teresa Guiccioli the Italian countess who becomes Byron's last mistress in 1819. Her relationship with Byron, though the centerpiece of the novel, is not her only adventure. The book also provides an interesting and fresh slant on the enigmatic figure of Byron.

Historical Accuracy: The basic outline of Guiccioli's history are faithfully observed.

ELIZABETH JANET GRAY
(PSEUD. OF ELIZABETH GRAY VINING, 1902-)

Born in Philadelphia, Vining graduated from Bryn Mawr College. Her novels include *I, Roberta*, *Flora: A Biography* (about Flora MacDonald), and *The Virginia Exiles*.

2555 *Meggy MacIntosh*

Date of Publication: 1930
Subject(s): American Colonies; Jacobite Rebellion
Fictional character(s): Meggy MacIntosh, Teenager
Historical character(s): Flora MacDonald, Immigrant, Leader (Jacobite Rebellion)
Time Period(s): 1770s (1775)
Locale(s): Edinburgh, Scotland; North Carolina, American Colonies

Summary: The title character is a young girl of 15 who flees Scotland intent on joining the rescuer of Bonnie Prince Charlie, Flora MacDonald, in the North Carolina colony. She achieves her desire, but not before adventure and romance interrupt her quest.

Historical Accuracy: The novel provides a faithful and accurate portrait of the Scottish immigrants who settled in Carolina before the American Revolution.

RICHARD GRAYSON
(PSEUD. OF RICHARD GRINDAL)

2556 *Crime Without Passion*

Date of Publication: 1983
Subject(s): Mystery

Fictional character(s): Jean-Paul Gautier, Police Officer (chief inspector); Denise de Richemont, Murderer (acquitted)
Time Period(s): 1900s
Locale(s): Paris, France

Summary: Denise de Richmont is acquitted in the murder of her lover, a prominent journalist, when she confesses to a crime of passion. The truth is more complex, as Inspector Gautier learns when his investigation reveals a link between the murder and the political unrest that has broken out in the Paris streets.

Historical Accuracy: Expertly detailed, the mystery has a vivid backdrop of period Paris.

2557 *Death En Voyage*

Date of Publication: 1986
Subject(s): Mystery
Fictional character(s): Jean-Paul Gautier, Police Officer (chief inspector); Mary Newbolt, Companion; Lady Dorothy Strathy, Noblewoman
Time Period(s): 1900s
Locale(s): Paris, France

Summary: When Lady Strathy is murdered, suspicion falls on her travelling companion, Mary Newbolt. Inspector Gautier learns that others may have a motive since Lady Strathy is connected with the Flower Girl Affair, a scandal which members of the French nobility are anxious to cover up.

Historical Accuracy: From fashionable salons to sinister backstreets, the author is convincing in his command of the period detail.

2558 *Death Off Stage*

Date of Publication: 1992
Subject(s): Mystery; Theatrical Life; Dance
Fictional character(s): Jean-Paul Gautier, Police Officer (chief inspector); Sophia Dashkova, Noblewoman (Russian princess)
Time Period(s): 1900s (1905)
Locale(s): Paris, France

Summary: The Russian Ballet is performing in Paris, and a prominent judge, who is romantically involved with one of the dancers, is attacked by another lover. When the judge is murdered, Gautier takes the case. He must step carefully because the tour sponsor, Sophia Dashkova, is also his mistress.

Historical Accuracy: The Parisian and theatrical background for the mystery are authentic and convincing.

2559 *Death on the Cards*

Date of Publication: 1988
Subject(s): Mystery
Fictional character(s): Jean-Paul Gautier, Police Officer (chief inspector)
Time Period(s): 1900s
Locale(s): Paris, France

Summary: The police receive a list of potential targets for assassination by a killer who intends to announce his victims with a playing card. Gautier surmises that the choice of card must be significant. His investigation takes him on a tour of the Belle Epoque, from the Longchamps races, to the Opera, to the fashionable salons.

Historical Accuracy: The period details are expertly and authentically presented.

2560 *The Monterant Affair*

Date of Publication: 1980
Subject(s): Mystery; Theatrical Life
Fictional character(s): Jean-Paul Gautier, Police Officer (chief inspector); Sophie Monterant, Actress; Clementine Lyse, Singer
Time Period(s): 1900s
Locale(s): Paris, France

Summary: On the first night performance of *Dame aux Camelias*, the young actress Sophie Monterant eats a poisoned chocolate and dies. There is no scarcity of suspects for Inspector Gautier, some of whom are very high up in the French government.

Historical Accuracy: The period details of turn of the century Paris are expertly delivered.

2561 *The Montmarte Murders*

Date of Publication: 1982
Subject(s): Mystery; Artistic Life
Fictional character(s): Jean-Paul Gautier, Police Officer (chief inspector); Theophile Delange, Artist, Heir
Time Period(s): 1900s
Locale(s): Paris, France; St. Tropez, France

Summary: Inspector Gautier searches for a missing painter, an ex-anarchist, who is the heir to a fortune and suspected of murder. The search takes Gautier from the bohemian enclave of Montmarte to fashionable salons, to the tiny fishing village of St. Tropez in the south of France.

Historical Accuracy: The period details are authentically re-created.

2562 *The Murder at Impasse Louvaine*

Date of Publication: 1978
Subject(s): Mystery
Fictional character(s): Jean-Paul Gautier, Police Officer (chief inspector); Josephine Hassler, Gentlewoman
Time Period(s): 1900s
Locale(s): Paris, France

Summary: In turn of the century Paris, a fashionable painter is found strangled to death with his wife, Josephine Hassler, bound and gagged at his side. She had been found in the bed of the French president on the night of his death as well, and Inspector Gautier investigates the case, trying delicately not to stir up an old scandal. Madame Hassler is hiding something, however, and someone powerful is protecting her.

Historical Accuracy: The novel offers a convincing re-creation of period Paris.

OWEN FRANCIS GRAZEBROOK
(1884-)

2563 *Nicanor of Athens: The Autobiography of an Unknown Citizen*

Date of Publication: 1947
Subject(s): Ancient Greece
Fictional character(s): Nicanor, Young Man
Time Period(s): 5th century B.C.
Locale(s): Athens, Greece

Summary: Nicanor, a wealthy Athenian, vividly re-creates Greece's golden age in his autobiography.

Historical Accuracy: Though the details of Athenian life are generally correct, the author fails to create a fully believable atmosphere.

ANNE GREEN (1899-)

Anne Green was a Georgia-born author, who, like her brother, novelist Julian Green, lived most of her life in France. Her novels include *Reader, I Married Him*, *The Silent Duchess*, and *The Lady in the Mask*. *With Much Love* is about her childhood in France.

2564 *The Lady in the Mask*

Date of Publication: 1942
Subject(s): Renaissance
Fictional character(s): Gregorio, Servant; Simonetta, Gentlewoman
Historical character(s): Leonardo da Vinci, Artist; Ludovico Sforza, Nobleman (Duke of Milan); Beatrice d'Este, Spouse (of Sforza), Gentlewoman
Time Period(s): 15th century (1494)
Locale(s): Milan, Italy

Summary: This story of late-Renaissance Italy takes place in the court world of Ludovico Sforza, ruler of Milan and patron of Leonardo da Vinci. The novel, filled with period characters and intrigue, concerns a young servant, Gregorio, who impersonates his dead master, a famous scholar. Sforza covets the beautiful Simonetta, who must escape his powerful grasp.

Historical Accuracy: The novel rarely reaches further than a costume romance in the depth of its historical presentation.

GERALD GREEN (1922-)

An American journalist and writer, born in Brooklyn, New York, Green graduated from Columbia University. He has worked as a producer for the "Today Show," "Chet Huntley Reporting," and several documentaries. Green won an Emmy Award for his screenplay for the TV series "Holocaust." He is best known for his novel *The Last Angry Man*.

2565 *Murfy's Men*

Date of Publication: 1981

Subject(s): American Revolution; Slavery; Battle of Rhode Island
Fictional character(s): Malachi Desmond Murfy, Military Personnel (army officer)
Historical character(s): Nathanael Greene, Military Personnel (general); John Sullivan, Military Personnel (army officer); Alexander Hamilton, Military Personnel (army officer)
Time Period(s): 1770s; 1780s (1775-1786)
Locale(s): Rhode Island; At Sea; Africa

Summary: This tale of the American Revolution depicts the role played by freed black slaves who fought for the American cause in the Battle of Rhode Island. The first black regiment in the U.S. Army is commanded by an Irish former slave-trader, Malachi Murfy. His adventures in the slave trade are combined with an authentic depiction of battle scenes.

Historical Accuracy: The novel provides a convincing description of period life and customs as well as an accurate account of the battlefield engagements.

2566 The Sword and the Sun: The Story of the Spanish Civil Wars in Peru

Date of Publication: 1953
Subject(s): Spanish Colonies; Inca Empire
Historical character(s): Francisco Pizarro, Military Personnel (conquistador); Diego de Almagro, Military Personnel (conquistador)
Time Period(s): 16th century (1537-1542)
Locale(s): Peru

Summary: Set during the civil war fought between rival Spanish factions contending for the spoils of the conquered Inca Empire, the novel dramatizes the events that pit Pizarro and his confederates against Diego de Almagro and his supporters.

Historical Accuracy: The events depicted are drawn from recognized sources on the period.

JULIAN GREEN (1900-)

Born of American parents living in Paris, Green is the first American novelist to choose French as his medium of expression and the first American to be ranked as a distinguished French writer. He has published over 60 works: novels, essays, plays, and multiple volumes of his journals. Green fought in both world wars and is a member of the Academie Francaise.

2567 The Distant Lands

Date of Publication: 1987
Subject(s): Antebellum South
Fictional character(s): Elizabeth Escaridge, Gentlewoman; Jonathan Armstrong, Gentleman; Charlie Jones, Gentleman
Time Period(s): 1850s
Locale(s): Savannah, Georgia; Virginia

Summary: In the 1850s, Elizabeth Escaridge arrives in Georgia from England. She seeks refuge with wealthy relatives, and she is soon immersed in the South's aristocratic society. Her love affairs become a metaphor for dark secrets and

tragedies hidden beneath the refined and proud Southern facade.

Historical Accuracy: The novel is solidly grounded in the period's politics and convincing in its depiction of the period.

2568 The Stars of the South

Date of Publication: 1995
Subject(s): Civil War—U.S.; Antebellum South; Family Saga
Fictional character(s): Charlie Jones, Gentleman; Elizabeth Jones, Widow(er)
Time Period(s): 1860s
Locale(s): Savannah, Georgia; Prince William County, Virginia; Charleston, South Carolina

Summary: In this sequel to *The Distant Land*, the stories of the characters from the earlier novel are continued. The focus is on English widow Elizabeth Jones who is unable to conform to the standards of behavior set for a proper Southern lady.

Historical Accuracy: Based in part upon the remembrances of the author's mother, the novel provides an authentic and believable historical background.

PETER GREEN (1924-)

An English author born in London, Green graduated from Trinity College, Cambridge. He has worked as a professor of classics at the University of Texas. His novel *The Sword of Pleasure* won the Heinemann Award in 1957. Green is also a translator of Greek and Latin.

2569 Achilles His Armour

Date of Publication: 1967
Subject(s): Ancient Greece; Biography, Fictionalized; Peloponnesian War
Historical character(s): Alcibiades, Military Personnel (general), Political Figure; Pericles, Political Figure
Time Period(s): 5th century. B.C. (441-404 B.C.)
Locale(s): Athens, Greece

Summary: This biographical novel chronicles the life of Alcibiades, the great general of the Peloponnesian War. Early in his career Alcibiades wins the admiration of his countrymen but then he is censured during the turbulent years of Athens' struggle against Sparta.

Historical Accuracy: The story is based on fact. Where evidence is lacking, Green opts for the probable.

2570 The Laughter of Aphrodite

Date of Publication: 1966
Subject(s): Literary Life; Ancient Greece; Biography, Fictionalized
Historical character(s): Sappho, Writer (poet)
Time Period(s): 7th century B.C.; 6th century B.C.
Locale(s): Lesbos, Greece; Sicily, Italy

Summary: Sappho, the great Greek lyric poet and cult figure, tells her own story in retrospect. Now old, in debt, and disappointed in love, she chronicles her life from shy girl to great artist, wife, mistress, and political intriguer.

Historical Accuracy: The author admits that we know little about Sappho and that his version of her life has depended on many surmises and speculations. But he claims he invented incidents or characters only when historical evidence was lacking.

2571 Sword of Pleasure: Being the Memoirs of the Most Illustrious Lucius Cornelius Sulla

Date of Publication: 1957
Subject(s): Roman empire; Biography, Fictionalized
Historical character(s): Lucius Cornelius Sulla, Military Personnel (Roman general), Political Figure
Time Period(s): 1st century B.C.
Locale(s): Rome, Roman Empire

Summary: In the form of a memoir by the Roman general Sulla, this novel recounts the dictator's career, including his motivation for voluntarily withdrawing from power. Sulla portrays himself as a complex blend of skill, talent, generosity, and butchery.

Historical Accuracy: The novel provides an authentic and believable portrait of first century B.C. Rome.

ERIC ROLFE GREENBERG (1945-)

Born in New York City, Greenberg attended the University of Wisconsin and NYU. He was a publicist for Columbia Pictures, a public relations and marketing representative for the *National Lampoon*, and a journalist for the U.S. Navy.

2572 The Celebrant

Date of Publication: 1983
Subject(s): Sports; Baseball
Fictional character(s): Jackie Kapp, Immigrant, Artisan (silversmith); Arthur Kapp, Businessman; Eli Kapp, Businessman (salesman)
Historical character(s): John McGraw, Sports Figure (baseball manager); Honus Wagner, Sports Figure (baseball player); Connie Mack, Sports Figure (baseball manager); Christy Mathewson, Sports Figure (baseball pitcher)
Time Period(s): 1900; 1910
Locale(s): New York, New York

Summary: The novel depicts the legendary sports career of America's first national baseball hero, Christy Mathewson. Connected to Mathewson's story is the tale of the Jewish immigrant Kapp family, whose fortunes become entwined with Mathewson's. The Kapps use baseball to assimilate into the culture of their adopted country and discover a dark underside corrupting the promise and possibility represented by the great Mathewson.

Historical Accuracy: The baseball figures and the games described are historical; the off-the-field incidents are invented.

JOANNE GREENBERG (1932-)

Born in Brooklyn, New York, Greenberg graduated from American University and was a professor of anthropology at

the Colorado School of Mines. Her most popular book is *I Never Promised You a Rose Garden*, the story of a young girl's battle against schizophrenia, based on the author's own struggle with mental illness. It was made into a popular film in 1977.

2573 The King's Persons

Date of Publication: 1963
Subject(s): Middle Ages; Jews; Religious Conflict
Fictional character(s): Abram, Young Man; Malabestia, Nobleman (baron)
Time Period(s): 12th century (1182-1190)
Locale(s): York, England

Summary: In 1182 Jewish refugees are received by the Jews of York, who have lived in peace with the Christian community for generations. As "the king's persons" they are under the crown's protection, but mob violence sweeps northward and culminates in a massacre. The novel chronicles the events and depicts the Jewish community at York during the siege.

Historical Accuracy: The framework of the story is factual.

LIZ GREENE (1946-)

Greene is the author of *The Puppet Master*.

2574 The Dreamer of the Vine

Date of Publication: 1981
Subject(s): Biography, Fictionalized
Historical character(s): Nostradamus, Doctor, Philosopher
Time Period(s): 16th century
Locale(s): France

Summary: Little is known of the enigmatic physician and astrologist Nostradamus, whose predictions have been interpreted in various way. The novel offers a fictional explanation for the source of his occult powers. His skills are linked to an underground pagan sect and the rites of the Templars.

Historical Accuracy: What is known provides the bare bones for this mainly fanciful speculation about Nostradamus.

MALCOLM W. GREENOUGH JR. (1926-)

An American novelist born in Boston, Greenough received his B.A. from Howard and his LL.B. from Boston University.

2575 Dear Lily

Date of Publication: 1987
Subject(s): Civil War—U.S.; Reconstruction Period
Historical character(s): Lily Violett, Gentlewoman; Violett Whelan, Gentlewoman; Malcolm Greenough, Gentleman
Time Period(s): 19th century; 20th century (1830s-1920s)
Locale(s): New Orleans, Louisiana; Philadelphia, Pennsylvania; Maine

Summary: Based on family letters and other materials, this novel is both a romance and a memoir. The story begins in New Orleans at the start of the Civil War, and Lily Violett reflects the war experience and the Reconstruction period. The scene shifts to fashionable Philadelphia and Maine in the 1890s for the love story between Lily's niece, Violett, and Malcolm Greenough.

Historical Accuracy: The documentary basis lends credibility and substance to a family story that reflects social history.

L.B. GREENWOOD
(PSEUD. OF LILLIAN BETHEL GREENWOOD, 1932-)

A Canadian writer and teacher, Greenwood lives in Kelowna, British Columbia, where she is a high school English teacher. Because of a childhood illness, most of her early schooling was done by correspondence, which created in her a love of reading and writing.

`2576` Sherlock Holmes and the Case of Sabina Hall

Date of Publication: 1988
Subject(s): Mystery; Victorian Period
Fictional character(s): Sherlock Holmes, Detective—Private; John H. Watson, Doctor
Time Period(s): 1880s
Locale(s): England

Summary: Holmes and Watson journey to Sabina Hall as a favor to a former acquaintance to assist Silas Andrew, the owner of the now abandoned Stowe mines. When they arrive, Silas is dead, and Holmes suspects foul play. His suspect list is a long one, and when one of the suspects is killed, the plot thickens into a complex tangle.

Historical Accuracy: The atmosphere is authentic.

`2577` Sherlock Holmes and the Case of the Raleigh Legacy

Date of Publication: 1986
Subject(s): Mystery; Victorian Period
Fictional character(s): Sherlock Holmes, Detective—Private; John H. Watson, Doctor
Time Period(s): 1880s
Locale(s): London, England

Summary: Holmes and Watson become involved in the mysterious events surrounding a legacy of an old college friend, an indecipherable Elizabethan letter that appears to have been written by Sir Walter Raleigh. Eventually, others show a great interest in the letter, and Holmes must solve a fascinating and intricate puzzle.

Historical Accuracy: The novel captures the Arthur Conan Doyle originals with solid period details.

`2578` Sherlock Holmes and the Thistle of Scotland

Date of Publication: 1989
Subject(s): Mystery; Victorian Period
Fictional character(s): Sherlock Holmes, Detective—Private; John H. Watson, Doctor; Caroline Mowbray, Gentlewoman
Time Period(s): 1890s (1890)

Locale(s): London, England

Summary: The title refers to a centuries-old jewel, originally a betrothal gift of Mary, Queen of Scots. In 1890 it is in the possession of Lady Caroline Mowbray, who has contracted a marriage of convenience with a shady businessman. On her wedding day, the jewel disappears from the clip in Lady Caroline's hair. Only Holmes could possible solve this "unsolvable crime.".

Historical Accuracy: The ingenuity of the mystery is matched by the expert rendering of the period.

JILL GREGORY

`2579` Lone Star Lady

Date of Publication: 1990
Subject(s): American West; Romance
Fictional character(s): Maggie Clay, Orphan, Rancher
Time Period(s): 1860s; 1870s
Locale(s): Texas

Summary: Set in Texas in the 1860s and 1870s, the novel follows the romantic adventures of Maggie Clay, who struggles to survive as a pregnant orphan of 16. When the father of her son returns, treachery, murder, and betrayal are obstacles that Maggie must overcome.

Historical Accuracy: The period details are accurate in setting the tone of the era.

LISA GREGORY
(PSEUD. OF CANDACE CAMP, 1949-)

Gregory was born in Texas and graduated from West Texas State University; she holds a law degree from the University of North Carolina. She has been a secondary school teacher and a lawyer in private practice in Texas. She wrote her first book at age 11 and completed her first novel while in law school. She credits her law school experience with giving her the discipline for her writing.

`2580` The Rainbow Promise

Date of Publication: 1989
Subject(s): American West; Romance
Fictional character(s): Julia Turner Dobson, Widow(er); James Bank, Doctor
Time Period(s): 19th century
Locale(s): Texas

Summary: Julia Dobson returns to her home town in Texas to try to make a new life for herself. She must face her feelings of inferiority and the man they kept her from years before.

Historical Accuracy: The period background is lightly sketched but convincing.

PHILIPPA GREGORY (1954-)

An English author born in Nairobi, Kenya, Gregory graduated from the University of Sussex and received a Ph.D. from the University of Edinburgh. She worked as a provincial journalist for a newspaper in England and as a radio journalist for the BBC. Her doctoral research was on the 18th century, which became the setting for her novels. Gregory finds it one of the most crucial periods of English history.

2581 *Fallen Skies*

Date of Publication: 1993
Subject(s): World War I
Fictional character(s): Lily Valence, Spouse (of Stephen), Singer; Stephen Winter, Veteran (World War I); Coventry, Veteran (World War I), Servant (orderly)
Time Period(s): 1920s
Locale(s): Portsmouth, England

Summary: The aftermath and legacy of World War I are explored in the relationship between army veteran Stephen Winter and Lily Valence. They marry, and Lily tries to cultivate her career as a singer while Stephen remains haunted by his war experience. The novel offers a compelling treatment of the war generation and survivor guilt.

Historical Accuracy: The author captures the era with conviction.

2582 *The Favored Child*

Date of Publication: 1989
Subject(s): Romance; Family Saga; Georgian Period
Fictional character(s): Julia Lacey, Gentlewoman; Richard MacAndrew, Gentleman; James Fortescue, Gentleman
Time Period(s): 18th century; 19th century
Locale(s): Sussex, England

Summary: In the sequel to *Wideacre*, the second generation continues the battle to possess this Sussex estate. Julia Lacey is to inherit the estate jointly with her cousin Richard. But she falls in love with Fortescue, a turn of events that puts the possession of Wideacre in doubt. *Meridon* continues Wideacre's story.

Historical Accuracy: The novel has an authentic period backdrop.

2583 *Meridon*

Date of Publication: 1990
Subject(s): Inheritance—Disputed; Family Saga; Regency Period
Fictional character(s): Meridon, Heiress; Will Tyacke, Businessman (estate manager); Clara Havering, Gentlewoman
Time Period(s): 1800s
Locale(s): Sussex, England

Summary: In the third volume of the Wideacre saga, Meridon is raised as a gypsy girl. She is, however, the heir of the Wideacre estate, and when she returns to claim her legacy, she becomes the target of the scheming Lady Havering.

Historical Accuracy: The novel effectively captures its era with authentic details.

2584 *A Respectable Trade*

Date of Publication: 1995
Subject(s): Business Building; Romance; Slavery
Fictional character(s): Josiah Cole, Trader; Frances Scott, Gentlewoman; Mehuru, Religious, Slave
Time Period(s): 1780s (1787)
Locale(s): Bristol, England

Summary: Josiah Cole, an ambitious trader, marries penniless but well-connected Frances Scott. She finds herself assisting her husband in the conversion of slaves to house servants. One of them, Mehuru, is a priest from the African kingdom of Yoruba. He provides a passionate lesson in power and freedom.

Historical Accuracy: This is an original and convincing look at the period and the slavery question.

2585 *Wideacre*

Date of Publication: 1987
Subject(s): Inheritance—Disputed; Georgian Period
Fictional character(s): Beatrice Lacey, Gentlewoman; Joan MacAndrew, Doctor
Time Period(s): 18th century
Locale(s): Sussex, England

Summary: Beatrice Lacey is determined to possess the great estate of Wideacre. She defies all conventions in a single-minded pursuit of her goal to become Wideacre's mistress, launching a chain of events that sweeps up everyone in her way. The Wideacre saga continues in *The Favored Child*.

Historical Accuracy: The novel's period background is convincing.

SUSANNA GREGORY

Susanna Gregory is a pseudonym of a Cambridge University fellow and a former police officer who lives in England.

2586 *An Unholy Alliance*

Date of Publication: 1996
Subject(s): Mystery; Middle Ages; Medical Profession
Fictional character(s): Matthew Bartholomew, Doctor; Brother Michael, Religious (monk)
Time Period(s): 14th century
Locale(s): Cambridge, England

Summary: Set two years after the Black Death decimates the population of England, this historical mystery introduces physician Matthew Bartholomew and his companion, Brother Michael. While trying to uncover the identity of a serial murderer who is stalking women in Cambridge, they uncover a sinister cult taking advantage of the despair caused by the plague.

Historical Accuracy: The story is thoroughly and believably grounded in details of medieval history, medicine, and religion. The author's notes indicate the historical basis for the story.

ANTHONY GREY (1938-)

An English author born in Norwich, Grey was a reporter and foreign correspondent in China. He was interned for 800 days in China, and his experiences are recorded in the autobiographical *Hostage in Peking*. Grey hosted a daily international current affairs program for the BBC World Service.

2587 *Peking: A Novel of China's Revolt*

Date of Publication: 1988
Subject(s): Revolution—China; Civil War—China
Fictional character(s): Jakob Kellner, Religious (missionary); Lu Mei-ling, Revolutionary
Time Period(s): 20th century (1921-1978)
Locale(s): Peking, China

Summary: The history of modern China is reflected in this dramatic story that begins with the Long March of the 1930s and ends with the events surrounding the death of Mao Tse-Tung and the overthrow of the Gang of Four in 1976. Jakob Kellner is a young English missionary captured by the Red Army at the beginning of the Long March. He endures enormous hardship and danger, sustained by a young revolutionary, Lu Mei-ling. Years later, Jakob returns to China for the terrible upheaval of the Cultural Revolution.

Historical Accuracy: The author captures with skill and conviction the Chinese background and the historical events that produce the novel's conflicts.

2588 *Saigon*

Date of Publication: 1982
Subject(s): Vietnam War; French Colonies
Fictional character(s): Joseph Sherman, Military Personnel (OSS agent), Journalist; Kieq Lan, Young Woman
Time Period(s): 20th century (1925-1975)
Locale(s): Saigon, Vietnam

Summary: The troubled history of Vietnam is chronicled from the perspective of young Joseph Sherman. The son of a Virginia senator, he first comes to Vietnam in 1925 on a game-hunting trip. He is destined to return in the 1930s as a pilot, during World War II as an OSS agent, and during the French Indochina War as a correspondent. His experiences capture the great events of Vietnam's modern history.

Historical Accuracy: Based on extensive research, the novel offers a reliable look at the events that shaped Vietnam's history.

ZANE GREY (1872-1939)

American western writer Grey was born in Ohio and practiced dentistry in New York City. He is credited with popularizing the American West as a subject for fiction and establishing the basic ingredients of the western novel. His most famous novels are *Riders of the Purple Sage* and *The Heritage of the Desert*. His western novels are marked by strong and accurate topographical details but largely romantic situations and stock characters.

2589 *Western Union*

Date of Publication: 1939
Subject(s): American West
Fictional character(s): Wayne Cameron, Frontiersman
Time Period(s): 1860s
Locale(s): West

Summary: This western novel's background is the creation of the first transcontinental telegraph, attempted in the 1860s. The massive project of stringing telegraph cables across the treeless western plains is dramatized through the experiences of young greenhorn Wayne Cameron.

Historical Accuracy: The novel provides a believable reconstruction of the period.

EDWARD GRIERSON (1914-)

An English writer born in Bedford, Grierson was a barrister and a justice of the peace in Northumberland. His books include *Far Morning*, *Dark Torrent of Glencoe*, and *The Second Man*.

2590 *Dark Torrent of Glencoe*

Date of Publication: 1960
Subject(s): Feuds; Glencoe Massacre; Royalty—England
Fictional character(s): Jamil Campbell, Military Personnel (lieutenant); Fiona MacIan, Young Woman
Historical character(s): William III, Ruler (King of England)
Time Period(s): 17th century (1692)
Locale(s): Highlands, Scotland; England

Summary: The novel dramatizes the story of the Campbell-MacDonald feud which culminates in the bloody massacre at Glencoe in 1692. When he learns of the king's secret command to destroy the MacDonalds of Glencoe, young Jamil Campbell, despite his clan loyalty, travels to London to intercede with the king to overturn his order.

Historical Accuracy: The basic details of the Glencoe Massacre are accurately depicted.

2591 *The Hastening Wind*

Date of Publication: 1953
Subject(s): Napoleonic Era; Espionage
Fictional character(s): Charles de Bellac, Diplomat
Historical character(s): Napoleon Bonaparte, Military Personnel (general); Joseph Fouche, Political Figure, Revolutionary
Time Period(s): 1800s (1803-1804)
Locale(s): Paris, France

Summary: This suspenseful tale set in the French Republic during Napoleon's ascendancy follows the attempt of Royalist Charles de Bellac to achieve the restoration of the Bourbons by secret, diplomatic means. Unknown to him, members of the conspiracy are planning a campaign of violence and assassination should Bellac fail.

Historical Accuracy: The novel is more exciting than it is accurate in its depiction of the period and its politics.

HENRY FARRAND GRIFFIN

2592　*The White Cockade*

Date of Publication: 1941
Subject(s): French Revolution; Vendee Uprising; Slavery
Fictional character(s): Jonathan Brewster, Sea Captain; Charles Stuart, Fugitive
Time Period(s): 1790s (1794)
Locale(s): Nantes, France; Dominican Republic (San Domingo); Pacific Northwest, North America

Summary: This wide-ranging adventure tale includes the supression of the uprising of the Vendee during the French Revolution, the slave revolt in San Domingo, and the American challenge to the British fur trade monopoly in the Pacific Northwest. American sea captain Jonathan Brewster rescues a fugitive who turns out to be the illegitimate son of Bonnie Prince Charles. The Scottish troops holding the English Pacific Northwest forts might be persuaded to revive the Stuart cause.

Historical Accuracy: The novel's plot is far-fetched, and its history is used primarily to accelerate the adventure.

ROBERTA GRIMES (1948-)

A 1968 graduate of Smith College who majored in religion, Grimes has been an accountant and economic consultant as well as a computer programmer and lawyer. The novelist lives in Plymouth, Massachusetts.

2593　*My Thomas: A Novel of Martha Jefferson's Life*

Date of Publication: 1993
Subject(s): American Revolution; American Colonies; Biography, Fictionalized
Historical character(s): Martha Jefferson, Gentlewoman, Spouse; Thomas Jefferson, Political Figure
Time Period(s): 1770s; 1780s (1770-1782)
Locale(s): Virginia

Summary: The novel takes the form of Martha Jefferson's journal from 1770, when the 22-year-old widow first meets Thomas Jefferson, a rising lawyer and legislator, until her death in 1782. Thomas and Martha marry in 1772 and struggle during the revolutionary years to build Monticello and raise their family. Jefferson resigns from politics in 1781, but Martha's death a year later drives him back.

Historical Accuracy: The research into the period is scrupulous, and the novel offers a convincing impersonation of Martha Jefferson's voice and ideas.

J.J.C. GRIMMELSHAUSEN (1621-1676)

Grimmelshausen German author whose picaresque novel *Simplicissimus* is a hallmark of early German fiction. Another of his novels was the basis for Bertold Brecht's *Mother Courage*.

2594　*Simplicissimus the Vagabond*

Date of Publication: 1669
Subject(s): Picaresque Adventure; Thirty Years War
Fictional character(s): Simplicissimus, Farmer (peasant), Courtier
Historical character(s): James Ramsay, Military Personnel
Time Period(s): 17th century (1616-1648)
Locale(s): Hanau, Germany; Cologne, Germany; Paris, France

Summary: This picaresque adventure takes Simplicissimus from his origin as a German peasant to Paris, Russia, and Japan before ending his career as a hermit. His experiences, sometimes marvelous, sometimes painfully realistic, illustrate the period of the Thirty Years War.

Historical Accuracy: This is the only fictional account in German of the Thirty Years War. Making Simplicissimus the nephew of James Ramsay is pure invention.

FRANCIS GRISWOLD (1902-)

Born in Albany, New York, Griswold lived in and wrote about the Carolina low country and is the author of *Sea Island Lady*.

2595　*The Tides of Malvern*

Date of Publication: 1930
Subject(s): Family Saga; Antebellum South; Civil War—U.S.
Fictional character(s): Gilbert Sheldon, Landowner
Time Period(s): Multiple Time Periods
Locale(s): Charleston, South Carolina

Summary: This novel chronicles seven generations of a family in Charleston, South Carolina, from colonial days to the period following World War I. The fortunes of the Sheldon family beginning with the arrival of John Sheldon from England are followed for three hundred years.

Historical Accuracy: The historical background is solidly constructed and believable.

LYNN GROH

Groh has worked for magazines, newspapers and in public relations and as the associate editor and East Coast correspondent for *Ships and Sea* magazine.

2596　*The Culper Spy Ring*

Date of Publication: 1969
Subject(s): American Revolution; Espionage
Historical character(s): Robert Townsend, Spy; George Washington, Military Personnel (army commander); Benjamin Tallmadge, Military Personnel (major)
Time Period(s): 1770s; 1780s
Locale(s): Long Island, New York; New York, New York; Connecticut

Summary: The novel dramatizes the working of American's first intelligence system as Quaker Robert Townsend provides essential information to General George Washington, assisted by a mysterious woman whose identity has remained a secret.

Historical Accuracy: The novel offers a plausible account of the making of the colonial intelligence system, which is clearly based on solid research.

MARY ELLEN GRONAU

`2597` *The Gentle Conqueror*

Date of Publication: 1989
Subject(s): Dark Ages; Romance
Fictional character(s): Lady Claudia, Captive; Angus McMahon, Warrior
Time Period(s): 10th century (987)
Locale(s): Brittany, France; England

Summary: Angus McMahon claims Lady Claudia as a prize of war. Despite a violent start to this relationship, friendship and love follow.

Historical Accuracy: The emphasis is on romance, but the period is suggested with details that create a plausible backdrop.

`2598` *Passionate Warriors*

Date of Publication: 1989
Subject(s): Dark Ages; Romance
Fictional character(s): Dorcas McMahon, Warrior; Neil McNeil, Warrior
Time Period(s): 10th century (987)
Locale(s): Ireland

Summary: In the prequel to the author's *The Gentle Conqueror*, clan warfare in 10th-century Ireland forms the novel's background. Dorcas McMahon marries Neil McNeil to bring peace to their respective feuding clans. Conflict must be overcome before love can flourish.

Historical Accuracy: The novel does provide some period elements that create a plausible backdrop for the action.

ELGIN GROSECLOSE (1899-1983)

An American economic and investment consultant and author, Groseclose taught at the University of Oklahoma and served as an economic adviser to the Iranian government. He performed refugee work in the Soviet Caucasus during the 1920s, which served as the basis for his novel *Ararat*, the winner of the 1939 National Book Award. His other books include *Comanche Country*, *The Simitar of Saladin*, and *Money: The Human Conflict*.

`2599` *The Carmelite*

Date of Publication: 1955
Subject(s): Religious Life
Fictional character(s): Sir Robert Sherley, Diplomat; Shamala, Royalty (princess)
Historical character(s): Juan Thaddeus, Religious (missionary); Clement VIII, Religious (pope)
Time Period(s): 17th century
Locale(s): Persia

Summary: The novel depicts the journey of a small group of Carmelite priests to Persia where Juan Thaddeus labors to win souls in the court of the Shah. The novel offers the contrast between the simplicity of the mendicant Carmelites and the luxurious Persian court.

Historical Accuracy: The novel shows the author's evident research in the history and customs of the Persians.

JOEL GROSS (1951-)

Born in New York City, Gross graduated from Queens College and Columbia University. He began writing at 19 and more than three million of his bestselling novels are in print.

`2600` *The Books of Rachel*

Date of Publication: 1979
Subject(s): Family Saga; Jews
Fictional character(s): Rachel Cuheno, Young Woman; Rachel Cohen, Young Woman; Rachel Kane, Young Woman
Time Period(s): Multiple Time Periods
Locale(s): Spain; Venice, Italy; Berlin, Germany

Summary: The Cuheno family in Spain control the sale of diamonds to the world. A 60-carat white diamond becomes the legacy of the first baby girl after the death of the last Rachel in the family. Over 500 years, each succeeding Rachel must face tests that range from the Spanish Inquisition to the Holocaust.

Historical Accuracy: The novel is remarkably accomplished in creating the period atmosphere of each era.

`2601` *The Lives of Rachel*

Date of Publication: 1984
Subject(s): Jews; Family Saga; Roman Empire
Fictional character(s): Rachel of Judea, Noblewoman; Rachel of Rome, Slave; Rachel of Byzantium, Gentlewoman
Time Period(s): Multiple Time Periods
Locale(s): Jerusalem, Israel; Rome, Roman Empire; Byzantine Empire

Summary: The novel examines the lives of women, all named Rachel, who play important roles in maintaining their heritage through 1,000 years of history. Rachel of Judea defies a half-mad king to save her husband's life; Rachel of Rome is sold into slavery but exacts revenge on her own master; and Rachel of Byzantium is a herder who helps stop the plague. Other Rachels play roles in Arthurian England and in a German pogrom.

Historical Accuracy: Each era is carefully and convincingly depicted.

`2602` *Maura's Dream*

Date of Publication: 1981
Subject(s): Immigrants; Women's Rights
Fictional character(s): Maura Dooley O'Connell, Widow(er), Immigrant; Patrick O'Connell, Immigrant
Time Period(s): 1890s (1897-1899)
Locale(s): Kerry, Ireland; New York, New York

Summary: When her husband dies on the crossing to America from Ireland, Maura O'Connell is thrown on her own resources. She survives enslavement in a brothel and grinding poverty by believing in her own integrity and the prospect of freedom in America.

Historical Accuracy: The details of turn-of-the-century New York life are convincing.

2603 *Sarah*

Date of Publication: 1987
Subject(s): Theatrical Life; Biography, Fictionalized
Historical character(s): Sarah Bernhardt, Actress
Time Period(s): 19th century (1840s to 1923); 20th century
Locale(s): Paris, France

Summary: Sarah Bernhardt was the last great 19th-century actress and the first 20th-century superstar; her legend was as strong and enduring as her on-stage performances. The novel attempts to explore this phenomenal woman's actual life.

Historical Accuracy: The novel imaginatively connects the facts of Bernhardt's life to her legend.

DAVIS GRUBB (1919-1980)

An American novelist and short-story writer, Grubb's stories chronicle the lives of the mountain dwellers of his native West Virginia. His most successful novel is *The Night of the Hunter*. Other books include *Shadow of My Brother*, *The Golden Sickle*, and *Fool's Parade*.

2604 *A Dream of Kings*

Date of Publication: 1955
Subject(s): Civil War—U.S.; Childhood
Fictional character(s): Tom Christopher Alexander, Orphan; Cathie Hornbrook, Foundling; Isaac Bone, Mountain Man
Time Period(s): 1850s; 1860s (1855-1864)
Locale(s): Virginia (western, now West Virginia)

Summary: A boy and a girl grow up on a river-bottom farm in western Virginia immediately before and during the Civil War. Tom Alexander, the narrator, is ten when Cathie Hornbrook shows up at his aunt's farm. Resentment and rivalry develop between the two children, but passion develops as well. Tom runs away into the mountains, then joins the Confederacy to fight under Stonewall Jackson. Finally he returns to his house and confronts his old problems.

Historical Accuracy: The novel is accomplished in rendering the background and experiences of the characters and developing the atmosphere that shaped them.

BERNARD GRUN (1901-1972)

A Czech-born composer, conductor, editor, and translator, Grun is the author of books on composers and other musical topics.

2605 *The Golden Quill: A Novel Based on the Life of Mozart*

Date of Publication: 1956

Subject(s): Musical life; Biography, Fictionalized
Historical character(s): Wolfgang Amadeus Mozart, Composer, Musician
Time Period(s): 18th century (1750s-1790s)
Locale(s): Vienna, Austria

Summary: This fictional life of the great composer Mozart is told in the form of a diary written by Mozart's sister Nannerl. She records Mozart's years as a musical child prodigy performing across Europe, his triumph as a composer, and his poverty-stricken death.

Historical Accuracy: The author's knowledge of the period and of Mozart is evident, creating a believable version of both, though some liberties have been taken with the facts.

STEPHAN GRUNDY

English author Grundy lives in Cambridge, where he is working on a Ph.D. thesis about the Norse god Woden.

2606 *Attila's Treasure*

Date of Publication: 1996
Subject(s): Dark Ages; Myths and Legends; Fantasy
Fictional character(s): Hagan, Royalty (prince)
Historical character(s): Attila the Hun, Ruler (King of the Huns)
Time Period(s): 5th century (415-417)
Locale(s): Europe

Summary: The conflict between the Huns and the Burgundians during the 5th century forms the backdrop for this imaginative reconstruction of the legendary tale of Hagan, a young Burgundian prince, who is sent to be a foster son to the great Attila. He learns the ways of the Huns, and discovers powers that become a threat to Attila.

Historical Accuracy: On occasion the author has let history step aside for legend. However, the novel's appendix points out the factual basis for the tale and the deviations chosen.

2607 *Rhinegold*

Date of Publication: 1994
Subject(s): Myths and Legends; Fantasy
Fictional character(s): Sigifrith, Warrior; Gundrun, Maiden
Time Period(s): Indeterminate Past
Locale(s): Europe (northern)

Summary: The novel is based on the early Northern European legend of Siegfried the Dragon-Slayer. At the center of the story is a vast hoard of gold that brings Sigifrith fame and power but ultimately causes the bloodshed that destroys him.

Historical Accuracy: The author explains that he attempted to link the historical with the legendary as much as possible.

LYNN GUEST (1939-)

American writer Guest lived for six years in Yokohama, Japan, where she researched her first novel. She now lives in Devon, England. Born in St. Louis, Missouri, she earned a B.A. in history and philosophy from Edinburgh University. She began writing by translating Japanese poetry and short stories. She is fascinated by Japanese culture and the concept of the Samurai. The accuracy of her works on Japan is due to her immersion in the country and its culture.

2608 *The Sword of Hachiman*

Date of Publication: 1981
Subject(s): Gempei Wars; Samurai; Japanese Empire
Fictional character(s): Shizuka, Dancer; Benkei, Religious (monk)
Historical character(s): Tairo Tamako, Gentlewoman, Spouse (of Benkei); Minamoto Yoshitshune, Warrior; Go-Shirakawa, Ruler (Emperor of Japan); Takakura, Ruler (emperor)
Time Period(s): 12th century
Locale(s): Japan

Summary: The novel describes the clash between two powerful warrior clans in medieval Japan, the Minamoto and the Taira. Yoshitshune, one of the most romantic and celebrated heroes of the Shogun era, is raised by monks and trained in the martial arts. His skills are quickly tested on the battlefield in the dynastic struggle of one clan against other.

Historical Accuracy: The novel is remarkably detailed and authentic.

2609 *Yedo*

Date of Publication: 1985
Subject(s): East/West Relations; Japanese Empire
Fictional character(s): Pev Fitzpaine, Diplomat; Umegawa, Prostitute; Tada Shom, Doctor
Time Period(s): 1860s
Locale(s): Yedo, Japan (modern Tokyo)

Summary: Pev Fitzpaine is a member of the first British legation in Japan in 250 years. To help him understand the strange ways of the Japanese, Fitzpaine depends upon the advice of Tada Shom, the Japanese doctor attached to the legation. Tada Shom must balance his loyalty to those who have sworn to eliminate all foreign influence in Japan and his curiosity about the West.

Historical Accuracy: Though fictional, many of the characters are based on actual historical figures, and the political events are authentic and accurate.

NICHOLAS GUILD (1944-)

Guild was born in San Mateo, California, and received his B.A. from Occidental College and Ph.D. from the University of California at Berkeley. He teaches English at Ohio State University and has written a number of novels, including *The Lost and Found Man* and *The Summer Soldier*.

2610 *The Assyrian*

Date of Publication: 1987
Subject(s): Assyrian Empire
Fictional character(s): Tiglath Ashur, Royalty (prince); Esharhamat, Royalty (princess)
Historical character(s): Esarhaddon, Warrior
Time Period(s): 7th century B.C.
Locale(s): Babylon; Nineveh, Mesopotamia

Summary: A young Assyrian prince, Tiglath, describes his relationship with Esarhaddon, his half-brother, best friend, and rival for the throne. One is destined to become king of Assyria, the other a famous warrior. Each will compete for Princess Esharhamat, who will wed one and become the lover of the other.

Historical Accuracy: The atmosphere and conditions of the time and place are remarkably authentic and convincing.

2611 *The Blood Star*

Date of Publication: 1989
Subject(s): Assyrian Empire
Fictional character(s): Tiglath Ashur, Royalty (prince), Outcast; Kephaolos, Servant
Historical character(s): Esarhaddon, Ruler (King of Assyria)
Time Period(s): 7th century B.C.
Locale(s): Nineveh, Mesopotamia; Egypt; Italy (Sicily)

Summary: In the sequel to the author's *The Assyrian*, Tiglath Ashur, deprived of the throne by his half-brother, Esarhaddon, is now in exile, pursued by assassins dispatched to hunt him down. His travels take him to Egypt and Sicily before he returns to Nineveh and a final confrontation with his brother.

Historical Accuracy: The novel presents a remarkably authentic picture of the ancient world.

BILL GULICK
(PSEUD. OF GROVER C. GULICK, 1916-)

American western novelist Gulick was born in Kansas City and attended the University of Oklahoma. His western novels are different from other novels in the genre in their characteristic setting in the Pacific Northwest, the emphasis on character development over action and violence, and the extensive research Gulick performs to create authenticity. Gulick has said that he never did "slam-bang action Western" because he knew too much about the real West.

2612 *Distant Trails*

Date of Publication: 1988
Subject(s): American West; Indians; Lewis and Clark Expedition
Fictional character(s): Matt Crane, Frontiersman; John Crane, Young Man; Tall Bird, Indian (Nez Perce)
Historical character(s): William Clark, Explorer; Meriwether Lewis, Explorer
Time Period(s): 19th century (1805-1836)
Locale(s): Pacific Northwest; St. Louis, Missouri

Summary: This is the first novel in a trilogy concerning the Nez Perce Indians and the encroachment of settlers into their territory. Matt Crane travels with Lewis and Clark to chart the Louisiana Purchase and falls in love with an Indian woman. Their son Tall Bird will cross paths with Crane's other son, John.

Historical Accuracy: Authentic in its background, the novel offers a believable depiction of period events.

2613 *Gathering Storm*

Date of Publication: 1988
Subject(s): American West; Indians
Fictional character(s): John Crane, Frontiersman; Tall Bird, Indian (Nez Perce)
Time Period(s): 19th century (1837-1868)
Locale(s): Pacific Northwest

Summary: In the second volume of the author's trilogy on the Nez Perce Indians half brothers John Crane and Tall Bird are unable to halt the rush of settlement in the Pacific Northwest that comes with the discovery of gold.

Historical Accuracy: The period and locale are sharply detailed and convincing.

2614 *The Hallelujah Train*

Date of Publication: 1965
Subject(s): American West; Wagon Trains; Indians
Fictional character(s): Thaddeus Gearhart, Military Personnel (colonel)
Historical character(s): Sojourner Truth, Abolitionist, Feminist; Ulysses S. Grant, Political Figure, Military Personnel
Time Period(s): 1860s (1867)
Locale(s): Colorado

Summary: This comic western is based on actual events surrounding a wagon train carrying cases of champagne and whiskey to Denver in the 1860s. Colonel Gearhart is charged with leading the train and protecting its contents from Indians and temperance leaguers. All factions in the story meet in a blinding sandstorm for the Battle of Whiskey Hills.

Historical Accuracy: Most of the characters are fictional, and actual characters are depicted fictionally, but the events are based on fact.

2615 *Liveliest Town in the West*

Date of Publication: 1969
Subject(s): American West
Fictional character(s): Gabe Walford, Frontiersman, Scout; Theodore Raff, Journalist
Time Period(s): 1870s
Locale(s): Dustville, Wyoming

Summary: The dull town of Dustville in the Wyoming territory is transformed overnight through the imagination of editor Theodore Raff into a legendary wild western scene complete with desperadoes and Indian attacks. As word spreads of the fame of Dustville, the town tries to match Raff's invention with comic results.

Historical Accuracy: This amusing send-up of western elements is given a convincing though farcical background.

2616 *Lost Wallowa*

Date of Publication: 1988
Subject(s): American West; Indians
Fictional character(s): John Crane, Frontiersman; Tall Bird, Indian (Nez Perce)
Time Period(s): 1860s; 1870s (1869-1879)
Locale(s): Pacific Northwest

Summary: This third volume of the author's trilogy concludes the story of the Nez Perce Indians and the encroachment of their territory by settlers. Half brothers John Crane and Tall Bird live through the aftermath of Custer's massacre and the eventual defeat of the Indians as they are forced into life on the reservation.

Historical Accuracy: Authentic and convincing, the novel captures the era with precision.

2617 *The Moon-Eyed Appaloosa*

Date of Publication: 1962
Subject(s): American West; Indians; Military Life—U.S. Cavalry
Fictional character(s): Burke Langdon, Military Personnel (corporal); Freddie Stahl, Military Personnel (private)
Time Period(s): 1860s
Locale(s): Idaho; Walla Walla, Washington

Summary: In the 1860s the U.S. Cavalry, in the mountain country of Idaho and Washington, finds itself outmanuevered by the swift-riding Indians. Corporal Burke Langdon suggests that the cavalry try the Indians own mounts, Appaloosas, and with Private Stahl, attempts to bring new mounts to Fort Walla Walla. Trouble from Oregon-bound settlers, Snake Indians, thieves, and deserters dog their trail.

Historical Accuracy: The setting and situation are authentic and realistic.

2618 *They Came to a Valley*

Date of Publication: 1966
Subject(s): American West; Indians
Fictional character(s): Andy Hale, Scout, Rancher; Levi, Indian (Delaware); Armand Kimball, Lawyer
Time Period(s): 1860s (1863-1868)
Locale(s): Idaho

Summary: The novel depicts the settling of Idaho through the experiences of Andy Hale, and the lawyer Armand Kimball. Andy, a wagon train guide, and his friend Levi travel to Idaho to raise cattle, and struggle to create a community on the frontier.

Historical Accuracy: The locale and the period are authentically presented.

2619 *Treasure in Hell's Canyon*

Date of Publication: 1979
Subject(s): American West
Fictional character(s): Walt Randall, Prospector; Ming Sen, Young Woman
Time Period(s): 19th century
Locale(s): Portland, Oregon; Snake River, Oregon

Summary: Walt Randall acquires a fortune at the poker table as well as a Chinese ''permanent companion.'' A month later, Ming Sen and his money are gone, and Randall sets out in search of gold on the Snake River. He heads towards Hell's Canyon and a fateful meeting with Ming Sen.

Historical Accuracy: The novel is authentic in its locale and period depictions.

NEIL GUNN (1891-1973)

A Scottish novelist, playwright, and short-story writer, Gunn was the son of a fishing captain. He published his first novel in 1926. It was followed by more than two dozen novels and much nonfiction.

2620 *Butcher's Broom*

Date of Publication: 1934
Subject(s): Rural Life—Scotland; Highland Clearances
Fictional character(s): Dark Mairi, Healer; Elie, Heroine
Time Period(s): 19th century (early)
Locale(s): Highlands, Scotland

Summary: This rich and haunting evocation of a tragic period of Scottish history depicts the destruction of traditional village life during the Highland clearances in the early 19th century. Dark Mairi is the strong center of a small community of crofters. Their stories illustrate a dismantled and dispossessed culture.

Historical Accuracy: The novel is a strong re-creation of a lifestyle uprooted by modern changes.

ALLAN GURGANUS (1947-)

Born in North Carolina, Gurganus graduated from Sarah Lawrence College and the University of Iowa. He is also an artist, whose paintings are represented in many private and public art collections. He began his *Oldest Living Confederate Widow Tells All* after he learned that his relatives had been slave owners. His short story "Minor Heroism" became the first story published in the *New Yorker* that depicted homosexual characters.

2621 *Oldest Living Confederate Widow Tells All*

Date of Publication: 1989
Subject(s): Civil War—U.S.; Battle of Antietam; Slavery
Fictional character(s): Lucy Marsden, Widow(er); Willie Marsden, Veteran (Civil War)
Historical character(s): Abraham Lincoln, Political Figure; Robert E. Lee, Military Personnel (Confederate commander)
Time Period(s): 19th century; 20th century (1860s-1980s)
Locale(s): South

Summary: Lucy Marsden's recollects the Civil War, the South, and the difficulty of coming to terms with the Civil War and a lifetime of memories.

Historical Accuracy: The author points out that history is his starting point. Abraham Lincoln's tour of Georgia is invented.

DAVID GURR (1936-)

A British-born novelist who emigrated to Canada in 1947, Gurr went to school in England, at Canada's Naval College, and at the University of Victoria. From 1954 to 1970 Gurr served as an officer and computer specialist in the Royal Canadian Navy. From 1971 to 1980 he ran his own company. Best known for espionage fiction and novels that

explore 20th-century history and culture, his novels include *An American Spy Story*, *The Action of the Tiger*, *A Woman Called Scylla*, and *Troika*. *The Ring Master* was shortlisted for the Commonwealth Prize for fiction in 1990.

2622 *The Ring Master*

Date of Publication: 1987
Subject(s): Nazis; Myths and Legends
Fictional character(s): Edwin Casson-Perceval, Nobleman; Edwina Casson-Perceval, Singer (opera)
Historical character(s): Adolf Hitler, Leader (Nazi), Political Figure; Richard Wagner, Composer; Winston Churchill, Political Figure
Time Period(s): 20th century
Locale(s): Germany; England

Summary: This elaborate exploration of Nazism and Hitler's Germany brings together history and myth in the suggestion that Wagner's Ring cycle provides a touchstone to explain Hitler's pervasive evil. The story concerns an obsessive love triangle involving Hitler; an English opera singer, Edwina Casson-Percival; and her brother Edwin, who is in search of the Holy Grail.

Historical Accuracy: The novel reshapes history into the theatrical and the archtypical. Actual events provide only a springboard for a fascinating exploration.

A.B. GUTHRIE JR. (1901-1991)

An American novelist who is generally considered one of the foremost writers on the American West, Guthrie was born in Indiana, but moved to Montana as an infant. He was a newspaper editor for twenty years in Lexington, Kentucky, before turning to fiction.

2623 *Arfive*

Date of Publication: 1970
Subject(s): American West; Settlement of the American Frontier
Fictional character(s): Benton Collingsworth, Teacher; Mort Ewing, Rancher; Sarge Kraker, Lawman (sheriff)
Time Period(s): 19th century
Locale(s): Arfive, Montana

Summary: The arrival of the new schoolmaster in the town of Arfive, Montana, represents the arrival of change and civilization and the passing of the rougher earlier times. The new and the old attitudes are represented by the schoolmaster, Collingsworth, and the rancher, Ewing, respectively. Each comes to acknowledge the appeal and the integrity of the other's ideas.

Historical Accuracy: Guthrie's details of life in a western community are convincing.

2624 *The Big Sky*

Date of Publication: 1947
Subject(s): American West; Settlement of the American Frontier; Indians

Fictional character(s): Boone Caudill, Mountain Man; Jim Deakins, Mountain Man; Teal Eye, Indian; Dick Summers, Mountain Man
Time Period(s): 1830s; 1840s (1830-1843)
Locale(s): West; Missouri; Kentucky

Summary: The closing of the American wilderness to hunters and trappers is depicted in the story of Boone Caudill and his friend Jim Deakins. They journey west by keel boat into Blackfoot country, and Caudill takes an Indian wife. Domestic troubles doom the friendship between Caudill and Deakins, casting an elegiac tone as the dream of frontier freedom and endless possibility sours.

Historical Accuracy: The characters' words and thoughts are expressed in frontier dialect, heightening the book's realistic effect.

2625 *Fair Land, Fair Land*

Date of Publication: 1982
Subject(s): American West; Settlement of the American Frontier
Fictional character(s): Dick Summers, Mountain Man, Guide; Boone Caudill, Mountain Man; Teal Eye, Indian
Time Period(s): 1850s
Locale(s): Pacific Northwest (Oregon, Washington, and Montana)

Summary: This sequel to *The Big Sky* and *The Way West* answers the questions of what became of Dick Summers after he guided the wagon train to Oregon; to Boone Caudill after he killed his best friend over the Indian woman, Teal Eye; and to Teal Eye herself, abandoned with her baby. The novel centers on Summers' search for the idyllic wilderness of his past and its gradual fading before the onrush of settlement.

Historical Accuracy: The authenticity of Guthrie's work stems from an abiding sense of the wilderness and the nation that was carved from it.

2626 *The Last Valley*

Date of Publication: 1975
Subject(s): American West; Settlement of the American Frontier
Fictional character(s): Benton Collingsworth, Teacher; Mort Ewing, Rancher; Ben Tate, Journalist
Time Period(s): 20th century (1920s-1940s)
Locale(s): Arfive, Montana

Summary: In this sequel to *Arfive*, Guthrie takes the story of the settlement of the West into modern times. Ben Tate purchases *The Arfive Advocate* with money saved from his military service in World War I. He turns the paper into a progressive journal. At the center of the tale is the sense of community and the enduring character of the land.

Historical Accuracy: Guthrie shows that he is as able to write convincingly about the modern West as the Old West.

2627 *These Thousand Hills*

Date of Publication: 1956
Subject(s): American West; Ranching; Cattle Drives

Fictional character(s): Lat Evans, Cowboy; Whitey, Cowboy; Little Runner, Indian
Time Period(s): 1880s
Locale(s): Oregon; Montana

Summary: Lat Evans signs on to drive cattle from Oregon to Montana. He is accompanied by a variety of western types who characterize the frontier experience. The novel is the third installment of Guthrie's epic depiction of the western frontier and its succeeding waves of mountain men, wagon trains, and cattlemen.

Historical Accuracy: Guthrie's western novels set the standard in important ways for believable Western fiction. His characters and situations define the archetype.

2628 *The Way West*

Date of Publication: 1949
Subject(s): American West; Settlement of the American Frontier; Wagon Trains
Fictional character(s): Dick Summers, Frontiersman, Guide; Lije Evans, Settler; Tadlock, Settler
Time Period(s): 19th century
Locale(s): Oregon Trail, United States (Independence, Missouri, to Oregon)

Summary: The novel chronicles a wagon train's journey west from Independence, Missouri, to Oregon. The train is filled with a variety of American types, all propelled by the dream of a better chance in the western wilderness. They are led by Dick Summers who remembers the former West of the mountain men and trappers. The wagon train's odyssey is filled with natural and human obstacles.

Historical Accuracy: Considered by some to be the best novel ever written on the subject, Guthrie's book is utterly convincing in both its characters and its details.

BEN HAAS (1926-1977)

Born in North Carolina, Haas worked as a proofreader, a clerk, a steel estimator, and a sales manager before becoming a full-time writer. He is a prolific author of novels about the South and West, having written more than 100 books, including *The Foragers*, *Look Away* and *Daisy Canfield*.

2629 *The Chandler Heritage*

Date of Publication: 1971
Subject(s): Family Saga; Reconstruction Period; Business Building
Fictional character(s): Lloyd Chandler, Businessman; Heath Chandler, Military Personnel (pilot)
Time Period(s): 19th century; 20th century
Locale(s): North Carolina; France

Summary: This family dynasty story spans three generations and begins with Lloyd Chandler, who grows up poor, but who, with determination, eventually dominates the cotton industry. His son Heath becomes a World War I pilot and ace who seeks his fortune out of his father's shadow until he is drawn back during the Depression. At the end it is an open question whether the family heritage is a blessing or a curse.

Historical Accuracy: The period background is effectively drawn.

2630 *The Foragers*

Date of Publication: 1962
Subject(s): Civil War—U.S.
Fictional character(s): Marshall Wales, Military Personnel (Confederate captain)
Time Period(s): 1860s
Locale(s): Virginia

Summary: This Civil War tale concerns Confederate Captain Marshall Wales, who is detached to pillage food for the hungry troops. When he chances upon the untouched and prosperous Red Oaks plantation, an ethical dilemma ensues.

Historical Accuracy: The novel's morality is cast in stark, melodramatic terms that undermine the realism and particularity of time and place.

HELLA S. HAASSE (1918-)

2631 *In a Dark Wood Wandering*

Date of Publication: 1989
Subject(s): Hundred Years War; Royalty—France; Royalty—England
Historical character(s): Charles VI, Ruler (King of France); Isabeau, Royalty (Queen of France); Louis, Nobleman (Duke of Orleans); Charles d'Orleans, Nobleman; Richard II, Ruler (King of England); Henry IV, Ruler (King of England); Henry V, Ruler (King of England); Joan of Arc, Warrior
Time Period(s): 14th century; 15th century (1394-1440s)
Locale(s): France; England

Summary: The novel is set during the Hundred Years War between France and England. It centers on the career of Charles d'Orleans who is an active participant in the great events of the period including the Battle of Agincourt.

Historical Accuracy: The novel is a masterful panorama of medieval life and times.

2632 *The Scarlet City*

Date of Publication: 1990
Subject(s): Renaissance
Historical character(s): Alexander VI, Religious (pope); Cesare Borgia, Diplomat, Military Personnel; Lucrezia Borgia, Noblewoman; Giovanni Borgia, Gentleman; Niccolo Machiavelli, Writer, Diplomat; Michelangelo Buonarotti, Artist; Vittoria Colonna, Noblewoman; Pietro Aretino, Writer
Time Period(s): 16th century
Locale(s): Italy

Summary: The Italian Wars during which French, Swiss, Spanish, and German armies vie for control of Italy is the background for the story's intrigue. At its center is Giovanni Borgia who may be the son or brother of Cesare Borgia. The novel is a panoramic depiction of the era that culminates in the sack of Rome in 1527.

Historical Accuracy: This is a monumental work of historical recreation.

2633 *Threshold of Fire*

Date of Publication: 1993
Subject(s): Roman Empire
Fictional character(s): Hadrian, Government Official (prefect); Marcus Anicius, Nobleman; Eliezar Ben Elijah, Gentleman
Historical character(s): Honorius, Ruler (Roman emperor); Claudius Claudianus, Writer (poet)
Time Period(s): 4th century; 5th century (380-414)
Locale(s): Rome, Italy; Ravenna, Italy

Summary: The novel explores the death throes of the Roman Empire. A variety of characters representing Rome's heroic past, disturbing present, and troubling future are dramatized. At the center is the court of the Emperor Honorius and the poet Claudian who chronicles the past age and the new one being born.

Historical Accuracy: The novel offers a canvas rich in historical details that rings with disturbing authenticity.

FRANCIS HACKETT (1883-1962)

An Irish historian and journalist, Hackett was born in Kilkenny and has worked as an editorial writer for newspapers and as the editor for *The New Republic*. He spent six years on the research and writing of his best-known work, *The Personal History of Henry the Eighth*.

2634 *Queen Anne Boleyn*

Date of Publication: 1939
Subject(s): Tudor Period; Royalty—England; Biography, Fictionalized
Historical character(s): Anne Boleyn, Royalty (queen consort of Henry VIII); Henry VIII, Ruler (King of England); Catherine of Aragon, Royalty (queen consort of Henry VIII); Sir Thomas Wyatt, Writer (poet), Courtier; Thomas Wolsey, Religious (cardinal); John Fisher, Religious; Thomas Cromwell, Government Official; Thomas Cranmer, Religious
Time Period(s): 16th century
Locale(s): England; Italy

Summary: The life and times of Anne Boleyn are depicted as she rises from relative obscurity to captivate Henry VIII. Refusing to be his mistress and insistent upon becoming his wife, she sets in motion the elaborate diplomatic maneuvering that leads to the Protestant Reformation and near civil war.

Historical Accuracy: Anne's early history is largely invented since many details are unknown. In other respects the author admits to having built upon the existing historical facts with sheer imagination.

DIANE HAEGER

2635 *Courtesan*

Date of Publication: 1993
Subject(s): Royalty—France
Historical character(s): Diane de Poitiers, Noblewoman (mistress of Henri II); Henri II, Ruler (King of France); Catherine de' Medici, Royalty (Queen of France)

Time Period(s): 16th century (1547-1569)
Locale(s): France

Summary: The love between France's Henri II and his mistress, Diane de Poitiers, is the novel's subject. Diane is Henri's great love who sustains him through his disastrous and unhappy marriage to Catherine de Medici.

Historical Accuracy: The novel is rich in historical details and well-developed and believable historical portraits.

LENNART HAGERFORS (1946-)

Hagerfors is a Swedish author who spent nine years in the Congo.

2636 *The Whales in Lake Tanganyika*

Date of Publication: 1989
Subject(s): Exploration; Frontier—Africa
Fictional character(s): John Shaw, Sailor
Historical character(s): Henry Morton Stanley, Explorer; David Livingstone, Explorer, Religious (missionary)
Time Period(s): 1870s (1871)
Locale(s): Africa

Summary: The novel provides an imaginative retelling of Henry Morton Stanley's 1871 expedition through Tanzania to find the explorer and missionary David Livingstone. Ironically revising the self-serving heroic account by Stanley himself, this chronicle, told by British sailor John Shaw, satirizes the pretensions of the imperialists' mission in Africa.

Historical Accuracy: This quirky satire does feature a closely observed period background.

H. RIDER HAGGARD

2637 *Cleopatra*

Date of Publication: 1889
Subject(s): Ancient Egypt; Royalty—Egypt
Fictional character(s): Harmachis, Religious (priest), Magician
Historical character(s): Cleopatra, Ruler (Queen of Egypt)
Time Period(s): 1st century B.C.
Locale(s): Egypt

Summary: This historical romance tells the story of a conspiracy of Egyptian nobles to overthrow Cleopatra and place Harmachis on her throne. Harmachis is intent on killing Cleopatra, but he falls in love with her as the plot unfolds.

Historical Accuracy: The novel is filled with many vivid and believable portraits of Egyptian life and culture.

EMILY HAHN (1905-)

American writer Hahn was born in St. Louis. She was the first woman to earn a degree from the University of Wisconsin's College of Engineering. Hahn lived in China for nine years and settled in Hong Kong, working as the *New Yorker*'s China Coast correspondent. Her novels include *Purple Passage*, *Love Conquers Nothing*, *Diamond*, and *The Tiger House Party*.

2638 *Purple Passage: A Novel about a Lady Both Famous and Fantastic*

Date of Publication: 1960
Subject(s): Restoration Period; Literary Life; Espionage
Historical character(s): Aphra Behn, Writer
Time Period(s): 17th century
Locale(s): Sussex, England; Suriname; London, England

Summary: This novel re-creates the life of Aphra Behn, the first female professional English writer. Although little is known of Behn's early life, the novel speculatively fills in the gaps to record her sojourn as a spy in the Dutch Wars and in Suriname during the slave revolt. Back in London society the unconventional Behn justifies her reputation as the George Sand of the Restoration period.

Historical Accuracy: The novel is part fiction and part invention, based on a sketchy factual record.

EDWIN HAINES (1877-)

2639 *The Exquisite Siren*

Date of Publication: 1938
Subject(s): American Revolution
Historical character(s): Margaret Shippen Arnold, Spouse; Benedict Arnold, Military Personnel (general), Traitor; John Andre, Military Personnel (British major), Spy
Time Period(s): 1770s
Locale(s): United States

Summary: This tale of the American Revolution concerns Peggy Arnold, the wife of Benedict Arnold, and her secret love for the British officer John Andre. The emphasis here is on romance and adventure rather than a careful delineation of character and motivation.

Historical Accuracy: Much of the plot is fanciful and does not reflect the actual events of the Arnold conspiracy.

WILLIAM WISTER HAINES (1908-1989)

Born in Iowa, Haines graduated from the University of Pennsylvania. A prolific author of adventure novels, plays, and film scripts, his best known work is *Command Decision*, which was made into a film starring Clark Gable.

2640 *The Winter War*

Date of Publication: 1961
Subject(s): American West; Indians
Historical character(s): Nelson Appleton Miles, Military Personnel (army commander); Sitting Bull, Indian (Sioux), Chieftain; George Armstrong Custer, Military Personnel (Cavalry officer); George C. Crook, Military Personnel (general); Crazy Horse, Indian (Sioux), Warrior
Time Period(s): 1870s (1876)
Locale(s): Montana

Summary: The campaign against Sitting Bull after the Battle of the Little Bighorn is dramatized in this account of the army's pursuit of the Sioux and the Cheyenne. General Nelson Miles is determined to avenge the army's defeat by Sitting

Bull and presses into the winter on a campaign that is doomed from the start.

Historical Accuracy: The novel offers a blend of fact and fiction. The romantic plot does not prevent an authentic depiction of the actual events.

LIN HAIRE-SARGEANT (1946-)

An American born in Kentucky, Haire-Sargeant graduated from Tufts University and has worked as an instructor in English at the University of Massachusetts and Boston University. Her novel on Emily Bronte's Heathcliff began as part of her academic work on the Brontes.

2641 *H.—: The Story of Heathcliff's Journey Back to Wuthering Heights*

Date of Publication: 1992
Subject(s): Victorian Period; Literary Life
Fictional character(s): Heathcliff, Outcast; Catherine Earnshaw, Gentlewoman; Edgar Linton, Gentleman
Historical character(s): Charlotte Bronte, Writer
Time Period(s): 1780s; 1840s (1844)
Locale(s): Yorkshire, England

Summary: The novel attempts to answer the literary mystery surrounding Heathcliff of Charlotte Bronte's *Wuthing Heights*. What became of Heathcliff after he fled Yorkshire and before he returns to Wuthering Heights as a man of means to finanace his campaign of vengeance fueled by his disappointed love of Catherine Earnshaw? Somewhat implausibly, in 1844 Charlotte Bronte receives a long letter written by Heathcliff 60 years before tracing the experiences that transform him from boy to gentleman.

Historical Accuracy: The novel is true to the spirit of Emily Bronte's novel and its period.

HARVEY HAISLIP (1889-1978)

Born in Virginia, Haislip attended the U.S. Naval Academy and held the rank of captain in the U.S. Navy when he began to write between the wars. His work as a technical adviser for several motion pictures led to a second career as a screenwriter. Haislip is best known for the Academy Award winning documentary *The Secret Land* about Richard Byrd's Deep Freeze expedition.

2642 *The Prize Master*

Date of Publication: 1959
Subject(s): Sea Story; American Revolution
Fictional character(s): Thomas Potter, Military Personnel (midshipman); Denise Milholme, Young Woman
Historical character(s): Benjamin Franklin, Political Figure
Time Period(s): 1770s
Locale(s): *Vixen*, At Sea

Summary: Thomas Potter, one of John Paul Jones' veterans during the American Revolution, is given command of the captured British ship *Vixen*. As the prize master, Potter must

deal with rebellious prisoners and an uncooperative crew and bring the *Vixen* into port safely. One of his greatest challenges is the young woman Denise Milholme.

Historical Accuracy: The nautical scene and details are convincingly depicted.

2643 *Sailor Named Jones*

Date of Publication: 1957
Subject(s): Sea Story; American Revolution
Fictional character(s): Thomas Porter, Military Personnel (sailor)
Historical character(s): John Paul Jones, Military Personnel (naval officer)
Time Period(s): 1770s
Locale(s): Brest, France; *Bonhomme Richard*, At Sea

Summary: The novel tells the story of John Paul Jones' struggle during the American Revolution to fashion the first American Navy. The action culminates in one of the most famous naval battles of all times when the *Bonhomme Richard*, undergunned and sinking, manages to defeat the powerful British frigate *Serapis*.

Historical Accuracy: Many of the scenes depicted are invented.

2644 *Sea Road to Yorktown*

Date of Publication: 1960
Subject(s): Sea Story; American Revolution; Battle of Yorktown
Fictional character(s): Thomas Potter, Military Personnel (midshipman)
Historical character(s): Francois Joseph Paul de Grasse, Military Personnel (naval officer)
Time Period(s): 1780s
Locale(s): *Princess*, At Sea (Chesapeake Bay); West Indies; Yorktown, Virginia

Summary: In the sequel to *The Prize Master*, young naval midshipman Thomas Potter joins the crew of a privateer, *Princess*, in action in the West Indies and with the French admiral, the Comte de Grasse, in the blockade that contributed to Cornwallis' defeat at Yorktown.

Historical Accuracy: The story is fanciful, but the period details and historical events are accurately described.

JOHN HALKIN

Halkin worked in education and journalism before becoming a producer for the BBC. He has also produced and directed documentaries and films and has worked as a screenwriter.

2645 *Kenya*

Date of Publication: 1983
Subject(s): Railroads; Frontier—Africa
Fictional character(s): John Andrewes, Engineer; Hester Andrewes, Spouse
Time Period(s): 1890s
Locale(s): Kenya

Summary: The novel concerns the experiences of engineer John Andrewes and his wife Hester who come to Kenya in the 1890s to help build the Uganda Railway. The obstacles they face in the wilds are described.

Historical Accuracy: The novel provides an authentic depiction of period Africa and the details of railroad construction.

ARTHUR DANA HALL (1893-)

2646 *The Golden Balance*

Date of Publication: 1955
Subject(s): Ancient Egypt; Pharaohs
Fictional character(s): Senmut, Young Man
Historical character(s): Hatshepsut, Royalty (Queen of Egypt)
Time Period(s): 15th century B.C.
Locale(s): Egypt

Summary: Set in ancient Egypt during the reign of the pharaohs Thothmes I, II, and III, the novel describes the rise to prominence of Senmut, a farmer's son whose wits take him to the pharaoh's court. When he becomes the lover of Queen Hatshepsut, rivals conspire to ruin him and the queen.

Historical Accuracy: The evident research is apparent, but the elements never reach the level of believability.

DESMOND HALL (1909-1992)

American writer and editor Hall served as assistant editor of *Astounding Stories of Super Science* from 1930-1933 and became editor of *Mademoiselle*.

2647 *I Give You Oscar Wilde*

Date of Publication: 1965
Subject(s): Biography, Fictionalized; Literary Life; Trials
Fictional character(s): Lawrence Young, Gentleman
Historical character(s): Oscar Wilde, Writer; Constance Lloyd, Spouse (of Wilde)
Time Period(s): 19th century; 20th century
Locale(s): London, England; United States; Paris, France

Summary: This biographical novel chronicles the scandal-ridden literary career of Oscar Wilde from his triumphs in the 1880s to his fall in one of the 19th century's most celebrated trials, followed by his imprisonment and self-exile in Paris. The novel offers a balanced and, on the whole, a sympathetic account of the controversial Wilde.

Historical Accuracy: The account mixes fact and fiction and the author admits to having added certain details and conversations.

DOUGLAS KENT HALL (1938-)

Born in Utah, Hall received his B.A. degree from Brigham Young University and an M.F.A. from the University of Iowa. He has worked as an instructor in creative writing and literature at the University of Portland. He is also a freelance photographer.

2648 *The Master of Oakwindsor*

Date of Publication: 1976
Subject(s): Artistic Life
Fictional character(s): David Harris, Artist; Kathy Dixon, Young Woman
Time Period(s): 1900s
Locale(s): England; Paris, France; Italy

Summary: The novel is a saga of two intertwined lives: David Harris, a young painter haunted by the mystery of his past, and Kathy Dixon, an independent woman. Their relationship is played out in colorful European settings ranging from the Dorset countryside to artistic Paris and the Italian Riviera.

Historical Accuracy: The emphasis is on the pair's relationship. However, the period background is convincingly depicted.

OAKLEY HALL (1920-)

Western novelist Hall was born in San Diego and graduated from the University of California at Berkeley and the State University of Iowa. A professor of English and creative writing, Hall won a Pulitzer Prize nomination for *Warlock*.

2649 *The Adelita*

Date of Publication: 1975
Subject(s): Mexican Revolution
Fictional character(s): Robert Macbean, Prospector; Adelita, Revolutionary
Time Period(s): 20th century (1913-1970)
Locale(s): Mexico; Texas; Tucson, Arizona

Summary: Robert MacBean is the son of a wealthy American oil tycoon and a Mexican heiress who, while prospecting in Mexico in 1913, is swept up in the events of the Mexican Revolution. He joins his mother's vaqueros in fighting the Federal troops. He also falls in love with a beautiful soldadera named Adelita.

Historical Accuracy: The details of Mexican life of the period are authentically reproduced.

2650 *Apaches*

Date of Publication: 1986
Subject(s): American West; Indians; Lincoln County War
Fictional character(s): Caballito, Indian (Apache), Chieftain; Johnny Angel, Cowboy; Jack Grant, Lawman (sheriff)
Time Period(s): 1880s
Locale(s): New Mexico

Summary: This western adventure is set during the Lincoln County Wars and links the fate of cowboy turned outlaw Johnny Angel with that of Apache chief Caballito. The story concerns swindles, Indian attacks, and a relentless pursuit.

Historical Accuracy: Few writers are better than Hall in making the western frontier scene more immediate and believable.

2651 *The Bad Lands*

Date of Publication: 1978
Subject(s): American West; Ranching

Fictional character(s): George Eustace Balater, Nobleman (Lord Machray), Businessman; Andrew Livingston, Banker, Political Figure; Yule Hardy, Rancher; Bill Driggs, Hunter
Time Period(s): 1880s (1883-1884)
Locale(s): Badlands, South Dakota

Summary: In the 1880s, the free-rangers battle those who would fence in the land and a Scottish lord launches a venture in the South Dakota Badlands to build a slaughterhouse to challenge the control of the Chicago meat-packers. The novel explores the conflict between the old and new West.

Historical Accuracy: The basis of the story comes from the South Dakota range wars. This novel captures the feeling of the times if not the actual historical events.

2652 *The Children of the Sun*

Date of Publication: 1983
Subject(s): Exploration; Spanish Colonies
Historical character(s): Alvar Nunez Cabeza de Vaca, Explorer; Alonso del Castillo, Explorer; Andres Dorantes, Explorer
Time Period(s): 16th century
Locale(s): Mexico; North America (Florida and the Southwest)

Summary: This story of the exploration of North America by the Spanish is written from the perspective of Andres Dorantes, one of the four survivors of the Narvaez expedition to Florida in the early 16th century. Dorantes takes part in Hernando Cortez's conquest of Mexico and Francisco Coronado's expedition in search of the seven cities of Cibola.

Historical Accuracy: Some historical liberties have been taken to accommodate all of the events to Dorantes' perspective.

2653 *Warlock*

Date of Publication: 1958
Subject(s): American West; Settlement of the American Frontier
Fictional character(s): Clay Blaisedell, Lawman (sheriff), Gunfighter; George Holloway, Judge
Time Period(s): 1880s (1880)
Locale(s): Warlock, Southwest

Summary: Warlock is a Southwest mining settlement that is besieged by cattle rustlers and desperadoes. The Citizens Committee hires Clay Blaisedell, a renowned gunman, to serve as their sheriff. But when he kills a man by mistake, it sets off a tragic train of events that includes lynchings, murders, and a showdown.

Historical Accuracy: This is a classic western tale with the scene convincingly detailed.

ROBERT LEE HALL (1941-)

Born in San Francisco, Hall attended the University of California, Berkeley, and the California College of Arts and Crafts. After a career as a public school teacher and painter, he turned to writing, beginning a short story that ''got out of hand.''

2654 *Benjamin Franklin and a Case of Artful Murder*

Date of Publication: 1994
Subject(s): Mystery; Artistic Life; Georgian Period
Fictional character(s): James Cavitty, Artist; Lady Shenstone, Gentlewoman; Nicholas Handy, Bastard Son (of Franklin)
Historical character(s): Benjamin Franklin, Political Figure, Inventor; William Hogarth, Artist
Time Period(s): 1750s
Locale(s): London, England

Summary: While Lady Shenstone is having her portrait done by James Cavitty, she leaves the famous Shenstone diamond with him to study for the painting. When she goes to reclaim the jewel, it has disappeared, and Lady Shenstone turns to Benjamin Franklin to solve the mystery of its whereabouts. His son, Nicholas, gains a position in the artist's studio where he witnesses forgery, murder, and romance.

Historical Accuracy: The background of 18th-century London is accurately detailed.

2655 *Benjamin Franklin and a Case of Christmas Murder*

Date of Publication: 1990
Subject(s): Mystery; Georgian Period
Fictional character(s): Frederick Fairbrass, Businessman (merchant); Nicholas Handy, Bastard Son (of Franklin)
Historical character(s): Benjamin Franklin, Political Figure, Inventor
Time Period(s): 1750s (1757)
Locale(s): London, England

Summary: A wealthy merchant dies while acting in a Christmas play. In the audience is Benjamin Franklin who is convinced that this is a case of murder. With his illegitimate son, Nicholas Handy, he begins an investigation that reveals a complicated intrigue carrying the two from the London banking world to its gaming rooms.

Historical Accuracy: Franklin is more a character invented out of his legendary traits than a historical figure. The realism is in the depiction of period London.

2656 *Benjamin Franklin Takes the Case*

Date of Publication: 1988
Subject(s): Mystery; Georgian Period
Fictional character(s): Nicholas Handy, Bastard Son (of Franklin)
Historical character(s): Benjamin Franklin, Political Figure, Inventor
Time Period(s): 1750s (1757)
Locale(s): London, England

Summary: While in London in 1757, pleading the case for American independence, Benjamin Franklin is called on to investigate the death of an old friend, apparently murdered by an American Indian. The trail of clues takes him into the dark alleyways of London and the great houses where Franklin's scientific method and inventiveness help him to unravel a complex tangle of deception.

Historical Accuracy: The novel is particularly strong in detailing period London life.

2657 *Exit Sherlock Holmes*

Date of Publication: 1977
Subject(s): Mystery; Victorian Period; Time Travel
Fictional character(s): Sherlock Holmes, Detective—Private; John H. Watson, Doctor, Writer; James Moriarty, Criminal, Professor
Time Period(s): 1930s; 19th century (1881-1895)
Locale(s): London, England; Sussex, England

Summary: In the 1930s Dr. John H. Watson records the final case of his celebrated friend, Sherlock Holmes. Different from his other narratives, in this one Watson answers many of the questions that have teased readers about Holmes: his early life, his relationship with his brother Mycroft, and most importantly, his relationship with his archenemy Moriarity. Watson tells all, including the climactic showdown between Holmes and Moriarity.

Historical Accuracy: The novel is adept in creating the atmosphere of Victorian England, but purists may object to the supernatural turn the story takes.

2658 *The King Edward Plot*

Date of Publication: 1980
Subject(s): Mystery; Royalty—England; Edwardian Period
Fictional character(s): Frederick Wigmore, Actor; Simon Bliss, Gentleman; Jack Merridew, Servant
Historical character(s): Edward VII, Ruler (King of England)
Time Period(s): 1900s (1906)
Locale(s): London, England; Norfolk, England (Sandringham, Edward VII's estate)

Summary: In 1906 Frederick Wigmore, a young actor and former Baker Street Irregular, and gentleman Simon Bliss uncover a plot to kill King Edward VII. In a desperate race against time, they manage to obtain an invitation to Sandringham where Edward is celebrating his birthday. There they devise the means to foil the plot and flush out the conspirators.

Historical Accuracy: The novel blends the fictional (Holmesiana) with the historical in a mind-bending mystery, filled with authentic period detail.

2659 *Murder at Drury Lane*

Date of Publication: 1992
Subject(s): Mystery; Theatrical Life; Georgian Period
Fictional character(s): Nicholas Handy, Bastard Son (of Franklin)
Historical character(s): Benjamin Franklin, Political Figure, Inventor; David Garrick, Actor; Sir John Fielding, Judge (magistrate)
Time Period(s): 1750s
Locale(s): London, England

Summary: When a heckler tumbles to his death during a performance at London's Drury Lane Theatre, Benjamin Franklin, on hand for the performance, is engaged by actor-manager David Garrick to look into the case. Franklin quickly finds himself in the middle of jealous actors and actresses and many motives for murder.

Historical Accuracy: The novel, like the entire series, excels in reproducing authentic period detail.

2660 *Murder at San Simeon*

Date of Publication: 1988
Subject(s): Mystery; Motion Picture Industry
Historical character(s): William Randolph Hearst, Publisher; Marion Davies, Actress; Charlie Chaplin, Actor
Time Period(s): 1930s (1933)
Locale(s): San Simeon, California; Hollywood, California

Summary: William Randolph Hearst is hosting one of his lavish parties at San Simeon. The luminaries of Hollywood are invited but also on hand are a disgruntled screenwriter, a Communist sympathizer, an ambitious starlet, and a dwarf with a hidden camera in his shoe. First an earthquake hits, then a murder occurs, and Hearst himself becomes the detective who must solve the crime while keeping a number of embarrassing secrets hidden.

Historical Accuracy: Few will confuse the actual Hearst with the character invented here, but the appeal is the conglomeration of well-known personalities and a suspenseful script.

2661 *Murder by the Waters*

Date of Publication: 1995
Subject(s): Mystery; Georgian Period
Fictional character(s): Nicholas Handy, Bastard Son (of Franklin); Emma Morland, Gentlewoman
Historical character(s): Benjamin Franklin, Diplomat, Scientist
Time Period(s): 1750s (1759)
Locale(s): Bath, England

Summary: Benjamin Franklin, sent to England to negotiate with the Crown on behalf of the American colonies, finds himself in the spa city of Bath where a series of crimes must be solved. When a man is found murdered, Franklin begins to suspect that his greatest enemy, the notorious Quimp, an English criminal mastermind, must be behind the intrigue.

Historical Accuracy: The novel offers an authentic portrait of the time in this ingenious period mystery.

RUBYLEA HALL (1910-)

Born in Greenwood, Florida, Hall attended Florida State University and the University of Florida. She has worked as a librarian at the University of Florida, as a teacher in Florida's public schools, and in business as a director of customer services. Her novels include *Davey*, *Flamingo Prince*, and *God Has a Sense of Humor*. *The Great Tide* has been in print continuously since its publication.

2662 *The Great Tide*

Date of Publication: 1947
Subject(s): Antebellum South; Disasters—Natural
Fictional character(s): Caline Cohran, Southern Belle
Time Period(s): 1830s; 1840s

Locale(s): Florida

Summary: In 19th century Florida Caline Cohran marries for money and learns to regret her choice. Her story is played out against a vivid backdrop of Florida history including a yellow fever epidemic and the tidal wave that destroyed St. Joseph.

Historical Accuracy: The novel is accurate in its regional and period elements.

RICHARD HALLET (1887-1967)

Born in Bath, Maine, Hallet was best known for his recounting of the Black Hawk wars in Illinois. His novels include *Michael Beam*, *Trial by Fire*, *The Rolling World*, and *Foothold of Earth*.

2663 *Michael Beam*

Date of Publication: 1939
Subject(s): Black Hawk War; Settlement of the American Frontier; Indians
Fictional character(s): Michael Beam, Frontiersman; Red Bloom, Indian (Algonquin); Charlessie Carteret, Young Woman
Time Period(s): 1820s; 1830s
Locale(s): Illinois; Wisconsin

Summary: This tale of frontier life during the Black Hawk War concerns frontiersmen Michael Beam, who is torn between the love of Red Bloom and Charlessie Carteret.

Historical Accuracy: Romance predominates here, with a plausible period backdrop.

WILLIAM F. HALLSTEAD (1924-)

An American born in Scranton, Pennsylvania, Hallstead has been a flight instructor and a senior highway designer. He has been the president of a real estate development company and has spent more than a decade working in public TV.

2664 *Conqueror of the Clouds*

Date of Publication: 1980
Subject(s): Aviation
Fictional character(s): Ben Horner, Pilot; Alex Horner, Blacksmith
Time Period(s): 1910s (1912)
Locale(s): United States

Summary: This novel of the early days of flying describes young Ben Horner who leaves his uncle's blacksmith shop to take up barnstorming. He becomes a stunt pilot and travels the country, fascinating crowds with his aerobatics.

Historical Accuracy: The novel captures the era of barnstorming with skill.

MAREK HALTER (1936-)

Born in Warsaw, Poland, Halter escaped the Nazis in the Warsaw ghetto. Since 1950 he has lived in France. He is also an artist and human rights activist.

2665 *The Book of Abraham*

Date of Publication: 1983
Subject(s): Jews; Roman Empire; Holocaust
Fictional character(s): Abraham, Writer (scribe); Abraham Halter, Printer
Time Period(s): Multiple Time Periods
Locale(s): Europe; Middle East

Summary: The novel covers the 2,000 year history of one Jewish family starting with the patriarch Abraham's flight from Jerusalem in 70 A.D. The story ranges throughout Europe, impacted by the great events of history: the Inquisition, the Crusades, and the Holocaust. This is a momentous work of imaginative recreation of the past.

Historical Accuracy: The novel effectively renders each of the historical periods with authenticity and conviction.

TOM HAM

2666 *Give Us This Valley*

Date of Publication: 1952
Subject(s): Settlement of the American Frontier
Fictional character(s): Elizabeth Stonecypher, Settler; George Washington Stonecypher, Settler
Time Period(s): 1830s (1837)
Locale(s): Pennsylvania; Georgia

Summary: Pioneer life in Georgia during the 1830s forms the background for this realistic novel describing the experiences of a young Pennsylvania couple—Wash and Elizabeth Stonecypher—who travel by wagon to their new valley home. The novel captures their struggle to put down roots in the wilderness.

Historical Accuracy: This is a believable portrait of pioneer life during the period.

JEAN HAMBURGER (?-1992)

Hamburger was a distinguished French medical researcher who pioneered kidney transplantation and was the president of the Institut de France, Academie des Sciences and a member of the Academie Francaise. He was the author of *The Power of the Family* and *Discovering the Individual*.

2667 *The Diary of William Harvey: The Imaginary Journal of the Physician Who Revolutionized Medicine*

Date of Publication: 1992
Subject(s): Medical Profession; Civil War—England
Historical character(s): William Harvey, Doctor; Sir Francis Bacon, Lawyer, Philosopher; Pierre Gassendi, Scientist, Philosopher
Time Period(s): 17th century (1647-1650)
Locale(s): England

Summary: This fictionalized diary of English physician William Harvey, the discoverer of the circulatory system, concentrates primarily on the period 1647-1650, 20 years after he announced his great discovery in 1628. The last events of the English Civil War and Charles I's execution provide the period backdrop for this examination of Harvey's genius and his scientific and philosophical observations.

Historical Accuracy: The novel is convincing in rendering both a realistic portrait of Harvey and 17th-century Europe.

CHARLES GRANVILLE HAMILTON
(1905-1984)

American novelist born in Pennsylvania, Hamilton graduated from Berea College, received his M.D. degree from Columbia University and his Ph.D. from Vanderbilt University. A clergyman for the Episcopal church in Mississippi, Hamilton served as a Mississippi state representative from 1940 to 1944. His books include *The North Wind Comes*, *A Single Star*, and *Our Yesterdays*.

2668　*Thunder in the Wilderness*

Date of Publication: 1949
Subject(s): Indians; Pontiac's Rebellion
Fictional character(s): Paul Duclos, Trader
Time Period(s): 1760s
Locale(s): Mississippi Valley, North America

Summary: This melodramatic tale of frontier life set during the time of Pontiac's War with the British during the 1760s is filled with the exciting details of wilderness life.

Historical Accuracy: The stark melodrama of the story undercuts the realism of the period and region. In addition, its characters are poorly developed.

JOAN LESLEY HAMILTON (1942-)

An American born in Hollywood, California, Hamilton is the daughter of actor John Leslie. She has worked for the Los Angeles Griffith Park Zoo as the assistant to the supervisor and veterinarian. She is a freelance writer and editor.

2669　*The Lion and the Cross*

Date of Publication: 1979
Subject(s): Dark Ages; Christianity; Myths and Legends
Historical character(s): Patrick, Captive, Religious
Time Period(s): 5th century
Locale(s): Ireland; England

Summary: This is the tale of Patrick, the patron saint of Ireland. He is captured by Celtic raiders and taken as a slave to Ireland. There he endures years in captivity in an Ireland wracked by civil war. He discovers a sustaining faith, and, when he finally escapes and returns home to England, he is drawn back to Ireland to begin his ministry.

Historical Accuracy: What little is known about the events of Saint Patrick's youth is used. The rest of the story is created within this historical framework.

TAMSIN HAMILTON

2670　*The Gypsy From Cadiz*

Date of Publication: 1977
Subject(s): Gypsies; Theatrical Life
Fictional character(s): Lola Sarita, Gypsy, Dancer; Rene Duvallier, Adventurer
Historical character(s): Louis Pasteur, Scientist; Guy de Maupassant, Writer; Edmond de Goncourt, Writer; Leopold II, Ruler (King of Belgium)
Time Period(s): 1890s
Locale(s): Cadiz, Spain; Tangier, Morocco; Paris, France

Summary: This romantic novel inspired by the tempestuous life of Caroline ''La Belle'' Otero, the famous courtesan, tells the story of Lola Sarita. Rescued from the squalor of Cadiz, she is kidnapped and winds up in the seraglio of the Pasha of Tangiers. She then escapes to celebrity status in Belle Epoque Paris.

Historical Accuracy: The novel is filled with exotic settings and situations anchored by a believable historical background.

WALLACE HAMILTON (1919-1983)

Born in New York City and a graduate of Harvard, Hamilton is a playwright and novelist whose books include *Christopher and Gay* and *Coming Out*. His work has concentrated on the gay scene and the gay experience.

2671　*David at Olivet*

Date of Publication: 1979
Subject(s): Biblical Story; Homosexuality
Historical character(s): David, Ruler (King of Israel); Absalom, Biblical Figure; Saul, Ruler; Jonathan, Biblical Figure; Bathsheba, Royalty (consort of David), Biblical Figure; Solomon, Royalty (King of Israel), Biblical Figure
Time Period(s): 10th century B.C.
Locale(s): Jerusalem, Israel

Summary: In old age King David awaits the destruction of Jerusalem by rebel troops led by his son, Absalom. The occasion causes David to reflect on his life and career, and the novel offers his meditations on his earliest days as a shepherd and his love for King Saul and Saul's son, Jonathan.

Historical Accuracy: Biblical sources from the basis of its story with some imagined interpretation.

JAMES HAMILTON-PATERSON (1941-)

An English teacher, journalist, and writer, Hamilton-Paterson was born in London and educated at Oxford University. He taught for a time in Tripoli, Libya, and worked as a freelance journalist for the *Times Literary Supplement* and the *New Statesman*. He won the Newdigate Prize for poetry in 1964 and the Whitbread Award in 1984 for *Gerontius*.

`2672` Gerontius

Date of Publication: 1984
Subject(s): Musical Life
Historical character(s): Edward William Elgar, Composer
Time Period(s): 1920s (1923)
Locale(s): Manaus, Brazil

Summary: The novel is based on an episode in the life of English composer and conductor Edward Elgar. In 1923 at the height of his fame, Elgar takes a cruise to the Amazon port city of Manaos. In despair about his lifework, there he is free to reevaluate his talent and his worth as a result of a brief reunion with his first fiancée.

Historical Accuracy: The portrait of Elgar is believable, though the author speculates and invents his thoughts and feelings.

SUYIN HAN (1917-)

Chinese author born in Sin Yang, Suyin graduated from the University of Brussels and London University. A physician in general practice, Suyin dramatized the problems of Eurasians in *A Many-Splendoured Thing*, which was made into a film in 1985.

`2673` The Enchantress

Date of Publication: 1985
Subject(s): East/West Relations; Chinese Empire
Fictional character(s): Colin Duriez, Young Man; Bea Duriez, Young Woman
Historical character(s): Voltaire, Philosopher
Time Period(s): 18th century (1750s-1780s)
Locale(s): Switzerland; China; Thailand

Summary: Set in the 18th century, the novel describes a brother and sister, Colin and Bea Duriez, who travel from Switzerland to China and Thailand. Colin has the skill to create precious clockwork machineries, and he is called on to repair the emperor's clockwork creations.

Historical Accuracy: The story is fanciful but filled with period elements that create a believable atmosphere.

PEGGY HANCHAR
(PSEUD. OF PEGGY HENSHAR)

`2674` Tomorrow's Dream

Date of Publication: 1989
Subject(s): American West; Romance; Gold Rush—Klondike
Fictional character(s): Kathleen O'Riley, Prospector; Hogan O'Shea, Prospector
Time Period(s): 1890s
Locale(s): Alaska; Canada

Summary: Set in the Yukon frontier during the Alaskan Gold Rush of the 1890s, this romantic adventure describes the career of Kathleen O'Riley. When her father is killed in an avalanche, she is forced to marry his partner, Hogan O'Shea, for protection. Romance ensues despite the violence and challenge of the Gold Rush era.

Historical Accuracy: The period details are authentic in this romantic adventure story.

FRANK BORDEN HANES (1920-)

Born in North Carolina, Hanes graduated from the University of North Carolina and has worked as a journalist and columnist. His books include *Abel Anders* and *The Seeds of Ares*.

`2675` The Fleet Rabble: A Novel of the Nez Perce War

Date of Publication: 1961
Subject(s): American West; Indians; Tribal Life—Native American
Fictional character(s): White Bird, Indian (Nez Perce), Warrior
Historical character(s): Chief Joseph, Indian (Nez Perce)
Time Period(s): 1870s (1877)
Locale(s): Idaho; Montana; Wyoming

Summary: The novel dramatizes the epic flight of the Nez Perce Indians led by Chief Joseph. They race to freedom in Canada pursued by the U.S. Army intent on restricting them to a reservation. The tragic destruction of the Nez Perce is one of the most ignoble events of Western Indian history.

Historical Accuracy: The details of the Nez Perce tragedy are rendered accurately.

LINDSEY HANKS

`2676` Outlaw Lover

Date of Publication: 1990
Subject(s): American West; Romance; Crime and Criminals
Fictional character(s): Samantha Savage, Journalist; Tyler Dalton, Fugitive (murder suspect)
Historical character(s): Butch Cassidy, Outlaw; The Sundance Kid, Outlaw
Time Period(s): 1890s (1897)
Locale(s): Collins, Wyoming

Summary: Newspaper woman Samantha Savage agrees to assist murder suspect Tyler Dalton's escape in order for her to write the story. She becomes his hostage, and they experience a series of adventures that are more than Samantha ever bargained for.

Historical Accuracy: The story is less than believable, and the period elements are only slightly developed.

EMILY HANLON (1945-)

An American born in New York City and a graduate of Barnard College, Hanlon worked as a teacher of mentally retarded adults and a writing teacher in elementary schools.

`2677` Petersburg

Date of Publication: 1988
Subject(s): Russian Revolution; Royalty—Russia

Fictional character(s): Alexei Kalinin, Businessman; Anna Orlov, Musician (pianist); Irina Rantzau, Gentlewoman, Revolutionary
Historical character(s): Nicholas II, Ruler (Czar of Russia); Sergei Witte, Political Figure; Maxim Gorky, Writer; Georgi Gapon, Religious (priest); Leon Trotsky, Revolutionary; U.K. Piehue, Government Official (Minister of the Interior); Nicolai Andreyevich Rimsky-Korsakov, Composer
Time Period(s): 1900s (1905)
Locale(s): St. Petersburg, Russia

Summary: Set during the first Russian Revolution of 1905, 12 years before the Bolshevik Revolution, the story is one of love and betrayal. As the wave of revolution is temporarily stemmed by the repressive Czarist forces, Anna Orlov, a gifted pianist, becomes involved with Alexei Kalinin, a former peasant who becomes one of Russia's wealthiest men.

Historical Accuracy: While the general chronology is accurate, the story is a work of fiction.

EDWARD B. HANNA

2678 *The Whitechapel Horrors*
Date of Publication: 1992
Subject(s): Mystery; Crime and Criminals; Victorian Period
Fictional character(s): Sherlock Holmes, Detective—Private; John H. Watson, Doctor; Mycroft Holmes, Gentleman
Historical character(s): Randolph Churchill, Nobleman; Edward, Prince of Wales, Royalty; Albert Edward, Duke of Clarence, Royalty (prince)
Time Period(s): 1880s (1888)
Locale(s): London, England

Summary: Sherlock Holmes investigates the Jack the Ripper murders in this homage to Arthur Conan Doyle's era and greatest creation. Holmes and Watson follow a trail of clues that leads directly to the House of Windsor. This brings about a crisis of conscience for Holmes as his attempts to expose a vicious murderer may bring down the monarchy.

Historical Accuracy: The novel is exact and exhaustive in evoking the period. Hanna offers both an authentic London scene and a Holmes true to Doyle's original.

EVA HEMMER HANSEN

2679 *Scandal in Troy*
Date of Publication: 1956
Subject(s): Ancient Greece; Trojan War; Myths and Legends
Fictional character(s): Helen of Troy, Noblewoman; Clytemnestra, Royalty (princess); Priam, Ruler (King of Troy); Agamemnon, Ruler (King of Greece); Ulysses, Warrior; Paris, Royalty (prince)
Time Period(s): Indeterminate Past
Locale(s): Troy, Ancient Civilization

Summary: The novel recounts the famous events of the Trojan War that stemmed from the elopement of Helen and Paris. The emphasis here is on the female perspective of the war, particularly Helen's view.

Historical Accuracy: The novel is a psychological and emotional exploration rather than a detailed historical or archaeological depiction.

RON HANSEN (1947-)

An American born in Omaha, Nebraska, Hansen is a graduate of Creighton University and the University of Iowa. He teaches at Cornell University. He is attracted to historical fiction because of the opportunity it offers to write about the Old West and philosophical questions. He has been praised as one of the finest stylists of American historical fiction.

2680 *The Assassination of Jesse James by the Coward Robert Ford*
Date of Publication: 1983
Subject(s): American West; Crime and Criminals
Historical character(s): Jesse James, Outlaw; Robert Ford, Murderer; Frank James, Outlaw
Time Period(s): 1880s; 1890s
Locale(s): Midwest; St. Joseph, Missouri; Kansas City, Missouri

Summary: In 1881 Jesse James is 34 years old and at the height of his criminal career. He becomes the obsession of young Robert Ford, the younger brother of a member of James' gang. Their relationship will end in James' murder in his own living room, and Ford will be labeled as the "dirty little coward who laid poor Jesse in his grave.".

Historical Accuracy: This is a remarkable telling of the familiar story that stays close to the facts but surprises with insights and originality.

2681 *Desperadoes*
Date of Publication: 1979
Subject(s): American West; Crime and Criminals
Historical character(s): Emmett Dalton, Outlaw; Robert Dalton, Outlaw
Time Period(s): 1880s (1887); 1930s (1937)
Locale(s): Coffeyville, Kansas; Hollywood, California; Indian Territory

Summary: Emmett Dalton, the lone surviving member of the Dalton gang after the infamous Coffeyville Raid of 1887, reflects back on the event 50 years later. He recalls the old days in the Indian Territory as the Daltons change from law enforcers to horse thiefs and outlaws.

Historical Accuracy: Although care was taken not to conradict the historical record, situations were altered and invented when the story required it.

2682 *Mariette in Ecstasy*
Date of Publication: 1991
Subject(s): Religious Life
Fictional character(s): Mariette Baptiste, Religious (nun)
Time Period(s): 1900 (1906)
Locale(s): New York

Summary: At the convent of the Sisters of the Crucifixion in upstate New York, a young postulant begins to bleed from her hands, feet, and sides, throwing the entire community into an uproar. Is Mariette a sham or is she truly blessed? The novel offers a look inside the world of the convent at the turn of the century.

Historical Accuracy: The novel is convincing in its portrait of a religious community.

BERTITA HARDING

`2683` *Magic Fire: Scenes around Richard Wagner*

Date of Publication: 1953
Subject(s): Biography, Fictionalized; Musical Life
Historical character(s): Richard Wagner, Composer; Cosima Wagner, Spouse
Time Period(s): 19th century
Locale(s): Germany

Summary: The novel offers a series of episodes from the life of German composer Richard Wagner, presenting a strong portrait of Wagner's genius and his times.

Historical Accuracy: The novel's invented dialogue sometimes fails to ring true. The admiration of the author for her subject sometimes causes her to avoid the less pleasant aspects of Wagner's life.

PAUL HARDING
(PSEUD. OF P.C. DOHERTY)

Paul Harding is one of several pseudonyms for P.C. Doherty, an English mystery writer who attended Liverpool and Oxford universities. He is currently headmaster of a school in northeast London.

`2684` *The Nightingale Gallery*

Date of Publication: 1991
Subject(s): Mystery; Middle Ages; Religious Life
Fictional character(s): Brother Athelstan, Religious (monk), Clerk; John Cranston, Gentleman, Government Official (coroner)
Historical character(s): John of Gaunt, Royalty
Time Period(s): 14th century (1336)
Locale(s): London, England

Summary: Brother Athelstan is a young monk serving medieval London's poorest parish and assisting Sir John Cranston, coroner of London, in his examinations. Murders at the home of one of John of Gaunt's followers occur, but someone at court does not want the investigation to continue. Athelstan and Cranston discover a web of intrigue that reaches directly to the throne of England.

Historical Accuracy: The novel features a remarkably detailed look at life in 14th- century London.

`2685` *Red Slayer: Being the Second of the Sorrowful Mysteries of Brother Athelstan*

Date of Publication: 1992
Subject(s): Mystery; Middle Ages; Religious Life
Fictional character(s): Brother Athelstan, Religious (monk), Clerk; John Cranston, Gentleman, Government Official (coroner)
Time Period(s): 14th century (1377)
Locale(s): London, England

Summary: There is a secret killer lurking in the Tower of London during the 14th century. The Constable's throat has been slit inside his locked room under the nose of his own guards. Brother Athelstan and his Falstaffian partner Sir John Cranston investigate a complex knot of intrigue and betrayal which will take all of Athelstan's considerable logic and his priestly eye for guilt to unravel.

Historical Accuracy: Harding's medieval atmosphere is solidly delivered and adds greatly to the interest of this historical mystery.

RICHARD LYNDEN HARDMAN
(1924-)

Seattle born Hardman graduated from the University of Washington, Seattle, and the University of California, Los Angeles. He has worked as a film producer for Paramount and Columbia Pictures. His books include *No Other Harvest*, *The Chaplain's Raid*, and *The Virgin War*.

`2686` *Fifteen Flags*

Date of Publication: 1968
Subject(s): Russian Revolution; Civil War—Russia; Railroads
Fictional character(s): Hunkpapa Jack Carlisle, Military Personnel (captain), Indian (Sioux); Harry Austin, Military Personnel (sergeant); Ira Leverett, Military Personnel (lieutenant)
Historical character(s): William S. Graves, Military Personnel (U.S. general); Aleksandr Kolchak, Military Personnel (admiral), Leader (of the White Russian forces); Grigori Semenoff, Military Personnel (Cossack); Ivan Kalmykoff, Military Personnel (Cossack)
Time Period(s): 1910s; 1920s (1918-1920)
Locale(s): Siberia, Russia

Summary: The novel's background concerns the American Siberian Expeditionary Force of 1918-1920 dispatched during the Russian Civil War to protect the Trans-Siberian Railroad. The novel recreates a little-known episode of American military history and follows the experiences of the American force while Siberia disintegrates into anarchy as white partisans vie with the Soviet military for control of the important railroad.

Historical Accuracy: The novel mixes fact and fiction, but the situation and many of the characters are drawn from history.

MICHAEL HARDWICK (1924-1991)

An English author born in Leeds, Hardwick worked in New Zealand as a government filmmaker and reporter before returning to England to join the BBC's drama department where he met his future wife. Hardwick is the author of numerous companions to literary authors, novelizations of films and TV series, and was an authority on both Charles Dickens and Arthur Conan Doyle's Sherlock Holmes. He described himself as a compulsive writer and his collaborations with his wife, Mollie Hardwick, as a near perfect arrangement.

2687 *Regency Royal*

Date of Publication: 1978
Subject(s): Regency Period; Royalty—England
Historical character(s): George, Royalty (Prince of Wales); Charlotte of Mecklenburg-Strelitz, Royalty (queen consort of George III); George III, Ruler (King of England); Maria Anne Fitzherbert, Gentlewoman; Mary Robinson, Actress; Caroline of Brunswick, Royalty (princess); Mary Hamilton, Governess; Richard Brinsley Sheridan, Writer, Political Figure; Charles James Fox, Political Figure; Frederick Augustus, Royalty (prince)
Time Period(s): 18th century; 19th century (1776-1830)
Locale(s): London, England; Brighton, England

Summary: The novel chronicles the career of George, Prince of Wales and later King George IV. Distrusted by his father, the prince is left with little to do but wait patiently for his turn to be king. He idles away his time in romantic liaisons and becomes the figurehead of the fashionable set as well as the focus of a conspiracy to wrestle the throne from the unstable George III.

Historical Accuracy: The novel is richly evocative of the Regency period, crammed with historical personalities.

2688 *The Revenge of the Hound*

Date of Publication: 1987
Subject(s): Mystery; Edwardian Period
Fictional character(s): Sherlock Holmes, Detective—Private; John H. Watson, Doctor
Historical character(s): Edward VII, Ruler (King of England)
Time Period(s): 1900s (1902)
Locale(s): London, England

Summary: It is 1902, the dawn of the Edwardian Age, and Sherlock Holmes is thinking of retiring. However, the sighting on Hampstead Heath of a creature similar to that of the infamous Hound of the Baskervilles, the apparently motiveless murder of a ship's steward, and a growing conspiracy that may topple the throne bring Holmes back for a final case.

Historical Accuracy: Richly evocative of both the period and Arthur Conan Doyle's original, the novel is a worthy Holmesian adventure.

MOLLIE HARDWICK

Born in Manchester, England, Hardwick was a BBC radio announcer and drama script editor and director in London, as well as a freelance writer and playwright. She won the Elizabeth Goudge Award in 1976 for the best historical novel for *Beauty's Daughter*. All of Hardwick's works are set in the 19th century or earlier because she is attracted to the research involved in recreating the past which she regards as the most exciting and rewarding part of a literary life.

2689 *Beauty's Daughter*

Date of Publication: 1977
Subject(s): Napoleonic Wars
Historical character(s): Emily Hart, Orphan; Lady Emma Hamilton, Gentlewoman
Time Period(s): 18th century; 19th century (1780s-1810s)
Locale(s): England; France

Summary: This is an account of Emily Hart, the daughter of Lady Emma Hamilton, who may or may not be the child of her mother's liaison with Horatio Nelson. Emily endures her childhood in a spartan boarding school before being called to London and being swept up into the fashionable world of Lady Hamilton who is unable to acknowledge Emily's identity, forcing Emily to make her own way.

Historical Accuracy: This is a novel based on fact that is to a large extent revealed here for the first time. A biographer of Lady Hamilton, the author has used information from her research to make her case.

2690 *Blood Royal*

Date of Publication: 1988
Subject(s): Tudor Period; Royalty—England
Historical character(s): Anne Boleyn, Royalty (queen consort of Henry VIII); Henry VIII, Ruler (King of England); Mary Boleyn, Gentlewoman; Francois I, Ruler (King of France); Thomas Boleyn, Gentleman; Sir Thomas Wyatt, Courtier, Writer
Time Period(s): 15th century; 16th century (1498-1592)
Locale(s): England; France

Summary: The fate of the Boleyn family is chronicled, particularly the children of Thomas Boleyn and Elizabeth Howard. Mary becomes the mistress of both Francois I and Henry VIII. Anne's marriage to Henry splits England and brings about the Protestant Reformation there. Thomas' unbridled ambition will have tragic consequences.

Historical Accuracy: The novel is quite convincing in its ability to evoke court and castle life during the Tudor period.

2691 *Charlie Is My Darling*

Date of Publication: 1977
Subject(s): Jacobite Rebellion
Fictional character(s): Dorothy Beaumont, Gentlewoman
Historical character(s): Charles Edward Stuart, Royalty (prince)
Time Period(s): 1740s (1745-1746)
Locale(s): London, England; Scotland; Paris, France

Summary: The novel features a love affair between Dorothy Beaumont and Prince Charles Edward Stuart as the Jacobite

Rebellion of 1745 runs its tragic course. Dorothy is committed to both the prince and his attempt to gain the English throne. However, the prince is doomed to failure and he abandons Dorothy to seek a bride of royal blood.

Historical Accuracy: The novel is richly evocative of the period, filled with convincing details of 18th century England.

2692 *The Crystal Dove*

Date of Publication: 1985
Subject(s): Victorian Period; Theatrical Life; Magic
Fictional character(s): Eleanore Carey, Gentlewoman; Manfred Pye, Gentleman; Merlin, Sorcerer
Time Period(s): 1860s
Locale(s): London, England

Summary: Eleanore Carey returns to London after growing up in India. She finds none of the exotic mystery she experienced in her childhood and grows restless living with her strait-laced aunts. She escapes into the world of magic and marvel as an assistant to a magician in the world of the Victorian theater.

Historical Accuracy: The story features a strong evocation of the world of magic and the Victorian theater.

2693 *The Duchess of Duke Street*

Date of Publication: 1976
Subject(s): Edwardian Period; Business Building; Servants
Fictional character(s): Louisa Leyton, Businesswoman, Cook; Augustus Trotter, Servant (butler); Charles Tyrrell, Nobleman (Lord Haslemere)
Historical character(s): Edward, Prince of Wales, Royalty
Time Period(s): 1890s; 1900s
Locale(s): London, England

Summary: Based on the BBC Television series created by John Hawksworth, the novel tells the story of Louisa Leyton. She rises from the servant class to become the best cook in England. She achieves notoriety that attracts the attention of the Prince of Wales and she uses her reputation to convert the Bentinck Hotel into the Edwardian period's most fashionable address.

Historical Accuracy: The story is partially based on fact and features a strong portrait of period London.

2694 *I Remember Love*

Date of Publication: 1983
Subject(s): War of the Roses; Victorian Period; Tudor Period
Fictional character(s): Yolande de Clifford, Gentlewoman; Joscelyn Conyers, Knight; Margery Burgoyne, Gentlewoman
Historical character(s): Richard Neville, Nobleman (Earl of Warkick); Edward IV, Ruler (King of England)
Time Period(s): Multiple Time Periods
Locale(s): England

Summary: The love between Yolande de Clifford, and Yorkist knight Joscelyn Conyers during the War of the Roses is tragically interrupted. It is resumed 70 years later during the Tudor Era by a couple who also find their happiness cruelly interrupted. Finally, in mid-Victorian London, a couple who are convinced that they are not strangers but do not know why fulfill the previous promises of love.

Historical Accuracy: The details of each era are convincingly drawn to sustain the fantasy elements.

2695 *Lovers Meeting*

Date of Publication: 1979
Subject(s): Regency Period; Romance; Theatrical Life
Fictional character(s): Jannie Sorrel, Dancer; Ivor Bryn, Entertainer; Sara Dell, Actress; Raymond Otway, Actor
Historical character(s): Joseph Grimaldi, Entertainer (clown)
Time Period(s): 1810s
Locale(s): England

Summary: The background for this novel is theatrical life during the Regency period and the tangled lives of four pantomime performers: Jannie Sorrel, a beautiful young dancer; Ivor Bryn, a Welsh clown; Sara Dell, an aging actress; and Raymond Otway, a fading tragedian. The action moves from the great London theaters to the provinces and performances in the stately great homes of the nobility. It features an appearance by Joseph Grimaldi, the greatest clown of the age.

Historical Accuracy: The evocation of the period and the theatrical background is genuine.

2696 *The Merrymaid*

Date of Publication: 1984
Subject(s): Tudor Period; Romance
Fictional character(s): Jacquette Valency, Entertainer; Margaretta Brandon, Widow(er); Alan Thornwood, Entertainer
Time Period(s): 16th century
Locale(s): England

Summary: When her father, a French jongleur or strolling entertainer, is killed in Dover, Jacquette is alone and stranded. Deemed at first an angel, then a devil and a mermaid by superstitious villagers, she is eventually adopted by the vulgar Margaretta Brandon. Betrothed to a wealthy merchant, Jacquette meets Alan Thornwood, a practitioner of her father's profession, and she must choose whether or not to return to the life of a travelling entertainer.

Historical Accuracy: The novel is richly evocative of the period.

2697 *Monday's Child*

Date of Publication: 1982
Subject(s): Victorian Period; Romance
Fictional character(s): Laura Diamond, Worker (shopgirl); Jim Broadbent, Gentleman
Historical character(s): Sigmund Freud, Doctor
Time Period(s): 19th century
Locale(s): London, England; Paris, France; Vienna, Austria

Summary: This is the story of a poor, uneducated shopgirl, Laura Diamond, who because of her great beauty gains access to high society and becomes the toast of London, Paris, and Vienna. She learns the obvious lesson that all that glitters can disappoint and that love is far more difficult to achieve than allure and attraction.

Historical Accuracy: The fairytale romantic elements are blended with a solid sense of the period.

2698 *The Shakespeare Girl*

Date of Publication: 1983
Subject(s): Edwardian Period; Romance; Theatrical Life
Fictional character(s): Miranda Heriot, Orphan, Actress; Andrew Craigie, Journalist
Time Period(s): 1900s; 1910s
Locale(s): Birmingham, England; Stratford-on-Avon, England; London, England

Summary: The novel describes a life transformed by the theater as Miranda Heriot, during a secret trip to Stratford, discovers the enticing conjunction of drama and dreams. She enters the world of the stage where love and disappointment are interwoven into a rich life.

Historical Accuracy: The details of theatrical life during the period are authentically rendered.

2699 *Willowwood*

Date of Publication: 1980
Subject(s): Victorian Period; Romance; Sports
Fictional character(s): Lilian de Wentworth, Gentlewoman, Invalid; Jack Ellershaw, Gardener; Leoline Bevis, Artist
Time Period(s): 1860s
Locale(s): Yorkshire, England; London, England

Summary: Lilian de Wentworth is a beautiful young invalid who is confined to her home by a childhood injury. Love comes to her unexpectedly from Jack Ellershaw, a gardener who is determined to become a professional cricketeer. Instead he becomes a hero by rescuing Lilian from entrapment by the devious artist Leoline Bevis, a member of the Pre-Raphaelite Brotherhood.

Historical Accuracy: The story is romantically fanciful but the period details of both country and town life are authentic.

THOMAS HARDY (1840-1928)

Hardy, the son of a stone mason, was born near Dorchester in Dorset and trained as an architect and church restorer. He soon turned to fiction writing, and although he is best known for his novels, his first love was poetry. His major works are *The Return of the Native*, *The Mayor of Casterbridge*, *Tess of the D'Urbervilles*, and *Jude the Obscure*. They are set against the harsh landscape of the southwest of England that Hardy called Wessex. After Hardy was attacked for immorality for *Jude the Obscure*, he abandoned the novel for poetry, publishing several volumes, including an historical epic on the Napoleonic Wars, *The Dynasts*.

2700 *The Trumpet Major*

Date of Publication: 1880
Subject(s): Napoleonic Wars
Fictional character(s): Anne Garland, Young Woman; John Loveday, Military Personnel (trumpet major); Festus Derriman, Farmer; Bob Loveday, Sailor
Time Period(s): 1800s
Locale(s): Dorset, England

Summary: Hardy's only attempt at historical fiction, this simple and largely pleasant tale is set during the Napoleonic Wars and concerns the wooing of Anne Garland. Her suitors include the trumpet-major of a regiment of dragoons, John Loveday, his sailor brother Bob, and the braggart yeoman Festus Derriman. In the story Festus is defeated; Bob eventually wins Anne, and John marches off to die in Spain during the Peninsular campaign.

Historical Accuracy: As a result of Hardy's painstaking research, the novel is alive with authentic period details and is one of the most convincing portraits ever drawn of England during the Napoleonic threat.

W.G. HARDY (1895-1979)

Canadian scholar and author Hardy was born in Ontario and graduated from the University of Toronto and the University of Chicago. A classicist, Hardy served as the head of the Department of Classics at the University of Alberta. His books include *The Unfulfilled*, *The Bloodied Toga*, and *Journey into the Past*.

2701 *All the Trumpets Sounded: A Novel Based on the Life of Moses*

Date of Publication: 1942
Subject(s): Biblical Story; Biography, Fictionalized; Ancient Egypt
Historical character(s): Moses, Biblical Figure
Time Period(s): 13th century B.C.
Locale(s): Egypt

Summary: This fictionalized biography of Moses describes his early life as a Prince of Egypt, having been adopted by the Pharaoh; his years of exile; and his leadership of the Hebrew exodus from Egypt. Moses' human side is emphasized in this account.

Historical Accuracy: Several historical events and Biblical tradition provide reference points for the novelist's imaginative reconstruction.

2702 *The City of Libertines*

Date of Publication: 1957
Subject(s): Roman Empire; Literary Life
Historical character(s): Gaius Valerius Catullus, Writer (poet); Clodia, Noblewoman; Marcus Tullius Cicero, Lawyer, Political Figure; Gaius Julius Caesar, Military Personnel, Political Figure; Publius Clodius Pulcher, Political Figure; Marcus Licinius Crassus, Political Figure; Pompey, Military Personnel (general)
Time Period(s): 1st century B.C. (62-54 B.C.)
Locale(s): Rome, Roman Empire

Summary: As the Roman Republic drifts toward dictatorship, the patician Clodia falls in love with the great Roman poet Catullus. Intrigue and betrayal mark their relationship as Clodia's deception and scheming involve her with Cicero and Caesar.

Historical Accuracy: The novel is based firmly on what is known of the life, history, and perspectives of the period. The author's sources include the private letters of Cicero and Catullus' poems.

`2703` *Turn Back the River*

Date of Publication: 1938
Subject(s): Roman Empire
Historical character(s): Clodia, Noblewoman; Catiline, Political Figure
Time Period(s): 1st century B.C. (75-25 B.C.)
Locale(s): Rome, Roman Empire

Summary: The final years of the Roman Republic are described from the vantage point of the noblewoman Clodia, daughter of a prominent Roman family and mistress of Cataline. Her experiences in love and politics reflect the state of affairs as Julius Caesar comes to power.

Historical Accuracy: Despite evident solid research, some liberties have been taken with the facts and scenes have been invented.

SHULAMITH HAREVEN

`2704` *The Miracle Hater*

Date of Publication: 1988
Subject(s): Biblical Story
Fictional character(s): Eshkal, Wanderer
Historical character(s): Moses, Biblical Figure
Time Period(s): 13th century B.C.
Locale(s): Egypt

Summary: Eshkar, a Hebrew born into slavery, takes part in the exodus from Egypt led by Moses. When Moses' miracles seem to bring only pain and death, Eshkar decides to go his own way. In the desert, Eshkar matures into a cynic and a loner.

Historical Accuracy: This philosophical meditation is convincing in its reconstruction of the atmosphere of the Biblical story.

LEONIE HARGRAVE
(PSEUD. OF THOMAS M. DISCH, 1940-)

Born in Iowa, Hargrave attended Cooper Union and NYU. He worked as a checkroom attendant, draftsman, and copywriter. He is the author of science fiction, poetry, historical novels, opera librettos, and computer-interactive fiction.

`2705` *Clara Reeve*

Date of Publication: 1975
Subject(s): Family Saga; Inheritance—Disputed; Victorian Period
Fictional character(s): Clara Reeve, Orphan; Niles Visconti, Gentleman; Zaide Visconti, Noblewoman
Time Period(s): 1850s
Locale(s): London, England; Naples, Italy

Summary: Clara Reeve is a poor English orphan who marries her cousin Niles and goes to live with him and his mother,

Zaide, in the decaying Villa Visconti in Italy. She inherits the fortune thought to be Niles' and finds herself trapped in fiscal and family intrigue.

Historical Accuracy: The details of period and Italian life are convincing.

SHEBA HARGREAVES (1882-)

Hargreaves' novels concentrate on Oregon family life in the 1840s.

`2706` *The Cabin at the Trail's End*

Date of Publication: 1928
Subject(s): American West; Settlement of the American Frontier; Indians
Fictional character(s): Rose Bainbridge, Settler
Time Period(s): 1840s (1843-1844)
Locale(s): Willamette Valley, Oregon

Summary: The experiences of the Bainbridge family's journey along the Oregon Trail and their first year on the frontier are depicted.

Historical Accuracy: The novel provides a dependable and faithful account of pioneer life in Oregon at the time.

`2707` *Heroine of the Prairies: A Romance of the Oregon Trail*

Date of Publication: 1930
Subject(s): American West; Wagon Trains
Fictional character(s): Salita Prentiss, Pioneer
Time Period(s): 1840s (1848)
Locale(s): Oregon Trail, United States

Summary: Life along the Oregon Trail in the 1840s is captured in the story of Salita Prentiss, who faces hardships to establish a home in a frontier community.

Historical Accuracy: The novel provides an authentic look at the period and the region.

DONALD HARINGTON (1935-)

Born in Little Rock, Arkansas, Harington grew up in the Ozarks. He graduated from the University of Arkansas and Boston University. He is a novelist and art historian.

`2708` *The Architecture of the Arkansas Ozarks*

Date of Publication: 1975
Subject(s): Rural Life—U.S.; Family Saga
Fictional character(s): Jacob Ingledew, Settler; Noah Ingledew, Settler; Eli Willard, Trader
Time Period(s): 19th century; 20th century
Locale(s): Stay More, Arkansas

Summary: The novel chronicles six generations of the Ingledew family over a span of 140 years, beginning when Jacob and Noah Ingledew come from Tennessee to found the town of Stay More in the Ozark mountains of Arkansas. The periodic visits of peddler Eli Willard bring news of the changing world outside Stay More.

Historical Accuracy: The novel is rooted in regional history and, according to the author, the more implausible the characters and situations, the more likely they are to mirror reality.

2709 *The Choiring of the Trees*

Date of Publication: 1991
Subject(s): Rural Life—U.S.; Crime and Criminals
Fictional character(s): Nail Chism, Convict; Viridis Monday, Artist, Journalist
Time Period(s): 1910s (1914)
Locale(s): Ozarks, Arkansas

Summary: In the backwoods of the Ozarks in 1914 a girl is raped, and Nail Chism is convicted of the crime and sentenced to the electric chair. However, his innocence is championed by Viridis Monday, the staff artist for an Arkansas newspaper. Their curious relationship is worked out in a moving story of two interesting eccentrics.

Historical Accuracy: The novel's regional details and period are authentically portrayed.

KAREN HARPER (1945-)

An American born in Ohio and a graduate of Ohio University and Ohio State, Harper is a high school English teacher in Ohio. She is the author of a series of royal histories, reflecting her love of England, where she visits regularly.

2710 *Circle of Gold*

Date of Publication: 1992
Subject(s): Romance; Victorian Period; Shakers
Fictional character(s): Rebecca Blake, Orphan; Adam Scott, Heir; Ramsey Sherborne, Nobleman
Time Period(s): 19th century (1823-1842)
Locale(s): Kentucky; England

Summary: The novel tells the remarkable story of Rebecca Blake, an orphaned mountain girl who is taken in by the Shakers. Their celibate ways produce conflict for Rebecca when she meets Ramsey Sherborne, a visiting British lord, who brings her to England. There Rebecca works to help the poor before returning to America.

Historical Accuracy: Most of the characters in the book are fictional, although they are inspired by historical research, particularly into the Shakers.

2711 *Eden's Gate*

Date of Publication: 1989
Subject(s): American Colonies; French and Indian War
Fictional character(s): Claire Chandon, Servant; Ethan Trent, Patriot
Time Period(s): 1750s
Locale(s): Mohawk Valley, New York, American Colonies

Summary: Set during the French and Indian Wars, this romantic adventure concerns Frenchwoman Claire Chandon who is

suspected of being a spy by Ethan Trent. He winds up falling in love with her as the events of the war bring them together.

Historical Accuracy: The period elements are suggested with some authenticity.

2712 *The Firelands*

Date of Publication: 1990
Subject(s): American Revolution
Fictional character(s): Althea Arnold, Young Woman; Morgan Glenn, Military Personnel (aide to Benedict Arnold)
Historical character(s): Benedict Arnold, Military Personnel (general)
Time Period(s): 1770s (1776)
Locale(s): American Colonies

Summary: This romantic adventure set during the American Revolution concerns a cousin of Benedict Arnold, Althea, who falls in love with the general's aide, Morgan Glenn. She must deal with jealousy and the ignominy of her cousin's treason.

Historical Accuracy: The story is invented but does interweave actual events and circumstances.

2713 *River of Sky*

Date of Publication: 1994
Subject(s): American West; Indians
Fictional character(s): Kate Craig, Widow(er); Blue Wing, Indian (Mandan); Stirling Mount, Naturalist; Randal MacLeod, Frontiersman
Time Period(s): 1830s
Locale(s): St. Louis, Missouri; Missouri River, United States

Summary: This tale of Indian and frontier life along the Missouri River concerns Kate Craig, wife of a St. Louis riverboat captain and Indian trader. When he dies, Kate is left only his riverboat, and she attempts to make a living by sailing the boat up the Missouri to trade for furs among the Mandans. She is introduced to the Indian way of life that is threatened by the rapacious fur trade.

Historical Accuracy: The author's notes indicate the factual basis for the story and the actual events that form the basis for the novel's plot.

2714 *The Wings of Morning*

Date of Publication: 1993
Subject(s): Romance; Victorian Period; Civil War—U.S.
Fictional character(s): Abigail Adair, Widow(er); Morgan West, Shipowner, Sea Captain
Time Period(s): 1850s; 1860s
Locale(s): St. Kilde, Scotland; England; Florida

Summary: When Abigail loses her child, she resolves to discover why other children o n the island of St. Kilde are dying as well. Her search brings her up against the island's conservative hierarchy and eventually takes her to London and Florida during the American Civil War.

Historical Accuracy: The novel's story is based on actual events and situations on St. Kilde, supported by solid research.

M.A. HARPER (1949-)

A novelist and playwright, Harper was born in Columbia, South Carolina, and attended Tulane University and the BMI Musical Theatre Workshop. Her career has included work as a stage manager with the La Mama Experimental Theatre Company in New York and as a commercial artist. She is the author, with Donald Oliver, of several plays for children.

2715 *For the Love of Robert E. Lee*

Date of Publication: 1992
Subject(s): Biography, Fictionalized; Civil War—U.S.; Fantasy
Fictional character(s): Garnet Laney, Young Woman
Historical character(s): Robert E. Lee, Military Personnel (army officer)
Time Period(s): 1960s; 19th century
Locale(s): South Carolina; Virginia

Summary: In the 1960s a young woman becomes obsessed with Confederate General Robert E. Lee. Her fantasies about his life are based on history books, family legends, and her own imagination. What emerges is an original portrait of a southern hero and his continuing hold on the imagination of his countrymen.

Historical Accuracy: Though the narrative is irreverent and at times zany, the history is accurate, and the events described are faithful to the facts.

ROBERT S. HARPER (1899-1962)

Born in Greenfield, Ohio, Haper worked as a journalist and served in the Pacific theater in World War II. He was an expert on Ohio history and wrote several histories and novels, including *The Road to Baltimore* and *Trumpet in the Wilderness*.

2716 *The Road to Baltimore*

Date of Publication: 1942
Subject(s): Stagecoaches
Fictional character(s): Beau Stark, Young Man
Historical character(s): Henry Clay, Political Figure
Time Period(s): 1830s (1836)
Locale(s): Wheeling, West Virginia; Washington, District of Columbia

Summary: This romantic tale of the age of the stagecoach is set in the 1830s. Beau Stark returns from the war in Texas and encounters Henry Clay and his young ward in a coach bound from Wheeling to Washington. Stark's search for a lost brother, his conflict with the ward's fiance, and a stagecoach holdup form the novel's complications.

Historical Accuracy: The novel shows evidence of considerable research into stagecoach travel during the period.

2717 *Trumpet in the Wilderness*

Date of Publication: 1940
Subject(s): War of 1812; Battle of Lake Erie

Fictional character(s): Jubal Johnson, Journalist
Time Period(s): 1810s
Locale(s): Detroit, Michigan; Ohio

Summary: In this novel set during the War of 1812, Jubal Johnson is a young college graduate who goes west to make his fortune. In Ohio he works on a newspaper before becoming involved in the military action. The novel's climax is the Battle of Lake Erie.

Historical Accuracy: The novel's story is supported by strong and believable period detail.

CYRIL HARRIS (1891-)

Nova Scotia-born Harris was an army officer, Episcopal priest, and teacher of English literature. He is descended from one of the Loyalist families that migrated to Canada after the American Revolution. His books include *One Braver Thing*, *Street of Knives*, and *The Trouble at Hungerford*.

2718 *Richard Pryne: A Novel of the American Revolution*

Date of Publication: 1941
Subject(s): American Revolution; Espionage
Fictional character(s): Richard Pryne, Spy
Time Period(s): 1770s
Locale(s): New York, New York, American Colonies

Summary: This story of espionage during the American Revolution is set in colonial New York and concerns the adventures of Richard Pryne. As the friend of one of Washington's officers, Pryne becomes a spy.

Historical Accuracy: The strength of the novel is the authentic background provided.

2719 *Trumpets at Dawn*

Date of Publication: 1938
Subject(s): American Revolution; Battle of Trenton
Fictional character(s): Horatio Wyatt, Businessman, Loyalist; Charles Townsend, Military Personnel (soldier); Sam Wyatt, Military Personnel (soldier)
Historical character(s): John Andre, Military Personnel (British soldier), Spy
Time Period(s): 1770s; 1780s (1775-1783)
Locale(s): New York, New York; New Jersey

Summary: The effects of the American Revolution on family and social life in British-occupied New York are examined in this novel that centers on the Loyalist Wyatt family. The novel dramatizes the campaigns in the Middle Atlantic States through the experiences of Sam Wyatt and Charles Townsend. They participate in the Battles of Brooklyn Heights, the crossing of the Delaware, and the Battle of Trenton, and are present when Benedict Arnold's treason is discovered and when Major Andre is hanged.

Historical Accuracy: The novel's period background is authentic and believable.

JOHN HARRIS (1911-)

MARGARET HARRIS (1912-)

John and Margaret Harris are a husband-and-wife writing team. John was president of the North American Association for the Preservation of Predatory Animals. He has lectured throughout the country on environmental awareness. Margaret Harris' books include *Arrow in the Moon* and *The Medicine Whip*.

2720 *Chant of the Hawk*

Date of Publication: 1959
Subject(s): American West; Indians; Settlement of the American Frontier
Fictional character(s): George Stroud, Mountain Man, Trapper; Jesse Reeshar, Mountain Man, Trapper
Time Period(s): 1840s
Locale(s): Oregon Trail, United States

Summary: Set in the American West when the era of the trappers and mountain men of the Rockies was giving way to the age of the settlers, the novel concerns the enmity between two trappers, George Stroud and Jesse Reeshar, and what happens when the two are trapped with two young squaws over a deadly winter. Stroud's vendetta with Reeshar leads to a trade war between the fur companies as Stroud attempts to recover a fortune in furs.

Historical Accuracy: The story is imagined, but its period background is genuine and convincing.

JOHN HARRIS (1916-1991)

English writer Harris worked as a clerk, reporter, cartoonist, sailor, airman, history teacher, and travel courier. He became a full-time writer in 1955. A prolific author of adventure stories, Harris had an abiding interest in military history.

2721 *Vardy*

Date of Publication: 1965
Subject(s): Franco-Prussian War; Paris Commune; Siege of Paris
Fictional character(s): Vardy Cutter, Bastard Daughter; Victor Weill, Gentleman; Max Cary de Lilly, Veteran (Confederate officer), Mercenary
Time Period(s): 1870s
Locale(s): Paris, France; Tours, France

Summary: The novel's background is the Franco-Prussian War, the seige of Paris, and Paris during the Commune. Vardy Cutter leaves England for a life in France that includes spurning the attention of wealty suitor Victor Weill and becoming the mistress of Colonel de Lilly. Marriage seems to secure Vardy the respectability she desires, but she is trapped in Paris during the Commune when Victor Weill returns in her life.

Historical Accuracy: The story is imagined against a vivid and convincing backdrop of period details.

JULIE HARRIS (1957-)

2722 *The Longest Winter*

Date of Publication: 1995
Subject(s): Aviation; Tribal Life—Eskimo
Fictional character(s): John Robert Shaw, Pilot
Time Period(s): 20th century (1920s-1950s)
Locale(s): Alaska

Summary: The novel offers a fictional autobiography of pilot John Robert Shaw. In 1926, attempting a solo flight record, Shaw crashes on an uncharted island off Alaska. The novel tells the story of his 17-year-stay among the Eskimos who adopt him into their tribe, and his struggle to survive in the harsh Arctic environment.

Historical Accuracy: The novel captures the locale with believable details.

LAURA B. HARRIS (1894-)

Harris was an American writer.

2723 *Bride of the River*

Date of Publication: 1956
Subject(s): Slavery; Underground Railroad; Antebellum South
Fictional character(s): Mary Marie Rutland, Southern Belle
Time Period(s): 19th century (1837-1860)
Locale(s): Ohio River, United States

Summary: The novel describes the experiences of a young Louisiana belle, Mary Rutland, who moves to an Ohio River town, where she marries a riverboat man. She must reconcile her conflicting loyalties when she becomes involved with abolitionist activities and the workings of the underground railroad.

Historical Accuracy: The period background is authentically presented.

MACDONALD HARRIS
(PSEUD. OF DONALD W. HEINEY, 1921-1993)

Born in California, Harris attended the U.S. Merchant Marine Academy, the University of Redlands, and UCLA. A professor of English, Harris' work is marked by elements of "magic realism," incorporating the fabulous, unreal, and the magical in a straightforward presentation. *The Balloonist* received a National Book Award nomination in 1977.

2724 *The Balloonist*

Date of Publication: 1976
Subject(s): Aviation
Fictional character(s): Gustave Crispin, Scientist; Luisa, Young Woman
Time Period(s): 1890s (1897)
Locale(s): Arctic; Paris, France

Summary: The novel describes an attempt by three men to reach the North Pole by balloon in the 1890s. Gustave Crispin is the Swedish leader of the expedition who narrates the story and interweaves his romantic memories of his affair with

Luisa that include a mishap-ridden balloon trip, an idyll in the Italian Lake District, and misadventures with the demimonde of 1890s Paris.

Historical Accuracy: The story is an inventive fantasy with credible evocation of the period and aviation details.

`2725` *Glowstone*

Date of Publication: 1987
Subject(s): Science
Fictional character(s): Claire Savarin-Decker, Widow(er); Blanco White, Rancher; Hermine Savarin-Decker, Young Woman
Historical character(s): Claude Monet, Artist
Time Period(s): 1900s (1906)
Locale(s): Paris, France

Summary: This is a story of love, independence, and science set in the Belle Epoque in Paris at the turn of the century. Claire Savarin-Decker and her husband are studying a new element they have discovered. Their scientific partnership is tragically interrupted when he is killed in a street accident. Claire continues on with her work, torn by the attraction of Coloradan rancher Blanco White and by the claims of her daughter.

Historical Accuracy: There are elements in the story from the real life of Marie and Pierre Curie but imaginatively repossessed.

`2726` *Herma*

Date of Publication: 1981
Subject(s): Aviation; Theatrical Life
Fictional character(s): Herma, Singer; Fred Hite, Businessman
Historical character(s): Enrico Caruso, Singer (opera); Marcel Proust, Writer
Time Period(s): 1890s; 1900s
Locale(s): Santa Ana, California; San Francisco, California; Paris, France

Summary: The novel tells the story of Herma, a young woman who rises from singing in the choir to stardom at the Paris Opera. Herma and her agent, Fred Hite, are propelled from California to Paris during the Belle Epoque of Caruso and Proust.

Historical Accuracy: The novel is fiction into which the events of the real world have been incorporated when necessary, although invariably in an altered state.

`2727` *Pandora's Galley*

Date of Publication: 1979
Subject(s): Napoleonic Era; Espionage
Fictional character(s): Malcolm Langrish, Sea Captain; Winifred Hervey, Gentlewoman; Zulietta, Lover
Time Period(s): 1790s (1797)
Locale(s): Venice, Italy

Summary: The novel describes the adventures of an American sea captain who serves as a mercenary in the Venetian navy as the intrigue from Napoleonic France sweeps south. No one seems to be who they truly are, as Langrish is entangled with an English girl, a French agent, and a Venetian courtesan.

Historical Accuracy: The novel is believably atmospheric in capturing the era.

MARILYN HARRIS
(PSEUD. OF MARILYN HARRIS SPRINGER, 1931-)

An American writer born in Oklahoma City, Harris is a graduate of the University of Oklahoma.

`2728` *American Eden*

Date of Publication: 1987
Subject(s): Family Saga; Ku Klux Klan
Fictional character(s): Mary Eden Stanhope, Gentlewoman; Burke Stanhope, Gentleman; Eve Stanhope, Actress
Time Period(s): 1880s; 1890s
Locale(s): Mobile, Alabama; Dallas, Texas; West

Summary: In the sixth volume of the Eden family saga, and the first set in America, the history of the emerging American nation is reflected in the story of the Stanhopes. Mary and her husband Burke battle the forces of the Ku Klux Klan as their daughter Eve heads west with a troupe of actors.

Historical Accuracy: The period details are convincing.

`2729` *Eden and Honor*

Date of Publication: 1989
Subject(s): Family Saga; Boer War; World War I
Fictional character(s): John Eden, Gentleman; Eve Stanhope, Actress; Geoffrey Eden, Military Personnel (soldier)
Time Period(s): 19th century; 20th century (1896-1916)
Locale(s): Devon, England; Mobile, Alabama; London, England

Summary: In the seventh volume of the Eden family saga, the events of the turn of the century are reflected in the experiences of the Eden family. John Eden rules his family with an iron determination that is challenged by the rush of history that includes the Boer War and World War I. The war alters forever family history and traditions that the Edens have carefully preserved.

Historical Accuracy: The elements of the period create a believable atmosphere for the domestic story.

`2730` *The Eden Passion*

Date of Publication: 1979
Subject(s): Family Saga; Victorian Period; Crimean War
Fictional character(s): John Eden, Heir; Harriet Eden, Gentlewoman
Time Period(s): 1850s; 1860s (1851-1861)
Locale(s): Devon, England; London, England; Crimea, Russia

Summary: In the third volume of the Eden family saga, John Eden brings his father's body back to the family estate for burial and begins to assert his claim as heir. An affair with his aunt, Harriet, brings on disaster and a ten-year search for his fortune and his honor that takes him to the Crimean battlefield and India follows.

Historical Accuracy: The period background is genuine and believable.

2731 *Eden Rising*

Date of Publication: 1982
Subject(s): Family Saga; Victorian Period
Fictional character(s): John Eden, Gentleman; Susan Mantle, Nurse; Elizabeth Eden, Convict
Time Period(s): 1870s (1874-1875)
Locale(s): Devon, England; Paris, France; London, England

Summary: As the Eden family saga continues into the 1870s, family patriarch John Eden is in decline and haunted by the past. He is nursed by Susan Mantle who assists him in a journey of self-discovery and expiation for past sins.

Historical Accuracy: As in all of the Eden family novels, the background and atmosphere of the period are authentic.

2732 *The Prince of Eden*

Date of Publication: 1978
Subject(s): Family Saga; Victorian Period
Fictional character(s): Edward Eden, Bastard Son, Heir; John Eden, Heir
Historical character(s): Thomas De Quincey, Writer
Time Period(s): 19th century (1836-1851)
Locale(s): London, England; Devon, England; Shropshire, England

Summary: The second volume of six tracing the family fortunes of the Edens focusses on the illegitimate Edward Eden, a disaffected maverick. Filled with reformer's zeal, he sells off parts of the Eden estate to help the poor, much to the family's alarm. He battles an opium addiction as well, and when he is killed in a tragic accident, his son, John, is brought to Eden Castle as heir.

Historical Accuracy: The novel is packed with romance elements. However, the period background is genuine and believable.

2733 *This Other Eden*

Date of Publication: 1977
Subject(s): Family Saga; French Revolution
Fictional character(s): Thomas Eden, Nobleman; Marianne Locke, Servant; Jane Locke, Young Woman
Historical character(s): Thomas Paine, Patriot; Lady Emma Hamilton, Gentlewoman; Horatio Nelson, Military Personnel (admiral)
Time Period(s): 1790s (1790-1798)
Locale(s): Devon, England; London, England

Summary: This is the first of a series of novels that trace the history of the Eden family from the 18th century to the present. The story begins in the 1790s during the turmoil of the French Revolution as Lord Thomas Eden pursues young Marianne Locke whose sister, Jane, assists in her sister's seduction. The novel is filled with the devices of romance: a dangerous smuggling ring, two marriage ceremonies, and an illegitimate heir.

Historical Accuracy: Despite the romantic orientation, the novel is framed by period details that are convincing.

2734 *The Women of Eden*

Date of Publication: 1980
Subject(s): Family Saga; Victorian Period
Fictional character(s): John Eden, Gentleman; Mary Eden, Gentlewoman; Burke Stanhope, Gentleman
Time Period(s): 1870s (1870-1871)
Locale(s): Devon, England; London, England

Summary: In the continuing saga of the Eden family, the time is the 1870s and patriarch John Eden, who has single-handedly rescued the family from financial ruin, comes into conflict with Lady Mary Eden. Her love for Burke Stanhope, a man John despises, causes her to question her family loyalty.

Historical Accuracy: The romantic elements and situation are anchored by some solid period backgrounds.

NORMA HARRIS

2735 *Trumpets of Silver*

Date of Publication: 1990
Subject(s): Jews; Religious Conflict
Fictional character(s): Shmuel Kaminsky, Worker; Sarah Kaminsky, Spouse
Time Period(s): 19th century; 20th century (1891-1947)
Locale(s): Odessa, Russia; Palestine; United States (Chicago, New York City)

Summary: The novel traces the Kaminsky family from the pogroms of Odessa and the Jewish Pate in the 1890s to America and the founding of Israel. Four generations are chronicled, whose faith and will to survive triumphs over enormous odds and the rush of history.

Historical Accuracy: Although the characters are fictitious, the historical events are factual. The author has taken some liberties with the sequence of dates.

HARRY HARRISON (1925-)

JOHN HOLM

Harrison is an American who is best known as a science fiction writer, especially as the author of the Stainless Steel Rat series. His *Deathworld* novels are considered classics in the genre. Also a playwright and an actor, he has won the Julie Harris Award and has acted on 19 episodes of the television series ''Hawaii Five-O.''

2736 *The Hammer and the Cross*

Date of Publication: 1993
Subject(s): Vikings; Dark Ages
Fictional character(s): Shef, Blacksmith; Brand, Warrior; Ivar, Warrior
Time Period(s): 9th century (865)
Locale(s): England

Summary: Shef is born to an Englishwoman raped by a Viking. His quest is to rescue his step-sister. On his way he meets Vikings who worship the old gods while praying for their eventual final battle. Shef develops new weapons, including the halberd and the crossbow, which he uses to lead his army against English enemies.

Historical Accuracy: The novel is fantasy-based rather than historical, using the atmosphere of 9th century England for imaginative purposes.

KATHRYN HARRISON (1961-)

American writer Harrison graduated from Stanford and is a former editor for Viking. Her other works include *Thicker than Water* and *Exposure*.

`2737` *Poison*

Date of Publication: 1995
Subject(s): Inquisition; Royalty—Spain
Fictional character(s): Francisca de Luarca, Young Woman
Historical character(s): Marie Louise de Bourbon, Noblewoman (niece of Louis XIV); Carlos II, Ruler (King of Spain)
Time Period(s): 17th century
Locale(s): Madrid, Spain

Summary: This novel of 17th-century Spain during the Spanish Inquisition links the stories of two women. Francesca is the daughter of a silk grower whose lover is a priest, and Marie Louise, niece of Louis XIV, contracts a loveless marriage with Carlos II and must take the blame for failing to produce an heir. The Inquistion works its way as these two women must find ways to surmount their destinies.

Historical Accuracy: Darkly atmospheric, the novel features a convincing period background.

RAY HARRISON (1928-)

Harrison is an English mystery writer who graduated from Cambridge University and for many years worked as a member of the fraud squad for the Department of Inland Revenue. His detective thrillers set in the Victorian period have been praised for their lively evocation of period atmosphere, convincing characters, and varied plots. Harrison believes that the use of a period setting should not just embellish the story but rather add to the reader's understanding of the past and the present as well.

`2738` *Counterfeit of Murder*

Date of Publication: 1986
Subject(s): Mystery; Victorian Period
Fictional character(s): Joseph Bragg, Police Officer (detective sergeant); James Morton, Police Officer (constable), Gentleman; Catherine Marsden, Journalist
Time Period(s): 1890s
Locale(s): London, England

Summary: Panic grips the government when a forged £1,000 note is passed at the Bank of England. Bragg and Morton's investigation must be discreet to avoid a financial panic. They penetrate a counterfeiting ring to uncover its leader.

Historical Accuracy: The period detail is expertly rendered.

`2739` *Death of a Dancing Lady*

Date of Publication: 1985
Subject(s): Mystery; Victorian Period
Fictional character(s): Joseph Bragg, Police Officer (detective sergeant); James Morton, Police Officer (constable), Gentleman; Catherine Marsden, Journalist
Time Period(s): 1890s (1892)
Locale(s): London, England; Galveston, Texas; Boston, Massachusetts

Summary: The ship *Dancing Lady* sinks under questionable circumstances south of Galveston, Texas. Lloyds of London is convinced that the ship was deliberately scuttled for the insurance. Constable Morton, on a visit to his American relatives, journeys to Galveston to investigate, while Sergeant Bragg follows leads closer to home.

Historical Accuracy: The period atmosphere is ably and interestingly developed.

`2740` *Deathwatch*

Date of Publication: 1986
Subject(s): Mystery; Victorian Period
Fictional character(s): Joseph Bragg, Police Officer (detective sergeant); James Morton, Police Officer (constable), Gentleman; Catherine Marsden, Journalist
Time Period(s): 1890s
Locale(s): London, England

Summary: James Morton shocks his well-bred family when he joins the police force as a constable. Sergeant Bragg suspects he is merely dabbling in crime-solving, but Morton proves his worth and sincerity in a case in which a young policeman's body is found impaled on a church railing. Meanwhile, Bragg finds himself behind bars, accused of raping a clergyman's daughter.

Historical Accuracy: The author is an expert in rendering the period details of late Victorian London.

`2741` *Harvest of Death*

Date of Publication: 1988
Subject(s): Mystery; Victorian Period
Fictional character(s): Joseph Bragg, Police Officer (detective sergeant); James Morton, Police Officer (constable), Gentleman
Time Period(s): 1890s
Locale(s): London, England; Dorset, England

Summary: After Sergeant Bragg is knifed by a burglar, he convalesces in the Dorset countryside at the home of his cousin. When a murder occurs there, Bragg begins an investigation that reveals the secrets and scandals beneath the surface of the idyllic English countryside.

Historical Accuracy: The author demonstrates his ability to portray Victorian rural scenes as well as Victorian London.

`2742` *Patently Murder*

Date of Publication: 1991
Subject(s): Mystery; Victorian Period

Fictional character(s): Joseph Bragg, Police Officer (detective sergeant); James Morton, Police Officer (constable), Gentleman
Time Period(s): 1890s
Locale(s): London, England

Summary: Is there a connection between the weapon used to kill a child prostitute and the one used to kill wealthy Andrew Livesey whose widow is the daughter of a Member of Parliament? Bragg and Morton reopen the Livesey case, despite the opposition of the M.P.

Historical Accuracy: The period details are sharply drawn and authentic.

2743   *A Season for Death*

Date of Publication: 1987
Subject(s): Mystery; Victorian Period
Fictional character(s): Joseph Bragg, Police Officer (detective sergeant); James Morton, Police Officer (constable), Gentleman; Catherine Marsden, Journalist
Historical character(s): Oscar Wilde, Writer; Edward, Prince of Wales, Royalty
Time Period(s): 1890s (1892)
Locale(s): London, England

Summary: A very clever blackmailer is at work plaguing some of England's most respectable citizens who have been caught in a variety of embarrassing situations. The latest victim is the Prince of Wales, and Sergeant Bragg and Constable Morton are called in to protect the reputation of the royals.

Historical Accuracy: The atmosphere of period London is well detailed.

2744   *Sphere of Death*

Date of Publication: 1990
Subject(s): Mystery; Victorian Period
Fictional character(s): Joseph Bragg, Police Officer (detective sergeant); James Morton, Police Officer (constable), Gentleman; Catherine Marsden, Journalist
Time Period(s): 1890s
Locale(s): London, England

Summary: Upon the mysterious disappearance of an American in London, Constable Morton poses as a Swiss anarchist in hopes of infiltrating a ring of European revolutionaries. He finds the missing American at the center of a conspiracy with the widest possible ramifications.

Historical Accuracy: The novel demonstrates the author's firm grasp of the period.

2745   *Tincture of Death*

Date of Publication: 1989
Subject(s): Mystery; Victorian Period
Fictional character(s): Joseph Bragg, Police Officer (detective sergeant); James Morton, Police Officer (constable), Gentleman
Time Period(s): 1890s
Locale(s): London, England

Summary: Sergeant Bragg and Constable Morton investigate the opium trade, which turns deadly.

Historical Accuracy: The period detail of London is convincingly described.

2746   *Why Kill Arthur Potter?*

Date of Publication: 1983
Subject(s): Mystery; Victorian Period
Fictional character(s): Joseph Bragg, Police Officer (detective sergeant); James Morton, Police Officer (constable), Gentleman; Belle Berkeley, Actress
Time Period(s): 1890s (1890)
Locale(s): London, England; France; Monte Carlo, Monaco

Summary: This is the first novel in a series involving London police officers Bragg and Morton. The murder of an obscure shipping clerk is the catalyst for a complex crime that takes Sergeant Bragg and Constable Morton, a society gentleman who has recently taken up police work, on a tangled trail that leads to Monte Carlo.

Historical Accuracy: The novel expertly establishes the period atmosphere.

SAMUEL BERTRAM HARRISON

2747   *The White King*

Date of Publication: 1950
Subject(s): Royalty—Hawaii
Historical character(s): Gerrit Parmalee Judd, Religious (missionary), Political Figure; Kamehameha III, Ruler (King of Hawaii)
Time Period(s): 19th century
Locale(s): Hawaii

Summary: Gerrit Judd goes to Hawaii in the 1820s as a missionary. Judd becomes a government official under King Kamehameha III and plays a leading role in gaining recognition of Hawaii as a sovereign state.

Historical Accuracy: The novel's history is accurately and thoroughly presented.

SUE HARRISON (1950-)

Born in Michigan, Harrison graduated from Lake Superior State University and has worked in public relations and as a instructor in writing. She spent three years researching, four years writing, two and a half years rewriting, and five years trying to get her first novel, *Mother Earth, Father Sky*, published.

2748   *Brother Wind*

Date of Publication: 1994
Subject(s): Prehistory; Tribal Life—Prehistoric
Fictional character(s): Kiin, Prehistoric Human; Kukutux, Widow(er), Prehistoric Human; Samiq, Hunter, Prehistoric Human
Time Period(s): 71st century B.C. (7038 B.C.)
Locale(s): Alaska, North America

Summary: In the last novel of a trilogy on prehistoric life of a native people of the Alaska peninsula, the fate of three individuals intertwine. Kiin is claimed by a brutal enemy; the widow Kuhutux faces the challenge of surviving on her own; and Samiq, the wounded hunter, must lead his people.

Historical Accuracy: The prehistoric elements are detailed and convincing.

2749 *Mother Earth, Father Sky*

Date of Publication: 1990
Subject(s): Prehistory; Tribal Life—Prehistoric
Fictional character(s): Chagak, Prehistoric Human, Indian (Aleut); Shuganan, Prehistoric Human, Indian (Aleut)
Time Period(s): 71st century B.C. (7056 B.C.)
Locale(s): Aleutian Islands, Alaska, North America

Summary: In this depiction of prehistoric tribal life among the Aleuts in Alaska, Chagak witnesses the massacre of her tribe. She survives with her infant brother, and they search for a place to live in the wilderness.

Historical Accuracy: Effective and convincing, the story provides some authentic looks at prehistoric life.

2750 *My Sister, the Moon*

Date of Publication: 1992
Subject(s): Tribal Life—Prehistoric; Prehistory
Fictional character(s): Kiin, Prehistoric Human; Amigigh, Indian (Aleut), Prehistoric Human
Time Period(s): 71st century B.C.
Locale(s): Aleutian Islands, Alaska, North America

Summary: In the prehistoric Aleutian Islands, Kiin is an unwelcomed girl-child whose father wants her killed so that a son can take her place. She is saved when the tribal chief claims her as a wife for his infant son, Amgigh, but her trials from abusive treatment continue.

Historical Accuracy: The novel's prehistoric elements are convincing.

WILLIAM HARRISON (1933-)

Harrison was born in Texas and is a graduate of Texas Christian and Vanderbilt universities. He is a professor of English at the University of Arkansas. Harrison is the author of the screenplay for the movie *Rollerball.*

2751 *Burton and Speke*

Date of Publication: 1982
Subject(s): Exploration; Frontier—Africa; Crimean War
Historical character(s): Sir Richard Francis Burton, Explorer, Writer; John Hanning Speke, Explorer
Time Period(s): 1850s; 1860s (1854-1864)
Locale(s): Africa; London, England; West

Summary: The novel dramatizes the friendship of explorers Richard Francis Burton and John Hanning Speke and the events that lead to the breakdown of that friendship. They collaborate in the search for the source of the Nile, but the trip goes tragically awry. The novel ranges from the wilderness of Africa, to the battlefields of Crimea, and to the American

West, presenting a masterful portrait of two fascinating Victorian eccentrics.

Historical Accuracy: The historical details and factual basis of the novel's story are strong and reliable.

CYNTHIA HARROD-EAGLES (1948-)

Born in London and educated at Edinburgh University and University College, London, Harrod-Eagles has written a long series of historical novels tracing the history of the fictional Morland family. The background to these novels is the real history of England, carefully researched and accurately recorded.

2752 *Anna*

Date of Publication: 1990
Subject(s): Napoleonic Wars; Russian Empire
Fictional character(s): Anne Peters, Governess; Sergei Kirov, Nobleman, Diplomat
Historical character(s): Napoleon Bonaparte, Ruler (French emperor), Military Personnel (army commander); Alexander I, Ruler (Czar of Russia)
Time Period(s): 1800s; 1810s
Locale(s): St. Petersburg, Russia; Moscow, Russia

Summary: The first volume of the author's Kirov Saga is set during the French invasion of Russia in 1812. Anne Peters accepts a position as the governess to the children of a Russian diplomat, Count Kirov. She becomes a member of the glittering salons of Russian society as the confrontation with Napoleon produces major changes.

Historical Accuracy: The novel is richly and believably detailed with period information.

2753 *Emily*

Date of Publication: 1992
Subject(s): Family Saga; Russian Empire; Russian Revolution
Fictional character(s): Emily Paget, Young Woman; Natasha Petrovna, Gentlewoman; Alexei Nikolayevitch, Gentleman
Historical character(s): Nicholas II, Ruler (Czar of Russia)
Time Period(s): 1900s; 1910s
Locale(s): England; St. Petersburg, Russia

Summary: In the final volume of the author's Kirov Saga, Emily Paget is rescued from her relatives' plans for her by her Russian grandmother who takes her back to Russia. There she discovers love for the first time with another woman's husband as the 1917 revolution breaks out with unexpected consequences and challenges.

Historical Accuracy: The details of the period are richly and authentically presented.

2754 *Fleur*

Date of Publication: 1991
Subject(s): Family Saga; Russian Empire; Crimean War
Fictional character(s): Fleur Hamilton, Gentlewoman; Sergei Kirov, Nobleman
Time Period(s): 1850s
Locale(s): St. Petersburg, Russia; Crimea, Russia; England

Summary: In the second volume of the author's Kirov Saga, it is the 1850s, and Fleur Hamilton falls in love with the enigmatic Count Kirov while visiting St. Petersburg. With the outbreak of the Crimean War, the scene shifts to the battle-field as Fleur attempts to solve the secret of Kirov and resolve her feelings for him.

Historical Accuracy: The details of the military engagements during the Crimean War are authentically presented.

2755 *I, Victoria*

Date of Publication: 1994
Subject(s): Victorian Period; Biography, Fictionalized; Royalty—England
Historical character(s): Victoria, Ruler (Queen of England)
Time Period(s): 19th century; 20th century (1820s-1900)
Locale(s): England

Summary: The novel is a fictional autobiography of Queen Victoria. Written at the end of her life in 1900, Victoria reflects back on her long reign and the various events in her public and private life. The novel attempts to provide a human portrait of the formidable Victoria.

Historical Accuracy: The novel stays close to the actual events and chronology of Victoria's reign, with a plausible imper-sonation of Victoria's voice and character.

ZSOLT DE HARSANYI (1887-1943)

Hungarian playwright and writer Harsanyi is the author of over 120 one-act plays. He is also the author of bestsellers based on the lives of various eminent historical figures such as Franz Liszt, Peter Paul Rubens, and Galileo Galilei.

2756 *Lover of Life*

Date of Publication: 1942
Subject(s): Biography, Fictionalized; Artistic Life
Historical character(s): Peter Paul Rubens, Artist, Diplomat
Time Period(s): 16th century; 17th century (1590-1640)
Locale(s): Antwerp, Belgium; Italy

Summary: Harsanyi offers a fictional account of the life and times of Flemish artist Peter Paul Rubens from his youth to his death in 1640. The novel traces Rubens' artistic develop-ment, diplomatic career, and personal life in a thorough presentation that brings both Rubens and his era to life.

Historical Accuracy: The novel invents little in its treatment of the facts.

2757 *The Star-Gazer*

Date of Publication: 1939
Subject(s): Science; Biography, Fictionalized; Renaissance
Historical character(s): Galileo Galilei, Scientist; Urban VIII, Religious (pope)
Time Period(s): 16th century; 17th century (1570s-1642)
Locale(s): Italy

Summary: This fictional life of Galileo traces his career from boyhood when he contemplated suicide because of his fa-ther's insistence that he make medicine his career. Enthusiam for science and invention brings him quickly into conflict with

orthodoxy, the vagaries of Medici rule, and papal politics. Galileo changes the way we see the world and the toll and cost of his quest for the truth are ably dramatized.

Historical Accuracy: The framework of the story is factual and close to history.

DYLAN HARSON

2758 *Kansas Blue*

Date of Publication: 1993
Subject(s): American West; Settlement of the American Fron-tier; Wagon Trains
Fictional character(s): Louise Danielle Coopersand, Settler; Austin Bourke, Veteran (Union cavalry officer), Wagonmaster
Time Period(s): 1860s (1867)
Locale(s): Kansas

Summary: In the aftermath of the Homestead Act of 1862, more and more wagon trains move west. Danni Coopersand is a member of a small wagon train guided by former Union cavalry officer Austin Bourke. They must contend with storms, floods, and ex-Confederate soldiers turned outlaws.

Historical Accuracy: The period and western details are con-vincing.

SCOTT HART

2759 *Eight April Days*

Date of Publication: 1949
Subject(s): Civil War—U.S.
Fictional character(s): Old Pine, Trader
Historical character(s): Robert E. Lee, Military Personnel (Confederate commander)
Time Period(s): 1860s (1865)
Locale(s): Virginia

Summary: The novel depicts the Confederate army's retreat from Petersburg that leads to Robert E. Lee's surrender at Appomattox. The story is told through the experiences of a female peddler named Old Pine, who meets others swept up in the final days of the Confederacy.

Historical Accuracy: The novel provides an authentic recon-struction of the period and the region and believably captures the spirit of the Confederate army.

DUFF HART-DAVIS (1936-)

An English writer born in London, Hart-Davis attended Eton and graduated from Oxford. He worked as a deckhand on a cargo boat along the West African coast and pioneered a motor route to Moscow from the Crimea. He is a feature writer and editor for London's *Sunday Telegraph*.

2760 *Horses of War*

Date of Publication: 1991
Subject(s): Russian Revolution; Horses; Romance

Fictional character(s): Joseph Clements, Jockey, Horse Trainer; Katya Mironov, Royalty (princess)
Time Period(s): 19th century; 20th century (1878-1920)
Locale(s): Russia; England

Summary: In this novel set during the Russian Revolution Joseph Clements is an English jockey and horse trainer who serves as the head of the Imperial stud farm. He meets and falls in love with Russian princess Katya Mironov as the terror of the Bolshevik revolt explodes. Joseph and Katya are separated while rescuing two prize horses, and Joseph is put to incredible tests to survive.

Historical Accuracy: The novel offers an interesting angle on the events of the period that are convincingly dramatized.

J.M. HARTLEY

2761 *The Way*
Date of Publication: 1944
Subject(s): Biblical Story; Roman Empire
Fictional character(s): Severus, Military Personnel (Roman centurion); Balthazar, Religious (priest), Biblical Figure
Time Period(s): 1st century
Locale(s): Israel

Summary: A Roman centurion, Severus, is sent by the emperor to spy on the Egyptian priest Balthazar, one of the Magi who celebrated the birth of Jesus 20 years earlier.

Historical Accuracy: The background is unconvincing and as fanciful as the novel's story.

JAN DE HARTOG

2762 *The Centurion*
Date of Publication: 1989
Subject(s): Time Travel; Fantasy; Roman Empire
Fictional character(s): Martinus Harinxma, Sea Captain; Sylvia Harinxma, Spouse; Mellarius, Military Personnel (centurion)
Time Period(s): 1980s (1986); 4th century (368)
Locale(s): England; Boston, Massachusetts; Germany

Summary: Two ages, 1986 and the 4th century, are juxtaposed in this meditative fanta sy. Martinus Harinxma turns explorer in time and follows the progress of a Roman centurion in Britain. The juxtaposition allows Martinus to work out for himself an explanation of his actions during the fateful encounter in World War II recorded in de Hartog's *The Captain*.

Historical Accuracy: This is an ingenious blend of modern and ancient times with a believable sense of the past.

2763 *The Peaceable Kingdom*
Date of Publication: 1971
Subject(s): Religious Life; Quakers; Settlement of the American Frontier
Fictional character(s): Boniface Baker, Settler; Caleb Martin, Settler
Historical character(s): George Fox, Religious (founder of the Quakers); Margaret Fell, Religious (founder of the Quakers)

Time Period(s): 17th century (1652-1653); 1750s (1754-1755)
Locale(s): Lancashire, England; Pennsylvania, American Colonies

Summary: This first volume of a trilogy that continues with the *The Peculiar People* and the *The Lamb's War* attempts collectively to offer an epic history of the Quakers. The story begins in 1652 with the persecution of Quaker founders George Fox and Margaret Fell. It continues with the Quaker settlement of Pennsylvania in the 18th century where the Friends encounter slavery and Indian uprisings and attempt to forge a harmonious community.

Historical Accuracy: This is a massive work of historical recreation, based on actual events and people.

2764 *The Peculiar People*
Date of Publication: 1992
Subject(s): Quakers; Indians
Fictional character(s): Mordecai Monk, Religious (Quaker preacher); Lydia Best, Young Woman; Ebenezer Stewart, Military Personnel (captain)
Time Period(s): 1830s (1832-1834)
Locale(s): Pendle Hill, Indiana; Philadelphia, Pennsylvania; Birmingham, England

Summary: The third volume of the author's epic of Quaker life in America takes place in the 1830s. Two members of the Society of Friends, or "Peculiar People," become involved with the U.S. Cavalry and a group of Indians who are being forced from their land. The Quakers and Indians unite to oppose the government.

Historical Accuracy: A clear bias in the description of the Quakers and the Indians does affect accuracy.

ALICE HARWOOD (1909-)
English writer Harwood was born in Staffordshire and graduated from Bedford College, University of London. She started her career doing secretarial work in a London hospital, and has worked as an editor and as an assistant in the educational books section for British prisoners of war.

2765 *The Lily and the Leopards*
Date of Publication: 1949
Subject(s): Tudor Period; Royalty—England
Historical character(s): Lady Jane Grey, Ruler (Queen of England), Noblewoman; Mary Tudor, Royalty (princess); Elizabeth Tudor, Royalty (princess); Edward Tudor, Royalty (prince); Henry VIII, Ruler (King of England); Jane Seymour, Royalty (queen consort of Henry VIII)
Time Period(s): 16th century
Locale(s): England

Summary: The tragic life of Lady Jane Grey is depicted. The granddaughter of Henry VIII's sister, she is a companion to both Mary and Elizabeth Tudor. Innocent and easily manipulated, Jane is swept up in the coup d'etat that puts her on the throne of England for nine days before she is executed. The novel captures the intrigue and color of this amazing period of English history.

Historical Accuracy: The story is close to the historical facts with some simplifications in the interest of the drama.

2766 *Merchant of the Ruby*

Date of Publication: 1950
Subject(s): War of the Roses; Royalty—England
Historical character(s): Edward IV, Ruler (King of England); Richard III, Ruler (King of England); Henry Tudor, Nobleman; Perkin Warbeck, Gentleman, Imposter; Catherine Gordon, Noblewoman; Margaret Tudor, Royalty (princess)
Time Period(s): 15th century
Locale(s): England; Scotland

Summary: Perkin Warbeck, who calls himself the Merchant of the Ruby, is the infamous pretender to the throne who challenges the Tudor victors in the War of the Roses. He claims to be Richard, Duke of York, one of the Princes in the Tower, and assembles a host of Yorkist supporters. The story of Warbeck's challenge to Henry VII is shown with a vast cast and a vivid recreation of dynastic power politics.

Historical Accuracy: The historical background is authentically drawn.

2767 *No Smoke Without Fire*

Date of Publication: 1964
Subject(s): Elizabethan Period; Royalty—Scotland
Historical character(s): James Stuart, Bastard Son, Nobleman (Earl of Moray); Mary, Queen of Scots, Ruler (Queen of Scotland); Henry Stewart, Nobleman (Lord Darnley); James Hepburn, Nobleman (Earl of Bothwell); James VI, Ruler (King of Scotland)
Time Period(s): 16th century
Locale(s): Scotland

Summary: In the shadow of his more famous younger sister, Mary, Queen of Scots, is James Stuart, Earl of Moray. Illegitimate, he is not eligible to reign. Instead he becomes enmeshed in Mary's troubled reign, serving after she is deposed as regent for Mary's son James VI, who vows to become James I of England. The novel brings to life the complex political world of the Scottish court.

Historical Accuracy: Remarkably detailed, the novel is essentially faithful to the facts of history.

2768 *Seats of the Mighty: A Novel of James Stuart, Brother of Mary, Queen of Scots*

Date of Publication: 1956
Subject(s): Royalty—Scotland
Historical character(s): James Stuart, Nobleman (Earl of Moray); Mary, Queen of Scots, Ruler
Time Period(s): 16th century
Locale(s): Scotland

Summary: This novel is based on the life of James Stuart, the illegitimate son of James V of Scotland and the half brother of Mary, Queen of Scots. James was at the center of the intrigue surrounding Mary's reign, and the novel captures the shifting allegiances and betrayals that mark the period.

Historical Accuracy: The novel is compelling in its re-creation of the past and presents believable portraits of very complex and contradictory individuals.

2769 *So Merciful a Queen, So Cruel a Woman*

Date of Publication: 1958
Subject(s): Elizabethan Period; Royalty—England
Historical character(s): Elizabeth I, Ruler (Queen of England); Mary I, Ruler (Queen of England); Lady Katharine Grey, Noblewoman; Robert Dudley, Nobleman (Earl of Leicester); Robert Cecil, Nobleman; Jane Seymour, Royalty (queen consort of Henry VIII); Mary, Queen of Scots, Ruler (Queen of Scotland)
Time Period(s): 16th century
Locale(s): England

Summary: The queen and woman is Elizabeth I, and the novel dramatizes her rise to the throne and the consolidation of her power which calls for dealing with Katharine Grey, sister of Lady Jane Grey, and Mary, Queen of Scots. Both are potential rivals. The intrigues of the period and Elizabeth's court are vividly reproduced.

Historical Accuracy: The novel is faithful to the facts and successful in creating a believable period atmosphere.

RONALD HARWOOD (1934-)

Born in Capetown, South Africa, Harwood attended the Royal Academy of Dramatic Art. He is an actor, novelist, playwright, and screenwriter, best known for the award-winning play, *The Dresser*.

2770 *Articles of Faith*

Date of Publication: 1973
Subject(s): Frontier—Africa; Family Saga
Fictional character(s): Johannes Henning, Religious (clergyman); Richard Thompson, Settler
Time Period(s): Multiple Time Periods
Locale(s): South Africa

Summary: The novel offers the epic history of South Africa from the end of the 18th century to the 1970s in the intermingled history of two families, the Dutch Hennings and the English Thompsons who reflect the original settlement by the Dutch, the arrival of the British, and the influx of Jews from Eastern Europe. All these elements, along with the Native Africans, produce the heritage of South Africa.

Historical Accuracy: The historical elements are cast into a convincing background for the drama.

2771 *Cesar and Augusta*

Date of Publication: 1978
Subject(s): Musical Life; Franco-Prussian War
Historical character(s): Cesar Augustine Franck, Musician, Composer; Augusta Holmes, Musician, Composer; Camille Saint-Saens, Musician
Time Period(s): 1870s
Locale(s): Paris, France

Summary: Set in Paris in the 1870s, the novel tells the story of French composer Cesar Franck who takes on as a pupil Augusta Holmes, who is determined to become the world's greatest female composer. By the end of the decade, Franck composes his Piano Quintet, the first of his major works, and the novel tells the story of how it comes to be written. The novel also authentically captures the musical ferment of the period.

Historical Accuracy: The basis of the story is historical, captured with care.

JACK HASHIAN

`2772` *Mamigon*

Date of Publication: 1982
Subject(s): Armenian Massacre; World War I
Fictional character(s): Mamigon, Military Personnel (soldier); Ahgavni, Spouse; Emily Hartnett, Teacher
Time Period(s): 20th century (1915-1946)
Locale(s): Anatolia, Turkey; Boston, Massachusetts

Summary: The background of the story is the Turkish massacre of Armenian Christians in 1915. Mamigon is a young soldier who tracks the killer of his family across his Anatolian homeland to America. The novel is a passionate tale of vengeance and of the love of Mamigon for his slain wife Ahgavni and the American school teacher Emily Hartnett.

Historical Accuracy: The details of the Turkish atrocities are based on British Foreign Office reports and eyewitness accounts.

MICHAEL HASTINGS
(PSEUD. OF MICHAEL BAR-ZOHAR, 1938-)

An Israeli novelist, Hastings was born in Bulgaria and graduated from Hebrew University of Jerusalem and the University of Paris. He has worked as a foreign correspondent in Paris for several newspapers and as the press and public relations attache for General Moshe Dayan. Hastings has been a member of the Israeli parliament. He is the winner of the Sokolov Prize (the Israeli equivalent of the Pulitzer) for *Ultra-Secret*. His *The Hunt for German Scientists* concerns efforts made by various countries to enlist the services of Germany's top scientists after World War II. He is also the official biographer of David Ben-Gurion.

`2773` *The Devil's Spy*

Date of Publication: 1988
Subject(s): World War I; Espionage; Jews
Fictional character(s): Ruth Mendelson, Spy; Saul Donsky, Spy
Historical character(s): T.E. Lawrence, Military Personnel (major); Edmund Henry Hynman Allenby, Military Personnel (British field marshal)
Time Period(s): 1910 (1917)
Locale(s): Palestine

Summary: This novel of espionage in Palestine during the First World War is based on the actual NILI Jewish espionage network that supplied British intelligence with information about the Turkish army. The story concerns the spying activities of Ruth Mendelson and her contact in British intelligence, Saul Donsky, a former Russian revolutionary and ardent Zionist.

Historical Accuracy: The story is derived from history with some slight alteration of the chronology of some of the events.

ROSEMARY HAUGHTON (1927-)

An English writer born in London, Haughton attended Queen's College, London, and is a writer, lecturer, and broadcaster on theology and spirituality.

`2774` *Elizabeth's Greetings*

Date of Publication: 1968
Subject(s): Middle Ages; Biography, Fictionalized
Historical character(s): Elizabeth of Hungary, Royalty (princess); Wolfram von Eschenbach, Writer (poet); Frederick II, Ruler (Holy Roman Emperor); Gottfried von Strassburg, Writer (poet)
Time Period(s): 13th century (1213-1231)
Locale(s): Germany

Summary: This biographical novel is the story of Elizabeth of Hungary, a canonized saint, who in medieval Germany struggles against the injustice of her time.

Historical Accuracy: The novel features a convincing use of period details and an authentic period background.

WALTER HAVIGHURST (1901-)

An American author and former professor at Miami University, Havighurst was born in Appleton, Wisconsin, and was educated at the University of Denver, King's College, London, and Columbia University. Although the majority of his books have focused on the old Northwest Territory, his earlier work draws on his experiences as a merchant seaman in such diverse location as London, Alaska, and Hong Kong. He is the author of *Land of Promise: The Story of the Northwest Territory, Voices on the River: The Story of the Mississippi Waterways, River to the West: Three Centuries of the Ohio*, and *Buffalo Bill's Wild West Show*, as well as several books for children.

`2775` *The Quiet Shore*

Date of Publication: 1937
Subject(s): Reconstruction Period; Business Building; Homesteading
Fictional character(s): Roger Bradley, Settler
Time Period(s): 1860s
Locale(s): Lake Erie, Great Lakes; Ohio

Summary: The Bradley family is the focus for this tale of homesteading along Lake Erie following the Civil War. The family's founder is Roger Bradley who reclaims swampland, while the next generation seeks its fortune in the increasing industrialization of Ohio.

Historical Accuracy: The novel features a vivid and believable period and regional background.

2776   *Winds of Spring*

Date of Publication: 1940
Subject(s): Settlement of the American Frontier
Fictional character(s): Jan Carl Sorensen, Naturalist, Pioneer; Margretta Sorensen, Spouse
Time Period(s): 19th century (1840s-1870s)
Locale(s): Wisconsin

Summary: The novel describes the opening of the virgin prairies and forests of Wisconsin from the perspective of Swedish immigrant Jan Carl Sorenson and his wife. Sorenson prefers the study of the region's rapidly vanishing wildlife to the task of acquiring land and money.

Historical Accuracy: The novel provides an authentic look at the region during the period.

DIANA HAVILAND

2777   *The Moreland Legacy*

Date of Publication: 1977
Subject(s): Romance; Politics; Slavery
Fictional character(s): Denise Chevillon, Southern Belle; Jason Moreland, Trader (slave), Adventurer
Time Period(s): 19th century (post Civil War)
Locale(s): Charleston, South Carolina; New York, New York; Hudson River Valley, New York

Summary: Denise Chevillon is a southern belle who marries the former slave trader Jason Moreland. He has built his fortune on the slave trade which becomes a dark legacy in his climb to success in business and politics. Theirs is a tempestuous union that must contend with infidelity and deceit.

Historical Accuracy: The novel captures the post-war world with some authenticity.

EDWARD HAVILL

2778   *Big Ember*

Date of Publication: 1947
Subject(s): Immigrants; Indians; Homesteading
Fictional character(s): Guri Erickson, Immigrant, Settler
Time Period(s): 1860s (1862)
Locale(s): Minnesota

Summary: This story of Norwegian immigrants homesteading in southern Minnesota depicts the struggle and calamities brought about by the Sioux Uprising of 1862.

Historical Accuracy: The novel offers an authentic look at pioneer life during the period.

ELLEN HAWKES

PETER MANSO (1940-)

Born in New York City, Manso graduated from Antioch College, Johns Hopkins, and the University of California, Berkeley, and has taught at Berkeley and Rutgers University. He wrote the screenplay for the documentary film *One by One*.

2779   *The Shadow of the Moth: A Novel of Espionage with Virginia Woolf*

Date of Publication: 1983
Subject(s): Mystery; World War I; Espionage
Historical character(s): Virginia Woolf, Writer; Leonard Woolf, Spouse; Roger Fry, Artist; Clive Bell, Writer; Vanessa Bell, Artist
Time Period(s): 1910s (1917)
Locale(s): London, England

Summary: In 1917, Virginia Woolf is recovering from a mental breakdown and a suicide attempt. She reads about the drowning death of a Belgian refugee and, in attempting to learn more about the incident, is plunged into a complex mystery and governmental espionage. The novel offers an ingenious puzzle for Woolf's Bloomsbury circle to solve.

Historical Accuracy: The novel borrows liberally from the facts of Woolf's life in creating the novel's atmosphere.

JACQUETTA HAWKES (1910-)

An English author and scholar, Hawkes was born in Cambridge and graduated from the university there. She has conducted archaeological research and excavations in England, Ireland, France, and Palestine. She is the author of many books on archaeology.

2780   *King of the Two Lands: The Pharaoh Akhenaten*

Date of Publication: 1966
Subject(s): Ancient Egypt; Pharaohs; Religious Conflict
Historical character(s): Akhenaton, Ruler (pharaoh); Nefertiti, Royalty (queen consort of Akhenaton)
Time Period(s): 14th century B.C.
Locale(s): Egypt

Summary: Set in ancient Egypt the novel recounts the story of the Pharaoh Akhenaton and his queen, Nefertiti. Akhenaton overthrows the old Egyptian deities, substituting his own faith in a single god. This act prompts a violent reaction from the priesthood of Amon, and Akhenaton slowly loses control of his kingdom.

Historical Accuracy: The novel is solidly researched, based on the historical record whenever possible, and offers plausible surmises otherwise.

2781   *A Quest for Love*

Date of Publication: 1980

Subject(s): Reincarnation; Time Travel
Fictional character(s): Jassa, Religious (priestess)
Time Period(s): Multiple Time Periods
Locale(s): Knossos, Greece; Tuscany, Italy; England

Summary: In a series of imaginative scenes and sensations, an unnamed heroine reenacts climactic moments of the lives she has lived in earlier incarnations from the dawn of history to the present. Scenes are depicted from the court of Minos at Knossos, Tuscany, and England during the reigns of Queens Matilda and Victoria.

Historical Accuracy: The flood of history rushes through the story, with each era captured with originality and believability.

JOHN HAWKESWORTH (1920-)

An English film and television writer and producer, Hawkesworth is best known in the U.S. for his work on the television series "Upstairs Downstairs" and "The Duchess of Duke Street."

2782 *Upstairs Downstairs*

Date of Publication: 1972
Subject(s): Edwardian Period; Servants
Fictional character(s): Richard Bellamy, Gentleman, Political Figure (M.P.); Lady Marjorie Bellamy, Noblewoman; Angus Hudson, Servant (butler)
Time Period(s): 1900s (1903-1909)
Locale(s): London, England

Summary: The novel is based on the successful television series, detailing the upstairs lives of the Bellamy family and the downstairs world of their servants at 165 Eaton Place, London. The two worlds collide with the arrival of a new servant.

Historical Accuracy: Like the TV series, the appeal is largely from the meticulous rendering of the particulars of domestic life of the time.

ANNE HAWKINS

2783 *To the Swift*

Date of Publication: 1949
Subject(s): American West; Pony Express
Fictional character(s): Sierra Dave Wagenet, Frontiersman; Haille Wagenet, Young Woman
Time Period(s): 1860s (1860)
Locale(s): West

Summary: The brief and colorful history of the Pony Express is chronicled in this adventure tale that centers on one of the Express riders, Sierra Dave Wagenet, and his young sister, Haille. Although the story is heavily burdened with cliches, it does do justice to the western relay that operated in 1860.

Historical Accuracy: The details of the operation of the Pony Express are documented with care.

PAUL HAWKINS

2784 *The Legend of Ben Tree*

Date of Publication: 1993
Subject(s): Indians; American West
Fictional character(s): Ben Tree, Mountain Man; Little Hoop, Indian (Crow), Spouse
Time Period(s): 1850s
Locale(s): Big Horn Mountains, Wyoming

Summary: Ben Tree leaves his father and brother for a visit to his mother's people, the Crow Indians of Wyoming. While there he meets and marries Little Hoop and becomes a member of the tribe. On his return home he finds that his father and brother have been killed by bandits and he sets off on a search for vengeance.

Historical Accuracy: The details of Indian life and culture are vividly and convincingly detailed.

HILDEGARDE HAWTHORNE
(1871-1952)

Born in New York City, Hawthorne was the granddaughter of Nathaniel Hawthorne. She wrote numerous books, including children's books, and was on the staff of *The New York Times*.

2785 *No Road Too Long*

Date of Publication: 1940
Subject(s): American West; Exploration
Fictional character(s): Jonathan Greenfall, Explorer, Frontiersman
Historical character(s): John C. Fremont, Explorer
Time Period(s): 1840s (1845)
Locale(s): California; Oregon; Utah

Summary: The story of John Fremont's third expedition into the far West in 1845 is dramatized, centering on young Jonathan Greenfall, a member of the party that surveyed along the Great Salt Lake and opened up the roads into Oregon and California.

Historical Accuracy: The novel's depiction of history is accurate. The presentation of Fremont's character is more heroic than other sources have recorded.

NATHANIEL HAWTHORNE (1804-1864)

An American novelist and short story writer, Hawthorne is one of the most important figures in 19th-century American literature. Hawthorne lived for a time in the Brook Farm commune before finally settling in Concord. His other novels include *The House of the Seven Gables*, *The Blithedale Romance*, and *The Marble Faun*.

2786 *The Scarlet Letter*

Date of Publication: 1850
Subject(s): American Colonies; Puritans

Fictional character(s): Hester Prynne, Spouse (adulterous), Outcast; Arthur Dimmesdale, Religious (minister); Roger Chillingworth, Doctor
Time Period(s): 17th century
Locale(s): Boston, Massachusetts, American Colonies

Summary: Hawthorne's masterpiece chronicles the effects of sin and guilt on four people: a woman accused of adultery, her vindictive husband, her daughter, and her guilt-ridden lover. The customs and conscience of the Puritans are detailed in this tale of the early days of the Massachusetts colony.

Historical Accuracy: Hawthorne presses his details to the service of the symbolic.

ERNEST HAYCOX (1899-1950)

Born in Portland, Oregon, and educated at Lewis and Clark College, Haycox served in World War I and then became a full-time writer. His work describes the construction of the Union Pacific, the Civil War, and Arizona life in the 1840s. His novels include *Bugles in the Afternoon*, *Trouble Shooter*, *Border Trumpet*, and *Sundown Jim*.

2787   *The Adventurers*

Date of Publication: 1954
Subject(s): American West
Fictional character(s): Mark Sheridan, Settler
Time Period(s): 1860s
Locale(s): Oregon

Summary: Settler Mark Sheridan arrives in Oregon in 1865 to seek his fortune. He must contend, not only with the challenge of the wilderness, but with the interests of big money intent on controlling the settlement and development of Oregon.

Historical Accuracy: The novel provides a convincing look at the region and the period.

2788   *Bugles in the Afternoon*

Date of Publication: 1944
Subject(s): American West; Battle of the Little Bighorn; Indians
Fictional character(s): Kern Shafter, Military Personnel (private)
Historical character(s): George Armstrong Custer, Military Personnel (Cavalry officer)
Time Period(s): 1870s (1875-1876)
Locale(s): Dakota Territory, United States

Summary: The events leading up to the Custer massacre are dramatized in this story concerning Kern Shafter, a private who enlists in Custer's command at Fort Lincoln in 1875. The action moves toward the climax at the Little Bighorn.

Historical Accuracy: The novel creates a believable atmosphere for the events of the Indian War with the Sioux.

2789   *The Earthbreakers*

Date of Publication: 1952
Subject(s): Settlement of the American Frontier; American West

Fictional character(s): Rice Burnett, Settler; Cal Lockyear, Settler
Time Period(s): 1840s (1845)
Locale(s): Oregon

Summary: The novel dramatizes the story of a year in the lives of a group of settlers in the Oregon Territory in 1845. The story centers on the rivalry between two former mountain men, Rice Burnett and Cal Lockyear, who are shown adjusting to the new ways of civilization encroaching on the wilderness.

Historical Accuracy: The novel provides an authentic portrait of wilderness life.

2790   *Long Storm*

Date of Publication: 1946
Subject(s): Civil War—U.S.; American West
Fictional character(s): Adam Musick, Sea Captain; Floyd Ringrose, Leader (Copperhead)
Time Period(s): 1860s
Locale(s): Portland, Oregon

Summary: The setting is Portland, Oregon, during the Civil War. Sea captain Adam Musick must put aside his struggle against the monopoly held on river traffic by the Navigation Company to battle Copperhead Floyd Ringrose who is plotting to force Oregon to withdraw from the Union.

Historical Accuracy: The novel captures the period and the region authentically.

2791   *Trouble Shooter*

Date of Publication: 1937
Subject(s): American West; Railroads
Fictional character(s): Frank Peace, Frontiersman
Time Period(s): 1860s (1868)
Locale(s): Cheyenne, Wyoming

Summary: Set in the rush to build the Union Pacific railroad and beat the Central Pacific to Salt Lake City, the novel's hero is Frank Peace, a trouble-shooter for the railroad.

Historical Accuracy: The atmosphere of the time and region is convincingly drawn.

MOLLY COSTAIN HAYCRAFT (1911-)

Canadian author Costain was born in Toronto and worked in the book and magazine trade. She is the daughter of historical novelist Thomas Costain.

2792   *Countess Carrots*

Date of Publication: 1973
Subject(s): Restoration Period; Royalty—England
Fictional character(s): Elizabeth Percy, Heiress
Historical character(s): Charles II, Ruler (King of England)
Time Period(s): 17th century
Locale(s): England; Netherlands

Summary: Redheaded Elizabeth Percy is the victim of her tyrannical grandmother who is determined to force Elizabeth into an undesirable marriage. In the end it is King Charles himself who alone can save Elizabeth from her grandmother.

Historical Accuracy: The story is fanciful, but the era is well presented and believable.

2793 *The King's Daughters*

Date of Publication: 1971

Subject(s): Middle Ages; Royalty—England

Historical character(s): Edward I, Ruler (King of England); Elizabeth Plantagenet, Royalty (princess); Joanna Plantagenet, Royalty (princess); Eleanor Plantagenet, Royalty (princess); Meg Plantagenet, Royalty (princess); Mary Plantagenet, Royalty (princess)

Time Period(s): 13th century

Locale(s): England; Netherlands

Summary: The story of the daughters of Edward I is dramatized from the point of view of Princess Elizabeth. She is married at age fourteen to the Count of Holland and is caught in the intrigues of the man who controls her husband. Her sisters' adventures are no less interesting and together they vividly reflect the time and place from a royal perspective.

Historical Accuracy: The period details are authentic and convincing.

2794 *The Lady Royal*

Date of Publication: 1964

Subject(s): Middle Ages; Royalty—England; Battle of Crecy

Historical character(s): Edward III, Ruler (King of England); Isabel, Royalty (princess); Edward, the Black Prince, Royalty (Prince of Wales)

Time Period(s): 14th century

Locale(s): England; France

Summary: Set during the reign of Edward III, the novel tells the story of Isabel, Edward's daughter, who journeys to France to be with her father as he fights the French. Isabel comes of age against the background of the important Battle of Crecy, the siege of Calais, the Jacquerie, and the effects of the Black Death.

Historical Accuracy: The era and its personalities are effectively and believeably presented.

2795 *My Lord Brother the Lionheart*

Date of Publication: 1968

Subject(s): Middle Ages; Royalty—England; Crusades

Historical character(s): Richard the Lionhearted, Ruler (King of England); Joan of Sicily, Royalty (Queen of Sicily); Berengaria of Navarre, Royalty (queen consort of Richard); Tancred, Knight, Ruler (King of Sicily)

Time Period(s): 12th century

Locale(s): Palestine; England

Summary: Joan is the daughter of Henry II and Eleanor of Aquitaine, and the favorite sister of Richard the Lionheart. She narrates her adventurous life that includes marriage at age twelve to the king of Sicily. She also accompanies Richard on the Crusades. After Richard is captured Joan wanders through Europe in disguise before returning home to England.

Historical Accuracy: As the author admits, very little was invented in telling this story, for the truth, in this case, is much stranger than fiction.

2796 *The Reluctant Queen*

Date of Publication: 1962

Subject(s): Tudor Period; Royalty—England

Historical character(s): Mary Tudor, Royalty (princess); Henry VIII, Ruler (King of England); Louis XII, Ruler (King of France); Thomas Wolsey, Religious (cardinal); Catherine of Aragon, Royalty (queen consort of Henry VIII); Charles Brandon, Nobleman (Duke of Suffolk)

Time Period(s): 16th century

Locale(s): England; France

Summary: The novel describes the life of Mary Tudor, the younger sister of Henry VIII. When Henry becomes king, Mary hopes to avoid an undesired state marriage to the prince of Flanders. Instead Henry insists that she marry the aging Louis XII of France. How Mary endures this bitter disappointment and eventually weds the man she truly loves forms the novel's story.

Historical Accuracy: The novel is based on fact with solid and believable period details.

2797 *Too Near the Throne*

Date of Publication: 1959

Subject(s): Elizabethan Period; Royalty—England

Historical character(s): Arabella Stuart, Gentlewoman; Elizabeth I, Ruler (Queen of England); Robert Devereux, Nobleman (Earl of Essex)

Time Period(s): 16th century

Locale(s): England

Summary: The novel dramatizes the story of Arabella Stuart, a cousin of Elizabeth I. Initially close to the Queen, Arabella falls out of favor when she falls in love with Essex. She soon discovers that her close kinship with the Queen is no advantage and that Elizabeth is a formidable foe.

Historical Accuracy: The novel mixes fact and fiction, but the essential details are accurate and the period scrupulously researched.

STERLING HAYDEN (1916-1986)

An American actor and author, Hayden was born in New Jersey and left school to become a seaman aboard fishing vessels and sailing ships out of ports throughout New England. He rose to the rank of captain. Hayden began acting in the 1940s, appearing in more than 50 films, notably as a hood in *Asphalt Jungle*, a deranged Air Force general in *Dr. Strangelove*, and a crooked police captain in *The Godfather*. He is the author of an autobiography, *Wanderer*.

2798 *Voyage: A Novel of 1896*

Date of Publication: 1976

Subject(s): Sea Story; Labor Movement; Gilded Age

Fictional character(s): Irons Saul Pendleton, Sea Captain; Simon Basil Harwar, Sailor

Time Period(s): 1890s (1895-1896)
Locale(s): *Neptune's Car*, At Sea; *Atalanta*, At Sea; San Francisco, California

Summary: This bold sea story is more than a nautical adventure. It is also a dramatic look at the Gilded Age of the robber barons as American class warfare between the haves and the have-nots reaches a crisis point. The novel details the maiden voyage of the four-masted square rigger *Neptune's Car* around the Horn to San Francisco. In counterpoint is the cruise of a luxurious yacht also bound for San Francisco on the eve of the Bryan-McKinley election.

Historical Accuracy: The period elements are authentic and give this novel a rich basis for its depiction of the past.

THOMAS HAYDEN (1928-1989)

An Irish writer and successful advertising executive in Dublin, Hayden spent ten years researching and writing *The Killing Frost*, and died not knowing that it would be published.

2799 *The Killing Frost*

Date of Publication: 1991
Subject(s): Independence—Ireland; Easter Rising
Fictional character(s): Myles Burke, Revolutionary (Fenian), Veteran (Civil War); Alexander Carew, Military Personnel (British officer); William Durkin, Journalist; Con Gallagher, Revolutionary
Time Period(s): 1910s (1916)
Locale(s): Ireland

Summary: The events leading up to the Irish Easter Uprising of 1916 are chronicled in the interlocking destinies of four main characters: Myles Burke, an aging Fenian rebel; Alexander Carew, a member of the Anglo-Irish aristocracy intent on crushing the rebellion; William Durkin, a cynical journalist; and Con Gallagher, a rebel. The turbulent events of the uprising are dramatized in the interplay of motive and characters.

Historical Accuracy: The characters are invented, but the atmosphere is authentic and reliable. There are few versions that more vividly capture the reality beneath the myths of the Easter Rebellion.

HOFFMAN REYNOLDS HAYS
(1904-1980)

Hays was born in New York and attended Cornell, Columbia, and the University of Liege. An educator, poet, translator, anthropologist, critic, and author, he is best known for his translations of Latin American poets, the Spanish poet Juan Ramon Jimenez, and the German playwright Berthold Brecht. Hays began his career as a playwright. His best known play, *The Ballad of Davy Crockett*, was restaged as *One Man From Tennessee*. His other works include *The Dangerous Sex: The Myth of Feminine Evil*, the novels *Stranger on the Highway* and *Lie Down in Darkness*, and *In the Beginning: Early Man and His Gods*.

2800 *Takers of the City*

Date of Publication: 1946
Subject(s): Spanish Colonies; Indians; Racial Conflict
Fictional character(s): Ricardo de la Fuente, Gentleman
Historical character(s): Bartolome de Las Casas, Religious (bishop)
Time Period(s): 16th century
Locale(s): Mexico

Summary: Mexico in the 16th century and the persecution of the Indians form the novel's background. The conquistadors are opposed by the Spanish missionaries led by Bishop Bartolome de las Casas, the Apostle of the Indies. A conventional romantic plot involving a young Spanish dandy, Ricardo de la Fuente, is interwoven with the efforts of Casas on behalf of the Indians.

Historical Accuracy: The novel is faithful to the works and efforts of Bishop Casas and the Dominican friars.

GERALD HEARD (1889-1971)

Heard is best known for his supernatural fiction, such as *The Great Fog, and Other Weird Tales* and *The Lost Cavern, and Other Tales of the Fantastic*.

2801 *The Gospel According to Gamaliel*

Date of Publication: 1945
Subject(s): Biblical Story
Historical character(s): Gamaliel the Elder, Scholar; Jesus Christ, Biblical Figure; Peter, Biblical Figure; Paul, Biblical Figure
Time Period(s): 1st century
Locale(s): Israel

Summary: This imaginative reconstruction of the life of Christ is told from the perspective of Jewish scholar and teacher of Paul, Gamaliel. The intention is to explore the relationship between the teaching of Jesus and Pharisaic teachings of the day. The novel features a reinterpretation of many of the familiar Gospel scenes.

Historical Accuracy: Despite the occasional use of colloquial speech, the novel offers a believable portrait of the period and the religious context for Jesus' teachings.

CONSTANCE HEAVEN (1911-)

An English author born in London, Heaven attended London College of Music and King's College, London. She has been an actress and operated a theater in Henley-on-Thames.

2802 *The Astrov Legacy*

Date of Publication: 1973
Subject(s): Russian Empire; Decembrist Uprising; Romance
Fictional character(s): Sophie Weston, Young Woman; Rilla Weston Kuragin, Noblewoman (countess); Leonid Astrov, Royalty (prince)
Time Period(s): 1820s
Locale(s): St. Petersburg, Russia

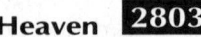

Summary: Young Sophie Weston travels to St. Petersburg to visit her sister, now Countess Kuragina. Sophie falls in love with the aristocratic Prince Astrov, causing antagonism with the proud Astrov family. The historical background is the Decembrist Uprising, a failed attempt at reform, which becomes the foreground action in the novel's complications.

Historical Accuracy: The period and details of Russian aristocratic life are vividly presented.

2803 *Castle of Doves*

Date of Publication: 1984
Subject(s): Romance
Fictional character(s): Charlotte Starr, Young Woman; Lorenzo Merenda, Nobleman (Marques de Merenda), Landowner; Guy Macalister, Manager
Time Period(s): 1830s
Locale(s): Seville, Spain

Summary: Charlotte Starr, a young English girl, accepts the invitation of her cousin to accompany him to Spain. In Seville, Spain is moving toward civil war between the child-queen Isabella II and her uncle Don Carlos. Charlotte is introduced to Spanish life and finds herself attracted to the aristocratic Don Lorenzo.

Historical Accuracy: The setting and atmosphere are colorful and authentic.

2804 *Castle of Eagles*

Date of Publication: 1974
Subject(s): Romance
Fictional character(s): Lisa Heron, Orphan, Musician; Julian Von Falkenburg, Nobleman (count)
Time Period(s): 1840s (1847)
Locale(s): Vienna, Austria; Carinthian Mountains, Austria

Summary: Lisa Heron journeys to Austria in 1847 on the eve of the revolution to develop her musical talent. When she falls in love with Count Julian Von Falkenburg, she is swept up in the sinister conspiracies surrounding Altburg, the ancestral home of his family.

Historical Accuracy: Romantic suspense is primary here, but there are convincing period details and atmosphere.

2805 *Daughter of Marignac*

Date of Publication: 1984
Subject(s): Romance; Franco-Prussian War; Siege of Paris
Fictional character(s): Pierre du Vallon, Artist; Louise du Vallon, Young Woman; James Delamaine, Gentleman
Time Period(s): 19th century (1854-1871)
Locale(s): England; Paris, France; Marignac, France

Summary: Louise du Vallon is the daughter of revolutionary French artist Pierre du Vallon who grows up in exile in England. When she returns to France, she must maintain her loyalty to her father and his cause while adapting to the world of the Second Empire which surrounds her. The action climaxes in the siege of Paris during the Franco-Prussian War.

Historical Accuracy: The atmosphere and period details are authentic and convincing.

2806 *The Fires of Glenlochy*

Date of Publication: 1975
Subject(s): Romance; Jacobite Rebellion
Fictional character(s): Marietta Gilmour, Young Woman; Richard Wynter, Military Personnel (captain)
Time Period(s): 1770s
Locale(s): Highlands, Scotland

Summary: After years of exile in Paris with Bonnie Prince Charlie, Marietta Gilmour returns home to Scotland to claim her legacy, Glenlochy Castle. She is swept up in bitter rivalry, as her kinsmen become her captors. Sustained by the love of English captain Richard Wynter, Marietta attempts to come to terms with present realities.

Historical Accuracy: The novel effectively evokes the Scottish Highland setting and customs.

2807 *Heir to Kuragin*

Date of Publication: 1979
Subject(s): Romance; Russian Empire
Fictional character(s): Anna Crispin, Spouse; Gregory Gadiani, Nobleman; Paul Kuragin, Military Personnel (officer)
Time Period(s): 19th century
Locale(s): Caucasus, Russia; St. Petersburg, Russia

Summary: This romantic novel features the exotic setting of the rugged Caucasus of Russia in the 19th century. Anna Crispin has hastily married the wealthy Gregory Gadiani, her opposite in temperament. Their marriage collapses quickly, and Gregory departs for his country estate. Anna, torn between her duty to Gregory and to the man she loves, obeys her husband's summons to join him. On her journey, she learns about Gregory's disappearance and about his family secrets.

Historical Accuracy: Although the action overshadows the historical period, the atmosphere of 19th-century Russia is convincing.

2808 *The House of Kuragin*

Date of Publication: 1972
Subject(s): Romance; Russian Empire
Fictional character(s): Rilla Weston, Governess, Companion; Andrei Kuragin, Nobleman (count)
Time Period(s): 1810s (1819)
Locale(s): St. Petersburg, Russia

Summary: Rilla Weston is an attractive English girl who takes a position as a companion and governess with the wealthy Kuragin family in Russia during the 1810s. She is quickly drawn into the intrigue of Czarist Russia and the secrets of the Kuragin clan.

Historical Accuracy: The romance is solidly anchored in convincing period details and a well-drawn atmosphere of Imperial Russia.

2809 *Lord of Ravensley*

Date of Publication: 1978
Subject(s): Romance

Fictional character(s): Alyne Aylsham, Foundling; Oliver Aylsham, Gentleman; Clarissa Fenton, Spouse (of Oliver)
Time Period(s): 1820s; 1830s (1829-1833)
Locale(s): East Anglia, England

Summary: This romantic novel is set in the fens of East Anglia in the 1830s and features the struggle to possess the Ravensley estate. Alyne is a foundling rescued from the fens as a child. She is determined to be mistress of Ravensley, deserting her childhood sweetheart, Oliver Aylsham, when it appears he has been supplanted by the return of his uncle. Disaster threatens Oliver's marriage to Clarissa as secrets and a peasant revolt complicate matters.

Historical Accuracy: Atmospheric and suspenseful, the novel masters the regional and period details.

2810 *The Queen and the Gypsy*

Date of Publication: 1977
Subject(s): Elizabethan Period; Royalty—England; Mystery
Historical character(s): Amy Robsart, Gentlewoman, Spouse (of Robert Dudley); Robert Dudley, Nobleman (Earl of Leicester); Elizabeth I, Ruler (Queen of England)
Time Period(s): 16th century (1560-1580s)
Locale(s): England

Summary: The novel explores the famous historical mystery that has puzzled investigators since Elizabethan times: How did Amy Robsart die? She was found dead at the foot of a steep staircase. Was she pushed or poisoned? Was her murderer her husband, who wanted to be free of his wife to marry Elizabeth I? The novel offers its own theory of this famous triangle and puzzle.

Historical Accuracy: The author admits that her version of the events are based on conjecture and unproven allegations from several sources.

2811 *The Wildcliffe Bird*

Date of Publication: 1981
Subject(s): Romance; Chartist Revolt
Fictional character(s): Juliet Prior, Young Woman; Sybil Chartley, Gentlewoman; Richard Chartley, Gentleman
Time Period(s): 1830s
Locale(s): London, England; North Country, England

Summary: Juliet Prior returns to London when her father is killed by a runaway carriage. She accepts a position with Lady Chartley and is soon swept up in a web of scandal involving the Chartley family. Richard Chartley is imprisoned when a young worker in the family's pottery factory is killed during Chartist agitation of the period.

Historical Accuracy: The period details are strongly and convincingly evoked.

2812 *The Wind From the Sea*

Date of Publication: 1991
Subject(s): Romance; French Revolution
Fictional character(s): Isabelle de Sauvigny, Refugee; Guy de Sauvigny, Refugee, Smuggler; Robert Kilgour, Nobleman (viscount)
Time Period(s): 1790s; 1800s (1793-1803)

Locale(s): England; Paris, France

Summary: Guy de Sauvigny and his sister, Isabelle, are refugees from the French Revolution forced to adapt to an English provincial life style. Guy soon becomes involved in dangerous smuggling raids across the channel. Isabelle must deal with the intrigues of London society, a persistent Frenchman, and a marriage that must endure attacks from all sides.

Historical Accuracy: The romantic complications predominate, but the period details are vividly presented.

ANN HEBSON (1925-)

Born in Alabama, Hebson graduated from Grinnel College and has worked as a social worker, an English instructor, and a public relations director. She won the Macmillan Fiction Prize in 1961 for *The Lattimer Legend*.

2813 *The Lattimer Legend*

Date of Publication: 1961
Subject(s): Civil War—U.S.
Fictional character(s): Kate Lattimer, Widow(er)
Time Period(s): 1950s; 1860s
Locale(s): Virginia

Summary: In this novel the breakup of a marriage in the years following the Korean War is juxtaposed with the story of a widow, Kate Lattimer, who loses her husband at Gettysburg and runs away with one of Morgan's Raiders.

Historical Accuracy: The Civil War material is realistic and believable.

PETER J. HECK (1937-)

Born in Baton Rouge, Louisiana, Heck received his B.A. from Louisiana State University. He has worked as a copywriter, copy editor, and creative director in advertising agencies. In addition to his historical novels, he has written nonfiction books with his wife, Suzanne Heck.

2814 *A Connecticut Yankee in Criminal Court*

Date of Publication: 1996
Subject(s): Mystery; Literary Life
Fictional character(s): Wentworth Cabot, Secretary
Historical character(s): Samuel L. Clemens, Writer; George Washington Cable, Writer
Time Period(s): 19th century
Locale(s): New Orleans, Louisiana

Summary: In the second of the author's mysteries employing Mark Twain as a sleuth, Twain arrives in New Orleans while on a lecture tour. There he joins forces with fellow writer George Washington Cable to prove the innocence of a black man who is accused of poisoning his wealthy employer.

Historical Accuracy: The novel features a colorful and convincing tour of period New Orleans.

2815 *Death on the Mississippi*

Date of Publication: 1995
Subject(s): Mystery; Riverboats
Fictional character(s): Wentworth Cabot, Secretary
Historical character(s): Samuel L. Clemens, Writer
Time Period(s): 1890s
Locale(s): Mississippi River; New York, New York

Summary: A dead man is found in New York City with Mark Twain's address in his pocket. The handwriting matches one of Twain's friends from his river boat days. Twain catches a riverboat for New Orleans. Aboard is a colorful collection of river life, including a killer.

Historical Accuracy: Twain's adventures are invented. The story does rely on a historically authentic period background.

URSULA HEGI (1947-)

German-born writer Hegi grew up in a small village near Dusseldorf and moved to the United States when she was 18. Once she realized that Americans knew far more about recent German history than she did, Hegi began to gain an understanding of what happened in Germany during the 20th century. She is currently a teacher of creative writing at Eastern Washington University.

2816 *Stones From the River*

Date of Publication: 1994
Subject(s): Nazis; Holocaust; World War II
Fictional character(s): Trudi Montag, Handicapped (dwarf), Librarian
Time Period(s): 20th century (1915-1952)
Locale(s): Bugdorf, Germany

Summary: The novel features the events and atmosphere of a small German town before, during, and after World War II. The central character is Trudi Montag, a dwarf who becomes the town's librarian and whose status as an outsider provides a unique point of view.

Historical Accuracy: The novel captures with clarity and insight small-town German life during the period.

VERNER VON HEIDENSTAM (1859-1940)

2817 *The Trees of the Folkungs*

Date of Publication: 1907
Subject(s): Middle Ages; Family Saga; Royalty—Sweden
Fictional character(s): Folke Filbyter, Adventurer, Warrior
Historical character(s): Valdemar, Ruler (King of Sweden)
Time Period(s): 11th century; 13th century
Locale(s): Sweden

Summary: This family saga is divided into two parts. The first shows the founding of the Swedish Folkungs family by an adventurer at the end of the 11th century. This brutal, heroic, and primitive age gives way to the history of the family in the 13th century in which descendants have risen to occupy the Swedish throne.

Historical Accuracy: Myth, legend, and fantasy are combined with history to create this panorama of a people and a nation.

MARCY MORAN HEIDISH (1947-)

Born in New York City, Heidish graduated from Vassar College and Catholic University. *A Woman Called Moses* was adapted for TV in 1978.

2818 *Miracles*

Date of Publication: 1984
Subject(s): Religious Life; Biography, Fictionalized
Fictional character(s): Thomas Chandler, Religious (priest)
Historical character(s): Elizabeth Ann Seton, Religious (nun), Teacher
Time Period(s): 18th century; 19th century (1776-1820s)
Locale(s): New York, New York; Baltimore, Maryland

Summary: The story of Elizabeth Seton, America's first canonized saint, is depicted. Her story is narrated from the perspective of a skeptical modern priest investigating her worthiness for sainthood. What emerges is the extraordinary story of her life, her conversion to Catholicism after the death of her husband, and her service as a nun and educator.

Historical Accuracy: Though based on historical fact, the author makes clear that the fictional elements prevent it from being regarded strictly as a biography.

2819 *The Secret Annie Oakley*

Date of Publication: 1983
Subject(s): American West; Theatrical Life
Historical character(s): Annie Oakley, Frontierswoman, Entertainer (sharpshooter); Frank Butler, Entertainer; Sitting Bull, Indian (Sioux), Chieftain; William F. Cody, Frontiersman, Entertainer
Time Period(s): 19th century; 20th century (1866-1906)
Locale(s): Newark, New Jersey; Ohio

Summary: This account of the life of Annie Oakley is told by her husband, Frank Butler, in 1905 when scandal surrounds the famous sharpshooter. Butler attempts to set the record straight and details the facts behind the legend of the frontierswoman who became one of the first great celebrities of the American West.

Historical Accuracy: Scrupulously based on fact and careful to separate the real Annie Oakley from her legend and publicity, the novel offers an authentic portrait of an American original.

2820 *Witnesses*

Date of Publication: 1980
Subject(s): American Colonies; Religious Conflict; Puritans
Historical character(s): Anne Hutchinson, Leader (religious); John Winthrop, Government Official (colonial administrator); John Cotton, Religious (clergyman)
Time Period(s): 17th century (1634-1638)
Locale(s): Boston, Massachusetts, American Colonies

Summary: The novel dramatizes the religious controversy involving Anne Hutchinson in the Massachusetts Bay Colony during the 1630s. She is considered a saint by some and an instrument of Satan by others, particularly the Puritan establishment. The novel details the controversy and makes a convincing case for Hutchinson as a heroic champion of religious freedom.

Historical Accuracy: The novel is based on actual events though the interpretation of the events and of the main character is at variance from sources not as sympathetic to Hutchinson.

2821 *A Woman Called Moses*

Date of Publication: 1976
Subject(s): Slavery; Civil War—U.S.; Underground Railroad
Historical character(s): Harriet Tubman, Slave, Abolitionist
Time Period(s): 19th century (1820s-1865)
Locale(s): Maryland (Eastern Shore)

Summary: Harriet Tubman tells her own story in this fictional memoir. The Civil War has ended and Tubman reflects back on her life as a fugitive slave who returned from freedom to lead as many as 300 fellow slaves north as the legendary conductor called Moses on the underground railroad.

Historical Accuracy: The events described are backed by facts. Some interpretation of Tubman's early years has been necessary to fill in gaps in the historical record.

GEORGE SIDNEY HELLMAN (1878-1958)

A New York City native, Hellman graduated from Columbia University and served in World War I. He worked as an editor and published several books of poems, plays, histories, biographies, and novels, including *Persian Conqueror* and *Peacock's Feather*.

2822 *Persian Conqueror*

Date of Publication: 1935
Subject(s): Persian Empire; Jews
Historical character(s): Cyrus the Great, Ruler (Persian king); Leah, Biblical Figure; Jeremiah, Biblical Figure; Aesop, Writer (storyteller); Croesus, Ruler
Time Period(s): 6th century B.C.
Locale(s): Persia; Babylon

Summary: The novel chronicles events surrounding the Persian Empire and the reign of Cyrus the Great. Cyrus' early years and his relationship with Leah are recounted. The novel also depicts the siege of Sardis and the captivity of the Jews in Babylon.

Historical Accuracy: The novel's historical events are a kind of patchwork of fact, legend, and romance with a diffuseness that undermines realism.

MARK HELPRIN (1947-)

An American novelist and short-story writer, Helprin is the author of *A Dove of the East and Other Stories* and the novel *Refiner's Fire: The Life and Adventures of Marshall Perl, a Foundling*. Helprin has contributed numerous short stories to the *New Yorker*. Helprin joined Bob Dole's 1996 campaign for president as a speechwriter.

2823 *A Soldier of the Great War*

Date of Publication: 1991
Subject(s): World War I
Fictional character(s): Alessandro Giuliani, Veteran (World War I)
Time Period(s): 20th century (1900s-1964)
Locale(s): Italy

Summary: In 1964 the 74-year-old Alessandro Giuliani finds himself walking the 70 kilometers from Rome to Monte Proto along with a young apprentice mechanic. On the way, Giuliani provides a luminous and harrowing account of his life and his experiences in World War I, which include his imprisonment as a deserter and his avoidance of a firing squad.

Historical Accuracy: Deeply felt and evocative, the story provides a convincing reconstruction of the period.

LOIS T. HENDERSON (1918-)

A native of Pennsylvania, Henderson graduated from Grove City College. She has been a high school teacher of political science. Henderson was born blind, and her writing began from a need to share her experiences with others.

2824 *Hagar*

Date of Publication: 1978
Subject(s): Biblical Story
Historical character(s): Abraham, Biblical Figure; Sarah, Biblical Figure; Hagar, Biblical Figure, Slave
Time Period(s): Indeterminate Past
Locale(s): Sinai Peninsula, Egypt

Summary: Based on the Genesis story of Abraham, the novel tells the story of 12-year-old Hagar who is given as a slave to Sarah, Abraham's wife. Sarah is too old to bear children, and Hagar agrees to have Abraham's child.

Historical Accuracy: The novel is close to the Biblical source, with some imaginative amplifications.

SHIRL HENKE

2825 *Night Wind's Woman*

Date of Publication: 1990
Subject(s): Spanish Colonies; Indians; Romance
Fictional character(s): Orlena Valdez, Gentlewoman; Night Wind, Indian (half Apache), Warrior
Time Period(s): 1770s
Locale(s): New Mexico

Summary: Set in Spanish New Mexico during the 1770s, Night Wind, a half-Apache warrior, sets out to kidnap the Spanish governor's son. Instead he takes the governor's niece, Orlena Valdez. Love ensues despite the cultural differences.

Historical Accuracy: The novel features convincing cultural details of the period.

VIRGINIA HENLEY (1935-)

An English writer born in Lancashire, Henley attended the University of Toronto. She worked as an executive secretary and an assistant buyer for Labatts Brewery. She began writing after her mother's illness caused both to begin reading historical romances in earnest.

2826 *The Falcon and the Flower*

Date of Publication: 1989
Subject(s): Middle Ages; Romance; Witchcraft and Sorcery
Fictional character(s): Jasmine, Bastard Daughter; Falcon de Burgh, Knight
Historical character(s): John, Ruler (King of England)
Time Period(s): 13th century
Locale(s): England

Summary: Set in the 13th century, this romantic novel concerns a young woman, Jasmine, who is trained in sorcery. She resists the wealthy Falcon de Burgh and the attentions of King John himself before finding true love.

Historical Accuracy: The period elements are suggested with some believable details.

2827 *The Pirate and the Pagan*

Date of Publication: 1990
Subject(s): Restoration Period; Romance; Pirates
Fictional character(s): Summer St. Catherine, Noblewoman; Ruark Helford, Pirate, Nobleman
Time Period(s): 17th century
Locale(s): England

Summary: Set during the Restoration Period, the romance involves the machinations of Lady Summer St. Catherine who comes to Charles II's court to find a husband to solve her financial problems. She settles on Lord Ruark Helford, but he is not what he seems, and Lady Summer finds herself in the center of political intrigue and piracy.

Historical Accuracy: Highly descriptive, the plot is less believable than the period elements.

MAX HENNESSY
(PSEUD. OF JOHN HARRIS, 1916-1991)

Englishman Hennessy worked as a clerk, reporter, cartoonist, sailor, history teacher, and travel courier before becoming a full-time writer in 1955. A prolific author of adventure stories, Hennessy actually began writing as a student during physics class.

2828 *Back to Battle*

Date of Publication: 1980
Subject(s): Sea Story; World War II; Civil War—Spain
Fictional character(s): Kelly Maguire, Military Personnel (naval officer)
Time Period(s): 1930s; 1940s
Locale(s): At Sea; Spain; England

Summary: The Lion at Sea Trilogy concludes with Kelly Maguire's experiences off the coast of Spain during the Spanish Civil War and in action during World War II.

Historical Accuracy: The novel provides an authentic look at the British Navy of the period.

2829 *Blunted Lance*

Date of Publication: 1981
Subject(s): Military Life; Boer War; World War I
Fictional character(s): Colby William Rollo Goff, Military Personnel (general); Dabney Goff, Military Personnel (cavalry officer)
Historical character(s): Horatio Herbert Kitchener, Military Personnel (general); Winston Churchill, Political Figure; David Lloyd George, Political Figure
Time Period(s): 19th century; 20th century (1898-1918)
Locale(s): Egypt; South Africa; France

Summary: In the second volume of the author's trilogy about the British cavalry in the days of the Empire, Colby Goff is now a general. He and his son Dabney see action against the Dervishes in Egypt, during the Boer War, and during World War I. In each engagement, the story offers the soldier's eye view.

Historical Accuracy: There are authentic details of engagements and a solid knowledge of military matters.

2830 *The Bright Blue Sky*

Date of Publication: 1982
Subject(s): World War I; Aviation
Fictional character(s): Nicholas Dicken Quinney, Pilot, Military Personnel; Cecil Diplock, Gentleman; Annys Toshack, Gentlewoman
Time Period(s): 1910s (1914-1918)
Locale(s): England; France

Summary: In the first novel of a trilogy on the history of the British R.A.F., we are introduced to Nicholas Quinney, a teenager with a passion for flying. With the outbreak of World War I, he rises from mechanic to navigator to one of the newly-formed R.A.F.'s most decorated aces. A romance with Annys Toshack and a rivalry with Cecil Diplock share the stage with the military action.

Historical Accuracy: The flying scenes are authentic and vividly presented.

2831 *The Challenging Heights*

Date of Publication: 1983
Subject(s): Aviation; Russian Revolution
Fictional character(s): Nicholas Dicken Quinney, Pilot, Military Personnel
Time Period(s): 1910s; 1920s (1919-1920)
Locale(s): Russia; Asia (China and India); Middle East

Summary: With World War I over, air ace Quinney seeks further adventures around the world. He battles the Bolsheviks in Russia and is present for Chiang Kai-Shek's rebellion in China, with stops along the way in Iraq and India. The adventure is non-stop as he continuously proves himself on land and in the air.

Historical Accuracy: The pace of the story is breakneck, too rapid for detailed looks at the historical events passing by. The atmosphere, however, is authentic, as are the aviation details.

2832 *The Crimson Wind*

Date of Publication: 1985
Subject(s): Mexican Revolution
Fictional character(s): Harley Marquis, Journalist; Angelica Ojarra, Young Woman
Historical character(s): Francisco Indalecio Madero, Political Figure; Emiliano Zapata, Revolutionary; Francisco Villa, Revolutionary, Outlaw
Time Period(s): 1910s
Locale(s): Mexico

Summary: Harley Marquis is a newspaperman sent to Mexico in the 1910s to cover the revolution. He finds himself swept up in the turmoil of events that follow the overthrow of Porfirio Diaz in 1911.

Historical Accuracy: The book is not meant to be history but fiction based on fact.

2833 *The Dangerous Years*

Date of Publication: 1979
Subject(s): Sea Story; Military Life—British Navy
Fictional character(s): Kelly Maguire, Military Personnel (naval lieutenant)
Time Period(s): 1920s
Locale(s): Russia; China; At Sea

Summary: In the second volume of the Lion at Sea trilogy, Lieutenant Maguire has a series of adventures in Russia, rescuing refugees from the Revolution, and in China.

Historical Accuracy: The period elements are authentically presented.

2834 *The Lion at Sea*

Date of Publication: 1978
Subject(s): World War I; Battle of Jutland; Military Life—British Navy
Fictional character(s): Kelly Maguire, Military Personnel (naval officer); Charlotte Upford, Young Woman
Time Period(s): 1910s (1911-1916)
Locale(s): England; At Sea

Summary: This is the first volume of the Lion at Sea Trilogy depicting the history of the British Navy during World War I and II. The protagonist is a young Anglo-Irishman who is determined to rise in the ranks. The story begins in 1911 when Kelly Maguire rescues a drowning man and is decorated for his courage. The climax of the story is the Battle of Jutland in 1916.

Historical Accuracy: The novel provides convincing and authentic period elements in describing the British Navy during the war.

2835 *The Medicine Whip*

Date of Publication: 1953

Subject(s): American West; Wagon Trains; Indians
Fictional character(s): Whip Braden, Frontiersman; Tracy Brown, Young Woman; Steve Chard, Military Personnel (major)
Time Period(s): 1860s
Locale(s): Wyoming

Summary: Set in the Wyoming territory in the years following the Civil War, the novel describes the triangular relationship between ox train driver Whip Bradon, Tracy Brown, and Army major Steve Chard. They are thrown together during a hazardous journey between Fort Laramie and Fort Gillian.

Historical Accuracy: This is a somewhat conventional romantic story, but it does have a believable period background.

2836 *Once More the Hawks*

Date of Publication: 1984
Subject(s): Aviation; World War II; Espionage
Fictional character(s): Nicholas Dicken Quinney, Pilot, Military Personnel; Cecil Diplock, Gentleman; Zoe Toshack, Pilot
Time Period(s): 1930s; 1940s
Locale(s): Europe; Africa; China

Summary: In the final volume of the author's R.A.F. trilogy, Nicholas Quinney is on the verge of retirement but with the onset of World War II he continues his adventures. They include intelligence work in Germany, a prison escape in France, and military action that takes him from Greece, to North Africa, and China.

Historical Accuracy: Though the pace prevents a thoughtful and full depiction of background and events, the novel does offer authentic military details.

2837 *Soldier of the Queen*

Date of Publication: 1980
Subject(s): Civil War—U.S.; Crimean War; Zulu War
Fictional character(s): Colby William Rollo Goff, Military Personnel (cavalry officer)
Historical character(s): Jeb Stuart, Military Personnel (Confederate officer)
Time Period(s): 19th century (1850s-1875)
Locale(s): Russia; Africa; United States

Summary: The novel details the military adventures of Colby Goff, cavalryman of the 19th Lancers. It chronicles his experiences with the Light Brigade at Balaclava during the Crimean War, his travels in America as a war correspondent riding with Jeb Stuart, his intelligence work during the Franco-Prussian War, and his close brush with death in the Zulu Wars.

Historical Accuracy: The details of military life and the actions described are authentic, even though Goff packs into one life the experiences of several.

FLORETTE HENRI (1908-1985)

An American historian and author, Henri's interest in the problems faced by blacks and American Indians are reflected in such works as *Bitter Victory: Black Soldiers in*

World War I and *Tenants at Will*. She is also the author of the historical drama *The Sword of Gideon*.

2838 *Kings Mountain*

Date of Publication: 1950
Subject(s): American Revolution; Battle of Kings Mountain
Fictional character(s): Reece MacDermott, Military Personnel (American captain); Colonel Ferguson, Military Personnel (British)
Time Period(s): 1780s (1780)
Locale(s): South Carolina

Summary: The novel tells the story of the Southern campaign of the American Revolution, particularly the events that culminate in the important Battle of Kings Mountain. The story centers on the personal duel between patriot captain Reece MacDermott and English officer Colonel Ferguson.

Historical Accuracy: The events described are close to the facts.

WILL HENRY
(PSEUD. OF HENRY ALLEN, 1912-1991)

Widely held to be one of the most preeminent western novelists, Henry was born in Kansas City and began his writing career in 1950 although he had begun submitting stories to magazines when he was 12. Henry left school and headed west to work as a cowhand, horse wrangler, and gold miner. He was determined to depict the West that he had come to know, not the version from the dime novels or Hollywood films. His more than 50 western novels are some of the most respected works in the genre.

2839 *Chiricahua*

Date of Publication: 1972
Subject(s): American West; Indians; Military Life—U.S. Cavalry
Historical character(s): Pa-nayo-tishn, Indian (Chiricahua), Warrior; Geronimo, Indian (Apache), Warrior; Flat Nose, Indian (Chiricahua), Warrior
Time Period(s): 1880s (1883)
Locale(s): Arizona

Summary: In 1883 a band of Chiricahua warriors sweeps up from Mexico on a six-day ride across Arizona. An Indian called Peaches by the whites finds himself caught between the rampaging Apaches and the U.S. Cavalry.

Historical Accuracy: Based on historical incidents, the story is true more to the spirit than to the letter of actual events.

2840 *Death of a Legend*

Date of Publication: 1954
Subject(s): Crime and Criminals; American West
Historical character(s): Jesse James, Outlaw; Frank James, Outlaw; Cole Younger, Outlaw
Time Period(s): 19th century
Locale(s): Missouri; Texas

Summary: The novel attempts a truthful portrait of Jesse James and his short, murderous career. Stripped of the romance that has surrounded the James legend, the novel presents the facts of Jesse James' life based on a solid knowledge of James' life and background.

Historical Accuracy: The novel is faithful to the facts surrounding Jesse James and realistically dismisses much of the glamour that has surrounded his legend.

2841 *From Where the Sun Now Stands*

Date of Publication: 1960
Subject(s): American West; Indians; Tribal Life—Native American
Fictional character(s): Heyets, Indian (Nez Perce), Warrior
Historical character(s): Chief Joseph, Indian (Nez Perce), Chieftain
Time Period(s): 1870s (1874-1877)
Locale(s): Idaho; Montana

Summary: Based on the actual events of the 18-day retreat of Chief Joseph and the Nez Perce Indians from White Bird Canyon in Idaho to the Bear Paws in Montana, the novel details the story from the perspective of an aging member of Chief Joseph's Wallowa band. The Indians fight five pitched battles with the army and must deal with the duplicity of government officials until their final tragic surrender.

Historical Accuracy: The speeches of Joseph and the army officers whom he meets in council are taken from the historical record.

2842 *The Gates of the Mountains*

Date of Publication: 1963
Subject(s): American West; Exploration; Lewis and Clark Expedition
Historical character(s): Meriwether Lewis, Explorer, Military Personnel (captain); William Clark, Explorer, Military Personnel (captain); Francois Rivet, Frontiersman; Sacajawea, Indian (Shoshone), Guide
Time Period(s): 1800s (1804-1806)
Locale(s): Pacific Northwest; Great Plains

Summary: The story of Lewis and Clark's expedition is told by Francois Rivet, a stowaway on the journey who does not return to St. Louis with the explorers. The novel offers his perspective of the journey and his love affair with Sacajawea, for whom he shares a rivalry with Captain Clark.

Historical Accuracy: The account of the expedition is authentic. However, nothing is known of Rivet and subsequently his story is entirely imaginary.

2843 *Journey to Shiloh*

Date of Publication: 1960
Subject(s): Civil War—U.S.; Battle of Corinth; Battle of Shiloh
Fictional character(s): Buck Curnet, Military Personnel (Confederate soldier)
Historical character(s): Albert Sidney Johnston, Military Personnel (Confederate general); Braxton Bragg, Military Personnel (Confederate general)

Time Period(s): 1860s (1862)
Locale(s): Tennessee

Summary: A company of Texas volunteers fight with the Confederacy and find themselves serving in the Army of the Mississippi. They are involved in the battles of Corinth and Shiloh.

Historical Accuracy: The events of the western campaign of the Civil War in 1862 are faithfully presented.

2844 *The Last Warpath*

Date of Publication: 1966
Subject(s): American West; Indians; Tribal Life—Native American
Historical character(s): Black Kettle, Indian (Cheyenne), Chieftain; Dull Knife, Indian (Cheyenne), Warrior; George Armstrong Custer, Military Personnel (cavalry officer); William Tecumseh Sherman, Military Personnel (general); John Milton Chivington, Military Personnel (colonel); George C. Crook, Military Personnel (general)
Time Period(s): 19th century (1850s-1890s)
Locale(s): Great Plains

Summary: The novel traces 40 years of warfare between the Cheyenne and the U.S. Army. The Cheyenne are slow to comprehend the motives of the federal government as settlement inevitably forces them to banishment on the squalid reservations. The great battles of the Indian Wars—Sand Creek, Washita, Rosebud, Little Big Horn, Powder River, and Wounded Knee—are all depicted.

Historical Accuracy: The events depicted are essentially true, with enough fictional cement supplied to bind the historical elements together.

2845 *Mackenna's Gold*

Date of Publication: 1963
Subject(s): American West; Indians; Treasure Hunt
Fictional character(s): Glen Mackenna, Prospector; Pelon, Indian, Outlaw
Time Period(s): 1890s (1897)
Locale(s): Arizona

Summary: Glen Mackenna, a prospector, becomes the sole possessor of the secret location of the famous Lost Adams Diggings—a fabulous deposit of gold. He is forced by Pelon, a half-breed outlaw, to lead him to the treasure. When they reach their destination, a showdown ensues.

Historical Accuracy: The story is fictional but convincing in its details of western life.

2846 *No Survivors*

Date of Publication: 1950
Subject(s): American West; Indians; Battle of the Little Bighorn
Fictional character(s): Colonel Clayton, Military Personnel
Historical character(s): Crazy Horse, Indian (Sioux), Warrior; George Armstrong Custer, Military Personnel (cavalry officer)
Time Period(s): 1870s (1876)
Locale(s): Dakota Territory, United States

Summary: The novel dramatizes the events of the Indian War that climax in the Battle of the Little Big Horn and the Custer massacre. The story is told from the perspective of Clayton, a white man adopted by Crazy Horse, who joins Custer in the great battle.

Historical Accuracy: Although the story has a fictional framework, the account of the period and its events are solidly based on fact.

2847 *One More River to Cross*

Date of Publication: 1967
Subject(s): American West; Racial Conflict
Fictional character(s): Matt Rash, Lawman
Historical character(s): Isom Dart, Cowboy, Gunfighter
Time Period(s): 1870s; 1880s
Locale(s): Fort Worth, Texas; Trinidad, Colorado

Summary: This is the story of real life African-American cowboy and gunfighter Isom Dart. Dart is a slave who runs away to the West and earns a reputation that grows into a western legend. The novel dramatizes the prejudice Dart encounters which he challenges in an epic confrontation.

Historical Accuracy: The essential facts of Dart's life are authentic.

2848 *San Juan Hill*

Date of Publication: 1962
Subject(s): Spanish-American War; Battle of San Juan Hill
Fictional character(s): Fate Baylen, Cowboy, Military Personnel (Rough Rider); Bucky O'Neill, Lawman
Historical character(s): Theodore Roosevelt, Military Personnel
Time Period(s): 1890s
Locale(s): Arizona; Cuba

Summary: The adventures of Teddy Roosevelt's Rough Riders in the Spanish-American War are dramatized. Fate Baylen joins up with Captain Bucky O'Neill, an Arizona sheriff. Through his eyes the Cuban campaign is detailed, including the magnetism of Roosevelt and the intense fighting that culminates in the heroic assault on San Juan Hill.

Historical Accuracy: The basic outline of the events described is accurate.

ANDREW HEPBURN (1899-1975)

Born in Massachusetts, Hepburn was educated at Harvard. During World War II, he spent five years serving on destroyers. He is an architect by profession.

2849 *Letter of Marque*

Date of Publication: 1959
Subject(s): War of 1812; Sea Story
Fictional character(s): Edward Stockton, Sailor
Time Period(s): 1810s (1812)
Locale(s): *The Shark*, At Sea

Summary: Set during the War of 1812, the novel describes the exploits of an American privateer. An insult from the British turns seaman Edward Stockton into an adversary. Aboard a refitted lugger, the *Shark*, Stockton attacks British shipping and dares the might of the British Navy.

Historical Accuracy: The naval action is realistically and authentically depicted.

ALAN PATRICK HERBERT (1890-1971)

An English social reformer, poet, lyricist, playwright, and novelist, Herbert was born in London and became a barrister. A member of Parliament from 1935 to 1950, his greatest achievement was the reform of the British divorce laws. Called the wittiest man of his time, Herbert's first successful book was an account of the horrors of the World War I Gallipoli campaign in which Herbert participated.

2850　*Why Waterloo?*

Date of Publication: 1953
Subject(s): Napoleonic Wars; Battle of Waterloo
Historical character(s): Napoleon Bonaparte, Ruler (French emperor)
Time Period(s): 1810s
Locale(s): Elba, Italy; France; Belgium

Summary: This historical adventure novel tells the story of Napoleon's exile on Elba, his escape, and the 100 days that culminate in Napoleon's final defeat at Waterloo. The novel reconstructs Napoleon's ten-month stay on Elba and the intricate naval mischances that allow his escape to Antibes.

Historical Accuracy: The novel is supported by considerable historical research. When facts are not known, the author supplies some plausible surmises.

KATHLEEN HERBERT

2851　*Bride of the Spear*

Date of Publication: 1988
Subject(s): Dark Ages; Myths and Legends; Celtic Britain
Fictional character(s): Loth, Ruler (King of Lothia); Taniu, Royalty (princess); Owen, Royalty (Prince of Cumbria)
Time Period(s): 7th century
Locale(s): England

Summary: Fifty years after the death of King Arthur his kingdom is split into warring factions battling for supremacy. Cumbria and Lothia intend to form an alliance through the marriage of Lothia's Princess Taniu and Cumbria's Prince Owain. Complications develop from within and without in this tale of treachery and romance.

Historical Accuracy: The details of ancient Britain lend credibility to this fictional tale.

2852　*Queen of the Lightning*

Date of Publication: 1983
Subject(s): Dark Ages; Myths and Legends; Celtic Britain
Fictional character(s): Riemmelth, Royalty (Celtic Queen of Cumbria); Oswy, Royalty (Prince of Northumbria)
Time Period(s): 7th century (641)
Locale(s): Cumbria, Scotland; Northumbria, England

Summary: In this tale of Celtic Britain in the 7th century, the country is controlled by a number of warring tribes anxious to protect their small kingdoms. Riemmelth is the last heir of the Cumbrian royal house, and to insure its survival she must marry a hated enemy, Oswy of Northumbria.

Historical Accuracy: This is an impressive re-creation of ancient Britain.

JOSEPH HERGESHEIMER (1880-1954)

Hergesheimer was an American writer of popular romances. His notable works include *The Lay Anthony*, *Gold and Iron*, and *Linda Condon*.

2853　*Balisand*

Date of Publication: 1924
Subject(s): Politics; Antebellum South
Fictional character(s): Richard Bale, Plantation Owner; Lavinia Roderick, Gentlewoman; Gawin Todd, Plantation Owner
Time Period(s): 1780s; 1790s (1782-1798)
Locale(s): Virginia

Summary: This romantic story of life in Virginia from Washington to Jefferson describes plantation owner Richard Bale's tragic love for Lavinia Roderick. Bale, an ardent Federalist, is opposed by Gawin Todd, a staunch Jeffersonian.

Historical Accuracy: The novel captures the post-Revolutionary period and its political conflicts convincingly.

2854　*Java Head*

Date of Publication: 1919
Subject(s): East/West Relations; Clipper Ships
Fictional character(s): Gerrit Ammidon, Sea Captain; Taou Yuen, Bride; Nettie Vollar, Gentlewoman
Time Period(s): 1840s
Locale(s): Salem, Massachusetts

Summary: The novel examines tragic cultural conflict as a Yankee sea captain brings home a Chinese bride in the days of the clipper ships. Each chapter is narrated from the viewpoint of a different character, lending depth of vision to a contrast of civilizations.

Historical Accuracy: The novel offers a good evocation of the era.

2855　*The Three Black Pennys*

Date of Publication: 1917
Subject(s): Business Building; Family Saga
Fictional character(s): Howat Penny, Businessman (ironmaster); Jasper Penny, Businessman; Howat Penny II, Businessman
Time Period(s): Multiple Time Periods
Locale(s): Pennsylvania (western)

Summary: The Penny family is of English descent except for a Welsh strain that comes out from time to time among descendants. Those possessing the strain are called Black Pennys. The novel is the story of three generations of Black Pennys who mirror the history of American culture from frontiersman to industrialist to effete aristocrat. The novel presents an interesting thesis of the rise and fall of a vibrant and volatile strain in American culture.

Historical Accuracy: There are good descriptions of the early steel mills in Pennsylvania and of frontier life.

RICHARD HERLEY (1950-)

An English author, Herley trained as a biologist.

2856 *The Earth Goddess*

Date of Publication: 1984
Subject(s): Prehistory; Tribal Life—Prehistoric
Fictional character(s): Paoul, Orphan, Heir; Rian, Young Woman
Time Period(s): 31st century B.C.
Locale(s): England

Summary: The final volume of The Pagans series concerns Paoul, the heir of the Valdor domain. He is sold into the priesthood, and the novel describes his disillusionment and illicit passion for his half-brother's wife.

Historical Accuracy: The novel provides a convincing reconstruction of the customs and beliefs of an ancient Neolithic culture.

2857 *The Flint Lord*

Date of Publication: 1981
Subject(s): Prehistory; Tribal Life—Prehistoric
Fictional character(s): Brennis Gehan Fifth, Chieftain, Prehistoric Human; Tagart, Warrior, Prehistoric Human
Time Period(s): 30th century B.C.
Locale(s): England

Summary: In the second volume of "The Pagans" trilogy, the war between Brennis Gehan Fifth, the lord of Valdoe and the nomadic tribes of Stone Age England continues. Tagart understands the danger represented by the Flint lord, but he must earn the might to lead the resistance before mounting a defense of his way of life.

Historical Accuracy: The novel captures with some skill the atmosphere of prehistoric life.

2858 *The Stone Arrow*

Date of Publication: 1978
Subject(s): Prehistory; Tribal Life—Prehistoric
Fictional character(s): Tagart, Warrior, Prehistoric Human; Segle, Prehistoric Human
Time Period(s): 30th century B.C.
Locale(s): England

Summary: This is the first volume of a trilogy called "The Pagans," set in Stone Age England. Tagart is the lone survivor of a savage attack by the new masters, settlers from continental Europe who begin to transform the former nomadic way of life by tilling the soil. Tagart embarks on a campaign of vengeance.

Historical Accuracy: The novel offers a plausible view of Stone Age Britain.

HANS HERLIN

2859 *Grishin*

Date of Publication: 1987
Subject(s): Russian Revolution
Fictional character(s): Lloyd Fleming, Diplomat; Mikhail Grishin, Spy
Historical character(s): Vladimir Ilich Lenin, Revolutionary
Time Period(s): 1910s (1918)
Locale(s): Russia

Summary: The turbulence of the early days of the Russian Revolution forms the backdrop for this political thriller. The British government sends Lloyd Fleming to negotiate with the Bolsheviks and assigns Mikhail Grishin the task of assassinating Lenin should the negotiations fail.

Historical Accuracy: The novel merges fact and fiction and takes a number of liberties with history to provide its suspense.

GEORGE HERMAN (1929-)

American-born novelist, short story writer, and children's fiction writer Herman taught English at Arizona State University and published several books on grammar and composition. He was also an actor, director, drama critic, and prize-winning playwright for over 40 years before beginning his first novel, *Carnival of Saints*, in 1994 at the age of 65.

2860 *Carnival of Saints*

Date of Publication: 1994
Subject(s): Theatrical Life; Renaissance
Fictional character(s): Vittorio Bracciolini, Actor; Colombia Fortini, Prostitute, Actress; Scapino Petrucci, Entertainer (juggler)
Historical character(s): Cesare Borgia, Nobleman, Military Personnel; Alexander VI, Religious (pope); Lucrezia Borgia, Noblewoman; Leonardo da Vinci, Artist, Inventor
Time Period(s): 16th century (1502)
Locale(s): Italy

Summary: The novel tells the story of the creation of commedia dell'arte—developed by a wanderer from the north called Harlequin who forms a company made up of a whore, a juggling pickpocket, Leonardo da Vinci's artistic assistant, and a host of other colorful period characters. Art falls foul of the treacherous Borgias who set out to suppress the new irreverant popular art form.

Historical Accuracy: The novel meticulously re-creates the period. The joy is the mixture of high and low characters, art and politics, in a bawdy and colorful romp through the past.

2861 *A Comedy of Murders*

Date of Publication: 1994
Subject(s): Mystery; Renaissance; Artistic Life
Fictional character(s): Niccolo, Entertainer

Historical character(s): Leonardo da Vinci, Artist, Inventor; Ludovico Sforza, Nobleman (Duke of Milan); Louis de Valois, Royalty (Duc d' Orleans)
Time Period(s): 15th century (1498)
Locale(s): Milan, Italy

Summary: In this witty and accomplished historical mystery, Leonardo da Vinci joins forces with a talented dwarf, Niccolo, to solve a series of baffling mysteries in the court of the Duke of Milan. An assassin ring is operating within the court itself, and a number of cardinals begin to die under odd circumstances. Leonardo must use his expertise in anatomy and his inventions, including a flying machine, to get to the bottom of the conspiracy.

Historical Accuracy: The knowledge of the period is shown with accomplishment.

`2862` The Tears of the Madonna

Date of Publication: 1996
Subject(s): Mystery; Renaissance
Historical character(s): Leonardo da Vinci, Artist
Time Period(s): 15th century (1499-1500)
Locale(s): Milan, Italy; Mantua, Italy; Venice, Italy

Summary: In this Renaissance-era mystery, the sleuth is Leonardo da Vinci who is asked to investigate the disappearance of a necklace called "The Tears of the Madonna." Suspicion falls on the Marquesa of Mantua, and Leonardo is soon embroiled in a series of deadly mysteries, including a decayed human head that might provide an answer to the whereabouts of the necklace.

Historical Accuracy: The novel is filled with authentic period color and a believable historical background.

MICHAEL HERR (1940-)

American writer Herr covered the war in Vietnam for *Esquire*. His experiences were collected in *Dispatches*, which has been called the best book written about the Vietnam War. He is the co-author of the screenplay for the film *Apocalypse Now*.

`2863` Walter Winchell: A Novel

Date of Publication: 1990
Subject(s): Journalism; Biography, Fictionalized
Historical character(s): Walter Winchell, Journalist (columnist); Damon Runyon, Writer; Ernest Hemingway, Writer; Sherman Billingsley, Businessman, Organized Crime Figure; Roy Cohn, Lawyer
Time Period(s): 1930s; 1940s (1939-1947)
Locale(s): New York, New York

Summary: Told in cinematic style, the novel depicts the life and times of Walter Winchell, the sharp-witted, hated, and hateful gossip columnist and star-maker who commanded a loyal daily audience of 50 million. Winchell's world, Table 50 at the Stork Club, is the locus for Herr's exploration of celebrity, gossip, and power.

Historical Accuracy: The novel is based on Winchell's biography and often uses his actual words.

LAMAR HERRIN (1940-)

A native of Atlanta, Georgia, Herrin graduated from the University of Kentucky, the University of Tennessee, and the University of Cincinnati. He is a professor of English at Cornell University. His books include *The Lies Boys Tell* and *American Baroque*.

`2864` The Unwritten Chronicles of Robert E. Lee

Date of Publication: 1991
Subject(s): Civil War—U.S.; Military Life
Historical character(s): Robert E. Lee, Military Personnel (Confederate commander); Thomas Jonathan Jackson, Military Personnel (Confederate general)
Time Period(s): 1860s (1863-1865)
Locale(s): Virginia

Summary: The novel provides a lyrical and psychological study of two of the leading figures of the Confederacy— Stonewall Jackson and Robert E. Lee. As the story opens, Jackson is victorious at Winchester and Lee assumes overall command of the Army of Northern Virginia. The action continues in a montage of letters and musings with an emphasis on character rather than fact and chronology.

Historical Accuracy: More impressionistic than thorough in its history, the novel does not provide an insider's perspective on the campaigns, but rather psychological portraits of Lee and Jackson.

VIRGINIA DAVIS HERSCH (1906-)

An American writer born in San Francisco, Hersch writes vivid novels teeming with historical detail. Her books include *Bird of God: The Romance of El Greco*, *Woman under Glass: St. Teresa of Avila*, and *The Seven Cities of Gold*.

`2865` The Seven Cities of Gold

Date of Publication: 1946
Subject(s): Exploration; Treasure Hunt
Fictional character(s): Carlos, Explorer
Historical character(s): Francisco Vasquez de Coronado, Explorer
Time Period(s): 16th century
Locale(s): Mexico; Southwest, North America

Summary: The novel provides a fictional account of the second of Spanish explorer Coronado's searches for gold in the Southwest. The journey is recounted by Carlos, a member of the expedition. Their journey takes them from Mexico into present day Texas and Kansas on a fruitless search for the fabled seven cities of gold.

Historical Accuracy: The novel is factual and authentic in its documentation of Coronado's expedition.

`2866` To Seize a Dream

Date of Publication: 1948
Subject(s): Biography, Fictionalized; Artistic Life

Historical character(s): Eugene Delacroix, Artist
Time Period(s): 18th century; 19th century (1798-1863)
Locale(s): France

Summary: This fictional biography traces the life and career of French painter Eugene Delacroix, considered the foremost painter of the romantic movement in France. The painter's artistic development and involvement with the art world of the 19th century are described.

Historical Accuracy: The basis for the novel's events and chronology is the painter's journal and letters, which creates a strong sense of authenticity.

MILDRED BARGER HERSCHLER

Born in West Virginia, Herschler's poems have appeared in *The Crisis*, and she is the author of *Frederick Douglass*, a biography for children.

2867 *The Walk into Morning*

Date of Publication: 1993
Subject(s): Civil War—U.S.; Slavery
Fictional character(s): Chap, Slave, Teenager; Anna, Slave; Blake Durand, Military Personnel (scout)
Time Period(s): 1860s (1862-1863)
Locale(s): New Orleans, Louisiana

Summary: Louisiana in 1862-1863 is depicted from the perspective of a young slave turned soldier. His experiences in battle are paralleled by the young slave woman, Anna, who has followed him out of slavery to shelter in a New Orleans where she experiences the Union occupation.

Historical Accuracy: The period elements are cast into a believable backdrop for the story.

JOHN HERSEY (1914-1993)

Born in Tientsin, China, the son of missionaries, Hersey returned to the U.S. with his family in 1925. He studied at Yale and Cambridge universities and served for a time as Sinclair Lewis' private secretary. Hersey worked as a journalist and won a Pulitzer Prize for his novel *A Bell for Adano*. He is most admired for his nonfiction work, particularly his coverage of the atomic bombing in *Hiroshima* and the race riots in Detroit in *The Algiers Hotel Incident*.

2868 *Antonietta*

Date of Publication: 1991
Subject(s): Musical Life
Historical character(s): Wolfgang Amadeus Mozart, Composer; Antonio Stradivari, Artisan (violin maker); Louis Hector Berlioz, Composer; Igor Stravinsky, Composer
Time Period(s): Multiple Time Periods
Locale(s): Cremora, Italy; Paris, France; Martha's Vineyard, Massachusetts

Summary: The novel tells the story of a Stradivarius violin over its 300-year odyssey from its creation through its possession by a variety of owners. The instrument is named An-

tonietta by its creator, the great Stradivarius, and it affects the lives of Mozart, Berlioz, Stravinsky, and others.

Historical Accuracy: The novel captures the world of music with conviction.

2869 *The Call*

Date of Publication: 1985
Subject(s): Chinese Empire; Religious Life; Revolution—China
Fictional character(s): David Treadup, Religious (missionary); Emily Treadup, Spouse
Time Period(s): 20th century (1900-1940s)
Locale(s): Syracuse, New York; China

Summary: The novel offers the fictional biography of an American missionary to China, David Treadup. Sent by the Y.M.C.A. to China in 1900, his experiences dealing with cultural differences and his own spirituality reflect as well the history of China in the early 20th century. Years of triumphs and frustration are dramatized in this vivid story of a time and a place.

Historical Accuracy: Obviously based on Hersey's own family experience, the novel captures China of the period with feeling and exactitude.

2870 *The Conspiracy*

Date of Publication: 1972
Subject(s): Roman Empire; Politics
Fictional character(s): Tigellinus, Military Personnel (commander, Praetorian Guard); Paenus, Government Official (tribune of secret police)
Historical character(s): Nero, Ruler (Roman emperor); Lucan, Writer (poet); Lucius Annaeus Seneca, Writer
Time Period(s): 1st century (64)
Locale(s): Rome, Roman Empire

Summary: The reign of the Roman emperor Nero is chronicled. Nero, who was once a friend of poets, is now dominated by the military and secret police, who are busy rooting out evidence of a conspiracy by men of letters, notably Lucan and Seneca. The novel is told in the secret communiques among government agents.

Historical Accuracy: The author points out that, while historical sources were consulted, the novel is intended as entertainment, not history.

OLGA HESKY (?-1974)

An English novelist and scriptwriter, Hesky was born in London and attended the University of London. Prior to 1949, she was a reporter, editor, and film and theater critic for newspapers in England and South Africa. Her books include *The Serpent's Smile* and *The Different Night*.

2871 *The Painted Queen*

Date of Publication: 1961
Subject(s): Biblical Story; Ancient Israel
Historical character(s): Jezebel, Biblical Figure; Ahab, Biblical Figure; Elijah, Religious (prophet)

Time Period(s): Indeterminate Past
Locale(s): Israel

Summary: In this version of the Biblical story of Jezebel, instead of being wicked, she is a loving wife and a patriot dedicated to a united and strong Israelite kingdom. Her nemesis is the fanatical prophet Elijah, who hates her because of her refusal to accept Yahweh as the one true god.

Historical Accuracy: The period elements are buttressed with some authentic details, but the author's interpretation seems particularly dominated by her own times.

WILLIAM HEUMAN (1912-1971)

An American writer born in Brooklyn, New York, Heuman worked as a clerk for 12 years before becoming a freelance writer in 1950. He contributed nearly 600 short stories and novellas to various magazines and wrote a large number of western novels.

2872 *Captain McRae: A Novel of the Northwest Frontier*

Date of Publication: 1954
Subject(s): American West; Indians
Fictional character(s): Brant McRae, Sea Captain (riverboat)
Time Period(s): 1870s
Locale(s): Missouri River, United States

Summary: Riverboat captain Brant McRae attempts to deliver guns to the soldiers at a remote outpost on the Missouri River. He must contend with natural obstacles and the Sioux, who are on the warpath.

Historical Accuracy: Romance and adventure predominate over careful documentation of the past.

GEORGETTE HEYER (1902-1974)

Heyer was an English romance novelist considered the Queen of the Regency Romance. Though her books are considered light and ''frothy'' entertainment, her scrupulous period backgrounds and authentic dialogue separate her novels from other Regency romances. She also wrote a number of mystery novels in a career that spanned almost fifty years.

2873 *April Lady*

Date of Publication: 1957
Subject(s): Mystery; Regency Romance
Fictional character(s): Giles Merion, Nobleman (Earl of Cardross); Nell Merion, Noblewoman (Countess of Cardross); Lady Letitia Merion, Noblewoman (Cardross' sister)
Time Period(s): 1810s
Locale(s): London, England

Summary: The most brilliant match of the London social season is the marriage between wealthy Lord Cardross and beautiful Lady Nell. But she has a secret from her husband: she is deeply in debt. When the priceless Cardross jewels disappear,

all the evidence points to Nell. Will the solution cost or reveal the newlyweds' love for one another?.

Historical Accuracy: This is an engaging combination of romance, mystery, and period detail, but some have criticized the novel for a series of period inaccuracies.

2874 *Arabella*

Date of Publication: 1949
Subject(s): Regency Romance
Fictional character(s): Arabella Tallant, Gentlewoman; Robert Beaumaris, Gentleman
Time Period(s): 1800s
Locale(s): London, England; Yorkshire, England

Summary: The novel is an amusing comedy of manners involving a poor parson's daughter thrust into the heart of fashionable London. All the ton are under the impression that she has a considerable fortune, which attracts the attention of a number of fortune-hunters and a wealthy leader of society.

Historical Accuracy: The novel offers a compendium of the lifestyles of the London rich and famous, including a party at Carleton House, the home of the Regent.

2875 *Bath Tangle*

Date of Publication: 1955
Subject(s): Regency Romance
Fictional character(s): Lady Serena Carlow, Noblewoman; Fanny Carlow, Widow(er), Noblewoman (Countess of Spenborough); Ivo Barrasford, Nobleman (Marquis of Rotherham)
Time Period(s): 1810s
Locale(s): Bath, England

Summary: Two young women, a recently widow and her stepdaughter, move to Bath in the hope of recovering from their bereavement. To her chagrin, Serena finds that her inheritance is controlled by the Marquis of Rotherham, whom she has recently jilted. In Bath, Fanny and Serena become entangled in a series of romantic complications, prompting the stern disapproval of the marquis, who has his own plans for both women, especially Serena.

Historical Accuracy: The romance is set in the background of Regency Bath, the idle playground of society.

2876 *Beauvallet*

Date of Publication: 1929
Subject(s): Sea Story; Elizabethan Period; Pirates
Fictional character(s): Nicholas Beauvallet, Pirate, Sea Captain; Dominica de Rada y Sylva, Noblewoman
Historical character(s): Elizabeth I, Ruler (Queen of England); Sir Francis Drake, Sea Captain; Philip II, Ruler (King of Spain); Martin Frobisher, Explorer, Sea Captain
Time Period(s): 16th century
Locale(s): England; *Venture*, At Sea (West Indies, Spanish Main); Spain

Summary: Sir Nicholas Beauvallet is an adventurer and pirate captain working the Spanish Main. He captures a Spanish lady and her father, returns them to Spain, and then returns in disguise to woo her and return with her to England.

Historical Accuracy: The novel is full of high-powered adventure, more Hollywood than Elizabethan, but the background of the period is adequate.

2877 *The Black Moth*

Date of Publication: 1929
Subject(s): Georgian Period; Crime and Criminals; Romance
Fictional character(s): John Carstares, Highwayman, Nobleman (Earl of Wyncham); Diana Beauleigh, Gentlewoman; Tracy Belmanoir, Nobleman (Duke of Andover), Rake
Time Period(s): 18th century
Locale(s): London, England; Bath, England

Summary: When his younger brother cheats at cards, John Carstares assumes the blame. Cast out of polite society, he becomes a highwayman. One night, he rescues Diana Beauleigh from abduction by the sinister Duke of Andover. Although he falls in love with her, John refuses to let Diana marry him because of his supposed disgrace. However, Andover's continued designs on Diana force John into a confrontation with the duke.

Historical Accuracy: In this costume romance the 18th-century atmosphere is cleverly recreated. The novel was considered somewhat old fashioned even when it was published in the 1920s.

2878 *Black Sheep*

Date of Publication: 1966
Subject(s): Regency Romance
Fictional character(s): Abigail Wendover, Gentlewoman; Stacy Calverleigh, Gentleman; Miles Calverleigh, Gentleman, Rake; Fanny Wendover, Heiress
Time Period(s): 1800s
Locale(s): Bath, England

Summary: In fashionable Bath at the height of the Regency Period, Abigail protects her niece from an apparent fortune-hunter only to encounter his eccentric uncle—the black sheep of the family—who seems to show up everywhere Abigail does, disturbing the social whirl of Bath.

Historical Accuracy: This is an amusing battle of wits set in fashionable Bath.

2879 *Charity Girl*

Date of Publication: 1970
Subject(s): Regency Romance
Fictional character(s): Cherry Steane, Ward; Ashley Carrington, Nobleman (Viscount Desford); Henrietta Silverdale, Gentlewoman
Time Period(s): 1810s
Locale(s): Hertfordshire, England; London, England

Summary: In this Heyer Regency romance, Lord Desford takes pity on poor Cherry Steane who comes to him with more than he bargains for: a needy grandfather and a rascally father. How to extricate himself from this charitable burden is the challenge that faces Desford.

Historical Accuracy: Heyer's blend of romance with realism of the period and customs is expertly delivered.

2880 *A Civil Contract*

Date of Publication: 1962
Subject(s): Regency Romance
Fictional character(s): Adam Deveril, Nobleman (impoverished viscount); Jenny Chawleigh, Heiress
Time Period(s): 1810s
Locale(s): England

Summary: The plot concerns a marriage of convenience between poor Adam Deveril and plain, though wealthy, Jenny Chawleigh.

Historical Accuracy: This is unusual Heyer in the sense that the novel's mercenary premise is decidedly unromantic, but romance is the novel's ultimate destination.

2881 *The Conqueror*

Date of Publication: 1931
Subject(s): Norman Conquest; Biography, Fictionalized; Middle Ages
Fictional character(s): Raoul de Harcourt, Nobleman, Knight; Edgar of Marwell, Nobleman (Saxon thegn)
Historical character(s): William the Conqueror, Ruler (Duke of Normandy); Harold II, Ruler (King of England); Robert I the Magnificent, Nobleman (Duke of Normandy); Matilda of Flanders, Noblewoman
Time Period(s): 11th century (1028-1066)
Locale(s): Normandy, France; Hastings, England; London, England

Summary: This fictionalized biography of William the Conqueror takes him from his birth as the bastard son of Count Robert, his youth, his wooing of and marriage to Matilda of Flanders, and the intrigues and battles with Kings Henry of France and Harold of England, culminating in the battle of Hastings. Throughout William is shown as a shrewd and driven man, yet one who is capable of earning the loyalty of men like Raoul de Harcourt, who becomes William's close friend and confidante.

Historical Accuracy: The novel is filled with authentic details of dress, speech, and customs of both the Normans and the Saxons.

2882 *The Convenient Marriage*

Date of Publication: 1934
Subject(s): Georgian Period
Fictional character(s): Horatia Winwood, Noblewoman; Robert Lethbridge, Nobleman (viscount), Rake; Marcus Drelincourt, Nobleman (Earl of Rule)
Time Period(s): 1780s
Locale(s): London, England

Summary: Seventeen-year-old Horatia Winwood rescues her older sister from an undesired marriage to Lord Rule by marrying him herself. She then falls prey to the advances of the rakish Lord Lethbridge who attempts to blackmail her. The major part of the story concerns Horatia's efforts to clear her reputation and to win the love of her husband.

Historical Accuracy: The novel is fast-paced with an interesting heroine with a stammer. There are good details of the lives of the English aristocracy.

2883 *Cotillion*

Date of Publication: 1953
Subject(s): Regency Romance
Fictional character(s): Kitty Charing, Heiress; Jack Westruther, Gentleman; Freddy Standen, Gentleman
Time Period(s): 1800s
Locale(s): London, England

Summary: In this comedy of manners, Kitty must marry one of her guardian's nephews in order to inherit his fortune. Her preference is for the handsome Jack, who is not interested. To force his hand, Kitty engineers an engagement to his frivolous cousin, Freddy. However, Freddy is more than he appears on the surface, and Kitty's mock engagement may turn out to be more than she had planned.

Historical Accuracy: This is classic Heyer, with a solid background of period detail.

2884 *Cousin Kate*

Date of Publication: 1968
Subject(s): Regency Romance
Fictional character(s): Kate Malvern, Orphan; Minerva Broome, Gentlewoman; Philip Broome, Gentleman; Torquil Broome, Mentally Ill Person
Time Period(s): 1800s
Locale(s): England

Summary: Kate Malvern is recently orphaned and unexpectedly receives an invitation from an unknown aunt to make her home at the Broome estate. Quite out of character, her aunt treats Kate with considerable kindness. Once a nephew arrives, the aunt's motive for bringing Kate to their home is revealed.

Historical Accuracy: A departure for Heyer, the novel is Gothic in tone, but includes her expected treatment of period detail.

2885 *Devil's Cub*

Date of Publication: 1932
Subject(s): Georgian Period; Romance
Fictional character(s): Dominic Alastair, Nobleman (Marquis of Vidal); Leonie Alastair, Noblewoman (Duchess of Avon); Mary Challoner, Gentlewoman; Justin Alastair, Nobleman (Duke of Avon)
Time Period(s): 1780s
Locale(s): London, England; Paris, France; Dijon, France

Summary: In this sequel to Heyer's *These Old Shades*, the Marquis of Vidal, son of the Duke of Avon, must flee to France after a duel. He plans to take along a young woman who thinks that the marquis can be trapped into marriage. However, her straightlaced sister, Mary, knowing that Vidal's intentions are not honorable, substitutes herself instead. Feeling that he has compromised a gentlewoman, Vidal attempts to force Mary into marriage and must chase his reluctant bride across France.

Historical Accuracy: The plot is fast-paced and true to the milieu of high-society customs.

2886 *False Colours*

Date of Publication: 1964
Subject(s): Regency Romance
Fictional character(s): Evelyn Fancot, Nobleman (Earl of Denville), Twin; Cressida Stavely, Gentlewoman; Christopher "Kit" Fancot, Twin, Diplomat; Amabel Fancot, Noblewoman (dowager countess of Denville), Parent (Evelyn and Kit's)
Time Period(s): 1810s
Locale(s): London, England

Summary: To restore his family's fortune, the Earl of Denville proposes marriage to a woman he does not love. When he mysteriously disappears just before an engagement to meet his fiancee's relatives, his identical twin brother, Kit, takes his place. The earl's continued absence forces Kit to keep up his impersonation. Complications follow when Kit falls in love with Cressida, his brother's intended bride.

Historical Accuracy: This improbable story is bolstered by expected detailed and accurate portraits of the period.

2887 *Faro's Daughter*

Date of Publication: 1941
Subject(s): Regency Romance
Fictional character(s): Max Ravenscar, Gentleman; Adrian Mablethorpe, Nobleman; Deborah Grantham, Gambler
Time Period(s): 1800s
Locale(s): London, England

Summary: Max Ravenscar sets out to break up the romance between his young cousin and a woman who runs a gambling house. However, he becomes attracted to her himself in this Regency romance set against the background of the gaming upper class.

Historical Accuracy: Heyer offers many details of high stylish life in London.

2888 *The Foundling*

Date of Publication: 1948
Subject(s): Regency Romance
Fictional character(s): Gillespie Vernon Ware, Nobleman (Duke of Sale); Belinda, Foundling; Lady Harriet Presteigne, Noblewoman, Fiance(e)
Time Period(s): 1810s
Locale(s): London, England; Bath, England

Summary: This is a fanciful comic tale of riches to rags, or at least a duke's desire to venture beyond fashionable London and Bath. He is guided by an entourage of commoners including the fair Belinda, a foundling, into a series of adventures, some comic, others dangerous.

Historical Accuracy: Heyer provides good details of fashionable life and country life.

2889 *Frederica*

Date of Publication: 1965
Subject(s): Regency Romance

Fictional character(s): Frederica Merrivale, Gentlewoman; Vernon Dauntry, Nobleman (Marquis of Alverstoke); Charis Merrivale, Debutante
Time Period(s): 1820s
Locale(s): London, England

Summary: Set at the height of Regency London's social season, this comedy of manners centers on the Merrivale family, respectable but without fortune. Twenty-four-year-old Frederica applies to a distant cousin for an introduction to society to afford her younger sister a chance in the marriage market. Soon the entire family begins to depend on Lord Alverstoke.

Historical Accuracy: There are interesting scenes of Regency England. Beyond the opera and balls, there is a scene of a balloon launching and a trip by steam down the Thames.

2890 *Friday's Child*

Date of Publication: 1946
Subject(s): Regency Romance
Fictional character(s): Anthony "Sherry" Sheringham, Nobleman (Viscount Sheringham); Hero Wantage, Orphan
Time Period(s): 1800s
Locale(s): London, England

Summary: In this fanciful Regency comedy, Lord Sheringham must marry to gain control of his fortune. Rejected by one woman, who considers him a rake, and criticized as a wastrel by his austere mother, he threatens to marry the next woman he sees. This turns out to be the orphaned Hero Wantage, a childhood friend. They elope, then go to London where the naive Hero learns society's ways, and they both learn the meaning of maturity, love, and marriage.

Historical Accuracy: This is a delightful comedy whose background of period details anchors a fairy-tale story.

2891 *The Grand Sophy*

Date of Publication: 1950
Subject(s): Regency Romance
Fictional character(s): Sophia Stanton-Lacy, Gentlewoman; Charles Rivenhall, Gentleman
Time Period(s): 1810s
Locale(s): London, England

Summary: Heyer's heroine is impulsive and head-strong, a far cry from the blushing, proper ladies of the ton. Sophy bursts on the fashionable London social scene to the shock of her proper aunt but to the delight and fascination of everyone else. Her overbearing cousin Charles eventually surrenders to her attractions.

Historical Accuracy: Heyer is at home in fashionable London, and she is able to expertly render the background for her comedy.

2892 *An Infamous Army*

Date of Publication: 1938
Subject(s): Napoleonic Wars; Battle of Waterloo
Fictional character(s): Barbara Childe, Noblewoman, Widow(er); Charles Audley, Military Personnel (member of Wellington's staff)

Historical character(s): Arthur Wellesley, Military Personnel
Time Period(s): 1810s (1815)
Locale(s): Brussels, Belgium; Waterloo, Belgium

Summary: The Hundred Days culminating at the Battle of Waterloo are seen through the eyes of a group of English aristocrats. The romance between the "Fatal Widow," Barbara Childe, and Charles Audley, a British army officer on Wellington's staff, plays out against this backdrop.

Historical Accuracy: Heyer is best in the social whirl prior to battle. Her preference for glamour at times clashes with the reality of the battlefield.

2893 *Lady of Quality*

Date of Publication: 1972
Subject(s): Regency Romance
Fictional character(s): Annis Wychwood, Gentlewoman; Lucilla Carleton, Heiress; Oliver Carleton, Guardian
Time Period(s): 1810s
Locale(s): Bath, England

Summary: The setting for this romance is Regency Bath with its dances, teas, and famous Pump Room. Miss Annis Wychwood is rich and independent, and, at 29, long past marriageable age. Into her life come 17-year-old heiress Lucilla and Lucilla's guardian, Oliver Carleton, considered to be the rudest man in London.

Historical Accuracy: The novel features a charming heroine and an irresistible hero in scenes that are filled with period color.

2894 *The Masqueraders*

Date of Publication: 1929
Subject(s): Georgian Period; Jacobite Rebellion; Identity—Concealed
Fictional character(s): Prudence Lacey, Imposter (aka Peter Merriot); Robin Lacey, Imposter (aka Kate Merriot); Sir Anthony Fanshawe, Nobleman; Robert Tremaine, Adventurer, Heir—Lost; Letitia Grayson, Heiress
Time Period(s): 1740s
Locale(s): London, England

Summary: In hiding because of his participation in the Jacobite Rebellion of 1745, Robin Lacey disguises himself as a woman, while his sister, Prudence, masquerades as a man. They save Letty Grayson from an elopement that turns into an attempted abduction. Complications ensue when Robin falls in love with Letty, who thinks he is a woman. Prudence falls for Sir Anthony Fanshawe, Letty's erstwhile fiance, who thinks she is a man. Adding to the confusion is the sudden appearance of Robin and Prudence's adventurer father, Robert Tremaine, who is suddenly claiming to be the long-lost heir to a noble title.

Historical Accuracy: The plot is more inventive than credible.

2895 *My Lord John*

Date of Publication: 1976
Subject(s): Middle Ages; Royalty—England

Historical character(s): John, Duke of Bedford, Royalty (prince); Henry IV, Ruler (King of England); Henry V, Ruler (King of England); Richard II, Ruler (King of England)
Time Period(s): 14th century; 15th century (1393-1413)
Locale(s): England; Scotland

Summary: This is the first and only volume completed of a proposed trilogy on the House of Lancaster. The story opens at the end of the reign of Richard II. Henry Bolingbroke seizes the throne, and his family is at the center of the drama, particularly his younger son John who fights for his father against the Scots and others disloyal to the crown.

Historical Accuracy: The novel is thoroughly researched, using period vocabulary. This is a meticulously detailed recreation.

2896 The Nonesuch

Date of Publication: 1963
Subject(s): Regency Romance
Fictional character(s): Sir Waldo Hawkridge, Nobleman, Philanthropist; Ancilla Trent, Governess
Time Period(s): 1800s
Locale(s): Yorkshire, England

Summary: A wealthy bachelor and leader of fashion, called the Nonesuch for his athletic prowess, inherits an estate in Yorkshire. His visit causes a general stir in village life, particularly among the females who look forward to the arrival of the ton in their rural world.

Historical Accuracy: The novel is something of a departure for Heyer who goes outside her normal fashionable London scenes for the details of English country life.

2897 The Quiet Gentleman

Date of Publication: 1952
Subject(s): Regency Romance
Fictional character(s): Gervais Frant, Nobleman (Earl of St. Erth); Drusilla Morville, Gentlewoman; Lucius Austell, Nobleman (Viscount Ulverston); Martin Frant, Gentleman (St. Erth's half-brother); Theodore Frant, Gentleman (St. Erth's cousin), Steward
Time Period(s): 1810s
Locale(s): England

Summary: A soldier returns from the Napoleonic Wars to claim his inheritance as the Earl of St. Erth. He discovers, however, that his return is not a joy to all, and a mystery ensues in which he survives several attempts on his life.

Historical Accuracy: The novel is a combination of mystery and historical romance. The period description is strong, although the characters are somewhat thin.

2898 Regency Buck

Date of Publication: 1935
Subject(s): Regency Romance
Fictional character(s): Judith Taverner, Heiress, Ward; Sir Peregrine Taverner, Nobleman, Ward; Julian Audley, Nobleman (Earl of Worth), Guardian
Historical character(s): William, Duke of Clarence, Royalty (brother of the Regent); George Bryan Brummell, Gentleman

Time Period(s): 1810s
Locale(s): Yorkshire, England; London, England; Brighton, England

Summary: Romantic complications follow a brother and sister who journey from Yorkshire to London to meet the guardian appointed by their eccentric father. Their treatment by the guardian is a mystery. All is confused until the final curtain.

Historical Accuracy: The novel is filled with period references and details.

2899 The Reluctant Widow

Date of Publication: 1946
Subject(s): Regency Romance
Fictional character(s): Elinor Rochdale, Governess; Edward Carlyon, Nobleman
Time Period(s): 1800s
Locale(s): Sussex, England

Summary: Elinor Rochdale arrives at the estate of Lord Carlyon by mistake. Instead of a job as a governess, she is offered a position as the wife of Carlyon's dying cousin. Carlyon presses her into accepting, and in short order Elinor finds herself widowed and in possession of an impoverished estate. She is also bedeviled by housebreakers, French spies, and her growing attraction to Lord Carlyon.

Historical Accuracy: The implausibility of the central conceit is at least anchored in the solid details of an English country estate.

2900 Royal Escape

Date of Publication: 1938
Subject(s): Civil War—England; Royalty—England
Fictional character(s): Jane Lane, Young Woman
Historical character(s): Charles, Prince of Wales, Royalty (later Charles II); George Villiers, Nobleman (Duke of Buckingham), Courtier; John Wilmot, Nobleman (Earl of Rochester), Courtier
Time Period(s): 17th century (1651)
Locale(s): Worcester, England

Summary: The novel is based on the historic events of Charles II, who invades England with a Scottish army and is defeated by Cromwell's forces at Worcester. In defeat, Charles escapes to France in disguise aided by loyal subjects including a beautiful girl.

Historical Accuracy: This is a believable and well-researched adventure story rooted in actual historical events.

2901 Simon the Coldheart

Date of Publication: 1925
Subject(s): Royalty—England; Middle Ages
Fictional character(s): Simon the Coldheart, Knight; Margaret of Belremy, Noblewoman; Raoul the Terrible, Nobleman
Historical character(s): Henry IV, Ruler (King of England); Henry V, Ruler (King of England)
Time Period(s): 15th century (1400-1417)
Locale(s): England (Cambridge, Shrewsbury, London); Wales; Normandy, France

Summary: This is a romantic historical novel set in the early 1400s during the reigns of Henry IV and Henry V. Simon, determined to rise in the world, goes from page to lord through his service to the crown. As a member of Henry V's invasion force in France, Simon lays siege to the castle of Lady Margaret, who loathes him at first. But when Simon rescues her from Raoul the Terrible, Margaret's affections are won.

Historical Accuracy: Heyer resisted re-issuing this early attempt because it is not as thoroughly researched and developed as her later books. It does, however, show Heyer's eye for period detail.

2902 *The Spanish Bride*

Date of Publication: 1940
Subject(s): Napoleonic Wars; Peninsular War; Battle of Waterloo
Historical character(s): Arthur Wellesley, Military Personnel; Harry Smith, Military Personnel; Juana Los Dolores de Leon, Noblewoman
Time Period(s): 1800s
Locale(s): Spain; Toulouse, France; London, England

Summary: Heyer's story is based on an actual romance during the Peninsular War in which an English officer rescues a Spanish girl from the destruction of Badajos. He marries her two days later. The story of this war romance concludes on the battlefield of Waterloo.

Historical Accuracy: The historical details of the military campaign are expertly rendered.

2903 *Sprig Muslin*

Date of Publication: 1956
Subject(s): Regency Romance
Fictional character(s): Amanda Smith, Gentlewoman, Runaway; Lady Hester Theale, Noblewoman; Sir Gareth Ludlow, Nobleman; Hildebrand Ross, Student
Time Period(s): 1810s
Locale(s): England

Summary: In this romantic tangle Amanda runs away from her grandfather who objects to her engagement to a young Army officer. Sir Gareth comes to her rescue with delightfully disastrous results. Finally the deceptions are uncovered, and romance is allowed to triumph.

Historical Accuracy: This is familiar Heyer territory with solid background and a fairly predictable romantic story.

2904 *Sylvester; or, The Wicked Uncle*

Date of Publication: 1958
Subject(s): Regency Romance
Fictional character(s): Sylvester Rayne, Nobleman (Duke of Salford); Phoebe Marlow, Gentlewoman, Writer; Edmund Rayne, Child (Sylvester's nephew)
Time Period(s): 1810s
Locale(s): London, England

Summary: In this period romance, Sylvester, Duke of Salford, is in the market for a wife and he fixes on Phoebe who dislikes him and rejects his offer. Phoebe has also written a Gothic

novel with a recognizable Sylvester as her villain. Delightful complications follow the publication of the novel.

Historical Accuracy: This comedy of manners features convincing dialogue that helps capture the period.

2905 *The Talisman Ring*

Date of Publication: 1937
Subject(s): Crime and Criminals; Georgian Period
Fictional character(s): Sir Tristram Shield, Nobleman; Sarah Thane, Gentlewoman; Eustacie de Vauban, Gentlewoman; Ludovic Lavenham, Nobleman, Smuggler
Time Period(s): 1790s
Locale(s): Sussex, England

Summary: In this adventure story set in England in the 1790s, the ingredients are an unsolved murder mystery, a band of smugglers, and a lost ring. Connected to these are the love affairs of a pretty young French girl and her English cousin.

Historical Accuracy: The novel is a swashbuckler with far more plot than is usual in a Heyer novel.

2906 *These Old Shades*

Date of Publication: 1926
Subject(s): Georgian Period; Identity—Concealed; Romance
Fictional character(s): Justin Alastair, Nobleman (Duke of Avon); Henri de Saint-Vire, Nobleman (comte de Saint-Vire); Leonie, Streetperson (disguised as a boy), Heiress—Dispossessed
Time Period(s): 1750s
Locale(s): Paris, France; England

Summary: The enigmatic Duke of Avon "buys" a Paris street urchin and makes him his servant. When "Leon" turns out to be Leonie, the stage is set for a confrontation with the Duke's arch-enemy, the comte de Saint-Vire.

Historical Accuracy: The novel is romantic make-believe, tethered lightly to the historical period.

2907 *The Toll-Gate*

Date of Publication: 1954
Subject(s): Regency Romance
Fictional character(s): John Staple, Military Personnel (retired soldier); Nell Stornaway, Heroine
Time Period(s): 1810s
Locale(s): England

Summary: Heyer leaves her normal milieu of high society in Regency London in this amusing tale of a retired army captain who accidently finds himself a toll-gate keeper and who becomes involved in a variety of intrigues that involve a highwayman and a Bow-Street runner, in addition to a beautiful heroine.

Historical Accuracy: Heyer shows her ability to depict both ordinary and criminal English life.

2908 *The Unknown Ajax*

Date of Publication: 1960
Subject(s): Regency Romance

Fictional character(s): Hugh Darracott, Heir, Military Personnel (former army officer); Anthea Darracott, Gentlewoman
Time Period(s): 1810s
Locale(s): England

Summary: The proud Darracott family learns that an unknown relative is heir to their grandfather's fortune. His mother was a weaver's daughter so all expect him to be a lower-class boor. He does not disappoint until a series of crises reveals his true blueblood.

Historical Accuracy: There is standard period background with much information about the development of the textile industry.

2909 *Venetia*

Date of Publication: 1959
Subject(s): Regency Romance
Fictional character(s): Venetia Lanyon, Gentlewoman; Jasper Damerel, Nobleman (baron), Rake; Aubrey Lanyon, Scholar, Teenager
Time Period(s): 1810s
Locale(s): England

Summary: Venetia is an unusual Regency romance heroine— competent, self-assured, and unwilling to settle for any marriage offer that comes her way. She holds out for Lord Damerel, a rake, who Venetia plots to win, risking her reputation in the process.

Historical Accuracy: A wealth of information about the period anchors this romance with its unusual heroine.

STEFAN HEYM

2910 *The King David Report*

Date of Publication: 1973
Subject(s): Biblical Story; Ancient Israel
Fictional character(s): Ethan, Historian, Writer
Historical character(s): David, Ruler (King of Israel); Solomon, Ruler (King of Israel)
Time Period(s): 10th century B.C.
Locale(s): Jerusalem, Israel

Summary: King Solomon commissions Ethan to write the official story of the reign of his father, King David of Israel. Ethan is faced with the challenge of presenting a truthful version of David's often violent and ambiguous years as king that will also be acceptable to Solomon.

Historical Accuracy: Events and figures from the Old Testament form a parallel with Stalinism, the uses and abuses of political power, and the rewriting of history to celebrate the reigning regime.

DUBOSE HEYWARD (1885-1940)

Born in Charleston, South Carolina, novelist and playwright Heyward grew up a member of the old Southern aristocracy with a vivid understanding of African Americans. His best known novel is *Porgy*, but he also wrote books for children and an historical novel, *Peter Ashley*.

2911 *Peter Ashley*

Date of Publication: 1932
Subject(s): Antebellum South; Civil War—U.S.
Fictional character(s): Peter Ashley, Gentleman
Time Period(s): 1850s; 1860s
Locale(s): Charleston, South Carolina

Summary: Young Peter Ashley has an ethical struggle on the eve of the Civil War. Recently returned from England, he is opposed to Secession. The novel's climax is the bombardment of Fort Sumter and Ashley's decision of which side he will follow.

Historical Accuracy: The novel achieves a high degree of realism in capturing life in Charleston at the time.

JACK HIGGINS
(PSEUD. OF HARRY PATTERSON, 1929-)

Jack Higgins is the pseudonym for English thriller writer Harry Patterson, born in Newcastle-on-Tyne and a graduate of the London School of Economics. Although a lecturer in history and economics, Higgins regards his role as a writer as that of an entertainer. Every one of his books since *The Eagle Has Landed* has been an international bestseller.

2912 *Luciano's Luck*

Date of Publication: 1981
Subject(s): Crime and Criminals; World War II
Fictional character(s): Harry Carter, Military Personnel (major); Maria Vaughan, Religious (nun); Don Antonio Luca, Organized Crime Figure (mafiosa)
Historical character(s): Charles "Lucky" Luciano, Organized Crime Figure; Albert Kesselring, Military Personnel (German field marshall); Dwight D. Eisenhower, Military Personnel (Allied army commander); Franklin Delano Roosevelt, Political Figure
Time Period(s): 1940s (1943)
Locale(s): Sicily, Italy; England

Summary: To insure the success of the Allied invasion of Sicily in 1943, General Eisenhower assigns Major Harry Carter to gain gangster Lucky Luciano's assistance in convincing Mafia Don Antonio Luca to support the Allied cause. The two convince a young nun, Maria Vaughan, the estranged granddaughter of Don Luca, to join them as they parachute into Sicily to convince her grandfather.

Historical Accuracy: The basis of the novel's story are persistent rumors that are imagined as historial by the author.

MONIQUE RAPHEL HIGH (1949-)

An American born in New York City and a graduate of Barnard College, High has worked as a public relations director and a writer. At the center of her work is the desire to tell a compelling story. English was the fourth language she learned, thus giving her writing a more stylized quality that seems better suited to past settings.

2913 *Between Two Worlds*

Date of Publication: 1989

Subject(s): Motion Picture Industry; Russian Revolution; Romance

Fictional character(s): Zeinab ''Zica'' Lazarevna, Gentlewoman; Yakov ''Yasha'' Luovitch, Young Man; Kyril ''Gredka'' Victorevitch, Young Man

Time Period(s): 20th century (1900s-1940s)

Locale(s): Russia; California

Summary: The novel tells the story of three friends caught up in the Russian Revolution: Zica, the pampered daughter of a rich and powerful Jewish Baron; Gredka, the son of a Cossack; and Yasha, the son of a peddler. Zica and Gredka become lovers, but when Zica becomes pregnant, it is Yasha who marries her and emigrates with her to California. They encounter Gredka again, and Zica can't resolve her feelings toward both.

Historical Accuracy: The period background is genuine, but the emphasis is on the complicated relationship over specific historical events.

2914 *The Eleventh Year*

Date of Publication: 1983

Subject(s): Russian Revolution; World War I; Romance

Fictional character(s): Lesley Aymes Richardson, Socialite; Jamie Lynne Stewart, Young Woman; Alexandre de Varenne, Nobleman

Time Period(s): 1910s; 1920s

Locale(s): St. Petersburg, Russia; Singapore; Paris, France

Summary: Set principally in the Paris of the 1920s, the story describes New York socialite Lesley Richardson who comes to Paris to become an artist. Instead she marries the aristocratic Alexandre de Varenne and finds romantic complications from a variety of sources.

Historical Accuracy: The scene is described with color and authenticity.

2915 *Encore*

Date of Publication: 1981

Subject(s): Theatrical Life; World War I; Dance

Fictional character(s): Natalia Oblonova, Dancer (ballet); Boris Kussov, Nobleman (count); Pierre Riazhin, Artist

Historical character(s): Serge Diaghilev, Businessman (impressario)

Time Period(s): 1900s; 1910s

Locale(s): St. Petersburg, Russia; Paris, France

Summary: Set in the world of Serge Diaghilev's famous Ballets Russes, the novel describes the young dancer Natalia Oblonova. Her career is depicted as well as her relationships which are at times in conflict with her need to dance. The action climaxes with the turmoil brought on by the outbreak of World War I.

Historical Accuracy: The author has assigned some famous roles to her fictional characters.

2916 *The Four Winds of Heaven*

Date of Publication: 1980

Subject(s): Russian Revolution; Jews; World War I

Fictional character(s): David de Gunzburg, Nobleman (baron); Sonia de Gunzburg, Noblewoman

Time Period(s): 1900s; 1910s

Locale(s): St. Petersburg, Russia; Paris, France; Kiev, Russia

Summary: The novel is set in the Russia of the Romanovs, on the brink of the turmoil of the Russian Revolution. The aristocratic Gunzburgs, the foremost Jewish family in Russia, are the novel's focus, specifically Sonia who is torn between her love for the son of her father's enemy and her loyalty to her heritage. The scenes range from the pogroms to the trenches of the Russian Front.

Historical Accuracy: The scene and period are evoked with authenticity.

MONICA HIGHLAND

(PSEUD. OF JOHN ESPEY, 1913- ; CAROLYN SEE, 1934- ; LISA SEE KENDALL, 1955-)

Monica Highland is a group pseudonym for a family trio of writers: John Espey, an American born in China of missionary parents and a professor of English at UCLA; Carolyn See, a writer and professor of English at UCLA; and their daughter, Lisa See Kendall. Together they seized upon the idea of writing an epic novel after viewing a TV mini series and deciding they could do better. Beside *Lotus Land* they are the authors of *110 Shanghai Road*.

2917 *Lotus Land*

Date of Publication: 1983

Subject(s): American West; Settlement of the American Frontier

Fictional character(s): Sung Wing On, Worker; Magdalena Ortiz, Young Woman; Clifford Creighton, Businessman

Time Period(s): 19th century; 20th century (1880s-1940s)

Locale(s): Los Angeles, California

Summary: The birth and growth of Los Angeles is depicted in the conjunction of three ethnic groups: Asian, Hispanic, and Anglo. The lives of three representatives—Sung Wing On, Magdalena Ortiz, and Clifford Creighton—dramatize Los Angeles' troubled and colorful history.

Historical Accuracy: The historical basis of the story's events are obvious from the author's detailed notes.

JAMAKE HIGHWATER (1942-)

Of Blackfoot and Cherokee Indian heritage, Highwater is a writer and lecturer at various universities in the U.S. and Canada. He has written more than a dozen books on American Indian culture and history, including novels and poetry on his own experiences as an Indian in America.

`2918` *Journey to the Sky: A Novel about the True Adventures of Two Men in Search of the Lost Maya Kingdom*

Date of Publication: 1978
Subject(s): Exploration; Mayan Empire
Historical character(s): Frederick Catherwood, Explorer, Archaeologist; John Lloyd Stephens, Explorer
Time Period(s): 1830s; 1840s (1839-1842)
Locale(s): Central America

Summary: Based on the actual 19th-century journey of explorers Catherwood and Stephens to discover the remnants of the lost Mayan civilization, the novel details their search by steamboat and mule into the jungles of Central America. There they stumble upon the remains of a civilization that had passed long before the Spanish invasion in the 16th century.

Historical Accuracy: The story is set solidly into a framework of fact.

`2919` *The Sun, He Dies: A Novel about the End of the Aztec World*

Date of Publication: 1980
Subject(s): Aztec Empire; Exploration; Tribal Life—Aztec
Fictional character(s): Nanautzin, Government Official
Historical character(s): Hernando Cortez, Explorer, Military Personnel (conquistador); Montezuma II, Ruler (Aztec emperor)
Time Period(s): 16th century
Locale(s): Mexico

Summary: The Spanish invasion of Mexico and Cortez's defeat of the Aztec Empire is described from the perspective of Nanautzin, an aide of Aztec emperor Montezuma. He tells of the events that precede the arrival of the Spanish and how Montezuma was torn between his dignity and pride as an Aztec and his religious fervor and belief in the return of the white god Quetzalcoatl that contributes to his people's downfall.

Historical Accuracy: The depiction of Aztec life and culture is convincing.

CAROL DE CHELLIS HILL (1942-)

An American writer, born in New Jersey, Hill graduated from Chatham College. She has worked as a publicist and book editor, as well as an actress.

`2920` *Henry James' Midnight Song*

Date of Publication: 1993
Subject(s): Mystery; Medical Profession; Psychology
Fictional character(s): Inspector LeBlanc, Detective—Police
Historical character(s): Sigmund Freud, Doctor; Edith Wharton, Writer; Henry James, Writer; Carl Jung, Doctor
Time Period(s): 1900s (1900)
Locale(s): Vienna, Austria

Summary: In fin de siecle Vienna women are dying mysteriously. One victim is found in Dr. Freud's study, but she quickly disappears. A number of suspects are identified including Edith Wharton and her travelling companion, Henry James. Inspector LeBlanc attempts to solve the case before the city's anti-Semitism explodes into a riot.

Historical Accuracy: The novel is a tour de force of ideas and history. The ingenuity of its cast is matched by the insights into turn-of-the-century Vienna that darkly mirror the contemporary scene.

DEBORAH HILL (1936-)

American author Hill was born in Massachusetts and graduated from the University of Pennsylvania and Villanova. She is a designer and builder of houses. She attempts in her historical novels to make the early years of America real for her readers.

`2921` *This Is the House*

Date of Publication: 1976
Subject(s): Family Saga; War of 1812
Fictional character(s): Molly Deems, Young Woman; Elijah Merrick, Sea Captain; Isaac Warden, Gentleman
Time Period(s): 18th century; 19th century
Locale(s): Cape Cod, Massachusetts

Summary: This family saga follows the fortunes of the Merrick family during the period immediately following the American Revolution through the War of 1812. The story begins with the marriage of Molly Deems to the seafaring Elijah Merrick and their creation of a shipping business on Cape Cod.

Historical Accuracy: The period elements and regional details are authentic and reliable.

ERNESTINE HILL (1899-1972)

Australian writer Hill was born in Queensland. Her books include *The Territory*, *Kabbarli*, and *The Passing of the Aborigines*.

`2922` *My Love Must Wait: The Story of Matthew Flinders*

Date of Publication: 1942
Subject(s): Biography, Fictionalized; Exploration
Historical character(s): Matthew Flinders, Explorer, Sea Captain
Time Period(s): 18th century; 19th century (1774-1814)
Locale(s): England; Australia (and present-day Tasmania)

Summary: The novel offers a biographical account of the life of English naval captain Matthew Flinders, who in voyages that circumnavigated Australia and Tasmania made valuable maps and charts of the water and the coastline. The novel captures the drama of Flinders' efforts to penetrate the mysteries of a continent in an eight-foot boat.

Historical Accuracy: The novel is a carefully documented work of biographical fiction, faithful to the sources.

FIONA HILL
(PSEUD. OF ELLEN JANE PALL, 1952-)

An American born in New York City, Hill graduated from the University of California, Santa Barbara, and has worked as a teacher of French. She began her writing career by writing songs and pursued a career as a singer/songwriter. She became a writer after reading several Gothic novels while recovering from having her wisdom teeth removed and became convinced that she could do as well.

2923 *The Autumn Rose*
Date of Publication: 1978
Subject(s): Regency Romance
Fictional character(s): Lady Beatrice Romby, Noblewoman; Lady Caroline Wythe, Noblewoman; Lord Seabury, Nobleman
Time Period(s): 1810s (1817)
Locale(s): London, England

Summary: At age 22 Lady Caroline Wythe is judged too tall, too thin, and over the hill. She seems doomed to spinsterhood. Lady Beatrice, a well-known marriage consultant, comes up with an ingenious way to enhance Caroline's appeal. Soon she has more suitors than she can deal with and the courtship ritual becomes a delightful test and trial.

Historical Accuracy: This is an amusing Regency romp with some authentic period touches in passing.

2924 *The Country Gentleman*
Date of Publication: 1987
Subject(s): Regency Romance
Fictional character(s): Anne Guilfoyle, Gentlewoman; Maria Insel, Companion; Henry Highet, Gentleman
Time Period(s): 19th century (Regency period)
Locale(s): London, England; Cheshire, England

Summary: Anne Guilfoyle, a bluestocking living a very comfortable life in London, finds herself bereft of her fortune and forced to live in a Cheshire farmhouse. She is determined to succeed in the country but finds rural life a shock to her delicate civilized constitution.

Historical Accuracy: This is an original use of the Regency locale, reversing the usual direction from country to town. The scenes of country life are convincing.

2925 *The Stanbroke Girls*
Date of Publication: 1981
Subject(s): Regency Romance
Fictional character(s): Jeffrey de Guere, Rake; Amy Lewis, Gentlewoman; Lady Isabella Stanbroke, Noblewoman; Lady Elizabeth Stanbroke, Noblewoman
Time Period(s): 19th century (Regency period)
Locale(s): England

Summary: A large cast of characters engages in the courtship rituals of Regency England. At the center of the story are the two Stanbroke girls, romantic and dreamy Lady Isabella and practical Lady Elizabeth. Eventually, after mishaps and misunderstandings, the correct partners are assigned.

Historical Accuracy: This is all rather standard fare, with the expected period details supporting the time and setting.

2926 *Sweet's Folly*
Date of Publication: 1977
Subject(s): Regency Romance
Fictional character(s): Honoria Newcombe, Orphan, Ward; Emily Blackwood, Gentlewoman, Artist; Alexander Blackwood, Gentleman
Time Period(s): 19th century (Regency period)
Locale(s): England

Summary: Orphaned Honoria Newcombe discovers that she is a financial burden to her maiden aunts and decides that she must resolve this strain. When work is ruled out, the only alternative is marriage. But to whom? The novel details the comedy of errors that complicates Honoria's marriage plans.

Historical Accuracy: The Regency details are convincing.

PAMELA HILL (1920-)

Born in Nairobi, Kenya, to Scottish parents, Hill studied at the Glasgow School of Art and has worked as a pottery teacher, a biology instructor in Glasgow and Edinburgh, and a mink farmer in Galloway, Scotland. She began her productive writing career in 1951.

2927 *Artemia*
Date of Publication: 1989
Subject(s): Romance; Victorian Period; Crimean War
Fictional character(s): Artemia Wivenhoe, Companion (of Lady Catherine); Lady Catherine Feldman, Gentlewoman
Time Period(s): 1850s
Locale(s): England

Summary: Artemia Wivenhoe is Lady Catherine Feldman's companion during the 1850s. She has a depth of emotional resources unimagined by her employer until family tragedy strikes, and Artemia proves her inner strengths.

Historical Accuracy: The novel is evocative of the period.

2928 *Bride of Ae*
Date of Publication: 1983
Subject(s): Gothic Romance
Fictional character(s): Sara Ryder, Artist, Worker (milliner's assistant); Francis Atherstone, Nobleman; Helena Consett, Gentlewoman
Time Period(s): 19th century; 20th century
Locale(s): Sussex, England

Summary: Francis Atherstone must marry a workingclass woman to inherit his fortune in this Gothic romance. He proposes to Sara Ryder, an aspiring artist who works in a milliner's shop. She accepts the offer to escape her dreary life but finds herself trapped in a loveless marriage.

Historical Accuracy: The situation strains credibility, and the exact period is difficult to pin down.

`2929` *The Brocken*

Date of Publication: 1990

Subject(s): Gothic Romance; Victorian Period

Fictional character(s): Nicholas Crowbetter, Banker; Melanie Von Reichmanstaal, Noblewoman (countess); Athene Crowbetter, Spinster

Time Period(s): 19th century (1860s-1880s)

Locale(s): London, England; Vienna, Austria; Hartz Mountains, Germany

Summary: This story of sexual infidelity and betrayal is set in Victorian London with side trips to Vienna and the Hartz Mountains in Germany. In the mountains every year on Walpurgis Night, the eve of May Day, a devil's dance occurs. The novel traces a connection between the dance and a family of merchant bankers.

Historical Accuracy: The novel is witty and sophisticated with attitudes that seem more modern than Victorian.

`2930` *The Crown and the Shadow: The Story of Francoise d'Aubigne, Marquise de Maintenon*

Date of Publication: 1955

Subject(s): Royalty—France; Biography, Fictionalized

Historical character(s): Francoise d'Aubigne, Noblewoman, Royalty (consort of Louis XIV); Louis XIV, Ruler (King of France); Paul Scarron, Writer (poet); Francoise Athenais Rochechouart de Mortemart, Noblewoman; Marie-Therese, Royalty (consort of Louis XIV)

Time Period(s): 16th century; 17th century (1642-1719)

Locale(s): France

Summary: This biographical novel is based on the life of Francoise d'Aubigne and shows her rise in the glittering circles of the French court, first as the wife of the poet Paul Scarron and later as the second wife of Louis XIV. She is portrayed as an early feminist and a woman of greater substance than many who surrounded the French royals.

Historical Accuracy: The novel stays close to the facts, occasionally lapsing in the direction of hagiography in its admiration of Madame de Maintenon.

`2931` *Daneclere*

Date of Publication: 1978

Subject(s): Romance; Civil War—England

Fictional character(s): Honor Sawtrey, Widow(er); Maud Farmiloe, Gentlewoman; Richard Farmiloe, Gentleman

Time Period(s): 17th century

Locale(s): England; Scotland

Summary: Set during the tumultuous days of the English Civil War, the novel chronicles the intermingled fortunes of three families: the Sawtreys, the Thwaites, and the Farmiloes, each caught up in the great events in different ways.

Historical Accuracy: The novel features realistic and believable depictions of 17th century life among the gentry of the period.

`2932` *Fire Opal*

Date of Publication: 1980

Subject(s): Reincarnation; Fantasy

Fictional character(s): Fiona Tilney, Handicapped (deaf-mute); Fiammetta, Captive; Anthony Graham, Adventurer

Time Period(s): 16th century; 19th century

Locale(s): Scotland; Istanbul, Turkey

Summary: This romantic fantasy shuttles between 19th century Scotland and 16th century Turkey. Fiona Tilney is the reincarnation of Fiammetta, a child captured by the Turks and raised to wed the Sultan. Rescued by Anthony Graham, she falls in love with him and they share a love affair that continues across the centuries.

Historical Accuracy: The emphasis is on romantic fantasy, though the 16th and 19th centuries are vividly portrayed.

`2933` *The Green Salamander*

Date of Publication: 1977

Subject(s): Tudor Period; Royalty—Scotland; Royalty—England

Historical character(s): Margaret Douglas, Noblewoman; Henry VIII, Ruler (King of England); Henry Stewart, Nobleman (consort of Mary); Mary, Queen of Scots, Ruler (Queen of Scotland); Robert Dudley, Nobleman (Earl of Leicester)

Time Period(s): 16th century

Locale(s): London, England; Scotland

Summary: The novel tells the story of Margaret Douglas, the niece of Henry VIII, who nurtures ambition for her son, Darnley, who marries Mary, Queen of Scots. Margaret plays a dangerous game, pitted between rivals and conspirators both in England and Scotland. She is like the symbol of the salamander of her family crest, living in the heart of the fire.

Historical Accuracy: The political issues of the period are well detailed, if sometimes overly confusing rather than illuminating.

`2934` *The Heatherton Heritage*

Date of Publication: 1974

Subject(s): Gothic Romance

Fictional character(s): William Heatherton, Religious (clergyman); Marie Vanneau, Spouse (of William)

Time Period(s): 19th century

Locale(s): England; Edinburgh, Scotland

Summary: This story of family secrets and obsessions looks beneath the surface of the ostensibly proper life of the Reverend William Heatherton. The Gothic-style novel is filled with adultery, murder, and vengeance lurking behind the respectable facade of 19th-century life.

Historical Accuracy: The novel emphasizes the melodramatic rather than the historical, but does present some reasonably detailed period backgrounds.

`2935` *Here Lies Margot*

Date of Publication: 1958

Subject(s): Royalty—France; Royalty—Spain; Biography, Fictionalized

Historical character(s): Margaret of Burgundy, Noblewoman; Charles VIII, Ruler (King of France); Juan, Prince of the Asturias, Royalty (heir to the Spanish throne); Ferdinand V, Ruler (King of Aragon); Isabella I, Ruler (Queen of Castile); Philibert of Savoy, Nobleman (Duke of Savoy)
Time Period(s): 15th century
Locale(s): Netherlands; France; Spain

Summary: This autobiographical account chronicles the life of Margaret of Burgundy, who becomes a pawn in the political allegiances of 15th century Europe. She marries Charles VIII while still a child and is sent home at age eleven when a better match for the monarch is desired. She next marries the son and heir of the Spanish throne. When he dies, Margaret finally finds happiness with Duke Philibert of Savoy. The novel captures the intrigue of power politics in the 15th century.

Historical Accuracy: Margaret's voice is convincing, as are the period details.

2936 *The House of Cray*

Date of Publication: 1982
Subject(s): Family Saga; Artistic Life; Business Building
Fictional character(s): Enrico Bondone, Art Dealer; Marcus Cray, Businessman
Time Period(s): 19th century; 20th century
Locale(s): Italy; London, England

Summary: This generational saga follows the fortunes of two families, the Italian Bondones and the English Crays. Enrico Bondone is the founder of an art firm whose shifting fortune is affected by succeeding generations, covering the period from Garibaldi's Italy to the beginning of the First World War.

Historical Accuracy: The emphasis is on relationships rather than history, but the period background is believable.

2937 *The King's Vixen*

Date of Publication: 1954
Subject(s): Royalty—Scotland
Historical character(s): James IV, Ruler (King of Scotland); Janet Kennedy, Gentlewoman
Time Period(s): 16th century
Locale(s): Scotland

Summary: Janet Kennedy is a mistress of King James IV. The novel captures the atmosphere of court intrigue during a crucial period of Scottish history.

Historical Accuracy: The author provides some authentic period details.

2938 *The Malvie Inheritance*

Date of Publication: 1973
Subject(s): Romance; Inheritance—Disputed
Fictional character(s): Morven Doon, Heir—Dispossessed; Annabel Doon, Heiress; Godfrey Devenham, Gentleman
Time Period(s): 18th century
Locale(s): Scotland

Summary: Family rivalry and betrayal is the legacy of Malvie, a great Scottish estate. Having been robbed of his inheritance, Morven Doon takes his revenge on young Annabel, the Malvie heiress, and her weak-willed husband Godfrey Devenham.

Historical Accuracy: The scenes of Scottish life and period customs are well-detailed and plausible.

2939 *Marjorie of Scotland*

Date of Publication: 1956
Subject(s): Royalty—Scotland; Middle Ages
Historical character(s): Robert I, Ruler (King of Scotland); Marjorie Bruce, Royalty (princess)
Time Period(s): 14th century
Locale(s): Scotland; England

Summary: Almost nothing is known about Marjorie, the daughter of Robert I of Scotland, except that she was a prisoner of Edward I for eight years. Nevertheless, the novel provides a factual version of her life and times. Marjorie's entanglement in the political maneuverings of the day is placed in the context of a vivid reconstruction of medieval Scotland.

Historical Accuracy: The majority of the story is speculative, and the author's obvious partisanship on behalf of her heroine sacrifices objectivity.

2940 *My Lady Glamis*

Date of Publication: 1985
Subject(s): Royalty—Scotland; Tudor Period; Royalty—England
Fictional character(s): Jonet Douglas, Gentlewoman
Historical character(s): James V, Ruler (King of Scotland); Margaret Tudor, Royalty (Queen of Scotland); Henry VIII, Ruler (King of England)
Time Period(s): 16th century
Locale(s): Scotland; England

Summary: Jonet Douglas, the beautiful Lady Glamis, finds herself in the middle of a bitter blood feud between her family and the Scottish royal family. Her family rebels against and finally captures James V of Scotland. James escapes and exacts revenge, and although Jonet is innocent of the kidnapping, she falls under James' power.

Historical Accuracy: The historical background here is solidly developed and convincing.

2941 *Norah*

Date of Publication: 1976
Subject(s): Romance; Gypsies; Inheritance—Disputed
Fictional character(s): Jody Curle, Gypsy; Norah Curle, Heiress
Time Period(s): 18th century
Locale(s): Cumberland, England

Summary: A passionate rivalry forms between Norah Curle, an heiress, and Jody Curle, her half-gypsy cousin. Jody fights Norah for control of the family estate in a series of confrontations that become violent.

Historical Accuracy: The period atmosphere forms a credible backdrop to this romantic story.

`2942` *A Place of Ravens*

Date of Publication: 1981
Subject(s): Civil War—England; Romance
Fictional character(s): Clemency Holles, Gentlewoman; Nicholas Talmadge, Gentleman; David Lewellyn, Servant
Time Period(s): 17th century
Locale(s): England

Summary: Clemency Holles accepts the hand of a wealthy man whom she has never seen. Nicholas Talmadge, the owner of Ravensyard, is a disappointing husband, but his estate is worth saving from his cousins. David Lewellyn helps Clemency as the English Civil War breaks out, forming the novel's climax.

Historical Accuracy: This is fairly standard romantic intrigue, bolstered by some convincing historical period details.

`2943` *Stranger's Forest*

Date of Publication: 1978
Subject(s): Romance; Inheritance—Disputed
Fictional character(s): Primrose Tebb, Heiress; Andrew Farquharson, Adventurer
Time Period(s): 18th century
Locale(s): Scotland

Summary: Primrose Tebb becomes the child-bride of adventurer Andrew Farquharson in 18th century Scotland. Andrew dreams of growing a great forest with seeds collected in his travels in Canada. In need of land, he arranges an alliance with Primrose, heiress to a great estate. As she matures, conflicts develop within and outside their household.

Historical Accuracy: The novel is strong on Scottish details.

`2944` *The Sutburys*

Date of Publication: 1988
Subject(s): Romance; Victorian Period; Feuds
Fictional character(s): Felix Sutbury, Nobleman (Viscount Harmhill); Guy Sutbury, Gentleman
Time Period(s): 19th century (Victorian period)
Locale(s): England

Summary: A feud between two brothers breaks out over control of the family estate and the woman in their lives. Felix Sutbury is the elder, who is caught in the grip of his younger brother's enmity. Their feud will have major implications on the succeeding generations who inherit Fenfallow.

Historical Accuracy: The background of the story is the violent change in England during the 19th century, suggested here with authentic details.

`2945` *The Sword and the Flame*

Date of Publication: 1991
Subject(s): Tudor Period; Royalty—Scotland
Fictional character(s): Claudine de Vouvray, Noblewoman
Historical character(s): Mary of Guise, Royalty (queen consort of James V); Mary, Queen of Scots, Ruler (Queen of Scotland)
Time Period(s): 16th century
Locale(s): Scotland; France

Summary: Told by a noblewoman attendant, the novel offers an intimate portrait of the tumultuous career of Mary of Guise, the wife of Scottish King James V and the mother of Mary, Queen of Scots. When James dies, Mary is determined to hold onto the throne for her daughter despite outside pressure from Henry VIII of England and internal dissension.

Historical Accuracy: Although the author admits to some manipulation of the chronology, the events are reasonably reliable and authentic.

`2946` *Tsar's Woman*

Date of Publication: 1977
Subject(s): Russian Empire; Royalty—Russia
Historical character(s): Catherine I, Ruler (Empress of Russia); Peter the Great, Ruler (Czar of Russia)
Time Period(s): 18th century
Locale(s): Russia

Summary: This is the story of the peasant girl who becomes Catherine I, Empress of Russia. She makes her way to Czar Peter's court, aided by a Russian soldier who is attracted to her beauty. There, she meets Peter, becomes his mistress, then wife, and after his death, Empress of all Russia.

Historical Accuracy: The story is convincing in its details of Imperial Russia.

`2947` *Vollands*

Date of Publication: 1990
Subject(s): Romance; Victorian Period
Fictional character(s): Anna Volland, Widow(er); James Volland, Landowner, Gentleman; Hubert Volland, Landowner, Gentleman
Time Period(s): 1840s
Locale(s): England

Summary: After her husband's bankruptcy and death, Anna Volland and her family come to live with her uncle at the estate of Volland. When he dies, the estate falls under the control of his stern son, James, and the family fragments under James' regime.

Historical Accuracy: The novel offers good period details of Victorian life.

`2948` *Whitton's Folly*

Date of Publication: 1975
Subject(s): Romance; Witchcraft and Sorcery
Fictional character(s): Edmund Whitton, Heir; Helen Stenhouse, Spouse (of Edmund)
Time Period(s): 1750s
Locale(s): Highlands, Scotland

Summary: Edmund Whitton returns home from India to claim his inheritance, an estate in the Scottish Highlands. He is immediately plunged into a gothic tangle of mystery, death, madness, and witchcraft.

Historical Accuracy: There are realistic and believable period details of Scottish life in this historical suspense novel.

2949 *The Woman in the Cloak*

Date of Publication: 1988

Subject(s): Middle Ages; Religious Life; Biography, Fictionalized

Historical character(s): Margaret of Metola, Religious (nun), Handicapped (blind)

Time Period(s): 13th century; 14th century

Locale(s): Castello, Italy

Summary: This is the biographical story of Margaret of Metola. Born blind, she is abandoned by her parents. She becomes a source of healing and goodwill among the needy, and eventually becomes a nun.

Historical Accuracy: The story is firmly rooted in accepted fact.

PORTER HILL

2950 *The War Chest*

Date of Publication: 1986

Subject(s): Sea Story; Military Life—British Navy; British Colonies

Fictional character(s): Adam Horne, Military Personnel (captain)

Time Period(s): 1760s (1761)

Locale(s): Bombay, India; Madagascar; Indian Ocean

Summary: Set during the British attempt in the 1760s to remove the French from the Indian sub-continent, the story continues the adventures of Adam Horne, captain of a motley band of ex-convicts, the East Indian Company's Bombay Marines. He is sent on a secret mission to Madagascar in an attempt to break the stalemate with the French.

Historical Accuracy: The story is fictional but the period backdrop is genuine.

RUTH BEEBE HILL (1913-)

Born in Cleveland, Hill graduated from Case Western Reserve University. She has worked as a news and feature writer and is the co-founder of the Women's Auxiliary California Institute for Cancer Research. She has always been fascinated by Indian life and culture, and her research for *Hanta Yo* took 32 years and was based on interviews of over 1,000 Indians. Hill was determined to experience Indian life first hand, and she mastered several Indian languages in the course of her research.

2951 *Hanta Yo*

Date of Publication: 1979

Subject(s): Indians; Tribal Life—Native American; Family Saga

Fictional character(s): Olepi, Indian; Ahbleza, Indian; Peta, Indian

Time Period(s): 18th century; 19th century (1750-1835)

Locale(s): West

Summary: Based on a document recorded on tanned hide by a member of the Mahto band of the Teton Sioux, the novel recounts the story of two families from the 1750s to the 1830s, before contact with the whites. The novel is a tour de force of ethnographic re-construction.

Historical Accuracy: The authenticity is compelling down to the linguistic component as the text was translated into the Sioux language and then retranslated into English using a dictionary of the early 19th century.

SUSAN HILL (1942-)

An English writer born in Yorkshire, Hill received her B.A. degree from King's College, London University. She won the 1971 Somerset Maugham Award for her novel, *I'm the King of the Castle*. She worked as a literary critic before devoting herself full-time to writing.

2952 *Strange Meeting*

Date of Publication: 1971

Subject(s): World War I

Fictional character(s): John Hilliard, Military Personnel (British officer); David Barton, Military Personnel (British officer)

Time Period(s): 1910s (1915)

Locale(s): France; England

Summary: This World War I era novel depicts the war on the Western Front and focuses on the relationship between two British officers, John Hilliard and David Barton. Their friendship develops during the lulls between offensives and is strengthened on the battlefield.

Historical Accuracy: The novel provides an authentic portrait of military life in the trenches.

AL HINE (1915-)

Born in Pennsylvania, Hine graduated from Princeton. He has worked as a copywriter and editor for *Holiday* magazine. Hine was the executive producer for the acclaimed film version of William Golding's novel *Lord of the Flies*.

2953 *Brother Owl*

Date of Publication: 1980

Subject(s): American Revolution; Indians; Biography, Fictionalized

Historical character(s): Joseph Brant, Indian (Mohawk), Chieftain; Sir William Johnson, Government Official

Time Period(s): 18th century (1740s-1780s)

Locale(s): New York, American Colonies; London, England

Summary: This is a fictional memoir of the remarkable Mohawk chief Joseph Brant who leaves his tribe at age 13 to live with his sister's lover, William Johnson, Britain's Indian superintendent, who educates him. Fiercely loyal to the British, Brant is a scout for the army and leads successful raids against the rebels. Later, he travels to London and translates the Book of Common Prayer into the Mohawk language.

Historical Accuracy: The author uses historical fact as a background, but the characters' motivations are his own.

CHARLOTTE HINGER (1940-)

Born in Kansas, Hinger attended Kansas State University and has worked as a sales clerk, bookkeeper, and an editor of history books. *Come Spring* won an award for the best first novel and was a Spur Award finalist for best historical novel.

2954 *Come Spring*

Date of Publication: 1986
Subject(s): Settlement of the American Frontier; American West
Fictional character(s): Aura Lee, Gentlewoman; Daniel Hollingworth, Farmer; Graham Chapman, Businessman
Time Period(s): 1880s
Locale(s): Kansas

Summary: Dispute between the homesteaders and town builders in 19th-century Kansas is the theme of this novel that also features the love story of beautiful young Aura Lee, who marries Daniel Hollingsworth and settles down to a life on the Kansas plains. She is pursued by Graham Chapman, a ruthless enterpreneur who covets both Aura and Daniel's land.

Historical Accuracy: The period and regional elements are convincing.

HARRIET HINSDALE (1900-)

Born in New York City, Hinsdale has been a motion picture story editor. Her books include *Robert Louis Stevenson, a Play*, *Confederate Gray*, and *Be My Love*.

2955 *Be My Love*

Date of Publication: 1950
Subject(s): American Colonies
Fictional character(s): Harry Frankland, Government Official; Agnes Surriage, Ward
Time Period(s): 1770s
Locale(s): Boston, Massachusetts, American Colonies

Summary: Boston in the years before the Revolution is the scene of this romantic novel. Harry Frankland, the Collector of the Port of Boston, takes under his wing a young ward, Agnes Surriage, and raises her Pygmalion-fashion into a woman of quality. The historical element of the story is the siege of Louisburg that breaks French power in the colonies.

Historical Accuracy: The author claims that the novel is all—or nearly all—true. Unfortunately, romance predominates and invalidates this claim.

RAYMOND HITCHCOCK (1922-)

Born in Calcutta, Hitchcock graduated from Cambridge University. He has worked as a research and development engineer as well as a freelance writer. He is the author of a number of radio and TV plays.

2956 *Attack the Lusitania!*

Date of Publication: 1979
Subject(s): World War I; Sea Story; Shipwrecks

Fictional character(s): Gavin Tweedman, Military Personnel (director of naval intelligence); Esmond Bone, Military Personnel (naval officer)
Historical character(s): Winston Churchill, Government Official (First Lord of the Admiralty); George V, Ruler (King of England)
Time Period(s): 1910s (1915)
Locale(s): London, England; At Sea (North Atlantic); Ireland

Summary: In this fanciful dramatization, the sinking of the *Lusitania*, with the loss of 1,201 lives, is imagined as a plot of the British to bring America into World War I as its ally. Director of Naval Intelligence Gavin Tweedman dreams up the idea and naval commander Esmond Bone is convinced to take on the deadly assignment.

Historical Accuracy: This is a historical fantasy. Though much surrounding the sinking of the *Lusitania* remains a mystery, there is little doubt that the attack came from the Germans.

JAMES E. HITT (1924-)

2957 *Tennessee Smith*

Date of Publication: 1979
Subject(s): Reconstruction Period
Fictional character(s): Stella McEverside, Widow(er); Tennessee Smith, Veteran (Confederate)
Time Period(s): 1860s (post Civil War)
Locale(s): Kentucky; Texas

Summary: After the Civil War, Stella McEverside finds her life destroyed by the notorious outlaw Krull clan. They rape her, kill her husband, and burn her home. She enlists the aid of an army veteran, Tennessee Smith, to help her track down the killers on a trail that takes them across the war-ravaged South to Texas in Indian country.

Historical Accuracy: The period elements here are authentically drawn.

WILLIAM HJORTSBERG (1941-)

Hjorstberg was born in New York City and graduated from Dartmouth College. Hjorstberg has always considered himself a writer, though he has worked at a number of jobs to support his writing. These include stints as a teacher in St. Croix, Virgin Islands, and as a draftsman. His novels include *Gray Matters* and *Toro! Toro! Toro!* Hjorstberg wrote the film adaptation for *A River Runs through It*. He has settled in Montana after many years living in Spain, the Virgin Islands, and Costa Rica.

2958 *Nevermore*

Date of Publication: 1994
Subject(s): Mystery; Spiritualism
Historical character(s): Arthur Conan Doyle, Writer; Harry Houdini, Magician; Damon Runyon, Journalist
Time Period(s): 1920s
Locale(s): New York, New York

Summary: On a tour of America promoting spiritualism, Arthur Conan Doyle becomes involved with magician Harry

Houdini in an investigation of a series of murders that seem to imitate those committed in the stories of Edgar Allan Poe. It appears the next victim will be Houdini himself, and all of Doyle's power, in both spiritualism and detection, are needed.

Historical Accuracy: The events are fanciful, but the novel does offer a believable period background and plausible versions of the real figures.

EDWARD HOAGLAND (1932-)

A novelist and essayist, Hoagland was born in New York City and graduated from Harvard. He is the author of award-winning essays on the world of nature and human interactions. A severe stutterer, Hoagland's restricted social contact in youth caused him to take long, solitary strolls in which he developed his skills as an observer.

2959 *Seven Rivers West*

Date of Publication: 1986
Subject(s): American West; Indians; Picaresque Adventure
Fictional character(s): Cecil Roop, Adventurer; Sutton, Prospector, Entertainer (circus performer)
Time Period(s): 1880s
Locale(s): West

Summary: This western picaresque adventure is set in the American West of the 1880s. Cecil Roop is on a quest to capture a grizzly bear cub to show on the vaudeville circuit and his friend Sutton is after gold. Together they face many dangers including unruly Indians, a mad trapper, and uncooperative grizzlies.

Historical Accuracy: The author explains that the novel is purely fictitious and that nothing in it is drawn from real life.

RUSSELL HOBAN (1925-)

Born in Pennsylvania, Hoban was an illustrator before becoming a writer. Since 1958, he has written over 50 books for children. His adult books include *The Lion of Boaz-Jachin and Jachin-Boaz*, *Kleinzeit*, *Turtle Diary*, and the acclaimed *Riddley Walker*.

2960 *Pilgermann*

Date of Publication: 1983
Subject(s): Middle Ages; Crusades; Jews
Fictional character(s): Pilgermann, Wanderer
Time Period(s): 11th century (1096-1098)
Locale(s): Palestine; Germany

Summary: At the time of the First Crusade, Pilgermann, a young Jewish man, is castrated for seducing the local tax collector's wife. He embarks on a pilgrimage to Jerusalem where he is captured by pirates and sold to a Turkish merchant. Pilgermann winds up in Antioch where he finds himself caught between the opposing armies of the Franks and the Turks.

Historical Accuracy: The novel's historical background provides a convincing setting for this meditation on history and the clash of beliefs among Christians, Jews, and Muslims.

MICHAEL P. HODEL

SEAN M. WRIGHT

2961 *Enter the Lion: A Posthumous Memoir of Mycroft Holmes*

Date of Publication: 1979
Subject(s): Mystery; Victorian Period
Fictional character(s): Mycroft Holmes, Detective—Private; Sherlock Holmes, Detective—Private; James Moriarty, Criminal, Professor
Historical character(s): William Gladstone, Political Figure; Benjamin Disraeli, Political Figure
Time Period(s): 1870s (1875)
Locale(s): London, England

Summary: In 1875 Mycroft Holmes, the older brother of the famous sleuth, becomes embroiled in a plot by a party of Americans in London to overthrow the United States and restore the Confederacy under British rule. The plot involves murder, kidnapping, and a threat to the British government. The novel also answers the vexing question about the animosity between Sherlock Holmes and his nemesis Moriarty.

Historical Accuracy: The novel is an ingenious puzzle with a convincing period background and echoes of the Arthur Conan Doyle originals.

JANE AIKEN HODGE (1917-)

An American writer and the daughter of poet Conrad Aiken, Hodge was educated at Somerville College, Oxford, and Radcliffe. She worked for a time as a researcher for *Life* magazine before devoting her career to fiction. She prefers historical novels, which she believes should be like icebergs in which there should be more than meets the eye. In her view, one should do vast amounts of research but let practically none of it show.

2962 *Escapade*

Date of Publication: 1993
Subject(s): Regency Romance; Napoleonic Wars; Regency Period
Fictional character(s): Charlotte Comyn, Gentlewoman; John Thornton, Gentleman; Beth Prior, Actress
Time Period(s): 1810s
Locale(s): London, England; Sicily, Italy

Summary: Charlotte Comyn runs away from a marriage of convenience and takes refuge with her mother's estranged friend, Beth Prior, an actress. The two travel to Sicily, which is alive with intrigue and danger. Their adventures there are set against the backdrop of political turmoil during the Napoleonic era.

Historical Accuracy: The story is fanciful but convincingly presents the atmosphere of its time and place.

2963 *First Night*

Date of Publication: 1989

Subject(s): Regency Period; Musical Life; Napoleonic Era
Fictional character(s): Martha Peabody, Heiress; Cristabel Sarum, Noblewoman
Time Period(s): 1800s
Locale(s): London, England; Paris, France; Venice, Italy

Summary: Napoleonic-era political intrigue and the Regency world are mixed in this romantic adventure. Lady Cristabel, the daughter of an English duke, and American heiress Martha Peabody escape Cristabel's conniving father. They flee to Paris, Vienna, and eventually the principality of Lissenberg, where the opening night of a new opera proves very important.

Historical Accuracy: The novel's story is fictional but does depend on a convincing evocation of the period and its customs.

2964 *Here Comes a Candle*

Date of Publication: 1967
Subject(s): War of 1812; Suspense
Fictional character(s): Kate Croston, Widow(er); Jon Penrose, Businessman (merchant)
Time Period(s): 1810s
Locale(s): Boston, Massachusetts; Washington, District of Columbia

Summary: This romantic suspense tale is set during the turmoil of the War of 1812. Kate Croston is a young British widow who is taken into the home of Boston merchant Jon Penrose and is plunged into a complex tangle of mystery and danger. The British attack on Washington provides the climax of the story.

Historical Accuracy: The novel provides a convincing period backdrop.

2965 *Judas Flowering*

Date of Publication: 1976
Subject(s): American Revolution; American Colonies
Fictional character(s): Hart Purchis, Plantation Owner; Mercy Phillips, Young Woman
Time Period(s): 1770s
Locale(s): Savannah, Georgia

Summary: The American Revolution is shown as more a civil war than the birth of a new nation in this novel set in colonial Savannah. Mercy Phillips is rescued by planter Hart Purvis from a vengeful mob that has just murdered her Tory father. She comes to live on his plantation and plays an important role in keeping it as the turmoil of the Revolution affects everyone's fortune.

Historical Accuracy: The Revolution is shown from an interesting angle that seems genuine.

2966 *The Lost Garden*

Date of Publication: 1982
Subject(s): Regency Romance; Napoleonic Wars
Fictional character(s): Caroline Thorpe, Gentlewoman
Time Period(s): 1800s
Locale(s): London, England; Norfolk, England

Summary: Caroline Thorpe is adopted at birth by a country vicar. When she is summoned as a child to live in a duke's household, she experiences a cold reception from the Duke's acknowledged heirs. Intrigue and danger are her principal legacies in this novel of romantic suspense set during the expected invasion of England by Napoleon.

Historical Accuracy: The novel's situation is loosely based on historical personalities and circumstances.

2967 *Marry in Haste*

Date of Publication: 1961
Subject(s): Regency Period; Napoleonic Wars; Suspense
Fictional character(s): Camilla Forest, Spouse (of Lavenham); Lord Lavenham Leominster, Nobleman
Time Period(s): 1800s
Locale(s): England; Portugal

Summary: Set during the Regency period and the war with Napoleon, the novel depicts the marriage of convenience between Camilla Forest and Lord Leominster. They are caught up in the intrigue that ensues when England joins forces with Spain in an attempt to save Portugal from Napoleon's armies.

Historical Accuracy: The story is fanciful, but the atmosphere and some of the details of the Peninsular War are authentic.

2968 *Polonaise*

Date of Publication: 1987
Subject(s): Napoleonic Wars; Independence—Poland
Fictional character(s): Jenny Peverel, Young Woman; Isobel Ovinska, Royalty (princess); Casimir Ovinska, Royalty (prince)
Historical character(s): Alexander I, Ruler (Czar of Russia); Charles Maurice de Talleyrand-Perigord, Diplomat
Time Period(s): 1800s; 1810s (1802-1815)
Locale(s): Paris, France; Warsaw, Poland; St. Petersburg, Russia

Summary: This tale of political and romantic intrigue is set during the Napoleonic era. A young Englishwoman, Jenny Peverel, joins her childhood friend, Polish princess Isobel Ovinska. Isobel's young son, Casimir, becomes a pawn in the multiple schemes of Alexander I of Russia, Napoleon, and the Brotherhood, a Polish loyalist sect which sees Casimir as its last hope for independence.

Historical Accuracy: The facts about historical events are accurate, although the author has taken some liberties with the historical personalities involved.

2969 *Rebel Heiress*

Date of Publication: 1975
Subject(s): Regency Romance; Napoleonic Wars
Fictional character(s): Henrietta Marchmont, Heiress
Historical character(s): George Bryan Brummell, Gentleman, Socialite
Time Period(s): 1810s (1812)
Locale(s): London, England

Summary: Henrietta Marchmont journeys from America to claim her place in the powerful Marchmont dynasty. She finds herself at the center of fashionable London where scandal is de rigeur, and her exploits become the talk of the town.

Historical Accuracy: The Regency details are authentic.

2970 *Savannah Purchase*

Date of Publication: 1971
Subject(s): Antebellum South; Identity—Concealed
Fictional character(s): Juliet Purchis, Young Woman; Josephine Purchis, Spouse; Hyde Purchis, Plantation Owner
Time Period(s): 1820s
Locale(s): Savannah, Georgia

Summary: Two cousins who might be twins decide to trade places to allow Josephine Purchis to launch a plot to free Napoleon from exile on St. Helena. Multiple complications ensue from the deception as the social scene of antebellum Savannah is depicted.

Historical Accuracy: The basic story is too fanciful to be believed; however the regional background is authentic.

2971 *Shadow of a Lady*

Date of Publication: 1973
Subject(s): Napoleonic Wars
Fictional character(s): Helen Telfair, Gentlewoman
Historical character(s): Sir William Hamilton, Diplomat, Gentleman; Lady Emma Hamilton, Spouse, Gentlewoman; Horatio Nelson, Military Personnel (admiral)
Time Period(s): 1790s
Locale(s): Naples, Italy

Summary: The novel describes the love affair of Lady Emma Hamilton and Lord Nelson, set amidst the glitter of the court of Naples. The story is told from the perspective of Helen Telfair the very dissimilar friend of Lady Hamilton.

Historical Accuracy: The novel is a blend of fact and fiction. The atmosphere of the period and place is genuine.

2972 *Whispering*

Date of Publication: 1995
Subject(s): Napoleonic Wars; Peninsular War
Fictional character(s): Caterina Gomez, Young Woman; Jeremy Craddock, Gentleman; Harriet Brown, Young Woman
Historical character(s): Arthur Wellesley, Military Personnel (army commander), Nobleman (Duke of Wellington)
Time Period(s): 1810s
Locale(s): Oporto, Portugal

Summary: When Caterina Gomez returns home to Portugal from England, she finds herself in the middle of the Peninsular Campaign against Napoleon. Accompanied by her English cousin, Jeremy Craddock, and her friend, Harriet Brown, Caterina is drawn into mounting intrigue between the English and the Portuguese.

Historical Accuracy: The period elements are authentic although the story is fanciful.

2973 *Wide Is the Water*

Date of Publication: 1981

Subject(s): American Revolution
Fictional character(s): Mercy Purchis, Spouse; Hart Purchis, Plantation Owner, Captive
Time Period(s): 1780s
Locale(s): London, England; Philadelphia, Pennsylvania; New England

Summary: Continuing the adventures of the hero and heroine of *Judas Flowering*, the novel is set in England and America at the end of the Revolution. Husband and wife Hart and Mercy Purchis are separated by the war. He is engaged in the intrigues of London society; she flees a blizzard in New England and colonial politics as she tries to be reunited with her husband.

Historical Accuracy: The novel is accomplished in rendering a convincing period atmosphere.

2974 *Windover*

Date of Publication: 1992
Subject(s): Romance; French Revolution; Georgian Period
Fictional character(s): Kathryn Pennam, Gentlewoman; Mark Weatherby, Teacher; Oliver Morewood, Gentleman
Time Period(s): 1780s; 1790s
Locale(s): England

Summary: In this romantic suspense story set in England during the French Revolution, Kathryn Pennam falls in love with Mark Weatherby despite opposition from her stepfather. Mark mysteriously disappears, and to avoid her stepfather's unwanted advances, Kathryn agrees to a marriage of convenience. News from revolutionary France causes Kathryn to flee to London, where she must surmount scandal and heartbreak.

Historical Accuracy: The novel's atmosphere is historical and convincing, but the emphasis is on suspense and adventure.

C. WALTER HODGES (1909-)

An English illustrator, designer, artist, and novelist, Hodges was an art student at London's Goldsmith College. He has done the illustrations for more than 70 children's books. He is also an authority on the structures of Elizabethan playhouses.

2975 *The Marsh King*

Date of Publication: 1967
Subject(s): Anglo-Saxon Period; Dark Ages; Vikings
Fictional character(s): Guthorn, Warrior (Viking)
Historical character(s): Alfred the Great, Ruler (King of Wessex)
Time Period(s): 9th century
Locale(s): England

Summary: This is a tale of the 9th-century combat between the Danes and the Saxons. King Alfred's Wessex is overrun, and he controls only the great marshes to which he retreats. His opponent is Guthorn, leader of the Danes, whom Alfred had once bested and set free. The novel details Guthorn's campaign in Wessex and the clash of two very different cultures.

Historical Accuracy: The story is imagined, but the atmosphere of the era is genuine.

SUSANNA HOE

`2976` *God Save the Tsar*

Date of Publication: 1978
Subject(s): Russian Revolution; Royalty—Russia; Alternate History
Historical character(s): Nicholas II, Ruler (Czar of Russia); Alexandra Feodorovna, Royalty (consort of Nicholas II); George V, Ruler (King of England)
Time Period(s): 1910s (1918-1919)
Locale(s): Russia; Constantinople, Ottoman Empire; Poland

Summary: This version of the fate of the Romanovs in 1918 imagines the royal family's escape from Ekaterinburg. The emphasis is on family relationships, and the pathos of the Romanovs' fallen state, with some glimpses of what brought them down.

Historical Accuracy: The novel begins with a scrupulously accurate account of what is known of the final days of Nicholas and his family.

PEGGY HOFFMANN (1910-)

Born in Ohio and educated at Miami University and the University of Chicago, Hoffman has worked as a free-lance writer. Her novels include *My Dear Cousin* and *A Forest of Feathers*. She is also the editor of 14 collections of choral music, reflecting extensive studies of organ music.

`2977` *My Dear Cousin*

Date of Publication: 1970
Subject(s): War of 1812
Fictional character(s): Lydia Hollingsworth, Gentlewoman; Augustus John Foster, Diplomat
Historical character(s): Jerome Bonaparte, Royalty; James Madison, Political Figure; Elizabeth Patterson, Gentlewoman; Dolley Madison, Spouse; John Randolph, Political Figure; Winfield Scott, Military Personnel (general)
Time Period(s): 1810s
Locale(s): Washington, District of Columbia; Baltimore, Maryland

Summary: Set during the War of 1812 and based on the personal letters and records of a prominent Federalist family, the novel describes the tragic romance between Lydia Hollingsworth, a Baltimore belle, and Augustus John Foster, a British ambassador to the U.S. The war puts them on opposite sides of the conflict.

Historical Accuracy: The novel interweaves the factual and the fictional, creating a convincing period background of real events and personalities.

RAY HOGAN (1908-)

Prolific American author Ray Hogan was born in Willow Springs, Missouri, and studied at the Hoosier Institute of Journalism. The author of over 125 books, Hogan also has written numerous television scripts and several hundred short stories. His novels include *The Hell Raiser*, *Lawman's Choice*, and *Outlaw's Pledge*.

`2978` *The Ghost Raider*

Date of Publication: 1960
Subject(s): Civil War—U.S.
Historical character(s): John Singleton Mosby, Military Personnel (Confederate soldier); Robert E. Lee, Military Personnel (Confederate commander); James Ewell Brown Stuart, Military Personnel (Confederate cavalry officer)
Time Period(s): 1860s
Locale(s): Virginia

Summary: Confederate raider, John Mosby is given the assignment of rescuing a Confederate officer who is being held as a Union prisoner. However, Mosby has sworn to kill the officer, who has sent a Confederate company needlessly to their death,.

Historical Accuracy: The situation is fictional and idealizes the exploits of Mosby and his Raiders.

`2979` *Mosby's Last Ride*

Date of Publication: 1966
Subject(s): Civil War—U.S.
Historical character(s): John Singleton Mosby, Military Personnel (Confederate soldier)
Time Period(s): 1860s
Locale(s): Virginia

Summary: This adventure tale set during the Civil War concerns the exploits of John Mosby and his group of Confederate raiders who strike deep behind the Union lines. The story concerns Mosby's Raiders final mission as the Confederate cause is lost.

Historical Accuracy: This is a fanciful story based on the actual exploits of Mosby and his men.

`2980` *Night Raider*

Date of Publication: 1964
Subject(s): Civil War—U.S.
Historical character(s): John Singleton Mosby, Military Personnel (Confederate soldier)
Time Period(s): 1860s
Locale(s): Virginia

Summary: This Civil War era adventure tale concerns the exploits of Confederate John Mosby and his daring Mosby's Raiders, who attempt to penetrate the Union lines and kidnap Union Brigadier General C.B. Stoughton.

Historical Accuracy: The story is based on two actual incidents in the life of John Mosby—the kidnapping attempt and the routing of an entire company of Union soldiers by Mosby and nine of his men. Some of the names, dates, and places are fictitious, as are some of the supporting episodes.

2981 *Soldier in Buckskin*

Date of Publication: 1996
Subject(s): American West; Biography, Fictionalized
Historical character(s): Kit Carson, Frontiersman; John C. Fremont, Frontiersman, Political Figure; Singing Grass, Indian (Arapahoe), Royalty (princess); Josefa Jaramillo, Gentlewoman, Spouse (of Carson)
Time Period(s): 1830s; 1840s (1831-1848)
Locale(s): West; California

Summary: This documentary novel chronicles the life of legendary frontiersman Kit Carson. He leads trapping expeditions, fights Indians, and guides John C. Fremont's expedition to survey and map the West. Carson emerges as a man of great resources and personal courage.

Historical Accuracy: The novel presents a blend of fact and legend to create a somewhat glorified portrait of Carson.

CECELIA HOLLAND (1943-)

An American writer, Holland's first historical novel was published when she was only 23. She has followed it by a series of impressive explorations of historical periods largely neglected by other writers. Her novels attempt to prove that there is more to historical thrillers than just sword play and seduction.

2982 *Antichrist: A Novel of the Emperor Frederick II*

Date of Publication: 1970
Subject(s): Middle Ages; Crusades
Historical character(s): Frederick II, Ruler (Holy Roman Emperor); al-Malik al-Kamil, Ruler (Sultan of Egypt and Palestine)
Time Period(s): 13th century
Locale(s): Sicily, Italy; Jerusalem, Palestine; Cyprus

Summary: The flamboyant life and times of Frederick II, Holy Roman Emperor and King of Sicily, are dramatized. Frederick is a magnetic and contradictory personality. Branded the AntiChrist and a heretic, he undertakes a crusade that leads to his taking Jerusalem and being crowned in Saint Sepulcher. The era is superbly rendered in capturing this unique historical figure.

Historical Accuracy: Despite occasional conjecture and invention, Holland succeeds in capturing a fascinating personality and his time and place.

2983 *The Bear Flag: A Novel of the Birth of California*

Date of Publication: 1990
Subject(s): Bear Flag Revolt; American West
Fictional character(s): Cat Reilly, Settler, Widow(er); Sergei Sohrakoff, Adventurer; Jesus Orozco, Military Personnel
Historical character(s): John C. Fremont, Military Personnel; Kit Carson, Military Personnel, Frontiersman; John A. Sutter, Settler, Businessman; John Bidwell, Miner; Robert Field

Stockton, Military Personnel; Thomas Larkin, Political Figure
Time Period(s): 1840s
Locale(s): Sutter's Fort, California; Sonoma, California; Monterey, California

Summary: Having survived the epic trek west to California in the early 1840s, widow Cat Reilly, gets involved in the battle for independence of California from Mexico. All of the important historical figures in the great Bear Flag Revolt are on hand, and the fighting and political maneuvering are dramatically shown.

Historical Accuracy: Holland admits to some meddling with her chronology, but the essential details of the Bear Flag Revolt are clearly shown and dramatically brought to life.

2984 *The Belt of Gold*

Date of Publication: 1984
Subject(s): Byzantine Empire
Fictional character(s): John Cerulis, Nobleman; Hagan, Nobleman
Historical character(s): Irene, Ruler (Byzantine empress)
Time Period(s): 9th century
Locale(s): Byzantium, Byzantine Empire (now Istanbul)

Summary: The scene is Byzantium in the 9th century. A Frankish knight journeying home from the Holy Land is introduced to court life. There he witnesses the splendour of Empress Irene's court as well as a contest of wills between Irene and Cerulis whose plots and counterplots prove murderous.

Historical Accuracy: The details of time and place are brilliantly rendered.

2985 *City of God: A Novel of the Borgias*

Date of Publication: 1979
Subject(s): Renaissance
Fictional character(s): Nicholas Dawson, Diplomat, Spy
Historical character(s): Cesare Borgia, Nobleman, Political Figure; Alexander VI, Religious (pope); Lucrezia Borgia, Noblewoman
Time Period(s): 16th century
Locale(s): Rome, Italy; Tuscany, Italy

Summary: The city of God is 16th-century Rome of the Borgias and the web of conflict and conspiracy in which the Spanish, French, and Papal forces plot to divide and control the wealth of Italy. In this mix operates Nicholas Dawson, secretary to the Florentine ambassador, spy for the Borgias, and go-between for the Spanish. His portrait as an opportunist and manipulator becomes a perfect metaphor for the age.

Historical Accuracy: Holland skillfully brings this moment in history to life in all its complexity.

2986 *The Death of Attila*

Date of Publication: 1973
Subject(s): Roman Empire; Barbarians

Fictional character(s): Dietric, Warrior; Tacs, Military Personnel
Historical character(s): Attila the Hun, Ruler
Time Period(s): 5th century
Locale(s): Germany; Europe (eastern)

Summary: The novel concerns the conjunction of cultures in the 5th century: Hun, Goth, and Roman; pagan and Christian; east and west. The cultural conflict is focussed on the friendship of two men, the son of a German chief and a Hun soldier. Each develops a respect for the other until the death of the great Attila splits them apart.

Historical Accuracy: Holland specializes in animating the little known periods of history with conviction.

2987 *The Earl*

Date of Publication: 1971
Subject(s): Royalty—England; Middle Ages
Fictional character(s): Rannulf, Knight
Historical character(s): Henry II, Royalty (prince); Fulk, Nobleman (Earl of Stafford); Thierry, Nobleman
Time Period(s): 12th century
Locale(s): Stafford, England; Tutbury, England

Summary: The novel's subject is the scramble for the English throne on the death of Henry I. Stephen claims the throne, and Henry II, Duke of Normandy and husband of Eleanor of Aquitaine, is determined to take it from him. England is in the grip of civil war. The novel focusses on the Earl of Stafford, a great Norman noble caught in the middle of shifting alliances.

Historical Accuracy: The novel offers a close psychological drama with few of the trappings and details of the period. Stafford is a convincing vassal.

2988 *The Firedrake*

Date of Publication: 1966
Subject(s): Middle Ages; Norman Conquest; Battle of Hastings
Fictional character(s): Laeghaire of Tralee, Knight
Historical character(s): William the Conqueror, Ruler (Duke of Normandy); Baldwin V, Ruler (Count of Flanders)
Time Period(s): 11th century
Locale(s): Flanders; Normandy, France; Hastings, England

Summary: The Norman invasion and conquest of England is dramatized through the experiences of an itinerant Irish knight. He becomes an officer of the court of Count Baldwin of Flanders where he meets William of Normandy and takes up his cause to win the throne of England. The novel culminates in the decisive Battle of Hastings.

Historical Accuracy: There are brilliantly described scenes of battle and action and a sure sense of period details. History is translated into moving human drama.

2989 *Great Maria*

Date of Publication: 1974
Subject(s): Middle Ages
Fictional character(s): Maria, Noblewoman; Richard, Knight
Time Period(s): 11th century
Locale(s): Italy

Summary: Southern Italy in the 11th century is a cauldron of conflict: Norman barons, Saracens, the Pope, and the Emperor all vie for power and influence. In the midst of all this, Maria, daughter of a Norman baron, marries a young knight, and together they attempt to build and protect a kingdom.

Historical Accuracy: With characteristic precision Holland renders the remote past with immediacy and compassion.

2990 *Jerusalem*

Date of Publication: 1996
Subject(s): Middle Ages; Crusades
Fictional character(s): Rannulf Fitzwilliam, Knight
Historical character(s): Baudouin IV, Ruler (King of Jerusalem); Sybilla, Royalty (princess), Widow(er); Saladin, Warrior, Ruler (sultan)
Time Period(s): 12th century (1187)
Locale(s): Jerusalem, Palestine

Summary: Set during the final years of the Kingdom of Jerusalem established by the leaders of the First Crusade, the novel dramatizes the political intrigue and religious fervor that grips the kingdom as it is hardpressed by Saladin. At the center of the story is Rannulf Fitzwilliam, a Knight Templar, who finds himself drawn into the political world of King Baudouin and his sister and heir, Sybilla.

Historical Accuracy: The novel is masterful in recreating the atmosphere of the period and the clash of cultures.

2991 *The Kings in Winter*

Date of Publication: 1968
Subject(s): Celtic Ireland; Vikings; Middle Ages
Fictional character(s): Muirtagh, Knight; Cearbhall, Knight
Historical character(s): Brian Boru, Ruler; Maelmordha, Ruler
Time Period(s): 11th century (1014)
Locale(s): Ireland

Summary: Ireland in the 11th century is the backdrop to this tale of clan feuds and power politics for control of all Ireland. Muirtagh is the a peace-loving head of a clan caught up in the High King Brian Boru's war with the Danes and other Irish rebels. Treachery and violence cause Muirtagh to join the opposition, and they join battle near Dublin.

Historical Accuracy: This is a powerful evocation of Irish history centered on the dramatic story of the central character.

2992 *The Lords of Vaumartin*

Date of Publication: 1988
Subject(s): Middle Ages; Inheritance—Disputed
Fictional character(s): Everard De Vaumartin, Orphan, Knight
Historical character(s): Philip VI, Ruler (King of France); Edward, the Black Prince, Royalty (prince); John, Royalty (prince)
Time Period(s): 14th century
Locale(s): Brittany, France; Paris, France

Summary: In this story of 14th-century France, a young man is done out of his inheritance and sent to war. He survives the Battle of Crecy and proceeds to Paris where he pursues a career as a scholar in anticipation of his return to Vaumartin and the restoration of his inheritance.

Historical Accuracy: The novel is particularly strong in evoking medieval Paris and its intellectual ferment and pageantry. Holland's scholarship in aid of her storytelling is exceptional.

2993 *Pacific Street*

Date of Publication: 1992
Subject(s): Gold Rush—California; Racial Conflict
Fictional character(s): Frances Hardhardt, Saloon Keeper/Owner; Tierney Rudd, Lawyer; Daisy, Entertainer, Saloon Hostess
Time Period(s): 1850s
Locale(s): San Francisco, California

Summary: The novel tells the story of San Francisco in 1850 through the creation and success of the Shining Light Saloon. Run by a tiny black woman named Frances Hardhardt, its principal attraction is the beautiful Daisy. The success of the Shining Light draws all to its doors, and the conjunction of types dramatizes frontier corruption, vigilante justice, and racial prejudice.

Historical Accuracy: Holland's angle of vision showing the San Francisco community of 1850 is interesting.

2994 *Pillar of the Sky*

Date of Publication: 1983
Subject(s): Prehistory; Tribal Life—Prehistoric
Fictional character(s): Landon, Chieftain; Moloquin, Outcast, Chieftain; Karella, Sorcerer (tribal storyteller and seer)
Time Period(s): Indeterminate Past
Locale(s): Stonehenge, England

Summary: Holland attempts a plausible explanation for the creation of Stonehenge and the customs and beliefs of the builders. Moloquin is the outcast heir to the tribal chieftainship who returns to claim his inheritance. He saves the People from starvation by bringing them the secrets of the forge and metals. As chief he begins the construction of a new ring of stones as a gateway between the present and the past.

Historical Accuracy: Since we know almost nothing about the prehistoric people who built Stonehenge, accuracy is less an issue here than consistency and credibility. On both counts Holland earns high marks in constructing a human story of an ancient people.

2995 *Rakossy*

Date of Publication: 1967
Subject(s): Turk-Magyr Wars
Fictional character(s): Janos Rakossy, Nobleman; Count Malencz, Nobleman; Catherine de Bunez, Gentlewoman
Historical character(s): Archduke Ferdinand, Ruler
Time Period(s): 16th century (1525)
Locale(s): Hungary; Vienna, Austria

Summary: Set during the Turk-Magyr wars in 16th-century Hungary, the title character is a ruthless and cynical baron preparing for the coming Turkish invasion. Political intrigue and romance complicates the story, taking Rakossy to Vienna to marry. The personal relationships climax with the Turkish war that is graphically described.

Historical Accuracy: This is an impressive recreation of a little known historical period.

2996 *The Sea Beggars*

Date of Publication: 1982
Subject(s): Pirates
Fictional character(s): Jan Van Cleef, Sailor, Pirate; Hanneke Van Cleef, Young Woman
Historical character(s): William, Duke of Orange, Nobleman; Fernando Alvarez de Toledo, Nobleman (Duke of Alba), Military Personnel
Time Period(s): 16th century
Locale(s): Antwerp, Belgium; England; *Wayward Girl*, At Sea (North Sea)

Summary: In this novel of the Dutch revolt against the Spanish in 16th-century Holland, the struggle of a brother and sister is the focus of the drama. He joins the Sea Beggars, Dutch pirates plundering the North Sea coast and attacking the Spanish fleet; she nurses her mother and endures the devastation of the Spanish at home. Both are swept up in a dramatic revolt for a nation's independence.

Historical Accuracy: Holland acknowledges certain tampering with some details in the interest of the narrative. This appears minor compared to the larger picture she brilliantly creates.

2997 *Two Ravens*

Date of Publication: 1977
Subject(s): Vikings; Middle Ages
Fictional character(s): Bjarni, Adventurer
Time Period(s): 12th century
Locale(s): Iceland; Hebrides, Scotland; England

Summary: This novel of 12th-century Iceland centers on Bjarni, who rejects the domination of his father to emigrate to Norway, prompted by tales of Viking strength and courage. He lands in the Hebrides and makes his way to England where he finds peace for a time before inevitably being drawn back to his homeland.

Historical Accuracy: Holland brings to life an austere primitive world split between Christianity and paganism and wracked with struggle and conflict.

2998 *Until the Sun Falls*

Date of Publication: 1969
Subject(s): Mongols
Fictional character(s): Psin, Ruler (of the Merkits tribe)
Historical character(s): Sabotai, Military Personnel (Mongol general); Batu Khan, Ruler; Quyuk, Ruler
Time Period(s): 13th century (1237)
Locale(s): Russia; Europe (eastern); Asia

Summary: The novel traces the events of the Mongol invasion of Russia and Eastern Europe. Historical figures like the great Mongol general Sabotai appear, but the novel centers on the fictional character, Psin, who represents a characteristic man of his age.

Historical Accuracy: The events described are solidly based on historical research. Holland brings a remote part of world history to life.

TOM HOLLAND

`2999` *Lord of the Dead: The Secret History of Byron*

Date of Publication: 1995
Subject(s): Vampires; Literary Life; Regency Period
Historical character(s): George Gordon Byron, Writer; John Cam Hobhouse, Gentleman; Percy Bysshe Shelley, Writer
Time Period(s): 1820s
Locale(s): Greece; London, England; Venice, Italy

Summary: Lord Byron becomes a vampire in this alternative version of his biography. While in Greece with his friend Hobhouse, Byron succumbs to the attractions of a fugitive slave who helps transform him into the world's most formidable vampire. Byron's sinister adventures across Europe are depicted.

Historical Accuracy: Although fantastic, the novel demonstrates a knowledge of the Byron biography and offers a convincing portrait of the period.

HELEN HOLLICK (1953-)

British writer Hollick left school at 16 and worked at a local library in the town of Chingford for 13 years, where she developed an interest in Arthurian history. She began writing *Pendragon's Banner*, the first of her historical novels about King Arthur, while working at a school cafeteria in the east London suburb of Walthamstow.

`3000` *The Kingmaking*

Date of Publication: 1994
Subject(s): Dark Ages; Myths and Legends; Arthurian Legends
Fictional character(s): Arthur, Warrior; Gwenhwyfar, Gentlewoman
Time Period(s): 5th century (450s)
Locale(s): England

Summary: In the first part of the Pendragon's Banner trilogy, the young Arthur is revealed as the new Pendragon, destined to lead the uprising of the Britons against an evil Italian tyrant. He and Gwenhwyfar become the partners in a political triangle, and Arthur is forced to choose between his kingship and the woman he loves.

Historical Accuracy: The author admits that she is no historian and that her story is her personal view of the Dark Ages. However, a few of the novel's events and characters are factually based. The novel's notes detail both the factual basis of the story and the author's departures.

`3001` *Pendragon's Banner*

Date of Publication: 1996
Subject(s): Dark Ages; Myths and Legends; Arthurian Legends
Fictional character(s): Arthur, Ruler (King of the Britons); Gwenhwyfar, Royalty (queen consort of Arthur)
Time Period(s): 5th century (459-466)

Locale(s): England

Summary: In this second novel of a trilogy on King Arthur and his reign, he wins the throne at the age of 24 and attempts to protect his kingdom from two enemies. One is Winifred, Arthur's first wife, who is determined to ensure the succession for her son and the other is Morgause, the malevolent priestess and Queen of the North. Domestic tragedy involving his queen Gwenhwyfar also tests the young leader.

Historical Accuracy: This is a version of the Arthurian story close in tone and detail to its period, stripped of the medieval elements of the more familiar versions. The author's notes indicate the historical sources and the deviations from them.

SHERI HOLMAN

Holman grew up in rural Virginia and now lives in Brooklyn, New York. *A Stolen Tongue* is her first novel.

`3002` *A Stolen Tongue*

Date of Publication: 1997
Subject(s): Mystery; Religious Life; Middle Ages
Historical character(s): Felix Fabri, Religious (priest)
Time Period(s): 15th century (1483)
Locale(s): Germany; Greece; Palestine

Summary: Based on the wanderings of Friar Felix Fabri, this mystery follows his adventures as he sets out on a pilgrimage to venerate the relics of Saint Katherine of Alexandria. On the journey from Germany to Mount Sinai, Fabri is thrust into a strange mystery as he discovers that Katherine's remains are being stolen from their holy resting place.

Historical Accuracy: The novel succeeds in believably recreating 15th-century life and customs.

MARJORIE HOLMES (1910-)

Born in Iowa, Holmes graduated from Cornell College. She is a freelance writer, columnist, and teacher. Her Biblical trilogy was intended to offer a human version of the story of Mary, Joseph, and Jesus.

`3003` *The Messiah*

Date of Publication: 1987
Subject(s): Biblical Story
Historical character(s): Jesus Christ, Biblical Figure; John the Baptist, Biblical Figure; Mary Magdalene, Biblical Figure; Mary, Biblical Figure; Lazarus, Biblical Figure; Peter, Biblical Figure; John, Biblical Figure
Time Period(s): 1st century
Locale(s): Nazareth, Israel; Jerusalem, Israel

Summary: The author concludes her fictional retelling of the life of Christ with the years of Jesus' ministry—as rabbi, leader, and finally martyr. The author renders the famous scenes of Jesus' miracles, his sermons, trial, and crucifixion with the novelist's eye for period details and plausible motives.

Historical Accuracy: The novel is a work of fiction, not an historical account. It presents what may have happened, given the facts of Jesus' life and times.

3004 *Three From Galilee: The Young Man From Nazareth*

Date of Publication: 1985
Subject(s): Biblical Story
Historical character(s): Jesus Christ, Biblical Figure; Mary, Biblical Figure; Joseph, Biblical Figure
Time Period(s): 1st century (12-30)
Locale(s): Nazareth, Israel

Summary: In the sequel to *Two From Galilee*, the author describes the "lost years" of Jesus, from the age of 12 when the New Testament describes his debate with the elders in the temple, to the of age 30 when he begins his ministry.

Historical Accuracy: Though obviously speculative, the novel vividly creates a convincing period background.

3005 *Two From Galilee: A Love Story*

Date of Publication: 1972
Subject(s): Biblical Story
Historical character(s): Mary, Biblical Figure; Joseph, Biblical Figure
Time Period(s): 1st century B.C.; 1st century
Locale(s): Galilee, Israel; Nazareth, Israel; Jerusalem, Israel

Summary: The story of Jesus Christ's birth is told through the love story of Mary and Joseph. They appear as two very human characters contending with the unexpected news of Mary's pregnancy.

Historical Accuracy: The author attempts to convey the human dimension of this great spiritual story. The customs of the times are convincingly demonstrated.

FELIX HOLT (1898-1954)

3006 *Dan'l Boone Kissed Me*

Date of Publication: 1954
Subject(s): Rural Life—U.S.
Fictional character(s): Duke Caldwell, Landowner
Time Period(s): 1840s (1845)
Locale(s): Kentucky

Summary: This story of life in western Kentucky during the 1840s centers on strong-willed and determined Duke Caldwell, who has built the best house and tobacco farm in the Jackson Purchase area. He is determined to control the lives of his family, and the novel's action offers him a lesson in humility.

Historical Accuracy: The novel captures the region and period believably.

HELENE HOLT
(PSEUD. OF LAURAN PAINE, 1916-)

Born in Minnesota, Paine is the author of some 900 books, under a variety of pseudonyms, making him arguably the most prolific author of our time. Paine has produced over 600 westerns, 125 romance novels, and 75 mysteries, in addition to numerous nonfiction works of history,

biography, espionage, and the occult. Paine has worked as a cowboy and rancher, and began his writing career producing a book a week.

3007 *Exiled*

Date of Publication: 1987
Subject(s): Religious Conflict; Puritans
Historical character(s): John Lothropp, Religious (clergyman); William Laud, Religious (Archbishop of Canterbury)
Time Period(s): 17th century (1630s)
Locale(s): England

Summary: Religious persecution of the Puritan separatists in England during the 17th century is dramatized in the experiences of John Lothropp, who resists the conformist doctrines of Bishop Laud. He is tried and exiled to America. At the novel's end, Lothropp and his family depart for Massachusetts. The novel makes a case that the Puritans of the 17th century paved the way for revolutionary thought in the 18th century.

Historical Accuracy: The novel is accurate and faithful to the complex religious issues of the time.

KARE HOLT (1917-)

Norwegian novelist Holt wrote about the occupation of Norway in World War II, the trade union movement, and medieval Norway.

3008 *The Race: A Novel of Polar Exploration*

Date of Publication: 1976
Subject(s): Exploration
Historical character(s): Roald Amundsen, Explorer; Robert Falcon Scott, Explorer
Time Period(s): 1910s (1911-1912)
Locale(s): Antarctica

Summary: This documentary novel chronicles the race between Englishman Robert Scott and Norwegian Roald Amundsen to be the first to reach the South Pole. Neither explorer emerges unscathed in this chronicle of their obsessive drive to be first. Amundsen is portrayed as devious and cold-blooded, while Scott is indecisive and a stickler for discipline.

Historical Accuracy: Only the private thoughts of the participants and an imaginary dialogue between Amundsen and Scott seem to be fiction. The bulk of the narrative is solidly based on the historical record.

TOM HOLT (1961-)

An English lawyer and author, Tom Holt was born in London and attended Wadham College, Oxford. Holt's comic novels blend his knowledge of mythology and the classics with lighthearted and ironic humor and have been compared to the works of P.G. Wodehouse. His books include *Expecting Someone Taller, Who's Afraid of*

Beowulf, and two continuations of E.F. Benson's Lucia series, *Lucia in Wartime* and *Lucia Triumphant*.

3009 *Goatsong*

Date of Publication: 1990
Subject(s): Ancient Greece
Fictional character(s): Eupolis, Farmer (goatherd), Writer
Historical character(s): Pericles, Political Figure; Euripides, Writer (playwright); Aristophanes, Writer (playwright); Sophocles, Writer (playwright); Socrates, Philosopher
Time Period(s): 5th century B.C.
Locale(s): Athens, Greece

Summary: Set during the Golden Age of Athens, this comic and wry look at the customs and politics of ancient Greece features Eupolis, a goat herder, who tells the story of his rise to fame and the glory and decline of Athens.

Historical Accuracy: Despite the satirical tone, the novel offers a convincing portrait of life in 5th century B.C. Athens.

3010 *The Walled Orchard*

Date of Publication: 1991
Subject(s): Ancient Greece
Fictional character(s): Eupolis, Farmer (goatherd), Writer
Historical character(s): Socrates, Philosopher
Time Period(s): 5th century B.C.
Locale(s): Athens, Greece

Summary: This sequel to *Goatsong* continues the reflections of former goat herder Eupolis, who achieves fame for his comic verse. He provides an irreverent account of the Golden Age of Greece and its fall from democracy to oligarchy.

Historical Accuracy: The novel's portrait of ancient Greek life and customs is well drawn and convincing.

VICTORIA HOLT
(PSEUD. OF ELEANOR HIBBERT, 1906-1993)

Victoria Holt is one of many pseudonyms of prolific British author Eleanor Hibbert. When she published her first novel, *Mistress of Mellyn*, under the name Victoria Holt, many thought that it was the creation of Daphne Du Maurier. The author once said that Victorian writers such as Charles Dickens and the Brontes were major influences on her suspense stories. Her other pseudonyms are Philippa Carr and Jean Plaidy.

3011 *The Captive*

Date of Publication: 1989
Subject(s): Gothic Romance; Pirates; Victorian Period
Fictional character(s): Rosetta Cranleigh, Gentlewoman; Simon Perrivale, Nobleman, Bastard Son
Time Period(s): 19th century
Locale(s): Mediterranean; Africa; England

Summary: Rosetta Cranleigh is shipwrecked and stranded on an island with Simon Perrivale in this 19th-century romantic adventure. She is captured by pirates and sold as a slave to a Turkish pasha. She finally makes her way back to England

and sets out to prove the innocence of Simon who has been wrongfully accused of murder.

Historical Accuracy: The novel is a miscellany of romantic and adventure elements with only the slightest hold on a particular historical period.

3012 *The Curse of the King*

Date of Publication: 1973
Subject(s): Victorian Period; Archaeology
Fictional character(s): Judith Osmond, Archaeologist; Tybalt Travers, Archaeologist; Sir Edward Travers, Archaeologist
Time Period(s): 19th century
Locale(s): England; Egypt

Summary: Judith Osmond, a young Englishwoman with a passion for archaeology, accompanies Sir Edward Travers and his son on a dangerous excavation in Egypt. Is their endeavor cursed? The archaeologists must discover why they are being threatened.

Historical Accuracy: Romantic suspense is all in this story, with little attempt to offer either a detailed period background or any historical basis.

3013 *The Demon Lover*

Date of Publication: 1982
Subject(s): Romance; Franco-Prussian War
Fictional character(s): Kate Collison, Artist; Baron Rollo de Centeville, Nobleman; Nicole St. Giles, Gentlewoman
Time Period(s): 1870s
Locale(s): Paris, France; Centeville, France; England

Summary: A young English woman rises to fame in France as a painter of miniatures. Baron Rollo de Centeville is responsible for promoting her, but he has ulterior motives. The novel is a romantic blend of secrets, deceits, murder, rape, and a touch of history.

Historical Accuracy: Holt does attempt to show some class conflict and some details about the Franco-Prussian War.

3014 *The Devil on Horseback*

Date of Publication: 1977
Subject(s): French Revolution; Romance
Fictional character(s): Minella Maddox, Teacher; Margot Delibe, Gentlewoman; Charles August Delibe, Nobleman
Time Period(s): 1780s
Locale(s): England; Paris, France

Summary: A young English schoolteacher falls in love with her best friend's father. When she and her friend travel to France to conceal her friend's pregnancy, they find themselves in the midst of the French Revolution. Death and deception abound as the Revolution surrounds them and threatens their lives. Whom should they trust? Who is the enemy?.

Historical Accuracy: The atmosphere of the French Revolution is clearly painted with numerous references to specific historical events and characters.

3015 *The Judas Kiss*

Date of Publication: 1981
Subject(s): Romance; Victorian Period
Fictional character(s): Francine Ewell, Gentlewoman; Pippa Ewell, Gentlewoman
Time Period(s): 19th century
Locale(s): Kent, England; Bavaria, Germany

Summary: When her sister Francine elopes with a Bavarian nobleman, Pippa Ewell is left in England to bear the wrath of her stern grandfather. Letters from her sister tell of her happy life, but suddenly the letters stop, and Pippa reads of the murder of a Bavarian nobleman and his English companion. Pippa is convinced that her sister was married and that there is a child, and she sets out to find the truth.

Historical Accuracy: The emphasis is on romantic suspense over a fully detailed historical period.

3016 *Lord of the Far Island*

Date of Publication: 1975
Subject(s): Romance; Edwardian Period
Fictional character(s): Ellen Kellaway, Orphan; Philip Carrington, Gentleman
Time Period(s): 1900s
Locale(s): London, England; Cornwall, England (Sea Isles)

Summary: Ellen Kellaway, a poor orphan in turn-of-the-century London, is surprised by a marriage proposal from Philip Carrington. Her future happiness is haunted by a premonition of doom connected to the secrets of her long-lost family. These secrets are revealed off the coast of Cornwall.

Historical Accuracy: The novel's Cornish setting is convincingly depicted.

3017 *My Enemy the Queen*

Date of Publication: 1978
Subject(s): Elizabethan Period; Royalty—England
Historical character(s): Letitia Knollys, Noblewoman; Robert Dudley, Nobleman (Earl of Leicester), Courtier; Robert Devereux, Nobleman (Earl of Essex), Courtier; Elizabeth I, Ruler (Queen of England)
Time Period(s): 16th century
Locale(s): London, England; Kenilworth, England; Chartley, England

Summary: The story is told by Letitia Knollys Devereaux, cousin of the queen. She forms a romantic alliance with Robert Dudley, Earl of Leicester, and becomes the queen's rival in love and consequently the queen's enemy.

Historical Accuracy: The novel offers many historical details of England during the reign of Elizabeth, including the treachery and passion of the era.

3018 *On the Night of the Seventh Moon*

Date of Publication: 1972
Subject(s): Romance; Franco-Prussian War; Victorian Period
Fictional character(s): Helena Trant, Young Woman; Maximilian Lokenburg, Nobleman
Time Period(s): 19th century (1859-1870)

Locale(s): Black Forest, Germany; England

Summary: On a visit to her mother's homeland in the Black Forest of Germany, Englishwoman Helena Trant finds herself in the middle of a haunting nightmare of seduction and betrayal. She attempts to resolve her relationship with the nobleman Maximilian, only to find herself gripped by jealousies, intrigue, and murder.

Historical Accuracy: The German locale is described with some realistic touches, but the emphasis here is romantic suspense rather than detailed history.

3019 *The Queen's Confession*

Date of Publication: 1968
Subject(s): Royalty—France; French Revolution
Historical character(s): Marie Antoinette; Royalty (Queen of France); Louis XVI, Ruler (King of France); Louis de Rohan, Religious (cardinal), Political Figure; Hans Axel von Fersen, Nobleman
Time Period(s): 1770s; 1780s
Locale(s): Versailles, France; Paris, France; Vienna, Austria

Summary: This biographical study of Marie Antoinette is written in the first person in the form of her memoirs of her life as queen. The novel is rich with historical detail and dramatic scenes. Unlike a mere re-telling of facts, the author surrounds the reader with the elegance, etiquette, filth, and crudeness of the era.

Historical Accuracy: The author's bibliography includes more than 50 works consulted, and the solidity of her research is evident.

3020 *Secret for a Nightingale*

Date of Publication: 1986
Subject(s): Romance; Victorian Period; Crimean War
Fictional character(s): Susanna Pleydell, Nurse; Aubrey St. Clare, Gentleman; Damien Adair, Doctor
Historical character(s): Florence Nightingale, Nurse
Time Period(s): 1850s
Locale(s): India; Crimea, Russia; Germany

Summary: Susanna Pleydell's marriage to Aubrey St. Clare ends in tragedy because of her husband's obsession with the occult and his weakness for opium. Susanna blames Dr. Damien Adair for Aubrey's fall, and she vows revenge. As a nurse in the Crimean War, working alongside Florence Nightingale, she reencounters Dr. Adair and experiences conflicting emotions.

Historical Accuracy: The nursing scenes in the Crimea are primarily plot contrivances rather than a plausible depiction of the period.

3021 *The Spring of the Tiger*

Date of Publication: 1979
Subject(s): British Colonies; Romance
Fictional character(s): Sarah Ashington, Heiress, Plantation Owner (tea plantation); Clinton Shaw, Gentleman; Clytie Blanford, Gentlewoman
Time Period(s): 19th century
Locale(s): England; Ceylon

Summary: A young English woman inherits a tea plantation from her father. After a whirlwind courtship with her father's young and impetuous friend, she marries him and they move to Ceylon where danger and mystery surround her. Sorcery, snakes, and a half-sister await her, along with the legendary family pearls and poison.

Historical Accuracy: The historical period is only dimly presented. Atmosphere is all in this romance.

3022 *The Time of the Hunter's Moon*

Date of Publication: 1983
Subject(s): Romance
Fictional character(s): Cordelia Grant, Teacher; Jason Verringer, Nobleman, Widow(er)
Time Period(s): 19th century
Locale(s): Canterton, England; Devon, England; Colby, England

Summary: A young schoolmistress is romantically pursued by a rich baron, who is a recent widower with a questionable reputation. This tale of mystery, intrigue, and murder is set at a girls' academy in the English countryside.

Historical Accuracy: There are few historical details or reference points to locate time or place. Romantic intrigue is all.

DONALD HONIG (1931-)

An American writer born on Long Island, New York, Honig is best known for his many baseball books, including *Baseball: When the Grass Was Green.* He is also the author of a number of western novels.

3023 *The Sword of General Englund*

Date of Publication: 1996
Subject(s): Mystery; American West; Military Life
Fictional character(s): Thomas Maynard, Military Personnel (captain); Billy Barrie, Military Personnel (sergeant); Alfred Englund, Military Personnel (general)
Time Period(s): 1870s (1876)
Locale(s): Dakota Territory, United States

Summary: The novel is set in a remote military post in the Dakota territory during the 1870s, where General Alfred Englund, alone in his office, is found stabbed to death. The solution to this locked-room puzzle is left to Captain Thomas Maynard. The investigation uncovers several suspects among the commander's five senior officers, each with a motive for murder, as well as the young wife of one of the officers, and an army scout who disappeared on the night of the murder.

Historical Accuracy: The novel's setting and period details are believable and create a plausible atmosphere.

3024 *Walk Like a Man*

Date of Publication: 1961
Subject(s): Civil War—U.S.; Coming of Age
Fictional character(s): Clay Taylor, Young Man; Jeff Taylor, Teenager; Pete Mariah, Teenager
Time Period(s): 1860s (Civil War period)
Locale(s): Long Island, New York; Virginia

Summary: This tale of a young boy's coming of age is set during the Civil War. Jeff Taylor's uncle Clay is accused of being a Confederate spy. To clear Clay's name and settle a family crisis, Jeff sets off on horseback for Virginia to bring Clay back. In the process, Jeff and his friend Pete learn much about the true nature of war and adulthood.

Historical Accuracy: The period is captured with intimacy and authenticity.

THOMAS HOOVER (1941-)

An American researcher and writer, Hoover was born in Texas and attended the University of Texas and Texas A & M. Hoover has traveled extensively in India and China.

3025 *Caribbee*

Date of Publication: 1985
Subject(s): Pirates; English Colonies; Slavery
Fictional character(s): Hugh Winston, Adventurer, Pirate; Katherine Bedford, Gentlewoman; Attiba, Slave
Time Period(s): 17th century (1638-1655)
Locale(s): West Indies; Barbados; Jamaica

Summary: The novel tells the story of life in the West Indies during the 17th century in which colonists escaping Cromwell's tyranny, pirates, and Puritans engaged in a battle for supremacy. The novel concerns Hugh Winston, an exiled aristocrat turned pirate, and Katherine Bedford, daughter of Barbados' governor. The story dramatizes the birth of American democracy 130 years before the Declaration of Independece.

Historical Accuracy: Many of the episodes in the novel are fictionalized renderings of actual events although some have been condensed for dramatic effect.

3026 *The Moghul*

Date of Publication: 1983
Subject(s): Mogul Empire
Fictional character(s): Brian Hawksworth, Military Personnel (British captain)
Time Period(s): 17th century
Locale(s): India

Summary: Captain Brian Hawksworth is sent by the East India Company to open up trade with India. He finds himself at the center of intrigue in the Moghul court.

Historical Accuracy: Mixing history and adventure, the novel offers an authentic look at 17th-century India.

JOSEPH G.E. HOPKINS (1909-)

Born in Brooklyn, New York, Hopkins is a graduate of Fordham and Columbia universities. He has worked as a teacher at preparatory schools and colleges in New York and was a book editor at Charles Scribner's Sons in charge of their reference works. He is the author of historical and biographical works as well as fiction.

3027   *Patriot's Progress*

Date of Publication: 1961
Subject(s): American Revolution; Battle of Lexington; Battle of Concord
Fictional character(s): John Frayne, Doctor; Alison Cunningham, Loyalist
Time Period(s): 1770s (1774-1776)
Locale(s): Wendham, Massachusetts, American Colonies; Concord, Massachusetts, American Colonies; Boston, Massachusetts, American Colonies

Summary: A young village doctor, John Frayne, must choose sides in the opening years of the American Revolution. He finally joins the Continental Army as a surgeon and is on hand at the battles of Lexington and Concord. The novel concludes with the siege of Boston.

Historical Accuracy: The evocation of the period is authentic, and the action is firmly rooted in fact.

3028   *The Price of Liberty*

Date of Publication: 1976
Subject(s): American Revolution; Medical Profession
Fictional character(s): John Frayne, Doctor (surgeon); Sarah Locker, Young Woman
Time Period(s): 1770s (1777-1778)
Locale(s): Bethlehem, Pennsylvania

Summary: In the winter of 1777-1778, John Frayne, Continental Army surgeon, is in charge of a military hospital tending the wounded from the Battle of Brandywine. He must contend with incompetence and dishonesty in high places, as well as the Moravian settlement of Bethlehem.

Historical Accuracy: The novel convincingly captures the era, with a background based on actual events.

3029   *Retreat and Recall*

Date of Publication: 1966
Subject(s): American Revolution; Espionage
Fictional character(s): John Frayne, Spy, Doctor
Historical character(s): George Washington, Military Personnel (army commander)
Time Period(s): 1770s (1776-1777)
Locale(s): New York, New York; Morristown, New Jersey

Summary: In this sequel to *Patriot's Progress*, the adventures of John Frayne, a young doctor from Massachusetts, are continued. He is captured by the British after the defeat at Fort Washington in New York. Frayne escapes and becomes a secret agent, posing as a Loyalist, and carries important intelligence to Washington via the Continental "underground."

Historical Accuracy: The historical events in the background of the story are authentic.

JAMES DAVID HORAN (1914-1981)

Journalist, historian, editor, producer, commentor, and author Horan was born in New York and attended Drake College. During his 30 years as a reporter and editor with the *New York Journal-American*, he won the Pulitzer Prize for public service for contributing to an article that resulted in

obtaining penicillin for a sick two-year-old child. A historian specializing in the Old West, Horan's books in that field include a trilogy, *The Authentic Wild West*, *Face and Voice of America's Wild, Wild West*, and *Matthew Brady: Historian with a Camera*. Horan's novels include *The Peking Agent*, *Ginerva*, and *The New Vigilantes*.

3030   *The King's Rebel*

Date of Publication: 1953
Subject(s): American Revolution; Indians
Fictional character(s): Esther Montour, Indian (Seneca); Ann Leslie, Young Woman
Historical character(s): Robert Carhampton, Military Personnel (British officer); William Howe, Military Personnel (general); Nathan Hale, Patriot; Joseph Brant, Indian (Mohawk), Chieftain
Time Period(s): 1770s
Locale(s): Mohawk Valley, New York, American Colonies

Summary: Captain Robert Carhampton of the Royal Welsh Fusiliers is sent during the American Revolution into the Mohawk Valley for scouting and espionage duties with the Indians. There he masters the Indian ways and slowly is won over to the rebel cause.

Historical Accuracy: The novel is based on the actual diaries, messages, and records of Carhampton.

3031   *Seek Out and Destroy*

Date of Publication: 1959
Subject(s): Civil War—U.S.; Sea Story; Espionage
Fictional character(s): Kit Dunboyne, Military Personnel (Confederate naval officer)
Time Period(s): 1860s (1865)
Locale(s): *Lee*, At Sea; England

Summary: This novel tale set during the Civil War is based on the actual exploits of the Confederate raider, the *Shenandoah* (here called the *Lee*), which harassed Union shipping and launched a desperate plan to disrupt the Union economy by attacking the New Bedford whaling fleet in the Pacific.

Historical Accuracy: The story alters the details of the *Shenandoah's* voyage and invents incidents that did not happen.

PAUL HORGAN (1903-1995)

An American novelist, biographer, and writer on natural, regional, and church history, Horgan was born in Buffalo, New York, and attended the New Mexico Military Institute. Horgan won a Pulitzer Prize for his classic study, *Great River*, in which he travelled the full length of the Rio Grande. He is also the author of *Lamy of Sante Fe*.

3032   *Distant Trumpet*

Date of Publication: 1960
Subject(s): American West; Indians; Military Life—U.S. Cavalry

Fictional character(s): Matthew Carlton Hazard, Military Personnel (army officer); Laura Greenleaf, Young Woman; White Horn, Indian (Apache)
Time Period(s): 19th century (1860s-1880s)
Locale(s): Fort Delivery, Arizona

Summary: Life in the Arizona territory in the 1880s is depicted in this story of Matthew Carlton Hazard, a West Point graduate who brings his wife Laura to Fort Delivery which is under constant threat by the Apaches. Life in the fort is chronicled.

Historical Accuracy: The story and characters are fictional but enhanced by a convincing sense of the past.

VINTILA HORIA (1915-)

Born in Romania, Horia served as the Romanian press attache in Rome and Vienna. Horia's books include *The Knight of Resignation*, *The Impossible Ones*, and *The Seventh Letter*. Horia received the Prix Goncourt in 1961 but it was withdrawn when it was learned that Horia collaborated with the Nazis.

【3033】 *God Was Born in Exile*

Date of Publication: 1961
Subject(s): Roman Empire; Literary Life
Historical character(s): Ovid, Writer (poet)
Time Period(s): 1st century (9-17)
Locale(s): Tomi, Romania

Summary: In 9 A.D. the poet Ovid is banished from Rome because of the corrupting influence of his erotic *Ars Amoris*. The novel offers an imagined account of his life in exile. The poet of secular love first tries to continue the life he led in Rome as an epicurean but eventually searches for more spiritual consolation.

Historical Accuracy: The novel freely adapts the facts of Ovid's biography to the service of the author's own contemporary outlook and insistence on a Christian message.

HARALD HORNBORG

【3034】 *Passion and the Sword*

Date of Publication: 1941
Subject(s): Religious Life
Fictional character(s): Martin Ryselius, Religious (pastor)
Time Period(s): 1730s
Locale(s): Finland

Summary: This tale of Finland in the 18th century describes the efforts of a young pastor, Martin Ryselius, who takes over a church in a remote northern community and attempts to win over the people of his parish despite the enmity his appointment creates.

Historical Accuracy: The period elements are provided primarily through the characterization, which is authentic.

HOWARD HORNE
(PSEUD. OF ROBERT PAYNE, 1911-1983)

Howard Horne is a pseudonym for the English novelist Robert Payne.

【3035】 *Concord Bridge*

Date of Publication: 1952
Subject(s): American Revolution; Battle of Lexington; Battle of Concord
Fictional character(s): Oliver de Lancey, Military Personnel (British officer); Eugenie de Malmedy-Armagnac, Spy
Historical character(s): Thomas Gage, Military Personnel (British officer); Joseph Warren, Doctor, Political Figure
Time Period(s): 1770s (1775)
Locale(s): Boston, Massachusetts, American Colonies; Concord, Massachusetts, American Colonies

Summary: The events leading up to the American Revolution are dramatized. The novel offers a sympathetic portrait of English general Gage, who tries to avoid violence. It also presents a romantic story involving a French-American spy, Eugenie de Malmedy-Armagnac, who finds herself in the center of historical events.

Historical Accuracy: The events leading up to the outbreak of hostilities are depicted accurately.

BILL HOTCHKISS (1936-)

Born in Connecticut, Hotchkiss attended the University of California, Berkeley, San Francisco State University, and the University of Oregon. He has worked as a fire fighter for the U.S. Forest Service and as a high school and college English teacher.

【3036】 *Ammahabas*

Date of Publication: 1983
Subject(s): Indians; Biography, Fictionalized; Tribal Life— Native American
Historical character(s): Jim Beckwourth, Indian (Crow), Chieftain
Time Period(s): 1830s (1834-1837)
Locale(s): Rocky Mountains; California

Summary: This sequel to *The Medicine Calf* continues the story of Jim Beckwourth, a son of a Virginia aristocrat and a mulatto slave girl, who becomes chief of the Montana Crows. Beckwourth's travels to California and visits relatives in Missouri are recounted as well as battles with the Cheyenne, Blackfoot, and white settlers.

Historical Accuracy: The novel stays as close as possible to the known facts about Beckwourth's life.

【3037】 *The Medicine Calf*

Date of Publication: 1981
Subject(s): Indians; Biography, Fictionalized; Tribal Life— Native American
Historical character(s): Jim Beckwourth, Indian (Crow), Chieftain

Time Period(s): 1820s; 1830s (1824-1833)
Locale(s): West

Summary: This is a biographical account of Jim Beckwourth, the son of a Virginia aristocrat and a mulatto slave girl, who is kidnapped by the Crows and adopted into the tribe. The novel covers Beckworth's life in the 1830s and 1840s when he becomes an important Indian leader.

Historical Accuracy: The story is faithful to the known facts about Beckworth's life and is based on his own account.

3038 *To Fell the Giants*

Date of Publication: 1991
Subject(s): American West; Family Saga
Fictional character(s): William Beard, Frontiersman; Califa Beard, Heiress; Raymondo Olivas, Businessman
Time Period(s): 19th century (1836-1855)
Locale(s): Russian River, California

Summary: Set in the redwood country of California during the 19th century, the novel follows the fortunes of the Beard family beginning when William Beard settles among the Indians and continuing through the annexation of California by the U.S. The threat to the redwoods is the catalyst for the Beards' determination.

Historical Accuracy: The fictional story stays close to the actual events of the period.

A.E. HOTCHNER (1920-)

An author, playwright, scriptwriter, and lawyer, Hotchner was born in St. Louis, Missouri, and attended Washington University. He wrote a popular biography, *Papa Hemingway*, and such novels as *The Man Who Lived at the Ritz* and *King of the Hill*. Hotchner is a business partner of Paul Newman in the Newman's Own line of foods.

3039 *Louisiana Purchase*

Date of Publication: 1996
Subject(s): Louisiana Purchase; Settlement of the American Frontier; French Colonies
Fictional character(s): Guy Laroule, Adventurer
Historical character(s): Louis XV, Ruler (King of France); Jeanne Antoinette Poisson, Noblewoman (Marquise de Pompadour), Lover (of the king); Mike Fink, Frontiersman; Armand-Jean Du Plessis, Religious (Cardinal Richelieu), Political Figure (Duc de Richelieu); Thomas Jefferson, Political Figure; James Monroe, Political Figure
Time Period(s): 18th century; 19th century (1750-1804)
Locale(s): France; New Orleans, Louisiana; St. Louis, Missouri

Summary: Guy Laroule is banished from France and attempts to rebuild his fortune in the New Orleans and Mississippi River region of North America before the Louisiana Purchase.

Historical Accuracy: The episodes described, including the founding and development of St. Louis , have their basis in fact. In some instances, the author has shortened time periods

and combined the features of several historical characters into one.

EMERSON HOUGH (1857-1923)

Born in Iowa, Hough graduated from the state university, and practiced law in New Mexico. He published articles about the preservation of the national parks and wildlife, and a series of stories for boys about cowboys and the passing of the Old West. His historical romances include *North of 36*, and *Covered Wagon*.

3040 *54-40 or Fight*

Date of Publication: 1909
Subject(s): Politics; Diplomacy
Historical character(s): John C. Calhoun, Political Figure; Sir Richard Pakenham, Political Figure, Diplomat; Baroness Helena von Ritz, Noblewoman
Time Period(s): 19th century
Locale(s): Washington, District of Columbia

Summary: This political novel dramatizes the controversy surrounding the Northwest boundary treaty and the annexation of Texas. Set in the drawing rooms of Washington, the novel features John C. Calhoun, English diplomat Sir Richard Pakenham, and the Russian Baroness Von Ritz as central players in this tale of power politics.

Historical Accuracy: The novel's story is rooted in fact, but involves considerable manipulation of detail.

3041 *Covered Wagon*

Date of Publication: 1922
Subject(s): American West; Wagon Trains
Fictional character(s): Molly Wingate, Pioneer
Time Period(s): 1840s (1848)
Locale(s): Oregon Trail, United States

Summary: The novel provides an account of a wagon train crossing from Missouri to Oregon in 1848. The story vividly chronicles the hardships along the way, the dissension among the company, and the fight for the hand of beautiful Molly Wingate.

Historical Accuracy: The account of the crossing is authentic and convincing.

3042 *North of 36*

Date of Publication: 1923
Subject(s): American West; Cattle Drives; Reconstruction Period
Fictional character(s): Taisie Lockhart, Orphan, Rancher
Time Period(s): 1860s
Locale(s): Texas

Summary: Set in Texas following the Civil War, the novel recounts the adventures of Taisie Lockhart, an orphan with a herd of cattle and no market for them in Texas. She conceives a desperate plan to drive the cattle north to Kansas, where the railroad has opened up a market. The novel describes the dangers of the journey.

Historical Accuracy: The story does have a basis in historical fact concerning the fate of Texas ranching following the Civil War.

FRANK OLNEY HOUGH (1899-1958)

`3043` *If Not Victory*

Date of Publication: 1939
Subject(s): American Revolution; American Colonies; Quakers
Fictional character(s): Abe Kronkhyte, Teenager, Military Personnel (soldier)
Time Period(s): 1770s (1776-1778)
Locale(s): Westchester County, New York

Summary: The impact of the American Revolution on a community along the Hudson River Valley is depicted through the experiences of 19-year-old Abe Kronkhyte who deserts his Quaker family to fight for the American cause. He develops into a valuable soldier in the Continental Army.

Historical Accuracy: The novel provides an authentic look on the war's impact on the ordinary soldier.

`3044` *The Neutral Ground*

Date of Publication: 1941
Subject(s): American Revolution
Fictional character(s): Robert Trowbridge, Young Man
Historical character(s): George Washington, Military Personnel (army commander)
Time Period(s): 1770s; 1780s (1775-1783)
Locale(s): Westchester County, New York

Summary: This novel of the American Revolution concerns the action surrounding Westchester County in New York, the so-called ''Neutral Ground'' between Tory and Rebel families.

Historical Accuracy: The author lists his minor tampering with the chronology of actual events.

`3045` *Renown*

Date of Publication: 1938
Subject(s): American Revolution; Biography, Fictionalized
Historical character(s): Benedict Arnold, Military Personnel (general)
Time Period(s): 18th century
Locale(s): American Colonies

Summary: This a sympathetic account of the career of Benedict Arnold, who emerges as a brilliant and courageous, though frustrated, military leader. The novel's account of the events surrounding Arnold's role in the American Revolution helps redress the balance of other portraits of Arnold as the consummate American villain.

Historical Accuracy: The novel keeps close to the known facts, inventing only the conversations.

HENRY BEETLE HOUGH (1896-1985)

Author and publisher Hough was born in New Bedford, Massachusetts. With his wife, Hough was the editor and publisher of the *Vineyard Gazette*. He received a special Pulitzer Prize in 1918 for service rendered to the American Press. His books about New England include *Singing in the Morning*, *Thoreau of Walden*, and *Whaling Wives*.

`3046` *The New England Story*

Date of Publication: 1958
Subject(s): Family Saga; Whaling; Feuds
Historical character(s): Enoch Adams, Sea Captain
Time Period(s): 19th century
Locale(s): New England; At Sea

Summary: This tale describes three generations of a New England whaling family. Based on the story of the legendary sea captain Enoch Adams, the novel looks behind the legend at the Adams family and a bitter feud that splits them apart.

Historical Accuracy: The novel is based on fact and captures the atmosphere of the period.

RICHARD HOUGH (1922-)

An English author born in Sussex, Hough served in the Royal Air Force as a fighter pilot during World War II. Besides his novels, he has published several books on motor racing and children's books under the pseudonym of Bruce Carter. He received a *Daily Express* Best Book of the Sea Award in 1972.

`3047` *Buller's Dreadnought*

Date of Publication: 1982
Subject(s): Sea Story; Military Life—British Navy; World War I
Fictional character(s): Whitney Campbell, Military Personnel (naval officer); Archibald Buller, Military Personnel (naval officer); Rod Maclewin, Military Personnel (naval officer)
Historical character(s): George V, Royalty (prince); Winston Churchill, Political Figure; John Arbuthnot Fisher, Military Personnel (admiral)
Time Period(s): 1900s; 1910s (1902-1915)
Locale(s): England; At Sea

Summary: The author continues the naval careers of Archy Buller and Rod Maclewin begun in *Buller's Guns* through the critical years leading up to World War I. Buller and Maclewin are on hand as naval observers of the Japanese defeat of the Russian fleet at Tsushima in 1905, and are involved in espionage to gauge the activities of the Imperial German Navy.

Historical Accuracy: The main events of the story are historical, though the novel does mix the factual with some imaginary interpretations.

`3048` *Buller's Guns*

Date of Publication: 1981
Subject(s): Sea Story; Military Life—British Navy; Victorian Period

Fictional character(s): Rod Maclewin, Military Personnel (seaman); Archibald Buller, Military Personnel (naval officer)
Historical character(s): George, Royalty (prince); Edward, Prince of Wales, Royalty
Time Period(s): 19th century; 20th century (1860s-1902)
Locale(s): England; At Sea

Summary: The Royal Navy during the Victorian period is depicted in the contrasting careers of two young seamen. Rod Maclewin comes from the slums of Tyneside, and Archy Buller is a member of a distinguished naval family. The former makes his way in the lower decks, the latter as a young officer. They are brought together in the heat of battle.

Historical Accuracy: Solid and convicing details of naval and military life of the period are featured here.

3049   *Buller's Victory*

Date of Publication: 1984
Subject(s): World War I; Military Life—British Navy; Battle of Jutland
Fictional character(s): Richard Buller, Military Personnel (naval officer); Archibald Buller, Military Personnel (naval officer)
Historical character(s): Winston Churchill, Political Figure; John Arbuthnot Fisher, Military Personnel (admiral)
Time Period(s): 1910s (1914-1918)
Locale(s): At Sea; Dardanelles, Turkey

Summary: Naval action during World War I is described through the experiences of Archy and Richard Buller. The events include the defeat of the British fleet off the coast of Chile, the Gallipoli invasion, the Battle of Jutland, and the final destruction of the German Pacific Squadron off the Falklands.

Historical Accuracy: The story is set against real events and features prominent figures of the times based on historical records and eyewitness accounts.

JAMES HOUSTON (1921-)

A Canadian author and artist, Houston lived with the Eskimos of the Canadian Arctic for 12 years, nine years of which he served as the first Civil Administrator of West Baffin Island. He has been a central force for the development of Eskimo arts.

3050   *Eagle Song*

Date of Publication: 1983
Subject(s): Indians; Tribal Life—Native American
Fictional character(s): John Jewitt, Sailor, Artisan (ironsmith); Siam, Indian (Nootkan); John Thompson, Sailor, Artisan (sailmaker)
Time Period(s): 1800s (1803-1805)
Locale(s): Pacific Coast, Canada

Summary: The novel is based on the true events of the massacre of the New England trading ship *Boston* by the Nootkan Indians of the Canadian Pacific coast. Two crew members survive, Jewitt and Thompson. The story depicts their two years in captivity.

Historical Accuracy: The author's familiarity with the customs of the Indians is evident, as is the authentic depiction of the period and locale.

3051   *Ghost Fox*

Date of Publication: 1977
Subject(s): French and Indian War; Indians; Frontier—Canada
Fictional character(s): Sarah Wells, Captive
Time Period(s): 1750s
Locale(s): New York, American Colonies; Canada

Summary: This is the account of a New England girl, Sarah Wells, stolen during the French and Indian War and forced into captivity by marauding Indians. She endures a grueling forced march into Canada, and her story is one of survival and the determination for freedom.

Historical Accuracy: The author states that every factual detail of this novel is based on historical records and his own research.

3052   *Running West*

Date of Publication: 1989
Subject(s): English Colonies; Frontier—Canada
Historical character(s): William Stewart, Frontiersman; Thandelthur, Indian (Dene), Young Woman
Time Period(s): 1710s
Locale(s): Hudson Bay, Canada

Summary: Based on historical fact, the novel describes the heroic trek across the northern wilderness of Hudson Bay by William Stewart and the Indian woman he loves, Thandelthur. Both are tested as they endure attack and near starvation in the wild.

Historical Accuracy: Gripping and authentic, the novel captures what actual life must have been like in the Canadian wilderness of the time.

3053   *The White Dawn*

Date of Publication: 1971
Subject(s): Indians; Tribal Life—Eskimo; Whaling
Fictional character(s): Avinga, Eskimo (skimo); Sarak, Eskimo (skimo), Hunter; Kakuktak, Sailor; Pilee, Sailor; Portagee, Sailor
Time Period(s): 1890s (1897)
Locale(s): Hudson Bay, Canada

Summary: This story set in 1897 tells what happens to the crew of a small whaleboat when a harpooned whale tows them north of Hudson Bay into the land of the Eskimos. They are nursed back to health and accepted by the Eskimos until, during the long arctic winter, trouble arises that produces a violent outcome in a cultural clash.

Historical Accuracy: The saga is based on true events told to the author when he lived with the Eskimos in the eastern Canadian Arctic.

JUNE DIMMIT HOUSTON

3054 *The Faith and the Flame*

Date of Publication: 1958
Subject(s): Royalty—France; Religious Conflict
Fictional character(s): Joanna de Brough, Gentlewoman
Historical character(s): Catherine de' Medici, Royalty; Henri of Navarre, Nobleman; Louis I de Bourbon, Military Personnel (general), Leader (Protestant)
Time Period(s): 16th century
Locale(s): France

Summary: Joanna de Brough, a lady-in-waiting to Catherine de' Medici, is a Catholic who falls in love with a Huguenot captain. She is caught up in the religious conflict between Catholics and Protestants.

Historical Accuracy: The period elements are developed effectively and convincingly with a number of realistic portraits of important figures in the drama.

MARGARET BELL HOUSTON

Houston began writing at the age of eight and had her first book published at eleven. She is the granddaughter of Sam Houston. Her books include *Yonder* and *Bride's Island*.

3055 *Cottonwoods Grow Tall*

Date of Publication: 1958
Subject(s): Ranching; American West
Fictional character(s): Rena Lyle, Young Woman
Time Period(s): 1900s (1900)
Locale(s): Texas

Summary: Domestic tragedy is the center of this story of Texas ranch life. The tale is set on the Cottonwood ranch in the hill country of Texas and describes the consequences when Rena Lyle is unfaithful to her husband.

Historical Accuracy: The region is captured convincingly.

ROBERT HOUSTON (1935-)

Born in Baltimore, Maryland, Houston graduated from the University of Maryland. A professor of photography, Houston's books include *Legacy to an Unborn Son*.

3056 *Bisbee '17*

Date of Publication: 1979
Subject(s): American West; Mining; Labor Movement
Fictional character(s): Elizabeth Gurley Flynn, Labor Organizer
Historical character(s): Mary Harris Jones, Labor Organizer; William "Big Bill" Haywood, Labor Organizer; Hary Wheeler, Lawman
Time Period(s): 1910s (1917)
Locale(s): Bisbee, Arizona

Summary: The novel tells the story of the strike in Bisbee, Arizona, in 1917 that pitted the Wobblies (I.W.W.) against the copper mine owners backed by an army of lawmen and private detectives determined to break the union.

Historical Accuracy: Though the major events actually occurred, details have been altered.

3057 *The Nation Thief*

Date of Publication: 1984
Subject(s): Independence—Central America
Historical character(s): William Walker, Adventurer
Time Period(s): 1850s
Locale(s): Nicaragua

Summary: William Walker's expedition to seize control of Nicaragua is dramatized in this documentary novel, which chronicles the activities of the ragtag group formed by Walker. Told in a series of monologues by the participants, the novel centers around the energies of Walker himself, who begins his adventure as a liberator and ends it by re-establishing slavery and sponsoring the carnage that eventually leads to his demise.

Historical Accuracy: The essential framework of events described is faithful to the facts.

SUSAN HOWATCH (1940-)

An English novelist of mysteries and family sagas, Howatch is a graduate of King's College, London. Howatch bases many of her characters on historical personages such as Henry II, Julius Caesar, and Cleopatra.

3058 *Cashelmara*

Date of Publication: 1974
Subject(s): Family Saga; Independence—Ireland
Fictional character(s): Edward De Salis, Widow(er), Landowner; Patrick De Salis, Young Man; Sarah De Salis, Spouse (of Patrick)
Time Period(s): 19th century (1859-1891)
Locale(s): Connacht, Ireland

Summary: This family saga concerns the De Salis family whose estate of Cashelmara becomes the focus of their lives and fortune. Edward De Salis is the patriarch who rules with an iron hand. His son Patrick brings change to the estate in an Ireland gripped by the growing wind of rebellion and independence.

Historical Accuracy: The period elements and regional details are convincingly captured.

FANNY HOWE (1940-)

An American poet, novelist, and short-story writer, Howe was born in Buffalo, New York, and attended Stanford University. Her works include the short-story collection *Forty Whacks* and the novels *In the Middle of Nowhere* and *The Lives of a Spirit*.

3059 *The White Slave*

Date of Publication: 1980
Subject(s): Slavery
Historical character(s): Peter McCutcheon, Bastard Son, Slave
Time Period(s): 19th century (1831-1854)

Locale(s): Missouri

Summary: This novel is based on the actual experiences of Peter McCutcheon, an illegitimate white infant who is handed over to a slave family to conceal his birth. McCutcheon is raised by his new family, marries a black woman, and goes from one slave-holding family to another before meeting his birth mother.

Historical Accuracy: The novel is based on an account written by McCutcheon's son and grandson and offers an authentic portrait of the age and the region.

HARVEY HOWELLS (1912-)

A Scottish writer born in Glasgow, Howells trained as an accountant and worked in a bank and in advertising. An author of TV plays and novels, Howells was the winner of the best TV comedy of 1956 for ''Goodbye Gray Flannel.'' Howells wrote his first play at age 12 and his first novel at 19. His works include *The Big Company*, *House of Glass*, and *The Braw and the Bonny*.

3060   *Bide Me Fair*

Date of Publication: 1968
Subject(s): Family Saga; World War II
Fictional character(s): Robert Boyd, Gentleman; Harriet Boyd, Spouse; Willie Boyd, Military Personnel (soldier), Actor
Time Period(s): 19th century; 20th century (1880-1941)
Locale(s): Scotland

Summary: This multi-generational saga, centering on Robert and Harriet Boyd, covers English history from the Boer War to the opening years of World War II. Robert Boyd is an honest Victorian whose wife, Harriet, is drawn to the new ideas of suffrage and equality. The great events of the 20th century are reflected in their family story.

Historical Accuracy: The novel makes good and authentic use of history as a catalyst for the domestic story.

EDWIN P. HOYT (1923-)

An American journalist and prolific writer of fiction and nonfiction, Hoyt was born in Portland, Oregon, and attended the University of Oregon. He is the author of several biographies, including ones on Charlie Chaplin and Oliver Wendell Holmes. Among his other nonfiction works are *The Nixons: An American Family* and *To the Marianas*. His novels include *Decatur's Revenge* and *The Tempting of Confucius*.

3061   *The Last Stand: A Novel about George Armstrong Custer and the Indians of the Plains*

Date of Publication: 1995
Subject(s): American West; Indians; Battle of the Little Bighorn
Historical character(s): George Armstrong Custer, Military Personnel (cavalry officer); Ulysses S. Grant, Military Per-

sonnel (chief general of U.S. Army); William Tecumseh Sherman, Military Personnel (general); Philip H. Sheridan, Military Personnel (general); Winfield Scott Hancock, Military Personnel (general); Elizabeth Bacon Custer, Spouse; Sitting Bull, Indian (Sioux), Chieftain; Sitting Red Cloud, Indian (Sioux), Chieftain
Time Period(s): 1860s; 1870s
Locale(s): Black Hills, South Dakota; Little Bighorn River, Montana

Summary: The novel chronicles the career of George Armstrong Custer, including its bloody climax at the Battle of the Little Bighorn, the last great Indian victory over the whites and the beginning of the end of the supremacy of the Plains Indians. The novel offers a context for the battle and a detailed look at the personalities involved, particularly the reckless and flamboyant Custer.

Historical Accuracy: Though based on actual events, conversations and circumstances are invented, offering a composite of the factual and the fictional.

3062   *The Voice of Allah*

Date of Publication: 1970
Subject(s): Biography, Fictionalized; Islam; Religious Life
Historical character(s): Mohammed, Religious (founder of Islam)
Time Period(s): 6th century; 7th century
Locale(s): Arabia

Summary: This is a sympathetic fictional biography of Mohammed, the Arab prophet and founder of Islam. The novel covers Mohammed's career as religious and military leader and includes a good deal of information on Muslim customs and beliefs.

Historical Accuracy: This is a reliable introduction to Mohammed's life and beliefs.

MARGARET ANN HUBBARD
(PSEUD. OF MARGARET HUBBARD PRILEY, 1909-)

An American author of juvenile fiction, mysteries, and novels, Priley was born in North Dakota. Her books include *Murder Takes the Veil* and *Sister Simon Murder Case*.

3063   *Flight of the Swan*

Date of Publication: 1946
Subject(s): Biography, Fictionalized; Literary Life
Historical character(s): Hans Christian Andersen, Writer
Time Period(s): 19th century (1805-1878)
Locale(s): Denmark

Summary: This fictional biography of Denmark's greatest author and storyteller covers Hans Christian Andersen's career from poverty to great acclaim. The novel captures both Andersen's gentle genius and the weaknesses that created a life which Andersen himself considered fairytale-like.

Historical Accuracy: The novel at times indulges in simplifications that reach the level of the sentimental.

RICHARD G. HUBLER (1912-)

Born in Pennsylvania, Hubler is a graduate of Swarthmore College. He has worked as a professor of English at California State University and in public relations. He has also been a radio broadcaster, editor, and foreign correspondent.

`3064` *Love and Wisdom: A Novel about Solomon*

Date of Publication: 1968
Subject(s): Biblical Story; Jews
Historical character(s): Solomon, Ruler (King of Israel), Biblical Figure
Time Period(s): 10th century. B.C.
Locale(s): Israel

Summary: The novel offers the life and times of King Solomon of Israel. He succeeds his father David and rules over the Hebrews for a halcyon period of 40 years. He builds the Temple and unites his people into a powerful nation. Solomon's legendary sagacity and human insight are depicted.

Historical Accuracy: The novel's extensive notes display the evident research and the historical basis of the novel's events and characterizations.

`3065` *The Soldier and the Sage: A Novel about Akiba*

Date of Publication: 1966
Subject(s): Roman Empire; Jewish Revolt
Fictional character(s): Rufus Teneius, Military Personnel (tribune)
Historical character(s): Akiba ben Joseph, Religious (rabbi); Hadrian, Ruler (Roman emperor); Trajan, Ruler (Roman emperor); Flavius Josephus, Historian, Military Personnel; Epictetus, Philosopher; Simon Bar Kokhba, Revolutionary
Time Period(s): 2nd century
Locale(s): Israel

Summary: The story of the Jewish Revolt against Rome that almost brought the empire of Hadrian down is depicted in the recollections of a Roman tribune, Rufus Teneius. Because of his friendship with the Jewish sage, Akiba Ben Joseph, Teneius is assigned as the emperor's personal legate to Judea. When Hadrian revokes Trajan's accommodation with the Jews, revolt and violence break out, and Teneius' friendship with Akiba is put to the test.

Historical Accuracy: The author explains that the story of Teneuis is largely apocryphal.

HAZEL HUCKER

Born in London where she received a degree in economics, Hucker has worked as a teacher and has lived in France, Germany, and Malaysia.

`3066` *Cousin Susannah*

Date of Publication: 1995
Subject(s): Georgian Period; Identity—Concealed

Fictional character(s): Susannah Trotter, Governess; James Manningford, Gentleman, Heir; Sedley Stacey, Religious (curate)
Time Period(s): 1790s (1794)
Locale(s): Hampshire, England

Summary: When Susannah Trotter, a yeoman farmer's daughter and governess, is seduced by James Manningford, her reputation is saved by linking her to an ambitious curate and introducing her as Manningford's cousin. James soon realizes his affections for Susannah are more than cousinly, and the novel records their efforts to undo the deception.

Historical Accuracy: The historical context and period elements are authentic and believable.

EDWARD HUEBSCH

`3067` *The Last Summer of Mata Hari*

Date of Publication: 1979
Subject(s): World War I; Espionage
Historical character(s): Margaretha Geertruida Zelle McLeod, Spy
Time Period(s): 1910s (1917)
Locale(s): France

Summary: The shadowy world of espionage and power politics is described in the climax of Mata Hari's career as a spy for both the Germans and the French, which ends in her execution. Mata Hari is seen primarily as a victim of a secret conspiracy of those in power who wish to see World War I continue.

Historical Accuracy: The facts surrounding Mata Hari's career as a spy are shrouded in controversy, and the novel offers a plausible, though by no means definitive, version of her story.

ETHEL HUESTON (1887-)

Born in Cincinnati, Ohio, Hueston attended public schools in Mt. Pleasant and Burlington, Iowa. She began writing as a sophomore at Iowa Wesleyan College and worked for a Chicago publisher until her marriage to a Presbyterian minister. She is the author of the Prudence and Ginger series, as well as *The Romance of the Lewis and Clark Expedition*, *Calamity Jane of Deadwood Gulch*, *Star of the West*, and *The Man of the Storm*.

`3068` *Calamity Jane of Deadwood Gulch*

Date of Publication: 1937
Subject(s): American West; Biography, Fictionalized
Historical character(s): Martha Jane Cannary Burk, Frontierswoman
Time Period(s): 19th century; 20th century (1875-1903)
Locale(s): Laramie, Wyoming; Deadwood, South Dakota

Summary: Despite its western serial title, this novel provides a realistic account of the life and times of Calamity Jane from her heyday in Laramie and Deadwood to her death in 1903. The novel captures the era of the South Dakota gold rush and the collision of Indians and prospectors.

Historical Accuracy: The novel is a blend of the known facts and an imaginative reconstruction.

3069 *The Man of the Storm*

Date of Publication: 1936
Subject(s): Lewis and Clark Expedition; Louisiana Purchase
Fictional character(s): Sally Dale, Orphan
Historical character(s): John Colter, Explorer, Frontiersman
Time Period(s): 1800s
Locale(s): St. Louis, Missouri

Summary: This historical romance involves John Colter, a member of the Lewis and Clark Expedition who is credited with the discovery of the Yellowstone River. The story is set largely in St. Louis during the French and Spanish occupation and the transition to American control following the Louisiana Purchase.

Historical Accuracy: The author does take liberties with the known facts of Colter's life to create the novel's romance.

3070 *Star of the West*

Date of Publication: 1935
Subject(s): American West; Lewis and Clark Expedition; Exploration
Historical character(s): Meriwether Lewis, Explorer; William Clark, Explorer; Sacajawea, Indian (shoshone), Guide
Time Period(s): 1800s (1803-1806)
Locale(s): Pacific Northwest; Rocky Mountains

Summary: The novel provides a factual account of the Lewis and Clark Expedition across the newly-acquired territory of the Louisiana Purchase to the Pacific. Based on the journals and the first-hand accounts of the journey, the novel stays close to the actual details of the trek.

Historical Accuracy: The novel's conversations have been invented, as well as some minor incidents.

CLAIRE HUFFAKER (1928-1990)

A Western writer of novels, short stories, and screenplays, Huffaker was born in Montana and attended Princeton and Columbia universities and the Sorbonne. Huffaker worked as an editor for *Time*, as a screenwriter, and head of his own film production company. Several of Huffaker's novels were made into films: *Seven Ways From Sundown*, *Posse From Hell*, and *The War Wagon*.

3071 *The Cowboy and the Cossack*

Date of Publication: 1973
Subject(s): Cattle Drives; Russian Empire
Fictional character(s): Levi Dougherty, Cowboy; Shad, Cowboy; Captain Rostov, Military Personnel (Cossack)
Time Period(s): 1880s
Locale(s): Siberia, Russia

Summary: Fifteen American cowboys arrive at Vladivostok in 1880 to drive a herd of cattle to a famine-stricken town thousands of miles inland through Siberia. They are joined by a band of Cossacks, and together they experience attacks by wolves and tigers, civil war, torrential rain, and a climactic battle with a Tartar army. They learn to depend on one another and bridge great cultural differences.

Historical Accuracy: The story is fanciful but also convincing in its details of Siberian and cowboy life.

LAURIE HUFFMAN (1916-)

American novelist Huffman was born in Oregon and attended the University of California. She worked as a pharmacist's assistant.

3072 *A House Behind the Mint*

Date of Publication: 1969
Subject(s): American West; Crime and Criminals
Fictional character(s): Ellen Scott, Young Woman; George Scott, Young Man
Historical character(s): Charles E. Bart, Outlaw (a.k.a. Black Bart)
Time Period(s): 1870s; 1880s (1875-1883)
Locale(s): San Francisco, California

Summary: Set in San Francisco in the 1870s and 1880s, the novel concerns the Scott family who are befriended by the mysterious Charles Bolton who plunges the family into a manhunt for the famous stagecoach robber Black Bart.

Historical Accuracy: Period San Francisco is captured with authority.

GLYN HUGHES (1935-)

Hughes is an English writer who lives in Yorkshire. He was born in Cheshire, England, and attended the Regional College of Art in Manchester. His first novel, *When I Used to Play on the Green* won the Guardian Fiction Prize and the David Higham First Novel Award in England. His other novels include *The Rape of the Rose* and *The Antique Collector*.

3073 *Bronte*

Date of Publication: 1996
Subject(s): Biography, Fictionalized; Literary Life
Historical character(s): Patrick Bronte, Religious (clergyman); Charlotte Bronte, Writer; Emily Bronte, Writer; Anne Bronte, Writer; Branwell Bronte, Artist
Time Period(s): 19th century
Locale(s): Haworth, England (in Yorkshire)

Summary: The novel provides a fictional account of the Bronte family that traces the development and forces at work that caused the Bronte children—Charlotte, Branwell, Anne, and Emily—to transfer their childhood fantasies into literature against a backdrop of domestic life more tragic than any novel.

Historical Accuracy: The author asserts painstaking accuracy in his portrait of the Brontes which he describes as an interpreted account. He differs in certain details from the accepted version.

RICHARD HUGHES (1900-1976)

An English writer of Welsh descent, Hughes attended Oxford, then spent time in the U.S., Canada, and the West Indies. His other novels include *In Hazard*, *A Moment of Time*, and *The Spider's Palace*. *The Fox in the Attic* is an historical novel set in the author's own time, culminating in World War II.

3074 *A High Wind in Jamaica*

Date of Publication: 1929
Subject(s): Pirates; Sea Story; Childhood
Fictional character(s): Emily Bas-Thornton, Child, Captive; Jonsen, Pirate, Sea Captain
Time Period(s): 19th century (early)
Locale(s): Jamaica; At Sea (in the West Indies); London, England

Summary: The novel is a psychological study of the seven Bas-Thornton children in Jamaica. They survive an earthquake and a hurricane, and then are captured by pirates. Their adventures aboard the pirate ship include witnessing death and murder. Eventually they are rescued and taken to England for the trial of the pirate captain. How culpable is he, and how guilty are the children themselves?.

Historical Accuracy: This is both an exciting adventure story and a study in psychological realism—a rare combination in an historical novel.

RUPERT HUGHES (1872-1956)

A Missouri-born author, Hughes is best known for his three-volume study of George Washington. He was also the author of many popular novels including *What Will People Say?*, *Souls for Sale*, and *No One Man*.

3075 *Stately Timber*

Date of Publication: 1939
Subject(s): American Colonies; Witchcraft and Sorcery; Puritans
Fictional character(s): Seaborn Fleet, Adventurer
Time Period(s): 17th century (1650s)
Locale(s): Massachusetts, American Colonies; Virginia, American Colonies; Barbados

Summary: This portrait of the Puritan Massachusetts Bay Colony tells the story of Seaborn Fleet, the son of a prosperous shipbuilder, who comes in conflict with the Puritan leaders by opposing the persecution of the Quakers. Exiled, Fleet embarks on a seafaring career, eventually wins a pardon, and returns home.

Historical Accuracy: The novel is filled with authentic period elements.

VICTOR HUGO (1802-1885)

Poet, dramatist, and novelist Victor Hugo was born in Besancon, France, the son of a general under Napoleon. A towering figure in 19th-century French literature, Hugo was considered by many to be the greatest poet of his day, but he is best known today for his novels, *Notre Dame de Paris*, *The Hunchback of Notre Dame* and *Les Miserables*. Two of his plays, *Hernani* and *Le Roi S'Amuse*, formed the basis for Giuseppe Verdi's operas *Ernani* and *Rigoletto*.

3076 *The Hunchback of Notre Dame*

Date of Publication: 1831
Subject(s): Middle Ages; Gypsies; Witchcraft and Sorcery
Fictional character(s): Quasimodo, Handicapped (hunchback); Esmeralda, Gypsy, Dancer; Claude Frollo, Religious (archdeacon)
Historical character(s): Louis XI, Ruler (King of France)
Time Period(s): 15th century (1482)
Locale(s): Paris, France

Summary: Hugo's classic novel of medieval Paris tells the story of the beautiful, hapless gypsy dancer, Esmeralda, the object of desire of three feckless and evil men. Betrayed by them and sentenced to death as a witch, Esmeralda unexpectedly comes under the protection of Quasimodo, the hunchback of Notre Dame, who carries her to sanctuary in the cathedral.

Historical Accuracy: Hugo has sharply rendered important aspects of medieval French society and all its passions, superstitions, and lack of free thought.

KATHRYN HULME (1900-1981)

An American writer born in San Francisco, Hulme studied at Columbia and Hunter College. She is best known for her bestselling *The Nun's Story* about a friend and business partner whom Hulme met while she was working with the U.S. Relief and Rehabilitation Administration in Bavaria. Hulme was an expatriate living in Paris before World War II but returned to California during the war to work as a welder in a shipyard. She wrote nine books mostly about her experiences.

3077 *Annie's Captain*

Date of Publication: 1961
Subject(s): Sea Story; Clipper Ships
Historical character(s): John Cavarly, Sea Captain; Annie Boles, Gentlewoman
Time Period(s): 19th century (1859-1895)
Locale(s): At Sea; San Francisco, California

Summary: Based on the experiences of the author's own grandparents, the novel tells the story of one of America's greatest sea captains, John Cavarly, who falls in love with passenger Annie Boles and marries her on the quarterdeck when his ship docks at San Francisco. Their life together is described in the flow of history and the changeover from sail to steam.

Historical Accuracy: The nautical details and period elements are convincing.

GEORGE FREDERICK HUMMEL
(1882-1952)

3078 *Joshua Moore, American*

Date of Publication: 1943
Subject(s): Immigrants; American Revolution; Settlement of the American Frontier
Fictional character(s): Joshua Moore, Immigrant
Time Period(s): Multiple Time Periods
Locale(s): United States

Summary: This family chronicle follows the history of English immigrant Joshua Moore and his descendants from the 17th century to modern times. Scenes include early life in the American colonies, the Revolution, settlement in Ohio and California, and the anti-slavery movement in Kansas.

Historical Accuracy: The novel's vast panorama works against a detailed portrait of the historical events covered.

WILLIAM HUMPHREY (1924-)

Humphrey was born in Texas. His novels include *Home From the Hill*, *The Ordways*, and *A Time and a Place*. He has been praised for his portraits of farm life and small-town America.

3079 *No Resting Place*

Date of Publication: 1989
Subject(s): Indians
Fictional character(s): Amos ''Noquisi'' Ferguson, Indian (Cherokee)
Time Period(s): 19th century; 20th century
Locale(s): Missouri; Georgia; Texas

Summary: The story of the removal of the Cherokees from their Georgia homeland is dramatized through the experiences of young Amos Ferguson, a mixed-breed Cherokee. He accompanies his grandparents on the march later to be known as the Trail of Tears. Amos serves his people as an interpreter and medical assistant while the Cherokees suffer countless indignities.

Historical Accuracy: The novel is unsparing in its criticisms of the whites and tends to sacrifice objectivity in its advocacy on behalf of the Indians.

CHRISTOPHER HUNT

3080 *The Bisley Boy*

Date of Publication: 1995
Subject(s): Elizabethan Period; Royalty—England; Identity—Concealed
Fictional character(s): John Neville, Imposter
Historical character(s): Edward Tudor, Royalty (prince); Robert Dudley, Nobleman; Philip II, Ruler (King of Spain); Mary I, Ruler (Queen of England); Robert Devereux, Nobleman (Earl of Essex); Sir Walter Raleigh, Courtier
Time Period(s): 16th century
Locale(s): England

Summary: The novel is based on a persistent rumor that Queen Elizabeth was in fact a man. The novel imagines this as true and dramatizes John Neville's successful impersonation of the young Princess Elizabeth who succeeds to the throne.

Historical Accuracy: The novel's premise is more ingenious than plausible, and the novel's very modern themes are cast into an Elizabethan atmosphere that is only partially convincing.

BLUEBELL MATILDA HUNTER

Born in London, Hunter's novels include *Death Dams the Tide* and *Big Ben Looks On*.

3081 *Manchu Empress*

Date of Publication: 1945
Subject(s): Chinese Empire; Royalty—China; Biography, Fictionalized
Historical character(s): Tz'u-hsi, Ruler (Dowager Empress of China)
Time Period(s): 19th century; 20th century
Locale(s): China

Summary: The novel presents a biographical portrait of the last empress of China, Tz'u Hsi. She rises to prominence as the consort of Emperor Hsien Feng and then holds onto power through intrigue and violence. Because of her profound conservatism, she resists foreign encroachment yet encourages the Boxer Rebellion. The novel captures the full flavor of Chinese court life and Tz'u Hsi's evil genius.

Historical Accuracy: The novel offers a balanced portrait of Tz'u Hsi and an authentic depiction of the period.

EVAN HUNTER (1926-)

American novelist Hunter was born in New York City. After graduating from Hunter College, Hunter taught in two vocational high schools, the basis for his novel, *The Blackboard Jungle*. As Ed McBain, Hunter is the author of the popular 87th Precinct series of mysteries. He has received a Grand Master Award for lifetime achievement from the Mystery Writers of America. Hunter is the recognized master of the police procedural crime novel.

3082 *The Chisholms*

Date of Publication: 1976
Subject(s): American West; Immigrants
Fictional character(s): Hadley Chisholm, Settler; Miverva Chisholm, Spouse
Time Period(s): 1840s (1844)
Locale(s): Appalachia, Virginia; West

Summary: In 1844 the Chisholm family leave their barren land in Virginia and head west to California. The novel details their dangerous and challenging trek during which they face hunger, fever, Indian attacks, and other settlers who prove to be unreliable and treacherous.

Historical Accuracy: The novel captures wilderness life with convincing details.

3083 *Lizzie*

Date of Publication: 1984
Subject(s): Crime and Criminals; Trials; Homosexuality
Historical character(s): Lizzie Borden, Young Woman, Criminal (accused)
Time Period(s): 1890s (1890-1892)
Locale(s): Fall River, Massachusetts; Europe; New Bedford, Massachusetts

Summary: The novel reconstructs America's most celebrated murder case in which Lizzie Borden's mother and father are viciously murdered. The novel creates a portrait of Lizzie Border as a frustrated spinster seething with rage who explodes into violence. The account alternates between her inquest and trial and a description of her trip to Europe that serves as a catalyst and an explanation for her crime.

Historical Accuracy: The inquest and the trial material is factual; Lizzie Borden's trip to Europe occurred, but the details are invented. Lizzie's lesbianism is also unsupported conjecture.

JACK D. HUNTER (1921-)

Born in Ohio, Hunter transferred from Infantry to Air Corps in World War II and trained and served as an undercover agent in Germany. Hunter worked as a news editor in Delaware and as the executive secretary to a Delaware congressman. Hunter won an Edgar Award in 1966 for *The Expendable Spy*. He is also a talented water colorist who specializes in action scenes from World War I and II. An expert in the history of aircraft of 1914-1918, his novel *The Blue Max* was made into a film in 1965.

3084 *The Blood Order*

Date of Publication: 1979
Subject(s): Nazis; Aviation
Fictional character(s): Bruno Stachel, Military Personnel (Luftwaffe officer), Pilot; Anna-Marie Elsbet Karlotte, Socialite, Noblewoman (Baroness Klingenhoff)
Historical character(s): Adolf Hitler, Political Figure; Paul Joseph Goebbels, Political Figure; Hermann Goering, Political Figure; Martin Bormann, Political Figure
Time Period(s): 1920s; 1930s
Locale(s): Germany

Summary: In the sequel to *The Blue Max*, World War I flying ace Bruno Stachel is recruited by the Nazis to help construct the mighty Luftwaffe. For Stachel it is a chance to fly again, but his foray takes him deep within the upper reaches of Nazi Party politics. He is forced to choose between the new era and his sense of old-world honor.

Historical Accuracy: The story is imagined but does offer convincing details of Nazi Germany.

3085 *The Blue Max*

Date of Publication: 1964
Subject(s): World War I; Aviation
Fictional character(s): Bruno Stachel, Military Personnel, Pilot (fighter pilot); Karl-Heinz Kettering, Military Personnel (officer); Hauptmann Otto Heidemann, Military Personnel (officer)
Time Period(s): 1910s (1918)
Locale(s): France (Western Front)

Summary: The German air force during the waning days of World War I is portrayed in the career of Bruno Stachel who covets the glory represented by winning the distinguished decoration the Blue Max. His monomaniacal pursuit of military success destroys all other human considerations as the novel reaches the level of an allegory on the origins of Naziism.

Historical Accuracy: The period flying elements are authentic.

ROLAND HUNTFORD

3086 *Sea of Darkness*

Date of Publication: 1975
Subject(s): Sea Story; Exploration; Alternate History
Fictional character(s): Jon Scolvessen, Sea Captain, Explorer
Historical character(s): Christopher Columbus, Explorer
Time Period(s): 15th century (1470s)
Locale(s): At Sea; Norway; Portugal

Summary: This story of the early sailing career of Christopher Columbus blends together actual accounts with an imagined voyage that Columbus takes with a Norwegian explorer, Jon Scolvessen (based on the real Johannes Scolvus). The expedition leaves Norway and reaches Newfoundland. On the journey Columbus learns how to cross the Atlantic, and, after studying some navigation aids from the King of Portugal, he is ready for his famous voyage.

Historical Accuracy: The voyage is apocryphal, but the nautical details are authentic and convincing.

BERNHARDT J. HURWOOD (1926-1987)

American writer Hurwood was born in New York City and graduated from Northwestern University. Hurwood worked as a merchant seaman and a film editor.

3087 *My Savage Muse: The Story of My Life: Edgar Allan Poe, an Imaginative Work*

Date of Publication: 1980
Subject(s): Literary Life; Biography, Fictionalized
Historical character(s): Edgar Allan Poe, Writer
Time Period(s): 19th century (1809-1847)
Locale(s): Richmond, Virginia; New York, New York; Baltimore, Maryland

Summary: The novel offers an "autobiography" of the tormented genius of American literature, Edgar Allen Poe. With evident solid research into Poe's life and work, the author presents a plausible evocation of Poe's voice and memories of childhood, and his struggle and anguish to produce his works while dealing with sizable personal problems.

Historical Accuracy: The notes suggest the extent to which the novel has kept to the historical record of Poe's life.

DARRELL HUSTED (1931-)

Born in Texas, Husted graduated from Columbia University and attended the Sorbonne. Husted has worked as a book editor. He enjoys the Regency period best because of its similarity to our age.

3088 *Louisa Brancusi*

Date of Publication: 1980
Subject(s): Theatrical Life; Dance; Regency Period
Fictional character(s): Louisa Brancusi, Dancer (ballet); Elizabeth Appelbaux, Noblewoman; Henry Thornton, Gentleman
Time Period(s): 1800s
Locale(s): Copenhagen, Denmark; London, England

Summary: Set during the Regency period, the novel describes the ballet career of Louisa Brancusi. Her success in the theatrical world is complicated by a deadly political intrigue connected with the question of Louisa's parentage. Is she the orpahaned daughter of two itinerant artists or the bastard daughter of the Prince Regent himself?.

Historical Accuracy: The story is fanciful, but filled with genuine period elements.

JANE HUTCHENS (1901-)

Born in Lathrop, Missouri, Hutchens attended William Woods College and the Central Missouri State Teachers College. A free-lance writer, she has published stories, articles, and two historical novels, *Timothy Larkin* and *John Brown's Cousin.*

3089 *Timothy Larkin*

Date of Publication: 1942
Subject(s): Civil War—U.S.
Fictional character(s): Timothy Larkin, Military Personnel (Union soldier), Scout
Time Period(s): 1850s; 1860s
Locale(s): Missouri

Summary: This picaresque story of a Missouri family in the years leading up to the Civil War centers on Timothy Larkin. He joins the Union army and is saved by his father, who left the family when Timothy was ten years old.

Historical Accuracy: The narration of Timothy's adventures carries the ring of reality, with an authentic period background.

LINDA HUTCHINS

3090 *Mortal Love: A Novel of Eleanor of Aquitaine*

Date of Publication: 1980
Subject(s): Middle Ages; Biography, Fictionalized
Historical character(s): Eleanor of Aquitaine, Royalty (Queen of France and England)
Time Period(s): 12th century; 13th century
Locale(s): France; England

Summary: This poetic first-person narrative provides the personal reminiscences of the remarkable Eleanor of Aquitaine. She reflects on her amazing career as queen of both France and England during one of the most turbulent periods of history. All the important events and personalities of Eleanor's life are touched upon.

Historical Accuracy: The novel features a meticulous reconstruction of its background, which is more convincing than Eleanor.

BETTY HALE HYATT (1927-)

American romance novelist Hyatt was born in Texas and attended the University of New Mexico. She is the author of The House of Lancien series for Playboy Paperbacks, and the novels *The Sapphire Lotus, The Jade Pagoda,* and *The Chevalier's Lady.*

3091 *The Shalimar*

Date of Publication: 1982
Subject(s): British Raj
Fictional character(s): Lady Summer Browne-Huntley, Gentlewoman
Time Period(s): 19th century
Locale(s): India

Summary: This romantic adventure story is set in 19th-century India and concerns Lady Summer Browne-Huntley, who flees to the country of her childhood from a forced marriage. The intrepid Lady Summer has a series of adventures in strife-torn India.

Historical Accuracy: The novel provides a colorful and convincing Indian background for its romantic adventures.

CHRISTOPHER HYDE

Born in Ottawa, Ontario, Hyde's novels include *Hard Target, Crestwook Heights,* and *Jericho Falls.*

3092 *A Gathering of Saints*

Date of Publication: 1996
Subject(s): World War II; Mystery
Fictional character(s): Morris Black, Detective—Police
Time Period(s): 1940s (1940)
Locale(s): London, England

Summary: Set during the London Blitz, this mystery thriller involves the pursuit of a serial killer who knows that the British have cracked Ultra, the Nazis' top secret military code. Scotland Yard detective Morris Black is given the task of finding the killer before a Nazi spy does.

Historical Accuracy: Although the story is fictional, it is based on some historical fact. All of the historical events took place as they are described.

SARA HYLTON

`3093` *In the Shadow of the Nile*

Date of Publication: 1993
Subject(s): Romance
Fictional character(s): Lavinia Levinson-Gore, Gentlewoman; Laura Levinson-Gore, Young Woman; Edward Burlington, Gentleman; Ahmed Hassan Farag, Royalty (prince)
Time Period(s): 1920s (1922)
Locale(s): Alexandria, Egypt

Summary: Laura Levison-Gore is a young woman being escorted by her mother to Egypt in 1922. The goal is to arrange a respectable match with eligible Edmund Burlington. But Laura meets Prince Farag and despite opposition on both sides, their relationship alters both of their lives.

Historical Accuracy: The rather conventional romance is relieved by the novel's exotic setting, authentically depicted.

TOM HYMAN

`3094` *Seven Days to Petrograd*

Date of Publication: 1988
Subject(s): Russian Revolution; World War I; Espionage
Fictional character(s): Harry Bauer, Spy
Historical character(s): Vladimir Ilich Ulyanov, Revolutionary; Winston Churchill, Political Figure; Woodrow Wilson, Political Figure (U.S. president)
Time Period(s): 1910s
Locale(s): St. Petersburg, Russia; Berlin, Germany; Zurich, Switzerland

Summary: This historical thriller concerns Lenin's famous journey to Russia, arrange d by the Germans, to begin the Russian Revolution and end Russia's involvement in World War I. Harry Bauer, an American intelligence officer, is given the job to infiltrate the party of revolutionaries aboard the train and kill Lenin at all costs.

Historical Accuracy: The Allied effort to stop Lenin's return to Russia is invented.

EVA IBBOTSON (1925-)

Born in Vienna, Ibbotson lives in England. She did honors work in physiology at the University of London and postgraduate research at Cambridge where she married a fellow student. Her novel, *The Magic Flutes*, won an award in Britain as the best romantic novel of the year. In her fiction, Ibbotson attempts to break down the barrier between serious and romantic novels.

`3095` *A Company of Swans*

Date of Publication: 1985
Subject(s): Romance; Theatrical Life
Fictional character(s): Harriet Jane Morton, Dancer; Romain Verney, Nobleman
Time Period(s): 1910s (1912)
Locale(s): Cambridge, England; Manaus, Brazil

Summary: Harriet Jane Morton is a Cambridge don's daughter who flees her home to join the corps de ballet of a travelling company that journeys to the exotic city of Manaus in South America to perform in its legendary opera house. Harriet is transformed by the experience and the attention of aristocratic exile Romain Verney.

Historical Accuracy: This is romantic make-believe with an interesting and authentic exotic setting in Manaus and a realistic depiction of the dance world.

`3096` *Madensky Square*

Date of Publication: 1988
Subject(s): Romance
Fictional character(s): Susanna Weber, Store Owner (dressmaker)
Time Period(s): 1910s (1911-1912)
Locale(s): Vienna, Austria

Summary: Vienna in the years before the outbreak of World War I is depicted through the perspective of Susanna Weber, the owner of a dressmaking shop on Madensky Square. Susanna reflects the milieu of the theatre and the opera of fashionable Vienna. Beneath the placid and frivolous surface are secrets and disruptions portending the changes that are to come.

Historical Accuracy: The period is vividly and authentically reproduced.

`3097` *Magic Flutes*

Date of Publication: 1982
Subject(s): Romance; Theatrical Life
Fictional character(s): Guy Farne, Businessman; Theresa-Maria of Pfaffenstein, Royalty (princess)
Time Period(s): 1920s (1922)
Locale(s): Vienna, Austria

Summary: Guy Farne is a foundling rescued from the Newcastle dockside who becomes a wealthy man. Theresa, an Austrian princess, leaves her family home to become a dresser in a Viennese opera house. Their paths cross in a complicated and romantic tale.

Historical Accuracy: The premise is more fairy tale than realistic, yet the period of postwar Vienna is accurately described.

ARI IBN-SAHAV (1899-)

Ibn-Sahav's books include *Jessica, My Daughter*.

`3098` *David and Bathsheba*

Date of Publication: 1951
Subject(s): Biblical Story; Ancient Israel
Historical character(s): David, Ruler (King of Israel), Biblical Figure; Bathsheba, Biblical Figure
Time Period(s): 10th century B.C.
Locale(s): Israel

Summary: In old age, as David is dying, he recalls the events of his life, particularly his relationship with his second wife, Bathsheba, the mother of Solomon. After his remarkable rise to become the second king of ancient Israel, David's decline begins with his adultery with Bathsheba and his murder of her husband. Revolt and the usurpation of his throne follow.

Historical Accuracy: David's story is given a modern spin in an over-sentimentalized and idealized retelling of the biblical story. Historical accuracy has been sacrificed in the interest of passion and pathos.

ALBERT E. IDELL (1901-1958)

Born in Philadelphia, Idell worked in many professions, including prize fighting, and he used his experiences in his novels.

3099 *Bridge to Brooklyn*

Date of Publication: 1944
Subject(s): Family Saga; Bridge Building
Fictional character(s): Jesse Rogers, Businessman; Augustina Rogers, Spouse
Time Period(s): 1870s; 1880s (1877-1883)
Locale(s): Pennsylvania; New York, New York

Summary: The novel continues the chronicle of the Rogers family during the period of the construction of the Brooklyn Bridge. Their experiences offer a colorful portrait of the age and the social customs of everyday life.

Historical Accuracy: The novel's social background is authentic and believable.

3100 *Centennial Summer*

Date of Publication: 1943
Subject(s): Family Saga
Fictional character(s): Jesse Rogers, Businessman; Augustina Rogers, Spouse
Time Period(s): 1870s (1875-1876)
Locale(s): Philadelphia, Pennsylvania; New York, New York

Summary: This story is set against the events of 1876 and the opening of the Centennial Exposition in Philadelphia. The various activities and experiences of the Rogers family offer a vivid and colorful view of the period.

Historical Accuracy: The story is set against a reliable period background.

3101 *The Great Blizzard*

Date of Publication: 1948
Subject(s): Disasters—Natural; Baseball; Family Saga
Fictional character(s): Jesse Rogers, Businessman; Augustina Rogers, Spouse; Ohio Ballou, Actress; Clint Weatherby, Sports Figure (baseball pitcher)
Time Period(s): 1880s (1884-1888)
Locale(s): New York, New York; Brooklyn, New York

Summary: Life in New York and Brooklyn, from 1884 to the Blizzard of '88 is described, a continuation of the fortunes of the Rogers family depicted in *Centennial Summer* and *Bridge to Brooklyn*. Several new members join the family including one of the first great underhand pitchers of the "Brooklyns" (later the Dodgers) and actress Ohio Ballou.

Historical Accuracy: The period elements are convincingly detailed.

3102 *Rogers' Folly*

Date of Publication: 1957
Subject(s): Family Saga
Fictional character(s): Jesse Rogers, Young Man; Augustina Borelli, Young Woman
Historical character(s): Phineas T. Barnum, Entertainer
Time Period(s): 1840s (1844-1849)
Locale(s): Bordentown, New Jersey; Philadelphia, Pennsylvania

Summary: Chronologically this is the first volume in a series chronicling the experiences of the Rogers family during the 19th century. The series begins with Jesse Rogers' courtship of Augustina Borelli, a member of the French emigre community of Bonapartists. The title refers to P.T. Barnum's bringing of the famous elephant, Jumbo, from Africa.

Historical Accuracy: The novel weaves fact and fancy together to present a convincing social chronicle of the times.

MICHAEL IGNATIEFF

Canadian-born writer Ignatieff worked for several years as a journalist and has taught history in British Columbia. He has been a celebrated critic and television commentator in London.

3103 *Asya*

Date of Publication: 1991
Subject(s): Russian Revolution
Fictional character(s): Asya Galitzine, Royalty (princess); Sergei Apollonovitch, Military Personnel (artillery officer)
Time Period(s): 20th century (1900s-1990s)
Locale(s): Russia; Paris, France

Summary: This love story is set against the backdrop of Russian history in the 20th century. Princess Asya Galitzine falls in love with Sergei Apollonovitch, an artillery officer. They are separated by the chaos of the Russian Revolution. Asya flees to Paris where Sergei reappears only to vanish again on the eve of World War II. Asya is haunted by her past, which she resolves in modern Russia.

Historical Accuracy: The details of Russian history are convincingly presented.

JAMES W. INGLES (1905-)

3104 *A Woman of Samaria*

Date of Publication: 1949
Subject(s): Biblical Story
Fictional character(s): Photina, Young Woman
Historical character(s): Jesus Christ, Biblical Figure
Time Period(s): 1st century
Locale(s): Samaria, Palestine

Summary: The novel is based on the Biblical story of the meeting of Jesus and the woman of Samaria. This version shows the woman, Photina, and her relationships with her five husbands and her Roman centurion lover.

Historical Accuracy: The period background is believable as is the description of the customs of the time.

GRACE INGRAM

(PSEUD. OF ELIZABETH GOUDGE, 1900-1984)

An English educator, artist, and author, Goudge was a prolific writer of books for children and adults, known for her depiction of small-town English life. Goudge taught handicrafts such as weaving, leatherwork, and embroidery. Her most famous novel was *Green Dolphin Street* , which was made into a film. Her other works include *Child from the Sea*, *The City of Bells*, *Towers in the Mist* , and *The Bird in the Tree*.

3105 *Gilded Spurs*

Date of Publication: 1978
Subject(s): Middle Ages; Witchcraft and Sorcery
Fictional character(s): Guy Armourer, Bastard Son; Reynald of Warby, Knight; Wulfrunt, Witch
Time Period(s): 12th century
Locale(s): England

Summary: Set in England during the 12th century before the reign of Henry II, the story depicts young Guy Armourer's quest to become a knight. As a bastard, the only means is to serve his father, Lord Reynald of Warby. Reynald practices black magic, and Guy is torn between serving his father and disapproving of his evil ways.

Historical Accuracy: There are many convincing period touches that support the novel's period and medieval atmosphere.

3106 *Red Adam's Lady*

Date of Publication: 1973
Subject(s): Middle Ages
Fictional character(s): Julietta de Montrigord, Gentlewoman; Red Adam, Nobleman (Lord of Brentborough)
Time Period(s): 12th century (1173)
Locale(s): Brentborough, England

Summary: In 12th century England Lady Julietta is abducted by Red Adam, the Lord of Brentborough, who astonishingly marries her after ruining her honor. Their relationship is depicted against a deftly portrayed and colorful medieval background of civil war, border raids, and intrigue.

Historical Accuracy: The central relationship is the most implausible aspect of the story; the medieval background is credible.

ROBERT INMAN (1931-)

Born in San Francisco and a graduate of Stanford and the University of Washington, Inman served in U.S. Army Intelligence in Germany. He has pursued careers as a linguist, teacher, editor, newspaperman, librarian, and historian.

3107 *The Blood Endures*

Date of Publication: 1981
Subject(s): Identity—Concealed; American West; Franco-Prussian War
Fictional character(s): Anthony Logan, Heir—Dispossessed, Adventurer; Anne Farleigh, Gentlewoman; Claire de Vignon, Prostitute (courtesan)
Historical character(s): Alexandre Dumas, fils, Writer
Time Period(s): 19th century (1839-1870)
Locale(s): Sussex, England; Paris, France

Summary: Anthony Logan is the offspring of a young English lord and a Castilian noblewoman. His true identity is concealed, and his search for fortune and his heritage takes him from a childhood in which he is raised as a groom on his father's estate to Germany as a courtier, the Paris of Napoleon III, Egypt during the building of the Suez Canal, Panama, San Francisco and Virginia City during the silver strike, and finally to a climax in Paris under the German siege.

Historical Accuracy: The author stresses that this novel is a work of fiction, and the characters are either the product of his imagination or used fictionally. Despite this, the hisorical background is sharply and convincingly depicted.

HAMMOND INNES (1913-)

An English novelist, Innes is widely regarded as one of the most popular adventure writers in the world. His books have sold some 40 million copies in over 50 different languages. Innes' most successful books include *The Blue Ice*, *The Doomed Oasis*, and *The Wreck of the Mary Deare*. A seafaring yachtsman, Innes travels around the world six months of every year gathering experiences for his novels.

3108 *The Last Voyage: Captain Cook's Lost Diary*

Date of Publication: 1979
Subject(s): Exploration; Sea Story
Historical character(s): James Cook, Explorer, Sea Captain
Time Period(s): 1770s
Locale(s): *Resolution*, At Sea; Hawaii

Summary: The novel invents a private journal that Captain James Cook might have kept on his fateful third voyage in search of a sea passage from the Pacific to the Atlantic across the top of North America. Blocked by walls of ice in the Bering Strait, Cook sails south to the Hawaiian Islands, where he is killed in a skirmish with natives over a stolen boat.

Historical Accuracy: The novel accurately portrays the facts of Cook's voyage. It attempts to offer a perspective on the events that might reveal the actual Cook, but is only partially successful.

PATRICK IRELAND

(PSEUD. OF BRIAN O'DOHERTY, 1934-)

An Irish artist, art critic, and novelist, O'Doherty adopted the pseudonym Patrick Ireland in 1972 to protest the presence of British troops in Northern Ireland.

3109 *The Strange Case of Madamoiselle P.*

Date of Publication: 1992
Subject(s): Medical Profession; Musical Life; Royalty—Austria
Historical character(s): Franz Anton Mesmer, Doctor, Scientist; Maria Theresa, Ruler (Empress of Austria); Maria Theresa von Paradies, Musician (pianist), Handicapped (blind)
Time Period(s): 18th century
Locale(s): Vienna, Austria

Summary: Based on an incident in the life of Franz Anton Mesmer, the celebrated discoverer of animal magnetism, the novel describes the case of Maria Theresa Paradies, a blind and gifted pianist. Her story becomes a tale of good versus evil and is steeped in the glitter and intrigue of the Hapsburg Court.

Historical Accuracy: The novel blends fact and fiction with a strong and believable period setting.

LUCILLE IREMONGER (1915-1989)

A political journalist and author, Iremonger was born in Jamaica. She is highly regarded for her examination of history, politics, and parapsychology in books and her contributions to the London *Times* and the *Evening Standard*. Her books include *The Ghost of Versailles*, *Love and the Princess*, *Creole*, and *Orphan of the Heart*. She also wrote an autobiography, *Yes, My Darling Daughter*.

3110 *How Do I Love Thee*

Date of Publication: 1976
Subject(s): Victorian Period; Literary Life; Biography, Fictionalized
Historical character(s): Elizabeth Barrett Browning, Writer (poet); Robert Browning, Writer (poet)
Time Period(s): 19th century
Locale(s): London, England; Italy

Summary: This novelized biography tells the story of the romance between English poets Robert and Elizabeth Barrett Browning. The novel dramatizes the well-known wooing by the younger Robert Browning of the reclusive Elizabeth Barrett and their 15-year marriage and life together in Italy.

Historical Accuracy: This is a more romantic than realistic portrait of the couple and their life together.

3111 *My Sister, My Love*

Date of Publication: 1981
Subject(s): Literary Life; Independence—Greece; Regency Period
Historical character(s): George Gordon Byron, Writer (poet), Nobleman; Augusta Leigh, Gentlewoman; Percy Bysshe Shelley, Writer (poet); Mary Wollstonecraft Godwin, Writer
Time Period(s): 1810s; 1820s (1811-1824)
Locale(s): England; Italy; Greece

Summary: This is a fictionalized account of Lord Byron's love affair with his half-sister, Augusta. This scandalous affair, though never proven in court, causes Byron to flee England for the Continent. Byron never sees Augusta after leaving England. His life in Italy and Greece is also described.

Historical Accuracy: The novel is based on letters, diaries, and records of the time. Although everything about Byron is filled with controversy and dispute, this is one plausible version of the famous poet's life.

LOLA IRISH

3112 *And the Wild Birds Sing*

Date of Publication: 1983
Subject(s): British Colonies; Frontier—Australia
Fictional character(s): Raurie Lorne, Young Woman; Brick O'Shea, Convict; Barbara Merrill, Gentlewoman
Time Period(s): 1840s
Locale(s): New South Wales, Australia

Summary: Life in Australia in 1841 is dramatized in the interconnected stories of three settlers. Raurie Lorne climbs up from Sydney's backstreets to a place in society. Brick O'Shea is a former convict who is determined to build an empire, and his affair with the genteel Barbara Merrill becomes the scandal of Sydney.

Historical Accuracy: The regional elements make a convincing period background for the story.

CLIFFORD IRVING (1930-)

An American novelist and journalist, Irving was born in New York City and is a graduate of Cornell University. He worked as a correspondent in the Middle East for NBC-TV. Irving created world-wide controversy for his involvement in the "Autobiography of Howard Hughes" hoax. Irving claimed that he had interviewed the reclusive financier, but they had never met.

3113 *Tom Mix and Pancho Villa*

Date of Publication: 1982
Subject(s): Mexican Revolution
Historical character(s): Tom Mix, Actor, Cowboy; Francisco Villa, Revolutionary, Outlaw; George S. Patton, Military Personnel (army officer); Emiliano Zapata, Revolutionary
Time Period(s): 1910s (1913-1916)
Locale(s): Mexico

Summary: The novel's premise is that cowboy actor Tom Mix, before his movie success, meets Pancho Villa and joins the revolutionaries in Mexico. Mix finds love and adventure and the horrors of the Mexican Revolution, including a confrontation with a young lieutenant, George S. Patton, Jr.

Historical Accuracy: The author describes the novel as a historical fantasy with efforts to be faithful to the facts of the Mexican Revolution and Pancho Villa's life.

3114 *The Valley*

Date of Publication: 1961
Subject(s): American West; Ranching

Fictional character(s): Clayton Roy, Young Man; Gavin Roy, Rancher; Laurel de Long, Spouse (of Gavin)
Time Period(s): 19th century (post Civil War)
Locale(s): New Mexico

Summary: Father-son conflict plays out in 19th-century New Mexico, as Clayton Roy grows to manhood in the shadow of his ruthless rancher father. Violence between ranchers and homesteaders erupts, and Gavin Roy's new bride produces a final confrontation between father and son.

Historical Accuracy: The period is detailed with some authenticity.

CONSTANCE IRWIN (1913-)

Born in Indiana, Irwin is a graduate of Indiana University and Columbia. She has worked as a librarian and book editor. *Strange Footprints on the Land* was named as one of the best books of 1989 by *School Library Journal*.

3115 *Gudrid's Saga*

Date of Publication: 1974
Subject(s): Vikings; Exploration
Historical character(s): Leif Eriksson, Explorer; Eirik Thurvaldsson, Explorer; Gudrid Thorbjornsdottir, Settler; Thorfinn Karlsefni, Trader
Time Period(s): 11th century
Locale(s): North America; Greenland

Summary: The novel attempts to reconstruct what might have happened in a Norse settlement in North America in the 11th century. Gudrid and her husband Karlsefni, an Icelandic merchant, lead a band of Norsemen and women across the Atlantic to begin the colonization of America.

Historical Accuracy: The real facts on which the novel is based have been filled in with well-researched suppositions.

MARGARET IRWIN (1889-1967)

English mystery and historical novelist Irwin was born in London. Her first novel, *None So Pretty*, won a competition organized by the publishing company Chatto & Windus.

3116 *The Bride*

Date of Publication: 1939
Subject(s): Royalty—England; Civil War—England
Historical character(s): James Graham, Nobleman; Louise Hallandine, Noblewoman (Countess Palatine); Charles II, Ruler (King of England); Edward Hyde, Lawyer, Government Official
Time Period(s): 1640s; 1650s
Locale(s): The Hague, Netherlands; Scotland

Summary: In the aftermath of the execution of Charles I, Charles II is in exile in The Hague rallying sympathizers to retake the English throne. Also living there are the exiled Queen of Bohemia and her unmarried daughters. The novel tells the story of Louise and her tempestuous love affair with the Marquis of Montrose, the hero of the King's army.

Historical Accuracy: The historical accuracy is assured by the use of the historical figures' actual words wherever possible.

3117 *Elizabeth and the Prince of Spain*

Date of Publication: 1953
Subject(s): Royalty—England; Elizabethan Period
Historical character(s): Elizabeth Tudor, Royalty (princess); Mary I, Ruler (Queen of England); Philip II, Ruler (King of Spain)
Time Period(s): 16th century
Locale(s): England

Summary: The novel depicts the girlhood of Elizabeth up to the beginning of her reign as queen. Elizabeth is a popular princess, regarded with suspicion by her half-sister, Queen Mary, and with increasing regard by Mary's husband, Philip of Spain, who wants to make Elizabeth his lover. After Mary's death, Elizabeth rejects Philip and sets in motion pivotal events with Spain.

Historical Accuracy: The novel stays within the framework of history here with elaboration and invention of scenes and dialogue.

3118 *Elizabeth, Captive Princess*

Date of Publication: 1948
Subject(s): Tudor Period; Royalty—England
Historical character(s): Elizabeth Tudor, Royalty (princess); Roger Ascham, Teacher, Scholar; Mary Tudor, Royalty (princess); Lady Jane Grey, Ruler (Queen of England); Philip II, Ruler (King of Spain)
Time Period(s): 16th century
Locale(s): England

Summary: The girlhood of Elizabeth I is depicted in this novel recreating this turbulent period of English history. She is a virtual prisoner and dependent on the ambivalent support of her half-sister, Mary, whom Elizabeth had supplanted with the succession of Elizabeth's mother Anne Boleyn, as queen. Now Mary comes to the throne, and Elizabeth must negotiate the treacherous shifts of her sister's affections.

Historical Accuracy: The novel is convincing in its re-creation of the era and the politics surrounding the succession to the English throne following the death of Henry VIII.

3119 *The Gay Galliard*

Date of Publication: 1942
Subject(s): Royalty—Scotland
Historical character(s): James Hepburn, Nobleman (Earl of Bothwell); Mary, Queen of Scots, Ruler; Henry Stewart, Spouse (consort of Mary), Nobleman (Lord Darnley); John Knox, Religious
Time Period(s): 16th century
Locale(s): Scotland

Summary: The novel describes the love affair between Mary, Queen of Scots and Bothwell, her third husband. Their union is tainted by the mysterious death of Mary's second husband, Darnley. Bothwell emerges as a far more sympathetic figure than in other historical and fictional treatments.

Historical Accuracy: The facts and incidents are drawn from contemporary records, as is much of the dialogue.

`3120` *The Proud Servant: The Story of Montrose*

Date of Publication: 1934
Subject(s): Royalty—England; Civil War—England; Biography, Fictionalized
Historical character(s): James Graham, Nobleman (Marquis of Montrose); Charles I, Ruler (King of England)
Time Period(s): 17th century (1612-1651)
Locale(s): England; Scotland

Summary: The novel chronicles the career of James Graham, Marquess of Montrose, loyal subject of Charles I and the king's faithful champion in the English Civil War that topples Charles from his throne. Montrose's military campaigns are described.

Historical Accuracy: All letters and documents quoted are authentic.

`3121` *Royal Flush: The Story of Minette*

Date of Publication: 1932
Subject(s): Royalty—England; Royalty—France; Restoration Period
Historical character(s): Henrietta Stuart, Royalty (princess); Charles II, Ruler (King of England); Louis XIV, Ruler (King of France); Philippe I, Duc d'Orleans, Royalty (prince)
Time Period(s): 17th century
Locale(s): England; France

Summary: The novel tells the story of Henrietta Stuart, princess of England, and daughter of Charles I and cousin of Louis XIV. Her story reveals the intimate details of two royal families and the motivations of two kings, Charles II and Louis XIV.

Historical Accuracy: The novel provides a remarkable reconstruction of the court world in England and France during the period.

`3122` *The Stranger Prince*

Date of Publication: 1937
Subject(s): Civil War—England; Royalty—England
Historical character(s): Rupert, Royalty (prince); Charles I, Ruler (King of England); Oliver Cromwell, Political Figure, Military Personnel
Time Period(s): 17th century
Locale(s): The Hague, Netherlands; England

Summary: Rupert is the third son of Elizabeth of Bohemia and fiercely loyal to the cause of his uncle Charles I. He becomes the king's champion in the Civil War, displaying great daring and military skill. He seems to have a charmed life though committed to a lost cause.

Historical Accuracy: Period details are convincingly portrayed.

`3123` *Young Bess*

Date of Publication: 1945
Subject(s): Tudor Period; Royalty—England
Historical character(s): Elizabeth Tudor, Royalty (princess); Thomas Cranmer, Religious; Mary Tudor, Royalty (princess)
Time Period(s): 16th century
Locale(s): England

Summary: The childhood of Elizabeth Tudor is chronicled in the first volume of a trilogy. At the age of 12, Elizabeth must contend with the intrigue of her father's court as the discredited daughter of Anne Boleyn.

Historical Accuracy: The novel's historical elements are plausible, though there is considerable invention of dialogue and circumstances.

CHARLES E. ISRAEL (1920-)

Born in Indiana and raised in Maryland, Israel served in the merchant marine in World War II. In 1950 Israel began working in Hollywood where he wrote radio and TV scripts. He subsequently moved to Toronto where he is one of Canada's best-known writers.

`3124` *Rizpah*

Date of Publication: 1961
Subject(s): Biblical Story; Ancient Israel
Fictional character(s): Rizpah, Slave (concubine)
Historical character(s): Saul, Ruler (King of Israel), Biblical Figure; David, Ruler (King of Israel), Biblical Figure; Samuel, Religious (prophet), Biblical Figure; Abner, Military Personnel (general), Biblical Figure
Time Period(s): 10th century B.C.
Locale(s): Israel

Summary: This novel of ancient Israel during the reign of Saul tells the story of Rizpah who at 16 is taken by Philistine raiders to be sold as a concubine. Trained as a courtesan, she is freed by the victorious Israelite army and comes to the attention of Saul, whose turbulent reign is depicted.

Historical Accuracy: The story is solidly depicted with a convincing sense of the period and the personalities.

`3125` *Who Was Then the Gentleman*

Date of Publication: 1963
Subject(s): Middle Ages; Peasants' Revolt
Historical character(s): Wat Tyler, Farmer (peasant), Revolutionary; Richard II, Ruler (King of England); John of Gaunt, Royalty; John Ball, Religious (priest), Revolutionary
Time Period(s): 14th century (1381)
Locale(s): England

Summary: This novel depicts the tragic Peasants' Revolt of 1381 as the despairing populace suffering under the crushing burden of the Poll Tax is led into rebellion by Wat Tyler and John Ball. Despite initial success, the revolt is eventually crushed.

Historical Accuracy: The novel is a fascinating account of the events of 1381 with an authentic sense of atmosphere and the personalities involved.

DONALD JACK (1924-)

English born and a resident of Canada, Jack has worked as a music critic, a salesman, an oil-field surveyor, and a scriptwriter. He has authored numerous stage, radio, and television plays, and over 50 film scripts.

3126 *It's Me Again*

Date of Publication: 1975
Subject(s): World War I; Aviation; Russian Revolution
Fictional character(s): Bartholemew Bandy, Military Personnel, Pilot
Historical character(s): David Lloyd George, Political Figure
Time Period(s): 1910s; 1920s
Locale(s): England; France; Russia

Summary: In the third volume of the Bandy Papers, unlikely military hero Bartholomew Bandy is back on the front in command of a fighter squadron. Shot down behind enemy lines, he steals a German plane only to be shot down again by his own side. Bandy is reassigned to Russia and sees action with White Russian troops.

Historical Accuracy: The novel is not attempting to document its period, rather to mine it for its comic possibilities. The period background is genuine.

3127 *Me So Far*

Date of Publication: 1989
Subject(s): Aviation
Fictional character(s): Bartholemew Bandy, Military Personnel, Pilot
Time Period(s): 1920s (1925-1926)
Locale(s): India

Summary: The seventh and final installment of the Bandy Papers is set in India in the 1920s as Bartholomew Bandy helps a maharajah to set up a new air force and defends against an attack by a neighboring state.

Historical Accuracy: Accuracy is not the point here. The period touches do, however, create a colorful and vivid backdrop to the comic action.

3128 *Me Too*

Date of Publication: 1983
Subject(s): Russian Revolution; Politics
Fictional character(s): Bartholemew Bandy, Adventurer, Political Figure (member of Parliament)
Time Period(s): 1910s; 1920s
Locale(s): Russia; Canada

Summary: In Book Five of the Bandy Papers, Bartholemew Bandy continues his adventures in Russia during the Revolution before heading home to Canada, where he becomes a Member of Parliament.

Historical Accuracy: The novel is a comic romp across the past with period details the grist for Bandy's comic interventions.

3129 *That's Me in the Middle*

Date of Publication: 1973
Subject(s): World War I; Aviation; Military Life
Fictional character(s): Bartholemew Bandy, Military Personnel, Pilot

Historical character(s): Winston Churchill, Political Figure; Lester Pearson, Political Figure
Time Period(s): 1910s (1918)
Locale(s): London, England; France; Dublin, Ireland

Summary: In the second volume of the Bandy Papers, World War I ace Bartholemew Bandy is now a lieutenant colonel and liaison officer in London for the Secretary of State for Air. Misadventures on the homefront send him back to France to join a bicycle brigade.

Historical Accuracy: More absurd than historical, the novel does offer some genuine period touches and a convincing background.

3130 *This One's on Me*

Date of Publication: 1987
Subject(s): Picaresque Adventure
Fictional character(s): Bartholomew Bandy, Adventurer
Time Period(s): 1920s
Locale(s): Reykjavik, Iceland; London, England

Summary: The sixth installment of the comic Bandy Papers follows Bartholomew Bandy, first to Iceland, and then to England, for a series of comic misadventures whose theme, common to the entire series, is the devastating effect of World War I on society.

Historical Accuracy: The novel presents an authentic, if at times absurd, look at post-war England during the 1920s.

3131 *Three Cheers for Me*

Date of Publication: 1973
Subject(s): World War I; Military Life; Aviation
Fictional character(s): Bartholemew Bandy, Military Personnel, Pilot
Time Period(s): 1910s
Locale(s): Canada; England; France

Summary: In the first of seven novels collectively called the Bandy Papers, the comic misadventures of young Canadian Bartholemew Bandy are recounted as he goes off to the Great War. His first night patrol produces an attack on his own lines and a transfer to the Royal Flying Corps. Adventures in the air cause him, improbably, to become an ace and face challenges among the officer class to which he is elevated.

Historical Accuracy: Accuracy seems beside the point in this comic send-up, but the period details are authentic, if skewed toward the absurd.

DOROTHY V.S. JACKSON (1924-)

Born in Brooklyn, Jackson attended Cooper Union, Brooklyn College, and Columbia University.

3132 *Walk with Peril*

Date of Publication: 1959
Subject(s): Battle of Agincourt; Royalty—England; Middle Ages
Fictional character(s): Robert Fairfield, Knight; Lewis Chappelle, Businessman (merchant); Constance Chappelle, Young Woman

Historical character(s): Henry V, Ruler (King of England)
Time Period(s): 15th century (1415)
Locale(s): England; France

Summary: Robert Fairchild is a poor squire who gives his service to Henry V. In London he is persecuted as a member of the Lollards, a heretical religious sect. He learns of a plot to kill the king, and accompanies Henry to France. The novel's action climaxes at the Battle of Agincourt.

Historical Accuracy: The novel's story is imagined, but it keeps close to the events of the era, which are captured with conviction.

EILEEN JACKSON (1906-)

Born in San Diego, California, Jackson attended San Diego State College and the University of Arizona. She worked as a reporter and editor on several newspaper, producing feature and travel articles.

3133 *Autumn Lace*

Date of Publication: 1976
Subject(s): Victorian Period; Romance; Servants
Fictional character(s): Miranda Courtney, Seamstress, Servant; Gethin Glendower, Landowner
Time Period(s): 19th century (Victorian period)
Locale(s): London, England; Wales

Summary: To avoid an unwanted marriage, Miranda Courtney takes a position as a seamstress on a wealthy Welsh estate. There she experiences the enmity of the Glendower family's servants.

Historical Accuracy: The novel captures the period with some authentic details of setting and locale.

3134 *Lord Rivington's Lady*

Date of Publication: 1976
Subject(s): Regency Romance
Fictional character(s): Peregrine Harvard, Gentleman; Penelope Harvard, Gentlewoman; Georgina Harvard, Gentlewoman; Alexander Rivington, Nobleman
Time Period(s): 1810s (1810)
Locale(s): London, England

Summary: The romantic plans of Penelope and Georgina Harvard are complicated by their family's straitened financial circumstances, due to gambling. Georgina, who believes in the emancipation of women, finds herself both attracted to and repelled by Lord Alexander Rivington. Happiness will depend on untangling the perilous fate of the Harvard family.

Historical Accuracy: Georgina's interest in a medical career is advanced enough to seem anachronistic.

MARIAN J.A. JACKSON
(PSEUD. OF MARIAN H. ROGERS, 1932-)

Born in Birmingham, Alabama, Jackson has worked as a manager of technical services for the Institute of Electrical and Electronics Engineers in New York City. She has been a

freelance writer since 1985 and is the author of the Miss Danforth mystery series.

3135 *Diamond Head*

Date of Publication: 1992
Subject(s): Mystery
Fictional character(s): Abigail Danforth, Detective—Private; Maude Cunningham, Companion
Time Period(s): 1900s
Locale(s): Oahu, Hawaii

Summary: The world's first female consulting detective, Abigail Danforth, has been asked to investigate the death by poison of a wealthy heir. Then suspicion for the murder of a member of the former Hawaiian royal family falls on her servant, Kincaid, who inexplicably confesses that he did it.

Historical Accuracy: Period life in Hawaii at the turn of the century provides a colorful and believable backdrop to the mystery.

3136 *The Sunken Treasure*

Date of Publication: 1994
Subject(s): Mystery
Fictional character(s): Abigail Danforth, Detective—Private; Maude Cunningham, Companion
Historical character(s): Erich Weiss, Magician
Time Period(s): 1900s (1900)
Locale(s): At Sea (Caribbean)

Summary: Consulting detective Abigail Danforth and her companion, Maude Cunningham, are on a Caribbean cruise aboard a millionaire's yacht. Other passengers include Erich Weiss, better known as Harry Houdini. Danforth must save the day when several people on board are found dead.

Historical Accuracy: The novel features authentic period details.

NAOMI JACOB (1884-1964)

British actress, educator, and author Jacob was born in Ripon, Yorkshire. A prolific writer, she began her career in the mid-1920s after ill health forced her to give up a successful acting career. Among her most popular stories were those that formed the Gollantz Saga, including *The Founding of the House*, *Gollantz: London, Paris, Milan*, and *Gollantz and Partners*.

3137 *The Irish Boy: A Romantic Biography*

Date of Publication: 1955
Subject(s): Biography, Fictionalized; Musical Life
Historical character(s): Michael Kelly, Singer (opera); Wolfgang Amadeus Mozart, Composer, Musician
Time Period(s): 18th century; 19th century
Locale(s): Dublin, Ireland; Italy

Summary: The novel presents a fictionalized account of the life and career of Irish opera singer Michael Kelly. The son of a Dublin wine merchant, Kelly rises to great acclaim in Italy and becomes a close friend of Mozart.

Historical Accuracy: The author admits to having taken liberties with the facts and inventing details of Kelly's early life.

HELEN HULL JACOBS (1908-)

An American writer born in Arizona, Jacobs was a national and international tennis star. She was a finalist at Wimbleton six times and won the singles championship in 1936. She is the author of an autobiography, *Beyond the Game*, and numerous books on tennis.

`3138` *Storm Against the Wind*

Date of Publication: 1944
Subject(s): American Colonies
Fictional character(s): Sheldon Hillard, Gentleman; Evelyn Buford, Gentlewoman
Time Period(s): 1770s
Locale(s): James River, Virginia, American Colonies

Summary: In the days preceding the American Revolution, a young aristocrat, Sheldon Hillard, rejects his family's Tory sentiments and sympathizes with the colonials. He is strongly influenced by Evelyn Buford, an ardent patriot.

Historical Accuracy: The novel achieves a high degree of authenticity in its period elements.

THORNWELL JACOBS (1877-)

Jacobs' books include *The New Science and the Old Religion*.

`3139` *Red Lanterns on St. Michael's*

Date of Publication: 1940
Subject(s): Civil War—U.S.
Fictional character(s): Peronneau Creston, Plantation Owner; Perry Poer White, Young Man
Time Period(s): 1860s
Locale(s): Charleston, South Carolina

Summary: This long Civil War tale takes place in Charleston, South Carolina, and depicts the city's role during the conflict. With a clear pro-Confederacy bent, the novel glamorizes the civilization that slavery and the landed class produced and which is destroyed by the war.

Historical Accuracy: The regional details are authentic, but the novel's point of view and the story's melodramatic arrangement destroy objectivity and realism.

SHELDON JACOBSON (1903-)

Born in New York City, Jacobson is a graduate of City College and earned his M.D. degree from Yale University. A pathologist in various New York hospitals, Jacobson has also worked as a professor of pathology at the University of Oregon.

`3140` *Fleet Surgeon to Pharaoh*

Date of Publication: 1971
Subject(s): Ancient Egypt; Sea Story; Medical Profession
Fictional character(s): Asa ben Abdiel, Doctor; Belnatan, Sea Captain
Time Period(s): 6th century (B)
Locale(s): Egypt; At Sea (along the coast of Africa)

Summary: The novel provides an account of the first sea voyage around the coast of Africa, a voyage briefly mentioned by Herodotus. The expedition's commander is the Phoenician captain Belnatan, and the central character is Asa ben Abdiel, a Jewish physician and priest, who has come to Egypt to advance his skills in medicine.

Historical Accuracy: The historical background of the story is authentic, and the details are based on solid research.

GLORIA JAHODA (1926-1980)

Historian and author Jahoda was born in Chicago. She graduated from Northwestern University and was an instructor in anthropology at Farleigh Dickinson University. Jahoda was the president of the Tallahassee Historical Society, and her book *River of the Golden Isis* was recognized by the Society of Midland Authors of Florida as the best history book of 1973.

`3141` *Annie*

Date of Publication: 1960
Subject(s): Restoration Period; Servants
Fictional character(s): Annie Warne, Orphan, Servant; Francis Bickley, Gentleman
Time Period(s): 17th century
Locale(s): Norfolk, England

Summary: Annie Warne is an orphan who comes to work for the Bickley family and serves them loyally for over 20 years. She eventually becomes Lady Bickley, a true member of the family.

Historical Accuracy: The backdrop of events of the 17th century is genuine and convincing.

`3142` *Delilah's Mountain*

Date of Publication: 1963
Subject(s): Indians; American Revolution; Settlement of the American Frontier
Fictional character(s): Delilah Winfield, Settler; Charles Bickley, Settler
Time Period(s): 18th century (1774-1794)
Locale(s): Clinch River Valley, Tennessee

Summary: Life in the Clinch River Valley of the Tennessee frontier during the American Revolution is described. White settlers arrive, in defiance of the treaties with the Indians, and then have to endure Indian attacks and the reassertion of British rule. Love between Charles Bickley and Delilah Winfield takes its long course, enduring trials and Indian capture.

Historical Accuracy: The period background is well-described and convincing.

JOHN JAKES (1932-)

American author Jakes was born in Chicago and worked for many years as a copywriter in advertising. Jakes had a long and somewhat obscure career as a writer of science fiction, mysteries, children's books, and suspense in the 1950s and 1960s before achieving phenomenal popular success with his American Bicentennial series of historical romances. None of the eight volumes in the series sold fewer than 3.5 million copies. Jakes has been justly praised for his narrative ability. He attributes his ability to capture scene and character to having a "gigantic cinemascope screen" in his head.

3143 *The Americans*

Date of Publication: 1980
Subject(s): Family Saga
Fictional character(s): Gideon Kent, Journalist, Publisher; Eleanor Kent Goldman, Actress; William Kent, Doctor
Historical character(s): Andrew Carnegie, Financier; Lucy Stone, Feminist; Joseph Pulitzer, Journalist, Publisher; Elizabeth Cady Stanton, Feminist; William Randolph Hearst, Journalist, Publisher; Theodore Roosevelt, Political Figure
Time Period(s): 1880s; 1890s
Locale(s): Boston, Massachusetts; New York, New York; Newport, Rhode Island

Summary: Jakes' Kent Family Chronicles concludes with the lives of Gideon Kent and his children. The novel ranges from the slums of New York to the opulence of the wealthy in Newport, offering a panorama of American society.

Historical Accuracy: The novel is largely successful in weaving the fictional and the historical into a large canvas that captures a major portion of American history.

3144 *The Bastard*

Date of Publication: 1974
Subject(s): American Revolution; Family Saga
Fictional character(s): Phillipe Charboneau, Bastard Son (aka Philip Kent), Heir—Dispossessed; Marie Charboneau, Innkeeper, Actress; Roger Amberly, Nobleman (Duke of Kentland)
Historical character(s): Benjamin Franklin, Diplomat, Patriot; Samuel Adams, Patriot, Revolutionary; Paul Revere, Artisan (silversmith), Patriot; Henry Knox, Military Personnel; Joseph Warren, Patriot, Doctor; Marie Joseph Paul de Lafayette, Nobleman (Marquis de Lafayette)
Time Period(s): 1770s (1771-1775)
Locale(s): Auvergne, France; England; Boston, Massachusetts, American Colonies

Summary: In this first volume of Jakes' American Bicentennial series of eight volumes, Frenchman Phillipe Charboneau, bastard son of English nobleman James Amberly, is prevented from claiming his birthright by his half brother. Phillipe travels to America and becomes involved in the Revolution in Boston in scenes that include the Boston Tea Party and Paul Revere's Ride.

Historical Accuracy: The second half of the novel is heavily dependent on faithfully described historical events.

3145 *California Gold*

Date of Publication: 1989
Subject(s): American West; Earthquakes; Motion Picture Industry
Fictional character(s): James Macklin "Mack" Chance, Adventurer; Nellie Ross, Journalist, Feminist; Walter Fairbanks, Lawyer
Historical character(s): William Randolph Hearst, Journalist, Publisher; Leland Stanford, Political Figure (Governor of California); Theodore Roosevelt, Political Figure; Edward Lawrence Doheny, Businessman (oilman); Collis Potter Huntington, Businessman (railroad executive); John Muir, Activist (conservationist)
Time Period(s): 19th century; 20th century (1886-1921)
Locale(s): San Francisco, California; Los Angeles, California; Riverside, California

Summary: The novel explores the lure and legends of California and charts its transformation from a frontier settlement to a modern state. The penniless wanderer James Macklin Chance struggles against the corruption of California politics, becomes involved in the early struggle of environmentalists, endures the terror of the 1906 San Francisco earthquake, invests in the movie business, and is caught up in the labor wars in the fields of the great central valley.

Historical Accuracy: The evident research into the period and its personalities establishes the novel's credibility.

3146 *The Furies*

Date of Publication: 1976
Subject(s): Family Saga; Texas Revolution; Battle of the Alamo
Fictional character(s): Amanda Kent, Hotel Owner; Luis Cordoba, Military Personnel (major in the Mexican army); Bart McGill, Sea Captain
Historical character(s): Davy Crockett, Frontiersman; Jim Bowie, Military Personnel (colonel in the Texas army); Antonio Lopez de Santa Anna, Military Personnel (Mexican general); Sam Houston, Military Personnel (commander of Texas army); Frederick Douglass, Writer, Abolitionist; William Cullen Bryant, Writer (poet), Journalist; Horace Greeley, Journalist, Political Figure
Time Period(s): 19th century (1836-1852)
Locale(s): San Antonio, Texas; San Francisco, California; New York, New York

Summary: This fourth installment of the Kent Family Chronicles (formerly the American Bicentennial series) features Amanda Kent, who keeps alive the Kent family spirit with her determination and ambition. Her journeys take her to the Battle of the Alamo, the California Gold Rush, and back East where she attempts to buy back the Kent family publishing company.

Historical Accuracy: The involvement in so many of the period's great events strains credibility, but the historical background is well detailed.

3147 *Heaven and Hell*

Date of Publication: 1987

Subject(s): Civil War—U.S.; Reconstruction Period; Family Saga

Fictional character(s): George Hazard, Veteran (Union army); Charles Main, Military Personnel (cavalryman), Trader; Madelaine Main, Widow(er)

Historical character(s): Andrew Johnson, Political Figure; George Armstrong Custer, Military Personnel (general); Wade Hampton, Military Personnel (Confederate general); Thaddeus Stevens, Political Figure, Abolitionist; Edwin Stanton, Government Official (Secretary of War); Simon Cameron, Political Figure

Time Period(s): 1860s; 1870s (1865-1876)

Locale(s): Charleston, South Carolina; Philadelphia, Pennsylvania; West

Summary: The final volume of Jakes' Civil War trilogy covers the events of the Reconstruction Period and the westward expansion. The focus is on the turmoil following the war and its effects on the Hazards of Pennsylvania and the Mains of South Carolina.

Historical Accuracy: The novel uses actual newspaper headlines and printed documents to help establish the novel's historical basis.

3148 *Homeland*

Date of Publication: 1993

Subject(s): Family Saga; Immigrants

Fictional character(s): Paul Crown, Immigrant; Julie Vanderhoff, Gentlewoman; Joseph Crown, Businessman (beer baron), Veteran (Civil War)

Historical character(s): Eugene V. Debs, Labor Leader; Theodore Roosevelt, Political Figure; Thomas Alva Edison, Inventor; Clara Barton, Nurse (organizer of the Red Cross); William F. Cody, Frontiersman, Entertainer

Time Period(s): 1890s; 1900s (1890-1900)

Locale(s): Chicago, Illinois

Summary: The first in a family chronicle concerning the Crown family of Chicago, the novel spans the decade of 1890-1900 when Joseph Crown and his family emigrate from Germany. Their experiences illustrate an America in the throes of technological change, social unrest, and political corruption.

Historical Accuracy: The novel is rich in historical events and characters that are accurately depicted.

3149 *The Lawless*

Date of Publication: 1978

Subject(s): Family Saga; American West

Fictional character(s): Gideon Kent, Labor Leader, Journalist; Jeremiah Kent, Murderer, Outlaw; Matthew Kent, Artist

Historical character(s): James Butler Hickok, Frontiersman, Lawman; Lucy Stone, Feminist; Martha Jane Cannary Burk, Frontierswoman, Entertainer; Edouard Manet, Artist; Paul Cezanne, Artist; James Abbott McNeill Whistler, Artist

Time Period(s): 1860s; 1870s (1869-1877)

Locale(s): Kansas; New York, New York; Paris, France

Summary: Jakes' seventh volume of the Kent Family Chronicles takes the reader from the Wild West to the sophisticated art studios of Paris. Matthew Kent befriends Manet, Cezanne,

and Whistler; Gideon Kent experiences corruption and worker agitation in New York and Chicago; and Jeremiah Kent turns murderer and fugitive.

Historical Accuracy: The novel goes into so many historical events that no one period or area is shown in great depth.

3150 *Love and War*

Date of Publication: 1984

Subject(s): Civil War—U.S.; Family Saga

Fictional character(s): George Hazard, Military Personnel (major); Orry Main, Military Personnel (colonel); Charles Main, Military Personnel (Confederate major)

Historical character(s): Abraham Lincoln, Political Figure (President of the U.S.); Jefferson Davis, Political Figure (President of the Confederacy); Edwin Stanton, Government Official (Secretary of War under Lincoln); Dorothea Dix, Nurse (superintendent of army nurses); Louisa May Alcott, Nurse, Writer; George Armstrong Custer, Military Personnel (U.S. Army Officer)

Time Period(s): 1860s (1861-1865)

Locale(s): Charleston, South Carolina; Richmond, Virginia; Pennsylvania

Summary: The second in a trilogy about the northern Hazard family and the southern Main family during the Civil War, the novel details the course of the war and its administration. Jakes' perspective is panoramic and includes scenes from the president's offices to prison camps.

Historical Accuracy: The novel effectively weaves the domestic story of the Hazards and Mains with an accurate picture of the period's major events.

3151 *North and South*

Date of Publication: 1982

Subject(s): Antebellum South; Civil War—U.S.; Slavery

Fictional character(s): George Hazard, Military Personnel (West Point cadet); Orry Main, Military Personnel (West Point cadet); Charles Orry, Orphan

Historical character(s): Robert E. Lee, Military Personnel (colonel in U.S. army); John C. Calhoun, Political Figure; Stephen A. Douglas, Political Figure

Time Period(s): 19th century (1841-1861)

Locale(s): West Point, New York; South Carolina; Newport, Rhode Island

Summary: The first novel in a trilogy, this story is a panoramic tale of two wealthy families during the years leading up to the Civil War. The Mains are plantation owners, and the Hazards are Pennsylvania industrialists. When George Hazard and Orry Main meet as West Point cadets, the lives of the two families become joined.

Historical Accuracy: The author has tried to capture the era by using historical facts from numerous sources, including the memoir of a West Point cadet, class of 1848.

3152 *The Rebels*

Date of Publication: 1975

Subject(s): Family Saga; American Revolution

Fictional character(s): Philip Kent, Military Personnel (formerly Phillipe Charboneau); Ann Kent, Spouse (of Philip Kent); Judson Fletcher, Gentleman
Historical character(s): George Washington, Military Personnel; Henry Knox, Military Personnel; Benjamin Franklin, Diplomat, Patriot; Thomas Paine, Writer, Patriot; John Adams, Political Figure; Joseph Warren, Doctor, Patriot; Marie Joseph Paul de Lafayette, Military Personnel (Marquis de Lafayette), Nobleman
Time Period(s): 1770s; 1780s (1775-1781)
Locale(s): Boston, Massachusetts; Virginia; Pittsburgh, Pennsylvania

Summary: The second in Jakes' Bicentennial series involves the Kent family, Philip and his wife Ann, in the Revolutionary War. The novel goes into the politics of the war as well as the domestic events of births, deaths, and the tragedies of war.

Historical Accuracy: Jakes' panorama is vast with authentic looks at all the major events and players.

`3153` *The Seekers*

Date of Publication: 1975
Subject(s): Indians; Family Saga; War of 1812
Fictional character(s): Abraham Kent, Military Personnel; Gilbert Kent, Publisher; Jared Kent, Military Personnel (sailor)
Historical character(s): Anthony Wayne, Military Personnel (general); William Henry Harrison, Military Personnel (aide to General Wayne); George Washington, Military Personnel (general), Political Figure; Thomas Jefferson, Diplomat, Political Figure; Meriwether Lewis, Military Personnel, Explorer; William Clark, Military Personnel, Explorer; George Rogers Clark, Frontiersman, Military Personnel
Time Period(s): 18th century; 19th century (1794-1814)
Locale(s): Boston, Massachusetts; Kentucky; Virginia

Summary: This third novel of Jakes' American Bicentennial series chronicles the second and third generations of the Kent family. Abraham Kent joins the army where he fights Indians and takes part in the early exploration of the West. His son, Jared, becomes the focus of the novel's action as a sailor on the *USS Constitution* during the War of 1812.

Historical Accuracy: The novel features much involvement with actual historical characters, who are, for the most part, accurately depicted.

`3154` *The Titans*

Date of Publication: 1976
Subject(s): Family Saga; Civil War—U.S.
Fictional character(s): Jared Kent, Journalist; Jephtha Kent, Journalist; Gideon Kent, Military Personnel (Confederate lieutenant)
Historical character(s): Abraham Lincoln, Political Figure (President of the U.S.); John Wilkes Booth, Actor; Jefferson Davis, Political Figure (President of the Confederacy); Robert E. Lee, Military Personnel (Confederate general); Clara Barton, Nurse, Activist (organizer of the Red Cross); James Ewell Brown Stuart, Military Personnel (Confederate cavalry officer); Allan Pinkerton, Detective (organized Secret Service), Military Personnel
Time Period(s): 1860s (1860-1862)

Locale(s): New York, New York; Washington, District of Columbia; Richmond, Virginia

Summary: The Kent family becomes involved in the beginnings of the Civil War. Some members of the family are Union sympathizers; others join the Confederacy. The novel details both sides in the conflict.

Historical Accuracy: The novel is convincing in its weaving together of the fictional and the historical.

`3155` *The Warriors*

Date of Publication: 1977
Subject(s): Family Saga; Civil War—U.S.; Railroads
Fictional character(s): Gideon Kent, Military Personnel (Confederate officer), Labor Leader (union organizer); Jeremiah Kent, Military Personnel (Union army officer); Michael Boyle, Railroad Worker
Historical character(s): Thomas Jonathan Jackson, Military Personnel (Confederate general); Jay Gould, Financier
Time Period(s): 1860s (1864-1868)
Locale(s): Atlanta, Georgia; United States; Midwest

Summary: The sixth of Jakes' Kent Family Chronicles details the end of the Civil War and the Reconstruction period with its continuing hatred between North and South over racial issues. The novel also begins to examine a changing America, emphasizing the developing of the West by the railroad barons and the emergence of unions for the protection of workers.

Historical Accuracy: The novel effectively captures the period.

DEANA JAMES
(PSEUD. OF MONA YOUNG SIZER, 1934-)

Romance novelist James was born in Arizona and has worked for 35 years as a high school English teacher. She won a *Romantic Times* award in 1988 for *Crimson Obsession* as the best Victorian romance and a Reviewer's Choice Award in 1991 for *Speak Only Love*. James rejects the notion that romance writers must live their books, since writers in other genres, like murder mysteries, obviously don't live theirs.

`3156` *Masque of Sapphire*

Date of Publication: 1990
Subject(s): Romance; War of 1812
Fictional character(s): Judith Talbot-Harrow, Businesswoman; Tabor O'Halloran, Businessman
Time Period(s): 1810s
Locale(s): England; United States

Summary: English-born Judith Talbot-Harrow arrives in America to help run her family shipping business. Competition and conflict with Tabor O'Halloran eventually lead to love, but major obstacles must be surmounted first.

Historical Accuracy: The emphasis is on romance over careful historical documentation, but there are sufficient period details to suggest the time and place.

DONALD JAMES

3157 *Once a Gentleman*

Date of Publication: 1987
Subject(s): World War I; Aviation
Fictional character(s): Claus von Hardenberg, Nobleman; Diana Winslow, Noblewoman, Pilot
Time Period(s): 20th century (1914-1934)
Locale(s): Cambridge, England; Nairobi, Kenya; Germany

Summary: Claus von Hardenberg, an impoverished German aristocrat, comes to England and embraces the myth of the English gentleman, even falling in love with his cousin, Lady Diana Winslow. World War I sends him back to Germany, but after the war he meets Diana again in Africa. She is a famous aviatrix, and events conspire to cure Claus of many of his illusions.

Historical Accuracy: The novel captures the era and the life-style of the English gentry class with assurance.

JANICE JAMES

3158 *A Lady of Repute*

Date of Publication: 1980
Subject(s): Victorian Period; Women's Rights; Identity—Concealed
Fictional character(s): Cecilia Ashworth, Gentlewoman; Laurence de Ford, Nobleman
Historical character(s): Edward, Prince of Wales, Royalty
Time Period(s): 19th century (Victorian period)
Locale(s): England

Summary: Few suspect that Miss Cecilia Ashworth, society hostess to nobility and royalty, is also the notorious Cecilia Andrews, whose best-selling novels shock the public with their progressive views on women's rights. Lord de Ford seeks to win Cecilia's hand, but to do so he must overcome several obstacles.

Historical Accuracy: The novel offers a colorful and convincing period background.

JOHN JAMES

Welsh author James is a graduate of Cambridge University and has worked as an English civil servant. His books, which include *Not for All the Gold in Ireland*, *The Bridge of Sand*, and *The Paladins*, are concerned with the unity of Great Britain.

3159 *The Lords of Loone*

Date of Publication: 1972
Subject(s): Rural Life—England
Fictional character(s): Robert Folland, Veteran; Jacob Kettlestang, Businessman (grain merchant), Banker; James Place, Farmer (vintner)
Time Period(s): 1700s
Locale(s): Wrackham, England

Summary: Who is Robert Folland? A smuggler, a Jacobite agent, or a government spy? He comes to Wrackham, England, a cast-off dragoon from Marlborough's army and a veteran of Malplaquet to associate with Jacob Kettlestang, the town's leading citizen. Folland becomes part of a tangled plot of incest and fratricide.

Historical Accuracy: The novel provides an authentic evocation of country-town life of the period.

3160 *Seventeen of Leyden*

Date of Publication: 1970
Subject(s): Monmouth's Rebellion; Espionage; Pirates
Fictional character(s): Richard Oliver Wormset, Doctor, Spy; Deborah Gadney, Young Woman
Time Period(s): 17th century (1680s)
Locale(s): England; West Indies

Summary: Dr. Richard Oliver Wormset is a physician and Number Seventeen of Leyden in the Knott, the formidable secret service of King James II. When his beloved is transported to the Indies for complicity in Monmouth's Rebellion, Wormset signs on as a ship's doctor to follow her. His adventures with a host of unorthodox characters follow.

Historical Accuracy: The period background is authentic.

3161 *Talleyman*

Date of Publication: 1986
Subject(s): Military Life; Independence—Ireland; Victorian Period
Fictional character(s): Thomas Talleyman, Military Personnel (naval officer)
Time Period(s): 1840s (1847)
Locale(s): Ireland

Summary: Thomas Talleyman, young naval lieutenant, is sent to Coulagh Bay in Ireland in 1847. There he witnesses the tensions between Catholic peasants and the Anglo-Irish gentry which explode into the Cabbage Patch Rebellion. Talleyman must choose between his loyalty to the crown and claims of friendship and love.

Historical Accuracy: The period and regional details create a convincing backdrop for the action.

3162 *Votan*

Date of Publication: 1966
Subject(s): Roman Empire; Myths and Legends
Fictional character(s): Photinus, Adventurer
Time Period(s): 2nd century
Locale(s): Germany

Summary: A Greek adventurer journeys north in search of a source of amber, the symbol of material wealth. He is rescued by a wild Germanic tribe and is hailed as their promised god, Votan. The novel records his story up to the sacking of Asgard by the Vandals and the destruction of Valhalla.

Historical Accuracy: The novel combines the legendary with the historical, offering an atmospheric portrait of the era and the region.

WILL JAMES (1892-1942)

A Western writer and illustrator of books for adults and children, James was born in Montana. Orphaned at the age of four, James was adopted by a French Canadian trapper and prospector. At the age of 13, he worked on cattle and horse ranches and later performed in rodeos and worked as an extra in the movies. His books include *The Three Mustangeers*, *Home Ranch*, and *Flint Spears, Cowboy Rodeo Contestant*.

3163 *The American Cowboy*

Date of Publication: 1942
Subject(s): American West; Ranching
Fictional character(s): Bill, Cowboy
Time Period(s): 19th century; 20th century (1830s-1940s)
Locale(s): Southwest

Summary: The novel dramatizes the history of the American cowboy from his earliest appearance in the 1830s to modern times through the experiences of three generations of cowboys named Bill. It captures the methods and ways of cattle ranching as well as the gradual transformation of the West.

Historical Accuracy: This is a highly romanticized portrait but filled with a good deal of authentic period elements.

OTTOKAR JANETSCHEK

3164 *The Emperor Franz Joseph*

Date of Publication: 1953
Subject(s): Biography, Fictionalized; Royalty—Austria; World War I
Historical character(s): Franz Josef I, Ruler (Emperor of Austria)
Time Period(s): 19th century; 20th century (1850s-1916)
Locale(s): Austria

Summary: The novel recounts the 68-year reign of Austrian emperor Franz Joseph. The years encompass the final days of the House of Hapsburg and the historical events that lead up to the Great War.

Historical Accuracy: This is a faithful account of Franz Joseph's life and reign.

ROSEMARY HAWLEY JARMAN (1935-)

English novelist Jarman was born in Worcester. She was educated until age 11 by her maternal grandmother at home. She is active in local politics and is a singer of lieder and oratorios. Her historical novels about the rulers of the 15th century have been widely praised for her mastery of the small expressive details that reveal the era.

3165 *The Courts of Illusion*

Date of Publication: 1983
Subject(s): Tudor Period; War of the Roses; Royalty—England

Fictional character(s): Nicholas Archer, Military Personnel (soldier)
Historical character(s): Henry Tudor, Ruler (King of England); Perkin Warbeck, Gentleman, Imposter
Time Period(s): 15th century (1490-1499)
Locale(s): England; Europe

Summary: After the defeat of Richard III at the Battle of Bosworth Field in 1485, the victor, Henry Tudor, tries to hold the throne against the claims of various rivals. The novel describes Nicholas Archer, a man bent on avenging the death of his father, which was ordered by Henry Tudor. Archer gives his support to one of the claimants, Perkin Warbeck, who insists that he is a Plantagenet and the true king of England.

Historical Accuracy: The medieval atmosphere is convincingly detailed in this story of insurrection and conspiracy.

3166 *Crown in Candlelight*

Date of Publication: 1978
Subject(s): War of the Roses; Royalty—England; Witchcraft and Sorcery
Fictional character(s): Hywelis, Witch
Historical character(s): Catherine of Valois, Royalty (princess), Spouse (queen consort of Henry V); Henry V, Ruler (King of England); Henry VI, Ruler (King of England); Owen Tydier, Military Personnel (squire)
Time Period(s): 15th century (1405-1438)
Locale(s): France; Wales; England

Summary: The novel details the reign of Henry V and his triumphs against the French. When Henry V dies unexpectedly, battle between the houses of York and Lancaster continues. The story also details the love affair between Henry's wife, Catherine of Valois, and the Welshman Owen Tydier (or Tudor), who together will produce the offspring who will resolve the dynastic struggle by establishing the House of Tudor.

Historical Accuracy: The atmosphere and events have a solid historical basis supplemented by a sense of the supernatural in the mystical romance of Wales.

3167 *The King's Grey Mare*

Date of Publication: 1973
Subject(s): War of the Roses; Royalty—England
Historical character(s): Edward IV, Ruler (King of England); Henry VII, Ruler (King of England); Elizabeth Woodville, Royalty (queen consort of Edward IV); John Grey, Gentleman
Time Period(s): 15th century (1452-1487)
Locale(s): France; England

Summary: The novel tells the story of Elizabeth Woodville of the House of Lancaster, who plays a pivotal role in the dynastic struggle of the War of the Roses. She leaves the court intrigue to marry John Grey, but their happy marriage ends when Grey is killed in battle. Elizabeth then becomes a pawn in a grab for power and a player in the backlash against Richard III when she marries her daughter to Harry Tudor.

Historical Accuracy: The historical record has depicted Elizabeth as either a helpless victim or a cruel manipulator. The author's portrayal is more balanced and consequently likely more realistic.

3168 *We Speak No Treason*

Date of Publication: 1971
Subject(s): War of the Roses; Royalty—England
Fictional character(s): Patch, Entertainer (jester)
Historical character(s): Richard III, Ruler (King of England)
Time Period(s): 15th century (1464-1485)
Locale(s): England

Summary: The enigmatic Richard III is described by a series of witnesses: a beautiful maiden whom he loves; his jester, Patch; and a man-at-arms who follows Richard dutifully. The king emerges not as the monster of Shakespeare, but as lonely, sensitive, honest, and just.

Historical Accuracy: The author states that the novel is based on historical fact and probability. She believes passionately in Richard's innocence and her advocacy drives her interpretation of the facts.

BENITA KANE JARO

3169 *The Key*

Date of Publication: 1988
Subject(s): Roman Empire
Fictional character(s): Caelius, Gentleman
Historical character(s): Gaius Valerius Catullus, Writer (poet); Julius Caesar, Military Personnel (army commander), Political Figure; Clodia, Gentlewoman
Time Period(s): 1st century B.C.
Locale(s): Roman Empire

Summary: The story behind Latin poet Catullus' love poems is imagined in this romantic tale set during the Roman Republic. Clodia, the sister of Clodius, a Roman nobleman and the bitter enemy of orator Cicero, inspires Catullus' passion.

Historical Accuracy: The author's descriptions are convincing even though she is inexact on the workings of Roman upper-class society.

MARJORIE JARRETT (1923-)

Born in Salt Lake City, Utah, Jarrett graduated from the University of Utah and did graduate study at Oxford. She is a therapist for schizophrenic autistic adolescents.

3170 *Wives of the Wind*

Date of Publication: 1980
Subject(s): American West; Mormons
Fictional character(s): Mellie Livingstone, Spouse; Sybil Livingstone, Spouse; Charlotte Livingstone, Spouse; Kolfinna Livingstone, Spouse; Harry Livingstone, Settler
Time Period(s): 19th century (1875-1890)
Locale(s): Utah

Summary: The novel depicts the lives of Harry Livingstone and his four wives. Members of the Mormon community of Utopia, they endure the pressure of the federal government to end polygamy. They struggle to survive flood, drought, Indian attacks, and government oppression. What emerges is a fascinating look at a community of women bound to one another in sharing a husband.

Historical Accuracy: The novel offers an authentic look at Mormon customs of the period.

TIM JEAL (1945-)

English writer Jeal was born in London and is a graduate of Christ Church, Oxford. He is the author of biographies of David Livingston and Robert Baden-Powell. Jeal is a recipient of the Llewellyn Rhys Memorial Prize for fiction.

3171 *For God and Glory*

Date of Publication: 1996
Subject(s): Victorian Period; Religious Life; English Colonies
Fictional character(s): Clara Musson, Young Woman; Robert Haslam, Religious (missionary); Francis Vaughan, Military Personnel (British officer)
Time Period(s): 1890s
Locale(s): England; Africa

Summary: This story of cultural conflict in Africa during the 1890s centers on the experiences of Clara Musson who leaves her life in Victorian England to join her missionary husband in Africa. There she discovers the Africans are split over their chief's possible conversion to Christianity. Civil war engulfs the community and produces the novel's crises for the various characters.

Historical Accuracy: The novel is exact and convincing in its period elements and the atmosphere of the times.

3172 *A Marriage of Convenience*

Date of Publication: 1979
Subject(s): Victorian Period; Trials
Fictional character(s): Clinton Danvers, Military Personnel (officer), Nobleman; Esmond Danvers, Gentleman; Theresa Simmonds, Actress
Time Period(s): 1860s
Locale(s): London, England; Ireland

Summary: The bitter and destructive rivalry of two brothers—Clinton and Esmond Danvers—forms this Victorian era drama. Clinton, the eldest, steals Esmond's love, the independent actress Theresa Simmonds, and Esmond sets out to bankrupt Clinton and destroy his career and reputation. Events conspire to produce one of the century's most scandalous court cases.

Historical Accuracy: The novel is remarkable in its ability to recreate the Victorian atmosphere and details of period life.

3173 *Until the Colors Fade*

Date of Publication: 1976
Subject(s): Victorian Period; Crimean War

Fictional character(s): Helen Goodchild, Gentlewoman; Thomas Strickland, Artist; Sir James Crawford, Military Personnel (admiral)
Time Period(s): 1850s
Locale(s): England; Crimea, Russia

Summary: This family drama is played out against a backdrop of Victorian England's tight code of conventions and honor and concerns a romantic triangle involving Helen Goodchild, Thomas Strickland, a young artist, and Sir James Crawford, a Rear Admiral in the British Navy. His sons take steps to prevent their father's affair as the events of the Crimean War place the domestic story in a larger context.

Historical Accuracy: The novel features a detailed and authentic evocation of the period.

BARBARA JEFFERIS (1917-)

An Australian journalist, novelist, and playwright, Jefferis attended the University of Adelaide and worked as a journalist in Sydney. Jefferis is the author of more than 100 documentaries, plays (for adults and juveniles), and children's serials for the Australian Broadcasting Commission. She has been the book critic for the Sydney *Morning Herald* and the *National Times*.

3174 *Beloved Lady*
Date of Publication: 1955
Subject(s): War of the Roses; Middle Ages
Fictional character(s): Margery Paston, Young Woman
Time Period(s): 15th century
Locale(s): England

Summary: This novel set during the political and social turmoil of the War of the Roses concerns a domestic crisis produced by young Margery Paston. She is determined to marry the man of her choosing, despite the strenuous objections of her family.

Historical Accuracy: The novel creates the atmosphere of the period with authority.

3175 *The Tall One*
Date of Publication: 1977
Subject(s): Middle Ages
Fictional character(s): Mary Mary, Young Woman
Time Period(s): 12th century
Locale(s): England

Summary: The novel chronicles the life of a medieval woman in the 12th century. As a child Mary Mary lives in the hovel of her villein father; she grows up to become a woman of property. In between, she is the serving maid of a lady, mistress of an alchemist, and wife of a dwarf fortune teller in a travelling circus.

Historical Accuracy: The novel evokes medieval life with conviction.

3176 *Time of the Unicorn*
Date of Publication: 1974

Subject(s): Middle Ages; Witchcraft and Sorcery
Fictional character(s): Clodagh, Young Woman; Walter Faber, Sea Captain; Simon de Baude, Knight
Time Period(s): 12th century
Locale(s): Portugal

Summary: The novel tells the story of 13 people, aristocratic Normans and English peasants, who in the 12th century are shipwrecked off the coast of Portugal. They trek northward in a 40-day struggle for survival that tests their faith in the Christian God and shows their descent into savagery and sorcery.

Historical Accuracy: The novel provides a convincing period background to the story.

H. PAUL JEFFERS (1934-)

Journalist and author Jeffers was born in Pennsylvania and graduated from Temple University and the University of Iowa. He has been an instructor of journalism at Boston University and a producer and newswriter for ABC-TV.

3177 *The Adventure of the Stalwart Companions*
Date of Publication: 1978
Subject(s): Mystery; Gilded Age
Fictional character(s): Sherlock Holmes, Detective—Private; William Hargreave, Detective—Police
Historical character(s): Theodore Roosevelt, Student—College
Time Period(s): 1880s (1880)
Locale(s): New York, New York

Summary: In 1880, Theodore Roosevelt, a young Harvard graduate, meets the great Sherlock Holmes while the detective is in New York in disguise performing in Shakespeare's *Twelfth Night*. A man is found shot to death in Gramercy Park, and Holmes realizes that this is no simple street crime. In the course of the ensuing investigation, Roosevelt, the future police commissioner of New York, is tutored by the master of detection.

Historical Accuracy: The depiction of period New York is authentic and convincing.

J.G. JEFFREYS
(PSEUD. OF BEN HEALEY, 1908-)

An Englishman born in Brighton, Jeffreys attended the Birmingham School of Art and the University of Birmingham and worked as a stage designer for the theater and an art designer for the film industry. Jeffreys wrote his first book in 1965 for his own entertainment. He favors stories set in historical periods and labors to acheive the desired accuracy of details by extensive reading of newspapers, journals, and biographies of the period.

3178 *Captain Bolton's Corpse*
Date of Publication: 1982
Subject(s): Mystery; Georgian Period; Sea Story

Fictional character(s): Jeremy Sturrock, Detective—Police (Bow Street Runner); Marie Lavalette, Gentlewoman; Isaac Bolton, Sea Captain
Time Period(s): 1800s
Locale(s): London, England

Summary: Jeremy Sturrock of the Bow Street Runners is asked to assist in two different, but related, cases. The brother of Marie Lavalette of New Orleans has disappeared and Captain Isaac Bolton discovers the body of a sailor hanging from the yardarm of his ship. Sturrock begins his investigation only to discover a complex conspiracy. The novel's climax is a sea battle.

Historical Accuracy: The novel excels in convincing period detail.

3179 *The Pangersbourne Murders*

Date of Publication: 1983
Subject(s): Mystery; Regency Period; Inheritance—Disputed
Fictional character(s): Jeremy Sturrock, Detective—Police (Bow Street Runner); Amelia Pangersbourne, Streetperson, Bastard Daughter
Time Period(s): 1810s (1815)
Locale(s): New Forest, England

Summary: The mystery surrounding the death of Lord Pangersbourne takes Bow Street Runner Jeremy Sturrock to a quiet village in England's New Forest. There he investigates the disposition of street urchin Amelia Pangersbourne's legacy.

Historical Accuracy: The novel blends an artful criminal puzzle with convincing period details.

3180 *The Thieftaker*

Date of Publication: 1992
Subject(s): Georgian Period; Mystery
Fictional character(s): Jeremy Sturrock, Detective—Police (Bow Street Runner)
Time Period(s): 1790s (1798)
Locale(s): London, England; Roehampton, England

Summary: The Bow Street Runners, England's first detectives and police force, are depicted in the story of Jeremy Sturrock. While in pursuit of a highwayman who has stolen a diamond necklace from a gentleman, Sturrock is faced with a ever-more complex and deadly series of crimes. It will take the new art and science of criminal detection to sift the various clues to solve the mystery.

Historical Accuracy: Although the characters are fictitious, the era is evoked with careful attention to historical details.

3181 *The Thistlewood Plot*

Date of Publication: 1987
Subject(s): Mystery; Regency Period
Fictional character(s): Jeremy Sturrock, Detective—Police (Bow Street Runner)
Time Period(s): 1820s (1820)
Locale(s): London, England

Summary: A dying man's final puzzling words and the corpse's sudden disappearance sets Jeremy Sturrock, Chief Officer of the Bow Street Runners on the trail of a crime that features additional murders and a threat to the entire nation. Sturrock's only clues are the man's dying words and a pouch of unusual tobacco.

Historical Accuracy: The period details of London life during the Regency era are expertly depicted.

3182 *A Wicked Way to Die*

Date of Publication: 1973
Subject(s): Georgian Period; Mystery
Fictional character(s): Jeremy Sturrock, Detective—Police (Bow Street Runner)
Time Period(s): 1800s (1800)
Locale(s): London, England

Summary: Jeremy Sturrock, the best of the Bow Street Runners, London's initial police force, investigates the apparent suicide of a young dandy in the ladies' dressing room of the Theatre Royal. Sturrock suspects murder, but he gets far more than he bargains for in an ingenious and complex mystery.

Historical Accuracy: Period details are authentically depicted.

PAMELA JEKEL (1948-)

Born in California, Jekel graduated from UCLA and the College of William and Mary. She received a Ph.D. from the University of Virginia. She was a teacher in Texas before becoming a full-time writer. She received a Best Historical Fiction Award from the Southwestern Booksellers Association for *Columbia* in 1987.

3183 *Bayou*

Date of Publication: 1991
Subject(s): Antebellum South; Civil War—U.S.; War of 1812
Fictional character(s): Olivia Doucet, Young Woman; Joseph Weitz, Businessman; Celisma, Slave
Time Period(s): Multiple Time Periods
Locale(s): Mississippi Delta, Louisiana; New Orleans, Louisiana

Summary: Spanning nearly 150 years, the novel is set in Louisiana's Delta country and New Orleans. Beginning in 1786, it tells the story of Cajun Olivia Doucet who marries Joseph Weitz and brings him home to the bayou. The novel offers scenes from the War of 1812, the Civil War, and the Jazz Age in New Orleans.

Historical Accuracy: The novel covers so much ground that the historical events rush by with scant attention. The locale description appears authentic.

3184 *Columbia*

Date of Publication: 1986
Subject(s): American West; Family Saga; Prehistory
Fictional character(s): Ilchee, Indian (Chinook), Royalty (princess); Caleb McDougal, Settler; Suzanne McDougal, Spouse
Time Period(s): Multiple Time Periods

Locale(s): Pacific Northwest, North America

Summary: The novel depicts the history of the Columbia River in the Pacific Northwest. Beginning 9,000 years ago, the narrative presents both a portrait of river life and a family chronicle that spans five generations and includes Indian life, settlement, and the building of the Grand Coulee Dam.

Historical Accuracy: The bulk of this work is historically accurate, although, as it is fiction, plot and theme considerations occasionally call for a deviation from fact.

`3185` Deepwater: A Novel of the Carolinas

Date of Publication: 1994
Subject(s): American Colonies; Family Saga
Fictional character(s): Leah Hancock, Settler
Time Period(s): 18th century
Locale(s): Carolinas, American Colonies

Summary: The background of this family saga that covers four generations is early life in the American colonies. Beginning with Roanoke's ''lost colony,'' the novel follows the lives of Leah Hancock and her four daughters, the beginning of Deepwater Plantation, and the founding of a family dynasty.

Historical Accuracy: The novel provides a credible historical backdrop for the family drama.

`3186` Natchez: A Novel of the Deep South

Date of Publication: 1995
Subject(s): Antebellum South; Civil War—U.S.; Family Saga
Fictional character(s): Martin Howard, Plantation Owner; Anne Lawrence, Southern Belle; Arden Lawrence, Southern Belle
Time Period(s): 18th century; 19th century (1729-1885)
Locale(s): Natchez, Mississippi

Summary: Four generations of Southern women are depicted in this novel of Mississippi plantation life. The domestic drama plays out against a historical background of the earliest settlers through the Civil War, Reconstruction, and the Great Flood of 1885.

Historical Accuracy: The novel features a convincing period backdrop for the fictional family chronicle.

`3187` Sea Star: The Private Life of Anne Bonny, Pirate

Date of Publication: 1983
Subject(s): Pirates
Historical character(s): Anne Bonny, Pirate
Time Period(s): 18th century
Locale(s): West Indies

Summary: This story interweaves romance with factual details about 18th- century pirate Anne Bonny's career.

Historical Accuracy: Facts concerning Bonny's career receive a good deal of fictional embellishing.

MIRKO JELUSICH (1886-1969)

German writer Jelusich is the author of the biographies *Oliver Cromwell* and *Hannibal.*

`3188` Caesar

Date of Publication: 1930
Subject(s): Biography, Fictionalized; Roman Empire
Historical character(s): Julius Caesar, Military Personnel (general), Political Figure
Time Period(s): 1st century B.C.
Locale(s): Roman Empire; Gaul (modern France)

Summary: This fictionalized biography offers a full-length account of the life and career of Julius Caesar from his boyhood days to his military campaigns and political maneuvering.

Historical Accuracy: The novel provides a believable portrait of Caesar with occasional lapses into artificial drama and romance.

BURRIS ATKINS JENKINS (1869-1945)

Born in Kansas City, Missouri, Jenkins was educated at Bethany College and Harvard University and became a clergyman. He wrote several books about religion as well as religious and historical novels, including *The Bracegirdle, The Beauty of the New Testament,* and *Torrent.*

`3189` The Bracegirdle

Date of Publication: 1922
Subject(s): Theatrical Life
Fictional character(s): Anne Bracegirdle, Actress; Richard Lovell, Gentleman
Historical character(s): William of Orange, Ruler (King of England); John Dryden, Writer; William Congreve, Writer (playwright); George Savile, Nobleman (Marquis of Halifax)
Time Period(s): 17th century
Locale(s): London, England

Summary: This romantic adventure tale is set during the reign of William and Mary and involves Richard Lovell's pursuit of Anne Bracegirdle, a celebrity on the London stage. To win her, Lovell must succeed at several romantic feats.

Historical Accuracy: Despite some inconsistencies, the novel achieves a high degree of authentic period atmosphere.

ELIZABETH JENKINS (1907-)

Jenkins, an English author born in Hertfordshire, worked as a school teacher. During World War II she joined the British civil service. She is the author of biographies of Lady Caroline Lamb and Jane Austen. In 1981 she was awarded an O.B.E.

`3190` Dr. Gully's Story

Date of Publication: 1972
Subject(s): Victorian Period; Medical Profession
Historical character(s): James Gully, Doctor; Florence Ricardo, Gentlewoman

Time Period(s): 1870s; 1880s
Locale(s): England

Summary: Based on the 1876 scandal that came to be known as ''The Balkan Affair,'' the novel details the relationship between respected physician Dr. James Gully and his patient Florence Ricardo, married and 40 years his junior. The affair is told from Gully's point of view and becomes a lesson in the stultifying effects of Victorian moral hypocrisy.

Historical Accuracy: The author has based the action and details on historical fact.

GWYN JENKINS (1919-)

Welsh teacher and writer Jenkins served in the Royal Air Force as a flying officer.

3191 *King David*

Date of Publication: 1961
Subject(s): Ancient Israel; Biblical Story
Historical character(s): David, Ruler (King of Israel), Biblical Figure; Saul, Ruler (King of Israel), Biblical Figure; Bathsheba, Royalty (queen consort of David), Biblical Figure; Solomon, Ruler (King of Israel), Biblical Figure
Time Period(s): 10th century B.C.
Locale(s): Israel

Summary: The career of the Old Testament hero David is chronicled from his humble origins as a shepherd to his reign as King of Israel. David wins the favor of King Saul, but Saul's love turns to hatred when David becomes a popular hero after slaying the Philistine champion Goliath. David's successes and failures in leading the nation are depicted.

Historical Accuracy: The novel attempts to create a full-bodied and realistic portrait of David and his age, based on extensive research.

KATHLEEN JENKS (1940-)

A native of Michigan, Jenks now lives in New York City but is a frequent visitor to Europe, Egypt, Israel, and the Far East. She is the author of *Journey of a Dream Animal*, a nonfictional study of dream symbols.

3192 *The River and the Stone: Moses' Early Years in Egypt*

Date of Publication: 1977
Subject(s): Biblical Story; Ancient Egypt; Pharaohs
Fictional character(s): Bak-Isis, Royalty (princess); Kia, Royalty
Historical character(s): Moses, Biblical Figure, Leader (Israelite); Miriam, Biblical Figure; Aaron, Biblical Figure
Time Period(s): 13th century B.C.
Locale(s): Egypt

Summary: This is the story of the young Moses as he grows up in the palace of Princess Bak-Isis, who rescued him from the Nile. She is determined that Moses should become a priest, devoted to the Egyptian gods. But Moses is influenced by Kia, the wife of the dead Pharaoh Akhenaton, to accept the concept of a single god, and by his sister Miriam, who helps Moses return to his people.

Historical Accuracy: Although this is a work of fiction, the author tries to remain within historical and biblical frameworks.

GARY JENNINGS (1928-)

Born in the Blue Ridge Mountains of Virginia, Jennings has worked in advertising, as a magazine editor and newspaper photographer, and served as an infantry correspondent in the Korean War before turning to writing full time. His historical novels, such as *Aztec* and *Raptor*, have been widely praised both for their great sweep and their meticulous attention to detail. To produce *Aztec*, Jennings lived in Mexico for ten years researching the book.

3193 *Aztec*

Date of Publication: 1980
Subject(s): Aztec Empire; Spanish Colonies
Fictional character(s): Mixtli, Nobleman (Aztec)
Historical character(s): Hernando Cortez, Explorer, Military Personnel (conquistador); Montezuma II, Ruler (Aztec emperor)
Time Period(s): 16th century
Locale(s): Mexico

Summary: This massive panoramic depiction of Aztec life and customs during the period of the Spanish conquest takes the form of the life story of Mixtli who rises from Aztec commoner to nobleman. With the arrival of the Spanish, he serves as Montezuma's envoy to Cortez. The novel provides a detailed portrait of Aztec society and life on the point of cultural collapse.

Historical Accuracy: The novel's evident research makes a strong and authentic period background for the story.

3194 *The Journeyer*

Date of Publication: 1984
Subject(s): Exploration; East/West Relations; Middle Ages
Historical character(s): Marco Polo, Explorer, Trader; Kublai Khan, Ruler (Emperor of China)
Time Period(s): 13th century; 14th century
Locale(s): Venice, Italy; China; Persia

Summary: The exploits of the great Venetian adventurer Marco Polo are described in this first person account that traces his travels east from Venice to the Levant, Persia, and then along the Silk Road to the court of the great Kubilai Khan. Throughout, Marco is irrepressible in his curiosity and appetite for new adventures.

Historical Accuracy: The novel is based in part on the actual accounts of Marco Polo with considerable embellishment and the author's own retracing of Polo's route from Venice to China.

3195 *Sow the Seeds of Hemp*

Date of Publication: 1976
Subject(s): Slavery; Crime and Criminals; Antebellum South

Historical character(s): John Murrell, Outlaw, Adventurer; Virgil Stewart, Outlaw
Time Period(s): 1830s
Locale(s): Natchez Trace, Mississippi

Summary: Based on fact, the novel describes the scheme of bandit leader John Murrell to steal a band of slaves in order to mount a revolution to make him the white emperor of a black empire in the Mississippi Valley. Murrell's exploits, and the role of Virgil Stewart, who is torn between his duty to society and his attraction to the charismatic Murrell, form the novel's intriguing story.

Historical Accuracy: Although based on actual historical events, the novel is composed of equal amounts of fact, legend, and imagination.

3196 *Spangle*

Date of Publication: 1987
Subject(s): Circus Life; Picaresque Adventure; Gypsies
Fictional character(s): Autumn Auburn, Entertainer (aerialist); Magpie Maggie Hag, Gypsy; Florian, Entertainer, Businessman; Zachary Edge, Veteran (Confederate)
Time Period(s): 19th century (post Civil War)
Locale(s): South; Europe (Italy, Russia, France)

Summary: The novel tells the story of a 19th-century circus troupe that travels from the post-Civil War South to the capitals of Europe. The impresario is the consummate showman Florian, who leads an eccentric company of entertainers. This picaresque tale details circus life and shows the revolutionary events and ideas that will produce modern Europe.

Historical Accuracy: This story offers a colorful rendition of time and place.

3197 *The Terrible Teague Bunch*

Date of Publication: 1975
Subject(s): American West; Crime and Criminals
Fictional character(s): L.R. Foyt, Cowboy; Karnes, Oil Industry Worker (oil rigger); Boudreaux, Worker; Wheeler, Veteran (Civil War)
Time Period(s): 1900s (1902-1905)
Locale(s): Louisiana; Texas

Summary: In 1905, a mixed group of men meet at Mme. Mattie Fouquet's Mahogany Parlor of Recreation, Diversion and Entertainment and hatch a plan to rob a train bringing money to a new bank in Teague, Texas. Their misadventures on their 150-mile journey involve cattle rustling, a tornado, and a beautiful woman. Just when they think it can't get any worse, it does.

Historical Accuracy: Acceptable portrayal of time and place.

JOHN EDWARD JENNINGS (1906-1973)

Born in Brooklyn, New York, Jennings began his writing career during the Depression. He attended the Colorado School of Mines, Columbia University, and the Washington Diplomatic and Consular Institute. He served in the U.S. Naval Reserve during World War II and was on active duty

as an officer in charge of the Naval Aviation History Unit. His novels include *Tattered Ensign* and *The Golden Eagle*.

3198 *Banners Against the Wind*

Date of Publication: 1954
Subject(s): Biography, Fictionalized; Independence—Greece
Historical character(s): Samuel Gridley Howe, Activist (social reformer); Julia Ward Howe, Writer
Time Period(s): 19th century
Locale(s): Massachusetts; Greece

Summary: Reformer and philanthropist Samuel Gridley Howe was involved in the struggle for Greek independence and the founding of the New England Asylum for the Blind. The author dramatizes Howe's life and career, including his marriage to writer Julia Ward.

Historical Accuracy: The novel stays close to the documentary sources; and the details of Howe's life are accurately portrayed.

3199 *Call the New World*

Date of Publication: 1941
Subject(s): Independence—South America; War of 1812
Fictional character(s): Peter Brooke, Adventurer
Time Period(s): 1810s; 1820s
Locale(s): United States; South America

Summary: West Point graduate Peter Brooke is court martialed but goes on to play a role in the struggle for South American independence.

Historical Accuracy: The novel convincingly masters its period background and geography.

3200 *Gentleman Ranker*

Date of Publication: 1942
Subject(s): French and Indian War; American Colonies
Fictional character(s): Stephen Trent, Gentleman, Military Personnel (soldier)
Historical character(s): Edward Braddock, Military Personnel (general)
Time Period(s): 1750s
Locale(s): London, England; Virginia, American Colonies

Summary: English gentleman Stephen Trent, because of his gambling debts and family circumstances, finds himself in the American colonies. There, in 1755, he joins General Braddock's army against the French. The novel traces his transformation and adjustment to life on the frontier.

Historical Accuracy: The story is fanciful but based on many accurate details of Braddock's campaign.

3201 *The Golden Eagle*

Date of Publication: 1958
Subject(s): Exploration; Spanish Colonies; Biography, Fictionalized
Historical character(s): Hernando de Soto, Explorer, Military Personnel (conquistador); Pedro Arias de Avila, Nobleman, Government Official (colonial governor); Francisco Pizarro,

Explorer, Military Personnel (conquistador); Luis de Moscoso, Explorer, Military Personnel (conquistador)
Time Period(s): 16th century (1500-1542)
Locale(s): Panama; Peru; North America

Summary: The novel tells the story of Don Hernando de Soto, who in the service of Don Pedro Arias de Avila, governor of Panama, begins his career as a conquistador in Central America. He amasses a fortune and obtains royal permission to explore in North America. His adventures, which culminate in the discovery of the Mississippi, are chronicled.

Historical Accuracy: Accounts of de Soto differ, and the author has chosen one version over others, telescoping some events, but altering none of the chronology in the interest of the drama.

`3202` *Next to Valour*

Date of Publication: 1939
Subject(s): French and Indian War; American Colonies
Fictional character(s): James Ferguson, Scout, Frontiersman
Time Period(s): 1750s
Locale(s): New Hampshire, American Colonies

Summary: James Ferguson, a Scot, goes to live with his uncle in New Hampshire. Trained in the wilderness by Indians, Ferguson participates in military campaigns against the French, including the battle for Quebec.

Historical Accuracy: This fictional story of Rogers' Rangers is convincingly integrated with actual events and an authentic period atmosphere.

`3203` *The Pepper Tree*

Date of Publication: 1950
Subject(s): Sea Story
Fictional character(s): Shubael Coit, Sea Captain; Abiezar Whipple, Shipowner; Jessie Whipple, Young Woman, Spouse (of Coit); Jon Shaw, Sailor
Time Period(s): 19th century
Locale(s): Beverly, Massachusetts; Java, Indonesia

Summary: This tale of the China trade tells the story of Captain Shubael Coit, who possesses the secret of where to find pepper in the Spice Islands of the East Indies. He uses his secret to marry shipowner Abiezar Whipple's daughter, Jessie. She is loved by young Jon Shaw who ships out with Coit on a voyage that ends in a destructive confrontation with the Malay natives.

Historical Accuracy: Missing.

`3204` *River to the West: A Novel of the Astor Adventure*

Date of Publication: 1948
Subject(s): Settlement of the American Frontier; Exploration
Fictional character(s): Rocheblave Xavier O'Rourke, Frontiersman, Trader; Deborah Drake, Young Woman
Historical character(s): John Jacob Astor, Financier; James Madison, Political Figure; Albert Gallatin, Political Figure; Washington Irving, Writer; Thomas Jefferson, Political Figure

Time Period(s): 1800s; 1810s (1808-1811)
Locale(s): Pacific Northwest; New York, New York

Summary: The novel tells the story of the Pacific Fur Company and John Jacob Astor's trading scheme in the Pacific Northwest. Frontiersman Rory O'Rourke describes the founding of Astoria on the Columbia River. The novel details Astor's negotiations to secure his fur trading monopoly in the Pacific Northwest, the recruitment of experienced voyageurs, and the hypothetical escape of the survivors of a doomed ship and their year-long walk back east across the continent.

Historical Accuracy: The novel's romantic treatment of events undermines the book's usefulness as an accurate reflection of its era and historical personages. The novel does show evidence of meticulous research in certain details.

`3205` *The Salem Frigate*

Date of Publication: 1946
Subject(s): Sea Story; Tripolitan War; War of 1812
Fictional character(s): Tom Tisdall, Doctor; Ben Price, Sailor
Time Period(s): 18th century; 19th century (1799-1810s)
Locale(s): Barbary Coast, Africa; Salem, Massachusetts; *Essex*, At Sea

Summary: Set during the early years of the young American nation, the novel describes naval adventures during the war against the pirates of Tripoli. Dr. Tisdall, the surgeon of the frigate *Essex*, narrates the action against the Barbary Pirates and his rivalry with seaman Ben Price who has married Tisdale's beloved.

Historical Accuracy: Though actual period details are featured, they are awash in a sea of implausible romance and improbable characterization.

`3206` *The Sea Eagles*

Date of Publication: 1950
Subject(s): Sea Story; American Revolution
Fictional character(s): Joshua Barney, Sailor; Kenny Boyle, Sailor
Historical character(s): George Washington, Military Personnel (army commander); John Paul Jones, Military Personnel (naval officer)
Time Period(s): 1770s; 1780s
Locale(s): Baltimore, Maryland; At Sea

Summary: The adventures of the young American navy during the Revolution are depicted in this story of two young adventurers, Joshua Barney and Kenny Boyle. They participate in a series of sea battles, escape from British prison ships, and finally take part in the most famous naval engagement of the war, the fight between the *Bonhomme Richard* and the *Serapis*.

Historical Accuracy: The period elements are convincing in this blending of actual details and invention.

`3207` *The Shadow and the Glory*

Date of Publication: 1943
Subject(s): American Revolution; Battle of Bennington; Battle of Bunker Hill

Fictional character(s): Davy Fergusson, Teenager, Military Personnel (soldier)
Historical character(s): John Stark, Military Personnel (general)
Time Period(s): 1770s (1774-1777)
Locale(s): Bennington, Vermont; Portsmouth, New Hampshire; New Jersey

Summary: The events of the early years of the American Revolution are depicted in the experiences of a teenager, Davy Fergusson of Portsmouth, New Hampshire. He joins the Patriots' cause in 1774 and is on hand at the Battle of Bunker Hill and the ill-fated Canadian expedition. He crosses the Delaware with Washington and serves at the battles at Princeton and Bennington.

Historical Accuracy: The novel's chronology of events is accurate, and the author excels in a realistic presentation of the battle scenes and the details of the colonial army.

3208   *Shadows in the Dusk*

Date of Publication: 1955
Subject(s): American West; Indians
Fictional character(s): Currito, Guide; Don Jode, Frontiersman; Don Yancey, Frontiersman
Time Period(s): 1830s (1837)
Locale(s): Santa Fe, New Mexico; Santa Rita, Texas

Summary: The novel dramatizes life in the Rio Grande Country of New Mexico in the 1830s as the Apaches take revenge for the treachery of some whites who try to collect government bounties on Indian scalps. Events culminate in the bloody siege of Santa Rita del Cobre and the exodus of 400 people across the New Mexican desert led by a Mexican scout called Currito.

Historical Accuracy: The novel's fictional story is set against a carefully detailed period backdrop and actual events.

3209   *The Strange Brigade*

Date of Publication: 1952
Subject(s): Frontier—Canada
Fictional character(s): Malcolm MacAllister, Teacher; Jeannie MacLean, Young Woman; Alec MacLean, Religious (clergyman)
Historical character(s): Thomas Douglas, Nobleman (Earl of Selkirk)
Time Period(s): 1810s (1813)
Locale(s): Manitoba, Canada

Summary: This is the story of a group of Scottish immigrants who, after being evicted from their land, join a Hudson's Bay Company expedition to create a settlement in the frontier of Manitoba. Their story is told by Malcolm MacAllister, the schoolmaster of the settlement.

Historical Accuracy: The novel blends the actual and the invented but provides a convincing period background for the action.

3210   *The Wind in His Fists*

Date of Publication: 1956
Subject(s): Sea Story; Battle of Lepanto

Fictional character(s): Dennis O'More, Adventurer
Time Period(s): 16th century
Locale(s): Mediterranean; Ireland; Spain

Summary: This swashbuckling tale describes the exploits of Irish adventurer Dennis O'More, who participates in Spain's battles against the Turks, the corsairs, and the Knights of Malta. The novel's climax is the Battle of Lepanto.

Historical Accuracy: The novel provides a believable historical backdrop of actual events for this high-speed adventure tale.

WILLIAM DALE JENNINGS (1917-)

Born in Amarillo, Texas, Jennings is a freelance writer for motion pictures (usually documentaries) and radio. He has developed a fascination for history as a result of his travels in China and Japan.

3211   *The Cowboys*

Date of Publication: 1971
Subject(s): Cattle Drives; American West; Ranching
Fictional character(s): Wil Anderson, Rancher; Charlie Smith, Teenager; Charlie "Slim" Honeycutt, Teenager
Time Period(s): 1870s (1877)
Locale(s): Missouri; Wyoming; Dakota Territory, United States

Summary: In 1877 a gold strike leaves rancher Wil Anderson with no cowhands to drive his herd to market. He recruits a group of schoolboys for the 400-mile drive, teaching them how to survive and do their job. The boys mature in their test, facing rustlers and hostile Indians.

Historical Accuracy: The western scene and the details of trail life are authentically depicted.

3212   *The Ronin*

Date of Publication: 1968
Subject(s): Samurai; Japanese Empire; Middle Ages
Fictional character(s): Ronin, Warrior
Time Period(s): 12th century
Locale(s): Japan

Summary: Called "a novel based on a Zen myth," the story chronicles the adventures of a nameless Ronin, or masterless samurai, who rises through his savagery and skills in warfare to a position of wealth and high status.

Historical Accuracy: The period Japanese scenes are authentic and convincing.

3213   *The Sinking of the Sarah Diamond*

Date of Publication: 1974
Subject(s): Sea Story; Civil War—U.S.
Fictional character(s): Jefferson MacBraugh, Sea Captain; Martyn Bolderman, Shipowner, Young Man; Margarita Gonzago y Cordoza, Noblewoman
Time Period(s): 1860s (1861)
Locale(s): *Sarah Diamond*, At Sea (South America to Boston); Brazil

Summary: Young Martyn Bolderman inherits a decrepit square rigger. The insurance will bring more if the ship is sunk, but Martyn is determined to resail the *Sarah Diamond* home from Brazil to Boston. With the help of Captain MacBraugh he sets out on the 5000-mile voyage, contending with a female general in love with Martyn, escaped convicts from Devil's Island, a Confederate privateer, and a catastrophic hurricane.

Historical Accuracy: The emphasis is on high-speed action over historical events, but the period is evoked with some care and ability.

JOHANNES VILHELM JENSEN
(1873-1950)

Danish novelist, poet, and essayist Jensen was awarded the Nobel Prize for Literature in 1944. He is known for his strong interest in myth and in travel, and for his Darwinian philosophy.

3214 *The Fall of the King*

Date of Publication: 1933
Subject(s): Royalty—Denmark
Fictional character(s): Mikkel Thoegersen, Student, Companion (of Christian II)
Historical character(s): Christian II, Ruler (King of Denmark)
Time Period(s): 16th century
Locale(s): Copenhagen, Denmark

Summary: The setting of the novel is Denmark in the early 16th century. The story follows the adventures of young Mikkel Thoegersen who begins as a poor student in Copenhagen but later becomes a companion and messenger for King Christian II.

Historical Accuracy: Despite the melodramatic nature of the novel's plot, it excels in vivid and convincing period description.

MURIEL MOLLAND JERNIGAN

Born in Nanking, China, the daughter of a missionary, Jernigan has devoted a lifetime to the study of Manchu and Chinese life. She lived in Peking until the Chinese Revolution.

3215 *Forbidden City*

Date of Publication: 1954
Subject(s): Chinese Empire; Boxer Rebellion; Royalty—China
Historical character(s): Tz'u-hsi, Ruler (Empress Dowager of China); Li Hung Chang, Government Official (viceroy); Jung Lu, Nobleman, Military Personnel
Time Period(s): 19th century; 20th century
Locale(s): China

Summary: The novel tells the story of the powerful Tz'u Hsi, the Empress Dowager. As the last of the Manchus, she wields great power through the turbulent period of Chinese history that culminates in the Boxer Rebellion. She comes to the Imperial Palace as a concubine but manages to wrest the throne from the dying monarch. Her love for her minister Jung Lu defies tradition but can not prevent her hatred of "foreign devils," which explodes in violence.

Historical Accuracy: The period background and the Chinese customs are authentic.

TEODOR JESKE-CHOINSKI (1854-1920)

A Polish author born in Warsaw, Jeski Choinski wrote historical fiction, sociological novels of contemporary life, and literary criticism. His books include *The Setting Sun*, *The Thorn and the Crown*, and *The Jacobins*.

3216 *The Last Romans*

Date of Publication: 1936
Subject(s): Roman Empire; Christianity; Battle of the Frigidus
Fictional character(s): Winfred, Nobleman (duke); Fausta Ausonia, Young Woman
Historical character(s): Theodosius the Great, Ruler (Roman emperor); Arbogast, Military Personnel (general); Alaric I, Ruler (King of the Visigoths)
Time Period(s): 4th century
Locale(s): Rome, Roman Empire

Summary: This story of the 4th-century clash between Christianity and paganism is set against the historical backdrop of the victory of the Emperor Theodosius over Arbogast in the Battle of the Frigidus. The fictional story centers on the love of Winfred, the Christian Duke of Italy, for the vestal Fausta Ausonia.

Historical Accuracy: The novel captures the period authentically with a fully realized background accurate in the smallest details and a host of historical characters convincingly rendered.

IRIS JOHANSEN

Iris Johansen is an American writer of romance novels. She is credited with stretching the boundaries of the romance genre and with tying books together with continuing characters. With fellow romance writers Kay Hooper and Fayrene Preston, she co-wrote a series of novels about the Delaney family.

3217 *Storm Winds*

Date of Publication: 1991
Subject(s): French Revolution; Romance
Fictional character(s): Juliette de Clement, Student, Gentlewoman; Jean Marc Andreas, Banker
Time Period(s): 1780s
Locale(s): France

Summary: In the second volume of the Wind Dancer Trilogy, the story of the legendary statue shifts to France during the Revolution, where powerful banker Jean Marc Andreas falls in love with young Juliette de Clement while working to retrieve the statue.

Historical Accuracy: The period elements are credibly depicted.

3218 *The Wind Dancer*

Date of Publication: 1991
Subject(s): Renaissance; Romance
Fictional character(s): Sanchia, Thief, Slave; Lionello Andreas, Nobleman, Mercenary
Time Period(s): 16th century (1503)
Locale(s): Italy

Summary: This is the first volume of the author's Wind Dancer Trilogy that follows the fate of a statue through history. When Lionello Andreas needs to retrieve his family's heirloom, he hires the female petty thief Sanchia. Loves ensues against the backdrop of Renaissance Italian treachery.

Historical Accuracy: The novel's story is ingenious and the period background convincing.

EVAN JOHN
(PSEUD. OF EVAN JOHN SIMPSON, 1901-1953)

Born in London, John was educated at Winchester and Oxford University. He served in the Intelligence Corps during World War II. He is the author of several histories and novels, including *King Charles I*, *King's Masque*, and *Ride Home Tomorrow*.

3219 *Crippled Splendour*

Date of Publication: 1938
Subject(s): Royalty—Scotland; Biography, Fictionalized; Royalty—England
Historical character(s): James I, Ruler (King of Scotland); Henry V, Ruler (King of England)
Time Period(s): 15th century
Locale(s): Scotland; England; France

Summary: This fictional biography of the first and greatest of the Stuart kings, James I, traces his career and accomplishments. The novel chronicles as well the social and political background of 15th-century Europe.

Historical Accuracy: The novel accurately captures the spirit and atmosphere of the era, if it is not exact in every detail.

3220 *King's Masque*

Date of Publication: 1941
Subject(s): Royalty—France; French Revolution; American Revolution
Historical character(s): Marie Antoinette, Royalty (queen consort of Louis XIV); Hans Axel von Fersen, Nobleman; Marie Joseph Paul de Lafayette, Nobleman (Marquis de Lafayette), Military Personnel (general); Honore Gabriel Riqueti, Revolutionary, Political Figure; Gouverneur Morris, Diplomat, Political Figure; Gustav III, Ruler (King of Sweden)
Time Period(s): 1780s; 1790s (1781-1791)
Locale(s): Paris, France; Yorktown, Virginia; Stockholm, Sweden

Summary: This panoramic novel covers the events of the American Revolution, the French Revolution, and the emergence of Sweden under Gustav III from feudalism. The story centers on the relationship between Swedish Count Axel von Ferson and Marie Antoinette.

Historical Accuracy: The novel offers a fair, if at times partisan, portrait of the age with a reliable framework of actual events.

3221 *Ride Home Tomorrow*

Date of Publication: 1951
Subject(s): Middle Ages; Crusades
Fictional character(s): Andrea Vaeringer, Knight
Time Period(s): 12th century
Locale(s): Palestine; England; Normandy, France

Summary: This tale of the Crusades follows Andrea Vaeringer first to Normandy, then to England where he encounters Robin Hood and Prince John, and finally to the Holy Land to expiate a sin he did not commit. Vaeringer takes part in the military defeat at Rattin where Saladin conquers the Latin Kingdom of Jerusalem.

Historical Accuracy: The novel is expert in its realism and depiction of period life, despite occasional lapses.

DAVID JOHNSON (1927-)

Johnson served in the British army as an infantryman, rising to the rank of lieutenant. His works include *Lanterns in Gascony*, *A Candle in Aragon*, and *Napoleon's Cavalry and Its Leaders*.

3222 *The Proud Canaries*

Date of Publication: 1959
Subject(s): Military Life; Napoleonic Wars
Fictional character(s): Charles LaSalle, Military Personnel (general)
Historical character(s): Andre Messena, Military Personnel (general); Louis Nicolas Davout, Military Personnel (marshal); Joachim Murat, Military Personnel (marshal)
Time Period(s): 1790s; 1800s
Locale(s): Europe

Summary: The novel tells the story of the French Hussar Cavalry, the mounted "Canaries" of the Grande Armee. The story centers on one of Napoleon's most gifted commanders, General Charles LaSalle. Day-to-day life of the mounted soldiers during the Napoleonic Wars is dramatized, as well as scenes of the great battles of Jena, Eylau, and Wagram.

Historical Accuracy: The novel is precise about the military details and the historical events depicted.

DOROTHY M. JOHNSON (1905-1984)

Born in Iowa, Johnson grew up in Montana and lived in New York City, where she worked as a writer of western stories and as a magazine editor. Johnson also was a professor of journalism at the University of Montana. She wrote many books and stories about the West and also the screenplays for three motion pictures—*A Man Called Horse*, *The Hanging Tree*, and *The Man Who Shot Liberty Valance*.

3223 *Buffalo Woman*

Date of Publication: 1977

Subject(s): American West; Indians; Tribal Life—Native American
Fictional character(s): Whirlwind, Indian (Sioux)
Historical character(s): Crazy Horse, Indian (Sioux), Warrior
Time Period(s): 19th century (1820-1877)
Locale(s): Great Plains

Summary: Whirlwind's experiences reflect the fate of the Sioux people. Born in the prosperity of the 1820s, she lives through encroachment by white settlers and d estruction of the Sioux's traditional ways. The novel portrays the events of the Indian Wars, including the Battle of Little Big Horn.

Historical Accuracy: The novel provides an authentic portrait of Indian life against a backdrop of actual historical events.

EYVIND JOHNSON (1900-1976)

A Swedish novelist and short-story writer, Johnson was the co-winner of the 1974 Nobel Prize for literature. Born in Saltsjobaden, Sweden, he was largely self-educated. Johnson served as a member of the Swedish UNESCO delegation during the late 1940s and was a member of the Nobel Council of the Royal Swedish Academy. Johnson's novels include *The Story of Olaf*, *The Days of His Grace*, and *Night Maneuvers*.

3224 *Return to Ithaca*

Date of Publication: 1952
Subject(s): Ancient Greece; Myths and Legends
Fictional character(s): Odysseus, Adventurer; Penelope, Spouse
Time Period(s): Indeterminate Past
Locale(s): Mediterranean; Ithaca, Greece

Summary: This version of Homer's *Odyssey* is cast in the form of a modern novel with psychological realism replacing the supernatural in the story of Odysseus' return home to Ithaca after 20 years of adventures following the end of the Trojan War.

Historical Accuracy: The novel is clearly at home with its Homeric sources and attempts a modernized, realistic reinterpretation of the familiar story.

GERALD WHITE JOHNSON (1890-1980)

An American journalist, professor of journalism, editor, writer, and news commentator, Johnson was born in New Jersey and attended Wake Forest College. During World War I, he served as an infantry soldier with the U.S. Army in France. A recipient of numerous awards and honors, Johnson's works include *Andrew Jackson: An Epic in Homespun*, a trilogy on American history for children, and a highly acclaimed trilogy on the U.S. government, *The Presidency*, *The Congress*, and *The Supreme Court*. These were followed by a fourth volume, *The Cabinet*.

3225 *By Reason of Strength*

Date of Publication: 1930
Subject(s): Antebellum South; Family Saga; Civil War—U.S.

Fictional character(s): Catherine Whyte, Settler
Time Period(s): 18th century; 19th century
Locale(s): North Carolina

Summary: This story of pioneer life in North Carolina covers the period immediately following the American Revolution to the Civil War. At the center of the family saga is Catherine Whyte who comes from Scotland to America and whose experiences reflect the history of the nation during the 19th century.

Historical Accuracy: This is a vivid and believable chronicle of life in North Carolina and of its Scottish settlers.

MARY ELLEN JOHNSON (1949-)

American writer Johnson was born in Hawaii and attended the University of Colorado. Johnson was a housewife until 1968 when she began her career as an author of historical fiction.

3226 *The Lion and the Leopard*

Date of Publication: 1985
Subject(s): Middle Ages; Royalty—England
Fictional character(s): Maria Rendell, Gentlewoman, Spouse; Phillip Rendell, Knight; Richard of Sussex, Nobleman
Historical character(s): Edward II, Ruler (King of England); Isabella of France, Royalty (queen consort of Edward II); Roger de Mortimer, Nobleman
Time Period(s): 14th century
Locale(s): England

Summary: Maria Rendell is married to the knight Phillip Rendell during the rise of Edward II in the 14th century. She falls in love with Richard of Sussex, the bastard brother of the king, while Phillip is off on the Crusades. Their fate is connected with the doomed reign of Edward, his ambitious queen, Isabella, and her lover, Roger de Mortimer.

Historical Accuracy: For the most part, the events portrayed are historically accurate, but some alterations have been made for literary purposes.

PAMELA HANSFORD JOHNSON
(1912-1981)

English writer Johnson was born in London and was the wife of novelist and scientist C.P. Snow. As a writer, Johnson concentrated on social and human concerns in contemporary society. She wrote 20 novels as well as critical studies of Thomas Wolfe, Charles Dickens, and Marcel Proust. Her novels include *The Good Husband*, *Night and Silence*, and *The Impossible Marriage*.

3227 *Catherine Carter*

Date of Publication: 1952
Subject(s): Victorian Period; Theatrical Life
Fictional character(s): Catherine Carter, Actress; Henry Peverel, Actor
Time Period(s): 1880s
Locale(s): London, England

Summary: The theatrical world of the Victorian period is portrayed in this love story between actress Catherine Carter and the greatest actor of the day, Henry Peverel. The novel vividly captures the theater of the time and creates a solid background for the novel's relationships.

Historical Accuracy: The theatrical world of 1880s London is evoked convincingly.

MARY JOHNSTON (1870-1936)

Johnston was born in Buchanan, Virginia, and much of her fiction is set during the state's colonial days. Her most successful historical romance was *To Have and To Hold*, set during the Indian massacre of Jamestown in 1622. It was the number one bestseller for 1900.

3228 *1492*

Date of Publication: 1922
Subject(s): Exploration
Fictional character(s): Jayme De Marchena, Sailor
Historical character(s): Christopher Columbus, Explorer
Time Period(s): 15th century; 16th century (1492-1506)
Locale(s): Spain; At Sea

Summary: Christopher Columbus' voyages of discovery are described, from his first crossing of the Atlantic until his death. The story is told from the perspective of Jayme De Marchena, a member of Columbus' crew. Columbus is portrayed as a heroic dreamer.

Historical Accuracy: The novel follows history closely in this chronicle of Columbus' career.

3229 *Audrey*

Date of Publication: 1902
Subject(s): American Colonies
Fictional character(s): Audrey Hanard, Orphan, Ward; Marmaduke Haward, Young Man; Evelyn Bird, Gentlewoman
Time Period(s): 18th century
Locale(s): Virginia, American Colonies

Summary: This sentimental historical romance is set in the Virginia colony in the early years of the 18th century. Marmaduke Haward rescues Audrey Hanard when her parents are killed by Indians. When Audrey matures, Haward pursues both Audrey and Evelyn Bird to the detriment of Audrey's reputation. A series of tragedies finally resolves their love for one another.

Historical Accuracy: The story is too filled with coincidence and the implausible to be taken as an effective rendering of the period.

3230 *Cease Firing*

Date of Publication: 1912
Subject(s): Civil War—U.S.
Fictional character(s): Edward Cary, Military Personnel (Confederate soldier); Desiree Gaillard, Southern Belle
Historical character(s): Robert E. Lee, Military Personnel (Confederate commander)

Time Period(s): 1860s (1861-1865)
Locale(s): Mississippi; Virginia

Summary: This panoramic account of the major engagements of the Civil War takes the Confederate point of view of the fighting and details such engagements as the Siege of Vicksburg, and the battles at Gettysburg, Chickamauga, and Missionary Ridge. The fortunes of a Confederate soldier, Edward Cary, and his beloved, Desiree Gaillard, provide the fictional story.

Historical Accuracy: The novel is exact and authentic in its chronology and the events of battles described.

3231 *Croatan*

Date of Publication: 1923
Subject(s): American Colonies; Indians .
Fictional character(s): Miles Darling, Young Man
Historical character(s): Virginia Dare, Settler
Time Period(s): 16th century
Locale(s): Roanoke Island, North Carolina, American Colonies

Summary: This romantic tale is based on the lost colony of Roanoke Island and of Virginia Dare, the first white child born in the American colonies. In this fanciful story, after the first settlement is destroyed by Indians, the colonists retreat to the mountains under the protection of the Croatan tribe. Virginia is captured by the Shawnees and rescued by her love, Miles Darling.

Historical Accuracy: The novel provides a highly idealized portrait of colonial life. Since nothing is known for sure about the fate of the Roanoke Colony, the novel's version is an imaginative and romantic speculation.

3232 *Drury Randall*

Date of Publication: 1934
Subject(s): Civil War—U.S.
Fictional character(s): Drury Randall, Gentleman
Time Period(s): 1850s; 1860s
Locale(s): Virginia

Summary: The experiences of Virginia gentleman Drury Randall are dramatized from his youth in the 1850s through the years of the Civil War. Randall refuses to take sides during the war, an act that will have important consequences.

Historical Accuracy: This is a lightly-sketched period piece with little to recommend it for its historical portrait.

3233 *Foes*

Date of Publication: 1919
Subject(s): Jacobite Rebellion
Fictional character(s): Alexander Jardine, Laird; Ian Rullock, Gentleman; Elspeth Barrow, Gentlewoman
Time Period(s): 18th century
Locale(s): Scotland

Summary: A love triangle splits two boyhood friends apart during the Stuart uprisings of the early 18th century. Elspeth Barrow comes between Alexander Jardine, the Laird of Glenfernie, and Ian Rullock.

Historical Accuracy: The novel's historical background is convincing.

3234 The Great Valley

Date of Publication: 1926
Subject(s): American Colonies; French and Indian War
Fictional character(s): John Selkirk, Religious (minister); Jeannie Selkirk, Spouse; Elizabeth Burke, Captive
Time Period(s): 18th century (1737-1759)
Locale(s): Shenandoah Valley, Virginia, American Colonies

Summary: The Selkirks, a pioneer family, cross the Blue Ridge to settle in the Shenandoah Valley of Virginia. The Selkirk's daughte, Elizabeth, endures many hardships as the French and Indian War breaks out and she becomes a captive of the Indians.

Historical Accuracy: The story tends towards romance rather than a realistic treatment of colonial life. The novel does, however, feature a believable atmosphere of the wilderness.

3235 The Hunting Shirt

Date of Publication: 1931
Subject(s): Indians; American Colonies
Fictional character(s): Myra Fontaine, Young Woman; Alastair MacLeod, Frontiersman
Time Period(s): 1770s; 1780s (1775-1780)
Locale(s): Virginia

Summary: While fleeing from an Indian raid, Myra Fontaine loses her necklace, which is found by a young Indian warrior. Alastair MacLeod, known as Hunting Shirt, vows to retrieve the necklace, a task that takes two years and many adventures to accomplish.

Historical Accuracy: The Virginia frontier setting provides a realistic and believable milieu for an otherwise overly sentimental adventure tale.

3236 The Long Roll

Date of Publication: 1911
Subject(s): Civil War—U.S.
Fictional character(s): Richard Cleave, Military Personnel (Confederate soldier); Maury Stafford, Military Personnel (Confederate soldier)
Historical character(s): Thomas Jonathan Jackson, Military Personnel (Confederate general)
Time Period(s): 1860s
Locale(s): Virginia

Summary: This historical romance depicts the military campaigns of Confederate General Stonewall Jackson against a romantic story of two Confederate volunteers vying for the love of the same woman. When Maury Stafford alters an order for Richard Cleave's regiment from General Jackson, Cleave is court-martialed and dismissed in disgrace. He re-enlists under an assumed name and distinguishes himself in battle.

Historical Accuracy: The emphasis here is on romantic adventure with a lightly sketched period background.

3237 Miss Delicia Allen

Date of Publication: 1933
Subject(s): Antebellum South; Civil War—U.S.
Fictional character(s): Delicia Allen, Southern Belle
Time Period(s): 19th century
Locale(s): Virginia

Summary: Plantation life in the years before and during the Civil War is depicted in the story of Delicia Allen and her aristocratic southern family who live in a magnificent house designed by Thomas Jefferson. Their gracious way of life is destroyed by the onrushing events of the war.

Historical Accuracy: A strong sense of unreality mars the presentation. The characters, customs, and situations are more stock than genuine.

3238 Prisoners of Hope: A Tale of Colonial Virginia

Date of Publication: 1898
Subject(s): American Colonies
Fictional character(s): Geoffrey Landless, Convict; Patricia Verney, Gentlewoman; Sir Charles Carew, Gentleman
Time Period(s): 17th century (1649-1651)
Locale(s): Virginia, American Colonies

Summary: This romantic tale set in the Virginia colony tells the adventures of an English colonist, Geoffrey Landless, who is sent as an indentured servant to Virginia. Landless becomes connected with the aristocratic Verney family and proves his worth during an Indian attack.

Historical Accuracy: The novel is a blend of romance and authentic elements that help capture the period.

3239 Silver Cross

Date of Publication: 1922
Subject(s): Tudor Period; Religious Life
Fictional character(s): Morgan Fay, Young Woman
Time Period(s): 16th century
Locale(s): England

Summary: Two abbeys vie for predominance in providing miracles to attract pilgrims. In the competition, the Abbey at Silver Cross is being eclipsed by what appear to be fraudulent relics at the Friary of Saint Leofric, and a solution needs to be found.

Historical Accuracy: The novel manages to produce a convincing atmosphere of the time.

3240 The Slave Ship

Date of Publication: 1924
Subject(s): American Colonies; Slavery; Sea Story
Fictional character(s): David Scott, Convict, Sea Captain
Time Period(s): 17th century (1660s)
Locale(s): Virginia, American Colonies; Africa

Summary: The slave trade in the American Colonies forms the background for this tale that describes the exploits of Jacobite David Scott who is exiled to Virginia. He escapes and takes refuge on a slave trader. Eventually he becomes its captain, despite his conscience and disapproval of slavery.

Historical Accuracy: The period elements are authentic and well-drawn.

3241 *To Have and to Hold*

Date of Publication: 1900
Subject(s): American Colonies; Indians
Fictional character(s): Ralph Percy, Settler; Patience Worth, Spouse (of Percy)
Time Period(s): 17th century (1621)
Locale(s): Virginia, American Colonies

Summary: This historical romance set in the early days of the Virginia colony tells of settler Ralph Percy taking a wife from the first shipload of eligible women sent to the colony.

Historical Accuracy: The novel captures colonial life convincingly, and the basis of the novel's circumstances is historically accurate.

TERRY C. JOHNSTON (1947-)

Born in Kansas, Johnson has worked as a roustabout, a history teacher, a printer, a paramedic, a dog catcher, and a car salesman. He has immersed himself in the history of the American West, the setting for all his best-selling novels.

3242 *Black Sun*

Date of Publication: 1991
Subject(s): American West; Indians; Military Life—U.S. Cavalry
Fictional character(s): Seamus Donegan, Scout, Veteran (ex-cavalry sergeant)
Historical character(s): William F. Cody, Frontiersman; James Butler Hickok, Lawman; George Armstrong Custer, Military Personnel (army officer)
Time Period(s): 1870s
Locale(s): Wyoming; Montana

Summary: Seamus Donegan, ex-soldier and army scout, is hired by Buffalo Bill Cody to scout for the Fifth Cavalry in their campaign against the Sioux and Cheyenne.

Historical Accuracy: The scene is both authentic and convincing.

3243 *Blood Song*

Date of Publication: 1993
Subject(s): American West; Indians; Military Life—U.S. Cavalry
Fictional character(s): Seamus Donegan, Military Personnel (cavalry scout)
Historical character(s): George C. Crook, Military Personnel (general); Philip H. Sheridan, Military Personnel (general); Joseph T. Reynolds, Military Personnel (colonel)
Time Period(s): 1870s (1876)
Locale(s): Wyoming; Montana

Summary: Frontier scout Seamus Donegan joins General Crook's cavalry force as the Great Sioux War breaks out,

culminating in the Battle of Powder Run. This is the eighth book in Johnston's series, The Plainsmen.

Historical Accuracy: The novel's fictional story is placed against an authentic depiction of actual historical events and figures.

3244 *Borderlords*

Date of Publication: 1985
Subject(s): American West; Indians
Fictional character(s): Scratch Bass, Mountain Man; Josiah Paddock, Mountain Man
Time Period(s): 1830s
Locale(s): Rocky Mountains

Summary: In the second volume of the trilogy that began with *Carry the Wind*, partners Scratch Bass and Josiah Paddock quarrel over a beautiful Crow woman. They go their separate ways, only to be reunited during the 1833 Green River Rendezvous.

Historical Accuracy: The novel's evocation of wilderness life is authentic and convincing.

3245 *Buffalo Palace*

Date of Publication: 1996
Subject(s): American West; Indians
Fictional character(s): Titus Bass, Mountain Man
Time Period(s): 1820s
Locale(s): St. Louis, Missouri; Great Plains; Rocky Mountains

Summary: In this installment of the life and adventures of mountain man Titus Bass, Bass sets out from St. Louis to seek his fortune hunting the great buffalo herds on the Great Plains. The novel chronicles his adventures as he journeys across the Plains into the Rockies.

Historical Accuracy: The novel provides an authentic depiction of the period and a carefully realistic background.

3246 *Carry the Wind*

Date of Publication: 1982
Subject(s): American West; Indians
Fictional character(s): Josiah Paddock, Frontiersman; Titus Bass, Mountain Man; Rotten Belly, Indian (Crow), Chieftain
Time Period(s): 1830s
Locale(s): Rocky Mountains

Summary: Life in the Rockies during the 1830s is portrayed through the adventures of young Josiah Paddock, who is instructed in survival by mountain man Titus Bass. Wild animals, fierce Indians, and an unforgiving environment all must be surmounted in this vivid depiction of the day-to-day life of the mountain man.

Historical Accuracy: The author is exact and convincing in the details of frontier life.

3247 *A Cold Day in Hell*

Date of Publication: 1996
Subject(s): American West; Indians; Military Life—U.S. Cavalry

Fictional character(s): Seamus Donegan, Military Personnel (cavalry scout)
Time Period(s): 1870s (1876)
Locale(s): Montana; Wyoming

Summary: Phil Sheridan mounts an offensive to capture Sioux warrior Crazy Horse during the disastrous winter campaign of 1876. Seamus Donegan is one of the scouts who join this campaign that culminates in the bloody Battle of Dull Knife.

Historical Accuracy: The historical elements are authentic and faithfully recorded.

`3248` Cry of the Hawk

Date of Publication: 1992
Subject(s): American West; Civil War—U.S.
Fictional character(s): Jonah Hook, Veteran (Confederate soldier); Shadrach Sweete, Mountain Man; Jubilee Usher, Renegade
Time Period(s): 1860s (1865-1868)
Locale(s): Platte Bridge, Wyoming; Republican River, Nebraska; Missouri

Summary: Confederate soldier Jonah Hook is captured in battle and sent to a prison camp, then released, after agreeing to serve on the frontier. He endures encounters with Indians before finally returning to his Missouri farm. There, he finds his wife and family have been abducted by renegade Jubilee Usher. With the help of mountain man Sweete, Hook sets out to find and free his family.

Historical Accuracy: The details of western frontier life of the period are authentically presented.

`3249` Dance on the Wind

Date of Publication: 1995
Subject(s): Settlement of the American Frontier; Riverboats
Fictional character(s): Titus Bass, Teenager
Time Period(s): 19th century
Locale(s): Mississippi River; St. Louis, Missouri; Great Plains

Summary: Titus Bass, the mountain man of the author's trilogy—Carry the Wind, Border Lords, and One-Eyed Dream—is shown in his youth, first in adventures on the Mississippi and later on the frontier of the Great Plains.

Historical Accuracy: The period and locale are depicted with authenticity.

`3250` Devil's Backbone

Date of Publication: 1991
Subject(s): American West; Indians; Military Life—U.S. Cavalry
Fictional character(s): Seamus Donegan, Military Personnel (sergeant); Ian O'Roarke, Rancher; Kientpoos, Indian (Modoc), Chieftain
Time Period(s): 1870s (1872-1873)
Locale(s): Tule Lake, Oregon

Summary: Cavalry sergeant Seamus Donegan, searching for his missing uncle, Ian O'Roarke, arrives in Oregon at the start of the Modoc War. He is drawn into a series of betrayals and broken promises during the Modoc's last stand.

Historical Accuracy: The period details are accurately depicted.

`3251` Dream Catcher

Date of Publication: 1994
Subject(s): American West; Indians
Fictional character(s): Jonah Hook, Veteran (Confederate soldier); Two Sleep, Indian (Shoshone), Warrior; Jubilee Usher, Renegade
Historical character(s): Brigham Young, Leader (Mormon), Religious
Time Period(s): 1870s (1875-1876)
Locale(s): Utah

Summary: Jonah Hook, who returned from the Civil War to find his wife and children kidnapped by the renegade Jubilee Usher, completes his quest to find them in a final confrontation with Usher. The trail leads to Utah and a punishing trek across the mountains.

Historical Accuracy: The author's western stories are all marked by impressive research, and this story is no exception.

`3252` Long Winter Gone

Date of Publication: 1990
Subject(s): American West; Indians; Military Life—U.S. Cavalry
Fictional character(s): Monaseetah, Indian (Cheyenne)
Historical character(s): George Armstrong Custer, Military Personnel (army officer); Philip H. Sheridan, Military Personnel (army general)
Time Period(s): 1860s (1868-1869)
Locale(s): Washita River, Oklahoma; Fort Dodge, Kansas

Summary: This first volume of a trilogy on the life of George Armstrong Custer, follows the exploits of the Civil War hero in the West up to the Battle of the Washita. The fictional plot centers on Custer's relationship with Monaseetah, a Cheyenne woman whom he makes his mistress, at the risk of his military career.

Historical Accuracy: The atmosphere and era are authentic, though the story is invented.

`3253` One-Eyed Dream

Date of Publication: 1988
Subject(s): American West
Fictional character(s): Scratch Bass, Mountain Man; Josiah Paddock, Mountain Man
Time Period(s): 19th century
Locale(s): Rocky Mountains; Taos, New Mexico; St. Louis, Missouri

Summary: In the final volume of the trilogy that includes Carry the Wind and Borderlands, mountain man Scratch Bass and his young partner, Josiah Paddock, are pursued by an Arapaho raiding party. They make their way to St. Louis, where a killer awaits.

Historical Accuracy: The novel provides an authentic period and regional portrait of wilderness life.

3254 *Reap the Whirlwind*

Date of Publication: 1994
Subject(s): American West; Indians; Military Life—U.S. Cavalry
Fictional character(s): Seamus Donegan, Military Personnel (sergeant), Scout
Historical character(s): George C. Crook, Military Personnel (army officer); Crazy Horse, Indian (Sioux), Warrior
Time Period(s): 1870s (1876)
Locale(s): Rosebud River, Montana

Summary: The Indian campaign during the summer of 1876 and the pivotal battle of Rosebud River, are depicted here. Seamus Donegan, the scout for Crook's column, meets the Sioux, led by Crazy Horse. The cavalry's defeat will have disastrous consequences for Custer's column at the Little Big Horn.

Historical Accuracy: The details of military strategy and the period are accurately captured.

3255 *Red Cloud's Revenge*

Date of Publication: 1990
Subject(s): American West; Indians; Military Life—U.S. Cavalry
Fictional character(s): Seamus Donegan, Military Personnel (sergeant), Scout; Rob North, Veteran (Confederate soldier), Renegade
Historical character(s): Jim Bridger, Frontiersman, Scout
Time Period(s): 1860s (1867)
Locale(s): Fort Phil Kearney, Wyoming; Fort C.F. Smith, Montana

Summary: In this tale of the Indian Wars, the Sioux mount a campaign to reclaim their hunting grounds and close the Bozeman Trail to settlers. Chief Red Cloud attacks the undermanned military posts, and Sergeant Donegan is in a fight for his life.

Historical Accuracy: The details of western life are authentic and convincing.

3256 *Seize the Sky*

Date of Publication: 1991
Subject(s): Battle of the Little Bighorn; Indians; Military Life—U.S. Cavalry
Fictional character(s): Monaseetah, Indian (Cheyenne); Yellow Bird, Indian (half-Cheyenne), Child
Historical character(s): George Armstrong Custer, Military Personnel (army officer)
Time Period(s): 1870s (1876)
Locale(s): Little Bighorn River, Montana; Fort Abraham Lincoln, Nebraska

Summary: The second volume of the author's trilogy based on the story of Custer shows the general in command of the Seventh Cavalry during the campaign of 1876. Unknown to Custer, his Cheyenne mistress, Monaseetah, and their child are in the Indian village on the Little Big Horn when he attacks.

Historical Accuracy: The story of Custer's mistress and child is invented. The details of the Battle of the Little Big Horn are credible.

3257 *The Shadow Riders*

Date of Publication: 1991
Subject(s): American West; Indians; Military Life—U.S. Cavalry
Fictional character(s): Seamus Donegan, Military Personnel (sergeant); Whitebear, Indian (Kiowa), Chieftain
Historical character(s): William Tecumseh Sherman, Military Personnel (general)
Time Period(s): 1870s (1873-1874)
Locale(s): Adobe Walls, Texas; Camp Supply, Oklahoma

Summary: In the last great uprising of·the southern Plains tribes, the Comanches, Kiowas, and Cheyennes attempt to drive out the whites in order to protect the buffalo herds from extinction. Buffalo hunters and U.S. troops, commanded by General Sherman, are equally determined to prevail. The action culminates in the Battle of Adobe Walls.

Historical Accuracy: The western scenery and atmosphere are realistically and believably depicted.

3258 *Sioux Dawn*

Date of Publication: 1990
Subject(s): American West; Indians; Military Life—U.S. Cavalry
Fictional character(s): Seamus Donegan, Military Personnel (cavalry sergeant), Scout
Time Period(s): 1860s (1866)
Locale(s): Bozeman Trail, United States

Summary: The opening battle in the Indian Wars—the Fetterman Massacre of 1866—is described through the experiences of army sergeant Seamus Donegan. This is the first book in Johnson's series, The Plainsmen.

Historical Accuracy: The novel provides a remarkably faithful version of the events and life during the period.

3259 *The Stalkers*

Date of Publication: 1990
Subject(s): American West; Indians; Military Life—U.S. Cavalry
Fictional character(s): Seamus Donegan, Military Personnel (sergeant), Scout
Historical character(s): George Forsyth, Military Personnel (army officer); Roman Nose, Indian (Cheyenne), Chieftain
Time Period(s): 1860s (1868)
Locale(s): Beecher's Island, Nebraska

Summary: Seamus is a member of a party of frontiersmen and army scouts led by Colonel George Forsyth that is searching for the Cheyenne. They are trapped on a rocky island in the dry bed of the Republican River and face an attack led by Chief Roman Nose.

Historical Accuracy: The novel mixes the historical with the fictional. The atmosphere and details are authentic.

3260 Trumpet on the Land

Date of Publication: 1995

Subject(s): American West; Battle of the Little Bighorn; Indians

Fictional character(s): Seamus Donegan, Military Personnel (scout); Samantha Donegan, Spouse

Historical character(s): William F. Cody, Frontiersman; Philip H. Sheridan, Military Personnel (general); George C. Crook, Military Personnel (general)

Time Period(s): 1870s (1876)

Locale(s): Montana; Wyoming

Summary: In the aftermath of the Custer massacre at the Little Big Horn, the U.S. army mobilizes for revenge. Total war is declared on the Cheyenne and the Sioux. The action centers on the experiences of Indian scout Seamus Donegan and details various encounters with the Indians.

Historical Accuracy: The author has mastered the period and locale and delivers convincing action.

3261 Whisper of the Wolf

Date of Publication: 1991

Subject(s): American West; Indians; Tribal Life—Native American

Fictional character(s): Yellow Bird, Indian (half-Cheyenne), Shaman; Preston Tripp, Military Personnel (army officer); Monaseetah, Indian (Cheyenne)

Time Period(s): 19th century (1876-1890)

Locale(s): South Dakota

Summary: The author's trilogy based on the life of George Armstong Custer concludes with the fictional story of Custer's son by a Cheyenne woman, Monaseetah. Yellow Bird grows up with the Cheyenne but is pursued by detectives Custer's widow hires. At the same time, the life of the Plains tribes is brought to a bloody end with the tragedy at Wounded Knee.

Historical Accuracy: Despite the fictional story of Custer's offspring, the details of Indian life are realistic and authentic.

3262 Winter Rain

Date of Publication: 1993

Subject(s): American West; Indians

Fictional character(s): Jonah Hook, Veteran (Confederate soldier); Jeremiah Hook, Captive, Child

Time Period(s): 1860s; 1870s (1868-1875)

Locale(s): Big Horn Mountains, Wyoming; Palo Duro Canyon, Texas

Summary: Jonah Hook's quest to recover his captive family continues. His sons have been captured by the Comanches, and Hook heads for Texas where he finds himself at the center of a war between the Comanches and federal troops and Texas Rangers. He must contend with their battle while still trying to rescue his sons.

Historical Accuracy: The details of western life of the period are plausibly presented.

VELDA JOHNSTON

American writer Johnston lives in Sag Harbor on Long Island, which appears frequently in her novels' settings. Her novels include *Along a Dark Path*, *The People on the Hill*, *Shadow Behind a Curtain*, and *Flight to Yesterday*.

3263 I Came to the Highlands: A Novel of Suspense

Date of Publication: 1974

Subject(s): Jacobite Rebellion; Suspense; Georgian Period

Fictional character(s): Elizabeth Logan, Gentlewoman

Historical character(s): Charles Edward Stuart, Royalty (prince)

Time Period(s): 1740s

Locale(s): Southampton, England; Highlands, Scotland

Summary: This novel of suspense, set during the period of Bonnie Prince Charlie's assault on the English throne, concerns Elizabeth Logan whose father is banished to Scotland for his loyalty to the Stuart cause. There her father dies, leaving Elizabeth alone with her hostile relatives until she is befriended by the Prince himself.

Historical Accuracy: Despite the obvious romantic invention, the novel's characters and background are believable.

3264 The Silver Dolphin

Date of Publication: 1979

Subject(s): Suspense; Trials; Whaling

Fictional character(s): Fiona MacWain, Spouse (of Torrance Ravencroft); Torrance Ravencroft, Gentleman; Brian Ravencroft, Sea Captain

Time Period(s): 19th century (first half)

Locale(s): Sag Harbor, New York

Summary: Set in the Long Island whaling village of Sag Harbor in the first half of the 19th century, the story concerns Fiona MacWain, the daughter of an indentured Scottish servant. Fiona marries rich old Torrance Ravencroft, it is said, for his money. When he dies, there is an inquest to determine whether it was an accidental death or murder, with Fiona the likely suspect.

Historical Accuracy: The period and locale details are authentic.

WILLIAM W. JOHNSTONE (1938-)

American author Johnstone has written over 85 novels since 1980. Although his best known works are Westerns, he has also produced books of fantasy and historical fiction.

3265 Blood on the Divide

Date of Publication: 1992

Subject(s): American West; Wagon Trains

Fictional character(s): Preacher, Mountain Man; Malachi Pardee, Outlaw; Betina Drum, Teacher

Time Period(s): 1830s (1838)

Locale(s): Oregon Trail, Wyoming

Summary: Trouble along the Oregon Trail is depicted in this western adventure. A gang of outlaws, teamed up with Indian outcasts, is victimizing immigrant wagon trains set up to fall into the outlaws' hands. Preacher, a mountain man, decides to intervene.

Historical Accuracy: The plot premise is a bit implausible, but the western scenes are believable.

3266 *Eyes of Eagles*

Date of Publication: 1993
Subject(s): American West; Indians; Texas Revolution
Fictional character(s): Jamie McAllister, Frontiersman, Captive; Tall Bull, Indian (Shawnee), Chieftain; Kate Olmstead, Frontierswoman
Time Period(s): 1830s; 1840s
Locale(s): Kentucky; San Antonio, Texas

Summary: Jamie McAllister is captured by Indians as a child and adopted by the tribe. When he returns to white society, he quarrels with and kills a man, and must flee west with Kate Olmstead, his intended. The two are pursued by bounty hunters and the Shawnees into Texas in the midst of the war with Mexico.

Historical Accuracy: The details of the period are accurate even though the story seems far too melodramatic to be believed.

3267 *Forty Guns West*

Date of Publication: 1993
Subject(s): American West
Fictional character(s): Preacher, Mountain Man; Elam Parks, Landowner; Dark Hand, Indian (Pawnee), Bounty Hunter
Time Period(s): 1830s
Locale(s): Ohio; Rocky Mountains, Colorado

Summary: The mountain man Preacher returns to his home in Ohio where he quarrels with and kills Elam Parks. Bounty hunters pursue him back into the Rockies. Once there, Preacher is more than a match for any number of bounty hunters.

Historical Accuracy: The novel offers some authentic details of western life.

3268 *Talons of Eagles*

Date of Publication: 1995
Subject(s): Civil War—U.S.
Fictional character(s): Jamie Ian MacCallister, Military Personnel (Confederate officer)
Historical character(s): Allan Pinkerton, Detective—Private; Abraham Lincoln, Political Figure; James Longstreet, Military Personnel (Confederate general)
Time Period(s): 1860s; 1870s
Locale(s): Tennessee; Virginia

Summary: The novel tells the adventures of Jamie Ian MacCallister who is raised by the Shawnee, fights in Texas, and becomes a legend in the West as a scout and gunfighter. As the Civil War begins, he is called to meet with President Lincoln. When the fighting starts, he leads his Confederate company into battle in many of the major events of the war.

Historical Accuracy: MacCallister is fictional, but the framework of the story and its chronology are based on fact.

ALEXANDRA JONES (1943-)

Jones was born in India and now lives in Kent, England.

3269 *Mandalay*

Date of Publication: 1987
Subject(s): English Colonies
Fictional character(s): Angela Featherstone, Fiance(e); Matthew Sinclair, Fiance(e), Government Official; Nathan de Veres-Vorne, Trader, Sea Captain
Time Period(s): 19th century; 20th century (1878-1945)
Locale(s): Mandalay, Burma

Summary: The scene is Mandalay, Burma, and the political turmoil surrounding the struggle for supremacy between the native queen and the British colonial forces. Angela Featherstone is a young Englishwoman engaged to marry Matthew Sinclair, a British civil service officer. She falls under the spell of American trader Nathan de Veres-Vorne. The novel's story extends from the 19th century to the end of World War II.

Historical Accuracy: The novel captures the exotic locale with convincing period details.

CLEO JONES

3270 *Sister Wives*

Date of Publication: 1984
Subject(s): American West; Mormons
Fictional character(s): Caledonia Spencer, Young Woman; Connie Spencer, Young Woman; Harley Crick, Settler
Historical character(s): Brigham Young, Leader (Mormon), Religious; Mark Twain, Writer; James Buchanan, Political Figure
Time Period(s): 1850s (1856)
Locale(s): Salt Lake City, Utah; Virginia City, Nevada

Summary: In the 1850s Caledonia Spencer vows to her parents that she will see her sister married in the Mormon tradition, and Connie becomes one of Harley Crick's three wives. Rivalry and bitterness result when Caledonia finds herself attracted to her sister's husband. She escapes to Virginia City, where she develops the strength to resist the Mormon patriarchy and to assert her freedom.

Historical Accuracy: The author insists that the Mormon traditions portrayed are based on books, newspapers, and journals of the time. She admits to some distortion of the actual chronology, however.

COURTWAY JONES (1923-)

Jones is a cultural anthropologist and ethnohistorian who earned his Ph.D. at Columbia. His trilogy, Dragon's Heirs, retells the Arthurian legend.

3271 *In the Shadow of the Oak King*

Date of Publication: 1991

Subject(s): Dark Ages; Myths and Legends; Arthurian Legends

Fictional character(s): Pelleas, Bastard Son; Arthur, Ruler (King of the Britons); Myrddin, Blacksmith

Time Period(s): 5th century (453-477)

Locale(s): England

Summary: In the first book of a proposed Arthurian trilogy called ''Dragon Heirs,'' the saga begins with the experiences of Pelleas, bastard son of Uther Pendragon, high king of the Britons. Arthur, a prince hidden since infancy, emerges to fulfill his destiny in the creation of Camelot.

Historical Accuracy: The story, which owes a great deal to Jones' anthropological research, is convincing in its authenticity.

3272 *Witch of the North*

Date of Publication: 1992

Subject(s): Dark Ages; Arthurian Legends; Myths and Legends

Fictional character(s): Arthur, Ruler (King of the Britons); Launcelot, Knight; Guinevere, Royalty (queen consort to Arthur); Morgan Le Fey, Sorceress

Time Period(s): 5th century (453-488)

Locale(s): England

Summary: This retelling of the Arthurian story focuses on Morgan Le Fey, the half-sister of King Arthur, who ventures to the northernmost reaches of England to establish a personal realm, while Arthur consolidates his rule as high king and forms the legendary Round Table.

Historical Accuracy: The author recounts Thomas Malory's tales from the perspective of the anthropologist, fashioning a more believable version of the legend.

DOUGLAS C. JONES (1924-)

Jones was born and raised in Arkansas, the setting for many of his works. He was a career officer in the military from 1943 until 1968 when he began his writing career. Many believe him to be one of the most knowledgeable and creative writers about the American West.

3273 *Arrest Sitting Bull*

Date of Publication: 1977

Subject(s): American West; Indians

Fictional character(s): Standing Elk, Indian; James McLaughlin, Government Official (Indian agent); Willa Mae Favoury, Teacher

Historical character(s): Sitting Bull, Indian (sioux), Chieftain

Time Period(s): 1890s

Locale(s): South Dakota; Standing Rock, North Dakota

Summary: It is the 1890s, and the ghost dance—the invocation of the power that will help the Indians destroy the white man—is sweeping through the Dakota reservation. Most troubling to the U.S. government is the aging Sitting Bull, who is attracting many fanatical followers. How can peace be maintained when the order is sent that Sitting Bull must be arrested?.

Historical Accuracy: This is an exciting and compelling drama that culminates in the tragedy of Wounded Knee. The attitude and the atmosphere are convincingly drawn.

3274 *The Barefoot Brigade*

Date of Publication: 1982

Subject(s): Civil War—U.S.; Military Life; Battle of Gettysburg

Fictional character(s): Noah Fawley, Military Personnel, Farmer; Zachery Fawley, Military Personnel, Farmer; Martin Hasford, Military Personnel, Farmer

Time Period(s): 1860s (1861-1865)

Locale(s): South (Arkansas, Virginia, Georgia, Tennessee); Gettysburg, Pennsylvania

Summary: The Civil War is depicted through the experiences of members of a mess unit of the Third Arkansas Infantry Regiment. The story tracks them from their recruitment, through training, to some of the pivotal campaigns of the war: Chickamauga, Gettysburg, the Wilderness, Spotsylvania, and the defense of Richmond.

Historical Accuracy: The emphasis here is not on political issues or military strategy, but on the common soldier's experience rendered in convincing and moving detail.

3275 *Come Winter*

Date of Publication: 1989

Subject(s): Rural Life—U.S.; Crime and Criminals

Fictional character(s): Roman Hasford, Political Figure, Businessman; Catrina Hasford, Heroine; Jared Dane, Murderer

Time Period(s): 19th century (1870-1894)

Locale(s): Gourdville, Arkansas

Summary: Roman Hasford returns to his hometown in the 1870s with a young woman whom he marries. His rise to prominence as a banker and political figure creates resentment that becomes a blood feud when Roman's childhood friend is murdered. A professional killer is called in to settle accounts.

Historical Accuracy: Jones' story ably portrays a time and place in the history of rural America.

3276 *The Court-Martial of George Armstrong Custer*

Date of Publication: 1976

Subject(s): Battle of the Little Bighorn; Trials; Alternate History

Fictional character(s): Asa B. Gardiner, Lawyer; Allan Jacobson, Lawyer

Historical character(s): William Tecumseh Sherman, Military Personnel; George Armstrong Custer, Military Personnel; Philip H. Sheridan, Military Personnel; Ulysses S. Grant, Political Figure, Military Personnel; Elizabeth Bacon Custer, Gentlewoman, Spouse

Time Period(s): 1870s

Locale(s): New York, New York

Summary: In this brilliant historical fantasy, Jones speculates on what might have happened had Custer survived the massacre at the Little Bighorn and faced a court-martial. The novel presents a taut courtroom drama that reveals much about the engagement and the men who fought in it, particularly the flamboyant and flawed Custer.

Historical Accuracy: This is a tour de force of historical speculation grounded by a solid knowledge of the events and the period.

3277 A Creek Called Wounded Knee

Date of Publication: 1978
Subject(s): Indians; Battle of Wounded Knee; Military Life—U.S. Cavalry
Fictional character(s): Quinton Tapp, Journalist
Historical character(s): Big Foot, Indian; George D. Wallace, Military Personnel; Widow Duncan, Journalist
Time Period(s): 1890s (1890)
Locale(s): Wounded Knee, South Dakota

Summary: The Seventh Cavalry's terrible revenge for Custer's massacre is exacted at Wounded Knee in 1890 in a media event with reporters from around the world anticipating the bloody climax. The novel provides a variety of perspectives on the events.

Historical Accuracy: Jones provides convincing details in this tragic story of the end of a way of life in the American West.

3278 Elkhorn Tavern

Date of Publication: 1980
Subject(s): Civil War—U.S.; Battle of Pea Ridge
Fictional character(s): Ora Hasford, Farmer; Roman Hasford, Farmer; Allan Eben Pay, Military Personnel
Historical character(s): James Butler Hickok, Frontiersman, Military Personnel; Philip H. Sheridan, Military Personnel
Time Period(s): 1860s (1862)
Locale(s): Elkhorn Tavern, Arkansas

Summary: A hill-country farming family of western Arkansas is caught up in the events of the Civil War. The Hasford family tries to survive pitted between the two contending armies. A love affair blossoms between the Hasford's daughter and a Union officer. The action culminates in the pivotal western battle of Pea Ridge.

Historical Accuracy: Jones is able to combine effectively the homefront experience of the Civil War with its military action.

3279 Gone the Dreams and the Dancing

Date of Publication: 1984
Subject(s): American West; Indians
Fictional character(s): Kwahadi Parry, Indian (Comanche); Liverpool Morgan, Frontiersman
Time Period(s): 19th century; 20th century (1875-1903)
Locale(s): Fort Sill, Oklahoma

Summary: The end of Indian traditions is dramatized in this sequel to *Season of Yellow Leaf*. Kwahadi, the son of a white girl taken by the Comanches, is a tribal leader who surrenders at Fort Sill. The novel depicts the Indians' integration into white civilization, and Kwahadi's search to learn the fate of his mother, ''rescued'' in 1854 by the Texas Rangers.

Historical Accuracy: Jones ably details the period of the closing of the Indian territories and sheds light both on Indian culture and that of the white victors in the battle for predominance.

3280 Remember Santiago

Date of Publication: 1988
Subject(s): Spanish-American War; Military Life—U.S. Army; Battle of San Juan Hill
Fictional character(s): Eben Pay, Lawyer, Military Personnel; Joe Mountain, Frontiersman, Military Personnel; Carlina Newton, Nurse
Historical character(s): Theodore Roosevelt, Military Personnel; Clara Barton, Nurse, Government Official; William R. Shafter, Military Personnel
Time Period(s): 1890s (1898)
Locale(s): Santiago, Cuba; Arkansas

Summary: Jones dramatizes the slapdash and bloody Cuban invasion of 1898 in a series of eyewitness accounts. The major players are represented, and the action follows two Arkansas volunteers—Pay and Mountain—from the invasion to the storming of San Juan Hill. Realism reduces military glory to tragic absurdity.

Historical Accuracy: The novel is absolutely convincing in its historical details, animated by a group of characters whose personal perspective brings the scenes to life.

3281 Roman

Date of Publication: 1986
Subject(s): American West; Indians; Railroads
Fictional character(s): Roman Hasford, Businessman; Roman Nose, Indian (Cheyenne); Crider Peel, Businessman
Historical character(s): Winfield Scott Hancock, Military Personnel; George Armstrong Custer, Military Personnel; Philip H. Sheridan, Military Personnel
Time Period(s): 19th century (1865-1880)
Locale(s): St. Louis, Missouri; Kansas

Summary: Roman Hasford, the young boy in Jones' *Elkhorn Tavern*, journeys west to Kansas where he gets an education in the corrupt world of railroad building. Disillusionment with the civilization he finds leads him farther west and into a confrontation with the Cheyenne at the Battle of Beecher's Island.

Historical Accuracy: Jones' details of western life are vividly painted, producing a realistic and unsentimental portrait of the American West.

3282 The Search for Temperance Moon

Date of Publication: 1991
Subject(s): Indians; American West; Crime and Criminals
Fictional character(s): Jewel Moon, Madam; Oscar Schiller, Lawman
Historical character(s): Isaac C. Parker, Judge
Time Period(s): 1890s
Locale(s): Fort Smith, Arkansas; Indian Nations, Oklahoma

Summary: The novel details a murder investigation surrounding the death of Temperance Moon, an Indian outlaw in the Indian Nations of Oklahoma in the 1890s. Her daughter, a Fort Smith madam, hires an ex-marshall to solve the mystery, revealing a tangled story of jealousy, blackmail, and deceit.

Historical Accuracy: Jones' story vividly brings to light the fading West with a cast of colorful frontier characters on the border between civilization and lawlessness.

3283 *Season of Yellow Leaf*

Date of Publication: 1983
Subject(s): American West; Indians; Tribal Life—Native American
Fictional character(s): Morfydd Annon Parry, Captive, Indian (adopted); Mendoza, Outlaw (commanchero); Iron Shirt, Indian (Comanche)
Time Period(s): 19th century (1830s-1854)
Locale(s): Texas; New Mexico

Summary: This is the tale of a 10-year-old white girl captured and raised by the Comanches. She learns their ways and becomes a tribal member, suffering the passing of a way of life as the white man encroaches on the Commanches' lands.

Historical Accuracy: The Comanches are portrayed as human beings, neither simplified nor idealized. Their customs and way of life are vividly described.

3284 *Shadow of the Moon*

Date of Publication: 1995
Subject(s): American Colonies; Immigrants; Settlement of the American Frontier
Fictional character(s): Old Sergeant Bobby Chesney, Immigrant, Settler; Nalambigi Chesney, Indian, Spouse; Young Bone Trudeau, Slave (freed); Noble Popjoy, Indian (half-Delaware), Guide
Historical character(s): Aaron Burr, Political Figure; James Wilkinson, Military Personnel (general)
Time Period(s): 18th century; 19th century (1770s-1820s)
Locale(s): Pennsylvania; Ohio Valley, United States

Summary: Scottish immigrant Old Sergeant Bobby Chesney and his Indian wife Nalambigi help tame the frontier of western Pennsylvania and the Ohio River Valley. Connected to their family story is a colorful cast of frontier types who begin to forge a common American identity in the wilderness.

Historical Accuracy: The novel is convincing in its depiction of the Young Republic and American frontier life.

3285 *This Savage Race*

Date of Publication: 1993
Subject(s): Settlement of the American Frontier; Indians
Fictional character(s): Boone Fawley, Settler; Molly Fawley, Settler
Time Period(s): 1800s (1808)
Locale(s): St. Louis, Missouri; Ozarks, Arkansas; Point of Rocks, Arkansas

Summary: The Fawley family travels from St. Louis into the wilderness of the Ozarks. There they face a number of unfore-

seen dangers and disasters, both from nature and the Indians they encounter.

Historical Accuracy: The novel expertly re-creates the time and place of the settlement of the American frontier.

3286 *Weedy Rough*

Date of Publication: 1981
Subject(s): Depression Era; Crime and Criminals; Rural Life—U.S.
Fictional character(s): Eben Pay, Lawyer; Barton Pay, Businessman; Duny Gene Pay, Young Man
Time Period(s): 1920s; 1930s
Locale(s): Weedy Rough, Arkansas (northwestern Arkansas)

Summary: In an Arkansas town during the Depression, Duny Gene Pay is implicated in a bank robbery that leaves two people dead. His grandfather, Eben Pay, defends the boy and in the process exposes the pettiness and prejudices of the town.

Historical Accuracy: Jones shows that he can convincingly portray a setting other than the Wild West. He expertly dissects the communal values of his Arkansas locale.

3287 *Winding Stairs*

Date of Publication: 1979
Subject(s): American West; Indians; Crime and Criminals
Fictional character(s): Eben Pay, Lawyer; Oscar Schiller, Lawman
Historical character(s): Isaac C. Parker, Judge
Time Period(s): 1890s
Locale(s): Fort Smith, Arkansas; Indian Nations, Oklahoma

Summary: Eben Pay, an idealistic lawyer, is educated in the ways of western life in the 1890s on the border of the Indian Nations. He is recruited as a member of a posse to investigate what becomes known as the Winding Stairs Massacre.

Historical Accuracy: Jones knows this territory well and fills the novel with the authentic sights and sounds of the period.

ELLEN JONES

3288 *Beloved Enemy: The Passions of Eleanor of Aquitaine*

Date of Publication: 1994
Subject(s): Middle Ages; Royalty—France; Royalty—England
Fictional character(s): Bellebelle, Prostitute
Historical character(s): Eleanor of Aquitaine, Royalty (Queen of France and England); Louis VI, Ruler (King of France); Louis VII, Ruler (King of France); Henry II, Ruler (King of England); Geoffrey of Anjou, Nobleman; Thomas Becket, Religious (archbishop)
Time Period(s): 12th century (1130-1162)
Locale(s): France; England; Palestine

Summary: The emphasis here is on the relationships of Eleanor of Aquitaine. Orphaned at 15, she is forced to marry the monkish Louis VII of France. She insists on accompanying him on a crusade, and on her return meets young Henry

Plantagenet, heir to the English throne. Their affair, an exciting mixture of power politics and sensuality, alters the course of English history.

Historical Accuracy: The story's background is thoroughly grounded in historical details, yet the foreground reaches the unhistorical level of the romance with somewhat embarrassing purple passages. Eleanor is depicted as a kind of proto-feminist.

3289 *The Fatal Crown*

Date of Publication: 1991
Subject(s): Middle Ages; Royalty—England
Historical character(s): Maud, Royalty (princess); Henry I, Ruler (King of England); Stephen, Nobleman
Time Period(s): 12th century (1125-1154)
Locale(s): France; England

Summary: This novel of dynastic conflict is based on the confused succession after the death of Henry I. He designates his daughter, Maud, his heir. Her rival for the throne is Stephen, her cousin and lover. He usurps the throne and plunges England into a bloody and protracted civil war.

Historical Accuracy: Jones' solidly researched story succeeds in combining the court intrigues of the period with the passions of believable human characters.

GARETH JONES (1951-)

3290 *Lord of Misrule*

Date of Publication: 1980
Subject(s): Jacobite Rebellion; Inheritance—Disputed
Fictional character(s): Gruffydd, Heir; Hywel Bevan, Religious (preacher)
Time Period(s): 1740s (1745)
Locale(s): Wales

Summary: In this tale of Wales in the 18th century, Gruffydd returns to the small village of his childhood determined to regain his birthright as owner of the Ystwyth Valley. Instead he is welcomed as the village's new conjurer, and what begins as a con becomes a much more serious game, while Gruffydd waits to claim Ystwyth.

Historical Accuracy: The period details of 18th-century Wales are authentic.

MADISON JONES (1925-)

American writer Jones has worked as a professor of English at Auburn University since 1956. He has also taught at the University of Tennessee. His books include *The Innocent*, *A Buried Land*, *An Exile*, *Season of the Stranger*, and *To the Winds*.

3291 *Forest of the Night*

Date of Publication: 1960
Subject(s): Settlement of the American Frontier
Fictional character(s): Jonathan Cannon, Teacher; Judith Gray, Settler

Time Period(s): 1800s (1802)
Locale(s): Tennessee

Summary: This is a story of disillusionment. Jonathan Cannon ventures west into Tennessee and is progressively stripped of his illusions about man's nobility in the wilderness. He is attacked by an Indian he helps, the woman he is determined to save refuses to be saved, and Jonathan finds brutality and injustice throughout his travels.

Historical Accuracy: This is a philosophically sobering novel that seems far more realistic than other treatments of the frontier experience.

MERVYN JONES (1922-)

English journalist and novelist Jones was born in London and attended NYU. He served in the British army during World War II and became a captain. Jones was the drama critic for the *London Tribune* and an assistant editor for the *New Statesman*. Jones' decidedly leftist orientation has been charged as a weakness in his ability to create fully believable characters. His novel *John and Mary* was made into a film in 1969.

3292 *Joseph*

Date of Publication: 1970
Subject(s): Biography, Fictionalized; Russian Revolution; World War II
Historical character(s): Joseph Stalin, Political Figure; Vladimir Ilich Lenin, Political Figure; Leon Trotsky, Political Figure
Time Period(s): 19th century; 20th century
Locale(s): Russia

Summary: This is a fictionalized biography of Joseph Stalin that traces his career. From a poor seminary student who exchanges Christ for Marx, through the turbulent events of the Russian Revolution, civil war, and party intrigue, he eventually emerges as one of the most powerful dictators of history. The novel attempts to trace the psychological pressures that created Stalin.

Historical Accuracy: The novel blends the known and the imagined. The author explains that some episodes are recounted exactly from scholarly works or contemporary accounts, but others are altered and some are invented. The invented passages are noted in an appendix.

3293 *Lord Richard's Passion*

Date of Publication: 1974
Subject(s): Romance; Boer War; World War I
Fictional character(s): Richard Somers, Nobleman (Duke of Berkshire); Ellie Colmore, Gentlewoman
Time Period(s): 19th century; 20th century (1875-1920s)
Locale(s): England

Summary: The novel is a love story and a picture of English aristocratic life. Both the love affair and the lifestyle are swept up in the unrest of the great events from 1875 to the 1920s. Richard Somers falls in love with Ellie Colmore, who is emotionally damaged by witnessing a country-house seduction. Their story is played out against a backdrop of English social life disrupted by the events of the Boer War, the Irish troubles, suffragette riots, and the Great War.

Historical Accuracy: The sense of history is captured with authenticity.

ROBERT F. JONES (1934-)

An American author of fiction and nonfiction, Jones was born in Milwaukee and graduated from the University of Michigan. He has worked as an editor for *Time* and as a writer for *Sports Illustrated*. Jones lives in Vermont, and his books include *Jake* and *Upland Passage*.

`3294` *Tie My Bones to Her Back*

Date of Publication: 1996
Subject(s): American West; Indians
Fictional character(s): Otto Dousmann, Young Man; Jenny Dousmann, Young Woman; Two Shields, Indian (Cheyenne)
Time Period(s): 1870s
Locale(s): Great Plains

Summary: The novel's background is the extermination of the buffalo herds in the 1870s that precipitates the great Indian War. Jenny Dousmann and her brother Otto head west to the buffalo range to recoup their fortune. After she is brutally raped and he is crippled, they seek refuge with a half-breed Cheyenne, Two Shields, in the Big Horn Mountains and begin a quest for revenge.

Historical Accuracy: The details of frontier life and the decimation of the buffalo herds are accurately presented.

ROD JONES (1953-)

Australian novelist Jones was born in Melbourne and graduated from the University of Melbourne. He has been an English teacher in Melbourne and Queenscliffe. His first novel, *Julia Paradise*, won the South Australia's Premier's Festival Award in 1988.

`3295` *Billy Sunday*

Date of Publication: 1996
Subject(s): Mystery; Spiritualism
Fictional character(s): Billy Sunday, Orphan, Teenager; Charles Van Schaick, Photographer
Historical character(s): Frederick Jackson Turner, Historian
Time Period(s): 1890s (1892)
Locale(s): Wisconsin

Summary: This tale of murder and spirituality is set in the Wisconsin woods during the 1890s. Orphaned vagabond Billy Sunday secures a job with photographer Charles Van Schaick who is attempting to photograph spirits with the help of a medium. When several local woman are killed, suspicion falls on Billy. Historian Frederick Jackson Turner becomes involved in the affair.

Historical Accuracy: This is an ingenious story with a believable atmosphere.

TED JONES (1937-)

Born in Oklahoma and a graduate of Fort Hays Kansas State College and Kansas State Teachers College, Jones is a superintendent of schools in Kansas. He considers himself a student of history and is particularly interested in anthropology, the Civil War, and World War II.

`3296` *The Fifth Conspiracy*

Date of Publication: 1995
Subject(s): Civil War—U.S.; Battle of Chickamauga; Espionage
Fictional character(s): Samuel Wade, Military Personnel (Union officer); Simon Thornton, Military Personnel (prisoner of war)
Historical character(s): Robert E. Lee, Military Personnel (Confederate commander); Abraham Lincoln, Political Figure
Time Period(s): 1860s (1863-1864)
Locale(s): Tennessee; Richmond, Virginia; Washington, District of Columbia

Summary: In the sequel to *Hard Road to Gettysburg*, Union officer Samuel Wade is separated from his troops during the Battle of Chickamauga. He heads south, impersonating a Confederate officer. Hearing of a plot to assassinate President Lincoln and that his brother is being held in Richmond's notorious Libby Prison, Wade is drawn back into clandestine operations behind enemy lines.

Historical Accuracy: The dialogue and specific incidents described in the novel are fictional and are not meant to be taken as real.

`3297` *Grant's War*

Date of Publication: 1992
Subject(s): Civil War—U.S.; Battle of Shiloh; Siege of Vicksburg
Fictional character(s): Arthur Kelly, Historian; Jeremiah Clemmens, Military Personnel; Jacob Gattlin, Military Personnel
Historical character(s): Ulysses S. Grant, Military Personnel (Union general); William Tecumseh Sherman, Military Personnel (Union general); Abraham Lincoln, Political Figure; Philip Sherman, Military Personnel (Union general)
Time Period(s): 1910s; 1860s
Locale(s): Galena, Illinois; Vicksburg, Mississippi

Summary: A historian, Arthur Kelly, travels around the country during the 1910s interviewing veterans of the Civil War for a study of General Grant. The witnesses he encounters review Grant's campaigns at Shiloh, Vicksburg, the Wilderness, Spotsylvania, and Appomattox, and present a portrait of Grant as a compassionate and courageous commander.

Historical Accuracy: The history is solidly researched, and the portrait both of Grant and other combatants is compelling and convincing.

`3298` *Hard Road to Gettysburg*

Date of Publication: 1993

Subject(s): Civil War—U.S.; Espionage; Battle of Gettysburg
Fictional character(s): Samuel Wade, Military Personnel (Union soldier); Simon Thornton, Military Personnel (Confederate soldier); Caroline Wade, Widow(er), Businesswoman
Historical character(s): Robert E. Lee, Military Personnel (Confederate commander); Thomas Jonathan Jackson, Military Personnel (Confederate general); Abraham Lincoln, Political Figure
Time Period(s): 1860s (1861-1863)
Locale(s): Gettysburg, Pennsylvania; Virginia

Summary: When Union officer Samuel Wade is captured in the fighting of the Seven Days, he recognizes an uncanny resemblance between himself and a Confederate lieutenant on Stonewall Jackson's staff. The solution of this mysterious resemblance leads him to uncover something significant about his past and into espionage for the Union Army.

Historical Accuracy: The situation is improbable and overly contrived. The details of the events and the period, however, are convincing.

ERICA JONG (1942-)

Jong is an American novelist and poet who achieved notoriety with her first novel, *Fear of Flying*, about the escapades of a woman in search of sexual fulfillment. Her other works include *How to Save Your Own Life*, *Parachutes and Kisses*, and *Fear of Fifty*. Her poetry is collected in three volumes.

3299 *Fanny: Being the True History of the Adventures of Fanny Hackabout-Jones*

Date of Publication: 1980
Subject(s): Crime and Criminals; Picaresque Adventure; Pirates
Fictional character(s): Fanny Hackabout-Jones, Outcast, Prostitute; Launcelot Robinson, Pirate
Historical character(s): Jonathan Swift, Writer, Religious; William Hogarth, Artist; John Cleland, Writer; Anne Bonny, Pirate
Time Period(s): 18th century (1730-1750)
Locale(s): Wiltshire, England; London, England; West Indies

Summary: Fanny is a female Tom Jones in this parody of Henry Fielding's 18th-century novel. Discovered on a doorstep, Fanny is forced to make her own fortune. She falls in with witches, highwaymen, and pirates. Her time in a brothel enables her to meet many leading figures of the day.

Historical Accuracy: There is a concerted effort to render the background of 18th-century life and atmosphere, but Fanny's sensibility is decidedly modern. Some characters and events have been manipulated to aid the narrative.

3300 *Serenissima: A Novel of Venice*

Date of Publication: 1987
Subject(s): Renaissance; Fantasy; Time Travel

Fictional character(s): Jessica Pruitt, Actress, Time Traveller; Shalach, Businessman
Historical character(s): William Shakespeare, Writer; Henry Wriothesley, Nobleman (Earl of Southampton)
Time Period(s): 20th century; 16th century
Locale(s): Venice, Italy

Summary: A popular Hollywood actress goes to Venice to be a judge in a film festival. She is transported back to the 16th century and meets Shakespeare, who is writing his *Merchant of Venice*. Her affairs with the English poet and his young, noble patron form the core of the novel's magic.

Historical Accuracy: Jong convincingly renders the atmosphere of Renaissance Venice, but depicts Shakespeare as a romance novel hero forever quoting his yet-to-be-written plays.

JAN JORDAN

Jordan was born in Illinois and served as a staff member in a congressional office in Washington.

3301 *Dim the Flaring Lamps*

Date of Publication: 1972
Subject(s): Civil War—U.S.; Theatrical Life; Biography, Fictionalized
Historical character(s): John Wilkes Booth, Actor, Murderer (assassin); Jefferson Davis, Political Figure; Belle Starr, Spy; Abraham Lincoln, Political Figure; John Yates Beall, Military Personnel (Confederate privateer)
Time Period(s): 19th century (1838-1865)
Locale(s): Philadelphia, Pennsylvania; Virginia; Washington, District of Columbia

Summary: This biographical novel on the life of John Wilkes Booth attempts to provide a more personal motivation for his assassination of Abraham Lincoln. Booth's life is chronicled from his acting career to his service as an agent of the Confederate Secret Service.

Historical Accuracy: Based on the actual events of Booth's life, the novel does resort to some interpretation and speculation.

3302 *Give Me the Wind*

Date of Publication: 1973
Subject(s): Indians; Biography, Fictionalized; War of 1812
Historical character(s): John Ross, Indian (Cherokee), Chieftain; Andrew Jackson, Political Figure, Military Personnel (general); George Washington, Political Figure; Abraham Lincoln, Political Figure
Time Period(s): 18th century; 19th century
Locale(s): Southeast; Cherokee Nation, Oklahoma (Oklahoma territory)

Summary: The novel tells the life story of John Ross, the son of a white father and Cherokee mother, who becomes chief of his people through his tribe's most turbulent period. He transforms the Cherokees into a genuine nation, rallies support for Andrew Jackson during the War of 1812, but then is betrayed by Jackson's Indian removal policy. During the Civil War, Ross fights on the side of the Union.

Historical Accuracy: The novel has a solid historical framework in building this panoramic story.

MILDRED A. JORDAN

(PSEUD. OF MILDRED JORDAN BAUSHER, 1901-1982)

A civil rights activist, editor, and author, Jordan was born in Chicago. She founded Camp Meo, a place for young mothers with special problems. Her novels include *Apple in the Attic*, *Miracle in Brittany*, and *Echo of the Flute*.

3303 *Asylum for the Queen*

Date of Publication: 1948
Subject(s): French Revolution; Royalty—France
Fictional character(s): Pierre de Michefalt, Patriot
Historical character(s): Louis XVI, Ruler (King of France); Marie Antoinette, Royalty (queen consort of Louis XVI)
Time Period(s): 1790s
Locale(s): France; Pennsylvania

Summary: This tale of the French Revolution tells the story of a plan to free Louis XVI and Marie Antoinette from imprisonment and bring them to freedom in the Pennsylvania wilderness town called Asylum. Pierre de Michefalt is the royalist patriot who intrigues against the French Republic. After the king and queen's execution, the dauphin is entrusted to his care.

Historical Accuracy: Despite the fanciful plot, the novel offers an authentic portrait of life in France and America during the period.

3304 *Echo of the Flute*

Date of Publication: 1958
Subject(s): American Colonies; American Revolution
Fictional character(s): Joshua Grunewald, Businessman; Juditha Grunewald, Spouse
Time Period(s): 18th century
Locale(s): Philadelphia, Pennsylvania

Summary: This family saga of the Grunewalds of Philadelphia chronicles the parts they play in the British occupation during the American Revolution and the effects of the yellow fever epidemic of 1793. At the center of the domestic story are the marital trials of Joshua and Judith Grunewald.

Historical Accuracy: The novel weaves a fictional story around a factual account of the period and its events.

3305 *One Red Rose Forever*

Date of Publication: 1941
Subject(s): Biography, Fictionalized; American Colonies
Historical character(s): Henry William Stiegel, Businessman (iron and glass manufacturer)
Time Period(s): 18th century
Locale(s): Pennsylvania, American Colonies

Summary: The novel is based on the life and career of German immigrant Henry William Stiegel who comes to America in 1750 and founds ironworks and glassworks in Pennsylvania. He is mostly known for the famous Stiegel glass and the first

manufacturing of flint glass in America. The novel dramatizes Stiegel's rise and fall.

Historical Accuracy: The novel combines the facts of Stiegel's life with some invented details. The details about glass-manufacturing are accurate.

NICHOLAS JOSE

3306 *The Rose Crossing*

Date of Publication: 1996
Subject(s): Civil War—England
Fictional character(s): Edward Popple, Scientist (horticulturist)
Time Period(s): 17th century
Locale(s): England; Indian Ocean

Summary: Unable to find employment at home, an English horticulturist embarks on a voyage of discovery sponsored by the Royal Society of Fellows. After a mutiny, he finds himself, with his stowaway daughter, on an island in the Indian Ocean. There they encounter a young pretender to the Chinese throne. A cultural clash ensues.

Historical Accuracy: The story is fanciful but the atmosphere of the era is convincingly evoked.

MARIE JOSEPH

English author born in Lancashire, Joseph is an accomplished short story writer. She has worked as an English civil servant. Her works are usually set in rustic northern England and attempt to portray the social history of the period. She is also the author of *One Step at a Time*, a non-fictional account of her battle against arthritis.

3307 *A Leaf in the Wind*

Date of Publication: 1982
Subject(s): Romance; Victorian Period
Fictional character(s): Jenny MaCartney, Worker (shopgirl), Servant (maid); Paul Tunstall, Gentleman, Landowner; Sarah Bleasdale, Gentlewoman
Time Period(s): 19th century
Locale(s): Lancashire, England

Summary: The romance between a wealthy landowner, Paul Tunstall, and a shopgirl, Jenny MaCartney, is dramatized. Though attracted to one another, their paths diverge: Jenny to a loveless marriage and Paul to a spoiled and selfish wife. They come together again when Jenny is engaged as a maid in Paul's household.

Historical Accuracy: This Cinderella-like romance is supported by strong regional details of Lancashire life of the period.

3308 *Maggie Craig*

Date of Publication: 1982
Subject(s): Victorian Period; Romance
Fictional character(s): Maggie Craig, Young Woman; Joe Barton, Worker

Time Period(s): 19th century (Victorian period)
Locale(s): Lancashire, England

Summary: Set in the 19th-century industrial northwest of England, the novel describes the travails of Maggie Craig, who commits the seemingly unpardonable sin of becoming pregnant by a man who cannot marry her. Maggie is forced to earn her living in the mills and suffers ostracism and the fanatical religious persecution of the times.

Historical Accuracy: The period and regional details are authentic and convincing.

ROSE JOURDAIN (1932-)

Born in Chicago, Jourdain graduated from Lake Forest College and worked as a researcher for Time, Inc. She was also a high school literature and history instructor.

3309 *Those the Sun Has Loved*

Date of Publication: 1978
Subject(s): Family Saga; American Revolution; Civil War—U.S.
Fictional character(s): Jacques Clavier, Military Personnel, Shipowner; Clay Clavier, Political Figure; Isabella Clavier, Young Woman
Time Period(s): Multiple Time Periods
Locale(s): New Bedford, Massachusetts; Charleston, South Carolina; Chicago, Illinois

Summary: The novel traces the history of an African-American family for nearly 200 years. The story begins with Jacques Clavier in New Bedford, who plays a role in assisting Washington's army during the Revolution. Succeeding generations become engaged in the later struggles of American history.

Historical Accuracy: The period background is effectively painted to create a plausible and authentic stage for the novel's drama.

CHARLES BURNET JUDAH (1902-)

Judah was a professor of government at the University of New Mexico.

3310 *Christopher Humble*

Date of Publication: 1956
Subject(s): Restoration Period; American Colonies
Fictional character(s): Christopher Humble, Adventurer; Mary Caprice, Servant (indentured)
Historical character(s): Nell Gwynne, Actress
Time Period(s): 17th century (1680s)
Locale(s): England; Virginia, American Colonies

Summary: This historical romance is set during the reign of Charles II and concerns adventurer Christopher Humble. Humble journeys from the Virginia Colonies to England and finds himself entangled with the Titus Oates plot. He must depend on the king's mistress, Nell Gwyn, for help.

Historical Accuracy: The realism of the story is undermined by a number of far-fetched historical coincidences woven around the romantic story.

CAMERON JUDD

3311 *Boone: A Novel Based on the Life and Times of Daniel Boone*

Date of Publication: 1995
Subject(s): Settlement of the American Frontier; American Colonies; Biography, Fictionalized
Historical character(s): Daniel Boone, Frontiersman
Time Period(s): 18th century (1755-1782)
Locale(s): Pennsylvania, American Colonies; Kentucky

Summary: This biographical novel traces the career of hunter, trapper, Indian fighter, and explorer Daniel Boone. He is shown possessing unmatched courage and resourcefulness and the vision that helped open up the continent as he cut the trail through the Cumberland Gap into Kentucky.

Historical Accuracy: Though the book is based on the actual experiences of Daniel Boone, the author has invented characters and plot.

3312 *The Border Men*

Date of Publication: 1992
Subject(s): American Revolution; Indians; Battle of Kings Mountain
Fictional character(s): Joshua Colter, Frontiersman; Elisha Brecht, Outlaw (renegade); Israel Coffman, Religious (itinerant preacher)
Time Period(s): 1770s; 1780s (1778-1783)
Locale(s): Tennessee

Summary: The Tennessee militia are involved in a two front war between the Cherokee and Chickamaugas, and British regulars and Tory sympathizers determined to subdue the southern colonies. The action, involving Colter and his band of patriots, culminates in the Battle of Kings Mountain.

Historical Accuracy: The novel is an authentic depiction of the period and its events.

3313 *The Canebrake Men*

Date of Publication: 1993
Subject(s): Settlement of the American Frontier; Indians
Fictional character(s): Owen Killefer, Teenager, Frontiersman; Emaline Killefer, Captive; Thomas Turndale, Military Personnel (British deserter)
Time Period(s): 1790s
Locale(s): Franklin, Tennessee

Summary: The Killefer family, settlers in the new state of Tennessee, are attacked by Chickamaugas Indians. Emaline is taken captive by renegade British ex-soldier Thomas Turndale. Her brother, Owen, sets out to rescue her.

Historical Accuracy: The details of frontier life of the period are vividly rendered.

3314 *Crockett of Tennessee: A Novel Based on the Life and Times of David Crockett*

Date of Publication: 1994

Subject(s): Settlement of the American Frontier; Biography, Fictionalized; Battle of the Alamo
Historical character(s): Davy Crockett, Frontiersman; Andrew Jackson, Political Figure; Elizabeth Crockett, Spouse
Time Period(s): 18th century; 19th century (1794-1836)
Locale(s): Tennessee; Virginia; Texas

Summary: In this novel based on the life and times of Davy Crockett, the frontiersman's career is traced from his frontier origins to his term as Congressman, and finally his achievement of legendary status at the Battle of the Alamo. The emphasis here is on a plausible rendering of the myth of Davy Crockett.

Historical Accuracy: The novel is an imaginative expansion upon the life of Davy Crockett. While adhering to the known facts, the story is supplemented by the imagined.

3315 *The Overmountain Men*

Date of Publication: 1991
Subject(s): American Colonies; Indians
Fictional character(s): Joshua Colter, Frontiersman; John Hawk, Indian (Cherokee), Warrior
Time Period(s): 18th century (1750-1777)
Locale(s): Tennessee

Summary: The novel describes the life of Joshua Colter on the Tennessee border country in the years prior to the American Revolution. Orphaned by an Indian massacre, he crosses the mountains into Tennessee where he finds himself caught in the struggle between Indians and settlers with the tensions leading up to the ensuing Revolution in the background.

Historical Accuracy: The atmosphere of wilderness life and the tensions of the period are convincingly evoked.

3316 *Passage to Natchez*

Date of Publication: 1996
Subject(s): Settlement of the American Frontier; Earthquakes; Disasters—Natural
Fictional character(s): Clardy Tyler, Frontiersman; Thias Tyler, Outlaw
Time Period(s): 18th century; 19th century (1798-1811)
Locale(s): Ohio River, United States; Mississippi River

Summary: Frontier life on the Ohio and the Mississippi is dramatized in the adventures of Clardy Tyler and his brother, Thias. The novel captures the color and the lawlessness of the frontier in a story that climaxes with the effects of the devastating New Madrid Earthquake of 1811.

Historical Accuracy: The story includes many real figures in secondary roles, and several incidents are closely based on actual events.

DENIS JUDD (1938-)

English historian and novelist Judd graduated from Oxford and Birbeck College, London. He has served as the head of the history department of the Polytechnic of North London. He is the author of numerous studies of 19th- and 20th-century topics, particularly the English royal family and events that have shaped modern England.

3317 *The Adventures of Long John Silver*

Date of Publication: 1977
Subject(s): Sea Story; Pirates
Fictional character(s): Long John Silver, Pirate; Billy Bones, Pirate; James Hawkins, Doctor
Time Period(s): 18th century
Locale(s): At Sea; West Indies

Summary: This elaboration of Robert Louis Stevenson's *Treasure Island* offers answers to a number of questions from the original story. How did Long John Silver lose his leg? Where did the treasure come from and why was it buried on Kidd's Island? And how did Billy Bones escape with the treasure map? The answers are provided by Dr. James Hawkins later in his life in this rousing recreation of the age of piracy and the great naval wars between Britain, France, and Spain.

Historical Accuracy: The novel is true to the Stevenson original and convincing in its evocation of the period.

3318 *Return to Treasure Island*

Date of Publication: 1978
Subject(s): Treasure Hunt; Pirates; American Revolution
Fictional character(s): Long John Silver, Pirate; James Hawkins, Doctor; Black Dog, Pirate
Historical character(s): Horatio Nelson, Military Personnel (naval midshipman)
Time Period(s): 18th century (1760s-1790s)
Locale(s): West Indies; Boston, Massachusetts; Valley Forge, Pennsylvania

Summary: The novel is a sequel to Robert Louis Stevenson's classic *Treasure Island* and answers the question of what happened to Long John Silver after he escaped from the *Hispaniola*. Silver returns to Kidd's Island to recover the remaining treasure. His further adventures take him to America at the time of the American Revolution where he becomes involved in a plot to murder George Washington. Eventually he returns to England during the Napoleonic Wars.

Historical Accuracy: Fanciful and inventive, the novel's period details are part of the fun.

JANE JULIAN
(PSEUD. OF DAVID WISEMAN, 1916-)

English author Julian was born in Manchester and graduated from Victoria University of Manchester. He worked as a high school teacher and principal and is the author of many adult, young adult, and juvenile novels that are set in the past.

3319 *Ellen Bray*

Date of Publication: 1985
Subject(s): Victorian Period; Mining
Fictional character(s): Ellen Bray, Young Woman
Time Period(s): 1860s; 1870s
Locale(s): Cornwall, England

Summary: On the eve of her family's departure for Australia to escape the brutal conditions of the mines of Cornwall, Ellen Bray's father and brother are killed in an explosion, leaving her on her own to survive as best she can. Her story is a struggle for independence against the background of stark labor conditions and the beginning of the struggle for women's suffrage and equality.

Historical Accuracy: The regional details are convincing and authentic.

ELLIS KADISON

Born in New Jersey, Kadison is a writer, director, and producer of more than 200 hours of television programming and 11 feature films.

3320 *The Eighth Veil*

Date of Publication: 1981
Subject(s): Roman Empire; Jews; Christianity
Fictional character(s): Daniel Bar Dineas, Revolutionary
Historical character(s): Salome, Dancer; Herod Antipas, Ruler (King of Judea); Paul, Religious; Peter, Religious; Nero, Ruler (Roman emperor); Barabbas, Revolutionary; Claudius I, Ruler (Roman emperor)
Time Period(s): 1st century (30-64)
Locale(s): Israel; Rome, Roman Empire

Summary: Set during the early years of the Christian church, the novel dramatizes the relationship between Jewish Zionist and, later, a member of the persecuted Christian sect David bar Dineas and Salome, whose dance before her stepfather King Herod results in the execution of John the Baptist. They meet first in Herod's palace and then 30 years later in Rome when Salome is married to a Roman senator and David aids the Christian leader Paul.

Historical Accuracy: The David-Salome love story is not historical, but the historical elements are faithful to the facts.

TOYOHIKO KAGAWA (1888-1960)

3321 *Behold the Man*

Date of Publication: 1941
Subject(s): Biblical Story; Biography, Fictionalized
Historical character(s): Jesus Christ, Biblical Figure; John the Baptist, Biblical Figure
Time Period(s): 1st century
Locale(s): Israel

Summary: The novel presents a fictional life of Jesus Christ beginning with the death of John the Baptist and ending a week after the Crucifixion. Based on the New Testament account, the novel fills in gaps with plausible surmises, capturing the spirit and atmosphere of the time.

Historical Accuracy: The novel is most interesting for the unusual perspective it offers. Occasionally, the novel's portraits are unconvincing and have no scriptural support.

ROBERTA KALECHOFSKY (1931-)

An American writer born in Brooklyn, New York, Kalechofsky earned her M.A. and Ph.D. from New York University. She has worked as an instructor in literature and writing and was the co-founder and general editor of Micah Publications. Her books include *George Orwell, Justice, My Brother*, and *Orestes in Progress*.

3322 *Bodin, 1349: An Epic Novel of Christians and Jews in the Plague Years*

Date of Publication: 1988
Subject(s): Middle Ages; Anti-Semitism; Plague
Fictional character(s): Will, Worker (peasant); Miriam, Outcast
Historical character(s): Edward III, Ruler (King of England)
Time Period(s): 13th century; 14th century (1260-1349)
Locale(s): England; Europe

Summary: This social portrait of medieval life concerns Will, a young peasant who flees a happy marriage when he discovers his wife, Miriam, may be a Jew. She is cast out and wanders through England and the continent in search of her true heritage. The novel offers a vivid and realistic portrait of medieval life, particularly of Christian persecutions of the Jews during the period.

Historical Accuracy: The novel is well-documented, with authentic period elements.

YVONNE KALMAN

3323 *After the Rainbow*

Date of Publication: 1989
Subject(s): English Colonies; Medical Profession
Fictional character(s): Rhys Morgan, Landowner; Daisy Morgan, Doctor; Andrew Rennie, Doctor
Time Period(s): 1850s
Locale(s): Christchurch, New Zealand

Summary: The novel continues the story of mid-19th-century New Zealand begun in *Mists of Heaven*. The marriage between Rhys Morgan and Lisabeth Rennie sends Rhys' disapproving daughter Daisy and Lisabeth's brother Andrew to Edinburgh. Daisy trains to become a doctor and returns to set up a medical practice, fighting long-standing prejudice.

Historical Accuracy: The New Zealand setting is captured with authority.

3324 *Greenstone*

Date of Publication: 1981
Subject(s): English Colonies; Frontier—New Zealand
Fictional character(s): Juliette Peridot, Young Woman; Evangeline Peridot, Settler
Time Period(s): 19th century (1837-1861)
Locale(s): New Zealand

Summary: The novel depicts life in the harsh wilderness of New Zealand during the 19th century, describing three decades of New Zealand's history in the story of Juliette Peridot. Her childhood ends when her mother, Evangeline, and her four siblings are murdered. Juliette embarks on a campaign to avenge the slaughter and is led into even greater torment.

Historical Accuracy: The scenes of New Zealand life during the period are convincing.

3325 *Mists of Heaven*

Date of Publication: 1987
Subject(s): English Colonies; Frontier—New Zealand; Coming of Age
Fictional character(s): Lisabeth Rennie, Settler, Orphan; Charles Stafford, Settler; Gwynne Stafford, Spouse
Time Period(s): 1850s
Locale(s): New Zealand

Summary: Pioneer life in mid-19th-century New Zealand is depicted in the coming-of-age story of Lisabeth Rennie, who upon the death of her mother is left to care for her infant brother. Taken in by the Staffords, they move to the South Island to start a new life. For Lisabeth the past proves to be a bitter legacy from which she gradually emerges.

Historical Accuracy: The novel is a convincing record of New Zealand pioneer life.

JEANNE KALOGRIDIS

3326 *Children of the Vampire: The Diaries of the Family Dracul*

Date of Publication: 1995
Subject(s): Vampires; Victorian Period; Myths and Legends
Fictional character(s): Arkady Tsepesh, Vampire; Prince Vlad Tsepesh, Royalty (prince), Vampire (aka Dracula); Abraham Van Helsing, Scientist, Vampire Hunter
Time Period(s): 19th century (1845-1872)
Locale(s): Amsterdam, Netherlands; Transylvania

Summary: This second volume in a trilogy exploring the Dracula legend opens 25 years before the start of Bram Stoker's novel. Arkady Tsepesh, now a vampire, attempts to prevent Prince Vlad Tsepesh, also known as Dracula, from claiming his son. Arkady enlists the help of Abraham Van Helsing to battle Vlad.

Historical Accuracy: The novel provides a convincing sense of place and atmosphere in recreating the Dracula legend.

3327 *Covenant with the Vampire: The Diaries of the Family Dracul*

Date of Publication: 1994
Subject(s): Vampires; Supernatural; Family Saga
Fictional character(s): Prince Vlad Tsepesh, Royalty, Vampire; Arkady Tsepesh, Gentleman; Mary Windham Tsepesh, Gentlewoman
Time Period(s): 1840s
Locale(s): Transylvania

Summary: Beginning 50 years before the start of Bram Stoker's novel, this story introduces Dracula's family, who

are bound to protect and serve him. The novel centers on the prince's great-nephew Arkady and his family, who come to manage the prince's estate. Arkady soon learns to his horror how else he must serve his relative.

Historical Accuracy: The novel is convincing in producing both the atmosphere of Gothic horror and the time and place of 19th-century Transylvania.

3328 *Lord of the Vampires: The Diaries of the Family Dracul*

Date of Publication: 1996
Subject(s): Vampires; Supernatural
Fictional character(s): Prince Vlad Tsepesh, Royalty, Vampire (aka Dracula); Abraham Van Helsing, Scientist, Vampire Hunter
Time Period(s): 1890s
Locale(s): Transylvania

Summary: The novel brings to a conclusion a trilogy that forms a prequel to and elaboration of Bram Stoker's *Dracula*. Events in this novel, which overlap with those in Stoker's book, provide some answers to the ambiguity of Stoker's text as the story moves to its climax and the final confrontation with Dracula.

Historical Accuracy: The novel blends fiction, history, and legend into a convincing story that is faithful to the Stoker original and considerably elaborates the original in provocative ways.

LAURA KALPAKIAN (1945-)

An American writer born in California, Kalpakian attended the University of California, Riverside, and the University of Delaware. She has worked as a clerk, a social worker, and an instructor of English and humanities at Lincoln University in Pennsylvania. She won *Stand* magazine's international short fiction competition in 1983 for "Veteran's Day." Her books include *Beggars and Choosers*, *Stand I*, and *Tiger Hill*.

3329 *Cosette: The Sequel to Les Miserables*

Date of Publication: 1995
Subject(s): Revolution of 1848
Fictional character(s): Cosette, Revolutionary, Orphan; Marius Pontmercy, Revolutionary; Jean Valjean, Criminal, Fugitive
Time Period(s): 19th century (1832-1867)
Locale(s): Paris, France

Summary: In the sequel to Victor Hugo's masterpiece *Les Miserables*, the story of Cosette, the adopted daughter of Jean Valjean, is continued through the period of the revolutionary 1830s and 1840s and into the decadent Second Empire of Louis-Napoleon. Cosette marries Marius Pontmercy, and together they publish a radical newspaper, a rallying cry for the social struggle that topples the monarchy. When the Republic is overthrown, Cosette goes into hiding, living among ragpickers' hovels and brothels.

Historical Accuracy: The novel uses an authentic period background and actual events as catalysts for the story.

3330 *These Latter Days*

Date of Publication: 1985
Subject(s): Family Saga; Mormons; American West
Fictional character(s): Ruth Douglass, Spouse; Samuel Douglass, Farmer; Lucius Tipton, Doctor
Time Period(s): 19th century; 20th century (1890s-1940s)
Locale(s): Idaho; California

Summary: This family saga of three generations of Mormons centers on the experiences of Ruth Douglass, born into genteel Salt Lake City society. She marries Samuel Douglass and endures life on the frontier of Idaho. When her husband goes mad, she moves her family to California to start a new life and passes the legacy of faith and struggle on to her children.

Historical Accuracy: The novel effectively captures the pioneer scene and the Mormon customs of the time.

STUART M. KAMINSKY (1934-)

An American writer born in Chicago, Kaminsky received degrees from the University of Illinois and Northwestern. He is a professor of speech and head of Radio/Television/Film at Northwestern. His mysteries set in 1940s Hollywood display his remarkable knowledge of trivia about the period. Kaminsky is also a biographer of Clint Eastwood and John Huston.

3331 *Bullet for a Star*

Date of Publication: 1977
Subject(s): Mystery; Motion Picture Industry
Fictional character(s): Toby Peters, Detective—Private; Sheldon Minck, Dentist
Historical character(s): Errol Flynn, Actor
Time Period(s): 1940s (1940)
Locale(s): Hollywood, California

Summary: In 1940 there is trouble at the Warner Brothers Studio. The studio's biggest star, Errol Flynn, is being blackmailed. Hollywood private detective Toby Peters is called in to protect Flynn in this nostalgic comic mystery set during the golden age of Hollywood and the hard-boiled private eye.

Historical Accuracy: This funny send-up of the hard-boiled mystery is filled with authentic period touches.

3332 *Buried Caesars*

Date of Publication: 1989
Subject(s): Mystery; World War II
Fictional character(s): Toby Peters, Detective—Private
Historical character(s): Douglas MacArthur, Military Personnel (general); Dashiell Hammett, Writer
Time Period(s): 1940s (1942)
Locale(s): Hollywood, California

Summary: Hollywood private detective Toby Peters is hired by General Douglas MacArthur to find one of his aides who has absconded with private papers that will wreck the general's political aspirations. Peters is joined by ex-Pinkerton operative and writer Dashiell Hammett in a journey into a dangerous world of hoods and conspiracy.

Historical Accuracy: Any resemblance to the historical is to be found in the details, not the events or the personalities.

3333 *Catch a Falling Star*

Date of Publication: 1981
Subject(s): Mystery; Circus Life
Fictional character(s): Toby Peters, Detective—Private; Sheldon Minck, Dentist; Jeremy Butler, Sports Figure (wrestler)
Historical character(s): Emmett Kelly, Entertainer (circus clown); Alfred Hitchcock, Director
Time Period(s): 1940s
Locale(s): Mirador, California

Summary: Trouble under the big top causes the famous circus clown Emmett Kelly to call in Toby Peters, private detective. Peters disguises himself as a clown to avoid the local marshall, and finds himself locked in a cage with a gorilla and handcuffed to the snake charmer and her snake.

Historical Accuracy: This is a humorous send-up of the hard-boiled detective novel with convincing period details.

3334 *Dancing in the Dark*

Date of Publication: 1996
Subject(s): Mystery; World War II; Motion Picture Industry
Fictional character(s): Toby Peters, Detective—Private; Arthur Forbes, Organized Crime Figure; Luna Martin, Dancer
Historical character(s): Fred Astaire, Actor, Dancer; Betty Grable, Actress; Rita Hayworth, Actress
Time Period(s): 1940s (1943)
Locale(s): Hollywood, California

Summary: Hollywood private eye Toby Peters is hired by Fred Astaire to protect him from the unwanted attentions of an ex-mobster and his moll who wants to become a dancer. Peters soon is on the trail of a killer while dancing himself onscreen with the likes of Rita Hayworth and Betty Grable.

Historical Accuracy: The novel is knowledgeable and believable in its period details and insider's look at the movie business.

3335 *The Devil Met a Lady*

Date of Publication: 1993
Subject(s): Mystery; World War II; Espionage
Fictional character(s): Toby Peters, Detective—Private
Historical character(s): Bette Davis, Actress
Time Period(s): 1940s (1943)
Locale(s): Hollywood, California

Summary: An attempted kidnapping of Bette Davis is connected to a wider Nazi plot to steal American plans for a top-secret bomber. Detective Toby Peters is hired to stop the Nazis and to keep the movie star out of danger. Peters penetrates the Nazi spy ring and the secrets of Hollywood during wartime.

Historical Accuracy: The atmosphere of the period is carefully and convincingly presented.

3336 *Down for the Count*

Date of Publication: 1985

Subject(s): Mystery; Sports; Boxing

Fictional character(s): Toby Peters, Detective—Private; Sheldon Minck, Dentist; Jeremy Butler, Sports Figure (wrestler)

Historical character(s): Joe Louis, Sports Figure (boxer)

Time Period(s): 1940s

Locale(s): Los Angeles, California

Summary: Detective Toby Peters finds his ex-wife's husband murdered on a deserted beach with boxing champion Joe Louis standing guiltily over the body. Toby agrees to investigate and protect the champ from the police and the press, and he finds himself deeply entangled in a boxing scam.

Historical Accuracy: Clever and funny, the novel is exact in capturing the period details.

3337 *The Fala Factor*

Date of Publication: 1984

Subject(s): Mystery; World War II

Fictional character(s): Toby Peters, Detective—Private; Sheldon Minck, Dentist; Jeremy Butler, Sports Figure (wrestler)

Historical character(s): Eleanor Roosevelt, Spouse (of the president); Buster Keaton, Actor

Time Period(s): 1940s (1942)

Locale(s): Los Angeles, California

Summary: Private detective Toby Peters is called in to assist First Lady Eleanor Roosevelt in 1942 when she is convinced that FDR's prized scottie Fala has been kidnapped and replaced by an imposter. Peters searches for Fala across a bizarre wartime Los Angeles.

Historical Accuracy: The novel is filled with authentic sights and sounds of the period, even if the story is comically absurd.

3338 *He Done Her Wrong*

Date of Publication: 1983

Subject(s): Mystery; Motion Picture Industry; World War II

Fictional character(s): Toby Peters, Detective—Private; Sheldon Minck, Dentist

Historical character(s): Mae West, Actress; Cecil B. DeMille, Director

Time Period(s): 1940s (1942)

Locale(s): Hollywood, California

Summary: Hollywood detective Toby Peters is hired by Mae West to track down her only copy of a tell-all autobiography that has been stolen. The trail of the actress' memoirs leads Peters into the middle of a family feud and a California sanitorium from which he must remove himself. The climax of the chase takes place at a war bonds party hosted by Cecil B. De Mille.

Historical Accuracy: The novel is filled with convincing period details.

3339 *High Midnight*

Date of Publication: 1981

Subject(s): Mystery; World War II

Fictional character(s): Toby Peters, Detective—Private

Historical character(s): Gary Cooper, Actor; Ernest Hemingway, Writer

Time Period(s): 1940s (1942)

Locale(s): Hollywood, California

Summary: Hollywood detective Toby Peters is hired by actor Gary Cooper to investigate blackmail, but Peters ends up investigating murder. Cooper and writer Ernest Hemingway find themselves under attack, and it takes Peters to save the day.

Historical Accuracy: More nostalgic than historical, the fun comes from an unusual, though by no means realistic, conjunction of figures and a firm sense of the period.

3340 *The Howard Hughes Affair*

Date of Publication: 1979

Subject(s): Mystery; Motion Picture Industry

Fictional character(s): Toby Peters, Detective—Private

Historical character(s): Howard Hughes, Financier; Basil Rathbone, Actor; Benjamin Siegel, Organized Crime Figure (aka Bugsy Siegel); Bertold Brecht, Writer (playwright)

Time Period(s): 1940s

Locale(s): Los Angeles, California

Summary: Hollywood detective Toby Peters is hired by Howard Hughes to investigate a bizarre series of unexplained circumstances. Unsavory characters are bent on stopping Peters, and Basil Rathbone is on hand to offer Sherlock Holmsian assistance.

Historical Accuracy: Comical and inventive, the mystery features a convincing picture of the period, even as the circumstances veer toward the ridiculous.

3341 *The Man Who Shot Lewis Vance*

Date of Publication: 1986

Subject(s): Mystery; Motion Picture Industry

Fictional character(s): Toby Peters, Detective—Private; Sheldon Minck, Dentist

Historical character(s): John Wayne, Actor; Charlie Chaplin, Actor

Time Period(s): 1940s (1942)

Locale(s): Los Angeles, California

Summary: Hollywood private eye Toby Peters finds himself in a Los Angeles hotel room beside a corpse, and John Wayne pointing a .38 revolver at him. It seems that someone has tried to involve Wayne in a scandal. Another corpse and attempts on Wayne's life widen the case and the challenge for Peters.

Historical Accuracy: The novel is filled with convincing period details.

3342 *The Melting Clock*

Date of Publication: 1991

Subject(s): Mystery; World War II; Artistic Life

Fictional character(s): Toby Peters, Detective—Private

Historical character(s): Salvador Dali, Artist

Time Period(s): 1940s (1942)

Locale(s): Los Angeles, California

Summary: In this case for Hollywood detective Toby Peters, he is hired by surrealist painter Savaldor Dali. Three of Dali's paintings have been stolen. Although Dali initially arranged for the theft as part of a publicity stunt, he wanted only two to disappear. If the third is seen by the public, the scandal could wreck Dali's career. Peters takes the case, which escalates into a series of mysterious murders.

Historical Accuracy: The implausibility is part of the fun here. The author is convincing in creating a sense of time and place.

3343   *Murder on the Yellow Brick Road*

Date of Publication: 1977
Subject(s): Mystery; Motion Picture Industry
Fictional character(s): Toby Peters, Detective—Private
Historical character(s): Judy Garland, Actress; Louis B. Mayer, Businessman (studio head); Clark Gable, Actor; Raymond Chandler, Writer
Time Period(s): 1940s (1940)
Locale(s): Hollywood, California

Summary: Hollywood in the 1940s is the setting for this burlesque of the private eye thriller. Detective Toby Peters is hired by Louis B. Mayer to investigate the murder of a Munchkin on the set of *The Wizard of Oz*. A plot is uncovered that threatens the life of young Judy Garland. Clark Gable and writer Raymond Chandler are on hand to assist in the detection.

Historical Accuracy: More absurdist than historical, the mystery is adept in capturing the period flavor.

3344   *Never Cross a Vampire*

Date of Publication: 1980
Subject(s): Mystery; Motion Picture Industry
Fictional character(s): Toby Peters, Detective—Private
Historical character(s): William Faulkner, Writer; Bela Lugosi, Actor; Boris Karloff, Actor
Time Period(s): 1940s (1942)
Locale(s): Hollywood, California

Summary: In the Hollywood of 1942, private detective Toby Peters takes on a case to clear Hollywood screenwriter William Faulkner of the murder of a literary agent. Meanwhile, Bela Lugosi has been receiving death threats. Both cases are ingeniously tied together.

Historical Accuracy: The mystery features convincing period details.

3345   *Poor Butterfly*

Date of Publication: 1990
Subject(s): Mystery; Musical Life; World War II
Fictional character(s): Toby Peters, Detective—Private; Jeremy Butler, Sports Figure (wrestler)
Historical character(s): Leopold Stokowski, Conductor
Time Period(s): 1940s (1942)
Locale(s): San Francisco, California

Summary: In 1942, in the midst of the Japanese scare, Leopold Stokowski decides to reopen the San Francisco Opera House with a new production of Puccini's *Madame Butterfly*, a decision that raises a storm of protest from the anti-Japanese faction. When a workman on the production falls from a scaffold and a series of death threats are received, Stokowski sends for Toby Peters to insure that the production goes forward.

Historical Accuracy: The novel is sharp and knowing in the period details and the atmosphere of the era.

3346   *Smart Moves*

Date of Publication: 1986
Subject(s): Mystery; World War II
Fictional character(s): Toby Peters, Detective—Private; Sheldon Minck, Dentist
Historical character(s): Albert Einstein, Scientist; Paul Robeson, Actor
Time Period(s): 1940s
Locale(s): New York, New York

Summary: Private detective Toby Peters is in New York to find a Nazi assasination sq uad that is trying to kill Albert Einstein and brand him as a traitor. Peters' path also crosses that of Paul Robeson who is appearing on stage in *Othello* .

Historical Accuracy: The story is implausible but fun, filled with clever period touches.

3347   *Think Fast, Mr. Peters*

Date of Publication: 1987
Subject(s): Mystery; Motion Picture Industry
Fictional character(s): Toby Peters, Detective—Private; Sheldon Minck, Dentist
Historical character(s): Peter Lorre, Actor
Time Period(s): 1940s (1942)
Locale(s): Hollywood, California

Summary: Hollywood detective Toby Peters is asked by his office partner, dentist Sheldon Minck, to find his wife, who has supposedly run away with actor Peter Lorre. When a Peter Lorre imitator is found killed, Peters is under suspicion, and he must find the killer, Mrs. Minck, and the real Peter Lorre.

Historical Accuracy: The novel is an amusing romp with authentic period details.

3348   *Tomorrow Is Another Day*

Date of Publication: 1995
Subject(s): Mystery; Motion Picture Industry
Fictional character(s): Toby Peters, Detective—Private
Historical character(s): Clark Gable, Actor
Time Period(s): 1930s (1938); 1940s (1943)
Locale(s): Hollywood, California; Los Angeles, California

Summary: The background for this Toby Peters vintage mystery is the filming of the burning of Atlanta on the set of *Gone with the Wind*. Peters is providing security, and when an extra is found dead, he notices Clark Gable showing an unusual interest in the corpse. Five years later, Peters encounters Gable again. This time the star is receiving death threats from someone killing people who were on the set in 1938.

Historical Accuracy: The mystery is clever and dependent on a sense of the period and its style.

▌3349 *You Bet Your Life*

Date of Publication: 1978
Subject(s): Mystery; Crime and Criminals
Fictional character(s): Toby Peters, Detective—Private
Historical character(s): Ian Fleming, Writer; Groucho Marx, Actor; Chico Marx, Actor; Al Capone, Organized Crime Figure; Richard Daley, Political Figure; Frank Nitti, Organized Crime Figure
Time Period(s): 1940s (1941)
Locale(s): Chicago, Illinois

Summary: Hollywood gum-shoe Toby Peters is called to Chicago in 1941 to help Chico Marx deal with a huge gambling debt to the mob. He is assisted by the unlikely group of Al Capone, Ian Fleming, and Richard Daley.

Historical Accuracy: The mystery is filled with period touches that capture the era with brio.

CAROL J. KANE (1952-)

▌3350 *Blood and Sable*

Date of Publication: 1988
Subject(s): Russian Revolution; Russian Empire
Fictional character(s): Anya Sidirov, Royalty (princess); Oleg Ivanov, Revolutionary; Adam Lowell, Widow(er), Diplomat
Time Period(s): 1910s
Locale(s): Petrograd, Russia

Summary: In this romantic tale set during the final days of the Russian aristocracy, Princess Anya Sidirov encounters the antagonistic Oleg Ivanov, a peasant who grows up to become a Bolshevik. When the Revolution comes, Anya and her husband, Adam Lowell, a Bostonian attached to the American legation, flee across the border to Finland trying to avoid the murderous Ivanov.

Historical Accuracy: The novel features an authentic period background.

HARNETT T. KANE (1910-1984)

Born in New Orleans, Kane was a journalist and author who concentrated on the experiences of the American South. He was educated at Tulane and was a frequent contributer of articles to *Reader's Digest*, *National Geographic*, and *Saturday Review*. Kane's books include *Louisana Hayride*, *Plantation Parade*, and *Natchez on the Mississippi*.

▌3351 *The Amazing Mrs. Bonaparte*

Date of Publication: 1963
Subject(s): Napoleonic Era
Historical character(s): Elizabeth Patterson, Spouse (of Jerome Bonaparte); Jerome Bonaparte, Royalty (younger brother of Napoleon); Napoleon Bonaparte, Ruler (Emperor of France); Arthur Wellesley, Military Personnel (English army commander), Nobleman (Duke of Wellington); Thomas Jefferson, Political Figure
Time Period(s): 19th century (1803-1829)
Locale(s): Baltimore, Maryland; Europe

Summary: This historical love story tells the implausible but true story of Betsy Patterson of Baltimore who meets, falls in love with, and marries Jerome Bonaparte, the youngest brother of the French emperor. Napoleon orders Jerome to return to France alone, and Betsy does not see her husband again, except for a fleeting glimpse years later with his new wife.

Historical Accuracy: The documentation is scrupulous, and the presentation is accurate and convincing.

▌3352 *Bride of Fortune*

Date of Publication: 1948
Subject(s): Civil War—U.S.; Biography, Fictionalized
Historical character(s): Varina Howell Davis, Spouse; Jefferson Davis, Political Figure (President of the Confederacy)
Time Period(s): 19th century (1843-1867)
Locale(s): Natchez, Mississippi; Washington, District of Columbia; Richmond, Virginia

Summary: The novel offers a fictionalized biography of Varina Howell Davis, the wife of Confederate president Jefferson Davis. She comes from a wealthy cotton planter family in Mississippi. She marries Davis and accompanies him to Washington and then to Richmond as the first lady of the Confederacy. She emerges out of the tall shadow of her enigmatic husband as a devoted and determined wife with an amazing strength under adversity.

Historical Accuracy: The author's list of sources is impressive, evidence of much research and the novel's factual basis.

▌3353 *The Gallant Mrs. Stonewall*

Date of Publication: 1957
Subject(s): Civil War—U.S.; Biography, Fictionalized
Historical character(s): Anna Morrison Jackson, Spouse; Thomas Jonathan Jackson, Military Personnel (Confederate officer)
Time Period(s): 1850s; 1860s (1853-1863)
Locale(s): Virginia

Summary: The married life of Anna and Thomas Jackson is described from her first meeting with the obscure soldier-professor until his tragic death, shot by his own troops after the great victory at Chancellorsville. Anna Jackson emerges as a strong and devoted supporter of her husband's considerable military genius.

Historical Accuracy: The novel is carefully researched and therefore credible in its version of the Jacksons' story.

▌3354 *The Lady of Arlington*

Date of Publication: 1953
Subject(s): Civil War—U.S.; Biography, Fictionalized
Historical character(s): Mary Custis Lee, Spouse (of Robert E. Lee); Robert E. Lee, Military Personnel (Confederate officer); Jefferson Davis, Political Figure; Varina Howell Davis, Spouse (of Jefferson Davis)
Time Period(s): 19th century (1840s-1870)
Locale(s): Arlington, Virginia; Richmond, Virginia

Summary: The novel offers a portrait of a marriage through the life of Mary Custis, wife of Robert E. Lee. When she accepts Lee, he is a lieutenant with scant prospects. Her devotion to him is strong from the start and continues through the great trials of the Civil War.

Historical Accuracy: The extensive bibliography and list of sources are evidence of the factual basis of the author's story.

3355 *New Orleans Woman: A Biographical Novel of Myra Clark Gaines*

Date of Publication: 1946
Subject(s): Biography, Fictionalized; Antebellum South
Historical character(s): Myra Clark Gaines, Heiress
Time Period(s): 19th century
Locale(s): New Orleans, Louisiana

Summary: In 1833, Myra Clark Gaines brings suit to establish her identity as the daughter of wealthy David Clark. The suit is not resolved until 1885, shortly before her death, when the Supreme Court finds in her favor. The novel offers a portrait of the unconventional Mrs. Gaines as well as a look at period New Orleans.

Historical Accuracy: The novel provides a faithful presentation of the Gaines case, as well as a meticulous re-creation of the period atmosphere.

3356 *Pathway to the Stars*

Date of Publication: 1950
Subject(s): Antebellum South; Slavery; Biography, Fictionalized
Historical character(s): John McDonogh, Landowner
Time Period(s): 1840s
Locale(s): New Orleans, Louisiana

Summary: This biographical novel describes the amazing career of John McDonogh, a Baltimore youth who journeys to New Orleans to make his fortune in the 19th century. He becomes one of the greatest landowners of the South. He reverses a reputation for harshness and sternness by mounting an innovative plan for slaves to earn their freedom and by endowing the public school system of Louisiana.

Historical Accuracy: The novel is based on a review of the extensive letters and record of McDonogh. The author uses this material advantagously, accurately capturing the man and the period.

3357 *The Smiling Rebel*

Date of Publication: 1955
Subject(s): Civil War—U.S.; Espionage
Historical character(s): Belle Boyd, Spy; Jefferson Davis, Political Figure; Thomas Jonathan Jackson, Military Personnel (Confederate officer)
Time Period(s): 1860s (Civil War period)
Locale(s): Virginia

Summary: This is the story of Belle Boyd, the Civil War's most glamorous spy. She begins her career at 17 when she shoots a Union soldier trying to raise the Union flag over her family's home. She soon turns to espionage, working for Stonewall Jackson and, though betrayed and imprisoned, she continues to captivate soldiers on both sides.

Historical Accuracy: The novel is largely based on eyewitness accounts of Boyd's exploits from contemporaries.

HARRIET KANE

ALBERT PERRY

3358 *The Scandalous Mrs. Blackford*

Date of Publication: 1951
Subject(s): Royalty—Russia; Russian Empire; Franco-Prussian War
Historical character(s): Harriet Blackford, Gentlewoman
Time Period(s): 1870s; 1880s
Locale(s): Paris, France; St. Petersburg, Russia

Summary: The love affair between an American minister's daughter, Harriet Blackford, and the Grand Duke Nicholas of Russia becomes a *cause celebre* in the 19th century. The novel is based on an actual scandal.

Historical Accuracy: The facts are based on information discovered by a Russian scholar, and the story is convincing.

MACKINLAY KANTOR (1904-1977)

An American novelist born in Iowa and educated in schools in Illinois and Iowa, Kantor was a reporter on various newspapers in Iowa and worked as a scenario writer for motion pictures. He was a war correspondent in Europe during World War II. He won an O. Henry Award in 1935 for "Silent Grow the Guns," and a Pulitzer Prize in 1956 for *Andersonville*. He ranks as one of the most respected historical novelists for his thorough research and realism.

3359 *Andersonville*

Date of Publication: 1954
Subject(s): Civil War—U.S.; Prisoners of War
Fictional character(s): Ira Claffey, Landowner; Harrell Elkins, Doctor; Eben Dolliver, Military Personnel (Union soldier), Prisoner
Historical character(s): John H. Winder, Military Personnel (Confederate general); Henry Wirz, Military Personnel (Confederate captain)
Time Period(s): 1860s (1863-1865)
Locale(s): Sumter County, Georgia

Summary: In 1863 the infamous Andersonville prison was built to house Union prisoners of war for the duration of the war. With little food or sanitation, the prisoners survived as best they could. Their stories, sufficient for a number of novels, fill in this canvas of heroism and survival.

Historical Accuracy: The novel can be credited as one of the most carefully documented and comprehensive books on the Civil War.

3360 *Arouse and Beware*

Date of Publication: 1936
Subject(s): Civil War—U.S.; Prisoners of War
Fictional character(s): Oliver Clark, Military Personnel (Union soldier); Prentiss Barlow, Military Personnel (Union soldier); Naomi, Fugitive
Time Period(s): 1860s (1864)
Locale(s): Belle Isle, Virginia

Summary: Two Union prisoners of war escape from Richmond's Belle Isle Prison in 1864. On the hazardous journey back to the Union lines along the Rapidan River they encounter a woman who is also fleeing from Richmond, and they make the journey together.

Historical Accuracy: The author's depiction of place and time is authentic.

3361 *Beauty Beast*

Date of Publication: 1968
Subject(s): Antebellum South; Slavery
Fictional character(s): Sidney Shallop, Plantation Owner; Beauty Beast, Slave
Time Period(s): 1850
Locale(s): Gulf Coast, United States

Summary: This portrait of slavery in the Antebellum South describes events at Apoxsee, a plantation on the Gulf Coast. Its owner, Sidney Shallop, acquires a male slave named Beauty Beast, and their relationship reveals the peculiar workings of the institution of slavery.

Historical Accuracy: The novel provides a penetrating and authentic insight into the atmosphere of the Antebellum South.

3362 *Long Remember*

Date of Publication: 1934
Subject(s): Civil War—U.S.; Battle of Gettysburg
Fictional character(s): Daniel Bale, Farmer; Tyler Fanning, Military Personnel (Union soldier); Adam Duffey, Doctor
Time Period(s): 1860s (1863)
Locale(s): Gettysburg, Pennsylvania

Summary: The novel constructs the scene of life in Gettysburg, Pennsylvania, on the first day of the decisive battle of the Civil War. Small town life is suddenly transformed as the town and surrounding countryside become a battlefield and two great armies collide. The human cost on the mostly civilian cast of characters is explored.

Historical Accuracy: The interesting angle of vision on the events is shaped by a careful and believable detailing of the actual.

3363 *Spirit Lake*

Date of Publication: 1961
Subject(s): Settlement of the American Frontier; Indians
Fictional character(s): Corn-Sucker, Indian; Rowland Gardner, Settler
Time Period(s): 1840s; 1850s
Locale(s): Iowa

Summary: The novel is set in Iowa in the 1850s and concerns the settlement of the frontier and the clash with the Indians that culminate in the Spirit Lake massacre in 1857. This huge novel populates the Iowa scene with a rich cross-section of settlers and Indians to create a sense of the entire community of the period.

Historical Accuracy: Although some of the characters and incidents are based on fact, most of the story is invented.

3364 *Valley Forge*

Date of Publication: 1975
Subject(s): American Revolution; Military Life
Historical character(s): George Washington, Military Personnel (army commander); Martha Washington, Spouse; Marie Joseph Paul de Lafayette, Nobleman (Marquis de Lafayette), Military Personnel (French general); Friedrich von Steuben, Military Personnel (Prussian general), Nobleman
Time Period(s): 1770s (1777-1778)
Locale(s): Valley Forge, Pennsylvania

Summary: This is a sweeping panorama of the American Revolution chronicling the terrible winter of 1777-1778 in which the American army struggled to survive at Valley Forge. They would emerge from the ordeal tested and resolute. The novel captures the scene from its commanders to its ordinary soldiers.

Historical Accuracy: Scrupulously documented, the novel blends fact and fiction in a comprehensive and authentic elaboration of the event and the period. This is a model of achievement for the historical novel.

BARRY JAY KAPLAN

3365 *Biscayne*

Date of Publication: 1988
Subject(s): Business Building; Family Saga
Fictional character(s): Clara Reade, Widow(er); Quentin McLeod, Sea Captain; F. Morrison Wheeler, Businessman
Time Period(s): 20th century
Locale(s): Miami, Florida

Summary: The novel details the growth of Miami, Florida, from a small frontier village in the early years of the 20th century to a great city. Clara Reade is a young widow from the Midwest who comes south and has a vision of the future. Her determination to see it fulfilled is shared with two men, a sea captain and a railroad mogul.

Historical Accuracy: The period and the region are captured with authenticity.

WALTER KARIG (1898-1956)

HORACE BIRD

An American writer born in New York City, Karig worked for the Newark *Evening News* and was the book editor for Washington's *Post* and *Time-Herald*. His books include *The Fortunate Islands*, *Zotz!*, and *Caroline Hicks*.

3366 *Don't Tread on Me*

Date of Publication: 1954
Subject(s): Sea Story; American Revolution; American Colonies
Fictional character(s): Manesseh Fisher, Military Personnel (midshipman)
Historical character(s): John Paul Jones, Military Personnel (naval captain)
Time Period(s): 1770s; 1780s (1773-1780s)
Locale(s): Martha's Vineyard, Massachusetts; *Bonhomme Richard*, At Sea

Summary: Narrated by midshipman Manesseh Fisher, the novel celebrates the exploits of John Paul Jones. Jones becomes captain of his first ship at age 20, and during the Revolution he bests the vaunted British navy from the capture of Nassau early in the Revolution to the epic victory over the *Serapis*.

Historical Accuracy: The framework of the story is factual, but there are some speculations and surmises.

PHYLLIS ANN KARR (1944-)

Born in Oakland, California, Phyllis Ann Karr attended Colorado State University and Indiana University. She has worked as a librarian and sales clerk for an antiquarian bookseller. She is the author of a column, "Thoughts from Oakapple Place," and the books *At Amberleaf Fair*, *The King Arthur Companion*, and *Wildraith's Last Battle*.

3367 *The Idylls of the Queen*

Date of Publication: 1982
Subject(s): Mystery; Dark Ages; Arthurian Legends
Fictional character(s): Sir Kay, Knight; Guenevere, Royalty (queen); Sir Gawaine, Knight
Time Period(s): 5th century
Locale(s): England

Summary: This mystery novel is set in the court world of Camelot. When one of the knights of the Round Table is poisoned, Sir Kay investigates as suspicion falls on Queen Guenevere.

Historical Accuracy: The novel shows an intimacy with the Arthurian legend that produces an effective and believable recreation.

JEAN KARSAVINA (1908-)

Born in Poland, Karsavina emigrated to the United States as a child. English is her fourth language, and she was educated at Smith College and Barnard. A magazine writer and a faculty member at NYU, she has published many children's books and is also the composer of opera librettos.

3368 *White Eagle, Dark Skies*

Date of Publication: 1974
Subject(s): Russian Empire; Independence—Poland
Fictional character(s): Adam Fabian, Revolutionary, Businessman; Wanda Borowska, Young Woman, Revolutionary

Time Period(s): 1890s; 1900s (1890-1905)
Locale(s): Warsaw, Poland

Summary: Poland under the iron rule of Russia at the turn of the century is the novel's subject. The story focuses on Adam Fabian, a young revolutionary. In order to become a successful businessman, he sacrifices his socialist convictions. The atmosphere of Tsarist repression, bread riots, and social life in Warsaw is vividly captured.

Historical Accuracy: The author drew on her family history for her story and modeled her central character on her father.

ELIZABETH KATA

An Australian of Scottish parents, Kata married into a Japanese family and lived for many years in Tokyo. Her first novel, *A Patch of Blue*, has been translated into nine languages and made into an award-winning film.

3369 *Kagami*

Date of Publication: 1992
Subject(s): Japanese Empire; Family Saga; Disasters—Natural
Fictional character(s): Kenichi Yamamoto, Scholar; Lady Masa, Spouse (of Kenichi); Renzo Yamamoto, Diplomat
Time Period(s): 19th century; 20th century (1850s-1923)
Locale(s): Japan

Summary: The novel is set in Japan after the arrival of Commodore Perry's ships in 1853 and the opening of Japan to the West. It tells the tale of three families caught in the turmoil that challenged traditional Japanese society. The scholar Yamamoto, his wife, the Lady Masa, and their son, Renzo, form the novel's domestic center in scenes set during the war with Russia, the First World War, and the great earthquake of 1923.

Historical Accuracy: The historical events that form the novel's core are accurately described, as are the Japanese customs.

FRED S. KAUFMAN (1902-)

3370 *Custer Passed Our Way*

Date of Publication: 1971
Subject(s): Indians; American West; Battle of the Little Bighorn
Historical character(s): George Armstrong Custer, Military Personnel (cavalry officer)
Time Period(s): 1870s (1873-1876)
Locale(s): Dakota Territory, United States; Little Bighorn River, Montana

Summary: This documentary novel assembles a great deal of information about the 7th cavalry in the Dakota Territory in the years leading up to the Battle of the Little Bighorn. Based on the diary kept by the author's father, a homesteader and government surveyor during Dakota Territorial days, the novel reconstructs the background for Custer's last stand.

Historical Accuracy: The novel is faithful to the events of history, as the novel's notes and documentation make clear.

PAMELA KAUFMAN

3371 *Banners of Gold*

Date of Publication: 1986
Subject(s): Middle Ages; Royalty—England
Fictional character(s): Alix of Wanthwaite, Gentlewoman, Adventurer; Bonel, Courtier (minister to Richard I); Robin Hood, Outlaw
Historical character(s): Richard the Lionhearted, Ruler (King of England); John, Royalty (prince); Eleanor of Aquitaine, Royalty (queen consort of Henry II); Henry Hohenstaufen, Ruler (Holy Roman Emperor); Leopold, Duke of Austria, Nobleman
Time Period(s): 12th century (1190s)
Locale(s): England; Germany; France

Summary: Alix of Wanthwaite, the young heroine of *Shield of Three Lions*, returns to assist Richard the Lionhearted, who is being held hostage. She finds herself at the center of intrigues to release Richard and then to restore him to power. The novel features an interesting portrait of Eleanor of Aquitaine and a cameo appearance by Robin Hood.

Historical Accuracy: Kaufman offers a fanciful speculation about the last decade of the 12th century. Some of her methods (reconstructing Eleanor's appearance through modern knowledge of dominant and recessive genes, for example) seem more a justification for her imagination than the solid recreation of historical characters and events.

3372 *Shield of Three Lions*

Date of Publication: 1983
Subject(s): Middle Ages; Crusades; Royalty—England
Fictional character(s): Alix of Wanthwaite, Orphan, Heiress—Dispossessed; Enoch Angus Boggs, Adventurer
Historical character(s): Richard the Lionhearted, Ruler (King of England)
Time Period(s): 12th century (1189)
Locale(s): England; Europe (France, Italy, Cyprus); Palestine

Summary: The novel is a fanciful tale of a young woman who is violently orphaned and goes to France disguised as a boy to seek help from Richard the Lionhearted. She is accompanied by a Scotsman bound for the Crusades. Richard takes the ''boy'' Alix on as his page and falls in love with him. They journey to Palestine, and Alix falls in love with her Scottish companion.

Historical Accuracy: There are good period details here bolstering this romantic adventure, more invented than reconstructed.

REBECCA KAVALER (1932-)

Born in Georgia, Kavaler graduated from the University of Georgia and worked as a freelance and science writer for the *Medical World News*.

3373 *Doubting Castle*

Date of Publication: 1984
Subject(s): Gothic Romance; Victorian Period

Fictional character(s): Ada Traherne, Student (medical)
Time Period(s): 1880s (1888)
Locale(s): England

Summary: Called a ''feminist gothic,'' the novel is set in 1888 as Ada Traherne is unjustly expelled from medical school. She travels to her father's home determined to clear up the mystery that seems to envelop him. The novel is replete with hidden staircases, suicide, and love affairs, all the ingredients of the conventional gothic, but featuring a most unorthodox heroine.

Historical Accuracy: The novel injects a modern sensibility into the period setting.

SUSAN KAY (1952-)

British author Kay is a graduate of Mather College of Education and has worked as a teacher in Manchester, England. *Legacy* received the Historical Novel Prize in memory of Georgette Heyer and the Betty Trask Prize from the Society of Authors.

3374 *Legacy*

Date of Publication: 1985
Subject(s): Elizabethan Period; Royalty—England
Historical character(s): Elizabeth I, Ruler (Queen of England); Robert Dudley, Nobleman (Earl of Leicester); William Cecil, Nobleman (Lord Burghley), Courtier; Robert Devereux, Nobleman (Earl of Essex); Sir Francis Walsingham, Government Official; Mary I, Ruler (Queen of England); Philip II, Ruler (King of Spain)
Time Period(s): 16th century; 17th century
Locale(s): England

Summary: The novel describes the remarkable career and reign of Elizabeth I. Elizabeth survives an uncertain childhood as the daughter of the fallen Anne Boleyn. On reaching the throne, Elizabeth establishes herself as an adroit wielder of political power. The novel captures all the intrigue of Elizabeth's reign while creating an intimate and astute portrait of the queen.

Historical Accuracy: Based on solid research, the novel offers a convincing portrait of the age and its leading figures.

3375 *Phantom*

Date of Publication: 1991
Subject(s): Theatrical Life; Gypsies
Fictional character(s): Erik, Handicapped (disfigured); Christine Daae, Singer
Time Period(s): 19th century (1831-1897)
Locale(s): Rome, Italy; Tehran, Persia; Paris, France

Summary: The novel tells the story of Erik, who is destined to become the Phantom of the Opera. The author places Gaston Leroux's 1911 story into a historical context, depicting Erik's life in a gypsy carnival sideshow, the court of the Shah of Persia, and the depths of the Paris Opera House.

Historical Accuracy: The novel offers a plausible historical context for the legendary figure of the Phantom.

M.M. KAYE (1908-)

An English author born in Simla, India, Kaye is a writer and a painter. An authority on India and its past, Kaye achieved an international success with *The Far Pavilions*. She has also authored children's books under the name of Mollie Kaye.

3376 *The Far Pavilions*

Date of Publication: 1978
Subject(s): British Raj; English Colonies
Fictional character(s): Ashton Pelham-Martyn, Military Personnel (British army officer); Anjuli, Royalty (Indian princess)
Time Period(s): 19th century
Locale(s): India; Afghanistan

Summary: Orphaned as a very young child, Ashton Pelham-Martyn spends his early years believing himself to be Indian and working as a servant in a rajah's palace. There he befriends Princess Anjuli, the lonely, neglected daughter of his master. Eventually, court intrigues force him to flee to the British, his own people. Years later he returns to India as a British army officer. His understanding of and sympathy for the Indians make him a controversial figure among his fellow officers. Assigned to escort two royal brides to their wedding, Ash is stunned when one of the women turns out to be his old childhood companion, Anjuli, with whom he falls in love. Ash and Juli are forced to choose between love and duty in this sweeping saga of life in India under the British Raj.

Historical Accuracy: The novel's romance and adventure are set against a realistic and convincing background of 19th-century India.

3377 *Shadow of the Moon*

Date of Publication: 1957
Subject(s): English Colonies; Indian Mutiny; British Raj
Fictional character(s): Alex Randall, Military Personnel (captain); Winter de Ballasteros, Gentlewoman; Conway Barton, Government Official (commissioner)
Time Period(s): 1850s (1857)
Locale(s): Lunjore, India; Delhi, India

Summary: The terrible events of the Indian Sepoy Mutiny of 1857 are reflected in the personal drama of Captain Alex Randall of the East India Company. He escorts young Winter de Ballasteros to India to wed the commissioner of Lunjore, Conway Barton, who is only interested in acquiring her fortune. They are soon swept up in the bloody revolution.

Historical Accuracy: The historical framework for the invented story is accurate and convincing.

3378 *Trade Wind*

Date of Publication: 1963
Subject(s): Slavery; Victorian Period
Fictional character(s): Hero Hollis, Young Woman; Rory Frost, Trader (slave)
Time Period(s): 1860s
Locale(s): Zanzibar

Summary: Set on the East African island of Zanzibar in the 19th century, the novel tells the story of Hero Hollis, niece of the American consul, who is rescued by a renegade English slaver, Rory Frost. Hero is subsequently torn between her loyalty to her family and her attraction to Frost as the island is swept by revolution and cholera.

Historical Accuracy: The events of the story are based on historical fact, but the author admits to having taken some liberties in compressing them into only one year.

SHEILA KAYE-SMITH (1887-1956)

Born in Sussex, England, Kaye-Smith published her first book before she was 21. She has written plays, short stories, ballad poems, a critical study of Jane Austen, and an autobiography, *Three Ways Home*. *Little England*, *Green Apple Harvest*, and *Joanna Godden* are considered her finest books.

3379 *Superstition Corner*

Date of Publication: 1934
Subject(s): Elizabethan Period; Religious Conflict
Fictional character(s): Catharine Alard, Gentlewoman
Time Period(s): 16th century (1588)
Locale(s): Sussex, England

Summary: The persecution of Catholics in Elizabethan England is the novel's subject. As the invasion by Catholic Spain seems imminent in 1588, persecution of England's Catholics grows. The novel tells the story of the Alard family, particularly young Catharine Alard. Called ''galloping Kate,'' she is a headstrong, quick-witted tomboy fervently devoted to her Catholic faith.

Historical Accuracy: The novel features a convincing evocation of the Elizabethan period and the conflicts of the times.

ELIA KAZAN (1899-)

Born in Turkey, Kazan emigrated to America at the age of four. He is a graduate of Williams College. Kazan directed four Pulitzer Prize-winning plays, including *Death of a Salesman*. He won Academy Awards for his films *Gentleman's Agreement* and *On the Waterfront*. Kazan has had one of the most distinguished careers on Broadway and in Hollywood.

3380 *America, America*

Date of Publication: 1962
Subject(s): Immigrants; Family Saga
Fictional character(s): Stavros Topouzoglou, Immigrant; Taomna Sinyosoglou, Young Woman
Time Period(s): 1890s
Locale(s): Anatolia, Turkey; New York, New York

Summary: The novel tells the story of Stavros, a 20-year-old immigrant from Anatolia, who is determined to succeed in America. He arrives in New York, and through an iron will he begins to make his way against tough odds. Stavros learns the facts of his new American life, but finally he is torn by homesickness and the cost of his monomaniacal drive.

Historical Accuracy: The scenes of immigrant life are captured convincingly.

3381 *The Anatolian*

Date of Publication: 1982
Subject(s): Immigrants; Family Saga
Fictional character(s): Stavros Topouzoglou, Immigrant; Althea Perry, Young Woman; Fernand Sarafian, Businessman
Time Period(s): 1900s; 1910s (1909-1919)
Locale(s): New York, New York

Summary: The author continues the story of young Greek Stavros Topouzoglou begun in *America America*. Stavros has met his family obligations by bringing his family to America. He finds himself in a battle between the familial duties of the old life and the promise and possibilities of America in early 20th-century New York.

Historical Accuracy: The period details create a plausible backdrop for this family saga.

3382 *Beyond the Aegean*

Date of Publication: 1994
Subject(s): Greco-Turkish War
Fictional character(s): Stavros Topouzoglou, Businessman, Immigrant; Thomna, Heroine
Historical character(s): Constantine I, Ruler (King of the Hellenes); Hadjianestis, Military Personnel (general)
Time Period(s): 1910s; 1920s (1919-1922)
Locale(s): Anatolia, Turkey; Smyrna, Turkey

Summary: The historical context of Kazan's novel is the ill-fated Greek campaign to reclaim Anatolia from Turkey in the 1920s. Stavros Topouzoglou has returned to Anatolia determined to create a life there. Instead he is caught up in the war, the betrayal of Greece's allies, and the racial hatred of the Turks.

Historical Accuracy: The history is effectively delivered but the central character is somewhat too limited to contain all the issues raised.

NIKOS KAZANTZAKIS (1883-1957)

A Greek novelist, playwright, and translator, Kazantzakis is one of the most important and controversial writers in 20th-century Greek literature. Born in Crete, he held various positions in the Greek government, including director general in the Ministry of Public Welfare, minister of state, and minister of national education. His novel *Zorba the Greek* brought him world acclaim and *The Last Temptation of Christ* produced a storm of controversy. All of Kazantzakis' works explore the conflict between man's physical, emotional, and spiritual values.

3383 *Freedom or Death*

Date of Publication: 1956
Subject(s): Revolution—Greece
Fictional character(s): Captain Michales, Revolutionary; Captain Polyxigis, Revolutionary; Emine, Young Woman
Time Period(s): 1880s (1889)

Locale(s): Crete, Greece

Summary: This is a story of an unsuccessful uprising of the Cretans against their Turkish rulers. Michales is the monomaniacal Cretan leader who risks all, even his life, for his devotion to Cretan independence. His tragic fall is shown in strong scenes of devotion to a cause and the progressive exclusion of all other human considerations.

Historical Accuracy: The novel is a vivid and authentic representation of a violent period in Cretan history and a tragic drama of a Cretan fighter.

3384 *The Last Temptation of Christ*

Date of Publication: 1960
Subject(s): Biblical Story
Historical character(s): Jesus Christ, Biblical Figure; Mary, Biblical Figure; Joseph, Biblical Figure; Mary Magdalene, Biblical Figure; Herod Antipas, Ruler (King of the Jews); Pontius Pilate, Government Official (Roman procurator); John the Baptist, Biblical Figure; Judas Iscariot, Biblical Figure; Lazarus, Biblical Figure
Time Period(s): 1st century
Locale(s): Israel

Summary: In this attempt to humanize the life of Jesus, the author offers an interpretation not of a confident Son of God with a prearranged plan, but a hesitant man who, to serve God, conspires with Judas to arrange his own execution. The details do not always parallel those in the Bible. Perhaps the most controversial suggestion is the treatment of Mary Magdalene, Jesus' greatest temptation, and the presentation of Lazarus, restored to life but not to health.

Historical Accuracy: The novel deviates from the Biblical narrative, but it does offer a very human interpretation of the familiar story.

3385 *Saint Francis*

Date of Publication: 1962
Subject(s): Religious Life; Middle Ages
Fictional character(s): Brother Leo, Religious (monk)
Historical character(s): Francis of Assisi, Religious (monk)
Time Period(s): 13th century
Locale(s): Assisi, Italy; Rome, Italy; Egypt

Summary: In this fictional account of St. Francis of Assisi, he struggles to gain sanctity of spirit through intensifying asceticism. This is a sympathetic account, not a psychological study of Francis' self-punishment. It celebrates his triumph of spirit and essential holiness. The narrative is from the perspective of Brother Leo, one of Francis' closest disciples, who chronicles their journeys.

Historical Accuracy: The novel is more an article of faith than a historical account.

JAMES KEENE

3386 *Justice, My Brother*

Date of Publication: 1957
Subject(s): American West; Ranching

Fictional character(s): Cord O'Dare, Rancher; Henry ''Smoke'' O'Dare, Cowboy
Time Period(s): 1900s (1903)
Locale(s): Cherokee Strip, Oklahoma

Summary: This novel is a study in family loyalties in the fight between ranchers and farmers during the 1900s in Oklahoma. The O'Dares build a thriving cattle ranch in the Cherokee Strip, but when a farmer is murdered, young Smoke O'Dare is torn·between his sense of justice and family allegiance.

Historical Accuracy: The novel captures the scene and the period with care.

CLARENCE BUDINGTON KELLAND
(1881-1964)

An American journalist, short story writer, novelist, and public relations executive, Kelland was born in Portland, Michigan, and worked as a reporter for the *Detroit News*, editor of *American Boy*, and lecturer at the University of Michigan. While at *American Boy*, Kelland published the popular Mark Tidd series as well as several other juvenile writings. Kelland began writing fiction for adults in 1921 with perhaps his most popular work being *Scattergood Baines*. Among his numerous other books are *The Great Crooner*, *Valley of the Sun*, *Stolen Goods*, and *Mark of Treachery*.

3387 *Arizona*

Date of Publication: 1939
Subject(s): American West; Civil War—U.S.; Business Building
Fictional character(s): Phoebe Titus, Young Woman, Baker; Peter Muncie, Frontiersman
Time Period(s): 1860s
Locale(s): Tucson, Arizona

Summary: This story of frontier life is set in Tucson, Arizona, during the years of the Civil War. It centers on the entrepreneurial spirit of young Phoebe Titus, who, unable to continue on to California, sets herself up in frontier Tucson selling pies and later managing a growing business.

Historical Accuracy: The novel provides a believable and realistic depiction of the region and the period.

3388 *Gold*

Date of Publication: 1931
Subject(s): Business Building; Railroads
Fictional character(s): Anneke Van Horn, Banker
Time Period(s): 1860s; 1870s
Locale(s): New York, New York

Summary: In the sequel to *Hard Money* and the second volume in the author's history of economic development in the U.S., the background for the novel is the struggle for control of the burgeoning railroad industry. Anneke Van Horn takes over her father's financial business and proves herself equally adept at speculation.

Historical Accuracy: Occasional anachronisms of tone mar the believability in the historical atmosphere.

3389 *Hard Money*

Date of Publication: 1930
Subject(s): Business Building
Fictional character(s): Jan Van Horn, Banker
Time Period(s): 19th century
Locale(s): New York, New York

Summary: In the first of a series of novels tracing the economic development of the U.S., Jan Van Horn, son of a Dutch peddler, arrives in New York intent on making his fortune. He is able to become one of the most powerful bankers of the period.

Historical Accuracy: The novel is an amalgam of factual elements and fictional invention, more romance than documentary history.

3390 *The Jealous House*

Date of Publication: 1934
Subject(s): Family Saga; Politics; Business Building
Fictional character(s): Jan Van Horn, Businessman
Time Period(s): 19th century; 20th century (1870s-1914)
Locale(s): New York, New York

Summary: This novel brings to a conclusion the author's chronicle of the Van Horn family. The story covers a 40 year period in the history of New York from the 1870s to the beginning of World War I. The central character is Jan Van Horn, whose struggles in business and love are dramatized.

Historical Accuracy: The novel does not create enough believable portraits of the characters or the times to be credible.

FAYE KELLERMAN (1952-)

Born in St. Louis, Kellerman graduated from UCLA. She is trained as a dentist and has worked as an independent investor and real estate manager. She has written mysteries that deal with ''gut level issues'' like life, death, murder, and deception.

3391 *The Quality of Mercy*

Date of Publication: 1989
Subject(s): Mystery; Elizabethan Period; Religious Conflict
Fictional character(s): Rebecca Lopez, Young Woman
Historical character(s): William Shakespeare, Writer, Actor
Time Period(s): 16th century (1593)
Locale(s): London, England; Spain

Summary: In parallel plots, William Shakespeare investigates the murder of a fellow actor, while Jews in England attempt to smuggle Jews out of Spain to escape the Inquisition. Rebecca Lopez is a *conversa*, a secret Jew posing as a Protestant. She escapes her home in search of romance and adventure and meets the young playwright Shakespeare. Together they venture to Spain to gain the release of Jews.

Historical Accuracy: The story is fictional, but the background and the Elizabethan customs are authentic.

WELBOURN KELLEY

3392 *Alabama Empire*
Date of Publication: 1957
Subject(s): Medical Profession; Indians
Fictional character(s): John Adam Fyfe, Doctor
Historical character(s): George Washington, Political Figure; William Augustus Bowles, Political Figure
Time Period(s): 1780s; 1790s (1789-1793)
Locale(s): New York, New York; Litte Tallasee, Alabama; Philadelphia, Pennsylvania

Summary: This novel of the early years of the new American republic is seen through the perspective of Dr. John Adam Fyfe, a Scottish doctor, who is sent to the Creek Nation as President Washington's emissary. The territory is claimed by the Spanish and the British as well as by the ambitious William Augustus Bowles, who is intent on creating an independent Alabama Empire.

Historical Accuracy: The novel's historical background is believable, but romance predominates.

ESTHER KELLNER (1909-1942)
Born in Indiana, Kellner won the Indiana University Novel Award in 1956 for *The Promise*. Her other books include *Mary of Nazareth*, *The Bride of Pilate*, and *The Devil and Aunt Serena*.

3393 *The Bride of Pilate*
Date of Publication: 1959
Subject(s): Biblical Story; Roman Empire
Fictional character(s): Claudia, Spouse (of Pilate); Decimus, Outlaw, Pirate
Historical character(s): Pontius Pilate, Government Official
Time Period(s): 1st century
Locale(s): Rome, Roman Empire; Jerusalem, Israel

Summary: Legend has it that the wife of Pontius Pilate was Claudia, a granddaughter of Augustus, who became the first woman to follow Christ. The novel dramatizes this legend, telling the story of Claudia's childhood exile, her return to Rome, her relationship with the outlaw Decimus, and her marriage to the ambitious Pontius Pilate. In Judea, Claudia is eventually drawn to the teachings of Jesus.

Historical Accuracy: The truthfulness of the novel's story resides primarily in its detailed portrayal of Roman life in the first century.

3394 *Mary of Nazareth*
Date of Publication: 1958
Subject(s): Biblical Story
Historical character(s): Mary, Biblical Figure; Jesus Christ, Biblical Figure
Time Period(s): 1st century
Locale(s): Israel

Summary: The story of Jesus is narrated from the perspective of his mother, Mary. The novel offers a version of Mary's thoughts and actions during the life of Jesus.

Historical Accuracy: This is a reverential blending of New Testament history and modern-day language.

3395 *The Promise*
Date of Publication: 1956
Subject(s): Biblical Story
Historical character(s): Abraham, Biblical Figure; Sarah, Biblical Figure
Time Period(s): Indeterminate Past
Locale(s): Ur, Mesopotamia; Middle East

Summary: The story of Abraham and Sarah is dramatized, including their years together in Ur, their long journey to Canaan, and the promise by God of many descendants and the creation of a great nation. Sarah's strength and determination justify her reputation as one of the great women in ancient times.

Historical Accuracy: The novel is particularly strong in capturing a believable sense of the customs and daily life of the period.

SUSANNAH KELLS

3396 *A Crowning Mercy*
Date of Publication: 1983
Subject(s): Civil War—England; Puritans
Fictional character(s): Dorcas Slythe, Young Woman; Toby Lazender, Young Man
Time Period(s): 17th century (1643)
Locale(s): London, England

Summary: The English Civil War is depicted from the perspective of a young Puritan woman, Dorcas Slythe, who yearns for escape from her dour father. Her deliverance comes when she is surprised by Toby Lazender, who dubs her "Campion." Her adventure begins with the discovery of a gold seal, one of four that will redeem a great treasure. The seal will subject her to peril, treachery, and captivity, and finally redemption and love.

Historical Accuracy: The period backdrop is authentic, even if the main emphasis here is romantic adventure.

3397 *The Fallen Angels*
Date of Publication: 1984
Subject(s): French Revolution; Suspense
Fictional character(s): Lady Campion Lazender, Noblewoman; Gitan, Gypsy
Time Period(s): 1790s
Locale(s): France; England

Summary: This suspenseful tale revolves around the efforts of Lady Campion Lazender to protect her fortune from the Fallen Angels, a secret society that attempts to spread the revolution across the channel into England. Lady Lazender is forced to turn to the enigmatic gypsy Gitan for aid.

Historical Accuracy: The novel features a believable portrait of the era of the French Revolution.

CARLA KELLY (1947-)

Born in Florida and a graduate of Brigham Young University, Kelly has worked as a park ranger and historian at the Fort Laramie National Historical Site. She began writing historical novels to correct the erroneous notions most tourists have about life in the West.

3398 *Daughter of Fortune*

Date of Publication: 1985
Subject(s): American West; Indians; Pueblo Revolt
Fictional character(s): Maria Espinosa, Orphan; Diego Masferrer, Rancher; Cristobal Masferrer, Rancher
Time Period(s): 17th century (1680)
Locale(s): Santa Fe, New Mexico

Summary: Set during the Pueblo Uprising of 1680 in Spanish New Mexico, the novel tells the story of Maria Espinosa, who travels to Santa Fe and survives a massacre by a band of Apaches. She is taken in by rancher Diego Masferrer. She is torn between her love for him and his half-Indian brother, Cristobal.

Historical Accuracy: The historical background for the story is factual.

ELEANOR KELLY

3399 *Richard Walden's Wife*

Date of Publication: 1950
Subject(s): Civil War—U.S.
Fictional character(s): Richard Walden, Settler; Aurora Walden, Spouse
Time Period(s): 19th century
Locale(s): Wisconsin

Summary: Set before and during the Civil War, the novel describes pioneer life in Wisconsin. The story focuses on the Waldens—Richard and Aurora—who come west from Maryland. The novel explores the tension between husband and wife as Aurora attempts to remain faithful to her southern background and while her husband has Union sympathies.

Historical Accuracy: Historical events are glimpsed only in passing, with the emphasis on the family drama. Period and regional atmosphere are convincing.

ERIC KELLY (1884-1960)

Born in Amesbury, Massachusetts, and educated at Dartmouth, Kelly worked as a journalist and English professor. He was active in several Polish organizations and wrote several books, including a life of Helen Modjeska.

3400 *Three Sides of Agiochook*

Date of Publication: 1935
Subject(s): American Revolution; American Colonies; Indians
Fictional character(s): Philip Brewster, Student—College
Historical character(s): Joseph Brant, Indian (Mohawk), Chieftain
Time Period(s): 1770s (1775)

Locale(s): Connecticut Valley, American Colonies

Summary: The novel describes the adventures of a young Dartmouth College student who agrees to carry a message from the President of Dartmouth to Indian leader Joseph Brant. The fate of the Connecticut Valley, which is threatened by Indian attacks, hangs in the balance.

Historical Accuracy: The framework of the story is real events and characters, mixed with a fictional tale.

JACK KELLY (1949-)

Kelly is the author of *Apalachin* and *Protection*.

3401 *Mad Dog*

Date of Publication: 1992
Subject(s): Depression Era; Crime and Criminals
Historical character(s): John Dillinger, Outlaw; Baby Face Nelson, Outlaw
Time Period(s): 1930s (1934)
Locale(s): Michigan; Chicago, Illinois

Summary: The story of John Dillinger, Public Enemy Number One, is reflected in the experiences of a small-time grifter who is mistaken one night for the famous outlaw. He starts a carnival show impersonating Dillinger and celebrating his exploits. The novel effectively brings to life the era of the Great Depression and its celebrity-criminals.

Historical Accuracy: The novel effectively and convincingly creates a believable period background.

ELMER KELTON (1926-)

An American born in Texas, Kelton received his B.A. degree from the University of Texas. He has worked as a farm and ranch editor for periodicals. He traces his interest in the Western from growing up around cowboys who talked about the good old days. His novels have been praised for their originality and avoidance of stereotypes. Kelton is one of the best of a new breed of western writers who are reshaping the genre.

3402 *Dark Thicket*

Date of Publication: 1985
Subject(s): Civil War—U.S.; American West
Fictional character(s): Owen Danford, Veteran (Confederate soldier); Phineas Shattuck, Military Personnel (Confederate home guard)
Time Period(s): 1860s
Locale(s): Texas

Summary: Owen Danford, a wounded Confederate soldier, returns home to Texas to find a community divided between Union loyalists and secessionist home guards. His loyalty is divided between the Confederate cause and his family, a conflict that is finally resolved by joining a band of Union guerillas.

Historical Accuracy: This rarely depicted aspect of the Civil War is captured with authentic details of the period.

3403 *The Day the Cowboys Quit*

Date of Publication: 1971
Subject(s): American West; Labor Movement; Ranching
Fictional character(s): Hugh Hitchcock, Cowboy; Rascal Mc-Ginty, Cowboy; Charlie Wade, Cowboy
Time Period(s): 1880s (1883)
Locale(s): Panhandle, Texas

Summary: The novel depicts a changing western scene in the 1880s when the wide-open frontier began to be fenced in, and the independence of the cowboy was challenged by a new ethic from the East. Hugh Hitchcock and his fellow cowboys participate in what comes to be known as the Canadian River Strike of 1883.

Historical Accuracy: The basis of the story is factual. The issues and the atmosphere are captured with skill.

3404 *The Far Canyon*

Date of Publication: 1994
Subject(s): American West; Cattle Drives; Ranching
Fictional character(s): Jeff Layne, Veteran (Confederate soldier), Rancher; Vesper Freed, Rancher; Crow Feather, Indian (Comanche), Warrior
Time Period(s): 1870s (1874)
Locale(s): Piedras, Texas

Summary: Jeff Layne, the young Confederate veteran and buffalo hunter of *Slaughter*, heads home to southern Texas to take up ranching. He finds, however, a fierce border war being waged between dispossessed Mexican ranchers and his longtime enemy, carpetbagger Vesper Freed. Jeff's goal, if he survives, is to drive his cattle north to a distant canyon remembered from his buffalo-hunting days.

Historical Accuracy: The novel captures, with skill, the time and the place.

3405 *The Good Old Boys*

Date of Publication: 1978
Subject(s): American West
Fictional character(s): Hewey Calloway, Cowboy; Spring Renfro, Young Woman
Time Period(s): 1900s (1906)
Locale(s): Texas

Summary: The closing of the American frontier is dramatized in the story of Hewey Calloway, a free-spirited cowboy who is torn between his freedom and increasing responsibilities and the implications of love. The West is changing, and Hewey must forge a sense of self as part of the new times.

Historical Accuracy: The time and place are evoked with skill and conviction.

3406 *The Pumpkin Rollers*

Date of Publication: 1996
Subject(s): American West; Cattle Drives; Coming of Age
Fictional character(s): Trey McLean, Rancher; Ivan Kerbow, Cowboy; Sarah Stark, Young Woman; Jarrett Longacre, Outlaw
Time Period(s): 1860s
Locale(s): Texas

Summary: The title refers to the term given to farmers who attempt to become ranchers, and this coming of age story describes the adventures of Trey McLean who leaves his family's East Texas cotton farm to take up ranching. He is cheated by a con man, meets the woman he is to marry, and sets out on a cattle drive to Kansas, plagued by the outlaw Jarrett Longacre.

Historical Accuracy: The novel presents an authentic portrait of ranching and cowboy life during the period.

3407 *Slaughter*

Date of Publication: 1992
Subject(s): American West; Indians
Fictional character(s): Crow Feather, Indian (Comanche), Warrior; Jeff Layne, Veteran (Confederate soldier)
Time Period(s): 1860s (post Civil War)
Locale(s): Texas

Summary: Jeff Layne, a young Confederate veteran, leads a party of hide hunters into Comanche Territory. There he will face Crow Feather, a Comanche warrior, who realizes that the encroaching whites threaten his tribe's existence by rapidly exterminating the buffalo.

Historical Accuracy: The locale and the period are sharply realized in appropriate background details.

3408 *The Wolf and the Buffalo*

Date of Publication: 1980
Subject(s): American West; Indians; Military Life—U.S. Cavalry
Fictional character(s): Grey Horse Running, Indian (Comanche), Warrior; Gideon Ledbetter, Military Personnel (cavalry soldier)
Time Period(s): 19th century (post Civil War)
Locale(s): Texas

Summary: This western story depicts the black cavalrymen known as, Buffalo Soldiers, ex-slaves who served on the American frontier as a buffer between the Indians and white settlers. The novel describes the violent confrontation between a young Comanche warrior, Grey Horse, and a soldier, Gideon Ledbetter.

Historical Accuracy: The depiction of the frontier is authentic and genuine.

BAYNARD KENDRICK (1894-)

Born in Philadelphia, Kendrick is best known for his mystery novels featuring the blind detective Duncan Maclain, who was based on a friend blinded in World War I. His expertise on blindness caused him to be asked to serve as a consultant on the training of blind veterans by the U.S. Army during World War II.

3409 *The Flames of Time*

Date of Publication: 1948
Subject(s): Spanish Colonies; Indians

Fictional character(s): Artillery Armes, Orphan; Dan Mc-Ketch, Outlaw; Ezekiel Buckhart, Outlaw
Time Period(s): 18th century; 19th century (1787-1812)
Locale(s): Florida (northern)

Summary: The setting is northern Florida under Spanish possession. Artillery Armes is an orphan raised by outlaws. Armes lives with the Indians and when his mentor, Dan McKetch, is betrayed by the Spaniards, he participates in the fighting that eventually joins Florida to the United States.

Historical Accuracy: The extensive research is clearly evident and lends this adventure story a sense of authenticity.

THOMAS KENEALLY (1935-)

Keneally is an Australian novelist whose impressive range has allowed him to produce novels with such diverse settings as an 18th-century penal colony, the American Civil War, and a World War II medical unit in Yugoslavia. Keneally's most famous work, *Schindler's List*, sparked controversy over whether the work should be regarded as nonfiction or fiction.

3410 *Bring Larks and Heroes*

Date of Publication: 1968
Subject(s): Crime and Criminals; Penal Colonies
Fictional character(s): Halloran, Military Personnel (corporal); Ann Rush, Young Woman
Time Period(s): 18th century
Locale(s): Pacific Ocean

Summary: Set in a South Pacific penal colony suggested by Sydney, Australia, in the late 18th century, the novel follows the career of Corporal Halloran who must deal with both his superior officers and his own conscience. The drama culminates in a violent prisoners' revolt.

Historical Accuracy: The novel blends fiction and fact to create a vivid picture of penal colony life.

3411 *The Chant of Jimmie Blacksmith*

Date of Publication: 1972
Subject(s): Governor's Rebellion; Aborigines; Racial Conflict
Fictional character(s): Jimmie Blacksmith, Worker; Gilda Blacksmith, Heroine; Mort, Worker
Time Period(s): 1900s (1900)
Locale(s): Breelong, Australia; New South Wales, Australia

Summary: Keneally re-creates the historical event of the so-called Governor's Rebellion. In 1900 an aborigine named Jimmie Governor took revenge for injuries inflicted by his employers and insults directed at his white wife. Keneally offers a penetrating study of racial conflict in the Australia of the time as his Jimmie Blacksmith is driven to madness, caught between his obsolete aboriginal ancestry and the white culture that excludes him.

Historical Accuracy: Keneally is sharply insightful in rendering the psychological and social background for this tragic story of racial hatred.

3412 *Confederates*

Date of Publication: 1979
Subject(s): Civil War—U.S.; Battle of Antietam
Fictional character(s): Usaph Bumpass, Military Personnel; Ephephtha Bumpass, Heroine; Dora Whipple, Spy, Widow(er)
Historical character(s): Thomas Jonathan Jackson, Military Personnel (general); James Longstreet, Military Personnel (general)
Time Period(s): 1860s (1862)
Locale(s): Virginia

Summary: The southern perspective of the Civil War is dramatized through the concurrent stories of four people: a member of the Stonewall Brigade, his wife, a southern widow who is also a Yankee spy, and a British journalist. The novel includes a strong portrait of Stonewall Jackson, and the military action culminates in the battle of Antietam.

Historical Accuracy: Keneally justifies the term epic in this novel's sweep of history and the personalities of the period. That Keneally is an Australian telling this preeminently American story is a testament to his imagination.

3413 *Gossip From the Forest*

Date of Publication: 1975
Subject(s): World War I; Politics
Fictional character(s): Matthias Erzberger, Diplomat
Historical character(s): Ferdinand Foch, Military Personnel (French commander); Maxime Weygard, Diplomat; Admiral Wemyss, Military Personnel
Time Period(s): 1910s (1918)
Locale(s): Compeigne, France

Summary: In November, 1918, Marshall Foch leads an Allied delegation to force the Germans to accept the crushing terms of the armistice. They meet in a train car in the forest of Compeigne, and the novel describes the meeting and its clash of cultures and motives that produces the end of World War I. Foch attempts to extract revenge, Admiral Wemyss tries to insure British naval sovereignty, and German diplomat Erzburger struggles to preserve his nation.

Historical Accuracy: This is a brilliant re-construction of the historical scene, based on fact and illuminated by an insightful sense of the period and personalities.

3414 *The Playmaker*

Date of Publication: 1987
Subject(s): Crime and Criminals; Penal Colonies; Frontier—Australia
Fictional character(s): Mary Brennan, Convict
Historical character(s): Ralph Clark, Military Personnel
Time Period(s): 1780s (1789)
Locale(s): New South Wales, Australia

Summary: The novel dramatizes an actual historical event: the production of the play *The Recruiting Officer* by a cast of convicts in the penal colony of New South Wales in 1789. The director is Ralph Clark, an officer of the Royal Marines. He, like his actors, must adjust to the demands of the new continent and the change that it brings about.

Historical Accuracy: The novel re-creates the early days of Australia through the personalities of its first citizens: convicts and their overseers.

3415 *A River Town*

Date of Publication: 1995
Subject(s): Frontier—Australia; Victorian Period
Fictional character(s): Tom Shea, Store Owner; Kitty Shea, Spouse; Bandy Habash, Herbalist
Time Period(s): 1890s (1899)
Locale(s): Kempsey, Australia (on the Macleay River)

Summary: The scene is an isolated town hundreds of miles north of Sydney in 1899. Tom Shea is a well intentioned shopkeeper who finds himself in conflict with the town leaders as English and Irish settlers define their community at the end of the Victorian period.

Historical Accuracy: The locale is masterfully and believable created.

3416 *Schindler's List*

Date of Publication: 1982
Subject(s): World War II; Holocaust; Jews
Historical character(s): Oskar Schindler, Businessman
Time Period(s): 1930s; 1940s (1939-1945)
Locale(s): Cracow, Poland

Summary: Keneally dramatizes the story of Oskar Schindler, a German industrialist who rescues thousands of Jews from extermination by creating in Cracow, Poland, a factory to shelter them. His story, based on the testimony of Schindler's survivors, details Schindler's negotiations with the Nazis and his moral courage in the midst of unspeakable horror and inhumanity.

Historical Accuracy: Based on eyewitness testimony, the novel brings to life an important episode in the war.

3417 *Victim of the Aurora*

Date of Publication:
Subject(s): Polar Exploration; Mystery
Fictional character(s): Eugene Stewart, Explorer; Victor Henneker, Journalist, Writer; Paul Gabriel, Scientist
Time Period(s): 1910s (1910)
Locale(s): Antarctica

Summary: In 1910 Captain Stewart and his 25-man team mount an expedition to the South Pole. During a blizzard, one of the company is savagely murdered. The story then combines polar adventure with the solution of a murder mystery. Both reveal the psychological depths of men pushed to the limit of their endurance.

Historical Accuracy: The author masterfully re-creates the details of polar exploration and the period.

JOHN P. KENNEDY (1795-1870)

Kennedy was an American writer and politician who was elected to Congress in 1838. He served as secretary of the navy and assisted William Makepeace Thackeray during his

visit to America with the regional details Thackeray later used in *The Virginians*.

3418 *Horseshoe Robinson, a Tale of the Tory Ascendancy*

Date of Publication: 1835
Subject(s): American Revolution; American Colonies
Fictional character(s): Horseshoe Robinson, Military Personnel, Blacksmith; Arthur Butler, Military Personnel; Mildrid Lindsay, Gentlewoman (loyalist's daughter)
Historical character(s): Charles Cornwallis, Military Personnel (British general)
Time Period(s): 1780s
Locale(s): North Carolina, American Colonies; South Carolina, American Colonies

Summary: The novel describes the effects of the American Revolution on the people of the Carolinas as if it were a civil war between patriots and loyalists. Major Butler, in love with the daughter of a loyalist, is betrayed by rebels secretly loyal to the British cause. The novel's climax takes place at the Battle of Kings Mountain.

Historical Accuracy: This tale is remarkably free from sentimentality and patriotic idealization, rendering a good depiction of a region divided.

LUCY KENNEDY

3419 *Mr. Audubon's Lucy*

Date of Publication: 1957
Subject(s): Biography, Fictionalized; Artistic Life
Historical character(s): John James Audubon, Artist, Scientist (ornithologist); Lucy Blackwell Audubon, Spouse; Andrew Jackson, Political Figure
Time Period(s): 19th century (1802-1830s)
Locale(s): Pennsylvania; Louisville, Kentucky; New Orleans, Louisiana

Summary: The novel depicts the trials and tribulations in the married life of Lucy Blackwell, who weds the intense Frenchman John James Audubon. He takes her across America in pursuit of the birds he is driven to paint. Audubon's passion is matched by Lucy's devotion, revealing a unique marital collaboration.

Historical Accuracy: The authenticity of the novel is derived from the use of journals, letters, and records of the Audubon family.

MARGARET KENNEDY (1896-1967)

Kennedy was a novelist, playwright, biographer, and critic.

3420 *A Night in Cold Harbor*

Date of Publication: 1960
Subject(s): Regency Period
Fictional character(s): Romilly Brandon, Gentleman; Dickie Cottar, Bastard Son
Time Period(s): 1810s

Locale(s): England

Summary: Young aristocrat Romilly Brandon searches for his illegitimate son who has joined the hordes of "Walking People" made up of ragged children and outcasts. The novel dramatizes the bridging of the social gap between father and son.

Historical Accuracy: The novel provides an authentic and believable portrait of English life and customs during the period.

3421 *Troy Chimneys*

Date of Publication: 1952
Subject(s): Regency Period
Fictional character(s): Miles Lufton, Political Figure
Time Period(s): 19th century
Locale(s): England

Summary: This novel takes the form of the discovered papers of a young member of Parliament, Miles Lufton, who reveals himself to have a dual personality. He becomes involved in two romances, both of which end unhappily.

Historical Accuracy: The novel captures the flavor of the period in a number of convincing details.

WILLIAM KENNEDY (1928-)

Born in Albany, New York, journalist, editor, screenwriter, professor of English, and novelist William Kennedy attended Siena College. He is a recipient of the 1984 Pulitzer Prize for fiction for his novel *Ironweed*, which he also adapted as a screenplay. Kennedy's other works include *O Albany!: An Urban Tapestry* and *Billy Phelan's Greatest Game*.

3422 *Legs*

Date of Publication: 1975
Subject(s): Crime and Criminals
Fictional character(s): Marcus Gorman, Lawyer
Historical character(s): Jack Diamond, Criminal
Time Period(s): 1920s; 1930s
Locale(s): New York, New York; Europe

Summary: This fictional portrait of gangster Legs Diamond is told by his friend, the lawyer Marcus Gorman, and concentrates on the last year and a half of Diamond's legendary career. The novel offers an ambiguous portrait of Diamond, who is in turn charming and repulsive.

Historical Accuracy: The various incidents depicted are faithful to the facts of Diamond's criminal career.

3423 *Quinn's Book*

Date of Publication: 1988
Subject(s): Civil War—U.S.; Immigrants; Draft Riots
Fictional character(s): Daniel Quinn, Orphan; Maud Fallon, Young Woman
Time Period(s): 19th century (1849-1864)
Locale(s): Albany, New York; Saratoga, New York

Summary: When Daniel Quinn rescues Maud Fallon from drowning in the Hudson River, the act sets in motion a chain of events that affects the fortunes of Quinn. In the process a good deal of history is reflected, including the working of the Underground Railroad, the Civil War and the Draft Riots, and the battle between natives and the Irish immigrants.

Historical Accuracy: The period elements are authentically portrayed as is the atmosphere of the locales.

ARDYTH KENNELLY

3424 *Good Morning, Young Lady*

Date of Publication: 1953
Subject(s): American West; Crime and Criminals
Fictional character(s): Dorney Leaf, Teenager
Historical character(s): Butch Cassidy, Outlaw
Time Period(s): 19th century
Locale(s): Salt Lake City, Utah

Summary: This romantic Western fantasy tells the story of teenager Dorney Leaf, who relieves the drudgery of her life in Salt Lake City by dreaming of being rescued by the famous outlaw Butch Cassidy. To Dorney all things are possible, and it is hardly surprising that her wish is partially fulfilled.

Historical Accuracy: The novel captures the era with some skill.

3425 *The Spur*

Date of Publication: 1951
Subject(s): Civil War—U.S.; Theatrical Life
Historical character(s): John Wilkes Booth, Actor, Murderer (assassin); Abraham Lincoln, Political Figure; Edwin Booth, Actor
Time Period(s): 1860s (1865)
Locale(s): Washington, District of Columbia

Summary: The novel dramatizes the conspiracy that causes the assassination of Abraham Lincoln and the motives of Lincoln's killer, John Wilkes Booth. A theatrical star, Booth drifts into the conspiracy to achieve a different kind of celebrity as the man who kills Lincoln. The novel offers a look at the inner workings of Booth, a man of great contradictions.

Historical Accuracy: The novel combines fact with fiction, offering plausible speculations based on valid research.

FRANCES KENNETT

Born in London, Kennett attended Oxford University, where she studied English and designed costumes for theatrical productions. After graduation, she worked as a fashion journalist, and has written several nonfiction books on the history of fashion.

3426 *A Woman by Design*

Date of Publication: 1987
Subject(s): Fashion Industry; Victorian Period
Fictional character(s): Alice Hardy, Businesswoman (couturiere)

Time Period(s): 19th century; 20th century (1885-1947)
Locale(s): England; New York, New York

Summary: This novel chronicles the rise of one of the first female couturieres. Alice Hardy rebounds from a failed marriage and strikes out on her own, becoming a fashionable dressmaker and eventually one of the most stylish lights of the Belle Epoque. She weathers the changes brought on by the Great War and leads the style revolution of the post-war world. Her strength of purpose as a designer and businesswoman is contrasted with her vulnerability in love.

Historical Accuracy: The world of fashion during the period is captured with authenticity.

ALEXANDER KENT
(PSEUD. OF DOUGLAS E. REEMAN, 1924-)

English novelist Reeman writes sea stories set in the 18th and 19th centuries. He writes under the name Alexander Kent and under Reeman. He served in the Royal Navy during the Second World War and began writing while with the London Metropolitan Police. Much travel and research goes into the creation of his books.

`3427` *Colors Aloft!*
Date of Publication: 1986
Subject(s): Sea Story; Military Life—British Navy; Napoleonic Wars
Fictional character(s): Richard Bolitho, Military Personnel (vice-admiral); Joubert, Military Personnel (French admiral)
Time Period(s): 1800s (1803)
Locale(s): *Helicon*, At Sea (Mediterranean)

Summary: The knighted Vice-Admiral Sir Richard Bolitho sails his squadron for the Mediterranean and an encounter with the French admiral Joubert. Again the politics and jealousy of command bedevil Bolitho. A climactic confrontation with his French nemesis concludes the novel.

Historical Accuracy: The tactics of the two worthy opponents make this one of the best of Kent's series.

`3428` *Command a King's Ship*
Date of Publication: 1973
Subject(s): Sea Story; Military Life—British Navy
Fictional character(s): Richard Bolitho, Military Personnel (captain)
Time Period(s): 1780s (1784)
Locale(s): *Undine*, At Sea; Madras, India

Summary: Bolitho is captain of the frigate *Undine* with orders to sail to India to protect the important East Indies trade. The peace settlement with France and Spain is tenuous at best, as the *Undine* discovers in naval action.

Historical Accuracy: Kent delivers not only accurate details of naval life but also history through the lens of the British Royal Navy.

`3429` *Enemy in Sight!*
Date of Publication: 1970

Subject(s): Sea Story; Military Life—British Navy; French Revolution
Fictional character(s): Richard Bolitho, Military Personnel (captain); Commodore Pelham-Martin, Military Personnel
Time Period(s): 1790s (1794)
Locale(s): *Hyperion*, At Sea (Bay of Biscay, Atlantic, Caribbean)

Summary: Bolitho and the *Hyperion* are on blockade duty to check the growing power of Revolutionary France. The squadron's commodore is no match for the French admiral, who eludes the blockade and forces a chase across the Atlantic and an encounter that tests Bolitho's mettle and seamanship.

Historical Accuracy: The strategies and the broadside battles are expertly rendered.

`3430` *The Flag Captain*
Date of Publication: 1971
Subject(s): Sea Story; Military Life—British Navy; French Revolution
Fictional character(s): Richard Bolitho, Military Personnel (captain); Lucius Broughton, Military Personnel
Time Period(s): 1790s (1797)
Locale(s): *Euryalus*, At Sea (Mediterranean)

Summary: Aboard the *Euryalus*, Bolitho joins a squadron to attack the French. As captain of the flag-ship for the Vice Admiral, Bolitho learns the tactics of combined naval action and the difficulties of command. A fortress needs to be taken, and the French fleet engaged.

Historical Accuracy: The strength of Kent's story is his ability to render the tactics and the technicalities of naval action understandable.

`3431` *Form Line of Battle!*
Date of Publication: 1969
Subject(s): Sea Story; Military Life—British Navy; French Revolution
Fictional character(s): Richard Bolitho, Military Personnel (captain); Thomas Herrick, Military Personnel
Time Period(s): 1790s (1793)
Locale(s): *Hyperion*, At Sea (Mediterranean); Cozar Island, France

Summary: Captain Bolitho takes command of the aging *Hyperion*, a 74-gun ship of the line at Gibraltar. His mission is to join Lord Hood in the monarchist-inspired occupation of Toulon to check the growing power of Revolutionary France. The adventure is a costly failure, but the outgunned and outnumbered *Hyperion* proves its worth.

Historical Accuracy: Kent is best with the scenes of sea combat, which are handled with assurance.

`3432` *Honor This Day*
Date of Publication: 1987
Subject(s): Sea Story; Military Life—British Navy; Napoleonic Wars
Fictional character(s): Richard Bolitho, Military Personnel; Somervell, Nobleman (viscount)

Time Period(s): 1800s (1804-1805)
Locale(s): Antigua-Barbuda; Gibraltar

Summary: Domestic troubles complicate matters as Bolitho is sent to the Caribbean to launch a daring raid on enemy fleets on the Spanish Main. He is able to take a fully-laden treasure ship before heading back to the Mediterranean for action against the Spanish fleet.

Historical Accuracy: Bolitho has grown as a full-bodied character during the series. The past increasingly affects his view of the present in this ably researched and described story.

3433 *In Gallant Company*

Date of Publication: 1977
Subject(s): Sea Story; Military Life—British Navy; American Revolution
Fictional character(s): Richard Bolitho, Military Personnel (Naval officer); Gilbert Brice Pears, Military Personnel
Time Period(s): 1770s (1777)
Locale(s): *Trojan*, At Sea (east coast of U.S., Caribbean)

Summary: Bolitho is a junior officer on the *Trojan*, assigned to prevent military supplies from reaching Washington's army and to engage French and American privateers. Bolitho acquits himself well in dealing with a hard and determined captain. In the end he earns his own command.

Historical Accuracy: Kent's naval details are first-rate, and the action is true to the period.

3434 *The Inshore Squadron*

Date of Publication: 1977
Subject(s): Sea Story; Military Life—British Navy; Battle of Copenhagen
Fictional character(s): Richard Bolitho, Military Personnel (rear admiral)
Time Period(s): 1800s (1800)
Locale(s): *Benbow*, At Sea (Baltic)

Summary: Bolitho is a newly appointed rear admiral who assumes command of his own squadron. He soon realizes that his talent for daring leadership is not the same skill needed to master the politics of leading others into battle. The action climaxes in the Battle of Copenhagen.

Historical Accuracy: The description of naval action is first-rate without being too technical.

3435 *Midshipman Bolitho and the Avenger*

Date of Publication: 1978
Subject(s): Military Life—British Navy
Fictional character(s): Richard Bolitho, Military Personnel (midshipman)
Time Period(s): 1770s (1773)
Locale(s): Cornwall, England

Summary: While on leave from sea duty in Cornwall, Midshipman Bolitho finds himself in the middle of a Cornish smuggling operation and murder.

Historical Accuracy: The period elements are authentic and convincing.

3436 *Passage to Mutiny*

Date of Publication: 1976
Subject(s): Sea Story; Military Life—British Navy
Fictional character(s): Richard Bolitho, Military Personnel (captain); Thomas Herrick, Military Personnel
Time Period(s): 1780s (1789)
Locale(s): Sydney, Australia; *Tempest*, At Sea (South Pacific)

Summary: Bolitho is dispatched to Sydney to protect the growing trade routes from pirates. When he sails into the South Pacific with the *Bounty* mutiny in mind, his command is challenged by the idyllic attraction of the Pacific islands. The French Revolution brings back the call to arms.

Historical Accuracy: The novel is solidly researched and detailed in its naval and period history.

3437 *Richard Bolitho—Midshipman*

Date of Publication: 1975
Subject(s): Sea Story; Military Life—British Navy
Fictional character(s): Richard Bolitho, Military Personnel (midshipman)
Time Period(s): 1770s (1772)
Locale(s): *Gorgon*, At Sea; England

Summary: Chronologically, this is the first novel in the series detailing the naval career of Richard Bolitho. The time is 1772, and the 16-year-old Bolitho is a midshipman aboard the *Gorgon*, investigating the slave trade on Africa's west coast.

Historical Accuracy: The novel is expert in rending period naval life.

3438 *Signal—Close Action!*

Date of Publication: 1974
Subject(s): Sea Story; Military Life—British Navy; Napoleonic Wars
Fictional character(s): Richard Bolitho, Military Personnel (commodore); Thomas Herrick, Military Personnel
Time Period(s): 1790s (1798)
Locale(s): *Lysander*, At Sea (Mediterranean)

Summary: Bolitho is the commodore of a small squadron that sails into the Mediterranean to seek out the rumored French armada. His squadron encounters violent weather and command rivalries. The action culminates in the pivotal Battle of the Nile against Napoleon's forces.

Historical Accuracy: The novel expertly details naval strategy and procedure during the Napoleonic wars.

3439 *Sloop of War*

Date of Publication: 1972
Subject(s): Sea Story; Military Life—British Navy; American Revolution
Fictional character(s): Richard Bolitho, Military Personnel (captain)
Time Period(s): 1770s (1778)
Locale(s): *Sparrow*, At Sea (east coast of U.S.); New York, New York

Summary: Bolitho, a 22-year-old captain, takes command of a sloop and is involved in the decisive naval action of the

American Revolution as the British and French fleets converge on the Chesapeake. Bolitho must train and motivate an untried and complacent crew.

Historical Accuracy: Kent's details of naval protocol and sailing are first-rate in this exciting adventure.

☐3440☐ *Stand into Danger*

Date of Publication: 1981
Subject(s): Sea Story; Military Life—British Navy
Fictional character(s): Richard Bolitho, Military Personnel (third lieutenant); Henry Vere Dumaresq, Military Personnel
Time Period(s): 1770s (1774)
Locale(s): *Destiny*, At Sea (Caribbean)

Summary: Appointed a third lieutenant at the age of 18, Bolitho joins a man-of-war on a secret mission to Rio de Janeiro and the West Indies where action with the Spanish, piracy, and conspiracy begin to steel Bolitho to the realities of life in the navy.

Historical Accuracy: Kent's details of naval service are convincing.

☐3441☐ *Success to the Brave*

Date of Publication: 1983
Subject(s): Sea Story; Military Life—British Navy; Napoleonic Wars
Fictional character(s): Richard Bolitho, Military Personnel; Belinda Bolitho, Spouse
Time Period(s): 1800s (1802)
Locale(s): *Achates*, At Sea (Atlantic, Caribbean); Boston, Massachusetts

Summary: Bolitho is sent on a diplomatic mission to turn over the island of San Felipe to the French as part of the peace Treaty of Amiens. He learns both the challenge of diplomacy and that the peace will not last long.

Historical Accuracy: There are interesting looks at the diplomatic issues of the period and a detour to Boston in 1802.

☐3442☐ *To Glory We Steer*

Date of Publication: 1968
Subject(s): American Revolution; Sea Story; Military Life—British Navy
Fictional character(s): Richard Bolitho, Military Personnel (captain); Thomas Herrick, Military Personnel
Time Period(s): 1780s (1782)
Locale(s): *Phalarope*, At Sea (Caribbean)

Summary: Bolitho is given command of a frigate, the *Phalarope*, and sent to the West Indies. He must get the ship into fighting trim and instill her men with a proper fighting spirit. An encounter with an American ship follows, and the action climaxes in the battle of Staines near Guadaloupe.

Historical Accuracy: The novel's details are well researched and presented, particularly the battle scenes.

☐3443☐ *A Tradition of Victory*

Date of Publication: 1982

Subject(s): Sea Story; Military Life—British Navy; Napoleonic Wars
Fictional character(s): Richard Bolitho, Military Personnel (rear admiral); Thomas Herrick, Military Personnel
Time Period(s): 1800s (1801)
Locale(s): Cornwall, England; *Styx*, At Sea

Summary: Bolitho's squadron, still suffering from damage inflicted during the Battle of Copenhagen, is pressed into action by news that the French are in motion from the Channel Ports to the Bay of Biscay. The challenge is to destroy the French invasion fleet and force them to sue for an armistice.

Historical Accuracy: Kent succeeds in placing Bolitho at the center of historical action without manipulating the facts and details of naval life that are shown in all their immediacy.

MADELEINE FABIOLA KENT

☐3444☐ *The Corsair: A Biographical Novel of Jean Lafitte, Hero of the Battle of New Orleans*

Date of Publication: 1955
Subject(s): Biography, Fictionalized; Pirates; War of 1812
Historical character(s): Jean Laffite, Pirate; Pierre Dominique Toussaint l'Ouverture, Revolutionary; Andrew Jackson, Military Personnel (general)
Time Period(s): 18th century; 19th century (1782-1832)
Locale(s): Haiti; New Orleans, Louisiana

Summary: French pirate Jean Lafitte tells his own story of his boyhood in Haiti during the slave revolt and his career as a pirate, culminating in assisting General Jackson in the victory over the British in the Battle of New Orleans. The novel makes a case that Lafitte is a genuine hero whom history has maligned.

Historical Accuracy: The novel's obvious partiality to Lafitte slants the presentation here. The period background is effectively captured.

F.W. KENYON (1912-)

An English author born in Preston, Kenyon was educated in England and New Zealand. He worked in a department store in Auckland and for four years travelled throughout Australia, New Zealand, and Europe. His novels have been translated into 11 foreign languages.

☐3445☐ *The Absorbing Fire: The Byron Legend*

Date of Publication: 1966
Subject(s): Literary Life; Biography, Fictionalized; Regency Period
Historical character(s): George Gordon Byron, Writer, Nobleman; Percy Bysshe Shelley, Writer; Mary Wollstonecraft Godwin, Writer; Lady Caroline Lamb, Noblewoman; Isabella Milbanke, Spouse (of Byron); Claire Clairmont, Gentlewoman
Time Period(s): 18th century; 19th century (1790s-1820s)

Locale(s): Aberdeen, Scotland; London, England; Italy

Summary: This biographical novel of the life of English poet Byron concentrates on his personal relationships in scenes at various points of his controversial career: as a lame boy living with his impoverished mother in Scotland, schooldays at Harrow and Cambridge, celebrity in London and on the continent. The novel attempts a rounded and apologetic portrait of the leading literary figure of his time.

Historical Accuracy: Clearly written by a Byron partisan, the novel is somewhat slanted toward the best possible interpretation of Byron and his actions.

3446   *The Consuming Flame: The Story of George Eliot*

Date of Publication: 1970
Subject(s): Literary Life; Victorian Period; Biography, Fictionalized
Historical character(s): Mary Ann Evans, Writer; George Henry Lewes, Writer; Charles Dickens, Writer; Thomas Carlyle, Writer; Herbert Spencer, Writer
Time Period(s): 19th century (1820s-1860s)
Locale(s): Coventry, England; London, England

Summary: This biographical novel of the life of George Eliot traces the great Victorian novelist's career up to the point of her first great literary success. She was the plain daughter of a conservative yeoman farmer whose progressive ideas alienated her family. She became that rarest of Victorian commodities: a female intellectual, shocking society by living with a married man who encouraged her to try her hand at writing.

Historical Accuracy: The novel is clearly based on solid research and the facts about Eliot's background.

3447   *The Duke's Mistress: The Story of Mary Ann Clarke*

Date of Publication: 1969
Subject(s): Regency Period; Royalty—England
Historical character(s): Mary Anne Clarke, Gentlewoman; Frederick Augustus, Royalty (Duke of York); George, Royalty (Prince of Wales); George III, Ruler (King of England)
Time Period(s): 1790s; 1800s
Locale(s): London, England

Summary: Mary Ann Clarke is a cockney beauty who becomes the mistress of Frederick, Duke of York, second son of George III. The novel chronicles her amazing story, telling how she captivates a royal and survives the King's disapproval. When she comes up with a scheme to sell commissions in the army, she produces one of the greatest royal scandals in English history.

Historical Accuracy: The novel artfully weaves fact and surmise, with a solid period backdrop.

3448   *Emma*

Date of Publication: 1955
Subject(s): Napoleonic Wars

Historical character(s): Lady Emma Hamilton, Gentlewoman, Spouse; Sir William Hamilton, Diplomat; Horatio Nelson, Military Personnel (naval officer)
Time Period(s): 18th century; 19th century
Locale(s): England; Naples, Italy

Summary: The novel tells the story of one of the most famous romances in English history. Emma Hamilton, the wife of British diplomat Sir William Hamilton, loves Horatio Nelson, the naval commander who would defeat Napoleon's navy. The affair is shown from Emma's point of view, depicting her marriage to Sir William and her passion for Nelson.

Historical Accuracy: There are a number of speculative leaps in interpreting motive and behind-the-scenes information. Other surmises might be equally valid in reconstructing the affair.

3449   *The Emperor's Lady: A Novel Based on the Life of the Empress Josephine*

Date of Publication: 1952
Subject(s): Napoleonic Era; Royalty—France; Biography, Fictionalized
Historical character(s): Josephine, Royalty (consort of Napoleon); Napoleon Bonaparte, Ruler (Emperor of France)
Time Period(s): 1790s; 1800s
Locale(s): Martinique; France

Summary: The novel describes the amazing life of the Empress Josephine, the daughter of an impoverished nobleman from the island of Martinique. She comes to France and survives the Revolution and Terror before captivating a young Corsican guard, Napoleon. She marries him to pay his debts but finds herself his empress.

Historical Accuracy: The novel is a blend of the factual and the invented with a plausible background of historical details.

3450   *The Glory and the Dream*

Date of Publication: 1963
Subject(s): Royalty—England; Glorious Revolution
Historical character(s): Anne, Ruler (Queen of England); John Churchill, Nobleman (Duke of Marlborough); Sarah Churchill, Noblewoman (Duchess of Marlborough); William III, Ruler (King of England); Mary II, Ruler (Queen of England)
Time Period(s): 17th century; 18th century (1688-1722)
Locale(s): England

Summary: The novel tells the story of the glamorous and ambitious couple John and Sarah Churchill, Duke and Duchess of Marlborough. He is the military genius responsible for the great victories at Blenheim and Ramillies and the leading British statesman of the era. She is called ''Queen Sarah'' for her hold on power and supremacy in court intrigues. Their career and era are vividly captured.

Historical Accuracy: The history is accurately described, with some dramatic blending of fact and fiction.

3451 *The Golden Years: A Novel Based on the Life and Loves of Percy Bysshe Shelley*

Date of Publication: 1959

Subject(s): Literary Life; Biography, Fictionalized; Regency Period

Historical character(s): Percy Bysshe Shelley, Writer; Mary Wollstonecraft Godwin, Writer; Leigh Hunt, Writer; George Gordon Byron, Writer, Nobleman; Jane Clairmont, Gentlewoman; Harriet Westbrook, Spouse (of Shelley)

Time Period(s): 1810s; 1820s

Locale(s): England; Geneva, Switzerland; Italy

Summary: This biographical novel tells the story of English Romantic poet Percy Shelley from his college days when he was expelled from Oxford for publically proclaiming his atheism, to his marriage to Harriet Westbrook and his affair with Mary Godwin. Shelley's circle, which includes Leigh Hunt and Byron, is also depicted.

Historical Accuracy: The novel offers a plausible account of Shelley and his fascinating career.

3452 *Imperial Courtesan*

Date of Publication: 1967

Subject(s): Royalty—France; Victorian Period

Historical character(s): Napoleon III, Ruler (Emperor of France); Elizabeth Ann Haryett, Gentlewoman; Alfred d'Orsay, Nobleman; Margaret Gardiner, Noblewoman (Countess of Blessington)

Time Period(s): 19th century

Locale(s): England; France

Summary: The novel chronicles the story of Elizabeth Ann Haryett, daughter of an English country squire, whose beauty propels her to social success in London as a member of Lady Blessington's Gore House set. In Brighton she meets the dashing Louis-Napoleon whose mistress she becomes, scheming with him to take the French throne as Napoleon III.

Historical Accuracy: The novel blends fact with fiction. The period atmosphere is convincing.

3453 *Marie Antoinette*

Date of Publication: 1956

Subject(s): Royalty—France; French Revolution; Biography, Fictionalized

Historical character(s): Louis XVI, Ruler (King of France); Marie Antoinette, Royalty (queen consort of Louis XVI)

Time Period(s): 18th century (1760s-1793)

Locale(s): France

Summary: This biographical novel chronicles the glittering career of Marie Antoinette from her arrival at the court of Versailles as the 14-year-old bride of the Dauphin who was to become Louis XVI. Extravagant and headstrong, Marie Antoinette is shown in love and gripped by the uncontrollable forces of history.

Historical Accuracy: The novel blends the actual and the imagined. A strong sense of the period makes it convincing.

3454 *Mary of Scotland*

Date of Publication: 1957

Subject(s): Elizabethan Period; Royalty—Scotland

Historical character(s): Mary, Queen of Scots, Ruler; James Stuart, Royalty (prince); Henry Stewart, Nobleman (Mary's second husband); Mary Seton, Gentlewoman; James Hepburn, Nobleman (Mary's third husband)

Time Period(s): 16th century

Locale(s): Scotland

Summary: The novel traces the story of Mary, Queen of Scots from her return to Scotland after the death of her first husband, Francois II of France. As a Catholic queen, Mary's hold on the throne is tenuous. She struggles at home and against the shrewd and devious Elizabeth I.

Historical Accuracy: Mary, Queen of Scots' reign has always been shrouded in mystery and controversy. The novel offers one plausible set of interpretations about her life, career, and motives. There are clearly other and different ones.

3455 *My Brother Napoleon: The Confessions of Caroline Bonaparte*

Date of Publication: 1971

Subject(s): Napoleonic Era; Royalty—France

Historical character(s): Caroline Bonaparte, Royalty (sister of Napoleon); Napoleon Bonaparte, Ruler (Emperor of France); Joachim Murat, Military Personnel (French marshal); Josephine, Royalty (consort of Napoleon); Marie Louise of Austria, Royalty (consort of Napoleon)

Time Period(s): 18th century; 19th century (1790s-1830s)

Locale(s): France; Italy

Summary: Caroline Bonaparte, Napoleon's sister, tells her own story and provides an insider's view of Napoleon's rise to power and the intrigues of Napoleon's court. Caroline defies her brother's wishes by marrying Joachim Murat who becomes one of Napoleon's greatest generals.

Historical Accuracy: The historical details are genuine.

3456 *The Naked Sword: The Story of Lucretia Borgia*

Date of Publication: 1968

Subject(s): Renaissance

Historical character(s): Lucrezia Borgia, Noblewoman; Rodrigo Borgia, Religious (pope); Giovanni Sforza, Nobleman (Lord of Pesaro); Cesare Borgia, Nobleman, Military Personnel; Giulia Farnesse, Gentlewoman; Ercole d'Este, Nobleman (Duke of Ferrara); Alfonso d'Este, Nobleman (Duke of Ferrara)

Time Period(s): 15th century; 16th century (1490s-1507)

Locale(s): Italy

Summary: The novel tells the story of Lucretia Borgia, the daughter of Pope Alexander VI and sister of Cesare Borgia, one of the most ruthless and ambitious men of the Italian Renaissance. Lucretia becomes a marriageable pawn in both her father's and brother's plans to dominate Italy. She marries three times, finding lasting happiness and escape from her dominating family in her third marriage to Alfonso, Duke of Ferrara, the most powerful man in the Italy of her time.

Historical Accuracy: This is a sympathetic look at the famous Lucretia Borgia who has been seen as a monster in some accounts. The novel offers a plausible case that she should be seen more as a victim.

3457 Passionate Rebel: The Story of Hector Berlioz

Date of Publication: 1972
Subject(s): Musical Life; Biography, Fictionalized
Historical character(s): Louis Hector Berlioz, Composer; Harriet Smithson, Actress; Alexandre Dumas, pere, Writer; Franz Liszt, Composer; Niccolo Paganini, Musician, Composer
Time Period(s): 19th century (1810s-1860s)
Locale(s): Paris, France; Italy

Summary: This biographical novel traces the career of the greatest composer of the French romantic school, Hector Berlioz. Pressured by his family to pursue a career in medicine, he escapes into the world of music and the theatre. The novel chronicles his musical successes and his numerous romances, including his passion for Irish actress Harriet Smithson.

Historical Accuracy: The facts of Berlioz's career and life form the novel's framework, while some surmises fill in gaps.

3458 The Questing Heart: A Romantic Novel about George Sand

Date of Publication: 1964
Subject(s): Literary Life; Musical Life; Biography, Fictionalized
Historical character(s): George Sand, Writer; Joachim Murat, Military Personnel (French marshal); Frederic Chopin, Musician, Composer; Franz Liszt, Musician, Composer; Prosper Merimee, Writer; Alfred de Musset, Writer (poet)
Time Period(s): 19th century (1810s-1849)
Locale(s): Paris, France

Summary: The novel tells the story of 19th-century French novelist George Sand. She was born Aurore Dupin, the daughter of an actress and an officer in Napoleon's army. She began to write for her own amusement and she established herself as a journalist and romantic novelist. She was perhaps as well-known, however, for her series of famous love affairs with Alfred de Musset, Prosper Merimee, and finally Frederic Chopin. The novel attempts to capture this extraordinary woman and her era.

Historical Accuracy: Well-researched and documented, the novel is based firmly on a framework of fact with certain fictional embellishments.

3459 Royal Merry-Go-Round

Date of Publication: 1954
Subject(s): Royalty—France
Historical character(s): Louis XV, Ruler (King of France); Jeanne Antoinette Poisson, Noblewoman (Marquise de Pompadour); Jeanne du Barry, Noblewoman (comtesse)

Time Period(s): 18th century
Locale(s): Versailles, France

Summary: The hedonistic court world of French King Louis XV is depicted. The emphasis is on the many loves of the king and on his most famous mistresses, Madame de Pompadour and the Comtesse Du Barry. As Louis indulges in his many vices, France loses most of its colonies, and the stage is set for the Revolution—the Deluge—that follows Louis' reign.

Historical Accuracy: The novel's picture of the French court is not always reliable in matching the facts or history.

3460 Shadow in the Sun: A Novel of Elizabeth I, the Virgin Queen

Date of Publication: 1958
Subject(s): Elizabethan Period; Royalty—England; Biography, Fictionalized
Historical character(s): Elizabeth I, Ruler (Queen of England); Robert Dudley, Nobleman (Earl of Leicester); Christopher Hatton, Nobleman; Robert Devereux, Nobleman (Earl of Essex); Jane Seymour, Royalty (queen consort of Henry VIII); Philip II, Ruler (King of Spain); Mary I, Ruler (Queen of England); William Cecil, Courtier, Nobleman; Robert Cecil, Courtier; Sir Francis Walsingham, Government Official
Time Period(s): 16th century; 17th century (1530s-1603)
Locale(s): England

Summary: This biographical novel traces the life and career of Elizabeth I from childhood until her death. Elizabeth emerges as clever and daring, a scholar and shrewd politician. Resisting marriage as a compromise of her power and authority, she nevertheless dominates a succession of the leading men of her age.

Historical Accuracy: The novel is solidly researched and convincing, even though not all the scenes or situations are factual.

3461 That Spanish Woman

Date of Publication: 1962
Subject(s): Royalty—France; Biography, Fictionalized; Victorian Period
Historical character(s): Eugenie, Royalty (consort of Napoleon III); Napoleon III, Ruler (Emperor of France); Victoria, Ruler (Queen of England)
Time Period(s): 19th century (1850s-1870s)
Locale(s): France; England

Summary: The Empress Eugenie, consort of Napoleon III, tells her own story in this biographical-historical novel. She is the trendsetter of the Second Empire, and her memoirs detail the intrigue and glamour of the French Court.

Historical Accuracy: The novel is dependably authentic in its research, a skillful blend of historical fact and fancy.

THEDA KENYON

Kenyon's novels include *Witches Still Live*, *Pendulum*, and *Something Gleamed*. She was born in Brooklyn, New York.

3462 *The Golden Feather*

Date of Publication: 1943
Subject(s): American Colonies; Religious Conflict
Fictional character(s): Gerald Stacey, Young Man; Ajax Stacey, Young Man; Clarissa Brinton, Young Woman
Historical character(s): Charles I, Ruler (King of England); William Laud, Religious (bishop); John Pym, Political Figure; Sir John Suckling, Writer (poet); Anne Hutchinson, Leader (religious)
Time Period(s): 17th century (1640s)
Locale(s): London, England; Virginia, American Colonies

Summary: Set during the reign of Charles I, this panoramic novel covers the tyranny of Bishop Laud and the religious persecution of Anne Hutchinson. At the center of the tale is a love story involving Ajax and Gerald Stacy who both fall in love with the scheming Clarissa Brinton. Both brothers are exiled to America for their opposition to Bishop Laud.

Historical Accuracy: This heavily-plotted melodrama is at odds with the reconstruction of the period that is largely effective and believable.

3463 *Something Gleamed*

Date of Publication: 1948
Subject(s): American Revolution; Military Life—British Army
Fictional character(s): Dorcas Spenser, Young Woman; Hal Nevins, Military Personnel (army officer); Roger Von Zweig, Military Personnel (soldier)
Time Period(s): 1770s
Locale(s): London, England; New York, New York

Summary: The novel is based on an actual circumstance of the American Revolution. The ''Jackson Whites'' are women pressed into the service of the British troops during the war. Dorcas Spenser finds herself forcibly taken from England to the colonies, where her experiences dramatize the fate of many.

Historical Accuracy: The novel is built on a solid framework of fact, the fruit of evident research.

3464 *That Skipper From Stonington*

Date of Publication: 1947
Subject(s): War of 1812; Biography, Fictionalized; Whaling
Historical character(s): Richard Fanning Loper, Sea Captain, Inventor
Time Period(s): 19th century
Locale(s): Stonington, Connecticut; At Sea

Summary: The novel is based on the life of Yankee whaling captain Richard Loper, the first shipbuilder to use iron frames, and the inventor of a screw propeller that may have preceded John Ericsson's. His life is chronicled from the time he runs away to sea to participate in the naval battles of the War of 1812 to his rise to sea captain and shipbuilder.

Historical Accuracy: The novel is based on authentic records, but the treatment is sentimentalized.

CHARLOTTE KEPPEL
(PSEUD. OF URSULA TORDAY, 1888-)

Charlotte Keppel is one of several pseudonyms for the prolific English author Ursula Torday, who was born in London and attended the London School of Economics and Oxford University. She has worked as a secretary and assisted in the placement of Jewish refugee children.

3465 *Loving Sands, Deadly Sands*

Date of Publication: 1974
Subject(s): Gothic Romance; Georgian Period
Fictional character(s): Margaret Walters, Housekeeper
Time Period(s): 1790s (1798)
Locale(s): England

Summary: Margaret Walters comes to serve as housekeeper to her wealthy cousin and his two daughters. She is almost immediately swept up in a series of events that leads her to the estate's hidden Bluebeard Room. Mystery and menace accompany her.

Historical Accuracy: The gothic elements are fairly standard here, with some period details to match the setting.

3466 *My Name Is Clary Brown*

Date of Publication: 1976
Subject(s): Theatrical Life; Romance; Georgian Period
Fictional character(s): Clary Brown, Actress; William Ringham, Gentleman
Historical character(s): David Garrick, Actor, Manager (theatrical)
Time Period(s): 18th century
Locale(s): London, England; Middleditch, England

Summary: Beautiful Clary Brown achieves renown on the stage as Diamond Brown. Pensioned off by the elderly aristocrat who makes her his mistress, Clary returns to the English village of her birth, where her father was hanged for poaching, and Clary was sent to a workhouse.

Historical Accuracy: The novel captures the era with convincing details, particularly its theatrical scenes.

3467 *The Villains: A Haunting Tale of the Marshes*

Date of Publication: 1981
Subject(s): Gothic Romance; Georgian Period
Fictional character(s): Nanette, Orphan; Leonie, Orphan
Time Period(s): 1730s; 1740s
Locale(s): England

Summary: Sisters Nanette and Leonie travel to Cudden Hall, a bleak mansion overlooking the marshes, to live with their aunt. The mansion has many secrets, and the novel shows the sisters slowly penetrating them and dealing with an eccentric group of inhabitants.

Historical Accuracy: The period details are only lightly suggested, with the priority gothic danger and threat.

BARBARA KER WILSON (1929-)

An English author born in Durham, Ker Wilson was educated in London and has lived in Australia since 1964. Ker Wilson has worked for publishing companies in England and Australia, and is the author of numerous books for young readers.

3468 *Antipodes Jane: A Novel of Jane Austen in Australia*

Date of Publication: 1985
Subject(s): Georgian Period
Historical character(s): Jane Austen, Writer
Time Period(s): 1800s (1799-1804)
Locale(s): Bath, England; Sydney, Australia

Summary: This what-if novel imagines a visit by Jane Austen, before she had achieved any literary success, to the colony of New South Wales. In response to a failed romance, Austen travels to Sydney in the early 1800s. The novel offers Jane Austen's imagined perspective on frontier Australia, as correspondences are worked out between well-ordered Georgian society and the former penal colony.

Historical Accuracy: Though Jane Austen's sojourn in Australia is imagined, the other details of her life are faithfully observed.

3469 *The Quade Inheritance*

Date of Publication: 1988
Subject(s): Inheritance—Disputed; Victorian Period
Fictional character(s): Imogene Quade, Heiress; Annette Duval, Governess; Nicholas Quade, Heir
Time Period(s): 19th century
Locale(s): Somerset, England; Australia; London, England

Summary: Imogene Quade goes to great lengths to possess Selbury Quade, a 16th-century state, including denying the claim of Nicholas Quade, the unexpected male heir. The novel dramatizes the interlocked fate of Imogene, Nicholas, and governess Annette Duval in scenes of Victorian England and colonial Australia.

Historical Accuracy: The novel uses an authentic period backdrop for this tangled domestic drama.

FRANCES CASEY KERNS (1937-)

Born in Arkansas, Kerns' early years were spent in the Ozarks. She graduated from the University of Colorado and worked as a proofreader for braille books.

3470 *This Land Is Mine*

Date of Publication: 1974
Subject(s): American West; Indians
Fictional character(s): Blake Westfall, Young Man; Hawk's Shadow, Indian, Warrior; Shy Fawn, Indian
Time Period(s): 1840s
Locale(s): Montana

Summary: Young Blake Westfall comes West with a wagon train, but he is captured by the Medicine River tribe in the Montana Territory. Adopted by the tribe, he learns Indian ways and marries the chief's daughter, Shy Fawn. He settles with his wife and fashions an idyllic life until tragedy strikes.

Historical Accuracy: The novel is fairly grounded in real history and geography, but some liberties were taken with dates and places to accommodate the story.

PHILIP KERR (1956-)

English writer Kerr has worked previously in law, advertising, and journalism. His books include *March Violets* and *A German Requiem*. He is also the editor of *The Penguin Book of Lies*.

3471 *The Pale Criminal*

Date of Publication: 1990
Subject(s): Mystery; Nazis
Fictional character(s): Bernie Gunther, Detective—Private
Time Period(s): 1930s (1938)
Locale(s): Berlin, Germany

Summary: Bernie Gunther, private detective, is hired by a widow to find out who is blackmailing her. Bernie then gets involved with a serial murderer who is on the loose in Nazi Berlin just before World War II begins.

Historical Accuracy: The novel excels in creating the menacing atmosphere of Berlin in that era.

ROBERT KERR (1899-)

3472 *The Stuart Legacy*

Date of Publication: 1973
Subject(s): Inheritance—Disputed; Jacobite Rebellion
Fictional character(s): Mary Beaton, Gentlewoman; Madeleine Campbell-Bannerman, Gentlewoman
Historical character(s): James Francis Edward Stuart, Royalty, Heir
Time Period(s): 17th century; 18th century
Locale(s): Scotland

Summary: When Jamie Stuart returns to Scotland from exile to claim his inheritance, he finds himself accused of a murder in which he had no part. His accusers are two women, Mary Beaton and Madeleine Campbell-Bannerman, and Jamie is soon running for his life.

Historical Accuracy: The novel's period background is authentic.

KEN KESEY (1935-)

W. KEN BABBS

Kesey is an American novelist from Oregon. His adventures as a counterculture figure are celebrated by Tom Wolfe in *The Electric Kool-Aid Acid Test*. Kesey's first novel, *One Flew Over the Cuckoo's Nest*, was a major success. His other works include *Sometimes a Great Notion* and *Demon Box*.

3473 *Last Go Round*

Date of Publication: 1994

Subject(s): American West; Rodeos

Historical character(s): George Fletcher, Cowboy, Rodeo Rider; Jackson Sundown, Indian, Rodeo Rider; Johnathan E. Lee Spain, Cowboy, Rodeo Rider; William F. Cody, Entertainer, Frontiersman; Frank Gotch, Sports Figure (wrestler)

Time Period(s): 1910s (1911)

Locale(s): Pendleton, Oregon

Summary: The novel offers an amusing recreation of the events of the original Pendleton, Oregon, Round Up in 1911 in which three cowboys—a black, a Nez Perce Indian, and a 17-year-old from Tennessee—compete to be the first world champion cowboy.

Historical Accuracy: This is a funny and authentic re-creation of the sights and sounds of the past western rodeo scene. Kesey's strengths are his dialogue and his ability to create frenetic, edgy excitement.

HERMANN KESTEN (1900-)

German novelist and playwright Kesten was born in Nuremburg and studied history and literature in German universities. Upon Hitler's rise to power, Kesten fled to Amsterdam, then to America. Already well known as a novelist in Germany, Kesten turned to writing historical fiction while in exile.

3474 *Ferdinand and Isabella*

Date of Publication: 1946

Subject(s): Biography, Fictionalized; Royalty—Spain; Inquisition

Historical character(s): Ferdinand V, Ruler (King of Spain); Isabella I, Ruler (Queen of Spain)

Time Period(s): 15th century; 16th century

Locale(s): Spain

Summary: This biographical novel dramatizes the reign of Ferdinand and Isabella and the events that created the kingdom of Spain, including the defeat of the Moors, the Inquisition, and the discovery of America. Isabella emerges as a complex blend of religious zeal and determination that produces a mixed legacy for Spain. Ferdinand is cast in a secondary and somewhat shadowy role.

Historical Accuracy: The facts are faithfully depicted. The author's interpretations are open to question.

3475 *I, the King*

Date of Publication: 1940

Subject(s): Biography, Fictionalized; Royalty—Spain

Historical character(s): Philip II, Ruler (King of Spain)

Time Period(s): 16th century (1550s-1590s)

Locale(s): Spain

Summary: The novel presents a fictional account of the reign and personality of Philip II from his mid-twenties to the end of his reign. The novel is steeped in its period and captures the major events of a reign that thrusts Spain firmly onto center stage of world affairs.

Historical Accuracy: The novel's facts and period details are authentic, even if the story is at times overburdened by both.

JOCELYN KETTLE (1934-)

A British journalist and author, Kettle was educated privately and at preparatory and boarding schools. She is the author of *Memorial to the Duchess*, *The Day of the Women* (under the name Pamela Kettle), and *A Gift of Onyx*.

3476 *The Athelsons*

Date of Publication: 1972

Subject(s): Family Saga

Fictional character(s): Justine Athelson, Young Woman; Athel Athelson, Heir

Time Period(s): 1890s; 1900s

Locale(s): England

Summary: Set at the turn of the century on the ancestral estate of the Athelsons on the north coast of England, the novel presents the challenges of love when Justine Athelson falls in love with her cousin Athel, heir to the estate.

Historical Accuracy: The novel offers convincing period and regional elements.

FRANCES PARKINSON KEYES
(1885-1970)

Born at the University of Virginia, where her father was head of the Greek department, Keyes studied under governesses and in private schools in Boston and Switzerland. She lived in Washington for 25 years while her husband, Henry Wilder Keyes, was a senator from New Hampshire. Her books sold more than 20 million copies. She gained popularity for her ability to evoke the atmosphere of aristocratic living. Keyes' writing was strongly influenced by her conversion to Catholicism; she wrote the biographies of several saints.

3477 *Blue Camellia*

Date of Publication: 1957

Subject(s): Rural Life—U.S.; Farming

Fictional character(s): Brent Winslow, Settler, Farmer (rice); Mary Winslow, Spouse; Lavinia Winslow, Young Woman

Time Period(s): 19th century; 20th century (1886-1900s)

Locale(s): Louisiana

Summary: Cajun life in rice-growing southwest Louisiana is the novel's subject. Brent Winslow and his wife, Mary, come from the north and achieve success after years of experimenting in rice breeding. The story of their daughter's love shares the stage with a realistic depiction of Cajun life and customs.

Historical Accuracy: The region is depicted with care and authenticity.

3478 *The Chess Player: A Novel of New Orleans and Paris*

Date of Publication: 1960

Subject(s): Civil War—U.S.; Chess; Antebellum South
Historical character(s): Paul Morphy, Sports Figure (chess champion); John Slidell, Government Official (Confederate), Diplomat; Pierre Gustave Toutant Beauregard, Military Personnel (Confederate general); Judah P. Benjamin, Political Figure, Government Official (Confederate cabinet)
Time Period(s): 19th century (1825-1884)
Locale(s): New Orleans, Louisiana; Paris, France

Summary: Chess champion Paul Morphy becomes a Confederate agent in Paris. He participates in the intricate diplomatic negotiations led by John Slidell to bring about France's recognition of the Confederate nation.

Historical Accuracy: The novel blends fact and fiction but relies heavily on documented sources.

3479 *I, the King*

Date of Publication: 1966
Subject(s): Royalty—Spain; Biography, Fictionalized
Historical character(s): Philip IV, Ruler (King of Spain); Isabel of Bourbon, Royalty (queen consort of Philip IV); Inez Calderon, Actress; Maria de Agreda, Religious (abbess); Mariana of Austria, Royalty (queen consort of Philip IV)
Time Period(s): 17th century (1615-1665)
Locale(s): Spain

Summary: This biographical novel is the story of Philip IV of Spain. A sportsman, poet, and musician, Philip was a patron of the arts, and he oversaw the golden age of Spanish culture. The novel details the women who most influenced his life, including Inez Calderon, an actress, and Sor Maria, the abbess whose correspondence with him over a period of 20 years is a record of a remarkable friendship.

Historical Accuracy: The author points out that most of the conversations in the book are imaginary, though all are based on fact.

3480 *Madame Castel's Lodger*

Date of Publication: 1962
Subject(s): Civil War—U.S.; Antebellum South; Reconstruction Period
Historical character(s): Pierre Gustave Toutant Beauregard, Military Personnel (Confederate general)
Time Period(s): 19th century
Locale(s): New Orleans, Louisiana; Manassas, Virginia; Charleston, South Carolina

Summary: This is a biographical novel of the life of Pierre Beauregard, the Confederate general who ordered the first shot fired on Fort Sumter and who led the Confederate army in its first great victory at Bull Run. There are scenes from his life in New Orleans as a member of the Creole gentry, his days at West Point, and his participation in the Civil War. After the war, Beauregard returns to New Orleans where he is reduced to taking humble lodgings.

Historical Accuracy: With its solidly documented background, the novel is more history and biography than fiction.

3481 *Steamboat Gothic*

Date of Publication: 1952

Subject(s): Family Saga; Reconstruction Period
Fictional character(s): Clyde Batchelor, Landowner; Lucy Page, Spouse (of Clyde)
Time Period(s): 19th century; 20th century (1870-1930)
Locale(s): Mississippi River; Louisiana

Summary: Clyde Batchelor rises from an orphan asylum and the mean streets of St. Louis to prominence. He owns a mansion on the Mississippi and marries into one of the finest families of Virginia. But his path to success is not smooth, nor are his achievements without some regrets.

Historical Accuracy: The novel captures with conviction the period and the locale.

WARREN KIEFER (1929-)

Born in New Jersey and a graduate of the University of New Mexico, Kiefer is a former Marine and commercial pilot. He has worked as a TV journalist and filmwriter and producer. His novel *The Lingua Code* won the Edgar Award in 1973. Kiefer is the writer for 25 documentary films produced in Africa, the Middle East, and Europe.

3482 *Outlaw*

Date of Publication: 1989
Subject(s): American West; Picaresque Adventure; Spanish-American War
Fictional character(s): Lee Oliver Garland, Adventurer
Historical character(s): Francisco Villa, Outlaw, Revolutionary; Theodore Roosevelt, Military Personnel (commander of the Rough Riders)
Time Period(s): 19th century; 20th century (1890s-1960s)
Locale(s): Southwest; Mexico; Cuba

Summary: This picaresque adventure tells the story of Lee Oliver Garland, whose family is killed by the Apaches. He becomes a cattle rancher and fugitive, a Rough Rider and participant in the charge up San Juan Hill, and a doughboy in World War I. The novel follows his many encounters with the historical events of the era.

Historical Accuracy: Although the author did considerable research to get the atmosphere right, he makes no claim to biographical accuracy.

MICHAEL KILIAN (1939-)

Born in Toledo, this noted writer on military and aviation affairs attended the University of Maryland. His prize-winning column for the *Chicago Tribune* is syndicated in more than 200 papers throughout the U.S. and Canada.

3483 *Dance on a Sinking Ship*

Date of Publication: 1988
Subject(s): Royalty—England; Espionage; Ocean Liners
Fictional character(s): C. Jamieson Spencer, Journalist; Nora Gwynne, Actress; Olga Maretzka, Spy
Historical character(s): Edward, Prince of Wales, Royalty; Wallis Warfield Simpson, Gentlewoman; Louis Mountbatten, Nobleman; Charles Lindbergh, Pilot
Time Period(s): 1930s (1935)

Locale(s): *Wilhelmina*, At Sea; Paris, France

Summary: Espionage and intrigue abound in this account of a transatlantic crossing in 1935. It features the Prince of Wales and his new mistress, Mrs. Simpson, and a cast of famous historical figures, including Charles Lindbergh, who reveals himself as one of America's greatest spies. Also on board are both Nazis and Stalinists intent on changing the course of history.

Historical Accuracy: Though fanciful, the novel is convincing in its period details. The apology for Lindbergh is a stretch of the known facts.

JOHN OLIVER KILLENS (1916-1987)

An American author, teacher, activist, and scholar, Killens founded the Harlem Writers Guild. He taught creative writing at Fisk, Howard, and Columbia universities. Killens was vice president of the Black Academy of Arts and Letters, and was a prominent figure in the African-American literary community. His novel *Youngblood* was nominated for a Pulitzer Prize.

3484 *Great Black Russian*

Date of Publication: 1989
Subject(s): Russian Empire; Literary Life; Biography, Fictionalized
Historical character(s): Aleksandr Sergeyevich Pushkin, Writer (poet); Alexander I, Ruler (Czar of Russia); Nikolai Gogol, Writer
Time Period(s): 18th century; 19th century (1799-1837)
Locale(s): St. Petersburg, Russia; Moscow, Russia

Summary: This biographical novel portrays the life of Russian poet Alexander Pushkin, considered the father of Russian literature. Pushkin's great-grandfather was an Ethiopian prince captured as a youth by the Turks. Pushkin's African heritage and his opposition to the absolute power of the czar, contribute to a unique perspective that results in conflict and banishment. His wife's love affair with a young Frenchman precipitates the duel that ends Pushkin's life.

Historical Accuracy: The novel is a believable integration of fact and fiction, a credible portrait of the great romantic poet.

GRACE KING (1852-1932)

Born in New Orleans, King was the daughter of a prosperous attorney. Her family fled the city during the Civil War and then returned to a life of poverty that they slowly overcame. Early in life King determined to travel and to become a writer. Many of her stories, collected in *Tales of a Time and Place* and *Balcony Stories* are based on her firsthand experience of the war and its aftermath.

3485 *La Dame De Sainte Hermine*

Date of Publication: 1924
Subject(s): Settlement of the American Frontier
Fictional character(s): Marie Alorge, Convict
Time Period(s): 1710s (1718)

Locale(s): New Orleans, Louisiana

Summary: The story of the founding and settlement of New Orleans is dramatized in the tale of Marie Alorge, who is exiled from France and sent as a prisoner to the governor of the colony. The novel depicts her struggle to adapt to the wilderness through a long series of adventures.

Historical Accuracy: Evident research provides an authentic background to the period.

JOAN KING (1930-)

An American writer born in Washington, D.C., King graduated from the University of Minnesota. She has worked as a paralegal. A painter who finds the art field rich with dramatic life, King is the author of *Sarah M. Peale: America's First Woman Artist* and a biography of the artist Charles M. Russell.

3486 *Impressionist: A Novel of Mary Cassatt*

Date of Publication: 1983
Subject(s): Biography, Fictionalized; Artistic Life
Historical character(s): Mary Cassatt, Artist
Time Period(s): 19th century; 20th century
Locale(s): United States; France

Summary: This biographical novel traces the artistic career of American painter Mary Cassatt. The daughter of a respectable American family, Cassatt embarks on a painting career that puts her at the center of the Impressionist movement.

Historical Accuracy: The novel stays close to the actual events of Cassatt's life and the artistic period.

LAURIE R. KING (1952-)

An American mystery novelist born in Oakland, California, King is a graduate of the University of California, Santa Cruz, and the Graduate Theological Union, Berkeley.

3487 *The Beekeeper's Apprentice, or, On the Segregation of the Queen*

Date of Publication: 1994
Subject(s): Mystery; World War I
Fictional character(s): Mary Russell, Detective—Amateur, Student; John H. Watson, Doctor; Sherlock Holmes, Detective—Private
Time Period(s): 1910s (1914-1918)
Locale(s): Sussex Downs, England

Summary: In 1914, an aging Sherlock Holmes meets 15-year-old Mary Russell. She becomes Holmes' apprentice and then his partner, bringing a female perspective to an ever-escalating series of cases.

Historical Accuracy: The novel's originality lies in teaming Holmes' Victorian sensibility with Russell's thoroughly modern outlook. The author is able to paint the period landscape with authenticity.

3488 *A Letter of Mary*

Date of Publication: 1996
Subject(s): Mystery
Fictional character(s): Sherlock Holmes, Detective—Private; Mary Russell, Detective—Private, Scholar
Time Period(s): 1920s (1923)
Locale(s): Sussex, England

Summary: In this third novel involving Mary Russell's relationship with Sherlock Holmes, the pair come into possession of a box that contains a letter that seems to be written by Mary Magdalene. The letter's contents could revolutionize biblical history. When the owner of the box dies in a traffic accident, Holmes and Russell take up the investigation.

Historical Accuracy: The novel provides an ingenious puzzle set against a background of Holmesian elements and the period.

3489 *A Monstrous Regiment of Women*

Date of Publication: 1995
Subject(s): Mystery
Fictional character(s): Mary Russell, Detective—Private, Scholar; Sherlock Holmes, Detective—Private
Time Period(s): 1920s (1920-1921)
Locale(s): London, England

Summary: In the second mystery involving Mary Russell, a student of the famous detective Sherlock Holmes, murder claims members of a charismatic sect, called the New Temple of God, in London during the 1920s.

Historical Accuracy: The novel weaves an ingenious plot and a convincing period backdrop.

MAGDALEN KING-HALL (1904-1971)

A British writer and novelist, Magdalen King-Hall was born in London, and was the daughter of an admiral in the Royal Navy. She attended Downe House and St. Leonards School in St. Andrews, Scotland. King-Hall was the first woman to take part in the BBC program ''Round Britain Quiz.'' She was the author of *The Noble Savages*, *The Fox Sisters*, and *Life and Death of the Wicked Lady Skelton*, which was filmed in 1947 as *The Wicked Lady*. She writes under the pseudonym Cleone Knox.

3490 *The Lovely Lynchs*

Date of Publication: 1947
Subject(s): Family Saga
Fictional character(s): Jenny Lynch, Young Woman; Dorothea Lynch, Young Woman
Time Period(s): 18th century; 19th century
Locale(s): Dublin, Ireland; London, England; Paris, France

Summary: Social customs and life in the 18th and early 19th centuries are depicted through the experiences of two Irish sisters, Jenny and Dorothea Lynch. Both make an impact on the fashionable society of the day.

Historical Accuracy: The period details are minutely and believably presented.

KATE KINGSBURY

3491 *Check-Out Time*

Date of Publication: 1995
Subject(s): Mystery; Edwardian Period
Fictional character(s): Cecily Sinclair, Hotel Owner, Detective—Amateur; Sir Richard Malton, Gentleman
Time Period(s): 1900s (1908)
Locale(s): England

Summary: While preparations are underway for the Midsummer Ball, Sir Richard Malton climbs up on the railing of his top-floor balcony like a tight-rope walker and plunges to his death. Was it an accident or murder? Cecily Sinclair, the owner of the Pennyfoot Hotel suspects the latter.

Historical Accuracy: The period atmosphere is authentic and believable.

3492 *Do Not Disturb*

Date of Publication: 1994
Subject(s): Mystery; Edwardian Period
Fictional character(s): Cecily Sinclair, Hotel Owner, Detective—Amateur; Madeline Pengrath, Herbalist
Time Period(s): 1900s (1906)
Locale(s): England

Summary: A guest at the Pennyfoot Hotel is surprised when a knock at his door reveals no one. A moment later he is dead. The police suspect poison, and suspicion falls on Cecily Sinclair's friend, Madeline, an avid herbalist. Cecily must find the real killer before there is another victim.

Historical Accuracy: The novel combines an ingenious mystery with authentic period details.

3493 *Eat, Drink, and Be Buried*

Date of Publication: 1994
Subject(s): Mystery; Edwardian Period
Fictional character(s): Cecily Sinclair, Hotel Owner, Detective—Amateur
Time Period(s): 1900s (1908)
Locale(s): England

Summary: May Day festivities at the Pennyfoot Hotel turn deadly when one of the guests is found strangled with the maypole ribbon. Cecily Sinclair takes up the investigation.

Historical Accuracy: The period is evoked with some skill.

3494 *Grounds for Murder*

Date of Publication: 1995
Subject(s): Mystery; Edwardian Period; Gypsies
Fictional character(s): Cecily Sinclair, Hotel Owner, Detective—Amateur
Time Period(s): 1900s (1908)
Locale(s): England

Summary: The peaceful Pennyfoot Hotel is disturbed by gypsies in a nearby woods. A young gypsy girl is found murdered and it is discovered that the murder weapon came from the hotel. Suspicion falls on the hotel staff and guests.

Historical Accuracy: The picture of the period is carefully integrated with the murder puzzle.

3495 *Room with a Clue*
Date of Publication: 1993
Subject(s): Mystery; Edwardian Period
Fictional character(s): Cecily Sinclair, Hotel Owner, Detective—Amateur; Lady Eleanor Danbury, Noblewoman
Time Period(s): 1900s (1906)
Locale(s): England

Summary: Cecily Sinclair is the owner of the seaside Pennyfoot Hotel. When Lady Eleanor Danbury falls four stories to her death, Cecily takes up the investigation before disaster strikes again.

Historical Accuracy: The Edwardian period details are convincing and authentic.

3496 *Service for Two*
Date of Publication: 1994
Subject(s): Mystery; Edwardian Period
Fictional character(s): Cecily Sinclair, Hotel Owner, Detective—Amateur
Time Period(s): 1900s (1907)
Locale(s): England

Summary: At Dr. McDuff's funeral, a stranger's body is found in the casket, a victim of murder. When one of the housemaids of the Pennyfoot Hotel tells Cecily Sinclair that she saw one of the victim's associates in the card room of the hotel, Cecily investigates.

Historical Accuracy: Good period details share the stage with an ingenious mystery.

CHARLES KINGSLEY (1819-1875)
An English writer and rector of a parish in Hampshire, England, Kingsley had a varied literary career. His principal novels, besides those listed below, are *Yeast*, *Alton Locke*, and *The Water Babies*.

3497 *Hereward the Wake*
Date of Publication: 1866
Subject(s): Middle Ages; Norman Conquest; Crime and Criminals
Fictional character(s): Lady Godiva, Noblewoman; Torfrida, Noblewoman
Historical character(s): William the Conqueror, Ruler; Hereward the Wake, Outlaw, Outcast
Time Period(s): 11th century
Locale(s): England; Scotland; Flanders

Summary: This is a tale of the final days of Anglo-Saxon England and the Norman invasion. Hereward is proclaimed a wake, or outlaw, by his mother and becomes an outcast. He has many adventures before returning home when he receives news of the Norman invasion. Fighting the Normans, he eventually makes peace with King William, but as one of the last of the Saxons, he is an enemy of the Norman conquerors.

Historical Accuracy: This is a remarkably realistic treatment of the Anglo-Saxon period. Kingsley's characters and story are believable.

3498 *Hypatia*
Date of Publication: 1853
Subject(s): Roman Empire; Jews; Christianity
Fictional character(s): Philammon, Religious (monk); Orestes, Government Official (Roman prefect)
Historical character(s): Hypatia, Philosopher (pagan)
Time Period(s): 5th century
Locale(s): Alexandria, Egypt; Rome, Roman Empire

Summary: At the time of the breakup of the Roman Empire, Hypatia, a female Greek philosopher, is one of the last worshippers of the Greek gods. The novel depicts her in the midst of the political and ideological conflicts between pagans, Christians, and Jews.

Historical Accuracy: There are good details of religious sects and factional turmoil.

3499 *Westward Ho!*
Date of Publication: 1855
Subject(s): Elizabethan Period; Sea Story; Inquisition
Fictional character(s): Amyas Leigh, Sailor; Rose Salterne, Gentlewoman; Don Guzman De Soto, Military Personnel
Historical character(s): Sir Francis Drake, Explorer, Sea Captain; Sir Walter Raleigh, Explorer, Courtier
Time Period(s): 16th century
Locale(s): Devon, England; Ireland; Caracas, Venezuela

Summary: In this romantic adventure set during the age of exploration, Amyas Leigh voyages with Drake around the world and fights the Spanish in South America and during the Armada. His personal vendetta is against a Spanish noble who captures the heart of his beloved. There are strong scenes of the horrors of the Spanish Inquistion.

Historical Accuracy: This is one of the best adventure stories in English literature: a superb blend of romance and history.

HENRY KINGSLEY (1830-1876)
Kingsley was an English author who was the younger brother of Charles Kingsley. He spent five years in Australia, the setting for his first novel, *Geoffry Hamlyn*. His other major works are *Austin Elliott*, *The Hillyars and the Burtons*, *Leighton Court*, and *Silcote of the Silcotes*.

3500 *Ravenshoe*
Date of Publication: 1862
Subject(s): Inheritance—Disputed; Family Saga; Crimean War
Fictional character(s): Charles Ravenshoe, Gentleman, Heir—Dispossessed; Mackworth, Religious; William Horton, Servant
Time Period(s): 19th century (1820-1855)
Locale(s): England; Crimea, Russia

Summary: This is a complicated tale of concealed identities and a disputed inheritance. Charles Ravenshoe is brought up by his nurse, the wife of the estate's gamekeeper, who also has a son, William. The boys are switched at birth; and William inherits the estate. Charles joins the army and fights in the Crimea, later to find that the mystery of his birth and inheritance is solved.

Historical Accuracy: The tale is slow-moving and more romance than history.

WILLIAM KINSOLVING

Kinsolving has worked as a screenwriter, actor, and singer.

3501 *Born with the Century*

Date of Publication: 1979
Subject(s): Family Saga; Business Building
Fictional character(s): Magnus Macpherson, Businessman; Mary Fleming, Spouse; Iris Fowler, Young Woman
Time Period(s): 20th century (1900-1971)
Locale(s): New York, New York; Canada

Summary: During his 70-year career, whiskey magnate Magnus Macpherson rises to power and respectability from the deadly competition created by Prohibition. He sacrifices his family to create his business empire.

Historical Accuracy: The story of business success and the destruction of a family is played out in scenes that capture the major events of the 20th century.

3502 *Mister Christian*

Date of Publication: 1996
Subject(s): Sea Story; Napoleonic Wars
Fictional character(s): Daphne Lewis, Captive
Historical character(s): Fletcher Christian, Military Personnel (naval officer), Fugitive; William Bligh, Military Personnel (naval officer); Horatio Nelson, Military Personnel (admiral); William Wordsworth, Writer; Samuel Taylor Coleridge, Writer; Dorothy Wordsworth, Writer
Time Period(s): 18th century; 19th century (1793-1811)
Locale(s): Pacific Ocean (South Pacific); England; At Sea

Summary: What if Fletcher Christian had not perished with his fellow *Bounty* mutineers on Pitcairn Island but made his way back to England? The novel explores the possibilities. Christian narrates his adventures as a fugitive, in the great sea battles of the Napoleonic War, with romantic poets Wordsworth and Coleridge, and in a final confrontation with his nemesis, William Bligh.

Historical Accuracy: The rumor and scanty evidence of Christian's survival and return to England provide the basis for this imagined reconstruction of the facts. The adventures too often push the boundary of credibility.

CEYSTA KINSTLER

Kinstler is a professor of philosophy, religion, and women's studies at American River College in Sacramento, California.

3503 *The Moon under Her Feet*

Date of Publication: 1989
Subject(s): Myths and Legends; Biblical Story; Witchcraft and Sorcery
Historical character(s): Jesus Christ, Biblical Figure; Mary Magdalene, Biblical Figure; Judas Iscariot, Biblical Figure
Time Period(s): 1st century
Locale(s): Israel

Summary: The novel offers an original retelling of the gospel story of Jesus Christ in which Mary Magdalene appears as a high priestess and sorceress and the lover of both Jesus (here Yeshua) and Judas. The novel combines the mythologies of paganism and Christianity into a fresh and daring repossession of the New Testament story.

Historical Accuracy: The novel departs radically from the received tradition although the book's notes establish its basis in mythological and historical sources.

KATE KIRBY

3504 *Scapegoat for a Stuart*

Date of Publication: 1975
Subject(s): Gunpowder Plot; Jacobean Period; Royalty—England
Fictional character(s): Harry Weaver, Bastard Son
Historical character(s): Robert Cecil, Courtier, Government Official; Guy Fawkes, Leader (of the Gunpowder Plot), Rebel; James I, Ruler (King of England); Elizabeth I, Ruler (Queen of England)
Time Period(s): 17th century (1603-1606)
Locale(s): England

Summary: Following the death of Elizabeth I and the succession of James I, a group of fanatics, including Guy Fawkes, plots to blow up Parliament in the notorious Gunpowder Plot. The fate of the Weaver Family, particularly young Harry Weaver, is connected with that of the royals and the court's ruling force, Sir Robert Cecil.

Historical Accuracy: The fictional story is set against a believable and authentic period backdrop.

ELITHE HAMILTON KIRKLAND (1907-)

3505 *Divine Average*

Date of Publication: 1952
Subject(s): American West; Mexican War; Texas Revolution
Fictional character(s): Range Templeton, Rancher
Time Period(s): 19th century (1838-1858)
Locale(s): Texas

Summary: The story of the development of Texas in the 19th century is told through the experiences of cattle king Range Templeton, the first to bring cattle to market in New Orleans and California. Templeton's obsession for land and power is displayed in his hatred of Mexicans and Indians and in the force he uses to subdue them both.

Historical Accuracy: The novel's documentation of the strife between the Americans and the Mexicans in Texas is authentic and believable.

3506 *Love Is a Wild Assault*

Date of Publication: 1959
Subject(s): Settlement of the American Frontier; Biography, Fictionalized; Texas Revolution
Historical character(s): Harriet Potter, Pioneer; Robert Potter, Political Figure
Time Period(s): 19th century
Locale(s): Texas

Summary: This biographical novel traces the life of Harriet Potter, a notorious figure in the years of the Texas Republic. A pioneer in the Texas wilderness, Harriet is a proud beauty who becomes involved with politician Robert Potter who is forced to flee North Carolina after to a sensational scandal.

Historical Accuracy: The novel is based on Potter's own autobiographical account and other contemporary letters, records, and first-hand reports.

PADDY KITCHEN (1934-)

An English writer born in London, Kitchen has worked for the Royal College of Art, the Chelsea School of Art, and the Tate Gallery in London. His books include the novels *A Fleshy School*, *Paradise*, and *A Pillar of Cloud*; a biography of Gerald Manley Hopkins; and the reference work *The Way to Write Novels*.

3507 *The Golden Veil*

Date of Publication: 1981
Subject(s): Victorian Period; Artistic Life; Biography, Fictionalized
Historical character(s): Dante Gabriel Rossetti, Writer (poet), Artist; Elizabeth Eleanor Siddal, Artist, Model; John Ruskin, Writer; Holman Hunt, Artist
Time Period(s): 19th century
Locale(s): London, England; France

Summary: This novel is based on the life of Elizabeth Siddal, Dante Rossetti's model. She becomes his mistress and dies under tragic circumstances. The novel traces her career from her youth to her involvement in the bohemian and artistic circle that includes John Millais, Algernon Swinburne, Holman Hunt, William Morris, and others.

Historical Accuracy: The novel's portraits of actual figures are unconvincing. However, the atmosphere of the period is captured with authentic touches.

JAMES ARTHUR KJELGAARD
(1910-1959)

Born in New York City, Kjelgaard worked as a trapper, teamster, surveyor's assistant, factory worker, and plumber's apprentice. He is best known for his books for children, featuring his two great loves: nature and dogs. He

is best remembered for his Big Red novels, three books about a champion Irish setter.

3508 *The Land Is Bright*

Date of Publication: 1958
Subject(s): Civil War—U.S.
Fictional character(s): Colin Campbell, Judge, Landowner; Jeannie Dare, Young Woman; Ling Stewart, Hunter, Mountain Man
Time Period(s): 1860s
Locale(s): Blue Ridge Mountains, Virginia

Summary: Divided allegiance in Civil-War-era Virginia is the novel's theme. Colin Campbell is a successful judge and landowner whose friendship with mountain man Ling Stewart suffers a severe test when they take opposite sides in the conflict.

Historical Accuracy: The novel presents the period and the locale with authority.

3509 *The Lost Wagon*

Date of Publication: 1955
Subject(s): American West; Immigrants; Wagon Trains
Fictional character(s): Joe Tower, Farmer; Emma Tower, Spouse
Time Period(s): 19th century
Locale(s): Oregon Trail, United States (Missouri to Oregon)

Summary: The novel describes the Tower family's trek West on the Oregon Trail. Joe and Emma and their six children fall behind the wagon train and are forced to make the journey on their own. The novel provides a vivid description of their difficult and dangerous passage to Oregon.

Historical Accuracy: The novel is convincing in its details of Western life.

P.F. KLUGE (1942-)

Born in New Jersey and a graduate of Kenyon College and the University of Chicago, Kluge was a Peace Corps volunteer and a speechwriter and political aide in Micronesia. Kluge also worked as a staff reporter for the *Wall Street Journal* and an assistant editor of *Life*.

3510 *Season for War*

Date of Publication: 1984
Subject(s): American West; Military Life—U.S. Cavalry; Spanish-American War
Fictional character(s): Henry Lawson, Military Personnel (army officer); Lucy Lawson, Spouse; Edwin Carter Morrison, Journalist
Time Period(s): 19th century (1885-1899)
Locale(s): Southwest; Philippines

Summary: The novel offers the story of career army officer Henry Lawson, his wife, Lucy, and journalist Edwin Morrison, who celebrates Lawson as "America's Foremost Fighting Soldier." Lawson commands the all-black 25th Cavalry against the Apaches and fights in the jungles of the Philippines in the Spanish-American War, becoming the embodiment of American imperialism.

Historical Accuracy: The period and historical events that drive the story are pictured accurately.

RICHARD KLUGER (1934-)

Born in New Jersey and a graduate of Princeton, Kluger worked for the *Wall Street Journal*, the New York *Post*, *Forbes* magazine, and the New York *Herald Tribune*, for which he was the literary editor. Kluger also worked as an executive editor at Simon & Schuster and editor-in-chief at Atheneum before turning to writing full time in 1973. His books include *Simple Justice*, a narrative on the Supreme Court's decision in Brown v. Board of Education; *When the Bough Breaks*; and *National Anthem*.

3511 *Members of the Tribe*

Date of Publication: 1977
Subject(s): Jews; Anti-Semitism; Trials
Fictional character(s): Noah Berg, Murderer (accused); Seth Adler, Lawyer
Time Period(s): 19th century; 20th century (1860s-1970s)
Locale(s): Savannah, Georgia

Summary: This novel is based on the actual murder case of Leo M. Frank of Atlanta, a Jew who was lynched after being convicted of murdering a Christian girl. This version of the case takes place in Savannah and centers on the Jewish lawyer, Seth Adler, who defends the accused murderer, Noah Berg.

Historical Accuracy: The novel draws freely on many historical events and personalities, and the trial of Noah Berg is based only loosely on the Frank case.

3512 *The Sheriff of Nottingham*

Date of Publication: 1992
Subject(s): Myths and Legends; Middle Ages; Royalty—England
Fictional character(s): Philip Mark, Government Official (sheriff), Mercenary; Robin Hood, Outlaw
Historical character(s): John, Ruler (King of England)
Time Period(s): 13th century (1208-1224)
Locale(s): Nottingham, England; Sherwood Forest, England

Summary: The Sheriff of Nottingham, best known as Robin Hood's legendary opponent, here is given a name and a history. King John sends Norman mercenary Philip Mark to Nottingham as sheriff in 1208. Philip must decide whether or not to carry out the King's commands when John orders him, against his own wishes, to execute 30 Welsh hostages.

Historical Accuracy: The novel's perceptive use of history is exact and convincing.

JOHN R. KNAGGS (1934-)

Knaggs worked as the Texas state capitol correspondent for UPI. He is a journalism graduate of the University of Texas.

3513 *The Bugles Are Silent: A Novel of the Texas Revolution*

Date of Publication: 1977
Subject(s): American West; Texas Revolution; Battle of the Alamo
Fictional character(s): Jason Gates, Military Personnel; Juan Calderon, Military Personnel (Mexican officer)
Historical character(s): Antonio Lopez de Santa Anna, Military Personnel (Mexican general); William Barret Travis, Military Personnel (officer); Jim Bowie, Frontiersman; Davy Crockett, Frontiersman; Sam Houston, Military Personnel (commander)
Time Period(s): 1830s (1835-1836)
Locale(s): Texas

Summary: Major events in the Texas war of independence from Mexico are depicted from the differing perspectives of combatants on both sides of the conflict. Jason Gates, a young courier to Sam Houston, and Juan Calderon, an officer on Santa Ana's staff, provide their views on the Alamo's defense and the climactic Battle of San Jacinto.

Historical Accuracy: The novel blends fictional characters with historical ones. The author made every effort to authenticate historical events.

ALANNA KNIGHT

An English author born in Durham, Knight began her career as a secretary. Research and writing on the life of Robert Louis Stevenson gave her clear insight into Victorian Edinburgh and paved the way for Knight's historical crime series featuring the detective Inspector Faro.

3514 *The Black Duchess*

Date of Publication: 1980
Subject(s): Elizabethan Period; Sea Story; Spanish Armada
Fictional character(s): Felipe Flores y Lennox Montreuse, Sea Captain, Pirate; Maeve O'Neill, Young Woman; Marie Jamesina Sibella Stewart, Gentlewoman
Historical character(s): Sir Francis Drake, Sea Captain
Time Period(s): 16th century (1588)
Locale(s): *Black Duchess*, At Sea; Orkney Islands, Scotland

Summary: The novel is a tale of sea adventure at the time of the Spanish Armada. Felipe Montreuse is the half-Scots godson of King Philip of Spain, a pirate captain who sails with the Armada and its reckoning with Drake. Aboard the *Black Duchess* is an Irish stowaway. Events carry the ship to the Orkney Islands and capture by the beautiful Lady Sibella.

Historical Accuracy: The emphasis here is romantic adventure not historical accuracy, but there are some convincing period details.

3515 *Blood Line*

Date of Publication: 1989
Subject(s): Mystery; Victorian Period
Fictional character(s): Jeremy Faro, Police Officer (detective inspector); Vincent Laurie, Doctor
Time Period(s): 1860s

Locale(s): Edinburgh, Scotland

Summary: An unidentified body found prior to Queen Victoria's visit to Edinburgh reminds Inspector Faro of a case 30 years ago which cost the life of his father. During repairs to Edinburgh Castle, the mummified remains of an infant from the 16th century are found in the wall of Mary, Queen of Scots' apartments. The identity of the child could have profound importance to the current queen.

Historical Accuracy: The novel vividly establishes the period atmosphere.

3516 *Castle of Foxes*

Date of Publication: 1981
Subject(s): Victorian Period; Suspense
Fictional character(s): Tanya Durris, Widow(er); Edward Durris, Heir, Nobleman
Historical character(s): Victoria, Ruler (Queen of England); Albert of Saxe-Coburg-Gotha, Royalty (prince consort of Victoria)
Time Period(s): 1850s
Locale(s): Highlands, Scotland

Summary: Set in the Scottish Highlands during the Victorian period, this suspenseful novel involves Tanya Durris, a young widow, who presents complications for Lord Edward, the heir to a great estate. When the Queen and Prince Albert come for a royal visit, danger and intrigue are afoot.

Historical Accuracy: The novel offers an odd and somewhat unbelievable conjunction between the historical and gothic suspense.

3517 *Deadly Beloved*

Date of Publication: 1990
Subject(s): Mystery; Victorian Period
Fictional character(s): Jeremy Faro, Police Officer (detective inspector); Vincent Laurie, Doctor; Melville Kellar, Doctor
Time Period(s): 1870s
Locale(s): Edinburgh, Scotland

Summary: Inspector Faro and Doctor Laurie, his stepson, attend a dinner party given by police doctor Kellar and his wife. The next day she takes a trip but never arrives at her destination. When her fur coat and a carving knife stained with blood are found, foul play seems certain. Suspicion points to Kellar.

Historical Accuracy: The novel offers an ingenious puzzle with period and local color.

3518 *Enter Second Murderer*

Date of Publication: 1988
Subject(s): Mystery; Victorian Period
Fictional character(s): Jeremy Faro, Police Officer (detective inspector); Vincent Laurie, Doctor
Time Period(s): 1870s (1870)
Locale(s): Edinburgh, Scotland

Summary: In the first of a series of mysteries set in Victorian Edinburgh, Inspector Jeremy Faro and his stepson, Doctor Vincent Laurie, re-open the sensational "Gruesome Convent Murders." The case leads them to a perilous investigation to

uncover secrets hidden beneath the surface of respectable Edinburgh society.

Historical Accuracy: The author shows a convincing mastery of the period and its locale.

3519 *Estella*

Date of Publication: 1986
Subject(s): Victorian Period
Fictional character(s): Estella Havisham, Young Woman; Bentley Drummle, Gentleman; Philip ''Pip'' Pirrip, Young Man
Time Period(s): 19th century
Locale(s): England

Summary: Based on the characters and situations of Charles Dickens' classic *Great Expectations*, the novel tells the story from the perspective of Miss Havisham's ward, Estella, who is raised by the bitter Miss Havisham to wreak vengeance on men and break their hearts. Estella's blighted life includes marriage to Bentley Drummle and poverty until she is finally reunited with the adoring Pip.

Historical Accuracy: The period details are accurate and the novel offers a credible echoing of the great Dickens' original.

3520 *Killing Cousins*

Date of Publication: 1992
Subject(s): Mystery; Victorian Period
Fictional character(s): Jeremy Faro, Police Officer (detective inspector); Vincent Laurie, Doctor; Francis Balfrey, Gentleman
Time Period(s): 1870s (1878)
Locale(s): Orkney Islands, Scotland

Summary: Vincent Laurie, Inspector Faro's stepson, hears from a school friend, Francis Balfrey, about his wife's illness. Faro's mother is Balfrey's housekeeper, and both Faro and Laurie decide to visit. The wife dies, and Vincent is convinced that she has been poisoned. When another person is killed, Faro must discover the identity of the killer before further deaths occur.

Historical Accuracy: The characters are believable, and the period is well-displayed.

BRIGID KNIGHT
(PSEUD. OF KATHLEEN H. SINCLAIR, 1905-)
Sinclair's books include *Walking the Whirlwind*.

3521 *The Covenant*

Date of Publication: 1943
Subject(s): Boer War; Afrikaaners; British Colonies
Fictional character(s): Stephen Barry, Landowner; Chris de Lange, Young Woman; Jannion Barry, Spouse (of Stephen)
Time Period(s): 1890s
Locale(s): South Africa

Summary: Relations between the Dutch and the English in South Africa during the Boer War form the background for this melodramatic tale concerning Englishman Stephen Barry, his wife Jannion, and the influence of Chris de Lange, a young Dutch woman. Stephen, who fights the Dutch, eventually recognizes his kinship with them in the mutual feeling for the land.

Historical Accuracy: The historical element takes a secondary place to the relationship between the Barrys and de Lange.

3522 *Not by Any Single Man*

Date of Publication: 1950
Subject(s): Napoleonic Wars
Fictional character(s): Catherine Gray, Young Woman; Madeleine Dallas, Bastard Daughter
Time Period(s): 1800s
Locale(s): Kent, England

Summary: This melodramatic tale set during the Napoleonic Wars centers on Catherine Gray, the daughter of a Kentish farmer. She loves a feckless adventurer who foists his bastard daughter Madeleine on her. Their conflict over the years forms the novel's implausible story.

Historical Accuracy: There are few period elements in this romance.

3523 *The Valiant Lady*

Date of Publication: 1948
Subject(s): Independence—Netherlands; Elizabethan Period
Fictional character(s): Anna von Breda, Gentlewoman
Time Period(s): 16th century
Locale(s): Netherlands; Cornwall, England

Summary: Set during the Dutch War of Independence against the Spanish during the 16th century, the novel describes the heroic efforts of Anna von Breda to protect her family from the violence of the period.

Historical Accuracy: The novel is faithful to the events of the period and accurately describes its manners and customs.

3524 *Westward the Sun*

Date of Publication: 1942
Subject(s): Frontier—Africa; Boers; Jameson Raid
Fictional character(s): Charlotte Durant, Young Woman; Adrian Durant, Young Man; Roderick Mason, Gentleman
Historical character(s): Paul Kruger, Political Figure
Time Period(s): 19th century (1877-1895)
Locale(s): South Africa

Summary: Events in 19th-century South Africa are enacted, focusing on Charlotte Durant and her brother Adrian, children of a mixed marriage of Boer and English parents. Conflicting loyalties and the rush of history affect their prospects. Scenes include the Jameson Raid of 1895 and a strong portrait of Boer leader Paul Kruger.

Historical Accuracy: The portrait of South African life of the period is convincing.

RUTH ADAMS KNIGHT (1898-1974)

Born in Ohio and educated at Toledo University, Knight began her writing career with the Toledo *Daily Times* and the Toledo *Sunday Times* as a reporter and drama and

literary editor. She was also a radio writer for national programs.

3525 *Certain Harvest: A Novel of the Time of Peter Cooper*

Date of Publication: 1960
Subject(s): Biography, Fictionalized; Railroads
Historical character(s): Peter Cooper, Financier, Inventor
Time Period(s): 19th century
Locale(s): New York, New York

Summary: This biographical novel on the life of Peter Cooper tells the story of the country farm boy who creates a business empire. Cooper establishes the Cooper Union to provide education for the working class, and his "Tom Thumb" locomotive spurs the success of the biggest railroad of its day, the Baltimore and Ohio. The novel also describes the growth and development of 19th-century New York.

Historical Accuracy: The novel is an accurate account of Cooper's remarkable career.

JOHN KNOWLES (1926-)

An American novelist born in West Virginia, Knowles graduated from Yale and worked as a newspaper reporter and magazine editor before becoming a full-time writer. His most popular and acclaimed novel is his first, *A Separate Peace*, which records the lives of schoolboys during the first years of World War II. It received the Faulkner Award. His other novels include *Peace Breaks Out*, *Indian Summer*, and *A Stolen Past*.

3526 *A Vein of Riches*

Date of Publication: 1978
Subject(s): Mining; Labor Movement; Oil Industry
Fictional character(s): Lyle Catherwood, Young Man; Virgil Pence, Labor Organizer
Time Period(s): 20th century (1909-1924)
Locale(s): West Virginia

Summary: The story of West Virginia's coal industry is dramatized from its heyday in 1909 through the union struggle to organize the miners, the dispute with the mine owners, the discovery of oil, and the collapse of the industry. The story centers on the experiences of young Lyle Catherwood, member of a prominent West Virginia family, and his exposure to the conflict.

Historical Accuracy: The novel offers believable and convincing period and regional details.

ALEXANDER KNOX (1907-)

Canadian actor and author Knox was born in Ontario and attended the University of Western Ontario. He has appeared in over 30 plays in England and the U.S. and in many films, including the distinguished 1944 film biography *Wilson*. His book *Night of the White Bear* records a journey of three Eskimos across the polar sea.

3527　*The Kidnapped Surgeon*

Date of Publication: 1977
Subject(s): Frontier—Canada; Indians; Medical Profession
Fictional character(s): Calvin Heggie, Trader; Ian Ogilvie, Doctor
Time Period(s): 1780s (1786)
Locale(s): Canada

Summary: Set in the Canadian lake region during the 1780s, the novel concerns Calvin Heggie, who is in charge of the Hudson Bay Company's trading post. Heggie's son is injured in an accident. To save him, Heggie must get to a young army surgeon, Ian Ogilvie, and persuade him to undertake a hazardous operation.

Historical Accuracy: The frontier setting of the period is convincingly captured.

CLEONE KNOX

(PSEUD. OF MAGDALEN KING-HALL, 1904-1971)

British author and novelist King-Hall was the first woman to take part in BBC's program, "Round Britain Quiz." Her book, *Life and Death of the Wicked Lady Skelton* was made into the film *The Wicked Lady*. Her other books include *Lady Sarah*, *Lord Edward*, and *The Fox Sisters*.

3528　*Gay Crusader*

Date of Publication: 1934
Subject(s): Middle Ages; Crusades
Fictional character(s): Sir Fulk de Lacy, Knight
Time Period(s): 12th century
Locale(s): England; Palestine

Summary: This romantic tale of the Crusades follows the adventures of English knight Sir Fulk de Lacy, who, to escape from an undesirable marriage, sets off for the Holy Land. His adventures in love and war are dramatized.

Historical Accuracy: The adventures are true to the history of the time, but the dialogue is modernized.

WERNER KOCH

3529　*Pontius Pilate Reflects*

Date of Publication: 1961
Subject(s): Biblical Story; Roman Empire
Historical character(s): Pontius Pilate, Biblical Figure, Government Official
Time Period(s): 1st century
Locale(s): Rome, Roman Empire; Jerusalem, Israel

Summary: At the end of his life, Pontius Pilate recalls the events that led up to the crucifixion of Jesus Christ. He has been dismissed from his government position and is living in Rome. The combination of past and present political intrigue pushes Pilate to the brink of insanity and forces a reassessment.

Historical Accuracy: Nothing beyond the few lines that mention Pilate in the New Testament is known. The novel's

imagined re-creation of Pilate's history and thoughts is set against a believable backdrop of Rome during the 1st century.

KARLEEN KOEN

3530　*Now Face to Face*

Date of Publication: 1995
Subject(s): American Colonies; Jacobite Rebellion; Georgian Period
Fictional character(s): Barbara Devane, Widow(er), Landowner
Historical character(s): George I, Ruler (King of England); George, Royalty (Prince of Wales); Robert Walpole, Political Figure; James Francis Edward Stuart, Royalty
Time Period(s): 1720s
Locale(s): London, England; Virginia, American Colonies

Summary: This sprawling romantic novel centers on Barbara Devane, a widow at 20, who struggles to develop the family tobacco plantation in colonial Virginia. When she returns to London, attempting to reestablish herself as a woman of property and distinction, she finds her social world exploding in political turmoil caused by the Jacobite challenge to the Hanoverian monarch.

Historical Accuracy: The novel features a believable period background that is interwoven with the fictional story.

3531　*Through a Glass Darkly*

Date of Publication: 1986
Subject(s): Romance; Royalty—France
Fictional character(s): Barbara Alderley, Gentlewoman; Roger Montgeoffrey, Nobleman (Earl of Devane)
Historical character(s): Philippe II, Duc d'Orleans, Royalty (regent of Louis XV); Louis-Francois-Armand de Vignerot du Plessis, Nobleman (Duc de Richelieu), Political Figure
Time Period(s): 1710s; 1720s
Locale(s): London, England; Paris, France

Summary: Barbara Alderley marries nobleman Roger Montgeoffrey, who propels her into 18th-century society in London and Paris. There she becomes involved in a world that is both elegant and duplicitous. Mysterious events and secrets lead up to a shattering betrayal.

Historical Accuracy: The period is suggested primarily by cameo appearances and by period references, which are accurate, if secondary to the novel's romantic intrigue.

ARTHUR KOESTLER

3532　*The Gladiators*

Date of Publication: 1939
Subject(s): Roman Empire; Servile War
Fictional character(s): Fulvius, Lawyer
Historical character(s): Spartacus, Gladiator, Leader (slave rebellion); Marcus Licinius Crassus, Military Personnel (general)
Time Period(s): 1st century B.C. (73-71 B.C.)
Locale(s): Roman Empire

Summary: Told from the perspective of a Roman lawyer named Fulvius, the novel records the events of the rebellion led by Spartacus in the 1st century B.C. With obvious parallels drawn between the Roman period and the modern world, the novel is best in its portrait of the cynical opportunist Crassus and the tragic failure of the humanitarian state dreamed of by Spartacus.

Historical Accuracy: The book effectively captures Roman life during the period.

MANUEL KOMROFF (1890-1974)

An American novelist, editor, and author of children's books and nonfiction works, Komroff was born in New York City and attended Yale University. During World War II, he was an adviser on the Writer's War Board. He has written a number of historical studies and travel books. His novels include *The Life, the Loves, the Adventures of Omar Khayyam*, *The Whole World Is Outside*, and *Jade Star*. He is also the author of *The Story of Jesus* and the editor of *Everyman's Bible*.

3533 *Feast of the Jesters*

Date of Publication: 1947
Subject(s): Napoleonic Era; Theatrical Life; Congress of Vienna
Fictional character(s): Sir Jonathan Parry, Gentleman; Jules Raymond, Actor
Historical character(s): Alexander I, Ruler (Czar of Russia)
Time Period(s): 1810s
Locale(s): Vienna, Austria

Summary: Amidst the glitter and intrigue of the Congress of Vienna, convened to redraw the boundaries of Europe after the defeat of Napoleon, a troupe of French actors and others come to Vienna for a variety of motives. The elaborate charade of power and manipulation ends with the news that Napoleon has escaped from Elba.

Historical Accuracy: The novel succeeds in its reconstruction of the atmosphere of the period and in its pithy portraits of some of the participants in the great gathering.

3534 *The Magic Bow*

Date of Publication: 1940
Subject(s): Biography, Fictionalized; Musical Life
Historical character(s): Niccolo Paganini, Musician (violinist)
Time Period(s): 19th century (1800-1840)
Locale(s): Italy

Summary: This biographical novel chronicles the story of Italian violin virtuoso Paganini. His story begins at age 18 when his prodigious talents are beginning to be recognized. The novel traces his rise to prominence as a legendary performer.

Historical Accuracy: The basic outline of the novel's background details is accurate though somewhat colored by a romanticized tinge to enhance Paganini's rise from poverty to prominence.

3535 *Two Thieves*

Date of Publication: 1931
Subject(s): Biblical Story; Roman Empire; Jews
Fictional character(s): Barzor, Outlaw; Rongus, Outlaw
Time Period(s): 1st century
Locale(s): Israel

Summary: The novel imagines the story of the two men who were crucified with Christ. Barzor is an Arab and Rongus a Jew who are united in their hatred of the Romans and embark on a plan to destroy Pontius Pilate.

Historical Accuracy: The novel is filled with period color, but there are errors in the topography and instances of anachronisms.

3536 *Waterloo*

Date of Publication: 1936
Subject(s): Napoleonic Wars; Battle of Waterloo
Historical character(s): Napoleon Bonaparte, Ruler (Emperor of France); Arthur Wellesley, Military Personnel (British general), Nobleman (Duke of Wellington)
Time Period(s): 1810s (1815)
Locale(s): Waterloo, Belgium; France

Summary: The story of Napoleon's Hundred Days that climax on the battlefield of Waterloo receives an anti-heroic and ironic treatment here. Napoleon's escape from Elba and his restoration to power, as well as the action on the battlefield, are illustrated through the added details and the experiences of dozens of the participants.

Historical Accuracy: The novel is filled with authentic details, but all is presented to diminish the heroic and emphasize the human.

HANS KONING

(PSEUD. OF HANS KONINGSBERGER, 1921-)

Born in Amsterdam, Koning escaped from occupied Holland and served in the British army during World War II. Since 1951 he has lived in the U.S. Primarily a novelist, he has also written plays and films. He has worked as a reporter-at-large for *The New Yorker* and was the first New York writer to visit China after the revolution.

3537 *Death of a Schoolboy*

Date of Publication: 1974
Subject(s): World War I; Assassination
Historical character(s): Gavrilo Princip, Student, Murderer
Time Period(s): 1910s (1914-1918)
Locale(s): Sarajevo, Bosnia-Hercegovina

Summary: The novel offers a fictional account of Bosnian student Gavrilo Princip who shot Archduke Franz Ferdinand, touching off World War I. Too young to be executed, Princip is sentenced to life in solitary confinement. From his cell, Princip reflects on his short life and his motives for murder.

Historical Accuracy: The circumstances are historical, but the interpretation and viewpoint are decidedly contemporary.

3538 *The Petersburg-Cannes Express*

Date of Publication: 1975

Subject(s): Railroads; Russian Empire; Espionage

Fictional character(s): Andrew Tolcheff, Revolutionary; Anna, Revolutionary, Teacher; Draskovich, Government Official

Time Period(s): 1900s (1900)

Locale(s): Europe (Poland, Austria, Italy); St. Petersburg, Russia

Summary: Two very amateurish young revolutionaries carry a message of great importance aboard the St. Petersburg-Cannes Express in 1900. They must match wits with a former Secret Police official in this story of high adventure and train-board romance.

Historical Accuracy: The period details are authentic.

3539 *A Walk with Love and Death*

Date of Publication: 1961

Subject(s): Middle Ages; Hundred Years War; Jacquerie

Fictional character(s): Heron of Foix, Student; Claudia, Noblewoman, Orphan

Time Period(s): 14th century (1358)

Locale(s): France

Summary: This medieval tale of love is set during the Jacquerie, the French peasants' revolt of 1358, and concerns Heron of Foix, a Parisian student, who, disgruntled by his life at the Sorbonne, sets off for Oxford. He encounters a wandering noblewoman displaced by the rebellion, and Heron sets himself up as her knight-protector. The two embark on a journey across the medieval landscape relieved by a mutual chivalric relationship.

Historical Accuracy: The background is unconvincing with modern phrases and attitudes intruding.

MICHAEL KORDA (1933-)

Born in London, editor and writer Michael Korda attended Magdalene College, Cambridge. He is the author of several bestsellers, including *Power! How to Get It, How to Use It*, and the novels *Queenie, Worldly Goods*, and *The Fortune*.

3540 *The Immortals*

Date of Publication: 1992

Subject(s): Motion Picture Industry; Politics

Historical character(s): John F. Kennedy, Political Figure; Marilyn Monroe, Actress; Robert F. Kennedy, Political Figure; J. Edgar Hoover, Government Official; Jimmy Hoffa, Labor Organizer

Time Period(s): 1960s

Locale(s): United States

Summary: The novel is a fictional retelling of the love affair between Marilyn Monroe and John F. Kennedy. To reconstruct the story, the novel stays close to the factual, providing a plausible interpretation of this controversial story.

Historical Accuracy: The many historical figures presented are convincing, and the story avoids the excesses of sensation in favor of a more careful documentation.

KEITH KORMAN (1956-)

An American born in New York, Korman is a graduate of Hobart College. He has worked as a disc jockey and a literary agent.

3541 *Secret Dreams*

Date of Publication: 1995

Subject(s): Medical Profession

Historical character(s): Sigmund Freud, Doctor; Carl Jung, Doctor

Time Period(s): 1930s

Locale(s): Zurich, Switzerland

Summary: Based loosely on the celebrated case of Sabrina Spielman, the novel describes the efforts of Carl Jung and Sigmund Freud to rescue Fraulein S. from madness that leaves her wrapped in a sheet like a corpse. As Jung unravels her hysteria, he falls in love with her and finds himself travelling back in time to an earlier era of rituals of birth and death at the core of the mystery of the human psyche.

Historical Accuracy: The author makes clear that this is a work of fiction and the incidents are either the product of his imagination or used fictionally.

ZOFJA KOSSAK-SZCZUCKA (1890-1968)

Born in Poland, Kossak's writings have been translated into many languages, including English. One of her best known historical novels is *The Meek Shall Inherit*, a fictionalized account of the seventeenth-century Pole Kazimierz Korsak. She was a recipient of the Knight of St. Lazarus Cross, the Polonia Restituta Cross, and the Golden Cross of Merit.

3542 *Blessed Are the Meek: A Novel about St. Francis of Assisi*

Date of Publication: 1944

Subject(s): Religious Life; Middle Ages; Crusades

Historical character(s): Francis of Assisi, Religious (monk); Jean de Brienne, Ruler (King of Jerusalem); Innocent III, Religious (pope)

Time Period(s): 13th century

Locale(s): Italy; Palestine

Summary: The novel captures events of the early 13th century that include the establishment of the Franciscan Order, the Children's Crusade, and the Crusade led by Jean de Brienne. Also chronicled are the activities of Francis of Assisi, including his attempt to convert the Muslim Sultan.

Historical Accuracy: Historically accurate for the most part, the novel mingles fact and fiction. The characters conform to the broadest outlines of their history, but the novel also invents scenes and situations.

3543 *The Covenant: A Novel of the Life of Abraham the Prophet*

Date of Publication: 1951

Subject(s): Biblical Story

Historical character(s): Abraham, Biblical Figure

Time Period(s): 20th century B.C.
Locale(s): Ur, Mesopotamia

Summary: Based on the story found in the Bible's book of Genesis, the novel recounts the development of the Hebrews' worship of a single god and their search, led by Abraham, for a homeland. Abraham resists the worship of the deities of King Hammurabi, and his longing for a higher purpose leads him to establish a covenant with the single god of the Hebrews and become a patriarch for a nation.

Historical Accuracy: The novel offers a convincing recreation of the Biblical era and customs of the times.

3544 *The Leper King*

Date of Publication: 1945
Subject(s): Middle Ages; Crusades
Historical character(s): Baldwin IV, Ruler (King of Jerusalem)
Time Period(s): 12th century (1180s)
Locale(s): Jerusalem, Palestine

Summary: The story of the final days of the Kingdom of Jerusalem established by the Crusaders is dramatized in this novel depicting the reign of Baldwin IV. Under almost constant attack by Saladin, Baldwin struggles to hold his kingdom together, even as his leprosy spreads rapidly.

Historical Accuracy: The novel features an abundance of accurate period details.

DAVID KOSSOFF (1919-)

Born in London, Kossoff has worked as a furniture designer, an actor for the BBC, and an illustrator. He co-starred in his own play, *On Such a Night*.

3545 *The Voices of Masada*

Date of Publication: 1973
Subject(s): Roman Empire; Siege of Masada; Jewish Revolt
Historical character(s): Vespasian, Military Personnel (general), Ruler (Roman Emperor); Titus, Ruler (Roman Emperor); Flavius Josephus, Historian; Eleazar ben Yair, Leader (of the Jewish rebellion)
Time Period(s): 1st century (73)
Locale(s): Masada, Israel; Jerusalem, Israel

Summary: The novel tells the story of the Jewish revolt against the Romans and the tragic siege and destruction of Masada, in which nearly 1,000 of the defenders killed themselves rather than be enslaved by the Romans. The novel offers a variety of perspectives, from those of guerrilla fighters to Roman generals, including Vespasian, who interrupts his attack on Masada to be made emperor after Nero.

Historical Accuracy: The novel blends the factual with the fictional, but the background is genuine and compellingly described.

DESZO KOSZTOLANYI (1885-1936)

A Hungarian writer who first made his reputation as a poet before turning to fiction and translation, Kosztolanyi is known as a supreme stylist.

3546 *Bloody Poet*

Date of Publication: 1928
Subject(s): Roman Empire
Historical character(s): Nero, Ruler (Roman emperor)
Time Period(s): 1st century
Locale(s): Rome, Roman Empire

Summary: In this version of the reign of Roman Emperor Nero, he is portrayed as a poet driven mad by his frustrated genius. The awful results of Nero's excesses and crimes are vividly portrayed.

Historical Accuracy: The novel is not reliable in its historical presentation.

NORMAN KOTKER (1931-)

An American born in Massachusetts, Kotker graduated from Harvard. He has worked as a reporter and book editor for Scribner's. His novel, *Miss Rhode Island*, examines the life of a beauty pageant contestant who longs to be crowned Miss America.

3547 *Herzl the King*

Date of Publication: 1972
Subject(s): Biography, Fictionalized; Religious Conflict; Jews
Historical character(s): Theodor Herzl, Leader (Zionist)
Time Period(s): 1890s; 1900s (1894-1904)
Locale(s): Vienna, Austria

Summary: This biographical novel chronicles the last ten years in the life of Theodor Herzl, the founder of modern Zionism. Based chiefly on Herzl's own diaries, the novel depicts Herzl's commitment to the cause of creating a Jewish homeland that leads him to neglect his family, fortune, and health.

Historical Accuracy: The essential details of Herzl's life are observed, though some alteration has been done.

ZANE KOTKER (1934-)

Born in Connecticut, Kotker is a graduate of Middlebury College and Columbia University. He has worked as a reporter and an editor.

3548 *White Rising*

Date of Publication: 1981
Subject(s): American Colonies; Indians; King Philip's War
Fictional character(s): Caleb Peck, Settler; Mama Strong, Settler, Widow(er)
Historical character(s): Metacomet, Indian (Wampanoag), Chieftain
Time Period(s): 17th century (1675-1676)
Locale(s): Massachusetts, American Colonies

Summary: The story of King Philip's War in the New England colonies during the 1670s is described from both the Indians' and the settlers' point of view. The confederacy of tribes known as the Wampanoag under the leadership of Metacomet, whom the English dubbed King Philip, leads the attack to halt the western spread of settlement and growing encroachment on Indian lands.

Historical Accuracy: The novel is solidly based on the historical record. Some liberties have been taken, and, particularly with the Wampanoag material, some invention has been employed.

WILLIAM KOTZWINKLE (1938-)

Born in Pennsylvania, Kotzwinkle attended Rider College and Pennsylvania State University. An author of novels as well as children's literature, Kotzwinkle's work features wildly funny imagery and a mingling of various genres: detective story, fairy tale, farce. He won the World Fantasy Award for best novel in 1977 for *Doctor Rat*.

3549 *Fata Morgana*

Date of Publication: 1977
Subject(s): Crime and Criminals; Magic; Mystery
Fictional character(s): Paul Picard, Detective—Police; Ric Lazare, Magician
Time Period(s): 1860s (1861)
Locale(s): Paris, France; Vienna, Austria; Hungary

Summary: Set in Paris during the Second Empire of Louis Napoleon and Empress Eugenie, the novel is a story of suspense and detection involving police inspector Picard and the enigmatic Ric Lazare. Is Lazare a criminal, a real magician, or worse, a reincarnation from another place and time? The answer takes Picard on a dangerous quest from Paris to Vienna and Hungary following a trail of deception and violent death.

Historical Accuracy: More fabulous than historical, the novel is nonetheless convincing in rendering its period atmosphere.

DALE KRAMER (1936-)

Born in South Dakota, Kramer received his Ph.D. from Western Reserve University. He is a professor of English at the University of Illinois. Kramer's books include *Charles Maturin* and *Thomas Hardy: The Forms of Tragedy*.

3550 *The Heart of O. Henry*

Date of Publication: 1954
Subject(s): Biography, Fictionalized; Literary Life
Historical character(s): William Sydney Porter, Writer, Journalist
Time Period(s): 19th century; 20th century (1880s-1910)
Locale(s): Ohio; Texas; New York, New York

Summary: The life and career of William Sydney Porter, the writer and journalist better known as O. Henry, is dramatized beginning with his youth in Ohio and his days in Texas. Porter serves a three-year prison sentence for embezzlement; while in jail, he begins to write. Upon his release, he settles in New York where he gains great literary success with his short stories and articles.

Historical Accuracy: The novel's facts are reliable and the presentation attempts to show O. Henry fully, as a flawed, though talented, writer.

PETER N. KRASSNOFF (1869-1947)

Russian writer Krassnoff served in the Russian Imperial Regiment and in 1911 became the commander of the First Siberian Cossack Regiment. During the Russian Revolution, he was arrested as a political prisoner and later raised an army of 50,000 to fight the Soviet regime. Krassnoff is the author of the fantasy novels *The Black Mass* and *The White Coat*.

3551 *Napoleon and the Cossacks*

Date of Publication: 1931
Subject(s): Napoleonic Wars; Russian Empire
Fictional character(s): Kousma Minaleff, Military Personnel (cossack); Evgueny Ogloblin, Nobleman
Historical character(s): Alexander I, Ruler (Czar of Russia); Napoleon Bonaparte, Ruler (Emperor of France)
Time Period(s): 1810s
Locale(s): Russia

Summary: This historical panorama depicts the events of Napoleon's invasion of Russia and the disastrous retreat from Moscow. The story concentrates on two figures—Kousma Minaleff, a young cossack, and Evgueny Ogloblin, a young Russian aristocrat—though both give way to the central conflict between Napoleon and Alexander I.

Historical Accuracy: The novel is filled with authentic period details.

RENE KRAUS (1902-1947)

Kraus is the author of such books as *Theodora, the Circus Empress* and biographies of Winston Churchill and Lady Randolph Churchill.

3552 *The Private and Public Life of Socrates*

Date of Publication: 1940
Subject(s): Ancient Greece; Biography, Fictionalized
Historical character(s): Socrates, Philosopher; Xanthippe, Spouse (of Socrates); Pericles, Political Figure; Plato, Philosopher
Time Period(s): 5th century B.C.; 4th century B.C.
Locale(s): Athens, Greece

Summary: The novel presents a fictionalized life of Greek philosopher Socrates that also attempts to bring to life Socrates' age and the political issues that surround him. The known facts are presented faithfully with some imaginative embellishments.

Historical Accuracy: The novel's facts are accurately depicted, and the atmosphere is brought to life convincingly.

ROBERT WILSON KREPPS (1919-1980)

American novelist Krepps was born in Pittsburgh and attended Westminster College. He is the author of *Fancy*, *Baboon Rock*, and with Barbara Van Tuyl, The Bonnie Books for Girls of All Ages. He also wrote novelizations of the films *El Cid*, *Taras Bulba*, and *Send Me No Flowers*.

Krepps has also written under the pseudonyms Beatrice Brandon and Jake Logan.

3553 *Earthshaker*

Date of Publication: 1958
Subject(s): Tribal Life—African
Fictional character(s): Gabriel Decker, Mercenary, Adventurer
Historical character(s): Lobengula, Ruler (African king)
Time Period(s): 19th century
Locale(s): South Africa

Summary: The background to this adventure story is the rebellion of the Matabele of South Africa under the leadership of King Lobengula, called ''Earthshaker.'' The fictional story involves adventurer Gabriel Decker who intends to steal Lobengula's cache of diamonds.

Historical Accuracy: The novel has much of the flavor of a western transplanted to Africa, succeeding, however, in a believable portrait of the Matabele and Lobengula and the desert warfare between the natives and the British.

LAURA KREY (1890-)

Born in Galveston, Texas, Krey also writers under the pen name of Mary Everett. She was educated at the University of Texas and is the author of *And Tell of Time*, *Reconstruction*, *Texas*, and *On the Long Tide*.

3554 *And Tell of Time*

Date of Publication: 1938
Subject(s): Reconstruction Period; Ku Klux Klan
Fictional character(s): Cavin Darcy, Veteran (Confederate soldier)
Time Period(s): 19th century (1865-1888)
Locale(s): Georgia; Texas

Summary: The experiences of Confederate veteran Cavin Darcy mirror the turbulent years of Reconstruction following the Civil War. They include Klan warfare, the planters' rebellion, and conflict with northern interlopers.

Historical Accuracy: The historical background is believable, but the tenor of the story is romanticized and idealized.

3555 *On the Long Tide*

Date of Publication: 1940
Subject(s): Texas Revolution
Fictional character(s): Jeffrey Fentress, Settler
Historical character(s): Sam Houston, Political Figure; Stephen F. Austin, Political Figure; William Barret Travis, Political Figure; Andrew Jackson, Political Figure
Time Period(s): 19th century (1812-1836)
Locale(s): Texas; Tennessee; New Orleans, Louisiana

Summary: The novel dramatizes the American settlement of Texas and the outbreak of the revolt that won independence from Mexico and created the Texas republic. The story follows the adventures of Jeffrey Fentress who leaves his grandmother's farm in Virginia for Tennessee, New Orleans, and finally Texas where he joins the struggle for independence.

Historical Accuracy: The novel's account of the events of the Texas Revolt are authentic, though the characters are too often pallid and shadowy.

HARRY HARRISON KROLL (1888-1967)

An Indiana-born novelist, teacher, and memoirist, Kroll wrote several novels about the South and the border states, including *Fury in the Earth*, *The Keepers of the House*, and *Rogue's Company*. His autobiography is entitled *I Was a Sharecropper*.

3556 *Darker Grows the Valley*

Date of Publication: 1947
Subject(s): Settlement of the American Frontier; Family Saga
Fictional character(s): Rachel Clinch, Pioneer; Charity Doaks, Pioneer; Josiah Clinch, Farmer
Time Period(s): Multiple Time Periods
Locale(s): Tennessee River Valley, United States

Summary: This novel provides a panoramic portrait of the Tennessee River Valley from the 1770s to the formation of the Tennessee Valley Authority and the electrification and modernization of the region. The story of the region is told in a series of character portraits whose perspectives illustrate the history of the area.

Historical Accuracy: The novel offers a genuine portrait of the region and the periods described.

3557 *Fury in the Earth: A Novel of the New Madrid Earthquake*

Date of Publication: 1945
Subject(s): Earthquakes; Disasters—Natural
Fictional character(s): Hogshead Bolivar, Frontiersman
Time Period(s): 1810s (1811-1812)
Locale(s): New Madrid, Missouri; Tennessee

Summary: The story of the devastating New Madrid earthquake is told from the viewpoints of some of those affected by the disaster. Frontier life at the time is captured in a study of the psychological effects of the disaster.

Historical Accuracy: The novel captures its scene accurately.

3558 *The Keeper of the House*

Date of Publication: 1940
Subject(s): Antebellum South; Civil War—U.S.
Fictional character(s): Lett Capers, Bastard Son
Time Period(s): 1850s; 1860s
Locale(s): Mississippi

Summary: Mississippi plantation life before and during the Civil War is the setting for this historical novel that concerns Lett Capers, the illegitimate son of a great plantation owner. During the Civil War, Lett helps the Yankees and gains possession of the estate.

Historical Accuracy: The novel provides a colorful and authentic period background.

3559 *Rogues' Company: A Novel of John Murrell*

Date of Publication: 1944
Subject(s): Crime and Criminals; Biography, Fictionalized
Historical character(s): John Murrell, Outlaw
Time Period(s): 1820s; 1830s
Locale(s): Natchez Trace, Mississippi

Summary: The novel provides a factual account of the life and times of outlaw John Murrell and his band who operated along the Natchez Trace during the 1820s and 1830s. The story follows his career as a "speculator" from his early teens to his trial for stealing and selling slaves.

Historical Accuracy: The novel stays close to the known facts about Murrell's notorious career.

JAAN KROSS (1920-)

Estonian author Kross was arrested by the Soviets in 1946 and spent nine years in exile in labor camps. He has published 11 works of fiction and four volumes of poetry.

3560 *The Czar's Madman*

Date of Publication: 1993
Subject(s): Independence—Russia; Russian Empire
Fictional character(s): Timotheus Von Bock, Veteran; Eeva Von Bock, Spouse
Time Period(s): 1820s; 1830s (1827-1837)
Locale(s): Estonia

Summary: In 1813, Colonel Timotheus Von Bock, a favorite of the Czar, returns a hero from the war with Napoleon. He scandalizes his fellow aristocrats by marrying a peasant girl and then by condemning Czar Alexander's tyrannical rule. He is imprisoned for nine years. The novel tells the story of his release and return to his impoverished estate and destitute wife as a new national awareness threatens the power of the Russian czar.

Historical Accuracy: The era is accurately rendered, particularly the Estonian elements.

YURI KROTKOV

3561 *The Red Monarch: Scenes From the Life of Stalin*

Date of Publication: 1979
Subject(s): Biography, Fictionalized
Historical character(s): Joseph Stalin, Political Figure
Time Period(s): 20th century
Locale(s): Union of Soviet Socialist Republics

Summary: The novel offers an account of the life of Joseph Stalin, chronologically organized into a series of vignettes of real and imagined incidents. Scenes include Mao's trip to the Soviet Union in 1949, the Teheran Conference, Stalin's wife's suicide, Stalin's death, and the power struggle that followed.

Historical Accuracy: The novel's mixture of fictional and historical scenes presents a humanized and believable portrait of Stalin.

MARY KRUGER

Writing under the name Mary Kinsley, Kruger is the author of a number of historical romances.

3562 *Death on the Cliff Walk*

Date of Publication: 1994
Subject(s): Mystery; Gilded Age
Fictional character(s): Matt Devlin, Detective—Police; Brooke Cassidy, Socialite
Time Period(s): 1890s (1895-1896)
Locale(s): Newport, Rhode Island

Summary: This first mystery in a series about homicide detective Matt Devlin and debutante Brooke Cassidy involves the murder of a wealthy woman who is found on Newport's famous Cliff Walk dressed in a maid's uniform. When evidence points to Brooke's scapegrace uncle, she joins forces with Devlin to find the real killer. She also finds romance along the way.

Historical Accuracy: The novel features a convincing depiction of the era and its customs.

3563 *Masterpiece of Murder*

Date of Publication: 1996
Subject(s): Mystery
Fictional character(s): Matt Devlin, Detective—Police; Brooke Devlin, Socialite
Historical character(s): Theodore Roosevelt, Political Figure
Time Period(s): 1890s (1896)
Locale(s): New York, New York

Summary: Husband-and-wife sleuths Matt and Brooke Devlin investigate the theft of several valuable paintings from the Manhattan Museum of Art and the murder of the museum's curator.

Historical Accuracy: The story is fictional but set against an authentic period background, as the author's notes make clear.

3564 *No Honeymoon for Death*

Date of Publication: 1995
Subject(s): Mystery; Gilded Age
Fictional character(s): Brooke Cassidy, Socialite, Spouse (of Matt); Matt Devlin, Detective—Police
Historical character(s): John Pierpont Morgan, Financier
Time Period(s): 1890s (1896)
Locale(s): *New York*, At Sea; New York, New York; London, England

Summary: In the second of the author's historical mysteries, socialite Brooke Cassidy is on her honeymoon with spouse Matt Devlin, aboard the *S.S. New York*. J.P. Morgan enlists their help to solve the mysterious disappearance of another financier. The pair must contend with a bumbling ship's detective and an actor who thinks he is Sherlock Holmes.

Historical Accuracy: The author's notes make clear the historical basis for the novel's period elements.

JAMES HOWARD KUNSTLER (1948-)

Born in New York City, Kunstler is a graduate of Brockport State College. He has worked as a feature writer for the *Boston Phoenix* and *Rolling Stone*.

3565 *An Embarrassment of Riches*

Date of Publication: 1985
Subject(s): Exploration; Indians; Picaresque Adventure
Fictional character(s): Samuel Walker, Explorer; William Walker, Scientist (botanist), Explorer
Historical character(s): Thomas Jefferson, Political Figure; Meriwether Lewis, Explorer; William Clark, Explorer
Time Period(s): 1800s (1803)
Locale(s): Ohio River, Ohio; Mississippi River

Summary: In 1803, William Walker, an esteemed botanist, and his nephew Samuel are given a commission by President Jefferson to search the southern wilderness for a live specimen of the giant ground sloth. So begins their picaresque comic adventure in the American frontier. They are beset by Indians and pirates, discover a log Versailles, the secret outpost of Bourbon France, and finally confront the giant sloth.

Historical Accuracy: The novel's comedy distorts and exaggerates history. The background, however, is historically convincing.

BJORN KURTEN (1924-)

Born in Finland, Kurten is a professor at the University of Helsinki and one of Europe's leading paleontologists. He has served as a lecturer in zoology at Harvard. Kurten writes technical as well as popular studies on human evolution and the Ice Age and is the author of *The Cave Bear Story*, *Not From the Apes*, and *Ice Age*.

3566 *Dance of the Tiger: A Novel of the Ice Age*

Date of Publication: 1980
Subject(s): Prehistory; Tribal Life—Prehistoric
Fictional character(s): Tiger, Prehistoric Human (Homo Sapien), Warrior; Sheck, Prehistoric Human (Homo Sapien), Warrior; Veyde, Prehistoric Human (Neanderthal), Leader
Time Period(s): Indeterminate Past
Locale(s): Europe

Summary: Set 35,000 years ago in Ice Age Europe, the novel tells the story of Tiger, son of the chieftain of a peaceful village of Homo Sapiens, who sets out in search of the warrior who killed his father. He is rescued by a Neanderthal clan and falls in love with Veyde, their beautiful leader. The novel poses a solution to one of prehistory's most vexing mysteries: Why did the Neanderthals disappear?.

Historical Accuracy: The novel is solidly rooted in research into the era.

3567 *Singletusk*

Date of Publication: 1986
Subject(s): Prehistory; Tribal Life—Prehistoric
Fictional character(s): Tiger, Prehistoric Human; Whitespear, Prehistoric Human
Time Period(s): Indeterminate Past
Locale(s): Europe

Summary: The sequel to *Dance of the Tiger* continues the story of Ice Age life and the cultural clash between *Homo sapiens* and Neanderthals. Tiger, one of the first *Homo sapiens* to join a Neanderthal community, is forced to send his son Whitespear into the unknown to bring back a powerful healer. The novel recounts Whitespear's journey through dangerous wilderness and his meetings with powerful shamans and fierce tribal leaders.

Historical Accuracy: The author, one of Europe's leading paleontologists, supports his narrative with impressive scholarship and detailed research into the period.

KATHERINE KURTZ (1944-)

An award-winning American fantasy writer, Kurtz was born in Florida and attended the University of Miami and UCLA, earning degrees in both chemistry and medieval English history. She worked as an instructional designer for the Los Angeles Police Academy before becoming a full-time writer. Kurtz is the author of the Deryni series, set in fantasy kingdoms that parallel 10th, 11th, and 12th century England; *Lammas Night*, a World War II thriller; and the science fiction novel *The Legacy of Lehr*.

3568 *Two Crowns for America*

Date of Publication: 1996
Subject(s): American Revolution; Jacobite Rebellion; Fantasy
Fictional character(s): Andrew Wallace, Leader (Jacobite); Simon Wallace, Military Personnel (major)
Historical character(s): George Washington, Military Personnel (army commander); Benjamin Franklin, Political Figure
Time Period(s): 1770s (1775)
Locale(s): American Colonies

Summary: During the American Revolution, a conspiracy of free masons connects the fate of the American colonies with the Jacobite Rebellion in England. At the center of the action is Masonic Master Andrew Wallace and his son, Simon, who is a member of George Washington's personal staff.

Historical Accuracy: The novel is an intriguing fantasy that depends on an authentic period background.

ALLEN KURZWEIL (1961-)

A history major while at Yale and a Fulbright scholar in Italy, Kurzweil was named one of the Best Young American Novelists by *Granta* in 1996. He is also a journalist.

3569 *A Case of Curiosities*

Date of Publication: 1992
Subject(s): Inventions

Fictional character(s): Claude Page, Inventor, Artisan (watchmaker)
Time Period(s): 1780s
Locale(s): Tourney, France; Paris, France

Summary: The novel details the adventures of Claude Page, who acquires the skills of a watchmaker and produces a masterpiece of design that proves to be his downfall. The novel captures the machine-obsessed 18th century and France on the edge of revolutionary change.

Historical Accuracy: The era is evoked with conviction.

DUNCAN KYLE
(PSEUD. OF JOHN FRANKLIN BROXHOLME, 1930-)

British journalist and author Kyle has worked as a newspaper reporter and magazine editor. He is known for writing intelligent thrillers featuring impeccable research.

3570 *The King's Commissar*

Date of Publication: 1983
Subject(s): Russian Revolution
Fictional character(s): Laurence Pilgrim, Banker; Horace Malory, Banker; H.G. Dikeston, Military Personnel
Historical character(s): Vladimir Ilich Lenin, Revolutionary, Political Figure; Leon Trotsky, Revolutionary, Political Figure
Time Period(s): 1910s (1918); 1980s
Locale(s): London, England; Russia

Summary: Shuttling between modern Russia and Russia in 1918, the novel involves a young American partner of a British bank, Laurence Pilgrim, who discovers a secret British mission to save the Czar in 1918. The revelation has profound implications for the fate of the bank and the Western world.

Historical Accuracy: The story is fanciful but solidly grounded in believable details.

ELIZABETH KYLE
(PSEUD. OF AGNES M.R. DUNLOP, ?-1982)

Born in Scotland, Kyle is the author of numerous adult and juvenile novels and nonfiction works, including *The White Lady*, *The Pleasant Dame*, *Queen's Evidence*, *Duet: The Story of Clara and Robert Schumann*, and *Great Ambitions: A Story of the Early Years of Charles Dickens*.

3571 *The Swedish Nightingale: Jenny Lind*

Date of Publication: 1966
Subject(s): Biography, Fictionalized; Musical Life
Historical character(s): Jenny Lind, Singer; Hans Christian Andersen, Writer
Time Period(s): 19th century (1820-1887)
Locale(s): Sweden; England; United States

Summary: This fictional biography of the Swedish soprano Jenny Lind dramatizes her musical career. The emphasis is on her early years and the factors that Lind needed to overcome

to develop her considerable musical talents, including her struggle to regain her voice.

Historical Accuracy: The novel stays close to the events of Lind's career and is more biography than fiction.

PETER S. KYNE (1880-1957)

A businessman turned author, Kyne produced 25 novles and 1,000 short stories. Born in San Francisco, he was educated in a two-room school, worked in his father's cattle business, and then turned to writing popular fiction featuring go-getting businessmen Cappy Ricks and Bill Peck.

3572 *Tide of Empire*

Date of Publication: 1928
Subject(s): American West; Gold Rush—California
Fictional character(s): Dermod D'Arcy, Young Man; Josepha Guerrero, Young Woman
Time Period(s): 1840s
Locale(s): California

Summary: This romantic adventure tale set during the California Gold Rush concerns a young Irishman, Dermond D'Arcy, who comes to California seeking his fortune. He falls in love with Josepha Guerrero, the daughter of a Spanish rancher, but conflicts ensue.

Historical Accuracy: The novel captures the historical moment with authenticity.

OLIVER LA FARGE (1901-1963)

Born in New York City, American educator, anthropologist, and author Oliver La Farge was educated at the Groton School and Harvard University. After winning a Pulitzer Prize in 1929 for his first novel, *Laughing Boy*, La Farge firmly established himself in American letters as an authority on Native American culture. The author of fiction and nonfiction, La Farge's works include the novels *Sparks Fly Upward*, *The Enemy Gods*, and *The Copper Pot*.

3573 *Long Pennant*

Date of Publication: 1933
Subject(s): War of 1812; Sea Story
Fictional character(s): Jonas Dodge, Sea Captain
Time Period(s): 1810s
Locale(s): Caribbean

Summary: This sea story set during the War of 1812 dramatizes the exploits of American privateer captain Jonas Dodge. When he takes a prize in the Caribbean, Dodge assigns a small crew to bring it home, but the two ships are separated in a storm. The story follows what happens to both ships on the homeward voyage.

Historical Accuracy: The novel's naval background is authentic.

PIERRE LA MURE (1909-1976)

A French-born author, La Mure came to the U.S. as a foreign correspondent for a French newspaper, and became a citizen in 1957. Besides his fiction, La Mure is the author of biographies of Thomas Edison and John D. Rockefeller.

3574   *Beyond Desire: A Novel Based on the Life of Felix and Cecille Mendelssohn*

Date of Publication: 1955
Subject(s): Musical Life; Biography, Fictionalized
Historical character(s): Felix Mendelssohn, Composer, Musician; Cecille Mendelssohn, Gentlewoman, Spouse; Maria Sala, Singer (opera); Frederic Chopin, Composer, Musician; Nathan Rothschild, Businessman, Financier; Victoria, Ruler (Queen of England); Richard Wagner, Composer; Robert Schumann, Composer, Musician
Time Period(s): 19th century (1820s-1840s)
Locale(s): Berlin, Germany; London, England; Paris, France

Summary: The life of Felix Mendelssohn, one of the outstanding musical talents of the 19th century, is dramatized in this novel. It is also the story of his love for the opera singer Maria Sala and his wife Cecille. Mendelssohn's life is dominated, however, by his music and his dedication to his predecessor, Johan Sebastian Bach.

Historical Accuracy: The novel offers a convincing portrait not only of the composer but of the era.

3575   *Clair De Lune: A Novel about Claude Debussy*

Date of Publication: 1962
Subject(s): Musical Life; Biography, Fictionalized
Historical character(s): Claude Debussy, Composer, Musician
Time Period(s): 19th century; 20th century (1860s-1918)
Locale(s): Paris, France; Russia; Rome, Italy

Summary: The novel is a fictional life history of musician and composer Claude Debussy. He is shown as the prototypical artist, totally devoted to his art with an almost complete lack of practicality. Chronically poor, he nevertheless manages a series of stormy love affairs.

Historical Accuracy: The novel is a faithful rendering of Debussy's life and times with a convincing portrait of France's history between the collapse of the Second Empire in 1870 and the end of the First World War.

3576   *Moulin Rouge: A Novel Based on Henri de Toulouse-Lautrec*

Date of Publication: 1950
Subject(s): Artistic Life; Biography, Fictionalized
Historical character(s): Henri de Toulouse-Lautrec, Artist; Edgar Degas, Artist; Camille Pissarro, Artist; Vincent Van Gogh, Artist; Pierre Tanguy, Artist; Jane Avril, Actress
Time Period(s): 19th century; 20th century (1872-1901)
Locale(s): Paris, France

Summary: The novel chronicles the life of the artist Toulouse-Lautrec. Crippled and deformed from childhood, he rejects his noble lifestyle for an artistic career. He divides his time in Paris between his studio, night clubs, and the brothels of Montmarte. The novel offers a sympathetic portrait of Toulouse-Lautrec's hunger for the romance which his deformity prevented and a colorful portrait of Paris in the 1880s and 1890s.

Historical Accuracy: The novel's period painting is convincing with many historical figures presented.

3577   *The Private Life of Mona Lisa*

Date of Publication: 1976
Subject(s): Artistic Life; Renaissance
Historical character(s): Lisa Gherardini Giocondo, Gentlewoman; Leonardo da Vinci, Artist; Lorenzo de Medici, Nobleman (patron of the arts); Charles VIII, Ruler (King of France); Girolamo Savonarola, Religious, Political Figure (reformer)
Time Period(s): 15th century; 16th century (1470s-1519)
Locale(s): Florence, Italy

Summary: The novel is a speculative history of the woman who posed for the most famous portrait of all time. Lisa Gioconda is shown as a Renaissance gentlewoman very much a part of her age. The period is shown in all its color, including the French invasion by Charles VIII and the fiery rise and fall of Savonarola. Finally, the novel offers a look at the genius of da Vinci and attempts to answer the mysteries as illusive as Mona Lisa's smile: why did he paint the portrait and for whom?.

Historical Accuracy: The novel is a brilliant and detailed recreation of Renaissance Italy. Although the history of Gioconda is mostly speculative, the atmosphere lends credibility to the situations.

BARBARA LACHMAN

3578   *The Journal of Hildegard of Bingen*

Date of Publication: 1993
Subject(s): Middle Ages; Religious Life
Historical character(s): Hildegard of Bingen, Religious (abbess)
Time Period(s): 12th century (1151-1153)
Locale(s): Germany

Summary: This is the imagined diary of the medieval abbess and mystic Hildegard of Bingen set during the period of a single liturgical year. The novel captures Hildegard's struggle to establish the first autonomous convent and her political battles with the paternalistic church hierarchy.

Historical Accuracy: The imaginary journal is firmly rooted in the facts of Hildegard's life and shows great familiarity with the period and the atmosphere of medieval life.

AL LACY

3579 *Beloved Enemy*

Date of Publication: 1994

Subject(s): Civil War—U.S.; Battle of Bull Run; Espionage

Fictional character(s): Jenny Jordan, Young Woman; Buck Brownell, Military Personnel (Union soldier)

Historical character(s): Abraham Lincoln, Political Figure; Joseph E. Johnston, Military Personnel (Confederate general); Pierre Gustave Toutant Beauregard, Military Personnel (Confederate general); George McClellan, Military Personnel (Union general)

Time Period(s): 1860s (1861)

Locale(s): Washington, District of Columbia; Virginia

Summary: This story, set against the background of the first major battle of the Civil War at Bull Run, describes the events leading up to the conflict with the fictional story of young Jenny Jordan, who supports her father's spy missions for the Confederacy but then must contend with a divided loyalty when she falls in love with a Union soldier.

Historical Accuracy: The details of the battle and the events leading up to it are authentic and reliable.

3580 *A Heart Divided*

Date of Publication: 1993

Subject(s): Civil War—U.S.; Battle of Mobile Bay

Fictional character(s): Ryan McGraw, Military Personnel (Confederate captain); Dixie Quade, Nurse; Victoria Manning Coffield, Spouse (of McGraw)

Historical character(s): Richard Page, Military Personnel (Confederate general); David Farragut, Military Personnel (Union admiral)

Time Period(s): 1860s (1864-1865)

Locale(s): Mobile, Alabama

Summary: Set against the backdrop of the events leading up to the Civil War Battle of Mobile Bay, the novel describes the triangular affair of Confederate Captain Ryan McGraw, army nurse Dixie Quade, and Victoria Coffield, McGraw's wife, who once abandoned him and suddenly returns to his life.

Historical Accuracy: The fictional story is interwoven with an authentic dramatization of the events surrounding the Battle of Mobile Bay.

3581 *Joy From Ashes*

Date of Publication: 1995

Subject(s): Civil War—U.S.; Battle of Fredericksburg

Fictional character(s): Layne Dalton, Military Personnel (Confederate major); Melody Dalton, Spouse

Historical character(s): Robert E. Lee, Military Personnel (Confederate commander); Ambrose E. Burnside, Military Personnel (Union general); James Longstreet, Military Personnel (Confederate general)

Time Period(s): 1860s (1862)

Locale(s): Fredericksburg, Virginia

Summary: This account of the Civil War Battle of Fredericksburg shares the stage with a fictional story of the experiences of Confederate Layne Dalton, who discovers his wife brutalized by three Union soldiers. Swearing vengeance, he finds himself their prisoner as the events of the battle reach their climax.

Historical Accuracy: The novel is precise and authentic in its treatment of the actual events surrounding the battle.

3582 *A Promise Unbroken*

Date of Publication: 1993

Subject(s): Civil War—U.S.; Battle of Rich Mountain

Fictional character(s): Abby Ruffin, Southern Belle; Web Steele, Military Personnel (Confederate soldier); Mandrake Steele, Slave

Historical character(s): Pierre Gustave Toutant Beauregard, Military Personnel (Confederate general); George McClellan, Military Personnel (Union general); William S. Rosecrans, Military Personnel (Union general)

Time Period(s): 1860s (1860-1861)

Locale(s): Virginia

Summary: The novel describes the outbreak of the Civil War and the action that culminates in the war's first major battle at Rich Mountain. The fictional story involves the experiences of a Virginia family, the Ruffins.

Historical Accuracy: The story is placed convincingly in the context of actual events and historical figures.

3583 *Shadowed Memories*

Date of Publication: 1994

Subject(s): Civil War—U.S.; Battle of Shiloh

Fictional character(s): Hannah Rose, Young Woman; Wayne Gordon, Military Personnel (Confederate captain), Amnesiac

Historical character(s): Ulysses S. Grant, Military Personnel (Union general); Albert Sidney Johnston, Military Personnel (Confederate general); Pierre Gustave Toutant Beauregard, Military Personnel (Confederate general); Nathan Bedford Forrest, Military Personnel (Confederate officer)

Time Period(s): 1860s (1862)

Locale(s): Tennessee

Summary: The events leading up to and including the Battle of Shiloh form the primary background for this Civil War tale that relates the fictional story of Confederate Captain Wayne Gordon, whose amnesia complicates his growing love for Hannah Rose.

Historical Accuracy: The novel's account of the actual events and battle is authentic and reliable.

GARALD LAGARD

3584 *Scarlet Cockerel*

Date of Publication: 1948

Subject(s): Civil War—U.S.

Fictional character(s): Lane Byrn, Military Personnel (Confederate soldier), Doctor

Historical character(s): John Singleton Mosby, Military Personnel (Confederate officer)

Time Period(s): 1860s

Locale(s): Virginia

Summary: This action-adventure novel set during the Civil War centers on Confederate soldier Lane Byrn who joins Mosby's Raiders. His love for the daughter of a Union general presents a variety of complications.

Historical Accuracy: The novel does make use of actual historical incidents and captures the Southern perspective on the war with skill.

PAR LAGERKVIST (1891-1974)

A Swedish playwright, poet, and novelist, Lagerkvist attended the University of Uppsala and won the Nobel Prize for Literature in 1951. He is considered one of the most significant figures of modern Swedish literature. His central concerns are the human soul and the problem of evil.

3585   *Barabbas*

Date of Publication: 1949
Subject(s): Biblical Story; Roman Empire
Fictional character(s): Sahak, Slave
Historical character(s): Jesus Christ, Biblical Figure; Barabbas, Biblical Figure, Outlaw
Time Period(s): 1st century
Locale(s): Jerusalem, Israel; Rome, Roman Empire

Summary: The novel dramatizes the life of the condemned thief whose place Jesus takes on the cross. After his release, Barabbas struggles with the meaning of Christ and the faith of his followers. Condemned to the mines, he is chained to Sahak, an ardent Christian. He then moves on to Rome, where he is finally crucified for his supposed membership in a group of believers.

Historical Accuracy: The novel's power is derived from the expertly described realistic scenes. The time and place are utterly convincing, even if the story is imagined.

SELMA LAGERLOF (1858-1940)

Lagerlof was the first woman to win the Nobel Prize for literature. Most of her novels depict peasant life in her native Varmland, Sweden.

3586   *The Story of Gosta Berling*

Date of Publication: 1894
Subject(s): Rural Life—Sweden
Fictional character(s): Gosta Berling, Religious (defrocked minister); Elizabeth Berling, Heroine
Time Period(s): 19th century (early)
Locale(s): Sweden

Summary: The novel offers the redemption story of Gosta Berling, a defrocked minister and drunkard who is eventually saved by love. It is told from the point of view of an old resident of a country town recalling events of long ago. The novel owes much of its vitality to its scenes of Swedish country life.

Historical Accuracy: Despite the distance of time, the past is brought to life here.

ANNABEL LAINE

3587   *The Melancholy Virgin*

Date of Publication: 1981
Subject(s): Mystery; Regency Period; Theatrical Life
Fictional character(s): Charles Dornay, Nobleman (Earl of Moriston); Francis Mervyn, Secretary; Katharine Kenwood, Singer (opera)
Time Period(s): 19th century (Regency period)
Locale(s): England

Summary: The prime suspect in the murder of a mysterious lady of easy virtue is Francis Mervyn, the private secretary of Charles Dornay, the Earl of Moriston. Dornay—aristocrat, diplomat, and occasional detective—begins to investigate, and the trail leads to the murdered girl's best friend, actress and singer Katharine Kenwood. Dornay finds himself falling in love with her even as he tries to solve the murder.

Historical Accuracy: The period detail, particularly of theatrical life, is exact and believable.

3588   *The Reluctant Heiress*

Date of Publication: 1978
Subject(s): Regency Romance; Mystery
Fictional character(s): Caroline Malcolm, Gentlewoman; Charles Dornay, Nobleman (Earl of Moriston)
Time Period(s): 19th century (Regency period)
Locale(s): England

Summary: The Earl of Moriston, who has a passion for solving mysteries, is attracted to the dilemma of Caroline Malcolm. She is searching for her father, and the only clue is that every year on her birthday she receives a gift of diamonds. Moriston begins to delve into the history of the Malcolm family, including the bizarre death of Caroline's mother, and uncovers a tangled web of deceit, blackmail, and murder.

Historical Accuracy: The period details are convincing in this novel of romantic suspense.

ALEXANDER LAING (1903-1976)

An American educator, librarian, poet, novelist, and author of nonfiction, Laing was born in New York City and graduated from Dartmouth. His books include *The Sea Witch*, *Dr. Scarlett*, and *American Ships*.

3589   *Matthew Early*

Date of Publication: 1957
Subject(s): Slavery; Abolition Movement; Sea Story
Fictional character(s): Matthew Early, Sea Captain; Barbara Channing, Young Woman
Time Period(s): 1790s; 1800s (1796-1802)
Locale(s): Newport, Rhode Island; At Sea

Summary: This adventure tale concerning New England sea captain Matthew Early takes him around the globe in a series of hedonistic adventures against the backdrop of the slave trade. Complicating matters is his love for Barbara Channing, an avowed abolitionist.

Historical Accuracy: Adventure is primary here, with only a slightly developed historical backdrop.

CHARLTON LAIRD (1901-)

An American journalist, English professor, and writer, Laird was born in Nashua, Iowa, and attended the University of Iowa, Columbia, Stanford, and Yale universities. His many nonfiction works include *A Writer's Handbook* and *Language in America.*

3590 *Thunder on the River*

Date of Publication: 1949
Subject(s): Black Hawk War; Indians
Fictional character(s): Mark Eldridge, Pioneer, Captive
Historical character(s): Black Hawk, Indian (Sauk), Chieftain; Daniel Boone, Frontiersman
Time Period(s): 19th century (1810s-1830s)
Locale(s): Illinois

Summary: The novel describes pioneer life through the experiences of a young Eastener, Mark Eldridge, who seeks his fortune in the Illinois wilderness and is captured by and adopted into the Sauk tribe.

Historical Accuracy: This is an authentic account of pioneer life and the Black Hawk Wars in Illinois.

3591 *West of the River*

Date of Publication: 1953
Subject(s): Settlement of the American Frontier; Indians
Fictional character(s): Paul Boudreau, Trader
Time Period(s): 1830s
Locale(s): Mississippi River

Summary: The fur trade on the Upper Mississippi during the 1830s is the background for this novel concerning Paul Boudreau, raised and educated by the Jesuits in Quebec. When his trading post is destroyed, Boudreau is hard pressed to survive in the wilderness.

Historical Accuracy: The novel shows a knowledgeable historical background and research into Indian customs.

ROSALIND LAKER
(PSEUD. OF BARBARA OVSTEDAL)

Rosalind Laker is the pseudonym for the English author Barbara Ovstedal who also produces Gothic novels under the name Barbara Paul. Laker's historical romances are marked by an unusual degree of historical accuracy.

3592 *Banners of Silk*

Date of Publication: 1981
Subject(s): Romance; Fashion Industry
Fictional character(s): Louise, Orphan, Seamstress
Historical character(s): Charles Worth, Designer (fashion); Eugenie, Royalty (French empress), Spouse (wife of Napoleon III)
Time Period(s): 19th century (1843-1880s)
Locale(s): Paris, France

Summary: Set in France during the Second Empire, the novel details the fashion industry from the perspective of a destitute orphan, Louise, and a young Englishman, Charles Worth, who will revolutionize the course of fashion. He rises from poverty to become the preferred fashion designer of the court.

Historical Accuracy: The subject matter is interesting and original. Laker's details and characterizations are convincing.

3593 *Circle of Pearls*

Date of Publication: 1990
Subject(s): Romance; Civil War—England; Family Saga
Fictional character(s): Julia Pallister, Gentlewoman
Historical character(s): Christopher Wren, Architect; Nell Gwynne, Lover (Charles II's mistress), Actress
Time Period(s): 17th century; 18th century (1641-1723)
Locale(s): Sussex, England; London, England

Summary: Julia Pallister is raised a confirmed Royalist as the English Civil War rages. She struggles to maintain the family estate and deal with love that comes from an unexpected source. Christopher Wren's career is connected with the romantic maneuverings of the story.

Historical Accuracy: The period details are present and play an important role in the novel's drama. Wren's presence in the romance is a bit strained, however.

3594 *Claudine's Daughter*

Date of Publication: 1978
Subject(s): Romance; Victorian Period
Fictional character(s): Lucy Di Castelloni, Widow(er), Gentlewoman; Richard Warwyck, Gentleman; Josh Barton, Gentleman
Time Period(s): 1850s (1850-1851)
Locale(s): Easthampton, England

Summary: An exotic and beautiful woman from Italy, Lucy di Castelloni, arrives at the seaside resort of Easthampton. However, she is anything but foreign. Born of English parents, she was married off to an elderly Italian, and has now returned home a widow. Her arrival will revive a decades-old scandal that will split the Warwyck family apart.

Historical Accuracy: The Victorian period details are slight in this romance with more secrets and adversity than insights into the era.

3595 *Gilded Splendour*

Date of Publication: 1982
Subject(s): Romance; Biography, Fictionalized; Georgian Period
Fictional character(s): Isabella Woodleigh, Gentlewoman
Historical character(s): Thomas Chippendale, Artisan (cabinet-maker)
Time Period(s): 18th century (1737-1777)
Locale(s): Yorkshire, England; London, England

Summary: This novel imagines a romance between Thomas Chippendale, the famous furniture maker, and a young lady of genteel birth, Isabella Woodleigh, who becomes his patron when prevented from being more. Their love is never acted upon as Chippendale fulfills his promise of becoming a great cabinet-maker.

Historical Accuracy: This fictional story is constructed around the very few facts known about the life of Thomas Chippendale. The author argues that this is how his life might have been.

3596 *The Golden Tulip*

Date of Publication: 1991
Subject(s): Romance; Artistic Life
Fictional character(s): Francesca Visser, Artist; Ludolf Van Deventer, Businessman
Historical character(s): Jan Vermeer, Artist; Rembrandt, Artist
Time Period(s): 17th century
Locale(s): Amsterdam, Netherlands; Delft, Netherlands

Summary: Set in the Netherlands of the 17th century, the novel follows the career of Francesca Visser, who desires to become a master painter. She is given the opportunity to study with Jan Vermeer, but she is also plagued by the obsession of businessman Ludolf Van Deventer, whose conspiracy threatens both Francesca and the Netherlands.

Historical Accuracy: The details about the artists and the era are solidly presented.

3597 *Jewelled Path*

Date of Publication: 1983
Subject(s): Romance; Business Building
Fictional character(s): Irene Lindsay, Gentlewoman, Designer (of jewelery); Edmund Lindsay, Jeweler
Time Period(s): 1890s
Locale(s): London, England; Paris, France; Monte Carlo, Monaco

Summary: Irene Lindsay is the daughter of an eminent London jeweler who wants a career as a jewelery designer. Her father just wants her to find a fashionable husband. Irene persists, however, and embarks on her career, stimulated by the new styles of Charles Tiffany, Peter Faberge, and Rene Lalique.

Historical Accuracy: The novel offers some interesting views of both the design business and the period of artistic explosion of the Belle Epoque.

3598 *Ride the Blue Riband*

Date of Publication: 1977
Subject(s): Romance; Horse Racing; Victorian Period
Fictional character(s): Tansy Marlow, Heiress, Gentlewoman; Dominic Reade, Gentleman
Time Period(s): 1840s (1847)
Locale(s): Hampshire, England

Summary: Tansy Marlow inherits an estate from her father that she never knew he owned. This is the first of many family secrets that continue to unfold. She finds herself at the center of a world of high-stakes gaming connected with one of the most famous racetracks in the world, Epsom Downs.

Historical Accuracy: The period details of Victorian life, particularly the world of the turf, are accurately portrayed.

3599 *The Silver Touch*

Date of Publication: 1987
Subject(s): Romance; Business Building
Fictional character(s): John Bateman, Artisan (goldsmith)
Historical character(s): Hester Bateman, Artisan (silversmith)
Time Period(s): 18th century (1721-1760s)
Locale(s): London, England

Summary: This unusual romance is based on the actual figure of Hester Bateman who became one of the premier silversmiths in the 18th century. It chronicles Hester's rise from a humble background to her introduction to the craft by the man she loves, as well as many invented romantic complications.

Historical Accuracy: The details of both London life and the silversmithing business seem reliable and authentic.

3600 *The Sugar Pavilion*

Date of Publication: 1994
Subject(s): Regency Romance; French Revolution; Business Building
Fictional character(s): Sophie Delcourt, Refugee, Businesswoman; Antoine De Jeneau, Ward, Heir; Tom Foxhill, Smuggler
Historical character(s): George, Prince Regent, Royalty; Maria Anne Fitzherbert, Lover (Prince Regent's mistress)
Time Period(s): 18th century; 19th century (1793-1823)
Locale(s): France; Brighton, England

Summary: Sophie Delcourt escapes from the ravages of the French Revolution to England with her charge, Antoine de Juneau, heir to his father's title and estate. They make their way to Brighton, home for other French emigres and the playground for the Prince Regent and his mistress, Mrs. Fitzherbert. Sophie enters the confectionery trade, is drawn to a dashing smuggler, and finds herself embroiled in court intrigue.

Historical Accuracy: Laker excels in creating the appropriate historical details for her romantic adventure story. The era is captured with mastery.

3601 *To Dance with Kings*

Date of Publication: 1988
Subject(s): Romance; Royalty—France; French Revolution
Fictional character(s): Marguerite Dremont, Gentlewoman; Jeanne Dremont, Worker (peasant); Jasmine, Gentlewoman
Historical character(s): Louis XV, Ruler (King of France); Louis XVI, Ruler (King of France); Marie Antoinette, Royalty (Queen of France)
Time Period(s): 17th century; 18th century (1664-1789)
Locale(s): France

Summary: Life at Versailles and in the courts of Louis XV and Louis XVI is the subject of this novel that chronicles three generations of women who are part of the royal entourage. Jeanne Dremont is a poor peasant, but it is prophesized that her daughter, Marguerite, will dance with kings. Marguerite fulfills this prophesy and her daughter, Jasmine, is born into privilege. Jasmine is exiled however, as the chaos of the Revolution brings the fairy-tale world of Versailles to a crashing end.

Historical Accuracy: Laker's ability to create convincing court scenes is impressive.

3602 *Tree of Gold*

Date of Publication: 1986
Subject(s): Romance; Napoleonic Wars; Feuds
Fictional character(s): Gabrielle Roche, Gentlewoman; Nicolas Devaux, Gentleman, Military Personnel
Time Period(s): 1800s; 1810s (1804-1815)
Locale(s): Lyon, France; London, England; Spain

Summary: Two prominent families in Lyons' thriving silk industry are bitter enemies. When Gabrielle Roche falls in love with Nicolas Devaux, the son of her father's greatest rival, complications abound which separate the lovers. Their desire for a reunion leads them across the battlefields of Europe.

Historical Accuracy: The novel sharply details the Napoleonic era. The reunion on the battlefield strains all but the most romantic sensibility however.

3603 *The Venetian Mask*

Date of Publication: 1993
Subject(s): Romance; Musical Life
Fictional character(s): Elena, Gentlewoman; Adrianna, Gentlewoman; Marietta, Gentlewoman
Time Period(s): 1770s; 1780s (1775-1780s)
Locale(s): Venice, Italy

Summary: Three girls become schoolfriends at the Ospedale della Pieta, a renowned music conservatory for orphaned girls in Venice during the 18th century. Adrianna gives up a promising operatic career to wed a Venetian maskmaker. Marietta weds a sworn enemy of her friend Elena. The three women share a supportive and enduring friendship.

Historical Accuracy: The details of 18th-century Venice and the period are authentically shown.

3604 *Warwyck's Woman*

Date of Publication: 1978
Subject(s): Romance; Boxing
Fictional character(s): Daniel Warwyck, Sports Figure (boxer), Heir; Kate Farringdon, Young Woman
Time Period(s): 1820s
Locale(s): Brighton, England; London, England

Summary: A farmer sells his wife at an auction to prize-fighter Daniel Warwyck. Warwyck hopes that the marriage will reinstate him as heir to Warwyck Manor and a fortune that is denied him because of his fighting. Kate proves a match for the dashing Warwyck, and she rises in society as he succeeds in becoming the English champion.

Historical Accuracy: The novel's premise is far-fetched from a historical perspective. Although wife-selling did occur, it is the least absurd of the novel's manipulations.

3605 *What the Heart Keeps*

Date of Publication: 1984
Subject(s): Romance; Immigrants; Motion Picture Industry

Fictional character(s): Lisa Shaw, Orphan, Immigrant; Peter Hagen, Immigrant; Alan Fernley, Businessman (movie industry)
Time Period(s): 20th century (1900-1920s)
Locale(s): Toronto, Ontario, Canada; London, England

Summary: Lisa Shaw is an orphan shipped off from England to a new home in North America. Before embarking she meets a fellow immigrant, Peter Hagen, but their paths divide. Lisa finds a harsh life with her adoptive family. She marries Alan Fernley, who is involved in the early years of the movie industry. A chance second meeting with Peter fulfills all her early dreams.

Historical Accuracy: The story offers some compelling details of struggles in Canada and the burgeoning film industry.

F. BRUCE LAMB (1913-)

An American writer born in Colorado, Lamb graduated from the University of Michigan and worked as an engineer and forester in the British West Indies and Brazil.

3606 *Kid Curry: The Life and Times of Harvey Logan and the Wild Bunch*

Date of Publication: 1991
Subject(s): American West; Crime and Criminals
Historical character(s): Harvey Logan, Outlaw; Butch Cassidy, Outlaw
Time Period(s): 19th century; 20th century (1880s-1904)
Locale(s): Colorado; New Mexico

Summary: The novel offers the life story of Kid Curry (Harvey Logan) from his cowboy days to his career as an outlaw, a member of the notorious Wild Bunch. Based on the stories Curry told the author's father, the story is a rousing tale of payroll busts, train robberies, and a daring prison escape.

Historical Accuracy: The documentation would be is appropriate for a biography, let alone a work of fiction. Invention fills in the gaps in the historical record.

HAROLD LAMB (1892-1962)

American historian and author Lamb was born in New Jersey and graduated from Columbia. After serving in the army and traveling extensively in the Near East, Lamb published a number of historical studies and biographies, including *Genghis Khan*, *Tamerlane*, *The Crusades*, and *Charlemagne*. Lamb produced stories and articles based on his travels and his attempts to retrace the paths of men like Marco Polo, Genghis Khan, and Alexander the Great. Movie adaptations of his works include *The Crusaders*, *The Plainsmen*, and *The Buccaneer*.

3607 *Alexander of Macedon: The Journey to World's End*

Date of Publication: 1946
Subject(s): Macedonian Empire; Biography, Fictionalized; Ancient Greece

Historical character(s): Alexander the Great, Ruler (King of Macedonia); Philip II, Ruler (king); Olympias, Royalty (consort of Philip)
Time Period(s): 4th century B.C.
Locale(s): Asia Minor; Persia; Greece

Summary: This biographical account of the remarkable career of Alexander the Great attempts to penetrate beneath the legend to arrive at a plausible portrait of the real Alexander who, before the age of 32, had conquered most of the known world. The author locates Alexander's peculiar mania in the split between his rational, skeptical Greek training as a pupil of Aristotle and his more exotic, mystical background from his mother, Olympias, who suggests that Zeus, not Philip of Macedon, was Alexander's true father.

Historical Accuracy: The details of Alexander's life and career are faithfully presented. However, the author's interpretations are open to question.

`3608` *Theodora and the Emperor*

Date of Publication: 1952
Subject(s): Byzantine Empire; Roman Empire
Historical character(s): Justinian I, Ruler (Byzantine emperor); Theodora, Royalty (empress consort of Justinian)
Time Period(s): 6th century (500-565)
Locale(s): Constantinople, Byzantine Empire

Summary: The novel portrays the end of the ancient world in the story of Justinian and Theodora and their reign over the Eastern Roman Empire. Their relationship and the intrigue of their court and kingdom are featured.

Historical Accuracy: The attention to historical details is impressive, despite some invented dialogue and scenes.

DEWEY LAMBDIN (1945-)

Born in California, Lambdin graduated from Montana State University. He has worked as a TV director and producer. He began writing nautical novels after reading all of C.S. Forester's and Alexander Kent's novels and deciding that he could do just as well. His books have been praised for their genuine 18th-century atmosphere.

`3609` *The French Admiral*

Date of Publication: 1990
Subject(s): American Revolution; Military Life—British Navy; Sea Story
Fictional character(s): Alan Lewrie, Military Personnel (midshipman); Caroly Chiswick, Young Woman
Time Period(s): 1780s
Locale(s): *Desperate*, At Sea (Chesapeake); Yorktown, Virginia

Summary: British midshipman Alan Lewrie finds himself in the middle of the concluding campaign of the American Revolution, fighting rebel partisans and trapped with Cornwallis' army at Yorktown.

Historical Accuracy: Some of the incidents are based on actual historical events.

`3610` *The Gun Ketch*

Date of Publication: 1993
Subject(s): Sea Story; Military Life—British Navy; Pirates
Fictional character(s): Alan Lewrie, Military Personnel (naval captain); Calico Jack Finney, Pirate
Time Period(s): 1780s (1786)
Locale(s): *Alacrity*, At Sea; Bahamas

Summary: Alan Lewrie captains the small two-masted ship *Alacrity*, whose job it is to protect British shipping from pirates in the Bahamas. Lewrie manages to upset polite society in Nassau before becoming absorbed in the pursuit of local hero-turned-pirate "Calico Jack" Finney, whom Lewrie intends to bring to justice.

Historical Accuracy: The period details are convincingly portrayed.

`3611` *H.M.S. Cockerel*

Date of Publication: 1995
Subject(s): Sea Story; Military Life—British Navy; French Revolution
Fictional character(s): Alan Lewrie, Military Personnel (naval lieutenant)
Historical character(s): Napoleon Bonaparte, Military Personnel (French officer); Sir William Hamilton, Diplomat; Lady Emma Hamilton, Spouse
Time Period(s): 1790s
Locale(s): Toulon, France; At Sea; Naples, Italy

Summary: During the French Revolution, Alan Lewrie participates in the battle for the French port of Toulon. Featured in the conflict is an obscure young military officer, Napoleon Bonaparte.

Historical Accuracy: Lambdin is a master at rendering a convincing period setting. The story is derived from actual events.

`3612` *The King's Coat*

Date of Publication: 1989
Subject(s): Sea Story; Military Life—British Navy; American Revolution
Fictional character(s): Alan Lewrie, Military Personnel (midshipman); Ezekiel Bales, Military Personnel (naval captain)
Time Period(s): 1780s
Locale(s): London, England; At Sea; West Indies

Summary: Alan Lewrie at the age of 17 is shipped off to the British navy after causing embarassments at home. He turns out to be surprisingly adept at sea and in warfare against the Dutch and the Americans. Lewrie is as resourceful at sea as he is prone to misadventure ashore.

Historical Accuracy: The novel excels at painting a convincing period picture of naval life and customs.

`3613` *A King's Commander*

Date of Publication: 1997
Subject(s): Sea Story; Military Life—British Navy

Fictional character(s): Alan Lewrie, Military Personnel (naval officer); Guillaume Choundas, Military Personnel (naval officer)
Historical character(s): Horatio Nelson, Military Personnel (naval officer); Samuel Hood, Military Personnel (admiral)
Time Period(s): 1790s
Locale(s): *Jester*, At Sea

Summary: In the seventh volume of the naval adventures of Alan Lewrie, Lewrie is in command of *H.M.S. Jester* and participates in the British victory over the French in the Battle of the Glorious First of June. Lewrie is dispatched to the Mediterranean to inform Admiral Hood of the French defeat and to help in Hood's capture of Corsica. Finally, alongside Horatio Nelson, Lewrie fights a series of fierce battles along the French coast and meets his nemesis, French commander Guillaume Choundas.

Historical Accuracy: The novel contains a background of actual historical events and features authentic nautical details.

`3614` *The King's Commission*

Date of Publication: 1991
Subject(s): Sea Story; Military Life—British Navy; American Revolution
Fictional character(s): Alan Lewrie, Military Personnel (naval officer); Lucy Beauman, Gentlewoman
Historical character(s): Horatio Nelson, Military Personnel (naval officer)
Time Period(s): 1780s
Locale(s): *Shrike*, At Sea; West Indies

Summary: Alan Lewrie has earned his commission and is the first officer aboard the brig-of-war *Shrike*, in action against the French and Spanish in the West Indies. Lewrie continues his pattern of competence at sea and mishaps on shore.

Historical Accuracy: The portrait of the British navy in the 18th century is authentic.

`3615` *The King's Privateer*

Date of Publication: 1992
Subject(s): Sea Story; Military Life—British Navy
Fictional character(s): Alan Lewrie, Military Personnel (naval officer)
Time Period(s): 1790s
Locale(s): London, England; *Telesto*, At Sea; Macao

Summary: As a lieutenant sailing on the *Telesto*, a vessel disguised as a merchant ship to keep watch on the Dutch, Spanish, and French in the China Seas. Lewrie experiences battle at sea and treachery ashore.

Historical Accuracy: The author has mastered the period details of nautical life.

ANTONY LAMBTON (1922-)

English author and politician, Lambton served as a British Member of Parliament from 1951 to 1973. He was the Parliamentary Private Secretary to the Foreign Secretary as well as the Parliamentary Undersecretary. He is the author of

Snow and Other Stories, *Pig and Other Stories*, and *The Mountbattens*.

`3616` *Elizabeth and Alexandra*

Date of Publication: 1985
Subject(s): Royalty—Russia; Russian Revolution; Russian Empire
Historical character(s): Alexandra Feodorovna, Royalty (consort of Nicholas II); Serge, Grand Duke of Russia, Royalty; Victoria, Ruler (Queen of England); Elizabeth, Grand Duchess Serge, Royalty; Nicholas II, Ruler (Czar of Russia)
Time Period(s): 19th century; 20th century (1864-1918)
Locale(s): Germany; St. Petersburg, Russia; Moscow, Russia

Summary: The novel offers the interesting story of Elizabeth, who like her older sister Alexandra, marries into the Russian royal family. Elizabeth marries the Grand Duke Serge of Moscow, a cruel man who is eventually assassinated. Elizabeth escapes only to be swept up in the violence of the Revolution, which ends in her death.

Historical Accuracy: The novel is a solidly recorded picture of Imperial Russia with appendices that attest to the novel's factual basis.

C.E. L'AMI (1896-)

An Irish-born journalist, poet, translator, and author who settled in Canada, L'Ami was born in Kilkenny, Ireland, and attended the University of Saskatchewan. During World War I, he served with the Canadian Army and afterwards worked as a newspaper reporter, editor, and writer in Canada, as well as a journalist for the Canadian Broadcasting Corporation. A Westminster Fiction Award winner for his novel *The Green Madonna*, L'Ami is also the author of *The Tipperary Stonethrowers*, a book of poems.

`3617` *The Green Madonna*

Date of Publication: 1952
Subject(s): Tudor Period; Religious Conflict
Fictional character(s): Lord Gisbert, Nobleman
Time Period(s): 15th century
Locale(s): England

Summary: Set during the reign of Henry VI, the novel dramatizes the religious and political turmoil of the period. The hero is Lord Gisbert who is sympathetic to the Lollards. Charged with heresy, Gisbert opposes a corrupt local abbot.

Historical Accuracy: The novel provides an authentic atmosphere of the period.

LOUIS L'AMOUR (1908-1988)

Born in North Dakota, L'Amour is one of the most popular American authors of all time. A prolific chronicler of the American West, L'Amour was a lecturer as well as a writer and during his life held numerous jobs, including longshoreman, lumberjack, miner, elephant handler, boxer, and fruit picker. He was a recipient of many awards, such as the Congressional Gold Medal and the Presidential Medal of

Freedom. Besides the many novels and short stories written under his own name, including the Sackett Family series, he was the author of the Hopalong Cassidy series under the pseudonym Tex Burns. L'Amour sold more books than almost any other contemporary novelist and wrote more.

3618 *The Californios*

Date of Publication: 1974
Subject(s): American West
Fictional character(s): Eileen Mulkerin, Widow(er); Sean Mulkerin, Sailor; Michael Mulkerin, Religious (monk)
Time Period(s): 19th century
Locale(s): Malibu, California

Summary: This story of Spanish California concerns an Irish family, the Mulkerins, who struggle to hold onto their ranch at Malibu against an assortment of enemies, aided by the Indians and the Spanish.

Historical Accuracy: The novel features an authentic historical background of the clash of cultures in California.

3619 *The Daybreakers*

Date of Publication: 1960
Subject(s): American West; Family Saga
Fictional character(s): Tyrel Sackett, Frontiersman, Gunfighter; Orin Sackett, Frontiersman, Lawman
Time Period(s): 1870s (1870-1872)
Locale(s): Tennessee; Great Plains

Summary: In this the sixth installment of the Sackett family saga, Tye Sackett and his brother Orin leave their Tennessee home for the western plains.

Historical Accuracy: The period elements are authentically drawn.

3620 *Jubal Sackett*

Date of Publication: 1985
Subject(s): American West; Settlement of the American Frontier; Family Saga
Fictional character(s): Jubal Sackett, Frontiersman; Itchakoma, Indian (Natchez), Royalty (princess); Keokotah, Indian (Kickapoo), Warrior
Time Period(s): 17th century (1620s)
Locale(s): Southwest, North America

Summary: In the fourth volume of the Sackett family saga, Jubal Sackett, son of Barnabas, sets out from the Carolinas to what is now New Mexico. He has numerous adventures and encounters with the Spanish and Indians who consider him a powerful medicine man. He wins the hand of Itchakoma, a Natchez Indian princess.

Historical Accuracy: The novel features a good deal of convincing lore about the Indians and life on the western frontier in the 17th century.

3621 *Lonely on the Mountain*

Date of Publication: 1980
Subject(s): American West; Cattle Drives; Family Saga

Fictional character(s): Tell Sackett, Frontiersman; Orin Sackett, Frontiersman; Tyrel Sackett, Frontiersman
Time Period(s): 1870s (1875-1879)
Locale(s): Dakota Territory, United States

Summary: This final installment of the Sackett family saga describes a cattle drive led by Tell, Tyrel, and Orin Sackett across the Dakota plains toward Canada. They must contend with the Sioux along an uncharted trail.

Historical Accuracy: The novel features authentic western and period elements.

3622 *The Man From Broken Hills*

Date of Publication: 1975
Subject(s): American West; Family Saga
Fictional character(s): Milo Talon, Outlaw
Time Period(s): 1870s
Locale(s): West

Summary: This installment of the Sackett family saga follows the adventures of outlaw Milo Talon who pursues the man who has betrayed his family.

Historical Accuracy: The novel features a dependable period background and customs.

3623 *Mustang Man*

Date of Publication: 1966
Subject(s): American West; Family Saga
Fictional character(s): Nolan Sackett, Fugitive
Time Period(s): 1870s (1875-1879)
Locale(s): New Mexico

Summary: In the 13th volume of the Sackett family saga, Nolan Sackett is on the run from a posse on a charge of murder, but his real problems stem from his involvement with two women.

Historical Accuracy: The period background is convincing and authentic.

3624 *Ride the Dark Trail*

Date of Publication: 1972
Subject(s): American West; Family Saga
Fictional character(s): Emily Talon, Rancher; Logan Sackett, Outlaw (rustler)
Time Period(s): 1870s (1875-1879)
Locale(s): West

Summary: In another installment of the author's Sackett family saga, Logan Sackett comes to the aid of his kin Emily Talon in a series of western adventures.

Historical Accuracy: The novel features dependable western action and a believable period background.

3625 *Ride the River*

Date of Publication: 1983
Subject(s): Family Saga
Fictional character(s): Echo Sackett, Young Woman
Time Period(s): 1840s; 1850s
Locale(s): Tennessee

Summary: This fifth novel in the Sackett family saga takes up the story of Echo Sackett who proves her mettle in the mountains of Tennessee against killers intent on cheating her of her inheritance.

Historical Accuracy: The period background is convincing.

3626 *Rivers West*

Date of Publication: 1975
Subject(s): American West
Fictional character(s): Jean Talon, Frontiersman; Richard Tourville, Nobleman
Time Period(s): 1820s (1821)
Locale(s): Pittsburgh, Pennsylvania; St. Louis, Missouri

Summary: This tale of frontier America concerns a young Canadian, Jean Talon, who journeys from Quebec to Pittsburgh where he hopes to build steam boats to work the rivers west into the frontier. He finds himself pitted against a band of cutthroats led by Baron Richard Tourville who is scheming to seize the Louisiana Territory as his private domain.

Historical Accuracy: The story is fictional but filled with authentic frontier details.

3627 *The Sackett Brand*

Date of Publication: 1965
Subject(s): American West; Family Saga
Fictional character(s): Tell Sackett, Frontiersman
Time Period(s): 1870s (1875-1879)
Locale(s): Southwest

Summary: In this 10th installment of the Sackett family saga, when Tell Sackett is attacked by a band of hired gunslingers, the rest of the Sackett clan is up in arms and hurries to the rescue.

Historical Accuracy: The western details and action are realistically and believably drawn.

3628 *Sackett's Land*

Date of Publication: 1974
Subject(s): Elizabethan Period; American Colonies; Family Saga
Fictional character(s): Barnabas Sackett, Fugitive, Settler
Time Period(s): 17th century (1600)
Locale(s): London, England; Virginia, American Colonies

Summary: In the first volume of the Sackett family saga, Barnabas Sackett is declared an outlaw, and flees Elizabethan London for the American colony of Virginia. On the way, he must contend with pirates before he deals with the challenges of the American wilderness.

Historical Accuracy: This is a romanticized version of the period with some authentic touches.

3629 *The Sky-Liners*

Date of Publication: 1967
Subject(s): American West; Family Saga
Fictional character(s): Galloway Sackett, Frontiersman; Flagon Sackett, Frontiersman; James Black Fetchen, Rancher
Time Period(s): 1870s (1875-1879)

Locale(s): New Mexico

Summary: In this installment of the Sackett family saga, when Galloway and Flagon Sackett run afoul of the powerful James Black Fetchen, they must contend with his wrath that comes in the form of a small army of expensive hired guns.

Historical Accuracy: The period elements are believable.

3630 *To the Far Blue Mountains*

Date of Publication: 1976
Subject(s): American Colonies; Settlement of the American Frontier; Indians
Fictional character(s): Barnabas Sackett, Fugitive, Settler; Abigail Sackett, Settler
Time Period(s): 17th century (1600s-1620s)
Locale(s): James River, Virginia, American Colonies

Summary: In the second volume of the Sackett family saga, Barnabas Sackett has escaped pursuit in Elizabethan London for the James River in the Virginia colony. There he and his wife Abigail begin to raise a family while contending with Indians and the wilderness.

Historical Accuracy: The period elements are captured convincingly.

3631 *Treasure Mountain*

Date of Publication: 1972
Subject(s): Family Saga; Treasure Hunt
Fictional character(s): Orin Sackett, Frontiersman
Time Period(s): 1870s (1875-1879)
Locale(s): New Orleans, Louisiana

Summary: In a search for a fortune in gold and his father, who disappeared 20 years before, Orin Sackett must contend with a group of competitors from New Orleans who also want the gold.

Historical Accuracy: The novel provides a believable period background for this adventure story.

3632 *The Walking Drum*

Date of Publication: 1984
Subject(s): Middle Ages; Byzantine Empire
Fictional character(s): Kerbouchard, Knight, Scholar
Historical character(s): Andronicus I Comnenus, Ruler (Byzantine emperor)
Time Period(s): 12th century (1176)
Locale(s): Constantinople, Byzantine Empire; Asia (southwest); Europe

Summary: Set during the 12th century, the novel chronicles the remarkable adventures of Kerbouchard. His quest for knowledge and fortune takes him across Europe and the Russian steppes to Byzantine Constantinople, where he is thrust into a web of conspiracy and tragedy.

Historical Accuracy: The place names, titles of books, authors, and dates are factual, and the description of names and people are based upon contemporary and historical sources, as well as personal observation.

3633 *The Warrior's Path*

Date of Publication: 1980
Subject(s): American Colonies; Family Saga
Fictional character(s): Kin-Ring Sackett, Young Man; Yance Sackett, Young Man
Time Period(s): 17th century (1620s)
Locale(s): Massachusetts, American Colonies; Northeast, American Colonies

Summary: In this installment of the Sackett family saga, when an Indian raiding party kidnaps a settler's daughter, Kin and Yance Sackett pursue the kidnappers along the Warrior's Path that leads north to what is now Boston.

Historical Accuracy: The novel features a good deal of believable period elements and a realistic setting.

GIUSEPPE DI LAMPEDUSA (1896-1957)

Italian novelist Lampedusa was a wealthy Sicilian prince who borrowed details from his own family's history to produce his only novel, *The Leopard*. Lampedusa died five days after receiving his publisher's rejection. The novel finally appeared posthumously and is regarded as a classic Italian novel. During World War I, Lampedusa was taken prisoner but succeeded in his second escape attempt and found his way back to Italy in disguise. He withdrew from public life after the rise of Mussolini and the Fascists.

3634 *The Leopard*

Date of Publication: 1959
Subject(s): Independence—Italy
Fictional character(s): Don Fabrizio Corbera, Royalty (Prince of Salina); Tancredi Falconeri, Royalty (Prince of Falconeri), Ward
Time Period(s): 19th century; 20th century (1860-1910)
Locale(s): Sicily, Italy

Summary: The novel is the story of the unification of Italy in the days of Garibaldi. It shows the effects of political and social change as experienced by Corbera, a philosophical Sicilian prince. Corbera watches Garibaldi's rise and awaits the outcome. His nephew, Tancredi, joins the fight, and Corbera involves himself in the debate during the plebiscite for unification.

Historical Accuracy: The novel features convincing characters, and as a version of the past, it goes beyond most historical fiction to comment on the universal human condition.

BRUCE LANCASTER (1896-1963)

Born in Worcester, Massachusetts, and educated at Harvard, Lancaster was a businessman and a foreign service officer in Japan. When developing a novel, Lancaster begins with the historical setting and the important figures of the time. He then adds fictional aspects.

3635 *The Big Knives*

Date of Publication: 1964

Subject(s): American Revolution; Battle of Vincennes
Fictional character(s): Markham Cape, Businessman (merchant); Oliver Pollock, Businessman (merchant); Leonard Helm, Military Personnel (army officer)
Historical character(s): George Rogers Clark, Military Personnel (American officer); Henry Hamilton, Military Personnel (British officer)
Time Period(s): 1770s (1778-1779)
Locale(s): Northwest Territory, United States (Ohio, Michigan, and Kentucky); Vincennes, Illinois

Summary: The novel describes the exploits of George Rogers Clark who in 1778 led a band of 200 Virginians and Kentuckians to capture settlements in Illinois. The action culminates in the pivotal Battle of Vincennes. Clark's campaign is interwoven with the fictional adventures of young Markham Cape, a merchant-adventurer trying to make his way back to Boston from New Orleans.

Historical Accuracy: The history is solidly detailed and exact.

3636 *Blind Journey*

Date of Publication: 1953
Subject(s): American Revolution; Sea Story; Battle of Yorktown
Fictional character(s): Ward Gratwick, Patriot
Historical character(s): Benjamin Franklin, Political Figure, Diplomat
Time Period(s): 1780s
Locale(s): At Sea; France; Yorktown, Virginia

Summary: Young American patriot Ward Gratwick is captured and sent to England. His ship, however, is waylaid, and he lands in France where he meets Benjamin Franklin. He sails back home in a French ship laden with gold and supplies for the American forces, and, after a series of adventures at sea, arrives in Virginia in time for the Yorktown campaign.

Historical Accuracy: The novel features an authentic background and a reliable account of the historical events featured, though the story itself is invented.

BRUCE LANCASTER (1896-1963)

LOWELL BRENTANO

Born in Worcester, Massachusetts, and educated at Harvard, Lancaster was a businessman and a foreign service officer in Japan. When developing a novel, Lancaster begins with the historical setting and the important figures of the time. He then adds fictional aspects.

3637 *Bride of a Thousand Cedars*

Date of Publication: 1939
Subject(s): Civil War—U.S.; Sea Story
Fictional character(s): Sally Cottrell, Young Woman; Trevor Wyeth, Blockade Runner
Time Period(s): 1860s
Locale(s): Bermuda

Summary: The novel's subject is the part played by the island of Bermuda during the American Civil War when southern blockade runners turned the island into an important trading area. Islander Sally Cottrell falls in love with Trevor Wyeth, a former British naval officer turned blockade runner, and the novel follows their experiences.

Historical Accuracy: The novel captures the period background and the region with skill.

BRUCE LANCASTER (1896-1963)

Born in Worcester, Massachusetts, and educated at Harvard, Lancaster was a businessman and a foreign service officer in Japan. When developing a novel, Lancaster begins with the historical setting and the important figures of the time. He then adds fictional aspects.

3638 *Bright to the Wanderer*

Date of Publication: 1942
Subject(s): Family Saga; Upper Canada Revolt
Fictional character(s): Gilbert Stenrood, Doctor
Historical character(s): William Lyon Mackenzie, Revolutionary
Time Period(s): 18th century; 19th century (1781-1840)
Locale(s): Toronto, Ontario, Canada; Albany, New York

Summary: The settlement of Upper Canada and the rebellion that broke out in the 1830s between the reformist advocates of self-rule and the small clique of the powerful known as the Family Compact are depicted. The conflict is seen through the experiences of the Stenrood family in Toronto.

Historical Accuracy: The historical details are accurately developed.

3639 *For Us the Living*

Date of Publication: 1940
Subject(s): Settlement of the American Frontier; Indians; Black Hawk War
Fictional character(s): Hugh Brace, Pioneer
Historical character(s): Abraham Lincoln, Political Figure
Time Period(s): 1820s; 1830s
Locale(s): Indiana; Illinois; Kentucky

Summary: Abraham Lincoln's early years in Indiana and Illinois are portrayed. Indian fights and frontier adventures are described, and Lincoln's commitment to democracy and nationalism emerges. The novel also offers a portrait of the New Salem community and the ethics of America's western frontier that were essential in the formation of Lincoln's character.

Historical Accuracy: Little is known for certain about Lincoln's early years, and the novel fills in the gaps with plausible and believable surmises.

3640 *Guns of Burgoyne*

Date of Publication: 1939
Subject(s): American Revolution; Battle of Saratoga; Military Life—British Army
Fictional character(s): Kurt Ahrens, Military Personnel (Hessian soldier)
Historical character(s): John Burgoyne, Military Personnel (general), Writer (playwright)

Time Period(s): 1770s (1777-1778)
Locale(s): Saratoga, New York

Summary: A young Hessian soldier, Kurt Ahrens, provides his viewpoint on the disastrous campaign of British General John Burgoyne that culminates in the Battle of Saratoga. The details of the flamboyant Burgoyne, called "Gentleman Johnny," who mounts the expedition in a style more suited to the drawing room than the American wilderness, are presented. The heroism of Burgoyne's troops emerges, even as the General's follies doom them to defeat.

Historical Accuracy: Some minor liberties with the chronology have been taken, but essentially the events are based on fact.

3641 *Night March*

Date of Publication: 1958
Subject(s): Civil War—U.S.; Military Life—U.S. Cavalry; Battle of Franklin
Fictional character(s): Kirk Stedman, Military Personnel (cavalry officer); Jake Pitler, Military Personnel (cavalry officer); Lynn Stockdale, Young Woman
Historical character(s): Ulrich Dahlgren, Military Personnel (Union officer)
Time Period(s): 1860s (1863-1864)
Locale(s): Richmond, Virginia; Nashville, Tennessee

Summary: The background of the story is the failed Kilpatrick-Dahlgren raid in the Civil War, meant to free Union soldiers being held in Richmond, Virginia. Two participants in the raid, Kirk Stedman and Jake Pitler, are captured and placed in Libby Prison. They escape and make their way behind enemy lines to Tennessee where they participate in the Battle of Franklin.

Historical Accuracy: Although the story is fictional, it is based on facts and documented evidence of the failed raid.

3642 *No Bugles Blow*

Date of Publication: 1948
Subject(s): Civil War—U.S.; Espionage; Siege of Vicksburg
Fictional character(s): Whipple Sheldon, Spy; Penn Grainger, Spy; Sharon McDaniel, Spy
Time Period(s): 1860s (1862)
Locale(s): Mississippi; Nashville, Tennessee; Alabama

Summary: Whipple Sheldon takes on the dangerous job of espionage work during the Civil War at the time of the sieges of Vicksburg and of Nashville and the Battle of Missionary Ridge. He works behind enemy lines maintaining contact with Union sympathizers.

Historical Accuracy: The military action described is historically correct.

3643 *Phantom Fortress*

Date of Publication: 1950
Subject(s): American Revolution
Fictional character(s): Ross Pembroke, Military Personnel (cavalry officer); Dorande van Kortenaer, Young Woman

Historical character(s): Nathanael Greene, Military Personnel (officer); Henry Lee, Military Personnel (officer); Francis Marion, Military Personnel (officer)
Time Period(s): 1780s (1780)
Locale(s): Carolinas, United States

Summary: The background of the story is the guerilla warfare mounted by Francis Marion in the Carolinas during the American Revolution. Ross Pembroke is a cavalry officer from Rhode Island who joins Marion's partisan fighters. He meets and falls in love with Dorande van Kortenaer, a refugee from a native uprising in the Dutch West Indies.

Historical Accuracy: The novel is based on actuality and attempts to capture the actual life of Marion's rebel army.

3644　Roll, Shenandoah

Date of Publication: 1956
Subject(s): Civil War—U.S.; Shenandoah Valley Campaign
Fictional character(s): Ellery Starr, Veteran (Union soldier), Journalist (war correspondent); Harry Gilmor, Military Personnel (Confederate cavalryman); Gillian Westlake, Young Woman
Historical character(s): Philip H. Sheridan, Military Personnel (Union officer); George Armstrong Custer, Military Personnel (Union officer)
Time Period(s): 1860s (1864)
Locale(s): Shenandoah Valley, Virginia; Chambersburg, Pennsylvania

Summary: Ellery Starr, a disabled Union veteran, is a war correspondent reporting on the Shenandoah Valley Campaign of 1864. He is on hand during the burning of Chambersburg and for General Sheridan's triumph at Opequon and Cedar Creek. His path crosses that of a dashing Confederate cavalryman, and he becomes involved with the daughter of a lay preacher.

Historical Accuracy: The novel artfully blends a fictional story and an accurate account of the Valley Campaign.

3645　The Scarlet Patch

Date of Publication: 1947
Subject(s): Civil War—U.S.; Battle of Antietam; Battle of Gettysburg
Fictional character(s): Jean de Merac, Military Personnel (Union soldier); Gail Shortland, Nurse; George Force, Military Personnel (Union soldier)
Historical character(s): Philip Kearney, Military Personnel (Union officer)
Time Period(s): 1860s (1861-1863)
Locale(s): Virginia; Pennsylvania

Summary: This Civil War novel details the military experiences of men in the Rochenbeau Rifles, a regiment of foreign-born volunteers who are involved in some of the greatest battles of the war. The story centers on Jean de Merac and his Yankee friend George Force.

Historical Accuracy: The Rifles are a fictional regiment but based on many such companies which were made up of foreign volunteers in the Union army. The military action is factually drawn.

3646　The Secret Road

Date of Publication: 1952
Subject(s): American Revolution; Espionage
Fictional character(s): Robert Townsend, Spy; Grant Ledyard, Military Personnel (intelligence officer); Polly Morgan, Spy
Historical character(s): Benjamin Tallmadge, Military Personnel (intelligence officer); John Andre, Military Personnel (British officer), Spy; Benedict Arnold, Military Personnel (American officer), Traitor
Time Period(s): 1780s (1780)
Locale(s): New York, New York; Connecticut; Long Island, New York

Summary: This is the story of the secret service during the American Revolution and the role it played in uncovering Benedict Arnold's treason. From occupied New York, information of Arnold's plot to surrender West Point to the British reaches Grant Ledyard, Major Benjamin Tallmudge's trusted courier. Ledyard finds himself at the center of John Andre's capture and the foiling of Arnold.

Historical Accuracy: The novel is an artful blend of fact and fiction: of what actually happened and what certainly could have happened.

3647　Trumpet to Arms

Date of Publication: 1944
Subject(s): American Revolution; Battle of Concord; Military Life
Fictional character(s): Ripley Mayne, Military Personnel (royal marine); Remembrance Morse, Young Woman
Historical character(s): John Glover, Military Personnel (army officer)
Time Period(s): 1770s; 1780s (1775-1780)
Locale(s): Concord, Massachusetts; Long Island, New York; Boston, Massachusetts

Summary: The novel follows Massachusetts' militia companies from the Battle of Concord to the campaigns of Trenton and Princeton when the ragtag state militias form the first American army. Ripley Mayne returns from impressment in the British Navy to use his skills in getting the Ticonderoga guns over the hump at Great Barrington for the Battle of Boston and at the rescue of Washington's army on Long Island.

Historical Accuracy: The novel's incidents are solidly rooted in actuality.

3648　Venture in the East

Date of Publication: 1951
Subject(s): East/West Relations; Japanese Empire
Fictional character(s): Trudi Van Os, Young Woman; Dirk Young, Young Man
Historical character(s): Francois Caron, Adventurer
Time Period(s): 17th century (1630s)
Locale(s): Japan

Summary: The story describes the events leading up to the Shimabara Rebellion of 1637 and the end of Japan's open relations with the west which lasted until Commodore Perry's treaty in 1854. Dirk Young is an Englishman employed by the

Dutch East Indian Company who falls in love with Trudi Van Os, who through a bribe, makes her way to Japan to avoid a distasteful marriage. Francois Caron, a liaison between the Dutch and the Japanese, plots to use Japanese soldiers aboard Dutch ships to seize the Philippines from the Spanish.

Historical Accuracy: The novel is solidly based on factual and historical evidence with probable surmises when the facts fail.

G.B. LANCASTER
(PSEUD. OF EDITH J. LYTTLETON, 1874-1945)

Born in Epping Forest, Tasmania, Lyttleton spent part of her childhood in New Zealand and later lived for a number of years in Australia. Her novel *Pageant* (1933) draws on her own family history in its depiction of a Tasmanian family between 1826 and the twentieth century. It won the Australian Literature Society's Gold Medal.

3649 *Grand Parade*

Date of Publication: 1943
Subject(s): English Colonies; War of 1812
Fictional character(s): Charnisay Cochrane, Young Woman
Time Period(s): 19th century (1800s-1880s)
Locale(s): Halifax, Nova Scotia, Canada

Summary: The novel depicts the history of Canada in the early years of the 19th century through the experiences of the Cochrane family of Halifax, Nova Scotia. The novel's focus is on the heroine, Charnisay Cochrane, whose experiences reflect the rise and fall of Halifax as Canada's military and social capital.

Historical Accuracy: The author explains that the history is as correct as diligent research could make it.

3650 *Pageant*

Date of Publication: 1933
Subject(s): Frontier—Australia; Family Saga
Fictional character(s): Robert Snow, Convict, Servant; Mab Comyn, Pioneer; Jenny Comyn, Young Woman
Time Period(s): 19th century
Locale(s): Tasmania, Australia

Summary: The novel details the settlement of Tasmania from the first settlers who come from England after the Peninsular War to the successive generations who participate in Australia's development. The story follows the fortunes of the Comyn family over the years.

Historical Accuracy: The novel is too overcrowded with character portraits to be fully satisfying, but it does capture the spirit of the place and its time.

SHEILA LANCASTER
(PSEUD. OF SHEILA HOLLAND, 1937-)

Born in London, England, Holland has published numerous books under her own name and has used the pseudonyms Laura Hardy and Charlotte Lamb, as well as Sheila Lancaster. Her novels under the latter pseudonym include *Sweet Park Wanton* and *The Tilthammer*.

3651 *Mistress of Fortune*

Date of Publication: 1982
Subject(s): Biography, Fictionalized; French Revolution
Historical character(s): Josephine, Spouse (of Napoleon); Napoleon Bonaparte, Military Personnel (army officer); Paul Barras, Revolutionary
Time Period(s): 18th century; 19th century (1778-1804)
Locale(s): Martinique; France

Summary: The novel dramatizes the early years of Josephine, from her childhood on a sugar plantation in Martinique to her marriage to a French aristocrat and her becoming the mistress of one of the leaders of the French Revolution. Finally, the novel depicts her fateful relationship with the ambitious young officer from Corsica, Napoleon Bonaparte.

Historical Accuracy: The novel is faithful to the facts of Josephine's life with some invented, though plausible, scenes and dialogue.

DORA LANDEY

ELINOR KLEIN

3652 *Triptych*

Date of Publication: 1983
Subject(s): Russian Revolution; Artistic Life; Family Saga
Fictional character(s): Sonya Poliakov, Revolutionary; Count Gregory Tolchin, Nobleman, Revolutionary; Delphi Stern, Artist
Time Period(s): 19th century; 20th century (1894-1945)
Locale(s): St. Petersburg, Russia; New York, New York; Italy (Siena, Florence)

Summary: This sweeping, panoramic novel ranges from revolutionary Russia, through bohemian Greenwich Village, to Italy and Paris of the 1920s. Sonya Poliakov and Count Tolchin are comfortable members of Imperial Russian society who reject their class. As immigrants in New York, they continue the struggle, opposed by their daughter Delphi, who pursues her own struggle through her art.

Historical Accuracy: The novel is a massive depiction of the 20th century's leading historical events blended into a compelling family chronicle.

JILL MARIE LANDIS

3653 *Sunflower*

Date of Publication: 1989
Subject(s): American West; Immigrants
Fictional character(s): Analisa Van Meeteren, Frontierswoman, Seamstress; Caleb Storm, Frontiersman, Indian (half Indian)
Time Period(s): 1870s
Locale(s): Iowa

Summary: Dutch immigrant Analisa Van Meeteren supports herself by dressmaking. Her child is half Indian, born of a rape during an Indian attack that killed Analisa's family. Into her life comes the half-Indian Caleb Storm. The novel examines the bitter conflict between the settlers and the Indians.

Historical Accuracy: The novel's period background is authentic.

CARL DANIEL LANE (1899-)

Born in Portland, Maine, Lane attended the New York School of Fine and Applied Arts, and worked as an interior decorator. He became a freelance writer of novels, juvenile books, and nonfiction in 1925.

3654 *The Fleet in the Forest*

Date of Publication: 1943
Subject(s): War of 1812; Battle of Lake Erie
Fictional character(s): Chid Alwyn, Worker (shipwright)
Historical character(s): Oliver Hazard Perry, Military Personnel (admiral)
Time Period(s): 1810s (1813)
Locale(s): Erie, Pennsylvania; Lake Erie, Great Lakes

Summary: The story of the building of Admiral Perry's fleet during the War of 1812 is dramatized through the experiences of a young Connecticut shipwright, Chid Alwyn, who begins his adventures aboard a privateer. The action includes scenes from the pivotal Battle of Lake Erie that made Perry a national hero.

Historical Accuracy: The author is convincing in delivering the life of the times and the details of boat construction and naval strategy.

JANE LANE
(PSEUD. OF ELAINE DAKERS)

3655 *Madame Geneva*

Date of Publication: 1945
Subject(s): Jacobite Rebellion
Fictional character(s): Michael Montague, Worker
Time Period(s): 18th century
Locale(s): London, England

Summary: London in the early years of the 18th century is the setting for this story of Jacobite Michael Montague who works for a London brewer while secretly working on behalf of the Stuart restoration. The novel offers a vivid portrait of the effect on the poor of the importing of cheap gin.

Historical Accuracy: The historical atmosphere is clearly and convincingly delivered.

3656 *Parcel of Rogues*

Date of Publication: 1948
Subject(s): Royalty—Scotland
Historical character(s): Mary, Queen of Scots, Ruler (Queen of Scotland); James Douglas, Nobleman (Earl of Morton); Henry Stewart, Nobleman (Mary's husband); David Rizzio, Musician; James Hepburn, Nobleman (Earl of Bothwell)
Time Period(s): 16th century (1542-1581)
Locale(s): Scotland

Summary: This novel based on the life of Mary, Queen of Scots records the tumultuous years of her reign from her return to Scotland and ascension to the throne to the death of Morton. The novel captures the court intrigue that haunted her reign and the plots and counterplots that lead to murder and betrayal.

Historical Accuracy: Faithful to the spirit of the times, the novel does indulge in some modifications of the facts. The novel offers a plausible interpretation concerning the famous Casket letters.

3657 *The Severed Crown*

Date of Publication: 1972
Subject(s): Royalty—England; Trials; Civil War—England
Fictional character(s): Jean de Montrevil, Nobleman; Thomas Herbert, Gentleman; Jack Ashburnham, Military Personnel (colonel)
Historical character(s): Charles I, Ruler (King of England); Oliver Cromwell, Political Figure
Time Period(s): 17th century (1646-1649)
Locale(s): England; France

Summary: Narrated by a variety of witnesses, the novel details the fall of Charles I—his imprisonment, trial, and execution. Charles is shown as the unmovable advocate of the absolute power of the monarchy who meets the irresistible force of Cromwell and the Parliament.

Historical Accuracy: The historical background is accurately depicted.

3658 *Thunder on St. Paul's Day*

Date of Publication: 1954
Subject(s): Popish Plot; Religious Conflict
Fictional character(s): Catherine Carrill, Gentlewoman; Charles Carrill, Student
Historical character(s): Titus Oates, Leader (of the Popish Plot)
Time Period(s): 17th century (1678)
Locale(s): London, England

Summary: During the religious hysteria created by Titus Oates and the sham Popish Plot, an English family, the Carrills, get caught up in the reign of terror that grips London.

Historical Accuracy: The story is fanciful but does present an authentic picture of London during the period and the facts concerning Oates and his conspiracy.

3659 *The Young and Lonely King*

Date of Publication: 1969
Subject(s): Royalty—England; Biography, Fictionalized; Jacobean Period
Historical character(s): Charles I, Ruler (King of England); Henrietta-Maria, Royalty (queen consort of Charles I); George Villiers, Nobleman (Duke of Buckingham), Courtier; James I, Ruler (King of England); Marie de' Medici, Ruler (Queen of France); Armand-Jean Du Plessis, Religious (Cardinal Richelieu), Political Figure (Duc de Richelieu)
Time Period(s): 17th century (1603-1649)
Locale(s): England; Spain; France

Summary: This biographical novel of Charles I covers his life from his early years to the birth of his first son, the future Charles II. As a young prince, Charles overcomes several physical handicaps. Later the influence of the Duke of Buckingham leads him to make some rash decisions that will have serious repercussions at home and abroad.

Historical Accuracy: The novel invents dialogue and some situations but is faithful to the general outline of Charles' life and career.

ROSE LANE (1887-1968)

Born in South Dakota, the daughter of writer Laura Ingalls Wilder, Lane's childhood experiences are celebrated in Wilder's classic "Little House" books. Lane worked as a newspaper reporter and feature writer as well as for the American Red Cross in Europe and the Near East. Lane won the O. Henry prize in 1922 for "Innocence.".

3660 *Free Land*

Date of Publication: 1938
Subject(s): American West; Farming; Homesteading
Fictional character(s): David Beaton, Settler
Time Period(s): 1880s (1880-1885)
Locale(s): South Dakota

Summary: Frontier life in South Dakota during the 1880s is depicted in the experiences of young David Beaton who travels west from his Minnesota home to a homestead on the western prairie. The novel describes his struggles and hardships.

Historical Accuracy: The incidents are historically correct, and the secondary characters are faithful to frontier types of the period.

JENNIFER LANG

3661 *The Peacock and the Pearl*

Date of Publication: 1992
Subject(s): Middle Ages; Royalty—England; Peasants' Revolt
Fictional character(s): Joanna Burgey, Young Woman; Tristram of Maudesbury, Knight
Historical character(s): Edward III, Ruler (King of England); John of Gaunt, Royalty; Henry Bolingbroke, Nobleman; John Ball, Revolutionary; Wat Tyler, Revolutionary; John Wycliffe, Religious
Time Period(s): 14th century (1371-1388)
Locale(s): Aquitaine, France; London, England; Maudesbury, England

Summary: This is a richly detailed novel of life in the 14th century. Joanna Burgey is a mercer's daughter who is rescued from a violent mob by a knight, Sir Tristram of Maudesbury, a retainer to John of Gaunt. In a case of mistaken identity, Tristram marries Joanna. She battles for survival in the treacherous world of city and royal politics.

Historical Accuracy: This is a very detailed depiction of 14th-century life and politics, all authentically presented.

THEO LANG

3662 *The Word and the Sword*

Date of Publication: 1974
Subject(s): Roman Empire; Biblical Story
Historical character(s): Pontius Pilate, Government Official, Biblical Figure; Flavius Josephus, Historian, Military Personnel; Tiberius, Ruler (Roman emperor); Caligula, Ruler (Roman emperor)
Time Period(s): 1st century
Locale(s): Rome, Roman Empire; Jerusalem, Israel; Capri, Roman Empire

Summary: The novel offers a portrait of Pontius Pilate, as a man and as a political operative. Reviled by history as the man with the blood of Jesus Christ on his hands, Pilate in this interpretation is as much a victim as a villain, caught between Roman politics and unrest in Judea. His tragedy is shown as the result of being in the wrong place at the wrong time.

Historical Accuracy: The period background is convincing, though the story is fictional.

ARTHUR L. LAPHAM (1922-)

Born in Houston, Texas, Lapham graduated from the Agricultural and Mechanical College of Texas and received his law degree from South Texas College of Law. He was in private practice in Victoria, Texas, for 20 years. In World War II, Lapham served as a bomber pilot in the South Pacific.

3663 *Justus*

Date of Publication: 1973
Subject(s): Biblical Story; Roman Empire
Fictional character(s): Justus, Military Personnel (Roman captain)
Historical character(s): Herod Antipas, Ruler (King of Judea), Biblical Figure; Jesus Christ, Biblical Figure
Time Period(s): 1st century
Locale(s): Jerusalem, Israel

Summary: This tale follows the life of Justus, the Roman captain of King Herod's guard. Originally an opponent of Jesus, Justus becomes one of his most ardent followers.

Historical Accuracy: The novel features some authentic period elements and a look at contemporary customs.

GILLES LAPOUGE (1923-)

A well-known French television journalist, Lapouge is the author of books on Brazil, piracy, and the Spanish anarchists. *The Battle of Wagram* won the Guttenberg Prize for historical fiction and was a runner-up for the Prix Goncourt.

3664 *The Battle of Wagram*

Date of Publication: 1986
Subject(s): Napoleonic Wars; Battle of Wagram

Fictional character(s): Clemence of Saxe-Salsa, Noblewoman; Otto Apfegrun, Young Man
Time Period(s): 1800s (1809)
Locale(s): Austria

Summary: This novel of the Napoleonic Wars is based on an actual episode during the Battle of Wagram in which an Austrian prince transfers his wife's young lover to a regiment on the opposite side of the conflict so he might be killed. The novel captures the spirit of the age and the court intrigue of the Hapsburgs under the pressure of Napoleon's conquest.

Historical Accuracy: The story interweaves the fictional and factual with a solid background of the period.

LINDA J. LAROSA (1951-)

3665 *Winter of the Heart*
Date of Publication: 1984
Subject(s): Romance; Franco-Prussian War
Fictional character(s): Jullienne Eisenstadt, Noblewoman, Spouse; Franz Eisenstadt, Nobleman (Count of Eisenstadt); Edward Atherton-Moore, Gentleman
Historical character(s): Franz Josef I, Ruler (Austrian emperor)
Time Period(s): 1860s; 1870s
Locale(s): Vienna, Austria; Paris, France

Summary: Set in Vienna and Paris in the 19th century, the novel tells the story of Jullienne Eisenstadt, caught in an abusive marriage to Franz, the Count of Eisenstadt. She flees with her children to Paris, where she assumes the indentity of a widowed Frenchwoman and works as a seamstress. She meets and falls in love with an Englishman, Edward Atherton-Moore. Against the background of the Franco-Prussian War, both must finally confront the past and Franz before managing a future together.

Historical Accuracy: The period background is authentically drawn.

ANTONIO LARRETA (1922-)

Born in Montevideo, Uruguay, Larreta is a playwright, actor, film critic, scriptwriter, and novelist.

3666 *The Last Portrait of the Duchess of Alba*
Date of Publication: 1988
Subject(s): Artistic Life; Royalty—Spain
Historical character(s): Maria Cayetana, Noblewoman (Duchess of Alba); Francisco Jose de Goya y Lucientes, Artist; Manuel de Godoy, Government Official, Nobleman (Duke of Alcudia)
Time Period(s): 1800s (1802); 1820s
Locale(s): Madrid, Spain; Bordeaux, France

Summary: In 1802, the notorious Duchess of Alba dies in her bed at the age of 40. Her death remains a mystery. The novel offers an ingenious speculation about her passing from the perspectives of Manuel de Godoy, her former lover and the royal minister charged with investigating the affair, and the

Duchess' most famous paramour, Francisco Goya. Was it suicide, a drug overdose, or royal intrigue that brought Spain's most famous femme fatale to her end?.

Historical Accuracy: The death of the Duchess of Alba is still a mystery, and this version of the facts is filtered through the subjective perspective of Godoy and Goya. Yet the novel does convince in its re-creation of the period and its personalities.

GAYLORD LARSEN (1932-)

An American mystery writer, Larsen was born in South Dakota and graduated from Sioux Falls College and UCLA. He has worked in film and TV as an editor and producer. Larsen is the author of the Joan Bradley mystery series. His novels are intended to reflect a Christian perspective.

3667 *Dorothy and Agatha*
Date of Publication: 1990
Subject(s): Mystery; Literary Life
Historical character(s): Agatha Christie, Writer; Dorothy L. Sayers, Writer; A.A. Milne, Writer; E.C. Bentley, Writer
Time Period(s): 20th century
Locale(s): England

Summary: When Dorothy Sayers discovers the corpse of a man slumped over her typewriter in what looks to be an elaborately staged suicide, the case is taken up by the Detectives Club and its most famous member, Agatha Christie.

Historical Accuracy: The author describes his novel as a "faction," a combination of fact and fiction. That the two great female mystery writers knew each other is certain, as was the existence of the Detectives Club. The rest is invented.

JEANNE LARSEN (1950-)

American scholar, teacher, and novelist Larsen was born in Washington, D.C., and graduated from Oberlin and Hollins colleges, and the University of Iowa. She is a professor of English at Hollins College and has taught in Taiwan and Japan. She is an authority on Tang and pre-Tang Shi-poetry, and has written critical studies of H.D. (Hilda Doolittle) and Emily Dickinson.

3668 *Bronze Mirror*
Date of Publication: 1991
Subject(s): Middle Ages; Chinese Empire; Fantasy
Fictional character(s): Pomegranate, Young Woman; Yellow Emperor, Ruler (mythical); Silkweb Empress, Ruler (mythical)
Time Period(s): 12th century
Locale(s): China

Summary: This fabulous tale set in 12th-century China tells the adventures of Pomegranate, who is engaged in a duel of wits in an epic storytelling competition. The world of medieval China emerges at the conjunction between the real and the imagined.

Historical Accuracy: Endlessly inventive and evocative, the novel creates a world in which the historical period emerges imaginatively.

3669 *Manchu Palaces*

Date of Publication: 1996
Subject(s): Chinese Empire; Coming of Age; Supernatural
Fictional character(s): Lotus, Young Woman
Time Period(s): 18th century
Locale(s): Peking, China

Summary: Set principally in the imperial court of the Manchu dynasty in China during the 18th century, the novel concerns the maturation of Lotus as she prepares for her life as a wife and daughter-in-law. A secondary plot records the spiritual pilgrimage of Lotus' dead mother.

Historical Accuracy: This inventive and provocative novel shows great skill in capturing the atmosphere of the period and its customs.

3670 *Silk Road*

Date of Publication: 1989
Subject(s): Chinese Empire; Magic; Supernatural
Fictional character(s): Greenpearl, Captive, Prostitute (courtesan)
Time Period(s): 8th century
Locale(s): China

Summary: This magical and fabulous tale of 8th-century China blends the real and the supernatural. Greenpearl, the daughter of a powerful T'ang dynasty general, is kidnapped by Tibetan raiders, sold to a caravan of traders along the Silk Road, and then forced into life as a courtesan.

Historical Accuracy: The novel is an inventive collection of narrative elements reflecting the real and the imaginary. The period atmosphere is genuine and convincing.

CHARLES R. LARSON (1938-)

Born in Iowa, Larson graduated from the University of Colorado and Indiana University. He worked as a high school teacher and a Peace Corps volunteer in Nigeria. A professor of literature at American University, Larson won an O. Henry Award in 1971 for "Up From Slavery," and is the author of the critical study *The Emergence of African Fiction*, as well as more than 300 reviews in a variety of periodicals.

3671 *Arthur Dimmesdale*

Date of Publication: 1983
Subject(s): American Colonies; Puritans
Fictional character(s): Arthur Dimmesdale, Religious (clergyman); Hester Prynne, Spouse, Outcast; Roger Chillingworth, Doctor
Time Period(s): 17th century (1640s)
Locale(s): Boston, Massachusetts, American Colonies

Summary: This is a retelling of Nathaniel Hawthorne's classic tale of 17th-century Puritans, *The Scarlet Letter*, from the viewpoint of the young minister Arthur Dimmesdale. His adulterous relationship with Hester Prynne produces guilt and a search for redemption. Hawthorne's characters all reappear with the focus on Dimmesdale's conflicts.

Historical Accuracy: The novel is a convincing echoing of the Hawthorne original, with a realistic depiction of the period.

RUTH LAUGHLIN (1889-)

3672 *The Wind Leaves No Shadow*

Date of Publication: 1948
Subject(s): Spanish Colonies
Historical character(s): Dona Tules Barcelo, Gentlewoman
Time Period(s): 19th century (1821-1846)
Locale(s): Santa Fe, New Mexico

Summary: Frontier life in Spanish colonial Santa Fe in the years before the Mexican War is described in this account of the career of Dona Tules. She rises from the life of a bound peon to become the mistress of the last Mexican governor and the proprietor of the most famous gaming house in Santa Fe.

Historical Accuracy: Existing historical records have been supplemented by the imagination in this convincing depiction of the period.

JONREED LAURITZEN (1902-)

Born in Utah, Lauritzen worked as a field representative for the U.S. Department of the Interior concerned with national parks, reclamation, public lands, and fish and game. He grew up on a ranch in Utah's canyon country and took high school correspondence courses while herding his father's sheep.

3673 *Captain Sutter's Gold*

Date of Publication: 1964
Subject(s): American West; Gold Rush—California; Biography, Fictionalized
Historical character(s): John A. Sutter, Settler
Time Period(s): 1830s; 1840s
Locale(s): California; Hawaii (Sandwich Islands)

Summary: This biographical novel depicts the career of Johann Sutter, who plays a pivotal role in opening up California. Sutter, once a captain of the elite Swiss Guard, comes to the U.S. in the 1830s. He dreams of establishing an empire in California. Eventually he builds a fort at the head waters of the Sacramento River and lays claim to a vast tract of coastal California. With the discovery of gold, he soon finds himself in violent conflict with the 49ers, who rush into his domain.

Historical Accuracy: The details of Sutter's life are accurately captured, as is the period background of life in California at the start of the gold rush.

3674 *The Cross and the Sword*

Date of Publication: 1965
Subject(s): American West; Indians; Spanish Colonies
Historical character(s): Juan Bautista de Anza, Explorer, Government Official; Junipero Serra, Religious (missionary)
Time Period(s): 1770s

Locale(s): California

Summary: The novel tells the story of the earliest Spanish settlement in California. It is the story of two men, Spanish soldier and explorer Anza and priest Junipero Serra, who travel up the California coast and found the settlement which becomes San Francisco.

Historical Accuracy: The essential facts and chronology are observed, but imagination was also employed to re-create personal experiences.

3675 *The Everlasting Fire*

Date of Publication: 1962
Subject(s): Mormons; Religious Conflict
Fictional character(s): Nathan Eyring, Judge; Myra Eyring, Young Woman; Rafael Eyring, Young Man
Historical character(s): Joseph Smith, Leader (Mormon), Religious; Brigham Young, Leader (Mormon), Religious
Time Period(s): 1840s
Locale(s): Nauvoo, Illinois; Iowa

Summary: The novel portrays the bloody migration of the early Mormons in Illinois, the murder of Joseph Smith, and Brigham Young's rise to leadership. The story centers on the Eyring family, who struggle with the challenge of committing to the Mormon faith under the pressure of enormous hostility and prejudice.

Historical Accuracy: The portrait offered of the Mormon migration and of the events of the period are accurate.

3676 *The Rose and the Flame*

Date of Publication: 1951
Subject(s): Spanish Colonies; Indians
Fictional character(s): El Tigre, Scout
Time Period(s): 17th century (1680)
Locale(s): Southwest, North America

Summary: The exiled Duke of Toledo treks to Monterey, whence he hopes to return to Spain and claim the throne. His journey is led by the Spanish swordsman El Tigre.

Historical Accuracy: The novel's convincing depiction of the Southwest under Spanish control compensates for thinly-drawn characters.

DAVID LAVENDER (1910-)

An American author born in Telluride, Colorado, Lavender attended Princeton University and Stanford. For many years he was a consultant to special collections at the library of the University of California, Santa Barbara, and to the California history section of the Oakland Museum. Among his many books are *The Big Divide*, *The Land of Giants*, *Nothing Seemed Impossible*, and *Bent's Fort*.

3677 *Red Mountain*

Date of Publication: 1963
Subject(s): Settlement of the American Frontier; Mining
Fictional character(s): John Ogden, Businessman
Time Period(s): 1880s

Locale(s): Colorado

Summary: Set during the Colorado silver boom of the 1880s, the novel describes the effort to build roads into the mountains. The story paints a vivid portrait of the era and the difficulties caused by the wild country and the ambitions of the prospectors.

Historical Accuracy: The novel's notes indicate the deviations from history. The primary sources, local newspapers of the time, provide an authentic period backdrop.

JANICE LAW
(PSEUD. OF JANICE LAW TRECKER, 1941-)

Born in Connecticut, Law is a graduate of Syracuse University and the University of Connecticut. She has worked as an elementary and high school teacher. Her books include *The Big Payoff*, *Gemini Trip*, and *Under Urion*.

3678 *All the King's Ladies*

Date of Publication: 1986
Subject(s): Royalty—France; Witchcraft and Sorcery
Historical character(s): Louis XIV, Ruler (King of France); Francoise Athenais Rochechouart de Mortemart, Noblewoman (Marquise de Montespan), Lover
Time Period(s): 17th century
Locale(s): France

Summary: Court life during the reign of Louis XIV is dramatized in the struggle for power of Athenais de Montespan. She accepts a position in the King's household and becomes, for a time, one of Louis' mistresses. She attempts to control the King with the aid of a sorceress.

Historical Accuracy: The novel blends actual events and historical figures with imagined material.

STEPHEN R. LAWHEAD (1950-)

Stephen R. Lawhead is an American writer of fantasy and historical fiction. He received his B.A. from Kearney State College in Nebraska and attended Northern Baptist Theological Seminary in Illinois. Much of his fiction is Christian-oriented. Lawhead's books include *In the Hall of the Dragon King* and *The Warlords of Nin*.

3679 *Arthur*

Date of Publication: 1989
Subject(s): Myths and Legends; Dark Ages; Arthurian Legends
Fictional character(s): Arthur, Ruler (King of the Britons); Merlin, Sorcerer; Gwenhwyvar, Royalty (queen consort of Arthur)
Time Period(s): 5th century
Locale(s): England

Summary: In the third volume of the author's Pendragon Cycle, Arthur comes to power and struggles to unite the British kings under his banner as High King, aided by Merlin. His success is short-lived as a new and greater challenge emerges to the peace and prosperity of his kingdom.

Historical Accuracy: The story is imagined, but its period atmosphere is authentic.

3680 *Byzantium*

Date of Publication: 1996
Subject(s): Byzantine Empire; Dark Ages; Religious Life
Fictional character(s): Aidan mac Cainnech, Religious (monk)
Time Period(s): 10th century
Locale(s): Ireland; Byzantium, Byzantine Empire

Summary: A young Irish monk, Aidan mac Cainnech, accompanies a small band to Byzantium and the Court of the Eastern Roman Empire to present the Book of Kells to the Emperor. The novel records his adventures among the Vikings and Saracens as a warrior, sailor, slave, and spy.

Historical Accuracy: The novel provides a believable evocation of the period and its customs.

3681 *Merlin*

Date of Publication: 1988
Subject(s): Myths and Legends; Dark Ages; Arthurian Legends
Fictional character(s): Merlin, Sorcerer; Uther, Ruler (King of the Britons)
Time Period(s): 5th century
Locale(s): England

Summary: In the second book of the author's Pendragon Cycle, Merlin, the son of the visionary Taliesin, prepares the way for Britain's new ruler, Arthur. Against a backdrop of tribal conflict, Merlin labors for a new age and the arrival of a great leader.

Historical Accuracy: Though more fantasy than historical, the novel does capture the atmosphere of Celtic Britain.

3682 *Pendragon*

Date of Publication: 1994
Subject(s): Dark Ages; Myths and Legends; Arthurian Legends
Fictional character(s): Arthur, Ruler (King of the Britons); Merlin, Sorcerer
Time Period(s): 5th century
Locale(s): England

Summary: In the fourth novel of the author's Pendragon Cycle, Arthur is king, but trouble arrives from all sides. His most trusted counselor, Merlin, is tested on a mystical journey back through his past leaving Arthur to contend with adversaries on his own.

Historical Accuracy: The novel is more fantasy than history, but it does create an atmospheric background of early Britain.

3683 *Taliesin*

Date of Publication: 1987
Subject(s): Myths and Legends; Dark Ages; Arthurian Legends
Fictional character(s): Charis, Royalty (princess); Taliesin, Minstrel
Time Period(s): 5th century

Locale(s): England

Summary: Book One of the author's Pendragon Cycle is set in Celtic Britain at the end of the Roman occupation. The story centers on Charis and Taliesin, whose vision of an earthly kingdom is pursued against a backdrop of the struggle of Celtic chieftains.

Historical Accuracy: The novel excels in capturing the spirit of mystery and magic of the Celtic period, though the elements are more imaginative than historical.

JOAN LAWRENCE

3684 *The Scapegoat: A Life of Moses*

Date of Publication: 1988
Subject(s): Biblical Story; Biography, Fictionalized
Historical character(s): Moses, Biblical Figure; Aaron, Biblical Figure; Miriam, Biblical Figure
Time Period(s): 13th century B.C.
Locale(s): Egypt

Summary: This imaginative recreation of the Jewish exodus from Egypt presents a portrait of its leader, Moses, as a divided man, torn between his devotion to God and his people. This autobiographical account offers a human side to the Biblical figure, who is beset by the arrogance of his brother Aaron and the contempt of his sister Miriam, and haunted by his brief marriage to a young Cushite woman.

Historical Accuracy: The novel provides an imaginative and realistic alternative to more heroic treatments.

MARGARET LAWRENCE

3685 *Hearts and Bones*

Date of Publication: 1996
Subject(s): Mystery
Fictional character(s): Hannah Trevor, Midwife; Daniel Josselyn, Veteran (American Revolution); Will Quaid, Lawman (constable)
Time Period(s): 1780s (1786)
Locale(s): Maine

Summary: This historical mystery is set in Maine in the years following the American Revolution. Hannah Trevor, a midwife, and Will Quaid, the local constable, investigate the rape and murder of a young woman. Among those accused of the crime is Daniel Josselyn, Hannah's one-time lover and the father of her illegitimate daughter. The investigation leads Hannah into dark and dangerous wartime secrets.

Historical Accuracy: The period details and the regional background are authentic and believable.

HALLDOR LAXNESS
(PSEUD. OF HALLDOR KILJAN GUDJONSSON, 1902-)

An Icelandic author of more than 50 books, Gudjonsson was born in Reykjavik. He has been the recipient of several awards, most notably the Literature Prize from the International Peace Movement and the Nobel Prize for literature. Despite his great acclaim, less than 15 of his books have been translated into English. He is the author of *The Great Weaver From Kashmir*, held by some critics to be his masterwork, *Independent People*, and *A Quire of Seven*.

3686 *Paradise Reclaimed*

Date of Publication: 1962
Subject(s): Mormons; Immigrants; American West
Fictional character(s): Steiner Steinsson, Farmer, Immigrant
Time Period(s): 19th century
Locale(s): Iceland; Utah; Denmark

Summary: The novel dramatizes the experiences of an Icelandic farmer, Steiner Steinsson, who is persuaded by a Mormon missionary to journey west to Utah.

Historical Accuracy: The novel is convincing in its depiction of Icelandic life and customs.

EDITH LAYTON

3687 *The Fireflower*

Date of Publication: 1989
Subject(s): Restoration Period; Romance
Fictional character(s): Mary Monk, Prostitute; Gideon Hawkes, Landowner
Time Period(s): 17th century (1666)
Locale(s): London, England

Summary: Following the Great Fire of London, young Mary Monk has no choice but to turn to prostitution to support herself. However, she falls in love with her first customer, Gideon Hawkes, a dispossessed Royalist landowner.

Historical Accuracy: The novel at least features a convincing atmosphere if not a full account of the period.

JOSEPH SHERIDAN LE FANU
(1814-1873)

Le Fanu was an Irish writer of mystery and horror. His most famous novel is *Uncle Silas*. Other works include *In a Glass Darkly*.

3688 *The House by the Churchyard*

Date of Publication: 1863
Subject(s): Crime and Criminals; Mystery
Fictional character(s): Mervyn, Nobleman, Detective—Amateur; Paul Dangerfield, Murderer
Time Period(s): 1790s
Locale(s): Dublin, Ireland

Summary: Set in 18th-century Dublin, the novel concerns an investigation of Mervyn, son of Lord Dunoran, who was executed for a murder he did not commit. Suspicion falls on wealthy Paul Dangerfield whose accomplice in the murder also turns up.

Historical Accuracy: Good period details help create the novel's ominous atmosphere.

ALAN LE MAY (1899-1964)

American author, film director, producer, screenwriter, and journalist Le May was educated at the University of Chicago. He has written more than a dozen highly regarded Western novels.

3689 *By Dim and Flashing Lamps*

Date of Publication: 1962
Subject(s): Civil War—U.S.
Fictional character(s): Shep Daniels, Cowboy; Julie Delorme, Young Woman; Roger Ashland, Landowner
Time Period(s): 1860s (1861)
Locale(s): Kansas; Missouri

Summary: Set during the Jayhawkers conflict in Kansas and Missouri in the 1860s and the opening of the Civil War, the novel dramatizes the feud between mule drivers Shep Daniels and Roger Ashland and Shep's doomed romance with Roger's cousin and fiancee, Julie Delorme.

Historical Accuracy: The background of the Kansas border war is authentically depicted.

3690 *Pelican Coast*

Date of Publication: 1929
Subject(s): Pirates; Crime and Criminals
Fictional character(s): Job Northrup, Smuggler
Historical character(s): Jean Laffite, Pirate
Time Period(s): 1810s
Locale(s): New Orleans, Louisiana

Summary: This story of pirate adventure describes New Englander Job Northrup, who joins Jean Lafitte's pirate gang and falls in love with the woman Lafitte has chosen. Lafitte must put down a rebellion and re-establish himself as the leader of the smuggling gang.

Historical Accuracy: The novel is more romance than carefully documented history.

3691 *The Searchers*

Date of Publication: 1954
Subject(s): American West; Indians
Fictional character(s): Amos Edwards, Cowboy; Martin Pauley, Cowboy
Time Period(s): 19th century
Locale(s): Texas; New Mexico

Summary: In a Western novel that has become a classic of the genre, Amos Edwards and Martin Pauley commit to a long desperate search to find a child captured by the Comanches. Their obsession takes them throughout the southwest in a series of adventures eventually climaxing in their success.

Historical Accuracy: The novel sets the standard for the pursuit Western. The details of western life of the period are authentically delivered.

3692 *The Unforgiven*

Date of Publication: 1957
Subject(s): American West; Indians

Fictional character(s): Rachel Zachary, Settler; Ben Zachary, Settler; Cassius Zachary, Settler
Time Period(s): 1870s
Locale(s): Panhandle, Texas

Summary: The Zachary family faces enormous obstacles—including an Indian raid—in trying to survive on the Texas frontier.

Historical Accuracy: The novel is effective in capturing the period and the details of western life.

HERBERT LE PORRIER

3693 *The Doctor From Cordova: A Biographical Novel about the Great Philosopher Maimonides*
Date of Publication: 1979
Subject(s): Biography, Fictionalized; Jews; Middle Ages
Historical character(s): Moses Maimonides, Philosopher, Doctor
Time Period(s): 12th century
Locale(s): Cordoba, Spain; Cairo, Egypt

Summary: The Spanish-Jewish philosopher and Talmudist, Maimonides, narrates the story of his life in a long letter to a friend in France. Maimonides describes his boyhood in Moorish Cordova, his exile from Spain, his travels in the Islamic world, and his final service as court physician to Saladin.

Historical Accuracy: The novel captures with skill the background of the period.

TOM LEA (1907-)

Born in El Paso, Texas, Lea drew on his home ground for his books on the Southwest. He studied art in chicago and used it to good effect in his panoramic pictures of his region. A painter and illustrator as well as a writer, Lea informed the genre of his historical novel *The Hands of Cantu*.

3694 *The Hands of Cantu*
Date of Publication: 1964
Subject(s): Spanish Colonies; Indians; Horses
Fictional character(s): Don Vito Cantu, Landowner; Toribio, Orphan
Time Period(s): 16th century
Locale(s): Mexico

Summary: The key to the Spanish conquest of Mexico were the horses that provided them with a means to assert their dominance. This tale of 16th century Mexico describes a Spanish rustler who is stealing horses and selling them to the Indians. He must be stopped, and the responsibility falls on Don Vito Contu, the best horseman in New Spain.

Historical Accuracy: The novel's depiction of the countryside and its horses is authentic and believable.

3695 *The Wonderful Country*
Date of Publication: 1952

Subject(s): American West
Fictional character(s): Martin Brady, Gunfighter
Time Period(s): 1880s
Locale(s): Puerto, Texas

Summary: This story of the southwestern border country of Texas during the 1880s follows the experiences of young Martin Brady and the clash of cultures—Mexican, American, and Indian—that divides the community.

Historical Accuracy: This is an authentic treatment of the period and region.

FRANCIS W. LEARY

3696 *Fire and Morning*
Date of Publication: 1957
Subject(s): War of the Roses; Royalty—England
Fictional character(s): John Flory, Gentleman, Military Personnel
Historical character(s): Richard III, Ruler (King of England); Anne Neville, Royalty (queen consort of Richard III); Elizabeth of York, Royalty (princess)
Time Period(s): 15th century (1470s-1480s)
Locale(s): England; France

Summary: The novel dramatizes the troubled reign of Richard III. Richard reaches the throne upon the mysterious disappearance of his two nephews, Edward and Richard, the princes in the Tower. As Richard attempts to hold onto power against a variety of warring factions, John Flory, gentleman and soldier, attempts to uncover the secret of the Tower. His research takes him to France and finally Bosworth Field.

Historical Accuracy: The historical elements here are genuine, but the speculation about the mystery of the Tower is open to other interpretations.

3697 *The Swan and the Rose*
Date of Publication: 1953
Subject(s): War of the Roses; Royalty—England
Fictional character(s): Arthur Adair, Military Personnel (soldier)
Historical character(s): Richard, Duke of Gloucester, Nobleman; Edward, Prince of Wales, Royalty; Margaret of Anjou, Royalty (queen consort of Henry VI); Anne of Warwick, Noblewoman
Time Period(s): 15th century (1471)
Locale(s): England

Summary: This tale set during the War of the Roses concerns young Arthur Adair who joins the Lancastrian cause and is on hand for the Battles of Tewkesbury and Barnet and the victory of the House of York.

Historical Accuracy: The novel is faithful to the events of the times and offers plausible interpretations of some of the leading figures.

3698 *This Dark Monarchy*
Date of Publication: 1949

Subject(s): Gothic Romance; Crime and Criminals; Victorian Period

Fictional character(s): Christine Carroll, Murderer

Time Period(s): 1850s; 1860s

Locale(s): Somerset, England; Paris, France

Summary: This Gothic tale of horror and murder is set in England during the 1850s and tells the grisly story of young Christine Carroll who rebels against her stepmother and former governess and murders her five-year-old step-brother.

Historical Accuracy: The novel is filled with atmosphere that captures the period setting with skill.

JAMES LEASOR (1923-)

An Englishman educated at the City of London School and Oriel College, Oxford, Leasor worked for London's *Daily Express* as a reporter and foreign correspondent. He is the author of numerous suspense novels, including *The Red Fort* and *The Millionth Chance*, which was chosen by the *New York Times* as one of the best 100 books of 1957-1959.

3699 *Follow the Drum*

Date of Publication: 1972

Subject(s): Indian Mutiny; British Raj; Victorian Period

Fictional character(s): Richard Lang, Military Personnel (British officer); Arabella MacDonald, Fiance(e)

Historical character(s): Victoria, Ruler (Queen of England); Henry John Temple, Political Figure (prime minister), Nobleman (Viscount Palmerston); James Andrew Broun Ramsay, Government Official (governor general of India), Nobleman (Marquis of Dalhouse); John Nicholson, Military Personnel (British officer)

Time Period(s): 1850s

Locale(s): India; England

Summary: This documentary novel chronicles the bloody Indian Mutiny, which began with the revolt of Indians in service to the East India Trading Company, as a result of English insensitivity and religious intolerance. The rebellion widens and threatens England's hold on its Indian empire. The events of the mutiny are detailed from the perspective of a young officer, Richard Lang, and his fiancee, Arabella MacDonald.

Historical Accuracy: The important incidents described are based on fact.

3700 *Mandarin Gold*

Date of Publication: 1974

Subject(s): East/West Relations; Chinese Empire; Opium War

Fictional character(s): Robert Gunn, Doctor, Trader

Historical character(s): Tao Kuang, Ruler (Chinese emperor); Robert Cornelis Napier, Military Personnel (general); William Jardine, Trader; James Matheson, Trader; Charles Elliot, Military Personnel (naval officer)

Time Period(s): 1830s

Locale(s): Canton, China

Summary: Intrigue in the Chinese opium trade is the novel's subject. Robert Gunn, a newly qualified doctor, arrives in Canton. A letter from shore sets him on a course to make a fortune, and he embarks on the lucrative and dangerous Coast

trade. The novel also depicts the delicate political negotiations between the Chinese and the English.

Historical Accuracy: The novel captures the era and its conflict with authenticity.

ANNE LEATON (1932-)

Born in Texas, Leaton graduated from Texas Christian University and did graduate work at the University of Vienna. She is an English instructor in Texas after having lived abroad for almost 20 years.

3701 *Pearl*

Date of Publication: 1985

Subject(s): American West; Crime and Criminals

Fictional character(s): Pearl Younger, Young Woman

Historical character(s): Belle Starr, Outlaw; Cole Younger, Outlaw

Time Period(s): 19th century; 20th century (1868-1925)

Locale(s): Texas; Arizona; Fort Smith, Arkansas

Summary: The life and times of Western outlaw Belle Starr are depicted from the perspective of her daughter, Pearl. Pearl witnesses her mother's adventurous life—her robberies, trials, and escapes. Her father is the outlaw Cole Younger, whom she sees killed. Finally, Pearl claims her mother's body after her violent death. On her own Pearl runs the most famous brothel in Texas.

Historical Accuracy: The background of the story is factual with some invention concerning Pearl's career.

DAVID LEAVITT (1961-)

Born in Pittsburgh, Leavitt is a graduate of Yale University and has worked as a reader and editor for Viking-Penguin. He won an O. Henry Award in 1984 for "Country Months" and is considered one of the most promising writers to emerge in the 1980s. He published his first short story in the *New Yorker* while still an undergraduate. His novel *Family Dancing* offers a depiction of homosexual life. *While England Sleeps* created a storm of controversy by basing some of its incidents on the life of English writer Christopher Isherwood.

3702 *While England Sleeps*

Date of Publication: 1993

Subject(s): Civil War—Spain; Homosexuality

Fictional character(s): Brian Botsford, Writer; Edward Phelan, Worker (London Underground), Activist (Communist); Philippa Archibald, Gentlewoman

Time Period(s): 1930s (1937)

Locale(s): London, England; Spain

Summary: The novel tells the story of the love affair between Brian Botsford, an upper-class writer, and Edward Phelan, an employee of the London Underground and a Communist party member. When Brian is convinced to give up this unorthodox love and settle down, Edward volunteers to fight

Franco in Spain. Brian pursues him across Europe and into the war.

Historical Accuracy: The novel generated considerable controversy by basing incidents on the life of English writer Christopher Isherwood. What is not contested is the author's ability to capture the period.

MICHAEL LECHNER

`3703` *My Beautiful White Roses*

Date of Publication: 1971
Subject(s): Middle Ages; Religious Life; Jews
Historical character(s): Francis of Assisi, Religious (monk); Innocent III, Religious (pope)
Time Period(s): 12th century; 13th century (1180-1213)
Locale(s): Assisi, Italy; Arles, France

Summary: This unusual account of the life of the founder of the Franciscan order, Francis of Assisi, attempts to show that Francis was a Jew, and that his persecution stems from this fact. To support this conjecture, the novel imagines a fully-realized biographical portrait.

Historical Accuracy: Despite the evident research into the period, the novel's contentions are speculative. The period is, however, evoked with authenticity.

ROSS LECKIE (1957-)

English writer Leckie was educated in Classics at Oxford. He has worked as a farm laborer, schoolmaster, and insurance broker.

`3704` *Hannibal*

Date of Publication: 1996
Subject(s): Punic Wars; Roman Empire; Biography, Fictionalized
Historical character(s): Hannibal, Military Personnel (general)
Time Period(s): 3rd century B.C.; 2nd century B.C.
Locale(s): Roman Empire; Carthage, Ancient Civilization

Summary: The story of the life and military career of Carthaginian general Hannibal is told in this first person account that covers Hannibal's childhood, his assumption of command of the Carthaginian army at the age of 18, and his invasion of Italy as he leads his army of mercenaries and elephants over the Alps in the middle of winter.

Historical Accuracy: Although based on classical sources for the life and times of Hannibal, the story does take some liberties with history, as the author freely admits.

CARYL LEDNER

`3705` *The Bondswoman*

Date of Publication: 1977
Subject(s): American Colonies; Pilgrims; Slavery
Fictional character(s): Hillaby, Slave, Servant; Robert Stanhope, Farmer; Abigail Stanhope, Spouse
Time Period(s): 17th century (1681)
Locale(s): Plymouth, Massachusetts, American Colonies

Summary: The setting is the Plymouth Colony in the 1680s. Hillaby, the daughter of an English father and slave mother from Barbados, is sold at auction to a pioneer farmer, Robert Stanhope. The novel describes their passionate relationship and the triangle created when Robert marries an inexperienced young bride.

Historical Accuracy: The emphasis is on passion rather than historical details. The Puritan setting is used to enhance the explosive and dangerous passions.

C.Y. LEE (1917-)

A Chinese writer born in Hunan, Lee came to the U.S. in 1942 and received an M.F.A. from Yale. Lee is best known as the author of *Flower Drum Song* which was adapted by Rodgers and Hammerstein as a Broadway musical and film. Lee has worked as an editor, writer, and teacher.

`3706` *China Saga*

Date of Publication: 1987
Subject(s): Boxer Rebellion; Revolution—China; Family Saga
Fictional character(s): Fong Tai, Government Official; Brigid Fong Yun, Young Woman
Historical character(s): Tsu Hsi, Ruler (Empress Dowager)
Time Period(s): 19th century; 20th century (1890s-1960s)
Locale(s): China; Boston, Massachusetts

Summary: This saga of four generations of a Chinese family begins in the 1890s during the Boxer Rebellion and continues through the Chinese Revolution to the Cultural Revolution of the 1960s. The story reflects a great deal of China's history and its effects on a variety of well-drawn characters.

Historical Accuracy: The novel is expert in capturing an authentic historical background.

`3707` *The Second Son of Heaven: A Novel of Nineteenth-Century China*

Date of Publication: 1990
Subject(s): Chinese Empire; Taiping Rebellion; East/West Relations
Historical character(s): Hung Hsiu-Ch'uan, Ruler (Chinese emperor); Charles George Gordon, Military Personnel (British officer)
Time Period(s): 19th century (1812-1864)
Locale(s): China

Summary: The novel describes the rise of Hung Hsiu-Ch'uan, leader of the Hans, who challenges the power of the Mandarin Dynasty in the Taiping Rebellion. Emerging victorious, he mounts the Dragon Throne and lays the groundwork for a new China. He is challenged by a Westerner, Major Charles Gordon, who allies himself with the Manchus and begins one of the bloodiest civil wars in Chinese history.

Historical Accuracy: The framework of the story is accurate in its chronology and events.

EDNA LEE

3708 *The Web of Days*
Date of Publication: 1947
Subject(s): Reconstruction Period
Fictional character(s): Hester Snow, Governess; St. Clair LeGrand, Plantation Owner
Time Period(s): 1860s (post Civil War)
Locale(s): Sea Islands, Georgia

Summary: Hester Snow is a Northerner engaged as a governess by an old Georgia plantation family in the years immediatly following the end of the Civil War. She experiences the reality of plantation life, which is very different from its romantic image. She is both attracted to and repulsed by her employer, St. Clair LeGrand. She marries him and sees first hand his cruelty and duplicity.

Historical Accuracy: The novel features a realistic and believable depiction of the period.

LILIAN LEE

3709 *Farewell to My Concubine*
Date of Publication: 1992
Subject(s): Revolution—China; Theatrical Life; World War II
Fictional character(s): Xiao Pouzi, Actor; Xiao Shitou, Actor
Time Period(s): 20th century (1930s-1980s)
Locale(s): Peking, China; Hong Kong

Summary: The novel, set in the theatrical world of the Peking Opera, describes the career of Xiao Pouzi, who is abandoned by his prostitute mother at age nine at the opera school where he learns and perfects his craft. His guardian, protector, and best friend is Xiao Shitou. The novel focuses on the love of Xiao Pouzi for his friend and the pressure of the great historical events that force them to betray each other.

Historical Accuracy: The novel features a convincing depiction of the historical events of the period.

TANITH LEE (1947-)

A British author of books for children and fantasy and science fiction for adults, Lee was born in London. Her adult novels include *The Birthgrave*, *Quest for the White Witch*, and *The Prince of Demons*. She has also written radio plays for the BBC.

3710 *The Gods Are Thirsty*
Date of Publication: 1996
Subject(s): French Revolution; Reign of Terror
Historical character(s): Camille Desmoulins, Revolutionary; Georges-Jacques Danton, Revolutionary; Maximilien Francois de Robespierre, Revolutionary
Time Period(s): 1780s; 1790s (1789-1794)
Locale(s): Paris, France

Summary: The novel captures the experiences of the French Revolution through the experiences of journalist, pamphleteer, and revolutionary Camille Desmoulins. Called the voice of the Revolution, Desmoulins is eventually sentenced to the guillotine during the Reign of Terror.

Historical Accuracy: The novel interweaves actual events and details with the imaginary to recreate the brooding and bloody atmosphere of the time.

VIRGINIA LEE (1927-)

Born in San Francisco, California, Virginia Lee attended San Francisco State University. She is the author of *The Magic North* and the co-author, with Craig Claiborne, of *The Chinese Cookbook*.

3711 *The House That Tai Ming Built*
Date of Publication: 1963
Subject(s): Family Saga; Gold Rush—California; Business Building
Fictional character(s): Tai Ming Kwong, Immigrant, Businessman; Lin Kwong, Young Woman
Time Period(s): 19th century; 20th century
Locale(s): China; San Francisco, California

Summary: This story of Chinese-American life describes four generations of a Chinese family. Beginning in the days of the California Gold Rush they find success in San Francisco with an importing business. The drama centers on Lin Kwong who falls in love with a westerner and must contend with the cultural conflict this causes.

Historical Accuracy: The novel provides a believable portrait of social customs and the atmosphere of the period.

WENDI LEE (1956-)

Author of the acclaimed Jefferson Bird series of westerns, Lee lives in Iowa.

3712 *The Overland Trail*
Date of Publication: 1996
Subject(s): American West; Wagon Trains; Indians
Fictional character(s): America Hollis, Pioneer
Time Period(s): 1840s (1846)
Locale(s): Oregon Trail, United States

Summary: The novel traces the adventures of America Hollis on the overland journey west in the late 1840s. She loses her husband and all her possessions early in the journey. Pregnant and alone, she is taken in by another family on the wagon train, but after she gives birth, the family leaves her for dead and takes her newborn daughter. America, with the help of a young Paiute woman, sets out to find her stolen child.

Historical Accuracy: The novel provides authentic details of period life.

JOHN LEEKLEY

3713 *The Blue and the Gray*
Date of Publication: 1982
Subject(s): Civil War—U.S.

Fictional character(s): Malachy Hale, Military Personnel (Union soldier); Luke Geyser, Military Personnel (Confederate soldier); John Geyser, Artist (draftsman)
Historical character(s): Ulysses S. Grant, Military Personnel (Union commander); Robert E. Lee, Military Personnel (Confederate commander)
Time Period(s): 1850s; 1860s (1856-1865)
Locale(s): Virginia; Vicksburg, Mississippi; Elmira, New York

Summary: The events of the Civil War split cousins apart. The Geysers live south of the Mason-Dixon line and side with the Confederacy; the Hales back the Union. In the middle is the idealist John Geyser who refuses to take sides and is labeled a traitor by his brothers.

Historical Accuracy: The novel provides an authentic period background and the accuracy of the events described is reinforced by the fact that Civil War historian Bruce Catton served as the book's historical consultant.

PETER LEFCOURT (1941-)

This American writer is also a television producer and scriptwriter. His other novels include *The Deal* and *The Dreyfus Affair*.

3714 *Di and I*

Date of Publication: 1994
Subject(s): Royalty—England; Fantasy
Fictional character(s): Leonard Schecter, Writer (screenwriter)
Historical character(s): Diana, Princess of Wales, Royalty; Charles, Prince of Wales, Royalty; Elizabeth II, Ruler (Queen of England); Margaret Rose, Royalty (princess); Philip, Duke of Edinburgh, Royalty (Duke of Edinburgh); Andrew, Duke of York, Royalty (prince); Sarah Margaret Ferguson, Royalty (Duchess of York); Juan Carlos I, Ruler (King of Spain); William of Wales, Royalty (prince); Henry of Wales, Royalty (prince); H. Ross Perot, Businessman
Time Period(s): 1990s (1994)
Locale(s): London, England; Florida; Rancho Cucamonga, California

Summary: This farcical fantasy describes what might happen if Diana, Princess of Wales, ran off with a Hollywood screenwriter. This implausible comedy pushes the definition of invasion of privacy, as Diana and the English royal family are coopted to play roles in the real world of McDonald's franchises and K-Mart shopping.

Historical Accuracy: Verisimilitude is supplied largely by mentioning brand names.

JOHN ADAMS LELAND (1907-1956)

Leland was an American writer.

3715 *Othneil Jones*

Date of Publication: 1956
Subject(s): American Revolution

Fictional character(s): Othnell Jones, Military Personnel (soldier)
Historical character(s): Francis Marion, Military Personnel (officer)
Time Period(s): 1780s (1781)
Locale(s): South Carolina; Tennessee

Summary: The military action of Francis Marion's raiders in the Carolina campaign of the American Revolution is depicted through the experiences of a young soldier, Othnell Jones. Part Cherokee Indian, Jones comes to maturity through the war.

Historical Accuracy: The novel provides a genuine depiction of the region and the history of the Carolina campaign.

JUDITH LENNOX-SMITH (1953-)

Lennox-Smith is an English writer born in Lancashire, where she graduated from the University of Lancashire. She was a civil servant and a full-time mother before she started her writing career. She set out to write the kinds of books that she liked to read: books that you could not put down. She gravitated to historical fiction because it offered the widest range for interesting characters, action, and romance.

3716 *The Glittering Strand*

Date of Publication: 1991
Subject(s): Renaissance; Slavery; Pirates
Fictional character(s): Serafina Guardi, Heiress; Thomas Marlowe, Sailor; William William, Sailor
Time Period(s): 16th century (1586-1599)
Locale(s): Marseilles, France; Barbary Coast, Africa; Italy (Livorno, Florence, Pisa, Genoa)

Summary: Serafina Guardi is the young heiress to her father's silk trading business in Marseilles. En route to Italy, she is kidnapped by Barbary pirates and taken into slavery for six years. On her escape, she mounts a determined effort to reclaim her lost position. Her story is intertwined with English traders involved in the lucrative but dangerous Mediterranean trade.

Historical Accuracy: The novel depicts the Mediterranean world of pirates and business building in vivid and authentic terms.

3717 *The Italian Garden*

Date of Publication: 1993
Subject(s): Renaissance; Artistic Life
Fictional character(s): Joanna Zulian, Orphan, Artist; Gaetano Cavazza, Artist; Martin Gefroy, Doctor
Time Period(s): 16th century (1500-1514)
Locale(s): Venice, Italy; France

Summary: Set in Renaissance Italy during the 16th century, the novel tells the story of independent Joanna Zulian. She is prevented from becoming a portrait painter and resists the roles of model, mistress, wife, or political pawn in the growing tension between Italy and France available to her. She achieves fulfillment designing an Italian garden France that captures her essence.

Historical Accuracy: The novel is able to build a convincing period background to which the story's unusual heroine reacts.

3718 *The Secret Years*

Date of Publication: 1994

Subject(s): World War I

Fictional character(s): Thomasine Thorne, Young Woman; Daniel Gillroy, Military Personnel (soldier); Nicholas Blythe, Military Personnel (soldier); Lally Blythe, Young Woman

Time Period(s): 20th century (1909-1928)

Locale(s): England

Summary: The relationship of four childhood friends is shattered by jealousy and suspicion in the summer of 1914. Their lives are irrevocably changed by the consequences of World War I. In the 1920s, the four come together again to resolve the past and attempt to cope with a disturbing present.

Historical Accuracy: The novel depends on a convincing depiction of the wartime atmosphere.

3719 *Till the Day Goes Down*

Date of Publication: 1991

Subject(s): Elizabethan Period

Fictional character(s): Arbel Forster, Orphan; Christie Forster, Orphan; Luke Ridley, Adventurer

Historical character(s): Sir Francis Walsingham, Government Official

Time Period(s): 16th century (1580s)

Locale(s): England; Scotland; France

Summary: The setting is the Scottish border country in the 16th century as England prepares for invasion from France, Scotland, and Spain on behalf of the imprisoned Mary, Queen of Scots. Loyalties split the Forster and Ridley families. The novel centers on two orphans, Arbel and Christie Forster, and the adventurer Luke Ridley, who are swept up in the tumult of the period.

Historical Accuracy: The novel is exact in its period elements.

PERRY LENTZ (1943-)

American professor and author Lentz was born in Alabama and graduated from Kenyon College and Vanderbilt University. He is a professor of English at Kenyon, and his books have been praised for their realism and historical accuracy. He sees his writing as more of an avocation, with his main goal to be an effective teacher.

3720 *The Falling Hills*

Date of Publication: 1967

Subject(s): Civil War—U.S.; Battle of Fort Pillow; Racial Conflict

Fictional character(s): Hamilton Acox, Lawyer, Military Personnel (Confederate officer); Jonathan Seabury, Military Personnel (Union officer)

Historical character(s): Nathan Bedford Forrest, Military Personnel (Confederate general)

Time Period(s): 1860s (1863-1864)

Locale(s): Fort Pillow, Tennessee

Summary: The novel dramatizes a little-known Civil War episode called the Fort Pillow Massacre. A Union fort manned largely by black troops is attacked by General Nathan Bedford Forrest, and most of the garrison is slaughtered. The novel focuses on Confederate officer Acox and Union officer Seabury and their reactions to the events that shockingly detail the racial hatred that underscores the conflict.

Historical Accuracy: The novel is exact in its scenes and action but is even more impressive in its realistic penetration of the motives and attitudes of the combatants.

HUGH LEONARD
(PSEUD. OF JOHN KEYES BYRNE, 1926-)

Leonard is an Irish writer and the author of many award winning plays, including the Tony-winning *Da*. He has written two volumes of memoirs, *Home Before Dark* and *Out After Dark*. Leonard has worked as an Irish civil servant, a script editor, and a literary editor for Dublin's Abbey Theatre. He began writing in his early thirties and has written numerous TV adaptations of classics by Flaubert, Dickens, and Dostoevsky.

3721 *Parnell and the Englishwoman*

Date of Publication: 1991

Subject(s): Politics; Independence—Ireland; Victorian Period

Historical character(s): Charles Stewart Parnell, Political Figure; Katherine O'Shea, Gentlewoman; William O'Shea, Political Figure

Time Period(s): 1880s; 1890s

Locale(s): London, England; Dublin, Ireland

Summary: The love affair between Charles Stewart Parnell, the leader of the Irish Home Rule Party, and Katherine O'Shea, the daughter of an English clergyman and the wife of a minor Irish politician, costs Parnell his position as Irish leader and splits the nation into those for and against the ''Uncrowned King of Ireland.'' The novel depicts the affair and its resulting scandal.

Historical Accuracy: The novel is precise in its historical details and accurate in capturing the time and the issues.

NATHAN LEONARD

3722 *Wind Like a Bugle*

Date of Publication: 1954

Subject(s): Slavery; Underground Railroad; Free Soil Movement

Fictional character(s): Susan Orr, Widow(er); Little David, Slave; Neal Geddes, Abolitionist

Time Period(s): 1850s

Locale(s): Kansas

Summary: Bloody Kansas and the conflict between abolitionists and slavery advocates is dramatized in this story involving a young and wealthy widow, Susan Orr; Neal Geddes, a protege of John Brown; and the slave Little David. The working of the Underground Railroad and the battle for control of Kansas are dramatized.

Historical Accuracy: The novel succeeds best in its evocation of the period atmosphere.

PHYLLIS LEONARD (1924-)

Born in Ohio, Leonard was her husband's partner in an insurance company in Phoenix. Her novels *Prey of Eagles* and *Phantom of the Sacred Well* have won prizes. A specialist in Latin American cultures and Amerindian civilizations, Leonard enjoys the archaeological and historical research she does for her books, particularly discovering little-known trivia.

`3723` *Tarnished Angel*

Date of Publication: 1980
Subject(s): Gold Rush—California; Sea Story
Fictional character(s): Lilly Randall, Singer; Benjamin Gray, Businessman; Nikolai Alexandrovski, Nobleman; Jake Thorpe, Sea Captain
Time Period(s): 1850s (1850-1851)
Locale(s): San Francisco, California; Hawaii; China

Summary: Set in Gold Rush San Francisco, the novel describes the adventures of Lilly Randall, who gains wealth and success as a singing sensation at the Golden Bonanza Casino. She is drawn to a variety of men, but her heart is lost to a flamboyant clipper ship captain, Wild Jake Thorpe. Lilly's adventures include abduction to Hawaii and a race to China.

Historical Accuracy: The era is captured vividly.

RHODA LERMAN

`3724` *Eleanor: A Novel*

Date of Publication: 1979
Subject(s): Biography, Fictionalized
Historical character(s): Eleanor Roosevelt, Spouse, Political Figure; Franklin Delano Roosevelt, Political Figure
Time Period(s): 1910s; 1920s (1918-1921)
Locale(s): Washington, District of Columbia

Summary: The novel offers a fictional account of the Roosevelts' marriage when Franklin Roosevelt was secretary of the navy and having an affair with Lucy Mercer. The period depicted begins in the post-war years and ends when F.D.R. is striken with polio.

Historical Accuracy: The factual basis of the novel is strong, based on private papers, oral histories, and interviews with family and friends.

JOHN T. LESCROART (1948-)

An American writer born in Houston, Texas, Lescroart attended the University of California, Berkeley, and worked for a time as a professional singer and guitarist in Los Angeles and San Francisco. He won the Joseph Henry Jackson Award for the novel *Sunburn* in 1978. His literary heroes include Ernest Hemingway, Lawrence Durrell, and

John Fowles. Among mystery writers, he most admires Sir Arthur Doyle, Rex Stout, John MacDonald, P.D. James, and Elmore Leonard.

`3725` *Rasputin's Revenge*

Date of Publication: 1987
Subject(s): Mystery; Russian Empire; Royalty—Russia
Fictional character(s): Auguste Lupa, Detective—Private; Jules Giraud, Sidekick
Historical character(s): Nicholas II, Ruler (Czar of Russia); Alexandra Feodorovna, Royalty (consort of Nicholas II); Grigori Efimovich Rasputin, Religious (monk)
Time Period(s): 1910s (1916-1917)
Locale(s): St. Petersburg, Russia

Summary: Sherlock Holmes' son, Auguste Lupa, is summoned to Russia and Czar Nicholas' court by Czarina Alexandra. He is asked to discover the identity of an assassin who is determined to eliminate the Czar's advisers one by one. Lupa and his associate Giraud are framed for espionage and barely escape the firing squad.

Historical Accuracy: The details of court life of the period are authentic.

`3726` *Son of Holmes*

Date of Publication: 1986
Subject(s): Mystery; World War I
Fictional character(s): Auguste Lupa, Detective—Private
Time Period(s): 1910s (1915)
Locale(s): Valence, France

Summary: Auguste Lupa, Sherlock Holmes' son, makes his sleuthing debut in this mystery set during World War I. A French intelligence agent, searching for clues to uncover a master assassin, is found dead in a French village. As a stranger in the village, Lupa is suspected. He identifies the killer and uncovers an ingenious sabotage plot.

Historical Accuracy: The protagonist is a worthy successor to his famous father, with all the familiar detective traits. The war setting is believable.

DORIS LESLIE
(PSEUD. OF HANNAH DORIS FERGUSSON, 1902-1982)

An English novelist and historian, Leslie was born in London and studied art and drama in London and Florence. Her novel *As the Tree Falls* was selected as the best historical novel in 1958 by Books and Bookmen. She was named Woman of the Year for Literature by the Catholic Women's League in 1970.

`3727` *The Prime Minister's Wife*

Date of Publication: 1961
Subject(s): Victorian Period; Politics
Historical character(s): Benjamin Disraeli, Political Figure; Mary Ann Evans, Spouse (of Disraeli); Victoria, Ruler (Queen of England); Albert of Saxe-Coburg-Gotha, Royalty (prince consort of Victoria); William Gladstone, Political Figure; Edward Bulwer-Lytton, Writer

Time Period(s): 19th century (Victorian period)
Locale(s): England

Summary: The novel dramatizes the life of Mary Anne Evans, the owner of a millinery shop who becomes the wife of Benjamin Disraeli, Prime Minister of England. Her rise to prominence is depicted, as well as the great events and figures of the Victorian period.

Historical Accuracy: The framework for the story is factual with some evident interpretations and speculations.

`3728` *Royal William*

Date of Publication: 1941
Subject(s): Royalty—England; Biography, Fictionalized
Historical character(s): William IV, Ruler (King of England)
Time Period(s): 18th century; 19th century
Locale(s): England

Summary: This novel offers a fictionalized biography of William IV, the third son of George III, who came to the English throne in 1830 on the death of his brother George IV. Called the "Sailor King," William served with distinction in the navy during the 18th century.

Historical Accuracy: Based on evident research, the novel provides an authentic portrait of the English ruler.

JENNETTE LETTON

FRANCIS LETTON

`3729` *The Robsart Affair*

Date of Publication: 1956
Subject(s): Elizabethan Period; Royalty—England
Historical character(s): Elizabeth I, Ruler (Queen of England); Robert Dudley, Nobleman (Earl of Leicester); Amy Robsart, Gentlewoman; William Cecil, Courtier, Government Official
Time Period(s): 16th century (1558)
Locale(s): England

Summary: The novel explores one of history's great mysteries: How did the young wife of Robert Dudley, Amy Robsart, lose her life? Was it an accident that left her dead at the foot of the stairs, or part of Dudley's plot to rid himself of his wife to share the throne with his lover, Elizabeth I? The novel offers some intriguing answers.

Historical Accuracy: The situation is factual; the surmises are open to debate.

`3730` *The Young Elizabeth*

Date of Publication: 1953
Subject(s): Tudor Period; Royalty—England
Historical character(s): Elizabeth Tudor, Royalty (princess); Mary I, Ruler (Queen of England); Thomas Seymour, Nobleman; William Cecil, Courtier, Government Official; Katherine Parr, Royalty (queen consort of Henry VIII)
Time Period(s): 16th century
Locale(s): England

Summary: The novel tells the story of Elizabeth Tudor in the years between the death of her father, Henry VIII, and the ascension to the throne of her half-sister, Mary. Elizabeth falls in love with Thomas Seymour, the fourth husband of her step-mother, Katherine Parr, and must negotiate between the attraction of the heart and the intrigue that surrounds her as a potential rival to her sister Mary's reign.

Historical Accuracy: The novel captures the period and its intrigues with care and authenticity.

CHARLES JAMES LEVER (1806-1872)

Lever was an Irish novelist who specialized in rollicking tales of military and sporting life. Well-known works include *Harry Lorrequer*, *Arthur O'Leary*, and *A Day's Ride*.

`3731` *Charles O'Malley*

Date of Publication: 1841
Subject(s): Napoleonic Wars
Fictional character(s): Charles O'Malley, Military Personnel
Historical character(s): Napoleon Bonaparte, Military Personnel, Ruler (Emperor of France)
Time Period(s): 1800s; 1810s (1808-1812)
Locale(s): Galway, Ireland; Dublin, Ireland; Europe (Portugal, Belgium)

Summary: The novel describes the army career of Irishman O'Malley, who takes to military life as another form of sport. A love affair at home interrupts his highjinks at the front.

Historical Accuracy: Lever was an unapologetic admirer of Napoleon; this accounts for the very romanticized version of the Napoleonic Wars with Napoleon as the central hero.

`3732` *Tom Burke of Ours*

Date of Publication: 1844
Subject(s): Napoleonic Wars
Fictional character(s): Tom Burke, Gentleman, Mercenary
Historical character(s): Napoleon Bonaparte, Military Personnel, Ruler (Emperor of France); Josephine, Royalty
Time Period(s): 1800s; 1810s
Locale(s): Dublin, Ireland; France; Europe

Summary: Lever offers a fast-moving adventure story about an Irish soldier of fortune who joins the French army and campaigns with Napoleon. The story covers Napoleon from his first consulship to his fall as emperor.

Historical Accuracy: Lever brilliantly re-creates Austerlitz, Jena, and the "Week of Glory," but his portrait of Napoleon is so idealized and worshipful that it defies credibility. The story's romance overwhelms its history.

JEAN LEVI (1948-)

Born in Paris, Levi is a prominent sinologist who studied in China during the Cultural Revolution and has published numerous articles on ancient China. His first novel, *The Chinese Emperor*, won the Goncourt Prize in France.

3733 *The Chinese Emperor*

Date of Publication: 1987
Subject(s): Chinese Empire; Royalty—China; Biography, Fictionalized
Historical character(s): Ch'in Shih Huang Ti, Ruler (Chinese emperor)
Time Period(s): 3rd century B.C.
Locale(s): China

Summary: Ch'in Shih Huang Ti establishes the first centralized Chinese state and attempts to extend imperial control throughout China. This biographical novel vividly describes court politics and intrigues during the Chin dynasty.

Historical Accuracy: This fictionalized account stays close to the known historical facts.

3734 *The Dream of Confucius*

Date of Publication: 1989
Subject(s): Chinese Empire; Royalty—China
Historical character(s): Liu Pang, Ruler (Chinese emperor)
Time Period(s): 3rd century B.C.
Locale(s): China

Summary: This novel continues the story, begun in *The Chinese Emperor*, of China's early history. In the third century B.C., Emperor Liu Pang succeeds the iron-handed Ch'in Shih Huang Ti and establishes the Han dynasty. He must contend with rebellion and a succession of robber barons.

Historical Accuracy: The novel is authoritative in its depiction of third century B.C. Chinese customs.

CURT LEVIANT (1932-)

3735 *The Man Who Thought He Was Messiah*

Date of Publication: 1990
Subject(s): Religious Life; Jews; Fantasy
Historical character(s): Nachman of Bratslav, Religious (rabbi); Ludwig van Beethoven, Musician, Composer
Time Period(s): 1800s (1800)
Locale(s): Vienna, Austria; Palestine

Summary: The novel provides a fictional recounting of the final years in the life of Rabbi Nachman of Bratslav, one of the greatest of the Hasidic teachers. In 1800 Nachman receives the calling to save the scattered nation of Israel. Failing to prove himself worthy for his important job, he loses his ability to read. Partially cured with the help of Beethoven, Nachman sets out for Palestine and his final destiny.

Historical Accuracy: The novel blends fact with fantasy to produce a convincing and compelling tale of a spiritual quest.

BENJAMIN H. LEVIN

Levin has been an illustrator, pharmacist, short story writer, and novelist.

3736 *Black Triumvirate: A Novel of Haiti*

Date of Publication: 1972
Subject(s): Independence—Haiti; French Colonies; Slavery
Historical character(s): Henri Christophe, Ruler (Haitian), Political Figure; Pierre Dominique Toussaint l'Ouverture, Revolutionary, Political Figure; Jean-Jacques Dessalines, Ruler (Haitian), Political Figure; Charles LeClerc, Nobleman; Pauline LeClerc, Spouse
Time Period(s): 18th century; 19th century (1790s-1820)
Locale(s): Haiti

Summary: The novel re-creates the turbulent slave revolt in the French colony of Haiti that created the first independent black nation in the Americas. Napoleon makes an expedition to Haiti to make his sister Pauline queen of the island and his brother-in-law, Charles Le Clerc, its ruler. He is opposed by three black men: Jean Dessalines, Pierre Toussaint L'Ouverture, and Henri Christophe. The story of their struggle is vividly depicted.

Historical Accuracy: The basic outline of the story is factual and reliable.

3737 *To Spit Against the Wind*

Date of Publication: 1970
Subject(s): French Revolution; American Revolution; Biography, Fictionalized
Historical character(s): Thomas Paine, Patriot, Philosopher; Benjamin Franklin, Diplomat; George Washington, Military Personnel (army commander); Georges-Jacques Danton, Revolutionary, Political Figure; Charlotte Corday, Revolutionary; Joel Barlow, Diplomat, Writer; Napoleon Bonaparte, Military Personnel (general); Thomas Jefferson, Political Figure; Marie Joseph Paul de Lafayette, Military Personnel (general), Nobleman (Marquis de Lafayette); Jean-Paul Marat, Revolutionary
Time Period(s): 18th century; 19th century (1750s-1809)
Locale(s): England; United States; France

Summary: This fictionalized biography traces the life and times of political thinker and advocate of the common man, Tom Paine. It traces his life from his impoverished childhood in England through the struggles of the American and French revolutions. The novel makes the case that Paine is not the drunkard of repute but a tragic genius and an uncompromising idealist.

Historical Accuracy: The novel is panoramic and captures the great events and figures of the period.

DAN LEVIN (1914-)

Levin is a Russian-born journalist, social worker, and editor whose books include *The Dream in the Flesh*, *Stormy Petrel: The Life and Work of Maxim Gorky*, and *Spinoza: The Young Thinker Who Destroyed the Past*.

3738 *Son of Judah*

Date of Publication: 1961
Subject(s): Roman Empire; Jews

Fictional character(s): Ben Yehudah, Military Personnel (Roman soldier); Marianne, Young Woman; Drosis, Young Woman
Time Period(s): 1st century
Locale(s): Alexandria, Egypt; Israel; Rome, Roman Empire

Summary: Set in the Roman Empire of the 1st century, the novel tells the story of Alexandrian Ben Yehudah, who becomes a Roman soldier and is sent to Judea to help put down an uprising. Inspired by the mystical leader of the band he is ordered to destroy, he sides with the rebels and becomes a wanderer in search of a meaningful life.

Historical Accuracy: The novel's story is invented, but the scene is set with authority.

LEE LEVIN

3739 *King Tut's Private Eye*

Date of Publication: 1996
Subject(s): Ancient Egypt; Mystery; Pharaohs
Fictional character(s): Eye, Government Official
Historical character(s): Tutankhamen, Ruler (Egyptian pharaoh); Nefertiti, Royalty
Time Period(s): 14th century B.C.
Locale(s): Egypt

Summary: Billed as the ''world's first murder mystery,'' the story set in the court world of Tutankhamen involves a former grand vizier of Akhenaten who is commanded by the young pharaoh to solve the mystery of his father's murder. He is given only seven days to find the murderer and is forbidden to use torture in his investigation.

Historical Accuracy: The novel combines authentic period elements with a thoroughly modern and anachronistic sensibility and style.

FAYE LEVINE (1944-)

Born in Connecticut, Levine is a graduate of Radcliffe College and Harvard. She has worked as a teacher of English in India and a newspaper reporter and is the author of the non-fictional *The Cultural Barons: An Analysis of Power and Money in the Arts.*

3740 *Solomon and Sheba*

Date of Publication: 1980
Subject(s): Biblical Story
Historical character(s): Solomon, Ruler (King of Israel), Biblical Figure; Queen of Sheba, Ruler, Biblical Figure; David, Ruler (King of Israel), Biblical Figure; Bathsheba, Royalty (queen consort of David); Hiram, Architect, Biblical Figure
Time Period(s): 10th century B.C.
Locale(s): Jerusalem, Israel

Summary: The meeting between Solomon, King of Israel, and the Queen of Sheba is dramatized. Solomon's dream is to build a temple in Jerusalem, and the story displays the political intrigue of 1000 B.C.

Historical Accuracy: The novel is a blend of the historical, based on archaeological and anthropological evidence, and the legendary.

SONIA LEVITIN (1934-)

An American novelist and writer of children's books, Levitin worked as a creative writer and an elementary school and adult education teacher in California. Her books include *Journey to America, Roanoke: A Novel of the Lost Colony,* and *A Season of Unicorns.*

3741 *The No-Return Trail*

Date of Publication: 1978
Subject(s): American West; Wagon Trains
Historical character(s): Nancy Kelsey, Pioneer
Time Period(s): 1840s (1841)
Locale(s): West

Summary: The novel re-creates the historical Bidwell-Bartleson Expedition by wagon train from Kentucky to California in 1841. The story is told from the perspective of Nancy Kelsey, the first woman to make the grueling overland journey from the southeast to California. The journey becomes a voyage of self-discovery for her as she struggles to survive the hardships of the crossing.

Historical Accuracy: The basic framework of the story is historical with some imagined elements to fill in the gaps in the record.

BARBARA LEVY

3742 *Adrienne*

Date of Publication: 1960
Subject(s): Theatrical Life; Biography, Fictionalized
Historical character(s): Adrienne Lecouvreur, Actress; Francois Marie Arouet, Writer (aka Voltaire), Philosopher
Time Period(s): 18th century
Locale(s): Paris, France

Summary: This fictional biography of the great French actress Adrienne Lecouvreur traces her rise from street urchin to celebrated actress of the Comedie Francaise and darling of French society before the Revolution. She is credited with helping to transform the acting techniques of the French stage to a more natural style. Her private life was tragic and ended in a mysterious death.

Historical Accuracy: Adrienne's death by poisoning is not entirely accepted by historians. However, the essential outlines of her career are accurate, and the depiction of French society of the period is masterful.

MARGARET LEWERTH

3743 *Stuyvesant Square*

Date of Publication: 1987
Subject(s): Social Chronicle

Fictional character(s): Noel Tremont, Gentlewoman; Ned Fitch, Young Man
Historical character(s): Caroline Restell, Criminal
Time Period(s): 1870s
Locale(s): New York, New York

Summary: New York City in 1878 is the setting for this story of love between upper-class beauty Noel Tremont and Englishman Ned Fitch. Connected with this story is the mysterious death of Caroline Restell, "the female abortionist.".

Historical Accuracy: The period setting of 1870s New York is captured with authority.

ADA COOK LEWIS

3744 *The Longest Night*
Date of Publication: 1958
Subject(s): Saint Bartholomew's Day Massacre; Huguenots; Royalty—France
Fictional character(s): Gervase d'Este, Young Man; Thalia d'Aire, Young Woman
Historical character(s): Charles IX, Ruler (King of France); Catherine de' Medici, Royalty; Gaspard de Coligny, Leader (Huguenot)
Time Period(s): 16th century (1570s)
Locale(s): Paris, France

Summary: The title refers to the infamous St. Bartholomew's Day Massacre of Huguenots masterminded by Catherine de' Medici. The novel's historical events are interwoven with a fictional romance between Gervase d'Este, whom Catherine unsuccessfully tries to recruit as an assassin of Protestant leader Gaspard de Coligny, and a young Huguenot woman, Thalia d'Aire.

Historical Accuracy: The novel provides a convincing portrait of the dissolute court of Charles IX and the events leading up to the massacre.

HILDA LEWIS (1896-1974)
Lewis is widely considered to be one of England's finest historical novelists. She excelled in scrupulous research to capture actual historical events and characters. She began a novel knowing what her characters did, then researched in an attempt to uncover why.

3745 *Call Lady Purbeck*
Date of Publication: 1961
Subject(s): Royalty—England; Jacobean Period
Historical character(s): George Villiers, Nobleman (Duke of Buckingham); John Villiers, Nobleman (Viscount Purbeck); Frances Coke, Spouse (of John Villiers); James I, Ruler (King of England); Charles I, Ruler (King of England)
Time Period(s): 17th century
Locale(s): England; France

Summary: Life in the Stuart court during the 17th century is dramatized through the story of Frances Coke, who is forced at the age of fifteen to marry the half-insane brother of the powerful Duke of Buckingham. Their union is never consum-

mated, and Frances takes a lover, a personal affront to Buckingham, who makes Frances pay for her affair.

Historical Accuracy: Based on fact, the novel is a detailed evocation of the Stuart period.

3746 *Catherine*
Date of Publication: 1966
Subject(s): Royalty—England; Restoration Period
Historical character(s): Charles II, Ruler (King of England); Catherine of Braganza, Royalty (queen consort of Charles II); Barbara Villiers, Noblewoman, Lover (Charles II's mistress); Nell Gwynne, Actress, Lover (Charles II's mistress)
Time Period(s): 17th century
Locale(s): England

Summary: The novel tells the story of a young princess from Portugal, Catherine of Braganza, who comes to England in 1662 to marry Charles II. Life in Charles' court and Catherine's endurance of the king's succession of mistresses are depicted. Intrigue over the succession; the threat of war with Spain, France, and the Netherlands; conspiracies of Protestants and Catholics; the Great Plague; and the Fire of London all form a colorful and dramatic background for this story of a royal relationship.

Historical Accuracy: The period is convincingly evoked.

3747 *The Gentle Falcon*
Date of Publication: 1957
Subject(s): Middle Ages; Royalty—England
Fictional character(s): Isabella Clinton, Teenager
Historical character(s): Richard II, Ruler (King of England); Isabella of France, Royalty (queen consort of Richard II); John of Gaunt, Royalty (Duke of Gloucester); Charles VI, Ruler (King of France); Henry Bolingbroke, Nobleman; Harry Monmouth, Nobleman
Time Period(s): 14th century
Locale(s): England

Summary: Set during the reign of Richard II, the novel tells the story of Princess Isabella of France who is brought to England at the age of seven to marry the king. Fifteen-year-old Isabella Clinton is also summoned to court as a companion to the queen. Mistress Clinton has a romance with a young follower of Bolingbroke as she tries to protect the queen during the rebellion that brings down Richard.

Historical Accuracy: Scrupulous in its period details, even as the romantic elements predominate, the novel is a convincing portrait of the personalities and period.

3748 *Harlot Queen*
Date of Publication: 1970
Subject(s): Middle Ages; Royalty—England; Homosexuality
Historical character(s): Edward II, Ruler (King of England), Homosexual; Isabella of France, Royalty (queen consort of Edward II); Piers Gaveston, Courtier, Homosexual; Edward III, Ruler (King of England); Roger de Mortimer, Nobleman
Time Period(s): 14th century
Locale(s): England

Summary: This is the story of the reign of Edward II from the perspective of Edward's queen, Isabella. Her place in her husband's bed is usurped by courtier Piers Gaveston. Isabella turns to Mortimer of Wigmore. Branded a harlot, Isabella mounts a campaign of revenge on her husband's paramours, confident that her son will avenge her honor.

Historical Accuracy: This is a frank and honest depiction of the period.

3749 *Harold Was My King*

Date of Publication: 1968
Subject(s): Middle Ages; Norman Conquest; Battle of Hastings
Fictional character(s): Edmund Edmundson, Knight (squire)
Historical character(s): Harold II, Ruler (King of England); Hereward the Wake, Rebel (Saxon), Outlaw; William the Conqueror, Nobleman (Duke of Normandy), Ruler (King of England)
Time Period(s): 11th century
Locale(s): Normandy, France; England

Summary: The story of the Norman Conquest is told from the perspective of Edmund Edmundson, King Harold's devoted page and squire. Edmund stands by Harold until his death at Hastings where Edmund loses everything to the Norman invaders and is forced to choose between his old life and the future under the new regime.

Historical Accuracy: Period details are authentic in this depiction of the disruption caused by the Norman invasion.

3750 *I Am Mary Tudor*

Date of Publication: 1971
Subject(s): Tudor Period; Royalty—England; Biography, Fictionalized
Historical character(s): Henry VIII, Ruler (King of England); Mary Tudor, Royalty (princess); Catherine of Aragon, Royalty (queen consort of Henry VIII)
Time Period(s): 16th century (1516-1558)
Locale(s): England

Summary: The tumultuous reign of Henry VIII is seen through the eyes of his first daughter, Mary. Her story follows the course of Henry's marriages and their effects on the princess. She emerges from the experience adamantly holding onto her Catholic faith with a lifetime of old scores to settle. When she takes the throne, she becomes the notorious ''Bloody Mary.''

Historical Accuracy: The novel is convincing in its depiction of the period and the perspective of Mary Tudor.

3751 *Wife to Great Buckingham*

Date of Publication: 1959
Subject(s): Royalty—England; Royalty—France; Jacobean Period
Historical character(s): James I, Ruler (King of England); George Villiers, Nobleman (Duke of Buckingham); Catherine Manners, Noblewoman, Spouse (to Buckingham); Charles Stuart, Royalty (prince); Anne of Austria, Royalty (queen consort of Louis XIII); Armand-Jean Du Plessis, Religious (cardinal), Government Official (minister); Diego Gondomar,

Diplomat (Spanish ambassador); Henrietta-Maria, Royalty (consort of Charles I)
Time Period(s): 17th century
Locale(s): England; France

Summary: Catherine Manners, one of the great heiresses of 17th century England, marries the handsome and profligate George Villiers, Duke of Buckingham. She is devoted to him despite the scandals of his love affairs, particularly his affair with Anne, Queen of France. The novel captures the intrigue and color of the court of James I.

Historical Accuracy: The characters are plausibly drawn and the period is convincingly portrayed.

3752 *Wife to Henry V*

Date of Publication: 1957
Subject(s): Royalty—England; Battle of Agincourt
Historical character(s): Catherine of Valois, Royalty (queen consort of Henry V); Henry V, Ruler (King of England); Owen Tudor, Gentleman; Charles VI, Ruler (King of France); Isabeau of Bavaria, Royalty (queen consort of Charles VI)
Time Period(s): 15th century
Locale(s): England; France

Summary: The novel describes the relationship between Henry V and Catherine of Valois, his queen and prize following his victory over the French at Agincourt. For Henry, his priority is his kingdom. For Catherine, love must wait for her second husband, the commoner Owen Tudor.

Historical Accuracy: The novel offers a rare unsympathetic portrait of Henry V as a self-absorbed egotist, with sympathy residing firmly on the side of Catherine. The honesty of the presentation is convincing.

3753 *Wife to the Bastard*

Date of Publication: 1966
Subject(s): Middle Ages; Norman Conquest; Royalty—England
Historical character(s): William the Conqueror, Nobleman (Duke of Normandy), Ruler (King of England); Matilda of Flanders, Noblewoman, Royalty (queen consort of William I); Baldwin V, Nobleman (Count of Flanders)
Time Period(s): 11th century
Locale(s): Flanders; Normandy, France; England

Summary: Matilda of Flanders is the first woman to be crowned queen of England. At the age of 15, she bears a child by a faithless lover. When William, the bastard son of Robert, Duke of Normandy, sues for her hand, her only choices are marriage or a convent. Together Matilda and William forge a strong alliance that results in the seizure of the English throne.

Historical Accuracy: Exact in it period depiction, the novel is also convincing in establishing believable characters.

3754 *The Witch and the Priest*

Date of Publication: 1970
Subject(s): Witchcraft and Sorcery; Trials
Fictional character(s): Samuel Fleming, Religious (clergyman)
Historical character(s): Joan Flower, Witch

Time Period(s): 17th century (1610s)
Locale(s): Leicestershire, England

Summary: Based on the true story of Joan Flower, an infamous 17th-century witch, the novel dramatizes how she recruits her two daughters in her schemes to exact revenge against a powerful nobleman. Filled with lore of 17th-century witchcraft, the novel culminates with the trial that brings Flower and her daughters to justice.

Historical Accuracy: The account is based on the actual records and the testimony of the Flowers' witchcraft trial.

JANET LEWIS (1899-)

An American novelist, poet, editor, and librettist, Lewis was born in Chicago and attended Lewis Institute and the University of Chicago. She has worked at the American Consulate in Paris and as a lecturer at the University of California, Berkeley, and at other colleges and universities. Her works include *The Invasion: A Narrative of Events Concerning the Johnston Family of St. Mary's* and the novels *The Wife of Martin Guerre* and *The Trial of Soren Quist*, as well as volumes of poetry.

■3755■ *The Ghost of Monsieur Scarron*

Date of Publication: 1959
Subject(s): Royalty—France
Fictional character(s): Jean Larcher, Businessman (bookbinder)
Historical character(s): Louis XIV, Ruler (King of France)
Time Period(s): 17th century (1690s)
Locale(s): Versailles, France; Paris, France

Summary: This story, based on an authentic event, is set during the reign of France's Louis XIV and concerns the search and prosecution by the police of those responsible for writing and publishing a pamphlet critical of the all-powerful Sun King. An innocent bookbinder becomes the victim of duplicity and betrayal and the incident's scapegoat.

Historical Accuracy: The novel provides a fascinating and authentic look at the workings of Louis XIV's court and the Paris of the period.

MATTHEW GREGORY LEWIS
(1775-1818)

Lewis was an English writer principally known for his Gothic romance, *The Monk*. He also wrote dramas as well as poetry that influenced Walter Scott's early work.

■3756■ *The Monk*

Date of Publication: 1795
Subject(s): Inquisition; Gothic Romance
Fictional character(s): Ambrosio, Religious (superior of the Capuchins); Antonia, Young Woman; Matilda de Villanegas, Witch
Time Period(s): 15th century
Locale(s): Madrid, Spain

Summary: This classic example of Gothic terror is set in Spain during the Inquisition. Ambrosio is a pious abbot who succumbs to lust for the evil Matilda. Demonic possession, passion, and violence follow his capitulation, until the Inquisition condemns him to death.

Historical Accuracy: The novel can hardly be called historical except that it reflects the English horror of Spanish Catholicism.

OSCAR LEWIS (1893-1992)

An American historian and writer, Oscar Lewis was born in San Francisco. During World War I, he served in the U.S. Army with the Ambulance Service of the American Expeditionary Forces. Lewis was best known for his works that chronicle the American West. His book, *The Big Four: The Story of Huntington, Stanford, Hopkins, and Crocker*, detailing the lives of the builders of the first transcontinental railroad, is considered an authoritative volume on the subject and has remained in print for over 50 years. Lewis' other works include *Silver Kings* and *High Sierra Country*.

■3757■ *The Lost Years: A Biographical Fiction*

Date of Publication: 1951
Subject(s): Alternate History; Fantasy; Reconstruction Period
Historical character(s): Abraham Lincoln, Political Figure
Time Period(s): 19th century
Locale(s): Washington, District of Columbia; California

Summary: This intriguing historical fantasy imagines what might have happened to Abraham Lincoln had he survived the attack by John Wilkes Booth. Lincoln finishes his second term disappointed and unpopular. Out of office, he leaves Washington for a visit to California where he is finally able to reclaim national attention.

Historical Accuracy: The fantasy works primarily because the author is able to capture the essence of Lincoln with subtle touches.

PAUL LEWIS
(PSEUD. OF NOEL B. GERSON, 1914-1988)

Paul Lewis is one of many pseudonyms for prolific author Noel B. Gerson. Gerson was born in Chicago and educated at the University of Chicago. During World War II, Gerson served in military intelligence. He was a newspaper reporter, radio and TV scriptwriter, and the author of over 100 books. His historical novels feature a lively and entertaining blend of fact and fiction.

■3758■ *The Gentle Fury: A Novel of Margaret of Austria*

Date of Publication: 1961
Subject(s): Royalty—France; Royalty—Spain; Biography, Fictionalized
Historical character(s): Margaret of Austria, Royalty (princess); Maximilian I, Ruler (Holy Roman Emperor); Charles

VIII, Ruler (King of France); Ferdinand V, Ruler (King of Spain); Isabella I, Ruler (Queen of Spain); Philibert of Savoy, Nobleman (Duke of Savoy)
Time Period(s): 15th century; 16th century (1483-1529)
Locale(s): Austria; Spain; Netherlands

Summary: The novel dramatizes the remarkable career of Margaret of Austria, daughter of Maximilian I, Holy Roman Emperor. She was married three times by the time she was 24, first to the heir to the French throne, then to Prince Juan of Spain, and finally to Philibert, Duke of Savoy. Initially only a pawn in political alliances, she gradually learns to rule and wins respect as the Regent of the Netherlands.

Historical Accuracy: The novel's chronology and events are accurately depicted.

3759 *The Nelson Touch*

Date of Publication: 1960
Subject(s): Sea Story; Biography, Fictionalized; Napoleonic Wars
Historical character(s): Horatio Nelson, Military Personnel (admiral); Lady Emma Hamilton, Gentlewoman
Time Period(s): 18th century; 19th century (1787-1805)
Locale(s): England; At Sea; Naples, Italy

Summary: The novel traces the personal and naval career of England's foremost naval hero, Horatio Nelson. His story includes his marriage while an obscure captain of the West Indies station, his love affair with Lady Hamilton, and his greatest victory over Napoleon at Trafalgar that cost him his life.

Historical Accuracy: More romantic novel than dependable biography, the novel is particularly adrift in documenting Nelson's naval activities.

PRESTON LEWIS

3760 *The Demise of Billy the Kid*

Date of Publication: 1995
Subject(s): American West; Crime and Criminals; Lincoln County War
Fictional character(s): H.H. Lomax, Businessman
Historical character(s): William Bonney, Outlaw, Gunfighter; Pat Garrett, Lawman
Time Period(s): 1880s
Locale(s): Lincoln County, New Mexico; Fort Sumner, New Mexico

Summary: Cowboy, bartender, drifter, and store clerk H.H. Lomax finds himself at the center of the events surrounding the final days of western legend Billy the Kid. Lomax survives the bloodshed of the Lincoln County Wars and Billy the Kid's battle with the Murphy-Dolan gang, but when Lomax falls in love with Billy's woman, the stage is set for a confrontation.

Historical Accuracy: The story is fictional, but the period background is authentic.

3761 *The Lady and Doc Holliday*

Date of Publication: 1989
Subject(s): American West
Historical character(s): John Henry Holliday, Gunfighter, Gambler; Lottie Dena, Gambler
Time Period(s): 1870s
Locale(s): Fort Griffin, Texas

Summary: The novel offers a factual depiction of Doc Holliday's early days on the Texas frontier. Doc Holliday earns his reputation as a gunfighter while pursuing a love affair with gambler Lottie Dena.

Historical Accuracy: The flavor of the era is captured with skill.

ROY LEWIS (1913-)

Born in Felixstowe, England, Lewis was educated in Birmingham and at University College, Oxford. As a journalist, Lewis has worked for *The Economist* and *The Times* as its Commonwealth correspondent. His bestselling historical satires include *The Evolution of Man* and *The Extraordinary Reign of King Ludd*.

3762 *Cock of the Walk*

Date of Publication: 1995
Subject(s): Victorian Period; Religious Conflict
Historical character(s): Pius IX, Religious (pope); Nicholas Wiseman, Religious (cardinal); Victoria, Ruler (Queen of England); Lord John Russell, Political Figure; Thomas Carlyle, Writer; Benjamin Disraeli, Political Figure; William Gladstone, Political Figure; Florence Nightingale, Nurse; Elizabeth Eleanor Siddal, Model; Dante Gabriel Rossetti, Writer, Artist
Time Period(s): 1850s
Locale(s): London, England

Summary: This satirical send up of mid-Victorian England takes as its historical background the appointment of Cardinal Wiseman as Archbishop of Westminster by Pope Pius IX. The act produces violent anti-popish sentiment and an occasion for satirizing England's Victorian establishment.

Historical Accuracy: The novel is a mixture of fact and fiction. The basic events are accurate, but considerable invention has been done to capture the spirit of the age and the imaginary conversations of many of the players.

SINCLAIR LEWIS (1885-1951)

One of the giants of American literature and the great satirist of middle-class American life, Sinclair Lewis was born in Sauk Centre, Minnesota, and was educated at Yale University. Lewis was the first American to win the Nobel Prize for literature (1930). He was also the first author in history to decline the Pulitzer Prize, which he was awarded for his 1936 novel *Arrowsmith*. Lewis' other books include *Main Street*, *Babbitt*, *Elmer Gantry*, and *Dodsworth*. The latter two novels were adapted into successful motion pictures.

3763 *The God-Seeker*

Date of Publication: 1949
Subject(s): Indians; Labor Movement; Racial Conflict
Fictional character(s): Aaron Gadd, Carpenter, Activist (labor union organizer)
Time Period(s): 1840s
Locale(s): Minnesota

Summary: This novel tells the story of carpenter Aaron Gadd who first serves as a missionary to the Sioux Indians. Later he organizes a union and fights for blacks to be included.

Historical Accuracy: Despite the evident research to produce a believable portrait of frontier society, the novel never achieves a high degree of conviction, with stock scenes and characters.

ALICE CHETWYND LEY (1913-)

Born in Yorkshire, Ley studied sociology at London University and is the past chairman of England's Romantic Novelists Association. She is the author of many Regency and Georgian romances.

3764 *A Fatal Assignation*

Date of Publication: 1987
Subject(s): Regency Period; Mystery
Fictional character(s): Anthea Rutherford, Gentlewoman, Detective—Amateur; Sir Aubrey Jermyn, Gentleman, Rake; Justin Rutherford, Gentleman, Detective—Amateur
Time Period(s): 19th century (Regency period)
Locale(s): London, England

Summary: Anthea Rutherford investigates first the disappearance and then the death of Sir Aubrey Jermyn, a notorious high-society womanizer. With her partner, Justin Rutherford, she discerns the secrets of some of London society's most influential personalities.

Historical Accuracy: The well-worn Regency period is portrayed with freshness and authenticity.

3765 *Masquerade of Vengeance*

Date of Publication: 1989
Subject(s): Mystery; Regency Period
Fictional character(s): Justin Rutherford, Gentleman, Detective—Amateur; Anthea Rutherford, Gentlewoman, Detective—Amateur
Time Period(s): 19th century (Regency period)
Locale(s): York, England; London, England

Summary: A revenge plot by a convict returned from Australia sets in motion a series of mysterious events and ''accidents'' that culminate at the masked ball given by Justin Rutherford and his niece Anthea. They must solve a puzzling mystery before the killer can strike again.

Historical Accuracy: The author has mastered both the crime detection genre and the Regency period.

3766 *A Reputation Dies*

Date of Publication: 1984

Subject(s): Regency Period; Mystery
Fictional character(s): Anthea Rutherford, Gentlewoman, Detective—Amateur; Justin Rutherford, Gentleman, Detective—Amateur
Time Period(s): 1810s (1816)
Locale(s): London, England

Summary: In this Regency detective romance, Justin Rutherford and his niece Anthea join forces to discover who has murdered Marmaduke Yarnton, the notorious gossip and scandalmonger, in Lady Windlesham's cloakroom during one of her soirees.

Historical Accuracy: The period details capture the era with conviction.

MARIE LEY-PISCATOR

3767 *Lot's Wife*

Date of Publication: 1954
Subject(s): Biblical Story
Fictional character(s): Ti-Sar, Royalty (princess; Lot's wife)
Historical character(s): Lot, Biblical Figure; Abraham, Biblical Figure
Time Period(s): Indeterminate Past
Locale(s): Tyre, Lebanon; Egypt; Sodom, Palestine

Summary: The wandering of Abraham and his nephew Lot is chronicled in this story based on the Book of Genesis. Their journey takes them into Canaan and Egypt until the pair separates, with Lot choosing to settle east of the Jordan River in Sodom. The novel details Lot's marriage to Ti-sar, princess of Tyre, and culminates in the destruction of Sodom.

Historical Accuracy: The novel faithfully adheres to the Biblical pattern outlined in Genesis.

SIMON LEYS
(PSEUD. OF PIERRE RYCKMANS, 1935-)

A Belgian art historian and author, Leys was born in Brussels and graduated from the University of Louvain. He is a noted sinologist who has taught art history at the Chinese University in Hong Kong and currently teaches Chinese literature at Australian National University.

3768 *The Death of Napoleon*

Date of Publication: 1991
Subject(s): Napoleonic Era; Alternate History; Fantasy
Historical character(s): Napoleon Bonaparte, Ruler (deposed Emperor of France)
Time Period(s): 1820s (1821)
Locale(s): Paris, France

Summary: This historical fable explores the scenario that the man who died in exile and captivity on St. Helena in 1821 was not the Emperor Napoleon, but a double. In this alternative version of history, Napoleon escapes and returns to France to confront the enigma of his legacy and his own identity. He revisits the battlefield at Waterloo, falls in with a group of veteran Bonapartists, and visits an asylum where most of the inmates think that they are Napoleon.

Historical Accuracy: The novel is more a philosophical excursion on the nature of identity and our public and private selves than an exploration of history and biography. However, the era and the enigma of Napoleon are authentically captured.

LESLIE LI (1945-)

Born in New York and educated at the University of Michigan, Li has written a novel, *Bittersweet*, and play for children, *The Magic Whip*. Her work has been anthologized, and has appeared in magazines and newspapers.

3769 *Bittersweet*

Date of Publication: 1992
Subject(s): Revolution—China; World War II
Fictional character(s): Bittersweet, Spouse (of Delin); Delin, Military Personnel, Political Figure
Time Period(s): 19th century; 20th century (1889-1989)
Locale(s): China

Summary: Inspired by the lives of the author's grandparents, the novel dramatizes 100 years of Chinese history. Bittersweet is a young woman who defies custom by arranging her own marriage to Delin, an officer in the newly formed republican army. As he rises to political power, Bittersweet struggles to keep her family together.

Historical Accuracy: The background and historical events that drive much of the story are genuine and convincing.

ELOISE S. LIDDON

3770 *Some Lose Their Way*

Date of Publication: 1941
Subject(s): Antebellum South; Indians; Theatrical Life
Fictional character(s): Adriana More, Actress
Time Period(s): 1830s
Locale(s): Montgomery, Alabama

Summary: Frontier life in ante-bellum Alabama in the 1830s is the backdrop for this historical romance involving a young English actress, Adriana More, who is rescued from the Creek Indians and falls in love with her rescuer. The course of love is complicated by her desire to become a successful actress.

Historical Accuracy: The novel offers a believable portrait of its era.

ALICE ALISON LIDE

MARGARET ALISON JOHANSEN

3771 *Dark Possession*

Date of Publication: 1934
Subject(s): American Colonies; Slavery; Witchcraft and Sorcery
Fictional character(s): Theo Halstad, Landowner; Regina Radney, Gentlewoman
Time Period(s): 1700s
Locale(s): Charleston, South Carolina, American Colonies

Summary: Colonial South Carolina in the early years of the 18th century is the setting for this tale that focuses on the lives of the Halstad family who create a prosperous holding on the wild, swampy island of Seagirt. The tangled love story of Theo Halstad and his cousin Regina Radney shares the stage with slavery, witchcraft, and Indian raids.

Historical Accuracy: The authors have drawn many of the scenes and characters from their own family history which helps insure an air of authenticity.

MARY LIDE

Born in Cornwall, England, Lide is a historian and award-winning poet who received an M.A. from Oxford University. She has taught in the history department at the University of Michigan, as well as other universities and secondary schools in the U.S. and abroad. Her academic specialty is the late medieval world.

3772 *Ann of Cambray*

Date of Publication: 1984
Subject(s): Middle Ages
Fictional character(s): Ann of Cambray, Gentlewoman; Raoul of Sedgemont, Nobleman
Historical character(s): Henry II, Ruler (King of England)
Time Period(s): 12th century
Locale(s): England; Wales

Summary: During the border wars between the Normans and the Celts, Ann of Cambray, the daughter of a Celtic princess and a warrior, is set upon by assassins and forced to seek protection from Raoul of Sedgemont. Their conflicts mirror the political crisis of the times.

Historical Accuracy: Although the story is imaginary, it is set against a vivid and believable period background.

3773 *Command of the King*

Date of Publication: 1990
Subject(s): Tudor Period; Royalty—England
Fictional character(s): Philippa de Verne, Gentlewoman, Heiress—Dispossessed
Historical character(s): Henry VIII, Ruler (King of England); Mary Tudor, Royalty (princess); Thomas Wolsey, Religious (cardinal), Government Official
Time Period(s): 16th century (1510s)
Locale(s): England

Summary: During the early years of the reign of Henry VIII, Philippa de Verne seeks to reclaim her estate, which has been stolen from her by her stepfather. She petitions the king and is plunged into the complex and dangerous world of Henry's court.

Historical Accuracy: The story is fictional but does offer a believable portrait of Tudor life and the court intrigues of the period.

3774 *Fortune's Knave: The Making of William the Conqueror*

Date of Publication: 1992
Subject(s): Middle Ages
Historical character(s): William I, Nobleman (Duke of Normandy); Matilda of Flanders, Royalty (queen consort of William I); Henri I, Ruler (King of France); Herleve, Worker (peasant mother of William); Baldwin V, Nobleman (Count of Flanders)
Time Period(s): 11th century (1035-1054)
Locale(s): Normandy, France; Paris, France; Rouen, France

Summary: When Robert of Normandy dies while on a pilgrimage to the Holy Land in the 11th century, he leaves his duchy in turmoil. The novel describes the rise to power of his illegitimate son, William, whose mother, the peasant Herleve, is determined that he will inherit Robert's domain. Through shrewd alliances with King Henry of France, Count Baldwin of Flanders, and his daughter Matilda, William achieves more than his mother could ever have imagined.

Historical Accuracy: The author explains that the sources for much of her book are records, chronicles, and documents whose conflicting legends she has attempted to put together in a logical sequence.

3775 *Isobelle*

Date of Publication: 1988
Subject(s): Tribal Life—African; Slavery
Fictional character(s): Isobelle, Captive; The Master, Chieftain (Berber)
Time Period(s): 1870s
Locale(s): Barbary Coast, Africa; Sahara Desert, Africa

Summary: This romantic adventure tale set in northern Africa in the 1870s describes the adventures of a young English girl, Isobelle, who is shipwrecked and taken into slavery by a caravan of desert raiders. She is claimed by a Berber chieftain known as ''The Master'' and must adapt to tribal life as a strong relationship grows between the two.

Historical Accuracy: The emphasis is on the exotic over the historical. However, period elements do appear and are convincing.

3776 *The Legacy of Tregaran*

Date of Publication: 1991
Subject(s): Family Saga; World War I
Fictional character(s): Paul Cradock, Lawyer; John Tregaran, Young Man; Alice Tregaran, Young Woman
Time Period(s): 1910s
Locale(s): Cornwall, England

Summary: In the prequel to the author's *Tregaran*, the origin of the family conflict and revenge that infected succeeding generations is explored in the relationship between John Tregaran and Alice Tregaran. Both of their families are determined to prevent the match and will resort to deception and manipulation to achieve their end.

Historical Accuracy: The novel is exact in its rendering of the period locale and customs.

3777 *A Royal Quest*

Date of Publication: 1987
Subject(s): Middle Ages; Royalty—England
Fictional character(s): Robert Sedgemont, Heir, Knight; Hue Sedgemont, Heir; Olwen Sedgemont, Heir; Taliesin, Royalty (Celtic prince)
Historical character(s): Henry II, Ruler (King of England); Eleanor of Aquitaine, Royalty (queen consort of Henry II); Richard the Lionhearted, Royalty (prince)
Time Period(s): 12th century
Locale(s): Wales; England; France

Summary: Set in the 12th century during the border wars between England and Wales, the novel tells the story of the heirs of Ann of Cambray and Raoul of Sedgemont. They are a Norman family whose fate becomes entangled with the schemes of Henry II and his queen, Eleanor of Aquitaine. Olwen is drawn to the Celtic Prince Taliesin and his campaign against the English forces.

Historical Accuracy: The novel's events are based upon history as much as possible. The author explains that she tried to fill the historical gaps with reasonable explanations to create a novel that gives an accurate impression of the time.

3778 *The Sea Scape*

Date of Publication: 1992
Subject(s): Victorian Period; Farming
Fictional character(s): Guinevere Ellis, Young Woman; Julian Polleven, Gentleman
Time Period(s): 1880s; 1890s
Locale(s): Cornwall, England

Summary: Set in 19th-century Cornwall, the novel describes the experience of Guinevere Ellis, raised on Penworth Farms on the Cornish moors. She escapes the toil of farm life when she falls in love with Julian Polleven, but circumstances complicate the relationship, including her mysterious past.

Historical Accuracy: The author excels at producing an authentic period locale.

3779 *Tregaran*

Date of Publication: 1989
Subject(s): Family Saga; World War II; Mining
Fictional character(s): Joycelyn Tregaran, Heiress; Philip Tregaran, Miner
Time Period(s): 20th century (1928-1940s)
Locale(s): Cornwall, England

Summary: Joycelyn Tregaran, heir to a magnificent Cornish estate, falls in love with the miner Philip Tregaran. The connection between Philip and the Tregaran family is uncovered, exposing past conflicts that ripped the family apart. When World War II further complicates the situation, the past threatens to repeat itself.

Historical Accuracy: The novel is convincing in its period Cornish setting.

SARA LIDMAN (1923-)

Swedish writer Lidman was educated at the University of Uppsala. Lidman contracted tuberculosis at the age of 14 and during a one-year hospitalization discovered literature and began to write. Her books include *Wearing the Mistletoe*, *I and My Son*, *With Five Diamonds*, and *Thy Servant Heareth*.

3780   *The Rainbird*

Date of Publication: 1962
Subject(s): Rural Life—Sweden
Fictional character(s): Linda Stahl, Young Woman; Egron Stahl, Farmer (peasant); Hanna Stahl, Spouse
Time Period(s): 19th century; 20th century (1890-1914)
Locale(s): Sweden

Summary: Linda Stahl is a love-starved girl among the peasant folk of northern Sweden at the turn of the century. Her father, Egron, is guilt-ridden, her mother weak and ineffectual. The tension between Egron and his daughter finally explodes, and she is cast out as an alien.

Historical Accuracy: This is a novel of character, searching for a level of universals, in which setting is relatively unimportant.

JUDITH LIEDERMAN (1927-)

Born in New York City, Liederman attended Syracuse University and Hunter College. She was an advertising copywriter before becoming a full-time writer.

3781   *The Moneyman*

Date of Publication: 1978
Subject(s): Family Saga; Business Building
Fictional character(s): Aaron Abel, Businessman; Jason Miller, Businessman; Jennie Abel, Young Woman
Time Period(s): 20th century (1920s-1950s)
Locale(s): New York, New York

Summary: Set in the New York nightclub world, the novel traces the rise of Aaron Abel, "the Hatcheck King," an ambitious young man from Brooklyn who makes his fortune setting up a network of entertainment concessions in Manhattan nightspots. His business partner is his nephew Jason Miller. His eldest daughter Jennie's desire for independence threatens the family and its business.

Historical Accuracy: The story is fanciful but filled with authentic elements that create a believable period background.

YUTANG LIN (1895-1976)

A Chinese novelist, translator, and scholar, Lin was born in Chanchow and educated at St. John's College, Harvard, and the University of Leipzig. He was the chancellor of Nanyang University, Singapore, and spent several decades preparing a Chinese-English dictionary of modern usage. In the 1930s Lin produced two best-selling nonfiction works, *My Country and My People* and *The Importance of Living*. He has been praised as one of the 20th century's best interpreters of the Chinese character for western readers.

3782   *Lady Wu*

Date of Publication: 1965
Subject(s): Chinese Empire; Royalty—China
Historical character(s): Wu Chao, Ruler (Empress of China); Gadtsung, Ruler (Emperor of China)
Time Period(s): 7th century
Locale(s): China

Summary: The novel chronicles the fascinating life of Lady Wu, T'ang Dynasty Empress, who ruled during the 7th century. She rises from obscurity to take the throne and holds it with ruthless power while overseeing a glorious period in Chinese culture.

Historical Accuracy: The novel's events are derived from the official histories of the T'ang Dynasty.

3783   *The Red Peony*

Date of Publication: 1961
Subject(s): Chinese Empire
Fictional character(s): Peony, Widow(er)
Time Period(s): 1890s
Locale(s): China

Summary: Set in China during the 1890s, the story concerns an unconventional young widow, Peony, who rebels against the traditional behavior expected of her.

Historical Accuracy: The novel provides a more modern perspective for its central character which clashes with the historical period portrayed.

JOSEPH C. LINCOLN (1870-1944)

FREEMAN LINCOLN (1900-1962)

An American writer born into a seafaring family in Brewster, Massachusetts, Joseph Lincoln is best known for his 40 novels and many short stories set on Cape Cod. His titles include *The Portugee*, *Fair Harbor*, and *Cape Cod Yesterdays*. Many of his books deal with the changing social structure of Cape Cod that resulted from economic changes in the late 19th and early 20th centuries. Freeman Lincoln was an editor and writer and the co-author of several books with his father, Joseph.

3784   *The New Hope*

Date of Publication: 1941
Subject(s): War of 1812; Sea Story
Fictional character(s): Isaiah Dole, Sea Captain; Jonathon Bangs, Sailor
Time Period(s): 1810s (1814)
Locale(s): Cape Cod, Massachusetts

Summary: This naval adventure story is set on Cape Code during the War of 1812. The Yankees concoct a plan to break the British blockade by outfitting the *New Hope* as a privateer. Murder and treachery complicate the plan.

Historical Accuracy: The novel features authentic and accurate period dialogue, details, and geography.

`3785` *Storm Signals*

Date of Publication: 1935
Subject(s): Civil War—U.S.; Sea Story
Fictional character(s): Benjamin Snow, Sea Captain
Time Period(s): 1860s
Locale(s): Cape Cod, Massachusetts

Summary: This sea tale is set during the early years of the Civil War. It involves a shipwreck of which the captain, Benjamin Snow, is the sole survivor.

Historical Accuracy: The period background is authentically presented.

VICTORIA LINCOLN (1904-1981)

Born in Massachusetts, Lincoln graduated from Radcliffe College and did graduate study at the University of Marburgh, Germany. She interrupted her work on her doctoral thesis to write a detective story, which led to her becoming a full-time writer. She is the winner of an Edgar Award for the best crime book in 1967 for *A Private Disguise*. Some of her fiction has been dramatized for Broadway, films, and TV.

`3786` *Charles*

Date of Publication: 1962
Subject(s): Victorian Period; Biography, Fictionalized; Literary Life
Historical character(s): Charles Dickens, Writer; Kate Dickens, Spouse
Time Period(s): 19th century (1820s-1870)
Locale(s): London, England

Summary: This biographical novel based on the life of Charles Dickens traces the novelist's career from his boyhood to literary success as one of England's greatest writers. The story concentrates on how Dickens overcame the traumas of his early years, dramatizing a series of events in Dickens' life.

Historical Accuracy: The novel is inspired by events in Dickens' life, but the author warns that it is not a biography.

`3787` *A Dangerous Innocence*

Date of Publication: 1958
Subject(s): American Colonies; Witchcraft and Sorcery; Puritans
Fictional character(s): Ann Archer, Spouse; Roger Evesham, Spouse
Time Period(s): 17th century (1692)
Locale(s): Salem, Massachusetts, American Colonies

Summary: This story of an early American marriage is set during the period of the Salem witchcraft trials and concerns Ann Archer who, although she loves another, marries the stern moralist, Roger Evesham. When their household is suspected of witchcraft, Roger stubbornly allows himself to be tried and killed in protest, and Ann is spared to be reunited with her true love.

Historical Accuracy: The story is less about 17th-century Puritans than about Ann's growing sense of life without love. The period elements, however, are handled believably.

HELMER LINDERHOLM (1916-)

Swedish writer Linderholm spent more than 20 years researching the experiences of Swedish settlers in the Delaware colony for *Land of the Beautiful River*. Until the age of 42, he owned and worked in a bakery.

`3788` *Land of the Beautiful River*

Date of Publication: 1963
Subject(s): American Colonies; Settlement of the American Frontier; Indians
Fictional character(s): Andreas Ramelius, Student (theological)
Historical character(s): Johan Printz, Government Official (colonial governor)
Time Period(s): 17th century (1647-1670s)
Locale(s): Delaware, American Colonies

Summary: This is an account of the Swedish colony in Delaware during the 17th century. The story follows the experiences of young Andreas Ramelius who becomes an assistant to Johan Printz, the governor of New Sweden, and is caught up in Printz's scheming against Peter Stuyvesant's Dutch settlement. Andreas is forced to flee and takes refuge with the Susquehanna Indians.

Historical Accuracy: The novel is obviously based on solid research and presents an authentic account of the period.

TORGNY LINDGREN (1938-)

`3789` *Bathsheba*

Date of Publication: 1989
Subject(s): Biblical Story; Ancient Israel
Historical character(s): David, Ruler (King of Israel), Biblical Figure; Bathsheba, Royalty (queen consort of David), Biblical Figure; Solomon, Ruler (King of Israel), Biblical Figure; Rabbah, Biblical Figure; Absalom, Royalty (prince), Biblical Figure
Time Period(s): 10th century (B)
Locale(s): Israel

Summary: The novel recounts the Biblical story of David and Bathsheba, who becomes the power behind the throne. David succumbs to Bathsheba's great beauty and forcibly takes her from her husband. She manages to keep David fascinated while realizing her greatest triumph: her son Solomon becomes David's heir.

Historical Accuracy: Derived from the scriptures, the novel creates believable characters and a plausible era.

AUDREY ERSKINE LINDOP (1920-1986)

An English actress, playwright, and novelist, Lindop was born in London and began her career as an actress in repertory companies in England. Her novels include *The

Singer Not the Song, Fortune My Foe, and *I Start Counting,* which received the French Prix Roman.

3790 *The Way to the Lantern*
Date of Publication: 1961
Subject(s): French Revolution; Theatrical Life
Fictional character(s): Philippe de Lambriere, Actor, Adventurer
Historical character(s): Georges-Jacques Danton, Revolutionary; Jean-Paul Marat, Revolutionary
Time Period(s): 1780s; 1790s
Locale(s): Paris, France; England

Summary: The French Revolution is seen from the perspective of a daring actor-confidence man named Philippe de Lambriere (also known as Roberts), who finds himself increasingly caught up in the violence of the revolution. His secret identity threatens to have him strung up on a lamp post as he encounters many of the important figures of the time and its violent events.

Historical Accuracy: The novel ingeniously weaves the fictional story of Roberts into a vivid and convincing backdrop of actual figures and events.

PHILIP LINDSAY (1906-1958)
An English writer born in Australia, Lindsay is the author of biographical and historical novels. His titles include *Morgan in Jamaica, Panama Is Burning,* and *Bride for a Buccaneer.*

3791 *The Gentle Knight*
Date of Publication: 1942
Subject(s): Middle Ages
Historical character(s): Geoffrey Chaucer, Writer
Time Period(s): 14th century
Locale(s): England

Summary: This fictional retelling of Chaucer's *Canterbury Tales* presents the story of the Canterbury pilgrims as they set out from London for Canterbury with elements added to Chaucer's story. The emphasis here is not on the pilgrims' tales as much as the pilgrims themselves in this vivid reconstruction of medieval life and customs.

Historical Accuracy: The novel's period elements are authentic, capturing the spirit of Chaucer's great work.

3792 *Here Comes the King*
Date of Publication: 1933
Subject(s): Tudor Period; Royalty—England
Historical character(s): Catherine Howard, Royalty (queen consort of Henry VIII); Henry VIII, Ruler (King of England)
Time Period(s): 16th century (1540-1542)
Locale(s): England

Summary: This account of the life of Catherine Howard, the fifth wife of England's King Henry VIII, covers the period from her marriage to Henry in 1540 to her execution less than two years later.

Historical Accuracy: The period and situation are captured accurately, with imaginative embellishment.

DAWN LINDSEY
Lindsey graduated from the University of Oklahoma and has worked in advertising, as a public relations director for several zoos, and as a marketing analyst.

3793 *The Duchess of Vidal*
Date of Publication: 1978
Subject(s): Regency Romance; Suspense
Fictional character(s): Dominique Forrester, Governess; Justin Vidal, Nobleman (duke)
Time Period(s): 19th century (Regency period)
Locale(s): England

Summary: Dominique Forrester is a young governess with a secret who meets and marries the Duke of Vidal. Determined to remain independent, Dominique attempts to keep her past concealed, as her husband begins an investigation that results in danger for Dominique and their relationship.

Historical Accuracy: The emphasis here is on romantic suspense with only a modicum of background painting.

JOHANNA LINDSEY (1952-)
American romance writer Lindsey was born in Frankfurt, Germany, and attended school in Hawaii. She began her writing career in 1977 and is the author of a succession of popular historical romances.

3794 *Defy Not the Heart*
Date of Publication: 1985
Subject(s): Middle Ages; Romance
Fictional character(s): Reina de Champeney, Noblewoman; Ranulf Fitz Hugh, Knight, Bastard Son; Lord Rothwell, Nobleman
Time Period(s): 12th century
Locale(s): England

Summary: In this romantic adventure novel set during the 12th century, the knight Ranulf is first the protector of Lady Reina de Champeney; then he abducts her to take her to Lord Rothwell for a forced marriage. Later her abductor becomes her intended as Lady Reina prefers Ranulf to the aging Lord Rothwell.

Historical Accuracy: The novel is unconvincing in its period backdrop, and the story is incredible.

3795 *Savage Thunder*
Date of Publication: 1989
Subject(s): American West; Romance
Fictional character(s): Jocelyn Fleming, Noblewoman (Duchess of Eaton), Widow(er); Colt Thunder, Guide, Indian (part Cheyenne)
Time Period(s): 1870s (1878)
Locale(s): Wyoming

Summary: Newly widowed English noblewoman Jocelyn Fleming journeys to the Wyoming territory of the 1870s, where she falls in love with the bitter Colt Thunder, whom she hires as a guide.

Historical Accuracy: It is difficult to take this as more than a romance. The period background is filled with idealization and cliches.

JOAN LINGARD (1932-)

Scottish author Lingard was born in Edinburgh and educated at the Moray House Training College, earning her teaching diploma. She is a teacher and writer of novels and TV scripts for Scottish television and the BBC. She began to write because she could not get enough to read.

3796 *Greenyards*

Date of Publication: 1981
Subject(s): Victorian Period; Immigrants; Frontier—Canada
Fictional character(s): Catriona Ross, Young Woman; Donald Munro, Young Man; Will Cruickshank, Nobleman
Time Period(s): 1850s (1852-1856)
Locale(s): Highlands, Scotland; Edinburgh, Scotland; Canada (Upper)

Summary: Set in Scotland in the 1850s, the novel concerns a rebellion mounted by those dispossessed of their land in the Highlands. The story centers on fiery Catriona Ross, who leads the rebellion and the emigration that follows. The scene shifts from the tenements of Glasgow and Edinburgh to the Canadian frontier.

Historical Accuracy: The novel creates a plausible background for the action.

ELIZABETH LININGTON (1921-1988)

Born in Illinois, Linington is perhaps best known as Dell Shannon, under which name she wrote three crime-detective series featuring police officer Luis Mendoza. She has been called the "Dean of Police Procedurals."

3797 *The King Breaker*

Date of Publication: 1958
Subject(s): Civil War—England; Royalty—England; Espionage
Fictional character(s): Ivor ap-Maddox, Spy
Historical character(s): Oliver Cromwell, Political Figure; Charles I, Ruler (King of England); George Villiers, Nobleman (Duke of Buckingham)
Time Period(s): 17th century
Locale(s): England

Summary: Set during the English Civil War and the conflict between Charles I and Cromwell, the novel describes the adventures of Royalist Ivor ap-Maddox who becomes a spy in Cromwell's household. Danger and intrigue connect all the characters, with Cromwell and the king overshadowing all.

Historical Accuracy: The emphasis is on thrilling intrigue and adventure over careful documentation of history, but the atmosphere of the time is convincing.

3798 *The Long Watch*

Date of Publication: 1956

Subject(s): American Colonies; American Revolution
Fictional character(s): James Bethune, Journalist; Robert MacDonald, Journalist
Time Period(s): 1770s; 1780s
Locale(s): New York, New York

Summary: The setting is colonial New York before and during the American Revolution. The novel dramatizes the efforts of two newspaper editors, James Bethune and Robert MacDonald, to keep their newspaper going during the British occupation of the city. The emphasis is on the day-to-day struggle of the time, realistically depicted.

Historical Accuracy: Although the story is fictional, the period is accurately portrayed.

3799 *Monsieur Janvier*

Date of Publication: 1957
Subject(s): Jacobite Rebellion; Georgian Period; Identity—Concealed
Fictional character(s): Ringan Monteith, Heir; Sir Alan Mackinnon, Gentleman; Claude de Chevereuil, Noblewoman (countess)
Time Period(s): 18th century
Locale(s): Paris, France; London, England; Scotland

Summary: When the third son of the Lord of the Monteith Clan, Ringan, learns that his father, sister and two brothers have been kidnapped and massacred by the English after the Battle of Culloden, he sets out to punish their betrayer, Sir Alan Mackinnon. Ringan returns from Paris to London in disguise as Monsieur Janvier for a series of high adventures in the fashionable salons of London.

Historical Accuracy: The adventures of Ringan are fictional, but the novel features a strong and authentic period background.

3800 *The Proud Man*

Date of Publication: 1955
Subject(s): Elizabethan Period; Royalty—Ireland; Royalty—England
Fictional character(s): Rory McGuinness, Military Personnel (soldier)
Historical character(s): Shane O'Neill, Nobleman (second Earl of Tyrone), Military Personnel; Elizabeth I, Ruler (Queen of England); Mary, Queen of Scots, Ruler; William Cecil, Nobleman (Baron Burghley), Government Official; Sir Francis Walsingham, Government Official
Time Period(s): 16th century (1559-1567)
Locale(s): Ulster, Ireland; London, England; Dublin, Ireland

Summary: The novel tells the story of the chieftain of the Clan O'Neill, Shane O'Neill, Prince of Ulster. O'Neill, a larger-than-life figure of boundless ambition, dreams of uniting Ireland as its High King and marrying Elizabeth Tudor to become King of England as well. What follows is a series of battles against the English and the Scots and a tangled chain of divided loyalties and tragic defeats.

Historical Accuracy: The novel is based on actual characters and events, although the author admits that the chronology was not followed too striclty.

GAIL LINK

3801 *Wolf's Embrace*
Date of Publication: 1989
Subject(s): Middle Ages; Romance
Fictional character(s): Duvessa O'Dalaigh, Gentlewoman; Hugh Fitzgerald, Gentleman
Time Period(s): 15th century (1476)
Locale(s): England

Summary: In the 15th century, Duvessa O'Dalaigh and Hugh Fitzgerald elope. This romantic novel examines the effect of their elopement on succeeding generations and features a look at the place of women in the social structure of the time.

Historical Accuracy: Different from other historical romances, the novel does attempt a convincing period background that assumes an equal priority to the novel's emotions.

ERIC LINKLATER (1899-1974)
Welsh writer Linklater graduated from the University of Aberdeen. A novelist, playwright, and biographer, his books include *The Wind on the Moon*, *The Crusader's Key*, and *Robert the Bruce*.

3802 *Husband of Delilah*
Date of Publication: 1962
Subject(s): Biblical Story
Historical character(s): Samson, Biblical Figure; Delilah, Biblical Figure
Time Period(s): Indeterminate Past
Locale(s): Israel

Summary: In this fictional re-creation of the Biblical story of Samson, several departures from the Old Testament version are taken. Despite her act of betrayal, the character of Delilah is rehabilitated in her great love for Samson. Samson himself emerges as a kind of Biblical folk hero, and the Philistines are transformed into modern proponents of progress who are ill-equipped to deal with the religious fanaticism of Samson.

Historical Accuracy: The ancient world is recast with a particularly modern bent.

GILLIAN LINSCOTT (1944-)
An English mystery novelist, Linscott was born in Windsor and received a degree in English from Somerville College, Oxford. She has worked as a journalist for a variety of newspapers and for the BBC. She has said about her devotion to the mystery genre that there are few books that could not be improved by dumping a body in them somewhere.

3803 *Crown Witness*
Date of Publication: 1995
Subject(s): Mystery; Women's Rights
Fictional character(s): Nell Bray, Suffragette, Detective—Amateur; Simon Frater, Gentleman
Time Period(s): 1910s (1910)

Locale(s): London, England

Summary: A Suffragette demonstration during George V's coronation leads to murder as Nell Bray's friend, Simon Frater, is discovered holding a gun beside the victim. He is arrested for murder, and Nell is taken in for obstructing justice. She sets out to prove Simon's innocence, while uncovering the wider political significance of the crime.

Historical Accuracy: The novel features authentic and convincing period elements.

3804 *Dead Man's Sweetheart*
Date of Publication: 1996
Subject(s): Mystery; Women's Rights
Fictional character(s): Nell Bray, Suffragette, Detective—Amateur
Time Period(s): 1910s (1913)
Locale(s): England

Summary: Nell Bray is on vacation at her brother's country home and finds herself involved in the case of a murdered mill owner. She unearths political conflicts surrounding the mill and a disturbing family secret.

Historical Accuracy: The novel provides a plausible period background and an authentic historical ambiance.

3805 *An Easy Day for a Lady*
Date of Publication: 1994
Subject(s): Mystery; Women's Rights; Mountaineering
Fictional character(s): Nell Bray, Suffragette, Detective—Amateur
Time Period(s): 1910s (1910)
Locale(s): Chamonix, France; Mont Blanc, France

Summary: Nell Bray, suffragette and amateur detective, is on a climbing holiday in the French Alps when a rescue team chips out of the ice the frozen remains of Englishman Arthur Mountford, who disappeared thirty years ago. Nell is recruited as an interpreter for the British family, but other skills are needed when it seems that the death might not have been accidental.

Historical Accuracy: The novel provides a lively and convincing evocation of the period.

3806 *Hanging on the Wire*
Date of Publication: 1993
Subject(s): Mystery; World War I; Medical Profession
Fictional character(s): Nell Bray, Suffragette, Detective—Amateur; Jenny Chesney, Nurse; Monica Minter, Gentlewoman
Time Period(s): 1910s (1916)
Locale(s): Wales

Summary: Women's Rights activist Nell Bray is asked by her friend Jenny Chesney to come to a small hospital in Wales during World War I and help stop the hospital's closing. Soon, what appears to be a murder occurs, and Nell takes up the investigation that is frustrated by the director of the hospital.

Historical Accuracy: The period details are authentic and convincing.

3807 *Murder, I Presume*

Date of Publication: 1990
Subject(s): Mystery; Victorian Period; Exploration
Fictional character(s): Peter Pentland, Explorer; Maud Stretton, Gentlewoman; Cecilia Bright, Gentlewoman
Time Period(s): 1860s (1864)
Locale(s): London, England

Summary: A feud among African explorers turns deadly in this Victorian mystery. Peter Pentland is the guardian of his two rivals' wives. When a former colleague out to ruin Peter's reputation is killed with a rare African poison, Peter and his charges become the prime suspects. Pentland must turn to sleuthing to clear his name.

Historical Accuracy: This is an ingenious mystery with an authentic period background.

3808 *Sister Beneath the Sheet*

Date of Publication: 1991
Subject(s): Mystery; Victorian Period; Women's Rights
Fictional character(s): Nell Bray, Suffragette, Detective—Amateur; Bobbie Fieldfare, Suffragette
Historical character(s): Emmeline Pankhurst, Feminist, Suffragette
Time Period(s): 1900s (1900)
Locale(s): Biarritz, France

Summary: Sent to Biarritz to collect a legacy left to the Women's Rights cause, suffragette Nell Bray finds herself investigating whether the benefactor committed suicide or was murdered. She also keeps an eye on one of her more volatile suffragette sisters, Bobbie Fieldfare, who is armed and setting her sights on a member of parliament.

Historical Accuracy: The novel offers some authentic period details, particularly on the suffragette movement.

3809 *Stage Fright*

Date of Publication: 1993
Subject(s): Mystery; Theatrical Life
Fictional character(s): Nell Bray, Suffragette, Detective—Amateur; Bella Flanagan, Actress; Lord Penwardine, Nobleman
Historical character(s): George Bernard Shaw, Writer
Time Period(s): 1900s (1909)
Locale(s): London, England

Summary: George Bernard Shaw asks suffragette and amateur sleuth Nell Bray to assist in his latest production. Shaw's leading lady is in danger, and the play, a scathing attack on English marital law, may be taken literally as a reflection of the actress' love-less marriage to Lord Penwardine. Apparently Penwardine is willing to do anything to keep his wife off the stage. Might he resort to murder? Nell Bray's task is to find out.

Historical Accuracy: The period is convincingly displayed.

ROBERT LITTELL (1935-)

American novelist and journalist Littell was formerly an editor for *Newsweek* based in Eastern Europe and the Soviet Union. An author of highly praised thrillers and mysteries, Littell won the Crime Writers Association Gold Dagger Award in 1974 and an Edgar Award the same year. His books include *The Sisters*, *The Once and Future Spy*, and *The October Circle*.

3810 *The Revolutionist: A Novel of Russia*

Date of Publication: 1988
Subject(s): Russian Revolution; Russian Empire; Espionage
Fictional character(s): Alexander Til, Revolutionary; Lili Yusupova, Royalty (princess); Ronzha, Writer (poet)
Historical character(s): Joseph Stalin, Political Figure; Vladimir Ilich Lenin, Political Figure, Revolutionary
Time Period(s): 20th century (1911-1950s)
Locale(s): Leningrad, Union of Soviet Socialist Republics; Moscow, Union of Soviet Socialist Republics

Summary: Blending fact and fiction, the novel details the course of the Russian Revolution and the creation of the Soviet state to the death of Stalin. The center of the story is the idealist Til, who is devoted to the creation of a free and just society. As he watches the defeat of his dream, he faces a bitter confrontation with Joseph Stalin.

Historical Accuracy: The author admits to having taken some liberties with the subject matter. He addresses the major alterations in an afterword.

NANCY LIVINGSTON (1935-)

Livingston is an English author who attended private schools in London and Manchester. She has worked as an actress, a secretary, a seamstress, and a production assistant for independent TV companies. She became a full-time writer in 1985. *The Trouble at Aquitaine* won the Poisoned Chalice Award in 1985; *Death in a Distant Land* won the Punch Award in 1988. She alternates between mysteries and sagas.

3811 *The Far Side of the Hill*

Date of Publication: 1987
Subject(s): Family Saga; Victorian Period
Fictional character(s): John McKie, Store Owner; Davie McKie, Young Man; Mary Hamilton, Young Woman
Time Period(s): 19th century; 20th century (turn of the century)
Locale(s): Scotland; Darlington, England

Summary: This story set in turn-of-the-century Scotland and England describes the experiences of John McKie and his brother, Davie, who leave their remote village for city life and hoped-for success. There, a young pregnant woman, Mary Hamilton, appears and creates conflict.

Historical Accuracy: The novel is convincing in its details of period life.

3812 *The Land of Our Dreams*

Date of Publication: 1988
Subject(s): Family Saga; World War I; Business Building
Fictional character(s): John McKie, Store Owner; Luke McKie, Student (medical); Jane McKie, Dancer
Time Period(s): 1910s
Locale(s): Darlington, England

Summary: In the sequel to *The Far Side of the Hill*, the success sought by a poor Scottish crofter family, the McKies, is realized. John McKie achieves prosperity with the Emporium, a small family department store. The family faces challenges from John's niece, Jane, an aspiring dancer, and all is altered by the horror of World War I.

Historical Accuracy: The family story is set against a convincing period and regional backdrop.

RICHARD LLEWELLYN (1907-1983)

A Welsh novelist best known for *How Green Was My Valley*, Llewellyn's other novels include *None but the Lonely* and *A Night of Bright Stars*.

3813 *How Green Was My Valley*

Date of Publication: 1940
Subject(s): Mining; Labor Movement
Fictional character(s): Huw Morgan, Hero; Gwilym Morgan, Miner; Beth Morgan, Heroine
Time Period(s): 19th century
Locale(s): Wales

Summary: The novel describes the life of a Welsh boy whose experiences, and those of his family, typify Welsh mining life in the 19th century. The family is divided by labor trouble and the hardships of their daily lives.

Historical Accuracy: The novel is an honest account of heroic, if non-glamorous endurance and fortitude.

ALAN LLOYD (1927-)

Born in London, Lloyd worked as a journalist until his first book was published in 1964. He is the author of novels and several biographies and historical studies, including *The Drums of Kumasi: The Story of the Ashanti Wars*, *The King Who Lost America*, and *The Maligned Monarch: A Life of King John of England*.

3814 *Trade Imperial*

Date of Publication: 1979
Subject(s): Chinese Empire; Opium War; English Colonies
Fictional character(s): Joshua Bishop, Trader; Edward Bishop, Gentleman, Businessman; Joel Bishop, Gentleman
Time Period(s): 1840s
Locale(s): England; Macao; Canton, China

Summary: The novel describes three generations of the Bishop family, who make their fortune in the illicit opium trade. The family fortune is started with Joshua Bishop, who amasses wealth buying opium in India and trading it for tea in China, then selling the tea in England. His son, Edward, rises to a position of respectability that his own son, Joel, exposes as hypocrisy.

Historical Accuracy: The period background is convincingly authentic.

ROBIN LLOYD-JONES (1934-)

Born in London, Lloyd-Jones spent his childhood in India. Lloyd-Jones is a graduate of Cambridge University and has taught history, geography, and social studies in secondary schools in England and Scotland. President of the Scottish Association of Writers, Lloyd-Jones published his first novel at age 48, writing two hours a day before work.

3815 *Lords of the Dance*

Date of Publication: 1983
Subject(s): Mogul Empire; Indian Empire; Picaresque Adventure
Fictional character(s): Thomas Coryat, Doctor; Brother Peter, Religious (monk)
Time Period(s): 16th century
Locale(s): India

Summary: The novel chronicles the picaresque adventures of two Englishmen, Thomas Coryat, a physician in search of a cure for his wife's illness, and Brother Peter, known as Frog, a Catholic missionary who has come to India to convert the heathens. Their adventures are set amidst the turmoil of the Mogul Empire and the dangers and spendors of India's royal court.

Historical Accuracy: The details of Indian life and culture of the time is convincingly displayed.

MORGAN LLYWELYN (1937-)

An American writer born in New York City, Llywelyn has worked as a fashion model and a dance instructor. She is also an amateur equestrian who trains and shows her own horses. Her lifelong interest in her Celtic background prompted her to write her first novel, the beginning of a proposed eight-volume history of the Celts from 700 B.C. to 1600.

3816 *Bard: The Odyssey of the Irish*

Date of Publication: 1984
Subject(s): Exploration; Witchcraft and Sorcery; Myths and Legends
Fictional character(s): Shinann, Young Woman, Minstrel (bard)
Historical character(s): Amergin, Writer (poet), Minstrel (bard)
Time Period(s): 4th century B.C.
Locale(s): Spain; Ireland

Summary: The novel offers a speculative history of the arrival in Ireland of the Celts, led by the great Bard of the Gauls, Amergin. His poetry inspires his people to embark into the unknown to conquer Erin, shrouded in mystery and magic. They encounter the Tuatha De Danann, and the mingling of cultures produces the heritage of the Irish.

Historical Accuracy: The story is speculative but based on evidence derived from both anthropological and archaeological sources.

3817 *Druids*

Date of Publication: 1991
Subject(s): Druids; Witchcraft and Sorcery; Roman Empire
Fictional character(s): Ainvar, Religious (Druid priest)
Historical character(s): Vercingetorix, Warrior, Ruler (King of the Celts)
Time Period(s): 1st century B.C.
Locale(s): Gaul

Summary: This is the story of Julius Caesar's campaign in Gaul, told from the Celtic perspective. The novel describes the experiences of Ainvar, a Druid priest and friend of the great Celtic leader Vercingetorix. Ainvar chronicles the Gallic rebellion that Caesar moves swiftly to put down. At the same time, he details the ancient beliefs and customs that he struggles to preserve in the face of the growing Roman threat.

Historical Accuracy: The novel blends the factual with the imaginary and succeeds in depicting in convincing terms the period and the people of ancient Gaul.

3818 *Finn Mac Cool*

Date of Publication: 1994
Subject(s): Myths and Legends
Fictional character(s): Finn Mac Cool, Warrior; Cormac, Warrior
Time Period(s): Indeterminate Past
Locale(s): Ireland

Summary: The exploits of the legendary Irish hero Finn Mac Cool are depicted. The mightiest of Irish warriors, the leader of the army of the Fionna, Finn is raised wild and fashions adventurous pursuits full of daring exploits and betrayals. The author attempts to find the human side of this legendary figure.

Historical Accuracy: The various tales that are the basis of the novel are more mythic than historical, yet the author is able to create a credible and authentic world.

3819 *Grania: She-King of the Irish Seas*

Date of Publication: 1986
Subject(s): Elizabethan Period; Pirates
Fictional character(s): Tigernan, Adventurer; Huw, Sailor
Historical character(s): Grace O'Malley, Chieftain (Irish), Pirate
Time Period(s): 16th century (1570s-1580s)
Locale(s): Connacht, Ireland

Summary: Grania is the real-life Irish chieftain turned pirate warrior Grace O'Malley. In 16th-century Ireland Grania wages a desperate struggle against the forces of Queen Elizabeth who intends to halt Grania's piracy and subjugate Ireland. Grania emerges as a forceful and determined female warrior.

Historical Accuracy: The novel mixes fact and fiction but captures authentically this period of Elizabethan Ireland.

3820 *The Horse Goddess*

Date of Publication: 1982
Subject(s): Bronze Age; Myths and Legends; Fantasy
Fictional character(s): Epona, Young Woman; Kazhak, Warrior (Scythian); Kernunnos, Religious (priest)
Time Period(s): 8th century B.C.
Locale(s): Europe

Summary: East meets West in the 8th century B.C. as Epona, a Celt, encounters Kazhak, a Scythian warrior and prince of the wild horsemen of the eastern plains. They are pursued across ancient Europe by Kernunnos, a Danish priest and shapechanger, a prototype of the first werewolf.

Historical Accuracy: Though a fantasy, the story is set in a clearly realized historical era, when horses were introduced to the early Celts by east Asian tribes.

3821 *The Last Prince of Ireland*

Date of Publication: 1992
Subject(s): Elizabethan Period; Royalty—Ireland
Historical character(s): Donal Cam O'Sullivan, Royalty (prince)
Time Period(s): 17th century
Locale(s): Ireland

Summary: The novel details the tragic defeat of the Gaelic clans by the English forces of Elizabeth I intent on breaking their power and subjugating Ireland. Donal Cam O'Sullivan, a historical figure, refuses to surrender after the disastrous battle of Kinsale. He retreats with his clan and must struggle against betrayal and treachery created by Elizabeth's bribery.

Historical Accuracy: Based on history, the story is a blend of fact and fiction.

3822 *The Lion of Ireland*

Date of Publication: 1979
Subject(s): Middle Ages; Vikings; Royalty—Ireland
Historical character(s): Brian Boru, Ruler (High King of Ireland); Gormlaith, Royalty (queen consort of Brian)
Time Period(s): 11th century
Locale(s): Ireland

Summary: The novel offers the story of Brian Boru, the greatest of the high kings of Ireland who in the 11th century came close to seeing his dream of a united Ireland realized. Boru is shown in combat with the invading Norsemen, culminating in the great victory at the Battle of Clontarf. Brian emerges as a hero and great Irish leader.

Historical Accuracy: The characters are taken from Irish and Norse history. The sources are often contradictory, and the author claims to have chosen those accounts which seemed most logical in the light of both historical and archaeological evidence.

3823 *Pride of Lions*

Date of Publication: 1996
Subject(s): Middle Ages; Royalty—Ireland
Fictional character(s): Cera, Religious (Druid), Young Woman

Historical character(s): Donough, Royalty (prince); Gormlaith, Royalty (queen consort of Brian Boru)
Time Period(s): 11th century
Locale(s): Ireland

Summary: This sequel to *Lion of Ireland* begins in the aftermath of Brian Boru's death in 1014. His son, Donough, is determined to succeed his father as High King of Ireland. To do so, he must contend with his mother, the treacherous Gormlaith, and put aside his love for the Druid Cera.

Historical Accuracy: The novel is expert in authentically presenting the period and its customs.

3824 Red Branch

Date of Publication: 1989
Subject(s): Myths and Legends; Royalty—Ireland
Fictional character(s): Cuchulain, Warrior; Deirdre, Young Woman
Historical character(s): Mac Nessa Conor, Ruler (Irish king); Maeve, Royalty (Queen of Connaught)
Time Period(s): 1st century B.C.
Locale(s): Ulster, Ireland

Summary: The pre-Christian Ireland of myth and legend is subject of this novel which chronicles the career of the legendary Irish warrior, Cuchulain. Based on the heroic tales of the warrior elite of Northern Ireland in the so-called Ulster Cycle, the novel tells the story of Cuchulain's prowess in combat, his deadly struggle with Queen Maeve, and the fatal beauty of Deirdre.

Historical Accuracy: The author explains that the novel tries to construct a skeleton of possible truth from the myths of ancient Ireland, where magic and truth are inextricably linked.

3825 The Wind From Hastings

Date of Publication: 1978
Subject(s): Norman Conquest; Royalty—England; Battle of Hastings
Historical character(s): Harold II, Ruler (King of England); Edyth, Royalty (queen consort of Harold II); Llywelyn ap Gruffydd, Royalty (Welsh prince)
Time Period(s): 11th century
Locale(s): England; Wales

Summary: The events of the reign of Harold II, the last Saxon king of England, and the Norman Conquest are dramatized from the perspective of Harold's wife Edyth. A pawn in the dynastic struggle of rival families, Edyth is first married to the Welsh Prince Griffith ap Llywelyn. After he is killed, Edyth is married to Harold only to see him defeated at the Battle of Hastings.

Historical Accuracy: The novel blends actual historical events with some inventions and speculation to create an authentic version of the period.

CHARLES O. LOCKE (1896-1977)

An American journalist, lyricist, scriptwriter, and novelist, Locke worked as a reporter in Toledo, Ohio, and New York City during the 1920s, and as a lyricist and radio scriptwriter

in the 1930s. During the 1950s, Locke wrote several adventure novels, the most successful of which was *The Hell Bent Kid.*

3826 The Last Princess

Date of Publication: 1953
Subject(s): Inca Empire; Spanish Colonies
Fictional character(s): Tacara-Mi, Royalty (Incan princess); Tacios, Young Man
Time Period(s): 16th century
Locale(s): Peru

Summary: The story of the conquest of Peru by the Spanish is described from the point of view of Incan princess Tacara-Mi and her lover Tacios. The drama shows the clash of cultures and the final days of a great civilization.

Historical Accuracy: Despite the modern idiom in telling the story, the novel successfully brings a primitive culture to life.

ROSS LOCKRIDGE JR. (1914-1948)

Lockridge was an American novelist whose sole book, *Raintree County*, was a bestseller. In the midst of the acclaim that Lockridge received, he committed suicide.

3827 Raintree County

Date of Publication: 1948
Subject(s): Civil War—U.S.; Slavery
Fictional character(s): John Wickliff Shawnessy, Teacher; Garwood B. Jones, Political Figure; Susanna Drake, Southern Belle
Time Period(s): 19th century (1840-1892)
Locale(s): Raintree County, Indiana; New Orleans, Louisiana; New York, New York

Summary: The novel examines a half century of American history through flashbacks that occur on a single day—July 4, 1892. John Shawnessy reflects on his life: and his tragic love affair with a woman from New Orleans; his service in the Civil War; and his return to Raintree County, disappointed and filled with a sense of loss and lost opportunities.

Historical Accuracy: Lockridge offers an interesting angle on 19th century American history.

SARAH LOCKWOOD (1882-)

Lockwood's books include *The Man From Mesabi* and *The Elbow of the Snake.*

3828 A Fistful of Stars

Date of Publication: 1947
Subject(s): Settlement of the American Frontier; Lumber Industry
Fictional character(s): Lint MacVey, Young Man
Time Period(s): 1880s
Locale(s): Wisconsin

Summary: Pioneer life in northern Wisconsin forms the background for this novel. The story centers on the experiences of

Lint MacVey in the Wisconsin logging camps and his domestic life.

Historical Accuracy: The novel provides an authentic look at the region during the period.

MARIA LODI

A French writer and author of strip cartoons and hundreds of short stories as well as a series of police stories for newspapers, Lodi's first novel, *Les Vagabonds*, was published to great acclaim.

3829 *Charlotte Morel*

Date of Publication: 1969
Subject(s): Romance
Fictional character(s): Charlotte Morel, Young Woman; Thomas Becque, Journalist
Time Period(s): 1860s
Locale(s): Paris, France

Summary: This historical romance, the first of a trilogy, is set in Paris during the 1860s as Napoleon III is rebuilding the city. Charlotte Morel is a young woman from the provinces who comes to the city with her husband but falls in love with Thomas Becque, a journalist.

Historical Accuracy: The novel features an authentic portrait of Paris under Napoleon III.

3830 *Charlotte Morel: The Dream*

Date of Publication: 1970
Subject(s): Romance
Fictional character(s): Charlotte Morel, Young Woman; Thomas Becque, Journalist
Time Period(s): 1860s
Locale(s): Paris, France

Summary: The novel continues the story of Charlotte Morel and her romantic relationship with journalist Thomas Becque. The setting is Paris during the 1860s as Becque is persecuted by the government for his writing.

Historical Accuracy: The novel's portrait of Paris during the period is convincing.

3831 *Charlotte Morel: The Siege*

Date of Publication: 1970
Subject(s): Franco-Prussian War; Romance
Fictional character(s): Charlotte Morel, Young Woman; Thomas Becque, Journalist
Time Period(s): 1870s
Locale(s): Paris, France

Summary: In this, the third and final historical romance concerning Charlotte Morel and journalist Thomas Becque, the setting is the siege of Paris during the Franco-Prussian War, which forms a backdrop for the resolution of their relationship.

Historical Accuracy: The period background is authentic and true to life and history.

HUBERTUS LOEWENSTEIN (1906-1984)

A German historian, politician, educator, journalist, and author, Loewenstein was one of Adolph Hitler's earliest opponents and one of the few members of the German nobility to speak out against the Nazis. He worked as an editorial writer in Germany until Hitler came to power, when he went into exile. With Thomas Mann and Sigmund Freud, Loewenstein headed the German Academy of Arts and Sciences in New York City. He returned to Germany after the war and served as a member of the West German parliament. He is the author of more than 40 books, including *After Hitler's Fall*, *The Germans in History*, and two autobiographical volumes, *Conquest of the Past* and.

3832 *The Eagle and the Crown*

Date of Publication: 1947
Subject(s): Roman Empire; Christianity
Fictional character(s): Marcius, Royalty (Irish prince)
Historical character(s): Tiberius, Ruler (Roman emperor)
Time Period(s): 1st century
Locale(s): Rome, Roman Empire

Summary: The sequel to *The Love of Longinus* tells the story of how an Irish prince, Marcius, carries the spear of Longinus that pierced Christ's side on the cross as a gift to the Emperor Tiberius and brings Christianity to Rome.

Historical Accuracy: The novel is marred by several anachronisms and is dominated by the author's Christian devotion.

3833 *The Lance of Longinus*

Date of Publication: 1946
Subject(s): Biblical Story; Roman Empire
Fictional character(s): Longinus, Military Personnel (Roman centurion)
Historical character(s): Jesus Christ, Biblical Figure
Time Period(s): 1st century
Locale(s): Jerusalem, Israel

Summary: The story of Jesus' passion and crucifixion is told from the perspective of the Roman centurion, Longinus, whose lance pierced Christ's side. Longinus' point of view offers an interesting angle on the last few weeks of Jesus' life.

Historical Accuracy: The novel's central character is imaginary, based on legend rather than fact. The overall framework of events, however, is based on the New Testament accounts.

NORAH LOFTS (1904-1983)

An English author born in Norfolk, Lofts was a prolific and bestselling author whose books sold more than one million copies in her lifetime. She is best remembered for her historical novels, many of which are set in the 19th century and feature English history in the background. Her work has been praised for its accuracy and ability to animate the past. She also wrote nonfiction and biographies, as well as several thrillers under the pseudonym Peter Curtis.

3834 *Afternoon of a Autocrat*

Date of Publication: 1956
Subject(s): Rural Life—England
Fictional character(s): Linda Shelmadine, Spouse; Sir Richard Shelmadine, Gentleman, Landowner; Damask Greenway, Young Woman
Time Period(s): 1790s
Locale(s): Suffolk, England; India

Summary: The historical background for this tale is the damage brought about by the laws of enclosure on a typical English community during the 1790s. Sir Richard Shelmadine returns from India, with his wife Linda, to take over the estate of Clevely. When he begins to enclose his property, conflict ensues.

Historical Accuracy: Despite detours toward the melodramatic, the novel does provide a convincing period portrait.

3835 *Bless This House*

Date of Publication: 1954
Subject(s): Elizabethan Period; Victorian Period
Fictional character(s): Tom Rowhedge, Landowner; Alice Rowhedge, Gentlewoman
Time Period(s): Multiple Time Periods
Locale(s): Suffolk, England

Summary: This is the story of a stately house built in 1577. The account of the house and its inhabitants covers nearly 400 years of English history. The major events of the English Civil War and the Restoration, Georgian, and Victorian periods are reflected, as are the changes brought on by the 20th century.

Historical Accuracy: The historical background is solidly presented.

3836 *Blossom Like the Rose*

Date of Publication: 1939
Subject(s): American Colonies; Indians; Religious Conflict
Fictional character(s): Philip Ollenshaw, Settler; Linda Seabrook, Young Woman; Judith Whistlecraft, Young Woman
Time Period(s): 17th century (1670s)
Locale(s): England; Salem, Massachusetts, American Colonies

Summary: This is the story of a young Scotsman, Philip Ollenshaw, who joins a group of religious fanatics in the 17th century and ventures to America, where he battles Indians and the intolerance of the Puritans.

Historical Accuracy: The novel offers some authentic period details and a convincing historical background.

3837 *The Brittle Glass*

Date of Publication: 1943
Subject(s): French Revolution; Napoleonic Wars
Fictional character(s): Sorrel Kingaby, Bastard Daughter, Heiress
Time Period(s): 1790s; 1800s
Locale(s): England

Summary: The novel describes the efforts of Sorrel Kingsby who becomes heiress to her father's whorehouse. Expected to sell the business, she decides instead to run it despite a series of personal setbacks.

Historical Accuracy: The novel makes use of period elements, but they are not essential to this romantic story whose contemporary attitudes show through its historical trappings.

3838 *A Calf for Venus*

Date of Publication: 1949
Subject(s): Regency Period; Crime and Criminals
Fictional character(s): Humphrey Shadbolt, Doctor; Letitia Rowan, Young Woman
Time Period(s): 1800s
Locale(s): Bury St. Edmonds, England

Summary: In this romantic tale, Dr. Henry Shadbolt falls in love at first sight with Letitia Rowan while aboard a coach heading for Bury St. Edwards. Letitia is travelling to join her aunt, the owner of a notorious coffee house. In an effort to save Letitia from danger, Shadbolt becomes involved in the deadly underworld of smuggling.

Historical Accuracy: The novel is filled with period elements that create a plausible background.

3839 *The Concubine*

Date of Publication: 1963
Subject(s): Tudor Period; Royalty—England; Biography, Fictionalized
Historical character(s): Anne Boleyn, Royalty (queen consort of Henry VIII); Henry VIII, Ruler (King of England); Thomas Wolsey, Religious (cardinal); Catherine of Aragon, Royalty (queen consort of Henry VIII); Clement VII, Religious (pope); Sir Thomas More, Government Official; Thomas Cromwell, Government Official; Thomas Cranmer, Religious (Archbishop of Canterbury)
Time Period(s): 16th century (1523-1536)
Locale(s): England

Summary: This story of Anne Boleyn, second wife of Henry VIII, whom the Spanish ambassador referred to as "the Concubine," follows Anne from her arrival at court as a 16-year-old lady-in-waiting to her marriage and eventual execution. Anne's story is reflected in the experiences of the major political figures and the political crisis wrought by Henry's divorce of Catherine of Aragon and marriage to Anne.

Historical Accuracy: The historical details are close to actuality.

3840 *Crown of Aloes*

Date of Publication: 1974
Subject(s): Royalty—Spain; Inquisition; Biography, Fictionalized
Historical character(s): Isabella I, Ruler (Queen of Castile); Ferdinand V, Ruler (King of Aragon); Tomas de Torquemada, Religious (Grand Inquisitor); Christopher Columbus, Explorer, Sea Captain
Time Period(s): 15th century; 16th century (1451-1504)
Locale(s): Spain

Summary: On her deathbed Isabella I of Spain reflects on her magnificent career. She overcomes great obstacles to reach the throne and then, in a remarkable political and personal union with Ferdinand of Aragon, unites their kingdom into the Spanish nation. She begins the great age of exploration by sponsoring Columbus and achieves great victories over the Portuguese and the Moors. The novel offers a unique look at this remarkable monarch.

Historical Accuracy: The author explains that although the book is based on fact, details of the characters were invented within a framework of known fact.

3841 *The Days of the Butterfly*

Date of Publication: 1979
Subject(s): Artistic Life
Fictional character(s): Daisy Holt, Servant, Dancer; Charles Overton, Gentleman; Jack Skelton, Artist
Time Period(s): 19th century
Locale(s): London, England

Summary: Daisy Holt's picaresque career begins when she is dismissed as a nursemaid. However, instead of the life in a brothel that she seems destined for, she becomes a dancer. When she catches the eye of painter Jack Skelton, she experiences romance as well as notoriety. This novel of early 19th-century life dramatizes Daisy's resolve and resourcefulness.

Historical Accuracy: The atmosphere and period details are convincingly presented.

3842 *Eleanor the Queen*

Date of Publication: 1955
Subject(s): Middle Ages; Crusades; Royalty—England
Historical character(s): Eleanor of Aquitaine, Royalty; Louis VII, Ruler (King of France); Henry II, Ruler (King of England); Richard I, Ruler (King of England)
Time Period(s): 12th century (1137-1190)
Locale(s): France; Palestine; England

Summary: The author describes her novel as the story of the most famous woman of the Middle Ages. She is Eleanor of Aquitaine, the queen of both France and England. Her career is chronicled from her unhappy marriage to Louis VII to her marriage to Henry, Duke of Normandy, whom she helps to claim the throne of England as Henry II.

Historical Accuracy: The novel blends an accurate historical background with speculation and imagination.

3843 *The Golden Fleece*

Date of Publication: 1944
Subject(s): Regency Period
Fictional character(s): Will Oakley, Innkeeper; Myrtle Oakley, Young Woman; Harriet Oakley, Young Woman
Time Period(s): 1810s (1817)
Locale(s): England

Summary: The novel describes a single day at an English inn during the Regency period. The landlord of the Golden Fleece, Will Oakley, and his daughter Harriet must contend with a blackmail attempt, while Harriet's sister, Myrtle, must resolve her romantic complications.

Historical Accuracy: The novel features many authentic details of period domestic life.

3844 *The Homecoming*

Date of Publication: 1975
Subject(s): Middle Ages; Crusades
Fictional character(s): Godfrey Tallboys, Knight; Sybilla Tallboys, Spouse; Tana, Young Woman
Time Period(s): 15th century
Locale(s): England

Summary: In the sequel to *Knight's Acre*, Sir Godfrey Tallboys returns from the Crusades to his home at Knight's Acre, bringing with him the young woman who saved his life. Her presence in the family shatters the peace and sends Godfrey off to war again as the houses of Lancaster and York battle for supremacy. The story concludes in *The Lonely Furrow*.

Historical Accuracy: The historical background is genuine and well used in this evocation of the period.

3845 *The House at Old Vine*

Date of Publication: 1961
Subject(s): Tudor Period; Family Saga; Civil War—England
Fictional character(s): Josiana Greenwood, Gentlewoman; Elizabeth Kentwood, Gentlewoman; Barbara Kentwood, Gentlewoman
Time Period(s): 16th century; 17th century (1496-1679)
Locale(s): England

Summary: The novel continues the story of the descendants of Martin Reed begun in *The Town House*. Reed's descendants struggle to hold on to the house at Old Vine, the symbol of their respectability, as they weather the shifts of English history from the 15th to the 17th century.

Historical Accuracy: The novel uses the genuine elements of history as a solid background for its domestic story.

3846 *How Far to Bethlehem?*

Date of Publication: 1965
Subject(s): Biblical Story
Fictional character(s): Melchior, Biblical Figure, Scientist (astronomer); Gaspar, Biblical Figure, Warrior; Balthazar, Biblical Figure, Scholar
Historical character(s): Jesus Christ, Biblical Figure; Mary, Biblical Figure; Joseph, Biblical Figure
Time Period(s): 1st century
Locale(s): Korea; Middle East; Bethlehem, Israel

Summary: The novel retells the Epiphany story of the Magi's journey to the Christ Child. Melchior, an aged astronomer, reads the message of the nativity in the sky and sets out from Korea to Bethlehem. He is joined by the warrior Gaspar and the scholar Balthazar on his fateful trek.

Historical Accuracy: The traditional story is given both a novelistic coloring and an authentic historical grounding.

3847 *The King's Pleasure*

Date of Publication: 1969

Subject(s): Tudor Period; Royalty—England; Biography, Fictionalized
Historical character(s): Catherine of Aragon, Royalty (queen consort of Henry VIII); Henry VIII, Ruler (King of England); Thomas Wolsey, Religious (cardinal)
Time Period(s): 15th century; 16th century (1485-1536)
Locale(s): Spain; England

Summary: This biographical story of Catherine of Aragon details the tormented career of the wife of Henry VIII whose inability to give the king the male heir he requires sets in motion the schism with the church that plunges England into near-civil war. Catherine stands firm against the king, unwilling to accept the divorce that the church would not sanction, and vainly waits for the vindication that does not come until too late.

Historical Accuracy: The novel is a vivid depiction of the period with careful attention to historical details.

3848 *Knight's Acre*

Date of Publication: 1975
Subject(s): Middle Ages; Crusades
Fictional character(s): Godfrey Tallboys, Knight; Sybilla Tallboys, Spouse
Time Period(s): 15th century (1450s)
Locale(s): England; Spain

Summary: Sir Godfrey Tallboys, the premier knight of his age, sees his castle, Knight's Acre, only half-completed before setting off on adventures in Spain, leaving his wife Sybilla to fend for herself. The novel details the adventures of both, one in war and the other in peace, before their reunion six years and many changes later. Their story continues in *The Homecoming*.

Historical Accuracy: The novel captures with real skill the period background of medieval life and times.

3849 *The Lonely Furrow*

Date of Publication: 1976
Subject(s): Tudor Period
Fictional character(s): Henry Tallboys, Landowner
Time Period(s): 15th century
Locale(s): England

Summary: In the third of the trilogy of novels that began with *Knight's Acre* and continued with *The Homecoming*, Sir Godfrey's son, Henry Tallboys, is now master of Knight's Acre. The novel is set at the end of the age of knighthood as Henry embarks on a life as a gentleman farmer and must contend with the political winds of the times.

Historical Accuracy: The novel offers an authentic portrait of ordinary life during the period.

3850 *The Lost Queen*

Date of Publication: 1968
Subject(s): Royalty—England; Royalty—Denmark
Historical character(s): Caroline-Matilda, Royalty (Queen of Denmark); Christian VII, Ruler (King of Denmark and Norway); Johann Frederick Struensee, Doctor, Political Figure
Time Period(s): 1760s; 1770s (1765-1775)

Locale(s): England; Denmark

Summary: Princess Caroline-Matilda is the sister of English King George III. Her marriage to Christian VII, King of Denmark and Norway, brings her unhappiness and disaster. Christian is an absolute monarch whose madness places Caroline-Matilda at the mercy of court intrigue and politics, and her secret love brings her to ruin.

Historical Accuracy: Although based on factual sources, the author admits that gaps in the historical record were filled in with logical speculation to create a coherent story.

3851 *Lovers All Untrue*

Date of Publication: 1970
Subject(s): Victorian Period
Fictional character(s): Marion Draper, Young Woman; Angela Taylor, Young Woman; Ellen Draper, Young Woman
Time Period(s): 19th century (Victorian period)
Locale(s): England

Summary: The novel offers a detailed portrait of a Victorian family whose domineering father stifles his daughters' youthful exuberance and produces conflict, frustratration, and finally, mental breakdown and murder.

Historical Accuracy: The novel's overheated melodrama undermines the book's effectiveness as a convincing portrait of the period.

3852 *The Lute Player*

Date of Publication: 1951
Subject(s): Crusades; Middle Ages; Royalty—England
Fictional character(s): Anna Apieta, Noblewoman
Historical character(s): Richard I, Ruler (King of England); Berengaria of Navarre, Royalty (queen consort of Richard I); Eleanor of Aquitaine, Royalty (queen consort of Henry II); Philip II, Ruler (King of France); Blondel de Nesle, Minstrel (troubadour)
Time Period(s): 12th century
Locale(s): Navarre, Spain; Palestine; Europe (Holy Roman Empire)

Summary: The novel tells the adventurous story of Richard the Lionhearted and the Third Crusade from the perspective of musician Blondel. Through Lady Anna, Duchess of Apieta, Blondel meets the beautiful Berengaria, destined to become Richard's queen. She convinces Blondel to accompany Richard on the crusade, and he provides an eyewitness account of the sacking of Cyprus, the seige of Acre, and the battle of Arsouf. Later he attempts to find the imprisoned Richard by playing his lute at every castle and tower throughout the Holy Roman Empire until acknowledged by the king.

Historical Accuracy: The novel is a blend of the actual, the legendary, and the fictional. The author is an unrepentant advocate of the essential heroism of Richard.

3853 *Madselin*

Date of Publication: 1983
Subject(s): Norman Conquest; Middle Ages
Fictional character(s): Madselin, Widow(er); Rolf, Knight (Norman)

Time Period(s): 11th century (1066)
Locale(s): England

Summary: Saxon versus Norman in the days following William's victory is the novel's theme, Madselin is the young widow of an aging Saxon lord killed in battle. She has lost her land to the Norman knight Rolf, but it is he who is eventually conquered by her nobility and determination.

Historical Accuracy: The period details are authentic.

3854   *Nethergate*

Date of Publication: 1973
Subject(s): Regency Period; French Revolution
Fictional character(s): Isabella de Savigny, Noblewoman, Refugee; Annabelle de Savigny, Young Woman
Time Period(s): 18th century; 19th century (1740-1816)
Locale(s): England

Summary: Isabella de Savigny is an aristocratic French refugee from the Reign of Terror who journeys to England and the old country estate of Nethergate. Her struggles with her daughters in Regency London are detailed in a series of adventures.

Historical Accuracy: Full of period touches, the novel offers a convincing and colorful historical romance.

3855   *The Old Priory*

Date of Publication: 1981
Subject(s): Elizabethan Period
Fictional character(s): Arthur Tresize, Sailor; Lettice Tresize, Young Woman
Time Period(s): 16th century; 17th century
Locale(s): Suffolk, England

Summary: This fanciful story tells the tale of a young sailor, Arthur Tresize, who, in exchange for gold, obliges a recently widowed lady in begetting an heir to ensure the retention of her title. Years later his grandson marries a girl cruelly rejected by a lord who is no other than the son Arthur Tresize sired years before.

Historical Accuracy: The novel's premise is farfetched. The period elements are convincing, however.

3856   *Out of the Dark*

Date of Publication: 1972
Subject(s): Crime and Criminals; Suspense; Victorian Period
Fictional character(s): Charlotte Cornwall, Teacher
Time Period(s): 19th century (Victorian period)
Locale(s): England

Summary: This novel of suspense and psychological drama is set in the 19th century and centers on the events surrounding a young English woman named Charlotte Cornwall. Her life is haunted as a result of an unsolved murder. The past returns in the form of another suspicious death.

Historical Accuracy: Part one of the story is based on an actual crime.

3857   *Pargeters*

Date of Publication: 1984
Subject(s): Civil War—England
Fictional character(s): Adam Woodley, Artisan (plasterer); John Mercer, Gentleman; Penelope Mercer, Young Woman
Time Period(s): 17th century
Locale(s): Minsham, England

Summary: Pargeting is ornamental plaster work, the skilled trade of Adam Woodley that gives its name to John Mercer's new house. When his daughter marries Adam, the two families are united. The novel describes the struggles during the period of the English Civil War in which Puritans fought Royalists.

Historical Accuracy: Rich in period detail, the novel offers an authentic look at the era.

3858   *A Rose for Virtue*

Date of Publication: 1971
Subject(s): Napoleonic Era; Royalty—France; Biography, Fictionalized
Historical character(s): Josephine, Royalty (empress consort of Napoleon); Napoleon Bonaparte, Ruler (Emperor of France); Hortense de Beauharnais, Spouse (of Louis Bonaparte), Royalty (Queen of Holland); Louis Bonaparte, Military Personnel (general), Royalty (King of Holland); Auguste Charles Joseph de Flahaut de la Billarderie, Military Personnel (general), Diplomat
Time Period(s): 18th century; 19th century (1796-1815)
Locale(s): France; Netherlands

Summary: This is the autobiographical account of Hortense, the daughter of Josephine and Napoleon's stepdaughter, who becomes swept up in the titanic power and manipulations of her stepfather. Hortense becomes the unhappy wife of Napoleon's brother, Louis, who is placed on the throne of Holland, and the lover of one of Napoleon's generals. Through the turbulence of the era she remains fiercely loyal to Napoleon and follows his rise and fall.

Historical Accuracy: The novel is an artful blend of the actual and the speculative. The period atmosphere is authentic.

3859   *Scent of Cloves*

Date of Publication: 1957
Subject(s): Civil War—England; Dutch Colonies
Fictional character(s): Julia Ashley, Orphan; Simon Vosmar, Plantation Owner (spice); Charles Youngman, Fugitive, Outlaw
Time Period(s): 17th century (1649-1664)
Locale(s): Amsterdam, Netherlands; Moluccas, Indonesia (Dutch East Indies)

Summary: When her titled family is massacred by Cromwell's troops, Julia Ashley is adopted by a Dutch sea captain and after his death is committed to the bleakness of an Amsterdam orphanage. After marriage by proxy to the son of a wealthy spice planter, Julia sets sail for the Moluccan islands. She falls in love with an exiled English Royalist and becomes an unwilling accomplice in a diabolical scheme devised by her charming, arrogant father-in-law, Simon Vosmar.

Historical Accuracy: The Battle of Naseby, Cromwell's campaign to conquer Ireland, and English-Dutch hostilities are described here. The cultural life of Amsterdam and the Dutch East Indies is also convincingly explored.

3860 *Silver Nutmeg*

Date of Publication: 1947
Subject(s): Business Building; Dutch Colonies; Slavery
Fictional character(s): Evert Haan, Landowner, Trader; Annabet Van Goens, Young Woman; Christy Ayrton, Trader
Time Period(s): 17th century (1650s)
Locale(s): Banda Islands, Indonesia (Dutch East Indies)

Summary: Against the background of the nutmeg trade in 16th-century Dutch East Indies, the novel tells the story of the English attempt to break the trading monopoly of the Dutch and the slave rising of those who use the dispute to try to gain their freedom. Annabet journeys from Holland to become the wife of black-market trader Evert Haan. Her love for the Englishman Christy Ayrton produces the novel's conflict.

Historical Accuracy: Though based on historical details, the author confesses that much of the novel is imaginary.

3861 *The Town House*

Date of Publication: 1959
Subject(s): Middle Ages; Family Saga
Fictional character(s): Martin Reed, Gentleman; Kate Reed, Spouse; Anne Blanchfleur, Gentlewoman
Time Period(s): 15th century
Locale(s): England

Summary: The novel chronicles the rise of a family in 15th century England from serfdom to prosperity. Martin Reed escapes bondage and the dominance of the feudal guilds to gain a fortune and become a man of property. Three generations of his family history are depicted with excellent details of medieval life. The story of his descendants continues in *The House at Old Vine*.

Historical Accuracy: The novel is loaded with convincing atmosphere and period details.

3862 *A Wayside Tavern*

Date of Publication: 1980
Subject(s): Roman Empire; Vikings; Tudor Period
Fictional character(s): Paulus, Veteran (Roman soldier); Cerdic, Religious (monk); Adam Gilderson, Innkeeper
Time Period(s): Multiple Time Periods
Locale(s): Suffolk, England

Summary: The novel traces the history of an establishment in Britain from its origins as a Roman wine shop through its subsequent transformations into an alehouse, coaching inn, hotel, and pub, from the fourth century to the 1970s. The inn, the possession of the Gilderson family, mirrors the history that passes outside its door and the history of its owners.

Historical Accuracy: The pace of the history here is too rapid for a full rendering, but the various eras are reflected with ingenuity.

3863 *Winter Harvest*

Date of Publication: 1955
Subject(s): Wagon Trains; American West; Donner Party
Fictional character(s): Cordy Warren, Settler; Nancy Jurer, Prostitute; Dave Glenny, Settler
Time Period(s): 1840s (1846)
Locale(s): Sierra Nevada Mountains, California

Summary: The story was inspired by the actual experiences of the tragic Donner Party, who in the 1840s were trapped in the Sierra Nevadas and resorted to cannibalism to survive. The novel offers a fictionalized version of the same predicament. A collection of travellers endure the western trek until the mountain blizzards and starvation cause them to degenerate into savagery.

Historical Accuracy: The novel captures life in the wilderness with conviction.

MARK LOGAN
(PSEUD. OF CHRISTOPHER NICOLE, 1930-)

British novelist Christopher Nicole was born in Georgetown, British Guiana (now Guyana). He has also written under the names Leslie Arlen, Robin Cade, Peter Grange, Carline Gray, Simon McKay, C.R. Nicholson, Christina Nicholson, Robin Nicholson, Alison York, and Andrew York. Logan regards himself as an historical novelist who also happens to be a romantic by nature, and he aims to retell history as entertainingly as possible.

3864 *Brumaire*

Date of Publication: 1977
Subject(s): French Revolution; Napoleonic Era
Fictional character(s): Nicholas Minnett, Gentleman; Anna Yealm, Widow(er)
Historical character(s): George Bryan Brummell, Gentleman; Robert Stewart, Nobleman, Political Figure; William Pitt the Younger, Political Figure; George, Royalty (Prince of Wales); Caroline of Brunswick, Royalty (consort of the Prince of Wales); Horatio Nelson, Military Personnel (admiral); Lady Emma Hamilton, Gentlewoman; Napoleon Bonaparte, Ruler (French emperor); Joachim Murat, Military Personnel (French marshal); Charles Maurice de Talleyrand-Perigord, Diplomat, Political Figure
Time Period(s): 1790s
Locale(s): England; France; Egypt

Summary: In the third volume of Nicholas Minnett's adventures during the period of the French Revolution and its aftermath, he is called out of retirement by Napoleon's invasion plans. He finds himself on a hazardous journey that takes him as far as Egypt, where he escapes from Napoleon only to be pursued by a squad of assassins.

Historical Accuracy: The emphasis is on high-speed adventure with a plausible period background and a large cast of actual figures.

3865 *Guillotine*

Date of Publication: 1976

Subject(s): French Revolution; Reign of Terror
Fictional character(s): Nicholas Minnett, Gentleman; Caroline Moncey, Spouse; Anna Yealm, Widow(er)
Historical character(s): George, Royalty (Prince of Wales); Frederick Augustus, Royalty (Duke of York); William Pitt the Younger, Political Figure; Napoleon Bonaparte, Military Personnel; George III, Ruler (King of England); Charlotte of Mecklenburg-Strelitz, Royalty (queen consort of George III); Horatio Nelson, Military Personnel (admiral); Charles James Fox, Political Figure; George Bryan Brummell, Gentleman; Robert Stewart, Nobleman, Political Figure; Joachim Murat, Military Personnel; Charles Maurice de Talleyrand-Perigord, Political Figure, Diplomat
Time Period(s): 1790s (1793)
Locale(s): England; France

Summary: In the second volume of the author's adventure series set during the French Revolution, Nicholas Minnett must travel to France at the height of the Reign of Terror. In Paris he sees the dangerous workings of the guillotine and is divided between his loyalty to his friends and his duty.

Historical Accuracy: The novel is filled with historical figures and a plausible historical background.

3866 *Tricolour*

Date of Publication: 1976
Subject(s): French Revolution; Sea Story
Fictional character(s): Nicholas Minnett, Gentleman
Historical character(s): William Pitt the Younger, Political Figure; George, Royalty (Prince of Wales); Marie Antoinette, Royalty (queen consort of Loius XVI); Charles James Fox, Political Figure; Frederick Augustus, Royalty (Duke of York); Louis XVI, Ruler (King of France); Camille Desmoulins, Political Figure; Maximilien Francois de Robespierre, Political Figure
Time Period(s): 1780s (1789)
Locale(s): England; France

Summary: This is the first of a series of historical adventure novels featuring Nicholas Minnett, an English gentleman and heir to the banking house of Minnett. The time is 1789, and the French Revolution has left England and France in turmoil. Nicholas finds himself at the center of intrigue that pits his skill and resources against the forces of the revolution.

Historical Accuracy: The background events and most of the main characters are factual.

HERBERT LOM (1917-)

Czech-born stage and film actor Lom has appeared in over 80 films, including *The Ladykillers*, *War and Peace*, and as Chief Inspector Dreyfuss in the Pink Panther series. He is the author of *Enter a Spy* about the double life of Christopher Marlowe.

3867 *Dr. Guillotine: The Eccentric Exploits of an Early Scientist*

Date of Publication: 1992
Subject(s): French Revolution; Science

Historical character(s): Joseph Ignace Guillotin, Scientist, Inventor; Jean-Paul Marat, Revolutionary; Charlotte Corday, Revolutionary, Murderer; Louis XVI, Ruler (King of France); Marie Antoinette, Royalty (queen consort of Louis XVI)
Time Period(s): 1780s; 1790s
Locale(s): Paris, France

Summary: Set during the French Revolution, the novel brings together Jean Paul Marat, Charlotte Corday, and the scientist Joseph Guillotin, whose new execution invention begins as a humanitarian device. The three are linked by their desire to improve their world. Instead, they destroy it through fanaticism and extremism.

Historical Accuracy: The novel ingeniously interweaves the factual and the fictional. The period background is geniune even if the story is a conceit.

JEFF LONG

3868 *Empire of Bones: A Novel of Sam Houston and the Texas Revolution*

Date of Publication: 1993
Subject(s): Texas Revolution; Battle of San Jacinto; Battle of the Alamo
Historical character(s): Sam Houston, Military Personnel (army commander); Davy Crockett, Frontiersman; Antonio Lopez de Santa Anna, Military Personnel (general)
Time Period(s): 1830s (1836-1837)
Locale(s): Texas

Summary: This novel of the Texas Revolution begins in the shattering aftermath of the Texans' defeat at the Alamo and centers on the so-called miracle of San Jacinto. The author shows that the battle that quickly supported the legend of the heroic Americans wresting Texas from the despotic Mexican empire was closer to a massacre and a moral turning point for Sam Houston.

Historical Accuracy: The basis for the novel is solid research that includes actual depositions in a slander suit brought by some survivors of San Jacinto.

WILLIAM STUART LONG
(PSEUD. OF VIVIAN STUART, 1914-)

Born in Rangoon, Burma, of American parents, Stuart attended the University of London and the University of Budapest. She is a prolific author of historical novels under a variety of pseudonyms. Her novels in the Australians series each sold a million copies.

3869 *The Adventurers*

Date of Publication: 1983
Subject(s): English Colonies; Frontier—Australia
Fictional character(s): Katie O'Malley, Settler; Rick Tempest, Settler; George De Lancey, Gentleman
Historical character(s): Lachlan Macquarie, Political Figure (governor); John MacArthur, Landowner
Time Period(s): 1820s
Locale(s): Sydney, Australia

Summary: In the fifth volume of the series, The Australians, the final years of Lachlan Macquarie's service as colonial governor are depicted. There is an influx of new settlers who are fleeing a Europe wracked by the Napoleonic Wars. The clash between powerful landowners and the settlers begins to dominate the political landscape.

Historical Accuracy: The period background and historical events are authentic.

3870 *The Colonists*

Date of Publication: 1984
Subject(s): English Colonies
Fictional character(s): Robert Willoughby, Settler; Joseph Van Buren, Settler; Alice Fairweather, Gentlewoman
Historical character(s): Ralph Darling, Political Figure (governor)
Time Period(s): 1820s
Locale(s): Australia

Summary: In the sixth volume of the author's series on the settlement of Australia, the colonial governor, Ralph Darling, struggles to balance the needs of the penal settlement against those of the powerful landowners and speculators. Robert Willoughby and Joseph Van Buren are opposed by Alice Fairweather, who battles for the rights of the original settlers.

Historical Accuracy: The period background is captured with conviction.

3871 *The Empire Builders*

Date of Publication: 1987
Subject(s): English Colonies; Maoris
Fictional character(s): Adam Vincent, Military Personnel; Kitty Broome, Spouse; Johnny Broome, Journalist
Time Period(s): 1860s
Locale(s): New Zealand

Summary: In the ninth volume of the series, The Australians, the scene shifts to the settlement of New Zealand. The exotic and dangerous world of the Maoris presents a considerable challenge.

Historical Accuracy: The depiction of the period New Zealand locale is convincing.

3872 *The Explorers*

Date of Publication: 1982
Subject(s): English Colonies; Frontier—Australia
Fictional character(s): Jessica MacClaine, Servant; Justin Broome, Adventurer; Jenny Hawley, Settler
Historical character(s): William Bligh, Political Figure (colonial governor), Military Personnel (naval officer); George Johnston, Military Personnel (colonel); Lachlan Macquarie, Political Figure (governor)
Time Period(s): 1810s
Locale(s): Australia

Summary: Volume four of the series, The Australians, describes the aftermath of the Rum Rebellion. The colony is now a quarter-century old and the rebels of the New South Wales Corps must be replaced. The community's second

generation comes of age and steps to the foreground of the action, which includes expeditions into the interior.

Historical Accuracy: The novel offers a blend of the fanciful and the historical. The period background is authentically delivered.

3873 *The Gallant*

Date of Publication: 1986
Subject(s): Frontier—Australia; Crimean War; Indian Mutiny
Fictional character(s): Kitty Cadogan, Heiress; Johnny Broome, Journalist; Jenny Broome, Young Woman
Time Period(s): 1850s
Locale(s): Australia; India

Summary: In the eighth volume of the series The Australians, trouble at home for the Broome family coincides with service on behalf of the Empire. There are scenes in Crimea and India, as well as in Tasmania, as pioneers push deeper into the unexplored outback.

Historical Accuracy: The adventures of the real-life characters are based in fact and exaggerated only occasionally.

3874 *The Gold Seekers*

Date of Publication: 1985
Subject(s): Victorian Period; Frontier—Australia
Fictional character(s): Luke Murphy, Adventurer; Mercy Bancroft, Young Woman; Elizabeth Tempest, Young Woman
Time Period(s): 1850s
Locale(s): Australia

Summary: In the seventh volume of the The Australians series, gold is discovered in Victoria and New South Wales. The story continues the history of the Broomses and Tempests and details the assorted villainies and betrayals prompted by the hunger for gold.

Historical Accuracy: The novel superimposes fictional characters and circumstances on actual events that are accurately presented.

3875 *The Imperialists*

Date of Publication: 1990
Subject(s): Frontier—Australia
Fictional character(s): Tolo Mason, Prospector; Java Gordon Mason, Spouse; Matthew Van Buren, Military Personnel (officer)
Time Period(s): 1900s
Locale(s): Australia; Papua New Guinea

Summary: In the 12th volume of The Australians, Tolo Mason explores the outback searching for gold, and the Broome family turns its attention to primitive New Guinea and a new field of opportunity.

Historical Accuracy: The period is captured with authenticity.

3876 *The Nationalists*

Date of Publication: 1989
Subject(s): Boer War

Fictional character(s): Rachel Java Gordon, Gentlewoman; Slone Shannon, Military Personnel (officer); Sianna De Hartog, Nurse
Time Period(s): 1890s; 1900s
Locale(s): Australia; South Africa; Sudan

Summary: In the 11th volume of the series The Australians, the push for independence and statehood dominates. The scene shifts from Australia to events in Africa: the war in the Sudan and the fight against the Boers.

Historical Accuracy: The novel is an artful blend of the fictional and the factual. The historical background is convincing.

3877 *The Seafarers*

Date of Publication: 1988
Subject(s): Sea Story; Clipper Ships; Disasters—Natural
Fictional character(s): Johnny Broome, Journalist; Kitty Broome, Spouse
Time Period(s): 1870s; 1880s
Locale(s): Australia

Summary: The Broomes, in the tenth volume of The Australians, are shown amidst their expanding shipping business that plies the South Pacific. The famous clipper ship *Cutty Sark* and the aftermath of the explosion of Krakatoa are depicted.

Historical Accuracy: *The Cutty Sark* scenes are imagined or rearranged to fit the fictional chronology.

3878 *The Settlers*

Date of Publication: 1980
Subject(s): English Colonies; Frontier—Australia; Penal Colonies
Fictional character(s): Jenny Taggart, Settler, Farmer; Frances O'Riordan Spence, Settler; Andrew Hawley, Military Personnel
Historical character(s): John MacArthur, Landowner; William Bligh, Political Figure, Military Personnel (naval officer)
Time Period(s): 1790s; 1800s
Locale(s): Australia

Summary: In the second volume of the author's series The Australians, tough times await the earliest settlers, who struggle to balance conflicting motives of the early penal colony. The story features a prominent role for William Bligh, the infamous captain of the *Bounty*.

Historical Accuracy: The novel blends the fictional and the historic, using actual characters and events to tell a dramatic story against a factual background.

3879 *The Traitors*

Date of Publication: 1981
Subject(s): English Colonies; Frontier—Australia; Rum Rebellion
Fictional character(s): Abigail Tempest, Heiress; Jenny Broome, Settler; Andrew Hawley, Political Figure
Historical character(s): William Bligh, Political Figure (colonial governor), Military Personnel (naval officer); John MacArthur, Landowner

Time Period(s): 1800s
Locale(s): Sydney, Australia

Summary: In volume three of the author's Australian series, the background is the Australian Rum Rebellion. The infamous William Bligh struggles to end the rum traffic engaged in by officers of the notorious New South Wales Corps, called the Rum Corps. The second generation of settlers is shown creating the thriving community of Sydney.

Historical Accuracy: The novel blends the fictional with the factual. The real characters and events are mostly historically accurate.

M.B. LONGMAN

3880 *The Power of Black*

Date of Publication: 1961
Subject(s): Family Saga; Oil Industry; Business Building
Fictional character(s): Homer Ashe, Landowner; Jay-Wade Ashe, Artist
Time Period(s): 19th century; 20th century
Locale(s): Texas; South Carolina

Summary: The novel chronicles three generations of a southern family who lose everything in the Civil War. They make a new fortune in the Texas oil fields, only to lose it all again in the Depression.

Historical Accuracy: The novel's depiction of the oil industry is authentic and believable.

STEPHEN LONGSTREET (1907-)

Born in New York City, Longstreet attended Rutgers and Harvard Universities and graduated from the New York School of Fine and Applied Art. Longstreet studied painting in Paris, Rome, and Berlin. He is a painter, writer, art critic, and lecturer on art. He is also the screenwriter of such films as *The Imposter*, *The Jolson Story*, *Duel in the Sun*.

3881 *All or Nothing*

Date of Publication: 1983
Subject(s): Immigrants; Family Saga; Earthquakes
Fictional character(s): George Fiore, Immigrant, Businessman; Tomas Velasquez, Heir
Time Period(s): 1890s; 1900s
Locale(s): San Francisco, California

Summary: This family saga begins with the arrival in San Francisco of Italian immigrant Gregorio Fiore who is able to found a banking dynasty. His rise to power follows the history of San Francisco from the turn of the century to the earthquake in 1906.

Historical Accuracy: Many of the incidents and events are based on historical fact, and the novel captures the history of San Francisco with skill.

3882 *The Bank*

Date of Publication: 1976
Subject(s): Business Building; Civil War—U.S.

Fictional character(s): Tyler Starkweather, Financier, Heir; Margo Crivelli, Artist; Howard Harrison Starkweather, Financier
Historical character(s): Ulysses S. Grant, Political Figure; Daniel Drew, Financier (railroad); William Marcy Tweed, Political Figure; John D. Rockefeller, Financier; Franklin Delano Roosevelt, Political Figure; Joseph P. Kennedy, Diplomat; Cornelius Vanderbilt, Financier; James Fisk, Financier; John Pierpont Morgan, Financier; Jay Gould, Financier
Time Period(s): 19th century; 20th century (1860s-1930s)
Locale(s): United States

Summary: The rise of a great American banking family, the Starkweathers, is dramatized, from the founding patriarch Howard Starkweather's gunrunning during the Civil War to his plot with the Goulds, Fisks, and Morgans to corner the gold market. His heir, Tyler, carries the story into the 20th century with scenes of the famous Wall Street bombing of 1912 and the Crash of 1929.

Historical Accuracy: The story weaves the fictional with the factual. The background is solidly based on fact.

3883 *The Burning Man*
Date of Publication: 1958
Subject(s): Artistic Life; Biography, Fictionalized; World War I
Fictional character(s): Julio Diaz Navarro, Artist
Historical character(s): Guillaume Apollinaire, Writer; Gertrude Stein, Writer; Henri Matisse, Artist
Time Period(s): 19th century; 20th century
Locale(s): Spain; Paris, France

Summary: After great hardships, Julio Diaz Navarro, a poverty-stricken young Spaniard, becomes one of the world's most controversial painters. The character of Navarro is based on Pablo Picasso.

Historical Accuracy: Although the novel observes the basic outline of Picasso's life, much is invented and often slips to the level of the cliched.

3884 *The Dream Seekers*
Date of Publication: 1979
Subject(s): Immigrants; Jews; Business Building
Fictional character(s): Alex Silverthorn, Immigrant, Businessman; Aaron Bendelbinder, Immigrant
Time Period(s): 19th century; 20th century (1880s-1920s)
Locale(s): Boston, Massachusetts; New York, New York; Russia

Summary: The story of two Jewish immigrant families, the Silverthorns and the Bendelbinders, is depicted from the 1880s, when one family settles in New York and the other in Boston, to the 1920s. The novel depicts their determination to achieve the American dream and their climb to positions of power and influence.

Historical Accuracy: The images and details of period life are authentically drawn.

3885 *Eagles Where I Walk*
Date of Publication: 1961

Subject(s): American Revolution; Medical Profession
Fictional character(s): David Cortlandt, Doctor, Military Personnel (officer); Roxanne Cortlandt, Spouse
Historical character(s): George Washington, Military Personnel (army commander); Henry Clinton, Military Personnel (British general); John Andre, Military Personnel (British officer), Spy; Benedict Arnold, Military Personnel (officer); Alexander Hamilton, Military Personnel (officer), Political Figure
Time Period(s): 1770s; 1780s (1774-1780)
Locale(s): New York; London, England

Summary: The second volume of a trilogy that begins chronologically with *War in the Golden Weather* is set during the American Revolution and depicts the experiences of a young surgeon in Washington's army during the New York campaign. The scenes include the actions of Benedict Arnold and the capture and execution of British secret agent John Andre. The trilogy concludes with *A Few Painted Feathers*.

Historical Accuracy: The novel mingles the factual and the imagined.

3886 *A Few Painted Feathers*
Date of Publication: 1963
Subject(s): American Revolution; Battle of Yorktown; Medical Profession
Fictional character(s): David Cortlandt, Doctor, Military Personnel (officer); Roxanne Cortlandt, Spouse; Toby Bowman, Spy
Historical character(s): George Washington, Military Personnel (army commander); Alexander Hamilton, Military Personnel (officer); Marie Joseph Paul de Lafayette, Nobleman (Marquis de Lafayette), Political Figure (general); Charles Cornwallis, Military Personnel (British general); Peter Blue Feather, Indian (Oneida), Spy; Horatio Gates, Military Personnel (general); Nathanael Greene, Military Personnel (general); Francis Marion, Military Personnel (officer); Daniel Morgan, Military Personnel (general)
Time Period(s): 1780s
Locale(s): Virginia; Charleston, South Carolina

Summary: The concluding volume of the trilogy that begins with *War in the Golden Weather* and *Eagles Where I Walk* depicts the military actions of the American Revolution through the Battle of Yorktown and Washington's resignation from the army. The story centers on David Cortlandt, Surgeon-General of the Continental armies in the South, and his wife.

Historical Accuracy: The historical background is genuine, and the depiction of a large cast of actual figures is credible.

3887 *Gettysburg*
Date of Publication: 1961
Subject(s): Civil War—U.S.; Battle of Gettysburg
Fictional character(s): Tjaden Hedrick, Military Personnel (Union officer); Alice Gross, Young Woman; Texas Chile, Military Personnel (Confederate soldier)
Historical character(s): Robert E. Lee, Military Personnel (Confederate army commander); James Longstreet, Military

Personnel (Confederate general); James Ewell Brown Stuart, Military Personnel (Confederate cavalry commander)
Time Period(s): 1860s (1863)
Locale(s): Gettysburg, Pennsylvania

Summary: The author takes up the subject of the Battle of Gettysburg that he previously treated in *Three Days* with a similar focus on the daily life of the townspeople of Gettysburg as the battle sweeps over them. The novel expands the author's previous treatment, developing both the events of the battle and the fictional lives of soldiers and non-combatants.

Historical Accuracy: The actual events are carefully and realistically drawn.

STEPHEN LONGSTREET (1907-)

ETHEL LONGSTREET

Born in New York City, Stephen Longstreet attended Rutgers and Harvard Univ ersities and graduated from the New York School of Fine and Applied Art. He is a painter, writer, art critic, screenwriter, and lecturer on art. A music gra duate of New York University, Ethel Longstreet conducted the popular T.V. progr am "Cavalcade of Records" and a lecture series, "Viewpoints.".

3888   *Man of Montmartre: A Novel Based on the Life of Maurice Utrillo*

Date of Publication: 1958
Subject(s): Artistic Life; Biography, Fictionalized
Historical character(s): Maurice Utrillo, Artist; Suzanne Valadon, Artist; Henri de Toulouse-Lautrec, Artist
Time Period(s): 19th century; 20th century (1883-1930s)
Locale(s): Paris, France

Summary: This fictional biography of the French painter Utrillo tells the extraordinary story of Utrillo's mother who by the time she was 18 had been a beggar, a circus performer, an artist's model, and finally a painter whom Degas pronounced "one of us." Maurice Utrillo is raised in the bohemian shadow of his mother. An alcoholic by the time he is 11, he turns to painting to release a number of demons not dulled by drugs and alcohol. The novel vividly captures Utrillo's life and times.

Historical Accuracy: Based on evident research and scholarship, the novel fills in gaps with surmise and speculation.

STEPHEN LONGSTREET (1907-)

Born in New York City, Longstreet attended Rutgers and Harvard Universities and graduated from the New York School of Fine and Applied Art. Longstreet studied painting in Paris, Rome, and Berlin. He is a painter, writer, art critic, and lecturer on art. He is also the screenwriter of such films as *The Imposter*, *The Jolson Story*, *Duel in the Sun*.

3889   *Masts to Spear the Stars*

Date of Publication: 1967
Subject(s): Sea Story; Shipbuilding; Clipper Ships
Fictional character(s): Ira Barraclough, Sailor
Time Period(s): 1840s (1843)
Locale(s): Nantucket, Massachusetts; *Flying Star*, At Sea; Canton, China

Summary: In the age of the clipper ships, young sailor Ira Barraclough keeps a journal of a trip in 1843 from Cape Cod to Canton. The novel captures the adventure and dangers of life at sea and the atmosphere of the China Run.

Historical Accuracy: The nautical details and period background are convincing.

3890   *Our Father's House*

Date of Publication: 1985
Subject(s): Family Saga; Motion Picture Industry; Business Building
Fictional character(s): George Fiore, Businessman
Time Period(s): 1920s
Locale(s): San Francisco, California; Los Angeles, California; New York, New York

Summary: In the sequel to *All or Nothing*, the story of George Fiore's financial empire is captured during the 1920s as it expands to include the motion picture industry in Hollywood, the oil industry in Texas, and speculation on Wall Street.

Historical Accuracy: The novel provides a convincing atmosphere of the times.

3891   *Three Days*

Date of Publication: 1947
Subject(s): Civil War—U.S.; Battle of Gettysburg
Fictional character(s): Linda King, Farmer; Lady, Military Personnel (rebel soldier)
Historical character(s): Robert E. Lee, Military Personnel (Confederate commander); George Meade, Military Personnel (Union commander)
Time Period(s): 1860s (1863)
Locale(s): Gettysburg, Pennsylvania

Summary: This unusual treatment of the climactic Civil War Battle of Gettysburg does not concern strategy or a comprehensive accounting of the military action. Rather it offers a series of impressions, the rippling reverberations from the battlefield, that sweep up soldier and citizen alike.

Historical Accuracy: The background action is authentically depicted.

3892   *War in the Golden Weather*

Date of Publication: 1965
Subject(s): French and Indian War; Indians; American Colonies
Fictional character(s): Will Cortlandt, Artist (painter), Military Personnel (soldier)
Historical character(s): George Washington, Military Personnel (major), Surveyor; Edward Braddock, Military Personnel (general)

Time Period(s): 1750s

Locale(s): Virginia, American Colonies; Northwest Territory, United States; New York, American Colonies

Summary: The first volume of a trilogy, the novel is set during the French and Indian War and involves a young painter who meets young army officer and surveyor George Washington and reluctantly takes up soldiering against the French and their Indian allies. The blunders of General Braddock, who insists that his men fight in strict military formation, are depicted. The trilogy continues with *Eagles Where I Walk* and *A Few Painted Feathers*.

Historical Accuracy: The period background is authentic.

3893 *The Young Men of Paris*

Date of Publication: 1967

Subject(s): Artistic Life; World War I; Biography, Fictionalized

Historical character(s): Amedeo Modigliani, Artist; Pablo Picasso, Artist; Henri Matisse, Artist; Marc Chagall, Artist; Maurice Utrillo, Artist; Guillaume Apollinaire, Writer (poet)

Time Period(s): 1900s; 1910s

Locale(s): Paris, France

Summary: This biographical novel about the artist Modigliani captures the atmosphere of bohemian Paris in the artistically vital years preceding World War I. Modigliani dedicates his life to art but indulges in every kind of excess during his brief, intense career.

Historical Accuracy: The novel's atmosphere of pre-World War I Paris and its artistic ferment is convincing.

NOEL M. LOOMIS (1905-1969)

American author and educator Loomis was born in Wakita, Oklahoma, and attended Clarendon College and the University of Oklahoma. His published works include 50 books and 400 short stories in the Western, science fiction, and mystery fields. Several of his books have been made into movies and television programs. He is the author of *Short Cut to Silver River*, a Western Writers of America and Silver Spur Award winner for best Western novel, *Bonanza*, and *Have Gun, Will Travel*.

3894 *The Twilighters*

Date of Publication: 1955

Subject(s): Settlement of the American Frontier; Crime and Criminals

Fictional character(s): Max Foley, Landowner

Time Period(s): 1800s

Locale(s): Kentucky; Natchez Trace, Mississippi

Summary: This story of banditry along the notorious Natchez Trace describes the experiences of Max Foley whose arrogance forces him to immigrate from Kentucky to Texas. On the way, his caravan encounters the bandits controlled by the notorious Mason and Harpe.

Historical Accuracy: The novel provides some authentic period element in capturing the era.

STANLEY LOOMIS (1922-1972)

Born in New York City, Loomis graduated from Columbia University and was a biographer, historian, and novelist.

3895 *The Fatal Friendship: Marie Antoinette, Count Fersen and the Flight to Varennes*

Date of Publication: 1972

Subject(s): Royalty—France; French Revolution

Historical character(s): Marie Antoinette, Royalty (queen consort of Louis XVI); Hans Axel von Fersen, Nobleman (count); Louis XVI, Ruler (King of France)

Time Period(s): 18th century (1774-1793)

Locale(s): France

Summary: In 1774 Marie Antoinette meets a young Swedish nobleman, Count Axel Fersen. This novel is the story of their friendship, as Marie Antoinette becomes the queen of France and Louis XVI is toppled in the French Revolution. Loomis provides answers to a variety of questions that have surrounded the affair: Were the queen and Fersen lovers? Did Louis know of the affair? And what was Fersen's part in the famous royal flight to Varennes?.

Historical Accuracy: More historical study than novel, the work does imagine invented conversations.

JOSE LOPEZ PORTILLO Y PACHECO
(1920-)

Born in Mexico City, Lopez Portillo received a degree and practiced law until 1960, when he entered public service. He served in a variety of appointed positions until 1976, when he became president of Mexico. He served until 1982. During Lopez Portillo's presidency, Mexico emerged as a major oil power.

3896 *They Are Coming: The Conquest of Mexico*

Date of Publication: 1987

Subject(s): Aztec Empire; Exploration; Spanish Colonies

Historical character(s): Hernando Cortez, Explorer, Military Personnel (conquistador); Montezuma II, Ruler (Aztec emperor)

Time Period(s): 16th century (1510s)

Locale(s): Mexico

Summary: The conquest of Mexico by Spanish conquistadors is dramatized through the juxtaposition of the perspectives of Montezuma, last emperor of the Aztecs, and Spanish leader Hernando Cortez. The novel depicts how 425 men and 16 horses defeated 30,000 Aztecs and conquered Mexico. The sympathies are clearly with the Indians in this version of the fall of the Aztec empire.

Historical Accuracy: The novel is solidly backed by evidence to support its truthfulness.

BETTE BAO LORD (1938-)

Born in Shanghai, Lord came to the U.S. in 1946 when her father, an officer of the Chinese government, was assigned here. She graduated from the Fletcher School of Law and Diplomacy. Lord returned to China in 1973 accompanied by her husband, Winston Lord, principal adviser to Henry Kissinger. She is the author of the acclaimed children's book *In the Year of the Boar and Jackie Robinson*. Her nonfiction book *Legacies* is an oral history of Chinese life based on dozens of taped interviews.

3897 *Spring Moon: A Novel of China*

Date of Publication: 1981
Subject(s): Chinese Empire; Chinese Revolution; Family Saga
Fictional character(s): Spring Moon, Young Woman; Bold Talent, Scholar, Writer (poet); Noble Talent, Military Personnel (soldier)
Time Period(s): 19th century; 20th century (1892-1970s)
Locale(s): Soochow, China; Peking, China

Summary: Traditional life in China undergoing the cataclysm of revolution is the novel's theme. It traces the experiences of the House of Chang from 1892 to the 1970s. At the center of the novel is Spring Moon, whose experiences frame a reflection of human life caught in the vortex of historical change.

Historical Accuracy: The novel is very convincing in its depiction of Chinese life and customs and the effects the historical events created.

ERNST LOTHAR

3898 *The Angel with the Trumpet*

Date of Publication: 1944
Subject(s): Family Saga; Social Chronicle
Fictional character(s): Hans Alt, Artisan (piano maker)
Time Period(s): 19th century; 20th century (1889-1938)
Locale(s): Vienna, Austria

Summary: The story of Austria from 1889, when the crown prince died, to 1938, when Austria was absorbed into the German Reich, is told through the experiences of the Alt family. A respectable family of piano makers, they become a personification of Austria's noble spirit of art and culture.

Historical Accuracy: The novel is based on fact, faithfully dramatizing the social history and pressures of the time.

MILTON LOTT (1919-)

Born in Idaho, Lott graduated from the University of California, Berkeley. He has worked as a welder in a West Coast shipyard and as a millwright. He is interested in portraying man in his novels as an animal, the equal, not the superior, of other animals on the planet. *The Last Hunt* was made into a film.

3899 *Dance Back the Buffalo*

Date of Publication: 1959

Subject(s): American West; Indians; Battle of Wounded Knee
Fictional character(s): Turning Hawk, Indian (Sioux), Warrior; Crazy Walking, Indian (Sioux), Young Man; Little Wound, Handicapped (blind and deaf), Indian (Sioux)
Time Period(s): 1880s; 1890s (1889-1890s)
Locale(s): South Dakota

Summary: This tale of the final chapter in the story of the Sioux Indians recounts the years of the Ghost Dance which the Indians hoped would bring back the past but prompted only a violent reaction from the whites. The clash is powerfully portrayed in the experiences of several Indian witnesses to the events that include the massacre at Pine Ridge.

Historical Accuracy: The novel is precise and authentic in its presentation of Indian customs and the historical events.

3900 *The Last Hunt*

Date of Publication: 1954
Subject(s): American West; Indians
Fictional character(s): Sandy MacKensie, Hunter (buffalo); Charley Gilson, Hunter (buffalo); Woodfoot, Cowboy
Time Period(s): 1880s (1882)
Locale(s): Great Plains

Summary: The novel depicts a small group of buffalo hunters at the end of the time of the great buffalo herds on the Great Plains. For Sandy MacKensie the slaughter of the buffalo is a business, a means to a more settled life as a homesteader. For Charley Gilson killing buffalo provides a form of emotional release. Their lives mirror the frontier experience.

Historical Accuracy: The novel effectively captures life on the Great Plains in the 1880s.

EILEEN LOTTMAN (1927-)

Born in Minnesota, Lottman attended school in Iowa and has worked as a press agent in the movie business, a publicity director, and a book editor and columnist for *The Village Voice*.

3901 *The Brahmins*

Date of Publication: 1982
Subject(s): Family Saga; American Revolution
Fictional character(s): Emily Stafford, Immigrant; Sarah Stafford, Patriot; Kate Stafford, Gentlewoman
Time Period(s): Multiple Time Periods
Locale(s): Boston, Massachusetts

Summary: Covering nearly three hundred years of American history, the novel chronicles the history of the Stafford family starting with Emily Stafford, who journeys to Boston in the 17th century. Her daughter, Sarah, risks all in support of the patriots' cause in the revolution. The family rises in stature to become one of the great Boston Brahmin families, a powerful legacy for succeeding generations.

Historical Accuracy: The novel covers far too much historical ground to be thorough; however, the events depicted are plausible.

MAUDE HART LOVELACE (1892-1980)

American writer Lovelace is best known for her Betsy-Tacy series of books for children. Lovelace relied on the personal journals of her own childhood to write her books.

3902 *The Black Angels*

Date of Publication: 1926
Subject(s): Theatrical Life
Fictional character(s): Roger Angel, Entertainer
Time Period(s): 19th century
Locale(s): Minnesota

Summary: Set during the pioneer days in the Minnesota territory, the novel chronicles the experiences of two generations of the Angel family who become travelling entertainers. Inspired by Jenny Lind's tour of America, the family, led by Roger Angel, tours the Middle West.

Historical Accuracy: The novel's period elements are convincing, as is its portrayal of the growth of concert entertainment in America.

3903 *Charming Sally*

Date of Publication: 1932
Subject(s): American Colonies; Theatrical Life; Quakers
Fictional character(s): Joel Ridgeway, Young Man; Meg Palmer, Actress
Time Period(s): 1750s (1752)
Locale(s): Virginia, American Colonies; Philadelphia, Pennsylvania, American Colonies

Summary: The novel dramatizes the adventures that befall one of the first theatrical companies to tour the American Colonies in the 1750s. Joel Ridgeway, a young Quaker, falls in with the troupe and, despite his Quaker upbringing, falls in love with one of the players, Meg Palmer.

Historical Accuracy: The novel captures the spirit of the time, if not the letter of the chronology.

3904 *Early Candlelight*

Date of Publication: 1929
Subject(s): Settlement of the American Frontier
Fictional character(s): Delia DuGay, Young Woman; Jasper Page, Trader (fur)
Time Period(s): 1830s
Locale(s): Fort Snelling, Minnesota (modern St. Paul)

Summary: This romantic adventure story involves Delia DuGay, the daughter of a French voyageur, who falls in love with fur-trader Jasper Page. The novel offers a look at the settlement that becomes St. Paul and frontier life in Minnesota.

Historical Accuracy: The novel achieves a high degree of believability in its recreation of the period and the region.

3905 *Gentlemen From England*

Date of Publication: 1937
Subject(s): Settlement of the American Frontier; Farming
Fictional character(s): Richard Chalmers, Settler

Time Period(s): 1860s; 1870s
Locale(s): Minnesota

Summary: The novel recounts the experiences of a group of English gentry who settle in Minnesota determined to make their fortune by bean farming. They must contend with a number of challenges.

Historical Accuracy: The novel features a believable historical background.

PETER LOVESEY (1936-)

Lovesey is an English mystery novelist who headed the education department at Hammersmith College until 1971 when he turned to writing full time. His specialty is period mysteries, largely set in the Victorian era.

3906 *Abracadaver*

Date of Publication: 1972
Subject(s): Mystery; Victorian Period; Theatrical Life
Fictional character(s): Sergeant Cribb, Police Officer; Edward Thackeray, Police Officer (constable)
Time Period(s): 1880s
Locale(s): London, England

Summary: Having set his first two Sergeant Cribb mysteries in the Victorian sporting world (*Wobble to Death* and *The Detective Wore Silk Drawers*), the author locates this mystery in a Victorian music hall where embarrassing practical jokes turn deadly. Cribb and Thackeray are on the case.

Historical Accuracy: The novel, like the series, excells in reproducing period atmosphere and details.

3907 *Bertie and the Crime of Passion*

Date of Publication: 1993
Subject(s): Mystery; Victorian Period; Royalty—England
Historical character(s): Edward, Prince of Wales, Royalty; Sarah Bernhardt, Actress; Henri de Toulouse-Lautrec, Artist
Time Period(s): 1890s (1891)
Locale(s): Paris, France

Summary: The Prince of Wales is in Paris to enjoy its shockingly non-Victorian pleasures when he takes up the investigation of a murder at the Moulin Rouge. His assistant is none other than Sarah Bernhardt and the crime-scene sketch artist is Toulouse-Lautrec. Bertie's investigation takes him inside Paris' demimonde and a determination that the French police have the wrong man in custody.

Historical Accuracy: Utterly fanciful, the novel is nonetheless anchored by authentic period details.

3908 *Bertie and the Seven Bodies*

Date of Publication: 1990
Subject(s): Mystery; Victorian Period; Royalty—England
Fictional character(s): Amelia Drummond, Gentlewoman, Widow(er); Queenie Chimes, Actress
Historical character(s): Edward, Prince of Wales, Royalty (later Edward VII); Alexandra of Denmark, Royalty (wife of the Prince of Wales)
Time Period(s): 1890s (1890)

Locale(s): Buckinghamshire, England

Summary: A killer is on the loose at a shooting party whose guests include the Prince of Wales. When an actress dies during the first night dinner party, a newspaper clipping with the single word "Monday" is the only clue. Edward takes up the investigation to decipher the killer's diabolic plan.

Historical Accuracy: The mystery's detective is certainly non-historical, but the depiction of the era and the mores is authentic.

3909 *Bertie and the Tinman*

Date of Publication: 1987
Subject(s): Mystery; Victorian Period; Royalty—England
Historical character(s): Edward, Prince of Wales, Royalty (later Edward VII); Victoria, Ruler (Queen of England); Charles Warren, Police Officer (commissioner); Joseph Edgar Boehm, Artist (sculptor); George Alexander Baird, Gambler, Gentleman; Christopher Sykes, Gentleman, Companion (to the Prince of Wales); Caroline Agnes Graham, Noblewoman (Duchess of Montrose), Widow(er)
Time Period(s): 1880s (1886)
Locale(s): England

Summary: England's greatest jockey, the Tinman, shoots himself, apparently deranged from typhoid fever. Edward, Prince of Wales, has his doubts and begins an investigation which leads him across the country.

Historical Accuracy: That the Prince of Wales could have functioned at all like this fictional version is the greatest inaccuracy here. Otherwise, the novel offers a masterful reconstruction of 19th-century England.

3910 *A Case of Spirits*

Date of Publication: 1980
Subject(s): Mystery; Victorian Period; Spiritualism
Fictional character(s): Sergeant Cribb, Police Officer; Edward Thackeray, Police Officer (constable)
Time Period(s): 1880s (1885)
Locale(s): London, England

Summary: At a fashionable London address, a medium is electrocuted during a seance. Sergeant Cribb and Constable Thackeray take the case and are plunged into the Victorian world of spiritualists and charlatans.

Historical Accuracy: The novel is remarkable for its ability to recreate the period.

3911 *The Detective Wore Silk Drawers*

Date of Publication: 1971
Subject(s): Mystery; Victorian Period; Sports
Fictional character(s): Sergeant Cribb, Police Officer; Edward Thackeray, Police Officer (constable); Henry Jago, Police Officer (constable), Sports Figure (boxer)
Time Period(s): 1880s (1880)
Locale(s): London, England

Summary: In the violent and illegal underground world of bare-fisted boxing matches, losers of fights are being disposed of by decapitation. Sergeant Cribb enlists the services of

Constable Jago, the police boxing champion, to penetrate the shady boxing circle.

Historical Accuracy: The novel offers a convincing reconstruction of the Victorian sporting world.

3912 *The False Inspector Dew*

Date of Publication: 1982
Subject(s): Mystery; Identity—Concealed; Ocean Liners
Fictional character(s): Walter Baranov, Dentist, Imposter (posing as Inspector Dew); Alma Webster, Gentlewoman
Time Period(s): 1920s (1921)
Locale(s): London, England; *Mauretania*, At Sea

Summary: It was supposed to be the perfect crime. In order to be with his lover, Alma Webster, Walter Baranov plots to kill his wife while they are sailing to America. After the murder, Alma poses as the wife while Baranov impersonates the famous Chief Inspector Dew, the man who solved the notorious Crippen murder case. When Mrs. Baranov's corpse is discovered, the ship's captain asks Baranov, as Inspector Dew, to look into the matter. The plot takes on a comic and surprising turn as Baranov must investigate his own crime.

Historical Accuracy: This black comedy is well detailed in its period elements.

3913 *Keystone*

Date of Publication: 1983
Subject(s): Mystery; Motion Picture Industry
Fictional character(s): Warwick Easton, Actor, Detective—Amateur
Historical character(s): Mack Sennett, Director; Roscoe "Fatty" Arbuckle, Actor; Mabel Normand, Actress
Time Period(s): 1920s
Locale(s): Los Angeles, California; Hollywood, California

Summary: Vaudevillian Warwick Easton lands a job as one of Mack Sennett's Keystone Cops—stunts and chases and five dollars a day. When murder occurs, the Keystone Cop finds himself both the principal detective on the case and the prime suspect. The investigation takes Easton through Hollywood and involves some of the silver screen's most important stars.

Historical Accuracy: Lovesey's ingenuity of plot is matched by his ability to recreate the period details and atmosphere.

3914 *Mad Hatter's Holiday*

Date of Publication: 1973
Subject(s): Mystery; Victorian Period
Fictional character(s): Albert Moscrop, Gentleman; Sergeant Cribb, Police Officer; Edward Thackeray, Police Officer (constable)
Time Period(s): 1880s (1882)
Locale(s): Brighton, England

Summary: Albert Moscrop, on holiday in Brighton, spends his time observing the seaside scene. His attention is drawn to the Prothero family. When a sensational murder occurs, Sergeant Cribb and Constable Thackeray arrive to investigate a baffling and macabre crime.

Historical Accuracy: The book offers an authentic depiction of Brighton in the 1880s.

3915 *Swing, Swing Together*

Date of Publication: 1976
Subject(s): Mystery; Victorian Period
Fictional character(s): Sergeant Cribb, Police Officer; Edward Thackeray, Police Officer (constable); Harriet Shaw, Student
Time Period(s): 1880s (1889)
Locale(s): Henley, England

Summary: Harriet Shaw defies school rules at Elfrida College for the Training of Female Elementary Teachers and goes skinny dipping. She is embarrassed to find that she has been observed, and at the same time becomes an important witness to murder. Cribb and Thackeray are called in to investigate three men in a boat and what Harriet saw.

Historical Accuracy: The novel is well-grounded and convincing in its period details.

3916 *The Tick of Death*

Date of Publication: 1974
Subject(s): Mystery; Victorian Period; Independence—Ireland
Fictional character(s): Sergeant Cribb, Police Officer; Edward Thackeray, Police Officer (constable); Rossanna McGee, Terrorist (Irish)
Time Period(s): 1880s (1884)
Locale(s): London, England

Summary: Irish terrorists are conducting a bombing campaign in London. Sergeant Cribb finds himself abducted at gun point and an unwilling member of the terrorist group that includes Rossanna McGee and the group's mysterious leader whose features are always concealed by a black hood. Cribb must act fast before the group's royal targets and Constable Thackeray are harmed.

Historical Accuracy: The Irish bombing campaign is historical. The novel, like the series, is authentic in its reconstruction of the period.

3917 *Waxwork*

Date of Publication: 1978
Subject(s): Mystery; Victorian Period
Fictional character(s): Miriam Cromer, Murderer (convicted); Sergeant Cribb, Police Officer; Edward Thackeray, Police Officer (constable)
Time Period(s): 1880s (1888)
Locale(s): London, England

Summary: As her execution draws near, something is not right with convicted murderer Miriam Cromer. Madame Tussaud's wants her image for its waxwork gallery of notorious felons, but she doesn't look the part, appearing composed and unafraid. A photograph arrives at the Home Office that casts doubt on her guilt, and Cribb is expected to explain away the awkward evidence. What he discovers raises questions about the official explanation of what happened and why.

Historical Accuracy: The novel is marked by a careful and realistic depiction of the period.

3918 *Wobble to Death*

Date of Publication: 1970
Subject(s): Mystery; Victorian Period; Sports
Fictional character(s): Sergeant Cribb, Police Officer; Edward Thackeray, Police Officer (constable)
Time Period(s): 1870s (1879)
Locale(s): London, England

Summary: In this, the first of Lovesey's Sergeant Cribb series, someone is killing contestants in a six-day walking race, or "wobble." As the race continues, Sergeant Cribb and Constable Thackeray investigate in this vivid reconstruction of the Victorian sporting world.

Historical Accuracy: The Wobbles depicted are based on fact as are many of the period details in this authentic Victorian mystery.

LEONE LOWDEN (1889-)

Born in Portland, Oregon, Lowden grew up in Indianapolis and earned B.A. and M.A. degrees from the University of Chicago. She taught grammar and high school in Indiana and Ohio, publishing short stories and historical novels.

3919 *Proving Ground: A Novel of Civil War Days in the North*

Date of Publication: 1946
Subject(s): Civil War—U.S.; Battle of Shiloh
Fictional character(s): William Neal, Artisan (cobbler)
Time Period(s): 1860s
Locale(s): Indiana

Summary: This story of the Civil War depicts life on the northern homefront of Indiana with its factional conflict provided by the Copperheads, Southern sympathizers in the North. The story follows the activities of William Neal, a cobbler who is actually a disgraced Virginia aristocrat. Scenes of Morgan's Raid and the battles of Shiloh, Missionary Ridge, and Lookout Mountain are included.

Historical Accuracy: The novel's background is authentic and believable.

JANICE LUCAS
(PSEUD. OF JANICE DREXLER)

Lucas lives in Ferndale, Maryland. Her first historical novel, *The Long Sun*, tells the story of the Tuscarora Indian tribe in 1700s western Pennsylvania. Tow of her grandparents were Cherokee.

3920 *The Long Sun*

Date of Publication: 1994
Subject(s): Settlement of the American Frontier; Indians; Tribal Life—Native American
Fictional character(s): Priscilla Ann Billips, Young Woman, Settler; Runs with the Wind, Indian (Tuscarora)
Time Period(s): 1700s (1703)
Locale(s): Pennsylvania, American Colonies (western)

Summary: In the mountainous frontier of western Pennsylvania, the Billipses are befriended by the Tuscarora Indians when menacing war parties attack their homestead. The family, particularly Priscilla Ann, are welcomed by the tribe and begin to learn Indian ways. When the Tuscarora offer her a place among them, a decision must be made.

Historical Accuracy: The novel offers a convincing depiction of the region and Indian customs.

CHARLES LUDWIG (1918-)

An American minister and writer, Ludwig was born in Illinois. The son of missionaries, he travelled to Kenya in 1927, where he remained for ten years. He graduated from Anderson College and has published over 1000 articles and short stories and nearly three dozen books. A minister in parishes in Pennsylvania, Illinois, Washington, Idaho, and Arizona, Ludwig has preached in many countries. His books include *General without a Gun: the Life of William Booth, Founder of the Salvation Army* and *Mama Was a Missionary*.

`3921` *Levi Coffin and the Underground Railroad*

Date of Publication: 1975
Subject(s): Slavery; Underground Railroad; Biography, Fictionalized
Historical character(s): Levi Coffin, Abolitionist
Time Period(s): 19th century
Locale(s): United States

Summary: This biographical novel traces the career of abolitionist Levi Coffin, called the "President of the Underground Railroad." A Quaker, Coffin dedicates his life to aiding slaves, assisting some 3,000 runaways on their journey to Canada.

Historical Accuracy: The novel is faithful to Coffin's history and is based in part on Coffin's autobiography.

`3922` *Queen of the Reformation*

Date of Publication: 1986
Subject(s): Religious Conflict; Biography, Fictionalized; Protestant Reformation
Historical character(s): Martin Luther, Religious; Katie Luther, Spouse
Time Period(s): 16th century
Locale(s): Germany

Summary: This biographical novel looks at the events of the Protestant Reformation in the 16th century from the perspective of Katie Luther, the wife of religious leader Martin Luther.

Historical Accuracy: Although based on historical events, the story is told with a romantic and ideological treatment that undermines its plausibility.

MARY M. LUKE (1919-1993)

An American writer and historian born in Massachusetts, Luke attended the Berkshire Business College and worked in advertising, oil, and tool firms in New York City, and then for a documentary film company during World War II. After the war she worked at RKO Pictures in Hollywood. She is best known for her biographies of Tudor royalty.

`3923` *The Ivy Crown: A Biographical Novel of Queen Katherine Parr*

Date of Publication: 1984
Subject(s): Tudor Period; Royalty—England; Biography, Fictionalized
Historical character(s): Katherine Parr, Royalty (queen consort of Henry VIII); Henry VIII, Ruler (King of England); Mary Tudor, Royalty (princess); Thomas Seymour, Nobleman; Elizabeth Tudor, Royalty (princess); Edward Tudor, Royalty (prince)
Time Period(s): 16th century (1524-1548)
Locale(s): England

Summary: Katherine Parr is remembered by history as the last of Henry VIII's wives and the only one not divorced or executed. She is portrayed in this biographical novel as one of the most brilliant women of her time. Though she never yearns to occupy the throne, when her opportunity comes, she reigns as Queen Regent with skill and compassion, becoming an affectionate stepmother to Mary, Elizabeth, and Edward Tudor. She even secures the release of Elizabeth, who was punished for questioning the execution of Anne Boleyn, her mother.

Historical Accuracy: The novel is effective and convincing in capturing the scene and its events.

`3924` *The Nonsuch Lure*

Date of Publication: 1976
Subject(s): Tudor Period; Reincarnation
Fictional character(s): Andrew Moffatt, Young Man; Chloe Cuddington, Gentlewoman
Time Period(s): Multiple Time Periods
Locale(s): London, England; Surrey, England

Summary: Andrew Moffatt finds a 17th century journal in a Williamsburg bookstore that introduces him to past events involving ancestral lands taken by Henry VIII. On a visit to England, Andrew journeys through hypnotic regression back in time, where a battle between good and evil is waged. The novel shuttles between the present and the past to reveal a love story that ranges over 400 years.

Historical Accuracy: The framework of the story is fantastical; however, the elements of Tudor life and customs are authentic.

ROBERT P. LUND (1915-)

Born in Utah, Lund worked in the U.S. merchant service as a chief engineer. He served as a commander during World War II. Lund has travelled the entire world and has lived in Alaska, Hawaii, and Mexico.

3925 *Daishi-San: A Novel*

Date of Publication: 1961
Subject(s): Japanese Empire; Elizabethan Period
Historical character(s): William Adams, Sailor; Tokugama Ieyasu, Ruler (shogun)
Time Period(s): 16th century; 17th century
Locale(s): Japan; England

Summary: Narrated by William Adams, the first Englishman to reach Japan, the novel tells the story of Adams' exploits in Elizabethan England, in trade along the Barbary Coast, and with Sir Francis Drake in the defeat of the Spanish Armada. In 1598 he sails with a Dutch fleet to the East, but only his vessel reaches Japan. Adams becomes an aide to the Shogun Iyeyasu and participates in the battle of Sekigehara, which ends the civil war in Japan. Adams spends his later years in the employ of the East India Company in numerous commercial ventures.

Historical Accuracy: The novel mixes the factual and the imaginary, creating a convincing atmosphere of Elizabethan England and feudal Japan.

3926 *The Odyssey of Thaddeus Baxter*

Date of Publication: 1957
Subject(s): American West; Picaresque Adventure
Fictional character(s): Thad Baxter, Wanderer
Time Period(s): 1870s
Locale(s): Wyoming; Texas; Utah

Summary: This comic western tale traces the journey of a young Texan, Thad Baxter, who is determined to leave the parched Pecos country of Texas in the 1870s for the promise of a new life in Wyoming. The story recounts his adventures and misadventures from Texas, through Mormon Utah, to the Wyoming territory.

Historical Accuracy: The novel features a variety of believable period elements.

DELLA LUTES (?-1942)

American writer Lutes was born in Jackson, Michigan, and worked as an editor for *American Motherhood Magazine*. Her books include an autobiography, *Homegrown*; *Millbrook*; and *The Country Schoolma'am*.

3927 *Gabriel's Search*

Date of Publication: 1940
Subject(s): Settlement of the American Frontier
Fictional character(s): Gabriel Reed, Settler; Deborah Cooper, Young Woman
Time Period(s): 1830s
Locale(s): Michigan

Summary: This portrait of pioneer life in southern Michigan tells the story of Gabriel Reed, who settles in a frontier community. Because of his early life in the home of a psalm-singing hypocrite, Gabriel lacks faith. However, events transpire that re-awaken his beliefs.

Historical Accuracy: The novel provides a number of authentic period elements that capture life in a frontier community.

GILES A. LUTZ (1910-1982)

A rancher specializing in Black Angus cattle, Lutz wrote fiction for pulp and popular magazines, producing over 60 novels and short stories. He wrote about gunfighters, homesteading families, abolitionism, and slavery. His best works are *The Magnificent Failure*, *The Long Cold Wind*, and *The Trouble Borrower*.

3928 *The Magnificent Failure*

Date of Publication: 1967
Subject(s): Red River Rebellion
Historical character(s): Louis Riel, Revolutionary
Time Period(s): 1870s; 1880s
Locale(s): Canada

Summary: The novel provides the story of Louis Riel, a French-Indian, who leads two rebellions in opposition to land measures by the Ottawa government. The revolts Riel leads in the Red River settlement and in Saskatchewan are quickly crushed, and Riel is hanged for treason.

Historical Accuracy: The novel presents the basic outlines of Riel's story, but it is overloaded with conventional western lore.

GAVIN LYALL (1932-)

An English writer, journalist, and TV director, Lyall graduated from Cambridge University. He has worked as the aviation editor for the *Sunday Times* and travelled as a staff journalist throughout Europe, the U.S., Libya, India, Pakistan, Nepal, and Australia. He is best known for his Mad Maxim series of spy thrillers.

3929 *Spy's Honour*

Date of Publication: 1993
Subject(s): Espionage
Fictional character(s): Matthew Ranklin, Military Personnel (captain), Spy; Conall O'Gilroy, Sidekick; Corinna Finn, Young Woman
Time Period(s): 1910s (1912)
Locale(s): London, England; Kiel, Germany

Summary: Set in the early years of the British Secret Service Bureau, the novel tells the story of Captain Matthew Ranklin, who chooses espionage over bankruptcy. Along with street-wise Conall O'Gilroy and American Corinna Finn, he stumbles into a plot that threatens peace.

Historical Accuracy: The novel's plot is fanciful, but the period is evoked with convincing details.

ELIZABETH LYLE

3930 *Cassy*

Date of Publication: 1981
Subject(s): Regency Romance; Theatrical Life
Fictional character(s): Cassy Loring, Actress, Orphan; Julian Allingham, Nobleman (marquis)
Time Period(s): 1810s (1813-1815)

Locale(s): London, England; Paris, France; Vienna, Austria

Summary: This spirited Regency romance tells the story of Cassy Loring, who turns to a career on the stage to avert an unwanted marriage. Her adventures take her to Paris before Napoleon's Hundred Days, to Vienna during the Congress, and to Brussels on the eve of Waterloo.

Historical Accuracy: The novel's setting and details are authentic to the period.

3931 *Claire*

Date of Publication: 1983
Subject(s): Romance; French Revolution
Fictional character(s): Claire de la Robiniere, Refugee; Vincent Carlow, Gentleman; Lord Milcroft, Nobleman
Historical character(s): George, Royalty (Prince of Wales)
Time Period(s): 1790s
Locale(s): Brighton, England

Summary: The novel is set in fashionable Brighton in the years after the French Revolution but before the outbreak of war between England and France. It describes the romantic adventures of Claire de la Robiniere, a French refugee who becomes a society sensation. However, she is secretly involved in the dangerous mission of smuggling her family's valuables out of France. She turns to Englishman Vincent Carlow for support as Lord Milcroft is determined to expose her.

Historical Accuracy: The period setting in Brighton and the world of the French fashionable refugees are well-presented and convincing.

DANIEL LYNCH (1946-)

Born in Elmira, New York, Lynch received his B.S. degree at Temple University in Philadelphia. He has worked on several newspapers and won awards for his journalism. He is the author of several novels, including *Deadly Ernest*, *A Killing Frost*, and *Yellow*.

3932 *Yellow: A Novel*

Date of Publication: 199
Subject(s): Civil War—Cuba
Historical character(s): Ambrose Bierce, Writer; Frederic Remington, Artist; Richard Davis, Journalist; William Randolph Hearst, Financier, Publisher; Joseph Pulitzer, Publisher
Time Period(s): 1890s
Locale(s): New York, New York; Cuba

Summary: The dying writer Ambrose Bierce recalls the story of journalist Richard Davis and artist Frederic Remington's trip to Cuba before the Spanish-American War. They meet with resistance forces to obtain a story for William Randolph Hearst. The action shifts from the revolutionary camp to the affairs of Hearst and Pulitzer, who are intent on making a war.

Historical Accuracy: The novel blends fact and fiction but does capture the atmosphere of the time.

FRANCES LYNCH
(PSEUD. OF D.G. COMPTON, 1930-)

English dramatist and novelist Lynch was born in London and attended Cheltenham College. Lynch is a former stage electrician, furniture maker, salesman, docker, and postman. He is the author of science fiction, crime novels, and romances, as well as stage plays and TV and radio dramas.

3933 *The Fine and Handsome Captain*

Date of Publication: 1975
Subject(s): Victorian Period; Romance; Aviation
Fictional character(s): Hester Malpass, Orphan; Captain Edward Deveraux, Adventurer (balloonist)
Time Period(s): 1880s
Locale(s): Bristol, England

Summary: Hester Malpass' great ambition is to becomes a typist, but training costs more than she can earn at the railway restaurant where she works. An opportunity arises, however, at the fairgrounds with the dashing balloonist Captain Deveraux, and Hester embarks on a romantic adventure.

Historical Accuracy: The scenes in the air are interesting and unusual. The era is captured with some skill.

3934 *Stranger at the Wedding*

Date of Publication: 1976
Subject(s): Romance; Identity—Concealed; Victorian Period
Fictional character(s): Katherine Furneau, Gentlewoman, Twin; Caroline Furneau, Gentlewoman, Twin; Bruno di Torrigiani, Nobleman
Time Period(s): 1840s
Locale(s): Italy; London, England

Summary: Identical twins Caroline and Katherine Furneau change places at the altar. They are quickly caught up in an elaborate series of misadventures, including murder, mistaken identity, and intrigue among Italian noblemen anxious to redeem their fortune at any cost.

Historical Accuracy: The story is implausible, and the emphasis is on romantic suspense over a fully documented period background.

FRANCIS LYNDE (1856-1930)

Born in Lewiston, New York, Lynde is the author of *The Grafters*, *The Real Man*, and *Young Blood*.

3935 *Mr. Arnold*

Date of Publication: 1923
Subject(s): American Revolution; Espionage
Fictional character(s): Dick Page, Military Personnel (captain), Spy
Historical character(s): Benedict Arnold, Military Personnel (general), Traitor; Alexander Hamilton, Military Personnel (officer); Henry Clinton, Military Personnel (British general)
Time Period(s): 1780s
Locale(s): New York

Summary: Set during the American Revolution, the novel dramatizes an attempt by the colonists to recapture Benedict Arnold and return him for trial for treason. Captain Dick Page agrees to defect to the British side to gain access to Arnold to deliver him to justice.

Historical Accuracy: The novel is fanciful, and the approach is more romanctic than historical.

ELINOR LYNLEY

3936 *Song of the Bayou*

Date of Publication: 1990
Subject(s): Antebellum South; Romance
Fictional character(s): Susanna Paxton, Southern Belle; Nicholas Jourdain, Widow(er), Plantation Owner
Time Period(s): 1850s (1854)
Locale(s): Louisiana

Summary: Cajun life during the 1850s forms the background of this romantic novel that describes the outcome of the love affair between aristocratic Susanna Paxton and Cajun Nicholas Jourdain. Vigilantes, black magic, and Cajun culture feature prominently in the story.

Historical Accuracy: The novel packs authentic ingredients of the period and the region into this romantic tale.

JACK LYNN (1927-)

Born in Baltimore, Lynn became a director of programming for TV and radio after a career in the theater. His other novels include *The Professor*, *The Turncoat*, and *The Factory*.

3937 *The Hallelujah Flight*

Date of Publication: 1989
Subject(s): Aviation; Racial Conflict
Historical character(s): James Herman Banning, Pilot; Thomas C. Allen, Pilot
Time Period(s): 1930s (1932)
Locale(s): United States (cross-country); in the Air

Summary: The novel tells the true story of James Herman Banning and Thomas C. Allen, who set out in 1932 to become the first black aviators to fly coast to coast across America. With no sponsorship and only 25 dollars, they leave from Los Angeles in an ancient, patched-up aircaft, the "Eagle Rock." The novel describes their odyssey that includes racial hatred and violence.

Historical Accuracy: The novel is based on contemporary newspaper reports, the actual flight log, and interviews with Thomas Allen.

KAREN LYNN
(PSEUD. OF KAREN MAXFIELD; LYNN TAYLOR)

Karen Lynn is the pseudonym of mother and daughter writing team Karen Maxfield and Lynn Taylorr. Lynn is a registered nurse and cosmetologist. Karen has taught physical education and music.

3938 *Double Masquerade*

Date of Publication: 1981
Subject(s): Regency Romance; Horses; Identity—Concealed
Fictional character(s): Georginna Danver, Noblewoman, Twin; George Danver, Nobleman (Earl of Danver), Twin; Charles Ashton, Nobleman (Marquis of Willerton)
Time Period(s): 1810s (1815)
Locale(s): England

Summary: Romantic conflicts involving twins Georgianna and George Danver form the dramatic matter of this Regency romance. Georgianna is attracted to George's best friend, the Marquis of Willerton, but he is attracted elsewhere, and is only interested in Georgianna when she masquerades as her twin brother.

Historical Accuracy: The novel offers fairly standard Regency fare with believable period touches but an essential core of make believe.

3939 *Dual Destiny*

Date of Publication: 1983
Subject(s): Victorian Period; Medical Profession; Romance
Fictional character(s): Samantha Salisbury, Doctor; Lord Belfort, Nobleman (duke)
Time Period(s): 1860s
Locale(s): Tucson, Arizona; London, England

Summary: After graduating from medical school, Samantha Salisbury learns that she has inherited the title and estate of the Earl of Helmcrest. She returns to England to marry the Duke of Belfort and contracts typhoid on the crossing. Samantha weds the duke, but he flees from her when he sees the ravages of the disease. Implausibly, a recovered Samantha sets out to win him back.

Historical Accuracy: The story strains credulity, and the emphasis is clearly on romance over historical documentation.

3940 *Midsummer Moon*

Date of Publication: 1985
Subject(s): Regency Romance; Battle of Waterloo; Napoleonic Wars
Fictional character(s): Larla Somerset, Widow(er); Jeremy Ainsworth, Military Personnel (officer)
Time Period(s): 1810s (1815-1818)
Locale(s): England; Belgium

Summary: During the Battle of Waterloo, Larla Somerset agrees to a death-bed wedding ceremony to Captain Jeremy Ainsworth. After the wedding night, Larla learns that the captain has died. Three years later, Larla, with her son, journeys to meet her husband's family. There she meets Captain Ainsworth's charming cousin who bears a haunting resemblance to her dead husband.

Historical Accuracy: The basics—setting and costumes—are authentic, but the story strains credibility.

3941 *The Rake*

Date of Publication: 1986
Subject(s): Regency Romance; Inheritance—Disputed

Fictional character(s): Sharisse Satterleigh, Heiress; Andrew Lindley, Rake
Time Period(s): 1810s (1819)
Locale(s): England

Summary: In this tangled romantic story set in 1819, Sharisse Satterleigh pretends her brother is still alive in order to hold onto the family estate, which otherwise would go to the next male heir. Complications naturally follow when the rakish Andrew Lindley arrives from India with her brother's effects and her brother's pregnant wife and mother-in-law visit anxious for news of him.

Historical Accuracy: The story is hard to take other than as a romantic frivolity.

3942 *The Scottish Marriage*

Date of Publication: 1982
Subject(s): Regency Romance
Fictional character(s): Ada Maplethorpe, Spouse; Vincent Maplethorpe, Nobleman
Time Period(s): 19th century (Regency period)
Locale(s): Gretna Green, Scotland; England

Summary: A chance encounter between Ada, a young English orphan, and Lord Maplethorpe results in a marriage ceremony. Ada accompanies Lord Maplethorpe back to London, where in a series of romantic complications both eventually fall in love with each other.

Historical Accuracy: The novel derives many of its complications from the arcane marriage laws of the period. Otherwise, the emphasis is clearly on romance over history.

MARGARET LYNN
(PSEUD. OF GLADYS STARKEY BATTYE, 1915-)

Born in Halifax, England, Battye was a textile designer and a hotelier before becoming a novelist. Under the pen name of Margaret Lynn, she has published *To See a Stranger* and *Mrs. Maitland's Affair.*

3943 *Free Soil*

Date of Publication: 1920
Subject(s): Settlement of the American Frontier; Free Soil Movement
Fictional character(s): John Truman, Settler; Ellen Truman, Settler
Historical character(s): John Brown, Abolitionist
Time Period(s): 1850s
Locale(s): Kansas

Summary: This story of the conflict in Kansas between free-soilers and slavery advocates dramatizes the experiences of a pioneer family, the Trumans, who journey west from New England and are plunged into the violence of the period.

Historical Accuracy: The story blends the fictional with the historical. The atmosphere is carefully and convincingly presented.

ANDREW LYTLE (1902-)
American novelist Lytle was born in Tennessee and graduated from Sewanee Military Academy and Vanderbilt University. He was a professor of English at the University of the South and the editor of the *Sewanee Review.*

3944 *At the Moon's Inn*

Date of Publication: 1941
Subject(s): Exploration; Indians; Spanish Colonies
Historical character(s): Hernando de Soto, Explorer
Time Period(s): 16th century
Locale(s): Florida

Summary: The story of Spanish explorer Hernando DeSoto's search for gold in Florida is dramatized. After a career spent in Peru, DeSoto sets out on his final expedition. The novel chronicles the events of the expedition, including the battle of Mauvilla.

Historical Accuracy: The atmosphere of the period and the events are rendered with skill and authenticity.

3945 *The Long Night*

Date of Publication: 1936
Subject(s): Civil War—U.S.; Crime and Criminals; Battle of Shiloh
Fictional character(s): Pleasant McIvor, Military Personnel; Tyson Lovell, Outlaw; Roswell Ellis, Military Personnel
Historical character(s): Albert Sidney Johnston, Military Personnel
Time Period(s): 1850s; 1860s (1857-1862)
Locale(s): Alabama; Michigan; Tennessee

Summary: A family conducts a campaign of personal justice against an outlaw gang (based on the historical Murrell Gang) that has murdered the family's patriarch. In the midst of their private vendetta, the Civil War begins. Pleasant McIvor is involved in the battle of Shiloh, where the personal drama climaxes with tragic consequences.

Historical Accuracy: This is a successful effort of historical imagination. The account of the battle of Shiloh is a first-rate piece of war reporting.

3946 *The Velvet Horn*

Date of Publication: 1957
Subject(s): Rural Life—U.S.; Reconstruction Period
Fictional character(s): Lucius Cree, Young Man; Captain Joe Cree, Landowner; Ada Belle Rutter, Frontierswoman
Time Period(s): 1870s (1879)
Locale(s): Cumberlands, Tennessee

Summary: The novel describes young Lucius Cree's search for identity in the wilderness of Tennessee after the Civil War. His legacy is violent deeds which have wiped out most of his family. But what is his true paternity? And how much of the past must be absorbed to determine the present? The novel offers a version of the modern southern Gothic filled with symbolic horrors and the wild poetry of place.

Historical Accuracy: The author constructs both a believable and poetic version of a region and a period.

AMIN MAALOUF

3947 *Leo Africanus*

Date of Publication: 1989
Subject(s): Renaissance; Biography, Fictionalized
Historical character(s): Leo Africanus, Writer; Leo X, Religious (pope)
Time Period(s): 16th century
Locale(s): Africa; Rome, Italy; Constantinople, Ottoman Empire

Summary: This fictional autobiography of the Moorish traveler and geographer Leo Africanus chronicles his childhood in Granada and Morocco, his capture by pirates, his conversion to Christianity by Pope Leo X, and his journeys through Africa and the Middle East. This fascinating story offers a vivid view of the West through Muslim eyes.

Historical Accuracy: The novel's version of Leo's life and times is dependable and convincing.

EDGAR MAAS

3948 *Don Pedro and the Devil*

Date of Publication: 1942
Subject(s): Spanish Colonies; Inca Empire; Inquisition
Fictional character(s): Don Pedro Cordova, Nobleman, Adventurer
Historical character(s): Francisco Pizarro, Military Personnel (conquistador), Explorer; Hernando Pizarro, Explorer, Military Personnel (conquistador); Diego de Almagro, Military Personnel (conquistador); Hernando Cortez, Explorer, Military Personnel (conquistador); Bartolome de Las Casas, Religious (missionary)
Time Period(s): 16th century
Locale(s): Spain; Panama; Peru

Summary: The destruction of the Inca Empire by the Spanish is dramatized in the story of a young Spanish nobleman, Don Pedro Cordova. After running afoul of the Inquisition, he sets out to make his fortune in the New World. There he meets the major figures in the conquest.

Historical Accuracy: The novel features a number of accurate details that form a convincing period background for the story.

3949 *Imperial Venus: A Novel of Napoleon's Favorite Sister*

Date of Publication: 1946
Subject(s): Biography, Fictionalized; Napoleonic Era
Historical character(s): Maria Paolina Borghese, Gentlewoman; Napoleon Bonaparte, Ruler (Emperor of France)
Time Period(s): 18th century; 19th century (1780-1825)
Locale(s): Europe; Corsica, France; Haiti

Summary: This fictional biography dramatizes the life of Pauline Bonaparte. Born on Corsica, she rises in the world with her brother's success. She accompanies her husband, General LeClerc, to Haiti and after his death marries a member of the Roman nobility. Pauline falls into disfavor with Napoleon,

but she shows considerably more loyalty than her other brothers and sisters.

Historical Accuracy: The novel features a thorough and detailed picture of Napoleon's family and background.

3950 *A Lady at Bay*

Date of Publication: 1953
Subject(s): Mystery; Royalty—France; Crime and Criminals
Historical character(s): Marie Madeleine Brinvilliers, Noblewoman
Time Period(s): 17th century (1670s)
Locale(s): France

Summary: This historical mystery novel is based on the actual case of the Marquise de Brinvilliers, a noblewoman in the court of Louis XIV, who is charged with poisoning her father and two brothers to secure a family fortune and to cover up her adulterous affairs. The novel offers a psychological re-creation of the crime and the motives for the poisonings.

Historical Accuracy: The novel is not greatly concerned with re-creating the period atmosphere. Rather, the emphasis is on the psychological basis for the crimes.

3951 *Magnificent Enemies*

Date of Publication: 1955
Subject(s): Middle Ages; Hanseatic League; Business Building
Fictional character(s): Simon Vann Utrecht, Businessman (merchant), Sea Captain; Klaus von Sissingen, Sea Captain
Time Period(s): 15th century
Locale(s): Europe

Summary: The warring and the intense rivalry and competition created by the Hanseatic League in the early 15th century are dramatized. This mercantile league, developed to protect trade, threatens the freedom of the seas. The ensuing conflict depicted centers on merchant traders Simon Vann Utrecht and Klaus von Sissingen.

Historical Accuracy: The historical elements are faithful to the times.

3952 *The Queen's Physician*

Date of Publication: 1948
Subject(s): Medical Profession; Royalty—Denmark
Historical character(s): Christian VII, Ruler (King of Denmark and Norway); Caroline-Matilda, Royalty (queen consort of Christian VII); Johann Frederick Struensee, Doctor, Courtier
Time Period(s): 18th century (1770s-1790s)
Locale(s): Copenhagen, Denmark

Summary: Set in the dissolute court of Christian VII of Denmark in the 18th century, the novel describes the rise to power of physician John Struensee. Struensee manages to become the king's doctor, confidant, and trusted adviser, and also the queen's lover. The novel shows his rise and eventual downfall and execution in a coup.

Historical Accuracy: The novel is a blend of fact and fancy, with the historical background solidly described.

3953 *World and Paradise*

Date of Publication: 1950
Subject(s): Thirty Years War
Fictional character(s): Karl Von Harrach, Nobleman (count)
Historical character(s): Albrecht von Wallenstein, Military Personnel (general); Johannes Kepler, Scientist (astronomer); Gustavus II Adolphus, Ruler (King of Sweden); Armand-Jean Du Plessis, Religious (Cardinal Richelieu), Political Figure (Duc de Richelieu)
Time Period(s): 17th century
Locale(s): Europe

Summary: This panoramic novel of the Thirty Years War ranges widely across Europe with appearances by several of the leading figures of the period. Dominating the drama is the Albrecht von Wallenstein. The novel's nominal hero is Karl, Count Harrach, but the real center of the novel is the political and religious chaos in Europe in the 1600s.

Historical Accuracy: Although the author displays an encyclopedic knowledge of period details, the whole is fashioned into a largely uncompelling melodrama.

MARY LOUISE MABIE

3954 *Prepare Them for Caesar*

Date of Publication: 1949
Subject(s): Roman Empire; Biography, Fictionalized
Historical character(s): Julius Caesar, Military Personnel (army commander), Political Figure
Time Period(s): 1st century B.C. (80-44 B.C.)
Locale(s): Rome, Roman Empire

Summary: The novel presents a case for the greatness of Julius Caesar, covering his career from his youth to his death. Episodic in approach, the novel offers both the highlights in an amazing career and some suggestions of Caesar's motivations and psychological make-up.

Historical Accuracy: The novel is based on authoritative sources, which provide many of the quotations. The background of Roman life and customs is authentic.

GERARD MAC

3955 *Pilgrims: A Novel of the Mayflower*

Date of Publication: 1994
Subject(s): American Colonies; Pilgrims; Sea Story
Fictional character(s): Daisy Mason, Teenager, Settler; Will Trefor, Settler
Historical character(s): Miles Standish, Leader (Pilgrim); John Carver, Leader (Pilgrim); John Alden, Leader (Pilgrim); William Bradford, Leader (Pilgrim)
Time Period(s): 17th century
Locale(s): London, England; *Mayflower*, At Sea; Plymouth, Massachusetts, American Colonies

Summary: The novel describes the fateful voyage of the *Mayflower* and the first desperate months of the Pilgrim colony in Plymouth from the perspective of young Daisy Mason, who leaves poverty in the London slums for a new life in America. The challenges of the voyage and settlement are vividly depicted.

Historical Accuracy: Based on solid research, the novel weaves the factual and the fictional into a dramatic narrative.

ROSE MACAULAY (1889-1958)

Macaulay was an English novelist, essayist and travel writer. Praised for her wit and satire, Macaulay is best remembered for her novels describing middle class life, such as *Told by an Idiot*, *The World My Wilderness*, and *The Towers of Trebizond*. She also wrote studies of John Milton and E.M. Forster. Macaulay was named a Dame of the British Empire in 1958.

3956 *The Shadow Flies*

Date of Publication: 1932
Subject(s): Literary Life
Fictional character(s): Julian Conybeare, Young Woman
Historical character(s): Robert Herrick, Writer (poet); John Milton, Writer; Abraham Cowley, Writer (poet); John Cleveland, Writer (poet); Richard Crashaw, Writer (poet)
Time Period(s): 17th century
Locale(s): Cambridge, England

Summary: This novel set in England just before the Civil War provides an occasion for displaying the literary figures of the time. Young Julian Conybeare accompanies her father and poet Robert Herrick to Cambridge where she meets Milton, Cranshaw, Cowley, and other poets of the time. She sees *Comus* performed and becomes involved with the fashionable poet John Cleveland who plays a role in a tragic turn of events.

Historical Accuracy: The novel captures both the customs and the literary milieu of the period.

GEORGE MACBETH (1932-1992)

Scottish broadcaster, editor, poet, and author, Macbeth was regarded as a powerful influence on modern British poetry, both through his own work and as the producer of BBC radio broadcasts featuring new poets during the 1960s and 1970s. He published nearly twenty volumes of poetry, including *The Broken Places* and *Trespassing*, as well as the novels *Anna's Book* and *Another Love Story*. He also wrote an autobiography, *A Child of War*.

3957 *Dizzy's Woman*

Date of Publication: 1986
Subject(s): Biography, Fictionalized; Victorian Period
Historical character(s): Benjamin Disraeli, Political Figure
Time Period(s): 1830s; 1840s
Locale(s): England

Summary: This novel imagines a correspondence between Benjamin Disraeli and his former mistress, the notorious Lady Londonderry. The letters capture the wit and the style of Disraeli in his hedonistic youth as well as the transition between the Regency era and the Victorian age.

Historical Accuracy: The novel achieves a sense of authenticity in capturing the voice of Disraeli and the atmosphere of the period.

3958   *The Lion of Pescara*

Date of Publication: 1984
Subject(s): Literary Life; Biography, Fictionalized
Historical character(s): Gabriele D'Annunzio, Writer
Time Period(s): 20th century
Locale(s): Italy; France

Summary: The novel provides a biographical portrait of the notorious Italian poet and author Gabriele D'Annunzio. His career is shown from the point of view of his secretary.

Historical Accuracy: The novel accurately reflects the life of D'Annunzio.

VICTOR MACCLURE

3959   *A Certain Woman: The Story of Mary Magdalene*

Date of Publication: 1951
Subject(s): Biblical Story
Historical character(s): Mary Magdalene, Biblical Figure; Lazarus, Biblical Figure; Martha of Bethany, Biblical Figure; Jesus Christ, Biblical Figure; Judas Iscariot, Biblical Figure
Time Period(s): 1st century
Locale(s): Israel

Summary: This Biblical tale dramatizes the story of Mary Magdalene. The author makes Mary the sister of Lazarus and Martha and tells the story of Christ's ministry through her perspective. Jesus is presented convincingly in non-dogmatic terms as a young carpenter before his public life.

Historical Accuracy: There is little historical basis for the facts of Mary's story presented here.

CATHERINE MACCOUN (1953-)

Born in Massachusetts, MacCoun graduated from Mundelein College and has worked as a management consultant at the University of Illinois, Chicago. She is a freelance business writer and an instructional designer.

3960   *The Age of Miracles*

Date of Publication: 1989
Subject(s): Middle Ages; Religious Life; Witchcraft and Sorcery
Fictional character(s): Ingrid Fairfax, Teenager, Healer; Jack Rudd, Adventurer
Time Period(s): 14th century (1345-1348)
Locale(s): Oxford, England

Summary: This romantic adventure story is set in 14th-century England and concerns young Ingrid Fairfax, thought to be a saint and miracle worker, who is seduced by Jack Rudd. Ingrid follows Jack out of her convent to Oxford, where secrets concerning Ingrid's past could result in a witch's death.

Historical Accuracy: The medieval period detail is genuine and convincing.

ISOBEL MACDONALD

3961   *The Buried Self: A Background to the Poems of Matthew Arnold*

Date of Publication: 1949
Subject(s): Biography, Fictionalized; Victorian Period; Literary Life
Historical character(s): Matthew Arnold, Writer
Time Period(s): 1840s; 1850s (1848-1851)
Locale(s): England; France

Summary: This biographical account attempts to provide a personal context for Matthew Arnold's development as a writer and for the creation of his poetry. The novel chronicles the important years between 1848 and 1851 when Arnold's travels and experiences were converted into his most important poetic work.

Historical Accuracy: The novel's notes make clear how close is this fictional account to the actual details of Arnold's life.

MALCOLM MACDONALD (1932-)

English novelist Macdonald also writes under the name Malcolm Ross. His novels are distinguished by a vivid recreation of history, based on Macdonald's admitted "obsession" with the past. He contends that he never invents a fact if the truth will serve as well.

3962   *Abigail*

Date of Publication: 1979
Subject(s): Victorian Period; Family Saga; Prostitution
Fictional character(s): Abigail Stevenson, Gentlewoman; Annie, Servant, Prostitute
Time Period(s): 19th century (1868-1890s)
Locale(s): London, England

Summary: Nora and John Stevenson have fought their way up the Victorian ladder to wealth and social prominence. Their daughter Abigail rebels against her parents' conformity and insists on experiencing the life respectable Victorians ignore. Her guide in discovery is the maid Annie who falls into prostitution. This is the fourth volume in the Stevenson family saga.

Historical Accuracy: Macdonald's central character illustrates the truth behind the Victorian veneer of respectability. She provides a modern perspective to reassess 19th century attitudes and customs.

3963   *All Desires Known*

Date of Publication: 1993
Subject(s): Victorian Period
Fictional character(s): Michael Raven, Doctor; Lucy Raven, Spouse; Diana Powers, Gentlewoman; Philip de Rinzi, Architect
Time Period(s): 19th century (Victorian period)

Locale(s): Dublin, Ireland

Summary: A complicated romantic tangle ensues when Lucy and Michael Raven accept an offer to open a sanatorium. Others involved in the project are connected with the pair romantically, and the novel explores the complex relationships that are acted out against the constraints of Victorian conventions.

Historical Accuracy: The novel captures the atmosphere with care.

`3964` For They Shall Inherit

Date of Publication: 1984
Subject(s): Business Building; Victorian Period
Fictional character(s): Clive Mortimer, Heir, Businessman; Freddy Oxley, Worker, Businessman; Ann Howard, Young Woman
Time Period(s): 19th century (1863-1892)
Locale(s): Midlands, England; South Africa; Vienna, Austria

Summary: The novel traces a friendship between the wealthy heir of a Victorian industrialist and a factory lad over a number of years as their careers take them around the world. They fall in love with the same woman, who rejects them both and makes her own way. The past acts as their nemesis to ruin them, and they must find an ingenious solution to their difficulties.

Historical Accuracy: The scenes in South Africa are solidly grounded and precise.

`3965` Goldeneye

Date of Publication: 1981
Subject(s): Family Saga; Business Building; World War II
Fictional character(s): Catherine Hamilton, Heroine; Burgo Macrae, Businessman
Time Period(s): 20th century (1910-1960)
Locale(s): Canada (western); Chicago, Illinois; England

Summary: This family saga begins after the Great War with the arrival of Catherine Hamilton to Goldeneye, a small town on the western plains of Canada. She marries the doctor's son, Burgo, and together they share a stormy relationship for 30 years that takes them through Canada, the U.S., and to Europe.

Historical Accuracy: The scenes are dramatically rendered, although without the level of detail of Macdonald's less panoramic novels.

`3966` Honour and Obey

Date of Publication: 1988
Subject(s): Romance; Business Building; Aviation
Fictional character(s): Julia Somerville, Businesswoman; George Somerville, Businessman; Eliot Baring, Engineer
Time Period(s): 1920s
Locale(s): London, England

Summary: When her husband becomes paralyzed in an accident, Julia Somerville must run the family business—an automobile manufacturing firm. She discovers that the company is badly in the red, and with determination and the assistance of a young American engineer, she begins building airplanes.

Historical Accuracy: The corporate maneuvering of this resourceful heroine is sharply drawn against a strong background of business life in the 1920s.

`3967` An Innocent Woman

Date of Publication: 1989
Subject(s): Romance; Prostitution; Victorian Period
Fictional character(s): Jane Hervey, Heiress; Esther Wilkinson, Prostitute; Vosper Scawen, Lawyer
Time Period(s): 1890s
Locale(s): Cornwall, England; Paris, France

Summary: Heiress Jane Hervey arrives at a Cornish village and attracts a number of suitors; however, she is drawn to the village's less reputable characters. Despite her innocence, she is intent on unravelling the mysteries of her past, which take her to Paris at the height of the Belle Epoque.

Historical Accuracy: The scenes here are well-managed and realistic, and the characters are carefully observed.

`3968` Kernow & Daughter

Date of Publication: 1995
Subject(s): Edwardian Period; Business Building
Fictional character(s): Barney Kernow, Businessman; Jessica Kernow, Businesswoman; Cornwallis Trelawney, Gentleman
Time Period(s): 1900s
Locale(s): Cornwall, England

Summary: Self-made businessman Barney Kernow is convinced that a woman's place is far from the family business. However, his daughter Jessica, out of love for Cornwallis Trelawney, is forced into a commercial venture that is shockingly daring for its day.

Historical Accuracy: The novel offers a convincing picture of the period and the region.

`3969` A Notorious Woman

Date of Publication: 1986
Subject(s): Romance; Rural Life—England
Fictional character(s): Johanna Rosewarne, Orphan; Hal Penrose, Gentleman; Nina Brookes, Gentlewoman
Time Period(s): 19th century
Locale(s): Cornwall, England

Summary: Johanna Rosewarne, an orphan, lives with her aunt and uncle in Cornwall until the threat of an arranged marriage causes her to become the companion of a sophisticated widow. Johanna's affair with her childhood friend produces a child, and she must struggle to earn a living and the respect of the Cornish villagers.

Historical Accuracy: The Cornish setting is accurately depicted and lends some depth to a fairly conventional romantic story.

`3970` On a Far Wide Shore

Date of Publication: 1986

Subject(s): Inheritance—Disputed; Romance; Victorian Period

Fictional character(s): Elizabeth Troy, Widow(er), Nurse; Morwenna Troy, Businesswoman

Time Period(s): 1880s (1889)

Locale(s): Cornwall, England

Summary: Elizabeth Troy, widowed on her wedding day, is surprised to learn that her husband has left her his entire Cornish estate—3,500 acres, tin mines, and a house full of treasures. She immediately comes into conflict with her sister-in-law, Morwenna, as Elizabeth attempts to revive the farms and mines and is branded a ''furinner.''.

Historical Accuracy: The Cornish scenes are expertly rendered.

3971   *The Rich Are with You Always*

Date of Publication: 1976

Subject(s): Victorian Period; Business Building; Family Saga

Fictional character(s): John Stevenson, Businessman; Nora Stevenson, Businesswoman; Arabella Thornton, Gentlewoman; Walter Thornton, Businessman

Historical character(s): George Hudson, Businessman

Time Period(s): 1840s; 1850s (1845-1851)

Locale(s): England; Ireland; France

Summary: Macdonald continues his story of the Stevensons and Thorntons during the railway mania of the 1840s to the Victorian high-water mark, the Crystal Palace Exhibition of 1851. Business success and its costs are explored, as are the central Victorian contradictions: great wealth and grinding poverty, prudery and lust. This is the second volume in the Stevenson family saga.

Historical Accuracy: As Macdonald's historical postscript makes clear, the factual basis of his story is almost uncannily established.

3972   *The Silver Highways*

Date of Publication: 1987

Subject(s): Romance; Canal Building; Georgian Period

Fictional character(s): Mary Flinders, Heroine; Matt Sullivan, Engineer; Lord Tottenham, Nobleman

Time Period(s): 1790s

Locale(s): Clare, Ireland; London, England; Yorkshire, England

Summary: Set during England's canal-building mania of the 1790s, the novel concerns the adventures of a young Irish woman invited by her childhood sweetheart to join him in London. On the way she is robbed twice, assaulted, and nearly drowned. In London, she meets a handsome though evil nobleman. There are colorful scenes of the period, including duels, walking races, and regattas.

Historical Accuracy: Macdonald is assured in his setting and period. The story is a lively one with an interesting slant on the era.

3973   *Sons of Fortune*

Date of Publication: 1978

Subject(s): Family Saga; Victorian Period; Business Building

Fictional character(s): Boy Stevenson, Gentleman; Caspar Stevenson, Gentleman

Time Period(s): 1850s; 1860s (1854-1863)

Locale(s): Yorkshire, England; London, England; New York, New York

Summary: John and Nora Stevenson's assault on the business world is complete. Their next challenge is penetrating society. The emphasis shifts to their two sons, who must make their own way, balancing parental expectations and class prejudice. This is the third volume of the Stevenson family saga.

Historical Accuracy: The Victorian period details are convincing.

3974   *Tessa d'Arblay*

Date of Publication: 1983

Subject(s): Victorian Period; Crime and Criminals; Mystery

Fictional character(s): Tessa d'Arblay, Gentlewoman; Segal Rosen, Artist; Connie Saunders, Actress

Time Period(s): 1880s (1888)

Locale(s): London, England

Summary: The title character lives in London's East End and is bewildered over the death of a friend from an undetected brain tumor. She visits a prominent brain specialist for answers and through him meets a noted painter, a member of Oscar Wilde's decadent set. She also befriends a young actress. Tessa is swept up in a series of dreadful discoveries, including a plausible solution to the Jack the Ripper murders.

Historical Accuracy: The late Victorian atmosphere is convincing, even if the characters' attitudes seem decidedly modern.

3975   *To the End of Her Days*

Date of Publication: 1994

Subject(s): Rural Life—England; World War II; Romance

Fictional character(s): Jessica Lanyon, Widow(er); David Carne, Doctor; Lorna Sancreed, Widow(er)

Time Period(s): 20th century (1920s-1940s)

Locale(s): Cornwall, England

Summary: Framed by the two World Wars and set in Cornwall, the novel tells the story of widow Jessica Lanyon, who has cared for her husband during his long fatal illness. She turns to his doctor for solace but social constraints are too strong. It takes the arrival of war widow Lorna Sancreed to act as a catalyst for Jessica and her Cornish village.

Historical Accuracy: Macdonald is sure of his setting and the period. Both are convincingly presented.

3976   *The Trevarton Inheritance*

Date of Publication: 1996

Subject(s): Victorian Period

Fictional character(s): Cristobel Moore, Orphan; Marian Moore, Orphan; Teresa Moore, Orphan

Time Period(s): 1890s

Locale(s): Cornwall, England

Summary: This Victorian-era tale involves the family of Sabrina Trevarton who shocked her wealthy family by elop-

ing with a stable hand. When she and her husband die, it falls to Cristobel Moore to reunite her scattered family.

Historical Accuracy: The novel features a believable period background.

3977 *A Woman Possessed*

Date of Publication: 1972
Subject(s): Romance
Fictional character(s): Laura Nisbet, Gentlewoman; Maurice Petifer, Businessman; Giles Curnow, Gentleman
Time Period(s): 1900s
Locale(s): Cornwall, England

Summary: Laura Nisbit's parents convince her to give up her passion for ne'er-do-well Maurice Petifer to marry the solid, dependable Giles Curnow. Fourteen years later, Maurice returns to Cornwall after having made his fortune in South Africa. Laura must now battle her former feelings and her duty to her husband and family.

Historical Accuracy: Macdonald's Cornish setting adds some needed solidity to this romantic tangle.

3978 *A Woman Scorned*

Date of Publication: 1992
Subject(s): Romance; Mystery; Feuds
Fictional character(s): Judith Carty, Heroine
Time Period(s): 1880s (1881-1888)
Locale(s): Dublin, Ireland; London, England

Summary: A blood feud involving the Bellinghams of Castle Moore results in murder. One of the survivors, Judith Carty, returns to solve the mystery of the crime as well as to endure the marriage market of the Dublin social season. Both present complications.

Historical Accuracy: Macdonald ably renders the Irish upper class, torn between English ways and deep-seated Irish loyalties.

3979 *The World From Rough Stones*

Date of Publication: 1974
Subject(s): Victorian Period; Railroads; Business Building
Fictional character(s): John Stevenson, Businessman; Nora Stevenson, Worker, Businesswoman; Walter Thornton, Engineer
Time Period(s): 1830s (1839)
Locale(s): Midlands, England

Summary: During England's railroad construction mania, John Stevenson is driven to complete the world's longest railway tunnel. He marries his partner, an 18-year-old street urchin. She shows an amazing facility in business, and together they mount an assault on power and status. Their unconventional marriage is contrasted with that of the project's engineer. This is the first volume of the Stevenson family saga, which continues with *The Rich Are with You Always.*

Historical Accuracy: Sex and business are shown as the central metaphors of the Victorian period. The period details are colorful and convincing.

ROBERT S. MACDONALD (1925-)

Born in New York, MacDonald graduated from Syracuse University. He has worked as a mathematics teacher, an industrial engineer, and a technical writer. He began writing when he discovered among his grandmother's effects a packet of letters written by his grandfather when he was at sea in the 19th century. His novels are expansions on these letters, supplemented by newspaper accounts of maritime news of the time.

3980 *The Catherine*

Date of Publication: 1982
Subject(s): Civil War—U.S.; Sea Story
Fictional character(s): William Saudners, Businessman (shipbuilder), Sea Captain; Elias Saudners, Businessman (shipbuilder); Kit Cavanaugh, Sailor
Time Period(s): 1860s
Locale(s): Rhode Island; New Orleans, Louisiana; *Catherine*, At Sea

Summary: The Saudners of Rhode Island are a shipbuilding and trading family who, when the Civil War breaks out, are commissioned to build the *Catherine* to sail as a privateer preying on the Southern shipping lanes. The novel dramatizes the adventures of the *Catherine* in action from New England to New Orleans.

Historical Accuracy: The novel's nautical scenes and period background are convincingly realistic.

WILLIAM COLT MACDONALD
(1891-1968)

3981 *California Caballero*

Date of Publication: 1936
Subject(s): American West; Crime and Criminals
Fictional character(s): Branch Dillard, Cowboy; Mariposa Castameto, Captive
Time Period(s): 1860s
Locale(s): California

Summary: This tale of California in the 1860s features the conflict between the Mexicans and the Americans. Branch Dillard, a young Texas cowboy, gets into the middle of the conflict when he rescues a young senorita from kidnapping by outlaws.

Historical Accuracy: The novel features exciting western action with an authentic period flavor.

JOSEPH MACHLIS (1906-)

An American born in Riga, Latvia, Machlis has been a professor of music at Queens College and member of the graduate faculty at the Julliard School. He is the author of several books on music, including *Introduction to Contemporary Music* and *The Enjoyment of Music*, which sold more than two million copies and is considered a classic text in its field.

3982　*The Career of Magda V.*

Date of Publication: 1985
Subject(s): Musical Life; Nazis; World War II
Fictional character(s): Magda Volkman, Singer; Erich Schlesinger, Musician; Otto Dunsche, Military Personnel (SS general); Dan Lerner, Conductor
Time Period(s): 1930s; 1940s
Locale(s): Berlin, Germany; Warsaw, Poland; Vienna, Austria

Summary: The story of the pursuit of art and its cost is played out in Berlin during the 1930s. Magda Volkman pursues her gift as a singer in the world of the Nazis and the Holocaust. Magda is torn between her ambition and her convictions, her conscience and her drive for success.

Historical Accuracy: The novel convincingly captures the world both of art and the Nazis of the period.

COLIN MACINNES (1914-1976)

An English novelist and journalist, MacInnes is the son of novelist Angela Thirkell. MacInnes is best known as a chronicler of London in its postwar years in books such as *City of Spades*, *Mr. Love and Justice*, and *Absolute Beginners*, which was adapted into a movie musical in 1986.

3983　*Three Years to Play*

Date of Publication: 1970
Subject(s): Elizabethan Period; Theatrical Life
Fictional character(s): Aubrey of Epping, Actor
Historical character(s): William Shakespeare, Writer
Time Period(s): 16th century; 17th century (1599-1601)
Locale(s): London, England; Epping Forest, England

Summary: The novel provides a comic look at Elizabethan England, as well as a fanciful suggestion about the origin of Shakespeare's *As You Like It*. The story concerns the adventures of young Aubrey of Epping who comes to London to seek his fortune and winds up working for two of the largest brothels in the city. Seeking refuge in his native Epping, Aubrey tells his experiences to William Shakespeare who transforms them into *As You Like It*. Aubrey is recruited to play one of the play's female roles.

Historical Accuracy: The novel is an ingenious, though fanciful, recreation, filled with authentic details of the period.

3984　*Westward to Laughter*

Date of Publication: 1969
Subject(s): Slavery
Fictional character(s): Alexander Nairn, Slave
Time Period(s): 1750s
Locale(s): West Indies

Summary: The novel takes the form of the memoirs of Alexander Nairn, a young Scotsman who is forced into slavery on the West Indies island of Laughter during the 1750s. His attempts to free himself and his involvement in a slave uprising are described.

Historical Accuracy: The novel provides a believable period backdrop for the narrative.

LORN MACINTYRE (1942-)

Born in England, MacIntyre received his Ph.D. from the University of Glasgow for his thesis on Sir Walter Scott and the Highlands. He is a writer of poetry, short stories, and critical and historical articles.

3985　*The Blind Bend*

Date of Publication: 1981
Subject(s): Family Saga; Edwardian Period
Fictional character(s): Niall MacDonald, Laird; Mary Rose MacDonald, Spouse
Time Period(s): 1900s
Locale(s): Highlands, Scotland

Summary: The novel continues the story of the MacDonald family begun in *Cruel in the Shadow*. It is 1904 and Niall MacDonald, the laird of Invernevis, brings home his new bride, Mary Rose, who must contend with the family's dark past.

Historical Accuracy: The novel provides a convincing recreation of a Scottish laird's family of the period.

3986　*Cruel in the Shadow*

Date of Publication: 1979
Subject(s): Victorian Period; Boer War
Fictional character(s): Niall MacDonald, Military Personnel (soldier); Laura MacDonald, Gentlewoman
Time Period(s): 1890s; 1900s
Locale(s): Highlands, Scotland

Summary: This family drama set at the end of Queen Victoria's reign during the Boer War concerns the MacDonalds of Invernevis whose tranquility is shattered. The novel penetrates the placid veneer of the family to reveal its darker side.

Historical Accuracy: The novel captures convincingly the era and the atmosphere of the period.

MARGARET MACKAY

3987　*The Wine Princes*

Date of Publication: 1958
Subject(s): Business Building; Napoleonic Wars; Peninsular War
Fictional character(s): Peregrine Prince, Businessman; Johnathan Prince, Businessman
Time Period(s): 1790s
Locale(s): Oporto, Portugal

Summary: The novel tells the story of two English cousins, Peregrine and Johnathan Prince, who go to Portugal in the late 18th century to learn the wine business. Their adventures in business and love reach a climax as the invading French army is bested by an English and Portuguese force under Sir Arthur Wellsley, later the Duke of Wellington.

Historical Accuracy: This is a somewhat restrained romantic tale with a good deal of authentic period details and evidence of considerable research into the era and the region.

WALTER MACKEN (1915-1967)

An Irish actor, playwright, and novelist, Macken was born in Galway. He managed, acted, and wrote plays for Dublin's Abbey Theatre, starring in his own plays at the Abbey, on Broadway, and in London. His novel *Flight of Doves* was made into a movie in 1970.

3988 *The Scorching Wind*

Date of Publication: 1964
Subject(s): Independence—Ireland; Civil War—Ireland; Easter Rising
Fictional character(s): Dualta, Patriot; Dominic, Patriot
Time Period(s): 1910s; 1920s (1915-1920s)
Locale(s): Ireland

Summary: The Irish struggle for independence is dramatized in the experiences of two boys, Dualta and Dominic. With a small band of compatriots, they fight underground against the British, from the Easter Rebellion to the proclamation of the Irish Free State and the ensuing civil war that splits the country.

Historical Accuracy: The period background and events are close to reality.

3989 *Seek the Fair Land*

Date of Publication: 1959
Subject(s): Civil War—England; Independence—Ireland
Fictional character(s): Dominick MacMahon, Young Man; Murdoc, Revolutionary, Patriot; Sebastian, Religious (priest)
Time Period(s): 17th century (1640s)
Locale(s): Ireland

Summary: The trials and tribulations of Ireland under the iron grip of Oliver Cromwell's forces set the novel's background. Dominick MacMahon struggles on a long trek from his destroyed town in search of a new life. He is torn between the selflessness of the priest Sebastian and the Irish patriot Murdoc.

Historical Accuracy: The novel offers an authentic look at 17th-century Ireland under the repressive policy of Cromwell.

3990 *The Silent People*

Date of Publication: 1962
Subject(s): Independence—Ireland; Irish Potato Famine; Religious Conflict
Fictional character(s): Dualta, Patriot, Farmer; Cuan, Outlaw
Historical character(s): Daniel O'Connell, Political Figure
Time Period(s): 19th century
Locale(s): Galway, Ireland; Clare, Ireland

Summary: Set during a turbulent era of Irish history—the struggle for Catholic emancipation, the attempt to repeal the Act of Union, and the Great Famine—the novel describes the experiences of Dualta, who is unjustly driven from his Galway home. He takes up with Cuan and his gang of Tipperary men, who seek justice through violence. Dualta is persuaded of a different approach by Daniel O'Connell and his political party.

Historical Accuracy: The novel is convincing in creating a believable sense of the period and its great events.

MARY MACKEY (1945-)

Born in Indiana, Mackey graduated from Harvard and the University of Michigan. She is a professor of English and writer-in-residence at California State University at Sacramento.

3991 *A Grand Passion*

Date of Publication: 1986
Subject(s): Theatrical Life; Dance; Motion Picture Industry
Fictional character(s): Natasha Ladanova, Dancer; Tatiana Trey, Dancer; Alysa Rochina, Dancer
Time Period(s): 20th century (1911-1974)
Locale(s): St. Petersburg, Russia; New York, New York; Hollywood, California

Summary: This is the story of three generations of ballet dancers living in pre-revolutionary Russia, Hollywood in the 1950s, and New York in the 1970s. Natasha Ladanova finds success in the Imperial Ballet on the eve of the revolution. Her daughter goes to Hollywood for fame in the movies, and her granddaughter must deal both with her passion for the dance and her family's legacy.

Historical Accuracy: The novel establishes a convincing historical backdrop for the family drama, and a solid depiction of theatrical life.

3992 *The Last Warrior Queen*

Date of Publication: 1983
Subject(s): Prehistory; Tribal Life—Prehistoric
Fictional character(s): Inanna, Prehistoric Human, Ruler (queen)
Time Period(s): 37th century B.C.
Locale(s): Mesopotamia

Summary: Set in the distant past when great matriarchal cultures are on the verge of being overrun by nomads, the novel concerns Inanna, a young woman with psychic powers, who leaves her own people and travels to the City of the Dove. There she becomes queen and leads the city into battle, forcing her to choose between her own people and her adoptive home.

Historical Accuracy: Much about pre-Sumerian Mesopotamia is speculative, although the author points out that there is evidence that the Sumerians may have overrun and absorbed an earlier matriarchal culture.

3993 *The Year the Horses Came*

Date of Publication: 1993
Subject(s): Prehistory; Tribal Life—Prehistoric
Fictional character(s): Marrah, Religious (priestess), Prehistoric Human; Stavan, Warrior, Prehistoric Human
Time Period(s): 44th century B.C. (4372)
Locale(s): Europe

Summary: The story is set in the fifth millennium B.C. as Europe is on the brink of major cultural transformations.

Marauding nomads from the East bring horses and war to Europe, which had been at peace for thousands of years. Marrah is a young priestess who falls in love with Stavan, one of the invading warriors. Her experiences re-create primitive life in Europe.

Historical Accuracy: The details about the European Neolithic period are convincing.

JEANNE MACKIN (1951-)

American novelist and journalist Mackin was born in New York and graduated from Ithaca and Bennington colleges. She has worked as an instructor in journalism, and a dance and performance auditor for the New York State Council on the Arts.

3994 *Dreams of Empire*

Date of Publication: 1996
Subject(s): Napoleonic Era; Treasure Hunt; Ancient Egypt
Fictional character(s): Marguerite Verdier, Artist
Historical character(s): Napoleon Bonaparte, Military Personnel (army commander); Thomas Bruce, Nobleman (Earl of Elgin)
Time Period(s): 1790s (1799); 1st century B.C.
Locale(s): Cairo, Egypt

Summary: Napoleon's conquest of Egypt sets the background for this novel concerning the search for a valuable and powerful stela called the "Woman Carried Away." The search involves Marguerite Verdier, an illustrator accompanying Napoleon on his campaign. Others, including Lord Elgin, are after the prize as well, and Marguerite's fate depends on the outcome, as she is accused of plotting Napoleon's murder. The action shifts between Egypt in the 1790s and ancient times.

Historical Accuracy: The novel is convincing in rendering the Egyptian scene during the time of Napoleon.

3995 *The Frenchwoman*

Date of Publication: 1989
Subject(s): French Revolution; Settlement of the American Frontier
Fictional character(s): Julienne, Seamstress
Historical character(s): Marie Antoinette, Royalty (queen consort of Louis XVI)
Time Period(s): 18th century; 19th century (1774-1836)
Locale(s): Paris, France; Pennsylvania

Summary: Julienne, the illegitimate daughter of a Paris prostitute, becomes Marie Antoinette's favorite dressmaker. As the revolution threatens, she is entrusted by the queen for a secret mission that takes her to the actual log-cabin colony in America, called French Azilum, meant to become Marie Antoinette's new home. Danger threatens Julienne in her new life in America.

Historical Accuracy: The novel blends fiction and fact, but the period details are authentic and compelling.

3996 *The Queen's War: A Novel of Eleanor of Aquitaine*

Date of Publication: 1991
Subject(s): Middle Ages; Royalty—England
Fictional character(s): Lucie, Actress; Godfrey, Actor; Benoit, Knight
Historical character(s): Eleanor of Aquitaine, Royalty (queen consort of Henry II); Henry II, Ruler (King of England); Richard the Lionhearted, Royalty (prince)
Time Period(s): 12th century
Locale(s): Poitiers, France

Summary: Set in Eleanor of Aquitaine's Court of Love, the novel describes the adventures of a young peasant girl, Lucie, who becomes one of Eleanor's favorites and one of the most sought after maidens at court. Eleanor, cast off by her husband, Henry II, plots her revenge as her sons begin their rebellion against their father.

Historical Accuracy: The author points out that, although based on research, this is a work of fiction representing her opinion.

MEAGAN MACKINNEY

3997 *Fair is the Rose*

Date of Publication: 1993
Subject(s): American West; Crime and Criminals; Romance
Fictional character(s): Christal Van Alen, Gentlewoman; Macaulay Cain, Veteran (Confederate), Outlaw
Time Period(s): 1870s (1875-1876)
Locale(s): Wyoming

Summary: Christal Van Alen, framed for a crime she did not commit, flees west to the Wyoming Territory in 1876. Her stage coach is waylaid by ex-Confederate outlaws, and she is held for ransom by their leader, Macaulay Cain. Christal tries to keep her identity and past a secret while she finds herself dangerously attracted to the outlaw Cain.

Historical Accuracy: The period details are lightly sketched in this romantic adventure.

MARY LINEHAN MACKINNON

3998 *One Small Candle*

Date of Publication: 1956
Subject(s): Farming
Fictional character(s): Ellen Moynahan, Immigrant, Servant
Time Period(s): 1850s
Locale(s): New York

Summary: Set in the years before the Civil War, the novel describes life in a small farming community of upper New York state. The plot concerns the experiences of a young Irish immigrant, Ellen Moynahan, who marries a man she does not love. When she strays with another, her true feelings are revealed.

Historical Accuracy: The plot is stock but enlivened by a solid period backdrop.

ALISTAIR MACLEAN (1922-1987)

Bestselling Scottish novelist Alistair MacLean was born in Glasgow and was educated at the University of Glasgow. One of Britain's most popular novelists, MacLean is best know for his war adventures, including *The Guns of Navarone*, *Force Ten From Navarone*, and *Where Eagles Dare*, all of whic were adapted by him as screenplays and produced as motion pictures.

3999 *Breakheart Pass*

Date of Publication: 1974
Subject(s): American West; Indians
Fictional character(s): John Deakin, Outlaw; Nathan Pearce, Lawman (U.S. marshall); White Hand, Indian (Paiute), Chieftain
Time Period(s): 1870s
Locale(s): Rocky Mountains

Summary: This adventure tale is set on board an army relief train in the Rocky Mountains during the 1870s. Federal agent Nathan Pearce is pitted against a group of gunmen and thieves.

Historical Accuracy: This period thriller provides an authentic atmosphere.

ALISON MACLEOD (1920-)

Born in Canada and now living in England, Macleod has worked as a freelance journalist and teacher at the London College of Printing. Her short fiction and plays have been nominated for numerous awards, and her historical novels have been widely praised for their strong feeling of place and time.

4000 *The Changeling*

Date of Publication: 1996
Subject(s): American Colonies; Pirates
Historical character(s): Anne Bonny, Pirate
Time Period(s): 17th century; 18th century (1690s-1720s)
Locale(s): Ireland; South Carolina, American Colonies; West Indies

Summary: The novel offers a fictional account of the remarkable career of Anne Bonny, daughter of a 17th-century solicitor and his servant, who transforms herself into a "male" pirate.

Historical Accuracy: The novel blends the known with the imagined to create a fully realized portrait of Bonny, sustained by a convincing period atmosphere.

4001 *City of Light*

Date of Publication: 1969
Subject(s): Tudor Period; Religious Conflict
Fictional character(s): Tom Vaughan, Servant, Spy
Historical character(s): John Knox, Religious (Protestant leader); John Calvin, Religious (Protestant leader)
Time Period(s): 16th century
Locale(s): Venice, Italy; Geneva, Switzerland

Summary: In this continuation of the adventures of Tom Vaughan, spy for Henry VIII, Tom is in exile in Venice. His deepest desire is to see his son once more, and he journeys to Calvin's Geneva, which is caught in the grips of a spiritual fervour that produces a series of adventures for Vaughan.

Historical Accuracy: The novel offers far more than a simple period adventure. It captures the period and its complexity with some insight.

4002 *The Heretic*

Date of Publication: 1966
Subject(s): Tudor Period; Religious Conflict; Royalty—England
Fictional character(s): Nancy Scarlett, Servant; John Fox, Government Official
Historical character(s): Anne Askew, Religious (Protestant martyr); Henry VIII, Ruler (King of England); Katherine Parr, Royalty (queen consort of Henry VIII)
Time Period(s): 16th century (1540s)
Locale(s): England

Summary: Based on the account of the actual Protestant martyr, Anne Askew, the novel details Askew's two trials and torture on the rack. Told by her maid, the account presents Askew's great strength under adversity and Henry VIII's persecution of both Catholics and Protestants.

Historical Accuracy: Little is known of Anne Askew outside her own account, and many questions go unanswered. This story, like any account of Askew's life, whether fictional or historic, is based on speculation.

4003 *The Hireling*

Date of Publication: 1968
Subject(s): Tudor Period; Royalty—England
Fictional character(s): Tom Vaughan, Servant, Spy
Historical character(s): Henry VIII, Ruler (King of England); Catherine of Aragon, Royalty (queen consort of Henry VIII); Thomas Cromwell, Courtier; Reginald Pole, Religious (cardinal)
Time Period(s): 16th century
Locale(s): Huntingdonshire, England; London, England; Venice, Italy

Summary: Tom Vaughan, the orphan son of one of Catherine of Aragon's ladies-in-waiting, agrees to serve Henry VIII by spying on Catherine who is living in seclusion, separated from the king. At first his intelligence brings him royal favor and gifts, but he is shortly caught up in the unpredictable and shifting winds of Tudor politics.

Historical Accuracy: Vaughn is a believable character and the scene and period details are authentically delivered.

4004 *The Muscovite*

Date of Publication: 1971
Subject(s): Elizabethan Period; Russian Empire
Historical character(s): Jerome Horsey, Trader, Diplomat; Ivan IV, Ruler (Czar of Russia); Boris Godunov, Nobleman; Elizabeth I, Ruler (Queen of England)
Time Period(s): 16th century (1570s-1590s)

Locale(s): Russia; England

Summary: The novel tells the true story of Jerome Horsey, who in 1573, is sent by the Russia Company of London as a trader to the court of Ivan the Terrible. He spends the next eighteen years involved with Russia's rulers, amassing a fortune. His fellow Englishmen accuse him of embezzlement and high treason, while the Russians accuse him of spying. The novel explores the colorful and ambiguous career of Horsey and the tangled intrigue of the Elizabethan period and the Russian court.

Historical Accuracy: Horsey was an actual person, and his own accounts have been used to tell his story with surmises added to fill in the gaps. Except for the date of one murder and the year of Horsey's trial, no facts have been altered.

4005 *The Portingale*

Date of Publication: 1976
Subject(s): Restoration Period; Royalty—England; Biography, Fictionalized
Historical character(s): Charles II, Ruler (King of England); Catherine of Braganza, Royalty (queen consort of Charles II); Samuel Pepys, Writer; Andrew Marvell, Writer (poet); Aphra Behn, Writer
Time Period(s): 17th century
Locale(s): England; Portugal

Summary: This fictional biography of Charles II's queen, Catherine of Braganza, portrays her as a sympathetic and complex figure. Catherine is shown first in the narrow royal world of the Portugal of her youth. The novel's center is her relationship with Charles II whose almost chronic unfaithfulness is a source of great pain for Catherine.

Historical Accuracy: The novel provides an historically accurate portrait of the age and its leading figures.

4006 *Prisoner of the Queen*

Date of Publication: 1973
Subject(s): Elizabethan Period; Religious Conflict
Fictional character(s): Paul Calverley, Religious (Jesuit priest)
Historical character(s): Sir Francis Walsingham, Government Official
Time Period(s): 16th century
Locale(s): Italy; England

Summary: Set during the Catholic persecution in the reign of Elizabeth I, the novel tells the story of a young Jesuit priest, Paul Calverley, who returns to England intent on ministering to English Catholics. He finds conspiracy and betrayal on all sides, and is torn between Church and State. To side with one means betrayal of the other. Meanwhile, forces of invasion push the religious matter to a climax.

Historical Accuracy: This is a believable depiction of the era and the issues, recognizing the perspective of both sides in the conflict.

LE ROY MACLEOD

4007 *The Battle-Ax of God*

Date of Publication:
Subject(s): Crusades; Middle Ages
Fictional character(s): Orme, Young Man; Ralph, Earl of Clarendon, Nobleman
Time Period(s): 11th century
Locale(s): England; Palestine

Summary: Orme, the young son of a Saxon thane, makes an enemy of a powerful lord, Ralph, Earl of Clarendon, when he defends the honor of his aunt. To seek revenge, Orme strives to become a knight, joining the First Crusade for a series of perilous adventures.

Historical Accuracy: The period elements are authentic, and the historical framework of the factual story is true to historical fact.

4008 *The Crowded Hill*

Date of Publication: 1934
Subject(s): Reconstruction Period
Fictional character(s): Tyler Peck, Spouse; Evaline Peck, Spouse
Time Period(s): 1860s
Locale(s): Wabash Valley, Indiana

Summary: This sequel to *Years of Peace*, is set in the Wabash Valley area of Indiana following the Civil War. The story concerns the marriage of Tyler and Evaline Peck, whose opposite natures are tested by several challenges.

Historical Accuracy: The period and regional elements are authentic and believable.

4009 *Years of Peace*

Date of Publication: 1932
Subject(s): Reconstruction Period
Fictional character(s): Tyler Peck, Spouse; Evaline Peck, Spouse
Time Period(s): 1860s
Locale(s): Wabash Valley, Indiana

Summary: This is a tale of daily life in Indiana's Wabash Valley following the Civil War. It concerns the meeting of rebellious Tyler Peck and Evaline, his future bride.

Historical Accuracy: The novel provides an authentic portrait of regional and period life.

DUNCAN MACNEIL
(PSEUD. OF PHILIP MCCUTCHAN, 1920-)

A British adventure writer, McCutchan joined the Royal Navy in 1939. He served on every type of warship during the Second World War and ended as a lieutenant. A prolific writer of more than 60 books, he divides his output between sea stories and thrillers, as well as military novels under the pseudonym Duncan McNeil.

`4010` *By Command of the Viceroy*

Date of Publication: 1975
Subject(s): English Colonies; Military Life—British Army; Royalty—Russia
Fictional character(s): James Ogilvie, Military Personnel (army officer); Ian Ogilvie, Military Personnel (army commander)
Historical character(s): Elizabeth Fedorovna, Royalty (Russian grand duchess); Victor Bruce, Political Figure (Viceroy of India), Nobleman (Earl of Elgin); Victoria, Ruler (Queen of England); Robert Gascoyne-Cecil, Political Figure (prime minister), Nobleman (Marquis of Salisbury)
Time Period(s): 1890s
Locale(s): Khyber Pass, India; Kathmandu, Nepal

Summary: Captain Ogilvie becomes involved in state politics when given the task of escorting a Russian mission to Nepal across the northern frontier of British India. The Russian delegation includes Queen Victoria's granddaughter, Elizabeth, the wife of Grand Duke Sergius. Suspicion is rife on both sides during the long trek from the Khyber to Kathmandu.

Historical Accuracy: The story is fanciful but well-detailed by period and local color.

`4011` *Charge of Cowardice*

Date of Publication: 1978
Subject(s): English Colonies; Military Life—British Army; British Raj
Fictional character(s): James Ogilvie, Military Personnel (army officer); Ian Ogilvie, Military Personnel (army officer)
Historical character(s): Victor Bruce, Political Figure (Viceroy of India), Nobleman (Earl of Elgin)
Time Period(s): 1890s
Locale(s): North-West Frontier, India

Summary: Captain Ogilvie's regiment is sent to put down an insurrection, and he is involved in a series of blunders that could result in the catastrophic end of his military career. Ogilvie must act decisively to reverse circumstances which effect not only British Raj but the whole world. *Mai*ACC The novel is knowledgeable and convincing in detailing military customs and locales of the period.

`4012` *Cunningham's Revenge*

Date of Publication: 1980
Subject(s): British Raj; Religious Conflict; Victorian Period
Fictional character(s): James Ogilvie, Military Personnel (British captain)
Time Period(s): 19th century
Locale(s): Peshawar, India

Summary: In this adventure tale of the British in India during the 19th century, Captain James Ogilvie of the 114th Queen's Own Royal Strathspeys finds himself seconded to the Political Department to infiltrate embattled Peshawar and seek out its Pathan leader. At risk is British control of the Raj from the Afghan border to the Indus River.

Historical Accuracy: The story is fictional but filled with authentic period elements.

`4013` *Drums Along the Khyber*

Date of Publication: 1969
Subject(s): English Colonies; Military Life—British Army; British Raj
Fictional character(s): James Ogilvie, Military Personnel (army officer); Ian Ogilivie, Military Personnel (army commander)
Time Period(s): 1890s (1894)
Locale(s): Khyber Pass, India; North-West Frontier, India

Summary: In the first of a series of military adventures set in the India of the British Raj, James Ogilvie's regiment is sent to the Khyber Pass to contain an Afghan rebel. He is unsure of himself and his suitability for a career in the military and must contend with the expectations of his irascible father and the divisional commander of the North-West Frontier.

Historical Accuracy: The details of military life of the time and of colonial customs in India are exact and credible.

`4014` *The Gates of Kunara*

Date of Publication: 1973
Subject(s): English Colonies; Military Life—British Army; British Raj
Fictional character(s): James Ogilvie, Military Personnel (army officer); Jara Mahommed, Chieftain (Afghan)
Time Period(s): 1890s (1897)
Locale(s): North-West Frontier, India; Kawarja, Afghanistan; Khyber Pass, India

Summary: In this military adventure set in the North-West Frontier of India, Captain James Ogilvie is temporarily seconded to a sepoy battalion. The battalion is sent to relieve the British residents of Kawarja who are being held for ransom by an Afghan rebel. Ogilvie must return through the Khyber Pass to carry the chieftain's terms to the British authorities and bring the British residents to safety.

Historical Accuracy: The period details, particularly the military strategy and army customs, are strongly depicted.

`4015` *Lieutenant of the Line*

Date of Publication: 1970
Subject(s): English Colonies; Military Life—British Army; British Raj
Fictional character(s): James Ogilvie, Military Personnel (army officer); Mary Archdale, Gentlewoman
Time Period(s): 1890s
Locale(s): North-West Frontier, India; Simla, India

Summary: In the second story of the military adventures of James Ogilvie, the action shifts between dangerous patrols on the North-West Indian Frontier and the formal British colonial world at Simla where Ogilvie woos Mary Archdale. The action culminates in the battle for Fort Gazai where Ogilvie must act quickly and boldly to save his men.

Historical Accuracy: The author is convincing both in the military details and the world of the Indian colonials.

`4016` *The Mullah From Kashmir*

Date of Publication: 1976

Subject(s): British Raj; Military Life; Victorian Period
Fictional character(s): James Ogilvie, Military Personnel (British captain)
Time Period(s): 19th century
Locale(s): Peshawar, India; Kashmir, India

Summary: In this installment of the adventures of Captain James Ogilvie of the 114th Queen's Own Royal Strathspeys, complications are created by the arrival of the Viceroy to Peshawar, a city in the grips of religious unrest. Ogilvie is called on to slip into the city in native disguise to find a mullah who has come from Kashmir to foment trouble between Muslims and Hindus.

Historical Accuracy: The novel is filled with authentic period elements.

4017 *The Red Daniel*

Date of Publication: 1973
Subject(s): Boer War; Military Life—British Army; Espionage
Fictional character(s): James Ogilvie, Military Personnel (army officer)
Historical character(s): Douglas Haig, Military Personnel (army officer); Louis Botha, Military Personnel (Boer general); Horatio Herbert Kitchener, Military Personnel (army commander); Redvers Henry Buller, Military Personnel (army general)
Time Period(s): 1890s
Locale(s): Kimberley, South Africa

Summary: Instead of the home posting they expected, the 114th Queen's Own Royal Strathspreys are dispatched to South Africa during the Boer War to join the relief forces of besieged Kimberley. Captain Ogilvie is given a spying mission to penetrate behind the Boer lines. His passport into Kimberley is a unique rosy diamond, the Red Daniel.

Historical Accuracy: The military engagements described are historical and accurately depicted, though the story of Ogilvie's part is fanciful.

4018 *The Restless Frontier*

Date of Publication: 1979
Subject(s): English Colonies; Military Life—British Army; British Raj
Fictional character(s): James Ogilvie, Military Personnel (army officer); Hector Ogilvie, Government Official (working in India); Angela Ogilvie, Spouse (of Hector)
Time Period(s): 1890s
Locale(s): Waziristan, India (Afghan-India border)

Summary: The action in this installment of the military adventures of Captain James Ogilvie stems from a border dispute between rival tribes. The 114th is called in to arbitrate. Ogilvie, however, has even more pressing concerns as his cousin Hector's wife, Angela, is kidnapped by one of the tribes and held as a bargaining chip.

Historical Accuracy: The period and military details are authentic and convincing.

4019 *Sadhu on the Mountain Peak*

Date of Publication: 1973
Subject(s): English Colonies; Military Life—British Army; British Raj
Fictional character(s): James Ogilvie, Military Personnel (army officer); Mary Archdale, Gentlewoman
Time Period(s): 1890s
Locale(s): Khyber Pass, India; Peshawar, India

Summary: In this installment of the military adventures of Captain James Ogilvie, a revolt is brewing on the North-West Frontier led by a sadhu, or holy man. He plans to annihilate Peshawar as the first step towards driving the English out of India. Ogilvie, disguised as an arms seller, sets out to gain intelligence regarding the revolt and is quickly swept up in events that could spell the end of the British Raj.

Historical Accuracy: Fast-paced and exciting, the story is bolstered by authentic period details and a believable depiction of military customs of the time.

4020 *Subaltern's Choice*

Date of Publication: 1974
Subject(s): English Colonies; Military Life—British Army; British Raj
Fictional character(s): James Ogilvie, Military Personnel (army officer); Hamish Dewar, Military Personnel (subaltern)
Time Period(s): 1890s
Locale(s): Hindu Kush, India

Summary: A tribal insurrection in the foothills of the Hindu Kush sends the 114th in to restore the status quo. A patrol is massacred in the rebel-held stronghold of Kalundabad with only one survivor, new subaltern Haimish Dewar, who is as foolhardy as he is fearless. Captain Ogilvie must mount a relief effort while controlling the battalion's over-zealous recruit.

Historical Accuracy: The novel offers a remarkably detailed and authentic look at the locale and the military customs of British India.

4021 *The Train at Bundarbar*

Date of Publication: 1981
Subject(s): English Colonies; Military Life—British Army; British Raj
Fictional character(s): James Ogilvie, Military Personnel (army officer); Francis Fettleworth, Military Personnel (army general); Fiona Elliott, Gentlewoman
Time Period(s): 1890s
Locale(s): Patna, India

Summary: An Indian flood provides a series of obstacles and challenges for Captain Ogilvie. The Rawalpindi to Calcutta train is floodbound and under attack by the Patnas. On board is Fiona Elliott, the niece of the 114th's second-in-command, and 100,000 pounds in gold. Ogilvie is detached to rescue the train, save the passengers and protect and Raj's gold.

Historical Accuracy: High-speed adventure is featured along with accurate period details.

`4022` *Wolf in the Fold*

Date of Publication: 1977
Subject(s): English Colonies; Military Life—British Army; British Raj
Fictional character(s): James Ogilvie, Military Personnel (army officer); Horatio Soames, Military Personnel (army officer)
Time Period(s): 1890s
Locale(s): London, England; Peshawar, India

Summary: While on leave in London, Captain Ogilvie comes to the aid of a fellow soldier who is being held on a trumped up charge. Ogilvie's investigation leads him to the discovery of a traitor in the regiment who is conspiring with the mysterious North-West Frontier bandit, the Wolf of the Salt Range. Back in India, Ogilvie serves as the agent provocateur to flush out the traitor.

Historical Accuracy: Fast-paced and exciting, the novel, like the series, relies on solid period background and evident knowledge of military customs.

ROBERT MACNEIL (1931-)

For almost 20 years MacNeil was co-anchor on Public Television's award-winning "MacNeil/Lehrer Report." He retired in October 1995 to pursue in earnest his career as a novelist. He was born in Montreal and, after obtaining a degree in English from Carleton University in 1955, went to work for Reuters News Service in London. In 1960 he began working as a correspondent for NBC News, then returned to London to work for the BBC in 1967. To date he has written four novels plus his memoirs, *Wordstruck*, and several non-fiction works.

`4023` *Burden of Desire*

Date of Publication: 1992
Subject(s): World War I
Fictional character(s): Peter Wentworth, Religious (minister); Stewart MacPherson, Psychologist; Julia Robertson, Young Woman
Time Period(s): 1910s
Locale(s): Halifax, Nova Scotia, Canada

Summary: The novel is set in Halifax, Nova Scotia, during World War I. It is based on the actual explosion of a freighter carrying dynamite in Halifax harbor which destroyed an entire district of the city. A young minister, Peter Wentworth, finds a woman's diary in a bundle of donated clothing, which leads him and his friend psychologist Stewart MacPherson to Julia Robertson, a young woman whose husband is fighting in France. The three struggle with conflicting emotions amidst the wreckage of war.

Historical Accuracy: Though based on actuality, the story is fictional. The period details of Halifax are authentic, however.

SALVADOR DE MADARIAGA
(1886-1976)

A Spanish diplomat, author, and scholar, Madariaga was born in La Coruna, Spain, and was educated at the College Chaptal, the Ecole Polytechnique, and the Ecole Nationale Superieure des Mines in Paris. One of Spain's leading intellectuals, Madariaga served in the 1930s as Spanish ambassador to the U.S. and France, and a delegate to the League of Nations. He fled to Great Britain after the outbreak of the Spanish Civil War. One of the foremost critics of the Franco regime, Madariaga did not return to Spain until after Franco's death in 1975. His works include *Spain*, a history of his native country, and a biographical trilogy on South America comprised of.

`4024` *The Heart of Jade*

Date of Publication: 1944
Subject(s): Aztec Empire; Spanish Colonies
Fictional character(s): Xuchitl, Royalty (Aztec princess); Alonso Manrique, Nobleman; Ixcawatzin, Warrior, Religious (priest)
Historical character(s): Montezuma II, Ruler (Aztec emperor); Hernando Cortez, Explorer, Military Personnel (conquistador)
Time Period(s): 16th century
Locale(s): Mexico; Spain

Summary: Set during the period of the Spanish conquest of Mexico, the novel presents a panoramic look at Aztec life and culture as it is being impacted by the Spanish invasion. Dozens of invented and historical figures illustrate the clash of cultures. However, the situation is trivialized somewhat in the romance between the Aztec princess Xuchitl and Don Alonso Manrique, one of Cortez's lieutenants.

Historical Accuracy: Evident research into every aspect of Aztec customs creates an authentic and informative background for the historical events.

ROBIN MADERICH

`4025` *Faith and Honor*

Date of Publication: 1989
Subject(s): American Revolution; Romance; Espionage
Fictional character(s): Faith Mary Asher, Spy, Widow(er); Fletcher Irons, Military Personnel (British soldier), Nobleman
Time Period(s): 1770s; 1780s (1775-1781)
Locale(s): New England

Summary: This romantic adventure novel is set during the American Revolution. It describes the love affair between Faith Asher and British soldier Fletcher Irons, adversaries on different sides in the conflict.

Historical Accuracy: More realistic than most historical romances, the novel features a solid background of colonial life and customs.

LINDA MADL

`4026` *Sweet Ransom*

Date of Publication: 1989
Subject(s): Russian Revolution; Cossacks; Romance

Fictional character(s): Elise Chatham Polonsky, Noblewoman (countess), Captive; Nikholai Famin, Outlaw, Leader (Cossack)
Time Period(s): 17th century (1669)
Locale(s): Russia

Summary: The story is set in a primitive Russia's Cossack community of the 17th century. The Countess Polonsky is held for ransom by a dashing Cossack leader. Love follows as the countess is exposed to the different culture of the warring Cossacks.

Historical Accuracy: The emphasis is on romance and emotions, not historical documentation. There is, however, an effort to capture some of the customs of the Cossacks.

DAVID MADSEN (1929-)

An American novelist born in North Dakota, Madsen received degrees from the University of North Dakota and the University of Chicago. He is a professor of education at the University of Washington, Seattle.

4027 *Black Plume: The Supressed Memoirs of Edgar Allan Poe*

Date of Publication: 1980
Subject(s): Biography, Fictionalized; Literary Life
Historical character(s): Edgar Allan Poe, Writer; Virginia Clemm, Spouse (of Poe)
Time Period(s): 1830s; 1840s (1835-1847)
Locale(s): New York, New York

Summary: This fictionalized memoir re-creates the life of Edgar Allan Poe, including his strange marriage to his child-bride, his struggle to make a living, and his addiction to alcohol. Poe emerges as a prisoner of his sensual nature, indulging his passion in low-life experiences that include opium and murder. Poe finds himself on the trail of a killer in an exercise in terror that rivals many of his stories.

Historical Accuracy: The novel is a blend of fact and fiction with a solid biographical background.

KATHLEEN MAGILL (1948-)

Born in Pennsylvania, Magill is a graduate of Ohio University and the California Institute of Asian Studies. She is a freelance researcher and advertising copywriter in San Francisco, as well as a playwright and novelist.

4028 *Megan*

Date of Publication: 1983
Subject(s): Romance; American West
Fictional character(s): Megan Byers Moore, Young Woman
Time Period(s): 1880s (1889)
Locale(s): Nebraska (eastern); Idaho City, Idaho

Summary: Set in the West of the 1880s, the story follows the adventures of Megan Byers Moore from the tedium of her life on a Nebraska farm to her escape to an Idaho boomtown and a series of tests and challenges to her independence and resourcefulness.

Historical Accuracy: The novel captures with some skill the period background.

JAMES MAGNUSON

DOROTHY PETRIE MAGNUSON

4029 *Orphan Train*

Date of Publication: 1978
Subject(s): Religious Life
Historical character(s): Edward Symms, Religious (minister)
Time Period(s): 1850s (1853)
Locale(s): New York; Midwest

Summary: Based on actual events, the novel describes the attempt in the 1850s to relocate groups of orphans from the Northeast to the Midwest, an effort supervised by the Reverend Edward Symms.

Historical Accuracy: The novel is faithful to the facts.

MARY MAHER (1940-)

Born in Chicago, Maher was a journalist and feature writer for the *Chicago Tribune* before moving to Ireland and working for the *Irish Times*.

4030 *The Devil's Card*

Date of Publication: 1992
Subject(s): Mystery; Politics
Fictional character(s): Tom Martin, Journalist; Dick Huntley, Journalist
Time Period(s): 1880s (1880)
Locale(s): Chicago, Illinois

Summary: Set in 1880s Chicago, the novel is based on the actual disappearance of a prominant Irish doctor, P.H. Cronin. Young reporter Tom Martin investigates the case, and he is plunged into the Chicago Irish underground and a deadly secret society.

Historical Accuracy: The mystery is based on fact.

CECIL MAIDEN (1902-)

Born in England, Maiden was educated at Reading University, where he started writing. One of his early stories was sold to Paramount Pictures, which began his association with motion pictures. He has worked for both Walt Disney and Universal Studios.

4031 *Harp into Battle*

Date of Publication: 1959
Subject(s): Middle Ages; Royalty—England
Fictional character(s): Benfras, Minstrel
Historical character(s): Llywelyn the Great, Ruler (North Wales chieftain); John, Ruler (King of England); Joan, Royalty (princess), Bastard Daughter (of King John)
Time Period(s): 12th century
Locale(s): Wales; England

Summary: In 1194 Llewelyn returns to Wales from exile to take the throne as ruler of North Wales. The novel depicts his struggle to secure his Welsh realm against encroachment led by England's King John. Circumstances are further complicated by Llewelyn's romance with Joan, the illegitimate daughter of King John.

Historical Accuracy: The author states that while this work is based on certain historical facts of the life of Llewelyn the Great of Wales, some events have been omitted or altered.

`4032` *Man Before the Morning*

Date of Publication: 1977
Subject(s): Biblical Story
Historical character(s): Joseph of Arimathea, Biblical Figure; Mary, Biblical Figure; Pontius Pilate, Government Official, Biblical Figure
Time Period(s): 1st century
Locale(s): Jerusalem, Israel

Summary: The novel tells the Easter story of Jesus' crucifixion from the perspective of Joseph of Arimathea, who challenges the Sanhedrin to try to save Christ from execution and then attempts to recover his body when he has failed.

Historical Accuracy: The story is based on an imagined extension of the scriptural evidence, offering a plausible background for the familiar events.

PAUL L. MAIER (1930-)

Born in St. Louis, Maier is a graduate of Harvard, Concordia Seminary, and the University of Basel. He is a professor of ancient history at Western Michigan University.

`4033` *The Flames of Rome*

Date of Publication: 1981
Subject(s): Roman Empire; Christianity
Historical character(s): Flavius Sabinus, Military Personnel (Roman soldier); Claudius I, Ruler (Roman emperor); Nero, Ruler (Roman emperor); Peter, Biblical Figure, Religious; Paul, Biblical Figure, Religious
Time Period(s): 1st century
Locale(s): Rome, Roman Empire

Summary: The novel concerns ancient Rome during the reigns of Claudius and Nero. Flavius Sabinus returns home in triumph after the victory over the Britons. He finds a city tormented by excess and treachery. He turns to Christianity as Rome burns, and Nero is in need of a convenient scapegoat.

Historical Accuracy: The author states that he did not tamper with the known facts or invent characters. The factual framework is documented in his notes, some of which, he claims, reveal new historical data.

`4034` *Pontius Pilate: A Biographical Novel*

Date of Publication: 1968
Subject(s): Biography, Fictionalized; Biblical Story; Roman Empire

Historical character(s): Pontius Pilate, Government Official (procurator of Judea), Biblical Figure; Jesus Christ, Biblical Figure; Lucius Aelius Sejanus, Military Personnel (Roman general), Political Figure; Herod Antipas, Ruler (Tetrarch of Galilee); Caligula, Ruler (Roman emperor); Herod Agrippa I, Ruler (King of Judea); Procula, Spouse (of Pilate)
Time Period(s): 1st century
Locale(s): Rome, Roman Empire; Jerusalem, Israel

Summary: This biographical novel attempts to trace the life of Pontius Pilate before and after the trial of Jesus. Pilate is shown as a player in the political intrigue surrounding Tiberius Caesar, an able governor of Judea, who attempts to save Jesus' life before later condemning him. In Rome, Pilate returns to the shifting and dangerous arena of Roman politics of Caligula and Claudius.

Historical Accuracy: All the major events in the book are historical and supported by careful documentation as the extensive notes indicate. A blend of fact and fiction, the auther labels his work a "documented historical novel.".

NORMAN MAILER (1923-)

Celebrated American author Norman Mailer was born in Long Branch, New Jersey, and was educated at Harvard and the Sorbonne. His army experience in the Pacific during World War II resulted in his first novel, *The Naked and the Dead*, which became a critically acclaimed bestseller. Mailer's other books include the Pulitzer Prize-winning nonfiction work *Armies of the Night*, *American Dream*, and *Tough Guys Don't Dance*.

`4035` *Ancient Evenings*

Date of Publication: 1983
Subject(s): Ancient Egypt; Reincarnation; Pharaohs
Fictional character(s): Menenhetet, Wanderer, Military Personnel (soldier)
Historical character(s): Ramses II, Ruler (pharaoh)
Time Period(s): 13th century B.C.; 12th century B.C. (1290-1100 B.C.)
Locale(s): Egypt

Summary: Mailer's elaborate reconstruction of pharaonic Egypt is set during the nineteenth and twentieth dynasties and records the four lifetimes of Menenhetet who rises from peasant birth to become first charioteer to Ramses II. His later lives cast him as a general, harem master, magician, high priest, and grave robber. The novel is a tour de force of psychological reconstruction of the lives and culture of ancient Egypt.

Historical Accuracy: The novel has been called the best reconstruction of the far past since Gustave Flaubert's *Salammbo*. However, the whole is ruled by a decidedly modernist sensibility.

`4036` *The Executioner's Song*

Date of Publication: 1979
Subject(s): Crime and Criminals
Historical character(s): Gary Gilmore, Murderer
Time Period(s): 1970s (1976-1977)

Locale(s): Utah

Summary: This documentary novel dramatizes the life and times of Gary Gilmore, the first man executed after the reinstatement of the death penalty. The story covers the brief period between Gilmore's release from prison in 1976 to his execution for murder in 1977, with his marketing as a public figure as he awaits the death he demands in a Utah prison.

Historical Accuracy: The novel's documentary method sifts through a mountain of facts and details to arrive at an authentic portrait of Gilmore.

MARY MAIN

4037 *The Girl Who Was Never Queen:*
A Biographical Novel of Princess
Charlotte of Wales

Date of Publication: 1962
Subject(s): Royalty—England; Biography, Fictionalized; Regency Period
Historical character(s): Charlotte, Princess of Wales, Royalty; George, Royalty (Prince of Wales); Charles Hess, Military Personnel (captain); Frederick III, Royalty (prince); Leopold of Saxe-Coburg, Nobleman
Time Period(s): 1810s
Locale(s): London, England

Summary: This biographical novel chronicles the life of Princess Charlotte of Wales, the only daughter of George IV. Next in line to the throne, Charlotte should have reigned in place of Victoria. She stands up to her father in pursuit of love over the affairs of state, and her story vividly depicts life in Georgian England during the Regency.

Historical Accuracy: The basis of the story is factual with some slight surmises to fill in the gaps.

BERNARD MALAMUD (1914-1986)

Born in Brooklyn and educated at Columbia University, Malamud, whose parents were Russian-Jewish immigrants, is deemed one of the top Jewish American writers. He considered himself a universal writer who used Jewishness as a spiritual and moral attitude rather than a cultural heritage and religious creed. He authored a number of works that explore the ethnic conflict of American life and a search for meaning and values. His best known novel is *The Fixer*, which won the Pulitzer Prize in 1967. His other works include *The Magic Barrel*, *The Assistant*, and *Dubin's Lives*.

4038 *The Fixer*

Date of Publication: 1966
Subject(s): Russian Empire; Jews; Anti-Semitism
Fictional character(s): Yakov Bok, Worker (handyman), Murderer (accused)
Time Period(s): 1900s
Locale(s): Kiev, Russia

Summary: Based loosely on the life of a turn-of-the-century Russian Jew accused of the ritual murder of a Gentile child,

the novel traces the experiences of Yakov Bok, a handyman or fixer, who is coerced into confessing the crime and is used as an excuse by Tsarist officials to begin a pogrom. While incarcerated, Bok begins to reevaluate the meaning of his Jewishness. The novel ends with his fate in doubt as his trial begins.

Historical Accuracy: The novel is richly evocative of Jewish life in Tsarist Russia during the period.

MANOHAR MALGONKAR (1913-)

An Indian author born in Bombay and a graduate of Bombay University, Malgonkar has been a big-game hunter in India, an executive with the Indian Government Service, and the proprietor of a mining company. Malgonkar spent most of his life in a village deep in the Indian jungle. He is a noted wildlife conservationist.

4039 *The Devil's Wind: Nana Saheb's*
Story

Date of Publication: 1972
Subject(s): Indian Mutiny; British Raj; English Colonies
Historical character(s): Nana Saheb, Royalty (prince)
Time Period(s): 1850s
Locale(s): India

Summary: To the British the archvillain of the Sepoy Rebellion or Indian Mutiny is Nana Saheb, Indian prince and heir to the Maratha confederacy of North India. To Indians, Saheb is a heroic symbol in the struggle for national liberation. The novel offers an Indian perspective on the controversial leader of the rebellion as he offers his own revellations.

Historical Accuracy: The author has attempted to render Nana's story as he might have written it. The author states that although it is fiction, it takes no liberties with the facts.

FRANCOISE MALLET-JORIS

4040 *The Favourite*

Date of Publication: 1962
Subject(s): Royalty—France; Religious Life
Fictional character(s): Louise de La Fayette, Gentlewoman
Historical character(s): Armand-Jean Du Plessis, Religious (Cardinal Richelieu)
Time Period(s): 17th century
Locale(s): France

Summary: This novel of intrigue in the court of French King Louis XII depicts a battle by rival factions over Louise de La Fayette, a friend of the king. Cardinal Richelieu conspires to discredit her by employing as his agent Louise's confessor, whose job it is to convince her to enter a convent.

Historical Accuracy: More psychological study than historical, the novel offers a convincing portrait of the heroine, but the historical figures remain sketchy.

WILLIAM MALLIOL
(PSEUD. OF WILLIAM MCINENLY, 1932-)

English-born novelist Malliol was born in London and educated at Oxford, Princeton, and Columbia universities. He became an American citizen in 1969. Malliol has worked as an English teacher, an advertising copywriter, and a sea captain in Tahiti. Malliol received three Purple Hearts for service in Korea. He is an author of film scripts and short stories in addition to novels.

`4041` *Slave*

Date of Publication: 1986
Subject(s): Slavery; Tribal Life—African
Fictional character(s): Hadi Guwah Abbabba, Adventurer
Time Period(s): 19th century
Locale(s): Africa

Summary: The novel is set in Africa at the coming of the white man and the establishment of the slave trade. Hadi is a young man whose world is destroyed when his mother is condemned as a witch and his village is overrun by slave-traders. He moves north across the Sahara to Algeria, where he witnesses the battle of Bel-al-Din and the effort to expel the Foreign Legion.

Historical Accuracy: The basis for the story is factual. The period and the customs are rendered with conviction.

THOMAS MALLON (1951-)

Born in New York, Mallon graduated from Brown and Harvard universities. He is a professor of English at Vassar College. He has published a biography of the English writer Edmund Blunden and a book about diaries entitled *A Book of One's Own: People and Their Diaries.*

`4042` *Henry and Clara*

Date of Publication: 1994
Subject(s): Assassination; Civil War—U.S.
Historical character(s): Henry Rathbone, Military Personnel (Union soldier); Clara Harris Rathbone, Gentlewoman, Spouse; Abraham Lincoln, Political Figure; Mary Todd Lincoln, Spouse; Ulysses S. Grant, Political Figure; Ira Harris, Political Figure
Time Period(s): 19th century (1845-1883)
Locale(s): New York; Washington, District of Columbia; Europe

Summary: This is the story of Henry and Clara Rathbone, the young couple seated in the president's box at Ford's Theatre on the night of Lincoln's assassination. Their love affair and the tragic events that follow their proximity to the event that shocks a nation are dramatized in this remarkable effort of historical interpretation.

Historical Accuracy: Though solidly anchored in the documentary record, the story is a product of inference, speculation, and invention.

KATE MALLORY

`4043` *Sarton Kell*

Date of Publication: 1977
Subject(s): Romance; Suspense
Fictional character(s): Christopher Sarton, Heir; Olivia Sarton, Spouse
Time Period(s): 1890s
Locale(s): Lake Champlain, New York

Summary: Set on Lake Champlain in New York State in the 1890s, this romantic suspense novel dramatizes the experiences of Christopher Sarton and his bride, Olivia. They return to Sarton Kell, the huge marble mansion created by Milo Sarton before the Civil War when, with the help of Mohawk Indians, he established the richest mining operation in New York. Olivia is surrounded by family secrets and menace at every turn.

Historical Accuracy: The period setting is vividly and believably created.

EMMA LOUISE MALLY (1908-)

American writer and translator Mally was born in Dallas, Texas, and attended Barnard College and Columbia University. She is the author of *The Mockingbird Is Singing* and *Abigail*, and was the translator for the volume *Immortal Lieder: 800 Years of German Poetry.*

`4044` *The Tides of Dawn*

Date of Publication: 1949
Subject(s): Independence—Netherlands
Fictional character(s): Jacqueline Crois de Chatrois, Gentlewoman; Gerrit van Wagenen, Businessman (merchant)
Time Period(s): 16th century (1574)
Locale(s): Netherlands

Summary: The background for this story of Jacqueline Crois de Chatrois and Gerrit von Wagenen is the war of independence between the Netherlands and Spain. The conflict culminating in the liberation of Leyden in 1574 forms the novel's climax.

Historical Accuracy: The historical elements—actual events and the atmosphere of the period—are effectively and authentically delivered.

DOROTHEA MALM

`4045` *The Paper Mistress*

Date of Publication: 1959
Subject(s): Victorian Period
Fictional character(s): Sophronia Plattner, Young Woman; Alonzo Odell, Gentleman; Frederic Chichley, Gentleman
Time Period(s): 1850s
Locale(s): London, England; Venice, Italy; New York, New York

Summary: The adventures abroad of American Sophronia Plattner are depicted in this romantic story that follows Sophronia from New York to London and Venice. She attracts the attention of a variety of men who try to render her in their own image. Sophronia emerges as a strong and unique individual.

Historical Accuracy: The romance is anchored in a convincing background setting.

4046 *The Woman Question*

Date of Publication: 1957
Subject(s): Women's Rights
Fictional character(s): Phoebe Whitby, Young Woman; Mary Whitby, Teacher, Feminist; William Bonchurch, Gentleman
Historical character(s): Lucretia Mott, Feminist; Lucy Stone, Feminist, Editor; Susan B. Anthony, Feminist
Time Period(s): 1853
Locale(s): Renborough, Connecticut

Summary: This is an amusing look at domestic customs and the burgeoning women's rights movement that culminates in the first Women's Rights Convention in New York in 1853. Actual figures like Mott, Stone, and Anthony interact with an activist teacher from Connecticut, whose social views disrupt the sedate and conventional Whitby family.

Historical Accuracy: The period background is authentic.

DAVID MALOUF

4047 *An Imaginary Life*

Date of Publication: 1978
Subject(s): Roman Empire; Literary Life
Historical character(s): Ovid, Writer (poet)
Time Period(s): 1st century
Locale(s): Tomi, Romania (Constanta)

Summary: In 8 A.D. the Roman Emperor Augustus banished poet Ovid to the barren Black Sea village of Tomis. The novel imagines Ovid's life in exile, where the poet must come to terms with the strange contrast between his present life and his past in Rome.

Historical Accuracy: The novel is speculative of what Ovid's life must have been like and what the poet felt about his exile.

ERIC MALPASS (1910-)

An English novelist born in Derby, Malpass took a position at Barclay's Bank after leaving school in 1926. For 20 years, from 1947 to 1967, he wrote in the evenings after work. Malpass is the author of *Morning's at Seven*.

4048 *The Cleopatra Boy*

Date of Publication: 1974
Subject(s): Elizabethan Period; Theatrical Life; Biography, Fictionalized
Historical character(s): William Shakespeare, Writer, Actor; Anne Hathaway, Spouse; James I, Ruler (King of England); Ben Jonson, Writer; Henry Wriothesley, Nobleman; Richard Burbage, Actor
Time Period(s): 17th century
Locale(s): London, England; Stratford-on-Avon, England

Summary: In the second volume of the author's trilogy on the life of William Shakespeare, the playwright is shown in mid-career. The queen is dead, and massive changes are in store with the arrival of James Stuart from Scotland. Shakespeare has lost his youthful swagger and is turning away from comedies to the story of two ancient lovers in Egypt.

Historical Accuracy: The novel is an interweaving of fact and speculation. The era is captured vividly, and the interpretation offered is plausible.

4049 *A House of Women*

Date of Publication: 1975
Subject(s): Elizabethan Period; Theatrical Life; Biography, Fictionalized
Historical character(s): William Shakespeare, Writer; Anne Hathaway, Spouse
Time Period(s): 17th century
Locale(s): Stratford-on-Avon, England; London, England

Summary: In the final volume of the author's trilogy on Shakespeare's life, the playwright has returned to Stratford as a prosperous country gentleman. The story shifts to the dramatic relationship between Shakespeare and Anne Hathaway, and their daughters and the men they marry.

Historical Accuracy: Much of the story is invented. What we do know is here, and the background is plausibly created.

4050 *Sweet Will*

Date of Publication: 1974
Subject(s): Elizabethan Period; Theatrical Life; Biography, Fictionalized
Historical character(s): William Shakespeare, Writer, Actor; Anne Hathaway, Spouse (of William); Elizabeth I, Ruler (Queen of England); Henry Wriothesley, Nobleman; Edward Alleyn, Actor; Richard Burbage, Actor; Robert Dudley, Nobleman (Earl of Leicester); Robert Devereux, Nobleman
Time Period(s): 16th century; 17th century
Locale(s): Stratford-on-Avon, England; London, England

Summary: The first volume of this Shakespeare trilogy traces the life of William Shakespeare from his days in Stratford and early married life with Anne Hathaway to the rough and tumble of the London stage. It depicts Shakespeare's initial great success, propelled by a genius that was at odds with his obligations to his wife and family.

Historical Accuracy: The novel balances the facts we know about Shakespeare's life with a number of plausible surmises.

4051 *The Wind Brings Up the Rain*

Date of Publication: 1978
Subject(s): World War I; World War II
Fictional character(s): Nell Dorman, Widow(er); Benbow Dorman, Young Man
Time Period(s): 20th century (1914-1970s)
Locale(s): England

Summary: Set at the outbreak of World War I and continuing through World War II and beyond, this family story tells of a young widow, Nell Dorman, and her son, Benbow, whose lives are shaped by the war experience.

Historical Accuracy: The novel offers a convincing version of the war years and their effects.

ELONA MALTERRE

`4052` *Mistress of the Eagles*

Date of Publication: 1990
Subject(s): Middle Ages; Romance
Fictional character(s): Arrah O'Donnell, Noblewoman, Pirate; Seagan MacNamara, Nobleman
Time Period(s): 15th century (1446)
Locale(s): Ireland; France

Summary: Love and adventure are featured in this novel that describes the exploits of a female pirate captain who falls in love with Seagan MacNamara.

Historical Accuracy: The historical is given short shrift in this romantic adventure.

GLADYS MALVERN (?-1962)

A prolific American author of children's books, Malvern's career included work as an actress and as an advertising manager in Los Angeles. She wrote under the pseudonyms Sabra Lee Corbin and Vahrah von Kloop. Malvern is the author of *Valiant Minstrel*, *The Queen's Lady*, and *Heart's Conquest*.

`4053` *According to Thomas*

Date of Publication: 1947
Subject(s): Biblical Story; Jews
Historical character(s): Thomas of Antioch, Biblical Figure, Religious (one of the twelve apostles); Jesus Christ, Biblical Figure; Joseph of Arimathea, Biblical Figure
Time Period(s): 1st century
Locale(s): Israel

Summary: The story of Jesus is told through the perspective of the apostle Thomas, called the Doubter. He recounts the story from his prison cell as he awaits martyrdom. Thomas is depicted as a young Pharisee drawn to Jesus as a teacher and finally convinced by his miracles that he was in fact the Messiah.

Historical Accuracy: The novel includes the events chronicled in the New Testament and much authentic detail about Jewish social and religious customs.

CLAUDE MANCERON (1923-)

Manceron's books include *Austerlitz: The Story of a Battle* and *The French Revolution*.

`4054` *So Brief a Spring*

Date of Publication: 1958
Subject(s): Napoleonic Wars
Fictional character(s): Paul Toussaint, Young Man
Historical character(s): Napoleon Bonaparte, Ruler (Emperor of France)
Time Period(s): 1810s (1815)

Locale(s): France

Summary: The novel chronicles the brief and fateful "100 days" when Napoleon returned from exile on Elba hoping to resurrect his empire. The events are seen from the perspective of Paul Toussaint. The emphasis here is on the political forces at play as France is swept up in Napoleon's final dramatic moments on the world's stage.

Historical Accuracy: The results of the author's 15 years of research into the period are evident in this believable portrait of the era.

FREDERICK F. MANFRED (1912-)

Manfred was born in Iowa. After graduation from Calvin College in Michigan, he worked as a factory hand, newspaper editor, salesman, and professional baseball and basketball player before beginning his career as a writer and teacher. Manfred is of Frisian-Saxon heritage, and his novels are usually set in what he calls Siouxland, the region of the Big Sioux River valley. His five Buckskin Man Tales have been praised for their authenticity and attention to period detail.

`4055` *Conquering Horse*

Date of Publication: 1959
Subject(s): Indians; Tribal Life—Native American
Fictional character(s): No Name, Indian (Sioux), Warrior
Time Period(s): 19th century
Locale(s): West

Summary: This tale of a young Indian brave's initiation into manhood and the status of warrior follows the experiences of 17-year-old No Name who must undergo a series of challenges before winning his place in the tribe.

Historical Accuracy: The novel features an authentic account of Sioux tribal customs.

`4056` *Lord Grizzly*

Date of Publication: 1954
Subject(s): American West; Indians
Fictional character(s): Bending Reed, Indian (Sioux); John S. Fitzgerald, Mountain Man
Historical character(s): Hugh Glass, Mountain Man; Jim Bridger, Mountain Man
Time Period(s): 1820s (1823-1824)
Locale(s): South Dakota; Yellowstone River, Montana; Missouri River, United States

Summary: The novel offers the story of one of the West's most famous mountain men, Hugh Glass. Glass is mauled by a grizzly then left for dead by young Jim Bridger and John Fitzgerald. He sets his broken leg and hobbles 200 miles to a settlement. He then sets out for vengeance on the two who left him.

Historical Accuracy: The novel is based on the real life adventures of its hero. The author collected all the actual accounts and legends related to the life of Hugh Glass to make this authentic story of the West's famous mountain man.

4057 *The Manly-Hearted Woman*

Date of Publication: 1975
Subject(s): Indians; Tribal Life—Native American
Fictional character(s): Flat Warclub, Indian (Yankton Dakota), Warrior; Manly Heart, Indian (Yankton Dakota)
Time Period(s): 19th century
Locale(s): Minnesota

Summary: This novel of Indian life tells the story of two Yankton Dakotas in a fight against the Omahas. Flat Warclub is a young warrior, and Manly Heart is a Dakota woman who becomes a man for a time in fulfillment of a vision. Their relationship is set in the context of two very different visions.

Historical Accuracy: The Indian customs of the period are convincingly detailed.

4058 *Of Lizards and Angels: A Saga of Sioux Land*

Date of Publication: 1992
Subject(s): Settlement of the American Frontier; Family Saga; Farming
Fictional character(s): Tunis Freyling, Settler; Clara Freyling, Settler
Time Period(s): 19th century; 20th century (1880s-1960s)
Locale(s): Siouxland, United States (border of Iowa, Minnesota, and the Dakotas)

Summary: The novel tells the story of three generations of the Freyling family from the 1880s to the 1960s, beginning with settlers Tunis and Clara Freyling. They transform the wilderness into a prosperous farm, but their relationship is shadowed by the past. The novel offers a compelling portrait of the frontier and the personalities that took root in it.

Historical Accuracy: The novelist is an expert in the region, and he fashions a compelling and plausible story out of the fragments of several lives.

4059 *Riders of Judgment*

Date of Publication: 1957
Subject(s): American West; Ranching
Fictional character(s): Cain Hammett, Cowboy
Time Period(s): 19th century
Locale(s): Wyoming

Summary: The background of this western novel is the Johnson County range wars in the Wyoming cattle country. The novel centers on Cain Hammett, the eldest of three brothers, who must avenge the murder of his father, grandfather, and brother. When the cattle barons invade the territory, Cain enters the conflict on the side of the small stockman.

Historical Accuracy: The region and the period are captured convincingly.

WOLF MANKOWITZ (1924-)

English novelist, playwright, screenwriter, journalist, and poet, Mankowitz is a graduate of Cambridge University. He is the owner of the Pickwick Club, a restaurant and meeting place for London theater society. Besides his poems, plays,

and fiction, Mankowitz has written biographies of Edgar Allan Poe and Charles Dickens.

4060 *A Night with Casanova*

Date of Publication: 1991
Subject(s): Fantasy
Fictional character(s): Wandering Jew, Wanderer
Historical character(s): Giovanni Jacopo Casanova, Adventurer, Writer
Time Period(s): 1790s
Locale(s): Dux, Germany

Summary: At the end of his illustrious and amorous career, Casanova is plotting his escape from Dux, where he has spent his declining years writing his memoirs. He meets a stranger who reveals himself as the Wandering Jew of legend. Together they spend the evening lying to each other about the past.

Historical Accuracy: Inventive and colorful, this dramatic fantasy offers two very convincing impersonations.

HEINRICH MANN (1871-1950)

Born in Lubeck, Germany, Mann was a prominent social critic and novelist before immigrating to the United States to escape Nazi persecution. His greatest reputation is as a historical novelist. He is the brother of Nobel Prize winner Thomas Mann.

4061 *Henry, King of France*

Date of Publication: 1939
Subject(s): Royalty—France; Biography, Fictionalized
Historical character(s): Henri IV, Ruler (King of France)
Time Period(s): 16th century (1589-1610)
Locale(s): France

Summary: This sequel to *Young Henry of Navarre* continues the account of the first Bourbon king from his ascension to the throne to his death.

Historical Accuracy: The novel's history is reliable, though occasionally marred by an ideological bias.

4062 *Young Henry of Navarre*

Date of Publication: 1937
Subject(s): Royalty—France; Huguenots; Biography, Fictionalized
Historical character(s): Henri of Navarre, Nobleman; Marguerite de Valois, Royalty (queen consort of Henry)
Time Period(s): 16th century (1553-1589)
Locale(s): France

Summary: This fictional biography traces the rise to power of Henry of Navarre, the first of France's Bourbon Kings, from his childhood to his ascension to the throne in 1589. At the center of Henry's story is the violence and turbulence of the Wars of Religion against the Protestant Huguenots, of whom Henry was the nominal head. Henry rejects Protestantism to claim the throne, asserting "Paris is well worth a Mass.".

Historical Accuracy: The novel captures the spirit of the age and the actual details of Henry's life and times.

HELEN R. MANN

A native of Massachusetts, Mann graduated from Simmons College. She is a direct descendant of Hannah Duston, her main character in *Gallant Warrior*.

4063 *Gallant Warrior*

Date of Publication: 1955
Subject(s): Biography, Fictionalized; American Colonies; Indians
Historical character(s): Hannah Duston, Pioneer, Captive
Time Period(s): 17th century (1697)
Locale(s): Haverhill, Massachusetts, American Colonies

Summary: This is a biographical account of a Massachusetts pioneer woman, Hannah Duston, who is captured by Indians. The novel describes her experiences in captivity and the events that lead to her escape and revenge on her captors.

Historical Accuracy: This is an authentic version of the actual events as well as a convincing re-creation of pioneer life in the New England colonies.

KLAUS MANN (1906-1949)

Son of world famous novelist Thomas Mann, Klaus published several works in English, including his autobiography, *The Turning Point*.

4064 *Pathetic Symphony: A Novel about Tchaikovsky*

Date of Publication: 1948
Subject(s): Biography, Fictionalized; Musical Life
Historical character(s): Peter Ilyich Tchaikovsky, Composer
Time Period(s): 19th century (1840-1893)
Locale(s): Russia

Summary: The life and career of Russian composer Tchaikovsky is dramatized in this novel, which gives the basic highlights of his career. It attempts, through interior monologues, to portray what Tchaikovsky was thinking when composing and performing.

Historical Accuracy: The novel falls somewhere between reliable biography and subjective interpretation.

THOMAS MANN

4065 *Joseph of Egypt*

Date of Publication: 1936
Subject(s): Biblical Story; Ancient Egypt
Historical character(s): Joseph, Biblical Figure; Potiphar, Biblical Figure
Time Period(s): Indeterminate Past
Locale(s): Egypt

Summary: This third volume of four dramatizes the Old Testament story of Joseph and takes up the years of Joseph's life in Egypt as the slave of Potiphar. When Joseph reports the advances of Potiphar's wife, he is thrown into prison.

Historical Accuracy: The novel achieves a high level of psychological realism in its depiction of the characters and their background.

4066 *Joseph the Provider*

Date of Publication: 1943
Subject(s): Biblical Story; Ancient Egypt
Historical character(s): Joseph, Biblical Figure
Time Period(s): Indeterminate Past
Locale(s): Egypt

Summary: The fourth and final volume of the author's series on the Old Testament story of Joseph describes Joseph's imprisonment and eventual rise to power in the court of the pharaoh. The novel concludes with Joseph's reunion with his brothers and father and his death.

Historical Accuracy: The novel is best measured as a penetrating psychological study with a believable period backdrop.

4067 *Tables of the Law*

Date of Publication: 1945
Subject(s): Ancient Egypt; Biblical Story; Biography, Fictionalized
Historical character(s): Moses, Biblical Figure
Time Period(s): 13th century B.C.
Locale(s): Egypt

Summary: This reconstruction of the life of Moses follows his career from his youth to the discovery of his heritage, the exodus from Egypt, and the engraving of the Ten Commandments on Mt. Sinai.

Historical Accuracy: The novel interweaves Old Testament details with imagined scenes and interpretations.

4068 *The Tales of Jacob*

Date of Publication: 1933
Subject(s): Biblical Story
Historical character(s): Jacob, Biblical Figure; Rachel, Biblical Figure; Leah, Biblical Figure; Joseph, Biblical Figure
Time Period(s): Indeterminate Past
Locale(s): Middle East

Summary: In the first of four books based on the Biblical story of Jacob and his son Joseph, Jacob is deceived and tricked into marrying Leah when it is her sister, Rachel, whom he really loves.

Historical Accuracy: The novel develops the Biblical facts into an authentic and psychologically believable study.

4069 *Young Joseph*

Date of Publication: 1934
Subject(s): Biblical Story
Historical character(s): Jacob, Biblical Figure; Joseph, Biblical Figure
Time Period(s): Indeterminate Past
Locale(s): Middle East

Summary: In the second part of a tetralogy on the Biblical story of Joseph, his adolescence is dramatized. As his father's favorite, Joseph prompts his brothers' jealousy, leading them to sell him to an Ishmaelite trader.

Historical Accuracy: The novel develops the Biblical story into a believable psychological portrait.

ALEXANDRA MANNERS
(PSEUD. OF ANNE RUNDLE)

English writer Manners was a civil servant from 1942 until 1950. She is a romance novelist who uses several pseudonyms.

4070 *Cardigan Square*

Date of Publication: 1977
Subject(s): Romance
Fictional character(s): Sable Martin, Companion; Adam Hunter, Activist (social reformer); Morgan Hunter, Gentleman
Time Period(s): 19th century
Locale(s): London, England

Summary: Young Sable Martin is saved from drudgery when a lady of means takes her on as a companion. When she attracts the attention of two brothers, Sable is torn between passionate Morgan Hunter and social reformer Adam Hunter.

Historical Accuracy: The period background is only vaguely suggested as 19th century. The romantic complications predominate over historical detail.

4071 *Wilford's Daughter*

Date of Publication: 1978
Subject(s): Regency Romance; Crime and Criminals
Fictional character(s): Emma Wilford, Young Woman; Captain Ringan, Steward (estate manager)
Time Period(s): 19th century (Regency period)
Locale(s): London, England

Summary: This is an unusual Regency romance with a social conscience. Emma Wilford chooses life in the country over fashionable society life and becomes involved in distributing food to the women in Newgate prison. The novel depicts a darker side of Regency society.

Historical Accuracy: The realistic touches capture a more detailed and convincing Regency background than is common in most historical romances.

JASON MANNING

4072 *The Border Captains*

Date of Publication: 1995
Subject(s): Settlement of the American Frontier; Indians; War of 1812
Fictional character(s): Nathaniel "Flintlock" Jones, Frontiersman
Historical character(s): Tecumseh, Indian (Shawnee), Chieftain; Henry Clay, Political Figure

Time Period(s): 18th century; 19th century (1768-1812)
Locale(s): Kentucky

Summary: The second volume of the Flintlock trilogy tells the story of Tecumseh's revolt and the War of 1812. Settlers begin to push west, and the young nation struggles to govern itself. At the center of the story is frontiersman Nathaniel Jones.

Historical Accuracy: The period background is accurate and the foreground action, though imagined, is convincingly drawn.

4073 *Flintlock*

Date of Publication: 1994
Subject(s): American Revolution
Fictional character(s): Nathaniel "Flintlock" Jones, Frontiersman; Jonathan Groves, Military Personnel (naval officer)
Historical character(s): Aaron Burr, Political Figure, Military Personnel (general); Thomas Jefferson, Political Figure; Daniel Boone, Frontiersman; Andrew Jackson, Military Personnel (general)
Time Period(s): 1780s (1781); 1800s (1806)
Locale(s): Kentucky; Natchez Trace, Mississippi

Summary: *Flintlock* is the first novel of a trilogy featuring the character Nathaniel Jones. Jones, who comes of age during the American Revolution, is asked in 1806 to assist President Jefferson in pursuing the renegade Aaron Burr and his army across Kentucky and the Natchez Trace. Burr is determined to create his own private empire in the wilderness.

Historical Accuracy: The situation is primarily imaginary, but the wilderness details are authentic.

4074 *Gone to Texas*

Date of Publication: 1995
Subject(s): American West; Texas Revolution
Fictional character(s): Nathaniel "Flintlock" Jones, Frontiersman; Christopher Groves, Military Personnel (lieutenant)
Historical character(s): Thomas Jonathan Jackson, Political Figure; Martin Van Buren, Political Figure
Time Period(s): 1830s (1839)
Locale(s): Kentucky; Texas

Summary: In the third novel of the Flintlock trilogy, it is 1839 and former President Andrew Jackson calls Nathaniel Jones and his grandson, Cristopher Groves, into action to help Texas gain its independence from Mexico. On the trail from Kentucky to Texas they must contend with kidnappers, river pirates, and bounty hunters.

Historical Accuracy: The period background is authentic. The actual events depicted are fanciful, though realistically drawn.

4075 *High Country*

Date of Publication: 1993
Subject(s): Settlement of the American Frontier; American West
Fictional character(s): Zach Hannah, Mountain Man; Sean Devlin, Mountain Man; Morning Sky, Indian (Crow), Spouse
Time Period(s): 1820s (1825-1829)
Locale(s): St. Louis, Missouri; Three Forks, Montana

Summary: Zach Hannah from Tennessee heads west in the 1820s to become a fur trapper. He learns how to survive in the wilderness, meets and marries Morning Sky, and then must contend with a jealous rival, fellow trapper Sean Devlin.

Historical Accuracy: The scenes of wilderness life are vividly and convincingly evoked.

HELENE MANSFIELD

4076 *Contessa*

Date of Publication: 1982
Subject(s): Russian Revolution; Civil War—Spain; World War II
Fictional character(s): Valentina Nikolayeva, Noblewoman
Historical character(s): Edward, Prince of Wales, Royalty
Time Period(s): 20th century (1900-1944)
Locale(s): Paris, France; St. Petersburg, Russia; Spain

Summary: When she makes her debut in Paris in 1900, Valentina is a sensation, attracting the attention of the Prince of Wales. The novel shows Valentina's involvement in great events of the 20th century: the Russian Revolution, postwar Paris, Spain during the Civil War, and occupied Paris during World War II.

Historical Accuracy: History flies by in this romantic tale. The background is believable if thinly textured.

HILARY MANTEL (1952-)

Born in Derbyshire, England, Mantel attended the London School of Economics and the University of Sheffield. She has held in a variety of jobs, including a salesperson, a social worker in a geriatric hospital, a secondary school English teacher, and film critic for the *Spectator*. Mantel has lived and worked in Botswana and Saudi Arabia. She won the Shiva National Memorial Prize for travel writing in 1987.

4077 *A Place of Greater Safety*

Date of Publication: 1992
Subject(s): French Revolution; Reign of Terror
Historical character(s): Georges-Jacques Danton, Revolutionary; Camille Desmoulins, Revolutionary; Pierre Choderlos de Laclos, Writer (novelist); Maximilien Francois de Robespierre, Revolutionary; Marie Joseph Paul de Lafayette, Nobleman (Marquis de Lafayette), Military Personnel (general); Jean-Paul Marat, Journalist, Revolutionary; Louis-Antoine-Leon de Saint-Just, Writer, Revolutionary; Charlotte Corday, Murderer
Time Period(s): 1780s
Locale(s): Paris, France

Summary: The events of the French Revolution are dramatized, centering on the experiences of three men who lead the rebellion. Danton, Robespierre, and Desmoulins are obscure young men from the provinces who make their way to Paris, where they change the course of history. Along with the forces that topple the monarchy, they unleash pent-up violence and terror that cannot be easily controlled.

Historical Accuracy: This is a remarkable achievement in historical re-creation. Most of the characters are real people, and the book is closely tied to historical facts.

ALESSANDRO MANZONI (1785-1873)

Manzoni was an Italian romantic novelist, dramatist, and poet. His *The Betrothed* is one of the greatest Italian historical novels. Manzoni and Walter Scott greatly admired each other's work.

4078 *The Betrothed*

Date of Publication: 1826
Subject(s): Plague
Fictional character(s): Lorenzo, Artisan (silkmaker); Don Rodrigo, Nobleman; Lucia, Fiance(e)
Time Period(s): 17th century (1620s)
Locale(s): Milan, Italy; Venice, Italy; Lombardy, Italy

Summary: This exciting adventure story is one of the world's greatest historical novels. Set in the 1620s, when much of Italy was under Spanish rule, the novel concerns the separation of two lovers on the verge of their marriage by the evil Don Rodrigo.

Historical Accuracy: Manzoni fully and accurately reconstructs the world of 17th-century Lombardy.

PAMELA MARCANTEL

Born in Louisiana of a French Catholic family, Marcantel teaches English at the University of Virginia. She spent four years researching *An Army of Angels*, her first novel.

4079 *An Army of Angels: A Novel of Joan of Arc*

Date of Publication: 1977
Subject(s): Biography, Fictionalized; Middle Ages; Hundred Years War
Historical character(s): Joan of Arc, Religious, Military Personnel (army commander); Charles VII, Ruler (King of France)
Time Period(s): 15th century (1420s-1430)
Locale(s): Rouen, France; Orleans, France

Summary: This biographical novel describes the remarkable career of Joan of Arc, the French peasant maid who, at the age of 13, is visited by St. Michel and selected to save France, by leading its army against the English. In this reconstruction of her life, she must prove herself in her mission to the Church, to the King of France, and to herself.

Historical Accuracy: The novel observes the facts surrounding Joan as the author's notes made clear. She does invent plausible dramatic elements to fill in gaps in the narrative.

LUCIEN MARCHAL (1893-)

Belgian writer Marchal spent several years in Brazil as a coffee and cotton planter.

4080 *Sage of Canudos*

Date of Publication: 1954
Subject(s): Frontier—Brazil
Historical character(s): Antonio Marcel, Leader, Fanatic
Time Period(s): 1880s
Locale(s): Brazil

Summary: Based on a true episode in Brazilian history, the novel describes how a group of outlaws and mystics, led by the fanatical Antonio Marcel, establish a ''holy city'' in the wilds of Brazil. The sect grows to over 12,000, existing by raids of the surrounding communities that finally prompt the Brazil government to take action against them.

Historical Accuracy: The novel stays close to the facts.

CATHERINE MARCHANT
(PSEUD. OF CATHERINE COOKSON, 1906-)

Catherine Marchant is a pseudonym for the prolific English novelist Catherine Cookson. Cookson's *The Round Tower* won the Winifred Holtby Award for best regional novel in 1968. Her books are read in 30 countries.

4081 *Miss Martha Mary Crawford*

Date of Publication: 1976
Subject(s): Romance; Victorian Period
Fictional character(s): Martha Mary Crawford, Heroine; Harry Pippin, Doctor
Time Period(s): 1870s (1879)
Locale(s): Northumberland, England

Summary: Martha Mary Crawford is a young woman of 20 who, since her mother's death, has cared for her siblings and managed her father's property. When he dies, she discovers that he has squandered the family fortune on his mistress and has left the family without even the comforts of the faded gentility to which they had been reduced. She must salvage what she can of her family life while risking total self-sacrifice.

Historical Accuracy: The novel offers strong and authentic regional details.

4082 *The Slow Awakening*

Date of Publication: 1976
Subject(s): Victorian Period
Fictional character(s): Kirsten MacGregor, Orphan, Servant; Ma Bradley, Criminal (baby farmer); Hop Fuller, Gypsy (tinker); Colum Knutsson, Gentleman
Time Period(s): 1850s
Locale(s): Northumberland, England

Summary: Kirsten MacGregor is a child of bitterness and adversity. An orphan, she falls under the control first of a baby farmer, Ma Bradley, then of a trader, who impregnates her. The cast in her eye marks her as bad luck, and she is driven off. Finally, she is taken in by the wealthy Knutsson family, where jealousy and hatred erupt before some reconciliation is possible.

Historical Accuracy: The novel is filled with period and regional details that paint a picture of the hardships the heroine must endure.

RICHARD MARIUS (1933-)

An American writer and academic, Marius is a professor of history at the University of Tennessee and the editor of the Thomas More papers at Yale. His novel *The Coming of Rain* was named the best novel of 1969 by the Friends of American Writers. He is the author of biographies of Thomas More and Martin Luther.

4083 *Bound for the Promised Land*

Date of Publication: 1976
Subject(s): American West; Wagon Trains; Gold Rush—California
Fictional character(s): Adam Cloud, Young Man; Harry Creekmore, Adventurer
Time Period(s): 1850s
Locale(s): Great Plains; California

Summary: The novel re-creates the drama of a wagon train crossing the Western plains in the 1850s. Adam and Harry set out from their Tennessee hill farm in pursuit of Adam's father, who took off one night for the California gold fields. They join the Jennings family and endure the challenges of unbearable heat, a winter mountain crossing, hostile Indians, and dangerous drifters.

Historical Accuracy: The novel offers an authentic look at the era and its particulars.

4084 *The Coming of Rain*

Date of Publication: 1969
Subject(s): Mystery
Fictional character(s): Sam Beckwith, Young Man; Brian Ledbetter, Veteran (Union army)
Time Period(s): 1880s (1885)
Locale(s): Bourbonville, Tennessee

Summary: Set in a Tennessee town in the 1880s, the novel centers on Sam Beckwith and his family. Sam searches for the truth about his father, who drifted into town after the Civil War, married Sam's mother, and suddenly died. The secrets he uncovers reveal the impact of the divisions caused by the Civil War.

Historical Accuracy: Taut and original, the novel offers a plausible re-creation of the period.

GRACE MARK (1946-)

Mark was born in Washington, D.C. She received a B.A. from Marshall University in 1963 and an M.A. from the University of Kentucky in 1965. A literature and writing teacher before entering business as an advertising copywriter, she eventually founded an advertising company.

4085 *The Dream Seekers*

Date of Publication: 1992

Subject(s): Immigrants; Labor Movement; Chicago World's Fair

Fictional character(s): Hannah Chernik, Young Woman; Josef Chernik, Criminal; Isabelle Chadwick Woodruff, Gentlewoman

Historical character(s): William F. Cody, Entertainer; Jane Addams, Suffragette; Clarence Darrow, Lawyer; Eugene V. Debs, Activist; George Pullman, Inventor

Time Period(s): 1890s (1893)

Locale(s): Chicago, Illinois

Summary: Set during the 1893 Chicago World's Fair, the novel follows the stories of two women, Hannah Chernik, an immigrant's daughter, and Isabelle Woodruff, a wealthy socialite. Their story is interwoven with the events of the fair and the infamous Pullman Strike, as the dream of America's future must confront its sobering present.

Historical Accuracy: The novel blends the fictional and the factual, creating a believable period background.

KAMALA MARKANDAYA
(PSEUD. OF KAMALA TAYLOR, 1924-)

Indian author Markandaya attended the University of Madras and worked briefly at a small newspaper in India before emigrating to England in 1948. Her novel *Nectar in a Sieve* was named a notable book of 1955 by the American Library Association. Her work has been praised for its accurate depiction of Indian village life.

4086 *The Golden Honeycomb*

Date of Publication: 1977

Subject(s): British Raj; World War I; Indian Empire

Fictional character(s): Bawajira, Ruler (Maharajah of Devapur); Mohini, Young Woman; Rabi, Heir

Time Period(s): 19th century; 20th century (1890s-1910s)

Locale(s): Devapur, India

Summary: Set in the Indian princely state of Devapur, the novel tells the story of the Maharajah Bawajira. His love for a beautiful commoner, who becomes his concubine, produces a son and heir, Rabi. Rabi comes of age in the splendor of his father's court with the omnipresent manipulation of the British. Eventually, Rabi must choose between conflicting cultures.

Historical Accuracy: The novel is vivid and colorful in its evocation of Indian life and culture of the period.

GENE MARKEY (1895-1980)

An American film producer and writer, Gene Markey was born in Jackson, Michigan, and attended Dartmouth College and the Art Institute of Chicago. He served with the U.S. Army during World War I and with the U.S. Naval Reserve during World War II. Markey retired from the service a highly decorated rear admiral. His novels include *The Great Companions* and *Women, Women Everywhere*. Markey's first three marriages were to the actresses Joan Bennett, Hedy Lamarr, and Myrna Loy.

4087 *Kentucky Pride*

Date of Publication: 1956

Subject(s): Reconstruction Period

Fictional character(s): Aidan Kensal, Veteran (Confederate); Veach Doucain, Military Personnel (major)

Time Period(s): 1860s

Locale(s): Kentucky

Summary: The conflict between Aidan Kensal, a former Confederate major, and Veach Doucain for the possession of Oakenden, Kensal's Kentucky bluegrass estate, is played out in a series of exciting adventure scenes, including a fist fight, a duel, and a cross country chase.

Historical Accuracy: The emphasis is on romantic adventure in a careful and fully-realized period setting.

4088 *That Far Paradise*

Date of Publication: 1960

Subject(s): Settlement of the American Frontier

Fictional character(s): Jared Kensal, Veteran (American Revolution)

Time Period(s): 1790s (1794)

Locale(s): Virginia; Kentucky

Summary: Set in the years following the American Revolution, the novel follows the journey of General Jared Kensal and his family from their home in Virginia into the frontier of Kentucky. The novel dramatizes the adventures of their journey and their arrival in Kentucky. Added excitement is provided in the plot to imprison Anthony Wayne and regain French power in the Ohio Valley.

Historical Accuracy: The events of 1794 are accurately depicted.

MORRIS MARKEY (1899-1950)

Markey lived in New York City and wrote novels and travel books. His works include *Doctor Jeremiah* and *This Country of Yours*.

4089 *The Band Plays Dixie*

Date of Publication: 1927

Subject(s): Civil War—U.S.

Fictional character(s): Kirk Hale, Military Personnel (Union soldier); Anthony Hale, Military Personnel (Union soldier)

Time Period(s): 1860s

Locale(s): Fredericksburg, Virginia; Richmond, Virginia; Savannah, Georgia

Summary: This adventure novel set during the Civil War involves the rivalry between Kirk and Anthony Hale who, while in a prison hospital in Richmond, fall in love with the same woman. Escape follows, and further adventures, although the romantic complications are not resolved until the conclusion of the war.

Historical Accuracy: The Civil War background is accurately and believably depicted.

DAVID MARKISH (1938-)

Born in Moscow, Markish is the son of Yiddish writer Peretz Markish who was executed along with other Yiddish writers during the Stalinist purges. Markish emigrated to Israel and began serving in the Israel Defence Force in 1973. He is the author of *Maariv* and *A New World for Simon Ashkenazi*.

4090 *Jesters*

Date of Publication: 1988
Subject(s): Russian Empire; Royalty—Russia; Jews
Historical character(s): Peter the Great, Ruler (Czar of Russia)
Time Period(s): 18th century
Locale(s): Russia

Summary: The life and times of Russian czar Peter the Great are seen from the perspective of three Jews who become his trusted advisers. However, as Jews, they remain ''jesters,'' living only at the pleasure of the brilliant and brutal Peter.

Historical Accuracy: The novel provides a believable atmosphere of the times and character of Peter the Great.

GEORGE MARKSTEIN (1929-1987)

An American journalist, TV and film screenwriter, and novelist, Markstein was the author of many spy novels and thrillers. He wrote the screenplay for *The Odessa File* and the award-winning *Robbery*, which featured modern film's first car chase scene. At the request of Steve McQueen, Markstein devised a similar car chase scene for the film *Bullitt*. Markstein was also a military correspondent and a feature writer for a London daily newspaper.

4091 *Tara Kane*

Date of Publication: 1978
Subject(s): Gold Rush—Klondike
Fictional character(s): Tara Kane, Young Woman; Jefferson Smith, Businessman
Time Period(s): 1890s (1897)
Locale(s): Yukon Territory, Canada; Skagway, Alaska

Summary: The scene is the Klondike Gold Rush of 1897. Tara Kane searches for her husband while coping with a series of misfortunes and misadventures. She is pursued by the handsome scoundrel Jefferson Smith.

Historical Accuracy: The novel is filled with period details that create a plausible historical background for the novel's adventures and romance.

DEREK MARLOWE (1938-)

Born in London, Marlowe won the Foyle Award for the best play of 1961-62 for *The Scarecrow*. He is best known for his spy thrillers, most notably *A Dandy in Aspic*.

4092 *A Single Summer with Lord B.*

Date of Publication: 1970
Subject(s): Literary Life; Regency Period

Historical character(s): George Gordon Byron, Writer (poet), Nobleman; Percy Bysshe Shelley, Writer (poet); Mary Wollstonecraft Godwin, Writer; Claire Clairmont, Gentlewoman; John Polidori, Doctor
Time Period(s): 1810s (1816)
Locale(s): Lake Geneva, Switzerland

Summary: The summer is 1816, the scene Lake Geneva, and Lord B. is Lord Byron. The novel offers a dramatic version of the famous holiday party that included Shelley; Mary Godwin; Claire Clairmont, Byron's mistress; and John Polidori, Byron's personal physician. The novel offers a look at this famous literary friendship.

Historical Accuracy: The novel is based on evident research, and scenes and dialogue are supported by annotation.

STEPHEN MARLOWE (1928-)

American writer Marlowe graduated from the College of William and Mary. He is probably best known for his science fiction and crime novels featuring Chester Drum. His novels have been published in 14 languages.

4093 *Colossus: A Novel about Goya and a World Gone Mad*

Date of Publication: 1972
Subject(s): Artistic Life; Napoleonic Wars; Biography, Fictionalized
Historical character(s): Francisco Jose de Goya y Lucientes, Artist; Maria Cayetana, Noblewoman (Duchess of Alba); Napoleon Bonaparte, Ruler (Emperor of France), Military Personnel (French commander); Arthur Wellesley, Military Personnel (British army commander)
Time Period(s): 18th century; 19th century (1770s-1824)
Locale(s): Spain; Paris, France

Summary: The life and artistic career of Francisco Goya are depicted in this biographical novel that follows Goya's rise as the premier painter to the kings of Spain. He paints portraits of most of Madrid's aristocrats and falls in love with the Duchess of Alba, one of the most sought-after women in Spain. When Napoleon's invasion unleashes unprecedented devastation, Goya turns from painting portraits to capturing the horror of war in his Disasters of War drawings.

Historical Accuracy: The novel is built on a framework of fact with some evident interpretation and surmises added.

4094 *The Death and Life of Miguel De Cervantes*

Date of Publication: 1991
Subject(s): Literary Life; Biography, Fictionalized; Renaissance
Historical character(s): Miguel de Cervantes, Writer
Time Period(s): 16th century; 17th century (1547-1616)
Locale(s): Spain; Algeria

Summary: The novel provides a fictional account of the remarkable life of Cervantes, the author of *The Adventures of Don Quixote de la Mancha*. It begins with Cervantes' death and works its way back to his beginnings and the imaginative fermentation that eventually produces his classic novel. The novel in turn provides a colorful version of Renaissance Europe.

Historical Accuracy: This is a tour de force of imagination and a believable reconstruction of a place and time.

`4095` *The Lighthouse at the End of the World*

Date of Publication: 1995
Subject(s): Literary Life; Fantasy
Fictional character(s): Auguste C. Dupin, Detective—Police
Historical character(s): Edgar Allan Poe, Writer
Time Period(s): 1840s (1849)
Locale(s): Baltimore, Maryland; France

Summary: In 1849, the year of his death, Edgar Allan Poe resurfaces in a Baltimore hospital after a disappearance. The novel offers a surmise of what might have happened during this time, as Poe tells the story of his life. Meanwhile, his fictional creation, Inspector Dupin, traces Poe to America, exposing several secrets that haunt his creator.

Historical Accuracy: The novel is a tour de force of blended fact and fantasy. The era is created with convincing authenticity.

`4096` *The Memoirs of Christopher Columbus*

Date of Publication: 1987
Subject(s): Exploration; Inquisition; Royalty—Spain
Fictional character(s): Petenera, Young Woman
Historical character(s): Christopher Columbus, Explorer; Isabella I, Ruler (Queen of Castile and Aragon); Tomas de Torquemada, Religious (Grand Inquisitor); Ferdinand V, Ruler (King of Aragon); Amerigo Vespucci, Explorer; Rodrigo Borgia, Religious (pope)
Time Period(s): 15th century; 16th century
Locale(s): Spain; West Indies; Italy

Summary: In this fanciful memoir of Columbus, the great admiral's life expands in many imaginative directions. Columbus is enmeshed in the Italian court of the Borgias, voyages from Iceland to Africa, and enters Isabella's secret service at the fall of Granada, before embarking on his great venture. The novel celebrates not only the great explorer but the colorful multiplicity of his era.

Historical Accuracy: This is not intended as a factual but as an inventive, fictional life and times. Nevertheless, the period is convincingly drawn.

`4097` *The Shining*

Date of Publication: 1963
Subject(s): Ancient Greece
Fictional character(s): Hiero of Marathon, Young Man
Historical character(s): Alcibiades, Political Figure, Military Personnel (general); Euripides, Writer
Time Period(s): 5th century B.C.
Locale(s): Greece; Persia; Macedonia

Summary: This tale of ancient Greece in the 5th century B.C. follows the experiences of Hiero of Marathon who starts out as an actor for Euripedes, becomes a herald on the Sicilian Expedition of Athens, goes to Sparta and Persia, and participates in the March of Xenophon's Ten Thousand.

Historical Accuracy: The events described are based on history, though the fictional frame is insufficient to support the weight of the events depicted.

ELLEN MARSH (1922-)

Born in Germany, Marsh is the author of *Drink to the Hunted*, *Dull the Sharp Edge*, and *Unarmed in Paradise*.

`4098` *If This Be Magic*

Date of Publication: 1990
Subject(s): French Revolution; Romance
Fictional character(s): Townsend Grey, Gentlewoman; Ian Moncrieff, Nobleman (Duke of Boyne)
Time Period(s): 1780s; 1790s (1789-1790)
Locale(s): Norfolk, England; Versailles, France

Summary: Love and intrigue during the turmoil of the French Revolution are featured in this historical romance. Townsend Grey meets and marries Ian Moncrieff and accompanies him to the Court of Versailles. She is swept up in intrigue and danger, causing her to wonder why he has married her.

Historical Accuracy: There are some convincing period details that set a plausible backdrop for the romantic intrigue.

GEORGE TRACY MARSH (1876-1945)

An American lawyer and writer, Marsh was born in Lansingburgh, New York, and educated at Yale University and Harvard Law School. Marsh's books include *Toilers of the Trails*, *Sled Trails and White Waters*, and *The Whelps of the Wolf*.

`4099` *Ask No Quarter*

Date of Publication: 1945
Subject(s): American Colonies; Pirates; Indians
Fictional character(s): Hugh Jocelyn, Adventurer
Time Period(s): 17th century
Locale(s): Rhode Island, American Colonies

Summary: Colonial Rhode Island in the later 17th century is the scene for this action novel that dramatizes the adventures of Hugh Jocelyn. He rises from poverty to gain his fortune, overcoming the challenges of Indians and pirates.

Historical Accuracy: Action is the primary intent here, but the author does show familiarity with the period and the details of Rhode Island history.

JEAN MARSH
(PSEUD. OF EVELYN MARSHALL, 1897-)

Born in Worcestershire, England, Marsh obtained a certificate for teaching and taught in Halesown until 1919, then worked as a journalist for the Thomson and Leng groups until the late 1920s. She was a contract writer for the

Amalgamated Press until 1939 and a broadcaster during World War II. After the war, she returned to the romantic novels she had written earlier as magazine serials.

4100 *The House of Eliott*

Date of Publication: 1993
Subject(s): Business Building; Fashion Industry
Fictional character(s): Beatrice Eliott, Businesswoman, Seamstress; Evangeline Eliott, Businesswoman, Seamstress
Time Period(s): 1920s
Locale(s): London, England

Summary: When their father dies leaving them penniless, Beatrice and Evangeline Eliott must come up with a plan to make ends meet while contending with a number of adversities. Eventually, they establish themselves as sought-after seamstresses and founders of the fashionable couturier, the House of Eliott.

Historical Accuracy: The period details are accurate and convincing.

EDISON MARSHALL (1894-1967)

Born in Indiana, Marshall attended the University of Oregon. As a young man, Marshall was a big-game hunter and explorer in East Africa, Alaska, Siam, China, Japan, and Nepal. He won an O. Henry award in 1921 for "The Heart of Little Shikara.".

4101 *American Captain*

Date of Publication: 1954
Subject(s): Sea Story; Slavery
Fictional character(s): Homer Whitman, Sailor
Time Period(s): 1790s
Locale(s): Maine; Malta; Africa (Tripoli, Sudan, Capetown)

Summary: This adventure novel set in the 1790s takes American sailor Homer Whitman from his home in Maine to Malta, where he endures attack by Barbary pirates, and on to adventures in Africa.

Historical Accuracy: Adventure predominates over careful and full historical documentation.

4102 *Benjamin Blake*

Date of Publication: 1941
Subject(s): Sea Story
Fictional character(s): Benjamin Blake, Bastard Son, Sailor; Matt Grimes, Sailor
Time Period(s): 1770s
Locale(s): England; *Western Star*, At Sea; Pacific Ocean (South Pacific)

Summary: Benjamin Blake is the persecuted bastard son of an English squire. Benjamin escapes as a seaman on a ship bound for the South Seas, where he experiences a series of adventures.

Historical Accuracy: The novel is a rather old-fashioned historical story with more emphasis on romance and adventure than history.

4103 *Caravan to Kanadu: A Novel of Marco Polo*

Date of Publication: 1953
Subject(s): Chinese Empire; Exploration
Historical character(s): Kublai Khan, Ruler (Chinese emperor); Marco Polo, Explorer
Time Period(s): 13th century
Locale(s): Italy; China; Asia

Summary: Marco Polo narrates this intimate record of his travels. Different from the actual accounts, the novel attempts to breathe life into Marco Polo's adventures and create a believable and very human Marco Polo. The story follows Polo's amazing odyssey east to the lands of the great Kublai Khan.

Historical Accuracy: The author's notes give evidence of solid research.

4104 *The Conqueror: A Novel of Alexander the Great*

Date of Publication: 1962
Subject(s): Macedonian Empire; Biography, Fictionalized
Historical character(s): Alexander the Great, Ruler (King of Macedon); Philip II, Ruler (King of Macedon); Ptolemy, Military Personnel (general); Aristotle, Teacher, Philosopher
Time Period(s): 4th century B.C.
Locale(s): Macedonia; Persia; Egypt

Summary: The extraordinary career of Alexander the Great, the conqueror of half the known world before his death at age 32, is dramatized as Alexander tells his own story. Taught by Aristotle, the son of Philip of Macedon begins his military career with a string of improbable successes that continue until madness and hubris mar his great advancements. This biographical novel attempts to present a believable portrait of a flawed and human leader.

Historical Accuracy: The novel blends fact and speculation, but offers a plausible version of Alexander's extraordinary story.

4105 *Cortez and Marina*

Date of Publication: 1963
Subject(s): Aztec Empire; Spanish Colonies
Historical character(s): Hernando Cortez, Explorer, Military Personnel (conquistador); Marina, Guide; Montezuma II, Ruler (Aztec emperor)
Time Period(s): 16th century
Locale(s): Mexico; Spain

Summary: The novel describes the conquest of Mexico through the first-hand account of Hernando Cortez himself. He relates his expedition to Mexico and encounters with the Aztecs that culminate in the defeat of Montezuma. At the center of the story is Cortez's relationship with his Aztec mistress and interpreter, Marina.

Historical Accuracy: The novel is faithful to the accepted sources in this portrait of the period and the personalities described.

`4106` *Earth Giant*

Date of Publication: 1960
Subject(s): Myths and Legends; Ancient Greece
Fictional character(s): Hercules, Adventurer; Ismene, Shepherd
Time Period(s): 11th century B.C.
Locale(s): Thebes, Greece

Summary: The novel conjures the legendary Hercules as an actual historical figure who lives in Thebes around 1000 B.C. His great labors are depicted not as supernatural, but as humanly possible feats of primitive engineering as well as great strength.

Historical Accuracy: Based on legend, the novel attempts to find a realistic basis for the Hercules story.

`4107` *The Infinite Woman*

Date of Publication: 1950
Subject(s): Dance; Theatrical Life
Fictional character(s): Lola Montero, Dancer
Time Period(s): 19th century
Locale(s): England; India; France

Summary: Based loosely on the life of the great dancer and courtesan Lola Montez, the novel offers the autobiographical memoirs of Lola Montero. Raised in India, she becomes an adored dancer and celebrity in Europe. The novel is a romantic story of a woman of great vitality and talent.

Historical Accuracy: The period background is captured with authenticity.

`4108` *The Lost Colony*

Date of Publication: 1964
Subject(s): American Colonies; Indians
Fictional character(s): Martyn Sutton, Settler
Historical character(s): Sir Walter Raleigh, Courtier, Explorer; Virginia Dare, Settler
Time Period(s): 16th century (1580s)
Locale(s): Roanoke Island, North Carolina, American Colonies; England

Summary: The novel speculates on the fate of the settlers of Roanoke Island, North Carolina, a colony founded by Sir Walter Raleigh that vanished without a trace. The author proposes a solution to the mystery of what happened.

Historical Accuracy: The author's interpretation of events is imaginative but plausible, and the Indian customs are believable and supported by evident research.

`4109` *The Pagan King*

Date of Publication: 1959
Subject(s): Dark Ages; Myths and Legends; Arthurian Legends
Fictional character(s): Arthur, Ruler (King of the Britons); Merlin, Sorcerer (Druid); Modred, Knight
Time Period(s): 5th century
Locale(s): England

Summary: The story of Arthur's reign as king of the Britons is stripped of the chivalrous trappings and described as a realis-
tic history of Arthur's triumph over rivals and his attempts to unify his kingdom. Britain is beset by Picts in the north, Irish in the west, and Saxons in the east and south. Arthur's kingdom is threatened from within and without.

Historical Accuracy: The story, though imagined, is closer to the true England of Arthur's time than other versions of his mythical reign.

`4110` *Princess Sophia*

Date of Publication: 1958
Subject(s): Gold Rush—Klondike
Fictional character(s): Eric Anderson, Miner; Sophia Hill, Young Woman
Time Period(s): 19th century; 20th century (1898-1918)
Locale(s): Alaska

Summary: This romantic adventure story is set in the Klondike Gold Rush days. The novel captures the rowdy era of mining towns and gold fields and climaxes with the fate of the *S.S. Princess Sophia* in 1918.

Historical Accuracy: The characters are fictional, but the story of the *Princess Sophia* is based on fact.

`4111` *Seward's Folly*

Date of Publication: 1924
Subject(s): Politics; Reconstruction Period
Fictional character(s): Jeff Sharp, Veteran (Confederate soldier)
Historical character(s): William Henry Seward, Political Figure
Time Period(s): 1860s (1867)
Locale(s): Sitka, Alaska

Summary: This romantic tale is built around the negotiations to acquire Alaska as an American territory in 1867. Secretary Seward sends Confederate veteran Jeff Sharp to Sitka to block the deal between the Russians and the Hudson's Bay Company that stands in the way of Alaska's transfer to the U.S.

Historical Accuracy: The author warns that the reader should not take the novel's historical elements as a faithful reflection of fact.

`4112` *The Upstart*

Date of Publication: 1945
Subject(s): Georgian Period; Theatrical Life
Fictional character(s): Richard Price, Actor
Historical character(s): David Garrick, Actor
Time Period(s): 18th century
Locale(s): London, England

Summary: This tale of theatrical life during the 18th century in England follows the career of Richard Price who rises from the streets to become an actor in a touring troupe before seeking his fortune in colonial Georgia.

Historical Accuracy: The novel provides a convincing portrait of its era, particularly of stage customs.

`4113` *The Viking*

Date of Publication: 1951

Subject(s): Vikings; Dark Ages
Fictional character(s): Ogier, Slave, Adventurer; Morgana, Royalty (princess), Captive; Hastings, Nobleman
Time Period(s): 9th century
Locale(s): Denmark; England; Italy

Summary: Ogier, a youth of uncertain birth, rises from slavery to become a member of a Viking raiding party sailing to England. There he meets Morgana, the daughter of the King of Wales, held for ransom by Hastings. Ogier's adventures take him from England to Italy and back to England to participate in a great Viking invasion.

Historical Accuracy: The story emphasizes adventure over careful documentation of the past. However, the period details offered are plausible.

4114 *West with the Vikings*

Date of Publication: 1961
Subject(s): Exploration; Vikings; Sea Story
Historical character(s): Leif Eriksson, Explorer; Erik the Red, Explorer
Time Period(s): 11th century
Locale(s): North America; Greenland; Iceland

Summary: Leif Ericson, the younger son of Eric the Red, narrates his own story. One of the last of the great Viking sea rovers, he reputedly discovered America 500 years before Christopher Columbus. Life in 11th-century Greenland and Iceland is dramatized, as is Ericson's journey farther west to landfall in North America.

Historical Accuracy: Based in part on the Icelandic and Greenlandic sagas that are regarded by many as factual, the author offers a plausible speculation about the Viking discovery of North America.

4115 *Yankee Pasha*

Date of Publication: 1947
Subject(s): Pirates
Fictional character(s): Jason Starbuck, Frontiersman, Adventurer; Roxana Reil, Young Woman, Captive
Time Period(s): 1790s; 1800s
Locale(s): Salem, Massachusetts; Barbary Coast, Africa; Constantinople, Ottoman Empire

Summary: This exotic adventure story describes the exploits of backwoodsman Jason Starbuck who pursues his love, Roxana Reil, who is seized by Barbary pirates. Starbuck's adventures take him into the service of the Dey of Algiers and on a search of the harems and slave markets of north Africa and the Ottoman Empire.

Historical Accuracy: Any given incident is plausible, but the cumulative effect of so many adventures strains credibility.

ROSAMOND MARSHALL (1902-1957)

American novelist Marshall was educated in California, France, Austria, and Germany. Her novels include *Kitty*, *Duchess Hotspur*, *Rogue Cavalier*, and *None but the Brave*.

4116 *Captain Ironhand*

Date of Publication: 1957
Subject(s): Sea Story; Pirates
Fictional character(s): James Challoner, Sea Captain; Kit McKenna, Young Woman
Time Period(s): 1770s (1772)
Locale(s): London, England; Morocco

Summary: Romantic adventure among the Moors in the 1770s is in store for James Challoner, who is secretly commissioned to destroy the Moorish pirates preying on British shipping. He sails under the guise of Captain Ironhand, the pirate, and has a series of adventures, escapes, and romantic interludes.

Historical Accuracy: Romantic adventure is featured over a fully realized historical background.

WILLIAM MARSHALL (1944-)

Marshall was born in Sydney, Australia and graduated from the Australian National University in Canberra. He is the author of *The Fire Circle*, *Thin Air*, *Frogmouth*, and *The New York Detective*.

4117 *Faces in the Crowd*

Date of Publication: 1991
Subject(s): Mystery
Fictional character(s): Virgil Tillman, Detective—Police; Ned Muldoon, Detective—Police
Time Period(s): 1880s (1884)
Locale(s): New York, New York

Summary: Tillman and Muldoon, police detectives in 1880s New York, investigate the mystery surrounding a missing prostitute. Is she dead, or just missing? And why are there 187 wedding rings in her room? Their investigation leads to a much larger conspiracy involving a secret society.

Historical Accuracy: The atmosphere of period New York is faithfully presented.

BOB MARSHALL-ANDREWS (1944-)

Marshall-Andrews was born in London and educated at the University of Bristol.

4118 *The Palace of Wisdom*

Date of Publication: 1989
Subject(s): Renaissance; Espionage; Inquisition
Fictional character(s): Frederico Sforzi Credi, Gentleman
Historical character(s): Cosimo II de' Medici, Nobleman (grand duke)
Time Period(s): 17th century
Locale(s): Florence, Italy; France

Summary: Late 17th-century Florence at the end of the Italian Renaissance is the novel's setting. The story is told by an aging conspirator who recounts his life and the dangerous attempt to protect the fruits of scholarship from the intellectual persecution of the Grand Duke Cosimo de Medici.

Historical Accuracy: The novel captures with vivid details the atmosphere of Florence and the period.

EDWARD MARSTON

`4119` *The Dragons of Archenfield*

Date of Publication: 1995
Subject(s): Mystery; Norman Conquest; Middle Ages
Fictional character(s): Ralph Delchard, Military Personnel (soldier); Gervaise Bret, Lawyer
Time Period(s): 11th century (1086)
Locale(s): Herefordshire, England

Summary: In the third of the author's historical mystery series set in England just after the Norman Conquest, soldier Ralph Delchard and lawyer Gervase Bret are sent to the border country of Herefordshire to settle a land dispute. They find themselves in the domain of a Marcher lord who recognizes no law but his own. When a principal witness in the dispute is murdered and evidence destroyed, the pair begin a search for the killer with more than land and wealth as a motive for murder.

Historical Accuracy: The novel is rich in period details from an actual entry in the *Domesday Book.*

`4120` *The Laughing Hangman*

Date of Publication: 1996
Subject(s): Mystery; Elizabethan Period; Theatrical Life
Fictional character(s): Nicholas Bracewell, Manager (of a theatrical company)
Time Period(s): 17th century
Locale(s): London, England

Summary: Controversy over the performance of a scandalous play by the Lord Westfield's Men turns to enmity with their rivals, The Blackfriars, and then to murder when hangings begin to occur. The killings are called a divine retribution for the immorality of the theater, but Nicholas Bracewell undertakes to discover a more human solution.

Historical Accuracy: The era is authentically re-created, particularly the details of the Elizabethan stage.

`4121` *The Lions of the North*

Date of Publication: 1996
Subject(s): Middle Ages; Mystery
Fictional character(s): Ralph Delchard, Military Personnel (soldier); Gervaise Bret, Lawyer
Time Period(s): 11th century
Locale(s): Yorkshire, England

Summary: In the fourth mystery in the series set during the reign of William the Conqueror, soldier Ralph Delchard and lawyer Gervase Bret journey into Yorkshire to settle land claims and help compile the *Domesday Book.* At the castle of a wealthy merchant, an anonymous young man is killed by pet lions. Delchard and Bret's investigation uncovers a threat to their lives and the Crown.

Historical Accuracy: The novel provides an authentic evocation of the period.

`4122` *The Mad Courtesan*

Date of Publication: 1992

Subject(s): Mystery; Elizabethan Period; Theatrical Life
Fictional character(s): Nicholas Bracewell, Manager (theatrical); Sebastian Carrick, Actor; Lawrence Firethorn, Actor
Time Period(s): 16th century (1590s)
Locale(s): London, England

Summary: The murder of Sebastian Carrick, a member of the company, is investigated by Nicholas Bracewell. He learns that Sebastian had enemies besides those in the company, and as he digs for clues to the identity of Sebastian's killer he begins to untangle a conspiracy that leads directly to the queen herself.

Historical Accuracy: The novel expertly blends daily life, theatrical details, and court politics of the Elizabethans into a rousing performance.

`4123` *The Merry Devils*

Date of Publication: 1989
Subject(s): Mystery; Elizabethan Period; Theatrical Life
Fictional character(s): Nicholas Bracewell, Manager (theatrical); Lawrence Firethorne, Actor; Roper Blundell, Actor
Time Period(s): 16th century (1590s)
Locale(s): London, England

Summary: Disaster accompanies the premier by Lord Westfield's Men of a new play, *The Merry Devils.* Three devils appear on stage instead of one, to the shock of the company and the audience. At the second performance, only one devil appears; another lies dead beneath the stage. Nicholas Bracewell must investigate these mysterious goings-on. The answers are revealed at a performance before the company's patron, Lord Westfield.

Historical Accuracy: The details of Elizabethan theatrical life are scrupulously presented.

`4124` *The Nine Giants*

Date of Publication: 1991
Subject(s): Mystery; Elizabethan Period; Theatrical Life
Fictional character(s): Nicholas Bracewell, Manager (theatrical); Lawrence Firethorn, Actor
Time Period(s): 16th century (1590s)
Locale(s): London, England

Summary: Offstage complications test Nicholas Bracewell's ability to keep the theatrical company going. An apprentice is assaulted, the ownership of the Queen's Head Inn threatens to change, and finally a mangled corpse is discovered in the Thames. This may be connected to the string of bad luck the company is experiencing.

Historical Accuracy: The novel is brilliantly and entertainingly evocative of the era with a convincing depiction of theatrical life.

`4125` *The Queen's Head*

Date of Publication: 1988
Subject(s): Mystery; Elizabethan Period; Theatrical Life
Fictional character(s): Nicholas Bracewell, Manager (theatrical); Lawrence Firethorn, Actor
Historical character(s): Mary, Queen of Scots, Ruler (Queen of Scotland)

Time Period(s): 16th century (1587-1588)
Locale(s): London, England

Summary: Nicholas Bracewell is the stage manager of Lord Westfield's Men, a company of actors in Elizabethan England. In 1588, on the eve of the English victory over the Spanish Armada, one of the actors is murdered in a tavern brawl. Bracewell investigates while accidents, robberies, and other misfortunes plague the company, whose success attracts the attention of Queen Elizabeth herself. Is there a plot to sabotage the company or are much larger schemes at work?.

Historical Accuracy: The novel is remarkable in its ability to create an accurate sense of the time and place without sacrificing interesting and lively characters.

4126 *The Ravens of Blackwater*
Date of Publication: 1994
Subject(s): Mystery; Norman Conquest; Middle Ages
Fictional character(s): Hamo Fitzcorbucion, Nobleman; Ralph Delchard, Military Personnel; Gervaise Bret, Lawyer
Time Period(s): 11th century (1070s)
Locale(s): Maldon, England; London, England

Summary: The mystery's circumstances, drawn from the Domesday Book, involves the shady business dealings of Hamo Fitzcorbucion, Lord of Blackwater Castle, during the reign of William the Conqueror. Ralph Delchard and Gervaise Bret are members of a tribunal sent to investigate, and they immediately find themselves in the midst of Saxon versus Norman strife and dangerous goings-on.

Historical Accuracy: The mystery is steeped in local and period customs that serve to bring the era to life.

4127 *The Roaring Boy*
Date of Publication: 1995
Subject(s): Elizabethan Period; Theatrical Life; Mystery
Fictional character(s): Nicholas Bracewell, Manager (theatrical); Edmund Hoode, Writer (playwright); Simon Chaloner, Gentleman
Time Period(s): 16th century
Locale(s): London, England

Summary: A mysterious stranger presents the Westfield's Men with a manuscript called *The Roaring Boy*, based on the events surrounding the murder of a mathematician. The company presents it on stage and a riot ensues. When playwright Edmund Hoode is arrested for libel, Nicolas Bracewell must solve the murder on which the play is based to save his company.

Historical Accuracy: The details of Elizabethan London and theatrical life of the time are faithfully and convincingly presented.

4128 *The Silent Woman*
Date of Publication: 1994
Subject(s): Elizabethan Period; Mystery; Theatrical Life
Fictional character(s): Nicholas Bracewell, Manager (of a theatrical troupe); Lawrence Firethorne, Actor; Edmund Hoode, Writer (playwright)
Time Period(s): 16th century

Locale(s): England

Summary: In the sixth installment of the Elizabethan theatrical mysteries involving Nicholas Bracewell, manager of the Lord Westfield's Men, fire displaces the troupe from its London home, and Nicholas must manage the company on a tour of the countryside. The murder of a young woman, disguised as a man, involves Nicholas in the investigation of a mystery that sends him back to his childhood home.

Historical Accuracy: The novel features authentic historical details, particularly of the Elizabethan theater.

4129 *The Trip to Jerusalem*
Date of Publication: 1990
Subject(s): Mystery; Elizabethan Period; Theatrical Life
Fictional character(s): Nicholas Bracewell, Manager (theatrical); Lawrence Firethorn, Actor; Clarence Marmion, Gentleman
Time Period(s): 16th century (1590)
Locale(s): London, England; York, England

Summary: Plague causes Lord Westfield's Men to journey north to York. On the way, they learn that a rival company is stealing their best plays, and they become entangled in a spy network designed to root out Catholic traitors. All is not resolved until they reach their destination in York.

Historical Accuracy: The period detail of Elizabethan England as well the theater make this mystery, like the series, an exceptional one.

4130 *The Wolves of Savernake*
Date of Publication: 1993
Subject(s): Middle Ages; Mystery; Norman Conquest
Fictional character(s): Ralph Delchard, Military Personnel; Gervaise Bret, Lawyer
Time Period(s): 11th century (1086)
Locale(s): Wiltshire, England

Summary: Two of William the Conqueror's Domesday Book investigators, Ralph Delchard and Gervaise Bret, look into a questionable land claim in Wiltshire. A baffling mystery arises when the man whose claim has drawn them to Wiltshire is savaged by a wolf in Savernake Forest. Is this an act of God or man?.

Historical Accuracy: The period detail of English life during the days of the Norman Conquest are convincingly depicted.

GEORGE R.R. MARTIN (1948-)

Martin was born in New Jersey and graduated from Northwestern University. He was a VISTA volunteer and a tournament director for the Continental Chess Association. Martin was an instructor of journalism at Clarke College, Dubuque, Iowa. A prolific writer whose works span many genres, Martin has won three Hugo awards, 2 Nebula awards, and one Bram Stoker award. He has also written episodes for the television shows ''Beauty and the Beast'' and ''The Twilight Zone.''

4131 *Fevre Dream*

Date of Publication: 1982
Subject(s): Riverboats; Vampires; Antebellum South
Fictional character(s): Abner Marsh, Sailor (riverboat captain); Joshua York, Gentleman, Vampire
Time Period(s): 1850s (1857)
Locale(s): Mississippi River

Summary: The novel combines an inventive depiction of the steamboat era with a vampire story. Abner Marsh, a riverboat captain without a ship, joins forces with Joshua York, who builds him the fastest steamboat on the Mississippi. To Abner's horror, Joshua turns out to be a vampire on a mission to free his brethren from their search for blood.

Historical Accuracy: The period details make a plausible backdrop for this historical horror story.

L. JAY MARTIN

(PSEUD. OF MORTON GOLDING, 1925-)

Born in New York City, Golding was educated at the University of Denver and New York University. He worked for several magazines before becoming a full-time freelance writer. He has also written mystery and adventure fiction under the name M.M. Michaeles.

4132 *El Lazo*

Date of Publication: 1991
Subject(s): American West; Sea Story; Independence—California
Fictional character(s): John Clinton Ryan, Sailor; Quint Sharpentier, Sea Captain
Time Period(s): 1840s
Locale(s): Santa Barbara, California

Summary: When sailor John Clinton Ryan is blamed for the loss of his ship, he is cast ashore on the coast of Mexican California, which is on the verge of rebellion against Mexico and war with the United States. Ryan must adapt to strange customs in order to survive while guarding against Captain Quint Sharpentier, who has sworn to see him hanged.

Historical Accuracy: The era and the locale are captured with realistic details.

4133 *Rush to Destroy*

Date of Publication: 1992
Subject(s): American West; Mexican War; Independence—California
Fictional character(s): Ned Beale, Military Personnel (midshipman)
Historical character(s): John C. Fremont, Military Personnel (captain)
Time Period(s): 1840s (1846)
Locale(s): San Francisco, California

Summary: When war breaks out in California between the United States and Mexico, Ned Beale leads a party of naval volunteers to assist the command of Captain John C. Fremont. The Mexican forces are determined to halt the encroachment

of the Americans into their territory, and Beale and Fremont must contend with the feared California lancers.

Historical Accuracy: The story is fanciful, but a clear and convincing historical background is established.

MALACHI MARTIN

An Irish writer born in Kerry, Martin came to the U.S. in 1965. He attended Oxford University, Hebrew University, and received a doctorate in Semitic languages, archaeology, and history at the University of Louvain, Belgium. Martin has done archaeological research in the Middle East. He also worked as an editor for the Encyclopedia Britannica.

4134 *King of Kings: A Novel of the Life of David*

Date of Publication: 1980
Subject(s): Biblical Story; Ancient Israel; Biography, Fictionalized
Historical character(s): David, Ruler (King of Israel), Biblical Figure; Saul, Ruler (King of Israel); Bathsheba, Biblical Figure, Royalty (Queen Consort of David); Samuel, Biblical Figure, Religious (prophet); Jonathan, Biblical Figure
Time Period(s): 10th century B.C.
Locale(s): Israel

Summary: The novel blends fact, legend, and history to tell the story of David, the first great captain-king, who rises from a shepherd boy to become the leader of his people. The novel captures a complex David, a brilliant battlefield commander and astute lawmaker, with a passionate and restless sexuality. David is shown as one of the first of the great conquerors, a forerunner of Alexander, Caesar, and Napoleon.

Historical Accuracy: Much of the story is invented, but the period background and psychology of David are credible.

SYLVIA MARTIN (1913-1981)

An American editor and writer, Martin served as an assistant editor for *Christian Century* and as an editor for the Society for Cultural Relations with Latin America during the 1930s. She was a correspondent in South America in the 1940s, and collaborated with her husband on several travel guides.

4135 *I, Madame Tussaud*

Date of Publication: 1957
Subject(s): Biography, Fictionalized
Historical character(s): Marie Grosholtz Tussaud, Businesswoman
Time Period(s): 18th century; 19th century
Locale(s): Paris, France; London, England; Switzerland

Summary: The novel provides a biographical account of the career of Swiss wax modeler Marie Gresholtz who becomes famous as Madame Tussaud. She is imprisoned in Paris during the Reign of Terror where many heads are brought to her for modeling. When she inherits her uncle's museum, she emigrates to London where she establishes her famous exhibition. Madame Tussaud tells her own story when she is old and wealthy, looking back on a colorful career.

Historical Accuracy: The novel has drawn from Madame Tussaud's own memoirs, aided by letters and other documents to establish authenticity.

VALERIE MARTIN (1948-)

Born in Missouri, Martin received a B.A. degree from the University of New Orleans and an M.F.A. from the University of Massachusetts. She has been a visiting lecturer in creative writing at New Mexico State University, Las Cruces.

4136   *Mary Reilly*

Date of Publication: 1990
Subject(s): Supernatural; Servants; Victorian Period
Fictional character(s): Mary Reilly, Servant; Henry Jekyll, Doctor, Murderer (aka Edward Hyde)
Time Period(s): 19th century
Locale(s): London, England

Summary: In this retelling of Stevenson's famous supernatural psychological thriller, Mary Reilly, a servant in the household of Dr. Jekyll, assists the doctor in his experiments. Her journal entries show her concern rising as Dr. Jekyll becomes more and more debilitated by his strange illness.

Historical Accuracy: The novel captures convincingly both the period and the Stevenson original.

WILLIAM MARTIN (1950-)

Born in Boston, Martin is a graduate of Harvard, and he received an M.F.A. from UCLA. He has won acclaim for his novels set in New England. Martin is also the author of the screenplay *Humanoids of the Deep*, and the script for the TV program *George Washington: The Man Who Wouldn't Be King*. Martin prefers to set his stories in the past because he finds it a good place to study character.

4137   *Annapolis*

Date of Publication: 1996
Subject(s): Family Saga; Sea Story
Fictional character(s): James Stafford, Military Personnel (naval officer); Jack Stafford, Journalist
Time Period(s): Multiple Time Periods
Locale(s): Annapolis, Maryland

Summary: This massive multi-generational saga follows the history of the Stafford and Parrish families of Annapolis, Maryland, and their connection with the naval life that defines the city. The story encompasses the naval history of America from the Revolution to Vietnam.

Historical Accuracy: The novel's documentation of events, particularly the little known and obscure, is impressive.

4138   *Back Bay*

Date of Publication: 1979
Subject(s): Family Saga; Mystery

Fictional character(s): Horace Taylor Pratt, Businessman; Peter Fallon, Student (graduate)
Historical character(s): George Washington, Military Personnel (army commander); John Hancock, Patriot; Paul Revere, Patriot; Dolley Madison, Spouse (of James Madison), Political Figure
Time Period(s): Multiple Time Periods
Locale(s): Boston, Massachusetts

Summary: In 1789 George Washington is presented by the businessmen of Boston with a tea set fashioned by Paul Revere. In 1814 as the British troops advance on Washington the tea set mysteriously disappears. Did Horace Taylor Pratt arrange to have it stolen as revenge for government interference in his trade? In the 1970s Peter Fallon, a Harvard graduate student, reopens the case and uncovers the haunted legacy of a prominent old family.

Historical Accuracy: The novel excels at capturing the various eras of its ingenious story.

4139   *Cape Cod*

Date of Publication: 1991
Subject(s): American Colonies; Family Saga; Pilgrims
Fictional character(s): Geoff Hilyard, Heir; Jack Hilyard, Settler
Historical character(s): Miles Standish, Leader (Pilgrim); William Bradford, Leader (Pilgrim)
Time Period(s): Multiple Time Periods
Locale(s): Cape Cod, Massachusetts

Summary: This huge, multigenerational saga set in Cape Cod, Massachusetts, chronicles the history of the Hilyard and Bigelow families from their arrival on the Mayflower and the mysterious drowning that may have been the first murder in America. A bitter feud is passed down through the generations to the present as Geoff Hilyard becomes the heir to his family's last stretch of pristine coastline.

Historical Accuracy: The novel covers so much ground and has so many different targets that it is difficult to keep all in focus simultaneously. The setting and the eras are convincingly captured, however.

4140   *The Rising of the Moon*

Date of Publication: 1987
Subject(s): Independence—Ireland; Easter Rising; World War I
Fictional character(s): Padraic Starr, Patriot (Irish), Revolutionary; Tom Tracy, Political Figure; Rachel Levka, Activist
Time Period(s): 1910s (1916)
Locale(s): Boston, Massachusetts; Galway, Ireland

Summary: Set during the preparation for the Irish Easter Rising in 1916, the novel describes Padraic Starr's arrival in Boston to seek help to run guns to the rebels. He recruits Tom Tracy, a rising politician, and a Jewish girl, Rachel Levka. The three set sail with a cargo of arms across a dangerous Atlantic for the story's climax on the Galway Coast.

Historical Accuracy: The story is fanciful, but convincing in its period details.

FRANCIS MARTON

`4141` *Mrs. Betsy, or Widowed and Wed*

Date of Publication: 1955
Subject(s): Victorian Period
Fictional character(s): Betsy Jordan, Widow(er), Housekeeper
Time Period(s): 19th century (Victorian period)
Locale(s): England

Summary: In this modern version of a Victorian novel, the plucky career of Mrs. Betsy Jordan is chronicled. A widow at 28 with four children to care for, she takes a job as a housekeeper and later as a tavern keeper. In her positions she succeeds beyond all expectations, despite setbacks and complications.

Historical Accuracy: This is a rosy, nostalgic look at the past with some convincing period details.

JOHN MASEFIELD (1878-1967)

English poet and writer Masefield went to sea as a youth, and his first volumes of poetry, *Salt-Water Ballads* and *Ballads*, earned him the title "poet of the sea." He is best remembered for his long narrative poems "The Everlasting Mercy," "The Widow in Bye Street," "Dauber," and "Reynard the Fox." Masefield was also a novelist, playwright, and essayist. His novels include *Multitude and Solitude*, *Sard Harker*, and *The Bird of Dawning*.

`4142` *Basilissa: A Tale of the Empress Theodora*

Date of Publication: 1940
Subject(s): Byzantine Empire; Biography, Fictionalized
Historical character(s): Theodora, Royalty (empress consort of Justinian I); Justinian I, Ruler (Byzantine emperor)
Time Period(s): 6th century
Locale(s): Constantinople, Byzantine Empire

Summary: The novel offers a revisionist portrait of the Empress Theodora, co-ruler with Justinian I of the Byzantine Empire. She has been viewed by history as bloodthirsty and depraved, and the novel offers an alternative to this view: a woman of rare talents and a good Christian.

Historical Accuracy: The depiction of Theodora goes considerably beyond the range of historical sources.

A.E.W. MASON (1865-1948)

An English actor, politician, and writer, Mason was born in London and attended Dulwich College and Oxford University. He was an actor in provincial touring companies and served as a Member of Parliament. He was the author of a number of crime novels and plays.

`4143` *Fire over England*

Date of Publication: 1936
Subject(s): Elizabethan Period; Spanish Armada; Espionage
Fictional character(s): Robin Aubrey, Spy

Historical character(s): Elizabeth I, Ruler (Queen of England); Sir Francis Walsingham, Government Official
Time Period(s): 16th century (1580s)
Locale(s): England; Spain

Summary: This tale of espionage and adventure, set on the eve of the Spanish Armada's invasion of England, records the exploits of young Robin Aubrey. He is sent on a secret mission to Spain to affect the outcome of the Spanish attack.

Historical Accuracy: The story is fanciful, but colorful, and filled with believable period elements.

ANITA MASON (1942-)

An English novelist born in Bristol, Mason received a degree from St. Hilda's College, Oxford. In 1983 *The Illusionist* was shortlisted for the Booker Prize.

`4144` *The Illusionist*

Date of Publication: 1983
Subject(s): Roman Empire; Christianity; Magic
Historical character(s): Simon Magus, Magician; Peter, Biblical Figure; Nero, Ruler (Roman Emperor)
Time Period(s): 1st century
Locale(s): Israel; Rome, Roman Empire

Summary: Set in the decade after the crucifixion, the novel tells the story of the famous magician Simon Magus, who meets Peter and then must contend with a different sort of power. He journeys to Rome for a final test of power and illusion before Emperor Nero himself.

Historical Accuracy: The story is fanciful, but the era is captured with credibility.

F. VAN WYCK MASON (1901-1978)

An American novelist who had a distinguished military career, Mason served as the Chief Historian for General Dwight Eisenhower and the Allied Expeditionary Force. He produced more than 60 novels, many of them historical.

`4145` *Armored Giants: A Novel of the Civil War*

Date of Publication: 1980
Subject(s): Civil War—U.S.; Sea Story; Battle of the *Monitor* vs. the *Merrimac*
Fictional character(s): Dion O'Dea, Convict; Lionel Humphrey, Journalist; David Dexter, Military Personnel, Spy
Historical character(s): John Ericsson, Engineer
Time Period(s): 1860s (1861-1862)
Locale(s): Norfolk, Virginia; New York, New York; Bermuda

Summary: The novel offers an exciting story that culminates in the pivotal battle of ironclads which changed the course of naval warfare. A large cast includes an Irish escaped convict (O'Dea), a British journalist (Humphrey), and a Union naval lieutenant turned spy (Dexter) who joins the crew of the *C.S.N. Merrimac*. All are caught up in the intrigue that leads to the climactic battle between the *Merrimac* and the *Monitor*.

Historical Accuracy: Mason's story captures the era and the moment that served as a turning point in naval warfare.

4146 *Blue Hurricane*

Date of Publication: 1954
Subject(s): Civil War—U.S.; Sea Story; Military Life
Fictional character(s): Matt Hovey, Smuggler, Military Personnel; Phoebe Whidden, Gentlewoman
Time Period(s): 1860s (1861-1862)
Locale(s): Penobscot County, Maine; St. Louis, Missouri; Mississippi River

Summary: Matt Hovey is forced to flee his home in Maine. He winds up in St. Louis where he joins with a group of blockade runners on the Mississippi. When his love, Phoebe, is endangered, Hovey reconsiders his role in the war and enters military service. He serves during the "River War" of 1862, fighting the Confederacy for control of the Mississippi.

Historical Accuracy: Mason offers convincing details of the Civil War in the west and the atmosphere of St. Louis at the outset of the war.

4147 *Brimstone Club*

Date of Publication: 1971
Subject(s): Politics; Prostitution; Georgian Period
Fictional character(s): Jeremy Brett, Sea Captain, Gentleman; Dolly Lawton, Young Woman
Historical character(s): John Montagu, Nobleman (Earl of Sandwich), Political Figure; Benjamin Franklin, Political Figure; John Wilkes, Political Figure
Time Period(s): 1760s
Locale(s): London, England

Summary: Jeremy Brett, an American from Portsmouth, journeys to London to regain his family's shipping fortune. He finds himself marooned and penniless but gains access to the circle of the notorious Brimstone Club, a collection of upper-class libertines who include Lord Sandwich and Benjamin Franklin. At the center of the Club's activities is international intrigue.

Historical Accuracy: The novel is an exciting blend of authentic period details and fanciful invention and titillation. Franklin in particular is shown as far more the sensualist than history records.

4148 *Cutlass Empire*

Date of Publication: 1949
Subject(s): Pirates; Sea Story
Historical character(s): Henry Morgan, Pirate, Sea Captain; Charles II, Ruler (King of England)
Time Period(s): 17th century (1650s-1670s)
Locale(s): England; West Indies; Panama

Summary: The novel tells the story of the rousing life and times of British pirate Henry Morgan. Highpoints in his career, such as fleeing Oliver Cromwell's forces and his arrival as a castaway in the Caribbean are described. He becomes a great buccaneer captain, the scourge of the Spanish Main, and is eventually knighted for his efforts against England's enemies.

Historical Accuracy: Mason attempts to place Morgan on the same heroic level as Francis Drake and Robert Clive. He tries to draw an accurate and complete picture of the period without focusing on the brutality that occurred.

4149 *Eagle in the Sky*

Date of Publication: 1948
Subject(s): American Revolution; Medical Profession; Sea Story
Fictional character(s): Lucius Devoe, Doctor; Asa Peabody, Doctor; Peter Burnham, Doctor
Historical character(s): Friedrich von Steuben, Military Personnel, Nobleman; Benedict Arnold, Military Personnel
Time Period(s): 1780s (1780-1781)
Locale(s): Boston, Massachusetts; Grand Turk, West Indies; New York

Summary: Three young doctors end their apprenticeships and begin their medical careers as the American Revolution reaches its climax. The novel chronicles their different careers: one aboard a privateer, one on the staff of Benedict Arnold, and the third on the homefront. The action culminates on the battlefield of Yorktown.

Historical Accuracy: The novel features well-researched details of the period's medical practices and a solid depiction of the campaigns and events of the final year of the Revolution.

4150 *Golden Admiral*

Date of Publication: 1954
Subject(s): Elizabethan Period; Spanish Armada; Sea Story
Fictional character(s): Henry Wyatt, Sailor; Katherine Ibbott, Gentlewoman; Hubert Coffyn, Sailor
Historical character(s): Sir Francis Drake, Military Personnel; Elizabeth I, Ruler (Queen of England)
Time Period(s): 16th century (1580s)
Locale(s): Spain; London, England; *Primrose*, At Sea (West Indies)

Summary: Henry Wyatt, aboard the *Primrose*, is able to escape from the Spanish and return to England to alert Drake and the Queen to the looming Spanish threat. After a brief interlude with his sweetheart, Wyatt is off with Drake's armada to annoy the King of Spain and take Spanish treasure ships.

Historical Accuracy: Mason captures the period and the naval scene with conviction in this exciting and well-researched sea story.

4151 *Guns for Rebellion*

Date of Publication: 1977
Subject(s): American Revolution; Battle of Bunker Hill
Fictional character(s): Andrew Hunter, Military Personnel
Historical character(s): Ethan Allen, Military Personnel; Benedict Arnold, Military Personnel
Time Period(s): 1770s (1775)
Locale(s): Boston, Massachusetts, American Colonies; Ticonderoga, New York, American Colonies

Summary: The Battle of Bunker Hill and the fall of Boston to the rebels, are related through the experiences of Andrew

Hunter, a lieutenant aboard *H.M.S. Lively* in Boston Harbor in 1775. Torn between his duty to the king and his love for his country, Andrew finally chooses sides and helps equip Washington's army with the guns it needs to capture the city.

Historical Accuracy: The story is an exciting one with believable action scenes and a detailed depiction of the period.

`4152` *Harpoon in Eden*

Date of Publication: 1969
Subject(s): Sea Story; Whaling
Fictional character(s): Micajah Paddock, Sea Captain; Obediah Paddock, Sea Captain; Jedediah Paddock, Sea Captain
Time Period(s): 1830s
Locale(s): Nantucket, Massachusetts; *Gladiator*, At Sea (in the South Pacific); New Zealand

Summary: The great days of whaling and the nautical Paddock family from Nantucket are the novel's subjects. The family patriarch, Micajah, distributes his legacy to his children, whose conflict forms the background for an exciting voyage to the Pacific and primitive New Zealand.

Historical Accuracy: The whaling and nautical details are convincingly portrayed.

`4153` *Log Cabin Noble*

Date of Publication: 1973
Subject(s): Sea Story; American Colonies; Treasure Hunt
Historical character(s): William Phipps, Adventurer, Sea Captain; James II, Ruler (King of England)
Time Period(s): 17th century (1675-1685)
Locale(s): Maine; Boston, Massachusetts, American Colonies; Bermuda

Summary: The novel tells the story of William Phips, who rises from humble origins as the owner of a small shipyard in Maine to knighthood and eventually to the governorship of the Massachusetts Bay Colony. The novel chronicles the beginning of his career and his determination to recover a fortune in Spanish gold and silver.

Historical Accuracy: This exciting story is based on some of the facts of Phips' life although the fictional drama is largely Mason's invention.

`4154` *Manila Galleon*

Date of Publication: 1961
Subject(s): Sea Story; Military Life—British Navy
Fictional character(s): Nathaniel Wade, Sailor
Historical character(s): George Anson, Military Personnel; Peircy Brett, Military Personnel; Augustus Van Keppel, Military Personnel
Time Period(s): 1740s
Locale(s): At Sea; Canton, China

Summary: George Anson, considered the father of the British Navy, embarks on an expedition to the South Seas. His mission is to harass the Spanish and to capture if he can the richest treasure ship of all time—"the Prize of All the Oceans,"—the Manila Galleon. He sets sail with an ill-

equipped squadron that takes him around the world to uncharted seas, exotic ports, and great sea battles.

Historical Accuracy: The nautical details are admirably done and believable.

`4155` *Our Valiant Few*

Date of Publication: 1956
Subject(s): Civil War—U.S.; Sea Story; Military Life
Fictional character(s): Raphael Bryson, Sea Captain (aka "Rascal Rafe"), Blockade Runner; Alistair Bryson, Journalist; India Bryson, Gentlewoman
Time Period(s): 1860s (1862-1864)
Locale(s): Charleston, South Carolina; Savannah, Georgia

Summary: Charleston, South Carolina, is under siege by the Union naval blockade. Rafe Bryson is a dashing blockade runner, and his cousin is the managing editor of the *Charleston Argus*, intent on exposing the war profiteering that Rafe abets. Efforts to break the blockade are detailed, such as the use of "fish-boats," the prototype of the modern submarine.

Historical Accuracy: The novel is solidly researched and presented, exact in atmosphere and in the details of naval action.

`4156` *Proud New Flags*

Date of Publication: 1951
Subject(s): Civil War—U.S.; Sea Story; Military Life
Fictional character(s): Sylvia Seymour, Southern Belle; Samuel Seymour, Military Personnel; Coralita Menendez, Prostitute (courtesan); Kitty Pingree, Widow(er); Louise Cottier, Gentlewoman (Creole)
Time Period(s): 1860s (1861-1862)
Locale(s): Baltimore, Maryland; Norfolk, Virginia; New Orleans, Louisiana

Summary: The novel chronicles the Confederate Navy during the first year of the Civil War. The novel describes important naval events, such as the Confederates building ironclads on the Chesapeake, a run-in with a Union blockade in the Carribean, and a battle for control of the mouth of the Mississippi. The dramatic story focuses on Samuel Seymour, formerly of the U.S. Navy; his sister-in-law, a Southern belle from Savannah; and a trio of other loves whose romantic stories are connected to the naval adventures.

Historical Accuracy: Mason's details of the period and the naval engagements maintain authenticity even when the romance veers toward the melodramatic.

`4157` *Rascal's Heaven*

Date of Publication: 1964
Subject(s): American Colonies; Settlement of the American Frontier; Indians
Fictional character(s): Thad Burton, Orphan, Indian; John Musgrove, Trader; Winsome Brooks, Settler
Historical character(s): James Edward Oglethorpe, Military Personnel, Political Figure (founder of Georgia colony)
Time Period(s): 1730s; 1740s (1732-1741)
Locale(s): Savannah, Georgia, American Colonies; St. Augustine, Florida

Summary: Oglethorpe's Georgia colony is shown from a variety of perspectives, including that of a Tuscarora brave, a refugee from Boston, a trader, and Oglethorpe himself. The action follows the settlement of Savannah, skirmishes with the Indians, and the siege of St. Augustine held by the Spanish.

Historical Accuracy: Mason attempts to disprove the widely-held notion that the Georgia colony was made up exclusively of criminals and felons. The evident research in support of this thesis makes the novel a convincing portrait of the period and place.

4158 *Rivers of Glory*

Date of Publication: 1942
Subject(s): American Revolution; Sea Story
Fictional character(s): Andrew Warren, Military Personnel; Minga Allen, Gentlewoman
Time Period(s): 1770s (1778-1779)
Locale(s): Boston, Massachusetts; Savannah, Georgia; Jamaica

Summary: Mason continues his chronicles of the American Navy during the American Revolution in this story of Andrew Warren. One of America's first naval officers, Warren embarks on a dangerous voyage to Jamaica to secure medical supplies for the patriot army. His love for Minga Allen is interwoven with action that moves from Boston to New York, and climaxes with the pivotal siege of Savannah.

Historical Accuracy: The details of the period are thoroughly and convincingly presented.

4159 *The Sea 'Venture*

Date of Publication: 1961
Subject(s): Sea Story; Settlement of the American Frontier; American Colonies
Fictional character(s): Peter Agnew, Settler; Dolly Mellish, Saloon Hostess (barmaid), Settler
Historical character(s): George Somers, Settler; John Smith, Settler; Pocahontas, Indian; John Rolfe, Settler; James I, Ruler (King of England)
Time Period(s): 17th century (1609-1610)
Locale(s): Jamestown, Virginia, American Colonies; Bermuda; London, England

Summary: The story of the first settlement in Bermuda by George Somers is combined with a chronicle of the Jamestown colony. Somers sails from England with a relief squadron of colonists and supplies to aid John Smith and his struggling settlement. Somers' ship, the *Sea 'Venture*, is thrown off course and lands in Bermuda. The other ships reach Jamestown, and the personalities of the colony—Smith, Rolfe, and Pocahontas—are shown.

Historical Accuracy: The novel is filled with authentic details of the time and is both a rousing and informative story.

4160 *Silver Leopard*

Date of Publication: 1955
Subject(s): Middle Ages; Crusades
Fictional character(s): Sir Edmund de Montgomerie, Knight

Historical character(s): Bohemund, Nobleman (Duke of Otranto)
Time Period(s): 11th century (1095-1099)
Locale(s): San Severo, Italy; Byzantium, Byzantine Empire; Jerusalem, Palestine

Summary: This colorful adventure novel describes the events of the First Crusade through the experiences of English knight Edmund de Montgomerie. His adventures take him from Italy to Byzantium, and finally to the capture of Jerusalem.

Historical Accuracy: Although most of the characters and events are fictitious, the author has taken considerable efforts to re-create accurately the time and the motivations of the Crusaders.

4161 *Stars on the Sea*

Date of Publication: 1940
Subject(s): American Revolution; Sea Story
Fictional character(s): Desire Harmony, Outcast, Prostitute; Timothy Bennett, Military Personnel
Historical character(s): George Washington, Military Personnel; Nathanael Greene, Military Personnel (general); John Paul Jones, Military Personnel (naval officer)
Time Period(s): 1770s (1776-1777)
Locale(s): Newport, Rhode Island; Charleston, South Carolina; Bahamas

Summary: Desire Harmony, a young Quaker woman from Newport, is disgraced when she is left pregnant by her British lover. She makes her way, first as a prostitute, then as a traveling entertainer, to Charleston during the British siege. Her final destination is the Kentucky wilderness. The novel also continues Mason's depiction of the young American Navy, and details the rarely depicted attack on the Bahamas, which was the first expedition attempted by an American naval force.

Historical Accuracy: The novel's melodrama is at odds with the solidly researched depiction of the siege of Charleston and the naval action.

4162 *Three Harbors*

Date of Publication: 1938
Subject(s): American Revolution; Sea Story; Battle of Bunker Hill
Fictional character(s): Robert Ashton, Sailor; Katie Tryon, Saloon Hostess (barmaid)
Time Period(s): 1770s (1774-1775)
Locale(s): Boston, Massachusetts, American Colonies; Norfolk, Virginia, American Colonies; Charleston, South Carolina, American Colonies

Summary: The origins of the American Navy are chronicled in this story of merchant seaman Robert Ashton. Ashton realizes that the success of the American Revolution will depend on keeping the sea lanes open to trade. The action covers the East Coast in close encounters with the British. This is the first of a series of novels on the role of the American Navy in the American Revolution.

Historical Accuracy: Mason's in-depth research makes this a well-grounded and authentic story.

4163 *Trumpets Sound No More*

Date of Publication: 1975
Subject(s): Civil War—U.S.; Reconstruction Period; Treasure Hunt
Fictional character(s): Rodney Ajax Tilt, Military Personnel (Confederate officer); Margaret Forsythe, Gentlewoman; James Manlove, Military Personnel (Confederate officer)
Time Period(s): 1860s (1865-1866)
Locale(s): Virginia (western); Mexico (Gulf Coast)

Summary: Rodney Tilt, a Confederate officer discharged after Appomattox, returns to western Virginia with a group of irregulars. There he finds his home destroyed by the war and the land ravaged by Union patrols and marauding outlaws. To restore his fortune and to marry Margaret Forsythe, Tilt embarks with another Confederate veteran, Manlove, to retrieve a chest of gold taken from a sunken payship off the Mexican coast. The expedition turns into the last campaign of the Civil War.

Historical Accuracy: The details of the events immediately following the Civil War's end are vividly displayed.

4164 *Wild Horizon*

Date of Publication: 1966
Subject(s): American Revolution; Battle of Kings Mountain; Indians
Fictional character(s): John Sevier, Military Personnel; Samuel Mason, Doctor
Historical character(s): Tom Spencer, Frontiersman; James Robertson, Military Personnel
Time Period(s): 1770s; 1780s (1779-1780)
Locale(s): Kentucky; Tennessee

Summary: With the success of the British army in the South, a group of American patriots head west to begin a new life in Kentucky. The novel describes their trek, which includes Indian attacks, blizzards, and internal dissension. The action culminates in the Battle of Kings Mountain which, along with Saratoga and Yorktown, was a decisive battle of the Revolution.

Historical Accuracy: The novel is solidly grounded and graphically realistic in its re-creation of the historical events.

4165 *Young Titan*

Date of Publication: 1959
Subject(s): Settlement of the American Frontier; French and Indian War; Indians
Fictional character(s): Bartholomey Mayhew, Settler; Megan Mayhew, Settler
Time Period(s): 1730s; 1740s (1739-1745)
Locale(s): New England, American Colonies; Cape Breton Island, Nova Scotia, Canada (Louisburg); Boston, Massachusetts, American Colonies

Summary: Hardship and struggle in an American settlement during the French and Indian War is the novel's subject. The Mayhews, the central family of the novel, endure Indians and pitiless nature to begin to forge an American nation. The action climaxes in the attack on the French fortress of Louisburg, the first unified action of the burgeoning American nation.

Historical Accuracy: The details of frontier and Indian life are impressively authentic.

LISA MASON

Mason is a graduate of the University of Michigan Law School. She lives in the San Francisco Bay area and is the author of four science fiction novels: *Arachne*, *Cyberweb*, *Summer of Love*, and *The Golden Nineties*. She has published short fiction in numerous publications and anthologies, including *Omni*, *Year's Best Fantasy and Horror*, and *Sorceries*.

4166 *The Golden Nineties*

Date of Publication: 1995
Subject(s): Time Travel; Fantasy
Fictional character(s): Zhu Wong, Prisoner, Time Traveller
Time Period(s): 25th century; 1890s (1895)
Locale(s): San Francisco, California

Summary: In the 25th century Zhu Wong, a prisoner in China, must choose between standing trial for murder or volunteering for the Golden Nineties Project, a time-travel mission to San Francisco in 1895. There she must find a young Chinese girl and secure a brooch called an aurelia. She becomes an indentured servant of San Francisco's most famous madam and finds herself faced with choices with great consequences for her and the distant future.

Historical Accuracy: This ingenious fantasy does rely on some authentic period elements to create the sense of San Francisco in the 1890s.

ALLAN MASSIE (1938-)

Born in Singapore and raised in Scotland, Massie attended Trinity College, Cambridge, where he studied history. He is the *Scotsman's* lead fiction reviewer and a columnist and reviewer for the London *Daily Telegraph*. He contributes regularly to the *Times*, the *Spectator*, and the *Independent*. He lives in Scotland.

4167 *Augustus*

Date of Publication: 1986
Subject(s): Roman Empire; Biography, Fictionalized
Historical character(s): Julius Caesar, Military Personnel, Political Figure; Augustus, Ruler (Roman emperor); Livia, Spouse (of Augustus); Marcus Tullius Cicero, Political Figure, Lawyer; Marc Antony, Military Personnel (general); Cleopatra, Ruler (Queen of Egypt); Marcus Aemilius Lepidus, Political Figure; Marcus Junius Brutus, Political Figure; Gaius Cassius Longinus, Political Figure
Time Period(s): 1st century B.C.; 1st century
Locale(s): Rome, Roman Empire

Summary: Augustus, the son of Julius Caesar and Rome's first emperor, tells his own story in a memoir that dramatizes Julius Caesar's death and the civil war that it caused. Mark

Anthony, one-time friend of Augustus, becomes his opponent as Augustus tries to rule an empire and his family.

Historical Accuracy: Solidly researched, the novel's actions and characters are convincing.

`4168` *Caesar*

Date of Publication: 1993
Subject(s): Roman Empire; Biography, Fictionalized
Historical character(s): Julius Caesar, Military Personnel (Roman commander), Political Figure; Cleopatra, Royalty (Queen of Egypt); Marcus Tullius Cicero, Political Figure, Lawyer; Marcus Junius Brutus, Political Figure; Marc Antony, Military Personnel (general); Vercingetorix, Chieftain (of the Gauls)
Time Period(s): 1st century B.C. (49-44 B.C.)
Locale(s): Gaul; Rome, Roman Empire; Egypt

Summary: Juius Caesar's story, from the crossing of the Rubicon to his assassination, is told from the perspective of one of his comrades-in-arms. Caesar is shown as a charismatic leader whose ambition produces the counterweight of conspiracy and murder. A large cast of historical figures is shown in detail as fully realized human players in this grand political drama.

Historical Accuracy: Massie's portrait of Caesar and his age is fresh and presented with conviction.

`4169` *Tiberius: The Memoirs of the Emperor*

Date of Publication: 1990
Subject(s): Roman Empire; Biography, Fictionalized
Historical character(s): Tiberius, Ruler (Roman emperor), Military Personnel (general); Augustus, Ruler (Roman emperor); Caligula, Ruler (Roman emperor); Livia, Royalty (consort of Augustus); Lucius Aelius Sejanus, Military Personnel (general)
Time Period(s): 1st century B.C.; 1st century (42 B.C.-37 A.D.)
Locale(s): Rome, Roman Empire; Rhodes, Greece; Germany

Summary: The novel presents itself as the discovered autobiography of Roman emperor and general Tiberius. It offers a fully realized portrait of the energetic and troubled Tiberius, judged by some historians as a monster but by others as a great general and a capable emperor. Tiberius emerges here as a brooding and troubled leader, overwhelmed by a sense of duty.

Historical Accuracy: Tiberius' voice sounds authentic with a solid sense of place and an insider's familiarity with the Roman Empire's first family.

RENE MASSON (1922-)

Masson is a French writer whose books include *Green Oranges*.

`4170` *Landru*

Date of Publication: 1965
Subject(s): Crime and Criminals; World War I

Historical character(s): Henri Desire Landru, Murderer
Time Period(s): 1910s
Locale(s): France

Summary: This documentary novel, based on the case of a famous French serial killer, explores the psychology of Henri Landru. A man of refined taste and a rose fancier, he killed ten women and a boy between 1914 and 1919. Landru ingratiated himself with middle-aged women for their savings, disposing of his victims by strangulation.

Historical Accuracy: The novel is carefully based on the actual facts of the Landru case.

JOHN MASTERS (1914-1983)

English writer Masters was born in Calcutta, the son of an English captain of the Indian Army. He was educated at Wellington and Sandhurst and was a career officer in the Indian Army. He left India in 1947 for America, where he began to write historical novels based on Indian history and his own experiences. Masters' novels have been widely praised for his knowledge of India; he has been called the ''Kipling for our times.''.

`4171` *By the Green of the Spring*

Date of Publication: 1981
Subject(s): World War I; Family Saga
Fictional character(s): Richard Rowland, Businessman; Quentin Rowland, Military Personnel (British general); Christopher Cate, Landowner, Gentleman
Historical character(s): Winston Churchill, Political Figure
Time Period(s): 1910s (1918-1919)
Locale(s): England; France; Ireland

Summary: In the final volume of the author's Loss of Eden trilogy, the Great War comes to a close, and the wreckage after the peace is reflected in the experiences of the Rowlands and the Cates. The novel's many characters find themselves in a new world with changed relationships and a past that seems increasingly remote.

Historical Accuracy: As in the other volumes of the series, the period details offer a convincing backdrop for the family drama.

`4172` *Coromandel!*

Date of Publication: 1955
Subject(s): Family Saga; Indian Empire
Fictional character(s): Jason Savage, Adventurer
Time Period(s): 17th century (1630s)
Locale(s): India

Summary: In this chronologically first installment of the author's multi-volume account of the Savage family's experiences in India, Englishman Jason Savage searches for treasure in 17th-century India.

Historical Accuracy: This is a colorful adventure novel filled with authentic details of period India.

4173 *The Deceivers*

Date of Publication: 1952
Subject(s): English Colonies
Fictional character(s): William Savage, Government Official
Time Period(s): 1820s
Locale(s): India

Summary: The infamous Cult of Kali and its devotees, the Thugs or Deceivers, form the background for this adventure novel set in India in the 1820s. William Savage, a shy district collector, goes out in native disguise to penetrate and expose the Thugs.

Historical Accuracy: The period background for the story is authentic.

4174 *Heart of War*

Date of Publication: 1980
Subject(s): World War I; Family Saga; Easter Rising
Fictional character(s): Johnny Merritt, Military Personnel (American soldier); Quentin Rowland, Military Personnel (English colonel); Christopher Cate, Landowner, Gentleman; Guy Rowland, Military Personnel (RAF pilot)
Historical character(s): James Connolly, Revolutionary
Time Period(s): 1910s (1916-1917)
Locale(s): England; France; Ireland

Summary: In the second volume of the author's Loss of Eden trilogy, the Great War reaches its deadly middle years, and on the home front revolution breaks out in Ireland. These events impact the Rowlands and the Cates, forcing them to form new relationships.

Historical Accuracy: The period background is well-worked to offer a believable context for the family drama.

4175 *The Lotus and the Wind*

Date of Publication: 1953
Subject(s): British Raj
Fictional character(s): Robin Savage, Military Personnel (soldier); Anne Hildreth, Spouse (of Savage)
Time Period(s): 1870s (1879)
Locale(s): India; Afghanistan

Summary: The novel continues the chronicle of the Savage family in India, here concentrating on Robin Savage who is given a secret service assignment that sends him into the deserts of Afghanistan in search of an elusive Russian agent.

Historical Accuracy: The story depends on a solid reconstruction of the period atmosphere and the region.

4176 *Nightrunners of Bengal*

Date of Publication: 1951
Subject(s): British Raj; Indian Mutiny
Fictional character(s): Rodney Savage, Military Personnel (captain)
Time Period(s): 1850s (1857)
Locale(s): Bengal, India

Summary: This adventure tale is set against the vivid background of the Indian Sepoy Rebellion of 1857. The events of the mutiny that plunged India into civil war are seen through the experience of the Anglo-Indian community.

Historical Accuracy: This is an authentic reconstruction of the events and the effects of the rebellion.

4177 *Now, God Be Thanked*

Date of Publication: 1979
Subject(s): World War I; Family Saga
Fictional character(s): Harry Rowland, Gentleman, Businessman; Quentin Rowland, Military Personnel (English officer); Richard Rowland, Businessman
Time Period(s): 1910s (1914-1915)
Locale(s): England; Ireland

Summary: The first volume of the author's Loss of Eden trilogy is set at the beginning of World War I. The intertwined lives of three generations of English and American families are shown. They must contend with divided family loyalty, ambition, and adultery. The war becomes a catalyst for new relationships and new perspectives on older ones.

Historical Accuracy: The period details establish a plausible historical background for this domestic drama set in motion by historical events.

4178 *The Ravi Lancers*

Date of Publication: 1972
Subject(s): World War I; Military Life—British Army; British Raj
Fictional character(s): Warren Bateman, Military Personnel (British officer); Krishna Ram, Royalty (prince)
Time Period(s): 1910s (1914-1915)
Locale(s): India

Summary: Set during the First World War, the novel tells the story of a regiment trained in India and made up of Hindu troops that is sent to the killing grounds of the Western Front. The novel centers on Major Warren Bateman, who wants to prove that the Ravi Lancers can fit into the British army, and Prince Krishna Ram, who wishes to preserve the unique cultural identity of the regiment.

Historical Accuracy: The knowledge of Indian military life is evident, and the period background is believable.

4179 *The Rock: A Novel about Gibraltar*

Date of Publication: 1970
Subject(s): Prehistory; Roman Empire; Napoleonic Wars
Fictional character(s): Julius, Military Personnel (Roman commander); Rachel, Young Woman; Judah Conquy, Shipowner
Time Period(s): Multiple Time Periods
Locale(s): Gibraltar

Summary: The novel illustrates the social history of the island of Gibraltar from its formation eons ago to its successive occupation by prehistoric tribes, the Romans, and the Moors, and finally its roles as a strategic Mediterranean outpost for the British. In each era fictional characters dramatize the period and its political and social background.

Historical Accuracy: The various eras are authentically drawn and convincing.

BERKELY MATHER
(PSEUD. OF JOHN EVAN WESTON DAVIES, 1914-)

Mather was born in New South Wales, Australia, and attended Kings School and the Royal School of Artillery in Britain. He spent 30 years in the British army in India, the Far East, and the Middle East. Mather is the author of crime novels, radio plays, and screenplays such as *Dr. No* and *The Long Ships*.

4180 *The Midnight Gun*
Date of Publication: 1981
Subject(s): Boer War; Business Building; Boxer Rebellion
Fictional character(s): Ross Stafford, Businessman; Bard Stafford, Businessman, Adventurer
Time Period(s): 1900s (1900)
Locale(s): Hong Kong; Yangtze River, China; South Africa

Summary: The second volume of the author's Far East trilogy follows the adventures of young Bard Stafford, who turns gun-runner in scenes set during the Boxer Rebellion and the Boer War.

Historical Accuracy: The emphasis is on fast-paced action and adventure. The period details are reliable.

4181 *The Pagoda Tree*
Date of Publication: 1979
Subject(s): British Colonies; Business Building; Victorian Period
Fictional character(s): Neil Stafford, Convict, Highwayman; Ross Stafford, Orphan; Leonora Mascharenhas, Young Woman
Time Period(s): 1850s
Locale(s): Australia; Hong Kong; India

Summary: Set in the 1850s, the novel tells the story of two brothers' quest for fortune that takes them from Australia to Hong Kong and India. Neil Stafford is transported to Australia for robbery. He is followed by his brother, Ross, who is determined to help him escape. He succeeds, and they next become involved with the powerful East India Company and the beautiful Leonora. Their story continues in *The Midnight Gun*.

Historical Accuracy: The exotic setting and period are captured with some skill and authenticity.

4182 *The Road and the Star*
Date of Publication: 1965
Subject(s): Civil War—England; Pirates
Fictional character(s): Lord Bemford, Rake, Adventurer
Time Period(s): 17th century
Locale(s): London, England; Goa, India; Capetown, South Africa

Summary: Set during the 17th century, this romantic adventure novel traces the rake's progress of the hero as he escapes from Cromwell's minions to India and Turkey, retracing the caravan route of Marco Polo. Along the way there are pirate attacks and enough derring-do for a series of adventures.

Historical Accuracy: The historical background is lightly sketched with an emphasis on action over documentation.

JANET MATHEWSON

4183 *Michael Torey*
Date of Publication: 1962
Subject(s): Business Building
Fictional character(s): Michael Torey, Businessman; Plumbridge Vaughn, Gentleman
Time Period(s): 19th century; 20th century (1898-1929)
Locale(s): Pittsburgh, Pennsylvania; Connecticut

Summary: The novel traces Michael Torey's rise to success. From a humble background he becomes a Pittsburgh steel tycoon. His rise is fueled by his desire to match the wealth and power held by his college friend Plum Vaughn. All is not satisfying once Michael achieves his goal.

Historical Accuracy: The novel captures with convincing insights America's boom years in the opening decades of the 20th century.

THEODORE MATHIESON (1913-)

Born in California, Mathieson graduated from the University of California, Berkeley. He has worked as a high school teacher of English, journalism, and drama. His books include *The Door to Nowhere*, *The Sign of the Flame*, and *Island in the Sand*.

4184 *The Devil and Ben Franklin*
Date of Publication: 1961
Subject(s): Mystery; American Colonies
Historical character(s): Benjamin Franklin, Printer, Political Figure
Time Period(s): 1730s (1734)
Locale(s): Philadelphia, Pennsylvania, American Colonies

Summary: Set in colonial Philadelphia when Benjamin Franklin is a young local printer and bookseller, this period mystery story involves a curse laid upon Franklin that seems to have supernatural effects, including murder. The rational Franklin sets out to disprove a Satanic origin for the curse.

Historical Accuracy: The novel provides a convincing and authentic period background.

PETER MATHIESSEN

4185 *Killing Mister Watson*
Date of Publication: 1990
Subject(s): Crime and Criminals
Fictional character(s): E. J. Watson, Plantation Owner
Time Period(s): 1910s
Locale(s): Everglades, Florida

Summary: The Florida Everglades is the scene for this psychological inquiry into the life of an engineer, E.J. Watson. Was he the man who gunned down the former female outlaw Belle Star? Will he kill again? The novel demonstrates the way a community creates its own legends.

Historical Accuracy: The author explains that there is almost no actual history in the book, as most of the events are imagined. There is, however, nothing implausible or inconsistent with history.

CECILE HULSE MATSCHAT (1895-1976)

An American artist, botanist, and writer, Matschat was the author of a number of historical novels and horticulture books.

`4186` *Preacher on Horseback*

Date of Publication: 1940
Subject(s): Religious Life; Reconstruction Period
Fictional character(s): Janos Sandor, Religious (minister); Rica Sandor, Spouse
Time Period(s): 1860s; 1870s
Locale(s): Michigan; Mohawk Valley, New York

Summary: Set in the years following the Civil War, the novel depicts the experiences of a circuit-riding preacher and his wife in Michigan and the Mohawk Valley of northern New York State.

Historical Accuracy: Although the story and characters are fictional, the life and customs are authentic, based on the actual experiences of the wife of a circuit rider of the period.

`4187` *Tavern in the Town*

Date of Publication: 1942
Subject(s): American Colonies; French and Indian War
Fictional character(s): Michael Barre, Convict; Hope Hilton, Young Woman
Historical character(s): George Washington, Military Personnel (colonel)
Time Period(s): 1750s
Locale(s): Virginia, American Colonies

Summary: Set in Colonial Virginia, this romantic tale traces the experiences of an English convict, Michael Barre, who becomes involved with a plantation family, the Hiltons. The background is the French and Indian Wars and features the appearance of a young Colonel George Washington.

Historical Accuracy: The story is set plausibly against a backdrop of period details and actual events.

ANNE IRWIN MATTHEW

`4188` *Warm Wind, West Wind*

Date of Publication: 1956
Subject(s): Tudor Period
Fictional character(s): Crede Canynges, Young Woman; Robin Thorne, Trader

Historical character(s): Desiderius Erasmus, Writer; Sir Thomas More, Writer
Time Period(s): 16th century (1500s)
Locale(s): Bristol, England; London, England; Oxford, England

Summary: Set during the reign of Henry VII, the novel describes the Canynges and Thorne families. As their shipping and trading businesses expand the limits of the known world, the New Learning of the Humanists, such as Thomas More and Erasmus, extends the limits of intellectual interests. The novel paints a colorful and detailed portrait of English customs and beliefs during the period.

Historical Accuracy: The novel offers a convincing depiction of the era and the ferment of new ideas that ushered in the 16th century.

GREG MATTHEWS (1949-)

Born in Australia, Matthews left school at age 17 and worked as a freight loader, office cleaner, and parcel wrapper. He settled permanently in the U.S. in 1983.

`4189` *The Further Adventures of Huckleberry Finn*

Date of Publication: 1984
Subject(s): American West; Gold Rush—California
Fictional character(s): Huckleberry Finn, Adventurer; Jim, Adventurer, Slave (former)
Time Period(s): 1840s (1849)
Locale(s): Missouri; West; San Francisco, California

Summary: Huck and Jim indeed "light out for the territory," as indicated at the end of Mark Twain's classic novel. In this sequel, it is 1849, and the two head west across the Great Plains to California. Along the way they encounter Indians, whores, preachers, gamblers, and outlaws—a full chorus of Western types.

Historical Accuracy: Matthews gives a fairly convincing imitation of Twain's original voice, a remarkable achievement for an Australian. The Western scene is exuberantly described.

`4190` *Heart of the Country*

Date of Publication: 1985
Subject(s): American West
Fictional character(s): Joe Cobden, Frontiersman, Hunter (buffalo); Adeline Attucks, Madam; Noah Pike, Wanderer
Time Period(s): 19th century (1854-1880)
Locale(s): Kansas; St. Louis, Missouri

Summary: In the late 19th century the community of Valley Forge is created in the unsettled plains of Kansas. The founder has a son by an Indian woman and promptly abandons both. The boy, Joe Cobden, is raised in St. Louis, malformed as a hunchback. At age 15, he sets out West becoming a woodcutter, a bouncer at a brothel, a buffalo hunter, and bone gatherer. Finally, he returns to the place of his birth.

Historical Accuracy: Matthews avoids the expected romantic elements for a more realistic portrait of the times, stripped of hyperbole and idealization.

4191 *Power in the Blood*

Date of Publication: 1993
Subject(s): American West; Crime and Criminals
Fictional character(s): Zoe Dugan, Orphan; Clayton Dugan, Lawman, Orphan; Drew Dugan, Outlaw
Time Period(s): 19th century (1869-1885)
Locale(s): Colorado; West

Summary: A girl and her two brothers are orphaned and in 1869 are sent out West on one of the so-called orphan trains, which shipped household and farm help to pioneer families. The three are separated, adopted by couples in three different states. Their stories of Western life and eventual reunion contribute to the novel's charm.

Historical Accuracy: Matthews renders the Western scene with assurance and authenticity.

4192 *The Wisdom of Stones*

Date of Publication: 1994
Subject(s): World War II; Frontier—Australia; Ranching
Fictional character(s): Clive Bagnall, Rancher; Doug Farrands, Rancher; Valerie Lansdowne, Rancher
Time Period(s): 1930s; 1940s (1939-1940s)
Locale(s): Darwin, Australia; Singapore

Summary: Clive Bagnall arrives in Australia to claim his inheritance: a ramshackle cattle station in the bush. He is befriended by local Doug Farrands, and they join forces with his cousin Valerie. The trio tries to make the ranch succeed but are interrupted by the war. Clive and Doug meet again as prisoners of the Japanese and escape after a harrowing voyage over the open ocean.

Historical Accuracy: The novel is solidly grounded in period and regional details. The scenes in the prison camp are based on fact.

JACK MATTHEWS (1917-)

A Canadian writer born in Manitoba, Matthews is a graduate of Heidelberg College, Ohio University, and Ohio State University. He has worked as a professor of speech and theater arts.

4193 *Sassafras*

Date of Publication: 1983
Subject(s): Settlement of the American Frontier; Picaresque Adventure
Fictional character(s): Thad Burke, Scientist (phrenologist); Henry Buck, Indian, Companion
Time Period(s): 1840s
Locale(s): Maryland; Ohio; Kansas

Summary: Phrenologists believed that the size and shape of a person's head could tell much about that person's character and intelligence. This picaresque tale follows the travels of a young phrenologist, Thad Burke, as he reads skulls from town

to town in the 1840s from Ohio to Kansas. Along the way he meets a colorful assortment of frontier characters.

Historical Accuracy: The story features a convincing, albeit comic and at times absurd, look at the western wilderness.

RICHARD MATTURRO

A specialist in Shakespeare and classical literature, Matturro earned a Ph.D. from the State University of New York at Albany.

4194 *Troy*

Date of Publication: 1989
Subject(s): Trojan War; Myths and Legends; Ancient Greece
Fictional character(s): Helen of Troy, Noblewoman; Achilles, Warrior; Hector, Warrior; Odysseus, Warrior
Time Period(s): Indeterminate Past
Locale(s): Troy, Ancient Civilization

Summary: The novel reimagines the deeds of the Trojan War. The story is the familiar one of Homer's *Iliad* with Helen's great beauty the catalyst for the conflict. Achilles, the great Greek warrior, pursues Hector, and Odysseus' schemes prepare the Trojans' downfall. All is seen in psychological depth.

Historical Accuracy: The novel expands and elaborates on Homer's original, offering a parallel version of the story.

ROBIN MAUGHAM
(PSEUD. OF ROBERT C.R. MAUGHAM, 1916-1981)

An English writer and a nephew of Somerset Maugham, Robert Maugham was educated at Eton and Cambridge. His wounds from service in the army in North Africa during World War II left him with recurrent bouts of amnesia for the rest of his life and forced him to give up his career as a barrister. While recovering from his wounds, he began his first novel, *Come to Dust*, and decided to become a writer. He went on to write novels, plays, film scripts, and nonfiction, including an autobiography and two books about Somerset Maugham.

4195 *The Barrier*

Date of Publication: 1973
Subject(s): British Raj; British Colonies; Racial Conflict
Fictional character(s): Tom, Military Personnel (colonel); Anne, Spouse; Sunil, Servant
Time Period(s): 1890s
Locale(s): India

Summary: Class distinction and racial barriers form the theme of this novel that depicts the domestic life of a British officer and his wife in India during the 1890s. The marriage between Tom and Anne is loveless and troubled. When Anne pays too much attention to a native servant, the conflict grows to tragic proportions.

Historical Accuracy: The novel offers a realistic portrayal of Anglo-Indian life of the period.

4196 *The Last Encounter*

Date of Publication: 1973
Subject(s): Siege of Khartoum
Historical character(s): Charles George Gordon, Military Personnel (general)
Time Period(s): 1880s (1885)
Locale(s): Khartoum, Sudan

Summary: The story of the Siege of Khartoum is told through the imaginary diary of General Charles Gordon. Although ordered to evacuate, Gordon attempts to defeat the Sudanese forces of the Mahdi and endures a ten month siege before Khartoum falls and he is killed. The novel focuses on the final days of the siege and attempts to solve the enigma of Gordon.

Historical Accuracy: The basic facts of the siege are observed. The author's thesis to explain Gordon's personality is plausible, if not totally convincing.

WILLIAM SOMERSET MAUGHAM

4197 *Catalina*

Date of Publication: 1948
Subject(s): Inquisition; Religious Conflict
Fictional character(s): Catalina, Handicapped
Time Period(s): 15th century
Locale(s): Spain

Summary: Set in Spain during the Inquisition, this romantic tale involves a young crippled girl, Catalina, who is cured by a vision of the Virgin Mary. As news of the miracle spreads, the Carmelite and Dominican orders battle over Catalina.

Historical Accuracy: Providing a convincing period background clearly is not the novelist's main consideration.

4198 *Then and Now*

Date of Publication: 1946
Subject(s): Renaissance
Historical character(s): Niccolo Machiavelli, Writer, Political Figure; Cesare Borgia, Military Personnel, Diplomat
Time Period(s): 16th century (1502-1503)
Locale(s): Italy

Summary: The political education of Niccolo Machiavelli is dramatized in the intrigue of Cesare Borgia. The novel translates the political wisdom of Machiavelli's *The Prince* into actual and human terms. A knowing depiction of scenes, customs, and personalities of the period are also featured.

Historical Accuracy: The novel's strength lies in its re-created atmosphere, which captures the period convincingly.

A.M. MAUGHAN

An English novelist, Maughan has worked as a company director in Durham, England. Her books include *Young Pitt* and *The King's Malady*.

4199 *Harry of Monmouth*

Date of Publication: 1956

Subject(s): Royalty—England; Battle of Agincourt; Middle Ages
Historical character(s): Henry of Monmouth, Royalty (prince); Henry IV, Ruler (King of England); Catherine of Valois, Royalty (queen consort of Henry V); John of Gaunt, Royalty (prince); Henry Percy, Knight
Time Period(s): 15th century
Locale(s): England; France; Wales

Summary: Henry V lived only to age 35, but his life became the stuff of legend. He is shown in this novel transformed from a dissolute youth to one of England's greatest national heroes as he comes to the disputed throne that his father seized from Richard II and achieves the impossible victory at Agincourt when 6,000 British troops defeated a French army of 42,000. Henry's prize is the daughter of the French king, Catherine of Valois. The novel captures both the personality of Henry and the events that contributed to his legend.

Historical Accuracy: The basic framework of the story is the actual events of Henry's career, faithfully presented.

4200 *Young Pitt*

Date of Publication: 1974
Subject(s): Georgian Period; Politics
Historical character(s): William Pitt the Younger, Political Figure; Charles James Fox, Political Figure
Time Period(s): 18th century; 19th century
Locale(s): England

Summary: English parliamentary politics during the reign of George III are dramatized through this account of the career of William Pitt the Younger, who at age 24 becomes Prime Minister. His main opponent is Charles James Fox, and the novel provides a colorful portrait of their sparring and a look at 18th-century customs.

Historical Accuracy: The novel offers an accurate look at the period and its politics.

PATRICIA MAXWELL (1942-)

An American writer born in Los Angeles, Maxwell won the best historical romance novel of the year award in 1985 for *Midnight Waltz*. In 1987 she received a lifetime achievement award for romance fiction. Maxwell confesses to having a love affair with history, and she attempts to re-create the past as closely and convincingly as possible. Maxwell also writes under the pseudonym Jennifer Blake.

4201 *The Notorious Angel*

Date of Publication: 1977
Subject(s): Revolution—Central America
Fictional character(s): Eleanora Villars, Young Woman; Grant Farrell, Military Personnel (colonel)
Historical character(s): William Walker, Adventurer
Time Period(s): 1850s
Locale(s): New Orleans, Louisiana; Nicaragua

Summary: Set against the backdrop of William Walker's adventures in Nicaragua, this romantic adventure novel follows Eleanor Villar's pursuit of her brother who has joined

Walker's army of occupation. She becomes the mistress of Colonel Grant Farrell and her romantic complications are connected with Nicaraguan politics.

Historical Accuracy: The novel's historical background is authentic.

BEATRICE MAY

4202 *Sister to Jane: The Story of Lady Katharine Grey*

Date of Publication: 1983
Subject(s): Tudor Period; Royalty—England
Historical character(s): Lady Jane Grey, Ruler (Queen of England), Noblewoman; Lady Katharine Grey, Noblewoman
Time Period(s): 16th century
Locale(s): England

Summary: The novel concerns the political maneuvering following the death of Henry VIII and concentrates on the experience of Lady Katharine Grey, sister of Jane Grey who becomes queen of England for nine days before she is executed. The sisters are brought up as royal princesses but find themselves pawns in a highstakes game of dynastic politics.

Historical Accuracy: The novel is faithful to the events of the period and the atmosphere of the times.

ALBERT MAYER (1897-1981)

An American born in New York City, Mayer graduated from Columbia University and MIT. An architect and structural engineer, Mayer has worked as a housing planner.

4203 *Follow the River*

Date of Publication: 1969
Subject(s): Settlement of the American Frontier; Indians
Fictional character(s): Tom Morrow, Teacher, Frontiersman
Time Period(s): 1790s
Locale(s): Cincinnati, Ohio; Ohio Valley, Ohio

Summary: The novel depicts the settlement of Cincinnati and the Ohio Valley in the 1790s from the perspective of a young teacher, Tom Morrow, who ventures west and becomes involved in the expedition against the Indians along the Maumee River.

Historical Accuracy: The details of the story are factually-based, with the wilderness elements faithfully presented.

EVELYN WILDE MAYERSON (1934-)

Mayerson is an American born in New York City and a graduate of the University of Miami, Coral Gables, Goddard College, and Laurence University of California. She is a professor of English at the University of Miami and the author of many novels including *Well and Truly*.

4204 *Miami: A Saga*

Date of Publication: 1994

Subject(s): Settlement of the American Frontier; Family Saga; Reconstruction Period
Fictional character(s): Eulalie Coombs, Landowner (homesteader), Southern Belle; Caroline Hanna, Fugitive; Zalman Levy, Immigrant
Time Period(s): 19th century; 20th century (1886-1992)
Locale(s): Miami, Florida

Summary: The story of the development of South Florida and Miami is traced from the post-Civil War era to the present through the experiences of five families beginning with Eulalie and John Quincy Coombs who come as homesteaders and build their house on the site of what will become a great city. Later generations of immigrants and settlers contribute to Miami's vibrant history.

Historical Accuracy: The novel keeps to the actual events of the city's development as the basis for the novel's action.

4205 *Princess in Amber*

Date of Publication: 1985
Subject(s): Royalty—England; Victorian Period
Historical character(s): Beatrice, Royalty (princess); Henry of Battenburg, Royalty (prince); Victoria, Ruler (Queen of England); Edward, Prince of Wales, Royalty; Edward Jenner, Doctor; William Gladstone, Political Figure (prime minister)
Time Period(s): 19th century (Victorian period)
Locale(s): England

Summary: Princess Beatrice, the youngest daughter of Queen Victoria, is raised as a virtual royal prisoner. When Beatrice meets Prince Henry of Battenburg, Beatrice is torn between her mother and the prince.

Historical Accuracy: The novel is based on diaries, journals, letters, and extensive research into the period. But the author has taken the novelist's perogative of reading between the lines to yield the richer stuff of motivation and desire.

SARA MAYFIELD (1905-1979)

Born in Alabama, Mayfield is a journalist, editor, playreader, and theatrical casting director. She was a college classmate of Zelda Fitzgerald, about whom she wrote in *Exiles in Paradise*. Mayfield has also written a biography of H.L. Mencken, *The Constant Circle*.

4206 *Mona Lisa: The Woman in the Portrait*

Date of Publication: 1974
Subject(s): Renaissance; Biography, Fictionalized; Artistic Life
Historical character(s): Lisa Gherardini Giocondo, Noblewoman; Leonardo da Vinci, Artist, Inventor; Rodrigo Borgia, Nobleman, Religious (pope); Cesare Borgia, Nobleman, Military Personnel; Sandro Botticelli, Artist; Niccolo Machiavelli, Government Official; Michelangelo Buonarotti, Artist
Time Period(s): 15th century
Locale(s): Florence, Italy; Rome, Italy

Summary: The novel offers a fictional biography of the model for the world's most famous painting, the Mona Lisa. Lisa

Gherardini Giaconda was very much a figure of her times—the vibrant, creative times of the Italian Renaissance and the turbulent and dangerous age of the Borgias and the Medicis. The novel's subject offers a clear window on the culture and politics of the times.

Historical Accuracy: The story keeps to the factual for the most part, with some obvious surmises and inventions to fill in gaps and connections.

MARGARET MAYHEW (1936-)

Mayhew was born in England.

`4207` *The Railway King*

Date of Publication: 1979
Subject(s): Railroads; Victorian Period; Romance
Fictional character(s): Kirby England, Businessman, Guardian; Hester Gurney, Ward
Time Period(s): 1830s; 1840s (1833-1840s)
Locale(s): England

Summary: Set during England's railroad mania during the 1830s and 1840s, the novel tells the story of self-made man Kirby England, who is determined to make his fortune through the new railroad. When he becomes the guardian of a plain, religious girl, Hester Gurney, his plans must accommodate a variety of surprises.

Historical Accuracy: The story owes something to the life of George Hudson, the "Railroad King.".

KENNETH MAYNARD

Maynard is a former British army officer and expert in nautical matters.

`4208` *First Lieutenant*

Date of Publication: 1985
Subject(s): Sea Story; Military Life—British Navy; Napoleonic Wars
Fictional character(s): Matthew Lamb, Military Personnel (naval officer); Captain Slade, Military Personnel (naval officer)
Time Period(s): 1790s
Locale(s): *Adroit*, At Sea; West Indies; Jamaica

Summary: In the second volume dramatizing the naval exploits of Matthew Lamb, Lamb is bound for the West Indies, dreaming of rich prizes and promotion. Lamb's commander, Captain Slade, is given the task of storming a fort on a French-held island to rescue a British agent, and Lamb must test himself in savage fighting.

Historical Accuracy: The period nautical background is convincingly authentic.

`4209` *Lamb in Command*

Date of Publication: 1986
Subject(s): Sea Story; Military Life—British Navy; Napoleonic Wars
Fictional character(s): Matthew Lamb, Military Personnel (naval officer); Charlotte Brett, Gentlewoman

Time Period(s): 1790s
Locale(s): Jamaica; *Heron*, At Sea

Summary: In the third volume of a trilogy, British naval officer Matthew Lamb finally achieves his commission and a long-coveted captaincy of the mail packet *Heron*, bound for Antigua and Barbados. He must contend with difficult passengers, including Charlotte Brett, who has been forced to leave a lover and quickly captivates Lamb. Naval action includes an encounter with a French privateer.

Historical Accuracy: The details of naval life of the period are convincingly depicted.

`4210` *Lieutenant Lamb*

Date of Publication: 1984
Subject(s): Sea Story; Military Life—British Navy; Napoleonic Wars
Fictional character(s): Matthew Lamb, Military Personnel (naval officer); Captain Cutler, Military Personnel (naval officer)
Time Period(s): 1790s (1798)
Locale(s): *Sturdy*, At Sea (Mediterranean); Portugal

Summary: In the first volume of a trilogy involving British naval lieutenant Matthew Lamb, Lamb is shown in action against privateers and a large French frigate as as onshore in a daring raid in Portugal.

Historical Accuracy: The novel captures with precision the nautical and military details, as well as the period background, to create a believable historical adventure.

DRAYTON MAYRANT
(PSEUD. OF KATHERINE DRAYTON MAYRANT SIMONS, 1892-1969)

American poet and novelist Simons was born in Charleston, South Carolina, and attended Converse College. She was an American and French Red Cross worker during World War I and a radar warning worker with the U.S. Army Air Force during World War II. Simons published her first book of poetry, *Shadow Songs*, in 1912 under the pen name Kadra Maysi. She abandoned that pseudonym in the early 1940s, believing it to be Japanese. Simon's novels include *The Land Beyond the Tempest*, *Lamp in Jerusalem*, and *Always a River*.

`4211` *Always a River*

Date of Publication: 1956
Subject(s): American Colonies; Puritans; Witchcraft and Sorcery
Fictional character(s): Sandy Purbeck, Teacher; Nicole Lenoir, Young Woman
Time Period(s): 17th century (1695)
Locale(s): Massachusetts, American Colonies; Carolinas, American Colonies

Summary: During the witchcraft hysteria in the Massachusetts Colony a young Puritan schoolmaster, Sandy Purbeck, journeys south into Carolina to establish a mission. He find his strict Puritanism in conflict with the more worldly ways of the Carolina French Huguenots.

Historical Accuracy: The novel is realistic in its period details of New England and the Carolinas.

4212 *First the Blade*

Date of Publication: 1950
Subject(s): Roman Empire; Biblical Story; Christianity
Fictional character(s): Draco, Military Personnel (Roman tribune)
Historical character(s): Pontius Pilate, Government Official; Claudia Procula, Spouse (of Pilate)
Time Period(s): 1st century
Locale(s): Jerusalem, Israel; Rome, Roman Empire

Summary: Based on the briefest of reference to Pontius's wife in the gospel of St. Matthew, the novel has constructed a biographical background for the woman who advised Pilate not to condemn Jesus. The granddaughter of Augustus, Claudia Procula is tricked into marriage with the opportunistic Pilate.

Historical Accuracy: The Roman period elements are authoritative and believable.

4213 *The Land Beyond the Tempest*

Date of Publication: 1960
Subject(s): Sea Story; American Colonies
Fictional character(s): Tamar Gates, Young Woman
Time Period(s): 17th century
Locale(s): Cornwall, England; *Sea Venture*, At Sea; Jamestown, Virginia, American Colonies

Summary: Young Tamar Gates decides to join her father on a hazardous journey to America. The details of the trip are based on the actual voyage of the *Sea Venture* on the third supply expedition to the Jamestown Colony.

Historical Accuracy: The novel features a realistic and convincing depiction of 17th-century England, Bermuda, and the American colony at Jamestown.

4214 *The Red Doe*

Date of Publication: 1953
Subject(s): American Revolution
Fictional character(s): Lex Mourne, Military Personnel (soldier), Farmer; Evelyn Fay, Military Personnel (lieutenant)
Historical character(s): Francis Marion, Military Personnel (officer)
Time Period(s): 1780s
Locale(s): Santee, South Carolina

Summary: This novel concerns the southern campaign of the American Revolution and the guerrilla warfare fought by Francis Marion against the British under Lord Tarleton. The story features a young farmer whose experiences in war compete with his experiences in love.

Historical Accuracy: The background for the novel's events is faithful to history.

4215 *The Running Thread*

Date of Publication: 1949
Subject(s): Antebellum South; Civil War—U.S.

Fictional character(s): Dinah Corley, Young Woman; Maurice Bay, Plantation Owner
Time Period(s): 1850s; 1860s
Locale(s): Charleston, South Carolina

Summary: This Civil War-era novel is set in Charleston before and during the war and focuses on the experiences of Irish immigrant Dinah Corley who finds herself the object of southern gentleman Maurice Bay's affection. Her fate is connected with the costs of secession and emancipation.

Historical Accuracy: The novel is a romanticized version of the South with an unconvincing treatment of the events surrounding Charleston during the War.

GORDON MCALPINE (1921-)

4216 *Joy in Mudville*

Date of Publication: 1989
Subject(s): Depression Era; Baseball; Fantasy
Fictional character(s): Buddy Easter, Teenager; Loren Woodville, Scientist
Historical character(s): Abner Doubleday, Veteran (Civil War); Woody Guthrie, Singer, Songwriter; Al Capone, Organized Crime Figure; George Herman Ruth, Sports Figure
Time Period(s): 1930s
Locale(s): Chicago, Illinois

Summary: This imaginative fable is set in Chicago during the 1930s and shows how the characters' lives are changed when Babe Ruth hits a mammoth home run that travels from Chicago to California. Buddy Easter sets out to be there when it finally lands, encountering on the way Al Capone and Woody Guthrie.

Historical Accuracy: The novel is filled with authentic period elements that convincingly capture the era.

JAMES MCCAGUE

4217 *The Fortune Road*

Date of Publication: 1965
Subject(s): American West; Railroads
Fictional character(s): Jed Skylark, Journalist; Danny Dye, Young Man; Nancy Dye, Young Woman
Time Period(s): 1860s (post-Civil War)
Locale(s): Omaha, Nebraska; Cheyenne, Wyoming; Laramie, Wyoming

Summary: A brother and sister, Daniel and Nancy Dye, and a newspaperman, Jed Skylark, follow the railroad west after the Civil War. Their misadventures take them from Omaha to Wyoming, through a blizzard, an angry mob, and capture by a group of army deserters.

Historical Accuracy: The period details capture the western scene with conviction.

DAN MCCALL (1940-)

Born in California, McCall graduated from Stanford and Columbia universities. He is a professor of English and

American Studies at Cornell University. McCall's novel *Jack the Bear* has been adapted for film. Best known for his comic novels, McCall is also the author of critical studies of Richard Wright and Herman Melville.

4218 *Beecher: A Novel*

Date of Publication: 1979
Subject(s): Trials; Women's Rights; Religious Life
Historical character(s): Henry Ward Beecher, Religious (clergyman); Harriet Beecher Stowe, Writer; Victoria Claflin Woodhull, Activist (free-love); Susan B. Anthony, Suffragette
Time Period(s): 19th century (1850s-1870s)
Locale(s): Brooklyn, New York

Summary: The novel dramatizes one of America's greatest scandals of the 19th century, in which the celebrated pastor of Brooklyn's Plymouth Church, the eminent Henry Ward Beecher, was accused of seducing the wife of his protege. The novel re-creates the story of Beecher's trial with a large cast of characters that includes his sister, Harriet Beecher Stowe, free-love advocate Victoria Woodhull, and women's rights activist Susan B. Anthony.

Historical Accuracy: The novel's framework is factual with some manipulations and surmises.

HUGH WRAY MCCANN (1928-)

Born in Northern Ireland and educated at Queen's University in Belfast, the Indiana Institute of Technology, and the University of Michigan, McCann has worked as an engineer in South Africa and as a reporter for *Newsweek*.

4219 *"Utmost Fish!"*

Date of Publication: 1965
Subject(s): World War I; Sea Story
Fictional character(s): Ian Frazier, Military Personnel (naval commander); Thomas Cavanaugh, Military Personnel (naval surgeon); Oswald Humphreys, Military Personnel (engineer)
Historical character(s): Winston Churchill, Political Figure (First Lord of Admiralty); John Arbuthnot Fisher, Military Personnel (Admiral of the Fleet)
Time Period(s): 1910s (1915-1916)
Locale(s): Lake Tanganyika, Africa; London, England

Summary: The title refers to British slang for "fire all torpedoes." The story recounts the Naval Africa Expedition, in which a small group of English sailors and soldiers drag two torpedo boats a thousand miles overland to sink a German fleet on Lake Tanganyika. The expedition must contend with quarrels and jealousies as well as impossible natural obstacles.

Historical Accuracy: The basis of the story is historical, but the specifics are invented.

CHARLES MCCARRY (1930-)

An American novelist born in Pittsfield, Massachusetts, McCarry worked as an editor and reporter for newspapers in Ohio. He also served as an assistant secretary of labor, and

worked for the C.I.A. from 1958 to 1967. Since 1967 he has written *The Last Supper*, *The Tears of Autumn*, *The Better Angels*, and *Citizen Nader*.

4220 *The Bride of the Wilderness*

Date of Publication: 1988
Subject(s): American Colonies; Indians
Fictional character(s): Fanny Harding, Heroine; Philippe de Saint-Christophe, Military Personnel (French soldier)
Time Period(s): 17th century (1660s)
Locale(s): London, England; New England, American Colonies; Canada

Summary: This is a tale of life in London in the 1660s and in the New England wilderness. When Fanny Harding is pursued by her family's enemy, she flees to the Massachusetts Bay Colony, where she embarks on a journey into the wilderness. She eventually finds happiness with a young French soldier, Philippe de Saint-Christophe.

Historical Accuracy: The novel captures with some skill and authenticity life during the period.

CORMAC MCCARTHY (1933-)

Born in Providence, Rhode Island, American author Cormac McCarthy attended the University of Tennessee. McCarthy has been hailed as one of the finest contemporary American writers. A National Book Award winner for his novel *All the Pretty Horses*, McCarthy is also the author of *Outer Dark*, *Blood Meridian*, and *The Orchard Keeper*, which won the William Faulkner Foundation Award.

4221 *The Crossing*

Date of Publication: 1994
Subject(s): American West; Ranching; Coming of Age
Fictional character(s): Billy Parham, Teenager, Rancher; Boyd Parham, Child, Rancher
Time Period(s): 1930s
Locale(s): Southwest; Mexico

Summary: In this coming of age novel, Billy Parham must deal with a wolf that is ravaging his father's ranch. As Parham attempts to deliver the animal back to the wilderness, a bond and kinship with the animal develops. Later Billy and his younger brother must avenge the murder of their parents by a band of horse thieves from Mexico.

Historical Accuracy: The novel offers an authentic treatment of the period and region, raised to the level of the mythic and universal.

GARY MCCARTHY (1943-)

Born in California, McCarthy attended the University of California, Pomona College, and the University of Nevada. He has worked as an occupational specialist and a rehabilitation program supervisor and is an author of Western novels.

4222 *The American River*

Date of Publication: 1992
Subject(s): American West; Gold Rush—California; Donner Party
Fictional character(s): Morgan Beck, Adventurer, Frontiersman
Historical character(s): John A. Sutter, Adventurer, Settler
Time Period(s): 1840s; 1850s
Locale(s): Sutter's Fort, California

Summary: John Sutter and Morgan Beck venture into Mexican California to stake a claim on the American River. They must contend with threats of war, revolution, and the terrible fate of the Donner party. When Sutter makes his fateful gold discovery, the Gold Rush begins.

Historical Accuracy: The novel blends fact and fiction in this picture of California and the cross-currents of cultures that explode into conflict.

4223 *The Gila River*

Date of Publication: 1993
Subject(s): American West; Exploration; Indians
Fictional character(s): Miguel Santana, Explorer; Vitorio Santana, Indian (half-Pima), Warrior; Jacova, Spouse, Indian (Pima)
Time Period(s): 18th century
Locale(s): Casa Grande, Arizona

Summary: Miguel Santana, abandoned by his troop of Spanish explorers, settles along the Gila River, and becomes one of the Pima Indians. His daughter, Jacova, is the unwilling bride of an Apache Indian.

Historical Accuracy: The novel is a believable re-creation of tribal life and the West of the period.

4224 *The Russian River*

Date of Publication: 1991
Subject(s): American West
Fictional character(s): Anton Rostov, Military Personnel (Russian lieutenant), Frontiersman; Mitana, Indian (Pomo)
Time Period(s): 1840s
Locale(s): Fort Ross, California; Russian River, California

Summary: Dispatched by the Russian government to exploit the rich fur trade on the Russian River of northern California during the 1840s, Anton Rostov adapts to the work and the customs of the inhabitants. When he takes Mitana as his wife, his assimilation is complete, until a situation that divides his loyalty arises.

Historical Accuracy: The novel is convincing in its depiction of California during the period.

VINCENT MCCONNOR

An American writer, editor, and producer, McConnor worked in radio and TV before becoming a novelist in 1965. He is an author of mysteries and has contributed more than 30 short stories to various periodicals.

4225 *I Am Vidocq*

Date of Publication: 1985
Subject(s): Crime and Criminals; Mystery; Literary Life
Fictional character(s): Zebulon Pennypacker, Businessman
Historical character(s): Alexandre Dumas, pere, Writer; Honore de Balzac, Writer; Francois Eugene Vidocq, Police Officer (chief of the Surete)
Time Period(s): 1820s (1823)
Locale(s): Paris, France

Summary: Vidocq, the renowned chief of the Surete, has his hands full in the summer of 1823. Paris is abuzz with a series of baffling crimes and mysteries. The murder of a famous jeweler and an infamous courtesan, the theft of a diamond necklace, and the work of a blood-market thief called Le Diable Noir all must be sorted out.

Historical Accuracy: The novel captures the period with skill.

CHRISTIAN MCCORD
(PSEUD. OF RODNEY R. PICKERELL, 1938-)

McCord was born in Boise, Idaho, and received a B.A. from the University of Idaho in 1979. In 1968 his novel *Across the Shining Mountains* was published. He lives in Fremont, California.

4226 *Across the Shining Mountains*

Date of Publication: 1986
Subject(s): American West; Settlement of the American Frontier; Indians
Historical character(s): Nathaniel J. Wyeth, Mountain Man, Frontiersman; Jim Bridger, Frontiersman, Mountain Man; Tom Fitzpatrick, Frontiersman, Mountain Man; Milt Sublette, Frontiersman, Mountain Man
Time Period(s): 1830s
Locale(s): Oregon

Summary: This is the largely true story of mountain man Nathaniel Wyeth, a Boston ice merchant who journeys to the Oregon Territory of the 1830s to make his fortune in beaver pelts and Columbia River salmon. His story is one of great determination and resourcefulness in the face of incredible obstacles and danger in the western wilderness.

Historical Accuracy: The author explains that the story is substantially true, although some events and details are based on conjecture.

MAX MCCOY

4227 *Sons of Fire*

Date of Publication: 1993
Subject(s): Civil War—U.S.
Fictional character(s): Zach Fenn, Military Personnel (Confederate guerilla); Sarah Drake, Young Woman; Frank Fenn, Military Personnel (Union soldier)
Historical character(s): William Clarke Quantrill, Military Personnel (Confederate guerilla leader); Jesse James, Military Personnel (Confederate guerilla)
Time Period(s): 1860s (1860-1863)

Locale(s): Lawrence, Kansas

Summary: The Fenn family is split by the impending Civil War. Frank Fenn joins the Union army, while his brother Zach takes the Confederate side and joins Quantrill's guerillas, fighting alongside Jesse James on the Kansas frontier. Frank serves the Union loyally until his home is destroyed, then he urges his brother to desert the cause to salvage what is left of their family.

Historical Accuracy: The atmosphere of the period is realistically portrayed.

ROBERT MCCRAIG

`4228` *Crimson Creek: A Novel of the Early West*

Date of Publication: 1963
Subject(s): American West; Indians
Fictional character(s): Ben Logan, Engineer; Sol Arnst, Journalist; Kathleen Buckwell, Young Woman
Time Period(s): 1890s (1897)
Locale(s): Medicine Lodge, Montana

Summary: Engineer Ben Logan goes West in 1897 for his health. In Montana he is plunged into a bitter dispute between the settlers and the remnants of the Kettle River Tribe. Logan helps make their resettlement lands livable, which causes enmity among those determined to rid the West of all Indians. When a series of mysterious killings occurs, tensions build toward a murderous climax.

Historical Accuracy: The novel captures the era with some skill, and the period details present a convincing background for the drama.

LEW MCCREARY

`4229` *Mount's Mistake*

Date of Publication: 1987
Subject(s): Inventions; Picaresque Adventure
Fictional character(s): Jay Fielding Mount, Outcast
Historical character(s): Thomas Alva Edison, Inventor
Time Period(s): 1890s
Locale(s): Ohio; New York

Summary: This picaresque tale follows the erratic path of Jay Fielding Mount in turn-of-the century America. After being struck by lightning as a boy, Mount finds himself crossing paths with inventor Thomas Alva Edison and the wonders of his inventions harnessing electricity.

Historical Accuracy: This comic tale depends on a inventive evocation of the period.

JESS MCCRIEDE

`4230` *Colorado Ambush*

Date of Publication: 1989
Subject(s): American West; Ranching

Fictional character(s): James Hunter, Rancher, Veteran (ex-army officer)
Historical character(s): Ulysses S. Grant, Military Personnel (general), Political Figure (U.S. president)
Time Period(s): 1870s
Locale(s): Denver, Colorado

Summary: Jim Hunter is called from his Colorado ranch to protect the life of his old friend Ulysses S. Grant, now president of the U.S. Ex-Confederates have conspired to assassinate the president, and Hunter holds the key to foiling the plot.

Historical Accuracy: The story is invented with an emphasis on exciting action over careful documentation of the past.

GUY MCCRONE (1898-)

McCrone was born in England but spent his childhood in Ayrshire, Scotland.

`4231` *Aunt Bel*

Date of Publication: 1949
Subject(s): Victorian Period
Fictional character(s): Bel Moorhouse, Spouse; Arthur Moorhouse, Businessman (merchant)
Time Period(s): 1890s
Locale(s): Glasgow, Scotland

Summary: Social life in Glasgow, Scotland, in the 1890s is chronicled in this comedy of manners that centers on Bel Moorhouse, the social arbiter and central manipulator in a tangle of complicated family affairs. Matchmaking accompanies much of the drama in this comic social record of mores and manners.

Historical Accuracy: All is bathed in a rosy glow of nostalgia, but even without the hard edges, the period emerges as authentic.

`4232` *Red Plush: The Story of the Moorhouse Family*

Date of Publication: 1940
Subject(s): Victorian Period; Family Saga
Fictional character(s): Arthur Moorhouse, Businessman; Bel Moorhouse, Spouse
Time Period(s): 19th century (1870-1890s)
Locale(s): Glasgow, Scotland; Vienna, Austria

Summary: The novel offers a picture of Victorian Scottish family life. The Moorhouses, farmers in Ayrshire, have made their way to Glasgow. The novel details the complicated domestic relations of this extended family, headed by Arthur and Bel Moorhouse.

Historical Accuracy: The emphasis is on charming nostalgia with a colorful period background.

COLLEEN MCCULLOUGH (1938-)

Australian author McCullough attended the University of Sydney and has held jobs as a teacher, a library worker, and a bus driver in Australia's outback. She was a medical technician at Yale University's School of Internal Medicine when she completed her block buster *The Thorn Birds*. Before she began that novel she surveyed six female friends to find out what they liked when they read novels. They suggested ordinary people and tears.

4233 *Caesar's Women*

Date of Publication: 1996

Subject(s): Roman Empire; Politics

Historical character(s): Julius Caesar, Military Personnel (Roman general), Political Figure; Pompey, Military Personnel (Roman general); Marcus Tullius Cicero, Lawyer; Servilia, Gentlewoman; Publius Clodius Pulcher, Political Figure; Pompeia, Gentlewoman; Marcus Bibulus, Political Figure; Marcus Porcius Cato, Political Figure

Time Period(s): 1st century B.C.

Locale(s): Rome, Roman Empire

Summary: The novel depicts Julius Caesar's rise to political prominence from his return to Rome in 68 B.C. When he sets out to dominate the political battlefield in Rome as he has the battlefield of Gaul, the going is no less treacherous. Caesar targets Rome's noblewomen as well, wielding love like a weapon.

Historical Accuracy: The author's evident research provides a convincing foundation for the novel's interpretation and version of events.

4234 *The First Man in Rome*

Date of Publication: 1990

Subject(s): Roman Empire; Politics

Historical character(s): Julius Caesar, Political Figure, Military Personnel (army commander); Caius Marius, Political Figure, Military Personnel (general); Lucius Cornelius Sulla, Political Figure

Time Period(s): 2nd century B.C. (110-100 B.C.)

Locale(s): Rome, Roman Empire; Numidia, Africa; Gaul

Summary: This is the first novel in a trilogy on the downfall of the Roman Republic. Two men vie for the position of eminence: Marius, of low birth, who succeeds through a lion will and talent, and Sulla, a patrician cursed by poverty. The intrigue and maneuvering make ancient Rome a very real and dangerous arena. The trilogy continues with *The Grass Crown*.

Historical Accuracy: Scrupulous and well-researched, the novel is monumental in its massive reconstruction of the past.

4235 *Fortune's Favorite*

Date of Publication: 1993

Subject(s): Roman Empire; Politics; Servile War

Historical character(s): Lucius Cornelius Sulla, Military Personnel (general); Pompey, Political Figure, Military Personnel (general); Spartacus, Slave; Julius Caesar, Military Personnel (army commander); Marcus Licinius Crassus, Military Personnel (general)

Time Period(s): 1st century B.C. (83-71 B.C.)

Locale(s): Rome, Roman Empire; Spain

Summary: The author concludes her trilogy on the fall of the Roman Republic with the events of the last years of the great

general Sulla and the rise of Pompey and Julius Caesar. There is rebellion in Spain and in the East. At home Sparticus leads a slave revolt.

Historical Accuracy: The novel offers a unique portrait of Sparticus. As in all her Roman novels, McCullough is convincing in her research and animation of history into a compelling drama.

4236 *The Grass Crown*

Date of Publication: 1991

Subject(s): Roman Empire; Politics

Historical character(s): Lucius Cornelius Sulla, Military Personnel (general), Political Figure; Caius Marius, Political Figure, Military Personnel (general); Julius Caesar, Military Personnel (army commander), Political Figure; Marcus Tullius Cicero, Political Figure, Lawyer; Mithridates VI, Ruler (King of Pontus); Lucius Cornelius Cinna, Military Personnel (general), Political Figure

Time Period(s): 1st century B.C. (98-86 B.C.)

Locale(s): Rome, Roman Empire

Summary: The author continues her saga of the downfall of the Roman Republic begun in *The First Man in Rome*. Marius, six-time consul of Rome, seeks an unprecedented seventh consulship. His former apprentice, Sulla, once his valued comrade, is now his most dangerous rival. Against a background of impending civil war, invasion, and conspiracy, the two battle for control with Rome hanging in the balance. *Fortune's Favorite* concludes the trilogy.

Historical Accuracy: The novel is a superb evocation of a time and a place. The author creates an utterly believable setting and political scene that resonate with contemporaneous association.

4237 *The Ladies of Missalonghi*

Date of Publication: 1987

Subject(s): Frontier—Australia

Fictional character(s): Missy Wright, Gentlewoman; John Smith, Frontiersman

Time Period(s): 1910s

Locale(s): Blue Mountains, Australia

Summary: In a small town in the Blue Mountains, just before World War I, a mysterious stranger affects the lives of the Hurlingford clan, particularly Missy Wright, the youngest of the three ladies who live in the house called Missalonghi.

Historical Accuracy: The novel captures its era and the region convincingly.

EVELYN MCCUNE

4238 *Empress*

Date of Publication: 1994

Subject(s): Chinese Empire; Royalty—China

Historical character(s): Wu Chao, Ruler (Empress of China); T'ai Tsung, Ruler (Emperor of China); Kao Tsung, Ruler (Emperor of China)

Time Period(s): 7th century

Locale(s): China

Summary: The novel chronicles the remarkable rise to power of China's only empress, Wu Chao, who comes to the imperial palace as one of the emperor's new concubines. She earns the love and respect of Emperor Taitsung, and after his death becomes the wife of his son, Kaotsung. Wu Chao manages to rule in her own right, and the novel details her rise to supreme power.

Historical Accuracy: The novel's framework is factual. However, invention and imagination fill in the gaps in the historical record.

RUTHANNE LUM MCCUNN

An Amerasian born in San Francisco, McCunn grew up in Hong Kong where she attended both Chinese and British schools. She has worked as a librarian, teacher, and bilingual specialist. She is the author of *An Illustrated History of the Chinese in America.*

4239 *Thousand Years of Gold*

Date of Publication: 1981

Subject(s): Biography, Fictionalized; American West; Homesteading

Historical character(s): Lalu Nathoy, Slave, Settler

Time Period(s): 19th century; 20th century (1865-1933)

Locale(s): China; Idaho

Summary: This biographical novel tells the story of Lalu Nathoy, later known as Polly Bemis. She is born in China in the 1860s. As a child she is snatched from her family by bandits and shipped as a slave to America, where she is auctioned off to a Chinese saloon keeper in an Idaho mining camp. She gains her freedom and runs a boarding house, homesteading on the River of No Return.

Historical Accuracy: Some fictional figures have been added and the chronology adjusted for the sake of the narrative, but the essential story of Polly's life is accurate.

PHILIP MCCUTCHAN (1920-)

A British adventure writer, McCutchan joined the Royal Navy in 1939. He served on every type of warship during the Second World War and ended as a lieutenant. A prolific writer of more than 60 books, he divides his output between sea stories and thrillers, as well as military novels under the pseudonym Duncan McNeil.

4240 *Apprentice to the Sea*

Date of Publication: 1994

Subject(s): Sea Story; Military Life—British Navy; Victorian Period

Fictional character(s): Tom Chatto, Military Personnel (seaman)

Time Period(s): 19th century (late)

Locale(s): At Sea

Summary: The novel introduces a new series of nautical adventures set in the late 19th century. Its hero is Tom Chatto, a young apprentice seaman, who must learn his trade on a square-rigged windjammer. His voyage is filled with rough seas and adventures.

Historical Accuracy: The author is a master of the period naval adventure story, able to create a believable backdrop for his story.

4241 *Beware, Beware the Bight of Benin*

Date of Publication: 1974

Subject(s): Sea Story; Military Life—British Navy; Victorian Period

Fictional character(s): St. Vincent Halfhyde, Military Personnel (naval lieutenant); Prince Gorsinski, Military Personnel (admiral)

Time Period(s): 1890s (1891)

Locale(s): Benin (West Africa); At Sea

Summary: St. Vincent Halfhyde is given a secret mission to find out the disposition of the Russian navy in Benin, West Africa. He is captured by the Russians almost immediately upon landing and quickly finds himself in the middle of a mutiny, fighting on the side of the mutineers.

Historical Accuracy: The story is invented, but the period background and military details are genuine and convincing.

4242 *The Guns of Arrest*

Date of Publication: 1976

Subject(s): Sea Story; Military Life—British Navy; Victorian Period

Fictional character(s): St. Vincent Halfhyde, Military Personnel (naval lieutenant); Henry Bassinghorn, Military Personnel (naval captain); Inspector Todhunter, Detective—Police

Historical character(s): John Arbuthnot Fisher, Military Personnel (British admiral)

Time Period(s): 1890s

Locale(s): *Prince Consort*, At Sea; South Africa

Summary: Halfhyde is assigned to the battleship *Prince Consort*. His mission is to apprehend an Admiralty civilian who has fled to South Africa with secret plans for a naval construction project of vital interest to the Germans. The race is on to get to the traitor first.

Historical Accuracy: The high-speed adventure is backed by a plausible period background and convincing nautical details.

4243 *Halfhyde and the Admiral*

Date of Publication: 1990

Subject(s): Sea Story; Military Life—British Navy

Fictional character(s): St. Vincent Halfhyde, Sea Captain

Time Period(s): 1900s

Locale(s): *Taronga Park*, At Sea; Valparaiso, Chile

Summary: Halfhyde, as the captain of the steamer *Taronga Park*, is asked by the Admiralty to get involved in an attempted rescue of the commander-in-chief of the Chilean Navy, a former British admiral whose life is in danger. The novel details the events of the voyage to Chile and the complications that await Halfhyde when he arrives.

Historical Accuracy: The novel offers a convincing atmosphere of both the period and the naval details.

4244 *Halfhyde and the Chain Gang*

Date of Publication: 1985
Subject(s): Sea Story; Boer War; Military Life—British Navy
Fictional character(s): St. Vincent Halfhyde, Military Personnel (naval officer)
Time Period(s): 1890s
Locale(s): *Glen Halladake*, At Sea; Portsmouth, England

Summary: St. Vincent Halfhyde is charged with delivering a cargo of convicts from Dartmoor Prison to serve as labor battalions in South Africa during the Boer War. The chain gang mutinies during the ill-fated voyage, testing Halfhyde's ability to complete his mission.

Historical Accuracy: The period background is believable.

4245 *Halfhyde and the Flag Captain*

Date of Publication: 1980
Subject(s): Sea Story; Military Life—British Navy; Victorian Period
Fictional character(s): St. Vincent Halfhyde, Military Personnel (naval officer)
Time Period(s): 1890s
Locale(s): *Halcyon*, At Sea; Uruguay

Summary: In this installment of the naval adventures of Lieutenant St. Vincent Halfhyde of the British Navy, he is involved in a delicate struggle with the German Navy in South America. When a revolutionary coup threatens the British ambassador in Uruguay, the British fleet has a divided interest as they attempt to keep a British traitor out of the hands of the Germans.

Historical Accuracy: The novel offers an authentic look at the British Navy of the period.

4246 *Halfhyde and the Fleet Review*

Date of Publication: 1991
Subject(s): Sea Story; Military Life—British Navy; Victorian Period
Fictional character(s): St. Vincent Halfhyde, Military Personnel (naval officer); Admiral Watkiss, Military Personnel; Victoria Penn, Young Woman
Historical character(s): Victoria, Ruler (Queen of England)
Time Period(s): 1890s (1897)
Locale(s): Portsmouth, England; At Sea

Summary: On the occasion of Queen Victoria's Diamond Jubilee, Captain St. Vincent Halfhyde is assigned to keep the irascible and unpredictable Admiral Watkiss out of trouble during Her Majesty's review of the British fleet. Complications are many.

Historical Accuracy: The author is exact and convincing in building his period background.

4247 *Halfhyde for the Queen*

Date of Publication: 1978

Subject(s): Sea Story; Victorian Period; Military Life—British Navy
Fictional character(s): St. Vincent Halfhyde, Military Personnel (naval lieutenant)
Historical character(s): Victoria, Ruler (Queen of England)
Time Period(s): 1890s
Locale(s): Torremolinos, Spain; Highlands, Scotland; At Sea

Summary: Lieutenant Halfhyde uncovers a plot to assassinate Queen Victoria. Acting on this intelligence, he must stand against the British government, which wishes to avoid the diplomatic implications of the plot. Halfhyde's struggle to save Victoria's life takes him from Spain by sea to the Scottish Highlands and an audience with the queen.

Historical Accuracy: The novel's plot is invented, but the era is evoked with some skill and care.

4248 *Halfhyde Goes to War*

Date of Publication: 1986
Subject(s): Sea Story; Military Life—British Navy; Boer War
Fictional character(s): St. Vincent Halfhyde, Military Personnel (naval officer)
Time Period(s): 1890s (1899)
Locale(s): South Africa

Summary: St. Vincent Halfhyde, having brought a shipment of gold bullion to Africa in *Halfhyde and the Chain Gangs*, must escort it from Cape Town to Ladysmith aboard an armored train with a naval gun crew.

Historical Accuracy: The period elements are authentic in this military adventure tale.

4249 *The Halfhyde Line*

Date of Publication: 1984
Subject(s): Sea Story; Edwardian Period
Fictional character(s): St. Vincent Halfhyde, Sea Captain; Porteous Higgins, Businessman
Time Period(s): 1900s
Locale(s): *Taronga Park*, At Sea; Chile; Ireland

Summary: Halfhyde has left the navy and attempts to earn his living as the master of the merchant ship *Taronga Park*. On a trip from Sydney to Ireland, his ship is taken over by the cargo's owner, and the cargo itself is more sinister than expected. Halfhyde sets out for revenge on land in Connemara, Ireland.

Historical Accuracy: The novel's nautical details are authentic.

4250 *Halfhyde on the Amazon*

Date of Publication: 1988
Subject(s): Sea Story; Mystery
Fictional character(s): St. Vincent Halfhyde, Sea Captain; Inspector Todhunter, Detective—Police
Time Period(s): 1910s
Locale(s): Liverpool, England; *Taronga Park*, At Sea; Brazil

Summary: St. Vincent Halfhyde is in command of the merchant steamer *Taronga Park*. Aboard is a British diplomat on a mission to Brazil, where the Germans are attempting to establish a naval base. When a mutilated corpse is found on board, Detective Inspector Todhunter embarks with the ship to conduct the murder investigation.

Historical Accuracy: The story is supported by solid and convincing period details.

`4251` *Halfhyde on Zanatu*

Date of Publication: 1982
Subject(s): Sea Story; Military Life—British Navy; Victorian Period
Fictional character(s): St. Vincent Halfhyde, Military Personnel (naval lieutenant)
Time Period(s): 1890s
Locale(s): Zanatu, Pacific Islands (Polynesia)

Summary: Lieutenant Halfhyde joins a squadron in the Far East ordered to put down a rebellion on a Polynesian island crucial to the British in the chain of colonies between Hong Kong and Australia. Halfhyde quickly finds himself between determined and well-armed islanders and Russian battleships probing for weakness in Britain's trade routes.

Historical Accuracy: The background of Britain's imperial plans and its conflicts is convincingly depicted.

`4252` *Halfhyde Ordered South*

Date of Publication: 1979
Subject(s): Sea Story; Military Life—British Navy; Edwardian Period
Fictional character(s): St. Vincent Halfhyde, Military Personnel (naval lieutenant); Captain Watkiss, Military Personnel (naval captain)
Time Period(s): 1900s
Locale(s): *Meridian*, At Sea

Summary: Halfhyde is assigned to deliver the obsolete battleship *Meridian* to Chile. However, he soon learns that his real purpose is to safeguard British interests in South America from threat by the Germans. An exciting confrontation with the Germans follows in a race to Valparaiso.

Historical Accuracy: The author is able to weave an exciting adventure against a backdrop of convincing period details.

`4253` *Halfhyde to the Narrows*

Date of Publication: 1977
Subject(s): Sea Story; Military Life—British Navy; Victorian Period
Fictional character(s): St. Vincent Halfhyde, Military Personnel (naval lieutenant); Captain Watkiss, Military Personnel (naval captain)
Time Period(s): 1890s
Locale(s): At Sea (Dardanelles and Black Sea)

Summary: Halfhyde's first command is of a tiny torpedo boat on a mission to rescue a British merchant ship from the Russians. He must guide the boat through the fortified Dardanelles and then find a way to free the British ship from the Russian fleet. All must be done without provoking a diplomatic incident that could lead to war.

Historical Accuracy: This exciting naval adventure provides an authentic period background.

`4254` *Halfhyde's Island*

Date of Publication: 1975
Subject(s): Sea Story; Military Life—British Navy; Victorian Period
Fictional character(s): St. Vincent Halfhyde, Military Personnel (naval lieutenant); Henry Bassinghorn, Military Personnel (naval captain); Prince Gorsinski, Military Personnel (admiral)
Time Period(s): 1890s
Locale(s): Hong Kong; *Viceroy*, At Sea (off the coast of Japan)

Summary: A geological change has produced a new island in the Pacific that could be suitable as a naval base. The *Viceroy*, with Lieutenant St. Vincent Halfhyde as second-in-command, is dispatched to claim the island for Britain. The Russians, however, have the same idea, as does the Imperial Japanese Navy.

Historical Accuracy: The novel captures the naval details of the period.

`4255` *The Last Farewell*

Date of Publication: 1991
Subject(s): Sea Story; World War I; Ocean Liners
Fictional character(s): William Pacey, Sea Captain
Time Period(s): 1910s (1915)
Locale(s): *Laurentia*, At Sea

Summary: The *Laurentia*, a thinly disguised fictional version of the *Lusitania*, sets out from New York in 1915 with a passenger list that is a microcosm of British and American society. They do not know that the ship is also carrying war materials and that German U-boats are waiting. Captain William Pacey pilots the ship toward its fateful end.

Historical Accuracy: The period details of a great ocean liner of the period are authentic. As a dramatization of the fate of the *Lusitania*, the novel is less reliable.

`4256` *Outward Bound*

Date of Publication: 1983
Subject(s): Sea Story; Victorian Period
Fictional character(s): St. Vincent Halfhyde, Sea Captain
Time Period(s): 1890s
Locale(s): *Aysgarth Falls*, At Sea

Summary: Halfhyde, placed on half-pay following the adventures chronicled in *Halfhyde on Zanatu*, joins the crew of a merchant ship bound for Sydney. The crew is a rough lot, and bad weather and fighting complicate the trip. There is also a conspiracy involving a mysterious passenger to be picked up off Chile.

Historical Accuracy: The naval adventure is supported by solid and believable period nautical details.

`4257` *The Second Mate*

Date of Publication: 1996
Subject(s): Sea Story

Fictional character(s): Tom Chatto, Military Personnel
Time Period(s): 1900s
Locale(s): *Orvega*, At Sea

Summary: Young Tom Chatto finds himself aboard the steamship *Orvega* for a voyage that includes an influenza outbreak, engine trouble, and a perilous rounding of the Horn.

Historical Accuracy: The novel provides a genuine account of naval life during the period.

GEORGE BARR MCCUTCHEON
(1866-1928)

An Indiana-born newspaperman and novelist, McCutcheon wrote swashbucklers and realistic novels, such as *Graustark* and *Brewster's Millions*.

4258 *Viola Gwyn*

Date of Publication: 1922
Subject(s): Settlement of the American Frontier; Inheritance—Disputed
Fictional character(s): Kenneth Gwynne, Lawyer; Viola Gwyn, Young Woman
Time Period(s): 1830s
Locale(s): Lafayette, Indiana; Kentucky

Summary: Kenneth Gwynne arrives to claim the inheritance left to him by his father and to seek revenge on his father's widow, the woman Kenneth believes stole his father away. He falls in love with her daughter, who is apparently his half-sister.

Historical Accuracy: This is a romantic story with some period atmospherics.

EVA MCDONALD (1909-)

Born in London, McDonald attended the South London Commercial College. Her first novel, *Lazare the Leopard*, was written when she was 21 and was followed by, among other titles, *Lord Byron's First Love*, *Cromwell's Spy*, and *Queen Victoria's Prince*.

4259 *John Ruskin's Wife*

Date of Publication: 1979
Subject(s): Victorian Period; Literary Life; Artistic Life
Historical character(s): John Everett Millais, Artist; John Ruskin, Writer; Effie Gray, Spouse (of Ruskin)
Time Period(s): 19th century
Locale(s): London, England

Summary: The novel dramatizes the peculiar marriage of English critic and author John Ruskin and Effie Gray. When she models for Victorian artist John Everett Millais, a scandal ensues that reaches all corners of England. The novel traces the disintegration of their marriage and the controversy that embroiled them.

Historical Accuracy: The novel is faithful to the facts surrounding Ruskin's life and Gray's relationship with Millais.

4260 *The Lady From Yorktown*

Date of Publication: 1977
Subject(s): American Revolution; Battle of Yorktown
Fictional character(s): Cornelia de Vere, Gentlewoman, Loyalist
Historical character(s): Charles Cornwallis, Military Personnel (British general); George III, Ruler (King of England)
Time Period(s): 1770s; 1780s (1776-1781)
Locale(s): Yorktown, Virginia; London, England

Summary: In this romantic tale, loyalist Cornelia de Vere's fortunes become connected with those of British commander Lord Cornwallis, who is fated to lead the British into defeat at Yorktown.

Historical Accuracy: The historical elements are only lightly sketched, with the primary emphasis on romance.

KAY L. MCDONALD (1934-)

Born in Salem, Oregon, McDonald worked for the Pacific Northwest Bell Telephone Company. She has been writing short stories since high school.

4261 *The Brightwood Expedition*

Date of Publication: 1976
Subject(s): Settlement of the American Frontier; Indians
Fictional character(s): Joshua Brightwood, Pioneer, Settler; Marlette Brightwood, Pioneer, Settler; Ross Chestnut, Frontiersman, Guide
Time Period(s): 1840s; 1850s
Locale(s): Oregon

Summary: The events leading up to the American annexation of the Oregon Territory from the novel's background. The story centers on Joshua Brightwood, his daughter Marlette, and a group of six companions who leave their Philadelphia home to settle in Oregon. Their story, particularly that of Marlette and her relationship with the group's guide, Ross Chestnut, is dramatized as they contend with the wilderness and the Indians.

Historical Accuracy: The novel is rich in historical details and convincing regional material.

4262 *The Vision Is Fulfilled*

Date of Publication: 1983
Subject(s): American West; Wagon Trains; Indians
Fictional character(s): Ross Chestnut, Frontiersman; Marlette Brightwood, Pioneer
Time Period(s): 1840s (1846)
Locale(s): Oregon Trail, United States; Independence, Missouri; Willamette Valley, Oregon

Summary: In the final volume of a trilogy that includes *The Brightwood Expedition* and *The Vision of the Eagle*, Ross Chestnut is reunited with his wife, Marlette Brightwood, as he assumes leadership of a wagon train that sets out from Missouri to Oregon.

Historical Accuracy: The details of frontier life along the Oregon Trail are authentic and believable.

4263 *Vision of the Eagle*

Date of Publication: 1977
Subject(s): Indians; War of 1812; Earthquakes
Fictional character(s): Ross Gallagher, Frontiersman; Abigail Gallagher, Spouse
Historical character(s): Daniel Boone, Frontiersman; John McLoughlin, Government Official
Time Period(s): 1800s; 1810s
Locale(s): Missouri; Pacific Northwest

Summary: This tale of frontier life describes the experiences of Ross and Abigail Gallagher who head west. Abigail becomes the captive of a Sioux chieftain, and their son is raised as an Indian. The novel features scenes of the Battle of Tippecanoe and the New Madrid Earthquake of 1811.

Historical Accuracy: The novel's historical events and characters are authentic and well documented.

ROGER MCDONALD (1941-)

Born in New South Wales, Australia, McDonald attended the Scots College and the University of Sydney. He has worked as a teacher, an educational radio and TV producer, and in publicity. He is the author of several volumes of poetry.

4264 *1915: A Novel*

Date of Publication: 1980
Subject(s): World War I; Battle of Gallipoli
Fictional character(s): Billy MacKenzie, Military Personnel (soldier); Frances Reilly, Young Woman; Walter Gilchrist, Military Personnel (soldier); Diana Benedetto, Young Woman
Time Period(s): 1910s (1913-1915)
Locale(s): Gallipoli, Turkey; Australia

Summary: Australia at the outbreak of World War I is the backdrop for this novel which details the experiences of Billy MacKenzie and Walter Gilchrist, unlikely childhood friends who enlist and serve in the disastrous Gallipoli campaign. The story also focuses on two women, Frances Reilly and Diana Benedetto who are left to wait out the war at home. The novel offers a strong and vivid portrait of both love and war and the shattering of the illusions of both.

Historical Accuracy: Derived from real events, the story is fictional. The Gallipoli experience is based on the eyewitness accouts of several participants.

JAMES MCDONOUGH (1946-)

A graduate of West Point, McDonough served in the U.S. Army, rising to the rank of colonel, and as the Director of the School of Advanced Military Study. He is the author of *Platoon Leader*, an account of his experiences as a young lieutenant in Vietnam.

4265 *The Limits of Glory: A Novel of Waterloo*

Date of Publication: 1991

Subject(s): Napoleonic Wars; Battle of Waterloo; Military Life
Historical character(s): Napoleon Bonaparte, Military Personnel (French commander), Ruler (Emperor of France); Arthur Wellesley, Military Personnel (British commander); Gebhard Leberecht von Blucher, Military Personnel (Prussian field marshal); Michel Ney, Military Personnel (French marshal); James MacDonnell, Military Personnel (British officer); Magdalene de Lancey, Gentlewoman
Time Period(s): 1810s (1815)
Locale(s): Waterloo, Belgium

Summary: The strategies of the climactic battle of the 19th century, Waterloo, are described by the generals of both sides—Napoleon, and Wellington and Blucher—and through the perspectives of its many combatants. The author offers a vivid and convincing account of one of the most significant and bloody battles ever fought.

Historical Accuracy: The novel is faithful to the known facts. Where there is disagreement, the author has based his interpretation on the most plausible circumstance. The thoughts of the combatants and many of the conversations are invented though faithful to biography and situation.

JAMES MCEACHIN

McEachin is a noted actor who has appeared in motion pictures and on television. He was the first African-American actor to be the sole lead in a dramatic series (''Tenafly.'').

4266 *Tell Me a Tale: A Novel of the Old South*

Date of Publication: 1996
Subject(s): Slavery; Reconstruction Period
Fictional character(s): Archibald McBride, Plantation Owner; Moses, Slave; Ben, Slave
Time Period(s): 1860s
Locale(s): North Carolina

Summary: In the days following the Civil War and the emancipation of the slaves, a young black man named Moses, a former slave, returns to McMillan's General Store in North Carolina to spin a tale before an audience of four white men. He tells the story of the destruction of a great plantation and the powerful legacy and burden of the past.

Historical Accuracy: The novel offers a convincing evocation of the period and the region.

MARJORIE MCEVOY

An English novelist born in Yorkshire, McEvoy has worked as an assistant matron at a girls' boarding school and as an auxiliary nurse. She is the author of many historical romances which feature an authentic background. McEvoy is an enthusiastic world traveller.

4267 *Camelot Country*

Date of Publication: 1986
Subject(s): Romance

Fictional character(s): Deborah Rodgers, Nurse; Steven Treleaven, Heir; Justinian Rowse, Gentleman
Time Period(s): 1910s (post-World War I)
Locale(s): Cornwall, England

Summary: Following World War I, Deborah Rodgers who has lost her fiance and her parents in the war, takes a position in Cornwall as the nurse for a wealthy woman. She falls in love with the woman's heir, Steven Treleaven, but must deal with the sinister machinations of Justinian Rowse, which include murder and a miner's revolt.

Historical Accuracy: The emphasis is on romantic suspense, but the Cornish scenes are effectively presented.

4268   *Echoes From the Past*

Date of Publication: 1979
Subject(s): Romance; Victorian Period; Sea Story
Fictional character(s): Stephanie Chalmers, Widow(er); Adam Colvin, Landowner, Businessman
Time Period(s): 1860s
Locale(s): England

Summary: In 1861 Stephnie Chalmers comes to England to assume her place in her dead husband's family. She learns of an ancestral curse on the family, and Stephanie resists its efforts as she struggles to find her way in the family's shipping business. The action climaxes in the famous Grain Race to Australia.

Historical Accuracy: The period elements of the story are factual and convincing.

4269   *The Sleeping Tiger*

Date of Publication: 1983
Subject(s): British Colonies; British Raj; Indian Mutiny
Fictional character(s): Andhra Hilton, Young Woman; Ranjana, Royalty (prince)
Time Period(s): 1850s (1857)
Locale(s): Chandifur, India

Summary: Set in the days immediately preceding the Indian Mutiny, Andhra Hilton, the young daughter of a British army officer, falls in love with Prince Ranjana. Their passion for one another is tested as conflict between Britain and India reaches a climax.

Historical Accuracy: The romance is set against a convincing period background.

4270   *Star of Randevi*

Date of Publication: 1984
Subject(s): British Colonies; British Raj
Fictional character(s): Andhra Hilton, Spouse (of Ranjana), Royalty (princess); Ranjana, Royalty (prince)
Time Period(s): 1850s
Locale(s): India

Summary: In the sequel to *The Sleeping Tiger*, Andhra and Prince Ranjana are preparing to enjoy life together with past troubles behind them. However, they face sedition and insurrection and the loss of Andhra's memory.

Historical Accuracy: The details of Indian life and culture are vividly and believably presented.

4271   *Temple Bells*

Date of Publication: 1985
Subject(s): Romance
Fictional character(s): Chantra, Orphan, Royalty (princess); James Stuart, Military Personnel (British captain); Veena, Nurse
Time Period(s): 1760s (1769); 1900s (1906)
Locale(s): Thailand

Summary: Set in Thailand, then called Siam, in the 18th century and the early years of the 20th century, the novel dramatizes the complicated passion of Chantra, a cousin to the royal family raised within the confines of the royal palace. She seeks adventure in the outside world and meets James Stuart, a handsome British captain. Years later Veena, a Siamese nurse suffers a fate similar to that of her ancestress when she is torn between love and duty.

Historical Accuracy: The exotic scene and setting is believably created.

PHILIP MCFARLAND (1930-)

Born in Alabama, McFarland graduated from Oberlin College and Cambridge University. He has worked as a textbook editor and as an English teacher at Concord Academy. He is the author of *Sojourners*, a historical account of 19th century America.

4272   *Seasons of Fear*

Date of Publication: 1984
Subject(s): American Colonies; Racial Conflict
Fictional character(s): Charles Alexander Corimer, Nobleman (Earl of Cavendham)
Time Period(s): 1740s (1741)
Locale(s): New York, New York, American Colonies

Summary: Based on actual events in New York in 1741 surrounding the so-called "Negro Plot," the novel dramatizes the circumstances that led to 34 people being hanged or burned at the stake in a chain of rumors and mob violence. When items are stolen and fires break out, the citizens of New York fear a slave revolt and a hysterical search for the ringleaders follows in which innocent people are killed or deported.

Historical Accuracy: Though the authority with which the period is presented is obvious, the author admits to occasionally tampering with the historical research.

THOMASINE MCGEHEE (1888-)

McGehee's books include *People and Music: A Textbook in Music Appreciation*.

4273   *Journey Proud*

Date of Publication: 1939

Subject(s): Civil War—U.S.; Antebellum South; Reconstruction Period

Fictional character(s): Thomas Mackay, Plantation Owner; George Mackay, Military Personnel (Confederate soldier)

Time Period(s): 19th century (1845-1879)

Locale(s): Virginia

Summary: The declining fortunes of a Virginia tobacco plantation family, the Mackays, are chronicled from the period before the Civil War to the end of Reconstruction. The novel traces the passing of a way of life as the Mackays must adapt to the forces of history.

Historical Accuracy: The story is a truthful one that avoids inflation or idealization and ultimately attains a high standard of believability.

PATRICIA MCGERR (1917-1985)

Born in Nebraska, McGeer held degrees from the University of Nebraska and Columbia's School of Journalism. She did publicity work and edited a technical magazine. She is the author of best-selling mystery stories that features the reverse of the standard formula. McGerr identifies her murderer on page one and centers the mystery on discovering the identity of the victim.

4274 *Martha, Martha*

Date of Publication: 1960

Subject(s): Biblical Story

Historical character(s): Jesus Christ, Biblical Figure; John the Baptist, Biblical Figure; Judas Iscariot, Biblical Figure; Martha of Bethany, Biblical Figure; Mary, Biblical Figure; Lazarus, Biblical Figure; Peter, Biblical Figure; Salome, Biblical Figure

Time Period(s): 1st century

Locale(s): Israel

Summary: Little is known of Martha of Bethany, the sister of Mary whose brother Lazarus is raised from the dead by Jesus. The novel offers a portrait of what might have been in a depiction of Martha interspersed with Gospel scenes from her perspective.

Historical Accuracy: Most of the story is an invention or an amplification of the Gospel stories.

GLADYS MCGORIAN

4275 *The Prince Regent's Silver Bell*

Date of Publication: 1987

Subject(s): Regency Romance; Napoleonic Wars; Horse Racing

Fictional character(s): Kate Martin, Gentlewoman, Heiress; Edward Radburn, Nobleman (earl)

Time Period(s): 1810s (1814)

Locale(s): England

Summary: Tomboyish Kate Martin reluctantly agrees to the peculiar conditions of her uncle's will to receive a legacy. She must endure a year's probation with her aunt to be deemed a proper lady. This proves difficult for Kate who is only interes-

ted in horses and conducts herself with unladylike abandon. The climax comes in a race meeting to which the Prince Regent has contributed a silver bell as a trophy. Success may mean the end of her inheritance.

Historical Accuracy: This is an amusing Regency with a credible period backdrop.

ELOISE JARVIS MCGRAW (1915-)

Born in Texas, McGraw graduated from Principia College and did graduate work in painting and sculpture at Oklahoma and Colorado universities. She has worked as an art teacher.

4276 *Pharaoh*

Date of Publication: 1958

Subject(s): Ancient Egypt; Pharaohs; Royalty—Egypt

Historical character(s): Hatshepsut, Ruler (Queen of Egypt); Tutmose III, Ruler (pharaoh); Senmut, Courtier, Architect

Time Period(s): 16th century B.C.; 15th century B.C.

Locale(s): Egypt

Summary: The novel, set in ancient Egypt, dramatizes the fascinating reign of Queen Hatsheput who became the first female to wear the double crown of Pharaoh. She is convinced of her own divinity, and her absolute power sets the standard for future rulers. The novel details the palace intrigue and culture of ancient Egypt.

Historical Accuracy: Though based on solid research, the novel inevitably relies largely upon imagination.

IONA MCGREGOR (1929-)

An English teacher and writer, McGregor is a graduate of the University of Bristol. She has been a teacher of classics and Latin at schools in England and Scotland. Her novels are usually set in Scotland and she calls herself a period, rather than historical, novelist who uses setting as a lens to explore character with the distancing effect to pick up the patterns in past lives.

4277 *Death Wore a Diadem*

Date of Publication: 1989

Subject(s): Mystery; Victorian Period; Homosexuality

Fictional character(s): Margaret Napier, Teacher; Christabel Mackenzie, Student, Lesbian; Eleanor Stewart, Servant, Lesbian

Historical character(s): Eugenie, Royalty (Empress of France)

Time Period(s): 1860s

Locale(s): Edinburgh, Scotland

Summary: In 1860s the visit of the Empress Eugenie to Edinburgh is preceded by the potentially embarassing theft of a replica of her Grecian diadem. The jewels were to be worn by a student at the Scottish Institute for the Education of the Daughters of Gentlefolk. Margaret Napier, the Institute's superintendent, goes to great lengths to suppress the theft and a subsequent murder. Rebellious pupil Christabel MacKenzie searches for the identity of the killer.

Historical Accuracy: The novel is an amalgam of period elements and very modern consciousness.

MARGERIE MCINTYRE

4278 *The River Witch*
Date of Publication: 1955
Subject(s): Riverboats
Fictional character(s): Michael Riley, Sea Captain (riverboat); Cordellia Riley, Sea Captain (riverboat)
Time Period(s): 1850s
Locale(s): Missouri River, United States; Mississippi River

Summary: Based on the life of an actual riverboat captain's daughter, the novel describes the captain of the *Blue Teal*, Michael Riley. When his daughter Cordellia stows away, she is captivated with life on the river. Eventually she captains her own boat and is called the River Witch. The novel features a vivid depiction of river life during the period.

Historical Accuracy: The author has based her story on that of the original River Witch and has used her first-hand knowledge of the region.

ALLIS MCKAY

4279 *The Women at Pine Creek*
Date of Publication: 1966
Subject(s): Farming; Rural Life—U.S.
Fictional character(s): Mary Hollister, Settler; Althea Hollister, Settler
Time Period(s): 1910s
Locale(s): Columbia River Valley, Washington

Summary: In the apple-growing region of Washington state the two Hollister sisters—Mary and Althea—claim a small plot willed to them by their father. The novel dramatizes their experiences.

Historical Accuracy: The novel presents a believable portrait of the times and the region.

ALEXANDER MCKEE (1918-)
The son of a surgeon in the Royal Navy, McKee grew up in a sucession of port towns. He has worked as a documentary writer for the B.B.C. His non-fiction works include, *The Coal-Scuttle Brigade*, *Black Saturday*, *Strike From the Sky*, and *The Golden Wreck*. He is best known for his book *Death Raft: The Human Drama of the Medusa*, a study of the 1816 shipwreck which claimed hundreds of lives. McKee supervised the successful recovery amd raising in 1982 of the Tudor ship, the *Mary Rose*.

4280 *H.M.S. Bounty*
Date of Publication: 1963
Subject(s): Sea Story; Military Life—British Navy; Mutiny
Historical character(s): William Bligh, Military Personnel (naval captain); Fletcher Christian, Military Personnel (naval officer)

Time Period(s): 1780s; 1790s
Locale(s): *Bounty*, At Sea; Tahiti, French Polynesia

Summary: This retelling of the mutiny of the *H.M.S. Bounty* attempts to give a faithful picture of both sides in the conflict. The novel answers many of the questions that have persisted in various interpretations and accounts. Was the mutiny a well-planned coup or a spontaneous reaction to Captain Bligh's cruelty?.

Historical Accuracy: The novel makes excellent use of the principal source documents in its reconstructions of the voyage.

RUTH ELEANOR MCKEE (1903-)
Born in Bardsdale, California, McKee is the author of *After a Hundred Years*, *Under One Roof*, and *Storm Point*.

4281 *Christopher Strange*
Date of Publication: 1941
Subject(s): American West; Gold Rush—California
Fictional character(s): Christopher Strange, Lawyer, Political Figure
Time Period(s): 19th century; 20th century (1853-1901)
Locale(s): San Francisco, California

Summary: This novel of the development of San Francisco and California in the 19th century follows the career of Massachusetts lawyer Christopher Strange who heads west with others lured by the gold strike. He settles in San Francisco and turns from law to politics. His experiences reflect important events in California history, including the fight against the slave interests, the promotion of the transcontinental railroad, and the fight against the domination of California by the Big Four.

Historical Accuracy: The historical elements which form a strong background for the story are faithfully presented.

4282 *The Lord's Anointed*
Date of Publication: 1934
Subject(s): Religious Life
Fictional character(s): Constancy Williams, Young Woman
Time Period(s): 1820s
Locale(s): Hawaii

Summary: This tale of missionaries who come from Boston to the Hawaiian Islands in the 1820s is seen through the experiences of Constancy Williams who secretly rebels against the ideals of her missionary husband and his colleagues but accepts the hardships inherent in their lives.

Historical Accuracy: The background of island life is curiously lightly sketched.

RUTH MCKENNEY (1911-1972)
An American writer, McKenney was born in Indiana and educated at Ohio State University. She worked as a printer, salesperson, waitress, and newspaper reporter. She is best known for her first book, *My Sister Eileen*, which was made into a Broadway play, a musical, and a motion picture. She

won the best fiction book award from the Writer's Congress for *Industrial Valley.*

4283 *Mirage*

Date of Publication: 1956
Subject(s): Napoleonic Wars; Battle of the Pyramids; Battle of the Nile
Fictional character(s): Remi Saint-Victor, Scientist (chemist)
Historical character(s): Napoleon Bonaparte, Ruler (Emperor of France), Military Personnel (French commander); Josephine, Royalty (consort of Napoleon); Charles Maurice de Talleyrand-Perigord, Diplomat
Time Period(s): 1790s (1797)
Locale(s): Paris, France; Egypt

Summary: This large panoramic novel concerns Napoleon's Egyptian campaign. The novel centers on the experience of released prisoner Remi Saint-Victor, a chemist who accompanies the young general Napoleon as one of his secretaries. There are scenes of the great Battle of the Pyramids and Nelson's triumph over the French fleet at the Battle of the Nile.

Historical Accuracy: The novel blends fact and fiction, but the historical events are genuine.

MARTHA FERGUSON MCKEOWN
(1903-)

McKeown's books include *Them Was the Days* and *The Trail Led North.*

4284 *Mountains Ahead*

Date of Publication: 1961
Subject(s): Wagon Trains; American West
Fictional character(s): Harmony Harrow, Pioneer; Dan Harrow, Pioneer
Time Period(s): 1840s (1847)
Locale(s): Oregon Trail, United States

Summary: Hardships and struggles along the Oregon Trail in the 1840s are dramatized in this account of a western trek from Independence, Missouri, to Oregon. The story centers on the Harmony family.

Historical Accuracy: This is an authentic and convincing account of the lot of the pioneers heading west by wagon during the period.

HUGH MCLEAVE (1923-)

Scottish writer McLeave graduated from the University of Glasgow and has worked as a journalist in London, serving as the science correspondent for the *News Chronicle* and the *Daily Mail*, and the editor of a medical journal. His books include *The Risk Takers* and *The Damned Die Hard.*

4285 *A Man and His Mountain: The Life of Paul Cezanne*

Date of Publication: 1977
Subject(s): Biography, Fictionalized; Artistic Life

Historical character(s): Paul Cezanne, Artist
Time Period(s): 19th century; 20th century (1839-1906)
Locale(s): France

Summary: This fictional biography of French painter Paul Cezanne traces his career in Provence where he was born and in Paris where his reputation earned him an important place among the Impressionists. The author shows a great familiarity with the period and the artistic movement in France in which Cezanne played an important part.

Historical Accuracy: The authenticity of the material makes this a convincing version of Cezanne's life and times.

ALISON MCLEAY

4286 *Passage Home*

Date of Publication: 1990
Subject(s): American West; Coming of Age
Fictional character(s): Rachel Dean, Widow(er); Adam Gaunt, Frontiersman
Time Period(s): 19th century (1827-1853)
Locale(s): Liverpool, England; Newfoundland, Canada; Missouri

Summary: The novel offers the growth and development of Rachel Dean from her first girlhood meeting with the mysterious bear trapper Adam Gaunt. Their paths will cross numerous times over the next decades in locales ranging from Liverpool to the Missouri frontier.

Historical Accuracy: The novel offers some convincing period details in establishing setting and time period.

4287 *Sea Change*

Date of Publication: 1992
Subject(s): Civil War—U.S.; Romance; Riverboats
Fictional character(s): Kate Summerbee, Young Woman; Matthew Oliver, Gentleman; Adam Gaunt, Gentleman
Time Period(s): 1860s; 1870s (1862-1870)
Locale(s): New Orleans, Louisiana; Liverpool, England

Summary: Kate Sommerbee is a young ''riverat'' living on her father's riverboat in New Orleans. At the outbreak of the Civil War a fugitive stranger sets in motion a chain of events that takes Kate from the river to England at the center of a family rivalry.

Historical Accuracy: The emphasis is on romantic adventure but the novel's backgrounds are convincing.

THOMAS MCMAHON (1943-)

American scientist and author McMahon was born in Ohio and studied physics at Cornell University. He completed his Ph.D. in fluid mechanics at MIT. A professor of applied mechanics and biology at Harvard, McMahon is the author of *Principles of American Nuclear Chemistry.*

4288 *Loving Little Egypt*

Date of Publication: 1987
Subject(s): Science; Inventions

Fictional character(s): Mourly Vold, Scientist
Historical character(s): Nikola Tesla, Scientist, Inventor; Alexander Graham Bell, Inventor; Thomas Alva Edison, Inventor; William Randolph Hearst, Financier; Albert Einstein, Scientist; Sarah Bernhardt, Actress
Time Period(s): 1920s
Locale(s): Cape Breton Island, Nova Scotia, Canada; West Virginia

Summary: This comic fantasy imagines the adventures of Mourly Vold, a science prodigy who creates an underground telephone network among blind people nationwide. His discovery pits him against the establishment represented by William Randolph Hearst and Thomas Edison. Vold joins forces with physicist Nikola Tesla to outwit Hearst and Edison in a fanciful battle for the control of science.

Historical Accuracy: The rumor of an underground telephone network has its basis in fact, but most of the plot contrivances and many of the inventions attributed to Bell and Edison are fanciful.

4289 *McKay's Bees*
Date of Publication: 1979
Subject(s): Science; Slavery
Fictional character(s): Gordon McKay, Businessman; Colin, Engineer; William Sewall, Naturalist
Historical character(s): Louis Agassiz, Scientist; John Brown, Abolitionist; Abraham Lincoln, Political Figure
Time Period(s): 1850s
Locale(s): Boston, Massachusetts; Lawrence, Kansas

Summary: This novel of ideas and science is set on the eve of the Civil War as a wealthy Bostonian, Gordon McKay, leads an expedition to Kansas to perfect a process for scientific beekeeping. The occasion becomes an opportunity for an exploration of human failings, ambition, and slavery in a series of vignettes that includes John Brown avenging the destruction of Kansas and Abraham Lincoln mourning the death of his son.

Historical Accuracy: The novel is overflowing with provocative ideas and an odd though believable evocation of the period.

CLARK MCMEEKIN
(PSEUD. OF DOROTHY PARK CLARK, 1899- ; ISABEL MCMEEKIN, 1895-)

Clark McMeekin is the pseudonym for two writers, Isabel McMeekin, born in Louisville, Kentucky, and Dorothy Park Clark, a native of Iowa. Their books include *Show Me a Land*, *Red Raskall*, and *Black Moon*.

4290 *City of the Flags*
Date of Publication: 1950
Subject(s): Civil War—U.S.
Fictional character(s): Murray Andrews, Widow(er)
Time Period(s): 1860s
Locale(s): Louisville, Kentucky

Summary: This Civil War tale is set in Louisville, Kentucky, a city torn between loyalty to the North and the South. It centers on Murray Andrews, a young widow with abolitionist sympathies. She is pursued by a Kentucky senator, a Yankee profiteer, a Confederate cavalryman, and a night-rider.

Historical Accuracy: The novel is strong and believable on regional and period background.

4291 *The Fairbrothers*
Date of Publication: 1961
Subject(s): Reconstruction Period; Horse Racing
Fictional character(s): Tolley Fairbrother, Veteran (Civil War); Jenny Fairbrother, Widow(er); Maria Zion Hobbs, Young Woman
Time Period(s): 1860s; 1870s
Locale(s): Louisville, Kentucky

Summary: Life in post-Civil War Kentucky is depicted in the experiences of the Fairbrother family of Louisville. Their plan to run a school for girls collapses with the arival of the French teacher who turns out to be Zion, masquerading as her dead mother. Zion stays on in the family, and, with Tolley Fairbrother, becomes involved in horse breeding that culminates in the running of the first Kentucky Derby.

Historical Accuracy: The period elements are authentic and believable.

4292 *Reckon with the River*
Date of Publication: 1941
Subject(s): Settlement of the American Frontier
Fictional character(s): Ma'am Cambrin, Settler
Historical character(s): Aaron Burr, Political Figure; Johnny Appleseed, Frontiersman; Joseph Brant, Indian (Mohawk), Chieftain
Time Period(s): 1800s
Locale(s): Kentucky; Ohio River, United States

Summary: Frontier life in Kentucky and along the Ohio River during the early years of the 19th century is described. The story centers on the experiences of 80-year-old Ma'am Cambrin who guides her family on a journey from their home in New York to Kentucky. They encounter a number of historical figures.

Historical Accuracy: The historical background is convincingly depicted.

4293 *Show Me a Land*
Date of Publication: 1940
Subject(s): Antebellum South; Civil War—U.S.; Horse Racing
Fictional character(s): Dana Terraine, Southern Belle; Rike Galphine, Farmer; Eben Coates, Religious (minister)
Time Period(s): 19th century (1816-1875)
Locale(s): Virginia; Kentucky

Summary: Life in Virginia and Kentucky is dramatized from the pre-Civil War era to the Reconstruction period. Dana Terraine is the Virginian southern belle confident in her ability with men and horses. Her story offers plenty of both as well as politics of the period.

Historical Accuracy: The regional and period elements are presented in a believable background.

4294 *Tyrone of Kentucky*

Date of Publication: 1954
Subject(s): Reconstruction Period
Fictional character(s): David Tyrone, Veteran (Confederate soldier); Glen Ellen Saxton, Spouse (of Tyrone); Cottie Thomas, Young Woman
Time Period(s): 1860s (post Civil War)
Locale(s): Kentucky

Summary: The novel describes the conflicts of life in Kentucky during Reconstruction as Confederate veteran David Tyrone brings his young bride Glen Ellen home from Alabama. The marauding Regulators and Avengers who terrorize the countryside as the state is split by divided loyalties are vividly depicted.

Historical Accuracy: The story is fictional but features a credible period background.

LARRY MCMURTRY (1936-)

McMurtry is an American novelist who specializes in writing about the West and Texas. Many of McMurtry's books have been turned into films. He is the author of such books as *The Last Picture Show*, *Terms of Endearment*, and *Texasville*.

4295 *Anything for Billy*

Date of Publication: 1978
Subject(s): American West; Crime and Criminals
Fictional character(s): Billy Bones, Outlaw; Ben Sippy, Writer (dime novelist); Katie Garza, Outlaw
Historical character(s): John Henry Holliday, Gunfighter
Time Period(s): 1870s
Locale(s): Southwest; Mexico

Summary: This darkly comic take on the Billy the Kid legend features Billy Bones who is encountered at the beginning of his short, murderous career by a dime novelist who chronicles their misadventures. More an absurdist fantasy than an accurate period tale, the novel is filled with the odd and the bizarre, including a seven-foot African who rides a camel. The Kid is, in turn, endearing and brutal, a cross between a holy fool and Charles Starkweather.

Historical Accuracy: As in most of McMurtry's West, the legends are reevaluated, here more by irony and excess than in the lovingly recreated details of *Lonesome Dove*.

4296 *Buffalo Girls*

Date of Publication: 1990
Subject(s): American West; Wild West Show
Fictional character(s): No Ears, Indian; Bartle Bone, Mountain Man; Jim Kagg, Mountain Man
Historical character(s): Annie Oakley, Frontierswoman; Martha Jane Cannary Burk, Frontierswoman; William F. Cody, Frontiersman, Entertainer; Sitting Bull, Indian, Chief-

tain (Sioux); Edward, Prince of Wales, Royalty (prince); Ned Buntline, Writer
Time Period(s): 1880s (1887)
Locale(s): West (Montana, Wyoming, the Dakotas); London, England

Summary: The novel is set in 1887 when Buffalo Bill assembles a cast of frontier legends for performances of his Wild West Show in England to celebrate Queen Victoria's Golden Jubilee.

Historical Accuracy: More elegy than historical Western, McMurtry evokes a moving tone of lost legends and fading western dreams.

4297 *Dead Man's Walk*

Date of Publication: 1995
Subject(s): American West; Texas Revolution; Indians
Fictional character(s): Augustus McCrae, Lawman (Texas Ranger); Woodrow F. Call, Lawman (Texas Ranger); Buffalo Hump, Indian (Comanche), Chieftain
Time Period(s): 1840s
Locale(s): Texas; Santa Fe, New Mexico

Summary: In this story of the early days of Gus McCrae and Woodrow Call from the author's *Lonesome Dove*, the pair, not yet in their twenties, come of age in the Texas Republic. They enlist as Texas Rangers and participate in a scheme to seize Sante Fe from the Mexicans. They must cross hostile Indian territory to reach New Mexico, encountering the ferocious Comanche war chief Buffalo Hump.

Historical Accuracy: The era and the locale are created with authority and conviction.

4298 *Lonesome Dove*

Date of Publication: 1985
Subject(s): American West; Cattle Drives; Indians
Fictional character(s): Woodrow F. Call, Gunfighter (former Texas ranger), Rancher; Augustus McCrae, Gunfighter (former Texas ranger), Rancher; Lorena Wood, Prostitute
Time Period(s): 1880s
Locale(s): Southwest; Mexico; Montana

Summary: McMurtry's Pulitzer Prize-winning Western tells the story of the first cattle drive from south Texas into the Montana frontier by two former Texas Rangers and Indian fighters. The novel is a narrative stem-winder that includes dust storms, stampedes, pursuits, and outlaw and Indian attacks. There is a grim, murderous villain, the renegade Blue Duck, and strong female characters.

Historical Accuracy: McMurtry does more than assemble a colorful cast and expertly set this Western odyssey in motion. His eye for period detail makes the familiar seem fresh.

LARRY MCMURTRY (1936-)

DIANA OSSANA

McMurtry is the well-known writer of such works as *The Last Picture Show* and *Lonesome Dove*. Diana Ossana is a screenwriter, and *Pretty Boy Floyd* was written after the two collaborated on a film script about the character.

4299 *Pretty Boy Floyd*

Date of Publication: 1994
Subject(s): Crime and Criminals; Depression Era
Historical character(s): Charles Arthur Floyd, Criminal; J. Edgar Hoover, Lawman (director of the FBI); Melvin Purvis, FBI Agent
Time Period(s): 1920s; 1930s (1925-1935)
Locale(s): St. Louis, Missouri; Kansas City, Missouri; Oklahoma City, Oklahoma

Summary: Charley Floyd's rise from a baker's helper at the Kroger Bakery to public enemy is chronicled in this novel. Floyd is charming and likable, a Robin Hood to some, but an opportunity for J. Edgar Hoover and his FBI to claim some publicity. The novel offers an interesting meditation on the price of celebrity in America.

Historical Accuracy: The novel's dialogue sparkles with authenticity, as do the Depression-era details.

LARRY MCMURTRY (1936-)

McMurtry is an American novelist who specializes in writing about the West and Texas. Many of McMurtry's books have been turned into films. He is the author of such books as *The Last Picture Show*, *Terms of Endearment*, and *Texasville*.

4300 *Streets of Laredo*

Date of Publication: 1993
Subject(s): American West; Crime and Criminals
Fictional character(s): Woodrow F. Call, Lawman; Joey Garza, Outlaw; Pea Eye, Lawman
Historical character(s): John Wesley Hardin, Outlaw; Roy Bean, Judge; Charles Goodnight, Rancher
Time Period(s): 1890s
Locale(s): Southwest; Mexico

Summary: This sequel to *Lonesome Dove* is set more than fifteen years after the events of the earlier novel. Captain Call hunts two killers—a Mexican train robber and a psychopath who sets his victims on fire—through West Texas and Mexico.

Historical Accuracy: Less filled with details of western life than *Lonesome Dove*, the novel is populated by many violent eccentrics who test Call's monolithic strength at the end of an era.

LARRY MCMURTRY (1936-)

DIANA OSSANA

McMurtry is the well-known writer of such works as *The Last Picture Show* and *Lonesome Dove*. Diana Ossana is a screenwriter, and *Pretty Boy Floyd* was written after the two collaborated on a film script about the character.

4301 *Zeke and Ned*

Date of Publication: 1996
Subject(s): American West; Indians
Historical character(s): Ezekiel Proctor, Indian (Cherokee); Ned Christie, Indian (Cherokee); Isaac C. Parker, Judge
Time Period(s): 1870s
Locale(s): Cherokee Nation, Oklahoma; Ozarks

Summary: Set in the Cherokee Nation during the 1870s, the novel constructs a fictional story around two actual figures—Ezekiel Proctor and Ned Christie—Cherokees in defiance of white law who are both caught in the conflict of cultures.

Historical Accuracy: The novel weaves a fictional story around Proctor and Christie that is filled with authentic period elements.

TOM MCNAB (1933-)

A Scottish-born novelist, McNab is a runner and coach for the U.K. Olympic team and served as an adviser on the film *Chariots of Fire*. McNab has devoted his life to athletics. He is the Scotland national triple-jump record holder.

4302 *The Fast Men*

Date of Publication: 1986
Subject(s): American West; Sports
Fictional character(s): Buck Miller, Sports Figure (runner); Billy Joe Speed, Sports Figure (runner)
Historical character(s): Edwin Booth, Actor; Phineas T. Barnum, Entertainer; Leland Stanford, Financier
Time Period(s): 1870s
Locale(s): West

Summary: In what can be called a Sports Western, the novel describes Buck Miller and Billy Joe Speed and their footrace from Kansas City to Mexico in the 1870s. Their adventures take them across the West in the aftermath of the Custer Massacre and lead to encounters with both real and fictional characters.

Historical Accuracy: The situation is fictional, but the scenes of western life are credible.

4303 *Flanagan's Run*

Date of Publication: 1982
Subject(s): Depression Era; Sports
Fictional character(s): Charles C. Flanagan, Businessman (promoter); Kate Sheridan, Dancer; Doc Cole, Adventurer, Sports Figure (runner)
Historical character(s): Al Capone, Organized Crime Figure
Time Period(s): 1930s (1931)
Locale(s): United States (crosscountry from California to New York)

Summary: Inspired by the actual Great Bunion Derby, a 3,000 mile cross-country foot-race, the novel describes the promotion of Charles C. Flanagan: a race from Los Angeles to New York with $300,000 in prize money. A colorful cast of opponents flood to the race with various motives and abilities.

Historical Accuracy: This comic story borrows some actual details from fact, but the essence of the story is invented.

TOM MCNAMARA (1944-)

Raised in Boston, McNamara graduated from Boston University and Northeastern. He served in Vietnam as an ordnance officer and as an officer with the Army Missile Command. In 1974 he received nationwide publicity as the recipient of Presidential and Chicago Police Department commendations for capturing a mugger in downtown Chicago. He is the co-author of *America's Changing Workforce*. McNamara is also an amateur sailboat racing skipper.

`4304` Henry Lunt and the Ranger

Date of Publication: 1991
Subject(s): American Revolution; Sea Story; Espionage
Historical character(s): Henry Lunt, Spy; John Paul Jones, Military Personnel (naval officer)
Time Period(s): 1770s (1778)
Locale(s): England; Ireland

Summary: This espionage and adventure story is set during the American Revolution and concerns the naval engagements of John Paul Jones in the Irish Sea during 1778. Jones rescues his sailing comrade Henry Lunt from a Welsh prison and lands him ashore in Ireland to investigate the British Navy's activities in Belfast harbor. There Lunt is able to provoke the British into facing Jones aboard the *Ranger*.

Historical Accuracy: The novel is a blend of fact and fiction. The author's notes indicate the story's basis in fact and the events that have been invented.

THOMAS MCNAMEE (1947-)

`4305` A Story of Deep Delight

Date of Publication: 1990
Subject(s): Indians; Antebellum South; Civil War—U.S.
Fictional character(s): Tchula Homa, Indian (Chickasaw), Chieftain; Sylvester Woodson, Servant (stableboy), Slave; Wordlaw Corelli, Artist
Historical character(s): Andrew Jackson, Military Personnel (general), Political Figure; Nathan Bedford Forrest, Plantation Owner, Military Personnel (Confederate officer)
Time Period(s): 19th century; 20th century (1811-1980)
Locale(s): Kentucky; Tennessee

Summary: This family saga covers over 150 years of American history and details the groups and events that formed the American South including the Indians, the plantation system, and the aftermath of the Civil War. Three young men, Tchula Homa, a Chickasaw Indian, Sylvester Woodman, a stable boy, and Wordlaw Corelli, a descendant of Sylvester's owner, reflect the impact of time and place on character.

Historical Accuracy: The novel offers an authentic version of time and place.

ALAN DECKER MCNARIE (1954-)

Born in Missouri, McNarie graduated from Northwest Missouri State University and the University of Missouri.

He was a Peace Corps volunteer in Thailand. In 1992 McNarie was the winner of the Editor's Book Award for *Yeshua: The Gospel of St. Thomas*.

`4306` Yeshua: The Gospel of St. Thomas

Date of Publication: 1993
Subject(s): Biblical Story; Christianity
Historical character(s): Thomas, Religious (apostle), Biblical Figure; Jesus Christ, Biblical Figure
Time Period(s): 1st century
Locale(s): India; Israel

Summary: Forty years after Jesus' crucifixion, the apostle Thomas, while in an Indian prison, composes this fictional memoir of his youth in Galilee, Jesus' ministry, and the development of early Christianity. The novel offers both a re-creation of the Biblical events and a psychological portrait of Thomas' progression from skeptic to believer.

Historical Accuracy: The emphasis is on Thomas' psychological development with a somewhat unsatisfactory re-creation of the setting and the theological disputes of the early Christian church.

EVERETT MCNEIL (1862-1929)

McNeil wrote several biographies and novels, including *In Texas with David Crockett* and *With Kit Carson in the Rockies*.

`4307` Daniel Du Luth

Date of Publication: 1926
Subject(s): Exploration; Indians
Fictional character(s): Paul Douay, Young Man
Historical character(s): Daniel Du Luth, Explorer
Time Period(s): 17th century (1670s)
Locale(s): North America; Canada

Summary: The exploration of the Great Lakes from Montreal to Lake Superior by the French explorer Daniel Du Luth is dramatized through a fictional tale told by Paul Douay who sets out with Du Luth by canoe in search of his sister who has been stolen by Indians.

Historical Accuracy: The novel should not be read as factual history, but the atmosphere is genuine.

MILDRED MASTERSON MCNEILLY (1910-)

Born in Kittias County, Washington, McNeilly is the author of *Praise at Morning* and *Each Bright River*. She has also written magazine stories under the names Glenn Kelly and James Dewey.

`4308` Each Bright River

Date of Publication: 1950
Subject(s): American West; Settlement of the American Frontier
Fictional character(s): Kitty Gatewood, Young Woman; Sunset Lee, Mountain Man; Curt Fletcher, Pioneer

Time Period(s): 1840s (1845)
Locale(s): Oregon

Summary: A South Carolina woman, Kitty Gatewood, journeys to Oregon only to find her lover dead. The novel records her experiences in the wilderness and her relationship with two frontiersmen—Curt Fletcher and Sunset Lee.

Historical Accuracy: Although the story is fictional, it is based on solid knowledge of the period and the region.

4309 *Heaven Is Too High*
Date of Publication: 1944
Subject(s): Frontier—Alaska
Fictional character(s): Danilo Chernov, Nobleman (count)
Historical character(s): Aleksandr Baranov, Leader (colonial)
Time Period(s): 18th century; 19th century (1790-1810)
Locale(s): Alaska

Summary: The Alaskan wilderness in the 18th and early 19th centuries forms the setting for this adventure tale based on the attempt by Alexander Baranov to establish a fur-trading colony. The fictional story involves Russian nobleman Danilo Chernov, who flees the Empress Catherine's wrath to join the expedition, becoming Baranov's main assistant.

Historical Accuracy: The authenticity of the novel's background is assured by the use of original Russian sources.

4310 *Praise at Morning*
Date of Publication: 1947
Subject(s): Civil War—U.S.; Diplomacy; Sea Story
Fictional character(s): Matthew Steel, Sea Captain
Time Period(s): 1860s
Locale(s): New York, New York; St. Petersburg, Russia

Summary: This Civil War tale of naval action and international diplomacy is based on the arrival of the Russian fleet in San Francisco and New York in 1863 as a deterrent to Britain's recognition of the Confederacy. The Russian move is the work of Yankee sea captain Matthew Steel.

Historical Accuracy: The novel's historical events and elements are accurately presented though the connection between the historical and the fictional is contrived and ultimately unconvincing.

JAMES MCNEISH (1931-)

A New Zealand novelist and playwright, McNeish was born in Auckland. He has worked as a journalist, teacher, radio broadcaster, and documentary producer. McNeish wrote a biography of architect Danilo Dolci, *Fire under the Ashes*. His novels include *MacKenzie*, *The Glass Zoo*, and *Joy*.

4311 *Lovelock*
Date of Publication: 1986
Subject(s): Sports
Historical character(s): Jack Lovelock, Sports Figure (Olympic track medalist)
Time Period(s): 1930s; 1940s (1932-1949)
Locale(s): Oxford, England; Berlin, Germany; New York, New York

Summary: Jack Lovelock, the New Zealander who won the 1,500 meters at the Olympic Games in 1936 was called the first modern athlete by Roger Bannister. His systematic assault on the mile brought him success over the greatest field of milers ever assembled. But after his triumph in Berin he stopped running, and the remainder of his life is a mystery. The novel offers an interpretation of Lovelock's life in the form of a diary.

Historical Accuracy: Where facts are known, the author has included them; the rest is conjecture.

JOSEPH WALKER MCSPADDEN
(1874-1960)

Born in Knoxville, Tennessee, and a graduate of the Unversity of Tennessee, McSpadden worked as a literary editor and wrote numerous books, including *Shakespearean Synopsis*, and the historical novel *Storm Center*.

4312 *Storm Center: A Novel about Andy Johnson*
Date of Publication: 1947
Subject(s): Biography, Fictionalized; Politics; Reconstruction Period
Historical character(s): Andrew Johnson, Political Figure
Time Period(s): 19th century
Locale(s): Tennessee; Washington, District of Columbia

Summary: This novel is based on the life of Andrew Johnson who succeeds Abraham Lincoln after his assassination. His more tolerant Reconstruction policy prompts the wrath of radical Republicans and a vote for impeachment. The novel offers a positive view of Johnson, showing him as a loyal and able leader who faces enormous opposition.

Historical Accuracy: The novel offers a rather simplified version of Johnson's life and the issues of the day that were far more complex than suggested here.

ELLIS K. MEACHAM (1913-)

An American born in Tennessee and a graduate of the University of Chattanooga, Meacham earned his law degree from Vanderbilt University. He has been an attorney and judge in the municipal court in Chattanooga.

4313 *The East Indiaman*
Date of Publication: 1968
Subject(s): Sea Story; Military Life—British Navy
Fictional character(s): Percival Merewether, Military Personnel (naval officer)
Time Period(s): 1800 (1806)
Locale(s): *Rapid*, At Sea; Calcutta, India; Canton, China

Summary: This naval adventure is set during the period of the naval service of the East India Company, the so-called Bombay Buccaneers, who sailed in the the perilous waters of the Indian Ocean and the South China Sea. Captain Percival Merewether, born a bastard and lacking formal education, rises to command and is tested in a variety of naval adventures.

Historical Accuracy: The period elements and nautical details are authentic.

4314 *For King and Company*

Date of Publication: 1976
Subject(s): Sea Story; Military Life—British Navy; Napoleonic Wars
Fictional character(s): Percival Merewether, Military Personnel (naval officer); Caroline Merewether, Spouse
Time Period(s): 1810s
Locale(s): India; At Sea (Gulf of Aden, Bay of Bengal, South China Sea)

Summary: The third novel about the naval adventures of Percival Merewether in the East India Company's Bombay Marine has Merewether commanding an attack on a pirate citadel, escorting a convoy attacked by the French, and on a diplomatic mission involving the opium trade in China.

Historical Accuracy: The details of nautical life of the period are exact and convincing.

4315 *On the Company's Service*

Date of Publication: 1971
Subject(s): Sea Story; Military Life—British Navy
Fictional character(s): Percival Merewether, Military Personnel (naval officer)
Time Period(s): 1800s
Locale(s): Calcutta, India; *Rapid*, At Sea; Tehran, Persia

Summary: The adventures of the naval service of the East India Company are captured as Captain Percival Merewether, the acting commodore of the Bombay Marines, is further tested in a series of naval actions and political intrigue that take him from Calcutta to Teheran and the Russo-Persia border.

Historical Accuracy: The story is fanciful but supported by convincing period elements.

ROBERT DOUGLAS MEAD (1928-1983)

An English writer born in Birmingham, Mead was a graduate of Columbia and Cambridge universities. Mead worked in publishing and served as language arts editor for Harcourt Brace and J.B. Lippincott.

4316 *Heartland*

Date of Publication: 1986
Subject(s): American West; Indians
Fictional character(s): Isaac Pride, Hunter (buffalo)
Historical character(s): Jesse Chisholm, Frontiersman; Kit Carson, Frontiersman
Time Period(s): 1850s; 1860s
Locale(s): Saline River, Kansas; Wichita, Kansas

Summary: In 1859, Isaac Pride sets off from Iowa for Pike's Peak and the promise of gold. He winds up in Kansas instead and begins a booming buffalo fur trade business. When the era of the great herds is over, Pride rides the cattle trails with

Jesse Chisholm, establishes the Wichita settlement and one of the first banks in the west.

Historical Accuracy: The novel is fact and fiction in equal measure. It is faithful to known historical events, while the details of the characters' motives have been inferred by the author.

MARION MEADE (1934-)

An American born in Pennsylvania, Meade graduated from Northwestern and Columbia universities. A novelist and biographer, Meade is an expert on 12th-century Europe and the author of widely acclaimed biographies of Eleanor of Aquitaine, Madame Blavatsky, and Victoria Woodhull. She considers herself a feminist whose works reflect her point of view.

4317 *Stealing Heaven: The Love Story of Heloise and Abelard*

Date of Publication: 1979
Subject(s): Middle Ages; Religious Life
Historical character(s): Peter Abelard, Scholar (theologian), Philosopher; Heloise, Religious (abbess)
Time Period(s): 12th century
Locale(s): Paris, France

Summary: The novel describes the celebrated love affair between Heloise, a fiercely independent woman, and Peter Abelard, the renowned philosopher and theologian, who becomes her tutor. They fall in love and secretly marry, but the relationship is discovered, and the lovers are permanently separated. Abelard becomes a monk, and Heloise a famous abbess.

Historical Accuracy: The novel follows the outline of Heloise and Abelard's lives and uses nothing but historical facts, when those facts are known.

4318 *Sybille*

Date of Publication: 1983
Subject(s): Middle Ages; Albigensian Crusade; Religious Conflict
Fictional character(s): Sybille d'Astarac, Entertainer (troubadour), Writer (poet); Oliver de Ferrand, Knight
Historical character(s): Simon de Montfort, Nobleman
Time Period(s): 13th century
Locale(s): Provencal, France; Toulouse, France

Summary: Set during the Albigensian crusade in the 13th century instituted by the Catholic Church to put down the Cathari sect, the novel describes the life of Sybille d'Astarac who becomes a troubadour poet caught up in the sieges and massacres of the Inquisition and her love for the knight Oliver.

Historical Accuracy: The novel relies on a convincing period treatment.

STEPHEN WARREN MEADER (1892-)

An American writer born in Rhode Island, Meader graduated from Haverford College. He worked as the editor of *Country Gentleman* and as a copyeditor. His books include *Clear for Action*, *A Blow for Liberty*, and *Phantom of the Blockade*.

⬛ **4319** *Boy with a Pack*

Date of Publication: 1939
Subject(s): Settlement of the American Frontier
Fictional character(s): Bill Crawford, Teenager, Peddler
Time Period(s): 1830s (1837)
Locale(s): New Hampshire; Ohio

Summary: This frontier tale depicts the adventures of 17-year-old Bill Crawford from New Hampshire who travels as an itinerant peddler into the wilderness of Ohio. He encounters horse thieves in Vermont, canal life in New York, and fugitive slaves along the Underground Railroad.

Historical Accuracy: The novel features a colorful and believable evocation of the period.

DENIS MEADOWS

⬛ **4320** *Tudor Underground*

Date of Publication: 1950
Subject(s): Elizabethan Period; Religious Conflict
Fictional character(s): Hugh Rampling, Government Official
Historical character(s): Sir Francis Walsingham, Government Official (secretary to Elizabeth I); Robert Persons, Religious (priest); Edmund Campion, Religious (priest)
Time Period(s): 16th century (1577)
Locale(s): England; Rome, Italy

Summary: The title refers to Catholics during the Elizabethan period who were driven underground by persecution. The story centers on Francis Walsingham's young assistant, Hugh Rampling, a lapsed Catholic turned Catholic-catcher, who faces a test of divided loyalties.

Historical Accuracy: The details of the Catholic persecutions of the period are authentically presented.

MARDI OAKLEY MEDAWAR

⬛ **4321** *Death at Rainy Mountain*

Date of Publication: 1996
Subject(s): Mystery; American West; Indians
Fictional character(s): Tay-Bodal, Indian (Kiowa), Shaman
Time Period(s): 1860s (1866)
Locale(s): West

Summary: This historical mystery is set in the summer of 1866 as the separate bands of the Kiowa nation gather at the sacred Rainy Mountain to elect a new chief. When the nephew of one of the leading candidates is accused of killing the nephew of another, the act threatens to destroy the peace. Tay-bodal, a healer, decides to investigate and prove the guilt of the actual murderer.

Historical Accuracy: The story is based on the actual lives of historical figures.

TERESA MEDEIROS (1962-)

An American author, Medeiros worked as a registered nurse for nine years. She is a romance author who attributes her writing career to being an only child and an ''army brat'' who developed her imagination to entertain herself. She believes romance writers are true feminists, advocates of strong female characters and in favor of love and family.

⬛ **4322** *Lady of Conquest*

Date of Publication: 1984
Subject(s): Dark Ages; Romance
Fictional character(s): Gelina O'Monoghan, Warrior; Conn, Ruler (High King of Ireland), Warrior
Time Period(s): 2nd century; 123
Locale(s): Ireland

Summary: This adventure story set in second century Ireland tells the story of Gelina O'Manoghan who sets out to avenge the destruction of her family and falls in love with the man whom she holds responsible.

Historical Accuracy: The period elements are only lightly captured in this story which emphasizes passion.

ARTHUR MEEKER (1902-)

Born in Chicago, Illinois, Meeker attended both Princeton and Harvard before leaving to become a reporter. He is the author of *Jerry: The Adventures of an Army Dog*, *Frog, the Horse That Knew No Master*, and *The Silver Plume*.

⬛ **4323** *The Silver Plume*

Date of Publication: 1952
Subject(s): Identity—Concealed
Historical character(s): Tancrede de Rohan, Nobleman
Time Period(s): 17th century
Locale(s): France

Summary: In a story based on fact, Charles Potentjk learns that he is really Tancrede, Duc de Rohan, the head of one of the ancient houses of France who was kidnapped at a young age. Tancrede enters the aristocratic world where he finds himself in the center of events, only to be killed in his first battle, at the age of 18.

Historical Accuracy: This is a true story based on considerable original research.

BROWN MEGGS (1930-)

An American writer, Meggs grew up in Los Angeles and Connecticut and attended California Institute of Technology and Harvard. He worked as a story analyst for Warner Brothers Pictures and as an industrial-film writer. He has also worked as the chief operating officer of Capitol Records.

4324 *The War Train: A Novel of 1916*

Date of Publication: 1981

Subject(s): Coming of Age; Railroads; Mexican Revolution

Fictional character(s): Cassie McGill, Engineer, Railroad Worker; Miles Antrobus, Military Personnel (colonel); Olan Rose, Veterinarian

Time Period(s): 1910s (1916)

Locale(s): Southwest; Lincoln, Nebraska

Summary: In 1916, 18-year-old Cassie McGill conducts a special train carrying the 12th U.S. cavalry from South Dakota to join General Pershing's pursuit of Pancho Villa. The train is filled with a large cast of eccentrics who provide Cassie with a rite of passage to adulthood.

Historical Accuracy: The novel is fiction based on fact, based on the stories told by the author's grandfather.

GITA MEHTA

Mehta was born into a prominent Indian family and was educated in India and at Cambridge University. She is the author of *Karma Cola: Marketing the Mystic East*.

4325 *Raj*

Date of Publication: 1989

Subject(s): Independence—India; British Colonies; British Raj

Fictional character(s): Jaya Singh, Royalty (princess); Jai Singh, Ruler (maharajah); Victor Bahadur, Royalty (prince)

Time Period(s): 20th century (1910s-1950)

Locale(s): Balmer, India; Sirpur, India

Summary: Set during the British Raj, the novel details a woman's coming of age amidst the splendor of an Indian princely court. Jaya is the daughter of the maharajah of a desert kingdom resisting the encroachment of the British Empire. Married to the ruler of the kingdom of Sirpur, Jaya is torn between the traditions of the past and her admiration of Gandhi and the revolution he leads.

Historical Accuracy: The novel is believable in creating a sense of India during the period.

CORNELIA MEIGS (1884-1973)

An American author of childen's books and adult fiction and nonfiction, Meigs was born in Illinois and graduated from Bryn Mawr where she worked as a teacher of English. Meigs won the Drama League Prize in 1915 for *The Steadfast Princess* and literary prizes for *Invincible Louisa* and *The Trade Wind*.

4326 *Call of the Mountains*

Date of Publication: 1940

Subject(s): Rural Life—U.S.; Farming

Fictional character(s): Nathan Lindsay, Farmer

Time Period(s): 1830s

Locale(s): Vermont

Summary: Nathan Lindsay is driven from his inherited valley farm by a charge of murder. He sets out to clear his name and to make a life in the inhospitable wilderness.

Historical Accuracy: The novel captures the spirit of the era and the region with skill and conviction.

4327 *Railroad West*

Date of Publication: 1937

Subject(s): American West; Railroads

Fictional character(s): Philip Fox, Engineer; Ann Hale, Young Woman

Time Period(s): 1870s

Locale(s): West

Summary: The challenge of building the Northern Pacific railroad from Minnesota to the Yellowstone is depicted. The many difficulties encountered are dramatized along with the romance between Philip Fox, a young engineer, and Ann Hale.

Historical Accuracy: The novel provides an authentic picture of the times and the engineering details of early railroad construction.

4328 *Swift Rivers*

Date of Publication: 1932

Subject(s): Settlement of the American Frontier

Fictional character(s): Chris Dahlberg, Teenager

Time Period(s): 1830s (1835)

Locale(s): Minnesota; St. Louis, Missouri; Mississippi River

Summary: Young Chris Dahlberg floats down the Mississippi River to the market of St. Louis to raise funds for his grandfather. The novel records the adventure of the journey downriver.

Historical Accuracy: The historical background elements are authentic and believable.

IB MELCHIOR (1917-)

A Danish actor, stage manager, and director, Melchior was born in Copenhagen. He worked as a television writer, director, and producer for such programs as the ''Perry Como Show'' and the ''Eddy Arnold Show.'' Melchior was the winner of several awards for documentary films. He won the Hamlet Award in playwriting for *Hour of Vengeance*. Melchior drew on his own wartime experience in intelligence work for his novel *Eva*.

4329 *Eva*

Date of Publication: 1984

Subject(s): World War II; Fantasy; Alternate History

Fictional character(s): Woody Ward, Military Personnel (army intelligence officer)

Historical character(s): Eva Braun, Spouse; Adolf Hitler, Leader (Nazi), Political Figure (German dictator); Martin Bormann, Political Figure

Time Period(s): 1940s (1945)

Locale(s): Germany; Italy

Summary: This historical fantasy imagines what might have happened if the body found with Hitler outside his Berlin bunker in 1945 was not Eva Braun. In this version, a pregnant Eva is escorted by Martin Bormann and two S.S. officers to Italy where a ship is waiting to take her to Argentina. U.S. Army intelligence agent Woody Ward learns of the plot and sets out to spoil the plan.

Historical Accuracy: The plot is more ingenious than plausible, and the historical portraits are cliche-ridden.

ANNE MELVILLE
(PSEUD. OF MARGARET POTTER, 1926-)

A British author of romance, short stories, and children's books, Melville was educated at Oxford and became a teacher and magazine editor. She won the Romantic Novelist Association major award in 1966 for *The Truth Game*.

4330 *Alexa*

Date of Publication: 1979
Subject(s): Romance; Musical Life; Earthquakes
Fictional character(s): Alexa Lorimer, Singer (opera), Ward; Matthew Lorimer, Artist; Margaret Lorimer Scott, Guardian
Time Period(s): 1900s
Locale(s): England; Jamaica; San Francisco, California

Summary: Alexa Lorimer's pursuit of a career as an opera singer is entangled by family secrets that plague her and intrude on her happiness. Guided by her guardian, Margaret Scott, the heroine of the author's *The Lorimer Line*, the two travel throughout Europe to success in America before the novel's thrilling climax during the San Francisco earthquake.

Historical Accuracy: The novel establishes a believable historical background for the story.

4331 *Blaize*

Date of Publication: 1981
Subject(s): Family Saga; World War I; Russian Revolution
Fictional character(s): Brinsley Lorimer, Military Personnel (lieutenant); Margaret Lorimer, Doctor; Alexa Lorimer, Singer (opera)
Time Period(s): 20th century (1914-1947)
Locale(s): England; France; Russia

Summary: The novel continues the story of the Lorimer family during the years of the Great Wars. Events affect family members throughout Europe, including involvement with the fighting on the Western Front and the outbreak of the Russian Revolution. The family saga continues through the period of World War II.

Historical Accuracy: The novel provides a believable historical backdrop for the many permutations of the family's history.

4332 *The Lorimer Line*

Date of Publication: 1977
Subject(s): Victorian Period; Romance; Business Building

Fictional character(s): Margaret Lorimer, Gentlewoman; John Junius Lorimer, Banker; David Gregson, Banker (manager)
Time Period(s): 1880s
Locale(s): Bristol, England; London, England; Jamaica

Summary: Margaret Lorimer's wealthy world collapses around her as the secret life of her father, John Junius Lorimer, threatens to bring down her family's financial empire and destroy the Lorimer line. Margaret must struggle to defy prejudice and fashion a new life for herself.

Historical Accuracy: The period elements create a believable historical background.

HERMAN MELVILLE (1819-1891)

Melville was an American writer whose sea career provided the basis for many of his exotic romance̊s. *Moby Dick*, based on Melville's 18-month voyage to the South Seas aboard the whaler *Acushnet*, is considered one of the greatest American novels. Other notable works include *Pierre* and *The Confidence Man*. His last years were spent in poverty and obscurity, after his writing became more metaphysical and lost public favor.

4333 *Billy Budd*

Date of Publication: 1924
Subject(s): Sea Story; Military Life—British Navy
Fictional character(s): Billy Budd, Military Personnel (seaman); Starry Vere, Military Personnel (captain of British man-of-war); Claggart, Military Personnel (master-of-arms)
Time Period(s): 1790s (1797)
Locale(s): *Indomitable*, At Sea

Summary: Written shortly before Melville's death in 1891 and discovered in the 1920s, the novel dramatizes the conflict between natural goodness and absolute evil through the persecution of young sailor Billy Budd by master-of-arms Claggart. Their conflict forces Captain Vere to choose between conscience and duty.

Historical Accuracy: Details of naval life are based on Melville's own sea experience. They ground a deeply symbolic story of good and evil.

4334 *Israel Potter*

Date of Publication: 1855
Subject(s): American Revolution; Battle of Bunker Hill
Fictional character(s): Israel Potter, Military Personnel (soldier)
Historical character(s): Benjamin Franklin, Political Figure, Diplomat; John Paul Jones, Military Personnel (naval officer); Ethan Allen, Military Personnel (army officer)
Time Period(s): 18th century; 19th century
Locale(s): Massachusetts, American Colonies; England; France

Summary: This historical romance follows the adventure of a New Englander, Israel Potter, who joins the Revolution and participates in the Battle of Bunker Hill. Captured by the British, Potter is taken to England where he escapes and serves as a secret messenger to Benjamin Franklin in France.

Potter is befriended by John Paul Jones and is on hand for the battle between the *Bonhomme Richard* and the *Serapis*. After 45 years of exile, he returns to America vainly seeking a pension and dies in poverty.

Historical Accuracy: The novel is largely based on an anonymous memoir, *Life and Remarkable Adventure of Israel Potter* (1824), which purports to be truthful.

AUBREY MENEN (1912-1989)

Born in London of Indian and Irish parents, Menen attended University College, London, where H.G. Wells encouraged him to become a writer. He worked as the drama critic for *The Bookman* and was a script editor for Indian government films during World War II. His study, *The Prevalence of Witches*, about the difference between tribal and British law was a popular success.

4335 *Fonthill*

Date of Publication: 1974
Subject(s): Literary Life; Regency Period
Historical character(s): William Beckford, Writer
Time Period(s): 1820s (1822)
Locale(s): England

Summary: The novel is inspired by the notorious Regency writer William Beckford whose gothic fantasy, *Vathek*, shocked Britain. Beckford constructs the grandiose Fonthill Abbey as the proper setting for his unusual lifestlye. The novel depicts Beckford not as a immoral satyr but as a charming innocent who refuses to grow up.

Historical Accuracy: The factual basis of the story is strong, but some interpretation is also evident.

CHARLES MERCER (1917-1988)

Canadian journalist, editor, and author, Mercer was born in Ontario, and graduated from Brown University. He worked for 13 years as an editor of young adult books for G.P. Putnam's Sons, and is the author of 17 novels, including *The Rachel Code* about an American missionary in Africa, which sold more than 3 million copies and was translated into 14 foreign languages. He also wrote many nonfiction books and was a feature writer and TV commentator for the Associate Press.

4336 *Enough Good Men*

Date of Publication: 1960
Subject(s): American Revolution; American Colonies
Fictional character(s): Micah Heath, Military Personnel (soldier); Alex March, Lawyer; Philly Twillow, Servant
Historical character(s): Anthony Wayne, Military Personnel (general); Charles Lee, Military Personnel (general)
Time Period(s): 1770s
Locale(s): Philadelphia, Pennsylvania

Summary: Action around Philadelphia during the American Revolution is presented through the experiences of Alex March, a lawyer and patriot, and Micah Heath, a soldier in the

Continental Army. The book is effective in creating a sense of the political currents that divided America as the war forced loyalties into the open.

Historical Accuracy: The basic framework of the story is historical and convincingly described.

DMITRI MEREZHKOVSKI (1865-1941)

A Russian novelist and critic, Merezhkovski's studies of Leo Tolstoy and Fyodor Dostoevsky inspired his theory of the antithesis between the spirit and the flesh. His historical novels embody this theory, and he founded the Religious-Philosophic Society to promote it. Twice exiled, he left Russia permanently in 1918 in opposition to the Bolsheviks.

4337 *Akhnaton, King of Egypt*

Date of Publication: 1927
Subject(s): Ancient Egypt; Pharaohs; Religious Conflict
Historical character(s): Akhenaton, Ruler (Pharaoh of Egypt); Nefertiti, Royalty (queen consort of Akhnaton)
Time Period(s): 12th century B.C.
Locale(s): Egypt

Summary: Court life during the reign of Egyptian Pharaoh Akhnaton and his sister-wife Nefertiti is dramatized. The religious conflict that marked Akhnaton's reign serves to expose the spiritual emptiness of the pagan world that will be filled only by the coming of Christianity.

Historical Accuracy: The novel is dominated by its theme and turns the characters into little more than abstractions. The story is unrealiable as a careful documentation of the period and its history.

4338 *The Death of the Gods*

Date of Publication: 1896
Subject(s): Roman Empire; Christianity
Historical character(s): Constantius II, Ruler (Roman emperor); Julian the Apostate, Ruler (Roman emperor)
Time Period(s): 4th century
Locale(s): Rome, Roman Empire; Constantinople, Byzantine Empire; Asia Minor

Summary: Merezhkovski's thesis is that European civilization is a result of combining classical paganism and Christianity. This combination is illustrated in the life and career of Julian the Apostate, who as Roman emperor in the fourth century attempts to halt the spread of Christianity and revive paganism.

Historical Accuracy: The novel is a masterpiece of historical re-creation. It is panoramic in its effects and totally convincing in its details.

4339 *The Romance of Leonardo Da Vinci*

Date of Publication: 1902
Subject(s): Renaissance; Biography, Fictionalized; Artistic Life

Historical character(s): Leonardo da Vinci, Artist, Inventor; Cesare Borgia, Nobleman, Political Figure; Lisa Gherardini Giocondo, Model
Time Period(s): 15th century; 16th century (1494-1519)
Locale(s): Milan, Italy; Florence, Italy; France

Summary: In this fictionalized biography of the great Renaissance painter and thinker Leonardo Da Vinci, the author presents a full and vivid portrait of the Italian Renaissance. In settings as diverse as the royal courts, the Vatican, artists' studios, and alchemists' workshops a depiction of an entire culture emerges. Leonardo is shown as a great genius buffeted by the religious and political struggles of the time.

Historical Accuracy: This is one of the finest fictionalized biographies ever written. The novel totally captures both its famous subject and his era.

CHARLES MERGENDAHL (1919-1959)

Mergendahl was born in Lynn, Massachusetts. His novels include *Bramble Bush* and *The Next Best Thing*.

4340 *The Drums of April*

Date of Publication: 1963
Subject(s): American Revolution; Espionage; Battle of Bunker Hill
Fictional character(s): Tom Willetti, Spy; Anthony Quinn, Military Personnel, Spy; Jenny Martin, Young Woman
Historical character(s): Paul Revere, Patriot; George Washington, Military Personnel (army commander); Samuel Adams, Patriot; John Burgoyne, Military Personnel (British general)
Time Period(s): 1770s
Locale(s): Boston, Massachusetts; London, England

Summary: Tom Willetti arrives with Jenny Martin in colonial Boston at the outbreak of the American Revolution as a spy for the Crown. Jenny is held by the British to ensure that Tom carries out his assignment, and Tom is forced to play the role of double agent. The major events of the opening days of the Revolution—Paul Revere's ride, the battles of Lexington and Concord, and the charge at Bunker Hill—are all depicted.

Historical Accuracy: The historical events shown are captured effectively.

LOUISE MERIWETHER (1923-)

An American author, Meriwether graduated from NYU and UCLA. She has worked as a legal secretary, a newspaper reporter, and story analyst for Universal Studios. Her book *Daddy Was a Numbers Runner* describes the social death of a Harlem family. She also is the author of biographies of Daniel Hale Williams, an African-American heart surgeon, and of Rosa Parks.

4341 *Fragments of the Ark*

Date of Publication: 1994
Subject(s): Slavery; Civil War—U.S.; Sea Story
Fictional character(s): Peter Mango, Slave, Sailor; Rain Mango, Spouse

Time Period(s): 1860s
Locale(s): Sea Islands, South Carolina; Charleston, South Carolina

Summary: Set during the siege of Charlestown, South Carolina, during the Civil War, the novel describes how Peter Mango, slave and ship pilot, steals a gunboat and runs the gauntlet of Confederate forts to deliver it and its cargo of fugitive slaves to the Union Navy and freedom. Mango rises to the rank of captain in the Union Navy and must confront his former master on behalf of his family still kept behind enemy lines.

Historical Accuracy: The historical research that underpins the story was massive and is faithfully recorded.

ROBERT MERLE (1908-)

Born in Algeria, Merle is a novelist, dramatist, critic and biographer who lives in France. He has worked as a teacher of English and American literature at the Sorbonne. The author of several best-selling French novels, Merle is the winner of the Prix Goncourt in 1949 for *Weekend at Zuydcoate*, the story of the Dunkirk debacle from the French point of view.

4342 *Vittoria*

Date of Publication: 1990
Subject(s): Renaissance
Historical character(s): Vittoria Peretti, Noblewoman; Paolo Orsini, Nobleman (prince)
Time Period(s): 16th century
Locale(s): Italy

Summary: The novel offers several testimonial accounts of the celebrated Italian Renaissance beauty, Vittoria Peretti, who marries a cardinal's adopted son and then falls passionately in love with Prince Orsini, a passion which creates a tangle of intrigue, betrayals, and assassinations. Through her experience a vivid portrait of the age is created.

Historical Accuracy: The author attempts a far more sympathetic portrait of the celebrated beauty than in other versions.

REUBEN R. MERLISS (1915-)

An American born in New York City, Merliss graduated from Wayne State University and is a physician specializing in internal medicine. He is in private practice in California and a professor of medicine.

4343 *The Year of the Death*

Date of Publication: 1965
Subject(s): Medical Profession; Plague; Middle Ages
Fictional character(s): Noe Abrois, Doctor
Time Period(s): 14th century (1348)
Locale(s): Avignon, France; Granada, Spain; Garonne, France

Summary: The year is 1348 when the plague sweeps through Europe emptying entire cities. Noe Abrois is a young assistant to a wealthy physician who, when the plague strikes and his master flees, stays to try to treat the mysterious disease. His search for medical answers takes him to the royal court at Avignon and to the Moorish capital at Granada before he is captured by the Inquisition.

Historical Accuracy: The details of medieval life during the plague are faithfully captured.

EMMA MERRITT

4344 *Masque of Jade*

Date of Publication: 1990
Subject(s): War of 1812; Romance
Fictional character(s): Laura Talbot-Harrow, Debutante, Gentlewoman; Clay Sutherland, Gambler
Time Period(s): 1810s (1813)
Locale(s): Louisiana

Summary: The background of this romantic novel is the War of 1812 as Laura Talbot-Harrow defies society by falling in love with gambler Clay Sutherland. Their romance is marked by duels and treachery.

Historical Accuracy: The novel is more costume drama than a full historical rendering of the period.

BARBARA METZGER (1944-)

An American born in New York, Metzger graduated from Connecticut College. She has worked as a greeting card verse writer, an editor, and proofreader. She is also a craftsperson specializing in animal paintings and ceramics.

4345 *The Earl and the Heiress*

Date of Publication: 1982
Subject(s): Regency Romance
Fictional character(s): Noelle Armstrong, Heiress; Justin Wrenthe, Nobleman
Time Period(s): 19th century (Regency period)
Locale(s): London, England

Summary: When Noelle Armstrong unexpectedly inherits a London house and modest inheritance, she, her younger sister, and brother are able to enjoy the London season. To make a connection with the ton, Noelle advertises to sell five white Maltese puppies. The ad attracts Justin, Earl of Wrenthe, who soon finds himself captivated by the resourceful Noelle.

Historical Accuracy: The novel features some convincing period elements amidst the romance.

4346 *My Lady Innkeeper*

Date of Publication: 1985
Subject(s): Regency Romance
Fictional character(s): Lyndell Markham, Heiress
Time Period(s): 1800s
Locale(s): England

Summary: Society heiress Lyndell Markham gets mixed up in intrigue including smuggling and the passing of military secrets to the French. She poses as an innkeeper to catch the criminal and finds herself over her head in a dangerous adventure.

Historical Accuracy: The story strains credibility, but it is filled with believable period details.

4347 *Rake's Ransom*

Date of Publication: 1986
Subject(s): Regency Romance
Fictional character(s): Jacelyn Trevaine, Young Woman; Leigh Claibourne, Nobleman, Rake
Time Period(s): 1810s
Locale(s): Cambridgeshire, England; London, England

Summary: This Regency romance features a spirited country girl, Jacelyn Trevaine, who finds herself entangled with an earl and a reputed rake, war hero Leigh Claibourne. A scandal brings them together, but Jacelyn wants to earn the Earl's love, while he finds himself extricating her from a series of scrapes.

Historical Accuracy: This comedy of manners and mistakes is supported by some credible period elements.

NICHOLAS MEYER (1945-)

A highly successful American screenwriter and director, Meyer directed "The Day After," the most watched made-for TV movie ever produced. He also co-wrote the second and sixth "Star Trek" movies. Meyer credits his father-in-law, a psychologist, for drawing the connection between detection and psychology.

4348 *The Canary Trainer*

Date of Publication: 1993
Subject(s): Mystery; Musical Life
Fictional character(s): Sherlock Holmes, Detective—Private; John H. Watson, Doctor; Irene Adler, Singer
Time Period(s): 1890s (1891)
Locale(s): Paris, France

Summary: In this Sherlock Holmes adventure, the great detective is employed as a pit musician at the Paris Opera House. He is commissioned to protect a young soprano whose haunting voice obsesses the creature known as the "Opera Ghost," immortalized as the Phantom of the Opera, with whom Holmes must contend.

Historical Accuracy: The novel gets great mileage out of the conjunctions of two such familiar fictional figures, echoing the originals with skill.

4349 *The Seven-Per-Cent Solution*

Date of Publication: 1974
Subject(s): Mystery; Victorian Period
Fictional character(s): Sherlock Holmes, Detective—Private; John H. Watson, Doctor
Historical character(s): Sigmund Freud, Doctor
Time Period(s): 1890s (1890-1891)
Locale(s): London, England; Vienna, Austria

Summary: In this delightful pastiche of Sherlock Holmes, the master detective joins forces with Sigmund Freud to uncover a diabolical conspiracy and to kick his cocaine addiction.

Historical Accuracy: The novel echoes with skill the Doyle original and sets the scene in a believably created period Vienna.

4350 *The West End Horror*

Date of Publication: 1976
Subject(s): Mystery; Victorian Period; Theatrical Life
Fictional character(s): Sherlock Holmes, Detective—Private; John H. Watson, Doctor
Historical character(s): George Bernard Shaw, Writer; Ellen Terry, Actress; Bram Stoker, Writer; Henry Irving, Actor; Oscar Wilde, Writer; Frank Harris, Writer
Time Period(s): 1890s (1895)
Locale(s): London, England

Summary: In 1895 in London's theatrical West End the bizarre murder of a theatre critic is the beginning of an immensely complex mystery that involves some of the most fashionable and creative luminaries of the time, including Oscar Wilde and George Bernard Shaw. Sherlock Holmes is convinced that a clever maniac is on the loose and must be stopped.

Historical Accuracy: This pastiche of Holmes and history is fun and convincing.

MAAN MEYERS
(PSEUD. OF ANNETTE MEYERS; MARTIN MEYERS)

This husband and wife team of mystery writers has also produced mysteries separately. Annette Meyers has written the Smith and Wetzon series, and Martin Meyers, the Patrick Hardy series.

4351 *The Dutchman*

Date of Publication: 1992
Subject(s): Mystery; American Colonies
Fictional character(s): Pieter Tonneman, Lawman (sheriff), Widow(er); Racquel Mendoza, Spy
Historical character(s): Peter Stuyvesant, Government Official (colonial leader)
Time Period(s): 17th century (1664)
Locale(s): New Amsterdam, American Colonies

Summary: It is 1664 in New Amsterdam and the British are poised to invade. Pieter Tonneman, the Dutch Schout or sheriff, is confronted with a series of strange events: the apparent suicide of a popular tavern owner, a mysterious fire, and a moving corpse. The exotic Jewish beauty Racquel Mendoza may be part of a spy ring responsible for a series of murders.

Historical Accuracy: The details of colonial life are painstakingly created and authentic. However, the authors have taken some liberties for the sake of their story.

4352 *The Dutchman's Dilemma*

Date of Publication: 1995
Subject(s): Mystery; American Colonies; Jews
Fictional character(s): Pieter Tonneman, Businessman; Racquel Mendoza, Spouse (of Pieter)
Time Period(s): 17th century (1675)

Locale(s): New York, New York, American Colonies

Summary: The time is 1675, eleven years after Pieter Tonneman, the former sheriff of Dutch Manhattan, brought a brutal murderer to justice and married the Jewish widow Racquel Mendoza in *The High Constable*. Now a successful businessman in British New York, Tonneman is brought back to his past profession when the governor's prized stallion is ritualistically killed, and the city suspects devil worship and a conspiracy among the city's Jewish population. Tonneman's wife is a suspect, but she might also become the next victim.

Historical Accuracy: The novel, like the others in the series, is remarkably precise in its rendering of 17th-century New York in its look and feel.

4353 *The High Constable*

Date of Publication: 1994
Subject(s): Mystery
Fictional character(s): John Tonneman, Doctor, Government Official (coroner); Marianna Tonneman, Spouse; Jake Hays, Police Officer (high constable)
Historical character(s): Aaron Burr, Political Figure
Time Period(s): 1800s (1808)
Locale(s): New York, New York

Summary: It is 1808 in New York City, and John Tonneman, the hero of the authors' *The Kingsbridge Plot*, is now past sixty and ready to enjoy the pleasures of retirement with his family. However, all is not well domestically, and when a lady is discovered in the Collect, the pond where the city gets its drinking water, Tonneman joins his friend Jake Hays in tracking down the killer. The solution to the mystery involves solving two murders, thirty years apart.

Historical Accuracy: The period details of life in New York at the time are exceptionally well-detailed and exact, though some alterations are present. Aaron Burr was certainly not in New York in 1808.

4354 *The House on Mulberry Street*

Date of Publication: 1996
Subject(s): Mystery; Jews
Fictional character(s): John "Dutch" Tonneman, Detective—Police; Esther Breslain, Immigrant, Photographer
Historical character(s): Lillian Russell, Actress
Time Period(s): 1890s (1895)
Locale(s): New York, New York

Summary: Young police detective John "Dutch" Tonneman finds himself in the middle of city reformers, crooks, and corrupt politician as a suspicious waterfront blaze and a union rally threaten to erupt in violence. Meanwhile a Polish Jewish immigrant working as a photographer possesses the key to a deeper Manhattan mystery.

Historical Accuracy: The novel features authentic period details and an accurate historical background.

4355 *The Kingsbridge Plot*

Date of Publication: 1993
Subject(s): Mystery; American Colonies; American Revolution

Fictional character(s): John Tonneman, Doctor, Government Official (coroner); Mariana Mendoza, Young Woman
Historical character(s): George Washington, Military Personnel (army commander); David Bushnell, Engineer, Inventor
Time Period(s): 1770s (1775-1776)
Locale(s): New York, New York

Summary: One hundred years after the action of *The Dutchman*, Sheriff Pieter Tonneman's descendants are thriving in colonial New York, which teeters on the verge of revolution. John Tonneman, recently returned from his medical studies, investigates the murders of women from the Sephardic Jewish community and stumbles upon a plot to assassinate General Washington.

Historical Accuracy: The plot to kill Washington is factual. The scene is exactly set with some slight speculation and conjectures.

MANNY MEYERS

4356 *The Last Mystery of Edgar Allan Poe*

Date of Publication: 1978
Subject(s): Mystery; Literary Life
Fictional character(s): Hollis Beckwith, Detective—Police
Historical character(s): Edgar Allan Poe, Writer
Time Period(s): 1840s (1846)
Locale(s): New York, New York

Summary: In 1846 Hollis Beckwith, New York's Superintendent of Police, recruits a destitute Edgar Allan Poe, the creator of the modern mystery story, to assist in the search for a brutal killer. Two young society heiresses have been found slain on New York's waterfront with the number 13 scrawled above their heads in their own blood. The search for the killer takes the pair across the landscape of New York to the uncovering of an international plot that is both bizarre and stunning.

Historical Accuracy: The evocation of period New York is convincing.

MARY MIAN

4357 *Young Men See Visions*

Date of Publication: 1958
Subject(s): Social Chronicle
Fictional character(s): Mark Deming, Religious (minister); Mary Chatfield, Gentlewoman
Time Period(s): 1900s
Locale(s): Wendover, Massachusetts

Summary: Social life in a turn-of-the-century New England town is the novel's subject. Mark Deming, a young Congregational minister, comes to the complacent and prosperous community of Wendover, Massachusetts where he becomes a catalyst for exposing the hypocrisy of the self-satisfied townsfolk.

Historical Accuracy: The evocation of New England life during the period is convincing.

MICHAEL, PRINCE OF GREECE (1939-)

4358 *Sultana*

Date of Publication: 1983
Subject(s): Ottoman Empire; Pirates
Historical character(s): Aimee Dubuc, Royalty (sultana); Selim III, Ruler (Ottoman sultan); Mahmud II, Ruler (Sultan); Josephine, Royalty (Empress Consort of Napoleon)
Time Period(s): 18th century; 19th century (1781-1816)
Locale(s): Martinique; Constantinople, Ottoman Empire

Summary: Writing her memoirs at the approach of her death, Aimee Dubuc recounts her extraordinary life beginning with her childhood on Martinique where she is raised with her cousin Josephine who will later become Napoleon's Empress. Aimee is kidnapped by pirates and sent to the Sultan's harem as a gift. There she becomes the mistress of the old Sultan; the beloved of his heir, Selim III; and the mother of Mahmud II. Her story depicts life in the seraglio and court politics in the Ottoman Empire.

Historical Accuracy: The basic framework of the story is factual, with some obvious embroidery for purposes of the narrative.

BARBARA MICHAELS
(PSEUD. OF BARBARA MERTZ, 1927-)

Barbara Michaels is a pseudonym of American writer Barbara Mertz. Born in Canton, Illinois, Mertz received a Ph.D. from the University of Chicago Oriental Institute in 1952. An Egyptologist by training, she has written several nonfiction books on ancient Egypt, including *Temples, Tombs, and Hieroglyphs* and *Red Land, Black Land*. She also writes mystery novels under the name Elizabeth Peters.

4359 *Greygallows*

Date of Publication: 1972
Subject(s): Romance; Victorian Period
Fictional character(s): Lucy Cartwright, Orphan, Heiress; Jonathan Scott, Lawyer; Edward Clare, Nobleman (baron)
Time Period(s): 1840s
Locale(s): London, England; Yorkshire, England

Summary: Lucy Cartwright is a young heiress forced into a fashionable marriage with Baron Clare. There is a secret surrounding Clare which Lucy discovers at his estate in Yorkshire.

Historical Accuracy: Gothic suspense and threat are at the center of this story which only lightly relies on a full-scale historical backdrop.

4360 *Patriot's Dream*

Date of Publication: 1976
Subject(s): Romance; Time Travel; American Revolution
Fictional character(s): Janice Wilde, Young Woman; Jonathan Muller, Young Man
Time Period(s): 1970s (1976); 1770s (1775-1776)
Locale(s): Williamsburg, Virginia

Summary: The novel shuttles between Williamsburg in the 1970s and Colonial Willamsburg in the 1770s. Janice Wilde, who spends the summer with her elderly aunt and uncle, begins to dreams of the past. Her dreams gain strength and life causing her to fall in love with Jonathan Muller who lived two hundred years before.

Historical Accuracy: The evocation of colonial Williamsburg is convincing.

4361   *Wings of the Falcon*

Date of Publication: 1977
Subject(s): Risorgimento; Romance
Fictional character(s): Francesca Fairbourn, Orphan; Andrea Tarconti, Nobleman, Twin; Stefano Tarconti, Nobleman, Twin
Time Period(s): 1860s
Locale(s): Italy; England

Summary: Set in the Italy of the 1860s disrupted by Garibaldi and his Red Shirts, the novel tells the story of the orphan Francesca who accepts shelter from her mother's noble Italian family. She is immediately plunged into romantic adventures.

Historical Accuracy: Although the characters are fictional, some of the more improbable events are based on actual facts. The historical background of Italy in 1860 is accurate.

4362   *The Wizard's Daughter*

Date of Publication: 1980
Subject(s): Suspense; Victorian Period; Spiritualism
Fictional character(s): Marianne Ransom, Singer; Roger Carlton, Gentleman; David J. Holmes, Psychic (spiritualist)
Time Period(s): 1880s
Locale(s): England

Summary: Young Marianne Ransom goes from singing in a fashionable Victorian supper club to become the medium of her supposed "father," renowned spiritualist David Holmes. Gothic suspense awaits Marianne in the atmospheric sanctuary of the Duchess of Devenbrook.

Historical Accuracy: Gothic thrills predominate over a full historical portrait.

KASEY MICHAELS
(PSEUD. OF KATHRYN SEIDICK, 1943-)

An American born in Pennsylvania, Michaels has worked as a bank teller and is the author of romance novels mainly based in the Regency period. Her aspiration is to write a Regency with a title from every letter of the alphabet. She is also the author of *Or You Can Let Go* about a family in crisis when a child suddenly loses the use of his kidneys.

4363   *Bride of the Unicorn*

Date of Publication: 1993
Subject(s): Regency Romance; Espionage
Fictional character(s): Caroline Monday, Heiress—Lost, Noblewoman; Morgan Blakely, Nobleman (Marquess of Clayton), Spy
Time Period(s): 1810s

Locale(s): England; France

Summary: In this romantic Pygmalion story with a Regency background, Morgan Blakely discovers lost heiress Caroline Monday and turns her into a lady. Initially he means to use her to revenge himself on her cousin, but his plans go awry when he falls in love with her. Dark secrets form everyone's pasts threaten to destroy Morgan and Caroline's happiness.

Historical Accuracy: The plot contrivances are fanciful, but the period is evoked with some care and conviction.

JAMES A. MICHENER (1907-)

An American novelist born in New York City, Michener grew up in Pennsylvania and graduated from Swarthmore College. Michener has worked as a leading man in a traveling show, a sports columnist, and an editor. He won a Pulitzer Prize in 1948 for *Tales of the South Pacific*, the beginning of a remarkable career in which he has been called the "literary world's Cecil B. DeMille" for his immense epic tomes that feature extensive research. A solid craftsman, Michener has been called a "historical compacter" for his ability to present a full context for his varied studies of past life and culture.

4364   *Alaska*

Date of Publication: 1988
Subject(s): Prehistory; Exploration; Gold Rush—Klondike
Fictional character(s): Trofim Zhdanko, Government Official; Sheldon Jackson, Religious (missionary); Raven Heart, Indian (Tlingit)
Historical character(s): Aleksandr Baranov, Government Official; Peter the Great, Ruler (Czar of Russia); Vitus Bering, Explorer; James Cook, Explorer, Military Personnel (naval officer); William Bligh, Military Personnel (naval officer); Jefferson Davis, Political Figure, Military Personnel (general)
Time Period(s): Multiple Time Periods
Locale(s): Alaska

Summary: The long and fascinating history of Alaska is chronicled from prehistory to the present, beginning with the crossing of the Bering Strait by huge exotic animals and later by native peoples. The story leaps forward to the 18th century and Alaska's domination by Russia until its sale to the U.S. and the exploitation of the state's gold and oil wealth.

Historical Accuracy: The novel blends the fictional and the historical, and the author helpfully details which is which.

4365   *Caribbean*

Date of Publication: 1989
Subject(s): Pirates; Independence—Haiti; Slavery
Historical character(s): Christopher Columbus, Explorer; Sir Francis Drake, Sea Captain; Henry Morgan, Pirate; Ferdinand V, Ruler (King of Spain); Horatio Nelson, Military Personnel (admiral); Pierre Dominique Toussaint l'Ouverture, Revolutionary; Edward John Eyre, Government Official; Alfred, Lord Tennyson, Writer; Thomas Carlyle, Writer; John Stuart Mill, Writer, Philosopher; Fidel Castro, Political Figure
Time Period(s): Multiple Time Periods

Locale(s): Caribbean; Haiti; Barbados

Summary: The colorful history of the Caribbean islands is portrayed from early tribal conflicts to the arrival of Columbus and the establishing of Spanish control and conflict with the English. The novel details as well the age of the buccaneers, the slave revolt in Haiti, as well as later developments as modern nations rise.

Historical Accuracy: The author helpfully untangles the blending of the historical and the factual.

4366 *Centennial*

Date of Publication: 1974

Subject(s): American West; Settlement of the American Frontier; Indians

Fictional character(s): Lame Beaver, Indian (Arapaho); Pasquinel, Trapper, Trader; Levi Zendt, Settler; Oliver Secombe, Rancher; Paul Garrett, Rancher

Time Period(s): Multiple Time Periods

Locale(s): Colorado

Summary: The history of the North American West, especially Colorado, is examined from prehistory to the present. The first main character in a story with over 70 major characters is Arapaho Lame Beaver whose tribe has never seen a white man until they encounter French trader-trapper Pasquinal. He marries Lame Beaver's daughter and their half-breed sons harass the settlers moving west on the Oregon Trail. The story of Colorado's settlement is traced to the modern danger of unrestricted development.

Historical Accuracy: Although the characters and scenes are imaginary, certain background incidents and characters are real.

4367 *Chesapeake*

Date of Publication: 1978

Subject(s): American Colonies; Family Saga; American Revolution

Fictional character(s): Edmund Steed, Settler; Edward Paxmore, Landowner; Cudjo, Slave

Time Period(s): Multiple Time Periods

Locale(s): Chesapeake Bay, United States

Summary: The novel attempts to capture the 400-year history of the Chesapeake Bay and the Eastern Shore. Beginning with Edmund Steed who flees England in 1611 to join Captain Smith in the settlement of Viginia, the story continues with Edward Paxmore and his family in scenes from the American Revolution and the struggle over slavery.

Historical Accuracy: The period elements are based on actual events and circumstances.

4368 *The Covenant*

Date of Publication: 1980

Subject(s): Frontier—Africa; Tribal Life—African; Boer War

Fictional character(s): Willem Van Doorn, Settler; Nicholas Saltwood, Settler

Historical character(s): Shaka, Chieftain (Zulu); Cecil John Rhodes, Businessman; Paul Kruger, Political Figure; Redvers Henry Buller, Military Personnel (British general)

Time Period(s): Multiple Time Periods

Locale(s): South Africa; Zimbabwe

Summary: The tortuous history of South Africa is chronicled from the first arrival of European immigrants in the 15th century. The Dutch and English settlement and conflict with the native people are dramatized in scenes that include the epic Great Trek and the Boer War, as well as the creation of the modern nation of South Africa and its rigid system of apartheid.

Historical Accuracy: The facts of South African history are established as a clear framework for the fictional story.

4369 *The Eagle and the Raven*

Date of Publication: 1990

Subject(s): Texas Revolution; American West; Battle of San Jacinto

Historical character(s): Antonio Lopez de Santa Anna, Military Personnel (general); Sam Houston, Political Figure, Military Personnel

Time Period(s): 1830s (1836)

Locale(s): Texas; Mexico

Summary: The story of the Texas Revolution that wrested Texas away from Mexican control and created a new nation is told in the contrasting stories of Sam Houston and Antonio Santa Ana. Both are shown as heroic, larger than life, but flawed individuals. The novel's climax is the Battle of San Jacinto. The Mexican defeat ends Santa Ana's career; Houston goes on to become the first president of the Texas Republic.

Historical Accuracy: The novel is careful to stay close to the historical events and circumstances.

4370 *Hawaii*

Date of Publication: 1959

Subject(s): Tribal Life—South Pacific; Family Saga

Fictional character(s): Abner Hale, Settler; John Whipple, Religious (missionary); Rafer Hoxworth, Sea Captain, Businessman

Historical character(s): Tamatoa VI, Ruler (exiled king of Bora Bora); Kanakoa, Ruler (Queen of Hawaii)

Time Period(s): Multiple Time Periods

Locale(s): Hawaii; Bora Bora, French Polynesia; China

Summary: Michener chronicles the history of Hawaii in six parts: the formation of the volcanic islands; the arrival to the islands of South Sea Islanders from Bora Bora; the arrival of new England missionaries, sailors, and commercial interests; the impact of imported Chinese; the cultural and economic interests of the Japanese immigrants; and the status of the islands in modern times. A huge cast is created to illustrate the mixture of four different racial strains—Hawaiiian, Caucasian, Chinese, and Japanese—that defines the Hawaiian character.

Historical Accuracy: The novel's scale and perspective is so wide that it encompasses a compelling history of a place over vast stretches of time. The level of research is evident.

4371 *Journey*

Date of Publication: 1989
Subject(s): Gold Rush—Klondike
Fictional character(s): Lord Evelyn Luton, Nobleman; Harry Carpenter, Prospector (gold); Philip Henslow, Prospector (gold); Tim Fogarty, Servant
Time Period(s): 1890s (1897)
Locale(s): Klondike River Valley, Yukon Territory, Canada

Summary: In 1899 as gold fever grips men from around the world, Lord Evelyn Luton plans a perilous journey to Canada's gold field. He insists that his group travel north from Edmonton on the MacKenzie River on British soil rather than the easier route through American Territory. The novel depicts their journey and the consequence of blind obedience to rigidly-held values.

Historical Accuracy: The novel is accurate in its re-creation of wilderness life of the period.

4372 *Mexico*

Date of Publication: 1992
Subject(s): Aztec Empire; Mexican Revolution; Spanish Colonies
Fictional character(s): Norman Clay, Journalist; Antonio Palafox, Military Personnel (conquistador); Jubal Clay, Military Personnel (Confederate soldier), Expatriate
Time Period(s): Multiple Time Periods
Locale(s): Mexico; Spain; United States

Summary: This massive panoramic history of Mexico's past is seen through the experiences and research of journalist Norman Clay who comes to Mexico to cover the bullfights but begins to uncover the story of his Mexican ancestors who include an Aztec queen, a conquistador priest, and a Confederate expatriate. Through their collective stories, the turbulent history of Mexico is revealed.

Historical Accuracy: The novel interweaves a fictional story with a framework of actual events and an authentic atmosphere of the past.

4373 *Poland*

Date of Publication: 1983
Subject(s): Middle Ages; Independence—Poland; World War II
Fictional character(s): Count Cyprjan Lubonski, Nobleman; Szymon Bukowski, Government Official; Janko Buk, Farmer
Historical character(s): Genghis Khan, Warrior, Leader (Mongol); Batu Khan, Warrior; Jan II Kazimir, Ruler (King of Poland); Jan III Sobieski, Ruler (King of Poland); Muhammad IV, Ruler (Sultan); Franz Josef I, Ruler (Austro-Hungarian Emperor); Ignacy Paderewski, Political Figure
Time Period(s): Multiple Time Periods
Locale(s): Poland

Summary: Framed by conflict between Polish farmers and the Communists in the 1980s, the novel covers important periods of Polish history from the 13th century to the present. The history of Poland is a long story of invaders—Tartars, Germans, Swedes, Turks, and Russians—and the struggle to preserve Polish independence and self-rule. The novel fol-lows three families: the noble Lubonskis, the Bukowskis from the gentry class, and the peasant Buks.

Historical Accuracy: The novel blends the fictional and the historical which the author untangles for the reader.

4374 *The Source*

Date of Publication: 1965
Subject(s): Ancient Israel; Roman Empire; Jews
Historical character(s): Akiba ben Joseph, Religious (rabbi); David, Ruler (King of Israel), Biblical Figure; Herod the Great, Ruler (King of Israel); Vespasian, Ruler (Roman emperor); Flavius Josephus, Historian; Moses Maimonides, Philosopher
Time Period(s): Multiple Time Periods
Locale(s): Makor, Israel

Summary: Spanning 12,000 years, the novel tells the stories of 15 different settlements that occupied the site of an ancient spring in Israel. Using archaeological evidence as the starting point, the novel vividly recreates life and customs of various civilizations, including Canaanite, Hebrew, Egyptian, Babylonian, Assyrian, Persian, Greek, Roman, Arab, Crusader, Mameluk, Turkish, and British, down to the creation of the modern state of Israel.

Historical Accuracy: Makor and its inhabitants are fictional although the story is solidly based on historical research and facts established by the exploration of many actual sites in Israel.

4375 *Texas*

Date of Publication: 1985
Subject(s): American West; Texas Revolution; Civil War—U.S.
Fictional character(s): Jubal Quimper, Settler; Otto Macnab, Lawman (Texas Ranger)
Historical character(s): Alvar Nunez Cabeza de Vaca, Explorer; Francisco Vasquez de Coronado, Explorer; Stephen F. Austin, Political Figure; Sam Houston, Political Figure; Antonio Lopez de Santa Anna, Military Personnel (general); Davy Crockett, Frontiersman; Jim Bowie, Frontiersman
Time Period(s): Multiple Time Periods
Locale(s): Texas

Summary: This massive history of Texas begins in the early 1500s when the first Spanish explorers arrive. The tumultuous life of the state including independence from Mexico, the subduing of the Indians, and the Civil War is illustrated through the experiences of a number of immigrant families whose lives are interweaved with actual historical figures and events.

Historical Accuracy: The author helpfully unravels the historical and the fictional.

EARL SCHENCK MIERS (1910-1972)

An American editor and author, Miers was born with cerebral palsy and learned to type because he could not hold a pencil. He produced some 60 books, both fiction and non-fiction, covering such diverse topics as American history and sports.

4376 *Valley in Arms: A Novel of the Settlement of Connecticut*

Date of Publication: 1943

Subject(s): American Colonies; Indians; Settlement of the American Frontier

Fictional character(s): Joel Ames, Settler; Gertje Borst, Settler

Time Period(s): 17th century (1636-1638)

Locale(s): Wetherfield, Connecticut, American Colonies; Saybrook, Connecticut, American Colonies; Boston, Massachusetts, American Colonies

Summary: In 1686, Joel Ames, Gertje Borst, and others break away from the trading post settlements in Boston and Salem to seek homes in the wilderness of the Connecticut Valley. The novel describes the first settlers who push west, enduring Indian attacks and the challenge of the frontier.

Historical Accuracy: Although specific incidents have been invented, the story adheres faithfully to actual events.

GRAHAM MILES

4377 *Evil Mark*

Date of Publication: 1985

Subject(s): Victorian Period; Suspense; Crime and Criminals

Fictional character(s): Roger Benchly, Steward; Amelia Mortimer, Widow(er); William Southey, Gentleman

Time Period(s): 19th century (Victorian period)

Locale(s): London, England

Summary: Set in Victorian England, the novel is a suspenseful story involving a mysterious criminal known as the Dagger and the domestic intrigue of a county family, the Southeys, whose steward, Roger Benchley, rules the estate with an iron hand. He eventually marries the widow Amelia Mortimer whose son, William Southey, comes to realize that Benchley is not who he appears to be.

Historical Accuracy: The period elements in the story are convincing.

ROSALIND MILES

4378 *I, Elizabeth*

Date of Publication: 1994

Subject(s): Elizabethan Period; Royalty—England; Biography, Fictionalized

Historical character(s): Thomas Cranmer, Religious (Archbishop of Canterbury); Mary Tudor, Royalty (princess); Edward VI, Ruler (King of England); Elizabeth Tudor, Royalty (princess); Henry VIII, Ruler (King of England); Robert Cecil, Government Official; Robert Devereux, Nobleman (Earl of Essex); Mary, Queen of Scots, Ruler (Queen of Scotland); Sir Walter Raleigh, Courtier; Sir Francis Walsingham, Government Official

Time Period(s): 16th century; 17th century (1533-1601)

Locale(s): England

Summary: This is a fictional autobiography of Elizabeth I, detailing her exceptional life. Daughter of Anne Boleyn, Elizabeth is branded a bastard and leads a precarious life during the reigns of her half brother and half sister. When she becomes queen, she rules with a practical brilliance developed from the survival instincts she was forced to cultivate in childhood and avoids marriage which would challenged her absolute rule. Her incredible reign is seen through her interpretation of events and characters.

Historical Accuracy: Brilliantly detailed and accomplished in its grasp of the period, the author achieves an interesting as well as a solid history of Elizabeth's reign.

GEORGE MILLAR (1910-)

Scottish writer Millar is a graduate of Cambridge University. He has worked as an architect, newspaper reporter, Paris bureau chief, and war correspondent. During World War II, Millar's capture and daring escape as a prisoner of war and his experiences as a parchutist for the French Resistance served as material for *Waiting for the Night* and *Horned Pigeon*, considered two of the most exciting and intelligent books about World War II.

4379 *A Crossbowman's Story of the First Exploration of the Amazon*

Date of Publication: 1955

Subject(s): Exploration

Historical character(s): Francisco de Orellana, Explorer, Military Personnel (conquistador); Francisco de Isasaga, Explorer, Military Personnel (bowman); Gonzalo Pizarro, Explorer

Time Period(s): 16th century (1641)

Locale(s): Amazon River, South America

Summary: The novel chronicles the expedition of the first white men to descend the Amazon and accomplish the journey from the Pacific to the Atlantic across South America. Francesco de Orellana leads a small group that separates from Gonzalo Pizzaro's unsuccessful attempt to cross the continent in 1541. The story of Orellana's trek is described by his scrivener and crossbowman.

Historical Accuracy: The novel is backed up by impressive scholarship that establishes its authenticity.

CAROLINE MILLER (1903-)

Many of Miller's stories are set in the South, reflecting her childhood in Waycross, Georgia. As a high school teacher, she first began publishing to supplement her income. Called a historical realist, her novel *Lamb in His Bosom* won the Pulitzer Prize for Fiction in 1934.

4380 *Lamb in His Bosom*

Date of Publication: 1933

Subject(s): Antebellum South; Civil War—U.S.

Fictional character(s): Cean Carver, Settler; Lonzo Carver, Settler

Time Period(s): 19th century (1816-1860s)

Locale(s): Georgia

Summary: This tale of wilderness life in the back country of Georgia centers on the experiences of Cean Carver. As a bride she accompanies her husband to a cabin he has built in the wilds. Her story continues to the end of the Civil War.

Historical Accuracy: The novel captures the region and the period atmosphere with skill.

CISSIE MILLER

4381 *Tish*

Date of Publication: 1981
Subject(s): Regency Romance; Balloons
Fictional character(s): Lady Letitia Abbott, Noblewoman; Alec Ardenly, Nobleman (Earl of Ardenly)
Time Period(s): 1810s (1816)
Locale(s): Lake District, England

Summary: Lady Letitia Abbott, an avid balloonist, plans to fly across the English Channel to recoup the family fortune. She drops from the sky, literally, on top of the Earl of Ardenly. His pursuit forms the novel's airborne adventures.

Historical Accuracy: The period elements described are credible.

DALLAS MILLER

4382 *Passage West*

Date of Publication: 1979
Subject(s): Family Saga; Easter Rising; Labor Movement
Fictional character(s): Nora Shannon, Immigrant; Patrick Cassidy, Immigrant; Charles Molloy, Widow(er)
Time Period(s): 20th century
Locale(s): Dublin, Ireland; New York, New York; Hollywood, California

Summary: The lives of two Irish immigrants to America are chronicled in a story that spreads over a quarter of a century from the Easter Rising to New York's Irish Catholic society, the Labor movement, and the Communist scare of the 1930s. Nora Shannon rises to the top reaches of New York society, while Patrick Cassidy dedicates his life to the cause of labor.

Historical Accuracy: The novel interweaves the fictional and the factual. The actual events describes are believable.

HELEN TOPPING MILLER (1884-1960)

Born in Fenton, Michigan, Miller began writing for children's magazines when she was only ten. She published more than 400 short stories and 11 magazine serials in such publications as the *Saturday Evening Post*, *Good Housekeeping*, and *McCall's*. Most of her 50 novels focus on the Reconstruction period in the South.

4383 *After the Glory*

Date of Publication: 1958
Subject(s): Reconstruction Period

Fictional character(s): William Markland, Veteran (Union soldier); Jack Markland, Veteran (Confederate soldier); Sue Markland, Spouse (of Jack)
Time Period(s): 1860s (post Civil War)
Locale(s): Tennessee

Summary: The Reconstruction period in eastern Tennessee is depicted in this story of divided loyalties in the Markland family. William Markland, a Union veteran, returns home and attempts to help his family who sided with the defeated Confederacy. They face the challenge of rebuilding their lives in the harsh, postwar world.

Historical Accuracy: This is an effective drama with convincing and realistic period details.

4384 *Born Strangers*

Date of Publication: 1949
Subject(s): Settlement of the American Frontier
Fictional character(s): Fred Riggs, Settler
Time Period(s): 19th century
Locale(s): Michigan

Summary: Based on the author's own family history, the novel describes pioneer life in the Michigan wilderness from the 1840s through the Civil War. The novel follows the experiences of two families, the Wixoms and the Riggs, beginning when Fred Riggs travels into the territory with his pack on his back. He later establishes a thriving trading post with the Indians.

Historical Accuracy: Pioneer life is realistically and authentically described.

4385 *Christmas at Mount Vernon*

Date of Publication: 1957
Subject(s): American Revolution; Christmas
Historical character(s): George Washington, Military Personnel (army commander); Martha Washington, Spouse
Time Period(s): 1780s (1783)
Locale(s): Mount Vernon, Virginia

Summary: It is 1783, the first Christmas following the end of the American Revolution, and the novel shows George and Martha Washington's return to their Mount Vernon home.

Historical Accuracy: The domestic portrait of America's great hero is somewhat sentimental and simplified.

4386 *Christmas for Tad: A Story of Mary and Abraham Lincoln*

Date of Publication: 1956
Subject(s): Civil War—U.S.; Christmas
Historical character(s): Abraham Lincoln, Political Figure; Mary Todd Lincoln, Spouse; Tad Lincoln, Child
Time Period(s): 1860s (1863)
Locale(s): Washington, District of Columbia

Summary: The year is 1863, the worst period of the Civil War, and the novel depicts Christmas in the Lincoln White House. The president is shown enduring the pressures of his office, the war, and his wife's scolding.

Historical Accuracy: The portrait of the Lincolns is convincing, if somewhat simplified.

4387 *Christmas with Robert E. Lee*

Date of Publication: 1958
Subject(s): Civil War—U.S.; Christmas
Historical character(s): Robert E. Lee, Military Personnel (Confederate commander); Mary Custis Lee, Spouse
Time Period(s): 1860s (1865)
Locale(s): Lexington, Virginia

Summary: The novel describes the first Christmas following the end of the Civil War as the Lee family is reunited in Lexington, Virginia, where the General has accepted the post of president of Washington College. The emphasis is on portraying the Lee family as real people.

Historical Accuracy: Some of the incidents portrayed are based on facts.

4388 *Dark Sails*

Date of Publication: 1945
Subject(s): American Colonies; Battle of Bloody Marsh
Fictional character(s): Mary Delanay, Settler, Young Woman; Douglas Mackaill, Military Personnel (soldier)
Historical character(s): Charles Wesley, Religious (clergyman); James Edward Oglethorpe, Leader (colonial)
Time Period(s): 1730s; 1740s
Locale(s): St. Simons Island, Georgia, American Colonies

Summary: Life and times in 18th-century Georgia are depicted as James Ogelthorpe sends out settlers to an outpost colony on St. Simons Island where they must contend with the Spanish to the south. The action culminates in the pivotal Battle of Bloody Marsh that settled the fate of Spain in the Southeast.

Historical Accuracy: The action and atmosphere are believable, though the emphasis is on adventure over careful documentation of the past.

4389 *Her Christmas at the Hermitage: A Tale about Rachel and Andrew Jackson*

Date of Publication: 1955
Subject(s): Antebellum South; Politics; Christmas
Historical character(s): Andrew Jackson, Military Personnel (general), Political Figure; Rachel Jackson, Spouse
Time Period(s): 1820s (1823)
Locale(s): Tennessee

Summary: Christmas at the Jackson's new home, The Hermitage, is depicted as General Jackson has a rare domestic interlude. His beloved wife Rachel, with the scandal of her divorce hanging over the scene, convinces her husband that his niece and nephew's romance should be encouraged.

Historical Accuracy: The novel is bathed in a kind, nostalgic light, with some convincing period touches.

4390 *Mirage*

Date of Publication: 1949

Subject(s): Reconstruction Period; American West; Ranching
Fictional character(s): Dickson Channing, Veteran (Confederate soldier); Victoria Channing, Young Woman; Jeb Channing, Rancher
Time Period(s): 1860s (post-Civil War)
Locale(s): Texas

Summary: Following the Civil War the Channing family heads west into Texas from their devastated home in Alabama to rebuild their fortune. When patriarch Dickson Channing falls ill, it is young Jeb Channing who must master the cattle business and secure the family's future.

Historical Accuracy: The novel offers convincing details of the era and the locale.

4391 *No Tears for Christmas*

Date of Publication: 1954
Subject(s): Civil War—U.S.; Christmas
Fictional character(s): Teresa Hunter, Young Woman; David Hunter, Military Personnel (Confederate soldier)
Time Period(s): 1860s (1863)
Locale(s): Tennessee

Summary: Christmas at the Hunter family home in 1863 is dramatized. They are a Tennessee family who have already lost one son in battle. Another son is badly wounded and hiding in the house when Union troops occupy the plantation. The story explores how the spirit of Christmas breaks down enmity.

Historical Accuracy: The story is more romanticized than historical.

HELEN TOPPING MILLER (1884-1960)

JOHN DEWEY TOPPING

Born in Fenton, Michigan, Miller began writing for children's magazines at the age of ten. She published more than 400 short stories, 11 magazine serials, and 50 novels.

4392 *Rebellion Road*

Date of Publication: 1954
Subject(s): Reconstruction Period
Fictional character(s): Duncan Wade, Veteran (Confederate soldier); Marian Villerand, Gentlewoman
Time Period(s): 1860s (post Civil War)
Locale(s): Alabama

Summary: The Reconstruction era is depicted as Confederate soldier Duncan Wade returns to his Alabama plantation to find it in shambles. To rebuild he must contend with hostile Union troops, northern carpetbaggers, and the freedmen for whom freedom becomes a different form of slavery.

Historical Accuracy: The novel does provide a convincing atmosphere, even as the action is slightly too exaggerated to be plausible.

HELEN TOPPING MILLER (1884-1960)

Born in Fenton, Michigan, Miller began writing for children's magazines when she was only ten. She published more than 400 short stories and 11 magazine serials in such publications as the *Saturday Evening Post*, *Good Housekeeping*, and *McCall's*. Most of her 50 novels focus on the Reconstruction period in the South.

4393 *Shod with Flame*

Date of Publication: 1946
Subject(s): Civil War—U.S.
Fictional character(s): Caroline Peyton, Plantation Owner; Carr Peyton, Military Personnel (soldier)
Time Period(s): 1860s (1863)
Locale(s): Tennessee

Summary: This Civil War melodrama takes as its subject women without men. As the tide of war shifts in favor of the Union, Caroline Peyton attempts to maintain the southern tradition while hosting three women visitors, all of whom are in love with Caroline's cousin, Carr.

Historical Accuracy: The historical background is stronger and more believable than the romantic story it supports.

4394 *Sing One Song*

Date of Publication: 1956
Subject(s): Civil War—U.S.
Fictional character(s): Hume Harper, Banker; Tom Findly, Military Personnel (Confederate soldier); William Harper, Young Man; Horatio Nesbitt, Judge
Time Period(s): 1860s
Locale(s): Kentucky

Summary: This Civil War-era tale is set in the border state of Kentucky and dramatizes the divided loyalties of a community that is split apart during the conflict. Banker Hume Harper stands firmly for the Union. He is opposed by young Tom Findly who joins Morgan's Raiders and Judge Nesbitt whose southern sympathies lead to conflicts.

Historical Accuracy: The novel captures the atmosphere of the era and the region convincingly.

4395 *Slow Dies the Thunder*

Date of Publication: 1955
Subject(s): American Revolution; Battle of Kings Mountain
Fictional character(s): Elly Deaderick, Patriot; Mike Callaway, Military Personnel (soldier), Frontiersman
Historical character(s): John Sevier, Military Personnel (colonel)
Time Period(s): 1780s (1780)
Locale(s): Charleston, South Carolina

Summary: This romantic adventure novel is set against the backdrop of colonial Charleston and the southern campaign of the American Revolution. Young Elly Deaderick, whose father is a British officer, is drawn to the rebel cause and the love of backwoodsman and patriot Mike Callaway. Scenes include the bombardment of Charleston, Francis Marion's guerrilla campaign, and the Battle of Kings Mountain.

Historical Accuracy: The historical elements are faithfully presented.

4396 *The Sounds of Chariots: A Novel of John Sevier and the State of Franklin*

Date of Publication: 1947
Subject(s): Settlement of the American Frontier; American Colonies; American Revolution
Fictional character(s): Lisle Mariot, Loyalist, Young Woman; Giles Hanna, Military Personnel (soldier)
Historical character(s): John Sevier, Political Figure
Time Period(s): 1780s (1780)
Locale(s): Tennessee; Augusta, Georgia

Summary: After the British defeat at the Battle of Kings Mountain in 1780, the Mariots, a loyalist family from Georgia, flee to John Sevier's state of Franklin (present day Tennessee). The journey is perilous and the demands of the wilderness are harsh. The countryside is also filled with individuals hostile to loyalists.

Historical Accuracy: The perspective is original and faithful to the era and the locale.

4397 *Trumpet in the Sky*

Date of Publication: 1948
Subject(s): American Revolution
Fictional character(s): Hardee McClure, Landowner, Widow(er); Margaret Clay, Southern Belle
Time Period(s): 1770s (1775)
Locale(s): Savannah, Georgia, American Colonies

Summary: The scene is 1775 in Savannah, Georgia, as the American Revolution begins. Hardee McClure is a wealthy landowner and widower engaged to Margaret Clay, a society belle. When the city's powder magazine is robbed, McClure is suspected of being one of the ringleaders of the Sons of Liberty.

Historical Accuracy: The period atmosphere is realistic, though the emphasis is on romantic adventure, not careful documentation of the past.

ISABEL MILLER
(PSEUD. OF ALMA ROUTSONG, 1924-)

Born in Michigan, Miller is a graduate of Mihigan State University and has work ed as an editor. She has been active in the gay liberation movement since 1970 and won the ALA Gay Book Award in 1971 for *Patience and Sarah*.

4398 *Patience and Sarah*

Date of Publication: 1969
Subject(s): Homosexuality; Farming
Fictional character(s): Patience White, Lesbian; Sarah Dowling, Lesbian
Time Period(s): 1810s (1816)
Locale(s): Housatonic Valley, Connecticut

Summary: The novel describes the love story between two women, Patricia White and Sarah Dowling, as they contend with narrow Puritanism and their own feelings and relationship for which they have no precedents. The story was inspired by the life of American primitive painter Mary Ann Wilson.

Historical Accuracy: The novel offers a good evocation of the period and the social constraints on the unorthodox relationship.

LINDA LAEL MILLER (1949-)

Born in Spokane, Washington, Miller has written more than 20 novels with more than 5 million copies in print, including the bestselling *Princess Annie*, *The Legacy*, *Yankee Wife*, and *Daniel's Bride*.

4399 Knights

Date of Publication: 1996
Subject(s): Romance; Middle Ages; Time Travel
Fictional character(s): Gloriana Kenbrook, Gentlewoman, Time Traveller; Dane St. Gregory, Nobleman
Time Period(s): 13th century
Locale(s): England

Summary: In this romantic tale set in the 13th-century England, five-year-old Megan is transported back in time to become Gloriana, Lady of Kenbrook. She is betrothed to Dane St. Gregory, who returns home desiring another and wishing to annul their engagement. Their eventual attraction is threatened by a curse that besets the Kenbrook clan and the chasm of seven centuries as Gloriana must unwillingly return to the future.

Historical Accuracy: Romance dominates the story with the outward trappings of period details present primarily to create the right exotic atmosphere.

MAY MILLER (1899-)

An American born in Washington, D.C., Miller graduated from Howard University. She is a poet, educator, playwright, and novelist who has worked as a teacher in schools in Baltimore. Miller was an important figure in the theater.

4400 First the Blade

Date of Publication: 1938
Subject(s): Settlement of the American Frontier; Civil War—U.S.; Railroads
Fictional character(s): Amelie McNeil, Settler
Time Period(s): 1860s; 1870s
Locale(s): Missouri; San Joaquin Valley, California

Summary: The conversion of the San Joaquin Valley of California from a near desert to rich farming land is dramatized in the story of Amelie McNeil from her girlhood in Missouri during the Civil War to her maturity in California. The settlers must contend with San Francisco's robber barons and the railroad magnates to hold their land and create an irrigation system to make it fruitful.

Historical Accuracy: The period background of California history is authentic.

REX MILLER

4401 I, Paul

Date of Publication: 1940
Subject(s): Biblical Story; Biography, Fictionalized; Christianity
Historical character(s): Paul, Biblical Figure, Religious
Time Period(s): 1st century
Locale(s): Middle East; Mediterranean; Rome, Roman Empire

Summary: The life of Saint Paul is re-created as an autobiographical adventure. Paul narrates the events of his life, including his conversion experience, shipwreck, and ministry across the Mediterranean world. The novel is sketchy on the details of the period and silent regarding the interpretations of Paul's epistles that earned him the reputation of the principle Christian theologian.

Historical Accuracy: The novel stays close to what is known of Paul's life and ministry, but the period background is thinly developed.

STANLEY MILLER

4402 Mr. Christian!

Date of Publication: 1973
Subject(s): Sea Story; Mutiny; Military Life—British Navy
Historical character(s): William Bligh, Military Personnel (naval officer); Fletcher Christian, Military Personnel (naval officer), Leader (mutiny)
Time Period(s): 18th century
Locale(s): *Bounty*, At Sea; England

Summary: This account of the famous *Bounty* mutiny is told by Fletcher Christian himself. It draws upon the legend that Christian escaped from Pitcairn Island, became a ship captain in the U. S. sailing industry, and visited England before returning to his Pacific exile. The novel traces the events leading up to the mutiny and Christian's subsequent adventures.

Historical Accuracy: The novel's strength is in its faithful depiction of 18th-century seafaring. The story takes considerable license with the facts of the *Bounty* Mutiny, however, and Christian's adventures are based on legend rather than fact.

TERESA MILLER (1952-)

An American born in Oklahoma, Miller graduated from Northeastern and Oklahoma State University. She is a fourth generation resident of Oklahoma, who comes from a family of storytellers.

4403 Remnants of Glory

Date of Publication: 1981
Subject(s): American West; Family Saga

Fictional character(s): Kate Dexter, Teacher; Nathaniel Dunellen, Musician
Time Period(s): 20th century (1907-1979)
Locale(s): Oklahoma

Summary: The life of pioneer woman Kate Dexter, born in 1907 in the Oklahoma Territory on the eve of statehood is depicted. Kate is resilient and determined, admired by her family, but challenges are many when she falls in love with her sister's husband, Nathaniel Dunellen, and she raises her retarded daughter. The novel offers a realistic picture of a flawed but spirited heroine.

Historical Accuracy: The details of pioneer life are convincing.

LARRY MILLETT (1947-)

Millett has worked as a writer for the *St. Paul Pioneer Press* and is the author of *Lost Twin Cities* and two books dealing with Minnesota's architectural history.

4404 *Sherlock Holmes and the Red Demon*

Date of Publication: 1946
Subject(s): Mystery; Railroads
Fictional character(s): Sherlock Holmes, Detective—Private; John H. Watson, Doctor, Sidekick
Historical character(s): John J. Hill, Financier
Time Period(s): 1890s (1894)
Locale(s): Minnesota

Summary: The novel records Sherlock Holmes and Dr. Watson's adventures in Minnesota in 1894. They have come to find and stop a murderous arsonist known as the "Red Demon" who is threatening to destroy the Great Northern Railway. Holmes must contend with a host of frontier characters and the novel's fiery climax after a railroad chase.

Historical Accuracy: As the novelist's notes make clear, the story is firmly grounded in factual and historical details. The author points out the liberties taken with the historical record.

SARAH GERTRUDE MILLIN (1889-1968)

South African novelist Millin was born in Kimberly, Cape Province, South Africa. Of her many novels, *God's Step-Children*, a critically acclaimed story of a missionary in 19th century South Africa, has proven most popular with American audiences. She is also the author of *The South Africans* and *The Herr Witch Doctor*.

4405 *King of the Bastards*

Date of Publication: 1949
Subject(s): Frontier—Africa; Afrikaaners
Historical character(s): Coenraad de Buys, Settler
Time Period(s): 18th century; 19th century
Locale(s): South Africa

Summary: The novel is based on the life of Coenraad de Buys, the first white settler in the Transvaal and captures his struggle

for survival and his growing family. The title refers to his children by a Hottentot and several Kafir wives.

Historical Accuracy: The novel provides authoritative information about early African colonization.

CARLA J. MILLS

4406 *Three Rivers*

Date of Publication: 1988
Subject(s): American West; Ranching
Fictional character(s): Doreen Anderson, Heiress; Laramie Smith, Cowboy; Cary Williams, Companion
Time Period(s): 1870s (1878)
Locale(s): Jamesville, Wyoming

Summary: Doreen Anderson inherits her uncle's ranch in Wyoming. There she encounters cattle rustlers and hostile neighbors who do not expect her to survive. She is protected by ranch hand Laramie Smith but must endure a hard winter on her own.

Historical Accuracy: The novel features convincing details of western life.

CHARLES K. MILLS (1946-)

Mills is a native of Tucson, Arizona, who has worked as a librarian.

4407 *A Mighty Afternoon*

Date of Publication: 1980
Subject(s): Battle of the Little Bighorn; Military Life—U.S. Cavalry; Indians
Historical character(s): Alfred H. Terry, Military Personnel (general); George Armstrong Custer, Military Personnel (cavalry officer); Frederick Benteen, Military Personnel (cavalry officer); Marcus Reno, Military Personnel (cavalry officer); Tom Custer, Military Personnel (soldier)
Time Period(s): 1870s (1876)
Locale(s): Dakota Territory, United States

Summary: The novel tells the story of the Seventh Cavalry at the Battle of the Little Big Horn. It provides a convincing dramatization of what happened and why, and offers, in minute detail, a step-by-step account of the engagement.

Historical Accuracy: This is a meticulously researched and accurate presentation of the controversial Custer Massacre.

JAMES R. MILLS (1927-)

Born in California and a graduate of San Diego State University, Mills has worked as a public school teacher in San Diego and has served in the California state assembly and state senate. He has won more than 35 awards for his books on government and politics.

4408 *The Gospel According to Pontius Pilate*

Date of Publication: 1977

Subject(s): Biblical Story; Roman Empire
Historical character(s): Pontius Pilate, Government Official; Jesus Christ, Biblical Figure
Time Period(s): 1st century
Locale(s): Jerusalem, Israel

Summary: Pontius Pilate offers his recollection of the story of Jesus and the cult following that grew into the Christian Church. Pilate is positioned to offer a wide-angled view of the various political and cultural issues of the period and the difficulties of Roman government of an unstable Empire.

Historical Accuracy: The novel's historical atmosphere is convincing.

ROSELEEN MILNE (1945-)

A Scottish writer born in Aberdeen, Milne feels that a good historical novelist should bring the past alive. She enjoys the research she does for her books more than the actual writing.

4409 *Borrowed Plumes*

Date of Publication: 1977
Subject(s): Regency Romance; Identity—Concealed
Fictional character(s): Constance Osborne, Landowner; Noel Musgrave, Nobleman (a.k.a. Lord Chievely)
Time Period(s): 19th century (Regency period)
Locale(s): Hampshire, England; London, England

Summary: This romantic tale set in Regency England tells the story of the reluctance of Constance Osborne to sell her Hampshire estate to the rakish Earl of Chievely. Inspecting the property that he expects will be his, the earl is injured and assumes the identity of Noel Musgrave while being nursed by Miss Osborne. Love triumphs despite the inevitable confusion of identities.

Historical Accuracy: The story is farfetched, but the period details are credible.

4410 *The Ninth Statue*

Date of Publication: 1983
Subject(s): Royalty—England; Georgian Period
Historical character(s): Sarah Lennox, Gentlewoman; William Gordon, Nobleman
Time Period(s): 1750s; 1760s (1759-1761)
Locale(s): Suffolk, England; London, England

Summary: The novel offers a portrait of a Georgian rebel, Lady Sarah Lennox, who makes her own marriage choice, ignoring the interest of George III. A loveless marriage is followed by a scandal when she elopes with Lord William Gordon and endures eleven years of exile for following her heart's desire.

Historical Accuracy: The novel draws on Sarah Lennox's own published letters to establish an authentic background for the story.

MEADE MINNIGERODE (1887-1967)

Publishing executive, civil servant, and author of biographies and historical fiction, Minnigerode was born in London. His books include *The Fabulous Forties, Marie*

Antoinette's Henchman, and *Some American Ladies*. He is also renowned as the co-lyricist of Yale University's "Wiffenpoof Song."

4411 *Black Forest*

Date of Publication: 1938
Subject(s): Settlement of the American Frontier; American Revolution; American Colonies
Historical character(s): George Washington, Military Personnel (army officer); Daniel Boone, Frontiersman; Edward Braddock, Military Personnel (general); George Rogers Clark, Military Personnel (army officer)
Time Period(s): 18th century (1754-1780s)
Locale(s): Northwest Territory, United States

Summary: This panoramic novel is concerned with events in the American colonies' Northwest territory from the 1750s to the conclusion of the American Revolution. The novel begins with Braddock's defeat and includes the campaign of George Rogers Clark at Kaskaskia and Vincennes and the passing of the Ordinance of 1787 which and opens up the territory for full settlement.

Historical Accuracy: The novel blends a fictional story with the important events of the region's history, which are delivered authentically.

4412 *Cockades: A Romance*

Date of Publication: 1927
Subject(s): French Revolution; Royalty—France; Espionage
Historical character(s): Louis XVII, Royalty (Dauphin of France)
Time Period(s): 1780s
Locale(s): New Orleans, Louisiana

Summary: This historical fantasy imagines the fate of the "Lost Dauphin," Louis XVII, who in this version, is rescued by French loyalists and brought to America under the name of Francis Vincent. He becomes the target for agents of the French and Spanish who kidnap him and hold him as a political pawn.

Historical Accuracy: The novel evokes the atmosphere of the past, even though the story is imagined and farfetched.

4413 *Cordelia Chantrell*

Date of Publication: 1926
Subject(s): Antebellum South; Civil War—U.S.
Fictional character(s): Cordelia Chantrell, Southern Belle
Time Period(s): 1850s; 1860s
Locale(s): Charleston, South Carolina

Summary: Life in Charleston, South Carolina, is depicted before and during the Civil War in the story of Cordelia Chantrell. Her grandmother comes to Charleston from the island of Martinique and her marriage creates problems for her grandchildren.

Historical Accuracy: Although romance predominates over historical reality, the novel does provide a believable background for the story.

KIRK MITCHELL (1950-)

American born in California, Mitchell is a graduate of the University of Redlands and has worked as a police officer and a member of the SWAT team in Redlands, California. He has been a freelance writer since 1979 and has incorporated his police experience in his writing.

4414 *Shadow on the Valley*

Date of Publication: 1994
Subject(s): Civil War—U.S.; Shenandoah Valley Campaign; Crime and Criminals
Fictional character(s): Simon Wolfe, Doctor, Military Personnel (colonel); Rebekka Zelter, Widow(er)
Historical character(s): Philip H. Sheridan, Military Personnel (Union general); George Armstrong Custer, Military Personnel (Union general); Jubal Early, Military Personnel (Confederate general); Elizabeth Bacon Custer, Spouse
Time Period(s): 1860s (1864)
Locale(s): Shenandoah Valley, Virginia

Summary: In the midst of the murderous Civil War Shenandoah Valley campaign of 1864, a serial murderer is on the loose. Women of the Dunbar Church, a German pacifist sect have been murdered, and Colonel Simon Wolfe races to stop the killer who might be a Union officer.

Historical Accuracy: The novel is an interesting blend of accurate Civil War history and a thriller. The author captures the era and the personalities with clarity.

MARGARET MITCHELL (1900-1949)

An American novelist born in Atlanta, Mitchell attended Smith College and worked as a feature writer and columnist for the *Atlanta Journal*. She won a Pulitzer Prize in 1936 for *Gone with the Wind*, which sold a record 1 million copies in its first six months, going on to become the largest selling book in history with the exception of the Bible. It has been translated into 27 foreign languages and published in 37 countries. In essential ways, the novel defined the popular image of the South. Mitchell grew up in a southern household that knew everything about the Civil War except that the South had lost. Mitchell learned this fact when she was ten.

4415 *Gone with the Wind*

Date of Publication:
Subject(s): Antebellum South; Civil War—U.S.; Reconstruction Period
Fictional character(s): Scarlett O'Hara, Southern Belle; Rhett Butler, Adventurer, Blockade Runner; Melanie Hamilton, Gentlewoman; Ashley Wilkes, Gentleman, Plantation Owner
Time Period(s): 1860s; 1870s
Locale(s): Atlanta, Georgia; Georgia (Tara plantation)

Summary: The tempestuous, scheming Scarlett O'Hara, roughish Rhett Butler, gentle Melanie Hamilton, and idealistic Ashley Wilkes are caught up in the conflagration of the Civil War and the social confusion of the Reconstruction in what is

undoubtedly the most popular and beloved historical romance novel of all time.

Historical Accuracy: Although generally filtered through the points of view of the characters, several events of the Civil War are chronicled here. The author's portrait of Southern society, and with it Southern womanhood, remains one of the best ever rendered.

SILAS WEIR MITCHELL (1829-1914)

Physician and author Mitchell was born in Philadelphia and was a surgeon in the Union army in the Civil War. He achieved fame for his research and writings on clinical medicine, toxicology, and the nervous system. He was the author of poetry and several historical romances, the greatest being *Hugh Wynne, Free Quaker*.

4416 *Hugh Wynne, Free Quaker*

Date of Publication: 1897
Subject(s): American Revolution; Espionage; Quakers
Fictional character(s): Hugh Wynne, Military Personnel (soldier), Spy; Darthea Peniston, Young Woman
Historical character(s): Marie Joseph Paul de Lafayette, Military Personnel (general), Nobleman (Marquis de Lafayette); Benedict Arnold, Military Personnel (general); John Andre, Military Personnel (British major), Spy; George Washington, Military Personnel (army commander)
Time Period(s): 1770s; 1780s
Locale(s): Philadelphia, Pennsylvania

Summary: This historical romance set during the American Revolution tells the story of Hugh Wynne, the son of a puritanical Philadelphia Quaker merchant. Wynne escapes the domination of his father to become a ''Fighting Quaker'' and an officer on George Washington's staff. The atmosphere of Revolutionary Philadelphia and Wynne's adventures as a spy, a prisoner of the British, and a member of Lafayette's staff are depicted.

Historical Accuracy: The novel is a classic historical romance on the Revolution offering a believable atmosphere, if invented narrative.

NAOMI MITCHISON (1897-)

Scottish writer and playwright, Mitchison was born in Edinburgh and attended St. Anne's College, Oxford. She served as a volunteer nurse during World War I and intended to become a scientist. Mitchison's writing career spanned seven decades. Besides her writing highly praised historical novels, Mitchison helped establish England's first birth control clinics and became involved in political action with the counterrevolution in Austria during 1934 and with sharecroppers in Arkansas in 1935.

4417 *Blood of the Martyrs*

Date of Publication: 1948
Subject(s): Roman Empire; Christianity
Fictional character(s): Crispus Flavius, Political Figure; Beric, Young Man; Laiage, Dancer

Time Period(s): 1st century (64 A.D.)
Locale(s): Rome, Roman Empire

Summary: This tale of the persecution of the Christians under Roman Emperor Nero centers on the household of Roman Senator Crispus and his adopted son, Beric, a selfish young Briton. Beric undergoes dramatic changes as the novel progresses, eventually attaining a belief in the Christian faith so strong, he faces martyrdom to defend it.

Historical Accuracy: The novel offers a vivid and accurate portrait of the age and the persecution of the Christians after the collapse of the Piso conspiracy to assassinate Nero.

`4418` *The Conquered*

Date of Publication: 1924
Subject(s): Roman Empire; Gallic War
Fictional character(s): Meromic, Warrior, Chieftain
Time Period(s): 1st century B.C. (53-46 B.C.)
Locale(s): Gaul; Rome, Roman Empire

Summary: The story of the conquest of Gaul is told from the perspective of Meromic, a young Gallic chieftain. Meromic's life comes full circle from his resistance of the Roman invaders, to slavery in Rome, to his return to Gaul in battle against his own people.

Historical Accuracy: The novel excels in re-creating its era and background for the novel's actions and a set of believable characters whose motivations are firmly tied to this period.

`4419` *The Corn King and the Spring Queen*

Date of Publication: 1931
Subject(s): Ancient Greece; Witchcraft and Sorcery
Fictional character(s): Erif Der, Sorceress; Tarrik, Chieftain
Historical character(s): Kleomenes, Ruler (King of Sparta)
Time Period(s): 3rd century B.C.; 2nd century B.C. (228-187 B.C.)
Locale(s): Asia (on the Black Sea); Sparta, Greece; Egypt

Summary: Sorceress Erif Der marries Tarrik, the Corn King. She must use her magic to break his power and begin a quest of discovery that covers the Mediterranean world to Sparta and Egypt.

Historical Accuracy: The novel has been called the most complete and satisfactory recreation of Greek civilization written in this century. Enormously erudite and learned, the story is based on a good deal of evidence of actual ideas and happenings in all sorts of other times and places.

HELEN MITTERMEYER (1930-)

An American born in New York, Mittermeyer attended the University of Rochester and Nazareth College. She has worked as a swimming instructor for the physically and mentally challenged. She won a Reviewer's Choice Award in 1984 for *Homecoming*.

`4420` *Princess of the Veil*

Date of Publication: 1992

Subject(s): Romance; Vikings
Fictional character(s): Iona, Royalty (princess); Magnus, Chieftain
Time Period(s): 11th century (1048)
Locale(s): Orkney Islands, Scotland

Summary: Iona is a Viking princess who, due to the abuse she received from her Scottish uncle and the scar she carries, hates and distrusts all men. She establishes a sanctuary for women and children on one of the Orkney Islands. When a Scottish chieftain, Magnus, asserts his claim to the land, he defeats Iona's forces but is captivated by her.

Historical Accuracy: The story is fanciful and more romance than history.

TIMOTHY MO (1950-)

Born in Hong Kong, the son of an English mother and Cantonese father, Mo was educated there and in England. His first novel, *The Monkey King*, won the Geoffrey Faber Memorial Prize. His second, *Sour Sweet*, won the Hawthornden Prize. His work dramatizes the cultural clash between East and West.

`4421` *An Insular Position*

Date of Publication: 1986
Subject(s): Chinese Empire; Opium War; East/West Relations
Fictional character(s): Walter Eastman, Journalist; Gideon Chase, Journalist
Time Period(s): 1830s; 1840s
Locale(s): Macao; Canton, China; Hong Kong

Summary: Set before and during China's Opium Wars, the novel depicts two young Americans, Walter Eastman and Gideon Chase, whose opposition to the European countries' deceit and intrigue in the drug trade causes them to create an irreverant newspaper targeted at the complacency of the corrupt trading society. They witness the destruction caused by the Opium Wars and the creation of Hong Kong.

Historical Accuracy: The novel is a convincing blend of fact and fiction, with a clear knowledge of the period and events.

VILHELM MOBERG (1898-1973)

A Swedish novelist and playwright, Moberg was raised in a barren province of Sweden and worked as a farmhand, a forest worker, and a journalist. His autobiographical Knut Toring trilogy has been hailed as an important achievement in Scandinavian literature. In 1948, Moberg first visited America to begin his research on immigrant life that became a tetralogy that has been successfully adapted into two films, *The Emigrants* and *The New Land*.

`4422` *The Emigrants*

Date of Publication: 1957
Subject(s): Immigrants; Farming; Rural Life—Sweden
Fictional character(s): Karl Oskar Nilsson, Immigrant; Kristina Nilsson, Spouse, Immigrant; Robert Nilsson, Immigrant

Time Period(s): 1840s
Locale(s): Sweden

Summary: In the first volume of a tetralogy, life in rural Sweden in the 1850s is described focusing on the Nilssons, Karl Oskar, his wife Kristina, their children, and Karl's young brother Robert. Hard times and limited possibilities convince them to make a new life in America.

Historical Accuracy: The novel is convincing in its picture of rural Swedish life of the period.

4423 *Last Letter Home*

Date of Publication: 1961
Subject(s): Immigrants; Farming; Civil War—U.S.
Fictional character(s): Karl Oskar Nilsson, Farmer; Kristina Nilsson, Spouse
Time Period(s): 19th century (1860s-1890)
Locale(s): Minnesota

Summary: In the final volume of the author's tetralogy, the Nilssons contend with the events of the Civil War and the Sioux uprising which attempts to drive the settlers off the former Indian lands. Day-to-day struggle to survive is depicted as the settlement grows and the former immigrants become Americans.

Historical Accuracy: The novel features a vivid and faithfully recorded period background.

4424 *The Settlers*

Date of Publication: 1961
Subject(s): Immigrants; Farming; Settlement of the American Frontier
Fictional character(s): Karl Oskar Nilsson, Farmer; Kristina Nilsson, Spouse; Robert Nilsson, Prospector
Time Period(s): 1850s; 1860s
Locale(s): Minnesota

Summary: In the third volume of the author's tetralogy, Karl Osker Nilsson and his wife Kristina establish their home in the Minnesota wilderness. His brother Robert, impatient for the promise of wealth, heads further west to the gold fields of California. The novel features a vivid depiction of ordinary life and survival as the immigrants gradually are assimilated as Americans.

Historical Accuracy: The details of farm and wilderness life is genuine and convincing.

4425 *Unto a Good Land*

Date of Publication: 1954
Subject(s): Immigrants; Farming; Settlement of the American Frontier
Fictional character(s): Karl Oskar Nilsson, Immigrant; Kristina Nilsson, Spouse (Immigrant); Robert Nilsson, Immigrant
Time Period(s): 1850s
Locale(s): Minnesota

Summary: In the second volume of the author's tetralogy, the group of Swedish immigrants that include the Nilssons reaches New York in 1850. They head west to the Mississippi River and into Minnesota where their hardships and triumphs in the American wilderness are vividly depicted.

Historical Accuracy: The picture of immigrant life of the time is authentic.

GWEN MOFFAT (1924-)

Born in Sussex, Moffat was educated in English schools. A prominent mountaineer, Moffat was the first woman to be granted a guide's certificate from the British Mountaineering Council. She has worked as a radio and TV broadcaster.

4426 *The Buckskin Girl: A Novel of the California Trail in the Mid-Nineteenth Century*

Date of Publication: 1982
Subject(s): American West; Wagon Trains
Fictional character(s): Helen Weir, Young Woman
Time Period(s): 1850s
Locale(s): West; California

Summary: The novel describes the experiences of a small wagon train that sets out in the 1850s to cross the continent for California. The novel centers on young Helen Weir and describes the calamities the settlers must face along the way: cholera, buffalo stampedes, Indians, rivalry, and conflict as they race to cross the Sierras before winter traps them.

Historical Accuracy: The novel is based on the first-hand-experiences of the author who set out on the pioneer trail, captured in the nonfiction book, *Hard Road West*.

MIRIAM GRACE MONFREDO

4427 *Blackwater Spirits*

Date of Publication: 1995
Subject(s): Mystery; Indians; Racial Conflict
Fictional character(s): Glynis Tryon, Librarian, Feminist; Jacques Sundown, Indian (half-Iroquois), Lawman (deputy)
Time Period(s): 1850s (1857)
Locale(s): Seneca Falls, New York

Summary: When Seneca Falls' half-Indian deputy, Jacques Sundown, is accused of murder, his trial exposes the fear and prejudice the community feels toward the Indians. Glynis Tryon, Seneca Falls' librarian and progressive activist, finds herself at the center of this controversy as well as the hostile reaction to a young Jewish female doctor and the passions of the temperance movement.

Historical Accuracy: The novel relies on scrupulous historical details to establish a precise period background.

4428 *North Star Conspiracy*

Date of Publication: 1993
Subject(s): Slavery; Underground Railroad; Mystery
Fictional character(s): Glynis Tryon, Librarian, Feminist; Cullen Stuart, Police Officer (constable)
Historical character(s): Elizabeth Cady Stanton, Feminist

Time Period(s): 1850s (1854)
Locale(s): Seneca Falls, New York; Virginia

Summary: Glynis Tryon, an advanced woman for her age—an abolitionist and proponent of woman's rights—investigates the recent deaths of a freed slave and a slave catcher. The action includes the operation of the Underground Railroad and the trial of a woman who assisted a fugitive slave.

Historical Accuracy: The depiction of the ferment of new ideas in the cradle of the woman's rights movement in Seneca Falls is authentic.

`4429` Seneca Falls Inheritance

Date of Publication: 1992
Subject(s): Mystery; Women's Rights
Fictional character(s): Glynis Tryon, Librarian, Feminist; Cullen Stuart, Police Officer (constable)
Historical character(s): Elizabeth Cady Stanton, Feminist, Suffragette; Frederick Douglass, Abolitionist; Lucretia Mott, Feminist
Time Period(s): 1840s (1848)
Locale(s): Seneca Falls, New York

Summary: Glynis Tryon is the independent librarian of Seneca Falls, New York, recruited by Elizabeth Cady Stanton to help organize the first Woman's Rights Convention in 1848. Her work is interrupted when the body of Rose Walker is discovered in the canal behind the library. Other murders, burglary, and arson follow.

Historical Accuracy: The details of the Women's Rights Convention and the period are exactly rendered.

`4430` Through a Gold Eagle

Date of Publication: 1996
Subject(s): Mystery
Fictional character(s): Glynis Tryon, Librarian, Feminist
Historical character(s): Elizabeth Cady Stanton, Feminist, Suffragette; Frederick Douglass, Abolitionist; John Brown, Abolitionist
Time Period(s): 1850s (1859)
Locale(s): Seneca Falls, New York

Summary: Nineteenth-century librarian and feminist Glynis Tryon finds herself in the center of a mystery incorporating social and political issues of the day when a man is murdered on her train to Seneca Falls, New York. Tryon begins an investigation of several related murders in a case tied to funding John Brown's attack on Harper's Ferry and the efforts of abolitionists who wish to start the Civil War.

Historical Accuracy: The novel provides a believable account of the period and its political and social atmosphere.

NICHOLAS MONSARRAT (1910-1979)

British author Nicholas Monsarrat was born in Liverpool and attended Trinity College, Cambridge, where he graduated with honors in law. He worked in a solicitor's office in Nottingham for two years before giving up the law for a writing career in 1934. During World War II, Monsarrat served as a lieutenant commander in the Royal

Navy. His many books include *The Cruel Sea*, *The Ship That Died of Shame*, *The Story of Esther Costello*, and *Something to Hide*, all of which have been produced as motion pictures.

`4431` Darken Ship

Date of Publication: 1981
Subject(s): Sea Story; Battle of Trafalgar; Slavery
Fictional character(s): Matthew Lawe, Sailor
Historical character(s): Horatio Nelson, Military Personnel (British admiral)
Time Period(s): 19th century
Locale(s): At Sea

Summary: Left unfinished at the time of the author's death, this novel continues the naval adventures of Matthew Lawe in 1806 with the Battle of Trafalgar. Lawe then becomes captain of an illegal slave trader.

Historical Accuracy: The novel fills in the details with a variety of convincing period elements.

`4432` Running Proud

Date of Publication: 1979
Subject(s): Sea Story; Exploration; Pirates
Fictional character(s): Matthew Lawe, Sailor
Historical character(s): Henry Hudson, Explorer, Sea Captain; Henry Morgan, Pirate; James Wolfe, Military Personnel (British general); James Cook, Explorer
Time Period(s): 17th century; 18th century
Locale(s): At Sea

Summary: This ambitious sea story chronicles the 400 years of English naval predominance from the defeat of the Spanish Armada to Nelson's victory at Trafalgar. The story uses a single character to link the diverse historical episodes. Seaman Matthew Lawe is cursed to live forever until he can redeem himself for an act of cowardice. He sails with Hudson on his voyage to find the Northwest Passage, with pirate Henry Morgan, and with Captain Cook in the South Seas.

Historical Accuracy: This adventure tale features authentic details to illustrate its naval panorama.

`4433` The White Rajah

Date of Publication: 1961
Subject(s): Pirates; Victorian Period
Fictional character(s): Richard Marriott, Adventurer, Pirate
Time Period(s): 1850s; 1860s (1850-1861)
Locale(s): Asia; England

Summary: This action-adventure novel describes the exploits of Englishmen Richard Marriott who seeks his fortune in the East Indies. Initially a pirate, he then gains control of the island of Makassary in the Java Sea.

Historical Accuracy: The novel features a colorful adventure filled with believable details of its exotic setting.

JEANNE MONTAGUE
(PSEUD. OF JEANNE YARDE, 1925-)

An English writer born in Bath, Montague attended Bath College of Art. She attributes her interest in historical romances to having grown up in the Regency city of Bath.

4434 *The Castle of the Winds*

Date of Publication: 1986
Subject(s): Regency Romance
Fictional character(s): Mariana Crosby, Young Woman; Christopher St. Jules, Landowner, Gentleman
Time Period(s): 1810s (1816)
Locale(s): Yorkshire, England; London, England; Vienna, Austria

Summary: Romantic intrigue and suspense follow the marriage of Mariana Crosby and Christopher St. Jules. She is a farmer's daughter; he is an aristocrat with a secret. The truth comes out in passionate outbursts from Yorkshire to London to Vienna.

Historical Accuracy: There are some credible period elements, but they are only lightly sketched with the romantic suspense predominating.

4435 *The Clock Tower*

Date of Publication: 1983
Subject(s): Romance; Victorian Period
Fictional character(s): Nancy Gray, Orphan; Nell Sheldon, Orphan; Rebecca Smale, Orphan
Time Period(s): 1900s
Locale(s): Bristol, England; Alexandria, Egypt

Summary: Three orphans leave their orphanage outside Bristol, England, and vow to come to each other's aide as needed and return in ten years time to help the remaining children. The novel follows their various adventures in love and their careers.

Historical Accuracy: The period elements are convincing.

4436 *Midnight Moon*

Date of Publication: 1985
Subject(s): Romance; Georgian Period
Fictional character(s): Guy Beaumaris, Nobleman; Lallage Beaumaris, Spouse
Time Period(s): 1790s
Locale(s): Morocco; England

Summary: A young girl without an identity rescued from the Mediterranean becomes the object of affection of Guy, Lord Beaumaris, who marries the girl called Lallage. Her presence in Guy's family provides the novel's intrigue as her past comes back to affect them all.

Historical Accuracy: The emphasis is on suspense rather than a full period depiction.

CARLO MONTEROSSO

4437 *The Salt of the Earth*

Date of Publication: 1967
Subject(s): Biblical Story
Historical character(s): Jesus Christ, Biblical Figure; John the Baptist, Biblical Figure; Judas Iscariot, Biblical Figure
Time Period(s): 1st century
Locale(s): Israel

Summary: In this revisionist account of Jesus's ministry, it is John the Baptist who is credited as the source for Christianity, while Jesus is depicted as a glutton, drunkard, and a scoundrel who falsely manufactures the miracles, including the fakery of his own death and presumed resurrection.

Historical Accuracy: The story is a travesty of history with a sensational treatment of the biblical story that will be offensive to most readers.

JANINE MONTUPET (1919-)

Montupet heads the lace-making workshops of Bayeux, France, and co-wrote *Lace: The Elegant Web*, an illustrated history of lace-making during the last 400 years.

4438 *The Lacemaker*

Date of Publication: 1988
Subject(s): Religious Conflict
Fictional character(s): Gilonne Perdriel, Artisan (lacemaker); Morel d'Arthus, Businessman
Time Period(s): 17th century (1660s)
Locale(s): Alencon, France

Summary: The novel's background is Alencon, France, in the 17th century, the lacemaking capital of Europe. The story describes Gilonne Perdriel's introduction to the trade and emergence as a celebrated craftsperson. It is also the period of the persecution of Protestants by the government of Louis XIV, and Gilonne's marriage to a wealthy Protestant businessman ends tragically.

Historical Accuracy: The period elements are richly interwoven with the story to make a fascinating re-creation of an era.

BARBARA MOORE
(PSEUD. OF BARBARA LEE, 1934-)

An award-winning journalist, Moore was born in Tulsa and received a B.A. and M.A. from the University of Arizona. She has worked as a reporter on newspapers in Fort Worth, Denver, and San Antonio.

4439 *The Fever Called Living*

Date of Publication: 1976
Subject(s): Literary Life; Biography, Fictionalized
Historical character(s): Edgar Allan Poe, Writer
Time Period(s): 1840s (1844-1849)
Locale(s): New York, New York; Virginia

Summary: This biographical novel traces the last five years in the life of Edgar Allan Poe from his arrival in New York, the sale for $10 of his most famous poem, ''The Raven,'' and his vigil beside his beloved wife's deathbed. The novel attempts to go beyond Poe the myth to capture Poe the man.

Historical Accuracy: The novel is essentially faithful to the known facts of Poe's life.

4440 *Hard on the Road*

Date of Publication: 1974
Subject(s): American West; Crime and Criminals
Fictional character(s): Pepper Fairchild, Teenager; Emma Prosser, Journalist; Otis Wasum, Murderer
Time Period(s): 1880s
Locale(s): Louisiana; West

Summary: When 15-year-old Pepper Fairchild witnesses a murder in Louisiana he is branded a liar. He decides to strike out for the west in a photographer's traveling studio, which attracts a colorful group of misfits and is being trailed by the home-town murderer.

Historical Accuracy: The period elements in the story are credible.

BRIAN MOORE (1921-)

Born in Belfast, Moore emigrated to Canada in 1948. He has worked as a proofreader, reporter, and re-write man on the *Montreal Gazette*. Considered a writer's writer, Moore is best known for his novel *The Lonely Passion of Judith Herne*. His fascination with Catholicism is central to Moore's works, which employ miracles and the supernatural in the midst of realistic settings.

4441 *Black Robe*

Date of Publication: 1985
Subject(s): Indians; Religious Life; Frontier—Canada
Fictional character(s): Laforgue, Religious (Jesuit priest); Chomina, Indian (Algonquin)
Time Period(s): 17th century
Locale(s): Canada

Summary: The cultural clash between Indians and a Jesuit priest in the Canadian wilderness of the 17th century is depicted. Father Laforgue sets off on a mission to convert the savages that he knows may end in torture and martyrdom. The author provides a sympathetic look at both Laforgue and the faith that sustains him, as well as the Indians that accompany him to an uncertain future.

Historical Accuracy: The novel captures the wilderness scene and Indian life with authenticity.

JOHN TROTWOOD MOORE
(1858-1929)

An American writer born in Alabama, Moore graduated from Howard College. Moore's books include *Songs and Stories From Tennessee* and *Ole Mistis and Other Songs and Stories From Tennessee*.

4442 *Hearts of Hickory*

Date of Publication: 1926
Subject(s): War of 1812; Battle of New Orleans
Historical character(s): Andrew Jackson, Military Personnel (general); Jean Laffite, Pirate; Davy Crockett, Frontiersman
Time Period(s): 1810s
Locale(s): Tennessee; New Orleans, Louisiana

Summary: Frontier life and Indian fighting, as well as the action of the War of 1812, are featured in this novel that celebrates two of Tennessee's greatest heroes—Andrew Jackson and Davy Crockett. The novel features an abundance of local color and a plot that climaxes in the Battle of New Orleans.

Historical Accuracy: The novel's fictional story is carefully grounded in its period and setting.

RUTH MOORE

4443 *A Fair Wind Home*

Date of Publication: 1953
Subject(s): American Colonies; Sea Story
Fictional character(s): Nathan Ellis, Settler; Francis Carnavon, Businessman; Maynard Cantril, Artisan (ship builder)
Time Period(s): 18th century
Locale(s): Maine

Summary: The story of life in Maine in the years before the American Revolution is described through the experiences of a variety of characters. Together, they represent the contribution of Down Easters to the eventual westward experience.

Historical Accuracy: The novel accurately captures its era and the region during the period.

SUSAN MOORE (1944-)

Born in Lancashire and educated at the University of Sussex, Moore has worked in publishing.

4444 *Paths of Fortune*

Date of Publication: 1984
Subject(s): Regency Romance; Coming of Age; Canal Building
Fictional character(s): Kate Byford, Gentlewoman, Governess; Sophy Byford, Gentlewoman; James Fraser, Engineer (canal)
Time Period(s): 1800s
Locale(s): Wiltshire, England

Summary: This coming of age novel set during the Regency period follows the fortunes of two sisters, Kate and Sophy Byford, whose father's untimely death forces them to make their own way in the world. Kate takes a hated post as a governess. Sophy tries the affection of a self-made man, canal engineer James Fraser, and experiences the clash of class.

Historical Accuracy: The regional elements are strongly and believably described.

4445 *A World Too Wide*

Date of Publication: 1989
Subject(s): Regency Romance
Fictional character(s): Georgiana Michaelmas, Bastard Daughter; Charity Michaelmas, Servant, Prostitute; Tom Fraser, Gentleman
Time Period(s): 1810s; 1820s
Locale(s): London, England; Paris, France; Liverpool, England

Summary: In the sequel to the author's *Paths of Fortune* describing the Byford family, Georgiana Michaelmas is the bastard daughter of Charity Michaelmas, the Byford servant turned prostitute. Determined to provide for Georgiana, Charity sends her to Katie Byford in America as the orphaned heiress to a Virginia tobacco fortune. When she returns to Europe to finish her education, Georgiana falls in love with Tom Fraser, but Charity, bent on revenge, opposes the match and sets off a volatile train of events that threatens both Georgiana and the Byfords.

Historical Accuracy: This complex tale of love and revenge does feature a believable period background.

WILLIAM MOORE (1930-)

4446 *Bayonets in the Sun*

Date of Publication: 1974
Subject(s): British Raj; Sikh War; Military Life—British Army
Fictional character(s): Eldred Mallindine, Military Personnel (army officer); Paddy Gough, Military Personnel (army commander); Robert Leiston, Military Personnel (army officer)
Time Period(s): 1840s (1848-1849)
Locale(s): Punjab, India

Summary: The story of the Sikh War, 1848-1849, is told through the experiences of the British army officers who find themselves surrounded as they push into western India and the fierce Sikhs rise in opposition.

Historical Accuracy: The details of military life and the period are authetically pictured.

4447 *Bush War!*

Date of Publication: 1975
Subject(s): Zulu War; Battle of Ulandi; Military Life—British Army
Fictional character(s): Herbert Mallandine, Military Personnel (army officer); U'nkomo, Warrior (Zulu)
Historical character(s): Cetewayo, Chieftain (Zulu); Benjamin Disraeli, Political Figure
Time Period(s): 1870s (1879)
Locale(s): Zululand, South Africa; London, England

Summary: Herbert Mallandine, a young British officer, is on hand for the Zulu revolt led by Chief Cetewayo. The Zulus are defeated by the British Gatling guns in the Battle of Ulundi.

Historical Accuracy: Grim and realistic, this version of the events is based on fact.

FRANK MOORHOUSE (1938-)

Australian writer Moorhouse was born in New South Wales and attended the University of Queensland. He has worked as an itinerant journalist in Australia. His experimental techniques and discontinuous narratives have earned him the title "The Elder Statesman of the Australian avantgarde." His works include the novel *Forty-Seventeen*, and *Selected Stories*.

4448 *Grand Days*

Date of Publication: 1993
Subject(s): League of Nations; Diplomacy; Coming of Age
Fictional character(s): Edith Campbell Berry, Diplomat; Major Ambrose Westwood, Diplomat
Time Period(s): 1920s
Locale(s): Geneva, Switzerland

Summary: This coming of age story of Englishwoman Edith Campbell Berry is set in Geneva following the First World War and involves the newly created League of Nations. Edith meets Major Westwood as they both take up their posts in the League, and he takes her on a voyage of self-discovery and sexual awakening.

Historical Accuracy: Though the author asserts that the novel is a work of the imagination, all the historical and political events depicted are inspired by documentary sources.

MARTA MORAZZONI (1950-)

Italian author Morazzoni realized her passion for writing while working on a graduate thesis in philosophy at the University of Milan. Her first book, a collection of stories called *La Porta Bianca*, was published in 1988 and appeared in English as *Girl in a Turban*. Her recent books, which she wrote while working as a high school teacher of Italian and history in Gallarate (between Milan and Varese), are *His Mother's House* and *The Invention of Truth*.

4449 *The Invention of Truth*

Date of Publication: 1993
Subject(s): Middle Ages; Victorian Period; Artistic Life
Fictional character(s): Anne Elizabeth, Artisan
Historical character(s): John Ruskin, Writer
Time Period(s): 11th century; 1870s (1879)
Locale(s): Amiens, France

Summary: The novel weaves together two counterpointed historical events: the creation of the Bayeux tapestry depicting William the Conqueror's triumph in 1066 and the visit of the aging English art critic, John Ruskin, to Amiens where he reflects on his life and art and the famous cathedral that dominates the town. Both offer an opportunity for meditation on the creative process.

Historical Accuracy: The basis of the novel is the historical creation of the Bayeaux tapestry and Ruskin's visit to Amiens in 1879 but the episodes and the links in this narrative are purely imaginary.

CYNTHIA MORGAN

4450 *Court of Shadows*

Date of Publication: 1992
Subject(s): Elizabethan Period; Espionage; Inquisition
Fictional character(s): Kat Langdon, Gentlewoman; Lord Harwood, Nobleman
Historical character(s): Elizabeth I, Ruler (Queen of England); Sir Francis Walsingham, Government Official
Time Period(s): 15th century (1570s)
Locale(s): London, England; Paris, France; Spain

Summary: This tale of adventure and intrigue during the Elizabthan period features Kat Langdon whose nemesis is Lord Harwood. Harwood is suspected of conspiring to assassinate Elizabeth in order to put Mary, Queen of Scots on England's throne. Kat becomes Harwood's prisoner, and a mutual attraction complicates the intrigue in scenes that range from London's underworld to Paris during the Huguenot uprising and Spain during the Inquisition.

Historical Accuracy: The period elements are convincingly detailed.

KATHLEEN MORGAN

4451 *Child of the Mist*

Date of Publication: 1993
Subject(s): Romance; Witchcraft and Sorcery; Tudor Period
Fictional character(s): Anne McGregor, Witch; Niall Campbell, Laird
Time Period(s): 16th century
Locale(s): Scotland

Summary: Anne McGregor and Niall Campbell are married to end a clan feud in Scotland during the 16th century. They must contend with the continuing tension from their enemies while discovering their growing love for one another.

Historical Accuracy: The scenes of Scottish life and customs are authentically presented.

ROBERT MORGAN (1944-)

Author of poetry and fiction with a background of the Blue Ridge Mountains, Morgan is an English Professor at Cornell University. He has won the James B. Hanes Poetry Prize, the North Carolina Award in literature, and the *Jacaranda Review* fiction prize.

4452 *The Truest Pleasure*

Date of Publication: 1995
Subject(s): Rural Life—U.S.; Farming
Fictional character(s): Tom Powell, Farmer; Ginny Peace, Landowner
Time Period(s): 1900s
Locale(s): North Carolina

Summary: This story of a marriage is set at the turn of the century in western North Carolina. Ginny Peace agrees to marry Tom Powell out of both their needs: Tom for land of his own, Ginny for someone to manage her family's farm. The novel depicts their relationship and the adversities that underscore their deepest feelings for one another.

Historical Accuracy: The novel succeeds in capturing the atmosphere of the period and the region.

SPEER MORGAN (1946-)

Morgan grew up in Fort Smith, Arkansas, and graduated from the University of Arkansas and Stanford University. A former book reviewer for *Rolling Stone*, Morgan is the author of *Frog Gig and Other Stories*. He is a professor of English at the University of Missouri.

4453 *Belle Starr*

Date of Publication: 1979
Subject(s): American West; Crime and Criminals; Indians
Historical character(s): Belle Starr, Frontierswoman, Outlaw; Blue Duck, Indian, Outlaw
Time Period(s): 1880s (1889)
Locale(s): Cherokee Nation, Oklahoma; Fort Smith, Arkansas

Summary: The novel takes up the story of the final weeks in the life of western legend Belle Starr. She was seduced and abandoned by Cole Younger, and became one of the great eccentrics of the Old West, an outlaw and an activist. The novel, in scenes of wild humor and energy, dramatizes a true western original at the point of the passing of both her kind and the West she knew.

Historical Accuracy: The author explains that the novel is not an attempt to reconstruct accurately the last weeks of Belle Starr's life but to re-create her character, using both facts of history and imagination.

EDUARD FRIEDRICH MORIKE
(1804-1873)

Born in Ludwigsburg near Stuttgart, Germany, Morike was an ordained Lutheran minister who made his mark as a lyric poet and writer of short prose. He took leaves of absence from his pastoral duties because of his frail mental health. His best known fiction is a historical novel, *Mozart on the Way to Prague*.

4454 *Mozart on the Way to Prague*

Date of Publication: 1855
Subject(s): Biography, Fictionalized; Musical Life
Historical character(s): Wolfgang Amadeus Mozart, Composer, Musician
Time Period(s): 1780s
Locale(s): Czechoslovakia

Summary: The novel imagines an incident in the life of Mozart connected with the composition of *Don Giovanni*. Mozart drives with his wife to Prague for the production of his unfinished opera. He wanders onto the grounds of a local count's family estate and the encounter suggests the melody for his opera.

Historical Accuracy: The novel is knowledgeable about Mozart's life and the atmosphere of his times.

IRIS MORLEY (1910-1953)

Morley was the author of such books as *Soviet Ballet* and *A Thousand Lives: An Account of the English Revolutionary Movement 1660-1685.*

4455 *We Stood for Freedom*

Date of Publication: 1942
Subject(s): Monmouth's Rebellion
Fictional character(s): Diana Hayes, Gentlewoman; Saul Flecke, Activist
Time Period(s): 17th century
Locale(s): England

Summary: Set in England during the time of Monmouth's Rebellion, the novel is concerned with the experiences of Diana Hayes, lady-in-waiting to the Duchess of York. She is dismissed from her post and seeks safety in the countryside where she meets Saul Flecke. Eventually she joins him in his efforts to improve the conditions of the poor.

Historical Accuracy: The novel provides a modern tone and relevance to the historical background that at times seems anachronistic.

DAVID MORRELL (1943-)

Canadian author Morrell was born in Ontario and graduated from the University of Waterloo and Pennsylvania State University. He is a professor of American literature at the University of Iowa. Morrell is best known as the creator of John Rambo in the novel *First Blood*, the protagonist in the enormously popular action films starring Sylvester Stallone.

4456 *Last Reveille*

Date of Publication: 1977
Subject(s): American West; Mexican Revolution
Fictional character(s): Miles Calendar, Military Personnel (soldier), Scout
Historical character(s): Francisco Villa, Outlaw, Revolutionary
Time Period(s): 1910s (1916)
Locale(s): Columbus, New Mexico; Chihuahua, Mexico

Summary: Set in 1916 during Pancho Villa's raid on the New Mexican border, the novel describes the U.S. Cavalry's expedition into Mexico in pursuit of Villa. To find him, the army turns to 65-year-old Miles Calendar, a veteran of the Civil War and an Indian fighter, as its guide. His story of a lifetime in battle emerges as the expedition unfolds.

Historical Accuracy: The story is imagined, but the period details are convincing.

GILBERT MORRIS (1929-)

A native of Arkansas, Morris spent ten years as a pastor before becoming a professor of English at Ouachita Baptist University in Arkansas. A prolific writer, Morris has published over 25 scholarly articles, 200 poems, and more than 20 novels. He claims that his ambition is to write many novels with just a touch of the Christian viewpoint.

4457 *The Captive Bride*

Date of Publication: 1987
Subject(s): Family Saga; American Colonies; Puritans
Fictional character(s): Gilbert Winslow, Settler; Rachel Winslow, Spouse; Robert Howland, Settler
Time Period(s): 17th century (1659-1691)
Locale(s): Plymouth, Massachusetts, American Colonies; Salem, Massachusetts, American Colonies

Summary: Life in the Puritan settlement of the Massachusetts Bay Colony is described in the second volume of the author's House of Winslow series. At the center of the drama is the freethinking Rachel Winslow who must contend with the strict conformity of the Puritan hierarchy.

Historical Accuracy: Slightly more sensational than accurate, the novel does provide some convincing period painting.

4458 *The Crossed Sabres*

Date of Publication: 1993
Subject(s): American West; Indians; Battle of the Little Bighorn
Fictional character(s): Thomas Winslow, Veteran (Civil War), Government Official
Historical character(s): George Armstrong Custer, Military Personnel (cavalry officer)
Time Period(s): 1860s; 1870s
Locale(s): Dakota Territory, United States

Summary: In the 13th volume of the House of Winslow series, Thomas Winslow has survived the Civil War and must adapt to life at home during the period. He takes a job with the Department of Indian Affairs and travels across the Northern Plains. Eventually, he joins the Seventh Cavalry and participates in the campaign that climaxes at the Battle of the Little Bighorn.

Historical Accuracy: The actual chronology of events is observed and some effort has been taken to create a believable period atmosphere.

4459 *The Dixie Widow*

Date of Publication: 1991
Subject(s): Family Saga; Civil War—U.S.; Espionage
Fictional character(s): Belle Wickham, Widow(er), Spy; Whitfield Winslow, Military Personnel (captain); Davis Winslow, Military Personnel (soldier)
Historical character(s): Edwin Stanton, Political Figure; Salmon P. Chase, Political Figure; Abraham Lincoln, Political Figure; Mary Todd Lincoln, Spouse; Joshua Lawrence Chamberlain, Military Personnel (army officer); James Longstreet, Military Personnel (Confederate general)
Time Period(s): 1860s (1862-1867)
Locale(s): Washington, District of Columbia; Gettysburg, Pennsylvania

Summary: Confederate widow Belle Wickham, the daughter of Sky and Rebekah Winslow, loses her husband during the battle of Sharpsburg and vows revenge against the Union. She travels to Washington as a spy for the Confederacy. The action includes scenes from the Battle of Gettysburg.

Historical Accuracy: The almost constant proximity of the fictional characters to historical ones strains credibility.

4460 The Final Adversary

Date of Publication: 1992
Subject(s): Family Saga; Frontier—Africa; Religious Life
Fictional character(s): Barney Winslow, Sports Figure (prize fighter)
Time Period(s): 1890s; 1900s (1896-1900)
Locale(s): New York; Africa

Summary: This 12th volume of the House of Winslow series follows the exploits of prize fighter Barney Winslow both in the ring and as a missionary in Africa.

Historical Accuracy: The story is set against an only lightly-sketched historical background.

4461 The Gentle Rebel

Date of Publication: 1988
Subject(s): Family Saga; American Revolution; Battle of Bunker Hill
Fictional character(s): Nathan Winslow, Military Personnel (soldier), Patriot; Abigail Howland, Loyalist
Historical character(s): Samuel Adams, Revolutionary; Thomas Gage, Military Personnel (general); George Washington, Military Personnel (army commander)
Time Period(s): 1770s
Locale(s): Lexington, Massachusetts, American Colonies; Boston, Massachusetts, American Colonies; Fort Ticonderoga, New York, American Colonies

Summary: The fourth installment of the House of Winslow series depicts the American Revolution as Nathan Winslow gradually embraces the patriots' cause while falling in love with spoiled Tory Abigail Howland. Action includes the battles of Lexington, Breed's Hill, and Bunker Hill, as well as the siege of Fort Ticonderoga.

Historical Accuracy: The period details are authentic and convincing, if somewhat overstuffed with historical events.

4462 The Holy Warrior

Date of Publication: 1989
Subject(s): Family Saga; American West; Indians
Fictional character(s): Christmas Winslow, Frontiersman; Knox Winslow, Trader
Time Period(s): 1790s; 1800s
Locale(s): Missouri; West

Summary: In the sixth installment of the House of Winslow series, Nathan Winslow's two sons, Chris and Knox, head west with the expanding nation. Knox sets up a trading post in Missouri, while Chris heads further west into the wilderness.

Historical Accuracy: The period is suggested with some convincing touches.

4463 The Honorable Imposter

Date of Publication: 1986
Subject(s): Family Saga; American Colonies; Pilgrims
Fictional character(s): Gilbert Winslow, Religious (minister), Settler
Historical character(s): William Bradford, Leader (pilgrim); John Alden, Leader (pilgrim); Miles Standish, Leader (pilgrim)
Time Period(s): 17th century
Locale(s): England; *Mayflower*, At Sea; Plymouth, Massachusetts, American Colonies

Summary: In the first of the author's House of Winslow series, Gilbert Winslow is forced to become a minister. He agrees to infiltrate the Pilgrims to identify their leaders. He crosses the Atlantic on the *Mayflower* and takes up life in the Plymouth colony where he must decide between betrayal of his comrades or life among them.

Historical Accuracy: The period details are effectively delivered.

4464 The Indentured Heart

Date of Publication: 1988
Subject(s): Family Saga; American Colonies; French and Indian War
Fictional character(s): Adam Winslow, Farmer; Molly Burns, Servant (indentured)
Historical character(s): Benjamin Franklin, Printer; Jonathan Edwards, Religious (minister); Paul Revere, Artisan (silversmith); George Washington, Military Personnel (army officer); Edward Braddock, Military Personnel (general)
Time Period(s): 1740s; 1750s (1740-1755)
Locale(s): Boston, Massachusetts, American Colonies; Northampton, Massachusetts, American Colonies; Mount Vernon, Virginia, American Colonies

Summary: Set in the pre-Revolutionary American colonies during Jonathan Edwards' Great Awakening and the first stirring of independence, this third volume of the House of Winslow series describes farmer Adam Winslow who arranges to bring a former beggar, Molly Burns, to America as an indentured servant. Action includes combat during the French and Indian War.

Historical Accuracy: The credibility of the story is undermined when nearly every character encountered is an historical one.

4465 The Jewelled Spur

Date of Publication: 1994
Subject(s): Settlement of the American Frontier; American West; Theatrical Life
Fictional character(s): Laurie Winslow, Entertainer; Cody Rogers, Entertainer
Historical character(s): William F. Cody, Frontiersman, Entertainer; Sitting Bull, Indian (Sioux), Chieftain; Annie Oakley, Entertainer
Time Period(s): 1890s
Locale(s): Wyoming; Omaha, Nebraska

Summary: This 16th installment of the House of Winslow series follows the career of Laurie Winslow who joins Buffalo

Bill's Wild West Show to earn enough money to return to college. She also finds a place for Cody Rogers whose past pursues him.

Historical Accuracy: The story is a fanciful one but does display some authentic period elements to capture the atmosphere of the Wild West Show.

4466 *The Last Confederate*

Date of Publication: 1990
Subject(s): Civil War—U.S.; Family Saga
Fictional character(s): Sky Winslow, Plantation Owner; Rebekah Winslow, Spouse; Thad Novak, Young Man
Time Period(s): 1860s
Locale(s): Virginia

Summary: In the eighth installment of the House of Winslow series, Sky Winslow and his wife Rebekah have returned from Oregon City to take up plantation life in Virginia. As the nation plunges into the Civil War, the family must deal with a young northerner, Thad Novak, whose motives are suspect.

Historical Accuracy: The emphasis is on a fast-paced story over careful period documentation. The atmosphere is authentic, however.

4467 *The Reluctant Bridegroom*

Date of Publication: 1990
Subject(s): Family Saga; American West; Wagon Trains
Fictional character(s): Sky Winslow, Frontiersman; Rebekah Jackson, Young Woman; Rita Duvall, Entertainer (dance hall girl)
Time Period(s): 1830s (1838)
Locale(s): New York, New York; Oregon Trail, United States; Oregon City, Oregon

Summary: In the seventh installment of the House of Winslow series, Sky Winslow agrees to lead a wagon train of brides for the men of Oregon City across the dangerous Oregon Trail. Two of the women make an impact on Sky: Rebekah Jackson, who is hoping for a fresh start out west and Rita Duvall, a former dance hall girl.

Historical Accuracy: The period details are authentic if the action is on occasion incredible.

4468 *The Rough Rider*

Date of Publication: 1995
Subject(s): Spanish-American War; Family Saga; Battle of San Juan Hill
Fictional character(s): Aaron Winslow, Military Personnel (soldier); Gail Summers, Nurse
Historical character(s): William Randolph Hearst, Publisher; Stephen Crane, Writer; Theodore Roosevelt, Military Personnel (army commander)
Time Period(s): 1890s
Locale(s): New York, New York; Cuba

Summary: In this eighteenth installment of the House of Winslow series, Aaron Winslow returns home from the Klondike and joins his brother as one of Teddy Roosevelt's Rough Riders to fight the Spanish in Cuba.

Historical Accuracy: The period elements are accurately presented.

4469 *The Saintly Buccaneer*

Date of Publication: 1988
Subject(s): Family Saga; American Revolution; Sea Story
Fictional character(s): Nathan Winslow, Military Personnel (soldier), Patriot; Paul Winslow, Loyalist
Historical character(s): Francois Joseph Paul de Grasse, Military Personnel (French admiral)
Time Period(s): 1770s; 1780s
Locale(s): Valley Forge, Pennsylvania; At Sea

Summary: The American Revolution divides the Winslow family as Nathan Winslow fights with the Continental Army and endures the hardships of Valley Forge, while his cousin Paul remains opposed to the war. He is shanghaied by a British press gang to work aboard a naval frigate, and amnesia changes his personality.

Historical Accuracy: The story of Paul's transformation is implausible, but the period details are credible.

4470 *Song of a Strange Child*

Date of Publication: 1996
Subject(s): American Revolution; Battle of Bunker Hill; Family Saga
Fictional character(s): Dake Bradford, Patriot; Clive Gordon, Doctor, Loyalist; Jeanne Corbeau, Young Woman
Time Period(s): 1770s (1775-1776)
Locale(s): Massachusetts, American Colonies; Fort Ticonderoga, New York, American Colonies

Summary: In the second volume of the Liberty Bell series, the American Revolution has begun, and Dake Bradford and his cousin, Clive Gordon, find themselves on opposite sides in the conflict. Scenes include the Battle of Bunker Hill and the attack on Fort Ticonderoga.

Historical Accuracy: This is a fictional story set against the backdrop of actual events, accurately described.

4471 *Sound of the Trumpet*

Date of Publication: 1995
Subject(s): American Colonies; American Revolution; Family Saga
Fictional character(s): Daniel Bradford, Servant (indentured); Holly Blanchard, Young Woman
Historical character(s): George Washington, Military Personnel (army officer); Samuel Adams, Revolutionary
Time Period(s): 18th century (1743-1775)
Locale(s): England; Virginia, American Colonies; Boston, Massachusetts, American Colonies

Summary: This first volume of the Liberty Bell series follows the experiences of Daniel Bradford who comes to the American colonies as an indentured servant. Bradford and his family move from Virginia to Boston where the first shots are fired in the Revolution, and Bradford must resolve his divided loyalties.

Historical Accuracy: The story is fanciful but set against a background of actual events, accurately described.

4472 *The Sword of Truth*

Date of Publication: 1994
Subject(s): Tudor Period; Royalty—England
Fictional character(s): Robert Wakefield, Nobleman; Myles Morgan, Heir; Hannah Kemp, Young Woman
Historical character(s): Henry VIII, Ruler (King of England); William Tyndale, Scholar; Thomas Wolsey, Religious (cardinal); Sir Thomas Wyatt, Writer, Courtier; Anne Boleyn, Royalty (queen consort of Henry VIII); Catherine of Aragon, Royalty (queen consort of Henry VIII)
Time Period(s): 16th century (1513-1534)
Locale(s): London, England

Summary: Myles Morgan is surprised to be named the heir to Sir Robert Wakefield. He is thrown into the world of Henry VIII's court in the midst of the Reformation which makes an English translation of the Bible an act of sedition. Myles is forced to choose among loyalty, love, and faith.

Historical Accuracy: The novel is packed with personalities and details of Tudor life, making a credible period background for this imagined story.

4473 *The Union Belle*

Date of Publication: 1992
Subject(s): American West; Railroads
Fictional character(s): Mark Winslow, Gunfighter; Lola Montez, Young Woman
Historical character(s): Grenville Dodge, Engineer
Time Period(s): 1860s
Locale(s): Texas; Nebraska; Utah

Summary: In this installment of the House of Winslow, Mark Winslow is released from a Mexican prison and heads north to work for the Union Pacific Railroad. In Texas he is imprisoned and escapes with the help of Lola Montez. Together they follow the progress of the railroad across the continent.

Historical Accuracy: The details of the railroad are convincingly presented.

4474 *The Valiant Gunman*

Date of Publication: 1993
Subject(s): American West; Ranching
Fictional character(s): Dan Winslow, Rancher; Hope Rogers, Widow(er)
Time Period(s): 1870s
Locale(s): Wyoming

Summary: This 14th installment of the House of Winslow series concerns Dan Winslow, who journeys to Wyoming to begin a new life as a rancher. He finds that the powerful cattle barons are forcing the small ranchers and homesteaders out, and he offers them assistance.

Historical Accuracy: The period elements are believably presented.

4475 *The Wounded Yankee*

Date of Publication: 1991
Subject(s): Civil War—U.S.; American West
Fictional character(s): Zack Winslow, Veteran (Civil War)

Time Period(s): 1860s
Locale(s): Montana

Summary: This installment of the House of Winslow concerns Zack Winslow who survives the battles of Bull Run and Shiloh as well as disappointment at home where he is sent to recover from wounds. Disillusioned, Zack heads west to become a hermit in Montana. But there unwelcome visitors intrude.

Historical Accuracy: The novel provides a factual period backdrop and some authentic details of frontier life.

4476 *The Yukon Queen*

Date of Publication: 1995
Subject(s): Family Saga; Gold Rush—Klondike
Fictional character(s): Cassidy Winslow, Young Man; Serena Stevens, Orphan
Time Period(s): 1890s
Locale(s): Yukon Territory, Canada

Summary: In Book 17 of the House of Winslow series, Cassidy Winslow sets out for the Klondike gold fields bankrolled by a man who insists that Cass take along his daughter to share in what gold they find. Together they experience dangers and adventures in the Yukon.

Historical Accuracy: The novel offers some reliable period elements.

IRA J. MORRIS

Born in Moscow and educated in London and Paris, Morris worked for a London advertising agency and was the art editor of a woman's magazine.

4477 *The Fortune Hunter*

Date of Publication: 1971
Subject(s): Russian Empire
Fictional character(s): Nicholas Lavrin, Nobleman (count); Alexandra Sergeivna Lavrin, Noblewoman (countess), Heiress
Historical character(s): Mikhail Illarionovich Kutuzov, Military Personnel (general)
Time Period(s): 19th century
Locale(s): Moscow, Russia; Bucharest, Romania

Summary: When Nicholas Lavrin loses his fortune at the gaming tables, he is forced to marry his wealthy cousin Alexandra. They fall in love with each other but pride prevents either from admitting it. Russia's war against the Turks threatens to destroy any chance for their happiness.

Historical Accuracy: The novel is atmospheric and convincing in its historical elements, though the author admits to altering the chronology of events somewhat.

4478 *The Rake and the Rebel*

Date of Publication: 1967
Subject(s): Napoleonic Wars; Congress of Vienna
Fictional character(s): Sacha Orloff, Rake, Bastard Son; Lise de Montargis, Noblewoman; Honoria Smith, Explorer, Traveller

Time Period(s): 1810s (1811-1816)
Locale(s): Russia; Europe

Summary: Rakehell Sacha Orloff is exiled to his country estate following a shocking scandal. He accidently takes with him Lise de Montargis, his stepmother's ward. Lise's reputation is saved by a timely encounter with eccentric Englishwoman Honoria Smith. Sacha is too preoccupied with his mistress and his plans to regain the emperor's favor to see that Lise is in love with him. Lise eventually returns to her family in England but her path crosses Sacha's once again at the Congress of Vienna. This time Sacha, now a war hero, cannot help but notice that Lise is now a grown woman. Originally titled *The Troika Belle*.

Historical Accuracy: The period atmosphere is convincing, even if the story is fanciful.

JANE KESNER MORRIS
(PSEUD. OF JANE KESNER ARDMORE, 1915-)

An American writer, Morris graduated from the University of Chicago. She has worked as an editor, advertising copywriter, and freelance writer.

4479 *Julie*

Date of Publication: 1952
Subject(s): Victorian Period; Haymarket Riots; Labor Movement
Fictional character(s): Julie Corper, Gentlewoman; Philip McManus, Writer (playwright); Leon Dekker, Activist (labor organizer)
Time Period(s): 1850s
Locale(s): London, England; Chicago, Illinois

Summary: The story depicts the life of a young Victorian woman, Julie Cooper, and her two lovers, a young rebellious playwright and a social reformer. Julie is on hand for the Haymarket Riots and the growth of the American theater.

Historical Accuracy: The period elements are colorfully detailed.

LYNN MORRIS

GILBERT MORRIS

Gilbert Morris was born in Arkansas. An ordained Baptist minister, he is a professor of English at Ouachita Baptist University and is the author of a number of historical novels. Lynn Morris is his daughter.

4480 *A City Not Forsaken*

Date of Publication: 1995
Subject(s): Medical Profession; Reconstruction Period
Fictional character(s): Cheney Duvall, Doctor; Shiloh Iron, Nurse; Devlin Buchanan, Doctor
Historical character(s): Ulysses S. Grant, Military Personnel (general)
Time Period(s): 1860s (1866)
Locale(s): New York, New York

Summary: The novel is part of a continuing saga concerning 19th-century doctor Cheney Duvall. In this volume she has returned to her home in New York City in 1866 determined to go into private practice with Devlin Buchanan, a physician who has asked for her hand. He returns from London when an outbreak of cholera is expected to spread to New York. Cheney must deal with the conflict of treating the rich and the powerful or the poor as the epidemic hits the city.

Historical Accuracy: The novel features some convincing period elements. The main character's status as a doctor seems more modern than believable in the period setting.

4481 *Shadow of the Mountains*

Date of Publication: 1994
Subject(s): Medical Profession; Rural Life—U.S.
Fictional character(s): Cheney Duvall, Doctor; Shiloh Irons, Nurse
Time Period(s): 1860s
Locale(s): Ozarks, Arkansas

Summary: The novel continues the experiences of doctor Cheney Duvall, who journeys to the Ozarks, where she meets resistance and superstition among the mountain people.

Historical Accuracy: The novel provides some plausible period details to create a convincing atmosphere of the times.

SUZANNE MORRIS (1944-)

An American writer and lecturer, Morris was born in Texas and attended the University of Houston. She received the literary East Texas Award in 1979 for *Galveston*.

4482 *Galveston*

Date of Publication: 1976
Subject(s): Family Saga; Politics
Fictional character(s): Claire Becker, Young Woman; Serena Garret, Young Woman; Willa Frazier, Young Woman
Time Period(s): 19th century; 20th century (1877-1920)
Locale(s): Galveston, Texas; Houston, Texas

Summary: This generational saga is set in Galveston, Texas, and covers fifty years in the lives of three women whose past and secrets play out against the history of the city and the deceit and betrayal hidden behind the facade of the respectable people who live on Avenue L.

Historical Accuracy: The regional and period elements are genuine and create a believable backdrop for this drama.

4483 *Keeping Secrets*

Date of Publication: 1979
Subject(s): Espionage; World War I; Mexican Revolution
Fictional character(s): Electra Cabot, Gentlewoman; Camille Devera, Young Woman
Time Period(s): 1910s (1917-1918)
Locale(s): San Antonio, Texas

Summary: Set in San Antonio, Texas on the eve of America's entry in the First World War and against the threat of a revolution across the border in Mexico, the novel tells the story of intrigue and secrets surrounding Electra Cabot who has come to town to marry her childhood sweetheart. Suspicion and distrust compel young Camille Devera to uncover the secrets that surround Electra.

Historical Accuracy: The period and locale details are authentic and credible.

GERRY MORRISON (1927-)

Born in Chicago, Morrison has worked as a secretary and a writer. She describes her work as a reflection of her love of travel and adventure. She has written a historical novel, *Unvexed to the Sea*, a cookbook, and a textbook on writing.

4484 *Unvexed to the Sea: A Novel of the Vicksburg Campaign*

Date of Publication: 1961
Subject(s): Civil War—U.S.; Siege of Vicksburg
Fictional character(s): Malvina McClellan, Gentlewoman; Belle McClellan, Gentlewoman
Time Period(s): 1860s (1863)
Locale(s): Vicksburg, Mississippi

Summary: The story of the siege and eventual surrender of Vicksburg, the key strategic position for the control of the Mississippi during the Civil War, is dramatized from the perspective of the combatants and civilians on both sides of the violent and deadly campaign.

Historical Accuracy: The Civil War details are authentic and convincing.

LESTER M. MORRISON (1907-1991)

RICHARD G. HUBLER (1912-)

An Englishman born in London, Morrison was an M.D. and pioneer medical researcher. He was the author of 130 scientific publications. In the 1940s he served as chief of staff at Cedars of Lebanon Hospital in Los Angeles and pioneered the correlation between diet and heart disease. Huber is an American novelist, editor, columnist, foreign correspondent, and publisher. He worked as the foreign editor of *Newsweek*.

4485 *Trail and Triumph: A Novel about Maimonides*

Date of Publication: 1965
Subject(s): Middle Ages; Jews; Crusades
Historical character(s): Moses Maimonides, Philosopher, Doctor; Saladin, Ruler (Muslim)
Time Period(s): 12th century
Locale(s): Cordoba, Spain; Africa; Middle East

Summary: This panoramic novel depicts the life and times of Maimonides, rabbi, physician, and philosopher whose thinking exerted a profound influence on Jewish, Christian, and modern learning. Driven from his home in Spain, Maimonides journeys through northern Africa to the Middle East where he becomes the personal physician and adviser to Saladin the Great during the time of Moorish-Christian conflict.

Historical Accuracy: Though careful to keep the story faithful to the known facts, the authors admit to stretching the facts to meet the probabilities.

HONORE MORROW (1880-1940)

Born in Ottumwa, Iowa, and educated at the University of Wisconsin, Morrow was a prolific novelist whose works include *We Must March*, *On to Oregon!*, *Forever Free*, *The Last Full Measure*, *Beyond the Blue Sierra*, and *Let the King Beware!*.

4486 *Beyond the Blue Sierra*

Date of Publication: 1932
Subject(s): Exploration; Spanish Colonies
Historical character(s): Juan Bautista de Anza, Explorer
Time Period(s): 1770s (1775-1776)
Locale(s): Mexico

Summary: The novel chronicles the opening of the overland trail from Mexico to California and the founding of San Francisco by explorer and colonial leader Juan de Anza. The novel provides a vivid record of how and why the Spanish missions in California were founded.

Historical Accuracy: The historical elements are well-documented and convincing.

4487 *Forever Free*

Date of Publication: 1927
Subject(s): Civil War—U.S.; Politics
Historical character(s): Abraham Lincoln, Political Figure; Mary Todd Lincoln, Spouse
Time Period(s): 1860s (1861-1863)
Locale(s): Washington, District of Columbia

Summary: This first novel of a trilogy on the Lincoln presidency covers the period from Lincoln's inauguration to the issuing of the Emancipation Proclamation. The historical elements are enlivened by a fictional subplot involving a beautiful Southern spy living in the Lincoln household.

Historical Accuracy: The plausible historical portrait of Lincoln is at times undermined by the melodramatic and incredible espionage subplot.

4488 *The Last Full Measure*

Date of Publication: 1930
Subject(s): Civil War—U.S.; Assassination
Historical character(s): Abraham Lincoln, Political Figure; John Wilkes Booth, Murderer
Time Period(s): 1860s (1865)
Locale(s): Washington, District of Columbia

Summary: In the concluding volume of the author's trilogy chronicling the events of the Lincoln presidency, the end of the Civil War and the final months of Lincoln's life are depicted. The novel offers a full account of the Booth conspiracy and the assassination of Lincoln.

Historical Accuracy: The novel does not invent a fictional accompaniment to the actual events.

4489 *Let the King Beware!*

Date of Publication: 1936
Subject(s): American Revolution; Royalty—England; Diplomacy
Fictional character(s): Tristram Amory, Diplomat; Margot Stuart, Gentlewoman
Historical character(s): George III, Ruler (King of England); Frederick North, Political Figure; Charlotte of Mecklenburg-Strelitz, Royalty (queen consort of George III); Benjamin Franklin, Political Figure; Edmund Burke, Political Figure
Time Period(s): 1770s
Locale(s): England

Summary: The events leading up to the American Revolution are viewed from the perspective of some of the major English figures involved, including George III, Lord North, and Edmund Burke. An American loyalist, Tristram Amory, is in the thick of things as negotiations break down and rebellion breaks out.

Historical Accuracy: The portrait of George III and the interpretations of events are at odds with more traditional accounts. However, there is evidence that research backs the author's point of view.

4490 *On to Oregon!*

Date of Publication: 1926
Subject(s): American West; Wagon Trains
Fictional character(s): John Sager, Teenager
Time Period(s): 19th century
Locale(s): Oregon Trail, United States

Summary: The story of a pioneer trek along the Oregon Trail from Missouri to the Willamette Valley of Oregon is described through the experiences of young John Sager. When his father and mother die on the journey, he is left in charge of six brothers and sisters.

Historical Accuracy: The novel stays close to the known facts of life along the Oregon Trail during the period.

4491 *We Must March: A Novel of the Winning of Oregon*

Date of Publication: 1925
Subject(s): American West; Settlement of the American Frontier
Historical character(s): Marcus Whitman, Religious (missionary); Narcissa Whitman, Spouse
Time Period(s): 19th century
Locale(s): Rocky Mountains; Oregon

Summary: The opening of the western route to Oregon by a small band of pioneers is described. At the center of the drama are the actual figures of Marcus Whitman and his wife Narcissa who brave hostile Indians, the Hudson Bay Company, which is determined to stop settlement, and the seemingly impassable barrier of the Rockies.

Historical Accuracy: The historical elements are authentic and provide a realistic basis for the novel's narrative elements.

4492 *With Malice Toward None*

Date of Publication: 1928
Subject(s): Civil War—U.S.; Politics; Biography, Fictionalized
Historical character(s): Abraham Lincoln, Political Figure; Charles Summer, Political Figure
Time Period(s): 1860s (1864-1865)
Locale(s): Washington, District of Columbia

Summary: The novel continues the story of Abraham Lincoln's presidency begun in *Forever Free*. The action covers the last two years of the war and Lincoln's conflict with Charles Summer over reconstruction.

Historical Accuracy: The novel mingles actual events with imaginative suggestions about thoughts and conversations.

IAN MORSON

4493 *Falconer's Crusade*

Date of Publication: 1994
Subject(s): Middle Ages; Baron's War; Mystery
Fictional character(s): William Falconer, Teacher, Philosopher; Thomas Symon, Student—College
Time Period(s): 13th century (1264)
Locale(s): Oxford, England

Summary: In the midst of the Barons' Rebellion in the 13th century led by Simon de Montfort against Henry III, Oxford University is torn by shifting allegiances. In a crime seemingly unconnected to the great political events, a young servant girl is savagely murdered. William Falconer, Regent Master, teacher, and amateur detective investigates and is caught up in a complex conspiracy involving heresy, magic, and murder.

Historical Accuracy: The novel features a convincing period background.

4494 *Falconer's Judgement*

Date of Publication: 1995
Subject(s): Mystery; Middle Ages; Religious Conflict
Fictional character(s): William Falconer, Teacher, Philosopher
Historical character(s): Henry III, Ruler (King of England)
Time Period(s): 13th century (1264)
Locale(s): Oxford, England; London, England

Summary: In the second medieval mystery involving Oxford Regent Master William Falconer, conflict arises as Pope Alexander's impeding death causes a power struggle to name his successor. When the Papal Legate's brother is killed by an assassin, the blame falls on a university student, and other students are accused in a string of bizarre murders. Falconer must solve the crimes to save the students' lives.

Historical Accuracy: The events described have a basis in history as the author's notes make clear.

JOHN MORTIMER (1923-)

An English novelist and playwright, Mortimer was born in London and attended Brasenose College, Oxford. Mortimer is a barrister who was named to the Queen's Council in 1966. He is best known by Americans for his Rumpole of the Bailey series of legal mysteries, and for his autobiographical *A Voyage Round My Father*.

4495 *Will Shakespeare: The Untold Story*

Date of Publication: 1977
Subject(s): Elizabethan Period; Theatrical Life
Fictional character(s): Jack Rice, Actor
Historical character(s): William Shakespeare, Writer, Actor; Christopher Marlowe, Writer; Henry Wriothesley, Nobleman (Earl of Southampton); Anne Hathaway, Spouse (of Shakespeare); Elizabeth I, Ruler (Queen of England); Robert Devereux, Nobleman (Earl of Essex)
Time Period(s): 16th century
Locale(s): Stratford-on-Avon, England; London, England

Summary: Described by a one-time boy actor, Jack Rice, the novel depicts the life and times of William Shakespeare from his journey to London and his start as a horse-tender outside the Rose Theater to his amazing success and involvement with some of the age's great events and personalities.

Historical Accuracy: The novel is a blend of the known and the imagined.

STANLEY MORTON
(PSEUD. OF MORTON FREEDGOOD; STANLEY FREEDGOOD)

American suspense writer Morton Freedgood was born in Brooklyn, New York, and attended the City College of New York. A writer since 1947, Freedgood has also worked as an occasional publicist for film production companies. He is known for his tautly paced crime and adventure thrillers, the best-known of which is *The Taking of Pelham One Two Three*, which was made into a hit movie starring Walter Matthau. He is also the author of *Fatal Beauty*, *Nella*, and *The Snake*.

4496 *Yankee Trader*

Date of Publication: 1947
Subject(s): American Colonies
Fictional character(s): Nathan Turner, Sea Captain; Francis Cowper, Businessman
Time Period(s): 18th century
Locale(s): Connecticut, American Colonies

Summary: The rivalry between sea captain Nathan Turner and businessman Francis Cowper forms the drama in this novel set in pre-Revolutionary days in Connecticut. Nathan is determined to achieve wealth and power, and the novel recounts his gains and losses.

Historical Accuracy: The story is a familiar one with only an average sense of the period.

ROBERT MOSS (1946-)

Moss is the author of a number of best-selling suspense novels, including *Moscow Rules* and *Carnival of Spies*, as well as the American historical adventure *Fire Along the Sky*. Moss was born in Australia of Scottish, Cornish, Irish, and French ancestry. He has worked as a college professor of history and philosophy, a war correspondent in Vietnam, a magazine editor, and a syndicated columnist.

4497 *Fire Along the Sky: A Novel of America*

Date of Publication: 1990
Subject(s): French and Indian War; Indians; Pontiac's Rebellion
Fictional character(s): Shane Hardacre, Gambler; Lady Valerie Diarcy, Noblewoman
Historical character(s): Sir William Johnson, Government Official (superintendent of Indians); Pontiac, Indian (Ottawa), Chieftain
Time Period(s): 1750s; 1760s
Locale(s): Mohawk Valley, New York, American Colonies; Lake Erie, Great Lakes; Detroit River, United States

Summary: Shane Hardacre, a gambler and adventurer, flees London and seeks out his kinsman, Sir William Johnson, the king's superintendent of Indians and a major figure of British influence on the frontiers. The novel describes Shane's adventures in the French and Indian War that take him from Mohawk territory through the Great Lakes to Detroit and an encounter with the great chief Pontiac whose revolt is described.

Historical Accuracy: Hardacre's account is documented by solid historical details.

4498 *The Firekeeper*

Date of Publication: 1995
Subject(s): American Colonies; French and Indian War; Indians
Fictional character(s): Island Woman, Indian (Iroquois), Shaman
Historical character(s): Sir William Johnson, Government Official; Catherine Weissenberg, Spouse (of Johnson); George Washington, Military Personnel (major); Benjamin Franklin, Political Figure; Ephraim Williams, Military Personnel (soldier)
Time Period(s): 18th century
Locale(s): Mohawk Valley, New York, American Colonies

Summary: This epic treatment of the American frontier during the period of the French and Indian Wars is based on the story of William Johnson. Johnson comes to America from Ireland and serves the British colonies by convincing the Iroquois to fight against the French. The novel shows the cultural clash of Indians and settlers, particularly from the point of view of the Island Woman, an Iroquois shaman whose visions become connected with Johnson and the emerging American nation.

Historical Accuracy: As the writer acknowledges, where facts about historical events and characters are known, the novel has been faithful to the sources. When the facts are unknown, the author has filled in the gaps with invention and has revised the conventional accounts of well-known events. The notes make clear the sources and the deviations.

4499 *The Interpreter*

Date of Publication: 1997
Subject(s): French and Indian War; Indians; Settlement of the American Frontier
Fictional character(s): Island Woman, Indian (Mohawk), Shaman
Historical character(s): Conrad Weiser, Frontiersman, Government Official (Indian agent); Hendrick Forked Path, Indian (Mohawk), Chieftain
Time Period(s): 18th century (1709-1741)
Locale(s): New York, American Colonies; Pennsylvania, American Colonies; England

Summary: This novel of Indian and pioneer life in the American colonies during the years of the French and Indian Wars tells the story of Conrad Weiser, Pennsylvania's Indian agent. Weiser grows up in New York and participates in the revolt of German settlers against the British. He is sent by his father to live among the Mohawks, learning their language and customs. Eventually, he leads a group of dispossessed German settlers into the wilderness of Pennsylvania.

Historical Accuracy: The novel has a solid basis in historical fact as its notes make clear.

IGAL MOSSINSOHN

4500 *Judas*

Date of Publication: 1963
Subject(s): Biblical Story; Christianity
Fictional character(s): Andigones, Philosopher
Historical character(s): Judas Iscariot, Biblical Figure; Peter, Biblical Figure
Time Period(s): 1st century
Locale(s): Garamus, Mediterranean (island-city)

Summary: Ten years after the crucifixion of Jesus, Judas Iscariot is still active and living in obscurity on the island city of Garamus. He tells his own story of the ensuing conflict between Peter who wishes Judas to remain dead in fulfillment of the moral in the story of his betrayal of Christ and the philosopher Andigones who for his own reasons wants to turn Judas into a local saint.

Historical Accuracy: This is an ingenious blend of the Biblical tale and a moral speculation. The era of early Christianity is aptly rendered.

ANNETTE MOTLEY

A British writer of romances and historical novels, Motley's fiction is characterized by detailed historical background intertwined with a romantic story. Her books include *My Lady's Crusade*, *Green Dragon, White Tiger*, and *Men on White Horses*.

4501 *Green Dragon, White Tiger*

Date of Publication: 1986
Subject(s): Chinese Empire; Royalty—China
Historical character(s): Wu Chao, Ruler (Chinese empress)
Time Period(s): 7th century
Locale(s): China

Summary: The novel is set during the 7th century T'ang Dynasty in China and dramatizes the remarkable rise of Wu Chao, called Black Jade, from concubine to Empress of China, the only woman in Chinese history to reign as empress. To reach the throne, Wu Chao must show considerable gifts both in the arts of love and manipulation.

Historical Accuracy: The novel is convincing in its extensive research and its authentic period details.

4502 *The Quickenberry Tree*

Date of Publication: 1983
Subject(s): Civil War—England; Family Saga; Religious Conflict
Fictional character(s): Lucy Heron, Gentlewoman; Will Staunton, Sea Captain, Adventurer; Cathal O'Connor, Gentleman
Historical character(s): Henry Morgan, Pirate; Charles I, Ruler (King of England)
Time Period(s): 17th century (1641-1657)
Locale(s): England; Bruges, Belgium

Summary: This massive family saga is set during the English Civil War and concerns the Royalist Heron family. Young Lucy Heron is attracted to two very different men, her Irish cousin Cathal O'Connor and sea captain Will Staunton. Their story is connected to the deposition and execution of Charles I and the eventual restoration of Charles II.

Historical Accuracy: The novel's historical background is authentic and accurately presented.

4503 *The Sins of the Lion*

Date of Publication: 1979
Subject(s): Renaissance
Fictional character(s): Leone da Valenti, Royalty (prince); Mona Tilla, Royalty (princess), Captive
Time Period(s): 15th century
Locale(s): Montevalenti, Italy

Summary: The setting is Renaissance Italy, and the story concerns the love affair between Leone, Prince of Valenti, and Tulla, a beautiful Greco-Turkish princess who has been taken by pirates into slavery. Leone purchases her and comes both to rely on her and to love her independence and judgment, as he defends his principality against mercenaries.

Historical Accuracy: The story is fanciful but does employ a convincing period atmosphere.

ROBERTA JEAN MOUNTJOY
(PSEUD. OF JERRY SOHL, 1913-)

An American writer born in Los Angeles, Mountjoy attended Central College of Arts and Sciences in Chicago. Mountjoy has worked as a photographer, police reporter, critic, reviewer, and staff writer for "Star Trek" and "Alfred Hitchcock Presents.".

`4504` *Night Wind*

Date of Publication: 1981

Subject(s): American West; Indians; Gold Rush—California

Fictional character(s): Marcus Opalgate, Young Man; Night Wind, Indian (princess); Richard Opalgate, Young Man

Time Period(s): 1840s

Locale(s): California (northwestern)

Summary: Set in the redwood forests of northern California as gold brings fortune hunters to California threatening the traditional ways of the Indians, the novel dramatizes the fateful encounter of two of the 49ers, Richard and Marcus Opalgate, with Night Wind, an Indin princess.

Historical Accuracy: The story is more romance than history, with some period elements lightly sketched.

KENIZE MOURAD

`4505` *Regards From the Dead Princess: A Novel of a Life*

Date of Publication: 1987

Subject(s): Ottoman Empire; World War II

Historical character(s): Selma, Royalty (princess); Mourard V, Ruler (sultan)

Time Period(s): 20th century

Locale(s): Constantinople, Ottoman Empire; Beirut, Lebanon; India

Summary: The novel traces the amazing story of Princess Selma, the granddaughter of Mourard V, a Sultan of the Ottoman Empire. Her story begins in the final days of the Empire with exile in Beirut and an arranged marriage to a royal in India. Finally she finds her way to German-occupied Paris during World War II.

Historical Accuracy: Though based on the real-life Selma, many of the events and figures have been fictionalized for the purpose of the novel.

LLOYD M. MOXON

`4506` *Before the Wind*

Date of Publication: 1978

Subject(s): Sea Story; Napoleonic Wars; Military Life—British Navy

Fictional character(s): John St. John, Military Personnel (naval officer)

Time Period(s): 1790s (1795)

Locale(s): England; At Sea

Summary: British naval officer John St. John engages the French in a variety of actions in 1795. His adventures are related in a first-person account.

Historical Accuracy: The novel vividly describes period nautical customs.

HELEN PARKER MUDGETT (1900-)

`4507` *The Sea Stands Watch*

Date of Publication: 1944

Subject(s): Politics; Sea Story

Fictional character(s): John Noyes, Sea Captain; Julia Noyes, Spouse

Historical character(s): Charles Cornwallis, Political Figure (Governor of East India Company)

Time Period(s): 18th century; 19th century (1785-1812)

Locale(s): New England; At Sea; China

Summary: The novel is set between the American Revolution and the War of 1812 and describes the commercial development of the young republic. The story focuses on the naval career of a young seaman, John Noyes, whose journeys take him around the world in pursuit of trade.

Historical Accuracy: The novel creates a vivid and convincing period atmosphere.

MARIE MUIR (1904-)

English writer Muir publishes novels under her own name and under the pseudonyms Monica Blake and Barbara Kaye. Her other titles include *Captive of the Sun*, *The Mermaid Queen*, and *The Cup of Froth*.

`4508` *Dear Mrs. Boswell*

Date of Publication: 1953

Subject(s): Biography, Fictionalized; Literary life

Historical character(s): Margaret Boswell, Spouse; James Boswell, Writer

Time Period(s): 18th century

Locale(s): Edinburgh, Scotland; London, England

Summary: Writer James Boswell, considered by many the greatest biographer in Western literature, is seen through the eyes of his cousin and wife, Margaret. Her love for Boswell is strong despite his arrogance, heavy drinking, and womanizing. The novel is knowing in its ability to capture Boswell's circle and the era.

Historical Accuracy: The novel mixes fact and romance, with a convincing evocation of the period.

ROBERT MUIR

`4509` *The Sprig of Hemlock: A Novel about Shays' Rebellion*

Date of Publication: 1957

Subject(s): Shays' Rebellion

Fictional character(s): Isiah Tucker, Farmer; Abel Tucker, Farmer; Enoch Tucker, Young Man

Historical character(s): Daniel Shays, Revolutionary

Time Period(s): 1780s (1786-1787)

Locale(s): Massachusetts

Summary: In 1786, a group of Massachusetts farmers led by Daniel Shays mount a rebellion over high taxes. The novel depicts the effect of events on the Tucker family who find themselves in the center of the turmoil controlled by mob psychology.

Historical Accuracy: The basic framework of the story is the actual events of the Rebellion, captured with authenticity.

BHARATI MUKHERJEE (1940-)

Born in Calcutta, Mukherjee attended universities in Calcutta and Baroda where she received a master's degree in English and Ancient Indian culture. She received a Ph.D. in English from the University of Iowa. She has been a professor of English at Berkeley and at Skidmore College. *Days and Nights in Calcutta* is a journal written with her husband, Clark Blaise, of her return to India after living in Canada and the U.S.

4510 *The Holder of the World*

Date of Publication: 1993
Subject(s): American Colonies; Puritans; Mogul Empire
Fictional character(s): Hannah Easton, Young Woman; Beigh Masters, Young Woman
Time Period(s): 17th century; 20th century
Locale(s): Boston, Massachusetts; India

Summary: This is the story of the meeting of cultures between Puritan America and Mogul India. Hannah Easton, born in the Puritan colonies in 1670, is an exception to the Puritan society. She travels with her husband, an English trader, to Mogul India where she becomes the white consort of a Hindu raja. Her spiritual descendent is Beigh Masters, a 20th century New Englander who pieces together the details of Hannah's journeys and the connections between the two women.

Historical Accuracy: The novel is convincing in both the scenes in Puritan America and 17th century Mogul India.

FREDERIC MULLALLY (1920-)

Born in London, Mullally was educated at St. Xavier College. He worked as an editor and publicity director for several British newspapers before becoming a full-time writer in 1958. His books include *Clancy*, *The Malta Conspiracy*, and *Venus Afflicted*.

4511 *Hitler Has Won*

Date of Publication: 1975
Subject(s): World War II; Alternate History
Fictional character(s): Kurt Armbrecht, Veteran (German soldier), Writer
Historical character(s): Adolf Hitler, Leader (Nazi); Franklin Delano Roosevelt, Political Figure; Pius XII, Religious (pope)
Time Period(s): 1940s
Locale(s): Germany; Italy

Summary: This rather outlandish alternative history of World War II stops the actual war in 1941 and then goes on to imagine Hitler winning on all fronts, the U.S. remaining neutral, and culminating with Hitler's attempt to depose Pius XII and have himself proclaimed Pope Adolph I. He is op-

posed by young Kurt Armbrecht who sets out to stop the Fuhrer.

Historical Accuracy: This melodramatic fantasy cannot be taken seriously as a plausible scenario even though the workings of the Nazi bureaucracy have a certain credibility.

MARGARET MULLALLY (1954-)

4512 *A Crown in Darkness: A Novel about Lady Jane Grey*

Date of Publication: 1975
Subject(s): Tudor Period; Royalty—England; Biography, Fictionalized
Historical character(s): Lady Jane Grey, Ruler (Queen of England); Elizabeth Tudor, Royalty (princess); Mary Tudor, Royalty (princess); Henry VIII, Ruler (King of England); Edward Tudor, Royalty (prince); Robert Dudley, Nobleman (Duke of Northumberland)
Time Period(s): 16th century (1537-1554)
Locale(s): England

Summary: The short and tragic life of Lady Jane Grey is dramatized. She reigned as Queen of England for nine days before being executed at the age of seventeen. Lady Jane is shown largely as a victim of the schemes of a variety of self-interested parties, especially the Duke of Northumberland who contrives the marriage of his son and Lady Jane to gain her throne.

Historical Accuracy: The essential elements of the story are historical. The period background is convincingly described.

EDWIN MULLINS (1933-)

An English Medievalist, art critic, journalist, broadcaster, and television scriptwriter, Mullins graduated from Oxford University. He has written several books on painting and sculpture and has served as the BBC television art correspondent.

4513 *The Master Painter*

Date of Publication: 1988
Subject(s): Artistic Life; Middle Ages
Fictional character(s): Master Jan, Artist
Historical character(s): Philip, Duke of Burgundy, Nobleman; Jacqueline of Hainault, Noblewoman; Joan of Arc, Military Personnel (French army leader)
Time Period(s): 15th century
Locale(s): Netherlands; France

Summary: Inspired by the life of Flemish painter Jan van Eyck, the first psychological portrait painter, the novel tells the story of artist Master Jan whose skill in capturing the truth behind the human mask brings him to prominence in the court of Philip, Duke of Burgundy in the midst of his bitter rivalry with Jacqueline of Hainault.

Historical Accuracy: The author maintains that Master Jan is and is not Jan van Eyck. The story offers speculations backed by a measure of historical probability.

TALBOT MUNDY

`4514` *Purple Pirate*

Date of Publication: 1936
Subject(s): Roman Empire
Fictional character(s): Tros of Samothrace, Military Personnel
Historical character(s): Cleopatra, Ruler (Queen of Egypt)
Time Period(s): 1st century B.C. (46-44 B.C.)
Locale(s): Egypt; Mediterranean

Summary: The novel continues the adventures of Tros of Samothrace through the period of the civil war that follows the death of Julius Caesar. Tros, who brings Cleopatra out of Rome after Caesar's death, remains in Egypt to help bolster her hold on her throne.

Historical Accuracy: The novel's adventures are set solidly in an accurate historical framework.

`4515` *Tros of Samothrace*

Date of Publication: 1934
Subject(s): Roman Empire
Fictional character(s): Tros of Samothrace, Military Personnel (general)
Historical character(s): Julius Caesar, Military Personnel (army commander), Political Figure
Time Period(s): 1st century B.C.
Locale(s): Rome, Roman Empire; England; Gaul (modern France)

Summary: This tale of the Roman conquest of Britain by Julius Caesar focuses on one of his generals, Tros of Samothrace. For personal and religious reasons, Tros opposes Caesar's aspirations and tries to save Britain from Roman rule.

Historical Accuracy: The novel blends fact and fiction and captures with some accuracy the Roman world at the time of Caesar.

H. WARNER MUNN (1903-1981)

An American born in Massachusetts, Munn worked as a salesman, truck driver, deck hand, railroad brakeman, and factory worker. He established his reputation as an author of fantasy and horror stories.

`4516` *The Lost Legion*

Date of Publication: 1980
Subject(s): Roman Empire; Exploration
Fictional character(s): Manlius Varro, Military Personnel (Roman commander); Lilia, Young Woman
Historical character(s): Caligula, Ruler (Roman emperor)
Time Period(s): 1st century
Locale(s): Rome, Roman Empire; Middle East; China

Summary: The mad Emperor Caligula sends the crack XIIIth legion on an impossible mission: to follow the silk route deep into Asia to recover the standard of a Roman army that disappeared one hundred years before. The legion dutifully sets out beyond the limits of the Empire to the fabled lands of the East.

Historical Accuracy: The story is fanciful but does offer a convincing description of the period and its exotic locales.

HOPE MUNTZ (1907-)

A Canadian writer born in Toronto, Muntz attended private school and art schools in England and Canada. Muntz set out to be an artist and practiced commercial art for a time. She has also worked as a freelance journalist, and done aircraft and precision engineering, as well as office and civil defense work.

`4517` *The Golden Warrior: The Story of Harold and William*

Date of Publication: 1949
Subject(s): Middle Ages; Norman Conquest; Battle of Hastings
Historical character(s): Harold II, Ruler (King of England); William the Conqueror, Nobleman (Duke of Normandy); Edward the Confessor, Ruler (King of England); Edward the Atheling, Nobleman; Matilda of Flanders, Royalty (consort of William I)
Time Period(s): 11th century
Locale(s): Hastings, England; Normandy, France; London, England

Summary: The story of the Norman Conquest is described from the perspective of Harold II, the last Saxon King of England. Invincible before his defeat and death at the Battle of Hastings, Harold's great strengths are balanced with the weaknesses exploited by William to help bring about Harold's downfall.

Historical Accuracy: The author used contemporary sources, supplemented by those of the 12th and 13th centuries, for her facts and characters.

T.N. MURARI (1941-)

Born in Madras, India, Murari came to the U.S. in 1977. Having attended Madras University and McGill University, Murari has worked as a journalist in Canada and England.

`4518` *The Imperial Agent*

Date of Publication: 1987
Subject(s): Espionage; Independence—India
Fictional character(s): Kimball O'Hara, Spy; Colonel Creighton, Military Personnel
Historical character(s): George Nathaniel Curzon, Political Figure
Time Period(s): 1900 (1905)
Locale(s): India

Summary: The novel is a sequel to Rudyard Kipling's adventure classic *Kim*, in which Kimball O'Hara, now a young man, is recruited again by the enigmatic Colonel Creighton, but the Great Game has a different set of rules in 1905. The first stirring of Indian independence divides Kim's loyalties between his duty to England and India as they move closer to conflict.

Historical Accuracy: The novel captures India with authentic period details.

4519 *The Last Victory*

Date of Publication: 1988
Subject(s): British Colonies; World War I; Independence—India
Fictional character(s): Kimball O'Hara, Military Personnel (Indian soldier); Colonel Creighton, Military Personnel (British officer); Parvati, Young Woman
Historical character(s): Jawaharlal Nehru, Political Figure; Mohandas K. Gandhi, Political Figure
Time Period(s): 1910s (1910-1919)
Locale(s): India; France

Summary: In this sequel to the author's *The Imperial Agent*, the story of Rudyard Kipling's Kimball O'Hara is continued in the 1910s. Kim distances himself from the control of his mentor, the Colonel, and endures the hardship of prison and trench warfare during World War I only to become involved in the struggle for Indian independence. The action climaxes in the violent events of 1919 in which Kim must finally choose between his allegiance to England or India.

Historical Accuracy: The period background is effectively and convincingly delivered.

CLYDE FRANCIS MURPHY (1899-1946)

Born in Montana, Murphy was the son of an officer of the Anaconda Copper Mining Company. *The Glittering Hill* won the first Lewis and Clark Northwest book contest.

4520 *Glittering Hill*

Date of Publication: 1944
Subject(s): American West; Mining; Immigrants
Fictional character(s): Magnus Dunn, Mine Owner; Nick Stryker, Adventurer
Time Period(s): 1890s
Locale(s): Butte, Montana

Summary: The novel provides a colorful depiction of life in Butte, Montana during the 1880s at the height of the copper mining era. It captures the customs and fortunes of various Irish immigrants who come to Butte to make or lose their fortunes.

Historical Accuracy: The novel is convincing in its evocation of the period and the place.

EDWARD FRANCIS MURPHY (1914-)

Born in Tarrytown, New York, writer and sports magazine editor Edward Murphy attended the National Academy of Design, Columbia University, Fordham, and the Art Students League. He served as a staff sergeant with the U.S. Army during World War II. During his early career, Murphy was a radio vocalist and musician with Tex Ritter and others in New York City. He then pursued a career in publishing and became an editor and writer for *Sports Afield*.

4521 *Angel of the Delta*

Date of Publication: 1958
Subject(s): Reconstruction Period; Biography, Fictionalized; Civil War—U.S.
Historical character(s): Margaret Haughery, Activist (reformer); Benjamin Butler, Military Personnel (Union general)
Time Period(s): 19th century (1813-1878)
Locale(s): New Orleans, Louisiana; Ireland

Summary: This biographical novel chronicles the life and career of Margaret Haughery who comes from Ireland to New Orleans where she is a tireless advocate on behalf of orphan children. She endures the struggles of the Union occupation and the years following the Civil War with a determination to serve others.

Historical Accuracy: The novel is thoroughly based on the details of Haughery's life and times.

4522 *A Bride for New Orleans*

Date of Publication: 1955
Subject(s): French Colonies; Religious Life
Fictional character(s): Yvonne Delisle, Young Woman; Raymond Massy, Young Man
Time Period(s): 1720s (1727)
Locale(s): Paris, France; New Orleans, Louisiana

Summary: The novel tells the story of the Casket girls who journeyed from France to New Orleans in the 1720s to marry and help settle Louisiana. The story centers on Parisienne Yvonne Delisle's experience.

Historical Accuracy: The novel is masterful in capturing the religious work of the priests and nuns during the early period of New Orleans' history.

4523 *Road From Olivet*

Date of Publication: 1946
Subject(s): Biblical Story; Roman Empire
Historical character(s): Mary Magdalene, Biblical Figure
Time Period(s): 1st century
Locale(s): Israel; Italy

Summary: This devotional novel, the sequel to *The Scarlet Lily*, continues the story of Mary Magdalene after the crucifixion of Jesus. Based on the legend that she travelled with a group of early Christian missionaries to France, the novel dramatizes what happened to her in Italy before she set out for France.

Historical Accuracy: The novel is unconvincing both as a psychological portrait and as a historical re-creation of the early Christian church.

4524 *The Scarlet Lily*

Date of Publication: 1944
Subject(s): Biblical Story
Historical character(s): Mary Magdalene, Biblical Figure
Time Period(s): 1st century
Locale(s): Israel

Summary: The biblical story imagines a biographical account of Mary Magdalene that traces her life from early childhood to her encounter with Jesus. The novel offers a sympathetic account of her failings and the process of redemption offered by her devotion to Jesus.

Historical Accuracy: The novel mixes historical elements from the New Testament and invention, some of which are unconvincing.

JAMES F. MURPHY JR.

Murphy is an Associate Professor of English at the Massachusetts Maritime Academy in Buzzards Bay on Cape Cod.

`4525` *They Were Dreamers*

Date of Publication: 1983
Subject(s): Family Saga; Immigrants
Fictional character(s): Brendan McMahon, Immigrant, Farmer; Mary McMahon, Spouse; Kate Ahearn, Young Woman
Time Period(s): 19th century (1832-1874)
Locale(s): Ireland; Prince Edward Island, Canada; Boston, Massachusetts

Summary: The novel dramatizes the story of Irish immigrants to Canada and the United States in the 19th century. Brendan McMahon and his wife Mary settle on Prince Edward Island where Brendan helps establish a newspaper and enters politics. Later generations are shown dealing with prejudice in Boston, having to prove their worth once again in a strange and alien land.

Historical Accuracy: The period elements in the story are convincingly drawn.

WALTER F. MURPHY (1929-)

`4526` *Upon This Rock: The Life of St. Peter*

Date of Publication: 1987
Subject(s): Christianity; Roman Empire; Biography, Fictionalized
Fictional character(s): Quintus, Religious (early follower of Jesus)
Historical character(s): Peter, Biblical Figure, Religious; Paul, Biblical Figure, Religious
Time Period(s): 1st century
Locale(s): Rome, Roman Empire

Summary: The story of the early Christians and of St. Peter is told from the perspective of Quintus, a fictional follower of Jesus. His narrative begins as he and Peter are fleeing Rome to escape persecution. The novel captures Peter's strength as a religious leader, the bitter dispute between Jews and Gentiles in the early church, and Peter's eventual martyrdom.

Historical Accuracy: The novel, based on evident research in current New Testament scholarship, offers a plausible picture of the early church and the conflict of cultures Christians struggled to resolve.

D.L. MURRAY

`4527` *Commander of the Mists*

Date of Publication: 1938
Subject(s): Jacobite Rebellion; Georgian Period
Fictional character(s): Darthula Maceachern, Young Woman
Historical character(s): Charles Edward Stuart, Royalty
Time Period(s): 1740s; 1750s
Locale(s): Scotland

Summary: This romantic adventure tale is set against the background of the effort by Bonnie Prince Charlie to mobilize the Highland clans on behalf of his claim to the English throne in 1745. In this version, the woman behind the man is young Darthula Maceachern, who sacrifices everything on behalf of the prince's cause.

Historical Accuracy: The story is fanciful but does employ actual events in the history of the Stuart Rebellion.

`4528` *Trumpeter, Sound!*

Date of Publication: 1934
Subject(s): Victorian Period; Crimean War; Battle of Balaclava
Fictional character(s): Fancy Fawkes, Dancer; Mark Woodrofe, Bastard Son; Major Blackwater, Nobleman, Military Personnel
Time Period(s): 1850s
Locale(s): London, England; Crimea, Russia

Summary: This tale of the Crimean War offers a fictional solution to the mystery surrounding the ill-fated charge of the Light Brigade. Off the battlefield two brothers—Major Blackwater and Mark Woodrofe—compete for the affections of London dancer Fancy Fawkes.

Historical Accuracy: The historical background is accurately provided, though the fictional story dominates the facts surrounding the battle at Balaclava.

EARL MURRAY

`4529` *Free Flows the River*

Date of Publication: 1991
Subject(s): Indians; American West
Fictional character(s): Thane Thompson, Mountain Man; Jethro Thompson, Mountain Man; Many Berries, Indian (Crow)
Time Period(s): 1840s (1849)
Locale(s): Wind River, Wyoming; Yellowstone River, Wyoming

Summary: Jethro Thompson is the son of mountain man Thane Thompson and his Crow wife. Jethro is raised a Crow, and on his vision quest he meets an enemy whose life he spares with disastrous consequences to those he loves.

Historical Accuracy: The scenes of tribal life and Indian lore are authentic.

4530 *High Freedom*

Date of Publication: 1989

Subject(s): American West; Settlement of the American Frontier

Fictional character(s): Thane Thompson, Mountain Man; Morning Swan, Indian

Time Period(s): 1820s

Locale(s): Montana

Summary: Falsely accused of murder in Virginia, Thane Thompson flees west into the mountains of Montana. There he establishes himself among a rough company of mountain men and learns to survive in the frontier.

Historical Accuracy: The details of wilderness life of the period are convincing.

4531 *Song of Wovoka*

Date of Publication: 1992

Subject(s): Indians; American West; Battle of Wounded Knee

Fictional character(s): Mark Thomas, Religious (Jesuit priest); Fawn, Indian; Two Robes, Indian, Warrior

Historical character(s): Wovoka, Indian (Paute), Shaman

Time Period(s): 1880s; 1890s (1889-1891)

Locale(s): North Dakota; South Dakota

Summary: In the 1880s the Paute mystic Wovoka has a vision that if the Indians dance the Ghost Dance the buffalo will return; all the departed Indians will come back, and the white man will vanish from the earth. As the appeal of Wovoka's message reaches the Cheyenne River Sioux, Father Mark Thomas must deal with conflict that reaches a climax at Wounded Knee.

Historical Accuracy: All the characters and events portrayed in the book are fictitious, and any resemblance to real people is purely coincidental.

4532 *Thunder in the Dawn*

Date of Publication: 1993

Subject(s): Indians; Sioux War of 1876; Battle of the Rosebud

Fictional character(s): Mason Hall, Military Personnel; Ghostwind, Indian (Cheyenne), Shaman

Historical character(s): Crazy Horse, Indian (Sioux), Warrior; Sitting Bull, Indian (Sioux), Chieftain; George C. Crook, Military Personnel (Army general)

Time Period(s): 1870s (1876)

Locale(s): Montana; Wyoming

Summary: The novel's background is the Great Sioux War of 1876 and the Battle of the Rosebud, one week before the massacre at the Little Big Horn. Mason Hall joins the U.S. Army as an alternative to being hanged. Alone after a raid, he is captured by Indians and comes into contact with Ghostwind, a survivor of the battle at Washita. Both experience a test of divided loyalties.

Historical Accuracy: Solidly based on actual events, the novel offers a reliable interpretation of these events.

FRANCES MURRAY
(PSEUD. OF ROSEMARY FRANCES BOOTH, 1928-)

A Scottish writer born in Glasgow, Murray graduated from the University of St. Andrews. She has worked as a history teacher in secondary schools.

4533 *The Belchamber Scandal*

Date of Publication: 1985

Subject(s): Victorian Period

Fictional character(s): Amelia Belchamber, Governess; Quentin Cateret, Gentleman

Time Period(s): 1860s

Locale(s): England

Summary: In the 1860s, Amelia Belchamber is forced, due to a family disaster, to make her way as a governess to the trying Haggeth family in the north of England. She must endure unwanted amorous advances, eight wayward offspring, and finally a most serious challenge.

Historical Accuracy: The regional elements are convincing.

4534 *Brave Kingdom*

Date of Publication: 1983

Subject(s): Family Saga; Musical Life

Fictional character(s): Hannah Lindsay, Young Woman; Nick Innis, Composer; John Macadam, Musician

Time Period(s): 19th century; 20th century

Locale(s): Scotland; New Zealand

Summary: This family saga begins in the 1850s with Hannah Lindsay's search for her brother in New Zealand. A chain of events is set in motion that covers more than a century and four generations of a musically talented family whose talent is sustained through war, depression, and the rise and fall of family fortune.

Historical Accuracy: The emphasis is on family over history, but the various periods are sketched with skill.

4535 *Castaway*

Date of Publication: 1978

Subject(s): Sea Story; Inheritance—Disputed; Napoleonic Wars

Fictional character(s): Isabelle Audley, Orphan; Charles de Beaumanoir, Military Personnel (naval officer)

Time Period(s): 1800s (1804)

Locale(s): Guernsey, England

Summary: In 1804, Isabelle Audley is shipwrecked off the Isle of Guernsey on her way back to England from India to claim her inheritance. With no means to prove her identity, she finds an ally in Charles de Beaumanoir of the Royal Navy as Napoleon readies his army for invasion.

Historical Accuracy: The period elements are convincingly drawn.

4536 *The Heroine's Sister*

Date of Publication: 1975

Subject(s): Victorian Period

Fictional character(s): Flora Porteous, Singer (opera); Mary Porteous, Young Woman, Governess
Time Period(s): 1860s (1868)
Locale(s): Venice, Italy

Summary: Two English sisters find themselves stranded in Venice in 1868. Flora Porteous is a decidedly limited young opera singer left without employment, while her sister Mary finds a job as a governess. Venice is alive with plots and intrigue, chaffing under the rule of the Austrian military that threatens to overwhelm the sensible and determined Mary.

Historical Accuracy: The period background of Venice is captured with authenticity.

LINDA MURRAY

4537 *The Dark Fire*

Date of Publication: 1977
Subject(s): Artistic Life; Biography, Fictionalized
Historical character(s): Michelangelo da Caravaggio, Artist
Time Period(s): 16th century; 17th century (1590s-1612)
Locale(s): Rome, Italy; Valletta, Malta; Naples, Italy

Summary: The fascinating figure of Italian painter Caravaggio is dramatized in this biographical novel that traces the artist's life and times from his apprenticeship in Milan and the flourishing of his artistry in Rome. Caravaggio is plagued by violence and misadventure that cause him to flee to Malta and Naples. After a brawl leaves him so disfigured as to be unrecognizable, he dies of fever at age 39. A revolutionary figure in the history of art, Caravaggio, the man, is as less fascinating as his age, which is vividly portrayed.

Historical Accuracy: The novel intermixes fact and fiction with an emphasis on the former when it is known.

SHELLEY MYDANS (1915-)

An American born in California, Mydans was a Japanese prisoner of war during World War II and later a foreign correspondent during the American occupation. Her books include *The Open City* and *Violent Peace: A Report on Wars in the Postwar World.*

4538 *Thomas: A Novel of the Life, Passions, and Miracles of Becket*

Date of Publication: 1965
Subject(s): Middle Ages; Royalty—England; Religious Conflict
Fictional character(s): Elured Porre, Banker
Historical character(s): Thomas Becket, Religious (Archbishop of Canterbury); Henry II, Ruler (King of England); Theobald, Religious (Archbishop of Canterbury)
Time Period(s): 12th century
Locale(s): Canterbury, England; France; London, England

Summary: The novel traces the career of Thomas Becket, son of a prosperous London merchant, educated in the church, but trained as a knight, lawyer, and politician. Becket is both a protege of the saintly Archbishop Theobald and a boon companion of Henry II. When Henry maneuvers Becket's election

as Archbishop of Canterbury, he hopes to control the Church, but Becket is forced to choose between his loyalty to his friend the king and his duty and responsibility to the Church.

Historical Accuracy: Although the conversations are invented, the chronology and the circumstances are accurate.

4539 *The Vermilion Bridge*

Date of Publication: 1980
Subject(s): Japanese Empire; Royalty—Japan
Historical character(s): Hime Abe No, Ruler (Empress of Japan); Fujiwara Nakamaro, Government Official; Dokyo, Religious (Buddhist priest)
Time Period(s): 8th century (710-770)
Locale(s): Japan

Summary: This novel is set in Japan when Chinese influence was at its height and the young nation could have developed either into an autocracy of Buddhist priests or a powerful secular nation. The struggle is dramatized in the reign of the Princess Abe by the ambitious Nakamaro, a member of the rising Fujiwara family, and Dokyo, a Buddhist priest.

Historical Accuracy: The story's chronology is carefully researched and accurate with some slight alterations for the sake of the story.

AMY MYERS

Born in Kent, England, Myers received a degree in English literature and has worked as a director of a London publishing company. She also writes under the name of Harriet Hudson. Her novels include *Murder at the Masque* and *Murder in the Limelight.*

4540 *Murder Makes an Entree*

Date of Publication: 1992
Subject(s): Mystery; Victorian Period
Fictional character(s): Auguste Didier, Cook, Detective—Amateur; Egbert Rose, Detective—Police
Historical character(s): Edward, Prince of Wales, Royalty
Time Period(s): 1890s (1899)
Locale(s): Broadstairs, England

Summary: This Victorian-era mystery features master chef Auguste Didier as its detective. The annual dinner of the Society of Literary Lionizers meets at Broadstairs in Kent to honor Charles Dickens. Presiding as president of the society is the Prince of Wales. When, during the program, someone collapses and dies of poisoning, Didier's cooking is suspected. Didier, along with Inspector Rose of Scotland Yard, attempts to uncover the real culprit.

Historical Accuracy: The novel features convincing period and regional details.

HENRY MYERS

4541 *Our Lives Have Just Begun*

Date of Publication: 1939
Subject(s): Middle Ages; Crusades; Children's Crusade

Historical character(s): Stephen of Cloyes, Leader (Crusades)
Time Period(s): 13th century (1212)
Locale(s): France; Italy

Summary: The novel tells the story of the Children's Crusade inspired by a visionary French peasant, Stephen of Cloyes. Hoping that the young could succeed when their elders had failed, Stephen embarks with a band of children to the Holy Land with disastrous consequences.

Historical Accuracy: The novel is a blend of the factual and the legendary. The historical background is well developed and convincing.

4542 *Signorina*

Date of Publication: 1956
Subject(s): Musical Life; Biography, Fictionalized
Historical character(s): Maria Felicita Malibran, Singer (opera); Vincenzo Bellini, Composer (opera)
Time Period(s): 19th century (1808-1836)
Locale(s): Europe

Summary: This biographical novel traces the short but notorious career of operatic contralto Maria Felicita Malibran. Born in Spain of a talented musical family, Malibran made her debut in 1825 in Rossini's *Barber of Seville*. She was considered by many to be the greatest singer who ever lived, though she died at the young age of 29.

Historical Accuracy: The novel is at times overly enthusiastic about its subject and indulges in questionable interpretations, for example, that Bellini, whom Malibran met only once, was the love of her life.

JOHN MYERS (1906-)

American writer born in Northport, New York, Myers attended St. Stephen's College, Middlebury College, and the University of New Mexico. He worked as a newspaperman, writer of advertising copy, and a farmer. His narrative poems attempt to offer a full chronicle of America's frontier experience.

4543 *The Harp and the Blade*

Date of Publication: 1941
Subject(s): Dark Ages
Fictional character(s): Finnian, Minstrel
Time Period(s): 10th century
Locale(s): France

Summary: The novel describes the exploits of an Irish minstrel, Finnian, in 10th-century France. Cursed by a priest and forced to help everyone he meets, Finnian embarks on a series of romantic adventures.

Historical Accuracy: The novel's romance predominates over a carefully documented period background.

4544 *I, Jack Swilling*

Date of Publication: 1961
Subject(s): American West; Biography, Fictionalized
Historical character(s): Jack Swilling, Pioneer, Adventurer

Time Period(s): 19th century
Locale(s): Southwest; Phoenix, Arizona

Summary: This story of the American Southwest chronicles the exploits of Jack Swilling, a frontiersman whose reconstruction of a prehistoric irrigation system enables the development of Phoenix, Arizona. Swilling looks back on his long life and many adventures.

Historical Accuracy: The known facts surrounding Swilling's life are few, and a good deal of imaginative embellishment has been necessary to round out the story.

4545 *Out on Any Limb*

Date of Publication: 1942
Subject(s): Elizabethan Period; Mystery
Fictional character(s): Ingram Applegarth, Young Man
Time Period(s): 16th century
Locale(s): England

Summary: This adventure tale set in Elizabethan England describes the efforts of young Ingram Applegarth of Westmoreland to solve the mystery of the disappearance and possible murder of the father of a girl with whom Ingram has fallen in love. Since a protege of Essex, the Queen's favorite, is suspected, Ingram faces great danger in his quest for the truth.

Historical Accuracy: The novel provides a colorful portrait of the era, for the most part convincing and authentic.

4546 *The Wild Yazoo*

Date of Publication: 1947
Subject(s): Settlement of the American Frontier; Antebellum South
Fictional character(s): Mordaunt Fitzmaurice Godolphin, Landowner
Time Period(s): 1830s
Locale(s): Yazoo River, Mississippi

Summary: This novel of frontier life along the Yazoo River of Mississippi features the adventures of a young Virginian, Mordaunt Godolphin, who flees his native state after killing a man. The novel trace his rise to success.

Historical Accuracy: The novel offers convincing factual data on the opening up of the region and early pioneer life.

LEOPOLD HAMILTON MYERS
(1881-1944)

English novelist Myers was born in Cambridge and educated at Trinity College. He was a fourth-generation writer; his father was Frederic W.H. Myers, a well-known poet and essayist.

4547 *The Near and the Far*

Date of Publication: 1929
Subject(s): Indian Empire; Religious Conflict
Fictional character(s): Hari Khan, Chieftain
Historical character(s): Akbar, Ruler (Mogul emperor)
Time Period(s): 16th century

Locale(s): India

Summary: Set in the Mogul court of 16th-century India, the novel is part philosophical inquiry and part adventure tale. The Emperor Akbar, finding the faith of Islam unsatisfactory, develops his own religion embodying the best elements of many forms of faith. The results are not what the emperor expects.

Historical Accuracy: The setting and era are used more as a point of exotic departure than for careful documentation of history. The author claims to have used facts when they were useful and ignored them when they were inconvenient.

ROBERT J. MYERS (1924-)

An American born in Indiana, Myers received a Ph.D. from the University of Chicago. He is the co-founder and publisher of *The New Republic*. Myers has served as the president for the Carnegie Council on Ethical and International Affairs and is the author of numerous studies of governmental agencies and programs, as well as political satire.

4548 *The Cross of Frankenstein*

Date of Publication: 1975
Subject(s): Gothic Romance; Supernatural
Fictional character(s): Victor Frankenstein, Scientist (doctor)
Time Period(s): 1810s (1816)
Locale(s): London, England; United States

Summary: In this sequel to Mary Shelley's gothic classic, the novel takes up the story of Dr. Victor Frankenstein's deranged monster forty years later and involves another Victor Frankenstein, the doctor's illegitimate son, who learns of his father's experiments. Convinced to come to America, Frankenstein comes face-to-face with his father's creation.

Historical Accuracy: Original and ingenious, the novel blends American period elements in with the gothic horror.

4549 *The Slave of Frankenstein*

Date of Publication: 1976
Subject(s): Gothic Romance; Slavery; Supernatural
Fictional character(s): Victor Frankenstein, Scientist (doctor)
Historical character(s): John Brown, Revolutionary, Abolitionist
Time Period(s): 1850s (1859)
Locale(s): Virginia

Summary: Thirty years after the monster's first encounter with his creator's son Victor in*The Cross of Frankenstein*, this sequel, set in 1859, continues the story of the monster and his lust for power that involves a conspiracy to kidnap John Brown.

Historical Accuracy: The novel is an intriguing amalgam of fantasy and history with some convincing period elements.

VIRGINIA MYERS

4550 *This Land I Hold*

Date of Publication: 1951
Subject(s): American West
Fictional character(s): Magdalena Estrada, Young Woman
Time Period(s): 1830s
Locale(s): California

Summary: Set in California in the declining years of Mexican rule, the novel tells the story of Magdalena Estrada who returns home from a Mexican convent for a struggle with love and marriage. Her preference for wealth over love will affect the outcome of her life.

Historical Accuracy: The novel's story is conventional and commonplace. There is some attempt to present a truthful portrait of the era and the region.

YOSHIRO NAGAYA (1888-1961)

Nagayo was a Japaneses writer.

4551 *Bronze Christ*

Date of Publication: 1959
Subject(s): Japanese Empire; Christianity; Religious Conflict
Fictional character(s): Yusa Tagiwara, Artist (sculptor)
Time Period(s): 17th century
Locale(s): Japan

Summary: Religious conflict in medieval Japan is the theme in this novel that describes the fate of a young sculptor, Yusa Hagiwara, who is commissioned to cast a statue of Christ to be used as a ''treading picture'' to root out Christians. Those who refuse to step on the figure reveal their beliefs. Hagiwara is in turn suspected of being a Christian himself.

Historical Accuracy: The novel captures the period and customs effectively.

GINA BARKHORDAR NAHAI

4552 *Cry of the Peacock*

Date of Publication: 1991
Subject(s): Jews; Islam
Fictional character(s): Peacock, Heroine; Esther the Soothsayer, Psychic; Soloman the Man, Musician
Historical character(s): Reza Shah Pahlavi, Ruler (Shah of Iran)
Time Period(s): Multiple Time Periods
Locale(s): Tehran, Persia (modern Iran)

Summary: Peacock is 116 years old when she is jailed by the Islamic Revolutionary Guard. She spends her time telling her fellow inmates her life story as a fortune teller, a survivor of the plague, and particularly as a Jew in Persia who witnesses the transformation of an ancient country and culture into modern-day Shiite Iran.

Historical Accuracy: The story of the Persian Jews is a largely unchronicled one, here told with conviction and authenticity.

LARRY D. NAMES

4553 *The Cowboy Conspiracy*

Date of Publication: 1987
Subject(s): Mystery; American West
Historical character(s): Wyatt Earp, Lawman (retired); Charlie Siringo, Detective—Private (retired)
Time Period(s): 1910s (1912)
Locale(s): Harqua Hala, Arizona

Summary: In 1912 Wyatt Earp and former Pinkerton detective Charles Siringo come out of retirement to investigate the murder of an old friend. They quickly find themselves in the middle of an elaborate political conspiracy aimed at assassinating the Progressive candidate for president.

Historical Accuracy: The story is imagined, but the period atmosphere is convincing.

4554 *Ironclads: Man-of-War*

Date of Publication: 1995
Subject(s): Civil War—U.S.; Espionage
Fictional character(s): Rafael Sims, Military Personnel (naval officer); Robert Anderson, Military Personnel (major); Sarah Hammond, Spy
Historical character(s): James Buchanan, Political Figure
Time Period(s): 1860s (1860-1861)
Locale(s): Washington, District of Columbia; Charleston, South Carolina

Summary: This novel of political and military maneuvering before the outbreak of the Civil War describes the countdown to the firing on Fort Sumter. A number of characters are swept up in the coming conflict.

Historical Accuracy: This taut drama of intrigue is set against a plausible historical backdrop.

PRISCILLA NAPIER (1908-)

An English historian and author, Napier was raised in Egypt and educated at Oxford. She is the author of poetry, histories, and memoirs.

4555 *Imperial Winds*

Date of Publication: 1981
Subject(s): World War I; Russian Revolution; Russian Empire
Fictional character(s): Daisy Pelham, Governess; Misha Dubelsky, Young Man; Kolya Dubelsky, Young Man
Time Period(s): 1910s
Locale(s): Moscow, Russia

Summary: Daisy Pelham is a young woman who travels to Imperial Russia on the eve of the revolution to care for the children of the noble Dubelsky family. She is caught up in the glitter of the Romanov court, but when the Czar falls, Daisy must conduct her charges to the safety of the Dubelsky's country home on the Black Sea.

Historical Accuracy: The novel offers an authentic look at the period and its impact on an aristocratic Russian family.

N. RICHARD NASH (1913-)

Born in Philadelphia, Nash graduated from the University of Pennsylvania. He is a playwright, screenwriter, TV writer, and novelist. Nash has been an instructor in philosophy and drama at numerous colleges and universities, including Bryn Mawr and Princeton. His works include *The Rainmaker* and *East Wind, Rain*.

4556 *Behold the Man*

Date of Publication: 1986
Subject(s): Biblical Story
Historical character(s): Judas Iscariot, Biblical Figure; Mary Magdalene, Biblical Figure; Jesus Christ, Biblical Figure; Mary, Biblical Figure
Time Period(s): 1st century
Locale(s): Jerusalem, Israel; Alexandria, Egypt

Summary: The story of Jesus' ministry and crucifixion is seen through the eyes of Mary Magdalene and Judas Iscariot. Mary defies her heritage for the opulence of Rome, while Judas is consumed by hatred for the Romans and becomes a zealot determined to end Roman rule. Both are brought together through Jesus.

Historical Accuracy: The Gospels offer few facts about either Mary Magdalene or Judas; the novel freely imagines a plausible history for both.

SENA JETER NASLUND

4557 *Sherlock in Love*

Date of Publication: 1993
Subject(s): Mystery; Victorian Period
Fictional character(s): Sherlock Holmes, Detective—Private; John H. Watson, Doctor
Historical character(s): Ludwig II, Royalty (King of Bavaria)
Time Period(s): 1920s; 1880s
Locale(s): England

Summary: As Dr. Watson begins to write a biography of his departed friend, Sherlock Holmes, he receives anonymous threats on his life. Watson must solve a murder of intriguing puzzles connected with the mad King Ludwig of Bavaria and the identity of the mysterious figure who was Holmes' one true love.

Historical Accuracy: The novel captures the atmosphere of the Doyle original with conviction.

TEMA NASON

Born in Brooklyn, Nason graduated from Brooklyn College and Johns Hopkins University. She has worked as a union representative and a government and factory worker. She is now a research associate in the sociology department of Brandeis University.

4558 *Ethel: The Fictional Autobiography*

Date of Publication: 1990
Subject(s): Espionage; Cold War; Biography, Fictionalized

Historical character(s): Ethel Rosenberg, Spy; Julius Rosenberg, Spy
Time Period(s): 20th century (1931-1953)
Locale(s): New York, New York

Summary: The novel offers the fictional prison diaries of Ethel Rosenberg as she awaits her execution for passing atomic secrets to the Russians. In solitary confinement for over 26 months, she ponders her past and emerges as a complex individual driven by deep conflicts that serve to capture the Cold War period.

Historical Accuracy: In this fictional autobiography Ethel Rosenberg's opinions are imagined.

ROBERT NATHAN (1894-1985)

Born in New York City, American author Robert Nathan attended Harvard University. He was a lecturer, novelist, screenwriter, playwright, and poet whose writing is recognized for its sentimental and gently ironic fantasy; its wry, whimsical, and sometimes macabre touches; and its occasional melancholic and bitter elements. Among the most popular of Nathan's 41 novels are *Jonah*, *One More Spring*, *The Bishop's Wife*, and *Portrait of Jennie*. The latter three novels were adapted into successful films.

4559 *The Fair*

Date of Publication: 1964
Subject(s): Dark Ages; Anglo-Saxon Period; Supernatural
Fictional character(s): Penryhd, Orphan; Azael, Angel
Time Period(s): 6th century
Locale(s): England

Summary: This romantic tale of an England overrun by Saxon invaders describes the adventures of Penryhd who, after her father is killed in a Saxon raid, sets out with her tutor for safety at the Priory at Malmesbury. On the way she is visited by her guardian angel, Azael, who plays an important role in Penryhd's rescue when she is captured by a Saxon.

Historical Accuracy: The novel's fantasy is set in a believable frame of the period and its atmosphere.

PETER NEAGOE (1881-1960)

Romanian writer Neagoe was born in Transylvania and attended the University of Bucharest, the Romanian Academy of Fine Arts, and the National Academy of Design. Neagoe worked both as a translator and illustrator. He abandoned a promising artistic career to become a writer. Neagoe is best known for his short stories of Romanian peasant life.

4560 *The Saint of Montparnasse: A Novel Based on the Life of Constantin Brancusi*

Date of Publication: 1965
Subject(s): Biography, Fictionalized; Artistic Life
Historical character(s): Constantin Brancusi, Artist (sculptor); Amedeo Modigliani, Artist (painter)

Time Period(s): 19th century; 20th century
Locale(s): Romania; Paris, France

Summary: This novel, based on the life and times of Romanian sculptor Constantin Brancusi, captures his unique genius and his attempt to reflect his spiritual values in art.

Historical Accuracy: The novel provides an accurate and authentic portrait of the artist and his career.

LINDA NEALE

4561 *The Briar Rose*

Date of Publication: 1987
Subject(s): Middle Ages
Fictional character(s): Briallen, Gentlewoman; Robert de Lacey, Knight; Iago, Rebel
Time Period(s): 13th century (1287)
Locale(s): Welsh Marches, Wales; England

Summary: The novel is set in the 13th century on the Welsh Marches, the border between England and Wales, where the Celtic population resists the domination of the Norman knights. Briallen is a young Welsh woman who meets the Norman knight Robert de Lacey, and their growing love entangles her in a conflict of loyalties and a rebellion led by the fiery Celtic rebel Iago.

Historical Accuracy: The novel's action is based on an actual 13th-century revolt.

CHARLES NEIDER (1915-)

Born in Odessa, Russia, Neider was brought to the U.S. in 1920 and became a naturalized citizen in 1927. He was educated at City College in New York. A nonfiction writer, editor, and novelist, Neider's works include *The Frozen Sea: A Study of Franz Kafka* and the novels *The White Citadel*, *Naked Eye*, and *Overflight*.

4562 *The Authentic Death of Hendry Jones*

Date of Publication: 1956
Subject(s): American West; Crime and Criminals
Fictional character(s): Hendry Jones, Gunfighter, Murderer
Time Period(s): 1880s
Locale(s): California; Mexico

Summary: This western novel tells the story of gunman and outlaw Hendry Jones, who is known as the Kid. His exploits are a retelling of the story of Billy the Kid with a setting that is shifted from New Mexico to the California coast. The Kid's short and murderous career is realistically described.

Historical Accuracy: The parallels of the novel to the history of Billy the Kid are close but not exact.

SARAH NEILAN

English book editor and writer Neilan graduated from Oxford. She is the author primarily of suspense novels set in her favorite period, the first quarter of the 19th century.

Neilan enjoys historical research and takes pride in the authenticity of her novels' backgrounds.

4563 *An Air of Glory*

Date of Publication: 1977
Subject(s): Regency Romance; Jacobite Rebellion
Fictional character(s): Polly Forster, Young Woman; Augustus Fenwick, Government Official
Time Period(s): 1800s (1801)
Locale(s): Nova Scotia, Canada; At Sea; England

Summary: In 1801 Polly Forster accepts a dangerous and treasonable mission to carry an urgent and secret message to the remaining Jacobites among the Scottish settlers in Nova Scotia. The novel describes her fateful journey and the intrigue that it creates.

Historical Accuracy: The voyage described is based on an actual one, and the historical background is authentic.

4564 *The Braganza Pursuit*

Date of Publication: 1976
Subject(s): Regency Romance; Royalty—Portugal
Fictional character(s): Adelaide Smith, Orphan, Governess; Dom Martin, Nobleman
Time Period(s): 1820s (1822)
Locale(s): London, England; Brazil

Summary: Englishwoman Adelaide Smith takes a position as governess to the Portuguese ambassador to England. When her charges are endangered by the rivalry within the Braganza family, hereditary rulers of Portugal, Adelaide must deliver the children to their uncle, Dom Martin, in Brazil. The trip is a fateful one, and Adelaide becomes enmeshed in the secrets of the Braganzas.

Historical Accuracy: The story and characters are fanciful, but the novel is written with a background of real events and places.

4565 *The Old Enchantment*

Date of Publication: 1990
Subject(s): Romance; Edwardian Period; World War I
Fictional character(s): Peregrine Fenwick, Gentleman; Lizzie Fenwick, Spouse
Time Period(s): 20th century (1910-1970)
Locale(s): Northumberland, England; Ontario, Canada; London, England

Summary: The history of an English great house, the Old Hall in Northumberland, is chronicled from 1910 to 1970. Lizzie Fenwick is absorbed in the social orbit of the Delmaynes and will follow their fortune through peacetime and war in England and Canada.

Historical Accuracy: The family saga is set solidly in a convincing cultural and historical context.

4566 *Paradise*

Date of Publication: 1982
Subject(s): Frontier—Canada; Immigrants; Family Saga

Fictional character(s): Charles Clare, Settler; Rose Clare, Settler; Quality Clare, Young Woman
Time Period(s): 19th century (1812-1830)
Locale(s): Talbot Settlement, Canada

Summary: Immigrant life in eastern Canada in the opening decades of the 19th century is described in the family story of the Clares, who create their home in the Canadian wilderness. The novel centers on the Clares' daughter, Quality, who grows to womanhood facing challenges in the Canadian frontier.

Historical Accuracy: The novel excels in creating a believable picture of Canadian frontier life.

ROBERT NEILL

4567 *Black William*

Date of Publication: 1955
Subject(s): Jacobite Rebellion
Fictional character(s): Molly Lawley, Young Woman; John Lawley, Young Man
Time Period(s): 1710s (1714)
Locale(s): London, England; Northumberland, England

Summary: In 1714 the Hanover succession of George I causes a Jacobite Rebellion in favor of James Edward Stuart. The novel details the period conflict as young Molly Lawley tries to prevent her uncle John from getting involved in the hopeless Jacobite cause. When the plotters are endangered, Molly is forced to decide where her loyalties truly lie.

Historical Accuracy: The novel captures the issues and the period with authenticity.

4568 *Elegant Witch*

Date of Publication: 1952
Subject(s): Witchcraft and Sorcery
Fictional character(s): Margery Whitaker, Young Woman; Roger Nowell, Gentleman
Time Period(s): 17th century
Locale(s): England

Summary: Set in England during the 17th century, the novel presents a vivid portrait of the age's superstitions and fascination with witchcraft.

Historical Accuracy: This is an authentic look at the period and its customs.

4569 *The Golden Days*

Date of Publication: 1972
Subject(s): Royalty—England; Popish Plot; Monmouth's Rebellion
Fictional character(s): Sir Harry Burnaby, Gentleman, Political Figure (member of parliament)
Historical character(s): James II, Ruler (King of England); Charles II, Ruler (King of England); John Dryden, Writer
Time Period(s): 17th century (1679-1681)
Locale(s): England

Summary: The background of the novel is the Exclusion Crisis of the 17th century when England drifts toward civil war in opposition to the succession of Charles II's Catholic brother James, Duke of York. The anti-Catholic Popish Plot splits the country. The novel depicts the events as they affect Sir Harry Burnaby and his family. Their story continues in *Lillibullero*.

Historical Accuracy: The historical events are authentically captured.

4570 *Hangman's Cliff*

Date of Publication: 1956
Subject(s): Crime and Criminals; Georgian Period
Fictional character(s): Captain William Appleton, Landowner; Margaret Appleton, Young Woman
Time Period(s): 1780s
Locale(s): Channel Coast, England

Summary: Captain William Appleton and his daughter Margaret inherit a cottage with a sinister past. They soon find themselves involved with smugglers, a secret agent from the American colonies, and a murder mystery.

Historical Accuracy: The novel features a believable accumulation of period surface details.

4571 *Lillibullero*

Date of Publication: 1975
Subject(s): Royalty—England; Glorious Revolution
Fictional character(s): Sir Harry Burnaby, Gentleman; John Burnaby, Gentleman; Nicholas Burnaby, Lawyer
Historical character(s): James II, Ruler (King of England)
Time Period(s): 17th century (1680s)
Locale(s): England

Summary: In the continuation of the author's *The Golden Days*, the troubled reign of James II is depicted in its effects on the Burnaby family. Harry Burnaby, formerly loyal to king and country, finds it difficult to serve the Catholic James II as events move swiftly to the Glorious Revolution that puts William and Mary onto the throne.

Historical Accuracy: The confusing issues and events of the time are covered with authority.

4572 *The Mills of Colne*

Date of Publication: 1959
Subject(s): Chartist Revolt; Labor Movement; Victorian Period
Fictional character(s): John Phillips, Businessman (mill owner); Nicholas England, Businessman (mill owner); Robert Shaw, Businessman (mill owner)
Time Period(s): 1840s
Locale(s): Colne, England

Summary: Labor troubles during the early years of England's Chartist Revolt turn the town of Colne into a battlefield. The novel depicts the conflict between mill owners and workers stimulated by the Chartist demands for reform, the early stirring of the labor movement.

Historical Accuracy: The terrible labor unrest of the period is captured in believable scenes of the conflict.

4573 *Rebel Heiress*

Date of Publication: 1954
Subject(s): Restoration Period; Civil War—England
Fictional character(s): Robert Carey, Veteran (Royalist soldier), Landowner; Sir Giles Orton, Veteran (Royalist soldier), Landowner; Barbara Paget, Young Woman; Anne Paget, Young Woman
Time Period(s): 17th century (1660s)
Locale(s): England

Summary: Romantic complications ensue when two Royalist soldiers, Carey and Orton, return with the exiled Charles II to reclaim their property seized during the English Civil War. Intent on revenging themselves on the man who gained their lands, they are surprised to find instead his beautiful orphaned daughters.

Historical Accuracy: The novel's situation is plausible and believable in its period elements.

4574 *Traitor's Moon*

Date of Publication: 1952
Subject(s): Restoration Period; Popish Plot; Religious Conflict
Fictional character(s): John Leyburne, Artisan (clockmaker); Penelope Langley, Young Woman
Historical character(s): Charles II, Ruler (King of England); Titus Oates, Religious (clergyman), Leader (Popish Plot)
Time Period(s): 17th century (1679)
Locale(s): London, England; Lancashire, England

Summary: This romantic adventure tale takes as its historical background the anti-papist frenzy of the 17th century spurred by Titus Oates. Clockmaker John Leyburne loves Penelope Langley, whose family is harboring a Roman Catholic priest in disguise. This leaves them vulnerable to the evil machinations of a virulent anti-papist.

Historical Accuracy: The novel offers a vivid and believable portrait of the era and its conflicts.

WINTHROP NEILSON

FRANCES FULLERTON NEILSON

4575 *Edge of Greatness*

Date of Publication: 1951
Subject(s): French and Indian War; American Colonies
Historical character(s): Benjamin Franklin, Political Figure
Time Period(s): 1750s (1755)
Locale(s): Philadelphia, Pennsylvania, American Colonies

Summary: The novel is a dramatization of one day in the life of Benjamin Franklin. It is July 18, 1755, the day of General Braddock's notorious defeat during the French and Indian Wars. The event alters Franklin's life and begins his commitment to the cause of American independence.

Historical Accuracy: The novel creates a believable aura of local and historical background.

BETTY PALMER NELSON (1946-)

Born in Tennessee, Nelson graduated from Muskingum College. She is a professor of English at Volunteer State Community College in Gallatin, Tennessee.

4576 *Private Knowledge*

Date of Publication: 1990
Subject(s): Rural Life—U.S.; Antebellum South
Fictional character(s): Molly Hampton, Young Woman; Benjamin Pader, Young Man; Simon Henderson, Spouse (of Molly)
Time Period(s): 19th century
Locale(s): Spencer County, Tennessee

Summary: Life in rural Tennessee in the early 1800s is depicted in the first of the author's Harvest Women series. Molly Hampton holds her family together despite her profligate father. Seduced by Benjamin Pader, she is forced to marry Simon Henderson to conceal her pregnancy. When Pader's wife dies, Molly must decide whether to return to her former lover.

Historical Accuracy: The novel is authentic in its regional and period depiction.

4577 *Pursuit of Bliss*

Date of Publication: 1992
Subject(s): Rural Life—U.S.; World War I
Fictional character(s): Annie Bee Cutterfield, Young Woman; Ral Henderson, Young Woman
Time Period(s): 1910s (1913-1919)
Locale(s): Tennessee

Summary: In the third volume of the author's Harvest Women series, central Tennessee is being forced into the modern world by electricity and the First World War. The novel depicts this period and tells the human stories of Annie Bee Cutterfield, Ral Henderson, and the Gwaltney family.

Historical Accuracy: The novel excels in regional and period details that are drawn with authority.

EDNA DEU PREE NELSON

Born in Kansas, Nelson attended the University of California, Berkeley, and Columbia University. She has worked in public relations and as a freelance writer for magazines.

4578 *O'Higgins and Don Bernardo*

Date of Publication: 1954
Subject(s): Independence—South America
Historical character(s): Ambrosio O'Higgins, Government Official; Bernardo O'Higgins, Bastard Son, Revolutionary
Time Period(s): 18th century; 19th century
Locale(s): Chile; Peru

Summary: The novel tells the story of Ambrosio and Bernardo O'Higgins, father and son, who both played important roles in the history of South America. Ambrosio O'Higgins comes to South America from Ireland as a trader and is appointed governor of Chile and viceroy of Peru. Spanish law decrees that no man with children born of a native woman can hold high office in South America. The novel details Don Ambrosio's rise to power while attempting to hide his illegitimate son, Bernardo. Bernardo becomes a revolutionary leader in the war against the Spanish and is made dictator of Chile.

Historical Accuracy: The novel is somewhat declamatory in its approval, which undermines its credibility. Facts are altered or distorted to fit the novel's theme.

JAMES L. NELSON (1935-)

Born near the coast of Maine, Nelson developed an interest in sailing, which led to model-making and then to small boat building. After graduating from UCLA, he ran away to sea, serving as a seaman, rigger, boatsman, and officer aboard a number of square-rigged ships and schooners. For two years he sailed aboard the H.M.S *Rose*, a replica of a British frigate active in the Revolution.

4579 *By Force of Arms*

Date of Publication: 1996
Subject(s): Sea Story; American Revolution
Fictional character(s): Isaac Biddlescomb, Sea Captain; Ezra Rumstick, Patriot
Time Period(s): 1770s
Locale(s): *Judea*, At Sea

Summary: The American seaman's view of the American Revolution is dramatized in this story of sea captain Isaac Biddlescomb. His smuggling activities lead to pursuit by the Royal Navy and the loss of his ship. As a merchant seaman, Biddlescomb is captured and faces harsh conditions aboard the H.M.S. *Icarus*.

Historical Accuracy: The novel features authentic nautical details that create a believable portrait of the period at sea.

4580 *The Maddest Idea*

Date of Publication: 1997
Subject(s): American Revolution; Sea Story
Fictional character(s): Isaac Biddlescomb, Sea Captain; Edward Fitzgerald, Military Personnel (major)
Historical character(s): George Washington, Military Personnel (army commander)
Time Period(s): 1770s (1775)
Locale(s): At Sea; Bermuda; Boston, Massachusetts, American Colonies

Summary: In the second volume of the Revolution at Sea Trilogy, Captain Isaac Biddlescomb is sent by General Washington to Bermuda to capture a cache of gunpowder essential for the American troops. But the daring plan is a trap set by a traitor aboard ship. Biddlescomb must rely on his cunning and seamanship to free his captured men, rescue his ship, and get his precious shipment to the Continental Army near Boston.

Historical Accuracy: The novel's notes indicate the historical basis for the story, which is filled with authentic nautical and period elements.

RAY FARADAY NELSON (1931-)

An American freelance artist and writer, Nelson has worked as a signmaker, translator, and computer programmer. His books include *The Agony of Love*, *Girl with the Hungry Eyes*, *Blake's Progress*, and *Time Quest*.

`4581` *Dogheaded Death*

Date of Publication: 1989
Subject(s): Mystery; Roman Empire; Religious Conflict
Fictional character(s): Gaius Hesperian, Military Personnel (captain); Optio Mannus, Military Personnel (soldier)
Historical character(s): Mark, Biblical Figure, Religious (apostle); Annianus, Religious (bishop)
Time Period(s): 1st century
Locale(s): Alexandria, Egypt

Summary: In the first century, when a wealthy shipping magnate is murdered, Centurion Gaius Hesperian, a member of Emperor Nero's palace guard, is sent to Alexandria, Egypt, to solve the crime and apprehend the murderer. He finds himself in the center of conflict in Alexandria, where the upstart Christians battle the established religion.

Historical Accuracy: The novel creates a believable historical backdrop for the suspense story.

TRUMAN NELSON (1911-1987)

Born in Lynn, Massachusetts, Nelson has been an author and actor in a Shakespearean repertory company. He also served as the chief union steward at General Electric. Among his books are *Passion by the Brook* and *The Old Man: John Brown at Harper's Ferry*.

`4582` *The Sin of the Prophet*

Date of Publication: 1952
Subject(s): Slavery
Historical character(s): Theodore Parker, Religious (clergyman), Abolitionist; Wendell Phillips, Writer, Abolitionist; Anthony Burns, Slave
Time Period(s): 1850s (1854)
Locale(s): Boston, Massachusetts

Summary: This documentary novel describes actual events involving a runaway slave, Anthony Burns, who seeks refuge in Boston. Although defended by Theodore Parker, the abolitionist preacher, Burns is sent back to Virginia.

Historical Accuracy: The novel stays close to the actual facts.

`4583` *The Surveyor*

Date of Publication: 1960
Subject(s): Slavery
Historical character(s): John Brown, Abolitionist
Time Period(s): 1850s (1855-1856)
Locale(s): Kansas

Summary: Set in the years following the Kansas-Nebraska Act of 1854, the novel traces the development of the Free-Soil Movement and the activities of John Brown in the Kansas territory prior to the events at Harper's Ferry. Whether Kansas would be a free or slave state was to be determined by popular vote, and Missouri slave owners crossed the border just long enough to cast ballots. The effort is opposed by Brown, who eventually helps win the state for the abolitionists.

Historical Accuracy: The novel reconstructs the Kansas of the period in a mountain of convincing details. Objectivity is sacrificed somewhat by the author's clear partisanship toward Brown and tendency to demonize his opponents.

ALFRED NEUMANN (1895-1952)

Born in West Prussia (now Poland), Neumann's Jewish family moved to Berlin, where Neumann received a traditional university education. After seeing action in World War I, he began writing peotry and then short stories and novels, winning both popularity and critical acclaim for his historical vignettes in *The Devil* and *The Rebels*. In 1941, he escaped from Germany to the United States, where he worked at Hollywood studios.

`4584` *The Gaudy Empire*

Date of Publication: 1937
Subject(s): Royalty—France
Historical character(s): Napoleon III, Ruler (Emperor of France)
Time Period(s): 19th century (1856-1870)
Locale(s): France

Summary: The history of France's Second Empire and the gradual fall from power of Napoleon III is dramatized. The events include the war in Italy and the Mexican fiasco under Maximilian. At the center of the story is the vacillation of Napoleon.

Historical Accuracy: The novel is marred by several historical errors, such as the locating of Napoleon's tomb in the Pantheon.

`4585` *The Rebels*

Date of Publication: 1929
Subject(s): Independence—Italy; Carbonari Uprising
Fictional character(s): Gasto Guerro, Revolutionary; Maria Corleone, Young Woman
Time Period(s): 1830s
Locale(s): Tuscany, Italy

Summary: Set during the Carbonari Revolt in Italy in the 1830s, this novel of revolutionary intrigue centers on Gasto Guerro, leader of the secret Carbonari, his love Maria Corleone, and the plot to assassinate the Grand Duke.

Historical Accuracy: The particulars of time and place are left purposely vague and fragmented to suggest more universal themes.

DAVID NEVIN (1927-)

Born in Washington, D.C., Nevin attended Louisiana State University and Texas Technological College. A newspaper reporter and magazine writer, Nevin is the author of numerous books on public affairs and historical subjects.

4586 *1812*

Date of Publication: 1996
Subject(s): War of 1812; Battle of New Orleans
Fictional character(s): Sally McQuirk, Journalist
Historical character(s): James Madison, Political Figure; Dolley Madison, Spouse; Andrew Jackson, Military Personnel; Rachel Jackson, Spouse; Winfield Scott, Military Personnel (general); Henry Clay, Political Figure
Time Period(s): 18th century; 19th century (1790s-1810s)
Locale(s): United States

Summary: This sweeping panoramic drama of the War of 1812 captures the details of the campaigns and the principals, including the Madisons, the Jacksons, and a young Winfield Scott. The fictional frame is the story of Sally McQuirk, who is determined to report on the war as a correspondent.

Historical Accuracy: The story blends the fictional with the historical and renders the principle events accurately.

4587 *Dream West*

Date of Publication: 1983
Subject(s): American West; Civil War—U.S.; Biography, Fictionalized
Historical character(s): John C. Fremont, Explorer, Political Figure; Jessie Benton Fremont, Spouse; Thomas Hart Benton, Political Figure; Kit Carson, Frontiersman; Abraham Lincoln, Political Figure
Time Period(s): 19th century (1840s-1860s)
Locale(s): California; Panama; Washington, District of Columbia

Summary: The life and times of John Charles Fremont, explorer, soldier, and first presidential nominee of the Republican Party, are chronicled. Fremont was called the "Pathfinder to the West." He helped open up California for settlement, made and lost a fortune during the Gold Rush, married the spirited daughter of Missouri Senator Thomas Hart Benton, barely lost the presidential election, and commanded the Western department of the Union Army in the Civil War.

Historical Accuracy: The basic framework of the novel is factual. There are some surmises added to fill in the gaps in this remarkable story of an American original.

CHRISTOPHER NEW

Born in England, educated at Oxford and Princeton, New has been a professor of philosophy at Reading University and the University of Hong Kong.

4588 *Shanghai*

Date of Publication: 1985
Subject(s): Revolution—China; World War II
Fictional character(s): John Denton, Government Official (customs service), Trader; Su-Mei, Young Woman
Time Period(s): 20th century (1903-1948)
Locale(s): Shanghai, China

Summary: Set in Shanghai, China, during the first half of the 20th century, the novel follows the fortunes of Englishman John Denton, who enters the customs service and then becomes a wealthy trader. His career becomes inextricably linked with the turbulent modern history of China, the declining power of the Europeans, and the mounting discontent of the Chinese masses.

Historical Accuracy: The novel offers convincing reflections of the major historical events of the period.

KERRY NEWCOMB (1946-)

FRANK SCHAEFER (1952-)

Newcomb was born in Connecticut, graduated from the University of Texas at Arlington, and received an M.F.A. from Trinity University. He worked as a teacher in American Indian schools in Montana, and as a singer, entertainer, and director of plays. Schaefer is an American born in Switzerland and a director of feature motion pictures, including *Wire to Kill Headhunter*, and *Baby on Board*, as well as the documentary series *Whatever Happened to the Human Race?*.

4589 *The Ghosts of Elkhorn*

Date of Publication: 1982
Subject(s): American West; Crime and Criminals
Fictional character(s): Wind River Kid, Gambler, Recluse; Roman, Outlaw; Lainie, Outlaw
Time Period(s): 1920s (1927)
Locale(s): Elkhorn, Colorado

Summary: During the 1880s the Wind River Kid was a notorious gambler, but cowardice causes him to live as a hermit until 1927. He reemerges to find the Colorado of his youth transformed. He comes to the aid of two lovers, Roman and Lainie, who have stolen $10,000 from the Denver mob.

Historical Accuracy: The novel colorfully captures the region and its period with telling details.

KERRY NEWCOMB (1946-)

Newcomb was born in Connecticut, graduated from the University of Texas at Arlington, and received an M.F.A. from Trinity University. He worked as a teacher in American Indian schools in Montana, and as a singer, entertainer, and director of plays.

4590 *In the Season of the Sun*

Date of Publication: 1990
Subject(s): American West; Indians
Fictional character(s): Tom Milam, Outlaw; Jacob "Sun Gift" Milam, Captive; Coyote Kilkenny, Outlaw, Guide
Time Period(s): 1820s; 1840s
Locale(s): Montana

Summary: When their parents are killed by Indians, Tom and Jacob Milam are separated. Jacob is raised by Indians and becomes "Sun Gift," a respected Blackfoot warrior. Tom becomes an outlaw. When they both grow to manhood, a drastic confrontation is depicted.

Historical Accuracy: The details of frontier and Indian life are effectively drawn.

4591 *Ride of the Panther*

Date of Publication: 1992
Subject(s): American West; Civil War—U.S.
Fictional character(s): Jesse Redbow McQueen, Military Personnel (Union captain); Daniel Pacer Wolf McQueen, Military Personnel (Confederate soldier)
Time Period(s): 1860s (1863)
Locale(s): Chanta Creek, Missouri

Summary: Two brothers divided by the Civil War, Jesse and Daniel McQueen, take opposite sides in the conflict and become bitter enemies. In western Missouri they are brought together by a threat to their family. Their father has been murdered, and a band of night riders, the Knights of the Golden Circle, have sworn to eliminate the last of the McQueens.

Historical Accuracy: The novel offers a convincing portrait of the border wars and divided allegiances of the times.

4592 *Scalpdancers*

Date of Publication: 1990
Subject(s): American West; Indians
Fictional character(s): Lone Walker, Indian (Blackfoot), Shaman; Morgan Penmerry, Sea Captain; White Buffalo, Indian, Shaman
Time Period(s): 1810s (1814)
Locale(s): Astoria, Oregon; Elkhorn Creek, Pacific Northwest

Summary: Lone Walker, in disgrace from the Scalpdancer band of the Blackfoot Indians in the Pacific Northwest, saves the life of sea captain Morgan Penmerry, who is being hunted by a pirate crew. Penmerry joins with Lone Walker to defeat the shaman White Buffalo and save the tribe.

Historical Accuracy: The novel captures the scene of the Pacific Northwest with skill and authenticity.

4593 *Sword of Vengeance*

Date of Publication: 1991
Subject(s): Spanish Colonies; War of 1812
Fictional character(s): Kit McQueen, Military Personnel (army lieutenant); Patrick O'Keefe, Adventurer; Raven O'Keefe, Frontierswoman
Time Period(s): 1810s (1811-1814)
Locale(s): Springtown, Pennsylvania

Summary: Kit McQueen is stranded in Spanish-held Florida as the War of 1812 rages. He is helped by an Irish adventurer, Patrick O'Keefe. Later, McQueen is sent to find and kill O'Keefe, the man who saved his life. To complicate things, McQueen finds himself attracted to O'Keefe's daughter.

Historical Accuracy: The story emphasizes adventure, but with a plausible background of historical events and details.

4594 *Warriors of the Night*

Date of Publication: 1991
Subject(s): American West; Indians

Fictional character(s): Ben McQueen, Military Personnel (army lieutenant); Anabel Cordera de Tosta, Outlaw; Spotted Calf, Indian (Comanche), Chieftain
Time Period(s): 1840s (1845)
Locale(s): San Antonio, Texas

Summary: In the Texas Republic of the 1840s, army officer Ben McQueen finds himself caught between Texas Rangers; a band of Mexican raiders led by beautiful Anabel Cordera de Tosta, the daughter of a landowner who never accepted Texas Independence; and the Comanches, determined to drive both groups off their lands. Into the mix come the Warriors of the Night, descendants of an ancient tribe that practices human sacrifice.

Historical Accuracy: The story is fictional, but it is bolstered by an authentic rendering of the time and place.

KIM NEWMAN (1959-)

British film critic, novelist, lyricist, and playwright Newman was born in London and graduated with honors from the University of Sussex. He has been a performer and broadcaster, the director of the Peace and Love Corporation, and a member of City Limits Collective and Sheep Worrying Enterprises, for which he co-wrote the music album ''Sheep Worrying.'' Newman is the author of *Nightmare Movies*, a critical history of horror films since 1968, and the co-author of *Ghastly Beyond Belief*, a celebration of the most ridiculous moments in science fiction books and movies.

4595 *Anno-Dracula*

Date of Publication: 1992
Subject(s): Horror; Vampires; Alternate History
Fictional character(s): Vlad Tepes, Nobleman (also known as Count Dracula); Silver Knife, Murderer; Genevieve Dieudonne, Vampire; Charles Beauregard, Adventurer
Historical character(s): Victoria, Ruler (Queen of England)
Time Period(s): 1880s (1888)
Locale(s): London, England

Summary: This alternative historical thriller offers an intriguing speculation of what might have happened if Van Helsing had failed to stop Dracula in England in 1885, as depicted in Bram Stoker's classic novel. Queen Victoria has remarried Vlad Tepes, known as Count Dracula, and the vampire population in England is growing in influence. In Whitechapel a murderer known as Silver Knife is attacking vampire girls and two people take up the case: Genevieve Dieudonne, a vampire and social reformer, and Charles Beauregard, a young adventurer.

Historical Accuracy: The novel is a dizzying thriller with an invented, but intriguingly real, Victorian background.

4596 *The Bloody Red Baron*

Date of Publication: 1995
Subject(s): World War I; Fantasy; Vampires

Fictional character(s): Dracula, Military Personnel (commander-in-chief), Vampire; Edwin Winthrop, Military Personnel (intelligence officer); Kate Reed, Journalist, Vampire
Historical character(s): Edgar Allan Poe, Writer; Manfred von Richthofen, Military Personnel (Pilot); Mata Hari, Spy
Time Period(s): 1910s (1918)
Locale(s): France; Germany

Summary: The novel is the continuation of the author's *Anno Dracula*, which offered an alternative undead version of Victorian England. The scene is World War I and Graf von Dracula, expelled from Britain, is commander-in-chief of the Axis powers, as the war becomes a much wider confrontation between the living and the undead. A resurrected Edgar Allan Poe is commissioned to celebrate the exploits of Manfred von Richthofen.

Historical Accuracy: The novel combines fantasy and horror with a creative alternative version of history that derives from a careful understanding of the facts.

SHARAN NEWMAN (1949-)

Born in Michigan, Newman is a graduate of Antioch College and Michigan State University. She is a Ph.D. candidate in medieval history and has worked as an instructor of English as a second language.

4597 *The Chessboard Queen*

Date of Publication: 1983
Subject(s): Dark Ages; Myths and Legends; Arthurian Legends
Fictional character(s): Guinevere, Royalty (queen consort of Arthur); Arthur, Ruler (King of the Britons); Lancelot, Knight
Time Period(s): 5th century
Locale(s): England

Summary: The novel continues the story of Guinevere, now Arthur's queen, as she falls in love with Lancelot, the King's champion of Camelot. The familiar story of one of the most famous of all romances is given a fresh interpretation in this version.

Historical Accuracy: The novel offers a number of telling details that help reinvigorate this classic, though well-worn story.

4598 *Death Comes as Epiphany*

Date of Publication: 1993
Subject(s): Middle Ages; Mystery; Religious Life
Fictional character(s): Catherine Levendeur, Scholar (religious), Detective—Amateur; Abbe Sueer, Religious (abbot)
Historical character(s): Heloise, Religious (abbess); Peter Abelard, Teacher, Philosopher
Time Period(s): 12th century (1139)
Locale(s): Paris, France

Summary: Set in the 12th century, the novel tells the story of a young scholar, Catherine Levendeur, at the Convent of the Paraclete, whose abbess is the famed Heloise. A manuscript has disappeared, and it is feared that the book contains sacrilegious passages that will be used to condemn Heloise's

famous lover, Peter Abelard. Catherine sets out to find the lost manuscript and discover who has altered its text.

Historical Accuracy: The novel offers a convincing portrait of medieval convent life and the religious factional controversies of the period.

4599 *The Devil's Door*

Date of Publication: 1994
Subject(s): Mystery; Middle Ages; Religious Life
Fictional character(s): Catherine Levendeur, Scholar (religious), Detective—Amateur
Historical character(s): Heloise, Religious (nun)
Time Period(s): 12th century (1140)
Locale(s): France

Summary: When a wealthy countess is brutally beaten by unknown assailants Catherine Levendeur, the novice-scholar at the Convent of the Paraclete, vows to find out the identity of the woman's attacker. The cost of her quest for justice is high. Hanging in the balance is the fate of the convent.

Historical Accuracy: The period setting and atmosphere are convincingly rendered.

4600 *Guinevere*

Date of Publication: 1981
Subject(s): Dark Ages; Myths and Legends; Arthurian Legends
Fictional character(s): Guinevere, Young Woman; Sir Arthur, Knight; Gawaine, Knight
Time Period(s): 5th century
Locale(s): England

Summary: The novel tells the story of the childhood of Guinevere, blending fantasy with period details. Protected by her Roman parents from the wars with the invading Saxons, Guinevere experiences danger at home. The familiar figures of the Arthurian romances appear in their youth.

Historical Accuracy: This is an ingenious reworking of the Mallory original with some attempt to offer a plausible historical basis for the legend.

4601 *Guinevere Evermore*

Date of Publication: 1985
Subject(s): Dark Ages; Myths and Legends; Arthurian Legends
Fictional character(s): Guinevere, Royalty (queen consort of King Arthur); Arthur, Ruler (King of the Britons); Lancelot, Knight
Time Period(s): 5th century
Locale(s): England

Summary: The concluding volume of the author's series on the famous rise and fall of Camelot told from Guinevere's perspective takes the story from the discovery of Guinevere's love affairs with Lancelot to the final battle against the villainous Modred. The novel attempts to transform the legend into a human story with believable, flawed heroes.

Historical Accuracy: This is a fresh and original retelling of the familiar legend with sufficient realistic details to offer a convincing historical backdrop.

`4602` *Strong as Death*

Date of Publication: 1996
Subject(s): Middle Ages; Mystery
Fictional character(s): Catherine Le Vendeur, Spouse; Edgar Wedderlie, Nobleman
Historical character(s): Peter Abelard, Religious
Time Period(s): 12th century
Locale(s): France; Santiago de Compostela, Spain

Summary: In the fourth historical mystery involving Catherine Le Vendeur, she and her husband, Edgar, set out on pilgrimage to the monastery of Campostela to petition St. James for a child. On the way they encounter mad monks, crusaders, and a motley collection of pilgrims. When several of the pilgrims are murdered, evidence suggests revenge may be the motive, and Catherine's life is endangered.

Historical Accuracy: The period elements are authentic, aided by the author's own travels along the pilgrimage route from Le Puy to Compostela.

`4603` *The Wandering Arm*

Date of Publication: 1995
Subject(s): Mystery; Middle Ages; Jews
Fictional character(s): Catherine Le Vendeur, Gentlewoman; Eliazar, Businessman, Scholar
Time Period(s): 12th century (1141)
Locale(s): England; Paris, France

Summary: The mummified arm of St. Aldhelm has been stolen from England and hidden somewhere in Paris. Suspicion falls on the Jewish community and, in particular, Catherine Le Vendeur's friend Eliazar. As the fragile peace between medieval Paris' Christian and Jewish communities threatens to erupt into violence, Catherine and her husband set about to discover the whereabouts of the relic and the identity of a murderer.

Historical Accuracy: The book is placed as accurately as possible within its particular time and place in history; however, it is meant to be an entertainment story, not a text book.

ED NEWSOM (1908-)

Newsom is a writer of Westerns whose books include *Trail to Sonora* and *Ride the High Places*.

`4604` *Wagons to Tucson*

Date of Publication: 1954
Subject(s): American West; Wagon Trains; Civil War—U.S.
Fictional character(s): Dick Benteen, Veteran (Union officer), Scout; Dallas Forrester, Southern Belle
Time Period(s): 1860s
Locale(s): Arizona; Fort Reno, United States

Summary: This western tale depicts a group travelling by wagon from Kansas through Missouri to Arizona during the closing days of the Civil War. Their experiences with Indians

are described, as well as the growing relationship between scout Dick Benteen, an ex-Union officer, and Dallas Forrester, a Southern woman joining her husband, a captured Confederate officer, at Fort Reno in the Oklahoma territory.

Historical Accuracy: The novel presents the western scene accurately and provides a convincing treatment of the period.

JOHN EDWARD NEWTON

`4605` *The Rogue and the Witch*

Date of Publication: 1955
Subject(s): American Colonies; Religious Conflict; Witchcraft and Sorcery
Fictional character(s): John Henniker, Religious (minister); Glory Upshall, Young Woman
Historical character(s): Increase Mather, Religious (clergyman)
Time Period(s): 17th century (1670s)
Locale(s): Boston, Massachusetts, American Colonies; Salem, Massachusetts, American Colonies

Summary: The novel's background is the religious conflict between Puritans and Quakers in colonial Massachusetts. John Henniker, a Puritan minister, falls in love with Quaker Glory Upshall. Accused of witchcraft, John flees to an island off the Connecticut shore where he endures danger and hardship before being reunited with Glory.

Historical Accuracy: The novel provides authentic period elements.

PIERRE NEZELOF

`4606` *Mirabeau, Lover and Stateman*

Date of Publication: 1937
Subject(s): French Revolution; Biography, Fictionalized
Historical character(s): Honore Gabriel Riqueti, Revolutionary, Political Figure
Time Period(s): 18th century
Locale(s): France

Summary: This biographical novel offers a romanticized account of the career of French revolutionary leader Mirabeau. It captures both his early wild excesses and amours and his later career as the popular third estate spokesman known for standing fast when the States-General were ordered to disband.

Historical Accuracy: The emphasis here is on the romantic side of Mirabeau's fascinating career. His political contributions are only lightly sketched.

`4607` *Napoleon and His Son*

Date of Publication: 1936
Subject(s): Napoleonic Era; Biography, Fictionalized
Historical character(s): Napoleon II, Royalty; Napoleon Bonaparte, Ruler (Emperor of France)
Time Period(s): 19th century
Locale(s): France; Austria

Summary: This depiction of the Napoleonic era covers the period from Napoleon Bonaparte's second marriage to his son's death at the age of 22 from tuberculosis. Although Napoleon I's abdication in 1815 was in favor of his son, he never ruled, remaining a virtual prisoner in Austria until his death.

Historical Accuracy: The basic framework of the story is accurate history, but the treatment is shallow.

ROLAND NICHOLAS
(PSEUD. OF ARNOLD R. WALMSLEY, 1912-)

Born in Ceylon, the son of an Anglican priest, Walmsley was educated at Oxford University. He served as a member of the British Diplomatic Service as a consul in Jerusalem and as the director of the Middle East Center for Arab Studies in Lebanon. He received an OBE in 1946.

4608 *Who Came by Night*

Date of Publication: 1971
Subject(s): Biblical Story; Roman Empire
Historical character(s): Nicodemus, Biblical Figure; John, Biblical Figure
Time Period(s): 1st century (28-29)
Locale(s): Israel

Summary: Judea at the time of Jesus is dramatized from the perspective of Nicodemus, who reveals the complex political and cultural conditions that help explain the rise and fall of Jesus as a radical philosopher.

Historical Accuracy: The novel blends the factual and the fictional but offers a convincing evocation of the environment that defined the story of Jesus.

CHRISTINA NICHOLSON
(PSEUD. OF CHRISTOPHER NICOLE, 1930-)

A writer of historical romances, thrillers, mysteries, and books on West Indian history and cricket, Nicholson was born in Georgetown, British Guiana and worked as a clerk for the Royal Bank of Canada. *The Eliminator* was adapted for film under the title *Danger Route*. He has also written under the names Leslie Arlen, Robin Cade, Peter Grange, Carline Gray, Simon McKay, C.R. Nicholson, Christina Nicholson, Robin Nicholson, Alison York, and Andrew York.

4609 *The Power and the Passion*

Date of Publication: 1977
Subject(s): American Colonies; Royalty—England; Royalty—Russia
Fictional character(s): Lorna MacMahon, Heroine; James Butler, Sea Captain; Vassily Bogoljubov, Royalty (prince)
Historical character(s): William III, Ruler (King of England); Peter the Great, Ruler (czar); Augustus II, Ruler (King of Poland); Sarah Churchill, Noblewoman; Mary II, Ruler (Queen of England); Anne, Royalty (princess)
Time Period(s): 17th century

Locale(s): Maryland, American Colonies; London, England; St. Petersburg, Russia

Summary: The novel describes the romantic adventures of Lorna MacMahon, who becomes the lover of three monarchs in a career that takes her from the American Colony of Maryland in the 17th century to the courts of William and Mary, Peter the Great, and Augustus of Poland.

Historical Accuracy: The fictional story interweaves many historical personages, but the cumulative effect is overwrought and unconvincing.

MEREDITH NICHOLSON

4610 *The Cavalier of Tennessee*

Date of Publication: 1928
Subject(s): Biography, Fictionalized
Historical character(s): Andrew Jackson, Political Figure; Rachel Jackson, Spouse
Time Period(s): 18th century; 19th century (1789-1824)
Locale(s): Tennessee

Summary: This is a romanticized version of the early life of Andrew Jackson in Tennessee before his political career. Jackson receives the full heroic treatment, pictured as resourceful and determined and a staunch defender of his wife's honor.

Historical Accuracy: The novel inflates Jackson to idealized status and is only partially useful as a faithful treatment of Jackson's life.

LESLEY J. NICKELL (1944-)

English author Nickell attended London's College of Drama and Dance and worked as a teacher of drama. She became a member of the British Council in their Stratford on Avon office. Nickell sings for the city of Birmingham Symphony Orchestra Chorus. She tries to visit all the major locations of her novels and greatly prefers the 15th to the 20th century.

4611 *The White Queen*

Date of Publication: 1978
Subject(s): War of the Roses; Royalty—England
Historical character(s): Anne Neville, Royalty (queen consort of Richard III); Richard III, Ruler (King of England); Richard Neville, Nobleman; Edward IV, Ruler (King of England); Louis XI, Ruler (King of France)
Time Period(s): 15th century
Locale(s): England; France

Summary: "The White Queen" refers to Anne Nelville, the daughter of Warwick the Kingmaker, the only queen of England who served as a kitchen maid. Bullied by her formidable father, Anne becomes a pawn in the political intrigue during the War of the Roses. Anne prevails as the wife of Richard III.

Historical Accuracy: The author claims to have invented as little as possible, filling gaps with intelligent guess work.

C.W. NICOL

`4612` *Harpoon*

Date of Publication: 1987
Subject(s): Japanese Empire; Whaling
Fictional character(s): Jinsuke, Sailor (whaling harpooner), Spy; Sadayori, Nobleman
Time Period(s): 1850s; 1860s
Locale(s): Japan; Yangtze River, China

Summary: Set during the dramatic turning point in Japanese history when Commodore Perry arrives in Japan and initiates the violent struggle between old and new, the novel describes the lives of two protagonists. Jinsuke is a talented harpooner who is recruited on a spying mission. Sadayori is devoted to the old traditions but is savy enough to know that Japan must embrace the West to survive. Jinsuke becomes one of the first Japanese to risk death by travelling abroad.

Historical Accuracy: The story is fictional, but the period details and the events that lead to the Meiji Restoration and the death of the Shogunate are authentically detailed.

CHRISTOPHER NICOLE (1930-)

Born in Georgetown, British Guiana, Nicole was educated there and in Barbados. He has worked for the Royal Bank of Canada in their West Indies branches. His many adventure novels offer a full history of the West Indies. He has also written under the names Leslie Arlen, Robin Cade, Peter Grange, Carline Gray, Simon McKay, C.R. Nicholson, Christina Nicholson, Robin Nicholson, Alison York, and Andrew York.

`4613` *Black Dawn*

Date of Publication: 1977
Subject(s): Slavery
Fictional character(s): Richard Hilton, Plantation Owner; Anthony Hilton, Plantation Owner
Historical character(s): Henri Christophe, Revolutionary
Time Period(s): 1810s
Locale(s): Jamaica

Summary: The fourth novel of the author's dramatic saga of the history of the West Indies depicts the struggle for control of Hilltop, a Jamaican plantation. Richard Hilton battles his dissolute brother Anthony as the slave revolt spreads throughout the Caribbean.

Historical Accuracy: The period's historical events are accurately captured.

`4614` *Caribee*

Date of Publication: 1974
Subject(s): Pirates; French Colonies
Fictional character(s): Tom Warner, Adventurer, Settler; Edward Warner, Adventurer, Settler; Yarico, Young Woman
Time Period(s): 17th century
Locale(s): St. Kitts and Nevis; Antigua-Barbuda

Summary: The novel dramatizes the history of the West Indies beginning with the arrival in the 17th century of settlers who displace the Caribbean natives and battle the French and Spanish for control of the islands. The story centers on the adventures and rivalry of father and son Tom and Edward Warner on the islands of St. Kitts and Antigua.

Historical Accuracy: The historical background is convincingly described.

`4615` *The Devil's Own*

Date of Publication: 1975
Subject(s): Pirates; Slavery
Fictional character(s): Kit Hilton, Pirate; Marguerite Warner, Plantation Owner
Historical character(s): Henry Morgan, Pirate
Time Period(s): 17th century
Locale(s): Hispaniola, West Indies; Panama City, Panama; Antigua-Barbuda

Summary: The second of the author's series on the history of the West Indies describes the love affair between Marguerite Warner, mistress of the richest plantation in Antigua, and buccaneer Kit Hilton, who joins with pirate Henry Morgan in the sacking of Panama City. The novel also dramatizes the fate of the Caribbean natives, who try in vain to coexist with the colonists.

Historical Accuracy: The background of historical events is accurate and convincing.

`4616` *Iron Ships, Iron Men*

Date of Publication: 1987
Subject(s): Civil War—U.S.; Sea Story; Antebellum South
Fictional character(s): Jeremiah McGann, Sea Captain; Rob Bascom, Plantation Owner; Marguerite McGann, Spouse
Time Period(s): 1850s; 1860s (1858-1865)
Locale(s): New Orleans, Louisiana; At Sea; Mobile, Alabama

Summary: The friendship between sea captain Jeremiah McGann and Rob Bascom is split both by the Civil War and by their love for Marguerite, who is married to McGann but loves Bascom. Through the years of the Civil War, the two wage their personal war.

Historical Accuracy: The emphasis is on intrigue and adventure, but does feature a believable historical backdrop.

`4617` *Mistress of Darkness*

Date of Publication: 1976
Subject(s): Slavery; Independence—Haiti
Fictional character(s): Gislane Nicholson, Bastard Daughter; Robert Hilton, Plantation Owner; Matt Hilton, Young Man
Historical character(s): Henri Christophe, Revolutionary; Pierre Dominique Toussaint l'Ouverture, Revolutionary; Jean-Jacques Dessalines, Revolutionary
Time Period(s): 1780s
Locale(s): London, England; West Indies

Summary: In the third of the author's saga based on the history of the West Indies, the sugar planters have built an immense plantation system supported by slave labor in the 1780s. The story concerns a master, Gislane Nicholson, who is the bastard daughter of a white planter and an octoroon slave. She is abducted to prevent a liaison with Matt Hilton, cousin of the powerful planter Robert Hilton. The historical background is the Haitian slave revolt.

Historical Accuracy: The story weaves the factual and the fictional. The details of the revolt are plausibly drawn.

4618 *Old Glory*

Date of Publication: 1986
Subject(s): Sea Story; American Revolution
Fictional character(s): Harry McGann, Sea Captain
Time Period(s): 18th century
Locale(s): American Colonies; At Sea

Summary: In this first volume of four tracing the exploits of the seafaring McGann family, Harry McGann leaves Ireland for America where he plays an important role in the formation of the U.S. Navy during the American Revolution.

Historical Accuracy: The period elements are serviceable and believable in this high-seas adventure tale.

4619 *Ratoon*

Date of Publication: 1962
Subject(s): Slavery
Fictional character(s): Joan Dart, Plantation Owner; Jackey Reed, Slave; George Bonning, Plantation Owner
Time Period(s): 1820s (1823)
Locale(s): Demerara, Guyana (British Guiana)

Summary: Based on the actual event of the East Coast Slaves' Insurrection of 1823, the novel describes Joan Dart's involvement in the rebellion as the hostage of the slave army led by Jackey Reed.

Historical Accuracy: The author's use of contemporary records and eye witness accounts adds authenticity to the story.

4620 *The Regiment*

Date of Publication: 1988
Subject(s): Victorian Period; Boer War; Military Life—British Army
Fictional character(s): Murdoch Mackinder, Military Personnel (lieutenant)
Time Period(s): 19th century; 20th century (1899-1914)
Locale(s): South Africa; Bath, England

Summary: Life in the British army during the Boer War is depicted from the perspective of young second lieutenant Murdoch Mackinder in the Royal Dragoon Guard. Mackinder must prove himself as a soldier, and he is tested both in battle and when he is captured and wounded.

Historical Accuracy: The characters are invented, but the author states that the battle scenes are recounted as accurately as the story will allow.

4621 *The Sea and the Sand*

Date of Publication: 1988
Subject(s): War of 1812; Sea Story; Pirates
Fictional character(s): Toby McGann, Sailor
Time Period(s): 1810s

Locale(s): United States; At Sea; Barbary Coast, Africa

Summary: In the second of four novels depicting the naval exploits of the McGann family, Toby McGann fights pirates on the Barbary Coast and then participates in action against the British during the War of 1812.

Historical Accuracy: The action-adventure tale provides some believable period elements.

4622 *The Secret Memoirs of Lord Byron*

Date of Publication: 1978
Subject(s): Literary Life; Biography, Fictionalized; Regency Period
Historical character(s): George Gordon Byron, Nobleman, Writer; Lady Caroline Lamb, Noblewoman
Time Period(s): 18th century; 19th century (1788-1824)
Locale(s): England; Switzerland; Greece

Summary: Romantic poet and notorious English social lion Lord Byron tells his own story with an emphasis on his colorful love life. It includes his adulterous liaisons with members of the London aristocracy, including Lady Caroline Lamb, and his incestuous relationship with his half-sister.

Historical Accuracy: Fact and fantasy are interwoven. Notes are added to assist in identifying the former.

4623 *Sunset*

Date of Publication: 1978
Subject(s): Spanish-American War
Fictional character(s): Meg Hilton, Young Woman
Time Period(s): 1890s
Locale(s): Jamaica

Summary: This is the fifth and concluding novel in the author's history of the West Indies, from the first colonies to the Spanish-American War. Meg Hilton's involvement in the Cuban revolt causes her to lose the Hilltop plantation in Jamaica, as the colonial rule of the Caribbean erupts in violence.

Historical Accuracy: The backdrop is convincingly depicted, based on actual events.

4624 *Wind of Destiny*

Date of Publication: 1989
Subject(s): Sea Story; Spanish-American War
Fictional character(s): Joe McGann, Military Personnel (naval officer)
Time Period(s): 1890s
Locale(s): Cuba; At Sea; United States

Summary: In the final installment of a series on the history of U.S. naval actions, Joe McGann participates with the American forces in Cuba against the Spanish.

Historical Accuracy: The period elements are believable.

IPPOLITO NIEVO (1831-1867)

Born in Padua, Italy, Nievo was a poet, philosopher, and soldier. It is reported that he shielded Garibaldi with his own body at the Battle of Calatafini. He was lost at sea in 1861.

Castle of Fratta was written in eight months when the author was 27.

4625 *The Castle of Fratta*

Date of Publication: 1867
Subject(s): Independence—Italy; Napoleonic Wars; Risorgimento
Fictional character(s): Carlo Altoviti, Patriot; Pisana, Gentlewoman
Historical character(s): Napoleon Bonaparte, Ruler (French emperor), Military Personnel (army commander)
Time Period(s): 18th century; 19th century (1775-1858)
Locale(s): Italy; England

Summary: Carlo Altoviti, in his eighties, chonicles his life, which documents a dramatic picture of Italy in the period of the French Revolution, the rise of Napoleon, and the Risorgimento. Carlo grows up in a household of noble gentry who represent the dying feudal class. Carlo loves Pisana, a complex woman capable of both loyalty and betrayal. Carlo fights with the patriots in Rome and Naples, is in exile in London, and returns penniless to Venice in 1823.

Historical Accuracy: The novel offers a remarkable portrait of the period with character studies that are convincing.

BLAIR NILES

Born in Charlotte County, Virginia, Niles is the author of a number of novels, including *Maria Maluna*, *Journey in Time*, *Passengers to Mexico*, and *Condemned to Devil's Island*. She has been a contributor to *The New York Times* and a number of other publications.

4626 *East by Day*

Date of Publication: 1941
Subject(s): Slavery; Antebellum South
Fictional character(s): Lucy Giles, Gentlewoman
Time Period(s): 1830s (1839)
Locale(s): New Haven, Connecticut

Summary: The background for this novel is the notorious *Amistad* case, the mutiny of the crew of a slave ship captured off Long Island in 1830. The case is explored through its impact on Lucy Giles, a young woman with abolitionist sympathies who discovers that her family's fortune is built on the slave trade.

Historical Accuracy: The actual *Amistad* story is based on contemporary accounts, and no liberties have been taken with the historical facts or personages.

4627 *Passengers to Mexico: The Last Invasion of Mexico*

Date of Publication: 1943
Subject(s): Politics
Fictional character(s): Sara Yorke, Young Woman
Historical character(s): Maximilian, Royalty (Archduke of Austria), Ruler (Emperor of Mexico); Carlota, Royalty (consort of Maximilian); Benito Juarez, Political Figure; William Henry Seward, Political Figure

Time Period(s): 1860s
Locale(s): Mexico

Summary: The story of the Mexican reign of the Emperor Maximilian is dramatized from a variety of vantage points, forming a documentary of this period of Mexican history. The clash of motive and self-interest is dramatized in a story that vividly animates the past.

Historical Accuracy: The novel provides a faithful depiction of the period, creating a human version of this chapter of Mexican history.

HUGH NISSENSON (1933-)

Born in Brooklyn, New York, Nissenson graduated from Swarthmore College. He is an acclaimed short story writer who received an American Book Award nomination and an Ohioana Book Award for *The Tree of Life*.

4628 *My Own Ground*

Date of Publication: 1976
Subject(s): Immigrants
Fictional character(s): Jake Brody, Immigrant, Orphan; Hannele Isaacs, Prostitute
Time Period(s): 1910s (1912)
Locale(s): New York, New York

Summary: John Brody tells the story of his life on the Lower East Side of New York in 1912. John struggles to save Hannele Isaacs, the daughter of a rabbi, who is seduced by a Jewish pimp and becomes a prostitute. The novel captures the spiritual journey of Brody as well as immigrant life in New York of the period.

Historical Accuracy: The novel offers a convincing and authentic view of period New York and immigrant life.

4629 *The Tree of Life*

Date of Publication: 1985
Subject(s): Settlement of the American Frontier; Indians
Fictional character(s): Thomas Keene, Settler; Lettiele Shipman, Slave (freed)
Historical character(s): Johnny Appleseed, Frontiersman
Time Period(s): 1810s (1811-1812)
Locale(s): Richland County, Ohio

Summary: Pioneer life in Ohio in the early 1800s is described by diarist Thomas Keene, who tells the story of his survival in the wilderness and his obsession with the mysterious John Chapman, who becomes known as Johnny Appleseed. The drama of daily life on the frontier and attacks by the Delawares, who go on the warpath heeding Tecumseh's charge to exterminate the whites, are chronicled along with Tom's spiritual and emotional journey.

Historical Accuracy: The frontier scene is convincingly described.

PETER WILLIAM NISSER (1919-)

Nisser is a Swedish writer.

4630 *The Red Marten*

Date of Publication: 1957
Subject(s): Rural Life—Sweden
Fictional character(s): Simon Wessel, Farmer
Time Period(s): 1700s
Locale(s): Sweden

Summary: The novel portrays peasant life in the early years of the 18th century in Sweden. The action centers on Simon Wessel's dissatisfaction with his lot in life. He counters this dissatisfaction by becoming involved in adventures and affairs, and on the battlefield of the Swedish-Russian War.

Historical Accuracy: The novel is accomplished in its authentic treatment of the time and its customs.

MARIAN NIVEN

(PSEUD. OF MARY NIVEN ALSTON, 1918-)

Born in North Carolina, Niven graduated from Bryn Mawr and Columbia University. She has worked as a history teacher in Virginia and New Jersey.

4631 *The Altar and the Crown*

Date of Publication: 1971
Subject(s): Ancient Egypt
Fictional character(s): Lord Sesostris, Nobleman; Tenatos, Young Man
Time Period(s): 1st century B.C.
Locale(s): Egypt

Summary: The novel is set during the last years of the Ptolemaic dynasty in Egypt in the first century B.C. The story is the philosophical search for meaning and values by Lord Sesostris, an Egyptian high priest and contender for the throne, and the idealistic Tenatos, presumed nephew of the tyrannical King Ptolemy. Political intrigue and betrayal mark their search for a means to sustain civilization.

Historical Accuracy: The historical background elements are authentic.

HOLLISTER NOBLE (1900-)

Noble's books include *One Way to Eldorado*.

4632 *Woman with a Sword: The Biographical Novel of Anna Ella Carroll of Maryland*

Date of Publication: 1948
Subject(s): Civil War—U.S.; Biography, Fictionalized
Historical character(s): Anna Ella Carroll, Writer; Abraham Lincoln, Political Figure; Edwin Stanton, Political Figure; William Henry Seward, Political Figure; Ulysses S. Grant, Military Personnel (Union general); William Tecumseh Sherman, Military Personnel (Union general); Benjamin Franklin Wade, Political Figure
Time Period(s): 1860s (1860-1865)
Locale(s): Maryland; Washington, District of Columbia

Summary: This biographical novel tells the story of Anna Ella Carroll, crusading newspaperwoman and writer, who becomes one of the important advisers to the Union forces and helps to plan the western campaign in the early years of the Civil War. The politics of Lincoln's War Cabinet and their infighting are detailed.

Historical Accuracy: The novel is based on the historical record with opinions and sentiments taken from many public documents and personal letters.

MARGUERITE NOBLE (1910-)

Born in Arizona and a graduate of Arizona State University, Noble spent many years teaching languages in junior high school in Phoenix. She has been a cafe owner in Phoenix and the owner of a guest ranch. Noble is also the mother of novelist Cynthia Buchanan.

4633 *Filaree: A Novel of an American Life*

Date of Publication: 1979
Subject(s): American West; Ranching
Fictional character(s): Melissa Baker, Spouse, Cook; Ben Baker, Rancher; Ike Talbott, Cowboy
Time Period(s): 1910s (1910)
Locale(s): Arizona; California

Summary: Set in the Arizona Territory in 1910, the novel tells the story of Melissa Baker, who struggles through the drudgery of the barren cattle country married to a man she does not love. Her story shows the death of her son, the loss of her ranch, and finally the disintegration of her family against a realistic backdrop of frontier life.

Historical Accuracy: Based on the author's own recollections of her youth in the Arizona Territory, the novel's authenticity in setting and detail is convincing.

FREDERICK NOLAN (1931-)

A British writer of novels, children's books, non-fiction, and screenplays, Nolan was born in Liverpool. After attending school at Liverpool Collegiate, he worked in publishing in London and New York. His Call to Arms series traces the American Strong family from the War of Independence onwards. *White Nights, Red Dawn* is set in Tsarist Russia on the eve of the Revolution.

4634 *White Nights, Red Dawn*

Date of Publication: 1980
Subject(s): Russian Revolution; World War I; Royalty—Russia
Fictional character(s): Tatiana Makcheyeva, Noblewoman; Vladimir Smirnoff, Nobleman
Historical character(s): Helmuth Johannes Ludwig von Moltke, Military Personnel (chief of staff, German army); Erich Ludendorff, Military Personnel (German general); Grigori Efimovich Rasputin, Religious, Zealot; Nicholas II, Ruler (czar); Vladimir Ilich Lenin, Political Figure, Revolutionary

Time Period(s): 1910s (1913-1917)
Locale(s): St. Petersburg, Russia; Moscow, Russia

Summary: The end of the Romanov dynasty in Russia is chronicled through a rush of events, including the First World War and the rise of the Bolsheviks and the Russian Revolution. At the center of the drama is Tatiana Makcheyeva, who is pursued by a variety of men who desire her, including Vladimir, the playboy son of the rich Smirnoff family.

Historical Accuracy: The author admits that this is not an accurate account of history, but an imagined story in an actual time and place.

WILLIAM F. NOLAN (1928-)

An American author of science fiction, mystery, fiction, and nonfiction, Nolan was born in Kansas City and attended the Kansas City Art Institute, San Diego State College, and Los Angeles City College. His eclectic career has included work as a cartoonist, office clerk, aircraft inspector, movie actor, and book and magazine editor, as well as a freelance writer. His award-winning books include *Dashiell Hammett: A Casebook* and the mystery novel *Space for Hire*. He is the co-author of *Logan's Run*, which was filmed in 1976, and the author of two sequels to it.

4635 *The Black Mask Murderers*

Date of Publication: 1994
Subject(s): Mystery; Motion Picture Industry
Fictional character(s): Tony Richett, Organized Crime Figure
Historical character(s): Dashiell Hammett, Writer
Time Period(s): 1930s
Locale(s): Hollywood, California

Summary: Writer Dashiell Hammett plays detective when an aging film star seeks his help extricating herself from a gambling debt. Hammett uncovers that the roulette wheel was fixed, and murder quickly follows.

Historical Accuracy: The novel offers authentic historical and biographical details from Hammett's life and period Hollywood.

MICHAEL NOONAN (1921-)

New Zealand author Noonan was born in Christchurch and attended the University of Sydney. He is the author of the popular Flying Doctor series of adventure stories.

4636 *The Sun Is God*

Date of Publication: 1973
Subject(s): Biography, Fictionalized; Artistic Life; Regency Period
Historical character(s): J.M.W. Turner, Artist
Time Period(s): 18th century; 19th century
Locale(s): England

Summary: This biographical novel offers the story of England's greatest painter, J.M.W. Turner. He is lionized by the wealthy and the powerful but is forced to vanish for months at a time assuming false names and disguises to sustain his art.

The novel attempts to dramatize the strange double life of the painter who laid the foundation for modern art.

Historical Accuracy: The basis for the novel is factual, with some evident invention and interpretation.

CHARLES NORDHOFF (1887-1947)

JAMES NORMAN HALL (1887-1951)

American writers Nordhoff and Hall met while serving in World War I. After the war they moved to Tahiti and produced a number of popular novels including the *Mutiny on the Bounty* trilogy. Other works include *The Hurricane*, a novel about contemporary Polynesian life. Hall's solo work includes reflections on his World War I experiences, essays, and novels, including *Lost Island*, about the effects of war on a small Pacific island.

4637 *Botany Bay*

Date of Publication: 1941
Subject(s): Sea Story; Frontier—Australia; Penal Colonies
Fictional character(s): Hugh Tallant, Convict
Historical character(s): Arthur Phillip, Government Official (governor)
Time Period(s): 1780s
Locale(s): London, England; Botany Bay, Australia (New South Wales)

Summary: The story of the first fleet of convicts sent to the penal colony of Botany Bay in Australia is told through the experiences of Hugh Tallant who offers his personal account of the long voyage out, the struggle of the convict settlers, and his escape back to England.

Historical Accuracy: Though based on research on early Australian history, the authors admit to having taken liberties in matter of dates and incidents for dramatic effect.

4638 *Men Against the Sea*

Date of Publication: 1934
Subject(s): Sea Story; Military Life—British Navy
Historical character(s): William Bligh, Military Personnel (naval officer); Thomas Ledward, Doctor
Time Period(s): 1780s (1789)
Locale(s): At Sea

Summary: In the second volume of the Bounty trilogy, the epic voyage of Captain Bligh and the eighteen loyal men who are set adrift by the mutineers is described. They make a 3,600-mile voyage to the Dutch East Indies in a 23-foot open boat.

Historical Accuracy: The novel is based on Bligh's own log.

4639 *Mutiny on the Bounty*

Date of Publication: 1932
Subject(s): Sea Story; Military Life—British Navy; Mutiny
Fictional character(s): Roger Byam, Military Personnel (midshipman)

Historical character(s): William Bligh, Military Personnel (naval officer); Fletcher Christian, Military Personnel (naval officer)
Time Period(s): 1780s
Locale(s): *Bounty*, At Sea; Tahiti, French Polynesia

Summary: In the first volume of the trilogy that tells the full story of the infamous *Bounty* mutiny, the ship sets sail in 1787 bound for Tahiti, under the stern command of Lieutenant William Bligh. After discipline breaks down in Tahiti, the crew, led by Fletcher Christian, revolts, casting Bligh and eighteen loyal seamen adrift in an open boat.

Historical Accuracy: The narrative is drawn from examination of the Admiralty records, Bligh's journal, and the confessions of the mutineers.

4640 *Pitcairn's Island*

Date of Publication: 1934
Subject(s): Sea Story; Military Life—British Navy
Historical character(s): Fletcher Christian, Military Personnel (naval officer); Maimiti, Spouse (of Christian)
Time Period(s): 1790s; 1800s (1790-1808)
Locale(s): Pitcairn Island, Pacific Islands

Summary: In the concluding volume of the author's Bounty trilogy, the life of the mutineers on the isolated South Sea Pitcairn Island is described. Arriving in 1790, they remain undiscovered until 1808 when only one of the former mutineers is left alive; the others have died, most of the them violently. The novel describes the bloody clash of cultures in paradise.

Historical Accuracy: The authors' sources offer conflicting testimony, and they have adapted a chronology and sequence of events which seems to render more plausible the play of cause and effect.

LAWRENCE NORFOLK (1963-)

Norfolk is a British novelist who lives in London.

4641 *Lempriere's Dictionary*

Date of Publication: 1992
Subject(s): Georgian Period; Picaresque Adventure
Fictional character(s): John Lempriere, Scholar
Time Period(s): 1780s
Locale(s): England

Summary: This unusual novel, which has been described as a Gothic-historical fantasy-tragedy involves a young scholar, John Lempriere, who sets out to write a classical dictionary. The death of his father and his journey to London to settle his estate sets in motion an intricate plot involving a power struggle among the East India trading company, dispossessed heirs, and henchman in the service of a Indian Nawab.

Historical Accuracy: The novel is a tour de force of erudition, offering a great many historical references and details. Even the main character is based on an actual figure, who in fact composed a classical dictionary. That is, however, the extent of the connection to historical fact.

4642 *The Pope's Rhinoceros*

Date of Publication: 1996
Subject(s): Renaissance; Picaresque Adventure
Fictional character(s): Salvestro, Mercenary; Bernardo, Companion
Historical character(s): Leo X, Religious (pope)
Time Period(s): 16th century (1510s)
Locale(s): Rome, Italy; Africa

Summary: Based on the actual events of an unsuccessful attempt by the Portuguese to transport a rhinoceros to Rome by ship as a gift to Pope Leo X, the novel is a complex story of deceit and betrayal. The main characters are the mercenary Salvestro and his companion Bernardo, who lead a group of monks on a pilgrimage to Rome, get mixed up in the intrigue between the Portuguese and the Spanish, and undertake a hazardous journey to West Africa in quest of the rhino.

Historical Accuracy: The novel is encylopedic in its texture. Although the reader is likely to get lost in the labyrinthian tale, the novel cannot fail to impress by its ability to reconstruct a vibrant past.

CHARLES NORMAN

4643 *Mr. Oddity, Samuel Johnson*

Date of Publication: 1951
Subject(s): Biography, Fictionalized; Literary Life
Historical character(s): Samuel Johnson, Writer, Scholar
Time Period(s): 18th century
Locale(s): England

Summary: The novel presents a fictionalized biography of the great English lexicographer, critic, and author Samuel Johnson. The novel follows Johnson's life using some of the best conversations recorded by his biographer, James Boswell. The result is a straightforward and entertaining introduction to Johnson, his circle, and his times.

Historical Accuracy: The novel makes use of the appropriate sources without distortion.

DIANA NORMAN (1935-)

English journalist and writer Norman is the author of *Terrible Beauty*, a biography of Countess Markievicz.

4644 *Fitzempress' Law*

Date of Publication: 1980
Subject(s): Middle Ages; Time Travel; Royalty—England
Fictional character(s): Len, Farmer (serf); Pete, Knight; Sal, Ward
Historical character(s): Henry II, Ruler (King of England)
Time Period(s): 12th century
Locale(s): Hertfordshire, England

Summary: Three young English hoods find themselves transported back in time to the 12th century. Len becomes a swine herder, Pete a knight engaged in the King's wars, and Sal a royal ward about to be delivered to a convent when her marriage contract is not honored. Each needs recourse to the law to get back to their future, but the law belongs to Henry Fitzempress, Henry II of England.

Historical Accuracy: The novel is a creative and imaginitive blend of the modern and the medieval.

4645 *The Morning Gift*

Date of Publication: 1985
Subject(s): Middle Ages
Fictional character(s): Matilda de Risle, Heiress; Sigward, Knight
Time Period(s): 12th century (1134-1154)
Locale(s): Dungesey, England (Fens)

Summary: The gift the Norman heiress Matilda de Risle receives from her husband is the Fens of England. There she endures the civil war that rips England apart in the 12th century as King Stephen and Empress Maude vie for control.

Historical Accuracy: The historical background and medieval customs are genuine and convincingly displayed.

RICK NORMAN (1954-)

Born in Louisiana, Norman graduated from LSU and is an attorney in private practice in Lake Charles, Louisiana. He is the author of a 1983 treatise on corporate law and is a former federal prosecuter.

4646 *Fielder's Choice*

Date of Publication: 1991
Subject(s): Baseball; World War II; Sports
Fictional character(s): Andrew Jackson Fielder, Sports Figure, Military Personnel
Time Period(s): 1940s
Locale(s): Arkansas; St. Louis, Missouri

Summary: Andrew Jackson Fielder is a young unknown pitcher whose "gooseball" gets him to the St. Louis Browns in 1941, where he plays a important role in the Browns' loss to the Yankees for the American League Pennant. Enlisting after Pearl Harbor, Jackson becomes a prisoner of war and must face an inquiry into charges that he conspired with the enemy. The novel offers his defense and the chain of events that got him there.

Historical Accuracy: The novel is an inspired comedy with a compelling and convincing period background.

KATHLEEN NORRIS

4647 *Certain People of Importance*

Date of Publication: 1922
Subject(s): American West; Gold Rush—California
Fictional character(s): Robert Crabtree, Settler; Ella Crabtree, Spouse
Time Period(s): 19th century
Locale(s): San Francisco, California

Summary: The novel captures the development of San Francisco in the 19th century from its boom town days during the gold rush to its importance as a shipping capital. The city's

growth is shown through the experiences of the Crabtree family whose history parallels that of the city.

Historical Accuracy: The novel provides a convincing portrait of the period and the region.

STERLING NORTH (1906-1974)

American naturalist and author North was born in Wisconsin and graduated from the University of Chicago. He worked as a newspaper reporter and literary editor, as well as the MC for the radio program *Books on Trial*. He is an award-winning children's book author whose best-known book is *Rascal: A Memoir of a Better Era*.

4648 *The Wolfling: A Documentary Novel of the 1870s*

Date of Publication: 1969
Subject(s): Animals; Rural Life—U.S.
Fictional character(s): Robbie Trent, Child
Historical character(s): Thure Kumlien, Scientist (naturalist)
Time Period(s): 1870s
Locale(s): Wisconsin

Summary: The novel attempts to reconstruct life in Wisconsin during the 1870s. At the center of the story is the young boy Robbie Trent, who raises a wolf whelp assisted by the Swedish-American naturalist Thure Kumlien.

Historical Accuracy: The author calls the work a documentary novel. Considerable efforts are made to accurately depict life in the 1870s, based on the author's father's recollections.

ANDRE NORTON (1912-)

SUSAN SHWARTZ (1949-)

Prolific author Andre Norton was born Alice Mary Norton in Cleveland, Ohio. A librarian whose career has included work at the Library of Congress, Norton is best known for her science fiction and fantasy books. Her books include *Star Man's Son, 2250 A.D.*, *The Sword is Drawn*, and the Witch World fantasy series. Susan Shwartz was born in Youngstown, Ohio, and educated at Mount Holyoke College, Trinity College, Oxford, and Harvard. She is the author of *Habitats*, *Heritage of Flight*, and *Hecate's Cauldron*.

4649 *Empire of the Eagle*

Date of Publication: 1993
Subject(s): Roman Empire; Fantasy; Witchcraft and Sorcery
Fictional character(s): Quintus, Military Personnel (Roman tribune)
Time Period(s): 1st century
Locale(s): The Silk Road, Asia

Summary: This blend of history, fantasy, and adventure describes the defeat and capture of a Roman legion by the Parthians. The captives are sold into slavery to the Ch'in emperor and forced to march along the Silk Road, where they battle desert storms and black magic.

Historical Accuracy: The fantasy elements are at odds with a faithful rendering of the period, but the atmosphere does employ a number of convincing historical elements.

DUNCAN NORTON-TAYLOR
(1904-1982)

An American journalist, editor, and author, Norton-Taylor began as a reporter and became the editor of *Time* and *Fortune* magazines. His books include *With My Heart in My Mouth* and *The Celts*.

4650　*God's Man: A Novel on the Life of John Calvin*

Date of Publication: 1979
Subject(s): Biography, Fictionalized; Religious Conflict; Protestant Reformation
Historical character(s): John Calvin, Religious (theologian)
Time Period(s): 16th century
Locale(s): France; Geneva, Switzerland

Summary: This novel describes the career of French Protestant theologian John Calvin whose teachings played a central role in the Reformation. It attempts to capture this stern and compelling figure and the era in which he lived through an ingenious first-person account.

Historical Accuracy: The novel offers a plausible and factual account of Calvin's life and the issues that defined the period.

FRANCIS TYSEN NUTT

4651　*Three Fields to Cross*

Date of Publication: 1947
Subject(s): American Revolution; American Colonies; Espionage
Fictional character(s): John Blake, Veteran (French and Indian Wars); Giletta Blake, Spy
Historical character(s): William Howe, Military Personnel (British army commander)
Time Period(s): 1770s
Locale(s): Staten Island, New York, American Colonies

Summary: This novel of the American Revolution is seen through the experiences of a British family on Staten Island. The conflict between rebels and royalists is described and Giletta, the Blake's tom-boyish daughter, turns to espionage work, warning General Washington about British General Howe's false retreat.

Historical Accuracy: The novel best depicts the conflict between Tories and rebels. Otherwise, the story is unlikely.

NELSON CORAL NYE (1907-)

American Western writer Nye was born in Chicago and worked in publicity for newspapers and as a cow-puncher and ranch-hand. He has contributed over 700 articles to horse and livestock publications. His books have won the

Spur Award from the Western Writers of Ameria on several occasions.

4652　*Pistols for Hire*

Date of Publication: 1941
Subject(s): American West; Lincoln County War
Fictional character(s): Flick Farsum, Cowboy
Historical character(s): William Bonney, Outlaw
Time Period(s): 1870s
Locale(s): Lincoln County, New Mexico

Summary: The events of the Lincoln County War, a range war in New Mexico which brought Billy the Kid to prominence is dramatized. The story is told by Flick Farsum, who describes the killing of John H. Tunstall and the three-day siege of Lawyer McSween. Billy the Kid is presented as a true killer rather than a western hero.

Historical Accuracy: The novel stays close to the actual facts, and the historical figures are authentic and believable.

ROBERT NYE

4653　*Falstaff*

Date of Publication: 1976
Subject(s): Middle Ages; Battle of Agincourt; Battle of Shrewsbury
Fictional character(s): Jack Falstaff, Knight
Historical character(s): Henry V, Ruler (King of England); John of Gaunt, Royalty; Henry Percy, Nobleman
Time Period(s): 14th century; 15th century
Locale(s): England; France; Ireland

Summary: Shakespeare's Falstaff is here allowed to tell his version of his remarkable life in this factual autobiography. In bawdy and revisionist detail, Falstaff offers his own interpretation of the battles of Shrewsbury and Agincourt and his own unique assessment of Hotspur, John of Gaunt, and Henry V.

Historical Accuracy: This is a comic triumph of reconstruction both of the Shakespearean original and of the times. However, Falstaff is far from a reliable historian.

4654　*Faust*

Date of Publication: 1981
Subject(s): Myths and Legends; Witchcraft and Sorcery
Fictional character(s): Christopher Wagner, Servant
Historical character(s): John Faust, Magician
Time Period(s): 16th century (1540)
Locale(s): Germany; Italy

Summary: In this comic pastiche of the Faust legend, the year is 1540, the last year of Faust's bargain with the devil before his damnation, and Faust negotiates a new deal. If he can murder the pope, he can secure another 24 years on earth. The novel offers the story of Faust's murderous pilgrimage to Rome with a Rabelaisian cast of characters.

Historical Accuracy: More phantasmagorical than historical, the novel is a comic send-up of the Faust legend with some authentic elements that reconstruct the Faust story.

4655 *The Memoirs of Lord Byron*

Date of Publication: 1989

Subject(s): Literary Life; Biography, Fictionalized; Regency Period

Historical character(s): George Gordon Byron, Nobleman, Writer (poet); Percy Bysshe Shelley, Writer (poet); Lady Caroline Lamb, Noblewoman; Claire Clairmont, Gentlewoman; Augusta Leigh, Gentlewoman

Time Period(s): 1810s; 1820s (1818-1822)

Locale(s): England; Italy; Switzerland

Summary: Nye's novel is an imaginative reconstruction of Byron's memoirs, which were destroyed in 1824. In this account, Byron details his final six years, with references to his childhood, education, quarrels, friendships, and particularly his love affairs. Byron emerges convincingly as a brash figure of boundless energy and passion.

Historical Accuracy: The novel achieves a remarkably believable impersonation of Byron's voice and psychological insight into his genius. The details of Byron's life are faithfully presented.

4656 *Mrs. Shakespeare: The Complete Works*

Date of Publication: 1993

Subject(s): Elizabethan Period; Literary Life

Historical character(s): Anne Hathaway, Spouse (of Shakespeare); William Shakespeare, Writer

Time Period(s): 16th century

Locale(s): London, England

Summary: This comic send-up of Elizabethan life in general and William Shakespeare in particular takes the form of an account written by Anne Hathaway of a week she spends with her husband in London. Among other intimate secrets, she reveals that she is the Dark Lady of the Sonnets and that Shakespeare was an avid bisexual.

Historical Accuracy: There are a number of inaccuracies that undermine the novel's reliability as a faithful, if comic, reflection of Shakespeare and his times.

4657 *The Voyage of the Destiny*

Date of Publication: 1982

Subject(s): Sea Story; Jacobean Period

Historical character(s): Sir Walter Raleigh, Sea Captain, Courtier

Time Period(s): 17th century (1616)

Locale(s): At Sea

Summary: The novel takes the form of a first-person narrative of Sir Walter Raleigh describing his final voyage in 1616. Under a temporarily commuted sentence of death for treason, Raleigh describes his fateful voyage and recollects his relationship with Queen Elizabeth.

Historical Accuracy: The novel is an occasion for some very modern speculations on identity, history, and art that compete with the actual events of Raleigh's voyage.

JOYCE CAROL OATES (1938-)

An American novelist, short story writer, and critic, Oates was born in New York and graduated from Syracuse University and the University of Wisconsin. She is a writer in residence at Princeton University. In 1970, after two previous nominations, Oates won the National Book Award for *Them.* At 31 she was one of the youngest ever to receive that honor. She averages almost two books a year, dazzling in her versatility, producing novels, plays, reviews, criticism, essays, and short stories.

4658 *A Bloodsmoor Romance*

Date of Publication: 1982

Subject(s): Family Saga

Fictional character(s): Deirdre Zinn, Young Woman (kidnapee); Constance Philippa Zinn, Young Woman; Malvinia Zinn, Actress

Historical character(s): Mark Twain, Writer

Time Period(s): 19th century (1879-1899)

Locale(s): Bloodsmoor Valley, Pennsylvania

Summary: Described as "the other side of *Little Women,*" Oates' novel is a 19th-century romance with decidedly modern complications. She tells the story of the five Zinn women, daughters of an eccentric inventor. One is abducted in a balloon, another disgraces herself on her wedding night, another becomes an actress who attracts a dandy named Mark Twain. The fourth is content at home, and the fifth devotes herself to her father's great work.

Historical Accuracy: More a send-up of the 19th century than a faithful representation, the novel does however show the spirit of the age.

4659 *Mysteries of Winterthurn*

Date of Publication: 1984

Subject(s): Mystery; Crime and Criminals

Fictional character(s): Xavier Kilvarin, Detective—Police; Perdita, Heroine

Time Period(s): 19th century; 20th century

Locale(s): Winterthurn City, United States

Summary: The novel details three cases of detective Xavier Kilvarin, all in his hometown of Winterthurn. Each expose family and community secrets while Xavier struggles to deal with his passion for his enigmatic cousin Perdita.

Historical Accuracy: Time and place are more mythical than historical, yet the novel offers a faithful version of the 19th-century novel of crime and detectives.

HILTON OBENZINGER

4660 *Cannibal Eliot and the Lost Histories of San Francisco*

Date of Publication: 1993

Subject(s): American West; Earthquakes; Gold Rush—California

Fictional character(s): Juan Pablo Grijalva, Military Personnel (Spanish sergeant); Cannibal Eliot, Sailor, Adventurer; Martin de Landacta, Religious (Spanish priest)
Time Period(s): Multiple Time Periods
Locale(s): San Francisco, California

Summary: From ''found'' documents—diaries, memoirs, interviews, and other first-hand accounts—the novel traces the history of San Francisco from the first clash between Spanish soldiers and the Indians in 1776 to the Great Earthquake of 1906.

Historical Accuracy: The novel offers a blend of fact and fiction with an authentic sense of San Francisco's colorful past.

PATRICK O'BRIAN (1914-)

O'Brian is an English author who has written naval adventure novels and biographies of Pablo Picasso and Sir Joseph Banks. He has also translated many works from the French including the novels and memoirs of Simone de Beauvoir.

4661　*The Commodore*

Date of Publication: 1995
Subject(s): Sea Story; Military Life—British Navy; Napoleonic Wars
Fictional character(s): Jack Aubrey, Military Personnel (naval officer); Stephen Maturin, Doctor, Spy; Sophie Aubrey, Spouse
Time Period(s): 1810s
Locale(s): Hampshire, England; At Sea

Summary: Domestic problems plague both Aubrey and Maturin. Jack is made a commodore and given a small fleet, ostensibly to enforce the ban on shipping slaves out of West Africa. His true mission is to destroy a French fleet attempting to land troops and arms in Ireland.

Historical Accuracy: O'Brian is skillful at reproducing both the dialogue of the era and an exact and precise picture of life aboard ship and on land during the period.

4662　*Desolation Island*

Date of Publication: 1978
Subject(s): Sea Story; Military Life—British Navy; Napoleonic Wars
Fictional character(s): Jack Aubrey, Military Personnel (naval officer); Stephen Maturin, Doctor, Spy; Mrs. Wogan, Spy, Convict
Time Period(s): 1800s
Locale(s): *Leopard*, At Sea

Summary: The action moves to the South Pacific as Aubrey and Maturin become involved with an American woman, Mrs. Wogan, who is sentenced to an Australian penal colony on a charge of espionage. The naval action takes them to the bottom of the world into the waters of the Antarctic. They must brave storms and avoid the pursuit of superior forces.

Historical Accuracy: O'Brian's ability to render the minutia of everyday naval life is exceptional.

4663　*The Far Side of the World*

Date of Publication: 1984
Subject(s): Sea Story; Military Life—British Navy; War of 1812
Fictional character(s): Jack Aubrey, Military Personnel (naval officer); Stephen Maturin, Doctor, Spy
Time Period(s): 1810s
Locale(s): *Surprise*, At Sea (Pacific Ocean)

Summary: During the War of 1812, Captain Aubrey heads for Cape Horn to intercept a powerful American frigate that is harassing the British whaling fleet. The voyage is plagued with disasters as Aubrey and Maturin must contend with typhoons, castaways, shipwreck, murder, and the criminally insane.

Historical Accuracy: Thorough and convincing in the technicalities of sail and naval strategy, the novel and the series are unmatched in their realistic and believable portraits.

4664　*The Fortune of War*

Date of Publication: 1979
Subject(s): Sea Story; Military Life—British Navy; War of 1812
Fictional character(s): Jack Aubrey, Military Personnel (naval officer); Stephen Maturin, Doctor, Spy; Diana Villiers, Gentlewoman
Time Period(s): 1810s (1812-1813)
Locale(s): England; At Sea (east coast of North America)

Summary: In the Dutch East Indies, Captain Aubrey learns that he has been appointed to the command of the best-armed frigate in the Royal Navy. When the War of 1812 breaks out, Aubrey and Maturin are sent to England where they become entangled in political intrigue. They are then involved in the naval action off the American East Coast.

Historical Accuracy: What separates O'Brian's stories from others is his evident expertise in everyday life beyond the nautical technicalities. Aubrey and Maturin have become utterly convincing characters and their surroundings totally believable.

4665　*The Golden Ocean*

Date of Publication: 1956
Subject(s): Sea Story; Military Life—British Navy
Fictional character(s): Peter Palafox, Military Personnel (midshipman)
Historical character(s): George Anson, Military Personnel (naval commander)
Time Period(s): 1740s
Locale(s): At Sea; Ireland

Summary: The background for this sea story is the 1740 circumnavigation of the world by Commodore Anson, which charted unexplored seas and netted an uncalculable cache of captured Spanish treasure. Peter Palafox is a young Irishman who signs on for the voyage as a midshipman.

Historical Accuracy: O'Brian's details of naval life and the period are exact and authentic.

4666   *H.M.S. Surprise*

Date of Publication: 1973

Subject(s): Sea Story; Military Life—British Navy; Napoleonic Wars

Fictional character(s): Jack Aubrey, Military Personnel (naval officer); Stephen Maturin, Doctor, Spy; Diana Villiers, Gentlewoman

Time Period(s): 1800s

Locale(s): Bombay, India; *Surprise*, At Sea (in the Indian Ocean)

Summary: In the third Aubrey-Maturin story the scene is the East Indies as Aubrey, in command of the *Surprise*, attempts to protect the British merchant fleet from superior French forces. Aubrey and Maturin re-encounter the dangerous Diana Villiers in Bombay and she continues to drive a wedge between them.

Historical Accuracy: The author creates believable period settings whether on land or sea.

4667   *The Ionian Mission*

Date of Publication: 1981

Subject(s): Sea Story; Military Life—British Navy; Napoleonic Wars

Fictional character(s): Jack Aubrey, Military Personnel (naval officer); Stephen Maturin, Doctor, Spy; Diana Villiers, Gentlewoman

Time Period(s): 1810s

Locale(s): London, England; At Sea; Greece

Summary: Aubrey is in command of a line-of-battle ship stationed on blockade duty off the French port of Toulouse. Events, however, take Aubrey and Maturin on a hazardous mission to the Greek islands. Maturin's skill and Jack's legendary luck are both needed to snatch success out of seeming failure.

Historical Accuracy: The period details and the military and naval elements are authentic and convincing.

4668   *The Letter of Marque*

Date of Publication:

Subject(s): Sea Story; Military Life—British Navy; Napoleonic Wars

Fictional character(s): Jack Aubrey, Military Personnel (naval officer); Stephen Maturin, Doctor, Spy; Diana Villiers, Gentlewoman

Time Period(s): 1810s

Locale(s): *Surprise*, At Sea; France

Summary: Aubrey, struck off the list of post-captains for a crime that he did not commit, finds himself in disgrace. Maturin purchases Aubrey's former ship, the *Surprise*, for Aubrey to command as a privateer. The action features a daring raid on a French port to redeem Aubrey's reputation. Maturin's estranged wife, the fascinating Diana Villiers, reappears as well.

Historical Accuracy: The novel and the series offer unsurpassed authentic details of the naval and period scenes.

4669   *Master and Commander*

Date of Publication: 1968

Subject(s): Sea Story; Military Life—British Navy; Napoleonic Wars

Fictional character(s): Jack Aubrey, Military Personnel (naval officer); Stephen Maturin, Doctor, Spy; James Dillon, Military Personnel (naval officer)

Time Period(s): 1800s (1800)

Locale(s): *Sophie*, At Sea (in the Mediterranean); Minorca, Spain

Summary: In the first volume of the author's series on the naval adventures of Jack Aubrey and Stephen Maturin, the two meet as Aubrey receives his first command, the armed brig *Sophie*. Aboard is James Dillon, his first officer and an Irish rebel. Aubrey convinces Maturin, a sometime intelligence agent, to join him as his ship's surgeon. Aubrey is intent on making his reputation and gaining prizes. The action climaxes when the *Sophie* takes on the heavily gunned Spanish frigate *Cacafuego*.

Historical Accuracy: The period detail and technicalities of sailing are utterly convincing.

4670   *The Mauritius Command*

Date of Publication: 1977

Subject(s): Sea Story; Military Life—British Navy; Napoleonic Wars

Fictional character(s): Jack Aubrey, Military Personnel (naval officer); Stephen Maturin, Doctor, Spy; Sophie Aubrey, Spouse

Time Period(s): 1800s

Locale(s): At Sea (in the Indian Ocean); Mauritius; Reunion

Summary: In the fourth novel of naval adventures involving Jack Aubrey and Stephen Maturin, Aubrey is now married. He is rescued from domestic life when given command of a naval squadron with a mission to capture the French island bases of Reunion and Mauritius. Aubrey must negotiate the tricky challenge of command over very different captains in this high-stakes gamble. Success could mean a knighthood; failure could end Aubrey's career.

Historical Accuracy: The novel offers a riveting story told with a scrupulous eye for nautical and period details. The events described are factual.

4671   *The Nutmeg of Consolation*

Date of Publication: 1991

Subject(s): Sea Story; Military Life—British Navy; Napoleonic Wars

Fictional character(s): Jack Aubrey, Military Personnel (naval officer); Stephen Maturin, Doctor, Spy

Time Period(s): 1810s

Locale(s): New South Wales, Australia

Summary: The novel begins where *The Thirteen Gun Salute* ended, with Aubrey, Maturin, and the crew of the *Diana* shipwrecked on a remote island in the Dutch East Indies. They fashion a makeshift vessel and must deal with Malay pirates. In Batavia, they secure a new ship and sail to the penal colony of New South Wales in Australia. Maturin's revulsion at the conditions in which the convicts live prompts a near-diplomatic crisis.

Historical Accuracy: The details of period life and naval technicalities are remarkably exact and convincing.

4672 *Post Captain*

Date of Publication: 1972
Subject(s): Sea Story; Military Life—British Navy; Napoleonic Wars
Fictional character(s): Jack Aubrey, Military Personnel (naval officer); Stephen Maturin, Doctor, Spy; Diana Villiers, Gentlewoman
Time Period(s): 1800s (1803)
Locale(s): Sussex, England; At Sea (English Channel); France

Summary: During the brief Peace of Amiens, Captain Jack Aubrey takes refuge in France from his creditors. When Napoleon breaks the truce, Aubrey is interned and escapes to serve on blockade duty in the Channel. The fascinating, though dangerous, Diana Villiers tests the friendship between Aubrey and Maturin. The naval action includes a dangerous mission into a French-held harbor.

Historical Accuracy: O'Brian's ability to capture a convincing period setting is remarkable.

4673 *The Reverse of the Medal*

Date of Publication: 1986
Subject(s): Sea Story; Military Life—British Navy; Napoleonic Wars
Fictional character(s): Jack Aubrey, Military Personnel (naval officer); Stephen Maturin, Doctor, Spy
Time Period(s): 1810s
Locale(s): At Sea (West Indies); London, England

Summary: In an uncharacteristic land-locked adventure, Jack Aubrey returns home from protecting British whalers off the coast of South America. He is induced by an acquaintance to make certain investments based on insider information. He soon gets entangled in the London criminal underworld and the espionage shadow-world of Maturin.

Historical Accuracy: The author is equally convincing on land as on sea in delivering an authentic setting and situations.

4674 *The Surgeon's Mate*

Date of Publication: 1981
Subject(s): Sea Story; Military Life—British Navy; War of 1812
Fictional character(s): Jack Aubrey, Military Personnel (naval officer); Stephen Maturin, Doctor, Spy; Diana Villiers, Gentlewoman
Time Period(s): 1810s
Locale(s): At Sea (the Grand Banks); England

Summary: Action against the United States during the War of 1812 causes Aubrey and Maturin to return to England pursued by two privateers intent on capturing Maturin. An exhilarating chase through the fogs of the Grand Banks is followed by intrigue in England surrounding the ever-fascinating Diana Villiers.

Historical Accuracy: The author admits to some slight distortion of the historical sequence of naval command. Otherwise the authenticity is persuasive.

4675 *The Thirteen Gun Salute*

Date of Publication: 1989
Subject(s): Sea Story; Military Life—British Navy; Napoleonic Wars
Fictional character(s): Jack Aubrey, Military Personnel (naval officer); Stephen Maturin, Doctor, Spy
Time Period(s): 1810s
Locale(s): At Sea (Dutch East Indies)

Summary: Reinstated in the Royal Navy after his exploits as a privateer, Jack Aubrey, along with Stephen Maturin, embarks on a diplomatic mission to prevent links between Napoleon and the Malay princes that will endanger British merchant shipping. The novel features a duel of wits between Maturin and French envoys, as well as a devastating typhoon.

Historical Accuracy: The period and technical details are commandingly presented.

4676 *Treason's Harbour*

Date of Publication: 1983
Subject(s): Sea Story; Military Life—British Navy; Napoleonic Wars
Fictional character(s): Jack Aubrey, Military Personnel (naval officer); Stephen Maturin, Doctor, Spy
Time Period(s): 1810s
Locale(s): Malta; *Surprise*, At Sea (in the Mediterranean and Red Seas)

Summary: Aubrey awaits repairs to his ship in Malta, which is filled with Napoleon's agents intent on sabotaging his mission. Maturin must match wits with the enemy agents before setting sail for the Middle East.

Historical Accuracy: The period details and technical details of sailing are convincingly presented.

4677 *The Truelove*

Date of Publication: 1992
Subject(s): Sea Story; Military Life—British Navy; Napoleonic Wars
Fictional character(s): Jack Aubrey, Military Personnel (naval officer); Stephen Maturin, Doctor, Spy; Clarissa Harvill, Convict
Time Period(s): 1810s
Locale(s): At Sea; Tonga

Summary: A British whaler has been captured by a native chief in Tonga at France's instigation. Captain Aubrey is dispatched to restore order. Aboard is the fascinating and mysterious Clarissa Harvill. The action features a pitched battle against a band of headhunters.

Historical Accuracy: The setting and situation is bolstered by thorough knowledge and sure presentation.

4678 *The Unknown Shore*

Date of Publication: 1959

Subject(s): Sea Story; Military Life—British Navy; Georgian Period
Fictional character(s): Jack Byron, Military Personnel (midshipman); Tobias Barrow, Doctor (surgeon's mate)
Time Period(s): 1740s
Locale(s): *Wager*, At Sea; Valparaiso, Chile

Summary: A forerunner of O'Brian's Aubrey/Maturin series, this novel describes the adventures of the *Wager*, a British ship that is separated from Commodore Anson's circumnavigation of the globe in 1740. Off Cape Horn the *Wager* is wrecked, and two shipmates, Jack Byron and Tobis Barrow, younger versions of Aubrey and Maturin, struggle for survival.

Historical Accuracy: This early O'Brian novel shows the same characteristic concern for authentic detail and period accuracy as his later books.

4679 *The Wine-Dark Sea*

Date of Publication: 1993
Subject(s): Sea Story; Military Life—British Navy; Napoleonic Wars
Fictional character(s): Jack Aubrey, Military Personnel (naval officer); Stephen Maturin, Doctor, Spy
Time Period(s): 1810s
Locale(s): At Sea; Peru

Summary: In this episode of the Aubrey-Maturin series, the *Surprise* is in pursuit of an American privateer while on a mission to deliver Maturin to help foment revolution in Peru and Chile. A volcanic eruption, a daring open-boat journey, a chase through the Andes, and a climactic pursuit south of Cape Horn are featured.

Historical Accuracy: The author possesses a remarkable ability to capture the period and setting whether flora, fauna, or historical details.

4680 *The Yellow Admiral*

Date of Publication: 1996
Subject(s): Sea Story; Napoleonic Wars
Fictional character(s): Stephen Maturin, Doctor, Spy; Jack Aubrey, Military Personnel (naval officer), Landowner; Sophie Aubrey, Spouse
Time Period(s): 1810s (1814-1815)
Locale(s): England; At Sea

Summary: In this installment of the Aubrey-Maturin series, Jack Aubrey finds himself landlocked and beset by a series of domestic crises. At sea he captures a French privateer but faces a charge of deserting his post. Aubrey fears that he may be "yellowed," promoted to the rank of admiral but given no squadron to command. Rescue is provided by Maturin who returns from France with the news that the Chileans require a navy and the service of English officers. The novel concludes with the news that Napoleon has escaped from Elba.

Historical Accuracy: The novel is precise in its chronology and its ability to capture period details and customs.

KATE O'BRIEN (1897-1974)

An Irish novelist and playwright, O'Brien was born in Limerick and attended University College, Dublin. Her novels are mostly concerned with the Irish middle class and the emotional tensions created by Irish-Catholic puritanism. She is the author of *Without My Cloak*, *Mary Lavalle*, *The Flower of May*, and *As Music and Splendour*.

4681 *For One Sweet Grape*

Date of Publication: 1946
Subject(s): Royalty—Spain
Historical character(s): Philip II, Ruler (King of Spain); Ana de Mendoza, Royalty (princess)
Time Period(s): 16th century
Locale(s): Spain

Summary: The novel is set in the court of Philip II and describes the curious relationship between the king and Catholic princess Ana de Mendoza. Philip takes her love and submission for granted, and, when she has the effrontery to take a lover, he sets out to ruin her.

Historical Accuracy: The basic situation is historical, but the author's version that forms the novel's drama is invented and is aimed at universal rather than historical relevance.

SALIEE O'BRIEN

(PSEUD. OF FRANKIE-LEE JANAS, 1908-)

Born in Missouri, Janas attended the University of Texas. She has worked as a proofreader and writer and is active in amateur dramatics and radio work. She writes under several pseudonyms, including Lisa Bremer, Francesca Gree, and Saliee O'Brien.

4682 *Farewell the Stranger*

Date of Publication: 1956
Subject(s): Settlement of the American Frontier; Romance
Fictional character(s): Devora Griggs, Young Woman; Jerd Warner, Widow(er)
Time Period(s): 1800s (1808)
Locale(s): St. Louis, Missouri

Summary: Widower Jerd Warner arrives in St. Louis in 1808 in search of a wife to take back with him to the wilderness. Devora Griggs takes him up on his offer and deals well with the frontier, Indian attacks, and other dangers but must contend with Warner's indifference and his obsession with the memory of his dead wife.

Historical Accuracy: The details of wilderness life of the period are convincing.

VINCENT O'BRIEN (1916-)

Born in Scotland and educated at the University of Montreal and McGill University, O'Brien served in the Canadian Army in World War II. He worked in advertising and on teleplays on historical figures for the National Film Board of Canada. O'Brien is considered an authority on early Canadian history.

4683 *The White Cockade*

Date of Publication: 1963
Subject(s): Jacobite Rebellion; French and Indian War; Battle of Quebec
Fictional character(s): Gillian Kennedy, Military Personnel (French volunteer)
Historical character(s): James Wolfe, Military Personnel (British general); Patrick MacKellar, Engineer, Spy
Time Period(s): 1750s
Locale(s): Canada; Ticonderoga, New York, American Colonies

Summary: Gillian Kennedy is a survivor of the failed Jacobite Rebellion who finds his way to Canada as a French volunteer on the eve of the decisive struggle with the British which will decide control of North America. He serves with the Varennes Rangers, and his life is entangled with that of James Wolfe.

Historical Accuracy: The historical background to the story is exact and authentic.

RICHARD O'CONNOR (1915-1975)

An American born in Indiana, O'Connor attended schools in Milwaukee. He worked briefly as an actor, appearing on Broadway in two plays. He was also a newspaperman in Chicago, Detroit, New Orleans, Boston, Los Angeles, and New York. A novelist and an author of popular historical studies, O'Connor's biography *Bat Masterson* was the basis of the popular TV series.

4684 *Company Q*

Date of Publication: 1957
Subject(s): Civil War—U.S.; Battle of Atlanta; Espionage
Fictional character(s): Frank Archer, Military Personnel (Union major), Spy
Time Period(s): 1860s
Locale(s): Atlanta, Georgia

Summary: This Civil War novel concerns the experiences of a company of demoted Union officers who are given the opportunity to redeem themselves in difficult fighting. Frank Archer, a former major, proves himself on a spying mission into besieged Atlanta.

Historical Accuracy: The novel's story is fictional, but it does rely on an authentic period and military background.

4685 *Guns of Chickamauga*

Date of Publication: 1955
Subject(s): Civil War—U.S.; Battle of Chickamauga
Fictional character(s): Matthew Wayne, Military Personnel (Union soldier), Journalist; Elizabeth Ashley, Gentlewoman
Time Period(s): 1860s
Locale(s): Chattanooga, Tennessee

Summary: This Civil War story centers on the bloody events of the Battle of Chicamauga and concerns the exploits of Matthew Wayne. He is cashiered from the Union Army after Shiloh and becomes a reporter for a Chicago newspaper that sends him to cover the action of the Army of the Cumberland.

He finds himself in the middle of a conspiracy involving contraband Southern cotton.

Historical Accuracy: The novel offers an authentic historical background.

4686 *Officers and Ladies*

Date of Publication: 1958
Subject(s): Spanish-American War
Fictional character(s): Douglas Warriner, Military Personnel (captain); Philip Warriner, Military Personnel (officer)
Time Period(s): 1890s (1898)
Locale(s): Manila, Philippines

Summary: Two brothers' rivalry is dramatized against the background of the American Army in the Philippines in 1898. Captain Douglas Warriner is joined by his younger brother Phillip as the islands are in turmoil due to the Moro threat to drive the U.S. Army off the islands.

Historical Accuracy: The period details are convincingly drawn.

4687 *The Vandal*

Date of Publication: 1960
Subject(s): Byzantine Empire
Fictional character(s): Marius the Vandal, Military Personnel (adjutant to Belisarius)
Historical character(s): Belisarius, Military Personnel (general); Justinian I, Ruler (Roman emperor)
Time Period(s): 6th century
Locale(s): Byzantium, Byzantine Empire; Middle East

Summary: The conflict between the great general Belisarius and the Emperor Justinian is described from the vantage point of Marius the Vandal, a young aide to Belisarius. Justinian, jealous of Belisarius' popularity, schemes to bring him down.

Historical Accuracy: The story is fictional with no attempt to tell an actual story based on historical events. The atmosphere is, however, convincing.

JANET O'DANIEL (1921-)

An American born in Ithaca, New York, O'Daniel attended Ithaca College and worked as a newspaper reporter and city editor. She has published books for both adults and children.

4688 *O Genesee*

Date of Publication: 1957
Subject(s): Settlement of the American Frontier; War of 1812
Fictional character(s): Helen Fairchild, Young Woman, Settler; Marcus Hook, Trader
Time Period(s): 18th century; 19th century (1799-1813)
Locale(s): Genesee Valley, New York (near present day Rochester)

Summary: The story of the settling of the Genesee Valley of New York during the period before and during the War of 1812 is described through the experiences of young trader Marcus Hook. Hook's nonconformist attitude causes a strain in the community, particularly when Hook is accused of trading with the British, and worse, after the massacre at Lewiston by Indian allies of the British.

Historical Accuracy: The author admits that the chronology of certain historical events have been slightly tampered with for the sake of the narrative.

SCOTT O'DELL (1898-1989)

Born in Los Angeles, O'Dell attended Occidental College, the University of Wisconsin, Stanford University, and the University of Rome. He worked as a technical director for Paramount Studios and became a full-time writer in 1934. His young adult novel, *Island of the Blue Dolphins*, its a Newbery winner.

4689 *Hill of the Hawk*

Date of Publication: 1947
Subject(s): American West; Spanish Colonies; Mexican War
Fictional character(s): Grady Dunavant, Settler; Luz de Zubaran, Young Woman; Don Saturnino Zubaran, Landowner
Historical character(s): Kit Carson, Frontiersman; Stephen Watts Kearney, Military Personnel (general)
Time Period(s): 1840s
Locale(s): Los Angeles, California

Summary: The story of Spanish California and the war between Spanish landowners and American settlers is described in the experiences of Grady Dunavant and the Los Angeles stronghold of Don Saturnino. The clash of cultures explodes into violence as Kit Carson, Stephen Kearney, and John Fremont lead the American forces to seize the territory.

Historical Accuracy: The story is invented, but the historical background is mainly accurate.

MARIE OEMLER (1879-1932)

Born in Savannah, Georgia, Oemler's first short stories appeared in popular magazines. A mostly sentimental writer of romance and melodrama, Oemler's most serious work is the historical novel *The Holy Lover*, which deals with John Wesley's career as a missionary in Savannah, Georgia.

4690 *The Holy Lover*

Date of Publication: 1927
Subject(s): Biography, Fictionalized; American Colonies
Historical character(s): John Wesley, Religious (minister), Government Official
Time Period(s): 1730s (1735-1738)
Locale(s): Georgia, American Colonies

Summary: Based on the years religious leader John Wesley spent in Georgia as Secretary of Indian Affairs under Governor Oglethorpe, the novel offers a frank and at times unflattering portrait of Wesley, particularly in his dealing with his first and last love affair.

Historical Accuracy: The novel is solidly grounded in historical research and offers a realistic, if sometimes overly negative, view of colonial life and Wesley.

JULIA O'FAOLAIN (1932-)

An English writer, translator, and language teacher, O'Faolain is the daughter of writer Sean O'Faolain. She is a graduate of University College, Dublin, and did graduate study at the University of Rome and the Sorbonne. Her book, *No Country for Young Men* was short-listed for the Booker Prize.

4691 *Women in the Wall*

Date of Publication: 1973
Subject(s): Dark Ages; Religious Life
Historical character(s): Radegunde, Royalty (princess)
Time Period(s): 6th century (568-587)
Locale(s): Gaul

Summary: Set in 6th century Gaul, the story chronicles the life of Radegunde, a German princess, who is captured and raised by Clotair, a Frankish king she is later forced to marry. She escapes from the count and found a convent at Poitiers, where she hopes to provide a haven for herself and women like her. Unfortunately, the world and the flesh intervene.

Historical Accuracy: The story is solidly based on the actual story of Radegunde.

SEAN O'FAOLAIN (1900-1991)

An Irish writer of novels and short stories, O'Faolain depicted in his work conflict between Ireland's past and present. He also wrote important biographies of Eamon De Valera and Daniel O'Connell.

4692 *A Nest of Simple Folk*

Date of Publication: 1933
Subject(s): Independence—Ireland; Fenians; Espionage
Fictional character(s): Leo Foxe-Donnell, Patriot; Johnny Hussey, Police Officer, Spy; Johno O'Donnell, Patriot
Time Period(s): 19th century; 20th century (1854-1916)
Locale(s): Limerick, Ireland; Cork, Ireland; Dublin, Ireland

Summary: The novel details the fight for Irish independence in the 19th century. The central character is Leo Foxe-Donnell, a committed patriot. He is symbolically contrasted with Johnny Hussey, a British loyalist policeman. The two men represent the two sides of a divided country.

Historical Accuracy: There are good regional details of Irish life here.

LIAM O'FLAHERTY (1896-1924)

An Irish laborer, clerk, founder of the Irish Communist Party, screenwriter, and author, O'Flaherty was born in Inishmore on the Aran Islands off the Galway coast of Ireland. He attended Rockwell College, Blackrock College, and University College. O'Flaherty is best known as the author of *The Informer*, a novel of Ireland's civil war during the 1920s, which became an Academy Award-winning motion picture in 1935. Other works include *The Mountain Tavern and Other Stories* and *Insurrection*.

4693　*Famine*

Date of Publication: 1937
Subject(s): Irish Potato Famine; Disasters—Natural
Fictional character(s): Brian Kilmartin, Farmer
Time Period(s): 1840s
Locale(s): Ireland

Summary: The novel graphically and compellingly dramatizes the tragedy of the Irish Potato Famine in the 1840s. Brian Kilmartin and his family are devastated by the famine and by the injustices that lead to the death or immigration of 1,500,000 Irish.

Historical Accuracy: The novel's setting, characters, and period are utterly convincing.

ELISABETH OGILVIE (1917-)

An American writer of suspense fiction, historical, and children's fiction, Ogilvie's books include *High Tide at Noon*, *My World Is an Island*, and *When the Music Stopped*.

4694　*Jennie about to Be*

Date of Publication: 1984
Subject(s): Romance; Regency Period
Fictional character(s): Jennie Hawthorne, Young Woman; Nigel Gilchrist, Military Personnel (officer), Landowner; Alick Gilchrist, Young Man
Time Period(s): 1800s (1809)
Locale(s): London, England; Highlands, Scotland

Summary: In 1809, Jennie Hawthorne meets and marries a young officer in the Household Cavalry, Nigel Gilchrist, and accompanies him to his family estate in Scotland. There she is appalled to discover from his cousin Alick that her husband plans to turn out the crofters. A fight ensues between Alick and Nigel that causes both Jennie and Alick to flee, first south to England and then to America.

Historical Accuracy: The period background of the Highland Clearances is convincing and authentic.

4695　*Jennie Glenroy*

Date of Publication: 1993
Subject(s): Family Saga; Romance
Fictional character(s): Jennie Glenroy, Spouse; Alick Glenroy, Businessman (shipbuilder)
Time Period(s): 1820s (1827)
Locale(s): Whittier, Maine

Summary: In the third volume of the author's books on Jennie and Alick Glenroy, who fled the Scottish Highlands and began a life together in coastal Maine, they now have a prosperous life. The story features a succession of disturbing events that touch the Glenroy children, including a false accusation of crime and the influence of slavery.

Historical Accuracy: The novel is convincing in its regional and period details.

4696　*The World of Jennie G.*

Date of Publication: 1986

Subject(s): Romance
Fictional character(s): Jennie Gilchrist, Widow(er); Alick Gilchrist, Young Man
Historical character(s): Colin MacKenzie, Businessman
Time Period(s): 1800s (1809)
Locale(s): Maine

Summary: Life in coastal Maine in the early 1800s is depicted in the story of Jennie Gilchrist whose husband is killed in a fight with his cousin, Alick. They flee from Scotland to America where they live together as the Glenroys, but their past comes out, and they find themselves entangled in jealousies and suspicion.

Historical Accuracy: The depiction of period Maine is convincing.

DOROTHY OGLEY

MABEL CLELAND WIDDEMER
(1902-1964)

4697　*Iron Land*

Date of Publication: 1946
Subject(s): Settlement of the American Frontier; Mining
Fictional character(s): Burr Rowntree, Young Man; Ethan Rowntree, Young Man
Time Period(s): 1860s
Locale(s): Minnesota

Summary: The story of development of Minnesota's iron region during the 1860s is depicted in the tale of two brothers, Burr and Ethan Rowntree. Scenes of prosperity and the rush to exploit the riches of the Mesabi range are dramatized.

Historical Accuracy: The novel features a believable and authentic historical background and period details despite a largely melodramatic story.

LESLIE O'GRADY

4698　*The Artist's Daughter*

Date of Publication: 1979
Subject(s): Victorian Period; Romance; Artistic Life
Fictional character(s): Nora Woburn, Spouse; Oliver Woburn, Gentleman; Mark Gerrick, Gentleman
Time Period(s): 19th century (Victorian period)
Locale(s): London, England; Dartmoor, England; Devonshire, England

Summary: This tale of romantic suspense set during the Victorian period describes the unhappy married life of Nora Woburn, daughter of a prominent painter. After she endures a brutal relationship with Oliver Woburn, Nora escapes to Devonshire where she finds employment on the estate of Mark Gerrick, a man with a troubling past. Her discovery of a long-lost portrait of herself leads her into danger that exposes a dark and violent side to Victorian England.

Historical Accuracy: The regional elements are captured with authenticity.

4699 *Lady Jane*

Date of Publication: 1981
Subject(s): Chinese Empire
Fictional character(s): May Monckton, Young Woman; Dinah Quo, Servant; Alex Wolders, Adventurer
Time Period(s): 19th century
Locale(s): China

Summary: May Monkton is a young Englishwoman who grows up in China before returning to England to be married. When her marriage ends in tragedy and scandal, she returns to China only to find herself at the center of shady dealings in stolen Chinese treasures.

Historical Accuracy: The novel features believable details of Chinese life and customs.

4700 *Lord Raven's Widow*

Date of Publication: 1983
Subject(s): Victorian Period; Gothic Romance
Fictional character(s): Nora Raven, Widow(er); Drake Turner, Businessman; Ella Mason, Young Woman
Time Period(s): 19th century (Victorian period)
Locale(s): London, England; Dartmoor, England

Summary: Nora Woburn, the heroine of *The Artist's Daughter*, now Lady Raven, is left alone after the deaths of her husband and son. She finds herself attracted to Drake Turner who is interested in buying her shares of the Raven shipping interests. When a mysterious American arrives claiming to be the real Lady Raven, Nora does not know whom to trust.

Historical Accuracy: The setting is convincing in this Victorian suspense story.

4701 *The Second Sister*

Date of Publication: 1984
Subject(s): Victorian Period; Suspense
Fictional character(s): Cassandra Clark, Gentlewoman; Geoffrey Lester, Gentleman; Leonie Lester, Spouse (of Geoffrey)
Historical character(s): Edward, Prince of Wales, Royalty; Alexandra of Denmark, Royalty (wife of Edward)
Time Period(s): 19th century
Locale(s): Cairo, Egypt; London, England

Summary: In Cairo, Cassandra Clark receives word that her mother desires to see her, even though her mother had deserted the family years before and has not been heard from since. She returns to London to find herself embedded in intrigue surrounding her half-sister Leonie, the mistress of the Prince of Wales. Her affair produces a tangle of passionate complications.

Historical Accuracy: The story is imagined but filled with convincing period elements.

ROHAN O'GRADY
(PSEUD. OF JUNE O'GRADY SKINNER, 1922-)

Canadian writer O'Grady was born in Vancouver, British Columbia. She worked as a newspaper librarian before turning to writing full time. Her books include *Pippin's Journal* and *Let's Kill Uncle*.

4702 *O'Houlihan's Jest*

Date of Publication: 1961
Subject(s): Independence—Ireland
Fictional character(s): Mick Delahanty, Wanderer, Writer (poet); Sean O'Houlihan, Royalty (High King of Ireland); Molly Bawn, Young Woman
Time Period(s): 18th century
Locale(s): Ireland

Summary: This tale of Irish opposition to English rule involves Sean O'Houlihan, the last high king of Ireland, who opposes the commander of the English forces, known as ''The Man.'' Told with the simplicity of a folk tale, the novel also details a feud over Molly Brown.

Historical Accuracy: The novel is more a romantic hodgepodge than a careful historical reconstruction, and contains a number of evident anachronisms.

JOHN O'HARA (1905-1970)

An American novelist, short story writer, essayist, and playwright, O'Hara was born in Pennsylvania and worked as a reporter, a soda jerk, a freight clerk, and a press agent in Hollywood. He won the National Book Award in 1956 for *Ten North Frederick*, and in the 1950s and 1960s, was one of the most popular, prolific, and successful authors in the U.S.

4703 *From the Terrace*

Date of Publication: 1958
Subject(s): Family Saga; World War II
Fictional character(s): Raymond Alfred Eaton, Businessman; Samuel Eaton, Businessman
Time Period(s): 19th century; 20th century (1897-1947)
Locale(s): Pennsylvania; New York; Washington, District of Columbia

Summary: The novel chronicles fifty years in the life of Raymond Alfred Eaton who is ignored by his businessman father. Eaton serves during World War I and then makes a fortune as an airplane manufacturer, serving as Assistant Secretary of the Navy during World War II. Through his public and private life, Eaton is shown as a fundamentally decent and generous, but limited, man.

Historical Accuracy: The novel is a superb example of social commentary.

4704 *Ourselves to Know*

Date of Publication: 1960
Subject(s): Crime and Criminals
Fictional character(s): Gerald Higgins, Student (graduate); Robert Millhouser, Banker, Landowner; Hedwig Millhouser, Spouse
Time Period(s): 19th century; 20th century (1850s-1928)
Locale(s): Lyons, Pennsylvania

Summary: A young graduate student researches the life of a prominent banker who shoots and kills his wife in 1908. The relationship between husband and wife becomes the novel's central theme. In the process of dramatizing this theme,

O'Hara presents a wealth of information about life in east-central Pennsylvania from the Civil War to the 1920s.

Historical Accuracy: O'Hara's naturalistic method emphasizes realistic detail and authenticity of background.

JANETTE OKE (1935-)

Born in Alberta, Canada, Oke is a graduate of Mountain View Bible College. She has done parish church work in Indiana, and Alberta, Canada. She is the author of *Love's Long Journey*, which won the Golden Medallion Award from the Evangelical Christian Publication Association, *Quiet Places, Warm Thoughts*, and *Love's Lasting Legacy*.

4705 *A Bride for Donnigan*

Date of Publication: 1993
Subject(s): Immigrants
Fictional character(s): Kathleen O'Malley, Immigrant, Mail Order Bride; Donnigan Harrison, Farmer
Time Period(s): 19th century
Locale(s): Canada

Summary: This volume in the Women of the West series concerns the experiences of Kathleen O'Malley who journeys from Ireland as a mail-order bride. She contracts a marriage with a farmer, Donnigan Harrison, and the story depicts her adjustment to life on the frontier.

Historical Accuracy: The novel's background is only sketchily drawn though there are some believable period elements.

4706 *The Calling of Emily Evans*

Date of Publication: 1990
Subject(s): Religious Life
Fictional character(s): Emily Evans, Religious (missionary)
Time Period(s): 1900s
Locale(s): Prairie Provinces, Canada

Summary: This novel, part of the Women of the West series, describes the experiences of Emily Evans who sets out alone as a Ministry Sister to open a new church in a pioneering community on the Canadian Prairie.

Historical Accuracy: The novel is fictional but based on actual cases, as the author's notes make clear.

4707 *Drums of Change: The Story of Running Fawn*

Date of Publication: 1996
Subject(s): Indians; Religious Life
Fictional character(s): Running Fawn, Indian (Blackfoot), Young Woman; Martin Forbes, Religious (missionary); Silver Fox, Indian (Blackfoot), Young Man
Historical character(s): Louis Riel, Revolutionary; Sitting Bull, Indian (Sioux), Chieftain
Time Period(s): 1870s; 1880s
Locale(s): Alberta, Canada

Summary: The novel portrays the experiences of Blackfoot Indians in Alberta, Canada, during the 1870s and 1880s. Running Fawn, a young Blackfoot maiden, and Silver Fox,

the son of the chief, are chosen to attend the Mission Boarding School in Calgary. The novel depicts Running Fawn's adaptation to the changes brought about by the Indians' new life on the reservations.

Historical Accuracy: The story is fictional but it is set against actual historical events and involves actual personalities.

4708 *Julia's Last Hope*

Date of Publication: 1990
Subject(s): Frontier—Canada
Fictional character(s): Julia Harrigan, Spouse; John Harrigan, Spouse
Time Period(s): 19th century
Locale(s): Rocky Mountains, Canada

Summary: This addition to the Women of the West series concerns a small lumber town in the Canadian Rockies. When the mill closes, the town's existence is threatened. Eastern-raised Julia Harrigan is forced to play an important role in saving the town and her home.

Historical Accuracy: The period elements are vague and only slightly developed.

4709 *They Called Her Mrs. Doc*

Date of Publication: 1992
Subject(s): Medical Profession; Frontier—Canada
Fictional character(s): Cassandra Dell Winston, Young Woman; Samuel Smith, Doctor
Time Period(s): 19th century
Locale(s): Montreal, Quebec, Canada; Alberta, Canada

Summary: This novel, part of the Women of the West series, concerns the lot of Cassandra Dell Winston who forgoes her comfortable life in Montreal to become the wife of a doctor in Alberta. The novel describes her struggles to cope with the challenges of the frontier.

Historical Accuracy: The period is believably evoked and the Alberta setting is authentically drawn.

4710 *Too Long a Stranger*

Date of Publication: 1994
Subject(s): Frontier—Canada
Fictional character(s): Sarah Perry, Widow(er); Rebecca Perry, Young Woman
Time Period(s): 19th century
Locale(s): Canada

Summary: This relationship drama concerns Sarah Perry who, to survive after her husband's death, is forced to send her daughter to a boarding school. When Rebecca returns, mother and daughter must bridge their differences.

Historical Accuracy: The past is only sketchily drawn and plays only a slight role in the novel's story.

4711 *A Woman Named Damaris*

Date of Publication: 1991
Subject(s): Frontier—Canada
Fictional character(s): Damaris Withers, Young Woman, Abuse Victim

Time Period(s): 19th century
Locale(s): West, Canada

Summary: This volume in the Women of the West series concerns young Damaris Withers who flees her abusive father for life on the western frontier. The novel dramatizes her efforts to make it on her own and come to terms with her past.

Historical Accuracy: The period background is not developed with much depth.

BULAT OKUDZHAVA (1920-)

A Russian educator, journalist, editor, poet, singer, songwriter, and author, Okudzhava was born in Moscow and attended Tbilisi University. His works include several volumes of poetry and the novels *Poor Aurosimov,* and *Nocturne: From the Notes of Lieutenant Amrian Amilakhuari.*

4712 *The Extraordinary Adventures of Secret Agent Shipov in Pursuit of Count Leo Tolstoy in the Year 1862*

Date of Publication: 1973
Subject(s): Russian Empire; Espionage
Fictional character(s): Shipov, Spy
Historical character(s): Leo Tolstoy, Nobleman (count), Writer
Time Period(s): 1860s (1862)
Locale(s): Russia

Summary: In 1862 the Tsarist secret police search Tolstoy's house, prompted by reports that Tolstoy is involved in illegal activities. The chief agent, Shipov, invents the charges for the benefit of his superiors.

Historical Accuracy: This real incident in Tolstoy's life is the starting point for an essentially imaginary story that does capture the atmosphere of the period.

ZOE OLDENBOURG (1916-)

Born in Leningrad, Oldenburg grew up in Paris.

4713 *Cities of the Flesh*

Date of Publication: 1963
Subject(s): Middle Ages; Religious Conflict; Albigensian Crusade
Historical character(s): Roger de Montbrun, Knight, Courtier
Time Period(s): 13th century (1209)
Locale(s): France

Summary: The novel is an impressive re-creation of 13th-century medieval France that details the life and times of Roger de Montbrun, a knight and courtier caught up in the turmoil of the Albigensian Crusade. He tries to maintain his sense of self and a code of chivalry amidst almost continual civil war and treachery.

Historical Accuracy: The novel is an exact and utterly convincing evocation of the era, its values, and customs.

4714 *The Cornerstone*

Date of Publication: 1955
Subject(s): Middle Ages
Fictional character(s): Ansiau de Linnieres, Nobleman (Lord of Linnieres); Herbert Le Gros, Heir; Haguenier of Linnieres, Knight
Time Period(s): 13th century
Locale(s): Champagne, France; Palestine

Summary: The cumulative details of life in the middle ages are depicted in the story of three generations of the French Linnieres family. Not an adventure but rather a chronicle of ordinary life in the period, the novel renders, as few other historical novels have done as well, the minds and hearts of its characters. The patriarch, Ansiau de Linnieres, turns over his fiefdoms to his heir and sets out on a pilgrimage of repentance for his rough life. One son, nicknamed the Gross, is a brute, and the other son, Haguenier, represents the idealistic side of the medieval temperament.

Historical Accuracy: The details of medieval life and customs are completely believable. This is a model of historical reconstruction.

4715 *Destiny of Fire*

Date of Publication: 1960
Subject(s): Middle Ages; Religious Conflict; Albigensian Crusade
Fictional character(s): Ricord de Montgeil, Nobleman (Seigneur of Montgeil); Gentian, Gentlewoman; Arsen de Cadejac, Gentlewoman; Aicart de la Cadiere, Knight
Time Period(s): 13th century (1209-1229)
Locale(s): Toulouse, France

Summary: The novel details the fate of Ricord de Montgeil and his family who, as vassals of the Count of Toulouse, are swept up in the religious persecution of the Albigensian heresy, the so-called Fourth Crusade in which Toulouse was overrun by French crusaders in a pitiless war of annihilation.

Historical Accuracy: While the history is exact, great events are very much in the background of this very personal drama of survival and suffering.

4716 *The Heirs of the Kingdom*

Date of Publication: 1971
Subject(s): Middle Ages; Crusades
Fictional character(s): Marie Longbras, Artisan (weaver); Jacques, Artisan (weaver)
Time Period(s): 12th century (First Crusade)
Locale(s): France; Middle East; Jerusalem, Palestine

Summary: The novel tells the story of the First Crusade from the perspective of the mass of poor peasants who join the long and arduous trek to Jerusalem. The center of the story is a young teenage couple whose experiences mirror that of the hordes who braved misery, war, slavery, and death in pursuit of a ideal.

Historical Accuracy: The author attempts to portray the human condition, especially the condition of the poorer classes, here, and comes very near the truth.

CORA OLDER

4717 *Savages and Saints*

Date of Publication: 1936
Subject(s): American West; Religious Life; Indians
Fictional character(s): Pedro Lacey, Religious (priest)
Time Period(s): 1850s
Locale(s): California

Summary: This tale of Spanish California after the American conquest tells the story of a young priest, Padre Pedro Lacey. As a penance, he is sent by his archbishop to restore the Mission of Santa Lucia which has been abandoned for 40 years. Padre Lacey's life in the valley among the Indians and Spanish is depicted.

Historical Accuracy: The picture of Spanish California is idealized and sentimental.

BRUCE OLDS (1952-)

A native of Milwaukee, Wisconsin, Olds is a journalist who now lives in Bernardsville, New Jersey. *Raising Holy Hell* is his first novel.

4718 *Raising Holy Hell*

Date of Publication: 1995
Subject(s): Slavery; Antebellum South; Biography, Fictionalized
Historical character(s): John Brown, Fanatic, Abolitionist; Frederick Douglass, Abolitionist; Harriet Tubman, Abolitionist
Time Period(s): 1850s
Locale(s): Kansas; Harpers Ferry, Virginia

Summary: The enigmatic figure of John Brown who helped ignite the bloodbath of the Civil War to abolish slavery is depicted in a collage of private correspondance, diaries and journal excerpts, newspaper articles, songs, poems, interviews, speeches, internal monologues, and eyewitness recollections. Brown emerges as a mean-spirited fanatic who becomes one of the most powerful symbols in American history.

Historical Accuracy: The novel is a work of fiction, some of whose characters, settings, situations, and events were lifted from history, reconstituted, and redeployed. The novel's language occasionally contains anachronisms.

JANE OLIVER

(PSEUD. OF HELEN CHRISTINA REES, 1903-1970)

America born Oliver attended St. Leonard's School in St. Andrews, Scotland, the University of Lausanne, and Bedford Physical Training College. She worked in a bookshop and hospital, taught gymnastics, and served as a secretary to several authors. An ambulance driver during the London blitz of World War II, Oliver was married to writer John Llewelyn Rees who was killed on active duty with the Royal Air Force.

4719 *Alexander the Glorious*

Date of Publication: 1965
Subject(s): Middle Ages; Royalty—Scotland
Historical character(s): Alexander III, Ruler (King of Scotland); Henry III, Ruler (King of England)
Time Period(s): 13th century
Locale(s): Scotland; England

Summary: The novel tells the story of the 13th century Scottish king Alexander III who reigned for nearly 40 years, leading a brief golden age for independent Scotland before the English invasion. Alexander's role as a social and military leader is depicted.

Historical Accuracy: The novel is convincing in its period details of court and of Scottish life.

4720 *The Blue Heaven Bends Over All*

Date of Publication: 1971
Subject(s): Literary Life; Biography, Fictionalized
Historical character(s): Sir Walter Scott, Writer; George Gordon Byron, Writer, Nobleman
Time Period(s): 18th century; 19th century (1775-1831)
Locale(s): Scotland; England

Summary: This fictional life of Walter Scott traces the poet and novelist's career from his childhood of illness and lameness to his literary renown as a poet. Bankruptcy causes him to write novels to pay off his debts, and he becomes a master at using the past in the novel form.

Historical Accuracy: This is a workmanlike fictional biography of the great writer, aided by the authenticity of the period and customs from the author's evident familiarity of the Scottish scene.

4721 *Candleshine No More*

Date of Publication: 1967
Subject(s): Jacobite Rebellion; Battle of Culloden; Royalty—Scotland
Historical character(s): Charles Edward Stuart, Royalty (prince)
Time Period(s): 1740s (1745-1746)
Locale(s): Scotland; England; France

Summary: The tragic story of the Jacobite Rebellion of 1745 is chronicled in this novel. Charles Stuart lands in Scotland and calls the Highlanders to rise in support of his claim to the throne of Scotland and England. His forces march through Scotland and England to London where betrayal by the French forces them to retreat to the disastrous Battle of Culloden.

Historical Accuracy: The novel is faithful to the facts and the historical details of the rebellion.

4722 *Flame of Fire*

Date of Publication: 1961
Subject(s): Tudor Period; Religious Life; Biography, Fictionalized

Historical character(s): William Tyndale, Scholar; Desiderius Erasmus, Philosopher, Scholar; Martin Luther, Religious; Henry VIII, Ruler (King of England)
Time Period(s): 16th century (1502-1536)
Locale(s): England; Wittenberg, Germany

Summary: This fictionalized biography of the life of William Tyndale tells the story of his heroic struggle to produce an English translation of the Bible. At the time, the unlicensed possession of the Bible is a criminal offense, and the plan to widen the circulation of the scriptures is considered a radical and defiant political act. Struggling on in poverty and neglect, Tyndale labors at his life's mission, paying the price for his daring.

Historical Accuracy: The atmosphere and religious issues of the period are authentically depicted.

4723 *Isle of Glory*

Date of Publication: 1964
Subject(s): Dark Ages; Religious Life
Fictional character(s): Nalda, Nurse; Maeve, Young Woman; Tombul, Warrior
Historical character(s): Columba, Religious (missionary); Dermot, Ruler (High King of Ireland); Hedh, Ruler (High King of Ireland)
Time Period(s): 6th century
Locale(s): Scotland; Ireland

Summary: The novel recounts the story of Saint Columba in the 6th century, a descendant of the kings of Ireland who is a dreamer and a poet. He joins the church and leads a group of enthusiasts known as the Knights of Christ. Defiance of the High King of Ireland causes disgrace and exile to Scotland, where Columba introduces Christianity.

Historical Accuracy: There is historical evidence, or at least tradional ground, for the dramatic story of Saint Columba's life.

4724 *The Lion and the Rose*

Date of Publication: 1958
Subject(s): Elizabethan Period; Royalty—Scotland
Historical character(s): Mary, Queen of Scots, Ruler (Queen of Scotland); Henry Stewart, Spouse (of Mary, Queen of Scots), Nobleman; James Hepburn, Spouse (of Mary, Queen of Scots)
Time Period(s): 16th century (1562-1587)
Locale(s): Scotland; England

Summary: The tragic reign of Mary, Queen of Scots, is chronicled from her return to Scotland, the widow, at age 19, of the King of France. Her turbulent reign is described, including the mysterious death of Darnley and her implication, along with her lover, Bothwell, in the murder. After seven tumultuous years, Mary is forced to leave Scotland forever, facing imprisonment and her final destiny at the hands of Queen Elizabeth.

Historical Accuracy: The author is convinced of the innocence of Mary and Bothwell in the death of Lord Darnley, and her interpretation of the facts reflects this. Other sources disagree with her interpretation.

4725 *The Lion Is Come*

Date of Publication: 1957
Subject(s): Middle Ages; Royalty—Scotland
Historical character(s): William Douglas, Nobleman; Robert the Bruce, Ruler (King of Scotland); William Wallace, Patriot
Time Period(s): 14th century
Locale(s): Scotland

Summary: When the great Scottish king, Alexander III, dies in 1286 without an heir, a dynastic struggle ensues, pitting the Scottish nobles against the might of England, both sides anxious to fill the vacuum left by the disputed succession. The novel dramatizes the events of the period and the important figures of Wallace, Bruce, and Douglas.

Historical Accuracy: Well imagined and vividly portrayed, the novel authentically creates the era and its customs.

4726 *Mine Is the Kingdom*

Date of Publication: 1937
Subject(s): Royalty—Scotland; Royalty—England; Jacobean Period
Historical character(s): James VI, Ruler (King of Scotland); Anne of Denmark, Royalty (queen consort of James); Mary, Queen of Scots, Ruler
Time Period(s): 16th century; 17th century
Locale(s): Scotland; England

Summary: This biographical novel based on the life of Scotland's James VI, who became England's James I, traces his career from childhood to maturity. The novel offers a portrait of James' complicated character and the warring factions that vied to control his destiny.

Historical Accuracy: The novel provides a convincing and faithful portrait of the period and the king.

4727 *Sing Morning Star*

Date of Publication: 1956
Subject(s): Middle Ages; Royalty—Scotland; Norman Conquest
Historical character(s): Malcolm III, Ruler (King of Scotland); Margaret, Royalty (Queen of Scotland)
Time Period(s): 11th century
Locale(s): Scotland

Summary: The reign of Scottish King Malcolm III (the son of the murdered Duncan in Shakespeare's *Macbeth*) is chronicled in this historical novel. The novel takes up Malcolm's story where Shakespeare leaves off and dramatizes his relationship with Margaret, Princess of Hungary, who becomes his queen.

Historical Accuracy: The novel's history is exact and accurately rendered.

4728 *Sunset at Noon*

Date of Publication: 1963
Subject(s): Middle Ages; Royalty—Scotland
Historical character(s): James IV, Ruler (King of Scotland); Margaret Tudor, Royalty (queen consort of James IV); Margaret Drummond, Gentlewoman

Time Period(s): 15th century; 16th century (1480-1513)
Locale(s): Scotland

Summary: The reign of Scotland's James IV is dramatized in this novel that depicts the king as strong and able, a leader who brought stability and order to Scotland. James marries Margaret Tudor, daughter of Henry VII, but is devoted to Margaret Drummond. His reign collapses in the disastrous English invasion that culminates in the Battle of Flodden Field.

Historical Accuracy: The novel is filled with convincing details of the period.

MARINA OLIVER (1934-)

4729 *Masquerade for the King*
Date of Publication: 1976
Subject(s): Restoration Period; Royalty—England
Fictional character(s): Sanchia Lawson, Servant; Sir John Moriss, Gentleman
Historical character(s): Charles II, Ruler (King of England)
Time Period(s): 17th century
Locale(s): France; Belgium

Summary: This romantic tale set during the exile of Charles II before his restoration to the English throne involves a tavern wench, Sanchia Lawson, who comes to play an important role in the intrigue and conspiracy surrounding him.

Historical Accuracy: The story is fanciful and more romantic than historical.

THEODORE OLSEN (1932-)

An American writer born in Wisconsin, Olsen is a graduate of Stevens Point College. He is a freelance writer and author mainly of Westerns.

4730 *There Was a Season: A Biographical Novel of Jefferson Davis*
Date of Publication: 1972
Subject(s): Black Hawk War; Biography, Fictionalized
Historical character(s): Jefferson Davis, Political Figure, Military Personnel; Sarah Knox Taylor, Gentlewoman; Zachary Taylor, Military Personnel, Political Figure; Abraham Lincoln, Military Personnel (soldier), Political Figure
Time Period(s): 1830s
Locale(s): Prairie du Chien, Wisconsin

Summary: This biographical novel details the early years of Jefferson Davis when he is a promising army officer. On the western frontier during the Black Hawk War, Davis meets and falls in love with Sarah Knox Taylor, the second daughter of Zachary Taylor, his commanding officer. Despite Taylor's opposition and efforts to end the affair, Davis and Sarah Knox are married, though Davis' bride dies of malaria three months later.

Historical Accuracy: Although based on historical research, the novel does offer some speculative and invented characters, events, and situations.

TOBY OLSON (1937-)

An American born in Illinois, Olson graduated from Occidental College and Long Island University. He is a professor of English at Temple University and a poet as well as a novelist.

4731 *The Life of Jesus: An Apocryphal Novel*
Date of Publication: 1976
Subject(s): Biblical Story
Historical character(s): Jesus Christ, Biblical Figure; Mary, Biblical Figure; Joseph, Biblical Figure
Time Period(s): 1st century
Locale(s): Israel

Summary: This autobiographical novel retells the story of Jesus repossessed as legend. The mythology is constructed from a sense of the life of Jesus as received by a young boy in Catholic school from the Biblical stories of Irish nuns. The version of this familiar tale is both a poetic and symbolic journey of Jesus facing the difficulties of being neither completely God nor man.

Historical Accuracy: More magic realism than historical accuracy, the novel's time scheme shifts from the Biblical to the modern.

CAROLA OMAN
(PSEUD. OF CAROLA M. LENANTON)

4732 *Crouchback*
Date of Publication: 1929
Subject(s): War of the Roses; Royalty—England
Historical character(s): Richard III, Ruler (King of England); Anne Neville, Royalty (queen consort of Richard III); Richard Neville, Nobleman (Earl of Warwick)
Time Period(s): 15th century
Locale(s): England

Summary: The reign of Richard III is dramatized focusing on his queen, Anne Neville, who is the daughter of Richard's enemy the Earl of Warwick, or, the Kingmaker. The novel depicts the fate of the two princes in the tower, which brings Richard to the throne, and the turbulent era in which Anne's loyalties are severely tested.

Historical Accuracy: The book's incidents are faithful to the historical record, and the period background and customs are particularly authentic.

WALTER O'MEARA (1897-1989)

An American born in Minnesota, O'Meara was an advertising executive, a civil servant, and an author of many works that featured his native Minnesota, including *Grand*

Portage, The Savage Country, and *Daughters of the Country*.

4733 *The Devil's Cross*

Date of Publication: 1957
Subject(s): Middle Ages; Crusades; Children's Crusade
Fictional character(s): Hugh de Gys, Knight
Time Period(s): 13th century (1212)
Locale(s): Germany; Italy

Summary: The novel follows the adventures of knight Hugh de Gys, who is commissioned to find the daughter of a German count. She has taken up the cause of the Children's Crusade and must be found in order to be shipped to a Turkish harem.

Historical Accuracy: The action and its portraits are idealized and rarely convincing, despite occasional authentic period details.

4734 *The Duke of War*

Date of Publication: 1966
Subject(s): Dark Ages; Arthurian Legends; Roman Empire
Fictional character(s): Arthur, Warrior; Guenevere, Gentlewoman; Launcelot, Warrior
Time Period(s): 5th century
Locale(s): England

Summary: The story of Arthur is told without the chivalrous trappings. Arthur is shown as a Briton and military leader of the island's Roman tradition in the fading days of the Empire. England is being overrun by the Saxons and the fate of the nation rests on the single great battle that Arthur plans to force the Saxons to wage.

Historical Accuracy: Although much of the story is invented, it is based on a solid foundation of written and archaeological evidence and attempts to stay within the realm of probability.

4735 *The Spanish Bride*

Date of Publication: 1954
Subject(s): Spanish Colonies
Fictional character(s): Josefina, Actress, Dancer
Time Period(s): 18th century
Locale(s): Avila, Spain; New Mexico

Summary: This is a story of a beautiful Spanish actress from Avila who leaves her successful theatrical life to journey to the colony of New Mexico where she becomes the mistress of the Governor. The novel provides a vivid portrait of Spanish America in its final struggle to maintain a foothold in the Southwest.

Historical Accuracy: The novel captures the period and region with convincing details.

MICHAEL ONDAATJE (1943-)

A Canadian born in Ceylon, Ondaatje graduated from the University of Toronto and Queen's University. He is a professor of English at York University who is a poet and novelist whose works blend elements of both forms. He has

received considerable acclaim for *The Collected Works of Billy the Kid*.

4736 *Coming through Slaughter*

Date of Publication: 1976
Subject(s): Musical Life; Biography, Fictionalized
Historical character(s): Buddy Bolden, Musician (jazz)
Time Period(s): 20th century (1900s-1930s)
Locale(s): New Orleans, Louisiana

Summary: The novel recreates through memoirs, fantasy. history, and hallucinations the life and times of Billy Bolden, the first of the great trumpet players, called the originator of jazz. Bolden worked by day as a barber and at night played with several bands every evening. At the height of his career he dropped out of sight for two years and went made.

Historical Accuracy: The basic framework of the story is historical and authentic.

COTHBURN O'NEAL (1907-)

An American born in Texas and a graduate of Trinity University and the University of Texas, O'Neal has taught at various high schools and colleges in Texas. He is a former clarinetist in symphony orchestras and also a commercial airline pilot and flight instructor.

4737 *Hagar*

Date of Publication: 1958
Subject(s): Biblical Story; Ancient Egypt
Historical character(s): Hagar, Servant, Royalty (princess); Sarah, Spouse (of Abraham), Biblical Figure; Abraham, Biblical Figure; Ishmael, Biblical Figure
Time Period(s): Indeterminate Past
Locale(s): Egypt; Middle East

Summary: The Biblical story of Sarah's handmaiden, Hagar, who bears Abraham's son and heir, is recounted. Hagar is an Egyptian princess who finds herself attached to a wandering tribe of Hebrews. She serves Sarah in her plight to supply Abraham with an heir but she and her son Ishmael are cast out to continue a life of wandering.

Historical Accuracy: The novel embroiders on the Biblical evidence to present a plausible but largely imagined story.

4738 *Master of the World*

Date of Publication: 1952
Subject(s): Mongol Empire; Biography, Fictionalized
Historical character(s): Timur the Great, Ruler (of Mongolia)
Time Period(s): 14th century
Locale(s): Asia; Europe; Samarkand, Uzbekistan

Summary: The military and romantic exploits of the infamous Mongolian conqueror Tamerlane are dramatized. He rules Samarkand in the 14th century and comes close to conquering all of Asia and Europe. Tamerlane emerges as an unrepentant schemer whose manipulations in and out of the bedroom are vividly portrayed.

Historical Accuracy: The thoroughness of this biography is at times undercut by a preference for the sensational, which distorts the effect of otherwise solid and believable research.

4739　*Untold Glory*

Date of Publication: 1957
Subject(s): Civil War—U.S.; Espionage; Biography, Fictionalized
Historical character(s): Felicia Lee Cary Thornton Shover, Spy (Confederate), Southern Belle; Ulysses S. Grant, Military Personnel (Union general); William Tecumseh Sherman, Military Personnel (Union general); Robert E. Lee, Military Personnel (Confederate commander); William Joseph Hardee, Military Personnel (Confederate general); Nathan Bedford Forrest, Military Personnel (Confederate officer)
Time Period(s): 1860s
Locale(s): Memphis, Tennessee

Summary: Based on her diaries and letters, the novel provides a biographical account of the espionage activities of Felicia Shover. A descendant of a distinguished Southern family, she is recruited into espionage work for the Confederacy to smuggle needed medical supplies.

Historical Accuracy: The letters quoted are genuine, and the significant incidents are suggested by reference to the letters and diaries.

4740　*Very Young Mrs. Poe*

Date of Publication: 1956
Subject(s): Biography, Fictionalized; Literary Life
Historical character(s): Virginia Clemm, Spouse (of Edgar Allan Poe); Edgar Allan Poe, Writer
Time Period(s): 19th century
Locale(s): Baltimore, Maryland; Richmond, Virginia; New York, New York

Summary: The tortured genius of Edgar Allan Poe is reflected in this fictional biography of his wife, Virginia Clemm. She was only 13 when she married her cousin Edgar, and the novel chronicles their relationship and Virginia's role in helping Poe to develop his literary genius.

Historical Accuracy: The essential story is accurate and faithful to the facts, though this is a somewhat idealized portrait of the Poes' marriage.

REAGAN O'NEAL
(PSEUD. OF JAMES O. RIGNEY, 1948-)

An American writer born in Charleston, South Carolina, and educated at the Citadel, O'Neal worked as a nuclear engineer before becoming a freelance writer. As Robert Jordan he produces books in the Conan the Barbarian series.

4741　*The Fallon Blood*

Date of Publication: 1980
Subject(s): American Revolution; Battle of Cowpens; Battle of King's Mountain

Fictional character(s): Michael Fallon, Servant (indentured), Landowner; Elizabeth Carver, Gentlewoman; Thomas Carver, Businessman (merchant)
Historical character(s): Benjamin Franklin, Political Figure, Diplomat; Charles Cornwallis, Military Personnel (British general); Francis Marion, Military Personnel (American officer); Banastre Tarleton, Military Personnel (British colonel); William Moultrie, Military Personnel (colonel); Marie Joseph Paul de Lafayette, Military Personnel (General), Nobleman (Marquis de Lafayette)
Time Period(s): 18th century (1760s-1780s)
Locale(s): Charleston, South Carolina, American Colonies

Summary: Michael Fallon is a young Irishman who makes his way to South Carolina in 1765 as an indentured servant. He rises into the rice-planting aristocracy and then is swept up in the American Revolution in scenes that depict important figures in the course of the war in the South, as well as the battles of Cowpens, King's Mountain, and Eutaw Springs.

Historical Accuracy: The historical framework of the story is accurately depicted.

4742　*The Fallon Pride*

Date of Publication: 1981
Subject(s): War of 1812; Family Saga
Fictional character(s): Robert Fallon, Sea Captain, Bastard Son
Historical character(s): Aaron Burr, Political Figure; Thomas Jefferson, Political Figure; Jean Laffite, Pirate; Andrew Jackson, Military Personnel (general); James Wilkinson, Military Personnel (general), Political Figure
Time Period(s): 1800s; 1810s
Locale(s): New Orleans, Louisiana; France; *Osprey*, At Sea

Summary: The novel continues the saga of the Fallon family concentrating on the second generation's Captain Robert Fallon, the bastard son of Michael Fallon and the wife of a vengeful slave trader. Robert's exploits have him fighting pirates, helping to initiate the Louisiana Purchase, and participating in some of the key events of the War of 1812.

Historical Accuracy: More romantic than carefully documented, the story covers a great deal of historical material, however much of it is only lightly sketched.

CHARLES KENDALL O'NEILL (1909-)

O'Neill is the author of such books as *Wild Train: The Story of the Andrews Raiders*.

4743　*Morning Time*

Date of Publication: 1950
Subject(s): Wilkinson Plot
Fictional character(s): Theron Hawley, Veteran (American Revolution)
Historical character(s): James Wilkinson, Military Personnel (general); George Rogers Clark, Military Personnel (general)
Time Period(s): 1780s (1783-1789)
Locale(s): New England; Pennsylvania; Kentucky

Summary: The novel provides a look at the young American republic in the years immediately following the Revolution.

At the center of the story, involving a veteran of Washington's army, Theron Hawley, is General James Wilkinson's plot to conspire with the Spanish.

Historical Accuracy: The author's cited sources help secure authenticity, despite anachronistic dialogue.

KYLE ONSTOTT (1887-1966)

Born in Illinois, Onstott was a dog show judge and author. He is the author of a number of bestselling books, including the Falconhurst series that feature antebellum settings and interracial sexual relations and the violence that they engendered at the time.

4744 *Drum*

Date of Publication: 1962
Subject(s): Antebellum South; Slavery
Fictional character(s): Tamboura, Slave; Drumson, Slave; Drum, Slave
Time Period(s): 19th century
Locale(s): Cuba; New Orleans, Louisiana; Africa

Summary: The fortunes of three generations of slaves are depicted in a sweeping panorama that moves from Africa, to the sugar plantations of Cuba, to New Orleans society, and to Falconhurst, a slave breeding plantation. This is a version of the antebellum south stripped of any gentility with a concentration on the inhumanity of slavery that reaches the level of an expose.

Historical Accuracy: The details are so sensationalized that the novel can be viewed as more a potboiler than a documentary novel.

BARONESS EMMA ORCZY (1865-1947)

Orczy was an English writer who was born in Hungary, the daughter of Baron Felix Orczy. In 1894 she married the illustrator Montague Barstow, and together they produced several children's books. Her most famous novel, *The Scarlet Pimpernel*, was turned down by every publisher to whom it was submitted before a play based on it was staged and became a huge popular success. Baroness Orczy continued to write historical romances—eight of them Pimpernel sequels—at a rate of two or more a year.

4745 *The Scarlet Pimpernel*

Date of Publication: 1902
Subject(s): French Revolution; Reign of Terror
Fictional character(s): Sir Percy Blakeney, Nobleman, Adventurer; Marguerite Blakeney, Gentlewoman; Chavelin, Diplomat
Historical character(s): George, Prince of Wales, Royalty
Time Period(s): 1790s
Locale(s): Paris, France; London, England

Summary: "We seek him here, we seek him there..." Set during the French Reign of Terror, this classic costume adventure involves an English aristocrat who pretends to be a foppish dandy to conceal his true identity as the notorious Scarlet Pimpernel, the rescuer of French nobles from the vengeance of French revolutionaries. His secret is kept from his French wife who is beset by an evil French minister.

Historical Accuracy: This is a rousing tale of the lifestyles of the rich and famous, more fun than historical.

4746 *A Spy for Napoleon*

Date of Publication: 1934
Subject(s): Espionage; Franco-Prussian War
Fictional character(s): Gerard Paul de Lancy, Nobleman (vicomte); Juanita Lorendana, Dancer, Spy
Historical character(s): Napoleon III, Ruler (Emperor of France); Eugenie, Royalty (consort of Napoleon III)
Time Period(s): 1860s; 1870s
Locale(s): France

Summary: Set during the final years of Napoleon III's reign, this adventure-romance concerns the exploits of Vicomte Gerard Paul de Lancy who becomes an unwitting participant in a conspiracy against the emperor, for which he is forced to marry a spy and is banished. The climax of the story is the opening of the Franco-Prussian War which brings Gerard back to France.

Historical Accuracy: Romance is primary here, and the period is only superficially developed.

4747 *The Uncrowned King*

Date of Publication: 1935
Subject(s): French Revolution; Royalty—France
Fictional character(s): Louis XIX, Heir; Cyril Bertrand, Young Man
Historical character(s): Louis XVII, Royalty (Dauphin of France)
Time Period(s): 1860s
Locale(s): Europe

Summary: This romantic novel images a later life for Louis XVII, the lost dauphin, son of Louis XVI and Marie Antoinette. The novel concentrates on Louis XVII's heir, the child of Louis' marriage to an English widow. Since he is weak and ineffectual, his mother persuades her son by her first marriage, Cyril Bertrand, to impersonate the heir in a plot to reclaim the French throne in the 1860s.

Historical Accuracy: The historical material is considerably simplified into a largely glamorous backdrop for this fanciful tale of royal ambition.

LEWIS ORDE (1943-)

An English author born in Reading, Orde left school at age fifteen. Orde has worked as a reporter and editor for clothing publications. He sees himself primarily as a storyteller.

4748 *Dreams of Gold*

Date of Publication: 1993
Subject(s): Family Saga; Antebellum South; Civil War—U.S.
Fictional character(s): Nathan Solomon, Immigrant; Gershon Lowensohn, Businessman (cotton factor); Leonora Solomon, Young Woman

Time Period(s): 19th century (1851-1882)
Locale(s): London, England; New Orleans, Louisiana; Atlanta, Georgia

Summary: This family saga begins in Victorian London with the escape of Nathan Solomon and his cousin Leonora to America and antebellum New Orleans. There they discover a strikingly different world, and they are both drawn into the city's considerable temptations. When the Civil War begins, Nathan must declare his loyalties, and he and Leonora are forced to begin again in war-torn Atlanta where they must continue to struggle against prejudice.

Historical Accuracy: The details of southern life are authentically described.

4749 *Heritage*

Date of Publication: 1981
Subject(s): Family Saga; Boxing; Immigrants
Fictional character(s): Leah Boruchowicz, Young Woman; Shmuel Boruchowicz, Sports Figure (boxer); Lazar Boruchowicz, Young Man
Time Period(s): 1900s
Locale(s): Russia; London, England (East End)

Summary: This family saga set at the turn of the century follows the Russian Boruchowicz family from Russia to London's rough and tumble East End. Shmuel, the youngest brother, uses his physical prowess to achieve success in the boxing ring. He, like the others, must struggle to survive.

Historical Accuracy: The depiction of London life of the period is authentic.

4750 *The Lion's Way*

Date of Publication: 1981
Subject(s): Family Saga; Opera; World War II
Fictional character(s): Daniel Kerr, Singer (opera)
Time Period(s): 20th century (1920s-1970s)
Locale(s): New York, New York; London, England

Summary: This saga that spans over fifty years traces the rise of Daniel Kerr in the competitive world of opera, from New York during the Depression to war-torn London. He eventually achieves distinction as a world-acclaimed artist, but the cost is high.

Historical Accuracy: The musical details are convincing.

CZENZI ORMONDE (1913-)

Ormonde is the author of *Laughter From Downstairs* and co-wrote, with Raymond Chandler, the screenplay for *Strangers on a Train*, a film directed by Alfred Hitchcock. He also wrote the screenplay for *1001 Arabian Nights*.

4751 *Solomon and the Queen of Sheba*

Date of Publication: 1954
Subject(s): Biblical Story
Historical character(s): Queen of Sheba, Biblical Figure, Ruler; Solomon, Ruler (King of Israel), Biblical Figure
Time Period(s): 10th century B.C.
Locale(s): Jerusalem, Israel

Summary: The novel retells the Old Testament story of the Queen of Sheba's triumphant arrival in Jerusalem, and her attraction to King Solomon. He faces the challenge of strengthening his people's belief in God in order to resist the temptation of conquerors on all sides. Under the Queen's tempting demeanor is a rival monarch, yielding to whom might bring disaster.

Historical Accuracy: The novel offers a considerable expansion on the Biblical story, and is convincing in its re-creation of period life.

FRANK O'ROURKE (1916-1989)

Born in Denver, O'Rourke is the author of more than 60 books including westerns, mysteries, historical novels, and sports stories. Among his books are *Gun Hand*, *The Far Mountains*, and *New Departure*. O'Rourke also writes under the pseudonyms Kevin Connor, Frank O'Malley, and Patrick O'Malley.

4752 *Far Mountains*

Date of Publication: 1959
Subject(s): American West
Fictional character(s): Juan Obregon, Young Man
Time Period(s): 19th century (1801-1848)
Locale(s): Southwest; Taos, New Mexico

Summary: The novel details the development of an Irish-American orphan boy in the declining days of Spanish control of the Southwest. He learns frontier ways and has to pass as a Spaniard named Juan Obregon.

Historical Accuracy: The novel captures with skill its period and the details of frontier life.

4753 *A Mule for the Marquesa*

Date of Publication: 1964
Subject(s): Mexican Revolution
Fictional character(s): Augustus Grant, Rancher; Angelina Grant, Captive; China Eye Raza, Kidnapper, Outlaw; Henry Farden, Cowboy
Time Period(s): 1910s (1916)
Locale(s): Mexico

Summary: In 1916, when Angelina Grant is kidnapped by Mexican outlaw China Eye Raza, Henry Farden is hired to lead an assault on Raza's stronghold 150 miles south of the border. The novel details the taut story of this mission.

Historical Accuracy: The story is fanciful but credible in its details.

MYRON DAVID ORR (1896-1986)

Orr is a Michigan lawyer who grew up near Mackinac Island and spent 25 years researching *The Citadel of the Lakes*.

4754 *The Citadel of the Lakes*

Date of Publication: 1952
Subject(s): War of 1812
Fictional character(s): Marie Pasquelle, Young Woman

Time Period(s): 1810s
Locale(s): Mackinac Island, Michigan

Summary: The workings of John Jacob Astor's American Fur Company and its rapacious efforts to corner the fur trade in Michigan form the background for this historical romance. French-Canadian Marie Pasquelle seeks her father's murderer amongst British and American spies, trappers, and Astor's agents.

Historical Accuracy: The novel's romantic story is set in a solid and believable period and regional frame.

4755 *Mission to Mackinac*

Date of Publication: 1956
Subject(s): Settlement of the American Frontier
Fictional character(s): Claire La Salle, Young Woman; Greg Parks, Government Official
Time Period(s): 1810s
Locale(s): Mackinac Island, Michigan; Canada

Summary: The novel's background is the dispute between the English, French, and Americans over control of Mackinac Island and the important fur trade in the years before the War of 1812. The novel centers on Claire La Salle, the daughter of a French fur trader. Her father is revered by the French, feared by the English, and becomes a target for the Americans.

Historical Accuracy: The novel's connection to actual events is evident as its appendix shows, indicating where the original material that formed the basis for the story can be found.

ISABEL ORTEGA (1924-)

An American writer who was born in Westerville, Ohio, Ortega attended the University of San Carlos in Guatemala City. She has contributed non-fiction to the *Christian Science Monitor* and fiction to various anthologies.

4756 *Street of the Madwoman*

Date of Publication: 1978
Subject(s): Romance
Fictional character(s): Venetia Collins, Young Woman; Sir Philip Stratford, Nobleman; Sean Malone, Journalist
Time Period(s): 1890s (1896)
Locale(s): Mexico City, Mexico

Summary: Mexico in the 1890s is the background for this romantic suspense novel. Venetia Collins is torn between two men, English nobleman Philip Stratford and journalist Sean Malone. At the center of the novel's adventure is the mystery of the Plumed Serpent which Venetia must solve.

Historical Accuracy: The period Mexican details are convincing.

SARA ORWIG

4757 *Albuquerque*

Date of Publication: 1990
Subject(s): American West; Romance

Fictional character(s): April Danby, Actress, Singer; Noah McCloud, Frontiersman
Time Period(s): 1860s
Locale(s): Albuquerque, New Mexico

Summary: Singer April Danby is pursued by Noah McCloud who is convinced she has robbed his brother of the family's gold. The pursuit is complicated by their attraction to each other.

Historical Accuracy: The novel's setting is realistically depicted.

KAREN OSBORN

An award-winning poet, Osborn is the author of *Patchwork*.

4758 *Between Earth and Sky*

Date of Publication: 1996
Subject(s): Settlement of the American Frontier; American West
Fictional character(s): Abigail Conklin, Pioneer
Time Period(s): 19th century; 20th century (1867-1930)
Locale(s): New Mexico

Summary: This epistolary novel records life in the Southwest for more than sixty years. Abigail Conklin journeys west with her family after the Civil War for a new life in New Mexico. Struggles to survive, conflicts with the Mexicans and Indians, and a deep appreciation of the southwestern landscape dominate the narrative.

Historical Accuracy: The novel provides a convincing period background.

ANNE OSBORNE

Born in Washington, D.C., Osborne graduated from Balboa High School in the Panama Canal Zone and from the University of Georgia. She has contributed to Georgia newspapers and historical publications.

4759 *Wind From the Main*

Date of Publication: 1972
Subject(s): American Colonies; Pirates; Sea Story
Historical character(s): Anne Bonny, Pirate; Edward Teach, Pirate (aka Blackbeard); Stede Bonnet, Pirate
Time Period(s): 1710s; 1720s
Locale(s): Charleston, South Carolina, American Colonies; West Indies

Summary: In this version of the pirate career of Anne Bonny she emerges as a proto-feminist who rebels from the dreary conventions of colonial Charleston for the liberation of piracy. To make this case, the novel mingles what is know of Bonny's career with an imagined interpretation.

Historical Accuracy: Although based on fact, the author admits to inventing details of Bonny's early life in Carolina and her later life after she disappears from history in 1720.

MAGGIE OSBORNE (1941-)

Born in Hollywood, California, Osborne attended Fort Lewis Junior College. She has worked as a flight attendant for United Airlines and a secretary until becoming a full-time writer in 1977. Osborne received a Career Achievement Award from *Romantic Times* in 1991.

4760 *Chase the Heart*

Date of Publication: 1987
Subject(s): Elizabethan Period; Royalty—England
Fictional character(s): Nellanor Amesley, Gentlewoman, Widow(er); Will Steele, Gentleman
Historical character(s): Elizabeth I, Ruler (Queen of England)
Time Period(s): 16th century (1590s)
Locale(s): England; France

Summary: Set after the defeat of the Spanish Armada and the death of Robert Dudley, Queen Elizabeth's favorite, the novel concerns Dudley's ward who is charged by the queen to retrieve a casket of letters that contain a secret that could change the line of succession to the throne of England. Lady Nell joins with Lord Will Steele in a chase to find the letters that takes them to France and back with danger and romance at every turn.

Historical Accuracy: The story is an ingenious re-working of history but it includes a believable Elizabethan background.

CLAUDE JACK OSGOOD

4761 *Eagle of the Gredos*

Date of Publication: 1942
Subject(s): Middle Ages
Fictional character(s): Ramon del Aguila, Knight; Leonor de Garrega, Young Woman
Time Period(s): 13th century
Locale(s): Spain

Summary: This tale of medieval adventure concerns young Don Ramon del Aquila, known as the Eagle of the Gredos. His efforts in war and romance are depicted. His lady love is the proud Castilean Leonor de Garrega. Ramon distinguishes himself in battle against the Moors and against his rival for Leonor's hand.

Historical Accuracy: The novel presents a lively and authentic portrait of the period.

MICHAEL O'SHAUGHNESSY (1912-)

4762 *Monsieur Moliere*

Date of Publication: 1959
Subject(s): Literary Life; Theatrical Life; Biography, Fictionalized
Historical character(s): Moliere, Writer (dramatist); Jean Racine, Writer (dramatist)
Time Period(s): 17th century
Locale(s): France

Summary: This biographical novel dramatizes the career of French playwright Moliere. The novel is particularly convincing in its portrait of the French stage in the 17th century and the highlights of Moliere's remarkable theatrical career. The novel strings together a number of colorful anecdotes into a fully realized life.

Historical Accuracy: The novelist admits that this is neither an official biography nor an entirely imagined novel, but a personal impression based on the evidence of Moliere's own works and historical sources.

JOHN OSKISON (1874-1947)

Oklahoma-born Oskison was an editor on *Collier's Weekly* and wrote about Indian affairs for newspapers and magazines. A Cherokee, his novels are based on his early experiences in Indian territory. He served in World War I and began writing in the 1930s. His last novel, *Brothers Three*, is set on an Oklahoma ranch and has been praised for its earthy humor.

4763 *Black Jack Davy*

Date of Publication: 1926
Subject(s): Settlement of the American Frontier
Fictional character(s): David Dawes, Teenager
Time Period(s): 19th century
Locale(s): Arkansas; Southwest

Summary: This coming of age novel involves the Dawes family who migrate west to settle in Indian territory. The novel chronicles their experiences, particularly those of young David Dawes, nicknamed "Black Jack Davy", after an old ballad, by his romantic step-mother.

Historical Accuracy: The period elements are vividly and convincingly imagined.

4764 *Brothers Three*

Date of Publication: 1935
Subject(s): Farming; Rural Life—U.S.
Fictional character(s): Timothy Odell, Businessman (merchant); Roger Odell, Rancher; Henry Odell, Writer
Time Period(s): 19th century; 20th century (1873-1930)
Locale(s): Oklahoma

Summary: Life in rural Oklahoma from the 1870s to the 1930s is described in the story of the Odell family. The novel is divided into three sections, each devoted to the career of one of the Odell brothers: Timmy, a small-town merchant, Roger, a cattleman, and Henry, a writer.

Historical Accuracy: The portrait of the period and the region is sentimentalized and more nostalgic than realistic.

G.J.A. O'TOOLE (1936-)

Born in New York City, O'Toole worked for the Central Intelligence Agency before becoming a writer. He is the author of nonfiction works on American espionage history, including *The Spanish War* and *Honorable Treachery: A History of U.S. Intelligence, Espionage, and Covert Action*

From the Amerian Revolution to the CIA, considered the best one-volume history of the evolution of Amerian intelligence operations.

4765 *The Cosgrove Report*

Date of Publication: 1979
Subject(s): Civil War—U.S.; Politics
Fictional character(s): Michael Croft, Detective—Private; Nicholas Cosgrove, Detective—Private
Historical character(s): John Wilkes Booth, Actor; Abraham Lincoln, Political Figure; Edward Stanton, Political Figure (Secretary of War); Allan Pinkerton, Detective—Private; Ulysses S. Grant, Military Personnel (army commander)
Time Period(s): 1860s (1868)
Locale(s): Washington, District of Columbia; New York, New York

Summary: This imaginative re-creation of the Lincoln assassination begins with the discovery by modern-day private investigator Michael Croft of a 19th century manuscript by Pinkerton detective Nicholas Cosgrove who is hired in 1868 by Secretary of War Edward Stanton to prove that John Wilkes Booth is still alive. Cosgrove's investigation uncovers a enormous political scandal and ingeniously offers some solutions to questions that have dogged Lincoln's assassination from the beginning.

Historical Accuracy: The novel's solutions are more ingenious than believable, but they do rely on a knowing presentation of the period and its players.

4766 *Poor Richard's Game*

Date of Publication: 1982
Subject(s): American Revolution; Espionage
Fictional character(s): Desmond de Lawless, Military Personnel, Nobleman
Historical character(s): Benjamin Franklin, Diplomat; Frederick North, Political Figure (British prime minister); Benjamin Tallmadge, Military Personnel (chief of intelligence); Pierre Augustin Caron de Beaumarchais, Writer (dramatist)
Time Period(s): 1780s
Locale(s): London, England; Paris, France

Summary: After Cornwallis is defeated at Yorktown, Washington and Jefferson fear that they still may lose the war at the negotiating table. They dispatch an exiled Irish aristocrat, Major Lawless, to France to find the spy in the American consulate and to investigate the rumor that Benjamin Franklin himself is a traitor. Lawless uncovers an English plot to reverse the military defeat, but at the same time uncovers an awful secret about Franklin.

Historical Accuracy: The novel's annotations attest to the solidity of personalities and events. The situation is fictional, however.

OUIDA

(PSEUD. OF MARIE LOUISE DE LA RAMEE, 1839-1908)

Ouida was an English novelist, the daughter of a French teacher. Her 45 novels deal chiefly with fashionable life and idealized characters. Examples include *Puck, Moths,* and *A Village Commune.*

4767 *Under Two Flags*

Date of Publication: 1867
Subject(s): French Foreign Legion
Fictional character(s): Bertie Cecil, Gentleman, Military Personnel; Rake, Servant; Cigarette, Entertainer (singer/dancer)
Time Period(s): 1800s
Locale(s): London, England; Algeria

Summary: In this romantic adventure, Bertie Cecil, a nobleman's son, is forced to leave England in disgrace and join the French Foreign Legion. While with the Legion in Africa, he has various adventures with the Arabs and those who know his true identity.

Historical Accuracy: Ouida was one of the most widely read writers of her generation. Her stories of heroic adventure highlight her storytelling ability, which predominates over historical accuracy.

WILLIAM OVERGARD (1926-1990)

American cartoonist and novelist Overgard started drawing at age twelve. He is well known for his detailed, realistic cartoons and for several adventure novels.

4768 *A Few Good Men*

Date of Publication: 1988
Subject(s): Military Life
Fictional character(s): Smedley D. Butler, Military Personnel (general); K.L. Magnusson, Military Personnel (marine lieutenant); Richard Kelly, Diplomat
Historical character(s): Augusto Cesar Sandino, Revolutionary
Time Period(s): 1930s (1931)
Locale(s): Nicaragua

Summary: In 1931, when Augusto Cesar Sandino kidnaps the 13-year-old daughter of the American consul to Nicaragua, a mixed group of American heroes pursues the rebel. The novel depicts their chase across the Nicaraguan countryside as they encounter earthquakes, love, and rugged terrain.

Historical Accuracy: The story is fanciful but it does offer a convincing setting.

4769 *Shanghai Tango: A Novel of China*

Date of Publication: 1987
Subject(s): Chinese Empire; Crime and Criminals; Espionage
Fictional character(s): Adrian Reed, Heir; Lola Ryan, Dancer; Captain Bodine, Veteran (marine)
Time Period(s): 1930s (1931-1932)
Locale(s): Shanghai, China

Summary: Set in Shanghai in the 1930s, the story concerns the adventures of a group of Americans who pursue $1.5 million in gold and Japanese military secrets in the middle of the Chinese Civil War. Adrian Reed comes to Shanghai to unravel the mystery of a treasure lost by his father. He meets up with Lola, a nightclub dancer, and Bodine, an ex-marine, for non-stop action in the Chinese underworld.

Historical Accuracy: High-speed adventure is set against a believable period background.

DEAN OWEN

4770 *The Sam Houston Story*

Date of Publication: 1961
Subject(s): Biography, Fictionalized; Texas Revolution; Battle of San Jacinto
Historical character(s): Sam Houston, Political Figure, Military Personnel (general); Andrew Jackson, Political Figure; Antonio Lopez de Santa Anna, Military Personnel (general), Political Figure
Time Period(s): 19th century
Locale(s): Tennessee; Texas

Summary: The novel attempts to capture the remarkable career of Sam Houston from his days as an Indian fighter with Andrew Jackson to his abrupt resignation as the governor of Tennessee to his leadership in the fight for Texan independence against Mexico.

Historical Accuracy: The novel covers so much territory that history takes on a capsulized form. The events described are truthful as far as they go.

WILLIAM A. OWENS (1905-1990)

Born in Blossom, Texas, American folklorist, educator, administrator, and author William A. Owens was educated at Southern Methodist University and the State University of Iowa. A professor of English at Texas A & M University and Columbia University, Owens' novels include *Walking on Borrowed Land* and *Fever in the Earth*. Owens also wrote several books on American culture and is especially known for his work on the origins of American folk songs.

4771 *Look to the River*

Date of Publication: 1963
Subject(s): Picaresque Adventure
Fictional character(s): Jed, Teenager, Peddler
Time Period(s): 1910s
Locale(s): Red River, Texas

Summary: A teenager named Jed takes to the road with an itinerant peddler in a series of adventures that include a young black man's escape from a chain gain.

Historical Accuracy: The novel provides an authentic look at the region and the atmosphere of the period.

ROBERT B. OXNAM (1942-)

An American born in Los Angeles, Oxnam is an internationally recognized expert on China and the president emeritus of the Asia Society. He has worked as an professor at Columbia, and Williams College. His first novel was *Cinnabar.*.

4772 *Ming: A Novel of Seventeeth Century China*

Date of Publication: 1994
Subject(s): Politics; Chinese Empire
Fictional character(s): Meihua, Young Woman; Longyan, Young Man, Military Personnel
Time Period(s): 17th century
Locale(s): China

Summary: Life in 17th-century China and the decay of the Ming dynasty in the face of the invasion of the Manchus is the novel's subject. Two lovers, Meihua and Longyan, battle both convention and duty in the ensuing struggle as a great empire gives way to a new age. Meihua rebels against the social restrictions on education for women. Longyan makes his mark as a military commander but must decide whether to protect the decaying dynasty or join the new.

Historical Accuracy: The setting and details of 17th-century Chinese life and events are authentic and vividly presented.

ELIZABETH PAGE (1889-)

Page was a teacher, welfare worker, and novelist who wrote stories of pioneer life and the conflict between the Jeffersonians and the Hamiltonians.

4773 *The Tree of Liberty*

Date of Publication: 1939
Subject(s): American Colonies; American Revolution
Fictional character(s): Matthew Howard, Frontiersman; Jane Peyton, Young Woman; Peyton Howard, Military Personnel (American soldier)
Historical character(s): Thomas Jefferson, Political Figure; Patrick Henry, Patriot, Lawyer; John Adams, Political Figure; George Washington, Military Personnel (army commander), Political Figure; Marie Joseph Paul de Lafayette, Military Personnel (French general), Nobleman; Alexander Hamilton, Military Personnel (American officer), Political Figure
Time Period(s): 18th century; 19th century (1754-1806)
Locale(s): Williamsburg, Virginia; Philadelphia, Pennsylvania; New York, New York

Summary: This vast historical panorama covers the major events in the birth of the American nation from the 1750s to the early years of the 19th century. Filled with incidents and historical figures, the novel shows the effects of the great events on three generations of the Howard, Peyton, and Humphreys families.

Historical Accuracy: The framework of the novel's depiction of the events of the Revolution is accurate.

4774 *Wilderness Adventure*

Date of Publication: 1946
Subject(s): American Colonies; Indians
Fictional character(s): John Howard, Military Personnel (captain); Lisel Salling, Captive
Time Period(s): 1740s (1742)
Locale(s): Virginia, American Colonies; Mississippi River, North America

Summary: Captain John Howard's expedition to explore the western territory of the American colonies becomes a rescue mission when a young girl is abducted by Indians. Howard and a small band, including the girl's father and two suitors, pursue her west, down to New Orleans.

Historical Accuracy: Most of the events described are true based on the diary of John Peter Salling. Lisel, however, is an invention.

ROBIN PAIGE
(PSEUD. OF SUSAN WITTIG ALBERT, 1940- ; BILL ALBERT)

Susan and Bill Albert, who live in central Texas, are a wife-and-husband writing team. Born in New York, Bill Albert grew up in southern California and moved to England in 1964 where he taught history at the University of Norwich. Albert is active in the disability movement. His first novel was *Desert Blues*. After becoming the first female vice president of Southwest Texas State University in San Marcos, Susan Albert left academia in 1985.

4775 *Death at Daisy's Folly*

Date of Publication: 1997
Subject(s): Mystery; Victorian Period
Fictional character(s): Sir Charles Sheridan, Gentleman, Scientist (amateur); Kathryn Ardleigh, Writer
Historical character(s): Edward, Prince of Wales, Royalty
Time Period(s): 1890s
Locale(s): England

Summary: In this Victorian house-party mystery, a murderer is on the loose, and the Prince of Wales orders Sir Charles Sheridan and Kate Ardleigh, an American writer of penny dreadfuls, to solve the crime and avoid a scandal.

Historical Accuracy: The novel provides good period details.

4776 *Death at Gallows Green*

Date of Publication: 1995
Subject(s): Mystery; Victorian Period
Fictional character(s): Kathryn Ardleigh, Writer; Sir Charles Sheridan, Gentleman, Scientist (amateur)
Historical character(s): Beatrix Potter, Writer
Time Period(s): 1890s
Locale(s): Essex, England

Summary: In the second installment of the Victorian-era mysteries featuring American writer Kathryn Ardleigh, Kathryn investigates the brutal murder of a local constable and the disappearance of a child. She is ably assisted by Sir Charles Sheridan and a young Beatrix Potter.

Historical Accuracy: The novel features a convincing period background.

ELEANOR PAINTER (1891-1947)

Born in Walkerville, Iowa, Painter studied singing in Berlin and London, performing in light opera and later in grand opera in Europe and America. After retiring from singing,

she wrote a historical novel, *Spring's Symphony*, based on the lives of Robert and Clara Schuman.

4777 *Spring Symphony*

Date of Publication: 1941
Subject(s): Biography, Fictionalized; Musical Life
Historical character(s): Robert Schumann, Composer; Clara Wieck Schumann, Spouse; Friedrich Wieck, Musician (pianist)
Time Period(s): 1830s
Locale(s): Germany

Summary: This biographical novel dramatizes the relationship between German composer Robert Schumann and Clara Wieck, the daughter of piano master Friedrich Wieck. Their love affair and long betrothal begins when Clara is a child of eight. The novel captures the pair's relationship as well as large doses of musical background.

Historical Accuracy: The novel is best when it stays close to the factual sources of Clara and Robert's letters. Occasionally, it veers toward the sentimental.

CHARLES PALLISER (1947-)

Born in Massachusetts and a graduate of Oxford, Palliser is a lecturer in English and creative writing.

4778 *The Quincunx*

Date of Publication: 1989
Subject(s): Inheritance—Disputed; Mystery; Family Saga
Fictional character(s): John Huffam, Gentleman; Mary Clothier, Gentlewoman; Barney Digweed, Criminal
Time Period(s): 1820s
Locale(s): London, England

Summary: A young man from the north of England begins an investigation into the mystery of his birthright. At the center of the plot is a complicated Chancery lawsuit and a missing codicil. The solution of the novel's many secrets take John Huffam on a survey of late-Regency London, from its salons and staterooms to its corrupt underworld.

Historical Accuracy: The novel is a brilliant pastiche of the 19th-century novel, exhaustingly researched to provide scrupulously accurate period detail.

BRUCE PALMER (1932-)

JOHN CLIFFORD GILES

Palmer was born in Massachusetts and graduated from Williams College. He has worked as an English teacher.

4779 *Horseshoe Bend*

Date of Publication: 1962
Subject(s): Indians; Battle of Horseshoe Bend
Historical character(s): Andrew Jackson, Military Personnel (general); Sam Houston, Military Personnel (army officer); Davy Crockett, Frontiersman; William Weatherford, Indian (Creek), Chieftain

Time Period(s): 1810s (1814)
Locale(s): Alabama

Summary: The novel provides a reconstruction of the events of the Battle of Horseshoe Bend during the Creek Indian War. The conflict sets half-breed leader of the Creeks, William Weatherford, aka Chief Red Eagle, against the generalship of Andrew Jackson.

Historical Accuracy: The basic facts are historically accurate though there is some tampering with details to embellish the story.

MARIAN PALMER (1930-)

A Canadian author born in British Columbia, Palmer worked as an accountant and an office manager before becoming a full-time writer in 1968.

4780 *The White Boar*

Date of Publication: 1968
Subject(s): War of the Roses; Royalty—England
Historical character(s): Richard III, Ruler (King of England); Phillip Lovell, Gentleman; Francis Lovell, Gentleman
Time Period(s): 15th century (1465-1486)
Locale(s): England; Burgundy, France

Summary: The controversial figure of Richard III, the last of the Plantagenet kings, is depicted through the eyes of two devoted friends, Phillip and Francis Lovell. Their allegiance to Richard during his rise to power and his tragically short-ened reign, ending in defeat at Bosworth Field, illustrates the pomp of the royal court and the intrigue that helps bring Richard down.

Historical Accuracy: The atmosphere of the era is faithfully re-created through a perspective that is clearly pro-Richard.

4781 *The Wrong Plantagenet*

Date of Publication: 1972
Subject(s): Tudor Period; Royalty—England
Historical character(s): Perkin Warbeck, Imposter; Henry VII, Ruler (King of England)
Time Period(s): 15th century (1488-1499)
Locale(s): England; Burgundy, France

Summary: The novel chronicles the rise of Perkin Warbeck, the pretender who claimed to be the son of Edward IV, one of the princes in the Tower who survived. Simon Lovell be-comes a follower of the Pretender and takes part in his fatal attempt to seize the English throne.

Historical Accuracy: The novel provides an ingenious mixture of historical fact and conjecture. The story offers a plausible interpretation of Warbeck's background.

WILLIAM J. PALMER (1943-)

An American English professor and scholar, Palmer was born in Charlotte, North Carolina, and graduated from the University of Notre Dame and Ohio State University. He is a Professor of English at Purdue University where he is an expert on such writers as Charles Dickens and John Fowles.

Palmer's avocation is acting, and he describes his Mr. Dickens novels as being all about actors.

4782 *The Detective and Mr. Dickens*

Date of Publication: 1990
Subject(s): Mystery; Victorian Period; Literary Life
Historical character(s): Charles Dickens, Writer; Wilkie Collins, Writer; William Field, Detective—Police; Ellen Ternan, Actress
Time Period(s): 1850s (1851)
Locale(s): London, England

Summary: Set during the 1850s and recorded by Charles Dickens' young friend Wilkie Collins, the novel details the relationship between Dickens and police inspector William Field, one of England's first professional detectives. The two investigate a brutal murder connected with a Covent Garden production of *Macbeth*.

Historical Accuracy: Dickens' nocturnal adventures with the famous detective Field are based on fact, though this particu-lar adventure is invented.

4783 *The Highwayman and Mr. Dickens*

Date of Publication: 1992
Subject(s): Mystery; Victorian Period; Literary Life
Fictional character(s): Tally Ho Thompson, Highwayman; Henry Jekyll, Doctor
Historical character(s): Charles Dickens, Writer; Wilkie Collins, Writer; William Field, Detective—Police; Sir Richard Francis Burton, Explorer
Time Period(s): 1850s (1852)
Locale(s): London, England

Summary: Wilkie Collins records his friend Charles Dickens' second criminal investigation as the pair are reunited with Inspector Field in the investigation of a grisly murder. Two corpses are found, their faces frozen in terror, as if they had seen the Medusa of legend. Suspicion falls on the notorious house-breaker and highwayman Tally Ho Thompson whom Dickens is determined to prove innocent.

Historical Accuracy: The story is an ingenious invention, but the period details are accurate and convincing.

4784 *The Hoydens and Mr. Dickens*

Date of Publication: 1997
Subject(s): Mystery; Victorian Period; Literary Life
Historical character(s): Charles Dickens, Writer; Wilkie Collins, Writer; Angela Burdett-Coutts, Noblewoman (countess); William Field, Detective—Police; Ellen Ternan, Actress; Florence Nightingale, Gentlewoman, Nurse; Dante Gabriel Rossetti, Writer, Artist; Elizabeth Eleanor Siddal, Model, Artist; Mary Ann Evans, Writer (aka George Eliot)
Time Period(s): 1850s (1852)
Locale(s): London, England

Summary: In this Victorian mystery involving the sleuthing exploits of Charles Dickens and his friend Wilkie Collins, Angela Burdett-Coutts is being threatened, her family's bank is robbed, and a member of the Woman's Emancipation Society is found strangled. Suspicion falls on the young actress Ellen Ternan who has captivated Dickens. The pair of literary detectives sets out to prove her innocence.

Historical Accuracy: The story is fanciful but does rely on a convincing reconstruction of the period.

DANIEL PANGER (1926-)

Born in New York City, Panger graduated from the University of California—Los Angeles and New York University. He is a Unitarian minister and has been a pastor in churches in California and New Mexico. His books include *The Dance of the Witch Mouse* and *Armed Only with the Cross.*

4785 *Joanna the Pope*

Date of Publication: 1986
Subject(s): Middle Ages; Religious Life; Identity—Concealed
Historical character(s): John VIII, Religious (pope)
Time Period(s): 9th century
Locale(s): Germany; Rome, Italy; France

Summary: This historical novel is based on the medieval legend that during the 9th century a woman reigned as Pope John VIII. Joanna makes her way to Rome, disguised as a man for protection, and then finds herself at the center of church politics that lead to her ascension to the Chair of St. Peter.

Historical Accuracy: The factual basis for the novel is debatable, but the story does succeed in convincingly capturing 9th-century life and church politics.

4786 *Ol' Prophet Nat*

Date of Publication: 1967
Subject(s): Slavery; Antebellum South
Historical character(s): Nat Turner, Slave, Leader (slave revolt)
Time Period(s): 19th century
Locale(s): Virginia

Summary: A World War II sailor discovers the journal of Nat Turner in his Bible. The journal records Nat's life as a slave in Virginia and the events that lead to the only effective slave rebellion in U.S. history.

Historical Accuracy: The novel provides an accurate account of Turner's Rebellion.

JEAN PARADISE (1913-)

4787 *The Savage City*

Date of Publication: 1956
Subject(s): American Colonies; Racial Conflict; Pirates
Fictional character(s): Richard Tucker, Bastard Son, Privateer
Time Period(s): 1740s (1741)
Locale(s): New York, New York, American Colonies

Summary: The background for this tale is the hysteria that afflicted New York City in the 1740s when a servant leaked news of a conspiracy by slaves and the Spanish to murder whites in the city. The ensuing panic and violence is played

out against a romantic plot involving privateer Richard Tucker.

Historical Accuracy: The historical details are accurately described, despite the fanciful plot.

MARY PARADISE

4788 *Siege in the Sun*

Date of Publication: 1967
Subject(s): Boer War; Siege of Mafeking
Fictional character(s): Lizzie Willoughby, Young Woman, Nurse; Tom Wheeler, Journalist
Time Period(s): 1890s
Locale(s): Mafeking, South Africa

Summary: The 217-day siege of the frontier outpost of Mafeking during the Boer War is the scene for this taut drama of survival. Lizzie Willoughby has come to South Africa to escape an unhappy past in England. She endures the bombardment, nursing the dying while conducting a love affair with journalist Tom Wheeler.

Historical Accuracy: The period background of the siege is genuine.

VIOLA PARADISE (1887-)

4789 *Tomorrow the Harvest*

Date of Publication: 1952
Subject(s): Settlement of the American Frontier
Fictional character(s): Dorcas Willett, Young Woman; Melissa Sawyer, Young Woman
Time Period(s): 1780s
Locale(s): Maine

Summary: Set in a small Maine community in the years immediately following the American Revolution, the novel dramatizes the conflicts in the new nation, centering on the relationship between two young women—Dorcas Willett and Melissa Sawyer.

Historical Accuracy: The novel offers an authentic depiction of the period and the region.

SANDRA PARETTI

Born in Regensburg, Germany, Paretti studied in Munich, London, and Rome. A journalist and critic, she lives and works in Zurich. Paretti is known in Germany as the "writing daughter of Alexandre Dumas" for her many successful romances.

4790 *The Drums of Winter*

Date of Publication: 1972
Subject(s): American Revolution; Family Saga; Battle of Trent
Fictional character(s): Anna Haynow, Spouse; Gottfried Haynow, Nobleman (baron); Claus Haynow, Military Personnel
Time Period(s): 1770s; 1780s (1775-1780)

Locale(s): Hessia, Germany; Trenton, New Jersey

Summary: This family drama is set during the American Revolution and involves the powerful Haynow family of Hessia in Germany. The baron's wife Anna learns that her first husband, thought dead, is alive in America, a discovery that sets in motion a family conflict that is only resolved at the Battle of Trenton.

Historical Accuracy: The fictional story is interwoven with believable and actual details and events of the period.

4791 *The Magic Ship*

Date of Publication: 1979
Subject(s): World War I
Fictional character(s): Fred Vandermark, Sailor; Gloria Lindsay, Actress, Widow(er); Charley Polack, Sea Captain
Time Period(s): 1910s (1914)
Locale(s): Bar Harbor, Maine

Summary: As war breaks out in Europe in August 1914, the German ship *Cecilie* seeks safety from high seas in the resort town of Bar Harbor, Maine. The novel details the interaction of crew, passengers, and townspeople.

Historical Accuracy: The event is based on fact.

4792 *The Rose and the Sword*

Date of Publication: 1967
Subject(s): Napoleonic Era; Royalty—France
Fictional character(s): Caroline de la Romme Allery, Noblewoman (countess); Lord Fouche, Nobleman (Duke of Otranto)
Historical character(s): Napoleon Bonaparte, Ruler (Emperor of France); Charles Maurice de Talleyrand-Perigord, Diplomat, Government Official
Time Period(s): 1810s
Locale(s): Paris, France; Italy

Summary: This romantic adventure story set in the first years of Napoleon's reign as emperor features the captivating Countess Caroline de la Romme Allery who conquers Napoleon and is swept up into a web of intrigue that leads to a final confrontation with her adversary Fouche, Duke of Otranto, and uncovers conspirators against Napoleon and the empire.

Historical Accuracy: The story is fanciful but does depend on a genuine period background.

4793 *Tenants of the Earth*

Date of Publication: 1973
Subject(s): Railroads
Fictional character(s): John Tyler Matlock, Financier; Loftus Poynder, Financier; Craig Matlock, Young Man
Time Period(s): 1860s (1865-1866)
Locale(s): Connecticut; New York, New York

Summary: In this tale of the robber barons who built America's railroads, John Matlock controls most of the rail lines in New York state, but the vital link into New York City is held by his rival, Loftus Poynder. Matlock's methods to break Poynder force his son to side with his rival, and when Craig

Matlock inherits all of Poynder's holdings, the stage is set for a father-son showdown.

Historical Accuracy: The story is fanciful but does offer an authentic look at the Railroad Wars of the 1860s.

4794 *The Wishing Tree*

Date of Publication: 1975
Subject(s): Family Saga; Business Building; World War I
Fictional character(s): Camilla Hofman, Businesswoman; Fritz Hofman, Businessman
Time Period(s): 1900s; 1910s
Locale(s): Berlin, Germany

Summary: The trials and tribulation of the Hofman family in Germany in the first two decades of the the 20th century form the novel's subject. Fritz Hofman builds a business empire and a great house only to lose everything in bankruptcy. His daughter Camilla is determined to rebuild the family fortune, relaunching her father's business.

Historical Accuracy: The novel deals knowingly with the period background, creating a believable sense of place and time.

EDITH PARGETER (1913-1995)

Pargeter was born and raised in Shropshire, England and worked as a pharmacist's assistant and dispenser before becoming a full-time novelist and translator of prose and poetry from Czech and Slovak. She also served as a petty officer in the Woman's Royal Naval Service during World War II. Almost all of her works are set in her home region of Shropshire on the Welsh border. She achieved world-wide acclaim from her series of medieval mysteries written under the pseudonym Ellis Peters. Her most recent work under her own name was a series of novels set in World War II.

4795 *The Bloody Field*

Date of Publication: 1972
Subject(s): Middle Ages; Royalty—England
Historical character(s): Henry IV, Ruler (King of England); Harry Monmouth, Royalty (prince); Henry Percy, Nobleman
Time Period(s): 14th century; 15th century (1399-1403)
Locale(s): Shrewsbury, England

Summary: The clash at Shrewsbury, on the Welsh border, between Henry Bolingbroke, now Henry IV, and Henry Percy, known as Hotspur, is dramatized. Percy leads a rebel army in revolt against Henry's succession to the throne. Henry's dissolute son begins to emerge as the military leader he will become while reigning as Henry V.

Historical Accuracy: The depiction of the events and the atmosphere of the period are solidly and credibly presented.

4796 *The Brothers of Gwynedd*

Date of Publication: 1989
Subject(s): Middle Ages; Royalty—Wales
Historical character(s): Llywelyn ap Gruffydd, Royalty (prince); David ap Gruffydd, Royalty (prince)

Time Period(s): 13th century
Locale(s): Wales; England

Summary: This volume collects into one four of the author's novels—*Sunrise in the West*, *The Dragon at Noonday*, *The Hands of Sunset*, and *Afterglow and Nightfall*—which chronicle the descendents of Llewelyn the Great, notably Llewelyn ap Gruffydd and his brother David. As Llewelyn tries to create and maintain an independent Welsh nation, David proves to be his undoing.

Historical Accuracy: This is a remarkable re-creation of the period, convincing in every detail.

4797 *The Heaven Tree Trilogy*

Date of Publication: 1993
Subject(s): Middle Ages; Artistic Life
Fictional character(s): Harry Talvace, Artist (stonecarver); Adam Boteler, Adventurer; Ranf Isambord, Nobleman (Lord of Parfois)
Historical character(s): Llywelyn ap Gruffydd, Royalty (prince of North Wales)
Time Period(s): 13th century (1200-1234)
Locale(s): Welsh Marches, Wales; Shrewsbury, England

Summary: The author's three novels *The Heaven Tree*, *The Green Branch*, and *The Scarlet Seed* are collected in one volume and offer a sweeping panorama of life in 13th century England and Wales. At the center of this story of loyalty and betrayal amidst civil war and border battles is Harry Talvace, a brilliant stonecarver who tries to create while those around him are bent on destruction.

Historical Accuracy: Remarkably vivid and compelling, the novels can be read as a sourcebook on life, thoughts, and customs of the period.

4798 *Hortensius, Friend of Nero*

Date of Publication: 1937
Subject(s): Roman Empire
Fictional character(s): Hortensius, Gentleman
Historical character(s): Nero, Ruler (Roman emperor)
Time Period(s): 1st century (60s)
Locale(s): Rome, Roman Empire

Summary: This tale of Rome during the reign of Emperor Nero takes the form of a diary kept by Nero's friend Hortensius who is made to realize the growing madness of his former comrade. The novel takes place after the Great Fire, when Nero is rebuilding Rome.

Historical Accuracy: The novel is not successful in creating a convincing or accurate depiction of the times. There is a good deal of simplification and a number of liberties are taken to form the novel's romantic tragedy.

4799 *The Marriage of Meggotta*

Date of Publication: 1979
Subject(s): Middle Ages; Royalty—England
Historical character(s): Henry III, Ruler (King of England); Simon de Montfort, Nobleman; Richard de Clare, Heir, Nobleman; Meggotta de Burgh, Gentlewoman; Hubert de

Burgh, Nobleman (Earl of Kent); William Marshal, Knight, Nobleman (Earl of Pembroke)
Time Period(s): 13th century (1230-1238)
Locale(s): England

Summary: Set during the turbulent reign of Henry III in the 13th century, the novel describes the love affair between Richard de Clare, heir to the earldoms of Gloucester and Hartfield, and Meggotta, the daughter of the king's judicary, Hubert De Burgh. When Hubert loses favor with the king, Richard and Meggotta must contend with the political forces trying to separate them.

Historical Accuracy: The novel's historical background is exact and richly textured.

JAY PARINI (1948-)

Born in Pennsylvania, Parini is a graduate of Lafayette College and the University of St. Andrews. He is a poet and novelist who teaches English at Middlebury College.

4800 *Bay of Arrows*

Date of Publication: 1992
Subject(s): Exploration
Fictional character(s): Christopher Genovese, Professor, Writer; Susan Genovese, Spouse
Historical character(s): Christopher Columbus, Explorer
Time Period(s): 1990s; 15th century
Locale(s): Dominican Republic

Summary: In parallel stories, a college professor obsessed with writing a long poem about Christopher Columbus journeys to the Dominican Republic where Columbus landed 500 years ago and first met resistance in the New World. Juxtaposed to the present is the story of Columbus on his voyage.

Historical Accuracy: The novel is comically inventive, working out the connection between present and past.

4801 *The Last Station*

Date of Publication: 1990
Subject(s): Biography, Fictionalized; Literary Life; Russian Empire
Historical character(s): Leo Tolstoy, Writer; Sofya Andreyevna Tolstoy, Spouse; Vladimir Cherkkov, Gentleman
Time Period(s): 1910s (1910)
Locale(s): Astapovo, Russia

Summary: In 1910, Leo Tolstoy, the world's most famous author flees his family and his wealth for a desired life of poverty and chastity. He makes it as far as the tiny railroad station of Astapovo where he collapses. Newspapermen, family, and disciples wrangle over access to and control of the dying great man. The novel, narrated in different voices, captures the moment and the history of a literary genius.

Historical Accuracy: The basis of the novel is factual, based on eyewitness accounts. However, the author admits he has freely imagined what might have been said.

PAUL PARK (1954-)

Park was born in Massachusetts and educated at Hampshire College. He has travelled extensively and lived in Asia and India. Park has taught creative writing at Williams College and Johns Hopkins University. His books include *Soldiers of Paradise*, *Sugar Rain*, and *The Cult of Loving Kindness*.

4802 *The Gospel of Corax*

Date of Publication: 1996
Subject(s): Biblical Story; Roman Empire
Fictional character(s): Corax, Slave
Historical character(s): Jesus Christ, Biblical Figure; Pontius Pilate, Government Official; Barabbas, Biblical Figure, Thief; Mary, Biblical Figure
Time Period(s): 1st century
Locale(s): Arabia; India

Summary: This radical reinterpretation of the story of Jesus follows the adventures of Corax, an escaped slave who raises money for a trip to India as a healer in Palestine. To save himself from recapture, he betrays the Jewish rebellion and Jesus and becomes a marked man. Together Corax and Jesus flee east to the foothills of the Himalayas where Jesus attains enlightenment.

Historical Accuracy: The novel is a jumble of facts and fancy in which imagination finally triumphs over a believable reconstruction of the past. The novel goes considerably beyond Biblical sources and will offend many orthodox Christians.

CORNELIA STRATTON PARKER
(1885-1972)

An American writer born in California, Parker was the author of *An American Idyll: The Life of Carleton H. Parker* and *Wanderer's Circle*, an autobiography.

4803 *Fabulous Valley*

Date of Publication: 1956
Subject(s): Business Building; Oil Industry
Fictional character(s): Linda Rinn, Landowner; Davy Rinn, Heir
Time Period(s): 1850s (1850)
Locale(s): Pennsylvania

Summary: This romantic story is set against the backdrop of the first oil rush in history as oil is discovered in Pennsylvania. Young Davy Rinn becomes one of the first of the oil barons as he persuades his mother to part with some of her land for a million dollars. He enjoys the high life while the money lasts, but is soon forced to return to his cabin on Oil Creek to rethink his life and his priorities.

Historical Accuracy: The novel's story is fictional, but the period elements are factual and authentic.

F.A. PARKER

Parker worked as a land manager in Southeast Oregon where he was responsible for vast herds of sheep, cattle, and horses.

4804 *The Predators*

Date of Publication: 1990
Subject(s): American West; Mormons
Fictional character(s): Caroline Shepard, Young Woman; Sam Wilde, Trapper; Nathan Tolliver, Rancher
Time Period(s): 1850s (1859)
Locale(s): England; Utah

Summary: The background of this western story is the efforts of the Mormons to create a nation on the Utah frontier. Caroline Shepard is an Englishwoman recruited by a missionary to join other women in the journey west to the Mormon state. Nathan Tolliver, a Texas rancher, heads north in a search for a mate. Their paths connect as the party is set upon by Indians, armed troops, and desperados.

Historical Accuracy: The period background is authentic.

GILBERT PARKER (1862-1932)

Canadian author Parke was a professor of elocution, a playwright, and a novelist. He is best known as the director of American propaganda for the British during World War I. Parker's books include *The Battle of the Strong*, *The Judgment House*, and *The Trail of the Sword*.

4805 *The Power and the Glory*

Date of Publication: 1925
Subject(s): Exploration
Historical character(s): Rene-Robert Cavelier de La Salle, Explorer; Louis de Buade, Government Official (colonial governor)
Time Period(s): 17th century
Locale(s): Canada; France; North America

Summary: The novel chronicles the career of French explorer La Salle. His conflicts with the Jesuits and the French colonial administrators become as great a challenge as that of exploring the wilderness of North America.

Historical Accuracy: The novel is only partially successful in creating a fully-realized and believable portrait of the period.

NORTON S. PARKER

4806 *Table in the Wilderness*

Date of Publication: 1947
Subject(s): Biblical Story
Historical character(s): Joseph, Biblical Figure (Old Testament figure)
Time Period(s): Indeterminate Past
Locale(s): Egypt

Summary: The novel dramatizes the Old Testament story of Joseph beginning with his being sold into bondage in Egypt by his brothers. This fictional embellishment of the Biblical story follows his experiences there.

Historical Accuracy: This is a blending of fact, legend, history, and myth with an evident modernist tinge. There are some convincing period elements, however.

ROBERT B. PARKER (1932-)

An American mystery novelist, Parker was born in Massachusetts and is a graduate of Colby College and Boston University. He has worked as an advertising writer and a lecturer in English. Parker is best known as the author of the Spenser detective series, called the best hardboiled detective fiction since Ross Macdonald and Raymond Chandler. He won an Edgar Award in 1976 for *Promised Land.*.

4807 *Perchance to Dream*

Date of Publication: 1991
Subject(s): Mystery
Fictional character(s): Philip Marlowe, Detective—Private; Carmen Sternwood, Young Woman; Eddie Mars, Criminal
Time Period(s): 1930s (1939)
Locale(s): Los Angeles, California

Summary: In this sequel to Raymond Chandler's *The Big Sleep,* Carmen Sternwood, committed by her sister to a sanatorium, has disappeared, and Marlowe is asked by the Sternwood's butler to help find her and to try and keep gangster Eddie Mars from returning to control the Sternwoods' lives.

Historical Accuracy: The novel offers an impressive replication of the feel of the Chandler original as well as an authentic period Los Angeles.

THOMAS TREBITSCH PARKER (1943-)

An American writer, Parker's works include *Small Business*. He assisted baseball star Dave Winfield with his autobiography *Winfield: A Player's Life.*

4808 *Anna, Ann, Annie*

Date of Publication: 1993
Subject(s): Musical Life; World War II
Fictional character(s): Anna Moser, Musician (pianist); Jake Weigel, Businessman
Time Period(s): 20th century (1927-1956)
Locale(s): Vienna, Austria; London, England; New York, New York

Summary: The novel offers a portrait of Anna Moses that takes her from Vienna in the 1920s to London on the brink of World War II and America during the war and post-war years. Anna is a gifted pianist who must struggle for love and artistic achievement against a backdrop of war and peace.

Historical Accuracy: The novel's musical and period elements are convincing.

C. NORTHCOTE PARKINSON
(1909-1993)

An Englishman educated at Cambridge University, Parkinson received a Ph.D. in history from King's College, London. He taught for several years at the University of Malaya. Although trained as a naval historian, Parkinson is best known for the maxim known as Parkinson's Law—that work expands to fill the time available for its completion.

4809 *Dead Reckoning*

Date of Publication: 1978
Subject(s): Sea Story; Military Life—British Navy; Napoleonic Wars
Fictional character(s): Richard Delancey, Military Personnel (naval officer); Fiona Delancey, Spouse; Fabius, Spy
Time Period(s): 1800s; 1810s (1806-1812)
Locale(s): At Sea (East Indies); Madagascar; Mauritius

Summary: In the fourth volume of the sea adventures of Richard Delancey, he has been promoted to the rank of Post-Captain and given command of a frigate on duty in the East Indies. There he discovers his long-lost brother and tracks down the enemy agent Fabius. The story climaxes in a naval battle against two French frigates.

Historical Accuracy: The exotic locations are expertly rendered, as is the nautical background.

4810 *Devil to Pay*

Date of Publication: 1973
Subject(s): Sea Story; Military Life—British Navy; Napoleonic Wars
Fictional character(s): Richard Delancey, Military Personnel (naval officer)
Time Period(s): 1790s (1794)
Locale(s): Guernsey, England; Leon, Spain; France

Summary: The first novel in the author's series of naval adventures concerning Richard Delancey shows him in disgrace with the navy. He gains temporary command of a revenue cutter and a chance to restore his reputation. The action takes him to France and Spain to gain intelligence on Britain's adversaries.

Historical Accuracy: The period and naval details are thorough and believable.

4811 *The Fireship*

Date of Publication: 1975
Subject(s): Sea Story; Military Life—British Navy; Napoleonic Wars
Fictional character(s): Richard Delancey, Military Personnel (naval officer); Henry Trollope, Military Personnel (naval officer)
Time Period(s): 1790s (1797)
Locale(s): Portsmouth, England; At Sea (North Sea); Ireland

Summary: In the second volume of the author's series chronicling the naval adventures of Richard Delancey during the Napoleonic Wars, Delancey is involved in a mutiny and in defending a brother officer at the ensuing court-martial. He is given command of an old and undermanned fireship that he brings to bear in combat with a French ship of the line.

Historical Accuracy: The period details are credible, and the naval strategy expertly rendered.

4812 *The Guernseyman*

Date of Publication: 1982
Subject(s): Sea Story; Military Life—British Navy; American Revolution
Fictional character(s): Richard Delancey, Military Personnel (naval officer)
Time Period(s): 1770s; 1780s (1776-1782)
Locale(s): Liverpool, England; New York, New York; Charleston, South Carolina

Summary: Richard Delancey, a 16-year-old from Liverpool, joins the British Navy and rises to the rank of a commissioned officer through his exploits during the American Revolution and the Siege of Gibraltar. This is the first volume of a series on Delancey's naval adventures.

Historical Accuracy: The novel provides convincing period and nautical details in capturing the era and its events.

4813 *The Life and Times of Horatio Hornblower*

Date of Publication: 1970
Subject(s): Sea Story; Military Life—British Navy; Napoleonic Wars
Fictional character(s): Horatio Hornblower, Military Personnel (naval officer); Lady Barbara Wellesley, Noblewoman; William Bush, Military Personnel (naval officer)
Historical character(s): Arthur Wellesley, Military Personnel (army commander), Nobleman (Duke of Wellington)
Time Period(s): 18th century; 19th century (1776-1857)
Locale(s): Kent, England; At Sea

Summary: The novel offers a full-scale, fully documented biography of C.S. Forester's fictional character, Horatio Hornblower. Pieced together from Forester's twelve Hornblower novels, the novel traces Hornblower's entire career, filling in gaps through the chance discovery of a collection of Hornblower's papers that Mr. Forester never saw.

Historical Accuracy: This is an ingenious re-imagination of the Hornblower saga with a detailed and believable period background.

4814 *So Near So Far*

Date of Publication: 1981
Subject(s): Sea Story; Military Life—British Navy; Napoleonic Wars
Fictional character(s): Richard Delancey, Military Personnel (naval officer); Fiona Sinclair, Actress
Time Period(s): 1800s (1802)
Locale(s): Lake District, England; At Sea; Boulogne, France

Summary: In this installment of the naval adventures of Richard Delancey, the Treaty of Amiens provides a brief respite in the war with France. Delancey experiences challenges on land and sea as Napoleon mounts plans to invade England.

Historical Accuracy: The period and naval details are authentic.

4815 *Touch and Go*

Date of Publication: 1977

Subject(s): Sea Story; Military Life—British Navy; Napoleonic Wars
Fictional character(s): Richard Delancey, Military Personnel (naval officer)
Historical character(s): James Saumarez, Military Personnel (admiral)
Time Period(s): 1790s; 1800s
Locale(s): Mediterranean; Valletta, Malta; Algeciras, Spain

Summary: In the third of the author's naval adventures about Richard Delancey, he is posted to the Mediterranean on convoy duty. Delancey proves his mettle during the siege of Valletta and in the rescue of a young slave girl in North Africa. The story's climax is two great sea battles against the Franco-Spanish squadron off Algeciras and Cadiz.

Historical Accuracy: Filled with period and naval details. The atmosphere is authentic and convincing.

PHILLIP PAROTTI (1941-)

An American scholar and writer, Parotti is a professor of English at Sam Houston State University and a former officer in the United States Navy.

4816 *Fires in the Sky*

Date of Publication: 1990
Subject(s): Trojan War
Fictional character(s): Dymas, Military Personnel (Trojan general); Pharos, Teacher
Time Period(s): 12th century B.C.
Locale(s): Troy, Ancient Civilization; Scyros, Greece (island in Aegean Sea); Mysia, Asia Minor

Summary: A young Trojan general tells the story of his rise. Born a commoner, Dymus recounts his battles with Agamemnon and the Greeks. His military successes are compromised as he becomes increasingly involved with royal scandals and in intrigue.

Historical Accuracy: The story depends on an authentically-created period backdrop.

4817 *The Greek Generals Talk: Memoirs of the Trojan War*

Date of Publication: 1986
Subject(s): Trojan War
Fictional character(s): Thrasymedes, Military Personnel (Greek general); Diomedes, Military Personnel (Greek general); Achilles, Warrior (Greek); Agamemnon, Ruler (King of Mycenae)
Time Period(s): 12th century B.C.
Locale(s): Troy, Ancient Civilization

Summary: In a brilliant blend of history and legend, the author recreates the bloody Trojan War from the perspective of a number of Greek generals who give their account of the 10-year conflict on the plains of Troy.

Historical Accuracy: The story of the Trojan War, if it happened in fact, might have happened in the way described. The author's possession of the period is remarkable.

4818 *The Trojan Generals Talk: Memoirs of the Greek War*

Date of Publication: 1988
Subject(s): Trojan War
Fictional character(s): Merops, Military Personnel (general); Antiphus, Military Personnel (general); Polydamas, Military Personnel (general); Hector, Warrior (Trojan commander); Priam, Ruler (King of Troy)
Time Period(s): 12th century B.C.
Locale(s): Troy, Ancient Civilization

Summary: This companion volume to the author's *The Greek Generals Talk* gives the Trojan perspective on the 10-year siege. Ten aging Trojan generals offer their recollections nearly half a century after the fall of Troy. The novel offers a compelling look at Priam's Troy at the height of its power and at the moment of its fall.

Historical Accuracy: The story invents its history, but it is convincing nonetheless in capturing a genuine atmosphere.

ANNE PARRISH (1888-1957)

American writer Parrish was born in Colorado Springs, Colorado. With her brother Dillwyn Parrish, she wrote and illustrated a number of children's books and was the author of 12 novels, including *Pray for Tomorrow*, *Poor Child*, and *The Lucky One*. She won the Harper Prize in 1925 for *The Perennial Bachelor*.

4819 *A Clouded Star*

Date of Publication: 1948
Subject(s): Slavery; Underground Railroad; Antebellum South
Historical character(s): Harriet Tubman, Abolitionist
Time Period(s): 1850s; 1860s (1859-1860)
Locale(s): United States

Summary: The novel re-creates an imagined journey north on the underground railroad by a small group of fugitive slaves conducted by Harriet Tubman. The story is the reflections of a former slave named Samuel who as a child was separated from his parents.

Historical Accuracy: The novel occasionally falters to the level of an abolitionist tract and sacrifices the realistic details of the journey north.

RICHARD PARRY

4820 *The Winter Wolf: Wyatt Earp in Alaska*

Date of Publication: 1996
Subject(s): Gold Rush—Klondike
Fictional character(s): Nathan Blaylock, Bastard Son
Historical character(s): Wyatt Earp, Lawman
Time Period(s): 1890s; 1900s
Locale(s): Alaska

Summary: The novel explores lawman Wyatt Earp's experiences during the gold rush in Alaska. At the age of 50, Earp and his wife try to make a new life in Alaska, but the past reappears in the form Nathan Blaylock. Blaylock, the son of Earp's common-law wife, stalks Earp for the chance at a $20,000 reward if he murders his father.

Historical Accuracy: The novel mingles historical fact and fiction. Wyatt Earp did visit Alaska during the Klondike Gold Rush. The physical locations described and most of the characters Earp meets are based on fact.

NORMAN PARTINGTON

4821 *Master of Bengal: A Novel of Robert Clive of India*

Date of Publication: 1974
Subject(s): British Colonies; British Raj; Biography, Fictionalized
Historical character(s): Robert Clive, Military Personnel (general); Warren Hastings, Political Figure; Sir Francis Dashwood, Government Official (Chancellor of the Exchequer); Edward Maskelyne, Military Personnel
Time Period(s): 18th century (1743-1767)
Locale(s): India; London, England

Summary: The novel reconstructs the amazing life of Robert Clive and the beginning of the British Indian Empire. As a young man, Clive obtains a commission in the army of the East India Company and becomes a national hero. The novel recreates 18th-century India, a loose conglomeration of Muslim princely states that is fashioned into a great empire by British daring and greed, in which Clive plays no small part.

Historical Accuracy: The basic outline of the story is factual and faithfully presented.

4822 *The Sunshine Patriot: A Novel of Benedict Arnold*

Date of Publication: 1975
Subject(s): American Revolution
Historical character(s): Benedict Arnold, Military Personnel (American general); Charles Cornwallis, Military Personnel (British general); John Andre, Military Personnel (British officer), Spy; George Washington, Military Personnel (American commander); Elizabeth Shippen, Loyalist
Time Period(s): 18th century; 19th century (1738-1805)
Locale(s): New York

Summary: The fictional memoirs of Lord Cornwallis tell the story of Benedict Arnold from a decidedly British and sympathetic perspective. Arnold's decision to betray his country and surrender West Point to the British and alter the course of the Revolution is depicted along with vivid portraits of John Andre, Arnold's sister-in-law, Elizabeth Shippen, and George Washington.

Historical Accuracy: The novel attempts to present Arnold's case a little more fairly. Although some imagination has been used, in all important respects the book does not distort historical fact.

BELLAMY PARTRIDGE

4823 *The Big Freeze*

Date of Publication: 1948
Subject(s): Politics
Fictional character(s): David Wakemani, Engineer
Time Period(s): 1840s
Locale(s): New York, New York

Summary: This story of New York social and political life during the 1840s takes as its background the maneuvering to build New York's water system. The novel records the political infighting and corruption that dogged the project.

Historical Accuracy: Every incident of importance in the book actually happened, and the period background is faithfully recorded.

BORIS PASTERNAK (1890-1960)

A Russian poet, translator, and novelist, Pasternak was born in Moscow and graduated from Moscow University. He is regarded in Russia as one of the greatest post-revolution poets. His fame outside of Russia is based on his only novel, *Doctor Zhivago* which was banned in Russia until 1988 as anti-Soviet. Pasternak was awarded the Nobel Prize for literature in 1958.

4824 *Doctor Zhivago*

Date of Publication: 1958
Subject(s): Russian Revolution; World War I
Fictional character(s): Yurii Andreievich Zhivago, Doctor, Writer (poet); Antonina ''Tonia'' Gromeko, Spouse (of Zhivago); Larisa ''Lara'' Guishar, Spouse (of Antipov); Pavel Antipov, Revolutionary, Government Official; Victor Komarovsky, Lawyer
Time Period(s): 20th century (1903-1948)
Locale(s): Moscow, Russia; Siberia, Russia; Eastern Front, Russia

Summary: This great historical novel chronicles Russia's terrible years before and after the revolution from the perspective of Yurii Zhivago, doctor and poet. His life becomes intertwined with Lara, wife of revolutionary Pavel Antipov, who was seduced as a young girl by Victor Komarovsky. Zhivago is wounded at the front and nursed back to health by Lara, with whom he has an affair. Returning to Moscow after the October Revolution, to a city ravaged by riots and disease, Zhivago and his family journey across Russia to the Urals where he meets Lara again. They are separated when he is seized by Red partisans and forced to serve as their doctor. After his escape, he and Lara have a brief period of happiness together, but the forces of history part them once again.

Historical Accuracy: The novel is a remarkable work of honesty informed by a genuine historical imagination.

IRENE STEINMAN PATAI

4825 *The Valley of God*

Date of Publication: 1956
Subject(s): Biblical Story; Ancient Israel
Historical character(s): Hosea, Religious (prophet), Biblical Figure; Gomer, Biblical Figure, Prostitute
Time Period(s): 8th century B.C.
Locale(s): Israel

Summary: The novel provides a dramatization of the Old Testament story of the prophet Hosea and his love for the prostitute Gomer. After Gomer deserts Hosea, he remarries her, a parable for God's love of the wayward and adulterous Israel.

Historical Accuracy: The novel provides a convincing amplification of the Biblical story.

WALTER PATER (1839-1894)

An English writer and critic, Pater was associated with the Pre-Raphaelites. His *Study in the History of the Renaissance* served to define the late Victorian aesthetic movement.

4826 *Marius the Epicurean*

Date of Publication: 1885
Subject(s): Roman Empire
Fictional character(s): Marius, Philosopher; Cornelius, Military Personnel
Historical character(s): Marcus Aurelius, Ruler (Roman emperor); Galen, Doctor
Time Period(s): 2nd century
Locale(s): Rome, Roman Empire

Summary: In this story of the 2nd century, Pater offers a fictional rendering of his own search for a philosophy of life. Young Marius is exposed to the leading philosophical ideas of the time including mysticism, epicureanism, and Christianity.

Historical Accuracy: Historians have criticized Pater's facts, but most grant that he has captured the spirit of the time and the people.

ISABEL PATERSON (1885-1961)

4827 *The Fourth Queen*

Date of Publication: 1926
Subject(s): Elizabethan Period; Royalty—England
Fictional character(s): Jack Montagu, Gentleman
Historical character(s): Elizabeth I, Ruler (Queen of England)
Time Period(s): 16th century
Locale(s): England

Summary: Intrigue and romance in the royal court of Elizabeth I are featured. Jack Montagu is one of the queen's favorites, but his love, a lady-in-waiting, is decidedly not. The course of their love must withstand intrigue and scandal before Queen Elizabeth finally relents and blesses the pair.

Historical Accuracy: The novel's period color adds to the believability of this historical romance.

KATHERINE PATERSON (1932-)

An American born in China to missionary parents, Paterson was educated in China and the U.S. and graduated from King College in Bristol, England. She has worked as a public school teacher in Virginia and as a missionary to Japan from 1957-1962. Her writing is primarily for young adults. Her novel, *Bridge to Terabithia*, won the Newbery Award.

4828 *Rebels of the Heavenly Kingdom*

Date of Publication: 1983
Subject(s): Chinese Empire; Taiping Rebellion
Fictional character(s): Wang Lee, Revolutionary; Mei Lin, Young Woman
Time Period(s): 1850s; 1860s (1850-1864)
Locale(s): China

Summary: The novel tells the story of two people caught up in China's Taiping Rebellion that tried to oust the ruling Manchus and to reverse the influence of Westerners. Wang Lee and Mei Lin are swept up in the great dream of freedom and independence.

Historical Accuracy: The period background is convincingly detailed.

JILL PATON WALSH
(PSEUD. OF GILLIAN PATON WALSH, 1937-)

Born in London and a graduate of St. Anne's College, Oxford, Walsh has worked as a teacher and publisher as well as a writer. Walsh is known for her works which deal realistically with life, death, honor, and maturation. Her award-winning juvenile fiction includes *Fireweed* and *Gaffer Samson's Luck*. She is also the author of the adult novels *Lapsing* and *A School for Lovers*.

4829 *Farewell Great King: A Novel of Ancient Greece*

Date of Publication: 1972
Subject(s): Ancient Greece; Battle of Salamis
Historical character(s): Themistocles, Military Personnel (naval commander), Political Figure; Aristides, Political Figure, Military Personnel (general); Artaxerxes I, Ruler (King of Persia); Darius, Ruler (King of Persia); Sophocles, Writer; Solon, Political Figure; Xerxes I, Ruler (King of Persia)
Time Period(s): 5th century B.C.
Locale(s): Athens, Greece

Summary: Themistocles, the great Athenian general and political leader, narrates his rise to power on the eve of his intended suicide, having been betrayed by political enemies. Themistocles is a self-made leader who plays the key role in several victories over the Persians. His recollections capture life in Athens at a crucial point in the development of democracy.

Historical Accuracy: The novel is solidly researched and based on reliable sources, as the author's notes make clear.

WILLIAM PATRICK (1948-)

Raised in Texas, Patrick is a book editor who has worked with authors including Jane Goodall, Robert Bly, and Magic Johnson.

4830 *Blood Winter*

Date of Publication: 1990
Subject(s): Espionage; World War I
Fictional character(s): Eli Gordon, Doctor (surgeon); Andreas Schilling, Detective—Police; Margrethe Riesling, Young Woman, Lover
Historical character(s): Winston Churchill, Political Figure
Time Period(s): 1910s (1917)
Locale(s): Berlin, Germany

Summary: Faced with a stalemate on the Western Front, Germany rushes to develop a deadly secret weapon. American surgeon Eli Gordon is dispatched to Berlin to investigate. He joins forces with detective Andreas Schiller who is investigating the death of the commandant of chemical weapons production whose mistress, Margrethe Riesling, becomes the key in the rush to prevent catastrophe.

Historical Accuracy: The story is fanciful but the period background is faithfully depicted.

LEWIS B. PATTEN (1915-1981)

An award-winning writer of Western novels and short stories, Patten was born in Denver, Colorado, and attended the University of Denver. He wrote more than 100 books, including *Death of a Gunfighter*, which was filmed in 1969, *Vengeance Rider*, and *Giant on Horseback*.

4831 *Red Runs the River*

Date of Publication: 1970
Subject(s): American West
Fictional character(s): John Sessions, Rancher
Time Period(s): 1860s (1868)
Locale(s): Kansas

Summary: Rancher John Sessions returns to his Kansas home to find his wife scalped and his sons brutally murdered. He suspects Indians until he discovers the theft of his hidden savings, $3,000 in banknotes. Sessions sets out to track down the killers.

Historical Accuracy: The novel features believable period elements.

HARRY PATTERSON (1929-)

Patterson is an English novelist better known as Jack Higgins, under which pseudonym he is the author of numerous bestselling novels, including *The Eagle Has Landed*. Patterson has worked as a teacher of history and education.

4832 *Dillinger*

Date of Publication: 1983

Subject(s): Crime and Criminals
Fictional character(s): Rose de Rivera, Young Woman
Historical character(s): John Dillinger, Outlaw (bank robber); J. Edgar Hoover, Government Official (FBI Director)
Time Period(s): 1930s (1934)
Locale(s): Indiana; Mexico

Summary: The background for the novel's events is the actual spectacular escape of bankrobber John Dillinger from Lake County Jail, Indiana. What happened to him following his escape has been a subject of speculation, and the novel offers an imaginative version as Dillinger heads to Mexico and an encounter with the Mexican police and a beautiful half-Spanish, half-Chinese woman.

Historical Accuracy: The background is authentic, but the story itself is invented.

ORLANDO PATTERSON (1940-)

A Jamaican scholar and writer, Patterson came to the U.S. in 1970, having graduated from the University of the West Indies. He is a professor of sociology at Harvard. He has written *Slavery and Social Death: A Comparative Study* and *The Children of Sisyphus.*.

4833 *Die the Long Day*

Date of Publication: 1972
Subject(s): Slavery
Fictional character(s): Quasheba, Slave
Time Period(s): 18th century
Locale(s): West Indies

Summary: The slave culture of the 18th century West Indies is depicted in the story of Quasheba, a slave, who rebels against her hideous plantation owner. The other slaves are immobilized by fear and her strength of character against a cruel and destructive system forms the novel's vivid drama.

Historical Accuracy: The historical elements in the depiction of the West Indies of the period are authentic.

BARBARA PAUL
(PSEUD. OF BARBARA OVSTEDAL, 1931-)

Barbara Paul is one of several pseudonyms of the English author Barbara Ovstedal, which also include Rosalind Laker. Under Paul, Ovstedal produces Gothic novels; under Laker, historical romances.

4834 *A Cadenza for Caruso*

Date of Publication: 1984
Subject(s): Mystery; Opera; Theatrical Life
Historical character(s): Enrico Caruso, Singer (opera); Giacomo Puccini, Composer; Emmy Destinn, Singer (opera); Arturo Toscanini, Conductor; David Belasco, Manager (theatrical)
Time Period(s): 1910s (1910)
Locale(s): New York, New York

Summary: In 1910, the opera world eagerly awaits the premier of Puccini's *La Fanciulla del West* with Enrico Caruso. But murder stalks the Met when an impressario is found stabbed to death, and Puccini himself is charged with the killing. Caruso comes to his friend's defense and sets out to discover the true murderer.

Historical Accuracy: The novel remarkably recreates New York and the opera world in 1910.

4835 *A Chorus of Detectives*

Date of Publication: 1987
Subject(s): Mystery; Opera; Theatrical Life
Historical character(s): Enrico Caruso, Singer (opera); Geraldine Farrar, Singer (opera); Emmy Destinn, Singer (opera)
Time Period(s): 1920s (1920)
Locale(s): New York, New York

Summary: Someone is systematically eliminating members of the chorus at the Metropolitan Opera House. Caruso and soprano Geraldine Farrar are joined by all of the soloists of the company to investigate the murders, though none can agree who is the guilty party.

Historical Accuracy: This offers convincing details of New York of the period, and the world of the opera.

4836 *Devil's Fire, Love's Revenge*

Date of Publication: 1976
Subject(s): Romance
Fictional character(s): Delia Gilmore, Fiance(e); Aaron Hart, Heir
Time Period(s): 19th century
Locale(s): Lancashire, England

Summary: This gothic-style romance concerns Delia Gilmore's fascination with Halewood Hall, a forbidding estate in Lancashire. It seems to cast a pall on everyone, but Delia is strongly drawn to the house and eventually its enigmatic owner, Aaron Hart.

Historical Accuracy: The novel is only slightly placed in a particularly time and place. The emphasis is on gothic thrills, not history.

4837 *The French Woman*

Date of Publication: 1977
Subject(s): Romance; Napoleonic Wars
Fictional character(s): Juliette Delahousse, Young Woman
Time Period(s): 19th century
Locale(s): Norfolk, England

Summary: Juliette Delahousse is the daughter of an English mother and a French soldier father. She is sent to England to marry a man she has never met. There she is suspected for her French blood and must endure life in a house full of eerie secrets.

Historical Accuracy: The period elements are somewhat stronger here, but the prime interest is suspense.

4838 *Prima Donna at Large*

Date of Publication: 1985
Subject(s): Mystery; Opera; Theatrical Life

Historical character(s): Enrico Caruso, Singer (opera); Geraldine Farrar, Singer (opera)
Time Period(s): 1910s (1915)
Locale(s): New York, New York

Summary: When someone replaces the baritone's throat spray with ammonia during a performance at the Metropolitan Opera House, Enrico Caruso is ready to mount an investigation. He is forced to recruit the famous soprano Geraldine Farrar to lead the investigation which she does with typical prima donna aplomb.

Historical Accuracy: The novel is delightfully witty and informed both as to New York and the opera scene of the period.

4839 *To Love a Stranger*

Date of Publication: 1978
Subject(s): Romance; Victorian Period
Fictional character(s): Beth Stewart, Orphan, Artist
Time Period(s): 1870s (1870)
Locale(s): Norway

Summary: Beth Stewart is a Scottish orphan whose books of wild flower illustrations allow her to journey to her mother's Norwegian birthplace. There she finds both danger and romance, as well as the attraction of the haunting landscape.

Historical Accuracy: The novel captures the Norwegian scene convincingly.

CHARLOTTE PAUL (1916-1989)

Born in Seattle, Washington, journalist and author Charlotte Paul attended Wellesley College and began her career in 1940 as an assistant foreign news editor for the *Chicago Times*. She later worked as an editorial assistant with the Esquire Corporation. Drawing on her experiences as a mother, writer, and co-owner of a small newspaper, Paul wrote the bestselling nonfiction book *Minding Your Own Business* and its sequel, *And Four to Grow*. Her novels include the bestselling *Phoenix Island* and *A Child Is Missing*.

4840 *The Cup of Strength*

Date of Publication: 1958
Subject(s): Lumber Industry; American West
Fictional character(s): Merrie Cowen, Spouse; Jim Cowen, Spouse
Time Period(s): 1890s
Locale(s): Snoqualmie Valley, Washington

Summary: Merrie Cowen, pregnant and dependent on the kindness of others, arrives in a primitive Snoqualmie Valley logging camp in search of her feckless husband. The novel offers a convincing look at the region and the logging industry of the period and Merrie's attempts to work out her complicated marital relations.

Historical Accuracy: Although the story is fictional, incidents and characters are drawn from real life, and the atmosphere has been recreated faithfully.

4841 *Gold Mountain*

Date of Publication: 1953
Subject(s): American West
Fictional character(s): Katherine Duncan, Teacher
Time Period(s): 19th century
Locale(s): Snoqualmie Valley, Washington

Summary: In a small wilderness community near Seattle, a young schoolteacher, Katherine Duncan, attempts to convince the wilderness families of the value of education. The novel describes hop ranching and features the impact of a smallpox epidemic on the Indians.

Historical Accuracy: The novel's authentic background is provided by several eyewitness accounts that form the basis for its depiction of the community and its history.

LOUIS PAUL

4842 *Dara, the Cypriot*

Date of Publication: 1958
Subject(s): Ancient Israel; Biblical Story
Fictional character(s): Dara ben Kition, Wanderer
Historical character(s): Jezebel, Biblical Figure; Ahab, Biblical Figure; Elijah, Biblical Figure, Religious (prophet)
Time Period(s): 9th century B.C.
Locale(s): Cyprus; Mediterranean; Jerusalem, Israel

Summary: This tale of Dara ben Kition, wanderer and maker of charms, recounts his travels throughout the world of the eastern Mediterranean. He is an eyewitness to the struggles surrounding Jezebel, Ahab, and the prophet Elijah.

Historical Accuracy: The novel features a believable reconstruction of ancient life and its customs, particularly its religious rites.

RAYMOND PAUL (1940-)

An American born in New Jersey, Paul graduated from Princeton and Columbia universities. He has worked as a professor of English at Montclair State College. He is a collector of memorabilia of old murders—trials, transcripts, and broadsides—from 19th century America. He finds the material an excellent resource to illustrate the social history of the past.

4843 *The Thomas Street Horror*

Date of Publication: 1982
Subject(s): Mystery; Trials
Fictional character(s): Lon Quinncannon, Lawyer; Davy Cordor, Journalist (cub reporter)
Time Period(s): 1830s (1835-1836)
Locale(s): New York, New York

Summary: Helen Jewett, a notorious prostitute, is murdered in New York in the 1830s. This actual and unsolved case is given a careful reconstruction and an ingenious solution by Davy Cordor, a cub reporter for the New York *Sun* and Lon Quinncannon, rogue attorney, who defends the person charged with the crime.

Historical Accuracy: The facts of the case and the period are carefully detailed.

4844 *The Tragedy at Tinkerton: An Historical Novel of Murder*

Date of Publication: 1984
Subject(s): Mystery; Crime and Criminals; Trials
Fictional character(s): Lon Quinncannon, Lawyer; Christy Randolph, Companion
Historical character(s): Ephraim Avery, Religious (minister); Sarah Maria Cornell, Worker (mill)
Time Period(s): 1830s (1832)
Locale(s): New York, New York; Hoboken, New Jersey; Fall River, Massachusetts

Summary: A note alerts authorities that Sarah Cornell's death was no suicide and points to the Reverand Avery, who is charged with her murder, the first minister in American history to face the charge. Quinncannon defends him, convinced that he did not commit the deed.

Historical Accuracy: The facts of this case are based on documented evidence of the actual case.

BARBARA ANNE PAULEY (1925-)

Born in Nashville, Tennessee, Pauley moved east where her father published movie magazines. She attended Wellesley College and started writing when her husband was attending Harvard Medical School.

4845 *Blood Kin*

Date of Publication: 1972
Subject(s): Civil War—U.S.; Suspense
Fictional character(s): Lesley Hallam, Teenager
Time Period(s): 1860s (1864)
Locale(s): Nashville, Tennessee

Summary: This romantic suspense novel is set in Tennessee during the Civil War. Eighteen-year-old Lesley Hallam visits her cousins, the Farringtons, at their plantation, Sycamore Knob, where she must contend with family pressures and intrigue as Union and Confederate soldiers clash all around them.

Historical Accuracy: The period and regional elements are convincing.

DIANA L. PAXSON

Born in California and educated at Mills College and the University of California, Berkley, Paxson is a specialist in the medieval period. She founded the Society for Creative Anachronism, an organization dedicated to recreating medieval arts and activities. Her work includes historical, contemporary, and futuristic novels.

4846 *The Serpent's Tooth*

Date of Publication: 1991
Subject(s): Celtic Britain; Iron Age

Fictional character(s): Leir Blatonikos, Chieftain (Celtic); Gunarduilla, Royalty (princess); Rigana, Royalty (princess); Cridilla, Royalty (princess)
Time Period(s): 5th century B.C.
Locale(s): England

Summary: The story of Shakespeare's King Lear is retold placed in the historical context of early Iron Age Britain. The Celtic chieftain Leir Blatonikos conquers three kingdoms and fathers a daughter on a woman from each—Gunarduilla, Rigana, and Cridilla. The story traces the cultural collision that is played out on the family and political level in a tale of loyalty and betrayal when he hands over his power to his daughters.

Historical Accuracy: The atmosphere of Iron Age Britain is authentic and convincing.

4847 *The White Raven*

Date of Publication: 1988
Subject(s): Myths and Legends; Dark Ages
Fictional character(s): Tristan, Knight (aka Drustan); Isolde, Royalty (aka Esseilte); Mark, Ruler (aka Marc'h); Branwen, Servant (handmaiden)
Time Period(s): 6th century
Locale(s): England; Ireland

Summary: The novel attempts to place the Tristan and Iseult legend in the context of the history of the 6th century. Marc'h is one of King Arthur's direct descendants, an aging king of the Britons who is betrayed by Drustan (Tristan) his most trusted knight with Esseilte (Isolde). The novel chronicles this ill-fated love story, but also captures the atmosphere of 6th-century Britain.

Historical Accuracy: The story is legendary, but the atmosphere is plausible and realistically described.

4848 *The Wolf and the Raven*

Date of Publication: 1993
Subject(s): Dark Ages; Myths and Legends; Fantasy
Fictional character(s): Brunahild, Royalty, Warrior; Sigfrid, Mythical Creature (shapechanger), Warrior
Time Period(s): 5th century
Locale(s): Europe

Summary: The novel offers a retelling of the early adventures of Sigfrid and Brunahild, the heroes of the Germanic *Nibelungenleid*. Set in a 5th century Europe ravaged by tribal warfare, the novel describes Brunahild, a Hun princess and Sigfrid, who comes from a race of shapechangers. While Sigfrid becomes a smith's apprentice and warrior-in-training, Brunahild is raised by a group of witches and instructed in the ways of sorcery. They come together as future leaders of their people.

Historical Accuracy: The novel is true to its mythical and legendary basis, with a convincing depiction of 5th century Germany.

ROBERT PAYNE (1911-1983)

Payne was born in Cornwall and educated at St. Paul's School, the University of Capetown, the University of

London, the University of Liverpool, and the Sorbonne. He worked as a tax inspector, a shipwright, a London *Times* correspondent during the Spanish Civil War, and an English professor. Payne conspired to assassinate Hitler during the occupation of Vienna. He began his writing career as a poet but established his reputation as the author of popular biographies of Karl Marx, Charlie Chaplin, Greta Garbo, Adolph Hitler, and others. His novels, including *Forever China* and *The Palace of Peking* focus on East/West relations.

4849 *Alexander the God*

Date of Publication: 1954
Subject(s): Macedonian Empire; Biography, Fictionalized; Ancient Greece
Historical character(s): Alexander the Great, Ruler (King of Macedon); Thaissa, Royalty (queen consort of Alexander); Darius, Ruler (King of Persia)
Time Period(s): 4th century B.C.
Locale(s): Greece; Persia

Summary: This biographical novel tells the story of Alexander the Great, from his conquest of Tarsus to his death in Babylon. Besides offering vivid depictions of the battles of Issus and Arbela, the burning of Persepolis, and Alexander's march through the desert, the novel also offers the romantic story of the Athenian flute girl, Thaissa, whom Alexander elevates to the position of his mistress-queen.

Historical Accuracy: The novel brings to vivid and believable life the era and the many personalities in Alexander's overpowering wake.

4850 *Blood Royal*

Date of Publication: 1952
Subject(s): Mogul Empire
Fictional character(s): Stephen Taverner, Gentleman
Historical character(s): Shah Jehan, Ruler (Mogul emperor)
Time Period(s): 17th century
Locale(s): India

Summary: Continuing the story begun in *The Young Emperor*, the novel chronicles the decline of Mogul emperor Shah Jehan's reign and the scramble for succession to his throne. Englishman Stephen Taverner, who has settled in India and married a Persian princess, narrates the tale.

Historical Accuracy: This exotic tale is given an authentic period atmosphere.

4851 *Caravaggio*

Date of Publication: 1968
Subject(s): Renaissance; Artistic Life; Biography, Fictionalized
Historical character(s): Michelangelo da Caravaggio, Artist
Time Period(s): 16th century
Locale(s): Rome, Italy

Summary: The short, intense life of Italian painter Caravaggio is depicted in this biographical novel that traces the effects of Caravaggio's genius in 16th-century Rome. He is very much a creature of his times, enjoying and enduring a series of patrons, lovers, and intrigues until, after accidentally killing a young nobleman, he is forced to flee to Malta where he dies at age 36.

Historical Accuracy: The essential details of Caravaggio's life are captured faithfully.

4852 *The Chieftain: A Story of the Nez Perce People*

Date of Publication: 1953
Subject(s): American West; Indians
Historical character(s): Chief Joseph, Indian (Nez Perce), Chieftain
Time Period(s): 1870s (1877)
Locale(s): United States

Summary: The author dramatizes the heroic and ultimately tragic story of the Nez Perce Indians' attempt to reach safety in Canada. Chief Joseph manages a masterful 1,000-mile journey until his tribe is stopped only thirty miles short of the Canadian border by U.S. troops.

Historical Accuracy: This account of the Nez Perce odyssey and military engagements stays close to the facts.

4853 *A House in Peking*

Date of Publication: 1956
Subject(s): Chinese Empire; Royalty—China
Fictional character(s): Red Jade, Slave (concubine); Lien, Royalty (prince)
Historical character(s): Ch'ien Lung, Ruler (Chinese emperor)
Time Period(s): 18th century
Locale(s): China

Summary: This story of Imperial China at the end of Manchu Emperor Ch'ien Lung's reign takes the reader inside the court. It follows the tragic consequences of a love affair between Prince Lien, whom the emperor picks as his successor, and the concubine Red Jade.

Historical Accuracy: The novel is convincing in its presentation of the imperial court and its customs.

4854 *The Lord Jesus*

Date of Publication: 1964
Subject(s): Biblical Story
Historical character(s): Jesus Christ, Biblical Figure
Time Period(s): 1st century
Locale(s): Israel

Summary: The novel describes the life of Jesus from the time of the calling of his first disciples to his final parting from them after his crucifixion. The emphasis is on Jesus the man, conscious of both his responsibility and his doubts about his strength and faith.

Historical Accuracy: The novel stays close to the Biblical sources, amplified by a convincing depiction of the era.

4855 *The Shepherd*

Date of Publication: 1959

Subject(s): Biblical Story; Roman Empire
Historical character(s): Yeshua, Biblical Figure; Joseph, Biblical Figure; Mary, Biblical Figure; Yona, Biblical Figure
Time Period(s): 1st century
Locale(s): Nazareth, Israel

Summary: The novel offers a fictional reconstruction of the hidden years in the life of Jesus from his childhood as the son of the carpenter Joseph to the time of his baptism and the beginning of his ministry. The emphasis is on telling a realistic story of the growth of a young Jewish prophet during the ferment of the Roman occupation of Judea.

Historical Accuracy: The sources for the story include Eastern tradition, the Talmud, early Christian tradition, and the Dead Sea Scrolls.

4856   *The Yellow Robe: A Novel of the Life of Buddha*

Date of Publication: 1948
Subject(s): Biography, Fictionalized; Religious Life
Historical character(s): Siddhartha Gautama, Religious, Philosopher
Time Period(s): 6th century B.C.; 5th century B.C.
Locale(s): India

Summary: This novel is a fictional account of the life of the founder of Buddhism. Siddhartha Gautama forsakes his life as a prince to become an ascetic pilgrim and preacher in search of enlightenment.

Historical Accuracy: Much of Buddha's life is surrounded by legend. The novel is a blend of fact and legend that creates a colorful, if at times overly reverential, portrait.

4857   *The Young Emperor*

Date of Publication: 1960
Subject(s): Indian Empire; Mogul Empire
Fictional character(s): Stephen Taverner, Adventurer
Historical character(s): Shah Jehan, Ruler (Indian emperor)
Time Period(s): 17th century
Locale(s): India

Summary: The rise to power of Prince Shah Jehan in 17th century India is depicted through the experiences of Englishman Stephen Taverner, who journeys to Hindustan to make his fortune as an armourer in the service of the prince. As war breaks out between the prince and his enemies, Taverner becomes one of the prince's trusted officers and is on hand when he becomes emperor and lays plans for the construction of the Taj Mahal.

Historical Accuracy: The framework of the story is accurate, though most of the actual events are invented.

ROBERTO PAZZI (1946-)

Italian poet and novelist Pazzi has published several collections of poetry, including *Calm of Wind* and the novels *The Princess and the Dragon* and *The Illness of Time*. Pazzi is also a literary critic and editor of the magazine *Sinopia*.

4858   *Searching for the Emperor*

Date of Publication: 1988
Subject(s): Russian Revolution; Royalty—Russia
Fictional character(s): Prince Ypsilanti, Royalty, Military Personnel (army commander)
Historical character(s): Nicholas II, Ruler (Czar of Russia); Alexandra Feodorovna, Royalty (consort of Nicholas II)
Time Period(s): 1910s (1918)
Locale(s): Siberia, Russia

Summary: The novel recreates the final days of the Romanov family. As Czar Nicholas and his family are held captive in Siberia, Prince Ypsilanti, commander of the Czar's regiment, sets off to try and rescue them. Against impossible obstacles, Ypsilanti watches his regiment dissolve, and Nicholas and his family alternate between hope for rescue and despair.

Historical Accuracy: The novel's story is fanciful, but it does capture the atmosphere of the period effectively.

MAX PEACOCK

4859   *The King's Rogue*

Date of Publication: 1947
Subject(s): Restoration Period; Crime and Criminals
Fictional character(s): Christopher Hallam, Young Man
Historical character(s): Thomas Blood, Outlaw; Charles II, Ruler (King of England)
Time Period(s): 17th century
Locale(s): England

Summary: This picaresque tale set during the reign of Charles II tells the story of the outlaw Thomas Blood, an Irishman who is deprived of his estate and vows vengeance on the king. Blood attempts to steal the crown jewels in a rollicking tale of attractive villainy.

Historical Accuracy: The novel blends the actual and the fanciful with the aura of romance predominating.

MARY E. PEARCE (1932-)

An English author born in London, Pearce has been widely praised for her careful depiction of rural English life.

4860   *Apple Tree Lean Down*

Date of Publication: 1876
Subject(s): Family Saga; Rural Life—England; Victorian Period
Fictional character(s): Beth Tewke, Young Woman; Jack Mercybright, Farmer
Time Period(s): 19th century; 20th century (1886-1920)
Locale(s): England

Summary: This family chronicle set in rural England follows several families from the 1880s to the 1920s. Beth Tewke grows to womanhood while Jack Mercybright works to reclaim the land on a neglected farm. Beth's hard-working ethic is challenged by the events of World War I.

Historical Accuracy: The details of rural life of the period are convincingly captured.

`4861` *Cast a Long Shadow*

Date of Publication: 1977
Subject(s): Victorian Period
Fictional character(s): Ellen Wainwright, Spouse (of Lancy); Richard Lancy, Businessman (miller)
Time Period(s): 1870s
Locale(s): England

Summary: A troubled Victorian marriage is dramatized in the relationship of Ellen Wainwright to Richard Lancy, a skilled miller and grain dealer. Richard's attitude about money produces domestic problems as Ellen and their young son struggle to deal with Richard's increasing eccentricities.

Historical Accuracy: The details of rural life of the period are effectively presented.

`4862` *The Land Endures*

Date of Publication: 1978
Subject(s): Rural Life—England; Depression Era
Fictional character(s): Stephen Wayman, Lawyer, Farmer; Betony Izzard, Teacher; Gwen Wayman, Spouse
Time Period(s): 1920s
Locale(s): England

Summary: The sequel to *Apple Tree Lean Down* tells the story of Stephen Wayman who leaves his law practice and moves with his wife and children to Holland Farm. There they struggle to run a small farm through the Depression.

Historical Accuracy: The period details are authentic.

`4863` *Polsinney Harbour*

Date of Publication: 1983
Subject(s): Victorian Period
Fictional character(s): Maggie Care, Young Woman; Brice Tallack, Fisherman; Gus Tallack, Fisherman
Time Period(s): 1860s (1869)
Locale(s): Cornwall, England

Summary: Stranger Maggie Care is slowly accepted by the people of a Cornish village until a sudden revelation from her past destroys Maggie's hopes and severs her relationship with her new-found friends. Help comes from an unexpected source.

Historical Accuracy: The Cornish scenes are convincing.

`4864` *Seedtime and Harvest*

Date of Publication: 1982
Subject(s): Rural Life—England; World War II
Fictional character(s): Linn Mercybright, Spouse; Charlie Truscott, Farmer
Time Period(s): 1930s; 1940s
Locale(s): England

Summary: In the sequel to the Mercybright story of *Apple Tree Lean Down*, the author concludes her chronicle of English family life from the 1880s to the Second World War. Linn Mercybright's marriage to farmer Charlie Truscott dramatizes the challenge of family life during wartime.

Historical Accuracy: The novel excels in presenting the period and its challenges.

`4865` *The Two Farms*

Date of Publication: 1985
Subject(s): Rural Life—England; Victorian Period
Fictional character(s): John Sutton, Farmer; Morris Riddler, Farmer; Jim, Child, Worker
Time Period(s): 1840s
Locale(s): Gloucestershire, England

Summary: This tale of two adjoining farms is set in Gloucestershire during the 1840s. John Sutton's farm is a thriving one, while Morris Riddler's farm struggles to produce a meager crop. When a wandering urchin, Jim, arrives to work for the Suttons, a disagreement sends him to help Riddler run his failing farm.

Historical Accuracy: The details of rural life of the period are convincing.

MICHAEL PEARCE (1931-)

Pearce is the author of the successful series featuring the adventures and investigations of Gareth Owen, the head of the secret police in British-ruled Cairo at the turn of the century.

`4866` *The Mamur Zapt and the Donkey-Vous*

Date of Publication: 1990
Subject(s): Mystery; Edwardian Period
Fictional character(s): Captain Cadwallader Owen, Government Official
Time Period(s): 1900s (1908)
Locale(s): Cairo, Egypt

Summary: Set in Egypt under British rule in the 1900s, the novel continues the investigations of the Mamur Zapt, Captain Cadwallader Owen, who is responsible for law and order in Cairo. When two tourists disappear from the terrace of Shepheard's Hotel, Owen investigates. Is this a political act to embarass the British and why the sudden interest of the royal Khedive?.

Historical Accuracy: The period is captured with authority.

`4867` *The Mamur Zapt and the Girl in the Nile*

Date of Publication: 1992
Subject(s): Mystery; Edwardian Period
Fictional character(s): Captain Cadwallader Owen, Government Official; Narouz, Royalty (prince)
Time Period(s): 1900s
Locale(s): Cairo, Egypt

Summary: When a young girl is found drowned in the Nile, a series of perplexing questions must be answered by Cadwallader Owen, the Mamur Zapt, or head of British-ruled Cairo's secret police. Who is the girl and what was she doing aboard a boat hired by Prince Narouz, son of the Khedive, ruler of Egypt? Owen's search takes him across Edwardian Egypt.

Historical Accuracy: The period elements in the story are authentic.

4868 The Mamur Zapt and the Men Behind

Date of Publication: 1991
Subject(s): Mystery; Edwardian Period
Fictional character(s): Captain Cadwallader Owen, Government Official
Time Period(s): 1900s (1909)
Locale(s): Cairo, Egypt

Summary: In 1909 Cairo is shocked by a series of attacks on British and Egyptian civil servants by a group of shadowy men in European dress. Cadwallader Owen, the Mamur Zapt, or head of Cairo's secret police, is determined to uncover the truth.

Historical Accuracy: The story is fanciful, but the atmosphere of Edwardian Egypt is authentic and believable.

4869 The Mamur Zapt and the Night of the Dog

Date of Publication: 1989
Subject(s): Mystery; Edwardian Period; Religious Conflict
Fictional character(s): Captain Cadwallader Owen, Government Official; Jane Postlewaite, Gentlewoman; Mahmoud, Lawyer
Time Period(s): 1900s
Locale(s): Cairo, Egypt

Summary: When a dead dog is found in a Coptic tomb, a Muslim insult, Cairo's Mamur Zapt, head of the political CID during British rule, finds himself responsible for preventing religious warfare. Things get worse when Captain Owen, while escorting Jane Postlewaite, niece of a visiting M.P., to see dancing dervishes, sees one of them stabbed to death. Owen must solve the murder soon or risk a catastrophe and his own career.

Historical Accuracy: The period background of Egypt under the British is authentic.

4870 The Mamur Zapt and the Return of the Carpet

Date of Publication: 1988
Subject(s): Mystery; Edwardian Period
Fictional character(s): Captain Cadwallader Owen, Government Official; Mahmoud el Zaki, Lawyer
Time Period(s): 1900s (1908)
Locale(s): Cairo, Egypt

Summary: In the first in a series of investigations by the head of Cairo's secret police, the Mamur Zapt, Cadwallader Owen, terrorists threaten the city as it prepares for its principal religious festival, the return of the Holy Carpet from Mecca.

Historical Accuracy: The author has stayed close to fact and depicted Cairo much as it was in 1908. The position of Mamur

Zapt really existed although the character in this book is invented.

4871 The Mamur Zapt and the Spoils of Egypt

Date of Publication: 1992
Subject(s): Mystery; Edwardian Period
Fictional character(s): Owen Cadwallader, Government Official (head of secret police); Miss Skinner, Gentlewoman
Time Period(s): 1900s (1908)
Locale(s): Cairo, Egypt

Summary: Owen Cadwallader, the head of British-ruled Cairo's secret police, is charged with protecting Miss Skinner, whose uncle might be the next president of the United States. Miss Skinner is on a mission to keep Egypt's antiquities in Egypt, and as Cadwallader trails after her from one excavation site to another, he encounters a series of baffling deaths.

Historical Accuracy: The novel is exact and convincing in capturing the period atmosphere of British Egypt.

RICHARD PEARCE (1909-)

An American born in Oklahoma, Pearce graduated from the University of Oklahoma and worked in Oklahoma City as a newspaper reporter and in San Francisco as the editor for the editorial page of the *San Francisco Examiner*.

4872 The Impudent Rifle

Date of Publication: 1951
Subject(s): Settlement of the American Frontier; Indians
Fictional character(s): Philip Royall, Military Personnel (lieutenant)
Time Period(s): 1830s
Locale(s): Arkansas

Summary: This novel describes frontier life in the Arkansas territory during the 1830s. The story centers on the experiences of a young West Pointer, Philip Royall, who battles corrupt Indian agents.

Historical Accuracy: Although the historical background is authentic, the presentation is more melodramatic than realistic.

4873 The Restless Border

Date of Publication: 1953
Subject(s): Texas Revolution; Indians
Fictional character(s): Alexander Prince, Military Personnel (captain)
Time Period(s): 1830s (1839)
Locale(s): Red River, Texas

Summary: Warfare against the Mexican forces of Santa Ana and the Commanches is described in this story set along the Red River in 1839. The central character is Alexander Prince, captain of a squadron assigned to protect the border.

Historical Accuracy: This is an authentic treatment of the period and the region.

ROBERT BRAINARD PEARSALL (1920-)

An American scholar and author, Pearsall has worked as a professor of English at several colleges and universities. He is the author of biographies and literary studies of Robert Browning, Frank Harris, Rupert Brooke, and Ernest Hemingway.

4874 *Young Vargas Lewis*

Date of Publication: 1968
Subject(s): Paraguayan War
Fictional character(s): Vargas Lewis, Engineer, Military Personnel (captain); Ella Lynch, Young Woman; Cedric Templeton, Military Personnel (colonel), Businessman
Historical character(s): Francisco Lopez, Military Personnel, Political Figure (Paraguayan dictator)
Time Period(s): 1860s (1865)
Locale(s): Buenos Aires, Argentina; Paraguay; Rio Plata, South America

Summary: During the American Civil War, army captain Vargas Lewis escapes the fighting to make his fortune as an engineer in South America. Instead he finds himself in the bloody Paraguayan War, the so-called War of the Triple Alliance, in which Paraguayan dictator Francisco Lopez challenged and fought the combined powers of Argentina, Brazil, and Uruguay in a war that almost destroyed Paraguay.

Historical Accuracy: The basic details of the period are captured faithfully.

DIANE PEARSON

(PSEUD. OF DIANE MCCLELLAND, 1931-)

A book editor in London, Pearson has worked as a senior editor for Transworld Publishers and in the production department of Jonathan Cape, Ltd. Her books include *Bride of Tancred*, *The Marigold Field*, and *Voices of Summer*.

4875 *Csardas*

Date of Publication: 1975
Subject(s): Family Saga; World War I; Austro-Hungarian Empire
Fictional character(s): Malie Ferenc, Young Woman; Eva Ferenc, Young Woman
Time Period(s): 20th century (1910s-1940s)
Locale(s): Hungary

Summary: This family saga of the Ferencs in the crumbling world of the Austro-Hungarian Empire follows the experiences of Malie and Eva Ferenc and their relatives through the calamitous history of the 20th century. The family is scattered and struggles to survive two World Wars and the emerging communist regime.

Historical Accuracy: The pressure of history on the family is captured with skill and believability.

4876 *The Marigold Field*

Date of Publication: 1969
Subject(s): Victorian Period; Boer War; Family saga

Fictional character(s): Anne-Louise Pritchard, Servant; Jonathan Whitman, Worker
Time Period(s): 1890s; 1900s
Locale(s): Kent, England; London, England; South Africa

Summary: A housemaid in a Kentish rectory, Anne-Louise Pritchard, loves Jonathan Whitman, an estate worker. He marries another, and, after service in the Boer War, returns to find his wife dead. Anne-Louise maneuvers him into marriage, with serious consequences.

Historical Accuracy: The attempt to paint a realistic portrait of period life is too often disrupted by a penchant for the melodramatic and the sentimental.

4877 *The Summer of the Bashinskeys*

Date of Publication: 1984
Subject(s): Edwardian Period; World War I; Russian Revolution
Fictional character(s): Sophie Willoughby, Gentlewoman; Galina Bashinskey, Young Woman; Edwin Willoughby, Gentleman
Time Period(s): 1900s; 1910s (1902-1919)
Locale(s): Kent, England; Moscow, Russia; St. Petersburg, Russia

Summary: The summer of the title is 1902, which is marked by the end of the Boer War and the coronation of Edward VII. It is a summer of repose before sweeping changes arrive. For the Willoughby family in Kent, England, the arrival of the Bashinskeys from Russia will introduce those dangers that are followed through war and revolution in England and Russia.

Historical Accuracy: The period elements are captured authentically.

JOHN PEARSON (1930-)

An English historian, novelist, and biographer, Pearson worked for the London *Times* as a staff reporter, columnist, and feature writer. He has also worked as a script writer for the B.B.C. and is the author of *The Life of Ian Fleming* and *Edward the Rake*. His most recent work has concentrated on the British royal family.

4878 *The Bellamy Saga*

Date of Publication: 1976
Subject(s): Family Saga; Edwardian Period; World War I
Fictional character(s): Richard Bellamy, Gentleman, Political Figure (M.P.); Lady Marjorie Bellamy, Noblewoman; James Bellamy, Military Personnel (officer), Gentleman
Time Period(s): 19th century; 20th century (1884-1929)
Locale(s): London, England

Summary: The Upstairs story popularized in the TV series "Upstairs, Downstairs," is described in biographical form. The family history of the Bellamys is traced from 1884 to 1929 showing Richard Bellamy's rise from a minor parliamentary figure to a minister and confidante of the Prince of Wales. This version adds much to the story that the series overlooked.

Historical Accuracy: This version depends on a carefully constructed sense of the period.

MICHAEL PEARSON

Pearson is an English author whose father-in-law was the third member of the family to direct Harrod's in London for an uninterrupted period of 68 years from 1891-1959. He is the author of nonfiction works, including *Those Damned Rebels*, a controversial British view of the American Revolution.

4879　*The Store*

Date of Publication: 1981
Subject(s): Victorian Period; Business Building; Edwardian Period
Fictional character(s): Thomas Kingston, Businessman
Time Period(s): 19th century; 20th century (1869-1915)

Summary: The novel describes the founding of a great merchantile dynasty as Thomas Kingston, a former draper's assistant, opens a store which grows into a vast business empire. A microcosm of Britain's larger empire, Kingston's experiences reflect many of the great events of the 19th and early 20th century—the Boer War, the women's suffrage movement, and World War I.

Historical Accuracy: History is effectively captured in this family and business story.

DONALD CULROSS PEATTIE
(1898-1964)

An American novelist born in Chicago and a graduate of Harvard, Peattie worked as a nature writer and as a botanist for the U.S. Department of Agriculture. Author of nature columns for the *Washington Evening Star* and the *Chicago Daily News*, Peattie's most successful book was *An Almanac for Moderns*, which attempted to combine his interest in poetry with scientific fact. He published an autobiography, *The Road of a Naturalist*.

4880　*Forward the Nation*

Date of Publication: 1942
Subject(s): Lewis and Clark Expedition; Exploration
Historical character(s): Sacajawea, Indian (Shoshone), Guide; Meriwether Lewis, Explorer; William Clark, Explorer; Toussaint Charbonneau, Frontiersman
Time Period(s): 1800s (1805)
Locale(s): Missouri River, United States; Rocky Mountains; Pacific Northwest

Summary: The novel offers the story of Lewis and Clark's expedition up the Missouri and across the Rockies to the Pacific with the invaluable assistance of the Shoshone Indian guide Sacagawea. This is a lyrical rather than a documentary account with an emphasis on heroism rather than on realism.

Historical Accuracy: Based on fact, the novel is most convincing in its natural descriptions. The dialogue is at times stilted.

4881　*Up Country: A Story of the Vanguard*

Date of Publication: 1928
Subject(s): American Colonies; Settlement of the American Frontier; American Revolution
Fictional character(s): Brandon Calverly, Plantation Owner
Time Period(s): 18th century
Locale(s): Charleston, South Carolina

Summary: Englishman Brandon Calverly builds a plantation in South Carolina. Disappointed with the social scene and his wife's flirtatiousness, he sells out and heads west into the frontier. The effects of the American Revolution on Calverly's attempts at homesteading are dramatized.

Historical Accuracy: The novel presents a plausible look at frontier life during the period.

RICHARD PECK (1934-)

Born in Illinois, Peck started writing while posted at an army base in Germany and has continued as a journalist, novelist, and educator. He writes regularly on architecture and travel for the *New York Times* and his poetry has appeared in the *Saturday Review*.

4882　*Amanda/Miranda*

Date of Publication: 1980
Subject(s): Edwardian Period; Servants
Fictional character(s): Mary Cooke, Servant; Amanda Whitehall, Gentlewoman
Time Period(s): 1900s (1911-1912)
Locale(s): Wight, England

Summary: Young Mary Cooke takes a position in Amanda Whitehall's household where she is rechristened "Miranda" and functions as a kind of double for the manipulative Amanda. The novel is a psychological thriller set in the upstairs/downstairs world of the fading Edwardian period.

Historical Accuracy: The era and the atmosphere are captured effectively.

4883　*The Family of Women*

Date of Publication: 1983
Subject(s): Earthquakes; Victorian Period; World War I
Fictional character(s): Lena Wheatley, Settler; Eve Freeman, Actress; Constance Nichols, Gentlewoman
Time Period(s): 19th century; 20th century (1850s-1939)
Locale(s): Virginia City, Nevada; London, England; San Francisco, California

Summary: Moving from London to San Francisco and various points in between, the novel offers a panoramic story of a group of women whose lives span the period from the 1850s through two World Wars. Lena Wheatley begins the story on a wagon train west. Eve, the next narrator, becomes a celebrated actress. Subsequent descendants take the story into the 20th century.

Historical Accuracy: The novel's various historical eras are captured convincingly.

ROBERT NEWTON PECK (1928-)

An American born in Vermont, Peck joined the 88th Infantry Division at age 17 during World War II. After the war, he attended Rollins College. Peck is the author of the bestselling *A Day No Pigs Would Die*. His special interest is the history of Fort Ticonderoga and the American Revolution. Peck sings in a barbershop quartet and plays ragtime piano.

4884 *Eagle Fur*

Date of Publication: 1978
Subject(s): French and Indian War; American Colonies
Fictional character(s): Abbott Coe, Servant (indentured); Skinner Benet, Trader (fur); Owen McKee, Military Personnel (English soldier)
Time Period(s): 1750s (1754)
Locale(s): Albany, New York, American Colonies

Summary: It is 1754, and the French and Indian War has begun as young Abbott Coe arrives in Fort Albany, the indentured servant of fur trader and Hudson Bay Company representative Skinner Benet. Benet teaches Coe how to survive in the wilderness, and in a trading expedition deep upriver, Coe comes of age.

Historical Accuracy: The details of wilderness life of the period are convincing.

4885 *Fawn*

Date of Publication: 1978
Subject(s): French and Indian War; Indians
Fictional character(s): Fawn, Indian (Mohawk)
Historical character(s): Benedict Arnold, Military Personnel (soldier)
Time Period(s): 1750s (1758)
Locale(s): Fort Ticonderoga, New York, American Colonies

Summary: The attack on Fort Ticonderoga in 1758 during the French and Indian War forms the novel's background which accurately relates the assault by British forces and their Mohawk allies from the perspective of Fawn, the son of a French Jesuit and the grandson of a fierce Mohawk warrior. Fawn is the ultimate outsider, in the midst of battle between two hostile forces for control of the country that neither could rightfully claim.

Historical Accuracy: The details of the military action are faithfully depicted.

4886 *Hang for Treason*

Date of Publication: 1976
Subject(s): American Revolution
Fictional character(s): Abel Booker, Military Personnel (soldier); Mary Comfort, Young Woman
Historical character(s): Ethan Allen, Patriot, Military Personnel
Time Period(s): 1740s (1745); 1770s (1775)
Locale(s): Vermont, American Colonies; Fort Ticonderoga, New York, American Colonies

Summary: Ethan Allen's Green Mountain Boys and the capture of Fort Ticonderoga form the historical background for this story of an American family split by divided loyalties during the American Revolution. The novel centers on the maturation of young Abel Booker who is transformed by his experiences into adulthood.

Historical Accuracy: The background of events are historical and accurately depicted.

4887 *The Horse Hunters*

Date of Publication: 1988
Subject(s): Horses
Fictional character(s): Ladd Bodeen, Teenager
Time Period(s): 1930s (1932)
Locale(s): Florida

Summary: Young Ladd Bodeen sets out alone on a 100-mile trek to bring back a near-legendary white stallion and a herd of wild mares to earn his brother's respect and to save the Buckle Tee Ranch. The adventure tests Ladd's resolve and provides a maturing test for the teenager.

Historical Accuracy: The setting is authentic.

4888 *The King's Iron*

Date of Publication: 1977
Subject(s): American Revolution
Fictional character(s): Cotton Wilty, Military Personnel (soldier)
Historical character(s): Henry Knox, Military Personnel (colonel); George Washington, Military Personnel (army commander)
Time Period(s): 1770s (1775)
Locale(s): New York, American Colonies; Massachusetts, American Colonies

Summary: To defend Boston during the American Revolution, General Washington needs artillery, and the captured cannon at Fort Ticonderoga in New York will supply the need. The novel dramatizes the actual struggle to transport 60 tons of cannon across Massachusetts by Colonel Henry Knox and a group of settlers.

Historical Accuracy: The circumstances are based on fact; the particulars are largely invented.

SAMUEL ANTHONY PEEPLES (1917-)

4889 *The Dream Ends in Fury*

Date of Publication: 1949
Subject(s): American West; Crime and Criminals; Gold Rush—California
Historical character(s): Joaquin Murieta, Outlaw
Time Period(s): 1840s
Locale(s): California

Summary: Based on the Mexican bandit Joaquin Murieta during gold rush days, the novel chronicles his search for revenge. When his brother and wife are murdered, Murieta embarks on a life of crime and violence.

Historical Accuracy: The novel captures its period and the essential facts about Murrietta's life, though his story is imaginatively embellished.

MARIO PEI (1901-1978)

An Italian-born academic and scholar, Pei was born in Rome and came to the United States in 1908. He became a U.S. citizen in 1925. A professor at Columbia University, Pei devoted his career to the study of linguistics. Pei spoke four languages fluently, was competent in twelve others, and could understand thirty more. A champion of the cause of a universal language, Pei's *The Story of Language* is considered by many as one of the best introductions to linguistic studies. Pei also wrote novels and books on world politics.

4890 *Swords of Anjou*

Date of Publication: 1953
Subject(s): Myths and Legends; Middle Ages
Fictional character(s): Thierry of Anjou, Knight; Roland, Knight
Time Period(s): 8th century
Locale(s): Spain

Summary: This medieval tale set during the conflict with the Moors in Spain is based on the *Song of Roland* and other *chansons de geste*. The story centers on young Thierry of Anjou, a follower of Roland, and records his heroism against great odds and challenges.

Historical Accuracy: The novel is based not on history but on the legendary tales of many writers who have previously elaborated the Roland legends. The author has duplicated some of their inaccuracies and anachronisms to recapture the spirit of the medieval *chansons de geste*.

SYLVIA PELL

Sylvia Pell is an English author who has worked in libraries and bookstores. She served as the Information Officer for the Booksellers Association.

4891 *The Shadow of the Sun*

Date of Publication: 1978
Subject(s): Royalty—France
Historical character(s): Louis XIV, Ruler (King of France); Maria Theresa, Royalty (queen consort of Louis XIV); Louise de La Valliere, Noblewoman, Lover; Francoise Athenais Rochechouart de Mortemart, Noblewoman, Lover; Francoise Scarrow, Gentlewoman, Governess
Time Period(s): 17th century (1660-1673)
Locale(s): France

Summary: The novel dramatizes court life under Louis XIV, the Sun King. Louis is shown in 1660 with his bride, the infanta Maria Theresa. The King's romantic interests are three other women: Louise de la Valliere, the cunning and deceitful Athenais de Montespan, and Francoise Scarrow, a governess to Louis' children, who becomes his principal

companion in his later years, The life of the French court is brought vividly to life.

Historical Accuracy: For the most part the events described are accurate and the atmopher convincing.

JUDITH PELLA

4892 *The Dawning of Deliverance*

Date of Publication: 1995
Subject(s): Russian Empire; Family Saga; Russo-Japanese War
Fictional character(s): Mariana Remizou, Noblewoman, Nurse; Daniel Trent, Journalist; Sergei Fedorcenko, Royalty (prince); Anna Fedorcenko, Spouse (of Sergei)
Historical character(s): Nicholas II, Ruler (Czar of Russia); Alexandra Feodorovna, Royalty (consort of Nicholas II); Vladimir Ilich Lenin, Revolutionary
Time Period(s): 1900s
Locale(s): St. Petersburg, Russia; Manchuria, China; Geneva, Switzerland

Summary: Set against a backdrop of the Russo-Japanese War, the novel continues the family saga of the Fedorcenkos and Remizous in pre-Revolutionary Russia. Mariana Remizou turns her back on the life of a high-society debutante to take up nursing on the military front. Revolutionary forces gain momentum, and violence threatens Mariana and her family.

Historical Accuracy: The family's story is set against an authentic period backdrop.

4893 *Heirs of the Motherland*

Date of Publication: 1993
Subject(s): Family Saga; Russian Empire
Fictional character(s): Dmitri Remizou, Nobleman (count); Mariana Remizou, Heiress—Lost; Anna Fedorcenko, Spouse (of Sergei); Sergei Fedorcenko, Royalty (prince)
Historical character(s): Nicholas II, Ruler (Czar of Russia); Alexandra Feodorovna, Royalty (consort of Nicholas II)
Time Period(s): 19th century; 20th century (1881-1900)
Locale(s): St. Petersburg, Russia; Katyk, Russia

Summary: The fourth volume of The Russians series takes up the story of Count Dmitri Remizou. He returns from exile to reclaim his daughter who has been raised as a peasant by Sergei and Anna Fedorcenko, who are hiding from the Russian government in Katyk.

Historical Accuracy: The period background is authentic and believable.

HUGH PENDEXTER (1875-1940)

A Teacher, journalist, and novelist, Pendexter was born in Massachusetts, but spent most of his life in Rochester, New York. He wrote many historical novels including *Harry Idaho*, *The Red Road*, *Red Belts*, and *A Virginia Scout*.

4894 *Harry Idaho*

Date of Publication: 1926

Subject(s): American West; Mormons
Fictional character(s): Harriet Idaho, Young Woman; Shoshoni Hale, Frontiersman
Time Period(s): 1860s
Locale(s): Idaho

Summary: Western adventure and the pursuit of a lost gold mine are featured in this novel depicting the "avenging angels," the Danite Sect of the Mormons who pursue the hero Shoshoni Hale and heroine Harriet "Harry" Idaho.

Historical Accuracy: This western adventure tale is filled with authentic details of pioneer life and facts of the period.

`4895` Kings of the Missouri

Date of Publication: 1921
Subject(s): Settlement of the American Frontier
Fictional character(s): Etienne Prevost, Trader (fur)
Historical character(s): Jim Bridger, Frontiersman; Jim Baker, Scout
Time Period(s): 1830s
Locale(s): St. Louis, Missouri; Missouri River, United States

Summary: The fur trade in Missouri during the 1830s is the focus for this novel that depicts the rivalry between the American Fur Company and the Rocky Mountain Fur Company. They compete in an epic fur-gathering expedition up the Missouri River.

Historical Accuracy: The novel captures with skill and authenticity the atmosphere of the times and the customs of the fur traders.

`4896` Old Misery

Date of Publication: 1924
Subject(s): Gold Rush—California; Indians
Fictional character(s): Old Misery, Mountain Man; Joseph Gilbert, Settler
Time Period(s): 1850s (1853)
Locale(s): California

Summary: California in the 1850s is the scene for this western adventure novel recording the exploits of a frontiersman named "Old Misery." His foil is the greenhorn Joseph Gilbert, and their experiences present a vivid portrait of the period including the gold rush's mining camps, outlaws, and Indian raids.

Historical Accuracy: The novel succeeds in rendering the period and characters in accurate historical terms.

`4897` Red Belts

Date of Publication: 1920
Subject(s): Settlement of the American Frontier
Historical character(s): John Sevier, Frontiersman, Political Figure
Time Period(s): 1780s
Locale(s): Tennessee

Summary: This novel tells of the struggle of the American settlers against Indians and renegades fighting on behalf of Spain. John Sevier is the principle figure, a pioneer whose daring and heroism help save the territory for the young Union.

Historical Accuracy: The basic situation of the period and region is accurately described.

`4898` The Red Road: A Romance of Braddock's Defeat

Date of Publication: 1927
Subject(s): French and Indian War
Fictional character(s): Black Brond, Scout
Historical character(s): Edward Braddock, Military Personnel (general); George Washington, Military Personnel (colonel)
Time Period(s): 1750s; 1760s (1754-1763)
Locale(s): Northwest Territory, United States

Summary: The story of General Braddock's defeat on the Menongahela during the French and Indian Wars is depicted here. In this romantic tale of adventure, English scout Black Brond, who carries messages to Braddock, enters Fort Duquesne disguised as a Indian and is on hand during the battle when Colonel Washington takes command.

Historical Accuracy: The novel mixes accurate period elements with a fanciful adventure story.

`4899` A Virginia Scout

Date of Publication: 1922
Subject(s): Indians
Fictional character(s): Basdel Morris, Frontiersman
Time Period(s): 18th century
Locale(s): Virginia

Summary: This tale of Indian warfare on the Virginia frontier features frontiersman Basdel Morris, a messenger for Governor Dunsmore. He is involved in a series of escapes, is captured, and battles with the Indians. The story's climax takes place in the final battle, which secures peace for the mountain settlers.

Historical Accuracy: The novel captures with skill and believability Indian warfare of the period.

TOM PENDLETON

`4900` The Seventh Girl: A Romantic Tale of Civil War Texas

Date of Publication: 1970
Subject(s): Civil War—U.S.; American West
Fictional character(s): Harper Chandler, Cowboy; Troy Chandler, Cowboy; Kate McKensie, Young Woman
Time Period(s): 1860s
Locale(s): Texas

Summary: Texas at the outbreak of the Civil War is the setting for this adventure novel concerning brothers Harper and Troy Chandler and Kate McKensie, a girl-of-all work in Dode Clancy's Saloon & Hide House. As the war creates conflict among kinsman, the three are caught up in a series of adventures that test each of them.

Historical Accuracy: The western details are captured with a convincing realism.

WILDER PENFIELD (1891-1976)

Penfield was born in Spokane, Washington, and became a Canadian citizen in 1934. Educated at Princeton and Oxford as a Rhodes Scholar, Penfield received his M.D. degree from Johns Hopkins. He served as the director of the Montreal Neurological Institute and as a past president of the Royal College of Physicians and Surgeons of Canada and the American Neurological Society.

4901 *No Other Gods*

Date of Publication: 1954
Subject(s): Biblical Story
Historical character(s): Abram, Biblical Figure
Time Period(s): 21st century B.C.
Locale(s): Ur, Mesopotamia; Canaan, Palestine

Summary: This Biblical story imagines the history of Abraham before his appearance in Genesis. Abram, as he is called here, is a scholar searching for the one true God. The novel depicts Abram's spiritual journey, which concludes with his leading the Hebrews into the Land of Canaan.

Historical Accuracy: The novel is an imaginary reconstruction with some plausibe capturing of the atmosphere of the times.

4902 *The Torch*

Date of Publication: 1960
Subject(s): Ancient Greece; Medical Profession
Historical character(s): Hippocrates, Doctor
Time Period(s): 4th century B.C.
Locale(s): Greece

Summary: The status of the medical profession in ancient Greece is dramatized in this story that focuses on Hippocrates, the father of modern medicine. He develops his novel approach to healing and the study of the patient and symptoms by observing cases of epilepsy and other diseases.

Historical Accuracy: The novel is particularly strong and believable in re-creating the atmosphere of ancient Greece and its medical practices.

SHARON KAY PENMAN

American novelist Sharon K. Penman writes historical novels set in various periods of British history. Her first novel, *The Sunne in Splendour*, is considered to be one of the best novels about Richard III.

4903 *Falls the Shadow*

Date of Publication: 1988
Subject(s): Middle Ages; Royalty—England; Wales—England Conflict
Historical character(s): Llywelyn ap Gruffydd, Royalty (Prince of North Wales); Henry III, Ruler (King of England); Simon de Montfort, Nobleman, Military Personnel
Time Period(s): 13th century (1231-1267)

Locale(s): France; Wales; England

Summary: This story of 13th-century England and Wales details the reign of Henry III and the controversial figure of Simon de Montfort, a French-born English national hero. Penman sees him as a kind of Shakespearean tragic hero damned by his many flaws while aspiring to a certain greatness by the courage of his convictions. The novel traces his downfall in the twisted intrigue of Henry's court. *Falls the Shadow* is the second title in Penman's series on medieval Wales, following *Here Be Dragons*. The series concludes with *The Reckoning*.

Historical Accuracy: Penman details in her afterward her slight modifications of some of the facts. The depth of her research brings the era to striking life.

4904 *Here Be Dragons*

Date of Publication: 1985
Subject(s): Middle Ages; Royalty—England; Wales-England Conflict
Historical character(s): Llywelyn ap Iowerth, Royalty (Prince of Gwynedd); John, Ruler (King of England); Joan, Royalty (princess), Bastard Daughter (aka Joanna); Eleanor of Aquitaine, Royalty
Time Period(s): 12th century; 13th century (1183-1234)
Locale(s): England; Wales; France

Summary: The novel dramatizes a tribal Celtic world besieged by Norman feudal society in the 12th and 13th centuries. John is king of England with aspirations to conquer Wales. He arranges a marriage between his bastard daughter Joanna and Llewelyn of Wales. Llewelyn, although John's vassal, has aspirations of his own for an independent Welsh kingdom. Their marriage and the intrigue reflected in the power politics of the era create the book's rousing drama. Penman's Welsh trilogy continues with *Falls the Shadow*.

Historical Accuracy: Penman has documented sources for most of the occurences in the book, although little is known about the Wales of the period, and imagination has filled in many of the gaps.

4905 *The Queen's Man*

Date of Publication: 1996
Subject(s): Mystery; Middle Ages
Fictional character(s): Justin de Quincy, Bastard Son
Historical character(s): Eleanor of Aquitaine, Royalty (queen consort of Henry II)
Time Period(s): 12th century (1192-1193)
Locale(s): Winchester, England; London, England

Summary: The discovery of a dying man on the road out of Winchester by Justin de Quincy leads him into a tangled web of murder and intrigue at the heart of the court surrounding England's dowager queen, Eleanor of Aquitaine. De Quincy comes into possession of a document that will settle the whereabouts of England's King Richard and is pivotal in the conflict over his successor.

Historical Accuracy: The novelist's notes indicate her departures from historical fact. The story is bolstered by a solid knowledge of the period.

4906 *The Reckoning*

Date of Publication: 1991
Subject(s): Middle Ages; Royalty—England; Wales-England Conflict
Historical character(s): Edward I, Ruler (King of England); Llywelyn ap Gruffydd, Royalty (Prince of North Wales); David ap Gruffydd, Nobleman
Time Period(s): 13th century (1271-1283)
Locale(s): England; Wales

Summary: Following *Here Be Dragons* and *Falls the Shadow*, this novel brings to a conclusion Penman's story of Wales beset by England's desire to extend its domain westward to the sea. Wales is led by two men, Llewelyn ap Gruffyd and his brother Davydd, who must confront the schemes and power of Edward I.

Historical Accuracy: Penman's inventions are minimal, and she has filled in the gaps with an imagination schooled by her research.

4907 *The Sunne in Splendour*

Date of Publication: 1982
Subject(s): War of the Roses; Royalty—England
Historical character(s): Richard, Duke of Gloucester, Royalty (later Richard III); Edward IV, Ruler (King of England); Anne Neville, Noblewoman
Time Period(s): 15th century (1459-1485)
Locale(s): London, England; England (Durham, Ludlow, Yorkshire, Warwick, Coventry)

Summary: In this massive, revisionist view of Richard III, Penman attempts to recast Richard in the role of hero instead of the villain promulgated by the Tudor apologists. In her version, Richard is a stalwart supporter of his flamboyant brother and tragically in love with a woman he is forbidden to marry, Anne Neville.

Historical Accuracy: Penman is scrupulous in the details of her story and the customs of the times. It is her interpretation of Richard that will remain open to debate.

4908 *When Christ and His Saints Slept*

Date of Publication: 1995
Subject(s): Middle Ages; Royalty—England
Historical character(s): Maud, Royalty (heiress to the English throne); Geoffrey of Anjou, Nobleman, Spouse (of Maude); Stephen of Blois, Ruler (King of England); Henry II, Ruler (King of England); Eleanor of Aquitaine, Royalty (queen consort of Henry II)
Time Period(s): 12th century (1135-1154)
Locale(s): England; France; Wales

Summary: The title refers to 20 dark years of anarchy and civil war in England when violence and enmity were the norm. The novel chronicles the result of Henry I's naming of his daughter, Maude, Empress of Germany, as his heir. Her trusted cousin Stephen betrays her, seizing the throne, and civil war begins. Maude and Stephen destroy each other and wreak painful vengeance on England.

Historical Accuracy: The novel is a marvel of careful and compelling historical re-construction.

JOSEPH STANLEY PENNELL

Born in Junction City, Kansas, Pennell attended the University of Kansas and Pembroke College, Oxford. He worked for a sucession of newspapers.

4909 *The History of Rome Hanks*

Date of Publication: 1974
Subject(s): Civil War—U.S.; Battle of Shiloh; Battle of Gettysburg
Fictional character(s): Rome Hanks, Military Personnel (captain); Clinton Belton, Political Figure, Military Personnel (brigadier); Pinckney Harrington, Military Personnel (Confederate soldier); Lee Harrington, Young Man
Time Period(s): 19th century
Locale(s): Kansas; Tennessee

Summary: Young Lee Harrington assembles and records the history of his ancestors, particularly Captain Romulus Hanks, captain of the 117th Iowa. Hanks' experiences during the Civil War, including action at Shiloh and Gettysburg, are featured, as well as his service in Kansas in the years following the war, until 1900.

Historical Accuracy: The anachronisms are deliberate reflecting a narrative that is filtered through several characters.

ISAAC RUSLING PENNYPACKER
(1852-1935)

Born in Pennsylvania, Pennypacker was a prolific author, one of the leading authorities on the history of the Civil War. In addition to histories, he wrote extensive poetry and prose and worked as a newspaper editor.

4910 *The Redemptioner*

Date of Publication: 1972
Subject(s): American Revolution; American Colonies
Fictional character(s): Richard Holt, Young Man
Time Period(s): 1770s (1774)
Locale(s): Pennsylvania, American Colonies

Summary: The picaresque adventures of Richard Holt who journeys to America to seek his fortune in the tumultuous year of 1774 are depicted. Holt arrives penniless and his transformation from an English lord into a loyal American is described. The novel is full of colorful scenes of what life must have been like at the inception of the American nation.

Historical Accuracy: The period elements are convincingly depicted.

ELEANOR PERENYI (1918-)

An American born in Washington, Perenyi attended Phillips Gallery of Art School. She has worked as a magazine editor and as the managing editor for *Mademoiselle*. She received a National Book Award nomination in 1974 for her book, *Lizt: the Artist as Romantic Hero.*

4911 *The Bright Sword*

Date of Publication: 1955
Subject(s): Civil War—U.S.; Battle of Franklin; Battle of Nashville
Historical character(s): John Bell Hood, Military Personnel (Confederate general)
Time Period(s): 1860s (1863-1864)
Locale(s): Richmond, Virginia; Tennessee

Summary: This Civil War novel focuses on Confederate General John Bell Hood. The story follows his career from Richmond society to his Tennessee campaigns, including the battles of Franklin and Nashville.

Historical Accuracy: The novel captures the events of the period, but fails to bring its central character to believable life.

BENITO PEREZ GALDOS (1843-1920)

A Spanish novelist and playwright, Perez Galdos has been called the greatest Spanish novelist since Cervantes. His *Episodios Nacionales* consists of 48 novels in five series that chronicle Spanish history from 1805 to the end of the 19th century.

4912 *Saragossa*

Date of Publication: 1874
Subject(s): Napoleonic Wars; Peninsular War
Fictional character(s): Don Jose de Montoria, Gentleman, Patriot; Antonio de Montorio, Hero; Mariquilla, Heroine
Time Period(s): 1800s (1808-1809)
Locale(s): Saragossa, Spain

Summary: The novel tells a tragic story of blighted love and heroism set during the second siege of Saragossa by Napoleon's troops. The young son of a Spanish patriot falls in love with a miser's daughter. The father's eventual charge of treason separates the lovers and dooms their love.

Historical Accuracy: The novel features an accurate description of the siege and clear pictures of the era.

JACOB RANDOLPH PERKINS
(1878-1959)

Perkins' books include *Trails, Rails, and War: The Life of General G.M. Dodge.*

4913 *Antioch Actress: A Novel of Pagan Against Christian*

Date of Publication: 1946
Subject(s): Roman Empire; Religious Conflict; Christianity
Fictional character(s): Cynthia Mamuta, Actress
Time Period(s): 1st century
Locale(s): Antioch, Syria

Summary: In his attempt to weaken Syrian Christians, the Emperor Trajan orders the actress Cynthia Mamuta, a former Christian, to present theatricals ridiculing Christianity. She stirs up religious conflict but eventually repents and is accepted back into the church.

Historical Accuracy: Although the novel demonstrates a solid period background, the elements are too often superficial and theme-dominated.

4914 *The Emperor's Physician*

Date of Publication: 1974
Subject(s): Biblical Story; Medical Profession; Roman Empire
Fictional character(s): Sergius Cumanus, Doctor; Mary Omri, Dancer
Historical character(s): Jesus Christ, Biblical Figure; Luke, Biblical Figure, Doctor; Pontius Pilate, Government Official
Time Period(s): 1st century
Locale(s): Israel

Summary: Jesus as a miraculous healer is the focus of this Biblical story that details the experiences of two doctors sent by the Emperor to investigate conditions in Palestine. Sergius Cumanus is the Emperor's personal physician and a scientific materialist; Luke Galen is a mystic.

Historical Accuracy: The story is fanciful but does depend on a convincing depiction of the era.

BARRY PEROWNE
(PSEUD. OF PHILIP ATKEY, 1908-1985)

An English writer born in Wiltshire, Perowne is best known for his popular crime and mystery books that revived the fictional career of the gentleman burglar A.J. Raffles, a character originated by E.W. Hornung.

4915 *A Singular Conspiracy*

Date of Publication: 1974
Subject(s): Literary Life
Fictional character(s): General Aupick, Military Personnel
Historical character(s): Edgar Allan Poe, Writer; Charles Pierre Baudelaire, Writer (poet)
Time Period(s): 1840s (1844)
Locale(s): New York, New York; Paris, France

Summary: Biographers of Edgar Allan Poe cannot account for Poe's whereabouts during the first four months of 1844. The novel offers a speculative account of this period, imagining Poe's journey to Paris to fight with the army of Poland against the Russians. He meets French poet Charles Baudelaire, and together they join forces against Baudelaire's stepfather, General Aupick, to free Baudelaire's inheritance.

Historical Accuracy: This is an ingenious fictional account of what might have happened had the two geniuses joined forces.

E.G. PERRAULT

Perrault is a Canadian author who was born and raised in Vancouver, British Columbia. He is a writer and producer of film documentaries.

4916 *The Kingdom Carver*

Date of Publication: 1968
Subject(s): Frontier—Canada

Fictional character(s): Dave Laird, Young Man; Johnny George, Indian; Jim McKillop, Frontiersman (logger)
Time Period(s): 1910s (1917)
Locale(s): Vancouver, British Columbia, Canada; Pacific Northwest, Canada

Summary: The opening of the Pacific Northwest timberland is depicted in this coming of age story involving young Dave Laird who accompanies his father far up the barren Pacific coast. There their lives are connected with a variety of individuals who epitomize the frontier spirit that conquered the territory.

Historical Accuracy: The details of wilderness life of the period are effectively presented.

ROBERT PERRIN (1939-)

English journalist and author Perrin was born in Portsmith and worked as a journalist for its *Sunday Pictorial*, the *Daily Herald*, and the *Sun*. He joined the BBC in 1965, where he has served as a series journalist and a chief editor of the World Service News.

4917 *Jewels*

Date of Publication: 1977
Subject(s): Royalty—England; Homosexuality; Crime and Criminals
Historical character(s): Frank Shackleton, Gentleman, Thief; Richard Gorges, Military Personnel (captain), Homosexual; Sir Arthur Vicar, Nobleman; Edward VII, Ruler (King of England)
Time Period(s): 1900s (1900-1907)
Locale(s): Dublin, Ireland; South Africa; London, England

Summary: The story is based on the theft of the Irish Crown Jewels in 1907, one of the world's greatest unsolved crimes. The author reconstructs the tangled intrigue and the conspiracy to avoid a homosexual scandal involving the king's brother-in-law that prevented the crime from being solved.

Historical Accuracy: The story is based on a close examination of the contemporary records. The author explains that many of the private conversations are invented, although some are based on official diaries and police statements.

ANNE PERRY (1938-)

Anne Perry is a London-born mystery writer with a somewhat colorful past. Frequently ill as a child, she moved to the Bahamas, then to New Zealand. At the age of 15, Perry and a girlfriend murdered the friend's mother after a quarrel. Perry served over five years in prison and returned to England after her release. She held a series of jobs in both England and the United States before finally becoming a full-time writer. She has lived in Scotland since 1989.

4918 *Ashworth Hall*

Date of Publication: 1997
Subject(s): Victorian Period; Mystery; Independence—Ireland

Fictional character(s): Thomas Pitt, Detective—Police; Charlotte Pitt, Spouse, Gentlewoman
Time Period(s): 1890s (1890)
Locale(s): England

Summary: In this installment of the Victorian-era mysteries featuring Superintendent Thomas Pitt and his wife Charlotte, the scene is an English country home where Irish Catholics and Protestants are meeting to negotiate home rule for Ireland. When the meeting's moderator is found murdered in his bath, the Pitts investigate as tensions threaten to erupt above and below stairs.

Historical Accuracy: The novel is less convincing in rendering the issues of English-Irish conflict than in the more human details of life at an English country estate during the period.

4919 *Belgrave Square*

Date of Publication: 1992
Subject(s): Mystery; Victorian Period
Fictional character(s): Thomas Pitt, Police Officer (inspector); Charlotte Pitt, Spouse, Gentlewoman; Sholto Byam, Nobleman
Time Period(s): 1890s
Locale(s): London, England

Summary: When a moneylender is found murdered, the chief suspect, Lord Byam, asserts his innocence. Inspector Pitt begins an investigation and learns that this was no ordinary moneylender but rather a vicious blackmailer whose list of victims includes some of London's most distinguished gentlemen. With the help of Charlotte and her social connections, a tangle of scandal is exposed.

Historical Accuracy: The novel captures the period in convincing detail.

4920 *Bethlehem Road*

Date of Publication: 1990
Subject(s): Mystery; Victorian Period
Fictional character(s): Thomas Pitt, Police Officer (inspector); Charlotte Pitt, Spouse, Gentlewoman; Florence Ivory, Suffragette
Time Period(s): 1890s
Locale(s): London, England

Summary: A Member of Parliament is found on Westminster Bridge with his throat cut, amidst a London falling apart from social unrest. Suspicion falls on suffragist Florence Ivory. Inspector Pitt tries to prove the case against her, while his wife Charlotte attempts to show that Florence is innocent.

Historical Accuracy: The novel offers an ingenious mystery set in an authentically drawn period London.

4921 *Bluegate Fields*

Date of Publication: 1986
Subject(s): Mystery; Victorian Period
Fictional character(s): Thomas Pitt, Police Officer (inspector); Charlotte Pitt, Spouse, Gentlewoman
Time Period(s): 1880s
Locale(s): London, England

Summary: When a boy's body is found in the sewers of Bluegate Fields, one of London's most dangerous slums, Inspector Pitt is shocked to learn that the boy is from an upperclass family. The family is uncooperative in supplying answers to Pitt's questions, and Charlotte must try to get behind the respectable facade of this proper Victorian family.

Historical Accuracy: The details of lowerclass and upperclass life are authentic and convincing.

4922   *Cain and His Brother*

Date of Publication: 1995
Subject(s): Mystery; Victorian Period
Fictional character(s): William Monk, Detective—Police, Amnesiac; Genevieve Stonefield, Gentlewoman; Caleb Stonefield, Gentleman
Time Period(s): 19th century (Victorian period)
Locale(s): London, England

Summary: The disappearance of Genevieve Stanfield's husband causes police detective William Monk to search through Victorian London's business community and slums. It looks like a case of murder with the chief suspect Caleb Stonefield, the missing man's vicious brother, whose whereabouts are also unknown. As Monk gets closer to the truth, his reputation and career are jeopardized.

Historical Accuracy: Perry's Victorian mysteries are all marked by an impressive re-creation of the period, and this novel is no exception.

4923   *Callander Square*

Date of Publication: 1981
Subject(s): Mystery; Victorian Period
Fictional character(s): Thomas Pitt, Police Officer (inspector); Charlotte Pitt, Spouse, Gentlewoman
Time Period(s): 1880s
Locale(s): London, England

Summary: Two murders in fashionable Callandar Square in London prompt Charlotte to meddle in the business of her husband, Police Inspector Thomas Pitt. Using her intimacy with fashionable life, Charlotte is able to uncover the secrets behind this wealthy and seemingly respectable preserve.

Historical Accuracy: The novel is convincing in its period details.

4924   *Cardington Crescent*

Date of Publication: 1987
Subject(s): Mystery; Victorian Period
Fictional character(s): Thomas Pitt, Police Officer (inspector); Charlotte Pitt, Spouse, Gentlewoman; Emily March, Gentlewoman
Time Period(s): 1880s
Locale(s): London, England

Summary: George March is poisoned, and suspicion, especially that of the March family, falls on his jealous wife, Emily. Emily has a strong advocate in her relative, Charlotte Pitt, wife of Inspector Pitt. Both investigate and discover others with motives for murder.

Historical Accuracy: The Victorian customs and period details of London are authentically presented.

4925   *The Cater Street Hangman*

Date of Publication: 1979
Subject(s): Mystery; Victorian Period
Fictional character(s): Emily Ellison, Gentlewoman; Charlotte Ellison, Gentlewoman; Thomas Pitt, Police Officer (inspector)
Time Period(s): 1880s (1881)
Locale(s): London, England

Summary: In the first of the author's Inspector Pitt series, the Ellisons are a respectable upperclass family whose two daughters—Charlotte and Emily—are expected to make fashionable marriages like their older sister did. This does indeed seem to be Emily's desire, but Charlotte shocks her family when, after a servant is murdered, she seems more than a little interested in the police inspector assigned to the case.

Historical Accuracy: The period details are authentic and convincing.

4926   *A Dangerous Mourning*

Date of Publication: 1991
Subject(s): Mystery; Victorian Period
Fictional character(s): William Monk, Detective—Police (inspector), Amnesiac; Hester Latterly, Nurse; Basil Moidore, Gentleman
Time Period(s): 1850s (1856)
Locale(s): London, England

Summary: The daughter of wealthy gentleman Basil Moidore is found stabbed to death, and Inspector Monk proves that only someone inside the house could have done it. His friend Hester Latterly, a nurse who served with Florence Nightingale during the Crimean War, takes a position in the household. Monk is hampered by bouts of amnesia and the meddling of his inept and jealous supervisor.

Historical Accuracy: The novel is exact and convincing in its depiction of Victorian manners and mores.

4927   *Death in the Devil's Acre*

Date of Publication: 1985
Subject(s): Mystery; Victorian Period
Fictional character(s): Thomas Pitt, Police Officer (inspector); Charlotte Pitt, Spouse, Gentlewoman
Time Period(s): 1880s (1887)
Locale(s): London, England

Summary: A grisly murder occurs in a section of London called the Devil's Acre. Soon there are three more bodies, all marked by a stab wound in the back and mutilated in the same way. Inspector Pitt, joined by his wife Charlotte, investigates.

Historical Accuracy: The novel expertly delivers a convincing portrait of Victorian London.

4928   *Defend and Betray*

Date of Publication: 1992
Subject(s): Mystery; Victorian Period; Trials

Fictional character(s): William Monk, Detective—Police (inspector), Amnesiac; Thaddeus Carlyon, Military Personnel (British general); Alexandria Carlyon, Gentlewoman; Hester Latterly, Nurse; Oliver Rathbone, Lawyer
Time Period(s): 1850s
Locale(s): London, England

Summary: General Carlyon dies at a London dinner party, and his wife Alexandra confesses to the murder. Inspector Monk, with the assistance of nurse Hester Latterly and lawyer Oliver Rathbone, scrambles against time to discover the truth. The climax includes courtroom revelations.

Historical Accuracy: The novel offers an authentic depiction of the Victorian legal system.

4929 *The Face of a Stranger*

Date of Publication: 1990
Subject(s): Mystery; Victorian Period
Fictional character(s): William Monk, Detective—Police (inspector), Amnesiac; Hester Latterly, Nurse
Time Period(s): 1850s (1856)
Locale(s): London, England

Summary: Inspector Monk struggles with amnesia while investigating the brutal murder of a Crimean War hero. He must contend with his flagging grasp of his detective skills, aided by friend and nurse Hester Latterly.

Historical Accuracy: The novel is marked by an authentic recreation of Victorian London.

4930 *Farriers' Lane*

Date of Publication: 1993
Subject(s): Mystery; Victorian Period; Anti-Semitism
Fictional character(s): Thomas Pitt, Police Officer (inspector); Charlotte Pitt, Spouse, Gentlewoman; Samuel Stafford, Judge
Historical character(s): Oscar Wilde, Writer
Time Period(s): 1890s
Locale(s): London, England

Summary: When Judge Stafford dies at the theater, Inspector Pitt investigates a tangled mystery involving a previous case the judge was trying to reopen. Complicating the investigation are the judge's adulterous wife and the spectre of anti-Semitism.

Historical Accuracy: The details of late Victorian life are authentically displayed.

4931 *Highgate Rise*

Date of Publication: 1991
Subject(s): Mystery; Victorian Period
Fictional character(s): Thomas Pitt, Police Officer (inspector); Charlotte Pitt, Spouse, Gentlewoman; Dr. Shaw, Doctor
Time Period(s): 1880s (1888)
Locale(s): London, England

Summary: In the quiet London suburb of Highgate, an arsonist has burned down Dr. Shaw's house and killed his wife. Was she or the doctor the intended victim? Inspector Pitt investigates with the aid of his wife, Charlotte, who ferrets out the

gossip surrounding the dead woman. Together they begin to unravel a complex conspiracy.

Historical Accuracy: This novel, like all of the author's Victorian mysteries, is distinguished by a remarkable grasp of the period.

4932 *Paragon Walk*

Date of Publication: 1981
Subject(s): Mystery; Victorian Period
Fictional character(s): Thomas Pitt, Police Officer (inspector); Charlotte Pitt, Spouse, Gentlewoman; Emily Ashworth, Gentlewoman
Time Period(s): 1880s
Locale(s): London, England

Summary: A young woman is brutally raped and murdered in Paragon Walk, where Charlott Pitt's sister, Emily Ashworth, lives. While Inspector Pitt mounts the official investigation, Charlotte and Emily penetrate the fashionable neighborhood for inside information.

Historical Accuracy: The novel accurately captures the respectable, but at times hypocritical, mores of Victorian society.

4933 *Pentecost Alley*

Date of Publication: 1996
Subject(s): Mystery; Victorian Period
Fictional character(s): Thomas Pitt, Detective—Police; Charlotte Pitt, Spouse, Gentlewoman
Time Period(s): 1890s
Locale(s): London, England

Summary: In London's Whitechapel, two years after the Jack the Ripper murders, a prostitute is found murdered wearing a Hellfire Club badge with the name of a powerful man's son inscribed on it. Police Superintendent Thomas Pitt is called in to find someone else to charge with the crime. Pitt, however, persists with the help of his wife Charlotte and untangles a complicated puzzle.

Historical Accuracy: The novel features an authentic atmosphere of 19th-century London and period police work.

4934 *Resurrection Row*

Date of Publication: 1981
Subject(s): Mystery; Victorian Period
Fictional character(s): Thomas Pitt, Police Officer (inspector); Charlotte Pitt, Spouse, Gentlewoman
Time Period(s): 1880s
Locale(s): London, England

Summary: When a man is found dead in an empty hansom cab, Inspector Pitt is shocked to learn that the man was no cabby but the dead and previously buried Lord Augustus Fitzroy-Hammond. Who would have wanted to unearth the old boy?.

Historical Accuracy: This baffling mystery is well-documented in its period details.

4935 *Rutland Place*

Date of Publication: 1984

Subject(s): Mystery; Victorian Period
Fictional character(s): Thomas Pitt, Police Officer (inspector); Charlotte Pitt, Spouse, Gentlewoman; Caroline Ellison, Gentlewoman
Time Period(s): 1880s (1886)
Locale(s): London, England

Summary: Caroline Ellison, Charlotte Pitt's mother, loses a locket that contains a compromising picture. This is the beginning of a series of bizarre events that lead to murder. Secrets buried deep in fashionable Rutland Place come to light as the Pitts investigate this baffling mystery.

Historical Accuracy: The novel offers authentic period details.

4936   *Silence in Hanover Close*

Date of Publication: 1988
Subject(s): Mystery; Victorian Period
Fictional character(s): Thomas Pitt, Police Officer (inspector); Charlotte Pitt, Spouse, Gentlewoman; Veronica York, Widow(er), Gentlewoman
Time Period(s): 1880s (1887)
Locale(s): London, England

Summary: Inspector Pitt is asked to reopen the three-year-old murder case of Robert York, an official of the Foreign Office who was apparently killed in a burglary attempt in fashionable Hanover Close. When a maid who seems to know a great deal is also murdered, it is apparent that something more than simple burglary is going on.

Historical Accuracy: The nuances of Victorian social mores and customs are accurately depicted.

4937   *The Sins of the Wolf*

Date of Publication: 1994
Subject(s): Mystery; Victorian Period
Fictional character(s): Hester Latterly, Nurse; William Monk, Detective—Police, Amnesiac; Mary Farraline, Gentlewoman; Oliver Rathbone, Lawyer
Time Period(s): 1850s
Locale(s): Edinburgh, Scotland

Summary: Hester Latterly accepts a position as a nurse/companion for elderly Mary Farraline. When Mary is found dead on the train to London and a missing brooch is found in Hester's possession, Hester is charged with murder. Investigator William Monk must try to uncover motive and method among the Farraline clan while lawyer Oliver Rathbone must direct the trial from the sidelines of the Scottish courts.

Historical Accuracy: The period detail makes this an authentic Victorian period mystery.

4938   *A Sudden, Fearful Death*

Date of Publication: 1993
Subject(s): Mystery; Victorian Period; Trials
Fictional character(s): William Monk, Detective—Police, Amnesiac; Hester Latterly, Nurse
Historical character(s): Florence Nightingale, Nurse
Time Period(s): 1860s
Locale(s): London, England

Summary: In a London hospital, one of Florence Nightingale's nurses is strangled to death. William Monk, no longer a police officer but a private investigator, is engaged to solve the murder. Aided by his friend Hester Latterly, he discovers much about the victim and a web of conspiracy that is finally sorted out in a climactic courtroom scene.

Historical Accuracy: The atmosphere and period details are ably woven into this suspense novel.

4939   *Traitors Gate*

Date of Publication: 1995
Subject(s): Mystery; Victorian Period
Fictional character(s): Thomas Pitt, Police Officer (inspector); Charlotte Pitt, Spouse, Gentlewoman; Arthur Desmond, Gentleman
Time Period(s): 1880s
Locale(s): London, England

Summary: Police Inspector Thomas Pitt must investigate a case of treason when it is learned that someone in the Colonial Office is passing information to Germany about England's Africa policy. The traitor must be one of several distinguished public servants. This case becomes connected to the mysterious death of Pitt's childhood mentor, Arthur Desmond.

Historical Accuracy: The period details are exact and detailed, offering a convincing portrait of the era.

KATHRIN PERUTZ (1939-)

Born in New York City, Kathrin Perutz attended Barnard College and New York University. Her writings include *Mother Is a Country, Beyond the Looking Glass: Life in the Beauty Culture*, and *Marriage Is Hell*. Her work has been collected in several anthologies as well.

4940   *Reigning Passions*

Date of Publication: 1978
Subject(s): Biography, Fictionalized; Literary Life; Sexuality
Historical character(s): Leopold Ritter von Sacher-Masoch, Writer
Time Period(s): 19th century
Locale(s): Austria

Summary: This biographical account of Austrian writer Leopold Sacher-Masoch for whom the term ''masochism'' was coined describes his life and sexual exploitations against a background of the decaying Hapsburg Empire.

Historical Accuracy: The novel succeeds in capturing the atmosphere of the times; it is less successful in creating a believable portrait of Sacher-Masoch.

LEO PERUTZ (1882-1957)

Born in Prague, Czechoslovakia, Perutz was a world-class mathematician, and an algebraic equation that he formulated bears his name. In 1938 Perutz fled Austria for Israel where he was employed as a statistician in an insurance company until he took up writing in the 1950s.

`4941` *Leonardo's Judas*

Date of Publication: 1989
Subject(s): Renaissance; Artistic Life
Fictional character(s): Joachim Behaim, Businessman (merchant); Boccetta, Businessman (usurer); Niccola, Young Woman
Historical character(s): Leonardo da Vinci, Artist
Time Period(s): 15th century (1490s)
Locale(s): Milan, Italy

Summary: The novel imagines Leonardo da Vinci's artistic process in finishing his *Last Supper*. Without a suitable model for Judas, da Vinci finds inspiration in German merchant Joachim Behaim. While feuding with usurer Boccetta, Behaim falls in love with Boccetta's daughter Niccola. Behaim's decision to sacrifice love for vengeance becomes the source for the artist's depiction of Judas' betrayal of Jesus.

Historical Accuracy: The novel's story is fanciful, but effective in creating a believable portrait of the age and the artistic process.

`4942` *The Marquis of Bolibar*

Date of Publication: 1960
Subject(s): Napoleonic Wars; Peninsular War
Fictional character(s): Marquis of Bolibar, Nobleman
Time Period(s): 1810s (1812)
Locale(s): La Bisbal, Spain

Summary: This historical fantasy is set during the Peninsular Campaign of 1812 and centers on the efforts of the mysterious Marquis of Bolibar to defeat the German force holding the fortified town of La Bisbal against attack by a band of Spanish guerrillas. He promises to deliver the town into the guerrillas' hand and enters it disguised as a mule driver. Exploiting the rivalry among the German officers, the Marquis facilitates the Germans' fall, but the question of who the mysterious Marquis is remains.

Historical Accuracy: The story is a fanciful one, but does produce a convincing atmosphere of the period and the region.

`4943` *The Swedish Cavalier*

Date of Publication: 1980
Subject(s): Identity—Concealed; Crime and Criminals
Fictional character(s): Christian von Tornefeld, Fugitive; Fowl-Filcher, Criminal (thief)
Time Period(s): 1700s
Locale(s): Poland; Germany; Sweden

Summary: A thief known as "The Fowl-Filcher" steals the identity of Christian von Tornefeld and becomes a Swedish cavalier while struggling to prevent his daughter from learning his secret past.

Historical Accuracy: The novel provides a genuine background for this story that combines the fantastic with the realistic.

DAVID PESCI

Connecticut writer Pesci's work has appeared in the *New York Times*, the *National Review*, and the *Hartford Courrant*. *Amistad* is his first novel.

`4944` *Amistad: The Thunder of Freedom*

Date of Publication: 1997
Subject(s): Slavery; Trials
Historical character(s): John Quincy Adams, Political Figure; Singbe-Pieh, Slave, Rebel; Grabeau, Slave, Rebel; Martin Van Buren, Political Figure
Time Period(s): 1830s (1839)
Locale(s): *Amistad*, At Sea; Connecticut; Havana, Cuba

Summary: A group of slaves led by a Mende rice farmer named Singbe-Pieh stage a rebellion on board the *Amistad*, a Spanish slaver from Cuba. The *Amistad* is seized by the U.S., and a trial is held to determine the fate of the rebels. They are defended by former U.S. President John Quincy Adams.

Historical Accuracy: The majority of the events presented are faithful to historical fact although some characters and dialogue have been invented.

DANIEL PETERS (1948-)

American novelist Peters was born in Wisconsin and graduated from Yale and the University of British Columbia. He has worked as a teacher of creative writing. Peters conducted extensive research for his trilogy on three different pre-Columbian civilizations.

`4945` *The Incas*

Date of Publication: 1991
Subject(s): Inca Empire
Fictional character(s): Cusi Huaman, Warrior; Micay, Spouse (of Cusi); Huayna Capac, Chieftain
Time Period(s): 16th century (1511-1530)
Locale(s): Cuzco, Peru; Machu Picchu, Peru

Summary: This is an immense reconstruction of the history of the Incas of Peru during the last years of the 16th century when they are overwhelmed by the Spanish. The story focuses on two characters, Cusi, a young warrior, and Micay, a young woman. Both come of age in scenes on the battlefield, in the royal court, and the temples as a panoramic picture of Incan life and culture emerges.

Historical Accuracy: The novel offers a convincing look at Incan customs.

`4946` *The Luck of Huemac: A Novel about the Aztecs*

Date of Publication: 1981
Subject(s): Aztec Empire; Spanish Colonies
Fictional character(s): Huemac, Warrior; Chimalman, Sorcerer
Historical character(s): Montezuma II, Ruler (Aztec)
Time Period(s): 15th century; 16th century (1428-1520)
Locale(s): Mexico

Summary: This massive reconstruction of the world of the Aztecs spans four generations and almost 100 years. The story centers on Huemac's experiences as he searches for his place in the treacherous world of court politics. Huemac becomes an Eagle Warrior and wins fame as a player of the sacred ball game. The action rushes toward the arrival of Cortez and the Spanish Conquest.

Historical Accuracy: The novel is filled with evidence of solid research, re-creating the Aztec culture with conviction.

4947 *Tikal: A Novel about the Maya*

Date of Publication: 1983
Subject(s): Mayan Empire
Fictional character(s): Balam Xoc, Rebel; Pacal Balam, Government Official (royal steward); Akbal Balam, Artist; Kinich Kakmoo, Warrior
Time Period(s): 8th century; 9th century (785-810)
Locale(s): Tikal, Central America (present-day Guatemala)

Summary: This is an imaginative re-creation of the ancient Mayan civilization that flourished for over 500 years in the tropical rain forests of Central America and then disappeared leaving only ruins to mark its vanished culture. The novel dramatizes the rebellion of Balam Xoc, who defies tradition and questions authority. His rebellion sweeps a number of characters up in the challenge of change.

Historical Accuracy: The background of Mayan culture is expertly and believably presented.

ELIZABETH PETERS
(PSEUD. OF BARBARA MERTZ, 1927-)

American historian and writer Mertz was born in Illinois and graduated from the University of Chicago. Mertz is the author of books on Egyptology as well as over 45 romance and suspense novels. In 1989 her book *Naked Once More* won a prize for the best mystery novel. Her romance novels are written under the pseudonym of Barbara Michaels.

4948 *The Curse of the Pharaohs*

Date of Publication: 1981
Subject(s): Mystery; Victorian Period; Archaeology
Fictional character(s): Amelia Peabody, Archaeologist; Radcliffe Emerson, Archaeologist
Time Period(s): 1890s
Locale(s): England; Luxor, Egypt

Summary: English archaeologist Amelia Peabody is happily called from her domestic routine in England to Egypt, where at a recently discovered tomb in Luxor Sir Henry Baskerville has died under bizarre circumstances that the press is calling "the Curse of the Pharaohs." Amelia takes up the investigation.

Historical Accuracy: The sense of place and time is authentic.

4949 *The Deeds of the Disturber*

Date of Publication: 1988
Subject(s): Mystery; Archaeology; Victorian Period

Fictional character(s): Amelia Peabody, Archaeologist; Radcliffe Emerson, Archaeologist
Time Period(s): 1890s
Locale(s): London, England

Summary: When a number of the British Museum staff apparently succumb to a mummy's curse, Amelia Peabody Emerson mounts an investigation. Her husband, Radcliffe, is determined to prevent his wife from becoming the next victim.

Historical Accuracy: The novel features a very well-researched period locale.

4950 *The Hippopotamus Pool*

Date of Publication: 1996
Subject(s): Mystery; Archaeology; Victorian Period
Fictional character(s): Amelia Peabody, Archaeologist; Radcliffe Emerson, Archaeologist
Time Period(s): 1890s; 1900s (1899-1900)
Locale(s): Egypt

Summary: In the eighth historical mystery involving archaeologist Amelia Peabody, she and her husband sail for Thebes in search of the hidden tomb of Queen Tetisheri, prompted by a mysterious stranger with a valuable scarab from the tomb. They encounter murders, kidnappings, grave robbers, and ancient Egyptian curses. Amelia must match wits with a nefarious art dealer and a master of disguises.

Historical Accuracy: The novel manages to animate its period convincingly.

4951 *The Last Camel Died at Noon*

Date of Publication: 1991
Subject(s): Mystery; Archaeology; Victorian Period
Fictional character(s): Amelia Peabody, Archaeologist; Radcliffe Emerson, Archaeologist; Willoughby Forth, Explorer
Time Period(s): 1890s (1897)
Locale(s): Nubian Desert, Sudan

Summary: English archaeologists Amelia and Radcliffe Emerson intend to spend the winter excavating in the Sudan. They interrupt their plan to search for explorer Willoughby Forth, who disappeared 14 years before in the Nubian desert with his new wife.

Historical Accuracy: The locale and period are captured convincingly.

4952 *Lion in the Valley*

Date of Publication: 1986
Subject(s): Mystery; Archaeology; Victorian Period
Fictional character(s): Amelia Peabody, Archaeologist; Radcliffe Emerson, Archaeologist; Ramses Emerson, Child
Time Period(s): 1890s (1895-1896)
Locale(s): Egypt

Summary: It is the 1895-1896 excavation season, and archaeologists Amelia and Radcliffe Emerson with their son, Ramses, are at work on a small pyramid in Egypt. Their work is interrupted by a disguised robber and a brilliant master criminal, who must be unmasked before he threatens Amelia's life and something even more precious.

Historical Accuracy: The novel captures with authority period Egypt and the world of archaeology.

`4953` *The Mummy Case*

Date of Publication: 1985
Subject(s): Mystery; Victorian Period; Archaeology
Fictional character(s): Amelia Peabody, Archaeologist; Radcliffe Emerson, Archaeologist
Time Period(s): 1890s
Locale(s): Egypt

Summary: Victorian Egyptologist Radcliffe Emerson is denied permission to dig at the pyramids of Dahshoor. Instead he is given the pyramids at Mazghunah, a place devoid of interest—until a murder takes place. The victim is an antiquities dealer killed in Cairo, and a sinister figure on the scene winds up in Mazghunah. Amelia takes up his trail.

Historical Accuracy: The novel is a witty and convincing recreation of period Egypt and the world of competitive archaeology.

`4954` *The Snake, the Crocodile, and the Dog*

Date of Publication: 1992
Subject(s): Mystery; Victorian Period; Archaeology
Fictional character(s): Amelia Peabody, Archaeologist; Radcliffe Emerson, Archaeologist
Time Period(s): 1890s (1898)
Locale(s): Egypt

Summary: In 1898 Amelia Peabody and her husband, Radcliffe, travel up the Nile, combining a second honeymoon with a search for Nefertiti's tomb. Present-day danger and mystery intervene when the couple uncovers a kidnapping plot and suspects that the villain is one of their party.

Historical Accuracy: The novel is convincing in capturing period Egypt.

ELLIS PETERS
(PSEUD. OF EDITH PARGETER, 1913-1995)

Ellis Peters is the pseudonym used by English novelist Edith Pargeter, most notably for her Brother Cadfael series of medieval mysteries. Peters worked as a chemist's assistant prior to serving in the Women's Royal Navy Service during Wolrd War II. She wrote modern-day thrillers before combining her love of mystery and history. She won an Edgar Award from the Mystery Writers of America in 1963 and the Crime Writers Association Silver Dagger in 1981. In addition, she has translated a number of books from Czech into English.

`4955` *Brother Cadfael's Penance*

Date of Publication: 1994
Subject(s): Middle Ages; Mystery; Religious Life

Fictional character(s): Brother Cadfael, Religious (monk), Detective—Amateur; Olivier De Bretagne, Knight; Yves Hugonin, Knight; Philip FitzRobert, Nobleman
Historical character(s): Stephen, Ruler (King of England)
Time Period(s): 12th century (1145-1146)
Locale(s): Shrewsbury, England; Coventry, England

Summary: In the most personal of Brother Cadfael's adventures, he learns that his son, Olivier, conceived years before Cadfael became a monk, is being held captive by a renegade nobleman who has broken his allegiance to the Empress Maud. Cadfael must break his vows and leave the cloister to search for his missing son. In Coventry, he encounters Olivier's brother-in-law. Cadfael must save him from danger while gaining entrance to the dungeon that holds his son.

Historical Accuracy: The novel is remarkable for its depiction of the period, its politics, and customs.

`4956` *The Confessions of Brother Halvin*

Date of Publication: 1988
Subject(s): Mystery; Middle Ages; Religious Life
Fictional character(s): Brother Cadfael, Religious (monk), Detective—Amateur; Brother Halvin, Religious (monk)
Time Period(s): 12th century (1142)
Locale(s): Shrewsbury, England

Summary: Brother Halvin falls from an icy roof and is injured badly enough to make a deathbed confession to Brother Cadfael, an admission of wickedness difficult to forgive. But Halvin recovers and undertakes a journey of expiation accompanied by Cadfael. Revenge and murder await them.

Historical Accuracy: The medieval era is vividly depicted.

`4957` *Dead Man's Ransom*

Date of Publication: 1984
Subject(s): Mystery; Middle Ages; Religious Life
Fictional character(s): Brother Cadfael, Religious (monk), Detective—Amateur; Hugh Beringar, Government Official (sheriff); Gilbert Prestcote, Gentleman
Time Period(s): 12th century (1141)
Locale(s): Shrewsbury, England

Summary: The civil war between King Stephen and Empress Maud rages on. In the battle of Lincoln, the sheriff of Shropshire is captured, and the king himself is being held by his enemies. An exchange of prisoners is arranged, but when one dies under mysterious circumstances, Brother Cadfael investigates.

Historical Accuracy: The historical background of Welsh border conflict and civil war is factual and along with the details of daily life provides a strong historical foundation for the mystery.

`4958` *The Devil's Novice*

Date of Publication: 1983
Subject(s): Mystery; Middle Ages; Religious Life
Fictional character(s): Brother Cadfael, Religious (monk), Detective—Amateur; Meriet Aspley, Religious; Peter Clemence, Political Figure
Time Period(s): 12th century (1140)

Locale(s): Shrewsbury, England

Summary: A young novice in Brother Cadfael's order creates so much disorder that he is called the Devil's Novice. When a political envoy on a mission to end England's civil war between King Stephen and the Empress Maud disappears, Cadfael investigates the mystery of which the young novice appears to be a part.

Historical Accuracy: The daily routine of monastic life is solidly detailed, as is the historical period.

4959 *An Excellent Mystery*

Date of Publication: 1985
Subject(s): Mystery; Middle Ages; Religious Life
Fictional character(s): Brother Cadfael, Religious (monk), Detective—Amateur; Brother Humilis, Religious (monk); Brother Fidelis, Religious (monk)
Time Period(s): 12th century (1141)
Locale(s): Shrewsbury, England

Summary: Brothers Humilis and Fidelis are refugees from the dynastic struggle between King Stephen and Empress Maud. Cadfael wonders about the curious allegiance of the pair. Soon a second mystery, the disappearance and the presumed murder of a girl, becomes connected with the pair.

Historical Accuracy: The era is sharply presented as are the details of monastic daily life.

4960 *The Heretic's Apprentice*

Date of Publication: 1990
Subject(s): Mystery; Middle Ages; Religious Life
Fictional character(s): Brother Cadfael, Religious (monk), Detective—Amateur; Gerbert, Religious; Elave, Servant (squire)
Time Period(s): 12th century (1143)
Locale(s): Shrewsbury, England

Summary: After his death, William of Lythwood is brought to the abbey for burial by his squire, Elave. William was once charged with heresy and Elave is overheard voicing the same views. When a murder occurs, Cadfael investigates both that crime and the heresy allegations.

Historical Accuracy: The period details are expertly rendered.

4961 *The Hermit of Eyton Forest*

Date of Publication: 1988
Subject(s): Mystery; Middle Ages; Religious Life
Fictional character(s): Brother Cadfael, Religious (monk), Detective—Amateur; Richard Ludel, Nobleman; Cuthred, Recluse (hermit)
Time Period(s): 12th century (1142)
Locale(s): Shrewsbury, England

Summary: On the death of Richard Ludel, his son (also named Richard) succeeds to power but resists the domination of his grandmother. When Richard disappears and a corpse is found in the forest where a hermit enjoys the protection of Richard's grandmother, Cadfael takes up the investigation.

Historical Accuracy: The medieval details are meticulously and convincingly presented.

4962 *The Holy Thief*

Date of Publication: 1992
Subject(s): Mystery; Middle Ages; Religious Life
Fictional character(s): Brother Cadfael, Religious (monk), Detective—Amateur; Brother Herlvin, Religious (monk); Brother Tutilo, Religious (monk)
Time Period(s): 12th century (1144)
Locale(s): Shrewsbury, England

Summary: The Abbey of St. Peter and St. Paul is visited by two brothers soliciting funds to restore Ramsey Abbey. Cadfael marks one of the brothers, Tutilo, as someone to watch. Cadfael's hunch is rewarded when a theft and a murder follow, and Tutilo is the prime suspect. But did he do it?.

Historical Accuracy: Meticulously researched, the daily life of a 12th-century abbey is vividly presented.

4963 *The Leper of St. Giles*

Date of Publication: 1981
Subject(s): Mystery; Middle Ages; Religious Life
Fictional character(s): Brother Cadfael, Religious (monk), Detective—Amateur; Jocelin Lucy, Nobleman; Iveta, Royalty (princess)
Time Period(s): 12th century (1139)
Locale(s): Shrewsbury, England

Summary: Brother Cadfael comes to the defense of two thwarted lovers—a princess about to be married to a man she does not love and a young nobleman who is charged with the murder of the prospective bridegroom. Cadfael sets out to prove Jocelin's innocence, and the answer to the mystery comes from an unexpected source: the leper house of St. Giles.

Historical Accuracy: The medieval atmosphere is convincingly created.

4964 *Monk's Hood*

Date of Publication: 1980
Subject(s): Mystery; Middle Ages; Religious Life
Fictional character(s): Brother Cadfael, Religious (monk), Detective—Amateur; Gervase Bonel, Gentleman; Mistress Bonel, Gentlewoman; Edwin Gurney, Gentleman
Time Period(s): 12th century (1138)
Locale(s): Shrewsbury, England

Summary: Gervase Bonel, a guest at the Abbey of St. Peter and St. Paul, and the husband of the woman that Cadfael once loved, is found poisoned by a dose of Cadfael's own potion of monkshood. Suspicion falls on Bonel's stepson whom Cadfael defends out of his past concern for his mother.

Historical Accuracy: The historical grounding of the story is remarkable.

4965 *A Morbid Taste for Bones*

Date of Publication: 1977
Subject(s): Mystery; Middle Ages; Religious Life
Fictional character(s): Brother Cadfael, Religious (monk), Detective—Amateur; Robert Pennant, Religious
Time Period(s): 12th century (1130s)

Locale(s): Shrewsbury, England; Wales

Summary: The novel introduces the chronicles of Brother Cadfael, a former Crusader turned Benedictine monk. The ambitious prior of Cadfael's order decides to appropriate the sacred remains of Saint Winifred from her proper resting place in Wales. The Welsh Cadfael goes to translate and is soon investigating a murder.

Historical Accuracy: The novel and the series provide a meticulous reconstruction of medieval life and customs.

4966 *One Corpse Too Many*

Date of Publication: 1979
Subject(s): Mystery; Middle Ages; Religious Life
Fictional character(s): Brother Cadfael, Religious (monk), Detective—Amateur; Hugh Beringar, Government Official (sheriff); Aline, Young Woman
Historical character(s): Stephen, Ruler (King of England)
Time Period(s): 12th century (1138)
Locale(s): Shrewsbury, England

Summary: The historical fall of Shrewsbury Castle in the dynastic struggle between King Stephen and Empress Maud provides the background and conflict for Brother Cadfael's second chronicle. He is asked to administer last rites to a number of hanged prisoners and discovers one corpse too many. There's been a murder as well as an execution.

Historical Accuracy: The historical as well as the daily life of a medieval abbey and town are precisely and convincingly rendered.

4967 *The Pilgrim of Hate*

Date of Publication: 1984
Subject(s): Mystery; Middle Ages; Religious Life
Fictional character(s): Brother Cadfael, Religious (monk), Detective—Amateur; Rhun, Traveller (pilgrim); Alice Weaver, Worker
Time Period(s): 12th century (1140s)
Locale(s): Shrewsbury, England

Summary: Pilgrims flock to the Benedictine Abbey at Shrewsbury to venerate the sacred relics of St. Winifred. Brother Cadfael establishes a link between the murder of a knight and a pair of pilgrims. A miracle cure and love complicate the mystery.

Historical Accuracy: The medieval era and its customs are convincingly detailed.

4968 *The Potter's Field*

Date of Publication: 1990
Subject(s): Mystery; Middle Ages; Religious Life
Fictional character(s): Brother Cadfael, Religious (monk), Detective—Amateur; Sulien Blount, Religious
Time Period(s): 12th century (1140s)
Locale(s): Shrewsbury, England

Summary: A field previously owned by a potter and his lovely wife is transferred to the Abbey of St. Peter and St. Paul. When the monks begin to plow it, they turn up the body of a young woman thought to be the potter's wife. Cadfael must

solve the crime that becomes entangled with the arrival of a young novice.

Historical Accuracy: Expertly researched, the novel brings the medieval world to dramatic life.

4969 *The Raven in the Foregate*

Date of Publication: 1986
Subject(s): Mystery; Middle Ages; Religious Life
Fictional character(s): Brother Cadfael, Religious (monk), Detective—Amateur; Hugh Beringar, Government Official (sheriff); Father Ailroth, Religious (parish priest)
Time Period(s): 12th century (1141)
Locale(s): Shrewsbury, England

Summary: Father Ailroth is assigned to the parish of the Holy Cross, known as the Foregate. His zeal and devotion quickly alienate him from his parishioners. When his body is discovered in the millpond, there is no shortage of suspects, but there are few clues for Brother Cadfael.

Historical Accuracy: The novel offers a solid depiction of the historical period.

4970 *The Rose Rent*

Date of Publication: 1986
Subject(s): Mystery; Middle Ages; Religious Life
Fictional character(s): Brother Cadfael, Religious (monk), Detective—Amateur; Judith Perle, Landowner, Widow(er); Brother Eluric, Religious (monk)
Time Period(s): 12th century (1142)
Locale(s): Shrewsbury, England

Summary: The widow Judith rents her cottage and garden to the abbey for the price of a single rose per year. Brother Eluric is entrusted to make the annual payment, but he is killed and the widow disappears. Cadfael must investigate a variety of likely suspects who might wish to break the contract and acquire Judith's holdings as part of a dowry.

Historical Accuracy: The details of ordinary life during the Middle Ages are scrupulously delivered.

4971 *St. Peter's Fair*

Date of Publication: 1981
Subject(s): Mystery; Middle Ages; Religious Life
Fictional character(s): Brother Cadfael, Religious (monk), Detective—Amateur; Emma Vernold, Young Woman
Time Period(s): 12th century (1130s)
Locale(s): Shrewsbury, England

Summary: St. Peter's Fair is an annual celebration in Shrewsbury, a holiday mingling of knights, gentry, and merchants. In the midst of the festivities, a wealthy merchant is murdered. His niece is left with a perilous task and is embroiled in a dangerous conspiracy, which Brother Cadfael must untangle before another death occurs.

Historical Accuracy: The texture and color of medieval life are vividly and convincingly presented.

4972 *The Sanctuary Sparrow*

Date of Publication: 1983

Subject(s): Mystery; Middle Ages; Religious Life
Fictional character(s): Brother Cadfael, Religious (monk), Detective—Amateur; Liliwin, Entertainer (acrobat)
Time Period(s): 12th century (1140)

Summary: An itinerant acrobat is accused of robbery and murder and seeks sanctuary at St. Peter and St. Paul's. Cadfael is not convinced of the boy's guilt, and he sets out to investigate. His inquiries reveal some dark family secrets.

Historical Accuracy: The period details lend solidity to the mystery.

4973 The Summer of the Danes

Date of Publication: 1991
Subject(s): Mystery; Middle Ages; Religious Life
Fictional character(s): Brother Cadfael, Religious (monk), Detective—Amateur; Brother Mark, Religious (monk)
Historical character(s): Owain Gwynmead, Royalty (Welsh prince); Cadwaladr Gwynmead, Royalty (Welsh prince)
Time Period(s): 12th century (1144)
Locale(s): Shrewsbury, England; Wales

Summary: Brother Cadfael embarks on an ecclesiastical mission to his native Wales. There, he is caught up in a deadly dispute between rival Welsh princes and an army of Danish mercenaries. Cadfael is captured, and his freedom depends on bringing a murderer to justice.

Historical Accuracy: Descriptions of the era are solidly grounded in fact.

4974 The Virgin in the Ice

Date of Publication: 1983
Subject(s): Mystery; Middle Ages; Religious Life
Fictional character(s): Brother Cadfael, Religious (monk), Detective—Amateur; Hugh Beringar, Government Official (sheriff)
Time Period(s): 12th century (1130s)
Locale(s): Ludlow, England; Shrewsbury, England

Summary: The dynastic struggle between King Stephen and Empress Maud drives two orphans and their chaperones into the wintry landscape where they are lost without a trace. Cadfael is called in to help locate them. Evidence of murder is discovered, linked to the priory of Bronfield.

Historical Accuracy: The novel, like the series, is an ingenious blend of accurate history, medieval period details, and first-rate suspense.

MAUREEN PETERS (1935-)

Welsh writer Peters was born in Caernarvon and is a graduate of the University College of North Wales. She has worked as a teacher of English to mentally retarded children. Her novels show her interest in the influence of the past on the present, though her main object is to tell a good story. Peters also writes under the names Veronica Black, Catherine Darby, Judith Rothman, and Sharon Whitby.

4975 Henry VIII and His Six Wives

Date of Publication: 1971
Subject(s): Tudor Period; Royalty—England
Historical character(s): Henry VIII, Ruler (King of England); Catherine of Aragon, Royalty (queen consort of Henry VIII); Anne Boleyn, Royalty (queen consort of Henry VIII); Jane Seymour, Royalty (queen consort of Henry VIII); Anne of Cleves, Royalty (queen consort of Henry VIII); Katherine Howard, Royalty (queen consort of Henry VIII); Catherine Parr, Royalty (queen consort of Henry VIII); Thomas Wolsey, Religious (cardinal); Thomas Cromwell, Religious (Archbishop of Canterbury); Mary Tudor, Royalty (princess); Thomas Cranmer, Religious (archbishop)
Time Period(s): 16th century
Locale(s): England

Summary: As King Henry VIII lies dying, he relives his past, the succession of six wives that caused the English Reformation, and his endless search for a male heir. Queen Isabella's daughter and Henry's brother's wife, Catherine of Aragon, is first, then Anne Boleyn, who produces the religious and constitutional crisis. Jane Seymour follows; she dies giving Henry his male heir. Anne of Cleves, Katherine Howard, and Catherine Parr are next.

Historical Accuracy: The novel covers so much ground that there is obvious compression of details. The chronology is accurate.

4976 Katheryn, the Wanton Queen

Date of Publication: 1967
Subject(s): Tudor Period; Royalty—England
Historical character(s): Catherine Howard, Royalty (queen consort of Henry VIII); Henry VIII, Ruler (King of England); Thomas Culpepper, Gentleman; Henry Madox, Gentleman; Francis Derham, Gentleman
Time Period(s): 16th century
Locale(s): England

Summary: The novel describes the life and times of Catherine Howard, Henry VIII's fifth wife. Prior to her marriage, Catherine is loved by other men, a fact Henry will use to charge her with wantonness and an excuse for having her beheaded.

Historical Accuracy: The novel is faithful to historical facts with some scenes and the dialogue invented.

NIS PETERSON

4977 Street of the Sandalmakers: A Tale of Rome in the Time of Marcus Aurelius

Date of Publication: 1933
Subject(s): Roman Empire; Christianity
Fictional character(s): Ruth, Slave; Marcellus, Writer (poet)
Time Period(s): 2nd century
Locale(s): Rome, Roman Empire

Summary: This story of daily life in Rome during the reign of Marcus Aurelius portrays the thoughts, conversations, and aspirations of ordinary folk. The novel concentrates on Ruth, a Jewish slave girl, and Marcellus, the son of a merchant. Marcellus is a poet whose encounter with Christianity sets up a conflict between sacred and profane love.

Historical Accuracy: The novel is filled with authentic period elements that produce a convincing backdrop.

GLEN PETRIE

Born in Glasgow and raised in the English Lake District, Petrie was educated at Oxford, Exeter University, and London University's Institute of Historical Research. He taught for many years before turning to writing full time.

4978 *The Branch-Bearers*

Date of Publication: 1973
Subject(s): Suspense; Victorian Period; Artistic Life
Fictional character(s): Rufus Chalmers, Gentleman; Clementina Wainwright, Model (artist's)
Time Period(s): 1860s
Locale(s): London, England

Summary: Set in the Victorian art world, this suspense novel records Rufus Chalmers' deadly attraction to artist's model Clementina Wainwright. When her husband disappears, Clementina is suspected but cleared after he is found drowned. When Rufus discovers that Clementina's two previous lovers died under similarly mysterious circumstances, he begins to wonder whether he will be next.

Historical Accuracy: The novel features a convincing depiction of the Victorian art world.

4979 *The Fourth King*

Date of Publication: 1986
Subject(s): Russian Empire; Royalty—Russia; Literary Life
Historical character(s): Aleksandr Sergeyevich Pushkin, Writer (poet); Natalya Pushkin, Spouse; Nicholas I, Ruler (Czar of Russia)
Time Period(s): 1820s; 1830s (1826-1837)
Locale(s): St. Petersburg, Russia

Summary: The life and tragic marriage of Aleksandr Pushkin, Russia's greatest poet, are described. Czar Nicholas I calls Pushkin back from exile, provided he will settle down and write harmless poems and novels. Pushkin marries the young Natalya, a great beauty who attracts interest, including the czar's. Her flirtations lead to tragedy.

Historical Accuracy: Though based on history, the novel is a blend of the historical and the imagined.

4980 *Hand of Glory*

Date of Publication: 1980
Subject(s): Crime and Criminals; Georgian Period
Fictional character(s): Leonie Croasdale, Young Woman, Heiress
Time Period(s): 1770s (1778)
Locale(s): Cumberland, England

Summary: London heiress Leonie Croasdale journeys to a remote village to seek peace and quiet. She finds instead a harsh land inhabited by smuggling gangs and secret societies, and she is determined to fight back.

Historical Accuracy: The novel is authentic in its period and regional depiction.

4981 *Marianne*

Date of Publication: 1977
Subject(s): Crime and Criminals; Victorian Period
Fictional character(s): Marianne Jenkins, Gentlewoman, Murderer; Simon Tufnell, Clerk; William Rowlands, Gentleman
Time Period(s): 19th century (Victorian period)
Locale(s): Cumbria, England

Summary: A love triangle turns deadly as Englishwoman Marianne Jenkins manipulates both her lover and fiance until a respectable marriage is threatened by blackmail. The story is inspired by the celebrated Madelaine Smith case that shocked Glasgow in the 1850s.

Historical Accuracy: Marianne Jenkins is a fictional creation, and the book is not intended to serve as a guide to the notorious Madelaine Smith murder case.

ALEXANDRA PHILLIPS

4982 *Forever Possess*

Date of Publication: 1946
Subject(s): American Colonies; Leisler's Rebellion
Fictional character(s): Annetje Hoosen, Spouse (of Devalon); Henri Devalon, Landowner
Time Period(s): 17th century (1690s)
Locale(s): Hudson River, New York, American Colonies

Summary: Colonial life on the great Hudson River estates during the 1690s is the scene for this novel. The story involves the married life between Annetje Hoosen, the daughter of a New York merchant, and the aristocratic Henri Devalon. Their happiness is disrupted by the events of Leisler's rebellion.

Historical Accuracy: The novel features a painstakingly accurate period background.

CARYL PHILLIPS (1958-)

Born in St. Kitts, West Indies, Phillips was raised in England and educated at Oxford. She has written numerous fiction scripts. *The First Passage* was the winner of the Malcolm X award. *The European Tribe*, a book of nonfiction, was the 1987 Martin Luther King Memorial prize winner. Phillips taught English at Amherst College.

4983 *Cambridge*

Date of Publication: 1991
Subject(s): Slavery
Fictional character(s): Emily Cartwright, Gentlewoman; Arnold Brown, Steward (estate manager); Cambridge, Slave
Time Period(s): 19th century
Locale(s): West Indies; England

Summary: The novel shows a clash of perspectives and cultures between 19th-century England and the West Indies. Gentlewoman Emily Cartwright travels to the Caribbean to inspect her father's sugar plantation. She is introduced to the alien world of slavery through the brutish estate manager, Arnold Brown, and the proud and fearless slave Cambridge, whose perspective provides a counterpoint to Emily's.

Historical Accuracy: The period elements are faithfully rendered.

4984 *Crossing the River*

Date of Publication: 1993
Subject(s): Slavery; Racial Conflict
Fictional character(s): Nash Williams, Religious (missionary); Martha Randolph, Settler
Time Period(s): Multiple Time Periods
Locale(s): United States; Liberia; Yorkshire, England

Summary: The novel begins with the confession of a man who sold his children into slavery. It then follows the lives of three of his descendants over 250 years. One is a missionary in Liberia in the 1830s; another ventures to the American West; the third is an American GI in England during World War II. Each is connected to the others by the burden of suffering and the crisis of identity wrought years before.

Historical Accuracy: The voices from different historical periods are all convincingly delivered, forming a compelling chorus on the themes of race and identity.

JILL M. PHILLIPS (1952-)

Born in Detroit, Phillips has also lived in Wyoming and New Mexico. A professional writer since the age of 14 when she wrote campaign speeches for local politicians, she has worked as a typist, editor, and ghost writer.

4985 *The Rain Maiden*

Date of Publication: 1987
Subject(s): Middle Ages; Royalty—France; Royalty—England
Historical character(s): Philip II, Ruler (King of France); Isabel of Hainault, Royalty (queen consort of Philip II); Richard the Lionhearted, Ruler (King of England); Henry II, Ruler (King of England); John, Royalty (prince)
Time Period(s): 12th century (1180-1192)
Locale(s): France; Flanders; England

Summary: The novel describes the reign of Philip II, France's greatest ruler until Louis XIV. When Philip marries young Isabel of Hainault, Philip's rival for her love is Richard the Lionhearted of England. The novel dramatizes the court intrigue and politics between France and England during the times of the Crusades.

Historical Accuracy: The historical elements are accurate and vividly captured.

4986 *Walford's Oak*

Date of Publication: 1990
Subject(s): Georgian Period; Supernatural

Fictional character(s): John Walford, Murderer, Spirit
Historical character(s): Samuel Taylor Coleridge, Writer (poet)
Time Period(s): 1790s (1797)
Locale(s): Over Stowey, England; Somerset, England

Summary: Samuel Taylor Coleridge, having recently moved to Over Stowey, becomes interested in the local ghost, John Walford, who was hanged for a year and a day after being convicted of murdering his pregnant wife. Walford's spirit will not be stilled.

Historical Accuracy: The novel features good regional descriptions.

MICHAEL PHILLIPS (1946-)

JUDITH PELLA

Michael Phillips is a graduate of Humboldt State University and owns a Christian bookstore in California. He is the editor of the George MacDonald Classic Reprint series and is MacDonald's biographer. Judith Pella has a nursing degree and a B.A. in the social sciences.

4987 *The Crown and the Crucible*

Date of Publication: 1991
Subject(s): Russian Empire; Family Saga; Servants
Fictional character(s): Anna Yevnovna Burenin, Servant; Katrina Fedorcenko, Royalty (princess)
Historical character(s): Alexander II, Ruler (Czar of Russia)
Time Period(s): 1870s
Locale(s): St. Petersburg, Russia

Summary: Anna Burenin is a peasant girl who leaves her village to work in a prince's palace in St. Petersburg. There she befriends the Princess Katrina. Their relationship is played out aginst a backdrop of war and revolt.

Historical Accuracy: The novel provides an authentic depiction of the period's events and atmosphere.

4988 *A House Divided*

Date of Publication: 1992
Subject(s): Russian Empire; Family Saga; Servants
Fictional character(s): Anna Yevnovna Burenin, Servant; Paul Burenin, Revolutionary; Sergei Fedorcenko, Royalty (prince); Katrina Fedorcenko, Royalty (princess)
Time Period(s): 1870s; 1880s (1879-1880)
Locale(s): St. Petersburg, Russia

Summary: The story of the servant girl Anna Burenin, who works for the aristocratic Fedorcenko family in St. Petersburg, is continued against the backdrop of the war with Turkey and the growing peasant rebellion.

Historical Accuracy: The novel provides a faithful account of the historical background during the period.

4989 *My Father's World*

Date of Publication: 1990
Subject(s): Gold Rush—California; Wagon Trains

Fictional character(s): Corrie Belle Hollister, Pioneer
Time Period(s): 1850s (1852)
Locale(s): Oregon Trail, United States; Sacramento, California

Summary: In the first volume of The Journals of Corrie Belle Hollister, set during the California Gold Rush, Corrie is left on her own during a wagon train crossing to California and must bring her brothers and sisters into a raucous mining camp in search of their uncle.

Historical Accuracy: The novel provides a solid and believable depiction of the period and background.

MICHAEL PHILLIPS

`4990` *Sea to Shining Sea*

Date of Publication: 1992
Subject(s): American West; Civil War—U.S.
Fictional character(s): Corrie Belle Hollister, Journalist; Cal Burton, Political Figure
Time Period(s): 1860s (1860)
Locale(s): San Francisco, California; Sacramento, California

Summary: This installment of the Journal of Corrie Belle Hollister centers on the fateful events of 1860 as the nation rushes toward the Civil War. Carrie find herself working for Lincoln and the Republicans, risking conflict with the Hollister clan.

Historical Accuracy: The novel's historical background is believable.

MICHAEL PHILLIPS (1946-)

JUDITH PELLA

Michael Phillips is a graduate of Humboldt State University and owns a Christian bookstore in California. He is the editor of the George MacDonald Classic Reprint series and is MacDonald's biographer. Judith Pella has a nursing degree and a B.A. in the social sciences.

`4991` *Travail and Triumph*

Date of Publication: 1992
Subject(s): Family Saga; Russian Empire; Servants
Fictional character(s): Anna Yevnovna Burenin, Servant; Katrina Fedorcenko Remizou, Royalty (princess); Sergei Fedorcenko, Royalty (prince)
Historical character(s): Alexander III, Ruler (Czar of Russia)
Time Period(s): 1880s (1880-1881)
Locale(s): St. Petersburg, Russia; Siberia, Russia

Summary: The novel continues the saga of two Russian families during the 1880s—the aristocratic Fedorcenkos and the Burenins, peasants from Katyk. Their experiences are set against a backdrop of growing unrest and rebellion.

Historical Accuracy: The novel is precise in its treatment of actual events during the period and in the creating of an accurate historical atmosphere.

J.B. PICK (1921-)

English writer Pick attended Emmanuel College, Cambridge. During World War II he volunteered to work in coal mines. After the war, Pick moved to the northern Highlands of Scotland and began to write professionally. His novel, *The Last Valley*, was made into a film starring Michael Caine.

`4992` *The Last Valley*

Date of Publication: 1960
Subject(s): Thirty Years War
Fictional character(s): Vogel, Wanderer
Time Period(s): 17th century
Locale(s): Europe

Summary: This philosophical novel set during the Thirty Years War explores one man's nature and capacity for violence. An idealistic wanderer, Vogel, attempts to persuade a band of mercenary soldiers to resist destroying a village in the last valley the war has left untouched. The characters are pressed to the level of ideal types in a philosophical debate on war and history.

Historical Accuracy: The historical background is used primarily for its thematic effect rather than for a depiction of history.

ROBERT PICK (1898-1978)

An Austrian novelist, editor, and translator, Pick was born in Vienna and received his doctorate from the University of Vienna. Pick served as an editor and a member of the board of Alfred A. Knopf, Inc. and a reviewer for the Book-of-the-Month Club and *Saturday Review of Literature*. He is also the author of a biography of Maria Theresa.

`4993` *The Escape of Socrates*

Date of Publication: 1954
Subject(s): Trials; Ancient Greece
Historical character(s): Socrates, Philosopher
Time Period(s): 4th century B.C. (399 B.C.)
Locale(s): Athens, Greece

Summary: In 399 B.C. the aging philosopher Socrates is put on trial for introducing new divinities offensive to all pious Athenians and for corrupting the youth of the city by his teaching. He can escape the death penalty if he is willing to forswear his teachings, but he refuses. This fictional version of Socrates' trial and final days attempts to re-create the spirit of the age and to make understandable the significance of Socrates' trial.

Historical Accuracy: The author uses his sources well and offers an authentic sense of the place and the period.

CARL VON PIDOLL (1888-)

`4994` *Eroica: A Novel about Beethoven*

Date of Publication:
Subject(s): Musical Life; Biography, Fictionalized

Historical character(s): Ludwig van Beethoven, Composer
Time Period(s): 18th century; 19th century (1792-1827)
Locale(s): Germany; Vienna, Austria

Summary: This biographical novel captures the life and musical accomplishments of Beethoven from the time he came to Vienna until his death in 1827. The novel dramatizes equally well Beethoven's creative drive and the effects of his deafness on his life and music.

Historical Accuracy: Impeccably researched, the novel stays close to the actual facts of Beethoven's biography.

ARTHUR STANWOOD PIER (1874-1966)

An American novelist, editor, and biographer, Pier was the author of several books for boys as well as adult fiction.

4995 The Young Man From Mount Vernon

Date of Publication: 1940
Subject(s): Biography, Fictionalized; American Colonies; French and Indian War
Historical character(s): George Washington, Military Personnel (soldier); George William Fairfax, Gentleman; Sally Fairfax, Gentlewoman
Time Period(s): 1740s; 1750s
Locale(s): Virginia, American Colonies; Northwest Territory, United States

Summary: This biographical novel of the life of George Washington covers his formative years during the 1740s and 1750s when the essential elements of Washington's personality and leadership qualities begin to emerge. The novel follows his complicated romantic life as well as the campaigns during the French and Indian Wars in which Washington's talent as a soldier are revealed.

Historical Accuracy: The author employs an awkward though truthful mechanism to point out the novel's deviations from fact as two historians offer commentary on the story.

GLENN PIERCE
(PSEUD. OF GLENN S. DUMKE, 1917-1989)

American educator and writer Pierce is credited with unifying the sixteen separate California state college campuses into the country's largest single state university system. Pierce is the author of several textbooks and novels, including *The Condor* and *Cavern of Silver*.

4996 The Tyrant of Bagdhad

Date of Publication: 1955
Subject(s): Dark Ages; Persian Empire
Fictional character(s): Count Eric of Normandy, Nobleman, Diplomat
Historical character(s): Harun al Raschid, Ruler
Time Period(s): 9th century (800)
Locale(s): Bagdhad, Persia

Summary: This novel of exotic adventure involves Count Eric, who is sent as the envoy of Charlemagne to the court of Harun

al Raschid in Baghdad. It features a series of court intrigues that force Eric to match wits with a wicked rival.

Historical Accuracy: The novel is guilty of a number of anachronisms in its period depiction.

OVID WILLIAMS PIERCE (1910-)

Born in North Carolina, Pierce graduated from Harvard and has worked as a professor of English at East Carolina University. He was the winner of the Sir Walter Raleigh Award for Fiction in 1960 for *On a Lonely Porch*.

4997 On a Lonesome Porch

Date of Publication: 1960
Subject(s): Reconstruction Period
Fictional character(s): Ellen Gray, Widow(er), Gentlewoman; Lucy Gray, Widow(er); Ward Caldwell, Veteran (Confederate)
Time Period(s): 1860s (1865)
Locale(s): North Carolina

Summary: In this story of the Reconstruction South, survivors of the Civil War attempt to pick up the threads of their old lives and adjust to the new. Ellen Gray and her daughter-in-law, both widows, return to Cherry Hill Plantation, which has been ransacked. They begin the long process of burying the past and rebuilding.

Historical Accuracy: The novel features a solidly realized period background and realistic detail.

MARGE PIERCY (1936-)

American poet and novelist Piercy was born in Detroit, Michigan, and attended the University of Michigan and Northwestern. A recipient of numerous awards and honors for her work, Piercy's novels include *Small Changes*, *Woman on the Edge of Time*, and *Braided Lives*.

4998 City of Darkness, City of Light

Date of Publication: 1996
Subject(s): French Revolution
Historical character(s): Claire Lacombe, Revolutionary; Manon Philipon, Revolutionary; Pauline Leon, Revolutionary; Maximilien Francois de Robespierre, Revolutionary; Georges-Jacques Danton, Revolutionary; Nicholas Condorcet, Revolutionary; Camille Desmoulins, Revolutionary; Louis XVI, Ruler (King of France); Marie Antoinette, Royalty (queen consort of Louis XVI); Thomas Paine, Revolutionary, Writer
Time Period(s): 1780s; 1790s (1780-1794)
Locale(s): Paris, France

Summary: The French Revolution is depicted from the perspectives of several actual figures, including Robespierre and Danton, but also women like Claire Lacombe and Pauline Leon, who play important parts in the unfolding events. The novel captures the sweeping events of the period and its atmosphere.

Historical Accuracy: The majority of events and biographies of the novel's viewpoint characters are faithful to the facts, though some invention has been used and some deliberate anachronisms included in the interest of creating living characters.

ARTURO USLAR PIETRI (1906-)

Author of novels, plays, essays, and short stories, Pietri is one of South America's most distinguished men of letters. Born in Venezuela, he received his Ph.D. in political science at the Universidad Central of Venezuela. He became a diplomat in Paris and secretary to the Venezuelan delegation to the League of Nations. He later served as Minister of Education, Finance, and the Interior and has been a professor of Spanish-American literature at Columbia University.

`4999` *The Red Lances*

Date of Publication: 1963
Subject(s): Independence—South America
Fictional character(s): Fernando Fonta, Plantation Owner; Presentacion Campos, Overseer
Time Period(s): 1810s; 1820s (1811-1821)
Locale(s): Venezuela

Summary: Set during the Venezuelan war of independence, the novel centers on the conflict between Fernando Fonta, son of a plantation owner, and the plantation overseer, Presentacion Campos. When Campos rebels and joins forces with the Royalists, Fonta joins the Republicans and dies for the cause.

Historical Accuracy: The novel mixes convincing regional elements with a tendency toward the melodramatic that undermines its realism and documentation of the period.

DAVID PILGRIM

(PSEUD. OF JOHN LESLIE PALMER, 1885-1944)

British writer Pilgrim was born in Oxford and worked as a drama critic and editor of the *Saturday Review of Literature*. He served as a member of the British delegation to the Paris Peace Conference in 1919 at the end of World War I. His books include *No Common Ground*, *The Great Design*, and *The Emperor's Servant*. One of his books was adapted by Alfred Hitchcock as *Spellbound*.

`5000` *So Great a Man*

Date of Publication: 1937
Subject(s): Napoleonic Era
Fictional character(s): Felix Marbot, Young Man
Historical character(s): Napoleon Bonaparte, Ruler (Emperor of France); Alexander I, Ruler (Czar of Russia); Marie Walewska, Noblewoman (countess); Charles Maurice de Talleyrand-Perigord, Diplomat; Joseph Fouche, Political Figure; Josephine, Royalty (consort of Napoleon)
Time Period(s): 1800s (1808-1809)
Locale(s): France; Spain

Summary: This panoramic novel set during the Napoleonic Wars covers a ten month period from 1808 to 1809 when

Napoleon is at the apex of his power but the first hints of the fall to come appear. The fictional story used to animate the historical events is that of a young Frenchman, Felix Morbat, who is charged with escorting Napoleon's mistress, the Countess Walewska, from Warsaw to Paris. He becomes a page in the Emperor's household and an observer of the leading figures of the period.

Historical Accuracy: The characterization of the historical figures is plausible as are the novel's created scenes.

ROBERT H. PILPEL (1943-)

Born in New York City, Pilpel received a B.A. from Stanford and his law degree from Yale. He served in the Air Force and was awarded a Fulbright Scholarship to study comparative criminal law in Rome. Pilpel began writing professionally in 1971. In his novels he is concerned with the relationship between history and individual moral choice.

`5001` *Between Eternities*

Date of Publication: 1985
Subject(s): Roman Empire
Fictional character(s): Lucius Celer, Sports Figure (retired runner and trainer)
Historical character(s): Marcus Aurelius, Ruler (Roman emperor); Lucius Aelius Aurelius Commodus, Ruler (Roman emperor)
Time Period(s): 2nd century
Locale(s): Rome, Roman Empire

Summary: This is the fictional journal of a retired runner and trainer, Lucius Celer, whose patron was the Roman emperor Marcus Aurelius. Celer recalls his past experiences, as well as his present difficulty with the Emperor Commodus, Marcus Aurelius' son, whom Celer opposed as the emperor's successor.

Historical Accuracy: The novel provides a believable depiction of Roman life and customs. The novel's alteration of history is at least plausible.

`5002` *To the Honor of the Fleet*

Date of Publication: 1971
Subject(s): World War I; Sea Story; Battle of Jutland
Fictional character(s): Benjamin Gehlman, Military Personnel (American naval officer); Harris Maltbie, Military Personnel (American naval officer)
Historical character(s): Edward House, Military Personnel (colonel), Political Figure; Woodrow Wilson, Political Figure; Wilhelm II, Ruler (German kaiser); Sir Edward Grey, Political Figure, Government Official (British foreign secretary); Winston Churchill, Political Figure, Government Official (First Lord of the Admiralty); Franklin Delano Roosevelt, Political Figure, Government Official; John Arbuthnot Fisher, Military Personnel (British admiral); John Rushworth Jellicoe, Military Personnel (British admiral)
Time Period(s): 1910s (1915-1916)
Locale(s): Washington, District of Columbia; London, England; Scotland

Summary: This thriller is set during World War I and concerns the attempt to keep America out of the conflict and to avoid the impending clash between the British and German fleets. A plan is worked out by Colonel Edward House that involves two American naval officers. Plot and counterplot follow involving many of the leading strategists on both sides of the conflict and culminating in the decisive Battle of Jutland.

Historical Accuracy: The story is fictitious, but it is made believable by authentic details of the period and convincing portraits of the combatants.

JOSEPHINE PINCKNEY (1895-1957)

Born in Charleston, South Carolina, Pinckney wrote poetry and novels about her native South, drawing on its folklore, and excelling in character development and conflict. Novels such as *Hilton Head* and *Three O'Clock Dinner* deal with the aristocracy of the old South and the challenges of industrialization.

5003 *Hilton Head*

Date of Publication: 1941
Subject(s): American Colonies; Medical Profession
Historical character(s): Henry Woodward, Doctor
Time Period(s): 17th century
Locale(s): South Carolina, American Colonies; Barbados

Summary: Colonial life in South Carolina is described through the experiences of a young doctor, Henry Woodword, who comes to America from England by way of Barbados. The novel recounts his actual adventures.

Historical Accuracy: The novel offers a high standard of truthfulness in its depiction of the period and the atmosphere of the times.

JEAN PLAIDY
(PSEUD. OF ELEANOR HIBBERT, 1906-1993)

Jean Plaidy is the pseudonym of the prolific English author Eleanor Hibbert, who also wrote romances as Victoria Holt and Philippa Carr. As Jean Plaidy, Hibbert produced a remarkable series of historical novels covering the entire range of English history. All her novels are lively entertainments with careful historical research.

5004 *The Bastard King*

Date of Publication: 1974
Subject(s): Norman Conquest; Battle of Hastings; Royalty—England
Historical character(s): William the Conqueror, Ruler (King of England); Matilda of Flanders, Royalty (queen consort of William); Robert II Curthose, Royalty (prince); William Rufus, Royalty (prince); Henry, Royalty (prince); Harold II, Ruler (King of England)
Time Period(s): 11th century (1060s)
Locale(s): Normandy, France; England

Summary: William the Conqueror is the natural son of a nobleman and a commoner. His rise to the throne of England

is dramatized, seen primarily as a domestic story of his love for Matilda of Flanders and their children. Family concerns are played out, as William's children must attempt to live up to the destiny that his ambition thrusts upon them.

Historical Accuracy: Historically accurate, the period is vividly re-created.

5005 *The Battle of the Queens*

Date of Publication: 1978
Subject(s): Middle Ages; Royalty—England; Royalty—France
Historical character(s): Isabella of Angouleme, Royalty (queen consort of King John); John, Ruler (King of England); Blanche de Castille, Royalty (queen consort of Louis VIII); Louis VIII, Ruler (King of France); William Marshal, Nobleman, Knight; Hugh de Burgh, Nobleman; Henry III, Ruler (King of England); Simon de Montfort, Nobleman
Time Period(s): 13th century (1216-1246)
Locale(s): England; France

Summary: The tangled careers of two dominating women, Isabella, Queen of England, wife of King John, and mother of Henry III; and Blanche, wife of Louis VIII and mother of Louis IX, are played out in this novel. The two are opposites who share a common ambition and a common hatred of the other. The novel details the turbulent court intrigues in both England and France.

Historical Accuracy: The historical details are convincing and authentic.

5006 *Beyond the Blue Mountains*

Date of Publication: 1948
Subject(s): Family Saga; Frontier—Australia; Penal Colonies
Fictional character(s): Kitty Kennedy, Gentlewoman; Caroline Haredon, Convict, Servant; Katherine Masterman, Gentlewoman
Time Period(s): 18th century; 19th century
Locale(s): London, England; Australia

Summary: This is the generational saga of life in early Australia. At the center of the drama is convict Caroline Haredon, who is transported to Australia to serve as a maidservant in the Marston household. She is determined to gain her freedom and a future. The sins of the past, however, will be visited upon her daughter, Katherine.

Historical Accuracy: The era is colorfully evoked.

5007 *The Captive of Kensington Palace*

Date of Publication: 1972
Subject(s): Royalty—England
Historical character(s): Victoria, Royalty (princess); William IV, Ruler (King of England); Maria Louisa Victoria, Duchess of Kent, Royalty; Sir John Conroy, Gentleman; Albert of Saxe-Coburg-Gotha, Royalty (prince)
Time Period(s): 1830s
Locale(s): England

Summary: Victoria is depicted in the 1830s during the reign of William IV. The period is a tense waiting game to determine whether she will be the next monarch. A virtual prisoner protected by her overbearing mother, the Duchess of Kent, Victoria becomes a pawn in her mother's power struggle with William.

Historical Accuracy: The political scene is ably described and thoroughly depicted.

5008 *The Captive Queen of Scots*

Date of Publication: 1963
Subject(s): Royalty—Scotland; Elizabethan Period
Historical character(s): Mary, Queen of Scots, Ruler (Queen of Scotland); George Douglas, Nobleman; William Douglas, Nobleman; Elizabeth I, Ruler (Queen of England)
Time Period(s): 16th century (1567)
Locale(s): Scotland; England

Summary: The story of Mary, Queen of Scots in captivity is chronicled. First, Mary, with the help of George and William Douglas escapes from her prison at Lochleven disguised as a laundress. After the Battle of Longside, Mary flees to England and places herself under the protection of her rival, Queen Elizabeth. A succession of royal prison cells leads up to her final stay at Fotheringay.

Historical Accuracy: The period details are faithfully depicted.

5009 *Caroline the Queen*

Date of Publication: 1968
Subject(s): Royalty—England
Historical character(s): George II, Ruler (King of England); Caroline of Ansbach, Royalty (queen consort of George II); Robert Walpole, Political Figure (prime minister)
Time Period(s): 18th century
Locale(s): England

Summary: The novel chronicles the reign of George II and his remarkable queen, Caroline of Ansbach. She knows that if she is to keep her place she must never cross George's will or incite his choleric temper. Hiding her intelligence to play the role of the docile and helpless wife, Caroline endeavors to control the king with the aid of Prime Minister Robert Walpole.

Historical Accuracy: The era is invoked with color and conviction, though at times simplified for heightened drama.

5010 *The Courts of Love*

Date of Publication: 1987
Subject(s): Royalty—England; Royalty—France; Biography, Fictionalized
Historical character(s): Eleanor of Aquitaine, Royalty (queen of Henry II & Louis VII); Louis VII, Ruler (King of France); Henry II, Ruler (King of England); Thomas Becket, Religious (Archbishop of Canterbury); William Marshal, Nobleman, Knight; Richard I, Ruler (King of England); John, Royalty (prince)
Time Period(s): 12th century
Locale(s): France; England

Summary: Told in the first person by the remarkable Eleanor of Aquitaine, the novel offers a chronicle of one of the most fascinating women of the Middle Ages. She participates in the Second Crusade, marries first the king of France, then assists

Henry II in succeeding to the throne of England, becoming his queen in the process. Her children, Richard and John, will make important marks on English history. Eleanor dominates her age, and her story proves it.

Historical Accuracy: The voice of Eleanor in this fictional autobiography is convincing with an authentic sense of the period.

5011 *Daughter of Satan*

Date of Publication: 1952
Subject(s): American Colonies; Witchcraft and Sorcery; Pilgrims
Fictional character(s): Tamar, Witch (suspected); Bartle Cavill, Adventurer; Humility Brown, Settler
Time Period(s): 16th century; 17th century
Locale(s): Plymouth, England; Plymouth, Massachusetts, American Colonies

Summary: In this tale of the Puritans and the Plymouth settlement, Tamar attracts the attention of both a gentleman-adventurer, Bartle Cavill, and a Puritan, Humility Brown. She is suspected of being a witch and must contend with mistreatment in the old world and the new.

Historical Accuracy: The scenes in both Plymouth, England and Plymouth, Massachusetts are authentic and convincing.

5012 *Epitaph for Three Women*

Date of Publication: 1983
Subject(s): Royalty—England; Hundred Years War
Historical character(s): Henry VI, Ruler (King of England); Catherine of Valois, Royalty (queen consort of Henry V); Joan of Arc, Warrior; Eleanor of Gloucester, Noblewoman; Humphrey, Duke of Gloucester, Nobleman; Henry Beaufort, Religious (bishop)
Time Period(s): 15th century
Locale(s): England; France

Summary: In the power struggle that follows the death of Henry V and the succession of Henry's infant son, three women's lives reflect the age. Catherine, Henry V's queen, is destined to establish the Tudor dynasty. Joan of Arc leads the French in battle against the invading English. Eleanor, first the Duke of Glouchester's mistress, then his wife, is the victim of a murder plot.

Historical Accuracy: The author's ability to depict the age with vivid and telling details is exceptional.

5013 *Evergreen Gallant*

Date of Publication: 1963
Subject(s): Royalty—France; Religious Conflict; Huguenots
Historical character(s): Henri of Navarre, Nobleman; Catherine de' Medici, Royalty (queen consort of Henri II); Margot, Royalty (queen consort of Henri IV); Marie de' Medici, Royalty (queen consort); Catherine de Sauves, Gentlewoman; Charlotte de Montmorency, Gentlewoman
Time Period(s): 16th century; 17th century
Locale(s): France

Summary: The reign of French King Henri of Navarre is chronicled. Henri, a Protestant, is swept up in the conflict of the Catholic persecution of the Huguenots. Reputed to have more mistresses than any other king of France, Henri's life was a series of romantic liaisons, giving him the nickname, the ''Evergreen Gallant.''.

Historical Accuracy: The history is helpfully detailed and convincingly presented.

5014 *The Follies of the King*

Date of Publication: 1980
Subject(s): Middle Ages; Royalty—England
Historical character(s): Edward II, Ruler (King of England); Piers Gaveston, Political Figure; Isabella of France, Royalty (queen consort of Edward II); Roger de Mortimer, Nobleman; Robert I, Ruler (King of Scotland)
Time Period(s): 13th century
Locale(s): England; Scotland

Summary: The troubled reign of Edward II is chronicled. Edward, under the influence of Piers Gaveston, makes a number of enemies, including his queen, Isabella. She and her lover, Roger Mortimer, seek vengeance on the king. Their plotting produces one of history's most horrific murders, committed in Berkeley Castle.

Historical Accuracy: The details of the complicated political forces are described accurately with careful attention to the facts.

5015 *Gay Lord Robert*

Date of Publication: 1955
Subject(s): Elizabethan Period; Royalty—England
Historical character(s): Robert Dudley, Nobleman (Earl of Leicester); Elizabeth I, Ruler (Queen of England); Amy Robsart, Spouse (of Dudley); Robert Cecil, Government Official; Sir Francis Bacon, Political Figure, Philosopher; Sir Francis Walsingham, Government Official
Time Period(s): 16th century
Locale(s): England

Summary: The title refers to Robert Dudley, the most powerful man in the Elizabethan period. Dudley's love affair with Elizabeth might have culminated in marriage except for Amy Robsart, his wife. The intrigues of the ambitious Dudley and the cautiousness of Elizabeth, who resisted compromising her power by marriage, are dramatized.

Historical Accuracy: This is a vivid and convincing version of the famous pair.

5016 *Goddess of the Green Room*

Date of Publication: 1971
Subject(s): Royalty—England; Theatrical Life; Georgian Period
Historical character(s): Dorothy Jordan, Actress; William, Duke of Clarence, Royalty; Richard Brinsley Sheridan, Writer; George, Royalty (Prince of Wales); Charlotte of Mecklenburg-Strelitz, Royalty (queen consort of George III)
Time Period(s): 18th century; 19th century (1790s-1810s)
Locale(s): England

Summary: William, Duke of Clarence, the younger brother of the Prince of Wales, falls in love with the comic genius of the

Drury Lane Theatre, Dorothy Jordan. The affair unexpectedly lasts for 23 years and is truly a marriage in all but name, producing ten children. Dorothy stands firmly loyal to the duke despite the royal family's efforts to drive them apart.

Historical Accuracy: The period is accurately rendered with an authentic look at both the royals and the theatrical scene of the time.

5017 *The Goldsmith's Wife*

Date of Publication: 1950
Subject(s): Middle Ages; Royalty—England
Historical character(s): Jane Shore, Young Woman, Lover (Edward IV's mistress); Edward IV, Ruler (King of England); Richard, Duke of Gloucester, Nobleman
Time Period(s): 15th century
Locale(s): England

Summary: The title refers to Jane Shore, the wife of a respectable London goldsmith, who becomes Edward IV's mistress and the most important figure in his court. The novel depicts Jane's unlikely rise and offers a sympathetic portrait of Richard, Duke of Gloucester, the brother of the king and later Richard III, that is very different from Shakespeare's depiction of him as villainy incarnate.

Historical Accuracy: The details of period life and the politics of the era are authentic.

5018 *Hammer of the Scots*

Date of Publication: 1979
Subject(s): Middle Ages; Royalty—England
Historical character(s): Edward I, Ruler (King of England); Llywelyn ap Gruffydd, Royalty (Prince of Wales); Edward, Royalty (prince); William Wallace, Patriot
Time Period(s): 13th century
Locale(s): England; Wales; Scotland

Summary: The novel chronicles the reign of Edward I, called Longshanks. He is one of England's greatest kings, a strong ruler whose mission is to unite the kingdoms of England, Scotland, and Wales. Tragedy falls when he passes the crown on to his dissolute son, Edward II.

Historical Accuracy: The historical details are accurate and vividly presented.

5019 *A Health Unto His Majesty*

Date of Publication: 1972
Subject(s): Restoration Period; Royalty—England; Fires
Historical character(s): Charles II, Ruler (King of England); Barbara Villiers, Noblewoman; Catherine of Braganza, Royalty (queen consort of Charles II); George Villiers, Nobleman (2nd Duke of Buckingham); Titus Oates, Religious (clergyman), Leader (of the popish plot)
Time Period(s): 17th century (1660s)
Locale(s): England

Summary: The Restoration period and the court of Charles II are depicted in this novel which looks at Charles in his middle years through the perspectives of his queen, Catherine of Braganza, and his mistress, Lady Castlemaine. The story of the two women's battle for dominance over Charles is dramatized against the backdrop of the age's major events: the plague, the fire of London, and the conspiracy of Titus Oates.

Historical Accuracy: The author admits that some may charge that her interpretation is overly generous to Charles. The portrait is far more flattering than the one history has accorded him.

5020 *The Heart of the Lion*

Date of Publication: 1977
Subject(s): Middle Ages; Royalty—England; Crusades
Historical character(s): Richard I, Ruler (King of England); Eleanor of Aquitaine, Royalty (queen consort of Henry II); John, Royalty (prince); Berengaria of Navarre, Royalty (queen consort of Richard I); Saladin, Ruler (Muslim); Philip II, Ruler (King of France)
Time Period(s): 12th century
Locale(s): England; Palestine

Summary: The novel chronicles the adventurous reign of Richard I, England's most famous and most romantic monarch. Richard comes to the throne and vows to win back Jerusalem, committing himself to a daring crusade. Berengaria is his queen, but it is his mother Eleanor of Aquitaine who remains an important source of power.

Historical Accuracy: The highlights of Richard's career are clearly and convincingly depicted.

5021 *Here Lies Our Sovereign Lord*

Date of Publication: 1957
Subject(s): Restoration Period; Royalty—England; Monmouth's Rebellion
Historical character(s): Charles II, Ruler (King of England); Nell Gwynne, Actress; George Villiers, Nobleman (Duke of Buckingham); Charles Sackville, Gentleman; Louise de Keroualle, Noblewoman (Duchess of Portsmouth); Hortense Mancini, Gentlewoman
Time Period(s): 17th century
Locale(s): England

Summary: The scene is Charles II's court, and the story details his succession of mistresses who include actress Nell Gwyn; Louise de Keroualle, Duchess of Portsmouth, who is actually a spy of Louis XIV's; and Hortense Mancini, who is regarded as the most beautiful woman in the world. Charles' liaisons are set against the intrigue and rebellion that plague his reign.

Historical Accuracy: The court of Charles II is vividly portrayed. The author grants more concessions to the king than history has.

5022 *In the Shadow of the Crown*

Date of Publication: 1988
Subject(s): Tudor Period; Royalty—England; Biography, Fictionalized
Historical character(s): Mary I, Ruler (Queen of England); Elizabeth, Royalty (princess); Henry VIII, Ruler (King of England); Philip II, Ruler (King of Spain); Catherine of Aragon, Royalty (queen consort of Henry VIII); Anne Boleyn, Royalty (queen consort of Henry VIII)
Time Period(s): 16th century (1510s-1550s)

Locale(s): England

Summary: This autobiographical account of the life and reign of Mary Tudor dramatizes her dangerous childhood as the daughter of Henry VIII and Catherine of Aragon. When her parents divorce and her mother is set aside, Mary sees her own position as princess usurped, for a time, by her half-sister, Elizabeth. When Mary succeeds to the throne, her adamant Catholicism and her persecution of Protestants earns her the nickname ''Bloody Mary.''.

Historical Accuracy: The voice of Mary Tudor is convincingly re-created.

5023 *It Began in Vauxhall Gardens*

Date of Publication: 1955
Subject(s): Romance; Victorian Period
Fictional character(s): Melisande St. Martin, Orphan; Charles Trevenning, Gentleman; Caroline Trevenning, Gentlewoman
Time Period(s): 19th century
Locale(s): London, England; France

Summary: Melisande St. Martin is rescued from a French orphanage to become the companion of an English gentlewoman. She has great beauty and innocence, a combination that leads her to tragedy as she discovers she has no one to protect her.

Historical Accuracy: The period setting is ably developed.

5024 *The Italian Woman*

Date of Publication: 1952
Subject(s): Royalty—France; Religious Conflict; St. Bartholomew's Day Massacre
Historical character(s): Catherine de' Medici, Royalty (queen consort of Henri II); Henri II, Ruler (King of France); Henri of Navarre, Nobleman; Jeanne of Navarre, Noblewoman; Gaspard de Coligny, Religious (leader of the Huguenots); Margot, Royalty (queen consort of Henri IV); Antoine de Bourbon, Nobleman
Time Period(s): 16th century
Locale(s): France

Summary: Catherine de Medici is portrayed in the middle stage of her life, as the powerful mother of kings. She rules as regent for her son Henri, ruthlessly holding onto power, at the beginning of her transformation into the monstrous figure of villainy portrayed in history.

Historical Accuracy: Although based on historical fact, Catherine's motives and actions are speculative.

5025 *Katharine: The Virgin Widow*

Date of Publication: 1961
Subject(s): Tudor Period; Royalty—England
Historical character(s): Catherine of Aragon, Royalty (consort of Arthur and Henry VI); Arthur, Prince of Wales, Royalty; Henry, Royalty (prince); Henry VII, Ruler (King of England); Ferdinand V, Ruler (King of Spain)
Time Period(s): 15th century; 16th century
Locale(s): England; Spain

Summary: The novel is an account of Catharine of Aragon's ill-fated first marriage to Henry VII's heir, Arthur, Prince of Wales. She becomes part of a diplomatic union between Spain and England, but when Arthur dies suddenly and her dowry remains unpaid, Katharine becomes an exile in England. It will take Arthur's brother, Henry, the king to be, to restore her position.

Historical Accuracy: This account of the first half of Katharine's tragic life is filled with solid research and convincing period details.

5026 *The King's Pleasure*

Date of Publication: 1949
Subject(s): Tudor Period; Royalty—England
Historical character(s): Henry VIII, Ruler (King of England); Anne Boleyn, Royalty (queen consort of Henry VIII); Sir Thomas Wyatt, Gentleman, Writer (poet); Sir Thomas More, Political Figure; Catherine of Aragon, Royalty (queen consort of Henry VIII); Jane Rochford, Gentlewoman; Thomas Cromwell, Political Figure; Mark Smeaton, Musician
Time Period(s): 16th century
Locale(s): England

Summary: The story of Anne Boleyn and Henry VIII is described from Anne's first meeting with Henry in the rose garden at Hever to her final betrayal and execution on the block in the Tower. Anne proves to be a successful mistress but a fatal queen. At the center of it all is the complex figure of King Henry.

Historical Accuracy: The period is authenically depicted, and the stage is crowded with historical personalities.

5027 *The King's Secret Matter*

Date of Publication: 1962
Subject(s): Tudor Period; Royalty—England
Historical character(s): Henry VIII, Ruler (King of England); Catherine of Aragon, Royalty (queen consort of Henry VIII); Anne Boleyn, Gentlewoman; Thomas Wolsey, Religious (cardinal), Government Official; Mary Tudor, Royalty (princess); John Fisher, Religious (bishop); Sir Thomas More, Government Official (lord chancellor)
Time Period(s): 16th century
Locale(s): England

Summary: When Henry VIII's 20-year marriage to Catherine of Aragon fails to produce the male heir that Henry demands, the King begins secret negotiations with his chief adviser, Cardinal Wolsey, to annul the marriage. The novel captures the ensuing power struggle that culminates in England's break with the Catholic Church.

Historical Accuracy: The novel offers a believable version of the events surrounding Henry's first divorce.

5028 *The Lady in the Tower*

Date of Publication: 1986
Subject(s): Tudor Period; Royalty—England; Biography, Fictionalized
Historical character(s): Henry VIII, Ruler (King of England); Anne Boleyn, Royalty (queen consort of Henry VIII);

Thomas Wolsey, Religious (cardinal), Government Official; Catherine of Aragon, Royalty (queen consort of Henry VIII)
Time Period(s): 16th century (1500s-1536)
Locale(s): England; France

Summary: Anne Boleyn offers her own interpretation of her remarkable life. She is the daughter of an ambitious father. When she comes to court and bewitches Henry, Anne refuses to be just his mistress and insists on becoming his wife. When Henry is unable to obtain a divorce, he breaks with the Catholic Church, a move that divides the nation. When Anne is unable to supply Henry with the son he requires, tragedy awaits.

Historical Accuracy: Anne's voice is convincing, and the period details are authentic.

5029 *Light on Lucrezia*

Date of Publication: 1958
Subject(s): Renaissance
Historical character(s): Lucrezia Borgia, Noblewoman; Alfonso d'Este, Nobleman (Duke of Ferrara); Alexander VI, Religious (pope); Cesare Borgia, Nobleman, Military Personnel; Isabella d'Este, Noblewoman
Time Period(s): 15th century; 16th century
Locale(s): Italy

Summary: The novel attempts a more sympathetic and less villainous portrait of the notorious Lucrezia Borgia. Her father, Pope Alexander VI, and her brother, Cesare Borgia, struggle to unite Italy under their control. Lucrezia is torn between her loyalty to them and to her husband.

Historical Accuracy: The novel evokes the period with much color and authority. The interpretations of the characters are original if debatable.

5030 *Lilith*

Date of Publication: 1954
Subject(s): Victorian Period; Servants
Fictional character(s): Amanda Leigh, Gentlewoman; Lilith Tremorney, Servant
Time Period(s): 19th century
Locale(s): Cornwall, England; London, England

Summary: The novel describes the unusual friendship between Amanda Leigh, the only child of a stern and pious Victorian aristocrat, and Lilith Tremorney, a poor and uncouth servant. Lilith is unwilling to settle for her allotted place in life and ventures out into the larger world of London for some unexpected adventures.

Historical Accuracy: The period details are convincingly presented.

5031 *The Lion of Justice*

Date of Publication: 1975
Subject(s): Norman Conquest; Royalty—England; Middle Ages
Historical character(s): Henry I, Ruler (King of England); William Rufus, Ruler (King of England); Robert II Curthose, Royalty (prince); Ranulf Flambard, Nobleman, Religious; Matilda, Royalty (princess); Stephen, Nobleman

Time Period(s): 11th century; 12th century
Locale(s): England; Normandy, France

Summary: At his death William the Conqueror divides his realm among his three sons. To William Rufus he bequeathes the throne of England; to Robert, Normandy; and to Henry, five thousand pounds in silver. In this novel the actions of the three sons are described. Robert seeks glory on a crusade; Rufus is openly homosexual and grows increasingly unpopular with his subjects. It is Henry who seizes his opportunity and the throne.

Historical Accuracy: The tangled politics of the period are authentically depicted.

`5032` *Louis the Well-Beloved*

Date of Publication: 1959
Subject(s): Royalty—France; Biography, Fictionalized
Historical character(s): Louis XV, Ruler (King of France); Louis XIV, Ruler (King of France); Andre Hercule de Fleury, Political Figure, Religious (cardinal); Armand-Jean Du Plessis, Political Figure (Duc de Richelieu), Religious (Cardinal Richelieu); Jeanne Antoinette Poisson, Noblewoman (Madame de Pompadour); Charles Edward Stuart, Royalty (prince)
Time Period(s): 18th century
Locale(s): France

Summary: The novel provides a biographical portrait of the early life of Louis XV. Only five years old when he succeeds his father Louis XIV on the throne, Louis is dominated by a series of powerful women. The novel captures the court world of France as it heads toward the breakup of the Revolution.

Historical Accuracy: The novel is faithful in its basic outline to the events of history, with some imaginative embellishments and invention added.

`5033` *Madame Serpent*

Date of Publication: 1951
Subject(s): Royalty—France
Historical character(s): Catherine de' Medici, Royalty (queen consort of Henri II); Henri II, Ruler (King of France); Diane de Poitiers, Noblewoman; Mary Stuart, Ruler (Queen of Scotland)
Time Period(s): 16th century
Locale(s): France

Summary: At age 14, Catherine de Medici leaves Italy to marry Henri of Orleans, the second son of the King of France. She is a reluctant bride, and Henri is an unfaithful husband. As Henri's queen, Catherine mounts her career of revenge and her relentless pursuit of power and control.

Historical Accuracy: The book depicts the era accurately and presents a plausible psychological portrait of the monstrous Catherine.

`5034` *Madonna of the Seven Hills*

Date of Publication: 1958
Subject(s): Renaissance

Historical character(s): Lucrezia Borgia, Noblewoman; Rodrigo Borgia, Nobleman, Religious (pope); Cesare Borgia, Nobleman, Military Personnel
Time Period(s): 15th century
Locale(s): Italy

Summary: The story of the infamous Borgia family is dramatized through the life and times of Lucrezia Borgia. She is shown not as the monster of legend, but as a creation of her times. Her father, who becomes Pope Alexander VI, deemed "the most carnal man of his age," and her brother, Cesare, who wished to unite all of Italy under his rule, are both brought to vivid life.

Historical Accuracy: The novel mixes fact and speculation. The author's interpretation of Lucrezia's character is controversial.

`5035` *The Murder in the Tower*

Date of Publication: 1964
Subject(s): Royalty—England; Witchcraft and Sorcery; Crime and Criminals
Historical character(s): James I, Ruler (King of England); Anne of Denmark, Royalty (queen consort of James I); Henry Frederick Stuart, Royalty (Prince of Wales); Frances Howard, Noblewoman; Thomas Overbury, Gentleman, Writer (poet); Robert Carr, Gentleman; Robert Devereux, Nobleman (Earl of Essex)
Time Period(s): 17th century
Locale(s): England

Summary: This is story of treachery and betrayal in the court of James I. Robert Carr becomes the king's favorite, but his dangerous liaison with Frances Howard, Countess of Essex, spells disaster and produces a charge of murder. Witchcraft and poisonings break out in James' court.

Historical Accuracy: The novel is faithful to the facts and vivid in its presentation.

`5036` *Murder Most Royal*

Date of Publication: 1949
Subject(s): Tudor Period; Royalty—England
Historical character(s): Henry VIII, Ruler (King of England); Anne Boleyn, Royalty (queen consort of Henry VIII); Catherine Howard, Royalty (queen consort of Henry VIII)
Time Period(s): 16th century
Locale(s): England

Summary: The novel dramatizes the bloody course of Henry VIII's marriages to Anne Boleyn and Catherine Howard. Both end in executions, and both women are portrayed as being caught up in the dangerous role of the king's wife. At the center of the story is Henry himself, a complex amalgam of hypocrisy, shrewdness, sentimentality, and ruthlessness.

Historical Accuracy: The details and the politics of the period are accurately detailed.

`5037` *Myself My Enemy*

Date of Publication: 1983
Subject(s): Royalty—England; Civil War—England; Biography, Fictionalized

Historical character(s): Henrietta-Maria, Royalty (queen consort of Charles I); Charles I, Ruler (King of England); Charles, Royalty (Prince of Wales); Oliver Cromwell, Political Figure; George Villiers, Nobleman (Duke of Buckingham)

Time Period(s): 17th century

Locale(s): England; France

Summary: This is an autobiographical account of Henrietta Maria, the wife of Charles I. She is fiercely loyal to the king and stands by him as England drifts toward civil war, as Parliament battles the Crown, and as Cavaliers oppose Roundheads.

Historical Accuracy: The voice of the queen is authenic and her perspective is an interesting and illuminating slant on this important period.

5038 *Passage to Pontefract*

Date of Publication: 1982

Subject(s): Middle Ages; Royalty—England; Peasants' Revolt

Historical character(s): Richard II, Ruler (King of England); John of Gaunt, Royalty (Duke of Lancaster); Henry Bolingbroke, Nobleman; Wat Tyler, Revolutionary; Anne of Bohemia, Royalty (queen consort of Richard II); Robert de Vere, Nobleman; Isabella of France, Royalty (queen consort of Richard II); Edward III, Ruler (King of England); Edward, the Black Prince, Royalty (Prince of Wales)

Time Period(s): 14th century

Locale(s): England

Summary: The novel describes the turbulent reign of Richard II. When Edward, the Black Prince dies before his father, Edward III, young Richard becomes heir to the throne. When he comes to power, he must contend with the Peasants' Revolt and the intrigues of his uncle, John of Gaunt. When Richard banishes John's son, Henry Bolingbroke, he seals his fate.

Historical Accuracy: The author is accomplished in reducing the myriad complexity of the period's politics into an understandable and convincing drama.

5039 *The Passionate Enemies*

Date of Publication: 1976

Subject(s): Royalty—England; Middle Ages

Historical character(s): Henry I, Ruler (King of England); Stephen, Ruler (King of England); Matilda, Royalty (Empress of Germany)

Time Period(s): 12th century

Locale(s): England

Summary: Who will rule after Henry I? The next in line is Henry's nephew, Stephen, but the king surprisingly names his daughter, Matilda, as his successor. Stephen and Matilda are lovers, and the succession question will make them bitter enemies. The novel depicts their fight to rule that plunges England into civil war.

Historical Accuracy: The period is authentically depicted.

5040 *Perdita's Prince*

Date of Publication: 1969

Subject(s): Royalty—England; Theatrical Life; Georgian Period

Historical character(s): George, Royalty (Prince of Wales); George III, Ruler (King of England); Mary Robinson, Actress; Charles James Fox, Political Figure; Richard Brinsley Sheridan, Writer (dramatist); Elizabeth Linley, Singer

Time Period(s): 1780s

Locale(s): London, England

Summary: The novel describes the love affair of the young Prince of Wales, not yet 21, and Mary Robinson, a young actress. George, lost in passion for Mary, fails to contend with political factions who attempt to exploit the uneasy relationship between the prince and the king and to set up a rival court with the prince at its head.

Historical Accuracy: The research and meticulous attention to details convince the reader of the authenticity of the historical facts here.

5041 *The Plantagenet Prelude*

Date of Publication: 1976

Subject(s): Royalty—England; Middle Ages; Religious Conflict

Historical character(s): Eleanor of Aquitaine, Royalty (queen consort of Henry II); Henry II, Ruler (King of England); Thomas Becket, Political Figure, Religious (Archbishop of Canterbury)

Time Period(s): 12th century

Locale(s): England

Summary: The beginning of the Plantangenet dynasty is dominated by Eleanor of Aquitaine who divorces the King of France to marry Henry Plantagenet. Their passionate and stormy relationship is jarred by the equally strong friendship between Henry and Thomas a Becket, who, as Archbishop of Canterbury, battles with the king over the power of church versus state.

Historical Accuracy: The period is colorfully and vividly presented with convincing details.

5042 *The Pleasures of Love*

Date of Publication: 1991

Subject(s): Royalty—England; Restoration Period; Biography, Fictionalized

Historical character(s): Charles II, Ruler (King of England); Catherine of Braganza, Royalty (queen consort of Charles II)

Time Period(s): 17th century (1650s-1690s)

Locale(s): Portugal; England

Summary: Catherine of Braganza tells the story of her unhappy marriage to Charles II. Their wedding is delayed when his father, Charles I, is deposed. After the monarchy is restored and Charles becomes king, they finally marry. Their relationship is soured by Charles' many infidelities and Catherine's inability to produce an heir.

Historical Accuracy: The voice of Catherine is authentic in this fascinating re-creation of the period.

5043 *The Prince and the Quakeress*

Date of Publication: 1968

Subject(s): Royalty—England; Georgian Period; Quakers
Historical character(s): George, Royalty (Prince of Wales); Hannah Lightfoot, Young Woman; George II, Ruler (king of England); William Pitt the Elder, Political Figure (secretary of state); Joshua Reynolds, Artist
Time Period(s): 1750s; 1760s
Locale(s): London, England

Summary: The novel describes the love affair between George, Prince of Wales (the future George III) and a young Quaker girl, Hannah Lightfoot. She is a virtuous maiden who is willing to become the Prince's mistress in secret in an affair that is doomed to disaster.

Historical Accuracy: Whether the affair occurred and even the existence of Hannah Lightfoot have been debated. The author based her novel on the available evidence and the character of the king.

`5044` *The Prince of Darkness*

Date of Publication: 1978
Subject(s): Royalty—England; Middle Ages
Historical character(s): John, Ruler (King of England); Arthur, Prince of Wales, Royalty; William Marshal, Nobleman, Knight; Isabella of Angouleme, Royalty (queen consort of King John)
Time Period(s): 12th century; 13th century
Locale(s): England; France

Summary: The troubled reign of King John, certainly one of the most reviled kings of England, is described. He conspires to defeat his rival, Arthur, whose murder becomes the rallying cry for John's numerous enemies. England comes under Papal Interdict, and John reluctantly compromises his powers in order to keep the throne at Runnymede, where he signs Magna Carta.

Historical Accuracy: The details of the period are credibly presented.

`5045` *The Princess of Celle*

Date of Publication: 1967
Subject(s): Royalty—Germany; Royalty—England; Georgian Period
Historical character(s): Sophia Dorothea, Royalty (queen consort of George I); George I, Ruler (King of England); Philip Christopher Konigsmarck, Nobleman (count)
Time Period(s): 17th century; 18th century
Locale(s): Celle, Germany; Hanover, Germany

Summary: Intrigue in the German court is depicted in the loveless marriage between Sophia Dorothea, Princess of Celle, and George of Hanover, the future king of England and the first of the four Georges. Sophia's affair with Count Konigsmarck ends in her tragic exile.

Historical Accuracy: The details of the period are convincingly described.

`5046` *The Queen and Lord M*

Date of Publication: 1973
Subject(s): Victorian Period; Royalty—England

Historical character(s): Victoria, Ruler (Queen of England); William Lamb, Nobleman (Viscount Melbourne), Political Figure; Robert Peel, Political Figure; Maria Louisa Victoria, Duchess of Kent, Royalty (Duchess of Kent); Sir John Conroy, Gentleman; Albert of Saxe-Coburg-Gotha, Royalty (prince)
Time Period(s): 1830s; 1840s
Locale(s): England

Summary: When Victoria succeeds to the throne in 1837, she is an 18-year-old, dominated and isolated by her mother (she sleeps alone for the first time on the night she becomes queen). Victoria is instructed by her Prime Minister, the worldly and cynical Lord Melbourne, on how to rule. The pair make an odd but effective partnership, the source of some gossip as Victoria begins to be called Mrs. Melbourne.

Historical Accuracy: The atmosphere and the politics of the period are accurately depicted.

`5047` *The Queen From Provence*

Date of Publication: 1981
Subject(s): Middle Ages; Royalty—England; Baron's War
Historical character(s): Eleanor of Provence, Royalty (queen consort of Henry III); Henry III, Ruler (King of England); Simon de Montfort, Nobleman
Time Period(s): 13th century
Locale(s): France; England; Scotland

Summary: Eleanor, daughter of the Count of Provence, becomes the wife of Henry III who tries to repair the damage inflicted upon England by his father King John. However, when he levies heavy taxes in order to lavish gifts on his queen, rebellion ensues. Simon de Montfort directs the rebellion, which produces England's first true parliament.

Historical Accuracy: The novel's period details and presentation of the historical facts are solid and dependable.

`5048` *Queen in Waiting*

Date of Publication: 1967
Subject(s): Royalty—England; Jacobite Rebellion; Georgian Period
Historical character(s): Caroline of Ansbach, Royalty (queen consort of George II); George I, Ruler (King of England); George Augustus, Royalty (Prince of Wales and Hanover); Robert Walpole, Political Figure, Nobleman (Earl of Orford)
Time Period(s): 18th century (1700s-1727)
Locale(s): Hanover, Germany; England

Summary: The novel chronicles the marriage between Caroline of Ansbach and George Augustus, Elector of Hanover and Prince of Wales, who is destined to become George II. Caroline comes to England with George and dutifully awaits the day when she will reign as his queen. She must balance the conflicting demands of George I and her husband, the prince.

Historical Accuracy: The atmosphere and the politics of the day are convincingly detailed.

`5049` *Queen Jezebel*

Date of Publication: 1958

Subject(s): Royalty—France; St. Bartholomew's Massacre; Huguenots

Historical character(s): Catherine de' Medici, Royalty (queen consort of Henri II); Henri of Navarre, Nobleman; Margot, Royalty (queen consort of Henri IV); Gaspard de Coligny, Religious (leader of the Huguenots); Henri de Guise, Nobleman

Time Period(s): 16th century (1572)

Locale(s): Paris, France

Summary: Catherine de Medici is shown at the height of her villainous career, surrounded by intrigue and murder. The campaign against the Huguenots climaxes in the butchery of the St. Bartholomew's Massacre. At the center of it all is the diabolical Catherine, for whom power is an all-consuming passion.

Historical Accuracy: The scene is vividly depicted.

5050 Queen of This Realm: The Story of Queen Elizabeth I

Date of Publication: 1984

Subject(s): Elizabethan Period; Royalty—England; Biography, Fictionalized

Historical character(s): Elizabeth I, Ruler (Queen of England); Henry VIII, Ruler (King of England); Mary I, Ruler (Queen of England); Robert Dudley, Nobleman (Earl of Leicester); Robert Devereux, Nobleman (Earl of Essex); Sir Francis Walsingham, Government Official

Time Period(s): 16th century; 17th century

Locale(s): England

Summary: Elizabeth tells her own story beginning with the death of her father, Henry VIII. She succeeds to the throne after the reign of her half-sister, Mary, and her own reign defines the age. Wary of any sacrifice of her hard-won power, Elizabeth resists marriage but not love. Her affair with the ambitious Robert Dudley is followed by great triumph in the defeat of the Spanish Armada and murderous practicality in the elimination of Mary, Queen of Scots.

Historical Accuracy: The novel offers a convincing portrait of the queen. The novel is filled with telling period details.

5051 The Queen's Favourites

Date of Publication: 1966

Subject(s): Royalty—England

Historical character(s): Sarah Churchill, Noblewoman (Duchess of Marlborough); John Churchill, Nobleman (Duke of Marlborough); Anne, Ruler (Queen of England); Abigail Hill, Gentlewoman, Courtier; Robert Harley, Gentleman

Time Period(s): 18th century

Locale(s): England

Summary: As Queen Anne comes to power in the 18th century, two women contend for control over her. One is the indomitable Sarah Churchill; the other is the unlikely challenger, Abigail Hill, whom Sarah has brought to court. The two vie for the queen's favor and affection as the question of who will succeed her begins to dominate political debate.

Historical Accuracy: This interesting period of English history is authentically captured.

5052 The Queen's Husband

Date of Publication: 1978

Subject(s): Victorian Period; Royalty—England; Crimean War

Historical character(s): Victoria, Ruler (Queen of England); Albert of Saxe-Coburg-Gotha, Royalty (prince consort of Victoria); William Lamb, Nobleman (Viscount Melbourne), Political Figure; Henry John Temple, Nobleman (Viscount Palmerston), Political Figure; Edward, Prince of Wales, Royalty; Victoria Adelaide Mary Louise, Royalty (princess); Robert Peel, Political Figure

Time Period(s): 19th century (1830s-1850s)

Locale(s): England

Summary: The marriage of Victoria and Albert defines in essential ways the Victorian period itself. Victoria falls in love with Albert, the younger son of a minor German nobleman in 1839. The difficult first years in which Victoria reluctantly gives over some of her powers of state are replaced by a working partnership that sees the two through some of the greatest events of the 19th century, including the Crimean War, the Indian Mutiny, and the Great Exhibition.

Historical Accuracy: The details of the domestic lives of the royal family are carefully and convincingly rendered.

5053 The Queen's Secret

Date of Publication: 1987

Subject(s): Royalty—England; Middle Ages; Biography, Fictionalized

Historical character(s): Catherine of Valois, Royalty (queen consort of Henry V); Henry V, Ruler (King of England); Henry VI, Ruler (King of England); Owen Tudor, Gentleman; Joan of Arc, Warrior; Charles VI, Ruler (King of France); Charles VII, Ruler (King of France)

Time Period(s): 15th century

Locale(s): France; England

Summary: This autobiographical novel allows Catherine of Valois, the daughter of Charles VI of France and Henry V's prize after his victory at the battle of Agincourt, to tell her own story. Her happiness as Henry's queen is short-lived when Henry dies, and Catherine languishes in isolation until she meets Owen Tudor and with him creates the Tudor dynasty.

Historical Accuracy: The voice of Catherine is authentic, and the period details are convincing.

5054 Red Rose of Anjou

Date of Publication: 1982

Subject(s): War of the Roses; Royalty—England

Historical character(s): Henry VI, Ruler (King of England); Margaret of Anjou, Royalty (queen consort of Henry VI); Richard Neville, Nobleman; Edward IV, Ruler (King of England)

Time Period(s): 15th century

Locale(s): England

Summary: Set during the War of the Roses, the novel dramatizes the troubled reign of Henry VI who lacked the will to rule that his wife, Margaret of Anjou, possessed. Conflict with

Warwick is described as he schemes to produce a Yorkist victory to put the young Edward IV on the throne.

Historical Accuracy: The period is convincingly detailed with the complicated political situation somewhat simplified for dramatic effect.

5055 *The Regent's Daughter*

Date of Publication: 1971
Subject(s): Royalty—England; Regency Period
Historical character(s): Charlotte, Princess of Wales, Royalty; George, Prince Regent, Royalty; George III, Ruler (King of England); Frederick Augustus, Royalty (Duke of York); Caroline of Brunswick, Royalty (wife of the Prince Regent); Leopold of Saxe-Coburg, Royalty (prince)
Time Period(s): 1810s
Locale(s): England

Summary: This is the story of Princess Charlotte, heir to the throne and the unhappy offspring of George, Prince Regent, and his wife, Princess Caroline. Charlotte is caught between her feuding parents but stands firm to marry for love. Her happiness with Prince Leopold ends tragically with her death in childbirth.

Historical Accuracy: The period is authentically rendered.

5056 *The Reluctant Queen: The Story of Anne of York*

Date of Publication: 1990
Subject(s): Royalty—England; War of the Roses; Biography, Fictionalized
Historical character(s): Anne Neville, Royalty (queen consort of Richard III); Richard III, Ruler (King of England); Richard Neville, Nobleman (Earl of Warwick)
Time Period(s): 15th century
Locale(s): England

Summary: Anne of York becomes a pawn in her father, the Earl of Warwick's gamble to maintain his role as the Kingmaker. In defiance of her father, Anne marries Richard, Duke of Gloucester, Edward IV's younger brother. This thrusts her back into the turbulence of the dynastic struggle when Richard becomes king.

Historical Accuracy: Anne's voice is authentic, as are the period and political details.

5057 *The Revolt of the Eaglets*

Date of Publication: 1977
Subject(s): Middle Ages; Royalty—England
Historical character(s): Henry II, Ruler (King of England); Eleanor of Aquitaine, Royalty (queen consort of Henry II); Richard the Lionhearted, Royalty (prince); Berengaria of Navarre, Royalty (consort of Richard); Henry Plantagenet, Royalty (prince); Philip II, Ruler (King of France); Rosamund Clifford, Gentlewoman
Time Period(s): 12th century
Locale(s): England; France

Summary: Following the murder of Thomas a Becket, Henry II must contend with the enmity of his wife, Eleanor of Aquitaine, when she discovers his infidelity with Rosamund Clifford. Henry's powers begin to fail, and he also must contend with the growing strengths of his sons, the eaglets of the title.

Historical Accuracy: The period details are authentically presented.

5058 *The Rose Without a Thorn*

Date of Publication: 1993
Subject(s): Royalty—England; Tudor Period; Biography, Fictionalized
Historical character(s): Catherine Howard, Royalty (queen consort of Henry VIII); Henry VIII, Ruler (King of England); Anne of Cleves, Royalty (queen consort of Henry VIII); Thomas Culpepper, Gentleman
Time Period(s): 16th century (1540s)
Locale(s): England

Summary: Catherine Howard, the fifth wife of Henry VIII, tells her story. Born into an impoverished branch of the Howard family, she comes to court as a lady-in-waiting to Anne of Cleves. Her main interest, however, is her cousin, Thomas Culpepper. She catches the eye of Henry VIII and agrees to marry him, but she cannot forget Thomas, and her betrayal of the king leads to her death.

Historical Accuracy: The voice of Catherine is authentic-sounding, and the period details are convincing.

5059 *Royal Road to Fotheringay*

Date of Publication: 1955
Subject(s): Elizabethan Period; Royalty—England; Royalty—Scotland
Historical character(s): Mary, Queen of Scots, Ruler (Queen of Scotland); Henri II, Ruler (King of France); Henry Stewart, Nobleman (Lord Darnley); James Hepburn, Nobleman (Earl of Bothwell)
Time Period(s): 16th century
Locale(s): France; Scotland; England

Summary: The amazing life of Mary, Queen of Scots, is depicted. She was queen of both France and Scotland and finally ran afoul of Elizabeth I, the powerful Queen of England. Her life at the French court, the intrigues in Scotland, her marriage to Darnley, his murder, and her affair with Bothwell are all dramatized. The novel climaxes with Mary's imprisonment by Elizabeth.

Historical Accuracy: Historians disagree on Mary's motives and actions. The author's interpretation of events is a blend of fact and speculation.

5060 *St. Thomas's Eve*

Date of Publication: 1954
Subject(s): Tudor Period; Royalty—England; Religious Conflict
Historical character(s): Henry VIII, Ruler (King of England); Sir Thomas More, Government Official; Thomas Wolsey, Religious (cardinal), Government Official
Time Period(s): 16th century
Locale(s): England

Summary: The dramatic confrontation between Henry VIII and his chancellor, Sir Thomas More, is chronicled. Henry's marriage to Anne Boleyn begins the Protestant Reformation in England, redefining the religious power of the monarch. In defiance of Henry, More stands firm, paying the ultimate price for his convictions.

Historical Accuracy: The period details are sharply and vividly presented.

5061 *The Scarlet Cloak*

Date of Publication: 1957
Subject(s): Elizabethan Period; Inquisition; Spanish Armada
Fictional character(s): Blasco Carramadino, Adventurer; Domingo Carramadino, Adventurer
Historical character(s): Philip II, Ruler (King of Spain); Henri III, Ruler (King of France); Elizabeth I, Ruler (Queen of England)
Time Period(s): 16th century (1572-1588)
Locale(s): Andalusia, Spain; Paris, France; Devon, England

Summary: In the 16th century, Philip II of Spain mounts a holy war against Protestants abroad and heretics at home. Blasco Carramadino and his brother Domingo are swept up in Philip's plot to overthrow Elizabeth I of England. Their adventures take them from quiet Andalusia to Paris and finally England as the Spanish Armada sails north.

Historical Accuracy: The period details are convincing.

5062 *The Shadow of the Pomegranate*

Date of Publication: 1962
Subject(s): Tudor Period; Royalty—England
Historical character(s): Catherine of Aragon, Royalty (queen consort of Henry VIII); Henry VIII, Ruler (King of England); Ferdinand V, Ruler (King of Spain); Thomas Wolsey, Religious (cardinal), Government Official; Elizabeth Blount, Gentlewoman; Francisco Ximenes de Cisneros, Religious (cardinal)
Time Period(s): 16th century (1510s)
Locale(s): England; Spain

Summary: The title refers to the insignia of Catherine of Aragon, the pomegranate, which is an Arabic sign for fertility. And therein lies her downfall, as the novel explores the consequences of her failure to provide her husband, Henry VIII, with the male heir to the throne that he requires. Their infant son dies, and Catherine suffers a series of miscarriages that makes Henry consider another wife.

Historical Accuracy: The period detail of the political intrigue of Henry's court is convincing.

5063 *The Sixth Wife*

Date of Publication: 1953
Subject(s): Tudor Period; Royalty—England
Historical character(s): Henry VIII, Ruler (King of England); Catherine Parr, Royalty (queen consort of Henry VIII); Thomas Seymour, Gentleman; Elizabeth Tudor, Royalty (princess); Lady Jane Grey, Ruler (Queen of England)
Time Period(s): 16th century (1543-1548)
Locale(s): England

Summary: The tragic story of Henry VIII's sixth wife, Catharine Parr, is dramatized. Catharine is the fiance of Henry's brother-in-law, Sir Thomas Seymour, yet Henry brings her to his court and proposes to her. Knowing the troubled and tragic fate of those who preceeded her, Catharine enters into what would prove to be one of Henry's most tempestuous marriages.

Historical Accuracy: Although Catharine's story appears more fictious than factual, the author has, for the most part, based her account on fact.

5064 *The Spanish Bridegroom*

Date of Publication: 1954
Subject(s): Tudor Period; Royalty—Spain; Inquisition
Historical character(s): Philip II, Ruler (King of Spain); Mary Tudor, Royalty (princess); Elizabeth Tudor, Royalty (princess); Don Carlos de Austria, Royalty (prince, son of Philip II); Elisabeth of Valois, Royalty (princess)
Time Period(s): 16th century
Locale(s): Spain; England

Summary: Few figures so dominated his age as did Philip II of Spain. Viewed by some as a fanatic and a tyrant, he is held by others as dutiful and devout. Philip remains a historical enigma. The novel attempts to arrive at the essential and real Philip, following his marriages to Mary Tudor and Elisabeth of Valois.

Historical Accuracy: The historical period is vivid, colorful, and authentically imagined.

5065 *The Star of Lancaster*

Date of Publication: 1981
Subject(s): Royalty—England; Battle of Agincourt; War of the Roses
Historical character(s): John of Gaunt, Royalty (Duke of Lancaster); Henry IV, Ruler (King of England); Henry, Royalty (prince); Isabella of France, Royalty (queen consort of Richard II); Henry Percy, Knight; Catherine of Valois, Royalty (queen consort of Henry V); John Oldcastle, Gentleman
Time Period(s): 14th century; 15th century
Locale(s): England; France

Summary: Henry IV deposes Richard II amd seizes the throne. Civil war breaks out, and Henry must try to hold onto power as his son, Prince Hal, emerges from his reckless youth to become a great national hero on the battlefield of Agincourt.

Historical Accuracy: The ground covered is well-researched and documented.

5066 *The Sun in Splendour*

Date of Publication: 1982
Subject(s): Royalty—England; War of the Roses
Historical character(s): Elizabeth Woodville, Royalty (queen consort of Edward IV); Edward IV, Ruler (King of England); Richard Neville, Nobleman (Earl of Warwick); Richard, Duke of Gloucester, Royalty; George, Duke of Clarence, Royalty; Jane Shore, Gentlewoman, Lover (Edward IV's mistress)
Time Period(s): 15th century

Locale(s): England

Summary: The Yorkist triumph during the War of the Roses and help from the Earl of Warwick put Edward IV on the throne. Edward falls in love with Elizabeth Woodville and makes her his queen, which shakes the foundation of his friendship with Warwick. Edward's greatest supporter is his brother Richard, Duke of Gloucester, and his worst enemy his brother George, Duke of Clarence. The novel follows the reign up to Richard's defeat at Bosworth Field, the end of the Plantagenet dynasty.

Historical Accuracy: The novel is dense with history but all is reliably argued and presented.

5067 Sweet Lass of Richmond Hill

Date of Publication: 1970
Subject(s): Royalty—England; Georgian Period
Historical character(s): George, Royalty (Prince of Wales); George III, Ruler (King of England); Maria Anne Fitzherbert, Gentlewoman; Charles James Fox, Political Figure; William Pitt the Younger, Political Figure; Charlotte of Mecklenburg-Strelitz, Royalty (queen consort of George III); Fanny Burney, Writer
Time Period(s): 1780s
Locale(s): England

Summary: The novel describes the scandalous affair between the Prince of Wales and Mrs. Maria Fitzherbert. Without his father's permission to marry, George contracts a secret marriage that becomes important when the king's madness is used as an excuse for political factions to seize the throne for the Prince.

Historical Accuracy: The period is evoked with care and attention to both the details and the facts.

5068 The Third George

Date of Publication: 1969
Subject(s): Royalty—England; American Revolution; Georgian Period
Historical character(s): George III, Ruler (King of England); Charlotte of Mecklenburg-Strelitz, Royalty (queen consort of George III); George, Royalty (Prince of Wales); William Pitt the Younger, Political Figure; Charles James Fox, Political Figure; Fanny Burney, Writer
Time Period(s): 18th century (1760-1780)
Locale(s): England

Summary: The German princess Charlotte is considered too plain and dull to keep the philandering young King George III in check. Their marriage is, however, happy and strong enough to endure the shock of political setbacks, family trouble, and the on-set of the king's madness.

Historical Accuracy: The novel's subject is so grand and sweeping that the story is forced to offer brief snapshots of the personalities and issues, all done well and accurately, but deserving of greater elaboration.

5069 The Thistle and the Rose

Date of Publication: 1963

Subject(s): Royalty—Scotland; Tudor Period; Royalty—England
Historical character(s): Margaret Tudor, Royalty (princess); James IV, Ruler (King of Scotland); Henry, Royalty (prince); Henry VII, Ruler (King of England); James, Royalty (prince)
Time Period(s): 15th century
Locale(s): England; Scotland

Summary: Princess Margaret Tudor marries James IV of Scotland to bring the two nations together. The plan goes awry as Margaret is barely accepted by James and conflict leads to the defeat of the Scots at Flodden Field. Margaret becomes Regent of Scotland and must contend with treachery and betrayal in the fight for custody and control of her son, James V.

Historical Accuracy: The period details are convincingly displayed.

5070 The Three Crowns

Date of Publication: 1965
Subject(s): Royalty—England; Restoration Period; Monmouth's Rebellion
Historical character(s): Charles II, Ruler (King of England); James, Royalty (Duke of York); James Scott, Nobleman (Duke of Monmouth); William of Orange, Royalty (prince); Mary, Royalty (princess, daughter of James II); Elizabeth Villiers, Gentlewoman
Time Period(s): 17th century
Locale(s): England; Netherlands

Summary: Although restored to the throne of England, Charles II has no heir. The heir-presumptive is his brother, James, Duke of York, but he is a Catholic, and multiple factions begin to plot for the throne, including James, Duke of Monmouth and William of Orange. William is married to Mary, James, the Duke of York's daughter, and he forces Mary to decide between loyalty to him and to her father.

Historical Accuracy: The politics of the period are insightfully presented with convincing portraits of the major players.

5071 Uneasy Lies the Head

Date of Publication: 1982
Subject(s): Royalty—England; Tudor Period
Historical character(s): Henry VII, Ruler (King of England); Elizabeth of York, Royalty (queen consort of Henry VII); Henry, Royalty (prince); Catherine of Aragon, Royalty (consort of Henry VIII)
Time Period(s): 15th century; 16th century (1486-1509)
Locale(s): England

Summary: The novel chronicles the reign of Henry VII, who tries to rule fairly and well but is weakened by failing health, corrupt advisers, and pretenders to the throne. He is also eclipsed by the magnetic power of his son, the Prince of Wales. When Henry VII's queen, Elizabeth, dies, father and son compete for the hand of the Spanish princess, Catherine of Aragon.

Historical Accuracy: The author provides a reliable interpretation of the events and a convincing re-creation of the period details.

5072 *Victoria in the Wings*

Date of Publication: 1972
Subject(s): Royalty—England
Historical character(s): George, Prince Regent, Royalty; Victoria, Royalty (princess); William, Duke of Clarence, Royalty (prince)
Time Period(s): 19th century (1815-1830)
Locale(s): England

Summary: The novel describes the precarious early years of Victoria, daughter of Prince Edward. She is considered far too remote in the line of succession to be assured the crown but too close to be ignored. She becomes a target for those who have their own ideas about who should succeed George IV and his brother William.

Historical Accuracy: The complicated politics of the period are authentically delivered.

5073 *Victoria Victorious*

Date of Publication: 1985
Subject(s): Royalty—England; Victorian Period; Crimean War
Historical character(s): Victoria, Ruler (Queen of England); Albert of Saxe-Coburg-Gotha, Royalty (prince consort of Victoria); Edward, Prince of Wales, Royalty; William Gladstone, Political Figure; Benjamin Disraeli, Political Figure
Time Period(s): 19th century; 20th century (1810s-1900s)
Locale(s): England

Summary: Told as an autobiography, Queen Victoria relates the details of her reign, the longest in English history, during which England becomes a modern world power. Victoria comes to the throne as a young, inexperienced girl and becomes the emblem of her age. The novel offers her perspective on the great events of the century and its greatest figures.

Historical Accuracy: This is an impressive achievement in historical reconstruction. Victoria emerges as a convincing personality.

5074 *The Vow on the Heron*

Date of Publication: 1980
Subject(s): Royalty—England; Hundred Years War; Battle of Crecy
Historical character(s): Edward III, Ruler (King of England); Philippa of Hainault, Royalty (queen consort of Edward III); Robert of Artois, Nobleman; Edward, the Black Prince, Royalty (prince); Isabella of France, Royalty (queen consort of Edward II); John of Gaunt, Royalty (Duke of Lancaster)
Time Period(s): 14th century
Locale(s): England; France

Summary: The novel chronicles Edward III's fascinating reign. His father is murdered by his mother and her lover. He marries Philippa of Hainault as a teenager, fathers the Black Prince, and brings prosperity to England before his reign is disrupted by the beginning of the Hundred Years War.

Historical Accuracy: The novel is detailed and accurate in its depiction of the period and the personalities.

5075 *The Wandering Prince*

Date of Publication: 1956
Subject(s): Royalty—England
Historical character(s): Charles Stuart, Royalty (prince), Heir; Louis XIV, Ruler (King of France); Lucy Walter, Gentlewoman, Lover; Henrietta Anne of England, Royalty (princess)
Time Period(s): 17th century
Locale(s): England; France

Summary: The early years of Charles Stuart, later King Charles II, are portrayed through the perspectives of two women in his life—Lucy Walter, his mistress, and Henrietta Anne, his sister, whose affair with Louis XIV turns her into a spy against her royal brother.

Historical Accuracy: The author's portrait of Charles is far more flattering than most sources record.

5076 *The Widow of Windsor*

Date of Publication: 1974
Subject(s): Victorian Period; Royalty—England
Historical character(s): Victoria, Ruler (Queen of England); Henry John Temple, Nobleman (Viscount Palmerston), Political Figure; William Gladstone, Political Figure; Benjamin Disraeli, Political Figure; Edward, Prince of Wales, Royalty; John Brown, Servant; Alexandra of Denmark, Royalty (wife of the Prince of Wales)
Time Period(s): 19th century; 20th century (1850s-1902)
Locale(s): England; Scotland

Summary: The novel dramatizes Queen Victoria's years alone after the death of Prince Albert. Determined to mourn him for the rest of her life, Victoria is slowly pulled back into public life by affairs of state. She sits on the throne while England is transformed into a modern nation.

Historical Accuracy: The novel illustrates many of the important events and personalities with care and precision.

5077 *William's Wife*

Date of Publication: 1993
Subject(s): Royalty—England; Religious Conflict; Biography, Fictionalized
Historical character(s): Mary II, Ruler (Queen of England); James II, Ruler (King of England); William of Orange, Royalty (prince)
Time Period(s): 17th century
Locale(s): England; Netherlands

Summary: Mary II of England tells the story of her forced marriage to the dour and power-hungry William of Orange in order to guarantee a Protestant succession. William is uninterested in Mary's affection, and she must choose between her filial devotion to James II and her duty to her husband, James' greatest enemy.

Historical Accuracy: Richly textured and convincing, the novel offers a plausible portrait of Mary.

BELVA PLAIN (1919-)

Bestselling American novelist Belva Plain was born in New York City, and was educated at Barnard College. Her first novel, *Evergreen*, was the first of Plain's many bestsellers and was produced as a television miniseries. Her other books include *Eden Burning*, *The Golden Cup*, and *Tapestry*.

5078 *Crescent City*

Date of Publication: 1984
Subject(s): Civil War—U.S.; Jews
Fictional character(s): Miriam Raphael, Immigrant; Eugene Mendes, Gentleman
Time Period(s): 19th century
Locale(s): New Orleans, Louisiana

Summary: This romantic story set in New Orleans before and during the Civil War describes the life of a Jewish family who flees from Europe. Their life in New Orleans produces crisis and conflict.

Historical Accuracy: The novel provides an authentic portrait of the period and New Orleans.

ROBERT PLAYER

5079 *Oh! Where Are Bloody Mary's Earrings?*

Date of Publication: 1972
Subject(s): Royalty—England; Mystery; Victorian Period
Historical character(s): Mary I, Ruler (Queen of England); Victoria, Ruler (Queen of England); Sir Henry Ponsonby, Government Official (private secretary); Edward, Prince of Wales, Royalty; Philip II, Ruler (King of Spain); Elizabeth Tudor, Royalty (princess)
Time Period(s): 16th century (1554); 1880s (1887)
Locale(s): London, England

Summary: Philip of Spain's wedding gift to his bride Mary I of England is a pair of diamond earrings, given to insure a male heir to the throne. The fate of those earrings is dramatized across the centuries from the Tudor period to the Victorian era as they become part of the delicate negotiations between Queen Victoria and her profligate son Edward, the Prince of Wales.

Historical Accuracy: The story is completely imaginary.

HENRY PLEASANTS (1884-1963)

American writer Pleasants received his B.A. degree from Haverford College and his M.D. from the University of Pennsylvania. Pleasants worked as a doctor in general practice until his retirement in 1949. His books include *Anthony Wayne*, *The Tragedy of the Crater*, and *Thomas Mason, Adventurer*.

5080 *Mars' Butterfly*

Date of Publication: 1942
Subject(s): American Revolution; Espionage

Historical character(s): John Andre, Military Personnel (British major), Spy; Benedict Arnold, Military Personnel (general); Margaret Shippen Arnold, Spouse (of Arnold), Spy
Time Period(s): 1770s; 1780s
Locale(s): New York

Summary: The career of British spy Major John Andre is dramatized. Andre's adventures, including his negotiations with Benedict Arnold to surrender West Point to the British, are chronicled, as well as his capture and execution in 1780.

Historical Accuracy: The novel relies on the familiar story of Andre's exploits, combining the factual with the legendary, and includes some obvious inaccuracies to heighten the drama.

LEON POIRIER

5081 *Saint Paul: A Historical Novel of His Life*

Date of Publication: 1961
Subject(s): Biography, Fictionalized; Religious Life; Christianity
Historical character(s): Paul, Religious
Time Period(s): 1st century
Locale(s): Middle East; Rome, Roman Empire

Summary: This biographical treatment chronicles the career of Saint Paul from his conversion to Christianity through the years of his ministry throughout the Mediterranean world. This is a devotional rendering of Paul's life and the early history of the Christian church.

Historical Accuracy: The novel is faithful to the chronology of Paul's life.

JOOST POLDERMANS

5082 *Vincent: A Novel Based on the Life of Van Gogh*

Date of Publication: 1962
Subject(s): Artistic Life; Biography, Fictionalized
Historical character(s): Vincent Van Gogh, Artist; Theo Van Gogh, Businessman; Pierre Tanguy, Artist; Paul Cezanne, Artist; Paul Signac, Artist; Henri de Toulouse-Lautrec, Artist; Paul Gauguin, Artist
Time Period(s): 19th century (1863-1890)
Locale(s): Netherlands; France

Summary: Based on letters, diaries, and reminiscences, the novel re-creates the short, tragic life of artist Vincent Van Gogh. This version of Van Gogh's story is stripped of romance, and Van Gogh is shown as a troubled youth, a misfit in business and society, and an enigma to his friends. At the novel's center is the curious and ambiguous relationship between Vincent and his brother Theo.

Historical Accuracy: Though based on recorded fact, this is not a biography. The letters and dialogue are inventions of the author.

DANIEL A. POLING (1884-1968)

An American clergyman, lecturer, and writer, Poling was the prohibition candidate in the Ohio gubernatorial race in 1912. He was an editor of the *Christian Herald*, the most widely circulated religious magazine in America. His radio talks were published in three volumes.

5083 *He Came From Galilee*

Date of Publication: 1965
Subject(s): Biblical Story
Historical character(s): Jesus Christ, Biblical Figure; Mary, Biblical Figure; Judas Iscariot, Biblical Figure; Pontius Pilate, Government Official
Time Period(s): 1st century
Locale(s): Nazareth, Israel; Jerusalem, Israel

Summary: The novel offers a dramatic retelling of the Biblical story of Jesus' life and ministry.

Historical Accuracy: The story stays close to the Biblical sources but is informed by an expressive feeling for its locale and the era.

MADELEINE POLLAND (1918-)

Polland was born in Ireland and grew up in England. She is the author of novels for adult and young readers, mainly historical, based on events and people in European, especially Irish, history. Polland makes a point of visiting all the sites of her books, walking the paths of her historical figures. Since the late 1960s she has lived on the Mediterranean coast of Spain.

5084 *All Their Kingdoms*

Date of Publication: 1981
Subject(s): Victorian Period; Family Saga
Fictional character(s): Celia Healey, Young Woman; Matthew O'Connor, Young Man
Time Period(s): 19th century (Victorian period)
Locale(s): Galway, Ireland; Dublin, Ireland

Summary: This family saga set in 19th-century Ireland begins with the romantic match between Celia Healey of Galway and Dubliner Matt O'Connor. Once married, Celia is thrust into Dublin life where conflict and fortune produce major climaxes through three generations.

Historical Accuracy: The novel is authentic in its rendering of the period and the Irish elements.

5085 *No Price Too High*

Date of Publication: 1984
Subject(s): Romance
Fictional character(s): Isabella Frost, Young Woman; Liam Power, Doctor; Angus Frost, Mine Owner
Time Period(s): 1920s
Locale(s): England; Chile

Summary: Isabella Frost is the daughter of a Scottish mine owner in Chile. When an earthquake kills her mother and cripples her father, Isabella is left penniless and is forced to make her own way as a clerk and servant before marrying an ambitious schoolmaster. When her father reappears in her life, Isabella must choose between duty and passion.

Historical Accuracy: The emphasis is on the emotional over the historical. However, there are accurate 1920s elements.

5086 *Sabrina*

Date of Publication: 1979
Subject(s): Romance; World War I
Fictional character(s): Sabrina Heron, Young Woman; Gerrard Moynihan, Gentleman
Time Period(s): 1910s
Locale(s): County Cork, Ireland

Summary: In Ireland just before World War I, Sabrina Heron meets and falls in love with Gerrard Moynihan. Her mother intends for her to become a nun, and Sabrina must summon the courage to oppose her mother's iron will.

Historical Accuracy: The novel offers a convincing re-creation of the place and the period.

FRANK POLLARD

5087 *East Indiaman*

Date of Publication: 1936
Subject(s): Georgian Period
Fictional character(s): John Adams, Sailor; Georgina Tibbles, Gentlewoman
Time Period(s): 1790s (1793)
Locale(s): London, England

Summary: This tale of London life during the 1790s concerns a young seaman, John Adams, who contracts a marriage of convenience to gain a vessel of his own. He must come to the aid of his true love, a servant girl, who picks up a diamond brooch and is charged with theft. She must be saved from the gallows by the intrepid Adams.

Historical Accuracy: The novel offers a remarkably detailed and authentic depiction of the London of the period and its customs.

ALYCE POLLOCK

RUTH GOODE (1905-)

Born in Brooklyn, New York, Goode graduated from Smith College and worked as a newspaper reporter and editor. She also has served as a ghostwriter for professionals in a variety of fields.

5088 *Don Gaucho*

Date of Publication: 1950
Subject(s): Independence—South America
Fictional character(s): Don Miguel, Cowboy
Time Period(s): 19th century
Locale(s): Argentina

Summary: This tale of life in Argentina during the 19th century features the adventures of Don Miguel, nicknamed

Don Gaucho. He and his cowboys save Buenos Aires from a British invasion. His participation in a series of revolts, duels, and ambushes are depicted to illustrate his romantic career.

Historical Accuracy: The novel features an authentic atmosphere of the period and the customs of life on the pampas.

NAPOLEON BACCINO PONCE DE LEON (1947-)

Born in Montevideo, Uruguay, Ponce de Leon is a literary critic. *Five Black Ships*, his first novel, received the Novela Casa de las Americas Award in 1989.

5089 *Five Black Ships: A Novel of Discoverers*

Date of Publication: 1990
Subject(s): Exploration; Sea Story
Fictional character(s): Juanillo Ponce, Entertainer (jester)
Historical character(s): Ferdinand Magellan, Explorer
Time Period(s): 16th century (1519-1521)
Locale(s): At Sea (circumnavigation of the globe); Seville, Spain

Summary: This fictional account of the epic voyage of discovery undertaken by Portuguese navigator Ferdinand Magellan is narrated by Juanillo Ponce, a jester who joins the expedition to find a western route to the Spice Islands, a journey that becomes the first circumnavigation of the globe. Juanillo's account captures the rigors and struggles of the voyage that Magellan would not survive.

Historical Accuracy: The dates and events of the voyage and the majority of the events described coincides with what is known of Magellan's voyage from other sources.

DARRYL PONICSAN (1938-)

Born in Pennsylvania, Ponicsan is a graduate of Muhlenberg College and Cornell University. He has worked as a high school English teacher. He is the author of *The Last Detail* and *Cinderella Liberty*, both of which were turned into popular films.

5090 *Tom Mix Died for Your Sins*

Date of Publication: 1975
Subject(s): American West; Motion Picture Industry
Historical character(s): Tom Mix, Cowboy, Actor
Time Period(s): 20th century (1904-1939)
Locale(s): Oklahoma; Hollywood, California

Summary: The life and times of Tom Mix, Hollywood's greatest movie cowboy, are described from his early rodeo and ranching days to his success in Hollywood, where his incredible stunts brought him great wealth and world fame.

Historical Accuracy: The chronology and events of Mix's life are accurate.

ERNEST POOLE

5091 *The Nancy Flyer*

Date of Publication: 1949
Subject(s): Stagecoaches; Underground Railroad; Civil War—U.S.
Fictional character(s): Sam Hubbard, Young Man; Bob Gale, Step-Parent
Time Period(s): 19th century (1835-1860s)
Locale(s): New Hampshire

Summary: Sam Hubbard's widowed mother marries Bob Gale, a daring stagecoach driver. Gale introduces Sam to the ways of the road. However, the heyday of the stagecoach will soon give way to the age of the railroad.

Historical Accuracy: The novel's documentary material on coaches and life in New Hampshire before the railroad is authentic.

LYNN POOLE (1910-1969)

GRAY POOLE (1906-)

Lynn Poole was born in Iowa and graduated from Western Reserve University. She worked as an administrator at Johns Hopkins University and a lecturer at its School of Medicine. Gray Poole was born in Philadelphia, attended Johns Hopkins, and worked as a newspaper reporter and fashion copywriter.

5092 *The Magnificent Traitor: A Novel of Alcibiades and the Golden Age of Pericles*

Date of Publication: 1968
Subject(s): Ancient Greece; Peloponnesian War
Historical character(s): Alcibiades, Political Figure, Military Personnel (general); Pericles, Political Figure; Socrates, Philosopher
Time Period(s): 5th century B.C. (450-405 B.C.)
Locale(s): Athens, Greece

Summary: The novel traces the life and career of Alcibiades, the ward of Athenian statesman Pericles and the city's golden boy. A devoted attendant of Socrates and confidant of Phidias, Alcibiades is a hero of the Olympic Games and an army commander in the Peloponnesian War. When betrayed at home, he turns traitor to gain revenge.

Historical Accuracy: The author claims that all characters, places, and events in this novel are real and based on historical fact.

DUDLEY POPE (1925-)

An Englishman born in Kent, Pope served as a midshipman in the British Merchant Navy before being invalided out of the service. He next worked as a naval correspondent and naval historian. Widely regarded as a legitimate successor to C.S. Forester in his depiction of the British Navy under sail,

Pope's knowledge of naval lore adds greatly to the authenticity of his novels. He lives year-round on an ocean-cruising ketch, the *Ramage*.

5093 *Buccaneer*

Date of Publication: 1984
Subject(s): Sea Story; Pirates
Fictional character(s): Ned Yorke, Plantation Owner, Pirate
Historical character(s): Sir Thomas Whetstone, Nobleman
Time Period(s): 17th century (1650s)
Locale(s): Barbados; Jamaica

Summary: Set in the Caribbean, a battleground among the Spanish, English, French, and Dutch, the novel traces the naval adventures of a young English royalist planter forced by Oliver Cromwell's men into buccaneering. The action shows the British capture of Jamaica and the famous raid on Santiago.

Historical Accuracy: The novel is much more historically authentic than other novels about pirates on the Spanish Main.

5094 *Drumbeat*

Date of Publication: 1968
Subject(s): Sea Story; Military Life—British Navy; Napoleonic Wars
Fictional character(s): Nicholas Ramage, Military Personnel (naval lieutenant); Gianna di Volterra, Noblewoman (marchesa)
Time Period(s): 1790s (1796-1797)
Locale(s): Mediterranean; Cartagena, Colombia

Summary: The naval adventures of Nicholas Ramage during the Napoleonic Wars continue in action leading up to the Battle of Cape St. Vincent. Adventure afloat and ashore is featured as Ramage attempts to discover the battle plans of the enemy fleet.

Historical Accuracy: The period and naval strategy are convincingly depicted.

5095 *Galleon*

Date of Publication: 1986
Subject(s): Sea Story; Pirates
Fictional character(s): Ned Yorke, Plantation Owner, Pirate; Aurelia Yorke, Spouse; Thomas Whetstone, Plantation Owner, Pirate
Time Period(s): 17th century
Locale(s): Jamaica

Summary: After the death of Oliver Cromwell and the restoration of Charles II, Ned Yorke, leader of the royalist buccaneers, and his second-in-command, Thomas Whetstone, begin to rebuild their plantations in Jamaica. The new colonial governor sent from England lowers the island's defenses, however, and the buccaneers are forced back into action along the Spanish Main.

Historical Accuracy: Full of period details, the author's grasp of the locale and the naval atmosphere is solid and convincing.

5096 *Governor Ramage, R.N.*

Date of Publication: 1973
Subject(s): Sea Story; Military Life—British Navy; Napoleonic Wars
Fictional character(s): Nicholas Ramage, Military Personnel (naval officer); Jebediah Goddard, Military Personnel (naval officer)
Time Period(s): 1790s
Locale(s): West Indies; At Sea

Summary: This novel is set in the West Indies, where Ramage encounters his nemesis, Rear Admiral Goddard. Aboard the *H.M.S. Triton*, Ramage survives a hurricane and action with French privateers. A master of every situation, Ramage sets himself up as the governor of the Spanish island he has captured and must defend himself at a court-martial on which his career and honor depend.

Historical Accuracy: Filled with action, the novel is convincing in its evocation of the period and the navy under sail.

5097 *Ramage*

Date of Publication: 1965
Subject(s): Sea Story; Military Life—British Navy; Napoleonic Wars
Fictional character(s): Nicholas Ramage, Military Personnel (naval lieutenant); Gianna di Volterra, Noblewoman (marchesa)
Historical character(s): Horatio Nelson, Military Personnel (naval commander)
Time Period(s): 1790s (1796)
Locale(s): Mediterranean; Italy

Summary: In the first of the author's sea stories set during the Napoleonic Wars, Nicholas Ramage, a young naval lieutenant is introduced. When his captain dies, Ramage must take command of a secret mission to rescue an Italian noble sympathetic to the British cause. The action features adventures on land and sea and romance with a marchesa.

Historical Accuracy: The novel is filled with authentic naval and period details.

5098 *Ramage and the Dido*

Date of Publication: 1989
Subject(s): Sea Story; Napoleonic Wars; Military Life—British Navy
Fictional character(s): Nicholas Ramage, Military Personnel (naval officer)
Time Period(s): 1800s
Locale(s): Martinique; *Dido*, At Sea

Summary: British Naval Captain Nicholas Ramage is given command of the *Dido*, one of the most formidable ships of the line. His maiden voyage on the *Dido* takes him to the West Indies and to Martinique where he faces the French.

Historical Accuracy: The nautical elements described are authentic.

5099 *Ramage and the Guillotine*

Date of Publication: 1975

Subject(s): Sea Story; Napoleonic Wars; Military Life—British Navy
Fictional character(s): Nicholas Ramage, Military Personnel (naval officer)
Time Period(s): 1800s (1801)
Locale(s): England; France

Summary: As Napoleon prepares to mount an invasion of England, Nicholas Ramage is given a spying mission to discover the strength of the French forces preparing for the invasion.

Historical Accuracy: The period background is close to actuality.

`5100` *Ramage and the Rebels*

Date of Publication: 1982
Subject(s): Sea Story; Napoleonic Wars; Military Life—British Navy
Fictional character(s): Nicholas Ramage, Military Personnel (naval officer)
Time Period(s): 1800s
Locale(s): West Indies; *Calypso*, At Sea

Summary: Nicholas Ramage, on duty in the West Indies aboard the *Calypso*, pursues a French privateer that has captured a British ship and murdered the entire crew and all its passengers. The pursuit takes Ramage to several hostile ports on the Spanish Main.

Historical Accuracy: The period nautical details are authentic and convincing.

`5101` *Ramage and the Saracens*

Date of Publication: 1988
Subject(s): Sea Story; Napoleonic Wars; Military Life—British Navy
Fictional character(s): Nicholas Ramage, Military Personnel (naval officer)
Time Period(s): 1800s (1806)
Locale(s): Mediterranean; *Calypso*, At Sea; Naples, Italy

Summary: After the battle of Trafalger, Nicholas Ramage is ordered into the Mediterranean. Instead of the expected duty escorting merchant shipping, he is given a mission to rid the seas around Sicily of Barbary Coast pirates.

Historical Accuracy: The novel succeeds in capturing the atmosphere of the period and providing authentic nautical elements.

`5102` *Ramage at Trafalgar*

Date of Publication: 1986
Subject(s): Sea Story; Napoleonic Wars; Battle of Trafalgar
Fictional character(s): Nicholas Ramage, Military Personnel (naval officer)
Historical character(s): Horatio Nelson, Military Personnel (admiral)
Time Period(s): 1800s (1806)
Locale(s): Cadiz, Spain; *Calypso*, At Sea; England

Summary: Nicholas Ramage is ordered by Admiral Nelson to join the fleet under Nelson's command in the blockade of the French and Spanish Navies off Cadiz. The novel's climax is the Battle of Trafalgar.

Historical Accuracy: All the facts concerning Nelson and the Battle of Trafalger are true; only the events surrounding Ramage are fictional.

`5103` *The Ramage Touch*

Date of Publication: 1984
Subject(s): Sea Story; Military Life—British Navy; Napoleonic Wars
Fictional character(s): Nicholas Ramage, Military Personnel (naval officer)
Time Period(s): 1800s
Locale(s): *Calypso*, At Sea (in the Mediterranean)

Summary: Ramage is ordered to the Mediterranean where he is given command of a captured French frigate. Flying false colors, his ship is ordered to attack the French deep within their territory and raid Napoleon's garrisons.

Historical Accuracy: The period and nautical details are authentically drawn.

`5104` *Ramage's Devil*

Date of Publication: 1982
Subject(s): Sea Story; Napoleonic Wars; Military Life—British Navy
Fictional character(s): Nicholas Ramage, Military Personnel (naval officer)
Time Period(s): 1800s
Locale(s): France; Cayenne, French Guinea

Summary: During the brief peace after the Treaty of Amiens, Nicholas Ramage honeymoons in France. When war breaks out, Ramage must hide from Napoleon Bonaparte's secret police. A British brig in the harbor at Brest could offer a means of escape.

Historical Accuracy: The novel is convincing in its period elements.

`5105` *Ramage's Diamond*

Date of Publication: 1976
Subject(s): Sea Story; Napoleonic Wars; Military Life—British Navy
Fictional character(s): Nicholas Ramage, Military Personnel (naval officer)
Time Period(s): 1800s
Locale(s): Martinique; *Juno*, At Sea

Summary: Nicholas Ramage is given a new command, the *Juno*, and ordered to take up blockade duty off the coast of Martinique. He must marshal an inexperienced and unruly crew before taking on the French fleet and French privateers.

Historical Accuracy: The novel masters its nautical elements with authenticity.

`5106` *Ramage's Mutiny*

Date of Publication: 1977
Subject(s): Sea Story; Napoleonic Wars; Military Life—British Navy

Fictional character(s): Nicholas Ramage, Military Personnel (naval officer)
Time Period(s): 1800s
Locale(s): Antigua-Barbuda; Venezuela; *Calypso*, At Sea

Summary: In this installment of the naval adventures of Nicholas Ramage, a mutiny and desertion has occurred on board one of His Majesty's frigates. She is being held by the Dons of Santa Cruz in one of the most impregnable harbor fortresses in the West Indies, and Ramage is dispatched to rescue her.

Historical Accuracy: The period elements are authentic.

5107 *Ramage's Prize*

Date of Publication: 1974
Subject(s): Sea Story; Military Life—British Navy; Napoleonic Wars
Fictional character(s): Nicholas Ramage, Military Personnel (naval officer)
Time Period(s): 1790s; 1800s
Locale(s): West Indies; Jamaica; At Sea

Summary: During the war with Napoleon, communication between England and the West Indies is suddenly and mysteriously cut, and Ramage must solve the disappearance of the Post Office packets. The cause may be French privateers or a new secret weapon.

Historical Accuracy: The story is based on true events.

5108 *Ramage's Signal*

Date of Publication: 1980
Subject(s): Sea Story; Napoleonic Wars; Military Life—British Navy
Fictional character(s): Nicholas Ramage, Military Personnel (naval officer)
Time Period(s): 1800s
Locale(s): Mediterranean; *Calypso*, At Sea

Summary: As Napoleon's hold on the Mediterranean tightens, Nicholas Ramage and the *Calypso* are sent on a lone foray against his might in the region.

Historical Accuracy: The events described are fictional, but the atmosphere and the period elements are convincing and authentic.

5109 *Ramage's Trial*

Date of Publication: 1984
Subject(s): Sea Story; Napoleonic Wars; Military Life—British Navy
Fictional character(s): Nicholas Ramage, Military Personnel (naval officer)
Time Period(s): 1800s
Locale(s): West Indies; *Calypso*, At Sea

Summary: In this installment of the adventures of British naval captain Nicholas Ramage, he is assigned convoy duty to escort a fleet of merchant ships bound for England from Barbados. An incident occurs that causes him to be sent before a full naval court martial when he reaches England.

Historical Accuracy: The details of naval life of the period are authentic and believable.

5110 *The Triton Brig*

Date of Publication: 1969
Subject(s): Sea Story; Military Life—British Navy; Napoleonic Wars
Fictional character(s): Nicholas Ramage, Military Personnel (naval officer)
Time Period(s): 1790s
Locale(s): London, England; West Indies; At Sea

Summary: Ramage is ordered to take command of the brig *Triton*, sail to the West Indies, and capture privateers that are raiding English shipping. His challenges are great as the crew has mutinied, and Ramage must use all his resources to gain control and accomplish his mission.

Historical Accuracy: The naval details are authentic and believable.

EDITH POPE (1905-1961)

Born in St. Augustine, Florida, Pope wrote *The Black Lagoon*, a book of poems, and *Old Lady* under her maiden name of Edith Everett Taylor. Her other books include *Colcorton*, *The Biggety Chameleon*, and *River in the Wind*.

5111 *River in the Wind*

Date of Publication: 1954
Subject(s): Indians; Seminole Wars
Historical character(s): Osceola, Indian (Seminole), Chieftain
Time Period(s): 1830s; 1840s (1835-1842)
Locale(s): St. Augustine, Florida

Summary: Life in Florida during the 1830s is portrayed as the settler's encroachment explodes into the violence of the Seminole Wars. The novel offers a colorful view of St. Augustine during the period.

Historical Accuracy: The incidental details are accurate and the general account of events is authentic.

DONALD PORTER (1939-)

Born in New Orleans, Porter graduated from the University of the South and Cambridge University. He is the head of his own successful investment company in New York.

5112 *Jubilee Jim and the Wizard of Wall Street*

Date of Publication: 1990
Subject(s): Business Building; Railroads
Fictional character(s): Annabelle Stokes, Gentlewoman
Historical character(s): James Fisk, Financier; Jay Gould, Financier; Cornelius Vanderbilt, Financier; Josie Mansfield, Gentlewoman; Ulysses S. Grant, Political Figure
Time Period(s): 1860s
Locale(s): New York, New York

Summary: The novel dramatizes the so-called Railroad Wars in the 1860s that pitted Cornelius Vanderbilt against upstarts Jay Gould and his partner Jim Fisk, a poor boy from Vermont who transforms himself into a major force to be reckoned with. Their battle involves the Grant administration and the crash of the gold market.

Historical Accuracy: The story is a mixture of fact, speculation, and fiction. Events and characters have been freely altered.

DONALD CLAYTON PORTER

5113 *Ambush*

Date of Publication: 1983

Subject(s): Indians; American Colonies; French and Indian War

Fictional character(s): Ghonkaba, Indian (Seneca), Warrior; To-Sha-Be, Indian (Seneca), Captive; Ludona, Indian (Erie), Warrior

Historical character(s): Louis Joseph de Montcalm, Military Personnel (French commander); George Washington, Military Personnel (army officer)

Time Period(s): 1750s (1759)

Locale(s): New York, American Colonies; Virginia, American Colonies; Quebec, Quebec, Canada

Summary: In book eight of the White Indian saga, Ghonkaba, grandson of Renno, has divided loyalties. He desires vengeance against the English for having stolen the woman he loves, yet has sworn to honor the Senecas alliance with the British in the war with the French.

Historical Accuracy: Depiction of the period is more atmospheric than reliably historical.

5114 *Apache*

Date of Publication: 1987

Subject(s): Indians; Treasure Hunt; American West

Fictional character(s): Renno, Indian (Seneca), Chieftain; Beth Beaumont, Gentlewoman; Father Sebastian, Religious (priest)

Time Period(s): 1780s (1786)

Locale(s): Southwest

Summary: A fortune in lost gold lies hidden deep inside Apache territory. Father Sebastian is sent by the Spanish to retrieve it, while Renno leads a small group in a race to prevent the Spanish from gaining the gold.

Historical Accuracy: The emphasis is on exciting action with some simplified historical details.

5115 *Cherokee*

Date of Publication: 1984

Subject(s): Indians; American Colonies; American Revolution

Fictional character(s): Ghonkaba, Indian (Seneca), Chieftain

Historical character(s): George Washington, Military Personnel (army commander); Daniel Boone, Frontiersman

Time Period(s): 1770s

Locale(s): Kentucky

Summary: As he assisted George Washington in campaigns against the British, Ghonkaba faces the penalty for having broken the Seneca alliance with the English: banishment.

Along with his family, he sets out west into the land of the Cherokee where a series of challenges await.

Historical Accuracy: The atmosphere of both the frontier and the period is convincing.

5116 *Choctaw*

Date of Publication: 1985

Subject(s): Indians; American Revolution

Fictional character(s): Renno, Indian (Seneca), Warrior; Rattlesnake, Indian (Choctaw), Warrior; Emily Johnson, Gentlewoman

Time Period(s): 1780s

Locale(s): Tennessee

Summary: As the American Revolution concludes, the focus of the White Indian series shifts to the second Renno, great-grandson of the legendary Seneca leader. He exults in the new alliance among the Senecas, the Cherokee nation, and the new American nation. The Choctaws, however, disrupt the peace, led by Rattlesnake the half-breed son of a British spy, and Renno faces a variety of tests.

Historical Accuracy: The atmosphere is authentically depicted, if simplified for dramatic purposes.

5117 *Father and Son*

Date of Publication: 1993

Subject(s): Indians

Fictional character(s): Renno, Indian (Seneca), Chieftain; Ta-Na, Indian (Seneca), Teenager; Gao, Indian (Seneca), Teenager

Time Period(s): 1800s

Locale(s): Ohio Valley, Ohio

Summary: While Renno and his son Little Hawk fight in Portugal, their cousins Gao and Ta-Na grow to maturity in the Ohio Valley. When Ta-Na protects a young girl from assault, he makes a powerful enemy that has grave consequences in the struggle to come.

Historical Accuracy: The details of frontier and Indian life are solid, if the historical period is somewhat simplified.

5118 *Father of Waters*

Date of Publication: 1989

Subject(s): Indians

Fictional character(s): Renno, Indian (Seneca), Chieftain; Egan Kirk, Gunfighter, Frontiersman; Atarho, Indian (Cherokee), Warrior

Time Period(s): 1780s

Locale(s): New Orleans, Louisiana; Yucatan, Mexico; Tennessee

Summary: When renegade Indians kill his family, Egan Kirk mounts a campaign of revenge. Atarho, the Cherokee leader, escapes into Mexico taking with him five abducted women to sell into slavery. Renno joins the chase to hunt them down and avoid a bloody war between the settlers and the peaceful Cherokees.

Historical Accuracy: The story is fanciful with a premium on action and adventure over historical accuracy.

5119 *Hawk's Journey*

Date of Publication: 1992
Subject(s): Indians; Lewis and Clark Expedition; Louisiana Purchase
Fictional character(s): Renno, Indian (Seneca), Chieftain; Little Hawk, Indian (Seneca), Chieftain
Historical character(s): Aaron Burr, Political Figure; Thomas Jefferson, Political Figure; James Madison, Political Figure
Time Period(s): 1800s (1805)
Locale(s): Pacific Northwest; Washington, District of Columbia

Summary: Renno attempts to stop Aaron Burr, former Vice President of the U.S., who has hatched a plot to conquer Mexico, create a new empire, and back a revolt against America. Meanwhile, Little Hawk is sent by President Jefferson to discover the fate of the Lewis and Clark Expedition.

Historical Accuracy: The story blends historical fact and fiction, and the author warns that details have been simplified for the sake of the drama.

5120 *Manitou*

Date of Publication: 1988
Subject(s): Indians; Sea Story; Slavery
Fictional character(s): Renno, Indian (Seneca), Chieftain; Beth Huntington, Spouse (of Renno); Hodano, Indian, Shaman
Historical character(s): George Washington, Political Figure
Time Period(s): 1780s (1788)
Locale(s): Jamaica

Summary: Renno sails to Jamaica to assist in a slave revolt, while Hodano, his nemesis, intends to lure him to destruction after kidnapping his wife and employing the powerful Voodoo arts of the Caribbean.

Historical Accuracy: The action is a pastiche of romantic adventure with little direct historical documentation.

5121 *Red Stick*

Date of Publication: 1994
Subject(s): Indians
Fictional character(s): Little Hawk, Indian (Seneca); Calling Owl, Indian; Gao, Indian (Seneca)
Historical character(s): Tecumseh, Indian (Cherokee), Chieftain; James Madison, Political Figure; William Henry Harrison, Political Figure
Time Period(s): 1810s (1811)
Locale(s): Ohio Valley, Ohio

Summary: Tecumseh's prophecy is fulfilled, signalling the beginning of the great Indian revolt to drive the settlers from their land. Gao, Renno's nephew, is unjustly accused of a crime that he did not commit, and Little Hawk is called to assist President Madison.

Historical Accuracy: The novel covers so much ground that breadth takes precedence over depth.

5122 *The Renegade*

Date of Publication: 1980

Subject(s): Indians; American Colonies; French and Indian War
Fictional character(s): Renno, Indian (Seneca), Warrior; Adrienne Bartel, Young Woman; Alain de Gramont, Military Personnel (French officer)
Historical character(s): John Churchill, Nobleman (Duke of Marlborough); Mary II, Ruler (Queen of England); William III, Ruler (King of England); John Dryden, Writer
Time Period(s): 17th century (1680s)
Locale(s): New England, American Colonies; Quebec, Quebec, Canada; London, England

Summary: In the second installment of the author's White Indian series, Renno, now a tribal leader, finds himself in London where he has an audience with William and Mary and inspires poet and playwright John Dryden. In America, an escalation of the conflict between the French and English occurs, with the Senecas between both warring nations.

Historical Accuracy: The scenes at the royal court are unconvincing.

5123 *Renno*

Date of Publication: 1981
Subject(s): Indians; American Colonies; French and Indian War
Fictional character(s): Renno, Indian (Seneca), Chieftain; Jo-Gonh, Indian (Seneca), Warrior; Goo-Ga-Ro-No, Indian (Seneca)
Time Period(s): 1720s
Locale(s): Springfield, Massachusetts, American Colonies; New York, American Colonies

Summary: In the fifth book of the author's White Indian saga, civil war among the Iroquois League threatens Renno, Sachem of the Senecas, and he must attempt to stop a plot that could destroy the American colonies.

Historical Accuracy: The emphasis is on action with some authentic period and locale painting.

5124 *The Sachem*

Date of Publication: 1981
Subject(s): Indians; American Colonies; French and Indian War
Fictional character(s): Renno, Indian (Seneca), Warrior; Alain de Gramont, Military Personnel (French officer); Ghonkaba, Indian (Seneca), Chieftain
Historical character(s): John Churchill, Nobleman (Duke of Marlborough); Sarah Churchill, Noblewoman (Duchess of Marlborough); Anne, Ruler (Queen of England)
Time Period(s): 1700s (1702)
Locale(s): Boston, Massachusetts, American Colonies; Quebec, Quebec, Canada; London, England

Summary: While his father, Ghonka, and wife, Betsy, journey to England to plead the Indian cause, the white Indian Renno becomes the Sachem of the Senecas. Meanwhile, peace is being undermined by both the French and the Spanish.

Historical Accuracy: More atmospheric than accurate. The English scenes in particular strain credibility.

5125 *Sachem's Son*

Date of Publication: 1990
Subject(s): Indians
Fictional character(s): Renno, Indian (Seneca), Chieftain; Little Hawk, Indian (Seneca); El-i-chi, Indian (Seneca), Shaman
Time Period(s): 1790s
Locale(s): Maumee Valley, Ohio

Summary: Two events move Renno to exile himself from the Senaca he has ruled for so long. First, his people turn against El-i-chi, Renno's brother, when he marries an Anglo woman. Second, he must fulfil his promise to his dead wife to rear their son, Little Hawk, as a white man. His intentions are good, but the transition between the Senaca and Anglo worlds proves to be filled with deadly peril.

Historical Accuracy: The details of tribal life are convincing.

5126 *Seminole*

Date of Publication: 1986
Subject(s): Indians
Fictional character(s): Renno, Indian (Seneca), Warrior; Emily Johnson, Fiance(e), Captive; Ben Whipple, Military Personnel, Murderer
Historical character(s): George Washington, Political Figure
Time Period(s): 1780s (1783)
Locale(s): Florida; Tennessee

Summary: On the eve of her marriage to Renno, Emily Johnson is kidnapped and taken into the remote Seminole territory of southern Florida. While she struggles to survive her captivity, Renno goes in search of her, contending with pirates, Seminoles, and the perils of the Everglades.

Historical Accuracy: Washington's intervention in the dispute between the settlers and the Senecas and Cherokees is fanciful.

5127 *Seneca*

Date of Publication: 1984
Subject(s): Indians; American Colonies; American Revolution
Fictional character(s): Ghonkaba, Indian (Seneca), Chieftain; Toshabe, Indian (Seneca)
Historical character(s): Alexander Hamilton, Military Personnel (army colonel); George Washington, Military Personnel (army commander); Samuel Adams, Patriot; John Adams, Political Figure; Abigail Adams, Spouse; Martha Washington, Spouse
Time Period(s): 1770s
Locale(s): New York, American Colonies; New Jersey, American Colonies; Boston, Massachusetts, American Colonies

Summary: As the American Revolution breaks out, Ghonkaba is divided between his hatred for the British and the Seneca's traditional alliance with them. To join the rebellious colonies, he must betray his heritage. Serving Washington's troops, he guides them to safety in a series of harrowing escapes. He is involved in the famous crossing of the Delaware and the attack on Trenton, New Jersey as well.

Historical Accuracy: The novel is a blend of the fictional and the factual with an emphasis on fast-paced action rather than careful historical documentation.

5128 *Spirit Knife*

Date of Publication: 1988
Subject(s): Indians; Sea Story; Whaling
Fictional character(s): Renno, Indian (Seneca), Chieftain; Beth Huntington, Spouse (of Renno); Hodano, Indian, Shaman
Historical character(s): George Washington, Political Figure; Benjamin Franklin, Political Figure
Time Period(s): 1780s (1787)
Locale(s): Northeast; At Sea

Summary: Set at the time of the ratification of the U.S. Constitution, the novel deals with threats to the young republic from a variety of unexpected sources, primarily from renegade tribes that form a secret alliance with the British. Renno finds himself in the center of the dispute that includes a whaling excursion.

Historical Accuracy: The novel covers so much ground that the historical details are only mentioned in passing and considerably simplified in favor of the action.

5129 *Tomahawk*

Date of Publication: 1982
Subject(s): Indians; American Colonies; French and Indian War
Fictional character(s): Renno, Indian (Seneca), Chieftain; Ja-Gonh, Indian (Seneca), Warrior; Gray Fox, Indian (Huron), Warrior; Ah-Wen-Ga, Indian (Seneca), Fiance(e)
Historical character(s): Louis XV, Ruler (King of France)
Time Period(s): 1730s
Locale(s): Quebec, Quebec, Canada; Paris, France

Summary: In the sixth volume of the White Indian saga, the Huron agent to the French, Grey Fox, intends to win French support for a plan to gain control of the colonies. To do so, he chooses a young woman to present to Louis XV. His choice, Ah-Wen-Ga, is the fiancee of Ja-Gonh, son of Renno, however, and Ja-Gonh pursues Grey Fox across the Atlantic.

Historical Accuracy: The novel's strength is fast-paced frontier adventure. The scenes in France strain credibility.

5130 *War Chief*

Date of Publication: 1980
Subject(s): Indians; American Colonies
Fictional character(s): Renno, Indian (Seneca), Warrior; Betsy Ridley, Young Woman; Consuelo Mirador, Captive
Time Period(s): 17th century
Locale(s): New England, American Colonies; Virginia, American Colonies; West Indies

Summary: In book three of the White Indian series, the action shifts to Virginia where Renno acts as a peace mediator between the Pimlico Indians and the Virginia settlers. He also finds a wife in Betsy Ridley and is drawn into the struggle for Florida between Spanish pirates and the Seminoles.

Historical Accuracy: The focus is on action and adventure with some period painting.

5131 *War Clouds*

Date of Publication: 1994
Subject(s): Indians; Sea Story; War of 1812
Fictional character(s): Renno, Indian (Seneca), Chieftain; Little Hawk, Indian (Seneca), Warrior
Historical character(s): Tecumseh, Indian (Cherokee), Chieftain; Meriwether Lewis, Political Figure, Explorer; William Henry Harrison, Political Figure
Time Period(s): 1800s
Locale(s): Ohio Valley, Ohio

Summary: As the British Navy wages war on American shipping, Little Hawk, the son of Renno, is impressed into service aboard the *H.M.S. Cormorant.* Meanwhile, Tecumseh has created a great Indian union whose aim is to forge an alliance with the British against the U.S. Renno finds himself at the scene of the mysterious death of Meriwether Lewis.

Historical Accuracy: Some liberties with the chronology have been taken in order to connect Renno with the investigation of the death of Meriwether Lewis.

5132 *War Cry*

Date of Publication: 1983
Subject(s): Indians; American Colonies; French and Indian War
Fictional character(s): Renno, Indian (Seneca), Chieftain; Ja-Gonh, Indian (Seneca), Warrior; Ghonkaba, Indian (Seneca), Warrior
Historical character(s): George Washington, Military Personnel (army officer)
Time Period(s): 1750s (1755)
Locale(s): Ohio Valley, United States; New York, American Colonies; Virginia, American Colonies

Summary: As Renno, the White Indian, tries to rally the tribes against the French invaders, his young grandson, Ghonkaba, turns renegade. By challenging the wisdom of his father, Ja-gonh, Ghonkaba threatens to split the tribe apart and could help decide the future of the American colonies.

Historical Accuracy: More fictional than factual, the story is convincing in its atmosphere.

5133 *War Drums*

Date of Publication: 1986
Subject(s): Indians
Fictional character(s): Renno, Indian (Seneca), Chieftain; Emily Johnson, Spouse; El-i-chi, Indian (Seneca), Guide
Historical character(s): Andrew Jackson, Military Personnel
Time Period(s): 1780s
Locale(s): Tennessee; Mississippi River

Summary: Renno joins forces with Andrew Jackson against the Chickasaws and the Spanish in a battle that decides the fate of the southeastern American frontier. Jackson is shown as a hot-tempered commander with a destructive prejudice against the Indians.

Historical Accuracy: Although the outline of history has been followed, it is clear that certain details and events have been simplified.

5134 *White Indian*

Date of Publication: 1979
Subject(s): Indians; American Colonies; Tribal Life—Native American
Fictional character(s): Renno, Indian (Seneca), Warrior; Deborah Alwin, Young Woman, Captive
Time Period(s): 17th century
Locale(s): Connecticut Valley, American Colonies; Springfield, Massachusetts, American Colonies; Mohawk Valley, New York, American Colonies

Summary: This novel begins the White Indian series, which chronicles over 200 years of American history. It describes Renno, a white child raised by the Senecas, and his adventures as he becomes a warrior. Conflict with the settlers is featured, as well as Renno's attraction to captive Deborah Alwin.

Historical Accuracy: The atmosphere seems authentic, if the story at times is overly melodramatic and action-oriented.

JANE PORTER (1776-1850)

An English author of two successful novels, Porter was also the writer of less successful plays.

5135 *The Scottish Chiefs*

Date of Publication: 1810
Subject(s): Middle Ages; Royalty—England
Historical character(s): William Wallace, Gentleman, Patriot; Edward I, Ruler (King of England); Robert the Bruce, Royalty (heir to the Scottish throne)
Time Period(s): 13th century; 14th century (1296-1305)
Locale(s): Scotland; London, England

Summary: The novel offers the story of a great Scottish national hero, Sir William Wallace, who fought heroically against the English to achieve Scottish independence. Betrayed by jealousy and intrigue, Wallace is turned over to the English to be executed as a traitor. However, he achieves his goal of restoring a King of Scotland to his throne.

Historical Accuracy: Porter based her research on sources now considered inaccurate, yet few modern historical novels are as detailed and thorough in representing historical customs.

5136 *Thaddeus of Warsaw*

Date of Publication: 1803
Subject(s): Independence—Poland
Fictional character(s): Thaddeus Sobieski, Patriot (Polish), Military Personnel; Pembroke Somerset, Military Personnel
Historical character(s): Thaddeus Kosciuszko, Military Personnel (general), Political Figure
Time Period(s): 1790s (1792)
Locale(s): Warsaw, Poland; London, England

Summary: This is a romantic story of Poland's fight against Russia for independence. Thaddeus Sobieski is a young patriot who fights nobly for the lost cause and then journeys to England as a political refugee, adapting to the strange customs of a different land.

Historical Accuracy: The novel offers a romantic blend of factual history and invention.

MARGARET EVANS PORTER (1959-)

Porter was born in Macon, Georgia. She received her B.A. from Agnes Scott College in 1980 and her M.A. from the University of Georgia in 1983. Porter lives and works in Littleton, Colorado.

5137   *Heiress of Ardara*

Date of Publication: 1988
Subject(s): Romance; Georgian Period
Fictional character(s): Aurora Donellan, Heiress; Lord Gavin Briavel, Nobleman
Time Period(s): 18th century
Locale(s): Dublin, Ireland

Summary: Set in 18th-century Ireland, this romance features a young heiress, Aurora Donellan, who reluctantly falls in love with nobleman Gavin Briavel. Complications stem from a scandal that has caused the two families to feud for years. Could revenge be a prime motive for Lord Briavel?.

Historical Accuracy: The period elements and the Irish scene are convincingly detailed.

STANLEY DAVID PORTEUS (1883-)

An Australian psychologist, educator, and prolific author on the subject of psychology, Porteus was born in Melbourne and was educated at the Melbourne Educational Institute and Melbourne University. His works include an award-winning book on Hawaii, *And Blow Not the Trumpet*; *Guide to the Porteus Maze Tests*; *Maze Test and Clinical Psychology*; and an autobiography, *A Psychologist of Sorts*.

5138   *Restless Voyage*

Date of Publication: 1948
Subject(s): Sea Story
Historical character(s): Archibald Campbell, Sea Captain
Time Period(s): 19th century
Locale(s): At Sea; Hawaii

Summary: Based on the autobiography of seaman Archibald Campbell, the novel recounts his life at sea and in Hawaii in the early 19th century. Campbell's account is recast into an exciting adventure and period story.

Historical Accuracy: The novel reworks Campbell's original account into a more exciting narrative.

CHARLES PORTIS (1933-)

Born in Arkansas, Portis graduated from the University of Arkansas. He has worked as a newspaper reporter and foreign correspondent in London. He is best known for his western novel *True Grit*, which was made into a successful film with an Academy Award-winning performance by John Wayne as Rooster Cogburn.

5139   *True Grit*

Date of Publication: 1968
Subject(s): American West; Crime and Criminals

Fictional character(s): Mattie Ross, Teenager; Rooster Cogburn, Lawman (marshall); Tom Chaney, Outlaw, Murderer
Historical character(s): Isaac C. Parker, Judge
Time Period(s): 1880s
Locale(s): Fort Smith, Arkansas; Indian Territory

Summary: Fourteen-year-old Mattie Ross sets out from Fort Smith, Arkansas, to bring her father's murderer to justice. She convinces one-eyed Rooster Cogburn, U.S. Marshall, to accompany her. Their adventure when they meet a gang of outlaws forms the novel's exciting story.

Historical Accuracy: The period elements in this western adventure are convincing and realistically drawn.

ABEL POSSE (1939-)

Argentinian writer Posse is a career diplomat in the Argentine Foreign Service. In 1987 his book *The Dogs of Paradise* received the Romulo Gallagos Prize for the best Spanish novel.

5140   *Daimon*

Date of Publication: 1992
Subject(s): Exploration; Spanish Colonies; Alternate History
Historical character(s): Lope de Aguirre, Explorer, Military Personnel (conquistador)
Time Period(s): 15th century; 16th century
Locale(s): Peru

Summary: The author continues his story of the early contact between Europeans and Native Americans, begun in *The Dogs of Paradise*, with the tale of Lope de Aguirre. One of Pizarro's lieutenants on an expedition in the Amazon, he slays his comrades, betrays his commander, and attempts to establish the Maranon Empire with dreams of besieging Peru, reconquering Spain, and taking over the world. In history Aguirre fails. In this reimagining of his story, Aguirre lives on after death as a disturbing presence.

Historical Accuracy: The novel blends history and fantasy, offering an alternative view of the facts, but a truthful account nonetheless.

5141   *The Dogs of Paradise*

Date of Publication: 1987
Subject(s): Exploration; Sea Story; Royalty—Spain
Historical character(s): Cristobal Colon, Explorer; Ferdinand V, Ruler (King of Castile and Leon); Isabella I, Ruler (Queen of Castile and Leon); Henry IV, Ruler (King of Castile and Leon); Juan II, Ruler (King of Aragon); Tomas de Torquemada, Religious (Inquisitor General); Alexander VI, Religious (pope)
Time Period(s): 15th century (1461-1499)
Locale(s): Spain; North America

Summary: The story of Columbus' voyage of discovery is imagined through the lens of magical realism. The novel describes the decadent Spanish court of Ferdinand and Isabella and Columbus' discovery of a tropical earthly paradise.

Historical Accuracy: The framework of the story is historical but with a fantastical twist on events and personalities. Posse concerns himself more with universals than with historical documentation.

JEREMY POTTER (1922-)

An English author educated at Oxford, Potter worked as the managing director of England's *TV Times*. His mysteries reflect his personal interests in art, field hockey, and publishing.

5142 *The Dance of Death*

Date of Publication: 1968
Subject(s): Mystery; Victorian Period; Artistic Life
Fictional character(s): Rowlandson Jones, Art Dealer
Time Period(s): 19th century (Victorian period)
Locale(s): London, England

Summary: This Victorian-era tale of murder in the art world tells the story of Rowland Jones, a London art dealer who is devoted to the works of 18th-century artist and caricaturist Thomas Rowlandson. When his young gallery assistant is found dead on his study floor, Jones conceals the crime, and the death toll mounts.

Historical Accuracy: The period details are authentic and convincing.

5143 *A Trail of Blood*

Date of Publication: 1970
Subject(s): Mystery; Tudor Period; Royalty—England
Fictional character(s): Brother Thomas, Religious (monk), Detective—Amateur
Historical character(s): Robert Aske, Rebel
Time Period(s): 16th century (1550s)
Locale(s): England

Summary: The novel is based on English history's greatest unsolved mystery: Who killed the Plantagenet princes in the Tower? Was it their uncle, Richard III? Or their brother-in-law Henry Tudor? Brother Thomas, the archivist at Croyland Abbey, joins forces with rebel Robert Aske and uncovers evidence that could topple Henry VIII's rule and help preserve the church in England. In their search for a Plantagenet heir they must deal with spies and threats of torture.

Historical Accuracy: The novel is a work of fiction based on historical fact.

FERNAND POUILLON (1912-)

French architect and writer Pouillon studied architecture in Paris and Marseilles and constructed his first building at age 22. In 30 years of professional activity, he put up buildings in Europe, Asia, and Africa that would be the equivalent of ten cities of 15,000 inhabitants each. In temporary retirement in 1960, he turned to writing. He produced *The Stones of the Abbey*, his memoirs, and a study of Cistercian abbeys.

5144 *The Stones of the Abbey*

Date of Publication: 1970
Subject(s): Middle Ages; Religious Life; Architecture
Fictional character(s): Guillaume Balz, Religious (monk), Architect
Time Period(s): 12th century (1161)
Locale(s): Provence, France

Summary: In 1161 master builder and monk Guillaume Balz is sent back to his birthplace to build his last and greatest achievement, an abbey in Provence, France. Told in diary form, the novel details the course of the construction. Storms threaten the foundation, sickness and accidents afflict the small force of lay brothers, but the masterpiece of the Cistercian Order is created.

Historical Accuracy: The notes accompanying the novel make it clear that the story is backed by a solid knowledge of both the period and the Cistercian Order.

ARTHUR POUND (1884-1966)

An American journalist, author, and historian, Pound served as the editor of the *Atlantic Monthly* and as the official historian for New York state. He was the founder and first president of the Society for Colonial History. His books include *The Iron Man in Industry*, *Native Stock*, and *Lake Ontario*.

5145 *Hawk of Detroit*

Date of Publication: 1939
Subject(s): Exploration; French Colonies
Historical character(s): Antoine de La Mothe Cadillac, Explorer
Time Period(s): 17th century
Locale(s): Detroit, Michigan; Paris, France

Summary: The novel describes the founding of Detroit by the French explorer and colonial administrator Antone de La Mothe Cadillac. He first petitions Louis XIV for a grant to authorize the Detroit settlement, and in Quebec, recruits a company of settlers for the endeavor. The novel features a vivid depiction of the various and conflicting forces—Church, state, and trading companies—responsible for the settlement of the interior of North America.

Historical Accuracy: The novel is tentative about reaching any conclusions regarding Cadillac's motivation and character, which leaves it unfocused but with a good deal of plausible period details.

DEBORAH POWELL

5146 *Bayou City Secrets*

Date of Publication: 1991
Subject(s): Mystery; Homosexuality
Fictional character(s): Hollis Carpenter, Journalist (crime reporter), Lesbian; Lily Delacroix, Lesbian
Time Period(s): 1930s
Locale(s): Houston, Texas

Summary: After dining with her newspaper's owner to discuss the story she is working on, reporter Hollis Carpenter discovers her apartment has been ransacked. Going for help, she finds the corpse of her friend, policeman Joe Mahon. The case becomes increasingly dangerous.

Historical Accuracy: The period details lend atmosphere.

RICHARD POWELL (1908-)

Born in Philadelphia, Powell graduated from Princeton. He worked at the Philadelphia *Evening Ledger* for 10 years, then in public relations. Powell is a tournament bridge player.

`5147` *I Take This Land*

Date of Publication: 1962
Subject(s): Railroads; Disasters—Natural; Social Chronicle
Fictional character(s): Ward Campion, Businessman (land promoter); Joel Emmet, Farmer; Rush Lightburn, Hunter
Historical character(s): Henry B. Plant, Financier (railroad)
Time Period(s): 19th century; 20th century (1895-1946)
Locale(s): Florida (southern)

Summary: The story of the development of southern Florida is depicted through the experiences of a variety of characters from 1895 to 1946. Ward Campion, a land promoter, wins a railroad in a poker game. Joel Emmet is a farmer, dedicated to the land, and Rush Lightburn is a hunter in the Everglades.

Historical Accuracy: Much of the book is based on real events, but the characters and places are mainly fictional.

`5148` *Whom the Gods Would Destroy*

Date of Publication: 1970
Subject(s): Trojan War; Mycenean Civilization
Fictional character(s): Helios, Servant (kitchen boy); Achilles, Warrior; Odysseus, Warrior; Hector, Warrior; Paris, Royalty (prince); Helen of Troy, Noblewoman; Aeneas, Warrior; Cassandra, Royalty (princess); Agamemnon, Leader (Greek forces), Ruler (King of Mycenae)
Time Period(s): 13th century B.C.
Locale(s): Troy, Ancient Civilization

Summary: The story of the Trojan War is told from the perspective of a Trojan kitchen boy, Helios, who may be the bastard son of King Priam. The story begins two years before the Trojan War and continues until Troy falls. All of the characters from Homer's *Iliad* are depicted with an emphasis on a realistic and psychologically valid rendering of the mythical and the heroic.

Historical Accuracy: The novel offers a believable re-creation of the mythical tale of the fall of Troy.

WILLIAM POWELL (1949-)

Born in the U.S., Powell spent most of his childhood in Europe. He has worked at various jobs including theater manager, bartender, book store manager, and grave digger. For two years he worked on the trans-Alaskan pipeline. His first book, *The Anarchist Cookbook*, was a bestseller.

`5149` *The First Casualty*

Date of Publication: 1979
Subject(s): World War I; Austro-Hungarian Empire; Politics
Historical character(s): Franz Ferdinand, Royalty (Archduke of Austria); Gavrilo Princip, Revolutionary, Murderer
Time Period(s): 1910s (1914)
Locale(s): Sarajevo, Bosnia-Hercegovina

Summary: The first casualty in the First World War was the Austrian Archduke Franz Ferdinand. His assassination by Bosnian nationalists in 1914 sets in place the complicated interlocked alliances that led to war. The novel re-creates the events leading up to and immediately following the assassination.

Historical Accuracy: The author calls this novel a work of fiction.

ANNE POWERS
(PSEUD. OF ANNE POWERS SCHWARTZ, 1913-)

Born in Minnesota, Powers has worked as a writing instructor. Her books include *Rachel*, *Royal Consorts*, and *Young Empress*.

`5150` *The Ironmaster*

Date of Publication: 1951
Subject(s): Politics; Business Building; French Revolution
Fictional character(s): Martin Rafferty, Businessman (ironworks); Jill Lansing, Young Woman
Historical character(s): Alexander Hamilton, Political Figure; George Washington, Political Figure; Marie Joseph Paul de Lafayette, Nobleman (Marquis de Lafayette), Military Personnel (French general); Anthony Wayne, Military Personnel (general)
Time Period(s): 1780s (1788)
Locale(s): New York; Paris, France; Ohio

Summary: The novel is set in the turbulent years immediately following the end of the American Revolution. The battle over the ratification of the Constitution shakes the new nation from within and the British with their Indian allies threaten it from without. At the center of the story is Martin Rafferty, an ironmaster who goes on a perilous mission to Fort Niagara and into the Ohio wilderness for the action at Fallen Timbers, called "the last battle of the Revolution.".

Historical Accuracy: The basic framework of the story is historical and accurately depicted.

`5151` *No King but Caesar*

Date of Publication: 1960
Subject(s): Roman Empire
Fictional character(s): Quintus Flavius, Nobleman; Diana Vincenzus, Gentlewoman
Historical character(s): Lucius Aelius Sejanus, Military Personnel (general), Political Figure; Tiberius, Ruler (Roman emperor); Caligula, Ruler (Roman emperor); Pontius Pilate, Government Official
Time Period(s): 1st century
Locale(s): Rome, Roman Empire; Israel

Summary: This tale of romance and intrigue during the reigns of Tiberius and Caligula concerns the love of a Roman nobleman, Quintus Flavius, for Diana Vincenzus. They are caught up in the turbulence of the Roman court. Scenes include Jesus' crucifixion, seen from the Roman perspective.

Historical Accuracy: The story is fanciful but full of convincing period atmosphere and an actual chronology of historical events.

5152 *No Wall So High*

Date of Publication: 1949
Subject(s): Elizabethan Period; Spanish Armada
Fictional character(s): Maurice Quain, Businessman (merchant); Lady Katherine Perrot, Noblewoman
Time Period(s): 16th century (1580s)
Locale(s): England

Summary: This novel, set at the time of the defeat of the Spanish Armada, concerns the relationship between Maurice Quain, a wealthy merchant, and Lady Katherine Perrot. Maurice gives up everything to help rescue Katherine from a false charge of conspiracy.

Historical Accuracy: The novel provides a good deal of vivid period color, but the story does not rise above standard romance.

5153 *Rachel*

Date of Publication: 1973
Subject(s): Biography, Fictionalized; Theatrical Life
Historical character(s): Elisa Felix, Actress (aka Rachel); Alfred de Musset, Writer; Alexandre Dumas, pere, Writer; Louis Napoleon Bonaparte, Royalty (prince)
Time Period(s): 19th century
Locale(s): France

Summary: This first-person account of the legendary French actress Rachel traces her early struggle for fame, achievements, numerous love affairs, and later years of recurring illnesses. Her lovers included Alfred de Musset and Prince Louis-Napoleon.

Historical Accuracy: The novel rarely reaches beyond the romantic and melodramatic.

5154 *Ride East! Ride West!: A Romance of the Hundred Years' War*

Date of Publication: 1947
Subject(s): Hundred Years War; Independence—Ireland; Battle of Crecy
Fictional character(s): Thomas Gilman, Clerk
Time Period(s): 14th century
Locale(s): England; Ireland; France

Summary: This tale of intrigue in the court of Edward III at the beginning of the Hundred Years War involves clerk and agent of the king, Thomas Gilman. He accompanies the English invasion to France and is on hand for the Black Prince's triumph at the Battle of Crecy. After the battle the scene shifts to Ireland where Thomas' true identity is revealed in the nascent struggle for Irish independence.

Historical Accuracy: The period background is well detailed and authentic.

5155 *The Thousand Fires*

Date of Publication: 1957
Subject(s): Napoleonic Wars; Battle of Austerlitz; Battle of Waterloo
Fictional character(s): Alan de Lacey, Military Personnel (soldier); Christine de Bruyere, Gentlewoman
Historical character(s): Napoleon Bonaparte, Ruler (French emperor); Joseph Fouche, Revolutionary; Michel Ney, Military Personnel (French marshal)
Time Period(s): 1810s; 1820s
Locale(s): France; Austria; Russia

Summary: The novel dramatizes the rise and collapse of Napoleon and the French Empire. Alan de Lacey becomes a member of Napoleon's general staff and begins an affair with Christine de Bruyere, an aristocrat trapped in a distasteful marriage.

Historical Accuracy: History is captured in broad swatches of color at a frenetic pace, somewhat undermining careful documentation of events including the battles of Wagram, Austerlitz, and Waterloo.

TIM POWERS (1952-)

Born in Buffalo, Powers has lived in southern California since the age of seven. He graduated from California State University, Fullerton, and is an acclaimed science fiction and fantasy writer. Powers' novels have been recognized for their intricate plots and well-rounded, though outlandish, characters. Many of his works feature time travel and encounters with actual historical figures. Both *The Anubis Gate* and *Dinner at Deviant's Palace* won the Philip K. Dick Memorial Award.

5156 *On Stranger Tides*

Date of Publication: 1987
Subject(s): Pirates; Fantasy; Sea Story
Fictional character(s): John Chandagnac, Accountant, Pirate
Historical character(s): Blackbeard, Pirate
Time Period(s): 1710s (1718)
Locale(s): West Indies; Florida

Summary: In this blend of fantasy and history, the time is 1718 and bookkeeper John Chandagnac becomes pirate Jack Shandy. He has a series of adventures on the high seas, including a journey to Florida in search of the fountain of youth, a sea battle with the British navy, and an encounter with sunken ships crewed by zombies.

Historical Accuracy: There are convincing period elements, but the emphasis is on comic fantasy, not history.

5157 *The Stress of Her Regard*

Date of Publication: 1989
Subject(s): Fantasy; Regency Period; Literary Life
Fictional character(s): Michael Crawford, Doctor

Historical character(s): George Gordon Byron, Writer; Percy Bysshe Shelley, Writer; John Keats, Writer; Mary Wollstonecraft Shelley, Writer
Time Period(s): 1810s; 1820s (1816-1822)
Locale(s): England; Venice, Italy; Rome, Italy

Summary: In this blend of history, legend, and fantasy set during the Regency period, Dr. Michael Crawford flees England to avoid being charged with his wife's murder. A strange force seems to haunt him, and England's greatest Romantic poets—Byron, Shelley, and Keats—help him understand what it is.

Historical Accuracy: The emphasis is on the fantastical rather than the historical, though the appearance by the Romantic poets is convincing.

DAVID POWNALL (1938-)

English novelist and playwright Pownall lives in South Africa.

5158 *The White Cutter*

Date of Publication: 1989
Subject(s): Middle Ages; Architecture; Religious Conflict
Fictional character(s): Hedric Herbertson, Architect; Henry de Reyns, Artisan (master of the royal masons); Herbert of Garstang, Artisan (gilder)
Historical character(s): Henry III, Ruler (King of England); Simon de Montfort, Nobleman
Time Period(s): 13th century (1250s)
Locale(s): Ireland; England

Summary: Hedric Herbertson, the greatest 13th-century builder, tells the story of his education and apprenticeship. Heresies and intrigue surround him and his two mentors, his father and Henry de Reyns, Master of the Royal Masons.

Historical Accuracy: The novel is exact and convincing in its re-creation of the Middle Ages. It shows how medieval buildings made political as well as spiritual statements.

JOHN COWPER POWYS (1872-1976)

A Welsh educator, critic, novelist, and poet, Powys was a lecturer in literature at several universities in England, including Oxford and Cambridge. He published his first novel at the age of 43, and continued as a prolific writer into his eighties. Many of his books, such as *The Glastonbury Romance*, deal with myths, cosmic fantasies, and the elemental forces of nature.

5159 *Owen Glendower*

Date of Publication: 1940
Subject(s): Independence—Wales; Middle Ages
Historical character(s): Owen Glendower, Revolutionary, Nobleman
Time Period(s): 15th century
Locale(s): Wales

Summary: This massive two-volume historical novel concerns the rebellion led by Welshman Owen Glendower in the 15th century. Shifting alliances and betrayals mark the drama as

the novel sets the political scene in the context of Welsh nationalism and mysticism.

Historical Accuracy: The novel is full of accurate details from history, but frequently moves beyond the historical to legend and invention. There are many inaccuracies concerning religious matters.

DAVID POYER (1949-)

Born in Pennsylvania, Poyer is a graduate of the U.S. Naval Academy and a career naval officer. He has worked as an engineer and a consultant while continuing his writing career.

5160 *The Only Thing to Fear*

Date of Publication: 1995
Subject(s): Suspense; World War II
Fictional character(s): Lauren Wolfe, Actress
Historical character(s): Franklin Delano Roosevelt, Political Figure (President of the U.S.); John F. Kennedy, Military Personnel (naval officer)
Time Period(s): 1940s (1945)
Locale(s): Washington, District of Columbia; Europe; Warm Springs, Georgia

Summary: In this thriller set in 1945, John Fitzgerald Kennedy, a young navy lieutenant convalescing from action in the Pacific, is transferred to the president's personal staff. There is the possibility of an assassin within FDR's circle. Kennedy and actress Lauren Wolfe race against time to foil the plot.

Historical Accuracy: The situation is fanciful.

JOE POYER (1939-)

Born in Michigan, Poyer is a graduate of Michigan State University and has worked as a director of public information, a proposal writer, and a military affairs consultant for a Los Angeles TV station. He has written the series A Time of War as well as other novels and nonfiction works on military subjects.

5161 *Devoted Friends*

Date of Publication: 1982
Subject(s): Russian Revolution; Russian Empire; Royalty—Russia
Fictional character(s): William Hughes Evans, Diplomat; Nikolai Sheremetiev, Military Personnel (captain)
Historical character(s): Grigori Efimovich Rasputin, Religious (monk), Zealot; Nicholas II, Ruler (czar); Alexandra Feodorovna, Royalty (czarina); Tatiana, Grand Duchess of Russia, Royalty
Time Period(s): 1910s; 1920s (1916-1920)
Locale(s): Petrograd, Russia; Moscow, Russia

Summary: Set during the turmoil of the Russian Revolution, the novel dramatizes an unlikely romance between an American diplomat, William Hughes Evans, and the daughter of Russian Czar Nicholas II. They are pursued by Nikolai Sheremetiev, a former royal soldier recruited into the Cheka.

Historical Accuracy: The novel blends fact and speculation. The author admits to taking certain liberties with the time frame and the personalities of the major characters.

AMANDA PRANTERA (1942-)

English author Prantera attended the University of London and has worked as a translator and television writer in London. She is a versatile writer who combines conventions from various literary genres in her modern Gothic novels. Manipulating trappings of the romance in *Strange Loop*, the thriller in *The Cabalist*, and the biography in *Conversation with Lord Byron on Perversion, 163 Years After His Lordship's Death*, she creates fantastic yet credible scenarios that are acclaimed for their suspense and for her elegant prose and quick wit.

5162 *The Side of the Moon*

Date of Publication: 1991
Subject(s): Roman Empire
Historical character(s): Lucius Aelius Aurelius Commodus, Ruler (Roman emperor); Galen, Doctor; Dio Cassius, Historian, Political Figure
Time Period(s): 2nd century
Locale(s): Rome, Roman Empire

Summary: The novel offers an alternative view of the short reign of the Roman Emperor Commodus, the son of Marcus Aurelius. History has treated Commodus as either stupid or a sadist. This version, narrated by the Greek physician Galen, paints him as misunderstood and sensitive. Court politics conspire to produce a very different official history to justify Commodus' assassination.

Historical Accuracy: The novel's rewriting of history makes its point about history and truth and who controls both. The atmosphere of the period is convincing, if the interpretations are dubious.

VASCO PRATOLINI

5163 *Metello*

Date of Publication: 1960
Subject(s): Labor Movement
Fictional character(s): Metello Salani, Worker
Time Period(s): 19th century; 20th century
Locale(s): Florence, Italy

Summary: The novel describes the plight of the Italian worker and the incipient labor movement in the early years of the 20th century. The story focuses on the motivation and career of Metello Salani who serves an apprenticeship as a bricklayer and becomes one of the leaders in a strike to better the lot of the Italian working class.

Historical Accuracy: The strike is based on an actual event, and the era is captured convincingly.

THEODORE PRATT (1901-1969)

Born in Minnesota, Pratt attended Colgate and Columbia universities. He has worked as a theater reviewer for *Variety* and as a newspaper columnist and European correspondent for the New York *Sun*. Many of his books are set in Florida. His trilogy—*The Barefoot Mailman*, *The Flame Tree*, and *The Big Bubble*—tells the history of the state from 1880 to 1924. Pratt has been called the Literary Laureate of Florida.

5164 *Seminole*

Date of Publication: 1954
Subject(s): Indians
Fictional character(s): Gideon Sauny, Young Man
Historical character(s): Osceola, Indian (Seminole), Chieftain
Time Period(s): 1830s
Locale(s): St. Augustine, Florida

Summary: Osceola, the great Seminole chief, leads his people in revolt against the encroachment of settlers in Florida during the 1830s. The story of Osceola's rebellion is told through the perspective of young Gideon Sauny, who is caught up in the conflict.

Historical Accuracy: The novel blends fact and fiction, with the major events as close to history as possible.

JOHN PREBBLE (1915-)

English journalist and writer Prebble attended public schools in Canada and England. He has worked as a reporter, columnist, and feature writer for various magazines and newspapers in London. He is the 1960 winner of the best historical novel award for *The Buffalo Soldiers*.

5165 *The Buffalo Soldiers*

Date of Publication: 1959
Subject(s): American West; Indians; Military Life—U.S. Cavalry
Fictional character(s): Garrett Byrne, Military Personnel (cavalry lieutenant); Annie Norvall, Widow(er); Quasia, Indian (Comanche), Warrior
Time Period(s): 1860s (post-Civil War)
Locale(s): Fort Sill, Indian Territory

Summary: The novel tells the story of Lieutenant Garrett Byrne, assigned to Fort Sill in Indian Territory after the Civil War. He is placed in charge of a group of black recruits whose mission it is to escort a band of Comanches on their last buffalo hunt before being confined to the reservation. They are tested by adversity, and Byrne learns to respect both the Comanches and his men.

Historical Accuracy: The period background is effective and believable.

CHARLOTTE PRENTISS

5166 *Children of the Ice*

Date of Publication: 1993
Subject(s): Tribal Life—Prehistoric; Prehistory

Fictional character(s): Laena, Prehistoric Human
Time Period(s): Indeterminate Past
Locale(s): Asia; North America

Summary: This tale of prehistoric life describes the initial settlement of North American from Siberia. The story centers on Laena who survives family tragedy to become a tribal leader before she is cast out and begins a journey from Siberia to North America.

Historical Accuracy: The novel offers a believable recreation of prehistoric life and customs.

`5167` *Children of the Sun*

Date of Publication: 1995
Subject(s): Prehistory; Tribal Life—Prehistoric
Fictional character(s): Nisha, Prehistoric Human
Time Period(s): 10th century B.C.
Locale(s): Southwest, North America

Summary: The novel completes the trilogy depicting prehistoric life in North American following the Ice Age. The story concerns a peaceful tribe of cave dwellers of the Southwest. When her husband and son are murdered by a band of nomads, Nisha vows revenge.

Historical Accuracy: The novel is based on evident archeological and anthropological evidence that creates a believable period background.

`5168` *People of the Mesa*

Date of Publication: 1995
Subject(s): Prehistory; Tribal Life—Prehistoric
Fictional character(s): Mara, Prehistoric Human
Time Period(s): Indeterminate Past
Locale(s): Southwest, North America

Summary: The novel offers a story of prehistoric times in the North American Southwest following the Ice Age. The story focuses on the leadership and survival instinct of Mara who resists destruction by nature and human enemies.

Historical Accuracy: The evocation of prehistoric customs is convincing.

H.F.M. PRESCOTT (1896-1972)

An English writer born in Cheshire, Prescott graduated from Oxford University and Manchester University. She was a research fellow at Royal Holloway College, Surrey, and was a distinguished author of historical studies and novels. She was also the author of a prize-winning biography, *Mary Tudor*.

`5169` *The Lost Flight*

Date of Publication: 1928
Subject(s): Middle Ages; Crusades
Fictional character(s): Adam de Morteigne, Knight
Time Period(s): 13th century (1220s)
Locale(s): Lorraine, France; Rome, Italy; Jerusalem, Palestine

Summary: Adam de Morteigne, a knight of Lorraine, is excommunicated by a vindictive bishop. He ventures to Rome

to plead his case and then joins the Sixth Crusade. The novel traces his adventures and features a convincing psychological and historical portrait of the age.

Historical Accuracy: The novel is a masterful reconstruction of the age, its customs, and its beliefs.

`5170` *The Man on a Donkey*

Date of Publication: 1952
Subject(s): Tudor Period; Religious Conflict; Royalty—England
Fictional character(s): Christabel Cowper, Religious (prioress); Thomas Darcy, Nobleman (Lord Darcy); Gilbert Dawe, Religious (priest)
Historical character(s): Henry VIII, Ruler (King of England); Catherine of Aragon, Royalty (queen consort of Henry VIII); Anne Boleyn, Royalty (queen consort of Henry VIII); Mary Tudor, Royalty (princess); Sir Thomas More, Political Figure; Thomas Cranmer, Religious (Archbishop of Canterbury); Thomas Wolsey, Religious (cardinal); Thomas Cromwell, Political Figure
Time Period(s): 16th century
Locale(s): England

Summary: In 1536, during the North Country rebellion, a group called the Pilgrims of Grace tries to save the monasteries from suppression by Henry VIII. Several people offer their testimony—prioress Christabel Cowper, Lord Darcy, and priest Gilbert Dawe. Together they paint a vivid picture of life in early 16th-century England.

Historical Accuracy: Many, but not all, of the events are based on factual evidence. The level of authenticity is impressive, with Prescott noting any deviation from the facts.

`5171` *Son of Dust*

Date of Publication: 1932
Subject(s): Middle Ages
Fictional character(s): Fulcun Geroy, Knight; Alde de Fervacques, Gentlewoman; Mauger de Fervacques, Gentleman
Historical character(s): William the Conqueror, Nobleman (Duke of Normandy)
Time Period(s): 11th century
Locale(s): Normandy, France

Summary: This is a tale of profane and sacred love told against the backdrop of 11th-century Normandy where Duke Guillelm, whom history knows as William the Conqueror, kept his court at his castles of Caen and Falaise. Fulcan Geroy is in love with Alde, and both are caught between the dictates of conscience and desire.

Historical Accuracy: Few other writers have matched this author in her ability to give substance and life to the medieval world with full and rich detail.

`5172` *The Unhurrying Chase*

Date of Publication: 1925
Subject(s): Middle Ages
Fictional character(s): Yves of Rifaucon, Heir, Mercenary

Historical character(s): Richard the Lionhearted, Royalty (prince)
Time Period(s): 12th century
Locale(s): France

Summary: Yves of Rifaucon is the young heir to a small fiefdom that has been besieged by Count Richard of Poitou, later to become Richard the Lionhearted of England. Yves, resentful over the loss of his legacy, joins the ranks of dispossessed, nomadic mercenaries. His eventual redemption after a career of killings and sacrilege is described.

Historical Accuracy: The novel is a remarkably detailed and realistic portrait of the age.

JOHN PRESCOTT (1919-)

A native of Michigan, Prescott graduated from Lawrence College and has worked in advertising and as a freelance writer. His novels include *Valley of Wrath*, *Lion in the Hills*, and *Treasure of the Black Hills*. He has also been a contributor to several Western anthologies.

5173 *Journey by the River*

Date of Publication: 1954
Subject(s): American West; Wagon Trains; Indians
Fictional character(s): Aaron Davis, Hunter, Frontiersman
Time Period(s): 1840s (1848)
Locale(s): Missouri; Kansas; Fort Laramie, Wyoming

Summary: This western novel describes a wagon train's westward progress from Missouri along the Oregon Trail into Wyoming. Trouble stalks the crossing, and the story focuses on the efforts of frontiersman and game hunter Aaron Davis to insure the survival of the pioneers.

Historical Accuracy: The novel's adventures are believable, and the story's period details are authentic.

DON PRESTON (1930-)

SUE PRESTON

Sue Preston is a designer of children's clothing, a craftsperson, and an administrator of a college-level craft program. Don Preston is a long-time book editor.

5174 *Crazy Fox Remembers*

Date of Publication: 1981
Subject(s): American West; Picaresque Adventure
Fictional character(s): Jack Knight, Adventurer; Crazy Fox, Indian (Potawatomie); Charles Knight, Rancher
Historical character(s): James Butler Hickok, Frontiersman, Gunfighter; William F. Cody, Frontiersman, Entertainer; George Armstrong Custer, Military Personnel (cavalry officer); John Wesley Hardin, Outlaw; Annie Oakley, Frontierswoman, Entertainer; Martha Jane Cannary Burk, Frontierswoman
Time Period(s): 1870
Locale(s): West

Summary: In the 1870s, Jack Knight, the son of one of the richest ranchers in Texas, travels to the West wearing a black mask to conceal his identity until he can reclaim his honor. His Indian companion is the much more sensible Crazy Fox, who accompanies Knight on his Don Quixote-like adventures. They meet many important Western figures and stumble upon some of the most famous incidents in frontier history.

Historical Accuracy: The background of the story is historically accurate, but the emphasis is on humor.

HUGH PRESTON

5175 *Feast in the Morning*

Date of Publication: 1975
Subject(s): Tudor Period; Royalty—England
Historical character(s): John Dudley, Nobleman (Viscount Lisle), Military Personnel (Lord Admiral of England); Edward Seymour, Nobleman (Earl of Hertford); Sir William Paget, Nobleman (Baron Paget of Beaudesert); Henry VIII, Ruler (King of England); Thomas Wriothesley, Nobleman (Earl of Southampton), Government Official (lord chancellor); Edward VI, Ruler (King of England); Lady Jane Grey, Noblewoman, Ruler (Queen of England)
Time Period(s): 16th century (1544-1553)
Locale(s): England; France

Summary: In the tangled conspiracy following the death of Henry VIII, John Dudley, Viscount Lisle and Lord Admiral of England, casts his lot with Sir William Paget and Edward Seymour, whose ambition leads to tragedy when the boy King Edward VI succeeds his father.

Historical Accuracy: Historians have traditionally portrayed Dudley as an amoral and cunning intriguer. This version presents a more sympathetic and rounded portrait, convincing in its period details.

CHARLES F. PRICE (1938-)

5176 *Hiwassee: A Novel of the Civil War*

Date of Publication: 1996
Subject(s): Civil War—U.S.; Battle of Chickamauga
Fictional character(s): Madison Curtis, Farmer; Sarah Curtis, Spouse; Oliver Price, Military Personnel (Confederate soldier)
Time Period(s): 1860s
Locale(s): Hiwassee River, North Carolina; Georgia

Summary: This Civil War novel describes life in western North Carolina centering on the Curtis family who fall prey to a gang of Union partisans led by a vicious bushwacker. The novel also depicts the scene on the battlefield at Chickamauga.

Historical Accuracy: The novel is based in part on the history of western North Carolina and of the author's family. Events are either accurately depicted and authentic or invented but consistent with the history of the region.

EUGENIA PRICE (1916-1996)

An American novelist born in Charleston, West Virginia, Price attended Ohio University and Northwestern as a dental student. She worked for a time as a serial writer for radio dramas. She has said that she spends every effort making certain that the history in her novels is accurate. Her books have been translated into 16 foreign languages and have become world-wide bestsellers, exceeding combined sales of 15,000,000.

5177 *Beauty From Ashes*

Date of Publication: 1995
Subject(s): Antebellum South; Civil War—U.S.
Fictional character(s): Anne Couper Fraser, Widow(er); John Couper Fraser, Gentleman; John Fraser Demere, Military Personnel (Confederate soldier)
Time Period(s): 19th century (1845-1864)
Locale(s): St. Simons Island, Georgia; Marietta, Georgia

Summary: In the concluding volume of the author's Georgia Trilogy, the story of the Couper and the Fraser families of St. Simons Island resumes in the 1840s and continues through the Civil War years. The story centers on the experiences of Anne Fraser, who survives the death of her parents and husband and the loss of her home as a prelude to the disaster of the Civil War. With strong Union sentiments, Anne finds her life disintegrating as her son and grandson join the Confederate cause.

Historical Accuracy: The period details and the locale are convincingly depicted, even as the action veers toward the melodramatic.

5178 *Before Darkness Falls*

Date of Publication: 1987
Subject(s): Antebellum South; Mexican War
Fictional character(s): Natalie Browning Latimer, Southern Belle; W.H. Stiles, Political Figure; Jonathon Browning, Gentleman
Time Period(s): 1840s (1842-1849)
Locale(s): Savannah, Georgia

Summary: In the third volume of the author's Savannah Quartet, the story of the Browning, Mackay, and Stiles families is continued during the 1840s. Domestic troubles share the stage with growing political tensions caused by the Mexican-American War and the increasing threat of civil war.

Historical Accuracy: The details of southern life during the period are exact and authentic. Occasionally, however, there are inaccuracies. For example, one character reads *Wuthering Heights* at a time when few in America would have heard of the book or its author.

5179 *The Beloved Invader*

Date of Publication: 1965
Subject(s): Biography, Fictionalized; Family Saga; Reconstruction Period
Historical character(s): Anson Dodge, Veteran (Union soldier), Religious (clergyman); Ellen Dodge, Spouse; Anna Dodge, Spouse

Time Period(s): 19th century (1870s-1890s)
Locale(s): St. Simons Island, Georgia

Summary: The first of the author's St. Simons trilogy, but the last chronologically, is a fictional biography of Anson Dodge, a Union veteran who comes to St. Simons in 1879. He becomes an Episcopal minister driven to rebuild his war-torn church and community.

Historical Accuracy: Based on solid and extensive research, the locale and the period are genuinely drawn.

5180 *Bright Captivity*

Date of Publication: 1991
Subject(s): War of 1812; Family Saga; Antebellum South
Fictional character(s): Anne Couper, Gentlewoman; John Fraser, Military Personnel (British soldier)
Historical character(s): Sir Walter Scott, Writer
Time Period(s): 1810s (1815-1817)
Locale(s): St. Simons Island, Georgia; London, England; Scotland

Summary: Book One of the author's Georgia Trilogy is set on St. Simons Island during and following the War of 1812. Anne Couper, the young daughter of a prominent St. Simons family, falls in love with a British officer on a mission to free the slaves. He returns after the war to marry Anne, and their life together takes them to England and Scotland while they struggle with the decision whether to make their lives in Europe or America.

Historical Accuracy: Strong on locale and period painting, the novel is a convicing look at the era.

5181 *Don Juan McQueen*

Date of Publication: 1974
Subject(s): Spanish Colonies; Antebellum South
Historical character(s): John McQueen, Veteran (Revolutionary War), Plantation Owner; Anne McQueen, Spouse
Time Period(s): 18th century; 19th century (1791-1807)
Locale(s): Savannah, Georgia; Florida

Summary: In Book One of the author's Florida Trilogy, John McQueen, a distinguished Revolutionary War veteran, is forced to flee into Spanish Florida to avoid debtor's prison. McQueen tries to keep the peace along the violent Georgia-Florida border while his wife Anne endures this period of forced separation.

Historical Accuracy: The novel is based on actual historical figures and shows evidence of thorough research into the period and its personalities.

5182 *Lighthouse*

Date of Publication: 1971
Subject(s): Antebellum South; Family Saga
Historical character(s): James Gould, Landowner; Jane Harris Gould, Spouse
Time Period(s): 1800s; 1810s
Locale(s): St. Simons Island, Georgia

Summary: Chronologically the first of the author's St. Simons trilogy, the novel begins the story of the real James Gould and his family. The period is the opening years of the 19th century as Gould, from Massachusetts, settles on St. Simons, drawn there by his dream of building a lighthouse.

Historical Accuracy: Based on extensive research into the Gould family, the novel captures the period and the locale convincingly.

5183 *Margaret's Story*
Date of Publication: 1980
Subject(s): Antebellum South; Civil War—U.S.; Reconstruction Period
Historical character(s): Margaret Seton Fleming, Plantation Owner; Lewis Fleming, Plantation Owner
Time Period(s): 19th century (1830s-1880s)
Locale(s): St. John's River, Florida

Summary: This, the final volume of the author's Florida Trilogy, tells the story of the personal fortunes of Margaret Seton Fleming, who settles on a plantation along the St. John's River in northern Florida. Her life is chronicled from the 1830s through the hardships of the Civil War and its aftermath.

Historical Accuracy: The novel is solidly based on period records and authentic details.

5184 *Maria*
Date of Publication: 1977
Subject(s): American Revolution; Antebellum South; Spanish Colonies
Fictional character(s): Maria Evans, Midwife, Spouse (of Fenwick); David Fenwick, Military Personnel (British officer)
Time Period(s): 1760s; 1770s
Locale(s): St. Augustine, Florida

Summary: Book Two of the author's Florida Trilogy is set in British occupied Florida during the conflict with Spain and the opening years of the American Revolution. Maria Evans is a young midwife from South Carolina who marries a British soldier, David Fenwick, and accompanies his regiment to St. Augustine where she faces hardship in the political upheavals of the Revolution.

Historical Accuracy: Strong on period color, the novel is bolstered by convincing research into the locale and era.

5185 *New Moon Rising*
Date of Publication: 1969
Subject(s): Antebellum South; Civil War—U.S.; Slavery
Historical character(s): Horace Gould, Landowner; Deborah Gould, Spouse
Time Period(s): 19th century (1830s-1860s)
Locale(s): St. Simons Island, Georgia

Summary: The second novel of the author's St. Simons trilogy covers the period from the 1830s through the Civil War. The story follows the career of Horace Gould, who comes of age in the decade before the war. An outsider, Gould struggles with the impact the devastating disruption of the Civil War has on his life and the traditions of his home.

Historical Accuracy: The characters are all based on actual people, developed from extensive research.

5186 *Savannah*
Date of Publication: 1983
Subject(s): Antebellum South; War of 1812; Family Saga
Fictional character(s): Mark Browning, Gentleman; Caroline Browning, Spouse
Time Period(s): 1810s; 1820s (1812-1822)
Locale(s): Savannah, Georgia

Summary: In the first volume of the author's Savannah Quartet, life in Savannah, Georgia during the War of 1812 and immediately following is described. Savannah is seen through the experiences of Mark Browning, an outsider who makes his way in Georgia society.

Historical Accuracy: The novel is a blend of the fictitious and the actual, derived from the social history of Savannah and its great families.

5187 *Stranger in Savannah*
Date of Publication: 1989
Subject(s): Antebellum South; Family Saga; Civil War—U.S.
Fictional character(s): Mark Browning, Landowner; Jonathon Browning, Military Personnel (Confederate soldier); Eliza Mackay, Gentlewoman
Time Period(s): 1850s; 1860s
Locale(s): Savannah, Georgia

Summary: The final volume of the author's Savannah Quartet takes the Browning, Mackay, and Stiles families into the Civil War. Divided loyalties rip the families apart. The effects of the war are dramatized as the past continues to give way to an unsettled future.

Historical Accuracy: Strong on period details, the atmosphere and the locale are authentically drawn.

5188 *To See Your Face Again*
Date of Publication: 1985
Subject(s): Antebellum South; Family Saga
Fictional character(s): Natalie Browning, Southern Belle; Burke Latimer, Young Man
Time Period(s): 1830s
Locale(s): Savannah, Georgia

Summary: In the second volume of the author's Savannah Quartet, the saga of the Browning, Mackay, and Stiles families continues with an emphasis on young Natalie Browning. She meets her match when she is rescued from a steam packet explosion by mysterious Burke Latimer. When he disappears, urging Natalie not to look for him, she searches for him anyway.

Historical Accuracy: The novel blends fact and fiction with an authentic look at period Savannah.

5189 *Where Shadows Go*
Date of Publication: 1993
Subject(s): Family Saga; Antebellum South; Slavery

Fictional character(s): John Fraser, Plantation Owner; Anne Couper Fraser, Spouse; Fanny Kemble Butler, Actress, Abolitionist
Time Period(s): 1820s; 1830s (1825-1839)
Locale(s): St. Simons Island, Georgia

Summary: In the second volume of the author's Georgia Trilogy, John Fraser, the former British officer, has returned with his wife Anne to her family's plantation on St. Simons Island. There he begins to learn about coastal planting and to adjust to life as a slave owner. A famous English actress, Fanny Butler, who is an outspoken abolitionist, challenges Anne's assumptions about the morality of slavery.

Historical Accuracy: The locale and the period are authentically drawn.

JERAMIE PRICE

`5190` *Katrina*

Date of Publication: 1955
Subject(s): Russian Empire; Royalty—Russia
Historical character(s): Peter the Great, Ruler (Czar of Russia); Catherine I, Royalty (consort of Peter the Great); Aleksandr Menshikov, Military Personnel (field marshal), Political Figure
Time Period(s): 1710s; 1720s
Locale(s): Russia

Summary: The novel captures life in Russia during the reign of Peter the Great. The focus is on the relationship between the czar and his second wife, Catherine, who was born a peasant. Captured by Russian soldiers, she becomes the mistress of Aleksandr Menshikov and meets and marries Peter. After he dies without an heir, Menshikov and the imperial guard raise her to the throne as Catherine I.

Historical Accuracy: The author has taken liberties with the historical background, which is at variance with standard accounts.

WILLARD PRICE (1887-)

A Canadian explorer, naturalist, and writer, Price was born in Ontario. He has travelled to over 140 countries on expeditions for the National Geographic Society and the American Museum of Natural History. His books have been published in 25 different languages.

`5191` *The Barbarian*

Date of Publication: 1941
Subject(s): Japanese Empire; East/West Relations
Fictional character(s): Jonathan Boone, Sailor
Time Period(s): 1850s
Locale(s): Japan

Summary: The opening up of Japan to the West is dramatized in the experiences of Jonathan Boone, a young American midshipman who travels to Japan with Commodore Perry in 1853. He returns five years later in his own ship determined to establish trade. Although successful, he is caught up in the anti-western sentiment that grips Japan.

Historical Accuracy: The essential details of the period are accurately presented.

TIM PRIDGEN (1899-)

Pridgen's books include *Courage* and *Tory Oath*.

`5192` *West Goes the Road*

Date of Publication: 1944
Subject(s): Settlement of the American Frontier; Indians; Wilkinson Plot
Fictional character(s): Caesar Brown, Frontiersman
Historical character(s): Aaron Burr, Political Figure
Time Period(s): 1790s; 1800s
Locale(s): Pennsylvania; Ohio

Summary: Set in the years following the American Revolution, the novel tells the story of frontiersman Caesar Brown. He is involved in skirmishes with the Spanish, French, and Indians. Brown joins up with Aaron Burr but later opposes James Wilkinson and Burr's schemes.

Historical Accuracy: The novel's presentation of its historical background is uneven. Some of the scenes are mere sketches in the onrush of events; others are plausible and authentic.

FREDERIC PROKOSCH (1908-1989)

An American poet and novelist born in Wisconsin, Prokosch graduated from Haverford College and Yale University. His first novel, *The Asiatics*, was an immense popular and critical success. He won the Harper Novel Award in 1937 for *The Seven Who Fled*.

`5193` *The Dark Dancer*

Date of Publication: 1964
Subject(s): Mogul Empire; Royalty—India
Historical character(s): Shah Jehan, Ruler (Mogul emperor of India); Mumtaz Mahal, Spouse (of Jehan)
Time Period(s): 17th century
Locale(s): India

Summary: Set during the time of India's Mogul Empire, the novel dramatizes the reign of Shah Jehan and his relationship with his wife. After her death, Jehan builds the Taj Mahal for her. The novel provides a poetic rendering of the exotic setting and period.

Historical Accuracy: The novel is more atmospheric than accurate about characters or events.

`5194` *The Missolonghi Manuscript*

Date of Publication: 1968
Subject(s): Literary Life; Biography, Fictionalized
Historical character(s): George Gordon Byron, Writer; Percy Bysshe Shelley, Writer; Anne Louise Germaine de Stael, Writer
Time Period(s): 1820s
Locale(s): Missolonghi, Greece; England; Italy

Summary: The dying Lord Byron offers an examination of his past in a series of notebook entries. Contemplating his scandal-filled life, Byron records his loves—both heterosexual and homosexual—and his friendships with some of the most famous figures of the period. All is cast in the elegiac tone of Byron's growing intimations of his own mortality.

Historical Accuracy: Occasionally the author's imagination dominates the biographical facts, leaving open the question of whether the novel captures Byron's proclivities and concerns or the author's.

5195　*A Tale for Midnight*

Date of Publication: 1955
Subject(s): Renaissance; Trials; Crime and Criminals
Historical character(s): Beatrice Cenci, Noblewoman, Murderer; Francesco Cenci, Nobleman; Lucrezia Cenci, Spouse (of Francesco)
Time Period(s): 16th century (1590s)
Locale(s): Rome, Italy

Summary: The novel reconstructs a notorious murder case in Renaissance Italy. Roman nobleman Francesco Cenci's cruel treatment of his daughter, Beatrice, and her stepmother, Lucrezia, leads to his murder. The grim and violent events, as well as Beatrice's trial for patricide, are vividly dramatized.

Historical Accuracy: The novel features an authentic portrait of Renaissance Rome and a sensuous reconstruction of the past.

LOZANIA PROLE
(PSEUD. OF URSULA BLOOM, 1893-1984)

Born in Nether Wallop, Hampshire, England, British journalist and author Ursula Bloom wrote more than 500 books, which makes her one of England's most prolific literary figures. Among her many novels are *Secret Lover*, *The Rose of Norfolk*, and *Judas Iscariot, Traitor?* Bloom also wrote several volumes of nonfiction as well as plays for the stage and radio.

5196　*The Little Victoria*

Date of Publication: 1957
Subject(s): Royalty—England; Victorian Period
Historical character(s): Victoria, Ruler (Queen of England); Edward, Duke of Kent, Royalty; George IV, Ruler (King of England); Victoria, Duchess of Kent, Royalty
Time Period(s): 19th century
Locale(s): England; Germany

Summary: The novel dramatizes the marriage of Edward, Duke of Kent to Victoria of Saxe Coburg, sister of Leopold I of Belgium. Their daughter, Victoria, is to become heir to the throne of England, and the novel captures her childhood up to her marriage.

Historical Accuracy: The novel is faithful to the facts of Victoria's life, with fictional embellishments.

5197　*Marlborough's Unfair Lady*

Date of Publication: 1965
Subject(s): Royalty—England

Historical character(s): Anne, Ruler (Queen of England); Sarah Churchill, Noblewoman (Duchess of Marlborough); John Churchill, Nobleman (Duke of Marlborough)
Time Period(s): 17th century; 18th century (1660-1714)
Locale(s): England

Summary: The novel portrays the career of Sarah Jennings, who marries the Duke of Marlborough and ascends to a position of great power and influence that extends to the crown itself. As the Duchess of Marlborough, she becomes the power behind the weak Queen Anne.

Historical Accuracy: This is a simplified version of a much more complex story. The basic outline of the narrative is close to actual facts.

5198　*Sweet Marie-Antoinette*

Date of Publication: 1969
Subject(s): Royalty—France; French Revolution; Biography, Fictionalized
Historical character(s): Marie Antoinette, Royalty (queen consort of Louis XVI); Louis XVI, Ruler (King of France)
Time Period(s): 18th century
Locale(s): Austria; France

Summary: This biographical portrait captures the career of Marie-Antoinette, the ninth child of the Empress of Austria, who at the age of 15 is betrothed to the Dauphin of France, later Louis XVI. Reviled by her adopted country, she is swept up in the forces of the Revolution that topples her family.

Historical Accuracy: This is a simplified and idealized portrait of the personalties and the era. The basic facts are, however, observed.

5199　*The Ten-Day Queen*

Date of Publication: 1972
Subject(s): Tudor Period; Royalty—England
Historical character(s): Lady Jane Grey, Ruler (Queen of England); Edward VI, Ruler (King of England); Thomas Cranmer, Religious (archbishop); Mary Tudor, Royalty (princess); Elizabeth Tudor, Royalty (princess)
Time Period(s): 16th century (1540s-1550s)
Locale(s): England

Summary: The novel dramatizes the short and tragic life of Lady Jane Grey who becomes a pawn in the political struggle that follows the deaths of Henry VIII and the boy-king Edward VI. Pushed forward, she occupies the throne for only a few days before she is executed.

Historical Accuracy: The novel invents scenes and conversations but is faithful in essentials to history.

BILL PRONZINI (1943-)

Born in California, Pronzini has worked as a newspaper reporter. He is a well-known critic and award-winning mystery and horror novelist. He is the author of the Nameless Detective series.

5200　*Firewind*

Date of Publication: 1989

Subject(s): American West; Fires
Fictional character(s): Matt Kincaid, Rancher; Austin Trace, Landowner
Time Period(s): 19th century
Locale(s): California (northern)

Summary: This Western thriller involves a cache of illegal weapons and ammunition being collected by lumber baron Austin Trace to exterminate the Nez Perce Indians. Outlaws set off a forest fire that threatens a community whose only escape is via the train that conceals the explosive cache of arms and ammunition. Rancher Matt Kincaid helps organize the evacuation and then must contend with the perilous journey through the forest fire.

Historical Accuracy: The novel is a gripping adventure with a convincing period backdrop.

5201 *The Gallows Land*

Date of Publication: 1983
Subject(s): American West; Crime and Criminals
Fictional character(s): Ray Boone, Widow(er), Wanderer; Jennifer Todd, Abuse Victim, Murderer
Time Period(s): 19th century
Locale(s): Arizona

Summary: After the death of his young wife, Ray Boone drifts west, encountering the battered Jennifer Todd. When his revolver disappears, it seems clear that she has used it to murder her husband. Ray sets out in pursuit, pursued himself by outlaws. He eventually serves as Jennifer's protector, and the two avoid several deadly encounters.

Historical Accuracy: The western setting is convincingly detailed.

5202 *The Hangings*

Date of Publication: 1989
Subject(s): American West; Mystery
Fictional character(s): Lincoln Evans, Lawman (constable)
Time Period(s): 19th century
Locale(s): Tule Bend, California

Summary: When a man is found hanging from a tree behind the saddlery shop in Tule Bend, Constable Lincoln Evans has little to go on but the sense that the killer could strike again if Evans doesn't act first. This is an ingenious mystery set in the Old West.

Historical Accuracy: The period details and a convincing background make this a believable historical mystery.

5203 *The Last Days of Horse-Shy Halloran*

Date of Publication: 1987
Subject(s): American West; Mining; Crime and Criminals
Fictional character(s): Horse-Shy Halloran, Outlaw; Sam Quarternight, Detective—Private (Wells Fargo); Faye Turnblow, Young Woman
Time Period(s): 1870s (1878)
Locale(s): Helena, Montana

Summary: The comic misadventures of one Horse-Shy Halloran form the basis of this Western novel set in the Montana Territory of 1878. Halloran hatches a scheme to rob the Wells Fargo stagecoach of its gold and then transport the gold (using a buckboard) to the nearest railhead. Halloran's obstacles include Wells Fargo detective Sam Quarternight, a gang of robbers, and a banker's daughter.

Historical Accuracy: This amusing Western tale is authentic in its period details.

ELINOR PRYOR

Pryor lives in Wichita, Kansas, where her husband is in the oil business. An ardent American historian, Pryor has long been interested in Indians.

5204 *And Never Yield*

Date of Publication: 1942
Subject(s): Mormons; Religious Conflict
Fictional character(s): Lindsey Allen, Young Woman; Nathan Welles, Religious (Mormon)
Time Period(s): 1830s; 1840s
Locale(s): Illinois; Missouri

Summary: The novel describes the persecution of the Mormons through the experiences of Lindsay Allen and her husband, Nathan Wells. The story presents the trek of a small group of Mormons through Illinois and Missouri. They experience the siege of DeWitt, the massacre at Haun's Mill, and the death of Joseph Smith.

Historical Accuracy: The novel blends a fictional story with the actual events of the Mormons' experiences in the Midwest.

5205 *The Double Man*

Date of Publication: 1957
Subject(s): Indians; Tribal Life—Native American; French and Indian War
Fictional character(s): Tsani, Indian (Cherokee), Chieftain (also known as Mark Caldwell); Nakwisi, Indian (Shawnee), Captive; Hannah Warren, Gentlewoman
Historical character(s): William Pitt the Elder, Political Figure; George Washington, Military Personnel (colonel)
Time Period(s): 1740s; 1750s (1749-1755)
Locale(s): Charleston, South Carolina, American Colonies; London, England

Summary: This tale of Indian life in the American colonies is told from the perspective of English-born Mark Caldwell, who is raised by Indians and becomes a Cherokee war chief. He is sent by his people to England to plead their cause. When he returns, he is faced with divided loyalties as war breaks out between the Cherokees and the colonists.

Historical Accuracy: The story is imagined but does employ a convincing period background and some actual events.

JOHN J. PUGH

5206 *Captain of the Medici*

Date of Publication: 1953
Subject(s): Renaissance
Fictional character(s): Pietro Lucca, Military Personnel (captain)
Time Period(s): 16th century
Locale(s): Florence, Italy

Summary: This historical action-adventure is set in the world of Renaissance Italy and describes the career of a blacksmith's son, Pietro Lucca, who rise to become an army captain. The novel's pivotal historical moment is the ultimate collapse of the last of the Italian republics.

Historical Accuracy: The novel is more melodramatic than realistic in its depiction of the period. Its hero is too flawless to be believed, and the period backdrop is far too thin to be convincing.

5207 *High Carnival*

Date of Publication: 1959
Subject(s): Renaissance; Espionage
Fictional character(s): Malatesta Greppia, Mercenary; Riccardo Del Buoncorso, Adventurer
Time Period(s): 16th century (1570)
Locale(s): Venice, Italy

Summary: This melodramatic tale of intrigue and violence is set in 16th- century Venice at the height of the city-state's naval and mercantile power. The exciting plot concerns treason, torture, poisoning, and imprisonment. There are at least three villains, one of whom, Malatesta Greppia, repents and joins the side of virtue, which is most thoroughly tested.

Historical Accuracy: The novel provides an authentic background, though it is marred by naval anachronisms and a preference for piling on implausibilities, which undermines its believability.

CHARLES K. PULSE

5208 *John Bonwell*

Date of Publication: 1952
Subject(s): Civil War—U.S.; Settlement of the American Frontier
Fictional character(s): John Bonwell, Settler
Time Period(s): 19th century (1818-1862)
Locale(s): Ohio; Kentucky

Summary: Frontier life in Kentucky and Ohio is described through the experiences of settler John Bonwell, who migrates west from Virginia in 1818. The story depicts his adaptation to life in the frontier.

Historical Accuracy: The novel features a wealth of convincing historical details that capture the historical period.

NORA PURTSCHER-WYDENBRUCH
(1894-1959)

Purtscher-Wydenbruch is the author of *Rilke: Man and Poet* and an autobiography, *My Two Worlds.*

5209 *Woman Astride*

Date of Publication: 1934
Subject(s): Thirty Years War; Civil War—England; Identity—Concealed
Historical character(s): Judith von Loe, Noblewoman
Time Period(s): 17th century
Locale(s): Europe; Turkey

Summary: The novel offers a partly factual, partly imaginative account of Judith von Loe who, disguised as a man, fights during the Thirty Years War in the army of Gustavus Adolphus. Her extraordinary career continues on a diplomatic mission to Turkey where she is held captive in a Turkish harem.

Historical Accuracy: Although the Turkish adventure is fanciful, the bulk of the heroine's amazing exploits have a factual basis.

ALEXANDER PUSHKIN (1799-1837)

A Russian writer considered the national poet of Russia, Pushkin's works consist of lyrical and narrative poems and a novel in verse, *Eugenii Onegin,* his masterpiece.

5210 *The Captain's Daughter*

Date of Publication: 1837
Subject(s): Russian Empire; Cossacks
Fictional character(s): Peter Grineff, Military Personnel; Maria Ivanovna, Young Woman
Historical character(s): Catherine II, Ruler; Emelyan Pougatcheff, Revolutionary
Time Period(s): 1770s (1774)
Locale(s): Russia

Summary: The novel offers a picture of army life in the Russian steppes during the reign of Catherine the Great. A young soldier, Grineff, falls in love with his captain's daughter and both survive a rebel Cossack uprising. Eventually, Grineff's name is cleared by a petition to the Empress Catherine herself.

Historical Accuracy: Pushkin's position as crown historian enabled him to gather details from the state archives and the private papers of Catherine.

NINA WILCOX PUTNAM (1888-1962)

Born in New Haven, Connecticut, Putnam was the author of *In Search of Arcady,* *The Impossible Boy,* and *The Inner Voice.*

5211 *The Inner Voice*

Date of Publication: 1941
Subject(s): Quakers; Slavery; Abolition Movement
Fictional character(s): Jonathan Pickett, Landowner

Time Period(s): 19th century
Locale(s): North Carolina; Indiana; Kansas

Summary: The role that the Southern Quakers played in the Abolitionist Movement is described in this tale of Jonathan Pickett. Rather than help support slavery, Jonathan gives up his land in North Carolina and ventures west to Indiana and finally Kansas. Refusing violence, Pickett and other Quakers are helpless before the fighting that pits the Free Soilers against pro-slavery advocates.

Historical Accuracy: The novel's background is historical, even if the story itself is more romance than fact.

MICHAEL KENNETH PYE (1946-)

A journalist, novelist, broadcaster and historian, Pye is the author of several books, including *Maximum City: The Biography of New York*. He was a staff writer for *The Scotsman* from 1967 to 1971 and for the *Sunday Times* from 1971 to 1978.

5212 *The Drowning Room*

Date of Publication: 1995
Subject(s): American Colonies
Fictional character(s): Anthony the Turk, Sailor
Historical character(s): Gretje Reynier, Prostitute
Time Period(s): 17th century
Locale(s): New Amsterdam, American Colonies; Amsterdam, Netherlands

Summary: The novel re-creates the life and career of Gretje Reynier, prostitute, money lender, and pelt dealer in the Dutch colonial city of New Amsterdam. Her life in Amsterdam, love for a sailor called Anthony the Turk, and her journey to New Amsterdam are described.

Historical Accuracy: Although Reynier is historical, the author admits that this is only one version of her colorful story.

AMANDA QUICK

(PSEUD. OF JAYNE ANN KRENTZ, 1948-)

American romance novelist Quick graduated from the University of California, Santa Cruz, and San Jose State University. She has worked as a librarian and is the author of many romances under a variety of pseudonyms.

5213 *Dangerous*

Date of Publication: 1993
Subject(s): Regency Romance; Mystery; Supernatural
Fictional character(s): Prudence Merryweather, Detective—Private; Sebastian Fleetwood, Nobleman (Earl of Angelstone), Detective—Private
Time Period(s): 1810s
Locale(s): London, England

Summary: This unusual Regency romance draws its excitement from other-worldly phenomena. Prudence Merryweather is an investigator of ghosts and spirits who finds herself in a romantic tangle with the Earl of Angelstone.

Historical Accuracy: This is an amusing mix of genres with period elements that create a believable backdrop.

5214 *Deception*

Date of Publication: 1993
Subject(s): Regency Romance; Treasure Hunt
Fictional character(s): Olympia Wingfield, Spinster; Jared Ryder, Nobleman (Viscount Chillhurst), Imposter
Time Period(s): 1810s
Locale(s): Dorset, England; London, England

Summary: This Regency romance features Olympia Wingfield, who divides her time between raising her nephews and researching ancient legends for clues leading to hidden treasures. Nobleman Jared Ryder, posing as a scholarly tutor, is on the same trail of hidden treasure, and love blossoms amidst murder, deception, and feuds.

Historical Accuracy: This high-speed adventure romance is not slowed down by excessive concentration on the period.

5215 *Mistress*

Date of Publication: 1994
Subject(s): Regency Romance; Crime and Criminals
Fictional character(s): Iphigenia Bright, Spinster, Teacher; Marcus Valerius Cloud, Nobleman (Earl of Masters)
Time Period(s): 19th century (Regency period)
Locale(s): London, England

Summary: To foil a blackmail plot, spinster schoolteacher Iphigenia Bright poses as the mistress of the infamous Earl of Masters, whose disappearance seems connected with the blackmailer. She creates a sensation among London society, particularly when the earl returns to meet his ''mistress.''.

Historical Accuracy: The Regency period is lightly but believably sketched in this ingenious entertainment.

5216 *Ravished*

Date of Publication: 1992
Subject(s): Regency Romance; Paleontology
Fictional character(s): Harriet Pomeroy, Naturalist (fossil collector), Spinster; Gideon Westbrook, Nobleman (Viscount St. Justin)
Time Period(s): 1810s
Locale(s): England

Summary: Fossil collector Harriet Pomeroy discovers smugglers disturbing her investigation. She enlists the help of the absent estate owner, Gideon Westbrook. Together they must deal with the smugglers while unraveling a buried secret.

Historical Accuracy: The historical setting is lightly sketched with an emphasis on romance and suspense.

5217 *Reckless*

Date of Publication: 1992
Subject(s): Regency Romance
Fictional character(s): Phoebe Layton, Noblewoman; Gabriel Banner, Nobleman (Earl of Wylde), Writer
Time Period(s): 1810s
Locale(s): England

Summary: Phoebe Layton enlists Gabriel Banner in her quest to recover a rare medieva l manuscript. Gabriel, however, is not the knight in shining armor Phoebe imagi nes him to be. He has a score to settle with the Layton family, but his plans go awry when he finds himself falling in love with Phoebe.

Historical Accuracy: How authentic can any novel that employs a gentleman pirate be?.

5218 *Rendezvous*

Date of Publication: 1992
Subject(s): Regency Romance
Fictional character(s): Augusta Ballinger, Noblewoman; Harry Fleming, Nobleman (Earl of Graystone), Spy
Time Period(s): 1810s
Locale(s): England

Summary: Free spirit Augusta Ballinger attempts to clear her brother's name with help from Harry Fleming, who is secretly the spy called Nemesis. Together they find themselves in a number of dangerous predicaments, and Augusta must reassess her vow never to marry.

Historical Accuracy: This fast-paced romantic thriller does offer some convincing period details.

5219 *Scandal*

Date of Publication: 1991
Subject(s): Regency Romance
Fictional character(s): Emily Faringdon, Spinster; Simon Traherne, Nobleman (Earl of Blade)
Time Period(s): 1810s
Locale(s): England

Summary: Emily Faringdon becomes a pawn in Simon Traherne's revenge plot. Emily proves to be no easy dupe, eventually convincing Simon that love is preferable to revenge.

Historical Accuracy: The novel is a fanciful tale but has a convincing period background.

5220 *Seduction*

Date of Publication: 1990
Subject(s): Regency Romance
Fictional character(s): Sophy Dorring, Spinster, Gentlewoman; Julian Sinclair, Nobleman (Earl of Ravenswood), Widow(er)
Time Period(s): 1810s
Locale(s): England

Summary: A conflict of wills ensues when widower Julian Sinclair hopes to remarry. He chooses free-thinking Sophy Dorring, who intends to remain independent.

Historical Accuracy: The emphasis is on romance over history, but the novel does feature some convincing period details.

5221 *Surrender*

Date of Publication: 1990
Subject(s): Regency Romance
Fictional character(s): Victoria Huntington, Spinster; Lucas Colebrook, Nobleman (Earl of Stonevale)

Time Period(s): 1810s
Locale(s): England

Summary: Lucas Colebrook is in the marriage market and chooses independent Victoria Huntington, who has no intention of marrying. However, romance does lead to a reconsideration when they find themselves in a compromising situation.

Historical Accuracy: This is fairly well-trod territory with credible period elements.

HERBERT QUICK (1861-1925)

Born on a farm in Iowa, Quick taught school for a number of years, was admitted to the Iowa bar, and worked as a journalist. He also served as mayor of Sioux City, Iowa.

5222 *The Hawkeye*

Date of Publication: 1923
Subject(s): Farming
Fictional character(s): Fremont McConkey, Young Man
Time Period(s): 19th century (1857-1878)
Locale(s): Iowa

Summary: The story of an Iowa farm during the 19th century is described in the life of Fremont McConkey. The novel captures the politics and struggles of pioneer life.

Historical Accuracy: The novel provides an accurate historical background.

5223 *Vandemark's Folly*

Date of Publication: 1922
Subject(s): Settlement of the American Frontier; Underground Railroad; Erie Canal
Fictional character(s): Jacobus Vandemark, Farmer
Time Period(s): 19th century (1840s-1860s)
Locale(s): Iowa; New York

Summary: This autobiographical account of Jacobus Vandemark chronicles life on the Erie Canal and pioneer days in Iowa. Vandemark is born in New York and works on a boat on the Erie Canal. He sets off for Iowa in search of his mother, where he becomes a farmer. The events of the conflict leading up to the Civil War are depicted.

Historical Accuracy: The details of pioneer life and times are captured accurately.

JOHN QUIGLEY (1927-)

Scottish journalist and writer Quigley started in journalism at age 17. After his first book was published he devoted his time to his writing and to a Scotch whiskey business he started when he discovered an ancient recipe. Quigley has worked as the director of a Scottish exporting company. He is also the proprietor of a pub in Scotland.

5224 *King's Royal*

Date of Publication: 1975
Subject(s): Business Building; Family Saga; Victorian Period

Fictional character(s): Fergus King, Saloon Keeper/Owner; Robert King, Businessman
Time Period(s): 1870s
Locale(s): Scotland

Summary: The birth of the Scottish whiskey industry is seen through a generational struggle within the King family. Fergus King is a hard-working publican who rises to respectability, while his son Robert is determined to introduce a superior blended whiskey and export it to the world.

Historical Accuracy: The novel offers fascinating period and regional elements that create a believable background for the story.

5225 *Queen's Royal*

Date of Publication: 1977
Subject(s): Family Saga; Victorian Period; Business Building
Fictional character(s): Fiona Fraser King, Gentlewoman; Robert King, Businessman; Douglas Dunbar, Businessman
Time Period(s): 1890s (1897)
Locale(s): Scotland; London, England

Summary: The novel, a sequel to *King's Royal*, continues the King family's saga. Robert King, now head of the family and its whiskey empire, turns his attention to London politics. Fiona Fraser King struggles to maintain the family ascendency in the industry while locked in conflict with her husband's nemesis, Douglas Dunbar.

Historical Accuracy: The period detail is authentic and convincing.

SIR ARTHUR THOMAS QUILLER-COUCH (1863-1944)

DAPHNE DU MAURIER (1907-1989)

Educated at Oxford, Quiller-Couch taught English literature at Cambridge. In addition to writing novels, poetry, short stories, romances and literary criticism, he edited the *Oxford Book of English Verse*. Daphne Du Maurier is best known for her classic gothic novel *Rebecca*. Quiller-Couch and Du Maurier shared an interest in Cornwall, where *Castle Dor* is set: he was born there, and she wrote a book about the region.

5226 *Castle Dor*

Date of Publication:
Subject(s): Romance; Victorian Period
Fictional character(s): Linnet Lewarne, Young Woman; Amoyot Trestane, Sailor
Time Period(s): 1840s
Locale(s): Cornwall, England

Summary: The novel provides an updated version of the tragic love affair of Tristan and Iseult set in Cornwall in the 1840s. Linnet Lewarne is a young woman married to a man many years older. She falls in love with a Breton sailor, Amoyot Trestane. The novel traces the dark consequences of their passion.

Historical Accuracy: The Cornwall period background is authentic.

PETER QUINN (1948-)

Quinn was raised in the Bronx and became a speech writer for former Governor Mario Cuomo. He is currently chief speech writer for Time-Warner, Inc. and lives in Brooklyn. *Banished Children of Eve* is his acclaimed first novel.

5227 *Banished Children of Eve*

Date of Publication: 1994
Subject(s): Civil War—U.S.; Draft Riots; Immigrants
Fictional character(s): Jimmy Dunne, Thief; Jack Mulcahey, Entertainer (minstrel show); Charles Bedford, Stock Broker
Historical character(s): Stephen Foster, Songwriter, Composer; George McClellan, Military Personnel (general)
Time Period(s): 1860s (1863-1864)
Locale(s): New York, New York

Summary: The title refers to the Irish-Americans of New York who emigrated from the famine at home and fought to protect their precarious place on the social ladder against the perceived competition of freed slaves during the Civil War. The novel ingeniously weaves a number of characters' stories—a thief, minstrel performers, businessmen—into an urban panorama culminating in the Draft Riots.

Historical Accuracy: Quinn's novel is an impressive performance, integrating convincing research with a flair for the human side of history.

THOMAS H. RADDALL (1903-)

Born in England, Raddall has lived in Canada since childhood. He has worked as an accountant for a wood pulp and paper firm in Nova Scotia. In the 1930s his short stories began to appear regularly in magazines. Raddall has an absorbing interest in Nova Scotian history and his many works on the subject offer a re-creation of Nova Scotian life from 1749 to the 20th century.

5228 *The Governor's Lady*

Date of Publication: 1960
Subject(s): Biography, Fictionalized; American Revolution
Historical character(s): John Wentworth, Political Figure (governor); Frances Wentworth, Spouse
Time Period(s): 18th century
Locale(s): Nova Scotia, Canada; New Hampshire, American Colonies; London, England

Summary: This biographical novel set around the time of the American Revolution describes the life and career of John Wentworth, the governor of New Hampshire, who when the revolution breaks out returns to London. There his restless and ambitious wife, Frances, involves herself in intrigue that nets Wentworth a post in the colonial administration of Nova Scotia, where Frances continues her manipulations and seductions.

Historical Accuracy: The novel is a blend of fact and fiction.

5229 *Hangman's Beach*

Date of Publication: 1966
Subject(s): Napoleonic Wars
Fictional character(s): Ellen Dewar, Young Woman; Michel Cascamond, Military Personnel (sailor)
Historical character(s): Peter McNab, Landowner; John Wentworth, Political Figure (governor)
Time Period(s): 1810s
Locale(s): Halifax, Nova Scotia, Canada

Summary: In the early years of the 19th century, Halifax, Nova Scotia, is the lone British fortress and naval base in North America during the Napoleonic Wars. In this colonial town live Peter McNab and his family and Michel Cascamond, the sailor responsible for firing the shell that killed Lord Nelson at Trafalgar.

Historical Accuracy: The novel blends historical fact with romantic elements and invented characters. Although Ellen Dewar and Michel Cascamond are invented, the author claims that their adventures might well have happened.

5230 *His Majesty's Yankees*

Date of Publication: 1942
Subject(s): American Revolution
Fictional character(s): Davy Strang, Young Man
Time Period(s): 1770s
Locale(s): Nova Scotia, Canada

Summary: When the American Revolution breaks out, Yankees living in Nova Scotia face a difficult test of divided loyalties. This novel narrated by young Davy Strang captures the perspective of both the Loyalists and the Patriots.

Historical Accuracy: The period and regional elements are convincing and authentic.

5231 *Pride's Fancy*

Date of Publication: 1946
Subject(s): Sea Story; Pirates
Fictional character(s): Nathan Cain, Sea Captain
Time Period(s): 1790s (1793)
Locale(s): West Indies; Nova Scotia, Canada

Summary: Young Nathan Cain commands *Pride's Fancy*, a privateer from Nova Scotia, on a cruise that takes him throughout the 18th-century West Indies.

Historical Accuracy: The story is imagined but does employ convincing period details.

5232 *Roger Sudden*

Date of Publication: 1945
Subject(s): French Colonies; Indians; American Colonies
Fictional character(s): Roger Sudden, Adventurer
Time Period(s): 18th century
Locale(s): Nova Scotia, Canada

Summary: Conflict between the English and the French in Nova Scotia during the 18th century forms the background for this novel. It follows the adventures of Englishman Roger Sudden, a Jacobite exiled after the Battle of Culloden, who seeks his fortune in the colonies.

Historical Accuracy: The author is exact and convincing in his period elements and historical atmosphere.

MAX RADIN (1880-1950)

Born in Kempen, Poland and brought to the U.S. in 1884, Radin was educated at jCity College, New York, New York University, and Columbia, where he received his Ph.D. He was a professor of law and wrote several books on legal history, biblical subjects, and philosophy.

5233 *Epicurus My Master*

Date of Publication: 1949
Subject(s): Roman Empire
Historical character(s): Titus Pomponius Atticus, Nobleman
Time Period(s): 1st century B.C.
Locale(s): Rome, Roman Empire

Summary: The novel imagines what might have been said if Titus Pomponius Atticus, friend and correspondent of Cicero, and one of the wealthiest and most celebrated men of his age, had written his memoirs. An elaboration of Atticus' Epicurean philosophy as well as reflections on the Rome of Pompey and Marc Anthony are featured.

Historical Accuracy: It is not clear how devoted an Epicurean Atticus was. The novel's impersonation of Atticus' voice and his era are nonetheless convincing.

CATHERINE M. RAE

5234 *Afterward*

Date of Publication: 1992
Subject(s): Fires
Fictional character(s): Angela Evans, Young Woman; Maud Evans, Young Woman
Time Period(s): 1910s
Locale(s): New York, New York

Summary: In 1904 a fire breaks out aboard the ferryboat *General Slocum* during an excursion on New York's East River. More than 1,000 people die in one of the worst shipping disasters in U.S. history. In this novel, Maud and Angela Evans, who lose their mother and three brothers on the ship, struggle with their grief and attempt to survive on the edge of poverty.

Historical Accuracy: The details of period New York are authentic and believable.

5235 *Flight From Fifth Avenue*

Date of Publication: 1995
Subject(s): Suspense; Romance; Fires
Fictional character(s): Maida Jardine, Gentlewoman; Edmund Ormley, Nobleman
Time Period(s): 1910s (1911)
Locale(s): New York, New York

Summary: This romantic suspense novel concerns the youngest daughter of a prominent banker. She rejects an arranged marriage with a British nobleman for her own uncertain prospects, which include a journey on an "orphan train" and a job in the ill-fated Triangle Shirtwaist factory before a final confrontation with her family secret.

Historical Accuracy: The novel is packed with convincing details of 1911 New York.

`5236` *Sarah Cobb*

Date of Publication: 1990
Subject(s): Romance
Fictional character(s): Henry Cobb, Gentleman; Sarah Cunningham, Spouse (of Cobb)
Time Period(s): 1910s (1910)
Locale(s): New York, New York

Summary: This romantic tale set in New York in the years before and during World War I tells the story of Sarah Cunningham, who marries widower Henry Cobb. Sarah must contend with the domineering Cobb family and a family secret that could destroy them.

Historical Accuracy: Period New York is believably suggested.

`5237` *The Ship's Clock*

Date of Publication: 1993
Subject(s): Business Building; Family Saga
Fictional character(s): John Ferguson, Businessman (shipping company); Robert Ferguson, Banker; Ellen Ferguson, Young Woman
Time Period(s): 19th century (1810-1885)
Locale(s): Hamburg, Germany; New York, New York

Summary: In 1810 Philip Manor rebels against his tyrannical father, assumes the identity of John Ferguson, and establishes a successful shipping company that rivals his father's business. The novel details how his children struggle to establish their own identities and deal with the strange legacy of their father's past.

Historical Accuracy: The period elements in the novel are credible.

HUGH C. RAE (1935-)

A Scottish writer born in Glasgow, Rae has worked as an antiquarian bookseller and as a lecturer in creative writing at the University of Glasgow. He is the co-author with Margaret Coghlan of novels under the pseudonym Jessica Stirling.

`5238` *Harkfast: The Making of the King*

Date of Publication: 1976
Subject(s): Dark Ages; Druids; Celtic Britain
Fictional character(s): Harkfast, Religious (Druid); Ruan, Orphan
Time Period(s): 3rd century
Locale(s): England

Summary: After the departure of the Romans, Britain is a collection of scattered tribes vulnerable to marauders. Harkfast is the last remaining Druid and sets out to unite the clans by establishing a new line of kings. He selects an orphan

Pictish boy, Ruan, and sets out to gain the talismans of Celtic legend whose magical power will insure Harkfast's dream.

Historical Accuracy: The story is imagined but convincing in its version of Celtic Britain.

`5239` *The Rookery: A Novel of the Victorian Underworld*

Date of Publication: 1975
Subject(s): Victorian Period; Crime and Criminals
Fictional character(s): Charley Cobbold, Thief; Badger Gregson, Thief; Sarah Gregson, Young Woman; Cooney, Thief
Time Period(s): 1850s
Locale(s): Yorkshire, England

Summary: Charley Cobbold is a skilled cracksman, but his night raid on the Ashcrofts' farm in Yorkshire goes awry. Badger Gregson is taken and fellow thief Cooney abducts Gregson's daughter, Sarah. Since Sarah is also the heir to Gregson's hoard of loot hidden in London, Cobbold pursues the pair to a violent climax at a rural slum, or rookery.

Historical Accuracy: The novel is authentic in its depiction of Victorian low-life.

MILLIE J. RAGOSTA (1931-)

Born in Pennsylvania, Ragosta began writing in 1966 as a 35-year old mother of ten to do something for herself. She began with gothic romances but soon moved on to historical fiction.

`5240` *Druid's Enchantment*

Date of Publication: 1985
Subject(s): Celtic Ireland; Druids; Dark Ages
Fictional character(s): Marda, Royalty (princess); Lucat-mael, Religious (Druid); Keagh, Doctor
Historical character(s): Patrick, Religious (missionary)
Time Period(s): 5th century
Locale(s): Ireland

Summary: Marda, the daughter of the High King of Ireland, attempts to break her engagement to the king's chief Druid, Lucat-mael. She journeys with her lover, Keagh, to the north of Ireland to seek the assistance of a man named Patrick who is preaching a new religion to challenge the power of the Druids.

Historical Accuracy: The story is fanciful but convincing in its 5th-century details.

`5241` *Gerait's Daughter*

Date of Publication: 1981
Subject(s): Tudor Period; Romance
Fictional character(s): Magheen Fitzgerald, Young Woman; Gerait Fitzgerald, Nobleman (Earl of Kildare); Sir Piers Roe, Gentleman
Time Period(s): 15th century
Locale(s): Dublin, Ireland

Summary: In the aftermath of the Tudor victory in the War of the Roses, Gerait Fitzgerald is ordered by Henry VII to marry his daughter to his family's sworn enemy. Megheen reluctantly agrees to marry Sir Piers to save her father's life and honor, but she resolves to despise him.

Historical Accuracy: The novel has some colorful period details that set a credible background for the drama.

5242 The House on Curtin Street

Date of Publication: 1979
Subject(s): Suspense; Architecture
Fictional character(s): Minerva Stewart, Architect; Anthony Richmond, Architect; Jon Boswell, Doctor
Time Period(s): 1890s
Locale(s): Bellefonte, Pennsylvania

Summary: Architect Minerva Stewart is commissioned to design a summer home for a mining engineer. Accidents, disappearances, and finally a destructive fire plague the construction, and Minerva must finally confront the cause of her troubles.

Historical Accuracy: The novel creates a credible setting and time period in this unusual suspense story.

5243 The Winter Rose

Date of Publication: 1982
Subject(s): War of the Roses; Royalty—England
Fictional character(s): Anne de Syon, Young Woman; Sir Adam Booth, Knight
Historical character(s): Edward IV, Ruler (King of England)
Time Period(s): 15th century (1482)
Locale(s): England

Summary: In 1482 convent-bred Anne de Syon is summoned by King Edward IV to join his court. She shortly learns the story of her heritage and is immersed in the complicated intrigue that surrounds the king.

Historical Accuracy: The story is imagined but believable in its depiction of the period.

5244 Witness to Treason

Date of Publication: 1977
Subject(s): Middle Ages; Suspense; Royalty—England
Fictional character(s): Katherine de Mer, Amnesiac, Ward
Historical character(s): Edward I, Ruler (King of England); Robert the Bruce, Nobleman (Earl of Carrick)
Time Period(s): 13th century; 14th century
Locale(s): Highlands, Scotland; England

Summary: As a child Katherine de Mer is shipwrecked on the Scottish coast and raised by the mighty Bruce family. When accompanying Robert Bruce to the court of Edward I to secure peace between England and Scotland, Katherine learns that she is a ward of the king and has witnessed the queen's murder. Divided loyalties, court intrigue, and the queen's murderer, who is still at large, create the novel's suspense.

Historical Accuracy: The story is fanciful but does feature a believable look at English-Scottish relations of the period.

JAMES S. RAND
(PSEUD. OF BERNARD ATTENBOROUGH)

English freelance writer Rand attended the University of Birmingham.

5245 The Great Sky and the Silence

Date of Publication: 1979
Subject(s): Frontier—Africa; Tribal Life—African; Afrikaaners
Fictional character(s): Pieter Hayden de Morgan, Landowner; Robert Queen, Hunter, Adventurer; Joachim Van Zyl, Young Man
Time Period(s): 1890s
Locale(s): Africa (southeast)

Summary: Set in southeast Africa in the closing years of the 19th century, the novel tells the story of three men struggling to subdue the African frontier. Pieter Hayden de Morgan is an Afrikaner who rules hundreds of square miles of territory with absolute authority. In search of more land, he mounts a trek into the unknown. Leading the trek is hunter and adventurer Robert Queen, and accompanying him is Joachim Van Zyl, son of a Boer father and Zulu mother. They are tested by challenges from the land, its tribal people, and each other.

Historical Accuracy: The author declares that only the names of the main characters are fictional; the events are firmly based on actuality.

RONA RANDALL (1911-)

Born in Cheshire, England, Randall spent three years in repertory theaters and on the London stage. She began her writing career after her marriage. An author of popular romance novels, Randall received the Romantic Novelists Association Major Award in 1969.

5246 Dragonmede

Date of Publication: 1974
Subject(s): Gothic Romance; Victorian Period
Fictional character(s): Julius Kershaw, Heir; Eustacia Rochdale, Young Woman, Spouse (of Julius)
Time Period(s): 1890s
Locale(s): London, England

Summary: In this suspenseful gothic romance set during the late 19th century, Eustacia Rochdale's scheming mother arranges a marriage for her daughter to Julius Kershaw, heir to Dragonmede. Eustacia arrives at Dragonmede as a new bride and is met with suspicion. Accidents occur, and she begins to wonder if her life is in danger.

Historical Accuracy: The emphasis is on gothic thrills, with the period background secondary and lightly sketched.

5247 The Drayton Legacy

Date of Publication: 1985
Subject(s): Romance; Georgian Period; Canal Building

Fictional character(s): Joseph Drayton, Artisan (potter); Simon Kendall, Worker (coal digger), Engineer; Mark Gibson, Worker
Time Period(s): 1740s; 1750s
Locale(s): Staffordshire, England

Summary: The novel's background is the industrializing of the potteries of Staffordshire, England, in the 18th century. Joseph Drayton is a master potter who runs his family business with narrow-minded efficiency. He is challenged by young Martin Gibson and a young coal digger, Simon Kendall, whose vision and skill as an engineer will transform the pottery trade.

Historical Accuracy: The character of Simon Kendall was inspired by James Brindley.

5248 *The Eagle at the Gate*

Date of Publication: 1978
Subject(s): Edwardian Period; Suspense; Theatrical Life
Fictional character(s): Aphra Coleman, Actress; Charles Coleman, Actor, Manager (theatrical); David Hillyard, Gentleman
Time Period(s): 1900s (1902)
Locale(s): Kent, England

Summary: This suspenseful story set during the Edwardian period concerns the travelling Thespian Players, who are invited to give a performance at a stately home in Kent. Aphra Coleman, daughter of Charles Coleman, the famous actor-manager of the company, is entranced by the surroundings and by David Hillyard. But he and the house are filled with secrets and danger.

Historical Accuracy: The novel captures its era with authenticity.

5249 *The Ladies of Hanover Square*

Date of Publication: 1981
Subject(s): Edwardian Period; World War I; Romance
Fictional character(s): Dulcima Howard, Socialite; Deborah Yorke, Young Woman; Delia Ashleigh, Actress
Time Period(s): 1900s; 1910s
Locale(s): London, England

Summary: Dulcima Howard, the mistress of a nobleman, receives a magnificent house on Hanover Square as a gift from her lover. She turns the house into a fashionable gaming salon and launches her assault on London's high society. Deborah Yorke, a parson's daughter, and Delia Ashleigh oppose Dulcima's ascent, which is halted by the onset of World War I.

Historical Accuracy: The novel offers convincing scenes of the Edwardian period and the Great War.

5250 *The Mating Dance*

Date of Publication: 1979
Subject(s): Victorian Period; Theatrical Life; Romance
Fictional character(s): Lucinda Grainger, Actress, Bastard Daughter; Clementine Boswell, Actress
Time Period(s): 1880s
Locale(s): London, England

Summary: Two aspiring actresses become rivals on the stage and in love. Lucinda Grainger is the daughter of a theatrical dresser, and Clementine Boswell is the self-indulgent daughter of the Boswell Theatre's director-manager. Each woman competes for the prize of the Boswell Theatre itself.

Historical Accuracy: The novel effectively re-creates the world of the Victorian theater.

ROBERT J. RANDISI (1951-)

Born in Brooklyn, New York, Randisi worked as a civilian police administrative aide. He is the founder of Private Eye Writers of America and is a prolific author of mysteries and westerns.

5251 *The Ham Reporter*

Date of Publication: 1986
Subject(s): Crime and Criminals; Sports; Boxing
Historical character(s): William Barclay "Bat" Masterson, Journalist (sports writer), Lawman; Damon Runyon, Journalist, Writer
Time Period(s): 1910s (1911)
Locale(s): New York, New York

Summary: In 1911, after a career as a gunfighter and marshal, "Bat" Masterson heads east to New York City to work as a sportswriter. While covering a heavyweight bout, Masterson discovers that the fight has been fixed, and he soon finds himself investigating the dangerous underworld of racketeers, gamblers, and crooked politicians.

Historical Accuracy: The story is based on Masterson's actual experiences writing for New York's *Morning Telegraph*.

KEVIN D. RANDLE (1949-)

Under the pseudonym Eric Helm, Randle is the author of the bestselling Vietman: Ground Zero series. He lives in Cedar Rapids, Iowa.

5252 *Spanish Gold*

Date of Publication: 1990
Subject(s): Civil War—U.S.; American West; Battle of Gettysburg
Fictional character(s): David Travis, Veteran (Civil War)
Time Period(s): 1860s (1863)
Locale(s): Texas

Summary: This western tale concerns the search for Spanish gold lost in the West Texas hills. David Travis, embittered by his experience at Gettysburg, sets out into the mountains to see if the tale of a lost gold-laden wagon train is true.

Historical Accuracy: The novel features a believable and authentic period and regional background.

CHRISTOPH RANSMAYR (1954-)

Austrian writer Christoph Ransmayr studied philosophy in Vienna and eked out a living driving luxury Mercedes cars from Munich to customers in Damascus, Syria, and Riyadh, Saudi Arabia.

5253 *The Last World: A Novel with an Ovidian Repertory*

Date of Publication: 1990
Subject(s): Roman Empire; Literary Life
Fictional character(s): Maximus Cotta, Gentleman
Time Period(s): 1st century
Locale(s): Tomi, Romania

Summary: Maximus Cotta journeys to the Black Sea town of Tomi to find the Roman poet Ovid, who is banished there. He does not find Ovid but finds a living version of the poet's masterpiece, *Metamorphoses*. The novel concerns the power of literature and its ability to transform reality.

Historical Accuracy: The work is more a fable and a novel of ideas than a fully documented historical novel.

MARK RASCOVICH (1918-1976)

Born in San Francisco and educated in Europe, Rascovich served as a pilot in World War II. He is best known for his Cold War novel *The Bedford Incident*, which was turned into a motion picture.

5254 *Falkenhorst*

Date of Publication: 1974
Subject(s): Franco-Prussian War
Fictional character(s): Tessa von Falkenhorst, Gentlewoman, Spouse; Albrecht von Falkenhorst, Gentleman, Military Personnel (Prussian officer); Gustaf von Falkenhorst, Military Personnel (Prussian officer)
Historical character(s): Otto von Bismarck, Political Figure (German chancellor); Helmuth Johannes Ludwig von Moltke, Military Personnel (German general)
Time Period(s): 1870s (1870-1871)
Locale(s): Germany; France

Summary: Describing the German perspective during the Franco-Prussian War, this panoramic novel centers on Tessa von Falkenhorst, who is torn between her husband, whom she does not love, and his brother, a young Prussian officer. The romantic story is intertwined with the events of the Prussian military's crushing and humiliating victory over the French.

Historical Accuracy: The events of the war and its leading players are authentic.

EVERETT RATTRAY (1932-1980)

Rattray was a 12th generation native of East Hampton, Long Island. After studies at Dartmouth and Columbia and service in the navy, Rattray took over his family's newspaper, *The East Hampton Star*, in 1958 and established its national reputation. He is also the author of *The South Fork: The Land and People of Eastern Long Island*, a winner of the 1985 Editor's Book Award.

5255 *The Adventures of Jeremiah Dimon: The Novel of Old East Hampton*

Date of Publication: 1985
Subject(s): Picaresque Adventure; Sea Story
Fictional character(s): Jeremiah Dimon, Teenager
Time Period(s): 1880s (1887)
Locale(s): East Hampton, New York (Long Island)

Summary: This picaresque coming-of-age story is set on Long Island's South Fork during the 1880s. Jeremiah Dimon is a teenager with a case of wanderlust. His travels and experiences dramatize a time and place on eastern Long Island more than a century ago.

Historical Accuracy: The novel is filled with authentic elements that create a believable period and regional narrative.

JULIAN LEE RAYFORD (1908-)

Born in Mobile, Alabama, Rayford is the author of *Cottonmouth*, *Child of the Snapping Turtle*, and *Mike Fink*.

5256 *Child of the Snapping Turtle, Mike Fink*

Date of Publication: 1951
Subject(s): Biography, Fictionalized; Riverboats
Historical character(s): Mike Fink, Frontiersman
Time Period(s): 18th century; 19th century
Locale(s): Ohio River, United States; Mississippi River

Summary: This novel, based on the life of frontiersman, Indian fighter, keel boatman, and trapper Mike Fink, traces his career in the wilderness of the Ohio Valley. The novel vividly captures life along the rivers between Pittsburgh and New Orleans.

Historical Accuracy: The novel provides an authentic historical background, effectively capturing frontier life and life on the river.

CHET RAYMO

An avid naturalist, Raymo is a professor of physics and astronomy at Stonehill College and a science columnist for the *Boston Globe*. He is the author of several books exploring the relationship of science, nature, and the humanities. His works include *365 Starry Nights*, an introduction to astronomy, and *Written in Stone: A Geological and Natural History of the Northeastern United States*.

5257 *In the Falcon's Claw: A Novel of the Year 1000*

Date of Publication: 1990
Subject(s): Middle Ages; Religious Conflict
Fictional character(s): Ailerman, Religious (abbot); Melisane, Gentlewoman
Historical character(s): Sylvester II, Religious (pope)
Time Period(s): 10th century; 11th century (998-1000)

Locale(s): Ireland; France

Summary: As the millennium approaches in the year 1000, the church seeks to assert its absolute authority. Ailerman, the abbot of a monastery off the coast of Ireland, is charged with heresy by his fellow monk Gerbert, now Pope Sylvester II. Ailerman reviews his past and his troubled relationship with Melisane before standing trial.

Historical Accuracy: The characters are fictional, but the story is based in part on historical events.

ERNEST RAYMOND (1888-1974)

A French novelist, essayist, playwright, and biographer, Raymond was ordained as an Anglican priest but later resigned. Many of his books concern the search for faith and fulfillment. His first and most popular book, *Travel England*, was based on his experiences in school and in World War I. He produced more than 50 books, including a long series of novels called A London Gallery, of which *We the Accused* is considered his finest.

`5258` *A Georgian Love Story*

Date of Publication: 1971
Subject(s): Romance
Fictional character(s): Stewart O'Murray, Young Man; Raney Wayburn, Young Woman
Time Period(s): 1900s
Locale(s): London, England

Summary: The novel is a love story set in London in the years before World War I. Upperclass, respectable Stewart O'Murray falls in love with Raney, an inhabitant of the notorious neighborhood called Hollen Dene. Stewart's stuffy father is ill-prepared for their romance and the clash of classes that it represents.

Historical Accuracy: The story captures the pre-war world with intimacy and authenticity.

CLAIRE RAYNER (1931-)

English writer Rayner was born in London and is a former nurse. She has had her own TV program on consumer affairs and makes weekly appearances on TV's *Good Morning Britain*. In 1988 Rayner was named one of the women "most British women would regard as a role model.".

`5259` *Bedford Row*

Date of Publication: 1977
Subject(s): Crimean War; Medical Profession; Theatrical Life
Fictional character(s): Martha Lackland, Nurse; Alexander Laurence, Doctor; Lydia Mohun, Actress
Historical character(s): Florence Nightingale, Gentlewoman, Nurse
Time Period(s): 1850s
Locale(s): London, England; Scutari, Albania

Summary: In the fifth volume of The Performers series, the backdrop is the Crimean War. Martha Lackland, unfulfilled by working in her father's clinic, travels to the war zone in the Crimea, where she encounters Florence Nightingale. In London, Lydia Mohun continues as an irritant to the family.

Historical Accuracy: The period elements that form the novel's background are authentic and convincing.

`5260` *Charing Cross*

Date of Publication: 1979
Subject(s): Victorian Period; Medical Profession; Theatrical Life
Fictional character(s): Sophie Lackland, Orphan, Doctor (surgeon); Gilbert Stacey, Actor; William Brotherton, Gentleman
Time Period(s): 1870s
Locale(s): London, England

Summary: The seventh installment in The Performers series continues to trace the tangled fortunes of two families, one medical and the other theatrical. In the late 19th century Sophie Lackland stands to inherit a fortune provided she becomes a surgeon and does not give up the Lackland name. She must contend with medical prejudice and her affection for Gilbert Stacey and William Brotherton.

Historical Accuracy: The period background is authentic.

`5261` *Chelsea Reach*

Date of Publication: 1982
Subject(s): Edwardian Period; Theatrical Life; Family Saga
Fictional character(s): Lucas O'Hare, Actor; Lettice Lackland, Young Woman
Time Period(s): 1900s
Locale(s): London, England

Summary: In Book Nine of the Performer series, Letty Lackland, disillusioned with her arduous life, falls under the spell of an aspiring actor, Luke O'Hare, and helps set up the Chelsea Reach theater.

Historical Accuracy: The novel features a convincing period background.

`5262` *Covent Garden*

Date of Publication: 1978
Subject(s): Victorian Period; Medical Profession; Theatrical Life
Fictional character(s): Amy Lucas, Actress; Freddy Caspar, Doctor; Fenton Lucas, Actor
Time Period(s): 1860s
Locale(s): London, England

Summary: This sixth novel in The Performers series continues the intertwined stories of two families and two professions. In the 1860s Amy and Fenton Lucas struggle for success on the stage, while a dispute over an inheritance causes conflict between the Lucas and Lackland families.

Historical Accuracy: The details of both theatrical and medical life of the period are convincing.

`5263` *The Enduring Years*

Date of Publication: 1981
Subject(s): Jews; Family Saga
Fictional character(s): Hannah Lazar, Seamstress

Time Period(s): 19th century; 20th century (1885-1980)
Locale(s): London, England

Summary: The novel captures the Jewish immigrant experience in England over nearly 100 years from 1885 to 1980. It concerns three families, the descendants of two sisters-in-law who exchanged children and separated in the Diaspora many centuries before. The story focuses on the experiences of Hannah Lazar, who rises from the slums of London's East End to become an internationally famous fashion designer.

Historical Accuracy: The novel sets a credible background of period and customs.

5264 *Gower Street*

Date of Publication: 1973
Subject(s): Family Saga; Theatrical Life; Medical Profession
Fictional character(s): Abel Lackland, Doctor; Lilith Lucas, Actress
Time Period(s): 1830s
Locale(s): London, England

Summary: This is the first novel in The Performers series, which traces the history of two family dynasties. It begins with the careers of Abel Lackland and Lilith Lucas, who come out of London's notorious Seven Dials. Abel's experiences as a body-snatcher lead him to a career in the new art of surgery while Lilith becomes an actress.

Historical Accuracy: The period elements are captured with authority and conviction.

5265 *The Haymarket*

Date of Publication: 1974
Subject(s): Family Saga; Medical Profession; Theatrical Life
Fictional character(s): Abel Lackland, Doctor; Lilith Lucas, Actress; Jonah Lackland, Young Man; Celia Lucas, Young Woman
Time Period(s): 1830s
Locale(s): London, England

Summary: In the second volume of The Performers series, the story of Abel Lackland and Lilith Lucas and their medical and theatrical careers continues. Abel's son Jonah falls under the spell of the theater and of Lilith and her daughter Celia. Abel continues to expand the frontiers of medical knowledge.

Historical Accuracy: The period background is convincingly drawn.

5266 *Paddington Green*

Date of Publication: 1975
Subject(s): Victorian Period; Family Saga; Medical Profession
Fictional character(s): Abel Lackland, Doctor; Lilith Lucas, Actress
Time Period(s): 1840s
Locale(s): London, England

Summary: In the third novel of The Performers series, the saga of the Lucas and Lackland families continues. The medical and theatrical worlds of Abel Lackland and Lilith Lucas form the backdrop to this family saga.

Historical Accuracy: The period elements of domestic Victorian life are convincing and authentic.

5267 *Piccadilly*

Date of Publication: 1984
Subject(s): Family Saga; Theatrical Life; Nazis
Fictional character(s): Leah Landis, Spouse (of Harry); Harry Lackland, Gentleman; Peter Lackland, Gentleman
Time Period(s): 1930s
Locale(s): England; Germany

Summary: The 11th book of The Performers series centers around a theatrical tour of Nazi Germany in 1938. Peter Lackland takes more than a familial interest in Leah Landis and the Landis family worries about the fate of their cousins in Hitler's Germany.

Historical Accuracy: The novel provides a convincing period background of the attitudes and events leading up to the outbreak of World War II.

5268 *Soho Square*

Date of Publication: 1976
Subject(s): Victorian Period; Medical Profession; Theatrical Life
Fictional character(s): Lydia Mohun, Actress; Jonah Lackland, Gentleman; Phoebe Lackland, Young Woman
Time Period(s): 1850s (1851)
Locale(s): London, England

Summary: The fourth volume of The Performers series, occurs on the eve of the Great Exhibition in 1851. Jonah Lackland is concerned about the arrival of his sister-in-law Lydia Mohun, an actress on the rise and the daughter of Lilith Lucas. Jonah's own daughter, Phoebe, comes under the influence of her Aunt Lydia's theatrical salon, setting in motion a series of complications.

Historical Accuracy: The period elements are authentic and convincing.

5269 *The Strand*

Date of Publication: 1981
Subject(s): Victorian Period; Medical Profession; Family Saga
Fictional character(s): Lewis Lackland, Doctor; Claudette Lucas, Actress; Miriam da Silva, Heiress
Time Period(s): 1890s (1892)
Locale(s): London, England

Summary: The eighth book in The Performers series, continues the story of the Lackland and Lucas families. It focuses on relationships between young Australian doctor Lewis Lackland, actress and ''Gaiety Girl'' Catherine Lucas, and young heiress Miriam da Silva.

Historical Accuracy: The novel offers a convincing look at both high society and London street life.

D.A. RAYNER (1908-)

Rayner's books include *The Long Haul*, and the novel *The Enemy Below*, which was made into a 1957 movie starring Robert Mitchum.

5270 *The Long Fight*

Date of Publication: 1958
Subject(s): Sea Story; Napoleonic Wars; Military Life—British Navy
Fictional character(s): George Nicholas Hardinge, Military Personnel (naval captain); William Dawson, Military Personnel (naval officer); Captain Epron, Military Personnel (French captain)
Time Period(s): 1800s (1808)
Locale(s): At Sea (Indian Ocean)

Summary: The epic 1808 battle in the Indian Ocean between the British *San Fiorenzo* and the French *Piemontaise* is described by this novel. The *Piemontaise* threatens merchant shipping in British India, and the *San Fiorenzo* battles her for three gripping days that are described in minute detail.

Historical Accuracy: The novel is a fictional story but is based on records of the period and on similar naval engagements.

WILLIAM RAYNER (1929-)

English teacher and author Rayner was born in Yorkshire and educated at Oxford. His novels include *The Reaper*, *The Barebones*, and *The Last Days*. He is also the author of a distinguished history of South Central Africa, *The Tribe and Its Successors*. He has worked as an English teacher in England and Africa.

5271 *The Knifeman: A Novel of Judas Iscariot*

Date of Publication: 1969
Subject(s): Biblical Story
Historical character(s): Judas Iscariot, Biblical Figure; Peter, Biblical Figure
Time Period(s): 1st century
Locale(s): Israel

Summary: The novel tells the story of Judas Iscariot after he betrays Jesus. Judas relates his experiences while in hiding during the final days leading up to his death. The novel attempts to create a believable psychological portrait of Judas beyond his symbolic role as the ultimate betrayer.

Historical Accuracy: The period elements here are strong and credible.

5272 *The Last Days*

Date of Publication: 1969
Subject(s): Jewish Revolt; Roman Empire; Siege of Masada
Fictional character(s): Gorion, Young Man; Joshua, Religious
Historical character(s): Jesus Christ, Biblical Figure; Peter, Biblical Figure
Time Period(s): 1st century
Locale(s): Jerusalem, Israel

Summary: This imaginative novel recounts the fall of Jerusalem and Masada to the Romans during the Jewish Revolt of 66-73 AD. It places the story of Jesus in the context of Jewish Zealot conflict. The events leading up to the apocalyptic defeat at Masada are related by Joshua, a holy man, and Gorion, a young man from a rich Alexandrian merchant family.

Historical Accuracy: The main events of the story are historically accurate.

5273 *The World Turned Upside Down*

Date of Publication: 1970
Subject(s): American Revolution; Slavery
Fictional character(s): James Blackford, Military Personnel (British major)
Time Period(s): 1780s (1781)
Locale(s): Prince Edward County, Virginia

Summary: In 1781 during the American Revolution, British Major James Blackford's company is ambushed and massacred by the rebels. He is the lone survivor. To escape through the American wilderness and reach the British lines, he stains his skin to pass as a slave. The novel describes his journey, in which he is captured by British deserters, physically abused, and unjustly accused of rape and murder.

Historical Accuracy: The period is described with authenticity, though the story is fictional.

JEAN RAYNES

5274 *Legacy of the Wolf*

Date of Publication: 1977
Subject(s): Victorian Period; Suspense
Fictional character(s): Olivia Selkirk, Accountant (bookkeeper), Teacher; Francis Sinclair, Nobleman
Time Period(s): 19th century
Locale(s): Scotland

Summary: Olivia Selkirk leaves her position as a teacher in a convent school to assume a post as bookkeeper for the Countess of Dunkeith. She finds herself caught up in the mystery surrounding Duncragie Castle and its sinister Wolf Tower. Her sudden marriage to nobleman Francis Sinclair does not allay her suspicions about her husband's sincerity, and her discoveries prove potentially deadly.

Historical Accuracy: The gothic elements predominate here, though some of the period background is credible.

ROBERT RAYNOLDS (1902-1964)

Born in New Mexico, Raynolds was a novelist, poet, and essayist. *Brothers in the West* was a Harper Prize novel.

5275 *The Sinner of Saint Ambrose*

Date of Publication: 1952
Subject(s): Roman Empire; Christianity; Barbarians
Fictional character(s): Gregory Julian, Nobleman
Historical character(s): Alaric I, Warrior (Goth); Ambrose, Religious (Bishop of Milan)
Time Period(s): 5th century
Locale(s): Rome, Roman Empire; England

Summary: Roman aristocrat Gregory Julian, in a variety of guises—politician, soldier, priest and bishop—is on hand for the decisive events in the collapse of the Empire.

Historical Accuracy: The novel convinces in its portrait of the political, social, and domestic details of the period.

STEVEN RAYSON (1932-)

Born in Somerset, England, Rayson attended Cambridge and Bristol universities. He practices medicine in Cornwall. While at school, Rayson developed an interest in the prehistory of Great Britain.

5276   *The Crows of War*

Date of Publication: 1974
Subject(s): Roman Empire; Celtic Britain
Fictional character(s): Airmid, Young Woman; Beothainn, Chieftain (Celtic)
Historical character(s): Vespasian, Military Personnel (commander of Roman Legion)
Time Period(s): 1st century (43)
Locale(s): England

Summary: The clash of cultures between Celtic Britain and its Roman invaders in 43 A.D. forms the background of this story. The Roman legion under the command of future emperor Vespasian struggles to capture a fortified hill town. Airmid, the daughter of a Celtic chieftain, faces the invasion fortified by a strange power that she does not fully understand.

Historical Accuracy: As the author's notes make clear, the novel is supported by thorough research into the period and its customs.

PIERS PAUL READ (1941-)

English writer Read was brought up in Yorkshire and educated at Ampleforth College, a Catholic school run by Benedictine monks, and Cambridge. Best known for his nonfiction bestseller, *Alive: The Story of the Andes Survivors*, Read has spent the majority of his career writing fiction. He won the Geoffrey Faber Memorial Prize for *Junkers* and the Hawthornden Prize for *Monk Dawson*. His first novel, *Game in Heaven with Tussy Marx*, was published in 1966.

5277   *The Free Frenchman*

Date of Publication: 1986
Subject(s): World War II
Fictional character(s): Bertrand de Roujay, Nobleman, Military Personnel (free French soldier)
Historical character(s): Charles de Gaulle, Military Personnel (general), Political Figure
Time Period(s): 19th century; 20th century (1890-1949)
Locale(s): France; London, England; Algiers, Algeria

Summary: French history from the end of the 19th century to 1950 is captured through the experiences of French aristocrat and civil servant Bertrand de Roujay. Roujay joins de Gaulle when France falls, and his experiences in London and Algiers

are contrasted with those of his family and friends who remain in France.

Historical Accuracy: The novel weaves a fictional story around actual events and personalities into a convincing portrait of the era.

5278   *Polonaise*

Date of Publication: 1976
Subject(s): Family Saga; World War II
Fictional character(s): Stefan Kornowski, Young Man; Krystyna Kornowski, Young Woman
Time Period(s): 20th century (1914-1958)
Locale(s): Poland; Paris, France; Cornwall, England

Summary: This family drama follows the lives of Polish brother and sister Stefan and Krystyna Kornowski, who must make their own way when their aristocratic father becomes bankrupt. World War II separates the siblings until they are brought together in the 1950s on a significant occasion.

Historical Accuracy: The novel interweaves a fictional family story with accurate glimpses of various eras and events.

CHARLES READE (1814-1884)

Reade was an English novelist who was an ardent social reformer. His works such as *It Is Never Too Late to Mend* and *Hard Cash* reflect his social concerns. All his novels are marked by scrupulous documentation.

5279   *The Cloister and the Hearth*

Date of Publication: 1861
Subject(s): Middle Ages
Fictional character(s): Denys, Knight; Gerard Eliason, Artist; Margaret Brandt, Young Woman
Historical character(s): Desiderius Erasmus, Scholar
Time Period(s): 15th century
Locale(s): Rotterdam, Netherlands; Europe (Germany, Italy, France)

Summary: The careers of a young Dutch artist and his beloved are depicted in scenes that take the characters throughout Europe. Denys is one of the most entertaining characters in English literature. The novel is a compendium of medieval literary forms and offers a close and interesting portrait of the medieval church.

Historical Accuracy: Reade provides near photographic detail of 15th-century European life.

5280   *Griffith Gaunt*

Date of Publication: 1866
Subject(s): Crime and Criminals
Fictional character(s): Griffith Gaunt, Gentleman; Kate Peyton, Gentlewoman; Mercy Vint, Maiden (innkeeper's daughter)
Time Period(s): 18th century
Locale(s): Cumberland, England

Summary: Griffith Gaunt marries Kate Peyton, a Roman Catholic, whom he suspects is having an affair with her priest. He leaves home and bigamously marries an innkeeper's daughter. When a disfigured body is discovered, Kate is tried for the murder of her husband.

Historical Accuracy: When the novel first appeared it was soundly criticized as immoral. Today it only appears sensational.

5281 *Peg Woffington*

Date of Publication: 1853
Subject(s): Theatrical Life; Georgian Period
Fictional character(s): Harry Vane, Businessman; Charles Pomander, Nobleman
Historical character(s): Peg Woffington, Actress; Colley Cibber, Actor, Writer (critic)
Time Period(s): 18th century
Locale(s): London, England

Summary: Backstage life in the English theater of the 18th century is the subject of this novel in which the famous actress Peg Woffington is loved by both a businessman and a nobleman. Their rivalry and Peg's hesitant affection form the novel's drama.

Historical Accuracy: The behind the scenes glimpses of theatrical life are realistic and witty.

FRANCISCO REBOLLEDO (1950-)

Born in Mexico City, Rebolledo taught chemistry until age 38 when he became a full-time writer. He serves as the literary editor for the VID Editorial Group of magazines. *Rasero* is his first novel and won the 1994 Pegasus Prize for Literature.

5282 *Rasero*

Date of Publication: 1996
Subject(s): French Revolution; Napoleonic Era; Enlightenment Period
Fictional character(s): Fausto Rasero, Nobleman
Historical character(s): Denis Diderot, Writer, Philosopher; Francois Marie Arouet, Philosopher, Writer (aka Voltaire); Jeanne Antoinette Poisson, Noblewoman (Madame de Pompadour); Francois Boucher, Artist (painter); Antoine Laurent Lavoisier, Scientist (chemist and physicist); Wolfgang Amadeus Mozart, Composer; Jean Jacques Rousseau, Philosopher, Writer; Maximilien Francois de Robespierre, Revolutionary; Francisco Jose de Goya y Lucientes, Artist (painter)
Time Period(s): 18th century; 19th century (1749-1812)
Locale(s): Paris, France

Summary: A young Spanish nobleman, Fausto Rasero, comes to Paris during the intellectual ferment of the Enlightenment. Given to apocalyptic visions, Rasero attempts to reconcile his visions with the promises of the rational Enlightenment. He meets many important figures of the period on his journey toward wisdom.

Historical Accuracy: The novel captures the era with skill.

BETTY LAYMAN RECEVEUR (1930-)

An American writer born in Kentucky, Receveur has worked as an antiques dealer. She has a fascination with the past, which has drawn her to writing historical novels and romances.

5283 *Kentucky Home*

Date of Publication: 1995
Subject(s): Politics; War of 1812
Fictional character(s): Roman Gentry, Political Figure (senator); Kitty Gentry, Spouse
Historical character(s): Aaron Burr, Political Figure; Alexander Hamilton, Political Figure; Thomas Jefferson, Political Figure
Time Period(s): 18th century; 19th century (1792-1825)
Locale(s): Philadelphia, Pennsylvania; Kentucky

Summary: The novel continues the story of Kitty and Roman Gentry begun in *Oh, Kentucky!* Roman is now a U.S. senator, and the Gentrys inhabit the political world of Philadelphia until renewed hostility with the British and their Indian allies calls them back to Kentucky.

Historical Accuracy: The novel captures the flavor and atmosphere of the early years of the American republic and the outbreak of hostilities during the War of 1812.

5284 *Oh, Kentucky!*

Date of Publication: 1990
Subject(s): American Colonies; Settlement of the American Frontier; Indians
Fictional character(s): Kitty Gentry, Settler; Roman Gentry, Settler
Historical character(s): Daniel Boone, Frontiersman; George Rogers Clark, Military Personnel (officer)
Time Period(s): 1770s; 1780s (1775-1785)
Locale(s): Boonesborough, Kentucky

Summary: The story of the frontier settlement of Boonesborough is depicted through the experiences of Kitty Gentry. Her family journeys through the Cumberland Gap to settle in the wilderness that is the sacred hunting ground of the fierce Shawnee.

Historical Accuracy: The period details of a Kentucky frontier settlement's struggle for survival are authentically depicted.

ISHMAEL REED (1938-)

An American teacher, poet, and novelist born in Tennessee, Reed attended the State University of New York at Buffalo. He was nominated for a Pulitzer Prize in 1973 for his novel *Mumbo Jumbo.* His fiction is marked by folk traditions put to the service of provocative subjects.

5285 *Flight to Canada*

Date of Publication: 1976
Subject(s): Civil War—U.S.; Slavery
Fictional character(s): Raven Quickskill, Slave, Fugitive; Arthur Swille, Plantation Owner
Historical character(s): Abraham Lincoln, Political Figure
Time Period(s): 1860s
Locale(s): Virginia

Summary: This comic novel tells the story of fugitive slave Raven Quickskill, who during the Civil War escapes from his master, Arthur Swille, determined to reach Canada and safety. Swille pursues Quickskill, enlisting Abraham Lincoln's assistance.

Historical Accuracy: The emphasis is on farce and dark comedy over historical documentation. However, the novel does employ convincing period elements.

WALTER REED

5286   *She Rode a Yellow Stallion*

Date of Publication: 1950
Subject(s): Settlement of the American Frontier; Farming
Fictional character(s): Jerry Bent, Rancher (horsebreeder); Margot McCann, Young Woman
Time Period(s): 19th century (1840s-1890s)
Locale(s): Sheboygan, Wisconsin

Summary: The novel describes life in southeastern Wisconsin in the 19th century. Centering on horsebreeder Jerry Bent and Margot McCann, the story depicts rural life among the immigrant settlers and the development of the cheese industry.

Historical Accuracy: The novel provides a believable portrait of the period and the region.

DOUGLAS E. REEMAN (1924-)

Born in Surrey, England, Reeman left school at 16 to join the Royal Navy, serving on destroyers and small craft in World War II from 1940 to 1946. He began writing while serving in the London Metropolitan Police Department, first as a patrolman and later as a detective. As Alexander Kent, Reeman is the author of the popular Richard Bolitho series of naval adventures. His books have been translated into 22 languages and have sold over 12 million copies.

5287   *Badge of Glory*

Date of Publication: 1982
Subject(s): Victorian Period; Military Life—British Army; Crimean War
Fictional character(s): Philip Blackwood, Military Personnel (Marine captain)
Time Period(s): 1850s
Locale(s): Africa (western); Crimea, Russia

Summary: Set during the 1850s, the novel depicts Captain Philip Blackwood's command of a company of Royal Marines ordered to West Africa to put down the slave trade. He deals with the challenge of leadership and a military tradition under pressure from the new Steam Age.

Historical Accuracy: The Crimean war scenes are believable and convincingly described.

5288   *The First to Land*

Date of Publication: 1984
Subject(s): Military Life—British Army; Victorian Period; Boxer Rebellion

Fictional character(s): David Blackwood, Military Personnel (captain)
Time Period(s): 1890s; 1900s (1899-1901)
Locale(s): China

Summary: Set during the explosive Boxer Rebellion in China, the novel describes the exploits of Captain David Blackwood. He commands the Royal Marines, one of the first units to meet a fanatical Chinese army determined to rid China of "foreign devils." Blackwood is ordered to escort a German countess to safety and then must face wave after wave of suicidal Chinese attacks.

Historical Accuracy: The story is fictional, but the period background is believably established.

GILBERT REES

5289   *I Seek a City*

Date of Publication: 1950
Subject(s): American Colonies; Biography, Fictionalized; Puritans
Historical character(s): Roger Williams, Religious (clergyman)
Time Period(s): 17th century (1603-1683)
Locale(s): England; Rhode Island, American Colonies; Salem, Massachusetts, American Colonies

Summary: This fictional autobiography records the career of Roger Williams: his childhood in London, his years as a minister in Salem, Massachusetts, and his founding of Providence, Rhode Island. The novel offers a vivid portrait not only of colonial life but of the spirituality and motivation of Williams.

Historical Accuracy: The author bases most of the events portrayed on Williams' own journals.

JOAN REES (1927-)

Born in London, Joan Rees attended the University of London. Her books include *Jane Austen: Woman and Writer*, *Shelley's Jane Williams*, and *Profligate Son: Branwell Bronte and His Sisters*. She has also written novels under her own name and under the pseudonyms June Avery, Ann Bedford, and Susan Strong.

5290   *The Queen of Hearts*

Date of Publication: 1974
Subject(s): Biography, Fictionalized
Historical character(s): Louise de Stolberg-Gedern, Royalty (princess); Charles Edward Stuart, Royalty (prince); Vittorio Alfieri, Writer (poet and dramatist)
Time Period(s): 18th century; 19th century
Locale(s): Brussels, Belgium; Florence, Italy

Summary: This biographical novel chronicles the career of Princess Louise of Stolberg-Gedern who marries Charles Edward Stuart and falls in love with Italian poet Vittorio Alfieri. The novel records her disappointing marriage to Bonnie Prince Charlie, who is more than 30 years her senior and obsessed by his failed attempt to regain the English throne in

1745, and her final happy relationship with one of Italy's greatest poets.

Historical Accuracy: The novel is faithful to the biographical facts.

VICTOR STAFFORD REID (1913-)

Born in Kingston, Jamaica, Reid has worked as a reporter, editor, and foreign correspondent, as well as in advertising and in printing. He is the author of several novels, including *New Day*, *The Leopard*, and *The Jamaicans*.

5291 *New Day*

Date of Publication: 1949
Subject(s): English Colonies
Fictional character(s): John Campbell, Landowner
Time Period(s): 19th century; 20th century (1865-1944)
Locale(s): Jamaica

Summary: The history of Jamaica from the rebellion of 1865 to the winning of self-government in 1944 is portrayed from the perspective of John Campbell, who recalls the events of his long life.

Historical Accuracy: The novel is true to historical fact in its panoramic story.

A.R. REIFE

5292 *Salt Lake City*

Date of Publication: 1989
Subject(s): American West; Religious Conflict; Mormons
Fictional character(s): Gideon Catton, Farmer, Settler
Historical character(s): Brigham Young, Religious (Mormon leader), Political Figure
Time Period(s): 1840s (1847)
Locale(s): Nauvoo, Illinois; Salt Lake City, Utah

Summary: Gideon Catton is a follower of Brigham Young and makes the trek westward out of Illinois into the Utah Territory. He faces Indians, deserts, and the hostility of settlers along the way. In Utah, Gideon must defend his home and family from the U.S. Army's determination to suppress the Mormons.

Historical Accuracy: This depiction offers a heroic portrait of Mormon struggles. Most of the story is backed by historical evidence.

ROBERT REILLY (1922-)

Born in Lowell, Massachusetts, Reilly received an A.B. from Suffolk University in 1947. He served in the U.S. Army and then did graduate work at Boston University, receiving an M.A. in 1948. He has worked in advertising and has taught courses in Irish and Russian literature. His books include *Red Hugh, Prince of Donegal*, *Massacre at Ash Hollow*, and *Rebels in the Shadows*.

5293 *The God of Mirrors*

Date of Publication: 1986
Subject(s): Literary Life; Victorian Period; Homosexuality
Historical character(s): Oscar Wilde, Writer; Lord Alfred Bruce Douglas, Nobleman, Writer (poet); George Bernard Shaw, Writer; Walter Pater, Writer, Scholar; Sarah Bernhardt, Actress; Frank Harris, Writer; Robert Ross, Gentleman; John Sholto Douglas, Nobleman (Marquis of Queensberry)
Time Period(s): 1890s
Locale(s): London, England; Paris, France

Summary: The novel details the sensational career of Oscar Wilde. It focuses on his relationship with Lord Alfred Douglas, which explodes in a lurid court trial that sends Wilde to prison and destroys his career.

Historical Accuracy: The author declares that many Wilde biographers have provided the facts but not the emotions. This novel, combining the factual with the imagined, attempts to redress the balance.

RICHARD REINHARDT (1927-)

Born in California, Reinhardt graduated from Stanford and Columbia universities. He has worked as a reporter, in public relations, and as a lecturer. Reinhardt lived for over 18 months in Greece and Turkey doing historical research for *The Ashes of Smyrna*.

5294 *The Ashes of Smyrna*

Date of Publication: 1970
Subject(s): Greco-Turkish War
Fictional character(s): Christos Trigonis, Businessman; Eleni Trigonis, Young Woman; Abdullah Pasha, Young Man
Historical character(s): Mustafa Kemal, Military Personnel (Turkish general); Eleutherios Venizelos, Political Figure (Greek premier)
Time Period(s): 1910s; 1920s (1919-1922)
Locale(s): Smyrna, Turkey; Athens, Greece; Ankara, Turkey

Summary: The historical framework for the novel is the Greco-Turkish War of 1919-1922 and the battle for the Turkish town of Smyrna. The story focuses on the Greek Trigonis family and the Turkish sons of Hilmi Pasha.

Historical Accuracy: This solidly researched novel captures with authority the major battles and political intrigues of the war, culminating in the Turkish recapture of Smyrna and the fire which destroys three-fifths of the town.

MARY RENAULT
(PSEUD. OF MARY CHALLANS, 1905-1983)

Born in London, Renault was educated at St. Hugh's College, Oxford. She decided at an early age to become a writer but to gain experience for her work enrolled in nursing school. Her experience provided material for her first novel, *Promise of Love*. During World War II, Renault continued her nursing while writing in her spare time. She is best known for her historical novels set in the ancient world, which are widely praised for their erudition and illumination of the formative stages of our civilization.

5295 *The Bull From the Sea*

Date of Publication: 1962
Subject(s): Myths and Legends; Ancient Greece
Fictional character(s): Theseus, Ruler (King of Athens); Hippolita, Ruler (Queen of the Amazons); Phaedra, Royalty (daughter of Minos of Crete), Spouse (of Theseus); Hippolytos, Bastard Son
Time Period(s): 20th century B.C.
Locale(s): Greece

Summary: In this sequel to *The King Must Die*, the author continues her examination of the dawn of Hellenic civilization. It is the story of the manhood and old age of Theseus, King of Athens, and of the incestuous love of Phaedra for Hippolytos. The mythic material is deepened in Renault's treatment to encompass an entire age of believable personalities.

Historical Accuracy: Renault's sources are mythical rather than historical, but within these constraints she offers convincing realistic details.

5296 *Fire From Heaven*

Date of Publication: 1969
Subject(s): Macedonian Empire
Historical character(s): Alexander the Great, Ruler (King of Macedonia); Philip II, Ruler (King of Macedonia); Olympias, Royalty (queen consort of Philip II); Aristotle, Philosopher, Teacher; Hephaestion, Companion (of Alexander); Demosthenes, Political Figure (orator)
Time Period(s): 4th century B.C.
Locale(s): Macedonia

Summary: The novel tells the life story of Alexander the Great from childhood to the age of 20, when he succeeds his murdered father, Philip II of Macedon. Covering nearly two-thirds of Alexander's brief life, the novel traces his development, his conflicting feelings towards his father, his early Spartan training, his schooling under Aristotle, and his first experiences of war and leadership.

Historical Accuracy: The novel blends the known with the imagined and the invented, though there are few historical novelists better at creating a believable period background.

5297 *Funeral Games*

Date of Publication: 1981
Subject(s): Macedonian Empire
Historical character(s): Alexander the Great, Ruler (King of Macedonia); Perdikkas, Military Personnel (general); Antipatros, Government Official (regent of Macedon); Kassandros, Nobleman; Ptolemy, Military Personnel (staff officer); Antigonus I, Military Personnel (general); Olympias, Royalty (queen consort of Philip II)
Time Period(s): 4th century B.C.; 3rd century B.C. (323-286 B.C.)
Locale(s): Macedonia; Babylon

Summary: As Alexander lies dying, his only heir is his unborn child. He sinks into a coma and dies without naming a successor to the kingdom he has created that stretches over half of the known world. The novel depicts the scramble for power that follows Alexander's death, as his generals and former loyal vassals compete for a share of the spoils of Alexander's conquests.

Historical Accuracy: The novel's background is reliably drawn from the known sources.

5298 *The King Must Die*

Date of Publication: 1958
Subject(s): Myths and Legends; Ancient Greece
Fictional character(s): Theseus, Royalty (Prince of Troizen); Medea, Sorceress; Minos, Ruler (King of Crete); Ariadne, Royalty (daughter of Minos)
Time Period(s): 20th century B.C.
Locale(s): Athens, Greece

Summary: The novel details the legendary story of Theseus: his encounter with Medea; his love for Ariadne, who helps him defeat the Minotaur on Crete; and his return trip to Athens, where forgetting to hoist the white sail of a safe return causes his mother to kill herself, convinced that he has perished. Renault treats this legendary material as historical fact and turns Theseus into a convincing historical personality.

Historical Accuracy: With inventiveness and authenticity, the author converts fragments of archaeological details and fashions a realistic panorama of the past.

5299 *The Last of the Wine*

Date of Publication: 1956
Subject(s): Ancient Greece
Fictional character(s): Alexias, Young Man; Lysis, Young Man
Historical character(s): Socrates, Philosopher; Plato, Philosopher; Kritias, Political Figure; Alcibiades, Military Personnel (general); Phaedo, Philosopher
Time Period(s): 5th century (430-402 B.C.)
Locale(s): Athens, Greece

Summary: Athens in the declining years of the Periclean Age is depicted as it battles with Sparta for the control of Greece. The story is told by Alexias, a young Athenian of a good family. A pupil under Socrates, he mingles with the group that surrounds the great philosophers—Plato, Phaedo, and Kritias. As a soldier he fights against Sparta and endures the horrors of the Spartan siege.

Historical Accuracy: The book is clearly the result of sound scholarship and a creative imagination that help revive a past age and convert historical fiction into a vehicle for both art and truth.

5300 *The Mask of Apollo*

Date of Publication: 1966
Subject(s): Ancient Greece; Theatrical Life
Fictional character(s): Nikeratos, Actor
Historical character(s): Plato, Philosopher; Dion, Philosopher, Military Personnel; Dionysios the Younger, Political Figure

Time Period(s): 4th century B.C.
Locale(s): Athens, Greece; Syracuse, Ancient Civilization

Summary: Life in Greece in the fourth century B.C. is described through the experiences of actor Nikeratos, whose devotion to his art is challenged by his involvement in the intrigues of despotic Syracuse. Dion, with the help of his friend Plato, tries to persuade the dictator Dionysios the Younger to moderate his policies. The clash between Dion and Dionysios explodes into violence that culminates in the burning and sacking of the city.

Historical Accuracy: The period elements are authentically drawn and are based on actual events.

`5301` *The Persian Boy*

Date of Publication: 1972
Subject(s): Macedonian Empire; Homosexuality
Historical character(s): Alexander the Great, Ruler (King of Macedonia); Bagoas, Slave, Companion (of Alexander); Darius, Ruler (King of Persia); Hephaestion, Companion (of Alexander)
Time Period(s): 4th century B.C.
Locale(s): Persia

Summary: The novel takes up the life and times of Alexander the Great six years after the conclusion of *Fire From Heaven*. Alexander is now 26, and the story of the rest of his life is narrated by his young lover, Bagoas. Alexander has conquered Persia, and his last seven years are described showing his humanity in his deep affection for Bagoas.

Historical Accuracy: All public acts of Alexander here recounted are based upon historical sources, the most dramatic being the most authentic.

`5302` *The Praise Singer*

Date of Publication: 1978
Subject(s): Ancient Greece; Literary Life
Historical character(s): Simonides, Writer (poet); Hipparchos, Political Figure
Time Period(s): 6th century B.C.; 5th century B.C.
Locale(s): Athens, Greece; Samos, Greece; Sicily, Italy

Summary: At the end of his life the Greek poet Simonides reflects on his career from his apprenticeship to his success in Athens at the court of Pisistratus, under the patronage of Hipparchos. Murder and betrayal sweep Simonides up in the turmoil of the era until his retirement in Sicily. His experiences reflect the inextricable connection between politics and poetry.

Historical Accuracy: The novel's historical background is reliable and authentically drawn.

MORRIS RENEK

`5303` *Bread and Circus*

Date of Publication: 1987
Subject(s): Politics; Draft Riots; Reconstruction Period
Historical character(s): William Marcy Tweed, Political Figure (Tammany Hall boss); Augusta Cordell, Gentlewoman; Jay Gould, Financier; Cornelius Vanderbilt, Financier; John Morrissey, Sports Figure (boxer); John Carmel Heenan, Sports Figure (boxer); Thomas Nast, Artist (political cartoonist)
Time Period(s): 1860s; 1870s (1863-1878)
Locale(s): New York, New York

Summary: The novel traces the rise and fall of "Boss" William Tweed, who runs New York during the period following the Civil War with his powerful Tammany Hall political machine. The novel depicts events in New York's history, including the Draft Riots of 1863, the financial war between Jay Gould and Cornelius Vanderbilt, and the bare-knuckle championship boxing match between Morrissey and Heenan.

Historical Accuracy: The novel is an ingenious blend of fact and fiction, capturing authentic details of New York City in the 1860s and 1870s.

PERCEVAL RENIERS

`5304` *Roses From the South*

Date of Publication: 1959
Subject(s): Social Chronicle
Fictional character(s): Lelia Barringer, Southern Belle
Time Period(s): 1880s
Locale(s): White Sulphur Springs, West Virginia; Saratoga, New York; New York, New York

Summary: Social life in the 1880s around America's famous resort spas is dramatized in the husband-hunting adventures of Lelia Barringer. Her assault on society takes her from West Virginia's White Sulfur Springs to New York City and Saratoga.

Historical Accuracy: The novel's period background is authentic and believable.

MARIE R. RENO

Born in Pennsylvania, Reno graduated from the University of Illinois and has been a magazine, book-club, and paperback editor. She was the editor-in-chief of Pyramid Books. Her first novel, *The Final Proof*, was nominated for an Edgar award in 1976.

`5305` *When the Music Changed*

Date of Publication: 1980
Subject(s): Civil War—U.S.
Fictional character(s): Miranda Chase, Young Woman; Damon McMaster, Military Personnel (Union soldier); Cort Adams, Journalist; Richard Schuyler, Gentleman
Time Period(s): 1860s (1860-1865)
Locale(s): New York, New York

Summary: Miranda Chase is transformed by the Civil War from an immature and reckless girl to a determined woman devoted to the Northern cause. She experiences conflict over the affections of three different men in her life.

Historical Accuracy: Reno captures the Civil War's homefront with skill and believability.

EVAN H. RHODES (1929-)

Born in New York City, Rhodes graduated from Brooklyn College and NYU and has worked as an editor, script reader, and advertising copywriter. His research for *An Army of Children* involved retracing 25,000 miles of the Crusaders' route from Germany to Jerusalem. It took him eight weeks, travelling mainly by car, but walking over 500 miles of the route.

5306 *An Army of Children*

Date of Publication: 1978
Subject(s): Middle Ages; Crusades; Children's Crusade
Fictional character(s): Roger, Teenager; Jonathan, Teenager; Laurelle, Teenager
Historical character(s): Nicholas, Leader (of the Children's Crusade)
Time Period(s): 13th century (1212)
Locale(s): Europe; Middle East

Summary: The novel recounts the story of the 13th-century Children's Crusade, in which an army of over 20,000 children from Germany and France marched across Europe to the Holy Land. The story focuses on two teenage boys, Roger and Jonathan, one Christian and the other Jewish, as they participate in one of the most extraordinary mass youth movements in world history.

Historical Accuracy: The author's description of events is based on primary sources and bolstered by his retracing of the route taken.

JAMES A. RHODES (1909-)

DEAN JAUCHIUS

Born in Coalton, Ohio, Rhodes was governor of the state in the 1960s and 1970s. He is the author of books on education and society, and of two novels, *The Court-Martial of Commodore Perry* and *The Trial of Mary Todd Lincoln*.

5307 *The Court Martial of Commodore Perry*

Date of Publication: 1961
Subject(s): War of 1812; Biography, Fictionalized; Battle of Lake Erie
Historical character(s): Oliver Hazard Perry, Military Personnel (admiral)
Time Period(s): 1810s (1813-1817)
Locale(s): Lake Erie, Great Lakes

Summary: The novel begins with a description of Oliver Hazard Perry's great naval victory in the War of 1812 at the Battle of Lake Erie. The plot reconstructs the conspiracy against him that resulted in a trial and a duel.

Historical Accuracy: The novel mixes the fanciful and the factual and cannot be read as a reliable reconstruction.

5308 *Johnny Shiloh*

Date of Publication: 1959
Subject(s): Civil War—U.S.; Battle of Shiloh
Historical character(s): John Lincoln Clem, Military Personnel (Union soldier); Ulysses S. Grant, Military Personnel (Union general)
Time Period(s): 1860s
Locale(s): Ohio; Tennessee

Summary: The novel recounts the Civil War career of nine-year-old John Clem, the youngest soldier ever to serve in a major war. Clem wins his nickname, Johnny Shiloh, from Ulysses S. Grant for his courage during the Battle of Shiloh. The novel follows his career through the war.

Historical Accuracy: The novel is based in large measure on the actual record but with fictional embellishments.

5309 *The Trial of Mary Todd Lincoln*

Date of Publication: 1959
Subject(s): Trials
Historical character(s): Mary Todd Lincoln, Spouse (of Abraham Lincoln); Robert Todd Lincoln, Lawyer
Time Period(s): 1870s
Locale(s): Illinois

Summary: The novel offers a reconstruction of the hearing that judged Mary Todd Lincoln insane and sent her to an asylum. The novel's theory is that the hearing and its finding were fraudulent and done for political reasons, casting the Lincoln family and supporters in a very damaging light.

Historical Accuracy: The novel's theory is not supported by historical fact. The depiction of the hearing is constructed on the premise that efforts to prove Mary Todd Lincoln insane were contested.

JEWELL PARKER RHODES

Born in Pittsburgh, Rhodes is an English professor at California State University, Northridge. She has received a National Endowment for the Arts award in fiction and is the author of many published short stories.

5310 *Voodoo Dreams: A Novel of Marie Laveau*

Date of Publication: 1993
Subject(s): Witchcraft and Sorcery; Voodoo
Fictional character(s): John, Magician (voodoo doctor)
Historical character(s): Marie Laveau, Witch (voodoo queen)
Time Period(s): 19th century (1822-1881)
Locale(s): New Orleans, Louisiana

Summary: The novel is based on the life of 19th-century voodoo queen Marie Laveau. Marie is raised in the Louisiana bayou and comes to New Orleans, where she falls under the spell of voodoo doctor John and begins her career.

Historical Accuracy: Since little is known about Marie Laveau, most of the story is an invention.

RICHARD RHODES (1937-)

Born in Kansas City and educated at Yale, Rhodes worked as a propagandist, a road repairer, a surgical assistant, a journalist, a book editor, and a chicken farmer. His *The Inland Grand* was named by the *New York Times* as one of the 100 best-known books of 1970. Most of his books feature a Midwestern setting.

5311 *The Ungodly: A Novel of the Donner Party*

Date of Publication: 1973
Subject(s): American West; Wagon Trains; Donner Party
Historical character(s): George Donner, Leader (wagon train); James Frazier Reed, Settler; Pat Breen, Settler
Time Period(s): 1840s (1846)
Locale(s): Sierra Nevada Mountains, California; California Trail, United States

Summary: Told in diary form, the novel depicts the tragic story of the ill-fated Donner Party that leaves Independence, Missouri, in 1846 to follow the California Trail. They choose an untried short cut that leaves them snow-bound for seven months in the Sierra Nevadas, 70 miles from their destination. To survive, the Donner Party descends to extremes of inhumanity.

Historical Accuracy: Though based on historical fact and actual letters, diaries, and quotes, the novel is a work of fiction.

JEAN RHYS (1890-1979)

Rhys was born and raised in Dominica, West Indies. Her father was a Welsh doctor, her mother a Creole. Rhys came to England at 16, married a Dutch poet, and later lived in Vienna and Paris. She authored five novels, three collections of short stories, and an unfinished autobiography. Her work was neglected until critic Alfred Alvarez praised Rhys as one of the finest British writers of this century.

5312 *Wide Sargasso Sea*

Date of Publication: 1966
Subject(s): Victorian Period
Fictional character(s): Edward Rochester, Gentleman; Antoinette Bertha Cosway, Spouse
Time Period(s): 19th century
Locale(s): Jamaica; England

Summary: The author brilliantly re-imagines the classic Victorian novel *Jane Eyre* from the perspective of Antoinette Bertha Cosway, the madwoman hidden in the attic of Rochester's Thornfield Hall. The novel tells the story of Antoinette's childhood and her marriage to Rochester. Her tragic story offers an alternate view of the class and culture described by Charlotte Bronte.

Historical Accuracy: The novel is convincing in its psychologically penetrating depiction of a Jamaican family ruined by the emancipation of slaves and a clash of cultures.

ANNE RICE (1941-)

An American writer born in New Orleans, Rice graduated from San Francisco State College and held a variety of jobs including waitress, cook, usher, and insurance claims examiner before achieving success as a bestselling author of horror fiction. She is best known for her Vampire Chronicles series, including *Interview with the Vampire*. Rice is credited with updating and providing a modern spin on the vampire tradition by identifying with the vampire instead of the victim. Rice also writes under the pseudonyms Anne Rampling and A.N. Roquelaure.

5313 *Cry to Heaven*

Date of Publication: 1982
Subject(s): Musical Life
Fictional character(s): Guido Maffeo, Singer; Tonio Treschi, Singer
Time Period(s): 18th century
Locale(s): Naples, Italy

Summary: The novel portrays the world of the 18th-century Italian castrati, male singers whose unique soprano voices are the result of boyhood castration. The novel concerns the relationship of two castrati—Guido Maffeo and Tonio Treschi. The latter aims to become one of the greatest singers while achieving revenge on his father who caused his mutilation.

Historical Accuracy: The novel demonstrates extensive research into the world of the castrati and the period which creates an authentic background for this lavish story.

5314 *The Feast of All Saints*

Date of Publication: 1979
Subject(s): Antebellum South; Racial Conflict
Fictional character(s): Marcel Ste. Marie, Young Man
Time Period(s): 1840s
Locale(s): New Orleans, Louisiana

Summary: Antebellum New Orleans is the setting for this novel that describes the precarious status of the city's "free people of color." The story centers on Marcel Ste. Marie, a quadroon who struggles to maintain his rights and dignity.

Historical Accuracy: The story is fictional, but the period background is authentic with a number of actual figures mentioned and the details of New Orleans' Free People of Color accurately described.

5315 *The Mummy; or Ramses the Damned*

Date of Publication: 1989
Subject(s): Ancient Egypt; Pharaohs; Supernatural
Fictional character(s): Julie Stratford, Young Woman
Historical character(s): Cleopatra, Ruler (Queen of Egypt); Ramses II, Ruler (Pharaoh of Egypt)
Time Period(s): 1910s (1914)
Locale(s): London, England; Cairo, Egypt

Summary: In this horror tale, Ramses II, who has discovered the secret of eternal life, awakens in 1914 London, where his sarcophagus has been transported. Julie Stratford, the young daughter of the mummy's discoverer, accompanies Ramses to Egypt where his life-giving elixir is used to raise the dead Cleopatra.

Historical Accuracy: Horror is central here with little effort to provide a carefully worked historical background. The portrayal of Egyptians is faithful to the theatrical rather than the historical.

ROBERT RICE (1945-)

Rice is a lawyer and lives with his family on a farm in Montana. He earned his M.A. in International Affairs at American University and did several years of graduate work in Latin American studies at the University of Florida. In 1990 he won the Oregon State Poetry Contest.

5316 *The Last Pendragon*

Date of Publication: 1991
Subject(s): Dark Ages; Arthurian Legends; Anglo-Saxon Period
Fictional character(s): Arthur, Ruler (King of the Britons); Bedwyr, Knight; Irion, Knight
Time Period(s): 6th century (540s)
Locale(s): England (southwestern)

Summary: The novel is set 11 years after the fall of King Arthur. Bedwyr—the last of the Knights of the Round Table—has returned from serving as a mercenary in the Roman Army. He joins Arthur's grandson, Irion, in a final battle against the Saxon warlord Ceawlin to determine the fate of Arthur's kingdom.

Historical Accuracy: The novel blends the imagined and the actual, against a convincing historical background.

SILE RICE

English author Rice left school at age 15 to work in a toy factory and as a wardrobe mistress. She has taught English to foreign students. Rice spent ten years writing *The Saxon Tapestry*.

5317 *The Saxon Tapestry*

Date of Publication: 1991
Subject(s): Middle Ages; Norman Conquest; Anglo-Saxon Period
Fictional character(s): Muirheal, Sorceress
Historical character(s): Edward the Confessor, Ruler (King of England); Hereward the Wake, Rebel, Outlaw; Harold Godwinesson, Ruler (King of England); William the Conqueror, Nobleman (Duke of Normandy), Ruler; Matilda of Flanders, Royalty (queen consort of William I)
Time Period(s): 11th century
Locale(s): England; Ireland

Summary: The story of Anglo-Saxon England's end and the horror of the Norman Conquest is told in this tale of legendary outlaw Hereward the Wake. Though he is an earl's son,

Hereward is born with a birthmark that sets him apart and is wrongly banished by King Edward. When William beats Harold at Hastings, Hereward refuses to accept defeat and becomes a rebel hero.

Historical Accuracy: The period details are captured with authority, and the historical background is accurately presented.

ELIZABETH RICHARDS

5318 *The Ravishers*

Date of Publication: 1992
Subject(s): Independence—Ireland; English Colonies
Fictional character(s): Medbeth, Ward; James Exforth, Sea Captain, Smuggler; Brockton Nowell-Grey, Plantation Owner
Time Period(s): 1730s (1733)
Locale(s): Ireland; Barbados

Summary: This romantic adventure story begins during the 1730s in an Ireland still reeling from repressive British policies instituted after Cromwell's 1649 invasion. Medbeth, the ward of a British noble, flees her uncle's unwelcome advances as a stowaway aboard a ship to America. When the ship puts in for repairs on Barbados, an island colony under harsh British rule, love and adventure ensue.

Historical Accuracy: The novel captures the scenes in Ireland and the West Indies with authenticity.

CONRAD RICHTER (1890-1968)

Richter was an American writer who won a Pulitzer Prize for *The Town* in 1951. He also wrote *The Trees*, *The Field*, *Tracey Cromwell*, *The Waters of Kronos*, and *A Simple Honorable Man*.

5319 *The Fields*

Date of Publication: 1946
Subject(s): Settlement of the American Frontier
Fictional character(s): Sayward Wheeler, Backwoodswoman; Portius Wheeler, Lawyer, Backwoodsman
Time Period(s): 1820s
Locale(s): Ohio; Kentucky

Summary: The novel is the second in Richter's trilogy that chronicles the development of a pioneer settlement in Ohio. The woods slowly give way to farms, cabins, and schools as a community is created. The focus is on the Wheeler family and the matriarch Sayward who resists the pull of settlement as her husband assumes a larger role as teacher and lawyer in the new community.

Historical Accuracy: The details of pioneer life are accurately captured.

5320 *Free Man*

Date of Publication: 1943
Subject(s): American Colonies; Immigrants; American Revolution

Fictional character(s): Henry Free, Immigrant, Servant (indentured)
Time Period(s): 18th century
Locale(s): Pennsylvania, American Colonies

Summary: German immigrant Henry Free (born Herner Dallicher) escapes indentured servitude for life in Pennsylvania Dutch country. When the Revolution comes, Henry joins the rebellion. He later marries his former mistress.

Historical Accuracy: The novel is convincing in its recreation of the period.

5321 *The Lady*

Date of Publication: 1957
Subject(s): American West; Ranching
Fictional character(s): Elena Sessions, Spouse; Albert Sessions, Judge
Time Period(s): 1890s (1893)
Locale(s): New Mexico

Summary: Elena Sessions, the daughter of an English father and a Mexican mother, is the wife of a judge in the New Mexico territory. Her arrogance and impulsiveness lead to violence. When a rancher is killed driving a herd of steers across her garden, Elena's brother is accused of the crime. But did he or Elena pull the trigger? This is only the initial instance in the train of violence that follows.

Historical Accuracy: Richter excells at both recovering the past and in creating a compelling human drama out of the facts of history.

5322 *The Light in the Forest*

Date of Publication: 1953
Subject(s): American Colonies; Indians
Fictional character(s): John Butler, Captive
Time Period(s): 1760s (1765)
Locale(s): Pennsylvania, American Colonies; Ohio

Summary: This tale of the frontier in Pennsylvania and Ohio is set during Henry Bouquet's expedition to rescue captives held by the Tuscaroras Indians. The story concerns John Butler who, after being rescued from the Indians, attempts to rejoin his lost Indian family.

Historical Accuracy: The author's intent is not to write a historical novel but to give an authentic depiction of life in early America.

5323 *The Sea of Grass*

Date of Publication: 1936
Subject(s): American West; Ranching; Homesteading
Fictional character(s): Colonel Jim Brewton, Rancher; Hal Brewton, Doctor; Brice Chamberlain, Lawyer
Time Period(s): 19th century; 20th century (1885-1910)
Locale(s): Southwest

Summary: The novel dramatizes the dispute between cattlemen and homesteaders from the cattleman's perspective. The novel tells the story of Colonel Brewton, his wife and her son who is the child of his wife's rival, the lawyer, Chamberlain. The boy becomes an outlaw, and the homesteaders fail due to the blistering heat and the sand introduced by the plowing of the sod.

Historical Accuracy: This is a moving and dramatic depiction of an important era of the settling of the West that shows the competing claims of two sides, one destroying the world of the other.

5324 *Tacey Cromwell*

Date of Publication: 1942
Subject(s): American West; Mining
Fictional character(s): Tacey Cromwell, Young Woman
Time Period(s): 1890s
Locale(s): Arizona

Summary: The scene for this novel is an Arizona copper mining town during the 1890s. Tacey Cromwell leaves the management of a sporting club to take up housekeeping in Brisbee's Brewery Gulch, where the forces of civilization and respectability cost her the man she loves.

Historical Accuracy: The novel captures the era convincingly.

5325 *The Town*

Date of Publication: 1950
Subject(s): Settlement of the American Frontier
Fictional character(s): Sayward Wheeler, Backwoodswoman; Portius Wheeler, Lawyer; Chancey Wheeler, Writer
Time Period(s): 1850s
Locale(s): Americus, Ohio

Summary: In this third novel of Richter's trilogy about the settlement of the American frontier, the emphasis shifts to Sayward and Portius' children and the growth of their Ohio town. Despite the development of civilization, the appeal of the wilderness is strongest to Sayward who provides the novel's link with the past.

Historical Accuracy: The novel and the trilogy as a whole are less concerned with the flow of historical events than in the depiction of ordinary people, their customs, speech, and everyday life.

5326 *The Trees*

Date of Publication: 1940
Subject(s): Settlement of the American Frontier; Indians
Fictional character(s): Worth Luckett, Backwoodsman; Sayward Luckett, Backwoodswoman; Portius Wheeler, Lawyer, Backwoodsman
Time Period(s): 18th century; 19th century (1790s-1810s)
Locale(s): Pennsylvania (western); Ohio

Summary: This is the first novel of a trilogy tracing the growth of a pioneer settlement in the seemingly impenetrable virgin forest of the old Northwest Territory west of the Alleghenies and north of the Ohio River. Worth Luckett brings his family west from Pennsylvania, and the care of the family falls to his daughter Sayward. The novel concerns their struggle to survive Indians, nature, and the loneliness of the American wilderness.

Historical Accuracy: The story uses the vernacular of the pioneers to help portray what the early settlers must have felt and thought.

ANTONIA RIDGE (?-1981)

A Dutch author born in Amsterdam, Ridge wrote books, plays, and songs and worked as a broadcaster for the BBC, where she was best known for her tales and narratives on BBC radio's *Women's Hour*. She also authored books for children, including *The Little Red Pony*.

5327 *The Royal Pawn*

Date of Publication: 1962
Subject(s): Middle Ages; Royalty—France; Royalty—England
Historical character(s): Catherine of Valois, Royalty (queen consort of Henry V); Henry V, Ruler (King of England); Charles VI, Ruler (King of France); Isabeau, Royalty (queen consort of Charles VI); Owen Tudor, Knight; Humphrey, Duke of Gloucester, Nobleman; Henry VI, Ruler (King of England); Guillemette Giguet, Nurse
Time Period(s): 15th century (1401-1485)
Locale(s): France; England

Summary: This novel is based on the extraordinary life of Catherine of Valois. She is the daughter of French King Charles VI, the wife of Henry V, and the mother of Henry VI. With her second husband Owen Tudor she establishes the Tudor dynasty and is the grandmother of Henry VII. The novel shows Catherine as the pawn of her ambitious mother Queen Isabeau and at the mercy of a dynastic power play after Henry V's death.

Historical Accuracy: The framework of the story is historically accurate. The author makes some surmises to fill in the gaps and to create a more seamless narrative.

BARBARA RIEFE (1925-)

Born in Connecticut, Riefe graduated from Colby College. He wrote 26 network TV programs, including *Pulitzer Prize Playhouse* and *Studio One*. He worked for eight years as a staff writer for *Masquerade Party*. He has been writing since age seven.

5328 *For Love of Two Eagles*

Date of Publication: 1994
Subject(s): American Colonies; Indians; Tribal Life—Native American
Fictional character(s): Margaret Addison, Frontierswoman, Gentlewoman; Two Eagles, Indian (Oneida), Warrior
Time Period(s): 1700s (1700)
Locale(s): New York, American Colonies; Boston, Massachusetts, American Colonies

Summary: In the sequel to *The Woman Who Fell From the Sky*, Englishwoman Margaret Addison has married Oneida warrior Two Eagles. When he is reportedly killed, Margaret begins a perilous trek to Boston to return to her family in England. She must elude the Mohawks, who have sworn vengeance on all allies of the Oneidas.

Historical Accuracy: The novel features a vivid and historically sound depiction of the region and of Indian customs.

5329 *Mohawk Woman*

Date of Publication: 1996
Subject(s): American Colonies; Queen Anne's War; Indians
Fictional character(s): Singing Brook, Indian (Mohawk), Spouse (of Sky Toucher); Sky Toucher, Indian (Mohawk), Spouse (of Singing Brook); Two Eagles, Indian (Oneida), Warrior
Time Period(s): 1710s
Locale(s): New York, American Colonies; Canada

Summary: The Mohawk warrior Sky Toucher leaves his new bride, Singing Brook, to fight with the British against the French in Queen Anne's War for control of the North American colonies. Betrayed by those he trusts, he is captured and forced to endure a grueling trek into Canada where he faces execution for treason. Singing Brook, along with his cousin, Two Eagles, mounts a rescue mission.

Historical Accuracy: The historical background is realistic and faithful to the facts.

5330 *The Woman Who Fell From the Sky*

Date of Publication: 1994
Subject(s): Indians; Tribal Life—Native American; American Colonies
Fictional character(s): Margaret Addison, Gentlewoman, Frontierswoman; Two Eagles, Indian (Oneida), Warrior
Time Period(s): 17th century
Locale(s): New York, American Colonies; Quebec, Canada

Summary: Margaret Addison, the sole survivor of a Mohawk massacre, is rescued and adopted by the Oneidas. They agree to escort her to Quebec, where her French fiance awaits her. During the journey, Margaret learns the ways of the Indians and falls in love. Finally, she must decide whether to honor her engagement or to share her lover's culture.

Historical Accuracy: The novel features accurate depictions of Indian life and culture.

JEAN RIKHOFF

Rikhoff is the founder-editor of the literary magazine *Quixote*. She lives in upstate New York and teaches at Adirondack Community College.

5331 *Buttes Landing*

Date of Publication: 1973
Subject(s): Settlement of the American Frontier; Family Saga; Indians
Fictional character(s): Odder Buttes, Settler; Emily Guthrie Buttes, Spouse; Guthrie Buttes, Farmer; Cobus Buttes, Military Personnel (Union soldier), Farmer
Time Period(s): 19th century
Locale(s): Adirondacks, New York

Summary: The story of life in the 19th-century Adirondack wilderness is told through three generations of the Buttes family. It begins with patriot Odder Buttes, who settles on a remote lake in the wilderness. His son, Guthrie, is raised by an Indian midwife, and Guthrie's son, Cobus, returns to Buttes Landing after the Civil War, attracted by the power of the land.

Historical Accuracy: The regional depiction is authentic and convincing.

5332 *One of the Raymonds*

Date of Publication: 1974
Subject(s): Reconstruction Period; Family Saga
Fictional character(s): Mason Raymond Buttes, Orphan; Worth Hart, Hunter
Time Period(s): 1870s
Locale(s): Adirondacks, New York; North Carolina

Summary: This continuation of the Buttes and Raymond family sagas centers on "summer boy" Mason Raymond Buttes. He is city-educated and must come to terms with the Adirondack wilderness and his family legacy, tutored by hunter Worth Hart. Mason embarks on a rite of passage into the Reconstruction-era South.

Historical Accuracy: The 19th century background is convincingly depicted.

5333 *The Sweetwater*

Date of Publication: 1976
Subject(s): Coming of Age; Family Saga; Indians
Fictional character(s): John Buttes, Farmer, Prospector; Mason Raymond Buttes, Orphan; Pepper Tom, Cowboy
Time Period(s): 1870s (1876)
Locale(s): Oregon Trail, United States

Summary: In the third volume of the author's trilogy on the Buttes and Raymond families, the scene shifts from the Adirondacks to the Oregon Trail. John Buttes and his cousin head to the Black Hills in 1876 in search of gold. Both come of age, instructed in the ways of the West by black cowboy Pepper Tom.

Historical Accuracy: The trilogy portrays the Adirondack setting and the western scene with equal clarity.

JUDITH MERKLE RILEY (1942-)

Born in Maine, Riley graduated from the University of California, Berkeley, and Harvard. She is a professor of government at Claremont McKenna College and the author of both historical fiction and works on political theory.

5334 *In Pursuit of the Green Lion*

Date of Publication: 1990
Subject(s): Middle Ages; Hundred Years War; Witchcraft and Sorcery
Fictional character(s): Margaret of Ashbury, Widow(er), Heiress; Gilbert de Vilers, Religious (friar); Brother Malachi, Religious (monk)
Time Period(s): 14th century (1356)

Locale(s): England; France

Summary: In the sequel to *A Vision of Light*, Margaret of Ashbury is newly married to unfrocked monk Brother Gregory, who turns out to be Gilbert de Vilers. He joins the campaign in France during the Hundred Years War and is lost without a trace. Margaret sets out with an herbalist and an alchemist, intent on finding the Green Lion, the secret of transmutation.

Historical Accuracy: The story features a strong and authentic period background.

5335 *The Oracle Glass*

Date of Publication: 1994
Subject(s): Witchcraft and Sorcery; Royalty—France
Fictional character(s): Genevieve Pasquier, Psychic (fortune teller)
Historical character(s): Louis XIV, Ruler (King of France); Marie-Therese, Royalty (Queen of France); Catherine Montvoisin, Sorceress; Francoise Athenais Rochechouart de Mortemart, Noblewoman (mistress to Louis XIV)
Time Period(s): 17th century (1670s)
Locale(s): Paris, France

Summary: Genevieve Pasquier is a young girl with the ability to read fortunes in the swirling waters of an oracle glass. She is taken up by La Voisin, a society fortune teller who heads a secret society of witches with influence in Louis XIV's court. As the 150-year-old Madame de Morville, Genevieve assumes a new identity with an unexpected power.

Historical Accuracy: The basis of the novel is fictional; the coven of Paris witches, however, is historical and based on actual records of the time. This is a fascinating glimpse into the dark and corrupt side of the Sun King's court.

5336 *The Serpent Garden*

Date of Publication: 1996
Subject(s): Tudor Period; Artistic Life
Fictional character(s): Susanna Dallet, Artist, Widow(er)
Historical character(s): Henry VIII, Ruler (King of England); Thomas Wolsey, Religious (cardinal); Mary Tudor, Royalty (princess)
Time Period(s): 16th century (1510)
Locale(s): England; France

Summary: The plot to put an English heir onto the throne of France, mounted by Henry VIII and Cardinal Wolsey, owes a good deal to the accomplished miniaturist Susanna Dallet whose portrait of Mary Tudor causes the proposed match to go forward. Susanna finds herself a member of the princess' entourage to the court of France and in possession of the key to a secret that swirls around the French court.

Historical Accuracy: The novel's situation is fanciful but convincing in its detailing of period customs.

5337 *A Vision of Light*

Date of Publication: 1989
Subject(s): Middle Ages; Medical Profession; Witchcraft and Sorcery

Fictional character(s): Margaret of Ashbury, Gentlewoman; Brother Gregory, Religious (friar)
Time Period(s): 14th century
Locale(s): England

Summary: In England during the 14th century, the novel's heroine, Margaret of Ashbury, dictates her life story to Brother Gregory, a renegade Carthusian friar. The story Margaret tells offers a full portrait of the era and of an extraordinary person.

Historical Accuracy: The novel is an impressive and convincing period portrait.

ALEXANDRA RIPLEY (1934-)

An American romance writer born in Charleston, South Carolina, Ripley graduated from Vassar College. She was an obvious choice to write the sequel to Margaret Mitchell's classic *Gone With the Wind*. Ripley undertook the project despite the storm of controversy it caused. Her historical novels have been praised for their period accuracy.

5338 *Charleston*

Date of Publication: 1981
Subject(s): Romance; Reconstruction Period; Civil War—U.S.
Fictional character(s): Elizabeth Tradd, Southern Belle
Time Period(s): 19th century (1863-1898)
Locale(s): Charleston, South Carolina

Summary: The novel is set during the Civil War and its aftermath in Charleston, South Carolina. Elizabeth Tradd, a pleasure-loving society belle must adjust to the grim realities of war as she takes charge of the family business and deals with a variety of sobering romantic challenges.

Historical Accuracy: The period background is authentic and convincing.

5339 *From Fields of Gold*

Date of Publication: 1994
Subject(s): Business Building; Reconstruction Period
Fictional character(s): Francesca Standish, Southern Belle; Nate Richardson, Plantation Owner
Time Period(s): 19th century (1875-1890s)
Locale(s): Virginia; North Carolina; London, England

Summary: In the post-Civil-War South, the modern tobacco industry is emerging. Francesca "Chess" Standish, born into the wealthy Tidewater society destroyed by the Civil War, allies herself with ambitious Nate Richardson to create a tobacco empire.

Historical Accuracy: The novel is convincing in its period details and remarkably restrained for a historical romance.

5340 *A Love Divine*

Date of Publication: 1996
Subject(s): Biblical Story; Roman Empire

Historical character(s): Joseph of Arimathea, Biblical Figure; Herod the Great, Biblical Figure, Ruler (King of the Jews); Jesus Christ, Biblical Figure
Time Period(s): 1st century
Locale(s): Palestine; Rome, Roman Empire; England

Summary: Joseph of Arimathea is mentioned in the New Testament only as a wealthy man who gave his tomb for the burial place of Jesus. The novel imagines a fuller story of Joseph based on the legend that suggests that he was a seaman and trader. The novel records his adventures across the ancient world and his role in Jesus' crucifixion.

Historical Accuracy: The historical characters and events are accurate. However, there is no evidence that Joseph's involvement actually occurred.

5341 *New Orleans Legacy*

Date of Publication: 1987
Subject(s): Antebellum South; Romance
Fictional character(s): Mary McAlister, Orphan; Valmont Saint-Brevin, Gentleman
Time Period(s): 1850s (1851)
Locale(s): New Orleans, Louisiana

Summary: A young orphan searches for her identity and heritage in antebellum New Orleans in the 1850s. Mary McAlister journeys from a convent boarding school to New Orleans overcoming several obstacles in establishing her in dependence, while falling in love with Valmont Saint-Brevin.

Historical Accuracy: The author admits to altering the chronology of New Orleans' yellow fever epidemic for the purposes of her story.

5342 *Scarlett*

Date of Publication: 1991
Subject(s): Fenians; Reconstruction Period; Family Saga
Fictional character(s): Scarlett O'Hara, Businesswoman, Landowner; Rhett Butler, Businessman (mine owner); Father Colum O'Hara, Leader (Fenian), Religious
Time Period(s): 1870s
Locale(s): Charleston, South Carolina; Savannah, Georgia; Meath, Ireland

Summary: The sequel to *Gone With the Wind* picks up the life of Scarlett O'Hara, who is unwelcome at Tara, ostracized by Atlanta society, and spurned by Rhett. During a visit to her mother-in-law in Charleston, Scarlett seeks out her O'Hara relatives in Savannah. Accompanied by her cousin, Father Colum O'Hara, she moves to Ballyhara, Ireland, where she buys and renovates a manor house on O'Hara land, gives birth to a daughter by Rhett, and becomes "The O'Hara"—the leader of the clan.

Historical Accuracy: The period customs and culture of Charleston, Savannah, the Irish, and the English have been painstakingly researched. The Fenian movement also figures prominently in the novel.

5343 *The Time Returns*

Date of Publication: 1985
Subject(s): Renaissance; Artistic Life

Fictional character(s): Ginevra de Pazzi, Gentlewoman
Historical character(s): Lorenzo de Medici, Ruler (Florentine); Sandro Botticelli, Artist; Michelangelo Buonarotti, Artist
Time Period(s): 15th century (1469-1492)
Locale(s): Florence, Italy

Summary: The story, set in 15th-century Florence, dramatizes the love affair between nobleman and patron of the arts Lorenzo de Medici and Ginevra de Pazzi. The lovers struggle to preserve the honor and grandeur of the Florentine Republic against threats from all sides.

Historical Accuracy: The book is based on realistic details of Lorenzo de Medici's life, but the character of Ginevra is invented.

CLEMENTS RIPLEY (1892-1954)

Born in Tacoma, Washington, Ripley was educated at Yale, served in the U.S. Army in World War I, and then took up farming and writing. He concentrated on stories of French court life and colonial Virginia, featuring historical figures such as George Washington, Thomas Jefferson, Patrick Henry, and John Paul Jones. His novels include *Mississippi Bell* and *Clear for Action*.

5344 *Clear for Action: A Novel about John Paul Jones*

Date of Publication: 1940
Subject(s): Sea Story; American Revolution
Fictional character(s): Angus Lowrie, Clerk
Historical character(s): John Paul Jones, Military Personnel (naval captain); George Washington, Military Personnel (army commander); John Adams, Political Figure; Benjamin Franklin, Diplomat; Patrick Henry, Patriot, Lawyer
Time Period(s): 1770s
Locale(s): *Bonhomme Richard*, At Sea; England; Paris, France

Summary: The story of John Paul Jones is told from the perspective of his clerk, Angus Lowrie, a fictional character who chronicles Jones' career as a slave-trader and a virtual one-man American navy. Jones is shown ''invading'' Britain, becoming the toast of Paris society, and battling the *Serapis*.

Historical Accuracy: The author admits that in the interest of drama he occasionally diverges from the historical record.

5345 *Gold Is Where You Find It*

Date of Publication: 1936
Subject(s): American West; Gold Rush—California; Farming
Fictional character(s): Colonel Virginius Ferris, Rancher; Serena Ferris, Young Woman
Time Period(s): 1870s
Locale(s): California

Summary: The scene is California during the second gold rush in the 1870s. The story concerns the conflict between ranchers and miners as Colonel Virginius Ferris attempts to maintain the old system of farming against the encroachment of the new fruit growing industry.

Historical Accuracy: The novel presents the historical background of the period and the region convincingly.

5346 *Mississippi Belle*

Date of Publication: 1942
Subject(s): Antebellum South; Identity—Concealed
Fictional character(s): Caitlin Preswald, Singer (as Kate Ryan), Widow(er); Buck Preswald, Gentleman
Historical character(s): Andrew Jackson, Political Figure
Time Period(s): 1830s
Locale(s): New Orleans, Louisiana; Memphis, Tennessee

Summary: New Orleans and Memphis in the 1830s are the setting for this story of Caitlin Preswald, who leads a curious double life as a respectable young widow and as the notorious Kate Ryan, torch singer in a gambling house. Caitlin struggles to live down her past, assisted by the aging Andrew Jackson.

Historical Accuracy: The novel's narrative premise strains credibility as a convincing reflection of the time period.

CLARA RISING

Rising is a native of Mississippi.

5347 *In the Season of the Wild Rose*

Date of Publication: 1986
Subject(s): Civil War—U.S.; Battle of Shiloh; Antebellum South
Historical character(s): John Hunt Morgan, Military Personnel (Confederate general); Albert Sidney Johnston, Military Personnel (Confederate general); Nathan Bedford Forrest, Military Personnel (Confederate cavalry officer); Henry Thomas Hines, Spy; Braxton Bragg, Military Personnel (Confederate general)
Time Period(s): 19th century (1833-1864)
Locale(s): Lexington, Kentucky; Ohio

Summary: This panoramic novel of the Civil War examines the years leading up to the conflict from the perspective of Kentucky's Hunt and Morgan families. It focuses on cavalry officer John Hunt Morgan's exploits, including his famous 1863 raid on the outskirts of Cincinnati.

Historical Accuracy: The author lists the few instances where she deviates from the historical record.

C.T. RITCHIE (1914-)

Born in Nova Scotia, Ritchie is a graduate of Dalhousie University. He has worked in a shipyard and as a clerk in a slaughter house before moving to New Brunswick where he operated a general store and a salmon fishing camp. As a consulting geologist, he has divided his time between exploration and writing. He is the author of *The First Canadian: The Story of Champlain*.

5348 *Black Angels*

Date of Publication: 1959
Subject(s): Monmouth's Rebellion; American Colonies; Indians

Fictional character(s): Gilbert of Axford, Captive; Wilhelmina Roebury, Young Woman; Silas Vetch, Government Official
Historical character(s): Sir George Jeffreys, Government Official (Lord Chief Justice)
Time Period(s): 17th century (1685)
Locale(s): Wiltshire, England; Jamaica; Wabenaki Territory, North America

Summary: In the aftermath of Monmouth's Rebellion in 1685, Wilhelmina Roebury and her betrothed, Gilbert of Axford, flee from the persecution of Silas Vetch, the agent of Lord Jeffreys, Chief Justice of England. Instead of safety with the Prince of Orange, they find themselves taken as prisoners to the New World: Wilhelmina to New Hampshire, Gilbert to a cruel planter in Jamaica. The novel tells the story of what happens to them, including Wilhelmina's abduction by Indians, and Gilbert's being stranded on a Bahamian island while escaping from Jamaica.

Historical Accuracy: The details of day-to-day events and the precise expressions of thought and action are derived from the author's imagination supported by historical records of the period.

5349 *The Willing Maid*

Date of Publication: 1958
Subject(s): French and Indian War; American Colonies; Siege of Louisburg
Fictional character(s): Corbet Sigourney, Student—College; Elizabeth Perry, Young Woman
Time Period(s): 1740s
Locale(s): Nova Scotia, Canada; Boston, Massachusetts, American Colonies

Summary: This romantic adventure tale set during the French and Indian Wars describes the experiences of Harvard student Corbet Sigourney who is falsely accused of murder. He escapes to Nova Scotia where he is on hand for the attack on and fall of Louisburg.

Historical Accuracy: Although the story itself is fictional, the historical events depicted and many of the characters, both major and minor, are real.

MARGARET RITTER

Ritter was born in Oklahoma and has lived in New York, Madrid, and London.

5350 *Women in the Wind*

Date of Publication: 1985
Subject(s): American West; Indians; Oil Industry
Fictional character(s): Reanna MacClaren, Spouse; Andrew MacClaren, Rancher; Jane Beauvaise, Indian
Time Period(s): 20th century (1905-1930s)
Locale(s): Oklahoma

Summary: Reanna MacClaren is a young bride who accompanies her new husband, Andrew, to the Indian Territory of Oklahoma in the early years of the 20th century. Instructed by Andrew's adoptive mother, Jane Beauvaise, an Indian tribal matriarch, Reanna witnesses the end of the Indian nation, the coming of statehood, and the discovery of oil.

Historical Accuracy: The period elements here are believably portrayed.

STEPHEN J. RIVELE (1949-)

An American author and film director, Rivele was born in Pittsburgh and graduated from Swarthmore and the University of Paris. He is the winner of numerous awards for nonfiction works and documentary films. Rivele is the coauthor of the screenplay for Oliver Stone's *Nixon*. His works include *The Plumber: The True Story of How One Good Man Helped Destroy the Entire Philadelphia Mafia*, *Lieutenant Ramsey's War*, and *Dark Genius*. *A Booke of Days* is his first novel.

5351 *A Booke of Days: A Journal of the Crusade by Roger, Duke of Lunel*

Date of Publication: 1996
Subject(s): Middle Ages; Crusades
Fictional character(s): Roger, Duke of Lunel, Nobleman
Historical character(s): Bohemond I, Royalty (Prince of Antioch), Leader (of the First Crusade)
Time Period(s): 11th century (1096-1100)
Locale(s): Provence, France; Palestine

Summary: The journal of a young French nobleman, Roger, Duke of Lunel, details the First Crusade that culminates in the attempt to recapture Jerusalem. Roger is plagued by religious doubt and guilt over a past sin as he endures a campaign filled with betrayal, deceit, and greed.

Historical Accuracy: This account of the First Crusade is close to historical reality. The chronology is reliable.

FRANCINE RIVERS (1947-)

American author Rivers was born in California and attended the University of Nevada and California State University at Hayward. A freelance writer since 1977, Rivers has also worked as a flight attendant, research librarian, and with the Special Case Division of the Internal Revenue Service on its investigation of mob involvement in Nevada's gambling establishments. Her titles include *Sarina*, *Sycamore Hill*, *A Voice in the Wind*, and *An Echo in the Darkness*.

5352 *As Sure as the Dawn*

Date of Publication: 1995
Subject(s): Christianity; Roman Empire
Fictional character(s): Atretes, Warrior (German), Gladiator; Rizpah, Widow(er)
Time Period(s): 1st century
Locale(s): Roman Empire

Summary: Atretes, a German warrior and gladiator, wins his freedom and sets out find his son and return to Germania. The child has been adopted by the widow Rizpah, and Atretes must overcome many complications and challenges to regain the boy. As a new Christian, Atretes must also come to terms with his new faith.

Historical Accuracy: The novel is more atmospheric than actual in its depiction of the era in this fictional story.

AUGUSTO ANTONIO ROA BASTOS
(1917-)

Paraguayan journalist and writer Roa Bastos was born in Iturbe, Paraguay, and attended school in Asuncion. He spent more than 40 years in exile in Argentina and France during and after Paraguay's civil war which began in 1947. Generally regarded as the finest Paraguayan author, Roa Bastos' fiction contains a distinctive blend of myth, fantasy, and realism that mirrors his native country's tumultuous political and military history while emphasizing the redemptive power of human suffering. He is the author of *Thunder Among the Leaves*, *Son of Man*, and short story anthologies, including *Antologia Personal*.

`5353` *I, the Supreme*

Date of Publication: 1986
Subject(s): Biography, Fictionalized; Independence—South America
Historical character(s): Jose Gaspar Rodriguez de Francia, Ruler (dictator of Paraguay)
Time Period(s): 19th century
Locale(s): Paraguay

Summary: The novel presents a fictional version of the life of Paraguay dictator Jose Gaspar Rodriguez de Francia who ruled as "perpetual dictator" from 1816 to his death in 1840. The story is told through a series of conversations between El Supremo and his secretary, as well as through statements from Francia's private notebooks and historical documents.

Historical Accuracy: The novel is assembled from a variety of fragments that contribute to a believable portrait of Francia and his era.

GARLAND ROARK (1904-1985)

Born in Texas, Roark apprenticed as an illustrator. He was an advertising sales manager and worked in various stores in Texas from 1924 to 1946 when he quit to become a full-time writer. Roark's oil paintings are part of the permanent collection of the Sam Houston Room in Nacogdoches, Texas. Two of Roark's books, *Wake of the Red Witch* and *Fair Wind to Java*, were made into films.

`5354` *Fair Wind to Java*

Date of Publication: 1948
Subject(s): Sea Story
Fictional character(s): Robert Culver, Businessman; Captain Boll, Sea Captain, Adventurer
Time Period(s): 1870s; 1880s (1879-1886)
Locale(s): Boston, Massachusetts; Indonesia (Dutch East Indies)

Summary: Ruthless Captain Boll of the *Gerrymaker* hatches a daring scheme to become rich by matching wits with the Dutch; his employer, Robert Culver; and the powerful Radja Mataram.

Historical Accuracy: Exotic adventure in the Dutch East Indies is emphasized over careful historical documentation.

`5355` *Hellfire Jackson*

Date of Publication: 1966
Subject(s): Texas Revolution; Religious Life
Fictional character(s): Horatio Jackson, Religious (preacher)
Historical character(s): Sam Houston, Political Figure, Military Personnel; Stephen F. Austin, Political Figure
Time Period(s): 1820s; 1830s
Locale(s): Texas

Summary: Set during the Texas Revolution, the novel depicts the adventures of Horatio Jackson, a former lawyer and soldier whose religious calling sends him to Texas. Posing as a surveyor to avoid the ban on non-Catholics in Mexican-controlled Texas, Jackson ministers to the community while becoming involved in the revolution.

Historical Accuracy: The main story is invented, but the historical context is based on fact.

`5356` *The Lady and the Deep Blue Sea*

Date of Publication: 1958
Subject(s): Sea Story; Clipper Ships
Fictional character(s): Philip Broadwinder, Sea Captain; Jenny Broadwinder, Spouse; George Cartwright, Shipowner
Time Period(s): 1850s (1856)
Locale(s): Boston, Massachusetts; At Sea (Boston to Melbourne)

Summary: This adventure tale, set during the era of the clipper ships, dramatizes a race from Boston to Melbourne. If Philip Broadwinder, captain of the *Calcutta Eagle*, can win the race, he can claim half the ownership of his ship. Also aboard are his wife, Jenny, and George Cartwright, owner of the shipping line.

Historical Accuracy: The nautical elements of the story are authentic.

`5357` *Rainbow in the Royals*

Date of Publication: 1950
Subject(s): Sea Story; Clipper Ships
Fictional character(s): James Quick, Sea Captain; Bill Quick, Sea Captain; Ellen Appleton, Gentlewoman
Time Period(s): 1850s (1850)
Locale(s): At Sea (around Cape Horn to San Francisco); Boston, Massachusetts; San Francisco, California

Summary: Set during the clipper ship era, the novel describes a race between two brothers, James and Bill Quick, from Boston around the Horn to San Francisco. The winner will marry the woman they both love, Ellen Appleton, daughter of the shipping line's owner.

Historical Accuracy: Though the emphasis is on high-speed adventure, the nautical elements are convincing.

5358 *Star in the Rigging: A Novel of the Texas Navy*

Date of Publication: 1954
Subject(s): Sea Story; Texas Revolution
Fictional character(s): Jeremiah H. Brown, Sea Captain
Time Period(s): 1830s (1832-1836)
Locale(s): Texas; Vera Cruz, Mexico; New Orleans, Louisiana

Summary: The little-known role of the ''Texas Navy'' in the revolution against Mexico is depicted in the story of Captain Jeremiah H. Brown, who breaks the Mexican embargo on Texas shipping. Brown battles the Mexican navy in his raid on Vera Cruz.

Historical Accuracy: The author admits to some tampering with facts in the interest of drama.

5359 *The Witch of Manga Reva*

Date of Publication: 1962
Subject(s): Sea Story; Witchcraft and Sorcery
Fictional character(s): Jason Hind, Sea Captain
Historical character(s): Honore Laval, Religious (priest)
Time Period(s): 19th century (1833-1854)
Locale(s): Mangareva, Pacific Islands (Gambier Islands, French Polynesia)

Summary: This tale of South Sea adventure is based on the historical Honore Laval, a priest who built a cathedral on the tiny Polynesian island of Mangareva and exerted an uncanny power over its inhabitants. The fictional story pits Laval against sea captain Jason Hind in a scramble for wealth.

Historical Accuracy: The general outline of the story is historical, but the details are invented, with an emphasis on the exotic.

MIKE ROARKE

5360 *Shadows on the Long House*

Date of Publication: 1994
Subject(s): American Revolution; Indians
Fictional character(s): Sam Watley, Frontiersman, Trapper; Thad Watley, Frontiersman, Trapper
Time Period(s): 1770s; 1780s (1775-1781)
Locale(s): Adirondacks, New York

Summary: In the third installment of the First Frontier Series the American Revolution splits the ancient Iroquois Confederacy. Sam Watley and his son Thad find themselves in the middle of the conflict, deep in the wilds of the Adirondack Mountains.

Historical Accuracy: The period and frontier elements are plausible and convincing.

5361 *Silent Drums*

Date of Publication: 1994
Subject(s): American Colonies; Pontiac's Rebellion; Indians
Fictional character(s): Sam Watley, Frontiersman, Trapper; Thad Watley, Frontiersman, Trapper
Historical character(s): Pontiac, Indian (Ottawa), Chieftain

Time Period(s): 1760s (1763-1765)
Locale(s): Ohio Valley, United States; Detroit, Michigan

Summary: In the second book of the First Frontier Series, the Northwest Territory erupts in the violence of Pontiac's Rebellion. Trapper Sam Watley and his son, Thad, come to the Ohio River Valley to trade with the native tribes, but Sam becomes a captive, first of the Ottawas, and then the Chippewas, while Thad attempts to free him.

Historical Accuracy: The story is a fictional one but does make use of an authentic period setting and actual events.

5362 *Thunder in the East*

Date of Publication: 1993
Subject(s): French and Indian War; Indians; American Colonies
Fictional character(s): Sam Watley, Frontiersman, Trapper; Thad Watley, Frontiersman, Trapper; Red Hawk, Indian (Mohawk), Warrior
Time Period(s): 1750s (1756)
Locale(s): New York, American Colonies

Summary: Set during the French and Indian Wars in the frontier of New York State, the novel centers on father and son Thad and Sam Watley. When the French stir up the Indian tribes against the British, the Watleys support the British cause and must contend with the personal attack of Red Hawk, leader of a Mohawk war band.

Historical Accuracy: The story features a believable period background and an authentic look at the New York frontier and customs.

KAREN ROBARDS (1954-)

Born in Kentucky, Robards is a graduate of the University of Kentucky. She has won awards from *Romantic Times* and *Affaire de Coeur* for *To Love a Man*, *Wild Orchids*, and *Loving Julia*.

5363 *Nobody's Angel*

Date of Publication: 1992
Subject(s): American Colonies; Romance
Fictional character(s): Susannah Redman, Spinster; Ian Connelly, Nobleman (marquis), Servant (indentured)
Time Period(s): 1760s
Locale(s): Beaufort, South Carolina, American Colonies; London, England

Summary: Set in the Carolina Colony of the 1760s, this romantic tale tells the story of spinster Susannah Redman. She acquires the services of indentured servant Ian Connelly, who is actually a marquis. Their relationship takes them from coastal Carolina to fashionable London.

Historical Accuracy: The novel's situation strains credibility, and is more romance than convincing history.

CANDACE M. ROBB (1950-)

Robb, a medieval scholar, lives in Seattle. Her Owen Archer mysteries, set in medieval York, have been British bestsellers.

5364 *The Apothecary Rose*

Date of Publication: 1993
Subject(s): Mystery; Middle Ages
Fictional character(s): Nicholas Wilton, Apothecary; Owen Archer, Military Personnel (soldier), Detective—Amateur; Lucie Wilton, Young Woman
Historical character(s): John Thoresby, Religious (archbishop)
Time Period(s): 14th century (1363)
Locale(s): York, England; Kenilworth, England

Summary: In 1363 an herbal remedy proves fatal to the ward of the lord chancellor of England. Owen Archer goes to York to investigate the apothecary who provided the medicine. He promptly falls in love with the apothecary's wife, who is one of the suspects.

Historical Accuracy: This medieval story is solidly grounded in historical knowledge of the time and place. Slight modifications of the chronology are admitted to by the author.

5365 *The King's Bishop*

Date of Publication: 1996
Subject(s): Middle Ages; Mystery; Religious Conflict
Fictional character(s): Owen Archer, Veteran (soldier), Detective—Amateur
Historical character(s): Edward III, Ruler (King of England)
Time Period(s): 14th century (1367)
Locale(s): Windsor, England; York, England

Summary: In the fourth case for medieval detective Owen Archer, the background is a dispute between the Pope and Edward III over the authority of the king in religious appointments. Archer is sent on a mission to convince powerful abbots to support the king's nominee for the next Bishop of Winchester. Murder interrupts, and Archer must prove his friend innocent of the crime.

Historical Accuracy: The novel is precise in its use of authentic historical elements and period details.

5366 *The Lady Chapel*

Date of Publication: 1994
Subject(s): Mystery; Middle Ages
Fictional character(s): Owen Archer, Military Personnel (soldier), Detective—Amateur; Gilbert Ridley, Trader (of wool); Lucie Archer, Spouse
Historical character(s): Edward III, Ruler (King of England); John Thoresby, Religious (Archbishop of York)
Time Period(s): 14th century (1365)
Locale(s): York, England

Summary: In 1365 Archbishop Thoresby asks Owen Archer to investigate a grisly murder within the Mercers' Guild of wool traders in York. Archer uncovers a complex conspiracy possibly involving the king's desire to manipulate the wool trade and further his aspirations in France.

Historical Accuracy: The period details and atmosphere are exceptionally well-drawn and authentic.

5367 *The Nun's Tale*

Date of Publication: 1995
Subject(s): Mystery; Middle Ages
Fictional character(s): Owen Archer, Veteran (soldier), Detective—Amateur; Lucie Walton, Spouse (of Owen)
Historical character(s): Geoffrey Chaucer, Spy, Writer
Time Period(s): 14th century (1365-1366)
Locale(s): Yorkshire, England

Summary: A young nun who dies of fever apparently is resurrected, but murder quickly follows her assertions of the miraculous. Archer looks into her claims and encounters a trail of corpses. A meeting with Geoffrey Chaucer, a spy for King Edward, uncovers connections with wide-ranging consequences.

Historical Accuracy: The novel is exact in its historical background and presents a plausible version of medieval life.

JENNIFER ROBERSON (1953-)

Born in Kansas City, Missouri, Roberson is a graduate of Northern Arizona University. She has worked as an investigative reporter and is a teacher of dog obedience, as well as an exhibitor of Labrador retrievers and Cardigan Welsh corgis. Roberson is the author of many science fiction and fantasy novels, including the Sword Dancer Saga and the Chronicle of Cheysuli series.

5368 *Lady of the Forest*

Date of Publication: 1992
Subject(s): Middle Ages; Romance; Myths and Legends
Fictional character(s): Robert of Locksley, Knight; Marian of Ravenskeep, Gentlewoman
Time Period(s): 13th century
Locale(s): Nottinghamshire, England; Sherwood Forest, England; Ravenskeer, England

Summary: This synthesis of the Robin Hood legend concentrates on the origin of the conflict that drives Robin to his career as outlaw and fugitive. Robert of Locksley returns from the Crusades to find life in Nottinghamshire changed dramatically during King Richard's two-year absence. The novel places the familiar characters and situations in the context of 13th-century conventions and customs.

Historical Accuracy: This is one of the more believable modern adaptations of the Robin Hood story, faithful to historical background and convincing psychologically.

5369 *Lady of the Glen*

Date of Publication: 1996
Subject(s): Romance; Glencoe Massacre; Jacobite Rebellion
Fictional character(s): Catriona Campbell, Young Woman; Alasdair Og MacDonald, Young Man
Time Period(s): 17th century (1680s-1690s)
Locale(s): Scotland

Summary: Set in the turmoil of 17th-century Scotland, the novel dramatizes a love story between Catriona Campbell and Alasdair Og MacDonald. They must overcome their families' feud and the threat of England's King William, who is intent on putting down the supporters of the Stuart claim to the throne.

Historical Accuracy: Most of the historical events described are real and many of characters actually lived.

ANN VICTORIA ROBERTS

5370 *Louisa Elliott*

Date of Publication: 1989

Subject(s): Victorian Period; Romance

Fictional character(s): Louisa Elliott, Bastard Daughter; Edward Elliott, Gentleman; Robert Duncannon, Gentleman

Time Period(s): 1890s (1892-1899)

Locale(s): England

Summary: This romantic novel set during the Victorian period involves heroine Louisa Elliott, who struggles against Victorian attitudes about her illegitimate birth. She is loved by her cousin Edward Elliott and by Robert Duncannon.

Historical Accuracy: The novel skillfully captures 19th-century Victorian attitudes.

5371 *Morning's Gate*

Date of Publication: 1991

Subject(s): World War I; Romance

Fictional character(s): Zoe Clifford, Artist; Steven Elliott, Sea Captain; Liam Elliott, Military Personnel (Australian soldier); Georgina Duncannon, Nurse

Time Period(s): 1990s; 1910s (1913-1917)

Locale(s): York, England; France; Australia

Summary: In this sequel to *Louisa Elliott*, Zoe Clifford and her cousin Stephen are researching their family's history. They discover their ancestor Liam Elliott's World War I romance with Georgina Duncannon, which is interrupted by action at Gallipoli and the Somme. Parallels between past and present abound.

Historical Accuracy: An Australian soldier's diary written in 1916 inspired the book.

CAREY ROBERTS (1935-)

REBECCA SEELY

Roberts was born in North Carolina and attended Agnes Scott College and Emory University. A lecturer in speed reading and time management, Roberts has always loved history and the sense of past lives. Seely was born in Pennsylvania and is a graduate of Pennsylvania State University and George Washington University. She has worked as an advertising executive.

5372 *Tidewater Dynasty: A Biographical Novel of the Lees of Stratford Hall*

Date of Publication: 1981

Subject(s): Biography, Fictionalized; American Revolution; American Colonies

Historical character(s): Francis Lightfoot Lee, Patriot, Political Figure; Henry Lee, Political Figure (Governor of Virginia); Richard Henry Lee, Political Figure, Patriot; John Adams, Political Figure; George Washington, Military Personnel (army commander), Political Figure

Time Period(s): 18th century; 19th century (1718-1810)

Locale(s): Tidewater, Virginia; Philadelphia, Pennsylvania

Summary: The novel offers a biographical history of the remarkable Lee family of Virginia. Stratford Hall, established in the 1720s on the Potomac, becomes the stronghold for three generations of Lees. Francis and Richard Henry Lee play central roles in the revolution, defiantly signing the Declaration of Independence, while Light-Horse Harry Lee becomes a war hero and major political figure in the life of the new nation.

Historical Accuracy: The period background and family history are solidly established and accurate.

CECIL ROBERTS (1892-1976)

A British journalist, literary editor, poet, and author, Roberts is best known for his historical travel books.

5373 *The Remarkable Young Man*

Date of Publication: 1954

Subject(s): Artistic Life; Literary Life

Historical character(s): Joseph Severin, Artist (painter); John Keats, Writer (poet)

Time Period(s): 1820s

Locale(s): Rome, Italy

Summary: The novel dramatizes the friendship between English painter Joseph Severin and poet John Keats. They journey together to Rome, where Keats succumbs to tuberculosis at the age of 25 in 1821.

Historical Accuracy: The novel is authoritative and convincing in depicting Rome of the period as well as the literary atmosphere.

CYNTHIA S. ROBERTS

Born in Wales, Roberts worked as a teacher, journalist, and broadcaster before becoming a writer. She is a member of the Welsh Academy.

5374 *The Fox-Red Hills*

Date of Publication: 1991

Subject(s): Victorian Period

Fictional character(s): Carne Harvard, Orphan; Mostyn Harvard, Orphan; Penry Vaughan, Religious (clergyman)

Time Period(s): 19th century (Victorian period)

Locale(s): Wales

Summary: This is the story of two brothers who are orphaned when their father, distraught over the death of his wife, kills himself. Carne and Mostyn Harvard are left penniless, and their home, Great House, is sold to pay the family debts. The novel chronicles the boys' growth to manhood fueled by their determination to reclaim Great House and their inheritance.

Historical Accuracy: The period elements are convincingly drawn.

DOROTHY JAMES ROBERTS (1903-1990)

REBECCA SEELY (1935-)

Born in West Virginia, Roberts is a graduate of Barnard College. She is known for her historical romances and interpretations of Arthurian legends as well as contemporary novels like *Durable Fire* and *Mountain Journey*. Seely was born in Pennsylvania and is a graduate of Pennsylvania State University.

5375 *Fire in the Ice*

Date of Publication: 1961
Subject(s): Middle Ages
Fictional character(s): Hallgerda Hoskuldsdaughter, Heroine; Gunnar, Chieftain
Time Period(s): 10th century
Locale(s): Iceland

Summary: Life in 10th-century Iceland is dramatized in this story of Hallgerda, whose struggle for power brings her three husbands. The last of them, Gunnar of the Lord Isles, proves to be her match.

Historical Accuracy: The novel is loosely based on two Icelandic sagas and features a credible picture of daily routine in medieval Iceland.

DOROTHY JAMES ROBERTS (1903-1990)

An American writer born in West Virginia, Roberts graduated from Barnard College. She is best known for her historical romances embued with the Arthurian legend. Roberts also wrote a mystery novel, *If a Body Kill a Body*, in 1946 under the pseudonym Peter Mortimer.

5376 *Kinsmen of the Grail*

Date of Publication: 1963
Subject(s): Middle Ages; Myths and Legends; Arthurian Legends
Fictional character(s): Arthur, Ruler (King of the Britons); Sir Perceval, Knight; Sir Gawin, Knight
Time Period(s): 12th century
Locale(s): Wales

Summary: Roberts sets the Arthurian legend in 12th-century Wales and focuses on two questing knights, Sir Perceval and Sir Gawin. Gawin is torn between his duty to King Arthur and his desire to locate the Holy Grail. His experiences contrast with those of the young and spiritual Perceval.

Historical Accuracy: The novel finds a realistic basis for its mythic elements in a careful rendering of the 12th century landscape and atmosphere.

5377 *Return of the Stranger*

Date of Publication: 1958

Subject(s): Myths and Legends; Dark Ages
Fictional character(s): Etain, Young Woman
Time Period(s): Indeterminate Past
Locale(s): Ireland

Summary: This legend of pagan Ireland tells the story of Etain, a young woman of unknown origin. Adopted by a farmer, she is courted but determined to become a bride of the high king of Ireland and mistress of the Seat of Kings at Tara. The novel dramatizes how Etain discovers her identity and achieves her destiny.

Historical Accuracy: More make believe than historical, the novel does provide a convincing atmosphere of pagan Ireland.

ELIZABETH MADOX ROBERTS
(1886-1941)

An American poet and novelist, Roberts was raised in the Kentucky farming region that she described in her work. Her re-creation of folk customs and speech is notable in such works as *Jingling in the Wind*, *A Buried Treasure*, and *He Sent Forth a Raven*.

5378 *The Great Meadow*

Date of Publication: 1930
Subject(s): Settlement of the American Frontier; American Revolution; Indians
Fictional character(s): Diony Jarvis, Farmer; Berk Jarvis, Farmer, Military Personnel; Evan Muir, Farmer
Time Period(s): 1770s; 1780s (1775-1783)
Locale(s): Virginia (western); Harrodsburg, Kentucky

Summary: The daily concerns of a pioneer woman form the central drama of this novel of life in the Kentucky wilderness during the Revolution. Diony marries Berk Jarvis and accompanies him across the Appalachian Trail. They endure an Indian attack, and Berk, who sets out with a party to aid George Rogers Clark in fighting the British, is taken by the Indians and believed dead. Diony marries another man only to find that Berk has survived. She then must decide whom to recognize as her true husband.

Historical Accuracy: The novel provides an excellent treatment of ordinary life on the frontier, rendered poetically through the thoughts of the central character.

JOHN MADDOX ROBERTS

5379 *The Catiline Conspiracy*

Date of Publication: 1991
Subject(s): Mystery; Roman Empire
Fictional character(s): Decius Caecilius Metellus, Nobleman, Detective—Amateur
Historical character(s): Marcus Tullius Cicero, Political Figure, Philosopher; Lucius Sergius Catilina, Nobleman
Time Period(s): 1st century B.C. (70 B.C.)
Locale(s): Rome, Roman Empire

Summary: Amidst great foreign triumphs for the Roman Republic there is internal dissent. High-born civil servant and amateur detective Decius Metellus is convinced that a conspiracy is afoot bent on overthrowing the government. The cost of cracking the cabal is murder.

Historical Accuracy: The historical elements are authentic and convincing, as are the details of ordinary life during the period.

5380 *The Sacrilege*

Date of Publication: 1992
Subject(s): Mystery; Roman Empire
Fictional character(s): Decius Caecilius Metellus, Nobleman, Detective—Amateur
Historical character(s): Julius Caesar, Military Personnel (Roman commander), Political Figure; Pompeia, Spouse (of Caesar)
Time Period(s): 1st century B.C. (70 B.C.)
Locale(s): Rome, Roman Empire

Summary: During the reign of Julius Caesar, a religious rite overseen by Pompeia, Caesar's wife, is disrupted by a patrician dressed in female garb. Decius Metellus, a fledgling senator and amateur detective, sees a connection between this sacrilege and four bizarre murders that follow. His investigation takes him from the lowest depths of the Roman underworld to the highest reaches of the Roman elite.

Historical Accuracy: The novel is convincing in re-creating both high and low life of the period.

5381 *SPQR*

Date of Publication: 1990
Subject(s): Mystery; Roman Empire
Fictional character(s): Decius Caecilius Metellus, Nobleman, Detective—Amateur
Historical character(s): Julius Caesar, Military Personnel (Roman commander), Political Figure
Time Period(s): 1st century B.C. (70 B.C.)
Locale(s): Rome, Roman Empire

Summary: Set in the 1st century B.C. during the turbulent days at the end of the Roman Republic, this is the first mystery featuring a patrician amateur detective, Decius Metellus, who investigates the garroting of an ex-slave and the disembowelment of a foreign merchant. The crimes lead to the uncovering of official corruption at the highest levels of government.

Historical Accuracy: The period is constructed with evident expertise.

5382 *The Temple of the Muses*

Date of Publication: 1992
Subject(s): Mystery; Roman Empire; Ancient Egypt
Fictional character(s): Decius Caecilius Metellus, Detective—Amateur, Nobleman; Metellus Creticus, Diplomat
Time Period(s): 1st century B.C.
Locale(s): Alexandria, Egypt

Summary: While on a diplomatic mission to Alexandria, Decius Metellus investigates the suspicious death of a philosopher at the insistence of the Egyptian pharaoh. When the corpse of a murdered courtesan turns up in Metellus' bed, he

finds himself at the center of a conspiracy that could topple the Empire.

Historical Accuracy: The period background is authentic and realistic delivered.

KENNETH ROBERTS (1885-1957)

Roberts was born in Maine, the setting for many of his novels. He served as an army captain in the intelligence section from 1918 to 1919. After working as a correspondent for the *Saturday Evening Post* from 1919 to 1928, he left journalism to write historical fiction. Meticulous research distinguishes his historical novels.

5383 *Arundel*

Date of Publication: 1930
Subject(s): American Revolution
Fictional character(s): Steven Nason, Military Personnel (colonial soldier); Phoebe Marvin, Young Woman
Historical character(s): Benedict Arnold, Military Personnel (general); Henri de Sabreuois, Nobleman (marquis)
Time Period(s): 1770s (1775)
Locale(s): Arundel, Maine; Quebec, Quebec, Canada; Abenaki Country, Maine

Summary: Narrated by Benedict Arnold's chief of staff, this is the story of the march led by Arnold in 1775 northward through the Maine wilderness to Quebec. Arnold puts together an army of untrained colonials and conducts one of the most difficult and dangerous military campaigns of the war.

Historical Accuracy: The basis for the novel's adventures is historical, though the specifics are largely imagined.

5384 *Boon Island*

Date of Publication: 1956
Subject(s): Sea Story
Fictional character(s): Neal Butler, Sailor, Actor; John Dean, Sea Captain; Christopher Langman, Sailor (first mate)
Time Period(s): 1710s (1710-1711)
Locale(s): Greenwich, England; Portsmouth, New Hampshire, American Colonies; Boon Island, New Hampshire, American Colonies

Summary: Fourteen men are shipwrecked for 24 days on an island of sheer rock off the coast of New Hampshire in 1710. Desperate to survive, the sailors and passengers resort to cannibalism. They also begin to represent moral types in terms of their response to adversity.

Historical Accuracy: This gripping and realistic story is authentic in terms of its psychological insights and period elements.

5385 *Captain Caution*

Date of Publication: 1934
Subject(s): Sea Story; War of 1812; Slavery
Fictional character(s): Daniel Marvin, Sailor; Corunna Dorman, Young Woman; Lurman Slade, Sea Captain
Time Period(s): 1810s
Locale(s): England; France; At Sea

Summary: During the War of 1812, young Maine merchant seaman Daniel Marvin is forced to serve on a British warship. Marvin fights to retake the ship from his captors, escapes to France, and has a climactic confrontation with enemy Lurman Slade, captain of an American slave-brig.

Historical Accuracy: The novel's period elements are authentic.

5386 *The Lively Lady*

Date of Publication: 1931
Subject(s): War of 1812; Sea Story
Fictional character(s): Richard Nason, Sea Captain, Prisoner; King Dick, Prisoner
Time Period(s): 1810s (1812)
Locale(s): *Lively Lady*, At Sea; Dartmoor, England

Summary: This sea adventure, set during the War of 1812, describes the lot of American privateers. Richard Nason, a young American sea captain, is captured and imprisoned in notorious Dartmoor, where survival becomes a test of determination and character.

Historical Accuracy: The period elements are convincingly described.

5387 *Lydia Bailey*

Date of Publication: 1947
Subject(s): Independence—Haiti; Tripolitan War
Fictional character(s): Lydia Bailey, Gentlewoman; Albion Hamlin, Lawyer
Historical character(s): Tobias Lear, Political Figure; William Eaton, Military Personnel (general); Henri Christophe, Revolutionary, Slave; Jean-Jacques Dessalines, Slave, Ruler (of Haiti); Pierre Dominique Toussaint l'Ouverture, Revolutionary, Slave
Time Period(s): 1800s (1800-1805)
Locale(s): United States; Haiti; Africa

Summary: This tale of adventure covers a wide range of places and events, including the controversy over the Alien and Sedition Laws in the United States, the Haitian rebellion, battles with the Barbary pirates, and the treachery of American politician Tobias Lear. Narrator Albion Hamlin is a young Maine lawyer who falls in love with Lydia Bailey through her portrait. They meet in Haiti and eventually move to Northern Africa.

Historical Accuracy: Despite the novel's range, its details are carefully authentic, particularly the scene in Haiti. Roberts' interpretation of Tobias Lear is defensible, but open to question.

5388 *Northwest Passage*

Date of Publication: 1936
Subject(s): American Colonies; French and Indian War; Indians
Fictional character(s): Langdon Towne, Artist, Military Personnel (soldier)
Historical character(s): Robert Rogers, Frontiersman, Military Personnel (major)
Time Period(s): 1750s (1759)
Locale(s): St. Francis, Quebec, Canada; American Colonies (northeast)

Summary: This tale of the French and Indian Wars describes the experiences of Harvard-educated artist Langdon Towne, who joins Rogers' Rangers. Major Rogers drives his men mercilessly in the overland march to attack St. Francis.

Historical Accuracy: Period details are credible and believable in this classic frontier adventure.

5389 *Oliver Wiswell*

Date of Publication: 1940
Subject(s): American Revolution; Battle of Long Island; Battle of Bunker Hill
Fictional character(s): Oliver Wiswell, Loyalist, Military Personnel (British officer); Thomas Buell, Loyalist, Military Personnel
Historical character(s): William Howe, Military Personnel (British commander); Benedict Arnold, Military Personnel (general); Henry Clinton, Military Personnel (general)
Time Period(s): 1770s; 1780s
Locale(s): Boston, Massachusetts; New York, New York; Paris, France

Summary: The Loyalist side of the American Revolution is described sympathetically, through the experiences of Oliver Wiswell and his friend Thomas Buell. The revolution is seen not as a conflict between the English and the Americans, but as a true civil war over conflicting ideals and principles.

Historical Accuracy: The novel's sympathetic treatment of the Loyalist side is original, while its framework of events is historically accurate.

5390 *Rabble in Arms*

Date of Publication: 1933
Subject(s): American Revolution; Battle of Saratoga
Fictional character(s): Cap Huff, Military Personnel (soldier); Steven Nason, Military Personnel (soldier)
Historical character(s): Benedict Arnold, Military Personnel (general); Horatio Gates, Military Personnel (general)
Time Period(s): 1770s (1775-1777)
Locale(s): Quebec, Quebec, Canada; Lake Champlain, New York; Saratoga, New York

Summary: This sequel to *Arundel* continues the story of Benedict Arnold's Northern Army. It describes the disastrous retreat from Quebec, the building of the first American navy, and the climactic defeat of General Burgoyne at Saratoga. Arnold emerges as a genuine hero, despite his later betrayal.

Historical Accuracy: The story's framework is historical.

RICHARD EMERY ROBERTS (1903-)

Roberts' books include *Star in the West*.

5391 *The Gilded Rooster*

Date of Publication: 1947
Subject(s): American West; Indians
Fictional character(s): Jed Cooper, Mountain Man
Time Period(s): 1860s (1863)

Locale(s): Wyoming

Summary: Action against the Sioux in an unfinished fort in Wyoming territory is featured in this western novel. Jed Cooper, one of the last of the mountain men, and known as ''The Gilded Rooster,'' is on hand to lend his expertise in the conflict.

Historical Accuracy: The background elements are accurately presented.

WALTER ADOLPHE ROBERTS
(1886-1962)

A Jamaican novelist, poet, and historian, Roberts is the author of such books as *The Caribbean: The Story of Our Sea of Destiny, Jamaica: The Portrait of an Island,* and *Havana: The Portrait of a City.*

5392 *Creole Dusk*

Date of Publication: 1948

Subject(s): Canal Building; Medical Profession; Panama Canal

Fictional character(s): Yvon Olivier, Doctor; Dora Boothby, Gentlewoman; Rachele Capello, Singer (opera)

Time Period(s): 1880s

Locale(s): New Orleans, Louisiana; Jamaica; Panama

Summary: The novel continues Roberts' study of New Orleans Creole society begun in *Royal Street.* Young doctor Yvon Olivier journeys to Panama where he deals with disease and revolution connected to the building of the Panama Canal. The story dramatizes Louisiana politics and the gradual integration of the Creoles into the larger life of New Orleans and the state.

Historical Accuracy: The novel is authentic in its portrait of the period and the region.

5393 *Royal Street*

Date of Publication: 1944

Subject(s): Antebellum South

Fictional character(s): Victor Olivier, Gentleman; Cherie Lamott, Gentlewoman

Time Period(s): 1840s

Locale(s): New Orleans, Louisiana

Summary: Life in Creole New Orleans during the 1840s forms the background for this novel that attempts to capture the conflicts leading to the Civil War in the struggle between the Creoles and Northern business interests. The central characters are Victor Olivier, the son of a wealthy Creole exporter, and Cherie Lamott, the daughter of an aristocratic family.

Historical Accuracy: The novel features an authentic look at the period and the region.

5394 *The Single Star*

Date of Publication: 1949

Subject(s): Independence—Cuba; Spanish Colonies; Spanish-American War

Fictional character(s): Stephen Lloyd, Revolutionary

Historical character(s): Theodore Roosevelt, Military Personnel; Calixto Garcia y Inigues, Revolutionary; Jose Miguel Gomez, Revolutionary, Political Figure

Time Period(s): 1890s

Locale(s): Cuba

Summary: This tale of the Cuban revolution and the American invasion during the Spanish-American War is seen through the experiences of Stephen Lloyd, a Jamaican descendent of a Confederate family. He joins the rebels and lives with them until the surrender of Santiago and the end of the war.

Historical Accuracy: The novel's history is accurately presented, avoiding the sensational or partisanship on behalf of the Americans who are presented as being as insensitive to the Cubans as the Spanish.

CONSTANCE ROBERTSON (1896-1985)

Canadian-born author Constance Robertson attended the University of Wisconsin. She was the author of short stories, poetry, and historical novels, taking a particular interest in the history of New York. She published three ''autobiographies'' of the Oneida Community, which was founded by her grandfather. Her novels include *The Unterrified, The Golden Circle, Six Weeks in March,* and *Go and Catch a Falling Star.*

5395 *Fire Bell in the Night*

Date of Publication: 1944

Subject(s): Slavery; Underground Railroad; Abolition Movement

Fictional character(s): Mahalia North, Young Woman; Dallas Ord, Abolitionist; John Palfrey, Young Man

Time Period(s): 1850s

Locale(s): Syracuse, New York

Summary: The abolitionist movement and the workings of the underground railroad are the concerns of this novel set in Syracuse, New York, during the 1850s. The heroine, Mahalia North, finds herself torn between two lovers, Dallas Ord, a prominent abolitionist leader, and John Palfrey, an opponent of the movement.

Historical Accuracy: The novel offers an accurate account of the period.

5396 *The Golden Circle*

Date of Publication: 1951

Subject(s): Civil War—U.S.; Copperhead Movement; Espionage

Fictional character(s): Zachary Granger, Spy; Gina Deyo, Young Woman; Asa Ormerod, Revolutionary (conspirator)

Historical character(s): Clement Vallandigham, Political Figure; John Hunt Morgan, Military Personnel (Confederate general)

Time Period(s): 1860s (1863)

Locale(s): Ohio

Summary: The background of this Civil War novel is the Copperhead Movement in Ohio, northerners opposed to the Union cause. Zachary Granger is a Union espionage agent charged with infiltrating the conspirators' Golden Circle as they plot to form the Northwest Confederacy and attempt to elect Copperhead Clement Vallandigham governor of Ohio.

Historical Accuracy: The framework of the story is authentic, interweaving the fictional and the factual.

5397 *The Unterrified*

Date of Publication: 1946
Subject(s): Civil War—U.S.; Copperhead Movement; Espionage
Fictional character(s): Ranyard King, Spy
Historical character(s): Clement Vallandigham, Political Figure; Horatio Seymour, Political Figure
Time Period(s): 1860s (1863)
Locale(s): New York

Summary: The homefront battles during the Civil War are dramatized in the Copperhead Movement of New York. The son of a senator, Ranyard King takes up spying for the South. The novel offers a look at Copperhead leader Vallandigham and the New York draft riots.

Historical Accuracy: The fictional story is connected to actual figures and events of the period.

DON ROBERTSON (1929-)

Born in Cleveland, Robertson attended Harvard and Western Reserve universities. He has worked for the *Cleveland News* and Cleveland *Plain Dealer* as a sports and police reporter. Robertson is well-known for his historical novels and his trilogy on Morris Bird III.

5398 *By Antietam Creek*

Date of Publication: 1960
Subject(s): Civil War—U.S.; Battle of Antietam
Fictional character(s): Omar Tipton, Military Personnel (Confederate soldier); Sam Leonard, Military Personnel (Union officer); Elizabeth Platt, Widow(er)
Time Period(s): 1860s (1862)
Locale(s): Maryland

Summary: This novel chronicles the bloodiest battle in the history of America. As in *The Three Days*, the emphasis is not on battle strategies but on the experiences of ordinary soldiers and civilians caught up in the turmoil and test of battle.

Historical Accuracy: The novel accurately captures both the actual tactics and the real experiences of the combatants.

5399 *Paradise Falls*

Date of Publication: 1968
Subject(s): Reconstruction Period; Business Building
Fictional character(s): C.P. Wells, Businessman; Irene Hollingshead, Businesswoman, Madam; Ike Underwood, Banker, Publisher
Time Period(s): 19th century; 20th century (1865-1900)
Locale(s): Paradise Falls, Ohio

Summary: This social chronicle of the fictional Ohio community of Paradise Falls recounts 35 years of town history from the conclusion of the Civil War to the dawn of the 20th

century. A huge cast dramatizes the emergence of the modern American nation.

Historical Accuracy: The details of regional and period life are convincing and authentic.

5400 *Prisoner of Twilight*

Date of Publication: 1984
Subject(s): Civil War—U.S.
Fictional character(s): Jasper Tidwell, Military Personnel (Confederate soldier); Sergeant Patterson, Military Personnel (Confederate soldier); John T. Clewellyn, Military Personnel (Confederate soldier)
Time Period(s): 1860s (1865)
Locale(s): Richmond, Virginia

Summary: It is April 1865, and a ragged group of Confederate soldiers comes together near Richmond, Virginia, trying to comprehend defeat. Each chapter offers the perspective of a different character who reveals himself as the story moves towards its inevitable violent climax.

Historical Accuracy: The story is imagined, but it is an authentic look at the conclusion of the war from the perspective of the defeated Confederacy.

5401 *The River and the Wilderness*

Date of Publication: 1962
Subject(s): Civil War—U.S.; Battle of Antietam; Battle of Fredericksburg
Fictional character(s): George Peters, Actor, Military Personnel (Union major); Martin Slocum, Farmer, Military Personnel (Confederate soldier); Henrietta Blackstone, Actress
Historical character(s): Thomas Jonathan Jackson, Military Personnel (Confederate general)
Time Period(s): 1860s (1862)
Locale(s): Virginia

Summary: This massive Civil War novel details the events of 1862 and includes action at the battles of Antietam, Fredericksburg, and Chancellorsville. The events are depicted through the experiences of combatants on both sides of the conflict, offering a panoramic cross section of military history.

Historical Accuracy: The framework of the story is accurate and based on actual events.

5402 *The Three Days*

Date of Publication: 1959
Subject(s): Civil War—U.S.; Battle of Gettysburg
Fictional character(s): Alf J. Castetter, Military Personnel (Union officer); Rufus Patterson, Military Personnel (Confederate soldier); Leon Marshall Strong, Military Personnel (Union sergeant)
Time Period(s): 1860s (1863)
Locale(s): Gettysburg, Pennsylvania

Summary: The title refers to the Battle of Gettysburg in July 1863 that decided the Civil War. The novel focuses on several combatants on both sides who play varying roles in the conflict. The emphasis is not on the strategy or the generals but the lot of the ordinary soldiers.

Historical Accuracy: The novel captures the action at Gettysburg from the realistic vantage point of ordinary combatants.

DEREK ROBINSON (1932-)

Born in Bristol, England, Robinson served in the RAF, then graduated from Cambridge with a degree in modern history. He worked in advertising in London and New York until 1966 when he became a full-time writer and broadcaster. His *Goshawk Square* was the runner-up for the Booker Prize in 1971.

5403 *Goshawk Squadron*

Date of Publication: 1972
Subject(s): World War I; Aviation
Fictional character(s): Stanley Woolley, Military Personnel (major)
Time Period(s): 1910s (1918)
Locale(s): France

Summary: Aerial combat during World War I is often idealized in contrast to the unglamorous trench war fare. Here, however, the air war receives realistic teatment, as Major Woolley, a cynical commander, and his small squadron are pressed into service as meaningless and as deadly as the war in the trenches.

Historical Accuracy: The novel features authentic details about flying during the period and a hard-boiled, though realistic, treatment of combat.

5404 *War Story: A Novel*

Date of Publication: 1987
Subject(s): Aviation; World War I; Battle of the Somme
Fictional character(s): Oliver Paxton, Military Personnel, Pilot
Time Period(s): 1910s (1916)
Locale(s): England; France

Summary: Young Oliver Paxton, fresh from public school and on his first solo flight, leads a convoy of biplanes across the Channel to the World War I battlefront. The five-hour flight takes five days, and every plane is lost. This misadventure is followed by his participation in the catastrophic Battle of the Somme.

Historical Accuracy: The novel is fiction built on a framework of fact. Technical details of the airwar are authentic and based on evident research.

KATHLEEN ROBINSON
(PSEUD. OF CHAILLE HOWARD ROBINSON, 1948-)

Born in San Jose, California, Robinson graduated from the University of California, Berkeley. She has worked at several administrative positions, authored several teleplays and treatments for television dramas, and written two novels, *Dominic* and *Heaven's Only Gift*.

5405 *Dominic*

Date of Publication: 1991
Subject(s): Roman Empire; Picaresque Adventure

Fictional character(s): Dominic Dio, Orphan, Entertainer; Kevin Dunkaldir, Singer
Time Period(s): 4th century (397)
Locale(s): Rome, Roman Empire; Gaul; Alexandria, Egypt

Summary: Set during the collapse of the Roman Empire, this picaresque adventure traces the journey of Dominic Dio, an orphaned dwarf from Gaul who travels with a circus troupe and is befriended by Danish singer Kevin Dunkaldir. Their adventures take them from Rome to Alexandria to Constantinople.

Historical Accuracy: The period elements are convincingly detailed.

5406 *Heaven's Only Daughter*

Date of Publication: 1993
Subject(s): Roman Empire
Fictional character(s): Galla Placidia, Royalty (princess); Atawulf, Warrior (Goth)
Time Period(s): 5th century
Locale(s): Rome, Roman Empire

Summary: When Rome falls to the Gauls in the fifth century, Imperial Princess Placidia finds herself the prisoner of Atawulf. They are complete opposites who attract, and the novel tells the story of their unusual relationship and the clash of culture it represents.

Historical Accuracy: The author makes it clear that all of the events and characters in this novel are entirely fictitious.

LYNDA S. ROBINSON

American mystery novelist Robinson has a Ph.D. in anthropology concentrating on archaeology from the University of Texas. She is an accomplished romance writer under the name of Suzanne Robinson.

5407 *Murder at the Feast of Rejoicing*

Date of Publication: 1996
Subject(s): Mystery; Ancient Egypt; Pharaohs
Fictional character(s): Lord Meren, Nobleman, Government Official
Historical character(s): Tutankhamen, Ruler (Egyptian pharaoh)
Time Period(s): 14th century B.C.
Locale(s): Nile Valley, Egypt

Summary: Lord Meren, the eyes and ears of Pharaoh Tutankhamun, is charged with transporting the remains and treasures of Akhenaton and Nefertiti to protect them from disgruntled priests. At a feast at his home, two of his guests are found murdered and his secret mission is compromised. Meren must investigate the crime for which one of his relatives or guests might be responsible. The solution is wrapped up in the court intrigues of the time.

Historical Accuracy: In recreating the world of Tutankhamun, the author has opted for interpretations that seem the most logical and probable or that best fit with the fictional circumstances.

`5408` *Murder at the God's Gate*

Date of Publication: 1995
Subject(s): Mystery; Pharaohs; Ancient Egypt
Fictional character(s): Lord Meren, Nobleman, Government Official; Kysen, Companion (son of Meren)
Historical character(s): Tutankhamum, Ruler (Egyptian pharaoh)
Time Period(s): 14th century B.C.
Locale(s): Egypt

Summary: The 14-year-old Pharaoh Tutenkhamum is beset by the Hittites abroad and the priests at home, who are angry at Akhenaten for trying to end their control. Lord Meren, the pharaoh's confidential agent, uncovers unrest and threats to Tut's life. When one of his spies is killed at the temple at Thebes, danger escalates.

Historical Accuracy: Like its predecessor, *Murder in the Place of Anubis*, this novel features a closely drawn picture of domestic, political, and religious life in early Egypt.

`5409` *Murder in the Place of Anubis*

Date of Publication: 1994
Subject(s): Mystery; Ancient Egypt; Pharaohs
Fictional character(s): Lord Meren, Nobleman, Government Official
Historical character(s): Tutankhamen, Ruler (Egyptian pharaoh); Akhenaton, Ruler (Egyptian pharaoh)
Time Period(s): 14th century B.C.
Locale(s): Thebes, Egypt

Summary: In the fifth year of the Pharaoh Tutenkhamum's reign one body too many is discovered by the embalmer priests at Thebes. Lord Meren, confidant of the pharaoh, investigates and must prevent the priestly class from using the incident to undermine Tutankhamum's authority.

Historical Accuracy: The atmosphere and details of court life are fully described and add much to the enjoyment of this unusual murder mystery.

MARGARET A. ROBINSON (1937-)

Born in Connecticut, Robinson graduated from the University of Vermont and the University of Wisconsin. She is a teacher of English. Her book *Arrivals and Departures* was inspired by her husband bringing home a stray dog.

`5410` *Courting Emma Howe*

Date of Publication: 1987
Subject(s): Rural Life—U.S.; Homesteading
Fictional character(s): Emma Howe, Spinster; Arthur Smollett, Settler
Time Period(s): 1900s (1905)
Locale(s): North Falls, Washington

Summary: Emma Howe travels from Vermont to Washington's North Falls to marry Arthur Smollett, whom she knows only through his letters. They each must adjust to the reality of homesteading life.

Historical Accuracy: The period and regional elements are authentically depicted.

RONY ROBINSON (1944-)

English writer Robinson is a graduate of Oxford University and has worked as an announcer on a local radio program.

`5411` *The Beano*

Date of Publication: 1988
Subject(s): World War I
Fictional character(s): Mr. Owen, Artist; Miss Tidmarsh, Worker
Time Period(s): 1910s (1914)
Locale(s): Scarborough, England

Summary: Ten days before the outbreak of World War I, the members of Britlings Imperial XXX Brewery embark on the Beano, their annual July seaside outing. This year the excursion is to Scarborough, where a number of characters flirt with each other, imbibe, and listen to the Spa Orchestra, dramatizing ordinary life on the brink of change ushered in by the war.

Historical Accuracy: The novel is clever and insightful in depicting life in a particular time and place.

SUZANNE ROBINSON (1951-)

Robinson has a Ph.D. in anthropology with a specialty in Middle Eastern archaeology.

`5412` *Lady Defiant*

Date of Publication: 1992
Subject(s): Elizabethan Period; Romance; Treasure Hunt
Fictional character(s): Oriel Richmond, Gentlewoman, Heiress; Blade Fitzstephen, Spy
Time Period(s): 16th century (1564-1565)
Locale(s): England (northern); Loire Valley, France

Summary: Set during the Elizabethan Period, this romance features court intrigue, mystery, and a treasure hunt, as well as passion between heiress Oriel Richmond and one of Queen Elizabeth's spies, the roguish Blade Fitzstephen. He is sent to seduce Oriel to extract an important secret. Circumstances send them to France to stop a conspiracy aimed at the throne of England.

Historical Accuracy: The story is fanciful, but filled with period atmosphere.

`5413` *Lady Gallant*

Date of Publication: 1992
Subject(s): Elizabethan Period; Romance; Espionage
Fictional character(s): Eleanora Becket, Noblewoman, Spy; Christian de River, Nobleman, Spy
Time Period(s): 16th century (1558)
Locale(s): England

Summary: This is a story of intrigue surrounding Queen Elizabeth I's succession to the throne. Eleanora Becket and Christian de River are both secret agents, unknowingly working on the same side in support of Elizabeth's claim. Differences lead to romance as they begin to trust one another, joining forces to deal with threats.

Historical Accuracy: The novel offers an ingenious adventure story with some authentic period details.

5414 *Lady Hellfire*

Date of Publication: 1992
Subject(s): Victorian Period; Romance
Fictional character(s): Katherine Grey, Heiress; Alexis de Granville, Nobleman (Marquess of Richfield), Rake
Time Period(s): 1850s (1854-1855)
Locale(s): England

Summary: Romance blossoms between an outspoken American heiress, Katherine Grey, and the Marquess of Richfield, Lord Alexis de Granville. For the Marquess women are little more than idle playthings, but Katherine forces him to reconsider.

Historical Accuracy: The period is suggested with some authentic details.

LUCIA ST. CLAIR ROBSON (1942-)

Born in Baltimore, Maryland, Robson completed graduate work at Florida State University. She served in the Peace Corps and taught in the Brooklyn Public Schools. She is the author of several novles about the West, including *Ride the Wind*, *Walk in My Soul*, and *Mary's Land*.

5415 *Mary's Land*

Date of Publication: 1995
Subject(s): American Colonies
Fictional character(s): Margaret Brent, Plantation Owner; Sparrow Anicah, Servant (indentured)
Time Period(s): 17th century (1638-1648)
Locale(s): Maryland, American Colonies

Summary: The novel is set in the early days of Maryland. It depicts the experiences of two women: Margaret Brent, who desires to practice her Catholic faith openly, and Sparrow Anicah, a teenage street urchin who comes to America as an indentured servant.

Historical Accuracy: Meticulously researched, the novel offers a convincing look at colonial times and customs.

5416 *Ride the Wind*

Date of Publication: 1982
Subject(s): American West; Indians
Historical character(s): Cynthia Ann Parker, Captive; Quanah Parker, Indian (Comanche), Chieftain
Time Period(s): 19th century; 20th century
Locale(s): Southwest

Summary: This is the story of Cynthia Ann Parker who is kidnapped by the Comanches in 1836. She eventually marries a Comanche and bears a son who becomes one of the tribe's greatest chiefs, Quanah Parker. The novel tells Cynthia's story from her kidnapping to her death, along with the fate of Quanah and the Comanches.

Historical Accuracy: The basic framework of the story is factual, enhanced by some imaginary events.

5417 *The Tokaido Road: A Novel of Feudal Japan*

Date of Publication: 1991
Subject(s): Japanese Empire; Samurai
Fictional character(s): Lady Asano, Noblewoman (aka Cat); Tosano Hanshiro, Warrior (ronin); Kasane, Companion (of Cat), Worker (peasant)
Time Period(s): 1700s (1702)
Locale(s): Japan

Summary: This tale, set during the years of the fifth Tokugawa shogun, is the story of Lady Asano. After the forced suicide of her father, she vows to avenge his death and restore her family's honor. To do so, she sets out with a peasant companion on a dangerous 300-mile journey to Kyoto in search of the leader of the samurai of the Asano clan. The novel details her adventures along the way.

Historical Accuracy: The novel is exact and convincing in capturing the customs and details of the period. The factual basis for the story is indicated in the author's notes.

5418 *Walk in My Soul*

Date of Publication: 1985
Subject(s): Indians; Tribal Life—Native American; Settlement of the American Frontier
Historical character(s): Tiana Rogers, Indian (Cherokee), Religious (priestess); Sam Houston, Frontiersman
Time Period(s): 19th century (1809-1830s)
Locale(s): Hiwassee River, Tennessee; Arkansas; Cherokee Nation, Oklahoma

Summary: Life among the Cherokees in the early years of the 19th century is described in this story of young Tiana, priestess, warrior, healer, and teacher. Her story involves a relationship with the young Sam Houston, who runs away from his family's general store in Tennessee to live among the Cherokees. Conflicts develop as Houston prepares to face his destiny, which is at odds with the Indians he has come to admire.

Historical Accuracy: The story is largely an invention, with a convincing evocation of the period, region, and Indian customs.

PHILLIP ROCK (1927-)

Born in Hollywood, California, Rock moved to England with his family at age seven. He is a novelist and screenwriter.

5419 *Flickers*

Date of Publication: 1977
Subject(s): Motion Picture Industry
Fictional character(s): Earl P. Donovan, Businessman
Time Period(s): 1920s
Locale(s): Hollywood, California

Summary: Earl P. Donovan, now in his eighties, looks back on the world of Hollywood in the 1920s. Donovan, a confidence man and a huckster, captures the departed era of the first great flowering of the movie business.

Historical Accuracy: The period elements of early Hollywood are authentic and convincing.

5420 *A Future Arrived*

Date of Publication: 1985
Subject(s): World War II
Fictional character(s): Derek Ramsey, Gentleman; Martin Rilke, Gentleman, Writer; Jennifer Wood-Lacy, Young Woman; Victoria Wood-Lacy, Young Woman
Time Period(s): 1930s; 1940s (1930-1940)
Locale(s): England; Berlin, Germany

Summary: The generation that came of age in the 1930s is the subject of this saga that connects a number of characters centered around an aristocratic English family. They are the post-World War I generation who watch the new war approach.

Historical Accuracy: The novel captures post-World War I England with convincing details.

5421 *The Passing Bells*

Date of Publication: 1978
Subject(s): World War I; Servants
Fictional character(s): Anthony Greville, Nobleman (Earl of Stonemore); Charles Greville, Military Personnel (soldier), Gentleman; Martin Rilke, Gentleman, Journalist
Time Period(s): 1910s; 1920s (1914-1920)
Locale(s): London, England; Gallipoli, Turkey; France

Summary: World War I changes the aristocratic Greville family as barriers between the classes come down and values are questioned.

Historical Accuracy: The novel features a convincing look at the wartime atmosphere and a faithful reflection of the actual events.

CLAUDE HENRI ROCQUET

A French professor of aesthetics and art history at the Ecole Nationale Superieure des Arts Decoratifs in Paris, Rocquet has published widely on art, literature, and the theater.

5422 *Bruegel, or, The Workshop of Dreams*

Date of Publication: 1991
Subject(s): Biography, Fictionalized; Artistic Life
Historical character(s): Pieter Brueghel, Artist
Time Period(s): 16th century (1525-1569)
Locale(s): Antwerp, Belgium; Netherlands

Summary: The novel provides a portrait of the Flemish painter Pieter Brueghel. The story mixes historical and fictional events to capture the essence of Brueghel's artistic genius as well as a general history of the Netherlands and Belgium in the 16th century.

Historical Accuracy: The novel excludes the aspects of Brueghel's life beyond his Flemish and Dutch experiences, therefore is limited as a portrait of the artist.

HOWARD A. RODMAN (1920-1985)

Primarily known as a Hollywood script writer, Rodman also wrote for television's "Playhouse 90." In 1976, he was honored with the Writer's Guide's Laurel Award for lifetime achievement.

5423 *Destiny Express*

Date of Publication: 1990
Subject(s): Nazis; Motion Picture Industry
Historical character(s): Fritz Lang, Director (movie)
Time Period(s): 1930s (1933)
Locale(s): Berlin, Germany

Summary: This is the story of film director Fritz Lang's final days in Nazi Germany before his escape and exile to America. Lang is transformed from a detached artist to one who embraces a darker political motive, as can be seen in his final film made in Germany, "The Testament of Dr. Mabuse." Hitler ultimately bans the film, and Lang's life slowly unravels as he is engulfed by Nazi Germany.

Historical Accuracy: The novel is truthful to the biographical facts of Lang's life and accurate in the details of German movie making during the period.

E.P. ROESCH
(PSEUD. OF ETHEL ROESCH; PAUL ROESCH)

E.P. Roesch is a pseudonym for the husband and wife writing team of Ethel and Paul Roesch.

5424 *Ashana*

Date of Publication: 1990
Subject(s): Indians; Fur Trade
Fictional character(s): Ashana, Indian (Athabascan)
Historical character(s): Aleksandr Baranov, Hunter, Trader (fur)
Time Period(s): 18th century; 19th century
Locale(s): Alaska

Summary: When Russian fur traders cross the Bering Strait to hunt the untapped riches of Alaska in the 1790s, Athabascan Indian Ashana is taken hostage by trader Aleksandr Baranov. Although she bears him two children, she dreams of her return to her Indian husband and culture.

Historical Accuracy: The novel is based on a true incident.

MARTHA ROFHEART (1925-)

Born in Louisville, Kentucky, Rofheart's early years were spent in the theater. Familiarity with Shakespeare's plays inspired her to write her first novel.

5425 *The Alexandrian*

Date of Publication: 1976
Subject(s): Ancient Egypt; Roman Empire; Biography, Fictionalized
Historical character(s): Cleopatra, Ruler (Queen of Egypt); Julius Caesar, Military Personnel (army commander); Marc

Antony, Military Personnel (general); Gaius Octavius, Military Personnel
Time Period(s): 1st century B.C.
Locale(s): Alexandria, Egypt; Rome, Roman Empire

Summary: Cleopatra tells the story of her ambitious rise to power propelled by an iron will and legendary beauty. Her romances with Julius Caesar and Marc Antony, her final gamble for power, and her defeat and suicide are depicted.

Historical Accuracy: The novel's basic outline is accurate and close to reality.

5426 *Fortune Made His Sword*

Date of Publication: 1972
Subject(s): Royalty—England; Battle of Agincourt; Middle Ages
Fictional character(s): Morgan ap Owen, Bastard Daughter
Historical character(s): Henry V, Ruler (King of England); Catherine of Valois, Royalty (queen consort of Henry V); John of Gaunt, Royalty; Richard II, Ruler (King of England)
Time Period(s): 15th century
Locale(s): England; Wales; France

Summary: The novel offers a portrait of the life and times of Henry V. Told from the perspective of a variety of characters—Henry, his queen, his Welsh mistress, the king's fool, and a loyal knight—the novel attempts to offer a balanced picture of the English hero-king who succeeded in welding England, Wales, and France into a single kingdom.

Historical Accuracy: The author attempts to find a balance between Elizabethan hero worshippers and modern detractors of Henry V.

5427 *Glendower Country*

Date of Publication: 1973
Subject(s): Middle Ages; Peasants' Revolt
Fictional character(s): Nathan ben Arran, Doctor; Sibli, Entertainer (bardic singer)
Historical character(s): Owen Glendower, Revolutionary, Royalty (prince); Geoffrey Chaucer, Writer; Richard II, Ruler (King of England); Wat Tyler, Revolutionary; Henry IV, Ruler (King of England); Harry Monmouth, Royalty (prince)
Time Period(s): 14th century; 15th century
Locale(s): Wales; London, England

Summary: The novel concerns the English-Welsh conflict and the last Welsh prince, Owen Glendower. The Welsh charismatic hero's story is told by six first-person narrators, including Owen himself, his wife, his daughter, his friend Geoffrey Chaucer, a Jewish physician, and a bardic poet. The novel culminates in the Welsh revolt ruthlessly put down by Henry IV and his son, later Henry V.

Historical Accuracy: Little is known precisely about Owen Glendower. There are only scattered, contradictory records and accounts. The author explains that she invented Owen's character from these scraps, rejecting most of the conflicting legends.

5428 *Lionheart!: A Novel of Richard I, King of England*

Date of Publication: 1981
Subject(s): Royalty—England; Middle Ages; Crusades
Fictional character(s): Blondelyn, Musician
Historical character(s): Richard I, Ruler (King of England); Henry II, Ruler (King of England); Eleanor of Aquitaine, Royalty (queen consort of Henry II); Berengaria of Navarre, Royalty (queen consort of Richard I)
Time Period(s): 12th century; 13th century (1157-1204)
Locale(s): England; France; Palestine

Summary: Various characters, both real and imagined, bear witness to the life and times of England's most romantic and heroic king, Richard I. His childhood, career, and loves are depicted in this full portrait of the period.

Historical Accuracy: Blondelyn is an invention. The other characters are historical, and the novel stays very close to the known facts.

5429 *My Name Is Sappho*

Date of Publication: 1974
Subject(s): Literary Life; Ancient Greece
Historical character(s): Sappho, Writer (poet), Singer; Alkaios, Writer (poet); Aesop, Writer; Thales, Philosopher; Pittakos, Military Personnel, Political Figure
Time Period(s): 7th century B.C. (612 B.C.)
Locale(s): Lesbos, Greece; Pyrhha, Greece

Summary: This novel of the life of Sappho shows her as a player in the brutal wars and political intrigue of 7th-century archaic Greece. Multiple narrators—including Sappho herself, her fellow poet Alkaios, and Sappho's sister-in-law—tell the tale of Sappho's artistic achievement, her involvement in a plot to overthrow a tyrant, her exile, and her eventual return to Lesbos to establish a school for women poets.

Historical Accuracy: Although the background facts are true, much of the story is invented.

5430 *The Savage Brood*

Date of Publication: 1978
Subject(s): Family Saga; Theatrical Life; Motion Picture Industry
Fictional character(s): Edward Savage, Actor; Miranda Savage, Actress; Joseph Peace Savage, Actor
Historical character(s): David Garrick, Actor, Manager (theater manager); Peg Woffington, Actress; Nathan Hale, Patriot; Richard Nixon, Political Figure; Charles Cornwallis, Military Personnel (general)
Time Period(s): Multiple Time Periods
Locale(s): London, England; San Francisco, California; Florence, Italy

Summary: The novel offers a history of the theatrical Savage family from the Tudor period to the 1970s. Their story takes them from London, to Florence, to Revolutionary America, to the early days of the fledgling movie business. Important historical figures and events and theatrical history round out this family saga.

Historical Accuracy: So much history is covered that the book gives only sketchy details. The particulars given, however, are convincing.

GARET ROGERS

An American writer born in Ohio, Rogers graduated from Transylvania College, Purdue University, and the University of Southern California. A lawyer in private practice, Rogers ran for mayor of Los Angeles in 1961. His novels include *Prisoner in Paradise*, *Scandal in Eden*, and *Oath of Dishonor*.

5431 *Lancet*

Date of Publication: 1956
Subject(s): Medical Profession; Georgian Period
Historical character(s): William Hunter, Doctor; John Hunter, Doctor
Time Period(s): 18th century
Locale(s): London, England

Summary: The medical profession in the 18th century is dramatized in this novel that centers on the Scottish brothers William and John Hunter, who were famous anatomists and surgeons. The novel illustrates their careers with many detailed depictions of medical practices of the time.

Historical Accuracy: The novel mixes fact and fiction, but the research into the period and the medical elements are copious and credible.

GAYLE ROGERS (1923-)

An American born in California, Rogers graduated from the University of California, Los Angeles and California Lutheran College. She has worked as a high school teacher of history and minority studies in Los Angeles. Since she was pronounced "dead" at age seven, Rogers has experienced a number of psychic incidents, including memories of past lives. Her novel, *The Second Kiss*, is claimed to be an account of one such past life.

5432 *The Second Kiss*

Date of Publication: 1972
Subject(s): American West; Indians; Tribal Life—Native American
Fictional character(s): Maria Frame, Captive; Nakoa, Indian (Blackfoot), Warrior
Time Period(s): 1840s (1846)
Locale(s): Oregon

Summary: The novel describes the result of an Indian attack on a wagon train heading to Oregon. All are massacred except Maria Frame, who is captured by the Blackfoot. She learns to adapt to Indian ways and must decide whether to become the wife of her captor.

Historical Accuracy: The novel is believable in its depiction of frontier life and Native American customs.

PETER-THOMAS ROHRBACH (1926-)

American writer Rohrbach was born in New York City and educated at Catholic University. He is a former Roman Catholic priest and was a master at the Discalced Carmelite Seminary in Washington, D.C. His other books include *Conversation with Christ*, *The Search for St. Therese*, *Journey to Carith*, and *The Disillusioned*.

5433 *Bold Encounter: A Novel Based on the Life of St. John of the Cross*

Date of Publication: 1960
Subject(s): Religious Life; Biography, Fictionalized
Historical character(s): Theresa of Avila, Religious (nun); John of the Cross, Religious, Writer (poet)
Time Period(s): 16th century
Locale(s): Spain

Summary: This is the biographical account of Saint John of the Cross, the 16th-century Spanish religious figure who helped lead the age's monastic revival. John is shown from his student days and his discontent as a Carmelite to his meeting with St. Theresa and his founding of the first Discalced monastery.

Historical Accuracy: The novel authentically captures the atmosphere of 16th-century Spain and the religious sentiment and conventions of the period. The principal scenes are historical; some fictional characters and minor scenes have been invented.

O.E. ROLVAAG (1876-1931)

A Norwegian-born writer who emigrated to the U.S. in 1896, Rolvaag is justly renowned for his trilogy depicting the life of Norwegian immigrants on the northwestern frontier of the U.S. *His Letters from America* is a semi-autobiographical account of his own adjustment as an immigrant to his adopted country.

5434 *Giants in the Earth*

Date of Publication: 1925
Subject(s): Settlement of the American Frontier; Immigrants; American West
Fictional character(s): Per Hansa, Settler; Beret Hansa, Settler
Time Period(s): 1870s (1873)
Locale(s): Dakota Territory, United States; Minnesota

Summary: The settling of the American frontier is dramatized in the story of a small company of Norwegian farmers in the Dakota Territory. Per Hansa contends with adversity with a stoical determination and steely resolve. In contrast, his wife falters under the strain and loneliness of prairie life. Their family's story continues in *Peder Victorious*.

Historical Accuracy: The novel is an epic of pioneer life. The cost of settling the frontier is made compellingly clear in this convincing story.

5435 *Peder Victorious*

Date of Publication: 1929

Subject(s): Immigrants; Settlement of the American Frontier; American West
Fictional character(s): Beret Holm, Settler; Peder Victorious Holm, Farmer; Susie Doheny, Heroine
Time Period(s): 1890s
Locale(s): Dakota Territory, United States

Summary: This sequel to *Giants in the Earth* takes place 20 years later, and its theme is less survival than the adaptation of the Norwegian immigrants to a new American society. Beret, the matriarch, wishes to keep her family's Norwegian heritage pure. Her son, however, pushes for assimilation, which culminates in his marriage to an Irish-American. Their story concludes in *Their Fathers' God*.

Historical Accuracy: Rolvaag, himself a Norwegian immigrant, understands and dramatizes the tension between homeland and life in a new country.

`5436` *Their Fathers' God*

Date of Publication: 1931
Subject(s): Settlement of the American Frontier; American West; Religious Conflict
Fictional character(s): Peder Victorious Holm, Farmer, Political Figure; Beret Holm, Farmer; Susie Holm, Farmer
Time Period(s): 1890s
Locale(s): Dakota Territory, United States

Summary: In the concluding volume of Rolvaag's trilogy, the subject is the cultural and religious conflict between Peder's Irish wife, Susie, and his mother, Beret. Beret secretly has her grandson baptised as a Lutheran. Peder enters politics on behalf of the Republican opposition to William Jennings Bryan, and personal matters become public with tragic consequences.

Historical Accuracy: The novel's period details are strong, and the author is to be commended for avoiding easy happy endings.

MARY TERESA RONALDS (1946-)

A native of Yorkshire and London, Ronalds teaches in a secondary school in London. She won the Silver Pen Award in 1969 for *Myself My Sepulchre*.

`5437` *Nero*

Date of Publication: 1969
Subject(s): Roman Empire; Biography, Fictionalized
Historical character(s): Nero, Ruler (Roman emperor); Lucius Annaeus Seneca, Writer; Agrippina, Royalty
Time Period(s): 1st century
Locale(s): Rome, Roman Empire

Summary: The Roman emperor Nero tells his own story, portraying himself not as the madman or monster of other accounts, but as a compelling figure who begins his reign at age 16 loved by the people and supported by the senate and the army. He is soon plunged into a struggle for power that consumes him.

Historical Accuracy: The story plays fair with the facts, but the novel's interpretations are open to question.

DAPHNE ROOKE (1914-)

A South African writer of short stories and novels for adults and children, Rooke was born in Boksburg, Transvaal. She is the author of *The Sea Hath Bounds*, *Boy on the Mountain*, and *Margaretha de la Porte*.

`5438` *Wizards' Country*

Date of Publication: 1957
Subject(s): Tribal Life—African; English Colonies
Fictional character(s): Thunzi, Warrior (Zulu)
Time Period(s): 1870s (1879)
Locale(s): Zululand, Africa

Summary: Set during the Zulu Wars of the 1870s, the novel describes the conflict from the Zulu perspective focusing on a tribal village's experiences during the conflict. The novel offers a sympathetic view of the culture and the customs of the Africans.

Historical Accuracy: The story and the characters are fictitious but do reflect actual historical events such as the enforcement of marriage laws, the war, and the death of the Prince Imperial.

LEON ROOKE (1934-)

A native of North Carolina who moved to Victoria, British Columbia, Rooke has been a writer-in-residence at the University of North Carolina, the University of Victoria, and the University of Toronto. He won the 1981 Best Paperback Novel of the Year award for *Fat Woman*. Rooke is considered one of the most imaginative fiction writers currently practicing in Canada.

`5439` *Shakespeare's Dog*

Date of Publication: 1983
Subject(s): Literary Life; Elizabethan Period; Dogs
Fictional character(s): Mr. Hooker, Animal (dog)
Historical character(s): William Shakespeare, Writer
Time Period(s): 17th century
Locale(s): Stratford-on-Avon, England

Summary: A dog's eye view of Elizabethan England and William Shakespeare is offered in this humorous story. Mr. Hooker is the Bard's canine colleague and rival in important matters.

Historical Accuracy: The Elizabethan details and the elements reflecting Shakespeare's life are authentic, if somewhat skewed in pursuit of comedy and the novel's unique perspective.

PHILIP ROONEY (1907-1962)

An Irish novelist and radio playwright, Rooney was born in Collooney, County Sligo. He worked as a bank clerk for 15 years, writing short stories in his spare time. Rooney specialized in Irish historical novels that featured action and romance. His titles include *All Out to Win*, *Overnight Entry*, and *The Long Day*.

5440 *Captain Boycott, a Romantic Novel*

Date of Publication: 1946
Subject(s): Independence—Ireland
Historical character(s): Charles Cunningham Boycott, Manager (land agent)
Time Period(s): 1880s
Locale(s): Ireland

Summary: This tale is built around the story of land agent Captain Charles Boycott whose ruthlessness in evicting tenants prompts the Irish to refuse all cooperation with him and his family, thus orignating the term "boycott.".

Historical Accuracy: The novel constructs a fanciful story around the authentic presentation of the lot of the Irish peasant during the period.

5441 *The Golden Coast*

Date of Publication: 1949
Subject(s): Sea Story; Pirates
Fictional character(s): Rich Sheridan, Sailor
Time Period(s): 17th century
Locale(s): Dublin, Ireland; *Ouzel*, At Sea

Summary: This nautical adventure tale is set during the 17th century and consists of the exploits of a young Dublin shipbuilder. He is pressed into service aboard the *Ouzel* as ship's carpenter for four years, and experiences escalating adventures and narrow escapes from sea hazards and pirates.

Historical Accuracy: The novel provides accurate details of sailing during the period.

ELLIOTT ROOSEVELT (1910-1990)

An American writer, Roosevelt was the son of Franklin and Eleanor Roosevelt. He travelled extensively with his father during his presidency. His three volume tell-all family history, *An Untold Story*, created considerable controversy and estrangement from his siblings. Toward the end of his life, he turned to mystery writing.

5442 *A First Class Murder*

Date of Publication: 1991
Subject(s): Mystery; Ocean Liners
Historical character(s): Eleanor Roosevelt, Spouse (First Lady), Detective—Amateur; Charles Lindbergh, Pilot; Jack Benny, Entertainer; Josephine Baker, Entertainer; John F. Kennedy, Teenager
Time Period(s): 1930s (1938)
Locale(s): *Normandie*, At Sea (Atlantic crossing)

Summary: After a visit to France in 1938, Eleanor Roosevelt is on the voyage home aboard the *Normandie* with a distinguished group of passengers. When one is found poisoned and a Russian ballerina is accused of the crime, Eleanor takes up the investigation.

Historical Accuracy: The atmosphere of the period is authentically created.

5443 *The Hyde Park Murder*

Date of Publication: 1985
Subject(s): Mystery
Fictional character(s): Alfred Doolittle Hannah, Businessman; Adriana Van der Meer, Gentlewoman
Historical character(s): Eleanor Roosevelt, Spouse (First Lady), Detective—Amateur; Franklin Delano Roosevelt, Political Figure (President of the U.S.); Joseph P. Kennedy, Government Official; Fiorello La Guardia, Political Figure (Mayor of New York City); Sam Rayburn, Political Figure (congressman); Louis Brandeis, Judge
Time Period(s): 1930s (1935)
Locale(s): Hyde Park, New York; New York, New York; Washington, District of Columbia

Summary: A Hyde Park neighbor of the Roosevelts, Alfred Hannah, is accused in a multi-million dollar stock swindle that threatens the upcoming marriage of Adriana Van der Meer. When Hannah is found dead in an apparent suicide, Eleanor Roosevelt suspects murder. In her investigation, she seeks help from some of the period's best and brightest.

Historical Accuracy: This is a delightfully detailed mystery with a full and accurate flavor of the period.

5444 *Murder and the First Lady*

Date of Publication: 1984
Subject(s): Mystery; World War II
Fictional character(s): Pamela Rush-Hodgeborn, Secretary
Historical character(s): Eleanor Roosevelt, Spouse (First Lady), Detective—Amateur; Franklin Delano Roosevelt, Political Figure (President of the U.S.); Lyndon Baines Johnson, Political Figure; J. Edgar Hoover, Government Official
Time Period(s): 1930s (1939)
Locale(s): Washington, District of Columbia

Summary: In 1939 when a White House staffer is murdered, Eleanor Roosevelt's young English secretary is charged with the crime. The First Lady proves to be a dogged and intrepid investigator: she fights to prove Pamela's innocence, going undercover and tangling with both the F.B.I. and Scotland Yard.

Historical Accuracy: The mystery features an insider's view of the Roosevelt White House and its first family.

5445 *Murder at the Palace*

Date of Publication: 1987
Subject(s): Mystery; World War II; Royalty—England
Fictional character(s): Anthony Brooke-Hardinge, Gentleman
Historical character(s): Eleanor Roosevelt, Spouse (First Lady), Detective—Amateur; Mary of Teck, Royalty (queen consort of George V); Winston Churchill, Political Figure (Prime Minister of England); Elizabeth, Royalty (princess); Margaret Rose, Royalty (princess)
Time Period(s): 1940s (1942)
Locale(s): London, England

Summary: While visiting England at the request of her husband, Eleanor Roosevelt must solve a murder in Buckingham Palace. One of the king's equerries, Sir Anthony Brooke-Hardinge, is found dead with a roomful of likely suspects.

Eleanor uncovers Sir Anthony's double life and his connection with the London underworld.

Historical Accuracy: While the novel is further afield from the insider look at the Roosevelt White House, there is some genuine period painting of wartime London and the royal family.

5446 *Murder in the Blue Room*

Date of Publication: 1990
Subject(s): Mystery; World War II
Historical character(s): Eleanor Roosevelt, Spouse (First Lady), Detective—Amateur; Franklin Delano Roosevelt, Political Figure (President of the U.S.); Vyacheslav Molotov, Diplomat; Nelson Rockefeller, Government Official
Time Period(s): 1940s (1942)
Locale(s): Washington, District of Columbia

Summary: Russian foreign minister Molotov is staying at the White House and displaying all the signs of extreme paranoia. When a young woman's battered corpse is discovered in the Blue Room, Eleanor Roosevelt suspects his fears are not imagined, and begins to look for answers.

Historical Accuracy: The novel features fascinating glimpses behind the scenes at the wartime White House.

5447 *Murder in the Chateau*

Date of Publication: 1996
Subject(s): Mystery; World War II
Historical character(s): Eleanor Roosevelt, Political Figure; Franklin Delano Roosevelt, Political Figure; Erwin Rommel, Military Personnel (German general); William J. "Wild Bill" Donovan, Spy; Gertrude Stein, Writer
Time Period(s): 1940s (1941)
Locale(s): France

Summary: A French/German resistance group's plot to assassinate Adolf Hitler sends Eleanor Roosevelt to a small chateau in the German-occupied French countryside. There Mrs. Roosevelt meets Erwin Rommel and Gertrude Stein and takes up spying when an SS colonel is found murdered.

Historical Accuracy: The plot is fairly far-fetched and more ingenious than historically grounded.

5448 *Murder in the East Room*

Date of Publication: 1993
Subject(s): Mystery; World War II
Fictional character(s): Vance Gibson, Political Figure; Amelia Gibson, Spouse
Historical character(s): Eleanor Roosevelt, Spouse (First Lady), Detective—Amateur; Franklin Delano Roosevelt, Political Figure (President of the U.S.); Alf Landon, Political Figure; Felix Frankfurter, Judge; Charlie Chaplin, Actor; Lyndon Baines Johnson, Political Figure; Greta Garbo, Actress; Henry Stimson, Political Figure
Time Period(s): 1940s (1940)
Locale(s): Washington, District of Columbia

Summary: In 1940, as the English face the Germans alone, FDR must make an unprecedented decision whether or not to seek a third term. At a state dinner at the White House,

Senator Vance Gibson excuses himself from the table complaining that he is ill. He is later found in the East Room on the floor in a pool of blood. Mrs. Roosevelt takes on the case, and uncovers a complex political mystery.

Historical Accuracy: The era and the details of White House life during the Roosevelt administration are expertly delivered.

5449 *Murder in the Executive Mansion*

Date of Publication: 1995
Subject(s): Mystery; Espionage
Historical character(s): Eleanor Roosevelt, Detective—Amateur, Spouse; Franklin Delano Roosevelt, Political Figure (President of the U.S.); Ernest Hemingway, Writer; William Faulkner, Writer; J. Edgar Hoover, Government Official (director of the FBI)
Time Period(s): 1930s (1939)
Locale(s): Washington, District of Columbia

Summary: On the eve of World War II, the Roosevelts entertain the King and Queen of England at the White House. When an assistant disappears and is found strangled in a White House linen closet, Eleanor Roosevelt begins an investigation that leads to a German spy ring.

Historical Accuracy: The author captures the atmosphere of the era and clearly has an insider's view of the Roosevelt White House which lends authenticity to the story.

5450 *Murder in the Oval Office*

Date of Publication: 1989
Subject(s): Mystery; Depression Era
Fictional character(s): Winstead Colmer, Political Figure; Amelia Colmer, Spouse
Historical character(s): Eleanor Roosevelt, Spouse (First Lady), Detective—Amateur; Franklin Delano Roosevelt, Political Figure (President of the U.S.); J. Edgar Hoover, Government Official; Lyndon Baines Johnson, Political Figure; Sally Rand, Dancer; Bob Hope, Entertainer; Bing Crosby, Entertainer; Felix Frankfurter, Lawyer, Professor
Time Period(s): 1930s (1934)
Locale(s): Washington, District of Columbia

Summary: An Alabama Congressman is found dead in the Oval Office with a pistol beside him and all the doors and windows locked from the inside. Is this a case of suicide? Eleanor Roosevelt suspects murder.

Historical Accuracy: The novel is filled with insider information and authentic period touches.

5451 *Murder in the Red Room*

Date of Publication: 1992
Subject(s): Mystery; Depression Era; Crime and Criminals
Historical character(s): Eleanor Roosevelt, Spouse (First Lady), Detective—Amateur; Franklin Delano Roosevelt, Political Figure (President of the U.S.); Charles Evans Hughes, Judge; Felix Frankfurter, Lawyer, Professor
Time Period(s): 1930s (1937)
Locale(s): Washington, District of Columbia

Summary: It's 1937 and FDR has just been inaugurated for his second term. During a White House dinner, a notorious Cleveland mobster is found stabbed to death in the Red Room. Eleanor takes on the case to discover how he got into the White House in the first place and who did not want him to leave.

Historical Accuracy: This is an ingenious mystery with insider period touches that appear to be authentic.

5452 Murder in the Rose Garden

Date of Publication: 1989
Subject(s): Mystery; Depression Era
Fictional character(s): Vivian Taliafero, Socialite
Historical character(s): Eleanor Roosevelt, Spouse (First Lady), Detective—Amateur; Franklin Delano Roosevelt, Political Figure (President of the U.S.); Mary McLeod Bethune, Teacher, Activist (civil rights); Charles Evans Hughes, Judge
Time Period(s): 1930s (1936)
Locale(s): Washington, District of Columbia

Summary: In 1936 a Washington society matron, Vivian Taliafero, is found murdered in the White House Rose Garden. She turns out to have been a blackmailer with a lot of enemies. Many of the suspects are high-ranking political figures, and Eleanor Roosevelt must be quick and discreet in getting to the truth.

Historical Accuracy: The novel offers informed period touches.

5453 Murder in the West Wing

Date of Publication: 1993
Subject(s): Mystery; Depression Era; Crime and Criminals
Fictional character(s): Paul Duroc, Government Official; Therese Rolland, Government Official
Historical character(s): Eleanor Roosevelt, Spouse (First Lady), Detective—Amateur; Franklin Delano Roosevelt, Political Figure (President of the U.S.); Fiorello La Guardia, Political Figure (Mayor of New York City); Albert Einstein, Scientist
Time Period(s): 1930s (1936)
Locale(s): Washington, District of Columbia

Summary: In 1936 Paul Duroc, special assistant to the president, is poisoned in the company of Therese Rolland, who drank from the same bottle yet felt no effect. She is accused of murder, and Eleanor Roosevelt takes up the case. Her search leads her to Washington's underworld and a possible connection with the assassination of Huey Long.

Historical Accuracy: The scene is sharply detailed with authentic touches.

5454 New Deal for Death

Date of Publication: 1993
Subject(s): Mystery; Politics; Depression Era
Fictional character(s): Jack "Blackjack" Endicott, Banker; Charlotte Wendell, Young Woman
Historical character(s): Franklin Delano Roosevelt, Political Figure; Meyer Lansky, Organized Crime Figure; Samuel Goldwyn, Businessman (movie executive); Jean Harlow, Ac-

tress; Cecil B. DeMille, Director; Benjamin Siegel, Organized Crime Figure
Time Period(s): 1930s (1932)
Locale(s): Hollywood, California

Summary: Blackjack Endicott, a Boston banker and close friend of F.D.R., is called to California to find out who is blackmailing the new Democratic presidential nominee. He mingles with mobsters and moguls and makes his way through dangerous Mafia connections where he learns that it's not blackmail but the murder of Roosevelt that is involved.

Historical Accuracy: Fanciful, the novel is rich in period details.

5455 The President's Man

Date of Publication: 1991
Subject(s): Mystery; Crime and Criminals; Assassination
Fictional character(s): Jack Endicott, Gentleman
Historical character(s): Franklin Delano Roosevelt, Political Figure (President of the U.S.); Arthur Flegenheimer, Criminal (aka Dutch Schultz); Al Capone, Criminal; Will Rogers, Entertainer; Charles "Lucky" Luciano, Criminal
Time Period(s): 1930s
Locale(s): Chicago, Illinois; New York, New York

Summary: In 1932, the governor of New York, Franklin D. Roosevelt, is a candidate for the presidency. His outspoken opposition to Prohibition has caused the wrath of bootlegging gangsters and threats of assassination. FDR calls on his old school friend, Jack "Blackjack" Endicott—pilot, gambler, sailor—to help him out. In his tour of the 1930s underworld, Endicott unravels a plot to murder Roosevelt.

Historical Accuracy: Tougher and seamier than the author's Eleanor Roosevelt detective series, the novel is convincing in its details and characterizations.

5456 A Royal Murder

Date of Publication: 1994
Subject(s): Mystery; World War II; Royalty—England
Historical character(s): Eleanor Roosevelt, Spouse (First Lady), Detective—Amateur; Franklin Delano Roosevelt, Political Figure (President of the U.S.); Edward, Duke of Windsor, Royalty (Duke of Windsor); Wallis Warfield Simpson, Noblewoman (Duchess of Windsor)
Time Period(s): 1940s (1940)
Locale(s): Washington, District of Columbia; Bahamas

Summary: Eleanor Roosevelt is sent by her husband to the Bahamas to help in the negotiations to establish air and naval bases on the islands. There she is warmly received by the exiled Duke and Duchess of Windsor. She shortly finds herself in the middle of dark and murderous conspiracies to turn the Bahamas and all of Latin America into a Nazi base of operation.

Historical Accuracy: Though fanciful, the novel is remarkable in its insider's details of the era.

5457 The White House Pantry Murder

Date of Publication: 1987
Subject(s): Mystery; World War II

Historical character(s): Eleanor Roosevelt, Spouse (First Lady), Detective—Amateur; Franklin Delano Roosevelt, Political Figure (President of the U.S.); Winston Churchill, Political Figure (Prime Minister of England)
Time Period(s): 1940s (1941)
Locale(s): Washington, District of Columbia

Summary: In 1941, during the first Christmas of the war, the White House prepares for the visit of Winston Churchill. Although security is tight, an intruder is found dead in the large walk-in refrigerator of the White House pantry. The corpse is unidentified, and Eleanor Roosevelt suspects a wider plot of assassination, perhaps even the destabilization of the Allies by the Nazis.

Historical Accuracy: The White House of the era is accurately depicted, and Churchill did make a visit in 1941.

JAMES ROOSEVELT (1907-1991)

SAM TOPEROFF (1933-)

Roosevelt was the eldest son of Franklin Delano and Eleanor Roosevelt. He graduated from Harvard and was his father's assistant throughout FDR's presidency. Roosevelt was a congressman from California and an ambassador to the United Nations. His recollections of his father were recorded in *Affectionately, F.D.R.: A Son's Story of a Courageous Man.* American academic and author Toperoff was born in Brooklyn, New York, and educated at Hofstra and Lehigh universities. He is a professor of English at Hofstra. His books include *All the Advantages*, *Crazy over Horses*, *Pilgrim of the Sun and Stars*, and *Porcupine Man.*

`5458` *A Family Matter*
Date of Publication: 1980
Subject(s): World War II; Politics
Historical character(s): Franklin Delano Roosevelt, Political Figure (President of the U.S.); Winston Churchill, Political Figure (British prime minister); James Roosevelt, Assistant (of FDR); Albert Einstein, Scientist (physicist); Leo Szilard, Scientist (physicist); Enrico Fermi, Scientist (physicist); J. Robert Oppenheimer, Scientist (physicist); Adolf Hitler, Political Figure (German fuhrer); Heinrich Himmler, Leader (Nazi); John Foster Dulles, Political Figure, Diplomat
Time Period(s): 1940s (1943-1945)
Locale(s): Washington, District of Columbia; Yalta, Russia; Los Alamos, New Mexico

Summary: James Roosevelt, his father's trusted assistant, gives an insider's view of the secret diplomatic maneuvering during World War II. He tells how the Allies argue over the peace once Hitler has been subdued and discusses Roosevelt's secret trump card, the atomic bomb. President Roosevelt makes a daring move to ensure a balance of power and a lasting peace.

Historical Accuracy: Given the author's privileged position as an eyewitness, the novel is convincing in its authenticity.

CORWIN ROOT

`5459` *An American, Sir*
Date of Publication: 1940
Subject(s): War of 1812
Fictional character(s): Jeremy Peabody, Young Man; Marilyn Hastings, Young Woman
Time Period(s): 1810s
Locale(s): Boston, Massachusetts; New Orleans, Louisiana

Summary: This historical romance illustrates the conflict between the Federalists and the Republicans over the wisdom of ''Mr. Madison's War.'' Young Jeremy Peabody goes to war to prove his love for Marilyn Hastings, taking to the sea aboard a privateer.

Historical Accuracy: Although ten years of research went into the background for this story, the author often sacrifices historical accuracy to the demands of the plot.

ROBERT A. RORIPAUGH (1930-)

Born in California, Roripaugh graduated from the University of Wyoming, where he has worked as a teacher of English. His career has included work as an oilfield roustabout, carpenter's helper, horse wrangler, and ranchhand. His novels, short stories, and poetry utilize the modern western experience.

`5460` *Honor Thy Father*
Date of Publication: 1963
Subject(s): American West; Ranching; Homesteading
Fictional character(s): Martin Tyrrell, Rancher; Ira Tyrrell, Young Man; Mart Tyrrell, Young Man
Time Period(s): 1880s; 1890s (1889-1890)
Locale(s): Sweetwater Valley, Wyoming

Summary: The novel dramatizes a father's conflict with his two sons in Wyoming during the late 1880s. Rancher Martin Tyrrell, who has won the battle against the Indians, now faces the challenge of homesteaders seeking land in the sprawling Sweetwater Valley. Ira Tyrrell turns against his father and rides with the homesteaders.

Historical Accuracy: The background and atmosphere are based on fact, but the events are imagined.

GEOFFREY ROSE (1932-)

Born in London, Rose left school at 17 for the stage, where he struggled for parts, working office jobs by day and writing by night.

`5461` *A Clear Road to Archangel*
Date of Publication: 1973
Subject(s): World War I; Espionage; Russian Revolution
Fictional character(s): Captain S., Spy
Time Period(s): 1910s (1917)
Locale(s): Russia

Summary: An unnamed young Englishman, a spy in Russia in the winter of 1917, attempts to reach safety in Archangel. He is pursued by Cossack troops across the frozen landscape of the collapsing Russian state.

Historical Accuracy: This period thriller is filled with authentic elements that create a convincing background of revolutionary Russia.

NORMA ROSEN (1925-)

An American author and professor of English, Rosen was born in New York and attended Mount Holyoke College and Columbia University. Rosen's books include the novels *Joy to Levine!* and *Touching Evil*, and a critically acclaimed volume of short stories and a novella, *Green*.

5462 *John and Anzia: An American Romance*

Date of Publication: 1989
Subject(s): Biography, Fictionalized
Historical character(s): John Dewey, Philosopher; Anzia Yezierska, Writer
Time Period(s): 1910s (1917)
Locale(s): United States

Summary: This love story is based on documented evidence that the renowned philosopher and educator John Dewey had an affair in 1917 with Polish immigrant and writer Anzia Yezierska.

Historical Accuracy: The novel's speculations are based, in large measure, on clues in Dewey's poetry and in Yezierska's tales of immigrant life. Dewey remains a secondary figure, and the novel's search for the truth at times compromises the interest of the novel's romance.

ANN B. ROSS

5463 *The Pilgrimage*

Date of Publication: 1987
Subject(s): American West; Wagon Trains; Identity—Concealed
Fictional character(s): Emma Louise Heath, Orphan, Imposter ("Emmett"); Jessie Heath, Orphan, Teenager; J.C. Garrett, Trapper, Mountain Man
Time Period(s): 1840s (1846)
Locale(s): Oregon Trail, United States

Summary: The story portrays the comic adventures of two orphan sisters who journey along the Oregon Trail without male protection. Emma Louise, a feisty 12-year-old tomboy, becomes "Emmett" with the aid of a haircut and men's clothing. Her sister's fervent spiritualism is tested when they encounter trapper J.C. Garrett.

Historical Accuracy: The novel is convincingly authentic by way of its believable period details.

BETTE M. ROSS (1932-)

Born in California, Ross graduated from UCLA and has worked as an elementary school teacher. An instructor in creative writing at Mt. San Antonio Community College,

Ross won the 1975 Henrietta C. Mears award for excellence in fiction. Her nonfiction work, *Our Special Child*, recounts her experiences as a parent of a mentally retarded child.

5464 *Gennie the Huguenot Woman*

Date of Publication: 1983
Subject(s): Huguenots; French and Indian War; Religious Conflict
Fictional character(s): Gennie Harmonie, Servant (indentured); Thomas Roebuck, Trapper
Time Period(s): 1740s (1744-1747)
Locale(s): Pennsylvania, American Colonies; France

Summary: Set during the Huguenot persecution in the 18th century, the novel tells the story of a young Frenchwoman, Gennie Harmonie, who comes to America after her father and brother are martyred for their Protestant faith. As an indentured servant in Pennsylvania during the French and Indian Wars, she falls in love with a young trapper named Thomas Roebuck. They are separated, and Gennie endures a loveless marriage, sustained by a deep religious belief.

Historical Accuracy: The novel offers some convincing period elements, consistent with the setting and era.

CAROLINE ROSS
(PSEUD. OF CATHERINE NICOLSON, 1948-)

Born in Lagos, Nigeria, Nicolson graduated from St. Anne's College, Oxford, and went on to work as a recording engineer, astrologer, model maker, cleaner, photographer, interior designer, publishing reader, editor, and proofreader.

5465 *Miss Nobody*

Date of Publication: 1981
Subject(s): Royalty—England
Fictional character(s): Rose, Orphan, Young Woman
Historical character(s): Charles, Prince of Wales, Royalty (Prince of Wales); Elizabeth II, Ruler (Queen of England); Elizabeth, the Queen Mother, Royalty
Time Period(s): 1990s
Locale(s): London, England; Scotland

Summary: This fairy tale romance involving a commoner and a prince uses the real English royal family in its story. In the years before Diana, Charles, the Prince of Wales, meets and falls in love with Rose. The queen is not amused, but the queen mother is sympathetic.

Historical Accuracy: The novel is a romantic fantasy, with the real lives of the royals only dimly suggested.

DANA FULLER ROSS

5466 *Arizona!*

Date of Publication: 1988
Subject(s): American West; Espionage; Horse Racing
Fictional character(s): Toby Holt, Frontiersman; Reed Kerr, Military Personnel (army officer); Henry Blake, Military Personnel (army officer), Spy

Time Period(s): 1870s
Locale(s): Arizona; Kentucky; Germany

Summary: In this installment of the Wagons West series, several plot threads are continued in action that ranges from the western U.S. to Europe. In Arizona, comancheros are terrorizing the territory. In Kentucky, Toby Holt deals with gangsters trying to take over the Kentucky horse-racing circuit. In Germany, Henry Blake finds himself in the center of intrigue.

Historical Accuracy: This is a collection of genres: western, spy thriller, and criminal detection, with the merest of historical backgrounds.

5467 *California!*

Date of Publication: 1981
Subject(s): American West; Gold Rush—California
Fictional character(s): Michael "Whip" Holt, Frontiersman; Rick Miller, Lawman (sheriff); Melissa Austin, Captive
Time Period(s): 1840s; 1850s
Locale(s): California

Summary: When gold is discovered in California, the rush is on, and settlers who flood into the gold fields become the prey of outlaws. Melissa Austin, a Texan beauty, finds herself sold into captivity, and former wagonmaster Whip Holt joins Sheriff Rick Miller to save her.

Historical Accuracy: The background of the story is historical, but the essential elements are fictional.

5468 *California Glory*

Date of Publication: 1991
Subject(s): Family Saga; Labor Movement
Fictional character(s): Tim Holt, Journalist; Toby Holt, Political Figure
Historical character(s): Clarence Darrow, Lawyer
Time Period(s): 1890s (1893-1894)
Locale(s): San Francisco, California; Chicago, Illinois; Portland, Oregon

Summary: In the fourth volume of the Holt family saga, the U.S. explodes into labor disputes and violence. Tim Holt, the owner of a San Francisco newspaper, goes east to cover the big story of the great Pullman strike.

Historical Accuracy: Historical events form only the skeleton for the story.

5469 *Carolina Courage*

Date of Publication: 1990
Subject(s): Family Saga; Racial Conflict
Fictional character(s): Janessa Holt Lawrence, Doctor; Joe Cheoh, Indian (Cherokee), Lawyer; Henry Blake, Government Official
Historical character(s): Liliuokalani, Ruler (Queen of Hawaii)
Time Period(s): 1890s (1891)
Locale(s): New York, New York; North Carolina; Hawaii

Summary: In this installment of the Holt family saga, a yellow fever epidemic breaks out on the sprawling Cherokee reservation. In Hawaii, unscrupulous planters resort to treachery and murder to topple the government and wrest the islands away from the native peoples.

Historical Accuracy: The pace is frenetic with some slight and simplified historical elements.

5470 *Celebration!*

Date of Publication: 1989
Subject(s): Politics
Fictional character(s): Toby Holt, Frontiersman; Henry Blake, Military Personnel (army officer); Cindy Holt Kerr, Young Woman
Time Period(s): 1870s (1876)
Locale(s): New York, New York

Summary: As America prepares to celebrate its 100th anniversary, Toby Holt is given a final mission in the 23rd and final novel in the Wagons West series. A group of anarchists plot to turn the centennial celebration into a bloodbath, and sweep up several strands of the series' extended family into their conspiracy.

Historical Accuracy: The story is imagined with some slight period background painting.

5471 *Colorado!*

Date of Publication: 1981
Subject(s): American West; Civil War—U.S.
Fictional character(s): Leland Blake, Military Personnel (general); Cathy Van Ayl, Spouse (of Leland); Luke Brandon, Scientist
Historical character(s): James Buchanan, Political Figure
Time Period(s): 1850s; 1860s
Locale(s): Denver, Colorado

Summary: Gold is discovered in Colorado as the nation comes apart during the Civil War. General Leland Blake embarks on a mission to make sure that Colorado stays in the Union. The boom town of Denver becomes a magnet for a varied cast of opportunists and scoundrels.

Historical Accuracy: The essence of the story is historical but the main elements are fictional.

5472 *Dakota!*

Date of Publication: 1983
Subject(s): American West; Indians; Railroads
Fictional character(s): Toby Holt, Frontiersman; Rob Martin, Engineer; Beth Martin, Spouse
Time Period(s): 1860s (1867)
Locale(s): Dakota Territory, United States; San Francisco, California; Sierra Nevada Mountains, California

Summary: Toby Holt finds himself at the center of the Indian Wars, led by Indians bent on the destruction of the U.S. Army and the prevention of the construction of the Northern Pacific Railroad. Meanwhile, Rob Martin oversees the building of the railroad through the Sierra Nevadas, and his wife Beth finds herself on trial for murder in San Francisco.

Historical Accuracy: The novel holds more action than is plausible, with a slight and simplified historical background.

5473 *Expedition!*

Date of Publication: 1993

Subject(s): Settlement of the American Frontier; Indians

Fictional character(s): Clay Holt, Frontiersman; Shining Moon, Indian (Sioux), Spouse (of Clay); Jefferson Holt, Frontiersman, Trapper

Time Period(s): 1800s (1809)

Locale(s): Yellowstone River, West; New York, New York

Summary: In the second volume of the author's Frontier Trilogy, Clay Holt, with his wife, Shining Moon, leads a perilous expedition up the Yellowstone River. Jeff Holt heads back east for an equally perilous quest in civilization.

Historical Accuracy: The details of frontier life are authentic and convincing.

5474 *Homecoming*

Date of Publication: 1994

Subject(s): Family Saga; Spanish-American War; Motion Picture Industry

Fictional character(s): Michael Holt, Businessman; Henry Blake, Military Personnel, Spy; Frank Holt, Adventurer

Time Period(s): 1890s (1899)

Locale(s): Taos, New Mexico; Manila, Philippines; Washington, District of Columbia

Summary: In the ninth volume of the Holt family series, the year is 1899 and in Taos, New Mexico, Michael Holt conceives of a new means of capturing the American West. In the Philippines, intelligence agent Henry Blake must choose between his country and his family in the military quagmire of the Spanish-American War.

Historical Accuracy: The formula in the series, including this novel, is as follows: action and adventure set in an historical period that is simplified to emphasize the drama.

5475 *Illinois!*

Date of Publication: 1986

Subject(s): Fires; Espionage; Franco-Prussian War

Fictional character(s): Toby Holt, Frontiersman; Henry Blake, Military Personnel (lieutenant), Spy

Time Period(s): 1870s (1871)

Locale(s): Chicago, Illinois; Germany

Summary: The Great Chicago Fire of 1871 is depicted, as Toby Holt plans to construct a new dynasty. Meanwhile, Lieutenant Henry Blake is in Germany on an espionage mission as Europe explodes into war.

Historical Accuracy: The scenery is authentic, but the historical details are considerably simplified in favor of the action.

5476 *Independence!*

Date of Publication: 1979

Subject(s): American West; Wagon Trains

Fictional character(s): Michael "Whip" Holt, Frontiersman; Claudia Humphries, Widow(er); Sam Brentwood, Wagonmaster; Cathy Van Ayl, Young Woman

Time Period(s): 1830s (1837)

Locale(s): Long Island, New York; Independence, Missouri

Summary: In the first of the author's Wagons West series, a party of settlers departs from Long Island to Independence, Missouri. This is only the first leg of a trek to Oregon, and the travellers are the first overland settlers. Wagonmaster Sam Brentwood is under secret orders from President Andrew Jackson to win the race with the British and the Russians to seize the Pacific Northwest for the U.S.

Historical Accuracy: Convincing in some of its frontier details, the emphasis is on a rousing story, not on fully documenting the historical period.

5477 *Kentucky!*

Date of Publication: 1987

Subject(s): Politics; Espionage

Fictional character(s): Toby Holt, Frontiersman; Henry Blake, Military Personnel (army officer), Spy

Time Period(s): 1870s

Locale(s): Kentucky; Germany

Summary: Toby Holt takes on an assignment to find an assassin plotting against President Grant. The trail leads to Kentucky. Meanwhile, Lieutenant Henry Blake continues his spying mission in Germany.

Historical Accuracy: The fictional predominates over the historical.

5478 *Louisiana!*

Date of Publication: 1985

Subject(s): Family Saga; Chinese Empire

Fictional character(s): Toby Holt, Young Man; Cindy Holt, Young Woman

Historical character(s): Ulysses S. Grant, Political Figure; Tz'u-hsi, Ruler (Dowager Empress of China)

Time Period(s): 1870s

Locale(s): New Orleans, Louisiana; China

Summary: This installment of the Wagons West series ranges widely in action, moving from the bustling port city of New Orleans to Hawaii and the Chinese imperial court of the dowager empress Tz'u Hsi. Toby Holt is sent on a diplomatic mission to China by President Grant. Meanwhile, Cindy Holt must prove herself in an adventure on the frontier.

Historical Accuracy: The historical elements are considerably simplified in favor of fast-paced action.

5479 *Montana!*

Date of Publication: 1983

Subject(s): American West; Ranching; Indians

Fictional character(s): Toby Holt, Frontiersman; Clarissa Sinclair, Spouse (of Toby); Beth Martin, Young Woman

Historical character(s): Andrew Johnson, Political Figure; Ulysses S. Grant, Military Personnel (general)

Time Period(s): 1860s (1866)

Locale(s): Fort Shaw, Montana

Summary: Toby Holt accepts a presidential assignment to assist in the construction of the Northwest railroad into the Montana territory. There he must contend with the Sioux and a deadly outlaw gang.

Historical Accuracy: This is mainly a fictional adventure with a basic historical orientation.

5480 *Nebraska!*

Date of Publication: 0
Subject(s): American West; Wagon Trains
Fictional character(s): Michael "Whip" Holt, Frontiersman; Cathy Van Ayl, Widow(er)
Time Period(s): 1830s (1837)
Locale(s): Nebraska; Independence, Missouri

Summary: In the second volume of the author's Wagons West series, 500 pioneers set off on a 2,200 mile trek to be the first wagon train to reach the Oregon territory. Leading the train is Whip Holt, who has convinced the widow Cathy Van Ayl to leave her family in Missouri. They endure Indians, flash floods, buffalo stampedes, and foreign espionage.

Historical Accuracy: The details of trail life are authentic and convincing.

5481 *Nevada!*

Date of Publication: 1982
Subject(s): American West; Civil War—U.S.
Fictional character(s): Leland Blake, Military Personnel (general); Michael "Whip" Holt, Frontiersman; Susanna Fulton, Editor
Historical character(s): William Gladstone, Political Figure; Henry John Temple, Political Figure, Nobleman; William Henry Seward, Political Figure; Abraham Lincoln, Political Figure; Salmon P. Chase, Political Figure; Winfield Scott, Military Personnel (general)
Time Period(s): 1860s (1861)
Locale(s): Virginia City, Nevada

Summary: As the Civil War breaks out, General Leland Blake undertakes a mission of utmost importance to the Union cause: transporting a shipment of silver from the Comstock Lode in Virginia City to New York. Aided by Whip Holt and a young newswoman, Blake leads the Silver Train east, contending with Confederate saboteurs and British agents.

Historical Accuracy: The action is fanciful, though a considerable number of historical figures make appearances.

5482 *Oklahoma!*

Date of Publication: 1989
Subject(s): American West; Indians
Fictional character(s): Toby Holt, Frontiersman; Alexandra Woodling, Southern Belle; Henry Blake, Military Personnel (army officer)
Time Period(s): 1870s
Locale(s): Oklahoma; Fargo, North Dakota

Summary: Homesteaders and ranchers are locked in a bitter range war in the Oklahoma territory. Toby Holt finds himself in the middle of the dispute while Captain Henry Blake is in the Dakotas for a rendezvous with Custer's Seventh Cavalry.

Historical Accuracy: This is history in passing, with a central interest on fast-paced action.

5483 *Oklahoma Pride*

Date of Publication: 1990
Subject(s): American West; Family Saga
Fictional character(s): Tim Holt, Journalist; Toby Holt, Political Figure; Peter Blake, Teenager
Time Period(s): 1880s (1889)
Locale(s): Guthrie, Oklahoma

Summary: The scene is the Oklahoma land rush of the 1880s as newspaperman Tim Holt and his 15-year-old cousin Peter Blake join the adventurers in the boom town of Guthrie. Tim hopes to establish a crusading newspaper, but powerful enemies attempt to stop him.

Historical Accuracy: The historical setting is colorfully depicted.

5484 *Oregon!*

Date of Publication: 1980
Subject(s): American West; Wagon Trains
Fictional character(s): Michael "Whip" Holt, Frontiersman; Cathy Van Ayl, Spouse (of Leland); Leland Blake, Military Personnel (lieutenant)
Historical character(s): Martin Van Buren, Political Figure; Winfield Scott, Military Personnel (general)
Time Period(s): 1830s
Locale(s): Oregon

Summary: America's first wagon train to the Pacific Northwest reaches the Oregon territory, where there is a clash between the American settlers, England, and Russia. Diplomatic manuevering explodes into open hostility, and Whip Holt and his party of settlers find themselves at the center of intrigue and rivalry with world-wide ramifications.

Historical Accuracy: The story is very loosely based on actual events, though considerably simplified and reduced to clear dramatic outlines.

5485 *Oregon Legacy*

Date of Publication:
Subject(s): Family Saga; Ranching; Mining
Fictional character(s): Toby Holt, Rancher; Tim Holt, Young Man
Time Period(s): 1880s (1887)
Locale(s): Dakota Territory, United States; Virginia City, Nevada

Summary: In the first volume of a series that continues the story of the Holt family, the scene is the Dakota territory in 1887 where rancher Toby Holt fights to save his new ranch during a brutal winter. His son, Tim, gets "silver fever" and heads west to the boom town of Virginia City.

Historical Accuracy: Like the Wagons West series, the emphasis is on fast-paced action with a simplified historical backdrop.

5486 *Outpost!*

Date of Publication: 1993
Subject(s): Settlement of the American Frontier; Indians; Crime and Criminals

Fictional character(s): Clay Holt, Frontiersman; Jefferson Holt, Frontiersman, Trapper; Shining Moon, Indian (Sioux), Spouse (of Clay)
Time Period(s): 1810s (1811)
Locale(s): Rocky Mountains; North Carolina

Summary: In the final volume of the author's Frontier Trilogy, Clay Holt sets out into the Northern Rockies to bring an outlaw to justice. Meanwhile in North Carolina, Jefferson Holt is stalked by a killer bent on destroying his family. The series concludes when the threat of war with Britain explodes into battle.

Historical Accuracy: The premium is on adventure with some solid period painting.

5487 *Pacific Destiny*

Date of Publication: 1994
Subject(s): Family Saga; Spanish-American War; Gold Rush—Klondike
Fictional character(s): Tim Holt, Journalist; Elizabeth Holt, Spouse, Suffragette; Frank Blake, Prospector
Time Period(s): 1890s (1898)
Locale(s): Yukon Territory, Canada; Cuba; Philippines

Summary: As war breaks out with Spain in 1898, the action ranges from prospecting in the Yukon gold fields to the military action of the Rough Riders in Cuba, to an espionage mission in the Philippines. Tim Holt travels to Cuba to cover the war and is reunited with his estranged wife Elizabeth.

Historical Accuracy: The historical details are trimmed and simplified to support the action.

5488 *Sierra Triumph*

Date of Publication: 1992
Subject(s): American West; Family Saga; Women's Rights
Fictional character(s): Tim Holt, Journalist; Elizabeth Emory, Suffragette; Frank Blake, Teenager
Time Period(s): 1890s (1895)
Locale(s): San Francisco, California

Summary: The year is 1895 as young Frank Blake strikes out on his own for the California oil fields. Meanwhile, newspaperman Tim Holt gets involved with suffragette Elizabeth Emory.

Historical Accuracy: The period setting is colorfully and convincingly detailed, but the emphasis is on action.

5489 *Tennessee!*

Date of Publication: 1986
Subject(s): Reconstruction Period
Fictional character(s): Toby Holt, Frontiersman; Clarissa Holt, Spouse; James Martinson, Political Figure
Time Period(s): 1870s
Locale(s): Memphis, Tennessee

Summary: Outlaws and renegades from the Civil War form a private army in Tennessee. Toby Holt is sent by the president to stop the threat to national security.

Historical Accuracy: The story is fictional with a simplified historical backdrop.

5490 *Texas!*

Date of Publication: 1980
Subject(s): Texas Revolution; American West; Wagon Trains
Fictional character(s): Leland Blake, Military Personnel (colonel); Michael "Whip" Holt, Frontiersman; Cathy Van Ayl Blake, Spouse (of Leland)
Historical character(s): Andrew Jackson, Political Figure; James K. Polk, Political Figure; Sam Houston, Political Figure; Andrew Johnson, Political Figure
Time Period(s): 1840s (1846)
Locale(s): Texas

Summary: As the Texas Republic struggles to survive, a band of Oregon volunteers journeys through Mexican territory, with Leland Blake leading a wagon train of future Texans from the east. Meanwhile, Whip Holt goes on a dangerous mission for Sam Houston.

Historical Accuracy: While the general outlines of history have been followed a few of the details of the record have been simplified.

5491 *Washington!*

Date of Publication: 1982
Subject(s): American West; Settlement of the American Frontier
Fictional character(s): Toby Holt, Veteran (Civil War); Caroline Brandon Holt, Spouse (of Toby); Beth Blake, Young Woman
Time Period(s): 1860s (1865)
Locale(s): Washington

Summary: As the Civil War ends, wounded veteran Toby Holt heads west to the Washington territory to claim a homestead. There he must deal with profiteers bent on exploiting the country's riches and seizing his land.

Historical Accuracy: The locale is colorfully presented.

5492 *Westward!*

Date of Publication: 1992
Subject(s): Settlement of the American Frontier; Lewis and Clark Expedition; Indians
Fictional character(s): Clay Holt, Frontiersman; Jefferson Holt, Frontiersman; Shining Moon, Indian (Sioux), Spouse (of Clay)
Historical character(s): Meriwether Lewis, Explorer; William Clark, Explorer; Thomas Jefferson, Political Figure
Time Period(s): 1800s (1806)
Locale(s): Ohio Valley, Ohio; Yellowstone River, West

Summary: This is the first volume of the author's Frontier Trilogy, that chronicles the forebears of wagonmaster Whip Holt of the Wagons West series. Clay Holt accompanies Lewis and Clark on their expedition to chart the West, and later, along with his brother Jefferson Holt, returns for adventures in the new land.

Historical Accuracy: The details of frontier life are authentic. The details of Lewis and Clark's expedition are invented.

5493 *Wisconsin!*

Date of Publication: 1987
Subject(s): Business Building; Franco-Prussian War
Fictional character(s): Toby Holt, Frontiersman; Henry Blake, Military Personnel (army officer), Spy
Time Period(s): 1870s
Locale(s): Milwaukee, Wisconsin; Germany

Summary: The lumber industry in Wisconsin during the 1870s is the setting for this installment of the Wagons West series. Toby Holt attempts to establish a lumber empire but must contend with corporate greed. Meanwhile, Lieutenant Henry Blake finds himself in a web of intrigue and romance in Germany.

Historical Accuracy: The novel's focus is wide and filled with adventure with some connection to its historical background.

5494 *Wyoming!*

Date of Publication:
Subject(s): American West; Wagon Trains; Indians
Fictional character(s): Michael "Whip" Holt, Frontiersman; Cathy Van Ayl, Widow(er); La-ena, Indian, Young Woman
Time Period(s): 1830s (1837)
Locale(s): Wyoming

Summary: America's first wagon train to the Pacific Northwest is attacked by Indians as it pushes through the Rockies. Survival depends on Whip Holt, who is torn between affection for Cathy Van Ayl and an Indian, La-ena.

Historical Accuracy: This is a rousing adventure story with some authentic details of period life.

5495 *Yankee*

Date of Publication: 1982
Subject(s): Espionage; Ottoman Empire
Fictional character(s): Jeremy Morgan, Privateer, Spy; Khana Tule Yasmin, Royalty (princess); Mary Ellis, Captive, Actress
Historical character(s): Alexander Hamilton, Political Figure; George, Royalty (Prince of Wales); Marie Joseph Paul de Lafayette, Nobleman
Time Period(s): 1780s; 1790s (1789-1791)
Locale(s): Constantinople, Ottoman Empire; London, England; Paris, France

Summary: Privateer Jeremy Morgan is sent as a secret agent by the young American government to Constantinople. There, he serves as guardian to Princess Khana Tule Yasmin, the key to a complicated diplomatic plot. Morgan is more interested in the English actress who is being held as Yasmin's slave.

Historical Accuracy: The story is farfetched but rousing. It should not be confused with real events or characters.

5496 *Yankee Rogue*

Date of Publication: 1984
Subject(s): French and Indian War; Battle of Quebec; American Colonies
Fictional character(s): Jared Hale, Military Personnel (lieutenant), Servant (indentured); Caroline Murtagh, Gentlewoman
Time Period(s): 1730s; 1740s (1739-1741)
Locale(s): London, England; Wilmington, Delaware, American Colonies; Quebec, Canada

Summary: A duel lands Jared Hale, an officer of the Royal Dragoons, in Newgate Prison. He is released from prison as an indentured servant to Caroline Murtagh in the American colonies. He wins his freedom in battle during the Quebec campaign in the French and Indian War.

Historical Accuracy: The situation is formulaic and well-worn, with some authentic period background painting.

DAVID WILLIAM ROSS (1922-)

5497 *Beyond the Stars*

Date of Publication: 1990
Subject(s): American West; Indians; Treasure Hunt
Fictional character(s): Andre Marcher, Adventurer; Benjamin Amiel, Adventurer; White River, Frontiersman; Ironfoot, Indian (Crow), Chieftain
Time Period(s): 19th century
Locale(s): Missouri River, United States (upper)

Summary: Three adventurers, Andre Marcher, Benjamin Amiel, and White River, set out into the Western frontier in search of an abandoned gold mine. They encounter an unforgiving landscape and Indians in this tale of their struggle for survival.

Historical Accuracy: The novel offers a genuine depiction of wilderness life in the West.

5498 *Eye of the Hawk*

Date of Publication: 1992
Subject(s): American West; Ranching; Indians
Fictional character(s): Seth Redmond, Rancher; Isabelle Redmond, Spouse; Blood Hawk, Indian (Comanche), Warrior
Time Period(s): 19th century (1841-1864)
Locale(s): Texas

Summary: Life on the Texas frontier before the Civil War is depicted in the family saga of the Redmonds, who build a horse ranch in the middle of Indian territory. The effects on the family of a Comanche raid and brutal rape are chronicled in a vivid depiction of frontier life.

Historical Accuracy: The details of life on the frontier are authentic and believable.

HUGH WILLIAMSON ROSS (1901-1978)

A prolific British nonfiction writer, novelist, and playwright, Ross was born in Hampshire, England, and attended the University of London. His career included work as a preparatory school master, an editor, a drama critic, a clergyman of the Church of England, and an actor. His writings include *The Princess a Nun!: A Novel Without Fiction*, *Historical Enigmas*, and *Letter to Julia*.

5499 *James, by the Grace of God*

Date of Publication: 1955

Subject(s): Royalty—England; Glorious Revolution
Historical character(s): James II, Ruler (King of England)
Time Period(s): 17th century (1680s)
Locale(s): England

Summary: The reign of English King James II is dramatized in the series of events that eventually lead to his ouster in the Glorious Revolution. James II, the second son of Charles I, is a Catholic, and, in the hysteria of the Popish Plot, is extremely unpopular. His autocratic tendencies and efforts to fill key government positions with Catholics do nothing to endear him to his subjects.

Historical Accuracy: The novel's defense of James II forces some debatable interpretations of history.

KATE ROSS

Ross is a trial lawyer with a Boston law firm.

5500 *A Broken Vessel*

Date of Publication: 1994
Subject(s): Mystery; Regency Period
Fictional character(s): Julian Kestrel, Gentleman, Detective—Amateur; Sally Stokes, Prostitute, Thief; Dipper, Servant (valet)
Time Period(s): 1820s
Locale(s): London, England

Summary: This Regency mystery features the elegant dandy Julian Kestrel, who becomes involved when his valet's sister, Sally Stokes, a prostitute and pickpocket, lifts handkerchiefs from three "clients" on a single evening. A stolen letter and an appeal for help from a woman who is later found dead supply the evidence. With Sally's help, Kestrel tracks down the three and solves the case.

Historical Accuracy: The novel features convincing period atmosphere.

5501 *Cut to the Quick*

Date of Publication: 1993
Subject(s): Mystery; Regency Period
Fictional character(s): Julian Kestrel, Gentleman, Detective—Amateur; Hugh Fontclair, Nobleman; Dipper, Servant
Time Period(s): 1820s
Locale(s): London, England

Summary: This mystery introduces the Regency dandy turned sleuth Julian Kestrel. When he rescues a young aristocrat, Hugh Fontclair, from a gaming house, Kestrel is invited to be the best man at Fontclair's wedding. At the Fontclair country house, he finds himself in the middle of family warfare that erupts into murder. With the help of his Cockney servant Dipper, a reformed pickpocket, Kestrel sets out to find the killer.

Historical Accuracy: The mystery is inventive and set convincingly in the Regency period.

5502 *Whom the Gods Love*

Date of Publication: 1995
Subject(s): Mystery; Regency Period

Fictional character(s): Julian Kestrel, Gentleman, Detective—Amateur; Barbara Falkland, Widow(er); Martha Gilmore, Servant (maid)
Time Period(s): 1820s (1825)
Locale(s): London, England

Summary: When Alexander Falkland is found in his study, his distraught family turns to Julian Kestrel for help. Kestrel has no end of suspects, but at the center of the case is the enigma of Falkland himself. Who was he really? A social reformer, or a rake with a secret?.

Historical Accuracy: The novel captures the era with telling details.

MALCOLM ROSS
(PSEUD. OF MALCOLM ROSS-MACDONALD, 1932-)

Malcolm Ross is a pseudonym used by this English author, best known for his historical novels.

5503 *The Dukes: A Novel*

Date of Publication: 1981
Subject(s): Victorian Period; Family Saga; Inheritance—Disputed
Fictional character(s): Alfred Boyce, Heir
Time Period(s): 19th century; 20th century (1849-1917)
Locale(s): England

Summary: This massive family saga tells the story of Alfred Boyce, a Victorian middle class box manufacturer who finds himself heir to a nearly bankrupt dukedom. With a rival heir lying in wait to make a claim, Boyce aspires to join Victorian high society.

Historical Accuracy: The novel is overstuffed with period references to events like the Crimean War and Jack the Ripper scandal that create a compelling and realistic background for the family drama.

ZOLA HELEN ROSS (1912-1989)

Born in Dayton, Iowa, and a graduate of MacMurray College, American educator and writer Zola Helen Ross was best known as the author of Westerns, mysteries, and children's books. She also wrote under the pseudonyms Helen Arre and Bert Iles.

5504 *The Green Land*

Date of Publication: 1952
Subject(s): American West; Railroads
Fictional character(s): Raleigh Mead, Doctor; Caroline Mead, Spouse
Time Period(s): 1870s
Locale(s): Pacific Northwest

Summary: This western melodrama is set in the Washington territory in the early 1870s as the Northern Pacific railroad works its way north to link the territory. Dr. Raleigh Mead and his wife Caroline face marital problems against a backdrop of land speculation, an earthquake, murder, and a near lynching.

Historical Accuracy: The period flavor is authentic, but the novel resorts to a considerable amount of implausible artifice to resolve the story's many elements.

5505　*A Land to Tame*

Date of Publication: 1956
Subject(s): American West; Indians; Settlement of the American Frontier
Fictional character(s): Rush Paxton, Scout; Theophilius Yates, Young Woman
Time Period(s): 1850s
Locale(s): Yakima Valley, Washington

Summary: Based on the actual Indian War in the Yakima Valley, the novel tells the story of white settlers who conspire to provoke a battle which will cost the Yakima Indians the land given them by treaty. Civilian scout Rush Paxton is caught in the middle between the Indians and the unscrupulous whites.

Historical Accuracy: The story is imagined but does depend on an actual period background.

LEONARD ROSSITER

Born in London and educated at Westminster, Rossiter served in World War I in the Middle East and France. After the war, he resumed his studies and became a barrister. Over the years he has made a study of Provence and the Middle Ages.

5506　*Bernadin, My Love*

Date of Publication: 1962
Subject(s): Middle Ages; Albigensian Crusade
Fictional character(s): Magali, Orphan, Heiress; Lord Rambaud, Nobleman; Bernadin, Minstrel (troubador)
Time Period(s): 13th century (1234)
Locale(s): Provence, France

Summary: Set in medieval Provence during the Albigensian heresy, the novel tells the romantic tale of Magali, who is forced into an arranged marriage with Lord Rambaud, a member of the Albigensian sect, who is sworn to celibacy. She is hidden away in a remote part of his castle, but she meets a childhood friend, the troubador Bernadin. She falls in love with him with serious consequences.

Historical Accuracy: This is not a book written for historians. The author has deliberately, for the sake of the essential unity of the story, altered dates, places, and persons.

JUDITH ROSSNER (1935-)

Born in New York City, Rossner attended City College. Her novels are concerned with women's lives, and she is best known for the bestselling *Looking for Mr. Goodbar*, inspired by a true-life murder committed by a man she met in a singles bar.

5507　*Emmeline*

Date of Publication: 1980

Subject(s): Mills and Millwork; Labor Movement
Historical character(s): Emmeline Mosher, Worker (factory)
Time Period(s): 1830s (1839)
Locale(s): Lowell, Massachusetts

Summary: The novel is based on the actual figure of Emmeline Mosher, who leaves her family's farm in Maine for a job in the fabric mills of Lowell, Massachusetts, in the 1830s. It is a haunting tale of seduction and betrayal that captures the grim reality of early industrialized America.

Historical Accuracy: The novel tells Mosher's story unadorned and is convincing in its period details.

THEODORE ROSZAK (1933-)

An American historian and cultural critic, Roszak graduated from UCLA and received his Ph.D. from Princeton. A professor of history at California State University, Roszak is best known for his study *The Making of a Counter Culture*.

5508　*The Memoirs of Elizabeth Frankenstein*

Date of Publication: 1995
Subject(s): Gothic Romance; Witchcraft and Sorcery
Fictional character(s): Victor Frankenstein, Scientist; Elizabeth Frankenstein, Gentlewoman; Robert Walton, Explorer
Time Period(s): 1790s
Locale(s): Switzerland

Summary: The novel is an imaginative counterpart to Mary Shelly's *Frankenstein*. It is the secret autobiography of Elizabeth Frankenstein, rescued as a child from the gypsies and raised as Victor Frankenstein's sister. They both are introduced to the occult and alchemy, which causes Victor to construct the Creature who will haunt Elizabeth's wedding night. The perspective offers a bold retelling of the familiar story.

Historical Accuracy: The novel captures with skill the atmosphere of Shelly's original and its period elements.

ABRAHAM ROTHBERG (1922-)

Born in New York City and a graduate of Brooklyn College, Rothberg has worked as a European correspondent for *The National Observer* and a special correspondent for the Manchester *Guardian*. Rothberg has received praise for his novels and his journalism.

5509　*The Sword of the Golem*

Date of Publication: 1970
Subject(s): Jews; Thirty Years War; Religious Conflict
Fictional character(s): Mordecai Mesler, Banker; Golem, Warrior
Historical character(s): Judah Low, Religious (rabbi)
Time Period(s): 16th century
Locale(s): Prague, Czechoslovakia

Summary: Set in the Prague ghetto in the 16th century, the novel tells the story of how Rabbi Low fashions a vengeful protector, a Golem, to defend his people and then must deal with the consequences of his creation. The rabbi is caught between Imperial forces on the outside and fanatism within and must decide when to resist and at what cost.

Historical Accuracy: The story is more fantasy than an accurate historical account. The period elements of life in the Prague ghetto are convincing.

CESAR J. ROTONDI (1926-)

Born in Brooklyn, New York, Rotondi attended City College, the Illinois Institute of Technology, and the University of Chicago. He has worked as a greeting card designer, manufacturer, retailer, and painter.

5510 *The Garden of Persephone*

Date of Publication: 1982
Subject(s): Middle Ages; Diplomacy; Religious Conflict
Fictional character(s): Julien FitzNigel, Scholar, Diplomat
Historical character(s): Roger II, Ruler (King of Sicily); Bernard of Clairvaux, Religious (mystic)
Time Period(s): 12th century
Locale(s): Sicily, Italy (Palermo, Salerno); Rome, Italy

Summary: Set in the court of Roger II, King of Sicily, the novel tells the story of young Julien FitzNigel. FitzNigel leaves a monastery in England to serve King Roger as his special envoy on a series of diplomatic missions to help achieve Roger's dream of consolidating all of southern Italy. The novel captures the color of medieval Sicily and the religious conflict of the period.

Historical Accuracy: The novel is authentic in its period elements and reflects actual events and circumstances.

JEAN ROUSSELOT (1915-)

Rousselot is a French writer whose books include *Blaise Cendars*.

5511 *Hungarian Rhapsody: The Life of Franz Liszt*

Date of Publication: 1961
Subject(s): Musical Life; Biography, Fictionalized
Historical character(s): Franz Liszt, Composer, Musician; Richard Wagner, Composer; Cosima Wagner, Spouse; George Sand, Writer; Alfred de Musset, Writer; Louis Hector Berlioz, Composer; Frederic Chopin, Composer, Musician
Time Period(s): 19th century (1811-1886)
Locale(s): Europe

Summary: This fictionalized biography of Hungarian musician and composer Franz Liszt traces his career from child prodigy to musical genius. His roles as teacher, finest pianist of his day, renowned composer, and passionate lover of women are dramatized. The novel's emphasis is on his long series of love affairs.

Historical Accuracy: The novel is careful with the biographical and musical data, though a few dates are wrong. Overall this is a rather romanticized version of Liszt's life.

EARL ROVIT (1927-)

Born in Boston, Rovit is a graduate of the University of Michigan and Boston University. He is a professor of English. His books feature intricate structures and themes and have evoked comparisons with Luigi Pirandello, James Joyce, and Bernard Malamud. His novels include *The Player King* and *A Far Cry*.

5512 *Crossings*

Date of Publication: 1973
Subject(s): Family Saga
Fictional character(s): Mayhew Enfield, Religious (minister); Elizabeth Enfield, Spouse; Prentiss Enfield, Young Man; Clovis Enfield, Young Woman
Time Period(s): 19th century (1865-1886)
Locale(s): Connecticut

Summary: This ingenious novel offers two points of view on a family tragedy in 19th-century Connecticut. One is the diary of Elizabeth Enfield, the other that of her minister husband, Mayhew. Perspectives converge on the crisis produced by the birth of their grandchild.

Historical Accuracy: The novel is a psychological study with a convincing depiction of the period.

JACK ROWE

Rowe was born in the Brandywine Valley of Delaware. His ancestors were among the early workers in the Du Pont gunpowder plant.

5513 *Brandywine*

Date of Publication: 1984
Subject(s): Business Building
Fictional character(s): Noreen Feeney, Young Woman; Patrick Gallagher, Artisan (stonemason); Francis Reardon, Religious (priest)
Historical character(s): Pierre Samuel Du Pont de Nemours, Businessman
Time Period(s): 19th century (1800-1837)
Locale(s): Brandywine River Valley, Delaware

Summary: The novel begins a trilogy on the Du Pont chemical empire. The Du Ponts, royalist refugees from revolutionary France, come to America and make their fortune making gunpowder. Several characters—a fiery Irish beauty, an Irish stonemason, and a Catholic priest—struggle for independence against the powerful influence of the Du Ponts' growing industrial empire.

Historical Accuracy: The novel blends a fictional story with the factual elements of the actual Du Pont family and their empire.

5514 *Dominion*

Date of Publication: 1986
Subject(s): Business Building; Civil War—U.S.; Mexican War
Fictional character(s): Michael Farrell, Immigrant

Historical character(s): Lammot Du Pont, Businessman, Scientist; Henry Du Pont, Businessman
Time Period(s): 19th century (1846-1873)
Locale(s): Brandywine River Valley, Delaware

Summary: In the second volume of the author's Du Pont trilogy, the story of the great chemical company is dramatized in the struggle of Lammot Du Pont to regain control of the explosives empire from his uncle, Henry Du Pont. Set during the Mexican and Civil Wars, the corporate intrigue reveals the inner workings of the massive Du Pont dynasty.

Historical Accuracy: The author is careful to follow documented sources, giving an authenticity to the family story and its era.

5515 *Fortune's Legacy*
Date of Publication: 1988
Subject(s): Business Building; Spanish-American War
Historical character(s): Alfred I. Du Pont, Businessman; Theodore Roosevelt, Political Figure
Time Period(s): 19th century; 20th century (1877-1902)
Locale(s): Brandywine River Valley, Delaware; Belgium

Summary: In the third volume of the author's trilogy on the history of the Du Pont family and its industrial empire, the focus is on Alfred I. Du Pont. He learns the family business from the bottom, steals a new munitions powder process by secretly infiltrating a Belgian company, and comes to the aid of the American war machine during the Spanish-American War.

Historical Accuracy: The period elements and the details of Du Pont family history are authentic.

PATRICIA ROWE

5516 *Children of the Dawn*
Date of Publication: 1996
Subject(s): Prehistory; Tribal Life—Prehistoric
Fictional character(s): Ashan, Prehistoric Human, Chieftain; Tor, Prehistoric Human, Hunter
Time Period(s): Indeterminate Past
Locale(s): Columbia River, North America

Summary: This sequel to the author's *Keepers of the Misty Time* continues the story of the Shahala people in the Pacific Northwest 9,000 years ago. Their chief is the woman Ashan who continues to face challenges as the Shahala struggle to survive.

Historical Accuracy: The novel is informed by evident research into the region and the history of prehistoric peoples of North America.

5517 *Keepers of the Misty Time*
Date of Publication: 1994
Subject(s): Prehistory; Tribal Life—Prehistoric
Fictional character(s): Ashan, Prehistoric Human, Chieftain; Tor, Prehistoric Human, Hunter
Time Period(s): Indeterminate Past
Locale(s): Pacific Northwest, North America

Summary: This story of prehistoric life in North America concerns the woman chieftain Ashan, who together with the hunter Tor, prepares for the changes that confront her people.

Historical Accuracy: The novel offers a believable version of prehistoric life and customs.

ADELAIDE C. ROWELL (1884-)
Born in Cleveland, Ohio, Rowell's family moved to Tennessee, where she graduated from the University of Tennessee. She was a librarian who wrote a number of one-act plays and a novle for young people in addition to *On Jordan's Stormy Banks*.

5518 *On Jordan's Stormy Banks*
Date of Publication: 1948
Subject(s): Civil War—U.S.; Espionage
Historical character(s): Sam Davis, Military Personnel (Confederate soldier)
Time Period(s): 1860s
Locale(s): United States

Summary: This Civil War story tells the tale of the actual Confederate scout Sam Davis who joins the Coleman's Scouts and in 1863 is captured and hanged as a spy. The novel dramatizes his adventures.

Historical Accuracy: The novel is based on solid research but is considerably enhanced by the melodramatic and sensational.

LAURA JOH ROWLAND
A granddaughter of Chinese and Korean immigrants, Rowland was born in Michigan.

5519 *Bundori*
Date of Publication: 1996
Subject(s): Mystery; Japanese Empire
Fictional character(s): Sano Ichiro, Warrior (samurai), Detective—Police; Yanagisawa, Government Official (court chamberlain); Adi, Religious (mystic)
Time Period(s): 17th century (1689)
Locale(s): Edo, Japan (modern Tokyo)

Summary: In the second case for the shogun's "Most Honorable Investigator of Events, Situations and People," Sano Ichiro, a war trophy, or *bundori*, of a severed head nailed to a plank and offered for public display, begins to panic the citizenry of feudal Edo, Japan. The victims are members of a noble clan and the killer appears to be carrying out an ancient grudge. Sano hunts for the killer who must be one of three powerful men.

Historical Accuracy: The novel excels in presenting a genuine and believable historical background.

5520 *Shin Ju*
Date of Publication: 1994
Subject(s): Mystery; Japanese Empire

Fictional character(s): Sano Ichiro, Warrior (samurai), Detective—Police

Time Period(s): 17th century (1689)

Locale(s): Edo, Japan (present day Tokyo)

Summary: This historical mystery is set in medieval Japan. When the bodies of a young man and woman are found bound together, it appears to be a case of *shinju*, a ritual double suicide by a pair of star-crossed lovers. Sano, a former samurai and now a police detective, begins an investigation and soon suspects murder. He pursues a trail of evidence that uncovers deceit and assassination that lead to the shogun himself.

Historical Accuracy: The novel's depiction of 17th-century Japan is convincing and authentic.

PETER ROWLAND (1938-)

English writer Rowland was born in London and graduated from the University of Bristol. He has worked as the administrative officer in the civil service departments of Highways & Transportation and Public Health Engineering.

5521 *The Disappearance of Edwin Drood*

Date of Publication: 1992

Subject(s): Mystery; Victorian Period

Fictional character(s): Sherlock Holmes, Detective—Private; John Jasper, Gentleman (choirmaster); John H. Watson, Doctor, Sidekick

Time Period(s): 1890s (1894)

Locale(s): England

Summary: At the urging of John Jasper, Sherlock Holmes is brought in to solve the mystery of Charles Dickens' last, uncompleted novel. Dickens' novel, set in mid-century, waits 40 years for Holmes' solution.

Historical Accuracy: The novel's two eras, Dickens' and Holmes', present an odd melange of Victorian backgrounds.

HELEN RUCKER

Born in Seattle, Washington, Rucker attended the National Park College, Cornish School of Allied Arts, and the University of Washington. A lifelong Seattle resident, Rucker has brought her Pacific Northwest background to her writing and is the author of *The Wolf Tree*.

5522 *Cargo of Brides*

Date of Publication: 1956

Subject(s): American West

Fictional character(s): Marianna Bancroft, Young Woman

Time Period(s): 1860s

Locale(s): Washington

Summary: In this historical romance, a shipload of young women journey to Washington to be married. The story centers on the romantic complications of Marianna Bancroft.

Historical Accuracy: Despite a solid regional depiction, the novel is marred by stock elements and characters, and excessive contrivance.

ROGER RUDIGOZ

5523 *French Dragoon*

Date of Publication: 1959

Subject(s): Napoleonic Wars

Fictional character(s): Claude Solassier, Military Personnel (cavalry captain)

Time Period(s): 1810s (1813)

Locale(s): France

Summary: Claude Solassier, a French cavalry captain, must make his way during the peace following the French defeat at Leipzig and Napoleon's abdication. Solassier must adjust to civilian life and to the new Royalist regime.

Historical Accuracy: The novel's period background is authentic and believable, although the plot is improbable.

E. RALPH RUNDELL

5524 *The Color of Blood*

Date of Publication: 1948

Subject(s): Independence—South America

Fictional character(s): Roberto "Blanco" Landerson, Young Man, Cowboy (gaucho)

Time Period(s): 1830s

Locale(s): Argentina

Summary: This adventure novel set in Argentina during the 1830s chronicles the exploits of a young half-English gaucho, Roberto "Blanco" Landerson, during the rise to power of Juan Manuel de Rosas. Landerson becomes a witness to most of the important events of Argentinean history during the period.

Historical Accuracy: The period elements are convincingly detailed and authentic.

KRISTINE KATHRYN RUSCH (1960-)

An American science fiction and fantasy writer and editor, Rusch was born in Oneota, New York. She attended Beloit College, Beloit, Wisconsin and graduated from the University of Wisconsin with a B.A. in History. She has worked as a journalist, editorial assistant, secretary, and owner of a frame shop. Since 1991, she has been the editor of *The Magazine of Fantasy and Science Fiction*. Rusch won the John W. Campbell Award as Best New Writer in 1990 and the Hugo Award in 1994.

5525 *The Gallery of His Dreams*

Date of Publication: 1991

Subject(s): Photography; Civil War—U.S.

Historical character(s): Matthew B. Brady, Photographer; Julia Brady, Spouse

Time Period(s): 19th century (1838-1887)

Locale(s): United States

Summary: While examining his pictures for an exhibition, Matthew Brady, pioneering photographer, reflects on his life and times. The novel dramatizes a range of Brady's experiences with a particular emphasis on his Civil War battlefield work.

Historical Accuracy: The novel is solidly based on the actual details of Brady's career.

WILLIAM RUSH (1887-1950)

Rush's books include *Wild Horses of Rainrock*, *Wild Animals of the Rockies*, and *Wildlife of Idaho*.

5526 *Red Fox of the Kinapoo*

Date of Publication: 1949
Subject(s): American West; Indians
Fictional character(s): Red Fox, Indian (Nez Perce)
Historical character(s): Chief Joseph, Indian (Nez Perce)
Time Period(s): 1870s (1872-1877)
Locale(s): Pacific Northwest

Summary: The story of the Nez Perce Indians and the leadership of Chief Joseph are dramatized through the experiences of Red Fox, who leaves a white school to return to his people. He becomes an aide to Chief Joseph and participates in the daring and eventually tragic attempt of the Nez Perce to avoid the U.S. Army and find refuge in Canada in 1877.

Historical Accuracy: The novel captures customs of the Nez Perce, their combat with the army, and the background of the period with conviction.

JANE GILMORE RUSHING (1925-)

Born in Texas, Rushing graduated from Texas Tech University. She has worked as a newspaper reporter and high school English teacher in Texas, as well as an instructor of English at the University of Tennessee, Knoxville.

5527 *Covenant of Grace*

Date of Publication: 1982
Subject(s): American Colonies; Puritans; Religious Conflict
Historical character(s): Anne Hutchinson, Leader (religious); John Winthrop, Government Official (colonial administrator); John Cotton, Religious (clergyman)
Time Period(s): 17th century (1630s)
Locale(s): Boston, Massachusetts, American Colonies

Summary: This biographical novel on the life of Anne Hutchinson dramatizes the antinomian controversy of the Massachusetts Bay Colony that sweeps Hutchinson up in a challenge to the leaders of New England's theocracy. Her dissent results in her banishment and excommunication. The novel captures both the heroism of its main character and the religious issues that produce the novel's tragedy.

Historical Accuracy: Although based on true events, the novel does take some liberties with the chronology and circumstances, which are detailed in the book's notes.

5528 *Hope of Earth*

Date of Publication: 1947
Subject(s): Settlement of the American Frontier
Fictional character(s): Amoret Phelps, Settler; Stephen Phelps, Settler; Joel Adams, Farmer, Religious (preacher)
Time Period(s): 1830s
Locale(s): Illinois

Summary: Pioneer life in the unsettled plains of Illinois during the 1830s is the novel's background. Amoret and Stephen Phelps journey west, where they grow apart under the strain of the wilderness. Amoret is sustained by the love of Joel Adams, a farmer-preacher.

Historical Accuracy: The details of wilderness life of the period are authentically presented.

5529 *Mary Dove*

Date of Publication: 1974
Subject(s): American West; Racial Conflict
Fictional character(s): Mary Dove, Young Woman; Red Jones, Cowboy
Time Period(s): 19th century
Locale(s): Texas (western)

Summary: Mary Dove is a young mulatto woman, raised in isolation by her protective father. When he dies, she is left on her own. After stranger Red Jones comes to visit, she begins to learn about her identity and its challenges.

Historical Accuracy: The novel is convincing in its period background.

5530 *Tamzen*

Date of Publication: 1972
Subject(s): American West; Homesteading; Railroads
Fictional character(s): Tamzen Greer, Settler; Arthur Field, Gentleman; Walter Hastings, Rancher
Time Period(s): 1890s
Locale(s): Texas (western)

Summary: West Texas in the 1890s is a battleground among the baronial ranchers, the railroad agents, and the homesteaders squatting on land while the government decides its fate. Tamzen Greer and her family are homesteaders, and she finds herself torn between a young rancher and the affections of a young Englishman.

Historical Accuracy: The novel captures the period and the locale with believable details.

5531 *Walnut Grove*

Date of Publication: 1964
Subject(s): American West
Fictional character(s): John Carlile, Young Man
Time Period(s): 1900s
Locale(s): Texas

Summary: Life in a frontier town in West Texas in the early years of the 20th century is depicted through the maturation of John Carlile. As he comes of age the cattle ranches give way to cotton farms and the railroad arrives, bringing more changes in its wake.

Historical Accuracy: This is a vivid and believable portrait of a community.

`5532` *Winds of Blame*

Date of Publication: 1983
Subject(s): Rural Life—U.S.; Crime and Criminals; American West
Fictional character(s): Joanna Doane, Young Woman; Isabel Doane, Young Woman
Time Period(s): 1910s (1916)
Locale(s): Greenfields, Texas

Summary: Set in a rural Texas town in 1916, the novel tells the story of a murder and frontier morality. The citizens of Greenfields close ranks to cover up the act and the truth. The curious story of the tragedy that befalls the Doane family paints a disturbing portrait of small town hypocrisy and deceit.

Historical Accuracy: The period elements are authentically evoked.

PAMELA REDFORD RUSSELL (1950-)

Born in California, Russell attended UCLA. She has worked as a fashion model, a tour guide, and a demonstrator of toys. She has written scripts for TV's "The Mary Tyler Moore Show.".

`5533` *The Woman Who Loved John Wilkes Booth*

Date of Publication: 1978
Subject(s): Civil War—U.S.; Assassination
Historical character(s): John Wilkes Booth, Murderer (assassin), Actor; Mary Eugenia Surratt, Criminal (conspirator)
Time Period(s): 1860s (1864-1865)
Locale(s): Washington, District of Columbia

Summary: The story of the conspiracy to assassinate Abraham Lincoln is told in the imagined diary of Mary Surratt, who becomes involved in the conspiracy through her attraction to the charismatic John Wilkes Booth. The novel captures both the personalities involved in the assassination and Washington in the period during the Civil War.

Historical Accuracy: The story of the assassination and the figures involved is accurately described.

RAY RUSSELL (1924-)

Born in Chicago, Russell attended the Chicago Conservatory of Music and the Goodman Theatre. Russell is a former magazine editor and occasional screenwriter. He is the author of short stories, poetry, and nonfiction. His work has been chosen to appear in more than 70 textbooks and anthologies.

`5534` *Princess Pamela*

Date of Publication: 1979
Subject(s): Victorian Period; Royalty—England

Fictional character(s): Pamela Summerfield, Gentlewoman; Giles O'Connor, Gentleman; Phoebe Summerfield, Gentlewoman
Historical character(s): Anthony Trollope, Writer; Douglas Jerrold, Writer; William IV, Ruler (King of England)
Time Period(s): 1830s (1837)
Locale(s): London, England

Summary: The novel takes the form of the diary of Pamela Summerfield written during the fateful year of 1837 as the old king, William IV, declines and the young Princess Victoria waits to be the next Queen of England. Pamela's diary records her contact with the great and fashionable and features startling disclosures, scandal, courtroom drama, violence, and an astonishing revelation.

Historical Accuracy: The period elements and the historical background serve to ground this story in a believable context.

EDWARD RUTHERFURD
(PSEUD. OF FRANCIS EDWARD WINTLE, 1948-)

Born in Salisbury, England, Rutherfurd was educated at Cambridge University and Stanford.

`5535` *Russka: The Novel of Russia*

Date of Publication: 1991
Subject(s): Social Chronicle; Russian Empire
Fictional character(s): Ivanushka, Landowner; Boris Bobrov, Landowner
Historical character(s): Peter the Great, Ruler (Czar of Russia); Ivan the Terrible, Ruler (Czar of Russia); Catherine the Great, Ruler (Empress of Russia)
Time Period(s): Multiple Time Periods
Locale(s): Russia

Summary: Over 1,800 years of Russian history are chronicled in the story of a small village and four ethnically diverse families who reflect the rich and complex panorama of Russian civilization. The story begins in A.D. 180 and continues into the 20th century, capturing the impact of Russia's rulers, including Ivan, Peter, and Catherine, and the Communist regime.

Historical Accuracy: The novel's portrait of Russian history is authoritative and convincing.

`5536` *Sarum: The Novel of England*

Date of Publication: 1987
Subject(s): Social Chronicle; Family Saga
Fictional character(s): Krona, Prehistoric Human, Warrior; Caius Porteus, Government Official; Richard de Godefroi, Gentleman
Historical character(s): Claudius I, Ruler (Roman emperor); Edward I, Ruler (King of England)
Time Period(s): Multiple Time Periods
Locale(s): Sarum, England (modern Salisbury)

Summary: The novel chronicles over 10,000 years of English history from the Ice Age to the modern period, focusing on the story of seven fictional families centered around the city of Sarum (modern Salisbury). The novel dramatizes the origins of Stonehenge, the invasion of Britain by the Roman Emperor

Claudius, the Norman Conquest, the Black Death, the Reformation, and World War II.

Historical Accuracy: Massive in concept, the novel displays an historically accurate portrait of the various ages depicted.

ADAM RUTLEDGE
(PSEUD. OF JAMES M. REASONER)

`5537` *Cannon's Call*
Date of Publication: 1993
Subject(s): American Revolution
Fictional character(s): Daniel Reed, Military Personnel (American officer)
Time Period(s): 1770s (1776)
Locale(s): Boston, Massachusetts

Summary: To assist in the siege of British-held Boston in 1776, the Continental Army of George Washington needs the captured artillery from Fort Ticonderoga. Daniel Reed undertakes the mission to bring the artillery across the rugged Berkshires while dealing with a traitor in his own command.

Historical Accuracy: The historical situation is accurately presented.

`5538` *Life and Liberty*
Date of Publication: 1993
Subject(s): American Revolution; Espionage
Fictional character(s): Daniel Reed, Military Personnel (American officer); Elliott Markham, Spy
Time Period(s): 1770s (1776)

Summary: The trials of the Continental Army continue for Daniel Reed, while double agent Elliott Markham maintains his dangerous secret mission.

Historical Accuracy: The story is invented but does depend on some accurately described historical events.

`5539` *Rebel Guns*
Date of Publication: 1992
Subject(s): American Revolution; Battle of Ticonderoga; Espionage
Fictional character(s): Daniel Reed, Military Personnel (soldier); Quincy Reed, Military Personnel (soldier); Murdoch Buchanan, Military Personnel (soldier), Frontiersman; Roxanne Darragh, Patriot, Spy
Historical character(s): Ethan Allen, Military Personnel (colonel)
Time Period(s): 1770s
Locale(s): Fort Ticonderoga, New York, American Colonies; Boston, Massachusetts, American Colonies

Summary: In the second volume of the author's series on the American Revolution, Daniel and Quincy Reed are with Ethan Allen and his Green Mountain Boys during the events surrounding the assault on Fort Ticonderoga. Meanwhile, in Boston, Roxanne Darragh is involved in an effort to capture a shipment of British munitions.

Historical Accuracy: The novel's essential historical framework is accurate though some liberties have been taken.

`5540` *Sons of Liberty*
Date of Publication: 1992
Subject(s): American Colonies; American Revolution
Fictional character(s): Daniel Reed, Student (law); Quincy Reed, Patriot; Roxanne Darragh, Patriot
Historical character(s): Nathan Hale, Patriot, Revolutionary; Samuel Adams, Patriot, Revolutionary
Time Period(s): 1770s (1773)
Locale(s): Boston, Massachusetts, American Colonies

Summary: The opening events of the American Revolution are dramatized in the story of Daniel Reed, a law student in Boston who finds himself caught up in the insurrection that culminates in the Boston Tea Party. His story is joined with those of his young brother, Quincy, and Roxanne Darragh.

Historical Accuracy: Although the period elements are accurate, certain minor details of history have been altered for dramatic purposes.

`5541` *Stars and Stripes*
Date of Publication: 1994
Subject(s): American Revolution
Fictional character(s): Daniel Reed, Military Personnel (American officer); Roxanne Darragh Stoddard, Young Woman; Cyril Eldridge, Spy; Elliot Markham, Patriot
Historical character(s): Thomas Jefferson, Political Figure; Benjamin Tallmadge, Military Personnel (American officer)
Time Period(s): 1770s (1776)
Locale(s): New York, New York; Virginia; Philadelphia, Pennsylvania

Summary: In the concluding volume of the Patriot Saga, an underground group of Tories plans a surprise attack on Washington's army. Daniel Reed serves as a bodyguard to Thomas Jefferson on a dangerous mission to Philadelphia, while Roxanne Darragh Stoddard must contend with the vengeance of English spymaster Cyril Eldridge.

Historical Accuracy: The story is invented but is set against a convincing backdrop of actual events.

EDWARD J. RYAN (1899-)
Born in Illinois, Ryan graduated from the University of Illinois and the Illinois Institute of Technology. He has worked as a newspaper reporter, college instructor, and dentist, and served as president of the Chicago Dental Society.

`5542` *Comes an Echo on the Breeze*
Date of Publication: 1949
Subject(s): Black Hawk War; Indians
Historical character(s): Abraham Lincoln, Military Personnel (army captain); Jefferson Davis, Military Personnel (army lieutenant); Zachary Taylor, Military Personnel (army colonel); Ann Rutledge, Young Woman
Time Period(s): 1830s (1832)
Locale(s): Illinois; Michigan

Summary: The novel provides a dramatic recreation of Abraham Lincoln's military experience during the Black Hawk

War. A number of other historical figures, such as Zachary Taylor and Jefferson Davis, are also depicted.

Historical Accuracy: The novel is historically accurate in most details. However, situations and dialogue have been invented.

VIKTOR RYDBERG (1829-1895)

A Swedish philosopher, poet, and novelist, Rydberg wrote *The Teaching of the Bible about Christ*, a refutation of fundamentalist Christian views. His poetry is noted for its majestic lyricism and for its sense of the mystery of human existence.

`5543` *The Last Athenian*

Date of Publication: 1859
Subject(s): Roman Empire; Religious Conflict; Christianity
Fictional character(s): Chrysanteus, Philosopher; Peter, Religious (bishop of Athens); Annaeus Domitius, Political Figure (Roman proconsul)
Time Period(s): 4th century
Locale(s): Athens, Greece

Summary: The novel concerns the factional battle between pagan and Christian sects during the reign of Roman Emperors Constantine and Julian. Peter, Bishop of Athens, is opposed by Chrysanteus, a pagan. The Roman proconsul Domitius tries to keep order as mobs from the different factions riot in the street. The message of the novel is a plea for religious tolerance.

Historical Accuracy: There are strong and convincing scenes of the early history of the Christian church.

REBECCA RYMAN

Rebecca Ryman lives in her native India.

`5544` *Olivia and Jai*

Date of Publication: 1990
Subject(s): British Raj; Indian Mutiny; English Colonies
Fictional character(s): Olivia O'Rourke, Young Woman; Jai Raventhorne, Bastard Son
Time Period(s): 1840s (1848)
Locale(s): Calcutta, India

Summary: Set during the British Raj in Calcutta, the novel describes the tragic romance between Olivia O'Rourke, a young American, and Jai Raventhorne, the half-caste bastard son of an Englishman and an Indian tribal girl. The novel traces Olivia's love and betrayal, set against the stifling customs of the English colonists.

Historical Accuracy: The period elements of colonial India are captured with authority.

`5545` *The Veil of Illusion*

Date of Publication: 1995
Subject(s): British Raj; English Colonies; Victorian Period
Fictional character(s): Olivia O'Rourke, Spouse; Maya Raventhorne, Young Woman; Christian Pendlebury, Gentleman

Time Period(s): 1870s
Locale(s): Calcutta, India

Summary: The dualities of Indian life under British rule in the 19th century are explored in this sequel to *Olivia and Jai*. It is 1871, 14 years after the Indian Mutiny in which Jai Raventhorne vanished, charged with a massacre that took the lives of over 200 European women and children. His wife, Olivia, is intent on proving his innocence, while their daughter Maya is caught up in the challenge of resolving conflicting cultural claims.

Historical Accuracy: The novel is expert in capturing the feeling of India under British rule.

RAFAEL SABATINI (1875-1950)

Italian-born Sabatini was educated in Switzerland and Portugal. He worked in the British War Office's Intelligence Department during World War I and was a playwright and short story writer as well as a novelist. The true successor of Andre Dumas, Sabatini is widely credited with sustaining the historical romance into the 20th century.

`5546` *Captain Blood*

Date of Publication: 1922
Subject(s): Sea Story; Pirates; Monmouth's Rebellion
Fictional character(s): Peter Blood, Doctor, Pirate; Arabella Bishop, Gentlewoman; Colonel Bishop, Plantation Owner, Government Official (deputy-governor of Jamaica)
Time Period(s): 17th century (1685-1689)
Locale(s): Bridgewater, England (Somerset); West Indies

Summary: After treating a lord wounded during Monmouth's rebellion, Doctor Peter Blood is arrested and deported as a slave to the Barbados plantation of the venal Colonel Bishop and the colonel's kind, upright niece, Arabella. Blood's adventures begin after he escapes and becomes the most shrewd, feared, and admired buccaneer of the West Indies.

Historical Accuracy: This swashbuckling tale is rich in period, political, and cultural detail concerning life in the West Indies and the buccaneers and colonial powers who waged war and trolled for treasure. Historical events that coincide with the story include the Duke of Monmouth's rebellion, and the result of England's "Glorious Revolution."

`5547` *The Carolinian*

Date of Publication: 1925
Subject(s): American Revolution
Fictional character(s): Sir Andrew Carey, Gentleman, Loyalist; Harry Latimer, Patriot, Military Personnel (major)
Historical character(s): William Moultrie, Military Personnel (colonel)
Time Period(s): 1770s
Locale(s): Charleston, South Carolina

Summary: The scene is Charleston during the American Revolution. Friendships are severed, and the conflict overwhelms a number of characters in this fast-paced adventure story.

Historical Accuracy: The fictional story is intermingled with actual events of the period.

5548 *Chivalry*

Date of Publication: 1935
Subject(s): Renaissance
Fictional character(s): Colombo De Siena, Nobleman, Mercenary
Time Period(s): 15th century
Locale(s): Italy

Summary: Colombo De Siena is the son of a disgraced nobleman who is hanged as a traitor in this romantic adventure novel set during the Italian Renaissance. Stripped of his title and fortune, Colombo becomes a soldier of fortune and his exploits in love, war, and political intrigue are cast into a fast-paced and colorful tale.

Historical Accuracy: The period elements form a believable backdrop for this essentially romantic adventure tale.

5549 *Columbus: A Romance*

Date of Publication: 1942
Subject(s): Exploration; Royalty—Spain; Sea Story
Fictional character(s): Beatriz, Dancer, Gypsy
Historical character(s): Christopher Columbus, Explorer, Sea Captain; Paoli dal Pozzo Toscanelli, Cartographer; Isabella, Ruler (Queen of Castile and Aragon); Ferdinand V, Ruler (King of Castile and Aragon)
Time Period(s): 15th century
Locale(s): Spain; Venice, Italy; At Sea

Summary: This romantic adventure story is built around Columbus' attempt to win support from Ferdinand and Isabella for his famous voyage of discovery. Possessing a valuable map from Italy's most famous cartographer, Columbus journeys to Spain. However, the Venetian doge is determined that the map must not fall into enemy hands and enlists a gypsy dancer, Beatriz, as the unwilling agent to destroy Columbus' plans. The novel includes a brief version of Columbus' fateful voyage.

Historical Accuracy: The story of Columbus is given Sabatini's patented adventure treatment, blending fact and fancy.

5550 *The Gamester*

Date of Publication: 1949
Subject(s): Royalty—France
Historical character(s): John Law, Financier
Time Period(s): 1710s
Locale(s): France

Summary: This unusual adventure story takes as its subject the exiled Scottish financier John Law, who wins control of the finances of France when the country is on the verge of bankruptcy after the death of Louis XIV. Louis' radical banking theories bring riches to the French people but enmity as well. Law must contend with a plot by members of the French parliament aimed at destroying his power.

Historical Accuracy: The novel is faithful to the facts of Law's remarkable career.

5551 *The Hounds of God*

Date of Publication: 1928
Subject(s): Inquisition; Elizabethan Period
Fictional character(s): Lady Margaret Trevanion, Noblewoman; Gervase Killegrew, Gentleman; Don Pedro de Mendoza y Luna, Nobleman
Historical character(s): Elizabeth I, Ruler (Queen of England); Philip II, Ruler (King of Spain); Sir Francis Drake, Sea Captain
Time Period(s): 16th century (1580s)
Locale(s): England; Spain

Summary: This romantic adventure tale concerns the fate of Lady Margaret Trevanion who gives shelter to a shipwrecked Spanish nobleman, Don Pedro, who then abducts her. On the voyage to Spain, she is revealed as a heretic and is subsequently exposed to the terrors of the Spanish Inquisition before being rescued by her devoted lover, Gervase Killegrew.

Historical Accuracy: The story is fanciful but does offer a sound historical background and believable portraits of Elizabeth I and Philip II.

5552 *King's Minion*

Date of Publication: 1931
Subject(s): Jacobean Period
Historical character(s): Robert Carr, Nobleman (Viscount Rochester); Frances Howard, Noblewoman (Countess of Essex)
Time Period(s): 17th century
Locale(s): England

Summary: This historical romance is based on the career of Robert Carr, a favorite of England's James I and the lover of Lady Frances Howard. Both are involved in the notorious murder of Sir Thomas Overbury.

Historical Accuracy: The facts of the Overbury case lend themselves to romantic treatment, and the novel provides a vivid and believable account.

5553 *Master-At-Arms*

Date of Publication: 1940
Subject(s): French Revolution; Chouan Revolt
Fictional character(s): Quentin de Morlaix, Gentleman; Germaine de Chesnieres, Gentlewoman
Time Period(s): 1790s
Locale(s): England; France

Summary: This swashbuckling adventure story is set during the French Revolution and depicts the gallant hero Quentin de Morlaix, fencing master and champion swordsman. His beautiful cousin, Germain de Chesnieres, convinces him to come to the aide of the Loyalists, or Chouans, in their fight for the lost king and the Bourbon cause.

Historical Accuracy: The essential story is invented but filled with convincing period elements.

5554 *Scaramouche*

Date of Publication: 1921

Subject(s): French Revolution; Theatrical Life; Identity—Concealed

Fictional character(s): Andre-Louis Moreau, Political Figure, Revolutionary; Marquis de la Tour d'Azur Gervais, Nobleman; Aline de Kercadiou, Noblewoman

Historical character(s): Georges-Jacques Danton, Lawyer, Revolutionary

Time Period(s): 1780s; 1790s

Locale(s): Rennes, France; Nantes, France; Paris, France

Summary: Andre-Louis Moreau is forced to flee because of his revolutionary activities and his public condemnation of the Marquis de la Tour d'Azur, who has murdered his best friend. He joins a theater troupe and takes the part of Scaramouche, a roughish stock character of the French drama. Further adventures place Moreau at the center of the French Revolution and reveal to him the dark secret of his parentage.

Historical Accuracy: The events of the French Revolution, told from the character's point of view, are skillfully woven into the plot. The author also provides interesting and convincing details concerning French drama, Italian *commedia dell'arte*, and fencing.

`5555` *Scaramouche the King-Maker*

Date of Publication: 1931

Subject(s): French Revolution; Reign of Terror

Fictional character(s): Andre-Louis Moreau, Lawyer, Revolutionary; Baron Jean de Batz, Nobleman, Revolutionary; Aline de Kercadiou, Noblewoman, Refugee

Historical character(s): Maximilien Francois de Robespierre, Revolutionary; Louis, Comte de Provence, Royalty (brother of Louis XVI), Government Official (Regent of France); Louis-Antoine-Leon de Saint-Just, Revolutionary; Camille Desmoulins, Revolutionary, Journalist; Francois Chabot, Revolutionary

Time Period(s): 1790s

Locale(s): Coblentz, Germany; Paris, France; Hamm, Germany

Summary: Aided and abetted by fellow emigre Jean de Batz and a group of royalists, Andre-Louis Moreau returns to Paris during the Reign of Terror. In Paris, he risks his life and jeopardizes his betrothal to Aline de Kercadiou as he conducts a clever campaign designed to destabilize the revolutionary government and pave the way for the restoration of the monarchy of France.

Historical Accuracy: The main historical characters and events of the Reign of Terror are intriguingly intermingled with the fictional conceit.

`5556` *Venetian Masque*

Date of Publication: 1934

Subject(s): Napoleonic Wars

Fictional character(s): Marc-Antoine Villiers de Melville, Adventurer

Time Period(s): 1800s

Locale(s): Venice, Italy

Summary: This romantic adventure tale is set during the final days of the Republic of Venice, before the French invasion led by Napoleon. The central figure is Marc-Antoine Villiers de Melville, part English and part French, who plays a dangerous double role as an earnest Royalist in the guise of a French partisan.

Historical Accuracy: Although the emphasis is clearly on romance, the novel does offer a believable period background.

FRED SABERHAGEN (1930-)

Born in Chicago, Saberhagen has worked as an electronics technician, a freelance writer, and an editor for the *Encyclopedia Britannica*. He is principally a science fiction writer, the author of the Berserker, Empire of the East, and Swords series.

`5557` *Seance for a Vampire*

Date of Publication: 1994

Subject(s): Edwardian Period; Vampires; Mystery

Fictional character(s): Sherlock Holmes, Detective—Private; John H. Watson, Doctor; Dracula, Vampire

Historical character(s): Grigori Efimovich Rasputin, Religious (monk), Zealot

Time Period(s): 1900s (1903)

Locale(s): London, England; St. Petersburg, Russia

Summary: An investigation by Sherlock Holmes into the claims of two psychics leads to a dead daughter's return as a vampire, a dead spiritualist, and the disapperance of Holmes. Watson must recruit the aid of Dracula in a baffling case that takes them to Russia and an encounter with the sinister Rasputin.

Historical Accuracy: The novel is an ingenious melange of forms: horror, mystery, and politics. The atmosphere of the period is convincing.

HENRY BARNARD SAFFORD (1883-)

`5558` *That Bennington Mob*

Date of Publication: 1935

Subject(s): American Revolution; Battle of Bennington; Indians

Fictional character(s): Joel Safford, Settler, Military Personnel (Green Mountain Boy)

Historical character(s): Ethan Allen, Military Personnel (leader of Green Mountain Boys)

Time Period(s): 1770s

Locale(s): New Hampshire, American Colonies; Bennington, Vermont, American Colonies; New York, American Colonies

Summary: The setting is New Hampshire in the years leading up to and during the American Revolution. The activities of Ethan Allen and the Green Mountain Boys are seen through the experiences of Joel Safford. He is captured by Indians, serves as a scout for the Green Mountain Boys, and participates in the attack on Fort Ticonderoga and the Battle of Bennington.

Historical Accuracy: The novel is based on letters, diaries, and the author's own family history. The author captures with authenticity the events of the early battles of the Revolution and the settlement of New Hampshire and Vermont.

5559 *Tory Tavern*

Date of Publication: 1942
Subject(s): American Revolution; Espionage
Fictional character(s): Roger Langalieve, Spy
Historical character(s): Benjamin Tallmadge, Military Personnel (intelligence officer)
Time Period(s): 1770s
Locale(s): Long Island, New York; New Jersey

Summary: During the American Revolution, Roger Langalieve, the son of a prominent Tory family on Long Island, after three-years' impressed service in the British Navy, agrees to become a spy for the rebels. He has a number of adventures as he slips back and forth through the British lines with intelligence about the projected British invasion from Canada and details of the Andre-Arnold plot.

Historical Accuracy: Though oriented toward the romantic, the novel does offer an accurate depiction of espionage work during the period.

5560 *Tristram Bent*

Date of Publication: 1940
Subject(s): American Colonies; Dutch Colonies; Espionage
Fictional character(s): Tristram Bent, Adventurer, Spy
Time Period(s): 17th century (1640)
Locale(s): American Colonies

Summary: The novel offers a compelling portrait of the early American colonies in the 1640s. Englishman Tristram Bent sets out for America and has a series of adventures, including spying on the Dutch.

Historical Accuracy: The novel is precise in its details of customs and the period.

WILLIAM SAFIRE (1929-)

Pulitzer Prize-winning journalist Safire attended Syracuse University and began his career as a reporter with the *New York Herald-Tribune* syndicate. He worked as a correspondent in Europe and the Middle East before serving in the U.S. Army. During the Nixon presidency, Safire worked as a special assistant to the president and as a speechwriter. He is currently a columnist for the *New York Times*, where he writes on politics and language.

5561 *Freedom*

Date of Publication: 1987
Subject(s): Civil War—U.S.; Battle of Antietam; Slavery
Historical character(s): Abraham Lincoln, Political Figure; George McClellan, Military Personnel (general); Salmon P. Chase, Political Figure; Edwin Stanton, Political Figure; Ulysses S. Grant, Military Personnel (general); John Cabell Breckenridge, Political Figure
Time Period(s): 1860s (1861-1862)
Locale(s): Washington, District of Columbia; Virginia; Tennessee

Summary: This massive panoramic novel covers the first two years of the Civil War. Abraham Lincoln and the nation face the question of how much freedom must be denied to protect and extend freedom to all. The novel traces the political forces in the administration of the war as Lincoln moves towards issuing the Emancipation Proclamation.

Historical Accuracy: As the author explains, if the scene deals with war or politics, it is fact; if it has to do with romance, it is fiction; if it is outrageously and obviously fictional, it is fact.

FRANCOISE SAGAN
(PSEUD. OF FRANCOISE QUOIREZ, 1935-)

French writer and film director, Sagan attended the Sorbonne. She was only 18 when she wrote *Bonjour Tristesse*, a novel which shocked the world. The novel won the Prix des Critiques in 1954.

5562 *The Still Storm*

Date of Publication: 1984
Subject(s): Literary Life; Servants
Fictional character(s): Flora de Margelasse, Orphan, Gentlewoman; Nicholas Lomont, Lawyer; Gildas Caussinade, Writer (poet); Martha, Servant
Time Period(s): 1830s
Locale(s): Angouleme, France

Summary: This triangulated love story is set in the 1830s in the French provincial town of Angouleme. It involves an aristocratic beauty, Flora de Margelasse, whose first conquest is the lawyer Lomont. She is then attracted to the peasant poet Gildas Caussinade, who in turn is captivated by Flora's maidservant, Martha.

Historical Accuracy: The novel is more psychological than historical, but does feature an authentic period background.

LEONARD ST. CLAIR (1916-1986)

California writer St. Clair has written over 250 radio and TV scripts. He began his writing career after serving as a vice president of the St. Clair Estate investment company. His novels include *A Fortune in Death* and *The Emerald Trap*.

5563 *The Seadon Fortune*

Date of Publication: 1977
Subject(s): Family Saga; Business Building
Fictional character(s): Val Seadon, Prospector; Cathlin Donahoe, Spouse (of Val); Ross Seadon, Heir
Time Period(s): 19th century; 20th century (1860s-1940s)
Locale(s): San Francisco, California; Sierra Nevada Mountains, California

Summary: This family saga set in California covers three generations and about 100 years of California history. The patriarch is Val Seadon, who is determined to prove that oil is on his land. With its discovery, he leaves to his family an ambiguous legacy of manipulation, betrayal, and corruption.

Historical Accuracy: The novel presents a convincing look at California during the period.

NICOLE ST. JOHN

An American writer and editor, St. John was born in New Jersey. She wrote her first book at age 12 and has been writing ever since. She has had careers in fashion, teaching, and publishing.

5564 *Wychwood*

Date of Publication: 1976
Subject(s): Civil War—U.S.; Suspense
Fictional character(s): Camille Jardine, Young Woman; Nell Jardine, Young Woman
Time Period(s): 1860s
Locale(s): Charleston, South Carolina; Wychwood, England

Summary: Camille Jardine, a young woman living in Charleston, South Carolina, at the outbreak of the Civil War, goes to England when her sister Nell is injured in an accident. The two sisters move to the village of Wychwood, where they have inherited a small cottage and are soon swept up in a mystery surrounding the Wychwood Token, a hidden jewel.

Historical Accuracy: The emphasis is on suspense with an authentic period backdrop.

CAROLA SALISBURY
(PSEUD. OF MICHAEL BUTTERWORTH, 1924-)

English author Salisbury served in the Royal Navy and has worked as a drawing tutor and as an art director and managing editor of a publishing company.

5565 *An Autumn in Araby*

Date of Publication: 1983
Subject(s): Victorian Period; Romance; Suspense
Fictional character(s): Suzanna Copley, Nurse; Justin Ormerod, Artist
Time Period(s): 1860s (1869)
Locale(s): Suffolk, England; At Sea; Egypt

Summary: Victorian nurse Suzanna Copley is hired to care for the child of one of England's most famous painters, Justin Ormerod. The scene shifts to Egypt when Justin is commissioned to record the opening of the Suez Canal, and family secrets surface. In this exotic setting, danger and romance are joined.

Historical Accuracy: The period setting is believably drawn.

5566 *A Certain Splendour*

Date of Publication: 1985
Subject(s): World War I; Romance
Fictional character(s): Faith Dangerfield, Gentlewoman; Jack Cummings, Military Personnel (naval officer); Natasha Chalmers, Gentlewoman
Time Period(s): 1910s (1911-1916)
Locale(s): Malta; London, England

Summary: Faith Dangerfield is the only daughter of a British naval commodore. She struggles through her father's disgrace, making a living as a cleaning woman at a Mayfair hotel. World War I intrudes as does the revelation of a secret that forces Faith to confront the disturbing new realities of her life.

Historical Accuracy: The basic situation strains credibility.

5567 *Count Vronsky's Daughter*

Date of Publication: 1981
Subject(s): Romance; Russian Empire
Fictional character(s): Anna Karenina, Heiress
Time Period(s): 1890s
Locale(s): Paris, France; St. Petersburg, Russia

Summary: Inspired by Leo Tolstoy's classic *Anna Karenina*, this novel offers a sequel as Anna learns that her real father is the Count Vronsky and her mother Anna Karenina. A quest to recapture her identity and heritage takes her to the artistic salons of Paris and St. Petersburg, pursued by the Tsar's secret police.

Historical Accuracy: The novel does reflect credibly the details of Russian Imperial rule and its class assumptions.

5568 *Dark Inheritance*

Date of Publication: 1975
Subject(s): Victorian Period; Romance; Suspense
Fictional character(s): Susannah Button, Young Woman
Time Period(s): 1840s (1845)
Locale(s): Cornwall, England; Venice, Italy

Summary: A deathbed revelation from her father connects a tavern-keeper's daughter, Susannah Button, with the great Cornish estate of Landeric. The novel follows the complications that take Susannah from Cornwall to Venice and discoveries about her identity and heritage.

Historical Accuracy: The novel manages to interweave believable period and regional details with the romantic suspense.

5569 *Dolphin Summer*

Date of Publication: 1977
Subject(s): Victorian Period; Romance; Suspense
Fictional character(s): Annabel Trewella, Companion, Orphan; Melloney Lumley, Invalid
Time Period(s): 1890s (1897)
Locale(s): *Dolphin*, At Sea (in the Mediterranean)

Summary: Aboard the steam yacht *Dolphin* on a summer cruise of the Mediterranean is orphan Annabel Trewella, companion to invalid Melloney Lumley. The cruise is supposed to be an idyllic holiday. Instead Annabel is plunged into a nightmare of family secrets and threats.

Historical Accuracy: The period elements are convincingly described.

5570 *The Pride of the Trevallions*

Date of Publication: 1975
Subject(s): Victorian Period; Romance; Suspense
Fictional character(s): Joanna Goodacre, Young Woman; Benedict Trevallion, Gentleman
Time Period(s): 1850s (1859)
Locale(s): Cornwall, England; Jamaica

Summary: Romantic suspense is featured in this novel set in mid-Victorian Jamaica and Cornwall. Joanna Goodacre, the daughter of a servant, accompanies Benedict Trevallion to his ancestral home in Cornwall. There, family secrets and mystery set the stage for romance.

Historical Accuracy: The emphasis is on romantic suspense with only a lightly sketched period background.

5571 *The Shadowed Spring*

Date of Publication: 1980
Subject(s): Victorian Period; Romance; Suspense
Fictional character(s): Clarissa Herbert, Teacher, Spinster; Lord Audubon, Nobleman
Time Period(s): 1870s (1878)
Locale(s): Cornwall, England; Paris, France; St. Petersburg, Russia

Summary: A broken engagement causes schoolmistress Clarissa Herbert to take a position as tutor for English Lord Audubon, her majesty's ambassador to the court of St. Petersburg. As European peace hangs in the balance, Clarissa accompanies Lord Audubon to Russia, where intrigue and romance await.

Historical Accuracy: The period elements in the story are convincing.

5572 *The Winter Bride*

Date of Publication: 1978
Subject(s): Victorian Period; Romance; Suspense
Fictional character(s): Charity Carew, Secretary; Martin Revesby, Writer (poet)
Time Period(s): 1850s (1856)
Locale(s): Cornwall, England

Summary: Gothic-style menace is afoot in Victorian Cornwall in this story of Charity Carew, who is hired as the private secretary of distinguished poet Martin Revesby. A sinister power seems to brood over his Cornish castle, sustained by the legend of The Beast, a creature that haunts the grounds.

Historical Accuracy: The story has all the required Gothic trappings, more remote and exotic than truly historical.

GEORGIA SALLASKA (1933-)

Born in Oklahoma and a graduate of Central State College in Edmond, Oklahoma, Sallaska has been a copywriter and illustrator for an advertising agency in Oklahoma. She was a recipient of the Tepee Award from the Oklahoma Writers Federation and the Friends of American Writers award of achievement.

5573 *Three Ships and Three Kings*

Date of Publication: 1969
Subject(s): Myths and Legends; Ancient Greece
Fictional character(s): Hippolochus, Hero; Bellerophon, Hero; Perseus, Hero
Time Period(s): Indeterminate Past
Locale(s): Greece; Mediterranean

Summary: Set in the Mediterranean Greek world, the novel describes the exploits of Hippolochus, Bellerophon, and Perseus and their adventures throughout the legendary world of the Greek myths.

Historical Accuracy: The novel owes its inspiration not to history but to Greek myth and legend.

SUSAN SALLIS (1929-)

A former teacher, Sallis is a successful author of novels for young adults. *April Rising* is her first adult novel, based on her own family in the West Country of England. Her *Only Love* was named the best book for young adults by the American Library Association in 1980.

5574 *April Rising*

Date of Publication: 1984
Subject(s): Family Saga; World War I
Fictional character(s): Will Rising, Tailor; Florence Rising, Spouse (of Will); April Rising, Young Woman
Time Period(s): 20th century
Locale(s): Gloucester, England

Summary: Set during the early years of the 20th century, the novel tells the story of the Rising family of Gloucester, England. Will Rising is a poor tailor, and the novel chronicles the family's attempt to escape poverty. The lives of the four Rising children are shown against a backdrop of war and its aftermath.

Historical Accuracy: The regional and period elements are convincingly detailed.

SHARON SALVATO (1938-)

Born in Columbus, Ohio, Salvato received her B.S.Ed. from the University of Cincinnati and went on to teach and write. Her first novel, *Briarcliff Manor*, was published in 1974.

5575 *The Drums of December*

Date of Publication: 1983
Subject(s): American Revolution; American Colonies
Fictional character(s): Elizabeth Manning, Plantation Owner; Andrew Manning, Patriot; Gwynne Manning, Spouse (of Andrew)
Historical character(s): Charles Cornwallis, Military Personnel (general)
Time Period(s): 1770s; 1780s (1773-1780)
Locale(s): South Carolina

Summary: In the sequel to *The Fires of July*, the story of the Manning family of South Carolina continues. The American Revolution breaks out and Drew Manning's support for the patriot cause splits the family and forces each to choose sides in the conflict.

Historical Accuracy: The fictional story is set against a convincing period background.

5576 *The Fires of July*

Date of Publication: 1983

Subject(s): American Colonies; American Revolution; Family Saga
Fictional character(s): Joseph Manning, Plantation Owner; Elizabeth Manning, Spouse; Andrew Manning, Young Man
Time Period(s): 1760s; 1770s (1767-1772)
Locale(s): South Carolina, American Colonies

Summary: The novel tells the story of the Manning family on their indigo plantation in South Carolina as events build up to the outbreak of the American Revolution. The family finds itself torn between loyalty to Britain and to the new American nation, involving them with the ''Regulations'' and the Cherokees.

Historical Accuracy: The novel convincingly captures the regional and period details.

5577 *Scarborough House*
Date of Publication: 1975
Subject(s): Family Saga; Erie Canal; Business Building
Fictional character(s): Marcella Paxton, Young Woman; Bradford Dalton, Heir
Time Period(s): 19th century (1825-1876)
Locale(s): Hudson River Valley, New York; New York, New York

Summary: Marcella Paxton, a child of New York's 19th-century slums, mounts her assault on respectability. Her vehicle is Bradford Dalton, the heir of the Hudson Valley estate of Scarborough House. Their affair scandalizes New York society and is played out over years that see the opening of the Erie Canal and the growth of New York City.

Historical Accuracy: The period elements of New York life are genuine.

STANLAKE SAMKANGE (1922-1988)
Born in Rhodesia, Samkange grew up in Bulawayo where his father was a Methodist minister. Educated at Waddilove Institution, Adams College, and Fort Hare University College in South Africa, Samkange was for many years the General Secretary of the African National Congress. Samkange worked for the liberation of British-ruled Rhodesia for three decades. He is the author of the historical study, *Origins of Rhodesia*, *African Saga*, *Year of the Uprising* and *On Trial for That U.D.I.*.

5578 *On Trial for My Country*
Date of Publication: 1966
Subject(s): English Colonies
Historical character(s): Cecil John Rhodes, Government Official (British colonial administrator); Lobengula, Ruler (Matabele king)
Time Period(s): 19th century
Locale(s): Rhodesia

Summary: The conquest and creation of Rhodesia forms the background for this novel that centers on the clash between Lobengula, the King of the Matabele and Cecil Rhodes. The novel recounts the political manuevering of Rhodes that suc-

ceeds in seizing the Matebele territory. Both sides—the African and the English—are represented.

Historical Accuracy: The novel is faithful to the details of African and Rhodesian history.

MAURICE SAMUEL (1895-1972)
A Romanian essayist, novelist, critic, and lecturer, Samuel became a U.S. citizen in 1921. Samuel was an interpreter of Jewish values and culture to Western readers. His novels include *The Outsider*, *The Devil that Failed*, and *The Second Crucifixion*.

5579 *The Second Crucifixion*
Date of Publication: 1960
Subject(s): Roman Empire; Anti-Semitism; Religious Conflict
Fictional character(s): Marcella Silana, Young Woman
Time Period(s): 2nd century
Locale(s): Rome, Roman Empire

Summary: The novel, set during the reign of Roman Emperor Hadrian, explores the origins of modern anti-semitism in the religious conflict between the Jews and the Christians. A Jewish girl, Marcella Silana, is adopted by a aristocratic Roman family and only later learns of her heritage. She then joins the Roman Jewish community during its persecution.

Historical Accuracy: The novel offers a believable re-creation of the period.

5580 *Web of Lucifer: A Novel of the Borgia Fury*
Date of Publication: 1947
Subject(s): Renaissance
Fictional character(s): Giacomo Orso, Young Man
Historical character(s): Cesare Borgia, Military Personnel, Diplomat; Niccolo Machiavelli, Political Figure, Writer
Time Period(s): 15th century
Locale(s): Italy

Summary: This tale of Renaissance Italy follows the adventures of a young peasant, Giacomo Orso, who vows vengeance on the murderers of his younger brother. Orso serves Cesare Borgia hoping for justice in a united Italy, but he eventually discovers Borgia's true identity.

Historical Accuracy: The author's re-creation of 15th-century Italy is accurate in its details, and the novel's fictional plot is interwoven with actual historical events.

THOMAS SANCHEZ (1944-)
A graduate of San Francisco State College, Sanchez' career has included participation in human rights organizations such as the Congress for Racial Equality and the United Farm Workers. He covered the 1973 takeover at Wounded Knee for Pacifica Radio, was the author and host of a five-part ABC-TV special on the California Hispanic community, and has lectured at several universities. Sanchez has been a contributor to anthologies, newspapers, and periodicals. A film documentary on Sanchez and the writing

of *Rabbit Boss* was produced by the University of California.

5581 *Rabbit Boss*

Date of Publication: 1973
Subject(s): Indians; American West
Fictional character(s): Gayabuc, Indian (Washo), Hunter; Captain Rex, Indian (Washo); Halleluiah Bob, Indian (Washo); Joe Birdson, Indian (Washo)
Time Period(s): 19th century; 20th century
Locale(s): Sierra Nevada Mountains, California; Lake Tahoe, California

Summary: The story of four generations of Washo Indians in California dramatizes the sad effects of white settlement on the Indians. The story begins with Gayabuc, whose first contact with whites is witnessing the disaster of the Donner Party. Other scenes show the effects of the California Gold Rush and the further decline of power and integrity of the Indians in Gayabuc's descendants. Joe Birdson, who becomes Rabbit Boss, a once honored position, is now reduced to keeping the vast ranches of the whites free of rabbits.

Historical Accuracy: The novel effectively weaves fictional and historical elements, capturing the atmosphere of Indian life and customs with conviction.

GEORGE SAND
(PSEUD. OF ARMANDINE DUPIN, 1804-1876)

Sand was a French novelist notorious for her affairs with Alfred de Muset and the Polish composer Frederic Chopin. Her novels include *Indiana*, *Lelia*, and *Jacques*.

5582 *Consuelo*

Date of Publication: 1842
Subject(s): Theatrical Life; Musical Life
Fictional character(s): Consuelo, Singer; Albert Rudolstadt, Nobleman; Porpora, Teacher (music master)
Historical character(s): Frederick the Great, Ruler (King of Prussia); Franz Joseph Haydn, Composer
Time Period(s): 18th century
Locale(s): Venice, Italy; Bohemia; Vienna, Austria

Summary: This is a romantic novel of the career of singer Consuelo that takes her from Italy to Germany and Austria, and a tragic affair with the son of a Bohemian count.

Historical Accuracy: Sand's intimate knowledge of music and musicians lends credibility to her romance.

CARL SANDBURG (1878-1967)

An American poet who fought in the Spanish-American War, Sandburg was a journalist, advertising writer, and Socialist party organizer. He attained recognition as a poet beginning in 1914. His verse is marked by colloquialism and a celebration of American democracy and the ordinary people.

5583 *Remembrance Rock*

Date of Publication: 1948
Subject(s): American Colonies; American Revolution; Civil War—U.S.
Fictional character(s): Oliver Windrow, Settler (Puritan), Artisan (woodcarver); Ordway Winshore, Printer; Omri Winwold, Farmer
Time Period(s): Multiple Time Periods
Locale(s): New Era, Illinois; Plymouth, Massachusetts; Philadelphia, Pennsylvania

Summary: Less a novel than a historical chronicle of America, *Remembrance Rock* connects three stories: the settling of Plymouth, the American Revolution, and the Civil War. Each section presents its era against a human backdrop of the American dream. Sandburg lifts the realism of America's past into the realm of the symbolic.

Historical Accuracy: This a panoramic sweep of American history whose power resides in the juxtaposition of the three eras.

JACQUIN SANDERS (1922-)

American author Sanders was born in Springfield, Ohio, and attended Pomono College. An associate editor for *Newsweek* since 1962, Sanders is the author of *Freakshow*, *The Fortune Finders*, and *A Night Before Christmas*.

5584 *Look to Your Geese: A Novel of the Deflowering of New England*

Date of Publication: 1959
Subject(s): American Colonies; Puritans; Indians
Fictional character(s): Thomas Hewitt, Young Man; Jason Ord, Judge; Hindfoot, Indian, Chieftain
Time Period(s): 17th century
Locale(s): Gruel, Massachusetts, American Colonies

Summary: This comic story of Puritan New England depicts the community of Gruel, Massachusetts, and its Indian neighbors. The novel offers a blend of melodrama, burlesque, and parody in capturing colonial life. The Indians emerge in the best light, and the true savages are the white settlers.

Historical Accuracy: The novel is as truthful as a caricature.

JOAN SANDERS (1924-)

Born in Montana, Sanders attended Stanford University. A former librarian and teaching assistant, Sanders lived in Uppsala, Sweden, for two years when her husband held a postdoctoral fellowship. She has explained her attraction to writing historical novel as a love of the "gossip of centuries." She has conducted extensive research on Louis XIV's court. She is the author of *La Petite: The Life of Louise de la Valliere*.

5585 *Baneful Sorceries, or The Countess Bewitched*

Date of Publication: 1969

Subject(s): Witchcraft and Sorcery
Fictional character(s): Margot Renard, Young Woman, Noblewoman (countess); Comte de Roc-sur-Besbre, Nobleman, Rake
Time Period(s): 17th century
Locale(s): Paris, France

Summary: The novel is set in the court of Louis XIV. Margot Renard is married to the Comte de Roc-sur-Besbre, a penniless rake, and is plunged into intrigue and a world of sorcery that threatens to destroy her marriage. The novel describes how Margot contends with the forces bent on her destruction.

Historical Accuracy: The period elements of life at court in the 17th century are believable.

`5586` *The Marquis*

Date of Publication: 1963
Subject(s): Royalty—France
Historical character(s): Louis XIV, Ruler (King of France); Louis-Henri de Pardailande Gondrin, Nobleman; Francoise Athenais Rochechouart de Mortemart, Noblewoman, Spouse (of Louis-Henri)
Time Period(s): 17th century
Locale(s): Paris, France

Summary: The scene is the court of Louis XIV, the Sun King. The Marquis de Montespan comes to Paris and finds a wife, Athenais, who becomes the king's mistress. Montespan dares to defy the king and assert his claim and honor. The novel features a vivid depiction of court life.

Historical Accuracy: The court scene is authentically captured.

JOHN SANDERS

`5587` *A Firework for Oliver*

Date of Publication: 1965
Subject(s): Civil War—England; Espionage
Fictional character(s): Nicholas Pym, Spy
Time Period(s): 17th century
Locale(s): England

Summary: Set during Oliver Cromwell's Commonwealth, this historical thriller concerns the espionage adventures of a Puritan spy, Nicholas Pym. Pym investigates the invention of the first percussion-bullet rifle that has come into the hands of Royalist opponents of Cromwell's regime.

Historical Accuracy: The novel's central situation is not historical, but the story offers many vivid period elements.

LEONARD SANDERS (1929-)

Born in Denver, Colorado, Sanders attended the University of Oklahoma. He worked as a journalist in Texas and Oklahoma and was fine arts editor for the *Fort Worth Star-Telegram* for 21 years.

`5588` *Fort Worth*

Date of Publication: 1984
Subject(s): American West; Family Saga; Oil Industry

Fictional character(s): Travis Spurlock, Lawyer, Political Figure; Reva Latham, Spouse (of Travis); Vern Spurlock, Military Personnel (pilot); Clay Spurlock, Oil Industry Worker (wildcatter)
Historical character(s): Theodore Roosevelt, Political Figure
Time Period(s): 19th century; 20th century (1860s-1940s)
Locale(s): Fort Worth, Texas

Summary: This multigenerational saga traces the transformation of Fort Worth, Texas, from a dusty frontier village into a commercial center. The story begins with Travis Spurlock, a young veteran of the Civil War who comes West and finds success as a trial lawyer and U.S. senator. His descendants are at the center of the Texas oil boom.

Historical Accuracy: Although the Spurlocks are fictional, the historical events of their times are factual. Fort Worth's past is presented with conscientious, if not complete, accuracy.

`5589` *Light on the Mountain*

Date of Publication: 1986
Subject(s): American West; Indians
Historical character(s): Isabel Crawford, Religious (missionary)
Time Period(s): 19th century; 20th century (1890s-1900s)
Locale(s): Oklahoma

Summary: The novel tells the true story of Isabel Crawford, who was raised on the Canadian frontier. She journeys to the Oklahoma Territory at the end of the 19th century to minister to the fierce Kiowas, who are defeated and dying following the Ghost Dance rituals. The novel details her hardships and struggles amidst the Oklahoma land openings.

Historical Accuracy: The period details are authentic, and the story stays close to the actual facts of Crawford's life and career.

`5590` *Star of Empire: A Novel of Old San Antonio*

Date of Publication: 1992
Subject(s): American West; Texas Revolution; Mexican War
Fictional character(s): Tad Logan, Political Figure; Carrie Logan, Spouse; Ramsey Cothburn, Gentleman
Historical character(s): Sam Houston, Political Figure; Mirabeau Buonaparte Lamar, Political Figure; Robert Potter, Political Figure; Thomas Jefferson Rusk, Political Figure
Time Period(s): 19th century (1830s-1860s)
Locale(s): San Antonio, Texas

Summary: This tale of the Texas Republic follows the lives of Carrie and Tad Logan in the 1830s and continues through the upheavals over statehood, war with Mexico, and the Civil War. Tad Logan serves in the Texas Congress, first as a protege of Sam Houston, then as his avowed enemy. When Mexico invades San Antonio, he is captured, and Carrie is consoled by former love Ramsey Cothburn.

Historical Accuracy: The novel interweaves a fictional story with accurate events of the period, faithfully presented.

SAMUEL SANDMEL (1911-1979)

A native of Ohio, Sandmel earned a B.A. at the University of Missouri and a Ph.D. from Yale. A rabbi, he served as a Navy chaplain during World War II. Sandmel has taught at Vanderbilt University and Hebrew Union College in Cincinnati. He is the past president of the Society of Biblical Literature.

5591 *Alone Atop the Mountain*

Date of Publication: 1973
Subject(s): Biblical Story; Ancient Egypt; Pharaohs
Historical character(s): Moses, Leader (Israelites), Biblical Figure
Time Period(s): 13th century B.C.
Locale(s): Egypt

Summary: Atop Mt. Pisgah, viewing the promised land, Moses reflects on his long life—his role in freeing the Israelites, and the long, wandering exodus that has finally ended. Moses emerges as a strong and determined leader yet possessing human failures and frailties.

Historical Accuracy: The novel elaborates on Biblical sources and invents a plausible psychological profile for Moses.

MARI SANDOZ (1896-1976)

American novelist and historian, Sandoz was born in Nebraska and has worked in various careers, including country school teacher, proofreader, and editor. She is the author of many nonfiction works and novels on the American West, including her Great Plains nonfiction series.

5592 *Miss Morissa: Doctor of the Gold Trail*

Date of Publication: 1955
Subject(s): Medical Profession; American West
Fictional character(s): Morissa Kirk, Doctor
Time Period(s): 1870s
Locale(s): North Platte River, Nebraska

Summary: The novel describes pioneer life in a small frontier community on the North Platte River of Nebraska during the 1870s. The story centers on the experiences of a woman doctor, Morissa Kirk.

Historical Accuracy: This is an authentic portrait of a pioneer settlement during the period.

5593 *Son of the Gamblin' Man: The Youth of an Artist*

Date of Publication: 1960
Subject(s): American West; Settlement of the American Frontier; Artistic Life
Historical character(s): Robert Henri, Artist; John Jackson Cozad, Settler, Gambler
Time Period(s): 19th century
Locale(s): Nebraska

Summary: Frontier life in Nebraska is depicted in the experiences of American artist Robert Henri, who follows his father, gambler and promoter John Jackson Cozad, west to the founding of Cozad, Nebraska. Robert comes of age as an artist in the midst of frontier violence and hardship, including conflict with cattlemen, droughts, blizzards, prairie fires, and grasshopper infestations.

Historical Accuracy: This documentary novel is reliable in its account of events and real personalities.

JOHN A. SANFORD (1929-)

Born in Camden, New Jersey, Sanford attended Kenyon College and the Episcopal Theological School. He served for nine years as a chaplain for the U.S. Army Reserve. After working as a rector for many years, Sanford became a private counselor, lecturer, and writer.

5594 *Song of the Meadowlark*

Date of Publication: 1986
Subject(s): American West; Indians; Tribal Life—Native American
Fictional character(s): Teeto Hoonod, Indian (Nez Perce); Rising Moon, Indian (Nez Perce)
Historical character(s): Chief Joseph, Indian (Nez Perce), Chieftain
Time Period(s): 1870s (1877)
Locale(s): Wallowa Valley, Oregon; Idaho; Montana

Summary: The novel tells the story of the Nez Perce War of 1877 and the tribe's epic 1,700 mile retreat across the Pacific Northwest in an effort to avoid the pursuing U.S. Army and to escape to Canada. The story is told by Indian Teeto Hoonod, whose love for Rising Moon is a tender counterpart to the tragedy of the Nez Perce.

Historical Accuracy: The basic outline of the historical events is accurately presented.

WILLIAM SARABANDE

Sarabande is an American science fiction writer who has set many of his stories in prehistoric times.

5595 *Beyond the Sea of Ice*

Date of Publication: 1987
Subject(s): Prehistory; Tribal Life—Prehistoric
Fictional character(s): Torka, Prehistoric Human, Hunter; Lonit, Prehistoric Human; Karana, Prehistoric Human, Orphan
Time Period(s): Indeterminate Past
Locale(s): North America

Summary: After his tribe is decimated by a series of natural disasters, Torka leads the survivors over the Arctic tundra eastward into North America to save the clan. They face animal attacks and encounters with rival bands. This is the first volume of The First Americans series.

Historical Accuracy: The story is based on evident research by archaeologists, paleontologists, and paleoanthropologists.

5596 *Corridor of Storms*

Date of Publication: 1988
Subject(s): Prehistory; Tribal Life—Prehistoric
Fictional character(s): Torka, Prehistoric Human, Hunter; Lonit, Prehistoric Human; Karana, Prehistoric Human, Shaman; Navahk, Prehistoric Human, Shaman
Time Period(s): Indeterminate Past
Locale(s): Bering Strait, Alaska, North America

Summary: In the second volume of the First Americans series, the prehistoric hunter Torka; his spouse, Lonit; and adopted son, Karana, journey across the frozen tundra to hunt the great mammoths. They encounter an evil seer, Navahk, who threatens to destroy Torka and his tribe.

Historical Accuracy: The story is filled with plausible details of Ice Age life.

5597 *The Edge of the World*

Date of Publication: 1993
Subject(s): Prehistory; Tribal Life—Prehistoric
Fictional character(s): Cha-Kwena, Shaman, Prehistoric Human; Ban-Ya, Prehistoric Human; Mah-Ree, Prehistoric Human
Time Period(s): Indeterminate Past
Locale(s): Great Plains, North America

Summary: In the aftermath of the ice age in North America, Cha-Kwena is intent on finding a land of plenty for his people. To do so he must violate a taboo, alienating his mate and his tribe.

Historical Accuracy: The details of tribal life and the setting are convincing.

5598 *Face of the Rising Sun*

Date of Publication: 1996
Subject(s): Prehistory; Tribal Life—Prehistoric
Fictional character(s): Warakan, Prehistoric Human, Wanderer; Jhadel, Prehistoric Human, Shaman
Time Period(s): Indeterminate Past
Locale(s): North America

Summary: At the end of the last Ice Age, Warakan, a chief's son, wanders in the primeval forest searching for the mysterious great white mammoth and its totemic power.

Historical Accuracy: The novel is supported by the author's evident research into Native American history and mythology.

5599 *Forbidden Land*

Date of Publication: 1989
Subject(s): Prehistory; Tribal Life—Prehistoric
Fictional character(s): Torka, Prehistoric Human, Hunter; Karana, Prehistoric Human, Shaman; Lonit, Prehistoric Human
Time Period(s): Indeterminate Past
Locale(s): Alaska, North America

Summary: The third volume of the First Americans series tells the story of the great hunter Torka, now the headman of a tribe that has come across the frozen sea. He struggles with his

family and a small band of followers on the new and forbidding continent.

Historical Accuracy: The novel offers a plausible version of what life must have been like during the Ice Age.

5600 *The Sacred Stones*

Date of Publication: 1991
Subject(s): Prehistory; Tribal Life—Prehistoric
Fictional character(s): Ysuna, Prehistoric Human, Religious (high priestess); Masau, Prehistoric Human, Hunter; Maliwal, Prehistoric Human, Hunter
Time Period(s): Indeterminate Past
Locale(s): North America

Summary: In this novel about prehistoric life, news that Maliwal has had success finding mammoths gives hope to his tribe that a white mammoth will be found that will return power to Ysuna and the People of the Watching Star.

Historical Accuracy: This version of prehistoric customs is convincing, clearly based on anthropological and archaeological research.

5601 *Shadow of the Watching Star*

Date of Publication: 1995
Subject(s): Prehistory; Tribal Life—Prehistoric
Fictional character(s): Cha-Kwena, Prehistoric Human, Shaman; Kosar-Eh, Prehistoric Human, Hunter
Time Period(s): Indeterminate Past
Locale(s): North America

Summary: The People, an Ice Age tribe, are ravaged by tribal fighting and have been abandoned by their spirits. The young shaman Cha-Kwena, who struggles to protect the last sacred herd of mammoths, must decide on a course of action to save the People.

Historical Accuracy: The novel presents a believable portrait of prehistoric life based on evident research in anthropological and archaeological sources.

5602 *Thunder in the Sky*

Date of Publication: 1992
Subject(s): Prehistory; Tribal Life—Prehistoric
Fictional character(s): Cha-Kwena, Prehistoric Human, Shaman
Time Period(s): Indeterminate Past
Locale(s): Great Plains, North America

Summary: Attempting to lead his people to safety and plenty, Cha-Kwena follows the legendary white mammoth on the Great Plains of North America. He is pursued by enemies.

Historical Accuracy: The novel is a thoughtful and convincing look at prehistoric times and tribal life.

5603 *Walkers of the Wind*

Date of Publication: 1990
Subject(s): Prehistory; Tribal Life—Prehistoric
Fictional character(s): Torka, Prehistoric Human, Hunter; Umak, Prehistoric Human, Twin; Manaravak, Prehistoric Human, Twin; Lonit, Prehistoric Human

Time Period(s): Indeterminate Past
Locale(s): North America

Summary: In the fourth volume of The First Americans series, Torka's leadership of the band he has led across the Arctic tundra is threatened from within by the deadly rivalry between twins Umak and Manaravak and without from a mysterious creature called the wanawut. Torka and Lonit embark on a dangerous journey to the home of the wind from which no one has ever returned.

Historical Accuracy: The story is based on evident research into the period.

5604   *Wolves of the Dawn*

Date of Publication: 1987
Subject(s): Prehistory; Tribal Life—Prehistoric
Fictional character(s): Balor, Wanderer, Prehistoric Human; Fomor, Chieftain, Prehistoric Human; Cethlinn, Religious (priestess), Prehistoric Human
Time Period(s): Indeterminate Past
Locale(s): England

Summary: The People of the Axe have exchanged their flint weapons for farm implements and are threatened by raiders. It is up to Fomor's son, Balor, to defend the clan.

Historical Accuracy: The novel is based on the lore and prehistory of Ireland, Scandinavia, and Britain.

LYNDA SARGENT

5605   *Judith Duchesne*

Date of Publication: 1979
Subject(s): Rural Life—U.S.
Fictional character(s): Judith Duchesne, Young Woman
Time Period(s): 1880s
Locale(s): New Hampshire

Summary: Set in 19th-century New Hampshire, the novel tells the story of Judith Duchesne. Condemned to a loveless marriage, Judith is abused and kept a near-prisoner in her small farming community. The community becomes an accomplice to her predicament.

Historical Accuracy: The novel offers a gripping and stark portrait of rural life of the period, chillingly convincing.

PAMELA SARGENT (1948-)

Born in New York, Sargent graduated from the State University of New York, Binghamton. She has worked as a freelance writer and editor. In 1983 she won the ALA Award for the best book for young adults for *Earthseed*.

5606   *Ruler of the Sky: A Novel of Genghis Khan*

Date of Publication: 1993
Subject(s): Mongol Empire; Chinese Empire; Biography, Fictionalized
Historical character(s): Temujin, Ruler (Mongols), Warrior; Hoelun, Parent (mother of Genghis Khan)

Time Period(s): 12th century; 13th century
Locale(s): Mongolia; China; Persia

Summary: This massive biographical novel traces the life and career of Temujin, whom history remembers as Genghis Khan. This story of the forging of one of the greatest armies in world history and the conquering of the known world from China to Persia is told with an emphasis on Genghis' military genius and individual character.

Historical Accuracy: Ably recorded and documented, the novel offers a compelling and convincing portrait of the age and its leading figure.

HERBERT RAVENEL SASS (1884-1958)

5607   *Look Back to Glory*

Date of Publication: 1933
Subject(s): Antebellum South; Civil War—U.S.
Fictional character(s): Richard Acton, Diplomat
Time Period(s): 1860s
Locale(s): South Carolina

Summary: The novel dramatizes the weeks leading up to the vote for Southern secession and the attack on Fort Sumter. The novel's moral vantage point is Southerner Richard Acton who returns to Charlestown convinced that the Southern cause is lost from the start. The action climaxes with the Union's attack on Fort Sumter in 1863.

Historical Accuracy: Evident research helps create an authentic and believable background for the story.

WALTER SATTERTHWAIT (1946-)

Born in Pennsylvania, Satterthwait attended Reed College and has worked as a bartender and bar manager. He became a full-time writer in 1968. He was attracted to writing crime books to try to figure out why people kill others.

5608   *Miss Lizzie*

Date of Publication: 1989
Subject(s): Mystery
Fictional character(s): Amanda Burton, Teenager
Historical character(s): Lizzie Borden, Murderer (accused), Spinster
Time Period(s): 1920s (1921)
Locale(s): Massachusetts

Summary: It is 1921, 30 years after the famous trial and acquittal of Lizzie Borden for the brutal murder of her parents. When 13-year-old Amanda Burton, on a summer vacation in Massachusetts, discovers the murdered remains of her stepmother and her elderly next-door neighbor, the notorious Lizzie Borden is the obvious suspect. Amanda and Lizzie set out to discover the truth and in the process uncover secrets concerning what happened in Fall River 30 years before.

Historical Accuracy: The novel offers an ingenious re-interpretation of the Borden case, clearly dependent on solid research.

`5609` *Wilde West*

Date of Publication: 1991
Subject(s): American West; Literary Life; Mystery
Fictional character(s): Robert Grigsby, Lawman (U.S. marshall)
Historical character(s): Oscar Wilde, Writer; John Henry Holliday, Gunfighter, Gambler; Horace Tabor, Businessman (mine owner); Elizabeth ''Baby Doe'' Tabor, Socialite, Fiance(e)
Time Period(s): 1880s (1882)
Locale(s): Colorado

Summary: While on his lecture tour of America, Oscar Wilde is a suspect in a series of savagely murdered prostitutes. Determined to clear his name, Wilde sets out to find the real killer while having an affair with the fiancee of Horace Tabor, the silver king, in this wildly inventive, comic western mystery.

Historical Accuracy: Wilde did visit America and met Tabor at dinner in his silver mine. Beyond that, the author admits, the plot is fictional.

DIANA SAUNDERS
(PSEUD. OF VIRGINIA COFFMAN, 1914-)

Born in San Francisco, Coffman graduated from the University of California at Berkeley in 1938. She worked as a secretary for a number of studios in Hollywood and wrote over 70 novels under various pen names. In addition to historical romances, she wrote gothic novels and detective fiction.

`5610` *The Passion of Letty Fox*

Date of Publication: 1986
Subject(s): Romance; Royalty—France
Fictional character(s): Letty Fox, Entertainer (impressionist); Max MacCroy, Government Official (security officer)
Historical character(s): Napoleon III, Ruler (Emperor of France); Eugenie, Royalty (wife of Napoleon III)
Time Period(s): 1870s
Locale(s): San Francisco, California; Paris, France

Summary: Letty Fox is a vaudeville performer in San Francisco during the 1870s, headlining as ''The Queen of the Impressionists.'' She bears an uncanny resemblance to the Empress Eugenie and is recruited as the public stand-in for the empress, who has been the target of assassination attempts. Letty plays her part only too well as conspiracy and danger threaten.

Historical Accuracy: The story is fanciful, but does employ some convincing period details that create a believable sense of the court world of Eugenie and Napoleon III.

KATE SAUNDERS (1960-)

Saunders works as a book reviewer, journalist, and columnist.

`5611` *Night Shall Overtake Us*

Date of Publication: 1994
Subject(s): World War I; Women's Rights
Fictional character(s): Aurora Carlington, Young Woman; Jenny Dalgleish, Young Woman; Francesca Garland, Young Woman; Eleanor Braddon, Young Woman
Time Period(s): 20th century (1907-1935)
Locale(s): England; Ireland

Summary: A pact among four schoolmates carries them into adulthood in scenes leading up to the outbreak of World War I and the war years. The novel dramatizes a friendship that is tested as the four endure many challenges from without and within.

Historical Accuracy: The period background is authentically presented.

RAYMOND M. SAUNDERS (1949-)

Saunders was a 1974 graduate of West Point, and he served in various military assignments in the U.S. and Korea. He is an avid student of military history.

`5612` *Fenwick Travers and the Forbidden Kingdom*

Date of Publication: 1994
Subject(s): Spanish-American War
Fictional character(s): Fenwick Travers, Military Personnel (lieutenant)
Time Period(s): 1900s (1900-1902)
Locale(s): Philippines

Summary: Fenwick Travers finds himself in the American-occupied Philippines following the defeat of Spain in the Spanish-American War. He comes upon a treasure map that leads him on a series of adventures.

Historical Accuracy: The novel's forte is an irreverent treatment of the past, supported by a believable period background.

`5613` *Fenwick Travers and the Panama Canal*

Date of Publication: 1995
Subject(s): Panama Canal; Canal Building; Espionage
Fictional character(s): Fenwick Travers, Military Personnel (cavalry officer)
Historical character(s): James ''Diamond Jim'' Brady, Financier; Theodore Roosevelt, Political Figure; Elihu Root, Political Figure
Time Period(s): 1900s (1903)
Locale(s): Panama; New York, New York

Summary: In the third adventure of the American rogue Fenwick Travers, gambling losses and involvement in a scandal cause Travers to head to Panama. He works as an agent provocateur in a rebellion against Columbia to facilitate the building of the Panama Canal. Travers' blundering gets him captured by Indians, which leads to an escape through the wilderness and a series of misadventures.

Historical Accuracy: Episodes in the novel are based on historical events, but dialogue and the actions of the fictional characters are the inventions of the author.

5614 Fenwick Travers and the Years of Empire

Date of Publication: 1993
Subject(s): Military Life; Spanish-American War; Boxer Rebellion
Fictional character(s): Fenwick Travers, Military Personnel (army officer)
Historical character(s): Theodore Roosevelt, Military Personnel, Political Figure; John J. Pershing, Military Personnel (army officer); William McKinley, Political Figure
Time Period(s): 1890s; 1900s
Locale(s): Cuba; China

Summary: This is the first volume of the memoirs of American rogue and soldier Fenwick Travers, whose adventures take him into action in Cuba during the Spanish-American War and to China at the time of the Boxer Rebellion. An unabashed egotist and adventurer with astounding luck, Travers romps across turn-of-the-century American history.

Historical Accuracy: The novel features genuine period elements and a faithful historical background. Travers, however, is a notoriously unreliable witness to history.

GEORGE SAVA
(PSEUD. OF GEORGE ALEXIS MILKOMANOVICH MILKOMANE, 1903-)

Born in Baku, Russia, Milkomane emigrated to England in 1932 and became a naturalized British citizen in 1938. He was educated at the Russian Naval Academy and the University of Paris, and received his medical degree from London's Royal College of Surgeons. A plastic surgeon as well as an author, Milkmane wrote a number of medical books as well as novels. His other works as George Sava include *Beloved Nemesis*, *Double Identity*, and *A Smile through Tears*.

5615 The Emperor Story: A Historical Romance

Date of Publication: 1959
Subject(s): Russian Empire; Royalty—Russia; Napoleonic Wars
Historical character(s): Alexander I, Ruler (Czar of Russia); Nadya Yurensky, Noblewoman (countess)
Time Period(s): 19th Century
Locale(s): Russia

Summary: The novel concerns the reign of Alexander I, Czar of Russia, and recounts his political and personal career as Napoleon's opponent and the revered savior of Russia from the French threat.

Historical Accuracy: The novel combines historical fact with the legends that have grown around Alexander. Certain liberties have been taken in treating some of these legends as truth.

CHRISTINA SAVAGE
(PSEUD. OF KERRY NEWCOMB, 1946- ; FRANK SCHAEFER, 1936-)

Newcomb and Schaefer first met in 1974 and decided to write a script for a horror movie together. When that did not work out, they co-authored a western before turning to romance novels. Newcomb was born in Connecticut and graduated from the University of Texas at Arlington and Trinity University. He has taught in a Native American school in Montana and has worked as a singer, entertainer, and director. Schaefer was born in New York and graduated from the Texas College of Arts and Industries and Trinity University. He has been an actor, director, radio announcer, and a Peace Corps volunteer in Costa Rica.

5616 Hearts of Fire

Date of Publication: 1984
Subject(s): American Revolution; Romance
Fictional character(s): Cassie Tryon, Young Woman, Heiress; Lucas Jericho, Military Personnel (colonial soldier), Pirate; Richard Tryon, Loyalist, Spy
Time Period(s): 1770s; 1780s
Locale(s): Philadelphia, Pennsylvania

Summary: Tory heiress Cassie Tryon finds herself in the middle of a deadly conflict between her lover, the rebel and former privateer Lucas Jericho, and her brother, a British spy and officer.

Historical Accuracy: The novel supplies a believable and well-developed wartime background.

DOUGLAS SAVAGE (1950-)

A practicing attorney and a farrier as well as a writer, Savage was born in Akron, Ohio, and received his law degree from Cleveland State University. He also attended the Ohio Horseshoeing School. Savage is a contributor to law and medical journals, an associate editor of the *Journal of Cranio-Mandibular Practice*, and a forensic medicine columnist for the *Ohio Family Physician*. Of his avocation, blacksmithing, Savage has said that he is very proud to have a "trade" along with his profession.

5617 The Court Martial of Robert E. Lee

Date of Publication: 1993
Subject(s): Civil War—U.S.; Battle of Gettysburg; Trials
Historical character(s): Robert E. Lee, Military Personnel (Confederate commander); Judah P. Benjamin, Political Figure; Jefferson Davis, Political Figure; James Longstreet, Military Personnel (Confederate general); James Ewell Brown Stuart, Military Personnel (Confederate general); A.P. Hill, Military Personnel (Confederate general)
Time Period(s): 1860s (1863)

Locale(s): Richmond, Virginia

Summary: This is a fascinating speculation about what might have happened if Robert E. Lee was court-martialed following the devastating defeat at Gettysburg. Lee is put on trial and forced to review and justify his famous campaigns. The novel is a fascinating study in tactical skill and human courage.

Historical Accuracy: Most of the dialogue is authentic, using the actual words of the speakers as detailed notes explain. This is an utterly convincing speculation.

▐5618▌ *The Sons of Grady Rourke*

Date of Publication: 1995
Subject(s): American West; Lincoln County War; Crime and Criminals
Fictional character(s): Patrick Rourke, Young Man; Sean Rourke, Young Man; Liam Rourke, Young Man
Historical character(s): William Bonney, Outlaw; John Chisum, Rancher; William Brady, Lawman
Time Period(s): 1870s (1878)
Locale(s): Lincoln County, New Mexico

Summary: The Rourke brothers return home and find themselves in the middle of the Lincoln County Wars. They are forced to choose sides in the fight in which the infamous Billy the Kid first makes his reputation.

Historical Accuracy: Nearly all the principal characters beside the Rourkes are real, and the framework for the action is based on actual events.

ELIZABETH SAVAGE (1918-)

Born in Massachusetts, Savage graduated from Colby College. She has worked as a freelance writer and contributor of short stories to the *Saturday Evening Post*, *Cosmopolitan*, and the *Paris Review*. Her books include *Summer of Pride*, *Happy Ending*, and *The Last Night at the Ritz*.

▐5619▌ *Willowwood*

Date of Publication: 1978
Subject(s): Artistic Life; Victorian Period
Fictional character(s): Will Little, Gentleman
Historical character(s): Dante Gabriel Rossetti, Writer (poet); Elizabeth Eleanor Siddal, Model (artist's), Artist; John Ruskin, Writer (art critic); William Morris, Artist; Fanny Cornforth, Model (artist's); Jane Burden, Spouse (of Morris)
Time Period(s): 1850s
Locale(s): London, England

Summary: The novel portrays the artistic and romantic world of the Pre-Raphaelite Brotherhood and Dante Gabriel Rossetti, whose innovations and pronouncements inspired an artistic revolution. Rossetti's complicated emotional life is dramatized, including his wife and model Elizabeth Siddal and his mistress Fanny Cornforth, as well as his circle that includes John Ruskin and William Morris.

Historical Accuracy: The novel depends on historical elements that are faithfully presented.

LES SAVAGE JR. (1922-1958)

Born in Alhambra, California, Savage wrote short stories for various magazines, including *Action Stories* and *Frontier Stories*. During the 1950s, he contributed a number of stories to *Zane Grey's Western Magazine*. He was a gifted historical novelist who excelled in evoking the terrain of the American West, and was painstaking in his research into fields such as mining, geology, dress, firearms, and anthropology. His best novels are *Doniphan's Ride*, set during the Mexican War, and his masterpiece, *The Royal City*, set in New Mexico during the Pueblo Revolt of 1680.

▐5620▌ *Doniphan's Ride*

Date of Publication: 1959
Subject(s): Mexican War; American West
Fictional character(s): Alexander Doniphan, Military Personnel (colonel); Nate Hatcher, Military Personnel (soldier); Inez Torreon, Gentlewoman
Time Period(s): 1840s (1846)
Locale(s): United States; Mexico

Summary: The adventures of Colonel Alexander Doniphan's First Missouri Volunteers during the War with Mexico are depicted. Doniphan is inexperienced and must contend with the Mexicans, Indians, and insubordination, including young Nate Hatcher's infatuation with Inez Torreon, the daughter of a powerful Mexican landowner.

Historical Accuracy: The novel uses convincing period elements.

▐5621▌ *The Royal City*

Date of Publication: 1956
Subject(s): Spanish Colonies; Pueblo Revolt; Indians
Fictional character(s): Luis Ribera, Nobleman; Barbara Cardenas, Gentlewoman; Toribio Quintano, Indian (half breed), Lawman
Time Period(s): 17th century (1680)
Locale(s): Santa Fe, New Mexico

Summary: The great Pueblo Revolt in 1680 is the background for this romantic adventure set in Santa Fe. Luis Ribera is an idealistic Spanish nobleman. He alone seems to grasp fully the unrest among the Pueblo Indians that will explode into violence.

Historical Accuracy: The background of this fictional story is accurate and authentic.

CAROL SAYLOR

▐5622▌ *The Equinox: A Novel of Rome in the Time of Commodus*

Date of Publication: 1966
Subject(s): Roman Empire; Christianity
Fictional character(s): Manlius Valerius, Young Man; Cleander, Servant

Historical character(s): Lucius Aelius Aurelius Commodus, Ruler (Roman emperor); Marcus Aurelius, Ruler (Roman emperor)
Time Period(s): 2nd century
Locale(s): Rome, Roman Empire

Summary: Manlius Valerius, a friend of the Roman emperor Commodus, becomes embroiled in the eunuch Cleander's intrigues and in a plot by the Christians to poison the emperor.

Historical Accuracy: Although little is known about the Rome of this period, the novel creates a believable atmosphere.

STEVEN SAYLOR (1956-)

Born in Texas, Saylor graduated from the University of Texas, Austin. His fascination with ancient Rome began when he saw the movie *Cleopatra* at a drive-in theater in Texas. He has worked as a magazine and newspaper editor in San Francisco. He has received high praise from critics for his Roma Sub Rosa series of historical mysteries.

5623 *Arms of Nemesis*

Date of Publication: 1992
Subject(s): Roman Empire; Mystery; Servile War
Fictional character(s): Gordianus the Finder, Detective—Private
Historical character(s): Marcus Licinius Crassus, Nobleman, Military Personnel (general)
Time Period(s): 1st century B.C. (72 B.C.)
Locale(s): Bay of Naples, Roman Empire

Summary: When is his estate overseer is murdered, Marcus Crassus blames two missing slaves who have run off to join the Spartacan Slave Revolt. In revenge, Crassus vows that unless the slaves are found, he will slaughter his remaining 99 slaves. Gordianus the Finder must solve the crime before the promised blood bath.

Historical Accuracy: The historical background of the Servile War is authentic and believable.

5624 *Catalina's Riddle*

Date of Publication: 1993
Subject(s): Mystery; Roman Empire
Fictional character(s): Gordianus the Finder, Farmer, Detective—Private
Historical character(s): Marcus Tullius Cicero, Lawyer, Political Figure; Lucius Sergius Catilina, Political Figure (senator)
Time Period(s): 1st century B.C. (63 B.C.)
Locale(s): Etruria, Roman Empire; Rome, Roman Empire

Summary: Gordianus is living on a farm in Etruria, in rustic retirement from the intrigues of Rome. He receives a messenger from his patron, Cicero, asking him to entertain a scheming senator, Catalina. A full measure of intrigue arrives, along with a headless corpse.

Historical Accuracy: The novel ingeniously recreates both the customs of the period and the atmosphere of the Roman Empire.

5625 *A Murder on the Appian Way*

Date of Publication: 1996
Subject(s): Mystery; Roman Empire
Fictional character(s): Gordianus the Finder, Detective—Private
Historical character(s): Marcus Tullius Cicero, Lawyer, Philosopher; Titus Milo, Nobleman
Time Period(s): 1st century B.C. (52 B.C.)
Locale(s): Rome, Roman Empire

Summary: Powerful populist politico Publius Clodius is murdered on the Appian Way. Gordianus the Finder joins the defense team led by Cicero for the prime suspect, Clodius' rival, Titus Milo. As Clodius' followers riot to avenge their slain leader, Gordianus must unravel a complex political tangle.

Historical Accuracy: The novel's details of Roman history are accurate and authentically presented.

5626 *Roman Blood*

Date of Publication: 1991
Subject(s): Mystery; Roman Empire
Fictional character(s): Gordianus the Finder, Detective—Private; Sextus Roscius, Landowner, Farmer
Historical character(s): Marcus Tullius Cicero, Lawyer; Lucius Cornelius Sulla, Political Figure (dictator), Military Personnel (Roman general)
Time Period(s): 1st century B.C. (80 B.C.)
Locale(s): Rome, Roman Empire

Summary: Gordianus the Finder is hired by Cicero to assist a client who is charged with murdering his father. Gordianus finds himself at the center of a conspiracy that reaches the dictator Sulla himself.

Historical Accuracy: The period details are well-drawn, if the lawyering and private detection are at times anachronistic.

5627 *The Venus Throw*

Date of Publication: 1995
Subject(s): Mystery; Roman Empire; Trials
Fictional character(s): Gordianus the Finder, Detective—Private; Dio of Alexandria, Diplomat
Historical character(s): Gaius Valerius Catullus, Writer (poet); Clodia, Gentlewoman; Marcus Tullius Cicero, Political Figure, Lawyer
Time Period(s): 1st century B.C. (56 B.C.)
Locale(s): Rome, Roman Empire

Summary: Gordianus the Finder is asked to help an old friend, Dio, the Egyptian ambassador, when several Egyptian envoys are viciously assassinated. Gordianus finds himself in the middle of dangerous political intrigue involving the notorious beauty Clodia, the poet Catullus, and a devious political opportunist. Poisoning, betrayals, and buried secrets confront Gordianus as the story climaxes in one of history's most famous trials.

Historical Accuracy: The period background is convincing.

JOHN SCALZO

Scalzo is a lawyer living in Omaha.

5628 *A Prince, a Piper, and a Rose*

Date of Publication: 1976
Subject(s): Jacobite Rebellion; Royalty—Scotland; Georgian Period
Fictional character(s): Richard Evereaux, Nobleman (Duke of Huntford); Ann D'Arcy, Gentlewoman
Historical character(s): Charles Edward Stuart, Royalty (prince)
Time Period(s): 1740s (1745)
Locale(s): England; Scotland

Summary: The glorious failure of the Stuart cause is dramatized from the perspective of Richard Evereaux, Duke of Huntford, who becomes a champion of Bonnie Prince Charlie. Evereaux loves Ann D'Arcy, whose devotion for him is misinterpreted as treachery against the prince. The decline of the Prince's Highland army and its ultimate destruction are portrayed.

Historical Accuracy: The basic historical outline of the story is authentic.

CARLO SCARFOGLIO (1887-)

Born in Rome, Scarfoglio worked as a writer and journalist in Naples and a war correspondent during World War I. He wrote about world politics.

5629 *The True Cross*

Date of Publication: 1956
Subject(s): Middle Ages; Crusades
Fictional character(s): Guido Acconciaiuoco, Knight
Time Period(s): 12th century (1177-1192)
Locale(s): Latin Kingdom of Jerusalem, Palestine

Summary: Events in the later stages of the Second Crusade are dramatized through the experiences of Guido, a young Knight Templar. He is shown from his induction into the Order of the Temple to his death on his way back to Italy 15 years later. The action takes place in the Latin Kingdom of Jerusalem and offers a balanced portrait of both the Crusaders and their Muslim enemies.

Historical Accuracy: The novel realistically depicts the time and place.

NATHAN SCHACHNER (1895-1955)

An American attorney, historian, and author, Schachner was born in New York City and practiced law from 1919 to 1933. He served as the director of public relations for both the American Jewish Committee and the national Council of Jewish Women. Shachner wrote over 100 science fiction stories. His books include *Aaron Burr*, *Alexander Hamilton*, *Thomas Jefferson*, and *The Founding Fathers*.

5630 *By the Dim Lamps*

Date of Publication: 1941

Subject(s): Civil War—U.S.; Reconstruction Period
Fictional character(s): Hugh Flint, Plantation Owner
Time Period(s): 1860s
Locale(s): New Orleans, Louisiana

Summary: New Orleans before, during, and after the Civil War is the setting for this novel that follows the impact of the war on the Flint family and their sugar plantations as well as on occupied New Orleans.

Historical Accuracy: The historical background of events, manners, and speech is faithfully rendered.

5631 *The King's Passenger*

Date of Publication: 1942
Subject(s): American Colonies; Bacon's Rebellion
Fictional character(s): Jeremy Wynne, Convict, Servant (indentured)
Historical character(s): Nathaniel Bacon, Leader (rebellion), Lawyer
Time Period(s): 17th century (1676)
Locale(s): Jamestown, Virginia, American Colonies

Summary: The story of Bacon's Rebellion in the Virginia Colony is dramatized through the experiences of a young Englishman whose sentence for treason is commuted into service as an indentured servant in Virginia. He comes to America on the same ship as the lawyer Nathaniel Bacon who will spearhead the rising of the colonists against the corrupt administration of Sir William Berkeley.

Historical Accuracy: The events of the rebellion are authentically drawn and believable.

5632 *The Sun Shines West*

Date of Publication: 1943
Subject(s): Settlement of the American Frontier; Free Soil Movement; Abolition Movement
Fictional character(s): Jonathan Ware, Settler, Professor; Delia Ware, Spouse; Susan Bowen, Pioneer
Time Period(s): 1850s; 1860s (1854-1861)
Locale(s): Kansas

Summary: This tale of pioneer life in "Bloody Kansas" in the years before the Civil War follows the domestic life of Harvard instructor Jonathan Ware and his wife Delia who, influenced by the Abolitionist cause, go west to settle in Kansas. There Delia finds the struggle of pioneer life overwhelming, while Jonathan finds himself, with the assistance of a young farm girl, Susan Bowen.

Historical Accuracy: The strength of the novel rests in the historical background, which is accomplished and believable.

5633 *The Wanderer: A Novel of Dante and Beatrice*

Date of Publication: 1944
Subject(s): Middle Ages; Literary Life
Historical character(s): Dante Alighieri, Writer; Beatrice Portinari, Gentlewoman
Time Period(s): 13th century
Locale(s): Florence, Italy

Summary: The novel, based on the biography of Italian poet Dante Alighieri, dramatizes his romance with Beatrice, the inspiration for his literary work. The novel features a colorful and authentic depiction of the period at this fascinating point in medieval Italian history.

Historical Accuracy: The novel stays close to the known biographical facts and makes good use of the evident historical research.

JACK SCHAEFER (1907-1991)

An American journalist and author, Schaefer was born in Cleveland, Ohio, and attended Oberlin College and Columbia University. With his first novel, *Shane*, Schaefer made a lasting mark on the genre of Western fiction. The novel has been hailed by many as one of the best novels about the Old West ever written. His other books include *Old Ramon*, *The Canyon*, and the nonfiction works *Heroes Without Glory: Some Goodmen of the Old West* and *An American Bestiary*.

5634   *Company of Cowards*

Date of Publication: 1957
Subject(s): American West; Civil War—U.S.; Indians
Fictional character(s): Jared Heath, Military Personnel (captain)
Time Period(s): 1860s
Locale(s): Virginia; New Mexico

Summary: In punishment for his cowardice during the Civil War Battle of the Wilderness, Captain Jared Heath is given command of a company made up of fellow cowards. They redeem themselves against the Indians in the New Mexico territory.

Historical Accuracy: The story is imagined, but relies on convincing period details.

5635   *Monte Walsh*

Date of Publication: 1983
Subject(s): American West; Ranching
Fictional character(s): Monte Walsh, Cowboy
Time Period(s): 19th century; 20th century (1872-1913)
Locale(s): West

Summary: The novel provides the life story of cowboy Monte Walsh who sees the time of the open range give way to the closing of the West during the early 1910s. It is a vivid portrait of western life as it must have truly been lived.

Historical Accuracy: This is a believable and accurate depiction of western life during the period.

SUSAN FROMBERG SCHAEFFER
(1941-)

Born in Brooklyn, New York, Schaeffer graduated from the University of Chicago. She is a professor of English at Brooklyn College, a novelist, and a poet.

5636   *Time in Its Flight*

Date of Publication: 1978
Subject(s): Medical Profession; Family Saga
Fictional character(s): John Steele, Doctor; Edna Dickinson, Spouse (of Steele)
Time Period(s): 19th century; 20th century (1865-1966)
Locale(s): Boston, Massachusetts; New York, New York

Summary: This massive family saga traces medical practice in the 19th century and its effects on both physicians and their families.

Historical Accuracy: The novel is convincing in its period details.

HENRY SCHINDALL (1916-)

5637   *Let the Spring Come*

Date of Publication: 1953
Subject(s): American Revolution; American Colonies
Fictional character(s): Peter Randolph, Young Man
Time Period(s): 1770s
Locale(s): Virginia

Summary: This historical romance set during the American Revolution describes the adventures of a young Virginian, Peter Randolph, during the first year of the war.

Historical Accuracy: This is more a costume romance than a carefully documented period drama.

ANN SCHLEE (1934-)

An English writer and Oxford graduate, Schlee is the author of several novels for older children. *Rhine Journey* was her first novel for adults.

5638   *The Proprietor*

Date of Publication: 1983
Subject(s): Victorian Period
Fictional character(s): Augustus Walmer, Gentleman; Amelia Pontefract, Gentlewoman
Time Period(s): 19th century (1836-1856)
Locale(s): England

Summary: Set during the Victorian period, the novel details the effort of idealist Augustus Walmer, the proprietor of a group of islands off the south coast of England, to improve the lot of the islands' inhabitants. His altruistic successes have personal costs.

Historical Accuracy: The locale is presented in convincing fashion.

5639   *Rhine Journey*

Date of Publication: 1980
Subject(s): Victorian Period
Fictional character(s): Charlotte Morrison, Spinster
Time Period(s): 1850s (1851)
Locale(s): Rhine River, Europe

Summary: The novel captures the fantasies and dreams of Charlotte Morrison as she makes a romantic journey with her family by paddle-steamer on the Rhine in 1851. One of the passengers recalls a man she gave up years before at her brother's insistence, and the memory sets in motion a rich and emotional response in contrast to the stifling conventions of the times.

Historical Accuracy: The psychological study is dependent on a solidly presented Victorian background.

GLADYS SCHMITT (1909-1972)

Born in Pittsburgh, Pennsylvania, Schmitt was educated at the University of Pittsburgh and worked as an editor for Scholastic Magazines and as a professor of English at Carnegie-Mellon University. Called by one critic the American Proust, Schmitt has also been compared to Willa Cather. She is the author of seven novels, including *Gates of Aulis*, a Dial Press Award winner.

5640 *Confessors of the Name*

Date of Publication: 1952
Subject(s): Roman Empire; Christianity
Fictional character(s): Favorinus Herennius, Nobleman
Time Period(s): 3rd century
Locale(s): Rome, Roman Empire

Summary: This story of Rome in the 3rd century centers on the experiences of the nephew of the emperor, Favorinus Herennius, who searches for meaning in his life. He turns to Christianity and is eventually martyred.

Historical Accuracy: Despite evident research to produce a plausible period background, this novel is more a psychological investigation than a typical historical novel.

5641 *David the King*

Date of Publication: 1946
Subject(s): Biblical Story; Ancient Israel
Historical character(s): David, Ruler (King of Israel), Biblical Figure; Saul, Ruler (King of Israel), Biblical Figure; Jonathan, Biblical Figure; Bathsheba, Biblical Figure; Absalom, Biblical Figure
Time Period(s): 10th century B.C.
Locale(s): Israel

Summary: The story of David's rise from shepherd boy to king of Israel is told in familiar Biblical scenes. David's relationships with King Saul and his beloved friend Jonathan, as well as his desire for the beautiful Bathsheba are dramatized. David emerges as a flawed but inspired leader.

Historical Accuracy: The novel provides plausible elaboration on the Biblical story.

5642 *The Godforgotten*

Date of Publication: 1972
Subject(s): Middle Ages; Religious Life
Fictional character(s): Father Albrecht, Religious (monk)
Time Period(s): 12th century (1100)

Locale(s): Cologne, Germany; St. Cyprian Island, Germany (Flemish coast)

Summary: Set in medieval Germany, the novel tells the story of the mysterious community of St. Cyprian. Father Albrecht, a dissident Benedictine monk, is sent by his superior to investigate the truth about the community. What he discovers is profoundly unsettling.

Historical Accuracy: The story features a convincing period background.

5643 *Rembrandt*

Date of Publication: 1961
Subject(s): Artistic Life; Biography, Fictionalized
Historical character(s): Rembrandt, Artist
Time Period(s): 17th century (1623-1669)
Locale(s): Leyden, Netherlands; Amsterdam, Netherlands

Summary: This biographical novel traces the career of Dutch painter and etcher Rembrandt. He is shown rising from his humble background to wealth and honor in the burgher society of Amsterdam. His unhappy marriage to an heiress and his relationship with a servant girl follow a path that leads to demoralization and bankruptcy before a final flourishing of his genius and his artistic vision.

Historical Accuracy: The novel stays close to the known facts of Rembrandt's life and time.

ERNST SCHNABEL (1913-)

Schnabel left school at 17 and was a merchant seaman for 12 years. He has written for radio and films. *The Voyage Home* was awarded the Fontone Prize.

5644 *The Voyage Home*

Date of Publication: 1958
Subject(s): Myths and Legends; Ancient Greece
Fictional character(s): Odysseus, Wanderer; Nausicaa, Noblewoman; Circe, Sorceress
Time Period(s): Indeterminate Past
Locale(s): Mediterranean

Summary: The novel offers an imaginative re-telling of the Homeric saga of Odysseus' long voyage home to Ithaca after the Trojan War.

Historical Accuracy: The novel depends on a convincing evocation of the ethos of *The Odyssey* .

YVONNE SCHOELL (1924-)

Schoell grew up in Denver and graduated from the University of Denver. She received her Master's degree from the University of the Pacific. A former college instructor in literature and composition, Schoell has extensively studied the early history of California.

5645 *The Argonauts*

Date of Publication: 1972
Subject(s): Gold Rush—California; American West; Wagon Trains

Fictional character(s): Goldie Baxter, Orphan, Pioneer; Darcy Dupres, Gentleman; Kevin Adams, Pioneer
Time Period(s): 1840s (1849)
Locale(s): Oregon Trail, United States; At Sea; California

Summary: The California Gold Rush of 1849 is the scene for this novel that traces the adventures of five young people who, drawn by gold fever journey by clipper ship around Cape Horn and by wagon train to California.

Historical Accuracy: This is an accurate historical account of the period.

KAREL SCHOEMAN (1939-)

Born in the Orange Free State of South Africa, Schoeman is regarded as one of South Africa's foremost contemporary writers. She is an author of travel books, television scripts, and translations of Dutch, German, and Irish works. Schoeman worked as a librarian, translator, and nurse in South Africa, Scotland, and Holland.

5646 *Another Country*
Date of Publication: 1991
Subject(s): Frontier—Africa
Fictional character(s): Versluis, Gentleman
Time Period(s): 1870s
Locale(s): Bloemfontein, South Africa

Summary: Set in South Africa during the 1870s, the novel depicts Dutchman Versluis, who comes to Bloemfontein seeking a cure for his tuberculosis. The novel explores his acceptance of African culture and his coming to terms with his own death.

Historical Accuracy: This psychological study creates a believable sense of time and place.

SUSAN CLARK SCHOFIELD (1958-)

Schofield was born in Chicago and grew up in Philadelphia, attending Bucknell and Penn State University. Her first novel, *Refugio, They Named You Wrong*, was runner-up in the 1991 Best First Novel Competition of the Western Writers of America.

5647 *Refugio, They Named You Wrong*
Date of Publication: 1991
Subject(s): American West; Crime and Criminals
Fictional character(s): Peter Jack Costello, Cowboy
Time Period(s): 19th century (late 1800s)
Locale(s): Texas (along the Mexican border)

Summary: This western tale concerns a young cattle driver, Peter John Costello, who is wanted for the murder of his father and brother. His experiences as a wanted man are dramatized. The author clearly sympathizes with Costello.

Historical Accuracy: The novel provides an authentic depiction of the time and place.

5648 *Telluride*
Date of Publication: 1993
Subject(s): American West; Mining
Fictional character(s): Gretel Coleman, Young Woman; Zachary "Cole" Coleman, Gunfighter
Time Period(s): 1890s (1891-1892)
Locale(s): Telluride, Colorado

Summary: A miner dies in a mysterious mine explosion after discovering gold. His son, Cole, is warned to stay away by his sister, Gretel. Cole returns to the mining town to uncover the truth and make peace with the past.

Historical Accuracy: The period elements are convincingly presented.

WILLIAM GREENOUGH SCHOFIELD (1909-)

An American journalist and author, Schofield was born in Rhode Island and attended Brown University. As a reporter and columnist for newspapers in Providence and Boston, journalistic assignments took him around the world. He was the founder of the Freedom Trail, the historic tour of Boston. His novels include *Treason Trail* and *Seek for a Hero*.

5649 *Ashes in the Wilderness*
Date of Publication: 1942
Subject(s): American Colonies; King Philip's War; Indians
Fictional character(s): Christian Painter, Military Personnel (officer)
Historical character(s): Roger Williams, Religious (clergyman); Benjamin Church, Military Personnel (captain)
Time Period(s): 17th century (1675-1676)
Locale(s): Rhode Island, American Colonies; Massachusetts, American Colonies

Summary: The events of King Philip's War between the Indians of southern New England and the colonists are described based on the war diary of colonial soldier Benjamin Church. Church took a leading part in the Great Swamp fight and finally hunted down and killed Philip. The novel also interweaves the romantic story of soldier Christian Painter whose love for a Quaker girl is finally blessed by Roger Williams, who marries them.

Historical Accuracy: The details of the campaign against the Indians are faithfully presented.

5650 *The Deer Cry*
Date of Publication: 1948
Subject(s): Biography, Fictionalized; Dark Ages
Historical character(s): Patrick, Religious (missionary)
Time Period(s): 4th century; 5th century (385-461)
Locale(s): England; Ireland

Summary: The novel offers a fictionalized biography of Saint Patrick and his mission to convert pagan Ireland to Christianity. Patrick's youth in England, his capture by Irish marauders, his escape after several years as a herdsman, and his eventual return to Ireland as a missionary are shown.

Historical Accuracy: The novel makes use of Patrick's own words from his autobiography to create a feeling of authority.

ALAN SCHOLEFIELD (1931-)

Born and educated in South Africa, Scholefield worked as a newspaperman and a defense correspondent. He is the author of historical, adventure, and suspense novels, many of which are set in his native South Africa.

5651 *The Alpha Raid*

Date of Publication: 1977
Subject(s): World War I
Fictional character(s): Edward Ross, Military Personnel (English officer); Justine Jumelle, Young Woman; Bagley, Military Personnel (commanding officer)
Time Period(s): 1910s (1917)
Locale(s): Lake Tanganyika, Tanzania (East Africa)

Summary: During World War I in East Africa, the Germans control Lake Tanganyika with their paddle-wheel steamer the *Afrika*. The novel details the English attempt to sink the *Afrika* by bringing two armed launches overland to mount the attack. In command is the martinet C.O. Bagley.

Historical Accuracy: The events are loosely based on the Naval Africa Expedition of 1915 but with liberties taken with the geography and the details.

5652 *The Eagles of Malice*

Date of Publication: 1968
Subject(s): Herrero Rising
Fictional character(s): Andrew Black, Police Officer, Military Personnel (soldier)
Time Period(s): 1900s (1904-1905)
Locale(s): Namibia (German Southwest Africa); Kalahari Desert, Africa

Summary: The background of the story is the Herrero Rising of 1904-1905, in which the African tribe was almost exterminated by the Germans who ruled Southwest Africa. The story is told from the perspective of a young colonial policeman, Andrew Black.

Historical Accuracy: The novel's historical elements are authentic.

5653 *Fire in the Ice*

Date of Publication: 1984
Subject(s): Russian Revolution; Trials
Fictional character(s): David Kade, Gentleman; Countess Cropotkin, Noblewoman
Time Period(s): 1910s; 1920s (1917-1920)
Locale(s): Siberia, Russia; Cape of Good Hope, South Africa; London, England

Summary: English gentleman David Kade is caught in the chaos of the Russian Revolution and flees for safety across Siberia. He is saved by the Countess Cropotkin in a series of events that are uncovered years later in a courtroom battle over the custody of Sir David's child.

Historical Accuracy: The story is invented but offers some gripping and authentic scenes of Russia during the period.

5654 *Great Elephant*

Date of Publication: 1967
Subject(s): Zulu Empire; Tribal Life—African
Fictional character(s): James Fraser Black, Convict; Robbie Black, Young Man; Mgobozi, Warrior (Zulu)
Historical character(s): Chaka, Ruler (Zulu Empire)
Time Period(s): 19th century (1817-1838)
Locale(s): Zululand, Africa

Summary: The title refers to the great Zulu warrior Chaka, and the novel tells the story of James Fraser Black, an escaped convict who brings his family to Zululand. There his son, Robbie, comes of age as his father takes up the primitive ways of the Zulus.

Historical Accuracy: The novel's backdrop is historical and convincing.

5655 *The Hammer of God*

Date of Publication: 1973
Subject(s): Victorian Period
Fictional character(s): Lord Lamming, Nobleman, Hunter; John Franklin, Guide, Veteran (ex-army officer)
Historical character(s): Theodore II, Ruler (King of Ethiopia)
Time Period(s): 1860s
Locale(s): Ethiopia

Summary: The story of Theodore II, King of 19th-century Ethiopia, is dramatized from the perspectives of a Victorian sportsman in search of hunting trophies and his guide, John Franklin, a former adviser to Theodore. The king, once a wise and rational ruler, is now half-mad, challenging the might of the English army at his mountain fortress Magdala.

Historical Accuracy: The novel interweaves the imagined and the historical. Theodore and his challenge to the might of Britain is factual.

5656 *Lion in the Evening*

Date of Publication: 1974
Subject(s): World War I; Railroads; Frontier—Africa
Fictional character(s): Richard Kendon, Engineer; Frederick Seaton Storey, Hunter; Margaret Storey, Young Woman
Time Period(s): 1910s (1916)
Locale(s): Kenya (British East Africa)

Summary: The setting is British East Africa during the Great War. Work on the spur line of the Uganda Railway to Kisimi is threatened both by the invasion of troops from German East Africa and by a man-eating lion. Engineer Richard Kendon joins forces with African hunter Frederick Storey to go after the lion while struggling with the challenges to complete the railway.

Historical Accuracy: The frontier and period setting is convincing.

5657 *The Lost Giants*

Date of Publication: 1989

Subject(s): American West
Fictional character(s): Margaret Dow, Traveller
Time Period(s): 1860s
Locale(s): California; Colorado

Summary: Set in the American West of the 1860s, the novel traces the adventures of a young Scottish woman, Margaret Dow, who joins a search for a legendary forest of great conifers. On the way she faces violent Indians and a fanatical religious group.

Historical Accuracy: The story is imagined but features convincing period details.

5658 *Wild Dog Running*

Date of Publication: 1971
Subject(s): Frontier—Africa
Fictional character(s): John Southgate, Settler, Immigrant; Charlotte Vicker, Settler, Immigrant
Time Period(s): 1820s
Locale(s): South Africa; Suffolk, England

Summary: This tale of the Southgate family, Suffolk farmers who escape England's Enclosure Act by emigrating to the Cape Colony of South Africa, focuses on the challenges that confront young John Southgate. When his father dies on the trek, John must battle the wilderness and the rapacity of a rich landowner who sets out to destroy the smaller homesteaders.

Historical Accuracy: The social and economic forces that produced emigration to South Africa are accurately described.

GABY VON SCHONTHAN

Austrian writer Gaby von Schonthan is the granddaughter of Franz von Schonthan and is a former actress, having worked at Vienna's Josef Statter Theatre and in Germany. Von Schonthan is married to historian and novelist Paul Frischauer.

5659 *Madame Casanova*

Date of Publication: 1968
Subject(s): Napoleonic Era
Fictional character(s): Felicine Elisa Maria Casanova, Adventurer
Historical character(s): Alexander I, Ruler (Czar of Russia); Charles Maurice de Talleyrand-Perigord, Diplomat; Napoleon Bonaparte, Ruler (Emperor of France)
Time Period(s): 18th century; 19th century
Locale(s): Europe

Summary: The novel provides a first-person account of a young lady who rises to the top of the social world of Europe during the Napoleonic era. Felicine Casanova, motivated by a desire to avenge the insult of being spurned by Napoleon, finds herself in the arms of such famous figures as Czar Alexander I and Talleyrand.

Historical Accuracy: The novel shows evident knowledge of the history of the period, but the main character is shallow, and her story is a light romantic fantasy based on some historical fact.

5660 *The Rose of Malmaison: The Turbulent Life of the Beautiful Josephine*

Date of Publication: 1966
Subject(s): Napoleonic Era; Biography, Fictionalized; French Revolution
Historical character(s): Josephine, Royalty (Empress of France); Napoleon Bonaparte, Military Personnel (army commander), Ruler (Emperor); Maximilien Francois de Robespierre, Revolutionary, Political Figure
Time Period(s): 18th century; 19th century (1779-1814)
Locale(s): Paris, France; Milan, Italy

Summary: Napoleon's Josephine tells her own extraordinary story, from her journey from Martinique to France to marry a vicomte she had never seen to becoming Empress Josephine of France. Once on the throne, she has to deal with Napoleon's greedy family intent on dislodging her and finally Napoleon's own affairs of state which lead him to divorce her to marry the archduchess of Austria. Josephine emerges as an extremely perceptive and practical adventuress.

Historical Accuracy: The novel quotes directly from Napoleon's own love letters to add to the novel's authenticity.

LAWRENCE SCHOONOVER (1906-1980)

Born in Iowa, Schoonover worked as a New York advertising executive. After 20 years, he quit to become an historical novelist. His books are set mainly in the 15th or 16th century. He is also the author of a contemporary novel on the advertising business, *The Quick Brown Fox*.

5661 *The Burnished Blade*

Date of Publication: 1948
Subject(s): Renaissance; Royalty—France; Hundred Years War
Fictional character(s): Pierre, Artisan (armorer), Adventurer
Historical character(s): Jacques Coeur, Financier; Joan of Arc, Warrior; Charles VII, Ruler (King of France)
Time Period(s): 15th century (1430s)
Locale(s): Rouen, France; Trebizond, Asia Minor

Summary: This adventure novel set in the 15th century follows the career of a foundling named Pierre. Pierre is taught the secrets of the armorer's trade and is sent on a mission to unmask a smuggling ring.

Historical Accuracy: The novel offers a richly evocative depiction of the period.

5662 *The Chancellor*

Date of Publication: 1961
Subject(s): Royalty—France; Renaissance
Historical character(s): Francois I, Ruler (King of France); Antoine Duprat, Political Figure (chancellor), Religious (cardinal); Charles, Duc de Bourbon, Nobleman; Benvenuto Cellini, Artist (sculptor), Writer
Time Period(s): 15th century; 16th century
Locale(s): France; Rome, Italy

Summary: The novel depicts the colorful reign of Francis I of France and the power behind his reign, his chancellor Antoine Duprat—warrior, cardinal, and financial wizard. The novel captures court intrigue and period details in scenes of high and low life with a colorful cast of players.

Historical Accuracy: The research shows in this fully-realized portrait of early Renaissance France.

5663 *The Gentle Infidel*

Date of Publication: 1950
Subject(s): Ottoman Empire
Fictional character(s): Michael da Montelupo, Military Personnel (captain); Aeshia, Young Woman; Angelica, Young Woman
Time Period(s): 15th century (1404-1453)
Locale(s): Constantinople, Ottoman Empire

Summary: This 15th-century adventure story depicts Michael da Montelupo, a young captain in the service of the Turkish emperor, during the siege and fall of Constantinople in 1453. It features the intrigue of Venetian merchants and the divided loyalties of Michael, torn between his service to the sultan and his allegiance to his Christian heritage.

Historical Accuracy: The novel combines the imagined and the historical. The picture of life in 15th-century Constantinople is authentic.

5664 *The Golden Exile*

Date of Publication: 1951
Subject(s): Middle Ages
Fictional character(s): Guy de Brunne, Nobleman; Elaine, Captive
Time Period(s): 13th century
Locale(s): England; Cambodia; Syria

Summary: This medieval adventure story is set during the 13th century and depicts the journey of young Guy de Brunne. On a pilgrimage to the Holy Land, Guy is cast adrift at sea as a leper, then rescued by an Arab trader. He makes his way as far as the jungles of Cambodia, where he is worshipped as a white god. Travelling to Syria, he rescues his beloved. Finally, Guy returns home to reclaim his lands.

Historical Accuracy: The novel packs in far more adventure than one person could reasonably expect. The settings are more exotic than historically based.

5665 *The Prisoner of Tordesillas*

Date of Publication: 1959
Subject(s): Royalty—Spain
Historical character(s): Juana I, Ruler (Queen of Spain); Ferdinand V, Ruler (King of Aragon and Castile); Isabella, Ruler (Queen of Aragon and Castile); Philip the Handsome, Royalty (Archduke of Austria); Charles V, Ruler (Holy Roman Emperor)
Time Period(s): 16th century
Locale(s): Spain; France; Flanders

Summary: The novel dramatizes the tragic life of Juana of Castile, known as the mad queen, who spent the last half of her life, nearly 50 years, imprisoned in the fortress of

Tordesillas. The daughter of Ferdinand and Isabella, Juana marries Philip the Handsome of Austria. Her husband's infidelities, and the indifference of her son, Charles V, bring on her madness and a tragic end.

Historical Accuracy: Juana's life and times are accurately depicted.

5666 *The Queen's Cross: A Biographical Romance of Queen Isabella of Spain*

Date of Publication: 1955
Subject(s): Royalty—Spain; Biography, fictionalized; Inquisition
Historical character(s): Isabella I, Ruler (Queen of Castile); Ferdinand V, Ruler (King of Aragon); Tomas de Torquemada, Religious (Grand Inquisitor); Christopher Columbus, Explorer
Time Period(s): 15th century
Locale(s): Spain

Summary: The fascinating reign of Isabella I of Spain is dramatized. She dares to unite Castile and Aragon by marrying Ferdinand, then launches the crusade that finally drives the Moors out of Spain, and creates modern Spain. A strong administrator and military genius, Isabella is shown contending with great challenges and disappointments, responsible for both Columbus' glorious discovery and the horror of the Inquisition.

Historical Accuracy: Called a "biographical romance," the novel combines factual material with fictional elaborations.

5667 *The Revolutionary*

Date of Publication: 1958
Subject(s): Sea Story; American Revolution; Biography, Fictionalized
Historical character(s): John Paul Jones, Military Personnel (naval officer); Benjamin Franklin, Diplomat; Catherine the Great, Ruler (Empress of Russia)
Time Period(s): 18th century (1747-1792)
Locale(s): Scotland; At Sea; Russia

Summary: This biographical novel depicts the career of naval officer John Paul Jones from his youth in Scotland to his days as a privateer in the American navy. It features the epic battle with the British frigate *Serapis* and Jones' final service in Russia at the court of Catherine the Great. Jones emerges as a genuine American hero.

Historical Accuracy: The novel provides a faithful recounting of Jones' career and times.

5668 *The Spider King*

Date of Publication: 1954
Subject(s): Royalty—France; Renaissance; Hundred Years War
Historical character(s): Louis XI, Ruler (King of France); Jean D'Armagnac, Nobleman; Charles VI, Ruler (King of France)
Time Period(s): 15th century
Locale(s): France

Summary: This is a biographical novel of the life of Louis XI, king of France in the 15th century. Louis is born with a misshapen body but shows great personal courage and principles in the endless conflict of the Hundred Years War. In Scoonover's treatment, Louis becomes a great but complex and brooding monarch.

Historical Accuracy: The novel is scrupulously researched, and Louis is interpreted far more generously than past historians have allowed.

5669 *To Love a Queen*

Date of Publication: 1973
Subject(s): Elizabethan Period; Royalty—England
Historical character(s): Elizabeth I, Ruler (Queen of England); Sir Walter Raleigh, Courtier, Gentleman; William Cecil, Nobleman, Government Official; George Villiers, Nobleman (Duke of Buckingham); James I, Ruler (King of England)
Time Period(s): 16th century; 17th century
Locale(s): England

Summary: Set in the Elizabethan and Stuart periods, the novel describes the remarkable career of Walter Raleigh—soldier, explorer, writer, and the favorite of Elizabeth I—who rises from obscurity to knighthood and ends his days disgraced as a traitor and executed on the block. The novel captures the rise and fall of Raleigh's fortune and the political and romantic intrigues that affected him.

Historical Accuracy: The novel is accurate for the most part in detailing both the career of Raleigh and his era.

MARK SCHORR (1953-)

An American author born in New York City, Schorr attended SUNY Binghampton and went to work as a journalist, bookstore manager, nightclub bouncer, private investigator, photographer, and international courier. A recipient of awards from the Associated Press and the Valley Press Club for his series on drug dealing, Schorr is the author of such mystery novels as *Red Diamond, Private Eye, Ace of Diamonds*, and *Diamond Rock*. He is also the author of *The Borzoi Control* under the pseudonym Scott Ellis.

5670 *Bully!*

Date of Publication: 1985
Subject(s): Mystery; Politics
Fictional character(s): Jim White, Cowboy
Historical character(s): Theodore Roosevelt, Political Figure
Time Period(s): 1900s (1903)
Locale(s): Washington, District of Columbia; New York, New York

Summary: When Teddy Roosevelt discovers a conspiracy aimed at thwarting his presidential aspirations, he turns for help to Jim White, ex-cowboy and Rough Rider. Together they uncover an assassination plot and crimes among the rich and powerful.

Historical Accuracy: The novel is curiously thin in period flavor, and the depiction of Roosevelt does not match what is known of his personality.

SAMUEL A. SCHREINER JR. (1921-)

A graduate of Princeton, Schreiner served with the OSS in China during World War II. He has been a reporter for the *Pittsburgh Sun-Telegraph*, managing editor of *Parade*, and senior editor of *Reader's Digest*.

5671 *Angelica*

Date of Publication: 1978
Subject(s): Artistic Life; Georgian Period
Historical character(s): Angelica Kauffman, Artist; Samuel Johnson, Writer; Joshua Reynolds, Artist; Henry Fuseli, Artist; Oliver Goldsmith, Writer; David Garrick, Actor; Antonio Zucchi, Artist; Johann Wolfgang von Goethe, Writer; Lady Emma Hamilton, Gentlewoman; Horatio Nelson, Military Personnel (admiral)
Time Period(s): 18th century; 19th century (1766-1807)
Locale(s): London, England; Italy

Summary: The novel is based on the life and times of Angelica Kauffman, Swiss-born portrait painter of the 18th century, whose clients and admirers included some of the most illustrious figures of the day: Joshua Reynolds, Samuel Johnson, and Johann Goethe. Kauffman scandalized her time by achieving success in a world dominated by men and rejecting society's assumption that she assume a secondary or supporting role.

Historical Accuracy: The author explains that although most of the characters and events in the novel are real, it was not intended to be historically accurate.

5672 *Thine Is the Glory*

Date of Publication: 1975
Subject(s): Business Building
Fictional character(s): Scott Shallenberger Stewart, Businessman
Historical character(s): John D. Rockefeller, Financier; Henry Clay Frick, Financier; Andrew Carnegie, Financier; Henry Thaw, Businessman
Time Period(s): 19th century; 20th century (1870s-1945)
Locale(s): Pittsburgh, Pennsylvania

Summary: The growth of American industry is described in the family fortunes of Scott Stewart, a country boy who creates a business dynasty in America's Golden Triangle in Pittsburgh. Stewart's story covers 75 years from the Gilded Age through World War II, reflecting some of the great events of the period, including the Homestead Strike, the stock market scare of 1907, and the Depression.

Historical Accuracy: The story is fictional but clearly based on actual events and personalities of the era.

DUANE PHILIP SCHULTZ (1934-)

Psychologist and author Schultz was born in Baltimore and attended Johns Hopkins and Syracuse universities. He received his Ph.D. from American University and is a professor of psychology at the University of North Carolina, Charlotte. The recipient of research grants from the National Institute of Mental Health and the Office of Naval Research,

Schultz has written on several aspects of his profession and has contributed numerous articles to psychology journals.

5673 *Glory Enough for All: The Battle of the Crater*

Date of Publication: 1993
Subject(s): Civil War—U.S.; Battle of the Crater
Historical character(s): Henry Pleasants, Military Personnel (Union colonel); George Meade, Military Personnel (Union general); Ulysses S. Grant, Military Personnel (Union general); Ambrose E. Burnside, Military Personnel (Union general); Robert E. Lee, Military Personnel (Confederate commander)
Time Period(s): 1860s (1864)
Locale(s): Petersburg, Virginia

Summary: In 1864 the Civil War has ground down to a stalemate in the trenches around Petersburg, Virginia. The key to the position is Cemetery Hill. The novel tells the story of the Union army's ingenious plan to break the stalemate: tunnel under Cemetery Hill and blow it up. The plan leads to the tragic Battle of the Crater and a story of the Union high command's blunders and racism that cause the massacre of the Fourth Division made up of black troops.

Historical Accuracy: The novel's history is accurate and convincingly presented.

MARY SCHUMANN (1950-)

Born in Youngstown, Ohio, Schumann attended Columbia University, and has written short stories and serial fiction for magazines. Her historical novels *Strife Before Dawn* and *My Blood and My Treasure* have an Ohio background.

5674 *My Blood and My Treasure*

Date of Publication: 1941
Subject(s): War of 1812; Battle of Lake Erie
Fictional character(s): Rufus Hazard, Military Personnel (soldier); Louise de La Verendrye, Indian (half-breed), Young Woman
Historical character(s): Oliver Hazard Perry, Military Personnel (naval officer); William Henry Harrison, Military Personnel (general)
Time Period(s): 1810s
Locale(s): Detroit, Michigan; Lake Erie, Great Lakes

Summary: Rufus Hazard, a lieutenant in the Ohio military, encounters several of the important figures of the War of 1812 and is on hand for the American defeat at Detroit and Perry's great victory at the Battle of Lake Erie.

Historical Accuracy: The novel excels in its presentation of Perry's triumph over the British fleet on Lake Erie. Otherwise, the background is thin.

5675 *Strife Before Dawn*

Date of Publication: 1939
Subject(s): Settlement of the American Frontier; American Revolution; Pontiac's Rebellion

Fictional character(s): Keith Maitland, Settler, Frontiersman; Jacqueline Norris, Settler; Hope Maitland, Spouse (of Keith)
Historical character(s): Simon Girty, Frontiersman; Pontiac, Indian (Ottawa), Chieftain; George Washington, Military Personnel (army officer); Sir William Johnson, Government Official
Time Period(s): 18th century (1764-1782)
Locale(s): Northwest Territory, United States (Ohio, Indiana, Illinois, Michigan, and Wisconsin); Fort Pitt, Pennsylvania, American Colonies

Summary: Covering the periods of Pontiac's Rebellion and the American Revolution, this fictional story focuses on Keith and Hope Maitland who are caught up in the historical events, and meet a number of historical figures along the way. Hope is captured by the Shawnees and bears a child by a Shawnee chief. Her return to civilization causes a number of crises for Keith.

Historical Accuracy: The battles, expeditions, and events closely follow the actual history of the period. The novel's preface indicates the author's sources and the few liberties she has taken with facts.

ISHA SCHWALLER DE LUBICZ (1885-)

5676 *Her-Bak: The Living Face of Ancient Egypt*

Date of Publication: 1954
Subject(s): Ancient Egypt; Pharaohs
Fictional character(s): Her-Bak, Child, Servant; Lord Menkh, Nobleman
Time Period(s): 13th century B.C.
Locale(s): Egypt

Summary: The novel offers a reconstruction of life in ancient Egypt through the experience of a child, Her-Bak. Her-Bak comes of age in the service of Lord Menkh and is taken into the Outer Temple as a novice before graduating to admission into the Inner Mysteries of the Temple.

Historical Accuracy: The novel is supported by solid research, as the novel's documentary appendix makes clear.

SUSAN SCHWARTZ

Schwartz received her M.A. and Ph.D. in Medieval English at Harvard. She is the author of *Silk Roads and Shadows* and has been nominated for both the World Fantasy and Nebula awards.

5677 *Shards of Empire*

Date of Publication: 1996
Subject(s): Byzantine Empire; Battle of Malazgirt
Fictional character(s): Leo Ducas, Nobleman
Time Period(s): 11th century
Locale(s): Constantinople, Byzantine Empire; Asia Minor

Summary: This tale of the slow decline of the Byzantine Empire follows the experiences of Leo Ducas, heir to a noble family, who fights the Turks abroad and discovers treachery and betrayal at home. He flees to the borders of the empire and discovers an alternative power to counter the corruption of Byzantium.

Historical Accuracy: As the novel's notes make clear, the story is built on a solid understanding of history that creates a believable period background.

LEONARDO SCIASCIA (1921-1989)

Born in Sicily, Sciascia worked as a functionary in a Fascist agency requisitioning produce from farms and as an elementary school teacher. He was member of both the Italian and the European parliaments.

5678 *The Council of Europe*

Date of Publication: 1966
Subject(s): Crime and Criminals
Fictional character(s): Abbot Giuseppe Vella, Criminal (forger); Francesco Di Blasi, Revolutionary
Time Period(s): 1790s
Locale(s): Sicily, Italy (Palermo)

Summary: Set in 18th-century Sicily, the novel concerns a forger, Giuseppe Vella, whose creations begin to get out of control. Vella's story becomes connected with that of Francesco Di Blasi, who attempts to import the ideas of the French Revolution for the creation of a Free Republic of Sicily. The authentic and the fraudulent compete in the surrealistic atmosphere of period Sicily.

Historical Accuracy: The novel brings together a convincing period background for a decidedly fictional version of the past.

JOANNA SCOTT (1960-)

Born in Greenwich, Connecticut, Joanna Scott attended Trinity College and Brown University. She teaches English at the University of Rochester. Her novels include *Fading, My Parmacheene Belle* and *The Closest Possible Union*.

5679 *Arrogance*

Date of Publication: 1990
Subject(s): Artistic Life; Biography, Fictionalized
Historical character(s): Egon Schiele, Artist
Time Period(s): 1900s; 1910s
Locale(s): Vienna, Austria

Summary: Based on the life of Austrian Expressionist painter Egon Schiele, the novel offers a montage of scenes from his life that functions as a meditation on the artist's place in society. The story covers the period from the turn of the century to World War I and is centered on Schiele's imprisonment in 1912 on charges of seducing a minor and selling pornography.

Historical Accuracy: The novel captures the atmosphere of turn-of-the-century Vienna and the major events in Schiele's life.

5680 *The Closest Possible Union*

Date of Publication: 1988

Subject(s): Sea Story; Slavery
Fictional character(s): Tom, Teenager (14 years old)
Time Period(s): 1850s
Locale(s): *Charles Beauchamp*, At Sea

Summary: Tom is the 14-year-old captain's apprentice on a voyage of the *Charles Beauchamp* in the 1850s. The crew think that they are on a whaling voyage, but the ship is bound for Africa for a cargo of slaves. Tom relates the events of the ship's Atlantic crossing.

Historical Accuracy: The period nautical details are convincing.

LESLIE SCOTT

5681 *Tombstone Showdown*

Date of Publication: 1957
Subject(s): American West; Crime and Criminals
Historical character(s): Johnny Ringo, Outlaw; Wyatt Earp, Lawman; Curly Bill Brocius, Outlaw; Joe Hill, Outlaw; Doc Holliday, Gunfighter
Time Period(s): 1880s
Locale(s): Tombstone, Arizona

Summary: This is the story of Tombstone, Arizona, during its heyday as a boom town, when it was a magnet for outlaws. The novel describes the short and violent career of outlaw Johnny Ringo.

Historical Accuracy: The novel captures the atmosphere of the era believably and provides a realistic portrait of Ringo's career.

PAUL SCOTT (1920-1978)

A British literary critic, playwright, poet, and novelist born in London, Scott served in the British and Indian Armies in the United Kingdom, India, and Malaya. Best known for the Raj Quartet, his novels about Anglo-India during and after World War II, Scott has written other novels with an Indian background: *The Alien Sky, The Birds of Paradise*, and *The Mark of the Warrior*. Scott often uses Indian settings because he finds them lively and dramatic and because of their usefulness as a metaphor for contemporary life. Critical acclaim for Scott's work was late in coming due to the slow pace of his novels.

5682 *The Day of the Scorpion*

Date of Publication: 1968
Subject(s): World War II; Independence—India; British Raj
Fictional character(s): Sarah Layton, Young Woman; Ahmed Kasim, Secretary (to Count Bronowsky); Count Dimitri Bronowsky, Government Official (chief minister); Ronald Merrick, Military Personnel (army captain); Hari Kumar, Journalist
Time Period(s): 1940s (1942-1944)
Locale(s): Pankot, India; Mirat, India; Calcutta, India

Summary: The second novel of the Raj Quartet chronicles events in the lives of members of the Layton Family. *The Day of the Scorpion* continues the story of hapless British-educated Indian Hari Kumar and parvenu army captain Ronald Merrick and introduces new characters. All of the characters figure prominently in the fate of the British in India and the growing Indian Independence movement.

Historical Accuracy: Scott's understanding of Indian culture and of British culture in India during this era is deep and illuminating.

5683 *A Division of the Spoils*

Date of Publication: 1975
Subject(s): Independence—India; British Raj
Fictional character(s): Guy Perron, Historian, Military Personnel (sergeant); Sarah Layton, Military Personnel (WAC sergeant); Ronald Merrick, Military Personnel (army colonel)
Time Period(s): 1940s (1945-1947)
Locale(s): Bombay, India; Pankot, India; Mirat, India

Summary: The postwar Indian Independence movement and the unrest accompanying it profoundly affect the lives of the characters in the fourth novel of the Raj Quartet. The final threads of the Manners case are examined as the past continues to exert its pressures on the present.

Historical Accuracy: The author has believably captured the atmosphere of postwar India and the effect of its approaching independence on the British nationals and administrators who lived and worked there.

5684 *The Jewel in the Crown*

Date of Publication: 1966
Subject(s): World War II; Independence—India; British Raj
Fictional character(s): Edwina Crane, Religious (Missionary); Daphne Manners, Young Woman; Hari Kumar, Journalist; Ronald Merrick, Government Official (superintendent of police)
Time Period(s): 1940s (1942)
Locale(s): Mayapore, India

Summary: When hospital worker Daphne Manners arrives in Mayapore, she is courted by the brutal, rigidly colonialist police superintendent Ronald Merrick but becomes romantically involved with the British-educated Indian, Hari Kumar. Racial turmoil is manifested in Daphne's rape by several Indians, Merrick's persecution of Hari Kumar, and the self-immolation of missionary Edwina Crane. This is the first book in the Raj Quartet.

Historical Accuracy: Scott has woven his story into Indian culture and politics of the era with great attention to historical accuracy.

5685 *The Towers of Silence*

Date of Publication: 1971
Subject(s): World War II; Independence—India; British Raj
Fictional character(s): Barbara Batchelor, Religious (missionary), Teacher; Captain Teddie Bingham, Military Personnel (army captain); Ronald Merrick, Military Personnel (army colonel)
Time Period(s): 1940s (1944-1945)
Locale(s): Pankot, India; Ranpur, India

Summary: Retired working-class missionary Barbara Batchelor is a less-than-welcome presence in the lives of the middle-class Layton family. The third volume of the Raj Quartet also tells the story of Teddie Bingham and his relationship with the Laytons and Ronald Merrick. Merrick continues to work on keeping the British colonial imperative secure in India and justifying his behavior during the Daphne Manners' rape case. The latter event and the death of Edwina Crane continue to affect the lives of the characters.

Historical Accuracy: British culture in India is convincingly rendered.

REVA SCOTT

5686 *Samuel Brannan and the Golden Fleece*

Date of Publication: 1944
Subject(s): Gold Rush—California; Mormons; Biography, Fictionalized
Historical character(s): Samuel Brannan, Leader (Mormon), Pioneer
Time Period(s): 19th century
Locale(s): California

Summary: Samuel Brannan, a Mormon leader, becomes famous as the individual who first spreads the word about the discovery of gold in California. A prominent figure in boomtown San Francisco, Brannan's early and later years are cloaked in obscurity.

Historical Accuracy: The novel blends the factual with the invented and should only be regarded as a partially authentic biographical treatment.

VIRGIL SCOTT (1914-)

Born in Washington, Scott graduated from Ohio State University. A professor of English at Michigan State University, Scott's books include *The Hickory Stick* and *The Savage Affair*.

5687 *I, John Mordaunt*

Date of Publication: 1964
Subject(s): Civil War—England; Restoration Period
Historical character(s): John Mordaunt, Nobleman; Charles II, Ruler (King of England)
Time Period(s): 17th century
Locale(s): England; West Indies

Summary: The novel chronicles the life and career of John Mordaunt, a Royalist conspirator during the Commonwealth. His conflict with Cromwell, imprisonment, exile, and eventual return to England as an aide to Charles II are detailed.

Historical Accuracy: Based on five years of research into the period, the novel captures England under Cromwell and Mordaunt's life as one of the "Malignants," with skill.

SIR WALTER SCOTT (1771-1832)

An English poet and novelist and towering literary figure of the first third of the 19th century, Scott turned to the novel late in his career as a means of best expressing his wide erudition and interest in Scottish customs and the past. His series of historical novels that began in 1814 created the genre of historical fiction, bringing to the past the same concentration on everyday life and realism that was the hallmark of the novel.

5688 *The Abbot*

Date of Publication: 1820
Subject(s): Elizabethan Period; Royalty—Scotland
Fictional character(s): Roland Graeme, Servant (page), Spy; Edward Glendinning, Religious (monk)
Historical character(s): Mary, Queen of Scots, Royalty
Time Period(s): 16th century (1567-1580)
Locale(s): Lochleven, Scotland

Summary: In this sequel to *The Monastery*, the basis of the story is the imprisonment of Mary, Queen of Scots at Lochleven Castle, her escape, and her supporters' defeat at the Battle of Longside. Roland Graeme is sent as a page to Mary in her imprisonment as a spy. Instead he assists in her escape.

Historical Accuracy: This is an interesting blend of romance with historical incident.

5689 *Anne of Geierstein*

Date of Publication: 1829
Subject(s): War of the Roses
Fictional character(s): Arthur De Vere, Nobleman; Anne of Geierstein, Noblewoman; Earl of Oxford, Nobleman
Historical character(s): Charles, Duke of Burgundy, Royalty; Margaret of Anjou, Royalty (wife of Henry VI); Rene of Provence, Nobleman
Time Period(s): 15th century (1461-1483)
Locale(s): Switzerland; Nancy, France; Westphalia, Germany

Summary: The Earl of Oxford and his son journey to Switzerland on behalf of the Lancastrians during the War of the Roses. Their mission is to gain the assistance of Charles the Bold. There is an interesting depiction of the secret tribunal of the Vehmgericht and the court of Rene, the king of the troubadours.

Historical Accuracy: This is Scott's characteristic blend of historical fact and romance and adventure.

5690 *The Antiquary*

Date of Publication: 1816
Fictional character(s): Jonathan Oldbuck, Scholar; Lovel, Bastard Son, Heir—Lost; Isabella Wardour, Gentlewoman
Time Period(s): 1790s
Locale(s): Scotland

Summary: Having stressed romance in his first novel (*Waverley*) and adventure in his second (*Guy Mannering*), *The Antiquary* is more a novel of manners. The plot concerns the mysterious past of Lovel whose dubious birth bars him

from winning the hand of a nobleman's daughter. A series of complications, including the anticipated invasion of the French, must be untangled either through coincidence or the diligence of the antiquarian Oldbuck.

Historical Accuracy: This is one of the most popular of Scott's novels primarily because of his characterization of Scottish peasants and his accurate dialogue that grounds an otherwise fanciful story in reality.

5691 *The Betrothed*

Date of Publication: 1825
Subject(s): Middle Ages; Crusades
Fictional character(s): Eveline Berenger, Gentlewoman; Hugo De Lacy, Nobleman; Damian, Nobleman
Time Period(s): 12th century
Locale(s): Wales

Summary: Set during the reign of Henry II, the novel concerns Eveline Berenger's rescue by the aging constable of Chester who leaves for the Crusades after a grateful Eveline agrees to marry him. Her heart, however, is lost to the constable's nephew, and their love causes complications, including a charge of high treason.

Historical Accuracy: Called one of the "Tales of the Crusaders," the novel has little to do with the Crusades.

5692 *The Black Dwarf*

Date of Publication: 1816
Subject(s): Gothic Romance; Supernatural
Fictional character(s): Elshender the Recluse, Outcast (dwarf); Grace Armstrong, Gentlewoman; Isabella Vere, Gentlewoman
Time Period(s): 1700s
Locale(s): Scotland

Summary: The novel is a Gothic tale of a grim and deformed dwarf who intercedes for good in the lives of several residents of a Scottish neighborhood.

Historical Accuracy: This is a romance with little of Scott's characteristic delineated personalities and customs.

5693 *The Bride of Lammermoor*

Date of Publication: 1819
Subject(s): Civil War—England; Inheritance—Disputed
Fictional character(s): Ravenswood, Heir—Dispossessed, Nobleman; Lucy Ashton, Gentlewoman; William Ashton, Nobleman, Lawyer
Time Period(s): 17th century
Locale(s): Scotland

Summary: This is a tragic tale of revenge and death in which the dispossessed Master of Ravenswood falls in love with the daughter of his family's enemy. Her mother plots to break up the affair with tragic consequences.

Historical Accuracy: This is a novel of passion, less concerned with verisimilitude.

5694 *Castle Dangerous*

Date of Publication: 1831

Subject(s): Middle Ages
Fictional character(s): John De Walton, Knight, Nobleman; Augusta of Berkeley, Gentlewoman
Historical character(s): James Douglas, Knight
Time Period(s): 14th century (1306)
Locale(s): Douglas, Scotland

Summary: The novel deals with the defense of Douglas Castle by Sir John de Walton against the fierce Scotsman Sir James Douglas. The Lady Augusta becomes a bargaining chip during the siege.

Historical Accuracy: The novel shows Scott at the end of his career and in decline. This is more a sketch than a full-scale treatment of a period.

5695 *Count Robert of Paris*

Date of Publication: 1831
Subject(s): Crusades; Middle Ages
Fictional character(s): Robert of Paris, Knight; Brenhilda, Gentlewoman (wife of Robert); Hereward, Knight
Historical character(s): Alexius I Comnenus, Ruler (Byzantine emperor); Anna Comnena, Royalty (princess); Nicephorus Briennius, Nobleman
Time Period(s): 11th century
Locale(s): Constantinople, Byzantine Empire

Summary: The novel is set in the court of Emperor Alexius Comnenus in Constantinople during the First Crusade and features the perilous adventures of a Frankish knight and his amazonian wife, as well as a plot to overthrow the emperor.

Historical Accuracy: This last of the Waverley novels was written by Scott in ill-health and shows his declining powers.

5696 *The Fortunes of Nigel*

Date of Publication: 1822
Subject(s): Jacobean Period; Crime and Criminals
Fictional character(s): Nigel Olifaunt, Nobleman; Margaret Ramsay, Young Woman; Dalgarvo, Nobleman
Historical character(s): James I, Ruler (King of England and Scotland); Charles, Royalty (prince; later Charles I)
Time Period(s): 17th century
Locale(s): London, England

Summary: Plots and counterplots surround the attempt of Nigel Olifaunt to recover from James I the repayment of a debt to secure his family estate in Scotland. Court intrigue and the criminal low-life of London are vividly depicted.

Historical Accuracy: Scott's multiplicity of characters and plots and his Scottish dialect make this novel difficult to untangle. Effort is repaid with some of Scott's best depictions of lower-class life and his finest historical portrait in James I.

5697 *Guy Mannering*

Date of Publication: 1815
Subject(s): Inheritance—Disputed; Gypsies; Crime and Criminals
Fictional character(s): Guy Mannering, Military Personnel; Meg Merrilies, Gypsy; Harry Betram, Heir—Dispossessed, Gentleman
Time Period(s): 1800s

Locale(s): Dumfries, Scotland; India

Summary: In this romance of a kidnapped heir, mistaken identities, and plots and counterplots, young Harry Betram loses and eventually regains his birthright to his Scottish estate and his true love.

Historical Accuracy: The plot is complicated by coincidences and surprises, but Scott's ability to create realistic characters, especially lower-class characters, causes the novel to be more than just a far-fetched adventure story.

5698 *The Heart of Midlothian*

Date of Publication: 1818
Subject(s): Crime and Criminals; Porteous Riot
Fictional character(s): Jeanie Deans, Heroine; Effie Deans, Prisoner; Meg Murdockson, Witch
Historical character(s): John Porteous, Military Personnel; Geordie Robertson, Outlaw; Caroline of Ansbach, Royalty (Queen of England)
Time Period(s): 1730s
Locale(s): Edinburgh, Scotland; London, England

Summary: The title refers to the Edinburgh Tolbooth, a prison known as the "Heart of Midlothian." This novel, considered Scott's best, is based on the historical Porteous Riot of 1736 at the prison. Scott ingeniously combines history with the story of Jeanie Deans' attempt to clear her sister of a charge of child murder that takes her on a perilous journey to London and an interview with the Queen.

Historical Accuracy: This is definitive Scott, blending suspense, mystery, and romance with Scottish life and customs.

5699 *Ivanhoe*

Date of Publication: 1819
Subject(s): Middle Ages; Jews
Fictional character(s): Wilfred of Ivanhoe, Knight; Rowena, Gentlewoman; Rebecca, Young Woman (Jewish); Robin Hood, Outlaw
Historical character(s): Richard I, Ruler (King of England); John, Royalty (prince)
Time Period(s): 12th century
Locale(s): Rotherwood, England; Ashby, England

Summary: This is Scott's most popular novel and the definitive treatment of romantic chivalry. Wilfred of Ivanhoe returns from the Crusades to triumph over a Norman knight at a tournament. He is nursed by the Jews Isaac and Rebecca, and they are captured by the Normans and rescued by the Saxons. A trial by combat provides the novel's stirring climax.

Historical Accuracy: Historians have disputed the enmity between Saxons and Normans that is the basis of Scott's drama.

5700 *Kenilworth*

Date of Publication: 1821
Subject(s): Elizabethan Period
Fictional character(s): Richard Varney, Servant; Edmund Tressilian, Gentleman
Historical character(s): Amy Robsart, Gentlewoman; Elizabeth I, Ruler (Queen of England); Robert Dudley, Nobleman

(Earl of Leicester), Courtier; Sir Walter Raleigh, Nobleman, Courtier
Time Period(s): 16th century (1575)
Locale(s): Oxford, England; Kenilworth, England

Summary: The novel concerns the intrigues of Elizabeth I's court and her changeable favor. The Earl of Leicester's marriage to Amy Robsart is concealed with disastrous consequences orchestrated by the villainous servant, Richard Varney.

Historical Accuracy: The plot here is thin, but Scott provides a detailed historical background and an interesting look at the court of Elizabeth.

5701 *The Monastery*
Date of Publication: 1820
Subject(s): Religious Life; Elizabethan Period; Supernatural
Fictional character(s): Halbert Glendinning, Gentleman; Edward Glendinning, Gentleman; Mary Avenel, Orphan
Time Period(s): 16th century
Locale(s): Tweed, Scotland

Summary: The reign of Elizabeth I, the spread of the Reformation to Scotland, and the resulting disruption of the monastic community form the backdrop to this novel. The plot concerns two sons' rivalry for the affection of Mary Avenel and an English knight who has sought refuge in Scotland from his intrigues on behalf of the Catholic interest.

Historical Accuracy: The supernatural elements here clash with the more realistic portraits of monastic life.

5702 *Old Mortality*
Date of Publication: 1816
Subject(s): Covenanters; Religious Conflict
Fictional character(s): Henry Morton, Gentleman; John Balfour, Fanatic (religious); Evandale, Nobleman
Historical character(s): John Graham of Claverhouse, Nobleman, Military Personnel
Time Period(s): 17th century; 18th century (1679-1702)
Locale(s): Glasgow, Scotland; Netherlands

Summary: Henry Morton is caught up in the rebellion of the Covenanters in 1679 that includes their decisive defeat at the Battle of Bothwell Bridge. Scott displays with considerable skill the excesses of religious fanaticism.

Historical Accuracy: This is one of Scott's better novels. The plot is dramatized with skill, and the characters are drawn with care.

5703 *Peveril of the Peak*
Date of Publication: 1823
Subject(s): Popish Plot; Religious Conflict
Fictional character(s): Geoffrey Peveril, Nobleman; Alice Bridgenorth, Gentlewoman; Julian Peveril, Gentleman
Historical character(s): Charles II, Ruler (King of England); George Villiers, Nobleman; Titus Oates, Revolutionary; Thomas Blood, Revolutionary; Geoffrey Hudson, Courtier (Queen's dwarf); Henrietta-Maria, Royalty (Queen of England)
Time Period(s): 17th century (1678)

Locale(s): Derbyshire, England; London, England

Summary: The novel features romantic complications and court intrigue during the period of Catholic persecution in England during the 17th century's "Popish Plot." Old animosity between Cavaliers and Puritans disturbs the Peveril and Bridgenorth families and the love between Julian and Alice. Alice falls into the hand of the licentious Duke of Buckingham, and Julian is imprisoned.

Historical Accuracy: Charles II and Buckingham are depicted in detail. Other historical figures are only glimpsed in passing.

5704 *The Pirate*
Date of Publication: 1821
Subject(s): Pirates
Fictional character(s): Mordaunt Mertoun, Gentleman; Clement Cleveland, Pirate; Ulla Troil, Mentally Ill Person
Time Period(s): 17th century
Locale(s): Shetland Islands, Scotland; Orkney Islands, Scotland

Summary: The arrival of a shipwrecked buccaneer captain complicates a love triangle between Mordaunt and two sisters. The denouement on the island of Orkney in which coincidence and surprise predominates, is arranged by the partially deranged Ulla Troil.

Historical Accuracy: Scott's local color was gathered on a voyage of the Scottish Lighthouse Commision on which he was a guest.

5705 *Quentin Durward*
Date of Publication: 1823
Subject(s): Middle Ages; Royalty—France
Fictional character(s): Quentin Durward, Military Personnel; Isabelle de Croye, Noblewoman, Heiress
Historical character(s): Louis XI, Ruler (King of France); Charles, Duke of Burgundy, Nobleman; William de la Marck, Outlaw; Tristan L'Hermite, Political Figure (marshal of France); Cardinal Jean Balue, Religious, Political Figure (French minister); Philippe de Commines, Writer
Time Period(s): 15th century (1468)
Locale(s): Liege, Belgium; Burgundy, France

Summary: A young Scotsman seeks his fortune in France and becomes a member of the Scottish Archers who protect King Louis XI. The novel details the dispute between the king and the Duke of Burgundy—the foreground drama to which is connected Quentin's passion for the Countess Isabelle. He wins his lady in scenes of exciting peril.

Historical Accuracy: This is the first of Scott's novels with a foreign setting. The authenticity is marred by some rearrangement of actual events.

5706 *Red Gauntlet*
Date of Publication: 1824
Subject(s): Jacobite Rebellion
Fictional character(s): Sir Edward Hugh Redgauntlet, Gentleman, Fanatic (Jacobite); Darsie Latimer, Nobleman (Sir Arthur Darsie Redgauntlet); Alan Fairford, Lawyer

Historical character(s): Charles Edward Stuart, Royalty (prince)
Time Period(s): 1760s
Locale(s): Edinburgh, Scotland; Dumfries, Scotland; Cumberland, England

Summary: The story concerns the fictitious return of Prince Charles Edward to England and the kidnapping of Darsie Latimer by his uncle, the fierce Jacobite Redgauntlet. Darsie's rescue and the failure of the insurrection form the novel's main action.

Historical Accuracy: The novel is a speculation about the ultimate failure of the Jacobite cause. It should not be read as historical truth, although it still has many notable characters and period details.

`5707` *Rob Roy*

Date of Publication: 1817
Subject(s): Crime and Criminals; Jacobite Rebellion
Fictional character(s): Frank Osbaldistone, Gentleman; Rasleigh Osbaldistone, Gentleman; Andrew Fairservice, Servant
Historical character(s): Rob Roy, Outlaw
Time Period(s): 1710s
Locale(s): Glasgow, Scotland; Highlands, Scotland; Northumberland, England

Summary: Frank Osbaldistone's fortune and feud with his father and cousin are connected with the adventures of Rob Roy, the Scottish Robin Hood, in the period immediately preceding the Jacobite Rising.

Historical Accuracy: This is one of Scott's most popular adventures and includes one of Scott's greatest portraits, the servant Andrew Fairservice, and exciting scenes of Scottish life.

`5708` *The Talisman*

Date of Publication: 1825
Subject(s): Middle Ages; Crusades
Fictional character(s): Sir Kenneth, Knight; Conrad, Nobleman (Marquis of Montserrat)
Historical character(s): Richard I, Ruler (King of England); Berengaria of Navarre, Royalty (Richard's queen); Saladin, Ruler (Muslim)
Time Period(s): 12th century
Locale(s): Palestine

Summary: During the Third Crusade, Richard the Lionhearted becomes ill and is assisted by a Scottish knight, Kenneth. Dissent among the Christian Council of Kings and Princes threatens Richard and Kenneth's lives. Disguises, hidden identities, love, mystery, and chivalry all make this novel one of Scott's best stories.

Historical Accuracy: Invented characters and situations are blended with real people and historical events.

`5709` *Waverley*

Date of Publication: 1814
Subject(s): Jacobite Rebellion

Fictional character(s): Edward Waverley, Military Personnel; Fergus MacIvor, Laird; Rose Bradwardine, Noblewoman
Historical character(s): Charles Edward Stuart, Royalty (prince)
Time Period(s): 1740s
Locale(s): Highlands, Scotland; Edinburgh, Scotland; England

Summary: Scott's first novel tells the tale of a young English army officer who journeys to Scotland at the time of the Jacobite Rising of 1745. Through Edward Waverley's experiences, Scott, for the first time in fiction, sympathetically and heroically dramatizes Scottish scenery, manners and customs, and the Stuart cause.

Historical Accuracy: Scott achieves a vivid depiction of the life of the past that had no precedent. His formula of romantic plot with realistic setting and psychology set the standard for the novel in the 19th century.

`5710` *Woodstock; or, The Cavalier*

Date of Publication: 1826
Subject(s): Civil War—England; Religious Conflict
Fictional character(s): Henry Lee, Nobleman (cavalier); Markham Everard, Military Personnel (Puritan); Alice Lee, Gentlewoman
Historical character(s): Oliver Cromwell, Political Figure; Charles, Royalty (prince)
Time Period(s): 17th century (1651)
Locale(s): Woodstock, England

Summary: The novel is set during the English Civil War and revolves around the famous escape of Prince Charles (later Charles II) from Cromwell at Woodstock. Charles in disguise complicates the love between a loyal cavalier's daughter and Everard, a Puritan.

Historical Accuracy: Historical inaccuracies suggest that this is history filtered through Scott's romantic imagination creating a rousing story of a royal in disguise, lovers in peril, spies, and intrigues.

PHILIP LIGHTFOOT SCRUGGS (1898-)

`5711` *Man Cannot Tell*

Date of Publication: 1942
Subject(s): American Colonies; Bacon's Rebellion
Fictional character(s): Jellis Holt, Servant (indentured); Anne Branch, Gentlewoman
Historical character(s): Nathaniel Bacon, Leader (of rebellion)
Time Period(s): 17th century
Locale(s): Virginia, American Colonies

Summary: The early years of the Virginia Colony are described through the experiences of Jellis Holt, who is sent there in 1670 as an indentured servant. He falls in love with his master's daughter and becomes involved in Bacon's Rebellion. The novel's climax is the capture of Lord Berkeley.

Historical Accuracy: This is a vivid and authentic portrait of colonial Virginia and the events of Bacon's Rebellion.

DONALD SEAMAN (1922-)

English writer Seaman has worked as a reporter and foreign correspondent for 25 years, serving as a war correspondent in Africa, the Middle East, and Cyprus. Seaman's best-known assignment was reporting the espionage scandal involving Guy Burgess and Donald MacLean, which Seaman wrote about in book form in *The Great Spy Scandal.*

5712 *Chase Royal*

Date of Publication: 1982
Subject(s): Victorian Period; Fenians; Espionage
Fictional character(s): Sean Donovan, Revolutionary (IRA); Wilberforce Evans, Spy; Sam Bass, Military Personnel (bomb disposal officer)
Historical character(s): Victoria, Ruler (Queen of England)
Time Period(s): 1860s (1867)
Locale(s): London, England; Highlands, Scotland

Summary: This thriller involves the Fenian bombings of the 1860s. The death of an informant leaves the British in the dark about the next Fenian targets. Wilberforce Evans attempts to infiltrate the Irish Republican Brotherhood, while Sam Bass finds himself the world's first bomb disposal officer as a royal target is exposed and must be saved.

Historical Accuracy: The author explains that the novel is a work of fiction based on actual events.

OUIDA SEBESTYEN

5713 *Words by Heart*

Date of Publication: 1979
Subject(s): Racial Conflict; Rural Life—U.S.
Fictional character(s): Lena Sills, Child
Time Period(s): 1910s (1910)
Locale(s): Southwest

Summary: Set in the Southwestern cotton country, in 1910, the novel tells of the adjustments young Lena Sills must make when she and her family move into a town where they are the only blacks. This coming-of-age drama explores the contradiction of freedom in the West.

Historical Accuracy: The regional and period elements are authentic.

CATHARINE MARIA SEDGEWICK
(1789-1867)

An American author and one of the most famous women writers of her day, Sedgwick was born in Stockbridge, Massachusetts. Active as a social reformer, Sedgwick organized the first free school in New York City for Irish immigrant children. Her novels *A New England Tale,* *Redwood,* and *Clarence* were internationally admired. Tea parties that she hosted were attended by James Fenimore Cooper, Nathaniel Hawthorne, William Cullen Bryant, Ralph Waldo Emerson, and Herman Melville.

5714 *Hope Leslie; or, Early Times in Massachusetts*

Date of Publication: 1827
Subject(s): American Colonies; Indians; Settlement of the American Frontier
Fictional character(s): Hope Leslie, Heroine; Magawisca, Indian; William Fletcher, Settler
Historical character(s): John Winthrop, Political Figure (colonial governor); William Pynchon, Judge
Time Period(s): 17th century (1660)
Locale(s): Boston, Massachusetts, American Colonies; Springfield, Massachusetts, American Colonies

Summary: Life among the Puritans and native Americans in 17th-century New England is the novel's subject. Hope Leslie is a rebellious individualist who defies the straight-laced morality of the Pilgrims in support of members of the Pequod tribe.

Historical Accuracy: The novel offers a convincing and realistic portrait of the period. The character Magawisca has been called the only Indian woman in early American literature invested with substance and strength.

KATE SEDLEY
(PSEUD. OF BRENDA CLARKE, 1926-)

A British-born author of romance and historical mystery novels, Sedley was a clerical officer in the British Civil Service for over 20 years before retiring to become a full-time writer. Her novels include *The Warrior King,* *The Queen and Mortimer,* and *Death and the Chapman.*

5715 *Death and the Chapman*

Date of Publication: 1992
Subject(s): Mystery; Middle Ages; War of the Roses
Fictional character(s): Roger the Chapman, Peddler, Detective—Amateur; Weaver, Government Official, Gentleman (alderman)
Historical character(s): Richard, Duke of Gloucester, Nobleman
Time Period(s): 15th century (1471)
Locale(s): England

Summary: In this historical mystery, Roger the Chapman has left a monastery for a life on the road. He is engaged by Alderman Weaver to find his son, who disappeared from the Crossed Head Inn. Roger discovers a wider conspiracy and danger in his investigation.

Historical Accuracy: England in the 15th century is artfully and authentically rendered with glimpses into the lives of ordinary people of the time.

5716 *The Eve of Saint Hyacinth*

Date of Publication: 1955
Subject(s): Middle Ages; Mystery
Fictional character(s): Roger the Chapman, Peddler, Detective—Amateur
Historical character(s): Edward IV, Ruler (King of England); Richard, Duke of Gloucester, Nobleman

Time Period(s): 15th century (1475)
Locale(s): London, England

Summary: In 1475, on the eve of Edward IV's planned invasion of France, Roger the Chapman, peddler and amateur sleuth, arrives in London and finds himself in the center of a royal mystery. Someone is planning to assassinate the Duke of Gloucester on the eve of Saint Hyacinth's feast. The duke trusts Roger alone to find the traitor in time.

Historical Accuracy: The novel features an ingenious plot set against a believable historical backdrop.

5717   *The Holy Innocents*

Date of Publication: 1994
Subject(s): Middle Ages; Mystery; War of the Roses
Fictional character(s): Roger the Chapman, Peddler, Detective—Amateur; Grizelda Harbourne, Young Woman
Time Period(s): 15th century (1475)
Locale(s): Totnes, England

Summary: Roger the Chapman, the 15th-century peddler and sleuth, is on the road again to Totnes, where a band of burglars is harassing the village. They are believed to be responsible for the disappearance of two village children, and Roger sets out to solve a baffling puzzle. How were the children taken in broad daylight, and where did they go? Are the outlaws the guilty party?.

Historical Accuracy: The author is expert in creating a believable period background involving ordinary people and customs.

5718   *The Plymouth Cloak*

Date of Publication: 1993
Subject(s): Mystery; War of the Roses; Middle Ages
Fictional character(s): Roger the Chapman, Peddler, Detective—Amateur; Philip Underdown, Gentleman, Government Official
Historical character(s): Richard, Duke of Gloucester, Nobleman
Time Period(s): 15th century (1473)
Locale(s): Plymouth, England

Summary: Roger the Chapman, peddler and detective, is asked by Richard, Duke of Gloucester, to accompany Philip Underdown on a mission to try to forestall an invasion from Brittany. Philip is a reluctant minister with a number of enemies that threaten to wreck the plan. Roger must try to keep him alive and accomplish their mission, which seems to have been discovered by Lancastrian rivals.

Historical Accuracy: The period details are strongly presented and convincing.

5719   *The Weaver's Tale*

Date of Publication: 1993
Subject(s): Middle Ages; Mystery
Fictional character(s): Roger the Chapman, Peddler, Detective—Amateur; Margaret Walker, Widow(er); Lillis Walker, Young Woman
Time Period(s): 15th century (1474)
Locale(s): Bristol, England

Summary: Roger the Chapman collapses with fever during the winter of 1474. He is nursed back to health by the widow Margaret Walker and her daughter, Lillis. He learns that a strange mystery haunts the Walker family: Margaret Walker's father disappeared, and a man was hanged for his murder, after which the old man returned home, unable to account for his disappearance. Roger investigates and uncovers a complex conspiracy of secret allegiances and rivalries among the townspeople.

Historical Accuracy: The author expertly details the ordinary life of the medieval period.

BRENDA LESLEY SEGAL

Segal was born in Philadelphia and graduated from Beaver College.

5720   *If I Forget Thee*

Date of Publication: 1983
Subject(s): Roman Empire; Jewish Revolt
Fictional character(s): Jara, Young Woman; Marcellus Quintus, Military Personnel (centurion)
Historical character(s): Simon Bar Kokhba, Leader (Jewish Revolt); Akiba ben Joseph, Religious (rabbi); Hadrian, Ruler (Roman Emperor)
Time Period(s): 2nd century
Locale(s): Israel

Summary: Following *The Tenth Measure* the author continues her depiction of the rebellion of the Jewish people against the domination of Rome in the revolt of Bar Kokhba, the second and final Jewish rebellion in the 2nd century. The story centers on Jara, the orphaned granddaughter of Eleazar ben Ya'ir, the leader at Masada, and Alexandra bat Harsom, the heroine of *The Tenth Measure*. Jara, like her grandmother before her, finds herself involved with the key figures in the revolt, including the legendary rebel Bar Kokhba.

Historical Accuracy: As the author's notes make clear, most of the figures and events depicted are historical.

5721   *The Tenth Measure*

Date of Publication: 1980
Subject(s): Roman Empire; Jewish Revolt; Siege of Masada
Fictional character(s): Alexandra bat Harsom, Gentlewoman
Historical character(s): Josef ben Matthias, Historian; Eleazar ben Yair, Leader (Jewish Revolt); Vespasian, Military Personnel (Roman general), Ruler (Roman Emperor)
Time Period(s): 1st century
Locale(s): Jerusalem, Israel; Masada, Israel

Summary: The novel's background is the 1st-century Jewish Revolt that culminates in the siege of Masada. The story centers on a young Jewish woman, Alexandra, who is caught up in the rebellion. She is connected with its principal figures, including the historian Josef ben Matthias and Eleazar ben Ya'ir, the dedicated leader of the band of Jews that resists the power of the Romans at Masada.

Historical Accuracy: The novel is careful to preserve the framework of the actual events and characters. However, as the author explains, in some cases it was necessary to use words and terms not in currency during the first century.

ROBERT J. SEIDMAN (1941-)

Born in Philadelphia and educated at Williams College and Oxford and Columbia universities, Seidman's screenplay *Touching Ground* won a prize at the 1970 Atlanta Film Festival.

5722 *One Smart Indian*

Date of Publication: 1977
Subject(s): American West; Indians; Civil War—U.S.
Fictional character(s): Tumbling Hawk, Indian (Cheyenne); Benjamin Hyde, Military Personnel (colonel)
Time Period(s): 19th century (1850s-1870s)
Locale(s): Great Plains, Nebraska; New York, New York; Washington, District of Columbia

Summary: Tumbling Hawk is a young Cheyenne Indian who on his first raiding party is captured by Colonel Benjamin Hyde. He is raised by Hyde to embrace the world of the whites. He is given an education at Yale and works in Washington for the Indian Bureau. Following the Civil War, Tumbling Hawk rejoins his tribe in Nebraska to resolve the cultural duel that his life has become.

Historical Accuracy: The novel captures its era with skill, interweaving the fictional story with actual events.

SHIRLEY SEIFERT (1889-1971)

Born in Missouri, Seifert graduated from Washington University, St. Louis. All of her many novels, except two, are based on real people living through times of crisis. She worked as a high school English Teacher and received a Pulitzer Prize nomination for *The Wayfarers*.

5723 *By the King's Command*

Date of Publication: 1962
Subject(s): American West; Spanish Colonies
Fictional character(s): Antonio Ibarbo, Rancher
Time Period(s): 1770s (1773-1779)
Locale(s): Texas

Summary: This story of Texas under Spanish rule in the 1770s is told through the experiences of Mexican rancher Antonio Ibarbo, who leads a group of settlers into Texas. Conflict with Indians and the Spanish government is depicted as well as the founding of Nacogdoches, Texas.

Historical Accuracy: The major events of the story are fact, but to give the book body, reality, and continuity, they have been enlarged upon and minor incidents have been invented.

5724 *Captain Grant*

Date of Publication: 1946
Subject(s): Mexican War; Civil War—U.S.; Military Life
Historical character(s): Ulysses S. Grant, Military Personnel (army officer); Julia Dent Grant, Spouse (of Grant)
Time Period(s): 19th century
Locale(s): Galena, Illinois; California; Mexico

Summary: The early life and career of Ulysses S. Grant are dramatized, from his entrance into West Point to the opening of the Civil War when Grant takes command of a regiment of Illinois volunteers. In between, Grant's courtship and marriage to Julia Dent and his service in Mexico and California are shown.

Historical Accuracy: The author claims to have resorted to little invention here, other than dialogue.

5725 *Destiny in Dallas*

Date of Publication: 1958
Subject(s): American West
Historical character(s): Alexander Cockrell, Settler; Sarah Cockrell, Spouse; Andrew Moore, Lawman
Time Period(s): 1850s (1858)
Locale(s): Dallas, Texas

Summary: Set in Dallas in the 1850s, the novel depicts the role played by Dallas' first citizen, Alexander Cockrell. Cockrell comes to Texas from Missouri as an illiterate teenager and helps shape the history of the state. The novel dramatizes what happens on a fateful day in 1858.

Historical Accuracy: The author explains that the fact pattern and sequence are true, but that some incidents were manipulated or invented to serve a storyteller's needs.

5726 *Farewell, My General*

Date of Publication: 1954
Subject(s): Civil War—U.S.; Military Life
Fictional character(s): Flora Cooke, Young Woman
Historical character(s): James Ewell Brown Stuart, Military Personnel (cavalry officer); Robert E. Lee, Military Personnel (Confederate commander)
Time Period(s): 1850s; 1860s (1855-1864)
Locale(s): Fort Leavenworth, Kansas; Virginia

Summary: The novel provides a fictional account of the military career of cavalry officer J.E.B. Stuart, from his Indian fighting days in Kansas in the 1850s to his becoming a Confederate cavalry officer and the "eyes" of Robert E. Lee's army. The author invents his married life and a devoted wife, Flora.

Historical Accuracy: The historic background is as accurate and as complete as the framework of the story allowed.

5727 *Let My Name Stand Fair*

Date of Publication: 1956
Subject(s): American Revolution
Historical character(s): Nathanael Greene, Military Personnel (general); Henry Lee, Military Personnel (officer); Anthony Wayne, Military Personnel (general); Alexander Hamilton, Military Personnel (officer); George Washington, Military Personnel (army commander); Catherine Greene, Spouse
Time Period(s): 18th century
Locale(s): Block Island, Rhode Island, American Colonies; Morristown, New Jersey, American Colonies; Charleston, South Carolina, American Colonies

Summary: This novel of the American Revolution reflects the events of the war from the perspective of Catherine Greene, wife of Washington's second-in-command, Nathanael Greene. She is shown from childhood on Block Island to her struggle alongside her husband in the campaigns of the Revolution.

Historical Accuracy: The novel is convincing in its depiction of the events and Greene's life story.

5728 *Look to the Rose*

Date of Publication: 1960
Subject(s): Civil War—U.S.; Antebellum South
Historical character(s): Willy Gordon, Businessman (cotton broker); Eleanor Kinzie Gordon, Spouse
Time Period(s): 19th century (1850s-1870s)
Locale(s): Savannah, Georgia

Summary: The novel dramatizes the married life of Willy and Nelly Gordon, parents of Juliette Gordon Low, the founder of the Girl Scouts. Their wedding is followed by the outbreak of the Civil War, and Willy joins the Confederacy. Nelly tries to keep the family together in the aftermath of Sherman's March and the Confederacy's defeat.

Historical Accuracy: Historic events and personal happenings are as close to the facts as possible. Dialogue and character delineation are invented and depend on the author's interpretations.

5729 *The Medicine Man*

Date of Publication: 1971
Subject(s): American West; Medical Profession; Biography, Fictionalized
Historical character(s): Antoine Saugrain, Doctor; James Wilkinson, Military Personnel (general)
Time Period(s): 1800s; 1810s
Locale(s): St. Louis, Missouri

Summary: French doctor Antoine Saugrain escapes the terror of the French Revolution to settle in St. Louis during the 1800s. There he confronts hostile Indians and the events of the War of 1812. The novel's climax is the threat of a smallpox epidemic that causes Saugrain to introduce the new vaccination to the western frontier of America.

Historical Accuracy: Based on solid research, the novel is derived from real events. However, as the author points out, not everything in the book happened as it is told, but it is at least probable.

5730 *Never No More: The Story of Rebecca Boone*

Date of Publication: 1964
Subject(s): Settlement of the American Frontier; Indians
Historical character(s): Daniel Boone, Frontiersman; Rebecca Boone, Spouse
Time Period(s): 1770s (1773-1774)
Locale(s): Virginia, American Colonies; Kentucky

Summary: This is the story of a year in the life of Daniel Boone and his wife, Rebecca. In 1773 the Boone family and

other settlers push through the wilderness to Kentucky, enduring an Indian attack in which the Boones' son James is killed. They eventually cross the Cumberland Mountains into Kentucky, despite Rebecca Boone's desire to hear of Kentucky "never no more.".

Historical Accuracy: The author stays close to the known facts in telling the Boones' story, supported by research into written sources and the author's own travels along the route the Boones took through the Cumberland Gap into Kentucky.

5731 *The Proud Way*

Date of Publication: 1948
Subject(s): Antebellum South
Historical character(s): Jefferson Davis, Widow(er), Political Figure; Varina Howell Davis, Southern Belle
Time Period(s): 1840s (1843-1844)
Locale(s): Natchez, Mississippi

Summary: The novel tells the story of the courtship of Jefferson Davis and Varina Howell in Natchez in the 1840s. Davis is in deep mourning for his wife, who died eight years before. Despite misunderstandings, family intrigue and interference, Varina breaks through Davis' reserve and becomes a full partner of the man who will become a congressman, cabinet member, senator, and finally president of the Confederacy.

Historical Accuracy: The liberties taken in shaping the story are chiefly the shifting of minor dates—never more than a few weeks—the enlargement of incident from the bare statistics of record, and the invention of some secondary characters.

5732 *River out of Eden*

Date of Publication: 1940
Subject(s): American Colonies
Fictional character(s): Andre Therriot, Adventurer
Time Period(s): 1760s (1763)
Locale(s): Mississippi River, North America

Summary: The novel describes a trip up the Mississippi River during the 1760s by Frenchman Andre Therriot, who journeys from New Orleans to the site of the future St. Louis. Along the way conflict and rivalries among the Spanish, French, Indians, and Americans are described.

Historical Accuracy: The novel is a fictional composite of events and details of the period and the region that accurately captures the scene.

5733 *The Senator's Lady*

Date of Publication: 1967
Subject(s): Politics; Civil War—U.S.; Biography, Fictionalized
Historical character(s): Stephen A. Douglas, Political Figure; Addie Cutts Douglas, Spouse (of Stephen); Abraham Lincoln, Political Figure
Time Period(s): 1850s; 1860s (1856-1861)
Locale(s): Washington, District of Columbia; Chicago, Illinois; Kansas

Summary: The novel tells the story of the romance between Senator Stephen Douglas and Addie Cutts. Douglas, a widower, meets Cutts during the fateful election year of 1856.

Their marriage shares the stage with politics of the day, the anti-slavery violence engendered by the Kansas-Nebraska Act of 1854, and the Lincoln-Douglas debates.

Historical Accuracy: The novel's depiction of Stephen Douglas and the period is based on solid research. However, the author's portrait of Addie Douglas is a composite taken from fragmentary references in period diaries.

5734 *Those Who Go Against the Current*
Date of Publication: 1943
Subject(s): Louisiana Purchase; Settlement of the American Frontier; Lewis and Clark Expedition
Fictional character(s): Manuel Lisa, Settler, Trader
Historical character(s): Meriwether Lewis, Explorer; William Clark, Explorer
Time Period(s): 18th century; 19th century (1772-1820)
Locale(s): St. Louis, Missouri

Summary: The exploration of the Upper Mississippi and the Missouri River and the founding of St. Louis are chronicled in the career of Spanish trader Manuel Lisa. He comes north from New Orleans and helps equip Lewis and Clark on their expedition following the Louisiana Purchase as control of the territory passes from the Spanish and French to the Americans.

Historical Accuracy: The novel is derived from a realistic depiction of the period.

5735 *The Three Lives of Elizabeth*
Date of Publication: 1952
Subject(s): Settlement of the American Frontier; Politics
Historical character(s): Elizabeth Moss, Young Woman; William Ashley, Political Figure; John Jordan Crittenden, Political Figure
Time Period(s): 19th century (1820s-1860s)
Locale(s): Missouri; Washington, District of Columbia; Kentucky

Summary: The novel tells the true story of Elizabeth Moss, from her life on the fron tier of the Missouri territory in the 1820s, through three marriages that bring her to prominence in St. Louis and Washington society, to the outbreak of the Civil War.

Historical Accuracy: Significant events and the personal history of the major characters follow the sequence of fact.

5736 *The Turquoise Trail*
Date of Publication: 1950
Subject(s): American West
Historical character(s): Samuel Magoffin, Settler; Susan Shelby Magoffin, Settler, Spouse
Time Period(s): 1840s (1846)
Locale(s): Independence, Missouri; Santa Fe, New Mexico

Summary: Based on the actual diary of pioneer woman Susan Shelby Magoffin, the novel tells the story of her overland journey from Independence, Missouri, to Santa Fe, New Mexico, in 1846. The novel records the hardships of the trip as the young newlywed Magoffins confront the challenges of both the frontier and married life.

Historical Accuracy: The novel retells the story of Susan Shelby from her diary, supplemented by the author's retracing of the actual route taken.

5737 *Waters of the Wilderness*
Date of Publication: 1941
Subject(s): Settlement of the American Frontier; American Colonies
Historical character(s): George Rogers Clark, Explorer, Military Personnel (colonel)
Time Period(s): 1770s; 1780s (1778-1780)
Locale(s): Ohio; St. Louis, Missouri

Summary: The novel describes George Rogers Clark's expeditions in Ohio and along the Mississippi during the 1770s. Clark must contend with the wilderness as well as the English and Spanish in St. Louis. Clark emerges as a hero of boundless resources on the western frontier of America at a critical time.

Historical Accuracy: The events depicted are mainly historical and convincingly depicted.

5738 *The Wayfarer*
Date of Publication: 1938
Subject(s): Biography, Fictionalized; Civil War—U.S.
Historical character(s): James Cotter, Trader
Time Period(s): 19th century
Locale(s): Missouri

Summary: The novel is a fictional biography of James Cotter, whose life includes whaling, trading in the West, action during the Civil War, and ranching in Missouri.

Historical Accuracy: The details of Cotter's remarkable life and times are based on the record.

OWEN SELA

5739 *The Petrograd Consignment*
Date of Publication: 1979
Subject(s): World War I; Russian Revolution
Fictional character(s): Caspar Ehrler, Military Personnel (intelligence officer); Alexander Helphand, Doctor
Historical character(s): Arthur Zimmerman, Government Official (foreign secretary); Vladimir Ilich Ulyanov, Revolutionary, Political Figure
Time Period(s): 1910s (1917)
Locale(s): Berlin, Germany; Zurich, Switzerland; Petrograd, Russia

Summary: This political thriller tells the mainly true story of how the German government encouraged the Russian Revolution in order to get Russia out of the war. The key is the revolutionary Ulyanov, later Lenin, who must be pursuaded to end his exile in Zurich. The taut novel details the twists and turns that result in the sealed railway car to the Finland Station that touches off the Revolution.

Historical Accuracy: The basic outline of history is observed, but the novel blends the fictional and the actual.

JOHN SELBY (1897-1980)

American editor and novelist Selby was born in Gallatin, Missouri, and attended Park College, the University of Missouri, and Columbia University. He was editor-in-chief of the publishing company Rinehart for 13 years. Previously he was the arts editor for the Associated Press and a music editor for the *Kansas City Star*. His novels include *Sam*, *Starbuck*, and *Madame*.

`5740` *Elegant Journey*

Date of Publication: 1944
Subject(s): Antebellum South; Slavery
Fictional character(s): Sereno Trace, Plantation Owner
Time Period(s): 19th century (1839-1857)
Locale(s): Wisconsin

Summary: Set in the years prior to the Civil War, the novel describes the experiences of plantation owner Sereno Trace, who frees his slaves and moves his family into the wilderness of Wisconsin to begin a new life.

Historical Accuracy: The novel provides a detailed and believable portrait of the era and the region.

ANNEMARIE SELINKO

`5741` *Desiree*

Date of Publication: 1953
Subject(s): Napoleonic Era; Napoleonic Wars
Historical character(s): Desiree Clary, Gentlewoman; Napoleon Bonaparte, Military Personnel (general), Ruler (French emperor); Jean-Baptiste Bernadotte, Military Personnel (general and marshal), Ruler (King of Sweden); Josephine, Royalty (French empress)
Time Period(s): 18th century; 19th century (1794-1829)
Locale(s): Marseilles, France; Paris, France; Stockholm, Sweden

Summary: This romantic historical novel is a fictionalized account of Desiree Clary. Clary is engaged to Napoleon but is jilted by him when he marries Josephine. She marries Bernadotte, one of Napoleon's most illustrious generals, and becomes Queen of Sweden. The novel covers the rise of Napoleon from the days of the Directory to his defeat at Waterloo and features a number of historical figures of the era.

Historical Accuracy: The novel is based on fact, but in a few instances the story departs from history.

RICHARD SELTZER (1946-)

Born in Clarksville, Tennessee, Seltzer attended Yale University and the University of Massachusetts. Author of *The Lizard of Oz*, Seltzer has also been a Russian translator and an editor of electronics magazines.

`5742` *The Name of Hero*

Date of Publication: 1981
Subject(s): Russian Empire; Chinese Empire; Boxer Rebellion

Fictional character(s): Sonya Vassilchikova, Gentlewoman; Aslalfetch, Young Woman; Chinese Sonya, Orphan
Historical character(s): Alexander K. Bulatovich, Military Personnel (Russian officer)
Time Period(s): 1890s; 1900s
Locale(s): Russia; Ethiopia; Manchuria, China

Summary: The novel is the first of a trilogy on the extraordinary life of soldier, explorer, and religious leader Alexander Bulatovich. His career takes him from Tsarist Russia to Ethiopia and the Manchurian Campaign during the Boxer Rebellion in 1900. Each stop is a test of Bulatovich's courage and passion, with a variety of romantic diversions along the way.

Historical Accuracy: The details of Bulatovich's career are accurately depicted.

FRANCIS SELWYN (1935-)

English author Selwyn was born in Sussex and educated at Oxford. A former research assistant for the BBC, Selwyn worked in book and magazine publishing and has written widely on criminal and military history. He is a regular contributor to *Penthouse Magazine*.

`5743` *Cracksman on Velvet*

Date of Publication: 1974
Subject(s): Mystery; Victorian Period
Fictional character(s): Sergeant William Verity, Police Officer; Verney Dacre, Criminal (cracksman)
Time Period(s): 1850s (1858)
Locale(s): London, England

Summary: The novel introduces Sergeant William Clarence Verity of Scotland Yard's newly created Private Clothes Detail in London. Verity is on the trail of something big when he is entrapped and then blackmailed by criminals to ensure his silence. A plot is afoot to steal half a ton of gold bullion from a train, bound for Dover. Verity must see to it that the plot is foiled.

Historical Accuracy: The novel's incidents are based on the actual Train Robbery Case of 1857.

`5744` *Sergeant Verity and the Blood Royal*

Date of Publication: 1979
Subject(s): Mystery; Victorian Period
Fictional character(s): Sergeant William Verity, Police Officer; Verney Dacre, Criminal (cracksman); Thomas Crowe, Military Personnel (captain)
Historical character(s): Edward, Prince of Wales, Royalty
Time Period(s): 1860s (1860)
Locale(s): United States

Summary: Sergeant Verity is off to America in 1860, where he must protect the Prince of Wales and catch an English criminal genius, Verney Dacre, who is plotting to rob the U.S. Mint at Philadelphia. Verity's adventures take him from the mean streets of New York to Niagara Falls and by steamboat down the Mississippi.

Historical Accuracy: The novel's period details are authentic.

5745 *Sergeant Verity and the Imperial Diamond*

Date of Publication: 1975
Subject(s): Mystery; Victorian Period; Indian Mutiny
Fictional character(s): Sergeant William Verity, Police Officer; Sergeant Martock, Police Officer
Historical character(s): Nana Sahib, Leader (Indian Mutiny)
Time Period(s): 1850s (1857)
Locale(s): India

Summary: Segeant Verity of Scotland Yard's Private Clothes Detail is sent to Imperial India at the time of the Indian Mutiny to discover the whereabouts of an English girl who has fallen into the hands of the leaders of the mutiny. Also lost is the Kaiser-i-Hind diamond, and Verity sets out with Sergeant Martock to recover both the gem and the girl.

Historical Accuracy: The details of the mutiny are accurately depicted.

5746 *Sergeant Verity Presents His Compliments*

Date of Publication: 1977
Subject(s): Mystery; Victorian Period
Fictional character(s): Sergeant William Verity, Police Officer
Time Period(s): 1860s (1860)
Locale(s): London, England

Summary: Sergeant Verity's case involves the violent death of a blackmailer and of an English lord. Verity's investigation leads him on a perplexing tour of Victorian low-life as he uncovers a madman's plot for revenge.

Historical Accuracy: The novel features convincing depictions of period London.

RICHARD SENNETT (1943-)

Born in Chicago, Sennett attended the University of Chicago and Harvard University. His books include works of urban history and social criticism. He teaches sociology at New York University and is the director of the Center for Humanistic Studies. His other novels include *The Frog Who Dared to Croak.*

5747 *Palais-Royale*

Date of Publication: 1986
Subject(s): Architecture; Religious Life; Victorian Period
Fictional character(s): Frederick Courtland, Architect; Charles Courtland, Religious (minister); Anne Mercure, Actress
Historical character(s): Victor Hugo, Writer
Time Period(s): 19th century (1828-1851)
Locale(s): Paris, France; London, England

Summary: The novel tells the story of two English brothers—Frederick and Charles Courtland—who come to Paris at the height of its romantic revolution. Frederick has been commissioned to assist in the construction of the Galerie d'Orleans in the Palais-Royale, and Charles, a lapsed country minister, follows him in search of purpose and fulfillment. Their stories play out against a backdrop of historical events—the 1830

July Revolution in Paris and the flowering of such artists as Hugo, George Sand, and Franz Liszt.

Historical Accuracy: The novel captures with care and conviction the era and its customs.

ANYA SETON (1904-1990)

An American novelist born in New York City, Seton was educated privately and at Oxford University. She preferred being called a biographical rather than a historical novelist to emphasize the degree of research and truthfulness she brought to each of her novels. *Foxfire* and *Dragonwyck* were made into successful films. Seton also wrote books for children, such as *The Mistletoe and Sword* and *Washington Irving.*

5748 *Avalon*

Date of Publication: 1965
Subject(s): Anglo-Saxon Period; Exploration
Fictional character(s): Rumon, Explorer; Merewyn, Young Woman
Historical character(s): Alfrida, Royalty (Queen of England); Edgar, Ruler (King of England)
Time Period(s): 10th century
Locale(s): England; North America

Summary: The novel tells the story of 10th-century England and the exploration of America. Roman, a descendant of Charlemagne and King Alfred, is a searcher for the Islands of the Blessed, King Arthur's Avalon. His quest takes him to the court of his cousin, King Edgar, where he meets Merewyn, whom he loses. His search for her leads him across the Atlantic.

Historical Accuracy: The story is fanciful, though based in part on folklore of the period.

5749 *Devil Water*

Date of Publication: 1962
Subject(s): Jacobite Rebellion; American Colonies
Historical character(s): Charles Radcliffe, Nobleman; Jenny Radcliffe, Gentlewoman; William Byrd, Nobleman
Time Period(s): 18th century (1709-1746)
Locale(s): Northumberland, England; Virginia, American Colonies; London, England

Summary: This story of the two Jacobite Rebellions features Charles Radcliffe and his daughter Jenny. Radcliffe is loyal both to his Catholic faith and the Stuart cause, and Jenny finds herself surrounded by intrigue in London and Virginia.

Historical Accuracy: The historical background of this fictional story is authentic.

5750 *Dragonwyck*

Date of Publication: 1944
Subject(s): Gothic Romance
Fictional character(s): Miranda Wells, Young Woman; Nicholas Van Ryn, Gentleman
Time Period(s): 1840s (1844)
Locale(s): Hudson River Valley, New York

Summary: This Gothic thriller is set in the Hudson River Valley during the 1840s and explores the consequences of Miranda Wells' invitation to live at Dragonwyck, the estate of her distant relative Nicholas Van Ryn.

Historical Accuracy: The author explains that she attempted to portray the historical framework and background details accurately.

5751 *Green Darkness*

Date of Publication: 1972
Subject(s): Tudor Period; Reincarnation
Fictional character(s): Stephen Marsdon, Young Man, Spouse; Celia Marsdon, Young Woman, Spouse
Time Period(s): 1960s (1968); 16th century (1552-1559)
Locale(s): England

Summary: A family secret originating in the 16th century is probed by two contemporary people, Richard and Celia Marsdon. She is able to go back in time 400 years earlier to become another Celia, Celia de Bohun, who with another Stephen Marsdon, is bound up in the turmoil of the Tudor period.

Historical Accuracy: The Tudor portion of the story is solidly rooted in historical fact, as is the depiction of the politics of the era.

5752 *Katherine*

Date of Publication: 1954
Subject(s): Middle Ages; Peasants' Revolt; Biography, Fictionalized
Historical character(s): Katherine Swynford, Gentlewoman; John of Gaunt, Royalty (Duke of Lancaster); Geoffrey Chaucer, Writer; Philippa de Roet, Spouse (of Chaucer); Wat Tyler, Revolutionary
Time Period(s): 14th century (1366-1396)
Locale(s): England; Spain; France

Summary: Set during the 14th century, this biographical novel tells the story of Katherine Swynford, the sister-in-law of Geoffrey Chaucer. Her love affair with John of Gaunt, Duke of Lancaster, is depicted amidst a fully realized portrait of medieval England on the brink of the War of the Roses.

Historical Accuracy: This book is full of suspenseful adventure, but also features a credible reconstruction of life in a fascinating period of English history.

5753 *My Theodosia*

Date of Publication: 1941
Subject(s): Politics
Historical character(s): Theodosia Burr Alston, Gentlewoman (daughter of Aaron Burr); Aaron Burr, Political Figure; Meriwether Lewis, Explorer; Dolley Madison, Spouse (of James Madison), Political Figure
Time Period(s): 1800s; 1810s (1800-1812)
Locale(s): New York, New York; Washington, District of Columbia; Richmond, Virginia

Summary: The novel tells the story of Aaron Burr's daughter Theodosia, who stands by her father after his fatal duel with Alexander Hamilton. Her love affair with Meriwether Lewis

is also depicted. The novel captures the politics of the period, the amazing daring and bravado of Burr, and the mystery that surrounds the short and colorful life of his daughter.

Historical Accuracy: Although this story is a fictional interpretation of Theodosia's life, the author has tried to be accurate in every detail. When accounts differ, the author has chosen the interpretation that seems to be the most truthful.

5754 *The Winthrop Woman*

Date of Publication: 1958
Subject(s): American Colonies; Puritans
Historical character(s): Elizabeth Fones Winthrop, Settler; John Winthrop, Political Figure (governor); Anne Hutchinson, Religious (leader)
Time Period(s): 17th century (1617-1655)
Locale(s): Boston, Massachusetts, American Colonies; Connecticut, American Colonies; England

Summary: This account of life in colonial America is based on the life of Governor John Winthrop's niece, Elizabeth, who settles in Massachusetts in 1631, a widow at 20. She rebels against the harsh theocratic Puritan government, befriends Anne Hutchinson, and challenges the authorities over the treatment of the Indians. She becomes, in the view of her stern uncle, his ''unregenerate niece.''.

Historical Accuracy: The author explains that this book is built on a framework of fact and claims never to have knowingly changed a date or circumstance.

MARY LEE SETTLE (1918-)

An American novelist born in West Virginia, Settle attended Sweet Briar College. She has worked as an editor for *Harper's Bazaar* and as the English correspondent for *Flair*. Settle won the National Book Award in 1978 for *Blood Tie*. She is also the author of an autobiographical account of her life in the WAAF during World War II, *All the Brave Promises*.

5755 *Know Nothing*

Date of Publication: 1960
Subject(s): Antebellum South; Slavery; Civil War—U.S.
Fictional character(s): Johnny Catlett, Young Man; Melinda Catlett, Young Woman
Time Period(s): 19th century (1837-1861)
Locale(s): Virginia (western)

Summary: Life on a western Virginia plantation in the years before the outbreak of the Civil War is dramatized in the story of Johnny Catlett and his cousin Melinda, who grow up together on the plantation of Beulah. Their story reflects the history of West Virginia and the great changes and turmoil that push the nation to war.

Historical Accuracy: The author is an expert in her locale and the period elements that create a vivid and convincing picture of the times.

5756 *O Beulah Land*

Date of Publication: 1956

Subject(s): Settlement of the American Frontier; French and Indian War; American Colonies
Fictional character(s): Jonathan Lacey, Frontiersman; Sal Lacey, Spouse
Time Period(s): 18th century (1754-1774)
Locale(s): Allegheny Mountains, Pennsylvania, American Colonies

Summary: The opening of the western wilderness of the Virginia Colony sets the backdrop for this panoramic social chronicle of frontier life and the forging of an American identity. At the center of the story is frontiersman Jonathan Lacey, a young Tidewater Virginian who, after the French and Indian Wars, pushes further west into the wilderness beyond the Alleghenies to a region he calls Beulah. The unfolding story of the country and this frontier community are vividly described.

Historical Accuracy: The period and regional elements are convincingly captured.

5757 *Prisons*

Date of Publication: 1973
Subject(s): Civil War—England
Fictional character(s): Jonathan Church, Young Man
Historical character(s): Oliver Cromwell, Political Figure
Time Period(s): 17th century (1640s)
Locale(s): England

Summary: Book One of the Beulah Quintet is set during the English Civil War. Johnny Church, a 16-year-old, leaves home in 1645 to fight on Cromwell's side in the war against the Crown. His revolutionary ideals are challenged by betrayal and execution.

Historical Accuracy: The story is set against an authentic evocation of the period.

5758 *The Scapegoat*

Date of Publication: 1980
Subject(s): Labor Movement; Mining
Fictional character(s): Dan Neill, Businessman; Lily Lacey, Activist
Historical character(s): Mary Harris Jones, Labor Leader
Time Period(s): 1910s (1912)
Locale(s): West Virginia

Summary: Set in West Virginia in 1912, the novel captures the tension of a coal miners' strike. The miners, many of which are Italian immigrants, are pitted against strikebreakers brought into the valley by a group of investors led by Captain Dan Neill. He is opposed by the legendary labor leader Mother Jones and Lily Lacey, a young Vassar graduate and daughter of one of the mine owners.

Historical Accuracy: The novel provides an authentic version of the period and the region.

FLORENCE A. SEWARD

5759 *Gold for the Caesars*

Date of Publication: 1961

Subject(s): Roman Empire
Fictional character(s): Gaius Julius Lacer, Slave, Architect; Penelope, Servant; Cornelius Classicus, Government Official (provincial governor)
Historical character(s): Domitian, Ruler (Roman Emperor); Trajan, Military Personnel (field marshal)
Time Period(s): 1st century (90s)
Locale(s): Rome, Roman Empire; Spain

Summary: This adventure novel is set during the 1st century in the reign of Emperor Domitian and concerns the search for gold in Roman Spain. Gaius Lacer is ordered into northern Spain for gold but must contend with both the treachery of the Roman governor, Classicus, and the Celtic warriors of the region.

Historical Accuracy: The story is invented but does employ authentic period elements.

MIRANDA SEYMOUR

5760 *The Bride of Sforza*

Date of Publication: 1975
Subject(s): Renaissance
Historical character(s): Beatrice d'Este, Gentlewoman; Ludovico Sforza, Nobleman (Duke of Bari); Leonardo da Vinci, Artist; Charles VIII, Ruler (King of France); Cecilia Gallerani, Gentlewoman
Time Period(s): 15th century
Locale(s): Milan, Italy

Summary: This novel of intrigue is set in Renaissance Italy during the French invasion of the late 15th century. Beatrice d'Este marries Lodovico, Duke of Bari, and comes to Milan, where she is swept up in the scheming of the Milanese court and her husband's efforts to replace his nephew as Duke of Milan.

Historical Accuracy: The historical background of the story is solid and convincing in its details of Italian court life and its intrigues.

5761 *Count Manifred*

Date of Publication: 1977
Subject(s): Gothic Romance; Literary Life
Fictional character(s): Lucy Emerton, Young Woman; Lord Ruthven, Nobleman
Historical character(s): George Gordon Byron, Nobleman (Lord Byron), Writer; Mary Wollstonecraft Shelley, Writer; Percy Bysshe Shelley, Writer; Claire Clairmont, Gentlewoman
Time Period(s): 1810s
Locale(s): Nottingham, England; London, England; Italy

Summary: This Gothic tale includes in its cast of characters Byron, Shelley, and Mary Godwin. The evil genious Lord Ruthven may be a specter or a vampire, and he has a dark hold on Byron that Lucy Emerton, out of her own passionate love for the poet, is determined to break.

Historical Accuracy: As unrealistic as the novel's supernatural elements are, it is solidly balanced with a reliable period background and actual details from Byron's life.

`5762` *Daughter of Shadows*

Date of Publication: 1977
Subject(s): Renaissance
Historical character(s): Lucrezia Borgia, Noblewoman; Cesare Borgia, Nobleman; Alexander VI, Religious (pope)
Time Period(s): 15th century
Locale(s): Italy

Summary: The novel describes the notorious Borgia family concentrating on the fate of Lucrezia Borgia who becomes the political pawn of her powerful father, Pope Alexander VI, and the victim of her brother Cesare's amorous attention and jealousy.

Historical Accuracy: The novel is based on fact and provides an authentic portrait of the age and a credible interpretation of the Borgias.

`5763` *The Goddess*

Date of Publication: 1979
Subject(s): Myths and Legends; Ancient Greece; Trojan War
Fictional character(s): Helen of Troy, Royalty (queen consort of Menelaus); Menelaus, Ruler (King of Sparta); Paris, Royalty (Trojan prince)
Time Period(s): Indeterminate Past
Locale(s): Greece; Troy, Ancient Civilization

Summary: The novel provides a psychological study of Helen of Troy and the consequence of her great beauty. Feared and desired by men, envied and hated by woman, Helen's destiny is to produce a cataclysm between two great nations. The novel recounts the mythical events with an emphasis on their human consequences.

Historical Accuracy: Based on a thorough reading of the mythological material, the novel provides an imaginary, though plausible, interpretation of the personalities and the era.

`5764` *Medea*

Date of Publication: 1982
Subject(s): Myths and Legends; Witchcraft and Sorcery; Ancient Greece
Fictional character(s): Medea, Murderer, Sorceress; Jason, Adventurer; Aegeus, Ruler (King of Athens)
Time Period(s): Indeterminate Past
Locale(s): Greece

Summary: The novel tells the mythical story of Medea, a woman whose passion exceeds all bounds. She falls in love with Jason and after helping him gain the Golden Fleece goes with him to Greece. Her second husband is Aegeus, king of Athens, who must judge Medea's actions based on passion, betrayal, and a relentless pursuit of revenge.

Historical Accuracy: The novel offers a modern interpretation of the mythic story with some convincing elements of the ethos of the Greek Heroic Age.

JEFF SHAARA (1952-)

Born in New Jersey, the son of Pulitzer Prize winning novelist Michael Shaara, Jeff helped his father in the research for *The Killer Angels* and served as a consultant for the movie version. *Gods and Generals* is his first novel.

`5765` *Gods and Generals*

Date of Publication: 1996
Subject(s): Civil War—U.S.; Battle of Fredericksburg; Battle of Chancellorsville
Historical character(s): Thomas Jonathan Jackson, Military Personnel (Confederate general); Winfield Scott Hancock, Military Personnel (Union general); Joshua Lawrence Chamberlain, Teacher, Military Personnel (Union officer); Robert E. Lee, Military Personnel (Confederate commander); James Longstreet, Military Personnel (Confederate general); James Ewell Brown Stuart, Military Personnel (Confederate officer); George McClellan, Military Personnel (Union commander)
Time Period(s): 1850s; 1860s (1859-1863)
Locale(s): Virginia

Summary: As a kind of prequel to his father's classic *The Killer Angels*, the author traces the careers of several of the major figures in the Battle of Gettysburg through the events that lead up to the conflict. The story concentrates on four men: Robert E. Lee, Joshua Lawrence Chamberlain, Winfield Scott Hancock, and Stonewall Jackson.

Historical Accuracy: The events and the presentation of the historical figures are convincing and detailed.

MICHAEL SHAARA (1929-1988)

Michael Shaara is an American novelist who worked as a merchant seaman, a police officer, and a professor of English. His novel *The Killer Angels* is widely regarded as one of the finest historical novels and the best novel about the Civil War ever written.

`5766` *The Killer Angels*

Date of Publication: 1974
Subject(s): Civil War—U.S.; Battle of Gettysburg; Military Life
Fictional character(s): Buster Kilrain, Military Personnel (Union sergeant)
Historical character(s): Joshua Lawrence Chamberlain, Military Personnel; Robert E. Lee, Military Personnel (general); James Longstreet, Military Personnel (general); George Edward Pickett, Military Personnel; John Buford, Military Personnel (cavalry officer); Winfield Scott Hancock, Military Personnel (general)
Time Period(s): 1860s (1863)
Locale(s): Gettysburg, Pennsylvania

Summary: Shaara offers one of the finest battle re-creations ever written. He describes the climactic struggle at Gettysburg from the multiple perspectives of the key participants on both sides. Lee, Longstreet, and Chamberlain emerge in depth. Shaara's battle scenes rival Leo Tolstoy's and Stephen Crane's.

Historical Accuracy: Few authors are able to deliver both military strategy and the human drama of combat. Shaara's re-creation of the Battle of Gettysburg is expertly and movingly rendered.

MAURICE SHADBOLT (1932-)

Born in New Zealand of English, Irish, Welsh, and Australian convict ancestry, Shadbolt is a short story and novel writer. He worked as a director for the New Zealand National Film Unit before becoming a freelance writer and journalist. *Season of the Jew* was selected by the *New York Times Book Review* as one of the best books of 1987.

5767 *Monday's Warriors*

Date of Publication: 1990
Subject(s): Maoris
Historical character(s): Kimball Bent, Military Personnel (soldier); Titokowaru, Warrior (Maori)
Time Period(s): 1840s
Locale(s): New Zealand

Summary: The novel tells the true story of American Kimball Bent from Maine who is dragooned into the English army and sent to help subdue the Maoris of New Zealand in the 1840s. Bent deserts his regiment and becomes the chief strategist of a Maori band that battles the British to a standstill in the bloodiest action of the Maori War.

Historical Accuracy: As the author explains, when this story most seems like fiction, it is true.

5768 *Season of the Jew*

Date of Publication: 1986
Subject(s): British Colonies
Fictional character(s): Kooti, Leader (Maori); George Fairweather, Military Personnel (captain)
Time Period(s): 1860s (1868-1869)
Locale(s): New Zealand

Summary: This tragic tale chronicles the efforts of a mission-educated Maori, Kooti, who leads an army of native New Zealanders against the English oppressors in an imitation of the Biblical Israelites. The conflict between the Maoris and the English settlers is seen through the eyes of Captain Fairweather, a British army officer.

Historical Accuracy: The narrative is derived from actual events with some condensation of incidents and fusing of historical figures into fictional composites.

GEORGE SHAFTEL

5769 *Golden Shore*

Date of Publication: 1943
Subject(s): American West
Fictional character(s): Mary Marquand, Young Woman; Arch Gillespie, Military Personnel (lieutenant); Michael O'Cain, Sea Captain
Time Period(s): 1840s (1840-1847)
Locale(s): California

Summary: The scramble for power and control of California between the Mexicans, the Americans, and the Russians is chronicled through the tangled story of Mary Marquand who finds herself married to two men at the same time. The novel depicts all the important events of the struggle, beginning with the Tepic Prison episode in which the Mexicans collected all the Americans in California and imprisoned them in Mexico.

Historical Accuracy: Although it is well-researched and depicts actual events, the novel is often too melodramatic and sentimental to be historically true.

MEIR SHALEV (1948-)

Israeli writer Shalev was writer-in-residence at Hebrew University of Jerusalem in 1994.

5770 *Esau*

Date of Publication: 1991
Subject(s): Family Saga; Jews
Fictional character(s): Abraham Levy, Baker; Sarah Levy, Spouse; Esau Levy, Writer
Time Period(s): 20th century (1910s-1970s)
Locale(s): Israel

Summary: The novel is a saga of several generations in the emerging state of Israel that spans the period from World War I and the inception of the British Mandate in Palestine through the mid-1970s. It is the story of Abraham Levy and his wife, Sarah, and their twin sons. The narrator, Esau, is disinherited and leaves home for a career as a writer in America.

Historical Accuracy: The novel captures with some skill the historical background of these pivotal years in the history of Palestine and Israel.

MOSHE SHAMIR (1921-)

Israeli novelist, essayist, and playwright Shamir's books include *Why Ziva Cried on the Feast of First Fruits*. He has had more of his plays produced than any other Israeli playwright.

5771 *David's Stranger*

Date of Publication: 1965
Subject(s): Biblical Story; Ancient Israel
Historical character(s): David, Biblical Figure, Ruler (King of ancient Israel); Bathsheba, Biblical Figure; Uriah, Biblical Figure
Time Period(s): 10th century B.C.
Locale(s): Israel

Summary: The novel offers a fictional recounting of the Old Testament story of King David ordering Bathsheba's husband, Uriah the Hittite, into the front lines at the seige of Rabbah in the hope that he would be killed. The story is seen through Uriah's perspective as he realizes the betrayal of his former comrade.

Historical Accuracy: The novel uses Biblical material to construct a very modern tale about loyalty and betrayal.

5772 *The King of Flesh and Blood*

Date of Publication: 1958
Subject(s): Ancient Israel
Historical character(s): Yannai, Ruler (King of Judea)
Time Period(s): 1st century B.C.
Locale(s): Israel

Summary: The novel dramatizes the reign of Alexander Jannaeus, or Yannai, the last king of an independent Israel. A grandson of Simon Maccabeus who had liberated Israel from the Syrians, Alexander has come to epitomize the excesses and evils of autocratic rule.

Historical Accuracy: The novel achieves a high degree of truthfulness in capturing the period and its customs.

DELL SHANNON
(PSEUD. OF ELIZABETH LININGTON, 1921-1988)

Born in Illinois, Linington wrote historical novels and mysteries. She has been called the ''doyenne of the police procedural'' for her popular mystery series featuring LAPD detective Luis Mendoza.

5773 *The Dispossessed*

Date of Publication: 1988
Subject(s): Rural Life—Ireland; Religious Conflict; Civil War—England
Fictional character(s): Fergal O'Breslin, Chieftain (clan); Hugh McFadden, Religious (monk); Kevin McCann, Outlaw
Time Period(s): 17th century (1651-1662)
Locale(s): Aran Islands, Ireland; Connacht, Ireland

Summary: Ireland in the 1650s is savaged by Oliver Cromwell's Act of Settlement, which requires many Irish to leave their ancestral homes to settle in the crowded and rocky province of Connacht. Fergal O'Breslin, a young clan chief, must struggle to survive the repression brought on by the English Parliament and the Puritans.

Historical Accuracy: The period background is authentically presented.

5774 *The Scalpel and the Sword*

Date of Publication: 1987
Subject(s): Napoleonic Wars; Medical Profession; Battle of Trafalgar
Fictional character(s): Con McDonagh, Doctor
Historical character(s): Horatio Nelson, Military Personnel (admiral)
Time Period(s): 1800s
Locale(s): Dublin, Ireland; London, England

Summary: During the Napoleonic Wars, Irish surgeon Con McDonagh, disillusioned with his homeland, departs for England and greater opportunity. After finding a job in a small hospital, he goes to sea with the Royal Navy. There he sees action at the Battle of Trafalgar and is on hand at the death of Lord Nelson. At home a number of romantic possibilities claim his attention.

Historical Accuracy: The period details of the story are authentic, and the historical events pictured are accurately described.

DORIS SHANNON (1924-)

Born in Elmira, New York, and raised in Ontario, Shannon attended the Napance Collegiate Institute. She worked for the Royal Bank of Canada during the 1940s and turned to writing in the 1960s. She is the author of *Hawthorne Hill* and *Cain's Daughters*. Shannon won the *Writer's Digest* creative writing award for her short story ''And Then There Was the Youngest.'' She writes the Robert Forsythe mystery series under the name E. X. Giroux.

5775 *Beyond the Shining Mountains*

Date of Publication: 1979
Subject(s): Settlement of the American Frontier
Fictional character(s): Laurie Woodbyne, Gentleman; Rowan Malone, Young Woman
Time Period(s): 1810s (1812)
Locale(s): Pacific Northwest, North America

Summary: Frontier survival in the Pacific Northwest is the novel's subject as two very different individuals' paths cross. Laurie Woodbyne is the son of an English aristocrat in pursuit of his wife's secret that has led to their estrangement. Woodbyne heads into the wilderness, where he meets Rowan Malone. She is a half-breed raised in a convent school who heads west when she loses her innocence. Their adventures together provide a test of survival.

Historical Accuracy: The novel features believable frontier details of the period.

5776 *Cain's Daughters*

Date of Publication: 1978
Subject(s): Civil War—U.S.
Fictional character(s): David Sevendor, Plantation Owner; Jemima Sevendor, Spouse
Time Period(s): 1860s
Locale(s): Georgia

Summary: Jemima, the daughter of a wealthy Northerner, falls in love with Georgian David Sevendor and returns with him to his plantation, Camelot, as the Civil War breaks out. She finds herself caught in the middle of the conflict, disowned by her family and distrusted by her in-laws. As the war proceeds, she comes to realize the dark underside of the Southern code of civility and honor.

Historical Accuracy: Social customs of the period are realistically drawn.

5777 *Hawthorn Hill*

Date of Publication: 1976
Subject(s): French Revolution; Romance
Fictional character(s): Mary Forrester, Young Woman; Comte du Levassoux, Nobleman
Time Period(s): 1790s; 1800s (1799-1807)
Locale(s): England; France

Summary: Independent Mary Forrester is forced to take a position in service at the height of the French Revolution. Then she meets the handsome and cruel Comte du Levassoux.

Historical Accuracy: The period elements are only lightly suggested in this romantic story.

MARGARET SHAW

5778 *Inherit the Earth*

Date of Publication: 1940
Subject(s): American Revolution; American Colonies
Fictional character(s): Desiree Phinney, Servant (indentured)
Time Period(s): 1770s
Locale(s): American Colonies; Nova Scotia, Canada

Summary: This historical romance set before and during the American Revolution follows the adventures of Desiree Phinny who, after her father is forced to leave England, follows him to America as an indentured servant. Romance ensues, including marriage to a loyalist that entails her moving to Nova Scotia.

Historical Accuracy: The historical background is often compromised by a preference for melodrama and sentiment.

PATRICIA SHAW

An Australian, Shaw has worked as a teacher and as a political journalist as well as a writer and historian.

5779 *Cry of the Rain Bird*

Date of Publication: 1994
Subject(s): Frontier—Australia
Fictional character(s): Corby Morgan, Plantation Owner; Jessie Morgan, Spouse; Mike Devlin, Manager
Time Period(s): 19th century
Locale(s): Queensland, Australia

Summary: Set on the "sugar" coast of Queensland, this novel of 19th-century Australian frontier life follows the fortunes of a husband and wife, Corby and Jessie Morgan, who attempt to run a sugar plantation with the help of manager Mike Devlin. Success depends on the help of Aborigines and laborers imported from South Sea islands.

Historical Accuracy: The novel provides an authentic period and regional background.

5780 *The Feather and the Stone*

Date of Publication: 1992
Subject(s): Frontier—Australia
Fictional character(s): Sibell Delahunty, Settler; Logan Conal, Sailor
Time Period(s): 19th century
Locale(s): Australia

Summary: A young and naive British woman named Sibell Delahunty is shipwrecked in Australia in the late 19th century. She is rescued by Logan Conal and taken to her only surviving relatives. Fleeing from an arranged marriage, Sibell goes to a cattle station, where she encounters Logan again and some surprising turns of events.

Historical Accuracy: The novel effectively captures the pioneering spirit of the Australian outback.

5781 *Where the Willows Weep*

Date of Publication: 1993
Subject(s): Victorian Period; Frontier—Australia; Aborigines
Fictional character(s): Laura Maskey, Young Woman; Amelia Roberts, Young Woman; Paul MacNamara, Rancher, Widow(er)
Time Period(s): 1860s
Locale(s): Queensland, Australia

Summary: The background for this story of life in Australia of the 1860s is the tumultuous history of Rockhampton, a goldrush town on Queensland's Fitzroy River. Laura Maskey is a daring young woman who resists her parents' attempt to arrange a conventional marriage, favoring Paul MacNamara instead. MacNamara is a widower and rancher who battles those attempting to divide Queensland and to rob the Aborigines of their ancestral homeland.

Historical Accuracy: The history of the period and the region is convincingly and authentically drawn.

STANLEY SHAW (1922-)

5782 *Sherlock Holmes Meets Annie Oakley*

Date of Publication: 1986
Subject(s): Victorian Period; Mystery
Fictional character(s): Sherlock Holmes, Detective—Private; John H. Watson, Doctor, Sidekick
Historical character(s): Annie Oakley, Entertainer, Frontierswoman; Edward, Prince of Wales, Royalty
Time Period(s): 1880s (1887)
Locale(s): London, England; Windsor, England

Summary: Buffalo Bill's Wild West Show tours England during Queen Victoria's Jubilee. Sherlock Holmes is summoned to Windsor Great Park, where the queen has ordered a command performance of the Wild West Show, to solve a mystery that involves Annie Oakley.

Historical Accuracy: The period elements are faithfully presented and many of the circumstances are based on fact.

EDITH SHAY (1894-)

KATHARINE SMITH (1838-1932)

Born in Manistique, Michigan, Edith Shay received her bachelor's degree from Wellesley College She joined the staff of *McClure's* as an advertising copywriter but soon turned to writing for *The New Yorker* and other magazines. Much of her work is set on Cape Cod.

5783 *The Private Adventures of Captain Shaw*

Date of Publication: 1945
Subject(s): French Revolution; Reign of Terror
Fictional character(s): Philander Shaw, Sea Captain
Time Period(s): 1790s (1793)

Locale(s): Paris, France; Cape Cod, Massachusetts

Summary: The adventures of a Cape Cod sea captain, Philander Shaw, in Paris during the Reign of Terror are described in this romantic novel. When Shaw's cargo is commandeered by a French man-of-war, Shaw sets off to Paris to demand restitution from Robespierre. He is quickly involved in the dangerous task of rescuing a young noblewoman from the guillotine.

Historical Accuracy: The novel provides a remarkably authentic period adventure.

ROBERT SHEA (1933-)

American writer Shea was born in New York City and attended Manhattan College and Rutgers University. After a long career in publishing as a copywriter and editor, Shea became a freelance writer. His works include *Illuminatus*, a novel Shea has described as a combination of science fiction, fantasy, political satire, and pornography. He is a member of the Social Revolutionary Anarchist Federation, the Coalition Against Registration and the Draft, the Richard III Society, and the Japanese Sword Society.

5784 *Shike: Time of Dragons*

Date of Publication: 1981
Subject(s): Japanese Empire; Chinese Empire
Fictional character(s): Jebu, Religious (monk); Lady Taniko, Noblewoman
Historical character(s): Kublai Khan, Ruler (Mongol emperor)
Time Period(s): 13th century
Locale(s): Japan; China

Summary: This tale of medieval Japan concerns the love affair between Jebu, a young monk from a Buddhist fighting sect, and the Lady Taniko. The two are separated and make their way to China where Kublai Khan is establishing his Mongol empire.

Historical Accuracy: The novel brings the times to life with authentic period elements.

J.A. SHEARS

5785 *Fire in the Sky*

Date of Publication: 1988
Subject(s): Indians; Frontier—Canada
Fictional character(s): Dan Locke, Frontiersman, Trapper; Loon Cry, Indian
Time Period(s): 1840s
Locale(s): Yukon Territory, Canada; Alaska

Summary: Dan Locke, a trapper in the Yukon Territory during the 1840s, takes the Indian woman Loon Cry away from her brutal husband. His kind act has tragic consequences as Loon Cry's tribe goes on the warpath for vengeance.

Historical Accuracy: The novel offers some convincing period elements and a believable frontier background.

VINCENT SHEEAN (1899-1975)

American journalist and writer Sheean was born in Illinois and attended the University of Chicago. He served as an intelligence officer in North Africa, Italy, and the Middle East with the U.S. Army Air Corps during World War II. As a journalist Sheean covered many of the important world events from the end of World War II to the Korean War. He is the author of the biographies *Dorothy and Red* (on Dorothy Thompson and Sinclair Lewis) and *Oscar Hammerstein I: The Life and Exploits of an Impressario*, and the novels *Lily* and *Rage of the Soul*.

5786 *Beware of Caesar*

Date of Publication: 1965
Subject(s): Roman Empire
Historical character(s): Nero, Ruler (Roman emperor); Lucius Annaeus Seneca, Political Figure, Writer
Time Period(s): 1st century
Locale(s): Rome, Roman Empire

Summary: Power politics during the reign of the Roman emperor Nero is the subject of this novel chronicling the excesses of imperial Rome. The story involves a plot to overthrow Nero, in which his former tutor Seneca is implicated. The story ends with Nero's demand that Seneca commit suicide.

Historical Accuracy: The novel is carefully based on actual events and details.

5787 *A Day of Battle*

Date of Publication: 1938
Subject(s): Battle of Fontenoy; Royalty—France; War of the Austrian Succession
Historical character(s): Maurice, Comte de Saxe, Military Personnel (French general); Francois Marie Arouet, Writer (aka Voltaire), Philosopher; Jeanne Antoinette Poisson, Noblewoman (Madame de Pompadour), Lover (of the king); Louis XV, Ruler (King of France)
Time Period(s): 1740s (1745)
Locale(s): Fontenoy, Belgium; France

Summary: This wide-ranging social chronicle focuses on a single day in 1745 when the French meet the British at the Battle of Fontenoy in Flanders. The action moves beyond the battlefield to the court of Louis XV.

Historical Accuracy: The novel is convincing in its ability to capture both the battle and the era that helps to explain it.

GRAHAM SHELBY (1939-)

English novelist Shelby has worked as a copywriter and book reviewer.

5788 *The Cannaway Concern*

Date of Publication: 1980
Subject(s): Family Saga
Fictional character(s): Charlotte Cannaway, Young Woman; Brook Henry Wintersill, Gentleman
Time Period(s): 1710s; 1720s (1719-1720)

Locale(s): Wiltshire, England; Bristol, England

Summary: In the second volume of the Cannaway family saga set in 18th-century England, Charlotte Cannaway's elopement with Brook Wintersill forms the novel's drama. Cut off from her family, Charlotte struggles to extricate herself from a disastrous marriage.

Historical Accuracy: The novel's fictional story is played against a convincingly detailed period background.

5789 *The Cannaways*
Date of Publication: 1978
Subject(s): Family Saga; Business Building
Fictional character(s): Byrdd Cannaway, Artisan, Businessman
Time Period(s): 17th century; 18th century (1697-1701)
Locale(s): Wiltshire, England; Paris, France; Vienna, Austria

Summary: This is the first novel of a trilogy that traces the fortunes of the Cannaway family. Their story begins with the adventures of Byrdd Cannaway, who is determined to become the greatest coach maker in England. He travels across Europe to learn his craft and eventually returns to England to begin his family dynasty.

Historical Accuracy: The novel is convincing in its ability to create a believable historical era.

5790 *The Devil Is Loose*
Date of Publication: 1974
Subject(s): Middle Ages; Royalty—England
Historical character(s): Richard the Lionhearted, Royalty (prince); John Lackland, Royalty (prince); Henry II, Ruler (King of England); Eleanor of Aquitaine, Royalty (queen consort of Henry II); William Marshal, Knight, Nobleman (Earl of Pembroke); Philip II, Ruler (King of France); Berengaria of Navarre, Royalty (consort of Richard)
Time Period(s): 12th century (1189-1199)
Locale(s): England; Normandy, France

Summary: The dynastic conflict of two Angevin princes—Richard the Lionhearted and John Lackland—is dramatized in the scramble for power at the death of Henry II. The novel offers a convincing portrait of the age as well as a chronicle of its dangerous political manuevering.

Historical Accuracy: The basic historical elements of the story are accurately presented.

5791 *The Kings of Vain Intent*
Date of Publication: 1970
Subject(s): Middle Ages; Crusades
Historical character(s): Richard the Lionhearted, Ruler (King of England); Berengaria of Navarre, Royalty (queen consort of Richard I); Frederick Barbarossa, Ruler (Emperor of Germany); Tancred, Ruler (King of Sicily); Saladin, Ruler (sultan); Conrad of Montferrat, Nobleman (marquis); Philip II, Ruler (King of France)
Time Period(s): 12th century (1187-1192)
Locale(s): Palestine

Summary: This sequel to *The Knights of Dark Renown* tells the story of the Third Crusade. After their catastrophic defeat at the hands of Saladin, the forces of the Christian Kingdom of Jerusalem are divided and feuding in anticipation of the arrival of Richard of England, Philip Augustus of France, and Emperor Frederick Barbarossa. At the center of the power struggle is the unscrupulous Conrad of Montferrat who holds the important stronghold of Tyre.

Historical Accuracy: The main events of the story are based on historical record.

5792 *The Knights of Dark Renown*
Date of Publication: 1969
Subject(s): Middle Ages; Crusades
Historical character(s): Reynauld of Chatillon, Nobleman; Saladin, Ruler (sultan)
Time Period(s): 12th century (1183-1187)
Locale(s): Palestine

Summary: This novel tells the story of the defense of Jerusalem by the Crusaders. At the center of the tale is Reynauld of Chatillon, whose bloody exploits culminate in the famous battle of the Horns of Hatton and a final confrontation with Saladin.

Historical Accuracy: The major events in this story are based on established historical record, but many of the researched incidents have been embellished.

5793 *The Wolf at the Door*
Date of Publication: 1975
Subject(s): Middle Ages; Royalty—England; Baron's War
Historical character(s): John, Ruler (King of England); Eleanor of Aquitaine, Royalty (queen consort of Henry II); Isabella of Angouleme, Royalty (queen consort of King John); William Marshal, Nobleman (Earl of Pembroke)
Time Period(s): 13th century (1200-1216)
Locale(s): England

Summary: The novel offers an unsympathetic portrait of King John of England, who succeeds his heroic brother, Richard the Lionhearted. John is shown as petty, cowardly, and unchivalrous. His excesses and inadequacies lead to revolt among his barons and force the concessions that produce Magna Carta.

Historical Accuracy: The period background and historical events are authentic and accurate.

SAMUEL SHELLABARGER (1888-1954)
Born in Washington, D.C., Shellabarger was a member of the English Department of Princeton as well as a writer.

5794 *Captain From Castille*
Date of Publication: 1945
Subject(s): Royalty—Spain; Aztec Empire; Inquisition
Fictional character(s): Pedro de Vargas, Gentleman, Military Personnel (conquistador); Catana Perez, Saloon Hostess; Diego de Silva, Landowner, Government Official; Juan Gar-

cia, Adventurer, Military Personnel (conquistador); Coatl, Slave, Chieftain (Zapotec)

Historical character(s): Hernando Cortez, Explorer, Military Personnel (conquistador); Montezuma II, Ruler (Aztec emperor); Charles I, Ruler (King of Spain)

Time Period(s): 16th century (1518-1522)

Locale(s): Jaen, Spain; Tenochtitlan, Mexico; Valladolid, Spain

Summary: After critically wounding the malevolent Diego de Silva, who has falsely denounced the de Vargas family as heretics, young Pedro de Vargas is forced to flee Spain. He becomes a captain in Cortes' company of conquistadors and with his lover, Catana Perez, and best friend, Juan Garcia, takes part in the conquest of Mexico. When the three are taken prisoner by the Aztecs, they must trust the mercy of Coatl, de Silva's escaped slave and a Zapotec chief. Upon Pedro's return to Spain, he must outwit de Silva, who has sworn revenge against him.

Historical Accuracy: The events of the Mexican conquest are recounted primarily from the point of view of the Spanish. The novel provides an interesting account of Aztec and Spanish Catholic culture of the era, although this is first and foremost a romantic adventure story.

5795 The King's Cavalier

Date of Publication: 1950

Subject(s): Royalty—France

Fictional character(s): Blaise de Lalliere, Military Personnel (soldier); Anne Russell, Gentlewoman; Jean de Norville, Gentlewoman

Historical character(s): Francois I, Ruler (King of France); Charles, Duc de Bourbon, Nobleman

Time Period(s): 16th century (1523)

Locale(s): France

Summary: The novel dramatizes the story of a young Frenchman and Englishwoman caught up in the plots and counterplots surrounding the Bourbon conspiracy against Francis I. Charles, Duke of Bourbon, is in league with Henry VIII and has launched a rebellion against the king. Francis I is intent on seizing the Bourbon provinces and eliminating the last of the French feudal states. Romance and intrigue follow both plots.

Historical Accuracy: Shellabarger's knowledge of the period is full and precise.

5796 Lord Vanity

Date of Publication: 1953

Subject(s): Georgian Period; French and Indian War; Battle of Quebec

Fictional character(s): Richard Morandi, Gentleman; Marcello Tromba, Gentleman; Maritza Venire, Dancer (ballet)

Historical character(s): James Wolfe, Military Personnel (British general); Carlo Goldoni, Writer (dramatist); Beau Nash, Gentleman; John Wesley, Religious (evangelical leader)

Time Period(s): 1750s (1757)

Locale(s): Venice, Italy; Bath, England; Quebec, Quebec, Canada

Summary: The novel offers a panoramic depiction of 18th-century life that moves from the fashionable salons of Venice to Bath, then on to a climax in North America as General Wolfe's armies engage the French in the Battle of Quebec. The novel shows the Age of Enlightenment on the verge of revolutionary change.

Historical Accuracy: Shellabarger's reach exceeds his grasp here as he attempts to render the age in as full a depiction as possible. Linking the various scenes convincingly is the problem.

5797 Prince of Foxes

Date of Publication: 1947

Subject(s): Renaissance

Fictional character(s): Andrea Orsini, Adventurer; Camilla Baglione, Noblewoman

Historical character(s): Cesare Borgia, Military Personnel, Political Figure

Time Period(s): 16th century

Locale(s): Venice, Italy; Ferrara, Italy; Rome, Italy

Summary: This swashbuckling romance in the cloak-and-dagger tradition is set during the High Renaissance and concerns peasant-born Andrea Orsini, who is taken in by Cesare Borgia's charms and his promises of a united Italy. He is launched on a number of dangerous assignments on behalf of the Borgia cause before being saved by the love of a noble lady.

Historical Accuracy: Even though exaggeration and contrivance fuel the novel's non-stop action, Shellabarger uses his considerable knowledge to present an authentic re-creation of the High Renaissance's look and spirit.

5798 Tolbecken

Date of Publication: 1956

Subject(s): Family Saga; World War I

Fictional character(s): Rufus Tolbecken, Judge; Jared Tolbecken, Student, Military Personnel (soldier)

Historical character(s): Woodrow Wilson, Scholar

Time Period(s): 19th century; 20th century (1898-1918)

Locale(s): Dunstable, Delaware; Princeton, New Jersey; France

Summary: The Tolbecken family is one of the most distinguished in Delaware. The patriarchal Judge Rufus Tolbecken expects his grandson to carry on the family legacy. The novel explores the grandson's education and growth, and how torn between the tradition he is expected to preserve and the new forces of change. He must endure the horrors of World War I before he is able to make peace with his identity and heritage.

Historical Accuracy: There are interesting and authentic scenes of period undergraduate life at Princeton and its idealistic president, Woodrow Wilson. War scenes are little more than a sketch.

GENE SHELTON

5799 *Brazos Dreamer*

Date of Publication: 1993
Subject(s): American West; Biography, Fictionalized; Indians
Historical character(s): Robert Simpson Neighbors, Lawman (Texas Ranger), Government Official (Indian agent)
Time Period(s): 1840s; 1850s (1849-1859)
Locale(s): Brazos River, Texas

Summary: This is the story of Robert Simpson Neighbors, a former Texas Ranger and Indian agent during the turbulent years in Texas history between the Mexican War and the Civil War. Neighbors attempts to keep peace between the settlers and Comanches who find their way of life threatened by westward expansion.

Historical Accuracy: The novel is a fictional story based on the career of Neighbors with efforts made to portray events as accurately as possible.

5800 *Captain Jack*

Date of Publication: 1991
Subject(s): American West; Biography, Fictionalized; Mexican War
Historical character(s): John Coffee Hays, Lawman (Texas Ranger)
Time Period(s): 19th century (1839-1848)
Locale(s): Texas; Mexico

Summary: This volume of the Texas Legends series dramatizes the career of John Coffee Hays, a young surveyor from Tennessee who joins the Texas Rangers in their early days and fights against outlaws, Comanches, and Mexicans.

Historical Accuracy: The novel mixes fact and fiction while portraying dates, locations, and biographical details as accurately as possible.

5801 *Last Gun: The Legend of John Selman*

Date of Publication: 1991
Subject(s): American West; Crime and Criminals
Historical character(s): John Selman, Gunfighter, Lawman; John Wesley Hardin, Gunfighter, Outlaw
Time Period(s): 19th century (1863-1896)
Locale(s): El Paso, Texas

Summary: The novel tells the story of gunfighter, outlaw, and lawman John Selman. His career is vividly depicted, including his showdown with the notorious John Wesley Hardin.

Historical Accuracy: The novel is authentic and historically based.

5802 *Rawhider*

Date of Publication: 1992
Subject(s): American West; Crime and Criminals; Biography, Fictionalized
Historical character(s): Isom Prenice "Print" Olive, Rancher, Gunfighter

Time Period(s): 19th century (1864-1886)
Locale(s): Texas; Colorado; Nebraska

Summary: This installment of the Texas Legends series dramatizes the career of gunman and rancher Print Olive, called the meanest rawhider in the West. Olive arrives in Texas after the Civil War, grabbing land and dispersing homesteaders with the help of a gang that includes a former slave and ex-Confederate soldiers.

Historical Accuracy: The novel is a work of fiction based on Olive's life. The story employs actual dates, locations, and biographical details accurately, supplemented by invention.

5803 *Tascosa Gun: The Story of Jim East*

Date of Publication: 1992
Subject(s): American West; Crime and Criminals
Historical character(s): Jim East, Lawman (sheriff); William Bonney, Outlaw; Pat Garrett, Lawman (sheriff)
Time Period(s): 1880s
Locale(s): New Mexico; Tascosa, Texas

Summary: The novel offers the story of Jim East, western lawman who began as a cowboy on the Texas Panhandle. When he joins a posse to hunt for a gang of rustlers that includes Billy the Kid, he takes up the career of manhunting. Eventually he is elected sheriff and tries to keep the peace between ranchers and homesteaders.

Historical Accuracy: Based on historical events, the novel offers an authentic look at the West and its lawmen.

STEPHEN SHEPPARD (1945-)

English author Sheppard was born in Bristol and educated at Dartington Hall, where he began painting and acting. He later attended the Royal Academy of Dramatic Arts and has worked as an actor and painter. Sheppard spent 18 months researching the plot by four Americans to defraud the Bank of England of $2 million, which became the novel *The Four Hundred*.

5804 *The Four Hundred*

Date of Publication: 1979
Subject(s): Victorian Period; Crime and Criminals
Historical character(s): Austin Biron Bidwell, Criminal; George Bidwell, Criminal; Edwin Noyes, Criminal; George MacDonald, Criminal; Allan Pinkerton, Detective—Police; Nathan Rothschild, Banker, Financier; Peregrine Francis, Businessman (Bank of England manager)
Time Period(s): 1870s (1872-1873)
Locale(s): London, England; Paris, France; New York, New York

Summary: Based on an actual case that shook the Victorian world, the novel tells the story of four young Americans who come to London with a daring scheme to rob the Bank of England of 400,000 pounds.

Historical Accuracy: The novel uses the attempted robbery of the Bank of England in the 1870s as a departure point for an imagined story based on fact.

JAMES SHERBURNE (1925-)

An American novelist born in Michigan, Sherburne attended Berea College and graduated from the University of Kentucky. He has worked as a copywriter in advertising.

`5805` *Hacey Miller*

Date of Publication: 1971
Subject(s): Slavery; Antebellum South; Underground Railroad
Fictional character(s): Hacey Miller, Teenager
Historical character(s): Cassius Marcellus Clay, Diplomat, Abolitionist; Frederick Douglass, Abolitionist; Thomas Wentworth Higginson, Abolitionist
Time Period(s): 1840s; 1850s (1845-1858)
Locale(s): Lexington, Kentucky; Boston, Massachusetts; Berea, Kentucky

Summary: The abolitionist agitation in the years preceding the Civil War is described in the experiences of young Hacey Miller, the son of a shopkeeper in Lexington, Kentucky. When he attends the trial of the slave girl accused of murdering Cassius Clay's infant son, he finds his life connected with Clay and the abolitionist movement. Scenes include the founding of Berea College and the internal division within the antislavery movement of the time.

Historical Accuracy: The historical elements in the story are accurate and based on solid research.

`5806` *Poor Boy and a Long Way Home*

Date of Publication: 1984
Subject(s): Picaresque Adventure; Labor Movement; Motion Picture Industry
Fictional character(s): Glen Hatton, Teenager, Con Artist; Jake Holmquist, Labor Organizer; M.P. Gebhart, Director (film)
Historical character(s): D.W. Griffith, Director (film)
Time Period(s): 1900s; 1910s
Locale(s): Washington; Oregon; California

Summary: This picaresque novel follows the adventures of teenage con man Glen Hatton. Hatton journeys west to Oregon and Washington, where he meets a leader of the Wobblies, Jake Holmquist. Hatton tries to balance his experiences as a con man with Holmquist's idealism and finds Holmquist's standards difficult to meet.

Historical Accuracy: The story blends a fanciful plot with actual events in the early labor movement and film industry and a convincing evocation of the period.

`5807` *The Way to Fort Pillow*

Date of Publication: 1972
Subject(s): Civil War—U.S.; Slavery
Fictional character(s): Hacey Miller, Teacher, Military Personnel (Union soldier)
Historical character(s): Cassius Marcellus Clay, Abolitionist; Thomas Wentworth Higginson, Abolitionist
Time Period(s): 1850s; 1860s (1859-1865)
Locale(s): Kentucky; Washington, District of Columbia; Fort Pillow, Tennessee

Summary: This sequel to *Hacey Miller* begins in 1859 with the closing of Berea College in Kentucky. Miller joins the Union Army, where he is put in command of black troops. The novel chronicles battlefield action, intrigue in wartime Washington, and the massacre of black troops at the Battle of Fort Pillow.

Historical Accuracy: The account of the events at Fort Pillow is the author's own interpretation of what probably happened, though reports differ.

ANNE-MARIE SHERIDAN (1948-)

French-born Sheridan received her B.A. from Cambridge University. During her college years she worked as a secretary and as a companion to a businesswoman. She became a freelance writer in the 1970s.

`5808` *The Far-Off Rhapsody*

Date of Publication: 1977
Subject(s): Victorian Period; Franco-Prussian War; Paris Commune
Fictional character(s): Tessa Thursday, Foundling, Actress; Oliver Craven, Entertainer
Time Period(s): 19th century
Locale(s): Cornwall, England; Paris, France

Summary: This is a romantic story of Tessa Thursday, who emerges from the poorhouse intent on achieving fame as an actress. Her mentor is the entertainer Oliver Craven, who assists her in gaining notoriety in France. There, adventures mount in scenes during the Franco-Prussian War and the siege of Paris, during which Tessa's true identity is revealed.

Historical Accuracy: Though the emphasis is on romantic adventure, there are credible historical details of the period.

`5809` *Summoned to Darkness*

Date of Publication: 1978
Subject(s): Suspense; Mystery
Fictional character(s): Giles Demaury, Gentleman; Meg Demaury, Young Woman; Lorenzo Giolitti-Crispi, Royalty (prince), Police Officer
Time Period(s): 1890s (1891)
Locale(s): Venice, Italy

Summary: The novel tells the story of reclusive patriarch Giles Demaury, who summons his clan to his palazzo in Venice to choose an heir to the family fortune. An impoverished cousin, Meg Demaury, arrives from England and becomes the prime suspect when one of the assembled guests dies of poisoning.

Historical Accuracy: The period atmosphere is convincingly presented.

JANE SHERIDAN
(PSEUD. OF PAULINE GLEN WINSLOW)

Popular English crime and mystery novelist Winslow was born in London but moved to New York, where she attended Hunter College, the New School, and Columbia University. She has worked as a freelance court reporter in New York City.

5810 *Damaris*

Date of Publication: 1978
Subject(s): Regency Period; Napoleonic Wars
Fictional character(s): Damaris Malfrey, Noblewoman (countess); d'Egremont, Nobleman (marquis); Howard Booth, Businessman, Political Figure
Time Period(s): 18th century; 19th century (1794-1817)
Locale(s): England; United States

Summary: Against the backdrop of Regency England during the Napoleonic era, scandal causes Damaris, Countess of Malfrey, to flee with her French lover, the Marquis d'Egremont to America. There amidst rough democratic values, Damaris builds a new life assisted by Yankee Howard Booth.

Historical Accuracy: The emphasis is on romantic complication rather than a full documentation of the period.

5811 *Love at Sunset*

Date of Publication: 1982
Subject(s): Edwardian Period
Fictional character(s): Clarissa Devereaux, Gentlewoman
Historical character(s): Edward VII, Ruler (King of England)
Time Period(s): 1900s; 1910s (1901-1910)
Locale(s): England; Germany; France

Summary: The novel continues the story of the St. Cloud women with the story of Clarissa Devereaux, the granddaughter of Damaris and the daughter of Amanda in *My Lady Hoyden*. Complications in love lead Clarissa to Germany and France, where the politics of the period share the stage with the affairs of the heart.

Historical Accuracy: The novel interweaves a fictional story with convincing period elements that create a plausible historical backdrop.

5812 *My Lady Hoyden*

Date of Publication: 1981
Subject(s): Victorian Period; Civil War—U.S.
Fictional character(s): Lady Amanda Heron, Gentlewoman
Historical character(s): Edward, Prince of Wales, Royalty; Florence Nightingale, Nurse, Gentlewoman
Time Period(s): 1860s; 1870s (1861-1871)
Locale(s): England; France; United States

Summary: The author continues the story of the St. Cloud women begun in *Damaris*. The time is the 1860s and Lady Amanda Heron, the daughter of Damaris, relentlessly pursues both a career as a nurse and the man she loves, even though he is her sister's husband. Her persistence takes her to America during the Civil War and to Imperial France.

Historical Accuracy: The novel offers a colorful period backdrop for this romantic story.

DAN SHERMAN (1950-)

Born in Los Angeles, Sherman attended the University of Oregon and graduated from the University of California, Northridge. He has worked as a freelance journalist and public relations copywriter.

5813 *The Man Who Loved Mata Hari*

Date of Publication: 1985
Subject(s): World War I; Espionage
Fictional character(s): Nicholas Gray, Artist
Historical character(s): Mata Hari, Spy (suspected), Dancer
Time Period(s): 1900s; 1910s (1904-1917)
Locale(s): Paris, France

Summary: The novel explores the colorful and tragic life of the dancer-courtesan called Mata Hari. Loved by important and influential men in Germany and France, she was executed in 1917 by the French as a spy. The novel is told from the perspective of a devoted lover, English painter Nicholas Gray. It makes a strong case that Mata Hari never was a spy and that she was set up with forged evidence by the British and French as a scapegoat for the failure of the Battle of the Somme.

Historical Accuracy: The author describes the novel as fiction extending from a core of truth. The case exonerating Mata Hari is based on an extensive review of the actual evidence, though the plot-line of the story is invented.

5814 *The Traitor*

Date of Publication: 1987
Subject(s): American Revolution; Espionage; Mystery
Fictional character(s): Matty Grove, Spy
Historical character(s): Benjamin Tallmadge, Military Personnel (intelligence officer); George Washington, Military Personnel (army commander); Paul Revere, Patriot
Time Period(s): 1770s; 1780s (1779-1780)
Locale(s): Morristown, New Jersey; Philadelphia, Pennsylvania

Summary: This espionage thriller is set during the American Revolution. Two lovers—an American seamstress and a young English officer, who are also spies for the rebels—are found brutally murdered. Washington's foremost spymaster, Benjamin Tallmadge, begins an investigation that leads to suspicion of traitors on Washington's closest staff.

Historical Accuracy: The novel is an inventive and imaginative story relying on a solid background of actual events and circumstances.

DELIA SHERMAN (1951-)

5815 *The Porcelain Dove*

Date of Publication: 1993
Subject(s): French Revolution; Mystery
Fictional character(s): Berthe Duvet, Servant, Orphan; Adele du Fourchet, Noblewoman; Duc de Malvoeux, Nobleman
Time Period(s): 18th century (1745-1789)
Locale(s): Paris, France; Jura Mountains, France

Summary: The life of French aristocrats in the years leading up to the French Revolution is portrayed in this story of a noble family dealing with a curse. The dark and broody scenery of the Jura mountains in France is original.

Historical Accuracy: The novel is vividly imagined and supported by clear evidence of research. The author brings a fresh slant on the period.

JORY SHERMAN (1932-)

Western and frontier novelist Sherman was born in Minnesota and attended San Francisco State University and the University of Minnesota. Sherman has worked as an advertising copywriter, computer programmer, actor, editor, and newspaper columnist. He attempts in his novels to break the mold of the Western novel and to take it in new directions. Sherman considers the novel of the American West to be America's native art form.

5816 *The Arkansas River*

Date of Publication: 1991
Subject(s): American West
Fictional character(s): Francisco Serrano, Farmer; Jacob Stonecipher, Mountain Man
Time Period(s): 19th century (1832-1858)
Locale(s): Arkansas River, Colorado; Taos, New Mexico

Summary: This is a panoramic saga of the settlers and mountain men who opened up the Arkansas River Valley of southern Colorado. The story focuses on the experiences of the Serranos, a family of farmers, and the Stoneciphers.

Historical Accuracy: The novel offers a convincing period background.

5817 *Eagles of Destiny*

Date of Publication: 1990
Subject(s): American West; Indians
Fictional character(s): Jeremiah York, Trader; Estrellita de Rojas, Heiress; Tecolote, Indian (Comanche), Warrior
Time Period(s): 1830s
Locale(s): Santa Fe, New Mexico; St. Louis, Missouri

Summary: Jeremiah York is a trader intent on making his fortune working the Santa Fe Trail between Missouri and the Mexican colonies. His greatest challenge comes when a headstrong Mexican heiress, Estrellita de Rojas, falls in love with him despite being betrothed to another. They must contend with the Comanches in their efforts to be together.

Historical Accuracy: The story paints solid and convincing period details into a believable portrait of the times.

5818 *The Grass Kingdom*

Date of Publication: 1993
Subject(s): American West; Ku Klux Klan; Ranching
Fictional character(s): Matt Baron, Rancher; Tom Casebolt, Rancher
Time Period(s): 1920s
Locale(s): Baronsville, Texas

Summary: During the 1920s, rancher Matt Baron and foreman Tom Casebolt contend with rustlers who have murdered a young cowhand. Baron and Casebolt hunt the killers down. Their code of the West comes in conflict with the period of Prohibition and the Ku Klux Klan.

Historical Accuracy: The novel convincingly juxtaposes the old ways of the West and the new era with many period details.

5819 *Horne's Law*

Date of Publication: 1988
Subject(s): American West; Ranching
Fictional character(s): Jackson Horne, Rancher, Mountain Man; Dan Reinhardt, Rancher
Time Period(s): 19th century (pre-Civil War)
Locale(s): Sky Valley, Colorado

Summary: Jackson Horne desires to be left alone on his land in Colorado. When Dan Reinhardt moves in to take the land and to threaten Horne, Horne must act to defend himself.

Historical Accuracy: The novel offers convincing Western elements and period details.

5820 *The Medicine Horn*

Date of Publication: 1991
Subject(s): American West; Settlement of the American Frontier
Fictional character(s): Lemuel Hawke, Frontiersman; Roberta Hawke, Spouse; Morgan Hawke, Child
Time Period(s): 18th century; 19th century (1793-1843)
Locale(s): Kentucky; St. Louis, Missouri; Mississippi Valley, United States

Summary: In the first of the Buckskinners Saga, Lemuel Hawke, a poor farmer from Virginia, heads west across the Cumberlands into the wilderness of Kentucky, then on to French St. Louis and the high plains. The story of Hawke, his wife Roberta, and his young son Morgan is told against the backdrop of life on the American frontier.

Historical Accuracy: The period background and elements of frontier life are authentic and convincing.

5821 *Rio Grande*

Date of Publication: 1994
Subject(s): American West; Spanish Colonies
Fictional character(s): Don Facundo Melgares, Military Personnel (Spanish officer); Matthew Caine, Mountain Man
Historical character(s): Zebulon Pike, Explorer
Time Period(s): 1800s (1805-1807)
Locale(s): Santa Fe, New Mexico; Rocky Mountains, North America

Summary: This volume of the Rivers West series is set in the American Southwest and the Rocky Mountains in the years immediately following the Louisiana Purchase. Matthew Caine, mountain man and U.S. agent, is assigned to make friendly overtures to the Indians in the Spanish territory. His adventures among both the Indians and the Spanish are dramatized.

Historical Accuracy: The period elements are credible.

5822 *Song of the Cheyenne*

Date of Publication: 1987
Subject(s): American West; Indians; Tribal Life—Native American
Fictional character(s): Sun Runner, Indian (Cheyenne), Warrior; Old Lodge, Indian (Cheyenne), Shaman
Time Period(s): 19th century

Locale(s): Great Plains

Summary: Cheyenne warrior Sun Runner comes of age during the last great days of the Plains Indians before the white migration that will change the Indians forever. Sun Runner is shown in battle against the Cheyenne's great enemies, the Pawnee.

Historical Accuracy: The details of Indian tribal customs are convincingly drawn.

`5823` *Trapper's Moon*

Date of Publication: 1994

Subject(s): American West; Settlement of the American Frontier

Fictional character(s): Lemuel Hawke, Frontiersman; Morgan Hawke, Frontiersman, Teenager; Major Angus MacDonald, Frontiersman

Time Period(s): 19th century

Locale(s): Rocky Mountains, North America

Summary: In Book Two of the Buckskinner's series, Lemuel Hawke and his teenage son journey to the rich and unexplored trapping grounds of the Rocky Mountains. Along the way they leave a dead enemy, and they are trailed by the dead man's family. They join a band of trappers and mountain men and become the target of Major MacDonald.

Historical Accuracy: The novel features convincing elements of frontier life of the period.

FRANCES SHERWOOD (1940-)

Born in Washington D.C., Sherwood holds a master's degree from Johns Hopkins. She has taught creative writing and journalism at Indiana University and has been a full professor there since 1994. Twice a recipient of the O. Henry Award for her short stories, she has published a collection of them called *Everything You've Heard Is True.* Her fictionalized biography of Mary Wollstonecraft, *Vindication*, was a Book of the Month Club selection and has been translated into eleven languages.

`5824` *Vindication*

Date of Publication: 1993

Subject(s): Literary Life; Georgian Period; French Revolution

Historical character(s): Mary Wollstonecraft Godwin, Writer; William Godwin, Writer; Henry Fuseli, Artist; William Blake, Writer

Time Period(s): 18th century; 19th century (1780-1800)

Locale(s): London, England; Paris, France; Yorkshire, England

Summary: This is a fictionalized biography of Mary Wollstonecraft, pioneering women's rights advocate. She makes her way first as a governess, then as a writer. Wollstonecraft has a series of ill-fated love affairs, including one with an American opportunist in France during the Revolution. The scenes and characters are historical, but the attitude is decidedly modern.

Historical Accuracy: There are many deviations in the novel from the actual history of Mary Wollstonecraft and her contemporaries.

VALERIE SHERWOOD

`5825` *Lisbon*

Date of Publication: 1989

Subject(s): Romance; Earthquakes; Disasters—Natural

Fictional character(s): Charlotte Vayle, Spouse (of Keynes); Rowan Keynes, Gentleman; Tom Westing, Sailor

Time Period(s): 18th century (1739-1755)

Locale(s): Lisbon, Portugal

Summary: This romantic novel set in 18th-century Lisbon tells the story of Englishwoman Charlotte Vayle. Separated from her seaman lover Tom Westing, she marries the elderly Rowan Keynes. With him she goes to Lisbon, where she is reunited with Westing and is forced to choose between her husband and her lover as disaster strikes the city.

Historical Accuracy: The period background of the story is authentic and forms a believable context for the novel's major dramatic situation.

FRANCES L. SHINE (1927-)

Born in Worcester, Massachusetts, Shine is a graduate of Radcliffe College and Cornell University. She is a novelist, short story writer, and poet. A short story earned her the National Fine Arts Award in 1952. Her first novel was *The Life-Adjustment of Harry Blake.*

`5826` *Conjuror's Journal*

Date of Publication: 1978

Subject(s): Magic; Theatrical Life; Picaresque Adventure

Fictional character(s): Joshua Medley, Entertainer, Magician

Time Period(s): 1790s (1793-1795)

Locale(s): New England

Summary: Life in New England during the 1790s is recorded in the journal of Joshua Medley, a mulatto magician and entertainer. He travels from town to town as he searches for the secret of his heritage. In the process the colorful life of the period is revealed.

Historical Accuracy: The details of theatrical conventions of the period are convincingly drawn.

GEORGE SHIPWAY (1908-)

An English author born in India, Shipway attended Sandhurst and was commissioned in the British cavalry, serving in India. Shipway retired from the army as a lieutenant-colonel and then worked as a schoolmaster in Hampshire, England.

`5827` *Free Lance*

Date of Publication: 1975

Subject(s): British Raj

Fictional character(s): Hugo Amaurey, Gentleman, Adventurer; Charles Marriott, Gentleman
Time Period(s): 1800s
Locale(s): India

Summary: In this swashbuckling adventure set in India during the early 19th century, two young Englishmen, Hugo Amaurey and Charles Marriott, enter service in the East India Company. Amaurey becomes an adventuring free lancer, captures an entire city, and defeats a notorious villain before returning to service.

Historical Accuracy: The novel is filled with color and convincing details of period India.

5828 *The Imperial Governor*
Date of Publication: 1968
Subject(s): Roman Empire
Fictional character(s): Suetonious Paulinus, Government Official (Roman governor)
Historical character(s): Nero, Ruler (Roman emperor)
Time Period(s): 1st century (60s)
Locale(s): England; Rome, Roman Empire

Summary: The Imperial Governor of Roman Britain in the first century, Suetonious Paulinus, offers his memoirs. He reflects on his career and the events that brought him to this outpost of the empire and battle with Britain's Queen Boadicea and the Druids. Corruption among the Romans and the final rebellion of the British tribes must be confronted by Paulinus.

Historical Accuracy: The novel's story is fictional, but the atmosphere of Roman Britain is convincing.

5829 *The Knight*
Date of Publication: 1970
Subject(s): Middle Ages
Historical character(s): Humphrey Visdelou, Knight; Geoffrey de Mandeville, Nobleman (count)
Time Period(s): 12th century (1135-1144)
Locale(s): England

Summary: After the death of Henry I in the 12th century, England is thrown into civil war by the dynastic struggle between Queen Matilda and King Stephen. During this period, the novel follows the experiences of one knight, Humphrey Visdelou, who is caught up in the conflict and in the wake of the ambitious Count Geoffrey de Mandeville.

Historical Accuracy: The historical background and events of the story are authentic, as are all of the major characters and most of the minor ones.

5830 *The Paladin*
Date of Publication: 1972
Subject(s): Middle Ages; Royalty—England
Historical character(s): Walter Tirel, Nobleman; William Rufus, Ruler (King of England); Robert II Curthose, Royalty (prince); Henry, Royalty (prince)
Time Period(s): 11th century; 12th century (1070-1100)
Locale(s): Normandy, France; England

Summary: Set against the maneuvering for power following the death of William the Conqueror, the novel follows the career of the actual, but shadowy, figure of Walter Tirel. Tirel is a young nobleman who comes into contact with William's ambitious three sons—Robert Curthose, William Rufus, and Henry. His allegiance shifts from one brother to the next until he attempts unsuccessfully to save the life of Rufus, who is killed mysteriously in England's New Forest.

Historical Accuracy: This tale is fiction embroidered in a historical patchwork. The story offers a debatable interpretation of the death of William II.

MAXINE SHORE

5831 *The Captive Princess*
Date of Publication: 1952
Subject(s): Roman Empire; Christianity
Fictional character(s): Gwladys, Royalty (princess)
Historical character(s): Caradoc, Ruler (King of Britain); Paul, Biblical Figure; Joseph of Arimathea, Biblical Figure
Time Period(s): 1st century
Locale(s): England; Gaul; Rome, Roman Empire

Summary: The novel dramatizes the Roman conquest of Britain and the spread of early Christianity. The story's central character is Gwladys, the daughter of Caradoc, King of Britain. After the conquest of Britain by the Romans, she is taken to Rome where she becomes a Christian and is renamed Claudia.

Historical Accuracy: The inspiration for the story comes from St. Paul's letter to Timothy which mentions Claudia. The period elements are authentic and drawn from the writings of Jerome, Tacitus, and Seneca.

EARL SHORRIS (1936-)

American comic writer Shorris was born in Chicago and attended the University of Chicago. He has held various jobs as a journalist and in advertising in Texas, California, and New York, and was named senior vice president of N.W. Ayer ABH International in New York City. As a novelist, Shorris is known for his black humor and strong sense of the absurd.

5832 *Under the Fifth Sun: A Novel of Pancho Villa*
Date of Publication: 1980
Subject(s): Mexican Revolution; Biography, Fictionalized
Historical character(s): Francisco Villa, Revolutionary, Outlaw; Francisco Indalecio Madero, Political Figure
Time Period(s): 19th century; 20th century (1878-1923)
Locale(s): Mexico

Summary: The novel dramatizes the career of Mexican revolutionary leader Pancho Villa and attempts to find an alternative to the American view of Villa as a drunken, illiterate bandit. Villa is shown as an unschooled peon who becomes a brilliant general and commands the only invasion of the continental

U.S. in the 20th century. As the revolution unravels, Villa sees its goals betrayed.

Historical Accuracy: Clearly a partisan on behalf of a heroic Villa, the author offers a version of the events of the Mexican Revolution shaped by the novel's thesis.

JOHN HENRY SHORTHOUSE
(1834-1903)

Shorthouse was an English novelist principally known for *John Inglesant* and other works of fiction of less importance.

`5833` *John Inglesant*

Date of Publication: 1881
Subject(s): Civil War—England; Religious Conflict
Fictional character(s): John Inglesant, Philosopher; Eustace Inglesant, Gentleman
Historical character(s): Charles I, Ruler (King of England); William Laud, Religious (Archbishop of Canterbury); John Milton, Writer
Time Period(s): 17th century
Locale(s): London, England; Ireland; Italy (Rome, Siena, Naples)

Summary: This historical-philosophical romance centers on the troubled reign of Charles I and the turmoil between Catholics and Puritans. Inglesant, of a philosophical and spiritual bent, agrees to serve the Jesuits as an agent for the king. He is eventually imprisoned and leaves for Italy when Charles is executed, both to find spiritual meaning and to solve the mystery of his brother's murder.

Historical Accuracy: This is one of the best pictures of the complicated political and ecclesiastical affairs of England in the 17th century. The historical appeal is now much stronger than the philosophical speculations.

EDWIN SHRAKE

`5834` *Blessed McGill*

Date of Publication: 1967
Subject(s): American West; Religious Life
Historical character(s): Peter Hermano McGill, Frontiersman
Time Period(s): 1880s
Locale(s): Southwest

Summary: Peter Hermano McGill, a frontiersman of the American West, was the first North American to be beatified by the Roman Catholic Church. This novel dramatizes his life, first as a lawless youth and later his repentance as he gives up his life to save a Franciscan mission.

Historical Accuracy: The details about McGill's life are based on a manuscript attributed to him. The story offers an authentic portrait of the West during the 1880s.

SUSAN RICHARDS SHREVE (1939-)

An American professor of literature, novelist, and children's author, Shreve was born in Toledo, Ohio, and attended the University of Pennsylvania and the University of Virginia.

Shreve's adult novels include *A Country of Strangers*, *Queen of Hearts*, and *Dreaming of Heroes*.

`5835` *Daughters of the New World*

Date of Publication: 1992
Subject(s): Family Saga; World War I
Fictional character(s): Anna Jermyn, Immigrant; Amanda Jermyn, Photographer
Time Period(s): 19th century; 20th century
Locale(s): United States; Europe

Summary: This multi-generational family saga begins in 1890 as Anna Jermyn comes to American from England as a servant. She makes her way in the wilderness of Wisconsin. Her daughter, Amanda, continues the story, as she follows her lover to the Western Front in World War I disguised as a man.

Historical Accuracy: The World War I elements are particularly unconvincing.

BERNARD SHRIMSLEY (1931-)

An English writer born in London, Shrimsley has worked as a newspaper editor.

`5836` *Lion Rampant*

Date of Publication: 1984
Subject(s): Royalty—England; Jacobean Period; Espionage
Historical character(s): Henry Frederick Stuart, Royalty (Prince of Wales); James I, Ruler (King of England); Frances Howard, Noblewoman; Robert Carr, Nobleman (Viscount Rochester)
Time Period(s): 17th century (1612)
Locale(s): England

Summary: Set in the court world of James I, the novel offers a provocative solution to one of history's greatest mysteries: What happened to Henry Frederick Stuart, Prince of Wales, who might have been crowned Henry IX? His story, including his love for the ambitious Lady Frances Howard, who juggles the affections of both the prince and the king's favorite, Robert Carr, is played out to its bloody conclusion.

Historical Accuracy: The period elements are convincing and authentic, though the novel's story involves some interpretations that are by no means unambiguous.

LINDA LAY SHULER

Born in Los Angeles, Shuler attended the University of California, Los Angeles and Southern Methodist University. She was the owner of a radio, and TV produc tion company and began writing when her husband retired.

`5837` *Let the Drum Speak: A Novel of Ancient America*

Date of Publication: 1996
Subject(s): Indians; Tribal Life—Native American; Prehistory
Fictional character(s): Antelope, Indian; Chomac, Indian
Time Period(s): 13th century
Locale(s): Southwest, North America

Summary: The third volume of the Time Circle Quartet on pre-Columbian Indian life in America takes up the adventures of Kwani's daughter, Antelope. She accompanies her husband, Chomoc, on a journey to Hasinai in what will become the state of Oklahoma. There she comes into conflict with ruler of the city who becomes her enemy.

Historical Accuracy: The novel is based on extensive archaeological and anthropological research that produces an authentic picture of the prehistoric past of Indian culture.

5838 *She Who Remembers*

Date of Publication: 1988
Subject(s): Indians; Tribal Life—Native American
Fictional character(s): Kwani, Indian (Anasazi), Wanderer; Kokopelli, Indian (Toltec), Shaman
Time Period(s): 13th century (1270)
Locale(s): Southwest, North America

Summary: This story of pre-Columbian Indian life in the 13th century involves Kwani, whose blue eyes suggest Viking ancestors. She is branded a witch and cast out of her tribe. Her wandering takes her throughout the Southwest and the Toltec kingdom to the south in pursuit of a new home, contending with betrayal and natural disasters.

Historical Accuracy: The author explains that the story is her version of what may have been, based on her own research.

5839 *Voice of the Eagle*

Date of Publication: 1992
Subject(s): Indians; Tribal life—Native American
Fictional character(s): Kwani, Indian (Anasazi), Shaman; Tolonqua, Indian, Spouse
Time Period(s): 13th century
Locale(s): Southwest, North America

Summary: The novel follows *She Who Remembers* and continues the story of Kwani, spiritual guide of the Anasazi tribe in the 13th century. Now with her husband, Tolonqua, and her newborn son, Kwani journeys west to Tolonqua's home, the last Pueblo city before the Great Plains. Marauding tribes threaten, and Kwani must persuade the townspeople to build a new fortified city while dealing with the tribe's suspicions about her and her powers.

Historical Accuracy: The novel is based upon the research of historians, anthropologists, and archeologists and offers a plausible version of life during the period.

SANDRA SHULMAN (1944-)

An American born in London, Shulman worked as a journalist and film researcher, as well as a broadcaster. She is a founding member of the Social Democratic Party and an ardent feminist whose novel's reflect the role of women in the past.

5840 *The Florentine*

Date of Publication: 1973
Subject(s): Renaissance; Identity—Concealed; Artistic Life
Fictional character(s): Francesca de Narni, Gentlewoman

Historical character(s): Lorenzo de Medici, Nobleman; Domenico Ghirlandajo, Artist; Leonardo da Vinci, Artist; Girolamo Savonarola, Religious (monk), Zealot; Sandro Botticelli, Artist; Giovanni Pico della Mirandola, Philosopher
Time Period(s): 15th century (1480s)
Locale(s): Florence, Italy

Summary: In Renaissance Florence, the only daughter of a wealthy family, Francesca de Narni, is caught up in the intrigue surrounding Lorenzo de Medici's rule. To survive she disguises herself as a boy and comes into contact with many of the leading figures of the time while pursuing her obsession for revenge and independence.

Historical Accuracy: The background of this fictional story is authentic and convincing.

GEORGE NAUMAN SHUSTER
(1894-1977)

Born in Lancaster, Wisconsin, journalist and educator Shuster was the author of books on 20th-century Germany, English literature, and education. He attended the University of Notre Dame, the University of Poitiers, and Columbia University and served in the Intelligence Section of the U.S. Army during World War II. A former president of Hunter College and assistant to the president of the University of Notre Dame, Shuster has been called an interpreter of Roman Catholicism to the modern world. His works include *The Catholic Spirit in Modern English Literature*, *The Germans*, and *Education and Moral Wisdom*.

5841 *Look Away!*

Date of Publication: 1939
Subject(s): Civil War—U.S.; Espionage
Fictional character(s): Robert Treloar, Lawyer, Spy; Edith Treloar, Spouse
Time Period(s): 1860s
Locale(s): Wisconsin

Summary: At the outbreak of the Civil War Kentuckian Robert Treloar is torn between his love for his northern wife and his loyalty to the Southern cause. He becomes a Confederate spy, and Edith Treloar struggles to maintain her family through the ensuing conflict.

Historical Accuracy: The novel is richly textured with authentic period elements and a convincing background.

SAM SICILIANO

5842 *The Angel of the Opera: Sherlock Holmes Meets the Phantom of the Opera*

Date of Publication: 1994
Subject(s): Mystery; Victorian Period; Theatrical Life
Fictional character(s): Sherlock Holmes, Detective—Private; Henry Verwien, Doctor; Eirik, Spirit (phantom)
Time Period(s): 1890s (1891)
Locale(s): Paris, France; Brittany, France

Summary: Sherlock Holmes is asked to exorcise the Paris Opera of its Phantom. Holmes is accompanied by his cousin Dr. Verwien and they enter the labyrinthian world of the Phantom for an operatic climax. Holmes is updated here, shorn of his Victorian proclivities and suffering the angst of modern life.

Historical Accuracy: The novel is filled with details about the Paris Opera. Traditionalists will find in this novel a Holmes for the 1990s.

WILLIAM SIDNEY
(PSEUD. OF WILLIAM DIETERLE)

Dieterle was the director of such classic American films as *The Devil and Daniel Webster*, *The Hunchback of Notre Dame*, *Juarez*, and *The Life of Emile Zola*.

5843 *The Good Tidings*

Date of Publication: 1950
Subject(s): Biblical Story
Historical character(s): John the Baptist, Biblical Figure; Salome, Biblical Figure; Herod Antipas, Ruler (King of Judea); Jesus Christ, Biblical Figure; Herodias, Spouse (of Herod)
Time Period(s): 1st century
Locale(s): Israel

Summary: The novel tells the story of John the Baptist and his ministry. After spending time in the desert, John receives a divine call to preach repentance in preparation for the coming of the Messiah. John's message and popularity lead to his tragic end at the hands of Herod, Herodias, and Salome.

Historical Accuracy: The dialogue is marred by anachronisms, and errors of Talmudic law and ancient Jewish customs abound.

BENJAMIN SIEGEL (1914-1991)

American writer Siegel was born in Brooklyn, New York. His novels include *Witch of Salem* and, as Matthew Benn, *Private Practice*. He also contributed short stories to *McCall's*, *Saturday Evening Post*, and other periodicals.

5844 *A Kind of Justice*

Date of Publication: 1960
Subject(s): Elizabethan Period; Jews
Fictional character(s): Andrew Bundy, Young Man
Time Period(s): 16th century (1580s)
Locale(s): London, England; Spain; Venice, Italy

Summary: When Andrew Bundy's wife is betrayed to the Inquisition by an English sailor, Andrew journeys to Elizabethan London to find and kill the man responsible for her death. As a Jew outlawed in England at the time, his life is in danger from the moment he arrives.

Historical Accuracy: The novel graphically and authentically delivers a realistic portrait of Elizabethan London.

5845 *The Sword and the Promise*

Date of Publication: 1959

Subject(s): Roman Empire; Jewish Revolt
Fictional character(s): Bias, Doctor; Gallus, Nobleman
Historical character(s): Hadrian, Ruler (Roman emperor); Simon Bar Kokhba, Revolutionary
Time Period(s): 2nd century
Locale(s): Rome, Roman Empire; Alexandria, Egypt; Israel

Summary: Set in the second-century world of the emperor Hadrian's Roman Empire, the novel follows the Greek physician Bias, whose story takes him from Imperial Rome to Alexandria and to Judea and involvement in the Jewish Revolt. Bias' nemesis is a decadent Roman aristocrat, Gallus, who causes Bias' search for a meaningful life against a backdrop of Roman oppression.

Historical Accuracy: Factual events are interwoven in this mainly fictional story with a plausible historical background.

HENRYK SIENKIEWICZ (1846-1916)

Internationally acclaimed Polish novelist and short story writer Sienkiewicz is the author of *Portrait of America*, a collection of letters describing his journey through the United States. He also wrote historical novels and was awarded the Nobel Prize for Literature in 1905.

5846 *The Deluge*

Date of Publication: 1886
Subject(s): Independence—Poland; Military Life
Fictional character(s): Andrei Kmita, Military Personnel; Olenka, Heroine
Historical character(s): Yanush Radziwill, Royalty (prince); Kordetzki, Religious; Boguslav, Royalty (prince)
Time Period(s): 17th century (1655-1657)
Locale(s): Poland; Lithuania; Prussia

Summary: The second novel of Sienkiewicz's trilogy is set against the bloody backdrop of the Swedish invasion of Poland in 1655. The emphasis is on exciting military action and the plots and counterplots of characters, real and imagined, working for and against independence for Eastern Europe. *The Deluge* follows *With Fire and Sword*. The trilogy concludes with *Fire in the Steppe*.

Historical Accuracy: The novel is a sweeping panorama of a time and a place that convinces in its details.

5847 *Fire in the Steppe*

Date of Publication: 1889
Subject(s): Independence—Poland; Military Life
Fictional character(s): Pan Volodyovski, Military Personnel; Basia, Heroine; Pan Zagloba, Military Personnel
Historical character(s): Jan III Sobieski, Nobleman
Time Period(s): 17th century (1668-1673)
Locale(s): Poland

Summary: *Fire in the Steppe* follows *The Deluge* as the concluding volume of Sienkiewicz's trilogy. The scene is the invasion of Poland by the Turks. East and West confront one another in an all-out battle of heroic action. The novel features a huge cast of characters meant to illustrate various personalities of the age.

Historical Accuracy: This is the most realistic of Sienkiewicz's novels. He has reduced his earlier idealization of military glory for a more realistic depiction.

5848 *Quo Vadis*

Date of Publication: 1895
Subject(s): Roman Empire; Christianity
Fictional character(s): Vinicius, Nobleman; Lygia, Royalty (princess)
Historical character(s): Nero, Ruler (emperor); Peter, Religious, Biblical Figure
Time Period(s): 1st century (64)
Locale(s): Rome, Roman Empire

Summary: The novel is a masterpiece of the historical recreation of the Roman Empire and the early years of the Christian church. A Roman patrician falls in love with a foreign Christian princess. First plotting to take her by force, Vinicius is subsequently converted to Lygia's faith. There are strong scenes of Nero's villainy and the fire of Rome.

Historical Accuracy: There are few better panoramic depictions of the Roman Empire, an exciting conjunction of history and a gripping dramatic story.

5849 *The Teutonic Knights*

Date of Publication: 1900
Subject(s): Middle Ages; Independence—Poland
Fictional character(s): Macko, Veteran; Zbyszko, Young Man
Time Period(s): 14th century; 15th century (1399-1410)
Locale(s): Poland

Summary: This epic of medieval life is set at the turn of the 15th century when a new ruling dynasty of Poland and Lithuania threatens the preeminence of the Teutonic Knights, a German religious brotherhood brought into the Baltic Sea area to quell the Prussian population. They quickly and ruthlessly subjugate the populace. The novel follows the adventures of Macko, a war veteran, and his young nephew, Zbyszko, as they struggle against the repressive Teutonic Knights.

Historical Accuracy: The range is panoramic, capturing the age, the customs of the knights, and important events, such as the Battle of Grunwald, with authority.

5850 *With Fire and Sword*

Date of Publication: 1883
Subject(s): Independence—Poland; Cossacks; Military Life
Fictional character(s): Pan Yan Skshetuski, Military Personnel; Bogun, Military Personnel; Helena Kurtsevich, Royalty (princess)
Historical character(s): Yeremi Vishnyevetski, Royalty (prince), Military Personnel
Time Period(s): 17th century (1647)
Locale(s): Poland; Ukraine

Summary: This is the first of three novels celebrating Polish military history in the 17th century. The events are the revolt of the Cossacks and the heroic defense of Zbarez by the Poles in the days of the Commonwealth. Pan Yan is a young Polish officer whose love for the Princess Helena is played out

against a backdrop of heroic military action. The trilogy continues with *The Deluge*.

Historical Accuracy: The emphasis is on military action, which is described with authenticity. Characterization is negligible, even though the trilogy has been called a "Polish *Gone With the Wind*."

ROBERTA SILMAN (1934-)

Born in Brooklyn, New York, Silman was educated at Cornell University and Sarah Lawrence College. She worked as a secretary and science writer for *Saturday Review* before becoming a freelance writer. She is the author of the novel *Boundaries*, a volume of short stories, *Blood Relations*, and *Somebody Else's Child*, a children's book.

5851 *Beginning the World Again*

Date of Publication: 1990
Subject(s): Science; World War II
Fictional character(s): Lisa Fialka, Spouse; Peter Fialka, Scientist (physicist); Jacob Wunderlich, Scientist (physicist)
Historical character(s): Enrico Fermi, Scientist (physicist); J. Robert Oppenheimer, Scientist (physicist)
Time Period(s): 1940s
Locale(s): Los Alamos, New Mexico

Summary: This novel takes us behind the scenes at the creation of the atomic bomb through the perspective of Lisa Fialka, the wife of one of the Manhattan Project's many scientists. She offers a personalized view of life at Los Alamos, but the novel attempts even more: a full treatise on the events and players in this critical period.

Historical Accuracy: The novel blends the imagined and the factual and convincingly captures the atmosphere of the period.

ALFRED SILVER (1951-)

Canadian writer born in Manitoba, Silver attended vocational school in Winnipeg. He has been an actor, musician, writer, cab driver, and guitar teacher.

5852 *Lord of the Plains*

Date of Publication: 1990
Subject(s): Indians; Tribal Life—Native American; Northwest Rebellion
Historical character(s): Gabriel Dumont, Indian (Metis), Leader; Madeline Dumont, Spouse; Louis Riel, Revolutionary, Leader (rebellion)
Time Period(s): 1880s (1885)
Locale(s): Northwest Territories, Canada

Summary: The novel tells the story of Canada's Northwest Rebellion during the 1880s when the Indians were starving on the reservations and a corrupt government in Ottawa ignored their pleas for assistance. At the center of the story are Gabriel and Madeline Dumont, leaders of the Metis, the half-Indian culture of the Great Plains.

Historical Accuracy: The framework for the story is historical, and the details of period life are believably captured.

ROBERT SILVERBERG (1935-)

American science fiction writer Silverberg was born in New York City and was educated at Columbia University. A writer since 1956, Silverberg has produced an immense body of work in several genres and under many pseudonyms. He is a multiple winner of the Nebula Award and the Hugo Award. Silverberg's novels include *Majipoor Chronicles*, *Valentine Pontifex*, and the *Conglomerated Cocktail Party*.

5853 *Gilgamesh the King*

Date of Publication: 1984
Subject(s): Sumerian Civilization; Fantasy; Myths and Legends
Historical character(s): Gilgamesh, Ruler (king)
Time Period(s): 26th century B.C.
Locale(s): Sumer, Mesopotamia (modern southern Iraq)

Summary: The novel retells the epic adventures of Gilgamesh, a Sumerian king who lived some 5,000 years ago. In this story of myth and magic, Gilgamesh journeys to the threshold of the gods causing their anger and retaliation.

Historical Accuracy: The novel combines historical elements with legends borrowed from the epic of Gilgamesh. The fanciful and fantastic events of these poems are interpreted in a realistic way to tell the story of Gilgamesh as though he were writing his own memoirs.

5854 *Lord of Darkness*

Date of Publication: 1983
Subject(s): Sea Story; Elizabethan Period; Tribal Life—African
Historical character(s): Andrew Battell, Sailor, Adventurer
Time Period(s): 16th century
Locale(s): Angola

Summary: Set during the Elizabethan Period, the novel tells the adventures of a young British seaman and adventurer who is captured by the Portugese and taken to the West African colony of Angola. There he is freed to serve as a ship's pilot in the slave trade and is increasingly drawn into the primitive rites of African tribal life.

Historical Accuracy: Although the main character actually existed, the author suggests that the work is more historical fantasy than history.

WILLIAM GILMORE SIMMS (1806-1870)

American writer born in Charleston, Simms began his career as a poet in imitation of Byron but turned to the novel making his reputation with romances of the frontier, the American Revolution, and South Carolina history. Called the Southern Cooper, Simms' novels recall Cooper in his use of stock figures and melodramatic plots. His books offer a more accurate though less poetic version of life.

5855 *The Yemassee*

Date of Publication: 1835
Subject(s): American Colonies; Indians
Fictional character(s): Sanutee, Indian (Yemassee), Chieftain; Gabriel Harrison, Settler
Time Period(s): 1710s (1715)
Locale(s): South Carolina, American Colonies

Summary: The South Carolina colonists' affairs with the Indians are portrayed in this romance. A Spanish agent is agitating the tribes against the settlers. Sanutee, a proud chief, is opposed to additional concessions to the whites, and open warfare breaks out.

Historical Accuracy: Simms' Native Americans are far more accurately portrayed than Cooper's more poetic interpretation.

EDITH SIMON (1917-)

German author Simon was born in Berlin. She is an artist, writer, and historian who has had a number of solo shows featuring her artwork.

5856 *The Golden Hand*

Date of Publication: 1952
Subject(s): Middle Ages
Fictional character(s): Edwin Widowson, Gentleman; Alfred Widowson, Religious (abbot)
Time Period(s): 14th century
Locale(s): England

Summary: England during the reign of Richard II is depicted through the experiences of the Widowson family. The novel eschews the usual historical romantic fare for a detailed look at ordinary daily life of the time.

Historical Accuracy: The setting and the spirit of the age are evoked with skill and authenticity.

5857 *The Twelve Pictures*

Date of Publication: 1955
Subject(s): Dark Ages; Myths and Legends
Fictional character(s): Siegfried, Warrior; Brunhilde, Maiden; Kriemhild, Widow(er)
Historical character(s): Attila the Hun, Ruler (King of the Huns)
Time Period(s): 5th century
Locale(s): Germany

Summary: The novel retells the *Nibelungenlied*—the saga of Siegfried and Brunhilde—with a psychological depth to the characters that is rare for such legendary material. This tale of revenge traces Siegfried's murder and the tragic consequences for Brunhilde and Siegfried's widow, Kriemhild, who marries Attila the Hun to further her plans of revenge.

Historical Accuracy: Although the basis for this story is legendary, the author provides a believable historical frame to capture the clash between the Christian and pagan worlds.

HARRY SIMONHOFF (1891-1966)

Historian and lawyer Simonhoff was born in Lithuania and grew up in Charleston, South Carolina, where he practiced law and served in the state legislature. He was a prominent

American Jewish leader. His books include *Under Strange Skies*, *The Chosen One*, and *Jewish Participants in the Civil War*.

5858 *And Abram Journeyed*

Date of Publication: 1967
Subject(s): Biblical Story
Historical character(s): Abraham, Biblical Figure
Time Period(s): Indeterminate Past
Locale(s): Middle East

Summary: Through the story of Abraham, the novel explores the origins of the Hebrews' faith in a single God. After searching for spiritual values different from the prevailing idol worship of the times, Abraham envisions a different God and embarks on a journey to Canaan.

Historical Accuracy: Although the story is speculative and invented, it features a believable reconstruction of the past.

ROSEMARY SIMPSON (1942-)

Educated in France and America, Simpson has travelled extensively throughout Europe and resides in Atlanta, Georgia. *The Seven Hills of Paradise* is her first novel.

5859 *The Seven Hills of Paradise*

Date of Publication: 1980
Subject(s): Middle Ages; Crusades; Byzantine Empire
Fictional character(s): Anne of Nanteuil, Religious (nun)
Historical character(s): Robert of Clari, Knight; Aleaumes, Religious (priest); Geoffrey of Villehardouin, Nobleman (marshal of Champagne)
Time Period(s): 13th century (1201-1205)
Locale(s): Constantinople, Byzantine Empire

Summary: The title refers to the Byzantine capital of Constantinople, and the novel tells the story of the Fourth Crusade in the 13th century. Although the goal was the liberation of the holy city of Jerusalem, greed and ambition take the crusaders to Constantinople instead. Their story is told through the experience of two brothers, Robert of Clari and Aleaumes, as well as a runaway nun, Anne of Nanteuil.

Historical Accuracy: The author's story of the Fourth Crusade is based on two eyewitness accounts.

MARIAN SIMS (1899-1961)

Born in Dalton, Georgia, Sims was a graduate of Agnes Scott College. She wrote fiction for popular magazines and published several novels, including *Beyond Surrender*, *Call It Freedom*, and *The City on the Hill*.

5860 *Beyond Surrender*

Date of Publication: 1942
Subject(s): Reconstruction Period
Fictional character(s): Denis Warden, Veteran (Confederate soldier)
Time Period(s): 1860s (post Civil War)
Locale(s): South Carolina

Summary: Denis Warden, a former major in the Confederate army, returns to his plantation in South Carolina and attempts to rebuild it, aided by a few loyal ex-slaves. The novel offers a vivid portrait of the political conflict of the Reconstruction period.

Historical Accuracy: The historical background is authentic and believable.

HAROLD SINCLAIR (1907-1966)

Born in Chicago, Sinclair left high school in his junior year and worked at a number of trades: telegraph operator, machinist, salesman, and musician.

5861 *The Cavalryman*

Date of Publication: 1958
Subject(s): American West; Wagon Trains; Indians
Fictional character(s): Jack Marlowe, Military Personnel (cavalry officer); Ruth Haynes, Immigrant
Time Period(s): 1860s (1864)
Locale(s): Badlands, North Dakota

Summary: In the sequel to the author's *The Horse Soldiers*, Jack Marlowe, now a general, is ordered to the Dakota Territory to guard a wagon train against one of the largest bands of Sioux warriors ever assembled on the Great Plains. He commands raw cavalry troops, many of them rebel deserters. At Killdeer Mountain they meet the Indians in the greatest Western battle up to that time.

Historical Accuracy: The fictional story is based on the Northwest Expedition against the Sioux, but should not be taken as an accurate description of that campaign.

5862 *The Horse Soldiers*

Date of Publication: 1956
Subject(s): Civil War—U.S.; Military Life—U.S. Cavalry
Fictional character(s): Jack Marlowe, Military Personnel (Union cavalry officer); Asa Bryce, Military Personnel (Union cavalry officer); Dick Gray, Military Personnel (Union cavalry officer)
Time Period(s): 1860s (1863)
Locale(s): Mississippi; Tennessee; Louisiana

Summary: Based on an actual Civil War episode known as Grierson's Raid, the novel depicts the exploits of Colonel Jack Marlowe's Union brigade that ventures deep within enemy territory in Mississippi to destroy the southern railway. Marlowe must lead his unit to safety, pursued by the Confederates.

Historical Accuracy: Though based on an actual incident, the novel is largely invented and is not to be taken as a realistic version of Grierson's Raid.

5863 *Westward the Tide*

Date of Publication: 1940
Subject(s): American Revolution
Fictional character(s): Philip Guard, Frontiersman
Historical character(s): George Rogers Clark, Frontiersman, Military Personnel (general)

Time Period(s): 1770s
Locale(s): Northwest Territory, United States

Summary: The novel describes the campaigns of George Rogers Clark in the old Northwest Territory and his expedition to capture Vincennes, which opened the way to Detroit and the territory between the Alleghenies and the Mississippi. The story is told by Philip Guard, a member of the expedition.

Historical Accuracy: The novel offers an authentic treatment of the period and the historical events with a fictional romance added.

JAMES SINCLAIR
(PSEUD. OF REGINALD THOMAS STAPLES, 1911-)

An English author born in London, Staples has worked as a magazine editor in London and regards his writing as a spare-time pleasure. He is the author of a number of historical novels under several pseudonyms, including James Sinclair and R. T. Stevens.

5864 *Canis the Warrior*

Date of Publication: 1979
Subject(s): Roman Empire; Celtic Britain
Historical character(s): Canis, Warrior; Suetonius Paulinus, Military Personnel (Roman governor); Cea, Royalty (princess)
Time Period(s): 1st century
Locale(s): England; Wales

Summary: The novel continues the story of the rebellion of Queen Boadicea's Iceni army begun in the *Warrior Queen*. After the defeat and death of Boadicea, Canis leads his surviving army into the mountains of Wales, pursued by the Roman legion that is determined to put down the rebellion.

Historical Accuracy: Little is known precisely of what happened to the Iceni following the death of Boadicea. The novel features a plausible speculation.

5865 *Warrior Queen*

Date of Publication: 1977
Subject(s): Roman Empire; Celtic Britain
Historical character(s): Canis, Warrior; Boadicea, Ruler (Queen of Britain)
Time Period(s): 1st century
Locale(s): England

Summary: The Celts versus the Roman Empire is the novel's subject dramatized in the story of Boadicea, Queen of the Britons, and her devoted warrior, Canis. Betrayal and the arrogance of Britain's conquerors cause Boadicea to rise in rebellion.

Historical Accuracy: The facts of the story are shrouded in legend, and the novel is a mix of the known and the imagined.

ISAAC BASHEVIS SINGER (1904-1991)

Born in Poland, Singer emigrated to the U.S. in 1935. He attended a rabbinical seminary in Poland and produced novels, short stories, children's books, and translations,

heralded as one of the foremost writers of Yiddish literature. Singer won a National Book Award for *A Crown of Feathers and Other Stories*, and in 1978, the Nobel Prize for Literature.

5866 *The Slave*

Date of Publication: 1962
Subject(s): Religious Life; Jews
Fictional character(s): Jacob, Scholar, Slave; Jan Bzik, Farmer; Wanda Bzik, Young Woman
Time Period(s): 17th century
Locale(s): Poland

Summary: In the 17th century, Jacob is a Jewish scholar who escapes from a Cossack raid only to be captured by Polish robbers and sold as a slave to Jan Bzik, a Gentile farmer. Jacob, a prisoner in a brutal Christian world, finds solace with Wanda, Bzik's daughter. Jacob's attempt to convert Wanda to his faith and thereby reconcile his love for her forms the novel's ethical dilemma.

Historical Accuracy: The novel is utterly convincing in recreating the ethos of the times.

ELSIE SINGMASTER
(PSEUD. OF E.S. LEWARS, 1879-1958)

An American novelist, Singmaster often wrote about her Pennsylvania Dutch background. Examples of her work include *Katy Gaumer*, *Basil Everyman*, and *Keler's Anna Ruth*.

5867 *A High Wind Rising*

Date of Publication: 1942
Subject(s): Settlement of the American Frontier; American Colonies; Indians
Fictional character(s): Anna Sabilla Schantz, Settler, Frontierswoman; Johann Sebastian Schantz, Frontiersman
Historical character(s): Conrad Weiser, Frontiersman, Scout; Henry Melchior Muhlenburg, Religious; Benjamin Franklin, Printer, Inventor
Time Period(s): 18th century (1728-1755)
Locale(s): Pennsylvania, American Colonies (western and Philadelphia)

Summary: This historical chronicle deals with the settling of western Pennsylvania and the struggle for control of the Ohio among the French, Indians, and English colonists. Anna Schantz and her grandson are at the center of the drama, which owes much of its appeal to its depiction of the day-to-day hardships of life in the wilderness.

Historical Accuracy: The novel offers a faithful picture of pioneer life that blends daily life with the larger flow of history.

5868 *I Speak for Thaddeus Stevens*

Date of Publication: 1947
Subject(s): Biography, Fictionalized; Civil War—U.S.; Reconstruction Period

Historical character(s): Thaddeus Stevens, Political Figure, Lawyer
Time Period(s): 19th century
Locale(s): Gettysburg, Pennsylvania; Washington, District of Columbia

Summary: This fictionalized biography of Thaddeus Stevens chronicles his career as a legislator from Pennsylvania and his rise to prominence during the Civil War. Stevens opposes Lincoln's moderate plan for Reconstruction and plays a decisive role in the impeachment proceedings against Andrew Johnson.

Historical Accuracy: Clearly favoring her central character, the author attempts to demonstrate Stevens' high principles.

5869 *Loving Heart*

Date of Publication: 1937
Subject(s): Civil War—U.S.; Underground Railroad; Battle of Gettysburg
Fictional character(s): Berry Pontifrac, Young Woman; James McIlvaine, Military Personnel (Union soldier)
Time Period(s): 1860s
Locale(s): Gettysburg, Pennsylvania

Summary: This Civil War-era tale describes the working of the Underground Railroad in Gettysburg, Pennsylvania, and the events leading up to the Battle of Gettysburg. The story concerns the roles played by two young lovers, Berry Pontifrac and James McIlvaine.

Historical Accuracy: This is a romantic tale that does feature some authentic period elements.

5870 *Swords of Steel*

Date of Publication: 1933
Subject(s): Civil War—U.S.; Battle of Gettysburg
Fictional character(s): John Deane, Teenager, Military Personnel (Union soldier)
Time Period(s): 1850s; 1860s
Locale(s): Gettysburg, Pennsylvania

Summary: Events in and around Gettysburg, Pennsylvania, are described through the experiences of young John Deane. The novel captures incidents leading up to the climactic Battle of Gettysburg, including John Brown's assault on Harper's Ferry.

Historical Accuracy: The description of the Battle of Gettysburg is accomplished and authentic.

C.L. SKELTON (1919-)

Skelton has made and directed motion pictures and worked in the London theater.

5871 *Beloved Soldiers*

Date of Publication: 1984
Subject(s): World War I; Family Saga; Military Life
Fictional character(s): Naomi Bruce, Bastard Daughter; Gordon Bruce, Military Personnel (lieutenant colonel); Donnie Cameron, Military Personnel (soldier)
Time Period(s): 1910s (1914-1916)

Locale(s): Highlands, Scotland; France

Summary: The third volume of the Regiment Quartet covers the first two years of World War I. The MacLaren Regiment mobilizes and is sent to France for the first engagements of the war. The younger generation of the MacLarens and the Bruces fight class privilege and social hypocrisy at home as well as the Germans on the battlefield.

Historical Accuracy: The fictional story is set against an authentic background of the actual engagements of the war.

5872 *Hardacre*

Date of Publication: 1976
Subject(s): Family Saga
Fictional character(s): Sam Hardacre, Worker, Businessman; Mary Hardacre, Spouse
Time Period(s): 19th century; 20th century
Locale(s): England

Summary: Sam Hardacre's business acumen overcomes poverty and creates a great commercial empire. With wealth, however, comes conflict with England's rigid social hierarchy. The fate of the Hardacre family mirrors the history of England from the Victorian to the modern periods.

Historical Accuracy: The focus on family matters is connected to a convincing background of actual events.

5873 *The Maclarens*

Date of Publication: 1978
Subject(s): Family Saga; Victorian Period; Military Life—British Army
Fictional character(s): Andrew Maclaren, Military Personnel (British officer); Maud Westburn, Young Woman; Willie Bruce, Military Personnel (sergeant)
Time Period(s): 19th century
Locale(s): India; Scotland

Summary: In the first volume of the author's Regiment Quartet, the story of the Maclaren family begins with Andrew Maclaren in the aftermath of the Indian Mutiny. He brings a survivor, Maud Westburn, back to his family's estate in Scotland and vies for her love with his childhood friend and companion Willie Bruce. Their stories dramatize the cost of empire in a succession of "little wars" that form the background of the novel's domestic drama.

Historical Accuracy: Though the 148th Regiment of Foot and the details of its battles are invented, the author states that the campaigns in the story are factual.

5874 *The Regiment*

Date of Publication: 1979
Subject(s): Boer War; Family Saga; Victorian Period
Fictional character(s): Donald Bruce, Military Personnel (soldier); Naomi Bruce, Bastard Daughter; Ian MacLaren, Military Personnel (soldier)
Time Period(s): 19th century; 20th century (1883-1901)
Locale(s): Scotland; South Africa; Egypt

Summary: In the second volume of the Regiment Quartet, the story of the MacLarens and the Bruces continues through the military events of the ebbing years of Victoria's reign. The story concentrates on the second generation, Donald and Naomi Bruce, Ian MacLaren, and others, who are tested during the great Imperial Wars in Africa.

Historical Accuracy: The author admits to taking liberties with the actual details of various campaigns. The fictional experiences of the MacLaren Highlanders are based on actions fought by some real Scottish Regiments.

ROBERT SKIMIN (1929-)

A native of Ohio, Skimin is a former army aviator, intelligence officer, and paratrooper. He attended the University of Georgia and the South Dakota School of Technology. Skimin has worked as a commercial artist and illustrator. He is the author of the Soldier for Hire paperback series. He has said of his historical novels that his quest for authenticity often leads to research that is as great a task as the writing itself.

5875 *Apache Autumn*

Date of Publication: 1992
Subject(s): American West; Indians
Fictional character(s): Carlota de Cardenas, Captive, Spouse; Rafael Murphy, Military Personnel (army officer); Lazaro, Indian (Apache), Chieftain
Historical character(s): Cochise, Indian (Chiricahua), Chieftain
Time Period(s): 19th century (1840s-1890s)
Locale(s): Santa Fe, New Mexico

Summary: Carlota de Cardenas is kidnapped by Apache raiders and forced to become the wife of Apache chief Lazaro. She escapes with her son and returns to marry American officer Murphy. The child eventually returns to the Apaches as they face extinction.

Historical Accuracy: The details of Apache life are well-displayed and believable.

5876 *Chikara!*

Date of Publication: 1984
Subject(s): Family Saga; World War II
Fictional character(s): Sataro Hoshi, Immigrant; Hiroshi Hoshi, Military Personnel (soldier); Itoko Hoshi, Spouse (of Sataro)
Time Period(s): 20th century (1907-1983)
Locale(s): Hiroshima, Japan; San Joaquin Valley, California

Summary: The novel is a saga of a Japanese family and covers many of the great events of the 20th century. The story begins in 1907 when Sataro Hoshi decides to immigrate to California in search of *chikara*, or power. The struggles of the Hoshi family are set against the background of historical events such as the Tokyo earthquake of 1923, the rape of Nanking, Pearl Harbor, Hiroshima, and Japan's economic recovery following the end of the war.

Historical Accuracy: The story is fictional, but it does employ an accurate sense of period history as the background.

5877 *Gray Victory*

Date of Publication: 1988
Subject(s): Civil War—U.S.; Confederate States of America; Battle of Gettysburg
Historical character(s): Salmon Brown, Abolitionist; John Singleton Mosby, Military Personnel (Confederate officer); James Ewell Brown Stuart, Military Personnel (Confederate officer); Abraham Lincoln, Political Figure; Robert E. Lee, Military Personnel (Confederate commander); Ulysses S. Grant, Military Personnel (Union general); James Longstreet, Military Personnel (Confederate general); George Edward Pickett, Military Personnel (Confederate general); Judah P. Benjamin, Political Figure (Confederate cabinet minister)
Time Period(s): 1860s (1866)
Locale(s): Richmond, Virginia

Summary: This fascinating what-if story speculates what might have happened had the South won the Civil War. The scene is Richmond, Virginia, in 1866 as General Stuart stands trial for the loss at Gettysburg, and a black revolutionary movement is gaining power to rekindle the war.

Historical Accuracy: To make the fictional premise work, the actual details must be believable. In this respect the author is convincing.

5878 *Ulysses: A Biographical Novel*

Date of Publication: 1994
Subject(s): Biography, Fictionalized; Civil War—U.S.; Military Life
Historical character(s): Ulysses S. Grant, Military Personnel (Union general), Political Figure; Julia Dent Grant, Spouse; James Longstreet, Military Personnel (Confederate general); Albert Sidney Johnston, Military Personnel (Confederate general); William Tecumseh Sherman, Military Personnel (Union general); Abraham Lincoln, Political Figure; Robert E. Lee, Military Personnel (Confederate commander); Joseph Pulitzer, Journalist
Time Period(s): 19th century (1839-1885)
Locale(s): United States

Summary: This biographical novel offers a full-scale treatment of the life and career of Ulysses S. Grant from his West Point days though the Civil War campaigns and his troubled presidency. The novel captures a complex leader, driven to succeed, yet filled with self-doubt.

Historical Accuracy: This is a remarkable biographical novel, detailed and convincing in its history and facts. The invented scenes and dialogue seem entirely plausible.

CONSTANCE SKINNER (1879-1939)

A Canadian-born novelist who wrote about the Far North, Skinner also wrote children's books and was the first editor of the Rivers of America series. Her novels include *Becky Landers: Frontier Warrior*, *The Search Relentless*, *Red Willows*, and *Pioneers of the Old Southwest*.

5879 *Becky Landers, Frontier Warrior*

Date of Publication: 1926

Subject(s): Settlement of the American Frontier; Indians
Fictional character(s): Becky Landers, Young Woman
Historical character(s): Daniel Boone, Frontiersman; George Rogers Clark, Military Personnel
Time Period(s): 18th century
Locale(s): Kentucky

Summary: In this adventure novel set in the Kentucky territory, Becky Landers is forced to defend her family when her father is killed and her brother is captured by Indians. She comes to the aid of the other settlers and helps to deliver her brother from captivity.

Historical Accuracy: The novel's melodrama predominates over detailed period elements.

JOSEF SKVORECKY (1924-)

Czech writer Skvorecky received his Ph.D. from Prague's Charles University and emigrated to Canada in 1969. He has worked as a professor of English at the University of Toronto. Skvorecky's first novel, *The Cowards*, though banned in Czechoslovakia, became a milestone in Czech literature and made him one of the country's most popular writers. Skvorecky won the Governor General's Award in Canada for *The Engineer of Human Souls* and in 1990 was awarded the Order of the White Lion, a prestigious Czech literary award.

5880 *The Bride of Texas*

Date of Publication: 1995
Subject(s): Civil War—U.S.; Immigrants
Fictional character(s): Linda Toupelik, Bride; Cyril Toupelik, Military Personnel (Union soldier)
Historical character(s): William Tecumseh Sherman, Military Personnel (Union general)
Time Period(s): 1860s
Locale(s): Savannah, Georgia; Bentonville, North Carolina; Chicago, Illinois

Summary: The novel offers an original portrait of the American Civil War from the vantage point of a group of Czech emigres who find themselves at the center of the war's chaos. Cyril Toupelik falls in love with a young slave woman, while his sister Linda marries a plantation owner's son.

Historical Accuracy: The novel's perspective is authentic and believable.

5881 *Dvorak in Love*

Date of Publication: 1986
Subject(s): Musical Life; Biography, Fictionalized
Historical character(s): Antonin Dvorak, Composer
Time Period(s): 1890s (1892-1895)
Locale(s): New York, New York; Spilville, Iowa; Czechoslovakia

Summary: The novel chronicles Czech composer Anton Dvorak's sojourn in America during the 1890s which culminates in the creation of the *New World Symphony*. The novel is told through vignettes by various people whose lives briefly intersect with the composer.

Historical Accuracy: The novel's multiple perspectives at time blur the focus on the central subject, casting Dvorak as a symbol rather than a complex historical figure.

SAM J. SLATE (1909-)

Born in Columbus, Georgia, Slate graduated from the University of Georgia. His career has included working for the United Press. He was also with CBS, serving as vice president in the radio division. He is the author of *It Sounds Impossible*, *As Long as the River Runs*, and *Satan's Backyard*, as well as numerous radio scripts.

5882 *As Long as the Rivers Run*

Date of Publication: 1972
Subject(s): Indians
Fictional character(s): Rafe Banks, Frontiersman
Historical character(s): Davy Crockett, Frontiersman; Andrew Jackson, Military Personnel, Political Figure; John Ross, Indian (Cherokee), Chieftain
Time Period(s): 1810s; 1820s
Locale(s): Tennessee

Summary: The historical background for this novel is the battle against the Creek Indians in 1813 in which the Cherokees join the side of the volunteers led by Andrew Jackson. Rafe Banks, who seeks revenge on the Creeks, grows in admiration for the Cherokee way of life. The novel features portraits of a number of the historical figures of the period.

Historical Accuracy: The historical background is accurate and captures the atmosphere of the time as well as several of the actual events.

FRANK G. SLAUGHTER (1908-)

American physician and author, Slaughter was born in Washington, D.C., graduated from Duke University, and received his M.D. degree from Johns Hopkins. Slaughter worked as a surgeon in Jacksonville, Florida, and is a prolific author of medical, biblical, and historical novels. More than 60 million copies of his books are in print in over 20 countries. Slaughter has been called the American Balzac. Slaughter also writes under the pseudonym C.V. Terry.

5883 *Constantine: The Miracle of the Flaming Cross*

Date of Publication: 1965
Subject(s): Roman Empire; Christianity
Historical character(s): Constantine I, Ruler (Roman emperor)
Time Period(s): 4th century
Locale(s): Roman Empire; Gaul

Summary: The novel chronicles the career of Constantine I, the first Christian emperor of Rome, who in battle against Maxentius, saw a fiery cross in the sky and took as his motto the phrase, "In this sign conquer." Constantine is shown giving Christianity equal status with paganism and constraining his military rivals and the Christain bishops who fight among themselves.

Historical Accuracy: The novel is a combination of the factual and the imagined.

5884 *The Curse of Jezebel: A Novel of the Biblical Queen of Evil*

Date of Publication: 1961
Subject(s): Biblical Story; Assyrian Empire
Fictional character(s): Michael, Warrior, Royalty (prince); Miriam, Gentlewoman
Historical character(s): Jezebel, Royalty (consort of King Ahab), Biblical Figure; Ahab, Ruler (King of Israel), Biblical Figure; Elijah, Religious (prophet), Biblical Figure
Time Period(s): 9th century B.C.
Locale(s): Israel

Summary: The novel dramatizes the story of King Ahab and his queen, Jezebel, recounted in the Old Testament Book of Kings. Jezebel has become a synonym for absolute evil, and her wickedness is depicted in her manipulation of Prince Michael and his beloved Miriam. In warfare with the Assyrians, Jezebel betrays her husband and her nation.

Historical Accuracy: Based on modern historical and archaeological research, the novel captures the era convincingly.

5885 *David: Warrior and King*

Date of Publication: 1982
Subject(s): Biblical Story; Biography, Fictionalized
Historical character(s): David, Ruler (King of Israel), Biblical Figure; Saul, Ruler (King of Israel), Biblical Figure; Bathsheba, Royalty (consort of David), Biblical Figure; Absalom, Royalty (prince), Biblical Figure; Solomon, Ruler (King of Israel), Biblical Figure; Samuel, Religious (prophet), Biblical Figure
Time Period(s): 11th century B.C.
Locale(s): Jerusalem, Israel

Summary: This fictional biography chronicles the career of the Biblical David, who grew up to unite the many tribes of Israel into a single nation. David achieves reknown for slaying the Philistine giant Goliath but is persecuted by King Saul. Upon Saul's death, David is crowned king, and he oversees a period of great glory and splendor in Israel.

Historical Accuracy: The novel mixes what is known with what might have been to tell David's story.

5886 *Divine Mistress*

Date of Publication: 1949
Subject(s): Renaissance; Inquisition; Medical Profession
Fictional character(s): Antonio Servetus, Teacher; Lucia Bellarmi, Young Woman; Clarice Strozzi, Model (artist's)
Time Period(s): 16th century (1562)
Locale(s): Padua, Italy; Venice, Italy; Spain

Summary: Set in Renaissance Italy and Spain, the story dramatizes the history of modern medicine through the experiences of a young soldier, Antonio Servetus, whose studies in anatomy lead to confrontation with the Inquisition. The details behind the creation of Sandro Botticelli's masterpiece *Birth of Venus* are also depicted.

Historical Accuracy: The medical history dramatized is based in part on historical precedents, but the author explains that it is primarily a romantic tale.

5887 *Flight From Avatchez*

Date of Publication: 1955
Subject(s): American Revolution; American Colonies
Fictional character(s): John Powers, Doctor, Loyalist; Faith Gordon, Young Woman; Stella Wright, Young Woman
Time Period(s): 1780s (1781)
Locale(s): Natchez, Mississippi; Pensacola, Florida; Georgia

Summary: This tale from the American Revolutionary period describes a group of Loyalists from Natchez who brave a 500-mile trek when conflict with the Spanish forces them into the wilderness. They brave famine and Indian attack before reaching sanctuary. Dr. John Powers leads the party. He is attracted to two very different young women, Faith Gordon and Stella Wright.

Historical Accuracy: The story is based on a historical incident.

5888 *The Galileans*

Date of Publication: 1953
Subject(s): Biblical Story
Historical character(s): Mary Magdalene, Biblical Figure
Time Period(s): 1st century
Locale(s): Israel; Alexandria, Egypt

Summary: The novel imagines a full, though melodramatic, life for Mary Magdalene before her encounter with Jesus and her role as reflected in the New Testament. In this version, she is a half-Greek, half-Jewish woman brutally persecuted by a Roman official and rescued by a young Jewish doctor.

Historical Accuracy: The story is invented and highly romantic, with some authentic details of the state of science at the time as well as some accurate period details.

5889 *God's Warrior*

Date of Publication: 1967
Subject(s): Christianity; Biography, Fictionalized; Roman Empire
Historical character(s): Paul, Religious
Time Period(s): 1st century
Locale(s): Damascus, Syria; Rome, Roman Empire; Corinth, Greece

Summary: This biographical novel traces the life of St. Paul, who is transformed from one of the most effective persecutors of the early Christians to the early church's greatest missionary and theologian. The novel follows Paul's career from Tarsus and the road to Damascus to his ministry through Greece, Rome, and Spain.

Historical Accuracy: The novel fills in the gaps in the documentary record with plausible surmises.

5890 *Golden Isle*

Date of Publication: 1947
Subject(s): Antebellum South; Slavery

Fictional character(s): Michael Stone, Doctor; Adam Leigh, Plantation Owner
Time Period(s): 19th century
Locale(s): Florida

Summary: The African slave trade in Spanish Florida in the early 19th century is dramatized in the story of Dr. Michael Stone who is kidnapped and forced to treat slaves being bred and trained by a villainous plantation owner.

Historical Accuracy: The novel's more blatant melodrama is supported by a solid knowledge of medical practice and the region during the period.

`5891` *In a Dark Garden*

Date of Publication: 1946
Subject(s): Civil War—U.S.; Espionage; Battle of Chickamauga
Fictional character(s): Julian Chisholm, Doctor; Jane Anderson, Widow(er); Lucy Sprague, Young Woman
Time Period(s): 1860s (1862)
Locale(s): Glasgow, Scotland; New York, New York; Vicksburg, Mississippi

Summary: Julian Chisholm is a young medical student who agrees to marry widow Jane Anderson to help her regain her property in Georgia. He joins the Confederacy as a field surgeon on the battlefields of Vicksburg and Chickamauga. He is torn between Jane and Lucy Sprague, the woman who rejected him to marry a wealthy Yankee senator.

Historical Accuracy: The story is imagined but does offer some accurate details of the events of the period.

`5892` *Lorena*

Date of Publication: 1959
Subject(s): Civil War—U.S.; Reconstruction Period; Ku Klux Klan
Fictional character(s): Lorena Selby, Southern Belle, Plantation Owner; Daniel Carroll, Military Personnel (Union soldier)
Time Period(s): 1860s
Locale(s): Georgia

Summary: Lorena Shelby's Georgia plantation is in the path of General Sherman's onrushing army during the Civil War. The novel describes her determined resistance in the face of the Confederate defeat and the challenge of Reconstruction with its nightriding Klansmen.

Historical Accuracy: The story is fictional but does feature a convincing period background.

`5893` *The Mapmaker: A Novel of the Days of Prince Henry, the Navigator*

Date of Publication: 1957
Subject(s): Exploration
Historical character(s): Henry the Navigator, Royalty (prince); Andrea Bianco, Cartographer
Time Period(s): 15th century (1450s)
Locale(s): Portugal

Summary: Set during the age of discovery in the 15th century, the novel centers on the actual figure of Andrea Bianco, who 50 years before the voyage of Columbus drew one of the first maps of the world. Bianco joins the learned collection of mapmakers, navigators, astronomers, mathematicians, and shipbuilders brought together by Prince Henry of Portugal. The beginning of Portugese exploration leads to the circumnavigation of Africa and the discovery of a water route to India, as well as providing the stimulus that sends Columbus westward in 1492.

Historical Accuracy: The novel provides a believable depiction of the era and its atmosphere.

`5894` *The Passionate Rebel*

Date of Publication: 1979
Subject(s): Civil War—U.S.; Espionage; Battle of Bull Run
Fictional character(s): Maritza Le Clerc, Noblewoman (countess), Spy
Historical character(s): Pierre Gustave Toutant Beauregard, Military Personnel (Confederate general)
Time Period(s): 1860s
Locale(s): Mobile, Alabama; Washington, District of Columbia; New Orleans, Louisiana

Summary: Civil War espionage is depicted in the experience of Maritza Le Clerc, who returns from France with a smuggled shipment of guns for the Confederacy. Her espionage work takes her to Washington and to occupied New Orleans.

Historical Accuracy: The story is imagined but does offer an authentic atmosphere of the period.

`5895` *Pilgrims in Paradise*

Date of Publication: 1960
Subject(s): Puritans; Religious Conflict
Fictional character(s): Paul Sutton, Doctor; Silas Sutton, Leader (Pilgrim), Zealot (religious); Anne Trevor, Fiance(e)
Time Period(s): 17th century (1647)
Locale(s): Bristol, England; Bahamas

Summary: Set in the 1640s among Puritan settlers in the Bahamas, the novel describes the iron rule of religious zealot Silas Sutton whose bigotry and superstition are finally opposed by his brother Paul. Paul falls in love with Silas' fiancee, Anne Trevor. Paradise is revealed as far more temporal and limited by human weakness.

Historical Accuracy: The historical backdrop of the invented story is plausible.

`5896` *The Purple Quest: A Novel of Seafaring Adventure in the Ancient World*

Date of Publication: 1965
Subject(s): Sea Story; Phoenicians
Fictional character(s): Straton, Sea Captain; Pygmalion, Ruler (King of Phoenicia); Elissa, Royalty (Queen of Phoenicia)
Time Period(s): 9th century B.C.
Locale(s): Tyre, Lebanon (Phoenicia); Carthage, Ancient Civilization

Summary: The novel dramatizes the story of Queen Elissa, or Dido, and the founding of Carthage. The story begins in the Phoenician city of Tyre and centers on the seafarer Straton, who must contend with royal intrigue as the Phoenicians prepare for war. After a palace revolt, a new kingdom is created in Africa.

Historical Accuracy: The events detailed have a strong basis in fact.

5897 The Road to Bithynia: A Novel of Luke, the Beloved Physician

Date of Publication: 1951
Subject(s): Biblical Story; Christianity; Medical Profession
Historical character(s): Luke, Biblical Figure, Doctor; Paul, Biblical Figure
Time Period(s): 1st century
Locale(s): Middle East

Summary: This Biblical novel tells of the early Christian church through the experiences of Luke. His youth, encounter with Paul, war experiences, and work as a physician are included. His conversion to christianity and decision to write the story of Jesus are also described.

Historical Accuracy: Much invention and a preference for surface color over historical substance mar this tale.

5898 Sangaree

Date of Publication: 1948
Subject(s): Antebellum South; Medical Profession
Fictional character(s): Tobias Kent, Doctor
Time Period(s): 1780s (1786)
Locale(s): Savannah River, Georgia

Summary: In coastal Georgia following the American Revolution, former indentured servant and doctor Tobias Kent attempts to carry out the will of his mentor and patron by creating a utopian community. Kent must contend with unreformed Tories and pirates as well as an epidemic of bubonic plague.

Historical Accuracy: Kent's utopian ideals are considerably ahead of the times and undermine the novel's credibility as a believable period portrait.

5899 Scarlet Cord: A Novel of the Woman of Jericho

Date of Publication: 1956
Subject(s): Biblical Story; Ancient Israel
Fictional character(s): Salmon, Doctor
Historical character(s): Rahab, Biblical Figure, Prostitute; Joshua, Biblical Figure
Time Period(s): 12th century B.C.
Locale(s): Jericho, Palestine

Summary: This biblical story from the Book of Joshua in the Old Testament is the tale of Rahab, a prostitute from Jerico. Her protection of Joshua's two spies saves her and her family from destruction. The hero of the tale is the physician, Salmon.

Historical Accuracy: The novel is filled with authentic data on life and customs of the period.

5900 The Sins of Herod: A Novel of Rome and the Early Church

Date of Publication: 1968
Subject(s): Roman Empire; Christianity
Fictional character(s): Prochurus, Government Official
Historical character(s): Caligula, Ruler (Roman emperor); Herod Antipas, Ruler (King of Judea); Herod Agrippa I, Ruler (King of Judea); John, Religious (apostle), Biblical Figure; Peter, Religious (apostle), Biblical Figure; James, Religious (apostle), Biblical Figure
Time Period(s): 1st century
Locale(s): Antioch, Syria; Rome, Roman Empire; Israel

Summary: The story of the early years of Christianity is told from the point of view of Prochurus, a Roman citizen of Judea, who is torn between the violence and intrigue of men like Herod Antipas, Herod Agrippa, and the mad Emperor Caligula, and the teaching of Jesus' disciples. Prochurus must choose between Rome and spiritual salvation.

Historical Accuracy: The novel is more about faith and spirit than history, though there are some credible period details.

5901 The Song of Ruth: A Love Story of the Old Testament

Date of Publication: 1954
Subject(s): Biblical Story
Historical character(s): Ruth, Biblical Figure; Naomi, Biblical Figure; Boaz, Biblical Figure
Time Period(s): 11th century B.C.
Locale(s): Israel

Summary: Based on the Biblical story, the novel dramatizes the fidelity of Ruth to her widowed mother-in-law, Naomi. After the death of her husband in Moab, Ruth returns with Naomi to Bethlehem where she marries Naomi's kinsman Boaz.

Historical Accuracy: The novel provides some elaboration on the Biblical story.

5902 The Stonewall Brigade: A Novel of the American Civil War

Date of Publication: 1975
Subject(s): Civil War—U.S.; Battle of Gettysburg; Battle of Antietam
Fictional character(s): David Preston, Doctor
Historical character(s): Thomas Jonathan Jackson, Military Personnel (Confederate general); Abraham Lincoln, Political Figure; Robert E. Lee, Military Personnel (Confederate commander); James Ewell Brown Stuart, Military Personnel (Confederate officer)
Time Period(s): 1860s (1861-1865)
Locale(s): Virginia; Washington, District of Columbia; Gettysburg, Pennsylvania

Summary: The history of the Stonewall Brigade, Stonewall Jackson's famous "foot cavalry," is chronicled from the early engagements at Harper's Ferry through Sharpsburg, Antietam, Chancellorsville, and Gettysburg. The novel mixes fact and fiction in the experiences of David Preston, a young medical officer.

Historical Accuracy: The depiction of the military engagements is authentic and close to the actual.

`5903` *Storm Haven*

Date of Publication: 1954
Subject(s): Civil War—U.S.; Cattle Drives
Fictional character(s): Christopher Clark, Doctor; Valerie Storm, Southern Belle
Time Period(s): 1860s
Locale(s): Florida

Summary: Florida during the Civil War is the scene for this romantic adventure novel involving Christopher Clark, a surgeon, cowboy, and Confederate medical officer. His outspoken opposition to slavery produces complications that cause Clark to flee to south Florida where he joins a cattle drive to the Georgia railhead to help feed the hard-pressed Confederate troops.

Historical Accuracy: Romance predominates thoughout. However, as in most of the author's books, there are reliable historical details of the life and customs of the time.

`5904` *The Stubborn Heart*

Date of Publication: 1950
Subject(s): Reconstruction Period; Medical Profession; Ku Klux Klan
Fictional character(s): Julian Chisholm, Doctor, Plantation Owner
Time Period(s): 1860s
Locale(s): Cape Fear, North Carolina

Summary: In this sequel to *The Dark Garden*, Doctor Julian Chisholm comes home to North Carolina after the Civil War. There he is beset by carpetbaggers and the Ku Klux Klan as he attempts to establish a model community at Chisholm Hundred.

Historical Accuracy: The novel is most believable on its medical elements. The historical elements provide a believable backdrop.

`5905` *The Thorn of Arimathea*

Date of Publication: 1959
Subject(s): Biblical Story; Roman Empire; Christianity
Fictional character(s): Quintus Volusianus, Doctor
Historical character(s): Peter, Biblical Figure; Caligula, Ruler (Roman emperor); Pontius Pilate, Government Official (Procurator of Jerusalem); Joseph of Arimathea, Biblical Figure; Veronica Giuliani, Biblical Figure
Time Period(s): 1st century
Locale(s): Jerusalem, Israel; Gaul; England

Summary: Quintus Volusianus is sent by the Emperor Tiberius to Jerusalem to investigate the power of the leader Jesus of Nazareth. He arrives too late, but becomes involved with Jesus' followers and Veronica of the Veil. This story of the earliest Christians ranges from Rome to Gaul and Britannia.

Historical Accuracy: The story is imagined, but skillfully creates a plausible atmosphere of the early church and the Roman Empire.

`5906` *Upon This Rock: A Novel of Simon Peter, Prince of Apostles*

Date of Publication: 1963
Subject(s): Biblical Story; Christianity; Roman Empire
Historical character(s): Peter, Biblical Figure, Religious; John the Baptist, Biblical Figure; Judas Iscariot, Biblical Figure; Mary Magdalene, Biblical Figure; Paul, Biblical Figure, Religious; Nero, Ruler (Roman emperor); Jesus Christ, Biblical Figure
Time Period(s): 1st century
Locale(s): Jerusalem, Israel; Rome, Roman Empire

Summary: The novel traces the life of Simon Peter as a humble fisherman, a disciple of Jesus, and finally a founder of the Christian church. Peter is shown as devoted to the church yet wracked with doubts. After the crucifixion of Jesus, Peter assumes leadership of the apostles and establishes the Christian church until his martyrdom at the hands of Nero.

Historical Accuracy: The background sources are scriptural, historical, and archaeological.

LINDA CHING SLEDGE (1944-)

Born in Hawaii, Sledge graduated from the University of California, Berkeley, San Francisco State College, and the City University of New York. She is a professor of English at Westchester Community College.

`5907` *Empire of Heaven*

Date of Publication: 1990
Subject(s): Chinese Empire; Taiping Rebellion
Fictional character(s): Rulan, Young Woman; Pao An, Captive; General Li, Military Personnel (Manchu general); Hung, Revolutionary
Time Period(s): 19th century (1847-1865)
Locale(s): China; Hong Kong; Hawaii

Summary: The novel dramatizes the events and effects of China's Taiping Rebellion, one of the bloodiest civil wars ever fought. A young villager, Rulan, meets the charismatic leader Hung and to aid the rebels serves as a spy in the house of the great Manchu general Li.

Historical Accuracy: Though based on extensive research, the author admits that the story is more imagination than fact.

RICHARD SLOTKIN (1942-)

American scholar and novelist, Slotkin was born in Brooklyn and graduated from Brooklyn College and Brown University. He is a professor of American Studies and English at Wesleyan University. Slotkin's childhood fascination with the Wild West led him to examine popular theories of its effects on society's development. He has published a trilogy of studies on the American frontier:

Regeneration through Violence, The Fatal Environment, and *Gunfighter Nation.*

5908 *The Crater*

Date of Publication: 1980
Subject(s): Civil War—U.S.; Battle of the Crater
Fictional character(s): Major Booker, Military Personnel (Union officer)
Historical character(s): Ambrose E. Burnside, Military Personnel (Union general); George Meade, Military Personnel (Union general)
Time Period(s): 1860s (1864)
Locale(s): Petersburg, Virginia

Summary: In an imaginative recreation of a tragic Civil War episode, the novel chronicles the Battle of the Crater, the result of a huge mine explosion under the Confederate trenches at Petersburg, Virginia, in 1864. Meant to break the stalemate and end the war, the battle leads to a massacre of black Union forces thrown into the breach after the great explosion.

Historical Accuracy: The novel's events and details closely follow the historical record, with some minor additions and alterations.

5909 *The Return of Henry Starr*

Date of Publication: 1988
Subject(s): American West; Crime and Criminals; Biography, Fictionalized
Historical character(s): Henry Starr, Outlaw (bank robber), Indian (Cherokee)
Time Period(s): 1910s
Locale(s): Oklahoma

Summary: This is a fictionalized biography of Cherokee outlaw Henry Starr. He attempts to reform from his criminal ways but slips back to his old habits.

Historical Accuracy: The novel offers a fascinating and informed picture of the turn-of-the-century West.

BERTRICE SMALL (1937-)

American romance writer Small was born in New York City. She has worked as a sales assistant.

5910 *Lost Love Found*

Date of Publication: 1992
Subject(s): Romance; Elizabethan Period
Fictional character(s): Valentine St. Michael, Widow(er), Noblewoman; Tom Ashburne, Nobleman
Time Period(s): 16th century
Locale(s): England; Constantinople, Ottoman Empire

Summary: Set in Elizabethan England, the novel follows Valentine St. Michael, a lady-in-waiting to the aging Elizabeth I, as she attempts to learn the secret of her identity. She journeys to Turkey, where she is abducted and threatened before finding love and answers to her quest.

Historical Accuracy: The period elements are only lightly sketched in this romance with an emphasis on the exotic.

5911 *A Moment in Time*

Date of Publication: 1991
Subject(s): Middle Ages; Norman Conquest; Romance
Fictional character(s): Wynne of Gwernach, Noblewoman; Madoc of Powys, Royalty (prince)
Time Period(s): 11th century (1060s)
Locale(s): Wales

Summary: Set in Wales during the Norman Conquest, this romantic story features reincarnation as Wynne and Madoc must contend with various forces opposing their love, including time and space, before happiness can be achieved.

Historical Accuracy: The period elements are secondary to the passion here.

5912 *The Spitfire*

Date of Publication: 1990
Subject(s): Romance; War of the Roses
Fictional character(s): Arabella Grey, Noblewoman; Tavis Stewart, Nobleman (Earl of Dummor)
Time Period(s): 15th century (1490s)
Locale(s): Scotland; England

Summary: Tavis Stewart's vengeance plot on the murderer of his betrothed involves kidnapping Arabella Grey and marrying her. Despite their beginning, the two fall in love. Complications develop as Arabella schemes to regain her lost estate.

Historical Accuracy: The situation is improbable, and the historical elements are secondary to the romance.

5913 *To Love Again*

Date of Publication: 1993
Subject(s): Dark Ages; Romance; Anglo-Saxon Period
Fictional character(s): Cailin Drusus, Captive, Fugitive; Wulf Ironfist, Warrior (Saxon); Flavius Aspar, Military Personnel (Byzantine general)
Time Period(s): 5th century
Locale(s): England; Constantinople, Byzantine Empire

Summary: The novel is a romantic adventure set in the 5th century that features Cailin Drusus, who marries a Saxon warrior, Wulf, but is sold to Aspar, a Byzantine general. When Wulf reappears as a gladiator, Cailin must deal with conflicting emotions, torn between love in primitive Britain and the luxury of the Byzantine Empire.

Historical Accuracy: The novel is an amalgam of competing eras that are only partially relevant to the novel's romance.

5914 *Wild Jasmine*

Date of Publication: 1992
Subject(s): Romance
Fictional character(s): Jasmine de Marisco, Royalty (princess); Rowan Lindley, Nobleman
Time Period(s): 17th century
Locale(s): India; England; Ireland

Summary: Set during the 17th century, the novel traces the career of Jasmine de Marisco, who is raised as a princess in India and is pursued by a number of noblemen whose intentions are far from honorable. She marries Rowan Lindley for a modicum of happiness and peace until tragedy strikes.

Historical Accuracy: The novel features more historical costumes than actual use of the period.

JANE SMILEY (1949-)

Born in Los Angeles, Smiley grew up in St. Louis and studied at Vassar and the University of Iowa, where she received her Ph.D. She is a professor of English at Iowa State University. A multiple recipient of the O. Henry award, Smiley is the author of the novels *Born Blind*, *At Paradise Gate*, and *Duplicate Keys* and a short story collection, *The Age of Grief*. All of her books share a concern for families and their troubles and have been been praised for capturing the rhythms of family life gone askew.

5915 *The Greenlanders*

Date of Publication: 1988
Subject(s): Middle Ages; Vikings
Fictional character(s): Asgeir Gunnarsson, Farmer; Margaret Asgeirsdottir, Young Woman; Gunnar Asgeirsson, Young Man
Time Period(s): 14th century
Locale(s): Greenland

Summary: Life in a remote Viking colony in Greenland during the 14th century is chronicled in the experiences of the family of Asgeir Gunnarsson. He is the patriarch whose fierce enmity toward his neighbors sets in motion a chain of events felt by his daughter, Margaret, and son, Gunnar.

Historical Accuracy: The novel offers a convincing presentation of a remote time and place.

A.C.H. SMITH (1935-)

British author and playwright Smith was born in Surrey and attended Cambridge University. His career has included work as a journalist, a television presenter and scriptwriter, and program compiler for the Royal Shakespeare Company. His novels include *Zero Summer*, *Treatment*, and *Extra Cover*. He has also written several movie novelizations including *The Dark Crystal* and *Lady Jane*.

5916 *Edward and Mrs. Simpson*

Date of Publication: 1978
Subject(s): Royalty—England; Biography, Fictionalized
Historical character(s): Edward, Prince of Wales, Royalty; Wallis Warfield Simpson, Socialite; Stanley Baldwin, Political Figure; George V, Ruler (King of England); Mary of Teck, Royalty (queen consort of George V); Winston Churchill, Political Figure; George, Duke of York, Royalty
Time Period(s): 20th century (1928-1940)
Locale(s): England; Europe

Summary: The novel, based on both the Thames Television Series written by Simon Raven and Lady Frances Donaldson's *Edward VIII*, dramatizes the relationship between Edward, Prince of Wales, and Wallis Simpson, which causes

Edward to choose between his heart and his duty. Their relationship produces a political crisis that leads to Edward's abdication.

Historical Accuracy: The novel is solidly based on fact with imagined conversations and scenes that are at least plausible if not historical.

ARTHUR DOUGLAS SMITH (1887-1945)

Born in New York City, historian and novelist Arthur Douglas Smith's books include *Commodore Vanderbilt: An Epic of American Achievement*, *John Jacob Astor: Landlord of New York*, and the novel, *Hate*.

5917 *The Doom Trail*

Date of Publication: 1922
Subject(s): American Colonies; Indians
Fictional character(s): Harry Ormerod, Trader (fur); Robert Juggins, Trader (fur)
Time Period(s): 17th century
Locale(s): London, England; American Colonies; Canada

Summary: This adventure tale depicts the conflict over the fur trade that pitted the French against the English and independent trappers against one another for control of the trade. Adventurer Harry Ormerod joins Robert Juggins against the Provincial Fur Company. The action takes place along the "Doom Trail," the secret route designed to get English manufactured goods into French trading posts to corner the Indian fur trade.

Historical Accuracy: The period and atmosphere are realistically and believably described.

5918 *Hate*

Date of Publication: 1928
Subject(s): War of 1812; Sea Story
Fictional character(s): Captain Fellowes, Military Personnel (naval officer)
Time Period(s): 1810s
Locale(s): Portugal; At Sea

Summary: This naval adventure tale set during the War of 1812 follows the exploits of American captain Fellowes. Shipwrecked off the coast of Portugal, Fellowes is imprisoned by the British on his way back to America. After escaping, Fellowes commands an American cruiser and sets out to settle his score with the British.

Historical Accuracy: The novel is an exciting mixture of romance, adventure, and history. The historical elements are authentic.

CHARD POWERS SMITH (1894-1977)

An American writer, poet, biographer, and editor, Smith was an attorney before giving up private practice to write. His works deal mainly with New England life. Two of his books, *Artillery of Time* and *The Housatonic* were bestsellers.

5919 *Artillery of Time*

Date of Publication: 1939
Subject(s): Civil War—U.S.; Farming
Fictional character(s): John Lathrop, Farmer; Isaac Lathrop, Farmer
Time Period(s): 1850s; 1860s
Locale(s): New York (upstate)

Summary: The novel concerns life in an upstate New York farming community in the years before and during the Civil War. The story centers on the experiences of the Lathrop family, particularly the two sons, Isaac and John.

Historical Accuracy: The novel features a faithful re-creation of the period and the region.

FREDERIC E. SMITH (1922-)

British writer Frederic Smith was born in Hull and began writing while living and working in South Africa for a steel company between 1947 and 1952. His writings include *A Killing for the Hawks*, *The Tormented*, and *Rage of the Innocent*. He is also the author of the *633 Squadron* series of novels, the first book of which was filmed in 1964.

5920 *Waterloo*

Date of Publication: 1970
Subject(s): Napoleonic Wars; Battle of Waterloo
Historical character(s): Napoleon Bonaparte, Ruler (Emperor of France), Military Personnel (army commander); Arthur Wellesley, Military Personnel (army commander), Nobleman (Duke of Wellington); Louis XVIII, Ruler (King of France); Michel Ney, Military Personnel (marshal of France)
Time Period(s): 1810s (1815)
Locale(s): Belgium; France

Summary: Based on the screenplay by H.A.L. Craig of the film *Waterloo*, the novel dramatizes the events of the Hundred Days after Napoleon's escape from Elba to the climatic battle of the Napoleonic era as Napoleon faces Wellington at Waterloo.

Historical Accuracy: The novel provides a believable record of the events of the battle from both the French and the British side.

HERBERT FRANCIS SMITH (1922-)

Smith was born in Buffalo and has worked as a factory worker, a technician, and a radio and TV instructor. Smith became a Jesuit priest in 1951. He has been a teacher as well as a writer and speaker for radio programs. His works include *The Lord Experience* and *Sunday Homilies*.

5921 *Hidden Victory: A Novel of Jesus*

Date of Publication:
Subject(s): Biblical Story
Historical character(s): Jesus Christ, Biblical Figure; Mary, Biblical Figure; Joseph, Biblical Figure; John the Baptist, Biblical Figure; Peter, Biblical Figure
Time Period(s): 1st century
Locale(s): Israel

Summary: The novel depicts the life of Christ in novel form, tracing his ministry and the events of the New Testament. It attempts to place Christ's story in both a historical and human context.

Historical Accuracy: The novel's events are rooted in the New Testament with the social and religious background based on research. Imagination has filled in some of the gaps, and certain minor characters, incidental dialogue, and minor events have been fabricated.

KAY NOLTE SMITH (1932-1993)

Born in Minnesota, Smith graduated from the University of Minnesota and the University of Utah. She worked as an actress under the stage name of Kate Gillian, a copywriter, and a communication consultant. She won an Edgar Award in 1980 for *The Watcher*.

5922 *A Tale of the Wind: A Novel of Nineteenth-Century France*

Date of Publication: 1991
Subject(s): Theatrical Life; Artistic Life; Paris Commune
Fictional character(s): Nandou, Actor; Jeanne Morel, Young Woman
Time Period(s): 19th century (1827-1885)
Locale(s): Paris, France

Summary: Set in the artistic ferment of Paris in the 19th century, the novel begins in the 1820s with the unlikely relationship between Nandou and a young girl from the street, Jeanne Morel. This odd attraction is followed through the revolutions of 1830 and 1848, the cholera epidemic, and the Paris Commune of the 1870s. Through it all, the conflicts between art and social conventions are vividly portrayed.

Historical Accuracy: The period elements captured are genuine and convincing.

MARTIN CRUZ SMITH (1942-)

Born in Pennsylvania, Smith graduated from the University of Pennsylvania. He has worked for local TV stations and as a journalist and correspondent for the Associated Press. His breakthrough novel was *Gorky Park*, a mystery set in Moscow employing a Russian detective. Smith spent eight years researching the novel. There have been two sequels, *Polar Star* and *Red Square*.

5923 *Rose*

Date of Publication: 1996
Subject(s): Victorian Period; Mining; Mystery
Fictional character(s): Jonathan Blair, Adventurer
Time Period(s): 19th century
Locale(s): Wigan, England

Summary: In this suspense novel set in Victorian England, American adventurer Jonathan Blair travels to the coal mining town of Wigan where he attempts to solve the mysterious disappearance of a young cleric, John Maypole, who had taken up with a pit girl. Maypole has disappeared on the same day that many men were killed in an explosion in a mine owned by the bishop.

Historical Accuracy: The novel features a highly believable period backdrop.

`5924` Stallion Gate

Date of Publication: 1986
Subject(s): Espionage; Science; World War II
Fictional character(s): Joe Pena, Military Personnel (sergeant), Indian
Historical character(s): Leslie R. Groves, Military Personnel (general); J. Robert Oppenheimer, Scientist (physicist)
Time Period(s): 1940s (1945)
Locale(s): Los Alamos, New Mexico

Summary: The historical background of this thriller is the development of the atomic bomb at Los Alamos in 1945. Sergeant Joe Pena is ordered by his superior to find or fabricate evidence that Robert Oppenheimer is a communist spy. Pena, an Indian, must also deal with the local Indian population disturbed by the mysterious activities in the area.

Historical Accuracy: The novel ingeniously re-creates a believable atmosphere and period background.

MARY-ANN TIRONE SMITH (1944-)

Born in Connecticut, Smith is a graduate of Central Connecticut State University. She was a Peace Corps volunteer in Africa and a kindergarten teacher. She has worked as a teacher at Fairfield University, and is best known for her first work, *The Book of Phoebe.*

`5925` Masters of Illusion: A Novel of the Connecticut Circus Fire

Date of Publication: 1994
Subject(s): Circus Life; Fires
Fictional character(s): Maggie Potter, Young Woman; Charlie O'Neill, Fire Fighter
Time Period(s): 1940s (1944)
Locale(s): Hartford, Connecticut

Summary: The novel re-creates the tragic Hartford circus fire that killed 169 people. Maggie Potter is a survivor who marries a Hartford fireman, Charlie O'Neill. Together they investigate the cause of the fire that haunts them both. The investigation strips away illusions and reveals some disturbing realities for both.

Historical Accuracy: The 1944 event is glimpsed with details that make the horror fresh and the disaster movingly real.

MASON MCCANN SMITH (1952-)

Born in California, Smith graduated from Pomona College. He has worked as a newspaper feature writer, has been a graduate student in anthropology, an assembly-line worker, a movie extra, and a motor home driver for Hollywood film companies.

`5926` When the Emperor Dies

Date of Publication: 1981
Subject(s): Victorian Period; Diplomacy
Fictional character(s): Rassam, Diplomat
Historical character(s): Theodore II, Ruler (King of Ethiopia); Robert Cornelis Napier, Military Personnel (British general); Henry John Temple, Political Figure, Nobleman (Viscount Palmerston); William Gladstone, Political Figure; Lord John Russell, Political Figure
Time Period(s): 1860s (1864-1868)
Locale(s): Massawa, Ethiopia; Magdala, Ethiopia; London, England

Summary: A perceived diplomatic slight felt by Theodore, Emperor of the Ethiopians, produces an international crisis that prompts the British to teach this mad despot a lesson. The novel chronicles the escalation to disaster that follows Theodore's presumption to be treated as an equal to Queen Victoria. Lord Napier's Indian Army mounts a full-scale invasion.

Historical Accuracy: The author insists that the story is very close to historical fact, but that some details were altered for the sake of the novel.

WILBUR SMITH (1933-)

Born in Northern Rhodesia (now Zambia), Smith is a graduate of Rhodes University. He considers himself a writer of entertainment fiction. Most of his adventure novels are set against a backdrop of southern Africa and concern the history of the land, wildlife, and people. *The Dark of the Sun* and *Gold Mine* were made into films.

`5927` Men of Men

Date of Publication: 1983
Subject(s): Family Saga; Frontier—Africa
Fictional character(s): Zouga Ballantyne, Settler, Businessman
Historical character(s): Cecil John Rhodes, Financier
Time Period(s): 1890s
Locale(s): South Africa

Summary: The Ballantyne family's fortune is tied to that of Cecil Rhodes, who establishes a commercial colossus while also setting in motion the confrontation and unrest that will mark relations between the Europeans and the native peoples in South Africa.

Historical Accuracy: The story of the Ballantyne family is invented, but the period elements are convincingly detailed.

`5928` River God

Date of Publication: 1993
Subject(s): Ancient Egypt; Pharaohs
Fictional character(s): Taita, Slave; Lostris, Young Woman; Tanus, Military Personnel (army officer)
Time Period(s): 20th century B.C.
Locale(s): Egypt

Summary: This absorbing and compelling story of ancient Egypt describes the interlocking destinies of Taita, a eunuch and slave; Lostris, an Egyptian lord's beautiful daughter; and

Tanus, a young army officer. Their story of passion and battle brings to life an ancient time and people.

Historical Accuracy: The novel's adventure is blended with solid research to present a convincing reconstruction of the past.

5929 *The Roar of the Thunder*

Date of Publication: 1966
Subject(s): Boer War; British Colonies
Fictional character(s): Sean Courteney, Adventurer
Time Period(s): 1890s (1899)
Locale(s): South Africa

Summary: The novel continues the adventures of Sean Courteney, ivory hunter, pioneer, and soldier of fortune, begun in *When the Lion Feeds*. Courteney takes to the battlefield as a British officer in the Boer War, fighting the burghers at their own game in guerrilla combat in the veld. Courteney's personal challenges play out against a backdrop of actual events of the Boer War.

Historical Accuracy: The novel's background of events and historical personalities is authentic.

5930 *Shout at the Devil*

Date of Publication: 1968
Subject(s): World War I; Sea Story
Fictional character(s): Flynn Patrick O'Flynn, Adventurer; Sebastian Oldsmith, Sailor; Herman Fleischer, Government Official
Time Period(s): 1910s
Locale(s): Africa

Summary: Set in East Africa at the outbreak of World War I, the novel describes adventurer Flynn Patrick O'Flynn's plan to sail into German territory and make off with a fortune in poached ivory. His nemesis, Herman Fleischer, sinks O'Flynn's small boat, and O'Flynn retaliates by attempting to destroy a German warship and with it Germany's stranglehold on East Africa.

Historical Accuracy: The story was suggested by action in World War I in which the German ship *Konigsberg* was sunk by the Royal Navy, but neither it nor its characters are meant to be taken as reflections of actual events or individuals.

5931 *When the Lion Feeds*

Date of Publication: 1964
Subject(s): Gold Rush—Africa; Zulu War; Frontier—Africa
Fictional character(s): Sean Courteney, Adventurer
Time Period(s): 1890s
Locale(s): South Africa

Summary: Sean Courteney joins the fight against the Zulus as a farmer-volunteer and then heads to the African gold fields, where a thousand-to-one shot makes his fortune. With wealth comes power, but the restless Courteney seeks more, returning to the wilderness in pursuit of ivory.

Historical Accuracy: The period and the region are captured with authenticity.

WILLIAM FIELDING SMITH

5932 *Diamond Six*

Date of Publication: 1958
Subject(s): Biography, Fictionalized; American West
Historical character(s): Wesley Smith, Veteran (Civil War), Rancher
Time Period(s): 19th century; 20th century (1844-1902)
Locale(s): Texas

Summary: This is the fictional biography of the author's grandfather, Wesley Smith, a veteran of the Civil War, Texas Ranger, sheriff, gun fighter, planter, and cattleman. Forced to leave Kentucky at the age of 15 for killing the man who murdered his father, Smith's adventurous life on the Texas frontier is described.

Historical Accuracy: The novel is truthful to the facts of Smith's life.

DAVID MYNDERS SMYTHE (1915-)

American historian and writer Smythe is a graduate of the University of Virginia. He was a career Foreign Service officer attached to the U.S. embassy in Paris prior to World War II. After the war he taught history at Loyola University in New Orleans. He is the author of the biography *Madame de Pompadour*.

5933 *Golden Venus*

Date of Publication: 1960
Subject(s): Biography, Fictionalized; Royalty—France
Historical character(s): Jeanne du Barry, Noblewoman (Comtesse du Barry); Louis XV, Ruler (King of France)
Time Period(s): 18th century
Locale(s): France

Summary: This biographical novel tells the remarkable story of the famous beauty and mistress of Louis XV, Madame du Barry. Her early life is spent in a convent school and on the streets of Paris selling ribbons. She rises to preside over a fashionable salon and captures the attention of the French king.

Historical Accuracy: The novel is based on solid research into the period and its personalities, but the gaps have been filled with interpretations that are a matter of opinion.

CAROLINE SNEDEKER

5934 *The Beckoning Road*

Date of Publication: 1929
Subject(s): Settlement of the American Frontier; Quakers
Fictional character(s): Dencey Coffyn, Settler
Historical character(s): Robert Owen, Leader (social reformer)
Time Period(s): 1840s
Locale(s): Indiana; Nantucket, Massachusetts

Summary: This tale of pioneer life describes the founding of the New Harmony Settlement in Indiana during the 1840s.

The novel describes the migration of a group of New England Quakers west from Nantucket to settle in Robert Owen's experimental community.

Historical Accuracy: The novel is based on the actual experiences of the New Harmony Settlement as derived from the memories of the author's grandmother.

5935 *Uncharted Ways*

Date of Publication: 1935
Subject(s): American Colonies; Religious Conflict; Quakers
Historical character(s): Mary Dyer, Religious (Quaker); John Cotton, Religious (minister)
Time Period(s): 17th century (1650s)
Locale(s): Boston, Massachusetts, American Colonies

Summary: Set in the Massachusetts Bay Colony during the 1650s, the novel dramatizes the religious persecution of the Quakers by John Cotton. The story is based on the actual experiences of Mary Dyer, a Quaker convert.

Historical Accuracy: The novel offers an authentic look at the period and the religious issues of the times.

LAURAINE SNELLING

5936 *An Untamed Land*

Date of Publication: 1996
Subject(s): Settlement of the American Frontier; Farming; Immigrants
Fictional character(s): Ronald Bjorklund, Immigrant; Ingeborg Bjorklund, Immigrant
Time Period(s): 1880s
Locale(s): Red River Valley, North Dakota

Summary: The novel describes the lot of Norwegian immigrants who journey west to settle in the Red River Valley of North Dakota during the 1880s. The novel characterizes the struggles of the Bjorklund family to make a home in the wilderness.

Historical Accuracy: The novel shows evidence of research into the period and the region that forms a convincing and authentic background for the story.

HELENA SOISTER

5937 *Prophecies*

Date of Publication: 1990
Subject(s): Religious Conflict; Mystery; Witchcraft and Sorcery
Fictional character(s): Sara Lathbury, Widow(er); Bess Marwick, Widow(er); Bartholomew Catlin, Businessman; Nicholas von Wouwere, Doctor, Occultist
Time Period(s): 16th century (1556)
Locale(s): Antwerp, Belgium

Summary: Sara and Beth are English widows of two merchants in search of a business manager in this tale of religious torment, guilt, and retribution. Evil is introduced by physician and black art practitioner Nicholas von Wouwere, a sinister monk, and an evil pauper.

Historical Accuracy: The novel is darkly atmospheric, derived from an effective period background.

LINDA SOLE

5938 *The Last Summer of Innocence*

Date of Publication: 1991
Subject(s): World War I
Fictional character(s): Emma Linton, Widow(er); Kate Linton, Young Woman
Time Period(s): 1910s (1913-1914)
Locale(s): Cambridgeshire, England; France

Summary: World War I is a catalyst in this story that begins in 1913 when the young widow Emma Linton sends her only child, Kate, to live in the Cambridgeshire fens to spare her from watching her mother die from consumption. Kate's first experiences of love are spoiled both by the outbreak of war and by revelations about her mother's past.

Historical Accuracy: The novel achieves a believable atmosphere of the period.

ARTHUR R.G. SOLMSSEN (1928-)

Born in New York, author and attorney Solmssen spent his early childhood in Berlin. He graduated from Harvard and the Law School of the University of Pennsylvania. His expertise in law and familiarity with main-line Philadelphia high society have produced a realistic backdrop for his novels featuring suspenseful courtroom battles and romantic entanglements. His novels include *Rittenhouse Square*, *The Comfort Letter*, and *Alexander's Feast*.

5939 *A Princess in Berlin*

Date of Publication: 1980
Subject(s): Wiemar Republic
Fictional character(s): Peter Ellis, Veteran (World War I), Artist; Christoph Keith, Veteran (German soldier); Bobby von Waldstein, Nobleman; Lili von Waldstein, Noblewoman
Time Period(s): 1920s (1922-1923)
Locale(s): Berlin, Germany

Summary: Germany after World War I is the backdrop for this novel that shows American patriot Peter Ellis' introduction to bohemian life in Berlin, with its radical politics of both Communists and Nazis. The story follows the crumbling lives of German aristocrats centering on the Von Waldstein family. Peter finds himself captivated by this dazzling life while also being swept up in political assassination and murder that threaten to change the old values.

Historical Accuracy: The story offers the color and period details of post-World War I Berlin to make a convincing backdrop for the fictional story.

RUTH FREEMAN SOLOMON (1908-)

Solomon was born in Kiev, Russia, received her education in the U.S. at Syracuse University, and pursued graduate work at the University of Vienna. Her novels include *The*

Eagle and the Dove, *The Ultimate Triumph*, and *The Wolf and the Leopard*.

5940   *The Candlesticks and the Cross*

Date of Publication: 1967
Subject(s): Russian Empire; Jews
Fictional character(s): Ronya Von Glasman, Young Woman; Boris Pirov, Nobleman
Time Period(s): 19th century; 20th century
Locale(s): Russia

Summary: Life in Russia for a wealthy Jewish family during the collapse of the Romanovs is depicted. The Von Glasmans are practicing Jews and landowners as well as advisers to the tsar. As such they are susceptible to the disaster that engulfs Russia when Rasputin rules the royal court and Tartars threaten to sack the Ukraine. At the center of the drama is the married life of Ronya Von Glasman and her Tartar husband, Boris Pirov.

Historical Accuracy: The characters are based on the author's ancestors, and the period is presented with believable details.

GREGORY SOLON (1923-1985)

Born in California, Solon served during World War II as a combat cameraman with the Eighth Air Force in North Africa and England and later as a tail gunner. He earned the Distinguished Flying Cross for his 175 bombing missions. After the war, he studied at the Sorbonne. He is the author of *Let Us Find Heroes*, a book about World War II.

5941   *The Three Legions*

Date of Publication: 1956
Subject(s): Roman Empire; Military Life
Fictional character(s): Quintillus Varus, Military Personnel (proconsul)
Time Period(s): 1st century (9)
Locale(s): Germany

Summary: While fighting German tribes, the three Roman legions under Proconsul Varus gradually disintegrate. Military life and the psychology of warfare are portrayed.

Historical Accuracy: The novel provides a convincing depiction of Roman customs.

ALEXANDER SOLZHENITSYN (1918-)

Born in Kislovodsk, Russia, Nobel Prize-winning author Solzhenitsyn emigrated to the United States in 1976, then returned to Russia after the collapse of the Communists. He attended the Moscow Institute of History, Philosophy, and Literature and the University of Rostov, where he received a degree in mathematics and physics. From 1945, when he was arrested for anti-Soviet activities while serving as a captain in the Soviet army, until his exile to the U.S., he was incarcerated in Soviet prisons and labor camps. He burst dramatically upon the literary scene with his 1962 novella *One Day in the Life of Ivan Denisovich*, the first published Soviet work of its kind exposing Stalin's camps. Among.

5942   *August 1914*

Date of Publication: 1971
Subject(s): World War I; Battle of Tannenberg; Russian Empire
Fictional character(s): Colonel Vorotyntsev, Military Personnel (Russian officer)
Historical character(s): Aleksandr Vasilyevich Samsonov, Military Personnel (Russian general)
Time Period(s): 1910s (1914)
Locale(s): East Prussia, Germany

Summary: The novel captures the events of the first two weeks of World War I on the Russian front and the disastrous Russian defeat at the Battle of Tannenberg. The event reveals the hollow core of Tsarism, and the staff blunders and incompetence that presage the fall of the Russian Empire in 1917.

Historical Accuracy: Clearly ideological imperatives are driving the presentation here, but the basic factual outline of the events is faithfully observed.

5943   *Lenin in Zurich*

Date of Publication: 1976
Subject(s): Politics; Russian Empire; Russian Revolution
Historical character(s): Vladimir Ilich Lenin, Revolutionary; Nadezhda Konstantinovna Krupskaya, Revolutionary
Time Period(s): 1900s; 1910s
Locale(s): Zurich, Switzerland

Summary: Lenin's life in Switzerland following the failed 1905 revolution in Russia is dramatized. The novel offers a day-to-day account of Lenin and his circle in which interior monologues reveal the revolutionary leader to be petty, self-righteous, and wrong-headed in predicting the course of the revolution. This unflattering picture is part of the author's larger portrait of Russia's collapse during World War I and its further corruption under the Communists.

Historical Accuracy: The depiction is clearly biased by the author's theme. The framework of events and situation is historical; the interpretation is clearly Solzhenitsyn's.

ROBERT SOMERLOTT (1928-)

Born in Huntington, Indiana, Somerlott was educated at Northwestern University, Michigan State University, and the University of Michigan. He worked as an actor and stage director before moving to Mexico in 1963 to become a freelance writer. His works include the novels *The Flamingos* and *The Inquisitor's House*, as well as many short stories and some nonfiction.

5944   *Death of the Fifth Sun*

Date of Publication: 1987
Subject(s): Aztec Empire; Spanish Colonies
Historical character(s): Hernando Cortez, Explorer, Military Personnel (conquistador); Montezuma II, Ruler (Aztec emperor); Ce Malinalli, Royalty (Aztec princess), Linguist (interpreter)
Time Period(s): 16th century
Locale(s): Mexico

Summary: This tale of the clash between the Aztecs and the Spanish under Cortez concerns Ce Malinalli, an Aztec princess who becomes the consort of Cortez and serves as his translator at the court of Montezuma.

Historical Accuracy: The novel features a convincing depiction of Aztec customs and the details of the Spanish conquest.

S.P. SOMTOW
(PSEUD. OF SOMTOW SUCHARITKUL, 1952-)

A Thai writer of science fiction and fantasy, Sucharitkul was born in Bangkok and attended St. Catherine's College, Cambridge. The winner of several literary awards, he originally worked in the music field as a conductor and avant-garde composer. Sucharitkul is the author of *Starship and Haiku*, *Light on the Sound*, and *The Aquiliad*.

`5945` *The Shattered Horse*
Date of Publication: 1986
Subject(s): Trojan War; Myths and Legends
Fictional character(s): Astyanax, Ruler (King of Troy)
Time Period(s): Indeterminate Past
Locale(s): Troy, Ancient Civilization

Summary: This tale of the aftermath of the Trojan War centers on Astyanax, the son of Hector, who survives the war to become King of Troy after the departure of the Greeks. Vowing revenge, Astyanax consults the gods and sets in motion the events leading to another conflict.

Historical Accuracy: The novel is informed by a strong knowledge of the period and the myths and legends of the time.

SUSAN SONTAG (1933-)

American novelist, short-story writer, critic, essayist, teacher, and filmmaker, Susan Sontag was born in New York City and attended the University of California, Berkeley, and Harvard University. An author of several collections of essays, including the prize winning *On Photography*, her works on modernist writing and Western culture have formed an important modern critical canon. Among her acclaimed nonfiction works are *Against Interpretation and Other Essays* and *Illness as Metaphor*. Her novels include *The Benefactor* and *Death Kit*.

`5946` *The Volcano Lover*
Date of Publication: 1992
Subject(s): Georgian Period; Napoleonic Wars
Historical character(s): Sir William Hamilton, Diplomat; Lady Emma Hamilton, Spouse, Gentlewoman; Horatio Nelson, Military Personnel (admiral)
Time Period(s): 18th century; 19th century
Locale(s): Naples, Italy

Summary: Based on the lives of Sir William Hamilton, his young and celebrated wife, Emma, and her lover, the great naval hero Horatio Nelson, the novel is an occasion for speculation on the causes of revolution, the condition of women, and the nature of love. Hamilton, a widower, selects and marries his nephew's former mistress. She blossoms under his care into a celebrated beauty who attracts the attention of the young British admiral Nelson.

Historical Accuracy: The author admits to a high degree of imaginative liberty in her depiction of character and events. Although based on actual figures, the novel is not constrained too tightly by the truth.

TROY SOOS (1957-)

Born in New Jersey, Soos lives in Boston. He did graduate work at Massachusetts Institute of Technology and worked in thermal physics research by day while writing baseball mysteries at night. He recently quit his job to write full time. A baseball buff and member of the Society for American Baseball Research, he considers himself the lone purveyor of historical baseball mysteries.

`5947` *Murder at Ebbets Field*
Date of Publication: 1995
Subject(s): Sports; Mystery; Baseball
Fictional character(s): Mickey Rawlings, Sports Figure (baseball player)
Historical character(s): Casey Stengel, Sports Figure (baseball player); Rube Marquard, Sports Figure (baseball player); Christy Mathewson, Sports Figure (baseball player); John McGraw, Sports Figure (baseball player)
Time Period(s): 1910s (1914)
Locale(s): New York, New York (Brooklyn); Coney Island, New York

Summary: In the second of the author's baseball mysteries, the year is 1914, and Mickey Rawlings is with the first-place New York Giants as they play the last-place Brooklyn Dodgers. When he discovers the nude body of the widow of the Dodgers' owner, Mickey finds himself entangled in a murder mystery that connects baseball and the fledgling movie business.

Historical Accuracy: The novel features convincing details of the period.

`5948` *Murder at Fenway Park*
Date of Publication: 1994
Subject(s): Mystery; Baseball; Sports
Fictional character(s): Mickey Rawlings, Sports Figure (baseball player); Robert Tyler, Businessman; Peggy Shaw, Entertainer
Historical character(s): Ty Cobb, Sports Figure (baseball player); Walter Johnson, Sports Figure (baseball player)
Time Period(s): 1910s (1912)
Locale(s): Boston, Massachusetts; New York, New York; St. Louis, Missouri

Summary: A rookie, Mickey Rawlings, reports to the Boston Red Sox at brand-new Fenway Park in 1912 and discovers a dead man battered beyond recognition. Mickey is a suspect, and he begins his own investigation. His inquiry leads him into the shady world of gambling, threats, and a number of suspects, including Ty Cobb.

Historical Accuracy: The novel is filled with authentic details about early baseball, on and off the field.

5949 *Murder at Wrigley Field*

Date of Publication: 1996
Subject(s): Mystery; Baseball; World War I
Fictional character(s): Mickey Rawlings, Sports Figure (baseball player)
Historical character(s): Shoeless Joe Jackson, Sports Figure (baseball player); Fred Merkle, Sports Figure (baseball player)
Time Period(s): 1910s (1918)
Locale(s): Chicago, Illinois

Summary: It is 1918 and America is at war, and anti-German sentiment is rampant, felt even in baseball. Mickey Rawlings is playing for the Cubs, and he agrees to help the owner investigate who might be trying to sabotage the team. Things turn deadly when a rookie named Willie Kaiser is shot dead in Wrigley Field on July 4th.

Historical Accuracy: The novel is expert at capturing the period and authentic details of baseball.

VIRGINIA SORENSEN (1912-1991)

An American author of books for adults and children, Sorensen was born in Provo, Utah, and attended Brigham Young University and Stanford University. She is best known for her award-winning children's books *Plain Girl* and *Miracles on Maple Hill*, which won the 1957 Newbery Medal. Her adult novels include *A Little Lower than the Angels* and *The Man with the Key*.

5950 *Kingdom Come*

Date of Publication: 1960
Subject(s): Religious Life; Mormons; Rural Life—Denmark
Fictional character(s): Hanne Dalsgaard, Young Woman
Time Period(s): 1850s
Locale(s): Denmark

Summary: Set in Denmark during the 1850s, the novel describes a group that converts to the Mormon faith and faces the decision to immigrate to America. The novel offers a realistic look at Danish life and the attraction of Mormonism that leads to breaking ties of home for a new life in America.

Historical Accuracy: The novel provides a believable portrait of customs and the period.

ARTHUR E. SOUTHON (1887-)

Born in London, Southon was a Methodist minister. He published a number of novels, including *On Eagle's Wings* and *Laughing Ghosts*.

5951 *On Eagles' Wings*

Date of Publication: 1937
Subject(s): Biblical Story; Biography, Fictionalized
Historical character(s): Moses, Biblical Figure
Time Period(s): 13th century B.C.

Locale(s): Egypt; Middle East

Summary: The novel presents a fictional re-creation of the story of Moses and the exodus of the Hebrews from Egypt. Borrowing from the Old Testament sources and evident research in the period and its customs, the novel provides a depiction of Moses as a man and a leader.

Historical Accuracy: The story offers a plausible period background and psychological characterization of Moses.

JOHN V.D. SOUTHWORTH (1904-1986)

Born in Syracuse, New York, Southworth graduated from Harvard and Columbia. He is the author of the nonfiction *The Story of the World*. He contributed to encyclopedias and was one of the authors on the radio series "Cavalcade of America." Southworth is the author of numerous nonfiction works and film and radio scripts, as well as a four-volume study of naval history, *War at Sea*.

5952 *The Pirate From Rome*

Date of Publication: 1965
Subject(s): Roman Empire; Pirates; Servile War
Fictional character(s): Marcus Lucius Paulus, Young Man, Pirate; Marcia, Young Woman
Historical character(s): Marc Antony, Military Personnel (general); Julius Caesar, Military Personnel (general); Pompey, Military Personnel (general)
Time Period(s): 1st century (B)
Locale(s): Rome, Roman Empire; Athens, Greece

Summary: The novel tells the story of the Pirate Brotherhood that dominated the Mediterranean during the 1st century B.C. Marcus Paulus is the son of a Roman senator who goes to Athens to finish his education. Instead he winds up joining the Pirate Brotherhood to save the captive Marcia. The novel features galley warfare, setting the pirates against the might of the Roman Republic.

Historical Accuracy: The historical framework of the story is authentic. The author is an expert in naval history, and the details of period warfare are faithfully presented.

ALBERT SPALDING (1888-1953)

Born in Chicago, Spalding studied violin in Florence and in the United States, debuting with the New York Symphony Orchestra in 1908. In addition to a long concert career, he wrote an autobiography, *Rise to Follow*, and a novel based on the life of Guiseppe Tartini, *A Fiddle, a Sword, and a Lady*.

5953 *A Fiddle, a Sword, and a Lady*

Date of Publication: 1953
Subject(s): Biography, Fictionalized; Musical Life
Historical character(s): Giuseppe Tartini, Composer, Musician (violinist)
Time Period(s): 18th century
Locale(s): Italy

Summary: This fictional story is based on the life of the greatest violin master of the 18th century, Giuseppe Tartini. Facts about the great musician and composer are interwoven with romance and adventure.

Historical Accuracy: The author's obvious knowledge of Tartini and his art lends authority to the fictional treatment.

ELIZABETH SPEARE (1908-)

Born in Massachusetts and a graduate of Boston University, Speare has taught English in high school and received two Newbery Awards for *The Witch of Blackbird Pond* and *The Bronze Bow*.

5954 *The Prospering*

Date of Publication: 1967
Subject(s): American Colonies; Settlement of the American Frontier; Indians
Fictional character(s): Elizabeth Williams, Young Woman; Ephraim Williams, Settler; John Sergeant, Religious (clergyman)
Historical character(s): Jonathan Edwards, Religious (minister)
Time Period(s): 18th century
Locale(s): Stockbridge, Massachusetts, American Colonies

Summary: The novel dramatizes the settlement of Stockbridge, Massachusetts, the colonists' relationship with the Indians, and the religious issues of the day. The story centers on the experiences of Elizabeth Williams and her father's rise and fall as a force in the community.

Historical Accuracy: The novel is based on facts and captures the period convincingly.

FRANK H. SPEARMAN

5955 *Carmen of the Rancho*

Date of Publication: 1937
Subject(s): Mexican War; Indians
Fictional character(s): Henry Bowie, Scout; Carmen Estrada, Young Woman
Time Period(s): 1840s
Locale(s): California

Summary: This tale of Spanish California during the conflict between America and Mexico involves a Texas scout, Henry Bowie. He rescues a young girl, Carmen Estrada, from the Indians and later reencounters her when he is captured by the Mexicans and sentenced to death as a spy.

Historical Accuracy: The romance elements predominate here over a carefully documented historical background.

JAN COX SPEAS

5956 *Bride of the MacHugh*

Date of Publication: 1954
Subject(s): Jacobean Period

Fictional character(s): Elsbeth Lamond, Gentlewoman; Alexander MacHugh, Laird
Time Period(s): 17th century
Locale(s): Scotland

Summary: Set during the reign of James I during his troubles with the Highland clans, the novel follows the adventures of Scottish-born but English-raised Elsbeth Lamond. Lamond journeys to the Highland seat of her kinsman, Duncan Campbell of Inverary. She is abducted by a highwayman, solves the secret of a long-lost brother, and becomes involved in the political turmoil of the period, eventually becoming the bride of Alexander, laird of the Clan MacHugh.

Historical Accuracy: The novel features a believable evocation of the period and its conflicts.

5957 *My Lord Monleigh*

Date of Publication: 1956
Subject(s): Civil War—England
Fictional character(s): Simon of Monleigh, Nobleman; Anne Lindsay, Orphan, Companion
Time Period(s): 17th century
Locale(s): Highlands, Scotland

Summary: This romantic tale set during Cromwell's rule tells the story of Anne Lindsay, who falls in love with Simon of Monleigh, a rebellious proponent of the Stuart cause. As the companion of a family of dour Scottish Presbyterians and Cromwellians, Anne must conceal her attachment to Monleigh before finally joining his rebellion against Cromwell.

Historical Accuracy: The novel's romance predominates over a full historical presentation. However, the atmosphere of the period and its conflicts are captured effectively.

5958 *My Love, My Enemy*

Date of Publication: 1961
Subject(s): War of 1812; Espionage; Sea Story
Fictional character(s): Page Bradley, Young Woman; Jocelyn Trevor, Nobleman (Viscount Hazard)
Time Period(s): 1810s
Locale(s): Washington, District of Columbia; Annapolis, Maryland; Bermuda

Summary: This romantic adventure story is set during the War of 1812 and involves the headstrong Page Bradley who helps rescue a young Englishman from a lynch mob. Capture by the British follows, and she learns that the man is a nobleman, Lord Hazard, and a possible British spy. The novel's climax is the British attack on Washington.

Historical Accuracy: Romantic adventure predominates over a careful and precise rendering of the period.

CATHY CASH SPELLMAN (1941-)

Born in New Jersey, Spellman attended Vassar College and the Art Students League. She has worked as a copywriter in advertising and was the creative director for Revlon who developed the marketing campaign for the popular Charlie brand of perfume. Spellman is the author of many bestselling novels.

5959 *An Excess of Love*

Date of Publication: 1984

Subject(s): Independence—Ireland; Easter Rising; Civil War—Ireland

Fictional character(s): Constance FitzGibbon, Patriot, Rebel; Beth FitzGibbon, Writer; Tierney O'Connor, Patriot, Rebel

Historical character(s): William Butler Yeats, Writer; Sean O'Casey, Writer; Constance Markievicz, Gentlewoman, Patriot; James Connolly, Patriot, Rebel; Patrick Henry Pearse, Patriot, Rebel; Michael Collins, Patriot, Political Figure; Eamon De Valera, Patriot, Political Figure

Time Period(s): 19th century; 20th century (1890s-1920s)

Locale(s): Ireland

Summary: The story of the Irish struggle for independence is told in the experiences of two sisters, Constance and Beth FitzGibbon. Constance marries the aspiring poet and revolutionary Tierney O'Connor and becomes involved in the events of the Easter Rising. Beth becomes a renowned author. Their story is connected with many of the important figures in the rush of events that leads to the creation of a free Irish nation.

Historical Accuracy: The author took painstaking care to accurately reflect the historical background of the story. However, the story is a biased one—written entirely from the point of view of the Irish. The story is not intended as a history that captures both sides of a complex situation.

5960 *Paint the Wind*

Date of Publication: 1989

Subject(s): American West; Civil War—U.S.; Indians

Fictional character(s): Fancy Deverell, Young Woman; Chance McAllister, Gambler; Hart McAllister, Artist

Historical character(s): Geronimo, Indian (Apache), Warrior

Time Period(s): 19th century (1862-1890s)

Locale(s): Colorado; New York, New York

Summary: This sweeping adventure novel follows the eventful life of Fancy Deverell, who leaves a southern plantation devastated by border raiders to journey west to the gold and silver fields of Colorado where she becomes involved with the McAllister brothers. One is a gambler, the other an artist. Fancy's story takes her to the New York stage and the final struggles of Geronimo and the Apache Nation.

Historical Accuracy: Though most of the characters are fictional, the spirit is factual. Despite some alterations of details, the author insists that it could have happened exactly this way.

HARTZELL SPENCE (1908-)

Born in Clarion, Iowa, American author Hartzwell Spence was educated at the University of Iowa. He worked for the United Press as a bureau manager of the Special Services Division, and in public relations before he became a freelance writer in 1946. During World War II, Spence served with the U.S. Army Air Forces, and was the founder and first editor of the Army weekly, *Yank*. His novels include *One Foot in Heaven*, *Radio City*, and *Vain Shadow*.

5961 *Bride of the Conqueror*

Date of Publication: 1954

Subject(s): Spanish Colonies

Fictional character(s): Dona Eloisa Canillejas, Noblewoman

Time Period(s): 16th century (1540s)

Locale(s): Peru; Panama

Summary: Spanish aristocrat Dona Eloisa journeys to the New World only to find her husband-to-be has died. With her great beauty and dowry, she finds herself a rich prize for a variety of suitors.

Historical Accuracy: This is a somewhat light-hearted romance with some convincing period elements added.

5962 *Vain Shadow*

Date of Publication: 1947

Subject(s): Exploration; Biography, Fictionalized

Historical character(s): Francisco de Orellana, Explorer

Time Period(s): 16th century

Locale(s): South America

Summary: This fictionalized biography of Francisco de Orellana, Spanish explorer of the Amazon River, chronicles his career in South America. A lieutenant of Francisco Pizarro, Orellana floats down the length of the Amazon when he is separated from the rest of his expedition. His tale of female warriors gives the Amazon River its name.

Historical Accuracy: Where provable facts are lacking, authentic elements have been invented to fill the gaps.

ARMSTRONG SPERRY (1897-1976)

American illustrator and author, Sperry was born in New Haven, Connecticut, and studied at the Yale School of Fine Arts, the Arts Students League, and the Academie Colarrossis in Paris. Although Sperry began his career solely as an illustrator, he eventually began to write his own books. Most of his books are based on his own experiences as a world traveller. *Call It Courage*, perhaps his most notable book, received the John Newbery Medal for the most distinguished children's book of 1941. His other books include *Storm Canvas* and *The Rain Forest*.

5963 *No Brighter Glory*

Date of Publication: 1942

Subject(s): American West

Fictional character(s): Mark Denny, Doctor; India de Chambord, Young Woman

Historical character(s): John Jacob Astor, Businessman; Kamehameha I, Ruler (king of the Hawaiian Islands)

Time Period(s): 1810s (1810-1812)

Locale(s): New York; Pacific Northwest; Hawaii

Summary: The novel recounts John Jacob Astor's fur trading expedition to establish an outpost on the Columbia River in 1810. Mark Denny is a young Vermont doctor who agrees to go on the trip out of his love for India de Chambord. Storms and Indian attack are only some of the obstacles they encounter.

Historical Accuracy: The novel provides a colorful and believable portrait of the period.

BART SPICER (1918-)

An American writer born in Virginia, Spicer worked as a journalist and radio writer. His books have been published in many European countries and Japan.

5964 *Brother to the Enemy*

Date of Publication: 1958
Subject(s): American Revolution; Espionage
Fictional character(s): John Champion, Military Personnel (sergeant-major), Spy
Historical character(s): Benedict Arnold, Military Personnel (general); Henry Lee, Military Personnel (cavalry commander)
Time Period(s): 1770s
Locale(s): New York, New York, American Colonies

Summary: Based on an actual incident recounted in the memoirs of Light-Horse Harry Lee, the novel dramatizes John Champion's attempt to enter the British encampment in New York as a spy to capture Benedict Arnold. Champion is based on Lee's actual Sergeant Major John Champe. The novel builds to the dramatic confrontation between the spy and the traitor Arnold.

Historical Accuracy: The novel considerably elaborates on the sketchy facts suggested by Lee.

5965 *The Day Before Thunder*

Date of Publication: 1969
Subject(s): American Colonies; American Revolution
Fictional character(s): James Coult, Businessman
Time Period(s): 1770s
Locale(s): London, England; New York, New York, American Colonies

Summary: Young James Coult embarks for colonial New York on a mission to rescue the faltering branch of his family's banking concern. He arrives on the brink of the American Revolution, and he is soon swept up in intrigue that represents a divided loyalty. James must decide between the family fortune and the larger promise of freedom offered by the rebels.

Historical Accuracy: The period details of revolutionary New York are believable.

5966 *The Wild Ohio*

Date of Publication: 1953
Subject(s): French Revolution; Settlement of the American Frontier
Fictional character(s): Duncan Crosbie, Military Personnel (colonel); Nicholas Blanchard, Military Personnel (lieutenant)
Time Period(s): 1790s (1790)

Locale(s): Gallipolis, Ohio

Summary: A company of French emigres fleeing from the terror of the French Revolution depart from Virginia and go west to the settlement of Gallipolis in the Ohio wilderness. Based on an actual incident, the novel chronicles their adventures and gradual adaptation to life on the frontier.

Historical Accuracy: The novel offers a solid and convincing historical background.

CARL J. SPINATELLI

5967 *Baton Sinister*

Date of Publication: 1959
Subject(s): Renaissance
Fictional character(s): Marco Doria, Bastard Son, Adventurer
Time Period(s): 16th century
Locale(s): Italy; Barbary Coast, Africa

Summary: This romantic adventure tale concerns the attempt of Marco, the illegitimate son of a murdered nobleman, to win a name for himself. He is captured by the Moors, escapes, captures Tunis almost single-handedly, and avenges his father's murder.

Historical Accuracy: This is an atmospheric romantic adventure story with only a hint of historical reality.

5968 *The Florentine*

Date of Publication: 1953
Subject(s): Renaissance; Artistic Life; Biography, Fictionalized
Historical character(s): Benvenuto Cellini, Artist (sculptor), Writer
Time Period(s): 16th century
Locale(s): Florence, Italy; Rome, Italy

Summary: This biographical novel dramatizes the career of Renaissance artist and writer Benvenuto Cellini. The novel traces his career from his youth in Florence and the beginning of his artistic reputation to his days in Rome under the patronage of Pope Clement VII and his imprisonment and escape from the Castle Sant' Angelo.

Historical Accuracy: The novel offers a dependable evocation of the period and Cellini's career, though not as lively nor as genuine as Cellini's own classic *Autobiography*.

ROSEMARY SPRAGUE

Sprague graduated from Bryn Mawr and Western Reserve University, where she earned her Ph.D. in English. She has worked as a professor at Longwood College. Sprague is lecturer on Shakespeare and an authority on children's literature. She is the author of a biography of Robert Browning, *Forever in Joy*, and her novels include *Northward to Albion*, *Heir to Kiloran*, and *The Jade Pagoda*.

5969 *Red Lion and Gold Dragon*

Date of Publication: 1967

Subject(s): Norman Conquest; Middle Ages; Battle of Hastings
Fictional character(s): Aelfred Ansculfson, Fugitive, Adventurer; Osric, Servant; Lady Adelaid, Gentlewoman
Historical character(s): William the Conqueror, Nobleman (Duke of Normandy)
Time Period(s): 11th century
Locale(s): England

Summary: The story of the Norman Conquest is described through the adventures of Aelfred Ansculfson, who is a victim of intrigue by his Norman step-brother. He flees his pursuers and joins the Saxon cause, fighting with King Harold up to the Saxon defeat at the Battle of Hastings. Aelfred finally wins the respect of William of Normandy.

Historical Accuracy: The novel blends what is known about the events of 1066 and offers plausible suggestions for what must be surmised.

EDOUARD A. STACKPOLE (1903-1993)

Born in Colorado and a graduate of the University of California, Los Angeles Stackpole was the curator of the Mystic Seaport Museum and an author of many books and articles about the sea, whatling, and New England history. He served for many years as the president of the Nantucket Historical Society.

5970 *Nantucket Rebel*

Date of Publication: 1963
Subject(s): American Revolution; Sea Story; Quakers
Fictional character(s): Stephen Starbuck, Sailor
Time Period(s): 1770s
Locale(s): Nantucket, Massachusetts, American Colonies

Summary: Dissension among the Quaker community of Nantucket forms the backdrop for this story of divided loyalties. Stephen Starbuck returns from a long whaling voyage and is forced to take sides in the growing conflict of the American Revolution. Opting to join the rebellion, he becomes a privateer.

Historical Accuracy: The story is imagined but features convincing details of period life.

DAVID STACTON (1925-1968)

Born in Nevada, Stacton graduated from the University of California. He is a poet and novelist whose historical novels examine rare and unfamiliar people and events from the past. Stacton's books helped launch a revolution in historical fiction by rejecting its most cherished conventions.

5971 *A Dancer in Darkness*

Date of Publication: 1962
Subject(s): Renaissance; Espionage
Fictional character(s): Bosola, Spy; Amelia, Noblewoman (Duchess of Amalfi); Roberto Sanducci, Religious (cardinal)
Time Period(s): 17th century (1611)
Locale(s): Amalfi, Italy

Summary: The author retells the story of John Webster's *The Duchess of Malfi*, a darkly violent tale of lust, selfishness, greed, and corruption in the Renaissance. At the center of the story is the spy Bosola, the ''dancer in darkness.'' He is drawn into the unscrupulous plotting of Cardinal Sanducci but becomes more a victim than an agent in the cardinal's schemes.

Historical Accuracy: Stacton is able both to reveal a past age and to use it to fashion a modern work of psychological and moral commentary.

5972 *The Judges of the Secret Court*

Date of Publication: 1961
Subject(s): Civil War—U.S.; Assassination; Trials
Historical character(s): John Wilkes Booth, Murderer, Actor; Edwin Booth, Actor; Edwin Stanton, Political Figure (Secretary of War)
Time Period(s): 1860s (1865)
Locale(s): Washington, District of Columbia

Summary: The novel dramatizes the events of the assassination of Abraham Lincoln, focusing on John Wilkes Booth and the aftermath of Lincoln's murder. The events are narrated in a coolly dispassionate manner which effectively captures the chain of events and the atmosphere of postwar Washington. Neither Booth nor Edwin Stanton are shown sympathetically.

Historical Accuracy: The novel suggests that Booth committed suicide in Richard Garrett's barn, a fact that historians dispute.

5973 *On a Balcony*

Date of Publication: 1958
Subject(s): Ancient Egypt; Pharaohs; Religious Conflict
Historical character(s): Akhenaton, Ruler (pharaoh); Nefertiti, Royalty (Queen of Egypt); Horemheb, Ruler (pharaoh)
Time Period(s): 14th century B.C.
Locale(s): Egypt

Summary: The controversial Pharaoh Akhenaton briefly imposes monotheism on ancient Egypt at a great cost. In this psychological study. Akhenaton emerges as a hysteric with a fanatical religious obsession and his wife/sister Nefertiti as a scheming manipulator.

Historical Accuracy: The novel provides an imaginative repossession of the era and its characters who are brought to vivid life.

5974 *People of the Book*

Date of Publication: 1965
Subject(s): Thirty Years War; Religious Conflict
Fictional character(s): Lars Larsen, Young Man; Hannale Larsen, Young Woman
Historical character(s): Axel Oxenstierna, Political Figure (chancellor of Sweden); Gustavus II Adolphus, Ruler (King of Sweden)
Time Period(s): 17th century (1635-1636)
Locale(s): Sweden; Germany

Summary: The novel describes the bloody religious conflict of the Thirty Years War in parallel stories. The first centers on the powerful Gustavus Adolphus, King of Sweden, and his chancellor, Axel Oxenstierna, through whom the events of the conflict at the state level are reflected. The second story is that of Lars Larsen and his young sister, Hannale, who search across a war-torn Europe for their only living relative.

Historical Accuracy: The depiction of the period and its events is authentic and convincing.

`5975` *Segaki*

Date of Publication: 1959
Subject(s): Religious Life; Japanese Empire
Fictional character(s): Muchaku Hojo, Religious (Buddhist priest); Yasumaro Hojo, Artist (painter); Lady Furikake, Gentlewoman
Time Period(s): 14th century (1333)
Locale(s): Japan

Summary: The novel's theme is the pursuit of *Satori*—intuitive enlightenment and serenity—by a Zen Buddhist priest during the civil wars in 14th-century Japan. The author's practice in this and other books is to place a small group of characters against a minor but revealing moment in history and examine the human spirit in conflict with circumstances and self. The monk Muchaku tries to resolve the spiritual crisis produced by the feudal conflict that surrounds him.

Historical Accuracy: The author shows a remarkable ability to render the historical period with precision and nuance.

`5976` *A Signal Victory*

Date of Publication: 1962
Subject(s): Mayan Empire
Fictional character(s): Guerrero, Sailor
Time Period(s): 16th century
Locale(s): Yucatan, Mexico

Summary: In 1511 Guerrero, a Spanish seaman, is shipwrecked on the coast of the Yucatan where he is taken in by the Mayans. He learns their language, marries a Mayan princess, and rises to a position of leadership. When the Spanish conquistadors arrive, Guerrero helps lead the Mayan resistance.

Historical Accuracy: The novel provides the occasion for a somber meditation on the clash of cultures. It succeeds in recreating the doomed world of the Mayans. However, the novel's Spaniards are far less believable in their unredeemed villainy.

`5977` *Sir William*

Date of Publication: 1963
Subject(s): Napoleonic Era
Historical character(s): Horatio Nelson, Military Personnel (naval admiral); Lady Emma Hamilton, Gentlewoman; Sir William Hamilton, Gentleman, Diplomat
Time Period(s): 18th century; 19th century (1782-1803)
Locale(s): Sicily, Italy; England

Summary: The novel tells the story of the famous love affair between Admiral Horatio Nelson and Lady Emma Hamilton from the viewpoint of Emma's aging husband, Sir William. He is surprisingly acquiescent of their affair, which helps the

author deflate the idealized aspects of the Nelson-Hamilton romantic legend.

Historical Accuracy: The author explodes the myths of this famous love affair and offers a realistic alternative that is convincing.

HILDA STAHL (1938-1993)

A writer, teacher, and lecturer, Stahl was born in Nebraska. She published 92 fictional titles and 450 short stories during her prolific career. In 1989 she won the Silver Angel Award for *Sadie Rose and the Daring Escape*. Among her works are *Undercover* and *Blackmail*, both part of the Amber Ainslie detective series, and *The Inheritance* and *The Covenant*, both part of the White Pine Chronicles.

`5978` *The Woman of Catawba*

Date of Publication: 1993
Subject(s): Antebellum South
Fictional character(s): Taylor Craven, Widow(er); Andrew Simons, Gentleman; Yates Marston, Widow(er)
Time Period(s): 18th century
Locale(s): Charleston, South Carolina

Summary: Set in South Carolina in the years following the American Revolution, the novel depicts the experiences of English widow Taylor Craven who is forced to flee from England to America. Aboard ship she meets a group of characters whose fate becomes connected with the plantation of Catawba in the South Carolina wilderness.

Historical Accuracy: The novel provides a believable period background for this romantic story.

ALFRED STANFORD (1900-1985)

An American newspaper executive, publisher, editor, and author, Stanford was born in East Orange, New Jersey, attended Amherst College, and served in the U.S. Naval Reserve during World War II. He was a recipient of the Legion of Merit and the Croix de Guerre for his war service. Stanford worked as editor and publisher of *Boats* and as second vice-president and advertising director of the *New York Herald Tribune*. His books include *Groundswell*, *A City out of the Sea*, and *Mission in Sparrow Bush Lane*.

`5979` *The Navigator: The Story of Nathaniel Bowditch*

Date of Publication: 1927
Subject(s): Biography, Fictionalized; American Colonies
Historical character(s): Nathaniel Bowditch, Sailor
Time Period(s): 1770s
Locale(s): Salem, Massachusetts, American Colonies

Summary: This fictional biography depicts the career of Nathaniel Bowditch, author of *The American Practical Navigator*. The novel features a vivid depiction of Salem, Massachusetts, before the American Revolution.

Historical Accuracy: The novel is faithful to the known facts of Bowditch's life.

HENRIK STANGERUP

`5980` *The Seducer*

Date of Publication: 1990
Subject(s): Biography, Fictionalized; Literary Life
Historical character(s): Peder Ludwig Moller, Writer
Time Period(s): 19th century
Locale(s): Denmark; Paris, France

Summary: Mixing history and fantasy, the novel provides a fictional portrait of Danish literary critic and libertine Peder Ludwig Moller. The novel blends direct quotations from Moller's writing with an imaginative flight into Moller's fantasies and dreams.

Historical Accuracy: The book is a novel, not a biography, although it contains authentic biographical material.

EDWARD STANLEY (1903-)

`5981` *The Rock Cried Out*

Date of Publication: 1949
Subject(s): Settlement of the American Frontier; Politics
Historical character(s): Aaron Burr, Political Figure; Harman Blennerhasset, Settler; Margaret Blennerhasset, Spouse
Time Period(s): 1790s; 1800s
Locale(s): Ohio Valley, United States

Summary: The novel traces the curious career of Harman and Margaret Blennerhasset. When Harman marries his niece in England, the couple is ostracized. They emigrate to America, where they settle on an island in the Ohio River. Blennerhasset advances money to Aaron Burr to further his scheme of establishing a western republic. The novel tells Blennerhasset's story from the couple's marriage through their part in Burr's treason and the decline of their fortune that follows.

Historical Accuracy: The novel stays close to the historical facts, but there are some rather glaring errors.

`5982` *Thomas Forty*

Date of Publication: 1947
Subject(s): American Revolution
Fictional character(s): Thomas Forty, Military Personnel (lieutenant), Printer
Time Period(s): 1770s; 1780s
Locale(s): Westchester County, New York

Summary: This novel set during the American Revolution follows the experiences of a young printer, Thomas Forty, who at first tries to maintain his neutrality, but eventually sides with the Colonists. He becomes a lieutenant in Armand's Partizan legion and plays an important role in the conflict.

Historical Accuracy: The novel offers an authentic look at the period.

FRANCES PATTON STATHAM (1931-)

American author Statham was born in South Carolina and graduated from Winthrop College and the University of Georgia. Statham was named Georgia's author of the year in 1978, 1979, and 1984. She is an award-winning artist and also a lyric-coloratura soprano. She began writing after taking a fiction writing course at Emory University and has specialized in romantic fiction.

`5983` *Trail of Tears*

Date of Publication: 1993
Subject(s): Indians
Fictional character(s): Laurel MacDonald, Indian (Cherokee), Teacher; Night Hawk, Indian (Cherokee)
Time Period(s): 1830s
Locale(s): Georgia

Summary: The story of the Indian removal policy that produced the forced emigration of the Cherokee Nation is told from the perspective of Laurel MacDonald. MacDonald is the daughter of a Cherokee chief and a teacher at a music school in Georgia. Her life is torn apart in the ensuing conflict, and she must choose between the white world and that of her people.

Historical Accuracy: The novel offers a convincing depiction of the era and the tragic effects of the government's Indian policy.

MARGUERITE STEEDMAN (1908-)

An American journalist, teacher, and writer born in Atlanta, Steedman worked as a book editor for the *Atlanta Times*. She is the author of *The South Carolina Colony*.

`5984` *Refuge in Avalon*

Date of Publication: 1962
Subject(s): Biblical Story; Druids
Historical character(s): Joseph of Arimathea, Biblical Figure; Jesus Christ, Biblical Figure
Time Period(s): 1st century
Locale(s): Israel; England

Summary: This Biblical tale connects the story of Christ with the Druids of ancient Britain. Joseph of Arimathea is shown as the grand-uncle of Jesus and is skeptical about the divinity of his nephew. He takes the 12-year-old to Britain, where Jesus is hailed by Druids as immortal. Only after the crucifixion, when Joseph seeks sanctuary in Britain, does he finally acknowledge Jesus as divine.

Historical Accuracy: The Greek and Roman background material is filled with inaccuracies.

DANIELLE STEEL (1947-)

Prolific bestselling romance novelist Danielle Steel was born in New York City and was educated in France, at the Parsons School of Design, and New York University. After producing a score of romance novels, which were generally dismissed by critics but almost always embraced by readers, Steel has been called a publishing phenomena. Her titles include *Now and Forever*, which was made into a movie,

Crossings, *Kaleidoscope*, *Fine Things*, *Changes*, *Daddy*, and *Palomino*, all of which were adapted for television.

5985 Zoya

Date of Publication: 1988
Subject(s): Russian Revolution; Russian Empire
Fictional character(s): Zoya Ossupov, Dancer; Clayton Andrews, Military Personnel (captain)
Time Period(s): 1910s
Locale(s): Russia; Paris, France; New York, New York

Summary: The struggles of romantic heroine Zoya Ossupov in the last days of Imperial Russia are dramatized. When the revolution comes, Zoya supports her family as a dancer with the Ballet Russe. A chance encounter with an affluent New Yorker, Captain Clayton Andrews, brings her to New York where tragedy follows.

Historical Accuracy: The novel's forte is romance with a serviceable, but hardly essential, period backdrop.

WILBUR DANIEL STEELE (1886-1970)

An American author, short story writer, and playwright, Steele was born in Greensboro, North Carolina, and attended the University of Denver, the Museum of Fine Arts in Boston, the Academie Julian in Paris, and the Art Students League. He is the author of several short story collections and the novels *Meat* and *The Way to the Gold*.

5986 Diamond Wedding

Date of Publication: 1950
Subject(s): American West; Settlement of the American Frontier
Fictional character(s): Skinner Gowd, Mountain Man, Scout
Time Period(s): 19th century; 20th century (1835-1919)
Locale(s): Denver, Colorado

Summary: The novel provides a portrait of mountain man and frontier scout, Skinner Gowd, over the course of his long and colorful career. Scenes include the founding of Denver and the settlement of Colorado.

Historical Accuracy: This is a believable tale with a convincing period background.

ROBERT STEELMAN (1914-)

Born in Ohio and a graduate of Ohio State University, Steelman served in the U.S. Navy Signal Corps and as a civilian electronics engineer. Steelman writes principally about the American West and attempts to make his backgrounds authoritative and true to the times, while endowing the Western story with some literary significance. His books include *Winter for the Sioux*, *Cheyenne Vengeance*, and *The Santee Massacre*.

5987 Call of the Arctic

Date of Publication: 1960
Subject(s): Exploration

Fictional character(s): Adam Burritt, Explorer
Historical character(s): Charles Francis Hall, Explorer
Time Period(s): 19th century
Locale(s): United States; Arctic

Summary: The novel dramatizes the Arctic expeditions of 19th-century American explorer Charles Francis Hall. Hall's three voyages into the Arctic are described by a young member of his team, Adam Burritt. Hall is a resolute and intrepid explorer, and the challenge of Arctic exploring is captured convincingly.

Historical Accuracy: The novel is a blend of solid research and accurate history with some imaginary elements. Hall's death by poisoning, instead of apoplexy, is fanciful.

MARGUERITE STEEN (1894-1975)

A British novelist, playwright, and biographer, Steen was born in Liverpool and was privately educated. A prolific writer, Steen's works include the novels *The Woman in the Back Seat* and *A Candle in the Sun*, a biography of Hugh Walpole, and two autobiographical volumes, *Looking Glass* and *Pier Glass*.

5988 The Sun Is My Undoing

Date of Publication: 1941
Subject(s): Georgian Period; Slavery; Family Saga
Fictional character(s): Matthew Flood, Trader (slave)
Time Period(s): 1760s
Locale(s): Bristol, England; Gold Coast, Africa; Cuba

Summary: Slave trader Matthew Flood's marriage to an abolitionist leads to problems. This is the first volume of a trilogy about the English Flood family.

Historical Accuracy: The novel believably captures its time period and various settings.

WALLACE STEGNER (1909-1993)

An American educator, environmentalist, editor, and writer, Stegner was born in Iowa and was renowned for his books on the American West. He won the Pulitzer Prize for *Angle of Repose* and the National Book Award in 1977 for *The Spectator Bird*. Stegner taught creative writing at Stanford for 26 years where he founded and led the university's writing program, one of the nation's best.

5989 Angle of Repose

Date of Publication: 1971
Subject(s): American West; Family Saga
Fictional character(s): Oliver Ward, Engineer; Susan Burling, Spouse (of Oliver)
Time Period(s): 19th century; 20th century (1860-1970)
Locale(s): West

Summary: The novel dramatizes the development of the American West through the story of four generations of an American family. Susan Burling leaves the East to marry mining engineer Oliver Ward, accompanying him from mining camp to mining camp throughout the West. Their hard life is recalled by their grandson as he sorts out the meaning of their suffering and strength.

Historical Accuracy: The period and the region are captured authentically.

HARRY STEIN (1948-)

Born in New York City, Stein attended Pomona College and Columbia University. He is a versatile journalist and author of biographies, social commentary, and historical fiction. His works include *One of the Guys: The Wising Up of an American Man*, a biography of the performer Tiny Tim, and a book of essays, *Ethics (and Other Liabilities): Trying to Live Right in an Amoral World*.

5990 *Hoopla*

Date of Publication: 1983
Subject(s): Sports; Baseball; Black Sox Scandal
Fictional character(s): Luther Pond, Journalist
Historical character(s): George "Buck" Weaver, Sports Figure (baseball player); John L. Sullivan, Sports Figure (boxer); Jim Jeffries, Sports Figure (boxer); Jack Johnson, Sports Figure (boxer); Ty Cobb, Sports Figure (baseball player); Ring Lardner, Writer, Journalist
Time Period(s): 1910s (1919)
Locale(s): Chicago, Illinois; New York, New York

Summary: The novel's story is told in alternating chapters narrated by fictional reporter Luther Pond and the actual Buck Weaver, a member of the infamous "Black Sox" who conspired to throw the World Series in 1919. Ranging from the Black Sox scandal itself to the fight of the century between Jack Johnson and Jim Jeffries, the novel brings to life America in the early years of the 20th century, when dreams faced a troubling reality.

Historical Accuracy: The novel's historical events and personalities are captured with authenticity.

JOHN STEINBECK

5991 *Cup of Gold*

Date of Publication: 1929
Subject(s): Sea Story; Pirates; Biography, Fictionalized
Historical character(s): Henry Morgan, Pirate
Time Period(s): 17th century (1635-1688)
Locale(s): Wales; Caribbean; Panama

Summary: The novel chronicles the life of English pirate Sir Henry Morgan, from his boyhood in Wales through his career as the scourge of the Spanish Main. Scenes include Morgan's sack of Panama and his respectable later years as the governor of Jamaica.

Historical Accuracy: The novel mixes the historical and the fanciful. The romance at times clashes with Morgan's actual biography.

MILTON STEINBERG (1903-1950)

A rabbi, Steinberg was the author of such books as *Anatomy of Faith*, *Basic Judaism*, *A Believing Jew*, and *The Making of the Modern Jew*.

5992 *As a Driven Leaf*

Date of Publication: 1940
Subject(s): Roman Empire; Jews
Historical character(s): Elisha ben Abuyah, Religious (rabbi)
Time Period(s): 2nd century
Locale(s): Palestine

Summary: Elisha ben Abuyah, a Jewish rabbi, is driven to renounce his faith and betray his people to the Roman governors of Palestine during the 2nd century's Jewish persecutions.

Historical Accuracy: The novel provides a convincing historical and scholarly background.

STENDHAL
(PSEUD. OF HENRI BEYLE, 1783-1842)

One of the greatest French novelists, Stendhal served in Napoleon's army and was present at the burning of Moscow. His masterpieces are *The Red and the Black* and *The Charterhouse of Parma*.

5993 *The Charterhouse of Parma*

Date of Publication: 1839
Subject(s): Napoleonic Wars; Battle of Waterloo
Fictional character(s): Del Dongo Fabrizio, Military Personnel, Adventurer; Gina Pietranera, Gentlewoman; Clelia Conti, Gentlewoman
Time Period(s): 1810s
Locale(s): Parma, Italy; France; Waterloo, Belgium

Summary: The novel concerns the adventures of a young Italian adventurer, Fabrizio, that take him to service in Napoleon's army at Waterloo and at home through intrigues of state, family, and lovers. He finally ends his career quietly at the Charterhouse, or monastery, in Parma.

Historical Accuracy: This is a classic novel of French romanticism. Social comedy competes with more serious speculations about the meaning of life.

RUTH WALGREEN STEPHAN (1910-)

An American writer and poet, Stephan was born in Chicago and attended Northwestern. She won the Friends of Literature Award in 1957 for *The Flight*. Her books include *My Crown, My Love*, *Poems for Nothing*, and *The Simple Sphere*.

5994 *The Flight*

Date of Publication: 1956
Subject(s): Royalty—Sweden; Biography, Fictionalized
Historical character(s): Christina, Ruler (Queen of Sweden)
Time Period(s): 17th century

Locale(s): Sweden; Innsbruck, Austria

Summary: The novel is cast in the form of an autobiographical account of the fascinating reign of Christina of Sweden. The daughter of Gustavus II, Christina reigned as the queen of Sweden until, weary of her royal duties and growing antagonism with her nobles, she abdicates, leaving Sweden dressed as a man. She converts to Catholicism and settles in Rome, later attempting in vain to regain her throne.

Historical Accuracy: The novel captures the atmosphere of the 17th-century Swedish court. To present Christina as the heroine of the novel, considerable embellishments of the facts were necessary create a more romantic figure than history records.

5995 *My Crown, My Love*

Date of Publication: 1960

Subject(s): Royalty—Sweden; Biography, Fictionalized

Historical character(s): Christina, Ruler (Queen of Sweden); Alexander VII, Religious (pope); Innocent XI, Religious (pope); Jules Mazarin, Religious (cardinal), Political Figure

Time Period(s): 17th century

Locale(s): Sweden; Rome, Italy

Summary: The author provides a second biographical account of the life of Queen Christina of Sweden. Not a sequel to its predecessor, *The Flight*, the novel is a reworking of the story of Christina's renunciation of her crown and search for spiritual meaning. In this version, Christina tell her own story.

Historical Accuracy: The novel shows evidence of exhaustive research into the period and the details of Christina's life.

JAMES STEPHENS (1882-1950)

Stephens was an Irish novelist and short story writer whose best-known work is the prose fantasy *The Crock of Gold.*

5996 *Deirdre*

Date of Publication: 1923

Subject(s): Celtic Ireland; Myths and Legends

Fictional character(s): Mac Nessa Conachur, Ruler (King of Ulster); Deirdre, Ward; Maeve, Noblewoman

Time Period(s): Indeterminate Past

Locale(s): Ulster, Ireland

Summary: Stephens attempts to revive ancient Gaelic legend in this story of the King of Ulster and his tragic passion for Deirdre, the daughter of his storyteller. It was foretold at Deirdre's birth that she would bring disaster to Ulster. She falls in love with a younger man who, with his kinsmen, resists the king's insistence that they be married. Tragedy follows.

Historical Accuracy: Although based in legend and fantasy, the story is anchored in realistic details.

PHILIP VAN DOREN STERN (1900-1984)

An American historian, editor, and author, Stern was born in Pennsylvania. He wrote more than 40 books, including several on the Civil War era. He is best known for the short story "The Greatest Gift," about a suicidal man who

rediscovers the joy of living. The story was adapted by Frank Capra as the film *It's a Wonderful Life.* Stern's books include *The Man Who Killed Lincoln, An End of Valor,* and *Secret Missions of the Civil War.*

5997 *The Drums of Morning*

Date of Publication: 1942

Subject(s): Civil War—U.S.; Slavery; Underground Railroad

Fictional character(s): Jonathan Bradford, Young Man

Historical character(s): John Brown, Abolitionist; Owen Lovejoy, Abolitionist

Time Period(s): 19th century (1837-1865)

Locale(s): United States

Summary: Jonathan Bradford's father is killed in the struggle for abolition. Bradford continues his father's work, becoming involved in the operation of the Underground Railroad, John Brown's activities, and the free-soil struggles in Kansas. He sees action in the Civil War and endures the horror of life in Andersonville prison.

Historical Accuracy: The novel provides a painstaking and believable re-creation of the abolitionist movement and the causes of the Civil War.

EMMA GELDERS STERNE (1894-)

Born in Birmingham, Alabama, teacher, editor, and author Emma Gelders Sterne attended Smith College, Columbia University, and the New School for Social Research. A member of the ACLU, the NAACP, CORE, the Women's International League for Peace and Freedom, and SNCC, Gelders has written books for adults and children. Her works include *His Was the Voice: The Life of W.E.B. Dubois, They Took Their Stand,* and *Benito Juarez: Builder of a Nation.*

5998 *The Drums of Monmouth*

Date of Publication: 1935

Subject(s): American Revolution; Battle of Monmouth; Biography, Fictionalized

Historical character(s): Philip Freneau, Writer (poet); George Washington, Military Personnel (army commander); Charles Lee, Military Personnel (general); Marie Joseph Paul de Lafayette, Military Personnel (general), Nobleman (Marquis de Lafayette)

Time Period(s): 18th century (1750s-1770s)

Locale(s): Monmouth, New Jersey, American Colonies; New York, American Colonies

Summary: This novel of the American Revolution centers on the career of poet Philip Freneau. It details his experiences and depicts the role of the Huguenots and Quakers in the war. The action culminates in the decisive Battle of Monmouth.

Historical Accuracy: Little is known of the early years of Freneau. The novel is a blend of the fictional and speculative as well as the historical.

5999 *No Surrender*

Date of Publication: 1932

Subject(s): Civil War—U.S.
Fictional character(s): Julia Thomas, Plantation Owner
Time Period(s): 1860s
Locale(s): Alabama

Summary: Beginning just after Lee's surrender at Appomattox, the novel depicts life on an Alabama plantation that has been stripped almost bare during the conflict. Julia Thomas struggles to survive, with her young children and a few faithful retainers.

Historical Accuracy: The atmosphere of the region and the period are drawn with conviction.

R.T. STEVENS
(PSEUD. OF REGINALD THOMAS STAPLES, 1911-)

Born in London, Staples attended secondary school in London and served as a sergeant in the British army during World War II. He worked in the shipping and publishing industries and as a managing director of a commercial photography firm, and has also served as chair on the board of directors of Vista Sports, Ltd. His historical novels include *Warrior Queen* (as James Sinclair), *The Professional Gentleman* (as Robert Tyler Stevens), and *Down Lambeth Way, Rising Summer,* and *The Trap* (as Mary Jane Staples).

6000   *Flight From Bucharest*

Date of Publication: 1977
Subject(s): World War I
Fictional character(s): Harry Phillips, Military Personnel (British captain), Captive (prisoner of war); Irena of Moldavia, Royalty (princess)
Time Period(s): 1910s (1918)
Locale(s): Bucharest, Romania; Belgrade, Yugoslavia; Italy

Summary: In the waning days of World War I, with the German and Austrian empires in shambles, a British prisoner of war agrees to smuggle a young princess out of Romania. The pro-German sentiments of Irene of Moldavia make her a target for socialist revolutionaries, and the novel features a chase across war-torn Europe.

Historical Accuracy: The depiction of Europe during the period is authentic in this historical thriller.

6001   *The Summer Day Is Done*

Date of Publication: 1976
Subject(s): Russian Empire; World War I; Russian Revolution
Fictional character(s): John Kirby, Spy
Historical character(s): Olga, Grand Duchess of Russia, Royalty; Nicholas II, Ruler (czar); Alexandra Feodorovna, Royalty (consort of Nicholas II)
Time Period(s): 1910s (1911)
Locale(s): Russia

Summary: The final years of the Romanovs are reflected in the experiences of John Kirby, a British secret agent who ingratiates himself with the Russian royal family, particularly Nicholas and Alexandra's eldest daughter, Olga. The idyllic respite crashes and turns to war and revolution.

Historical Accuracy: The story is fanciful but does depend on a convincing period backdrop of the Romanov court during its swan song.

6002   *A Woman of Texas*

Date of Publication: 1979
Subject(s): American West
Fictional character(s): Isabella Cordova, Landowner; Jason Rawlings, Adventurer; Colonel John B. Hendricks, Landowner
Time Period(s): 19th century
Locale(s): Texas

Summary: Set in Texas at the time of the Republic, the novel concerns a land dispute between Isabella Cordova and Colonel Hendricks. Into the volatile mix comes the English adventurer Jason Rawlings, who has his own plans.

Historical Accuracy: The period backdrop of frontier life of the times is convincingly presented.

JANET STEVENSON (1913-)

Born in Chicago, Stevenson attended Bryn Mawr and Yale University. She is a prize-winning novelist, critic, biographer, and playwright. She was the recipient of the International Bicentennial Playwriting Prize, the Friends of American Writers Award, and the National Arts of the Theatre Award.

6003   *The Ardent Years*

Date of Publication: 1960
Subject(s): Antebellum South; Theatrical Life
Historical character(s): Fanny Kemble, Actress; Pierce Butler, Gentleman, Plantation Owner
Time Period(s): 19th century
Locale(s): London, England; Philadelphia, Pennsylvania

Summary: In the years before the Civil War, famed English actress Fanny Kemble marries a wealthy American planter, Pierce Butler. Her opposition to slavery leads to conflict in their marriage.

Historical Accuracy: The novel stays close to the actual events of Kemble's life with plausible surmises in imagined conversations and situations.

6004   *Departure*

Date of Publication: 1985
Subject(s): Sea Story
Fictional character(s): Jonathan Bright, Sea Captain; Amanda Bright, Spouse
Time Period(s): 1850s (1851)
Locale(s): At Sea; Columbia River, Oregon; Portland, Oregon

Summary: The novel is based loosely on the actual adventures of a woman who travelle d from the Sandwich Islands to the west coast of America in the 1850s. Amanda Bright joins her husband, Jonathan, the captain of the *Maria M.*, on an around-the-world trading voyage. Circumstances force her into the unaccustomed position of command as she becomes captain and navigator of the ship on its voyage to the mouth of the Columbia River and the frontier of Oregon.

Historical Accuracy: The incident is based on fact but the story is considerably enhanced by the details of other women who accomplished comparable feats.

6005 *Sisters and Brothers*

Date of Publication: 1966
Subject(s): Antebellum South; Slavery; Quakers
Historical character(s): Angelina Grimke, Abolitionist; Sarah Grimke, Abolitionist
Time Period(s): 19th century
Locale(s): Charleston, South Carolina; Philadelphia, Pennsylvania

Summary: The Grimke sisters of Charleston, South Carolina, become Quakers and ardent anti-slavery crusaders. They face major opposition and a family crisis when Angelina Grimke learns that a young black man is the son of her brother.

Historical Accuracy: The novel's reconstruction of the details of the Grimkes' career and the atmosphere of the period are genuine and faithful to the facts.

6006 *Weep No More*

Date of Publication: 1957
Subject(s): Civil War—U.S.; Espionage
Historical character(s): Elizabeth Van Lew, Spy
Time Period(s): 1860s
Locale(s): Richmond, Virginia

Summary: This partly fictional account is based on the life of Elizabeth Van Lew of Richmond, Virginia, whose opposition to slavery leads to her serving as a Union spy. She helps Union soldiers escape from Libby Prison and constructs a plan for the Union capture of Richmond.

Historical Accuracy: The author's evident partisanship on behalf of her heroine and her cause compromises objectivity.

JOHN P. STEVENSON
(PSEUD. OF EDWARD GRIERSON, 1914-)

English writer Stevenson graduated from Exeter College, Oxford. Before becoming a novelist in 1952, Stevenson was a barrister. Several of his books have been made into American and British television productions.

6007 *Captain General*

Date of Publication: 1956
Subject(s): Independence—Netherlands
Fictional character(s): Juan, Spy; Catherine de Bleymont, Noblewoman
Historical character(s): Fernando Alvarez de Toledo, Nobleman (Duke of Alba), Military Personnel (general)
Time Period(s): 16th century
Locale(s): Netherlands

Summary: The background for this historical adventure novel is the Duke of Alba's mission to repress a Dutch rebellion against Spain at the request of Philip II. The duke's vicious-

ness produces a reaction when a lovely noblewoman, Catherine de Bleymont, is made a hostage, prompting the spy Juan to rescue her and join the opposition.

Historical Accuracy: The novel's story is fanciful but with a plausible historical background and atmosphere.

ROBERT LOUIS STEVENSON
(1850-1894)

Robert Louis Stevenson was a Scottish-born author who wrote essays, travel pieces, and poetry, as well as fiction. *Treasure Island* brought him fame. Compelled both by his love for adventure and health reasons, Stevenson traveled extensively throughout his life. He died unexpectedly of a cerebral hemorrhage while living in Samoa. His *The Strange Case of Dr. Jekyll and Mr. Hyde* (1886) defines the modern horror story.

6008 *The Black Arrow*

Date of Publication: 1888
Subject(s): War of the Roses; Middle Ages
Fictional character(s): Daniel Brackley, Nobleman; Dick Shelton, Ward, Orphan; Lawless, Outlaw
Historical character(s): Richard, Duke of Gloucester, Nobleman
Time Period(s): 15th century
Locale(s): England

Summary: This is a medieval tale of conspiracy and revenge set during the War of the Roses. It is centered on the villainy of Sir Daniel and the adventures of Dick Shelton. Mysterious bowmen appear with their signature black arrows to exact vengeance and help bring Sir Daniel to justice.

Historical Accuracy: Except for some archaic "ye's" and "thou's" there is little to place this adventure tale in any particular historical period, except a vague age of chivalry.

6009 *Catriona*

Date of Publication: 1893
Subject(s): Crime and Criminals; Jacobite Rebellion
Fictional character(s): David Balfour, Gentleman; Catriona Drummond, Heroine
Historical character(s): James Stewart, Laird; Alan Breck, Adventurer
Time Period(s): 1750s
Locale(s): Scotland; France; Netherlands

Summary: In this sequel to *Kidnapped*, David Balfour attempts to prove the innocence of James Stewart of the Glen in the murder of Colin Campbell, which was an actual historical event. David also falls in love with the daughter of a renegade Scottish outlaw.

Historical Accuracy: Stevenson repeats his blend of romance, adventure, and historical intrigue with Scottish customs that create an authentic sense of time and place.

6010 *Kidnapped*

Date of Publication: 1886

Subject(s): Jacobite Rebellion
Fictional character(s): David Balfour, Heir—Dispossessed, Orphan; Ebenezer Balfour, Kidnapper
Historical character(s): Colin Campbell, Laird; Alan Breck, Adventurer
Time Period(s): 1750s
Locale(s): Scotland

Summary: Set in the 1750s in Scotland and featuring the historical murder of Colin Campbell, the novel involves the kidnapping of David Balfour by his wicked uncle on a ship bound for America. During the voyage, a Scotsman, Breck, is rescued from a sinking ship only to be shipwrecked again. David and Alan return home together, witness the murder of Campbell, and, after a perilous Highland journey, succeed in uncovering Ebenezer's villainy and recovering David's property.

Historical Accuracy: Authentic settings and Scottish details have made this work a perennial favorite.

6011 *The Master of Ballantrae: A Winter's Tale*

Date of Publication: 1889
Subject(s): Jacobite Rebellion
Fictional character(s): James Durrie, Gentleman; Henry Durrie, Gentleman; Allison Graeme, Gentlewoman
Time Period(s): 1740s; 1750s
Locale(s): Scotland; New York, New York, American Colonies; France

Summary: Set against the turbulence of the Scottish Revolt of 1745 and the cause of the Young Pretender, Bonnie Prince Charlie, the novel details a family feud between two brothers. The elder and Master, James Durrie, fights for the Scottish cause in the battle of Culloden only to return home a wanted man. His younger brother, Henry, has taken his place and the woman he was to marry. James then embarks on a campaign of revenge that drives Henry mad and ultimately destroys both brothers.

Historical Accuracy: There are strong Scottish details in this perennial adventure favorite.

6012 *Treasure Island*

Date of Publication: 1883
Subject(s): Pirates; Sea Story; Treasure Hunt
Fictional character(s): Jim Hawkins, Sailor (cabin boy); Long John Silver, Pirate, Cook; Squire Trelawney, Gentleman
Time Period(s): 1740s
Locale(s): England; West Indies

Summary: Jim Hawkins, the young boy narrator of this classic adventure of pirates and buried treasure, obtains by accident a treasure map. In the voyage that follows to recover the treasure, disguised buccaneers, led by one-legged Long John Silver, mutiny and battle a small band for control of the island and possession of the treasure.

Historical Accuracy: The novel set the standard for pirate adventure, and its depiction is more romance than realistic.

WILLIAM STEVENSON (1924-)

Born in London and a graduate of Ruskin College, Oxford, Stevenson was a foreign correspondent for the *Toronto Star* and an executive producer of television documentaries for the Canadian Broadcasting Corporation. He was the host of ''Dateline,'' a nightly television newsmagazine, as well as a syndicated columnist. His *A Man Called Intrepid* was produced as a mini-series for the BBC and as a feature film. He is also the author of *Ninety Minutes at Entebbe*.

6013 *The Ghosts of Africa*

Date of Publication: 1980
Subject(s): World War I
Historical character(s): Paul Emil von Lettow-Vorbeck, Military Personnel (army commander)
Time Period(s): 1910s (1914-1918)
Locale(s): Africa (East Africa)

Summary: The novel chronicles the battle for control of East Africa during World War I through the experiences of Paul Emil von Lettow-Vorbeck, commander of the German forces. Known as the ''lion of Africa,'' Lettow-Vorbeck, using native soldiers, mounts a guerilla campaign against the British that forces them to commit many more troops to Africa than they intended.

Historical Accuracy: Despite the impressive research to render the period's events, the novel occasionally lapses into anachronisms of language and attitude.

BARBARA STEWARD

DWIGHT STEWARD

6014 *Evermore*

Date of Publication: 1978
Subject(s): Mystery
Historical character(s): Edgar Allan Poe, Writer
Time Period(s): 19th century
Locale(s): France; Austria

Summary: In this historical mystery novel, the premise is that Edgar Allan Poe did not die in 1849. Rather, he stages his own death and reemerges as Henri Le Rennet, detective. He is asked to investigate the series of events that leads to the deaths of Austria's Crown Prince Rudolph and Baroness Mary Vetsera at the royal hunting lodge.

Historical Accuracy: Beside the novel's unique premise, this is a rather ordinary whodunit, although it has a colorful period background.

6015 *The Lincoln Diddle*

Date of Publication: 1979
Subject(s): Civil War—U.S.; Assassination
Historical character(s): Edgar Allan Poe, Writer
Time Period(s): 1860s (1865)
Locale(s): Washington, District of Columbia

Summary: Edgar Allan Poe, disguised as detective Henri Le Rennet, is involved with the Lincoln assassination. First he fails to prevent Lincoln's murder, then he solves the mystery surrounding the conspiracy.

Historical Accuracy: Although much about the plot is fanciful, the basis is a well-researched evocation of the facts surrounding the Lincoln assassination.

DAVENPORT STEWARD

6016 *Rainbow Road*

Date of Publication: 1953
Subject(s): Settlement of the American Frontier; Indians
Fictional character(s): Steve Vickers, Frontiersman; Deborah Reeves, Gentlewoman
Time Period(s): 1820s
Locale(s): Georgia

Summary: The novel traces the tragic consequences of a gold rush into the Cherokee country of northern Georgia in the 1820s. A large cast of various frontier types is animated by greed and competition as gold fever grips the region.

Historical Accuracy: The novel provides a believable and authentic background.

6017 *Sail the Dark Tide*

Date of Publication: 1954
Subject(s): Civil War—U.S.; Sea Story
Fictional character(s): Wyck Talburt, Sea Captain, Blockade Runner
Time Period(s): 1860s
Locale(s): Nassau, Bahamas; *The Wanderer*, At Sea

Summary: This Civil War tale describes the attempt of blockade runner Captain Wyck Talburt to deliver a shipload of needed supplies to the Confederates in North Carolina. Intrigue in Nassau is followed by adventure at sea.

Historical Accuracy: The novel captures the atmosphere of the period in Nassau. The nautical details are convincing.

6018 *They Had a Glory*

Date of Publication: 1952
Subject(s): Settlement of the American Frontier
Fictional character(s): Munro Dunbar, Veteran (Revolutionary War)
Time Period(s): 1780s
Locale(s): Kentucky

Summary: Pioneer life on the Kentucky frontier is described through the experiences of Revolutionary War veteran Munro Dunbar, a former member of Francis Marion's raiders. When he is cheated of his inheritance in South Carolina he heads west with others to help settle new territory.

Historical Accuracy: The details of ordinary life in the wilderness are authentic. The overall story, however, veers toward the melodramatic and artificial.

SAMUEL M. STEWARD (1909-1993)

Born in Woodsfield, Ohio, Steward received his B.A., M.A., and Ph.D. from Ohio State University. An educator, author, and tattoo artist, Steward taught English at Loyola and DePaul universities from the 1930s to the 1950s, when he left the academic world to make a living as a tattoo artist under the name Phil Sparrow. Although he published a book of short stories and a novel, *Angels on the Bough*, in the 1930s, he did not return to writing until 1977, when he published *Dear Sammy: Letters From Gertrude Stein and Alice B. Toklas*. Steward was a friend of both writers. Much of his later writing career was spent publishing gay erotica under the pseudonym Phil Andros,.

6019 *The Caravaggio Shawl*

Date of Publication: 1989
Subject(s): Mystery; Literary Life
Historical character(s): Gertrude Stein, Writer; Alice B. Toklas, Writer
Time Period(s): 1930s (1937)
Locale(s): Paris, France

Summary: Someone has stolen a Caravaggio from the Louvre and replaced it with a forgery. Investigating the theft are the unlikely pair of Gertrude Stein and Alice B. Toklas.

Historical Accuracy: The novel captures 1930s Paris and the bohemian scene.

6020 *Murder Is Murder Is Murder*

Date of Publication: 1985
Subject(s): Mystery; Literary Life
Historical character(s): Gertrude Stein, Writer; Alice B. Toklas, Writer
Time Period(s): 1930s (1937)
Locale(s): France

Summary: While suffering from a case of writer's block, Gertrude Stein, along with Alice B. Toklas, finds herself in the middle of a mystery. They investigate the disappearance of the father of their young gardener.

Historical Accuracy: This is a fairly slight exercise with little in-depth presentation of the period or the famous couple.

A.J. STEWART (1929-)

A Scottish author and playwright, Stewart is a founding member of the Scottish Society of Playwrights. His plays include *The Man From Thermoplylae*. Stewart was the first recipient of the Wendy Wood Memorial Award.

6021 *Falcon: The Autobiography of His Grace James IV, King of Scots*

Date of Publication: 1970
Subject(s): Royalty—Scotland; Biography, Fictionalized; Battle of Flodden
Historical character(s): James IV, Ruler (King of Scotland)
Time Period(s): 15th century; 16th century

Locale(s): Scotland

Summary: In this biographical study, James IV tells his own story, facilitated presumably by the author's claim to have inhabited the body of the Scots king in a former life. One of the ablest and best loved of the Stuart kings, James' reign is documented to his death on the battlefield of Flodden.

Historical Accuracy: The novel's clear partisanship on behalf of James presents a one-sided portrait, but it does offer a convincing insight into the times and the tangled politics of the period.

CATHERINE POMEROY STEWART

6022 *Three Roads to Valhalla*

Date of Publication: 1948
Subject(s): Reconstruction Period; Racial Conflict
Fictional character(s): Kate Rider, Young Woman
Time Period(s): 1860s (Post-Civil War)
Locale(s): Jacksonville, Florida

Summary: The violence and turmoil of the Reconstruction period is captured in the story of Kate Rider from Hartford, Connecticut. She accompanies her father to Jacksonville, Florida, where he is to head up the Freedman's Bureau. Murder and hatred greet their arrival.

Historical Accuracy: The novel leans toward the sensational and the melodramatic, punishing the wicked and rewarding the virtuous in ways that undermine believability.

FRED MUSTARD STEWART (1932-)

Stewart was born in Indiana and graduated from Princeton with a degree in history. He worked as a concert pianist before travelling to Hollywood, where he wrote numerous screenplays, including *The Mephisto Waltz*, *Lady Darlington*, and *Six Weeks*.

6023 *Ellis Island*

Date of Publication: 1983
Subject(s): Immigrants
Fictional character(s): Jacob Rubinstein, Immigrant; Marco Santorelli, Immigrant; Tom Banicek, Immigrant, Miner
Time Period(s): 1900s; 1910s
Locale(s): New York, New York; Pennsylvania

Summary: This tale of immigrant life in American at the turn of the century follows the experiences of a group of young immigrants who arrive at Ellis Island, the first step in their progress to varied fortunes in America.

Historical Accuracy: The novel features a meticulous recreation of the period and its details.

6024 *The Magnificent Savages*

Date of Publication: 1996
Subject(s): Sea Story; Taiping Rebellion
Fictional character(s): Justin Savage, Bastard Son, Adventurer; Samantha Aspinal, Young Woman
Time Period(s): 1850s; 1860s

Locale(s): At Sea; China; England

Summary: This adventure story set during the mid-19th century involves Justin Savage, the illegitimate son of a New York shipping magnate. On a voyage to the east, he is marked for murder by his jealous half-brother, captured by pirates, and taken to China as a slave. His long struggle to reclaim his inheritance takes him to Victorian England, Italy under Garibaldi, and China during the violence of the Taiping Rebellion.

Historical Accuracy: The novel uses a framework of actual events that form a plausible backdrop for the novel's adventure.

6025 *Pomp and Circumstance*

Date of Publication: 1991
Subject(s): Civil War—U.S.; Antebellum South; English Colonies
Fictional character(s): Lizzie Desmond, Young Woman; Adam Thorne, Nobleman (Earl of Pontefract)
Historical character(s): Pierre Gustave Toutant Beauregard, Military Personnel (Confederate general); Benjamin Disraeli, Political Figure; Victoria, Ruler (Queen of England)
Time Period(s): 19th century (1850s-1874)
Locale(s): England; Virginia; India

Summary: When Adam Thorn becomes the Earl of Pontefract, he is forced into a loveless marriage, foregoing his passion for Lizzie Desmond. The novel follows their separate stories: Lizzie to the court of Louis Napoleon of France and then to a Virginia plantation; Adam to India of the British Raj. Each must deal with war and rebellion before they are reunited.

Historical Accuracy: The fictional story is set against genuine period events and details.

6026 *A Rage Against Heaven*

Date of Publication: 1978
Subject(s): Civil War—U.S.; Franco-Prussian War; Mexican Empire
Fictional character(s): Lew Crandall, Young Man; Elizabeth Butterfield, Young Woman
Time Period(s): 19th century (1848-1871)
Locale(s): Princeton, New Jersey; Mexico; Paris, France

Summary: World events between 1860 and 1870 are depicted through the experiences of Lew Crandall and Elizabeth Butterfield, including the Civil War, the Mexican Empire of Maximillian and Juarez, the corruption of the Grant administration, and the Franco-Prussian War.

Historical Accuracy: The historical backdrop of the story employs real events that are authentically detailed.

GEORGE RIPPEY STEWART (1895-1980)

An American educator and writer, Stewart was born in Pennsylvania and was educated at Princeton University, the University of California, and Columbia University. Stewart was affiliated with the University of California for nearly 40 years as an English professor. His fields of study included history, forestry, meteorology, and onomastics. In addition to his novel *Storm and Fire*, Stewart wrote nonfiction books, including *Pickett's Charge* and *The California Trail*.

6027 *East of the Giants*

Date of Publication: 1938
Subject(s): American West; Gold Rush—California
Fictional character(s): Judith Hingham, Young Woman
Time Period(s): 19th century (1837-1861)
Locale(s): California

Summary: On a trip to California, Judith Hingham, the daughter of a New England sea captain, marries a young Spanish ranch owner. Her experiences in the ensuing years reflect the development of the state.

Historical Accuracy: The novel features an accurate and convincing historical background.

6028 *Years of the City*

Date of Publication: 1955
Subject(s): Ancient Greece
Fictional character(s): Archias, Young Man; Bion, Military Personnel (soldier)
Time Period(s): 8th century B.C.; 7th century B.C. (750-600 B.C.)
Locale(s): Greece

Summary: The novel reconstructs the founding, growth, and eventual downfall of a fictional Greek colonial city. The experiences of a variety of characters collectively mirror the phases of the city's life over 150 years, from its youthful founding to its decline.

Historical Accuracy: The story is well founded in historical feasibility.

MARY STEWART (1916-)

Born in Durham, England, Stewart received her B.A. in literature from Durham University, where she worked as a lecturer. Her writing career was launched with the publication in 1954 of her first novel, *Madam, Will You Talk?*. In 1968 she was elected as a Fellow of the Royal Society of Arts. A master at what critics have called the labyrinthine modern-Gothic thriller, she turned to historical fiction in 1970 with *The Crystal Cave*, the first of three books on Merlin and the Arthurian legend.

6029 *The Crystal Cave*

Date of Publication: 1970
Subject(s): Dark Ages; Arthurian Legends; Witchcraft and Sorcery
Fictional character(s): Merlin, Bastard Son
Time Period(s): 5th century
Locale(s): England; Wales

Summary: Set in the half-mythical world of 5th-century Britain and Arthurian legend, the novel attempts to identify Merlin, the chief architect of the first united Britain. Merlin is the bastard son of Niniane, daughter of the king of South Wales, and an unknown father. The novel opens in Wales

when Merlin is seven and closes in Cornwall with the begetting of Arthur.

Historical Accuracy: *The Crystal Cave* is not a work of scholarship, and can obviously make no claims to be serious history.

6030 *The Hollow Hills*

Date of Publication: 1973
Subject(s): Dark Ages; Arthurian Legends; Witchcraft and Sorcery
Fictional character(s): Merlin, Sorcerer; Arthur, Young Man
Time Period(s): 5th century
Locale(s): England; Wales

Summary: The novel continues Merlin's chronicles of the Arthurian saga begun in *The Crystal Cave*. Set in 5th-century Britain, the boy Arthur is rejected by his father and is kept ignorant of his parentage. The novel describes his growth into manhood and his discovery of his strange power and destiny.

Historical Accuracy: The novel is a work of the imagination, firmly based in both history and legend, although perhaps not equally in both since so little is known about Britain in the fifth century.

6031 *The Last Enchantment*

Date of Publication: 1979
Subject(s): Dark Ages; Arthurian Legends; Witchcraft and Sorcery
Fictional character(s): Merlin, Sorcerer; Arthur, Ruler (King of Britons); Morgause, Witch; Guinevere, Royalty (queen consort of Arthur)
Time Period(s): 5th century
Locale(s): Camelot, England; Wales

Summary: The novel continues the story of Merlin and Arthur. Arthur is now king, at war with the Saxons and attempting to forge a united Britain. The novel also traces the domestic warfare of Arthur, his half-sister Morgause, and their son Modred, fulfilling Merlin's dark prophecies of betrayal and grief.

Historical Accuracy: The novel's main source is legend with every attempt to place the legend in the context of what is known about the historical Arthur.

6032 *The Prince and the Pilgrim*

Date of Publication: 1995
Subject(s): Dark Ages; Arthurian Legends; Witchcraft and Sorcery
Fictional character(s): Alexander, Royalty (prince); Morgan Le Fay, Sorceress; Alice, Wanderer
Time Period(s): 5th century
Locale(s): England

Summary: Young Prince Alexander seeks justice from King Arthur and vengeance for the death of his father. He is diverted from his quest by sorceress Morgan LeFay, who persuades Alexander to steal an enchanted silver cup which many believe is the Holy Grail. This leads him to a young pilgrim named Alice.

Historical Accuracy: The novel is effective in creating the Arthurian milieu.

6033 *The Wicked Day*

Date of Publication: 1983
Subject(s): Dark Ages; Arthurian Legends; Witchcraft and Sorcery
Fictional character(s): Modred, Bastard Son; Arthur, Ruler (King of Britons); Morgause, Witch; Guinevere, Royalty (queen consort of Arthur)
Time Period(s): 5th century
Locale(s): Orkney Islands, Scotland; Camelot, England

Summary: The author completes the retelling of the story of King Arthur from the perspective of his son Modred. Sent by his mother and Arthur's half-sister, Morgause, to be reared on the Orkney Islands, Modred is eventually thrust into the intrigues of Arthur's court and the tragic fate that awaits the dissolution of Camelot. The novel attempts to present Modred not as the evil villain of legend but rather as a victim of fate.

Historical Accuracy: The novel combines legendary sources with what little is known of the historic Arthur and 5th-century Britain.

RAMONA STEWART (1922-)

American writer Stewart was born in San Francisco and attended the University of Southern California. She is best known for her novels *Desert Town* and *The Possession of Joel Delaney*, both of which were made into films. She is also the author of *Seasons of the Heart* and *The Nightmare Candidate*.

6034 *Casey*

Date of Publication: 1968
Subject(s): Immigrants; Draft Riots; Civil War—U.S.
Fictional character(s): Dan Casey, Political Figure
Historical character(s): James Fisk, Financier; William Marcy Tweed, Political Figure
Time Period(s): 19th century (1860-1886)
Locale(s): New York, New York

Summary: Irish immigrant life in New York City is depicted through the career of Dan Casey, from the events of the Civil War Draft Riots to the heyday of Boss Tweed and Tamany Hall. Casey's rise to power is played out against the important events of the period.

Historical Accuracy: The depiction of period New York and its colorful cast of characters is authentic and convincing.

STANLEY N. STEWART (1931-)

Born in Minnesota, Stewart attended UCLA and received both his B.A. and Ph.D. there. He has taught acting and English at the University of California, Riverside, and written books and periodical articles on 17th-century English literature.

6035 *The King James Version*

Date of Publication: 1977
Subject(s): Jacobean Period; Royalty—England
Historical character(s): James I, Ruler (King of England); Frances Howard, Noblewoman (Countess of Essex); Robert Carr, Nobleman (Viscount Rochester)
Time Period(s): 17th century (1610s)
Locale(s): England

Summary: This tale of passion and betrayal is set in the court world of James I. Frances Howard, the most beautiful woman at court, sets her heart on Robert Carr, James I's favorite, though she is already married. She secures patrons to help her annul her marriage in a sensational trial and to secure Carr's love, but her plan for happiness goes dramatically awry.

Historical Accuracy: The history reflected in the story is accurate and reliable.

CAROLINE STICKLAND (1955-)

Born in Rintein, Germany, English novelist Caroline Stickland attended the University of East Anglia and has been a voluntary adult literacy tutor as well as a writer. *The Standing Hills* was nominated for several historical fiction awards. She lives in Dorset, the setting for several of her novels.

6036 *The Darkening Leaf*

Date of Publication: 1995
Subject(s): Victorian Period
Fictional character(s): Ellen Farebrother, Young Woman; Frederick North, Gentleman; Philobeth Alleyn, Young Woman
Time Period(s): 1840s
Locale(s): Dorset, England

Summary: In Dorset during the Victorian period, Ellen Farebrother, the mysterious survivor of a shipwreck, comes between two young lovers, Philobeth Alleyn and Frederick North, in this tale of revenge and betrayal.

Historical Accuracy: The novel features convincing period and regional elements.

6037 *The Darkness of Corn*

Date of Publication: 1990
Subject(s): Victorian Period; Rural Life—England
Fictional character(s): Daniel Fayerdon, Worker (miller); Beatrice Fayerdon, Spouse
Time Period(s): 19th century (Victorian period)
Locale(s): Dorset, England

Summary: The novel depicts an unhappy marriage in Victorian Dorset. Beatrice Fayerdon yearns for love while she endures a charge of infidelity. Labor unrest and the rural custom of wife-selling dramatize both the period and the plight of Victorian women.

Historical Accuracy: The period background is authentic as are the customs depicted, including wife-selling.

6038 *The Standing Hills*

Date of Publication: 1986
Subject(s): Victorian Period; Rural Life—England
Fictional character(s): Richard Webster, Religious (clergyman); Laura Delaford, Spouse (of Webster); Samuel Delaford, Gentleman; Rachel Cooper, Worker (milkmaid)
Time Period(s): 1860s
Locale(s): Dorset, England

Summary: Set in the Dorset countryside during the 1860s, the novel traces the relationships of four characters—clergyman Richard Webster; his young, naive wife, Laura; her brother, Samuel Delaford; and the innocent farm milkmaid Rachel Cooper, who is in love with Samuel. A tangle of motives and desires produces dramatic consequences.

Historical Accuracy: The author is able to render a period context that is convincing and believable.

JESSICA STIRLING

(PSEUD. OF MARGARET M. COGHLAN, 1920- ; HUGH C. RAE, 1935-)

Jessica Stirling was originally a pseudonym for Margaret M. Coghlan and Hugh C. Rae; since 1984, Rae has written under the name alone. Born in Glasgow, Scotland, Coghlan first began writing stories for magazines and wrote her first novel at Rae's suggestion. Also born in Glasgow, Rae was educated at Knightswood School, Glasgow. He worked as an antiquarian bookseller from 1952 to 1965; since then he has been a full-time writer. He is a lecturer in creative writing at the University of Glasgow.

6039 *The Asking Price*

Date of Publication: 1989
Subject(s): Edwardian Period
Fictional character(s): Kirsty Barnes, Orphan; Craig Nicholson, Police Officer; David Lockhart, Religious (minister)
Time Period(s): 1900s
Locale(s): Glasgow, Scotland

Summary: In the second of four novels set in Edwardian Glasgow, the troubled relationship of Kirsty Barnes and Craig Nicholson continues. Craig becomes increasingly committed to his police work, and the two drift further apart, as Kristy is drawn closer to David Lockhart.

Historical Accuracy: The details of Glasgow life of the period are authentic.

6040 *Call Home the Heart*

Date of Publication:
Subject(s): Victorian Period; Mining; Labor Movement
Fictional character(s): Merrin Stalker, Young Woman; Andrew Stalker, Student (law)
Time Period(s): 1870s
Locale(s): Blacklaw, Scotland

Summary: Labor conflicts in a Scottish mining village during the 1870s are depicted in the story of the Stalker family. Andrew Stalker is determined to become a lawyer and escape the grim life in Blacklaw. His sister Merrin, must decide whether to pursue a music hall career or marry the man she loves.

Historical Accuracy: The regional and period elements are convincingly presented.

6041 *Creature Comforts*

Date of Publication: 1986
Subject(s): Regency Period; Napoleonic Wars
Fictional character(s): Elspeth Patterson, Spouse (of Moodie); James Moodie, Businessman; Anna Patterson, Spouse (of Sinclair); Matt Sinclair, Gentleman
Time Period(s): 1810s (1812-1813)
Locale(s): Scotland

Summary: In the second volume of a trilogy beginning with *Treasures on Earth*, the marriages of the daughters of Gaddy Patterson are dramatized. Elspeth's marriage to James Moodie is loveless and clouded by a secret, while Anna awaits the return of a soldier from the Peninsular War in Spain with tragic consequences. *Hearts of Gold* concludes the trilogy.

Historical Accuracy: The story is fictional but does depend on a credible period background of actual events and customs.

6042 *The Dark Pasture*

Date of Publication: 1977
Subject(s): Victorian Period; Mining; Trials
Fictional character(s): Tom Armstrong, Farmer; Merrin Armstrong, Spouse; Andrew Stalker, Lawyer
Time Period(s): 1890s
Locale(s): Blacklaw, Scotland; Edinburgh, Scotland

Summary: Life in a mining village in Scotland during the 1890s is depicted, along with a murder trial. A young man is accused of murdering a constable during a bitter mining strike. The story revolves around Merrin and Tom Armstrong and Merrin's brother, Andrew Stalker.

Historical Accuracy: The period and regional elements here are convincing and faithfully presented.

6043 *The Good Provider*

Date of Publication: 1988
Subject(s): Edwardian Period; Crime and Criminals
Fictional character(s): Kirsty Barnes, Orphan; Craig Nicholson, Criminal; David Lockhart, Religious (missionary)
Time Period(s): 1900s
Locale(s): Glasgow, Scotland

Summary: In the first of four novels set in Edwardian-era Glasgow, the novel describes the troubled relationship of Kirsty Barnes and Craig Nicholson. Kirsty escapes her life as a servant to elope with her childhood sweetheart and live with him in a common-law marriage in Glasgow. Craig turns to crime, and Kirsty is attracted to David Lockhart, a young missionary.

Historical Accuracy: The novel features solid details of Glasgow life during the time.

6044 *Hearts of Gold*

Date of Publication: 1987
Subject(s): Regency Period; Mining
Fictional character(s): Elspeth Patterson, Spouse (of Moodie); Anna Patterson, Young Woman; Randall Bontine, Laird
Time Period(s): 1810s (1814)
Locale(s): Scotland

Summary: The novel follows *Creature Comforts* as the concluding volume of the trilogy describing the lives of Gaddy Patterson and her two daughters, Elspeth and Anna. Both daughters are in flight from bad relationships. Elspeth seeks sanctuary from her husband's agents with a mining family, and Anna, cast off by Randall Bontine, settles as a servant. She is determined to snare a new husband, with important consequences for herself and her sister.

Historical Accuracy: The novel's period elements are convincing and authentic.

6045 *Lantern for the Dark*

Date of Publication: 1992
Subject(s): Mystery; Georgian Period; Trials
Fictional character(s): Clare Kelso, Servant; Cameron Adams, Lawyer
Time Period(s): 1780s (1787)
Locale(s): Glasgow, Scotland

Summary: In this mystery set in 18th-century Scotland, Cameron Adams must defend Clare Kelso on a charge of murdering her son. Although Clare claims she is innocent, she is either unable or unwilling to provide an alibi.

Historical Accuracy: The details of period Scotland are effectively and convincingly depicted.

6046 *The Marrying Kind*

Date of Publication: 1996
Subject(s): World War II; Family Saga; Depression Era
Fictional character(s): Alison Burnside, Student (medical); Jim Abbot, Veteran (World War I); Howard McGrath, Gentleman
Time Period(s): 1930s
Locale(s): Glasgow, Scotland

Summary: In this coming-of-age novel, medical student Alison Burnside is torn between her loyalty to disabled World War I veteran Jim Abbot and her attraction to Howard McGrath. This is the sequel to *The Penny Wedding*.

Historical Accuracy: The novel provides an authentic period and regional background.

6047 *The Penny Wedding*

Date of Publication: 1994
Subject(s): Depression Era
Fictional character(s): Alex Burnside, Businessman (shipwright); Alison Burnside, Teenager, Student; Jim Abbott, Teacher
Time Period(s): 1930s
Locale(s): Glasgow, Scotland

Summary: The novel chronicles the experiences of the Burnside family whose prospects and prosperity are set back when the Depression spreads to Glasgow. The story centers on 17-year-old Alison who is faced with a choice between love and loyalty.

Historical Accuracy: The story is set against a fully-realized period and regional background.

6048 *Shadows on the Shore*

Date of Publication: 1993
Subject(s): Mystery; Regency Period
Fictional character(s): Clare Kelso, Gentlewoman; Frederick Striker, Rake
Time Period(s): 1800s (1802)
Locale(s): Ladybrook, Scotland

Summary: In this sequel to *Lantern for the Dark*, 13 years have passed since Clare Kelso was abandoned by her lover, Frederick Striker, to stand trial for their son's murder. Clare must deal with her past feelings and the mystery of Striker's relationship with two strangers who accompany him.

Historical Accuracy: The Scottish scene and period atmosphere are masterfully portrayed.

6049 *Treasures on Earth*

Date of Publication: 1985
Subject(s): Rural Life—Scotland
Fictional character(s): Gaddy Patterson, Wanderer; Coll Cochran, Farmer; Elspeth Patterson, Orphan
Time Period(s): 18th century; 19th century
Locale(s): Scotland

Summary: Rural life in Scotland during the 19th century is depicted in the story of Gaddy Patterson. Gaddy is an itinerant cattle dealer who discovers a dead girl and the girl's infant daughter, Elspeth. Gaddy raises the child, though scandal and tragedy pursue them, including the mystery of Elspeth's ancestry. Their story continues in *Creature Comforts*.

Historical Accuracy: The novel creates a believable portrait of Scottish rural life of the period.

6050 *The Welcome Light*

Date of Publication: 1991
Subject(s): Edwardian Period
Fictional character(s): Kirsty Barnes, Orphan; Craig Nicholson, Police Officer
Time Period(s): 1900s
Locale(s): Glasgow, Scotland

Summary: In the final volume of the author's Glasgow quartet, the troubled relationship of Kirsty Barnes and Craig Nicholson is resolved. Their son is stricken with polio, and events create a final epiphany for Kristy in her feelings toward Craig.

Historical Accuracy: The novel's period details are convincing.

JOCELYN STIRLING

6051 *Promises to Keep*

Date of Publication: 1986
Subject(s): War of 1812
Fictional character(s): Evangeline Bryant, Young Woman; Jason Farr, Military Personnel (army captain); Jessica Carbury, Fiance(e) (of Farr)
Time Period(s): 1800s; 1810s (1804-1814)
Locale(s): Boston, Massachusetts; Washington, District of Columbia

Summary: Set during the early years of the 19th century in America, the novel tells the story of Evangeline Bryant, who in 1809 comes to Boston to be the bridesmaid of her cousin, Jessica Carbury. She falls in love with the groom, Jason Farr, and when he keeps his promise to marry, Evangeline departs for Washington during the period of the War of 1812.

Historical Accuracy: The novel uses actual events as a plausible backdrop for this romantic story.

GRACE ZARING STONE (1891-1991)

Born in New York City, Stone attended the Sacred Heart Convent in New York and the Sacre Coeur in Paris. During World War II, Stone wrote under the pseudonym Ethel Vance to protect her daughter who was living in occupied Czechoslovakia, and her son-in-law who was a naval attache in France. Three of Stone's bestsellers, *The Bitter Tea of General Yen*, *Escape*, and *Winter Meeting*, were made into movies.

6052 *The Cold Journey*

Date of Publication: 1934
Subject(s): American Colonies; Indians
Fictional character(s): Evan Evans, Captive
Time Period(s): 1700s (1704)
Locale(s): Deerfield, Massachusetts, American Colonies; Quebec, Canada

Summary: A group of American colonists are captured in a raid by the French and their Indian allies in Deerfield, Massachusetts. They endure a forced march through the wilderness to Quebec.

Historical Accuracy: The story is a convincing description of frontier life during the period, with a believable contrast between the French and their Puritan enemies.

IRVING STONE (1903-1989)

Stone was born in California and graduated from the University of California, Berkeley, and USC. He began writing in 1926 after he abandoned work on his doctoral thesis and travelled throughout Europe. Exposure to the works of Vincent Van Gogh led him to write the bestseller *Lust for Life*. He followed it with a series of books that earned him a reputation as the master of the biographical novel. He preferred this form to straight biography because it allowed him to use his novelistic skills, developed in his early writing of plays. Stone is noted for his search for authenticity in his books. For example, he stayed in Van Gogh's asylum cell and in the room where he.

6053 *Adversary in the House*

Date of Publication: 1947
Subject(s): Biography, Fictionalized; Labor Movement
Historical character(s): Eugene V. Debs, Labor Organizer, Political Figure (socialist); Theodore Debs, Relative, Labor Organizer
Time Period(s): 19th century; 20th century
Locale(s): Indiana; Chicago, Illinois

Summary: This biographical novel depicts the career of union organizer and socialist leader Eugene V. Debs. Debs works first as a foreman for the Vandalia Railroad and begins to organize one of the first industrial unions, enduring two prison sentences for his beliefs. Debs is sustained by the devotion of his brother Theodore.

Historical Accuracy: The biographical details are based on solid research and documentation.

6054 *The Agony and the Ecstasy*

Date of Publication: 1961
Subject(s): Renaissance; Biography, Fictionalized; Artistic Life
Historical character(s): Michelangelo Buonarotti, Artist; Domenico Ghirlandajo, Artist; Lorenzo de Medici, Nobleman; Julius II, Religious (pope); Donato Bramante, Architect, Artist; Pius IV, Religious (pope)
Time Period(s): 15th century; 16th century (1490-1564)
Locale(s): Florence, Italy; Rome, Italy

Summary: The novel traces the long and troubled career of Michelangelo beginning with his apprenticeship at the age of 13 to the painter Ghirlandaio. The story follows his sponsorship by Lorenzo de' Medici, his exile to Rome, and his conflict with Pope Julius II over the painting of the Sistine Chapel. The novel concentrates on the torments of Michelangelo's genius and also offers a fully realized portrait of his age.

Historical Accuracy: The novel is the result of extensive research, including use of the first English translation of the entire body of Michelangelo's letters.

6055 *Depths of Glory*

Date of Publication: 1985
Subject(s): Biography, Fictionalized; Artistic Life
Historical character(s): Camille Pissarro, Artist; Gustave Courbet, Artist; Honore Daumier, Artist; Camille Corot, Artist; Claude Monet, Artist; Paul Cezanne, Artist; Paul Gauguin, Artist; Edgar Degas, Artist; Georges Seurat, Artist; Edouard Manet, Artist; Mary Cassatt, Artist
Time Period(s): 19th century
Locale(s): Paris, France

Summary: This biographical novel on the life and times of Camille Pissarro begins with the West Indian-born artist's arrival in Paris to study painting. He comes under the influence of Corot and the Barbizon School. He soon develops his own unique style that scandalizes the art establishment but becomes part of the Impressionist movement. Pissarro struggles through poverty and rejection while adhering to his artistic vision. The novel offers a full presentation of the Paris artist community and its principal figures during the era of the greatest artistic explosion since the Renaissance.

Historical Accuracy: The novel stays close to the biographical sources for the main outline of the story. Dialogue and some situations are invented.

6056 *The Greek Treasure*

Date of Publication: 1975
Subject(s): Archaeology; Biography, Fictionalized
Historical character(s): Heinrich Schliemann, Archaeologist; Sophia Schliemann, Archaeologist, Spouse
Time Period(s): 1870s
Locale(s): Greece; Turkey

Summary: The novel chronicles the remarkable career of Heinrich Schliemann and his wife, Sophia, as they search for the ancient city of Troy and the royal tombs of Mycenae. After having made his fortune in Russia and the California Gold Rush, Schliemann devotes the rest of his life to proving the historical basis of Homer's *Iliad*. With his young Greek wife, Schliemann takes to the field to prove the skeptics wrong.

Historical Accuracy: Much surrounding Schliemann remains controversial and disputed. This version of the facts offers one interpretation.

6057 *Immortal Wife*

Date of Publication: 1944
Subject(s): American West; Biography, Fictionalized; Politics
Historical character(s): Jessie Benton Fremont, Spouse; John C. Fremont, Frontiersman, Political Figure; Thomas Hart Benton, Political Figure; Kit Carson, Frontiersman; Abraham Lincoln, Political Figure
Time Period(s): 19th century
Locale(s): California; Washington, District of Columbia

Summary: The novel traces the remarkable life of Jessie Benton Fremont, daughter of U.S. Senator Thomas Hart Benton, who marries and accompanies John C. Fremont west during the conquest and development of California. Fremont's near capture of the presidency and the western campaign during the Civil War are portrayed.

Historical Accuracy: Although the basis of the story is factual, much of the dialogue is imagined and a few incidents are invented, though based on the author's sense of the probable.

6058 *Love Is Eternal*

Date of Publication: 1954
Subject(s): Biography, Fictionalized; Civil War—U.S.
Historical character(s): Abraham Lincoln, Political Figure; Mary Todd Lincoln, Spouse; Henry Clay, Political Figure
Time Period(s): 19th century
Locale(s): Springfield, Illinois; Kentucky; Washington, District of Columbia

Summary: The married life of Abraham Lincoln and Mary Todd is depicted. She is a beautiful, witty belle from a wealthy and prominent family in Kentucky whose courtship and marriage to the awkward country lawyer from Springfield, Illinois, is considered "not improbable but impossible" by her family. Instead, Mary Todd follows Lincoln to the White House and shares in his efforts to keep the Union together during the Civil War.

Historical Accuracy: The novel's period background and account of the actual events in the Lincolns' family and political history are accurately presented.

6059 *Lust for Life*

Date of Publication: 1934
Subject(s): Artistic Life; Biography, Fictionalized
Historical character(s): Vincent Van Gogh, Artist; Theo Van Gogh, Businessman; Paul Gauguin, Artist, Businessman; Emile Zola, Writer; Georges Seurat, Artist; Henri Rousseau, Artist; Henri de Toulouse-Lautrec, Artist; Paul Cezanne, Artist
Time Period(s): 19th century
Locale(s): Netherlands; France; London, England

Summary: The novel traces the extraordinary career of artist Vincent Van Gogh. His first calling is a religious one, working in the slums of London and the coal mines of Belgium. Excommunicated from the church, disowned by his family, Van Gogh discovers his gift as an artist and becomes one of the major participants in the great artistic renaissance of the 19th century. Tortured by his vision, Van Gogh's life is a testimony to a unique genius.

Historical Accuracy: The major details of Van Gogh's life and career are true. The dialogue is invented and there are occasional fictional elements.

6060 *The Origin*

Date of Publication: 1980
Subject(s): Biography, Fictionalized; Science; Victorian Period
Historical character(s): Charles Darwin, Scientist (naturalist); Charles Lyell, Scientist (geologist); Thomas Henry Huxley, Scientist (biologist)
Time Period(s): 19th century (1830s-1880s)
Locale(s): England; *Beagle*, At Sea

Summary: This biographical novel traces the career of Charles Darwin. At the age of 22 he is about to enter the clergy when he receives an invitation to sail on the *H.M.S. Beagle*'s as a naturalist on a cruise that will circle the globe. Darwin returns from the five-year voyage an expert naturalist with the germ of a theory about the origin of species that would shake the foundations of Victorian society. The novel traces the *Beagle*'s voyage, the controversies surrounding Darwin's work, and the personal side of this great innovative thinker.

Historical Accuracy: The novel is well grounded in fact in its depiction of Darwin's life and times.

6061 *The Passionate Journey*

Date of Publication: 1949

Subject(s): Artistic Life; Biography, Fictionalized
Historical character(s): John Noble, Artist (painter)
Time Period(s): 19th century; 20th century
Locale(s): Wichita, Kansas; Paris, France; New York, New York

Summary: American painter John Noble is chronicled in this fictional version of his life that begins when Noble is 18. He grows up on the Kansas prairie and after many difficulties, eventually achieves artistic success in Paris and New York.

Historical Accuracy: The novel accurately captures Noble's life and career with some fictional attempts to capture his inner conflicts and the nature of his genius.

6062 *The Passions of the Mind*

Date of Publication: 1971
Subject(s): Biography, Fictionalized; Medical Profession
Historical character(s): Carl Jung, Doctor (psychiatrist); Ernest Jones, Doctor (psychoanalyst); Martha Bernay, Spouse (of Freud); Sigmund Freud, Doctor (psychiatrist); Alfred Adler, Doctor (psychiatrist); Otto Rank, Doctor (psychoanalyst)
Time Period(s): 19th century; 20th century (1880s-1938)
Locale(s): Vienna, Austria; Paris, France; Zurich, Switzerland

Summary: This biographical novel tells the story of Sigmund Freud and the development of psychoanalysis. Freud's career is traced from the 1880s when as a promising pathologist his search for the causes of hysteria leads to the discovery of the unconscious and the science of psychoanalysis. Freud's private and professional life is documented up to his flight from the Nazis.

Historical Accuracy: The novel is based on six years of research and the cooperation of the families of many of the principals.

6063 *The President's Lady*

Date of Publication: 1951
Subject(s): Politics; War of 1812
Historical character(s): Andrew Jackson, Military Personnel (general), Political Figure; Rachel Jackson, Spouse
Time Period(s): 18th century; 19th century (1790s-1830s)
Locale(s): Tennessee; Washington, District of Columbia

Summary: The novel details the married life of Andrew and Rachel Jackson. Because Jackson marries Rachel before her divorce is finalized, their marriage is marred by charges of immorality. The vicious attacks on Rachel Jackson lead to her breakdown and death shortly before Jackson enters the White House.

Historical Accuracy: The history depicted is authentic; the interpretation of character is the author's. The dialogue is re-created, but it is based on a solid knowledge of the speaker as well as a variety of documented sources.

6064 *Those Who Love*

Date of Publication: 1965
Subject(s): American Revolution; Biography, Fictionalized; Politics

Historical character(s): John Adams, Political Figure, Lawyer; Abigail Adams, Spouse; Samuel Adams, Patriot; George III, Ruler (King of England); George Washington, Political Figure, Military Personnel (army commander); Thomas Jefferson, Political Figure
Time Period(s): 18th century; 19th century (1761-1801)
Locale(s): Massachusetts; Paris, France; London, England

Summary: The novel traces the married and professional lives of John and Abigail Adams from their courtship to Adams' election as the second president of the United States. When Abigail Smith marries John Adams in the 1760s, he is a hard-working lawyer who struggles to make a living for his growing family. Called "the Atlas of the Revolution," Adams is one of the central players in the birth of the new nation, and his career takes him to France and England before his election as president. Throughout, Abigail Adams is a true partner in her husband's work.

Historical Accuracy: The novel's period background is convincing, and the essential elements of the Adamses' story are faithfully depicted.

PHILIP D. STONG (1899-1957)

An American adult and children's author, Stong was born in Iowa and worked as a journalist and a writer in Hollywood. His books are mainly depictions of rural Iowa life and humorous boys' tales. They include *State Fair*, *Stranger's Return*, and *Buckskin Breeches*.

6065 *The Adventure of "Horse" Barnsby*

Date of Publication: 1956
Subject(s): Gold Rush—California; Mining
Fictional character(s): Horace "Horse" Barnsby, Teenager
Time Period(s): 1850s
Locale(s): California

Summary: The novel describes life in the California gold fields during the 1850s. The story centers on teenager Horse Barnsby who is taken in as a partner by a pair of miners in Dead Day Gulch. Horse's ingenuity and dead-eye with a rifle are needed to get them out of various adventures.

Historical Accuracy: This is a highly romanticized and idealized version of frontier life.

6066 *Forty Pounds of Gold*

Date of Publication: 1951
Subject(s): Gold Rush—California
Fictional character(s): John Warrick, Prospector; Clark Clayton, Prospector; Andy Milam, Prospector
Time Period(s): 1850s
Locale(s): Iowa; California; Panama

Summary: To earn enough to buy a farm in Iowa and marry, John Warrick sets out for the California gold fields in 1850. His journey takes him down the Mississippi to New Orleans, across Panama, and then, by ship, to San Francisco.

Historical Accuracy: This is an authentic portrait of the age, filled with believable period details.

HERBERT STOVER

6067 *Copperhead Moon*

Date of Publication: 1952

Subject(s): Civil War—U.S.; Battle of Gettysburg; Espionage

Fictional character(s): Coleman Jons, Military Personnel (Union soldier)

Time Period(s): 1860s

Locale(s): Pennsylvania

Summary: The Copperhead conspiracy during the Civil War—Northern Democrats opposed to the Lincoln government and the Union cause—is dramatized in this novel. A discharged Union soldier, Coleman Jons, returns to Pennsylvania to lead the fight against the Copperheads. They have hatched a plot to release and arm Confederate prisoners of war and capture Harrisburg.

Historical Accuracy: The suggestion of a military conspiracy fostered by the Copperheads is fanciful.

6068 *The Eagle and the Wind*

Date of Publication: 1953

Subject(s): American Revolution; American Colonies

Fictional character(s): Jeffry Claus, Artisan (gunsmith), Servant (bondsman); Mark Fultz, Trader

Time Period(s): 1770s

Locale(s): Pennsylvania

Summary: Set during the time of the American Revolution, the novel dramatizes the working of the bondage system in which a bondsman was property and could be sold or traded. Jeffry Claus, a gunsmith, is bound for four years to Mark Fultz, a kindly Pennsylvania trader. When he dies, his scheming nephew denies any knowledge of the bargain that should have granted Claus' freedom. He has little choice but to escape.

Historical Accuracy: The novel features an accurate and convincing rendering of the region and the period.

6069 *Men in Buckskin*

Date of Publication: 1950

Subject(s): American Revolution; Indians

Fictional character(s): Simon Braide, Engineer, Spy

Historical character(s): George Washington, Military Personnel (army commander)

Time Period(s): 1770s

Locale(s): Susquehanna Valley, Pennsylvania

Summary: This romantic tale of the American Revolution involves engineer and secret agent Simon Braide who is commissioned to chart the points of probable attack by British troops and their Senecan allies on the settlers of the Susquehanna Valley. When his valuable map disappears, Braide launches into a series of exciting adventures.

Historical Accuracy: The story blends the actual and the invented. It is evident that the story is based on the author's familiarity with the region and its history.

6070 *Powder Mission*

Date of Publication: 1951

Subject(s): American Revolution

Fictional character(s): Martin Jon Richtier, Frontiersman

Time Period(s): 1780s

Locale(s): Mississippi; Detroit, Michigan; Philadelphia, Pennsylvania

Summary: Frontiersman Martin Jon Richtier is given the task of leading an expedition from Fort Pitt down the Mississippi River to get gold and badly needed gunpowder for Washington's troops. Richtier's adventures takes him throughout the Northwest frontier.

Historical Accuracy: Romantic adventure predominates with history providing only embellishment.

6071 *Song of the Susquehanna*

Date of Publication: 1949

Subject(s): American Colonies; French and Indian War

Fictional character(s): Peter Grove, Military Personnel (soldier)

Historical character(s): John Bartram, Scientist (botanist); Gouverneur Morris, Diplomat; Conrad Weiser, Frontiersman; Michael Cresap, Frontiersman, Military Personnel (soldier)

Time Period(s): 1750s

Locale(s): Pennsylvania, American Colonies

Summary: Soldier Peter Grove fights Indians in colonial Pennsylvania during the French and Indian War.

Historical Accuracy: The novel features several historical figures as well as an authentic depiction of everyday life around the trading town of Lancaster.

HARRIET BEECHER STOWE (1811-1896)

Stowe was an American writer whose *Uncle Tom's Cabin* was a world-wide phenomenon. Her other works include *Dred*, *A Tale of the Great Dismal Swamp*, and *The Pearl of Orr's Island*.

6072 *Oldtown Folks*

Date of Publication: 1869

Fictional character(s): Horace Holyoke, Gentleman

Time Period(s): 1790s

Locale(s): Oldtown, Massachusetts (modeled on Natick)

Summary: This is one man's recollections of his boyhood in a Massachusetts town shortly after the Revolutionary War. The novel presents a vivid picture of New England life, particularly the religious movements which followed the collapse of the older Pilgrim-Puritan theocracy.

Historical Accuracy: Stowe drew heavily on her husband's hometown recollections for her portrait of Oldtown and its citizens.

THELMA STRABEL (1900-1959)

Born in Crown Point, Indiana, Strabel became a feature and fashion writer. She wrote several novels, including *Caribee* and *Reap the Wild Wind*.

`6073` *Storm to the South*

Date of Publication: 1944
Subject(s): Independence—South America
Fictional character(s): Star Shattuck, Young Woman; Marita, Revolutionary; Bart Winship, Diplomat (vice consul)
Time Period(s): 19th century
Locale(s): California; Lima, Peru

Summary: This romantic tale is set during the period of Simon Bolivar's revolution in Peru. The story concerns two cousins, Star Shattuck, the daughter of a California rancher, and Marita, an ardent Peruvian revolutionary. They vie for the attention of Bart Winship, the American vice consul in Lima.

Historical Accuracy: The novel constructs a believable period backdrop for the romantic action.

MICHAEL WHITNEY STRAIGHT
(1916-)

American economist, journalist, editor, publisher, and author, Straight was born in New York, and attended the London School of Economics and Cambridge University. During World War II, he served with the U.S. Army Air Forces. He worked as an economist for the U.S. State Department; correspondent, editor, and publisher of the *New Republic*; and held executive positions with the National Endowment for the Arts, the NAACP, and Amnesty International. He wrote the novel *Happy and Hopeless* and the nonfiction works *Trial by Television and Other Encounters* and *Twigs for an Eagle's Nest: Government and the Arts, 1965-1978.*

`6074` *Carrington*

Date of Publication: 1960
Subject(s): American West; Fetterman Massacre; Indians
Historical character(s): Henry Beebee Carrington, Military Personnel (colonel); W.J. Fetterman, Military Personnel (colonel)
Time Period(s): 1860s (1866)
Locale(s): Wyoming

Summary: This western novel examines the events surrounding the famous Fetterman massacre of 1866 in which 81 men under the command of Colonel W.J. Fetterman are massacred by the Sioux. Although Fetterman was acting in defiance of explicit orders of his commanding officer, Colonel Henry Carrington, it is Carrington who is ultimately held responsible for the disaster. The novel focuses on Colonel Carrington and the impact of the catastrophe on his career.

Historical Accuracy: The novel is based on Army records, dispatches, and congressional records, as well as letters and eyewitness accounts that provide an accurate and authentic treatment of the events.

`6075` *A Very Small Remnant*

Date of Publication: 1963
Subject(s): American West; Indians; Sand Creek Massacre

Historical character(s): Edward Wanshear Wynkoop, Military Personnel (major); John Milton Chivington, Military Personnel (colonel)
Time Period(s): 1860s (1864)
Locale(s): Sand Creek, Colorado

Summary: This novel of the Indian Wars provides an accurate depiction of the Sand Creek Massacre in which an unarmed village of Cheyennes were exterminated in a five-hour massacre. The story depicts the events and the futile efforts of Major Edward Wynkoop to abide by the treaty with the Indians.

Historical Accuracy: The novel stays close to the known facts and invents little in this version of a tragic chapter of American history.

JAMES H. STREET (1903-1954)

Born in Mississippi, Street became a minister in Missouri and then a journalist for the New York *World-Telegram*. He wrote nonfiction books about American history as well as fiction. His novels include *The Gauntlet*, set in Missouri, and its sequel, *The High Calling.*

`6076` *By Valour and Arms*

Date of Publication: 1944
Subject(s): Civil War—U.S.; Sea Story; Siege of Vicksburg
Fictional character(s): Wyeth Woodward, Military Personnel (Confederate gunner's mate); Simeon St. Leger Granville, Mercenary; Vespasian Gillivray, Military Personnel (Confederate sailor)
Time Period(s): 1860s
Locale(s): Natchez, Mississippi; Vicksburg, Mississippi; Mississippi River

Summary: The Mississippi River theater of the Civil War is depicted, from the building of the Confederate gunboat *Arkansas* to the fall of Vicksburg. The action revolves around three Confederate sailors—Woodward, Granville, and Gillivray—but includes many others, showing the Union occupation of Natchez and the siege of Vicksburg.

Historical Accuracy: The historical elements are faithfully observed even though the story itself is fictional.

`6077` *Captain Little Ax*

Date of Publication: 1956
Subject(s): Civil War—U.S.; Battle of Shiloh; Battle of Chickamauga
Fictional character(s): Little Ax Trowbridge, Military Personnel (Confederate soldier), Teenager
Time Period(s): 1860s
Locale(s): Tennessee

Summary: This Civil War story describes the experiences of teenager Little Ax Trowbridge. After his father dies in the Battle of Shiloh, Little Ax forms a "Cradle Company" of young volunteers to the Confederate cause and leads them in action that includes the Battle of Chickamauga.

Historical Accuracy: Although the story is imagined, the period elements are convincingly reproduced.

6078   *Mingo Dabney*

Date of Publication: 1950
Subject(s): Revolution—Cuba
Fictional character(s): Mingo Dabney, Adventurer; Rafaela Galban, Revolutionary
Time Period(s): 1890s (1895-1896)
Locale(s): Mississippi; Havana, Cuba

Summary: In this sequel to *Tomorrow We Reap* (co-authored with James Childers), Mingo Dabney leaves the Mississippi Valley for Cuba in search of revolutionary leader Rafaela Galban. He quickly becomes involved in the events of the Cuban Revolution of 1895-1896.

Historical Accuracy: The story shifts the Virginius episode from the Cuban Revolution of 1868-1870 to the Revolution of 1895-1896. The story is intended to be read as romantic adventure rather than as a faithful history of actual events.

6079   *Oh, Promised Land*

Date of Publication: 1940
Subject(s): Settlement of the American Frontier; War of 1812; Indians
Historical character(s): Davy Crockett, Frontiersman; Andrew Jackson, Military Personnel (general); Sam Dabney, Frontiersman
Time Period(s): 18th century; 19th century (1794-1817)
Locale(s): Alabama; Natchez, Mississippi; Georgia

Summary: The settlement of the Mississippi Territory is described through the experience of legendary frontier figure Sam Dabney, who leads the first pack train west from Georgia. Dabney becomes the most feared Indian fighter on the frontier, a slave trader, and speculator who organizes the first freight service over the Natchez Trace. The Indian war with Tecumseh is described, as well as Dabney's epic ride of 950 miles in seven days with a message for Andrew Jackson that decides the Battle of New Orleans.

Historical Accuracy: The novel offers a blend of the factual and the fictional, with a convincing period background.

6080   *Tap Roots*

Date of Publication: 1942
Subject(s): Civil War—U.S.
Fictional character(s): Hoab Dabney, Plantation Owner; Keith Alexander, Young Man; Morna Dabney, Young Woman
Time Period(s): 1850s; 1860s (1858-1865)
Locale(s): Jones County, Mississippi

Summary: This unusual Civil War story depicts the activities of anti-slavery Southerners in Mississippi. Hoab Dabney, a Southern planter, decides that if Mississippi can secede from the Union, then his county can secede from Mississippi. The novel follows the consequence of this decision as the Dabney clan attempts to hold out against the full weight of the Confederacy.

Historical Accuracy: Romantic elements compromise the novel's authenticity.

JAMES H. STREET (1903-1954)

JAMES CHILDERS (1899-)

Childers was born in Alabama. He was a flier in World War I and a Rhodes Scholar. He was a colonel in the Air Force during World War II. Street, born in Mississippi, was a minister and then a journalist for the New York *World-Telegram*. Childers was a fan of Street's Dabney novels, and they began their collaboration when Street became bogged down writing *Tomorrow We Reap*.

6081   *Tomorrow We Reap*

Date of Publication: 1949
Subject(s): Politics
Fictional character(s): Big Sans Dabney, Businessman; Mingo Dabney, Businessman
Time Period(s): 1890s
Locale(s): Mississippi

Summary: The novel continues the story of Mississippi's Dabney clan in this story concerning the lumber industry and political corruption. At the center of the story are brothers Big Sans and Mingo Dabney, who resist northern financial pirates threatening to encroach on traditional southern values.

Historical Accuracy: The story is fanciful but does depend on an effective portrayal of the period.

JAMES H. STREET (1903-1954)

Born in Mississippi, Street became a minister in Missouri and then a journalist for the New York *World-Telegram*. He wrote nonfiction books about American history as well as fiction. His novels include *The Gauntlet*, set in Missouri, and its sequel, *The High Calling*.

6082   *The Velvet Doublet*

Date of Publication: 1953
Subject(s): Sea Story; Exploration; Inquisition
Fictional character(s): Juan Rodrigo Bermejo, Sailor
Historical character(s): Christopher Columbus, Explorer
Time Period(s): 15th century
Locale(s): *Pinta*, At Sea; Spain

Summary: The sailor who claims to have been the first to sight the New World on Columbus' fateful voyage tells his story. The novel vividly captures the world of the late 15th century when the Moors still held Granada and the threat of the Inquisition was ever present. Juan Bermejo signs on for Columbus' voyage with the prize of a velvet doublet promised to the first man to see the new world.

Historical Accuracy: The novel is a fanciful reproduction of Columbus' voyage, but the period background of Spain during the time is authentic.

THOMAS S. STRIBLING (1881-1965)

Born in Clifton, Tennessee, Stribling was a lawyer and author best known for his 1932 Pulitzer Prize-winning novel *The Store*. After practicing law for one year, Stribling took a job in Nashville on the *Taylor-Trotwood Magazine* and then began writing stories for Sunday school and pulp magazines. His first novel, *Birthright*, was published in 1922. Stribling's other works include *The Sound Wagon*, a satirical novel about law and politics, and another satire, *These Bars of Flesh*, about educators and radicals at a fictional university.

6083 *The Forge*

Date of Publication: 1931
Subject(s): Antebellum South; Civil War—U.S.; Reconstruction Period
Fictional character(s): Jimmie Valden, Landowner
Time Period(s): 19th century
Locale(s): Alabama

Summary: The novel describes the lives of an Alabama family before, during, and after the Civil War. The Valdens are the center of this social chronicle that tries to provide a balanced portrait of the South under pressure of the war and the ignominy of the peace.

Historical Accuracy: The novel is only convincing in its parts rather than in its whole.

MYRTLE STRODE-JACKSON

English writer Strode-Jackson was educated at Oxford and published poetry, fiction, and biography. She has also written on religious subjects.

6084 *Tansy Taniard*

Date of Publication: 1945
Subject(s): Elizabethan Period; Royalty—England
Fictional character(s): Tansy Taniard, Young Woman; Rupert de Boscage, Nobleman (count)
Historical character(s): Elizabeth I, Ruler (Queen of England); Sir Francis Walsingham, Government Official
Time Period(s): 16th century
Locale(s): London, England; Paris, France

Summary: Young Tansy Taniard sacrifices her red hair for a wig meant as a gift for Queen Elizabeth. This leads Tansy into a series of adventures. The intrigue includes her lover, Count Rupert de Boscage's attempt to regain his family's castle in Lorraine.

Historical Accuracy: The novel is rich in period background but verisimilitude is sacrificed at several places by anachronisms.

FRANK STANLEY STUART (1904-)

Stuart's books include *City of Bees*, *Wild Wings*.

6085 *Caravan to China*

Date of Publication: 1941
Subject(s): Roman Empire; Chinese Empire
Fictional character(s): Simon of Cyrene, Adventurer
Time Period(s): 1st century
Locale(s): Asia; China

Summary: Set during the reign of the Roman emperor Tiberius, the novel recounts the adventures of a trading expedition to China. The trek is led by Simon of Cyrene, who takes the opportunity to search for a girl sold into slavery.

Historical Accuracy: Adventure predominates and the period authenticity is undercut by modern dialogue.

VIVIAN STUART (1914-)

Born in Rangoon, Burma, Stuart is a prolific novelist who was trained in science at the University of London and the University of Budapest. During World War II, she served with the Australian forces and the British Army in Burma. After the war, she published numerous books under a variety of pseudonyms. As William Stuart Long, she enjoyed million copy sales for each of the volumes in The Australians series.

6086 *Brave Captains*

Date of Publication: 1968
Subject(s): Crimean War; Sea Story; Battle of Balaclava
Fictional character(s): Phillip Hazard, Military Personnel (naval officer)
Time Period(s): 1850s
Locale(s): Balaclava, Russia; *Trojan*, At Sea (Black Sea)

Summary: The novel continues the military adventures of British naval officer Phillip Hazard as he takes part in the Battle of Balaclava.

Historical Accuracy: The main events described are historically accurate and based on actual reports of the fighting.

6087 *Hazard of Huntress*

Date of Publication: 1972
Subject(s): Crimean War; Sea Story; Military Life—British Navy
Fictional character(s): Phillip Hazard, Military Personnel (naval officer)
Time Period(s): 1850s (1855)
Locale(s): *Huntress*, At Sea; Odessa, Russia

Summary: In the fourth volume of the military adventures of Phillip Hazard, he is, as the new commander of *H.M.S. Huntress*, dispatched to Odessa under sealed orders for a series of clandestine adventures.

Historical Accuracy: The main events described are real and accurately described, although the espionage plot in Odessa is fabricated.

6088 *Hazard's Command*

Date of Publication: 1971
Subject(s): Crimean War; Military Life—British Navy; Sea Story
Fictional character(s): Phillip Hazard, Military Personnel (naval officer)
Historical character(s): Fitzroy Somerset, Military Personnel (British general), Nobleman (Baron Raglan)
Time Period(s): 1850s (1854)
Locale(s): Constantinople, Ottoman Empire; *Trojan*, At Sea

Summary: This third installment in the Phillip Hazard series is set in the aftermath of Balaclava and the tragic charge of the Light Brigade. The novel describes the circumstances that lead to Hazard's first command.

Historical Accuracy: The main events described are historically accurate.

`6089` *Massacre at Cawnpore*

Date of Publication: 1973
Subject(s): Indian Mutiny; British Raj; Victorian Period
Fictional character(s): Alexander Sheridan, Military Personnel (British cavalry officer); Emmy Sheridan, Spouse
Time Period(s): 1850s (1857)
Locale(s): Cawnpore, India

Summary: This is the third installment of the military adventures of Alex Sheridan of the East India Company's Bengal Cavalry. Sheridan is part of the defense of Cawnpore that faces destruction unless a relief force rescues them in time.

Historical Accuracy: The story is based on published accounts by the survivors of the siege of Cawnpore and is truthful to actual events.

`6090` *The Valiant Sailors*

Date of Publication: 1966
Subject(s): Crimean War; Military Life—British Navy; Sea Story
Fictional character(s): Phillip Hazard, Military Personnel (naval officer)
Time Period(s): 1850s (1854)
Locale(s): Sebastopol, Russia; *Trojan*, At Sea (Black Sea)

Summary: The first in a series, the novel introduces Phillip Hazard, a young British naval officer, who is involved in the action surrounding the siege of Sebastopol during the Crimean War.

Historical Accuracy: The background to the fictional story of Hazard and *H.M.S. Trojan* involves actual historical figures and events.

`6091` *Victory at Sebastopol*

Date of Publication: 1992
Subject(s): Crimean War; Battle of Sebastopol; Sea Story
Fictional character(s): Phillip Hazard, Military Personnel (naval officer)
Time Period(s): 1850s (1854-1855)
Locale(s): Sebastopol, Russia; *Huntress*, At Sea

Summary: In this installment of the military adventures of Phillip Hazard, he must chart a passage for the Allied squadron into the land-locked Sea of Azoff to break the siege at Sebastopol. Hazard also faces a court martial.

Historical Accuracy: Although the actions of the *Huntress* and its men are fictional, the overall background of events and characters have a basis in historical fact.

JEAN STUBBS (1926-)

Born in Lancashire, England, Stubbs attended Manchester School of Art. She won the Society of Authors award in 1964 for her short story "A Child's Four Seasons." She is best known for her mysteries featuring Inspector Lintott that show her interest in character over plot; why-done-it over who-done-it.

`6092` *By Our Beginnings*

Date of Publication: 1979
Subject(s): Family Saga; Georgian Period
Fictional character(s): Ned Howarth, Farmer; Dorcas Wilde, Gentlewoman
Time Period(s): 18th century (1760-1793)
Locale(s): Lancashire, England

Summary: The first volume in a series that traces the Howarth family from 1760 to the present is set in Lancashire on the brink of the Industrial Revolution. Ned Howarth is a yeoman farmer who marries the gentle Dorcas Wilde. Their experiences reflect the period, as their rural life is transformed by the coming of mills.

Historical Accuracy: The novel's period is accurately and convincingly detailed.

`6093` *The Case of Kitty Ogilvie*

Date of Publication: 1970
Subject(s): Crime and Criminals; Trials; Georgian Period
Fictional character(s): Thomas Ogilvie, Laird; Kitty Ogilvie, Spouse; Patrick Ogilvie, Gentleman
Time Period(s): 1760s
Locale(s): Scotland

Summary: A lovers' triangle leads to murder in this story set in Scotland during the 1760s. Kitty Ogilvie marries Thomas Ogilvie, the laird of East Mill, but the marriage proves an unhappy one, and Kitty falls in love with Thomas' brother Patrick. Eventually, Patrick is hanged for his part in his brother's murder, and Kitty also stands trial as the novel explores motive and consequences in this tragic love story.

Historical Accuracy: The atmosphere and the region are reproduced with care and believability.

`6094` *Dear Laura*

Date of Publication: 1973
Subject(s): Victorian Period; Mystery
Fictional character(s): Laura Crozier, Spouse; Theodore Crozier, Gentleman; Inspector Lintott, Detective—Police
Time Period(s): 1890s (1890)
Locale(s): England

Summary: Based on an actual Victorian-era scandal, the novel tells the story of a young wife, Laura Crozier, who learns of her older husband's secret affair from a sinister veiled lady. When Theodore Crozier dies suddenly, an inquest reveals he has received a lethal dose of morphine. Inspector Lintott investigates, while the entire Crozier household has something to hide. And who is the mysterious veiled woman?.

Historical Accuracy: The novel owes many of its details to an actual case.

`6095` *Eleanora Duse*

Date of Publication: 1970
Subject(s): Theatrical Life; Biography, Fictionalized
Historical character(s): Eleanora Duse, Actress; Sarah Bernhardt, Actress; Gabriele D'Annunzio, Writer (poet)
Time Period(s): 19th century; 20th century (1860s-1920s)
Locale(s): Italy; France; United States

Summary: This biographical novel dramatizes the career of the legendary actress Eleanora Duse. Born into a poor Italian theatrical family, Duse made her first great success on stage as Juliet at the age of 14. Her only rival for acting preeminence was Sarah Bernhardt and, like hers, Duse's offstage life was both passionate and tempestuous.

Historical Accuracy: This is a documentary novel, not a biography since the author has taken liberties which no biographers would permit themselves. The conversations are imagined, and some of the events are invented.

`6096` *The Golden Crucible*

Date of Publication: 1976
Subject(s): Mystery; Earthquakes; Theatrical Life
Fictional character(s): Inspector Lintott, Detective—Police; Felix Salvador, Magician; Bel Barak, Gentleman
Time Period(s): 1900s (1906)
Locale(s): San Francisco, California

Summary: When Inspector Lintott returns to San Francisco in 1906, he is hired to find the sister of a famous magician, Felix Salvador. Unscrupulous American millionaire Bel Barak's plans to avenge an old grudge against Salvador must be stopped. The San Francisco earthquake provides the novel's thrilling climax.

Historical Accuracy: The period elements are convincing, as are the novel's theatrical scenes.

`6097` *An Imperfect Joy*

Date of Publication: 1981
Subject(s): Family Saga; Luddites; Georgian Period
Fictional character(s): William Howarth, Businessman; Charlotte Howarth, Widow(er); Dick Howarth, Farmer
Time Period(s): 18th century; 19th century (1785-1812)
Locale(s): Lancashire, England

Summary: This novel follows *By Our Beginnings* and tells the story of the second generation of the Howarth family. Oldest son William strives for success in the newly created iron industry. His sister Charlotte opposes him because of the injustice created by the industry, and his brother Dick tries to maintain the old ways tending the family farm. The explosive Luddite revolt breaks out with devastating consequences for them all.

Historical Accuracy: The period elements of life in Lancashire are accurate and convincing.

`6098` *My Grand Enemy*

Date of Publication: 1967
Subject(s): Crime and Criminals; Georgian Period; Trials

Historical character(s): Francis Bandy, Lawyer; Mary Bandy, Gentlewoman; Willy Cranstoun, Gentleman
Time Period(s): 18th century
Locale(s): England

Summary: Based on an actual 18th century crime and murder trial, the novel tells a dark tale of passion. Lawyer Francis Bandy's daughter, Mary, is attracted to a fortune-hunter, Willy Cranstoun, for whom she does the unspeakable. When her father is poisoned, she stands trial for murder.

Historical Accuracy: The novel bases the details of the story on the actual trial transcripts.

`6099` *The Northern Correspondent*

Date of Publication: 1984
Subject(s): Victorian Period; Family Saga
Fictional character(s): Ambrose Longe, Editor (newspaper); William Howarth, Businessman; Naomi Blum, Gentlewoman
Time Period(s): 19th century (1831-1851)
Locale(s): Lancashire, England

Summary: The fourth volume of the author's saga about the Howarth family of Lancashire dramatizes the conflict between radical newspaper editor Ambrose Longe and his uncle William Howarth. Howarth finances the establishment *Lancashire Herald*, and the war of rival newspapers is affected by Naomi Blum's arrival.

Historical Accuracy: The Lancashire scene during the period is authentic.

`6100` *An Unknown Welshman*

Date of Publication: 1973
Subject(s): War of the Roses; Royalty—England
Historical character(s): Henry Tudor, Nobleman; Richard III, Ruler (King of England); Elizabeth of York, Royalty (queen consort of Henry VII)
Time Period(s): 15th century (1457-1486)
Locale(s): Wales; England

Summary: The tortuous and bloody route of Henry Tudor to the throne of England and the conclusion of the War of Roses are chronicled. The novel concentrates on the early years of Henry in Wales and his complex manuevering to gain power and to hold it.

Historical Accuracy: The essential outline of the novel is historical and faithfully presented.

`6101` *The Vivian Inheritance*

Date of Publication: 1982
Subject(s): Family Saga; Regency Period; Railroads
Fictional character(s): William Howarth, Businessman (ironmaster); Hal Vivian, Engineer; Anna Howarth, Young Woman
Time Period(s): 19th century (1815-1830)
Locale(s): Lancashire, England

Summary: In the third volume of the author's saga of the Howarth family, it is 1815 and the wars with Napoleon are over. Young engineer Hal Vivian pursues his dream of a future age of steam, transforming Wyndendale and the Howarth family with the railroad that accelerates the industrialization of Lancashire.

Historical Accuracy: The region and the period are captured with convincing details.

EDUARD STUCKEN (1865-1936)

German writer Stucken produced a number of exotic romantic works. He is best remembered for his trilogy of Aztec novels.

6102 *The Great White Gods*

Date of Publication: 1934
Subject(s): Spanish Colonies; Aztec Empire
Historical character(s): Montezuma II, Ruler (Aztec emperor); Hernando Cortez, Explorer, Military Personnel (conquistador)
Time Period(s): 16th century
Locale(s): Mexico

Summary: The novel dramatizes the final flourishing of the Aztec Empire that is ended by the Spanish invasion led by Cortez. Encyclopedic in its descriptions of Aztec life and customs, the novel chronicles the great events of the conquest with Montezuma and Cortez the principal figures, surrounded by a large and colorful supporting cast.

Historical Accuracy: The novel blends a high degree of evident research, both historical and anthropological, with some imagined scenes and events.

SHOWELL STYLES (1908-)

Prolific British writer Styles was born in Warwickshire and worked as a bank clerk early in his career. He served in the Royal Navy as a lieutenant commander during World War II. An avid mountaineer, Styles led three British climbing expeditions in the early 1950s and has written two standard works on mountain climbing. His books include *The Lee Shore, Stella and the Fireships*, and *The Malta Frigate*. Styles is also the author of murder mysteries under the pseudonym Glyn Carr.

6103 *The Frigate Captain*

Date of Publication: 1956
Subject(s): Sea Story; Napoleonic Wars; Military Life—British Navy
Historical character(s): Thomas Cochrane, Military Personnel (naval officer)
Time Period(s): 18th century; 19th century (1793-1814)
Locale(s): England; At Sea

Summary: The novel traces the adventures and contentious life of Captain Lord Cochra ne. Although his heroism rivals that of Horatio Nelson, Cochrane's reputation is clouded by his reformer's zeal in pursuing unpopular courses. His naval exploits include the taking of a Spanish frigate against impossible odds, the holding of a fort against a powerful French army, and a single-handed victory over a French fleet.

Historical Accuracy: The novel stays close to the actual events and personalities of Cochrane's life.

6104 *His Was the Fire*

Date of Publication: 1957
Subject(s): Napoleonic Wars; Biography, Fictionalized; American Revolution
Historical character(s): Sir John Moore, Military Personnel (British general)
Time Period(s): 18th century; 19th century
Locale(s): American Colonies; Spain

Summary: This fictional biography of British general Sir John Moore is told from the perspective of a variety of characters—a young rifleman, a British schoolboy, a professional officer, and a society lady—whose lives are affected by Sir John.

Historical Accuracy: The novel is based on the actual events of Moore's life.

6105 *The Sea Officer*

Date of Publication: 1961
Subject(s): Sea Story; Military Life—British Navy
Historical character(s): Edward Pellew, Military Personnel (naval officer), Nobleman (Viscount Exmouth); Horatio Nelson, Military Personnel (admiral); Robert Steward, Political Figure, Nobleman (Viscount Castlereagh); Robert Banks Jenkinson, Political Figure, Nobleman (Earl of Liverpool)
Time Period(s): 18th century; 19th century
Locale(s): England; At Sea

Summary: The novel describes the naval career of Edward Pellew, first Viscount Exmouth, Vice Admiral of England, regarded as the finest sea officer of his age. Pellew is the naval officer under whom the fictional Horatio Hornblower trained aboard the *Indefatigable*. Pellew is shown in action during the American Revolution and the Napoleonic War.

Historical Accuracy: All the chief events of the story are historical. Only the gaps between the bare bones of history have been filled with material suggested by the facts.

WILLIAM STYRON (1925-)

An American author born in Virginia and a graduate of Duke University, Styron has had a distinguished literary career. He won the 1968 Pulitzer Prize for *The Confessions of Nat Turner* and the American Book Award for *Sophie's Choice*. He has earned critical praise for his willingness to raise difficult but important issues.

6106 *The Confessions of Nat Turner*

Date of Publication: 1967
Subject(s): Slavery
Historical character(s): Nat Turner, Slave, Religious (preacher)
Time Period(s): 1830s (1831)
Locale(s): Southampton, Virginia

Summary: Jailed in 1831 and awaiting execution, Nat Turner, an educated slave and preacher who felt divinely ordained to

bring a violent end to slavery, reflects on his life and the bloody events of the slave revolt he led, the only effective slave rebellion in U.S. history.

Historical Accuracy: The known facts about Nat Turner and the revolt he led are accurate. However, in those areas where there is little knowledge in regard to Turner, his early life, and his motivation for the revolt, liberties have been taken to fill in the gaps with plausible surmises.

BENJAMIN SUBERCASEAUX (1902-1973)

Born in Santiago, Chile, Subercaseaux studied medicine at the Unversity of Chile and psychology at the Sorbonne. He has travelled and lived abroad, lectured in his native country, and authored several works of nonfiction and fiction.

6107 *Jemmy Button*

Date of Publication: 1954
Subject(s): Exploration; Sea Story
Fictional character(s): Jemmy Button, Indian (Fuegia); Fuegia Basket, Indian (Fuegia)
Historical character(s): Robert Fitz-Roy, Sea Captain; Charles Darwin, Scientist (naturalist)
Time Period(s): 1830s
Locale(s): Tierra del Fuego, Chile; England; At Sea

Summary: Based on the journals of Robert Fitz-Roy, the captain of the *H.M.S. Beagle*, the novel concerns Fitz-Roy's attempt to civilize some natives of Tierra del Fuego. The story chronicles what happened to four natives who are taken back to England. Their experiences in civilization and their return home are depicted. The novel offers a very different interpretation of the noble savage theme.

Historical Accuracy: The novel has re-cast the factual material from both Fitz-Roy and Darwin's journals with some imaginative invention.

CLIFFORD SUBLETTE (1887-1939)

Born in Charleston, Illinois, Sublette is the author of *Scarlet Cockerel*, *The Bright Face of Danger*, and *Greenhorn's Hunt*.

6108 *The Bright Face of Danger*

Date of Publication: 1926
Subject(s): American Colonies; Bacon's Rebellion
Fictional character(s): Francis Havenell, Young Man
Time Period(s): 17th century (1676)
Locale(s): Henrico County, Virginia, American Colonies

Summary: Set during the period of Bacon's Rebellion in the Virginia colony, this historical romance turns on the search for revenge by Francis Havenell for the murderer of his father and friend. He joins Nathaniel Bacon's cause and experiences trouble with the Indians and a slave revolt before achieving his goal.

Historical Accuracy: The historical background is only average in its effectiveness, with romantic adventure predominating.

CLIFFORD SUBLETTE (1887-1939)

HARRY HARRISON KROLL (1888-1967)

Born in Charleston, Illinois, Sublette is the author of *Scarlet Cockerel*, *The Bright Face of Danger*, and *Greenhorn's Hunt*. An Indiana-born novelist, teacher, and memoirist, Kroll wrote several novels about the South and the border states, including *Fury in the Earth*, *The Keepers of the House*, and *Rogue's Company*. His autobiography is entitled *I Was a Sharecropper*.

6109 *Perilous Journey: A Tale of the Mississippi River and the Natchez Trace*

Date of Publication: 1943
Subject(s): Settlement of the American Frontier
Fictional character(s): Jim Dalyrymple, Young Man
Time Period(s): 1820s (1821)
Locale(s): Mississippi River; Natchez Trace, Mississippi; New Orleans, Louisiana

Summary: Young Jim Dalyrymple sets out from Indiana down the Mississippi to New Orleans in search of his missing father. He must contend with river pirates and betrayal before finding his father and returning home.

Historical Accuracy: This is an authentic depiction of life along the Mississippi River and the Natchez Trace, with solid and convincing local color.

CLIFFORD SUBLETTE (1887-1939)

Born in Charleston, Illinois, Sublette is the author of *Scarlet Cockerel*, *The Bright Face of Danger*, and *Greenhorn's Hunt*.

6110 *Scarlet Cockerel*

Date of Publication: 1925
Subject(s): American Colonies; Huguenots
Fictional character(s): Blaise de Breault, Fugitive
Time Period(s): 17th century (1690s)
Locale(s): France; North Carolina, American Colonies

Summary: This historical romance takes as its background the French Huguenot settlement of Carolina. Young Blaise de Breault flees to America after killing a follower of the Duc de Guise. There he has many adventures with the Indians and the Spanish.

Historical Accuracy: The novel's colonial background is authentic and believable.

RUTH SUCKOW (1892-1960)

Born in Iowa, Suckow worked as an editor, beekeeper, and author of novels and short stories. In the 1920s, Suckow's short stories gained the attention of literary editor H.L. Mencken and subsequent national readership in Mencken's magazines. Set mostly in early 20th-century Iowa, Suckow's fiction won praise for its sociologically sound local color and psychologically acute character analysis. Her novels include *New Hope*, *Cora*, and *The Odyssey of a Nice Girl*.

6111 *Country People*

Date of Publication: 1924
Subject(s): Family Saga; Settlement of the American Frontier; Farming
Fictional character(s): August Kaetter-Henry, Farmer; Carl Kaetter-Henry, Farmer
Time Period(s): 19th century
Locale(s): Iowa

Summary: This novel chronicles the lives of three generations of a German-American family who come to America from Pomerania during the 1850s to settle in Iowa. The novel features a carefully documented portrait of ordinary life.

Historical Accuracy: This is a faithful and authentic depiction of daily life in the Iowa farmlands.

GWYNEDD SUDWORTH

6112 *Richard Whittington, London's Mayor*

Date of Publication: 1975
Subject(s): Middle Ages; Biography, Fictionalized; Peasants' Revolt
Historical character(s): Richard Whittington, Businessman, Political Figure; Richard II, Ruler (King of England); Wat Tyler, Revolutionary
Time Period(s): 14th century; 15th century
Locale(s): London, England; Gloucestershire, England

Summary: This biographical account of the life and career of Richard Whittington describes his rise to become Lord Mayor of London and a great benefactor to the citizens of London. Whittington's career connects with that of Richard II during the Peasant Revolt.

Historical Accuracy: The novel interweaves fact and legend, setting Whittington's story against a background of London in the 14th century.

ALAN SULLIVAN (1868-1947)

Born in Montreal, Sullivan worked on the Canadian Pacific Railroad as a surveyor and then went on to several different positions in mining and industrial enterprises. He wrote poetry, fiction, and history.

6113 *The Fur Masters*

Date of Publication: 1947
Subject(s): Frontier—Canada
Fictional character(s): Neil Campbell, Young Man; Angus Campbell, Trader
Time Period(s): 1800s (1804)
Locale(s): Canada

Summary: In early 19th-century Canada the rivalry between the Northwest Company and the Hudson Bay Company explodes into pitched battle. Against this backdrop a young

Scotsman, Neil Campbell, seeks his fortune and the father he hasn't seen since childhood.

Historical Accuracy: The novel's elements from Canadian history are accurate, but the story does not fully develop the sense of the era.

6114 *Three Came to Ville Marie*

Date of Publication: 1943
Subject(s): Frontier—Canada; Indians
Fictional character(s): Paul de Lorimer, Settler; Jules Vicotte, Settler
Historical character(s): Louis XIV, Ruler (King of France)
Time Period(s): 17th century
Locale(s): Canada; France

Summary: This tale of the early settlement of New France begins in the court of Louis XIV and continues in the wilderness in the battle against the Indians and nature. A love triangle dominates the romantic elements of the story.

Historical Accuracy: The novel provides a believable evocation of the period.

WALTER SULLIVAN (1924-)

American author Walter Sullivan was born in Nashville, Tennessee, and attended Vanderbilt University and the University of Iowa. A professor of literature at Vanderbilt, Sullivan is the author of books of literary criticism and the novel *The Long, Long Love*.

6115 *Sojourn of a Stranger*

Date of Publication: 1957
Subject(s): Civil War—U.S.; Slavery; Racial Conflict
Fictional character(s): Allen Hendrick, Plantation Owner
Time Period(s): 1850s; 1860s
Locale(s): Tennessee

Summary: This Civil War era story concerns the experiences of plantation owner Allen Hendrick whose father marries a fair-skinned octoroon from New Orleans. It is Allen, however, who must live with the consequences of his father's defiance of social conventions.

Historical Accuracy: The novel employs a believable period backdrop for this ethical drama.

RICHARD SUMMERS

Summers is an associate professor of English at the University of Arizona.

6116 *Vigilante*

Date of Publication: 1949
Subject(s): American West; Vigilantes
Fictional character(s): Lucky Langmeade, Government Official
Historical character(s): David Broderick, Political Figure
Time Period(s): 1850s (1856)
Locale(s): San Francisco, California

Summary: This story of California in the 1850s centers on the career of David C. Broderick—senator and opportunist—and the vigilante movement that brought him down. The novel's narrator is "Lucky" Langmeade who is deputized by the Committee of Seven to connect Broderick with the lawless element of San Francisco.

Historical Accuracy: This is an excessively fictionalized version of history with a 1940s sensibility imposed on the 1850s.

RACHEL SUMMERSON (1944-)

Born in Darlington, England, Summerson attended the Sorbonne, the University of Sussex, and the University of London. She has worked as a writer and director with theater companies in England.

6117 *Belgrave Square*

Date of Publication: 1981
Subject(s): Victorian Period; Romance
Fictional character(s): Flora Peat, Young Woman
Time Period(s): 1860s
Locale(s): London, England

Summary: This amusing tale traces the unlikely romantic success of Flora Peat, the eldest and least attractive of the four Peat sisters, who falls in love with London's most eligible bachelor.

Historical Accuracy: The novel is more fantasy than a realistic treatment of the period.

RICHARD SUMNER

6118 *Mistress of the Boards*

Date of Publication: 1976
Subject(s): Restoration Period; Theatrical Life; Fires
Historical character(s): Nell Gwynne, Actress, Lover (of the king); Charles II, Ruler (King of England)
Time Period(s): 17th century
Locale(s): London, England

Summary: This is a romanticized account of the liaison between English actress Nell Gwynne and Charles II. The novel features a vivid portrait of Restoration London and the events of the Great Fire of London.

Historical Accuracy: The novel's characterization owes more to a romantic imagination than history.

PER OLOF SUNDMAN (1922-)

Swedish novelist Sundman has been active in local government, serving as a member of the Swedish Parliament. His books have won the Swedish Great Novel Prize and the Prize of the Nordic Council.

6119 *The Flight of the Eagle*

Date of Publication: 1970
Subject(s): Aviation; Polar Exploration

Historical character(s): Salomon August Andree, Explorer (polar), Scientist
Time Period(s): 1890s (1896-1897)
Locale(s): Stockholm, Sweden; Arctic

Summary: This documentary novel dramatizes the 1897 attempt by Swedish scientist S.A. Andree to fly to the North Pole in a hydrogen balloon. After a 65-hour flight, Andree is forced to land on the ice, where he and his crew struggle to survive for months before dying. The death of the Andree party has been one of the great mysteries of the Arctic, and the novel offers a plausible solution to many of the puzzles of Andree's ill-fated expedition.

Historical Accuracy: To a great extent the book is a novel of imagination, but nothing in it that is imagined should conflict with the known historical facts.

PATRICK SUSKIND (1949-)

Suskind was born near Munich. A problem with his hands made it impossible for him to pursue his desired career as a concert pianist. He enrolled in the University of Munich, where he studied medieval and modern history. Suskind is a TV script writer, playwright, and novelist. *Perfume* won the World Fantasy Award in 1986 for best fantasy novel.

6120 *Perfume: The Story of a Murderer*

Date of Publication: 1986
Subject(s): Crime and Criminals
Fictional character(s): Jean-Baptiste Grenouille, Orphan, Murderer
Time Period(s): 18th century
Locale(s): Paris, France

Summary: The novel, set in 18th-century France, traces the bizarre story of foundling Jean-Baptiste Grenouille, who is gifted with the power to smell the very composition of objects and their history. He sets out to isolate the most perfect scent of all, life itself. In his quest he tries to extract from the most beautiful young virgin the ultimate perfume that can make him fully human.

Historical Accuracy: The story is a fascinating psychological study with a convincing period background.

ROSEMARY SUTCLIFF (1920-1992)

English author Sutcliff was born in Sussex and educated privately and at the Bideford School of Art. Sutcliff is considered one of the greatest writers of children's literature, though most of her books were meant for adult readers as well. Her historical novels feature scrupulous research. *The Mark of the Horse* and *Katherine* are considered her masterpieces. *The Lantern Bearer* won the Carnegie Medal in 1960.

6121 *Blood and Sand*

Date of Publication: 1987
Subject(s): Ottoman Empire; Napoleonic Wars
Fictional character(s): Anoud, Spouse (of Keith)

Historical character(s): Thomas Keith, Military Personnel (private); Tusson Bey, Nobleman
Time Period(s): 1800s
Locale(s): Cairo, Egypt; Arabia

Summary: The novel is based on the true story of an English private, Thomas Keith, who in the Egyptian campaign of the Napoleonic Wars is taken prisoner, converts to Islam, and rises to become emir of the holy city of Medina. Keith's adventures and his friendship with Tusson Bey, the young son of the Turkish viceroy of Egypt, are dramatized in desert campaigns to reclaim the holy places of Islam.

Historical Accuracy: The novel is authentic in its depiction of the scene and the era.

6122 *The Flowers of Adonis*

Date of Publication: 1969
Subject(s): Ancient Greece; Peloponnesian War
Historical character(s): Alcibiades, Military Personnel (general)
Time Period(s): 5th century B.C.
Locale(s): Athens, Greece; Sparta, Greece; Persia

Summary: This story of the Peloponnesian War focuses on the life of the Athenian military hero Alkibiades, who is exiled to Sparta after being condemned for sacrilege. His military career then thrusts him into war against his own country.

Historical Accuracy: The author writes that she followed historical accounts closely but filled in the gaps with speculation.

6123 *Lady in Waiting*

Date of Publication: 1957
Subject(s): Elizabethan Period; Royalty—England
Historical character(s): Sir Walter Raleigh, Gentleman, Courtier; Bess Throckmorton, Spouse (of Raleigh); Elizabeth I, Ruler (Queen of England); James I, Ruler (King of England)
Time Period(s): 16th century; 17th century
Locale(s): England

Summary: This is the story of Walter Raleigh's relationship with his wife, Bess Throckmorton. She is a lady in waiting to Queen Elizabeth, and he is one of the Queen's favorites. Their love survives Elizabeth's disfavor and the charges of treason from James I that lead to Raleigh's execution.

Historical Accuracy: The author is a master of the period, which is rendered in convincing fashion. The story stays close to history.

6124 *Rider on a White Horse*

Date of Publication: 1959
Subject(s): Civil War—England
Historical character(s): Thomas Fairfax, Military Personnel (Civil War leader); Anne Fairfax, Spouse
Time Period(s): 17th century
Locale(s): England

Summary: Set during the English Civil War, the novel tells the true story of military leader Sir Thomas Fairfax, who takes up the fight against King Charles I and the Cavaliers. His wife

Anne rejects her expected role of waiting at home for his return by joining her husband at the head of the rebel army.

Historical Accuracy: The story and its events are true and faithfully presented.

6125 *Sword at Sunset*

Date of Publication: 1963
Subject(s): Dark Ages; Myths and Legends; Arthurian Legends
Fictional character(s): Artos the Bear, Warrior; Ygerma, Royalty (princess); Bedwyr, Knight
Time Period(s): 5th century
Locale(s): England

Summary: The novel retells the Arthurian legend realistically, stripped of the medieval trappings. Artos the Bear is described, a fierce warrior-king who may well have been the historical King Arthur. His struggle to resist the onslaught of the Saxons after the departure of the Romans is depicted.

Historical Accuracy: As the author explains, the novel is an attempt to re-create Arthur's story from fragments of known facts, guesswork, and speculation.

VICTOR SUTHREN (1942-)

Born in Montreal, Suthren is the Deputy Curator of the Canadian War Museum and has written extensively on 18th- and 19th-century history. His sailing experience includes cruising on schooners while retracing the sailing routes of 18th-century wars.

6126 *Admiral of Fear*

Date of Publication: 1991
Subject(s): Sea Story; Military Life—British Navy
Fictional character(s): Edward Mainwaring, Military Personnel (naval officer); Rigaud de la Roche-Bourbon, Military Personnel (naval officer)
Historical character(s): George II, Ruler (King of England)
Time Period(s): 1740s (1742)
Locale(s): Toulon, France

Summary: In 1742, Edward Mainwaring goes into action against the French and Spanish over the Mediterranean fortress of Toulon. Opposing him is the cunning Rigaud de la Roche-Bourbon. Outnumbered and poorly armed, Mainwaring must storm the French fortress and prevent a major disaster for the British fleet.

Historical Accuracy: Toulon was historically a strategically pivotal point for the control of the Mediterranean. The novel's story is invented but its atmosphere is authentic.

6127 *The Black Cockade*

Date of Publication: 1977
Subject(s): Sea Story
Fictional character(s): Paul Gallant, Sea Captain
Time Period(s): 1740s (1745)
Locale(s): *Echo*, At Sea; Minorca, Spain; Algiers, Algeria

Summary: It is 1745 and France and Britain are locked in a struggle for control of North America. Paul Gallant's is the last French ship still afloat in the besieged harbor of Louisburg. He is ordered to run the British blockade and reach Toulon to secure reinforcements. His adventures include capture and imprisonment in the British naval base at Minorca, a visit to the court of the Dey in Algiers, and action against a British squadron.

Historical Accuracy: This fictional story is solidly grounded in convincing period elements.

6128 *Captain Monsoon*

Date of Publication: 1992
Subject(s): Sea Story; Military Life—British Navy
Fictional character(s): Edward Mainwaring, Military Personnel (naval officer); Lady Caroline Grenville, Noblewoman; Rigaud de la Roche-Bourbon, Military Personnel (naval officer)
Time Period(s): 1740s (1744)
Locale(s): Mauritius; *Pallas*, At Sea; Indian Ocean

Summary: In this installment of the naval adventures of the young American Edward Mainwaring, it is 1744 and war breaks out between England and France. Mainwaring is captured off the coast of Mauritius. He mounts a daring escape, and with a flotilla of ill-equipped ships, prepares to attack the French fleet. The outcome will decide the fate of English influence in the Indian Ocean.

Historical Accuracy: The story is fanciful but does rely on authentic period elements.

6129 *The Golden Galleon*

Date of Publication: 1989
Subject(s): Sea Story; Military Life—British Navy
Fictional character(s): Edward Mainwaring, Military Personnel (naval officer); Anne Brixham, Gentlewoman; Rigaud de la Roche-Bourbon, Military Personnel (naval officer)
Time Period(s): 1740s (1741)
Locale(s): *Diana*, At Sea; Marquesas Islands, French Polynesia

Summary: In this installment of the author's naval series involving American Edward Mainwaring of the British Navy, it is 1741, and Mainwaring, on his own initiative, pursues Spanish privateers who have kidnapped Anne Brixham. In the Pacific, Mainwaring chances upon the greatest prize of all, the fabled Manilla Galleon.

Historical Accuracy: Although the story is fanciful, it does feature authentic nautical and period details.

6130 *In Perilous Seas*

Date of Publication: 1983
Subject(s): Sea Story
Fictional character(s): Paul Gallant, Sea Captain; Marianne de Bezy, Noblewoman (marquise); Don Alfonso Castelar, Nobleman
Time Period(s): 1740s (1747)
Locale(s): Martinique; *Echo*, At Sea

Summary: In 1747 as France, Spain, and England fight for control of the seas and the riches of the New World, Acadian-born Paul Gallant is charged with accompanying a convoy of

ships to France. Marianne, Marquise de Bezy, a favorite cousin of Louis XV, is one of the passengers, and in command is the Spanish nobleman Don Alfonso. Gallant quickly finds himself in the middle of a double-cross and betrayal. He must also contend with a swarm of privateers and a British fleet of superior strength.

Historical Accuracy: The story is invented but based on what might have happened and given a plausible background.

6131 *A King's Ransom*

Date of Publication: 1981
Subject(s): Sea Story; Pirates
Fictional character(s): Paul Gallant, Sea Captain
Time Period(s): 1740s (1746)
Locale(s): Cape Breton Island, Nova Scotia, Canada; *Echo*, At Sea

Summary: Acadian sea captain Paul Gallant seeks to discover the whereabouts of a golden statue, the Nuestra Senora de la Concepcion, given by the King of Spain to the King of France to secure France's support. The ship carrying the priceless statue has disappeared along the Cape Breton coast of New France. Gallant sets out in pursuit and must match wits against both the English navy and buccaneers.

Historical Accuracy: The situation is imagined but plausible in its period atmosphere and nautical details.

6132 *Royal Yankee*

Date of Publication: 1987
Subject(s): Sea Story; Military Life—British Navy
Fictional character(s): Edward Mainwaring, Military Personnel (naval officer); Anne Brixham, Gentlewoman; Rigaud de la Roche-Bourbon, Military Personnel (naval officer)
Time Period(s): 1730s (1739)
Locale(s): *Athena*, At Sea

Summary: This naval action novel introduces Edward Mainwaring, an American naval officer serving in the British Navy. It is 1739, and Mainwaring, aboard the schooner *Athena*, participates in the British attack on the Caribbean harbor of Porto Bello. Mainwaring meets his love, Anne Brixham, and his nemesis, the Chevalier de la Roche-Bourbon.

Historical Accuracy: The novel features an authentic portrait of the British Navy during the period.

WILLIAM GILBERT VAN TASSEL SUTPEN (1861-1945)

American novelist Sutphen was born in Philadelphia. His books include *The Doomsman* and *Golficide, and Other Tales of the Fair Green*.

6133 *I, Nathanael, Knew Jesus*

Date of Publication: 1941
Subject(s): Biblical Story; Christianity
Historical character(s): Jesus Christ, Biblical Figure; Nathanael, Biblical Figure, Religious (apostle); Bartholomew, Biblical Figure, Religious (apostle)

Time Period(s): 1st century
Locale(s): Israel

Summary: The novel offers a fictional life of Jesus told from the perspective of the apostle Nathanael, who is at first skeptical but gradually accepts Jesus' divinity. Nathanael emerges as a modern skeptic offering an interesting gloss on the other versions of the story of Jesus.

Historical Accuracy: The novel, despite its clearly contemporary viewpoint, does offer an authentic version of the attitudes of first-century Christians.

VIRGINIA SWAIN (1899-)

6134 *The Dollar Gold Piece*

Date of Publication: 1942
Subject(s): Business Building
Fictional character(s): Cathie Brawne, Young Woman
Time Period(s): 1880s (1887-1888)
Locale(s): Kansas City, Missouri

Summary: The novel's subject is the livestock industry in Kansas City during the 1880s. The story is filled with period elements that capture the region and the vitality of the cattle boom.

Historical Accuracy: The novel provides an authentic look at the period.

LOIS SWANN (1944-)

Born in New York City, Swann graduated from Marquette University, where she studied drama.

6135 *The Mists of Manittoo*

Date of Publication: 1976
Subject(s): American Colonies; Indians; Tribal Life—Native American
Fictional character(s): Elizabeth Dowland, Young Woman; Wakwa Manunnappu, Indian, Warrior
Time Period(s): 1740s
Locale(s): Massachusetts, American Colonies

Summary: Set during the 18th century in colonial Massachusetts, the novel tells the story of Elizabeth Dowland's encounter with Indians. Rescued by Indian Wakwa Manunnappu, she eventually marries him and takes up Indian life while struggling to reconcile her family to her marriage.

Historical Accuracy: The novel offers a convincing look at the American colonies and Indian life.

6136 *Torn Covenants*

Date of Publication: 1981
Subject(s): American Colonies; Indians; Tribal Life—Native American
Fictional character(s): Elizabeth Dowland, Spouse (of Wakwa); Wakwa Manunnappu, Indian, Warrior
Time Period(s): 1740s (1748)
Locale(s): Massachusetts, American Colonies

Summary: This sequel to the author's *The Mists of Manittoo* continues the story of Elizabeth Dowland, who has married Indian Wakwa Manunnappu in colonial Massachusetts. Elizabeth must adjust to Indian life and deal with jealousy and resentment from some of the Indians. Threats from both Indians and whites endanger Elizabeth and Wakwa.

Historical Accuracy: The novel is authentic in its period background.

NEIL HARMON SWANSON (1896-1983)

American editor, journalist, and author Swanson was born in Minneapolis, Minnesota, and began his career at the *Minneapolis Journal* when he left the University of Minnesota during his junior year. After serving as a company commander with the U.S. Army in France during World War I, Swanson returned to the *Journal* and then went on to hold positions with other newspapers, including the *Baltimore Sun*, where he won three Pulitzer Prizes. Considered an expert on the War of 1812, Swanson wrote nine historical books, one of which, *The Unconquered*, was filmed by Cecil B. DeMille.

6137 *The First Rebel*

Date of Publication: 1937
Subject(s): American Colonies; Indians; French and Indian War
Historical character(s): James Smith, Frontiersman
Time Period(s): 1760s (1763-1767)
Locale(s): Pennsylvania, American Colonies

Summary: The story dramatizes the Scottish-Irish uprising in Pennsylvania in the 1760s led by John Smith. Many historical incidents are recounted including General Braddock's defeat and Smith's capture by the Indians.

Historical Accuracy: This is a careful and accurate documentary history cast in fictional form with an authentic period background.

6138 *The Forbidden Ground*

Date of Publication: 1938
Subject(s): American Revolution; Indians
Fictional character(s): Baril MacGregor, Trader (fur), Frontiersman
Time Period(s): 1770s
Locale(s): Detroit, Michigan; Northwest Territory, United States

Summary: This adventure tale is set in Detroit during the American Revolution and concerns the experiences of frontiersman and fur trader Baril MacGregor amongst the voyageurs, his French counterparts.

Historical Accuracy: The fictional story makes use of a well-researched and authentic period and regional background.

6139 *The Judas Tree*

Date of Publication: 1933
Subject(s): American Colonies; Pontiac's Rebellion; Indians

Fictional character(s): Arnett Leslie, Military Personnel (major), Trader; Diantha Gaillard, Servant (indentured)
Time Period(s): 1760s (1763)
Locale(s): Fort Pitt, Pennsylvania, American Colonies (modern Pittsburgh)

Summary: This adventure tale concerns the exploits of militia officer Arnett Leslie during the Indian siege of Fort Pitt during Pontiac's Rebellion. To save the fort, Arnett treks 70 miles through the hostile wilderness to bring the Scottish regiments to Fort Pitt's relief.

Historical Accuracy: The story is a fanciful one but filled with colorful period details. Arnett's role in the saving of Fort Pitt is invented.

6140 *The Phantom Emperor*

Date of Publication: 1934
Subject(s): Settlement of the American Frontier
Historical character(s): James Dickinson, Frontiersman
Time Period(s): 1830s (1836)
Locale(s): Northwest Territory, United States

Summary: The novel is based on an actual attempt by James Dickinson to proclaim himself Montezuma II and to conquer a kingdom to rule in the Northwest Territory. After raising a small army, Dickinson sets out through the Great Lakes to Duluth and the wilderness of Minnesota and Canada where the scheme collapses.

Historical Accuracy: The novel employs what is known about the Dickinson conspiracy and faithfully re-creates the frontier era.

6141 *The Silent Drum*

Date of Publication: 1940
Subject(s): American Colonies; Settlement of the American Frontier; Indians
Fictional character(s): Frederic Van Buren, Frontiersman
Time Period(s): 1760s
Locale(s): Pennsylvania, American Colonies

Summary: This massive adventure novel captures life in the Pennsylvania wilderness in the years preceding the American Revolution. Indian fighting and the struggle of the settlers on the western frontier are described.

Historical Accuracy: The novel is careful to link its fictional story accurately to a background of actual events during the period.

6142 *The Unconquered*

Date of Publication: 1947
Subject(s): American Colonies; Pontiac's Rebellion; Indians
Fictional character(s): Chris Holden, Frontiersman
Time Period(s): 1760s (1763)
Locale(s): Pennsylvania, American Colonies

Summary: This companion novel to *The Judas Tree* depicts events on the Pennsylvania frontier during Pontiac's Conspiracy of 1763 and the siege of Fort Pitt. Chris Holden attempts to warn the frontier forts of the Indian uprising.

Historical Accuracy: The novel is painstaking in its documentation of Indian lore and period elements.

GLENDON SWARTHOUT (1918-1992)

American action and western writer Swarthout was born in Michigan and received his Ph.D. from the University of Michigan. He has received several awards for his work, including the Theatre Guild Playwriting Award and the Spur Award from the Western Writers of America. Four of his novels have been made into films, most notably *The Shootist.*

6143 *The Homesman*

Date of Publication: 1988
Subject(s): American West; Settlement of the American Frontier
Fictional character(s): Mary Bee Cuddy, Frontierswoman (homesteader); George Briggs, Frontiersman
Time Period(s): 19th century
Locale(s): Nebraska

Summary: Mary Bee Cuddy must take on the job of "homesman," returning east with four women who have gone insane on the frontier. She is aided in the long, perilous journey by George Briggs, deserter and claimjumper.

Historical Accuracy: The novel's period elements are convincingly presented.

6144 *The Old Colts*

Date of Publication: 1985
Subject(s): American West; Crime and Criminals
Historical character(s): Wyatt Earp, Lawman; William Barclay "Bat" Masterson, Lawman; Walter Winchell, Journalist
Time Period(s): 1910s (1916)
Locale(s): New York, New York; Dodge City, Kansas

Summary: Two western legends and friends, Wyatt Earp and Bat Masterson, record their final adventure in 1916 in Dodge City. The action begins in New York City and moves out west, where the legendary pair are given a final opportunity to burnish their reputation.

Historical Accuracy: The story is fanciful but filled with authentic period elements.

6145 *The Shootist*

Date of Publication: 1975
Subject(s): American West; Crime and Criminals
Fictional character(s): John Bernard Books, Gunfighter
Time Period(s): 1900s (1901)
Locale(s): El Paso, Texas

Summary: At the turn of the century one of the last of the legendary gunfighters, J.B. Books, learns that his days are numbered. He decides to orchestrate his exit by arranging a final climactic gunfight, the last courageous act to define his legend. The novel follows Books to his moment of destiny.

Historical Accuracy: The details of the era are authentically recounted.

6146 *The Tin Lizzie Troup*

Date of Publication: 1972
Subject(s): Mexican Revolution; Military Life
Fictional character(s): Stanley Dinkle, Military Personnel (lieutenant)
Time Period(s): 1910s (1916)
Locale(s): Glenn Springs, Texas; Mexico

Summary: The novel describes the comic misadventures of the Philadelphia Light Horse Brigade of National Guardsmen who are mounted on Model T Fords during the Mexican-American border skirmishes. The dapper and naive members of this military club meet their match in U.S. Cavalry officer Lt. Stanley Dinkle.

Historical Accuracy: The story is based on actual events, with some details imagined and circumstances invented.

VERONICA GEOGHEGAN SWEENEY

Born in Paddington, New South Wales, Sweeney studied law, then began working towards an acting career. She has worked as a singer, actress, playwright, and scriptwriter. She is the great-great-granddaughter of Irish convicts in Australia.

6147 *The Emancipist: An Unforgettable Epic of Australia*

Date of Publication: 1985
Subject(s): Frontier—Australia; Irish Potato Famine; Penal Colonies
Fictional character(s): Aidan O'Brien, Convict, Landowner
Time Period(s): 19th century
Locale(s): Ireland; Tasmania, Australia (then Van Dieman's Land); New South Wales, Australia

Summary: Aidan O'Brien is an emancipist, the Australian term for an ex-convict. The novel chronicles his history, from Ireland during the famine to the penal colony of Van Dieman's Land, to eventual success as an Australian landowner and proprietor of a newspaper chain. O'Brien's career captures the colorful history of 19th-century Australia.

Historical Accuracy: The fictional story of O'Brien is set against a convincing period background.

WILLIAM SYERS (1914-)

A native of Texas, Syers attended St. Mary's University of San Antonio and the University of Texas. He has worked as a journalist and in public relations. Syers is a specialist in Texas' role in the Civil War.

6148 *The Devil Gun*

Date of Publication: 1976
Subject(s): Civil War—U.S.; American West; Battle of Glorieta
Fictional character(s): Lingston Slate, Military Personnel (lieutenant); Jim Clinton, Scout
Time Period(s): 1860s (1861-1862)
Locale(s): Texas; New Mexico

Summary: Confederate Major Henry Sibley leads a brigade on a 700-mile march from San Antonio into New Mexico. Their objective is to seize the West for the Confederacy. The action culminates in the little known Battle of Glorieta, called the Gettysburg of the West.

Historical Accuracy: The story interweaves the imagined with the factual. It is based on actual events which are accurately described.

ALLENE SYMONS (1944-)

American novelist Symons was born in California and attended San Francisco State College, Claremont Graduate School, and UCLA. She has worked in publishing, in sales, and as an editor for *Publisher's Weekly*. Nostradamus, the subject of her first novel, *Vagabond Prophet* seemed to Symons to be a perfect subject for fiction.

6149 *Vagabond Prophet*

Date of Publication: 1983
Subject(s): Renaissance; Religious Conflict; Inquisition
Fictional character(s): Alain Saint-Germain, Writer (poet)
Historical character(s): Michel de Nostredame, Doctor; Henri II, Ruler (King of France)
Time Period(s): 16th century (1518-1559)
Locale(s): France

Summary: The story of the prophet Nostradamus is told from the perspective of his boyhood friend, poet Alain Saint-Germain. Nostradamus' strange powers of divination are placed solidly within the context of the French Renaissance and the religious conflict of the times. Nostradamus faces the threat of heresy and endures years of exile while pursuing the secrets of the occult.

Historical Accuracy: The author's interpretation suggests that Nostradamus was authentic and attempts to explain him by placing his story within the context of his times, which are revealed faithfully.

JULIAN SYMONS (1912-)

English writer Symons was born in London and worked as an advertising copywriter before becoming a full-time writer in 1947. Symons produced book reviews, histories, biographies, as well as mysteries. His critical account of crime and detective fiction, *Bloody Murder*, is considered one of the classic texts of the genre.

6150 *The Blackheath Poisonings*

Date of Publication: 1978
Subject(s): Mystery; Victorian Period
Fictional character(s): Charles Mortimer, Businessman; Harriet Colland, Gentlewoman; Paul Vandervent, Gentleman
Time Period(s): 1890s
Locale(s): London, England

Summary: In the two mansions built by toy manufacturer Charles Mortimer unexpected death seems to be haunting the family business. On the surface things seem natural, but other evidence points to a more sinister view. Young Paul Vandervent is convinced that a murderer is on the loose.

Historical Accuracy: The novel features a meticulous reconstruction of the period.

6151 *The Detling Secret*

Date of Publication: 1982
Subject(s): Mystery; Victorian Period; Independence—Ireland
Fictional character(s): Bernard Ross, Political Figure (member of parliament); Dolly Detling, Gentlewoman; Sir Arthur Detling, Gentleman
Time Period(s): 1890s
Locale(s): London, England; Kent, England

Summary: Sir Arthur Detling is less than pleased when his daughter Dolly marries the young Liberal M.P. Bernard Ross. He seems to be linked to the revolutionary Fenians and is keeping secrets. Soon the family is swept up in murder and a mystery that will be unravelled at the Detlings' Christmas party.

Historical Accuracy: The mystery depends on an evocative and meticulous presentation of its era.

6152 *Sweet Adelaide*

Date of Publication: 1980
Subject(s): Mystery; Trials; Crime and Criminals
Historical character(s): Adelaide Blanche Bartlett, Bastard Daughter, Spouse; Thomas Edwin Bartlett, Businessman (grocer)
Time Period(s): 1880s
Locale(s): England

Summary: This "experimental crime story" is based loosely on an actual 19th-century murder case involving Adelaide Bartlett, who poisoned her grocer husband. The novel involves an elaboration of the case supplying motive and method that the actual facts of the case only suggest.

Historical Accuracy: The author helpfully separates the facts from the inventions.

ANDRZEJ SZCZYPIORSKI (1924-)

A Polish writer born in Warsaw, Szczypiorski fought in the resistance movement during the German occupation of Poland, took part in the Warsaw Uprising of 1944, and was imprisoned in a concentration camp until 1945. After the war he joined the opposition to Communist rule and helped found the Solidarity Congress of Polish Culture. He is the author of *The Beautiful Mrs. Seidenham.*

6153 *Mass for Arras*

Date of Publication: 1993
Subject(s): Religious Conflict; Witchcraft and Sorcery; Middle Ages
Fictional character(s): Jan, Gentleman
Time Period(s): 15th century (1461)
Locale(s): Arras, France

Summary: The background for this novel is the famous Vauderie d'Arras in 1461, in which Jews and witches were persecuted for heresy in an outbreak of rioting and looting. Jan is a young member of the intelligentsia who, when faced with escalating violence and his own downfall, must make important choices. The novel explores the personal and political consequences of fanaticism.

Historical Accuracy: The period elements are based on actual events.

HUGH TALBOT
(PSEUD. OF ARGENTINE FRANCIS ALINGTON, 1898-)

6154 *Gentlemen—The Regiment!*

Date of Publication: 1933
Subject(s): Victorian Period; Crimean War; Military Life
Fictional character(s): Alastair Chappell, Military Personnel (soldier); Katherine St. Quentyn, Gentlewoman
Time Period(s): 1850s
Locale(s): England; Crimea, Russia

Summary: This Victorian-era story describes a bitter feud between two proud military families. It is principally the story of young Alastair Chappell, who rebels against the traditions of his family and the regiment. The story comes to a climax during the Crimean War.

Historical Accuracy: The novel features believable period elements and an authentic version of historical events.

MICHAEL TALBOT (1937-)

6155 *To the Ends of the Earth*

Date of Publication: 1986
Subject(s): Crime and Criminals; Frontier—Australia
Fictional character(s): Joe Crabb, Convict, Veteran; Kitty Brandon, Actress, Convict; Ben Thorpe, Farmer, Convict; Abraham Levy, Doctor, Convict
Time Period(s): 1780s
Locale(s): London, England; Botany Bay, Australia; At Sea

Summary: In the first of a series of novels tracing the last 200 years of Australian history, the novel follows the second group of Europeans to reach Australia: condemned criminals transported to Botany Bay to begin the colonization of Australia. The novel dramatizes the experiences of four of the condemned criminals, a former sergeant in the British army, an actress, a farmer, and an Eastern European Jew.

Historical Accuracy: The novel is exact in rendering the period background and life in the Australian wilderness.

6156 *A Wilful Woman*

Date of Publication: 1989
Subject(s): Frontier—Australia; Penal Colonies
Fictional character(s): Joe Cribb, Military Personnel (sergeant), Convict; Kitty Brandon, Actress, Convict; Charles "Buck" Nash, Military Personnel (officer)
Time Period(s): 1780s
Locale(s): Botany Bay, Australia

Summary: The novel is part of the author's saga of the founding and rise of the Australian nation in the 18th century and depicts the arrival of the first shipload of convicted prisoners to Botany Bay. It describes the first settlement of the colony and the clash between Kitty Brandon, actress and murderess, and the scheming Charles Nash, who is determined to use the female convicts for profit.

Historical Accuracy: The novel offers a genuine version of life in the earliest days of the settlement of Australia.

REAY TANNAHILL (1929-)

Born and raised in Scotland, Tannahill was educated at the University of Glasgow, where she studied history and sociology. Tannahill is the author of the critically acclaimed studies *Food in History* and *Sex in History*.

6157 *In Still and Stormy Waters*

Date of Publication: 1992
Subject(s): Victorian Period; Inheritance—Disputed; Family Saga
Fictional character(s): Rachel Macmillan, Bastard Daughter, Heiress; Sophie Macmillan, Young Woman; Rainer Blake, Gentleman
Time Period(s): 19th century (1856-1880)
Locale(s): Scotland; Canton, China

Summary: Set during the Victorian period, this family saga details the conflict between two women over the inheritance of a Scottish estate and the love of the mysterious Rainer Blake. Rachel Macmillan is the illegitimate daughter of David Macmillan, who unexpectedly inherits Juran, the Macmillan's estate in Scotland. Her rival is Sophie Macmillan, who comes from China to contend with Rachel for possession of Juran.

Historical Accuracy: The novel offers a convincing period background.

6158 *Return of the Stranger*

Date of Publication: 1995
Subject(s): Victorian Period; Family Saga
Fictional character(s): Grace Smith, Gentlewoman; Max McKenzie, Heir
Time Period(s): 19th century; 20th century (1894-1905)
Locale(s): England

Summary: This Victorian-era family saga describes the fate of Grace Smith and her daughters who discovers that a will has left them at the mercy of a complete stranger, Max McKenzie.

Historical Accuracy: The novel provides authentic period detail as the backdrop for this tale of money and family betrayal.

6159 *The World, the Flesh, and the Devil*

Date of Publication: 1985
Subject(s): Royalty—Scotland; Religious Conflict
Fictional character(s): Ninian Drummond, Artist; Adam de Verve, Bastard Son

Historical character(s): Gavin Cameron, Religious (bishop); Columba Crozier, Religious (archdeacon); James I, Ruler (King of Scotland); Robert Stewart, Nobleman
Time Period(s): 15th century (1411-1437)
Locale(s): Edinburgh, Scotland; Rome, Italy

Summary: Scotland is divided by religious strife and dynastic struggle. Ninian Drummond is caught up in the intrigues of her surrogate father, Columba Crozier, who plots regicide and a civil war, assisted by his bastard son Adam de Verve. In opposition is Bishop Gavin Cameron, who struggles against Crozier as the fate of Scotland hangs perilously in the balance.

Historical Accuracy: The novel uses a genuine period backdrop and actual circumstances intermingled with the fictional story.

JANET TANNER

Born in England's coal-mining region, Tanner's father was a miner. Tanner has written for magazines.

6160 *The Hours of Light*

Date of Publication: 1981
Subject(s): World War I; Family Saga
Fictional character(s): Jack Hall, Military Personnel; Ted Hall, Military Personnel; Charlotte Hall, Parent
Time Period(s): 1910s; 1920s (1911-1921)
Locale(s): Hillbridge, England; France

Summary: The novel chronicles the struggles of the Hall family of England's coal-mining region during the years of the Great War. Charlotte Hall tries to save her son Jack from life in the pit, while Jack's brother, Ted, rebels against his lot as a carting boy. Both are swept up in the conflict of the First World War.

Historical Accuracy: The novel features an authentic evocation of country life from 1911 to 1921.

R.F. TAPSELL (1936-)

Born in England, Tapsell is a graduate in history from London University's School of Slavonic and East European Studies. He has travelled extensively in western Europe, the Balkans, Egypt, and Iraq and has served as a member of the administrative staff of the University of East Anglia. Tapsell's interests include military history, genealogy, and fencing.

6161 *The Unholy Pilgrim*

Date of Publication: 1968
Subject(s): Middle Ages; Crusades; Byzantine Empire
Fictional character(s): Tancred of Varville, Knight; Melinda of Ibelin, Gentlewoman; Eleanor, Young Woman
Time Period(s): 13th century
Locale(s): Mediterranean (Aegean Sea); Byzantine Empire

Summary: The novel depicts the adventures of Tancred of Varville, a young Norman knight on a pilgrimage to Jerusalem to recover his honor and inheritance. Tancred endures shipwreck, naval battles, and conspiracy until the climactic siege of Metos, where by his courage and daring, he achieves renown.

Historical Accuracy: The story is fictional but convincing in its historical elements.

6162 *The Year of the Horsetails*
Date of Publication: 1967
Subject(s): Mongol Empire; Dark Ages
Fictional character(s): Bardiya, Warrior; Kagan, Chieftain
Time Period(s): Indeterminate Past
Locale(s): Asia

Summary: The novel provides an imagined encounter between the horse people of the vast Eurasian Steppe and the agriculturists. The Tugors, led by Kagan, attempt to subdue the Drevichi. The latter are assisted by a renegade warrior, Bordiya, who teaches them how to defeat the Tugars.

Historical Accuracy: The time and setting employed are left undefined and lack historical specificity.

BOOTH TARKINGTON (1869-1946)
Tarkington was an American novelist from Indiana. Her two novels of life in the Middle West, *The Magnificent Ambersons* and *Alice Adams* won Pulitzer Prizes.

6163 *Monsieur Beaucaire*
Date of Publication: 1900
Fictional character(s): Victor M. Beaucaire, Nobleman (aka Louis-Philippe de Valois); Duke of Winterset, Nobleman; Mary Carlisle, Noblewoman
Historical character(s): Richard Nash, Gentleman, Socialite
Time Period(s): 18th century
Locale(s): Bath, England

Summary: This slight and romantic story is set in fashionable Bath, England, in the early 18th century. A barber in disguise penetrates fashionable society. The English Duke of Winterset is determined to unmask the social upstart. But who is he really?.

Historical Accuracy: In such a romp it probably is only a quibble to point out that two unhistorical duels are fought in Bath which had outlawed dueling at the time.

JUDITH TARR (1955-)
Born in Maine, Tarr graduated from Mount Holyoke College and Cambridge and Yale universities. She has worked as a high school Latin teacher. She has a respected reputation as a fantasy writer who depends on a expert knowledge of history in her novels. For Tarr, good fantasy requires the author to adhere as closely as possible to the actual historical events while incorporating elements of fantasy and alternatives to the actual.

6164 *Alamut*
Date of Publication: 1989
Subject(s): Fantasy; Middle Ages; Crusades

Fictional character(s): Aidan, Royalty (prince); Morgiana, Gentlewoman; Sinan, Knight
Historical character(s): Baldwin IV, Ruler (King of Jerusalem)
Time Period(s): 12th century (1176)
Locale(s): Jerusalem, Palestine; Middle East

Summary: Set in the Kingdom of Jerusalem between the Second and Third Crusades, the novel concerns Prince Aidan, the son of a human father and an immortal sorceress. When his nephew is slain at the command of Sinan, Aidan vows revenge, but he must contend with an assassin whose powers are greater than his own.

Historical Accuracy: The events of the novel are fairly equally divided between history and fantasy. The author's notes indicate the differences between the two.

6165 *The Eagle's Daughter*
Date of Publication: 1995
Subject(s): Byzantine Empire; Holy Roman Empire; Dark Ages
Fictional character(s): Aspasia, Royalty (princess), Widow(er); Ismail, Doctor
Historical character(s): Theophano, Royalty (empress, consort of Otto II); Otto II, Ruler (Holy Roman Emperor)
Time Period(s): 10th century (968-983)
Locale(s): Germany; Constantinople, Byzantine Empire; Rome, Italy

Summary: The novel tells the story of the Byzantine princess Theophano, who comes west to become the wife of Otto II, the Holy Roman Emperor. When Otto dies in battle, Theophano becomes regent for her infant son, Otto III, and must hold onto the throne despite one of the greatest wars of succession during the Dark Ages.

Historical Accuracy: Though most of the major characters are historical, the author admits taking considerable liberties with the settings and making occasional changes in chronology for sake of the story.

6166 *King and Goddess*
Date of Publication: 1996
Subject(s): Ancient Egypt; Pharaohs
Historical character(s): Hatshepsut, Ruler (Queen of Egypt); Senenmut, Architect; Thutmose II, Ruler (pharaoh)
Time Period(s): 14th century B.C.
Locale(s): Egypt

Summary: This dramatization of the life and times of Hatshepsut records her usurpation of the Egyptian throne and her reign, first as the regent for Pharaoh Menkheperaa Thutmose, then as a ruler in her own right. The novel is based on the memoirs of Hatsheput's lover, the architect Senenmut.

Historical Accuracy: The author has invented little in her narrative and has stayed close to what is known.

6167 *Lord of the Two Lands*
Date of Publication: 1993
Subject(s): Macedonian Empire; Ancient Egypt
Fictional character(s): Meriamon, Royalty, Religious

Historical character(s): Alexander the Great, Ruler (King of Macedonia)
Time Period(s): 4th century B.C.
Locale(s): Macedonia; Middle East; Egypt

Summary: This historical fantasy involves Alexander the Great, who after becoming king of Macedonia sets out to conquer the Persian Empire. Meanwhile in Egypt Alexander's protection is desired against the Persian threat.

Historical Accuracy: Atmospheric and full of adventure, the novel is not bound by the actual historical events.

6168 *Pillar of Fire*

Date of Publication: 1995
Subject(s): Ancient Egypt; Biblical Story; Pharaohs
Fictional character(s): Nofret, Servant
Historical character(s): Akhenaton, Ruler (Egyptian pharaoh); Tutankhamen, Ruler (Egyptian pharaoh); Moses, Biblical Figure; Nefertiti, Royalty (consort of Akhenaton); Ramses I, Ruler (pharaoh)
Time Period(s): 14th century B.C.
Locale(s): Egypt

Summary: The novel portrays the controversial reign of Egyptian pharaoh Akhenaton, who introduced monotheism to ancient Egypt. His troubled reign is connected with the plight of the captive Israelites and poses an ingenious interpretation. The novel suggests that the Egyptian royal family was related to the descendants of Joseph and that Moses was indeed a prince of Egypt.

Historical Accuracy: The author details her sources and her variations from history. Since so much of the ancient world is shrouded in mystery, most versions, whether fictional or historical, include much speculation.

6169 *Queen of Swords*

Date of Publication: 1997
Subject(s): Middle Ages; Crusades
Historical character(s): Melisende, Ruler (Queen of Jerusalem); Baldwin II, Ruler (King of Jerusalem); Fulk, Nobleman (Count of Anjou), Ruler (King of Jerusalem)
Time Period(s): 12th century (1129-1153)
Locale(s): Jerusalem, Palestine; Byzantium, Byzantine Empire

Summary: The novel describes the remarkable career of Melisende, the oldest daughter of Baldwin II, the Latin King of Jerusalem, following its capture in the Crusades. Married to Count Fulk of Anjou, who has been designated Baldwin's successor, it is instead Melisende who rules the city and rises to the challenge of holding the kingdom together.

Historical Accuracy: The novel sticks to actual facts in describing Melisende's story.

6170 *Throne of Isis*

Date of Publication: 1994
Subject(s): Roman Empire
Historical character(s): Cleopatra, Ruler (Queen of Egypt); Marc Antony, Military Personnel (general); Octavian, Military Personnel
Time Period(s): 1st century B.C. (41 B.C.)

Locale(s): Alexandria, Egypt; Antioch, Syria; Athens, Greece
Summary: The novel tells the story of Cleopatra, the love of Julius Ceasar and the mother of his only son. Upon Ceasar's death, she takes Marc Antony, Ceasar's greatest general, as her lover and consort. Together they conspire to unite Egypt and Rome. Their plan fails at the naval battle of Actum. The novel offers a retelling of this fateful time with Cleopatra emerging as a remarkably canny political leader who falls in love with the man she intended to use for her own purpose.

Historical Accuracy: The novel attempts to stay closer to the actual historical facts than the legends that have been attached to Cleopatra's story over time.

ALLEN TATE (1899-1979)

American poet, novelist, and critic, Tate was born in Tennessee and began his career as the editor of *The Fugitive*. Best known for his poetry, among his most famous poems is ''Ode to the Confederate Dead.'' He is also the author of interpretive biographies of Stonewall Jackson and Jefferson Davis. A major figure in the literary Southern Renaissance, Tate taught English at the University of Minnesota.

6171 *The Fathers*

Date of Publication: 1938
Subject(s): Civil War—U.S.; Family Saga
Fictional character(s): Lewis Buchan, Gentleman; George Posey, Gentleman
Time Period(s): 1860s (1860-1861)
Locale(s): Virginia; Washington, District of Columbia

Summary: The conflicts of Southern society during the Civil War are played out in a single family of Northern Virginians. Major Buchan, the patriarch, is an advocate of tradition and kinship, the foundation of Southern society. George Posey, his Northern son-in-law, is his opposite, fiercely resisting any other dictates than his own.

Historical Accuracy: The novel effectively portrays the private life and public actions of a family at a decisive moment in history.

JILL TATTERSALL (1931-)

Born in Tintagel, Cornwall, British novelist Tattersall was educated in England and Switzerland. Her diverse career has included work as a photographic model, receptionist, film extra, horse trainer, and nursery school teacher and owner. She was a member of the Association of Occupational Therapists and of the executive committee of the Red Cross in the British Virgin Islands, where she lives with her family. Her romantic suspense novels include *A Summer's Cloud* and *Enchanter's Castle*.

6172 *Damnation Reef*

Date of Publication: 1979
Subject(s): Suspense; Regency Period
Fictional character(s): Marina Derwent, Young Woman; Marcus Granville, Landowner

Time Period(s): 1800s (1805)
Locale(s): West Indies

Summary: This tale of suspense begins in 1805 when Marina Derwent sails to the West Indies to investigate why her closest friend has committed suicide. She survives a shipwreck and on the island of Antilla begins to discover the fate of her friend and the complicity of the brooding and dangerous Marcus Granville.

Historical Accuracy: The novel's setting is authentic.

6173 *Dark at Noon*

Date of Publication: 1978
Subject(s): Suspense
Fictional character(s): Mary Ramsey, Amnesiac; Lucian Castelmarten, Nobleman
Time Period(s): 19th century
Locale(s): Wales

Summary: In this romantic suspense tale, a young woman is the sole survivor of a coach accident. Affected with amnesia, she does not know whether she is Mary Ramsey or Victoria Marten, the recently widowed mistress of the Castelmarten estate. She is plunged into a tangle of intrigue and conspiracy in which few can be trusted and appearances are deceiving.

Historical Accuracy: The novel features a believable atmosphere of the period.

6174 *Midsummer Masque*

Date of Publication: 1972
Subject(s): Regency Period; Gothic Romance
Fictional character(s): Rowena Manville, Orphan, Companion; Adam Lyngate, Heir
Time Period(s): 1800s (1803)
Locale(s): England

Summary: Rowena Manville, who has been left on her own to fend for herself, seeks a position as a companion on the estate of Gryphons in the south of England. Her chilly reception is the beginning of her troubles, which center on the secrets that dominate Gryphons, particularly those surrounding the enigmatic heir, Adam Lyngate.

Historical Accuracy: This is familiar Gothic material set in a thinly realized Regency period.

MEREDITH TAX

Born in Wisconsin, Tax graduated from Brandeis University and studied on fellowships in London. She was one of the founders of Bread & Roses, a socialist and feminist group in Boston, and has been active in the Chicago Woman's Liberation Union.

6175 *Rivington Street*

Date of Publication: 1982
Subject(s): Immigrants; Labor Movement; Women's Rights
Fictional character(s): Hannah Levy, Immigrant; Sarah Levy, Labor Organizer; Ruby Levy, Businesswoman
Historical character(s): Mary Dreier, Labor Organizer; Alva Belmont, Suffragette; Abraham Cahan, Editor

Time Period(s): 1900s; 1910s
Locale(s): Russia; New York, New York

Summary: The novel captures life in New York in the years before World War I, centering on the immigrant Levy family. Their members survive the Triangle Factory fire in 1911, help organize a garment workers union, and are instrumental in the introduction of ladies' ready-to-wear and the invention of the brassiere. The novel offers a rich study of the interactions of the labor movement and the women's rights movement.

Historical Accuracy: The novel offers a blend of the imagined and the actual, with real figures mingling with the invented ones.

6176 *Union Square*

Date of Publication: 1988
Subject(s): Labor Movement; Fashion Industry
Fictional character(s): Hannah Levy, Immigrant; Sarah Levy Spector, Labor Organizer; Ruby Levy Berliner, Designer (dress)
Historical character(s): Chaim Arlosoroff, Activist (Zionist)
Time Period(s): 20th century (1919-1939)
Locale(s): New York, New York

Summary: In the sequel to *Rivington Street*, the story of the Levy family is continued from 1919 to 1939. Sarah Levy becomes a labor-union militant and wife of a leading communist; Ruby Levy achieves fame as a fashion designer and marries a department store heir. The garment wars of the 1920s, Zionism, and the increasing Nazi menace are all illustrated.

Historical Accuracy: The book's notes indicate its sources, which reflect actual events. The story employs a number of real figures in minor roles.

ANNA TAYLOR (1944-)

Born in Croyden, England, Taylor attended St. Anne's College, Oxford, but left at the end of her first year to devote her time to writing. She has done temporary factory, shop, and post office work to support herself while writing.

6177 *The Gods Are Not Mocked*

Date of Publication: 1968
Subject(s): Roman Empire; Celtic Britain; Druids
Fictional character(s): Becca, Sorceress; Lucius Valerius, Military Personnel (Roman tribune); Amergin, Religious (Druid)
Historical character(s): Julius Caesar, Military Personnel (general), Political Figure; Publius Clodius Pulcher, Political Figure; Gaius Valerius Catullus, Writer (poet); Clodia, Gentlewoman
Time Period(s): 1st century B.C. (55 B.C.)
Locale(s): England; Rome, Roman Empire

Summary: This tale combines scenes of the first Roman invasion of Celtic Britain and the first years of the Roman Empire. The cultural clash of Celts and Romans is described from the perspective of Becca, a Celtic girl with magical powers, and the ambitious Roman tribune Lucius Valerius.

Historical Accuracy: The story is imagined, interweaving some convincing period elements of Roman and Celtic life.

DAVID TAYLOR (1900-1965)

A Scottish author born in Aberdeen, Taylor graduated from the University of Aberdeen. He was a writer and producer for radio and wrote the radio show *Meet the MacMullens* for 11 years.

6178   *Farewell to Valley Forge*

Date of Publication: 1955
Subject(s): American Revolution; Espionage; Battle of Monmouth
Fictional character(s): Jonathan Kimball, Military Personnel (American captain), Spy; Elizabeth Ladd, Spy
Historical character(s): Charles Lee, Military Personnel (general); Friedrich von Steuben, Military Personnel (general); Marie Joseph Paul de Lafayette, Military Personnel (general), Nobleman (Marquis de Lafayette); Molly Pitcher, Patriot
Time Period(s): 1770s (1778)
Locale(s): Philadelphia, Pennsylvania; Valley Forge, Pennsylvania; Monmouth, New Jersey

Summary: Set during the desperate winter of 1778, the novel explores American General Charles Lee's plot to replace Washington as head of the army. The novel involves the espionage work of Jonathan Kimball and Elizabeth Ladd in Philadelphia, who uncover vital information that helps Lafayette out of a trap set by the British. The action climaxes with a description of the Battle of Monmouth.

Historical Accuracy: The background action and events are accurately described.

6179   *Mistress of the Forge*

Date of Publication: 1964
Subject(s): Alien and Sedition Acts; Pennamite Wars
Fictional character(s): Richard Braxton, Young Man; Charlotte Luken, Businesswoman
Historical character(s): Alexander Hamilton, Political Figure, Government Official; Robert Morris, Patriot, Financier
Time Period(s): 1790s (1798)
Locale(s): Pennsylvania

Summary: The turmoil of the young American nation in 1798 is the background for this story of the Tory revolt, the Alien and Sedition Acts, and the creation of the American iron industry. Richard Braxton undertakes a mission to investigate rumors of a Tory uprising. There he meets Charlotte Luken, the "mistress of the forge," who joins with him in the struggle that becomes known as the Pennamite War.

Historical Accuracy: The major historical events—the land struggle between the Connecticut settlers and the Pennsylvanians, the reign of terror in Philadelphia, the undeclared naval war with France, and the Tory plot to overthrow the Federal government—are all based on fact.

6180   *Storm the Last Rampart*

Date of Publication: 1960

Subject(s): American Revolution; Espionage; Battle of Yorktown
Fictional character(s): Bennett Paige, Military Personnel (American captain), Spy; Hannah Clements, Saloon Hostess, Spy
Historical character(s): Benedict Arnold, Military Personnel (general); John Andre, Military Personnel (British officer), Spy; George Washington, Military Personnel (army commander); Marie Joseph Paul de Lafayette, Military Personnel (general), Nobleman (Marquis de Lafayette); Nathanael Greene, Military Personnel (general); Alexander Hamilton, Military Personnel (colonel); Friedrich von Steuben, Military Personnel (general)
Time Period(s): 1780s (1780-1781)
Locale(s): Tarrytown, New York; Philadelphia, Pennsylvania; Virginia

Summary: The American Revolution's pivotal year of 1780 is described beginning with the conspiring of Benedict Arnold and ending with the climactic Battle of Yorktown. Bennett Paige, who enters Washington's secret service, and tavern maid and spy Hannah Clements find themselves at the center of Arnold's treachery. The action climaxes in the Battle of Yorktown.

Historical Accuracy: The story combines a fictional central story with accurate historical events as catalysts for the narrative.

6181   *Sycamore Men*

Date of Publication: 1958
Subject(s): American Revolution
Fictional character(s): Jewel May Ward, Gentlewoman; Dixon Blakely, Military Personnel (cavalry officer)
Historical character(s): Francis Marion, Military Personnel (American officer); Charles Cornwallis, Military Personnel (British general)
Time Period(s): 1780s (1780-1781)
Locale(s): South Carolina

Summary: This novel of the American Revolution depicts the Southern campaign of Francis Marion in South Carolina. Marion leads a guerrilla war against General Cornwallis. A romantic adventure involving cavalry officer Dixon Blakely and Jewel Ward shares the stage with scenes from battlefields at Camden, Kings Mountain, and Eutaw Springs.

Historical Accuracy: The description of the historical events is faithful to the facts.

GEORGIA ELIZABETH TAYLOR

6182   *The Infidel*

Date of Publication: 1979
Subject(s): Middle Ages; Religious Conflict
Fictional character(s): Abu Hasan, Nobleman
Historical character(s): Jimena Gomez, Noblewoman; Rodrigo Diaz de Vivar, Knight
Time Period(s): 11th century
Locale(s): Spain

Summary: This is a fictional account of the life of Jimena Gomez, the first wife of Rodrigo Diaz, whom the world knows as El Cid. Set during the conflict between Christians and Moors, the novel shows Jimena torn between the two worlds. When El Cid wrongs the powerful Abu Hasan, Hasan kidnaps Jimena and introduces her to the attractions of Moorish civilization.

Historical Accuracy: The fate of Jimena Gomez is shrouded in mystery and controversy; it is uncertain whether she ever existed. The novel invents a possible fate for her.

6183 *Lamia: A Witch*

Date of Publication: 1994
Subject(s): Witchcraft and Sorcery
Fictional character(s): Lamia, Witch; Giles de Sade, Nobleman; Marco Cellini, Businessman
Time Period(s): 16th century
Locale(s): Nevers, France

Summary: Lamia is a witch pursued and persecuted by the Church. She is befriended by various protectors, including a wealthy Italian merchant steeped in the dark arts and a young French nobleman prepared to give up everything for her love.

Historical Accuracy: The atmosphere of period France is rooted in historical details, though the sensibilities seen curiously modern.

JANELLE TAYLOR (1944-)

Born in Athens, Georgia, American romance author Janelle Taylor attended Augusta College and the Medical College of Georgia. She has worked as an orthodontic nurse and a medical research assistant. Taylor has taught and lectured on romance literature and creative writing. A prolific, best-selling novelist, Taylor is perhaps best known for her historical romances. Notable among these are the titles comprising her Ecstasy Saga series, which features an ongoing love story between a Sioux warrior and a pioneer woman. Taylor was honored at the Sioux National Celebration for the first five books in the saga. She is also the author of *First Love, Wild Love* and.

6184 *Chase the Wind*

Date of Publication: 1994
Subject(s): Romance; American West; Indians
Fictional character(s): Navarro Breed, Government Official; Bethany Wind, Government Official (aka Elizabeth Lawrence)
Time Period(s): 1880s (1886)
Locale(s): Tucson, Arizona

Summary: Set in the 1880s in the midst of Geronimo's heyday, the novel describes Navarro Breed's mission to stop a shipment of arms to the Apaches. His relationship with female agent Bethany Wind, to whom he pretends he is married, forms the novel's emotional center as intrigue and conspiracy compete with passion.

Historical Accuracy: The novel works more as romance than as historical fiction. The characters seem far more modern than authentic figures of the period.

6185 *Defiant Hearts*

Date of Publication: 1996
Subject(s): Romance; Civil War—U.S.; Espionage
Fictional character(s): Laura Adams, Spy; Jayce Storm, Military Personnel (Confederate lieutenant)
Time Period(s): 1860s
Locale(s): Richmond, Virginia; Arizona

Summary: Laura Adams, proprietress of a gentleman's social club, is also a Union spy determined to play a role in ending the Civil War. Her greatest challenge comes from Confederate officer Jayce Storm, producing a conflict of loyalties in a story that extends to the Arizona territory.

Historical Accuracy: The novel employs some believable period elements but the major emphasis is on romantic adventure.

LIZA PENNYWITT TAYLOR (1955-)

Born in Washington, D.C., Taylor is a flutist and a former research biologist who has worked in AIDS research at UCLA. She combined a love of history with her background in science to produce her first novel, *The Drummer Was the First to Die*. In the true story of 19th-century cholera researcher Dr. John Snow, she found a reflection of her work with AIDS, in which a disease can have a profound effect on relationships, society, ambition, and morality.

6186 *The Drummer Was the First to Die*

Date of Publication: 1992
Subject(s): Victorian Period; Medical Profession
Fictional character(s): Lillian Anysworth, Young Woman
Historical character(s): John Snow, Doctor
Time Period(s): 1850s (1854)
Locale(s): London, England; India

Summary: Based on the work of British anesthesiologist Dr. John Snow, the novel dramatizes his search for the causes of a devastating cholera epidemic that originates in India. His research takes him throughout Victorian London, where he develops an unorthodox theory of contagion.

Historical Accuracy: The cholera epidemic described and Dr. Snow's research in epidemiology and anesthesiology are historical; however, the majority of the novel's other events and characters are invented.

ROBERT TAYLOR (1941-)

American author Taylor was born in Oklahoma City, Oklahoma, and was educated at San Francisco State College, the University of Oklahoma, and Ohio University. An English professor as well as an author, Taylor's works include the novel *Fiddle and Bow*, and short stories that have appeared in anthologies and magazines.

6187 *Loving Belle Star*

Date of Publication: 1984
Subject(s): American West; Crime and Criminals
Historical character(s): Belle Starr, Outlaw; Jesse James, Outlaw; Frank James, Outlaw
Time Period(s): 19th century
Locale(s): West

Summary: This portrait of western outlaw Belle Starr, her family, and the James Gang offers an insight into the behavior of western outlaw families as the decline of the Indians and the growth of new towns in the western territories spell the end of lawlessness.

Historical Accuracy: The novel blends facts and popular legends to offer intimate portraits of Belle Starr and her cronies. The book does capture the period atmosphere with authenticity.

ROBERT LEWIS TAYLOR (1912-)

Born in Illinois, Taylor left a job on a newspaper in 1934 for Tahiti, where he stayed for two years, financing his stay as a correspondent. He has worked as a profile writer for the *New Yorker*. Taylor won a Pulitzer Prize in 1959 for *The Travels of Jaimie McPheeters*.

6188 *A Journey to Matecumbe*

Date of Publication: 1961
Subject(s): Reconstruction Period; Picaresque Adventure; Ku Klux Klan
Fictional character(s): Davey Burnie, Teenager, Orphan; Jim Burnie, Veteran (Confederate officer); Zeb, Slave (former), Servant
Time Period(s): 1860s (post-Civil War)
Locale(s): Kentucky; Mississippi River; Florida Keys, Florida

Summary: Shortly after the Civil War, Davey Burnie, his uncle Jim Burnie, and Jim's former servant during the war head down the Mississippi away from the Ku Klux Klan for the Florida Keys and a possible treasure. The novel details their adventures along the way in homage to Mark Twain.

Historical Accuracy: The story is lavishly detailed with period information.

6189 *Niagara*

Date of Publication: 1980
Subject(s): Social Chronicle
Fictional character(s): William Morrison, Journalist; Samantha Rutledge, Southern Belle; Frances Barclay, Waiter/Waitress
Historical character(s): James Gordon Bennett, Publisher (newspaper); Blondin, Entertainer (tight-rope walker)
Time Period(s): 19th century
Locale(s): Niagara Falls, New York; New York, New York; France

Summary: William Morrison is dispatched by a newspaper to report on the lifestyles of the rich and famous, who have gravitated to the newly-built resort town of Niagara Falls.

They are joined by a colorful collection of daredevils, con-artists, and suicides.

Historical Accuracy: The novel's cast of eccentrics is set within a believable context of the period.

6190 *The Roads to Guadalupe*

Date of Publication: 1964
Subject(s): Mexican War; Picaresque Adventure
Fictional character(s): Sam Shelby, Teenager, Military Personnel (soldier); Blaine Shelby, Military Personnel (soldier)
Time Period(s): 1840s (1845-1848)
Locale(s): Mexico

Summary: Events during the Mexican War are described through the misadventures of two brothers, Sam and Blaine Shelby, who for different reasons enlist in the U.S. Army. They join in the campaign that wrests Texas, New Mexico, and California from Mexico.

Historical Accuracy: The novel's fictional story is placed against a solidly recorded and authentic historical background.

6191 *A Roaring in the Wind*

Date of Publication: 1978
Subject(s): American West; Picaresque Adventure
Fictional character(s): Ross Nickerson, Student—College
Time Period(s): 1850s (1857)
Locale(s): Montana

Summary: The novel tells the story of Howard College student Ross Nickerson, who leaves school for adventure in Montana. His adventures take him into a territory filled with miners, mountain men, Indians, gamblers, and vigilantes.

Historical Accuracy: The description of life in Montana in the 1850s is believable.

THOMAS TAYLOR (1934-)

Born in Fort Leavenworth, Kansas, Taylor served in the U.S. Army and was discharged as a major in 1968, having served in Germany, Greece, Saudi Arabia, Panama, and Vietnam. His awards and honors include the Breadloaf Fellowship and the Corothers Prize in Literary Composition from the University of California. He is the author of *Born of War* and *A-18*.

6192 *Born of War*

Date of Publication: 1988
Subject(s): World War II; Biography, Fictionalized
Historical character(s): Orde Charles Wingate, Military Personnel (English general)
Time Period(s): 1930s; 1940s
Locale(s): Palestine; Burma

Summary: This biographical "docudrama" recounts the military exploits of British General Orde Wingate. The story covers Wingate's life from the 1930s in Palestine to his death in Burma in 1944 and attempts to provide a psychological basis for the general's colorful career.

Historical Accuracy: The historical background is believable, and the story sticks closely to the biographical facts.

WINCHOMBE TAYLOR

6193 *Ram: Being the Tale of One Ramillies Anstruther*

Date of Publication: 1960
Subject(s): American Colonies; War of the Spanish Succession
Fictional character(s): Ramillies Anstruther, Adventurer
Time Period(s): 18th century
Locale(s): England; India; Georgia, American Colonies

Summary: A deserted child is found on the battlefield of Ramillies and adopted by an English officer. As Ramillies Anstruther, his adventures takes him to India, to London where he narrowly escapes execution, and to the American colonies where he assists James Oglethorpe in establishing the colony of Georgia.

Historical Accuracy: The novel's portraits of the time and place are convincing, if somewhat inadequately developed in the interest of high-speed adventure.

JOHN WILLIAM TEBBEL (1912-)

Born in Michigan, Tebbel graduated from Central Michigan University and Columbia University. He has worked as an editor and feature writer for several newspapers and magazines and as a professor of journalism at New York University and Columbia. Tebbel wrote the novels *Touched with Fire* and *The Conqueror*; biographies of William Randolph Hearst, George Horace Lorimer, and Marshall Field; and the four-volume *A History of Book Publishing in the United States.*

6194 *The Conqueror*

Date of Publication: 1951
Subject(s): American Colonies; Indians; French and Indian War
Historical character(s): Sir William Johnson, Government Official
Time Period(s): 18th century
Locale(s): Mohawk Valley, New York, American Colonies

Summary: This novel is based on the life of Sir William Johnson, colonial leader and British superintendent general of Indian affairs in North America. It traces his career from his arrival in New York from Ireland to his overseeing of his uncle's vast lands along the Mohawk, and his management of Indian affairs and involvement in the French and Indian Wars.

Historical Accuracy: The novel uses actual historical events and creates a convincing period atmosphere.

6195 *Touched with Fire*

Date of Publication: 1952
Subject(s): Exploration

Fictional character(s): Philippe Brisson, Adventurer; Madeleine Lamoreaux, Young Woman; Anne De Chartes, Young Woman
Historical character(s): Rene-Robert Cavelier de La Salle, Explorer
Time Period(s): 17th century
Locale(s): New France, North America (present-day Quebec and Great Lakes region); Mississippi River

Summary: Based on the life of French explorer La Salle, the novel describes high intrigue in New France and La Salle's epic discoveries of the Great Lakes and the Mississippi. His nemesis is the ambitious Madeleine Lamoreaux, who loves the explorer but challenges his attempt to seize half of the North American continent for the French king.

Historical Accuracy: The novel combines the fictional with the factual. The essentials of La Salle's travels are faithfully described.

6196 *A Voice in the Streets*

Date of Publication: 1954
Subject(s): Social Chronicle; Civil War—U.S.; Draft Riots
Fictional character(s): Timothy Duncan Stevens, Editor
Time Period(s): 19th century (1830s-1860s)
Locale(s): New York, New York

Summary: This portrait of New York City follows the rise of a young Irishman, Timothy Duncan Stevens, who begins as a street waif and becomes the crusading editor of *The Guardian.* The novel's climax is New York's Draft Riots.

Historical Accuracy: The novel is scrupulously filled with period details that create a believable portrait of the era.

DARWIN LE ORA TEILHET (1904-1964)

Teilhet's books include *The Hawaiian Sword*, *The Big Runaround*, *Bright Destination*, and *Journey to the West.*

6197 *The Lion's Skin*

Date of Publication: 1955
Subject(s): Revolution—Central America
Fictional character(s): John Anderson, Adventurer
Historical character(s): William Walker, Adventurer, Revolutionary
Time Period(s): 1850s
Locale(s): Nicaragua

Summary: American character William Walker attempts to seize control of Nicaragua and get himself elected president in this adventure story. The action centers on John Anderson, a gold miner turned filibuster, who joins Walker's forces until he discovers Walker's true intentions.

Historical Accuracy: The novel sticks firmly to the actual chronology of events and is truthful even in its presentation of the minor personalities.

6198 *Retreat From the Dolphin*

Date of Publication: 1943
Subject(s): Independence—South America
Fictional character(s): Jim Porteous, Teenager

Time Period(s): 1810s; 1820s (1810-1820)
Locale(s): Chile

Summary: This coming of age story is set against the background of the Chilean revolution during the 1810s. Young Jim Porteous inherits the ship *The Dolphin* from his sea-going father. Porteous joins his mother on an island off the southern coast of Chile when she remarries. In the adventure that follows, Porteous escapes his stepfather and manages to sail the *Dolphin* back to Philadelphia.

Historical Accuracy: Adventure is the primary concern in this tale with a plausible period and regional background.

6199 *The Road to Glory*

Date of Publication: 1956
Subject(s): American West; Indians
Fictional character(s): Hugo Oconor, Adventurer
Historical character(s): Junipero Serra, Religious (missionary)
Time Period(s): 1780s (1783-1784)
Locale(s): San Jose, California; Mexico City, Mexico

Summary: The novel dramatizes the ministry of Father Junipero Serra among the Indians of California during his last years. A young opportunist, Hugo Oconor, is sent by the Viceroy in Mexico City on a mission to California. Its success will undermine Serra's attempt to give dignity and economic success to the California Indians.

Historical Accuracy: The author claims to have invented little in the story and to have stayed close to fact.

6200 *Steamboat on the River*

Date of Publication: 1952
Subject(s): Riverboats
Fictional character(s): Jim Owens, Engineer; Horace Owens, Young Man
Historical character(s): Abraham Lincoln, Political Figure
Time Period(s): 1830s
Locale(s): Sangamon River, Illinois; Cincinnati, Ohio

Summary: This tale of river boat life in Illinois during the 1830s involves a young Abraham Lincoln on a voyage to St. Louis aboard the steamboat *The Talisman*. Along the way, Horace Owens, the young son of the boat's builder, recently returned to Cincinnati from the East, encounters outlaws, resentful flat boatmen, and romance.

Historical Accuracy: The picture of a young Lincoln is improbable, and the description of Cincinnati is historically inaccurate.

EMMA TENNANT (1937-)

A British novelist, critic, and editor, Tennant was born in London. She has worked for the magazine *Queen* and British *Vogue*. Tennant's novels include *Hotel de Dream*, *The Bad Sister*, and *The House of Hospitalities*.

6201 *Pemberley, or Pride and Prejudice Continued*

Date of Publication: 1993

Subject(s): Regency Romance
Fictional character(s): Elizabeth Darcy, Gentlewoman; Fitzwilliam Darcy, Gentleman; Georgiana Darcy, Gentlewoman
Time Period(s): 19th century (Regency period)
Locale(s): Derbyshire, England

Summary: This sequel to Jane Austen's *Pride and Prejudice* begins one year after the marriage of Elizabeth Bennet and Mr. Darcy. The time has come for a visit from Elizabeth's mother, which grows into a full-scale reunion of virtually all of the original characters and a revival of the old issues of *Pride and Prejudice*.

Historical Accuracy: The evocation of the Austen original is authentic and convincing, as is the period atmosphere.

6202 *An Unequal Marriage; or Pride and Prejudice Twenty Years Later*

Date of Publication: 1994
Subject(s): Regency Period
Fictional character(s): Elizabeth Bennett, Spouse; Fitzwilliam Darcy, Gentleman
Time Period(s): 19th century
Locale(s): England

Summary: In this continuation of Jane Austen's *Pride and Prejudice*, problems concerning Elizabeth and Darcy's children dominate the story. Edward Darcy, a student at Eton, has fallen under bad influences and has gambled away most of the family estate.

Historical Accuracy: This ingenious re-creation of the Austen set gives the familiar characters new problems that are believably drawn against a realistic period background.

JOHN UPTON TERRELL (1900-1988)

Born in Chicago, Illinois, Terrell was a journalist, author, and award-winning historian of the Old West who ran away from home in the eighth grade to become a cowboy. He also worked as a reporter for the *San Francisco Chronicle*, west coast editor for the United Press, and a war correspondent for *Newsweek*. Although he wrote more than 40 books, including children's books and novels, Terrell is best remembered for his histories, such as *Life Among the Apaches* and *The Arrow and the Cross: A History of the American Indian and the Missionaries*.

6203 *Plume Rouge: A Novel of the Pathfinders*

Date of Publication: 1942
Subject(s): Settlement of the American Frontier
Fictional character(s): Benton McKenzie, Frontiersman; Alenn Johns, Young Woman
Time Period(s): 1830s
Locale(s): St. Louis, Missouri; Pacific Northwest

Summary: The novel describes a 4,000 mile trek from St. Louis to the Columbia River of the Pacific Northwest to open up the trading route to the West. The expedition is led by

Benton McKenzie, whom the Indians call "Plume Rouge." With him is a young woman, Alenn Johns, who is attempting to discover her past.

Historical Accuracy: The novel presents an authentic portrait of life in the wilderness.

CHARLES TERROT (1917-)

Terrot is the author of such books as *The Passionate Pilgrim*, *The Angel Who Pawned Her Harp*, and *The Stowaway From St.Tropez*.

6204 *The Passionate Pilgrim*

Date of Publication: 1949
Subject(s): Crimean War; Victorian Period; Medical Profession
Fictional character(s): Elizabeth Walker, Nurse
Historical character(s): Florence Nightingale, Gentlewoman, Nurse
Time Period(s): 1850s
Locale(s): Crimea, Russia

Summary: The story of Florence Nightingale's efforts to introduce women as nurses in military hospitals during the Crimean War is characterized in scenes that capture the incompetence and inefficiency with which Florence Nightingale and her nurses had to contend. The documentary aspect of the story is lightened by a romance story involving one of the nurses, Elizabeth Walker.

Historical Accuracy: Although many of the details and accounts depicted are faithful to history, there is a good deal of simplification and idealization.

C.V. TERRY
(PSEUD. OF FRANK G. SLAUGHTER, 1908-)

C.V. Terry is a pseudonym for the prolific bestselling author and physician Frank G. Slaughter, who was born in Washington, D.C., graduated from Duke University, and received his M.D. degree from Johns Hopkins. Slaughter worked as a surgeon in Jacksonville, Florida, and is a prolific author of medical, biblical, and historical novels. More than 60 million copies of his books are in print in over 20 countries. Slaughter has been called the American Balzac.

6205 *Buccaneer Surgeon*

Date of Publication: 1954
Subject(s): Pirates; Elizabethan Period
Fictional character(s): Bernal Fitzhugh, Doctor, Sea Captain; Dona Maria Andreda, Noblewoman
Time Period(s): 16th century (1580s)
Locale(s): West Indies; England; Spain

Summary: This adventure tale of the Spanish Main in the days of Sir Francis Drake involves the exploits of Bernal Fitzhugh, a surgeon turned buccaneer who becomes Drake's chief lieutenant. On a secret mission to Spain, Fitzhugh is apparently betrayed by Dona Maria Andreda, a lady-in-waiting to the Spanish queen. This prompts Fitzhugh to a course of revenge played out in New Spain.

Historical Accuracy: Romance predominates here, but the background is filled with vivid period elements.

6206 *The Deadly Lady of Madagascar*

Date of Publication: 1959
Subject(s): Sea Story; Pirates
Fictional character(s): Richard Douglas, Sea Captain; Bonita Damao, Young Woman
Time Period(s): 18th century
Locale(s): Madagascar; Indian Ocean; New York, New York

Summary: This tale of romance and adventure involves piracy and the East India Trade. Richard Douglas is an intrepid sea captain who gets involved with the pirates of Madagascar and the lovely Bonita Damao.

Historical Accuracy: The story is full of swashbuckling adventure with little direct reference to historical events or figures but still colorful and atmospheric.

JUDITH TERRY

Terry emigrated from England to British Columbia, where she teaches English at the University of Victoria. A Jane Austen scholar, she wrote the foreword to the Everyman's Library Edition of *Persuasion* that was issued to coincide with the release of the recent film version of the novel.

6207 *Version and Diversion*

Date of Publication: 1986
Subject(s): Regency Romance; Servants
Fictional character(s): Jane Hartwell, Servant (lady's maid); Julia Bertram, Gentlewoman
Time Period(s): 1810s (1815)
Locale(s): England

Summary: This novel offers a below-stairs view of the events of Jane Austen's *Mansfield Park*. Jane Hartwell is a lady's maid whose own drama coincides with the above-stairs pursuit of the handsome Henry Crawford by the Bertram sisters. Jane finds herself in a series of scandals that continue even after she escapes Mansfield Park, pursued by bounty hunters and outlaws, until she finally achieves success on the stage at Covent Garden.

Historical Accuracy: This is an ingenious alternative *Mansfield Park* with authentic period elements and a convincing echoing of the Austen original.

BRIGITTE VON TESSIN

6208 *The Bastard*

Date of Publication: 1959
Subject(s): Religious Conflict; Inheritance—Disputed
Fictional character(s): Gaston de Racon, Nobleman (count); Madeleine de Racon, Spouse; Martin de Racon, Bastard Son
Time Period(s): 17th century
Locale(s): France

Summary: Gaston de Racon attempts to prevent his illegitimate son, Martin, from usurping the inheritance of his other two sons. The domestic drama is set against a backdrop of Catholic-Huguenot conflict.

Historical Accuracy: The historical background is marred by bias, which undermines historical credibility.

JOSEPHINE TEY
(PSEUD. OF ELIZABETH MACKINTOSH, 1897-1952)

Scottish born playwright and novelist Mackintosh attended the Royal Academy at Inverness. She taught physical education at various schools during the 1920s. Mackintosh was a prolific author of stage and radio plays. Under the pseudonym Josephine Tey, her books include *The Privateer*, *Miss Pym Disposes*, *Brat Farrar*, and *The Singing Sands*.

6209 *The Daughter of Time*

Date of Publication: 1951
Subject(s): Royalty—England; Mystery; War of the Roses
Fictional character(s): Alan Grant, Detective—Police (Scotland Yard); Brent Carradine, Writer; Marta Hallard, Actress
Historical character(s): Richard III, Ruler (King of England); Cecily Neville, Noblewoman (mother of Richard III); Elizabeth of York, Royalty (queen consort of Henry VII)
Time Period(s): 15th century; 1950s
Locale(s): London, England

Summary: While recuperating in the hospital from a job-related injury, police detective Alan Grant enlists the aid of writer Brent Carradine and actress Marta Hallard to procure research materials that will help him deduce whether or not Richard III was in reality a malevolent schemer and the murderer of the young princes in the Tower.

Historical Accuracy: There is much information here on the War of the Roses and the reign and life of Richard III.

WILLIAM MAKEPEACE THACKERAY
(1811-1863)

This revolutionary English novelist and satirist helped create the novel as social criticism, puncturing hypocrisy and romantic falsification. His masterpiece, *Vanity Fair: A Novel Without a Hero*, established a standard for the novel in the 19th century, much as James Joyce's *Ulysses* did in the 20th.

6210 *Barry Lyndon*

Date of Publication: 1843
Subject(s): Military Life—British Army; Picaresque Adventure; Seven Years War
Fictional character(s): Redmond Barry, Adventurer, Rake; Lady Honoria Lyndon, Gentlewoman; Viscount Bullington, Heir, Nobleman
Time Period(s): 1750s; 1760s
Locale(s): Ireland; Germany; London, England

Summary: Thackeray offers a realistic alternative to the romantic treatment of rogues and outlaws by presenting a thorough-going scoundrel with no redeeming features. Barry

makes his fortune as a soldier, spy, gambler, and mercenary husband to a widowed countess during the Seven Years War.

Historical Accuracy: The novel's details of outre life (sharp practices, double dealing, and corruption) on the continent provide a realistic alternative to the usual historical romance of the period.

6211 *Denis Duval*

Date of Publication: 1864
Subject(s): Crime and Criminals
Fictional character(s): Denis Duval, Hero; Chevalier De la Motte, Nobleman, Smuggler
Time Period(s): 1770s
Locale(s): Rye, England

Summary: This unfinished novel takes place in the underworld of smuggling. After reporting the villainous intrigues of the smuggler De La Motte, Duval is ostracized and goes to sea. Thackeray planned to dramatize his sea adventures, including a sea battle with John Paul Jones and the defeat of Admiral Grasse's squadron.

Historical Accuracy: This unfortunately incomplete story has an intriguing setting and details.

6212 *Henry Esmond*

Date of Publication: 1852
Subject(s): Jacobite Rebellion
Fictional character(s): Henry Esmond, Military Personnel, Gentleman; Rachel Esmond, Gentlewoman; Beatrix Esmond, Gentlewoman, Femme Fatale
Historical character(s): Sir Richard Steele, Writer; Joseph Addison, Writer; Jonathan Swift, Writer
Time Period(s): 17th century; 18th century
Locale(s): Castlewood, England; London, England; Europe (Low Countries: Holland, Belgium)

Summary: The story intertwines the domestic drama of Henry Esmond's love for his guardian's wife and daughter with early 18th century literary, military, and royal history. Henry serves in Marlborough's campaigns from Blenheim to Malplaquet and becomes involved in the plot to put the Young Pretender on the throne.

Historical Accuracy: The novel vividly depicts 18th-century English society, but is overly sentimental in parts.

6213 *Vanity Fair*

Date of Publication: 1848
Subject(s): Regency Period; Victorian Period; Battle of Waterloo
Fictional character(s): Becky Sharp, Adventurer; George Osborne, Gentleman, Military Personnel; Amelia Sedley, Gentlewoman, Widow(er)
Historical character(s): William Dobbin, Military Personnel; Arthur Wellesley, Military Personnel
Time Period(s): 19th century (1815-1840)
Locale(s): Brussels, Belgium; London, England; Germany

Summary: Thackeray's masterpiece recreates the opening decades of the 19th century, showing how the Regency period gave way to the Victorian era. The plot centers on two pairs of school friends—Amelia Sedley and Becky Sharp and George Osborne and William Dobbin. Their careers are mapped in scenes that include the Duchess of Richmond's famous ball before the battle of Waterloo, court life in London, and spa life on the continent.

Historical Accuracy: By puncturing its tendency toward romance and idealization, Thackeray redefined the novel as an instrument of truth.

6214 The Virginians

Date of Publication: 1859
Subject(s): American Revolution; French and Indian War
Fictional character(s): Harry Warrington, Gentleman; George Warrington, Military Personnel; Baroness Beatrix Bernstein, Noblewoman (formerly Beatrix Esmond)
Historical character(s): James Wolfe, Military Personnel
Time Period(s): 18th century (1750-1790)
Locale(s): Virginia; London, England

Summary: This sequel to *Henry Esmond* follows Henry's two grandsons in the French and Indian Wars and the American Revolution. High and low life in England and conflicting political loyalties play an important role in both brothers' careers.

Historical Accuracy: There are vivid portraits of the period, particularly of English society.

ELSWYTH THANE (1900-)

Born in Iowa, Thane has been a journalist, playwright, and screenwriter as well as a prolific author of fiction. Her first novel, *Riders of the Wind*, was published in 1926. Thane is the wife of famous naturalist-explorer Dr. William Beebe.

6215 Dawn's Early Light

Date of Publication: 1943
Subject(s): American Revolution; American Colonies; Battle of Yorktown
Fictional character(s): Julian Day, Teacher
Historical character(s): George Washington, Military Personnel (army commander); Thomas Jefferson, Political Figure; Marie Joseph Paul de Lafayette, Military Personnel (general), Nobleman (Marquis de Lafayette); Nathanael Greene, Military Personnel (general); Francis Marion, Military Personnel (army officer); Johann de Kalb, Military Personnel (general)
Time Period(s): 1770s; 1780s (1774-1781)
Locale(s): Williamsburg, Virginia; Camden, New Jersey; South Carolina

Summary: The novel depicts action in the American Revolution, from the turmoil of colonial Williamsburg on the eve of hostilities to the Battle of Camden and the Carolina campaign with Francis Marion's Swamp Force. The action culminates in the battle of wits between Cornwallis and Lafayette that ends in the Battle of Yorktown and the British defeat.

Historical Accuracy: The essential chronology of events is observed, although some scenes and situations are imagined.

6216 Ever After

Date of Publication: 1945
Subject(s): Spanish-American War; Battle of San Juan Hill
Fictional character(s): Bracken Murray, Journalist; Fitz Sprague, Journalist
Time Period(s): 1890s
Locale(s): Williamsburg, Virginia; San Juan, Cuba; London, England

Summary: The events of the Spanish-American War are reflected in the experiences of war correspondent Bracken Murray and his cub reporter cousin Fitz Sprague. They are on hand to describe the makeshift invasion of Cuba at Daiquiri and the charge of the Rough Riders up Kettle Hill before San Juan.

Historical Accuracy: The description of the action in Cuba is authentic.

6217 Yankee Stranger

Date of Publication: 1944
Subject(s): Civil War—U.S.
Fictional character(s): Eden Day, Southern Belle; Cabot Murray, Military Personnel (Union officer)
Time Period(s): 1860s (1860-1865)
Locale(s): Williamsburg, Virginia; Richmond, Virginia

Summary: In this sequel to *Dawn's Early Light*, one of Thane's series of novels located in Williamsburg, Virginia, the scene is the American Civil War. Descendants of characters from the earlier book appear in this story that concerns a Yankee officer with whom Eden Day falls in love.

Historical Accuracy: Though the characters are fictional, care has been taken to place them with actual regiments in actual events.

STEVE THAYER (1952-)

A native of St. Paul, Minnesota, Thayer flunked out of Southwest State University in Marshall, Minnesota. He tried his hand at acting and writing in Hollywood before returning to St. Paul and taking a variety of jobs to support himself while writing his first novel *Saint Mudd*, about St. Paul in the 1930s.

6218 Saint Mudd

Date of Publication: 1992
Subject(s): Mystery; Crime and Criminals
Fictional character(s): Grover Mudd, Journalist
Historical character(s): John Dillinger, Criminal; Alvin Karpis, Criminal; Kate "Ma" Barker, Criminal; Arthur "Doc" Barker, Criminal
Time Period(s): 1930s
Locale(s): St. Paul, Minnesota

Summary: St. Paul, Minnesota, in the 1930s is the setting for this blend of fact and fiction. Grover Mudd is a newspaper man who becomes involved in the historical activities of Dillinger, Karpis, and the Barker gang.

Historical Accuracy: The novel offers an authentic look at the gangster 1930s that is rooted in the actuality of the locale.

HJALMAR P. THESEN (1925-)

South African writer Thesen was born in Knysna and was educated at the University of Cape Town. He was the director of Thesen & Co., Ltd. from 1950 to 1982. His books, which concern the interdependence of man and nature in Africa, include *The Castle of Giants*, *Master of None*, and *Country Days*.

6219 *The Echoing Cliffs*

Date of Publication: 1964
Subject(s): Tribal Life—African
Fictional character(s): Liklik, Wanderer, Hunter; Kwiknee, Young Woman
Time Period(s): 17th century
Locale(s): South Africa

Summary: This novel of tribal life in the forests of South Africa 300 years ago tells the story of Liklik, the sole survivor of an illness that wipes out his tribe. He joins another tribe and is accepted by them, but when the tribe is attacked, everyone but Liklik and his young wife are killed. Their wandering continues.

Historical Accuracy: The particularity of time and place are muted and shadowy. The novel proceeds like a folk tale rather than a realistic portrait of an age and its customs.

ANGELA THIRKELL (1890-1961)

An English novelist whose books found enthusiastic audiences in Britain and the U.S., Thirkell was the granddaughter of Pre-Raphaelite artist Edward Burne-Jones and a friend of the Kipling family. She and Kipling's daughter Josephine were the first trial audience for Kipling's *Just So Stories*. Her novels include *Before Lunch* and *Cheerfulness Breaks In*.

6220 *Coronation Summer*

Date of Publication: 1937
Subject(s): Victorian Period
Fictional character(s): Fanny Darnley, Gentlewoman
Time Period(s): 1830s (1837-1838)
Locale(s): London, England

Summary: Young Fanny Darnley accompanies her father to see Queen Victoria crowned in 1837. The novel provides a vivid account of the period and manners and customs in the first year of Victoria's long reign.

Historical Accuracy: Carefully researched and documented, the novel captures the events, customs, and sensibility of the period.

BODIE THOENE (1951-)

Thoene began her writing career as a teen journalist for her local newspaper and worked for a time as a writer and researcher for John Wayne. She is the author of *Writer to Writer* and a frontier fiction series, The Saga of the Sierras.

6221 *Danzig Passage*

Date of Publication: 1991
Subject(s): Holocaust; Jews
Fictional character(s): Peter Wallich, Young Man
Time Period(s): 1930s (1938)
Locale(s): Germany; Austria

Summary: In this installment of the Zion Covenant Series, the final days of prewar life in Germany are described as a number of Christians and Jews attempt to flee persecution for Danzig and the prospect of freedom.

Historical Accuracy: The novel captures its era effectively.

6222 *In My Father's House*

Date of Publication: 1992
Subject(s): World War I; Racial Conflict; Religious Conflict
Fictional character(s): Ellis Warne, Military Personnel (soldier); Birch Tucker, Military Personnel (soldier); Jefferson Canfield, Military Personnel (soldier)
Time Period(s): 1910s
Locale(s): France; United States

Summary: The novel dramatizes America's role in the fighting of World War I and the racial and religious conflict on the homefront after the war. Three soldiers from different backgrounds are brought together for the fighting, and their lives and that of their families become intertwined.

Historical Accuracy: The novel offers a believable portrait of the atmosphere of the age.

6223 *Jerusalem Interlude*

Date of Publication: 1990
Subject(s): Holocaust; Jews
Fictional character(s): Leah Feldstein, Young Woman; Shimon Feldstein, Young Man
Historical character(s): Hermann Goering, Military Personnel (German field marshall)
Time Period(s): 1930s (1938)
Locale(s): Jerusalem, Palestine; Germany

Summary: In the fourth volume of the Zion Covenant Series, as war prepares to sweep Europe, Leah and Shimon Feldstein have reached Palestine and what they hope will be a safe haven. Events, however, conspire to threaten their search for peace.

Historical Accuracy: The novel provides a believable backdrop of historical events and atmosphere of the times.

6224 *Munich Signature*

Date of Publication: 1990
Subject(s): Holocaust; Jews; Nazis
Fictional character(s): Elisa Murphy, Young Woman; Leah Feldstein, Young Woman
Time Period(s): 1930s (1938-1939)
Locale(s): Germany; Austria

Summary: In the third of the Zion Covenant Series, Europe is on the brink of war as Leah Feldstein attempts to escape Austria and Elisa Murphy is involved in international intrigue that could hold the key to stopping Hitler's domination of Europe.

Historical Accuracy: The story is a fanciful one but does serve to capture the spirit of the era convincingly.

6225 *Prague Counterpoint*

Date of Publication: 1989
Subject(s): Holocaust; Jews; Nazis
Fictional character(s): Elisa Lindhelm, Young Woman; Leah Feldstein, Young Woman
Time Period(s): 1930s
Locale(s): Prague, Czechoslovakia

Summary: In the second volume of the author's Zion Covenant Series, the Nazis have invaded Austria and threaten to do the same in Czechoslovakia. Elisa Lindhelm and Leah Feldstein work for the underground opposing the Nazis while attempting the rescue of two small boys.

Historical Accuracy: The novel's historical background is accurately described.

6226 *Say to This Mountain*

Date of Publication: 1993
Subject(s): Depression Era
Fictional character(s): Jefferson Canfield, Convict; Ellis Warne, Doctor
Time Period(s): 1920s; 1930s
Locale(s): Arkansas

Summary: The novel brings to a conclusion the author's Shiloh Legacy series of life in post-World War I Arkansas. A large cast of characters copes with the changes brought by the stockmarket crash, and Jeff Canfield, unjustly imprisoned for ten years, finds his way home.

Historical Accuracy: The novel's period elements are authentic and believable.

6227 *A Thousand Shall Fall*

Date of Publication: 1992
Subject(s): Racial Conflict
Fictional character(s): Birch Tucker, Veteran (World War I); Max Meyer, Journalist
Time Period(s): 1920s
Locale(s): New York, New York; Arkansas

Summary: The novel continues the chronicle begun in *In My Father's House* of the years following World War I. In 1920s, Birch Tucker and his family struggle in Arkansas, while Max Meyer, a financial columnist, reports on the boom times on Wall Street.

Historical Accuracy: The novel captures its era believably.

6228 *Vienna Prelude*

Date of Publication: 1989
Subject(s): Holocaust; Jews; Nazis
Fictional character(s): Elisa Lindhelm, Young Woman
Time Period(s): 1930s
Locale(s): Vienna, Austria

Summary: This first volume of the author's Zion Covenant Series concerns the efforts of Elisa Lindhelm, a Christian, to help Jews escape persecution in pre-World War II Austria.

Historical Accuracy: The novel captures the era effectively.

6229 *Warsaw Requiem*

Date of Publication: 1991
Subject(s): World War II; Holocaust; Jews
Fictional character(s): Peter Wallich, Young Man; Lori Ibsen, Young Woman; Jacob Kalner, Young Man
Time Period(s): 1930s (1939)
Locale(s): Warsaw, Poland; Danzig, Poland; London, England

Summary: In the finale of the author's Zion Covenant Series, war breaks out, threatening a group of refugees waiting in Danzig for a ship to England and Peter Wallich, who is with the Jews in the Warsaw ghetto.

Historical Accuracy: The historical timeline is accurate as is the atmosphere of the period.

JAMES ALEXANDER THOM (1933-)

An American novelist born in Indiana, Thom graduated from Butler University. He has worked as a newspaper and magazine editor, and conducts extensive research for his books. *From Sea to Shining Sea*, for example, required field work in 40 states. Thom has become proficient in the use of 18th-century tools and weapons.

6230 *The Children of the First Man*

Date of Publication: 1994
Subject(s): Indians; Middle Ages; Exploration
Fictional character(s): Stonecutter, Indian; Man Face, Indian
Historical character(s): George Catlin, Artist; Madoc, Royalty (prince), Explorer
Time Period(s): Multiple Time Periods
Locale(s): Wales; North America

Summary: The novel offers a possible interpretation of how the Welsh prince and explorer Madoc sailed to the east coast of North America in the 12th century and landed Welsh colonists. They may have worked their way to the Tennessee and Ohio Valleys where they mingled with Native American tribes. The novel explores the mixing of cultures and heritages that shaped our time.

Historical Accuracy: The research is convincing, though the author grants that there are skeptics who doubt the novel's assumptions of Madoc's settlement in America.

6231 *Follow the River*

Date of Publication: 1981
Subject(s): Indians; French and Indian War; American Colonies
Historical character(s): Mary Draper Ingles, Captive; George Washington, Military Personnel (officer)
Time Period(s): 1750s; 1760s (1755-1768)
Locale(s): Ohio River, United States; Virginia, American Colonies

Summary: Based on a true account, the novel describes the adventures of Mary Draper Ingles, who in 1755 is captured from her Virginia settlement by the Shawnees. She manages to escape her captors and, using the Ohio River as a guide, walks 1,000 miles through the wilderness to safety.

Historical Accuracy: The details of wilderness life of the period are convincing.

6232 *From Sea to Shining Sea*

Date of Publication: 1984

Subject(s): Settlement of the American Frontier; American Revolution; Lewis and Clark Expedition

Historical character(s): John Clark, Frontiersman; Ann Rogers Clark, Spouse; George Rogers Clark, Military Personnel; William Clark, Military Personnel, Explorer; Meriwether Lewis, Military Personnel, Explorer

Time Period(s): 18th century; 19th century (1773-1806)

Locale(s): Virginia; Ohio Valley, United States; West

Summary: The novel tells the story of the remarkable Clark family of Virginia. George Rogers Clark becomes a military hero in America's first western frontier, and his brother William, along with Meriwether Lewis, explores the territory of the Louisiana Purchase.

Historical Accuracy: The story is factually based and evinces much research, including the author's retracing of the Lewis and Clark expedition.

6233 *Long Knife*

Date of Publication: 1979

Subject(s): American Revolution; Settlement of the American Frontier; Indians

Historical character(s): George Rogers Clark, Military Personnel (officer)

Time Period(s): 18th century; 19th century (1777-1818)

Locale(s): Northwest Territory, United States

Summary: The novel tells the epic adventure story of George Rogers Clark, who leads a small army west from Virginia during the American Revolution to conquer all of the territory between the Ohio and Mississippi Rivers. The novel describes his battles with the British and treaties with the Indians, as well as his ultimate betrayal by the government he served.

Historical Accuracy: The author explains that the novel reflects the documented facts as they are revealed in the letters and memoirs of its principal characters.

6234 *Panther in the Sky*

Date of Publication: 1989

Subject(s): Indians; Biography, Fictionalized; Settlement of the American Frontier

Historical character(s): Tecumseh, Indian (Shawnee), Chieftain; William Henry Harrison, Military Personnel, Political Figure; Daniel Boone, Frontiersman; George Rogers Clark, Military Personnel (officer); Anthony Wayne, Military Personnel (general)

Time Period(s): 18th century; 19th century (1768-1813)

Locale(s): Ohio; Michigan; Kentucky

Summary: The novel presents a fictionalized biography of the great Shawnee chief Tecumseh, first an ally of the British, then a war leader in the long struggle against encroachment of settlers.

Historical Accuracy: The author points out that the book often takes the Native American perspective, which in some cases cannot be reconciled with that of white historians.

D.M. THOMAS (1935-)

Born in Cornwall, England, and educated at New College, Oxford, Thomas is also a poet and translator, well known for his translation of the Russian poet Anna Akhmatova. Thomas' breakthrough novel, *The White Hotel* won the Cheltenham Prize, the *Los Angeles Times* Book Award, and a Booker Prize nomination.

6235 *Eating Pavlova*

Date of Publication: 1994

Subject(s): Medical Profession

Historical character(s): Sigmund Freud, Doctor; Anna Freud, Doctor

Time Period(s): 1930s (1939)

Locale(s): London, England

Summary: In 1939 in London, Sigmund Freud is dying of cancer, attended by his daught er, Anna. The novel records his last thoughts and dreams. Family secrets and the eerie relationship between Freud and his daughter are revealed.

Historical Accuracy: The novel is accurate in its biographical treatment but inventive in its exorcising of Freud's and his daughter's peculiar demons.

6236 *Flying into Love*

Date of Publication: 1992

Subject(s): Assassination; Politics

Historical character(s): John F. Kennedy, Political Figure; Jacqueline Kennedy, Spouse; Lee Harvey Oswald, Murderer (assassin); John Connolly, Political Figure; J. Edgar Hoover, Government Official (director of the F.B.I.)

Time Period(s): 1960s (1963)

Locale(s): Dallas, Texas; Washington, District of Columbia

Summary: The events of the assassination of John F. Kennedy in Dallas in 1963 are depicted in a blending of fact and fiction that seeks to unravel the paradoxes and mysteries of the murder. The novel dramatizes the conjunction of myth and reality that adheres to the events in Dallas.

Historical Accuracy: Each book about the assassination of John F. Kennedy has mingled reality and ficiton, and this novel is no different.

6237 *The White Hotel*

Date of Publication: 1981

Subject(s): World War II; Holocaust; Medical Profession

Fictional character(s): Lisa Erdman, Young Woman

Historical character(s): Sigmund Freud, Doctor

Time Period(s): 20th century (1910s-1940s)

Locale(s): Vienna, Austria; Russia

Summary: This harrowing novel joins two central elements of 20th century consciousness, psychoanalysis and the Holocaust. It is centered on Lisa Erdman, who is seen through an imagined exchange of letters between Sigmund Freud and his disciples. Lisa's story unfolds to its tragic apotheosis at Babi Yar, where both history and the psyche are surmounted by the mythical.

Historical Accuracy: To describe the landscape of hysteria, which the author calls the terrain of the novel, the author uses Freud as one of his characters. The role played by Freud is entirely fictional, though based on the known facts of Freud's life and sometimes quoting from his works and letters.

DONALD THOMAS

Thomas has worked as a teacher at the University of Wales at Cardiff. He is the author of *Cardigan* and two collections of poems.

`6238` *Captain Wonder*

Date of Publication: 1981
Subject(s): Edwardian Period; Espionage
Fictional character(s): Captain Richard Gaudeans, Spy, Adventurer; Tonia Schroeder, Young Woman
Historical character(s): Helmuth Johannes Ludwig von Moltke, Military Personnel (general)
Time Period(s): 1900s (1907)
Locale(s): Berlin, Germany; London, England; Dublin, Ireland

Summary: Captain Wonder, alias Richard Gaudeans, a Boer War veteran, spy, and confidence man, is the central character in a rollicking story of espionage, plots, and betrayal set in the Edwardian period. Gaudeans finds himself in the middle of the search by German and British intelligence services for each other's plans, as well as King Edward VII's visit to Dublin in 1907, and the theft of the Irish crown jewels.

Historical Accuracy: The story of Gaudeans is fanciful but set against actual events of the period.

`6239` *The Flight of the Eagle*

Date of Publication: 1975
Subject(s): Napoleonic Wars; Regency Period; Battle of Waterloo
Fictional character(s): Charles Auguste Tollemache, Military Personnel (captain)
Historical character(s): Arthur Wellesley, Military Personnel (army commander), Nobleman (Duke of Wellington); George, Prince Regent, Royalty; Caroline of Brunswick, Royalty (princess consort of George); Matthew Gregory Lewis, Writer; Napoleon Bonaparte, Military Personnel (French commander), Ruler (Emperor of France); Michel Ney, Military Personnel (marshal)
Time Period(s): 1810s
Locale(s): London, England; Naples, Italy

Summary: The events in England and Europe in the months preceding the Battle of Waterloo are described from the perspective of Captain Charles Tollemache. After the Battle of Vitoria in Spain, Tollemache is dismissed by Wellington and is recruited by the Duke of York as a spy in the battle between Princess Caroline and her estranged husband, the prince regent. Tollemache sets off to prevent Caroline's conspiracy with Napoleon and is on hand for the events of the Hundred Days and Waterloo, seen from the French side of the battle.

Historical Accuracy: Tollemache is an invented character, but the events depicted are factual, modified only by Tollemache's view of them.

`6240` *Jekyll, Alias Hyde*

Date of Publication: 1988
Subject(s): Mystery; Victorian Period
Fictional character(s): Henry Jekyll, Doctor, Murderer (aka Edward Hyde); Alfred Swain, Detective—Police; Oliver Lumley, Police Officer (sergeant)
Time Period(s): 1890s (1891)
Locale(s): London, England

Summary: The author offers a "variation" on Robert Louis Stevenson's classic tale of the gentle physician Henry Jekyll who is also the sadistic murderer Edward Hyde. The case is re-explored by Scotland Yard's Inspector Swain and Sergeant Lumley. The oddities of Stevenson's original account become the basis for a different interpretation.

Historical Accuracy: The novel is a remarkable echoing of a literary classic with an authentic sense of time and place.

`6241` *Prince Charlie's Bluff*

Date of Publication: 1974
Subject(s): Jacobite Rebellion; French and Indian War
Fictional character(s): Lovat Fraser, Military Personnel
Historical character(s): Charles Edward Stuart, Royalty; George Washington, Military Personnel (colonel)
Time Period(s): 1750s; 1760s (1759-1761)
Locale(s): Virginia, American Colonies

Summary: The novel offers an intriguing alternative history in which General Wolfe loses the Battle of Quebec and Bonnie Prince Charlie secretly comes to Colonial Virginia. The Stuart clans reverse the defeat inflicted at the Battle of Culloden.

Historical Accuracy: Though the novel alters particular events, it does not alter the most important underlying situations. The author's historical notes detail the factual basis for the story.

`6242` *The Ripper's Apprentice*

Date of Publication: 1986
Subject(s): Mystery; Victorian Period
Fictional character(s): Alfred Swain, Detective—Police; Oliver Lumley, Police Officer (sergeant)
Time Period(s): 1890s (1891-1892)
Locale(s): London, England

Summary: A psychopathic killer is stalking the streets of London's Lambeth area in 1891. Called the Ripper's Apprentice in honor of the greater notoriety of Jack the Ripper in 1888, the killer is no less diabolical or clever. Investigator Swain and Sergeant Lumley are on his trail as he deviously dares the police to solve the case.

Historical Accuracy: The murders in Lambeth during 1891 and 1892 are historical, and this fictional account is rendered close to the facts.

ELIZABETH MARSHALL THOMAS
(1931-)

Born in Boston, Thomas is a graduate of Radcliffe College. As a researcher on animals and hunters around the world, she has traveled to Europe, Lebanon, Baffin Island, and Australia. She is the author of the nonfiction work *The Homeless People. Reindeer Moon* won the Hemingway Citation.

6243 *The Animal Wife*

Date of Publication: 1990
Subject(s): Prehistory; Tribal Life—Prehistoric; Animals
Fictional character(s): Kori, Prehistoric Human, Hunter; Swift, Prehistoric Human, Hunter
Time Period(s): Indeterminate Past
Locale(s): Central Siberia, Europe

Summary: A companion volume to the author's *Reindeer Moon*, this novel is set a few years later. It is narrated by Kori, a young mammoth hunter determined to become as great a hunter as his father, Swift. The novel's action stems from Kori's accidental encounter with what he believes to be an animal. The animal turns out to be a woman, whom he abducts and takes as his wife.

Historical Accuracy: The novel offers a plausible version of prehistoric life, informed by evident and substantial research.

6244 *Reindeer Moon*

Date of Publication: 1987
Subject(s): Prehistory; Tribal Life—Prehistoric; Animals
Fictional character(s): Yanan, Prehistoric Human, Teenager; Graylag, Prehistoric Human, Chieftain; Swift, Prehistoric Human, Hunter
Time Period(s): Indeterminate Past
Locale(s): Central Siberia, Europe

Summary: Set 20,000 years ago in Central Siberia, a cold version of the African savannah, the novel tells the coming-of-age story of Yanan, a young girl. Her experiences dramatize an entire culture of Paleolithic life: hunters, gatherers, and shamans, and especially the animals that form the locus of their lives.

Historical Accuracy: The novel offers a brilliant and knowledgeable reconstruction of prehistoric life, obviously shaped by thoughtful research.

MICHAEL M. THOMAS (1936-)

Born in New York City, Thomas attended Phillips Exeter Academy and Yale University, where he majored in art history. After graduation, he became a curator at the Metropolitan Museum of Art and in 1961 joined his father, an investment banker, at Lehman Brothers. He left to start his own financial consulting firm and eventually began

writing fiction. His first novel, *Green Monday*, was praised for its authentic treatment of Middle Eastern and American oil interests and politics. His novels have drawn on his experiences both as an art historian and investment banker.

6245 *Hanover Place*

Date of Publication: 1990
Subject(s): Business Building; Family Saga
Fictional character(s): Howland Warrington, Businessman; Morris Miles, Businessman; Arthur Lubloff, Financier
Time Period(s): 20th century (1924-1990)
Locale(s): New York, New York

Summary: This family saga ranges over several decades, from the 1920s to 1990, and concerns the history of Warrington & Co., a great Wall Street financial house. The company is dominated by two families, the Warringtons and the Mileses, and the novel follows their various members through the years of depression and war, capturing the world of high finance and society.

Historical Accuracy: The novel reflects the impact of historical events.

ROSIE THOMAS (1947-)

Born in Wales, Thomas graduated from Oxford in 1976 and published her first novel, *Love's Choices*, six years later. Her fourth novel, *Sunrise*, was named Romantic Novel of the Year by the Romantic Novelists' Association in 1985. She turned to historical fiction the same year with *The White Dove*. Her novel *Bad Girls, Good Women* is set in the London of the 1950s and 1960s.

6246 *The White Dove*

Date of Publication: 1986
Subject(s): Labor Movement; Civil War—Spain
Fictional character(s): Amy Lovell, Gentlewoman; Nick Penny, Labor Organizer
Historical character(s): Edward, Prince of Wales, Royalty (Prince of Wales)
Time Period(s): 1930s
Locale(s): England; Spain

Summary: England between the wars is depicted in the relationship of upper-class Amy Lovell and Nick Penny, a dedicated union organizer whose commitment to the socialist cause leads him to join the fighting in Spain. Their relationship is affected by historical events that underline their class differences.

Historical Accuracy: The novel captures the actual events of the period in a believable setting.

JOHN WILLIAMS THOMASON

6247 *Gone to Texas*

Date of Publication: 1938
Subject(s): American West; Reconstruction Period

Fictional character(s): Edward Cantrell, Veteran (Civil War), Military Personnel (lieutenant)
Time Period(s): 1860s (1868)
Locale(s): Rio Grande, Texas

Summary: In Texas following the Civil War, a young Civil War veteran, Edward Cantrell, is sent to serve on an army post along the Rio Grande. His experiences with the Mexicans and in the wilds form the novel's plot.

Historical Accuracy: The details of frontier life are convincingly depicted.

CHINA THOMPSON
(PSEUD. OF MARY LEWIS, 1907-1988)

An English writer, Lewis was born in Malaya, the daughter of a rubber planter. She was educated in India and England. Lewis is best known for her detective stories written as Christianna Brand, featuring Inspector Cockrill of the Kent County Police. Her books include *Death in High Heels*, *Heads You Lose*, and *Green for Danger*.

`6248` *Starrbelow*

Date of Publication: 1958
Subject(s): Georgian Period
Fictional character(s): Sophia Devigne, Young Woman
Time Period(s): 1760s (1764)
Locale(s): London, England

Summary: This romantic tale tells of young Sophia Devigne, who is brought from Venice to make a fashionable marriage to Baron Weyburn of Starrbelow. She ends up charged with fraud, wantonness, and murder.

Historical Accuracy: The story is improbable and contrived but does provide a look at London social life during the 1760s.

DANIEL PIERCE THOMPSON
(1795-1868)

Thompson was an American author and lawyer from Vermont, the subject of his fiction and his historical work. His novels show the strong influence of Sir Walter Scott and James Fenimore Cooper.

`6249` *The Green Mountain Boys*

Date of Publication: 1839
Subject(s): American Colonies; American Revolution
Fictional character(s): Charles Warrington, Settler, Patriot; Alma Hendee, Gentlewoman
Historical character(s): Ethan Allen, Military Personnel, Patriot; Benedict Arnold, Military Personnel
Time Period(s): 1770s (1775-1776)
Locale(s): Vermont, American Colonies; Fort Ticonderoga, New York, American Colonies

Summary: Set in the Vermont settlements immediately preceding the American Revolution, the story dramatizes the land disputes with authorities in New York led by the Green Mountain Boys. Warrington joins with Ethan Allen to take

Fort Ticonderoga and other garrisons, meeting his beloved in the process.

Historical Accuracy: In this classic novel of Vermont there are strong scenes of local color based on fact.

DAVID THOMPSON
(PSEUD. OF DAVID L. ROBBINS, 1940-)

Thompson's books include *Death Hunt*, *Prairie Blood*, and *Tomahawk Revenge*.

`6250` *Apache Blood*

Date of Publication: 1992
Subject(s): American West; Indians
Fictional character(s): Nathaniel King, Mountain Man, Trapper; Shakespeare McNair, Mountain Man, Trapper; Winona King, Indian (Shoshone), Spouse
Time Period(s): 1830s
Locale(s): Bent's Fort, Colorado; Santa Fe Trail, New Mexico

Summary: In the 1830s, mountain men Nathaniel King and Shakespeare McNair journey south into Mexican territory along the Santa Fe Trail. They find themselves in the middle of disputes with fellow American trappers, the Mexican authorities, and Apache raiders. King's wife, Winona, is taken prisoner, and a pursuit follows.

Historical Accuracy: The details of frontier life of the period are authentic.

`6251` *Blackfoot Massacre*

Date of Publication: 1992
Subject(s): American West; Indians
Fictional character(s): Nathaniel King, Mountain Man, Trapper; John Burke, Religious (missionary)
Time Period(s): 1830s
Locale(s): Rocky Mountains

Summary: Nathaniel King's peaceful life among the Shoshones is disrupted by missionary John Burke, who is determined to preach to the Blackfoot Indians. When Burke is captured deep within Blackfoot country, King mounts a daring rescue mission.

Historical Accuracy: The details of frontier life are believable.

`6252` *Blood Fury*

Date of Publication: 1991
Subject(s): American West; Indians
Fictional character(s): Nathaniel King, Mountain Man, Trapper; Sitting Bear, Indian (Crow), Warrior
Time Period(s): 1820s (1828)
Locale(s): Rocky Mountains

Summary: While on his own in the high Rockies, Nathaniel King encounters Sitting Bear, a Crow warrior banished from his tribe. When his famiy is kidnapped by a Ute war party, King finds himself in the middle of a tribal war.

Historical Accuracy: The details of Indian customs are effectively presented.

6253 *Blood Truce*

Date of Publication: 1993
Subject(s): American West; Indians
Fictional character(s): Nathaniel King, Mountain Man, Trapper; Winona King, Indian (Shoshone), Spouse
Time Period(s): 1830s
Locale(s): Rocky Mountains

Summary: It is up to Nathaniel King to try to work out a truce between the Utes and the shoshones before a full-scale tribal war erupts. He and his family are caught in the middle of the conflict with disasterous consequences if he should fail.

Historical Accuracy: The depiction of Indian life and customs is convincing.

6254 *Hawken Fury*

Date of Publication: 1992
Subject(s): American West
Fictional character(s): Nathaniel King, Mountain Man, Trapper; Adeline Van Buren, Heiress; Winona King, Indian (Shoshone), Spouse
Time Period(s): 1830s (1836)
Locale(s): Fort Bonneville, Idaho

Summary: When a figure from his past life in New York appears, Nathaniel King's mountain life is disrupted. Adeline Van Buren urges him to return to New York to help settle his father's estate. King must choose between his life in the mountains with Winona and a return to civilization with Adeline.

Historical Accuracy: The period background is believable.

6255 *King of the Mountain*

Date of Publication: 1990
Subject(s): American West
Fictional character(s): Nathaniel King, Teenager, Wanderer; Ezekiel King, Mountain Man, Trapper; Shakespeare McNair, Mountain Man, Trapper
Time Period(s): 1820s (1828)
Locale(s): Missouri; Rocky Mountains

Summary: In the first volume of the author's Wilderness Series on the frontier career of Nathaniel King, King comes West in 1828 in search of his uncle Ezekiel, who introduces him to the world of the Rocky Mountain trappers.

Historical Accuracy: The novel offers an authentic look at the frontier and the ways of the mountain men.

6256 *Lure of the Wind*

Date of Publication: 1990
Subject(s): American West; Indians
Fictional character(s): Nathaniel King, Mountain Man, Teenager; Shakespeare McNair, Mountain Man, Trapper
Time Period(s): 1820s (1828)
Locale(s): Rocky Mountains

Summary: In the second of the author's wilderness series, teenager Nathaniel King and trapper Shakespeare McNair encounter a raiding party of Blackfoot. The pair are rescued by the Shoshones, hereditary enemies of the Blackfoot, and King is tutored in Indian ways.

Historical Accuracy: The period elements and the depiction of Indian customs are authentic.

6257 *Mountain Devil*

Date of Publication: 1992
Subject(s): American West
Fictional character(s): Nathaniel King, Mountain Man, Trapper; Red Moon, Indian (Crow), Guide; Milo Menteen, Trapper
Time Period(s): 1830s
Locale(s): Rocky Mountains

Summary: An old Crow warrior, Red Moon, agrees to lead a party to a secret valley in the mountains where beavers are still plentiful. Mountain man Nathaniel King accepts a partnership in the plan despite the dangers, primarily to answer his doubts that the valley is guarded by a ''mountain devil.''.

Historical Accuracy: The novel offers a convincing look at frontier life.

6258 *Northwest Passage*

Date of Publication: 1992
Subject(s): American West; Wagon Trains
Fictional character(s): Nathaniel King, Mountain Man, Trapper; Simon Banner, Wagonmaster; Libbie Banner, Teenager
Time Period(s): 1830s
Locale(s): Oregon Trail, United States

Summary: Nathaniel King signs on to guide a small wagon train up the Oregon Trail to the Williamette Valley. They battle wild animals, bad weather, and hostile Indians. A secret plagues Libbie Banner, daughter of the party's leader, which may explain the Piegan war party that is following them.

Historical Accuracy: The details of trail life are authentic.

6259 *Tenderfoot*

Date of Publication: 1993
Subject(s): American West
Fictional character(s): Nathaniel King, Mountain Man, Trapper; Zach King, Child; Winona King, Indian (Shoshone), Spouse
Time Period(s): 1830s
Locale(s): Rocky Mountains

Summary: Nathaniel King takes his son into the mountains, to get to know him. His plans are shattered when King is captured by Indians, and only his son, Zach, can save him. The rescue tests the wilderness lessons Zach learned from his father.

Historical Accuracy: The period details of wilderness life are believable.

6260 *Tomahawk Revenge*

Date of Publication: 1991
Subject(s): American West; Indians

Fictional character(s): Nathaniel King, Mountain Man, Trapper; Shakespeare McNair, Mountain Man, Trapper; Winona King, Indian (Shoshone), Spouse
Time Period(s): 1820s (1828)
Locale(s): Rocky Mountains

Summary: When Blackfoot warriors capture his trapping companions, including the legendary Shakespeare McNair, Nathaniel King sets out in pursuit despite a serious wounding from a grizzly. King receives some unexpected assistance, and his plan for rescuing his friends requires him to run the deadly gauntlet.

Historical Accuracy: The details of Indian and wilderness life are authentic.

`6261` *Trapper's Blood*

Date of Publication: 1994
Subject(s): American West
Fictional character(s): Nathaniel King, Mountain Man, Trapper; Winona King, Indian (Shoshone), Spouse; Shakespeare McNair, Mountain Man, Trapper
Time Period(s): 1830s
Locale(s): Rocky Mountains

Summary: Peaceful mountain life is disrupted when a gang of white renegades rob and kill a number of victims, leaving their mutilated bodies to look like the work of Indians. King and his friends must band together to go after the killers.

Historical Accuracy: The novel is convincing in its depiction of the region and the period.

`6262` *Winterkill*

Date of Publication: 1993
Subject(s): American West
Fictional character(s): Nathaniel King, Mountain Man, Trapper; Winona King, Indian (Shoshone), Spouse; Selena Leonard, Criminal; Elden Leonard, Criminal
Time Period(s): 1830s
Locale(s): Rocky Mountains

Summary: Nathaniel King rescues Elden and Selena Leonard from a band of marauding Indians and takes them in for the winter. The Leonards are wanted criminals fleeing a murder charge in Missouri. They intend to make the King home their hangout, once they have disposed of the family.

Historical Accuracy: The details of wilderness life are effectively presented.

E.V. THOMPSON (1931-)

British writer E.V. Thompson held a variety of jobs before becoming a full-time writer in 1977, including serving in the Royal Navy for nine years. He was a founding member of the Bristol Police Force vice squad and an investigator with the British Overseas Airways Corporation. In Hong Kong he worked with the Hong Kong Police Narcotics Bureau, and in Africa he was chief security officer of the Rhodesia Department of Civil Aviation. He has set some of his novels in Africa, including the Retallick series. What is perhaps his best novel, *The Dream Traders*, is set in China at the time of the Opium Wars.

`6263` *Ben Retallick*

Date of Publication: 1980
Subject(s): Mining; Fishing; Rural Life—England
Fictional character(s): Ben Retallick, Miner; Jesse Henna, Heroine
Time Period(s): 1820s
Locale(s): Cornwall, England

Summary: The lives of Cornish miners and fishermen are described in this prequel to Thompson's *Chase the Wind*, describing the parents of that novel's Josh Retallick. Daily existence in a harsh and unforgiving landscape creates the drama here.

Historical Accuracy: The details of Cornish life are faithfully described.

`6264` *Chase the Wind*

Date of Publication: 1977
Subject(s): Labor Movement; Mining; Victorian Period
Fictional character(s): Josh Retallick, Miner; Miriam Trago, Heroine; William Thackeray, Religious
Time Period(s): 1850s
Locale(s): Cornwall, England

Summary: Set in the Cornish copper mining area in the 19th century, the novel tells of the birth of the trade union movement led by Josh Retallick. He makes an unfortunate match with the foundry manager's daughter, while his true love marries the icy and power-hungry preacher Thackeray. The domestic tangle is played out against the backdrop of labor struggle.

Historical Accuracy: The Cornish atmosphere and the era are fully and authentically depicted.

`6265` *Harvest of the Sun*

Date of Publication: 1979
Subject(s): Frontier—Africa; Business Building
Fictional character(s): Josh Retallick, Trader; Miriam Retallick, Young Woman; William Thackeray, Religious
Time Period(s): 1840s (1846)
Locale(s): Africa

Summary: In this sequel to *Chase the Wind*, Josh Retallick flees England after an unjust treason conviction with another man's wife—his sweetheart Miriam. Both are shipwrecked in South-West Africa. They trek inland and must contend with both Afrikaners and Herreros. The past reappears in the form of the aggrieved and vengeful husband, the Reverend Thackeray.

Historical Accuracy: The African background is solidly and convincingly described.

`6266` *Republic: A Novel of Texas*

Date of Publication: 1985
Subject(s): American West; Texas Revolution; Indians
Fictional character(s): Adam Rashleigh, Diplomat

Historical character(s): Mirabeau Buonaparte Lamar, Political Figure; Henry John Temple, Political Figure (Britih foreign secretary), Nobleman (Viscount Palmerston); Sam Houston, Political Figure
Time Period(s): 1830s (1838)
Locale(s): Texas; Mexico

Summary: The scene is the infancy of the Texas Rebellion in 1838 following Sam Houston's defeat of the Mexican Army. Englishman Adam Rashleigh is dispatched by Lord Palmerston to report on the prospects of the new country, and Rashleigh quickly finds himself drawn into a web of conflict and intrigue that forces him to change from observer to actor in the drama of the Texas Republic.

Historical Accuracy: The novel is effective in creating a plausible atmosphere, though the events of the novel are largely invented.

JOAN THOMPSON (1943-)

An American writer born in Boston, Thompson is a graduate of Colby College.

6267 *Marblehead*

Date of Publication: 1978
Subject(s): Coming of Age
Fictional character(s): Abigail Curtis, Young Woman; Burton Madison, Gentleman
Time Period(s): 1900s (1906)
Locale(s): Marblehead, Massachusetts; Boston, Massachusetts

Summary: This coming-of-age novel is set during the early years of the 20th century. Rebellious Abigail Curtis is banished from fashionable Boston to her aunt's house in Marblehead to protect her from a liaison with the rakish Burton Madison. There she matures under the wise tutelage of the ordinary folk in the Marblehead community.

Historical Accuracy: Although the novel attempts to be faithful to 1906 Boston and Marblehead, the author admits to a few necessary inaccuracies indicated in notes.

MAURICE THOMPSON (1844-1901)

An Indiana lawyer, poet, and author Thompson is best known for his romantic regional novels that include *A Tallahassee Girl* and *At Love's Extremes*.

6268 *Alice of Old Vincennes*

Date of Publication: 1900
Subject(s): American Revolution
Fictional character(s): Alice Tarleton, Young Woman; Gaspard Roussillon, Trader
Historical character(s): George Rogers Clark, Military Personnel (general), Frontiersman
Time Period(s): 1770s (1778)
Locale(s): Northwest Territory, United States

Summary: This historical romance is set in the Northwest Territory during the American Revolution and mainly concerns George Rogers Clark's capture of Vincennes. Alice Tarleton is abducted as a child and raised by a French trader,

Gaspard Roussillon. She comes to Clark's assistance, and the complications from her romance with one of Clark's officers is cleared up with the revelation of her parentage.

Historical Accuracy: The historical background is authentic, but the romance predominates.

MORTON THOMPSON

6269 *The Cry and the Covenant*

Date of Publication: 1949
Subject(s): Biography, Fictionalized; Medical Profession
Historical character(s): Ignaz Philipp Semmelweis, Doctor
Time Period(s): 19th century
Locale(s): Vienna, Austria; Hungary

Summary: This fictional biography of the Hungarian physician Ignaz Semmelweis dramatizes his medical discovery of the infectious nature of puerperal fever. His insistence on cleanliness and disinfection greatly reduced the mortality rate during childbirth. During his lifetime, Semmelweis was ridiculed, which eventually led to insanity and his suicide.

Historical Accuracy: This is a skillful and historically accurate portrait of Semmelweis and the medical issues of the period.

THOMAS THOMPSON

6270 *Crompton Way*

Date of Publication: 1947
Subject(s): Biography, Fictionalized; Inventions; Industrial Revolution
Historical character(s): Samuel Crompton, Inventor
Time Period(s): 18th century; 19th century
Locale(s): Lancashire, England

Summary: The novel recreates the life story of English inventor Samuel Crompton. As a young man in a cotton mill, Crompton recognizes the limitation of the current technology and is determined to create something better. After five years of secret work, Crompton produces the mule spinner or muslin wheel, an important innovation in the development of fine cotton spinning. Crompton is too poor to obtain a patent and sees little reward from his invention.

Historical Accuracy: The novel excels in evoking the atmosphere of period Lancashire.

ROBERT THOMSEN (1915-1983)

Born in Baltimore, Thomsen was a writer for motion pictures, TV, and most major magazines. An actor as well as a writer, Thomsen appeared in several Broadway plays and contributed scripts for the television series "Topper." His novel *Carriage Trade* was adapted for the stage. Among his nonfiction works was a 1975 biography of Alcoholics Anonymous founder William G. Wilson, *Bill W.*.

6271 *Carriage Trade*

Date of Publication: 1972
Subject(s): Civil War—U.S.; Battle of Gettysburg

Fictional character(s): Dr. Myer, Doctor; Miss Joy, Madam
Time Period(s): 1860s (1863)
Locale(s): Gettysburg, Pennsylvania

Summary: The novel provides a unique view of the events of the Battle of Gettysburg during the Civil War. A derelict doctor turns a brothel into a field hospital, saving the lives of many men wounded during the battle. The novel offers an interesting analysis of the nature of sensual immorality in the midst of the immorality of war.

Historical Accuracy: The novel's story is imagined, but the background of the events of the battle is authentic.

NICOLA THORNE

(PSEUD. OF ROSEMARY ELLENBECH)

Born in Cape Town, South Africa, Ellenbech worked as an editor before becoming a full-time writer. She has written under the pseudonyms Anne L'Estrange, Katherine Yorke, and Nicola Thorne.

6272 *Affairs of Love*

Date of Publication: 1983
Subject(s): Victorian Period; Theatrical Life; Medical Profession
Fictional character(s): Estella Abercrombie, Actress; Lindsey Abercrombie, Doctor
Historical character(s): Sigmund Freud, Doctor; Ellen Terry, Actress; Jean-Martin Charcot, Doctor
Time Period(s): 1880s; 1890s
Locale(s): England; Paris, France; Boston, Massachusetts

Summary: The late Victorian scene is reflected in the experiences of two sisters—Estella and Lindsey Abercrombie—whose pursuit of careers in theater and medicine puts them in contact with the leading figures of both worlds, including Ellen Terry and Sigmund Freud.

Historical Accuracy: The novel features a fictional story interwoven with actual figures and a believable historical background.

6273 *Cashmere*

Date of Publication: 1982
Subject(s): Business Building; Fashion Industry
Fictional character(s): Margaret Dunbar, Businesswoman, Model
Time Period(s): 20th century (1919-1951)
Locale(s): Scottish Borders, Scotland; London, England

Summary: The fate of Dunbar & Sons woolen mill in Scotland is affected by the headstrong Margaret Dunbar. She goes to London as a model to learn about clothes and design, then makes Dunbar & Sons the preeminent mill in Scotland by importing cashmere from China and weaving it into high-fashion clothing.

Historical Accuracy: The novel is authentic in its depiction of the Scottish woolen industry and the era.

6274 *Sisters & Lovers*

Date of Publication: 1981
Subject(s): Victorian Period; Crimean War
Fictional character(s): Caroline Vestry, Young Woman; Emily Vestry, Young Woman; Jane Vestry, Young Woman
Historical character(s): John Ruskin, Writer; Harriet Martineau, Writer; Karl Marx, Writer, Philosopher; Florence Nightingale, Nurse; Victoria, Ruler (Queen of England)
Time Period(s): 1850s
Locale(s): London, England; Crimea, Russia

Summary: The novel details events and personalities of the Victorian period through the experiences of three sisters—Caroline, Emily, and Jane Vestry—including the opening of the Crystal Palace and the action of the Crimean War in Florence Nightingale's hospital.

Historical Accuracy: The story mixes the fictional and the factual with a solid and believable period background.

LAWRENCE THORNTON (1937-)

American writer Thornton was born in Pomona, California, and attended the University of California, Santa Barbara, where he earned his Ph.D. He has taught at several American colleges and universities and was a writer-in-residence at the University of California, Irvine. He received several literary awards for his first novel, *Imagining Argentina*, published in 1987.

6275 *Ghost Woman*

Date of Publication: 1992
Subject(s): American West; Indians
Fictional character(s): Soledad, Indian; Henry Harper, Settler; Elizabeth Harper, Spouse; Fray Xavier Santos, Religious (priest)
Time Period(s): 19th century
Locale(s): Santa Barbara, California

Summary: Based on an actual historical event, the novel dramatizes the tragic consequences of an Indian woman, Soledad, who is forcibly introduced into the white community of Santa Barbara, California, during the 19th century. Soledad becomes the catalyst for crime and retribution affecting a Catholic priest, Father Santos, and a married couple, Henry and Elizabeth Harper.

Historical Accuracy: The period is sharply and believably captured.

RODERICK THORP (1936-)

Born in New York City and a graduate of the City College of New York, Thorp received the Theodore Goodman Memorial Short Story Award in 1957, the year he graduated from college. Thorp's novel *The Detective* was an international bestseller and was adapted for a 1968 film starring Frank Sinatra.

`6276` *Jenny and Barnum: A Novel of Love*

Date of Publication: 1981
Subject(s): Theatrical Life; Circus Life
Historical character(s): Phineas T. Barnum, Entertainer, Businessman; Jenny Lind, Singer; Tom Thumb, Entertainer
Time Period(s): 1860s
Locale(s): United States; Vienna, Austria; London, England

Summary: Based on the events surrounding P.T. Barnum's recruiting of Swedish soprano Jenny Lind to join his troupe, the novel dramatizes the affair between the irrepressible American promoter and the timid Lind, who became most unlikely lovers.

Historical Accuracy: The basic facts of the novel are true, but scenes and situations are invented.

`6277` *Westfield*

Date of Publication: 1977
Subject(s): Family Saga
Fictional character(s): Thomas Westfield, Political Figure; Kate Regan, Young Woman; Michael Westfield, Orphan
Time Period(s): 19th century; 20th century (1870s-1970s)
Locale(s): New York, New York

Summary: This generational saga is set in New York beginning in the 1870s and follows the career of Thomas Westfield, who enters politics and rises to wealth and respectability. His mistress, Kate Regan, and his adopted son, Michael, must deal with the ambiguous legacy of Westfield's success. The story follows later generations through the Prohibition Era and the Vietnam War.

Historical Accuracy: The novel's various historical moments and their impact are captured convincingly.

ADAM THORPE (1956-)

Born in Paris and brought up in India, Cameroon, and England, Thorpe attended Oxford University. He is a co-founder and actor with the Equinox Theatre and a teacher of mime in secondary schools in London. He is the author of two volumes of poetry: *Meeting Montaigne* and *Morning in the Baltic*, which won the Whitbread Prize for Poetry in 1989.

`6278` *Ulverton*

Date of Publication: 1992
Subject(s): Civil War—England; Social Chronicle
Fictional character(s): Gabby Cobbold, Farmer
Time Period(s): Multiple Time Periods
Locale(s): Ulverton, England (Wessex Downs)

Summary: Ranging over 300 years of English history, the novel is made up of monologues, diary entries, letters, conversations, and film scripts that create a dense and vivid portrait of the fictional village of Ulverton in the Wessex Downs. The story begins with a soldier in Cromwell's army who returns home to find his wife remarried. It continues with an 18th-century farmer's attempt to introduce scientific methods

while carrying on an affair with his maid, and concludes with a modern TV documentary.

Historical Accuracy: The novel is a tour de force of historical re-creation in a kind of symphony of authentic voices.

HELEN THORPE

`6279` *Elizabeth: Queen & Woman*

Date of Publication: 1971
Subject(s): Elizabethan Period; Royalty—England
Historical character(s): Elizabeth I, Ruler (Queen of England); Robert Dudley, Nobleman (Earl of Leicester); William Cecil, Nobleman (Baron Burghley), Government Official
Time Period(s): 16th century
Locale(s): England

Summary: The story of Elizabeth I's turbulent reign is dramatized in Elizabeth's relationship with Sir Robert Dudley, the Earl of Leicester, reportedly the one true love of Elizabeth's life. She is revealed as a complex individual, expressing characteristics of both her parents, Henry VIII and Anne Boleyn.

Historical Accuracy: The basic outline of the historical elements described are authentic.

FRANK TILSLEY (1904-1957)

English writer Tilsley served as a R.A.F. squadron leader during World War II. He is the author of novels, plays, and newspaper articles. His best known book is *Champion Road*.

`6280` *Mutiny*

Date of Publication: 1958
Subject(s): Sea Story; Military Life—British Navy; Mutiny
Fictional character(s): Captain Crawford, Military Personnel (naval officer); Lieutenant Scott-Paget, Military Personnel (naval officer)
Time Period(s): 1790s (1796)
Locale(s): Portsmouth, England; *Regenerate*, At Sea

Summary: The novel is set during the Napoleonic era and illustrates the conditions in the British navy that produced the mutinies of Spithead and Nore. It describes the conflict between Captain Crawford of the frigate *Regenerate* and the sadistic Lieutenant Scott-Paget, who terrorizes the crew. Events explode when the *Regenerate* captures an enemy frigate carrying a French officer and his Italian mistress.

Historical Accuracy: The characters and the incidents of the story are fictional, but the atmosphere and conditions at sea in the British navy of the period are historically authentic.

FELIX TIMMERMANS (1886-1947)

Timmermans was the author of the fantasy *The Triptych of the Three Kings*.

`6281` *The Perfect Joy of St. Francis*

Date of Publication: 1952

Subject(s): Religious Life; Middle Ages; Biography, Fictionalized
Historical character(s): Francis of Assisi, Religious (monk)
Time Period(s): 12th century; 13th century
Locale(s): Assisi, Italy

Summary: The life and career of St. Francis of Assisi is dramatized in this lyrical and devotional version of the saint's story. Francis' transformation from callow youth to self-effacing monk is shown.

Historical Accuracy: More devotional than historical, the novel shows the author's evident partiality in his portrait of Francis.

GILES TIPPETTE (1934-)

Born in Texas and a graduate of Sam Houston University, Tippette has held a variety of jobs including rodeo contestant, diamond courier, and gold miner in Mexico. He has written for *Time*, *Newsweek*, *Texas Monthly*, *Sports Illustrated*, and *Inside Sports*. Two of his novels, *Austin Davis* and *The Bank Robber*, were made into movies.

6282 *Heaven's Gold*

Date of Publication: 1996
Subject(s): Crime and Criminals; World War I
Fictional character(s): Wilson Young, Outlaw, Gunfighter; Lauren Young, Spouse
Time Period(s): 1910s (1916)
Locale(s): San Antonio, Texas

Summary: Fifty-eight-year-old former outlaw and gunslinger Wilson Young hopes to reverse the rush into the modern world by robbing a shipment of gold bars to the Federal Reserve Bank in San Antonio.

Historical Accuracy: The story is fanciful but filled with believable period and regional elements.

HAROLD TITUS (1888-)

Born in Traverse City, Michigan, Titus was educated at the University of Michigan. He contributed to popular magazines and is the author of *I Conquered* and *The Last Straw*.

6283 *Black Feather*

Date of Publication: 1936
Subject(s): American West
Fictional character(s): Rodney Shaw, Trader (fur)
Time Period(s): 19th century
Locale(s): Mackinac Island, Michigan

Summary: This adventure revolving around John Jacob Astor's fur company during the early years of the 19th century concerns Rodney Shaw who defies Astor's company. He wears a black feather indicating that he can lick any man on Mackinac Island.

Historical Accuracy: The novel provides a historically faithful portrait of the life and people of the Northwest in the early 19th century.

CATHERINE TODD

6284 *Bond of Honour*

Date of Publication: 1982
Subject(s): Norman Conquest; Middle Ages
Historical character(s): William the Conqueror, Nobleman
Time Period(s): 11th century
Locale(s): Normandy, France; England

Summary: This account of the career of William the Conqueror is told through a variety of narrative devices, including letters, diaries, and dialogue. Together the various sources record the long series of battles that climax with William's winning the English crown in 1066.

Historical Accuracy: The method helps create an authentic and believable texture of the age and the personalities.

HELEN TODD (1912-)

An American writer born in St. Louis, Todd's books include *High Places*, *So Free We Seem*, and *The Roots of the Tree*.

6285 *A Man Called Grant*

Date of Publication: 1940
Subject(s): Civil War—U.S.; Biography, Fictionalized
Historical character(s): Ulysses S. Grant, Military Personnel (Union commander), Political Figure
Time Period(s): 19th century
Locale(s): United States

Summary: The complex figure of Ulysses S. Grant is the subject for this fictional biography that follows his career as one of the nation's greatest military leaders and most decried political leaders. The novel invents conversations and explores Grant's thoughts to make him more understandable.

Historical Accuracy: The general outline of facts is accurate, though some simplifications have been done.

6286 *So Free We Seem*

Date of Publication: 1936
Subject(s): Settlement of the American Frontier
Fictional character(s): Ann Wingate, Frontierswoman; Blaize Ormandy, Wanderer
Time Period(s): 19th century
Locale(s): Indiana; Missouri

Summary: In this tale of pioneer life in the Missouri territory, Ann Wingate surprises her family by marrying the shiftless Blaize Ormandy and accompanying him to Missouri. Eventually he deserts her and their family, leaving her alone to run their farm. When he returns 14 years, later tragedy ensues.

Historical Accuracy: This is an authentic look at pioneer life and times.

RAY GRANT TOEPFER (1923-)

Born in Kansas, Toepfer graduated from the University of Wisconsin and the City University of New York. He has worked as a professor of English at Brooklyn College. His books include *The Second Face of Valor, Beat of a Distant Drum,* and *Endplay.*

6287 *The Scarlet Guidon*

Date of Publication: 1958
Subject(s): Civil War—U.S.; Battle of Gettysburg; Military Life
Fictional character(s): Dan Howells, Military Personnel (Confederate soldier)
Time Period(s): 1860s
Locale(s): Virginia; Gettysburg, Pennsylvania

Summary: This Civil War story follows the experiences of Company B of the 43rd Alabama Infantry through campaigns in the Shenandoah Valley, at Gettysburg, Fisher's Hill, and the Battle of Cold Harbor. The story centers on the maturation of young Dan Howell, the sole survivor of the 60-man company of volunteers.

Historical Accuracy: The background details are accurately depicted as is the common soldier's point of view.

6288 *The Second Face of Valor*

Date of Publication: 1966
Subject(s): Civil War—U.S.; Shenandoah Valley Campaign
Fictional character(s): Tom Tanner, Military Personnel (Confederate soldier); Alison West, Young Woman
Time Period(s): 1860s (1864)
Locale(s): Shenandoah Valley, Virginia

Summary: This Civil War story describes the maturation of young Tom Tanner and Alison West. Tanner serves in a Confederate artillery company during the Shenandoah campaign near the end of the war. The novel also depicts the experiences of a group of guerrilla fighters.

Historical Accuracy: The military action conforms to actual events and the operation of actual guerrilla units and the Union cavalry during the period.

HERMAN TOEPPERWEIN (1907-)

6289 *Rebel in Blue*

Date of Publication: 1963
Subject(s): Civil War—U.S.; Immigrants; Espionage
Fictional character(s): Alan Barry, Surveyor; Caroline Ritter, Young Woman
Time Period(s): 1860s (1861-1864)
Locale(s): Fredericksburg, Texas

Summary: This is the story of a group of German settlers in south-central Texas who remain staunchly loyal to the Union during the Civil War. The story concerns surveyor Alan Barry who participates in an undercover operation based in San Antonio.

Historical Accuracy: The background for the book is authentic, and the various events depicted are accurate.

FRANK XAVIER TOLBERT (1912-1984)

An American historian, journalist, and author, Tolbert worked for various newspapers, becoming a columnist for the *Dallas Morning News* in 1947, a position he retained for 30 years. A chili enthusiast, Tolbert's book, *A Bowl of Red*, inspired the first World Chili Cookoff. More than 2,000 cookoffs have been held since this inception in the 1960s. His books include *Bigamy Jones* and *An Informal History of Texas.*

6290 *The Staked Plain*

Date of Publication: 1958
Subject(s): American West; Indians
Historical character(s): Lonnie Nabors, Artisan (gunsmith)
Time Period(s): 1870s
Locale(s): Texas

Summary: Lonnie Nabors joins the Antelope Comanches of the Staked Plains in the Texas frontier of the 1870s. He participates in raids and becomes known as the "Minister of War" for the Comanches.

Historical Accuracy: Although Nabors is a real figure, the actual story is invented. The novel is authentic in detailing the life of the South Plains Indians.

RUBY C. TOLLIVER (1922-)

Born in Texas, Tolliver graduated from business college and has worked as a civil service clerk. She has written a number of Christian-oriented novels for young adults.

6291 *Muddy Banks*

Date of Publication: 1988
Subject(s): Civil War—U.S.; Slavery
Fictional character(s): Boy "Muddy" Banks, Slave (runaway); Bethel Banks, Widow(er)
Time Period(s): 1860s (Civil War period)
Locale(s): Sabine Pass, Texas

Summary: Boy, a young runaway slave, is taken in by the Widow Banks in Texas during the Civil War. Although he dreams of the freedom that will come with a Union victory, when he learns of an impending Union attack that threatens his friends and benefactor, he must resolve a divided loyalty.

Historical Accuracy: The novel is convincing in its period details.

EDWARD TOLOSKO

6292 *Sakuran: A Novel of Medieval Japan*

Date of Publication: 1978
Subject(s): Japanese Empire
Fictional character(s): Jujiro, Royalty (prince)
Time Period(s): 13th century
Locale(s): Japan

Summary: Prince Jujiro, son of the daimyo of Ikoma, seeks vengeance on a bandit leader who conquers Ikoma and makes himself the new daimyo. Jujiro's revenge is complicated when he falls in love with the bandit's daughter and must contend with the invasion of Kublai Khan's Mongol army.

Historical Accuracy: This is a vivid and largely convincing portrait of feudal Japan and the atmosphere of the period.

ALEXEY TOLSTOY (1883-1945)

A distant relative of Leo Tolstoy, Alexey Tolstoy attended the Petersburg Technological Institute. He worked as a military correspondent in World War I and wrote plays as well as novels.

6293 *Peter the Great*

Date of Publication: 1932
Subject(s): Russian Empire; Royalty—Russia
Fictional character(s): Ivan Brodkin, Farmer (serf)
Historical character(s): Peter the Great, Ruler (Czar of Russia); Catherine I, Ruler (Empress of Russia); Charles XII, Ruler (King of Sweden)
Time Period(s): 17th century; 18th century
Locale(s): Russia

Summary: This historical epic chronicles Peter the Great's reign and Russia's transformation from a backward medieval state to one of the great European powers. At the center of the story is the dominating character of Peter, who is driven to create a modern nation.

Historical Accuracy: The novel blends historical events with invented scenes and characters, offering a reliable atmosphere of the period.

6294 *Prince of Outlaws*

Date of Publication: 1927
Subject(s): Russian Empire; Royalty—Russia
Historical character(s): Ivan the Terrible, Ruler (Czar of Russia); Boris Godunov, Nobleman; Prince Serebryany, Royalty
Time Period(s): 16th century
Locale(s): Russia

Summary: During the bloody reign of Russia's Ivan the Terrible, Prince Serebryany opposes the Czar and is forced to head a band of outlaws. The novel provides a vivid depiction of the atrocities of the period.

Historical Accuracy: The period background is carefully and convincingly drawn.

LEO TOLSTOY (1828-1910)

A Russian novelist of noble birth, Tolstoy's fiction is among the greatest of the 19th century. His chief novels are *Anna Karenina*, *The Death of Ivan Ilyitch*, *The Kreutzer Sonata*, *Resurrection*, and *War and Peace*.

6295 *War and Peace*

Date of Publication: 1869
Subject(s): Napoleonic Wars

Fictional character(s): Pierre Bezuhov, Bastard Son, Gentleman; Andrey Bolkonsky, Royalty (prince); Natasha Rostov, Gentlewoman
Historical character(s): Napoleon Bonaparte, Military Personnel, Ruler (Emperor of France); Mikhail Illarionovich Kutuzov, Military Personnel (commander of the Russian army)
Time Period(s): 1800s; 1810s (1805-1813)
Locale(s): St. Petersburg, Russia; Moscow, Russia

Summary: Tolstoy's panorama of Russian life during Napoleon's invasion shows the interconnections of three families—the Bezuhovs, the Rostovs, and the Bolkonskys—particularly Pierre, Natasha, and Andrey. Their loves, domestic dramas, and involvement in the wider world illustrate Tolstoy's thesis that history is made up of the smaller influences of individuals.

Historical Accuracy: *War and Peace* is one of the greatest novels ever written. Tolstoy convincingly shows how everyday life can share the stage with great historical events.

NIKOLAI TOLSTOY (1935-)

English writer Tolstoy is a direct descendent of Leo Tolstoy. Count Nikolai Tolstoy is the author of several distinguished works of nonfiction, including *Victims of Youth*, *The Minister and the Massacres*, and *Stalin's Secret War*. He is one of the world's leading Arthurian scholars.

6296 *The Coming of the King*

Date of Publication: 1989
Subject(s): Dark Ages; Myths and Legends; Arthurian Legends
Fictional character(s): Arthur, Ruler (King of the Britons); Merlin, Sorcerer; Beowulf, Warrior, Chieftain
Time Period(s): 5th century
Locale(s): England

Summary: The story of Celtic Britain is told from the perspective of Merlin, not as a figure of fairy tales, but as a realistic figure of his time. As a child, Merlin must flee from the evil King Custennin. He learns his destiny by descending into the pit of Annufn and witnesses the final legendary battle between Beowulf and the Red Dragon.

Historical Accuracy: The novel is convincing in creating a believable atmosphere of Britain during the Dark Ages.

LEONARD TOURNEY (1942-)

An American author, Tourney is a professor of Elizabethan literature and drama who began writing his series of English Renaissance mysteries as an alternative to his scholarship and teaching.

6297 *The Bartholomew Fair Murders*

Date of Publication: 1986
Subject(s): Mystery; Elizabethan Period; Royalty—England
Fictional character(s): Matthew Stock, Businessman (clothier), Government Official (constable); Joan Stock, Spouse,

Detective—Amateur; Ned Babcock, Animal Trainer (bear trainer)
Historical character(s): Elizabeth I, Ruler (Queen of England); Robert Cecil, Government Official (secretary to Elizabeth I)
Time Period(s): 17th century (1600s)
Locale(s): London, England

Summary: The aging Queen Elizabeth decides to attend the Bartholomew Fair, the greatest festival in England. Also attending are Matthew and Joan Stock, up from Chelmsford. A puppeteer is found dead, and trouble surrounds Matthew's friend Babcock, the trainer of a very dangerous dog-fighting bear. Conspiracy is afoot that endangers the queen.

Historical Accuracy: Tourney's sense of time and place are admirable. The history is not sacrificed for the story or vice versa.

6298 *Familiar Spirits*

Date of Publication: 1984
Subject(s): Mystery; Elizabethan Period; Witchcraft and Sorcery
Fictional character(s): Matthew Stock, Businessman (clothier), Government Official (constable); Joan Stock, Spouse, Detective—Amateur; Ursula Tusser, Witch (suspected), Spirit
Time Period(s): 17th century (1602)
Locale(s): Chelmsford, England (in Essex)

Summary: In the town of Chelmsford in 1602, three people are hanged for witchcraft. One is Ursula Tusser, a young girl who refuses to rest in peace. Her spirit seems to haunt the town, terrifying the townspeople. Matthew Stock, the constable, must try to keep order and to explain the ever-stranger happenings that seem linked to Ursula's spirit.

Historical Accuracy: The novel draws on actual witch hangings which occured in Chelmsford, and convinces in its verisimilitude, even as the action veers toward the supernatural.

6299 *Frobisher's Savage*

Date of Publication: 1994
Subject(s): Mystery; Elizabethan Period; Exploration
Fictional character(s): Matthew Stock, Businessman (clothier), Government Official (constable); Joan Stock, Spouse, Detective—Amateur; Adam Nemo, Eskimo, Servant
Historical character(s): Martin Frobisher, Explorer
Time Period(s): 16th century (1576; 1595)
Locale(s): Greenland; Chelmsford, England (in Essex)

Summary: In 1576 English explorer Martin Frobisher brought an Eskimo from Greenland to England, proof that he had found the Northwest Passage. This factual event forms the basis for the novel. The Eskimo is given the name of Adam Nemo and made a servant of a wealthy landowner. When the landowner and his family are savagely murdered, the townspeople instinctively suspect the outsider. Matthew Stock and his wife are determined to see that justice is served.

Historical Accuracy: The period details are impressive, and the everyday life and customs are vividly presented.

6300 *Knaves Templar*

Date of Publication: 1991
Subject(s): Elizabethan Period; Mystery; Legal Profession
Fictional character(s): Matthew Stock, Businessman (clothier), Government Official (constable); Joan Stock, Spouse, Detective—Amateur; Robert Cecil, Government Official (secretary to Elizabeth I)
Historical character(s): John Donne, Religious, Writer (poet)
Time Period(s): 17th century (1600s)
Locale(s): London, England

Summary: In Elizabethan London someone is killing the law students of Temple Bar and making their murders appear to be suicides. Matthew and Joan Stock are called in to investigate. To do so, much of Elizabethan London must be sifted for clues.

Historical Accuracy: The novel is particularly sharp in its presentation of period detail that never obscures the story, only enhances it.

6301 *Low Treason*

Date of Publication: 1982
Subject(s): Mystery; Elizabethan Period
Fictional character(s): Matthew Stock, Businessman (clothier), Government Official (constable); Joan Stock, Spouse, Detective—Amateur; Thomas Ingraham, Apprentice
Historical character(s): Robert Cecil, Government Official (secretary to Elizabeth I)
Time Period(s): 17th century (1600s)
Locale(s): London, England; Chelmsford, England (in Essex)

Summary: While travelling from London to Chelmsford, Thomas Ingraham is accosted and disappears. His brother seeks the aid of his father-in-law, Matthew Stock, to investigate. Stock knows his way around London and has powerful friends, including the queen's secretary, Sir Robert Cecil. Stock uncovers treachery and conspiracy in the tangled labyrinth of Elizabethan London.

Historical Accuracy: The novel is evocative of the period and filled with persuasive details of the customs and daily life of the Elizabethans.

6302 *Old Saxon Blood*

Date of Publication: 1988
Subject(s): Mystery; Elizabethan Period
Fictional character(s): Matthew Stock, Businessman (clothier), Government Official (constable); Joan Stock, Spouse, Detective—Amateur; Frances Challoner, Gentlewoman
Historical character(s): Elizabeth I, Ruler (Queen of England); Robert Cecil, Government Official (secretary to Elizabeth I)
Time Period(s): 17th century (1601)
Locale(s): London, England; Derbyshire, England

Summary: Matthew and Joan Stock are summoned to London by Queen Elizabeth to investigate the drowning death of Sir John Challoner, the father of Elizabeth's favorite Maid of Honor, Frances. They are instructed to go in disguise to Derbyshire to investigate the death, becoming part of Challoner's large estate. They begin to unravel an elaborate and dangerous puzzle.

Historical Accuracy: The sense of period and the customs of the age make this work as much a glimpse of history as a rousing mystery.

6303 *The Players' Boy Is Dead*

Date of Publication: 1980
Subject(s): Mystery; Elizabethan Period; Theatrical Life
Fictional character(s): Matthew Stock, Businessman (clothier), Government Official (constable); Joan Stock, Spouse, Detective—Amateur; Henry Saltmarch, Gentleman
Time Period(s): 16th century
Locale(s): Chelmsford, England (in Essex)

Summary: The players' boy of a travelling theatrical company that has come to entertain Sir Henry Saltmarsh is found murdered. The death of such an unimportant person is no great matter except to the local constable, Matthew Stock, who sets about investigating the murder. This is the first of Tourney's series of Elizabethan mysteries.

Historical Accuracy: The details of Elizabethan life and times are solidly presented.

6304 *Witness of Bones*

Date of Publication: 1992
Subject(s): Mystery; Elizabethan Period
Fictional character(s): Matthew Stock, Businessman (clothier), Government Official; Joan Stock, Spouse, Detective—Amateur
Historical character(s): Robert Cecil, Government Official (secretary to Elizabeth I)
Time Period(s): 17th century (1600s)
Locale(s): Chelmsford, England (in Essex)

Summary: As Queen Elizabeth declines, the conspiracies to sieze control of her throne mount. Matthew and Joan Stock find themselves caught up in a devious scheme that involves grave-robbing. When a priest is murdered, Matthew is framed for the crime.

Historical Accuracy: The novel, like the series, shows an intimate knowledge of the period.

MICHEL TOURNIER (1924-)

Born in France, Tournier has degrees in both law and philosophy. He has worked as the literary director of one of France's largest publishing houses and as a radio and TV host. *Friday* won the 1967 Novel Prize from the Academie Francaise. Tournier has few rivals among contemporary French novelists in writing books that are both vivid and intellectually provocative.

6305 *Friday*

Date of Publication: 1969
Subject(s): Shipwrecks
Fictional character(s): Robinson Crusoe, Castaway; Friday, Indian
Time Period(s): 18th century
Locale(s): Chile (island off the coast)

Summary: In an alternative version of Daniel Defoe's classic adventure tale, Robinson Crusoe establishes colonial order over his savage paradise only to find his values challenged by the arrival of Friday. Soon Friday gains ascendancy over his master, and Crusoe becomes his servant's pupil in essential things.

Historical Accuracy: The novel is a satire on the modern mania for organization and on Western technology, more a parable than an attempt to render a past age.

SUE TOWNSEND (1946-)

English writer born in Leicestershire, Townsend has worked as a garage attendant, hot dog seller, dress shop clerk, and factory worker. She has been a full-time writer since 1982, best known as the creator of Adrian Mole, whose teenage musings are recorded in two books, a stage play, a TV series, and a magazine column.

6306 *The Queen and I*

Date of Publication: 1992
Subject(s): Royalty—England; Fantasy
Fictional character(s): Jack Barker, Political Figure (British prime minister); Beverley Threadgold, Gentlewoman; Violet Toby, Gentlewoman; Spiggy, Worker (carpet fitter); Harris, Animal (the queen's corgi)
Historical character(s): Elizabeth II, Ruler (Queen of England); Philip, Duke of Edinburgh, Royalty (prince consort of Elizabeth II); Charles, Prince of Wales, Royalty; Diana, Princess of Wales, Royalty; Elizabeth, the Queen Mother, Royalty; Margaret Armstrong-Jones, Royalty (sister of Elizabeth II)
Time Period(s): Indeterminate
Locale(s): London, England

Summary: On the night of the general election, Elizabeth II dreams that a newly elected republican government, headed by socialist prime minister Jack Barker, abolishes the monarchy and sends the now-penniless royal family to live a grim, bureaucratic existence in an appallingly run-down public housing project. The royals and the queen's one remaining corgi must learn to cope with their marginally law-abiding but good-hearted working-class neighbors.

Historical Accuracy: This is a comic, ironic fantasy which has historical significance for readers who may wonder what life would be like in the future for the royals if they were deprived of their pampered existence.

DON TRACY (1905-)

An American author born in Connecticut, Tracy worked as a journalist and rewrite man before becoming a freelance writer in 1941. During World War II, he served as an M.P. and Master Sergeant with the U.S. Army. His first book, *Round Trip*, was published in 1935. It was followed by more than 30 books, including *Death Calling Collect* and *High, Wide, and Ransom*. Tracy also writes under the pseudonym Roger Fuller.

6307 *Carolina Corsair*

Date of Publication: 1955
Subject(s): Pirates; American Colonies
Historical character(s): Edward Teach, Pirate
Time Period(s): 1710s
Locale(s): North Carolina, American Colonies; At Sea

Summary: The pirate career of buccaneer Edward Teach, better known as Blackbeard, is chronicled in this adventure novel. The pirate's lucrative trade preying on shipping along the Carolina and Virginia coast is depicted, climaxing in his downfall.

Historical Accuracy: The details concerning Blackbeard's end are accurately described, though embellished.

6308 *Crimson Is the Eastern Shore*

Date of Publication: 1953
Subject(s): War of 1812
Fictional character(s): Anthony Worth, Plantation Owner, Political Figure; Gracellen Worth, Young Woman; Task Tillman, Landowner
Historical character(s): George Cockburn, Military Personnel (admiral); Francis Scott Key, Writer
Time Period(s): 1810s
Locale(s): Eastern Shore, Maryland

Summary: The story of the War of 1812 on the Eastern Shore of Maryland is told through the experiences of planter and political kingpin Anthony Worth. Worth guards a dual secret about the basis of his fortune and his daughter Gracellen, who falls in love with Worth's neighbor and enemy, Task Tillman. Worth's story is told against a background of actual scenes of the conflict.

Historical Accuracy: Though peopled by actual figures and illustrating actual events, the book is not an authoritative history. The author has taken generous liberties with history in this effort to entertain.

6309 *The Last Boat out of Cincinnati*

Date of Publication: 1970
Subject(s): Civil War—U.S.
Fictional character(s): Hank Champelle, Teenager
Time Period(s): 1860s
Locale(s): Cincinnati, Ohio

Summary: This amusing tale describes the experiences of teenager Hank Champelle from Louisiana who is sent by his father up river to Cincinnati to buy a string of horses on the eve of the Civil War. The novel describes the misadventures of the naive country boy who becomes the victim of a number of individuals intent on taking advantage of his innocence.

Historical Accuracy: The novel provides a vivid and authentic period background.

6310 *On the Midnight Tide*

Date of Publication: 1957
Subject(s): Civil War—U.S.; Sea Story
Fictional character(s): Champ Grayson, Sailor (pilot); Sir Raymond Scott-Hobey, Sea Captain

Time Period(s): 1860s
Locale(s): Wilmington, North Carolina; *Queen's Own*, At Sea; Hamilton, Bermuda

Summary: This Civil War-era adventure tale describes the exploits of Confederate blockade runners involved in the dangerous trade between Bermuda and Wilmington, North Carolina. Champ Grayson is the daring blockade pilot who plays an important part in the Union assault on Fort Fisher.

Historical Accuracy: The story is fanciful but does provide an authentic period backdrop and is based on actual events surrounding the assault on Fort Fisher.

6311 *Roanoke Renegade*

Date of Publication: 1954
Subject(s): Elizabethan Period; American Colonies
Fictional character(s): Dion Harvie, Gentleman
Time Period(s): 16th century (1587)
Locale(s): Roanoke Island, North Carolina, American Colonies

Summary: The fate of the lost colony at Roanoke is explored in this adventure tale that postulates a possible solution to the mystery of what became of the first English settlement in America. Dion Harvie is an Elizabethan gentleman who escapes the Queen's wrath by going to America where he joins the Roanoke settlement. Relations with the Indians prove the colonists' undoing.

Historical Accuracy: The novel's plot is fanciful with a good deal of invention filling in the gaps surrounding the mystery of what really happened to the Roanoke colonists.

6312 *Sign of the Pagan*

Date of Publication: 1955
Subject(s): Roman Empire
Fictional character(s): Marcian, Military Personnel (Roman centurion)
Historical character(s): Attila the Hun, Ruler (King of the Huns); Theodosius II, Ruler (Eastern Roman emperor); Pulcheria, Royalty (princess)
Time Period(s): 5th century
Locale(s): Constantinople, Roman Empire; Europe

Summary: The Roman and Eastern Empires are under attack by Attila and the barbarian hordes in this melodramatic adventure tale. The novel features a large cast of characters, including Emperor Theodosius and his sister Pulcheria, the Roman centurion Marcian, and Attila himself.

Historical Accuracy: The novelist explains that historical chronology has been afforded cavalier treatment at times. This is an understatement given some rather glaring errors.

ARTHUR CHENEY TRAIN (1875-1945)

Boston-born and educated at Harvard University, Train was a lawyer, public official, and writer of popular stories and best-selling novels, including *Tassels on Her Boots*, *On the Trail of the Bad Men*, and *Mr. Tutt's Case Book*.

`6313` *Tassels on Her Boots*

Date of Publication: 1940
Subject(s): Politics
Fictional character(s): Barry Carter, Gentleman; Kathleen O'Carroll, Young Woman
Historical character(s): William Marcy Tweed, Political Figure; James Fisk, Financier; Ward McAllister, Gentleman, Socialite
Time Period(s): 1870s
Locale(s): New York, New York

Summary: Barry Carter makes his way in society and business in a New York dominated by the corruption of Tamany Hall and the Tweed Ring, and the financial manipulations of Jim Fisk. His love for Kathleen O'Carroll is linked with the machinations of Boss Tweed.

Historical Accuracy: Some of the events in the collapse of the Tweed Ring have been telescoped in the interest of clarity, but the essential accuracy of the period is painstakingly attempted.

NIGEL TRANTER (1909-)

Prolific Scottish novelist Tranter was born in Glasgow and attended schools in Edinburgh. He served as a lieutenant in the Royal Artillery of the British army during World War II. His historical program ''Towers of Strength'' has been broadcast on Scottish television, and other programs adapted from his works have been broadcast by the BBC. For his distinguished career, Tranter was awarded the Order of the British Empire.

`6314` *Chain of Destiny*

Date of Publication: 1964
Subject(s): Royalty—Scotland; Biography, Fictionalized; Tudor Period
Historical character(s): James IV, Ruler (King of Scotland); Perkin Warbeck, Imposter (pretender to English throne); Margaret Tudor, Royalty (princess)
Time Period(s): 15th century
Locale(s): Scotland; England

Summary: This biographical novel dramatizes the reign of one of the most popular rulers of Scotland, James IV. His career is described from the murder of his father at Bannockburn in 1488 to his ultimate defeat at the hands of the English on the Field of Flodden.

Historical Accuracy: The novel stays close to the known facts surrounding James IV and his reign.

`6315` *James, by the Grace of God*

Date of Publication: 1985
Subject(s): Royalty—Scotland; Tudor Period
Historical character(s): James V, Ruler (King of Scotland); David Beaton, Government Official (Lord Privy Seal); David Lindsay, Gentleman, Writer (poet); Margaret Tudor, Royalty (queen consort of James IV)
Time Period(s): 16th century
Locale(s): Scotland

Summary: The novel continues the story of the troubled region of Scotland's James V begun in *The Riven Realm* by ambitious conspirators and a covetous King Henry VIII in the south is ready to invade. The story focuses on James' advisors, David Lindsay and David Beaton, friends from school days who find themselves in conflict as they attempt to maintain order in the realm and keep James V on his throne.

Historical Accuracy: The basic outline of the novel's history is accurate and convincingly presented.

`6316` *The Master of Gray Trilogy*

Date of Publication: 1996
Subject(s): Elizabethan Period; Royalty—Scotland; Royalty—England
Historical character(s): Patrick Gray, Nobleman, Adventurer; James VI, Ruler (King of Scotland); Elizabeth I, Ruler (Queen of England); Sir Francis Walsingham, Government Official; Sir Philip Sidney, Writer (poet), Courtier; Mary, Queen of Scots, Ruler
Time Period(s): 16th century
Locale(s): Scotland; England

Summary: The three novels that make up this trilogy tell the story of one of the most remarkable Scottish adventurers of his era, Patrick, Master of Gray, son and heir of the 5th Lord Gray. His story includes efforts to free the imprisoned Mary, Queen of Scots, and conflict in the intrigues of Elizabeth I's court.

Historical Accuracy: The author has taken considerable liberties with the characters and dates. The trilogy represents the author's notion of Patrick Gray as he might have been, not necessarily as history records him.

`6317` *The Riven Realm*

Date of Publication: 1984
Subject(s): Royalty—Scotland; Tudor Period
Historical character(s): David Lindsay, Gentleman; David Beaton, Gentleman; James IV, Ruler (King of Scotland); James Stewart, Royalty (prince); Margaret Tudor, Royalty (queen consort of James IV)
Time Period(s): 16th century
Locale(s): Scotland

Summary: Power politics and intrigue in 16th-century Scotland are featured in this novel that follows the aftermath of the Scottish defeat at Flodden Field in 1513 that leaves the infant King James V on the throne as various forces assemble to seize the spoils. The story involves David Lindsay of the Mount, later to be famous as the author of *The Three Estates*, and David Beaton, who becomes one of the most execrated figures in Scotland's history.

Historical Accuracy: The novel offers a convincing depiction of the era and its complicated political circumstances.

`6318` *Robert the Bruce: The Path of the Hero King*

Date of Publication: 1970
Subject(s): Middle Ages; Independence—Scotland; Battle of Bannockburn

Historical character(s): Robert the Bruce, Ruler (King of Scotland); Elizabeth de Burgh, Royalty (queen consort of Robert I)

Time Period(s): 14th century

Locale(s): Scotland

Summary: In the second volume of the author's trilogy on the career of Scottish hero Robert the Bruce, Robert's kingdom is occupied by the invading English army, but Bruce continues the struggle. He seeks refuge in the Hebrides, where he launches a campaign to reclaim his kingdom. The story climaxes in the Battle of Bannockburn, where Robert defeats the mighty English army.

Historical Accuracy: The historical background for the story is authentic and believable.

6319   *Robert the Bruce: The Price of the King's Peace*

Date of Publication: 1971

Subject(s): Middle Ages; Independence—Scotland

Historical character(s): Robert the Bruce, Ruler (King of Scotland); Elizabeth de Burgh, Royalty (queen consort of Robert I)

Time Period(s): 14th century

Locale(s): Scotland

Summary: The third volume of the author's trilogy on the career of Robert the Bruce depicts the years following the great Scottish victory at Bannockburn. Conflict with the English invaders continues as Bruce struggles to force the English to acknowledge him as the sovereign king of Scotland.

Historical Accuracy: the historical elements are faithfully drawn.

6320   *Robert the Bruce: The Steps to the Empty Throne*

Date of Publication: 1969

Subject(s): Middle Ages; Independence—Scotland

Historical character(s): Robert the Bruce, Ruler (King of Scotland); Edward I, Ruler (King of England); Elizabeth de Burgh, Royalty (queen consort of Robert I); William Wallace, Patriot; Henry de Percy, Nobleman (Lord of Northumberland); John Comyn, Nobleman

Time Period(s): 14th century

Locale(s): Scotland

Summary: This first volume of a trilogy depicts the career of Scottish hero-king Robert the Bruce during the Scottish war of independence. With the death of Alexander III, there are numerous claimants to the Scottish throne, including Robert Bruce, whose hold on power is challenged by the might of Edward I of England. The novel describes Robert's climb to power and the series of defeats that result in an empty throne and the loss of his kingdom.

Historical Accuracy: The novel's historical elements are faithfully depicted.

6321   *A Stake in the Kingdom*

Date of Publication: 1966

Subject(s): Tudor Period; Royalty—Scotland; Royalty—England

Historical character(s): David Beaton, Religious (cardinal), Political Figure; James V, Ruler (King of Scotland); Margaret Tudor, Royalty (consort of James IV); Louis XII, Ruler (King of France); Mary Tudor, Royalty (Queen of France); John Stewart, Nobleman

Time Period(s): 16th century

Locale(s): Scotland; England; France

Summary: Set during the 16th century, the novel describes the rise to power of the ambitious David Beaton who uses the Church for his own ends to become the real ruler of James V's Scotland. The novel provides a look at court intrigue and power politics during the period.

Historical Accuracy: The novel stays close to the actual sources with some manipulation in the interest of the narrative.

6322   *True Thomas*

Date of Publication: 1981

Subject(s): Middle Ages; Royalty—Scotland

Historical character(s): Alexander III, Ruler (King of Scotland); Thomas Learmouth, Writer (poet)

Time Period(s): 13th century

Locale(s): Scotland

Summary: Set in Scotland during the reign of Alexander III, the novel tells the story of Thomas Learmouth, vassal of the Earl of Dunbar, the poet and prophesizer known as Thomas the Rhymer.

Historical Accuracy: Since there are gaps in the historical record concerning Thomas the Rhymer, the author has had to speculate frequently, but his inventions are based on evident knowledge of the period.

6323   *Unicorn Rampant*

Date of Publication: 1984

Subject(s): Jacobean Period; Royalty—England

Historical character(s): James I, Ruler (King of England); John Stewart, Nobleman (Duke of Lennox); George Villiers, Nobleman (1st Duke of Buckingham); Anne of Denmark, Royalty (queen consort of James I); Charles, Royalty (Prince of Wales); Sir Francis Bacon, Lawyer, Political Figure (lord chancellor)

Time Period(s): 17th century (1617)

Locale(s): Scotland; England

Summary: Life in the court world of James I is dramatized. In 1617 James returns to Scotland, his only return to his native country after succeeding Elizabeth on the throne. The visit does not live up to expectations. The experience is reflected by the young courtier John Stewart, who returns with the king to London and the intrigues of the court.

Historical Accuracy: The essential elements of the novel's historical events are truthful.

GEOFFREY TREASE (1909-)

An English writer born in Nottingham, Trease attended Queen's College, Oxford. He worked as a journalist and social worker before becoming a full-time writer in 1933. Best known for his children's books, Trease was one of the first 20th-century children's writers to approach the historical adventure genre seriously and establish accurate backgrounds for his stories. His adult novels include *Such Divinity*, *Only Natural*, and *So Wild the Heart*.

6324 *Snared Nightingale*

Date of Publication: 1958
Subject(s): Renaissance; Inheritance—Disputed
Fictional character(s): Niccolo Sannazaro, Heir
Time Period(s): 16th century
Locale(s): Italy; England

Summary: This amusing tale of cultural differences describes what happens when a young Englishman raised in Italy inherits an English duchy. Niccolo Sannazaro must make the transition to become an English lord.

Historical Accuracy: The novel features a believable period background that heightens the conflict between English and Italian sensibilities.

HENRY TREECE (1912-1966)

Born in England and educated at the universities of Birmingham, Liverpool, and Santander (Spain), Treece has worked as a broadcaster on the B.B.C. and as the writer of TV thrillers and history programs for schools. During World War II, he served with the Royal Air Force and as an intelligence officer. Treece has written both adult and juvenile historical novels and nonfiction, mysteries, radio plays and features, and several volumes of poetry. He has been praised for his formidable knowledge of history, anthropology, and archaeology.

6325 *Amber Princess*

Date of Publication: 1963
Subject(s): Myths and Legends; Ancient Greece.
Fictional character(s): Electra, Royalty (princess); Agamemnon, Ruler (King of Mycenae); Clytemnestra, Royalty (queen consort of Agamemnon); Orestes, Royalty (prince)
Time Period(s): Indeterminate Past
Locale(s): Mycenae, Greece

Summary: The novel retells the tragic story of the House of Atreus; of Clytemenestra's murder of her husband, Agamemnon, of her daughter and son, Electra and Orestes' revenge. The author attempts to paint a realistic portrait of the Royal House of Mycenae, solidly anchored in anthropological and archaeological research.

Historical Accuracy: This is a convincing, realistic picture of the legendary story.

6326 *The Dark Island*

Date of Publication: 1952
Subject(s): Roman Empire; Celtic Britain

Historical character(s): Caradoc, Royalty (prince); Cunobelin, Ruler (King of the Britons)
Time Period(s): 1st century (30-56)
Locale(s): England; Gaul

Summary: The story of the Roman invasion and defeat of the Celts is dramatized in the experiences of two young princes, Gwyndoc and Caradoc, who valiantly resist the Roman occupation. The cultural clash between the Celts and Romans is vividly illustrated.

Historical Accuracy: The basic historical outline of the story is accurate, but individual scenes are imaginary.

6327 *The Eagle King*

Date of Publication: 1994
Subject(s): Myths and Legends; Ancient Greece
Fictional character(s): Oedipus, Ruler (King of Thebes); Antigone, Royalty (princess)
Time Period(s): Indeterminate Past
Locale(s): Thebes, Greece; Corinth, Greece

Summary: The novel retells the famous story of Oedipus with an emphasis on historical realism over mythical significance. Oedipus tells his own story of his origin as a shepherd boy who is driven to be a hero and a king. He is introduced to the world of cattle-kings and city ways in his search for self-fulfillment and self-esteem.

Historical Accuracy: The novel is solidly placed in an archaeological and anthropological context.

6328 *The Golden Strangers*

Date of Publication: 1956
Subject(s): Prehistory; Tribal Life—Prehistoric
Fictional character(s): Garroch, Prehistoric Human, Chieftain; Isca, Prehistoric Human, Royalty (princess)
Time Period(s): 20th century B.C.
Locale(s): England

Summary: Prehistoric England of 4,000 years ago is depicted in the struggle of Garroch, the young chieftain of the Hill People, who must contend with the invading Golden Strangers. The flint of the Hill people are no match weapons of the invaders, and the sun-worshipping Golden Strangers' victory climaxes in the building of Stonehenge.

Historical Accuracy: The novel is a poetic and imaginative interpretation of prehistoric life supported by archaeological findings.

6329 *The Great Captains*

Date of Publication: 1956
Subject(s): Dark Ages; Myths and Legends; Arthurian Legends
Fictional character(s): Ambrosius, Nobleman (Count of Britain); Uther Pendragon, Chieftain (Celtic); Artos the Bear, Warrior (also known as Arthur)
Time Period(s): 6th century
Locale(s): England

Summary: The novel attempts to present a plausible account of King Arthur as a warrior leader in the fight against the Angles and the Saxons after the departure of the Romans. Ambrosius, the Count of Britain, is determined to form a confederation with Uther Pendragon in the west to preserve the remnants of Roman Britain. Pendragon's son is Artos the Bear, so called for his shaggy appearance and great strength. Artos' rise to power is shown with only slight glimpses of the Arthur of the legend.

Historical Accuracy: Though based on archaeological and anthropological research, this is a fictional account of a plausible orgin for the historical Arthur.

6330 *The Green Man*

Date of Publication: 1966
Subject(s): Dark Ages; Myths and Legends; Arthurian Legends
Fictional character(s): Amleth, Royalty (prince); Beowulf, Warrior (King of the Geats), Chieftain; Arthur, Ruler (King of the Britons)
Time Period(s): 6th century
Locale(s): Jutland, Denmark; England

Summary: The violent and savage world of 6th-century northern Europe is depicted in the adventures of Prince Amleth that take him from the court of King Beowolf in Jutland to that of Arthur in Britain. He is loved by three queens whose violent ends, so different from the popular conception of medieval love, are in keeping with a realistic view of the 6th century.

Historical Accuracy: The novel is an amalgam of historical, legendary, and realistic elements, convincing in its attempt to base the imaginary in a believable context.

6331 *Jason*

Date of Publication: 1961
Subject(s): Ancient Greece; Myths and Legends
Fictional character(s): Jason, Adventurer; Hypsipyle, Ruler (queen); Medea, Sorceress
Time Period(s): Indeterminate Past
Locale(s): Colchis, Greece; Lemnos, Greece; Corinth, Greece

Summary: The novel tells the story of Jason and his pursuit of the Golden Fleece in realistic terms. The story follows Jason from boyhood through his training as a warrior, his gold-seeking mission to Colchis, his meeting with the love of his life, Queen Hypsipyle at Lemnos, and his marriage to the witch-priestess Medea. After attaining the Golden Fleece, Jason returns to Corinth, where the decline of his fortunes follows.

Historical Accuracy: Despite the mythical nature of the story, Treece is convincing in establishing a believable historical basis.

6332 *Red Queen, White Queen*

Date of Publication: 1958
Subject(s): Roman Empire
Fictional character(s): Gemellus, Military Personnel (Roman soldier); Duatha, Warrior
Historical character(s): Boadicea, Ruler (queen of ancient Britain)
Time Period(s): 1st century

Locale(s): England

Summary: The background of this historical adventure novel is the campaign waged by Queen Boadicea against the Roman occupiers of ancient Britain. The fictional story centers on Gemellus, a Roman soldier, and his Celtic half-brother, Duatha, who are dispatched to kill Boadicea.

Historical Accuracy: The novel is believable in its re-creation of the battle scenes and the period customs.

ROSE TREMAIN (1943-)

English author of novels, short stories, and television and radio plays, Tremain teaches creative writing at the University of East Anglia. She has worked as an elementary school teacher of French and history in London and as an editor before becoming a full-time writer. In 1989 she won the Sunday Express Book of the Year Award and the Angel Literary Prize for *Restoration*.

6333 *Restoration: A Novel of Seventeenth-Century England*

Date of Publication: 1990
Subject(s): Restoration Period; Royalty—England; Medical Profession
Fictional character(s): Robert Merivel, Doctor; Celia Clemence, Spouse (of Merivel)
Historical character(s): Charles II, Ruler (King of England)
Time Period(s): 17th century (1660s)
Locale(s): England

Summary: Set in the court world of Charles II, the novel describes the career of Robert Merivel, who becomes the king's fool and doctor to the royal dogs. He agrees to a marriage of convenience to Celia Clemence, one of the king's mistresses. When Merivel falls in love with his wife, his punishment is banishment from the king's favors. He goes to work treating the insane in Bedlam while he attempts to cure himself of his obsessional love.

Historical Accuracy: The novel is a remarkable evocation of the period and the atmosphere of Charles II's court.

PETER TREMAYNE
(PSEUD. OF PETER BERRESFORD ELLIS, 1943-)

Born in Coventry, England, Ellis studied at Brighton College and has worked as a journalist and editor. A full-time writer since 1975, Ellis is the author of numerous novels of adventure, horror, and fantasy under a variety of pseudonyms. His books include *A Voice from the Infinite: The Life of Sir Henry Rider Haggard* and *The Hound of Frankenstein*. Ellis has also contributed articles on the problems of national minorities to journals in many countries.

6334 *Absolution by Murder*

Date of Publication: 1994
Subject(s): Mystery; Dark Ages; Religious Conflict

Fictional character(s): Sister Fidelma, Religious (nun); Brother Eadulf, Religious (monk); Oswy, Ruler (King of Northumberland)
Time Period(s): 7th century (664)
Locale(s): Whitby, England

Summary: In the seventh century at a synod convened by King Oswy of Northumberland to determine whether the Roman or Celtic form of Christianity should prevail, a leading spokesperson for the Celtic church is found murdered. Oswy turns to Sister Fidelma, a legal advocate as well as a nun, and Brother Eadulf to find the killer and prevent a religious crisis. Soon more murders are discovered, as well as a plot against the king.

Historical Accuracy: The period elements are convincingly detailed.

`6335` *The Revenge of Dracula*

Date of Publication: 1978
Subject(s): Victorian Period; Vampires
Fictional character(s): Upton Welsford, Government Official; Dracula, Vampire; Clara Clarke, Young Woman
Time Period(s): 1860s
Locale(s): London, England

Summary: Thirty-five years before the events of Bram Stoker's original Dracula story, an official of the British Foreign Office recounts his confrontation with the vampire and the link with an ancient Egyptian religious cult of blood sacrifice. Upton Welsford, in a memoir written from an asylum, records the series of horrifying encounters that leads him to Dracula himself.

Historical Accuracy: The novel is convincing in its atmosphere of Victorian horror.

EVE TREVASKIS

`6336` *The Lion of England*

Date of Publication: 1975
Subject(s): Middle Ages; Royalty—England
Historical character(s): Edward I, Ruler (King of England); Simon de Montfort, Nobleman, Political Figure
Time Period(s): 13th century (1257-1265)
Locale(s): England

Summary: This tale concerns the wild and arrogant youth of English King Edward I. Simon de Montfort's sons are determined to help their father teach Edward a lesson that will serve him well on the throne.

Historical Accuracy: The author states that all the incidents in the story are based on reports written by contemporary chroniclers or storymakers.

ROBERT TREVELYAN
(PSEUD. OF ROBERT FORREST-WEBB, 1929-)

English author Forrest-Webb was born in Nottingham. He worked as a journalist and editor and served as the chairman of Hemarvine Productions, a film company. Forrest-Webb has raced motorcycles in international competition and was

a British canoe champion. His sculptures have been exhibited in a major London gallery.

`6337` *Pendragon: Late of Prince Albert's Own*

Date of Publication: 1975
Subject(s): Victorian Period; Espionage; Crimean War
Fictional character(s): John Hawkdale Pendragon, Military Personnel (British officer), Spy
Historical character(s): James Thomas Brudenell, Military Personnel (general); Sidney Herbert, Government Official (war minister)
Time Period(s): 1850s
Locale(s): London, England; Crimea, Russia

Summary: The novel introduces John Hawkdale Pendragon, a survivor of the charge of the Light Brigade who agrees to become a spy in Victorian London. He is charged with solving the mysterious murder of a British spycatcher. Pendragon's investigation uncovers a complex conspiracy involving opium, explosives, and a threat to the British Empire itself.

Historical Accuracy: The novel is full of convincing atmospherics that create a believable period background.

`6338` *Pendragon. . .The Montenegran Plot*

Date of Publication: 1977
Subject(s): Victorian Period; Espionage
Fictional character(s): John Hawkdale Pendragon, Military Personnel (captain), Spy; Janez Krakar, Revolutionary (anarchist)
Time Period(s): 1850s
Locale(s): London, England

Summary: The visit to Victorian London of the King of Montenegro sets in motion a complex conspiracy. Also in London is the king's bastard half-brother, anarchist Janez Krakar, who is plotting assassination and more. Queen's agent Captain John Hawkdale Pendragon must stop him, and the ensuing adventures include a naval battle on the Thames and a full-scale cavalry battle in St. James Park.

Historical Accuracy: The novel goes beyond the range of the realistic, but the emphasis here is on action and adventure rather than a careful depiction of the period.

ELIZABETH BORTON DE TREVINO
(1904-)

Born in California, Trevino graduated from Stanford University and studied violin at the Boston Conservatory of Music. She later worked as a journalist, a publicist for the Mexico City Tourist Department, and First Violinist in the Vivaldi Orchestra. An author of books for adults and children, her best-known juvenile book is *I, Juan de Pareja*, which won the Newbery Medal in 1966. Her adult novels include *The Greek of Toledo: A Romantic Narrative about El Greco* and *Among the Innocent*.

6339 *Among the Innocent*

Date of Publication: 1981
Subject(s): Inquisition; Spanish Colonies; Religious Conflict
Fictional character(s): Guidmar, Young Woman; Juan Palomar, Adventurer; Gonzalo, Young Man
Time Period(s): 16th century (1585)
Locale(s): Spain; Mexico

Summary: The novel dramatizes the Spanish Inquisition in New Spain during the 16th century. Guidmar leaves her convent school for a reunion with her brother and father in Mexico. There she is caught up in the terror of the Inquisition which threatens Christians and Jews with the tortures of the auto-da-fe.

Historical Accuracy: The characters are fictional, but the atmosphere is based on history.

6340 *The House on Bitterness Street*

Date of Publication: 1970
Subject(s): Mexican Revolution
Fictional character(s): Marisa Estrada Brook, Young Woman
Time Period(s): 1910s (1910)
Locale(s): Mexico City, Mexico

Summary: Set during the tumultuous events of the Mexican Revolution, the novel chronicles Marisa Estrada Brook's experiences. She is a child of the aristocracy who becomes a camp follower in the guerilla war before forging a new sense of identity and faith in the future of her country.

Historical Accuracy: The novel does not pretend to be history, rather a picture of the kind of life lived by many women during the Mexican Revolution.

ELLESTON TREVOR (1920-)

English writer Trevor was an apprentice racing car driver for two years prior to World War II. During the war, he served in the Royal Air Force, and he began writing in off-duty hours in various Spitfire hangers, producing a novel every two weeks under a dozen pseudonyms. Trevor has written for the stage, and two of his novels, *Flight of the Phoenix* and *The Quiller Memorandum*, were made into popular films.

6341 *Bury Him Among Kings*

Date of Publication: 1970
Subject(s): World War I
Fictional character(s): Aubrey Talbot, Gentleman; Victor Talbot, Military Personnel (officer)
Time Period(s): 1910s (1914-1918)
Locale(s): England; France

Summary: The homefront and battlefront of World War I are dramatized over the course of the war from its outbreak in 1914 to the armistice in 1918. The war begins in confidence and patriotism, but the terrible reality of modern mechanized warfare soon produces a loss of innocence. The story centers on the experiences of the Talbots, who reflect the cost of the conflict on their generation.

Historical Accuracy: The novel captures the era with conviction.

MERIOL TREVOR (1919-)

A British novelist, poet, and biographer, Trevor was born in London and received her B.A. from St. Hugh's College, Oxford, in 1942. After World War II, she worked as a relief worker for the United Nations Relief and Rehabilitation Administration in Italy. Her first novel, *The Last of Britain*, was published in 1956. Trevor was awarded the James Tait Black Memorial Prize for biography in 1963.

6342 *The Fortunate Marriage*

Date of Publication: 1976
Subject(s): Regency Romance; Family Saga
Fictional character(s): Louisa Pierce, Gentlewoman; Sir Rowland Dynham, Gentleman; Hilary Tollington, Gentleman
Time Period(s): 19th century (Regency period)
Locale(s): London, England; Cornwall, England

Summary: In this Regency romance, Louisa Pierce is invited to join the household of her cousin Caroline, the wife of Sir Rowland Dynham. Their marriage is marred by temper and scandal, and when Caroline accidentally dies, Louisa must decide about Dynham's character while extricating herself from romantic complications.

Historical Accuracy: The story is set in a believable period context.

6343 *Last of Britain*

Date of Publication: 1956
Subject(s): Dark Ages
Fictional character(s): Lucius Candidianus, Nobleman
Time Period(s): 6th century (576)
Locale(s): Bath, England

Summary: The author imagines the world of 6th-century Britain as the last vestiges of Roman civilization face Saxon encroachment. Lucius Candidianus is called back to Bath after the death of his father to try to govern justly against enormous odds.

Historical Accuracy: The novel's story is speculative as to the way of life in the 6th century.

6344 *Shadows and Images*

Date of Publication: 1962
Subject(s): Religious Life; Victorian Period
Fictional character(s): Clemency Burnet, Gentlewoman; Augustine Firle, Gentleman
Historical character(s): John Henry Newman, Religious (cardinal), Scholar
Time Period(s): 19th century
Locale(s): England

Summary: Clemency Burnet, the daughter of an Anglican clergyman, becomes engaged to the Roman Catholic Augustine Firle. The scandal this creates serves as a vehicle to dramatize John Henry Newman's highly public conversion to the Roman Church and the controversy inspired by the Oxford High Church Movement.

Historical Accuracy: Biography and fiction are intermingled here. The details of Newman's conversion experience are based on Newman's own letters and autobiographical writings.

6345 *The Wanton Fires*

Date of Publication: 1979
Subject(s): Regency Romance; Napoleonic Wars; Family Saga
Fictional character(s): Georgiana Allison, Young Woman; Sir Miles Dynham, Gentleman; Lord Adrian Caynnes, Nobleman
Time Period(s): 1810s (1814-1815)
Locale(s): London, England; Devon, England

Summary: The novel continues the story of the Dynham family begun in *The Fortunate Marriage.* The unexpected marriage of Sir Miles Dynham to a North Devon trademan's daughter, Georgiana Allison, encounters complications, especially when she becomes enamored of Miles' cousin, Lord Caynnes.

Historical Accuracy: The drama makes good use of the period background, creating a believable portrait of the age.

ANTHONY TROLLOPE (1815-1882)

English novelist Anthony Trollope is often credited with having written more good novels than any other Victorian writer. He wrote more than 40 books while holding various responsible positions with the English postal service (Trollope help design the familiar red postal box). His major works include his series of Barsetshire novels about provincial and ecclesiastical life and the Palliser novels dealing with urban life and politics. Henry James claimed that Trollope's greatness stemmed from his complete appreciation of the usual. This allowed Trollope to produce a remarkable portrait of Victorian life and customs in novels distinguished by their sympathy and psychological perception.

6346 *La Vendee*

Date of Publication: 1850
Subject(s): French Revolution
Fictional character(s): Henri Larochejaquelin, Leader (Vendean); Marie de Lescure, Young Woman
Historical character(s): Maximilien Francois de Robespierre, Revolutionary, Political Figure
Time Period(s): 1790s (1793)
Locale(s): France

Summary: Trollope's only historical novel is set during the Vendean counter revolution of 1793 and concerns the fortunes of the Larochejaquelin family. The plot centers on the romantic complication between young Henri Larochejaquelin, the commander in chief of the Vendean forces and his cousin Marie. Robespierre brutally represses the revolt.

Historical Accuracy: Trollope observes the basic outline of historical events, though the story is mainly fanciful.

JOANNA TROLLOPE (1943-)

English novelist Trollope attended Oxford University, worked at the Foreign Office, and taught English at a German school. Trollope won the 1979 Historical Novel of the Year Award for *Parson Harding's Daughter.*

6347 *Eliza Stanhope*

Date of Publication: 1979
Subject(s): Napoleonic Wars; Regency Period; Battle of Waterloo
Fictional character(s): Francis Beaumont, Military Personnel; Pelham Howell, Military Personnel; Eliza Stanhope, Gentlewoman
Time Period(s): 1810s (1814-1815)
Locale(s): Hampshire, England; London, England; Waterloo, Belgium

Summary: Love and war during the Regency period are dramatized in this novel set in rural England, London society, and the battlefield of Waterloo. Eliza Stanhope meets Francis Beaumont and fellow officer Pelham Howell, recently returned from the Peninsular Campaign. A love triangle forms, to be resolved on the field of Waterloo.

Historical Accuracy: The period elements in the story are believably presented.

6348 *Leaves From the Valley*

Date of Publication: 1980
Subject(s): Victorian Period; Crimean War
Fictional character(s): Edgar Drummond, Military Personnel (army captain); Blanche Drummond, Gentlewoman; Sarah Drummond, Gentlewoman
Time Period(s): 1840s; 1850s (1842-1855)
Locale(s): Crimea, Russia; England

Summary: Set during the Crimean War, the novel describes the experiences of Captain Edgar Drummond, who serves his first commission in the Crimea, bringing his two sisters, Blanche and Sarah, with him. The war has profound effects on all three, yet only Sarah finds the courage to protest the horrors she discovers.

Historical Accuracy: The details of the war are effectively and believably presented.

6349 *Mistaken Virtues*

Date of Publication: 1979
Subject(s): Inheritance—Disputed; English Colonies; British Raj
Fictional character(s): Caroline Harding, Young Woman; Johnnie Gates, Gentleman
Time Period(s): 1770s
Locale(s): England; Calcutta, India

Summary: Set in the 1770s in England and India, the novel describes the experiences of Caroline Hodge, a parson's daughter, who in order to preserve an inheritance sails to India to become the bride of Johnnie Gates, her former admirer. Caroline must negotiate unfamiliar Indian society and domestic difficulty.

Historical Accuracy: The novel captures period India and its cutoms effectively.

6350 *The Steps of the Sun*
Date of Publication: 1983
Subject(s): Boer War; Victorian Period
Fictional character(s): Matthew Paget, Student—College; Hendon Bashford, Student—College; Frances Paget, Young Woman
Time Period(s): 1890s
Locale(s): Oxford, England; South Africa

Summary: The novel shifts from the world of Oxford to the Boer War in South Africa. Matthew Paget's conflict with Hendon Bashford, an expatriate social climber from South Africa, begins in Oxford and continues on the battlefield.

Historical Accuracy: The period elements are convincing.

6351 *The Taverners' Place*
Date of Publication: 1986
Subject(s): Family Saga
Fictional character(s): Tom Taverner, Heir, Landowner; Catherine Taverner, Gentlewoman
Time Period(s): 19th century; 20th century (1870-1938)
Locale(s): England; Crete, Greece; Africa (east)

Summary: This family saga traces three generations of the Taverner family from 1870 to the outbreak of the Second World War. Though the novel is centered on the family estate of Buscombe, the action ranges to Crete and East Africa and shows the influences of change in the 20th century on traditional values.

Historical Accuracy: The novel creates a believable historical context for the various eras and locales portrayed.

WILLIAM R. TROTTER (1943-)

A native of Charlotte, North Carolina, Trotter attended Davidson College and went on to work as a bookseller, buyer, editor, and writer with a special interest in music. He is the author of such nonfiction works as *Civil War in North Carolina*, *A Frozen Hell: The Story of the Russo-Finnish War of 1939-1940*, and *Life Begins at Forte: The Conductor as Musical Hobo*.

6352 *Winter Fire*
Date of Publication: 1993
Subject(s): World War II; Musical Life
Fictional character(s): Erich Ziegler, Military Personnel (German soldier), Conductor
Historical character(s): Jean Sibelius, Composer
Time Period(s): 1940s
Locale(s): Finland

Summary: Erich Ziegler is a gifted young conductor drafted into the German army during World War II who is assigned as a liaison officer to the Finnish forces under attack by the Soviets. He meets the Finnish composer, Jean Sibelius, and is faced with the mystery of Sibelius' refusal to present his long-awaited Eighth Symphony.

Historical Accuracy: The novel mixes the imagined and the factual in this graphic portrait of the era and the composer.

HENRI TROYAT (1911-)

Russian-born writer Troyat left Russia for France during the 1917 Revolution. A member of the Academie Francaise, Troyat is the author of biographies of Catherine the Great, Gogol, and Alexander I.

6353 *The Brotherhood of the Red Poppy*
Date of Publication: 1961
Subject(s): Napoleonic Wars
Fictional character(s): Nikolai Ozeroff, Military Personnel (lieutenant); Sophie de Champlittle, Widow(er)
Time Period(s): 1810s (1814-1815)
Locale(s): Russia; Paris, France

Summary: Set during the period of the fall of Paris to the Allied Armies in 1814, the novel tells the romantic story of a lieutenant in Czar Alexander's army who marries a French widow, Sophie de Champlittle. She is a member of an underground political organization called "The Brotherhood of the Red Poppy" opposed to both Napoleon and the restoration of the Bourbons.

Historical Accuracy: The novel features a fully realized and believable period background.

HOWARD WILLIAM TROYER (1901-)

An American educatior and writer, Troyer is the author of *Ned Ward of Grub Street: A Story of Sub-Literary London in the Eighteenth Century*.

6354 *The Salt and the Savor*
Date of Publication: 1950
Subject(s): Settlement of the American Frontier; Rural Life—U.S.
Fictional character(s): Perry Harman, Settler
Time Period(s): 19th century
Locale(s): Indiana

Summary: This chronicle of pioneer life in Indiana in the years preceding the Civil War is based on the reminiscences of Perry Harman who serves as the novel's main character. His experiences capture the daily life and customs of the early settlers and the development of the Grange movement.

Historical Accuracy: Although, as the author claims, every incident described has historical authenticity, some liberties have been taken in some details of the narrative.

THOMAS TRYON (1926-1991)

American actor and bestselling author Tryon was born in Hartford, Connecticut, and graduated from Yale University. Tryon was introduced to the theater after initially preparing for an art career and went to Hollywood in the mid-1950s. After a career as an actor on stage, TV, and in film (climaxed by his award-winning performance in *The Cardinal*), Tryon retired from acting to concentrate on writing. His first novel, *The Other*, was a bestseller.

6355 *In the Fire of Spring*

Date of Publication: 1992
Subject(s): Family Saga; Slavery
Fictional character(s): Georgiana Ross, Teacher; Sinjin Grimes, Sea Captain; Aurora Sheffield, Gentlewoman
Time Period(s): 1840s
Locale(s): Pequot Landing, Connecticut

Summary: In the second novel of the author's Kingdom Come sequence, the story of the feuding Talcotts and Grimeses is continued, shaped by the struggle over slavery that divides the Connecticut town of Pequot Landing in the 1840s. The arrival of an escaped slave provides the catalyst for old enmities.

Historical Accuracy: The novel offers authentic period elements.

6356 *The Wings of the Morning*

Date of Publication: 1990
Subject(s): Family Saga
Fictional character(s): Aurora Talcott, Young Woman; Sinjin Grimes, Sea Captain; Georgiana Ross, Servant
Time Period(s): 1820s
Locale(s): Pequot Landing, Connecticut; England; Macao

Summary: The first in a sequence of novels called Kingdom Come depicts two rival New England clans, the Talcotts and the Grimeses, during the 19th century. Aurora Talcott falls in love with Sinjin Grimes, and they are violently separated by their feuding elders. She is sent to England and he to Portuguese Macao and the China trade.

Historical Accuracy: The novel is convincing in its historical background and period details.

KUNIO TSUJI (1925-)

Tsuji was born in Tokyo and after studying French literature at Tokyo University studied at the Sorbonne. He has taught at several universities in Japan. His works of fiction have received numerous prizes. *The Signore* is his first novel to appear in English.

6357 *The Signore: Shogun of the Warring States*

Date of Publication: 1968
Subject(s): Japanese Empire; East/West Relations
Historical character(s): Oda Nobunaga, Nobleman
Time Period(s): 16th century
Locale(s): Japan

Summary: The struggle to unify 16th-century Japan is detailed from the perspective of a group of Portuguese missionaries. At the center of the story is the energetic young Lord Oda Nobunaga, engaged in a ruthless pursuit of supreme power.

Historical Accuracy: The novel is authentic in its depiction of feudal Japan.

NICCOLO TUCCI (1908-)

Born in Lugano, Switzerland, Tucci entered Mussolini's press and propaganda ministry, where he was reprimanded for inviting German Jews to air their political views.

6358 *Before My Time*

Date of Publication: 1962
Subject(s): Family Saga
Fictional character(s): Gross Mama Chen, Gentlewoman; Doctor, Doctor (narrator's father); Mary, Spouse (narrator's mother)
Time Period(s): 19th century; 20th century (1890-1908)
Locale(s): Rome, Italy; Paris, France; Berlin, Germany

Summary: This is a novel-memoir, both a fictional work and an account of Tucci's family history, detailing family intrigues and entanglements among the Russian wealthy class at the turn of the century. The story is dominated by the unidentified narrator's Russian grandmother, whose strength is drained by deceits and betrayals around her.

Historical Accuracy: Tucci's characters are carefully and convincingly imagined.

WILSON TUCKER (1914-)

Born in Illinois, Tucker is an author of mystery novels and science fiction and has won a Hugo Award for his work. He has been a contributor of short stories to magazines, sometimes under the pseudonym Bob Tucker, and was the editor and publisher of the *Science Fiction Newsletter*. His novels include *The Chinese Doll*, *Red Herring*, *Last Stop*, and *Ice and Iron*.

6359 *The Lincoln Hunters*

Date of Publication: 1956
Subject(s): Time Travel
Fictional character(s): Benjamin Steward, Time Traveller
Historical character(s): Abraham Lincoln, Political Figure
Time Period(s): 26th century (2578); 1850s (1856)
Locale(s): Bloomington, Illinois

Summary: In the 26th century, Benjamin Steward's job is to travel back in time and get historical information for clients. He is sent to Bloomington, Illinois, to record a speech by Abraham Lincoln in 1856, but an error on the part of the engineers who run the time machine puts his life in danger.

Historical Accuracy: The novel offers a believable portrait of both eras.

BEATRICE TUNSTALL

6360 *The Long Day Closes*

Date of Publication: 1934
Subject(s): Jacobite Rebellion

Fictional character(s): Giles Starmont, Gentleman; Christopher Church, Servant
Historical character(s): Dick Turpin, Highwayman; Charles Edward Stuart, Royalty
Time Period(s): 1740s (1745)
Locale(s): Chester, England

Summary: This tale of smuggling and the Jacobite conspiracy is set in the English Midlands and concerns the Starmont family, devoted Jacobites who await Bonnie Prince Charlie's arrival. Their story is narrated by the family's loyal retainer, Christopher Church, and features an appearance by notorious highwayman Dick Turpin.

Historical Accuracy: The novel is a romantic mixture of actual historical elements and fancy, with the later predominating.

H.C. TURK

Turk is an author of science fiction novels.

6361   *Black Body*

Date of Publication: 1989
Subject(s): Witchcraft and Sorcery
Fictional character(s): Alba, Witch, Ward; Lady Amanda Rathel, Noblewoman; Eric Denton, Gentleman
Time Period(s): 18th century
Locale(s): Isle of Man, England; London, England

Summary: The novel offers the memoirs of a white witch, Alba, who becomes the ward of Lady Rathel. Alba is brought to London in order to fall in love with Eric Denton as an act of revenge, since sexual contact between witches and humans can be fatal to the male. Alba comes to love Eric, though the price of their love is high.

Historical Accuracy: The novel mixes its fantasy/horror elements with a believable period backdrop.

AGNES SLIGH TURNBULL (1888-1982)

Born in Pennsylvania, Turnbull spent 12 years writing short stories, then began her career as a novelist with the epic work *The Rolling Years*. She followed that novel with others about the inhabitants of rural Pennsylvania: *Remember the Day*, *The Day Must Dawn*, and *The Bishop's Mantle*. All were popular successes due to her nostalgic look at life during the turn of the century. Espousing old-fashioned virtues and optimism, Turnball's novels are regarded by some as anachronistic. Her works have, however, been read widely and have appeared in foreign translations.

6362   *The Day Must Dawn*

Date of Publication: 1942
Subject(s): American Revolution; Indians
Fictional character(s): Sam Murray, Settler; Martha Murray, Spouse; Hugh McConnell, Young Man; Violet Murray, Young Woman
Time Period(s): 1770s
Locale(s): Pennsylvania

Summary: During the American Revolution in western Pennsylvania, the Murray family struggles to create a frontier community under harsh conditions and constant threat by the Indians.

Historical Accuracy: The novel excels in its convincing portrait of everyday life during the period.

6363   *The King's Orchard*

Date of Publication: 1963
Subject(s): American Revolution; Biography, Fictionalized
Historical character(s): James O'Hara, Military Personnel, Government Official; Guyasuta, Indian (Seneca), Chieftain; George Rogers Clark, Military Personnel (general); Anthony Wayne, Military Personnel (general); George Washington, Military Personnel (army commander)
Time Period(s): 18th century (1770s-1790s)
Locale(s): Fort Pitt, Pennsylvania

Summary: This is a fictional biography of James O'Hara, who comes to America in 1772 at age 20 from Ireland to reach Fort Pitt, then the farthest outpost of the American West. He becomes an Indian trader, an officer in the Revolution, and serves as the Quartermaster General of the U.S.

Historical Accuracy: The novel stays close to the actual facts of O'Hara's remarkable career.

6364   *The Richlands*

Date of Publication: 1974
Subject(s): Rural Life—U.S.
Fictional character(s): Jim Ryall, Farmer; Peggy Ryall, Spouse
Time Period(s): 19th century
Locale(s): Pennsylvania

Summary: Rural life in western Pennsylvania during the 19th century is celebrated in the story of Jim Ryall, who manages his family's farm. Jim's ambition for the farm becomes a driving obsession that alienates him from those who are closest to him.

Historical Accuracy: The novel features a believable regional and period background.

JUDY TURNER
(PSEUD. OF JUDITH SAXTON, 1936-)

English novelist Saxton was born in Norwich and published her first historical novel, *The Bright Day Is Done*, in 1974. Her other novels include *Princes in Waiting* and *Cousin to the Queen*, under the pseudonym Judy Turner.

6365   *Ralegh's Fair Bess: The Story of Bess Throckmorton*

Date of Publication: 1972
Subject(s): Elizabethan Period; Jacobean Period; Royalty—England
Historical character(s): Bess Throckmorton, Gentlewoman, Spouse (of Ralegh); Sir Walter Ralegh, Gentleman, Courtier; Elizabeth I, Ruler (Queen of England); James I, Ruler (King of England); Ben Jonson, Writer

Time Period(s): 16th century; 17th century
Locale(s): England

Summary: The married life of Walter Ralegh and Bess Throckmorton is depicted. Bess is a maid of honor in Queen Elizabeth's court, and the pair earn the queen's disfavor and are imprisoned for marrying. Their love endures disgrace and absence until Ralegh's execution by James I.

Historical Accuracy: The novel is a blend of fiction and fact, with the basic outline of Raleigh's life accurately depicted.

WILLIAM OLIVER TURNER (1914-)

Born in Oregon but raised in the Middle West, Turner is a former newspaperman. His books include *Thief Hunt* and *The Long Rope*. His novel *Maberly's Kill* was made into a 1969 movie starring Robert Redford.

6366 *Call the Beast Thy Brother*

Date of Publication: 1973
Subject(s): American West; Indians; Tribal Life—Native American
Fictional character(s): David Nails, Captive
Time Period(s): 19th century
Locale(s): Pacific Northwest

Summary: This tale of the Pacific Northwest follows the experiences of young David Nails who jumps ship in Vancouver. He falls in with mercenaries who are captured and held by the Haida Indians as slaves. Determined to escape, Nails discovers that he is part of the potlatch ceremony to determine who will become the next Haida chief.

Historical Accuracy: The story offers an authentic look at the tribal customs of the Haida.

HARRY N. TURTLEDOVE (1949-)

An American writer and academic, Turtledove holds a Ph.D. in Byzantine history from UCLA. He has taught ancient and medieval history at UCLA. He is now a full-time science fiction and fantasy writer. His Videssos Cycle draws on his field of expertise, as it follows the exploits of a Roman legion.

6367 *The Guns of the South*

Date of Publication: 1972
Subject(s): Civil War—U.S.; Fantasy
Fictional character(s): Andries Rhoodie, Inventor
Historical character(s): Robert E. Lee, Military Personnel (Confederate commander); Jefferson Davis, Political Figure
Time Period(s): 1860s (1864)
Locale(s): Virginia

Summary: This ingenious alternative history is set in 1864 as the Confederacy is on the brink of defeat. A mysterious stranger, Andries Rhoodie, offers Robert E. Lee a secret weapon: an AK-47. The result is a Confederate victory and an altered version of American history.

Historical Accuracy: The period elements and details about the Civil War are accurate and a solid foundation for the novel's fantasy.

GODFREY TURTON (1901-)

A British author born in Yorkshire, Turton graduated with first class honors from Balliol College, Oxford. He has worked as a reporter in Budapest, Hungary, and as the lead writer for the weekly magazine *Truth*. For many years Turton was on the staff of the Clarendon Press, working on the Oxford Latin Dictionary. His novels include *There Once Was a City*, *The Devil's Churchyard*, and *The Syrian Princess*. He is also the author of a nonfiction work, *Builders of England's Glory*.

6368 *The Emperor Arthur*

Date of Publication: 1967
Subject(s): Dark Ages; Arthurian Legends; Roman Empire
Fictional character(s): Arthur, Ruler (King of the Britons); Pelleas, Knight; Guinevere, Royalty (queen consort of Arthur); Lancelot, Knight; Merlin, Sorcerer
Time Period(s): 5th century
Locale(s): England

Summary: This version of the Arthur story is set in a Romanized Britain, with Arthur the last proponent of Latin order and manners against Celtic chaos and abandon. He holds off the invading Saxons but must contend with the betrayal of Merlin and Lancelot, who help initiate the dissolution of post-Roman England.

Historical Accuracy: The novel features the story of Arthur stripped of medieval fashions and bolstered by actual events of fifth-century England.

6369 *My Lord of Canterbury*

Date of Publication: 1967
Subject(s): Tudor Period; Religious Life; Biography, Fictionalized
Historical character(s): Thomas Cranmer, Religious (Archbishop of Canterbury); Henry VIII, Ruler (King of England); Anne Boleyn, Royalty (queen consort of Henry VIII); Thomas Cromwell, Political Figure (chancellor); Lady Jane Grey, Royalty; Mary Tudor, Royalty (princess); Elizabeth Tudor, Royalty (princess); Hugh Latimer, Religious (bishop); Nicholas Ridley, Religious (prelate and Protestant martyr)
Time Period(s): 16th century
Locale(s): England

Summary: This autobiographical novel is based on the life of Thomas Cranmer, the Archbishop of Canterbury. He was one of the principal architects of the annulment of Henry VIII's marriage to Catherine of Aragon and a leader of the English Reformation. The tumultuous events of Henry VIII's reign and the important figures of the period are seen from the perspective of Cranmer, who emerges as a complex figure in a dangerous period.

Historical Accuracy: The novel stays close to the known historical events. To fill the gaps, the author has treated some conjecture as fact.

FREDERIC TUTEN

6370 *Tallien: A Brief Romance*

Date of Publication: 1988
Subject(s): French Revolution; Reign of Terror
Historical character(s): Jean Lambert Tallien, Revolutionary; Maximilien Francois de Robespierre, Revolutionary, Political Figure; Napoleon Bonaparte, Military Personnel (army officer)
Time Period(s): 1780s; 1790s
Locale(s): Paris, France

Summary: The frame for this unusual meditation on politics and betrayal is a son's deathbed visit to his estranged father, a radical unionist who deserted his family. The story of Jean Lambert Tallien, a revolutionary betrayed, is then offered, with the reader expected to supply the connections between the present and the past.

Historical Accuracy: The juxtaposition here is not quite successful—it is more jarring than illuminating—but there is no question that the flavor and atmosphere of revolutionary France are captured with skill.

MARK TWAIN
(PSEUD. OF SAMUEL CLEMENS, 1835-1910)

An American writer who grew up in Hannibal, Missouri, Twain worked as a journeyman printer and on a steamboat. During the Civil War he fought briefly with a group of Confederate volunteers before heading west to Nevada. In 1870 he settled in Hartford, Connecticut. His principal works include *Tom Sawyer*, *The Adventures of Huckleberry Finn*, *Roughing It*, *Life on the Mississippi*, and *Pudd'nhead Wilson*.

6371 *A Connecticut Yankee in King Arthur's Court*

Date of Publication: 1889
Subject(s): Arthurian Legends; Middle Ages; Fantasy
Fictional character(s): Hank Morgan, Mechanic; Arthur, Ruler; Merlin, Sorcerer
Time Period(s): 6th century
Locale(s): Camelot, England (Arthur's legendary court)

Summary: In this satirical fantasy—a companion novel to Twain's *The Prince and the Pauper*—Twain measures feudalism by a modern, democratic standard when a Connecticut mechanic awakes to find himself in Camelot. Twain then exposes the golden age of chivalry as a fraud and as primitive barbarism. The Yankee, now called the Boss, refashions Camelot into a 19th-century democracy with tragic results.

Historical Accuracy: Twain's exposure of the feudal system makes his social point about the merit of democracy and its frailty.

6372 *Personal Recollections of Joan of Arc*

Date of Publication: 1896

Subject(s): Hundred Years War; Biography, Fictionalized; Religious Life
Fictional character(s): Sieur Louis de Conte, Secretary (to Joan)
Historical character(s): Joan of Arc, Warrior; Charles VII, Ruler (King of France)
Time Period(s): 15th century
Locale(s): France

Summary: Joan of Arc is seen through the eyes of Sieur Louis de Conte, a fictional page and secretary to Joan. The story follows the known facts of her life, including her childhood as a peasant, her audiences with Charles VII, her military career, and her trial and execution.

Historical Accuracy: The historical facts are closely followed. The work can be described as serious, though romanticized, history.

6373 *The Prince and the Pauper*

Date of Publication: 1882
Subject(s): Middle Ages; Tudor Period; Royalty—England
Fictional character(s): Tom Canty, Streetperson (beggar); Hendon Miles, Knight
Historical character(s): Edward Tudor, Royalty (Prince of Wales); Henry VIII, Ruler (King of England); Elizabeth Tudor, Royalty (princess); Mary Tudor, Royalty (princess)
Time Period(s): 16th century
Locale(s): London, England

Summary: Twain scrutinizes feudalism from a modern, democratic standpoint. The Prince of Wales exchanges identities with a poor street urchin with satirical results: the humanity of the Prince is illustrated, and the shallowness of the pomp and privilege of royalty are dramatized.

Historical Accuracy: The novel is more a moral fable than an historical account. Twain casts real figures in his fantasy, but they play their roles in the fable, not in history.

KATHLEEN TYNAN

Canadian journalist and author Tynan received her B.A. from Oxford University and has worked as a researcher for *Newsweek* and as a feature writer for the *Sunday London Times*. Her novel *Agatha* was begun as a documentary film and became both a novel and a feature film.

6374 *Agatha*

Date of Publication: 1978
Subject(s): Mystery; Literary Life
Historical character(s): Agatha Christie, Writer; Sir Max Mallowan, Archaeologist
Time Period(s): 1920s (1926)
Locale(s): Harrogate, England

Summary: This mystery novel explores what might have happened in 1926 when detective novelist Agatha Christie, in the midst of marital difficulties, disappeared for a time. When she was discovered at a resort hotel in Harrogate registered in the name of her husband's mistress, Christie claimed it was the result of a loss of memory. The novel offers another solution.

Historical Accuracy: The novel's situation is true; the interpretation and solution are questionable.

MABEL L. TYRREL

Born in Merthyr Tydfil, England, Tyrrell is a journalist who has written about withcraft, superstitions, and folklore.

6375 *The Affairs of Nicholas Culpepper*

Date of Publication: 1946
Subject(s): Biography, Fictionalized; Science
Historical character(s): Nicholas Culpepper, Herbalist
Time Period(s): 17th century
Locale(s): England

Summary: This biographical novel traces the career of the 17th-century English herbalist Nicholas Culpepper. Originally destined for the church, Culpepper instead studies the healing properties of plants. His eagerness to assist the ailing poor brings him into conflict with established physicians who regard his treatments as primitive superstitions.

Historical Accuracy: The novel incorporates all that is known of Culpepper's life, set against a convincing period backdrop.

KENNETH ULYATT (1920-)

English writer Ulyatt studied at the Croyden School of Art then pursued a career in advertising. Always interested in the American West from reading Western novels and factual accounts of the period, Ulyatt decided to write novels about the West as it really was. His books include the Portugee Phillips trilogy (*North Against the Sioux*, *The Longhorn Trail*, and *Custer's Gold*) and *The Day of the Cowboy*.

6376 *North Against the Sioux*

Date of Publication: 1965
Subject(s): American West; Indians
Historical character(s): Portugee John Phillips, Scout; Henry Beebee Carrington, Military Personnel (colonel); Red Cloud, Indian (Sioux), Chieftain
Time Period(s): 1860s (1866-1867)
Locale(s): Wyoming

Summary: The siege of Fort Phil Kearney by Red Cloud, chief of the Sioux nation, is dramatized. Colonel Carrington, the fort's commander, asks for a volunteer to bring relief, and Portugee Phillips, a cavalry scout, sets out on a 200-mile journey to save the fort.

Historical Accuracy: The characters and the events described are true.

CHARLES UNDERHILL
(PSEUD. OF REGINALD HILL, 1936-)

English author Underhill graduated from Oxford and has worked as a secondary school teacher and a lecturer in English literature. He became a full-time writer in 1982. He received an Edgar Award nomination in 1981 for *The Spy's Wife*.

6377 *Captain Fantom*

Date of Publication: 1977
Subject(s): Picaresque Adventure; Thirty Years War; Civil War—England
Fictional character(s): Carlo Fantom, Adventurer
Time Period(s): 17th century (1623-1647)
Locale(s): Saxony, Germany; London, England; Oxford, England

Summary: A reference in John Aubrey's *Brief Lives* records that Captain Carlo Fantom was "very quarrelsome and a qreat ravisher." This quote provides the basis for this novel, a portrait of a thoroughly amoral adventurer, in which Fantom tells his own story. He is a mercenary during the Thirty Years War and then in England, fighting first for Parliament and then for the king during the Civil War.

Historical Accuracy: The story is fictional but the period details are authentic.

SIGRID UNDSET (1882-1949)

Undset was a Norwegian novelist born in Denmark. Her *Kristin Lavransdatter* originally appeared in three volumes, and its successor, *The Master of Hestviken*, won her the Nobel Prize for Literature in 1928.

6378 *The Axe*

Date of Publication: 1925
Subject(s): Middle Ages; Crime and Criminals; Family Saga
Fictional character(s): Olav Audunsson, Knight, Nobleman; Steinfinn Toresson, Nobleman; Ingunn Steinfinnsdatter, Fiance(e)
Time Period(s): 13th century
Locale(s): Bergen, Norway; Oslo, Norway

Summary: This is the first volume of a tetralogy collectively called *The Master of Hestviken*. This great historical chronicle begins in the 13th century with a feud that affects future generations. Olav Audunsson attempts to wed his stepfather's daughter, and the crime that this causes sets the dramatic tension. The story continues in *The Snake Pit*.

Historical Accuracy: The novel begins a massive depiction of Norwegian history and customs, grounded in a human drama of conflict and medieval beliefs.

6379 *The Bridal Wreath*

Date of Publication: 1922
Subject(s): Middle Ages; Family Saga
Fictional character(s): Kristin Lavransdatter, Gentlewoman; Laurans Bjorgulfson, Knight, Landowner; Erlend Nikulausson, Knight, Landowner
Time Period(s): 14th century (first half)
Locale(s): Norway

Summary: The first volume of Undset's *Kristin Lavransdatter* trilogy chronicles Kristin's life from childhood to her marriage. Kristin resists an unwanted betrothal and while in Oslo at a convent school meets Erlend, with whom she falls in love without her father's blessing. She becomes his mistress and then his wife, despite her father's disapproval. Her story continues in *The Mistress of Husaby.*

Historical Accuracy: Undset's period details are authentic, and her delineation of character is impressively realistic.

6380 *The Cross*

Date of Publication: 1922
Subject(s): Middle Ages; Family Saga; Plague
Fictional character(s): Kristin Lavransdatter, Gentlewoman; Erlend Nikulausson, Knight, Landowner; Ulf, Servant
Time Period(s): 14th century (1340s)
Locale(s): Norway

Summary: In the final volume of Undset's trilogy, Kristin and Erlend return to her father's estate. They quarrel and scandal ensues involving the servant Ulf and Kristin's newborn child. Too late Erlend repents his mistreatment of his wife. Kristin enters a convent and is infected by the Black Death.

Historical Accuracy: As an accurate picture of medieval Norway, the novel and the trilogy are unsurpassed.

6381 *In the Wilderness*

Date of Publication: 1927
Subject(s): Middle Ages; Family Saga
Fictional character(s): Olav Audunsson, Knight, Nobleman; Eirik, Heir; Cecilia, Young Woman
Time Period(s): 14th century
Locale(s): London, England; Hestviken, Norway

Summary: In this third volume of *The Master of Hestviken* series, Olav mourns the death of his wife and for distraction embarks on a trading mission to England. His son Eirik grows wild and boastful, quarreling with his father. There are scenes of the invasion of Norway by Sweden. The story concludes in the *Son Avenger.*

Historical Accuracy: Undset superbly details the life and times of medieval Norway. The invasion of Norway by Duke Eirik is based on historical fact.

6382 *The Mistress of Husaby*

Date of Publication: 1922
Subject(s): Middle Ages; Family Saga
Fictional character(s): Kristin Lavransdatter, Gentlewoman; Erlend Nikulausson, Landowner, Knight; Simon Andresson, Landowner
Time Period(s): 14th century (first half)
Locale(s): Norway

Summary: In the second volume of Undset's trilogy, Kristin attempts to restore her husband's estate and bears seven sons. Erlend become involved in a conspiracy against the Swedish king. He is arrested and tried for treason. He emerges with his life but forfeits his lands. Their story concludes in the final volume of the trilogy, *The Cross.*

Historical Accuracy: Undset provides telling and convincing period details and accomplishes remarkable psychological insight.

6383 *The Snake Pit*

Date of Publication: 1925
Subject(s): Middle Ages; Family Saga; Crime and Criminals
Fictional character(s): Olav Audunsson, Knight, Nobleman; Ingunn Steinfinnsdatter, Noblewoman
Time Period(s): 13th century; 14th century
Locale(s): Hestviken, Norway; Oslo, Norway

Summary: The effect of Olav Audunsson's crime is chronicled in this second volume of *The Master of Hestviken* series. Unable to confess his crime to protect the wife he loves, Olav is a stricken man. His family is blighted by the past, and we watch as it infects the next generation. The third volume of the series is *In the Wilderness.*

Historical Accuracy: Undset presents a remarkably accurate portrait of a medieval man and his inner life as well as the manners and morals of his age.

6384 *The Son Avenger*

Date of Publication: 1927
Subject(s): Middle Ages; Family Saga
Fictional character(s): Olav Audunsson, Knight, Nobleman; Eirik, Heir; Cecilia, Young Woman
Time Period(s): 14th century
Locale(s): Hestviken, Norway; Oslo, Norway

Summary: In this final volume of the massive *The Master of Hestviken* saga, the sins of the father are passed on to the next generation and the psychological cost of passion and guilt is explored. Eirik, Olav's son, fails to become a monk, and Cecilia makes a disastrous marriage.

Historical Accuracy: This is a richly detailed evocation of the past.

FRITZ VON UNRUH (1885-1970)

Born in Koblenz, Unruh works are deeply influenced by his religious home and education. After fighting in the cavalry in World War I, he wrote several dramas and lived for several years in the United States.

6385 *The Saint*

Date of Publication: 1950
Subject(s): Religious Life; Biography, Fictionalized; Middle Ages
Historical character(s): Catherine of Siena, Religious (saint), Diplomat
Time Period(s): 14th century
Locale(s): Siena, Italy

Summary: This fictional biography of Italian mystic and diplomat Catherine of Sienna dramatizes a number of episodes from her life, including her spiritual visions and her involvement in the complex debate over the Papacy of the period.

Historical Accuracy: The novel's credibility is undercut by a persistent romantic manner that idealizes Catherine.

BARRY UNSWORTH (1930-)

Born in England and a graduate of Manchester University, Unsworth is a former teacher of English in Athens and Istanbul. His works include *The Partnership*, *The Greeks Have a Word for It*, and *Mooncranker's Gift*. *Sacred Hunger* won the Booker Prize in 1992. He has said that his main interest in writing fiction is to explore moral complexities and ambiguities.

6386 *The Idol Hunter*

Date of Publication: 1980
Subject(s): Ottoman Empire; Espionage
Fictional character(s): Basil Pascali, Spy; Anthony Bowles, Archaeologist
Time Period(s): 1900s (1908)
Locale(s): Asia Minor

Summary: This psychological novel of betrayal and deceit is set on a tiny Greek island off the coast of Asia Minor in the declining years of the Ottoman Empire. Basil Pascali is an informer for the Turks who begins to suspect that the islanders are aware of his deceit. Onto the island comes an English archaeologist, Anthony Bowles, with whom Pascali begins to suspect he has a good deal in common. What follows is a test of wills in an elaborate game of betrayal.

Historical Accuracy: The period background is effectively presented.

6387 *Morality Play*

Date of Publication: 1995
Subject(s): Middle Ages; Mystery; Theatrical Life
Fictional character(s): Nicholas Barber, Religious (priest)
Historical character(s): Richard de Guise, Nobleman
Time Period(s): 14th century
Locale(s): England

Summary: In this thriller set in 14th-century England, Nicholas Barber is a young priest on the run from the Church, having broken his vow of chastity. He falls in with a troupe of travelling players. When a murder takes place, the company gathers information about the murder to incorporate into its next performance, seizing on its topical interest. The drama comes close to the dangerous truth, attracting the attention of the powerful Lord de Guise.

Historical Accuracy: The story captures with conviction the period background.

6388 *The Rage of the Vulture*

Date of Publication: 1983
Subject(s): Ottoman Empire
Fictional character(s): Robert Markham, Government Official; Elizabeth Markham, Spouse
Time Period(s): 1900s (1908)
Locale(s): Constantinople, Ottoman Empire

Summary: Set during the decline of the Ottoman Empire in 1908, the novel centers on English government official Robert Markham, newly posted to Constantinople with his wife and son. For Markham it is a return visit. Twelve years before

during the Armenian massacre he stood by helplessly while his fiancee was raped and murdered. He sets out on a mission of redemption while the Turkish Third Army is on the verge of revolt, and Armenians, Jews, Bulgarians, and Turks are uniting to bring down the regime.

Historical Accuracy: The period elements are authentic and create a believable historical backdrop for this psychological drama.

6389 *Sacred Hunter*

Date of Publication: 1992
Subject(s): Slavery; Sea Story
Fictional character(s): William Kemp, Businessman (slaver); Matthew Paris, Doctor; Erasmus Kemp, Heir
Time Period(s): 1750s (1752)
Locale(s): Liverpool, England; At Sea; Miami, Florida

Summary: In 1752 Liverpool merchant William Kemp becomes a slaver, building and outfitting a ship to carry precious human cargo to America. The novel describes the disasterous voyage that includes disease and mutiny. The ship lands on the east coast of Florida where the survivors—whites, blacks, free men, and former slaves—form a secret community.

Historical Accuracy: The story is invented, but the period elements are believable.

BOYD UPCHURCH (1919-)

Born in Atlanta, Upchurch attended Atlanta Junior College and the University of Southern California. He worked for the Star Engraving Company in Los Angeles from 1947 until 1971 when he became a full-time writer. He is the author of *Scarborough Hall*, as well as many science fiction novels under the pseudonym John Boyd.

6390 *The Slave Stealer*

Date of Publication: 1968
Subject(s): Antebellum South; Slavery
Fictional character(s): Solomon Villaricca, Peddler; Melinda Blake Ricky, Slave
Time Period(s): 1850s (1858)
Locale(s): Cincinnati, Ohio; Georgia

Summary: This adventure story, set during the period before the Civil War, describes the efforts of a Jewish peddler, Solomon Villaricca, who is commissioned to bring back a young slave girl from Georgia by a man who has fallen in love with her. Their experiences on the trip north and their growing relationship are described against the background of the antebellum South.

Historical Accuracy: The novel offers a believable portrait of the period.

JOHN UPDIKE (1932-)

Born in Pennsylvania, Updike graduated from Harvard. From 1955 to 1957 he was a member of the staff of the *New Yorker*. One of the best-known and respected writers of his generation, he has won the Pulitzer Prize, the National Book

Award, and the National Book Critics Circle Award. He is the author of *The Poorhouse Fair*, *The Centaur*, *The Witches of Eastwick*, and the acclaimed Rabbit series of novels.

6391   *Memories of the Ford Administration*

Date of Publication: 1992
Subject(s): Politics
Fictional character(s): Alfred Clayton, Historian, Professor
Historical character(s): Gerald R. Ford, Political Figure; James Buchanan, Political Figure; Andrew Jackson, Political Figure; Edwin Stanton, Political Figure; Nathaniel Hawthorne, Writer, Diplomat
Time Period(s): 1970s; 1850s
Locale(s): New Hampshire; Washington, District of Columbia

Summary: Scholar and historian Alfred Clayton is asked for his memories of Gerald Ford's administration and produces recollections of a turbulent period in his personal life as well as pages of an unpublished book on the life of James Buchanan, the 15th president of the U.S. The alternating subjects of the present and the past provide an interesting contrast of life and social custom in two very different yet very similar eras.

Historical Accuracy: The novel is an amalgam of forms and themes with an ingenious and believable correspondence established between the eras.

MARK UPTON

(PSEUD. OF LAWRENCE SANDERS, 1920-)

American writer Sanders was born in Brooklyn, New York, and attended Wabash College. He served as a sergeant in the U.S. Marine Corps during World War II. A novelist since 1969, Sanders began his career working for various magazines as an editor and writer of war, men's adventure, and detective stories. His first novel, *The Anderson Tapes*, published in 1970, won an Edgar Award and was made into a motion picture starring Sean Connery. His best-selling novels include *The First Deadly Sin* and *Capital Crimes*.

6392   *The Dream Lover*

Date of Publication: 1978
Subject(s): Motion Picture Industry
Fictional character(s): Eli Hebron, Businessman; Charlie Royce, Businessman; Gladys Divine, Actress
Time Period(s): 1920s (1927)
Locale(s): Hollywood, California

Summary: Hollywood in 1927 on the eve of talking pictures is the novel's setting as Eli Hebron battles Charlie Royce for control of Magna Pictures. Hebron, an artist and idealist, is overmatched by the unscrupulous Royce, who uses starlet Gladys Divine to drive Hebron to disaster.

Historical Accuracy: The novel convincingly depicts the movie industry's transition from silent pictures to "talkies."

LEON URIS (1924-)

A bestselling and award-winning American novelist, Uris was born and raised in Baltimore, Maryland, and served in the U.S. Marine Corps during World War II. He is the author of such acclaimed novels as *Battle Cry*, *The Angry Hills*, *Exodus*, *Mila 18*, *Topaz*, and *The Haj*.

6393   *Redemption*

Date of Publication: 1995
Subject(s): Independence—Ireland; World War I; Battle of Gallipoli
Fictional character(s): Liam Larkin, Rancher (sheep); Rory Larkin, Revolutionary, Military Personnel (soldier)
Historical character(s): Winston Churchill, Political Figure
Time Period(s): 19th century; 20th century (1895-1916)
Locale(s): Ireland; England; New Zealand

Summary: The sequel to *Trinity* continues the story of the Larkin clan, centering on Liam, who emigrates to New Zealand where he becomes a successful sheep baron. His son, Rory, however, wishes to return to Ireland to join the conflict for independence inspired by his uncle Conor. The novel features scenes of the disastrous Gallipoli campaign during World War I and offers an insider's look at the politics of the period from the secret memoranda of Winston Churchill.

Historical Accuracy: Romance predominates over history here with many of the great events in the struggle for Irish independence taking place off center stage.

6394   *Trinity*

Date of Publication: 1976
Subject(s): Independence—Ireland; Irish Potato Famine; Easter Rising
Fictional character(s): Conor Larkin, Young Man; Frederick Weed, Businessman
Time Period(s): 19th century; 20th century (1840s-1916)
Locale(s): Ireland

Summary: This panoramic novel concerning the making of modern Ireland follows the interlocked fortunes of three families in the North of Ireland who collectively illustrate the cause and effect of Catholic-Protestant and wealthy-poor conflict. The central figure in an immense cast is young Conor Larkin who gradually is turned into a revolutionary. The novel spans the period from the Potato Famine to the Easter Rising.

Historical Accuracy: The novel excels in the presentation of authentic Irish customs and period life. The novel's history is not as thorough or as accurate.

ERROL LINCOLN UYS (1943-)

Born in Johannesburg, South Africa, Uys has been a newspaper reporter in South Africa and England and an editor at *Reader's Digest*. His first novel, *Brazil*, was praised by critics as a skillful synthesis of many epochal events in Brazil's history. Uys has said that in writing the novel he strove to avoid oversimplification and stereotypical images and hopes that the novel will increase public awareness of the pride and promise of Brazil.

6395 *Brazil*

Date of Publication: 1986
Subject(s): Family Saga; Portuguese Colonies
Fictional character(s): Nicolau Calvalcanti, Landowner; Inacio Calvalcanti, Religious (priest); Amador Flores da Silva, Prospector
Time Period(s): Multiple Time Periods
Locale(s): Brazil

Summary: This massive, panoramic novel captures five centuries of Brazil's history from its earliest colonial days to its emergence as a modern republic. The story centers on two families, the Calvalcantis and the da Silvas, who reflect the history of Brazil.

Historical Accuracy: The novel mixes the factual with the historical. Events such as the enslvav ement and massacre of the Brazilian Indians, the prospecting frenzy, the Paragu ayan War, rebellion, and the birth of Brasilia are faithfuly described within the context of the story.

LOUIS VACZEK (1913-1983)

A Hungarian scientist and author, Vaczek was born in Szeyed, Hungary, and attended McGill University. During World War II, he served as a pilot with the Royal Canadian Air Force. He combined his training as a chemist with an interest in exploring the relation between science and art. Vaczek served as a science editor for several encylopedias and authored a chemistry textbook. His work in the Middle East as a chemical factory manager, diplomat, and trading company director led him to write *Travelers in Ancient Lands: A Portrait of the Middle East.*

6396 *River and Empty Sea*

Date of Publication: 1950
Subject(s): Frontier—Canada
Fictional character(s): Paul Denys, Young Man
Time Period(s): 17th century (1670)
Locale(s): Quebec, Canada; Hudson Bay, Canada

Summary: Frontier life in Canada during the 17th century is depicted in this story of young Paul Denys who joins his family in Quebec and becomes the secretary to the Intendant. The action includes a long canoe trip to Hudson's Bay.

Historical Accuracy: Despite thinness of plot and character, the novel excels in its presentation of the frontier background of the period.

PHILIP VAIL

(PSEUD. OF NOEL B. GERSON, 1914-1988)

Vaughan is one of several pseudonyms of prolific American writer Noel B. Gerson. He was born in Chicago and educated at the University of Chicago. During World War II, Gerson served in military intelligence. He was a newspaper reporter, radio and TV scriptwriter, and the author of over 100 books. His historical novels feature a lively and entertaining blend of fact and fiction.

6397 *The Sea Panther: A Novel about the Commander of the U.S.S. Constitution*

Date of Publication: 1962
Subject(s): Sea Story; Military Life; War of 1812
Historical character(s): William Bainbridge, Military Personnel (naval officer); David Porter, Military Personnel (naval officer)
Time Period(s): 18th century; 19th century (1797-1813)
Locale(s): United States; *Constitution*, At Sea; Tripoli, Africa

Summary: The novel dramatizes the naval career of William Bainbridge, one of the first officers commissioned in the American navy, who was the commander of the first American ship-of-the-line, the U.S.S. *Constitution.* Bainbridge's daring and superb seamanship made him one of the most renowned naval figures of his era. His subordinates—Decatur, Porter, Jacob and James Lawrence—went on to distinguished naval careers after being trained by Bainbridge.

Historical Accuracy: The basic facts of the life and career of Commodore Bainbridge are accurate. Gaps in the historical record have been filled by the imagined, and some details have been altered to tell a smoother story.

6398 *The Twisted Saber: A Biographical Novel of Benedict Arnold*

Date of Publication: 1963
Subject(s): American Revolution; Biography, Fictionalized; Battle of Saratoga
Historical character(s): Benedict Arnold, Military Personnel (general); George Washington, Military Personnel (army commander); Horatio Gates, Military Personnel (general); John Andre, Military Personnel (major), Spy; Henry Clinton, Military Personnel (general)
Time Period(s): 18th century; 19th century (1756-1801)
Locale(s): United States; Quebec, Canada

Summary: The novel attempts to solve the enigma of Benedict Arnold. Although his name is synonymous with treason, Arnold was one of America's greatest generals, whose accomplishments on behalf of the American cause helped ensure eventual victory. The novel traces Arnold's life and military career, particularly his military campaigns at Quebec, Saratoga, and Ticonderoga.

Historical Accuracy: Although the basic facts in the novel are accurate, the dialogue and many of the book's episodes are invented.

CAY VAN ASH

Born in Sussex, England, Van Ash was attracted to the Far East by the Fu Manchu books. He has lived in Japan for about 20 years and teaches at Waseda University in Tokyo.

6399 *The Fires of Fu Manchu*

Date of Publication: 1987
Subject(s): Mystery; World War I
Fictional character(s): Petrie, Doctor; Nayland Smith, Gentleman; Dr. Fu Manchu, Criminal
Time Period(s): 1910s (1917)
Locale(s): Cairo, Egypt

Summary: The villainous Dr. Fu Manchu is at work in Egypt during World War I. A British scientist who has been working on a top-secret project known as Midnight Sun has disappeared. Dr. Petrie and Nayland Smith set out to determine whether the Germans are involved with Fu Manchu. Their search takes them to tunnels beneath the Step Pyramid, a torture chamber on an Egyptian estate, and a dramatic encounter at the site of Midnight Sun in the western desert.

Historical Accuracy: The novel captures the flavor of the original Fu Manchu books along with a serviceable period background.

6400 *Ten Years Beyond Baker Street*

Date of Publication: 1984
Subject(s): Mystery; Crime and Criminals
Fictional character(s): Sherlock Holmes, Detective—Private; Dr. Fu Manchu, Criminal
Time Period(s): 1910s
Locale(s): England; Wales

Summary: Sherlock Holmes comes out of retirement to match wits with the Chinese master criminal, Dr. Fu Manchu. In an investigation that takes him from London to Wales, Holmes is abducted, trapped in an abandoned coal mine, and besieged in a manor house before a climactic confrontation with Fu Manchu.

Historical Accuracy: The novel convincingly echoes the originals in tone and substance.

FREDERIC F. VAN DE WATER
(1890-1968)

American historian, journalist, critic, editor, and author Van de Water was born in New Jersey. Before turning to freelance writing, he worked variously as a reporter, night city editor, book critic, and special writer for such newspapers as the *New York American*, the *New York Tribune*, and the *New York Post*. Van de Water is the author of more than 35 books, including mysteries, novels, biographies, histories, travel books, and essays.

6401 *Catch a Falling Star*

Date of Publication: 1949
Subject(s): American Revolution
Fictional character(s): Olin Royden, Young Man; Faith Marshall, Young Woman
Historical character(s): Ethan Allen, Military Personnel (soldier), Leader (Green Mountain Boys); Ira Allen, Political Figure
Time Period(s): 1780s (1780-1781)
Locale(s): Vermont

Summary: The novel continues the author's history of Vermont during the early years of the 1780s as Ethan and Ira Allen struggle to maintain an independent Vermont republic. Grafted onto the historical background is a conventional love story in which Olin Royden, a follower of Ira Allen, pursues and finally rescues Faith Marshall.

Historical Accuracy: The author's familiarity with the locale and history lends a good deal of credibility despite the emphasis on romantic adventure.

6402 *Day of Battle*

Date of Publication: 1958
Subject(s): American Revolution; Battle of Ticonderoga; Battle of Bennington
Fictional character(s): Jeremy Shaw, Military Personnel (lieutenant); Jonas Holloway, Farmer, Military Personnel (soldier)
Time Period(s): 1770s (1777)
Locale(s): Vermont

Summary: The novel completes the author's cycle of novels presenting the story of Vermont's struggle for independence. Vermont's role in the Revolution from the fall of Fort Ticonderoga to the Battle of Bennington is described through the experiences of several combatants.

Historical Accuracy: The novel faithfully captures the events of the 1777 Saratoga Campaign.

6403 *Reluctant Rebel*

Date of Publication: 1948
Subject(s): American Revolution; Battle of Ticonderoga
Fictional character(s): Adam Corlaer, Young Man; Felicity Sherwood, Young Woman
Historical character(s): Ethan Allen, Leader (Green Mountain Boys)
Time Period(s): 1770s
Locale(s): Bennington, Vermont, American Colonies; New York, American Colonies

Summary: The novel tells the story of the border dispute between New York and Vermont and of Ethan Allen and the Green Mountain Boys during the American Revolution. The story focuses on the experiences of Adam Corlaer of Albany, who becomes a champion of the Vermonters' cause and serves as secretary to Allen. The story climaxes with Corlaer's espionage mission just before the capture of Fort Ticonderoga.

Historical Accuracy: The story is fictional, but it does depend on a realistic background and context of historical events.

6404 *Wings of the Morning*

Date of Publication: 1955
Subject(s): American Revolution; Politics
Fictional character(s): Job Aldrich, Farmer; Melissa Sprague, Young Woman; Silence Thayer, Young Woman
Time Period(s): 1770s (1774-1777)
Locale(s): Vermont, American Colonies

Summary: The story of the political dispute between Vermont and New York before and during the American Revolution is dramatized in the experiences of Massachusetts farmer Job

Aldrich. Aldrich claims his dead brother's land in southeastern Vermont and is slowly caught up in eastern Vermont's dispute with New York over the authority of its jurisdiction.

Historical Accuracy: The novel captures the issues of the border dispute accurately.

JAN VAN DORP
(PSEUD. OF OSCAR VAN GODTSENHOVEN)

6405 *The Sable Lion*
Date of Publication: 1954
Subject(s): Sea Story; Pirates; War of the Spanish Succession
Fictional character(s): Marinus DeBoer, Sea Captain
Time Period(s): 17th century; 18th century
Locale(s): Ostend, Netherlands; At Sea

Summary: Set during the years of the War of the Spanish Succession, this adventure novel describes the exploits of Dutch privateers in action against the English.

Historical Accuracy: The novel is set against a believable background of the period and its customs.

DALE VAN EVERY (1896-1976)
Born in Michigan, Van Every worked as a crime reporter, newspaper correspondent, motion picture writer, producer, editor, and cattle rancher. He began writing books about his primary personal interest, the early American frontier, producing numerous historical novels and histories, including the award-winning *American Frontier People*, a four-volume survey of the westward movement from 1754 to 1845.

6406 *Bridal Journey*
Date of Publication: 1950
Subject(s): Settlement of the American Frontier; American Colonies; American Revolution
Fictional character(s): Colby Gower, Frontiersman, Military Personnel (colonel); Marah Blake, Fiance(e)
Historical character(s): William Clark, Frontiersman; George Rogers Clark, Military Personnel (general); Joseph Brant, Indian (Mohawk), Chieftain; Simon Girty, Frontiersman; James Girty, Frontiersman
Time Period(s): 1780s (1781)
Locale(s): Ohio Valley, United States

Summary: Action in the western theater of the Ohio River Valley during the American Revolution is depicted. The catalyst is the capture of Colonel Colby Gower's fiancee by British and Indian forces and her attempted rescue. Many actual historical figures appear.

Historical Accuracy: The background of actual historical events is authentic.

6407 *The Captive Witch*
Date of Publication: 1951
Subject(s): Settlement of the American Frontier; American Revolution; American Colonies

Fictional character(s): Adam Frane, Scout, Frontiersman
Historical character(s): George Rogers Clark, Military Personnel (general)
Time Period(s): 1780s
Locale(s): Kentucky

Summary: Adam Frane is a young scout for George Rogers Clark's army who sets out along the Wilderness Road to escort a group of prisoners to Virginia. The scene is the western theater of the American Revolution, and the fate of Clark's army, threatened on all sides by the British and the Indians, is depicted.

Historical Accuracy: The essential outline of the historical events is faithful to the facts.

6408 *The Day the Sun Died*
Date of Publication: 1971
Subject(s): Indians; Battle of Wounded Knee
Fictional character(s): Stuart Kirk, Journalist; John Winthrop, Indian (Sioux)
Historical character(s): Sitting Bull, Indian (Sioux), Chieftain; Nelson Appleton Miles, Military Personnel (general); Frederic Remington, Artist; Wovoka, Indian (Paiute), Shaman; Red Cloud, Indian (Sioux), Chieftain
Time Period(s): 1890s (1890)
Locale(s): South Dakota

Summary: The novel dramatizes the 1890 campaign against the Indians that begins in a panic over a misinterpretation of the meaning of the Ghost Dance that is spreading among the Indians on the reservations. Fear of an Indian rising produces the tragic Indian massacre at Wounded Knee and the ultimate revenge of the Seventh Cavalry for Custer's defeat in 1876.

Historical Accuracy: The activities and personalities of the historical figures are accurate, though there is no evidence that Frederic Remington took as active a part in the Wounded Knee campaign as depicted.

6409 *Scarlet Feather*
Date of Publication: 1959
Subject(s): Settlement of the American Frontier; American Colonies; American Revolution
Fictional character(s): Betsey Slover, Teenager; Caleb Jordan, Military Personnel (colonel); Duncan Jordan, Frontiersman
Time Period(s): 1780s (1785)
Locale(s): Louisville, Kentucky; Ohio River, United States

Summary: The novel describes the adventures of a Virginia family who journey down the Ohio River to settle in the Kentucky wilderness near Louisville. The time is 1785, the middle of the conflict between the British and Indian forces during the American Revolution.

Historical Accuracy: The novel is convincing in its depiction of wilderness life and the events of the Revolution.

6410 *The Shining Mountains*
Date of Publication: 1948
Subject(s): Lewis and Clark Expedition; Indians; American West
Fictional character(s): Matt Morgan, Scout

Historical character(s): William Clark, Explorer; Meriwether Lewis, Explorer
Time Period(s): 1800s
Locale(s): West; Rocky Mountains

Summary: The opening of the western frontier of America is described through the adventures of one of Lewis and Clark's scouts, Matt Morgan, who must contend with the harsh terrain of the Rockies and capture by the Indians.

Historical Accuracy: The story is fanciful but authentic in its period details.

6411 *The Trembling Earth*

Date of Publication: 1953
Subject(s): Mining; Earthquakes
Fictional character(s): Martin Brown, Miner; Judith Ayres, Fiance(e); Jared Brown, Religious (minister)
Time Period(s): 1810s (1811)
Locale(s): Missouri

Summary: The scene is the lead mines of southeast Missouri in 1811. Martin Brown invests everything in his mine, and his fortune is affected by the great New Madrid earthquake of 1811, the most violent earthquake in American history. The disaster is the catalyst for a domestic drama involving Brown, his minister brother Jared, and his fiancee, Judith Ayres.

Historical Accuracy: The novel interweaves a fictional story with a faithful depiction of the Missouri scene in 1811.

6412 *The Voyagers*

Date of Publication: 1957
Subject(s): Settlement of the American Frontier; American Revolution; American Colonies
Fictional character(s): Abel Traner, Adventurer; Jasper Hedges, Adventurer
Historical character(s): George Rogers Clark, Military Personnel (general); James Wilkinson, Military Personnel (general)
Time Period(s): 1780s
Locale(s): Ohio Valley, United States; Mississippi River; New Orleans, Louisiana

Summary: This is the adventurous tale of Abel Traner, who on his wedding day flees to freedom in the wilderness. He journeys down the Ohio and the Mississippi as far as New Orleans, encountering Indians, river pirates, and English agents, as well as such actual figures as George Rogers Clark and General James Wilkinson.

Historical Accuracy: The novel is fanciful in its events and circumstances, but believable in presenting the frontier scene of the period.

ROBERT VAN GULIK (1910-1967)

Dutch born van Gulick entered the Netherlands Foreign Service in 1935, serving in China, Japan, East Africa, Egypt, and India. He was a world-renowned orientalist who began his series of Chinese detective stories involving Judge Dee as a hobby.

6413 *The Chinese Nail Murders*

Date of Publication: 1961
Subject(s): Mystery; Chinese Empire
Fictional character(s): Hoong Liang, Assistant (of Judge Dee); Ma Joong, Assistant (of Judge Dee)
Historical character(s): Dee Jen-dieh, Judge
Time Period(s): 7th century
Locale(s): Pei-Chow, China

Summary: This novel is one in a series of fictional detective cases of Judge Dee, an actual Chinese magistrate of the Tang dynasty. He has been appointed magistrate of Pei-Chow, a distant frontier district in the north. He must solve a fiendish murder involving the nude, headless body of a woman, the disappearance of a young woman in love, missing jewels, and a contentious boxing master.

Historical Accuracy: Although Judge Dee's cases are fictional, the period details of the Tang dynasty are authentic.

6414 *The Emperor's Pearl*

Date of Publication: 1963
Subject(s): Mystery; Chinese Empire
Fictional character(s): Hoong Liang, Assistant (of Judge Dee)
Historical character(s): Dee Jen-dieh, Judge
Time Period(s): 7th century
Locale(s): China

Summary: Judge Dee takes on a baffling fictional case. The drummer of the favorite boat in the Poo-yong dragon-boat races is poisoned. Then a beautiful young woman is cruelly murdered in a deserted mansion. Dee connects both deaths to the theft of the Emperor's pearl, stolen 100 years earlier.

Historical Accuracy: The mystery offers remarkably convincing details of the period.

6415 *The Haunted Monastery*

Date of Publication: 1969
Subject(s): Mystery; Chinese Empire
Fictional character(s): Tao Gan, Assistant (of Judge Dee)
Historical character(s): Dee Jen-dieh, Judge
Time Period(s): 7th century
Locale(s): China

Summary: Judge Dee, the author's Tang dynasty sleuth, finds himself stranded in a Taoist monastery in the mountains. During the night he solves three gruesome crimes, while confronting the strange figure of the Embalmed Abbot who sits in state in the monastery's underground crypt.

Historical Accuracy: The period detail of 7th-century Chinese life is expertly presented.

6416 *The Lacquer Screen*

Date of Publication: 1969
Subject(s): Mystery; Chinese Empire
Fictional character(s): Chiao Tai, Assistant (of Judge Dee)
Historical character(s): Dee Jen-dieh, Judge
Time Period(s): 7th century
Locale(s): China

Summary: To solve a baffling murder and two other complicated crimes Judge Dee goes incognito into the criminal underworld for information. He and his companion Chiao Tai share the life of a gangster boss and his mistress as they uncover the secrets hidden by four panels of a lacquer screen.

Historical Accuracy: The mystery offers many authentic details of life during the period.

6417 *The Monkey and the Tiger*
Date of Publication: 1965
Subject(s): Mystery; Chinese Empire
Fictional character(s): Tao Gan, Assistant (of Judge Dee)
Historical character(s): Dee Jen-dieh, Judge
Time Period(s): 7th century
Locale(s): China

Summary: The novel offers two of Judge Dee's more baffling cases. In the first, a gibbon draws Dee's attention to the puzzling murder of an old tramp, which he solves aided only by two clues: four amputated fingers and a gold ring. In the other, Dee solves the murder of a young girl with the help of a ghostly apparition on a moonlit balcony.

Historical Accuracy: Dee's cases are invented, but the period detail of the Tang dynasty are authentic.

6418 *Murder in Canton*
Date of Publication: 1966
Subject(s): Mystery; Chinese Empire
Fictional character(s): Chiao Tai, Assistant; Tao Gan, Assistant
Historical character(s): Dee Jen-dieh, Judge
Time Period(s): 7th century (680)
Locale(s): Canton, China

Summary: Judge Dee arrives in Canton to secretly investigate a mysterious disappearance. The trail leads Dee and his assistants, Chiao Tai and Tao Gan, from the mortuary of the Flowery Pagoda to the floating brothels of the Pearl River. They are pressed for time by an impending coup in the capitol and must solve three different cases of murder.

Historical Accuracy: The period details are exact and convincing.

6419 *Necklace and Calabash*
Date of Publication: 1967
Subject(s): Mystery; Chinese Empire
Fictional character(s): Lang Liu, Businessman; Third Princess, Royalty (emperor's daughter)
Historical character(s): Dee Jen-dieh, Judge
Time Period(s): 7th century
Locale(s): China

Summary: In this 7th-century Chinese mystery, Judge Dee's plans for some relaxation are spoiled when the cashier of his Inn is found in the river, tortured and murdered. At the same time a valuable pearl necklace is stolen from the emperor's daughter, the Third Princess. Can the two crimes be connected?.

Historical Accuracy: The mystery is filled with authentic period details.

6420 *The Phantom of the Temple*
Date of Publication: 1966
Subject(s): Mystery; Chinese Empire
Fictional character(s): Hoong Liang, Assistant (of Judge Dee); Ma Joong, Assistant (of Judge Dee)
Historical character(s): Dee Jen-dieh, Judge
Time Period(s): 7th century
Locale(s): China

Summary: Judge Dee, the author's 7th-century Chinese sleuth, is in a remote western border province where he investigates a series of brutal murders. The inquiry is complicated by a cryptic message from a dying woman and the theft of a fortune in gold from the imperial treasurer.

Historical Accuracy: The details of life in the Tang dynasty are convincing.

6421 *The Red Pavilion*
Date of Publication: 1964
Subject(s): Mystery; Chinese Empire
Fictional character(s): Ma Joong, Assistant (of Judge Dee)
Historical character(s): Dee Jen-dieh, Judge
Time Period(s): 7th century
Locale(s): China

Summary: Judge Dee is asked by an old friend to help wrap up what appears to be a routine case of suicide. Dee finds himself, however, in the middle of a baffling situation involving a beautiful courtesan, rape, murder, and a 30-year-old crime.

Historical Accuracy: The novel offers a detailed and convincing look at the period.

6422 *The Willow Pattern*
Date of Publication: 1965
Subject(s): Mystery; Chinese Empire
Fictional character(s): Ma Joong, Assistant (of Judge Dee); Chiao Tai, Assistant (of Judge Dee)
Historical character(s): Dee Jen-dieh, Judge
Time Period(s): 7th century
Locale(s): China

Summary: The author's 7th-century sleuth, the historical Judge Dee, solves three interlocking crimes: the murder of a wealthy merchant in his study, the death of a merchant who kills himself in a supposedly accidental fall, and the murder of a servant girl by a perverted nobleman. Dee finds the connection among the three ostensibly separate cases.

Historical Accuracy: Dee's cases are invented, but the period details are authentic and convincing.

ANTONIA VAN-LOON (1940-1993)
Van-Loon grew up in Connecticut and graduated from City College of New York. A former English professor at Thames Valley Technical College in Norwich, Connecticut,

Van-Loon lived in Colchester and wrote four historical novels.

6423 *For Love and Honor*

Date of Publication: 1978
Subject(s): Civil War—U.S.
Fictional character(s): Emily Stevens, Young Woman; Beth Shepherd, Nurse; Kent Wilson, Doctor
Time Period(s): 1860s
Locale(s): Massachusetts

Summary: This sequel to *For Us the Living* is set during the Civil War. It describes the homefront of Massachusetts and the restlessness of Emily Stevens, who defies convention by running her own store, starting a library, and getting involved in town politics. She trades her independence for marriage, and her adjustment to married life within the confines of her historical period is dramatized.

Historical Accuracy: The novel is accurate in capturing the historical and social forces at work in shaping the characters' lives.

6424 *For Us the Living*

Date of Publication: 1976
Subject(s): Civil War—U.S.; Battle of Gettysburg; Draft Riots
Fictional character(s): Beth Shepherd, Teacher, Nurse; Gregory Allister, Military Personnel (Union officer); Kent Wilson, Military Personnel (Union major), Doctor
Time Period(s): 1860s
Locale(s): New York, New York; Gettysburg, Pennsylvania

Summary: After an unfortunate love affair, upper-class New Yorker Beth Shepherd goes to live with relatives in Pennsylvania. There she serves as a nurse in a field hospital during the Battle of Gettysburg and meets military surgeon Kent Wilson. Both Wilson and Union officer Gregory Allister fall in love with Beth.

Historical Accuracy: The novel offers a detailed portrait of immigrant soldiers in the Union Army whose discontent leads to the New York Draft Riots.

6425 *Katherine*

Date of Publication: 1979
Subject(s): Romance
Fictional character(s): Katherine Wilson, Young Woman; Luke Sullivan, Doctor; Edward Madison, Businessman (mill owner)
Time Period(s): 1880s; 1890s
Locale(s): New York; Massachusetts

Summary: Katherine Wilson (the daughter of Beth and Kent Wilson of the author's *For Us the Living*) falls in love with Dr. Luke Sullivan, who is already married. Determined to forget Luke, Katherine contracts a disastrous marriage to Edward Madison, a Massachusetts mill owner. When their conflicts explode in a night of violence, Katherine finds herself back in New York and in Luke Sullivan's life again.

Historical Accuracy: The novel evokes its era with believable period details.

6426 *Sunshine and Shadow*

Date of Publication: 1981
Subject(s): Immigrants; World War I
Fictional character(s): Tracy Sullivan, Young Woman; Luke Sullivan, Doctor; Michael Ryan, Worker
Time Period(s): 19th century; 20th century (1890s-1910s)
Locale(s): New York, New York

Summary: Immigrant life on the Lower East Side of New York at the turn of the century is the background for this novel. It depicts the efforts of young Tracy Sullivan to pull herself and her family out of the misery that surrounds them. With the aid of a relative, Dr. Luke Sullivan (from the author's *Katherine*), she makes a start, but her past is not easily escaped.

Historical Accuracy: The period details are believable.

PHILIP VAN RENSSELAER

6427 *That Vanderbilt Woman*

Date of Publication: 1978
Subject(s): Biography, Fictionalized
Historical character(s): Gloria Morgan Vanderbilt, Socialite; Reginald Vanderbilt, Gentleman; William Randolph Hearst, Financier; Edward VIII, Ruler (King of England)
Time Period(s): 1920s; 1930s
Locale(s): New York, New York; Newport, Rhode Island; Monte Carlo, Monaco

Summary: The novel captures the opulent world of the rich and famous during the 1920s in the experiences of Gloria Morgan Vanderbilt, the convent-bred daughter of a diplomat. Gloria marries Reginald Vanderbilt, who launches her on a notorious lifestyle that culminates in a scandalous custody trial.

Historical Accuracy: The novel's story is faithful to the facts surrounding the Vanderbilts.

SEYMOUR VAN SANTVOORD
(1868-1943)

A Troy, New York, native, Van Santvoord was a graduate of Union College and a practicing lawyer. He wrote several historical novels, including *Octavia: A Tale of Ancient Rome*, *St. Francis, The Christian Exemplar*, and *The House of Caesar*.

6428 *Octavia: A Tale of Ancient Rome*

Date of Publication: 1923
Subject(s): Roman Empire; Christianity
Historical character(s): Nero, Ruler (Roman emperor); Octavia, Spouse (of Nero); Caligula, Ruler (Roman emperor); Claudius I, Ruler (Roman emperor)
Time Period(s): 1st century
Locale(s): Rome, Roman Empire

Summary: Imperial politics during the reigns of Caligula, Claudius, and Nero are dramatized, centering on the unhappy fate of Octavia. Her virtue stands in marked contrast to Nero, whom she is forced to marry. She endures countless indignities with consolation coming from her faith in Christ.

Historical Accuracy: The novel closely follows historical facts and features an elaborate depiction of Roman customs.

PETER VANSITTART (1920-)

British author Vansittart was born in Bedford and attended Worcester College, Oxford. He is the author of *Green Knights, Black Angels: A Mosaic of History*.

`6429` *A Choice of Murder*

Date of Publication: 1992
Subject(s): Ancient Greece
Historical character(s): Timoleon, Military Personnel (general)
Time Period(s): 4th century B.C.
Locale(s): Greece

Summary: This is a fictional retelling of Plutarch's biography of the Greek general Timoleon. In the 4th century B.C. Timoleon helped liberate Syracuse from despotic rule. As a young man he caused the death of his brother Timophanes. The novel explores the ethical issue of whether a successful career can redeem a past crime.

Historical Accuracy: The novel stays close to its source in Plutarch.

`6430` *The Lost Lands*

Date of Publication: 1964
Subject(s): Middle Ages
Fictional character(s): Talvas, Nobleman (count), Landowner
Time Period(s): 13th century
Locale(s): Angers, France

Summary: The novel describes the rush of history and its effect on the small fiefdom of Count Talvas. He tries to hold onto the past while France's Philip the Fair is expanding his power and challenging the powerful Knights Templar. The novel registers these changes on the fixed and obsessed viewpoint of Talvas, struggling to comprehend the storm that surrounds him.

Historical Accuracy: The novel captures with authenticity the era and its customs.

`6431` *The Siege*

Date of Publication: 1962
Subject(s): Religious Conflict; Anabaptists
Fictional character(s): Matthias, Fanatic, Leader (Anabaptist); Knipperdollink, Leader (Anabaptist)
Historical character(s): Jan of Leyden, Leader (Anabaptist)
Time Period(s): 16th century (1534)
Locale(s): Munster, Germany

Summary: The novel dramatizes the seizure of the city of Munster by Anabaptists, a radical religious sect that believed in polygamy and the abolition of money and private property. Almost from the moment the Anabaptists seize power, they are threatened by the troops of the Holy Roman Empire from without and terror and dissension from within. The novel shows the corruption that infects the Anabaptist leaders and the terror of the times.

Historical Accuracy: The novel is based on an actual event during the Protestant Reformation in the 16th century.

AGNES CARR VAUGHAN (1887-)

American author and translator Vaughan was born in New Jersey and received a Ph.D. from the University of Michigan. She was a professor of Greek at Smith College from 1926 to 1952. Research and study for her books led to extensive travel, with stays in Greece, Italy, and Paris. Her chief interests were archaeology and ancient life. Her books include *Evenings in a Greek Bazaar* and *The Genesis of Human Offspring: A Study in Early Greek Culture*.

`6432` *Bury Me in Ravenna*

Date of Publication: 1962
Subject(s): Roman Empire
Historical character(s): Galla Placidia, Ruler (empress); Alaric I, Ruler (King of the Visigoths); Ataulf, Ruler (King of the Visigoths); Honorius, Ruler (Roman emperor); Constantius III, Ruler (Roman emperor); Theodosius II, Ruler (Eastern Roman emperor); Valentinian III, Ruler (Roman emperor)
Time Period(s): 5th century
Locale(s): Ravenna, Roman Empire

Summary: Galla Placidia, Roman empress and daughter of Theodosius I, tells the story of her life. Captured by Alaric I, she is held by the Visigoths as a hostage, and she marries Ataulf. Rescued by her brother Honorius, she marries the general Constantius and becomes regent for her son Valentinian III. The novel captures the intrigue and conspiracies of the final years of the Roman Empire as well as the remarkable personality of Galla Placidia.

Historical Accuracy: The historical context of the story is accurate.

CARTER A. VAUGHAN
(PSEUD. OF NOEL B. GERSON, 1914-1988)

Vaughan is one of several pseudonyms of prolific American writer, Noel B. Gerson. He was born in Chicago and educated at the University of Chicago. During World War II, Gerson served in military intelligence. He was a newspaper reporter, radio and TV scriptwriter, and the author of over 100 books. His historical novels feature a lively and entertaining blend of fact and fiction.

`6433` *The Charlatan*

Date of Publication: 1959
Subject(s): Espionage
Fictional character(s): Elias Wheaton, Military Personnel (colonel); Marie Blanchard, Spy; Juliet de Ronzie, Young Woman
Historical character(s): John Churchill, Nobleman (Duke of Marlborough), Military Personnel
Time Period(s): 1700s (1702)

Locale(s): London, England; Brussels, Belgium; Paris, France

Summary: Adventure and intrigue during the reign of Queen Anne are featured in this novel. Captain Elias Wheaton, to redeem himself after having fallen under the influence of a French spy, agrees to help rescue the Duke of Savoy's illegitimate son from the French. His mission in disguise among the French is complicated by the attractions of the exotic Marie Blanchard and the lovely Juliet de Ronzie.

Historical Accuracy: The emphasis is on romantic adventure, but there are some attempts at accurate period painting.

6434 *Dragon Cove*

Date of Publication: 1964
Subject(s): American Revolution; Espionage; Sea Story
Fictional character(s): Jonathon Sherwood, Sea Captain; Holly Talbot, Spy; Faith Hopkins, Young Woman
Time Period(s): 1770s
Locale(s): Newport, Rhode Island

Summary: The story dramatizes the work of the Newport Underground, whose task it was to break the British blockade of the city of Newport. Jonathan Sherwood is a young sea captain whose privateer helps supply American troops. He is aided by two women, Holly Talbot and Quaker Faith Hopkins. The action culminates in a sea battle with the English fleet that determines the fate of Rhode Island in the Revolution.

Historical Accuracy: The period details and locale are sharply detailed.

6435 *Fortress Fury*

Date of Publication: 1966
Subject(s): American Revolution; Espionage; American Colonies
Fictional character(s): Will Markham, Spy, Frontiersman; Catherine Ramsay, Young Woman
Time Period(s): 1770s (1775-1776)
Locale(s): Detroit, Michigan; Pittsburgh, Pennsylvania, American Colonies

Summary: In this novel of adventure and espionage set during the American Revolution's western campaign, frontiersman Will Markham is given the mission to infiltrate Fort Detroit in anticipation of the Continental Army's offensive. He winds up a prisoner of the British, and all his skills are needed to escape the gallows and complete his mission.

Historical Accuracy: The locale and the period are colorfully depicted, but the emphasis is romantic adventure rather than careful historical documentation.

6436 *The Invincibles*

Date of Publication: 1958
Subject(s): French and Indian War; American Colonies
Fictional character(s): Gordon Fuller, Military Personnel (lieutenant)
Time Period(s): 1740s (1744-1745)
Locale(s): Boston, Massachusetts, American Colonies; Louisburg, Kentucky

Summary: A financial scheme gone sour causes Lieutenant Gordon Fuller to set out across the Atlantic in search of the man behind his lost fortune. Arriving in Boston, Fuller soon begins an expedition into the frontier to Louisburg, Kentucky. He finds himself in the middle of the climax of the French and Indian War.

Historical Accuracy: More atmospheric than directly historical, the focus of the novel is on adventure and action with history acting merely as period setting.

6437 *The River Devils*

Date of Publication: 1968
Subject(s): Louisiana Purchase; Politics
Fictional character(s): Andrew MacCullough, Frontiersman
Historical character(s): Thomas Jefferson, Political Figure; James Madison, Political Figure; John Adams, Political Figure; Napoleon Bonaparte, Ruler (Emperor of France); Charles Maurice de Talleyrand-Perigord, Diplomat
Time Period(s): 18th century; 19th century (1799-1803)
Locale(s): New Orleans, Louisiana; Paris, France; Mississippi River

Summary: The background for this romantic adventure is the tumultuous years before the Louisiana Purchase and the complicated diplomatic negotiations that preceded it. The story follows the experiences of Mississippi River adventurer Andrew McCullough as he fights the Spanish and the French in New Orleans.

Historical Accuracy: The novel blends fact and fiction. The locale and southern atmosphere is more convincing than the political plot.

6438 *Roanoke Warrior*

Date of Publication: 1965
Subject(s): American Colonies; Indians
Fictional character(s): Jonas Miller, Military Personnel, Captive; Lao-ke, Indian (Tuscarora), Young Woman
Time Period(s): 18th century
Locale(s): North Carolina, American Colonies

Summary: Jonas Miller, a former British army officer, comes to North Carolina to help the colonists in their battle against the warring Tuscaroras. He is captured and finds himself the slave of an Indian woman, Lao-ke.

Historical Accuracy: The emphasis here is on romantic adventure, not historical accuracy.

6439 *Scoundrels' Brigade*

Date of Publication: 1962
Subject(s): American Revolution; American Colonies; Espionage
Fictional character(s): Hugh Spencer, Servant (indentured), Military Personnel (intelligence officer); Sara Dean, Young Woman
Historical character(s): George Washington, Military Personnel (army commander); Benjamin Tallmadge, Military Personnel (intelligence officer)
Time Period(s): 1770s (1774-1777)

Locale(s): London, England; New York, New York, American Colonies; Rhode Island, American Colonies

Summary: Hugh Spencer is mistakenly implicated in a counterfeiting ring in England. Convicted and transported as an indentured servant to America, Spencer joins the rebellion and is made the head of the Scoundrels' Brigade, a special intelligence unit that tracks down counterfeiters who are helping to destabilize the Continental currency.

Historical Accuracy: The British plot to destroy the new American government through counterfeiting is historically based, and the operation in which Spencer is involved actually took place.

6440 *The Seneca Hostage*

Date of Publication: 1969
Subject(s): American Colonies; Indians
Fictional character(s): Jonathan Lewis, Adventurer, Captive
Historical character(s): Benjamin Franklin, Political Figure; George Washington, Military Personnel (army officer)
Time Period(s): 1750s (1753)
Locale(s): Philadelphia, Pennsylvania, American Colonies; Ohio Valley, United States

Summary: This romantic adventure, set in the American frontier of the Northwest Territory, tells the story of Jonathan Lewis. He travels to America to claim his inheritance, but is captured by the Senecas. His trials build his character and fuel his love for America.

Historical Accuracy: The novel is unconvincing as historical reporting. It does feature fast-paced and exciting adventure.

6441 *The Silver Saber*

Date of Publication: 1967
Subject(s): American Colonies; French and Indian War
Fictional character(s): Jared Hale, Servant (indentured), Military Personnel; Caroline Murtagh, Gentlewoman; Polly White, Servant (indentured)
Time Period(s): 1740s
Locale(s): Delaware, American Colonies; Quebec, Quebec, Canada; England

Summary: This romantic swashbuckling tale follows the career of Jared Hale from Newgate Prison to service as an indentured servant of Lady Caroline Murtagh in colonial Delaware. He escapes servitude to fight the French in the Quebec campaign, but must decide between the woman who owns him and a fellow servant, Polly White.

Historical Accuracy: The period is evoked authentically, but the main focus is on romance and action.

6442 *The Wilderness*

Date of Publication: 1959
Subject(s): American Colonies; French and Indian War; Espionage
Fictional character(s): Paul Ferrand, Spy; Haidee Bertomy, Spy; Jeanne Osgood, Young Woman
Time Period(s): 1740s (1745)
Locale(s): New England, American Colonies

Summary: Espionage during the French and Indian Wars is featured. The story concerns Paul Ferrand, who serves as a spy for the French but is actually a double agent assisting the English. His French accomplice, Haidee Bertomy, is jealous of Paul's interest in Jeanne Osgood and threatens the success of his double mission.

Historical Accuracy: More formula and costume drama than carefully drawn history, the novel nonetheless captures some of the color of the period.

6443 *The Yankee Brig*

Date of Publication: 1960
Subject(s): Sea Story; American Colonies
Fictional character(s): Isaiah Hazlitt, Sea Captain; Ann Parsons, Young Woman; Charles Knowles, Military Personnel (naval commander)
Time Period(s): 1740s
Locale(s): Boston, Massachusetts, American Colonies

Summary: Captain Isaiah Hazlett, a hero of the French and Indian War, must contend with a rival for Ann Parsons, namely the cunning British commodore of the port of Boston, Charles Knowles. The novel paints a picture of a Boston divided by mixed allegiances and moving toward open hostilities.

Historical Accuracy: The period is original and detailed, even if the main emphasis remains romantic rather than historical.

6444 *The Yankee Rascals*

Date of Publication: 1963
Subject(s): American Revolution; Espionage
Fictional character(s): Jeremy Ford, Military Personnel (captain)
Historical character(s): Alexander Hamilton, Military Personnel (army officer); Benjamin Tallmadge, Military Personnel (intelligence officer)
Time Period(s): 1770s (1777-1778)
Locale(s): United States

Summary: Set during the American Revolution, this is a romantic story of adventure and espionage involving Captain Jeremy Ford. His job is to effect the escape of American prisoners of war, a mission of great value to the war effort.

Historical Accuracy: The emphasis is on swashbuckling adventure although the period is colorfully evoked.

MATTHEW VAUGHAN

6445 *Major Stepton's War*

Date of Publication: 1978
Subject(s): Civil War—U.S.
Historical character(s): James Ewell Brown Stuart, Military Personnel (Confederate cavalry officer); Gervase Stepton, Military Personnel (Confederate officer); Thomas Jonathan Jackson, Military Personnel (Confederate general); Robert E. Lee, Military Personnel (Confederate commander); Cole Younger, Military Personnel (Confederate soldier), Outlaw;

William Clarke Quantrill, Military Personnel (Confederate guerilla leader)
Time Period(s): 1860s
Locale(s): Virginia; Massachusetts

Summary: This Civil War story is based on the experiences of Gervase Stepton, staff officer for Robert E. Lee. Stepton is captured and after escaping from Fort Delaware mounts a daring journey from Canada into northern Massachusetts to find and destroy the North's gold bullion reserves.

Historical Accuracy: The story is based on some facts, with fictional elements added.

ROBERT VAUGHAN (1937-)

Born in Missouri, Vaughan attended the College of William and Mary and served in the U.S. Army from 1955 to 1973 as a helicopter pilot in Korea, Germany, and Vietnam. He has worked as a TV talk show host, a publisher, and an editor.

6446 *Cold War*

Date of Publication: 1995
Subject(s): Politics; Korean War
Fictional character(s): Shaylin McKay, Journalist (war correspondent); Travis Jackson, Veteran, Pilot
Historical character(s): John F. Kennedy, Political Figure
Time Period(s): 1950s
Locale(s): United States; Korea

Summary: The seventh volume of the author's American chronicles attempts to capture the events of the 1950s. The Korean War, the beginning of the space race, the McCarthy Red Scare, and the Civil Rights Movement are portrayed in the fictional story of several characters, including war correspondent Shaylin McKay and aviator Travis Jackson.

Historical Accuracy: The novel effectively presents a believable historical context for the fictional story.

6447 *The Iron Curtain*

Date of Publication: 1994
Subject(s): World War II; Independence—Israel; Civil Rights Movement
Fictional character(s): Anna Gelbman, Patriot; Travis Jackson, Veteran, Pilot; Shaylin McKay, Journalist
Time Period(s): 1940s (1945-1949)
Locale(s): St. Louis, Missouri; Palestine

Summary: As a part of the author's series examining the social history of the 20th century, the novel chronicles the post-World War II world. Scenes include the creation of the State of Israel, the Communist witch-hunt, and the dawning of the Civil Rights Movement.

Historical Accuracy: The novel features fictional characters interacting with a plausible version of historical events.

6448 *Legacy*

Date of Publication: 1995
Subject(s): American Colonies; Pilgrims; King Philip's War
Fictional character(s): Richard Prouty, Military Personnel (naval midshipman); Damaris Torry, Settler

Historical character(s): Metacomet, Indian (Wampanoag), Chieftain; John Alden, Settler, Leader (pilgrim)
Time Period(s): 17th century (1666-1674)
Locale(s): Plymouth, Massachusetts, American Colonies

Summary: This story of the Pilgrims in the Plymouth settlement follows Richard Prouty, a midshipman who settles among the Pilgrims and joins in the fight for survival.

Historical Accuracy: The author explains that the events are based on fact when documentation could be found, but that they are more fictional than factual.

6449 *Over There*

Date of Publication: 1992
Subject(s): World War I; Shipwrecks; Russian Revolution
Fictional character(s): Lucinda Chetwynd-Dunleigh, Gentlewoman; Billy Canfield, Pilot; Eric Twainborough, Journalist
Historical character(s): Dwight D. Eisenhower, Military Personnel (officer)
Time Period(s): 1910s (1912-1919)
Locale(s): *Titanic*, At Sea; St. Louis, Missouri; Europe

Summary: The tumultuous years that begin with the sinking of the *Titanic* in 1912 through the destruction of World War I are chronicled in the experiences of a variety of fictional characters who encounter real events. This is the second volume of the author's social history of the 20th century.

Historical Accuracy: The historical background is authentic.

CLARKE VENABLE (1892-)

Born in Liberty, Missouri, Venable wrote, under the pen name Covington Clarke, *Aw Hell*, *All the Brave Rifles*, and *Mosby's Night Hawk*.

6450 *All the Brave Rifles*

Date of Publication: 1929
Subject(s): Texas Revolution; Battle of the Alamo
Historical character(s): Sam Houston, Political Figure; Davy Crockett, Frontiersman; Antonio Lopez de Santa Anna, Military Personnel (Mexican general)
Time Period(s): 1830s
Locale(s): Tennessee; Washington; Texas

Summary: The novel recounts the series of events that leads to the Texas War of Independence. Many of the major figures in the conflict appear, and the novel features a vivid presentation of the Battle of the Alamo.

Historical Accuracy: The novel stays close to the actual events of the period, with some embellishment.

ERICO VERISSIMO (1905-1975)

A Brazilian author, editor, and lecturer, Verissimo was born in Cruz Alta, Rio Grande do Sul, Brazil. He is regarded as one of Brazil's major 20th-century authors. He left high school to support his family but managed to find time to write short fiction while working at a variety of odd jobs. His first critical success was the novel *Crossroads*; his first commercial success was the best-selling *Consider the Lilies of the Field.* Verissimo's other works include the novels *Clarissa* and *The Rest Is Silence*, as well as two volumes of impressions of the United States and a biography of Joan of Arc.

6451 *Time and the Wind*

Date of Publication: 1951
Subject(s): Family Saga; Independence—South America
Fictional character(s): Licurgo Cambara, Landowner; Ana Terra, Pioneer; Captain Rodrigo Cambara, Adventurer
Time Period(s): 18th century; 19th century (1740s-1895)
Locale(s): Brazil

Summary: The novel portrays Brazilian life from the frontier days in the 1740s to the siege of Santa Fe in the Federalist-Republican wars of the 1890s. The focus is on a single family, the Terra-Cambaras, whose history is traced over several generations.

Historical Accuracy: This is a vivid and convincing portrait of the period and its events.

GLENN R. VERNAM (1896-1980)

Born in Kansas, Vernam moved with his family by covered wagon to Nebraska when he was seven years old. He worked as a cowhand, horse breeder, saddlemaker, and blacksmith before becoming a rancher and writer. A member of the Cowboy Hall of Fame, Vernam is the author of the award-winning nonfiction work *Man on Horseback, the Rawhide Years: A History of the Cattlemen and the Cattle Country*, and the novels *Incident at Bloody Axe* and *The Trail of the Jackal.*

6452 *Indian Hater*

Date of Publication: 1969
Subject(s): American West; Indians
Fictional character(s): Jim Falconer, Captive
Time Period(s): 1820s (1824)
Locale(s): Missouri River, United States

Summary: Jim Falconer is banished from sophisticated Philadelphia to an isolated trading post on the upper Missouri River. He dreams only of returning home, but his capture by the Sioux forces profound changes. He survives through his intense hatred of the Indians who treat him as a slave. Yet Jim finds himself slowly appreciating the Indians' perspective, and he begins to reevaluate his earlier assumptions.

Historical Accuracy: The novel presents a credible portrait of the frontier and Indian customs.

6453 *Pioneer Breed*

Date of Publication: 1972
Subject(s): American West; Indians
Fictional character(s): Rance Harding, Teenager, Orphan; Tenny Gatewood, Teenager, Orphan
Time Period(s): 1850s
Locale(s): Oregon

Summary: Rance Harding and Tenny Gatewood are orphaned by marauding Indians and must struggle together through the harsh winter in the Oregon Territory of the 1850s. On their isolated farmstead they manage to create a home, but they are under constant threat of Indian attack in a harsh and unforgiving wilderness.

Historical Accuracy: The novel offers an authentic look at survival in the frontier of the period.

6454 *The Talking Rifle*

Date of Publication: 1973
Subject(s): American West; Ranching
Fictional character(s): Brent Curley, Cowboy; Tom Little Bear, Cowboy
Time Period(s): 19th century
Locale(s): Wyoming

Summary: A mysterious fire sweeps the Wyoming range while cattle are being slaughtered and calves stolen. Suspicion points to a new arrival in town. Sidekicks Curley Brent and Tom Little Bear set out to track down the real villain, and they find themselves in the middle of a chain of violent events.

Historical Accuracy: The novel's mystery depends on a credible portrait of the era and western ways.

FRANCES VERNON (1963-1991)

Born in London, Vernon studied history at Cambridge University. *Privileged Children* was written by Vernon at the age of 17 and won an award for the most promising first novel of 1982 from the Authors Club. Her other novels include *Gentlemen and Players* and *The Marquis of Westmarch.*

6455 *Privileged Children*

Date of Publication: 1982
Subject(s): World War I; Artistic Life
Fictional character(s): Alice Molloy, Artist
Time Period(s): 20th century (1906-1931)
Locale(s): London, England

Summary: Set during the years before, during, and after the Great War, the novel centers on the artistic career of Alice Molloy who manages to break free from her uncle's tight control to create an independent life in London as a painter. The novel describes her world of artists and free-thinkers during the war years.

Historical Accuracy: The novel creates a believable period background.

JOHN VERNON (1943-)

Vernon was born in Massachusetts and graduated from Boston College and the University of California, Davis. He is a professor of English at State University of New York, Binghamton. A poet and novelist, Vernon's works include *La Salle, Lindbergh's Son,* and *Peter Doyle.*

6456 *All for Love: Baby Doe and Silver Dollar*

Date of Publication: 1995
Subject(s): American West
Historical character(s): Horace Tabor, Mine Owner; Elizabeth "Baby Doe" Tabor, Spouse (of Horace); Silver Dollar Tabor, Writer, Prostitute; Oscar Wilde, Writer
Time Period(s): 19th century; 20th century (1872-1935)
Locale(s): Leadville, Colorado; Denver, Colorado

Summary: The story of Baby Doe Tabor's amazing career has inspired several biographies, a 1932 film, and an opera. Now her story is told in a novel that traces her relationship with silver magnate Horace Tabor, owner of the Matchless Mine. When Tabor dies in 1899, he leaves Baby Doe penniless. The novel considers Baby Doe's career and that of her daughter, Silver Dollar, who wrote poetry and died tragically in 1925.

Historical Accuracy: The author claims that the events and dates represented in the novel are almost all factual.

6457 *Peter Doyle*

Date of Publication: 1991
Subject(s): Picaresque Adventure; Fantasy
Fictional character(s): Joseph Bonaparte Benton, Adventurer; Timothy Stokes, Entertainer; Peter Doyle, Young Man
Historical character(s): Emily Dickinson, Writer (poet); Walt Whitman, Writer (poet)
Time Period(s): 1870s; 1880s
Locale(s): New York; Colorado; Europe

Summary: This picaresque fantasy tale takes the form of the quest for Napoleon's dismembered penis which has accidentally fallen into the hands of young Peter Doyle. This comic conceit propels the story across the American continent and to Europe, and involves an imaginative meeting of America's greatest 19th-century poets, Emily Dickinson and Walt Whitman.

Historical Accuracy: This is a phantasmagoric version of history with a knowing sense of the past that is subverted comically.

6458 *La Salle*

Date of Publication: 1986
Subject(s): Exploration
Historical character(s): Rene-Robert Cavelier de La Salle, Explorer; Pierre Goupil, Cartographer
Time Period(s): 17th century (1682-1688)
Locale(s): Mississippi River; Quebec, Canada; Texas

Summary: This is the story of French explorer LaSalle's effort to chart the length of the Mississippi River and claim a wilderness kingdom for France. It is told from the alternating perspectives of LaSalle himself and his cartographer, Pierre Goupil. The New World is revealed as a mirror in which the 18th-century European mind examines a strange aspect of itself.

Historical Accuracy: The novel is solidly based on journals, letters, and secondary sources.

PATRICIA VERYAN
(PSEUD. OF PATRICIA V. BANNISTER, 1923-)

English romance writer Veryan worked as a secretary before beginning her writing career. Her novels include *The Lord and the Gypsy*, *The Dedicated Villain*, and *Pride House*.

6459 *Ask Me No Questions*

Date of Publication: 1993
Subject(s): Romance; Georgian Period
Fictional character(s): Ruth Allington, Widow(er), Artist; Gordon Chandler, Heir; Sir Brian Chandler, Gentleman; Gideon Rossiter, Gentleman
Time Period(s): 1740s (1748)
Locale(s): England

Summary: In this installment of the Tales of the Jewelled Men, Ruth Allington has found employment at the estate of Sir Brian Chandler by hiding her family background. Sir Brian Chandler and his son Gordon are a target of the League of Jewelled Men who are to determined to ruin his name and claim his estate. Ruth is caught up in the intrigue and her situation is complicated by her attraction to Gordon, who is openly hostile to her. Gideon Rossiter helps the Chandlers fight the League in a battle of wits.

Historical Accuracy: The romantic adventure features some convincing period elements.

6460 *Cherished Enemy*

Date of Publication: 1988
Subject(s): Georgian Period; Jacobite Rebellion
Fictional character(s): Rosamond Albriton, Gentlewoman; Charles Albriton, Religious (minister); Robert Victor, Doctor
Time Period(s): 1740s (1746)
Locale(s): England

Summary: In the fifth book of the Golden Chronicles, Rosamond Albriton finds herself involved in the Jacobite supporters' search for the cypher that will lead to Bonnie Prince Charlie's hidden treasure. An injury on board a ship to England brings her in contact with Dr. Robert Victor, and her feelings for him complicate her previous views.

Historical Accuracy: The story offers a fanciful view of the disposition of Prince Charles Stuart's treasure and is not intended to be interpreted as historical fact.

6461 *The Dedicated Villain*

Date of Publication: 1989
Subject(s): Georgian Period; Jacobite Rebellion
Fictional character(s): Roland Farleigh Mathieson, Gentleman, Rake; Fiona Bradford, Young Woman
Time Period(s): 1740s (1746)
Locale(s): England

Summary: In the sixth and final volume of the Golden Chronicles, notorious rake and mercenary Roland Farleigh Mathieson is recruited to the Jacobite cause through his attraction to Fiona Bradford, the daughter of the leader of a travelling theatrical troupe.

Historical Accuracy: The novel's plot is fanciful and is not intended to be taken as historical fact.

`6462` *Feather Castles*

Date of Publication: 1982
Subject(s): Regency Romance; Battle of Waterloo
Fictional character(s): Rachel Strand, Fiance(e); Claude Sanguinet, Gentleman; Tristram Leigh, Military Personnel
Time Period(s): 1810s (1815)
Locale(s): Waterloo, Belgium; England

Summary: This Regency romance begins on the battlefield of Waterloo as Rachel Strand accompanies her fiance in a search for one of the fallen. They encounter a young wounded soldier who saves them from plunderers. He can recall neither his name nor his nationality, but he plays an important role in the romantic complications that follow.

Historical Accuracy: The emphasis is on romantic complication rather than careful period documentation.

`6463` *Had We Never Loved*

Date of Publication: 1992
Subject(s): Georgian Period
Fictional character(s): Horatio Glendenning, Nobleman (viscount); Amy Consett, Gypsy
Time Period(s): 1740s
Locale(s): England; Scotland

Summary: In the second of the Tales of the Jewelled Men, the sinister League's victim is Lord Horatio Glendenning. He owes his survival to a gypsy maid, Amy Consett, and a missing heirloom pin.

Historical Accuracy: The novel's adventures are set against a believable period background.

`6464` *Journey to Enchantment*

Date of Publication: 1986
Subject(s): Georgian Period; Jacobite Rebellion
Fictional character(s): Prudence McTavish, Gentlewoman; Geoffrey Delacourt, Military Personnel (English captain); Ligun Doone, Fugitive (Jacobite)
Time Period(s): 1740s (1746)
Locale(s): Inverness, Scotland; England

Summary: The aftermath of Bonnie Prince Charlie's defeat at the Battle of Culloden is played out in the second installment of the Golden Chronicles series. Prudence McTavish resists the British Captain Geoffrey Delacourt in favor of Jacobite rebel Ligun Doone. She joins in a plan to rescue captured Scots and deliver to England a cypher to be used to find the location of Prince Charlie's legendary treasure.

Historical Accuracy: The story is fanciful but is set in an accurately described period background.

`6465` *Lanterns*

Date of Publication: 1996
Subject(s): Regency Romance
Fictional character(s): Marietta Warrington, Gentlewoman; Diccon Paisley, Spy

Time Period(s): 1810s (1818)
Locale(s): Sussex, England

Summary: The novel returns to the world of the Sanguinet Saga for this Regency-era tale that concerns the attraction felt by Marietta Warrington for a mysterious stranger who is suspected of being a smuggler.

Historical Accuracy: While romantic suspense predominates, the novel makes convincing use of its period elements.

`6466` *Logic of the Heart*

Date of Publication: 1990
Subject(s): Regency Romance
Fictional character(s): Susan Henley, Widow(er); Valentine Montclair, Gentleman
Time Period(s): 1810s
Locale(s): England

Summary: Susan Henley, the widow of a man who gambled away a fortune, has come to live in reduced circumstances on the grounds of Longhills Manor, the county seat of the Montclairs. Valentine Montclair is bewitched by the beautiful Susan, but can she be trusted? And is the series of odd accidents that occur evidence that someone is plotting against him?.

Historical Accuracy: The novel offers a complex mixture of adventure, romance, and some credible period details.

`6467` *Love Alters Not*

Date of Publication: 1987
Subject(s): Georgian Period; Jacobite Rebellion
Fictional character(s): Dimity Cranford, Gentlewoman; Horatio Glendenning, Fugitive (Jacobite); Anthony Farrar, Military Personnel (British officer)
Time Period(s): 1740s (1746)
Locale(s): England

Summary: In the fourth book of the Golden Chronicles, Dimity Cranford sets out to rescue her childhood companion Horatio Glendenning, a Jacobite sympathizer. When the wounded Glendenning is unable to deliver a crucial cypher, Dimity becomes the courier. She encounters infamous officer Anthony Farrar under an assumed identity that becomes increasingly difficult to maintain.

Historical Accuracy: The novel's emphasis is romantic adventure with a convincing period background.

`6468` *Love's Duet*

Date of Publication: 1979
Subject(s): Regency Romance
Fictional character(s): Lady Sophia Drayton, Gentlewoman; Camille Damon, Nobleman (marquis)
Time Period(s): 1810s
Locale(s): England

Summary: Lady Sophia Drayton finds herself strangely drawn to the man she holds responsible for her brother's enlistment in the wars against Napoleon and his subsequent loss of an arm in battle. There are momentary flashes of a different man behind his facade of cowardliness and cruelty, and Sophia begins to regret the revenge she has plotted against him.

Historical Accuracy: This is a familiar romantic situation featuring some authentic period details.

6469 *Married Past Redemption*

Date of Publication: 1983
Subject(s): Regency Romance
Fictional character(s): Lisette Van Lindsay, Gentlewoman; Justin Strand, Gentleman; James Garvey, Gentleman
Time Period(s): 1810s (1816)
Locale(s): London, England

Summary: Financial need causes Lisette Van Lindsay to marry the cold-hearted Justin Strand. When a former suitor, James Garvey, continues to pursue her, gossiping London society sets in motion a series of events that keeps the newlyweds at odds, narrowly escaping tragedy.

Historical Accuracy: The period background is believably presented.

6470 *Men Were Deceivers Ever*

Date of Publication: 1989
Subject(s): Regency Romance
Fictional character(s): Helena Hammond, Gentlewoman; Peter Clivedon, Military Personnel (lieutenant)
Time Period(s): 1810s (1811)
Locale(s): England

Summary: Helena Hammond marries Lieutenant Peter Clivedon to repair her shattered fortune. Eventually, she grows to love him, but the marriage is disrupted when Helena learns a terrible truth about Peter.

Historical Accuracy: The novel features some authentic period elements.

6471 *Mistress of Willowvale*

Date of Publication: 1980
Subject(s): Georgian Period; Jacobite Rebellion
Fictional character(s): Christopher Aynsworth, Nobleman; Leonie Haliwell, Fiance(e)
Time Period(s): 1740s
Locale(s): England

Summary: Christopher Aynsworth returns from the Jacobite Wars to find that his fiancee, Leonie Haliwell, has been thoroughly disgraced. Aynsworth refuses to withdraw from his commitment, and she refuses to release him. After marrying, they begin to rediscover their initial attraction, but their relationship is threatened by Haliwell's past and the hunt for fugitives from the Jacobite cause.

Historical Accuracy: The romantic elements are set within a believable context of the period.

6472 *Nanette*

Date of Publication: 1981
Subject(s): Regency Romance
Fictional character(s): Nanette Sanguinet, Gentlewoman; Sir Harry Redmond, Gentleman

Time Period(s): 1810s
Locale(s): London, England

Summary: The villainy of the notorious Parnell Sanguinet brings together his stepdaughter Nanette and Sir Harry Redmond. She, in disguise, attempts to escape her stepfather while investigating the death of her brother. Redmond is determined to discover the cause of his father's death and his lost family estate and fortune. Their quests converge, and when Nanette is kidnapped by her stepfather's agents, Redmond sets out to free her, becoming a hunted man.

Historical Accuracy: Fast-paced adventure is featured in this period story that does offer some convincing historical details.

6473 *Never Doubt I Love*

Date of Publication: 1995
Subject(s): Romance; Georgian Period
Fictional character(s): Zoe Grainger, Young Woman (farmer's daughter); Peregrine Cranford, Military Personnel (lieutenant)
Time Period(s): 1740s (1748)
Locale(s): London, England

Summary: The fifth volume of the Tales of the Jewelled Men is set in Georgian England. Zoe Grainger, a farmer's daughter, and Lieutenant Peregrine Cranford join forces in the fight against the traitorous League of Jewelled Men. In the process they find both romance and adventure.

Historical Accuracy: The story is strong on adventure with a convincing period backdrop.

6474 *The Noblest Frailty*

Date of Publication: 1983
Subject(s): Regency Romance
Fictional character(s): Yolande Drummond, Young Woman; Alain Devenish, Fiance(e); Craig Tyndale, Gentleman
Time Period(s): 1810s
Locale(s): England; Scotland

Summary: Romantic complications affect Yolande Drummond, who is engaged to marry her cousin Alain Devenish. His youthful pranks cause her to delay setting the date. When their cousin Craig Tyndale arrives from Canada, Yolande begins to fall in love with Alain's rival and is faced with several choices.

Historical Accuracy: The novel is a fairly conventional romance with some slight period details setting a believable backdrop.

6475 *Practice to Deceive*

Date of Publication: 1985
Subject(s): Georgian Period; Jacobite Rebellion
Fictional character(s): Penelope Montgomery, Gentlewoman; Quentin Chandler, Fugitive
Time Period(s): 1740s (1746)
Locale(s): England

Summary: This first volume of the Golden Chronicles tells the story of the search for the treasure amassed by Bonnie Prince

Charlie after his defeat at the Battle of Culloden. The series begins with the story of Penelope Montgomery, who comes to the aid of a fugitive Jacobite, Quentin Chandler. Together they journey across England to a small town where Quentin must deliver a cypher, part of a code that will reveal the location of Prince Charlie's fortune.

Historical Accuracy: The story is fanciful but does offer many authentic period elements.

6476 *Sanguinet's Crown*

Date of Publication: 1985
Subject(s): Regency Romance
Fictional character(s): Claude Sanguinet, Gentleman; Rachel Leith, Gentlewoman; Charity Strand, Gentlewoman; Mitchell Redmond, Gentleman
Historical character(s): George, Prince Regent, Royalty
Time Period(s): 1810s (1817)
Locale(s): Brighton, England; Hebrides, Scotland

Summary: The novel continues Claude Sanguinet's conspiracy against the British government, now aimed at the life of the Prince Regent himself. Sanguinet first arranges to kidnap Rachel Leith, his former fiance, but it is her sister, Charity Strand, who is abducted to the Hebrides instead. She and Mitchell Redmond, who rescues her, rush cross-country to Brighton to save the life of the Prince Regent.

Historical Accuracy: The author admits that in her depiction of the Royal Pavilion at Brighton in 1817 she has included some apartments that were not completed at that time.

6477 *A Shadow's Bliss*

Date of Publication: 1994
Subject(s): Romance; Georgian Period
Fictional character(s): Jennifer Britewell, Gentlewoman, Teacher; Jonathan Armitage, Outcast (also known as Crazy Jack); Lord Hibbard Green, Nobleman
Time Period(s): 1740s (1746)
Locale(s): Cornwall, England

Summary: Jennifer Britewell befriends the village idiot, Crazy Jack, who shows signs of intelligence and gallantry when he and Jennifer begin to uncover the secrets of his past. They become entangled in the dangerous dealings of the League of Jewelled Men, and Jennifer becomes a target of the lecherous Lord Hibbard Green.

Historical Accuracy: This pygmalion-like transformation of the village idiot is more fairy tale than historical.

6478 *Some Brief Folly*

Date of Publication: 1981
Subject(s): Regency Romance
Fictional character(s): Euphemia Buchanan, Gentlewoman; Garret Hawkhurst, Rake
Time Period(s): 1810s
Locale(s): England

Summary: On the road from London to Bath, Euphemia Buchanan's coach is overturned in a landslide. Her rescuer is the notorious rake Garret Hawkhurst, who is rumored to have been responsible for the deaths of his wife and child. Conva-

lescence takes place within the walls of Hawkhurst's country estate.

Historical Accuracy: This is a familiar romantic tangle with some convincing period elements.

6479 *Time's Fool*

Date of Publication: 1991
Subject(s): Georgian Period
Fictional character(s): Gideon Rossiter, Military Personnel (captain); Lady Naomi Lutonville, Gentlewoman
Time Period(s): 1740s (1748)
Locale(s): England

Summary: In the first of the Tales of the Jewelled Men, Captain Gideon Rossiter returns to England to find his fortune lost and his engagement to Lady Naomi Lutonville broken off. Rossiter vows to uncover the unknown cause of his misfortune. The plot is complicated by the disappearance of a jewelled figurine, which draws Lady Naomi into a sinister conspiracy.

Historical Accuracy: The novel offers an ingenious tangle of romantic adventure with a credible period background.

6480 *The Tyrant*

Date of Publication: 1987
Subject(s): Georgian Period; Jacobite Rebellion
Fictional character(s): Phoebe Ramsay, Gentlewoman; Meredith Carruthers, Gentleman
Time Period(s): 1740s (1746)
Locale(s): England

Summary: In book three of the Golden Chronicles, Phoebe Ramsay finds herself betrothed to a man she hardly knows, Meredith Carruthers, in order to safeguard the life of one of the outlawed supporters of the Jacobite cause. She finds herself working with Carruthers to avoid suspicion, which could lead to death.

Historical Accuracy: The period details and the backdrop of actual events create a believable historical presentation.

6481 *The Wagered Widow*

Date of Publication: 1984
Subject(s): Georgian Period; Jacobite Rebellion
Fictional character(s): Rebecca Parrish, Widow(er); Trevelyan de Villars, Gentleman; Sir Peter Ward, Gentleman
Time Period(s): 1740s (1746)
Locale(s): England

Summary: Rebecca Parrish is left an impoverished widow when her husband is killed in a duel. She sets out to find a new husband, but her flirtatiousness turns serious when the two men she loves are prepared to duel to the death over her. Meanwhile, the turmoil of the Jacobite Rebellion intervenes, and Rebecca attempts to save a fugitive Jacobite.

Historical Accuracy: The period background is authentic.

RICHARD VETTERLI

LEO V. GORDON (1942-)

6482 *Powderkeg*

Date of Publication: 1991
Subject(s): American West; Mormons
Historical character(s): James Buchanan, Political Figure; Jefferson Davis, Political Figure; Albert Sidney Johnston, Military Personnel (general)
Time Period(s): 1850s (1857-1858)
Locale(s): Utah; Washington, District of Columbia

Summary: In 1857, General Albert Sidney Johnston and an army of 3,000 are dispatched from Fort Leavenworth to the Utah Territory. There Johnston is to put down the rebellious Mormon settlers. But secession dreams complicate the picture, and the Union is threatened.

Historical Accuracy: The novel is a blend of truth and fiction. But the essential story is built on solid research.

DANIEL D. VICTOR (1944-)

Born in California, Victor graduated from the University of California, Berkeley, and the University of California, Los Angeles. He is a high school English teacher.

6483 *The Seventh Bullet*

Date of Publication: 1992
Subject(s): Mystery; Vampires
Fictional character(s): Sherlock Holmes, Detective—Private; John H. Watson, Doctor
Historical character(s): Theodore Roosevelt, Political Figure; William Randolph Hearst, Journalist, Publisher
Time Period(s): 1910s (1911)
Locale(s): New York, New York

Summary: The murder of a muckraking journalist brings Sherlock Holmes and Watson to New York to investigate. The body is riddled with six bullets, but the prescribed killer had a seventh for himself from a six-shot revolver. A wider conspiracy is detected involving vampires, Teddy Roosevelt, and William Randolph Hearst.

Historical Accuracy: The novel is an ingenious mystery with genuine period details.

GORE VIDAL (1925-)

American novelist and editor Vidal is one of the best known literary figures in America, as well as a two-time political candidate. He is the author of novels, plays, screenplays, essays, and reviews, all noted for their wit and biting satire.

6484 *1876: A Novel*

Date of Publication: 1976
Subject(s): Politics; Business Building
Fictional character(s): Charlie Schuyler, Writer; Emma d'Agrigente, Widow(er), Royalty (princess)

Historical character(s): Samuel Tilden, Political Figure; William Cullen Bryant, Writer; Mark Twain, Writer
Time Period(s): 1870s (1875-1876)
Locale(s): New York, New York; Washington, District of Columbia

Summary: Charles Schuyler returns to America in 1875 after a long self-imposed exile in Europe. He is intent on restoring his finances by arranging a suitable marriage for his daughter, Emma, the widowed Princess d'Agrigente. He finds himself in New York and Washington at the height of the corruption of the Grant Administration and during the 1876 election battle between Hays and Tilden.

Historical Accuracy: The real characters are depicted faithfully.

6485 *Burr*

Date of Publication: 1973
Subject(s): American Revolution; Politics
Fictional character(s): Charlie Schuyler, Journalist
Historical character(s): Aaron Burr, Political Figure; George Washington, Military Personnel (army commander), Political Figure; Thomas Jefferson, Political Figure; Alexander Hamilton, Political Figure; James Madison, Political Figure; Dolley Madison, Spouse; Andrew Jackson, Political Figure, Military Personnel (general); Martin Van Buren, Political Figure
Time Period(s): 18th century; 19th century (1775-1840)
Locale(s): United States

Summary: Aaron Burr was a hero of the American Revolution, served as Vice President under Thomas Jefferson, killed Alexander Hamilton in a duel, and was tried for treason when Jefferson accused him of plotting to make an empire of his own in the western territories. The novel offers a remarkably inventive depiction of the founding and struggles of the new United States from the perspective of one of its most brilliant and complex figures.

Historical Accuracy: The novel is based on the known facts with imagined conversations and some manipulations of the chronology that the author admits in the book's afterward.

6486 *Creation*

Date of Publication: 1981
Subject(s): Ancient Greece; Persian Empire; Chinese Empire
Fictional character(s): Cyrus Spitama, Diplomat
Historical character(s): Xerxes I, Ruler (Persian king); Confucius, Philosopher; Socrates, Philosopher; Darius, Ruler (Persian king); Pericles, Military Personnel (general), Political Figure
Time Period(s): 5th century B.C.
Locale(s): Greece; India; China

Summary: Cyrus Spitama provides insights into the ancient world of the 5th century B.C. in which many of our modern philosophical, political, and scientific ideas were created. Cyrus is brought up in the Persian court and undertakes a diplomatic mission that takes him to India and China. His search for meaning brings him in contact with Buddha, Confucius, and Socrates.

Historical Accuracy: The novel is masterful in providing a convincing synthesis of an enormous swathe of history and ideas.

6487 *Empire: A Novel*

Date of Publication: 1987
Subject(s): Politics; Spanish-American War
Fictional character(s): Caroline Sanford, Young Woman; Blaise Sanford, Businessman, Publisher
Historical character(s): William Randolph Hearst, Businessman, Publisher; William McKinley, Political Figure; Theodore Roosevelt, Political Figure; William Jennings Bryan, Political Figure; John Hay, Political Figure; Henry Adams, Writer; Henry James, Writer; Elihu Root, Political Figure
Time Period(s): 1890s; 1900 (1898-1904)
Locale(s): New York, New York; Washington, District of Columbia

Summary: This panoramic political novel is set in the aftermath of the Spanish-American War as America's manifest destiny begins to claim an empire. Young Caroline Sanford is propelled to the center of political and social power. Her half-brother, Blaise Sanford, and William Randolph Hearst are determined to thwart her ambitions.

Historical Accuracy: The historical figures are depicted in keeping with the historical record.

6488 *Hollywood: A Novel of America in the 1920s*

Date of Publication: 1990
Subject(s): Motion Picture Industry; Politics; World War I
Fictional character(s): Caroline Sanford, Businesswoman, Actress; Blaise Sanford, Businessman; James Burden Day, Political Figure
Historical character(s): Woodrow Wilson, Political Figure; William Randolph Hearst, Financier, Publisher; Eleanor Roosevelt, Spouse; Warren G. Harding, Political Figure; Franklin Delano Roosevelt, Political Figure; Henry Adams, Writer; Douglas Fairbanks, Actor; Edith Wilson, Spouse
Time Period(s): 1910s; 1920s (1917-1924)
Locale(s): Washington, District of Columbia; Hollywood, California

Summary: The rise of America's second power center, Hollywood, is chronicled, along with America's entry into World War I, Woodrow Wilson's campaign for the League of Nations, and the corruption of the Harding administration. Caroline Sanford, publisher, becomes Emma Traxler, movie star, in a Hollywood that, like Washington, is in the business of manufacturing the truth.

Historical Accuracy: Endlessly inventive and provocative, the novel is convincing in its depiction of the period.

6489 *Julian*

Date of Publication: 1964
Subject(s): Roman Empire; Christianity; Religious Conflict
Fictional character(s): Priscus, Philosopher, Editor (of Julian's memoirs); Libanius, Philosopher, Editor (of Julian's memoirs); Maximus, Sorcerer (soothsayer)

Historical character(s): Julian the Apostate, Ruler (Roman Emperor); Helena, Spouse (of Julian), Royalty
Time Period(s): 4th century (361-363)
Locale(s): Rome, Roman Empire; Athens, Greece; Persia

Summary: The novel is based on the life of Roman emperor Julian the Apostate. Though raised a Christian, Julian tries to turn the Empire back to the worship of pagan gods. To tell his story, Vidal uses three narrators: Julian himself and the philosophers Priscus and Libanius, who edit Julian's memoirs. Julian proves himself a great general in his defeat of Persia, but he overreaches himself in trying to conquer all Asia and to turn the clock back to the pre-Christian spiritual world.

Historical Accuracy: Vidal offers many discursive passages on curiosities of the times, convincing the reader that he is both a good historian and a good researcher.

6490 *Lincoln: A Novel*

Date of Publication: 1984
Subject(s): Politics; Civil War—U.S.
Fictional character(s): Charlie Schuyler, Journalist
Historical character(s): Abraham Lincoln, Political Figure; Mary Todd Lincoln, Spouse; William Henry Seward, Political Figure; Salmon P. Chase, Political Figure; George McClellan, Military Personnel (Union general); John Wilkes Booth, Murderer (assassin); Ulysses S. Grant, Military Personnel (Union general); David Herold, Spy
Time Period(s): 1860s (1861-1865)
Locale(s): Washington, District of Columbia

Summary: The Lincoln presidency is depicted from the perspectives of family and friends, political rivals, and his eventual assassins. Lincoln emerges in three dimensions as he tries to manage the war and preserve the Union while fighting off political challenges. The novel captures both Lincoln's greatness as a leader and his human side through some of the darkest days of the American nation.

Historical Accuracy: The historical figures portrayed have been based on letters, journals, newspapers, and diaries with only a few alterations for the sake of the story.

6491 *Live From Golgotha*

Date of Publication: 1992
Subject(s): Biblical Story; Fantasy
Historical character(s): Mary Baker Eddy, Religious; Jesus Christ, Biblical Figure; Shirley MacLaine, Actress, Writer; Oral Roberts, Religious; Timothy, Religious (bishop)
Time Period(s): 1st century (96); 1990s
Locale(s): Thessalonika, Macedonia; Jerusalem, Israel

Summary: In a phantasmagorical satire on TV and religion, Timothy, bishop of Macedonia, struggles to complete his version of the story of Jesus while, through a breakthrough in computer software, an NBC film crew is able to broadcast the Crucifixion to boost the network's ratings during sweeps week. Twentieth-century figures of various religious stripes struggle to appropriate the event.

Historical Accuracy: Clearly the author's intention is satirical rather than historical. The details are accurate, however, both modern and biblical.

6492 *A Search for a King: A 12th-Century Legend*

Date of Publication: 1950
Subject(s): Middle Ages; Royalty—England; Myths and Legends
Historical character(s): Blondel de Nesle, Entertainer (minstrel); Richard the Lionhearted, Ruler (King of England)
Time Period(s): 12th century
Locale(s): Europe

Summary: Blondel, Richard the Lionhearted's faithful minstrel, searches for the king after he is imprisoned in Austria. Based on the Chronicle of Rheims, the novel follows Blondel's adventurous journey across Europe to free the king.

Historical Accuracy: This story is more legendary than historical, making the background uncertain.

6493 *Washington, D.C.*

Date of Publication: 1967
Subject(s): Politics
Fictional character(s): James Burden Day, Political Figure (senator); Clay Overbury, Political Figure; Blaise Sanford, Businessman, Publisher
Historical character(s): Franklin Delano Roosevelt, Political Figure; Joseph McCarthy, Political Figure (senator)
Time Period(s): 20th century (1937-1952)
Locale(s): Washington, District of Columbia

Summary: Chronologically the third book in a trilogy that includes *Burr* and *1876*, the novel follows the ambitions of two politicians, James Burden Day, a conservative senator, and his young assistant, the opportunistic and amoral Clay Overbury.

Historical Accuracy: The fictional story is interwoven with actual events and believable portraits of individuals from the New Deal to the McCarthy era.

NICOLE VIDAL (1928-)

French author Vidal was born in Hanoi, where her father was an engineer. She later lived for four years in Egypt, where she developed her interest in ancient Egypt. She has written books for children and adults and has won literary awards for *La Main Droite*, *La Conspirations des Parasols*, and *Nom de la Guerre*.

6494 *The Goddess Queen: A Novel Based on the Life of Nefertiti*

Date of Publication: 1961
Subject(s): Ancient Egypt; Pharaohs
Historical character(s): Nefertiti, Ruler (Queen of Egypt); Amenhotep IV, Ruler (pharaoh)
Time Period(s): 14th century B.C.
Locale(s): Egypt

Summary: The reign of Nefertiti as queen of ancient Egypt is described. Married to her older brother Amenhotep, she becomes the virtual ruler of Egypt as Amenhotep (better known as Akhenaton) destroys the old gods in favor of monotheism, costing Egypt its empire. Nefertiti is shown as a forceful and capable ruler during a fascinating period of Egyptian history.

Historical Accuracy: The novel is convincing both in its atmosphere and its treatment of history.

ALFRED VICTOR DE VIGNY (1797-1863)

This poet, dramatist, and novelist was an early leader of the French Romantic movement. He translated Shakespeare and achieved success with his play *Chatterton*. He also published *Servitude et Grandeur Militaires*, three stories set during the Napoleonic Wars.

6495 *Cinq-Mars*

Date of Publication: 1826
Subject(s): Royalty—France
Historical character(s): Henri Coeffier-Ruze d'Effiat, Nobleman (Marquis de Cinq-Mars); Armand-Jean Du Plessis, Religious (Cardinal Richelieu), Political Figure; Louis XIII, Ruler (King of France); Anne of Austria, Royalty (queen of France)
Time Period(s): 17th century (1639-1641)
Locale(s): France

Summary: This exciting adventure of court intrigue and conspiracy has been called the first French historical novel. The Marquis of Cinq-Mars attempts to overthrow Cardinal Richelieu and wed his beloved, who is destined to become the Queen of Poland. Vigny's portrait of Richelieu is a fascinating study in wiliness.

Historical Accuracy: This is an exceptional rendering of actual historical events, convincing and compelling.

JOSE ANTONIO VILLARREAL (1924-)

The son of Jose Hiladio, a Mexican revolutionary, Villarreal was born in Los Angeles, California, and became a naturalized Mexican citizen in 1973. He is a graduate of the University of California, Berkeley, and has been a professor of English literature and creative writing in the U.S. and Mexico, as well as a radio and TV broadcaster. His acclaimed novels of Mexican and Chicano history include *Pocho* and *Clemente Chacon*.

6496 *The Fifth Horseman*

Date of Publication: 1974
Subject(s): Mexican Revolution
Fictional character(s): Heraclio Ines, Young Man
Historical character(s): Francisco Villa, Revolutionary
Time Period(s): 19th century; 20th century (1890s-1914)
Locale(s): Mexico

Summary: The Mexican Revolution of 1910 is seen through the experiences of Heraclio Ines, the fifth son of a family of accomplished horsemen. Raised under a strict code of honor, Heraclio finds his values tested in the Revolution as a member of Pancho Villa's army.

Historical Accuracy: The author warns that the novel should not be taken as an accurate history of the Mexican Revolution.

The events have been shaped to enhance the pattern of the story.

ELIZABETH VILLARS
(PSEUD. OF ELLEN FELDMAN, 1941-)

American author Ellen Feldman was born in Elizabeth, New Jersey, and attended Bryn Mawr College. She has worked as an advertising copywriter, a publicity director for a publishing company, and a freelance editor. Feldman has been a full-time writer since 1977 and is the author of *Looking for Love*, *A Woman Once Loved* (under the pseudonym Amanda Russell), and several novels under the pseudonym Elizabeth Villars, including *Lipstick on His Collar*.

6497 *The Normandie Affair*

Date of Publication: 1982
Subject(s): Ocean Liners
Fictional character(s): Emily Atherton, Young Woman, Journalist; Max Ballinger, Businessman; Anson Sherwood, Socialite
Time Period(s): 1930s (1936); 1940s (1942)
Locale(s): *Normandie*, At Sea

Summary: Aboard the fashionable ocean liner *Normandie* three central characters come together — Emily Atherton, a young journalist; Anson Sherwood, the scion of a wealthy family; and Max Ballinger, an industrialist. They work out their relationship against the splendor of the great liner as the world hovers on the brink of war.

Historical Accuracy: The period forms a convincing backdrop to this relationship drama.

6498 *One Night in Newport*

Date of Publication: 1981
Subject(s): Business Building
Fictional character(s): Amelia Leighton, Young Woman; Samuel Van Nest, Financier
Historical character(s): John Pierpont Morgan, Financier; Harry Houdini, Magician
Time Period(s): 1910s (1912)
Locale(s): Newport, Rhode Island

Summary: Newport in 1912 is the scene for this novel of love and money among the fashionable Leighton family. Samuel Van Nest attempts to outwit five of the richest men in America on behalf of the very richest, J.P. Morgan. The social proprieties are duly observed as passion for love and power dominates the social scene.

Historical Accuracy: Conspicuous consumption and financial dealings among the social elite of Newport are believably captured.

6499 *The Very Best People*

Date of Publication: 1979
Subject(s): Romance; Depression Era
Fictional character(s): Kathryn Owen, Young Woman; Tyson Enfield, Young Man

Time Period(s): 20th century (1917-1937)
Locale(s): Philadelphia, Pennsylvania; Washington, District of Columbia

Summary: Kathryn Owen is the daughter of a Philadelphia politico and a ladies' maid. Her love for mainline socialite Tyson Enfield is chronicled over a 20-year period. Their passion for one another endures separation, Ty's unhappy marriage, and Kate's career, which takes her into the inner circle of New Deal politics.

Historical Accuracy: The love-conquers-all theme is set against a believable period background.

BARBARA VINE
(PSEUD. OF RUTH RENDELL, 1930-)

English writer Vine was born in London and has worked as a newspaper reporter. Her mysteries have earned her the accolade of the new Agatha Christie. She is a master of the police procedural and psychological thriller genres, and writes a series featuring Chief Inspector Wexford.

6500 *Anna's Book*

Date of Publication: 1994
Subject(s): Mystery; Edwardian Period
Fictional character(s): Ann Eastbrook, Detective—Amateur
Time Period(s): 1900s (1905); 1990s
Locale(s): London, England

Summary: Ann Eastbrook, while reading through her grandmother's diary, discovers that a single entry has been cut out. The entry may shed light on both Ann's mother's birth and a gory unsolved murder during the summer of 1905. Ann sets out to learn the truth.

Historical Accuracy: The novel depends on a convincing sense of the Edwardian period.

ELIZABETH GRAY VINING (1902-)

Born in Philadelphia and educated at Bryn Mawr and the Drexel Institute, Vining served from 1946 to 1950 as the tutor to Japanese Crown Prince Akihito. Her experiences are recorded in the book *Windows for the Crown Prince*. Vining has won numerous awards for her work, including the 1943 Newbery Medal for *Adam of the Road*, the *Herald Tribune* Spring Festival Award in 1945 for *Sandy*, and the *Philadelphia Atheneum* Literary Award in 1964 for *Take Heed of Loving Me*.

6501 *I, Roberta*

Date of Publication: 1967
Subject(s): Suspense
Fictional character(s): Roberta Morelli, Spouse; Anthony Morelli, Gentleman
Time Period(s): 1890s (1895)
Locale(s): New Jersey

Summary: This intriguing character study set in a small New Jersey town at the end of the 19th century concerns Roberta Morelli, who discovers that her husband has been a bigamist.

The drama revolves around the fate of Roberta's five-year-old son and the reevaluation that her circumstances force on Roberta.

Historical Accuracy: The psychological examination is set within a believable period background that helps force the novel's crises.

6502 *Take Heed of Loving Me: A Novel about John Donne*

Date of Publication: 1963
Subject(s): Elizabethan Period; Jacobean Period; Literary Life
Historical character(s): John Donne, Writer (poet); Anne More, Gentlewoman; Elizabeth I, Ruler (Queen of England); James I, Ruler (King of England); Sir Walter Raleigh, Courtier; Ben Jonson, Writer; Robert Devereux, Nobleman (Earl of Essex)
Time Period(s): 16th century; 17th century (1597-1617)
Locale(s): England

Summary: This is the fascinating story of John Donne, libertine and poet, who became one of England's greatest preachers and the dean of St. Paul's Cathedral. His love for Anne More cost Donne his political career. His struggles in art, politics, and love are dramatized with the historical background vividly drawn.

Historical Accuracy: The novel stays close to the sources and faithful to the facts, with some imagined scenes and dialogue.

ANATOLII VINOGRADOV (1888-1946)

Vinogradov was a Russian writer.

6503 *The Black Consul*

Date of Publication: 1935
Subject(s): Independence—Haiti; French Revolution
Historical character(s): Pierre Dominique Toussaint l'Ouverture, Revolutionary; Antoine Laurent Lavoisier, Scientist; Andre Chenier, Writer (poet); Honore Gabriel Riqueti, Revolutionary; Maximilien Francois de Robespierre, Revolutionary; Napoleon Bonaparte, Military Personnel; Jean-Paul Marat, Revolutionary
Time Period(s): 1780s; 1790s
Locale(s): France; Haiti

Summary: This panoramic novel offers glimpses of the French Revolution and its impact on the rebellion led by Toussaint-L'Ouverture to abolish slavery and achieve independence in Haiti. Dozens of actual characters appear in a series of scenes that are both historical and imagined.

Historical Accuracy: Despite documentary evidence that provides the basis for many of the scenes, there are extensive inaccuracies.

ELFRIDA VIPONT
(PSEUD. OF ELFRIDA VIPONT FOULDS, 1902-)

Born in Manchester, England, Vipont studied history and music and became a professional singer, free-lance writer, and lecturer. During World War II, she served as the

headmaster at a Quaker school. She is the author of over 30 books. She is probably best known for *The Lark in the Morn* and its Carnegie Medal-winning sequel, *The Lark on the Wing.* Her other books for adults and young adults include *The Candle of the Lord* and *Swarthmore Hall.*

6504 *Bed in Hell*

Date of Publication: 1974
Subject(s): Jacobite Rebellion; Georgian Period
Fictional character(s): Maurice Lydiard, Gentleman; Jane Stuart, Young Woman
Time Period(s): 18th century
Locale(s): Wisbech, England

Summary: This novel of political intrigue, religious persecution, and social change in the early decades of the 18th century centers on Maurice Lydiard, whose physical deformity has produced in him a unique attitude toward life. Into his life comes the enigmatic Jane Stuart, who may be related to the Stuart claimants to the throne.

Historical Accuracy: The novel's story is imagined, but it does capture the flavor of the times believably.

ANGE VLACHOS (1915-)

Vlanchos is a Greek writer.

6505 *Their Most Serene Majesties*

Date of Publication: 1961
Subject(s): Byzantine Empire; Middle Ages
Historical character(s): John II, Ruler (emperor); Manuel I, Ruler (emperor); Andronicus I Comnenus, Ruler (emperor)
Time Period(s): 12th century
Locale(s): Constantinople, Byzantine Empire; Asia Minor

Summary: An unnamed chronicler records the lives and works of the last emperors of the House of Comnenus of the Byzantine Empire at the court of Constantinople. The decline and fall of the Byzantine Empire is shown with a colorful depiction of the political, military, and theological issues of the period.

Historical Accuracy: The novel is faithful to history and believable.

R.G. VLIET (1929-1984)

American poet and novelist Vliet was born in Chicago and attended Southwest Texas State College and Yale University. He was the recipient of numerous awards for his works, including the Texas Institute of Letters Fiction Award for *Solitudes.* Vliet is also the author of the critically acclaimed novel *Scorpio Rising,* published the year after his death, and the award-winning poetry collection *Events and Celebrations.*

6506 *Rockspring*

Date of Publication: 1973
Subject(s): American West; Crime and Criminals

Fictional character(s): Jensie, Teenager, Captive; Bernardino, Outlaw
Time Period(s): 1830s
Locale(s): Texas

Summary: The novel recounts the experiences of a young girl who is kidnapped by three Mexican outlaws. Her winter-long ordeal as a captive and her struggle to return home with the youngest outlaw provide a vivid western tale and coming of age drama.

Historical Accuracy: The novel creates a believable period atmosphere.

6507 *Solitudes*

Date of Publication: 1977
Subject(s): American West
Fictional character(s): Claiborne Sanderlin, Wanderer; Soledad Kincaid, Young Woman
Time Period(s): 1880s
Locale(s): Texas

Summary: The novel tells the tale of a drifter who kills a man and finds in the dead man's pocket a picture of a beautiful girl whom he sets out to meet. His search and eventual confrontation with the dead man's granddaughter is told in the authentic voices of Texas in the 1880s.

Historical Accuracy: The period elements in the story are authentic.

WILLIAM T. VOLLMANN (1959-)

6508 *Fathers and Crows*

Date of Publication: 1992
Subject(s): Exploration; Religious Conflict; Indians
Fictional character(s): Born Underwater, Indian (Micmac), Shaman; Born Swimming, Indian (Micmac)
Historical character(s): Samuel de Champlain, Explorer, Government Official; Jean de Brebeuf, Religious (priest)
Time Period(s): 17th century; 18th century (1610-1791)
Locale(s): Canada

Summary: The Seven Dreams series continues with a depiction of the conflict between the French Jesuits and the Indians in Canada. Two cultures collide, and the resulting clash is captured in myth, factual chronicle, drama, and the author's own personal experiences.

Historical Accuracy: Literal accuracy is not the author's goal but rather a symbolic history made up, in the author's words, from a tissue of speculations, prejudices, and falsehoods.

6509 *The Ice Shirt*

Date of Publication: 1990
Subject(s): Exploration; Vikings; Myths and Legends
Historical character(s): Leif Eriksson, Explorer; Freydis Eiriksdottir, Explorer, Bastard Daughter; Gudrid Thorbjornsdottir, Explorer
Time Period(s): 11th century
Locale(s): Greenland; North America; Iceland

Summary: In the first of the Seven Dreams series offering a symbolic history of North America, Norsemen from Greenland set out to claim new lands in America. Two women, Freydis and Gudrid, compete for control of the new land with the Indians, who find their world transformed by the power of the iron axes the Norsemen bring.

Historical Accuracy: The novel blends folklore, historical material, and contemporary observations into an imaginative if unconventional reconstruction of the past.

6510 *The Rifles*

Date of Publication: 1994
Subject(s): Exploration; Tribal Life—Native American
Historical character(s): Sir John Franklin, Explorer
Time Period(s): 1840s
Locale(s): Arctic; Canada

Summary: In the sixth of Vollman's projected seven-novel cycle examining the clash of Native Americans and European colonizers, the third and final Arctic expedition by Sir John Franklin becomes the occasion for a wide ranging meditation that shuttles back in time and forward to the present and the state of the Inuits in Northern Canada.

Historical Accuracy: The author calls the series a symbolic history in which untruths reveal a deeper sense of truth. The novel's notes indicate the factual basis for the novel's imaginative.

NICHOLAS VON HOFFMAN (1929-)

A columnist on political and economic matters, Von Hoffman was born in New York City. He began his career in Chicago, where he worked for nine years as associate director of the Industiral Areas Foundation, a grass-roots social activist organization. He subsequently worked as a journalist for the *Chicago Daily News* and the *Washington Post*. A syndicated columnist, Von Hoffman was also the Point-Counterpoint commentator on CBS's ''Sixty Minutes.'' He is the award-winning author of *Mississippi Notebook* and *We Are the People Our Parents Warned Us Against*, an unflinching portrait of discord among America's youth in the late.

6511 *Organized Crime*

Date of Publication: 1984
Subject(s): Crime and Criminals
Fictional character(s): Allan Archibald, Socialite, Student (graduate); Mona Jupiter, Young Woman; Irena Giron, Student (graduate)
Historical character(s): Frank Nitti, Organized Crime Figure; Anton Cermak, Political Figure (mayor of Chicago); Samuel Insull, Financier; George Mundelein, Religious (cardinal); Al Capone, Organized Crime Figure
Time Period(s): 1930s (1931)
Locale(s): Chicago, Illinois

Summary: Chicago in the 1930s is captured in a satire of vice and folly. Allan Archibald, a young socialite, is convinced to do field work on organized crime. He finds himself taken up by Frank Nitti of the Capone gang. Meanwhile, financier Samuel Insull must defend his financial empire from a raid, and Chicago Mayor Anton Cermak alienates the mob, which culminates in his assassination.

Historical Accuracy: The story mingles facts and inventions. The atmosphere of gangland Chicago is captured believably.

JOHN VORNHOLT (1951-)

A full-time writer who lives in Tucson, Arizona, Vornholt has written 13 Star Trek books as well as other science fiction novels.

6512   The Fabulist

Date of Publication: 1993
Subject(s): Fantasy
Fictional character(s): Xanthus, Professor
Historical character(s): Aesop, Writer, Wanderer
Time Period(s): 6th century B.C.
Locale(s): Greece; Egypt; Babylon

Summary: The legendary figure of Aesop is described. Raised as a mute slave, he acquires the gift of storytelling after an encounter with Isis. He becomes a gifted and well-travelled storyteller moving throughout the ancient world.

Historical Accuracy: There is little historical basis for the fantasy, but the atmosphere of the ancients is strong.

ETHEL LILLIAN VOYNICH (1864-1960)

A British composer and author, Voynich was born in Cambridge. She was 90 years old when she learned from a group of Soviet journalists that in the Soviet Union her fame as a novelist ranked with that of writers Mark Twain, Theodore Dreiser, and Charles Dickens. Her novel, *The Gadfly*, sold 2.5 million copies in the Soviet Union alone and was made into a film and an opera in Russia. Voynich's other novels include *Interrupted Friendship*.

6513   Put Off Thy Shoes

Date of Publication: 1945
Subject(s): Georgian Period
Fictional character(s): Beatrice Telford, Gentlewoman
Time Period(s): 18th century
Locale(s): Warwickshire, England; Cornwall, England

Summary: This character study is set during the reign of George III and traces the development of Beatrice Telford from her unhappy childhood to her adult life among the Cornish peasants.

Historical Accuracy: The novel offers a believable period and regional background.

THEODORE VRETTOS (1919-)

Born in Peabody, Massachusetts, Vrettos attended Holy Cross Greek Seminary and pursued graduate study at Tufts and Yale universities. He has been a writer-in-residence at Simmons College and received critical acclaim for his 1980

novel of Greece on the eve of Mussolini's invasion, *Birds of Winter*. His other novels include *Hammer on the Sea* and *Origen*.

6514   Lord Elgin's Lady

Date of Publication: 1982
Subject(s): Regency Period
Historical character(s): Thomas Bruce, Nobleman (Earl of Elgin), Diplomat; Mary Nisbet, Gentlewoman; Horatio Nelson, Military Personnel (admiral); Sir William Hamilton, Diplomat; Lady Emma Hamilton, Spouse, Gentlewoman; Selim III, Ruler (Ottoman sultan)
Time Period(s): 1790s; 1800s
Locale(s): Athens, Greece; Constantinople, Ottoman Empire; Sicily, Italy (Palermo)

Summary: The novel describes one of history's greatest art thefts. His Majesty's British Ambassador Thomas Bruce, Earl of Elgin, obtains the Turkish government's permission to dismantle the great sculptures of the Parthenon and ship them home to England. The negotiations and their aftermath are seen through the perspective of Lady Elgin, who watches her marriage disintegrate as Lord Elgin's obsession grows.

Historical Accuracy: The background of the story is accurate, but the plot mixes the fictional with the factual.

6515   Origen: A Historical Novel

Date of Publication: 1978
Subject(s): Biography, Fictionalized; Religious Life
Historical character(s): Origen Adamantius, Religious (theologian), Philosopher
Time Period(s): 3rd century
Locale(s): Alexandria, Egypt

Summary: This is a fictional account of the 3rd-century Christian philosopher and scholar Origen. Before St. Augustine, Origen was the most influential theologian in the Christian church. The novel attempts to capture the cultural and ecclesiastical turmoil of the day as well the genius of Origen.

Historical Accuracy: The novel shows evidence of painstaking research into the period that produces an authentic evocation of the era.

BARBARA FITZ VROMAN

Vroman was born in Chicago. Her first novel, *Tomorrow Is a River*, won the Leslie Cross Award.

6516   Sons of Thunder

Date of Publication: 1981
Subject(s): Independence—Ireland
Fictional character(s): Siobonna Covington, Young Woman; John Murphy, Religious (priest); Marietta Manning, Noblewoman (Duchess of Farleigh)
Time Period(s): 1790s (1797-1798)
Locale(s): Ireland

Summary: The story of the failed uprising by the United Irishmen led by Wolfe Tone is described from the perspectives of a young Irish girl and a village priest. The conflicting loyalties of the Anglo-Irish aristocracy are examined.

Historical Accuracy: Marietta Manning is based on a real figure, Maria Gunning, Duchess of Coventry. The depiction of battles and historical events is faithful to the facts.

HELEN WADDELL (1889-1965)

Born in Tokyo, Japan, the daughter of a British Presbyterian minister and missionary, Waddell was educated at Queen's University in Belfast, Northern Ireland. A playwright, translator, nonfiction writer, and novelist, Waddell was known for her expert translations of medieval Latin literature and her scholarship on the Middle Ages. An early book that received acclaim from both critics and general readers was *The Wandering Scholars*, a critical account of the classical Latin tradition in literature. Her other books include *Medieval Latin Lyrics*, the plays *The Spoiled Buddha* and *The Abbe Prevost*, and three children's books.

6517 *Peter Abelard: A Novel*

Date of Publication: 1933
Subject(s): Middle Ages; Religious Life
Historical character(s): Peter Abelard, Philosopher, Religious (monk); Heloise, Gentlewoman, Religious (abbess)
Time Period(s): 12th century
Locale(s): France

Summary: This is a retelling of the tragic medieval love story of Peter Abelard and Heloise who find themselves trapped in a series of circumstances that separate them and make the fulfillment of their love impossible. The novel captures with skill the customs and beliefs that underpin their tragedy.

Historical Accuracy: Although the novel is filled with authentic period elements, this is a rather simplified version of the Abelard and Heloise story.

CONSTANCE WAGNER (1903-)

Wagner's books include *Sycamore* and *The Major Has Seven Guests*.

6518 *Ask My Brother*

Date of Publication: 1959
Subject(s): Civil War—U.S.
Fictional character(s): Warren Randall, Military Personnel (Confederate soldier); Phoebe Randall, Southern Belle
Time Period(s): 1860s (1861-1865)
Locale(s): Virginia

Summary: The novel presents the events of the Civil War as experienced by members of a well-to-do Virginia family, the Randalls. The war on the homefront and the battlefield is reflected in a story that illustrates the divided loyalties of the period.

Historical Accuracy: The novel provides a believable account of the war years and their impact on a typical family of the period.

GEOFFREY WAGNER (1927-)

A Malaysian-born poet, novelist, nonfiction writer, translator, and college professor, Wagner became a naturalized American citizen. He attended Christ Church College, Oxford, and embarked on his teaching career at City College in New York after receiving his Ph.D. from Columbia University in 1954. His works include *Wyndam Lewis: The Portrait of the Artist as the Enemy* and the novels *The Wings of Madness: A Novel of Charles Baudelaire*, *The Innocent Grove*, and *The Sands of Valor*.

6519 *Sophie*

Date of Publication: 1957
Subject(s): Biography, Fictionalized
Historical character(s): Sophie Dawes Feucheres, Noblewoman
Time Period(s): 19th century
Locale(s): France

Summary: This is the tale of the actual daughter of a smuggler who rises from poverty on the Isle of Wight to become one of the most powerful women in France. The novel illustrates Sophie Dawes' meteoric rise as the mistress of Louis, Duke of Bourbon.

Historical Accuracy: The novel is accurate in its facts and period details.

JOHN WAGNER (1917-)

ESTHER WAGNER

John Wagner is a professor of English at the College of Puget Sound, Washington. Esther Wagner is a writer whose stories have appeared in *Atlantic*, *New Yorker*, and the *Saturday Evening Post*.

6520 *The Gift of Rome*

Date of Publication: 1961
Subject(s): Roman Empire; Trials
Historical character(s): Marcus Tullius Cicero, Lawyer; Cluentius, Businessman; Sassia, Gentlewoman
Time Period(s): 1st century B.C. (66 B.C.)
Locale(s): Rome, Roman Empire

Summary: Cicero is the lawyer for the defense in one of history's strangest murder cases. The defendant is Cluentius, a respected businessman who is accused of the murder of his stepfather. Cicero's investigation reveals much that is hidden. He must try his case in the Forum of Rome, newly freed from the dictatorship of Sulla and filled with menace and political maneuvering.

Historical Accuracy: The situation is inspired by a real event; and the depiction of the Roman Republic's atmosphere and customs is authentic.

DAVID WAGONER (1926-)

An American poet and professor of English at the University of Washington, Wagoner was born in Massillon, Ohio, and attended Pennsylvania State University and Indiana University. A highly regarded poet and novelist, Wagoner is the author of several poetry collections, including *Staying Alive*.

6521 *Tracker*

Date of Publication: 1975
Subject(s): American West; Crime and Criminals
Fictional character(s): Eli, Worker (stableboy); Tracker Byrd, Indian
Time Period(s): 1880s (1889)
Locale(s): Colorado

Summary: Set in Colorado during the 1880s, this western novel begins with a bank robbery. Stableboy Eli seizes the opportunity to become Tracker Byrd's apprentice in tracking down the criminal Worley Brothers.

Historical Accuracy: The novel offers an authentic version of the West and the period background.

6522 *Where Is My Wandering Boy Tonight?*

Date of Publication: 1970
Subject(s): American West
Fictional character(s): Arthur Jackson Holcomb Jr., Young Man; Fred Haskell, Young Man
Time Period(s): 1890s
Locale(s): Wyoming

Summary: This western tale, set in Wyoming during the 1890s, follows the experiences of Arthur Jackson Holcomb, Jr., the son of the local judge, and his friend Fred Haskell, the son of the local preacher. When Arthur's father leaves town, he also leaves title to half the town to his son. The novel follows the pair's maturation and the conflict between idealistic youth and small town corruption.

Historical Accuracy: The novel provides a believable portrait of the region and the era.

6523 *Whole Hog*

Date of Publication: 1976
Subject(s): American West
Fictional character(s): Zeke Hunt, Pioneer; Casper, Businessman (whiskey salesman)
Time Period(s): 1850s (1852)
Locale(s): Oregon Trail, United States

Summary: This tale of the Western frontier is set in the 1850s and involves the journey of Zeke Hunt and his parents who sell their Missouri farm and head west with a herd of hogs. When his parents are killed and all but three of the hogs are lost, Zeke makes his own way, hooking up with an itinerant whiskey salesman.

Historical Accuracy: The novel captures pioneer life and customs with skill.

R.G. WALDECK (1898-)

Waldeck's books include *Athene Palace*, *Europe between the Acts*, and *Prelude to the Past*, her autobiography.

6524 *The Emperor's Duchess*

Date of Publication: 1948
Subject(s): Napoleonic Era; Peninsular War
Historical character(s): Laure Junot, Noblewoman; Andoche Junot, Nobleman, Military Personnel (French general)
Time Period(s): 1800s; 1810s (1807-1813)
Locale(s): France

Summary: The scandals, intrigues, and politics of Napoleon's court are dramatized through the experiences of Laure Junot, the Duchesse d'Abrantes. Her husband is Napoleon's aide and the governor of Paris. Laure and her husband's life together follows the fortunes of Napoleon in the Peninsular War.

Historical Accuracy: Romance predominates in this picture of the period.

6525 *Lustre in the Sky*

Date of Publication: 1946
Subject(s): Napoleonic Era; Diplomacy; Congress of Vienna
Historical character(s): Charles Maurice de Talleyrand-Perigord, Diplomat; Clemens von Metternich, Diplomat; Alexander I, Ruler (Czar of Russia); Dorothea de Perigord, Noblewoman (countess)
Time Period(s): 1810s (1814-1815)
Locale(s): Vienna, Austria

Summary: This novel about the Congress of Vienna, called after the defeat of Napoleon to redraw the map of Europe, has as its central character the wily French ambassador Talleyrand. Although a Napoleon loyalist for years, he manages to stake his claim for power in the new regime. Away from the negotiating tables, Talleyrand embarks on an affair with his niece, Dorothea.

Historical Accuracy: The novel is best in capturing the glamour and atmosphere of the period. There are a number of historical inaccuracies.

FRANCIS WALDER

6526 *The Negotiators*

Date of Publication: 1959
Subject(s): Diplomacy; Religious Conflict; Huguenots
Fictional character(s): De Malassise, Diplomat
Historical character(s): Gaspard de Coligny, Leader (Protestant), Nobleman; Catherine de' Medici, Royalty (Queen Mother of France)
Time Period(s): 16th century (1570)
Locale(s): France

Summary: Catherine de Medici and the Comte de Coligny, a Huguenot leader, negotiate over the cession of four towns to the Protestant cause. Events are seen through the eyes of De Malassise, the chief diplomatic representative of the Catholic

side. Power politics and religious control are wrapped up in this subtle chronicle of the delicate art of diplomacy.

Historical Accuracy: The historical background to the diplomatic manuevering is authentic and accurately detailed.

EMERSON WALDMAN

6527 *Beckoning Ridge*

Date of Publication: 1940
Subject(s): Civil War—U.S.
Fictional character(s): Martin Glendower, Farmer; Lindsey Glendower, Spouse
Time Period(s): 1860s
Locale(s): Shenandoah Valley, Virginia; Blue Ridge Mountains, Virginia

Summary: The effect of the Civil War on a group of peaceful and prosperous Virginia farmers is depicted in this story that slowly but inevitably exposes the ravages of war on Martin and Lindsay Glendower. Living on a ridge overlooking the strategic Shenandoah Valley, they are caught between the contending armies and are reduced to war-like activities to survive.

Historical Accuracy: The novel captures the Virginia mountain setting with accuracy.

ANNA LEE WALDO (1925-)

Waldo was born in Montana and graduated from Montana State University and the University of Maryland. Waldo worked as a toxicologist and a research biochemist and as a professor of chemistry and physical science at St. Louis Community College. Her interest in the Lewis and Clark Expedition began when she moved to St. Louis.

6528 *Prairie*

Date of Publication: 1986
Subject(s): American West; Biography, Fictionalized
Historical character(s): Charles Button Irwin, Frontiersman
Time Period(s): 19th century; 20th century
Locale(s): West

Summary: This massive panorama of western life during the last decades of the 19th century and the beginning of the 20th focuses on the life of cowboy and rodeo star Charles Button Irwin. His experiences provide the basis for an almost encyclopedic presentation of western life and customs.

Historical Accuracy: The novel succeeds in filling in the background with authentic period details.

6529 *Sacajawea*

Date of Publication: 1978
Subject(s): Indians; American West; Lewis and Clark Expedition
Historical character(s): Sacajawea, Indian (Shoshone), Guide; Meriwether Lewis, Explorer; William Clark, Explorer; Jean Baptiste Charbonneau, Frontiersman
Time Period(s): 19th century

Locale(s): West

Summary: This is a massive fictional biography of Sacajawea, the Shoshone chief's daughter and the lone woman who accompanied Lewis and Clark on their trip to the Pacific. The novel imagines Sacajawea's life from her youth to her death in the 1880s and colorfully portrays a passing era.

Historical Accuracy: The novel mixes factual details with considerable speculation, particularly in the later stages of Sacajawea's life.

ROBERT WALES (1923-)

Born and educated in Scotland, Wales emigrated to Australia, where he worked as a cattle grazier and gold prospector before turning to writing. He is the author of the award-winning plays *The Holiday House*, *The Grotto*, and *The Cell*.

6530 *Harry: A Novel of Australia*

Date of Publication: 1985
Subject(s): Frontier—Australia
Fictional character(s): Harry Walford, Worker (ranchhand); Dan McKenzie, Rancher
Time Period(s): 1880s (1882)
Locale(s): Australia

Summary: Set in the Australian outback in the 1880s, the novel tells the story of one of the biggest cattle thefts of all time. Ranchhand Harry Walford attempts to drive 1,500 head of cattle across 1,200 miles of the outback. He is pursued by powerful rancher Dan McKenzie and a legendary Aborigine trapper.

Historical Accuracy: The novel features an authentic background and convincing setting in the Australian frontier.

MARGARET WALKER (1915-)

An American poet, novelist, and nonfiction writer, Walker was born in Birmingham, Alabama, and received her A.B. from Northwestern where she began writing *Jubilee*. After marrying and raising a family, she attended the University of Iowa where she received her Ph.D. and completed the novel on the 100th anniversary of Appomattox. Critics have called the novel the first truly historical black American novel. Walker is also the author of poetry collections and has been a contributor to many anthologies and periodicals.

6531 *Jubilee*

Date of Publication: 1966
Subject(s): Civil War—U.S.; Slavery; Reconstruction Period
Fictional character(s): Vyry Ware, Slave; John Dutton, Plantation Owner; Randall Ware, Blacksmith
Time Period(s): 19th century
Locale(s): Georgia

Summary: The antebellum, Civil War, and Reconstruction periods are dramatized from the perspective of Vyry, a slave on the Georgia plantation of John Dutton. Her life in service through the disaster of the war years and the bitter promise of Reconstruction is chronicled.

Historical Accuracy: The novel's story is based on the life of the author's great-grandmother.

MILDRED WALKER
(PSEUD. OF MILDRED W. SCHEMM, 1905-)

An American profeesor and author, Schemm was born in Philadelphia and graduated from Wells College and the University of Michigan. She worked as a copywriter before becoming a professor of English at Wells College. She received the Avery Hopwood Award from the University of Michigan for *Fireweed*. Her other books include *Unless the Wind Turns*, *Winter Wheat*, and *The Quarry*.

6532   *If a Lion Could Talk*

Date of Publication: 1970
Subject(s): Religious Life; Indians
Fictional character(s): Mark Ryegate, Religious (missionary); Harriet Ryegate, Spouse
Time Period(s): 19th century
Locale(s): Massachusetts; Missouri

Summary: A Massachusetts minister, Mark Ryegate, and his wife, Harriet, go into the wilderness of Missouri to convert the Indians. The tragic consequences of Ryegate's failure are explored.

Historical Accuracy: Although the characters and situations are based on actual figures and events, the author's treatment and interpretation are fictional.

ROBERT E. WALL (1940-)

Born in Brooklyn, Wall moved to Canada in 1970, settling in Quebec and becoming a Canadian citizen in 1976. A historian, Wall has taught at several universities including Concordia University in Montreal and has served as provost of Fairleigh Dickinson University.

6533   *Birthright*

Date of Publication: 1982
Subject(s): American Revolution
Fictional character(s): Stephen Norwell, Businessman, Loyalist
Time Period(s): 18th century (1765-1784)
Locale(s): Boston, Massachusetts; Canada

Summary: In the third volume of The Canadians series, Stephen Norwell is now middle aged and prosperous. He marries into a wealthy Boston family as the American Revolution produces a conflict of loyalties. His opposition to the American cause leads him to leave his son and home.

Historical Accuracy: The novel's period elements are authentic and convincing.

6534   *Blackrobe*

Date of Publication: 1981

Subject(s): American Colonies; Frontier—Canada; Indians
Fictional character(s): Stephen Norwell, Orphan; Karl Stieger, Mercenary
Historical character(s): Molly Brant, Indian (Mohawk)
Time Period(s): 1730s; 1740s (1730-1745)
Locale(s): North America

Summary: In the first volume of The Canadians saga, which chronicles the history of 18th and 19th-century North America, Stephen Norwell, an orphan, is raised by Jesuit priests who hide his identity from him. Norwell sets out to find his lost family across the landscape of the North American frontier at the crucial stage of English, French, and Indian conflict.

Historical Accuracy: The novel offers a blend of fictional and factual details with a believable historical background.

6535   *Bloodbrothers*

Date of Publication: 1981
Subject(s): American Colonies; French and Indian War
Fictional character(s): Stephen Norwell, Frontiersman; Karl Stieger, Mercenary
Historical character(s): Louis Joseph de Montcalm, Military Personnel (general); Molly Brant, Indian (Mohawk)
Time Period(s): 1740s; 1750s (1746-1759)
Locale(s): New York, American Colonies; Quebec, Quebec, Canada

Summary: The second volume of The Canadians saga continues the story of Stephen Norwell and his friendship with Swiss mercenary Karl Stieger through the years of the French and Indian Wars. The action of the novel culminates with the fall of New France on the Plains of Abraham.

Historical Accuracy: The novel interweaves the fictional story with authentic details of actual events and figures.

LEW WALLACE (1827-1905)

American writer Wallace's early career was spent in the military. He served in the Mexican War and in the Civil War, rising to the rank of major-general. He turned to writing in 1873 and his second novel, *Ben Hur*, is said to have sold over 2,000,000 copies. Wallace served as territorial governor of New Mexico and as minister to Turkey.

6536   *Ben Hur: A Tale of the Christ*

Date of Publication: 1880
Subject(s): Roman Empire; Jews; Christianity
Fictional character(s): Judah Ben Hur, Royalty (prince), Slave (galley); Messala, Military Personnel; Balthazar, Nobleman, Biblical Figure
Historical character(s): Jesus Christ, Biblical Figure
Time Period(s): 1st century (1-33)
Locale(s): Jerusalem, Israel; Rome, Roman Empire; Antioch, Syria

Summary: Wallace connects the story of Christ with the family history of the Ben Hurs. Judah Ben Hur, son of a rich Jewish family, is accused of treason by his former friend Messala. He becomes a galley slave and the adopted son of a

Roman consul. He returns to Antioch for revenge on Messala and encounters Jesus' final days in Jerusalem.

Historical Accuracy: Wallace provides evidence of great familiarity with the customs and details of ordinary life of the time. His characters, however, appear abstract and life-less.

`6537` *The Fair God*

Date of Publication: 1873
Subject(s): Exploration; Aztec Empire
Fictional character(s): Guatamozin, Nobleman
Historical character(s): Montezuma II, Ruler (Aztec emperor); Hernando Cortez, Explorer, Military Personnel (conquistador)
Time Period(s): 16th century
Locale(s): Mexico

Summary: The conquest of the Aztecs by the Spanish is dramatized in this historical romance which depicts the Emperor Montezuma as weak-willed and vacillating before the Spanish invaders. His son-in-law Guatamozin mounts a defense that fails.

Historical Accuracy: The novel offers an idealized and imagined portrait of the last days of the Aztec Empire that is more romantic than historically accurate.

RANDALL WALLACE

`6538` *Braveheart*

Date of Publication: 1995
Subject(s): Middle Ages; Royalty—Scotland; Independence—Scotland
Historical character(s): William Wallace, Knight, Patriot; Robert the Bruce, Nobleman; Philip IV, Ruler (King of France); Edward Longshanks, Ruler (King of England); Isabella of France, Royalty (queen consort of Edward II)
Time Period(s): 13th century; 14th century (1276-1314)
Locale(s): Scotland; London, England; France

Summary: The novel tells the heroic story of commoner William Wallace, who grows up while England's hold on Scotland is tightening and Scottish lords are stripped of many priveledges. As an adult, Wallace brings Scots together against the tyrannical English king, Edward Longshanks, in a battle for freedom.

Historical Accuracy: The author admits that William and his world are seen through the eyes of a poet, not a historian. The relationship between Wallace and Isabella is a fabrication since she was only nine at the time of his death and three years from becoming Edward II's queen.

WILLARD WALLACE (1911-)

Born in Maine, Wallace was a professor of history at Wesleyan University and the author of five non-fiction books, including *Appeal to Arms: A Military History of the American Revolution* and *Soul of the Lion: A Biography of General Joshua Chamberlain.*

`6539` *East to Bagaduce*

Date of Publication: 1963
Subject(s): American Revolution; Sea Story
Fictional character(s): Tom Dearborn, Military Personnel (American privateersman)
Historical character(s): Dudley Saltonstall, Military Personnel (American naval officer); Paul Revere, Military Personnel (American officer), Patriot
Time Period(s): 1770s (1779)
Locale(s): Bagaduce, Maine (New Castine)

Summary: The novel is based on the actual records of America's great naval disaster in the seige of British-headed Bagaduce (New Castine), Maine, by a ragged Revolutionary expeditionary force. The failed campaign is dramatized from the perspective of young privateer Tom Dearborn, aboard his ship, the *Dart*. The reputations of the commodore of the American fleet, Dudley Saltonstall, and Lieutenant-Colonel Paul Revere are tested.

Historical Accuracy: The novel is based on fact. The main character, Tom Dearborn, though invented, has historical prototypes.

`6540` *Jonathan Dearborn: A Novel of the War of 1812*

Date of Publication: 1967
Subject(s): War of 1812; Sea Story
Fictional character(s): Jonathan Dearborn, Lawyer, Military Personnel (privateersman); Ben Vail, Sea Captain
Time Period(s): 1810s (1813-1815)
Locale(s): Maine; *Argus*, At Sea; Hartford, Connecticut

Summary: The novel tells the story of a young lawyer, Jonathan Dearborn, who at the outbreak of the War of 1812 signs on with Captain Ben Vail of the *Argus* as a privateersman. His adventures take him through important events of the war and vividly depict the political issues surrounding the conflict, including the fateful Hartford Convention.

Historical Accuracy: The story is fictional but has factual precedents, as the author's historical notes point out.

`6541` *The Raiders: A Novel of the Civil War at Sea*

Date of Publication: 1970
Subject(s): Civil War—U.S.; Sea Story; Draft Riots
Fictional character(s): Scott Pettigrew, Military Personnel (naval lieutenant)
Historical character(s): Henry Adams, Writer
Time Period(s): 1860s (1862-1865)
Locale(s): At Sea; England; New York, New York

Summary: The story of the *C.S.S. Alabama* is told through the experiences of a young Maine-bred U.S. Navy lieutenant who becomes a crew member aboard the Confederate raider. The novel depicts the New York Draft Riots, the sinking of the *Alabama*, and the capture of Fort Fisher.

Historical Accuracy: The novel is solidly researched and offers a convincing depiction of the historical action.

IRA JAN WALLACH (1913-)

American author and dramatist Wallach was born in New York City and attended Cornell University. He served with the U.S. Army in the Pacific theater during World War II. Wallach is the author of *Hot Millions*, the screenplay for the film *Boy's Night Out*, and the novel *The Absence of a Cello*.

6542   *The Horn and the Roses: A Novel Based on the Life of Peter Paul Rubens*

Date of Publication: 1947
Subject(s): Biography, Fictionalized; Artistic Life
Historical character(s): Peter Paul Rubens, Artist, Diplomat
Time Period(s): 16th century; 17th century
Locale(s): Belgium

Summary: This fictionalized biography of the 17th-century Flemish painter and diplomat Peter Paul Rubens describes his rise to power and success. The novel endorses the controversial theory that many of Rubens' masterpieces were done not by him but by others in his workshop.

Historical Accuracy: The novel is best at evoking the atmosphere of the period and its artistic controversies. The debunking of Rubens' artistic genius is debatable.

LESLIE WALLER (1923-)

Born in Chicago, and a resident of Italy, Waller began writing as a crime reporter on a Chicago newspaper. His best-selling trilogy, *The Barber*, *The Family*, and *The American* won acclaim. Three of his books have been made into motion pictures: *A Change in the Wind*, *Dog Day Afternoon*, and *Hide in Plain Sight*.

6543   *Blood & Dreams*

Date of Publication: 1980
Subject(s): Oil Industry; Business Building
Fictional character(s): Kate Blood, Young Woman; Edmund Crozat, Gentleman
Time Period(s): 1880s (1888-1889)
Locale(s): New Orleans, Louisiana

Summary: This colorful story of New Orleans focusses on the impact of the discovery of oil. Kate Blood's affair with Edmund Crozat provides the romance, but the main drama is provided by the city itself, filled with clashing cultures and contradictions.

Historical Accuracy: The novel is convincing in its depiction of period New Orleans.

HUGH WALPOLE (1884-1941)

This English novelist is most noted for his four-novel historical sequence on the Herries family. His other well-known titles include *Maradick at Forty*, *Mr. Perrin and Mr. Traill*, *Prelude to Adventure*, *The Dark Forest*, and *The Green Mirror*.

6544   *The Fortress*

Date of Publication: 1932
Subject(s): Family Saga
Fictional character(s): Judith Paris, Gentlewoman; Walter Herries, Gentleman
Time Period(s): 1820s; 1830s
Locale(s): England

Summary: Part three of the Herries chronicle covers the later life of Judith Paris (nee Herries) and her quarrel with Walter Herries. He swears vengeance on those he holds responsible for slighting his proud, snobbish family; and the feud passes to the next generation.

Historical Accuracy: The novel offers a social panorama, powerful narrative and complicated genealogy.

6545   *Judith Paris*

Date of Publication: 1931
Subject(s): Family Saga
Fictional character(s): Judith Paris, Gentlewoman; George Paris, Smuggler, Gambler; William Herries, Gentleman
Time Period(s): 18th century; 19th century (1770-1815)
Locale(s): England; Paris, France

Summary: The second of four novels dealing with the Herries family, this volume focuses on Judith Herries, daughter of Rogue Herries and a young gypsy. Her first 40 years include a disastrous marriage and a growing family rift with her nephew, William Herries.

Historical Accuracy: This is a long and complex story with many references to the political and social background of the period.

6546   *Katherine Christian*

Date of Publication: 1943
Subject(s): Jacobean Period; Civil War—England; Family Saga
Fictional character(s): Katherine Christian, Gentlewoman; Nicholas Herries, Landowner
Historical character(s): James I, Ruler (King of England); Charles I, Ruler (King of England); Oliver Cromwell, Political Figure
Time Period(s): 17th century (1603-1643)
Locale(s): England

Summary: The author's final volume in the Herries family saga depicts forty years of turbulent English history during the reigns of James I and Charles I and the conflict that exploded into the English Civil War. Nicholas Herries witnesses the important events of the period; and the title character, the most beautiful woman in England, becomes a favorite at the royal court.

Historical Accuracy: The novel provides a colorful and genuine entry into the life of the period and its events.

6547   *Rogue Herries*

Date of Publication: 1930
Subject(s): Family Saga; Jacobite Rebellion

Fictional character(s): Francis Herries, Adventurer; Mirabell Starr, Gypsy, Actress
Time Period(s): 18th century (1730-1774)
Locale(s): Cumberland, England; Carlisle, Scotland

Summary: Francis Herries, called Rogue for his dissolute and unconventional lifestyle, falls in love with a young gypsy woman. This first volume of a tetralogy begins the story of an English family over 200 years.

Historical Accuracy: Walpole offers a generalized picture of English history, manners, and morals, along with specific scenes of the siege of Carlisle.

`6548` *Vanessa*

Date of Publication: 1933
Subject(s): Family Saga; Edwardian Period
Fictional character(s): Vanessa Paris, Gentlewoman; Benjamin "Benjie" Herries, Gentleman; Ellis Herries, Gentleman
Time Period(s): 19th century; 20th century (1875-1930)
Locale(s): London, England; Cumberland, England

Summary: The final novel in the Herries family chronicle ends in the 1930s. Vanessa Paris is torn between loving her unconventional cousin, Benjie, and Ellis Herries. Her marriage to the latter proves disastrous, and Benjie is revealed as the true spiritual descendent of the family patriarch, Rogue Herries.

Historical Accuracy: The novel is confusing in its multiple characters and relationships. However, it is still a satisfying social chronicle of the period.

MAURICE WALSH (1879-1964)

An Irish writer of popular romance and adventure novels, Walsh was born in County Kerry and worked as a customs officer in Scotland and Ireland. His short story, "The Quiet Man," was adapted into the 1952 John Ford film starring John Wayne. His books include *The Key Above the Door*, *While Rivers Run*, and *The Small Dark Man*.

`6549` *The Dark Rose*

Date of Publication: 1937
Subject(s): Religious Conflict; Covenanters; Wars of Montrose
Fictional character(s): Martin Somers, Military Personnel (soldier)
Time Period(s): 17th century (1644-1645)
Locale(s): Scotland

Summary: This novel describes the religious conflict of the Wars of Montrose and the fighting against the Covenanters through the experiences of a young English soldier.

Historical Accuracy: The period elements are authentic, and the era is convincingly described.

MIKA WALTARI (1908-1979)

Waltari was a Finnish writer whose novel *The Egyptian* catapulted him to worldwide success. He originally studied for the ministry, but while in school in Paris he became determined to write. He was a member of a radical literary

group called The Torch Bearers. He is the author of poetry, mysteries, short stories, plays, criticism, and screenplays, as well as novels.

`6550` *The Adventurer*

Date of Publication: 1950
Subject(s): Religious Conflict
Fictional character(s): Michael Bast, Adventurer, Bastard Son
Historical character(s): Martin Luther, Religious; Philippus Aureolus Paracelsus, Doctor (alchemist)
Time Period(s): 16th century
Locale(s): Europe

Summary: Set during the turmoil of the Protestant Reformation, the novel follows the adventures of Michael Bast throughout Europe. Born in Finland, Bast becomes a student in Paris, a clerk in Germany, and a doctor in Scandinavia, Italy, and France. Michael comes into contact with some of the central figures of the period.

Historical Accuracy: The novel accurately captures the atmosphere of Europe during the period.

`6551` *The Dark Angel*

Date of Publication: 1953
Subject(s): Byzantine Empire; Ottoman Empire
Fictional character(s): John Angelos, Heir; Anna Notaras, Gentlewoman
Historical character(s): Muhammad II, Ruler (Turkish sultan); Constantine XI Palaeologus, Ruler (Byzantine emperor)
Time Period(s): 15th century (1452-1453)
Locale(s): Constantinople, Byzantine Empire

Summary: The fall of Constantinople to the Turks in 1453, widely regarded as the beginning of the modern age, is described in the diary of John Angelos. Constantine XI attempts to overcome church and state rivalry in order to mount a desperate defense that ultimately fails, opening the way for the vast expansion of the Ottoman Empire and the end of an era.

Historical Accuracy: The novel is convincing in its historical elements.

`6552` *The Egyptian*

Date of Publication: 1949
Subject(s): Ancient Egypt; Pharaohs
Fictional character(s): Sinuhe, Doctor
Historical character(s): Akhenaton, Ruler (pharaoh); Horemheb, Ruler (pharaoh)
Time Period(s): 14th century B.C.
Locale(s): Egypt; Crete, Greece

Summary: From the perspective of Sinuhe, physician to the pharaoh, the world of ancient Egypt is revealed, through war, intrigue, murder, religious strife, and love. The novel features Pharaoh Akhenaton's attempt to establish a single diety for the Egyptians.

Historical Accuracy: The novel is remarkable in its ability to re-create the past convincingly.

6553 *The Etruscan*

Date of Publication: 1956
Subject(s): Etruscan Civilization
Fictional character(s): Lars Turms, Warrior, Pirate
Time Period(s): 5th century B.C.
Locale(s): Italy; Greece

Summary: The novel tells the story of Turms, an Etruscan warrior whose adventures in piracy, love, and war take him on a tour of the known world in the 5th century B.C. Little is known of the civilization that dominated the Italian penninsula before the Romans, and the novel attempts to fill in the shadowy past with a believable re-creation of customs and events.

Historical Accuracy: Though clearly speculative in places, the novel is convincing in its version of the past and the Etruscans.

6554 *The Roman*

Date of Publication: 1964
Subject(s): Roman Empire; Christianity
Fictional character(s): Minutus Lausus Manilianus, Military Personnel (Roman soldier), Government Official
Historical character(s): Nero, Ruler (Roman Emperor)
Time Period(s): 1st century
Locale(s): Antioch, Syria; Rome, Roman Empire; England

Summary: The novel is the memoirs of Minutus, a Roman nobleman who serves the Empire during the reign of Claudius and Nero. He travels from his house in Antioch to Rome and Britain. His career is interwoven with the burgeoning new sect of Christianity. Minutus helps Nero massacre hundreds of Christians in reprisal for the burning of Rome, but in his later years he discovers Christian consolation.

Historical Accuracy: The novel's story is fictional, but the background is authentic.

6555 *The Secret of the Kingdom*

Date of Publication: 1961
Subject(s): Biblical Story; Roman Empire
Fictional character(s): Marcus Mezentius Manilianus, Philosopher
Historical character(s): Jesus Christ, Biblical Figure; Pontius Pilate, Government Official; Mary, Biblical Figure; Mary Magdalene, Biblical Figure
Time Period(s): 1st century
Locale(s): Jerusalem, Israel

Summary: Marcus Manilianus, a young Roman seeking the meaning of life, is drawn to Judea by the promise of a Jewish messiah. He arrives in time to witness Christ's crucifixion, and Marcus stays to investigate the power of this crucified teacher. His quest brings him into contact with many who knew Jesus, including Mary, the apostles, and Pontius Pilate.

Historical Accuracy: The novel is more a philosophical inquiry than a full depiction of the period, but the atmosphere is authentic.

6556 *The Wanderer*

Date of Publication: 1951
Subject(s): Ottoman Empire; Picaresque Adventure
Fictional character(s): Michael Furfoot, Adventurer
Time Period(s): 16th century
Locale(s): Africa (north Africa); Balkan Peninsula; Middle East

Summary: In this sequel to *The Adventurer*, Michael Furfoot's adventures continue. Now a physician and converted Muslim called El-Hakim, Michael has a series of encounters with mighty personages during major events.

Historical Accuracy: The period background is evoked convincingly.

ELIZABETH WALTER

Born in London, Walter grew up in Hereford, near the Welsh border. She has worked in publicity for the Collins Crime Club, one of the most distinguished crime novel lists in British publishing. Her novels include *The More Deceived*, *The Nearest and Dearest*, and *A Season of Goodwill*. Walter received the Scott Moncrieff Translation Prize for her translation of Claire Gallois' *A Scent of Lilies*.

6557 *Homeward Bound*

Date of Publication: 1990
Subject(s): Ocean Liners
Fictional character(s): Angus Meiklejohn, Sea Captain; Nina Martin, Gentlewoman
Time Period(s): 1920s (1924)
Locale(s): Bombay, India; *Karachi*, At Sea

Summary: The novel examines the closed society of passengers aboard the *SS Karachi*, bound from Bombay to England. Many of them are English expatriates and casualties of the Great War brought together for a 25-day cruise during which secrets are revealed and a horrible crime is committed on board.

Historical Accuracy: The novel is believable in its portrait of the period and life at sea.

EVANGELINE WALTON
(PSEUD. OF EVANGELINE ENSLEY, 1907-)

Born in Indianapolis, Indiana, Walton studied under private tutors. She is the author of highly praised adaptations of ancient Celtic tales. Her best-known works are her *Mabinogion* novels, adaptations of four Welsh myths.

6558 *The Cross and the Sword*

Date of Publication: 1956
Subject(s): Dark Ages; Vikings
Fictional character(s): Sweyn Haraldsson, Young Man
Time Period(s): 10th century
Locale(s): Norway; England

Summary: Inspired by his father's tales of his adventures as a Viking raider in England, young Norseman Sweyn

Haraldsson journeys abroad. He converts to Christianity and plays a crucial part in King Aethelred's battle with the Danes.

Historical Accuracy: Although much of the story is imagined, the novel tries hard not to contradict established fact.

JAY WALZ (1907-1991)

AUDREY WALZ (1907-1983)

Jay Walz, born in South Bend, Indiana, worked as a newspaperman for the *Washington Post* and the *New York Times*. Audrey Walz, born in Mobile, Alabama, was the author of several mysteries under the pseudonym Francis Bonnamy.

6559 *The Bizarre Sisters*

Date of Publication: 1950
Subject(s): Crime and Criminals; Trials
Historical character(s): Richard Randolph, Gentleman; Judith Randolph, Spouse; Nancy Randolph, Gentlewoman
Time Period(s): 1790s
Locale(s): Virginia

Summary: This novel is based on the actual Randolph family scandal. In 1792 it was rumored that the 17-year-old Nancy Randolph bore a child by her brother-in-law Richard Randolph. The pair were charged with infanticide and were defended by Patrick Henry and John Marshall. After Richard Randolph mysteriously died, the feud between Randolph's wife and her sister, Nancy, continued, even after Nancy married Gouverneur Morris.

Historical Accuracy: This is an authentic version of the facts of the famous scandal.

6560 *The Undiscovered Country*

Date of Publication: 1958
Subject(s): Exploration; Spiritualism
Historical character(s): Margaret Fox, Psychic (medium); Elisha Kent Kane, Doctor, Explorer
Time Period(s): 1850s
Locale(s): Philadelphia, Pennsylvania; Arctic

Summary: The novel describes the fascinating story of the love affair between Dr. Elisha Kent Kane, America's first great Arctic explorer, and Maggie Fox, one of the famed Fox sisters, America's first spiritualist mediums, whose "spirit rappings" were a sensation in the 1850s. Kane, a semi-invalid, leads one of the most famous expeditions into the Arctic, but his love for Maggie Fox, a schoolgirl half his age, destroys both of them.

Historical Accuracy: The story finds itself in the strange but true category with the basic facts of biography and history observed.

ANDREW WARD (1946-)

Born in Chicago, Ward lived in India for six years as a photographer for the Ford Foundation in New Delhi. He is a former contributing editor at the *Atlantic Monthly* and the author of *Fits and Starts: The Premature Memoirs of Andrew Ward*.

6561 *The Blood Seed*

Date of Publication: 1985
Subject(s): British Raj; Independence—India; Indian Mutiny
Fictional character(s): Balbeer Rao, Wanderer, Servant; Natholi Rao, Widow(er); Josiah Weems, Religious (clergyman)
Time Period(s): 19th century; 20th century (1857-1947)
Locale(s): India

Summary: The novel takes the form of a memoir, the confessions of Balbeer Rao, who is born during the Indian mutiny. It traces his search for his father's identity and in the process reflects the history of the British Raj from the mid-19th century to Indian independence in 1947. Balbeer's journeys take him from the slums to a missionary orphange and involvement in the Kali Cult.

Historical Accuracy: The novel interweaves its fictional story with a plausible historical atmosphere.

CHRISTOPHER WARD (1868-1943)

Born in Delaware and educated as a lawyer, Ward later went into business and also built a reputation as a humorist and historian. In *Foolish Fiction*, he wrote parodies of bestselling novels. His historical fiction includes *Strange Adventures of Jonster Drums* and *Yankee Rover*.

6562 *Strange Adventure of Jonathan Drew*

Date of Publication: 1932
Subject(s): Picaresque Adventure
Fictional character(s): Jonathan Drew, Peddler, Wanderer
Time Period(s): 1820s (1821-1824)
Locale(s): New England; Midwest

Summary: Itinerant peddler Jonathan Drew travels throughout New England and the midwestern frontier of the 1820s. Drew hunts bear in the Ozarks, struggles with river pirates, captures runaway slaves, and wins a fortune at cards.

Historical Accuracy: The details and the descriptions of customs are authentic.

6563 *Yankee Rover*

Date of Publication: 1932
Subject(s): Picaresque Adventure
Fictional character(s): Jonathan Drew, Peddler, Wanderer
Time Period(s): 1820s (1824-1829)
Locale(s): Southwest

Summary: This sequel to *Strange Adventures of Jonathan Drew* continues the wanderings of the itinerant peddler. He travels south to White Sulphur Springs and Charleston and west on a 2,000-mile journey to Santa Fe before heading back to his native New England.

Historical Accuracy: The novel captures the atmosphere of the period and the details of frontier life.

REX WARNER (1905-1986)

A prolific British author, poet, translator of Greek, and professor of Classics and English, Warner was born in Birmingham, England, and graduated from Oxford University. His well-received early novels, including *The Wild Goose Chase* and *The Aerodrome*, were considerably influenced by Franz Kafka. His later novels show a greater concern for structure. He is also the author of numerous nonfiction works, including a biography of John Milton, *The Greek Philosophers*, and *Men of Athens: The Story of Fifth Century Athens*.

6564 *The Converts: A Historical Novel*

Date of Publication: 1967
Subject(s): Roman Empire; Religious Conflict
Fictional character(s): Alypius, Gentleman
Historical character(s): Augustine, Gentleman; Jerome, Religious, Scholar; Monica, Gentlewoman
Time Period(s): 4th century
Locale(s): Rome, Roman Empire; Milan, Roman Empire

Summary: The novel dramatically reconstructs the early years of Saint Augustine before his conversion to Christianity. Narrated by Alypius, a young intellectual and friend of Augustine, the story records the rapidly declining Roman Empire of the late 4th century beset by a bewildering pantheon of cults and deities. His journal records Augustine's struggle with himself and with his domineering mother before embracing Christianity.

Historical Accuracy: The novel is convincing in its depiction of the era and the essential details of Augustine's conversion.

6565 *Imperial Caesar*

Date of Publication: 1960
Subject(s): Roman Empire; Biography, Fictionalized
Historical character(s): Julius Caesar, Military Personnel (army commander), Political Figure
Time Period(s): 1st century B.C. (59-44 B.C.)
Locale(s): Rome, Roman Empire

Summary: In the sequel to the author's *Young Caesar*, the novel depicts the last 15 years of Julius Caesar's life. The novel is told in the form of recollections that pass through Caesar's mind during the sleepless night that precedes his assassination. Caesar reveals insights into his character and motivations, as well as a vivid portrait of the major figures of the period, such as Cicero, Pompey, Brutus, and Antony.

Historical Accuracy: This is a remarkable historical reconstruction. If the author's imagination is mostly responsible for rendering Caesar's thoughts, the results seem plausible and historically sound.

6566 *Pericles the Athenian*

Date of Publication: 1963
Subject(s): Ancient Greece; Biography, Fictionalized
Historical character(s): Pericles, Political Figure; Anaxagoras, Philosopher
Time Period(s): 5th century B.C.

Locale(s): Athens, Greece

Summary: The unique leadership of Pericles who ruled during Ancient Greece's Golden Age is examined in this biographical novel narrated by the philosopher Anaxagoras, Pericles' friend and teacher, who traces Pericles' youth and acquisition of power. It was Pericles' leadership that helps Athens reach the apex of its power, but Anaxagoras is troubled by the novel's central questions: Was Athens' greatness purchased at too great a cost? Was Pericles a tyrant and the source of Athens' downfall?.

Historical Accuracy: The novel is expert in creating a believable period background and in capturing the scene.

6567 *The Young Caesar*

Date of Publication: 1958
Subject(s): Roman Empire; Biography, Fictionalized
Historical character(s): Julius Caesar, Military Personnel (general); Pompey, Military Personnel (general); Marcus Tullius Cicero, Lawyer; Caius Marius, Military Personnel (general); Catiline, Political Figure
Time Period(s): 1st century B.C.
Locale(s): Rome, Roman Empire

Summary: In this biographical novel the mature Julius Caesar narrates the story of his youth and rise to power. More ambitious and perceptive than others, Caesar plans carefully and seizes his opportunity when it presents itself. The novel captures both Caesar's strengths and the challenges with which he was forced to contend.

Historical Accuracy: Although the voice of Caesar is imagined, his perspective stays close to the historical facts.

SYLVIA TOWNSEND WARNER
(1893-1978)

Warner was born in Middlesex, England, and privately educated. Having abandoned a career as a musicologist to pursue writing, Warner wrote novels, short stories, poetry, and nonfiction. She wrote biographies of authors T.H. White and Jane Austen and translated Marcel Proust's work. Warner is considered a fine stylist best known for her 12 collections of short stories.

6568 *The Corner That Held Them*

Date of Publication: 1949
Subject(s): Middle Ages; Religious Life
Fictional character(s): Cecily, Religious (nun); Walter, Religious (bishop)
Time Period(s): 14th century (1349-1382)
Locale(s): England

Summary: This novel of medieval life centers on the Convent of Oby in England between the years of the Black Death and the Peasants Revolt. It offers a vivid and authentic picture of life at the time, created out of the small details of ordinary life and the effects of larger events taking place outside the convent.

Historical Accuracy: This is a faithful and convincing depiction of abbey life during the 14th century.

6569 *The Flint Anchor*

Date of Publication: 1954
Subject(s): Family Saga; Victorian Period
Fictional character(s): John Barnard, Gentleman, Businessman; Julia Barnard, Spouse
Time Period(s): 19th century (1830s-1863)
Locale(s): England

Summary: The novel tells the tragic domestic tale of a tyrannical Victorian husband and father, John Barnard, who makes life miserable for his wife and children. The family's destruction under the supreme egotism and merciless abuse of Barnard is demonstrated.

Historical Accuracy: The characters are brought vividly to life and create a convincing period background.

CHARLES MARQUIS WARREN
(c. 1-1990)

An American producer, director, scriptwriter, and novelist, Warren was born in Baltimore, Maryland, and is remembered as the driving force behind the popular television series "Gunsmoke" and "Rawhide." A friend and protege of F. Scott Fitzgerald, Warren was a regular contributor to the *Saturday Evening Post* before breaking into films. He directed such Hollywood westerns as *Streets of Laredo*, *Pony Express*, and *Seven Angry Men*. His novels include *Bugles Are for Soldiers* and *Only the Valiant*, which was adapted into a 1950 film starring Gregory Peck.

6570 *Valley of the Shadow*

Date of Publication: 1948
Subject(s): American West; Indians; Military Life—U.S. Cavalry
Fictional character(s): John Reardon, Military Personnel (lieutenant); Deesohay, Indian (Apache), Chieftain
Time Period(s): 19th century
Locale(s): Southwest

Summary: The feud between cavalry lieutenant John Reardon and Apache chief Deesohay plays out to a disastrous conclusion as Reardon commits the forces of B Company in an attempt to destroy the Indians.

Historical Accuracy: The period elements are marred by inaccuracies. The Apaches did not wear feathered bonnets or warpaint, and scalping was not one of their customs.

LELLA WARREN (1899-1982)

An American government and public relations worker, journalist, short-story writer, and novelist, Warren was born in Clayton, Alabama. Her novels include *A Touch of Earth* and *Whetstone Walls*, a sequel to *Foundation Stone*.

6571 *Foundation Stone*

Date of Publication: 1940
Subject(s): Antebellum South; Civil War—U.S.; Slavery
Fictional character(s): Yarborough Whetstone, Plantation Owner; Gerda von Ifort, Spouse (of Whetstone)
Time Period(s): 19th century (1820s-1860s)
Locale(s): South Carolina; Alabama

Summary: The novel chronicles the experiences of Yarborough Whetstone, who marries Gerda von Ifort and moves from South Carolina to Alabama where he starts a plantation and a family dynasty.

Historical Accuracy: The novel offers a vivid and authentic look at southern life during the period.

ROBERT PENN WARREN (1905-1989)

Novelist, essayist, editor, playwright, critic, and teacher Robert Penn Warren has been described as America's dean of letters. Born in Guthrie, Kentucky, Warren attended Vanderbilt University, the University of California at Berkeley, Yale, and Oxford. He was the recipient of numerous honorary degrees, awards and prizes for his work, including three Pulitzer Prizes, and the Presidential Medal of Freedom. His most important novel is *All the King's Men*, which was adapted into a play and a film. In 1986, he was named the first official Poet Laureate of the United States.

6572 *Band of Angels*

Date of Publication: 1954
Subject(s): Antebellum South; Civil War—U.S.; Slavery
Fictional character(s): Tobias Sears, Military Personnel (Union officer); Amantha Starr, Slave, Orphan; Hamish Bond, Plantation Owner
Time Period(s): 19th century (1840s-1870s)
Locale(s): Kentucky; Kansas; New Orleans, Louisiana

Summary: The novel tells the story of Amantha Starr, the daughter of a Kentucky planter, who learns that her mother was a mulatto slave. Subject to seizure and sale by her father's creditors, she is purchased by a rich planter in New Orleans, and finally marries a Union occupation officer with whom she travels to St. Louis and to a succession of small towns in Kansas.

Historical Accuracy: Warren shows that he has a convincing historical imagination to capture the period.

6573 *Wilderness: A Tale of the Civil War*

Date of Publication: 1961
Subject(s): Civil War—U.S.
Fictional character(s): Adam Rosenzweig, Military Personnel (Union soldier)
Time Period(s): 1860s
Locale(s): Bavaria; United States

Summary: The novel tells the story of a crippled German Jew, Adam Rosenzweig, who leaves a Bavarian ghetto to join the Union army to fight for a just cause. The novel describes his adventures in America and the revision of his view of human nature and his place in the world. He is tested and grows to a deeper understanding of himself and his world through his experience of war.

Historical Accuracy: The novel is more a philosophical inquiry than a direct reflection of actual Civil War experience.

The horror of war and its impact, however, are artfully and convincingly rendered.

L.J. WASHBURN
(PSEUD. OF LIVIA REASONER, 1957-)

Washburn is an American writer whose books include *The Emerald Land*, *Epitaph*, *Red River Ruse*, and *Bandera Pass*.

6574 *Dead-Stick*

Date of Publication: 1989
Subject(s): Mystery; Motion Picture Industry
Fictional character(s): Lucus Hallam, Detective—Private, Actor (stuntman)
Time Period(s): 1920s
Locale(s): Hollywood, California

Summary: In 1920s Hollywood, someone is trying to sabotage the film that Lucus Hallam is working on. The studio hires him to discover who is doing it and why.

Historical Accuracy: The novel captures with skill period Hollywood and the movie business.

6575 *Dog Heavies*

Date of Publication: 1990
Subject(s): Mystery; Motion Picture Industry
Fictional character(s): Lucus Hallam, Detective—Private, Actor (stuntman)
Time Period(s): 1920s
Locale(s): Hollywood, California; Fort Worth, Texas

Summary: Hired to turn a New York actor into a cowboy star, Lucus Hallam, former Texas Ranger and occasional stuntman, takes the actor to a ranch in Texas. There he must contend with rustlers, Indians, and a dead body.

Historical Accuracy: The novel is accurate in its locale and its period elements.

JAKOB WASSERMANN (1873-1934)

A German novelist and short story writer, Wasserman was born in Fuerth, but he spent most of his life in Austria to avoid anti-semitism in Germany. His writing is known for its psychological depth and attacks on injustice. Shortly before his death, Wassermann's books were banned by the Nazis, and he was expelled from the Prussian Academy of Letters. His titles include *Dark Pilgrimage*, *Casper Hauser*, *The World's Illusion*, and *My Life as a German and a Jew*.

6576 *Alexander in Babylon*

Date of Publication: 1949
Subject(s): Macedonian Empire
Historical character(s): Alexander the Great, Ruler (Macedonian king); Hephaestion, Companion (of Alexander)
Time Period(s): 4th century B.C. (325-323 B.C.)
Locale(s): Babylon

Summary: The last two years of the life of Alexander the Great are dramatized, from his epic march across the Gedrosian Desert in southern Baluchistan to his death in Babylon. Alexander is shown slowly slipping into madness.

Historical Accuracy: The general course of historical events is roughly followed, but the characterizations are unreal and the true worth of the story is in its psychological study of madness.

HERBJORG WASSMO (1942-)

Scandinavia's leading woman novelist, Wassmo was awarded the Nordic Council Literature Prize in 1987 and named the "author of the Eighties" by Norwegian journalists. Her works have been published in a dozen languages around the world.

6577 *Dina's Book*

Date of Publication: 1989
Subject(s): Family Saga
Fictional character(s): Dina Holm, Young Woman; Jacob Gronelu, Landowner
Time Period(s): 1850s
Locale(s): Norway

Summary: This psychological tale concerns Dina Holm who is haunted by her role in the accidental death of her mother for which she is blamed by her father. She is brought up untamed and untaught. When she is married off to a wealthy landowner who dies under mysterious circumstances, Dina becomes mute, and the novel explores her gradual emergence from her traumas.

Historical Accuracy: The emphasis here is psychological rather than historical. The atmosphere of repression and guilt in the period is convincing.

FRANK WATERS (1902-)

American author Waters was born in Colorado Springs, Colorado, and attended Colorado College. During World War II, he served in the U.S. Army where he prepared training films on weapons. He is the author of *The Man Who Killed the Deer*, *Pike's Peak: A Family Saga*, and *River Lady*, which was made into a film in 1949.

6578 *Wild Earth's Nobility*

Date of Publication: 1935
Subject(s): American West; Mining
Fictional character(s): Joseph Rogier, Businessman
Time Period(s): 19th century; 20th century (1870s-1900)
Locale(s): Colorado

Summary: Joseph Rogier comes west to Colorado to make his fortune during the post-Civil War boom years. He succeeds by hard work until he succumbs to gold fever and loses everything.

Historical Accuracy: Great pains are taken to present a carefully detailed and authentic period background.

GLADYS WATERS

`6579` *Fairacres*

Date of Publication: 1952
Subject(s): Settlement of the American Frontier; Slavery
Historical character(s): James Shepherd, Settler; Catherine Shepherd, Settler
Time Period(s): 1820s (1826)
Locale(s): Independence, Missouri

Summary: The novel describes the founding of Independence, Missouri, through the experiences of James Shepherd and his wife, Catherine. The story captures the frontier and slavery activities in Missouri during the time.

Historical Accuracy: The author used the history of her own family for material in the novel, creating an authentic period background.

PAUL WATKINS (1964-)

Born in California and a graduate of Eton College and Yale University, Watkins has quickly gained a reputation for his dedication to research and for his vivid, detailed prose. *Night Over Day Over Night* was nominated for the Booker Prize. *Calm at Dawn* won Britain's Encore Prize for best second novel. Watkins was educated at Eton College and Yale University.

`6580` *In the Blue Light of African Dreams*

Date of Publication: 1990
Subject(s): Aviation
Fictional character(s): Charlie Halifax, Pilot; Ivan Konoualchik, Mechanic
Time Period(s): 1920s (1926-1927)
Locale(s): Morocco; Paris, France

Summary: American pilot Charlie Halifax survives service in World War I and finds himself in Africa flying for the French in their war with Arab tribesmen for control of Morocco. His way out and home is the Orteig Prize offered to the first man to fly between Paris and New York, and with his mechanic Ivan, a former officer in the Russian cavalry, he attempts to capture the prize.

Historical Accuracy: The novel is completely convincing in its locale and the details of flying.

`6581` *The Promise of Light*

Date of Publication: 1992
Subject(s): Independence—Ireland; Identity—Concealed
Fictional character(s): Ben Sheriden, Young Man
Time Period(s): 1920s (1921)
Locale(s): Ireland

Summary: Ben Sheriden searches for his identity in 1920s Ireland torn by conflict between the Irish Republican Army and the British Black and Tan. The son of an Irish immigrant, Sheriden learns that the man he thought was his father is not,

and he journeys to Ireland in search of his past, plunging into a dangerous present.

Historical Accuracy: The novel is authentic in its depiction of the period.

SHIRLEY WATKINS

Born in Rye, New York, Watkins attended Bryn Mawr College, worked at Philadelphia newspapers and *Publishers Weekly*, translated children's books, and authored several for girls, including *The Island of Green Myrtles*, *Nancy of Paradise Cottage*, and *The Prophet and the King*.

`6582` *The Prophet and the King*

Date of Publication: 1956
Subject(s): Biblical Story
Historical character(s): Saul, Ruler (King of Israel); Samuel, Religious (prophet)
Time Period(s): 11th century B.C.
Locale(s): Israel

Summary: This is a fictional version of the Bibilical story of the Old Testament prophet Samuel and Saul, the first king of the Hebrews. Samuel anoints Saul king but most of Saul's reign is spent in conflict with the Philistines. The novel ends with Saul's tragic death and the succession of David to the Israelite throne. Saul emerges as a towering figure with a fatal flaw that helps ensure his downfall.

Historical Accuracy: The novel stays close to the Old Testament sources, straightening out the inconsistencies of the Biblical account into a logical narrative. The period background, however, is very lightly sketched.

MARJORIE WATSON

`6583` *Heir to Polventon*

Date of Publication: 1973
Subject(s): Suspense; Georgian Period
Fictional character(s): Ben Polventon, Heir; Julie Polventon, Spouse
Time Period(s): 18th century
Locale(s): Cornwall, England

Summary: This romantic suspense novel in the Daphne DuMaurier mode tells the story of a young newlywed who comes to live at Polventon, an estate in ruins and haunted by pirates, smugglers, and hostile townspeople. Julie Polventon must cope with a distant husband, hostile surroundings, and a rival for her husband's love.

Historical Accuracy: More atmospheric than fully documented in its use of a historical setting, the novel does capture Cornish customs and flavor.

SALLY WATSON

`6584` *Highlands Rebel*

Date of Publication: 1954
Subject(s): Jacobite Rebellion; Battle of Culloden

Fictional character(s): Lauren Cameron, Young Woman
Historical character(s): Charles Edward Stuart, Royalty (prince)
Time Period(s): 1740s (1745)
Locale(s): Highlands, Scotland

Summary: This historical romance is set against the backdrop of the rebellion led by Bonnie Prince Charlie and centers on young Lauren Cameron, who longs to be a man in order to participate in the rebellion. After the Battle of Culloden, she plays an important part in the prince's escape.

Historical Accuracy: The novel is a fanciful story with an authentic Scottish atmosphere.

EVELYN WAUGH (1903-1966)

An English satirical novelist, Waugh's initial success came from the scathing indictment of the ''Bright Young Things''—the post-Great War generation—in the novels *Decline and Fall*, *Vile Bodies*, and *A Handful of Dust*. His autobiographically-based *Brideshead Revisited* has been justly praised as his most sustained work.

6585 *Edmund Campion*

Date of Publication: 1935
Subject(s): Biography, Fictionalized; Religious Conflict; Elizabethan Period
Historical character(s): Edmund Campion, Religious; Elizabeth I, Ruler (Queen of England)
Time Period(s): 16th century (1540-1581)
Locale(s): Oxford, England; Rome, Italy

Summary: The novel is a fictionalized biography of English Catholic martyr Edmund Campion who, during the time of Elizabeth I, became a Jesuit and returned to England to try to keep the Catholic faith alive. His efforts eventually lead to his martyrdom.

Historical Accuracy: Waugh is convincing in his portrait of Campion and his rendering of the period.

W.J. WEATHERBY

6586 *Chariots of Fire*

Date of Publication: 1981
Subject(s): Sports; Olympic Games
Historical character(s): Eric Liddell, Sports Figure (runner); Harold Abrahams, Sports Figure (runner); Edward, Prince of Wales, Royalty
Time Period(s): 1910s; 1920s (1919-1924)
Locale(s): England; Paris, France

Summary: Based on the screenplay by Colin Welland, the novel records the success of the English track and field team in the 1924 Olympic Games. The story concentrates on two gold medal winners, Harold Abrahams, a Jew from Cambridge, and Eric Liddell, a Scottish missionary who refuses to compete on a Sunday.

Historical Accuracy: The novel is based on fact with some modifications for dramatic purposes.

JEAN FRANCIS WEBB (1910-)

A professional writer since his graduation from Amherst College, Webb is the author of hundreds of magazine serials, articles, short stories, and over 30 novels. He has taught courses in writing at the University of Hawaii, Amherst, and Columbia University. His books include *Kaiulani: Crown Princess of Hawaii*, *The Cajuns*, *Tree of Evil*, and *The Bride of Cairngone*.

6587 *Somewhere Within This House*

Date of Publication: 1973
Subject(s): Gothic Romance
Fictional character(s): Ellen Sedgwick, Fiance(e), Governess; Ambrose Talmadge, Gentleman
Historical character(s): Kalakaua, Ruler (King of Hawaii)
Time Period(s): 1880s (1887)
Locale(s): Honolulu, Hawaii

Summary: Gothic-style threats and secrets plague a brooding Waikiki mansion in the waning days of the Kingdom of Hawaii. Ellen Sedgwick has sailed to the islands to prove that her fiance did not commit suicide. When she takes a position as a governess for the aristocratic Talmadge family, she uncovers family secrets and a sinister plot, as the island erupts in revolution.

Historical Accuracy: The Hawaiian civil conflict on which the action is based is faithfully described though the events of several months are compressed in time to a few weeks.

LILIANE WEBB

Born and raised in Germany, Webb worked as an interpreter for various French and American offices in Stuttgart until 1957. Her marriage to a Spanish Jew in 1958 spurred her interest in the history of the Spanish Jews.

6588 *The Marranos*

Date of Publication: 1980
Subject(s): Jews; Inquisition
Fictional character(s): Isabel Valderocas, Gentlewoman; Rafael Coates, Religious (friar)
Historical character(s): Philip IV, Ruler (King of Spain); Isabelle de Bourbon, Royalty (queen consort of Philip IV)
Time Period(s): 17th century (1632-1637)
Locale(s): Seville, Spain

Summary: Depicting the fate of the Spanish Jews, or *Marranos*, during the Inquisition, the novel tells the story of Isabel Valderocas, a descendant of a wealthy Christian family who discovers that she is in fact Jewish and as such will be condemned to death if discovered. Concealment of her identity is complicated by the king's interest in her and by her love for Rafael Coates, a friar determined to become the Grand Inquisitor.

Historical Accuracy: The story interweaves the fictional and the factual, employing a convincing period background.

LUCAS WEBB (1950-)

Born in Helena, Montana, Webb attended the University of Montana in Missoula. Webb has lived out of a pick-up truck and worked as a mechanic, ranch stock hand, and a cook.

`6589` *Eli's Road*

Date of Publication: 1971
Subject(s): Slavery; American West
Fictional character(s): Eli Russell, Lawman
Time Period(s): 19th century
Locale(s): Kansas; Montana

Summary: This western novel tells the colorful story of Eli Russell's adventurous career. Born in Kansas in the 1850s, Russell becomes involved in the Free Soil conflict with Missouri's pro-slave partisans. He later heads west to become a marshal in the Montana territory.

Historical Accuracy: The novel offers a blend of authentic period elements with a sometimes jarring modernist perspective.

MARY WEBB (1881-1927)

English novelist Webb's specialty is novels set in the English county of Shropshire. *Gone to Earth* and *Precious Bane* are the most well-known of her works.

`6590` *Precious Bane*

Date of Publication: 1924
Subject(s): Rural Life—England
Fictional character(s): Prudence Sarn, Fiance(e); Gideon Sarn, Farmer; Jancis Beguildy, Fiance(e)
Time Period(s): 19th century (mid-century)
Locale(s): Shropshire, England

Summary: This is a weird tale of English rural folkways, of a seemingly doomed family, the Sarns, of Gideon Sarn's monomaniacal plan for success, and his sister Prudence's long-suffering endurance of her brother's mastery. Rural life is stripped of social custom down to elemental forces that seem to control the characters' lives.

Historical Accuracy: The novel excels in depicting traditional folkways.

EVERETT WEBBER (1909-)

OLGA WEBBER

Webber is the auhtor of *Louisiana Cavalier, Escape to Utopia: The Communal Movement in America*, and an autobiography, *Backwoods Teacher*.

`6591` *Bound Girl*

Date of Publication: 1949
Subject(s): Civil War—U.S.
Fictional character(s): Rebecca Whitman, Servant

Historical character(s): Jesse James, Military Personnel (Confederate soldier); William Clarke Quantrill, Military Personnel (Confederate soldier)
Time Period(s): 1860s
Locale(s): Kansas; Missouri

Summary: This romance, set during the Kansas-Missouri border battles during the Civil War, tells the story of a pretty servant girl, Rebecca Whitman, who is bound to a rascally innkeeper. Several important figures of the period and the region, including Quantrill and a 17-year-old Jesse James, factor in the story.

Historical Accuracy: The novel features a graphic and accurate re-creation of the period and the region.

JAN WEBSTER (1924-)

Scottish author Jan Webster was born in Blantyre, Scotland, and attended Hamilton Academy. She has worked as a journalist since her teens before turning to full-time fiction writing. She once stated that her chief aim was to present the Scots as the exciting, ambitious "repressed romantics" they really are. Her novels include *Beggerman's Country* and *Due South*.

`6592` *Colliers Row*

Date of Publication: 1972
Subject(s): Victorian Period; Family Saga
Fictional character(s): Kate Kilgour, Housekeeper; James Galbraith, Religious (minister)
Time Period(s): 19th century (1840s-1880s)
Locale(s): Scotland

Summary: The novel follows the career of Kate Kilgour, the young housekeeper to minister John Galbraith. Local gossip forces her to give notice, and she begins a journey that will uncover her link to a wealthy pit-mining family. Marriage brings children who venture far from their Scottish home, as Kate finds her way back to the Reverend Galbraith.

Historical Accuracy: The novel is authentic in its period and regional elements.

`6593` *Saturday City*

Date of Publication: 1979
Subject(s): Victorian Period; Family Saga
Fictional character(s): Duncan Fleming, Gentleman; Sandia Kilgour, Young Woman
Time Period(s): 19th century; 20th century (1880-1918)
Locale(s): Glasgow, Scotland

Summary: The title refers to Glasgow, Scotland, the British Empire's second city during the period of the novel, 1880 to 1918. The history of the city through change and strife is reflected in the story of the Fleming and Kilgour families. Duncan Fleming is dedicated to improving the lives of coal miners, while Sandia Kilgour struggles to achieve independence.

Historical Accuracy: The novel captures with skill period Glasgow and the forces of change during the period.

HARRY E. WEDECK (1894-)

An English writer, editor, and translator, Wedeck was born in Sheffield and graduated from the University of Edinburgh and the Sorbonne. Wedeck served as the chairman of the department of classical languages at Erasmus Hall, Brooklyn, New York, and as a lecturer in classics and medieval studies at Brooklyn College and the New School.

6594 *Mortal Hunger: A Novel Based on the Life of Lafcadio Hearn*

Date of Publication: 1947
Subject(s): Biography, Fictionalized; Literary Life
Historical character(s): Lafcadio Hearn, Writer
Time Period(s): 19th century; 20th century (1860s-1904)
Locale(s): Greece; Japan; United States

Summary: This fictionalized biography depicts the career of Lafcadio Hearn, an American writer who helped introduce Japanese culture to the West. Hearn's boyhood in Greece, his schooling in Europe, his journalistic career in the U.S., and his exposure to Japanese life and culture are dramatized. Hearn goes to Japan in 1890 to write a series of articles. He spends the rest of his life there, becoming a Japanese citizen and writing his best work.

Historical Accuracy: Despite the framework of Hearn's life story, there are a number of alterations of facts for dramatic purposes.

ROBERT S. WEEKLEY (1932-)

An American scientist and writer, Weekley was born in Alabama. He has worked in Hollywood, writing for television and the movies. Weekley established the Turtle Bay Institute, which is engaged in studying behavioral sciences.

6595 *The House in Ruins*

Date of Publication: 1958
Subject(s): Reconstruction Period
Fictional character(s): Crawford Gauntry, Veteran (Confederate soldier)
Time Period(s): 1860s (1865)
Locale(s): Cold Forks, Mississippi

Summary: Crawford Gauntry leads a small band of Confederate guerillas. After the surrender at Appomattox, they return to their small town in Mississippi and mount a war of resistance against the Union troops occupying the area.

Historical Accuracy: The novel offers a convincing evocation of the region during the period.

HEBE WEENOLSEN

Born in England, Weenolsen subsequently moved to New York City. Her second novel, *To Keep This Oath*, has been described as one of the truly great historical novels. She is also the author of a story for young readers, *Mrs. Duck and the Milkman*.

6596 *The Last Englishman: The Story of Hereward the Wake*

Date of Publication: 1951
Subject(s): Norman Conquest; Biography, Fictionalized; Anglo-Saxon Period
Historical character(s): Hereward the Wake, Rebel, Outlaw
Time Period(s): 11th century
Locale(s): England

Summary: Anglo-Saxon rebel and folk hero Hereward the Wake returns from fighting the Saracens to resist the Normans. Until his death, Hereward leads a committed band of Saxons in rebellion against Norman control.

Historical Accuracy: Fictional elements round out the sketchy historical facts of Hereward's life and career in this plausible fictional biography.

6597 *To Keep This Oath*

Date of Publication: 1958
Subject(s): Medical Profession; Middle Ages
Fictional character(s): Jesu-Maria, Doctor
Historical character(s): Stephen, Ruler (King of England); Henry Plantagenet, Nobleman
Time Period(s): 12th century
Locale(s): England

Summary: Set during the 12th century and the dynastic struggle that led to the Plantagenet victory of Henry II, the novel tells the story of Jesu-Maria, a young barber who, after overcoming his horror of blood, becomes a practitioner of the art of healing. The novel offers a vivid account of the development of medicine in the Middle Ages.

Historical Accuracy: The novel is convincing in both its period elements and its depiction of medical customs during the 12th century.

6598 *The Trial of Jenny Sykes*

Date of Publication: 1990
Subject(s): Medical Profession; Trials
Fictional character(s): John Toller, Doctor; Jenny Sykes, Young Woman
Time Period(s): 17th century (1685)
Locale(s): Dorset, England

Summary: John Toller, a young country doctor, comes to the aid of a young woman on trial for concealing the birth and death of her illegitimate baby. His only hope is a new legal/medical test that determines if the baby was born dead. Toller searches for the test in time to save Jenny's life.

Historical Accuracy: The novel is based on the 17th-century discovery that the lungs of a deadborn infant would sink in water. This phenomenon, first observed in 1663, was introduced in a court case in 1682 in Saxony in a successful defense of a charge of infanticide.

JOY DEWEESE WEHEN

Born in Malaysia of an English father and American mother, Wehen was educated in America, Canada, and England. At age 19 she won an award for a short story for the *Writer's Digest* and has been writing steadily since then. She is the author of suspense fiction for young people as well as adults. Her novels include *Stranger at Golden Hill* and *The Singing Wind* (under the pseudonym Jennifer Wade).

6599 *So Far From Malabar*

Date of Publication: 1970
Subject(s): Pirates
Fictional character(s): Valli, Dancer, Slave
Historical character(s): Francis Xavier, Religious (Jesuit missionary)
Time Period(s): 16th century (1540s)
Locale(s): Goa, India; Malabar Coast, India

Summary: Valli is a young Indian temple dancer in Malabar on the Indian coast who is kidnapped by pirates and taken to the Portuguese colony of Goa where she is sold into slavery. Bought by one of the most influential men in Goa, she lives in great luxury but longs to return home. Jesuit missionary Francis Xavier plays a part in her eventual destiny.

Historical Accuracy: The events are imaginary, but they are based on historical possibility.

NATHANIEL NORSEN WEINREB

Born in New York City, Weinreb attended both New York University and City College. He worked for the *New York Mirror* and is the author of numerous radio scripts and stories. He has also worked as a story analyst for Twentieth Century Fox.

6600 *The Babylonians*

Date of Publication: 1953
Subject(s): Babylonian Empire; Biblical Story; Medical profession
Fictional character(s): Beladar, Doctor, Companion (to Nebuchadnezzar)
Historical character(s): Jeremiah, Religious (prophet), Biblical Figure; Nebuchadnezzar II, Ruler (King of Babylon)
Time Period(s): 6th century B.C.
Locale(s): Babylon; Jerusalem, Israel

Summary: Beladar is a physician and companion to Babylonian ruler Nebuchadnezzar who is exiled from Babylon and sent on a mission to the prophet Jeremiah in Jerusalem to persuade him to foment rebellion. Beladar's efforts lead to the siege of Jerusalem.

Historical Accuracy: The essential story is fictional but based on the actual events of the fall of Jerusalem to Babylon in 586 B.C.

6601 *Esther*

Date of Publication: 1955
Subject(s): Biblical Story; Ancient Israel
Historical character(s): Hadassah, Royalty (Persian queen), Biblical Figure; Xerxes I, Ruler (King of Persia), Biblical Figure; Haman, Biblical Figure, Courtier; Mordecai, Biblical Figure

Time Period(s): 5th century B.C.
Locale(s): Persia

Summary: The novel offers a fictionalized version of the Biblical story of Esther. She is a Jewish woman who is chosen as the queen of the Persian King Xerxes I. Esther and her cousin Mordecai prevent the wicked courtier Haman from bringing about the massacre of the Jews. The events of the deliverance of the Jews are celebrated in the feast of Purim.

Historical Accuracy: The novel mixes fiction and fact borrowed from the Biblical account.

6602 *The Sorceress*

Date of Publication: 1954
Subject(s): Biblical Story; Ancient Israel
Historical character(s): Deborah, Religious (prophet), Biblical Figure; Barak, Biblical Figure
Time Period(s): Indeterminate Past
Locale(s): Israel

Summary: The story of the conquest of Canaan by the tribes of Israel is described. At the center of this victory is Deborah who is thought by her townspeople to be a sorceress. She trains Barak to help unite the disorganized tribes of the Israelites to challenge the might of Canaan.

Historical Accuracy: The source for the characters and events is the Bible's Book of Judges.

THERESA WEISER

6603 *Music for God*

Date of Publication: 1951
Subject(s): Biography, Fictionalized; Musical Life
Historical character(s): Anton Bruckner, Composer, Musician
Time Period(s): 19th century
Locale(s): Vienna, Austria

Summary: This biographical novel traces the life and musical career of Austrian composer Anton Bruckner. First acknowledged as a virtuoso organist, Bruckner becomes the court organist in Vienna and slowly gains a reputation as a composer of distinction.

Historical Accuracy: Bruckner is shown as a flawless genius which undercuts the novel's usefulness as an objective and historically accurate portrait.

DAVID WEISS (1909-)

Born in Philadelphia, Pennsylvania, Weiss was educated at Temple University and the New School for Social Research. He has worked at more than 50 jobs during his career, including stevedore, story editor for David O. Selznick, actor, ghost writer, and basketball and swimming instructor. His historical and biographical novels attempt to capture the feel and flavor of the times in which his protagonists lived. His most popular book was *Naked Came I*, but his greatest critical success was *Sacred and Profane*.

6604 *The Assassination of Mozart*

Date of Publication: 1970
Subject(s): Musical Life
Fictional character(s): Jason Otis, Musician, Composer; Deborah Otis, Spouse
Historical character(s): Ludwig van Beethoven, Composer
Time Period(s): 1820s
Locale(s): Salzburg, Austria; Vienna, Austria

Summary: When Mozart dies suddenly and unexpectedly in 1791, his body disappears into an unknown grave amidst rumors of poison and foul play. The novel investigates the mystery of Mozart's death using a fictional young American musician and composer, Jason Otis, and his bride, Deborah. They set out in 1823 to piece together the facts, and their inquiry takes them throughout Europe, meeting with individuals who help develop a possible solution to the mystery.

Historical Accuracy: The facts of the case are authentic, but the solution to the mystery is speculative and open to question.

6605 *I, Rembrandt*

Date of Publication: 1979
Subject(s): Artistic Life; Biography, Fictionalized
Historical character(s): Rembrandt, Artist; Baruch Spinoza, Philosopher
Time Period(s): 17th century (1654-1656)
Locale(s): Amsterdam, Netherlands

Summary: In 1654, Dutch painter Rembrandt is 48 years old, in debt, and in disfavor, but on the verge of undertaking some of his greatest work. He tells his own story, particularly of his relationship with the Dutch philosopher Spinoza.

Historical Accuracy: The relationship between Rembrandt and Spinoza is speculative, based on facts that suggest that a friendship was probable.

6606 *Myself, Christopher Wren*

Date of Publication: 1973
Subject(s): Architecture; Royalty—England; Biography, Fictionalized
Historical character(s): Christopher Wren, Architect; Charles I, Ruler (King of England); Charles II, Ruler (King of England); Oliver Cromwell, Political Figure (Lord Protector of England); Giovanni Lorenzo Bernini, Artist (sculptor), Architect; John Milton, Writer (poet); Nell Gwynne, Actress; Isaac Newton, Scientist
Time Period(s): 17th century (1636-1708); 18th centruy
Locale(s): London, England

Summary: This immense novel traces the extraordinary life and times of Christopher Wren, the architect who helped rebuild London after the Great Fire. The novel provides a full rendering of Wren's remarkable life, following him through the reign of Charles I, the English Civil War, and the Restoration period, as he struggles to complete his masterwork, St. Paul's Cathedral.

Historical Accuracy: The novel offers invented scenes and imagined dialogue, but stays close to the facts of Wren's life and the events of the various periods his career spanned.

6607 *Naked Came I: A Novel of Rodin*

Date of Publication: 1963
Subject(s): Artistic Life; Biography, Fictionalized
Historical character(s): Auguste Rodin, Artist (sculptor); Camille Claudel, Model, Artist; Edgar Degas, Artist; George Bernard Shaw, Writer; Claude Monet, Artist; Pierre Auguste Renoir, Artist; Victor Hugo, Writer; Emile Zola, Writer; Rainer Maria Rilke, Writer (poet)
Time Period(s): 19th century; 20th century (1840-1917)
Locale(s): France

Summary: This biographical novel traces the life and career of French sculptor Auguste Rodin, the most admired sculptor since Michelangelo. Rodin was a rebel and innovator who battled the conventional throughout his life. His era and those who created the artistic fervor of France in the 19th century are captured.

Historical Accuracy: The novel stays close to the actual details of Rodin's life, with some invented dialogue and scenes.

6608 *Physician Extraordinary: A Novel of the Life and Times of William Harvey*

Date of Publication: 1975
Subject(s): Medical Profession; Royalty—England; Science
Historical character(s): William Harvey, Doctor, Scientist; Galileo Galilei, Scientist; Elizabeth I, Ruler (Queen of England); Charles I, Ruler (King of England); James I, Ruler (King of England); Sir Walter Raleigh, Courtier; William Shakespeare, Writer; Sir Francis Bacon, Writer (essayist), Philosopher; John Donne, Writer, Religious (dean of St. Paul's)
Time Period(s): 16th century; 17th century
Locale(s): England; Padua, Italy

Summary: The novel depicts the career of ground-breaking doctor and scientist William Harvey, whose heretical theory that the blood circulates from the heart challenged custom and orthodoxy. His career is dramatized, including his school days at Cambridge, his studying of medicine at Padua, where he lived with Galileo, and his service as physician to Elizabeth I, James I, and Charles I.

Historical Accuracy: The novel is faithful to the facts of Harvey's career and the historical events of his lifetime.

6609 *Sacred and Profane: A Novel of the Life and Times of Mozart*

Date of Publication: 1968
Subject(s): Musical Life; Biography, Fictionalized
Historical character(s): Wolfgang Amadeus Mozart, Composer, Musician; Maria Theresa, Ruler (Empress of Austria); Johann Wolfgang von Goethe, Writer, Scientist; George III, Ruler (King of England); Franz Joseph Haydn, Composer; Johann Sebastian Bach, Composer
Time Period(s): 18th century (1756-1791)
Locale(s): Austria; Germany; England

Summary: The novel offers a biographical account of Mozart, including his years as a performing child prodigy, his unparalleled creative explosion as a composer, and his death at the age of 35. His story is also that of the 18th century and the Age of Enlightenment.

Historical Accuracy: All the physical facts are real, and the events occur in the correct chronological order. Situations, conversations, and motivation had to be imagined and interpreted.

6610 The Spirit and the Flesh: A Novel Inspired by the Life of Isadora Duncan

Date of Publication: 1959
Subject(s): Theatrical Life
Fictional character(s): Leonora Malcolm, Dancer
Time Period(s): 19th century; 20th century (1878-1927)
Locale(s): United States; Europe

Summary: This biographical novel follows the known facts in the life of dancer Isadora Duncan. Her story is told through the experiences of Leonora Malcolm, who transcends a strict and repressive background to become an acclaimed dancer and greatly influence the development of modern dance.

Historical Accuracy: The novel is set in a largely fictional frame which does not allow the story to be read as a complete parallel to the life of Isadora Duncan.

6611 The Venetian

Date of Publication: 1976
Subject(s): Artistic Life; Renaissance; Biography, Fictionalized
Historical character(s): Titian, Artist; Michelangelo Buonarotti, Artist; Paul III, Religious (pope); Philip II, Ruler (King of Spain)
Time Period(s): 15th century; 16th century (1477-1576)
Locale(s): Venice, Italy

Summary: In this biographical novel, an elderly Titian recalls his long and distinguished career as the master of the Venetian School of the High Renaissance. Famous for his use of color and his choice of subject, Titian emerges as an artistic genius, capturing the vivid and tumultuous era of the 16th century.

Historical Accuracy: The novel is reliable in its summary of Titian's career and the historical background of the Italian Renaissance.

MANLY WADE WELLMAN (1903-1986)

American author Wellman was born in Angola, the son of a medical officer and scientist. After attending the Municipal University of Wichita, Kansas, he went on to work as a journalist, book and motion picture reviewer, project supervisor for the WPA Writers Project, and a college instructor in creative writing. Wellman published more than 85 books, many of them in the fantasy and science fiction genre. He received a Pulitzer Prize nomination in 1958 for his Civil War study, *Rebel Boast: First at Bethel, Last at Appomattox.* Wellman's novels include *The Lost and the*

Lurking, The Voice of the Mountain, and many children's novels.

6612 Candle of the Wicked

Date of Publication: 1960
Subject(s): Reconstruction Period; Crime and Criminals
Fictional character(s): Spanish McCready, Veteran (Confederate soldier)
Time Period(s): 1870s (1873)
Locale(s): Kansas

Summary: Civil War veteran Spanish McCready attempts to find land in Kansas in 1873. The action takes place around a tavern on the road between Fort Scott and Independence where McCready encounters the murderous Bender family.

Historical Accuracy: The novel features a believable period background and an accurate account of what is known about the Bender clan, with a plausible theory about the family's ultimate fate.

PAUL I. WELLMAN (1898-1966)

American historian and novelist Wellman was born in Enid, Oklahoma, but spent the first eight years of his life in Angola, West Africa, where his father worked as a health officer at mission stations. Wellman spent the rest of his youth in Utah and subsequently attended Fairmont College in Kansas. During World War I, he served as a sergeant in the U.S. Army Signal Corps. Several of his novels of the Old West, including *Bronco Apache, The Commancheros,* and *Jubal Troops,* were adapted into motion pictures.

6613 Angel with Spurs

Date of Publication: 1942
Subject(s): Civil War—U.S.
Fictional character(s): Clay Bennett, Military Personnel (Confederate captain); Merit Hampton, Young Woman
Historical character(s): Joseph Orville Shelby, Military Personnel (Confederate general)
Time Period(s): 1860s
Locale(s): Southwest; Mexico

Summary: The novel is based on the march of General Joseph Shelby and 1,000 Confederate soldiers who, instead of surrendering after the Civil War, trekked to Mexico to join Maximilian. A love story between Captain Clay Bennett and a young Southern woman, Merit Hampton, shares the stage with the events of the dangerous journey.

Historical Accuracy: The actual events of Shelby's march are authentically presented.

6614 Broncho Apache

Date of Publication: 1936
Subject(s): American West; Indians; Crime and Criminals
Historical character(s): Massai, Indian (Apache), Warrior
Time Period(s): 1880s (1886)
Locale(s): Illinois; Southwest

Summary: Massai, an Apache Warrior, escapes from the prison train carrying Geronimo and his band to exile in Florida. Massai returns from Illinois to Arizona, where he is betrayed by his people, is captured, and escapes again. He becomes a "broncho," or wild outlaw, and starts a one-man war of vengeance against the Mexicans and Americans, along with his own people.

Historical Accuracy: This is a fictionalized account of the known facts about Massai.

6615 *The Buckstones*

Date of Publication: 1967
Subject(s): Picaresque Adventure; Crime and Criminals
Fictional character(s): Bion B. Buckstone, Veteran (of the War of 1812), Convict; Prudence Buckstone, Young Woman
Historical character(s): Thomas Hart Benton, Political Figure; Andrew Jackson, Political Figure
Time Period(s): 1830s
Locale(s): Tennessee; Washington, District of Columbia

Summary: When "Colonel" Bion B. Buckstone, masquerading as a close friend of Andrew Jackson, is imprisoned for debt, his daughter Prudence sets off for Washington to enlist the aid of the U.S. President. On the way she is captured by a band of robbers, escapes with the help of a runaway slave, is recaptured, and finally reaches her goal in this comic adventure story.

Historical Accuracy: The story strains credibility in pursuit of comedy. However, the period backdrop is effective.

6616 *The Comancheros*

Date of Publication: 1952
Subject(s): American West; Indians
Fictional character(s): Paul Regret, Gambler; Tom Gatling, Lawman (Texas Ranger); Eloise Grailhe, Young Woman
Historical character(s): Sam Houston, Political Figure
Time Period(s): 1840s
Locale(s): New Orleans, Louisiana; Texas

Summary: Paul Regret, a New Orleans gentleman gambler, joins the Texas Rangers through a twist of fate during the years of the Texas Republic. He joins forces with veteran Ranger Tom Gatling to stop the Comanches and their white allies, the Comancheros.

Historical Accuracy: The characters, except for Houston, are fictional as are their adventures.

6617 *The Female: A Novel of Another Time*

Date of Publication: 1953
Subject(s): Byzantine Empire
Historical character(s): Justinian I, Ruler (Byzantine emperor); Theodora, Royalty (empress consort of Justinian)
Time Period(s): 6th century
Locale(s): Constantinople, Byzantine Empire

Summary: The title refers to the Empress Theodora and the subtitle to the 6th century. The novel dramatizes the court intrigue surrounding the Byzantine Empire's capital at Constantinople, an exotic setting for a novel of passion and politics. Theodora emerges as a vibrant individual who rose from courtesan to become an empress.

Historical Accuracy: The novel is a combination of authentic historical elements and fictional events.

6618 *The Iron Mistress*

Date of Publication: 1951
Subject(s): Biography, Fictionalized; Texas Revolution; Battle of the Alamo
Historical character(s): Jim Bowie, Frontiersman; John James Audubon, Scientist (ornithologist); Jean Laffite, Pirate
Time Period(s): 19th century
Locale(s): Louisiana; Texas

Summary: This fictional biography of frontiersman James Bowie chronicles his life in Louisiana and his arrival in Texas in 1828. There he becomes a leader among the American settlers who oppose the Mexican government. When the revolt begins, Bowie is made a colonel, and dies at the Alamo.

Historical Accuracy: The author has invented scenes and details connected to Bowie's early life. The Texas scenes and atmosphere are authentic and clearly based on solid research.

6619 *Magnificent Destiny*

Date of Publication: 1962
Subject(s): War of 1812; Texas Revolution; Politics
Historical character(s): Andrew Jackson, Military Personnel (general), Political Figure; Sam Houston, Political Figure, Leader (of the Texas Revolution); Rachel Jackson, Spouse; Henry Clay, Political Figure; John C. Calhoun, Political Figure; James K. Polk, Political Figure
Time Period(s): 19th century (1813-1843)
Locale(s): New Orleans, Louisiana; Washington, District of Columbia; Texas

Summary: The novel records the friendship and relationship between Andrew Jackson and Sam Houston beginning with Jackson's Indian-fighting days when he met Houston, through the Battle of New Orleans, Jackson's presidency, the events of the Texas Revolution, and Texas' entry into the U.S. Both men emerge as capable and determined leaders who overcome major obstacles and tower above other men of the times.

Historical Accuracy: The story is largely seen through the perspective of Jackson whose biases are obvious. Some minor events have been transposed in the interest of a smooth narrative.

6620 *Ride the Red Earth*

Date of Publication: 1958
Subject(s): Spanish Colonies; French Colonies
Historical character(s): Louis Juchereau St. Denis, Nobleman (chevalier)
Time Period(s): 1710s
Locale(s): Southwest, North America; Mexico

Summary: The background for this novel is the conflict between France and Spain for control of Texas. French chevalier Louis Juchereau St. Denis tells the story of his role in the conflict that includes capture by the Santa Hermondad and imprisonment by the Inquisition.

Historical Accuracy: The novel is authentic in capturing the atmosphere of the period.

EVELYN WELLS

Born in California, Wells began her career as a reporter for a San Francisco newspaper. She has worked as a journalist, editor, and teacher of creative writing. A recipient of the Christopher Award, Wells is the author of *What to Name the Baby*, a biography of the Egyptian queen Hatshepsut, and the novels *Men at Their Worst* and *Jed Blaine's Woman*, both of which were made into films.

6621 *A City for St. Francis*

Date of Publication: 1967
Subject(s): Spanish Colonies; Exploration
Historical character(s): Juan Bautista de Anza, Military Personnel (general); Junipero Serra, Religious (priest); Susana Galvan, Spouse; Don Angel Galvan, Gentleman
Time Period(s): 1770s (1775)
Locale(s): San Francisco, California

Summary: The novel describes the founding of San Francisco and the 1,000-mile trip north from Mexico led by General Juan de Anza. The company endures Apache raids, starvation, and other hardships before reaching their goal. Susana Galvan, a member of the expedition, fears its conclusion with its expected reunion with the fiery Father Junipero Serra.

Historical Accuracy: Events of Susana's story are based on fact, but her joining Anza's second expedition is speculative.

LAWRENCE WELLS (1941-)

A native of Alabama, Wells received his Ph.D. from the University of Mississippi. Wells has edited several nonfiction books, including *William Faulkner: The Cofield Collection*. He operates the Yoknapatawpha Press in Oxford, Mississippi.

6622 *Rommel and the Rebel*

Date of Publication: 1986
Subject(s): Military Life; Civil War—U.S.; World War II
Fictional character(s): Max Speigner, Military Personnel (lieutenant), Linguist
Historical character(s): Erwin Rommel, Military Personnel (German field marshal); William Faulkner, Writer
Time Period(s): 1930s (1937); 1940s (1942)
Locale(s): New York, New York; Mississippi; Africa

Summary: This what-if story imagines what might have happened if the future German Field Marshal Erwin Rommel had been one of the German officers who actually visited the United States in the 1930s to study Confederate battle strategy. Rommel is introduced to American life by his interpreter, Max Speigner. Four years later, Max's knowledge of the man may give the Allies an edge in predicting and outwitting Rommel's maneuvers in North Africa.

Historical Accuracy: The story is speculative and imagined, though clearly based on a solid knowledge of both the Civil War and Rommel's North Africa campaign.

EUDORA WELTY (1909-)

Distinguished American novelist and short-story writer Eudora Welty was born in Jackson, Mississippi, and attended Mississippi State College for Women, the University of Wisconsin, and Columbia University Graduate School of Business. She was the winner of the 1973 Pulitzer Prize in fiction for her novelette *The Optimist's Daughter* and won the American Book Award in 1981 for *The Collected Stories of Eudora Welty* and in 1984 for *One Writer's Beginnings*. Welty is also a recipient of the Presidential Medal of Freedom and the National Medal of the Arts. Her novels include *Delta Wedding* and *The Ponder Heart*.

6623 *The Robber Bridegroom*

Date of Publication: 1942
Subject(s): Crime and Criminals
Fictional character(s): Jamie Lockhart, Outlaw; Rosamond Musgrove, Gentlewoman
Historical character(s): Mike Fink, Frontiersman
Time Period(s): 19th century
Locale(s): Mississippi River; Natchez Trace, Mississippi

Summary: This tale set in the early years of the 19th century along the Mississippi and the Natchez Trace tells the story of how the bandit Jamie Lockhart steals a wilderness planter's beautiful daughter for his bride.

Historical Accuracy: The novel combines a believable period atmosphere with surrealistic touches that turn the story into a modern fairy tale or moral fable.

PATRICIA WENDORF (1928-)

Born in Somserset, England, Wendorf began writing seriously at the age of 50 and published her first novel, *Peacefully: In Berlin*, in 1983. She is also the author of the novels *Leo Days* and *Larksleve*.

6624 *Double Wedding Ring*

Date of Publication: 1989
Subject(s): Victorian Period; Immigrants; Civil War—U.S.
Fictional character(s): Rhoda Greypaull, Immigrant, Orphan; George Salter, Businessman
Time Period(s): 19th century (1850-1889)
Locale(s): Somerset, England; Wisconsin

Summary: An orphan leaves England to marry her dead cousin's husband, George Salter, in America. Her diary reveals her experiences in love, marriage, and family while reflecting as well the events that shape her life: the Civil War and Chicago's Great Fire.

Historical Accuracy: The novel provides an authentic period background.

FRANZ WERFEL (1890-1945)

Born in Prague, Werfel fled from Nazi-occupied Austria to France and then the United States. Besides several volumes of poetry, his work includes plays, the comedy *Jacobowsky and the Colonel*, and the novel *The Forty Days of Musa Dagh*, a recounting of the struggle between the Armenians and the Turks during World War I.

6625 *The Song of Bernadette*

Date of Publication: 1941
Subject(s): Religious Life
Historical character(s): Bernadette Soubirous, Religious; Dean Peyramale, Religious (parish priest); Marie Therese, Religious (nun)
Time Period(s): 19th century (1858-1875)
Locale(s): Lourdes, France

Summary: This is the story of Bernadette's vision at Lourdes and the skepticism that resulted before many were convinced that a miracle had occurred. Werfel wrote the book in fulfillment of a vow he had made while hiding from the Nazis in the church of St. Bernadette at the beginning of World War II. More than a religious story or a testament of faith, the novel is a moving account of humans confronted by the unknown.

Historical Accuracy: All of the facts here are drawn from the historical records.

LAEL TUCKER WERTENBAKER (1909-)

American author Wertenbaker was born in Bradford, Pennsylvania, and attended the University of Louisville. Her varied career has included work with the Theatre Guild, as a foreign correspondent during World War II, and in publishing. Her novel, *Death of a Man*, written under the name Lael Tucker, was adapted by playwright Garson Kanin as *A Gift of Time*. She is also the author of *The Afternoon Women* and *Unbidden Guests*.

6626 *The Eye of the Lion: A Novel Based on the Life of Mata Hari*

Date of Publication: 1964
Subject(s): World War I; Espionage; Theatrical Life
Historical character(s): Mata Hari, Dancer, Spy
Time Period(s): 19th century; 20th century (1878-1917)
Locale(s): Netherlands; France; Germany

Summary: The novel attempts to uncover the reality behind the enigmatic and mysterious Mata Hari, whose name has become synonymous with glamor and intrigue. Born Geertruida Zelle in Holland, her skill as a performer and dancer leads to notoriety and intrigue that eventually costs Mata Hari her life in 1917, when she is executed by the French on a charge of espionage, which she denies.

Historical Accuracy: The novel is solidly based on fact and captures the flavor of the times with conviction.

EUGENIA LOVETT WEST (1923-)

Born in Boston, West was educated at Chatham Hall and Sarah Lawrence College. A resident of Connecticut, West has been a contributor to local newspapers and the editor of the *Playhouse Square Gazette*.

6627 *The Ancestors Cry Out*

Date of Publication: 1979
Subject(s): Inheritance—Disputed; Slavery
Fictional character(s): Marietta Jackson, Young Woman; James Thaw, Landowner
Time Period(s): 1880s
Locale(s): Jamaica

Summary: Marietta Jackson visits Repose, a sugar plantation in Jamaica, to complete the drama that began in the 1830s for her grandmother when a slave rebellion swept the island. The past refuses to stay buried as Marietta confronts both the great charm of the island and its violent past.

Historical Accuracy: The depiction of period Jamaica is convincing.

JESSAMYN WEST (1902-1984)

Born in Indiana of Quaker parents, West was educated in California at Whittier College, the University of California at Berkeley and in England at Oxford University. She was a teacher and lecturer at many colleges and universities, as well as a writer of novels, nonfiction, screenplays, and an opera libretto. She is the award-winning author of such short-story collections as *Love, Death, and the Ladies Drill Team* and *Crimson Ramblers of the World, Farewell*. Her first work, *The Friendly Persuasion*, was adapted by her as a screenplay and filmed in 1956. Other filmed screenplays include *The Big Country* and *Stolen Hours*.

6628 *Except for Me and Thee*

Date of Publication: 1969
Subject(s): Civil War—U.S.; Quakers; Underground Railroad
Fictional character(s): Jess Birdwell, Farmer; Eliza Birdwell, Farmer
Time Period(s): 1850s; 1860s
Locale(s): Indiana

Summary: The novel offers scenes in the life of a Quaker family, the Birdwells of Indiana, before, during and after the Civil War. The courtship and marriage of Jesse and Eliza are shown, as well as their settling on a farm in the Indiana frontier and their assistance with the Underground Railroad. The war years and their aftermath are also dramatized.

Historical Accuracy: The novel features a convincing period background and evident familiarity with the region.

6629 *The Friendly Persuasion*

Date of Publication: 1945
Subject(s): Civil War—U.S.; Quakers

Fictional character(s): Jess Birdwell, Farmer; Eliza Birdwell, Farmer, Religious (minister); Josh Birdwell, Military Personnel (Union soldier)
Time Period(s): 1860s
Locale(s): Indiana

Summary: The life of a Quaker family, the Birdwells, in Indiana is depicted. Daily life and rural customs are described as well as the conflict that arises when son Josh joins the Union cause in the Civil War to stop Morgan's Raiders at Finney's Ford.

Historical Accuracy: The region and the period are captured with authenticity.

6630 *Leafy Rivers*

Date of Publication: 1967
Subject(s): Settlement of the American Frontier
Fictional character(s): Leafy Rivers, Bride; Reno Rivers, Settler
Time Period(s): 1810s (1818)
Locale(s): Cincinnati, Ohio

Summary: Life in the Ohio territory around Cincinnati in the 1810s is chronicled through the experience of a young bride, Leafy Rivers, and her husband, Reno. The novel offers a vivid description of wilderness life in the woods of America's first western frontier.

Historical Accuracy: The novel creates a convincing historical backdrop for this fanciful story.

6631 *The Massacre at Fall Creek*

Date of Publication: 1975
Subject(s): Indians; Trials; Settlement of the American Frontier
Fictional character(s): Hannah Cape, Young Woman; Charlie Fort, Lawyer
Historical character(s): James Monroe, Political Figure; John C. Calhoun, Political Figure
Time Period(s): 1820s (1824)
Locale(s): Indiana

Summary: Based on an actual incident, the novel tells the story of a brutal murder of Seneca Indians on the frontier of Indiana. The novel dramatizes the story of the massacre and the subsequent trial of the five white men charged in the crime largely from the perspective of Charlie Fort, the lawyer for the defense.

Historical Accuracy: Though based on fact, the novel freely invents characters and details to tell a wider story of the relationship between Indians and whites.

KEITH WEST
(PSEUD. OF KENNETH WESTMACOTT LANE)

6632 *Winter Cherry*

Date of Publication: 1944
Subject(s): Chinese Empire
Fictional character(s): Winter Cherry, Young Woman
Time Period(s): 8th century

Locale(s): China

Summary: The novel provides a look at the court world of China's T'ang dynasty during the 8th century. The story concerns Winter Cherry, a reluctant mistress of the Emperor whose adventures include an escape from court disguised as a boy, return to the Emperor's entourage, and eventual marriage to the man of her choice.

Historical Accuracy: The novel succeeds in convincingly capturing the customs and details of Chinese life during the period.

PAMELA ELIZABETH WEST (1945-)

West is an American writer.

6633 *Madeleine*

Date of Publication: 1983
Subject(s): Victorian Period; Trials
Historical character(s): Madeline Hamilton Smith, Murderer (accused); Sir James Wellwood Moncrieff, Lawyer
Time Period(s): 1850s (1857)
Locale(s): Scotland

Summary: The novel dramatizes the actual murder trial of Madeline Hamilton Smith who was charged in 1857 with the poisoning death of her lover. She pleads not guilty, admitting to only a passing acquaintanceship with the victim but witnesses and other evidence contradict her story. The novel offers a fascinating re-creation of Victorian restraint and passion.

Historical Accuracy: The novel uses the actual murder testimony as the basis for a full and authentic exploration of the era and its psychological impact.

PAUL WEST (1930-)

6634 *Lord Byron's Doctor*

Date of Publication: 1989
Subject(s): Regency Period; Literary Life
Historical character(s): George Gordon Byron, Writer, Nobleman; Percy Bysshe Shelley, Writer; Mary Wollstonecraft Shelley, Writer; John Polidori, Doctor, Companion (of Byron)
Time Period(s): 1810s (1816)
Locale(s): Switzerland; Italy

Summary: The novel is cast as the diary of John Polidori, Byron's doctor and travelling companion, as he records Byron's European tour of 1816. Polidori becomes the lens for viewing the genius of Byron and Shelley and their personal competition over the claims of genius.

Historical Accuracy: The atmosphere of the period is genuine, and the chronology is faithful to the facts.

6635 *Sporting with Amaryllis*

Date of Publication: 1996
Subject(s): Literary Life; Myths and Legends
Historical character(s): John Milton, Writer (poet)

Time Period(s): 17th century

Locale(s): Cambridge, England; London, England

Summary: This exploration of creative genius and sexuality centers on the young John Milton. As a student at Cambridge he becomes infatuated with a woman who may be a prostitute, a witch, or a myth come to life. The novel probes the psychology of an artist caught in the web of sensuality.

Historical Accuracy: The novel is an imaginative exploration with a detailed period background that captures its era.

6636 *The Tent of Orange Mist*

Date of Publication: 1995

Subject(s): Sino-Japanese Conflict, 1937-1945

Fictional character(s): Scald Ibiz, Teenager, Prostitute

Time Period(s): 1930s (1937)

Locale(s): Nanking, China

Summary: Scald Ibiz is the teenage daughter of an eminent scholar. When the Japanese invade Nanking, she is forced to work in a bordello as a prostitute in order to survive. The novel traces the ways she is transformed through the experience.

Historical Accuracy: The novel provides an authentic look at the horrors of the Japanese invasion.

6637 *The Very Rich Hours of Count von Stauffenberg*

Date of Publication: 1980

Subject(s): World War II; Assassination; Nazis

Historical character(s): Adolf Hitler, Political Figure; Claus von Stauffenberg, Military Personnel (German officer), Nobleman (count)

Time Period(s): 1940s (1944)

Locale(s): Germany

Summary: This is an imaginative reconstruction of an attempt on the life of Adolph Hitler by a cadre of aristocratic conspirators. Claus von Stauffenberg, one of the conspirators, tells the story after his death.

Historical Accuracy: The novel is a well-researched and believable account of the conspiracy, with a genuine evocation of the period and personalities.

6638 *The Women of Whitechapel and Jack the Ripper*

Date of Publication: 1991

Subject(s): Victorian Period; Crime and Criminals; Royalty—England

Fictional character(s): Annie Crook, Model; Marie Kelly, Prostitute

Historical character(s): Walter Richard Sickert, Artist (painter); Albert Edward, Duke of Clarence, Royalty (prince); Sir William Gull, Doctor

Time Period(s): 1880s

Locale(s): London, England

Summary: In this version of the Jack the Ripper mystery, Queen Victoria's grandson Eddy is introduced to the forbidden pleasures of London's bohemian life by painter Walter Sickert. When he fathers a child by shopgirl and model Annie Crook, the royals step in to put a end to Eddy's affair. When a group of prostitutes threaten blackmail, the personal physician to the royal family, Sir William Gull, hunts them down.

Historical Accuracy: The novel's ingenious, though historically debatable, solution to the Ripper killings is taken from Stephen Knight's *Jack the Ripper: The Final Solution*. The novel is most impressive in capturing the atmosphere and setting of London's underworld.

REBECCA WEST (1892-1983)

English journalist, novelist, biographer, and critic, West has been hailed as one of the 20th century's finest writers. A feminist, historian, and political commentator, her book *The Thinking Reed* is generally considered her finest novel. She was awarded an Order of the British Empire in 1959.

6639 *The Fountain Overflows*

Date of Publication: 1956

Subject(s): Family Saga

Fictional character(s): Piers Aubrey, Journalist; Claire Aubrey, Musician (ex-concert pianist); Cordelia Aubrey, Musician

Time Period(s): 1900s

Locale(s): London, England

Summary: Life at the turn of the century is portrayed in this story of the gifted but troubled Aubrey family. Piers Aubrey is a journalist whose passion for gambling keeps the family in poverty. Cordelia Aubrey strives to achieve success as a musician though her talent is insufficient. The appeal of the novel is its ability to evoke with clarity the rich details of life at the turn of the century.

Historical Accuracy: The novel is an exceptionally fine recreation of the past.

GLENWAY WESTCOTT (1901-)

An American writer from Wisconsin, Westcott was known for his writings about his native region, although he lived mainly abroad. *The Grandmothers* is his best-known work. He also published poetry, short stories, and essays.

6640 *The Grandmothers*

Date of Publication: 1927

Subject(s): Family Saga; Settlement of the American Frontier

Fictional character(s): Alwyn Tower, Hero; Henry Tower, Settler; Rose Tower, Settler

Time Period(s): 19th century; 20th century (1830-1925)

Locale(s): Wisconsin

Summary: A young boy, Alwyn Tower, assembles his heritage by learning the history of his ancestors and relatives. Much of the history of the 19th century is reflected in the struggles of the pioneer Tower family.

Historical Accuracy: The characters are vivid and authentic, and the frontier past is accurately re-created.

JAN WESTCOTT (1912-)

Born in Philadelphia, Westcott attended Swarthmore College. Westcott is best known for novels about the Tudor-Stuart periods of English history.

6641 *The Border Lord*

Date of Publication: 1946
Subject(s): Elizabethan Period; Royalty—Scotland
Historical character(s): Francis Hepburn, Nobleman (Earl of Bothwell); Anne Galbraith, Gentlewoman; James VI, Ruler (King of Scotland)
Time Period(s): 1590s
Locale(s): Scotland

Summary: Francis Hepburn, the Earl of Bothwell, is the uncrowned king of Scotland in the 1590s. The novel dramatizes his career: his escape from a prison cell in Edinburgh Castle, his challenge to James VI, and his love for Anne Galbraith.

Historical Accuracy: More romantic adventure than history, the novel does employ a credible atmosphere of the times, if the actual events are largely imagined.

6642 *Captain Barney*

Date of Publication: 1951
Subject(s): American Revolution; Sea Story
Fictional character(s): Joshua Barney, Military Personnel (American naval officer); Lady Douglass Harris, Gentlewoman
Time Period(s): 1780s
Locale(s): Philadelphia, Pennsylvania; Stacia, West Indies

Summary: Set during the American Revolution, the novel tells the adventurous story of Captain Joshua Barney, a daring privateer and officer in the fledgling American Navy in Philadelphia and the West Indies. A love story involving a high-spirited Englishwoman, Lady Douglass Harris, is joined to the scenes of naval action.

Historical Accuracy: The story is fictional and features more romance than authentic history.

6643 *Captain for Elizabeth*

Date of Publication: 1948
Subject(s): Elizabethan Period; Sea Story
Historical character(s): Thomas Cavendish, Explorer (navigator), Sea Captain; Sir Francis Drake, Explorer, Sea Captain; Elizabeth I, Ruler (Queen of England)
Time Period(s): 16th century
Locale(s): London, England; *Desire*, At Sea

Summary: The novel tells the story of English navigator and sea captain Thomas Cavendish's third voyage around the world. Leaving Elizabeth's court, Cavendish reaches Mexico in the *Desire* and, off the southern tip of California, captures the great Spanish galleon *Santa Anna*.

Historical Accuracy: The account of Cavendish's third trip around the world is taken from the journal of one of the members of Cavendish's company which appeared in Richard Hakluyt's *Voyages*.

6644 *Condottiere*

Date of Publication: 1962
Subject(s): Renaissance; Military Life
Historical character(s): Bartolomeo Colleoni, Mercenary; Francesco Sforza, Nobleman (Duke of Milan)
Time Period(s): 15th century
Locale(s): Italy

Summary: After his father and patron are murdered Renaissance mercenary Bartolomeo Colleoni begins a quest to become one of the most powerful men in Italy. He achieves success as a soldier of fortune in the wars between Venice and Milan, changing sides when opportune. The novel offers a vivid look at a remarkable figure during a fascinating, though violent, period in history.

Historical Accuracy: The novel is accurate in summarizing Colleoni's career and the events which shaped his fortune.

6645 *The Hepburn*

Date of Publication: 1950
Subject(s): Royalty—Scotland
Historical character(s): James IV, Ruler (King of Scotland); Patrick Hepburn, Nobleman (Earl of Bothwell); Lady Jane Gordon, Noblewoman
Time Period(s): 15th century
Locale(s): Scotland

Summary: Set during the reign of Scotland's James IV, this historical romance is centered on the romantic pursuit by Patrick Hepburn, the king's right-hand man, of the rebellious Lady Jane Gordon, the king's cousin. The border war with England and court intrigue share the stage.

Historical Accuracy: The novel features an authentic re-creation of the period and the atmosphere of court life.

6646 *The Queen's Grace*

Date of Publication: 1959
Subject(s): Tudor Period; Royalty—England
Historical character(s): Henry VIII, Ruler (King of England); Catherine Parr, Royalty (queen consort of Henry VIII); Thomas Seymour, Nobleman, Diplomat; Jane Seymour, Royalty (queen consort of Henry VIII); Mary Tudor, Royalty (princess); Edward Tudor, Royalty (prince); Elizabeth Tudor, Royalty (princess)
Time Period(s): 16th century (1529-1548)
Locale(s): England; Scotland

Summary: The novel tells the story of Henry VIII's sixth and final wife, Catherine Parr. She was a border lord's daughter who was married four times but whose true love was the rakish Thomas Seymour, brother of Henry VIII's third wife. Catherine's circuitous route to the throne, the final years of Henry's reign, and her life as the Dowager Queen are described.

Historical Accuracy: For the most part, the story captures the events in Catherine's life with accuracy.

6647 *The Tower and the Dream*

Date of Publication: 1974

Subject(s): Elizabethan Period; Royalty—England
Historical character(s): Elizabeth I, Ruler (Queen of England); Mary, Queen of Scots, Ruler; Elizabeth Shrewsbury, Noblewoman
Time Period(s): 16th century; 17th century (1532-1608)
Locale(s): England

Summary: The novel describes the remarkable career of Elizabeth Shrewsbury, considered second only to Queen Elizabeth as the most powerful woman in Elizabethan England. The novel dramatizes the struggle for dominance among Elizabeth Shrewsbury; Mary, Queen of Scots; and Queen Elizabeth.

Historical Accuracy: The history is authentic with some manipulation for the sake of the story.

6648 *The White Rose*
Date of Publication: 1969
Subject(s): War of the Roses; Royalty—England
Historical character(s): Richard, Duke of Gloucester, Nobleman; Henry VI, Ruler (King of England); Edward IV, Ruler (King of England); Elizabeth Woodville, Noblewoman; Richard Neville, Nobleman (Earl of Warwick)
Time Period(s): 15th century (1460s-1490s)
Locale(s): England

Summary: The novel dramatizes the tempestuous and fateful love affair between Edward IV and Elizabeth Woodville. Their relationship sets the powerful Earl of Warwick in opposition to the king and prompts a bloody struggle. The novel covers a 30-year period of English history with a cast that includes King Henry VI and his treacherous brother, who would become Richard III.

Historical Accuracy: The basic outline of history is observed in re-creating this fascinating story.

6649 *A Woman of Quality*
Date of Publication: 1978
Subject(s): Romance; Servants; Victorian Period
Fictional character(s): Anna Theros, Gentlewoman; Edward Theros, Gentleman; Kaatje, Housekeeper
Time Period(s): 1890s
Locale(s): Amsterdam, Netherlands; London, England

Summary: Set in Amsterdam in the 1890s, the novel tells the romantic story of the upstairs and downstairs world of a rich burgher household. Anna is married to a dashing Greek adventurer; Kaatje is a valued upstairs maid who falls in love with her mistress' brother-in-law.

Historical Accuracy: The period elements are convincingly presented.

MICHAEL WESTON

Weston was born in Devon, England. *The Cage* won Britain's Historical Novel Prize in memory of Georgette Heyer in 1986.

6650 *The Cage*
Date of Publication: 1986
Subject(s): Victorian Period; Mining; Rural Life—England

Fictional character(s): Ralph Fletcher, Religious (clergyman); Welland Halt, Miner
Time Period(s): 1880s (1887)
Locale(s): Cornwall, England

Summary: The discovery of a human skull in the fragments of an iron cage by a road marker leads Reverend Fletcher to reconstruct the events surrounding the death of the skull's owner. The answers are found in the story of Welland Halt who enters the lives of an isolated community of miners and whose past catches up with him.

Historical Accuracy: The novel constructs a believable period and regional backdrop for the story.

JUNE WETHERELL (1909-)

Born in Bellingham, Washington, Wetherell began writing for her college annual at the University of Washington. She then worked as a journalist and college professor. She is the author of *Every Ecstasy*, *Run with the Pack*, *But That Was Yesterday*, and *The Glorious Three*.

6651 *The Glorious Three*
Date of Publication: 1951
Subject(s): American West
Fictional character(s): Emily Ashburn, Pioneer; Jim Riley, Pioneer
Time Period(s): 1840s
Locale(s): Puget Sound, Washington

Summary: Prompted by her husband, Emily Ashburn reluctantly sets out on the Oregon Trail. When he and their children die on the road, Emily gets together with Jim Riley who is attempting to make a fresh start after his wife has been unfaithful.

Historical Accuracy: The genuine details of frontier life during the period are occasionally undercut by melodrama and sentiment.

EDITH WHARTON (1862-1937)

Edith Wharton was raised in a distinguished New York family, the milieu of many of her works, and specialized in sophisticated comedies of manners such as *The House of Mirth* and *The Age of Innocence*. *Ethan Frome*, a short novel set in New England, is considered her greatest tragic story.

6652 *The Old Maid*
Date of Publication: 1924
Subject(s): Social Chronicle
Fictional character(s): Delia Ralston, Gentlewoman; Charlotte Lovell, Gentlewoman; Tina Lovell, Ward
Time Period(s): 1850s
Locale(s): New York, New York

Summary: The parallel lives of two women are studied against the conservative conventions of New York society in the 19th century. Delia Ralston chooses stability over passion; her cousin Charlotte opts for passion and must pay the price for her recklessness. At the center of the drama is a young orphan girl named Tina.

Historical Accuracy: Wharton's strengths are her ability to realistically capture characters and the social environment that determines their choices.

6653 *The Valley of Decision*
Date of Publication: 1902
Subject(s): Politics; Independence—Italy
Fictional character(s): Odo Valsecca, Nobleman, Political Figure; Trescorre, Government Official (minister of state); Orazio Vivaldi, Philosopher
Time Period(s): 18th century
Locale(s): Lombardy, Italy; Switzerland

Summary: Odo Valsecca is a young Italian nobleman with liberal sympathies whose rise to power tests those sympathies. His support of the philosopher Vivaldi proves difficult to sustain under the pressure of the conservative aristocratic and clerical classes. Disillusioned in love and politics, Odo is unable to share the revolutionary fervor when the influence of the French Revolution shakes his region.

Historical Accuracy: The novel captures the politics of the period and interestingly shows the decline of the liberal ideal in the face of reality.

DENNIS WHEATLEY (1897-1977)
Born in London, Wheatley served as an officer in World War I. After the war he entered his family's wine business. Wheatley left the trade in 1932 to take up writing and achieved great success with his first novel, *Forbidden Territory*, followed by numerous bestsellers, earning him the reputation of "prince of the thriller-writers" and one of the 20th century's most prolific and best-selling authors. His other novels include *The Eunich of Stamboul, Uncharted Waters*, and *The Devil Rides Out*.

6654 *The Man Who Killed the King*
Date of Publication: 1965
Subject(s): French Revolution; Royalty—France; Espionage
Fictional character(s): Roger Brook, Spy; Athenais, Captive
Historical character(s): Louis XVI, Ruler (King of France); Marie Antoinette, Royalty (queen consort of Louis XVI); Napoleon Bonaparte, Military Personnel (officer); Charles Maurice de Talleyrand-Perigord, Diplomat, Political Figure; Maximilien Francois de Robespierre, Revolutionary; Gouverneur Morris, Diplomat; Louis Charles, Royalty (dauphin)
Time Period(s): 1790s
Locale(s): France; Spain

Summary: The novel takes place during the French Revolution and features the swashbuckling hero Roger Brook, a British agent sent to France to save the royal family. His mission as a double agent brings him into contact with the Royals, the inner circle of the Revolution, and a young Napoleon. The novel features a fictional solution to the mystery surrounding the disappearance of the heir to the French throne.

Historical Accuracy: The emphasis is on exciting adventure with a plausible historical backdrop.

GUY WHEELER
Born in Bengal, India, Wheeler is a Cambridge-educated career soldier. He served as a member of the army staff assigned to the British embassy in Washington, D.C. and was appointed aide-de-camp to Queen Elizabeth in 1972.

6655 *Cato's War*
Date of Publication: 1980
Subject(s): American Revolution; Battle of Yorktown
Fictional character(s): Philip Cato, Military Personnel (British colonel)
Historical character(s): Charles Cornwallis, Military Personnel (general); George Washington, Military Personnel (army commander); Henry Clinton, Military Personnel (general); George III, Ruler (King of England); Banastre Tarleton, Military Personnel (British officer)
Time Period(s): 1780s
Locale(s): England; South Carolina; Virginia

Summary: The British perspective on the American Revolution is dramatized as Colonel Philip Cato is sent to South Carolina to recruit loyalist supporters. The novel chronicles Cornwallis' southern campaign that culminates in his surrender at Yorktown. Cato faces a series of moral choices and divided loyalties in this alternate version of heroism during the Revolution.

Historical Accuracy: The novel is solidly grounded by sources including the generals' own accounts of the campaigns.

RICHARD S. WHEELER (1935-)
Born in Milwaukee, Wisconsin, Wheeler attended the University of Wisconsin at Madison. He worked as an editorial writer, copyeditor, reporter, and book editor from 1961 until 1987. Since 1988 he has been a full-time writer whose specialty is the western historical novel. Wheeler concentrates on the 1840s and 1850s, which he says were the most colorful decades in the settlement of the West.

6656 *Beneath the Blue Mountain*
Date of Publication: 1979
Subject(s): American West; Homesteading
Fictional character(s): Nathaniel Hapgood, Settler; Don Ignacio Olivera, Landowner
Time Period(s): 1870s (1873)
Locale(s): Arizona

Summary: The novel records the clash of cultures during the struggle for control of the Southwest. New Englander Nathaniel Hapgood stakes a homestead claim in the Arizona territory of the 1870s. He must contend with Don Ignacio Olivera, a Spanish nobleman who refuses to recognize the U.S.'s claim to land that his family has held for over 100 years.

Historical Accuracy: The novel offers a genuine look at the period and the region.

6657 *Dodging Red Cloud*
Date of Publication: 1987

Subject(s): American West; Indians
Fictional character(s): Hannah Holt, Young Woman; Colonel Wiley Smart, Trader (horse); Linc Larrimer, Orphan
Historical character(s): Sitting Bull, Indian (Sioux), Chieftain; Red Cloud, Indian (Sioux), Warrior
Time Period(s): 1860s (1868)
Locale(s): Bozeman Trail, United States

Summary: Three travellers on the Bozeman Trail attempt to keep out of the way of Sioux warrior Red Cloud. Hannah Holt is coming from Virginia City with a fortune in silver. She is forced to join forces with horse trader Wiley Smart and twelve-year-old Linc Larrimer for safety. They face stolen horses, food shortages, and captivity in a Crow Indian village.

Historical Accuracy: The novel, though imagined, offers a believable portrait of the period.

6658 *The Far Tribes*

Date of Publication: 1990
Subject(s): American West; Indians
Fictional character(s): Barnaby Skye, Mountain Man; Elkanah Morse, Scientist
Time Period(s): 19th century (pre-Civil War)
Locale(s): Rocky Mountains, Montana

Summary: Easterner Elkanah Morse wishes to study the ''Far Tribes,'' Indians who live in the Rockies. He engages Barnaby Skye to lead a small expedition into the wilderness. Skye must use all his skills to survive.

Historical Accuracy: The period elements are convincingly presented.

6659 *Fool's Coach*

Date of Publication: 1989
Subject(s): American West
Fictional character(s): Aristotle Scrimshaw, Businessman; Angelica Ramirez, Prostitute; Randolph Figaro, Gambler
Time Period(s): 1860s (1863)
Locale(s): West

Summary: Three travellers attempt to make it across the plains from Nevada to Salt Lake City on a trail populated by road agents poised to set upon whomever is foolhardy enough to travel into their domain. The novel records their adventure.

Historical Accuracy: The premium here is action and adventure with some accurate period painting.

6660 *Goldfield*

Date of Publication: 1995
Subject(s): Mining; American West
Fictional character(s): Maude Arbuckle, Prospector; Big Sam Jones, Trader; Delia Favor, Young Woman; Hannibal Dash, Professor, Scientist (geologist)
Time Period(s): 1900s
Locale(s): Nevada

Summary: A gold strike in Nevada in the 1900s is the scene for this western novel that assembles a colorful cast of characters who rush into southwestern Nevada in pursuit of their dreams. They include Maude Arbuckle, a veteran prospector; Big Sam

Jones, a con-man selling wildcat stocks; Delia Favor, a beauty in search of a husband; and Hannibal Dash, a geology professor who gives up everything to strike it rich.

Historical Accuracy: The novel provides a convincing portrait of the period and the region.

6661 *Montana Hitch*

Date of Publication: 1990
Subject(s): American West
Fictional character(s): Abner Dent, Rancher; Eve Dent, Spouse
Time Period(s): 19th century
Locale(s): Montana

Summary: Abner Dent brings his wife Eve to his Montana ranch only to be beset by cattle thieves and a neighboring cattleman's unwanted attentions towards his wife and his ranch. Dent must take action and failure could mean the loss of everything he loves.

Historical Accuracy: The novel convinces in its period elements and the regional portrait.

6662 *Richard Lamb*

Date of Publication: 1987
Subject(s): American West; Indians
Fictional character(s): Richard Lamb, Trader; Joseph Partridge, Military Personnel (captain)
Time Period(s): 1870s (1877)
Locale(s): Montana

Summary: When the U.S. Army, under the direction of Captain Joseph Partridge, enforces an order to place all Indians on the reservation, it must contend with trader Richard Lamb. For over 40 years Lamb has lived in Montana among the Blackfeet whom he regards not as hostiles but as kin. The novel describes Lamb's resistance in the face of overwhelming pressure to change.

Historical Accuracy: The details of frontier and Indian life are authentic.

6663 *The Two Medicine River*

Date of Publication: 1993
Subject(s): American West; Indians
Fictional character(s): Peter Kipp, Trader; Marie Therese Paris, Indian (Blackfoot)
Time Period(s): 1850s; 1860s
Locale(s): Rocky Mountains; St. Louis, Missouri

Summary: This novel, part of the ''Rivers West'' series, centers on events along the Two Medicine River in the eastern Rocky Mountains in Blackfoot territory. Two characters, Marie Therese Paris and Peter Kipp, come into conflict with forces determined to destroy the Indians. The action culminates in the Baker massacre.

Historical Accuracy: The central characters are fictional, but the story is set against real events, though the historical record has been altered in minor ways.

6664 *Where the River Runs*

Date of Publication: 1990
Subject(s): American West; Indians
Fictional character(s): Jed Owen, Military Personnel (army captain); Susannah, Frontierswoman, Fiance(e)
Time Period(s): 1840s (1849)
Locale(s): Montana (upper Missouri River)

Summary: On a peace mission to the Indians, Captain Jed Owen becomes the lone survivor of a massacre. He struggles back to civilization as his fiancee, Susannah, journeys up the Missouri in search of him.

Historical Accuracy: The details of wilderness life of the period are believable.

6665 *Winter Grass*

Date of Publication: 1983
Subject(s): American West; Ranching
Fictional character(s): John Quincy Putnam, Rancher; Nicole Aumont, Lawyer
Time Period(s): 1880s (1886-1887)
Locale(s): Montana

Summary: This story of ranching in Montana during the 1880s captures the period of the introduction of barb wire to the range, an event that explodes into a range war as neighbors ignore the boundaries of John Quincy Putnam's ranch and threaten to destroy his supply of winter grass.

Historical Accuracy: The setting and the novel's atmosphere are authentic and believable.

SESSIONS S. WHEELER (1911-)

A biologist and conservationist, Wheeler graduated from the University of Nevada, and served as executive director of the Nevada Fish and Game Commission. He is the coauthor of an outdoor sportsman column in the *Reno Evening Gazette* and of two conservation textbooks.

6666 *Paiute*

Date of Publication: 1965
Subject(s): American West; Indians
Fictional character(s): Julian Chadmore, Gentleman; Sarah Martin, Singer
Historical character(s): Numaga, Indian (Paiute), Chieftain
Time Period(s): 1850s; 1860s (1859-1860)
Locale(s): Nevada

Summary: The novel captures the period of Nevada's history that includes the discovery of the Comstock Lode and the Paiute massacre at Pyramid Lake. Julian Chadmore arrives in the territory and gets involved with the mining frenzy brought about by the gold and silver discovery and in the conflict with the Indians.

Historical Accuracy: The events described are authentic, and, where sources disagree, the most plausible version has been chosen.

JERE HUNGERFORD WHEELWRIGHT (1905-1961)

Born in Baltimore and educated at Princeton, Wheelwright served in the Navy during World War II, devoting himself to writing at the end of the war. His other novels include *The Strong Room* and *The Wolfshead*.

6667 *Draw Near to Battle*

Date of Publication: 1953
Subject(s): Napoleonic Wars; Battle of Eylau
Fictional character(s): Ridley Howard, Military Personnel (soldier); Cary Gilmore, Gentlewoman; Cecilie Von Hulsen, Noblewoman
Historical character(s): Napoleon Bonaparte, Ruler (emperor of France); Charles Maurice de Talleyrand-Perigord, Diplomat
Time Period(s): 1800s
Locale(s): Europe

Summary: This story dramatizes the adventures of a young American in Napoleon's army. It combines some fairly conventional romance with historically authentic battlefield descriptions. The climax of the novel is the bloody Battle of Eylau, in which 50,000 Russian and French troops were lost during a single day of fighting.

Historical Accuracy: The novel's convincing settings and accurate presentations of historical events are somewhat at odds with its romantic scenes.

6668 *Gentlemen, Hush!*

Date of Publication: 1948
Subject(s): Civil War—U.S.; Reconstruction Period
Fictional character(s): Harry Ashwood, Veteran (Confederate soldier); Tom Stewart, Veteran (Confederate soldier); Stacey Harris, Veteran (Confederate soldier)
Time Period(s): 1860s
Locale(s): Virginia

Summary: Three Confederate soldiers meet near Appomattox two days before Lee's surrender. The trio return to Harry Ashwood's home in Virginia and struggle to build a new life. The novel dramatizes the conditions in the South following the war and during Reconstruction.

Historical Accuracy: The novel provides a believable portrait of the period.

6669 *The Gray Captain*

Date of Publication: 1954
Subject(s): Civil War—U.S.; Military Life
Fictional character(s): Thomas Brice, Military Personnel (lieutenant); Captain Stowell, Military Personnel
Time Period(s): 1860s (1864)
Locale(s): Virginia

Summary: The experiences of a company of infantry from Maryland in the Army of Northern Virginia during the summer of 1864 are the focus of the novel. Lieutenant Thomas Brice is the newcomer who is introduced to the various personalities of the company, including its leader, Captain Stowell.

Historical Accuracy: The Civil War details are authentic and accurate.

6670 *Kentucky Stand*

Date of Publication: 1951
Subject(s): Indians; American Revolution; Settlement of the American Frontier
Fictional character(s): James Cheston, Young Man
Historical character(s): Daniel Boone, Frontiersman; Simon Kenton, Frontiersman; Thomas Jefferson, Political Figure
Time Period(s): 1770s (1777)
Locale(s): Boonesborough, Kentucky; Maryland

Summary: A young ex-schoolboy from Baltimore journeys west to join his uncle in Kentucky. He is the sole survivor of an Indian attack and makes it to Daniel Boone's settlement. There he becomes a trapper and Indian fighter as the western settlement contends with hostile Indians and the British.

Historical Accuracy: The novel interweaves a fictional story with an authentic background of actual events and a convincing frontier atmosphere.

6671 *The Strong Room*

Date of Publication: 1948
Subject(s): Tudor Period; Royalty—England
Fictional character(s): John Aumarle, Nobleman
Historical character(s): Mary I, Ruler (Queen of England); Elizabeth Tudor, Royalty (princess)
Time Period(s): 16th century
Locale(s): England

Summary: Aristocrat John Aumarle is imprisoned in the Tower of London by Henry VIII because of his close relationship with the royal family. When Mary I comes to the throne he is pardoned but becomes involved in a plot to prevent the Queen from wedding Philip II of Spain.

Historical Accuracy: The novel ingeniously connects its fictional story with the historical events of the period.

6672 *Wolfshead*

Date of Publication: 1949
Subject(s): Elizabethan Period; Sea Story; Pirates
Fictional character(s): John Aumarle, Pirate
Time Period(s): 16th century
Locale(s): At Sea; France; England

Summary: This sequel to *The Stray Room* recounts the adventures of John Aumarle as an outlaw in France and as a pirate on the high seas during the reign of Mary Tudor. With the accession of Elizabeth to the English throne, Aumarle's criminal career is ended.

Historical Accuracy: The novel features a thorough and believable period backdrop for the story's adventures.

MAURINE WHIPPLE (1910-)

Born in St. George, Utah, American author Maurine Whipple attended the University of Utah and the University

of California. A teacher as well as a writer, she is the author of *This Is the Place* and has been a contributor to numerous magazines.

6673 *The Giant Joshua*

Date of Publication: 1941
Subject(s): American West; Mormons
Fictional character(s): Clory MacIntyre, Young Woman, Orphan; Abijah MacIntyre, Settler
Historical character(s): Brigham Young, Religious (Mormon leader)
Time Period(s): 1860s
Locale(s): Utah

Summary: The novel describes the founding of Dixie Mission in the Utah desert by a band of Mormon settlers who brave flood, famine, and Indian attack. The story centers on young Clory MacIntyre, an orphan who is "sealed" as the third wife of Abijah MacIntyre. She is torn between her fear of Abijah, her faith in Mormonism, and her desire for beauty and gaiety.

Historical Accuracy: Many of the events depicted are true and are based on actual diary entries and eyewitness accounts.

BEATRICE WHITE (1902-1986)

Born in Cambridgeshire, British educator, editor, and author Beatrice White was an authority on Chaucer, Shakespeare, and Mary Tudor. She spent the last 30 years of her academic career at the University of London where she served as the vice-president of Westfield College and professor of English literature. White served as the editor of *The Year's Work in English Studies* and *The Vulgaria of Robert Whittington*, and was the author of *Mary Tudor*.

6674 *Royal Nonesuch: A Tudor Tapestry*

Date of Publication: 1936
Subject(s): Tudor Period; Royalty—England
Historical character(s): Henry VIII, Ruler (King of England); Mary Tudor, Royalty (sister of Henry VIII); Charles Brandon, Nobleman (Duke of Suffolk)
Time Period(s): 16th century
Locale(s): England

Summary: This story of Tudor court life dramatizes the relationship between Henry VIII, his beloved sister Mary, and her husband, Charles Brandon, Duke of Suffolk. The novel offers a vivid and authentic look at the period and life at court.

Historical Accuracy: The novel captures the Tudor scene faithfully.

ETHEL WHITE

White is a former schoolteacher.

6675 *Bear His Mild Yoke*

Date of Publication: 1966
Subject(s): American Colonies; Quakers; Puritans
Historical character(s): Mary Dyer, Young Woman; Anne Hutchinson, Religious; George Fox, Leader (Quaker)

Time Period(s): 17th century (1635-1660)
Locale(s): American Colonies; England

Summary: The novel is the journal account of Quaker minister Mary Dyer who, inspired by the religious convictions of Anne Hutchinson and George Fox, opposes the religious intolerance of the Puritan theocracy in the Massachusetts colony. Her journal recounts her growing religious fervor and determination to accept persecution on behalf of the principles of religious freedom and freedom of speech.

Historical Accuracy: The story of Mary Dyer is reconstructed from a variety of sources. When dates and facts conflicted, those that fit the narrative were used. When no facts were available conjecture was employed.

HELEN CONSTANCE WHITE (1896-1967)

An American author, educator, and diplomat, White was born in New Haven, Connecticut, and educated at Radcliffe College and the University of Wisconsin. The recipient of numerous awards and honors, White is the author of *Tudor Books of Saints and Martyrs*, *Dust on the King's Highway*, and *Not Built with Hands*.

`6676` *Bird of Fire: A Tale of Francis of Assisi*

Date of Publication: 1958
Subject(s): Religious Life; Middle Ages; Biography, Fictionalized
Historical character(s): Francis of Assisi, Religious (friar)
Time Period(s): 12th century; 13th century
Locale(s): Assisi, Italy

Summary: Born to a wealthy merchant, Francis eventually founded the religious order named after him. This novel dramatizes his tranformation from a boisterous youth to a pious, self-effacing religious figure.

Historical Accuracy: Though he interweaves legend and fact, the author manages to present a vivid portrait of the age and a convincing psychological picture of Francis.

`6677` *Dust on the King's Highway*

Date of Publication: 1947
Subject(s): Spanish Colonies; Religious Life; Indians
Fictional character(s): Francisco Garces, Religious (priest)
Historical character(s): Juan Bautista de Anza, Explorer, Government Official
Time Period(s): 1770s
Locale(s): Mexico; California

Summary: Missionary life in Mexico and California is the subject for this novel that chronicles the experiences of a Franciscan priest, Francisco Garces, among the Indians. He finds himself in the middle of conflict between the Spanish and the Indians for control of California.

Historical Accuracy: The novel provides a number of authentic scenes of period life.

`6678` *The Four Rivers of Paradise*

Date of Publication: 1955
Subject(s): Roman Empire; Christianity
Fictional character(s): Hilary of Bordeaux, Young Man
Historical character(s): Augustine, Religious (bishop); Jerome, Religious (bishop)
Time Period(s): 5th century
Locale(s): Rome, Roman Empire; Bordeaux, France

Summary: Hilary of Bordeaux, heir of a great Aquitainian landowner, journeys to Rome just prior to Alaric's invasion. He is on hand for the sack of Rome and meets St. Augustine and St. Jerome who help set him on a religious path.

Historical Accuracy: The novel is best in capturing the mood and atmosphere of the times.

`6679` *Not Built with Hands*

Date of Publication: 1935
Subject(s): Middle Ages
Historical character(s): Gregory VII, Religious (pope); Matilda of Tuscany, Noblewoman (countess); Henry II, Ruler (Holy Roman Emperor)
Time Period(s): 11th century
Locale(s): Italy

Summary: The novel dramatizes the epic battle waged in the 11th century by Matilda, Countess of Tuscany and Pope Gregory VII against Henry II of Germany. Matilda sides with Gregory in his attempt to consolidate the power of the church and root out corruption, represented by the unscrupulous Henry.

Historical Accuracy: The novel is faithful to the events of history and accurately portrays the historical figures and the times.

`6680` *To the End of the World*

Date of Publication: 1939
Subject(s): French Revolution; Reign of Terror
Fictional character(s): Michel de la Tour d'Auvergne, Religious (priest)
Time Period(s): 18th century
Locale(s): France

Summary: The role of the Church during the French Revolution is this novel's theme. It traces the experiences of a young priest who struggles for a role to play during the turmoil of the period. Michel de la Tour d'Auvergne, the son of a noble family, first wishes to become a monk and revise the medieval traditions. Later he becomes a parish priest and struggles to maintain the position of the Church against the forces of the Revolution and the Terror.

Historical Accuracy: The novel's authenticity is at times undermined by a colloquial tone and anachronistic terms. Yet the novel avoids the romantic cliches of many other fictionalized versions of the French Revolution.

HILDA CRYSTAL WHITE (1917-)

Born in Oklahoma City, White published poetry in magazines when she was eight. She attended public schools in Chattanooga, Tennessee, and was the organizer and leader of the Shrub Oak Writer's Workshop. She is the author of *Song Without End: The Love Story of Robert and Clara Schumann*, as well as children's plays and musicals.

6681 *Wild Decembers: A Biographical Portrait of the Brontes*

Date of Publication: 1957
Subject(s): Literary Life; Biography, Fictionalized; Victorian Period
Historical character(s): Charlotte Bronte, Writer; Emily Bronte, Writer; Anne Bronte, Writer; Branwell Bronte, Artist; Patrick Bronte, Religious (clergyman)
Time Period(s): 19th century
Locale(s): Haworth, England (in Yorkshire)

Summary: The novel tells the story of the Bronte family and the four children—Charlotte, Branwell, Emily, and Anne—who are raised by their brooding clergyman father, Patrick Bronte. With little outside stimulation the four turn to their imaginations which become the basis of the three Bronte sisters' literary efforts. Tragedy dogs the family even on the eve of Charlotte Bronte's great success with *Jane Eyre*.

Historical Accuracy: The novel stays close to the sources, primarily Elizabeth Gaskell's biography of Charlotte Bronte.

LESLIE TURNER WHITE (1903-)

A Canadian born in Ottawa, White has worked as a rancher, county sheriff, and movie cameraman, and has been a professional hunter, served in the military, and a member of a carnival troupe. He became a full-time writer in 1932. Three of his books have been made into films.

6682 *The Highland Hawk*

Date of Publication: 1952
Subject(s): Civil War—England
Fictional character(s): Davy Dugald, Servant (groom), Military Personnel (colonel); Olivia Westmoreland, Gentlewoman
Historical character(s): Oliver Cromwell, Political Figure
Time Period(s): 17th century
Locale(s): Highlands, Scotland

Summary: During the English Civil War, Scottish groom Davy Dugald goes off to war against the Royalists. In a few short months he finds himself laird of the clan and a colonel in Cromwell's parliamentary army and wins the hand of the daughter of the Earl of Westmoreland. Dugald's quick wits, bravery, knowledge of the Highlands, and colorful cast of companions facilitate his rise.

Historical Accuracy: The novel offers exciting and colorful action against a plausible historical backdrop.

6683 *His Majesty's Highlanders*

Date of Publication: 1964
Subject(s): French and Indian War

Fictional character(s): Bruce Fletcher, Military Personnel (British soldier); Wendy Mason, Young Woman
Historical character(s): James Wolfe, Military Personnel (British general)
Time Period(s): 1750s
Locale(s): Lake George, New York, American Colonies; Quebec, Canada

Summary: A fight over a woman who jilted him causes Bruce Fletcher to join a Highlander regiment in the campaign against the French and Indians in America. Bruce is taken captive, into Canada, where he gains important information that leads to the British victory over the French in Quebec. The story also features a romance between Bruce and Wendy Mason.

Historical Accuracy: The story is largely invented, but does feature some convincing period elements.

6684 *Log Jam*

Date of Publication: 1959
Subject(s): Lumber Industry
Fictional character(s): Barnabas Ward, Businessman (timber); Bull Rau, Businessman (timber); Walt Devers, Businessman (timber)
Time Period(s): 1870s
Locale(s): Saginaw Valley, Michigan

Summary: Set in Michigan's lower penninsula the novel dramatizes the conflict in the timber industry between the timber kings and the forces of change attempting to break their monopoly and introduce new logging methods. Walt Devers is convinced that the old logging methods are no longer useful, and he must confront intractable Bull Rau.

Historical Accuracy: The novel offers a convincing portrait of the timber industry of the time.

6685 *Look Away, Look Away*

Date of Publication: 1944
Subject(s): Civil War—U.S.; Reconstruction Period
Fictional character(s): Dan Beals, Sailor
Time Period(s): 1860s (1866)
Locale(s): Amazon River, Brazil

Summary: After the Civil War a group of Confederate refugees take a Mississippi river-boat to South America where they plan to create a colony along the Amazon. The rag-tag group of Southern aristocrats and poor whites contends with a hurricane and the inevitable crises in dealing with the South American wilderness.

Historical Accuracy: The story adheres closely to actual facts, incorporating some of the dialogue from actual letters and records.

6686 *Lord Fancy*

Date of Publication: 1960
Subject(s): Boxing; Georgian Period; Sports
Fictional character(s): Darcy Scott, Sports Figure (boxer); Matt Burnham, Blacksmith
Historical character(s): George, Prince of Wales, Royalty
Time Period(s): 18th century

Locale(s): London, England

Summary: The novel tells the story of young Englishman Darcy Scott and his determination to become the boxing champion of England in the 18th century. He must first triumph over an assortment of obstacles, including being thrown into prison. Eventually he faces the most feared fighter in England, the Slasher.

Historical Accuracy: The novel is atmospheric but not convincing. The period is created largely through quaint archaisms of speech.

6687 *Lord Johnnie*

Date of Publication: 1949
Subject(s): Crime and Criminals; Georgian Period; American Colonies
Fictional character(s): Johnnie Rogue, Outlaw; Lady Leanna Somerset, Gentlewoman
Time Period(s): 1750s
Locale(s): London, England; American Colonies

Summary: This romantic adventure story is based on the 18th-century custom in which a gentlewoman could escape her debts by marrying a condemned felon. But what might happen if the condemned man survives his intended execution? This premise drives the drama as Johnny Rogue marries Lady Leanna and escapes into piracy and conspiracy in the conflict between the French and the English in colonial America.

Historical Accuracy: The story is fanciful with an emphasis on romantic adventure over careful historical documentation.

6688 *Magnus the Magnificent*

Date of Publication: 1950
Subject(s): Elizabethan Period; Sea Story
Fictional character(s): Magnus Carter, Sea Captain, Privateer
Time Period(s): 16th century
Locale(s): England; At Sea

Summary: Magnus Carter is a privateer who returns home from a successful voyage to find disappointment in love. After losing his money and his beloved, he returns to sea where he wins fame and the favor of Elizabeth I.

Historical Accuracy: Although swashbuckling adventure receives pride of place here, there is evidence of authentic language and customs.

6689 *Monsieur Yankee*

Date of Publication: 1957
Subject(s): French Revolution; Reign of Terror
Fictional character(s): William Dudley Tayloe, Doctor; Andre Guillet, Gentleman
Time Period(s): 1790s (1793)
Locale(s): Paris, France

Summary: Set during the Reign of Terror in France, the story describes the adventures of Will Tayloe, who comes to Paris at the urging of his friend, Andre Guillet, who cannot be found when Tayloe arrives. Will is mistaken for a famous British spy and finds himself involved in conspiracy, duels, and chases.

Historical Accuracy: The emphasis is on adventure and derring-do, with some convincing period elements.

6690 *Scorpus the Moor*

Date of Publication: 1962
Subject(s): Roman Empire; Christianity
Fictional character(s): Ahmed Ben Mourouane, Entertainer (aka Scorpus the Moor); Libba, Young Woman
Historical character(s): Nero, Ruler (Roman emperor); Peter, Biblical Figure
Time Period(s): 1st century
Locale(s): Rome, Roman Empire

Summary: Life in Nero's Rome is described through the experiences of Ahmed Ben Mourouane who survives a sea disaster and is forced to live by his wits in Rome as Scorpus the Moor. He succeeds with a trained flea act that attracts the attention of the Emperor and leads to a job in the Circus Maximus. When Libba, a young Christian, is imprisoned and sentenced to be served to the leopards, Ahmed must use all his resources to save her.

Historical Accuracy: The Roman background is more colorful than carefully documented. The emphasis here is on the sensational rather than the realistic.

6691 *Sir Rogue*

Date of Publication: 1954
Subject(s): Elizabethan Period; Russian Empire
Fictional character(s): Sir Guy Spangler, Gentleman
Historical character(s): Ivan the Terrible, Ruler (Czar of Russia)
Time Period(s): 16th century (1570s)
Locale(s): England; Russia

Summary: This swashbuckling historical adventure describes the exploits of Sir Guy Spangler who is charged with delivering a beautiful young girl to Russian Czar Ivan the Terrible.

Historical Accuracy: Fast-paced adventure is primary here, with only a serviceable period atmosphere.

6692 *Wagons West*

Date of Publication: 1964
Subject(s): American West; Wagon Trains
Fictional character(s): John Jackson, Doctor; Blacky Dupre, Settler; Merry Dupre, Young Woman
Time Period(s): 1840s (1848)
Locale(s): Boston, Massachusetts; Missouri; Fort Laramie, Wyoming

Summary: The novel describes the western adventures of Boston doctor John Jackson, who accompanies a family travelling in a Conestoga wagon. Jackson becomes a competent frontier ranger, gunfighter, temporary rancher, and head of a Mormon wagon train when its leader is killed in a Comanche attack.

Historical Accuracy: The novel is so packed with adventures that credibility is strained.

MAX WHITE
(PSEUD. OF CHARLES W. WHITE, 1906-)
Max White is the pseudonym of Charles White. He is the author of *Tiger Tiger*.

6693 *In the Blazing Light*
Date of Publication: 1946
Subject(s): Biography, Fictionalized; Artistic Life
Historical character(s): Francisco Jose de Goya y Lucientes, Artist (painter); Maria Cayetana, Noblewoman (Duchess of Alba)
Time Period(s): 18th century
Locale(s): Madrid, Spain

Summary: This fictionalized life of Spanish painter Goya records his successes as a prominent court painter as well as his 20-year love affair with the Duchess of Alba. The painter emerges in all his complexity against a well-realized period background of the dissolute court of the Bourbons.

Historical Accuracy: The novel can be charged with oversimplification to create stronger contrasts than the facts allow.

6694 *The Midnight Gardener: A Novel about Baudelaire*
Date of Publication: 1948
Subject(s): Biography, Fictionalized; Literary Life
Historical character(s): Charles Pierre Baudelaire, Writer (poet)
Time Period(s): 19th century
Locale(s): Paris, France

Summary: The novel provides a fictional biography of French poet and critic Charles Baudelaire. His life and literary career are chronicled from his youth to the eve of his departure for Brussels where he died in 1867.

Historical Accuracy: While the novel observes the main facts of Baudelaire's life and times, the interpretations are overly psychoanalytical and debatable.

NELIA GARDNER WHITE (1894-1957)
The daughter of a Pennsylvania clergyman, White wrote fiction based on her experience in *No Trumpet Before Him* and *The Fields of Gomorrah*. *Daughter of Time* is a fictionalized biography of writer Katherine Mansfield.

6695 *Daughter of Time*
Date of Publication: 1942
Subject(s): Biography, Fictionalized; Literary Life
Historical character(s): Katherine Mansfield, Writer; John Middleton Murry, Editor, Writer; D.H. Lawrence, Writer
Time Period(s): 19th century; 20th century (1890s-1923)
Locale(s): New Zealand; France; England

Summary: This novel offers a fictionalized biography of writer Katherine Mansfield from her childhood in New Zealand to her death. The author paints a vivid and convincing portrait of the artist who was, through her art, able to momentarily transcend her isolation and pain.

Historical Accuracy: The novel is faithful to the events of Mansfield's life and succeeds in creating a vivid interior view. It is less successful in creating believable portraits of the men in Mansfield's life.

OLIVE WHITE (1899-)
Born in New Haven, Connecticut, and educated at Radcliffe College, White became an English professor at Wellesley and then Bradley University in Peoria, Illinois. She is the author of *The King's Good Servant* and *Late Harvest*.

6696 *The King's Good Servant*
Date of Publication: 1936
Subject(s): Tudor Period; Biography, Fictionalized; Religious Conflict
Historical character(s): Sir Thomas More, Political Figure, Writer; Henry VIII, Ruler (King of England); Thomas Cranmer, Religious (archbishop); John Fisher, Religious (bishop); Thomas Cromwell, Political Figure; Thomas Howard, Nobleman (Duke of Norfolk); Stephen Gardiner, Religious (prelate)
Time Period(s): 16th century (1529-1535)
Locale(s): England

Summary: This biographical novel chronicles the last six years in the life of Sir Thomas More from his return to England after securing the Peace of Cambrai and his assumption of the chancellorship under Henry VIII. The King seeks More's support in his plan to marry Anne Boleyn producing More's crisis of conscience, which leads to his execution.

Historical Accuracy: The novel is historically accurate in its depiction of the events surrounding More's life, as well as in a series of believable portraits of the major figures of the era.

6697 *Late Harvest*
Date of Publication: 1940
Subject(s): Elizabethan Period; Religious Conflict
Historical character(s): Edmund Campion, Religious (priest)
Time Period(s): 16th century; 17th century (1580-1603)
Locale(s): England

Summary: The background for this novel is the Catholic persecution during the reign of Elizabeth I. At the center of the novel's drama is Edmund Campion who helps sustain the Catholic faith in England, though his life is constantly threatened. The novel concentrates on the ordinary life of Catholics during the period.

Historical Accuracy: The period is rendered with a convincing authenticity.

PATRICK WHITE (1912-1990)
An English novelist, playwright, memoirist, and short story writer, White was educated at Cambridge and received the Nobel Prize for Literature in 1973. His novels are dense with symbols, myths, and allegories marking a unique artistic vision. His novels *The Tree of Man*, *Voss*, and *The Solid Mandala* are among the most important novels of this century.

6698 *Voss*

Date of Publication: 1957
Subject(s): Exploration; Frontier—Australia
Fictional character(s): Johann Ulrich Voss, Explorer; Laura Trevelyan, Gentlewoman
Time Period(s): 19th century (1840s-1860)
Locale(s): Australia

Summary: The novel contrasts life in Sydney, Australia, in the 1840s and 1850s with the exploration of Australia's unknown interior. The two central characters are the indomitable Johann Voss, who endures hardships in the long trek across the Australian desert, and Laura Trevelyan, who loves him and endures no less a trial and process of maturation in civilized Sydney.

Historical Accuracy: The novel is strongest in the details of social life of the period. The author shows the suffering the men undergo but does not develop the landscape with sufficient detail.

SIMON WHITE

6699 *Clear for Action!*

Date of Publication: 1978
Subject(s): Sea Story; Napoleonic Wars; Military Life—British Navy
Fictional character(s): Jethro Cockerill Penhaligon, Military Personnel (naval captain); Clarissa Campden, Gentlewoman
Time Period(s): 1800s
Locale(s): Naples, Italy; *Avenger*, At Sea (in the Mediterranean)

Summary: In the sequel to *The English Captain*, the roguish Captain "Cocky" Penhaligon finds himself in difficulty after eloping with a flag officer's daughter and landing in a Neapolitan jail. Meanwhile, the French Navy at Toulon has been instructed to destroy Penhaligon's *Avenger*.

Historical Accuracy: Swashbuckling adventure is balanced by a convincing picture of naval life and strategy during the age of sail.

6700 *The English Captain*

Date of Publication: 1977
Subject(s): Sea Story; Napoleonic Wars; Military Life—British Navy
Fictional character(s): Jethro Cockerill Penhaligon, Military Personnel (naval captain)
Historical character(s): Lady Emma Hamilton, Gentlewoman; Sir William Hamilton, Diplomat; Horatio Nelson, Military Personnel (admiral)
Time Period(s): 1800s (1800)
Locale(s): *Avenger*, At Sea (in the Mediterranean); Naples, Italy

Summary: The novel introduces swashbuckling naval captain Jethro "Cocky" Penhaligon who is ordered by Lord Nelson to stop a French ship that is harassing British merchant vessels in the Mediterranean. To do so, Penhaligon must also solve the mystery of who is passing secret information on naval maneuvers to Napoleon's fleet.

Historical Accuracy: The novel convincingly depicts naval strategy and details of naval life.

STEWART EDWARD WHITE (1873-1946)

A Grand Rapids, Michigan, native, White was educated at the University of Michigan and Columbia Law School. He prospected for gold in South Dakota and used that as background for his novels, including *The Westerners* and *The Claim Jumpers*.

6701 *Folded Hills*

Date of Publication: 1934
Subject(s): American West; Mexican War
Fictional character(s): Andy Burnett, Frontiersman, Rancher; Carmel Burnett, Spouse
Time Period(s): 1840s
Locale(s): California

Summary: The novel concludes the author's trilogy on the adventures of frontiersman Andy Burnett, covering the years leading up to California statehood. Burnett is now married and a hildago on his ranch in Southern California. The novel describes the American occupation during the war with Mexico and the ensuing conflict with the Spanish settlers.

Historical Accuracy: The author's considerable research into the period is evident, and his conclusions are at variance from other accepted interpretations.

6702 *The Long Rifle*

Date of Publication: 1930
Subject(s): American West
Fictional character(s): Andy Burnett, Frontiersman
Historical character(s): Daniel Boone, Frontiersman
Time Period(s): 1820s
Locale(s): Rocky Mountains

Summary: Life in the western wilderness is depicted in this story, the first in the author's second series of novels on western and California history. The scene is the Rocky Mountains in the 1820s and the trials of frontiersman Andrew Burnett.

Historical Accuracy: The novel's depiction of the wilderness and frontier customs is plausible and authentic.

6703 *Ranchero*

Date of Publication: 1933
Subject(s): American West
Fictional character(s): Andy Burnett, Frontiersman
Time Period(s): 1830s (1832)
Locale(s): California

Summary: The novel is the second volume of a trilogy that begins with *The Long Rifle* and concludes with *Folded Hills*. The story continues the adventures of frontiersman Andy Burnett, who crosses the Sierras into California where he makes friends among the Spanish settlers.

Historical Accuracy: The novel is marked by a high degree of reliability in portraying the period's customs and speech.

TERENCE DE VERE WHITE (1912-)

An Irish author and literature professor, White was born in Dublin and educated at Trinity College. A former solicitor, White's works include a biography of Oscar Wilde's parents and the novels *The March Hare* and *The Distance and the Dark.*

6704 *Johnnie Cross*

Date of Publication: 1983
Subject(s): Victorian Period; Literary Life
Fictional character(s): Colin Cathcart, Writer
Historical character(s): John Walter Cross, Spouse (of George Eliot); George Eliot, Writer
Time Period(s): 1880s
Locale(s): London, England

Summary: The novel reconstructs the story of George Eliot's seven-month marriage at age 61 to Johnnie Cross, 20 years her junior. The marriage shocks Victorian England, coming after Eliot's mourning for George Henry Lewes, the married man she had lived with for 24 years. Cross, in his eighties, shares his recollections with a writer.

Historical Accuracy: The novel is a mixture of actual biographical details, psychological speculation, and literary gossip.

T.H. WHITE (1906-1964)

Born in Bombay, White came to England in 1911 and graduated from Cambridge. He worked as a teacher in a prep school in England. White is best known for his tetralogy *The Once and Future King*, which was adapted for stage and screen as *Camelot.*

6705 *The Once and Future King*

Date of Publication: 1958
Subject(s): Myths and Legends; Dark Ages; Arthurian Legends
Fictional character(s): Arthur, Ruler (King of the Britons); Guenevere, Royalty (queen consort of Arthur); Lancelot, Knight
Time Period(s): Indeterminate Past
Locale(s): England

Summary: This omnibus of White's four novels, *The Sword and the Stone, The Witch in the Wood, The Ill-Made Knight,* and *The Candle in the Wind* retells the Arthurian story from Arthur's early days to his final battle and death. White refashions Thomas Malory's material into a tragic statement of considerable power.

Historical Accuracy: An expert medievalist is evident in the details of hawking, hunting, tilting, and archery, even though there are certain anachronisms.

BARBARA WHITEHEAD (1930-)

Born in Sheffield, England, Whitehead was educated at the Sheffield College of Arts and Crafts. She has worked as a post office worker and as an adult education teacher. She intends in her books to show other people how people in past times lived and thought.

6706 *The Caretaker Wife*

Date of Publication: 1978
Subject(s): Regency Romance; Napoleonic Wars
Fictional character(s): Richard Welby, Military Personnel (naval lieutenant); Caroline Hill, Spouse (of Welby)
Time Period(s): 1800s
Locale(s): England

Summary: As the Peace of Amiens ends and the war with Napoleon resumes, Lieutenant Richard Welby is posted to service with Lord Nelson's navy. Before departing, he marries Caroline Hill and leaves her to take care of his children by his first wife and his estate. Caroline must attempt to bury the ghost of her predecessor, Lady Kitty.

Historical Accuracy: The novel depends on an accurate backdrop of actual events of the period.

6707 *Quicksilver Lady*

Date of Publication: 1979
Subject(s): Regency Romance
Fictional character(s): Arabella Hill, Gentlewoman
Time Period(s): 1810s
Locale(s): London, England

Summary: The trials and tribulations of the London season are dramatized in the experiences of young gentlewoman Arabella Hill who, disappointed in love, looks for a cure in the London social whirl. She encounters a social climbing maid, a mysterious gentleman with a secret, and an army officer who cannot be trusted. Arabella must sort out the truth and learn whom she can trust before love is possible.

Historical Accuracy: This is fairly standard Regency fare with some effort to create a meaningful period backdrop.

6708 *Ramillies*

Date of Publication: 1983
Subject(s): Regency Romance
Fictional character(s): Henry Akeham, Teacher, Heir; Laetitia Elmet, Gentlewoman; Hannah Clare, Teacher
Time Period(s): 1820s (1820)
Locale(s): Yorkshire, England

Summary: When the ninth Earl of Ainsty dies, schoolmaster Henry Akeham is the unlikely heir to the title and the Yorkshire estate of Ramillies. But who will become the new earl's wife? Laetitia, Countess of Elmet, and Hannah Clare, the local school mistress, are the two contenders.

Historical Accuracy: This is a pleasant enough romantic story with a serviceable period backdrop.

ARCH WHITEHOUSE
(PSEUD. OF ARTHUR GEORGE WHITEHOUSE, 1895-1979)

Born in Northampton, England, Whitehouse came to the U.S. at the age of nine. In 1914 he joined the British forces and served with the infantry and later with the Royal Flying Corps. He was credited with 16 air victories as an aerial gunner and fighter pilot. Whitehouse worked as an official U.S. war correspondent and a screenwriter. He is the author of several military histories.

6709 *The Casket Crew*

Date of Publication: 1971
Subject(s): World War I; Aviation
Fictional character(s): Grahame Townsend, Military Personnel (lieutenant)
Time Period(s): 1910s (1918)
Locale(s): Cassel, France; London, England

Summary: The novel tells the story of Handley Page Bomber NS C 9711, a twin-engine bomber, during the final years of World War I. The plane's company, known as "the Casket Crew," participate in the effort to cripple Germany through a program of nightly bombing raids on military targets.

Historical Accuracy: The story is fictional but based on actual circumstances.

6710 *Playboy Squadron*

Date of Publication: 1970
Subject(s): World War I; Aviation
Fictional character(s): Ellis Burdon, Military Personnel (lieutenant)
Time Period(s): 1910s (1918)
Locale(s): London, England; France

Summary: This novel of aerial combat during World War I follows a group of American college students who set out to gain glory fighting in the air. When their orders are lost, Lieutenant Ellis Burdon manages to get them attached to the Royal Flying Corps. In France they discover the reality behind the image of the dashing air war.

Historical Accuracy: The story of what could have happened to a group of American Aviation cadets is fiction, but based on fact.

6711 *Squadron Forty-Four*

Date of Publication: 1965
Subject(s): World War I; Aviation
Fictional character(s): Hoyt, Military Personnel (captain); G.K. Patterson, Military Personnel (lieutenant)
Time Period(s): 1910s (1918)
Locale(s): Amiens, France

Summary: Set during the German spring offensive of 1918, the novel depicts life in the Royal Flying Corps during World War I. Lieutenant Patterson is a new recruit from America with visions of glamorous combat and the chivalry of the air. What he finds is little glory and more danger in ground support, escort duty, and low-level bombing and strafing missions. It becomes veteran Captain Hoyt's responsibility to try to keep Patterson alive.

Historical Accuracy: The aviation elements are convincing and authentic.

6712 *Squadron Shilling*

Date of Publication: 1968
Subject(s): World War I; Aviation; Espionage
Fictional character(s): Cynthia Pollard, Spy; Ralph Macintosh, Military Personnel (pilot); Bartley Crispin, Military Personnel, Pilot
Time Period(s): 1910s (1916-1917)
Locale(s): England; France

Summary: Aerial combat and espionage during World War I are featured in this story about two Princeton graduates who find their way into combat in the skies over Europe, one a war hero, the other a traitor. The novel describes the role played by the air corps in espionage work during World War I.

Historical Accuracy: The characters and situation are fictional but based on actual experiences and with an authentic background.

6713 *Wings for the Chariots*

Date of Publication: 1973
Subject(s): World War I; Aviation; Battle of Cambrai
Fictional character(s): Keith Clement, Military Personnel (captain); Chuck Bower, Military Personnel (tank commander)
Time Period(s): 1910s (1917)
Locale(s): Cambrai, France

Summary: The novel recreates the first large-scale use of tanks in combat during the attack on Cambrai in 1917. The story is told from the perspectives of Captain Keith Clement of the Royal Flying Corps, an ex-cavalry officer who sees the new weapon as far more valuable than the airplane, and Lieutenant Chuck Bower, an American tank commander, who wishes he could transfer to the Flying Corps.

Historical Accuracy: The details of the Battle of Cambrai are faithful to the facts.

BRAND WHITLOCK (1869-1934)

An Urbana, Ohio, native, Whitlock grew up in Methodist parsonages in Ohio and was deeply affected by his father's religious teachings and his love of literature. A professional man of letters and political activist, Whitlock wrote biographies, memoirs, and novels, including *The Stranger on the Island*, *The Thirteenth District*, and *Her Infinite Variety*.

6714 *The Strangers on the Island*

Date of Publication: 1933
Subject(s): Mormons
Fictional character(s): Pierre Lenoir, Frontiersman
Time Period(s): 1850s
Locale(s): Lake Michigan, Great Lakes (Beaver Island)

Summary: The story concerns the adventures of French-Canadian Pierre Lenoir, who after a brawl, seeks refuge on Beaver Island in Lake Michigan. There he encounters a group of exiled Mormons and falls in love with one of the young wives of the group's leader.

Historical Accuracy: The novel offers a realistic portrait of the period and the region that is noticeably free of sentimentality.

JANET WHITNEY (1894-)

American writer Whitney was the author of a biography of Abigail Adams and the books *Elizabeth Fry, Quaker Heroine, Jennifer,* and *Judith.*

6715 *Intrigue in Baltimore*

Date of Publication: 1951
Subject(s): Civil War—U.S.; Politics
Fictional character(s): Roger Fitzroy Bathurst, Young Man
Historical character(s): Abraham Lincoln, Political Figure
Time Period(s): 1860s
Locale(s): Illinois; Baltimore, Maryland

Summary: The novel captures events surrounding the presidential election of 1860 as the victory of Abraham Lincoln seems to guarantee the outbreak of the Civil War. The plot involves the fate of the border state of Maryland. Will it stay loyal to the Union or secede?.

Historical Accuracy: The novel captures the atmosphere of the period with skill.

PHYLLIS A. WHITNEY (1903-)

A prolific and popular adult and juvenile writer, Whitney was born in Yokohama, Japan. She attended public schools in Chicago, and, since the publication of her first novel, *A Place for Ann,* in 1941, Whitney has published over 50 books, earning the reputation of "America's queen of romantic suspense." Over 40 million copies of her novels are in print. Titles include *Willow Hill, Woman Without a Past,* and *Ebony Swan.*

6716 *The Quicksilver Pool*

Date of Publication: 1955
Subject(s): Civil War—U.S.
Fictional character(s): Lora Tyler, Spouse; Wade Tyler, Military Personnel (Union soldier)
Time Period(s): 1860s (1862-1863)
Locale(s): Staten Island, New York

Summary: Set during the Civil War on Staten Island, New York, this romantic novel tells the story of Lora Tyler, a southern girl who marries Union soldier Wade Tyler. She must contend with a haughty mother-in-law, the memory of Wade's first wife, a disturbed stepson, and Copperhead intrigue.

Historical Accuracy: The picture of the time and place is believable, though the heroine is a bit overidealized and stock.

6717 *Sea Jade*

Date of Publication: 1964
Subject(s): Sea Story; Clipper Ships
Fictional character(s): Miranda Heath, Orphan; Brock McLean, Sea Captain
Time Period(s): 1870s
Locale(s): New England; At Sea

Summary: This romantic tale is set during the heyday of the New England clipper ships and the lucrative China Trade. The novel concerns the experiences of a young orphan girl, Miranda Heath, who takes refuge with a sea captain and is introduced to the life of a clipper ship captain's wife.

Historical Accuracy: The portrait of the New England shipping industry of the time is believable and forms a plausible backdrop for this romantic tale.

DENTON WHITSON

6718 *The Governor's Daughter*

Date of Publication: 1953
Subject(s): French and Indian War; American Colonies
Fictional character(s): Clytie Delancey, Young Woman; Adam Appleton, Military Personnel (captain)
Historical character(s): George Washington, Military Personnel (army officer); Benjamin Franklin, Printer
Time Period(s): 18th century
Locale(s): New York, American Colonies

Summary: This historical adventure is set during the French and Indian War. Its central characters are Clytie Delancey, the daughter of the governor of New York, and Captain Adam Appleton of the colonial troops. The story blends combat, Indian attacks, and whiskey bootlegging but is primarily a romance.

Historical Accuracy: The novel's adventure and romantic elements are occasionally interrupted for an authentic period detail.

TYLER WHITTLE
(PSEUD. OF MICHAEL TYLER-WHITTLE, 1927-)

English author Whittle graduated from Cambridge University and served in the Royal Marines during World War II. He has devoted his career to writing and painting. The author of a number of adult novels under the pseudonym Mark Oliver, Whittle is also the author of many children's books.

6719 *Albert's Victoria*

Date of Publication: 1972
Subject(s): Victorian Period; Biography, Fictionalized; Royalty—England
Historical character(s): Victoria, Royalty (Queen of England); Albert of Saxe-Coburg-Gotha, Royalty (prince consort of Victoria); William Lamb, Political Figure (prime minister), Nobleman (Viscount Melbourne); Henry John Temple, Political Figure, Nobleman (Viscount Palmerston)

Time Period(s): 19th century (1840-1861)
Locale(s): England

Summary: The second volume of three on the reign of Queen Victoria depicts her married years with Prince Albert. Disliked by the English and married to a queen who is reluctant to share or diminish her power, Albert becomes an indispensible partner to Victoria, and helps her shape and define the period.

Historical Accuracy: The novel is based on fact, and the small liberties taken to bridge gaps in the documentary evidence are within historical probability.

`6720` *Bertie, Albert Edward, Prince of Wales*

Date of Publication: 1974
Subject(s): Victorian Period; Royalty—England; Biography, Fictionalized
Historical character(s): Edward, Prince of Wales, Royalty; Victoria, Ruler (Queen of England); Albert of Saxe-Coburg-Gotha, Royalty (prince consort of Victoria); Alexandra of Denmark, Royalty (consort of Edward VII)
Time Period(s): 19th century; 20th century

Summary: In the first part of a two-volume biographical novel on Edward VII, his years as Prince of Wales are dramatized. The novel chronicles Edward's scandals as well as his troubled relationship with his mother, Queen Victoria, and her ministers.

Historical Accuracy: As in the author's other novels, the characters and events are faithful to the known facts. Some slight liberties have been taken to bridge gaps in the documentary evidence.

`6721` *Edward*

Date of Publication: 1975
Subject(s): Edwardian Period; Royalty—England; Biography, Fictionalized
Historical character(s): Edward VII, Ruler (King of England); Alexandra of Denmark, Royalty (queen consort of Edward VII)
Time Period(s): 1900s (1901-1910)
Locale(s): England

Summary: In the final volume of the author's biographical study of the reigns of Victoria and Edward, the Prince of Wales finally ascends to the throne. Committed to pleasure, Edward is now too old to change his love of opulence and good times. As the uncle to so many European sovereigns, Edward becomes a major figure in the complicated diplomatic manueverings within Europe in the opening decade of the century.

Historical Accuracy: The novel is solidly backed-up by believable documentary evidence.

`6722` *Richard III: The Last Plantagenet*

Date of Publication: 1970
Subject(s): War of the Roses; Royalty—England
Historical character(s): Richard III, Ruler (King of England); Edward IV, Ruler (King of England); George, Duke of Clar-

ence, Nobleman (brother of Edward and Richard); Anne Neville, Royalty (queen consort of Richard III)
Time Period(s): 15th century (1459-1485)
Locale(s): England

Summary: The career of Richard III is traced from the time he is taken captive during the War of the Roses at age seven to his death in battle 25 years later. The documentary novel attempts to show the real Richard, somewhere between the monster of the Tudor historians and the noble hero of later apologists. Richard's character emerges in his relationships with his two brothers and his wife, Anne Neville.

Historical Accuracy: Although a fictional treatment, the author has been faithful to the known facts. Nothing has been distorted or omitted.

`6723` *The Widow of Windsor*

Date of Publication: 1973
Subject(s): Victorian Period; Royalty—England; Biography, Fictionalized
Historical character(s): Victoria, Ruler (Queen of England); Beatrice, Royalty (princess); Randall Davidson, Religious (Dean of Windsor); John Brown, Servant; William Gladstone, Political Figure (prime minister); Benjamin Disraeli, Political Figure (prime minister); Jane Churchill, Noblewoman; Edward, Prince of Wales, Royalty
Time Period(s): 19th century; 20th century
Locale(s): England

Summary: In the concluding volume of the author's trilogy on the life of Queen Victoria, her years alone after the death of Prince Albert are shown. Victoria remains in mourning for the rest of her life and only gradually returns to public life. The private and public sides of this remarkable monarch are vividly presented.

Historical Accuracy: The novel is faithful to the known facts.

`6724` *The Young Victoria*

Date of Publication: 1971
Subject(s): Royalty—England; Biography, Fictionalized; Victorian Period
Historical character(s): George IV, Ruler (King of England); William IV, Ruler (King of England); Victoria, Royalty (princess), Ruler (Queen of England); Victoria, Duchess of Kent, Royalty (mother of Queen Victoria); Sir John Conroy, Gentleman; William Lamb, Political Figure (prime minister), Nobleman (Viscount Melbourne); Arthur Wellesley, Military Personnel (army commander), Political Figure; Albert of Saxe-Coburg-Gotha, Royalty (prince consort of Victoria)
Time Period(s): 19th century (1820s-1840s)
Locale(s): England

Summary: In the first of a trilogy on the life of Queen Victoria, the novel depicts her early years as a young princess who was not expected to succeed to the throne. Cloistered by her mother, the Duchess of Kent, Victoria comes to the throne at age 18 and astounds everyone by her sophistication and skills. But by the end of her first year, she has become so unpopular that the monarchy is imperiled. The novel offers both the public and private side of Victoria's remarkable reign.

Historical Accuracy: The author's grasp of the period is impressive. Victoria emerges as a believable and convincing character.

JACK WHYTE

This award-winning Canadian author was born in Scotland.

6725 *The Singing Sword*

Date of Publication: 1996

Subject(s): Dark Ages; Myths and Legends; Arthurian Legends

Fictional character(s): Caius Publius Varrus, Warrior; Luceiia, Spouse (of Varrus)

Time Period(s): 5th century

Locale(s): England

Summary: This is the second volume of the Camulod Chronicles, tracing the origins of the Arthurian legend in the collapse of Roman Britain. The novel continues the story of Arthur's great-grandfather, Publius Varrus, and his British-born and Roman-raised wife, Luceiia, who struggle to hold onto a stronghold which will one day be known as Camelot.

Historical Accuracy: The historical background for the fictional story is authentic, and the major political events described are accurate.

6726 *The Skystone: The Forging of Arthur's Britain*

Date of Publication: 1996

Subject(s): Roman Empire; Dark Ages; Arthurian Legends

Fictional character(s): Caius Britannicus, Military Personnel (soldier); Caius Publius Varrus, Military Personnel (soldier); Luceiia, Noblewoman

Time Period(s): 4th century; 5th century (367-448)

Locale(s): England

Summary: The novel traces the origins of King Arthur in a story that begins with Arthur's grandfather, Roman soldier Caius Publius Varrus. When the declining Roman Empire abandons Britain, Varrus decides to remain and preserve civilization on the island. With the Celtic noblewoman Luceiia, he founds a dynasty and forges the sword that will become Excalibur.

Historical Accuracy: The events around which this fictional story is based are real.

PHILIPPA WIAT

(PSEUD. OF PHILIPPA FERBRIDGE, 1933-)

An English novelist, Wiat was born in London and has worked as a writer since 1972. She is the author of a number of historical novels, including *Queen-Gold*, *Fair Rosamond*, and *The King's Vengeance*.

6727 *The Heir of Allington*

Date of Publication: 1973

Subject(s): Tudor Period; Royalty—England

Historical character(s): Sir Thomas Wyatt, Writer (poet), Courtier; Henry VIII, Ruler (King of England); Anne Boleyn, Royalty (queen consort of Henry VIII); Jane Seymour, Gentlewoman, Royalty (queen consort of Henry VIII); Thomas Cranmer, Religious (archbishop)

Time Period(s): 16th century

Locale(s): England

Summary: The novel dramatizes the rumored relationship between Sir Thomas Wyatt, courtier, poet, and diplomat, and Anne Boleyn. The story reconstructs the court world of Tudor England and the dangerously temperamental Henry VIII.

Historical Accuracy: It is by no means certain that Wyatt was in fact Anne Boleyn's lover as the story suggests.

ANNA WIBBERLEY

6728 *Time and Chance*

Date of Publication: 1973

Subject(s): Independence—Ireland; Civil War—Ireland

Fictional character(s): Caithlin Carroll, Young Woman; Davy Carroll, Rebel (IRA member)

Time Period(s): 1920s

Locale(s): Cork, Ireland

Summary: The events of the Troubles in Ireland in the years preceding the creation of the Irish Republic are reflected from the point of view of the Carroll family in Cork. The family struggles to survive amidst raids from the Black and Tans, retaliation from the IRA, and the Irish Civil War.

Historical Accuracy: The novel is convincing in interweaving an authentic atmosphere with this fictional story.

LEONARD WIBBERLEY (1915-1983)

Born in Dublin, Wibberley came to the U.S. in 1943. He attended schools in both England and Ireland. A journalist and an author, Wibberley worked as well as a street violinist, a security guard, and ship builder. He wrote more than 100 books, including stories for children, historical novels, satires, plays, and mysteries. Wibberley is best known for his Mouse trilogy, political satires set in the fictional Duchy of Grand Fenwick that included *The Mouse That Roared*, *The Mouse on the Moon*, and *The Mouse That Saved the West*. The first novel was made into a film starring Peter Sellers in 1958.

6729 *The Centurion*

Date of Publication: 1966

Subject(s): Roman Empire; Biblical Story

Fictional character(s): Longinus, Military Personnel (centurion)

Historical character(s): Jesus Christ, Biblical Figure; Pontius Pilate, Government Official; Peter, Biblical Figure; James, Biblical Figure; Mary, Biblical Figure; John the Baptist, Biblical Figure

Time Period(s): 1st century

Locale(s): Israel

Summary: The Roman centurion mentioned in the Gospels who officiated at the crucifixion of Jesus is the focus for this novel. Longinus, a veteran of many military campaigns, finds himself part of the occupying Roman army in Judea, and he provides an interesting point of view on Jesus' ministry and final days.

Historical Accuracy: The atmosphere of the times and customs are convincingly detailed in this blend of fancy and the New Testament events.

`6730` *The Testament of Theophilus*

Date of Publication: 1973
Subject(s): Roman Empire; Christianity
Fictional character(s): Theophilus, Slave, Businessman
Historical character(s): Jesus Christ, Biblical Figure; Tiberius, Ruler (Roman emperor); Caligula, Ruler (Roman emperor); Pontius Pilate, Government Official
Time Period(s): 1st century
Locale(s): Rome, Roman Empire; Jerusalem, Israel

Summary: The story of Jesus and the early days of the Christian church is seen through the perspective of Theophilus, a former slave turned successful businessman in Imperial Rome, whose contact with Jesus proves to be a turning point in his life. The novel offers a dramatic look at Rome under Tiberius and Caligula.

Historical Accuracy: The novel's story is imagined but the period is evoked with some conviction and credibility.

LEE WICHELNS

`6731` *The Shadow of the Earth*

Date of Publication: 1987
Subject(s): Biography, Fictionalized; Elizabethan Period; Literary Life
Historical character(s): Christopher Marlowe, Writer; Thomas Kyd, Writer; Sir Walter Raleigh, Courtier; Robert Greene, Writer; Sir Francis Walsingham, Political Figure
Time Period(s): 16th century
Locale(s): England

Summary: This biographical account of the life and times of English poet and playwright Christopher Marlowe traces his career from university days at Cambridge to his success in London and his controversial death in a tavern quarrel.

Historical Accuracy: The novel stays close to the facts of Marlowe's life with some imaginative embellishments.

LORI WICK

`6732` *The Knight and the Dove*

Date of Publication: 1995
Subject(s): Tudor Period
Fictional character(s): Lord Bracken of Hawkings Crest, Nobleman (duke); Lady Megan, Noblewoman; Lady Marigold, Noblewoman
Historical character(s): Henry VIII, Ruler (King of England)
Time Period(s): 16th century (1531-1542)
Locale(s): England

Summary: King Henry VIII orders Lord Vincent to marry one of his daughters to Lord Bracken. The choice falls on his younger daughter, Megan, when his older daughter, Marigold, spurns the offer. However, when Bracken is made a duke, Lady Marigold's jealousy drives her to scheme against her sister.

Historical Accuracy: There are a number of convincing period elements in this fanciful tale of the Tudor period.

TOM WICKER (1926-)

A respected *New York Times* columnist and writer, Wicker was born in Hamlet, North Carolina, and was educated at the University of North Carolina. During his long career as a journalist, he has published several works of fiction and nonfiction, including the award-winning *A Time to Die*, a chronicle of his experience as a mediator and observer during the 1971 Attica prison uprising. His novels include the bestselling *Facing the Lions* and *So Fair, So Evil*, written under the pseudonym Paul Connolly.

`6733` *Unto This Hour*

Date of Publication: 1984
Subject(s): Civil War—U.S.; Battle of Second Bull Run/Manassas
Fictional character(s): Hugh Williams, Military Personnel (Union soldier); Hoke Arnall, Military Personnel (Confederate general); Micah Duryea, Military Personnel (Union captain)
Historical character(s): Robert E. Lee, Military Personnel (Confederate commander); James Longstreet, Military Personnel (Confederate general); John Pope, Military Personnel (Union general); Joseph Hooker, Military Personnel (Union general); Abraham Lincoln, Political Figure; Thomas Jonathan Jackson, Military Personnel (Confederate general)
Time Period(s): 1860s (1862)
Locale(s): Virginia

Summary: The events of the 1862 Civil War battle of Second Bull Run or Manassas are recounted through the perspective of both the strategists and the common soldiers. Lee, faced by a larger Union force, does the unthinkable. He splits his force and sends General Jackson on a secret march around Union General Pope's right flank producing a stunning Confederate victory.

Historical Accuracy: The novel blends fictional characters and real ones, but the events described are accurate. Every remark by a historical figure has been authenticated. The author's postscript lists his sources.

MARGARET WIDDEMER (1897-)

An American novelist and poet, Widdemer was born in Pennsylvania and graduated from the Drexel Institute. The author of novels, short stories, and poetry, Widdemer began writing as a child and continued to write until 1968 when she published her last book at the age of 84. Although a bestselling novelist, Widdemer is best remembered for her poetry.

6734 *Buckskin Baronet*

Date of Publication: 1960
Subject(s): American Colonies; Indians
Fictional character(s): Julian Tynedale, Nobleman (baronet); Brigid Scott, Young Woman
Historical character(s): Benjamin Franklin, Political Figure; Joseph Brant, Indian (Mohawk), Chieftain; Samuel Adams, Revolutionary
Time Period(s): 1770s (1773)
Locale(s): Albany, New York, American Colonies; England; Ohio

Summary: Julian Tynedale, a young English baronet, undertakes a mission to America for the British prime minister on the eve of the American Revolution. There he encounters political intrigues and relations with the Indians that help explain the origin of the Revolution.

Historical Accuracy: The novel's essential story is fictional and emphasizes romantic adventure, yet there is a strong effort to root the background in solid historical fact.

6735 *The Golden Wildcat*

Date of Publication: 1954
Subject(s): French and Indian War; American Colonies; Indians
Historical character(s): Sir William Johnson, Government Official (colonial official); Mary Johnson, Young Woman; Joseph de St. Castine, Indian (half breed), Warrior
Time Period(s): 1750s
Locale(s): Oswego, New York, American Colonies

Summary: Set during the first two years of the French and Indian War, the novel offers an answer to why Oswego, the all-important outpost of the English and Iroquois, was lost to the French. Mary, the daughter of Sir William Johnson, undertakes the perilous journey to Oswego to insure the loyalty of the Iroquois and Mohawks. Along the way she is captured by a band of French led by the half-breed Joseph de St. Castine.

Historical Accuracy: The novel's times, dates, and events are factual. Some of the evidence suggested to explain the loss of Oswego is circumstantial and based on conjecture.

6736 *Lady of the Mohawks*

Date of Publication: 1951
Subject(s): American Colonies; Indians
Historical character(s): Sir William Johnson, Government Official (English Indian commissioner); Molly Brant, Indian (Mohawk)
Time Period(s): 1740s
Locale(s): Mohawk Valley, New York, American Colonies

Summary: Set in colonial New York State in the years preceding the French and Indian War, the novel describes the efforts to maintain the Covenant Chain that kept the Iroquois allied with the English. At the center of the story is the Indian princess Deyonwadonti, also known as Molly Brant. A

daughter of a Mohawk sachem, she was educated at an English school and was the niece of Sir William Johnson's wife.

Historical Accuracy: The action is imagined but the atmosphere is believable and does depend on actual circumstances and figures.

6737 *Red Cloak Flying*

Date of Publication: 1950
Subject(s): American Colonies; Jacobite Rebellion
Fictional character(s): Rosamund Cantillon, Young Woman; Geoffrey Tynedale, Military Personnel (captain); Ian Craigvalloch, Fugitive
Historical character(s): Sir William Johnson, Government Official
Time Period(s): 1740s (1745-1747)
Locale(s): New York, American Colonies

Summary: This historical romance tells the story of heroine Rosamund Cantillon who is loved by two men, Geoffrey Tynedale and his former prisoner, Jacobite Ian Craigvalloch.

Historical Accuracy: The characters are more idealized than believable, and the historical elements are rather shadowy.

JAN WIDGERY (1920-)

Born in Philadelphia, Widgery graduated from Chatham College and received her master's degree from Radcliffe. She has taught English, speech, and drama in high school and college, serving as chair of the department of English at the Winchester-Thurston School in Pittsburgh.

6738 *The Adversary*

Date of Publication: 1966
Subject(s): Dark Ages; Vikings
Fictional character(s): Eadwin, Nobleman (earl); Wulfric, Blacksmith
Time Period(s): 9th century (841)
Locale(s): East Anglia, England

Summary: Set during the period when the Danish Northmen were beginning their devastating raids on the English coast, the novel tells the story of two brothers, an idealistic English earl and his more practical blacksmith brother. When the Danes attack, the earl must put himself into the hands of the Viking raiders in an attempt to save his village.

Historical Accuracy: The author has grounded the story in the known and has tried never to assume anything which is inconsistent with the available historical and archaeological facts.

6739 *Trumpet at the Gate*

Date of Publication: 1970
Subject(s): War of the Roses; Royalty—England
Fictional character(s): Michael Frye, Young Man; Elizabeth Hammond, Gentlewoman
Historical character(s): Richard II, Ruler (King of England); Henry Bolingbroke, Royalty
Time Period(s): 14th century (1399)
Locale(s): England

Summary: As Henry Bolingbroke contends for the throne with Richard II and initiates the War of the Roses, Michael Frye searches for vengeance against a powerful nobleman. He discovers a secret that sweeps him up into the center of the age's violent political current.

Historical Accuracy: The novel is effective in capturing the chaos and the intrigue of the period.

WILLIAM WIEGAND (1928-)

Born in Detroit, Wiegand graduated from the University of Michigan and Stanford University. He has worked as a professor of English at San Francisco State College. He won the Mary Roberts Rhinehart Award for *At Last, Mr. Tolliver* and the Joseph Henry Jackson Award in 1958 for *The Treatment*.

6740 The Chester A. Arthur Conspiracy
Date of Publication: 1983
Subject(s): Politics; Reconstruction Period; Civil War—U.S.
Historical character(s): Ulysses S. Grant, Military Personnel (general), Political Figure; James A. Garfield, Political Figure; John Wilkes Booth, Murderer (assassin); Chester Alan Arthur, Political Figure; Edwin Booth, Actor
Time Period(s): 1860s
Locale(s): New York, New York; Washington, District of Columbia

Summary: The novel's premise is that John Wilkes Booth, the assassin of Abraham Lincoln, did not perish in the barn where he was hiding. Instead he makes his way to New York and becomes involved with the political career of Chester A. Arthur, a New York Custom House official who rises to occupy the White House. Plots and schemes abound in this historically rich exploration of conspiracy, assassination, and politics.

Historical Accuracy: The plot is scrupulously based on historical possibilities and facts.

WILLARD WIENER

6741 Morning in America
Date of Publication: 1942
Subject(s): American Revolution; Battle of Monmouth
Fictional character(s): Israel Eusopus, Military Personnel (soldier)
Historical character(s): Nathanael Greene, Military Personnel (general); Marie Joseph Paul de Lafayette, Military Personnel (French general), Nobleman (Marquis de Lafayette); Charles Lee, Military Personnel (general); Anthony Wayne, Military Personnel (general); George Washington, Military Personnel (army commander)
Time Period(s): 1770s; 1780s
Locale(s): New Jersey; New York

Summary: This story of the American Revolution takes as its subject American general Charles Lee who is presented as an early American fascist. The story of Lee's betrayal of the American cause and his undermining of General Washing-ton's command, particularly at the Battle of Monmouth, is told from the perspective of a young American soldier who serves as Lee's aide.

Historical Accuracy: The author admits to tampering with some of the facts in his story but the essential truth remains.

SUSAN WIGGS
Wiggs attended school in Brussels and Paris. She has a master's degree from Harvard.

6742 Circle in the Water
Date of Publication: 1994
Subject(s): Tudor Period; Romance
Fictional character(s): Juliana Romanov, Royalty (princess), Gypsy; Stephen de Lacey, Nobleman (baron)
Historical character(s): Henry VIII, Ruler (King of England)
Time Period(s): 16th century (1530s)
Locale(s): England

Summary: Punishment proves to be a surprising reward when Henry VIII orders Baron Stephen de Lacey to marry a gypsy girl who tries to steal his horse. She turns out to be a Russian princess, and the secret of her past could destroy them both.

Historical Accuracy: The story's premise strains credibility, but the novel does offer some convincing Tudor elements.

6743 Jewel of the Sea
Date of Publication: 1993
Subject(s): Romance; Spanish Colonies
Fictional character(s): Will, Musician; Paloma, Slave; Armando, Adventurer
Time Period(s): 16th century
Locale(s): South America; At Sea; England

Summary: In this adventure romance, fate joins three renegades together—Paloma, a slave; Armando, an adventurer; and Will, a musician. They find new lives in the Spanish colonies.

Historical Accuracy: The novel is a panoramic and effective treatment of early life in the Americas, despite the primary emphasis on romance and adventure.

6744 Kingdom of Gold
Date of Publication: 1994
Subject(s): Elizabethan Period; Romance; Sea Story
Fictional character(s): Annie Blythe, Young Woman; Evan Carew, Sea Captain
Historical character(s): Elizabeth I, Ruler (Queen of England); Sir Francis Drake, Sea Captain
Time Period(s): 16th century (1568-1580)
Locale(s): England; Caribbean

Summary: Intrigue and conspiracy surround Annie Blythe, the daughter of an Englishman and a Spanish, noblewoman when she joins in the war against the Spanish treasure ships directed by Elizabeth I.

Historical Accuracy: More than most romance novels, the story is filled with period elements that create a believable historical context.

6745 *The Lily and the Leopard*

Date of Publication: 1991
Subject(s): Middle Ages; Romance; Battle of Agincourt
Fictional character(s): Lilianna, Noblewoman, Heiress; Enguarrand Fitzmarc, Knight
Historical character(s): Henry V, Ruler (King of England)
Time Period(s): 15th century (1414-1415)
Locale(s): England; France

Summary: Fleeing from an arranged marriage, Lilianna of France runs from her castle in Normandy straight into the arms of the English knight to whom she is bethrothed. Their love story is set against the action of Henry V's war with France and his triumphant victory at Agincourt.

Historical Accuracy: The historical events depicted are accurate.

6746 *The Raven and the Rose*

Date of Publication: 1992
Subject(s): Napoleonic Era; Romance
Fictional character(s): Lorelei Du Clerc, Young Woman; Daniel Severin, Mercenary
Historical character(s): Napoleon Bonaparte, Ruler (Emperor of France); Josephine, Royalty (consort of Napoleon)
Time Period(s): 1800s (1800)
Locale(s): Paris, France; Switzerland

Summary: Mercenary Daniel Severin is sent by the Empress Josephine on a mission into Switzerland. He is caught in an avalanche in the Alps and is nursed by Lorelei Du Clerc, a young woman raised by the monks of St. Bernard. They fall in love, but her past threatens the very foundations of Napoleon's empire.

Historical Accuracy: The novel depends on a fully realized historical context, including portraits of Napoleon and Josephine.

FREDERICK WIGHT (1902-1986)

An art critic, museum curator, educator, painter, and author, Wight was born in New York City. As a professor of art and director of the galleries of UCLA, Wight played a major role in building the university's art collection into one of the most prestigious in academia. In 1972, the UCLA galleries were named after Wight. His writings include the novel *Kindling* and various articles and books on art, including *Van Gogh*, *Goya*, and *The Potent Image: Art in the Western World From Cave Paintings to the 1970s*.

6747 *Verge of Glory*

Date of Publication: 1956
Subject(s): Biography, Fictionalized; Artistic Life; World War I
Historical character(s): Amedeo Modigliani, Artist
Time Period(s): 1910s
Locale(s): Paris, France

Summary: This fictional account of the life of Modigliani is set during World War I and depicts the artist's struggle for recognition and the excesses of drugs and alcohol that eventually lead to his premature death from tuberculosis.

Historical Accuracy: The story follows the events of Modigliani's life closely.

STELLA WILCHEK

Born in Vienna, Wilchek was educated there until the outbreak of World War II. A refugee from Hitler, Wilchek fled to South America, where she remained for eight years before emigrating to America. Her other works include *Ararat* and *Tale of a Hero*.

6748 *Judith*

Date of Publication: 1969
Subject(s): Biblical Story; Babylonian Empire
Fictional character(s): Judith, Biblical Figure, Widow(er); Holofernes, Biblical Figure, Military Personnel (general)
Historical character(s): Nebuchadnezzar II, Ruler (Babylonian king)
Time Period(s): 6th century B.C.
Locale(s): Bethel, Palestine

Summary: The novel recounts the Biblical story of Judith, a Jewish widow of great beauty who attempts to save her people when besieged by the Babylonian army under Nebuchadnezzar. She enters the enemy camp, gains the favor of Holofernes, and beheads him while he is drunk. The novel offers an elaboration of the Biblical story enhanced with historical details.

Historical Accuracy: The novel attempts to establish a factual and historical basis for this Biblical folk tale. The direct connections with the Babylonians and the reign of Nebuchadnezzar are speculative and by no means certain.

JENNIFER WILDE
(PSEUD. OF TOM E. HUFF, 1938-)

Writing under a variety of pseudonyms, including Edwina Marlow, Beatrice Parker, Katherine St. Clair, and Jennifer Wilde, American author Huff has made his career penning gothic novels for women. A former high school teacher, Huff began turning out novels when he was a high school student, but it was many years before he found his market with *Danger at Dahlkari*. Other novels include the bestselling *Dare to Love* and *Marabelle*.

6749 *Love's Tender Fury*

Date of Publication: 1976
Subject(s): Romance; American Colonies
Fictional character(s): Marietta Danver, Servant (indentured); Derek Hawke, Landowner
Time Period(s): 1770s
Locale(s): London, England; Carolinas, American Colonies; Natchez Trace, United States

Summary: In this historical romance set in the American colonies, Marietta Danver is raped by her aristocratic employer, falsely accused of theft, and shipped off as an indentured servant to America. There she is sold to a plantation owner, Derek Hawke, with whom she falls in love while being pursued by two men.

Historical Accuracy: The romance predominates over the history in this emotional story.

ROBERT WILDER (1901-1974)

An American novelist, journalist, and playwright, Wilder was born in Virginia. He worked as a reporter, columnist, and correspondent in Mexico, where he lived for a number of years. His novel *Written in the Wind* was made into a film in 1956.

`6750` *Bright Feather*

Date of Publication: 1948
Subject(s): Indians; Seminole Wars
Fictional character(s): Clay Hammond, Heir
Historical character(s): Osceola, Indian (Seminole), Chieftain
Time Period(s): 1830s; 1840s (1835-1842)
Locale(s): Florida

Summary: The Indian removal policy drives the Seminoles out of their land in northern Florida. Clay Hammond, the heir to a great plantation, is the childhood friend of the Seminole Osceola. Clay finds himself drawn into the Indians' struggles. In the end, his plantation is in ruins and Osceola is in prison.

Historical Accuracy: The novel offers an authentic reconstruction of the forces that created the tragedy, including wealthy landowners, land speculators, settlers, the Indian agency, and the U.S. Army.

`6751` *Wind From the Carolinas*

Date of Publication: 1964
Subject(s): Family Saga; American Revolution; Civil War—U.S.
Fictional character(s): Ronald Cameron, Plantation Owner; Caroline Cameron, Young Woman; Bruce Raleigh, Gentleman
Time Period(s): Multiple Time Periods
Locale(s): Bahamas

Summary: The story depicts the settlement of the Bahamas by Tory loyalists from Georgia, the Carolinas, and Virginia after the American Revolution. Ronald Cameron leaves the American colonies to re-create the plantation life he left behind. The novel traces the story of his family over several generations and almost 140 years.

Historical Accuracy: The novel is fictional, and some liberties have been taken, though the basic facts of the settlement and development of the Bahamas are authentic.

THORNTON WILDER (1897-1975)

An American novelist and playwright, Wilder achieved fame with *The Bridge of San Luis Rey*, which won the Pulitzer Prize in 1927. He is probably best known for his plays *Our Town*, *The Matchmaker*, and *The Skin of Our*

Teeth. He was awarded the first National Medal for Literature in 1965.

`6752` *The Bridge of San Luis Rey*

Date of Publication: 1927
Subject(s): Spanish Colonies; Disasters
Fictional character(s): Marquesa de Montemayor, Noblewoman; La Perichole, Actress; Pio, Actor
Time Period(s): 1710s (1714)
Locale(s): Peru

Summary: In 1714 the bridge of San Luis Rey, the most famous bridge in Peru, collapsed killing five travellers. Their stories, full of interesting sidelights of the days of Peru as a Spanish colony, form the novel's scheme that poses fascinating questions about each individual's influence on others and the true meaning of a disaster.

Historical Accuracy: Wilder's character sketches are memorable as is his ability to dramatize the period and its customs.

`6753` *The Ides of March*

Date of Publication: 1948
Subject(s): Roman Empire; Politics; Assassination
Historical character(s): Julius Caesar, Military Personnel, Political Figure; Marcus Junius Brutus, Nobleman; Gaius Valerius Catullus, Writer (poet); Cleopatra, Ruler (Queen of Egypt); Marc Antony, Military Personnel; Marcus Tullius Cicero, Political Figure, Philosopher
Time Period(s): 1st century B.C. (45 B.C.)
Locale(s): Rome, Roman Empire

Summary: Told in the form of letters exchanged by leading figures of Roman society in 45 B.C., the last year of Julius Caesar's life, Wilder's novel paints a complex picture of Roman life and politics. At the center is Caesar himself, the supreme egotist. The conspiracy that is determined to bring him down builds to the novel's dramatic climax.

Historical Accuracy: Wilder does take some liberties with the chronology here, giving life and voice to historical figures who were already dead by 45 B.C.

`6754` *Woman of Andros*

Date of Publication: 1930
Subject(s): Romance
Fictional character(s): Simo, Trader; Chrysis, Teacher, Philosopher; Pamphilius, Student
Time Period(s): 1st century B.C.
Locale(s): Brynos, Greece

Summary: Wilder presents a philosophical fable about the emptiness of the classical world on the brink of profound changes that will be ushered in by the birth of Christ. Two outsiders on a small Greek island force a reassessment of assumptions and philosophies and a redefinition of love and happiness.

Historical Accuracy: Wilder's tale is based on Terence's Latin comedy. He uses his classical setting to explore deeper philosophical issues rather than historical ones.

RICHARD WILEY (1944-)

Born in California, Wiley graduated from the University of Puget Sound, Sofia University in Tokyo, and the University of Iowa's Writers' Workshop. His first novel, *Soldiers in Hiding* won the Pen/Faulkner Award for the best novel of 1986. He is a professor of English at the University of Nevada, Las Vegas.

6755 *Fools' Gold*

Date of Publication: 1988
Subject(s): Gold Rush—Klondike
Fictional character(s): Finn Wallace, Prospector; Kaneda, Prospector; John Hummel, Prospector
Time Period(s): 1890s (1894)
Locale(s): Alaska

Summary: A varied cast of characters is drawn to the Alaskan gold fields by the dreams that gold might bring. They include Finn Wallace, an Irishman with an ambition to build a town, and Kaneda, a Japanese prospector who speaks no English. The action covers a few months when various discoveries are made.

Historical Accuracy: The novel swerves toward the offbeat and comic with a setting and period that serve symbolic functions as much as historical ones.

WILLIAM VAUGHAN WILKINS
(1890-1959)

Born in London, Wilkins was educated at the Merchant Taylors' School. A writer for several newspapers, he is the author of *Seven Tempest, Crown Without Sceptre, Being Met Together, Lady of Paris,* and *A King Relucant.*

6756 *Being Met Together*

Date of Publication: 1944
Subject(s): Napoleonic Era
Fictional character(s): Anthony Purvis, Adventurer
Historical character(s): Robert Fulton, Engineer, Inventor; Napoleon Bonaparte, Ruler (Emperor of France)
Time Period(s): 18th century; 19th century
Locale(s): Virginia; Europe

Summary: This enormous historical panorama traces the exploits of Anthony Purvis, who is goaded by his British-hating grandmother in Virginia to come to the aid of Napoleon. His adventures take him to Europe and climax with an unsuccessful attempt to rescue Napoleon from St. Helena by submarine.

Historical Accuracy: Although the climactic incident is fictional, it is based on a possibility that the British were afraid could have happened. The novel's grasp of the period is impressive.

6757 *Consort for Victoria*

Date of Publication: 1959
Subject(s): Victorian Period; Royalty—England
Fictional character(s): Fancy Eves, Gentlewoman; Major Richard Houldway, Gentleman

Historical character(s): Victoria, Ruler (Queen of England); Albert of Saxe-Coburg-Gotha, Royalty (prince consort of Victoria)
Time Period(s): 1840s
Locale(s): England

Summary: This tale of conspiracy and blackmail during the early years of the reign of Queen Victoria involves an attempt to suggest that Prince Albert is an illegitimate member of the House of Saxe-Coburg and thus discredit Victoria. The story recounts the conspiracy and how it was foiled.

Historical Accuracy: Although the story itself is invented, the period elements are remarkably authentic.

6758 *Crown Without Sceptre*

Date of Publication: 1952
Subject(s): Jacobite Rebellion
Historical character(s): Vittorio Alfieri, Writer; Charles Edward Stuart, Royalty
Time Period(s): 1770s
Locale(s): Italy; England

Summary: The story dramatizes the declining fortunes of Charles Stuart, the young Pretender. During the 1770s the best years of the prince are behind him. Instead of thrones to conquer, the emphasis is on a succession of romantic misadventures involving the Earl of Deverly; his niece, Charles Stuart's third wife; and her lover, Count Vittorio Alfieri.

Historical Accuracy: The novel blends facts and fiction, and, though fanciful, it does offer some authentic period elements.

6759 *A King Reluctant*

Date of Publication: 1953
Subject(s): French Revolution; Royalty—France; Alternate History
Fictional character(s): Virginia Traill, Guardian; Richard Saguenary, Nobleman (Duc de Brignoles)
Historical character(s): Louis XVII, Royalty (heir to the throne of France)
Time Period(s): 1790s
Locale(s): Wales

Summary: This historical fantasy imagines the fate of the "lost dauphin," Louis XVII. In this version, the heir to the French throne arrives in Wales by balloon where he is raised by a young American girl. An historically authentic French raid on the coast of Wales is connected with the fate of the dauphin and the decision of whether or not he is to rule.

Historical Accuracy: This is a fanciful tale but one that provides plausible if romanticized characters and situations, anchored in an authentic depiction of the period.

6760 *Lady of Paris*

Date of Publication: 1957
Subject(s): French Revolution; Reign of Terror
Historical character(s): Jeanne Marie Therese de Cabarrus, Noblewoman; Jean Lambert Tallien, Revolutionary; Paul Barras, Revolutionary
Time Period(s): 1780s; 1790s
Locale(s): France

Summary: During the French Revolution Therese Cabarrus is rescued from prison by Revolutionary leader Tallien whom she marries. She is involved in the downfall of Robespierre and becomes the consort of the leader of the Directory, Paul Barras. She finally reaches the pinnacle of her power as the Princess de Chimay.

Historical Accuracy: Historical events are at times casually treated, but the period elements and atmosphere are masterfully rendered.

`6761` *Seven Tempest*

Date of Publication: 1942
Subject(s): Victorian Period
Fictional character(s): Seven Tempest, Heir; Anne Louise of Limburg, Noblewoman (duchess)
Historical character(s): Leopold I, Ruler (King of Belgium); Albert of Saxe-Coburg-Gotha, Royalty (prince)
Time Period(s): 19th century
Locale(s): England

Summary: Seven Tempest, the result of his father's experiment to find a worthy heir, by chance encounters Anne Louise, a niece of King Leopold of Belgium. She is fleeing an unwanted arranged marriage. The ingenious plot shows how Tempest aids Anne Louise and, with Prince Albert's assistance, bests King Leopold.

Historical Accuracy: This fanciful adventure plot is placed securely in an historical background that is convincing in its details and its use of actual figures who behave as history suggests they should.

FRANK WILKINSON

A graduate of Princeton University, Wilkinson has worked as an editor in a publishing company.

`6762` *Bygones*

Date of Publication: 1981
Subject(s): Family Saga; World War I
Fictional character(s): Gwyneth Evans, Young Woman; Benjamin Biddle Whisten, Gentleman, Heir
Time Period(s): 19th century; 20th century (1880s-1940s)
Locale(s): Philadelphia, Pennsylvania; New York, New York; Paris, France

Summary: In this family saga that stretches from the 1880s to World War II, the catalyst for the drama is the illicit love between aristocratic Benjamin Biddle Whisten and Gwyneth Evans, a farmer's daughter. The tangled relationships that result are played out against a historical backdrop of *Belle Epoque* Paris, the Western Front during World War I, the Great Depression, and the rise of the Nazis.

Historical Accuracy: The novel's period elements create a believable background.

ALAN WILLIAMS (1935-)

Son of the actor-playwright Emlyn Williams, Alan Williams has worked as a journalist in Vietnam, Israel, Ireland, and Beirut, where he encountered the spy Kim Philby the day before he defected to Moscow. His novels include *Long Run South*, *The Tale of the Lazy Dog*, and *The Beria Papers*.

`6763` *Gentleman Traitor*

Date of Publication: 1974
Subject(s): Espionage
Fictional character(s): Barry Cayle, Journalist
Historical character(s): Harold "Kim" Philby, Spy
Time Period(s): 1970s
Locale(s): Russia; Europe

Summary: The novel is constructed around an intriguing speculation: What if Kim Philby, the famous British spy for the Soviet Union, returned to the life of an active intelligence agent? Journalist Barry Cayle tracks down Philby in Russia. The implication of the encounter takes Cayle around Russia and Europe to Rhodesia, where conspiracy and terrorism provide the novel's climax.

Historical Accuracy: The novel offers a believable set of plausible scenarios, though they are all fanciful.

BEN AMES WILLIAMS (1889-1953)

Williams has written poetry and novels and is a professor of English at the University of Denver.

`6764` *Come Spring*

Date of Publication: 1940
Subject(s): American Colonies; American Revolution
Fictional character(s): Philip Robbins, Settler; Joel Adams, Settler
Time Period(s): 1770s; 1780s (1770-1784)
Locale(s): Maine

Summary: The novel describes the founding of a town in Maine during the American Revolution. Hardship and fierce determination mark this depiction of ordinary life during the time. The novel offers a vivid account of what the colonist faced during the period.

Historical Accuracy: Most of the major incidents described actually happened, and the characters are based on real people.

`6765` *House Divided*

Date of Publication: 1947
Subject(s): Civil War—U.S.; Battle of Gettysburg
Fictional character(s): Travis Currain, Military Personnel (Confederate soldier); Cinda Currain, Southern Belle
Historical character(s): James Longstreet, Military Personnel (Confederate general); Robert E. Lee, Military Personnel (Confederate commander); John Brown, Abolitionist, Revolutionary; Abraham Lincoln, Political Figure
Time Period(s): 1850s; 1860s (1859-1865)
Locale(s): Virginia

Summary: This massive novel offers the Southern perspective on the Civil War. Divided loyalties are exposed when a proud Southern family learns that their patriarch was also the grandfather of Abraham Lincoln. The novel depicts many of the great battles of the war.

Historical Accuracy: The novel is a marvel of historical reconstruction that offers a believable panorama of the era and its major figures.

6766 *Owen Glen*

Date of Publication: 1950
Subject(s): Labor Movement; Mining; Spanish-American War
Fictional character(s): Owen Glen, Teenager, Labor Leader
Time Period(s): 1890s (1890-1898)
Locale(s): Ohio

Summary: Set in a small town in the southern Ohio coalfields, the novel follows the growth and development of young Owen Glen who works in the mines and becomes an officer in the new United Mine Workers of America union. The novel attempts to show the maturation of America into a modern nation under the pressure of labor conflict and the catalyst of the Spanish-American War.

Historical Accuracy: The period and regional elements are convincingly portrayed.

6767 *Thread of Scarlet*

Date of Publication: 1939
Subject(s): War of 1812; Sea Story
Fictional character(s): David Swain, Sailor; Damaris Coffin, Young Woman
Time Period(s): 1810s
Locale(s): Nantucket, Massachusetts

Summary: Nantucket during the War of 1812 is the setting for this adventure novel that depicts the conflict between an American privateer and a British frigate. Conditions in Nantucket at the time bring the struggling islanders close to seceding from the United States. Young seaman David Swain is forced to declare his loyalty when the British interfere off the coast.

Historical Accuracy: The novel is accurate in its depiction of conditions on Nantucket during the period.

6768 *The Unconquered*

Date of Publication: 1953
Subject(s): Reconstruction Period; Business Building; Politics
Fictional character(s): Travis Currain, Veteran (Confederate soldier); Lucy Currain, Young Woman
Historical character(s): James Longstreet, Military Personnel (Confederate general), Veteran
Time Period(s): 1860s; 1870s (1865-1874)
Locale(s): New Orleans, Louisiana

Summary: The novel continues the story of the Currain family chronicled in *A House Divided* into the aftermath of the Civil War and the Reconstruction period. The action surrounds the corrupt politics of Louisiana and the attempt by Confederate General James Longstreet to pursue a moderate accommodation policy. The intrigue of the military government that controls New Orleans of the period as well as the development of the cotton-seed oil industry are depicted.

Historical Accuracy: The factual events of New Orleans after the Civil War are faithfully presented.

CHANCELLOR WILLIAMS (1905-)

An American historian, sociologist, and author, born in South Carolina, Williams is a graduate of Howard University. He taught in public schools and served in various U.S. government posts, including section chief of the Census Bureau. As a professor at Howard, Williams conducted field research in Ghana in the 1950s and throughout Africa in the 1960s. His novels include *Have You Been to the River?* and *The Second Agreement with Hell.*

6769 *The Raven*

Date of Publication: 1943
Subject(s): Biography, Fictionalized; Literary Life
Historical character(s): Edgar Allan Poe, Writer; Virginia Clemm, Spouse (of Poe)
Time Period(s): 19th century (1809-1849)
Locale(s): Richmond, Virginia; Baltimore, Maryland; New York, New York

Summary: This biographical novel recounts the life and career of Edgar Allan Poe. The novel attempts to arrive at a true depiction of Poe's character in a narrative that conforms to the known facts about his life. Poe emerges as a driven genius contending with internal and external demons.

Historical Accuracy: The essential facts of Poe's life are observed with some fictional surmises.

GORDON WILLIAMS (1934-)

Scottish author Williams worked as a reporter for a newspaper in Scotland. Author of more than a dozen mystery, science fiction, and spy novels, Williams has earned a reputation as one of the most innovative postwar Scottish novelists. He is best known for his third novel, *The Man Who Had Power Over Women*, which was made into a film. His novel *The Siege of Trencher's Farm* was made into the film *Straw Dogs.*

6770 *Pomeroy*

Date of Publication: 1982
Subject(s): Edwardian Period; Espionage
Fictional character(s): John Stockley Pomeroy, Adventurer, Spy
Historical character(s): Theodore Roosevelt, Political Figure
Time Period(s): 1900s (1903)
Locale(s): London, England

Summary: The exploits of American hustler and adventurer John Stockley Pomeroy are described as he is chosen to act as President Theodore Roosevelt's personal undercover agent on a dangerous mission to Edwardian London. Pomeroy finds himself in the center of a dangerous game of political intrigue with the stakes the control of Europe.

Historical Accuracy: The story is fanciful with an emphasis on diplomatic maneuvering that has a certain air of authenticity.

JAY WILLIAMS (1914-1978)

Born in Buffalo, Williams attended the University of Pennsylvania, Columbia University. and the Art Students' League. He is the author of over 60 books for adults and children. His novels include *The Good Yeoman, The Rogue From Padua, The Siege, The Witches,* and *Solomon and Sheba.* He received more than 1,000 letters a year from children, each of which he answered himself. His historical novels have been praised for their adherence to the period.

6771 The Good Yeomen

Date of Publication: 1948
Subject(s): Middle Ages; Myths and Legends
Fictional character(s): Robin Hood, Outlaw; Little John, Outlaw; Friar Tuck, Religious, Outlaw
Time Period(s): 14th century
Locale(s): Nottinghamshire, England

Summary: The novel retells the story of Robin Hood and the outlaws of Sherwood Forest. This version suggests that the real brains behind the operation are Friar Tuck and Little John, who emerge as serious political thinkers.

Historical Accuracy: The novel's ingenious reappraisal of the legendary story does not diminish the story but makes it more believable.

6772 The Rogue From Padua

Date of Publication: 1952
Subject(s): Religious Conflict; Protestant Reformation; Peasants' War
Fictional character(s): Arminius, Adventurer
Time Period(s): 16th century (1525)
Locale(s): Germany

Summary: While on his way home to Italy, itinerant charlatan Arminius finds himself caught up in the Germany of the Peasants' War and the Lutheran Rebellion during the Reformation. The conflict becomes an opportunity for Arminius to capture a fortune and win respectability.

Historical Accuracy: The novel convincingly creates a plausible atmosphere of the time.

6773 The Siege

Date of Publication: 1955
Subject(s): Middle Ages; Albigensian Crusade; Religious Conflict
Fictional character(s): Jocelin Peirot, Knight; Guy of Nissan, Knight; Aumeric of Montjoie, Knight
Time Period(s): 13th century
Locale(s): France

Summary: In medieval France, three knights embark on the crusade to destroy the Albigensian heretics. The novel's drama stems from how each reacts to the conflict and their love for the daughter of their liege lord.

Historical Accuracy: The novel excels in its authentic battle scenes and its portrait of medieval country life.

6774 Solomon and Sheba

Date of Publication: 1959
Subject(s): Biblical Story; Ancient Israel
Historical character(s): Queen of Sheba, Biblical Figure; Solomon, Ruler (King of Israel), Biblical Figure; David, Biblical Figure, Ruler (King of Israel)
Time Period(s): 10th century B.C.
Locale(s): Israel

Summary: This biblical story about the reign of Solomon describes how Solomon strayed from the worship of the Hebrew god and how he met the Queen of Sheba.

Historical Accuracy: The author's depiction of Israel during the 10th century B.C. is authoritative.

6775 Tomorrow's Fire

Date of Publication: 1964
Subject(s): Middle Ages; Crusades
Historical character(s): Richard the Lionhearted, Ruler (King of England); Denys de Courtebarbe, Entertainer (troubador)
Time Period(s): 12th century
Locale(s): England; Cyprus; Jerusalem, Palestine

Summary: This tale of the Third Crusade is told in excerpts from the journal of the wandering trouvere Denys de Courtebarde, who comes under the magnetic power of Richard the Lionhearted. The king is presented as insecure and alternatively compassionate and dismissive, a combination guaranteeing a difficult time for the trouvere.

Historical Accuracy: The novel provides an authentic portrait of personalities and the events of the period.

6776 The Witches

Date of Publication: 1957
Subject(s): Royalty—Scotland; Espionage
Fictional character(s): Vinolas, Spy
Time Period(s): 16th century
Locale(s): Edinburgh, Scotland

Summary: This historical adventure novel is based on an actual conspiracy against Scottish King James IV. French Huguenot exile Vinolas is sent by the Scottish Privy Council to investigate rumors of a Popish plot against the king.

Historical Accuracy: The novel effectively creates a plausible historical backdrop.

JEANNE WILLIAMS (1930-)

American writer Williams was born in Kansas and attended the University of Oklahoma. She is a novelist and teacher.

6777 Home Mountain

Date of Publication: 1990
Subject(s): American West; Ranching
Fictional character(s): Katie MacLeod, Teenager, Singer; Bill Radnor, Cowboy; Ed Larrimore, Rancher
Time Period(s): 1880s (1881)
Locale(s): Arizona

Summary: Katie MacLeod takes over an Arizona ranch after the death of her parents. She is befriended by cowboy Bill Radnor and must contend with Apache raids and natural disasters as well as a hostile takeover plan by neighboring rancher Ed Larrimore.

Historical Accuracy: The period elements in the story are authentic and convincing.

`6778` Home Station

Date of Publication: 1995
Subject(s): Railroads
Fictional character(s): Lesley Morland, Young Woman; Adam Benedict, Financier (railroad tycoon); Jim Kelly, Worker (wagon driver)
Time Period(s): 1900s
Locale(s): Oklahoma; Bountiful, Kansas

Summary: The novel concerns the impact of the railroad on a small Kansas community. Young Lesley Morland's father takes the position of station master in Bountiful, Kansas. When tragedy strikes, Lesley must take over for her father. She must also resolve her feelings for two men: railroad magnate Adam Benedict and wagon driver Jim Kelly.

Historical Accuracy: The author's notes indicate the factual basis and sources for her reconstruction of the period.

`6779` The Island Harp

Date of Publication: 1991
Subject(s): Highland Clearances
Fictional character(s): Mairi MacLeod, Young Woman; Magnus Ericson, Sailor; Iain MacDonald, Military Personnel
Time Period(s): 1830s
Locale(s): Highlands, Scotland

Summary: The novel dramatizes the infamous Highland Clearances of Scotland. Greedy landlords force tenant farmers off the land they have worked for centuries, creating the end of a community and a culture. This tragic end is dramatized in one family's plight; led by Mairi MacLeod, they must find a new home.

Historical Accuracy: Williams' Scottish details are exactly rendered with a glossary of terms to help translate the dialect and events.

`6780` Lady of No Man's Land

Date of Publication: 1988
Subject(s): American West; Immigrants
Fictional character(s): Kirsten Mordal, Orphan, Seamstress; Patrick O'Brien, Farmer, Rancher (cattleman); Ash Bowden, Businessman
Time Period(s): 1880s (1884)
Locale(s): Kansas; Texas

Summary: Swedish orphan Kirsten Mordal comes to America with her sister to homestead. Her sister dies from the arduous journey, and Kirsten, to save enough money to build a home, becomes a traveling seamstress on the trail from Dodge City across the panhandle to Texas. She befriends two men and must choose between love and security.

Historical Accuracy: The novel is convincingly recorded and filled with period information.

`6781` The Longest Road

Date of Publication: 1993
Subject(s): Depression Era; World War II
Fictional character(s): Laurie Field, Young Woman; Buddy Field, Young Man; Johnny Morrigan, Migrant Worker
Time Period(s): 1930s; 1940s
Locale(s): Kansas; Oklahoma; California

Summary: In this Depression Dust Bowl story the Field family heads west from Kansas for the promise of California. The family is broken up, and Laurie Field and her brother hop the rails for California. Laurie tries to find a new home for her family as the Depression gives way to the outbreak of war.

Historical Accuracy: The setting and details of life on the road in the 1930s are convincing.

`6782` No Roof but Heaven

Date of Publication: 1990
Subject(s): American West
Fictional character(s): Susanna Alden, Teacher; Asa McCanless, Rancher; Matt Rawdon, Doctor
Time Period(s): 1870s (1875)
Locale(s): Mason-Dixon, Kansas (western Kansas)

Summary: In 1875, having lost both her fiance and her father to the Civil War, Susanna Alden travels from her home in Ohio to the Kansas prairie. She starts a school and becomes a member of the prairie community, still split by the war and struggling to exist.

Historical Accuracy: Williams' novel is thoroughly recorded and convincing, and her prairie community is elaborately detailed.

`6783` The Unplowed Sky

Date of Publication: 1994
Subject(s): Depression Era; Farming
Fictional character(s): Hallie Meredith, Housekeeper, Cook; Garth McLeod, Farmer; Quentin Raford, Businessman
Time Period(s): 1920s (1924)
Locale(s): Kansas (western)

Summary: Hallie Meredith leaves her job as housekeeper to wealthy Quentin Raford during the Depression to become a cook for the MacLeod threshing outfit, which travels through western Kansas threshing wheat. The security of this life on the prairie is threatened when Raford puts MacLeod's business at risk.

Historical Accuracy: The details of prairie life of the period are believably presented.

JOEL WILLIAMS
(PSEUD. OF JOHN EDWARD JENNINGS, 1906-1973)

Born in Brooklyn, New York, Jennings attended the Colorado School of Mines, New York University, Columbia University, and the Washington Diplomatic and Consular

Institute. He served in the U.S. Naval Reserve during World War II and was on active duty as an officer in charge of the Naval Aviation History Unit. His novels include *Tattered Ensign* and *The Golden Eagle* (as John Jennings) and *The Sultan's Warrior* and *Tide of Empire* (as Bates Baldwin).

6784 *Coasts of Folly*

Date of Publication: 1942
Subject(s): Independence—South America
Fictional character(s): Paul Cartier, Revolutionary; Lucia Salas y Montalva, Gentlewoman
Historical character(s): Francisco Miranda, Military Personnel (general)
Time Period(s): 1800s (1808)
Locale(s): Venezuela; New York, New York

Summary: General Francisco Miranda and a small band of revolutionaries mount an expedition to liberate South America. Paul Carter joins the expedition, fired not by patriotism or hope of gain, but by love for the beautiful Dona Lucia.

Historical Accuracy: Romance and adventure predominate, and the historical elements are only lightly sketched.

JOHN WILLIAMS

Born in Texas, Williams graduated from the University of Denver and received his Ph.D. from the University of Missouri. Williams has worked as a professor of English at the University of Denver.

6785 *Augustus*

Date of Publication: 1972
Subject(s): Roman Empire; Biography, Fictionalized
Historical character(s): Augustus, Ruler (Roman emperor); Julius Caesar, Military Personnel (general), Political Figure; Marc Antony, Military Personnel (general); Cleopatra, Ruler (Egyptian queen); Tiberius, Ruler (Roman emperor)
Time Period(s): 1st century B.C.; 1st century (45 B.C.-55 A.D.)
Locale(s): Rome, Roman Empire

Summary: Told in the form of letters, journal entries, and memoirs of Augustus and his contemporaries, the novel offers a multi-dimensional portrait of Rome's first emperor. The nephew of Julius Caesar, Augustus avenges the murder of his uncle and holds onto power despite intrigue and conspiracy. Augustus emerges both as he is seen by others and as he sees himself.

Historical Accuracy: Some of the errors of fact in the book are deliberate. The order of some events has been changed, and the novel's primary documents are invented.

6786 *Butcher's Crossing*

Date of Publication: 1960
Subject(s): American West
Fictional character(s): Will Andrews, Student—College; Miller, Hunter, Frontiersman
Time Period(s): 19th century
Locale(s): Kansas; Colorado

Summary: Harvard student Will Andrews has come out west to hunt buffalo. He convinces frontiersman Miller to lead him to a herd in a hidden valley in Colorado, where they stay through the summer annihilating the herd. Staying too long, they are caught by the first blizzard, and they must spend the winter before trying to make their way back in the spring. The novel describes Will's coming of age and celebrates the connection between death and life.

Historical Accuracy: The novel is exact in its details of wilderness life, pushed to the level of universals and the mythical.

LAWRENCE WILLIAMS (1916-1983)

A playwright and author of such novels as *The Fiery Furnace* and *The Smoke-Filled Boudoir*, Williams adapted his fictional autobiography, *I, James McNeill Whistler*, for the stage as a one-man show performed by the Hartford Stage Company in 1981.

6787 *I, James McNeill Whistler*

Date of Publication: 1972
Subject(s): Artistic Life; Biography, Fictionalized
Historical character(s): James Abbott McNeill Whistler, Artist; John Ruskin, Writer; Dante Gabriel Rossetti, Writer, Artist
Time Period(s): 19th century (1850s-1890s)
Locale(s): Paris, France; London, England

Summary: This fictional autobiography of artist and wit James McNeill Whistler covers his life from his arrival in Paris, after being discharged from West Point for failing chemistry, to his art career in London. The novel features the notorious lawsuit Whistler brought against John Ruskin for defamation of character.

Historical Accuracy: The novel is generally reliable in its chronology and portrait of the age and of Whistler and his circle.

MARY FLOYD WILLIAMS

6788 *Fortune, Smile Once More*

Date of Publication: 1946
Subject(s): American West; Gold Rush—California; Crime and Criminals
Fictional character(s): Sam Watkins, Convict
Time Period(s): 1850s (1851)
Locale(s): Australia; San Francisco, California

Summary: San Francisco during the boom time of the California Gold Rush forms the background for this romantic story of Australian convict Sam Watkins who escapes and arrives in San Francisco in 1851. Watkins makes his way in the wide-open town until his past catches up with him.

Historical Accuracy: The novel offers a strong evocation of the period and convincing regional details.

MASLYN WILLIAMS (1911-)

English-born of Irish parents, Williams was reared in Australia on sheep ranches. He became a film editor/writer on documentary films, a job which has taken him on location around the world.

6789 Dubu: A Novel of New Guinean Conquest

Date of Publication: 1971
Subject(s): Tribal Life—New Guinean; English Colonies
Fictional character(s): Thomas Goffett, Government Official (colonial administrator); Jack Galmon, Trader; Father Henri, Religious (priest)
Time Period(s): 1870s (1878)
Locale(s): Papua New Guinea

Summary: Cultural conflict between Westerners and native New Guineans during the 1870s is described from the perspectives of a colonial administrator, a trader, and a French priest who longs for martyrdom. Conflict between Western and tribal values culminates in a fierce battle for supremacy.

Historical Accuracy: The novel is believable in its description of place and period.

THAMES ROSS WILLIAMSON (1894-)

Born on the Nez Perce Indian Reservation in Idaho, Williamson ran away from home at 14 and worked as a circus hand, cabin boy, reporter, and secretary to the warden of the Iowa State Prison. He graduated from the University of Iowa and Harvard. Williamson's books include *The Woods Colt: A Novel of the Ozark Hills*, *Problems in American Democracy*, *Far North Country*, and *The Earth Told Me*.

6790 The Gladiator

Date of Publication: 1948
Subject(s): Roman Empire; Christianity
Fictional character(s): Faljan, Gladiator
Time Period(s): 1st century
Locale(s): Rome, Roman Empire

Summary: Life in Nero's Rome is described through the adventures of a gladiator, Faljan. His experiences illustrate the corruption of Nero's court, the growing Christian community, and the burning of Rome.

Historical Accuracy: The novel is not successful in rendering a fully-realized period portrait.

ANNE C. WILLIMAN

6791 Mary of Magdala

Date of Publication: 1990
Subject(s): Biblical Story
Historical character(s): Mary Magdalene, Biblical Figure; Jesus Christ, Biblical Figure
Time Period(s): 1st century
Locale(s): Israel

Summary: This tale of Jesus' ministry and crucifixion is told from the perspective of Mary Magdalene. A devoted follower of Jesus, Mary accompanies him through the trials of his ministry up to his death.

Historical Accuracy: The story is largely invented, but faithful to New Testament sources.

TED WILLIS (1918-1992)

Born in London, playwright, novelist, and screenwriter Ted Willis left school at 15 and worked as an office boy, delivery boy, and news boy. During World War II, he wrote films and documentaries for the War Office. His first play, *Buster*, was produced in 1944. He followed its success with numerous plays for stage and screen and was hailed by the *Guinness Book of World Records* as the world's most prolific scriptwriter. In 1963, he was made a life peer. His novels include the suspense thrillers *Death May Surprise Us* and *The Buckingham Palace Connection*.

6792 The Buckingham Palace Connection

Date of Publication: 1978
Subject(s): Russian Revolution; Royalty—England
Fictional character(s): James Tremayne, Government Official; John Story, Engineer; Kasakov, Military Personnel (general)
Historical character(s): George V, Ruler (King of England); David Lloyd George, Political Figure
Time Period(s): 1910s (1918); 1970s (1976)
Locale(s): Siberia, Russia; England

Summary: In 1918, England's George V mounts a rescue mission to save his cousin, Tsar Nicholas II, from the Bolsheviks. Young Englishman James Tremayne, American construction engineer John Story, and White Russian general Kasakov set off across Siberia in an armored train to retrieve the imperial family. The novel offers a solution to one of history's great mysteries: What became of the Romanovs?.

Historical Accuracy: The novel has no basis in fact but is an ingenious dramatization of what might have happened.

6793 The Green Leaves of Summer

Date of Publication: 1989
Subject(s): World War I
Fictional character(s): Rosie Carr, Widow(er)
Time Period(s): 1910s; 1920s
Locale(s): London, England

Summary: During World War I, Rosie Carr's resourcefulness enables her to rise from poverty in London's East End to prosperity and distinction.

Historical Accuracy: The novel captures both the period and the locale with authenticity.

6794 Spring at The Winged Horse

Date of Publication: 1983
Subject(s): Edwardian Period

Fictional character(s): Rosie Carr, Orphan
Time Period(s): 1900s
Locale(s): London, England

Summary: Rosie Carr is a penniless Cockney orphan working at the Winged Horse, a London pub. This is the first of a series of novels about Rosie's life and career.

Historical Accuracy: The novel provides a believable portrait of London life during the period.

A.N. WILSON (1950-)

An English writer born in Staffordshire, Wilson is a graduate of New College, Oxford, where he has worked as a lecturer in English. A former literary editor of the *Spectator*, Wilson's books include the novels *Wise Virgin* and *Scandal* and biographies of Hilaire Belloc and John Milton. Wilson is best known for his farcical novels on British life.

6795 *Gentlemen in England*

Date of Publication: 1986
Subject(s): Victorian Period
Fictional character(s): Maudie Nettleship, Teenager; Lionel Nettleship, Religious (priest); Timothy Lupton, Artist
Historical character(s): Walter Pater, Writer; Anthony Trollope, Writer; George Eliot, Writer
Time Period(s): 1880s
Locale(s): London, England

Summary: Upper-middle class life in Victorian London is dramatized in this saga of the Nettleship family. The tension between manners and passion is played out in a household in which the family patriarch has not exchanged a word with his wife in 15 years. Their son converts to Catholicism and becomes a slum priest, and young Maudie Nettleship discovers how difficult it is to express the heart's longing. The Nettleships' affairs become intertwined with appearances by several eminent Victorians.

Historical Accuracy: The novel offers a comic and satirical but believable portrait of the age and its neuroses.

CHARLES MORROW WILSON (1905-)

Prolific American author Charles Morrow Wilson was born in Fayetteville, Arkansas, and was educated at the University of Arkansas and Oxford University. His career has included work as a journalist and as a special assistant to the president of the United Fruit Company. His books include *Geronimo*, *The Dred Scott Decision*, and *The Commoner: William Jennings Bryan*.

6796 *A Man's Reach*

Date of Publication: 1944
Subject(s): Settlement of the American Frontier; Biography, Fictionalized; Mexican War
Historical character(s): Archibald Yell, Political Figure
Time Period(s): 19th century
Locale(s): North Carolina; Alaska

Summary: The novel provides a fictional portrait of one of the early governors of Arkansas, Archibald Yell. It traces his career as a soldier, lawyer, congressman, governor, and as an officer in the War with Mexico.

Historical Accuracy: The novel's historical background is well drawn and authentic.

DEREK WILSON (1935-)

A graduate of Cambridge University, Wilson has been a history teacher in Nairobi, Kenya, an historian, and a broadcaster with the B.B.C. Primarily known for his books on the Tudor period, Wilson has written textbooks on world and African history. Some of his books include: *Sweet Robin: A Biography of Robert Dudley*, *The Tower*, *England in the Age of Thomas Moore*, and *White Gold: The Story of African Ivory*.

6797 *Her Majesty's Captain*

Date of Publication: 1978
Subject(s): Elizabethan Period; Royalty—England; Sea Story
Historical character(s): Robert Dudley, Nobleman; Elizabeth I, Ruler (Queen of England); Sir Walter Raleigh, Courtier, Sea Captain
Time Period(s): 16th century (1574-1590s)
Locale(s): England; At Sea (West Indies); Cadiz, Spain

Summary: Robert Dudley, Duke of Northumberland—explorer, admiral, diplomat, and author—tells his own story. He is the son of Queen Elizabeth's favorite, the Earl of Leicester, and one of the queen's maids of honor. When the great earl dies, Dudley inherits his fortune. Lured by tales of El Dorado, Dudley sails under Sir Walter Raleigh, earning the lasting enmity of the formidable Raleigh. Dudley distinguishes himself in action against the Spanish during a victorious raid on Cadiz, the greatest naval battle of the era.

Historical Accuracy: The novel is particularly strong in its details of Elizabethan maritime affairs.

DOROTHY CLARKE WILSON (1904-)

Born in Maine, Wilson graduated from Boston College. She has taught courses in writing religious drama in Mexico City and Alexandria, Egypt. She has declared that her purpose in writing is to inspire her readers.

6798 *Alice and Edith: A Biographical Novel of the Two Wives of Theodore Roosevelt*

Date of Publication: 1989
Subject(s): Biography, Fictionalized; Politics
Historical character(s): Theodore Roosevelt, Political Figure; Alice Lee Roosevelt, Spouse; Edith Roosevelt, Spouse
Time Period(s): 19th century; 20th century (1870s-1940s)
Locale(s): New York, New York; Boston, Massachusetts; Washington, District of Columbia

Summary: This biographical novel chronicles the life of Theodore Roosevelt from the perspective of the two women in his life. Edith Carow is Roosevelt's childhood friend who rejects his marriage proposal. Roosevelt marries instead the vivacious Alice Lee from Boston, and she shares with him the beginning of his political career until the day Roosevelt's mother dies of typhoid and Alice dies during childbirth. Edith waits patiently for Roosevelt to emerge from grief, helping him all the way to the White House.

Historical Accuracy: The details of history are observed in this biographical novel.

6799 *The Brother*

Date of Publication: 1944
Subject(s): Biblical Story
Historical character(s): James, Biblical Figure; Jesus Christ, Biblical Figure
Time Period(s): 1st century
Locale(s): Israel

Summary: This Biblical story provides a portrait of James, who, after the crucifixion, becomes, with Peter, head of the young church. Based on scant evidence, the novel offers a new interpretation of the familiar Christian story.

Historical Accuracy: Biblical events supply a convincing backdrop for this non-traditional gospel story.

6800 *The Gifts: A Story of the Boyhood of Jesus*

Date of Publication: 1957
Subject(s): Biblical Story
Historical character(s): Jesus Christ, Biblical Figure; Mary, Biblical Figure; Joseph, Biblical Figure
Time Period(s): 1st century
Locale(s): Nazareth, Israel; Jerusalem, Israel

Summary: The novel provides a picturesque reconstruction of the boyhood of Jesus. The story centers on his 12th birthday and the gifts of the Magi, and features a vivid portrait of everyday life during the period.

Historical Accuracy: The novel offers an authentic presentation of the customs of the period and the region.

6801 *The Herdsman*

Date of Publication: 1946
Subject(s): Biblical Story; Biography, Fictionalized; Ancient Israel
Historical character(s): Amos, Religious (prophet)
Time Period(s): 8th century B.C.
Locale(s): Israel

Summary: This Biblical-era novel imagines the life story of the Hebrew prophet Amos. Based on scant Biblical references, the novel elaborates Amos' life as the son of a poor farmer, his youthful rebellion against injustice, and his questioning of God's existence. The story traces the development of Amos' revolutionary concept of God and his philosophy of social justice.

Historical Accuracy: Because so little is known about the historical Amos, the book is largely fictional, but the details accurately reflect what is known of the historical background,

customs, and social conditions of Israel in the middle of the 8th century B.C.

6802 *Jezebel*

Date of Publication: 1955
Subject(s): Biblical Story
Historical character(s): Ahab, Ruler (King of Israel); Jezebel, Royalty (queen consort of Ahab); Elijah, Biblical Figure, Religious (prophet); Micaiah, Biblical Figure, Religious (prophet)
Time Period(s): Indeterminate Past
Locale(s): Israel; Tyre, Lebanon

Summary: The novel dramatizes the story of Jezebel, the woman whose name becomes synonymous with evil. She is a Phoenician princess who agrees to marry the Israelite King Ahab to seduce him and his people away from the worship of Jahweh for a god of blood and war. To accomplish her goal, she is willing to plot her own son's death, to murder her enemies, and to betray her husband and her people. Her opposition comes from the prophets of Israel, Elijah and Micaiah.

Historical Accuracy: The story is based on the Biblical story with considerable elaboration.

6803 *Lady Washington*

Date of Publication: 1984
Subject(s): Biography, Fictionalized; American Revolution; American Colonies
Historical character(s): George Washington, Military Personnel (army commander), Political Figure; Martha Washington, Spouse; Daniel Parke Custis, Landowner
Time Period(s): 18th century; 19th century (1750s-1802)
Locale(s): Virginia

Summary: The life and times of Martha Washington are depicted in this biographical novel. The tomboy daughter of a genteel Virginia family, she marries her godfather, Daniel Parke Custis. She is widowed at 27 and meets the young military officer George Washington, whom she marries and shares life with for the next 40 years. The novel describes Martha Washington's tireless efforts on behalf of her husband and the fledgling nation.

Historical Accuracy: The novel offers a faithful portrait of its subjects, staying close to the known facts.

6804 *Lincoln's Mothers: A Story of Nancy and Sally Lincoln*

Date of Publication: 1981
Subject(s): Biography, Fictionalized; Settlement of the American Frontier
Historical character(s): Thomas Lincoln, Farmer; Nancy Hanks, Spouse (of Thomas Lincoln); Abraham Lincoln, Political Figure; Sally Bush, Spouse (second wife of Thomas Lincoln)
Time Period(s): 19th century
Locale(s): Illinois

Summary: This biographical novel tells the story the two women to whom Lincoln said he owed all that he was. The first is his actual mother, Nancy Hanks, who encourages her son to become more than a farmer. Nancy dies when Lincoln is nine, and his father marries Sally Bush, who, though she is unable to read, also encourages her stepson. The novel offers a vivid portrait of frontier life.

Historical Accuracy: The novel keeps close to the known facts, though the friendship between Nancy Hanks and Sally Bush is fanciful.

6805 *Prince of Egypt*

Date of Publication: 1949
Subject(s): Biblical Story; Ancient Egypt; Pharaohs
Historical character(s): Moses, Biblical Figure
Time Period(s): 13th century B.C.
Locale(s): Egypt

Summary: The novel dramatizes the life of Moses from his youth in the Egyptian court until his discovery of his true identity and his kinship with the Hebrew slaves. He then leads his people on their exodus in the desert in pursuit of the promised land.

Historical Accuracy: Although most of the details of Moses' life are the stuff of legend rather than history, the novel is convincing in its depiction of the period and consistent with the Biblical story.

6806 *Queen Dolley: The Life and Times of Dolley Madison*

Date of Publication: 1987
Subject(s): Biography, Fictionalized; War of 1812; Politics
Historical character(s): James Madison, Political Figure; Dolley Madison, Spouse; Thomas Jefferson, Political Figure
Time Period(s): 18th century; 19th century (1778-1849)
Locale(s): Washington, District of Columbia; Philadelphia, Pennsylvania

Summary: This biographical novel chronicles the remarkable career of Dolley Madison. She was raised a strict Quaker, forbidden all earthly amusements. A widow with a young son at the age of 25, she becomes the wife of James Madison, many years her senior. In Washington, she becomes the capital's dominating hostess combining both social grace and enormous political savvy. During the War of 1812 and the burning of the White House she shows her mettle.

Historical Accuracy: The novel is faithful to the facts of Madison's life and times.

ERLE WILSON (1898-)

Wilson was born in Dundee, Scotland, and was educated both in Scotland and England. He later emigrated to New South Wales, Australia. His works include *Churinga Tales*, a compilation of Aboriginal myths, and the nature novels *Minado* and *Coorina*.

6807 *Adams of the Bounty*

Date of Publication: 1958
Subject(s): Sea Story; Military Life—British Navy; Mutiny

Historical character(s): John Adams, Military Personnel (seaman); William Bligh, Military Personnel (naval captain); Fletcher Christian, Military Personnel (naval officer)
Time Period(s): 18th century
Locale(s): *Bounty*, At Sea; Tahiti, French Polynesia; Pitcairn Island, Pacific Islands

Summary: The story of the *Bounty* mutiny and the fate of the mutineers on Pitcairn Island is told from the point of view of seaman John Adams. In this version, it is Adams who plans the mutiny and manages to triumph in the violence that splits the Pitcairn settlement.

Historical Accuracy: The novel's revisionist view of other accounts is believable in its assessment of Captain Bligh and reasonable in its theory about Christian's role in the mutiny.

JEANNE WILSON (1920-)

An English actress and author, Wilson was born in London and educated in private schools and drama schools in London. She has worked as a nurse and a teacher of speech and drama. Wilson has performed in more than 100 radio and stage plays and has written several plays. She was motivated to write historical fiction by her deep love of history.

6808 *The Golden Harlot*

Date of Publication: 1980
Subject(s): French Revolution; Georgian Period
Fictional character(s): Topaze Barrett, Foundling; Justin Barrett, Plantation Owner
Time Period(s): 18th century; 19th century (1782-1801)
Locale(s): England; Jamaica

Summary: The career of a mulatto foundling named Topaze is chronicled. Rescued from a life of prostitution by Justin Barrett, a wealthy West Indian planter, whom she marries, Topaze seeks revenge on a former lover who kills her husband in a duel. Forced to flee to Jamaica, she is caught up in the turmoil of the impact of the French Revolution in the Caribbean.

Historical Accuracy: The novel offers a colorful depiction of the past with a believable portrait of Caribbean life of the period.

6809 *Weep in the Sun*

Date of Publication: 1976
Subject(s): Restoration Period
Fictional character(s): Richard Vane, Fugitive, Servant; Colonel Walter Wells, Plantation Owner; Charlotte Wells, Gentlewoman
Time Period(s): 17th century; 18th century (1662-1700)
Locale(s): Jamaica

Summary: With the return of Charles II to the thrown, Richard Vane, a supporter of Cromwell, is forced to flee England. Captured by a pressgang, he is sold as an indentured servant to a wealthy planter, Walter Wells. Vane's adventures and struggle to create a plantation out of the tropical wilderness are described.

Historical Accuracy: The novel is convincing in its portrait of Jamaica during the period.

LESLIE WILSON (1952-)

Born in Nottingham, Wilson has lived in England, Germany, and Hong Kong. She has worked in adult education and as a translator.

6810 *Malefice*

Date of Publication: 1992
Subject(s): Witchcraft and Sorcery; Puritans; Civil War—England
Fictional character(s): Alice Slade, Witch
Time Period(s): 17th century (1655)
Locale(s): England

Summary: Set against the background of Puritan fanaticism and the English Civil War, the novel describes the effects on a small English village of the persecution of Alice Slade on a charge of witchcraft. A variety of perspectives presents a riveting portrait of communal guilt.

Historical Accuracy: This psychological study is set against an authentic period and regional background.

6811 *The Mountain of Immoderate Desires*

Date of Publication: 1994
Subject(s): Victorian Period; English Colonies; Royalty—England
Fictional character(s): Samuel Pink, Bastard Son, Gentleman; Lily, Young Woman
Time Period(s): 19th century; 20th century (1880s-1900s)
Locale(s): Hong Kong; England

Summary: Turn-of-the-century Hong Kong is the scene of this novel which imagines the existence of an illegitimate son of Queen Victoria, Samuel Pink, whose entanglement with the Chinese Lily sheds a light on the Victorian colonial world.

Historical Accuracy: The public events correspond to actual events of the period, but the main characters are invented.

MARGARET WILSON (1882-1973)

Wilson is best known for her works focusing on themes of religion, women's rights, and justice. She enlisted as a Presbyterian church missionary in 1904 and served for six years in India. This experience later informed several of Wilson's novels and inspired a series of short stories. Her first three novels, published between 1923 and 1926, are set in America and explore the effects of society's rigidity and the absurdity of domestic laws. The most successful of these, *The Able McLaughlins* earned a Pulitzer Prize in 1924. She is also the author of *Daughters of India* and *The Law and the McLaughlins*.

6812 *The Able McLaughlins*

Date of Publication: 1923

Subject(s): Reconstruction Period
Fictional character(s): Willy McLaughlin, Veteran (Union soldier); Christie McNair, Young Woman
Time Period(s): 1860s
Locale(s): Midwest

Summary: Wally McLaughlin returns from the Civil War to find his sweetheart, Christie McNair, has been violated by the community's scoundrel. Wally marries Christie, accepts the blame for the early birth of her child, and seeks revenge on the real father.

Historical Accuracy: The novel convincingly portrays the atmosphere of the period and the region.

SANDRA WILSON (1944-)

Welsh author Wilson worked for the British Civil Service before becoming a writer.

6813 *The Lady Cicely*

Date of Publication: 1974
Subject(s): Royalty—England; Tudor Period
Historical character(s): Cicely Plantagenet, Royalty (princess); Henry VII, Ruler (King of England)
Time Period(s): 15th century (1490s)
Locale(s): England

Summary: In the final volume of a trilogy on the life of Cicely Plantagenet, daughter of Edward IV, Henry VII sits uneasily on the throne of England threatened by the claims of Perkin Warbeck, who claims to be one of the princes in the Tower. Cicely discovers the truth about Warbeck with disastrous consequences for her marriage and happiness.

Historical Accuracy: The novel captures the atmosphere of the era with authenticity.

6814 *Less Fortunate than Fair*

Date of Publication: 1974
Subject(s): Royalty—England; War of the Roses
Historical character(s): Cicely Plantagenet, Royalty (princess); John of Gloucester, Bastard Son (of Richard III); Richard III, Ruler (King of England)
Time Period(s): 15th century (1480s)
Locale(s): England

Summary: The novel is the first volume of a trilogy on the life of Cicely Plantagenet. At 14 Cicely learns that her parents' marriage is invalid and that she and her siblings are illegitimate. Cecily falls in love with her cousin, John of Gloucester, the illegitimate son of Richard III. The story of their love is told against the backdrop of Richard III's reign.

Historical Accuracy: The story is not meant to be taken as historical but as a romance with a convincing period background.

6815 *The Queen's Sister*

Date of Publication: 1974
Subject(s): Royalty—England; Tudor Period
Historical character(s): Cicely Plantagenet, Royalty (princess); John of Gloucester, Bastard Son (of Richard III); Henry

VII, Ruler (King of England); Elizabeth of York, Royalty (princess)
Time Period(s): 15th century (1485)
Locale(s): England

Summary: The story of Cicely Plantagenet, the daughter of Edward IV, continues in the aftermath of Richard III's defeat and death at Bosworth and the succession of Henry Tudor to the throne. Henry plans to marry Richard's niece Elizabeth, Cicely's sister. Meanwhile, the man Cicely loves, John of Gloucester, is in the hands of the new Tudor king, and Henry has another husband in mind for Cicely.

Historical Accuracy: This is a historical romance, not intended for the serious historian. The atmosphere, rather than the events, is accurate.

TIMOTHY R. WILSON

`6816` *Beauty for Ashes*
Date of Publication: 1992
Subject(s): Victorian Period; World War I
Fictional character(s): Hannah March, Young Woman; Isabel Goodwin, Gentlewoman; Frank Holland, Revolutionary, Worker (brickmaker)
Time Period(s): 19th century; 20th century (1877-1918)
Locale(s): Fens, England

Summary: The setting is England's Fens from the Victorian period to the conclusion of World War I. The novel features the bitter rivalry between Hannah March and wealthy Isabel Goodwin. Their childhood bond is shattered both by romantic rivalry and the modern age, represented by Frank Holland, brickmaker and revolutionary.

Historical Accuracy: The novel is convincing in its depiction of the region and the period.

`6817` *Master of Morholm*
Date of Publication: 1986
Subject(s): Georgian Period; Family Saga
Fictional character(s): Mary Hardwick, Orphan; George Hardwick, Heir, Gentleman; James Hardwick, Gentleman
Time Period(s): 1770s
Locale(s): Fens, England; London, England

Summary: The death of the patriarch of the Hardwick family is the catalyst for this family saga set during the Georgian period. The passing of Joseph Hardwick and the arrival of an orphaned cousin, Mary, create tensions that surrounded the great house of Morholm in England's Fens.

Historical Accuracy: The region and the period are accurately depicted.

WILLIAM EDWARD WILSON
(1906-1988)

An American educator, journalist, and prolific author, Wilson was born in Bloomington, Indiana, and attended Harvard University. He served as a lieutenant commander in the U.S. Navy during World War II. His books include *The*

Wabash, Crescent City, The Angel and the Serpent: The Story of New Harmony, and *Every Man Is My Father*.

`6818` *Abe Lincoln of Pigeon Creek*
Date of Publication: 1949
Subject(s): Biography, Fictionalized; Settlement of the American Frontier
Historical character(s): Abraham Lincoln, Political Figure
Time Period(s): 19th century (1817-1830)
Locale(s): Indiana

Summary: The novel depicts Abraham Lincoln's youth in southern Indiana, from the arrival of his stepmother from Kentucky to his return from his trip down the Mississippi.

Historical Accuracy: Events are based on authenticated reports of Lincoln's early years in Indiana. The author captures the flavor of Hoosier speech and frontier customs.

`6819` *The Raiders*
Date of Publication: 1955
Subject(s): Civil War—U.S.
Fictional character(s): Henry Clayburn, Gentleman
Time Period(s): 1860s (1863)
Locale(s): Ohio River, United States

Summary: Henry Clayborn attempts to save a southern Ohio River town during the Civil War. The novel depicts the conflicting loyalties along the border between the Union and the Confederacy that is constantly under the pressure of attack by Morgan's Raiders.

Historical Accuracy: The novel vividly and believably re-creates life in a border town of the period.

JANICE WOODS WINDLE (1938-)

Born in San Antonio, Windle attended the University of Texas. She has held positions in government that include Texas state representative and director of the El Paso Bicentennial and Community commissions and has directed senate, gubernatorial and mayoral political campaigns. Her first novel, *True Women*, was the basis for the CBS mini-series of the same name.

`6820` *True Women*
Date of Publication: 1993
Subject(s): American West; Family Saga; Texas Revolution
Historical character(s): Euphemia Texas Ashby King, Settler, Activist; Georgia Virginia Lawshe Woods, Southern Belle; Bettie Moss King, Young Woman; Sam Houston, Political Figure
Time Period(s): 19th century; 20th century (1830s-1940s)
Locale(s): Texas

Summary: Based on the author's ancestors, the novel chronicles the history of Texas from the Texas Revolution to World War II. The story celebrates the determination and survival skills of the women in the author's family tree. The novel shows them contending with the Mexican army, the Comanches, Yankee carpetbaggers, and the Ku Klux Klan.

Historical Accuracy: The novel is a remarkable and believable re-creation of its eras.

MARK WINEGARDNER (1961-)

Born in Bryan, Ohio, Winegardner attended Miami University and George Mason University. He is a professor at John Carroll University. Winegardner is the author of the nonfiction books *Elvis Presley Boulevard* and *Prophet of the Sandlots*.

6821 *The Veracruz Blues*

Date of Publication: 1996
Subject(s): Baseball
Fictional character(s): Frank Bullinger, Journalist; Theolic "Fireball" Smith, Sports Figure (baseball player)
Historical character(s): Ernest Hemingway, Writer; George Herman Ruth, Sports Figure (baseball player); Diego Rivera, Artist; Frida Kahlo, Artist
Time Period(s): 1940s (1946)
Locale(s): Mexico

Summary: In 1946 a number of prominent white ball players join the Mexican league for the first fully-integrated baseball season in history. The story of that season is told by journalist Fred Bullinger, who captures the atmosphere and flavor of the postwar period.

Historical Accuracy: The novel blends the actual with the imaginary, using real and fictional characters to capture the era.

KATHLEEN WINSOR (1919-)

Winsor was born in Minnesota and graduated from the University of California. She worked as a reporter and receptionist for the *Oakland Tribune* in Oakland, California and has acted as a story consultant for the television series "Dreams in the Dust." She is best known for her novel *Forever Amber*, which caused a nationwide scandal and was banned as obscene and offensive in Boston, but which proved a popular success, with bookstores not able to keep up with demand. When the film rights to *Forever Amber* were purchased, it was reported that Winsor earned several times more than was paid to Margaret Mitchell for.

6822 *Forever Amber*

Date of Publication: 1944
Subject(s): Restoration Period; Fires; Plague
Fictional character(s): Amber St. Clare, Adventurer, Bastard Daughter; Lord Bruce Carleton, Nobleman
Historical character(s): Charles II, Royalty (King of England); Barbara Villiers, Noblewoman (Countess of Castlemaine)
Time Period(s): 17th century
Locale(s): London, England

Summary: Beautiful, tempestuous Amber St. Clare, the illegitimate daughter of two aristocrats, becomes the mistress of handsome Lord Bruce Carleton whom she loves with a consuming passsion. Carleton refuses to marry her and goes off to sea, prompting Amber to bed and wed a variety of men,

including a highwayman and an earl. Amber's adventures include incarceration in Newgate Prison and a glittering career on the London stage before she finally finds and loses favor at the court of Charles II.

Historical Accuracy: Although primarily a romance, the novel faithfully presents the culture and customs of the Restoration era.

6823 *Wanderers Eastward, Wanderers West*

Date of Publication: 1965
Subject(s): American West; Settlement of the American Frontier; Business Building
Fictional character(s): Zack Fletcher, Prospector; Lisette Devlin, Young Woman; Joshua Ching, Financier
Time Period(s): 19th century (1861-1883)
Locale(s): Montana; New York, New York

Summary: This massive panoramic novel depicts the settlement of the Montana territory over a span of twenty years as the railroad comes to Butte and brings to a close the territory's frontier existence. Dozens of characters are linked in the pursuit of fortunes in gold, silver, and copper. The novel shuttles between the Montana mining camps and the world of New York's financiers.

Historical Accuracy: Despite evident research into the period and the region, the novel exists more on the plane of myth than historical reality.

DAOMA WINSTON (1922-)

Born in Washington, D.C., Winston received an A.B. degree from George Washington University in 1946. She writes two types of novels: long historical novels and shorter works that are predominantly mystery stories.

6824 *The Fall River Line*

Date of Publication: 1983
Subject(s): Ocean Liners; Family Saga
Fictional character(s): Marcus Kincaid, Businessman; Augusta Kincaid, Young Woman; Luke Wakefield, Sailor, Businessman
Time Period(s): 19th century; 20th century (1847-1937)
Locale(s): Fall River, Massachusetts

Summary: The novel tells the story of four generations of a family that runs a shipping line ferrying passengers between Boston and New York. Marcus Kincaid and his wife are the original founder of the line, and their children's lives are shaped by the business.

Historical Accuracy: The novel is based on an accurate depiction of the shipping business of the period.

6825 *Gallows Way*

Date of Publication: 1976
Subject(s): Antebellum South; Underground Railroad; Slavery
Fictional character(s): Marietta Garvey, Plantation Owner; Lafe Flynn, Plantation Owner
Time Period(s): 1850s (1858)

Locale(s): North Carolina

Summary: In the South on the eve of the Civil War, Marietta Garvey marries Lafe Flynn, a man she does not love, in order to keep Galloway, the tobacco plantation with which she is obsessed. Flynn's involvement with the Underground Railroad begins to force Marietta to choose between the old South and a new life with the man she has slowly learned to love.

Historical Accuracy: The novel blends a principally romantic story with a plausible historical background.

6826 The Golden Valley

Date of Publication: 1975
Subject(s): American West
Fictional character(s): Anitra Martinez, Young Woman; Leigh Ransome, Adventurer
Time Period(s): 1870s
Locale(s): New Mexico

Summary: Set in the New Mexico territory during the 1870s, the novel dramatizes the clash of Spanish, Anglo, and Indian cultures. Anitra Martinez, the daughter of one of the largest Spanish landowners, meets and marries an adventurer from Texas, Leigh Ransome. Ransome's actions force Anitra to defend her Spanish heritage.

Historical Accuracy: The region and the period elements are captured believably.

6827 The Haversham Legacy

Date of Publication: 1974
Subject(s): Civil War—U.S.; Reconstruction Period; Family Saga
Fictional character(s): Miranda Haversham, Young Woman; John Haversham, Businessman; Reed Haversham, Veteran (Civil War)
Time Period(s): 1860s
Locale(s): Washington, District of Columbia

Summary: Political, social, and business life in Washington following the end of the Civil War and the assassination of President Lincoln are described, centering on the fortunes of the fashionable Haversham family. Miranda is an impoverished member of the family who comes to hold a key position as the events of the post-Civil War period produce dramatic consequences.

Historical Accuracy: The novel relies on a plausible depiction of the period.

6828 Mills of the Gods

Date of Publication: 1979
Subject(s): Labor Movement; Business Building
Fictional character(s): Victoria Davelle, Young Woman; Leslie Winton, Teacher; Richard Cavendish, Businessman (mill owner)
Time Period(s): 1900s (1901)
Locale(s): Fall River, Massachusetts

Summary: Set in 1901, the novel depicts life in Fall River, Massachusetts, and the conflict between its wealthy industrialists and the fledgling labor movement. Englishwoman Victoria Davelle visits her wealthy American cousin, Richard Cavendish. He overpowers her and forces an undesired marriage, and Victoria must struggle to win her independence regardless of the consequences.

Historical Accuracy: The novel is precise in describing the region and its milieu.

FRANCES WINWAR

6829 Ardent Flame

Date of Publication: 1927
Subject(s): Middle Ages
Historical character(s): Francesca da Rimini, Gentlewoman; Paolo Malatesta, Gentleman
Time Period(s): 13th century
Locale(s): Italy

Summary: Winwar reworks the story, immortalized in Dante Alighieri's Divine Comedy, of the ill-fated love affair between Francesca da Rimini and Paolo Malatesta. Francesca is contracted to marry the hunchbacked Lord of Rimini, Giovanni Malatesta. His brother, Paolo, falls in love with Francesca; and they are both killed by the jealous Giovanni.

Historical Accuracy: The novel convincingly captures the atmosphere of the period.

6830 The Eagle and the Rock

Date of Publication: 1953
Subject(s): Napoleonic Era; Biography, Fictionalized; French Revolution
Historical character(s): Napoleon Bonaparte, Military Personnel (army commander), Ruler (Emperor of France); Josephine, Royalty (empress consort of Napoleon); Joseph Bonaparte, Nobleman
Time Period(s): 18th century; 19th century
Locale(s): Europe

Summary: This fictional life of Napoleon stays close to the biographical sources and follows Napoleon's rise to power from corporal to emperor and the scourge of Europe. The novel is successful in presenting the well-known figures with fresh and original insights and capturing the atmosphere of the age with skill.

Historical Accuracy: The novel is reliable in its facts and makes good use of evident research into the period.

6831 Gallows Hill

Date of Publication: 1937
Subject(s): American Colonies; Witchcraft and Sorcery; Puritans
Fictional character(s): Bridget Bishop, Widow(er); Mary Bishop, Young Woman
Historical character(s): Cotton Mather, Religious (minister)
Time Period(s): 17th century
Locale(s): Salem, Massachusetts, American Colonies

Summary: This tale of colonial Salem captures the history of the witchcraft trials in the late 17th century. Cotton Mather investigates claims that the devil has infected townspeople.

The frenzy of accusations targets the widow of the town's innkeeper, accused out of jealousy for her finery and distrust for her independence. Her fate and that of her daughter, Mary, is dramatized.

Historical Accuracy: The novel presents a convincing backdrop of the customs and atmosphere of the times, though the novel's human story is less successful.

6832　*Last Love of Camille*

Date of Publication: 1954
Subject(s): Musical Life
Historical character(s): Marie Duplessis, Model; Franz Liszt, Composer, Musician
Time Period(s): 1840s
Locale(s): Paris, France

Summary: The novel dramatizes the romance between composer Franz Liszt and the famous courtesan and model Marie Duplessis, who is known as the Lady of the Camellias. The novel captures the atmosphere of 19th-century Paris and the circle that revolved around Liszt and one of the most notorious beauties of the time.

Historical Accuracy: The novel's romanticism sometimes conflicts with the story's realism.

G. CLIFTON WISLER (1950-)

Born in Oklahoma, Wisler graduated from Southern Methodist University. He has been a high school and middle school teacher of journalism and English in Texas. In 1980 he was nominated for the American Book Award for *My Brother, the Wind*. He is the author of juvenile, young adult, and western novels.

6833　*Lakota*

Date of Publication: 1989
Subject(s): American West; Indians; Tribal Life—Native American
Fictional character(s): Tecante, Indian (Sioux), Warrior
Historical character(s): Crazy Horse, Indian (Sioux), Chieftain
Time Period(s): 19th century (1850-1880)
Locale(s): Black Hills, South Dakota; Wyoming

Summary: Tecante is a Sioux warrior who earns his reputation and name "Buffalo Heart" in the tribal wars against the Crow and the Pawnee. The new war, however, will be against the white man, and it is doomed to failure.

Historical Accuracy: The novel offers an authentic look at Indian tribal life.

TADEUSZ WITTLIN (1909-)

A Polish author and translator, Wittlin was born in Warsaw. During World War II, he spent two years as a prisoner of war in Germany and Russia. Upon his release from a Siberian labor camp, Wittlin joined the Polish forces under British command in the Middle East and took part in the Italian campaign in 1944 and 1945. During the 1950s, he worked as an editor, radio script writer, and freelance writer for the

Voice of America and Radio Free Europe, as well as a lecturer at several U.S. colleges and universities. He is the author of *A Reluctant Traveler in Russia*, *Commissar: The Life and Death of Lavrenty Pavlovich Beria*, and *The Last Bohemid*.

6834　*Modigliani: Prince of Montparnasse*

Date of Publication: 1964
Subject(s): Biography, Fictionalized; Artistic Life
Historical character(s): Amedeo Modigliani, Artist
Time Period(s): 19th century; 20th century
Locale(s): Italy; Paris, France

Summary: The novel presents a biographical study of Italian artist Modigliani. The emphasis is on the psychological dimension of Modigliani's genius. He is viewed as seriously damaged, tied to his mother, and unable to establish any meaningful relationships while slowly destroying himself with drink and drugs.

Historical Accuracy: The novel is based in part on interviews with Modigliani's family and friends, which helps lend credibility to the imagined conversations and events depicted.

BURTON WOHL

6835　*Soldier in Paradise*

Date of Publication: 1977
Subject(s): American Colonies; Biography, Fictionalized
Historical character(s): John Smith, Leader (Jamestown Colony)
Time Period(s): 16th century; 17th century
Locale(s): Jamestown, Virginia, American Colonies; England

Summary: The novel provides a biographical account of the adventurous career of Captain John Smith, the leader of the English colony at Jamestown. Different from his heroic portrait of legend, the novel offers a more realistic view of Smith as a driven adventurer with his eye firmly on the main chance for his own advancement. He is shown during his mercenary career, during the struggle of the colony, and later in life after achieving acclaim as an explorer and historian.

Historical Accuracy: Despite the novel's realistic perspective, Smith rarely achieves believability as a historical figure.

CHRISTA WOLF (1929-)

A German novelist, essayist, and scriptwriter, Wolf was born in Landsberg an der Warthe in Germany and attended the University of Jena and the University of Leipzig. She has worked as a magazine editor and in a factory manufacturing railroad freight cars. She is the author of *Divided Heaven*, *The Quest for Christa T*, which was attacked in her native East Germany for its perceived emphasis on Western psychology over Marxist politics, and the autobiographical work *Pattern of Childhood*.

6836 *No Place on Earth*

Date of Publication: 1982
Subject(s): Literary Life
Historical character(s): Heinrich von Kleist, Writer; Karoline von Gunderode, Writer
Time Period(s): 1800s (1804)
Locale(s): Germany

Summary: The novel imaginatively recounts a fictional meeting between two German writers—Heinrich von Kleist and Karoline von Gunderode—who come together at an afternoon literary party. The relationship between art and society dominates their conversation.

Historical Accuracy: The meeting and the conversation between Gunderode and Kleist are invented. All the other figures and their opinions are real.

JOAN WOLF

6837 *Born of the Sun*

Date of Publication: 1989
Subject(s): Myths and Legends; Dark Ages; Anglo-Saxon Period
Fictional character(s): Niniane, Royalty (Celtic princes), Captive; Guthfrid, Royalty (queen consort of Cynric)
Historical character(s): Cynric, Ruler (West Saxon King), Bastard Son; Ceawlin, Royalty (prince), Ruler (West Saxon King)
Time Period(s): 6th century (555-577)
Locale(s): Winchester, England

Summary: The scene is Anglo-Saxon England in the 6th century. Niniane is a Celtic princess captured and brought to the court of Cynric, King of the West Saxons. There she becomes involved in treacherous court intrigue involving Cynric's illegitimate son, Ceawlin. When Ceawlin kills the legitimate heir in a duel, both Ceawlin and Niniane flee into exile to return years later bringing peace and prosperity with them.

Historical Accuracy: The novel is detailed and convincing in its period elements.

6838 *Daughter of the Red Deer*

Date of Publication: 1991
Subject(s): Prehistory; Tribal Life—Prehistoric
Fictional character(s): Mar, Warrior, Prehistoric Human; Atlaw, Chieftain, Prehistoric Human; Alin, Young Woman, Prehistoric Human
Time Period(s): 13th century B.C. (paleolithic times)
Locale(s): Vezere, France

Summary: Set during paleolithic times in the Pyrenees, the novel describes the conflict that results when tainted waters fatally poison the women of the tribe of the Horse. The clan's young men set out on a raid to kidnap new women from the matriarchal tribe of the Red Deer. Their success produces conflict with the tribes' elders, complicating the love that develops between Mar, the leader of the young men, and Alin, daughter of the Red Deer priestess and chief.

Historical Accuracy: The paintings, tools, and weapons described are based on actual artifacts. The culture is appropriate for that of the Magdalenian. The depiction is based on evident research into that period.

6839 *The Edge of Light*

Date of Publication: 1990
Subject(s): Dark Ages; Anglo-Saxon Period; Vikings
Historical character(s): Elswyth, Royalty (princess), Spouse (consort of Alfred); Alfred the Great, Ruler (King of Wessex); Ethelwulf, Ruler (King of Wessex)
Time Period(s): 9th century (856-878)
Locale(s): Wessex, England

Summary: The novel celebrates the career of Alfred the Great, whose kingdom of Wessex was the only English kingdom that was successful in resisting the Danes. Alfred comes to rule unexpectedly as the fifth son of Ethelwulf. The novel interweaves the actual details of Alfred's struggle with the Danes with his relationship with his wife, Elswyth.

Historical Accuracy: The novel combines the known and the imagined, filling the story out into a convincing re-creation of the age. Details of Elysworth are invented, as historians know nothing about her but her name.

6840 *The Horsemasters*

Date of Publication: 1993
Subject(s): Prehistory; Tribal Life—Prehistoric
Fictional character(s): Ronan, Prehistoric Human; Nel, Prehistoric Human
Time Period(s): Indeterminate Past
Locale(s): Pyrenees, France

Summary: This prehistoric tale describes the mastery of the horse that was to have a devasting effect on Cro-Magnon Man. Ronan, a member of the Tribe of the Red Deer, is cast out and discovers a fierce band of northerners who have mastered the art of horsemanship and are moving south as conquerors. Ronan attempts to forge an alliance of tribes to resist invasion and tame a herd of wild horses.

Historical Accuracy: The novel is based on archaeological and anthropological research that creates a believable portrait of prehistorical life.

6841 *The Reindeer Hunters*

Date of Publication: 1994
Subject(s): Prehistory; Tribal Life—Prehistoric
Fictional character(s): Alane, Prehistoric Human, Young Woman; Nardo, Prehistoric Human, Young Man
Time Period(s): Indeterminate Past
Locale(s): France (southern)

Summary: Set 25,000 years ago among the Cro-Magnon people of southern France, the novel dramatizes prehistoric life in a story that centers on the resolution of tribal disputes through the forced marriage between Alane, the Norakamo chief's daughter, and Nardo, the son of the chieftain of the Kindred. The proud Alane resists the union but is slowly drawn to Nardo as the success of their tribes depends on the outcome of their marriage.

Historical Accuracy: The novel offers a plausible portrait of prehistoric life and customs.

6842 *The Road to Avalon*

Date of Publication: 1988
Subject(s): Myths and Legends; Dark Ages; Arthurian Legends
Fictional character(s): Arthur, Ruler; Merlin, Sorcerer; Morgan Le Fay, Gentlewoman; Gwenhwyfar, Gentlewoman
Time Period(s): 5th century (446-470)
Locale(s): England; Wales

Summary: In this re-imagining of the Arthurian legend, Arthur, true heir to the High King of Britain, is rescued from exile by Merlin and brought to Avalon. There he falls in love with Merlin's youngest daughter, Morgan, who turns out to be Arthur's mother's half-sister. Their marriage would be incestuous and mean forfeiture of the throne. Instead Arthur marries the scheming Gwenhwyfar, but his forsaken love will determine the destiny of Camelot.

Historical Accuracy: The novel provides an intriguing alternative version of the familiar story, offered against a credible period background.

GENE WOLFE (1931-)

Born in Brooklyn, New York, Wolfe attended Texas A & M and the University of Houston. He has worked as a project engineer for Proctor & Gamble, an editor, and a writer. Wolfe has won many awards for his science fiction stories. His tetralogy, The Book of the New Sun, has earned him a reputation as one of the major contemporary writers of science fiction.

6843 *Soldier of the Mist*

Date of Publication: 1986
Subject(s): Ancient Greece; Myths and Legends; Supernatural
Fictional character(s): Latro, Mercenary, Amnesiac
Time Period(s): 5th century B.C. (479 B.C.)
Locale(s): Greece

Summary: Set in the world of pre-classical Greece, the novel describes the adventures of mercenary soldier Latro, who loses his memory after suffering a head wound in battle. The injury gives him the ability to see and converse with the invisible gods, goddesses, demons, and werewolves which inhabit the ancient world.

Historical Accuracy: Though filled with fantastic elements, the novel is authentic in its details of life during 479 B.C.

NELSON WOLFORD

SHIRLEY WOLFORD

Nelson Wolford was born in Texas and grew up on a ranch. Shirley Wolford grew up in New Jersey. Both worked for the film industry until the publication of their first novel.

6844 *The Southern Blade*

Date of Publication: 1961
Subject(s): American West; Civil War—U.S.
Fictional character(s): Russell Ekridge, Military Personnel (Union captain); Ann Wilmot, Captive; Dorrit C. Sawling, Military Personnel (Confederate lieutenant)
Time Period(s): 1860s (1865)
Locale(s): New Mexico

Summary: As the Civil War draws to a close, a group of Confederate prisoners of war escapes from Fort McCabe in New Mexico. They are pursued by a Union Army captain, Russell Ekridge, who is determined to subdue the rebels and to rescue their hostage, Ann Wilmot.

Historical Accuracy: The story is fanciful but convincing in its western elements.

STANLEY WOLPERT (1927-)

American historian and writer Wolpert was born in Brooklyn, New York, and graduated from City College and the University of Pennsylvania. A professor of history at the University of California, Los Angeles, Wolpert is best known for his biographical study *Jinnah of Pakistan*.

6845 *An Error of Judgment*

Date of Publication: 1970
Subject(s): British Raj; Independence—India
Fictional character(s): Rex, Military Personnel (general)
Time Period(s): 1910s (1919)
Locale(s): Amritsar, India; Lahore, India

Summary: In 1919 in the Punjab city of Amritsar at a meeting ground known as Jallionwala Bagh, a British general ordered a company of Gurkha Rifles to fire into a tightly packed crowd, killing several hundred unarmed Indians. The novel reenacts the circumstances surrounding the event and the motivation of the general, known as Rex in the novel, for ordering the massacre.

Historical Accuracy: The events of the Amritsar massacre are depicted accurately based on the evidence of the official inquiry and eyewitness accounts.

6846 *Nine Hours to Rama*

Date of Publication: 1962
Subject(s): Assassination; Independence—India
Historical character(s): Mohandas K. Gandhi, Political Figure; Natu Godse, Murderer (assassin); Guruji, Political Figure; P.K. Shankaracharyarau, Political Figure
Time Period(s): 1940s
Locale(s): India

Summary: This is a fictional account of the assassination of Gandhi that focuses on the assassin, Natu Godse, a religious and nationalist zealot who sacrifices himself for his cause. The characters that surround Godse and Gandhi collectively illustrate the tension and political issues of the period as India becomes an independent nation.

Historical Accuracy: This is a compelling rendering of history although it is less successful at interpreting the historical events.

BARBARA WOOD (1947-)

English writer Wood attended the University of California, Santa Barbara, and has worked as a surgical technician. She has been a full-time writer since 1977.

`6847` *Domina*

Date of Publication: 1983
Subject(s): Medical Profession
Fictional character(s): Samantha Hargrave, Doctor
Historical character(s): Elizabeth Blackwell, Doctor; Emily Blackwell, Doctor; Ulysses S. Grant, Political Figure
Time Period(s): 1880s; 1890s (1881-1895)
Locale(s): New York, New York; London, England; San Francisco, California

Summary: The novel tells the story of Samantha Hargrave who is born into the slums of London and struggles to enter the all-male profession of medicine. Rejection and disappointment lead her to America and the fulfillment of her career goals in New York and San Francisco.

Historical Accuracy: The central character is a composite of several women doctors in the second half of the 19th century. All the incidents are invented, though inspired by actual events.

`6848` *The Dreaming: A Novel of Australia*

Date of Publication: 1991
Subject(s): Frontier—Australia; Aborigines; Ranching
Fictional character(s): Joanna Drury, Heiress; Hugh Westbrook, Rancher
Time Period(s): 1870s; 1880s (1871-1886)
Locale(s): Melbourne, Australia

Summary: Set in Australia in the 19th century, the novel tells the story of Joanna Drury, who has come to Australia to claim property left to her by her mother. She falls in love with Hugh Westbrook, a prosperous sheep rancher, and then begins to delve into her family's past and its connection with the native Aborigines.

Historical Accuracy: The depiction of Australian life of the period and aboriginal customs are authentic.

`6849` *Green City in the Sun*

Date of Publication: 1988
Subject(s): Family Saga; Medical Profession
Fictional character(s): Grace Treverton, Doctor; Mama Wachera, Healer (medicine woman); Deborah Treverton, Doctor
Time Period(s): 20th century (1919-1988)
Locale(s): Nairobi, Kenya

Summary: In the early 1900s, the Treverton family settles in Kenya and must deal with their effect on the native peoples. A curse on the Treverton family from a local medicine woman must be worked out over the years and the generations.

Historical Accuracy: The depiction of African life is genuine and convincing.

`6850` *Soul Flame*

Date of Publication: 1987
Subject(s): Roman Empire; Medical Profession
Fictional character(s): Selene, Orphan, Healer; Mera, Healer; Andreas, Doctor (surgeon)
Historical character(s): Claudius I, Ruler (Roman emperor)
Time Period(s): 1st century
Locale(s): Antioch, Syria; Rome, Roman Empire; Alexandria, Egypt

Summary: The novel provides a dramatic history of the ancient healing arts through the experiences of Selene of Antioch, who learns primitive healing from Mera, a healer-woman, and Andreas, a surgeon with whom she falls in love. Selene's search for him takes her throughout the ancient world, to Babylon, Persia, Egypt, and Rome as the beginning of modern medicine takes shape.

Historical Accuracy: The novel is well researched and convincing in its depiction of ancient medicine.

MARTIN WOODHOUSE (1932-)

ROBERT ROSS

English author Martin Woodhouse has been a pilot, parachutist, computer expert, inventor, and creator of the popular TV series "The Avengers." Robert Ross worked as creative director for a leading New York advertising firm. They share a fascination for the Renaissance and Leonardo da Vinci.

`6851` *The Medici Emerald*

Date of Publication: 1976
Subject(s): Renaissance
Fictional character(s): Bianca Visconti, Noblewoman
Historical character(s): Lorenzo de Medici, Ruler (of Florence); Leonardo da Vinci, Artist; Sixtus IV, Religious (pope)
Time Period(s): 15th century (1478)
Locale(s): Rome, Italy; Venice, Italy; Florence, Italy

Summary: In the ongoing conflict among the Italian city-states, Venice is desperate to obtain an emerald on which is inscribed a vital military secret that could shift the balance of power in the Mediterranean. The emerald is in the possession of one of Lorenzo de Medici's most trusted agents, the artist Leonardo da Vinci. He must decipher the emerald's secret while rescuing his mistress.

Historical Accuracy: The story is fanciful but filled with colorful and believable period elements.

`6852` *The Medici Guns*

Date of Publication: 1975
Subject(s): Renaissance

Fictional character(s): Bianca Visconti, Noblewoman
Historical character(s): Leonardo da Vinci, Artist; Lorenzo de Medici, Ruler (Florence); Sixtus IV, Religious (pope); Rodrigo Borgia, Religious (cardinal)
Time Period(s): 15th century (1477)
Locale(s): Florence, Italy

Summary: In the conflict between the Florentine republic and the papal army of Sixtus IV and Cardinal Borgia, the fortress of Castelmonte has been seized by Rome, which threatens all of Florence. Lorenzo de Medici's army has failed to breach the fortress' impregnable walls, and Lorenzo places the fate of the campaign in the hands of a young artist and inventor, Leonardo da Vinci.

Historical Accuracy: The novel is an imaginary story based on fragments taken from da Vinci's notebooks.

6853　The Medici Hawks

Date of Publication: 1978
Subject(s): Renaissance
Fictional character(s): Bianca Visconti, Noblewoman; Girolamo Riario, Nobleman
Historical character(s): Lorenzo de Medici, Ruler (of Florence); Leonardo da Vinci, Artist; Sixtus IV, Religious (pope); Muhammad II, Ruler (Turkish sultan)
Time Period(s): 15th century (1480)
Locale(s): Otranto, Italy; Florence, Italy; Rome, Italy

Summary: The invasion fleet of Turkish sultan Muhammed II has captured the Italian coastal city of Otranto. In response Pope Sixtus IV names his nephew, Riario, to command an army from the city-states to oust the invaders. Leonardo da Vinci, Riario's enemy, is in charge of the Florentine contingent, the Medici gunners. Leonardo's inspiration when observing hawks in flight revolutionizes warfare.

Historical Accuracy: The background to this fanciful story is based on Leonardo's notebooks and the actual capture of Otranto by Muhammed II.

SARAH WOODHOUSE

6854　The Native Air

Date of Publication: 1990
Subject(s): Napoleonic Wars
Fictional character(s): Alexander French, Doctor; Ann Gerard, Gentlewoman
Time Period(s): 1800s (1803)
Locale(s): Norfolk, England; France

Summary: In the sequel to *The Peacock's Feather*, Dr. Alexander French decides to leave England for India. Before departing, he returns to Norfolk for a final visit. He is involved in a kidnapping and the ensuing search in France and England, where an invasion from Napoleon's army is expected.

Historical Accuracy: The novel is set against a plausible and authentic period backdrop.

6855　The Peacock's Feather

Date of Publication: 1988
Subject(s): Georgian Period; Inheritance—Disputed
Fictional character(s): Alexander French, Doctor; Jardine Henry Savage, Gentleman
Time Period(s): 18th century
Locale(s): Suffolk, England

Summary: Set in 18th-century Suffolk, England, the novel depicts a scandal over an inheritance. A stranger, Savage, returns from India to live in a beautiful but dilapidated house. At the center of the conflict is the irascible Dr. French, who must contend with the gossip and scandal that fill the country village.

Historical Accuracy: The novel is convincing in its period background and regional elements.

6856　A Season of Mists

Date of Publication: 1984
Subject(s): Georgian Period
Fictional character(s): Ann Mathick, Heiress, Landowner; Sir Harry Gerard, Gentleman, Landowner
Time Period(s): 1790s; 1800s
Locale(s): Norwich, England

Summary: Young Ann Mathick inherits the estate of Thorn. Her relationship with her landed neighbor, Sir Harry Gerard, forms the novel's romantic drama.

Historical Accuracy: The novel provides an authentic portrait of the age and the region.

RICHARD WOODMAN (1944-)

English author Woodman served in the British merchant navy as a midshipman and navigator. He was a junior officer on cargo liners and ocean weather ships and the commander of the vessel *Patrician*. Woodman won the Barbara Harmer Award in 1978 for *Keepers of the Sea*. His nautical historical novels aim for absolute historical accuracy.

6857　1805

Date of Publication: 1985
Subject(s): Sea Story; Battle of Trafalgar; Military Life—British Navy
Fictional character(s): Nathaniel Drinkwater, Military Personnel (naval officer); Edouard Santhonax, Military Personnel (naval officer)
Historical character(s): Pierre de Villeneuve, Military Personnel (French admiral); Horatio Nelson, Military Personnel (English admiral)
Time Period(s): 1800s (1804-1805)
Locale(s): Channel Coast, France; *Antigone*, At Sea; Gibraltar

Summary: The events leading up to the momentous Battle of Trafalgar are portrayed in this installment of the naval series featuring Nathaniel Drinkwater. Recently promoted post-captain, Drinkwater participates in the naval blockade to prevent Napoleon's threatened invasion of England. When French squadrons slip through, events move swiftly to the climax at Trafalgar in which Drinkwater plays an important role. This account provides a rare sympathetic look at Nelson's adversary, French Admiral Villeneuve.

Historical Accuracy: The author states that he has not consciously meddled with history but has used artistic liberty to interpret some of the major events and characters. Written or recorded words and opinions of the combatants have been used to preserve historical accuracy.

6858 *Arctic Treachery*

Date of Publication: 1987
Subject(s): Sea Story; Napoleonic Wars; Whaling
Fictional character(s): Nathaniel Drinkwater, Military Personnel (naval officer)
Time Period(s): 1800s (1803)
Locale(s): London, England; *Melusine*, At Sea; Greenland

Summary: Following his promotion for bravery at the Battle of Copenhagen, Nathaniel Drinkwater is given command of the H.M.S. Melusine that is to escort the British whaling fleet on its annual voyage to Greenland and the Arctic Ocean. Drinkwater must contend with resentful whaling skippers, a vessel ill-fitted for the punishing waters, and hazards from the cold and from the French.

Historical Accuracy: The period elements are solidly based on reliable sources, as the author's notes make clear.

6859 *Baltic Mission*

Date of Publication: 1986
Subject(s): Napoleonic Wars; Sea Story; Espionage
Fictional character(s): Nathaniel Drinkwater, Military Personnel (naval captain); Edouard Santhonax, Military Personnel (French general)
Historical character(s): Napoleon Bonaparte, Ruler (French emperor); Alexander I, Ruler (Czar of Russia)
Time Period(s): 1800s (1807)
Locale(s): *Antigone*, At Sea (Baltic Sea); Tilsit, Russia

Summary: The background of this installment of the adventures of Captain Drinkwater during the Napoleonic Wars is the Treaty of Tilsit between France and Russia in 1807. Drinkwater is aboard the *H.M.S. Antigone* in the Baltic when a chance interception of a coded message sends him on an espionage mission to the raft in the middle of the river Nieman where Napoleon and Alexander I are meeting to decide the fate of Europe.

Historical Accuracy: History is unclear about exactly how the British government learned of the secrets in the Treaty of Tilsit. Staying close to the known facts, the novel explores some intriguing possibilities of what could have happened.

6860 *The Bomb Vessel*

Date of Publication: 1984
Subject(s): Sea Story; Napoleonic Wars; Battle of Copenhagen
Fictional character(s): Nathaniel Drinkwater, Military Personnel (naval officer); Edward Drinkwater, Gentleman
Historical character(s): Horatio Nelson, Military Personnel (admiral)
Time Period(s): 1800s

Locale(s): *Virago*, At Sea; England

Summary: Lieutenant Drinkwater is given command of the *Virago*, a tender that must be turned into a fighting ship to join the Baltic campaign against Napoleon. Drinkwater labors with his ship while also trying to save his brother from the gallows and survive the antagonism of Lord Nelson. The action culminates in a crucial role for the *Virago* in the Battle of Copenhagen.

Historical Accuracy: Though the story is fictional, it is based on records of similar vessels playing similar roles in the Copenhagen campaign.

6861 *Decision at Trafalgar*

Date of Publication: 1985
Subject(s): Sea Story; Napoleonic Wars; Battle of Trafalgar
Fictional character(s): Nathaniel Drinkwater, Military Personnel (naval officer); Edouard Santhonax, Military Personnel (admiral)
Historical character(s): Horatio Nelson, Military Personnel (admiral); Pierre de Villeneuve, Military Personnel (admiral)
Time Period(s): 1800s (1804-1805)
Locale(s): *Antigone*, At Sea

Summary: The story of the epic battle at Trafalgar is depicted from the perspective of Nathaniel Drinkwater aboard the frigate *Antigone*. His ship is involved in the blockade of the French and Spanish ports, the search for the combined fleets of France and Spain, and the great confrontation off Cape Trafalgar. The novel offers a rare sympathetic view of Nelson's opponent, Villeneuve.

Historical Accuracy: All of the major events took place as described. Some interpretation has been supplied to fill in some gaps.

6862 *In Distant Waters*

Date of Publication: 1988
Subject(s): Sea Story; Military Life—British Navy
Fictional character(s): Nathaniel Drinkwater, Military Personnel (naval officer); Dona Ana Maria, Gentlewoman
Time Period(s): 1800s (1807-1808)
Locale(s): *Patrician*, At Sea; West Coast, North America; California

Summary: British naval officer Captain Nathaniel Drinkwater in the cruiser *Patrician* voyages around Cape Horn to the Pacific coast of North America. There he captures a Spanish frigate, meets the daughters of the Commandante of San Francisco, and finds himself caught in colonial intrigue between the Spanish and Russians.

Historical Accuracy: The background details of the Russians on the Pacific coast of North America are factual.

6863 *A Private Revenge*

Date of Publication: 1989
Subject(s): Sea Story; Military Life—British Navy; Chinese Empire
Fictional character(s): Nathaniel Drinkwater, Military Personnel (naval officer)
Time Period(s): 1800s (1808-1809)

Locale(s): *Patrician*, At Sea (South China Sea); China; Asia (Borneo)

Summary: In the aftermath of a typhoon British naval captain Nathaniel Drinkwater finds himself in one of the sideshows of the Napoleonic Wars, the British occupation of Macao and the attack on Canton. On convoy escort to Penang, Drinkwater's encounter with an old nemesis climaxes in the rain forest of Borneo.

Historical Accuracy: As the author's notes make clear, the details of the novel's imagined story are accurate, down to the weather in 1808.

WILLIAM HOWARD WOODS (1916-)

Born in New York City, Woods graduated from the University of North Carolina and the University of Iowa. His books have been translated into many European languages.

6864 *Riot at Gravesend: A Novel of Wat Tyler's Rebellion*

Date of Publication: 1952
Subject(s): Middle Ages; Peasants' Revolt; Royalty—England
Fictional character(s): Tom Kybbet, Gentleman
Historical character(s): Wat Tyler, Revolutionary; Richard II, Ruler (King of England); John Ball, Religious (priest), Revolutionary
Time Period(s): 14th century (1381)
Locale(s): London, England

Summary: The background of this historical novel is the Peasants' Revolt of 1381 led by Wat Tyler and John Ball. They direct a peasant army to London to demand the end of serfdom. The action of the rebellion is connected to a love story involving Tom Kybbet, a gentleman who sides with the peasants.

Historical Accuracy: The novel shows only brief images of England in the 14th century. Most of the novel's time is spent on a conventional love story that could have taken place in any period.

ANN WOODWARD

6865 *The Exile Way*

Date of Publication: 1996
Subject(s): Mystery; Japanese Empire
Fictional character(s): Lady Adi, Gentlewoman
Time Period(s): 11th century
Locale(s): Japan

Summary: Set in Japan in the later years of the Heian Period at the beginning of the western 11th century, the novel concerns intrigue and murder in the Imperial palace. Lady Adi is the detective who must sort through a tangled network of betrayal and deception.

Historical Accuracy: The novel features a convincing period backdrop and authentic customs of the times.

VIRGINIA WOOLF (1882-1941)

English novelist and critic Virginia Woolf is one of the foremost modernist writers of the 20th century. Her experimentation with techniques such as interior monologue and stream of consciousness in such novels as *Mrs. Dalloway* and *To the Lighthouse* moved the reader into the character's psyche to concentrate on moment by moment subjective experience.

6866 *Orlando*

Date of Publication: 1928
Subject(s): Sexuality; Fantasy
Fictional character(s): Orlando, Gentleman
Historical character(s): Elizabeth I, Ruler
Time Period(s): Multiple Time Periods
Locale(s): London, England; Constantinople, Turkey

Summary: The novel is a biographical fantasy of a man who awakes to find himself a woman. In the course of his/her 350-year history much of English history is encountered in scenes that include the royal courts of Elizabeth, Anne, and Victoria.

Historical Accuracy: The novel is a tour de force of historical and philosophical musings unfettered by restraints of time and place.

PERSIA WOOLLEY (1935-)

Woolley is a journalist and scholar specializing in the Dark Ages.

6867 *Child of the Northern Spring*

Date of Publication: 1987
Subject(s): Myths and Legends; Dark Ages; Arthurian Legends
Fictional character(s): Guinevere, Royalty (princess); Arthur, Ruler (King of the Britons)
Time Period(s): 5th century
Locale(s): England

Summary: The novel is the first volume of a trilogy on King Arthur's Camelot as seen from the perspective of Guinevere. The story depicts her youth as a Celtic princess. When she is chosen to be Arthur's queen, she finds the realm in revolt with Saxons and Celts uneasily allied under Arthur's tenuous control. Guinevere must play an active role in keeping the peace.

Historical Accuracy: The novel attempts to find a realistic basis for the Arthurian legend, with convincing period elements.

6868 *Guinevere: The Legend in Autumn*

Date of Publication: 1991
Subject(s): Dark Ages; Myths and Legends; Arthurian Legends
Fictional character(s): Arthur, Ruler (King of the Britons); Guinevere, Royalty (queen consort of Arthur); Lancelot, Knight; Modred, Knight, Royalty (prince)
Time Period(s): 5th century
Locale(s): England

Summary: In the concluding volume of the author's Guinevere trilogy, Guinevere's reign as queen of Camelot is coming to an end as her affair with Lancelot breaks the ideals of the Round Table. The novel describes the quest for the Holy Grail, Guinevere's trial for treason, and her sentencing to being burned at the stake.

Historical Accuracy: The novel emphasizes the realistic basis for the legendary story; the period elements are believably drawn.

6869　*Queen of the Summer Stars*

Date of Publication: 1990
Subject(s): Dark Ages; Myths and Legends; Arthurian Legends
Fictional character(s): Arthur, Ruler (King of the Britons); Guinevere, Royalty (queen consort of Arthur); Lancelot, Knight
Time Period(s): 5th century
Locale(s): England

Summary: In the second volume of the author's trilogy on Guinevere, she falls in love with the noble Lancelot, risking the ideals of the Round Table. Arthur's knights battle the Saxons in a realistic version of the famous legendary story.

Historical Accuracy: Effective use is made of period elements to ground the story in its time and place.

ANNE WORBOYS

Born in Auckland, New Zealand, Worboys won the Mary Elgin Prize in 1975 for *The Magnolia Room* and *The Lion of Delos*. She also won the Romantic Novelist Award in 1977 for *Every Man a King*. Worboys travels extensively to research her novels. *Every Man a King* was written after riding a horse across the Sierra Nevadas.

6870　*Aurora Rose*

Date of Publication: 1988
Subject(s): English Colonies; Frontier—New Zealand; Family Saga
Fictional character(s): Nicholas Le Grys, Heir; Rose Snape, Young Woman
Time Period(s): 19th century (1826-1850s)
Locale(s): New Zealand; England

Summary: The 19th-century beginnings of the New Zealand colony are depicted in the tangled love story of aristocratic Nicholas Le Grys and Rose Snape, the granddaughter of the great house's butler. Defending Rose from rape, Nicholas kills the village smithy and is forced to leave the country with a new wife in tow. Unbeknownst to Nicholas, Rose is on board his ship bound for the New Zealand colony. The drama is played out against a backdrop of conflict with the Maoris and the settlement of the New Zealand wilderness.

Historical Accuracy: The novel's characters are fictitious, but the depictions of the first frontier years of the New Zealand colony are based on actual events and real people, including the author's relatives.

DON WORCESTER (1915-)

An American writer born in Arizona, Worcester graduated from the University of California. He has spent time on an Apache reservation working in pueblo ruins and riding with Apache cowboys. He is a professor of history.

6871　*Gone to Texas*

Date of Publication: 1993
Subject(s): American West; Texas Revolution
Historical character(s): Ellis Bean, Frontiersman, Rancher
Time Period(s): 19th century (1800-1850)
Locale(s): San Antonio, Texas; Mexico City, Mexico

Summary: This is a fictionalized history of Ellis Bean, who comes to Texas when he is 17. Captured and imprisoned by Spanish troops, Bean goes on to become a soldier and statesman, first in the battle for an independent Mexico and then for the Republic of Texas.

Historical Accuracy: Worcester, a historian, is able to convince with his research and dramatize a colorful story of an important period of Western history.

6872　*Man on Two Ponies*

Date of Publication: 1992
Subject(s): American West; Indians
Fictional character(s): Running Elk, Indian (Sioux), Teenager
Time Period(s): 1870s
Locale(s): South Dakota

Summary: Running Elk is sent from his Dakota home to the Carlisle Indian School, where he learns the ways of the whites. When he returns to Dakota, he is mistrusted both by the white world that will not fully accept him and by his own people. Caught between two cultures, he is immersed in the death throes of the Sioux in the tragic era of the Ghost Dawn.

Historical Accuracy: The novel captures the period as well as the psychological impact of the clash of cultures.

HERMAN WOUK (1915-)

American novelist Herman Wouk was born in New York City of Russian Jewish heritage. He graduated from Columbia University and began his career as a gag writer for radio comedians. He started writing in earnest in 1943, while serving in the Pacific. His war experiences were the basis for *The Caine Mutiny*, which won the Pulitzer Prize in 1952. He followed this success with such bestsellers as *Marjorie Morningstar* and *Youngblood Hawke*. After years of research, Wouk produced his epic of World War II, *The Winds of War* and *War and Remembrance*. It has been said that in the last decade more Americans have learned about World War II through Wouk's account than from any other source.

6873　*The Glory*

Date of Publication: 1994
Subject(s): Jews; Independence—Israel; Yom Kippur War

Fictional character(s): Zev Barak, Military Personnel (army officer), Diplomat; Benny Luria, Military Personnel (Air Force general); Sam Pasternak, Military Personnel (intelligence officer); Don Kishote, Military Personnel (general)
Historical character(s): Golda Meir, Political Figure; Moshe Dayan, Military Personnel (general); Anwar Sadat, Political Figure; Henry Kissinger, Political Figure; David Elazar, Military Personnel (army commander); Menachem Begin, Political Figure
Time Period(s): 20th century
Locale(s): Israel; United States

Summary: The novel continues the story of modern Israel begun in *The Hope*. The focus is on the effects of such events as the Six Day War, the Yom Kippur War, the Entebbe rescue, and the signing of the Camp David accords.

Historical Accuracy: The novel's notes indicate the relationship between fact and fiction in the story. Despite invented scenes and dialogue, great effort has been made to provide a truthful version of events.

6874 *The Hope*

Date of Publication: 1993
Subject(s): Jews; Six-Day War; Independence—Israel
Fictional character(s): Zev Barak, Military Personnel (army officer); Benny Luria, Military Personnel, Pilot (fighter pilot); Sam Pasternak, Military Personnel (intelligence officer); Don Kishote, Military Personnel (army officer)
Historical character(s): David Ben Gurion, Political Figure; Moshe Dayan, Military Personnel (general); Yitzhak Rabin, Political Figure
Time Period(s): 20th century (1948-1967)
Locale(s): Israel; United States

Summary: This panoramic novel of the history of modern Israel covers the period from the War of Independence to the Six-Day War of 1967. The turbulent events on the battlefield and at the negotiating table are reflected in the fictional story of four Israeli army officers.

Historical Accuracy: The novel attempts to present a truthful portrait of Israel's history and the author's notes indicate any deviations from fact.

6875 *War and Remembrance*

Date of Publication: 1978
Subject(s): World War II; Holocaust; Jews
Fictional character(s): Victor Henry, Military Personnel (naval officer); Byron Henry, Military Personnel (naval officer); Natalie Jastrow, Spouse (of Byron); Aaron Jastrow, Scholar (Jewish)
Historical character(s): Franklin Delano Roosevelt, Political Figure; Harry S Truman, Political Figure
Time Period(s): 1940s (1941-1945)
Locale(s): Europe; United States

Summary: The novel continues the story of the Henry family during World War II. Aaron Jastrow and his niece Natalie experience the horrors of the Holocaust. Action includes major events in both the European and Pacific theaters.

Historical Accuracy: The novel's details about the war are accurate and authentic. The words and acts of the actual historical figures are either fictional or derived from accounts of their behavior in similar situations.

6876 *The Winds of War*

Date of Publication: 1971
Subject(s): World War II; Nazis; Jews
Fictional character(s): Victor Henry, Military Personnel (naval officer); Natalie Jastrow, Young Woman; Byron Henry, Young Man; Aaron Jastrow, Scholar (Jewish)
Historical character(s): Franklin Delano Roosevelt, Political Figure; Adolf Hitler, Leader (Nazi), Political Figure; Joseph Stalin, Political Figure
Time Period(s): 1930s; 1940s
Locale(s): Europe; United States

Summary: This panoramic story presents the events leading up to the outbreak of World War II. The focus is on the military and diplomatic career of naval officer Victor "Pug" Henry and on his family's experiences, including his son Byron's relationship with Natalie Jastrow, the niece of a prominent Jewish scholar.

Historical Accuracy: The novel interweaves the fictional story of the Henry family with an accurate history of the events leading up to America's involvement in the war.

CONSTANCE WRIGHT (1897-1987)

Born in Brooklyn, New York, Constance Wright attended Vassar College, Columbia University, and the Sorbonne. She is the author of *Fanny Kemble and the Lovely Land*, *Beautiful Enemy*, and *A Royal Affinity*.

6877 *A Chance for Glory*

Date of Publication: 1957
Subject(s): French Revolution
Historical character(s): Marie Joseph Paul de Lafayette, Nobleman (Marquis de Lafayette), Military Personnel (general); Justus Erich Bollman, Adventurer, Doctor; Francis Kinloch Huger, Adventurer
Time Period(s): 1790s
Locale(s): Austria

Summary: During the French Revolution, the Marquis de Lafayette flees France only to become a captive of the Austrians. The novel describes the attempt made by German doctor Justus Bollman and young American Francis Huger to free the American Revolutionary War hero from an Austrian prison.

Historical Accuracy: As the author's notes makes clear, the story is backed up by sources and evident research.

DON WRIGHT

6878 *The Captives*

Date of Publication: 1987
Subject(s): American Revolution; Settlement of the American Frontier

Fictional character(s): Morgan Patterson, Backwoodsman, Military Personnel; Susan Patterson, Heroine; James Southampton, Military Personnel
Historical character(s): Henry Bird, Military Personnel
Time Period(s): 1780s (1780)
Locale(s): Kentucky; Ohio; Michigan

Summary: Woodsman Morgan Patterson returns in 1780 to rescue his wife and daughter taken in the British attack on Kentucky forts. At the center of the drama is the desire for revenge on Morgan by British officer Southampton, wed to the woman who bore Morgan's son. This family drama is played out against a backdrop of the American wilderness.

Historical Accuracy: While the relational drama is pure invention, the events of the Revolutionary action in the Kentucky wilderness are based on fact.

6879 *The Last Plantation*

Date of Publication: 1990
Subject(s): Civil War—U.S.
Fictional character(s): Clayton Harris, Military Personnel (Confederate soldier), Gentleman; Lettie Billingsley, Southern Belle; Cotton Ferris, Military Personnel (Confederate soldier)
Time Period(s): 1860s
Locale(s): Gallatin, Tennessee

Summary: This Civil War-era saga concerns the interlocking fate of a large group of characters including Clayton Harris, a Northern aristocrat who comes to Tennessee and reluctantly fights for the Confederacy.

Historical Accuracy: The author's notes indicate the factual basis for most of the novel's events and several of the story's fictional characters.

6880 *The Woodsman*

Date of Publication: 1984
Subject(s): French and Indian War; Settlement of the American Frontier; Indians
Fictional character(s): Morgan Patterson, Frontiersman, Military Personnel; Judith Cornwallace, Noblewoman; Susan Spencer, Servant
Historical character(s): George Washington, Military Personnel (army officer); Edward Braddock, Military Personnel (general)
Time Period(s): 1750s (1755)
Locale(s): Ohio; Pennsylvania, American Colonies

Summary: Morgan Patterson, General Braddock's scout, survives the Battle of the Wilderness in 1755 but is cut off from the retreating British with three women to escort through the wilderness to safety. They endure attacks by Indians and the French, disease, and starvation. In the end they reach safety and Morgan gains a bride.

Historical Accuracy: The scenes of the American wilderness are convincing.

PATRICIA WRIGHT (1932-)

Born in Surrey, England, Wright has worked as an agricultural surveyor and agent as well as a teacher of

history and economics. She won the Georgette Heyer Historical Novel Prize in 1987 for *I Am England.*

6881 *I Am England*

Date of Publication: 1987
Subject(s): Vikings; Middle Ages; Tudor Period
Fictional character(s): Edred, Warrior; Ralf D'Escoville, Knight; Francis Wyse, Worker
Historical character(s): William the Conqueror, Ruler (Duke of Normandy)
Time Period(s): Multiple Time Periods
Locale(s): Sussex, England

Summary: Five linked episodes form a history of Sussex over 1,500 years, involving Celt, Saxon, Norman, and Elizabethan. The intention is to show continuity and connections over time while defining an English national character.

Historical Accuracy: This is a remarkably authentic look at very different ages of English history, each convincingly delineated.

6882 *Journey into Fire*

Date of Publication: 1977
Subject(s): Russian Revolution; World War II
Fictional character(s): Kolya Berdeyev, Musician; Anna Dmitreyevna, Spouse (of Kolya)
Historical character(s): Georgi Konstantinovich Zhukov, Military Personnel (marshal); Konstantin Rokossovsky, Military Personnel (general)
Time Period(s): 20th century (1911-1945)
Locale(s): Leningrad, Union of Soviet Socialist Republics; Moscow, Union of Soviet Socialist Republics

Summary: The history of Russia in the 20th century from the Revolution to World War II is depicted from the perspective of Kolya Berdeyev and his wife, Anna. The novel offers a graphic depiction of life under the Communist regime before and during the War.

Historical Accuracy: The basic framework of events and figures is factual with some simplification that attempts to avoid falsifications.

6883 *The Near and Distant Place*

Date of Publication: 1988
Subject(s): Civil War—England; Georgian Period
Fictional character(s): Daniel Gage, Bastard Son; General Braybon, Landowner; John Smith, Pilot
Time Period(s): Multiple Time Periods
Locale(s): Sussex, England

Summary: The novel tells the story of the events and personalities in an English village over nearly 350 years. The story begins in the 17th century with the political turmoil of the Civil War. A century later the village is beset by organized smugglers; 80 years later it is the conflict between landowners and tenants. Finally, the story reaches modern times with the permanence of the land the one enduring feature.

Historical Accuracy: This is an interesting dramatic compression of English history as seen in local history. The period elements are convincing.

6884   *A Space of the Heart*

Date of Publication: 1976
Subject(s): Russian Empire; Crimean War
Fictional character(s): Eleanor Lovell, Gentlewoman; Nicolai Berdeyev, Military Personnel (officer)
Time Period(s): 1850s (1852-1855)
Locale(s): England; St. Petersburg, Russia; Kharkov, Ukraine

Summary: A young woman is sent from her English home to Russia, where she is forced to make her way. The novel dramatizes her education in Russian life and customs that are in the grips of major changes. She also finds herself behind enemy lines when war breaks out in the Crimea.

Historical Accuracy: Wright's story is based on the experiences of a relative who went to Russia as a governess. The background is solidly painted and documented.

6885   *The Storms of Fate*

Date of Publication: 1981
Subject(s): Restoration Period
Fictional character(s): Arabella Sperling, Gentlewoman; Harry Cornish, Artisan; Adam Furnival, Bastard Son
Time Period(s): 17th century; 18th century (1660s-1704)
Locale(s): London, England

Summary: London life during the Restoration is the subject of this novel that follows the careers of two characters, Arabella Sperling, a goldsmith's daughter, and Harry Cornish, an alderman's son. Arabella intends to succeed in Charles II's court, while Harry is committed to defending Londoners' rights against the king.

Historical Accuracy: The appeal here is a solid sense of London that anchors the characters' story to a fully realized time and place.

6886   *While Paris Danced*

Date of Publication: 1982
Subject(s): World War I
Fictional character(s): Eve Ottoway, Nurse; Rick Dwyer, Journalist; Hugo Von Kobis, Military Personnel, Diplomat
Time Period(s): 1910s (1919)
Locale(s): Norfolk, England; West Prussia, Germany; Paris, France

Summary: Paris after the armistice following World War I is the scene of this story of the war generation immediately after the conflict. Paris is the hub for both the peace negotiations that will guarantee another war and for a young, inexperienced American girl, who is drawn into the city's considerable attractions and dangers.

Historical Accuracy: This is a fascinating period of power politics as the modern world takes shape after World War I. Wright ingeniously weaves many plot threads to create a convincing panorama.

NICHOLAS E. WYCKOFF

6887   *The Braintree Mission*

Date of Publication: 1957
Subject(s): American Revolution; American Colonies
Fictional character(s): Edward Humbird, Nobleman (Earl of Hemynge); Giuseppe Tempkins, Clerk
Historical character(s): William Pitt the Elder, Political Figure; John Adams, Political Figure; Abigail Adams, Spouse; Benjamin Franklin, Political Figure
Time Period(s): 1770s (1770-1771)
Locale(s): London, England; Boston, Massachusetts, American Colonies

Summary: The novel explores what might have happened if William Pitt had been able to persuade George III to an attitude of moderation toward the American colonies. Edward Humbird is sent on a peace mission to elevate several American colonists to the peerage, seat them in the House of Lords, and then negotiate through them for the establishment of American boroughs with seats in the House of Commons. The novel describes the failure of the mission; coming too late, it only serves to commit the American patriots to the cause of independence.

Historical Accuracy: The novel presents, through an imaginary situation, a convincing picture of life in Boston during the period and a compelling understanding of the basic differences in the struggle for American independence.

6888   *The Corinthians*

Date of Publication: 1960
Subject(s): Mormons
Fictional character(s): Simon Weddle, Young Man; Clorinda Weddle, Spouse
Time Period(s): 1850s
Locale(s): Illinois; Missouri

Summary: The impact of the Mormons western migration is examined in the story of Simon Weddle. Assisting a band of Mormons leads to a double life with his childless wife Clorinda in Illinois and with his sister-in-law down river in Missouri. The novel acts out an American version of the Abraham-Sarah-Hagar story.

Historical Accuracy: The period background is accurately documented and convincing.

I.A.R. WYLIE

6889   *Ho, the Fair Wind*

Date of Publication: 1945
Subject(s): Civil War—U.S.
Fictional character(s): Hebron Allyn, Farmer; Ellen Frosbie, Young Woman
Time Period(s): 1860s
Locale(s): Martha's Vineyard, Massachusetts

Summary: Set on the island of Martha's Vineyard at the end of the Civil War, the novel captures island life and customs, particularly some of the islanders' narrow religious beliefs, which are challenged by new arrivals.

Historical Accuracy: This is an authentic look at the region during the period.

OSWALD WYND (1913-)

Born in Tokyo, Wynd was the son of Scottish missionaries. He attended the University of Edinburgh and served in the British Intelligence Corps during World War II. He began to write while he was a prisoner of war in Japan. Wynd's novels include *The Blazing Air* and thrillers under the pen name Gavin Black. He estimates that he has written about 2,000,000 words in his many adventure and suspense books.

6890 *The Ginger Tree*
Date of Publication: 1977
Subject(s): East/West Relations; Earthquakes; Chinese Empire
Fictional character(s): Mary Mackenzie, Spouse; Kentaro, Nobleman; Richard Collingsworth, Diplomat
Time Period(s): 20th century (1903-1942)
Locale(s): Peking, China; Tokyo, Japan

Summary: A series of letters records the experiences of a young Scotswoman who comes to China to be married and conducts an adulterous affair with a Japanese nobleman. She is cast out by the British in Peking and must make her way in Japan during the years that include the Tokyo earthquake of 1923 and the outbreak of World War II.

Historical Accuracy: The novel is convincing in its depiction of period customs and the effects of actual events.

ANNABEL WYNNE

6891 *A Lady in Doubt*
Date of Publication: 1979
Subject(s): Victorian Period; Romance; Inheritance—Disputed
Fictional character(s): Alice Lacey, Gentlewoman; Sir Geoffrey Lacey, Gentleman; Matthew Vale, Gentleman
Time Period(s): 19th century (mid-Victorian period)
Locale(s): London, England

Summary: When her half-brother, Sir Geoffrey Lacey, proves that Alice Lacey's father never married her mother, her lands and fortune are taken from her. The novel describes her effort to adjust to her new circumstances and her attempt to find a means of restoring her birthright.

Historical Accuracy: The period elements are convincing in setting the novel's background.

IRVIN D. YALOM (1931-)

An American doctor and author, Yalom was born in Washington, D.C., and graduated from George Washington University and the Boston University School of Medicine. A professor of psychiatry at the Stanford University School of Medicine, Dr. Yalom is the author of the classic textbooks

The Theory and Practice of Group Psychotherapy and *Inpatient Group Psychotherapy*. He is noted for his existential approach to psychotherapy, linking anxieties and phobias to basic human issues of death, freedom, and isolation.

6892 *When Nietzsche Wept: A Novel of Obsession*
Date of Publication: 1992
Subject(s): Medical Profession
Historical character(s): Friedrich Nietzsche, Philosopher, Writer; Josef Breuer, Doctor; Lou Salome, Writer; Sigmund Freud, Doctor; Bertha Pappentheim, Young Woman
Time Period(s): 1880s (1882)
Locale(s): Vienna, Austria

Summary: The birth of psychotherapy is imagined in the fanciful encounter between pioneering physician Josef Breuer and philosopher Friedrich Nietzsche. Nietzsche's suicidal despair after the end of his love affair with Lou Salome leads him to Dr. Breuer for treatment. The two men discover that they share much in common as their relationship grows into friendship.

Historical Accuracy: The meeting between Nietzsche and Breuer is invented, but the essential details of the major characters' lives are grounded in fact.

AGUSTIN YANEZ (1904-1980)

A Mexican teacher, political figure, and author, Yanez held numerous positions in the Mexican government, including under-secretary to the president and secretary of education, as well as governor of the state of Jalisco. Yanez is widely regarded as one of Mexico's first modernist novelists, best known for *The Edge of the Storm* and *The Lean Lands*. His novels give a psychological perspective on the social and cultural changes brought about by the Mexican Revolution.

6893 *The Edge of the Storm*
Date of Publication: 1963
Subject(s): Revolution—Mexico
Fictional character(s): Micaela Rodriguez, Young Woman; Maria, Revolutionary
Time Period(s): 1900s; 1910s (1909-1910)
Locale(s): Guadalajara District, Mexico

Summary: The novel offers a panoramic view of life in a provincial Mexican village during the final days of the Diaz regime and the beginning of the Mexican Revolution. Rebelling against their repressive villages, the women illustrate social reasons for the Revolution.

Historical Accuracy: The description of ordinary life is both poetic and typical.

CHELSEA QUINN YARBRO (1942-)

An American novelist born in Berkeley, California, Yarbro has written books in a number of genres: fantasy, gothic, science fiction, Western, and suspense. She is best known for her historical vampire novels. A believer in the occult, Yarbro often incorporates magic and mysticism into her stories, but rarely is the historical sacrificed. Yarbro also writes under the pseudonym Quinn Fawcett.

6894 *Better in the Dark*

Date of Publication: 1993
Subject(s): Supernatural; Vampires; Dark Ages
Fictional character(s): Comte de Saint-Germain, Nobleman (aka Francois Ragoczy), Vampire; Ranegonda, Noblewoman; Pentacoste, Noblewoman
Time Period(s): 10th century (937)
Locale(s): Saxony, Germany

Summary: Comte de Saint-Germain is shipwrecked in Saxony. He is held for ransom in a fortress ruled by the indomitable Ranegonda with whom he falls in love. Saint-Germain helps her fight off the besieging Danes and Pentacoste, her brother's embittered former wife.

Historical Accuracy: What separates Yarbro's vampire stories from other Gothic thrillers is her successful attempt at providing a solid historical background.

6895 *A Candle for D'Artagnan*

Date of Publication: 1989
Subject(s): Supernatural; Vampires
Fictional character(s): Atta Olivia Clemens, Noblewoman, Vampire; Niklos Aulirios, Servant; Charles D'Artagnan, Military Personnel (musketeer)
Historical character(s): Jules Mazarin, Religious (cardinal), Political Figure (prime minister of France); Armand-Jean Du Plessis, Religious (Cardinal Richelieu), Political Figure (minister of Louis XIII); Louis XIV, Ruler (King of France)
Time Period(s): 17th century (1637-1644)
Locale(s): Rome, Italy; Paris, France

Summary: The final adventure in the 1,500-year career of Yarbro's female vampire Olivia Clemens sends her to France and Alexandre Dumas' territory. She is embroiled in the intrigues of Cardinal Richelieu who is trying to hold on to power against the rising Mazarin. She has a fateful affair with a young Gascon musketeer who should be familiar to the reader.

Historical Accuracy: Yarbro attempts to use convincingly the historical personages behind Dumas' inventions in this tale of the 17th century that features an authentic atmosphere of the period.

6896 *Charity, Colorado*

Date of Publication: 1994
Subject(s): American West; Mystery
Fictional character(s): Jason Russell, Lawman
Time Period(s): 19th century (post-Civil War)
Locale(s): Charity, Colorado

Summary: The unusual English sheriff Jason Russell returns in this western mystery novel. Unlike most Western Lawmen, Russell depends on his sleuthing ability rather than on firearms to bring justice to Charity, Colorado. Russell must con-

tend with a serial killer and a land dispute that threatens to escalate into a full-scale range war.

Historical Accuracy: This is a refreshing departure from the standard Western fare offering a believable alternative to most Wild West depictions.

6897 *Crusader's Torch*

Date of Publication: 1988
Subject(s): Supernatural; Vampires; Middle Ages
Fictional character(s): Atta Olivia Clemens, Noblewoman, Vampire; Valence Rainaut, Knight; Niklos Aulirios, Servant
Time Period(s): 12th century; 13th century (1189-1214)
Locale(s): Tyre, Lebanon; Cyprus

Summary: Olivia Clemens, Yarbro's benign vampire, is living in Tyre intent on returning home to Rome when the Mediterranean world explodes in war brought on by the Crusades. She makes the perilous journey accompanied by a young knight who has fallen in love with her. Together they contend with pirates, bandits, and renegade Christian knights.

Historical Accuracy: The supernaturalism of Yarbro's story is secondary to the historical adventures that have a solid grounding in the period.

6898 *Darker Jewels*

Date of Publication: 1993
Subject(s): Supernatural; Vampires; Russian Empire
Fictional character(s): Comte de Saint-Germain, Nobleman, Vampire; Xenya Evgeneiva, Noblewoman; Atta Olivia Clemens, Noblewoman, Vampire
Historical character(s): Ivan IV, Ruler (Czar of Russia); Istvan Bathory, Ruler (King of Poland); Boris Godunov, Nobleman
Time Period(s): 16th century (1582-1586)
Locale(s): Moscow, Russia

Summary: In 16th-century Russia, Ivan the Terrible murders his oldest son and is driven nearly insane by guilt. Saint-Germain, on a diplomatic mission for the King of Poland, assists the Czar in seeking relief from his guilty conscience. In the tangled Kremlin world of treachery and intrigue, Saint-Germain also finds love with the beautiful Xenya.

Historical Accuracy: Many of the characters are based on historical figures and, although presented fictionally, are as accurately portrayed as the constraints of the plot will allow.

6899 *A Flame in Byzantium*

Date of Publication: 1987
Subject(s): Supernatural; Vampires; Byzantine Empire
Fictional character(s): Atta Olivia Clemens, Noblewoman, Vampire; Niklos Aulirios, Servant; Drusus, Military Personnel
Historical character(s): Belisarius, Military Personnel (general); Justinian I, Ruler (Byzantine emperor)
Time Period(s): 6th century (545)
Locale(s): Rome, Roman Empire; Byzantium, Byzantine Empire

Summary: With Rome occupied by the Ostrogoths and the Empire crumbling, Olivia Clemens, Yarbro's historical vampire, must flee the city, aided by General Belisarius and a young soldier, Drusus. Upon arriving in Byzantium, Olivia is plunged into the city's intrigue.

Historical Accuracy: Although the characters are based on actual historical figures, they are used fictionally and should not be construed as representing actual persons.

`6900` *Hotel Transylvania*

Date of Publication: 1978
Subject(s): Vampires; Supernatural
Fictional character(s): Comte de Saint-Germain, Nobleman, Vampire; Madelaine de Montalia, Gentlewoman, Vampire
Time Period(s): 1740s (1743)
Locale(s): Paris, France

Summary: The novel introduces Yarbro's genteel and humane vampire, Le Comte de Saint-Germain, Oxford-educated and 3,000 to 4,000 years old. Arriving in Paris in 1743 amidst the dazzling opulence of the court of Louis XV, he falls in love with the beautiful Madelaine and battles a coven of devil-worshippers.

Historical Accuracy: Yarbro's Gothic supernaturalism is bolstered by a solidly detailed historical background rare in this genre.

`6901` *The Law in Charity*

Date of Publication: 1989
Subject(s): American West; Crime and Criminals
Fictional character(s): Jason Russell, Lawman (sheriff); Coffin Mayhew, Outlaw
Time Period(s): 19th century
Locale(s): Charity, Colorado

Summary: Jason Russell is a different kind of western lawman: an Englishman who uses his wits instead of an arsenal. He succeeds in maintaining order in the town of Charity, but will his methods be a match for the notorious outlaw Coffin Mayhew? Their final showdown provides the novel's climax.

Historical Accuracy: The novel is a refreshing departure from the Western genre. Unfortunately, brain over brawn seems unhistorical.

`6902` *Mansions of Darkness*

Date of Publication: 1996
Subject(s): Vampires; Spanish Colonies; Inquisition
Fictional character(s): Comte de Saint-Germain, Nobleman, Vampire; Acanna Tupac, Noblewoman (Incan)
Time Period(s): 17th century (1694)
Locale(s): Peru

Summary: In this installment of the adventures of the vampire Saint-Germain, he travels to Peru in the 17th century where he meets Acanna Tupac, a Incan noblewoman, and must contend with the Spanish conquerors and their Inquisition.

Historical Accuracy: Many of the characters are composites of actual historical figures, and the customs are faithful to the period.

`6903` *Out of the House of Life*

Date of Publication: 1990

Subject(s): Ancient Egypt; Vampires; Supernatural
Fictional character(s): Comte de Saint-Germain, Nobleman, Vampire; Madelaine de Montalia, Gentlewoman, Vampire; Egidius Maximillian Falke, Doctor
Time Period(s): 1820s (1825-1828); Indeterminate Past
Locale(s): Thebes, Egypt

Summary: Madelaine de Montalia, Yarbro's courtly vampire and le Comte de Saint-Germain's greatest love, has come to Egypt to investigate the secret history of her lover, who lived in Egypt centuries before. Grave robbers, smugglers, and scorpions hinder her investigation.

Historical Accuracy: Yarbro has been careful to represent the Egypt of the period and its understanding of pharaonic Egypt.

`6904` *The Palace*

Date of Publication: 1978
Subject(s): Supernatural; Vampires; Renaissance
Fictional character(s): Comte de Saint-Germain, Nobleman (aka Francesco Ragoczy), Vampire; Atta Olivia Clemens, Noblewoman, Vampire
Historical character(s): Lorenzo de Medici, Nobleman; Sandro Botticelli, Artist; Girolamo Savonarola, Religious, Political Figure
Time Period(s): 15th century (1490)
Locale(s): Florence, Italy

Summary: Vampires versus 15th-century Florence is the subject in this second novel about the humane vampire Saint-Germain, here called Francesco de San Germano Ragoczy. He is opposed by the fanatical Savonarola, and Saint-Germain risks all to save Olivia Clemens from certain death.

Historical Accuracy: The conjunction of the supernatural and the historical is surprisingly entertaining. Yarbro handles both competently.

`6905` *Path of the Eclipse*

Date of Publication: 1981
Subject(s): Supernatural; Vampires; Mongol Empire
Fictional character(s): Comte de Saint-Germain, Nobleman, Vampire; T'en Chih-Yu, Warlord; Tamasrajasi, Royalty (princess), Religious (priestess of Kali)
Time Period(s): 13th century (1216)
Locale(s): China; Tibet; India

Summary: Saint-Germain, Yarbro's well-traveled, genteel vampire, is in the Far East during the Mongol invasion of China. First he comes to the aid of a woman warlord in a battle with the Mongols. Then, on the trek home, he visits a Tibetan monastery and later falls under the power of an Indian princess and priestess of Kali, the evil goddess of lust and depravity.

Historical Accuracy: Yarbro's exotic settings and adventures are surprisingly well-anchored in accurate historical details.

`6906` *Tempting Fate*

Date of Publication: 1982
Subject(s): Supernatural; Vampires
Fictional character(s): Comte de Saint-Germain, Nobleman, Vampire; Laisha Vlassevna, Orphan, Ward; Madelaine de

Montalia, Gentlewoman, Vampire; Irina Ohchenov, Noblewoman; Gudrun Ostneige, Widow(er)
Time Period(s): 1910s; 1920s (1917-1928)
Locale(s): Austria; France; Germany

Summary: In post-World War I Europe, Saint-Germain becomes the guardian of a Russian war orphan and aids three others: an exiled Russian duchess, a young widow, and his great love, Madelaine de Montalia. His actions could lead to his final death.

Historical Accuracy: The novel, like the series, features convincing details of the period.

ELIZABETH YATES (1905-)

An American lecturer and author, Yates was born in Buffalo, New York. She has won several awards for her children's books and has been honored by several U.S. colleges. She is the author of *The Seventh One*, *Silver Lining*, and an autobiographical trilogy entitled *My Diary*.

6907 *Hue and Cry*

Date of Publication: 1953
Subject(s): Crime and Criminals; Rural Life—U.S.
Fictional character(s): Danny O'Dare, Outlaw (horse thief); Melody Austin, Young Woman
Time Period(s): 1830s (1836-1837)
Locale(s): New Hampshire

Summary: Life in rural New Hampshire in the 1830s is the scene for this novel that describes the working of the Hue and Cry, a volunteer association on the lookout for horse thieves. The Austin family, members of the Hue and Cry, are tested by the arrival of Irishman Danny O'Dare.

Historical Accuracy: The novel's regional portrait is vivid and convincing.

FRANK YERBY (1916-1991)

Yerby was a prolific African-American historical novelist, whose first novel, *The Foxes of Harrow*, was a bestseller. He maintained his appeal for the next twenty years. During the 1950s, he was probably the most widely-read American novelist and had an overseas reputation that rivaled Ernest Hemingway's and William Faulkner's. Today his novels seem more costume romances with an emphasis on sensational melodrama than accurate novels of the past.

6908 *Benton's Row*

Date of Publication: 1954
Subject(s): Antebellum South; Family Saga; World War I
Fictional character(s): Tom Benton, Plantation Owner; Sarah Benton, Young Woman; Roland Benton, Military Personnel
Time Period(s): 19th century; 20th century (1842-1920)
Locale(s): Louisiana; France

Summary: The novel follows four generations of the Benton clan from 1842, when Tom Benton arrives in Louisiana ahead of a Texas posse, until World War I, when great-grandson Roland serves in France. The story covers the expected con-

fused family tree, an illicit Cajun branch, and sufficient sex and violence to ignite the plot and provide some illumination of this family through the generations.

Historical Accuracy: Yerby is best in his Louisiana scenes and less convincing as he moves farther afield.

6909 *Bride of Liberty*

Date of Publication: 1955
Subject(s): American Revolution; Battle of Lexington; Valley Forge
Fictional character(s): Polly Knowles, Patriot; Ethan Knowles, Military Personnel, Patriot; Kathy Knowles, Loyalist, Fiance(e)
Historical character(s): Paul Revere, Patriot, Artisan (silversmith); George Washington, Military Personnel (general); Anthony Wayne, Military Personnel
Time Period(s): 1770s; 1780s (1774-1781)
Locale(s): New York, New York; Boston, Massachusetts; Valley Forge, Pennsylvania

Summary: Polly Knowles, the daughter of a prominent New York Tory, is drawn to the rebel cause out of her love for her sister's fiance, Ethan. Her pursuit of him causes her to meet many prominent figures and experience many of the American Revolution's most memorable moments.

Historical Accuracy: The story's connection with historical events is contrived and improbable.

6910 *Captain Rebel*

Date of Publication: 1956
Subject(s): Civil War—U.S.; Sea Story
Fictional character(s): Tyler Meredith, Sea Captain, Blockade Runner; Susan Drake, Southern Belle
Historical character(s): Benjamin Butler, Military Personnel (military governor)
Time Period(s): 1860s (1861-1865)
Locale(s): New Orleans, Louisiana; Havana, Cuba; Liverpool, England

Summary: In this Civil War tale about the adventures of a Confederate blockade runner, Tyler Meredith must maneuver between the Yankees and the three women in his life.

Historical Accuracy: The novel features exciting action scenes but more romance and melodrama than historical details.

6911 *The Dahomean*

Date of Publication: 1971
Subject(s): Coming of Age; Tribal Life—African; Slavery
Fictional character(s): Nyasanu, Warrior, Chieftain
Time Period(s): 1830s; 1840s
Locale(s): Dahomey (West Africa)

Summary: This coming-of-age novel concerns 17-year-old Nyasanu, the son of a Dahomean chief in West Africa, and the slave trade that destroys the culture and traditions of tribal life. It is one of Yerby's finest efforts at historical reconstruction.

Historical Accuracy: Yerby convincingly creates the customs, details, and feel of West African life.

6912 *A Darkness at Ingraham's Crest: A Tale of the Slaveholding South*

Date of Publication: 1979
Subject(s): Antebellum South; Slavery
Fictional character(s): Wes Parks, Slave; Pamela Bibbs, Southern Belle
Time Period(s): 1850s
Locale(s): Natchez, Mississippi

Summary: In this sequel to *The Dahomean*, Nyasanu, now Wes Parks, endures slavery in the antebellum South. Wes is a tower of strength and integrity, compared to the petty and weak-willed white overseers at Ingraham's Crest, who include a northern-educated mistress of the sprawling plantation. The story is action-packed, with a poisoning, duels, trickery, and a final conflagration.

Historical Accuracy: Yerby's theme here is the corrupting influence of slavery. His preference for his main character elevates Nyasanu into the realm of myth and symbol.

6913 *The Devil's Laughter*

Date of Publication: 1953
Subject(s): French Revolution; Reign of Terror
Fictional character(s): Jean Paul Marin, Gentleman
Historical character(s): Jean-Paul Marat, Revolutionary; Louis XVI, Ruler (King of France); Marie Antoinette, Royalty (Queen of France); Georges-Jacques Danton, Revolutionary, Political Figure; Camille Desmoulins, Revolutionary, Political Figure; Maximilien Francois de Robespierre, Revolutionary, Political Figure
Time Period(s): 1780s; 1790s (1784-1794)
Locale(s): Paris, France

Summary: Jean-Paul Marin is swept up in the events of the French Revolution and Reign of Terror. The major players appear as characters.

Historical Accuracy: There are strong scenes of great events, but the novel is more an overheated melodrama than a useful historical depiction.

6914 *Devilseed*

Date of Publication: 1984
Subject(s): American West; Gold Rush—California
Fictional character(s): Mireille Duclos, Heroine; Alain Curtwright, Gentleman; Andrew MacFarland, Gentleman
Time Period(s): 1850s
Locale(s): San Francisco, California

Summary: San Francisco during the 1850s Gold Rush provides the setting for this novel about a New Orleans woman who is a kind of frontier Moll Flanders.

Historical Accuracy: The San Francisco scenes seem authentic, but the melodramatic story reads more like wish-fulfilment than history.

6915 *Fairoaks*

Date of Publication: 1957
Subject(s): Antebellum South; Slavery; Civil War—U.S.

Fictional character(s): Guy Falks, Plantation Owner; Beeljie, Slave (Arabian); Guiletta, Singer (opera)
Time Period(s): 18th century; 19th century (1780-1884)
Locale(s): New Orleans, Louisiana; Caribbean; Africa (west Africa)

Summary: This is the story of Guy Falks, an antebellum Southern aristocrat and plantation owner. The slave trade is depicted in action that moves from the South to the Caribbean, Africa, and Europe.

Historical Accuracy: Falks' redemption seems more romantic than historically plausible.

6916 *Floodtide*

Date of Publication: 1950
Subject(s): Antebellum South; Slavery; Business Building
Fictional character(s): Ross Pary, Businessman; Morgan Brittany, Southern Belle; Conchita Izquierdo, Revolutionary (Cuban)
Time Period(s): 1850s
Locale(s): Natchez, Mississippi; Havana, Cuba; New Orleans, Louisiana

Summary: Ross Pary climbs from Natchez-Under-the-Hill, home of cutthroats, thieves, and rivermen to Natchez-on-the-Hill, home of gentlemen planters. His appeal is primarily to women, and he is drawn to three—a heartless Southern belle, a Cuban refugee who draws him into rebellion, and a common country girl.

Historical Accuracy: The South at the floodtide of its fortunes is captured in a variety of portraits and scenes, some authentic, many too idealized to be taken seriously.

6917 *The Foxes of Harrow*

Date of Publication: 1946
Subject(s): Antebellum South; Slavery; Civil War—U.S.
Fictional character(s): Stephen Fox, Gambler, Plantation Owner; Odalie Fox, Southern Belle
Time Period(s): 19th century (1825-1865)
Locale(s): New Orleans, Louisiana

Summary: Set in New Orleans and the surrounding bayou country before and during the Civil War, the novel features the charming rogue and gambler, Stephen Fox, who, starting with nothing, becomes a New Orleans aristocrat. The novel is loaded with period color: duels, southern belles, riverboat gambling, and Creole life.

Historical Accuracy: The novel is more a costume drama than a full depiction of the past. Its strength is a non-stop rousing story and intimate knowledge of the locale.

6918 *The Garfield Honor*

Date of Publication: 1961
Subject(s): Reconstruction Period; Business Building
Fictional character(s): Roak Garfield, Rancher; Hannah Furniss, Rancher; Gwendolyn Heindrichs, Teacher
Time Period(s): 1870s; 1880s
Locale(s): Texas

Summary: A penniless and disillusioned Civil War veteran, Roak Garfield, creates for himself a life of wealth and social prominence in Texas. Three women compete for his affections with expected melodramatic complications.

Historical Accuracy: Despite the emotional hyperbole, there are good details of Texas life, particularly the Mexican influences.

6919 *The Girl From Storyville: A Victorian Novel*

Date of Publication: 1972
Subject(s): Prostitution
Fictional character(s): Fanny Turner, Prostitute; Philippe Sompayac, Gentleman (Creole), Doctor
Time Period(s): 1890s; 1900s (1895-1903)
Locale(s): New Orleans, Louisiana

Summary: The story is set in New Orleans at the turn of the century. Fanny Turner, the daughter of a famous madam in New Orleans' notorious Storyville red light district, becomes a prostitute after a failed love affair.

Historical Accuracy: There are many details of New Orleans and period life. Yerby employs a curiously modern perspective in narrating the tragic story of a fallen but indomitable woman.

6920 *Goat Song: A Novel of Ancient Greece*

Date of Publication: 1967
Subject(s): Peloponnesian War; Ancient Greece
Fictional character(s): Ariston, Warrior, Captive (slave, prostitute)
Historical character(s): Socrates, Philosopher, Teacher; Alcibiades, Military Personnel; Euripides, Writer; Sophocles, Writer; Aristophanes, Writer; Critias, Political Figure, Writer
Time Period(s): 5th century B.C.
Locale(s): Sparta, Greece; Athens, Greece

Summary: The protagonist is a young Spartan warrior, Ariston, who is captured during the Peloponnesian War and sent back to Athens as a slave and later a prostitute. He finally becomes one of the most powerful men of Athens.

Historical Accuracy: The frank depiction of Greek sexual mores is original, but still the novel seems more a costume pageant than an historical recreation.

6921 *The Golden Hawk*

Date of Publication: 1949
Subject(s): Sea Story; Pirates
Fictional character(s): Kit Gerardo, Pirate, Sea Captain; Don Luis, Nobleman (Spanish)
Time Period(s): 17th century (1690-1697)
Locale(s): Jamaica; Cartagena, Colombia; Caribbean (at sea)

Summary: A West Indies pirate adventure, this is the story of buccaneer Kit Gerardo, who sets out to win power, the love of a female pirate, and revenge in the New World.

Historical Accuracy: The novel is heavy on cartoon-like adventure and light on historical details.

6922 *Griffin's Way*

Date of Publication: 1962
Subject(s): Civil War—U.S.; Reconstruction Period; Ku Klux Klan
Fictional character(s): Paris Griffin, Plantation Owner; Candace Trevor, Nurse; Bruce Randolph, Teacher
Time Period(s): 1860s; 1870s
Locale(s): Vicksburg, Mississippi

Summary: Amnesiac Paris Griffin returns home from the Civil War to his Mississippi plantation. This family saga is dramatically heightened by the violence of the Reconstruction with its night riders, Klu Klux Klan activities, and racial hatred.

Historical Accuracy: The novel is overfilled with period details serving a conventional story.

6923 *Jarrett's Jade*

Date of Publication: 1959
Subject(s): American Revolution; Family Saga
Fictional character(s): James Jarret, Laird; Jarl Jarret, Patriot, Military Personnel
Historical character(s): John Wesley, Religious (founder of Methodism); James Edward Oglethorpe, Military Personnel, Political Figure; George Washington, Military Personnel
Time Period(s): 18th century (1717-1783)
Locale(s): Savannah, Georgia; Highlands, Scotland; London, England

Summary: In Savannah, Georgia, a Scottish aristocrat ruthlessly pursues his dynastic dream, using the love of a Scottish girl, an English aristocrat, a Southern belle, and a slave girl, who all fall prey to his attractions. Eventually, he battles his son during the American Revolution.

Historical Accuracy: The novel is an over-heated patriarchal saga.

6924 *McKensie's Hundred: A Tale of the Old Dominion*

Date of Publication: 1985
Subject(s): Civil War—U.S.; Family Saga
Fictional character(s): Rosa Ann McKensie, Southern Belle, Spy; Colin Claiborne, Gentleman
Historical character(s): Robert E. Lee, Military Personnel; Thomas Jonathan Jackson, Military Personnel; Count Ferdinand von Zeppelin, Nobleman; Abraham Lincoln, Political Figure; Mary Todd Lincoln, Gentlewoman (first lady)
Time Period(s): 1860s
Locale(s): Richmond, Virginia; Paris, France; New York, New York

Summary: The novel begins in 1861 when Rosa Ann McKensie is sent home from her Boston finishing school to her Virginia homestead. She is a passionate and fiery Southern belle who, with the rest of her family, gets caught up in the Civil War. She becomes a notorious spy.

Historical Accuracy: This is unquestionably a fast-paced and exciting story, but the historical figures aren't integrated well into the romance.

6925 *Pride's Castle*

Date of Publication: 1949
Subject(s): Business Building; Gilded Age
Fictional character(s): Pride Dawson, Businessman; Sharon O'Neill, Seamstress (dressmaker)
Time Period(s): 19th century (1870-1891)
Locale(s): New York, New York; Pennsylvania; Colorado

Summary: Taking place in the New York City of the Gilded Age of robber barons, stock swindles, labor riots and strikes, the novel traces the financial rise of Pride Dawson from penniless dreamer to multi-millionaire, with the inevitable mixed results when Pride's dreams are realized.

Historical Accuracy: The history here is delivered in newspaper headlines without real integration into what is essentially a timeless family saga.

6926 *The Saracen Blade*

Date of Publication: 1952
Subject(s): Middle Ages; Crusades
Fictional character(s): Pietro di Donati, Knight; Iolanthe, Noblewoman; Zenobia, Slave
Historical character(s): Otto of Brunswick, Royalty (prince); Frederick II, Ruler (Holy Roman Emperor); Philip II, Ruler (King of France)
Time Period(s): 12th century; 13th century (1194-1250)
Locale(s): Sicily, Italy; Europe (France, Germany); Palestine

Summary: This novel recounts the medieval adventures of Pietro di Donati, the Sicilian son of an armorer who is improbably linked to the Holy Roman Emperor. Pietro's journey takes him throughout Europe and the Holy Land where he falls in love with Iolanthe, a baron's daughter, and Zenobia, a Greek slave girl.

Historical Accuracy: Full of color and pageantry, the novel is unconvincing as a reliable portrait of the past. There are several historical inaccuracies, despite documentary footnotes.

6927 *Serpent and Staff*

Date of Publication: 1958
Subject(s): Medical Profession; Family Saga
Fictional character(s): Duncan Childers, Doctor (surgeon); Jenny Greenway, Nurse
Time Period(s): 19th century; 20th century (1885-1905)
Locale(s): New Orleans, Louisiana; Vienna, Austria

Summary: In turn-of-the-century New Orleans, Duncan Childers claws his way up from the gutter to become the city's most fashionable surgeon before returning to his roots as a healer of the poor.

Historical Accuracy: Yerby's strength is depicting the atmosphere and details of life in post-war New Orleans.

6928 *The Treasure of Pleasant Valley*

Date of Publication: 1955
Subject(s): American West; Gold Rush—California
Fictional character(s): Bruce Harkness, Settler, Prospector; Hailey Burke, Settler, Prospector; Rufus King, Gambler
Time Period(s): 1840s; 1850s (1849-1850)
Locale(s): San Francisco, California; Sacramento, California

Summary: In this novel of the California Gold Rush, two Southerners journey west away from loved ones to encounter new loves in a land of misfits, gamblers, outlaws, and dreamers.

Historical Accuracy: There are good period details of California life, marred by melodramatic romantic complications.

6929 *The Vixens*

Date of Publication: 1948
Subject(s): Reconstruction Period
Fictional character(s): Laird Fournois, Veteran (Civil War); Sabrina Fournois, Spouse
Time Period(s): 1860s; 1870s
Locale(s): New Orleans, Louisiana

Summary: Laird Fournois, a Southerner who fought for the Union in the Civil War, returns home from Andersonville to riots and hardships in Reconstruction-era New Orleans. He marries Sabrina, whose cousin is one of the city's most notorious exploiters. Their relationship is doomed in the wake of the violence that follows the end of military hostilities.

Historical Accuracy: Yerby is sure of his New Orleans setting, but the melodrama overwhelms the period details.

6930 *Western: A Saga of the Great Plains*

Date of Publication: 1982
Subject(s): American West; Settlement of the American Frontier
Fictional character(s): Ethan Lovejoy, Settler; Anne Jeffreys, Settler
Historical character(s): James Butler Hickok, Lawman
Time Period(s): 19th century (1866-1888)
Locale(s): Kansas (Abilene, Topeka, Wichita)

Summary: The novel tells the story of Ethan Lovejoy, who homesteads in Kansas after the Civil War, eventually becoming one of the state's biggest landholders. Yerby includes a romantic triangle and Civil War guilt in the story of Lovejoy's rise.

Historical Accuracy: There is strong western color in his details of prairie life.

6931 *A Woman Called Fancy*

Date of Publication: 1951
Subject(s): Crime and Criminals
Fictional character(s): Fancy Williamson, Heroine; Court Brantley, Businessman
Time Period(s): 1880s
Locale(s): South Carolina; Augusta, Georgia; Savannah, Georgia

Summary: In the deep South of the 1880s, a 19-year-old backwoods Carolina girl aspires to become a great lady. The novel follows her path up and down the social ladder.

Historical Accuracy: Implausible dialect and cliches abound.

ROBERT YORK

English screenwriter York has written several novels under a pseudonym, many of which have been made into films.

6932 *My Lord the Fox*

Date of Publication: 1984
Subject(s): Elizabethan Period; Tudor Period; Espionage
Fictional character(s): Anthony Woodcott, Spy
Historical character(s): William Cecil, Government Official; Elizabeth I, Ruler (Queen of England); Robert Dudley, Nobleman (Earl of Leicester)
Time Period(s): 16th century (1560s)
Locale(s): England

Summary: The novel explores two of history's most vexing mysteries: Was Elizabeth Tudor's father really Henry VIII, and what was the truth behind the death of Amy Robsart, the wife of Lord Robert Dudley, Elizabeth I's supposed lover? Anthony Woodcott, secret agent for his master, Sir William Cecil, the Queen's powerful secretary, investigates both cases with some startling discoveries.

Historical Accuracy: The novel offers a plausible solution for both of these historical mysteries.

6933 *The Swords of December*

Date of Publication: 1978
Subject(s): Middle Ages; Royalty—England
Fictional character(s): William of Colchester, Gentleman
Historical character(s): Thomas Becket, Religious (Archbishop of Canterbury); Henry II, Ruler (King of England); Eleanor of Aquitaine, Royalty (queen consort of Henry II)
Time Period(s): 12th century (1160s)
Locale(s): England; France

Summary: This ingenious historical re-creation offers an alternative interpretation of Henry II and his Archbishop of Canterbury, Thomas Becket. The novel is the chronicle of William of Colchester and portrays both Henry and Becket as heretics, and Becket's murder in Canterbury Cathedral as part of a ritual sacrifice. The novel's evidence is compelling in this fresh and original look at Henry, Eleanor of Aquitaine, and Becket.

Historical Accuracy: The central thesis of the novel is speculative and more entertaining than credible. The period atmosphere is authentic and helps to make the story believable.

EIJI YOSHIKAWA (1892-1962)

Born near Tokyo, Yoshikawa began his literary career at the age of 22. He worked as a journalist while earning a reputation as one of Japan's most popular novelists.

6934 *The Heike Story*

Date of Publication: 1956
Subject(s): Japanese Empire
Historical character(s): Taira Kiyomori, Leader (clan), Government Official
Time Period(s): 12th century
Locale(s): Kyoto, Japan

Summary: In the Imperial city of Kyoto in the 12th century, Kiyomori of the Heike clan rises to power and becomes the emperor's chief counselor. Kiyomori's success and that of the Heike aggravate relations with a rival clan, the Genji. Betrayal, intrigue, and violence follow.

Historical Accuracy: The novel's period background is painted with skill and authenticity.

6935 *Musashi: An Epic Novel of the Samurai Era*

Date of Publication: 1981
Subject(s): Japanese Empire; Battle of Sekigahara
Historical character(s): Miyamoto Musashi, Warrior (samurai)
Time Period(s): 16th century; 17th century
Locale(s): Japan

Summary: The novel recounts the real-life exploits of Musashi Miyamoto, the son of a country samurai. Musashi finds himself on the losing side of the decisive Battle of Sekigahara, which establishes the Shogunate of Tokugama Ieyasu. He is saved from execution by a Zen priest and begins the training to become Japan's greatest swordsman. His travels take him throughout Japan, and the novel features a vivid depiction of feudal customs and classes.

Historical Accuracy: The novel accurately captures the Japan of the period and stays close to the known facts of Musashi's life and the events of the time.

6936 *Taiko*

Date of Publication: 1967
Subject(s): Japanese Empire
Historical character(s): Toyotomi Hideyoshi, Ruler (military ruler); Oda Nobunaga, Warlord; Tokugama Ieyasu, Warlord
Time Period(s): 16th century (1536-1582)
Locale(s): Japan

Summary: This massive novel of feudal Japan in the 16th century depicts the chaos that ensues as the shogunate crumbles and Japan is plunged into near constant civil war. Rival warlords battle for supremacy and three leaders emerge—Nobunaga, Ieyasu, and Hideyoshi—who struggle to unite Japan under their control. It is finally Hideyoshi who succeeds to become *Taiko*, the absolute ruler of Japan in the emperor's name.

Historical Accuracy: The novel, though based on actual figures and events, is idealized.

MARLY YOUMANS (1953-)

A native of South Carolina, Youmans is a poet and short story writer, and the author of *Little Jordan*.

6937 *Catherwood*

Date of Publication: 1996
Subject(s): American Colonies
Fictional character(s): Catherwood Lyte, Immigrant, Settler
Time Period(s): 17th century (1676-1678)
Locale(s): Albany, New York, American Colonies

Summary: This story of survival in the wilderness of the American colonies concerns recent immigrant Catherwood Lyte who, on a short visit to her nearest neighbor, becomes lost with her one-year-old daughter. She and her child struggle to stay alive while searching for signs of human habitation.

Historical Accuracy: This is a graphic and believable account of wilderness life during the period.

AGATHA YOUNG

A native of Cleveland, Young trained as a nurse and wrote a history of surgery entitled *Scalpel*. She served on the faculty of Yale as the head of the department of costuming at the university theater.

6938 *The Hospital*

Date of Publication: 1970
Subject(s): Medical Profession
Fictional character(s): Sue Ward, Doctor; Matthew Chapin, Doctor
Time Period(s): 1880s
Locale(s): New England

Summary: The novel continues the author's history of the medical profession from the Civil War to the present begun in *I Swear by Apollo*. Sue Ward, the adopted daughter of Matthew Chapin, is the first woman to join the surgery staff of New England's prestigious Joseph Linklighter Memorial Hospital. The novel dramatizes the prejudices she faces and the conflict between her personal and professional lives.

Historical Accuracy: The depiction of the period and the medical profession is authentic and believable.

6939 *I Swear by Apollo*

Date of Publication: 1968
Subject(s): Civil War—U.S.; Medical Profession
Fictional character(s): Matthew Chapin, Doctor
Historical character(s): Oliver Wendell Holmes, Lawyer, Judge
Time Period(s): 1860s; 1870s
Locale(s): Virginia; Boston, Massachusetts; New York, New York

Summary: Matthew Chapin is a young medical orderly during the Civil War. The novel dramatizes his career as a doctor in a small country practice in Vermont, in a primitive hospital in Ohio, at the Harvard Medical School, and in his first professional appointment, as a surgeon in New York's Bellevue Hospital. Chapin must contend with the major medical issue of the day, applying Dr. Lister's theories of antisepsis to surgery techniques.

Historical Accuracy: The details of the medical profession of the time are authentic and convincing.

FRANCIS BRETT YOUNG

6940 *The City of Gold*

Date of Publication: 1939
Subject(s): Frontier—Africa; Boer War; Jameson Raid
Fictional character(s): Janse Grafton, Prospector
Historical character(s): Paul Kruger, Political Figure; Cecil John Rhodes, Government Official (British colonial admistrator)
Time Period(s): 1890s
Locale(s): South Africa

Summary: The novel continues the story of South African history begun in the author's *They Seek a Country* centering on the descendents of John Grafton and his Dutch wife, Lisbet. Events include the founding of Johannesburg, the Jameson Raid, and the events leading up to the first Boer War.

Historical Accuracy: The novel's strength is its faithful depiction of the era and the historical events that shape the characters' lives.

6941 *They Seek a Country*

Date of Publication: 1937
Subject(s): Frontier—Africa
Fictional character(s): John Oakley, Convict; Lisbet Prinsloo, Young Woman
Time Period(s): 1830s
Locale(s): South Africa; England

Summary: Englishman John Oakley, is transported from England to South Africa for poaching. He escapes his convict ship and takes refuge on a Boer farm, where he shares the family's fortunes, participates in the Great Trek, and finally marries the Prinsloos' daughter Lisbet.

Historical Accuracy: The novel is a distinguished attempt to create a believable portrait of the region and the period.

STANLEY YOUNG (1906-1975)

An American educator, poet, playwright, literary critic, and novelist, Young was born in Indiana and graduated from the University of Chicago and Columbia University. He taught at William College. Young is the author of *Tippecanoe and Tyler, Too!* and four plays that were produced on Broadway, including *Bright Rebel* and *Mr. Pickwick*.

6942 *Young Hickory*

Date of Publication: 1940
Subject(s): Settlement of the American Frontier; Biography, Fictionalized
Historical character(s): Andrew Jackson, Military Personnel, Political Figure; Rachel Jackson, Spouse
Time Period(s): 18th century (1779-1792)
Locale(s): North Carolina; Tennessee

Summary: The novel chronicles the early years of Andrew Jackson from his boyhood in North Carolina to his experiences in Tennessee, including his days as a circuit lawyer. The story takes Jackson's life to the start of his political and military career.

Historical Accuracy: The historical record of Jackson's early years is scanty and speculative. Occasionally, speculations have been delivered as facts.

STARK YOUNG (1881-1963)

An American writer of poetry, plays, criticism, and fiction, Young's novels include *Heaven Trees*, *The Torches Flare*, and *River House*.

6943 *Heaven Trees*

Date of Publication: 1926
Subject(s): Antebellum South
Fictional character(s): George Clay, Plantation Owner
Time Period(s): 1850s
Locale(s): Mississippi

Summary: Life on a Mississippi plantation in the years before the Civil War is depicted in this story of George Clay and his family. A contrast of life styles is provided by the arrival of a young kinswoman from Vermont.

Historical Accuracy: The novel reconstructs with skill plantation life before the Civil War.

6944 *So Red the Rose*

Date of Publication: 1934
Subject(s): Civil War—U.S.; Rural Life—U.S.; Slavery
Fictional character(s): Malcolm Bedford, Plantation Owner; Hugh McGehee, Plantation Owner; Duncan Bedford, Military Personnel
Historical character(s): William Tecumseh Sherman, Military Personnel
Time Period(s): 1860s (1860-1865)
Locale(s): Natchez, Mississippi

Summary: This is an interesting novel of the Civil War whose focus is the homefront and the effect of the war on two plantation families. Southern plantation life is shown in detail before, during, and after the war.

Historical Accuracy: The novel is a good rendering of the effects of the war among the non-combatants.

STEVEN YOUNT

Yount is a former archivist for the University of Texas.

6945 *Wandering Star*

Date of Publication: 1994
Subject(s): American West
Fictional character(s): Tom Greer, Teenager; Sam Adams, Editor (newspaper); Brother Nicholas, Religious (charismatic preacher)
Time Period(s): 1910s (1910)
Locale(s): High Plains, Texas

Summary: The passing of the era of the Old West is dramatized by the events surrounding the arrival of Halley's Comet in 1910 in a small Texas town. Tom Greer, the young narrator, is attracted to the larger world introduced to him by the newspaper editor Sam Adams, but is also swept up in the town's hysteria fomented by the charismatic Brother Nicholas, who predicts the coming Armageddon.

Historical Accuracy: The novel features many period elements that create a believable historical backdrop.

MARGUERITE YOURCENAR

6946 *The Abyss*

Date of Publication: 1976
Subject(s): Medical Profession; Religious Conflict
Fictional character(s): Zeno, Philosopher, Doctor
Time Period(s): 16th century (1510-1569)
Locale(s): Europe

Summary: The novel captures as few other historical novels have the intellectual ferment of 16th-century Europe. It follows the career of its central character, Zeno, a physician, alchemist, engineer, and philosopher. Raised for a career in the church, Zeno seeks knowledge unconstrained by orthodoxy. He mixes with both kings and the poor as his quest takes him across a Europe torn by religious and social upheaval.

Historical Accuracy: As the author's extensive notes make clear, the novel stays remarkable close to actual events and details. The few distortions are listed and explained.

6947 *Hadrian's Memoirs*

Date of Publication: 1954
Subject(s): Roman Empire
Historical character(s): Hadrian, Ruler (Roman emperor)
Time Period(s): 2nd century (138)
Locale(s): Rome, Roman Empire

Summary: This beautifully written philosophical novel is in the form of a lengthy letter from the Emperor Hadrian to his adopted grandson and successor, Marcus Aurelius. On the brink of death, Hadrian reviews his career and in the process takes the reader inside the thoughts and beliefs of important figures of the time.

Historical Accuracy: The author lists her sources and tells where and why she took minor liberties with chronology and characters. This is a model of thoughtful and imaginative re-creation of the past.

LOUIS ZARA

Born in New York and educated in Chicago, Zara has worked in advertising and publishing and as an editor-in-chief. His novel *This Land Is Ours* won the Foundation of Literature award in 1940, and *Blessed Is the Land* won an award in 1955.

6948 *Against This Rock*

Date of Publication: 1943
Subject(s): Biography, Fictionalized; Holy Roman Empire
Historical character(s): Charles V, Ruler (Holy Roman Emperor)
Time Period(s): 16th century

Locale(s): Europe

Summary: This biographical novel dramatizes the life and reign of Charles V, King of Spain, Naples, Sicily, and the Netherlands. A deeply religious man of justice and peace, Charles continually struggles against various factions determined to split his kingdom.

Historical Accuracy: Though occasionally too sentimental in its portrait of Charles, the novel faithfully presents the facts of his life and times.

6949 *Blessed Is the Land*

Date of Publication: 1954
Subject(s): American Colonies; Jews; Religious Conflict
Historical character(s): Ashur Levy, Leader (Jewish)
Time Period(s): 17th century
Locale(s): New Amsterdam, American Colonies

Summary: The novel dramatizes the story of the first Jewish settlers who came from Brazil to New Amsterdam. They are led by Ashur Levy, who narrates the story, providing a firsthand account of Jewish customs and religious prejudices in the colonial period.

Historical Accuracy: The story is accurate in capturing the atmosphere of the time and many of the events of the period.

6950 *Dark Rider*

Date of Publication: 1961
Subject(s): Literary Life; Biography, Fictionalized
Historical character(s): Stephen Crane, Writer
Time Period(s): 19th century; 20th century (1870s-1900)
Locale(s): New Jersey; New York, New York; Cuba

Summary: The life and literary career of American writer Stephen Crane are depicted. Crane astounds the literary world at the age of 23 when he publishes one of the greatest novels about war ever written, *The Red Badge of Courage*, despite having no direct experience with combat. The development of Crane's considerable literary gifts and his short and tortured career are captured with an emphasis on the many personal demons that haunted this literary genius.

Historical Accuracy: The novel relies on considerable research to offer a faithful interpretation of Crane's life and career.

6951 *In the House of the King*

Date of Publication: 1952
Subject(s): Royalty—Spain; Biography, Fictionalized
Historical character(s): Philip II, Ruler (King of Spain); Charles V, Ruler (Holy Roman Emperor); Mary I, Ruler (Queen of England)
Time Period(s): 16th century (1537-1598)
Locale(s): Spain; England

Summary: This biographical novel traces the career of Spanish King Philip II from his boyhood to his death. The emphasis is on the king's amorous affairs and political maneuvering in one of history's most colorful periods.

Historical Accuracy: The novel offers a vivid and believable portrait of the 16th century, though the authenticity is marred by a preference for invented intimacy and an anachronistic Freudian bias.

6952 *Rebel Run*

Date of Publication: 1951
Subject(s): Civil War—U.S.; Espionage
Fictional character(s): James Andrews, Military Personnel (Union captain), Spy
Time Period(s): 1860s (1862)
Locale(s): Tennessee

Summary: Based on an actual Civil War incident, the novel dramatizes the efforts of Union Captain James Andrews to disrupt Confederate communications between Atlanta and Chattanooga. The story recounts his part in a raid in which he seizes a train and heads north pursued by the Confederates.

Historical Accuracy: Although the incident is historical, the details are for the most part invented.

6953 *This Land Is Ours*

Date of Publication: 1940
Subject(s): French and Indian War; American Revolution; War of 1812
Fictional character(s): Andrew Benton, Frontiersman, Military Personnel (soldier)
Historical character(s): George Rogers Clark, Frontiersman, Military Personnel (general); Pontiac, Indian (Ottawa), Chieftain; Anthony Wayne, Military Personnel (general)
Time Period(s): 18th century; 19th century (1755-1835)
Locale(s): Susquehanna Valley, Pennsylvania; Mississippi River

Summary: The novel depicts 80 years of American frontier experience through the character of Andrew Benton, who takes part in most of the great border events. He is captured by the Shawnees as a youth, is with George Rogers Clark in the capture of Kaskaskia and Vincennes, fights with Anthony Wayne at the Battle of Fallen Timbers, marches with William Henry Harrison to Tippecanoe, and survives the Fort Dearborn massacre.

Historical Accuracy: The novel is faithful to the events depicted in this 80-year panorama of American history.

NANCY ZAROULIS

6954 *Call the Darkness Light*

Date of Publication: 1979
Subject(s): Immigrants; Labor Movement
Fictional character(s): Sabra Palfrey, Worker (textile)
Time Period(s): 19th century (1840s-1861)
Locale(s): Lowell, Massachusetts

Summary: Set in industrial Lowell, Massachusetts, in the years before the Civil War, the novel depicts the grim lives of mill workers. Women work 14-hour days in the mill in unsafe conditions. Sabra Palfrey is the central character and victim of an industrial system that exploits women and blights many lives.

Historical Accuracy: The novel is convincing in its period elements and description of the condition of the textile workers of the period.

6955 *The Last Waltz*

Date of Publication: 1984
Subject(s): Family Saga
Fictional character(s): Isabel January, Gentlewoman; Marian Childs, Gentlewoman
Time Period(s): 1900s
Locale(s): Boston, Massachusetts; Newport, Rhode Island

Summary: The novel is set in the world of wealth and power in Boston and Newport at the turn of the century. It tells the story of the unconventional loves of Isabel January and Marian Childs, who are bound by convention and marry men that they do not love. Unrequited love pushes both to unfortunate consequences against a backdrop of a society in which public scandal is the greatest sin.

Historical Accuracy: The milieu of wealthy New England and society during the period is believably presented.

6956 *Massachusetts: A Novel*

Date of Publication: 1991
Subject(s): American Colonies; American Revolution; Family Saga
Fictional character(s): Bartholomew Revell, Orphan, Settler; Ebenezer Revell, Patriot
Historical character(s): John Carver, Leader (pilgrim); Samuel Adams, Patriot; Paul Revere, Patriot; Thomas Gage, Military Personnel (general); William Howe, Military Personnel (general)
Time Period(s): Multiple Time Periods
Locale(s): Massachusetts

Summary: This massive saga covers over 350 years of Massachusetts and American history, from the *Mayflower* to the present. The story centers on the Revell family, whose history is interwoven with the great moments of American history, including the Pilgrims' settlement, the American Revolution, the China trade, the Civil War, and the labor movement in response to the second wave of Irish immigrants in the 19th and 20th centuries.

Historical Accuracy: The novel offers a panorama of historical events authentically detailed, though overly compressed to accommodate the novel's immense scale.

ROGER ZELAZNY (1937-)

GERALD HAUSMAN (1945-)

Zelazny was born in Cleveland and graduated from Case Western Reserve University and Columbia University. He is considered one of the most popular contemporary science fiction writers, noted for his Amber series. Hausman was born in Baltimore and is a teacher of English, a poet, and a collector of native American and ethnic tales.

6957 *Wilderness*

Date of Publication: 1994
Subject(s): American West; Indians
Historical character(s): John Colter, Mountain Man; Hugh Glass, Mountain Man
Time Period(s): 1800s (1808); 1820s (1823)
Locale(s): Yellowstone River, Wyoming

Summary: The novel offers the linked tales of two mountain men in two different eras. Colter is a surveyor for the Lewis and Clark expedition, captured by the Blackfoot Indians in 1808. Glass is mauled by a grizzly bear in the Yellowstone 20 years later. Both are survivors whose tales dramatize life in the wilderness.

Historical Accuracy: The novel is vivid and authentic in its details of wilderness life.

CHAYYM ZELDIS (1927-)

Born in Buffalo, New York, Zeldis attended the University of Michigan where he won the Avery Hopwood Award in poetry. In 1948, Zeldis settled in Israel, living on various agricultural settlements, including a kibbutz. He is the author of a volume of poetry, *Seek Haven*, and the novels *Golgotha* and *The Marriage Bed*.

6958 *The Brother*

Date of Publication: 1979
Subject(s): Biblical Story; Roman Empire; Jews
Fictional character(s): Rabbi, Religious; Vespasian, Government Official (proconsul); Enoch, Rebel
Time Period(s): 1st century
Locale(s): Nazareth, Israel

Summary: This struggle between good and evil centers around a Nazareth brothel patronized by Romans and Jews alike. A number of characters' fates are connected in the struggle against Roman oppression and the search for meaning.

Historical Accuracy: The novel's period elements are convincingly portrayed.

ERIC ZENCEY (1954-)

Zencey is a professor of history at Goddard College and a contributing editor of the *North American Review*.

6959 *Panama*

Date of Publication: 1995
Subject(s): Mystery
Fictional character(s): Miriam Talbott, Young Woman
Historical character(s): Henry Adams, Historian, Writer
Time Period(s): 1890s (1892)
Locale(s): Paris, France

Summary: In Paris, historian Henry Adams searches for an American woman studying there. Her disappearance is connected with the scandalous Panama Affair, brought on by the bankruptcy of the French Panama Canal Company, which has bribed members of the Chamber of Deputies to push its

interests. Adams' search leads him directly into the tangled political scene.

Historical Accuracy: Although the story is imagined, the period background is authentic.

STEFAN ZEROMSKI (1864-1925)

Zeromski was born in Poland but spent much of his life in exile from his native land. The revolutionary idealism of his work is marked by a pessimistic strain, the result of family tragedies and emotional troubles. Most of his works are fiercely nationalistic.

6960 *Ashes*

Date of Publication: 1904
Subject(s): Napoleonic Wars; Peninsular War
Fictional character(s): Raphael Olbromski, Military Personnel; Helen, Heroine; Prince Gintult, Royalty
Time Period(s): 18th century; 19th century (1796-1812)
Locale(s): Warsaw, Poland; Saragossa, Spain

Summary: The novel tells the story of young Raphael Olbromski: his childhood on his uncle's estate in Poland, his schooling, and his tragic love affair with Helen. Raphael enlists in Napoleon's army and sees action against the Austrians. There are also scenes of the battle of Saragossa in Spain.

Historical Accuracy: This is more a series of unconnected scenes than a narrative. The scenes of some of Napoleon's campaigns are precise and realistic.

ISABELLE GIBSON ZIEGLER (1904-)

American author and journalist Ziegler was born in Columbus, Ohio, and was educated at Ohio State University, the University of Chicago, and the University of Vienna. Ziegler worked and travelled as a syndicated columnist for the Carlisle Crutcher Syndicate, and was once jailed for 48 hours by Nazi troops in Czechoslovakia. She was the author of television plays for CBS and in 1975 published *The Creative Writer's Handbook: What to Write, How to Write It, Where to Send It.*

6961 *Nine Days of Father Serra*

Date of Publication: 1951
Subject(s): Spanish Colonies; Indians; Religious Life
Historical character(s): Junipero Serra, Religious (missionary)
Time Period(s): 1760s (1769)
Locale(s): San Diego, California

Summary: This novel about the creation of the California coast missions by missionary Father Serra is based on an actual incident in 1769. Serra has begun a mission in San Diego, but the military commander is preparing to abandon the expedition and return to Mexico since the needed supply ship has not arrived. Father Serra convinces him to wait nine days for relief to come. During this time the fate of Spanish California hangs in the balance.

Historical Accuracy: The novel blends fact and speculation into a plausible period story that captures the atmosphere of early California history.

LAJOS ZILAHY (1891-)

Hungarian novelist and playwright Zilahy is the author of *The Dukays* and *The Angry Angel.*

6962 *Century in Scarlet*

Date of Publication: 1965
Subject(s): Napoleonic Wars; Crimean War
Fictional character(s): Antal Dukay, Nobleman (count), Twin; Albert Dukay, Nobleman (count), Twin
Historical character(s): Clemens von Metternich, Diplomat
Time Period(s): 19th century; 20th century (1814-1914)
Locale(s): Europe; United States

Summary: The novel attempts nothing less than a full depiction of the major events of the 19th century beginning with the Congress of Vienna and ending with the outbreak of World War I. The novel follows the careers of twin Hungarian aristocrats Antal and Albert Dukay. Antal is conservative and loyal to the Hapsburg monarchy; Adalbert is dedicated to revolutionary change and an independent Hungary. The action ranges across Europe and includes scenes set in Poland under Russian occupation, the court of Czar Nicholas, revolutionary Paris, and the U.S.

Historical Accuracy: The novel establishes a believable period backdrop and traces with some skill the effects of the historical events on the characters' stories.

URSULA ZILINSKY

Born in Germany, Zilinsky lived in Munich until she was 16. She came to New York in 1949 and attended New York University.

6963 *Before the Glory Ended*

Date of Publication: 1967
Subject(s): Social Chronicle
Fictional character(s): Jean Riebeck, Spy, Military Personnel (officer); Istvan Halyi, Military Personnel (officer)
Time Period(s): 20th century (1918-1957)
Locale(s): Paris, France; Vienna, Austria; Budapest, Hungary

Summary: The breakup of Europe between the wars is depicted in the lives of two men—Frenchman Jean Riebeck and his cousin Istvan Halyi, a Hungarian. The action moves across Europe and includes scenes from the Hungarian Uprising and the death camp at Buchenwald. The novel attempts to show the passing of tradition and the collapse of society against the onrush of history.

Historical Accuracy: The period elements create a believable historical backdrop for the drama.

6964 *The Long Afternoon*

Date of Publication: 1984
Subject(s): World War I; Edwardian Period

Fictional character(s): Felix Von Landeck, Heir; Toby Altondale, Gentleman; David Harvey, Gentleman
Time Period(s): 20th century (1902-1920s)
Locale(s): England; France

Summary: The novel describes the effects of World War I on the friendship of three childhood friends—Felix, a German industrial heir; Toby, son of a British aristocrat; and David, the son of a poor English vicar. Their lives together are altered by the events of war and the world created in its aftermath. The novel captures the protected pre-war world forever changed by the conflict.

Historical Accuracy: The pre-war and post-war atmospheres are captured believably.

NORMAN ZOLLINGER (1921-)

Born in Chicago, Illinois, Zollinger attended Cornell College. He has been the president and chair of the board of AZI, Inc. and a bookstore owner in New Mexico. He is the author of *Riders to Cibola* and *Medal of Honor*.

6965 *Chapultepec*

Date of Publication: 1995
Subject(s): Independence—Mexico; Mexican Revolution
Fictional character(s): Jeremiah James, Military Personnel (colonel); Sarah Kent Anderson, Young Woman
Historical character(s): Maximilian, Ruler (Emperor of Mexico); Carlota, Royalty (Empress of Mexico); Francoise-Achille Bazaine, Military Personnel (commander of French forces); Benito Juarez, Political Figure; Porfirio Diaz, Military Personnel (general)
Time Period(s): 1860s

Locale(s): Mexico

Summary: The novel is set against the background of the Mexican Revolution and the ill-fated reign of Maximilian and Carlota. Jeremiah James, an American colonel in the French Foreign Legion, and Sarah Alexander, a girlhood friend of the Empress Carlota, are caught in the conflict between the French and the Mexicans. Sarah is forced to choose between her sympathy for Juarez and the republican movement and her friendship with the royal family.

Historical Accuracy: The story is true to the historical events that form its background.

6966 *Not of War Only*

Date of Publication: 1994
Subject(s): Mexican Revolution
Fictional character(s): Jorge Martinez, Revolutionary; Corey Lane, Lawman; Dona Luisa Lopez y Montenegro, Gentlewoman
Historical character(s): Francisco Villa, Revolutionary; Emiliano Zapata, Revolutionary
Time Period(s): 1910s (1914-1917)
Locale(s): Mexico

Summary: This tale of the Mexican Revolution centers on the parallel stories of two Americans, Jorge Martinez and Sheriff Corey Lane, who pursues Martinez across the Mexican border on a special assignment for the U.S. State Department. Each finds love and disappointment as the events of Mexico's revolution intrude.

Historical Accuracy: The novel provides a genuine and convincing portrait of its period with actual events and figures believably integrated into the fictional story.[/gs]